A MANDAIC DICTIONARY

A MANDAIC DICTIONARY

BY

E. S. DROWER, Hon. D.Litt. Oxon,
Hon. D.D. Uppsala,
HON. FELLOW OF THE SCHOOL OF ORIENTAL AND AFRICAN STUDIES, UNIVERSITY OF LONDON

AND

R. MACUCH, Ph.D.
PROFESSOR OF SEMITICS
FREIE UNIVERSITÄT, BERLIN

WIPF & STOCK • Eugene, Oregon

Wipf and Stock Publishers
199 W 8th Ave, Suite 3
Eugene, OR 97401

A Mandaic Dictionary
By Drower, E. S. and Macuch, Rudolf

Softcover ISBN-13: 978-1-7252-7204-0
Publication date 8/11/2020
Previously published in English by Oxford University Press, 1963

This edition is a scanned facsimile of the original edition published in 1963.

This reprint is published by arrangement with Oxford University Press.

PREFACE

A PALAEOLITHIC ancestor, asked why he had made a stone axe, might have replied that he had often wanted such an implement, and our dictionary has grown out of our needs in much the same casual way. Working independently on the Mandaean language, we came together eventually at short notice and with limited time to put the results of our labour into publishable shape.

Three collections have served as the basis of the dictionary: our own separate collections, and that of the late Professor Mark Lidzbarski, which consisted of index-cards kept loosely together in two cigar boxes. The cards, written in cursive Hebrew script, were not in good order, as they had been frequently moved from place to place. Permission to use them was granted by Professor Johannes Fück of Halle University, and at the friendly suggestion of Professor Kahle it was arranged that one of Professor Fück's pupils should copy out the entries, transposing the cursive script into square Hebrew characters and rearranging them when necessary.

As a life-work of so great a scholar as Lidzbarski, these cards were extremely valuable, and we are grateful to Professor Fück. In actual word-treasure our own collections were richer of course, as in Lidzbarski's day only about a quarter of the texts since brought to Europe were available, but the meticulous care with which Lidzbarski had given exact references to lines and pages of manuscripts and published works enhanced the value of his material. We have tried to give references in the same manner, but this was not always possible. It would have been theoretically preferable to have waited until the whole body of Mandaean texts had been published, but this would have meant too long a postponement. The majority of the classical texts are, in fact, now in print: of the manuscripts which remain in the Bodleian Library (the Drower Collection), and in Berlin and London, some may eventually reach publication, but many are corrupt texts which could hardly merit presentation in published form. Nevertheless in such texts there are gleanings which should not be overlooked in such work as ours. A few invite the curiosity of the scholar and should be published in the future.

The reasons why precise references are often omitted are various. Some manuscripts are illustrated, and the illustrations interrupt and intermingle with the text.[1] The index-cards and note-books which grew with the Drower Collection were originally intended for private use and the owner contented herself with citing the name or number of a manuscript or page of her transliterations: moreover, part of these had been lost during the war. Since the dictionary was undertaken, faults of omission have been repaired where possible, but to track down words and short phrases in long manuscripts is a tedious and often impossible task.

In the dictionary verbal roots are printed in capital letters to assist identification and reference. Derived words are a source of considerable difficulty, since

[1] DC 7 and DC 8 contain more illustrations than text.

the Mandaic dialect is still in a fluid state. Many influences (for example, the weakness and continual loss of guttural sounds, aphaeresis, apocope, syncope, metathesis, epenthesis, and so on) have contributed to confusion, so that words often assume unexpected shapes; they are, therefore, entered both briefly in the lists of derived words following each root, and fully under their first letter (whether prefixed or radical) in their proper alphabetical places.

Not all available material is of equal value. The exact date of many texts is unknown, and the oldest have suffered from editing, neglect, and deterioration; the colophons themselves sometimes bear witness to these processes. Magical texts, especially short phylacteries and those dealing with black magic, have so often been copied by semi-literate scribes that they bristle with corruptions (for example, the town called *Burṣip* 'Borsippa' in earlier copies has in later books become *parṣupa* 'countenance'). We have grudgingly quoted examples worth an entry or a reference and have omitted much that is doubtful or obviously corrupt. We have inserted a representative number of proper names, including some of the best known, especially those of angels and demons, which are legion; and **-ˁil** may be attached to almost any verbal root to create such names.

We regret that for reasons of economy Mandaic type could not be used, but see no reason for using Hebrew characters, since these are inadequate, and the Latin alphabet with a few subsidiary letters and signs (such as **ᶜ**, **h̲**, **d̲-**, and ع) answers every purpose. Further, the customary and abundant *scriptio plena* of Mandaic texts makes the use of the Latin script preferable. We have been unable to find any satisfactory method of transliteration capable of indicating the pronunciation and have adopted the system of 'a single letter, a single sign', disregarding aspiration; and we have throughout used **u** and **i** for semi-vowels, whether they are pronounced as vowels or as consonants. Capital **W** and **Y** are used only to indicate original consonants in unvocalized verbal roots, e.g. **DWR** 'to lead' (opposed to **DUR** 'to dwell'), **HWA** 'to show' (opposed to **HUA** 'to be'), **YDA** 'to know' &c. A table showing the system of transliteration which we have used will be found on p. xii.

It remains for us to express gratitude to scholars who have encouraged us by taking active interest in our work and putting their specialized knowledge at our disposal when we asked for it. Amongst these are Professors O. R. Gurney, W. B. Henning, Paul Kahle, Sydney Smith (who gave the work its first impetus), and G. Widengren. We should like to pay a special tribute to the staff of the Oxford University Press, and particularly to Dr. J. P. Naish of the Reading Department, who gave us invaluable help with his time, his erudition, and his experience, at all stages of production. Thanks are due also to Teheran University for granting two years (1956–58) of special leave to Dr. Macuch; and to Oxford University for the invitation which procured for him such a favour.

On the financial side, the editorial expenses of the dictionary were most generously supported by the British Academy, Leverhulme Research Awards, the British School of Archaeology in Iraq, and by the Iraq Petroleum Company and the Basrah Petroleum Company, on various occasions. To them and to those who approached them on our behalf we tender grateful thanks.

Above all, we are grateful to Professor G. R. Driver, C.B.E., who, with endless patience and unfailing resourcefulness, has piloted our dictionary through many a shoal from the moment of its launching in card-index form, to its final harbour—publication. Never once has he failed in support and help.

Finally, conscious of many imperfections in our work, we take refuge in a well-worn Mandaic phrase:

Haṭaian uhauban uskilatan utiqlatan ušabašatan šbuqlan ('Forgive us our sins, misdoings, foolish errors, stumblings and mistakes')!

E. S. DROWER
R. MACUCH

July 1963

[*A Personal Note*]

Lady Drower would like to express her especial thanks for the never wearying kindness and help of the learned Sheikh Nejm eṣ-Ṣâbiya of Baṣrah, Iraq.

ABBREVIATIONS

abstr., abstract.
adj., adjective.
AF, Rosenthal, F., *Die aramäistische Forschung seit Th. Nöldeke's Veröffentlichungen*, Leiden, Brill, 1939.
af., afel.
AIT, Montgomery. J. A., *Aramaic Incantation Texts from Nippur*, Philadelphia, 1913.
Akk., Akkadian.
Akk. Fw., s. Zimmern.
AM, *Aspar Malwâšia*, ed. E. S. Drower, London 1949 (Cf. BZ).
antep., antepenultimate.
AO, *Archiv Orientálni*.
Ap., Appendix.
Ar., Arabic.
Aram., Aramaic.
ATŠ., *Alf Trisar Šuialia*, Transliteration, Translation and Commentary by E. S. Drower, Berlin, Akademie-Verlag, 1960.
Bab., Babylonian.
Bartholomae, Bartholomae, *Altiranisches Wörterbuch*, Straßburg, 1904.
Bez., Bezold, C., *Babylonisch–Assyrisches Glossar*, Heidelberg, 1926.
Brockelm., Brockelmann, C., *Grundriß der vergleichenden Grammatik der semitischen Sprachen*, Berlin 1908–13.
BZ, *The Book of the Zodiac*, translation and commentary of AM., Royal Asiatic Society, London, 1949.
Chr.-Pal., Christian-Palestinian.
cod., codex.
col., column.
coll., colloquial.
coloph., colophon.
comp., compound.
Coron., *The Coronation of the Great Šišlam*, trsl. E. S. Drower, facsimile text, Brill, 1962.
CP, *The Canonical Prayerbook of the Mandaeans*, edited and translated with notes by E. S. Drower (E. J. Brill, Leiden, 1959).
DAb., E. S. Drower, *Diwan Abatur*. Text and translation, Città del Vaticano, 1950 (ST 151).
DC, The Drower Collection of Mandaean manuscripts in the Bodleian Library, Oxford.

1. Codex, fragmentary collection of liturgical prayers, undated.
3. Codex, collection of canonical prayers, slightly imperfect with copied additions to complete. Undated.
6. Roll, five of the seven parts of Alf Trisar Šuialia. In several hands and much repaired. Date of one part A.H. 969.
7. Roll, Diuan ḏ-Nahrauata. Illustrated account of rivers and mountains. Date, A.H. 1259.
8. Roll, Diuan Abatur, s. DAb. Undated, 16th cent.
9. Roll, s. HG.
10. Roll, s. *J.R.A.S.* 1943, pp. 177 ff.
12. Roll, Pašar Haršia. Date A.H. 1196. (Colophon attached is copied from another MS. on account of its historical interest.)
18. Roll, Zrazta ḏ-Šuba Šibiahia, modern copy, corrected from an older MS.
20. Roll, Šafta ḏ-Dahlulia, modern copy, corrected from an older MS.
21. Roll, Šafta ḏ-Pišra (*or* Pašar) Ainia. *J.R.A.S.* 1937, pp. 590–597.
22. Codex, Sidra Rba ḏ-Mara ḏ-Rabuta: Ginza Rba. A.H. 1253.
23. Roll, Pašar Sumqa. On reverse, Qmāha Gasṭata. A.H. 1226.
24. Roll, Šarḥ ḏ-Paruanaiia. A.H. 1248.
27. Roll, Zihrun Razia Kasia. Illustrated. A.H. 1088.
30. Codex, Drašia ḏ-Yahia. A.H. 1166.
31. Loose-leafed codex, Spar Maluašia, cf. AM. A.H. 1247.
33. Roll; three *qmahia*: Šuba lbišna, ʿsirna htimna, bYawar Ziua nišimtai (also in D.C. 43).
34. Roll, illustrated. Diuan Malkuta ʿlaita. A.H. 1204.
35. Roll, Diuan Maṣbuta ḏ-Hibil-Ziwa. A.H. 1247.
36. Roll, Alf Trisar Šuialia, cf. ATŠ. All seven parts with Haran Gawaita as eighth part. A.H. 1088.
38. Codex, Šarḥ ḏ-Qabin ḏ-Šišlam Rba. A.H. 1217. Cf. ŠQ.
39. Roll, Šafta ḏ- Qaština. A.H. 1216.
40. Roll, Pašar Mihla. A.H. 1247.
41. Roll. Alma Rišaia Rba. A.H. 1220.
42. Roll, Šarḥ ḏ-Ṭabahata. A.H. 2148.
43. Roll, a collection of exorcisms and phylacteries: A. Ṣir Sahria; B. Qmaha ḏ-Šaiul; C. Šuba lbišna, ʿsirna htimna, bYawar Ziua (cf. D.C. 33); D. Šalhafta ḏ-mahria; E. Qmaha ḏ-Dahlulia; F. Qmaha ḏ-Gasṭata; G. Qmaha ḏ-br ʿngaria, & br ʿngaria zuṭa; H. Qmaha ḏ-Yurba; I. Qmaha ḏ-Šuba; J. Šafta ḏ-Qaština.
44. Zrazta ḏ-Hibil Ziua; in five sections. Cf. Morg.
45. Fragmentary codex, magical, cf. *J.R.A.S.* 1943, pp. 149–81.
46. Codex, book of magic, modern copy. Cf. *J.R.A.S.* 1943, pp. 149–81.
48. Roll, Alma Rišaia Zuṭa. Illustrated. A.H. 972.
50. Roll, Šarḥ ḏ-Maṣbuta Rba; Hamša Maṣbutiata; Raza Rba ḏ-Zihrun. A.H. 1284.
51. Roll, Pišra Pugdama ḏ-Mia. A.H. 1277.
53. Codex, (loose-leaved) Collection of liturgical prayers and hymns. (The canonical prayer-book.)
54. Roll, Taraṣa ḏ-taga ḏ-Šišlam Rba.

DER. Derivative(s).
DLZ, *Deutsche Literatur Zeitung.*
EB, *Encyclopaedia Britannica.*
Eg., Egyptian.
encl., enclitic(s).
Ephem., Lidzbarski, M., *Ephemeris für semitische Epigraphik*, Gießen, 1900–2.
ERE, Hastings's *Encyclopaedia of Religion and Ethics.*
Eth., Ethiopic.
ethpe., ethpeel.
ethpa., ethpaal.
ettaf., ettafal.
expr., expression.
fem., feminine.
fig., figurative.
Fränkel, S., *Die aramäischen Fremdwörter im klassischen Arabisch*, Leiden 1886.
Germ., German.
Ges., Gesenius-Buhl, *Hebräisches u. aramäisches Handwörterbuch zum Alten Testament.*
Ginzā, Lidz., Mark, *Ginzā, der Schatz oder das große Buch der Mandäer, übersetzt u. erklärt*, Göttingen, 1925.
Gl., Glossarium Sabico-Arabicum, University Library, Leiden.
Gs, Ginza smala (Left Ginza).
Gy, Ginza iamina (Right Ginza).
H., Hebrew.
HG, *The Haran Gawaita*, ed. Drower (together with the Baptism of Hibil-Ziwa), Città del Vaticano, 1953 (ST 176).
hif., hif'il (Hebrew).
HpGn, Bousset, W., *Hauptprobleme der Gnosis*, Göttingen, 1907.
HW, Schulthess, *Homonyme Wurzeln im Syrischen*, Berlin, 1900.
IM, Pognon, H., *Inscriptions mandaïtes des coupes de Khouabir*, Paris, 1898.
imp., imperfect.
impt., imperative.
Ind., index.
ISK, *Iranisch-semitische Kulturbegegnung in der parthischer Zeit*, Geo. Widengren (Arbeitsgemeinschaft für Forschung des Landes Nordrhein-Westfalen: Heft 70), 1960.
J., Jastrow, Marcus, *A Dictionary of the Targumim, Talmud Babli and Yerushalmi, and the Midrashic Literatur*, 2 vols. New York, 1950.
JA, *Journal Asiatique.*
JAOS, *Journal of the American Oriental Society.*
Jb, *Das Johannisbuch der Mandäer*, ed. by M. Lidzbarski, Gießen, 1915.
Jb ii, *Translation and Commentary of the Johannisbuch.*
JbPTh, *Jahrbücher für protestantische Theologie.*
Jew., Jewish.
J.R.A.S., *Journal of the Royal Asiatic Society.*
KAT, Schrader, E., *Die Keilinschriften u. das Alte Testament*, 3. Auflage von Winckler u. Zimmern.
l., line.
Lat., Latin.
Leid., Leiden copy of *Ginza Rba.*
Lidz., Lidzbarski.
loan-w., loan-word.
Lond., MS. of British Museum in London.
Löw, Löw, A. P., *Aramäische Pflanzennamen*, Leipzig, 1881.
LS, Brockelmann, C., *Lexicon Syriacum*, 2nd ed., Halle, 1928.
Macl., Maclean, A. J., *A Dictionary of the Dialects of Vernacular Syriac*, Oxford, 1901.
masc., masculine.
MG, Nöldeke, Th., *Mandäische Grammatik*, Halle, 1875.
MHenb, Henning, W. B., *Das manichäische Henochbuch*, SBAW, Phil.-hist. Klasse, München, 1934, pp. 27–34.
Mishn., Mishnaic Hebrew.
ML, Lidzbarski, M., *Mandäische Liturgien, mitgeteilt, übersetzt und erklärt*, Berlin, 1920.
MMII, Drower, E. S., *The Mandaeans of Iraq and Iran*, Oxford, 1937, Leiden, Brill, 1962.
MO, Monde Oriental.
mod., modern.
Morg., Morgan, J. de, *Études Linguistiques*, IIe partie: Textes mandaïtes, Paris 1904 (Mission scientifique en Perse, V).
mparth, middle Parthian.
MR, Brandt, W., *Die mandäische Religion, ihre Entwicklung und geschichtliche Bedeutung*, Leipzig, 1912, 1st ed., 1889.
MSchr, Brandt, W., *Mandäische Schriften*, Göttingen, 1893.
MSt. Pallis, S. A., *Mandaean Studies*, London, 1926.
Nab., Nabataean.
nom. act., nomen actionis.
nom. ag., nomen agentis.
Nöld., Nöldeke.
nom., nominal.
Norb., Matth. Norberg, *Codex Nasaraeus.*
occ., occasionally, occasional.
OLZ, *Orientalistische Literaturzeitung.*
OP, Old Persian.
Or., *Orientalia*, vol. 15, Nova series, Fasc. 3.
OSt., *Orientalische Studien Th. Nöldeke zum siebzigsten Geburtstag gewidmet*, Gießen, 1906.
Oxf., MS. of Oxford in the Bodleian Library without further indication refers to the liturgical MS. edited by Lidzb. as the last part of ML, designated by Nöld. as Oxf. III.
P., Persian.
pa., pael.
P.A., Père Anastase Marie's collection of Mand. MSS.
paen., penult., penultimate.
Pahl., Pahlavi.
panp., panp(el).
Par., MS. of Bibliothèque Nationale, Paris.
part. pres., present participle.
PD, the Paris Diwan (containing two parts of ATŠ), Lidz. *Pariser Diwan.*
pe., peal.
Pet., Petermann's edition of *Ginza* or *Sidra Rba*: Thesaurus sive liber magnus vulgo liber Adami appelatus, opus Mandeorum summi ponderis, Leipzig, 1867.
pf., perfect.
Phoen., Phoenician.
Phon., Phonetic.
pi., pi'el (Hebrew).

pl., plural.
PNC *A Pair of Naṣoraean Commentaries* (DC 41 and DC 48). Text with translation and notes by E. S. Drower (Brill, Leiden, 1963).
PRE, *Protestantische Realencyklopädie.*
prep., preposition.
procl., proclitic(s).
pron., pronounced, pronunciation.
PSm., Payne Smith, J. A., *A Compendious Syriac Dictionary*, Oxford, 1903.
pt., participle.
Q., Euting, J., *Qolasta oder Gesänge von der Taufe und dem Ausgang der Seele*, Stuttgart, 1867.
qm., qmaha.
Qur., Qur'ān.
q.v., *quod vide.*
rad., radical.
RD, Diwan of Rome (containing the text of DAb; Lidz. *Römischer Diwan*).
refl., reflexive.
REJ, *Revue d'Études Juives.*
rel., related.
rt., root.
SA, Drower, E.S., *The Secret Adam*, A Study of Naṣoraean gnosis, Oxford, 1960.
Ṣâb., MSS. belonging to Nâṣer Ṣâbūri, Ahwaz, Persia.
SBAW, Sitzungsberichte der bayerischen Akademie der Wissenschaften.
scr. def., scriptio defectiva.
scr. pl., scriptio plena.
sg., singular.
Sh. 'Abd., the copy of the Ginza belonging to Shaikh 'Abdullah Khaffaji, Ahwaz.
Siouffi, Siouffi, M. N., *Études sur la religion des Soubbas ou sabéene*, Paris, 1880.
Soghd., Soghdian.
SsSs, Chwolsohn, D., *Die Ssabier und der Ssabismus*, i–ii, St. Petersburg, 1856.
st. abs., status abstractus, absolute state.
st. emph., status emphaticus, emphatic state.
Steing. Steingass, *Persian-English Dictionary*, New York, 1957, reprint.
suff., suffix.
Syr., Syriac.
ŠQ, *Šarḥ ḏ-Qabin ḏ-Šišlam Rba*, text transliterated, translated and commented by E. S. Drower, Roma—Pontificio Istituto Biblico, 1950.
Talm., Talmudic.
Taraṣa, *The Coronation of Šišlam-rba*, Drower, E. S. (Brill, Leiden, 1962).
Targ., Targumic.
ThLZ, *Theologische Literaturzeitung.*
Toch., Tocharic.
ult., ultima.
var., variant.
varr., variants.
WedF., Wedding Formulary (text corresponding to ŠQ, Lidzb. *Mand. Hochzeitsformular*).
Wid., Widengren, Geo.
WiW, Drower, E. S., *Water into Wine*, Murray, London, 1956.
ZA, *Zeitschrift für Assyriolgie.*
ZDMG, *Zeitschrift der Deutschen Morgenländischen Gesellschaft.*
Zimmern, Zimmern, H., *Akkadische Fremdwörter als Beweis für babylonischen Kultureinfluß*, Leipzig, 1917.
Zotb., Zotenberg, *Catalogue des manuscrits syriaques et sabéens (mandaïtes) de la Bibliothèque Nationale*, Paris, 1874.
ZS, *Zeitschrift für Semitistik.*

MANDAEAN ALPHABET WITH LATIN AND HEBREW TRANSLITERATIONS

MANDAEAN	LATIN	HEBREW
ࡀ	a	א
ࡁ	b	ב
ࡂ	g	ג
ࡃ	d	ד
ࡄ	h	ה
ࡅ	u	ו
ࡆ	z	ז
ࡇ	h̲	ח
ࡈ	ṭ	ט
ࡉ	i	י
ࡊ	k	כ
ࡋ	l	ל
ࡌ	m	מ
ࡍ	n	נ
ࡎ	s	ס
ࡏ	ʿ	ע
ࡐ	p	פ
ࡑ	ṣ	צ
ࡒ	q	ק
ࡓ	r	ר
ࡔ	š	ש
ࡕ	t	ת
ࡖ	ḏ- (as procl., in ࡗ as kḏ)	ד̌

A

a the first letter of the alphabet, MMII 241; as a vowel sign called *halqa*, ibid. 243. Its normal round form (AF 247 n. 1) becomes triangular when attached to the preceding letter. Used very often as a mere prosthetic vowel not only when the word begins with two consonants but also with a single consonant as well as after proclitic prepositions. It always has a mere vocal value; its guttural value was lost in the prehistoric period of the language. Often instead of ʿ and vice versa, e.g. **amrat** = **ʿmrat** etc., MG 15:16 f. Transition to a front vowel, MG § 89 b; transition to a back vowel by labialization, MG § 19; wavering between central and front vowels, MG § 15; omission of an initial **a** by aphæresis, MG § 34; contraction of two successive **a**'s, MG § 35.

-a 1 Gen. Aram. ending of the st. emph. masc. sg. and of the st. abs. fem. sg., MG § 126.

-a 2 a rarer ending of the st. abs. fem. pl. inst. of the normal **-an**, MG § 131, p. 162:7.

-a 3 suff. of the 3rd p. fem. sg., sometimes written **-ah**, usually replaced by the masc. suff. **-ẖ**, MG § 62, p. 68 nn. 3–4, § 76 p. 88:8.

ab- 1 a rare form of the prep. **b-** (with a prosthetic **a**), MG 25:23. **ḏ-abuhun mistakra uauda nišmatun** Sh. ʿAbd.'s copy's var. of Gy 25:4 (Pet. **ḏ-bhun**) by which the souls are imprisoned and perish; **abmambugia** Q 13: ult.; MG 25:ult.

ab 2 (אָב, ܐܒ Bab. *abu*) month under the rule of Leo called **auual gaiṭa,** corresponding to August, see MMII 84; SsSs ii 28: *Fihrist* آب. See also MMII 84, from which the phrase 'under the rule of Leo' becomes understandable.

ab 3, aba (Gen. Sem.) father. St. abs. not used. Pl. **abahata** fathers, parents, ancestors. Sg. with suff. **ab** my father MG 175:10; **abuk** thy father MG 99:7, 177:8; **abuia** his father; **abu** her father MG 177:27 f.; **abun** our father MG 179:12; but also **abuhan** ibid. n. 1; **abukun** your father MG 179:21; **abuhun** (var. **abhun**), **abaihun, abuihun** their father MG 181:21 f. Pl. with suff. **abahatai** my fathers (or my Father, when referring to the Life) MG 176:19; **abahatan** our fathers MG 178:ult. Rarer forms: **abuẖ, abẖ** his father, **abuian** our, their father. **aba ḏ-ab** (often in lists of copyists) my grandfather; **aba ḏ-ʿm** (AM 255:18) my maternal grandfather; **abahatan qadmaiia** our forefathers; **abahatai ḏ-niṣbun** Gy 78:8 my Father (: the Life) who created (lit. planted) me, Lidzb. Ginzā 77 n. 1; **utaiaba tub ʿlan ia abuhan** DC 34 and, Compassionate One, take pity on us, O our father; **abuhan** Gy 248:paen. a var. of **abuhun** their father; **bit abu** Gy 75:3, 98:10, 99:6, 101:18, 208:10, 209:20 paternal home MG 182 n. 3 (Bab. *bît abûti* Ginzā 303 n. 1) **aba saba rba** Gy 190:13 great old father; **aba ḏ-ʿutria** (often) father of the uthras; **ab abuian aiar uʿmian iardna hu** DC 34. 166 my father, our father, is the Ether and our mother the Jordan.

ABA I, ʿBA I (עבי) to be thick, become thick, dense, dark (cf. עבב).

Pe. Pf. **abiat** (a *qmâhâ*) she became thick (or dark). Imper. Pe. with encl. **l** + pers. suff. **abulẖ** condense him; **aba abulẖ** DC 43 G 39 make his darkness thick.

Af. Pf. with suff. **akuat daiua usahra ukarsa aubuk** DC 43 as devil, demon, and calamity condensed (?) thee.

Der.: **aba, abia, ababia, aububa.**

ABA II, ʿBA II, ʿBB (אבב) 1. to bring out, come out, swell out: only in Der.: **aba II, ʿbiba.** 2. to grow hot, shine forth, glow.

Pe. Pf. **aba** he glowed: **aba uham ziua** DC 50 radiance glowed and became warm.

aba I (rt. **ABA I**) darkness, thickness, denseness: **aba ḏ-aiba** DC 46 darkness of a cloud.

aba II (rt. **ABA II**) 1. product. **aminṭul ḏ-kul aba ḏ-ʿutria mn kimṣa dakia** DC 6 because each product of the uthras is from the pure storehouse. 2. swelling: **aba ukiba bhiuaniata** AM 185:16 swelling and disease amongst cattle.

ababa = **baba.**

ababia (rt. **ABA I**) thickets, dense growth. **uqal aria ḏ-nahim bababia** DC 45 & 46 and the voice of the lion that roareth in the thicket.

abagada A–B–C–D, alphabet. **asrin uarba hugiania ḏ-abagada** twenty-four letters of the alphabet MG 1; **ṭabagada** (DAb) of the A–B–C–D. Cf. SA 17–20.

abada varr. **ʿbada, ʿubada,** mod. **bada** (rt. עבד) work, performance, rite. **ʿbad hazin abada** DAb perform this rite.

abara 1 (אֲבָרָא, ܐܒܪܐ) lead MG 115:4. St. abs. **abar. kdublẖ lṭasa ḏ-abar** DC 13, 15, 44 write it on a plate of lead; **anka uabara** DC 44. 1086 tin and lead; **šušlata ḏ-abara** DC 8, 26, 40 chains of lead; **abara ʿl libaihun** DC 44. 614 lead on their hearts.

abara 2 (ܥܒܪܐ) bank, riverside. **ḏ-abara iadlalun umia ḏ-mrabilun** ATŠ I no. 269 which the riverside brings forth and the water (that) nurtures them. According to the form it corresponds to אֲבָרָא, according to the meaning to עִבְרָא.

abara 3 (cf. אַבְרוּרֵי) rampart, outer wall. Pl. **abaria. ahdirulia šuba šuria ḏ-parzla lbaitai . . . ušuba abaria ḏ-nhaša** DC 19, Par. xxvii 13a 'put round my house seven walls of iron . . . and seven ramparts of copper'.

abara 4 (עֲבָרָא) bolt. Pl. **abaria. ahud babik gauaiia ušraibun abaria** Jb 127:ult. close thine inner doors and undo the bolts (read **šadibun,** rt. **ŠDA II** 'fasten', cf. Jb ii 126 n. 6;

see also **halša**); **abaria tabrinun** DC 44. 1035 f. = Morg. 263/16:1 breaks the bolts.

abara 5 = **habara** darkness. With suff. **babaran** in our darkness, **uabarkun** and your darkness, **abarun** their darkness MG 61:14, but Lidzb. as **abara 1** Jb ii 148 n. 5. **abarak mn gangaratun** DC 37. 38 thy obstruction (?) from their throat.

abara 6 a var. of **abira** = **bira** (v.s. **abira**).

abarai, barai (rt. **BRR**) period of isolation for, women (during menstruation and childbirth). **gubria ḏ-iuma qadmaia ḏ-šaia zauaiun ḏ-abarai dilẖ qarbia luaẖ** DAb men who approach their wives the first day of the period of isolation; **ʿnšia ḏ-daštana ḏ-abarai lagṭan** DAb women that observed isolation during menstruation.

abararia DC 46. 79:13 = **bararia.**

abaš iasdid ṭibian Gy 383:17 (var. Sh. ʿAbd.'s copy **baš**): an early Iranian king: Abbâs Yazdagart the Aθwyânian (Gray ZA 19/1905–6, 286).

abatar, less often **batar,** 1. prep. after, behind (ܒ+ܐܬܪ with a prosthetic **א**, see Nöldeke MG § 32). With suff. **abatrai** after me, behind me, **abatrak** after thee, **abatrẖ** after him, etc., **labatru** after them; **mn abatraiun** with their followers, with their train. **uanašia mn abatraiun napqia** AM 263:10 and the people go forth with their followers; **abatar haka** thereupon, thereafter MG 204:5; **abatar rišẖ** DC 46 headlong, head downwards; **niriṣunẖ abatar rišẖ** DC 31 they will hurl him headlong; coll. *bâθerīšī* (so pron.) after him, behind him (cf. P پشت سر). **kul man ḏ-lhama abatar napaqa nikal** ATŠ II no. 345 whoever eateth (ritual) food (after death) for the (soul of the) departed. 2. conj. and adv. **abatar** (**ḏ**-) after (that), later. **abatar qiniana malka nimṭia** AM 241:10 after he will attain princely property.

abatur (very often) an outstanding Mand. genie sitting between the purgatories and the worlds of light and weighing souls in his scales, keeper of the last maṭarta, Gy XIII, Gs IV; Pallis MSt 73, 111 ff. An analogy of the Iranian Rašnu, Kraeling JAOS 1933, 163, 165. An Iranian etymology proposed by Andreas: ***aβā̆*** "he that has" + ****turā*** "balance, scale", cf. Brandt, *Die jüdischen Baptismen* 147, Jb xxix, MSt 111 f. Popular etymology: **ab atur** father of wealth, **aba ḏ-ʿutria** father of the uthras MG 182 n. 3, MR 51, cf. **aba ḏ-ʿutria hatiqa rama kasia nṭira** CP 48:7, ML 64:2 father of the uthras; the old, lofty, hidden, safeguarded; and **abatur hatiqa rama kasia unṭira** CP 15:4, ML 16:13, CP 66:13, 104:13, etc.; **abatur ḏ-muzania** Q 37:14, 39:15, Morg. 116:2, etc., Ābatur of the Scales . . .

abgan, bgan (ܚܪܡ) anathema, curse. Used only in st. abs. & cstr. A st. emph. (ܚܪܡܐ) is unknown. The noun occurs often in elliptic sentences: **abgan hiia uabgan manda ḏ-hiia** ATŠ I no. 5, etc. (often) the curse of the Life and the curse of M.–ḏ–H.; **tlatma ušitin zibnia abgan hiia qra** ATŠ I no. 42 he cursed the curse of the Life 360 times; **abgan hiia ʿlik ruha** Jb 164:2 anathema of the Life (be) upon thee, Rūha. Frequent in magical texts, cf. Pognon IM no. 25, p. 75 and Gl.

ABD I, ʿBD, AWD, ʿWD (עבד, ܥܒܕ) to do, perform, do work, act, make.

Pe. Pf. **abad** he did, they did, **abdat, ʿbdat** she did, **abadt** thou didst, neg. **labadt** thou didst not, **abdit, ʿbdit** I did, **abadiun** they did, **abadtun** ye did, **abadnin** we did MG § 179; with encl. **abadubak** they did to thee, with thee, **abadilun** I did to them, **abadnalẖ** we did to him MG ibid. Impf. **nibad, tibad, ʿbad** (var. **ʿbid**), **nibdun, tibdun** he (will) do, etc., MG ibid.; with encl. **nibidulẖ** they (will) do to him, we (shall) do to him, **tibidulẖ** ye (will) do to him, her MG ibid., but also shorter forms as **nibdulẖ** AM 21, 25, etc. Impt. **ʿbid, abid, ʿbad, abud, ʿbud, ʿubud** do! MG § 179, p. 242. Act. pt. **abid**, later **qabid** he is doing, will be doing, **abda**, later **qabda** she is doing, etc., **abdin, qabdin** they (will) do, **(q)abdit** thou art doing, **(q)abidna** I am doing, etc., **(q)abditun** ye (will) do, **(q)abdinin** we (shall) do (cf. MG 243). Pass. pt. **ʿbid(a)** made MG 243. Inf. **mibad, ibid.** With suff.: Pf. **ʿbdẖ** he made him, her, it, **ʿbduia, ʿbduiẖ** they made him, they did it, **ʿbdu** they made her, **abadtẖ, ʿbadtẖ** thou didst it, I did it, **abadnẖ** we made him, her, it, etc.; Impf. **nibdẖ, tibdẖ, ʿbdẖ**, etc. Impt. **ʿbdẖ, ʿubdẖ**, pl. **ʿbduia** (Gy 101:4) make him, her, it MG § 200.

Af. only pt.: act. **mabid** making do, pass. **mabad** made MG § 180, p. 243.

Ethpe. Pf. **ʿtbid**, f. **ʿtibdat** was done, made. Impf. **nitbid.** Pt. **mitbid**, f. **mitibda** ibid.

Šaf. Pf. **šabid** he made a slave. Pt. pres. **mšabidna** (DAb) I enslave.

Eštaf. Pf. **ʿštabad** became subservient. Impf. **ništabdun** they (will) become slaves MG p. 244.

ḏ-abadnin udabdinin Morg. 209/5:8 what we have done and what we are doing; **ʿbidata rurbata abid uluat anašia ṭabuta abid** AM 17:20 he performeth mighty deeds and is a benefactor (lit. does good) to men; **ubada ḏ-parzla abid** ibid. he will be an ironsmith (perform iron work); **labdilẖ** AM 41:12 they omit to do (this) to him; **kḏ abid abdilun** Gy 187:8 as they do will be done to them; **adam mahu ḏ-yada** (var. **ʿda**) **mibadbẖ balma** Gy 100:antep. f. what does Adam know how to do in the world?; **bṣubiana ḏ-bišia laʿbidlia** Gs 103:3 I acted not according to the will of the wicked; **kul ḏ-ʿbid umabad baṭil** Jb 46:9 all that is done and performed will come to naught; **anat balhudak mahu abdit** ibid. thou alone, what wilt thou do?; **haršia ḏ-ʿbidan bšauṭa** DC 46 sorceries performed with a whip; **anatun ʿu abditun zakitun** Jb 11:8 ye, if ye did (it), would succeed; **man ʿtbidbẖ mn qadmaiia kḏ ḏ-biušamin ʿtbidẖ** (var. **ʿtibdẖ**) ibid. who, from earliest times, was treated as Yushamin was treated?; **ha ʿbid** (var. Sh. ʿAbd. **ʿbad**) **uha mibad** (read **mabad**) Gy 368:9 *ecce factum, ecce performatum*; **la ʿbid ula la mibad** Gy 368:15 neither what was done nor what was performed; **abdia umabdia hiia bkušṭa** CP 118:8, ML 144:1 they make and create life in the Truth (cf. Lidzb., ibid. n. 1).

IDIOMS: **qabin abad** to perform a marriage (s. **qabin**); **zipa abid** Gy 391:23 he lies; **buta abad** to pray; **d̠-nitun buta nibdun ʿlai** that they (may) come and pray for me. (Mod. use of **abad** in idiomatic expressions corresponds to that of the P. کردن: **bad ʿbad** = P. کار کرد he worked; **tilipun ʿbad** = P. تلفن کرد he 'phoned; **taršuma ʿbad** = P. ترجمه کرد he translated, etc.).

DER.: **abada, abda, bada, mabada, ʿbada, ʿbidata** (pl.), **ʿubada, šabadata** (pl.). (**abad ukšar** Gy 151:9, 152.15 'he-worked-and-succeeded' is used as a pr. n.).

ABD II (עֲבַד Jastrow 3, ܥܒܕ PSm, J) to pass time, stay, sojourn. **unibdun bmdin mdin** AM and they will tarry awhile in many a city. Not really a separate word, but a special meaning of **ABD I**, see Dalman s.v. 6, Brockelmann LS s.v. 23.

ABD III, AWD, ʿUD (אבד, ܐܒܕ) to perish, be lost, go astray.

PE. Pf. **abad** was lost, perished. With suff, **ʿudun** Gy 96:25 to me they're dead; **abadtinkun** DC 40 she destroyed you (= I destroyed you). Impf. **laniuad ulanistakar** DC 41. 237 neither strays nor is hindered; **(la) niudun** Gs 62:12 they will (not) perish. Act. pt. (often with pass. meaning): **abid, auid** perished, f. **audu** Gs 41:15, pl. **audia** Gy 327:3, 346:14, etc.

ETHPA. Pf. **ʿtauda** Q 34:10 they (f.) are dead.

mindam d̠-abad mitaška AM 143:10 something that was lost will be found; **tibil d̠-audia** Gy 328:7 the perishable world; **auid** (var. DC 22 **abid**) **dahba rhima** Gy 370:11 f. beloved gold will perish; **qabid qurba d̠-ʿmak** DC 41 the approach of thy mother will pass away; **nibulak** DC 37 they will bring thee to naught; **audubun lʿšiul** Gy 313:15 they will perish in the Sheol (or AF.: they will bring them to naught in Sheol); **psiqia uaudia** Gs 65:8 they are cut off and perish; **šuta d̠-audia** Gy 347:4, 11 speech of those who perish.

DER.: **abdana** = **audana, abdunia** = **ʿbdunia** (pl.), **auda 1, mabudia** (pl.).

abda 1 (rt. **ABD I**) slave MG § 89, p. 100:10. Pl. **abdia** AM 17, etc., mod. pl. **abdania** or **abid** AM 199:15 (= Ar. عُبَيد). Gl. 73:12, 121:5. **abda mšauilh̠ br haria ubr haria mšauilh̠ abda** Gy 264:2 f. *sclavum faciunt liberum et liberum faciunt sclavum*; **lanisbat babdia bnih̠** Gy 355:3 f. she did not make his sons slaves; **abdia uamata** (often) slaves and handmaidens; **gabra ṭaba d̠-rahimih̠ abdania** AM a good man beloved by his servants; **abdia kšiṭia** Gy 14:17 true servants.

abda 2 (rt. **ABD I**) deed, work, action. Pl. **abdia** Gs 71:16.

abdala, later **ʿabdala,** عبد الله 'Abdullah. **abdula arabaia** (var. **arbaia**) Gy 229:18, 230:1, 232:13, 233:1, 19 'Abdullah the Arab (= Muḥammad the son of 'Abdullah, cf. Lidzb. Ginzā 223:11); **abdia uamata d̠-abdala** Gy 230:4, 232:20, DAb, etc. slaves and handmaidens of 'Abdullah.

abdana (rt. **ABD III**). 1. perdition, loss, ruin. 2. lost waste, ends of the earth, Abaddons, place of desolation, land of the lost, wilderness. Pl. **abdania,** var. **abdunia, ʿbdunia, ʿubdania, bdunia** MG 49:5 n. 2, 140:6; **udiatbia baudania** Gy 391:9 and those who dwell in desolate places; **ʿbdunia titaiia** Gy 208:5, Gs 27:18, Q 24:1, 8, etc. the lower Abaddons; **ʿbdunia ʿlaiia** Gy 205:7, 206:3 the upper Abaddons; **lbaba d̠-bit ʿbdunia** (var. **bdunia**) Gs 136:15 in the door of the house of Abaddons, Lidzb. Ginzā 206 n. 5; **ṭabdana ṭura** Gy 54:12 Mount-of-Perdition, cf. Ginzā 49 n. 2.

abhar = **bhar** (P. بهار) spring.

abual (Ar. أبوال) offspring, young creature (s. **hurpa 2**).

abugdana, abugbana (Pognon IM no. 25, DC 40. 578 etc.) *Pater Fortunatus* (name of genie mentioned in exorcisms).

abu danab AM 273:13, **abudanab** AM 276:2; **bu danab** AM 273:19 (translit. of Ar. أبو ذَنَب) a comet.

abuzubʿa, abuzaubʿa, buzaubʿa, zaubʿa AM 270:22 (Ar. زَوبَعة) hurricane.

abuṭia s. **habuṭia**.

abula (אַבּוּלָא < Akk. *abullu*) gate, gateway. Pl. **abulia. lgaṭ ʿlai abulia d̠-labṭunan bʿuhra . . . upta ʿlai abula** Gs 130:16 f, antep. f. they locked the gate before me to retain me on the road . . . and he opened for me the gate; **alma labulia babil mṭit** DC 3. 194:15, DC 53. 188:15 I reached the gates of Babylon.

aburia 1 (ܚܨܝܪܐ) reed-mat. **umsabṭia kd̠ aburia** (Jb 156: 12, DC 30: **aubria**) and were joined together like a reed-mat.

aburia 2 Jb 274:8 a pl. of **abara 4**.

aburnaiia (בּוּרְנִי = λιβυρνίς?); or (cf. P. آبرانه) travellers by water? Doubtful) light ships, sailing-boats. **utlatma ušitin aburnaiia ʿtlh** DAb it has 360 small sailing-ships.

aburnaita, abrunaita (cf. אִבְרְיָיתָא) rural place, prairie, grass plain; or (P. آب روان) river. **utlatma ušitin aburnaita ʿtbh̠** DAb and there are 360 prairies (or rivers) in it.

ABṬ I, ʿBṬ (עבט) to bind, fetter, take captive, hold fast.

PA. Pf. **abṭun** DC 43. 1:135 they were captured (?). Impf. (only) with suff. **nʿiabṭh̠** Gs 94:19 we fetter him; **nabṭunik** Gs 77:10 they fetter thee (f.); **labṭunan** Gs 130:7 they fetter me (an unsure form without suff. **niabaṭ** AM 92:antep. prob. a miscopying of **niabad,** cf. BZ 59 n. 6). Pass. pt. **mabaṭ** bound.

ETHPA. **ʿtiabaṭ** (often in exorcisms) was bound, is bound. Impf. **nitiabaṭ,** pl. **nitiabṭun.** Pt. **mitiabaṭ** is, will be, bound.

niabṭh̲ bgu arqa DC 30 we shall hold him captive in the earth; **d̲-la nabṭunik bit maksia** Gs 77:10 so that they do not fetter thee in the custom-house; **ʿsira umabṭa** CP 455:13 bound and captive; **haša maṭarta d̲-man hʿ ulman naṭra uman mabaṭbh̲** Gy 182: 12 f., etc., whose is this purgatory, and whom does it guard, and who is held captive in it?; **kul man d̲-napiq mn pagrh̲ adinqia raza d̲-aba uʿma nitiabaṭ** ATŠ whosoever departeth from the body without the 'mystery of the Father and the Mother' will be held captive; **d̲ mabṭin uqaimin bmaṭarta** Gy 226:15 f.; **nišmata d̲-bgauaiun nitiabṭun** DC 8 souls that are held captive therein; **bhazin maṭarta . . . mitiabṭia umištaiilibh̲ halin gubria d̲-** DC 8 in this purgatory . . . are held captive and put to the question those men who . . .

Der.: **iabaṭṭa, ʿbṭa.**

ABṬ II = **HBṬ** (q.v.) to grind, gnash, clash (?), to shake, brandish (?).

Pa. Pt. pl. **miabṭia (sikinia)** DC 44. 973 they brandish knives. Inf. **abuṭia** DC 13 gnashing (of teeth).

ABṬ III (ܥܒܛ) to grow thick.

Pe. Impf. **nibuṭ zira nišpur umnh̲ nibuṭ** DC 31 seed will thrive and some of it will grow thickly.

abia (= ܥܒܝܐ, **ABA I**) thick, crass, swelling. Fem. sg. st. abs. **abia** MG 110:paen. f., f. pl. st. abs. **abian. abia mn dilh̲** Gy 84:6 that was thicker than himself; **masputita d̲-abia mn kulh̲ alma** Gy 94 a fetter that was stronger than the whole world; **uʿsph̲ abian** DC 31 and his lips (will be) thick.

abid (rt. **ABD I**) slave (used also as pl., s. **abda**): **bṣir kd̲ abid** DC 31 as lowly as a slave.

abihdia (בַּהֲדֵי MG 33:14, 195:10) with, together with, next to. With suff. **abihdh̲** with him, **abihdai** with me, etc.; **ʿlianak uṣbatak d̲-abihdia ʿlianak** CP 93:28 thy thumb and the finger next to thy thumb; **ularaṭin abihdh̲ bildbabh̲** DC 31. 23 and his enemies (will) not speak with him; **abihdia zauaiin** DC 6 together with their husbands; **latiṭaibun abihdh̲** ibid. do not partake (of ritual food) with him; **alipnin abihdan mandaiia** DC 50 we joined the Mandaeans to us; **abihdia nišan** AM 266:11 with the sign; **abihda qaimin** Gy 146:6 they stood by her; **šahqa abihdia ʿsqta** Gy 147:14 she worried about the ring.

abinia = **binia** (בֵּינֵי) between, amongst MG 33:13 f.; **abinia dilh̲ labatur** DAb between him and Abatur; **abinia ahh̲** DC 31 amongst his brethren; **mn binia mania** Gy 336:11 f. from amongst the *mânas*.

abiqata DAb = **biqata** pl. of **biqita** (q.v.).

abira = **bira** (q.v.), var. **abara 6** pit, waterhole, grave, well. **kd̲ mia bhaṣubia ubabiria** DC 44 like water in the waterpot-stands and in the water-holes; **alma d̲-babira atuia** DC 30 until they put me in the grave; **ubabiran** (var. **ubabaran**) **hšuka našk(a)bh̲** DC 22. 445 = Gs 57:18 f. and he shall find darkness in our pit; **babira atunia atnuia** Jb 125:13 f. they put (: thrust) him into the mouth of the stove.

ABL, ʿBL (אבל, ܐܒܠ) to mourn, to wail.

Pe. No pf. found. Impf. **niblun** AM 21:2 they (will) mourn. Pass. pt.: **ʿbil(a)**.

Der.: **ʿbilia, ʿblia** (pl.), f. **ʿbilata** (pl.).

abla = **bla** (q.v.) without.

ablaṭina anbilaṭ DC 44 a spirit invoked in an exorcism.

abluš Gl. 36:7 ابلوج sugar, شكر sweetening.

abliaiil DC 40. 871 an angel.

abna (Akk. *abnu*, Can. אבן) stone. Pl. **abnia 1,** var. **bnia 2. šidiuk kd̲ abna d̲-mihla** DC 21 they cast thee down like rock-salt; **bbnia rigmun** CP 175:4 they stoned me with stones.

abnia 2 = **bnia 1** sons, children MG 183:22, Zotb. 229a: upper text.

ABQ s. **ʿBQ.**

ABR I, ʿBR (עבר, ܥܒܪ) to get over, cross over, pass over, step over, pass through; Af. to bring across, (of illness) to get over, recover; to remove.

Pe. Pf. **abar** (identical with Af.) he crossed; f. **abrat**, etc., pl. **abariun**, neg. **labariun** Jb 186:4 they did not get across; with suff. **abrh̲** he went over (it). Impf. **nibar** ML 59:12 *transi(e)t*; neg. with suff. **labrh̲** Gs 403:5 *non transeam eum* MG 35:13. Impf. **sahra . . . d̲-hazin ṣurta nibar** DC 43, A 13 the devil who crosses this (magic) circle. Impt. pl. with suff. **ʿubruia** (Gy 18:19, var. **ʿbruia**) go across (it) MG 278:23 f. Pt. **abar**, participial pres. **abarna** I (shall) cross, etc.

Af. Pf. as pe., with suff. **abran** he brought me across MG 270:antep.; **abrinun** he brought them across MG 277:13; **abruia** they led him across; **abarth̲** I brought him across MG 277:13 f.; **abirtunh̲** ATŠ II no. 171 ye have ferried her over. Impf. & jussive: **niabar** (often in AM) he will get over; with suff.: **latabrh̲** Gy 218:5 do not transgress (it); **tabrinkun** may she bring you across MG 280: paen. f. Pt. **mabar**, f. **mabra** who carries across, (of illness) recovers; **bišuta d̲-abrat ʿlauaihun** AM 267:23 evil things which have befallen them; **(kd̲) bra ana d̲-man mana smira abritun** DC 6 (ATŠ II no. 164) (when) ye have gone through the prayer 'Whose son am I? Of the Guarded Mana!'; **mabarlun d̲-maṭilh̲ lʿšumia** ATŠ II no. 235 he leads them over until he brings him [*sic*] to heaven; **mambarta d̲-mabra bhiria tabrinkun** CP 79 ult. a ferry-boat that takes over the elect will take you over.

Idioms: Af. with **mahra, kiba** (frequent in AM) to get over an illness; **mabar mahra niabar, tiabar kiba**, etc. Pe. sometimes 'to transgress, deviate'. **man d̲-mn miniltak abar** Gy 33:8 f. who deviated from thy word; **latabrh̲ bʿbidatak** Gy 218 do not transgress in thy actions; **rahmai nibar** DC 34 he neglecteth the devotions; **abar šiqa ʿlh̲** s. **ziqa** b. Gl. 7:9 f. انتقل *transire* نقل كرد ; 18:15 f. ادخل *intro-ducere* اندرون كرد ; 114:7 f. عبر *transire* *pertransire* بنشت ; 152:7 f. من *permittere, possibile esse* گذاشت ; 179:13 f. دخل د *introire* داخل شد.

DER.: **abara 2, abrana, ambura, mabar, mabra, mabrana, mambarta, ʿbra 1.**

ABR II (cf. Akk. *abāru* to be strong) to impress: **ʿuhauqa d̠-rbia abar ʿlh̠** ATŠ and impress upon him (the novice) fear (respect) of his master.

abr(a) = **bra** (q.v.) son MG 25:19, Zotb. 220a: 11, Gl 26:5, 36:9 f., 41:8 (always with a prosthetic a).

abram (אַבְרָם) Abram, mentioned together with the following: **abraham** (אַבְרָהָם) Abraham; **abram uabraham** DC 43 (invocation in an exorcism); **abrahim** (id.) Gy 381:16, Jb 74:12 Abraham; **brahim, ʿbrahim, abrahim nbiha d̠-ruha** Gy 45:14, 46:7 Abraham the prophet of Rūha.

abraš (Ar. أَبْرَش) spotted, parti-coloured, dappled. **humar abraš** AM 129:10 a dappled he-donkey.

abrata = **brata** daughter. **anat abratai dilia** DC 30 thou art my daughter.

abrunaita a var. of **aburnaita**, cf. DAb 10 n. 1.

abrundiata, brundiata (Pl. Etym. unknown) RD 5:360 a kind of fish. (Sg. **brunda** = **prunda**? V. s. **prunda**.)

abruṣa = **bruṣa**.

abrišam, abrišum (P. ابريشم) silk. **gaz uabrišam** WedF 60 = ŠQ 19:8 gauze and silk; **tulita d̠-abrišam** ATŠ I no. 279 silkworm; **abrišum d̠-šuba launia** DC 12. 195, Lond. R. 6412 silk of seven colours.

abrʿil AM (Ṣâb.) a genie.

aga 1 (T.-P. آغا) AM 256:40 Sir, Mr.

aga 2 (var. **auga** = עוגא), used only in pl. **agia** furrows, ruts (often with **ṢRA** to plough and **pdana** the plough, cf. Lidzb. Ginzā 109 n. 6). **bmiṣai agia** CP 121:6 from the middle of the ruts.

aga 3 (cf. Mishn. אגא 'thorn', Löw 146), us. in pl. **agia** twigs: **agia d̠-asa** (frequent) myrtle-twigs, Lidzb. Ginzā 109 n. 6; Drower MMII 105, 121 n. 14, DC 40. 664.

aga 4 (perh. a mere metaph. use of 3), pl. **agia** beams, rays. **agia d̠-nhura** DC 34. 914, CP 342:6 (often) channels of light.

agaiia (הֲגִיָּה, rt. **HGA**) recitations, study: **agaiia d̠-šapir ladakrit** Jb 146:6 thou pronouncest not recitations which are lovely.

agam(a) = **gam(a)** mod. prep. for. **agam arasa** (varr. **agama arasa, agama arsa**) AM 252 (cf. Transl. 69 n. 5) for the bride (Sh. 'Abd.)

agama a var. of **agma**.

agambia, aganbia varr. gambia, ganbia (אַגַּב) prep. beside, over, at the side of, back of. **agambia mia** Gy 380:19 over the water; **mn aganbaiin** (var. **gambaiin**) from beside them; **ʿl agambia, lagambia** to the side of MG 33:16 ff., 196:9, 197:15; **aganbia d̠-kraiia uligria** DC 46. 78:16 the sides of limbs and legs; **ʿl aganbia kušṭa dilak hualan ruhṣana** CP 50:15 = ML 66:4 at the side of thy Kušṭa there is confidence for us, cf. Lidzb. n. 1; **ʿl aganbia ʿušana šadruia** Gy 338 (the Life) sent him on the back of a mare.

agania (ܐܓܢ̈ܐ, אַגָּנָא) plu. bowls, wine-pots, vessels. **mazga agania** Gs 30:21; **agania d̠-rugza mzigan bzmaihun milian** DC 3 vessels of wrath mixed with their blood are filled; **agania hamra** ibid. bowls of wine; **agania d̠-zma mlʿian** DC 44. 554 = Morg. 200:1 bowls full of blood; **aganun** DC 44. 556 their vessels.

aganbia s. **agambia**.

aganpa Jb 44:4 var. of **ganpa**.

agapra a var. of **aqapra** = **apra** (q.v. MG 72 antep.).

agar st. abs. of **agara 1** and **agra**.

agara 1 (rt. **AGR II**), st. abs. (& cstr.) **agar** tie, bond, fastening. **uagar d̠-rišaia (u)mharšaia** DC 44 and a bond of the chief sorcerer; **usidma uagara llišania** DC 43. 138 and a lock and fastening on his tongue.

agara 2 (nom. act. of **AGR I**) hirer, employer.

AGD, ʿGD (אגד) to bind together.

ETHPE. Pf. **ʿtigid kanph̠** JRAS 1937 37:594 her bosom was constricted.

agzaiil DC 40. 879 f. name of an angel.

agzara (rt. **GZR**) being cut-off, banishment, exile, a cut-off (desolate, inaccessible) place. **kd̠ ʿmbra maiit bagzarh̠** AM 26:1 like a sheep (which) dies in an inaccessible place (cf. Transl. 21 n. 5).

agzaraiia, gziraiia (rt. **GZR**) DC 44. 543 those who give a verdict, issue a decree, officers-at-law, v.s. **gziraiia**.

agzarta (nom. act. **GZR**) judgement, condemnation, verdict, sentence. Gl. 121:15 عذاب *supplicium*. Gy 237:14, Gs 19:8, Q 25:14. **ukulman d̠-ʿsura uagzarta nirmibh̠** DC 36 and everyone whom they cast into bonds and condemn; **agzar agzarta** (often) he delivered judgement, or Impt.: deliver judgement!; **rgala uagzarta** DC 43 A 153 fetter and condemnation; **šamadta . . . uagzarta** DC 43 A 59, **šamadta uagzarta** DC 43 A 111 desolation and condemnation.

agzʿil a byname of Sin (the moon). **agzʿil d̠-sin qarilh̠** Gy 120:paen. f. Agziel whom they call Sin.

agla 1, (**ʿgla**) (אגלא) gate. **aglaikun nṭar, nṭar aglaikun** Jb 180:3 f. guard your gates.

agla 2 (גַּלָּא, ܓܠܠܐ), pl. **aglauata** wave(s). Nöld. MG 167:3 f. knew only pl.: Gy 129:16, Q 53:23. **maria agla aglauata** DC 51. 764 f. lord of wave and waves.

agma, var. **agama** (Akk. *agammu*, Syr. ܐܓܡܐ) marsh, swamp, pool, lagoon. Pl. **agmia** and **agmata**, var. **agamata**. **ṣaida d̠-sliq mn agma** DC 21 fisherman who rises from the marsh-pool; **lṭuria uagmata** DC 46. 205:15 mountains and swamps; **agmia d̠-zifa** Jb 149:3 swamps of deception.

AGN (עגן, ܥܓܢ) to cast down, imprison, suppress.

AF. Part. pres. with encl. **mauginiatlh̠** DC 48. 269 thou castest it down.

Ethpe. **umitignat** (read **ʿtignat**) **ʿšata d̲-plan** DC 45 & 46 and the fever of — was suppressed, cast off.

AGR I (**אגר**, ܐܓܪ, اجر, Akk. *agāru*) to hire, employ, reward a service rendered; to give a wage or fee.

Pe. Act. pt. **agar, agra** employer; pass. pt. **ʿgir(a)**, pl. **ʿgiria** hired (servant), hireling, employee. Inf. **migar. mn luṭta d̲-ʿgira uagra d̲-agrh̲ gzilh̲** AO 9, 96:10 and from the curse of the hireling whose employer cuts his wages; **šapir l . . . migar ʿgira** AM 140:14 propitious for hiring a slave; **agra d̲-ʿgira** Gy 19:1, 38:3 etc. wage of a hireling; **gira bagra** DC 12. 299 hireling with employer.

Der.: **agra, ʿgira, agara 2.**

AGR II (cf. **אגר** II J. Rel. to **AGR I**) to tie, bind, cf. ZDMG xxxii 402.

Pe. Pf. **agar**, suff. **agarlh̲, agarlun.** Impf. **nigar.** Pass. pt. **agir. agarlun malalun bpumaihun** Gy 177:9 they became tongue-tied (var. DC 22. 170 **agarlh̲ mamla bpumh̲** sg.); **uagar malalun bpumaiun . . . d̲-badmu ligia mamlilia** Gy 177:8 they became tongue-tied . . . so that they spoke like stammerers; **agir lišanun bpumaihun** DC 44. 1346 their tongues in their mouths were tied; **unigar pkar kul minilia bišata** DC 44 he ties and binds fast all evil words.

Der.: **agara.**

agra (rt. **AGR I**) reward, fee, hire, wage MG 100:10. St. abs. **agar. agra uzidqa** (often) fee and pious gift MMII 189. **agra d̲-ʿgira** s. **AGR I**; **d̲-masia ulanasib** (var. **ulanisib**) **agra** Gy 332:2 f. who heals and takes no reward; **ʿbidata uagria** DC 36 works and wages, rights and dues; **kd̲ ʿubadh̲ uagrh̲** Jb 176:13 like his work is his reward.

agran = **gran** (q.v.) costly, dear, expensive, at a high price. **zabnit agran umzabnit arzan** AM 157:16 f. thou buyest dearly and sellest cheaply.

agrania (P. گرانی with a prosthetic **a**) high price (abstr. noun from **agran** = **gran**). **miṭra mipsiq uagrania nihuia** AM 264:12 rain will be cut off and there will be high market price(s).

agrida = **grida** (q.v.).

ad (**עד**, ܥܕ) while, so far as, until MG 209:12. Neg. **adla** before ibid. ff., cf. also n. 6. **admṭininin** Gy 151:12 until we came, until we reached MG 368:12, 376:11 ff. & n. 2, 466:ult. Gl. 37:1 اذ *ecce, si* حالاً; 130:7 فَإِن *quoniam, si* اگر; 148:10 لَمّا *cum* چون; belong rather s. **d̲** = ܕ q.v.

ADA I, ʿDA I (**עדא**, ܥܕܐ, H. **עדה**) to pass over, pass by, through, make a pass (with the hand).

Pe. Pf. **ada, adat, adit** = **ʿdit** MG 257, pl. **ʿdun** they passed through, **adinin** we passed; with suff. **adaith̲, adith̲** I passed by it MG 288:8, neg. (**ʿl ʿdai**) **ladan** Gy 192:1 did not pass (through my hands); pl. with encl. **adiubh̲** DC 6 they passed with him. Impf. **nidia** ML 82:3, pl. **nidun** *transeunt* MG 259:2; **tidun** *transitis* (formally = **ʿDA** = **ידע** to know). Pt. **adia**, pl. **adin** Gy 252:15 *transeunt(es)*.

Af. Pf. **adia** he brought over, **adit** thou hast brought over MG § 192 (p. 260:26, 261:5); with encl. **adilh̲, adilak** I brought him, thee, over MG 261:9; with suff. **adian** he brought me across, he made me pass by MG 284: antep.; **adih̲** he made him pass by MG 287:10; **adith̲** I made him pass by MG 288:12. Impf. **nadia** he bringeth over MG 261:antep.; with suff. **nadian** he bringeth me over MG 285:5; **nadiak** and **lʿiadiak, ʿiadiak** he bringeth, I bring thee over MG 286:23 ff.; with encl. **ʿiadilh̲, ʿiadilak** I (shall) take him, thee, over. Impt. **adia, adun** Gy 37:16 bring over, make pass! Pt. **madia**, pl. **madin**; part. present **madit, maditun** ATŠ II no. 164 *transportan(te)s*.

udla ada parzla ʿlh̲ latiklun Gy 38:23 *quod ferrum non transiit ne edatis*; **adit mn binataihun** Gy 259 I passed through them; **gabra d̲-ada binaian** CP 179:7 the being who passed between us; **tum adia banpak hatamta d̲-napšak** AM then make a pass across thy face, thy own signing; **uʿl taturaqa latidun** CP 110:15 = ML 136:4, **ʿiadilh̲ ʿdai lganbh̲** Gy 160:6 I pass my hand over his side; **unadia lsikina lraza ṣaurh̲** DC 24 and he shall pass the knife across the mystery of his throat (i.e. cut his throat).

Idioms: Af. to make a ritual pass (**adaita**, pl. **adiata**); with **miša** to anoint. **uadia tlata ad(a)iata** DC 41: 320, ML 57:11 and make three (ritual) passes, cf. n. 2; **kul man d̲-nadia minh̲ mn hazin miša** CP 31:13 = ML 35 any man anointed by this oil (lit. whoever letteth pass on himself some of this oil), cf. ML 35 n. 3; **bruk lmiša uadun** Gy 37:16 say a blessing over the oil and sign yourselves therewith, cf. Brandt MSchr. 67, Lidzb. Ginzā 36 n. 4. Sh. ʿAbd. translates **adia** as 'he gave'. This semantic development 'to pass' = 'to give' (common to many languages) is attested by **ʿdilun** Gy 70:21 I shall give them.

Der.: **adaita (adaiia, adaiata, adiata, ʿdiata), adia, ʿdia, ʿuda.**

ADA II (Pa. **עַדִּי**) to disconnect, sever, remove, detach.

Pa. (identical with Af.). Pf. **adia** DC 41 it disconnected. Impf. pl. **niudun** (read **niadun**) they stray. Impt. pl. **adun. atar uadun napšaikun mn** Gy 179:12, 16 sever and detach yourselves from . . . ; **la niudun mn hdadia** ATŠ I no. 244 let them not stray from one another (if not from **ABD III** = **AUD I** let them not perish from one another, or together).

adadia Sh. ʿAbd.'s copy Gs 17:10 a var. of **adidia.**

adaita (**daita**) (rt. **ADA I** = **ʿDA**, **אַעֲדִיתָא**), pl. **adaiia, adiata, (a)daiata** (**אַעֲדָיָתָא**). (*a*) a pass, a sign made by the finger-tip, signing with the finger-tip, (*b*) pl. means of passage over, rites. Ritual action of the priest when he passes the tip of the forefinger of his right hand from right to left touching the person or thing so signed. (Corresponds to the sign of the cross of the Christians, but is horizontal only.) ML 57 n. 2. (*a*) **ukd̲ madit tlata diata** DC 41 and when thou performest 3 passes; **rušmia udaiata** ATŠ II no. 117 the signs and passes; (*b*) **halin masqata . . . uadiata uᶜkilta d̲-nišimta bgauh̲ mitqaima** DC 34 the *masiqtas* (etc.) . . . are means of passage (*rites de passage*) and sustenance whereby a soul is raised up; **adaita d̲-ma d̲-bh̲** ATŠ II no. 163 the pass at that which is with her.

adakas (= **adam kasia** 'the Hidden Adam') the mystic or occult Adam, Brandt MR 36 n. 2, MSchr. 36, Bousset HpGn 34, 218, Pallis MSt 108 no. 3, Lidzb. Ginzā Ind. s.v., Drower MMII 54, 73, 253. **adakas mana** MR 36 f., Gy 102:6, 127:19, 131:15, 243:8, 244:6 & 13, 245:14 & 18; **adakas ziua** Gy 104:4 ff., 235:25, 241:21, etc.; **adakas malala** Gy 235:17, 236:5, ATŠ (trs.) 237 n. 1; CP 441:8.

adakata, adakiata Gy 69:4 (= **dakiata**, fem. pl. of **dakia** q.v.) *purae*.

adala = **iadala**.

adam (אָדָם) Adam: **adam gabra qadmaia** CP 44:11, 46:11, RD 14 (DAb) Adam the first man; **adam uhaua** Gy 12:22, 100 f. (their creation) Adam and Eve; **adam br adam** Gy 115:25 Adam son of Adam ERE viii 382; **adam kasia** CP 119:13, 361:2, ML 145:3, 269:3 the Occult Adam MMII Ind., HpGn Ind. SA, esp. 21–38; **adam d̲-pagria** Gy 241:4, 337:4 the Physical Adam ibid.; **adam malka d̲-utria** Gy 108:12 Adam the king of the uthras; **adam shaq rba** DAb Adam the Great Shaq (He-was-bright); **malka adam shaq ziua** Morg. 5:3; **adam br ptahil** DAb; **adam rba** Gy 272:2 & 23; **adam riša d̲-šurbta haita** Gy 26:7 Adam the head of the living generation; **škinta d̲-adam** DAb (celestial) dwelling of Adam, etc. Lidzb. Mand. Gl.

adar, dar (אֲדָר, ܐܕܳܪ Bab. *addaru, adāru*) month under the rule of Pisces, called **miṣai situa** MMII 84, SsSs: *Fihrist* آذار.

adar(a) = **dara** (q.v.). **iahbilh̲ ladara** AM 156:1 they give him a dwelling.

adarin (ܐܕܪܘܢ, P. آذريون) camomile Löw 41 f. **aitilh̲ adarin d̲-hu apiun miṣria** AM 128:1 bring him camomile which is an Egyptian drug.

adatan uiadatan two spirits of light (occurs often). Formation ML Ind. & 42 n., DLZ 1913 col. 1805, Jb ii 198 no. 4, Ginzā Ind. According to MMII two 'pointing stars' at the North MMII 246. **ᶜutria d̲-ᶜpaqad liardna qadmaia šumaihun adatan uiadatan** Gy 292 f. the uthras who were set over the first jordan, their name is A. and Y.; **adatan uiadatan d̲-iatbia ᶜl baba d̲-hiia ubaiin lruhia unišmata batra d̲-nhura** CP 23:18 A. and Y. who sit at the door of the Life and pray for spirits and souls in the place of light. Further references Lidzb. Mand. Gl.

aduga, duga 2 (ܐܘܓܐ) fire-oven, furnace. Fem. Gy 111:7, masc. Gy 216:14, MG 159:16 f. Pl. **adugia**. **aduga d̲-nura** Gy 117:10 ἡ κάμινος τοῦ πυρός (Matt. 13:50); similarly **adugia d̲-ᶜšata** Gy 80:16 fire-ovens, and **adugia šrigata** Gy 111:7 heated ovens.

adunai (H. אֲדֹנָי) Adonai, a name given esp. to the sun (Jews being represented as worshipping the sun), used often in exorcisms with **iahu** (יַהְוֶה), cf. Glossaries to IM and AIT. **adonai** = **šamiš** Gy 23:15, 45:11 ff., MR 126:17, MSt 121 f., MMII xxiii n. 2; **šamiš d̲-adunai qarilh̲** Gy 120:14 etc. Š. (: Sun) whom they call Adonai; **adunai ᶜṣṭuna** Gy 333:11 A. the pillar (one of the 7 pillars of Jerusalem); **baba d̲-qra adunai** Gy 120:15 *porta* (: *secta*) *quam creavit A.*; **adunai ṣbabut** DC 43 J 204 f. (frequent) = יְהוָה צְבָאוֹת; **hauma d̲-adunai** DC 36 the heat of A. (= the sun).

adupia, dupia (cf. Akk. *edēpu 'wüten'* Bez., Targ. דּוּפְיָא 'damage to reputation' J. Apparently inf. af. of ***DPA** otherwise not used) rage, fury, ill-repute (?). **šihia adupia** Jb 180:8 eager to fury (Lidzb. Jb ii 178 does not translate the word, cf. n. 3).

adia (rt. **ADA I**) DAb transitory things.

adiaura 1, diaura, diara (mparth. *aδyāvar*) ISK 89. Kessler PRE 167, MG 418 n. 2. Pl. **adiauria**. Used only in st. emph. (A st. abs. or cstr. only in the name **iauar ziua** MG ibid.). (*a*) helper, assistant: **adiaurih̲** Gy 127:18 his helpers; **ulnṣab ziua ᶜhabunun badiauria** CP 170:15 and they gave them to N.Z. as helpers; **adiaura d̲-masiqta** ATŠ ii no. 150 assistant at the *masiqta*; **adiaurih̲ trin tarmidia** DC 42 his assistants are two priests; **mara adiaurh̲** DC 50 the chief celebrant, (*b*) aid, assistance: . . . **uᶜlmasqata uadiauria uzidqa brika d̲-iumia** ATŠ no. 130 . . . and about the *masiqtas* and aids (i.e. means of aiding souls after death) and the Blessed Oblation of the feast-days.

adiaura 2 (from **DUR** by influence of **adiaura 1**) inmate. **adiauria d̲-minh̲ ᶜtigbil** Gy 32 f. inmates that were formed therefrom.

adiauruta, adiaruta, ᶜdiaruta (abstr. n. from **adiaura 1**) help, aid.

adiata = **adaiata** pl. of **adaita**.

adidia (MG 71:4, 312:3 ܥܐ̈ܕܐ 'festivals'; Lidzb. 'oracle-tellers' pointing to עֲדוֹן of the Zkr-inscription ML 22 n. 5; prob. from עדד 'to cut, strip') CP 20:11 priests who cut up victims of sacrifice or animals slaughtered by ritual slaughterers, or plunderers, despoilers. Both meanings may be incorporated in **kumria zabia uadidia** Gy 28:15, Gs 17:10, 27:20 priests (double meaning of *consumers*) slaughterers (double meaning of wolves) and priests that cut up slaughtered victims (double meaning of *despoilers*).

adarbaigan a var of **adirbaiigan**.

adinqia (*עֲדִי + נקי 'free from' Nöld.) without MG 197 n. 3.

adirbaiigan AM 202; **adirbaiišan** AM 283:7 (آذربيجان) Azerbaijan.

adkarta (nom. act. **DKR**) invocation. **adkarta nidkar** DC 40 will pronounce an invocation.

adla (עד + לא) conj. before (followed by impf. as Lat. *antequam* by subj.). **adla niquš uadla nihšuk uadla niqmun bnia minh̲ zuṭia ušiṭuata bnpᶜš nibidulh̲** (Gs 6:15 ff.) before he becometh grey-haired: ere (before) he becometh senile and ere his young children rise up and put him to much shame. But the same construction can refer to the past as well: **adla nihuia hazin daura adla nihuia hazin hua adla nihuia šamiš usira** DC 30 before there was this abode, before (all) this existed, before there were the sun and the moon.

adma = **dma** (q.v.) blood. Gl. 183:6 دم *sanguis* خون.

admasa = **dmasa.**

admu = **dmu** (s. **dmuta**) used with the prep. **b** as a prepositional expression **badmu** like, representing, standing proxy for. **badmu qupia** Gy 225 like apes; **badmu aiar** DC 50 representing (as proxy for) Ayar; **badmu manda d̲-hiia** ibid. representing M–d̲–H. The original meaning 'in the likeness of' could still remain, at least in certain expressions: **badmu hiia asmkuia** CP 92:2 they gave her support in the likeness of the Life, cf. n. 2; **ailu badmu hiia** CP 69:3 they brought her into the likeness of the Life (cf. n. 3, ML 84).

admuta DC 36 no. 284 = **dmuta.**

admᶜil (adam with a theophorous affix) DAb a heavenly being.

adqata s. **dqata.**

adra (אְדְרָא) skin, hide. Pl. **adria. daiua amar duktai badrh̲ d̲-mia hauia** DC 46. 121:6 the demon said: 'my place is in water-skins'. Gl. 70:11 جزيه *census* باج ; 85:3 زوان *zizania* علف ; 137:7 فرض *mutuum.*

adraiia = **draiia** (s. **dra**). ᶜl **ᶜdai** uᶜl **atrin adraiia** DC 30 on my hands and both arms.

adrakta = **drakta** (q.v.). **adrakta** ᶜl **ligrai uhaila lligrai** DC 51. 397 stepping forward to my feet and strength to my feet.

adraša = **draša** (q.v.). **adrašia d̲-malkia** DC 30, Zotb. 226 left col. recitations of kings.

adšir pabugan (آردشير پاپكان) Gy 383:21 Ardeshir (226–41) Ochser ZA 19, p. 76 n. 5, Arṯašīr the Kayān (called Vohuman) son of Spendāṯ of Bahman Yašt iii 17, Gray ZA 19, p. 282.

aha 1 (אַחָא, ܐܚܐ Gen. Sem.) brother. Pl. **ahia** brethren, before suff. **ahu-** MG 99:8, 182:15. With suff. **ahai** my brother(s) MG 176:8, **ahuk** thy brother MG 177:9, **ahak** thy brothers MG 177:10, **ahik** thy (f.) brother MG 177:21, **ahuia** his brother ibid. antep., **ahu** her brother ibid. paen., **ahh̲** his brothers MG 178:13, **ahan** our brothers MG 179:5, **ahun** id. or sg. our brother ibid. 12, **ahukun** your brother ibid. 21, pl. **ahaikun** cf. ibid. p. 180, **ahuhun** var. **ahun** their brother MG 181:22, **aha hurina** (in colophons) half-brother; **ahia d̲-bisra** Gy 18:10 brothers by birth; **ahia d̲-kušṭa** ibid. spiritual brothers (cf. Matt. 12:50). (Gl. 27:14 **aha** اخ *frater* برادر).

aha 2 (from **ha**, cf. Mod. Syr. ܐܗܐ) mod. demonstr. this.

ahab(a) (rt. **AHB** = **YHB**) presentation, giving. **ahab zidqa** Zotb. 226 b:9 the giving of alms; **ahaba d̲-mania** DC 24 the presentation of garments (a form of **zidqa brika** for those who have died not wearing the ritual garment) MMII 214 ff.

ahara = ***hara** (?). **kd̲** (var. **akuat**) **ahara bgunda ukd̲** (var. **uakuat**) **libna bšita** DC 40. 343 f. (var. ibid. 470 f.) '(bound . . .) like a freeman (?) in the army and like a clay brick in the wall'. Doubtf.

aharan DC 9 & 36 = **haran.**

ahata (f. of **aha**) sister MG 99:8, pl. **ahuata** less often **ahauata** MG 168:4. With suff. **ahat** my sister, **ahuat** my sisters MG 175:12 f.; **ahatak** thy sister MG 177:5; **ahath̲** his sister, **ahuatan** our sisters etc.

AHB a later form of **YHB**, **ᶜHB** to give, bestow. Forms with an initial **a** (without ᶜ) are used in the Cl. esp. in the impt. **ahub**, with the encl. **l**: **(a)hablan** give us, **(a)hablia** give me, **(a)hbulia** *date mihi* MG 246:15 ff., while in Mod. Mand. **ahab** he gave, **ahbat** she gave, etc., are the only forms used. Mod. impt. is always **hab** give, **hablan** give us (as often in the Cl., cf. MG ibid.). Gl. 3:15 f. **AHB** اوحى, اعطا [sic] *manifestare, dare* وحى كرد ; 5:9 f. id. اذن *reddere, solvere* ربحا آورد ; 26:1 f. اوف *offerre* نزديك شد ; 60:1 f. جازى *retribuere* جزا داد ; 93:9 سل *tradere* داد ; 131:7 f. (synonymous with **QMA**) قدّم *offerre* پيش برد ; 173:11 f. (synonymous with **WFA**) *reddere, solvere, vendere* ادا كرد ; 180:5 f. دنا *permittere, appropinquare* نزديك شد , گذشت ; ibid.:9 f. دفع *tradere, dimittere, dare, committere* دفع كرد.

Pe. Act. pt. pl. with encl. **ahbilh̲ dnuta** Gy 9:ult. they make submission to him.

Der.: **ahab(a).**

ahbulia = **hbulia**: Gl. 34:9 ارباح *lucrum* فايده ميكند.

AHD (אחד, ܐܚܕ) to close, fasten, shut up, hold fast, grasp, to take over, receive MG § 179, p. 242 & n. 1.

Pe. Pf. with suff. **ahadtinun** Gy 145:19A (var, BCD **ahidtinun** would be a pa.) I shut them MG 282:24; with encl. **uhadulia (babia)** Gs 85:7 and they shut (the doors) in my face; **ahidtulia** (as pa.) DAb ye shut in my face. Impf. **ᶜhud (baba)** Gy 188:2 I shall shut (the door); with suff. **(baba) nihdunh̲** AM 216:9 they (will) close (the gate). Impt. **ahid** (as pa.) MG 242:23 f. **ahud (babik)** close (thy door). Act. pt. **ahid** holding (the hand), helping (idiomatic, below). Pass. pt. **(baba) ᶜhida** CP 51:ult. (a) closed (door). **ᶜt-d̲-babaiun ahid** CP 168:ult. there are (those) who close their doors; **uahid klilak** Gs 78:ult. and grasp thy wreath.

Idioms: **ahid ᶜda** holding the hand (in order to help), helper MG 363 n. 1, Brockelm. LS s.

ܥܡ; ʿ**da** can be omitted: **ahid ʿda uparuanqa** CP 119:13 (often) a helper and saviour; **rahmilh̲ uahidibh̲** DC 31 they are fond of him and help him; **unihdun bʿda minaihun** ATŠ II no. 433 and they should helpfully co-operate with them; **anat tihuilun bahid ʿda** CP thou wilt be a helper to them; **ahid ʿda usimaka** CP 174:4 f. a helper and a support; **ahid bauata d̲-ruhia** ML 12:2, 142:8 he receives (into keeping) the prayers of spirits. (CP 10:14 has **ahib** for **ahid**).

ahda = **hda.** Gl. 177:2 **ahda** واحد, *unus* یکی, ibid.: 5 id. وحد, *seorsus* تنها.

ahdara = **hdara.** Gl. 182:12 **ahdr** دار *atrium* حیاط.

ahu (P. آهو) gazelle, gazelle-skin. **kdub bkaṭa d̲-ahu** DC 46. 226:17 write on a strip of gazelle-(skin).

ahuaz (اهواز) AM 198 Ahwaz, a town in Khuzistan (Southern Iran).

ahudia (apparently an inf. pa. of **AHD**) close to, touching, close against, and not a miscopying of **ahuria**. **uiatib damad ahudia kilta** DC 38 and the bridegroom sits close against the veil, (in contact with) the veil (mosquito-net).

ahuria, ʿ**huria,** ʿ**uhuria** (Talm. אֲחוֹרֵי, Jer. Talm. חורי) behind MG 194:16. **ahuria tarmidia laqaimin** Gy 287:ult. (DC 22. 280: **ahuria d̲** . . .) and they stand not behind the priests.

aḥuš (Ar. حوش, coll.) cattle (as collective). **uaḥuš maitin** DC 31 and cattle (will) die.

ahṭa (rt. **HṬA**) sin. **nišbuq** ʿ**lh̲ ahṭa** (var. **aiṭa**) Jb 61:3 we will loose sin (var. vexation) upon him.

ahiaiil a surname given to Yahweh in an exorcism, alluding to the popular etymology אֶהְיֶה אֲשֶׁר אֶהְיֶה (Ex. 3:13). **iahu iahu d̲-ahiaiil ṣbabut** ʿ**l šidai gabra aziza** DC 40. 949 Y.Y. that (is) Ahiaiil Sebaoth El Shaddai, the powerful being.

ahid ʿ**da** (s. **AHD**) a helper. Always sg.

AHK, ʿ**HK** (Talm. אחך, orig. פ״ע = *עחך = צחק, ضحک, doublet **GHK**) to laugh MG 73 n. 2, 241 n. 1.

Pe. Pf. ʿ**hkat** she laughed MG 241:11; ʿ**hkit, ahkit** I laughed MG 73 n. 2, 241:15; with encl. ʿ**hikibun** I laughed at them 241:17. Impf. not found. Act. pt. f. **ahka** CP 65:9 she laughs, pl. **uahkia** and they laugh.

Af. Pt. **mahik** he laughs; **mahikna** I laugh MG 244:19.

Der.: ʿ**hka.**

AHL (אהל) to spread tent-like, shade, bend over, overshadow.

Only refl.: Pt. **mitahlia. uṭulaihun biardna mitahlia** DC 36 and their shadows overshadow the running water.

ahl (Ar. أهل) people. **ahl pisad** (= اهل فساد) AM 280:13 people of corruption.

ahla (Talm. אֲהָלָא from Akk. *uḫulu*) soapwort, Löw, no. 11, p. 42. **šaipia** ʿ**daihun bahla ṭaba uṣabun** DC 38 and they shall rub their hands with good soapwort and soap; **hauariun** ʿ**daihun bahla ṭaba** DC 34. 1133 they washed their hands with good soapwort.

ahmaṭ (احمد) pers. n. Aḥmad (in colophons, sometimes **ahmad**). **ahmaṭ br bizbaṭ** (var. **biṣbaṭ**) Aḥmad (= Muḥammad) son of the wizard B, cf. Ginzā 30 n. 3.

ahriaiil DC 40. 1001 a genie.

ahrima (rt. **HRM**), pl. **ahrimia** banned, excluded, excommunicated. **bnia ahrimia** DC 40 outlawed sons.

AWA I (cf. ܐܘܐ, a supposed rt. of **auana**). Pe. impf. **ulaniuia bišia** DC 37. 515 and the evil (spirits) will not remain.

AWA II (עָוָה, ܥܘܐ) to howl, cry.

Pe.? Impf. ʿ**iai tuiia** ʿ**lak** DC 43 I 102 'Woe' thou wilt bewail thyself.

Nom. ag. Pa.: **mauiana** PD 807 howler.

Der.: **auata.**

auaza (אַוְזָא, ܘܙܐ, ܘܐܙܐ Ar. وَزّ, إِوَزَّة) goose, f. **uauaza mnaktalik** JRAS 1938 2:20 and a goose shall bite thee (f.).

aual (Ar. أوّل, mod. & coll.) the first. Sometimes with the Ar. article ʿ**l aual** AM 261:34, or **al aual** (ٱلأوّل), or **laual** (ٱلأوّل). **tišrin** ʿ**l aual** AM 261:34 ܬܫܪܝ ܩܕܝܡ (Oct.), **kanun aual** (ܟܢܘܢ ܩܕܝܡ) (Dec.) **aual situa** first month of winter (Šabaṭ), **aual bhar** first month of spring (Ayar), **aual gaiṭa** first month of summer (Ab), **aual paiiz** first month of autumn (Mašrwan) MMII 84; **ium aual,** or **auali** (coll.) the first day.

auana (OP *avahana*, Pahl. *avan*, Aram. ܐܘܢܐ, אַוְנָא) quarter, precinct, dwelling-room MG 136 no. 1. Found only in pl. **auania. bauania manda** CP 122:16 in the precinct of the cult-house; **bauania d̲-hilbunia** DC 34, ATŠ II no. 318 in the dwelling-rooms of the houses; **bauania auania** ʿ**tiksun** Gy 333:1 f. they hid in various quarters; **bauania d̲-iardna** in the neighbourhood of the river.

auar (P. *apar* = اوار) devastation, ruin, oppression MG xxxii. 305:10 f. No st. emph. **bqiniana ubanašuta auar nihuia** Gy 385:7 devastation will take place amongst cattle and people (var. **auad** DC 22); **auar banašia nišbuq** Gy 385:13 and he will loose devastation amongst people.

auata (rt. **AWA II**) DC 43 griefs, wailing, mourning.

aubaria 1, aubria, ʿ**buria, auburia** (עֲבוּרָא, ܥܒܘܪܐ) AM 167:19, var. **ababia** (cf. BZ 104 n. 8). **aububa** Par. 26 dense undergrowth, plants, vegetation. Us. in pl. or collective.

aubaria 2 = **abara** 4. **aubaria blišanun usikia bpumaiun** DC 26. 588 & 44. 611 bolts on their tongues and wedges in their mouth.

aububa, aubura s. **aubaria** 1.

auburia = **aubaria.**

aubiria s. **aubra.**

aubra, ʿubra (< ܥܘܩܒܪܐ) mouse (still used); (possibly **ab ʿbra** 'father of needles') porcupine, mentioned in lists of animals with the hedgehog BZ 173 n. 2. Var. **aubiria** (pl.). **aubra uqunpud dairia bhabara** ATŠ I no. 255 the porcupine (or the mouse) and the hedgehog dwell in darkness; **uaşlunia uaubra uqunpud . . . daiuia minaihun naidia** ATŠ I no. 256 and owls and porcupine and hedgehog . . . devils fear them.

augia (עוּגְיָא) DAb a rare but better var. of **aga, agia 2** furrows, ruts.

augunlia, auginia (cf. preceding) ploughed fields; (cf. Talm. אוגייא), beds (of plants), spaces of land divided by irrigation ditches. **bdišta ḏ-radia pdana auginia bmişai agia** AM 121:6 f. (var. Şâb.'s copy **bdišta bdukta ḏ-radia pdana ʿlḥ auguniia**) in the track which the plough drives in ploughed fields in the midst of the furrows.

AWD = **ABD III.**

AUD (עוד, ܥܘܕ, cf. Ar. تَعَوَّدَ) to exist, continue to be, occur, persist. Mod. The only form found: Pt. ethpa. **mitauad: ʿlat bpagrḥ mitauad** DC 46. 64:8 disease persists in his body; **ḏ-ʿlat ukiba mitauadbun** ibid. 65:2 so that disease and pain continue in them.

auda 1 (rt. **ABD III** = **AWD**), pl. **audia** transitory, perishable things, things which cause to perish, sg. loss. **umparqilḥ mn audia** DC 40 & 50 and he will deliver him from (causes of) destruction.

auda 2, ʿuda (ܐܘܕܐ) kindling-wood, (fire-)brand; (Ar. عود) staff, stick (s. **ʿuda**). **zibna biuma auda** CP 28:7 once a day (needs) a firebrand. **audak** DC 44. 1967 s. **ʿuda.**

audana (rt. **AWD** = **ABD III**) wilderness. Pl. **audania** MG 49:5, 136:6. **uanašia ḏ-hauin baudania uazlin ʿl anašia ḏ-iatbia bbatia** Gy 389:19 and the people who are in the wilderness march against the people that dwell in houses.

AUṬ, ʿUṬ (ܥܘܛ, a supposed rt. of **aiṭa**).

auira, ʿuira blind. Gl. 30:4 **auira** اعمى *caecus* كور.

AUL I, ʿUL (עול, supposed rt. of **aula 1** = **ʿula 1, aulana**).

AUL II = **ALL** (transition from ע״ע to ע״ו in certain forms, s. **ALL**). **unišimta mn pagra lʿiil** ML 80:8 and he brings the soul out of the body, cf. n. 2, is a mistranslation as appears in CP 64:ult to 65:1 **ḏ-šaria ruha unišimta mn pagra ʿl ʿiil** who freeth spirit and soul from the body, up there (etc.).

aula 1, ʿul(a) 1 (עַוְלָא, ܥܘܠܐ) evil, iniquity, crime, injury MG 7:20, 23:22. **aula uṭiba uglala tihuia** Gy 385:22 there will be injury and drowning and hail; **aula ušiqra** Gy (DC 22. 53) evil and deceit; **şauma ḏ-aula** Gs 35:8 abstention from iniquity; **bnia aula** Gy 179:21 wrongdoers, criminals.

aula 2, ʿula 2 (עוּלָא) embryo, fœtus. **ʿnšaihun aulaihun niahṭa** DC 31 and their women will miscarry their embryos.

aulana (from ܥܘܠܐ, with a nominal suff. **-na**) wrongdoer, miscreant, criminal MG 138: antep. Var. **ʿulana 1** (s.v.). **aulana damia rumana . . .** Gy 216:1 f. the wrongdoer resembleth a pomegranate . . .

auma 1 JRAS 1937 590:13 a var. of **alma** (P. Anastase's copy).

auma 2 DC 22. 85 a var. of **hauma** Gy 91:3.

aumara (Ar. أُمَرَاء, pl. of أمير) the princes. **ulagiṭlu ʿl aumara ḏ-aqamḥ** AM 283:38 and he will captivate princes he encountereth.

AUP, ʿUP, APP (ܥܘܦ) to double (s. **APP**).

Der.: **aupa 5, ʿupapa.**

aupa 1 (אוּפְיֵי, אופיא, ܥܘܦܐ) branch, stem, foliage MG 100:20. Pl. **aupia**, later **aupania** leaves, foliage. Per. ext. sprouting, output. **aupa ḏ-gupna** (often) the stem of the vine; **auph ʿutria** Gs 37:20, ML 72:9 his branches are the uthras; **anpiš aupaihun parsia** ML 203:3 f. = CP 167:ult. their foliage was far outspread, **mn aupa ḏ-šušma hiura** ATŠ II no. 317 some of the output of the white sesame-plant.

aupa 2 (metaphor. ext. of **aupa 1**) hair. **aupia rišiḥ** JRAS 37 591 the hair of his head, cf. ibid. 600 n. 2; **mbaṭal auph mana rba ḏ-brišḥ ḏ-daiua** DC 37. 182 f. spoilt is his hair, the great (head-)dress that is on the demon's head.

aupa 3 (אופי) character, disposition. **auph uparşuph** ATŠ II no. 353 his character and his personality.

aupa 4 (אופיא) foam, froth. **aupia mia** DC 40 (often, cf. l. 141) the foam of the water.

aupa 5 (rt. **AUP** = ܥܘܦ) increase, intensification, doubling. **mn aupia ḏ-ziua umn ʿupapia ḏ-nhura** CP 402:7 from intensification of radiancy and from redoublings of light.

AUQ, HUQ I = **HQQ II, ʿUQ** (ܥܘܩ) to be anxious, worry. Used only in act. pt. pe. ***aiiq**, f. **aiqa**, m. pl. **aiqia.** (Coll. *wayyeq*, cf. *χolqedî wayyeq* = P. خلقش تنگ است he is anxious.) All other forms are from **HUQ** MG 71:17 ff. As an impers. verb used in f.: **laiqia ḏ-aiqalun** Gy 369:4 to the anxious who are anxious MG 365:14 f.

Der.: **aqa (aqata) 1 & 2, aquta (aqu, aqut), aqta.**

AUR I & II, ʿUR I & II, YUR (the double weak rt. עור to awake, waken, was completely confused with יהר to shine, so that both are represented by the same rt. of double meaning. Even the context often admits either meaning, cf. Lidzb. ZDMG 61 697 n. 2, ML 88 n. 3.) (*a*) to stir up, arouse, awaken, (*b*) to shine, enlighten, brighten, dazzle.

Pe. Pf., impf., and impt. are replaced by **ATR** (q.v.), a secondary rt. formed from the ethpe. MG 251 n. 2. Act. pt. pl. **airin** they awake MG 250:11.

Pa. (identical with Af.). Pf. with suff. **airḥ** he woke him, **aiartḥ** I woke him, **airuia** they woke him up MG 253:1 f.; **airuiḥ lbuna** Gs 1:10 they woke to life the edifice (: the body). Impf. (with ʿ before the 1st rad.) **ʿiaiar** I wake

MG 244:15. Impt. with suff. **airẖ (lkulẖ ginzak) ʿlan** CP 348:14 let (all thy treasure) shine upon us. Pt. act. & pass. **maiar** he awakens, or (is) awakened MG 252:ult.; with encl. **(ulibẖ) maiarlẖ** Jb 109:1 (and his heart) awakeneth him; **(la) maiarlun (libaihun)** CP 128:3 (their heart) awakeneth them (not), pl. with encl. **mairilin** Gy 288:6 they arouse, or enlighten, them. Inf. **aiuria** to arouse, or to enlighten.

Af. (mostly identical with Pa.). Pf. with suff. **airinun (lkulhun tušlimiẖ)** CP 386:15 he awakened (all his perfections). Impf. with suff. **nairẖ (lkulẖ ginzẖ)** DC 36 he shall let (all his treasure) shine forth. Nom. ag. **mairana, maiirana** awakener (s.v.).

Ethpe. Pf. **mazruta ʿtirat ḏ-baiia mašpal lmarba** DC 41.434 the semen awoke, seeking to fall in the womb. Pt. pl. **mitirin** ATŠ II no. 14, fem. **mitiran** *excitatae sunt* (var. **mtairan** ethpa.) MG 251:anteantep.

Ethpa. (with ʿ = i before the 1st rad.): **ʿtiaiar (minaihun trin anašia)** Gy 380 there survived, or were waked to life, revived (from them two persons); a shorter (haplological) form **ʿtiar (mia hiia lškinatun)** CP 73:4 = ML 90:1 (the living water) shone (in its *škina*), cf. MG 62 n. 2, f. **(nišimta uruha) ʿtiairat** DC 47 (the soul and the spirit) was [*sic*] awakened, (without ʿ before the 1st rad.:) **(ruha) ʿtairat** DC 34 (the spirit) was awakened; with encl. **uʿtiarlia (libai)** Gy 130:15, 16 (and my heart) was awakened within me; **tʿaiarbun** Gy 238 was illuminated by them. Impf. **nʿtiaiar** MG 5:17, **(ḏ-nihuia) unitiaiar (unitqaiam alma hazin)** DC 22. 160 (so that this world) might (come to existence) and be awakened (and be established); **nitiaira (halin nišmata)** DC 42 = CP 72:6 (these souls) shine, or are illumined, or called to life; the same form with a sg. **nitiaira nišimta** ML 89:9 may the soul shine (where one would expect **titiaiar**, cf. n. 2). Impt. **ʿtiaiar**, special pl. **ʿtiairun**. 292:antep., etc., be awakened, attentive! Pt. **(uminaihun dilun) mitiaiar (alma)** Gy 245:7 (and from them the world) came to life, f. **mitaira**, pl. **mitairia, mitairin** revived, awakened, vigilant, enlightened, f. pl. **mitairan, mtairan** MG 251:antep.; **šinta lamitiaria škibun** DC 34. 776 they slept a sleep from which they will not waken. Inf. **ʿtiaiuria (mia hiia)** CP 72:5 = ML 88:8 (with) the shining (of the living water), or as (the living water) shines; **lmitaiuria** ML 182:6 with a better var. **lmitiaiuria** CP 152:3 to rouse; **ulamaprišilin ulamauralin** (var. DC 22. 283. **ulamaurilin**) **ulamairilin** Gy 288:6 and they neither teach them, nor instruct them or arouse (or enlighten) them; **hin airin umitiairin umaiarlun mana** Gy 290:12 if they awake and are vigilant and the Mana instructeth (or enlighteneth) them . . .

Der.: **aiar 3, airuta, aria 2,** cf. **iura, ʿura, ʿra,** pl. **ʿria 1, 3, ʿruta,** fem. **ʿrta.**

AWR, ʿWR (with a mobile cons. ו, ܥܘܰܪ, عَوِرَ, H. עִוֵּר) to (be) blind, dazzled (by light).

Pe. **nʿuar, niuar** will be blind MG 242:3 f., 247 n. 2, **niurun** they are blinded. Pass. pt. **ʿuira, auira** (s. vv.).

Pa. Pf. **(ḏ-bʿdẖ) auar (ainẖ man hauilẖ asia)** Jb 182:12 f. (he who, with his own hand,) blinded (his eyes, who shall be his healer?); with suff. **aurinun lainẖ** Gy 151:19 he blinded his eyes, **auartinun lainẖ** Gy 145:8 I blinded his eyes (formally identical with 'she blinded', 'thou didst blind', var. **auritinun** DC 22. 140 only 'I blinded'). Impf. with suff. **atiaurinun** (read **tiaurinun**) **lainaihun** DC 44 thou blindest, or she blindeth their eyes. Impt. **auar aina ḏ-daiua** ibid. blind the eyes of the demon!; with suff. **aurinun (lainẖ)** Gy 151:17 blind (his eyes) MG 282:13. Pt. (act. and pass.) **mauar,** f. **maura,** f. pl. id. **maura ainaihun** Gy 180:7 their eyes are blinded. Participial pres. with suff. **tiaurninun** [*sic*, read **miaurinun**!] **umitaršinun** DC 44 we blind and deafen them.

Af. Impf. with suff. **naurunan** Gs 75:8 they (may) blind me.

Ethpa. Pf. (without **t** in the pref.) **ʿiauar** was (or were) blinded MG 213:19. Pt. pl. **mitauria (libia hadua)** Gy 370:12 f. (rejoicing hearts) are blinded (DC 22. 366 f. has **matauria lilbẖ hadẖ,** read **hadia** 244:21).

Der.: **auira, ʿuira.**

auraita a var. of **ʿuraita** Gy 56:8 (Sh. 'Abd.'s copy).

auruz, aurus (cf. אורוס of Jewish bowls Lidzb. Mand. Gl.) Gy 59:5, 7 Oros, Oreus MSchr. 97 n. 2, Jb ii 20, Ginzā 52 n. 6, OLZ 25 col. 54 (identified with Orpheus = Christ by Lidzb. Cf. S. A. Cook, *Schw. Lect.* Pl. xxxix. 3).

auša (Ar. أَوْج) AM 286:8 zenith, apogee.

aušpiza a var. of **ašpinza** (q.v.).

auta a var. of **ata** (q.v.).

autrana, atrana (עוּתְרָא, ܥܘܬܪܐ 'wealth' + nominal suff. **na**) prosperity, plenty, wealth. **autrana lmašqiana** Or 332:7 prosperity to him that administers the potion.

az 1 (rt. **AZZ** = **ʿZZ**) power. **baz** DC 22. 51:2 with power (?, var. Gy 54:20 **baṭla**!).

az 2 (rt. **AZZ** = **ʿZZ**, an abbr. of **aziz 2** q.v.) name of a spirit: **baz rba** ML 22:5 by the Great Az ML Ind.

(**AZA I** s. Af. **ZHA I.**)

(**AZA II** mod. s. **ZGA** = Af. **SGA.**)

azabid, var. **azbid** (Ar. أَزَابِيد pl. of زَبَد) mod. DC 31 & 46 butter, cream.

azahʿil DC 48 (illustration) a personified banner.

azazan (rt. **AZZ**) DC 40 name of a spirit.

azaziaiil, azaziʿl, azazʿl & varr. (rt. **AZZ** = **ʿZZ** with a theophorous ending) Gy 129:2, 167:9, 173:21 an uthra.

azara Gl. 32:15 ازار *sindon* كفن ; 84:5 ردا *pallium,* 147:11 لِفَافَه *sindon.*

AZB, ʿZB (עזב) to forsake, abandon. Pa. to release, relieve, remove.

Pe. Impf. (optative) **latizbinan** CP 106:17 = ML 132:4 do not abandon us (Lidzb. read **latizlinan** do not despise us, cf. n. 1).

Pa. Impt. with and without suff. **azbun azib rugun** DC 40. 951 relieve them, remove their anger (read rugzun).

Der.: **ʿziba**, f. **ʿzibta** (originally pass. pt. pe.).

azga (ࡀࡆࡂࡀ) a vault. Var. **zga** s.v. **d-sagdia lazga ulibna** CP 106:10 = ML 131:14 who worship a vault and a brick, similarly Jb 140:9 f., cf. ii 114 n. 2; **zabnanak azga bnpiš** DC 30 I shall buy thee a vault at a high price. (Here the *vault* can be used metaphorically for the *bier*, a usage which might be influenced by Aram. רבע 'to lie down').

azgauaia (from **azgauita** with nominal suff. **-aia**) glass-blower, a man with an unclean trade MG 142:4. Pl. **azgauaiia**. **minilia hakima lsakla aiak mania hiuaria lazgauaia** Gy 217:13 (var. DC 22. 210 **azgauaiia**) words of a wise to a fool are like white clothes for a glass-blower (var. glass-blowers).

azgauita = **zgauita, zgagita**. Var. **azgauaita**. **mania d-azgauita** Gy 281:10 glass vessels; **minziz kd azgauaita** ATŠ I no. 200 will be brittle like glass; **gupta d-azgauaita** DC 44. 1, **kapta d-azgauita** Morg. 225/27: ult. (= **kapta d-zgauita** Q 24:31) a glass receptacle, cup.

azdai a genie IM Gl., AIM Gl.

azuʿlaʿil DC 22 & 43 etc. a spirit of power.

AZZ, ʿZZ (עזז, ܥܙܙ) to strengthen, refresh, make powerful, invigorate. Used only in pa. and derivatives.

Pa. Act. pt. **maziz** strengthening, reviving, refreshing MG 71:2, 131:10, 244:16; **mazaz** DC 22. 9 not a pass. pt. but a var. of **maziz** Gy 9:9 **aziṭ** (read **azit**) **uzakit** DC 44 thou gavest power and victory (treated as ל״י by influence of the following **zakit**).

Der.: **az, azazan, azazʿil, aziz(a)**,

azihiata for **aziliata** (rt. **AZL III**) ? **aziliun tlata azihiata** [*sic*] **d-mia** DC 50. 257 they stirred the water thrice (three stirrings: **aziliata** for **azihiata**).

aziza, abs. **aziz** (rt. **AZZ** = **ʿZZ** ࡏࡆࡆ) strong, harsh, powerful. Fem. **azizta, aziztia**. Pl. **azizia**, later **azizana, azizania**. Fem. pl. **azizata**. **mihla azizta** DC 40. 902 powerful salt; **qašiša uazizia** (read **uaziza**) **utaqipa** AM 32:16 stern, harsh, and domineering; **ʿnšia azizata zidniata** IM nos. 16 & 17 powerful and violent women; **malkia azizania utaqipia** DC 40. 963 powerful and mighty spirits; **dina aziza** Jb 176, DC 48. 396. Used as name of a spirit; **baz rba ubaziz rba** CP 20:9, by the great Az and by the Great Aziz (prob. identical with the Aram. deity עזיז ML Ind.); **libat azizta** DC 40. 643 powerful Venus.

aziṭ s. **AZZ**.

azil (Ar. عزل) AM 155:9 retiring, loving solitude BZ 97 n. 5.

aziqum (read **azirum**, P. آزرم) courtesy, respect. **aziqum lhdadia lanibdun** AM 217:3 they show no courtesy to one another, BZ 132 n. 1.

AZL I (**ʿZL III**) (אזל, ࡀࡆࡋ) to go, move on, set, leave, depart.

Pe. Pf. **azal** (worse var. **azil** identical with pt.) he went, they went, special pl. form **azaliun** they went, **azlat, ʿzlat** she went, **azalt** thou didst go, **azlit, ʿzlit** I went MG 241. Impf. **nʿzal, nizal, nizil** *i*(*bi*)*t*, *i*(*bi*)*mus*, **tizal**, rarely **tʿzal** *i*(*bi*)*s*, **ʿzal** I (shall) go, pl. **nizlun, tizlun** they, ye (will) go MG 242. Impt. **ʿzil**, worse varr. **azil, ʿzal** go! ibid. Pt. **azil**, f. **azla**, m. pl. **azlin, azlia**, f. pl. **azla(n)**. Participial pres. **azilna**, f. **azlana** I (shall) go, with neg. **lazlana** I (f.) do not go, **azlinalh**, var. **azlanalh** I go to her MG 231, **azlinin** we (shall) go MG 14:22, 35:24, 242:ult. Inf. **mizal** going MG 243:2; with suff. **mizlai** my going MG 176:18, **mizlak** thy going, **mizlh** his going MG 178:3, **mizlaikun** Gy 17 your going; **uazlit ʿzlit** Gy 138 I (definitively) went; **asgia ʿzil** go, depart! (s. **SGA**); **pahra uazil** Gy 102:10 fleeth and goeth away (s. **PHR I**); **asgit luat abahatai mizlai** Gy 352:15 I went, my going (was) to my fathers (: my Father) MG § 269 with further examples; **ʿuhra d-ahia kulhun zlibh** Gs 56:13 (Sh. 'Abd.'s copy) the way all my brothers go (pt. with aphaeresis of the 1st rad. and with encl.); **azla mia** (s. **ZHA**); **šapir . . . bʿuhra mizal** DC 3 & 31 prosperous for travelling by road; **udukrania mn tibil azilh uʿt d-azilh kd gira** ATŠ i no. 291 and the commemorations are going from the earth and some of them go like an arrow (**azilh** = **azilia** pro **azlia**, **azlin** by analogy of the sg.); **aziliun . . . luat ṭura d-sinai uaziliun luat kinta d-ruha** HG they set off towards Mount Sinai, and they kept going to the community of Rūha.

Idioms: **azal l** or **ʿl** to attack, march against (aside from 'to go to' or 'for'): **malka lbild-babh nizal** DC 31 and the king will go out against his enemy; **azla zban** DC 3 occasionally, on occasion; **lkul ṭabu azla** ML 69:1 it suiteth anything.

Der.: cf. **ʿzlat**.

AZL II (Ar. عزل) to retire, abdicate. **malka d-babil iazul** (var. Ṣâb.'s copy **iazal**) **mn atrh** AM 264:26 the king of Babylon will abdicate from his position, cf. BZ 167 n.; **malka d-marba iiuzul lṭau**ع **hurina** a king of the west will enter into a new submission.

AZL III, (**ʿZL I**) (עזל, ܥܙܠ) to twist round, twine, spin, weave; to stir (around).

Pe.: **ʿzlat** she span. Inf. with suff. **mizlun** DC 36 their weaving, twisting.

Pa. Participial pres. **mazilna mia** Gy 191 I stir water, **mia mazlit** DC 27. 102 thou stirrest the water round.

Der.: **azla, ʿzala**, cf. **ʿzlat**.

azla (rt. **AZL III** = **ʿZL**) net. Pl. **azlia**. **kulhun azlia uaqia ulihia** Jb 156 all the meshes, garotting-nets and fishing-nets.

azma = **zma**.

azmiuz a place-name? **azmiuz hamra** CP 178:16, ML 218:4 wine of Azmiuz, cf. n. 2.

aznaqita (cf. H. זנק, Syr. ܙܢܩ to cast, hurl) a caster-down, a binder (?). Fem. **la huatalak ruha baznaqita** CP 457:17 Rūha was not for thee a binder (?), or R. did not hold thee in thrall (?, cf. J. s.v. 2), CP 291 n. 2.

AZP = **YZP.**

AZQ (עזק) to compress, lay low. **aziq mn qudamaihun malkauata ḏ-ruhmaiia** Morg. 263/16:41 before them the kingdoms of the Romans are laid low (?) MMII 18 n. 8.

azrun name of a genie IM Gl.

-ah (־ָהּ) a rare form of the suff. of the 3rd p. sg. fem., v.s. **-a** 3 and **-h̠.**

AṬA I (ܥܛܐ, H. עטה) to cover, hide. **mahu ṭaṭat marba** DC 3 what is that which the womb conceals?

AṬA II (טעי, ܛܥܐ) to seduce. **nsabth̠ ulibh̠ aṭa** JRAS 1937 597:6 she took him and his heart was seduced.

aṭaualqan (Ṣâb.'s copy of AM) = **ṭaualqan** a city in the climate of Mercury.

aṭaṭa: **ṭaṭa** (ܐܛܛܐ from אטד, اطد) thorn, thorn-bush, thistle MG 43:3. **kuba uaṭaṭa** Gy 12:10, Gs 13:17, Jb 45:15 thorn and prickle, thistle and thorn.

aṭama for **ṭama** 1 in **aṭaman** Gy 309:3 our judgement.

aṭar (rt. **ʿṬR** I) for a long time, as long as (correlative of **alma ḏ**) MG 203:1, 221:6, 238 n. 2. **aṭar huitbh̠** (var. DC 22. 321 **ahuitbh̠**) **urbitbh̠ alma ḏ-hnatalh̠ labuk** Gy 323:16 thou didst stay in it and enjoy it as long as it pleased thy father; similarly Gy 324:1 f.; **aṭar siblit udaribh̠ balma** Gs 42:6 f. for a long time I suffered and dwelt in the world; similarly Gs 45:16; **aṭar madkarlh̠ lšuta ḏ-utria** Gy 115:21 remembering for a long while the speech of the uthras.

aṭaria, ṭaria (rt. **ṬRA**) shaking down, or out. Doubtf. **uṭarilun minh̠ mn aṭaria** Jb 155:9 and beat them (: the fish) out of it (: net) with shaking-out (?), cf. Jb ii 158 n. 2.

aṭarpa = **aṭirpa** (q.v.).

aṭarpan, aṭirpan a demon Ginzā Ind. **aṭarpan ulupan trin singiania ḏ-alma** Gy 98:1 A. and L. the two viceroys of the world.

aṭunia (ܐܛܘܢܐ) thongs, straps. **apkartinun baṭunia kaprun** Jb 148:3 f. I bound them with thongs (: ropes) of fibre (ropes are made of palm-fibre in ʿIrāq).

aṭirpa (אטרפא, ܛܪܦܐ) leaf, pl. **aṭirpia** leaves, foliage MG 33:6 & n. 1, 100:ult. Var. **aṭarpa**, pl. **aṭarpia.** Also nutriment, food. **baṭirpia ḏ-klilak mitgadlia** CP463:12 they are intertwined with the leaves of thy wreath; **ulaiit ziua ḏ-šamiš ḏ-damilh̠ lhad aṭirpa ḏ-klilh̠** ATŠ I no. 98 and there is no ray of the sun comparable with one leaf of his wreath; **aṭirpia ḏ-klila** Gy 5:21 foliage of the wreath; **aṭirpa ḏ-bina** DC 37 a tamarisk leaf; **mn aṭirpia ʿhablia minh̠** Jb 173:5 he gave me of its leaves; **lqurqubana** [*sic*] **ulšuba aṭirpia ḏ-ʿtbh̠** DC 48. 26 f. to the stomach and its seven nutriments.

aṭlala Gy 67:ult. = **ṭlala.**

aṭma (עָטָם, ܥܛܡܐ) thigh, side, flank, hip, loin, upper part of the thigh Ginzā 29 n. 1. Pl. **aṭmata** (ܥܛܡܬܐ) found only in Gl. 129:13 **aṭma, aṭmata** فخذ, افخاذ *crus* باشند. **kiba nihuilh̠ baṭma** AM 27:penult. he will have pain in his thigh; **hirbia laṭmai rmalia** DC 13 he put his sword on my thigh; **alma laṭmai qamit bmia** Gy 337:13 up to my thighs I stood in the water, id. Gy 338:7; **aṭmaihun** Gy 28:5, **aṭmaiun** Gy 226:14 their thighs; **alma lrubaia ḏ-aṭmak** ML 20:12 up to a fourth of thy thigh(s); **šingdunia baṭma** v.s. **šingdunia.**

aṭnupia = **ṭnupia**: **aṭnupia udaštana** Jb 96:1 uncleanness and menstruation.

AṬP I, ʿṬP I (ܥܛܦ) to turn, turn back, return.

Pe. Pf. **aṭap** he turned back, they turned back MG 241:6. Impf. Act. pt. fem. **aṭpa** (**nišimta**) DC 41. 525 (the soul) returns.

AṬP II, ʿṬP II (YṬP) (עָטַף, ܥܛܦ, H. עטף I) to wrap oneself in, clothe oneself.

Af. 1. (as from פ״א = פ״י) Pf. **auṭip** (**banhura kalalh̠**) Morg. 245/77:9 = Q 42:25 he covers his wreath with light. 2. (as from פ״ע) (**balbuš ḏ-nura lbišna**) **umaṭpinabh̠** (one would expect **umaṭipnabh̠**) DC 44 (I clothe myself in a garment of fire) and I wrap myself therein.

Der.: **aṭpia.**

AṬP III (related to **AṬP II**, cf. H. עטף II) to droop, languish, be lax, loose. **aṭap unpaṣ ṭunaihun** DC 34 they drooped and shed their fruit.

aṭpia (rt. **AṬP II**) veils, coverings, shroudings. Only in pl. **ʿuṣrai ḏ-šrabh̠ hiia baṭpia šaduih̠** (var. **ašduih̠**) Gs 39:5 my mind, in which life dwelt, here they cast into a shrouding; **aṭpia habara** Jb 100:6 shroudings of darkness.

AṬR I, ʿṬR (עֲטַר) to go back, to drive away, be driven away, go away, go off, disappear, come to an end; with **mn** to sever, be severed from.

Pe. Pf. (**uʿbilia umalia**) **aṭar** (**minh̠**) Gs 24:11 and dispelled (her grief and lamentation). Impf. **nʿṭar, niṭar** he goes away, off MG 221:6, pl. **niṭrun** (**uniṭbarun**) DC 43 = Oxf. roll 177 they shall be driven away and cast off; (**ninzun**) **uniṭrun minh̠** ML 37:7, CP 33:17 they shall be (detached) and driven out of him. Impt. (**zha**) **aṭar** (a *qmâhâ*) (Avaunt!) Begone! **aṭar** (**ukbuṣ**) CP 22:3 be off with you (and shrink)! **aṭar uadun napšaikun mn zipa uhrara ḏ-hazin alma** Gy 179:12 and sever yourselves and cut yourselves away from the deception and illusion of this world!

Af. Pf. **aṭar** (אַעְטַר) he put aside, he neglected; **anpia iuma laṭar** Jb 213:6 he did not neglect the morning (devotions).

Idiom: **AṬR** = **ʿṬR** with the verb of existence and the co-ordinative **alma ḏ-** means 'as long as': **ʿṭar ʿhuia uʿdarbh̠ alma ḏ-hinialh̠ lab** Gs 50:6 I shall stay and dwell in it as long as it pleases my father. With **HWA** in the pf. **aṭar** does not change and became a conjunctional expr.

Der.: **aṭar.**

AṬR II (cf. עֲטַר, ܥܛܪ) a rt. of **aṭra.**

aṭra (rt. **AṬR II**), pl. **aṭria** vapours, exhalations, spots. **ubṭuria aṭria ḏ-gaunia gaunia uznia znia** DC 6 and in the mountains (there are) vapours (exhalations) of various colours and kinds. Gl. 123:4 aṭra(i) عيب *macula*, 168:14 id. نجس *spurcitia, macula.*

aṭrušia Jb 198:8 AC a var. of **ṭrušia.**

aṭšia (ܐܛܫܐ) crops (generally), agricultural produce, fruits, cereals MG 42:23. Only in pl. **aṭšia ubazrunia** (var. **bazirunia**) Gy 201:15, 339:10 etc. (often, esp. in AM) crops and seedlings; **aṭšia usaria** Gy 389:16 crops and barley. **aṭšia d̠-gaiṭa** AM 212:3 summer crops.

-ai possessive suff. of the 1st p. sg. MG 88:7; as **-ia** in **lia** ܠܝ and **dilia** ܕܝܠܝ, rarely with nouns.

aia (ܝܐ with a superfluous prosth. vowel) vocative particle: O, Aye, Yea. **aia darata d̠-babai** ŠQ 19:18 O my daddy's portresses!

aiauar AM 169:11 a var. of **aiar 2**, cf. BZ 105 n. 4.

aiak (ܐܝܟ) like, as if, in manner that . . ., to such a degree that . . ., like unto . . . MG 21 f., 32:19, an original conjunction which became a prep. MG 195 n. 2, 209:4, never as an interrogative adv. MG 453:7 f. & n. 2. **aiak lihdaia d̠-laiit muma** DC 27 like a leader without fault; **mitgirbia aiak aklia bisra d̠-maitia** AM 267:23 they will be plundered to such a degree that they will devour the flesh of the dead.

aiala, aila (ܐܝܠܐ, Akk. *aialu*) deer, hart. Pl. **aialia** DC 12:90, Lond. roll. 6:185. **ailia** (q.v.) is more frequent.

aialta (rt. **AUL II = ALL = ʿLL**) income. **aialta napša uapaqta qalia** AM 51:3 (and he will have) much income and little expense.

-aian (aside from **-an, -n**) possessive suff. of the 1st p. pl. MG 32:19

aiar 1 (ἀήρ) the upper atmosphere, air, ether, wind MG xxx 19; as Ar. اير ,هير blowing, wind ibid. n. 2; used as masc. MG 160:8 & n.; often as pr. n., always in st. abs. MG 305:8, MR 22 f.; εὖρος Fränkel 285 (accord. to Fleischer to Levy's 106). When personified (= Zoroastrian Vayu): the genie of the Upper Air, often called **aiar ziua** 'the Radiant Ether', **aiar ziua rba** Gy 76:1 'the Great Radiant Ether', **aiar rba d̠-hiia** 'the Great Ether of Life' (the counterpart of the Great Mana), **aiar gupna** (**br piriauis gupna**) Gs 37:18 the Ether-Vine (son of Piriawis-Vine), **aiar gupna dakia** CP 117:13, ML 143:4 Ether the Pure Vine, **gupna aiar** Gy 116:12 the Vine-Ether, **malka aiar dakia** Morg. 7:8 the King (: Angel) Pure Ether, **malka aiar sagia** Morg. 7:9 the King Abounding Ether, etc. Lidzb. Mand. Gl. & Indd. to his translations, cf. Kessler PRE 164, Brandt ERE viii 382, Bousset HpGn 135, 292, Drower MMII 58 n. 13, 249, etc. **ʿu aiar mhambil lškinta** ATŠ I no. 61 if wind ruins the cult-hut; **akuat aiar d̠-ʿlana našim** ibid. when a wind bloweth the tree; **aiar ziqa** Gy 101:5, 221:13, 281:10, 283:4, Jb 56:5, etc. air, wind, cf. Ginzā 15 n. 7; **aiar iaqra** Gy 360:18 the dear (= venerable) ether; **klil aiar** Gy 320:14, 335:2, Gs 107:24, 109:6 the wreath of ether; **aiar bgu aiar** Gy 68:22, 69:17 ether in ether (= pre-emanational state); **arqa d̠-aiar** Gy 292:15, Jb 14:8, 16:4 ff. earth of ether (= place of beings of light); **malka d̠-raqa d̠-aiar** Gy 360:24 king of the earth of ether; **kinia aiar** Gy 116:13 veils of ether, cf. Ginzā 129 n. 7; **malka d̠-aiar** Gy 328:7 the king of the ether; **arqa d̠-aiar hiuartia** Gy 346:5 the white earth of ether (cf. above); ¶ **nhur aiar qaiimna** Oxf. 3 a I stand on the light of ether; **aiar baraia** Gy 172:19, 188:10, Gs 37:22, Q 5:28, 56:33, 57:6, etc. the outer ether; **aiar stana, aiar ʿstana** Gy 283:3 ff., Gs 108:7 f. 10, etc. the north wind.

aiar 2 (ܐܝܪ, Bab. *Ayaru*) month under the rule of Taurus called **aual (a)bhar** corresponding to May MMII 84, SsSs ii 25: *Fihrist* اَيار.

aiar 3 (pt. and adj. from **AUR I & II = ʿUR I & II = YUR**). (*a*) vigilant, (*b*) brilliant, dazzling, radiant. **šaiar uaiar ṣṭunh̠** DC 6 his body is strong and radiant; **aiar ldaura d̠-nʿhia šribh̠** Gy 275:9 dazzling is the dwelling in which the mild dwell, cf. Ginzā 272 n. 5.

aiat (Ar. آية) AM verse of the Qur'ān.

aiba (עיבא, ܥܝܒܐ) cloud, fog, mist, darkness MG 7:19. **aiba ʿkuma** Gy 385:3 a dark cloud; **aba d̠-aiba bšumia** Lond. roll B 172 darkness of the cloud in the sky; **kababta d̠-aiba** AM 32:13 a burning cloud, a hot cloud; **aiba umiṭra** AM 169:penult. cloud and rain; **aiba napša nihuia uaiba d̠-šidta ʿkuma nihuia** AM 231:19 there will be much cloud and the mist of the year will be black; **aiba d̠-šidta mrahib** AM 232:6 and the darkness of the year will be widespread.

(**aida** = **ʿda** Gl. 178:3 **aida** يد *manus* دست).

-aihun, fem. **-aihin** (s. **-hun,** fem. **-hin**) possessive suff. of the 3rd p. pl.

aium a personage mentioned in a prophecy. **brh̠ d̠-aium d̠-siph̠ mn alma d̠-saṭana hua luath̠** DC 36 the son of A., whose sword from the world of Satan is with him. (**d̠-aium** = **daium** q.v. is a byname of Rūha).

-aiun (fem. **-aiin**, v.s. **-hun,** fem. **-hin**) possessive suff. of the 3rd p. pl.

aizla s. **ʿzla.**

aiṭa 1 (ܚܐܛܐ, cf. Ar. غَيْظ, rt. **AUṬ = ʿUṬ**) contumely, indignation, resentment, provocation, annoyance, vexation. No. st. abs.; only sg. **aiṭa ukariuta** Gy 19:12, Gs 21:5, 17 resentment and sadness; **aiṭa mištbiq** Gs 351:1 provocation is loosed; **aiṭa d̠-bišia** CP 88:9 = ML 109:1 the resentment of the wicked; **baiṭa maiit** AM 149:5 he will die in vexation; **aiṭaikun** Jb 61:10, 62:2 your resentment; **aiṭa uridpa** Jb 268:8 annoyance and persecution; **ridpa d̠-tibil uaiṭh̠ uaiṭh̠ d̠-bišia** DC 34. 180 persecution of the world and its vexation and the vexation of the wicked.

aiṭa 2 (Ass. *ḫaṭṭu*, Jew.-Aram. עיטא) prob. an iron instrument for writing, chisel, graver, stylus. . . . **uplanza linzarara ʿthib uaiṭa lsindirka** DC 34. 379 . . . steel was given to the lote-tree and stylus (?) to the date-palm.

-aiik (ܝܟܝ, ܝܟܝ) a rare form of the possessive suff. of the 2nd p. sg. after pl. nouns MG 177:23.

-aiin s. **-aiun.**

aiit s. **ait.**

-aiit (ܐܝܬ) adv. ending (rarer than in Syr.) MG 200 f.

-aikun (-akun), fem. -aikin (-akin) (s. -kun, fem. -kin) possessive suff. of the 2nd p. pl.

-ail (s. -ˁil) ending of theophorous names.

aila (s. aiala) deer. Found only in pl. ailia, fem. ailata hinds, does MG 120:3, 303:antep. **raqdia kd̲ ailia** Gy 174:14, 21, Q 52:14, 19 they skip like deer; **uailata bdbar mšahṭia** (read **mšahṭa**[n]) ˁ**ulaihun** (read ˁulaihin) ibid. and does in the field cast their young.

aimanuta (var. ˁmanuta, ˁumanuta ܐܘܡܢܘܬܐ abstr. n. from Akk. *ummānu*) profession, handicraft, trade, pursuit. **aimanuta ialip** AM 90:3 he is skilled in handicraft; **aimanuth̲ ramia** AM 97:15 his pursuit is fraud.

ain (s. ˁ**in 2**) yea, indeed (affirmatory exclamation). **uain hazin** AM 200:4 yea, and (even) these . . .

aina (עֵינָא, ܥܝܢܐ), st. abs. & cstr. ˁin 1 (s.v.) MG 100:20 f. Used as fem. MG 157:15 f. 1. eye, pl. **ainia** eyes MG 170:17 f.; with suff.: **ainai** Gy 337:11 my eyes, **ainak** Gy 96:4 thy eyes, **ainik** thy (f.) eyes MG 177:22 f., **ainh̲, ainih̲, ainia** (all three frequent) his eyes, **ainan** our eyes MG 179:5, **ainaikun** (often) your eyes, **ainaihun** (often), **ainaiun** Morg. 256:33, etc., their eyes; **pišra d̲-aina** exorcism of the (evil) Eye (DC 21, publ. in JRAS 1937 589–611); **aina bišta ukauihta** ibid. Evil and Dimmed Eye; **aina zruqtia** ibid. Blue Eye, cf. 597 n. 5; **aina bruqtia** ibid. eye with white cataract; **aina qliqtia** ibid. eye affected by a white film; **aina** ˁ**kiltia** ibid. Corroded Eye; **mlia ainak b . . .** s. **MLA I**; **pihtit ainai bnhura** ˁ**timlia** Gs 50:15 I opened my eyes, they (were) filled with light; **ainia lagiṭ** s. **LGṬ**; **uainai bainaiun lanapla baiina l**ˁ**utria bnai hinun bainai lanapla** Jb 39 and my eyes meet not theirs, I seek for the uthras, my sons, but they do not meet my eyes, cf. also s. **NPL**; **baina ṣbat** s. **BUN.** (Gl. 120:4 **aina,** pl. **ainai** [read **ainia**] عين، عيون *oculus* چشم). 2. well-spring, fountain, source, fig. origin, beginning, personified as the female aspect of Creation with the **sindirka** (male), pl. **ainata** (ܥܝܢܬܐ), **ainaniata** MG 170:17 f., **aininiata** MG 21:6, 136:10, **ainiata** DC 36. 16, **ainanita** AM 216:3, **ainanata, ain**ˁ**anata** etc. **duktai bainiata** DC 46. 80:8 f. my place is in the well-springs; **mn aina ltit** DC 34 from the source (beginning) downwards; **nahlia zabia uainanata** DC 40 rivers, streams and springs; **aina d̲-ziua** Gy 336:22 f. the well-spring of radiance; **aina rabtia** Gy 145:3, Q 62:28, etc., the great well-spring; **aina rabtia kasita** Morg. 112:3, etc. the great hidden well-spring; **šuma d̲-aina rabtia** Q 21:14 the name of the great well-spring; **sumqaq aina rabtia d̲-hšuka** (often in DAb, etc.) S. (s.v.), the Great Well-spring of Darkness; **aina d̲-mia** ˁ**kumia** Gy 139:15, 145:4 the well-spring of black waters, identified with **aina rabtia**; **tlat ainaniata d̲-ziua** CP 356: ult. three well-springs of radiance; **aina usindirka** cf. above and s. **sindirka** Lidzb. Mand. Gl. 3. fig. a bud (on a stem), a knot (or roughness in coarse silk), a knee-cap (?), pl. **ainaniata. kd̲ aina d̲-piršat bhanata gupna** CP 413:13 like the bud which appeared on that Vine; **taga d̲-šaraia d̲-ainaniata litbh̲** ATŠ I no. 16 the crown (fillet) of silk, in which there are no knots (or coarse threads); **ainaniata d̲-burkia** Or 327:3 kneecaps (?).

airan (ايران) AM 186 Iran, Persia.

airuta s. ˁ**ruta.**

ait- with pers. suff., independently **aiit** (אִית, ܐܝܬ particle of existence) there is, exists. Neg. **lait-**, independently **laiit** (s.v.) there is not. Varr. ˁ**iit**, ˁ**it**, with encl. ˁ**t-** (s.v.), neg. **lit-**, Pt (s.v.). With suff. **aitan** I am, I exist, **aitak** thou art, existest, **aith̲** he is, she is, **aita** she is, **aitinan** (bad var. **aitinin**) we are, **aitinkun** ye are, **aitinhun, aitinun** they are MG 295; **d̲-ana haka aitan** Gy 138:2 that I was there; **aitak mn iuma qadmaia** Gy 7 thou existest from the first day; **aith̲ bsakia** Gy 4:3 he has qualities, cf. Ginzā 4:3; **kma d̲-aita** ˁ**mh̲** AM as long as his mother lives; **kma d̲-aita bpagrh̲** ATŠ II no. 9 as long as he exists (read **aith̲**) in the body; **ukianh̲ biša aith̲** Gy 155:15 and his nature is bad; **uhinun almia d̲-nhura bsakia d̲-napšia aitinhun** Gy 9:16 *et ei mundi lucis existunt in multis speciebus*, cf. Ginzā 4:3; **lia aitinun** Gy 150:5 where are they?; **duktak triṣa kd̲ d̲-aita** ATŠ I no. 293 thy place is set up as it was; **haiman bmalka d̲-nhura d̲-aita** Gy 213:24 believe in the king of light that he existeth; **balma hazin d̲-ldilia aitan bgauh̲** Gs 3: 9, 12 in this world, in which I live (var. DC 22. 394 **aitin**). Without suff. **kd̲ aiit dmutun** Gy 99:12 as their likeness (existeth).

aita (אִיתָא st. emph. of the preceding verbal substantive) being, existence, Lidzb. ZS 1/1922 p. 1. St. abs. ˁ**it. ulatitarh̲ aith̲** ATŠ I no. 224. Translation doubtful (ATŠ p. 166 a paraphrase).

-ak (ךָ, ـَـك, after vocal endings only **-k** s.v.) suff. of the 2nd p. sg. MG §§ 76–77 p. 88.

aka 1 (אית + כא), more frequently ˁ**ka 1**, rarely **ka** there is MG 204:5. Neg. **lika, l**ˁ**ka, laka** (s. vv.) there is not. Interr. **miaka** (and varr. s. mi-), **aka** is there? **aka d̲-gabir minan** Gy 80:24 (if) there is one who is greater than we; **aka d̲-npal bmia urahtia mia siauia** Gy 165: paen. it happens that when he falls into the water the black waters boil.

aka 2 (not from **AUQ** = ˁ**UQ**, Nöld. MG 40 n. 2 suggested ܥܩܐ, perhaps from **NKA**) distress, affliction, calamity, need. Var. ˁ**ka 2.** No st. abs., no pl. ˁ**ka aka** ˁ**lik dilik** Gy 156:8 there will be hardship for thee (fem.). (**aka umkika** Jb 263:10 humble and submissive, read **maka umkika** with Lidzb. ii 236 n. 1).

akabir (Ar. pl. اكابر), bad var. **akabar** people of rank. **akabir tišpur** AM 277:6 folk of high degree will prosper; **akabir uašrap** AM 257:7 (Ar. اكابر واشراف) people of rank and the nobles.

akala (nom. ag. Pe. of **AKL**) eater, glutton,

fond of eating. **akala ušataia hauia** AM 98:8 he will be fond of eating and drinking.

akalta = **akilta** = **ʿkilta** (q.v.).

akandẖ, akandia, akandit, kandia, kandit (cf. Talm. אכתי, Mand. **kdi** Morg. 250/87:23) while as yet, as yet, whilst still MG 44:14, 202:10. Still used (pron. *kandī, kandiye*). With neg. **akandit la** not yet MG 202:11, Gl. 45:3 **knda** [*sic*] بعد *adhuc* از آن بعد. **akandit ʿutria mianqia anatun** Jb 11:7 f. (for) as yet ye are youthful uthras; **akandit taga brišẖ ḏ-rba matnẖ** DC 41. 544 f. whilst he still has to place the crown on the head of his teacher; **uakandit lasaqim srin uhda rahmia** ATŠ I no. 136 and as yet he has not completed his twenty-one 'devotional prayers'.

akasta (nom. act. af. of **KSS**) reproach, reproof, rebuke, confutation, spite, fury, wrath. **akasta makislun** Gs 53:20 rebuking them, cf. Gs 54:14; **iahbit akasta** Q 53:9 I rebuked; **ḏ-iahbilan akasta** Gy 362:6 f. those who rebuke us; **ubakasta makislun** Gs 53 and he set them right with a rebuke; **umištria haršia bišia uakasta ḏ-harašata** (var. **harašiata**) DC 45 & 40. 146 and loosed will be evil spells and the fury of the witches; **akasta mn riša ḏ-iahra** DC 43 D 66 the rebuke of the beginning of the month (?).

akar (ܟܪ?) at once, immediately, forthwith, without delay: **akar lalma šubqẖ** Jb 57:10 forsake the world forthwith, cf. Jb ii 61 n. 5; **akar šibqẖ** Jb 72:2 he left her immediately; **akar nišmatak ahbalia** Gs 112:14 f. give me thy souls at once!

akara s. **ʿkara**: Gl. 34:3 **akara** اجراء *mercenarii* بغلها [*sic*] (read بقّالها, all three should be sg.), 124:7 id. غارس *agricola* نشاننده; 128:3 **akara**, pl. **akarai** (read **akaria**) فاعل, فعله *operarii* عوامّ.

akbar 1 (Ar. اخبار) news, tidings. **aršap uakbar napša nihuia** AM 282:14 there will be alarming tidings and much (evil) news.

akbar 2 for **akabir** (s.v.). **rabania uakbar** AM 216:7 great men and chieftains.

akuaṣta, kuaṣta (cf. אכוזא, עכוז) buttocks (?). St. abs. **akuaṣat** DC 25. 54. **kauba uzinipta uakuaṣta** DC 12. 163, **kiba zanaptẖ uakuaṣtẖ** DC 43 & 46, Lond. roll. B 331 pain in his tail and his buttocks (?).

akuat, kuat (כְּנָת, ܐܟܘܬ) like, as like unto, just as, as if, whenas, thus MG 195:8. Strengthened by **ha**: **hakuat** (s.v.), **haakuat** ibid. f. Rarely used with the original meaning 'thus' MG 206 f., Ginzā 62 n. 1. ʿ**akuat** thus, like this. **akuat ḏ-** conj. as MG 210:5 ff. **akuat damit lgabra** Gy 180:15 thou art like unto a man; **ṣilmia ḏ-kuatun** DC 22. 174 (var. Pet. Gy 181:21 & Norb. **akuatun**) their own images; **man nihuia ḏ-akuatak** Gy 88:4 who will be like unto thee?; **akuat ḏ-amar** Gy 11 as (someone) said.

akula Gl. 33:10 اكول *vorator, vorax* بسيار خور.

akum = **ʿkum** in **la akum, lakum** Gy 6:19 will not become black (an influence of the preceding a ?) MG 125:18: **uakum lbušiẖ** ATŠ I no. 173; **rušmaihun ʿtbar uakum** s. **BRR**.

akilta a var. of **ʿkilta** (q.v.) Ginzā 234 n. 4.

akin ḏ (כֵּן, ܗܟܢ + ד, ܕ) thus, in such manner as, (or) that. **azil lkulhun bnat anašia akin ḏ-bla zibnaihun** . . . DC 43 D 10 he attacks all the children of men in such manner that before their time . . . (they die).

akinda a var. of **akandẖ** DC 22. 437 (where Pet. Gs 48:15 has **akandẖ**).

akir, kir (Ar. أخير) final, last (postcl. and mod.): **kanun akir** AM 272:4 ܟܢܘܢ ܐܚܪܝ (January); **akir situa** last winter-month, **akir bhar** last spring-month, **akir gaiṭa** last summer-month, **akir paiiz** last autumn-month MMII 84. Gl. 28:11 **akir (akra)** آخر *novissimus* آخرين; 30:13 **akira** اقاصى *fines* حد; 33:1 **akira, alakirai** [*sic*] ابد الآباد *saecula saeculorum* هميشه; 37:5 **akira** أخيراً *postea* آخرين.

AKL I, ʿKL (אכל, ܐܟܠ) to eat, consume, devour, absorb.

Pe. Pf. **akal** he ate, **aklat** she ate, **akalt** thou didst eat, **aklit** I ate MG 241, special pl. form **akaliun** they ate; with suff. **ʿklẖ** he ate it, **akaltẖ** she ate it, etc.; with neg. **lakaltan** she did not eat me MG 271:24 f. Impf. **nikul, nʿkul**, but also **nikal** he eateth, will eat, or we (shall) eat, **tikul, tikal** she eateth, will eat, or thou eatest, wilt eat, **niklun** they (will) eat, **tiklun** ye (will) eat MG 242; with suff. **niklẖ** we (shall) eat him or it, **tiklẖ** thou eatest or wilt eat, **ʿklẖ** I (shall) eat MG 275:20 f., **tiklan** she eats me MG 271:3; with pl. suff. **nikilinun**, varr. **nikalinun, niklinun** he eats them, **tikilinun** she eats them (formally identical with 'thou eatest them') MG 281:antep. Impt. **akul ʿkul** eat!; MG 28:7, 242:20, **akul pihtak** (often in ritual prescriptions) eat thy pihtha (sacramental bread)!, pl. **akuliun** ATŠ II no. 334; sg. with suff. **ʿklẖ** eat it!; Act. pt. **akil** he eateth, will eat MG 242:paen., neg. **lakil** he will not eat, enjoy, etc.; **lahma grida agrida akil** AM 5:7 he will make a meagre living; **lahma šapira akil** ibid. he will make a fine living; **lhama mn bunka akil** AM 7:10 he will be supported from his native place; **ulhama umia mn anašia akil** AM 8:5 ibid. and he will be entertained by people; fem. **akla** she will eat, neg. **lakla** she will not eat; **ukisa uqiniana gabrẖ akla** AM 57:9 and she will use up her husband's purse and property; pl. **aklia hbulia** (*often*) they take interest (Germ. *sie fressen Zins*); **aklin** Gy 387:10 they last (**AKL II**); **qaklia** DAb they eat; with encl. **aklilun** Gy 187:8 they eat them. Participial pres. **akilna** I eat MG 242:ult., fem. **aklana** Gy 220:2 I last (**AKL II**), neg. **laklana** I do not eat MG 231:19, **aklit** thou eatest, wilt eat MG 242:ult. Pass. pt. **ʿkila** (*often*) eaten, corroded. Inf. **mikal** eating, to eat MG 243:2; with suff. **miklaikun** Gy 17:17 your eating; with encl. **miklinhun** to eat them MG 293:10, 386:22.

Af. Pf. **aukil** he gave to eat, he fed; with

suff. **aukiltinun** I fed them, **aukiltinkun** I fed you MG 243:22, 281:5; **aukluih̲** ATŠ they gorged on it. Act. pt. **maukil** he gives food; with encl. **maukilh̲** (var. DC 22. 402 **makulh̲**) **man uman mašqilh̲** Gs 11 ult. who will feed it and who will give it drink? Participial pres. with encl. **maukilnalkun** Gy 233:11 I (shall) feed you.

Ethpe. **ʿtkil** he was eaten, **ʿtiklat** she was eaten etc. Pt. **mitkil** he is eaten MG 243:6, pl. **mitiklin, mitiklia** they are eaten, fem. **mitiklan** they (fem.) are eaten, may they be eaten MG 243:12; **utikal ʿkilta balma** Gy 33:14 and it (: the fire) will consume in the world; **kd̲ akal aklilun** Gy 187:8 as they ate, let them eat them; **ʿl miklaikun ulmištiaikun** Gy 17:17 when you eat and when you drink (with your eating and with your drinking); **umn mikal d̲-ʿkuria udqaṭil aria udiba udgisa udmita latiklun** CP 32:47 f. . . . from eating from the pagan shrines, and do not eat from what the lion and the wolf killed and from what was cast forth and what died (cf. 1 Cor. 8:1); **latiklun zma d̲-hiuaniata uladmaita** (: **uladmita**) **uladbaṭna** Gy 18:3 do not eat the blood of animals nor those which died or were pregnant (cf. Lev. 17, 11:39 f.); **briš hapura mitkil** Gs 3:11 first the aftermath will be eaten; **tiklan nura** Jb. 104:6 (may) fire consume me; **sindirka d̲-nura akalth̲** ATŠ I no. 187 a palm-tree which fire hath consumed; **miša udubša maukilnalkun** Gy 233:11 (varr. DC 22 **maukanalkun**, Sh. 'Abd.'s copy **maukinalkun**) I feed you both with oil and honey; **hakima d̲-la ʿkilak pihta mn paturai** Jb 26 how long is it since thou atest (pass. pt. with encl.) no morsel from my platter?

Idioms: With **lahma, lhama, kisa, qiniana** above s. act. pt. With **baita** to occupy: **baita d̲-lau dilh̲ akil** AM 15:11 he will occupy a house which is not his own. With **hbulia** above s. act. pt. pl. **akil pirṣa** s. **pirṣa**; **aklia šauṭa** s. **šauṭa**. Mod. **gam akal** (pron. *yam aχal*) he worried (cf. P. غصّه خورد).

Gl. 6:7 f. اكل *manducare* خورد; 109:9 f. طعم *pascere* چشيد.

Der.: **akala, akla, aklaia, akalta, akilta, ʿkilta, mikla, makulta, maukalta, makalata ʿkula** (& var.), **ʿkila**, fem. **ʿkiltia**.

AKL II (יכל=אכל) to occupy space, last, endure for, complete. Prob. related to **KUL** MG 241 n. 1, 481. Forms identical with those of **AKL I**. **uʿtitlh̲ ladam gabra mikal alpa d̲-šnʿ** Gy 26:13 it is determined for A. the man to complete a thousand years, cf. Ginzā 27 n. 3; **uakla alpa d̲-šnʿ bduhna** Gy 27:8 and it endureth (fem.) for a 1,000 years; **alma d̲-akaliun** DHG 7 f. until they came to an end; **haizak akil malka d̲-hardubaiia tlatma ušitin šnia** HG so the kingdom (*pars pro toto*) of the Sasanians (?) lasted 360 years; **akil kiuan btrisar maluašia** AM Saturn lasteth with the 12 signs of the Zodiac . . .; **šibiahia aklia luat trisar maluašia** Gy 379 the planets last with the 12 signs of the Zodiac.

akla 1 (act. pt. of **AKL I** st. emph. masc. & st. abs. fem.) consuming, devouring. **nura akla** (*often*) the consuming fire, cf. Jb 11–15; **akla** alone with the meaning of 'consuming fire' in Gs 55: 6, 15, Jb 188:10, ML 143:8, cf. Jb ii 166 n. 7, ML 143 n. 2, Ginzā 447 n. 2; **mia aklia** (often) a designation of the water of the underworld, Ginzā 15 n. 5.

Gl. 31:3 **akl** اكل *manducatio* خوردن.

akla 2 (ܐܟܠܐ) a mace, club, pestle. **akla unarga** Jb 273:15 a club and an axe; **akla d̲-zahba** RD 29 a mace of gold; **akla d̲-nhaša** ibid. a mace of copper; **akla d̲-parzla** Morg. 194:2, etc. an iron club; **akla (rba) d̲-ziua** (very often) may be sometimes rendered by 'the (great) consuming ray of light' (**AKL I**), or 'the (great) encircling of radiance', but the meaning 'mace' is supported by its occurrence with **MHA**: **bakla d̲-ziua mha** Gy 303:23 he beat with the mace of radiance; **mhith̲ bakla d̲-ziua** Gy 333:5 I beat him with the mace of radiance, cf. **bhalin aklia mahilun** RD 28e = DAb they beat them with those maces. (Similar semantics as Engl. 'beam' = 'timber' and 'ray'.)

aklaṭ (Ar. اخلاط) the four humours of the body. **mn aklaṭ hu zma hu** AM 286:11 he is of the (four humours) of the body, he is the blood.

aklaia (rt. **AKL I**) eater, man fond of eating: **aklaia ušataia** (AM 98:18 has **akala**) a man fond of eating and drinking.

AKM, (ʿKM) (אכם, ܐܘܡ) to become black, turn black, blacken, get black.

Pe. Pf. **akum** he became black, **akimiun** ATŠ II no. 178, var. **ʿkumiun** (Lidzb. Mand. Gl.) they were blackened. Pt. **akum**, fem. **akma** (both used adjectivally). **d̲-akum lbušaihun** ATŠ so that their dress has become (i.e. is) black; **d̲-kd̲ nura hilpat ʿlh̲ uakum** ibid. which, when fire passes over it, turns black; **akma mn zimta** Gy 182:18 blacker than a hair (see also s. **akum**).

Der.: **akum, ʿukma, ʿkum.**

akma = **kma**: Gl. 145:1 **akma** كم *quantus* چند; 145:3 **akmai** [*sic*] كم *quot* چند است (cf. coll. *kemye*); 145:4 **akma šita** كم مرّة *quoties* چند بار; 162:15 **akma** ما *quantus* يا (?).

AKS = **KSS II** (cf. s. **ʿkisa**).

aksa (cf. عكس) name given to the vowel **i** (because of its graphical form ◌), used in spelling MMII 243 n. 2.

AKṢ (עקץ, ܚܡܨ) to hurt, trouble, grieve. Used as impersonal verb **akṣalia** it chagrins me MG 40:1, 45 n. 4, 365:ult.; **akṣat ukarialia** it chagrins and afflicts me MG 365:paen. f. See also **KṢA**.

AKR I, ʿKR I (עכר, ܥܟܪ) to detain, retain, hold back, restrain, obstruct.

Pe. Pf. with suff. **akartinun landašatkun ʿlai** Jb 62:5 I restrained your plots against me. Impf. with suff. **nikrunan** (var. **nakrunan**) they hold me back MG 273:1, with a pl. suff. **tikirinun lhanath̲ ruhia bišata uhumria taqipata minh̲** DC 48 thou wilt hold back those evil spirits and powerful amulet-spirits from him.

PA. (Pf. would be identical with pe.). Pass. pt. (**kpar**) **makarna** Gs 41:14 (haply) I shall be delayed (var. DC 22. 430 **makirna** would be an act. pt.).

DER.: **ʿkarta 2, ʿkira.**

AKR II, ʿKR II (עכר, عَكَرَ) to make turbid or to hold back (i.e. **ḏ-nikiriia** [*sic*] **ʿl prat ziua** DAb who make turbid (?) *or* hold back the Light-Euphrates.)

AKR III, (ʿKR III) (אכר, ܐܟܪ) to plough, dig, cultivate.

DER.: **akara, ʿkara, ʿkarta.**

akra s. **kraiia**: Gl. 30:7 **akra** ارجل *pedes* پايان; 84:1 id. رجل *pes* پا.

akraba = **kraba.**

akrad (prob. اكراد, pl. of كُرد) AM 202 a place-name, Kurdistan (?). **nura titlia utiqlia ʿl akrad** AM 264:28 fire will be set and destroy the cultivation (read **akrab**?) cf. BZ 167 n. 5.

akrah (Ar. اكره) diseased, sickly. **akrah il atmar** AM 282:17 (اكره الاثمار) fruit will be diseased (Ṣâb.'s copy has **tukras atmar**, read تُكَرَّه اثمار?).

akšalta (nom. act. **KŠL**) stumbling down, cause of error, stumbling-block. **akšalta makšlith̲** Gy (DC 22. 349, missing in Pet.) thou makest him stumble.

akšar (pe. of **KŠR**) 'He-Succeeded' used as a pr. n. of beings of light. **akšar uabad** (often) 'He-Succeeded-and-Performed'; **akšar iauar ziua** Gy 151:9 Y.Z.-Succeeded.

akšilana s. **makšilana.**

akt-, ʿkt- with pers. suff. — a mod. form of **ait-** (אית, ܐܝܬ): **aktinan** (DC 51:coloph.) we are.

aktiar, ktiar, var. **aktiir** (Ar. اختيار, postcl. & mod.) selection, choice, free decision. **aktiar ḏ-iumia ḏ-iahra** AM selection of days of the month; **aktiar ḏ-iumia ṭabia** AM selection of good days; **aktiar** (var. **aktiir**) **bzibnh̲ uzabunh̲ hauilh̲** AM 19:5 he will be independent in his buying and selling.

aktilap (Ar. اختلاف) AM 275:36 dissension.

al- 1 (often for **l** and **ʿl**, see both) to, for, against, or a simple *nota accusativi*. Always procl. **alak** ܠܟܘܢ, **almana** (var. **lmana**) *spiritum*, **šlama alak** *pax tecum*, and regularly in **alanpia** (q.v.) MG § 158 p. 193.

al- 2 (أل, postcl. & mod.) Ar. article used in transliterations of Ar. nouns, sometimes also with Mand. nouns. Often written **ʿl**, or simple **l** (آل). **šaعir alšin** AM 129 (شعير الجن), **altania** AM 261:37 (الثانى), **altiعlab** AM 130 (الثعلب). With Mand. nouns: **ubalmania hidutia uhiduti(ni)ata** DC 49:30 f. and in the clothes of bridegrooms and brides.

al 3 (آل): Gl. 33:3 **al** آل *familia.*

ALA, ʿLA II, ALL III, YLL (Gen. Aram.) to shriek, wail, howl, lament MG 241 n. 1.

PE. Pt. **bakia alia** Gs 74:antep. she weeps and wails, pl. **ualin bakin kḏ ʿnšia** Gy 353:15 and they will wail and weep like women. Participial pres. **ualma alit** DC 44 and why wailest thou?

AF. from **YLL.**

DER. **alia, malia 3, ʿlita.**

ala 1 (Talm. אֲלָה lance, fork) a projecting piece of wood (or, perhaps, **ʿla**, above). **lala tlilh̲** AM 128 hang it on a peg! (or, above).

ala 2 (إلى) until: Gl. 36:15 **ala** الى *usque ad, in* تا; 38:10 **ala šita** الى زمان *usque ad tempus* تا زمان; 38:11 **ala ʿmqa** [*sic*] الى العمق *in altum* عمق.

ala 3 (الله ?) DC 26.438 name of a demon.

alaha (Gen. Sem.) a god, pl. **alahia** (false) gods. Used of false gods, evil deities ML xv, OSt 545, MSt 38, MR 211 f., differently only in the moral codex Gy 13–26, ERE viii 384, MSchr. 24–43. No. st. abs. sg. St. abs. pl. **alihin, alihun, alihan** MG 305:antep., 310:4; **alaha alihin, alaha alihun** (often) God of gods cf. ML 199 n. 2; **alahakun, alahkun** your god MG 65:13; **alahun** (often) their god; **alahia bʿkuraihun** CP 103:1 gods in their shrines; **alahia mn ʿkuraihun** Q 24:18 gods from their shrines; **bit alahia** (often) house of gods, pagan temple; **alahia mitiqria kulhun mdiniata ubit alahia dahna** Gy 392:3 gods will be esteemed; all cities and temples of gods will flourish; **udahil alahia hauia** (often in AM) and he will be god-fearing; **alahia zikria uʿstirata nuqbata** (often in exorcisms) male gods and female astartes; **šum alaha lanadkar** Gy 329:18 he will not mention the name of God (here with the meaning of the 'true God' cf. Ginzā 338 n. 2); **mlakia ḏ-alahun** DC 26. 156 f. angels of their god.

alahuta (abstr. noun from **alaha**) idolatry, worship of false gods, divinity, allah-dom, divinities (us. evil). **rupʿil asia rba ḏ-mlakia ḏ-alahuta** (an exorcism) Raphael, the great healer of the angels of (false) divinity; **titpik kulh̲ alahuta ḏ-baita** DC 43 J 116 all the divinities of the House (: the world) shall be turned against him; **parṣupa ḏ-alahuta nihuilh̲** AM 93:1 he will have a godlike appearance; **qarqalta ḏ-alahuta ḏ-baita** Gy 180:31 the overthrow of the gods of the House (: world).

alauia, alau- with pers. suff. = **ʿlauia, ʿlau-**: **alauh̲** upon him, **alauan** upon us (rarer than with an initial **ʿ**); **alauak balpa ḏ-zuzia** ŠQ 7:5 thou shalt bestow (on her) a thousand *zuzim.*

alai (עַל with the suff. of the 1st p. sg.) interj. woe on me! alas! Us. repeated **alai alai** MG 81 n. 2.

alak ḏ (עַל with the suff. of the 2nd p. sg.) upon thee that . . ., thou art responsible for . . .: **alak ḏ-halin kušṭa bgauh̲ nṭiria** ATŠ I no. 141 thou art responsible that these keep their word (are held to their promise).

alaka s. **alka.**

alal AM 199 a pl.n., possibly Alân BZ App. II s.v.

alalta (ܡܚܝܠܘܬܐ) feebleness. **uʿburia alalta nihuibun** AM 236:13 and crops will be feeble.

alam st. abs. & cstr. of **alma** (q.v.).

alana = **ʿlana**: Gl. 35:14 **alana**, pl. **alani(a)** شجرة, اشجار *arbores* چوب.

alanpia (إلقى) towards MG 193:18 ff., as to, as regards. **rgaz šuba alanpai** CP 3:1 the Seven raged against me; **paruanqa d̲-atia alanpai** CP 133:12 the Deliverer that cometh towards me; **ubhiria alanpia napqia** ML 207:6 and the elect will go towards him; **alanph̲ d̲-šganda npaq** Jb 52:7 he went forth towards the messenger; **alanpaiin d̲-nišmata** DAb towards the souls.

alaṣa = **hlaṣa. alaṣa ungada** Jb. 191:8 torture and torment.

albar = **lbar, ʿlbar** (s. **bar**) without, except, outside.

albuša = **lbuša** (q.v.). St. abs. **albuš**, pl. **albušia. balbuš dakia qaiimna** CP 401:5 in pure clothing do I stand; **balbušia d̲-hirbia sipia uʿuṣṭamumia** DC 37. 313 with armaments of blades, swords, and poisoned darts; **albušia anania mia lbiš** Gy 29:6 he (: Anuš-Uthra) is clothed with clothes of water-clouds.

ALG (علج, H. עלג) to be dumb, or have impaired or stammering speech. Occurring only in pt. **algia** *balbutientes* MG 107:15.

alga (rt. **ALG**) dumb, tongue-tied, stammerer. Pl. **algia** (s. **ALG**), with suff. **algaiun** Gy 107:4 their stammerers. **alga . . . uʿšiqa** Jb 105:6 dumb . . . and deaf; **algia udugia** Jb 193:7, 274:12, 275:13 etc. *balbi et surdi*; **utariṣ malala bpumaihun d̲-algia** DC 46 and establisheth speech in the mouths of the dumb; **mn algia zikria umn algia nuqbata** DC 37. 512 from male and female demons of dumbness.

aldudu AM 203:11 a place-name (not identified).

aldilia = **ldilia** (s.v.) Zotb. 226 left col.: 6.

alhud (s. **balhud**) alone, separate(ly).

alua (אלא Buxtorf, cf. עֲלָא = H. עָלֶה, Akk. *alû, elû*) tendril, leaf. No st. abs. sg. Pl. **aluata** MG 170:paen. f., st. abs. & cstr. **aluat. gauaza d̲-lgiṭ bʿdh̲ kulh̲ alua mn riš briš** Jb 173:4 f. the staff which he held in his hand was in leaf from end to end, similarly Gy 358:6; **kana d̲-alip alip hauin aluath̲** DC 51 a Stem, from which there sprang a thousand thousand offshoots; **aupa d̲-gupna ziua ualuath̲ nhura** Jb 132:1 the branches of the Vine are radiance and its foliage is light; **gupna d-aluath̲ hua kd̲ aluata d̲-asa hadta** DC 3 a vine whose tendrils are like tendrils of fresh myrtle; **knara d̲-hazin d̲-tlatma ušitin aluatia** JRAS 1938 3:8 this lote-tree, which (hath) 360 leaves; **upira rba uʿlaia brakinun lšitlia d̲-aluatia** CP 426:5 and the great and lofty Fruit(-Tree) blessed its offspring, that is its foliage; **aluath̲ pasimkia d̲-nhura** Gs 37:20 his branches are lamps alight.

alual (perh. P. آل Steing.) a kind of fish, whale. **umahilun kauaria brundia ualuai** Jb 148:9 and they strike the fish, the small fish (s. **brunda**) and the big fish (?); **ukauaria ualuai lalagṭia** Jb 148:12 and they catch no (little) and no big fish (?, Lidzb. ii 151 is mistaken).

aluaia s. **ʿluaia**.

aluaita s. **aluita**.

aluana s. **ʿluana**.

aluat, luat, ʿluat (לְוָת, ܠܘܬ) with or without suff. — with, towards, in company with, amongst, in the presence of. With suff. **aluat, aluatai** with me, towards me, **(a)luatak** with thee, towards thee, etc. (cf. **luat**). **mn aluatai** (often) from my presence, from my home; **uliliata d̲-aluat** DC 43 and the liliths that are with me (i.e. 'haunt me'); **unibsum šumak urihak aluat mana rba kabira** CP? thy name and thine odour will be fragrant before the great and mighty Mana; **ʿutria aluatak kanpia** CP 418:11 the uthras assemble before thee; **ukanpia kulhun ʿutria aluath̲ d̲-iauar** CP 419:1 f. and all the uthras assemble before Yawar.

aluata, aluatia pl. of **alua**.

***aluka** (perh. rel. to Ass. *alâku* 'to kindle', Ginzā 80 n. 2) flame. Found only in pl. st. abs. **alukin** Gy 80:17 (var. **lukin**, Leid. **ʿlukin**), **alukʿn, alkin** Gs 107:2 f., 11 (var. DC 22. 489 **alukrin** read **alukʿin**) and only in the sentence: **nura d̲-saliq alukin (alukʿn)** ibid. fire the flame of which ascendeth (constructed as sg.).

alupa = **ialupa**.

aluita DC 22. 483 = **luita** GS 100:6 f.

alzur, lzur Gy 383:17 a king of ancient Iran (cannot be Ἀλέξανδρος, since this is called **sandar**) Gray ZA 19/1905, 286.

alia, ʿlia = **lia: ab alia** (varr. **alia, ʿlia, lia**) **azlinin** (var. **azlinin**) DC 22. 130 (= GY 134: 18) my father, whither do we go?; **alia azlin ualia atin umdurtun alia** DC 22. 194 whither go they, whence come they, and where will be their habitation?; **alia nizal ualia** (Pet. **ulia**) **nihuilak ruhṣana** DC 22. 415 = Gs 24:18 whither shall we go and where wilt thou find confidence?

alia 2 Zotb. 227b:ult. = **alai**.

aliam (obscure, perh. from עלם 'to tie up') a tether (?) **aliam ʿl hiuaniata badmu himiana dilkun** ATŠ I no. 253 a tether for the animals like your girdle, s. footn. ATŠ 183.

aliana, ʿliana (אֲלְיוֹנָא, אַלְיוֹן) thumb (cf. s. **ʿliana**). **ṣbitak d̲-aqama ʿlianak** CP 93:28 the finger that is before (next) thy thumb.

aliha = **liha: pihtit mn alihun** DC 22. 446 I escaped from their net.

alihan s. **alaha**.

alihda, alihdia (לְחוֹד, ܠܚܘܕ, cf. s. **lihdaia**) alone, unique. **udinba d̲-kulh̲ maiit alihdia** ATŠ I no. 249 at the end of it all, it dies alone; **bhak ʿṣṭuna d̲-alihda mitlabša** ATŠ II no. 262 it is clothed in that body which is unique.

alihdai (**alihda** + pers. suff. of the 1st p. sg.) towards, near, close to me. Us. repeated **alihdai alihdai. alihdai alihdai anpai** Jb 144:11 close to me, close to my face; **alihdai alihdai arbai**

Jb 144:14 near me, close to my boat (Lidzb. *dicht an dicht an*).

alihun, alihin s. **alaha.**

alikta (a later form of **alita 2**) sheep's tail. **alikta** (var. **alita**) **udubša aukiltinkun** DC 22. 228 = Gy 234:4 I fed you with sheep's fat and honey.

alip s. **alpa.**

alita 1 (עִלִּיתָא, ܥܶܠܺܝܬܳܐ) upper part. **ata ʿlalita ḏ-ʿudnẖ** AM 98:6 a mark on the upper part of his ear.

alita 2 (אליתא = אַלְיָה) sheep's tail-fat (the upper part or base of a sheep's tail which is all fat and upon which it can live for some time in a grassless place). **umn alita ḏ-tata** ATŠ II no. 317 and some lamb's tail-fat.

ALL I, AUL II, ʿLL, ʿUL (עלל, ܥܠܠ) to enter, go (or) come in; af. to bring in, introduce (with transitions from ע״ע to ע״ו, cf. below).

Pe. Pf. **al** he entered MG 284:4; **al luataihun** Gy 152 he entered to them; **al hauqa lʿuṣraihun** DC 34. 336 fear entered their minds; **lal** Gs 103:5 he did not enter MG 35:12 f.; **alat** she entered MG 248:10; **alit** I entered MG 248:ult. (without ref.); **aliun kulhun . . . lškinta** DC 38 all of them entered the cult-hut; **alnin** we entered MG 249:4. Impf. **niul, niiul, nʿiul, niʿiul** *intra(bi)t, intra(bi)mus* MG 6:22 f., 8:19, 249:12, **tiul, tiiul, tʿiul** *intra(bi)s* MG 69:paen., 249:12, **tiʿiul** AM 242:13 id., **ʿiul** I (shall) enter MG 249:13, **ʿiul uʿdurbẖ bhazin ʿṣṭuna** Gs 62:paen. I shall enter this column (: the body) and dwell in it (should be impt. **ʿul** 'enter!' as in DC 22. 450). Impt. **ʿul** MG 250:7; **ʿul ʿl bimanda** DC 40 enter into the cult-hut! Act. pt. **aiil** *intra(bi)t* MG 112: 13, 250:13; **qaiil** (often in later texts) id., fem. **aila** (later **qaila**) *ea intra(bi)t* MG 7:19, 250:8, pl. **ailia** MG 250:9; **a(i)lin** DAb they (will) enter, fem. **ailan** DAb *eae intra(bu)nt.* Participial pres. **alit** I enter MG 82 n. 2; **aiiltun** DAb ye (will) enter (mod. **alinin** pron. *alenni* 'let us go!'). Inf. **mʿial** entering, to enter MG 250:ult., less regular **mʿiil**, cf. **mʿiil habšaba** CP 180:7 at the entry of Sunday **ʿṣṭuna ḏ-baiia mʿiil bgauẖ** DC 34. 162 the body into which he seeks to enter.

The forms of pa. and af. are completely confused: Pf. **aiil** he brought in MG 253:23; **aiil šdun** Gs 14:17 they brought and threw me in; **ailat** she brought in etc.; with suff. **ailẖ** he brought him in MG 275:7 f.; **ailan** he brought me in MG 253:paen.; **ailuia** they brought him in; **ailu** they brought her in MG 279:15 f.; **rahmuiẖ lplanita uailuiẖ blibẖ ḏ-plan** DC 46 (a love-charm) they will make him love (*pf. propheticum*) N (woman) and put her into the heart of N (man); **šabšat aiiltẖ** Gy 115:17 she duped (him and) made him enter; **aiiltun** ye brought (me) in (identical with the form without suff.) MG 253:paen. f., pl. with **-n-**: **ailunak** (var. **ailunan**) they brought thee (var. me) in MG 274:17; with encl. **ailibẖ** I brought therein MG 253:anteantep. Impf. **taiil**, neg. **lataiil hasiruta ʿl ʿuṣrak** Jb 36 and let not error enter thy mind!; **uganabia lharia nailun** AM bandits will attack noblemen (idomatic, cf. below); with suff. **nailak** (he will bring thee in), we (shall) bring thee in MG 253:ult.; **nʿiaulak, naulak** id. MG 215: 21 f.; **nailẖ** we (shall) bring him in MG 275: 31; **nailinak** they bring thee in MG 254:1; **nailinun** they bring them in, ibid.; **ʿiailak** I (shall) bring thee in MG 273:18 f. Impt. with suff. **ailẖ** Gy 135:13 bring him in! Act. pt. **maiil** he bringeth in MG 131:ult. Pass. fem. **maila** *introducta est* (formally identical with the act.) MG 253:anteantep. Participial pres. **mailit** thou bringest in MG 253:antep.; with suff. **maililẖ** they bring him in, ibid.

taiil ḏ-razia DC 36 thou shalt enter (be initiated) the arcana; **ʿiul lbit ginzai** Gy 144:3 I shall enter my treasure-house; **al bgu pagra** Gs 59:20 it went into the body; **umaililẖ bpagra ulaila** Gs 74:antep., they (seek to) put it into the body, but it entereth not the body.

Idioms: Af. with **b** sometimes 'to invade, attack', cf. **umata bmata tiiul** AM and town will invade town; with **l, ʿl** 'to attack, oppose': **ʿul lkulhun razia** DC 40 attack all the mysteries; **ʿiul ʿzil ldaiua** DC 44. 2063 I shall attack (and) go against the demon; **bhad traṣa ḏ-razia ḏ-had mn habrẖ la nipuq ulaniul ʿlẖ** DC 27. 392 in a single celebration of mysteries, of which not one is disassociated from or in opposition to another; **anat šambra ʿiil kuhrania ltit . . . tiul bṭab** DC 48 thou, Rue, attack maladies (send them) below . . . thou shalt come in with benefit, Or, p. 325: antepenult.

Der.: **mala 2.**

ALL II (אלל, ܐܠܠ) rt. of **alalta.**

ALL III = YLL I.

ALL IV = YLL II.

ALM I (אלם, cf. Targ. & Talm. אִלְמָא, אִילְמָא mute, ignorant) to make dumb, foolish, to bemuse. Pe. Pt. pl. with suff. **almilun** (**lanašia**) Gy 389:7 they make (people) foolish.

ALM II, ʿLM (עלם to be strong) rt. of **almana** = **ʿlimana.**

alma 1 (עָלְמָא, ܥܳܠܡܳܐ) world. St. abs. & cstr. **alam** (often as) *αἰών* age, eternity, Ginzā 46 n. 4. Pl. **almia** (often as) beings, persons, people, Ginzā 6 n. 1, ML 5 n. 1, MSchr. 3 n. 3. **alma ḏ-nhura** (often) world of Light, **alma ḏ-hšuka** (often) world of Darkness (two dualistic principles: world of celestial and of infernal beings); **alma ḏ-kušṭa uhaimanuta ḏ-kadba unikla litbẖ** Gy 32:1 a world of faithfulness and belief without lie and deception; **alma ḏ-busmania ḏ-riha saina litlẖ** Gy 31:ult. world of perfumes with no stink; **almun** their world MG 181:2; **lalam** (often) *εἰς τοὺς αἰῶνας*; **lalam almia** (often) *εἰς τοὺς αἰῶνας τῶν αἰώνων*; **mn lalam** Gy 274:14 from ever; **hašta lalam iuma** DC 54 now and evermore.

alma 2 (לְמָא + עַד = ܥܕܡܐ) until, till (often with **ḏ** or **ld** as **alma ḏ-, alma ld-**) MG 210:10 ff. Syntactic construction MG 423 f., 446. **alma liumai** Gy 162:ult. until today; **alma ḏ-bi miṣria** Gy 152 until the frontier; **alma lšub šnia** Gy 149 until seven years, only after seven years.

alma 3 (Talm. אלמא < על מא) why, wherefore, about what? (also **almahu**, ꞉l **mahu** = + על הו + מא) MG 207. **alma bakitun** Gy 173:20 why do ye weep?

almana = ꞉limana.

ALS, ALṢ II (אָלַס) pa. to bite, snap with teeth.
PA. Act. pt. **malis** AM 121:ult. (var. Ṣâb's copy **maliṣ**) he will bite (of a madman).

ALP, YLP, ꞉LP (אלף = ילף, ܝܠܦ) pe. (from **YLP**) to learn, practise, train oneself, to practise with skill; af. to teach, instruct MG 83 f.
PE. All forms from **YLP**.
PA. Pf. **alip** (mod. *allef*) he taught; with suff. **alpinun** he taught them MG 281:20; **alpun** ATŠ II no. 11 they taught me. Impf. **nalip** *doce(bi)t* MG 244:18. Pt. **malip** id. ibid.; with encl. **maliplun hukumta d̲-kadba** DC 34. 348 he teaches them false wisdom. Participial pres. (pass.) **malpit** thou wert taught MG 244:19; **kd̲ malpit burkh̲ ꞉l bit anašak qadmaia** CP 131:16 as thou wert taught, bless thy first home!; **kul d̲-malpilh̲ ula ialip** ATŠ I no. 235 everyone whom they teach and he learneth not; **malpilun** DAb they (will) teach them; **malpinalak bṣaidia** Jb 153:10 we shall make thee known to the fishermen; **hukumta usibruta malpatlun** CP 200:15 thou teachest them wisdom and the faith; **malpitulun** Gy 22 *bis*. Inf. **malupia** teaching, to teach; with suff. **malpinun** to teach them MG 293:12.
Gl. 10:9 f. **alip** اعلم *nuntiare* بشارت داد; 113:9 f. **ALP** (pa.) علّم *docere* آموخت.
DER.: **alupa** (= **ialupa**), **malpana, malpanaiit,** (**iulpana** s. **YLP**).

ALP II, LUP I, LPP (s. **LUP**) to wrap, enfold. **alpat** Gy 183:4 she wrapped.

alpa (אלפא, ܐܠܦܐ) thousand MG 190:6. St. abs. **alip, alp.** Pl. **alpia. šita alpia** 6,000 MG 190:7; **trisar alpia šnia** 12,000 years; **hanatin alip šnia** those thousand years; **tmanima alpia ruban ꞉utria** 8,000,000,000 uthras MG 347:1 ff.; **hazin alpa batraiia** this last thousand; **hda alpa** one thousand; **alpa d̲-zibnia** 1,000 times; (**hda**) **alpa d̲-šnia** = **alip šnia** = **šnia alpa** 1,000 years; **trin alpia šnia** 2,000 years etc. MG 348; **alpa anilh̲** a thousand answered to him; **alip alip** a thousand thousand MG 346:14 f.

ALṢ, ꞉LṢ (ܐܠܨ) to press, torture MG 241 n. 1.
PE. Pf. **alaṣ** he pressed. Pass. pt. **꞉liṣ** compressed, narrow. **nišma bhakimuta ṭupra l꞉ngirta alaṣ** CP 90:10 the soul in her wisdom pressed her nail down on (the seal of) the letter; **biria ꞉liṣa** CP 110:16, Q 56:12 a narrow street.
DER.: **alaṣa, hlaṣa, ꞉ulṣana.**

am JRAS 1939 590:13 = ꞉**m.**

ama 1 (עַמָּא, ܥܡܐ) people, nation, folk MG 100:13. Pl. **amamia** nations MG 31:23, 163:9. **ama d̲-iahuṭaiia** Gy 120:19 the Jewish people, the Jews; **ama d̲-iazuqaiia** s. **iazuqaiia**; **ama d̲-bit ꞉sraiil** Gy 120:15 f. the people of Israel; **ama d̲-naṣuraiia** Gy 234:12, etc. (the people of) the Naṣoraeans; **bit ama** Jb 67:7, 93:8, 12, ML 210:1, 211:3 the synagogue; **amamia taumia ulišania** Gy 220:18, Gs 75:11, etc. peoples, nations and tongues; **amamia udaria** Gy 173:20, 175:10 peoples and generations; **amamia ubabia** Gy 24:2 peoples and sects; **amamia trisar** Gy 58:5 the 12 peoples; **lbar mn šita ušaba amamia** CP 156:7 beyond the six or seven peoples, cf. n. 1, MR 60; **marguš d̲-amamia** CP 162:4 the tumult of the nations (used as גּוֹיִם Ps. 2:1); **ama nukraia** AM 218:11 a foreign people.

ama 2 (אַמָּא; ܐܡܐ, ܐܡܬܐ H. אַמָּה) ell, forearm. Pl. **amia, amamia** ells MG 163 n. 2. ꞉**urkh̲ tlatma amia** Gy 380:12 its length 300 ells; **mn ainaniata d̲-burkh̲ umn ginia d̲-amh̲** DC 48 from his knee-caps and from his armpits.

ama 3 = **ma 2** (q.v.).

amai (mod., perh. < יוֹמֵי) today (pron. *â mây*). ꞉**hai qašaplia amai bišia qamdalia amai ṭabia** CP 234:5 f. = ŠQ 18:3 lo, the wicked are abased today, the good are raised up today!

amakuta (rt. **MKK**) = **makuta 1**: **bṭuria d̲-arqa bamakuta ub꞉umqa titaia** DC 43 J 21 within mountains of earth, in the depths and in the lower profundity.

amalia Gs 95:5 a var. of **malia 2** (q.v.).

amamia a pl. of **ama 1, 2.**

amamit, mamit (rt. **AMM**?) a female deity of the underworld, a name of Libat (Venus). **zauak amamit** Gy 138:10 thy wife A.; **libat amamit** = **ruha** Gy 28:17, cf. MSchr. 457, Ginzā Ind. I; **amamit** (var. **mamit**) **ṣṭartia** HG (var. DC 36) the little Amamit; **amamit brath̲ d̲-qin** DC 27 A. daughter of Q.

aman꞉l, varr. **amanu꞉il, amun꞉l, amun꞉il,** ꞉**muna꞉l** (עִמָּנוּ אֵל *Ἐμμανουήλ*) Gy 28:17, etc. Emmanuel.

amar (Ar. آمار) affairs, aspects, amount. **amar madnia** AM 152 astrological aspects; **amar d̲-zidqa** Zotb. 219 left col.: 30 amount of the alms.

amara, var. **aumara** (Ar. أُمَرَاءُ) AM 262:12 the princes BZ 164 n. 3.

amaria (etym. unknown) bier. The form seems to be with the suff. (i.e. **amarh̲**) not pl. **kd̲ d̲-amaria abdia kulman d̲-luath̲ qarib nisih̲ mia unidakia napšh̲** ATŠ 6 (ATŠ 36 II no. 332 has **kd̲ d̲-amamia abdia**) (of funeral practices:) when they make his bier, any person that approaches it shall wash in water and purify himself.

amarit ('thou-causest-to-dwell' **AMR**?) a name given to Mother Earth ATŠ I no. 249. (ATŠ 6 has **amamit**: see under).

amata pl. of **amta.**

amat꞉ta a genius MZ 5, AIT Gl. A.

ambara = ꞉**mbra**

ambuba, anbuba (ܐܢܒܘܒܐ, אבובא, Ar. loan-w. انبوب) tube, flute, (reed-)pipe MG 50:19 & n. 3, 135:3, AramFw 23 f. Pl. **ambubia** (var. **anbubia**) flutes, tubes. **ambuba d̲-libh̲** Oxf. roll g 635, **ambubia d̲-libh̲** Or. 327:2 the tube(s) of his heart; **ṭiblia uambubia** Gy 60:5, 112:8, Gs 14:3 drums and flutes; **zmara**

uambubia Gy 225:4 singing and flutes; **kinara uambuba** Gy 176:23 harp and flute; **biluria uambubia** Gs 75:14 cymbals and flutes; **šipuria uambubia** Gy 105:8 horns and flutes.

ambura (cf. ܚܒܘܪܐ cord?) **hatma ḏ-hu a-m-b-u-r-a** DC 41 (in a passage about the symbolism of ritual in the *masiqta*) the seal which is a cord (? context suggests 'umbilical cord').

ambra = ʿmbra. Gl. 69:8 **anbra** خروف *ovis* گوسفند ; 85:8 **anbraria** رعية *grex* رعيت.

AMD (ܥܡܕ) to perform a Christian baptism, baptize in cut-off water. Used only in pa. (pt.). **ubmia psiqia mamidilun** Gy 57:1 and he baptizes them with cut-off water, Ginzā 51 n. 1; **mamidilhun** Gy 226:8 they baptize them.

Der.: **mamiduta.**

amhata a pl. of **amta.**

amu, mu (< על מאהו, mod. **qamu** pron. *qâmû*) why, wherefore? MG 61:25, 94:5. **amu** = ʿl **mahu** Gs 55:18. **amu qrun mn atrai** Gs 38:ult. wherefore did they call me from my place?

amud = **mud**: **uamud piš mn mandaiia ʿtabadariun** (Ṣâb.'s AM:coloph.) *et quodcumque remansit ex Mandaeis dispersi sunt*; **ṣauirtẖ amud ḏ-mṣia hailai** DC 7 right side:94 I pictured it as well as I could; **kidbit minẖ amud mṣit** ATŠ I no. 297 I wrote from it as much as I could; **ukdab minẖ amud mṣa hailẖ umadihtẖ** ATŠ II no. 409 and he wrote from it as well as his capacity and judgement permitted; **kidbit amud hzat ainai** ATŠ II no. 409 I wrote as faithfully as my eyes could see.

amuza (cf. Löw s. ܓܘܙܐ & ISK 89) walnut MMII 188. **šigdia ušukar uamuza lmhadiania** ŠQ 8:23 almonds, sugar, and walnuts for the wedding guests. (Frequent in lists of ritual meals.)

amunʿil, amunʿl s. **amanʿl.**

amuq, ʿmuq (rt. **ʿMQ**) deep MG 125:8 f. No st. emph. sg. found, pl. **amuqia** *profundi*. **ruianẖ ʿmuq ukibša blibẖ** AM 74:2 her thought will be depressed and she will be down-hearted; **ubit ainẖ unhirẖ amuq** AM 83:14 and her eye-sockets and her nose (will be) deep-set (flat?); **nahlia amuqia** Or. 327:11 deep rivers; **umia ḏ-iama amuqia** DC 22. 176 and the water of the sea is deep.

amuta s. **amta.**

amin (אָמֵן) Amen. **amin amin sala** (אָמֵן אָמֵן סֶלָה) (a frequent terminal of exorcisms) MMII 27.

amin glaita DC 43 J 164 f. a demon.

amin hambukaita DC 43 J 165 a demon.

amintul, mintul (Talm. אמטול, Syr. ܡܛܠ) conj. for, because (of); prep. **amintulat-** (with pers. suff.) because of, for the sake of MG 33:14 f., 51:15 f., 195:5 f.; **amintul l** s. **l 2**; **amintul ḏ, ʿl amintul ḏ-** because, on account of MG 210:7. 465:28 ff.; **amintul mindam ḏ-** because of that what (s. **mindam**). With suff. **amintulatak** CP 191:1, 4, 7 for thy sake; **amintulatik nišimta** Gs 76:11 for thy sake, o soul; **lau amintul ḏ-dilkun atit** Gs 69:10 not on your account did I come; **amintul lnaṭuria ḏ-adam** Gs 76 (in order) to guard A.

amir (Ar. أمير) AM 155:9 prince. Gl. 36:5 **amira** امير *princeps*.

amlak (أَمْلاك) possessions, fields. **ʿtabadariun bamlak** (Ṣâb.'s AM:coloph.) they were dispersed in the fields.

amlaiia, mlaiia (rt. **MLA**) full(ness). **nišra . . . ḏ-ganpẖ amlaiia ḏ-alma** Jb 141 an eagle . . . whose wings are world-wide (span the world).

amlaš (Ar. أُمْلوج) AM 287:3 wild dates, sugar candy.

amlia = **mlia**: Gl. 144:7 **amlia** كامل *plenus* تمام.

AMM (עמם rel. to עמי, ܥܡܐ) to grow dim. A rt. of **amamit**? **amamit aina mṣuṣtia ḏ-libat** JRAS 1937 596:16 thou art extinguished, peeping eye of Libat (Venus).

AMN (אמן, ܐܡܢ) to be firm, true. Haf. to believe, Ettaf. to be found true, firm, worthy of trust, faithful.

Pe. used only in the pass. pt. **amin** firm, strong, trustworthy. **had šliha ḏ-amin** DC 37. 568 a trustworthy messenger; **mia amin mia nišar** DC 51 the water is efficacious, the water preserves.

Haf. Pf. **haimin** MG 244:4, **haiman** MG 211:22, 244:22 he, they believed; with encl. **haimanubẖ** they believed in him MG 211:22; **haimanubak bspia mhaimanata** Gy 5:10 they confessed thee with faithful lips; **haiminubia, haimanubia** they believed in me, **haimanabak** we believe(d) in thee MG 244:4 ff. Impf. **nihaimnun** they (will) believe, with encl. **tihaiminubẖ, tihaimanubẖ** ye (shall) believe in him MG 244: 6 f., pl. id.; **haiman blibaikun** Gy 21 *credite in cordibus vestris!* pl. with encl. **haiminubẖ, haimanubẖ** believe in him! MG 244:8. Pt.: act. **mhaimin** believing, believer; pass. **mhaiman** (found) trustworthy MG 132:4; **mhaiman mn iahuṭaiia** Gy 29 he finds believers among the Jews.

Ettaf. Pf. **ʿthaiman bhiia rurbia** DC 48. 137 he believed in the Mighty Life; **ʿthaimanin** we became firm MG 244:10. Pt. **mandaia ḏ-mšalam haka hu ḏ-mn tarmidia mithaiman** DC 36 a perfect Mandaean is one who is found faithful by the priests. Impt. **ʿthaiman** be firm! MG 244:10.

Gl. 6:15 f. **HYMN** امن *credere* ايمان آورد, 52:1 f. id. تيقن *certus esse* يقين شد.

Der.: **mhaimna, haimanuta, amin.**

amna 1 = **mna. amna atit** Jb 129:ult. whence comest thou?

amna 2 = **mna. la tihun amna hšuka** Jb. 49:8 be not the portion of darkness!

amsia = **msia** (q.v.).

AMṢ, ʿMṢ (עמץ, ܥܡܨ) to close, shut up, shut in.

Pe. Pf. with encl. **amaṣlẖ** (var. **amiṣlia**) **lpumẖ** Gy 394 (var. DC 22. 389) he closed up his mouth. Impf. with suff. **nimṣunẖ** (**bṣuṣt-mia ḏ-mia**) DC 43 they shall shut him in (with barriers of water). Pass. pt. **ʿmiṣ(a)**, pl. fem. **ʿmiṣan (ainaihun)** Jb 168:9 f. (their eyes) are shut.

Der.: **amṣa, ʿumṣa.**

amṣa (rt. **AMṢ**) conclusion, end. Gl. 143:12 **amṣa** كمال *consummatio* آخر.

AMR I (אמר, ܐܡܪ) to say, speak, talk, narrate, discuss, command.

Pe. Pf. **amar** he said, **amrat, ʿmrat** she said MG 241, neg. **lamrat** Gy 5:17 she did not say, **amart** thou didst say, **ʿmrit** I said MG 241, **ana mrit** Zotb. 228 left col.:7 = **ana amrit** ibid. 8 id., special pl. form **amariun** they said, **amartun**, fem. **amartin** ye said, **amarnin** we said MG 241; with encl. **amaralẖ, amaralia, amarilun** she said to him, to me, to them, **amarilẖ, amarilkun, amarilun** I said to him, to you, to them (Gy 75:3), **amartulia** ye said to me, **amarnalẖ, amarnalak** we said to him, to thee MG 241. Impf. **nimar** he says, will say, we (shall) say, **timar** thou sayest, wilt say, **ʿmar** I (shall) say, **nimrun** they (will) say, **timrun** ye (will) say MG 241; with encl. **nimarlẖ** Gy 330:9, 17 he said to her, **timarlun** Gy 330:3 she said to them (both as past, cf. below), **nimirbun** Jb 224: he will command them, **nimrulia, nimirulia, nimurulia** they (will) say to me, **nimrulẖ, nimirulẖ** they (will) say to him, **timirulẖ, timirulun** ye (will) say to him, to them MG 242. Impt. **amar, amur** say! MG 242:20 (& n. 4), pl. id.: **amar bpumaikun** Gy 21 speak with your mouths!, special pl. form **amuriun (ḏ-la mitmar)** DC 31 tell (that which is not being talked about); **uamuriun (zhara kḏ amritun briš)** DC 50 and repeat (the rubric as ye said [it] at the beginning); with encl. **amarulia** speak to me, **amarulẖ, amurulẖ** speak to him MG 242:23 f. Act. pt. **amar** he says, will say MG 57:16, 149:8, 242:paen., **amra** she says, will say MG 149:8, **amria, amrin** they (will) say MG 3:antep., 149:8; participial pres. **amrit** thou sayest, wilt say, **amarna, amirna** I (shall) say MG 15:27. Pass. pt. **ʿmir** *dictus* MG 243:1. Inf. **mimar** saying, to say MG 243:2.

Ethpe. Pf. **ʿtmar** was said MG 70:8, 243:5; with encl. **la ʿtmarlia** Gy 94:20 it was not told me. Impf. **nitmar** it is (will be) told me MG 380:3, **raza nitmar** AM 218:2 the secret will be told. Pt. **mitmar** *dictus* MG 132:12, 243:5, (= **nitmar**) MG 380:3. The impf. is often used as a historical pres.: **timar utaudẖ** Gy 82:2 she said and instructed him; **malil ḏ-nimar** (often) = تكلّم يقول etc. MG 371; act. pt. in the same way: **šailit uamarilia** Gy 181:9 etc. I asked and they answered me; **tnat ʿhailat uamra** Gy 93:5 for the second time she got strength and said MG 375. The pers. suff. can be used inst. of the encl.: impt. **ʿumrẖ** say to him, tell him! MG 276:12. **ʿštalṭit mimar** s. **ŠLT**; **ʿlkun amirna umaprišna** Jb 224 to you I say and you I instruct; **kadba amritun** Gy 390 ye lie; **dina mitmar mn** often) judgement is pronounced by . . .

Gl. 3:5 f. **AMR** اجاب *respondere*, 5:5 f. اقال *dici* گفته شد, 48:1 f. تكلّم *loqui* گفت, 63:9 f. **AMR** with encl. **l** حرّك *concitare* بجنگ انداخت, 131:3 f. **AMR** قال *dicere* گفت.

Der.: **amar, ʿmra, mimra.**

AMR II, ʿMR (ܥܡܪ, عمر) to dwell, live in, stay in, refl. to settle down, inhabit.

Pe. Pf. (**kḏ hda biša uṭaba ḏ-**) **amar** (**ʿl mia hiia**) ATŠ (like one were the evil and the good that) dwelt upon the living waters; (**ubalmia ḏ-nhura razia šnia bpagra laiit ḏ-timar kḏ btibil**) **amrit** ATŠ I no. 288 (and in the worlds of light there are no transitory bodily mysteries, that thou canst live as) thou didst live (on earth). Impf. **timar** (above ATŠ I). Act. pt. **amar** he dwells MG 242:paen.; **ḏ-amar bdaria malkuta** Gy 3:15 who dwelleth in habitations of kingliness. Participial pres. (**ana haka mitkamran**) **amrana** (**latrai**) DC 34. 84 (and here I am turned back, so) I shall stay (in my place).

Ethpe. Pf. (**uhanatun hatmia alsabria mn hiia**) **la ʿtmar** ATŠ I no. 8 (and those sealings of the believers) abode not (with the Life), without **t** in the pref. (**alma hazin ḏ-**) **ʿmar** DC 22. 166 this world that is inhabited.

amra 1 (עֲמְרָא, ܥܡܪܐ) wool, fleece. Doublet **aqamra** s.v. **amra hiuara** DC 23. 774 white wool.

amra 2 (עֲמְרָם) Amram, father of Moses. **miša br amra** Gy 50:15 (DC 22. 47, DC 44 etc.) Moses son of Amram.

amrazuta a corruption of **mzarzuta**. **qum bamrazutak** (a talisman) rise in thy armour (equipment).

amriduta s. **mriduta.**

AMŠ, ʿMŠ (עמש, ܥܡܫ, غمس) to submerge, plunge into (or under), to souse thoroughly.

Pe. Pf. **amaš** Gy 160: 10 he plunged, **amaš braza ulanbaṭ** ATŠ II no. 289 he plunged into a mystery and did not emerge (again); **amašiun bimanda** DC 41. 167 they soused the cult-hut; with suff. **amaštinun** Gy 351:17 (var. Sh. ʿAbd.'s copy **amištinun**) I plunged them MG 282:25. Impf. **nimuš** he plunges. Act. pt. **amiš** ATŠ I no. 41, pl. (**nagdia tum**) **amšia** DC 7 (they flow out and then) they dive under; (**uminaihun ḏ-**) **amšin atutia** ibid. (and some of them that) plunge beneath. Pass. pt. **ʿmiš** dipped: **kḏ ʿmiš bzma ḏ-hizura** AM 131:8 f. when dipped in pig's blood. (See also **ʿMŠ**.)

Der.: **ʿumušiata** (var. **ʿumi-**).

amta (אמתא, ܐܡܬܐ LS), var. **amuta** maid-servant, bondswoman, handmaiden. Pl. **amata** MG 98:7, **amhata** (s.v.). **uamta ʿu armalta tištamulẖ** AM 82:6 and a maid-servant or a widow will serve her; **abdia uamaṭa** (often) slaves and bondswomen.

-an 1 Gen. Aram. ending of the st. abs. fem. pl. (often only **-a**, s. **-a 2**) MG 162:7.

-an 2 suff. of the 1st p. pl. MG § 145.

ANA I, ʿNA I (עני, ܥܢܐ, H. ענה) to answer, reply, respond.

Pe. Pf. with suff. **anan** he answered me MG 284:22, **ʿnian** id. MG 284:24, **anatẖ** she answered him MG 287:antep., **anun** they answered me MG 285:paen., **ʿniun** id. MG 286:3, **ʿniuia** they answered him (her) MG 288:22. Impf. with suff. **ninian** *responde(bi)t mihi* MG 285:1, **niniẖ** *responde(bi)t ei*, (*respondebimus ei*) MG 287:15, **ʿniak** I (shall) answer thee MG 286:21 f., **ʿninkun** Gy 261:1 I (shall) answer you, **niniuk** they (will) answer thee MG 287:4. Impt. with suff. **ʿunian** answer me! MG 285:5, **ʿunian ab ʿunian** CP 122:21 ff. answer me, my Father, answer me!, **ʿuniun** *respondete mihi!* MG 286:21. Participial forms with encl. **anʿlun** DAb he answereth them, **aniḻẖ** Gy 6:ult. they answer him.

Der.: **ʿniana.**

ANA II, ANH, ʿNA II, TNA II, TNH (אנח, ܐܢܚ, Akk. *anâḫu*), to sigh, groan, lament.

Ettaf. Pf. ***ʿtana** (not found). Impf. (**ʿl kma**) **ʿtana** Jb 33 (how) I must sigh! Pt. **mitana** Gs 49:19 he groans.

Der.: **tinta.**

ana 1 (אֲנָא, ܐܢܐ) I (pers. pron.) MG 28:8, 86:8. Gl. 28:7 **ana** انا *ego* من.

ana 2 (var. of **aqna** q.v.) sheep, herd, flock MG 73:1. Pl. **ania** DAb. transl. 11 n. 9. **ʿla ḏ-anai ḏ-ganian bišlum** Jb. 41:8 f. however, my flock was lying down in peace.

anaia = **naia.**

anamia (נְעָמֵי, cf. نغم, نغمة ; ܢܥܡܬܐ) tunes, melodies, songs. Var. **anmia.** Sg. unknown MG 26:10. **zmaria uanamia** Gy 218:12 (var. DC 22. 211 **anmia**) songs and melodies.

anana (עֲנָנָא, ܥܢܢܐ), st. abs. & cstr. **anan 2** (B. Aram עֲנָן). (*a*) cloud MG 115:4 f., (*b*) spouse, wife, consort, woman, (*c*) often personified, Lidzb. Ginzā Ind. I, Uthra 544. Used as fem. MG 159:anteantep. Pl. **anania, ananʿ(ia).** **anan ziua** Gy 304:1 the cloud of radiance; **anana ksaita** Q 25:4 the hidden cloud; **qaimia banania** Gy 2:13 who stand in the clouds (i.e. the higher beings Ginzā 6 n. 3); **anana ḏ-nhura** Gy 31 etc. the cloud of light; **durdia ḏ-anania** s. **durdia**; **bnat anania** s. **bnat**; **anan nṣab** (often) a spirit (Lidzb.'s suggestion Ginzā Ind. "I take **anan** as a verbal form 'he granted me', 'he heard [my prayer]'" is improbable); **tartin anania ḏ-nṣab uanan nṣab ʿhablun** Gy 374:13 the two wives (Lidzb. 'clouds') which they gave to Nsab and Anan-Nsab; **iasmus anana, tatagmur anana, šaškiʿil anana, mašqlʿil anana** ibid. etc. pr. nn.; **anania šapirata** (often) lovely women (us. as synonym of priests' women: wives and daughters); **anana ptula** Gy 374:4 the virgin. With suff. **ananai** DAb. my spouse(s), **ananẖ** his spouses. The st. abs. is sometimes used as masc.: **uanan raza ḏ-bhura gla** Jb 9:11 f. and Anan revealed the secret of the light; **anan anan gabra** Gy 374:25 Anan-Anan the man; **bauata ḏ-anan ḏ-anan gabrẖ** DC 36 the prayers of the Spouse, whose husband is Anan. (Cf. Aram. עֲנָן as masc. MG 159:anteantep.) Here could belong also **anan nṣab** (above) 'Anan-planted'. Further pr. nn. in Lidzb.'s Mand. Gl. Mand. priests add the following meanings: (*d*) rain (semantic development of (*a*), cf. **anania miṭra** Gy 10:5 rain clouds), (*e*) house, building (prob. a confusion of **banana** 'in the cloud' with **biniana** 'building', cf. **mn riš banana** and **briš banana** s. **banana**), (*f*) ark, boat, ship (cf. H. אֳנִיָּה, but more prob. a metaphor: 'cloud-boat'), (*g*) cover, protection (metaph.), (*h*) earth, ground (doubtful), (*i*) ears (a mod. pl. of **ʿudna**, coll. pron. *onna*), (*j*) the poor, the miserable (a later pl. of **ania 1**).

ananai = **nanai** (q.v.): **kul ruhia ukul ruh ananai** . . . Or. 331:3 all (evil) spirits and every spirit of Nanai (Venus) . . .; **šria ananai btaga šria libat lʿubada** DC 12 & 29 loosed is Nanai with her crown, loosed is Venus for her works.

anapqa, napqa (Iranian, cf. *anapak* Bartholomae 123a, Horn: *Grundr. d. pers. Etym.*, no. 1015, Talm. loan-w. אַנְפָּקָא, אַנְבְּגָא, Gr. ἄμβικος, cf. ISK 89), cup, drinking-vessel. Meaning unknown to Lidzb. Ginzā 116 n. 1. Found only in pl. **anapqia**, var. **anapuqia, -iqia. ušatia anapqia** DC 43 J 197; and they drink (from) cups; **nirig aitla anapqia** (varr. **anapuqia, anapiqia**) **kulhun** Gy 106:13 (varr. Sh. 'Abd.'s copy & DC 22. 101) Nirig (Mars) brought all drinking-cups.

anaqia (rt. **ANQ** = ܐܢܩ) groaners. **nuqbata bakian kḏ anaqia** Jb 251:5 the female (demons) cry like groaners.

anaša, naša (אֱנָשָׁא, ܐܢܫܐ) human being. Sg. in the gen. construction **br (a)naša**, later also **barnaša** a man, an individual, pl. **anašia**, var. **anašiʿ** Gy 49:18 AB people, **bnia anaša**, less often **bnat anaša, bnat anašia** human beings, individuals, people MG 182 f. St. abs. sg. **ʿniš** (s.v.). Mod. **naš, naša**, pl. **ʿnšia** (pron. *nâš, nâša, enšî*) people, **barnaša 1** (pron. *barnâša*) see above. **bit anašak** thy family-house, **bit anašaihun** their family-house.

anašata (**anaš** with the pl. end. **-ata**) family, kinsfolk; with suff. **anašatkun** your family, **anašatun** their family MG 183:6 ff.

anašuta (ܐܢܫܘܬܐ Nöld. ZDMG xxii 519) humanity, human beings, people. **ubanašuta** . . . **nišanqia nišauun** Gy 384:antep., they shall show forth signs amongst people; **tumria uanašuta nišiprun** AM 251:2 dates and people will flourish.

anat 1 (differently from ܐܢܬ, אַתְּ > אַנְתְּ) pers. pron. thou MG 32:17, 86:antep. ff. (53 n. 1), but mod. **at** (pron. *ât*).

anat 2 a rare pl. of **anta** woman. With suff. **anatun** their wives. **abdia mn maraihun uzauaiun** (read **zauia**) **mn anatun** DC 35 slaves with their masters, husbands with their wives.

anatan an infernal being, husband of Qin

MSchr. 146 n. 2, Ginzā Ind. I, DAb Ap. I. Accord. to Kessler PRE 181 the Old-Bab. *Anat.* **anatan qarabtana d̲-hšuka uzauh̲ qin** Gy 140:2, cf. 1.7, the warrior of Darkness and his wife Q.; **anatan mlaka rba d̲-hšuka** DC 43 A. the great angel of Darkness; **iaqut d̲-anatan** DAb the ruby of A.

anatata (a pl. of **anta** by adding a further **-ta** to the fem. end.) the females. See also **ntata. gadia uanatata** ATŠ I no. 256 the goats and nanny-goats.

anat hiia ('Thou-art-the-Life'; Lidzb. suggested a connexion with ענת of the papyri Ginzā Ind. I) Gy 108:1 a higher female being. Used also as a *malwâša* woman's name.

anatun (differently from ܐܢ̱ܬܘܢ, אתון) pers. pron. of the 2nd p. pl. you, ye MG 32:17, 86:antep. ff. (53 n. 1), but mod. **atun** (pron. *atton*), cf. Gl. 28:8 **atun** انتم *vos* شما, تو.

anbaza (P. همباز) AM partner, mate.

anbar AM 198 a city on the Euphrates in neo-Babylonian and Moslem times BZ Ap. II.

anbuba s. **ambuba.**

anbia = **nbiha, nbiia.** Gl. 168:1 **anbia** نبى *propheta* پيغمبر.

anga (rt. **NGA II**) injury, affliction. Pl. **angia. mutana utigra uhamid auanga hauibh̲** AM 166:16 there will be mortality, strife, wrath, and affliction in it; **kṣurta umaskinuta uangia** AM 160 sickness, poverty, and afflictions.

angauia, ʿngauia (Targ. אַנְגְוָון) islands MG 166 n. 2. No sg. found. **angauia iama** Gy 175:2, 5 the islands of the sea; **nihtit angauia d̲-girba** DC 40. 28 f. I came down to the northern islands (?).

angara 1, ʿngara (ܐܶܓܳܪܳܐ roof) occurring only in pl. and in the gen. constr. **br angaria** AM 120:12 (var. Ṣâb.'s copy **ʿngaria**) roof-demons, lunatic demons (cf. ܐܶܓܳܪܳܐ ܒܰܪ) and **bnia angaria** DC 37. 36, 94, 146 etc. id.

angara 2. Gl. 36:6 **angara** انجر *ancora* لنگر. Found in no text.

anguza (cf. Löw s. ܓܘܙܐ & ISK 89, P. گوز, Ar. loan-w. جوز, H. אֱגוֹז, Talm. אַמְגוּזָא) nuts, almonds; **ʿnbia uanguza** (often in lists of ritual food) raisins (grapes) and nuts.

Gl. 75:9 **anguza**; جوز *nux* گردو.

angulana s. **anglia.**

angiʿil s. **angʿil.**

anglia pl., later pl. **angulana** (cf. עִגְלָא, ܥܶܓ̈ܠܶܐ) prob. calves. Found only in pl. **uankus iaminh̲ anglia** AM 121:20 (var. Ṣâb.'s copy **uankis iaminh̲ d̲-angulana**) and let his right hand slaughter calves (?).

angʿil a name given to Bel-Jupiter. **angʿil** (var. **angiʿil**) **d̲-bil qarilh̲** Gy 121:13 (var. DC 22. 116) A. whom they call Bel (Jupiter).

ANDA (**ADA I,** influenced by the af. **NDA**; forms with suff. identical with the af. of **NUD** 'to shake') to pass by, through, on, into, pass out, remove: **anda biama . . . anda bnura** CP 40:4, 16; 41:9, Q 17:24, 33, 18:8 he passed into the sea . . . he passed into the fire. With suff. **uiahibia niaria lšganda uandinun** ATŠ II no. 103 and they give the bowls to the assistant and he passes them (out?); **gargla ʿlaia ʿl kulhun garglia andinun** DC 34. 290 the upper sphere surpassed (i.e. is over) all spheres.

andaza, andazta (P. اندازه, verb **ANDZ**) measure, quantity, measuring, assessment, summing up, setting-up, collecting, set piece, calculation. MG 127:11. **andaza lnapšh̲ abda ubnia ubnata mitqaimilh̲** AM 75:8 she will take care of herself (idiom.) and will rear sons and daughters; **andazta rba** [*sic*] Jb 177:3 a great summing up; **bandazta rabtia d̲-hʿ mambarta d̲-bhiria zidqa mitqiria** ATŠ II no. 378 in the Great Assessment which is called the Transit of the Righteous Elect; **abatar andazta** (often in ATŠ) after calculation, after assessment (refers to menstrual periods, examination of the candidate for priesthood, etc.); **kd̲ msaiak mn andazta šualia** CP 349:9 when the assessment of the novice is finished; **andazta d̲-mṣararlh̲ lmamla umasbarlh̲ lišana** DC 34 (which is) the instrument (P. انداز) formed for speech and teacheth the tongue.

andalus (اندلوس) Am 204 Andalusia, Spain.

andalima AM 205 (varr. **andarima, andirima, andarma**) a place-name BZ Ap. II.

andašta (P. انديشه) meditation, carefulness, consideration, pondering, care, careful thought, anxious thought, anxiety MG 127:10. Pl. **andašata,** with suff. **andašatak** Jb 23:3 thy meditations, **andašatan** ATŠ colophon, our worries, **andašatkun** Jb 62:5 your anxious plannings; **andašata d̲-lašalman** Jb 58:8 never-ceasing anxieties; **andašata d̲-hazin alma** Jb 61:2 *αἱ μέριμναι τοῦ αἰῶνος* (Mark 4:19); **andašata uhauqa** ATŠ II no. 112 cares and fear; **bandašata (d̲-libaihun) d̲-ʿutria** ATŠ II nos. 53, 235 in the thoughts (of the hearts) of the uthras; **ridpan uandaštan nupša bla kila uminiana** ATŠ II no. 441 our affliction and anxiety augmented without measure or count; **uʿpilbh̲ bandašata d̲-lbuša baṭla** Gs 62:17 f. and I (must) fall into the anxieties of the perishable garment (i.e. the body); **kulhun bandašata anpal** Gs 63:12 f. all of them fell into anxious thought; **bandašata d̲-napša** Jb 25:5 f. with much anxious care.

andulus AM 202 = **andalus.**

ANDZ (P. انداز, انداختن) to measure off, cut off a quantity, set forth, assess, sum up, mark off, mark out, (of a manuscript:) copy from, compare with another, assemble, gather, collect, recite (a set book). Used only as af. and ettaf. MG 211 f. Pf. **andiz** DC 34. 24 he set forth, special pl. **andiziun** Oxf. 144 b, Lond. roll A 62; with suff.: **andizth̲** Oxf. 14 b. Impf. **unandiz mn šumaihun ʿl kbiš hšuka** Lond. roll A 117 and he recites (the set book) from '(In) the name of' to 'Darkness is crushed'. Impt. **andiz** Lond. roll A 61, 117. Act. pt. **(tum) mandiz (kul ginzih̲)** DC 6 & 36 (then) he shall set out (all his treasures, i.e. ritual objects); **umandiz alma lkbiš hšuka**

CP 349:1 and he shall recite (the allotted prayers) until the 'Darkness is crushed' (a prayer). Pass. pt. **mandaz** MG 211:antep.: **tum hua hazin sidra mandaz mn sidra ḏ-** (often in the colophons) so this book was copied from . . .; **lamandaz bgauẖ kudkia** RD B 15, Jb 184:12, Gs 13:11, 84:10 no milestones were erected in it (: it is not marked out by milestones). MG 305, pl. **mandizia** (as from act. pt.): **tum mandizia halin diuanan** DC 36 and so these scrolls were copied; **tum halin bauata mandizia** DC 9: coloph., and so these prayers were copied. Inf. (haf.) **handuzia** ML 144:9, Gy 366:19 measuring, to measure MG 211:ult. f. Ettaf. only pt. pl. **mitandizia** Jb 175:13 *bis* they shall be allotted MG 211:paen., 230:20. Nom. act. **andazta** s. **andaza.**

andim AM 197 a place-name BZ Ap. II.

andiruna (s. **andruna**) a ritual hut built for marriage rites and the consecration of a priest MMII 149 ff.

andirima AM 197 s. **andalima.**

andruna, ʿndruna (P. اندرون, Parthian *andrun* 'in' MBBb 107, ISK 33), varr. **andiruna** (q.v.), **ʿndiruna** chamber, booth. Gl. 183:13 **andrun** داخل *intra* اندرون.

ANDŠ (P., cf. nom. act. **andašta,** Manich. Soghd. *andišn*, Pahl. *handēš*) to be anxious, think carefully about.

Af. Pf. **landišt** Jb 20:14, 21:1 thou wast unreflecting MG 212:2, 222:27; special pl. **andišiun** PD 53. Participial pres. (**umn sikina ḏ-parzla**) **lamandišan** Jb 41:8 and they are not troubled (about an iron knife).

ANH I, ANA II, ʿNA II, TNA II, TNH (אנח, انس Akk. *anâḫu* LS) to sigh, groan.

Ettaf. Pt. **umitanha nišmatun** Gy 253: antep., and their souls groan.

Der.: **tinuhta, tinihta.**

ANH II = ANA I, ʿNA I. Exceptional. **anihat uamralia** DC 13 & 44 she answered and said to me.

anhar a *malwâša* woman's name. **anhar ziua** Gy 108:3 a supernatural female being, Ginzā Ind. I; **anhar ziua haua** Gy 108:5 id., born of Eve; **anhar zauẖ** Morg. 88:11 his (: John the Baptist's) wife; **anhar** DAb = RD 7 identified with Libat.

anhura = nhura: Gl. 168:9 **anhura** نور *lux.*

anhimta = nhimta 1: anhimtẖ anhinta ḏ-ʿnšia Gy 91:1 I made him shriek a womanish shriek.

anhin (with bad varr.) a rare form of **anin** MG 87:5.

anhira = nhira: G. 161:6 **anhira** منخر *nasus* بينى.

anuš, ʿnuš (Bibl. אֱנוֹשׁ) an outstanding uthra, called also **anuš ʿutra**, Biblical Anoš (very often); one of the triad of spirits Hibil, Šitil, and Anuš, cf. Ginzā Ind. I, ML Ind., DAb Ind., MMII Ind., MHenb 28 ff., HpGn Reg. s. Henoch, MSt 29, 126 f., EB s. Mandaeans, MR 124 & n. 2, 130:4 ff. **hibil ušitil uanuš** Gy 157:8, Q 60:11, **hibil ušitil uanuš utria** Gy 101:25 the uthras H., Š., and A.; **anuš ʿutra šliha** Gy 289:10, 14 A.-U. the Apostle (cf. ἄνθρωπος ἀπεσταλμένος John 1:6, AF 251 n. 1, Wid. V 75 no. 1); **maṭarta ḏ-anuš brẖ ḏ-ptahil** DAb the watch-house (: purgatory) of A. son of P.; **anana ḏ-anuš ʿutra** Gy 329:24, 330:9, 17, 331:10 the cloud of A.-U.; **raza usidra ḏ-anuš rba** Gy 249:10 The Mystery and the Book of the Great A. (title of the 11th book of Gy Ginzā 250:2 ff.); **anuš rba br šitil rba** Gy 272:22 A. the Great, son of Š. the Great; **anuš zuṭa brẖ** Gy 270:ult. the little A., his (: Manda-ḏ-Hiia's) son; **anuš br danqa** HG 141, 147 f., 150 a personage from Mand. history in early Islamic times.

anuta a var. of **anašuta** (or pl. of **ana 2** q.v.).

anzaba, ʿnzaba, nzaba (cf. **zaba 1**), torrent, flood MG 43 n. 3. Pl. **anzabia,** var. **anzibia. latra ḏ-anzabia mia** Jb 243:5 to the place of water-torrents, Jb ii 223 n. 2; **anzabia mia** (often); **pt ʿnzaba pšira pt aina rabtia ḏ-nzaba** DC 40. 199 daughter of the unloosed torrent, daughter of the great fountain-head of the torrent (var. **pt anzaba kšira** daughter of the busy [?] torrent, prob. wrong).

anzrara, ʿnzrara (ܚܙܪܘܪܐ, cf. Löw no. 229 pp. 283 ff.) sorb(-apple). **rumana uanzrara . . . uabara lrumana ʿthib uplanza linzrara** DC 34. 376, 379 the pomegranate and the sorb-apple . . . and lead is bestowed on the pomegranate and steel on the sorb.

anṭakia AM Antioch BZ Ap. II.

anṭalia AM 198 a place-name, Anatolia BZ Ap. 11.

ania 1 (עַנְיָא, עַנְיָיא) poor MG 124:12 f. Pl. **aniia** the poor MG 165:12. **ania udania** (in colophons) poor and lowly; **litbẖ lmismak aniia** Jb 127:11 f. there is nothing in it to support the poor; **aniia udaniia** DC 27. 9 pl.

ania 2 (Act. pt. of **ANA I** used adjectivally) answering, attentive, helper, attendant. **huilẖ ania ʿunian** DC 24 be attentive to me (read **-lia**), answer me!; **ania usmaka** DC 41 helper and support; **nihuia lanašia mandaiia ania** ATŠ I no. 234 will be attentive to Mandaean people; **kḏ iadla iadalta man hauila ania** Gs 10 when a woman bears a child, who will be her helper (var. **hauilun ania** will be an attendant for them?, cf. Ginzā 431 n. 4).

ania 3 pl. of **ana 2.**

-ania (P. ـَان) Postcl. and mod. pl. ending MG § 136, pp. 169 f.

aniaha = niaha: **umn aniahun šrun lʿuṣrai** DC 22. 338 and imparted some of its (i.e. the Life's) calm to my thought.

aniuta 1 (עַנְיוּתָא) lowliness, poverty MG 146: 18.

aniuta 2 (ܥܢܝܘܬܐ) answer, response. **nimar anitak ganzibra nimar aniutak lhiia umanda ḏ-hiia** ŠQ 6:20 he shall say 'I answered thee'; the ganzibra shall say 'Thy answer be to the the Life and to M.-ḏ-H.'.

anizta a miscopying of **azizta. mn qudam libat anizta** (= **azizta,** as it occurs later on) DC 40 before the powerful Venus.

anin, an'n (אנן, less often אנין. Chr. Pal. ܐܢܢ) Pers. pron. we MG 16:10, 28:8, 63:14, 86: paen., 87:4 & n. 1. Var. anhin s.v., a dittographical form **anin'n** MG 87:9. Gl. 148:14 **anin** لاننا (*quod, ut*) *nos* ما (براى اینکه).

anka (ܐܢܟܐ from Akk. *anâku*, Ar. loan-w. آنك Fränkel 153) tin MG 112:9. Only st. emph. sg. **tasa d̲-anka** JRAS 1937 595 a tin bowl; **anka uabara** DC 37. 88, DC 44. 1086, DC 43 A 68 etc. tin and lead.

anmia DC 22. 211 a var. of **anamia** (q.v.).

an'n s. **anin.**

ansata (rt. **NSA II**) = **asata 1. ansit mn ansata d̲- . . .** (often in colophons) I copied from the copy of . . .

anpia (אפי, אנפי, ܐܦ̈ܐ) face, presence MG 51:15, 100:9. Used as masc. MG 158:2 ff. With suff. **anpai, anpak,** fem. **anpik, anpih̲ (anph̲)** etc., my, thy, his face. In the Cl. always with **n**; a mod. form is **apa** (pron. *appâ*). **anpia iuma** the early dawn (used as sg. MG 187:5 f.; not the eve of the day, for the Mandaean day begins with the rising of the sun); **alanpia** s.v. **kidbit mn anph̲ d̲-, ansit mn anpia** (or **anph̲**) **d̲-** (both in colophons) I wrote (I copied) from (the face of); **latišpur banpia** Gy 40 do not flatter (idiomatic, s. **ŠPR**), similarly Q 72:5; **kursiat anpia** s. **kursiat; anpia sbar ginza** Gy 319:18 they understand very well (idiom s. **SBR**); **tarbaṣia anpaikun** Gy 345:11 the features of your faces; **anpia trin uanpia tlata** Jb 111:1 the morn of the second (day) and the morn of the third (day); **d̲-anpia d̲-iuma la'dun** Gs 37:13 f. who know not (the prayer) at dawn (cf. above); **anpia iuma d̲-iaqir šumh̲** Jb 84:8, 94:13, 112:4, CP 188:2, ML 223:1 the dawn of the day whose name is dear (Lidzb.'s conception Jb ii 68 n. 4, ML Nachtr. needs correction); **habšaba uanpia iuma** Jb 78:1, 213:5 Sunday and the Dawn of the Day; **šamrun anpia iuma** Jb 64:9 observe morning devotions (: **rahmia d̲-anpia iuma** prayers to be recited before the sunrise); **anpia anašia** DC 44 (var. **anpia d̲-anašia** Morg. 260/12:16 f.) before people; **banpia, banph̲** (often) in his presence, before him, opposite to him, against it, compared to it; **anpia šapiria uparṣuph̲ rauzia** (often) a beautiful face and blooming countenance; **nihzia anpia hdadia** Gy 390:23 let us see face to face (cf. 2 Kings 14:8, Ginzā 417 n. 2); **'niš banpaihun lalgaṭinun** Gy 246:12 and no one favoured them (idiomatic, s. **LGṬ**); **ahdia banpan** Gy 253:5 they close (the doors) in our face; **anph̲ nipṣunun** DC 38 his presence gladdens them; **uanpaihun saipia** DC 8 and they will perish; **anpia luat qaria d̲-qrun** ML 5:1, CP 3:5, my face towards the Creator who created me; **banph̲ ṭabia** DC 44. 720 favourably.

anpiš = **npiš.**

anṣab = **nṣab.**

anqa = **aqna.**

anqia (cf. עִנְקָא, عنق) perh. nooses, loops, holes (in a fish-net), fish-traps. Only in pl. and only in Jb, cf. ii 158 n. 9. **anqia ulihia** Jb 156:3 webs and nooses; **lanqia blihia d̲-ṣbia** Jb 157:9 to the holes in submerged nets (?).

anšasa only in Gl. 36:8 انجاص [*sic*] *pixa* [*sic*].

anšil 1 = **anšir: kdub 'la anšil** DC 46. 229:4 write on a fig; **šuba anšil akil gabra umištria** DC 46 the man will eat 7 figs and be freed.

anšil 2 (Ar. انجيل) Gospel. DC 46 in an Ar. talisman in Mand. letters.

anšir (P. انجير) fig. **parahiata d̲-hilapa uanšir lklila d̲-damad** DC 38. 7:25 (they shall bring seven) sprigs of willow and fig for the bridegroom's wreath. Gl. 53:6 **anišira** [*sic*] تين *ficus* انجير.

anta = **'nta**: Gl. 31:11 **anta** انثى *femina* ماده.

as a higher being. **bas rba ubasin rba ubas iama** CP 20:10, ML 22:5 f., by As the Great, by Asin the Great and by the sea As. ML Ind.

ASA I (Pa. אַסִּי, ܐܣܝ) to heal, make whole, strengthen MG 241 n. 1, MMII 200 n. 2.

Pe. Inf. **misia** Jb 135:2, var. **masia** ACD af.

Pa. Pf. **asia** he healed MG 260:25, with suff. **asih̲** he healed him, **asiak,** fem. **asiik** he healed thee MG 286:16 f., **asith̲** Gy 332:1 I healed her MG 288:4. Impf. with suff. **nasian** he healeth me MG 285:3. Impt. with suff. **asian mn** DC 24. 59 preserve me from; **kušṭa asiak qaimak** (baptismal formula) the Troth preserve and establish thee!; **kušṭa asiak ṭaba uasia lmalala d̲-mamliltbh̲** Gy 91:18 etc. Troth preserve thee, Good One, and preserve the word thou hast spoken (an old greeting formula, Ginzā 95 n. 2); **kušṭa asinkun** (often) Troth preserve you!; pl. with suff. **asiuia** DC 43 D 13, 42 heal it (: the body). Pt. **masia** healing MG 131:12; **masia qirsana** Gy 29 he healeth the sick; with encl. **(kul hšuka mahilh̲ nhura) masilh̲** ATŠ I no. 155 (every person that the Darkness strikes, the Light) will cure him. Inf. **asuiia, asuia** healing, to heal MG 143;ult. & n. 2, 263:12; **asuiia mn muta** DC 51. 127 to preserve him from death.

Af. Inf. **masia** s. pe.

Ethpa. Pf. **'tasia** he was made whole MG 263:21; **(nišimta hak mn kibia umumia) 'tasiat** DC 48. 395 (that soul) was healed (from her diseases and blemishes). Impf. **nitasia** *sana(bi)tur, sana(bi)mur* MG 264:antep. f.; **umn pišra usa(ma)nia nitasia** AM 13:1 and he will be cured by exorcisms and simples; **nitasun** *sana(bu)ntur* MG 244:22, 265:7; **titasun** *sana(bi)mini* MG 265:11; with encl. **nitasubkun** they will be healed by you MG 265:8. Impt. **'tasia** ML 27:10 = CP 25:6 be made whole!

Idiom: With the meaning 'to strengthen' the verb might have been used as pe., cf. inf. **misia** in **atit lmisia lmiriai** Jb 135 I have come to strengthen Miriai but af. (see varr.) conveys meaning better.

Der.: **asia 1, asuta, masia, misia, masta, asa 2, asata 3.**

ASA II (formal and material confusion of **ASA I** with **SAA** = ܣܚܐ) to wash, cleanse, purify. Forms identical with **ASA I. urmia bmia uasia uašqh̲ minaihun** AM 121:19 and put (it) in the water and wash him and give him some of it (: the water) to drink!; **unisia mia unidakia napšh̲** ATŠ II no. 332 he shall wash in water and purify himself; **unasia iardna sama d̲-ˁlauia kulhin asuata** ATŠ I no. 53 and he shall wash in the jordan, the medicine above all medicines (or means of purification, both meanings implied); **nisiun** (pe.) **mia unapšaihun nidakun** ATŠ II no. 208 they shall wash with water and cleanse themselves; **asia d̲-masia rahmih̲ asinan mn haṭaian** Gy 62 Healer (or Cleanser) that healeth (or cleanseth) his friends, cleanse us from our sins! (both meanings implied).

Der.: **asata 2, asuta 2.**

ASA III, ASS (עסא, ܥܨܐ; Nöld. حز MG 45 n. 1) to press, press down, tread down, oppress, to press the teeth together (?), gnash (?). **ˁusiana ubusiana d̲-asin ubasin bišia lšalmania** Gy 215:23 f. the oppression and contempt wherewith the wicked tread down and despise the perfect; **guh̲ umitgauh̲ d̲-asin** DC 44 they are kept deep within it (: the Purgatory), so that they gnash (the teeth?; prob. the subj. of **asin** is omitted: so that they, i.e. the Purgatory demons, tread them down!); **d̲-ˁsaiun** DC 37 that oppress me.

Der.: **asaita, asita, ˁusiana.**

ASA IV (a mistake for **BSA** Ginzā 24 n. 2) to despise. **ˁlauaihun la tisun ulatigihkun** Gy 23 do not despise them and do not mock at them!

ASA V, YSA (ANSA = NSA II) a rt. of **asata 1**: **hzia d̲-uṣrak daianak d̲-iasit bˁdh̲ d̲-manu naplit lhalin razia** DC 36 let thine intelligence judge (decide) into whose hands that which thou copiest may fall.

asa 1 (אָסָא, ܐܳܣܳܐ) myrtle Löw pp. 50 f., MMII 36. **klila d̲-asa** (often) a myrtle wreath; **kd̲ asa asa bgninia d̲-hibil ruaz** CP 142:14, ML 146:5 when the myrtle, the myrtle flourished in H.'s gardens, cf. ibid. n. 2.

asa 2 (rt. **ASA I**) healing. Exceptional. **hazin baba asa gam ˁnta d̲-mula** DC 45 & 46 this is a healing charm for a pregnant woman.

asauata Pl. of **asuta** MG 167:paen. f. and of **asia 1** MG 166.

asaita (rt. **ASA III**) oppression. **maskinuta uangia uasaita d̲-šulṭania** AM poverty and afflictions and oppression by the rulers.

asamta (rt. **SUM**) **d̲-ˁda** ATŠ no. 181 the laying-on of hands (a ritual expr.).

asar ten, fem. of asra (q.v.).

asara 1 (אֱסָרָא, ܐܶܣܳܪܳܐ rt. **ASR**) bond, tie, fetter, fastening, bondage MG 115:22. St. cstr. **asar**, pl. **asaria. tiparqh̲ utipaqh̲ mn atutia asar ˁdaihun d̲-bišia** DC 51 thou wilt deliver him and loose him from bondage at the hands of wicked persons; **giṭria uasaria** (often) knots and bonds; **mlakia d̲-šarin asaria d̲-bnia anašia** PA 12 angels that loosen the bonds of the children of men; **asarun mgaṭirlh̲** DC 46 their bond (: spell) ties him; **asarh̲ mia** ML 87:4 its bond is the water (cf. n. 1), CP 71:8.

asara 2 (nom. ag. **ASR**) a binder, one who binds. St. cstr. **asar. asar haṭaiia nihuilun** Gy 290 they will have a binder of sins.

asarun (اسارون, ἄσαρον Löw 369:paen. ff.) DC 46. 123:6 nard, spikenard.

asata 1 (rt. **ANSA = ASA V = NSA II**) copy. No pl. found. **asata alma lhaka huat** DC 31 the copy was to here (: this part); **hazin asata d̲-diuan d̲-gadana rabtia** DC 9, 36, & 42 this is a copy of the Great Scroll of Destiny; **ukd̲ d̲-abad bdilh̲ basath̲** DC 22. 178 as he did, so in like manner they will do to him.

asata 2 (rt. **ASA II**) washing, purifying, cleaning. **baiia mimar d̲-asata mia** DC 27 he wishes to speak of the washing in water.

asata 3 (rt. **ASA I**) healing. Var. **asita. asath̲ marai** Morg. 241/70:7 healing of my Lord.

asabata (rt. **NSB** q.v.) accidents, mishaps.

asga 1 (s. **azga**) vault. **uazlin luat asga ulibna sagdia** DC 8 and they go towards a vault and worship a clay brick.

asga 2 (etm. unsure, cf. Mishn. חָסַךְ 'to diminish', Syr. ܚܣܟ 'to prohibit, retain') trouble, tiresomeness, grief. **uhad minaihun asga marira šumh̲** ATŠ and the name of one of them is bitter trouble; **d̲-asga umuma litbh̲** CP 136:12, Gs 80:4 f., ML 158:9 in which there is no trouble nor fault (Lidzb. ML 158 n. 9 needs correction: the word is not a hapaxl.).

asgia = sgia. asgia ldaura taqna CP 130:13 go to the durable habitation.

asdag DC 22. 379 s. **asdahag.**

asdahag Gy 382:20 a king of early Iran, Av. Aži Dahāka, cf. Gray ZA 19/1905 276 f., ضحّاك of Ar. writers.

asdiˁl DC 43 D 33 an angel.

ashaq s. **shaq.**

asuta 1 (אָסְיוּתָא, ܐܳܣܝܽܘܬܳܐ, rt. **ASA I**) healing, cure, remedy MG 145:19, MM II 200, Fränkel 261. Cl. st. cstr. only in **asut malka** title of a salutation prayer; mod. forms *sut, suta.* Pl. **asauata**, rarely **asuata**, means of healing MG 167:paen. f. Used regularly as fem., but often as masc. esp. in the formula **asuta uzakuta nihuilak** (very often) healing and vindication be thine! **uasuta lnapša tibad uasuta maška** AM 79:ult. and she will perform a cure and find healing; **maraihun d̲-kulhun asauata** (often) Lord of all remedies. Gl. 96:7 misspelt with ṣ سلامة *pax.*

asuta 2 (rt. **ASA II**) purification. **lbaita asuth̲ šapir** DC 3 propitious for purifying a house.

asutara s. **astara.**

asṭaṭ Ṣâb.'s AM — a var. of **qusṭaṭ.**

asṭaruan (etym. unsure, acc. to Andreas prob. from P. ستاره, hence *Sternbaum* Ginzā 406 n. 5) a mystical tree. **asṭaruan ˁlana** Gy 377:21, var. **ṣṭaruan** DC 22. 37 the tree Asṭarwan (personified).

asia 1 (אָסְיָא, ܐܳܣܝܳܐ, rt. **ASA I**) healer Fränkel 261. Pl. (**anat asia d̲-ˁlauaihun**) **asauata** Q 24:14 (thou art a healer over all) healers.

asia 2 (אָסְיָא, ܐܳܣܝܰܐ) Asia. **d̲-amsinun lṭuria asia d̲-msuta bgauaihun** DC 50 that solidified the mountains of Asia so that solidity was in them.

asiuta (rt. **ASA III**) Q 72:2 oppression.

asin a spirit mentioned with as (q.v.).

asinuara Morg 265/21:36 = **sinuara.**

asita 1, sita (rt. **ASA III**) prison, imprisonment. **uʿl hda asita mhabšin** DC 21 (JRAS 1937 594:18) and they are imprisoned in one prison.

asita 2 DC 6 & 36 a var. of **asata 3.**

asiptan a kind of demons (with a mod. pl. ending **-an**) of either gender. **mn asiptan zikria umn asiptan nuqbata** DC 37. 511 from male asifta(n)s and from female asifta(n)s.

askilata (nom. act. af. **SKL**) Gs 103:1 trespass(ing), follies. **askilatan** (often) our trespasses MG 134:10 f.

aslita = **slita, silata. aslitak litbh̲ ašla** Jb 162:2 there is no draw-string in thy draw-net.

asmala, ʿsmala = **smala** MG 25:anteantep.

asmar (rt. **SMR**) heedful, observant, studious BZ 13 n. 4. **ʿu bmiṣai hauia asmar uialip sipra** AM 14:6 if born in the middle (of the Sign) he will be studious and skilled in writing.

asmukia (inf. of **SMK**) to support. **asmukia ʿdaihun d̲-gubria šalmania** DC 43 to support the hands of righteous men.

ASS (= **ASA III** ܥܣܣ) to press down, tread down. Only pa. impf. with encl. found: **ʿiasbh̲** DC 31 I tread him (: the demon) down, **latiasbh̲ lanana** DC 22. 312 do not press the Cloud down! (However, Pet. Gy 314:12 **latʿiahiqh̲ lanana** do not affright the Cloud!).

Der.: s. **ASA III.**

asعar (Ar. أَسْعَار, pl. of **siعir** q.v.) AM 259:32 current prices.

aspag 1 a var. of **spag 1** in **br (a)spag** DC 22. 122 = Gy 126 a name given to the demon Karkum.

aspag 2 Gy 382:20, var. **spag 2** (Sh. ʿAbd.'s copy) father of **asdahag.**

aspand = **spand: aspand ʿkuma** DC 46. 107:10 f. black rue.

aspas, aspasa, spasa (P. سپاس) gratitude, kindness, reciprocation. **uabid aspas banašia uanašia sanilh̲** AM 9:6 he performs kindnesses to people, but people hate him; **kul d̲-abda aspash̲ lamqablia** AM whatever she does, people are ungrateful to her.

aspar, ʿspar = **spar 1** st. (abs & cstr. of **sipra** (q.v.)). **aspar** (or **spar**) **maluašia** Book of the Zodiac (title of the most famous Mand. astrological codex); **aspar diuta d̲-alahia** Gy 205:19 f. the book in ink of the gods; **aspar dukranai** Gy 205:2 my book of remembrance (cf. סֵפֶר זִכָּרוֹן Mal. 3:16, סֵפֶר הַזִּכְרֹנוֹת Esther 6:1, סְפַר דָּכְרָנַיָּא Ezra 4:15 Ginzā 206 n. 1); **aspar hilmia uaspar hizuania** Jb 67:15 ff. the book of dreams and the book of visions; **baspar sidria** Gy 245:8 s. **sidra b-.**

aspind AM 204: paen. a place-name, Asfand (a district to the south-east of Nîshâpûr, in Khorâsân) BZ Ap. II.

aspara (Ar. إِسفَار ?) splendour, brilliance. **aspara uharuta uʿqara nihuilia** DC 46 splendour and nobility and honour be there for me.

aspindiar, spandiar (P. اسفنديار) Gy 383:8 name of Ardeshir's father.

aspinta = **spinta.** Gl. 161:14 misspelt with ṣ مركب *navis* كشتى.

asprʿil Ṣâb.'s AM a higher being.

ASQ, ʿSQ (עסק, ܥܣܩ) to take pains with, take trouble about, be vexed, be grieved, be occupied with, restrain, constrain.

Pa. Pf. **lnapšaihun asiq** ATŠ I no. 258 they are vexed about themselves; with suff. **kbaštinkun uasiqtinkun** DC 43 I subdued you and restrained you; **bkušṭa biniuih̲ uasquih̲ ušalmuih̲ uasquih̲ lbit rahmia** DC 8 they cultivated it conscientiously and took pains with it and made it perfect and raised it up to the House of Mercies (the second **asquih̲** af. of **SLQ**). Pt. **masiq anašia dagalia hauia** DC 31 he will restrain deceitful people; pl. **umlakia d̲-hšuka unišmata masqin lginzaihun** DC 43 and the angels of darkness keep the souls (delete **u**) back in their treasures. Inf. **asuqia** DC 26. 147.

Ethpa. Pf. with encl. **npišan šiṭuata d̲-hšuka . . . mn qudam nhura ʿtasaqlh̲** ATŠ I no. 253 many were the shameful deeds of Darkness . . . before the Light resisted it.

Der.: **asqa.**

asqa (ܥܣܩܐ, rt. **ASQ**) constraining, heavy. **ʿuṣṭamumia d̲-asqa** DC 31 heavy bonds.

ASR, ʿSR (אסר, ܐܣܪ) to bind, tie up, tie on, gird on, fasten, secure, fetter, take captive MG 240 n. 1.

Pe. Pf. **asar (klila)** DC 43 he tied (the wreath); with suff. **asrh̲, ʿsrh̲, ʿsrih̲** he tied him, her MG 275:2, **asran, ʿsran** he tied me MG 270:24, **asarinhan** he bound us MG 279:24, **asartinun** I bound them MG 282:25; with encl. **lbil taga d̲-hirba asarlh̲** DC 22. 349 on Bel he tied (: set) a crown of destruction. Impf. **nisar** (s. Idiom), **ʿsar** I (shall) tie MG 242:7; with suff. **nisrunak,** varr. **nisarunak, nisirunak** they (will) bind thee MG 274:19 f.; **ʿsirh̲,** varr. **ʿsrh̲, ʿsarh̲** I (shall) bind him MG 275:21; with encl. **nʿsirulh̲, nisirulh̲, nasirulh̲** they (will) bind him MG 242:15 & n. 1. Impt. **asar** *liga(te)* MG 242:22; with suff. **ʿusrh̲** bind him MG 276:12, **ʿusruia** *ligate eum* MG 278:23, **asrinun** DAb tie them, **ʿsrunin, ʿsurunin** (with worthless varr.) *ligate eas* MG 283:24 f. Pt. pl. **asrin** DAb they tie. Pass. pt. **ʿsir** bound 423:1, pl. **ʿsirin** (often) *ligati*; with encl. pers. pron. **ʿsirna htimna mn iaminai . . . mn smalai** DC 37 (often) I am secured and sealed on my right . . . and left, **ʿsiritun** (often in exorcisms), ye are bound; with encl. prep. (& act. meaning) **šuba himiania d̲-ziua bhalṣai ʿsirlia** DC 44 I bind (gird on) seven girdles of light on my loins; with encl. pers. pron. and pers. suff. (with act. meaning) **ʿsirnak** I gird thee MG 291:21, 381:8. Inf. **misar** tying, to tie.

Ethpe. Pf. **ᶜstar** Gy 355:3 he was captured MG 70:15; **bᶜsuria ḏ-alaha ᶜstar** Gy 34 he was fettered with God's fetter; (without metathesis) **bšapta rmaith ḏ-ᶜtisrat** (var. **ᶜtasrat**) **uᶜzdarat** DC 44 I put it (: the talisman) into a case, so that it was fastened up and (read **ᶜzdahrat**) kept safe; with encl. (**masputita**) **ḏ-ᶜstartbh** Gy 94:14 f.; (the fetter) with which thou wert fettered. Impf. **asaria lmalka nistar** AM 215:1 bonds will be fastened to the king; **nistar** Gy 12:ult., **ᶜstar** Gs 76:3 I am (or shall be) captured MG 243:7 f.; (without metathesis) **nitisrun** (**alahia umalakia**) DC 40 (gods and angels) are bound (by enchantment). Impt. **ᶜstar** Gy 75:21 be captured MG 243:7. Pt. **mitisrin** *vincti sunt*, **mitisra** *vinctae sunt*; with encl. pers. pron. **mitisrit** thou art (or wilt be) captured MG 243:13 f.

Ettaf. **ᶜtasarbun** (with encl.) Morg. 265/21:16 corrupt.

Less regular forms: Certain pe. forms (above) could be taken rather as pa. or af., but esp. **ᶜiasar** (**mn lbušia ḏ-ᶜšata haita**) DC 22. 92 I gird myself (with a garment of living flame); ethpa. (or ettaf.) **mitasar** DC 8 is secured; Ar. forms: Impf. with the pref. **i-**: **iaṣir** AM 284:27, **iiasar** (cf. BZ 192 n. 7) he will be taken prisoner.

Idiom: to be prohibited ritually or by religious law: **laiit ᶜsira ᶜlauaikun** Gy 226 there is nothing prohibited for you; **kul tarmida ḏ-napših nisar** any priest who has disqualified himself by pollution.

Gl. 17:11 f. **ASR** (read so) انشق *scindi* شکافته شد; 47:11 f. id. تشق *rumpi*, (P. as 17:11); 32:6 **aṣira** [*sic*] اسير *vinctus*.

Der.: **asara, asra 2, msir, ᶜsara, ᶜsir, ᶜsura, ᶜstura.**

asra 1, fem. **asar** (עַסְרָא, ܥܣܪܐ) ten MG 188. **asra uhda** (or **hdisar** s.v.) eleven, **asra utrin,** fem. **asar utartin** (or **trisar, ᶜtrisar** s. vv.) twelve, **tlasar,** fem. **asar utlat** thirteen etc. MG 188 f. Gl. 125:9 misspelt with **s** عشره *decem* ده.

asra 2 (rt. **ASR**) bond, fetter. Pl. **-ia. asrh ḏ-karkum** Gy 382:23 Karkum's bond(s).

asraiil, asriaiil, asrᶜiil, ᶜsraiil, sraiil (*a*) (rt. **ASR**) name of an exorcizing spirit, DC 40. 884:965, (*b*) (יִשְׂרָאֵל) Israel: **bit ᶜsraiil** HG 8 the House of Israel; **bnia asraiil** Gy 52:ult. the children of Israel.

asriaia, asriiaia (ord. number from **asra**) tenth MG 192.

asrin, ᶜsrin, srin (ܥܣܪܝܢ) twenty.

asrᶜiil (s. **asraiil**) DC 43 D 25 an angel.

astad, ᶜstad, stad (P. استاد) a skilled person or workman. Often in colophons.

astara (ܣܬܪܐ) decay, corruption, (of teeth) caries. **ruha hᶜ ḏ-iatba lkakia ušinia umitiqria astara** Or 328:16 f. that spirit that settleth on the back teeth and front teeth and is called Caries.

astira, ᶜstira 1 (ܐܣܛܝܪܐ, στατήρ) a gold coin. Pl. **astiria,** used as fem. MG 160:15. **bit kabiṣia ḏ-bazra bhamiš astiria** (var. Sh. ʻAbd.'s copy **ᶜstiria**) **nibia** Gy 237:2 f. one καπίθη of seed will be sought for five gold coins.

ap 1 (אַף, ܐܦ, Pal. אוף, ܐܘܦ) conj. also, moreover, **uap** and also MG 208:1 & no. 1.

ap 2 AM 203 a place-name BZ Ap. II.

APA I (אֲפֵי, ܐܦܐ) to bake (still used, pron. *afâ*).

Pe. Pf. **lašiun uapun lahma** DC 41. 169 they kneaded and baked bread. Impf. **napia** Lond. roll A 554. Participial forms: **apin** Gy 226:2, **qapin** DAb (cf. 37 n. 6) they bake, **apinin** Jb 150:1 we will bake; with encl. **apilh** Gy 231:14 they bake it.

Der.: **apaiia.**

APA II (עפי, cf. MG 264:19) to be healed, be cured, recover. A different derivation by Lidzb., s. **TPA I.**

Only Ethpa.: Pf. **ᶜtapun** Gy 275:6 they were healed. Impf. **libai ḏ-kaiub nitapa** CP 171:11, ML 208:3, (and) my aching heart shall be healed. Pt. **mitapa** AM (will be) cured.

apa 1 (אַפָּא) mod. form of **anpia.** Gl. 176:3 misspelt with **b** وجه, *facies* رو.

apa 2 (אַפָּא, cf. MG 58 n. 2:ult.) AM hyæna (?).

apaiia (ܦܐܐ, rt. **APA I**) bakers (found only in pl.) MG 64:5.

apakta (nom. act. pa. **APK**) turning round or aside, reversion, perversion, revolution, perversity MG 122:6. **qala ḏ-qra daula huat minh apakta** Gy 124:10 from the cry which Aquarius gave there proceeded perversity.

apana mod. pl. of **apa 1. asrug pira upihla apana ananai** DC 12. 173 Lond. roll 6:353 doubtful. See **SRG.**

apapa (rt. **APP**) roll of manuscript. **ansh mn šuba ṭupsia had apapa anuš . . . had apapa mabu zuqbad . . .** DC 21:coloph. he copied it from seven exemplars, one of the roll of A. . . . one of the roll of M.Z. . . .

apaqta (rt. **NPQ**) expense, outlay. **uaialta napša uapaqta qalia** AM 51:3 and his income is plentiful and his outlay small.

apat (Ar. آفة) pest, disaster, calamity, plague, infirmity. **uᶜl hiṭia usaria afat maṭilun** AM 282:7 and a pest will attack the wheat and barley.

apuna 1 (< ܦܘܢܐ) hill, palace, *palatium*. **apuna ḏ-parzla** DC 43 I 138 a hill of iron.

apuna 2 a name. **apuna br apuna** Lond. roll G 1045 A. son of A.

aputa 1, puta (אַפּוּתָא) forehead, face, countenance. Still used (pron. *fottâ*). **uzuṭ rišh uzuṭa aputh** AM 8:15 and his head is small and his face is small; **uputh pta urab** AM 4:13, and his countenance is open and large; **tlata šumia ḏ-ṣiria ᶜl aputh** DC 41 three names that are graven on her forehead.

aputa 2 (rt. **PTA**) opening, mouth (of a vessel). **tlata rušumia ḏ-ᶜl aputa ḏ-šiša hinun** DC 41 three signs that are on the mouth of the bottle.

APZ (אָפַז) to leap, sport, dance. Doubtful.

Af. Pf. **aupiz** DC 43 he maketh dance.

apiun (P. افيون) drug, opium. **apiun miṣria** AM 128:1 an Egyptian drug.

apisqupa (ἐπίσκοπος through ܐܦܝܣܩܘܦܐ) bishop MG xxix:25. Miscopyings **apisquna** DC 22, **apisupa** Sh. ʿAbd.'s copy (varr. to Gy 227:2).

apiṣ (אֲפִיץ, ܥܦܨܐ, عفص) gall-nut. **apiṣ ušahpa d̲-zaitun** DC 46 gall-nut and olive-leaves.

apiqia, hapiqia (Bibl. אֲפִיקֵי־מַיִם, Syr. ܐܦܩܐ) Gy 70:16 f., 295:15, Gs 90:6, Jb 206:7 f. etc. Streams (*plurale tantum*), waters separating the world of Light from this world MG 71:15 f., MR 76, Ochser ZDMG lxii 170 n. 1, MSt 23 f., Jb xviii footn., Brand *Jahrb. f. prot. Theol.* xviii 405, 427 ff., Ginzā 67 no. 2. Gl. 30:3 terribly misspelt امسواج *fluctus* موجها.

APK, ʿPK I (אֲפַךְ, הפך, ܗܦܟ, Akk. *abâku*) to turn, reverse, turn back, pervert, turn from, twist, reject, convert, overturn; with **mn** to evade, avoid, flee from, be false to, MG 61:9, 241 n. 1.

Pe. Pf. (identical with pa.) **apak** ML 162:2 he turned, **apak a(n)paihun** Gy 177:3 they turned their faces, **d̲-apak miṣria** ATŠ II no. 55, 238 etc. that changed boundary-lines, neg. **d̲-lapak mn rušumaiun** DC 42 who did not turn from (or were not false to) their Sign, **apakt** Q 52:16 thou didst turn MG 241:14, **urazia d̲-brišia apkit brišia** DC 44 and I turned (: confused) in his head the secrets that were in his head; with suff. **ʿpkh̲** (diff. from pa.) he turned him, it MG 275:3; **apku** (varr. **apkuia, apkia**) he turned her (varr. him) MG 279:11 f.; **ulapkith̲** (var. DC 22. 429 **ulapakth̲** pa.) **lšutai mn šuta d̲-ab** Gs 51:4 I did not make my speech a perversion of my father's speech. Impf. **baṭinata nipkun** AM 238:10 pregnant women will miscarry (or will be in labour, cf. **ʿPK II**, BZ 152 n. 9), **tipkun** ye (will) turn MG 242:12; with suff. (**la**) **tipkuia** (do not) pervert it (**tipkunh̲** would be admissible) MG 278:19. Pt. **apik** he turneth, **apik banašia hauia** AM he will be changeable (?) with people; **uapik umšauia ama lnapših̲** HG etc. and he perverted and made over a people to himself (hist. pres.); **uhad mn** (read **man**) **apik mn kušṭa uhad d̲-apik mn abiuh̲ uʿmh̲** ATŠ and one that turneth (: is false to) his pact (: marriage vow) and one that turneth from his father and mother; **ukul daiua d̲-apik mn qmahia uasaria** AM and any demon that evades talismans and bonds; fem. **ʿnta d̲-apka** DC 20 woman in travail; **apka bgubria hauia** AM she will turn (: be attractive to) the men; pl. **apkia** (*often*), **apkʿ** MG 5:19 they turn; **apkin** (**miṣria**) DAb = RD C 26 they change (the boundary-lines); **ia apkia halia lmarira umarira lhalia** Gy 176 O (ye) who turn sweet into bitter and bitter into sweet; fem. **ʿnšia d̲-apkan** AM women who are in labour; with encl. **apkilh̲ ʿl libaihun** Gy 25:4 f. they pervert their hearts; **anašia apkibh̲** AM people will be changeable (?) with him (cf. above s. sg.). Pass. pt. **ʿpik, ʿpika** (*often*) overturned, perverse, (with act. meaning) perverting, deluding, destructive, pl. masc. **ʿpikia** Gs 55 *perversi*, pl. fem. **ainia ʿpikata** Gs 69:4 perverted eyes; with encl. (& act. meaning) **la ʿpiklia miṣria** Gs 103:8 I did not change the boundary lines.

Pa. Pf. identical with pe., forms with suff. diff. from pe. **apakʿnin** (: **ʿl malalia d̲-nhura**) DC 36 he perverted them (: the words of light); **ulapakth̲** DC 22. 439 a var. of **ulapikth̲** Gs 51:4 (pe. above); **apaktinun malalun** DC 36 I have turned aside their word. Pt. **mapik** perverting, pl. **mapikia** Gs 55 *pervertentes* (or *perversi*). Nom. act. **apakta** (s.v.).

Ethpe. Pf. **ʿtpik** Gy 355:1 they were overturned, **ʿtpik uʿtirgil uʿthambal sahria** DC 26 & 40 the demons are turned back, hobbled, and destroyed, special pl. **utpikiun** HG and they became perverted. Impf. **nitpik ʿlh̲ kulh̲ alahuta d̲-baita** DC 43 every divinity of the House (: the world) shall be turned against him; **uatra mn atra titpik** AM and town will turn against town; **nitipkun** AM 192 they will become perverse; id. DC 26 & 40 they are overturned; with encl. **nitpikubh̲** DC 44 they will be overturned by it. Pt. **mitpik** overturned, perverted MG 132:13, 243:6; **malka d̲-miṣraiia mitpik mn malkia** AM the king of the Egyptians will be dethroned; **ʿu šarualh̲ mitpik** ATŠ if his leggings are reversed; **uzauh̲ mitipka minh̲** ATŠ II no. 3 and his wife is estranged from him, pl. **mitipkia** Gy 75:9 they curl.

Ethpa. Pf. **ʿtapak** CP 160:14 ML 126:2 they curled, **ʿtapaktun** ye (were) turned MG 244:21. Impf. **nitapkun** a var. of **nitipkun** (above s. ethpe.). Pt. **mitapak biardna kd̲ klauata mia** DC 34 they writhe in the jordan like waves of water (should be pl. **mitapkia**); a less regular form (**mn mirta**) **mitapik** DC 46 is turned (from the bile), pl. **mitapkia** Gy 75:19 they writhe MG 244:21; **anašia mitapkia mn hdadia** AM people become estranged from one another. Inf. **ltapukia** (i.e. **lʿtapukia**) to overturn MG 144:14 f., 244:22.

Gl. 52:3 f. **APK** تضلّ *seduci* گمراه كرد; 62:1 f. **APK** حرج *advolvere, revolvere*; 133:5 f. قلب *evertere, subvertere* پيچيد.

Der.: **apakta, apkuta, ʿpika, ʿpikuta.**

apkuta (rt. **APK**) jaws (?). **kaupa d̲-apkuta** DC 41 convexity of the jaws (?).

aplaga = **plaga.**

aplaiia (cf. Talm. אַפְּלָא, אפילא) the second-season crops. **ʿburia haripia d̲-šidta nišiprun uaplaiia nihamblun** AM 251:5 the early crops of the year will be fair, but the later will be ruined.

aplanza = **plinza.** Var. **aplinza. parzla uanka unirba uaplanza** DC 43 J 172 iron and tin and brass (?) and bronze.

apliṭus AM 202 a place-name BZ Ap. II.

aplinza a var. of **aplanza, plinza.**

apna DC 31 a miscopying of **apka. apna bgubria hauia** AM 64:4 she will be attractive (read **apka** as the var.) to men.

apsad var. **psada** (rt. **PSD**) diminishment, spoliation, loss, deterioration. **upsada lhusrana hauia** AM 185:10 there will be diminishment to the point of (total) loss; **apsad bbnia mšauia** AM 84:12 she will lose children; **apsad bhamra nihuia** AM 265:19 there will be loss in the vintage.

apsaq(a) = **psaqa**. Gl. 74:1 misspelt ختان *circumcisio* سنت كرد.

apsus (P. افسوس) (*a*) jest, joke, (*b*) woe. (*a*) **latibad apsus ulatighuk lšalmania** Gy 213:ult. do not make fun of or laugh at the righteous; (*b*) **apsus dilia** DC 23. 639 woe to me!

APP, ʿPP (ܥܦܦ) to double, redouble, fold over, wrap, enfold, swathe, bend.

Pe. Pf. **apun (krikiun pandama lpumaihun)** DC 41. 169 they wrapped (and wound the face-cloth over their mouths); with suff. **uapth̲ ʿl arba ʿpia** Gy 84:2 and I wrapped it in 4 thick webs; **uarba ʿpia apth̲** Gy 167:6 and in 4 thick webs I wrapped it. Pass. pt. **ʿpip** folded, doubled, pl. **ʿpipia** *duplices* MG 250:21 f.

Pa. Pt. **mapip** doubling, doubled MG 244:16 f. Participial forms: **apip umapip balpia d̲-iutrana** (DC 22 ibid. **ʿutranh̲**) Gy 214:paen. a merchant who doubled and redoubleth a thousand times his wealth; **mipa** (?) **ʿpipa nišimta** Jb 123:ult. the soul is wrapped up and muffled.

Der.: **apapa, ʿupia, ʿpia, ʿpipia.**

apṣa (etym. unknown) shore (?). **niṭrup aṣaṣia uapṣa d̲-iama** DC 40. 134 he will be dashed against stones and the sea-shore.

APQ (ܥܦܩ) to embrace.

Pa. Pt. **ʿnšia mapqia** (read **mapqa**) **mn hdadia** DC 46 women embracing each other (Lesbians).

apquta = **pquta** neck. Pl. **apqutata. d̲-hu tabar apqutatun d̲-ʿlamania** (a *qmâhâ*) which broke the necks of the strong; **bapquth̲** DC 47 & 51 in his throat.

APR I (עפר) to scatter (dust).

Pa. **apra aprith̲ lʿšumia** DC 44 I scattered its dust to the heavens.

Ethpe. Impf. **nitipkun unitiprun alahia** DC 40. 655 the gods will be turned away and become dust (?).

Der.: **apra, apraiia** (?).

APR II s. **PRA II.**

APR III s. **PRR.**

apra (עַפְרָא, ܥܦܪܐ) (*a*) dust, ashes, desert herbage MG 72:ult. Pl. **aprauata** ashes, (*b*) adj. dusty, ashen, pale (?). (*a*) **apra mn ʿlauia agia** AM 121:8 dust from the top of the furrows; **apra ugibar sumqa** AM 271:29 ash and red dust; **hila uapra** AM 208:penult. fine dust and dust; **ugamṣia nitun apra niklun** AM 174:10 and locusts will come and eat the desert herbage; **apra d̲-mihrab d̲-masgda** AM 133:8, dust from the *mihrab* of a mosque; **uaith̲ apra** (var. **aprauata**) DC 44 and bring the ashes; (*b*) adj. pl. masc. **apria**, pl. fem. **aprata. mia apria** Gy 141:6 turbid water; **ʿšata aprata** Gs 59:9 perh. conflagration (Lidzb. read **aprath̲** and took it as a verb of a doubtful meaning Ginzā 483 n. 2). Gl. 120:11 **apra** غبار *pulvis*.

aprahia (BZ 16 n. 9) = **prahia.**

apraiia (formed as an adj. from **apra**) hapaxl. of unknown meaning. **ʿl anašia apraiia nimṭun** Gy 386:2 *apraiia* will come on people (Ginzā 413 n. 5: *kaum 'Staubgeborene'*).

apranš (افرنج) AM 206:5, var. (Ṣâb.'s copy) **aprinš** Europe.

apras (rt. **PRS**) palm (of hand). Only in st. cstr. in **apras iamina** (or **iaminh̲**) Morg. 232/51:10, Gy 237:7, DC 51. 147 etc. the palm of the (or his) right hand.

aprašta 1 (nom. act. af. **PRŠ II**) teaching, doctrine, explanation MG 134:8. Var. **aprišta.** pl. **aprašata, aprišata. aprašta ugalalta** Gy 289:19 the explanation and revelation; **aprašata d̲-madnia** AM 148:10 explanations of horoscopes; **aprašta ugalalta** Gy 282:19 the explanation and revelation; **aprašata d̲-alma hazin** Gy 198:4 ff. explanations about this world; **sidra uaprašta** Gy 219:8 book and commentary; **sidria uaprišata** Gy 371:20, id. pl. **hukumta uaprašta** Gy 213:9 wisdom and explanation; **mgalilak ʿl aprašata** Jb 29:6 *revela(bi)t tibi explanationes*; **aprašata . . . mitaprišia** Gy 299:15 *explanationibus . . . docebuntur*; **aprašata d̲-ptahil** DC 7 teachings about P.; **aprišta d̲-ahaba d̲-mania** DC 42 an explanation of the giving of garments (title of the scroll); **ukulan aprišata lman aprišuih̲** CP 384:4 and to whom did they give all explanations. Gl. 30:15 misspelt (with **b**) امثال *parabolae* حكايت, افسانه; 158:3 misspelt مرآه [*sic*] *contradictio* خلاف.

aprata Gs 59:9 s. **apra.**

aprunaiia (**PRA I**?). **haizak hamša hurinia d̲-hinun aprunaiia** DC 41. 469 then there are five other (gates of the body) which are . . .?

apruqa = **pruqa.**

apriqia (אַפְרִיקְיָא, افريقيا) AM 204:10 Africa.

aprišuta = **prišuta.**

aprišta Gy 213:19 etc. **aprašta.**

apt a var. of **aput(a).**

aptahil Jb 5:6 = **ptahil.**

aptiliata s. **ptiliata.**

aṣamata (Sh. ʿAbd.'s copy of Ginzā) a var. of **aṣmata** Gy 283:2.

aṣaṣa, ṣaṣa, ʿṣaṣa (חֲצָצָא, ܚܨܨܐ) gravel, pebble, boulder, stone. Pl. **aṣaṣia** MG 61:15, **aṣaṣʿ** MG 5:20. **tišrun miša mn aṣaṣa** ATŠ I no. 241 do ye wring out oil from a stone?; **zim kd̲ nunia baṣaṣa** DC 45 pent back like fishes by a boulder; **hazin aṣaṣa mna ʿlh** Gy 257:3 whence cometh this stone? (Ginzā 256 n. 4); **humria uaṣaṣia** Gy 10:22 beads and pebbles (: false jewels, cf. MG 61 n. 2, Ginzā 61 n. 2); **mn nangaria uaṣaṣia** Gs 26:14 (var. Sh. ʿAbd.'s copy **uṣaṣia**) from graves and rocky places (Nöld. MG 61 n. 1 thought of ܨܨܐ 'needles', Lidzb. left untranslated but doubted the meaning, Ginzā 444 n. 1).

aṣaṣan a higher being. **aṣaṣan gupna rba qadmaiia** DC 40 A. the first great Vine.

aṣara (rt. **ṢRA**) maceration, laceration. **aṣara mitiṣria ˁl hirba** DC 8 they shall be lacerated on the sword.
aṣba a var. of **ˁṣba** (**ˁuṣba**). **aṣba d̲-nhura** gleam of light (lit. colour of light, v. **ˁṣba**).
aṣur AM 204 a place-name BZ Ap. II.
aṣira (Mishn. צְצִירָה BZ 91 n. 1) obstruction (of an orifice), constipation, closing up. **uialda d̲-hauia lˁmh̲ aṣira rba hauilh̲** AM 143:3 and the babe that is born (to its mother) will have constipation (?).
aṣlunta, aṣluntina (perh. from **ṢLA**) owl BZ 80 n. 4. Pl. **aṣlunia, aṣluntia, (a)ṣluniata. šultanh̲ uaṣluntia raza d̲-aiar lgaṭiun** ATŠ I no. 254 the bats and owls took the mystery of the air; **šultina uaṣlunia uaubra uqunpud** ibid. the bat, owls, the mouse, and the hedgehog; **bnaiun d̲-aṣluniata** AM 124:penult. the fledgelings of (female) owls.
aṣmata (*אַצְמְחְתָא, rt. **ṢHM**) shining, radiance. Varr. **(a)ṣamata, ṣamah(a)ta, ṣahamata, ṣahamta** MG 64:11, 134:9. St. abs. and cstr. **aṣmat. ulahauialun aṣmat lkulhun kukbia** Gs 56:5 (Pet. miscopied as **ahmat**) and none of the stars will shine; **tuqna lsira uaṣmata lkukbia** Gy 283:2 (Sh. ˁAbd.'s copy **aṣamata** s.v.) brightness to the moon, glittering to the stars.
AṢR, ˁṢR (עֲצַר, ܥܨܰܪ) to squeeze, wring out, press out.
Pe. Impf. **unišar miša** Lond. roll A 553 and (he) presses out oil; **tišrun miša mn aṣaṣa** s. **aṣaṣa.** Impt. **aṣur**, var. **ṣur** MG 221:10, 242:18 f. Part. pres. **kd̲ aṣrit mia** AM 287:15 when thou pressest out juice.
Pa. Pf. with suff.: **aṣirth̲** DC 46. 96:8 I squeezed him.
Ethpa. Impf. **niṭasar** Gy 391:24 is pressed down.
Gl. 116:9 f. misspelt عصر *succum educere, extrahere succum* زاند.
Der.: **aṣira, maṣirana, ˁuṣrana.**
aṣta = **ˁuṣta.**
aqa 1 (rt. **AUQ**) distress, adversity, grief, poverty, harm, narrowness **mn aqa lruaha** (often) from distress to alleviation. St. emph. **aqta** s.v.
***aqa 2** (rt. **AUQ**) adj. harmful, (of eye) evil. Fem. **aqta**, pl. **aqata.** Masc. not found (by coincidence). **aina aqta** DC 21 (often) evil eye; **ruhia bišata aqata zadaniata** CP 22:2 evil, harmful, malicious spirits.
aqalata (cf. ܚܡܳܠܳܐ) griping pains? Sg. not found. **hqilat aqalata riba** DC 43 E 54 she twisted (them with) gripings of famine (doubtful) (var. differs completely).
aqam, aqama, aqamia = qam (q.v.). **aqamh̲** before him MG 33:12, 44:8; **laqamh̲** (often) onwards; **mn haka ulaqamh̲** Gy 380:20 from here on; **mn aqamak** Gs 40:1 from thee onwards; **aqamai** (often) before me; **aqamia purat** AM 262: 13 from the Euphrates onwards (BZ 164 n. 5); **laqam kul man** ML 124:1 before whomsoever; **umn palgaiin d̲-šnia laqamh̲ ualma d̲-qašiš** AM 10:6 and for a number of years and on until he is aged; **alpa aqamia sagdia** AM 13:6 thousand bow before him; **ahia d̲-aqamia** AM his older brothers (i.e. brothers who were born before himself). In Mod. Mand. **aqam** = **qam** is used also with the meaning 'for': **ktabinun aqam br zandita** DC 40. 1115 I wrote them for Bar Ž.
aqamra (doublet of **amra 1**, cf. Egyptian Aram. קמר Ges.) wool, fleece MG 72:antep. **hiuaniata d̲-aqamra** AM wool-bearing animals; **himiana d̲-aqamra d̲-br tata hiuara** ATŠ I no. 15 the girdle (woven) of the wool of a male lamb of a white ewe; **zahrˁil mn aqamrh̲ šuba ṣibunia šauiat** ATŠ I no. 248 Z. made seven dyed robes from its fleece; **aqamra d̲-halin hiuaniata** Gy 243:15 f. the fleece of these animals.
aqapra, qapra (doublet of **apra**), var. **agapra** dust, soil MG 72:21. **aqapra lpumaihun d̲-yahuṭaiia** CP 173:16 dust on the mouths of the Jews!; **arqa kd̲ msa aqapra mn mia siauia** DC 6 the earth, when it congealed into soil from the black waters; **aqapra uqira** ATŠ I no. 255 dust and pitch; **hala uaqapra** ATŠ sand and dust; **aqapra ˁkul** Gy 211:23 eat dust; **aqapra laklia** Gy 212:1 they eat not dust; **aqapra d̲-mita** Gy 228:3 the dust of the dead.
aqar 1, varr. **ˁqar(ia), ˁqria** = **qar** (q.v.) prep. with or without suff. MG 195 f. **aqar hdadia** AM 209:4 by one another, together; **mn aqaran** AM 230:ult. from our house; **aqarh̲** near him; **(a)qarak** near thee, in thy house; **aqarai** near me, with me, in my house etc. (s. **qar**).
aqar 2 (rt. **QRR**) cold. **ziqa nitia aqar** AM 207:5 the wind will be(come) cold.
aqara 1, qara (etym. unsure Jb ii 42 n. 4) treachery, faithlessness. **d̲-qara unikla litbh̲ litbh̲ aqara unikla** DC 22. 444 = Gs 60:4 there is no treachery or cunning in it; in it there is no treachery or cunning; **baqara d̲-pumai** Jb 39:10 through the treachery of my mouth.
aqara 2 (cf. s. **AQR**) root (?). Pl. **aqaria. d̲-aqaria aqria** DC 8 = RD C 5 that eradicate roots (: perform castration?); **halin d̲-darilh̲ lsimat hiia uaqara biardna aqrin** DC 8 those that bear the treasure of life and eradicate the root (?) in the Jordan.
aqariata (cf. ܩܘܼܢܳܝܬܳܐ), varr. **aqiriata, aqraiata, qraiata, arqaiata**, outcry, uproar, dissensions, provocations, contentious cries, crying out upon, curses, invectives. Sg. **(a)qraita** (s.v.). **aqariata** (varr. **aqraiata, qraiata**) **taqipata** DC 31 grievous dissensions; **luṭata uaqariata ušqupta** DC 40. 253, 43 etc. curses, uproars, and buffet(ing).
aqarta (rt. **AQR**) a barren woman, barrenness. **kd̲ aqarta d̲-lahualh̲ bra** Jb 54:9 f. like a barren woman who hath no son; **uṭuba d̲-aqarth̲ tišul** Par. 26 (DC 31 has **ṭabia**) and she will seek a boon (: cure) for her barrenness.
aqata pl. of **aqta.**
AQB, ˁQB (עקב, ܥܩܰܒ) rt. of **aqba, ˁqba.**
aqba 1 (rt. **AQB**) curb. **zim . . . kd̲ susia baqbia pikta** DC 46 held back . . . like a horse by his curb rein.
aqba 2 (rt. **AQB**) postpositional prep. after, in consequence of (?). **alanpia hizuai utiratai**

aqba ʿpika arqa lʿšumia DC 46 before my glance and in consequence of my vigilance the earth is turned from the heavens (doubtful).

aqbal = **qbal. mn aqbal** DC 22. 261 a var. of **mn qbal** Gy 265:antep. for the reason . . .

AQD (עקד, ܥܩܕ) to secure to, affix, tie on. Only pe. pf. with suff. found: **uqarnia aqdh̲ lnapših̲** ATŠ I no. 254 and affixed horns to itself; **uziqna lnapših aqdh̲** ibid. and tied to himself a beard; **uaqda gusparta** ATŠ I no. 255 and he (: the cock) affixed [*sic*] a comb.

aqdana DAb = **iaqdana.**

aqu (ܥܩܘ) st. abs. of **aquita** (q.v.).

aquza, ʿquza, quza (rt. QZZ = קצץ, ܩܨ) short. St. abs. **ʿquz** MG 125:antep. Frequent esp. in AM. **ʿrikia aquzia** RD C:12 broad and short.

aquta (ܥܩܘܬܐ, rt. **AUQ** = **ʿUQ**) distress, adversity, need, evil, ill will, envy, harm. St. cstr. **aqut** in **aqut ainia** Jb 77:12, 171:8, 213:1, Gy 357:5 etc. (ܥܩܘܬ ܥܝܢܐ) envious eye, envy, jealousy, Evil Eye MG 71:19. (Sh. ʿAbd.'s copy has **aquta aina** as a var. to Gy 357:5). St. abs. **aqu** MG 7:13. **hrig laqu** Gy 186:12 pushed (lit. rubbed) to frightening.

aqiriata s. **aqariata. luṭata uaqariata** DC 40. 232, 249 curses and invective abuse.

AQL s. **ʿQL.**

aqlida, qlida (κλεῖδα through אקלידא, ܩܠܝܕܐ, ܐܩܠܝܕܐ, Ar. loan-w. اقليد Fränkel 15, P. كليد) key. Pl. **aqlidia. aqlida ṣaliaʿl šumh̲** DAb the key named Ṣ.

aqlis a pr. n. **aqlis ʿmaihun d̲-harašata** DC 12. 222, 227, DC 40. 169 f. A. mother of witchcraft.

aqna (Bab. Aram. קנא, doublet **ana 2** עָנָא, ܥܢܐ), var. pl. **anqia** Gs 30:31 sheep, flock MG 73:1 & n. 1. Fem. MG 156:anteantep. Sg. Jb 40:7, 43:1, 44:13, Gy 184:12, pl. **aqnia** Gy 191: 2. **aqnai** Jb 42:9, 43:2, 5, 8 my sheep, my flock; **kd raia ṭaba ʿl aqn(i)h̲ d̲-ldibnaihun dabarlun** Gy 177:21 like a good shepherd who leadeth his sheep to their fold.

aqṣiaiil mlaka DC 40. 883 an angel.

AQR, ʿQR (עקר, ܥܩܪ) to uproot, tear loose, tear away, eradicate, detach, destroy, exterminate, break down, tear down.

Pe. Pf. **aqar apra** AM 270:26 dust is whirled off (idiom below); **aqar ʿkuria** DC 44 they uprooted the high places (: pagan temples); **uarqa bšihh̲ aqar** Gy 166:12, 171:13 and (he) tore up the ground in his vehemence; special pl. **uaqariun ziqia** Jb 41:11 and winds broke loose (idiom below). Impf. (**ʿu nibasar bgauh̲**) **uniqar bgauh̲ aqara** ATŠ II no. 356 (if he deducts from it) or eradicates something; **niqar bunka** DC 46 he will uproot his foundation; with suff. **niqrh̲** we (shall) uproot MG 275:20. Impt. **aqur** DC 21 root out; **aqar aqur halšak uabarak** Jb 130:5 tear loose thy bar(s) and thy bolt(s); special pl. **auquru kursaikun** DC 43 J 56 tear down your thrones!; with suff. **ʿuqruia**, var. **ʿqruia** *eradicate eum!* MG 278:bottom. Act. pt. **uaqar pugdamia** ATŠ II no. 308 and (he) breaks down commandments, pl. **aqrin; aqria** s. **aqara; ziqia aqria** Jb 42:1 the winds break loose (*idiom below*). Pass. pt. **arza mn gintai ʿqir** Gs 111:16 a cedar was uprooted from my garden. Inf. **miqar** Gy 271:8 (B **miraq** is correct).

Af. Impf. **d̲-ʿiaqirlh̲ banpai mn ridpai** DC 22. 462 = Gs 76:3 f. that I may pluck it out before my persecutors. Certain forms were influenced by **YQR**, cf. **ʿbidata nisakrh̲ uʿbidata nauqrh̲** ATŠ I no. 88 he will stop the rites and destroy the ceremonies; **uʿiaqirinkun mn gaṭlai** DC 22. 352 and I shall tear you away from my murderer(s). Pt. with suff. **mauqirinun (mn aklia d̲-nunia)** Jb 159 tearing them away (from the fish-eaters), or making them evade (**ARQ** ?). Part. pres. (pass.) **umbaritun umaqritun mn pagrai** DC 43 A 98 ye are expelled and uprooted from my body.

Ethpe. Pf. ***ʿtqar** MG 380:1; **ʿtiqrat** she was rooted out MG 243:11. Impf. **umalka mn dukth̲ nitqar** AM 243:15 and the king shall be ousted from his position; **nitiqrun** AM 210:18 they will be extirpated. Pt. **mitqar** *eradica(bi)tur* MG 234:5, pl. **mitiqria** *eradica(bu)ntur* MG 243:11 f.

Idioms: With **apra** to be whirled off. With **ziqa** to break loose. With **malka** as a subj. to be dethroned etc. (all as semantic developments of 'to uproot'). **aqria bmia** Jb 44:10, **aqara biardna aqria** (s. **aqara 2**) very obscure (cf. Jb ii 49 n. 4; hardly related to Ar. عكّر 'to trouble the water'). Confusions with other roots frequent.

Gl. 48:13 **AQR** تنقلع *eradicare* كند; 93:5 f. سلب *despoliare aliquid* شكافت; 132:11 f. قلع *eradicare* كند; 166:15 f. نزع *auferre* كند.

Der.: **aqara** (1?, 2), **aqarta, ʿqara 2.**

aqra 1, arqa 4 (ἄκρα, אקרא, Syr. ܚܩܪܐ a place-name, Ar. loan-w. عقر Fränkel 233) fortress, stronghold MG 71 n. 2. Pl. **aqria.** With suff. **arqaihun** Gs 95:7 and **arqun** (the same page several times) their fortress MG 182:6 f.; **škinata uaqria** DC 22. 10 = Gy 10 (Pet. **arqia**) dwellings and fortresses (Ginzā 13 n. 2); **aqria d̲-bnak mitpasasia** Jb 27 thy sons' strongholds are destroyed.

aqra 2 (rt. **QRA**) creature. Pl. **aqria. aqria d̲-iušamin** DC 8 creatures of Y.

aqra 3 (rt **AQR** = **ʿQR**) barren, sterile, impotent. Fem. **aqarta** (s.v.). Pl. **aqria bnaṣiruta** DC 36.

aqraiata s. **aqariata: luṭata uaqraiata d̲-alahia uanašia** Or. 331:9 curses and abuse of gods and men; **luṭata uaqraiata** DC 51 curses and imprecations.

aqraita DC 43 A 59, CP 33:10 = **qraita** ML 89:5 (sg. of **aq[a]riata**).

aqšia Jb 180:7 = **qšia** (ibid. var.).

aqta (עקתא, ܥܩܬܐ) distress, need, adversity, hardship, penury, want, privation MG 110:13. St. abs. **aqa** (s.v.). Pl. **aqata** as adj. fem. **uaqta nisbal** AM 31:16 and he will endure hardship; **bišuta uaqta** ibid. evil and distress;

aqta nihuilẖ ibid. she will meet with adversity; **tlata razia aqta** DC 34. 994 three mysteries of deprivation (?); **ruhia bišata aqata zadaniata** DC 3 and CP 22:3 = ML 24:6 the evil, distressing, wrathful spirits.

ARA (אֲרַע, ܐܪܥ) to meet, encounter, point out, indicate, behold.

Pe. Act. pt. **hazin aria šadiriata** DC 8 this one indicates the ropes.

arab 1 st. abs. of **arba** 1 MG 107:16. **larab** Gy 382:4 no ship, without ship MG 302:3.

arab 2 a place-name, **mdinta arab** AM 219:19 the town A. BZ 133 n. 10.

arabaiia (ܥܪܒܝܐ) Arabs (*often*).

arabata 1, varr. **arauata, aruahata** (cf. **rahbata** and **rahuata**) perh. food-offerings, trays of ritual food (Sh. Nejm indicated the **ṭariana** for a **zidqa brika** as **rahbata**; Lidzb. ML 122 n. 1 did not dare to propose any meaning). See CP p. 67 n. 5. **ušaba arabata** CP 95:8, ML 121:13 = **ušaba arauata** DC 3, **ubšaba arabata** CP 95:13, ML 122:4 = **ubšaba arauata** DC 3; **uginza hamšiaia ḏ-arabata hinun** and the fifth treasure concerns the ritual trays (?).

arabata 2 (cf. Syr. sg. ܥܪܘܒܐ) sponsor. **abahata ḏ-hinun arabata mitqirian** DC 27. 349 the parents who are called the sponsors (the pl. **arabata** is adjusted to **abahata**).

arabata 3 (rt. **ARB I**) DC 48. 242 *rites de passage*, rites of transit.

arabigar a var. of **arqa bigal** (q.v.).

arada 1 (עֲרָדָא, ܥܪܕܐ) wild ass MG 28:5 f., 115:4. Pl. **aradia**. **aradia nigirbun unitgaṭlun bdibraihun** AM 190:1 wild asses will be raided and killed in their plains; **ušria aialia ušria aradia** DC 12. 90 and loose the deer and loose the wild asses; **ṭabiia uaradia** Gy 387:16 gazelles and wild asses.

arada 2 (ܥܪܕܐ, عرّادة) punt-pole Jb ii 155 n. 7. **habšaba lagiṭ arada** Jb 152:1 f. Sunday (personified) grasps the punt-pole.

arada 3 a place-name BZ Ap. II.

aradaiia 1 Gy 121:15 (cf. Akk. *rêdû*) a kind of dignitaries Ginzā 136 n. 3.

aradaiia 2 the people of **arada** BZ Ap. II.

arahata AM 283:36 a phonetic writing of **arqahata** lands, territories.

arauata DC 44. 1037 a var. of **arabata** 1 Morg. 263/16:2.

aramata, ramata pl. of **ramta** MG 33:8. **paqata uaramata mištarhizia** DC 15 valleys and crags are shaken with fear; **ṭuria uaramata hinun** ATŠ I no. 236 they are mountains and heights; **mn aramata ḏ-ʿlauia aramata** DC 51 from peaks above peaks; **uṭba ṭuria uṭba aramata** Gy 380:18 and inundated the hills and inundated the peaks; **bpaqata ubaramata** Or. 331:17 in valleys and heights; **aramata ḏ-nhura** Gy 352:12 the heights of light.

aramla s. **ramla**.

arasa (rt. **ARS**) betrothal. **agam arasa** AM 152:10 for betrothal; **hazin hušbana amar larasa ušutapa** AM 152:17 this is the calculation of aspects concerning a betrothal or partnership.

araqa = **aruqa**. **araqa ḏ-niraq** DC 31 a fugitive that escapes.

ARB I, ʿRB I, HRB II (ערב, ܥܪܒ H. ערב IV Ges.) to go down, set (sun, moon, or star), fall down, founder, come over.

Pe. Pf. **arab** it set MG 241:7, as desiderative **šidta ḏ-qabibiliun arabaiia arab alma ʿlauaihun** (in every colophon after the year) year of the Arabs (: Moslem era) — may the world founder upon them (a pun). Impf. **nihuta ḏ-ṭabia tibarlak** Gs 16:20 may the calm of the good come over thee!; **limalia ḏ-ʿrub ʿlauakun** Gs 65:14 why should I go down to you? (Nöld. MG 242:4 *ich bürge*, but cf. Lidzb. Ginzā 492 n. 3). Act. pt. neg. masc. **larab** doth not set. MG 19:2, fem. **atra ḏ-larba šamšia** CP 193:4, ML 227:8 etc. the place whose sun setteth not.

Der.: **arabaiia, arbaia** 1, **mariba** 2, **marba** 1, **mrubia, ʿurupta**.

ARB II, ʿRB II (ערב, ܥܪܒ H. ערב II) to mix, intermix, mingle, add to, join to, press into.

Pe. No pf. found. Impf. **nirab iamina mn smala usmala mn iamina** ATŠ I no. 261 he must join the right (brick) to the left and the left to the right; **nirbun** they mix, mingle, fem. **nirba** id.; **latirbun minaihun** Gy 46:4 mix not with them! Impt. with suff. **arbinun** AM 287:30 mix them!; **uʿspintak ʿurbẖ bspintan** Jb 154:1 and join thy ship with ours! Act. pt. **arib mia** ATŠ II no. 36. DC 41. 261 he mingles water; pl. **mia bqira larbia** Gy 79 water mixeth not with pitch; with encl. **arbilẖ** Gy 112:14 he mixeth it, **arbibhun** Gy 25 they mix with them. Pass. pt. **ʿriba**, pl. **ʿribia** (s.v.). Inf. **mirab** ATŠ II no. 134.

Pa.? Inf.? **raza ḏ-mrubia** ATŠ II no. 143 mystery of commingling.

Ethpa. Pf. **ʿtarab . . . bihdadia** Gy 291:41 it mixed together; **ʿtarab hu urbẖ bhalin trin agia** ATŠ II no. ? he and his master are joined together (?) by those two myrtle twigs. Impf. **nitarab** Q 28:6 will be mingled. Pt. pl. **mitarbia** Gy 293:13, 388:5 (DC 22. 298 has **mitrabia** for the former) they (will) mingle, mix. Inf. **ʿtarubia** to be mixed, mingled MG 144:15, inf. abs. **ʿtarubia hamra bmia** Q 28:6 as the wine mixeth with the water MG 398 & n. 3.

Some forms are formed as from **RBA**, cf. **mitrabia** as a var. of **mitarbia** and **mraba** AM 287:22, **muraba** AM 287:32 mixed; as from **RBB**: (**ʿurbana**) **mrablẖ** s. **ʿurbana**.

Der.: **arba 2, 3, mariba, muraba, ʿurbana, ʿriba**.

arba 1 (עַרְבָּא, ܥܪܒܐ) boat, ford, ferry, ferry-boat MG 3:19:paen., 107:16, Fränkel 218, st. abs. **arab** 1 (s.v.). Fem. MG 158:10. **kḏ arba ḏ-ʿl mia azla** Gy 221:22 like a boat that goeth on the water; **qamit ʿl ramta ḏ-arba** Jb 44:2 f. I stood on the high part of the ford (or ferry-boat); **iatibna barba ḏ-ziua** Jb 144:5 I sit in a boat of light. Pl. **arbia . . . kabšan uldilia sagdan** Jb 152:6 the boats . . . bowed and worshipped me. Gl. 125:4 غراب *navigium* كشتى.

arba 2 (rt. **ARB II** = **ʿRB II**) mixture, mixing-bowl, dish (?). **asqunh̲ ... darba** [*sic*] **mišṭahan** DC 37. 196 ff. make him drink ... of the filthy mixture (?). Pl. **arbata**?, cf. **ʿstadar masiqta barbata d̲-šitil** DC 6 the *masiqta* is arranged in Shitel's mixing-bowls.

arba 3 (rt. **ARB II** = **ʿRB II** ?) woman of mixed (racial) origin? Lidzb. as fig. use of **arba 1** Jb ii 127 n. 8. **arba mzanaita** Jb 129:13, 130:4 a debauched woman of mixed race (?), Lidzb. *verhurter Trog*.

arba 4 (אַרְבְּעָא, ܐܪܒܥܐ) masc.; **arbia**, rarely **arba** (אַרְבַּע, ܐܪܒܥ) fem. the number four MG 187. **arba habšaba** Wednesday (P. چهارشنبه); **arba ziqia d̲-baita** Gy 13:3 f., 33:12, Jb 46:7, 79:8 the four winds of the House (i.e. the world, cf. s. **baita**, Bab. *irbitti šāri*, ἐπὶ τὰς τέσσαρας γωνίας τῆς γῆς Apoc. 7:1; Enoch 18:2); **arba zauiata d̲-baita** ML 9:8 CP 8:8 the four corners of the House (= cardinal points). Gl. 36:12, **arba** اربعة *quattuor* چهار.

arba 5 a poor spelling of **rba**. **šaialta ašualia uarbh̲** Zotb. 231 left col. 2nd text — the question of the novice and his teacher.

arbagan ʿšata DC 37. 252 a fever spirit (s. **arbgan**).

arbaia 1 (rt. **ARB I** = **ʿRB I**) adj. westerly, western, Arab. Pl. **arbaiia** (and **arabaiia** s.v.) Gy 385:6, 14 etc. **ziqa arbaia** AM 195:ult. westerly wind; **nbiha arbaia** (var. **arbaiia**) Gy 61:4 the Arab prophet = **mhamad bizbaṭ arbaia** s. **mhamad** identified with his father **abdala arbaia** Gy 229:22, 231:22, 232:14, 233:1, 18; **malka d̲-arbaiia** Gy 385:6 the king of the Arabs; **malkia arbaiia** Gy 390:6 the Arab kings; **bit arbaiia** AM etc. the country of the Arabs, Arabia; **arbaia d̲-šibqh̲ hilqh̲** Jb 120:12 an Arab that abandoned his *qesmat* (i.e. fatalism, cf. ii 117 no. 6).

arbaia 2 a var. of **arbiaia**.

arbaiaia id. **arbaima** a var. of **arbima** MG 189 n. 3.

arbana (cf. **ʿurba 1**) perh. crow. **uailik arbana pasa** Jb 158:8 woe to thee, black-and-white crow (? Lidzb. ii 160:8 transcribed the word, cf. also n. 6 and **pasa 1**).

arbasar (Talm. ארביסר, Syr. ܐܪܒܥܣܪ) fourteen MG 188 (fem. **asar uarbia** MG 189).

arbgan, arbigan an evil spirit. **lak bšumak d̲-napšak qraitak arbgan** DC 37. 204 and later I have called thee by thy own name A.

arbia fem. of **arba** four; but Gy 393:21 C for **arbin** forty (MG 189:18).

arbiaha a rare var. of **arbiaia** MG 56:15, 192:2. **bit arbiaha** Gs 42 the House of the Fourth (Ginzā 459 n. 3); **ṭupsa arbiaha** DC 36 the fourth type.

arbiaia (רְבִיעָאָה, ܪܒܝܥܝܐ), var. **arbaia(ia)**, **arbiaha** fourth MG 192:2. Fem. **arbiaita** *quarta*. Pl. **arbiaiia** (occ. sg.).

arbiaiil DC 40. 871 an angel.

arbigal, arbigar s. **arqabigal**.

arbigan s. **arbgan**.

arbila? (אַרְבִּילָא) in **ulabarbilaiun hizura** DC 44. 596 f., 624 corrupt (read **ulau barbilaiun hizra** s. **hizura 2**).

arbima, var. **arbaima** four hundred MG 189: ult. and n. 3.

arbin forty MG 189:12.

arbita, rbita (cf. s. **rbita 2**) sea, lagoon, ocean, any large expanse of water, salt or fresh. **mn trin kipia d̲-(a)rbita** DC 22. 183 = Gy 192:9 from the two banks of the lagoon; **šria arbita d̲-mia** DC 12. 82 loose the sea of water (from enchantment).

arbkan (cf. **arkban**) DC 43 I 151 an angel.

arga DC 6 = **arqa 2**.

argazta (nom. act. **RGZ**) wrath, anger, condemnation (often). **samarta uargazta** DC 43 banishment and condemnation.

argba (cf. Ass. *argaman*[*n*]*u* 'red purple', Aram. loan-w. אַרְגְּוָן, Hittite loan-w. *arkammana* 'tribute'. The expr. **argba uminuna** [below] might originally have been one word.) money, possessions MG 50 n. 1, 128:3. **argba uminuna** Gy 24:17, 112:5, 220:8, 363:10, Jb 212 etc. money and possessions; with suff. **argban ... minunan** Gy 368:7 our money ... our possessions; **laargbaiun ulaminunun** Gy 17:13 neither their money nor their wealth; **argbaihun** CP 128:10 their money. See CP trs. p. 94 n. 3.

argiuat a name given to Libat (Venus). **argiuat marat alahia uanašia** DC 44. 1082 f. A. mistress of gods and men.

arda (Ar. ارض) earth, land, soil. **uaitunh̲ lbaitai uardh̲ umath̲** DC 46 and bring ye him to my house and his land and his country! (charm to make a lover return).

ardaban a var. of **ardban**, q.v.

ardaga (cf. P. اردگان 'certain figures in astrology') an astrological symbol. **uardaga d̲-šaraia glipa mn halṣh̲** DC 43 A 10 f., 125, and (take) the graven symbol of exorcism from his loins; **uardaga d̲-šaraia glipa lman d̲-mahia ušadih̲** DC 43 A 15 and an exorcizing symbol (is) graven on him whom he (the demon) striketh and woundeth.

ardba (ארדבא, ܐܪܕܒܐ, ἀρτάβη) a measure, measuring-pot. Pl. **ardbia**. **saria lpumh̲ d̲-ardba atin** AM 172:12 the barley will come up to the mouth of the measuring-pot; **nasbia bardbia rurbia uiahbia bardbia dirdqia** Gy 186:ult. f., Gs 32:10 they take in great measure and give in small measure.

ardban Gy 383:18, varr. **ardaban, arduan** Artabanus V (*ca.* 213–27, Gray ZA 19/1905 286), HG 5 Artabanus III (12–*ca.* 38).

arduan s. **ardban**.

ardupa (rt. **RDP**) taskmaster, overseer. Only a form with suff. **ardupai** DAb my taskmaster.

ardikla (אַרְדִּיכְלָא, אַרְדְּכְלָא, ܐܪܕܝܟܠܐ, ܐܪܕܟܠܐ) architect, master-mason, builder, compiler. Var. **rdikla**. Pl. **ardiklia**. **ardikla rama d̲-naṣiruta** (*often in colophons*) an exalted master-mason of priestly knowledge; **kul had nsab raza d̲-baiia d̲-nihuia ardiklh̲** ATŠ II no. 189 each one took the mystery of which he sought to be the master-builder; **ardiklia banaiia** ATŠ I no. 261 master-builders, master-masons; **uardiklh̲ minh̲ sliq** Jb 63:15 f. and its architect has (left it and) risen up; **libh̲ nihuilh̲ ardikla** Gy 357:1 his heart is his master-builder; **ardiklia d̲-ṭina** Gy 6:5 builders of clay.

ardšir br aspindiar Gy 383:8 Arṯašir the Kayān called Vohūman son of Spendāṯ (Bahman Yast III 17, Gray ZA 19/1905 282). **ardšir pabugan** Gy 383 اردشير بابكان. Var. **adšir.**

arhamta = **rhamta.**

arhum Gy 182 the keeper of a *maṭarta* (together with Yur and Yahur) Ginzā Ind. I.

arua a phonetic writing of **arba 1. hinqai uaruai** DC 46 p. 37:8 f. my snare and my net (?).

aruaz gupna = **ruaz gupna.**

aruana (ארונא, ܐܪܘܢܐ) ark, chest, coffer. **mihla . . . pt aruana d̲-arqa** DC 40. 438 salt . . . daughter of the ark of the earth.

arudan gaimuraṭ Gy 382:15 (var. **arduan gaimiraṭ**) a Parthian king, Gayamarətan (Yasna xxiii:2 etc.) Gray ZA 19/1905 247 f., Ochser ibid. 74 n. 2, Ginzā 411 n. 1.

aruzban DC 43 I 18 name of a supernatural being.

aruita = **ruita.**

aruk (rt. **ARK**) AM 259:13 long.

arumaiia = **rumaiia. mahuza d̲-arumaiia** Ṣâb.'s AM a Byzantine town.

aruqa (rt. **ARQ I**) often in AM a person escaping, a fugitive.

arza 1 (אַרְזָא, ܐܪܙܐ Löw 56) cedar MG 100:10. Pl. **arzia. gṭul arzia** Gy 265:11, 380:10 cut down cedars!; **arza rama** Gy 116:11 a high cedar; **arzia bliban** Q 52:13, 18, **arzia blilban** Gy 174:17, 24 אַרְזֵי־הַלְּבָנוֹן (Ps. 29: 5); **arzia ramia uašuhia** DC 44. 773 etc. lofty cedars and female cedars. Gl. 35:5 **arz** ارز *cedrus.*

arza 2, arzia (Talm. אַרְזֵי) dryness, dry thorns, firewood: **ualma kulh̲ arza** (var. **arzia**) **maṭilh̲** Gy 384:21 and all the world will be overtaken by dryness; **nura d̲-arzia** DC 44 a fire of dry thorns.

arzabania (P. آرزو 'desire'? Targ. ארזובא 'hammer' makes no satisfactory sense). **mn raza urimza uarzabania d̲-baita** DC 51 from mystery and signal and desires of the House (: world). Or, s. **arzibana.**

arzan 1 (P. ارزان) cheap, cheaply. **zabnit arzan umzabnit gran** AM 157:16 thou wilt buy cheaply and sell dearly.

arzan 2 name of a supernatural being.

arzania (P. ارزانى an abstr. noun from **arzan 1**) low price. **uarzania nihuia** AM 259:29 etc. and there will be low prices; **arzania d̲-asʿar** AM 259:31 f. low market prices.

arzapana (Targ. אַרְזוּבָא) hammer, mallet. **uatina mibia zmim uarzapana** DC 46. 136:2 and I came to ask a bridle and a hammer.

arzubta = **arzibta.**

arzun AM 198 a place-name BZ Ap. II.

arzibana (cf. **arzapana**) smiter. **arzibana anpai** DC 43 G 23 the smiter of my face.

arzibta (Targ. ארזובא) DC 43 hammer, mallet.

arzingan AM 198 a place-name, Arzanjân BZ Ap. II.

arṭazta (a miswriting of **argazta**). **arṭazta udahalta** DC 43 E 41, DC 20. 91 wrath (?) and fear.

arṭalana a var. of **arṭilana.**

arṭil (ܥܪܛܠܝ) naked, nakedly MG 128:5, 141: anteantep., 200:bottom. **arṭil šlihia** Gy 226 stripped naked; **arṭil lalma atalia** Gs 97:9 *nudum me apportavit* (*mater mea*) *in mundum* (cf. Job 1: 21); **arṭil qam** Jb 69:14 he stood up naked.

arṭilaia (from **arṭil**) Gy 16:1, 3 naked MG 141:anteantep. Var. **arṭlaia.**

arṭilana (from **arṭil**), var. **arṭalana** naked MG 137:14. **man malbišlh̲ larṭilana** Gs who will clothe the naked?

arṭlaia = **arṭilaia** (a var. to Gy 16:1 in Sh. 'Abd.'s copy).

arṭlaiit (adv. from **arṭil**) bare, naked(ly). **arṭlaiit kd̲ ianqa d̲-napiq mn kras ʿmh̲** DC 34. 352 naked as a new-born babe; **arṭlaiit qam** DC 34. 338 they stood bare.

aria 1 (אַרְיָא, ܐܪܝܐ) lion, pl. **ariauata,** the Zodiacal sign Leo, MG 166 f., MM II 74. **aria mhambla aria mrida** Gs 14:8 the despoiling (: ravening) fierce lion: **aria mrida** Jb 41:5 the fierce lion; **aria mrida marda** Gs 75:22 the fierce furious lion; **aria haṭipa** Gs 9:12 the predatory lion; **aria makšilana** Gy 287:22 the lion hurtling down; **qupa uaria** DAb the ape and the lion; **dmut d̲-aria** DAb = RD 32 the picture of a lion; **trin ariauata** DAb = RD C 13 two lions; **ariauata mhamblania** Gy 179:17 the ravening lions. Gl. 36:1 **aria** اسد *leo* شير.

aria 2 (rt. **AUR**) s. **ruta.**

ariaiil DC 40. 879 name of a spirit.

arika (rt. **ARK**) long. St. abs. **arik.** Pl. **arikia. arikia quzia hauin** DC 8 the long shall become short.

arisa (rt. **ARS**) betrothed, fiancé. Gl. 66:11 misspelt with **ṣ** خطيب *sponsus.*

ARK, ʿRK (אֲרַךְ, ܐܪܟ) to be long, prolonged, lengthy, last a long time. Pt. fem. **arka kṣurth̲** AM (often) his illness will be prolonged. Pass. pt. **ʿrik, ʿrika** s.v. Gl. 109:7 f. طال *elongare* دراز كرد; 109:13 f. طال *crescere, increscere* دراز كرد.

Der.: **aruk, arika, ʿrika, ʿurka.**

arkan (Ar. اركان) minister of state. **ʿmara uarkan daula** AM 161 translit. of أُمَرَاءُ وأَرْكَانُ الدَّوْلَةِ.

arkban DC 43 I 144 an angel-name (cf. **arbkan**).

arkun, arkuna (אַרְכוֹן, אַרְכוֹנָא, ܐܪܟܘܢ, ܐܪܟܘܢܐ, ἄρχων) elder, ruler, governor, Prince of Darkness, evil spirit, Furlani, *I Nomi* 435. Pl. **arkunia** Gy 279:5. **ubit alahia lanihirbun**

uarkuna niridpun AM 219:7 and they will not ruin the house of the gods, but they will harass the governor. In DC 44 citadel (?), cf. **qamit bgauh̲ d̲-arkuna** I stood in the interior of the citadel (?), **umlagṭia mlakia mn arkuna** and they seize the angels from the citadel (?).

arkubia a var. of **rkubia** s. **SAR II.**

armalta (אַרְמַלְתָּא, ܐܪܡܠܬܐ) widow. Pl. **armalata, armlata. armalta d̲-hauia hiduta** Jb 107:3 f. a widow that becomes a bride. Gl. 22:1 written defectively ارملة *vidua* بيوه.

arman Armenia. **arman ʿṣṭartia** AM 203 Armenia Minor.

armanaiia Armenians. **ṭura d̲-armanaiia** AM 202 Armenian mountains; **alma lsihil d̲-diria d̲-armanaiia** AM 205:3 up to the coast of the Armenian Sea.

armania Armenia. **armania gauaita** AM 203 Inner Armenia.

armila = **armla.**

ARML (verb denom. from **armla, armalta** as ܐܬܐܪܡܠ) to become a widow(er). **armlat** she became a widow MG 27:6, 222:14.

armla (אַרְמְלָא, ܐܪܡܠܐ) widower. Pl. **armilia, armlia. gabra armla kdiblh̲** AM 103:3 it is written that she shall have a widower as husband; **armlia uarmlata** Gs 11:18 (var. DC 22. 401 **armilia uarmalata**) widowers and widows.

armʿil RD 41 a supernatural being.

arnab (Ar. أَرْنَب) hare. **aitilh̲ kulai d̲-arnab** AM 131:ult. bring him the kidneys of a hare.

ARS (ארס, عرس, der. עַרְסָא, ܥܪܣܐ) to bind, connect, join (in marriage), betroth.

Pe. Pf. **kd̲ laras ulamkar** Gs 11:20 when they were still unwed; with suff. **gabra d̲-arsan** Gy 147:15 the man who betrothed me; with encl. **man araslh̲ lhiduia . . . hibil araslh̲ lhiduia** ŠQ 19:11 f. who wedded the bridegroom? . . . H. wedded the bridegroom. Pt. pass. **arisa** s.v. Inf. **lmiras ʿnta** AM 138:1 to betroth a woman.

Af. (?) Pt. **mauris** DC 37. 550 binding.

Gl. 46:15 f. misspelt with ṣ تزوج *uxorem ducere* كدخدا شد; 165:1 f. misspelt with ṣ نكح Lat. and P. as before.

Der.: **arasa, arisa, arsa.**

arsa (v. **ARS**) bed, couch, marriage-bed, betrothal, joining-together; (astrological) conjunction; Cassiopeia or the four stars that form the 'bed' or 'bier' in Ursa Major. Fem. **arsa d̲-puria** (var. **purai**) Gy 376:21 couch of pillows; **kd̲ mahra barsa** Gy 43:4 like illness in bed; **uqirsa barsa hauilh̲** AM 17:3 and he will be ill in bed; **ubarsa npil** DC 21 and he fell on his couch; **arsaiun d̲-baṭinata** Jb 4:6, 6:5 bed of pregnant women; **šaltik anhar barsa qadmaita d̲-šakbinabh̲** Jb 113:7 I have asked thee, Anhar, by the first (: nuptial) couch in which we both slept; **arsak qadmaita hzia** Jb 111:2, 4 behold thy nuptial bed; **uarsa uhitra ušataputa** AM and betrothal and legal ceremony and pairing-off; **arsa d̲-ʿlauai** (read **ʿlauh̲**) **gnina** DC 37 the bed on which I sleep.

arsauan DC 44. 627 = Morg. 259/10:28 a supernatural being. More usual **arsapan, arspan** (q.v.).

arsaiia (patronymic from Ἀρσάκης Arsaces) Arsacides, Parthians, Medes: **ṭura d̲-arsaiia** HG 141 the uplands of the Arsacides (= **ṭura d̲-midai** HG 6 Median hills).

arsam (ܐܪܣܡܐ) AM 22:6 swelling, inflammation, pleurisy. St. emp. unknown.

arsapan, arspan (var. **arsauan** s.v.) a supernatural being. CP 194:10, 356:6, **arsapan** (**arspan** ML) **rabia ṭalia** ML 229:2, 264:4 A., a boy of tender years (cf. ML Ind.). **kursia arspan** DAb = RD 30 the throne of A. (cf. DAb Ap. I).

arpala AM 208 a var. of **arpila.**

arpila (עַרְפִּילָא, ܥܪܦܠܐ) with aphaeresis **rpila** (s.v.) cloud, darkness, mildew on plants. Fem. in spite of masc. pl. **arpilia** MG 34:20, 159:22. About the formation cf. MG 128:14. With procl. prep. **barpilia, brpilia** in the clouds MG 11:7. **arpilia d̲-habara** Jb 223:1, **rpilia d̲-hšuka** Jb 99:4, 223:9, 249:3, Gy 301:4, 377:15 etc. clouds of darkness; **arpilia rurbata d̲-hšuka** Gy 148:17 great clouds of darkness; **arpila sumaqtia** AM 208:6 a reddish cloud; **iarqana uarpila ʿl aṭšia d̲-šidta napil** AM 214:12 mildew and smut will attack the annual fruit-crops.

arṣia (from עֲרַץ, ܥܪܨ) accidents, mischances. Sg. not found. **haršia uarṣia ukibia** DC 51. 674 f. spells, mischances, and pains.

ARQ I (עֲרַק, ܥܪܩ) to escape, flee from, evade; pa. to drive away.

Pe. Pf. **araq** he, they fled away. Impf. **niraq** AM 260:16, var. **niruq** *fugi(e)t*. Pt. **kul d̲-ariq mikṣar** AM 271:24 whoever escapes will be cut off; **udariq bʿuhra** AM 140:15 and that escapeth by road; pl. **uanašia arqan** [*sic*] **mn hak gabra** AM 265:5 f. and people (will) escape from that man; **ʿsiria arqa kd̲ iauna** DC 43 the bound escape like a dove; with encl. pers. pron. **ana ariqna minaihun** Gy 265:22 I evade them. Inf. **miraq** evading, fleeing, escaping.

Pa. Impt. **arqh̲ sruta mn škintak** Jb 37:7 drive corruption away from thy dwelling. Pt. **susia marqan** horses are driven.

Af. Impf. with suff. (as from פ״א) **uʿiauriqinkun mn gaṭlia** Gy 354 and I shall free you from the murderers.

Der.: **araqa, aruqa, arqa 3.**

ARQ II (orig. ע״י, cf. ריקא, ܣܪܝܩܐ Akk. *râqu* 'to be empty', *rêqu* 'empty', used only as pa. פ״א) to pour (from one vessel to another). Still used (pron. *arreq*).

Pa. Pf. **ariq mia** Lond. roll A 667 etc. he poured water. Pt. **ganzibra nasibh̲ lqanina d̲-hamra . . . umariq bkasa** CP 464:4 the g. taketh the bottle of wine . . . and poureth it into the cup. Gl. 12:7 f. **ARQ** افاض *fundere,* *liquefacere* ریخت از سر; 92:15 f. id. سبك *spergere* ریخت; 104:3 f. صبّ *fundere* ریخت.

arqa 1 (אַרְקָא Jer. 10: 11) earth, land, field MG 73:12, 100:10. Fem. MG 159:ult. Pl. **arqahata** lands MG 171:13, 183:15. No. cl. st. abs. and cstr. **arqa titaita ḏ-hšuka** Gy 127:3 the lower earth of Darkness; **arqa slmat armʿil** DAb = RD 41 the land of S.A.; **arqa ḏ-ruha** DAb = RD F 1 the land of Rūha; **arqa ḏ-ptahil** DAb = RD A 1 the land of Ptahil; **arqa ḏ-miṣraiia** Gy 381:17, 21 the land of Egyptians, Egypt; **arqa ḏ-tibil** or **arqa tibil** תֵּבֵל אֶרֶץ MG § 221 end; **arqa nahirta** Gy 281:14 the shining earth; **babil arqa, arqa babil, arqa ḏ-babil** the land of Babylon MG 319 bottom; **arqa ḏ-nhaša** Gy 160:1, 11 ff. the copper earth; **arqa ḏ-aiar** Gy 178:18, 292:15, 360:18 the earth of ether; **arqa ḏ-iušamin** Gy 360:17 the land of Y.; **arqa hiuartia** Gy 9:15, 379:9 the white land; **bihram arqa** DAb = RD A 1 the land of B.; **arqa ḏ-ṭina** Dab = RD B 30 the clay earth; **arqa ḏ-taruan dakita** Gy 306:3 the clean land of T.; **arqa ḏ-nṣab rba** Gy 360:21 the land of the great N.; **ʿtit lalma ḏ-arqa tiniana** Gy 260:26 (var. Sh. ʿAbd.'s copy **ḏ-tiniana**, read with the Leid. **ḏ-qra tiniana**) I came to the land which the Second created Ginzā 381 n. 4; **arqa qadmaita** Q 66:24 f. the first earth; **arqa ḏ-nhura** (*often*) the earth of Light; **arqa qadmaita ḏ-nhaša** DAb = RD B 26 f. etc. the first earth of copper; **arqa batraita ḏ-parzla** ibid. the last earth of iron; **arqahata udištata** AM 177:10 fields and deserts.

arqa 2 (עַרְקָא J. 2 ܥܪܩܐ) thong, tie. Pl. **arqia. arqia msanun** CP 11:penult., ML 13:5, 144:12 the thongs of their sandals; **blimitun bsara arqa** DC 26 (read with DC 40 **basara arqa**) ye are gagged with a bond, a strap; **kḏ arqa ḏ-parzla luatai** DC 44 is about me like an iron band.

arqa 3 (rt. **ARQ I**) = **araqa: nipqa kḏ arqa** DC 43 she cometh out like a runaway.

arqa 4 an inversion of **aqra 1** (ἄκρα). Pl. **aqria. mitpasasia aqria** CP 170:1 ML 206:2 s. PSS. **barqia ṭuria** Morg. 266/22:26 in the strongholds of the hills.

arqa 5, arqia (a shortened form of **rqiha**) sky, firmament MG 171 n. 3. **usalqia srutun umaṭia arqa** Sh. ʿAbd.'s copy of Gy 323:5 and its (i.e. of **mia** the water's) stink goeth up and reacheth the firmament; **arqaihun** Gy 8:ult. their firmament.

arqaba an exceptional form of **arqba. mašaruan arqaba** Zotb. 230 left col. 4 (the month) Mašarwan (under the sign of) Scorpio.

arqabata (ארקפטא, ἀργαπέτης) Persian high dignitary: **kursia rama ḏ-ldabahata ḏ-hinun arqabata** ATŠ II no. 133 a lofty throne that belonged to the ancestors, who were high dignitaries (?).

arqabigal (< אַרְקָא בְּרְגַל), varr. **arqabigar, arbigal, arbigar, arabigar, rabigar, abigal, arqabaigar, rabigal, bigar** etc. humble servant (lit. earth on the foot تراب اقدام, in each coloph. after the name of the copyist) MG 79 & n. 2. **atinia ḏ-nihuilak arqa bigar** DC 22. 335 = **atinin lmihuilak rabigar** Gy 339:19 f. we came to become thy servants; **ana hauin arqa bigar dilẖ** Jb 76:8 I will be his slave; **hauilak arqa bigar** Jb 154:10 they will be thy slaves.

arqaha a var. of **rqiha** MG 171 n. 3. **ʿl arqahaihun** Gy 8:9 (var. B **arqihun**) on their firmaments (var. firmament) MG 409:13 & n. 1, MSchr. 15, MSt 57:5 ff.

arqahata pl. of **arqa 1**.

arqaita AM 227:3 a var. of **aqraita, aqariata** (read **aqraita**). DC 3 **aqraita ḏ-kadba** has **arqaita** in CP 33:10 lying accusation (?): ML 39:5 has **aqraita.**

arqba (inversion of עקרבא, ܥܩܪܒܐ) scorpion MG 74:4, 128:2. Sign of the Zodiac Scorpio Nöld. ZDMG xxv 256 ff., MMII 74. Fem. MG 156:antep. Pl. **arqbia** and **arqbata.** A rare var. **aqraba** s.v. **arqbia urihšia bišia** AM 182:penult. scorpions and evil vermin; **uarqbia maitin** AM 269:4 and scorpions will die; **murat** (var. **ʿumrara**) **arqba gauaita ḏ-hšuka** Gy 209:2 the poison of the inner scorpion of darkness. Gl. 123:13 **arqba** with masc. and fem. pl. عقرب, عقارب *scorpio* کژدم.

arqia, = **arqa 5** MG 171 n. 3. **arqaihun** Gy 8:9 their firmament MSt 57. Gl. 100:6 **arqia** سماء *coelum* آسمان.

arqiha = **rqiha: arqihun** v.s. **arqaha.**

arqsa (inversion of ἄκρος?) top? **barqsa aiiltun** DAb = RD B 77 ye brought me on the top (?).

aršaiata (cf. רְשׁוּתָא) powers, authorities, (cf. רְשְׁעוּתָא) evil powers. Sg. not found. **ušuba udauraiun udaiuaiun . . . aršaiata nihun** ATŠ I no. 293 and the Seven and their abode and their devils . . . are the evil powers.

aršap (Ar. ارجاف) alarming news. **aršap uakbar napša nihuia** AM 282:14 there will be much alarming rumour and news.

arta, ʿrta (rt. **AUR I & II = ʿUR**) awake, shining. Only fem. found. **šurbta haita arta** Jb 278:11 the living, awake, race.

ašagta (nom. act. **ŠUG**) washing(-water). Var. **ašgata** (s.v.). **urmun ašagta atutia margnaihun** DC 50. 445 and they cast the washing-water beneath their staves.

ašaiata pl. of **ašita** (q.v.). **ašaiatun** Gy 10 their walls.

ašamta (nom. act. **ŠUM**) the laying (of hands). **ašamta ḏ-ʿda ʿl ašualania** ATŠ I no. 181 the laying of hands on postulants.

ašanai = **šanai.**

ašaq br ašqan Gy 383:16 a king of early Iran (Ashkanian dynasty).

ašar 1 (rt. **ŠRR**) adv. well, thoroughly, firmly, plenteously. **ašar ṣban ṣabuiia** Morg. 215/18:2, ML 84:8 = CP 69:7, Q 31:20 well did the Baptizer baptize me; **ašar nasbia ʿukuma** DC 22. 452 they became thoroughly black.

ašar 2, var. **šar,** AM 204 a place-name BZ Ap. II.

ašariʿil DC 43 D 31 an angel.

ašaša (ܐܫܫܐ) raft. Still used in marshes for a bundle of reeds as a raft. **iama d̲-larab ulašaša** Gy 382:3 (var. B **lašaš** st. abs.) the sea with no ferry and no raft MG 302:4.

ašata s. **ašita.**

ašga, ašgan malka Gy 383:11 a king of early Iran (an eponym of Ashkanian or Parthian dynasty, Gray ZA 19/1905 284).

ašganda (Sum. *aš-gan-da*, Akk. *ašgandu*) helper, assistant, servant; the Messenger (syn. of **šliha** Wdg. iii 50); name given to the boy or young man assisting the priest in the rituals RO ii 463; ML 231:7 a pr. name, cf. n. 3. **ašgandai ṭaba d̲-nhura** ML 172:2, CP 144:5, has **šgandai** my good Messenger of Light, cf. n. 1; **šadrh̲ lbihdad ašganda** DC 41 he sent B. as a messenger. Gl. 99:11 written defectively شماس *diaconus.*

ašgar (Ar. اشقر) roan, sorrel: **hisan ašgar** AM 129:9 a roan stallion (حصان اشقر).

ašgata (var. of **ašagta**) rinsing, water for washing. **ukd̲ ašgata tlitaita lniarak ašigth̲** DC 47 and when thou hast given thy bowl a third rinsing.

AŠD (אֲשַׁד, ܐܫܕ) to pour down, pour out (water, rain, tears, blood) MG 241 n. 1.

Pe. Pf. **ašad** he poured MG 241:7. Impf. **nišud** he poureth MG 242: 8; with suff. **ʿšidh̲** I pour him out MG 275:22; with encl. **uništdilh̲ miša** CP 92:19 and drop down oil upon him. Act. pt. **daula d̲-mia d̲-malia ušid** AM 10:16 a water-bucket that is full and flows over; pl. **zma btibil ašdia** Gs 36:21 they shed blood on earth, **ašdia zma** Gy 122:4. Inf. **lmišad zma** Gy 122:5 to shed blood.

Ethpe. Pf. **ʿštid** was poured MG 70:14. Impf. **ništid** AM 178:12 is shed. Inf. **mištaduia, maštaduia,** to be shed MG 13:bottom.

Ethpa. Impf. **uzma bmia ništad** AM 172:18 and the rivers will run with blood.

Ettaf. Only pt. found: **bakia ualia umitašida** Gs 74:23 she weepeth and waileth and sheddeth tears; pl. **mitašidia** Gy 232:5 they are dissolved (in tears), **mitašidin** Gy 229:15, Jb 251:3 id., cf. Jb ii 227 n. 2. Part. pres. **alma d̲-mitašidit** JRAS 1943 171:3 why dost thou shed (tears)?

Idioms: Ettaf. is regularly used with the meaning of shedding tears, being dissolved in tears. Certain forms were confused with **ŠDA** and acquired the meaning 'to throw, reject', cf. **man ašdan bhasiruta ubṣiruta** Gs 40:8 f. who hurled me into the deficiency and defect; **umagzirania latišdinan** CP 113:13 and the condemning (judges) shall not reject us.

ašdum s. **šdum.**

ašha s. **ašuha 2.**

ašualia, šualia (Talm. שְׁוָלְיָא) pupil, disciple, novice for priesthood, pl. **(a)šualania** MG 170:2 f., RO ii 464, ML 6 n. 2, DAb 24 n. 2. Fem. pl. **šaualata** s.v. **palig bnaṣuraiia uašualania** HG 120 schism ensued amongst the Naṣoraeans and the disciples.

ašuat 1 (Targ. אַשְׁוָתָא cstr. אַשְׁוַת) tricks, evasion, circumlocution, subterfuge. St. emph. not found. **baiina d̲-tigalalia adinqia ašuat** ATŠ I no. 37 I ask that thou reveal to me without evasions; **ašuat naṣiruta,** PD 1033, 1107, **ašuat naṣirut** PD 1419, **ašuat naṣrut** PD 477, DC 34. 32, **ašuat naṣruta** PD 975, ATŠ trs. p. 122 n. 6 priestly circumlocutions, ambiguities concealing true meaning.

ašuat 2 (H. שַׁבָּת Akk. *šabattu*) Sabbath. **biuma d̲-šubaia d̲-ašuat** ATŠ coloph. on the seventh day, that is Saturday.

ašuha 1, šuha (אשוחא, ܫܘܚܐ Löw 60) fir-tree MG 379:bottom & n. 3, female cedar Jb ii 157 n. 4, Ginzā 215 n. 3, Meissner, *Mitteilungen d. Vorderasiat. Gesellsch.* 1913 35. Pl. **ašuhia, šuhia. arza mn gintai ʿriq uašuha qpil mn bunkh̲** Gs 111:17 a male cedar was torn up from my garden and a female cedar felled from its place (Nöld., loc. cit.: a cedar and a fir-tree); **arzia mn arqa d̲-libnan uašuhia mn ṭura d̲-(i)atur** Gy 265:12 cedars from the land of Lebanon and female cedars from the mountain of Atur; **arzia mn haran uašuhia libnan** Gy 380:11 cedars from the Harran and female cedars of Lebanon (Nöld. compared **arzia uašuhia** to ארזים וברושים 'cedars and cypresses', cf. Löw 60); **arzia ramia uašuhia umšauia ʿlania** DC 44 lofty cedars and female cedars and levelled trees.

ašuha 2, or **ašha** (etym. and meaning unknown). **ašhia litbh̲ d̲-nikla hauilh̲ lnunia d̲-ʿuria** Jb 162:3 obscure, cf. ii 163 no. 3.

ašultina, ašlutina = **šultana**. **ašultina uaṣluntia raza d̲-aiar lgaṭiun** ATŠ I no. 254 (var. DC 6 **šultana uaṣluntai**) the bat and the owls took to the mystery of the air.

ašuma (rare) = **šuma. ašumak** Jb 163:9 thy name.

ašia (אַשְׁיָן?) hard? **d̲-ašia lagiṭna** DC 46. 113:2 so that I seize him hard (? corrupt).

ašiunta a miscopying of **ašultina**? **ašiuntai hu** Bodl. 12 this is . . . (accompanied by a picture which makes the meaning completely doubtful).

ašimiaiil DAb a supernatural being.

ašiqa = **ʿšiqa. sahra ašiqa d̲-lahazia** DC 51 a blind demon that seeth not; **uʿl ašiqa hulh̲ paruanqa** Gy 15:16 and to a blind one be a leader, cf. ZS 1922 2.

ašita (אֻשְׁיְתָא, ܫܝܬܐ Ar. loan-w. آسية) wall, pl. **ašiata,** worse varr. **ašata, ašaiata** MG 113:6. **libna mn ašita** Gy 387:7 the clay brick from the wall; **aqria bašita sliq** Gy 115:6 he climbed the fortress by the wall (differently from Lidzb. Ginzā 127:ult. & n. 5); **ʿtala ašiath̲ unpal** Gs 15:14 its walls fell apart and it fell (var. DC 22. 468 **ʿtla ašith̲** its wall split apart), similarly Gs 83:1 f. (DC 22. 405 **ʿšaith̲**); **lašath̲** Gy 67:24 (var. DC 22. 62 **lašiath̲**) for its walls; **ṣaliba d̲-naqšia bašiata** Jb 109:3 f. the cross which they fix on the walls; **ṣilmia d̲-ʿl ašiata ṣiria** Jb 274:1 the images pictured on the walls.

ašitiaiil a var. of **ašimiaiil.**

aškal (Ar. اشكال) AM 257:27 the shapes, phenomena.

aškaṣta (rt. ŠKṢ = Ar. شكس, شكص) indigence, poverty, penury. **uaškaṣta rabtia bmdiniata d̲-babil nihuia** AM 232:2 (Ṣâb.'s copy **aškaṣuta**) and there will be great indigence in the cities of Babylonia.

aškarta (Middle P. *[h]ašākert*, Mod. P. شاگرد) (*a*) maid-servant, **aškarta bbakth̲** (varr. **brapth̲, brabth̲, brakth̲, bikth̲, birikta** etc.) **bdagaluta masgia** Gy 389:3 and the maid-servant acteth deceitfully with her mistress, Ginzā 416 no. 1. (*b*) (miswritten) **pum bit aškarta d̲-aith̲ lriš sura** HG 80 Pumbeditha, the Academy situated at the end of Sura (?), cf. p. 10 no. 3.

aškinta = **škinta** MG 25:bottom. Gl. 144:11 written defectively (but with a prosth. **a**) كنيسة *ecclesia* كليسا.

aškita 1, škita (nom. act. af. **ŠKA I**) finding, discovery, something found, settling down, rest, tranquillity. **aškita maška** AM 36, 67, 73 etc. (*often*) will make a discovery.

aškita 2 (nom. act. af. **ŠKA II**) complaint, lament MG 104:5 & no. 1. **ʿlita uaškita** Gy 183:9 wailing and lamenting.

ašla (rt. **ŠLA I**) draw-string, rope for pulling, tow-rope, cable, path (?). **aslitak litbh̲ ašla** Jb 162:2 there is no draw-cord in thy net; **ašlh̲ ašlia d̲-ziua** Jb 151:ult. its ropes are ropes of light; **ušdilun ašlai lṭabia** Jb 149:6 and he threw my rope to the good ones; **uašlia** (var. **uašla**) **d̲-nhura rmibh̲** Gy 273:16 (var. DC 22. 268) and a cable of light is cast into it; **utlatma ušitin alpia ašlia ʿtlia** DC 8 and it has 360,000 paths. Gl. 66:13 **ašla** جلاء *transmigratio*.

ašlamata (rt. **ŠLM**), var. **šalamata** surrenderings (cf. تسليم), tyrannous requisitions. **uqiria unidria uašlamata** DC 40. 234 and accidents and (evil?) vows and surrenderings (forfeitures).

ašlanda = **šlanda.**

ašlutina s. **ašultina, šultana.**

ašlia = **šlia.** Gl. 124:8 **ašli** عريان *rudus* برهنه; 125:11 id. على عرية *in nudo* برهنه.

ašlimun = **šlimun.**

ašma Gl. 26:11 اسم *nomen* نام.

ašmuiil Jb 85 n. 3 Ismael (cf. **šumʿil**).

ašnia (Talm. אשוני, אָשִׁין, עָשִׁין) tough, coarse, rough. **iarqunia rgigia mitklia mn qudam ašnia** Gs 3:13 the tender green stuff will be eaten before the coarse.

AŠP (ܐܫܦ, Akk. *ašipu* LS) to use magical arts, exorcize, read incantations. Only in the Qm.-d̲-H.Z.

Pe. Impf. **kd̲ miša . . . ʿšup** DC 44. 644 like Moses . . . I employ magical arts, **ʿšup ʿpuq uʿzkinun** ibid. I exorcize, I banish (lit. go out) and vanquish them. Pass. Pt. **ašip pumaihun** DC 44 their mouths were exorcized.

ašpur = **špur** MG 26:8.

ašpula, emph. **ašpulta** (rt. **ŠPL**) lowest part, latter end, latter part. **ašpulta udnabta d̲-alma** DC 47 the latter part and end of the world. Gl. 159:9 defectively and without ending منحدر *radix* بيخ.

ašpinza = **špinza.**

AŠQ, ʿŠQ (עָשַׁק, ܥܡܗ) to oppress, to blind Lidzb. ZS 1922 2.

Pe. Pf. **ašaq ašaq asip asip nbu** DC 43 J 68 he blinded, he blinded, he destroyed, he destroyed N. Pass. pt. **asiqa, ʿsiqa** (s.v.).

Ettaf. Pf. **ʿtašaq ulahzun** CP 128:2, ML 155:4 they were blind and did not see.

Der.: **asiqa, ʿsiqa, ʿsqa.**

ašqa = **šaqa: ašqik gupnia aiar** DC 22. 111 (for **šaqik** Gy 116:12) thy (fem.) limbs are airy vines.

ašqan father of **ašaq.**

ašraia Gl. 54:3. تحلية *solutio, liberatio* گذاشتن; 129:9 فاتحه *apertio* كشاده.

ašrap (Ar. اشراف) noblemen. **akabir uašrap** s. **akabir.**

ašria = **šria:** Gl. 158:12 **ašri** [*sic*] محلول *dimissus, inclinatus* رفته; 160:7 id. مفتوح *apertus* باز; 161:2 id. منطلق *nolens, fugiens* گريزنده.

AŠŠ (אשש) a rt. of **mašašta** (q.v.).

aššar (Ar. اشجار) trees; **aššar ṭiʿam uhamra qalia nihuia** AM 280:36 trees, food, and vintage will be scanty.

aštargan, štargan (ܐܫܛܪܓܢ, اشترغان Löw p. 37; middle, 251 f., P. اشترگان) camel-foot (?). **marua aštargan** Gy 106:20, 22, Jb 232:5 a kind of giant fennel Ginzā 116 n. 3. **margna d̲-hiduia mn aštargan ʿlana** ŠQ 15:12 the staff of the bridegroom is of camel-thorn.

at a mod. form of **anat: at masiqta d̲-šum qria ʿlh̲** ATŠ II no. 74 (DC 6), thou, read thou the *masiqta* of Šum (: Shem) for him. Gl. 28:9 **at** انت *tu* تو.

-at 1 (or **-ut, -it**) Gen. Aram. ending of the st. cstr. fem. sg. (*-ăt*) and pl. (*-ât*) MG 162.

-at 2 (or **-it**) encl. pers. pron. of the 2nd p. sg. MG 87.

-at 3 pers. ending of the 3rd p. fem. sg. pf. MG 222.

ATA I, ʿTA I (אֲתָא, ܐܬܐ) to come, arrive; pa. & af. to bring, MG 241 n. 1.

Pe. Pf. **ata** he came MG 28:4, 257:2, **atat** she came MG 257:6, **atit, ʿtit** thou hast come, I have come MG 257:bottom, **atun, ʿtun** they came MG 258:2, **ʿtitun** ye came MG 258: middle, **atin(in)** we came MG 258:bottom; with encl. **atalan** he came to us Lidzb. ZDMG lxi 693, **atatalun, atatlun** she came to them MG 275:16 f., **atatalan** she came to us ibid., **ʿtitlh̲** I came to him MG 258:1, **atulik** they came to thee (fem.) MG 258:10. Impf. **nitia** *veni(e)t* MG 258:paen., **titia** *ea veni(e)t, veni(e)s* MG 258:ult., **ʿtia** I (shall) come MG 259:1, **nitun, nʿtun** they (will) come MG 259:2, **nit(a)ian** Gs 7:ult. *eae veniunt*, ***titun** ye came MG 259 n. 2; with encl. **nitubh̲** they (will) come in it. Impt. **ata**, fem. **atai**, pl. **atun**, fem. pl. **atian** come! MG 259:middle. Pt. **atia** he cometh, will come MG 259:18; participial pres. **atina** I (shall) come, fem. **latiana** I do not come, **atit** *veni(e)s* MG 259:

bottom, **atina, qatina** (often) I (shall) come, **atinin** we (shall) come, **atitun** ye (will) come, **atin, qatin** (often) they (will) come; with encl. **atitubẖ** ye (will) come in it MG 259:anteantep. Inf. **mitia** the coming, to come MG 260:13; with suff. **mitiai** my coming MG 176:18, **mitiak** thy coming MG 177:7, (**lmizlaikun**) **ulmitiaikun** Gy 17:17 (at your going) and at your coming.

Pa. & Af. Pf. **aitia** (af.) he brought MG 243:bottom, 7:17 f., **atiat** (pa.) she brought MG 243:bottom, 261:1, **aitit** (af.) & **atit** (pa.) I brought MG 261:7, **aitun, aitu** (af.) they brought MG 261:middle; with encl. (all as af.) **aitilak, aitilun, aititilun, aitit(i)lkun** I brought thee, them (twice), you MG 261:8, 11, **aitulẖ** they brought (to) him MG 261: middle; with suff. **atian** (pa.) he brought me MG 243:bottom, 284:anteantep. (Nöld. mistakenly af.), **atiak** (pa.) he brought thee MG 286:middle (Nöld. as af.), **atiiẖ, atiẖ** (pa.), **aitiẖ** (af.) he brought him MG 287:9 (Nöld. all as af.), **atiun** (pa.) they brought me, neg. **latiun** they brought me not, **aitiun** (af.) they brought me MG 286:top, **atitẖ** (pa.) thou hast brought him MG 288:5 (mistakenly as af.), **aititẖ** I brought him, her MG 288:13, **atiuia** (pa.), **aituia** (af.), **atiunẖ** (pa.), **aitunẖ** (af.) they brought him MG 288:bottom (all s. af.), **atinkun** he brought you MG 290:2, **aitinun** he brought them MG 290:middle, **aititinun** I brought them MG 291:3, **atunun** they brought them MG 291:9. Impf. **naitia** (often) *apporta(bi)t*, **ʿiatia** I (shall) bring MG 262:1, **naitun** (*often*) they (will) bring; with suff. **ʿiatẖ** I (shall) bring him MG 287:17; with encl. **taitilan** ML 140:6 bring (to) us, **ʿiaitilak** ML 226:5 I (shall) bring (to) thee. Impt. fem. **aitai, atai,** pl. **aitun, atun** bring! MG 262: middle; with suff. **atiẖ** (pa.) bring him MG 287:bottom (Nöld. as af.), pl. **atiuia, atuia** (both pa.) *apportate eum* MG 289:top (Nöld. as af.). Pt. **maitia, matia** *apporta(bi)t* (the latter preferred as a fem. form) MG 262:18; pl. **matin** they bring MG 243:antep.; with encl. **matilẖ** they bring (to) him MG 262:18; Participial pres. **maititun** ye (will) bring MG 263:1; with suff. **maitinun** I (shall) bring them MG 291:anteantep.; with encl. **matiatlia** *apporta(bi)s me* MG 262:anteantep. Inf. **(m)aituiia** bringing, to bring MG 144:9, 263:14; with encl. **maitilkun** (read **maituiil-kun**) to bring (to) you MG 263:middle. Nom. ag. **matiana** someone who brings MG 138:9.

atun niškub luat hdadia Gy 392:11 come, let us sleep with one another; **mn ziuak taitilan** ML 140:6 bring us from thy brilliance; **mitiẖ ḏ-adam mn bit hiia** Gs 68:ult. when A. came from the House of Life MG 388 f.; **lmatin** (var. **lmitin**) **dirdqunia luat rabaiun** AM for taking children to their teachers; **lmitin ulmiqrublẖ qurbana** AM for bringing and offering a gift; **lšum ḏ-ata ulšum ḏ-atia** Gy 196:15 in the name of him who came, and in the name of him who will come.

Idioms: With **ʿl, l** 'to attack'. With **b** 'to accuse' (influenced by **ATA II**).

Gl. 8:11 f. **ATA** اتى *duci* آورد; 16:11 f. id. اتاا (read آتى) *adducere* آورد; 48:7 f. id. تعال *venire* آمد; 56:1 f. جاب *parare, afferre* آورد; 56:3 f. جاء *accedere, venire* آمد; 63:7 f. جاا به [sic] *adducere* آورد; 64:1 f. حدث *accidere* بهم رسيد; 79:11 f. with encl. **l** زمع *futurus esse* خواهد آمد; 132:9 f. **ATA** قدّم *adferre* آورد; 171:7 f. هات *afferre* آورد; 175:15 f. وافا (read وافى) *attulere* [sic] آورد.

Der.: **ʿtia, matiana.**

ATA II, ʿTA II (pa. ࡏࡕࡀ) to accuse: **atibun qala akuat iušamin atibẖ qala** DAb accusing them, just as Y. was accused.

Der.: **atiauata.**

ata 1 (אָתָא, ࡀࡕࡀ) mark, sign MG 110:middle. Pl. **atuata** MG 167:5, rarely **atauata. uata lhadiiẖ** AM he will have a mark on his breast.

ata 2 (Targ. איתא, איתתא) a mod. form of **ʿnta.**

-ata (or **-auata, -uata, -iata**) Gen. Aram. ending of the st. emph. fem. pl. MG 162:6 f.

atana 1 (אֲתָנָא, ࡀࡕࡀࡍࡀ; Nöld. supposed a reduplication of **t**, which vanished as in all فعّال-forms, pron. *aθâna*) she-ass MG 121:6 ff. **qudša ḏ-atana ḏ-arba ligria** Gy 226:11 the sacrament of a four-legged she-ass.

atana 2, ʿtana (Ass. *itannu, itanu*) mesh, network Jb ii 153 no. 2. **akma šapir atana ḏ-ʿtbẖ** Jb 149:11 how beautiful is the mesh that is in it; **latanak litbẖ humria** Jb 149:12 there are no stones (: weights) in thy mesh; **uabaria batana ramia ʿtana ʿtana ḏ-nadir minẖ mn alma** Jb 155:2 f. she has to put lead (weights) into the mesh, a mesh that is heavier than the world.

atar st. abs. & cstr. of **atra. batar atar** (*often*) in many places, **ḏ-atar atar** (*often*) of many places; **lkul atar** Gy 4:6 etc. to every place; **atar zadiq** Gs 123:24 a just place; **ʿl atar** Gs 94:22 on the spot; **atra ksia** Gy 73:22 etc. a hidden place MG 302:bottom; **atar nhur** (*very often*) place of the Light, synonymous with **atar hiia** place of the Life.

atuat 1 st. abs. of **ʿnta** MG 183:11 ff.; used also as a determined noun, later also for pl. **kḏ atuat ḏ-ṭariana tarṣa ʿl libat** ATŠ II no. 211 like a woman that setteth up a table to Venus; **ʿl kul atuat** Gy 22:3 f. about every woman; **kḏ atuat ḏ-ialda lamrabia** Jb 54:13 like a woman who doth not bring up her child; **ula amrat atuat** Gy 5:17 and no woman said . . .; **atuat harašata** DC 40. 639 witch-woman; **atuat hakimta harašata** DC 40. 1095 the wise witch-woman; **halin atuat lhdadia ladamian** DC 40 these women do not resemble one another; **halin atuat ḏ-lašihan** DAb those women that are unworthy; **atuat ḏ-šabqalẖ lzauẖ qadmaia** DAb a woman that leaveth her first husband; **špur atuat** Gy 365:15 beauty of women.

atuat 2, atuata pl. of **ata 1. umandaia umanda atuat ḏ-braza qadmaia ḏ-ʿma qaimin** ATŠ I no. (?) and 'Mandaean' and 'Manda' are symbols arising from the mystery of the

Mother; **atuat ḏ-ziqa** AM portents of wind; **uatuat ḏ-mhamblata** DC 51 and signs of corruptive qualities; **atuata ḏ-šupra** Gy 10:6 signs of beauty. (Sometimes difficult to distinguish from **atuat** 1, cf. **ʿsiria haršia ḏ-atuat harašata** DC 26, DC 40 etc. bound are the spells of magic symbols, or of women enchantresses (?))

atun a mod. form of **anatun.**

atuna (אַתּוּנָא, ܐܬܘܢܐ, Ar. loan-w. أَتُّونُ Fränkel 26) furnace, oven MG 125:7 & n. 3. Pl. **atunia. ṣibia ḏ-atunia** Jb 97:11 oven fuel; **daula hiuara br atuna ḏ-lamšarai** DC 51 a white water-pitcher, fresh from the furnace, never used; **lpumaiun ḏ-atunia** Gs 29:19 into the apertures of the stoves.

atuniana a miscopying of **atiniana** = **tiniana. bpaṭira atuniana** ATŠ II no. 124 in the second unleavened loaf (read with DC 6 **bpagra atiniana** in the second body).

atutia, tutia (Talm. תּוּתֵי < תְּחוּתֵי, ܬܚܘܬ) beneath, under, underneath, below MG 63:13, 194:8. With other prepositions: **mn atutia** from beneath, from below, from amongst, **latutia, ʿl atutia** beneath, under the authority of, under the eye of MG 197:2. Could possibly be constructed also with **ḏ**, cf. **atutia adabara** CP 176:16 [*sic*] a var. of **atutia abara** ML 215:6 under the lead; **ʿniana ḏ-atutia** DC 3 the prayer (given) below; **uʿl atutia ḏ-šar gupna amarulia kma alpia ʿutria iatbin** Jb 2:15 f. and tell me how many thousands of uthras dwell under the rule of Shar Gufna; **ʿl atutia alahia ʿdilna atutia alahia mrabina** DC 13 I was born under (the eye of) the gods, under (the supervision of) the gods was I reared.

atiauata (rt. **ATA II**) villainies, frauds, knavery. **umardita uatiauata banaša tihuia** AM 246:1 and there will be rebellion and knavery amongst men.

atiaruta = **tiaruta** MG 145:11.

atid (עֲתִיד, ܥܬܝܕ) ready, prepared. Only once in MA, the rt. being otherwise used as **ATT.**

atiniana = **tiniana: muta atiniana** DC 22. 219 the second death.

atiqa (עַתִּיקָא, ܥܬܝܩܐ), doublet. **hatiqa** old, ancient MG 71:16. **kdaba atiqa** (often) an old writing. Gl. 28:6 **atiqa** اوّل , اوّلين *antiquus.*

atitia miscopying of **atutia.**

atlata = **tlata.**

atmar (Ar. أَثْمَار) AM 263:35 fruits.

atminaia = **tmanaia** MG 192:7.

ATNA I (אַתְנַח), אִיתְנָחָא √נוח: see Epstein: *Gr. Bab. Aram.*, p. 931 Qidd. fol. 45b) to put, place, lay, set MG 84:6. Used as af. and ettaf.

Af. Pf. **atna** he put MG 84:6; **atnatun** ATŠ II no. 165 ye have set; **atnun** they put MG 237:17; with suff. **ʿu šga latnẖ hamra bmia** ATŠ I no. 198 if he mistook (and) did not put wine into the water; **ʿu šga umindam latnẖ** ATŠ I no. 194 if he mistook and did not place something; **atnatẖ** I put him MG 84:7. Impf. **umaka ltaqipa latatnun** Gy 14 and do not leave a weak one to a strong one; with suff. **natnẖ** he will put him, it, putteth him, it; neg. **ʿda ḏ-kušṭa bʿdaiun lanatnẖ** ATŠ I no. 165 he shall not place the hand of *kušṭa* (: the ritual handclasp) in theirs; **latatnẖ lʿutria blihia** Gy 305:11 do not bestow it on foolish uthras; **šuṭaihun ḏ-biaminaiun natnulia** DC 44 their whips which are in their right hands they hand over to me. Impt. **atna** (**ʿdak lrišiẖ**) Morg. 215/17:5 f. put (thy hand on his head); with suff. **atnun** DAb place them! Pt. (act. & pass.): **matna** (often) he putteth, is put; with encl. pers. pron. **matnit** AM 287:14 thou wilt put; with encl. prep. **sandlia ḏ-ziua bligrai matnalia** JRAS 1939 399:5 sandals of radiance are put on my feet; **lkadpẖ matnalẖ** Gy 187 is placed on her shoulder. Pl. **matnin** ATŠ II no. 112. Part. pres. **matnitun** ATŠ II no. 166 ye place.

Ettaf. Pf. **muma bgauaihun ʿtatna** ATŠ I no. 184 blemish hath been set upon them; **uhad ʿsiqta ʿtatnat ʿlauaihun** DC 34 and one seal was set upon them. Pt. **mitatna** ATŠ II no. 365 is placed.

Note: Certain forms are confused with **NTN** 'to give', cf. **nitnulak binta ʿšumia larqa** DC 37 they will place thee between heaven and earth (formal confusion); **ḏ-lamṣia ḏ-natnẖ lkulẖ zidqa nitin lpalgia ḏ-zidqa** ATŠ who is unable to bestow all the oblation shall give half the oblation (formal and material confusion); **šlama ʿl nbihia latitnul(h)un** Gy 223:14 (var. **tatnalhun** Sh. 'Abd.'s copy) greet not (false) prophets.

ATNA II = **TNA: atna ganzibra ḏ-nimarlẖ** DC 38. 6:25 the ganzibra repeats and says.

ATR I, ʿTR II (secondary rt. from ܐܬܬܥܝܪ, cf. Sam. ࠀࠕࠏࠕࠓ MG 84 n. 1) to awake, call to life MG 84:top

Pe. Pf. **ʿtar** he awoke MG 251:antep.; **ʿtirat nišimta tarmidia bihdadia** DC 27. 314 the soul of priests was roused in each other. Impf. **nitar apra** Gy 97 (synonymous with **sliq aqapra** ibid.) the dust rose. Inf. **mitar** to (a)wake, (a)wakening.

Pa. **atar** he wakened MG 84:4; **had had razia atartun** ATŠ II no. 159 ye awakened all mysteries; with suff. **atrẖ** he wakened him, ibid.; **atartẖ** she wakened him MG 84:5, 276:22; **latrun** they did not waken me MG 84:6; **nišimta atirtinun lrazia** DC 34. 777 the soul awakened the mysteries. Impf. with suff. **nʿiatran** he will awaken me MG 84:5, 271:4. Pt. **matarlẖ mn šinta** Gs 10:2 who wakened him from his sleep; **matrana ḏ-matralun** DC 34 awakener that will waken them; **matrilun** DC 48. 246 they awake them. Nom. ag. **matrana** (s.v.).

Der.: **matrana.**

ATR II, ʿTR, YTR (עֲתַר, ܥܬܪ) to become rich, enrich, be prosperous, be plenteous, abounding. Pa. and ethpa. formed from **YTR** (יְתַר, ܝܬܪ).

Pe. Pf. **ʿtar, tar** Gy 79:7 he abounded MG 245:3 f.; **ḏ-mitar ʿtar ulahasar** 75:22 that was surpassingly rich without lacking; **atar hšuka atar** DC 22 the darkness abounded, it abounded. Pass. pt. **atira. ubiatiria d̠-lau bhasiria** CP 108:1 as having plenty and not as lacking. Inf. **mitar** Gy 75:22 (above).

PA. (as ܐܬܪ) Impf. with suff. **niatrh̠ lšurbth̠** DC 22. 101 we shall increase his race. Pt. **miatar, miatra** (s.v.).

ETHPA. Pt. **mitiatar** (often) he will become enriched.

DER.: **autrana, atrana, miatra, lutrana, ʿutra, iatir.**

atra (אַתְרָא, ܐܬܪܐ) place, region. St. abs. & cstr. **atar** (s.v.) MG 152:9. Used first as masc., later as fem. 159:7 f. Pl. **atrata** MG 170:antep., **atrauata** (ܐܬܪܘܬܐ) miscopied as **atraiata** AM 194:ult. With suff. **atrai** my place, **atrak** thy place etc. **batrata atrata** AM 248:5 in many a place; **atra ʿl atra napla** Gy 50:21 one land will attack another; **batra d̠-** in the place where, **latra d̠-** to the place where, **atra d̠-** (in) the place where MG 450 f.; **atra d̠-hšuka** (often) the place of darkness.

atrana a var. of **autrana. atrana lmašqiana** DC 48 prosperity to him who administereth the potion.

atraṣa ATŠ I no. 8 = **traṣa.**

atrunga DC 48. 282 = **trunga.**

atrin = trin. **atrin zibnia** Jb 13:4 twice; **atrin mutia** Jb 57:2, 7 two deaths.

atrisar = **trisar.**

ATT, ʿTT (עתד, ܥܬܕ) to prepare, make ready, foreordain, destine. Used esp. in the pass. pt. **ʿtit, ʿtita** s.v. **ʿtitlh̠ lmihuia** ATŠ I no. 110 it is destined to be; **ʿtitlh̠ ladam** Gy 26 it is destined to A.; **ʿtitilh̠** (*often*) they are prepared for him; **lbušia ʿtitinlh̠** (var. **ʿtitnulh̠** Sh. ʿAbd.'s copy) Gy 250:7 garments are prepared for him MG 53 n. 2. **ʿtatna** Gy 240:5 I am ready.

B

b the second letter of the alphabet, MM II 241. Phon. value: plosive *b*, or aspirated *β*. Phon. changes: **b** < **p** before **g** and **b** > **p** MG 47, **b** > **u** MG 49, syncope of **b** after **au-** in the af. of **YBL**, final **b** > **m** MG 49:bottom.

b– (Gen. Sem.) prep. in, by, with, by means of etc., used proclitically before nouns and pronouns, enclitically after verbs. **ubmanda d̠-hiia saipibh̠** Gy 229:21 and they have no more portion in M.-d̠-H.; **d̠-bh̠ rauibh̠ almia** Gy 112:3 by which people become intoxicated; **bʿdak** in thy hand MG 4:18, **bilanun** in their tree MG 4:24, **biblia** in sorrow ibid., **bisura** (varr. **bʿsura, bʿusura**) in the bond MG 4:25; **bdnab** at the end, **bdbar, badbar, bidbar** in the desert etc. MG 10. **bzma** in the blood MG 11:1, **brpilia, barpilia** in the clouds MG 11:7, **brqba, barqba** in Scorpio MG 11:8, **bh̠ biuma hanath̠** Gy 293:2 in that day, **bmalia ʿhšibh̠** Gy 221:1 I shall consider it as full. With adverbs: **(b)sarhabaiit** swiftly, **(b)nihaiit** softly, **(b)npiš** much etc. MG 201. In oaths: **bhaiak** by thy life MG 482:3. To form adverbial expressions: **bhaṭaiia** Gy 14 in a sinful way, as sinners.

ba– often for **b-**, even when the noun needs no prosthetic vowel: **babaita** = **bbaita** in the house, **babauata** = **bbauata** in the prayers MG 32:12 f., **bahamša** = **bhamša** on the fifth.

ba (cf. Egyptian *bꜣ* represented by 𓅡) a ritual word for the dove sacrificed at the *masiqta*, and the sacred dove's meat consumed by the priests at the same, MMII Ind. Masc. **uaitun ba mn yauna urauṭa d̠-asa mn ginta d̠-lania** DC 27 and they brought Ba from the dove and a twig of myrtle from the garden of trees; **dirh̠ palga d̠-ba** CP 71:19 (**durh̠** etc. DC 3) bring a fragment of the dove's flesh; **matna lqina ba uamuza . . .** DC he will put on the pile (i.e. the unleavened bread upon which the scraps of ritual food are placed) the dove's flesh, walnut etc.; **ʿu šga uprat ba mn qudam . . .** ATŠ I no. 179 if he mistook and divided up the dove before . . .; **uba d̠-masiqta minh̠ hua** ATŠ I no. 246 and the *ba* (dove) of the *masiqta* was from her (: **simat hiia**).

BAA (בְּעֵי, ܒܥܐ) to ask, demand, desire, want, seek, pray, beg, wish.

PE. Pf. **ba** he wanted, sought MG 257:3, contracted in **blmihuia** Gy 276:10 (var. B **bilmihuia**) sought to be, was going to be (cf. Idioms) MG 11 n. 2, **bat** she wanted, sought MG 257:7, **bit** *volui*(*sti*), *quaesivi*(*sti*) MG 257: bottom; **bit buta mn hiia qadmaiia** ML 18:7 = CP 16:ult. I prayed a prayer to the First Life; **bit d̠-tiklh̠** Gy 86 thou didst want to devour the whole world; **bit mšauinun** Gy 171:4 I wanted to make them; **bun** they wanted, sought MG 258:2, **baitun** ye wanted, sought MG 258:13, **bitun** (often) id., **bin, banin** we asked; **bin uaškinin** Morg. 218/23:8 f. we sought and found; with encl. **b**: **bauata d̠-babin adam** Gy 376:2 the prayers wherewith A. prayed; with suff. **bun** they sought me MG 285:paen. f., **bʿiun, biun** id. MG 286:3 f., **biiuk, biuk** they sought thee MG 287:2. Impf. **nibia** *roga*(*bi*)*t*, *desidera*(*bi*)*t*, or we (shall) ask, seek MG 258:paen., **tibia** *ea desidera*(*bi*)*t*, *desidera*(*bi*)*s* MG 258:ult., **ʿbia** I (shall) seek MG 259:1, **ʿbiia** Gy 366:21 I shall pray, **nibun**, fem. **nibʿian, nibiian, nibian, nibʿiian** they (will) seek MG 259:4; **nibiia mia** DC 3 they (fem.) beg for water; **tibun** ye (will) seek MG 259:7; with suff. **nibʿih̠** he asketh him, her MG 287:15, **ʿbiih̠** I seek him, her MG 287:16. Impt. **bʿ** MG 259:11, **bia uaška** CP 42:23, ML 50:11 seek and find; pl. **bun** MG 259:20; with suff. **buiia** seek him MG 287 bottom; **hazin buta buia** CP 151:penult. ML 182:3 pray this prayer; **binun** CP 17:10, ML

19:4 pray them (: the prayers), **buiuia** ŠQ 27:1 *quaerite eum* (?) MG 289:2. Pt. **baiia** he seeketh, will seek MG 259:18; **man d̲-baiia buta minaikun** Gy 42 when somebody addresseth a petition to you; **baiia buta** Gy 189:11 praying a prayer, fem. **bahia** MG § 64: end, pl. **baiin** MG 69:ult. Participial pres. **baiina**, fem. **baiana** I seek, **baiit** thou seekest MG 259:bottom; **baiit mapqit lqirsa** AM 135 thou wantest to expel the malady; **baiinin** we (shall) seek, **baiitun** ye (shall) seek MG 259: bottom, **baiitun umaškitun** Gy 135:11 seek and find!; with suff. **baiinak**, fem. **baianak** I seek thee MG 291:bottom; with encl. **baiinalh̲** we seek him MG 15:12, 259:bottom, **baiitulh̲** ye seek him MG 259:bottom. Inf. **mibia** MG 129:20, 260:13, **lmibia rahmia** CP 152:1, ML 182:5 to pray the Devotions.

Ethpe. Only participial forms: **mibia** is required MG 265:24, **mibᶜia** *quaesita* MG 214:7, **mitbᶜia** id. MG 5:antep.; with encl. **mibilh̲** is necessary to him MG 265:bottom; pl. **mibilia** are necessary to me ibid., **mibilak** Jb 14:11 he is accessible to thy prayer.

mn butun bun lnapšaihun Gy 238:12 he (: the Life) prayed one of his prayers to himself; **kul zban tibunan tiškunan** Gy 269:ult. whenever ye seek me, ye shall find me (cf. Matt. 7:8); **anat buiia ulhaka atih̲** CP 276:6 ML 261:6 seek him out and bring him here; **mn tam bun ᶜlan uanin mn haka nibia ᶜlauaikun** CP 12:12 ML 14:1 pray ye from there for us, and we shall pray from here for you; **anat bᶜ mn tibil uanin nibia napšia ukabiria** Gs 66:17 pray thou for us from the world, and we shall pray (prayers) abounding and great.

Idioms: 'To invite, summon': **kd̲ baiilak abuk qudamh̲** Gy 203:6 when thy father summoneth thee before himself. Pt. + inf. to describe the future (P. خواهد + inf.) or to express an intention: **d̲-mihuia mibilh̲** Gy 196: 16 who will come into existence; **baiit midirih̲ bmarbak umidilih̲ lᶜur** Gy 156:10 f. thou wilt bear in thy uterus and bring forth Ur; **ldilia labaiit mihzian** Gy 156:12 f. thou wilt see me no more; **hazinin mahu d̲-baiinin lmibad** Gy 165:ult. we shall see what to do.

In mod. Mand. the verb became **ABA** (*abâ* he wanted), cf. Gl. 3:1 f. **ABA** اخذ , اراد *accipere, velle* گرفت ; 5:7 f. id. اشتهى *concupiscere, desiderare* خواست ; 9:11 f. انبض (?) *oportere* لايق بود ; 117:1 عرض *accidere* عارض كرد (doubtful); 171:5 f. هوا [sic] *desiderare* خواست .

Der.: **buta.**

baba 1 (בָּבָא, ܒܒܐ) gate, door, entrance, portal; sect; versicle, paragraph, verse, portion, part. St. abs. & cstr. **bab.** Masc. MG 108:11, 149:paen. Pl. **babia,** mod. pl. **babania.** With the meaning 'sect' Gy 224:9, 22 ff. **baba rba** Q 28:27 f. the great gate; **baba d̲-bil** Gy 231:3 the gate (: sect) of Bel; **baba d̲-qra bil** Gy 121:13 the sect which Bel created; **baba d̲-hiia** Q 59:11 the gate of Life; **baba d̲-bit hiia** Gy 368:24 the gate of the House of Life; **baba rba d̲-bit abatur** Q 36:26 the great gate of the House of A.; **baba d̲-iasana** Gy 272:13, 273:18 ff. the gate of Y.; **baba d̲-libat** Gy 224:23, 225:24 the gate of Venus; **baba d̲-sin** DAb = RD 35 the gate of Sin (: Moon); **baba d̲-qra agzᶜil** Gy 120:23, 121:12 the sect which A. created; **baba d̲-qra sin** Gy 121:1, 231:18 the sect which S. created; **baba d̲-qra nirig** Gy 121:23, 122:9, 231:22 the sect which Mars created; **baba d̲-qra šamiš** Gy 120:13 the sect which the Sun created; **baba d̲-qra adunai** Gy 120:14 f. the sect which Adonai created; **baba d̲-qra kᶜiuan** Gy 121:5 the sect which Saturn created; **baba d̲-tlata malkia** Gy 141:5 the gate of three kings; **baba laima šauia** Gy 91:5 he made a gate for the world; **babia trisar** (*often*), Gy 288:5 f., 301:5, 13 etc., **babia d̲-trisar** Jb 266:10; **trisar babia** Gy 188:1 the twelve gates, the sects of the Twelve (: Planets); **bit babia trisar** Gy 18:6 the house of twelve gates, cf. MR 93:bottom, MSchr 40 n. 3; **srin uarba babia** Gy 86:5, 7 twenty-four sects; **babia d̲-hšuka** Gy 155:15 the gates of darkness; **babia d̲-qra mšiha** Gy 120:7 the sects which Christ produced; **babia d̲-qrat ruha** Gy 120:2 f. the sects which Rūha produced; **mšania babia d̲-šinta** Gy 186:12 who removes the gates of sleep; **kulhun babia** Gy 120:19 all the gates; **amamia ubabia** Gy 24:2 peoples and sects; **lbab almia** Jb 2:6, **ᶜl bab almia** Jb 6:9, Gs 27:17 at the gate of the world; **lbab almia kulhun** Oxf. roll 119, Gy 114:3 at the gate of all the worlds; **ᶜl bab nhura lanihlup** Gy 40:15 he shall not pass by the gate of light; **babia uhatmia akuat mitiqria asbar** ATŠ teach sections and 'sealings' as they are recited; **zahba ukaspa ubabaihun** DC 34 gold and silver and similar things; **baba ᶜhida** CP 51 ult., ML 67:8 a closed door; **baba d̲-rhamta** DC 45 & 46 (*often*) love-charm; **baba d̲-rahmia** AM Gate-of-Mercies BZ 104 n. 6; **baba d̲-buta** CP 24:ult., ML 27:5 gate of prayer (Lidzb. n. 2: *viell. das Tor des Tempels*; actually toward the north, which is the Mand. *qibla*); **baba d̲-haṭaiia** CP 48:15, ML 64:6, 65:8 the gate of sins; **baba d̲-nhura** CP 48:15 f., ML 64:7, 65:9 the gate of light; **tlata babania d̲-qmaha d̲-šaiul** DC 43 b:36 f. the three sections of the phylactery of Sheol; **bab ᶜšumia** DC 44. 733 f. the gate of the heavens; **baba hadia** DC 46. 70:1 (an expression for 'breast', cf. **tarbaṣa** (*b*)).

baba 2 (P. بابا) father MG 171 n. 1. **baba umama** DC no. 249 Daddy and Mummy (Papa and Mamma); **baba iardna hu uᶜma arqa hᶜ** ATŠ I no. 249 flowing water is the father and the earth is the mother.

baba 3 (semantic development of **baba 2**?) a designation of the male in **tata ubaba** ATŠ I no. 249 ewe and ram.

babanuš, babnuš (P. 'Father of Anuš') IM 98, 102 personal name IM Gl.

babariata s. **riata.**

babil 1 (בָּבֶל, ܒܒܠ, Bab. *Bâbilu*) Babylonia, Babylon, sometimes Baghdad BZ Ap. II, IM Gl. **babil arqa** Gy 387:1 *passim* the land of Babylonia; **mdinta d̠-babil** (often) the city of Babylon; **malka d̠-babil lbabil nitia** Gy 385:17 f. the king of Babylonia will come to Babylon; **malka d̠-babil** Gy 385:4; **malkia d̠-babil** Jb 127:6 the kings of Babylonia; **ʿbra d̠-babil** Gy 390:4 f., 8 the sea-coast of Babylonia.

babil 2 (a theophorous name from בָּבֶ?) an angel? **babil malaka rba d̠-alahia** DC 37. 44 f. Babel, the great angel of gods (read **bbil** 'by Bel'; s. **bil**).

babita DAb read **rabita** (q.v.).

babnuš s. **babanuš**.

babta (ܒܒܬܐ) entrance, entrance-hall, passage-way. Pl. **babata. uzanga tlila ʿl babta** Jb 156:6 and a bell is hung at the entrance; **uagania ... lbabataiun triṣ** DC 44 and vessels are set up at their entrance-halls.

baga (P. باغ) garden. **miqar ziqla mn baga** DC 21 a palm-tree is uprooted from the garden.

bagal (Ar. بغل) mule. **ṣurat lbagal** (translit. of صورة البغل) AM 278:4 likeness of a mule.

bagdad (بغداد) AM 198 Baghdad, in HG Babylonia.

bada (mod. form of **ʿbada**), st. abs. & cstr. **bad** work. **basit bada** Zotb. 227 left col.:22 I disliked the work; **bad biad gumiaiil** DC 44 a work by the hand of G.; **ʿz umal ubada hu** AM 254:17 it (portends) might, wealth, and work; **maria badh̠** Zotb. 219 left col.:1 his task master; **bada lhiia lasaliq** Zotb. 228 left col.:4 the work does not ascend to the Life. Gl. 72:6 **bada** خدمة *ministerium* خدمت; 129:1 id. فعل *operatio* كار.

badam (P. بادام) almond. **badam halia hu** DC 41 (illustration) it is a sweet almond.

baduia a miscopying of **baduia d̠-kulhun dmauata** Gy 2 Creator of all the appearances.

badušnam DC 23. 126 ff. a devil.

badim = **badam. miša d̠-sandal umiša badim** DC 46. 129:1 sandalwood oil and almond oil.

badmu (ܒܕܡܘ) s. **admu**.

bahar (a pt. of **BAR I** q.v.) shining MG 62:paen. & n. 3.

baḥar (Ar. بَحر) AM 287:3 sea.

bahuš (P. باهوش ?) DC 40 a supernatural being cited with **huš**.

bahima (H. בְּהֵמָה Ar. بهيمة) beast of burden, donkey, ass. Fem. **bahimta** she-ass. **ṭupra d̠-bahima** AM 127:12 the hoof of a donkey; **bahimia maitia** AM donkeys (will) die; **bahimta marqala kalṣat** Morg. 274:21 the she-ass farted; **damia kd̠ bahima** DC 46. 113:11 it resembles a donkey. Gl. 31:13 fem. written defectively اتان *asina* خر, 71:1; masc. written defectively جحش (?) *pullus asinei* خر كره; 75:12 id. حمار *asinus* خر.

bahmʿil DC 43 D 36, DAb an angel (possessor of an incense-brazier).

bahram, bahran, bihram, bihran (P. بهرام from *Varahrân, Verethragma*) a P. name, s. **bihram** MG xxxii n. 1. **bahran** (var. **bihran**) **malka** Gy 383 the king Bahran, Vahram I Gray ZA 19/1905 285, Vahram V (420–38) Ochser ZA 19/1905 16 n. 8.

bidraq. bedraq (?) **alaha d̠-lšidra udaiuia mšalaṭ** DC 40. 927 (by?) the god Y. who ruleth devils and demons.

bihrun a spirit of light. **bhir ubihrun** CP 140 (d):4.

bahtuta (rt. BHT, cf. בַּהְתְּתָא, ܒܗܬܬܐ) shame, confusion, disgrace. **qaimun bbahtuta** DC 36 they were occupied in a shameful proceeding; **iahba ... anph̠ d̠-napša bbahtuta** DC 51 she lent her countenance (: connived) at shameful actions; **qlalun ubahtutun** DAb = RD B 70 their shameful ways and disgraceful practices; **ʿtriṣiun bbahtuta** Q 53:10 they were raised in shame.

bauaba (formed as فعّال) janitor, doorkeeper. Gl. 43:1 defectively بوّاب *ianitor, ostiarius* دربان.

bauar (P. باور) belief. No st. abs. MG 305:11. **bauar laʿhab** Gy 278:21 they did not believe (a phrase still used).

bauata pl. of **buta** (q.v.).

baz 1, biz a purgatory demon. **baz daiua** DAb = RD 35 the demon Baz.

baz 2, baza (Ar.-P. باز) Oxf. xii (with a picture of a) falcon.

baz 3 ('with power'?) s. **az 1**.

baza 4 (rt. **BZA**) crevice, hole, rent. **bazai** JRAS 1938 3:27 read **baza** (with PA's copy).

bazar (P. بازار) market, bazaar. **duktai bazar hauia** DC 46. 82:8 my haunt is the bazaar. Gl. 96:4 **bazar** (with a fem. pl.!) سوق *forum* بازار.

bazara a var. of **baz(i)ra** (v.s. **gizar**).

bazargania, bazirgania (P. بازرگان) tradesmen, traders, shop-people. Found only in pl., another pl. is **bazirganan** AM 288:19. **halin tarmidia d̠-azlin ʿl bazirgania** DAb those priests that go to tradesmen.

bazgaraiia ATŠ I no. 248 a shortened form of **bazargania**.

bazuna (בָּזוּנָא) in **abu bazuna** ATŠ II no. 440 a name given to the king of Persia.

bazira, bazra (< בַּר זַרְעָא, ܒܪ ܙܪܥܐ) seed MG 55:3, 187:3, Fränkel 138. Pl. **bazrania**, or **bazrunia** (s.v.). **mn zirh̠ d̠-lilia umn bazirh̠ d̠-ʿumama** DC 43 J 202 from his semen at night and his seed by day; **qinianai ubazirai bdibrai** DC 40 my property and my seed-ground(s); **bazira d̠-aba** ATŠ I no. 169 the semen of the father.

bazirgania s. **bazargania. gabra ṭaba d̠-rahmih̠ abdania uzirh̠ uziruth̠ ubazirgania** AM 154: penult. a good man beloved by his servants, offspring, progeny, and tradesmen.

baznaqata part of name of a being invoked in exorcisms. **ana hu hanzaqa abugdana baznaqata gabra qašiša** DC 26 & 40. 745 I am H.A.B., a sacred being.

baznaqita (etym. unknown) Jb 155:9 f., 157:11 a kind of fish-trap.

bazra (בִּזְרָא, see also **bazira**) seed, metaph. sowing, seed-time. **biahra d̲-bazra qadmaia d̲-hu adar** ATŠ I no. 209 in the month of the first seed-time, which is Adar; **biahra d̲-bazra tiniana d̲-hu nisan** ATŠ II no. 221 in the month of the second seed-time, which is Nisan; **bazra uraza** ATŠ I no. 280 seed and mystery.

bazrania pl. of **bazira, bazra** seeds, green crops, grain. **aṭšia ubazrania** (Pet. **bazrunia**) **upiria** DC 22. 192 = Gy 201:15 produce, grain, and fruits.

bazrgania a var. of **bazargania, bazirgania.**

bazrunia (diminutive of **bazira, bazra**) seedlings, seeds MG 140:10. **aṭšia ubazrunia** DC 12 fruit-crops and grain (see also s. **bazrania**); **samania ubazrunia** Jb 232:7 healing herbs and seedlings; **bazrunia d̲-arqa šapir nihuia** AM 270:13 the grain of the country will be excellent; **bazrunia bakria baṣria** AM 282:15 early seedlings will fail; **bazrunia upiqunia** Gy 33:16 seeds and flowers.

baṭil st. abs. of **baṭla** (below).

baṭin, baṭina, fem. **baṭinta, baṭintia** (ܒܛܝܢ, ܒܛܝܢܬܐ with transition to בַּטִּין) pregnant MG 110 n. 1. Masc. pl. **baṭinia,** fem. pl. **baṭinata,** var. **baṭinita** AM 216:4, **baṭin** AM 279:18 (Ar. بطِين) big-bellied, abdominous. **mia . . . ubaṭinia uiadalia** DC 51. 311 f. the waters . . . conceive and bring forth; **ʿu hauia baṭintia** ATŠ I no. 79 if she be a pregnant woman; **baṭinta biṭnat** s. **tiniana**; **baṭinata niabṭan** AM 214:12 pregnant women will miscarry.

baṭla, abs. **baṭil** (rt. **BṬL**) vain, idle, useless, futile, transitory, null, void, innocuous, perishable, unavailing, good-for-nothing, illusory. Pl. **baṭlia. mšiha baṭla** Gy 223:12 the pseudo-Christ; **hiia rbia d̲-labaṭlia** (*often*) the Great Life which is eternal (unending); **pagra baṭla** Jb 51:15 the perishable body (a contrast of **nišimta** MS 94); **gdulia baṭlia** DC 37 illusory phantoms.

baṭna (rt. **BṬN**) large belly, pregnant belly, pregnant (s. **BṬN**). Gl. 72:9 written defectively حبل *gravitatio* آبستنى.

baia, biia (orig. pl. of **bita,** used also as a sg.) egg(s). **kdub hazin baba lbaia** (var. **ala biia**) **d̲-zagata** DC 45 (var. DC 46. 1) write this charm on a hen's egg.

baiad, biiad, biaid (Ar. بياض) white(ness). **lbaiad algašaua d̲-ainia** AM 287:14 for whiteness and a film over the eyes; **tum lilbiiad** (var. **lilbiaid**) **lʿain** AM 287:27 then, for a whiteness over the eyes; **baiad d̲-aina** AM 287:14 the white film; **lilbaiad bla aiba** AM 277:28 into cloudless daylight.

baian (often in coloph.) a *malwâša* man's name.

baidukt Morg. 265/20:26 = DC 44. 1353 a higher female being.

baiha Gs 125:5, 16 pt. fem. pe. of **BAA.**

baiuazig Gy 231:12 partizans of a sect (ascribed to Sin), Ginzā 232 n. 3.

baiin (obscure) in **ulaʿhablia baiin biad** CP 79:1, ML 97:1 but he gave me not the . . . into my hand (one would expect 'palm branch', cf. *בָּאיִין J.). (Delete 'not'?).

baiinšnia AM 202, var. **baiinšria** a place-name BZ Ap. II.

bainai var. **baina** (often in coloph.) a (*malwâša*) man's name.

bainia ATŠ I no. 8b = **binia.**

baita 1 (בַּיְתָא, ܒܰܝܬܳܐ) house MG 150:2, 183:17. A frequent designation of the earthly world (taken over from Parsism) Jb ii 7 n. 5, CP trs. p. 1 n. 2, ML 4 n. 3, Ginzā 15 n. 6, MS 31. St. cstr. **bit** (s.v.). Pl. **batia,** bad var. **baitia** MG 183:19 f., later also **bait(a)uata** (mod. pl. pron. *bêθwôθa*). **br baita** Jb 245:15 a son of the world; **bbaita, babaita** in the house MG 32:12; **arba ziqia d̲-baita, arba zauiata d̲-baita** s. **arba 4**; **baita napla** Gs 82:25, 95:18 the falling House (: the world); **marh d̲-baita napla** s. **mara**; **ʿubadia d̲-baita** Q 29:3 worldly actions; **humria baita** Gy 316:13 the amulet-spirits of the House; **duktia . . . bbaitauata hauia** DC 46. 65:14 (*and often*) my place is in houses; **baita d̲-muqadas** AM 202, **bait lmuqadas** AM 198, **bait almuqadas** (بيت المقدس) Jerusalem (cf. Mand. **bit mqadšia** s. **mqadšia**).

baita 2 = **bita.**

bakru (Ar. بَكْر) AM 129:15 a firstling.

bakša (P. بخشيش) gift. Pl. **bakšan. bakš(a) ubakšan** Gy 187:2 gift and gratuities (Lidzb. *Prozent und Prozentprozente*).

bakt, bakta var. **bikta** (cf. Mod. Syr. ܒܟܬܐ Macl.) lady, mistress, housewife. **bakt lilit** DC 43 the lady Lilith; **aškarta bbakth̲** (with many varr. and miscopyings) s. **aškarta.**

baktara (P. بختيار) happy, lucky, prosperous, fortunate (miscopyings **barkta** BZ 29 n. 11, **birikta, birukta** BZ 25 n. 3 'blessing'). **baktara bzibnh̲ uzabunh̲ hauilh̲** AM 39:17 he will prosper in his commercial transactions; **uzabunh̲** (read **zibnh̲**) **uzabunh̲ baktara** AM 32:3 and his buying and selling will be prosperous.

baktiar (P. بختيار) RD D 2, 8 etc. a *malwâša* man's name (frequent in coloph.).

bal, bala 1 (ܒܠܐ, بَال) heart, mind(fulness), state, condition, preoccupation. **ubalak lmaṣbutak** CP 25:28, ML 29:5 and thy baptism be thy preoccupation; **ubalak mn riš ualma ldinba** CP 42:18, ML 50:7 f. and be mindful from beginning till end; **hiia lbalun lanasib** CP 106:13, ML 132:2 he careth not about the Life; **lanisbun lbalun** CP 168:2, ML 203:5 they care not about me; **bbala** (often) mindfully, with intention; **nitraṣ balai luat manda d̲-hiia** ATŠ I no. 222 may he raise my mind to M.-d̲-H.; **ubalh̲ lnišimta nihuia** ATŠ and the soul will be his (chief) preoccupation; **bla bala** DC 40 without mind; **adinqia bala hauin** Gy 389:7 f. they will be heedless; **balai uʿuṣrai** Gs DC 22. 445:2 my mind and thought; **ubalh̲ mn manda d̲-hiia lašania** CP 482:5 and his mind doth not stray from M.-d̲-H.; **balak haqar** v.s. **HQR II** pa. impt.

bala 2 (בָּלָא, בָּאלָא) prairie, land outside towns, uncultivated ground. **hiua bala** Gy 18:4, 100:10 f., AM 209:17 etc. wild animals, wild beast(s).

bala 3 a var. of bilur. **zgig utaqun badmu bala** DC 22. 9 (var. Gy 9 **bilur**) transparent and lucent like a gem.

baladbaba a var. of **bildbaba**. **bit baladbabai** DC 22. 449 (var. Gs 61:11 **bildbabai**) the house of mine enemies.

balaiat (Ar. بَلَايَة) misfortune. **balaiat nihuia lganabia** AM 281:41 thieves will meet with misfortune.

balaš malka hurnig (var. **hurmig**) **br sabur** Gy 383:paen. (var. Leid.) a Persian king Hormizdas I, cf. Gray ZA 19/1905 285.

balgam, balgama (*φλέγμα* by the intermediary of بَلْغَم not that of ܦܠܓܡܐ) phlegm, watery humours, mucus. Var. **balguma. uraṭabuta ubalgam nihuilh̲** AM 29:9 and he will have a watery humour and phlegm; **riša h^c balgam h^c** AM 286:25 she (Venus) governs the head and phlegm; **balgam uruṭba** AM 286:35 watery humours and dampness; **arba razia . . . zma umirta uziqa ubalgam** DC 41. 438, DC 34. 285 the four mysteries; blood and gall and wind and mucus; **zma umirta ubalguma** HG blood, gall, and mucus.

bald d̲-rum AM 202 a place-name BZ Ap. II.

balda (Ar. بَلَد in an Aram. st. emph.) AM 205: 13 land, country.

baldbaba a var. of **bildbaba** Gs 61:22 (Sh. ʿAbd.'s copy).

balhud (ܒܠܚܘܕ) with or without pers. suff. alone, separately, individually, singly, one by one, MG 207:bottom. **uhad rušuma ʿl kulaikun balhud lhud** ATŠ II no. 156 and one sign upon all of you, individually; **balhudai** by myself, I alone MG 176:11; **balhudia, balhudih̲, balhudh̲** (often) by himself, by herself, alone, singly; **kul had msadar ṭarianh̲ balhudh̲** DC 24 each one will arrange his own table for himself.

baluda (בְּלוּט, בְּלוּטָא, ܒܠܘܛܐ, Ar. loan-w. بَلُّوط) oak-tree. Masc. **baluda hu** DC 7 & 41 it is an oak-tree.

baliuz (mod.) consul, British agent. **baliuz big mistar ṭilar** DC 35:coloph. the consul-beg Mr. Taylor.

baliqa (rt. **BLQ II**) greedy. **d̲-karsh̲ baliqa** DC 46 whose belly is greedy (?).

balk (بَلْخ) AM 203 a place-name, Balkh.

balɛuma (Ar. بُلْعُوم, بُلْعُم, mod.) gullet. **ubalɛuma d̲-anašia lagiṭna** DC 46. 117:10 and I seize on the gullet of people.

bamar a var. of **bimar** (q.v.).

ban 1 AM 187 name of a city in Khorasan BZ Ap. II.

ban 2, bana 1 (בָּנָא, pt. pe. of **BNA** = **BNN II**, cf. MG 83 n. 3) builder, mason. With suff. **banai** my builder MG 83:18. **baita labna bana** DC 8 the House (which) no builder built; **lban šumia uarqa** DC 22. 267 for the builder of heaven and earth.

bana 2 (rt. **BNA** = **BNN II**, doublet of **biniana**) building, construction. **nipqit mn bana d̲-banan rbia** CP 157:15 I came out of the building which the Great (Life) built; **bana** CP 157:3, ML 190:3 s. **banana.**

banaia (בַּנָּאֵי, ܒܢܝܐ) builder MG 83:15. Pl. **banaiia. banaia d̲-binth̲ qudamh̲ labna** Jb 170:9 f. the builder who built no building for himself.

banana 1 (nom. ag. from **BNN II**) builder, edifier. Pl. **banania. banania d̲-nasqinun** DC 48:241 builders that elevate them.

banana 2 (doublet **bnana,** rt. **BNN II** related to **BNA**) building, edifice. **mn riš banana nipqit minak daura taqna** CP 157:14, ML 190:2 at the beginning of construction (creation) I went out from thee, Abiding Abode (**banana** = **daura**); **banth̲ ubaninth̲ . . . utirṣit briš banana** CP 160:9 **bana bananth̲** = ML 194:6 I built and edified him . . . and raised him on the top of the building; **bana** CP 157:3, ML 190:3 is a shortened form of **banana** (Lidzb. n. 1, as well as his transl. of the phrases just quoted, is mistaken).

banana 3 a (*malwāša*) woman's name.

banapša, var. **bnapša** (P. بنفشه) violet. **miša d̲-banapša** AM 130 violet oil.

bangania Zotb. 221 right col:18 a cognomen.

band d̲-magrib AM 205 a place-name.

***banuna** (a nom. ag. of **BNN II** rel. to **BNA,** cf. ܒܢܘܝܐ; doublet of **banana**) 1 builder ML 135 n. 2. Pl. **banunia. banunia d̲-baninit** CP 109:18, ML 135:4 o builders whom I edified!

banunia (inf. of **BNN I**) begetting, to beget. **banan banunia** Gy 21:ult. beget children!

bania (rt. **BNA**) (*a*) builder (s. **BNA**), (*b*) a reed shroud for a corpse MMII Ind.

bas (cf. **baz 1**) DC 41. 468 f. a demon .

basada DC 37. 400 f. a var. of **bisada** (q.v.).

basim, basima (בְּסִימָא, ܒܣܝܡܐ) pleasant, pleasing, goodly, friendly, agreeable, sweet, fragrant, kindly, fair. Pl. **basimia.** Fem. **basimta** (var. **bisimta**), **basimtia** MG 154:16. **rihh̲ basim** MG 30:1 f. its fragrance is pleasing; **basima damia lṭura d̲-pirunia** Gy 215:4 f. the friendly (man) resembleth a hill of blossoms; **riha d̲-hiia basim** (said whenever inhaling perfume of a flower or tree) the perfume of Life is goodly; **uziqa basima ninšum ʿlh̲** AM 65:1 and a kindly wind shall breathe on her; **h^c zriztia b^cbidath̲ hauia ubisimta** AM (missing in DC 31) she will be keen in her work and good-tempered; **nihuta uliba basima** AM 284:10 ease and a glad heart. Gl. 33:8 Pl. misspelt اصحاء *sani* صختمند.

basimta (cf. ***pasanta**) the palm of the hand. **arbiaiia basimta d̲-ʿda** DC 41:461 the fourth is the palm of the hand.

basin DC 41. 467 ff. a demon quoted together with **bas** (q.v.).

basmaniata (rt. **BSM**) delights, things pleasant, or fragrant, or lovely. Found only in fem. pl. **umn ʿbidatun umn rabutun umn basmaniatun**

JRAS 1938 6:16 from their works and their majesty and their delights.

basraia (adj. from BSR) scornful, contemptuous, disdainful. **lau tišaia hu basraia** AM 156:12 he is not affable, but disdainful.

bastirqa, bistirqa (בִּיסְתַּרְקָא, בִּסְתַּרְקָא from Phl., Pâzend *vastarg*, Mod. P. بستر) a woollen robe, cushion, pillow, couch, mattress of carded wool MG xxxii n. 1. **bastirqun** JRAS 1938 6:16 their fleecy robes; **bastirqa mirmilh̲** ATŠ II no. 111 a woollen robe they placed on him; **bastirqa d̲-mara d̲-rabuta** ATŠ II no. 123 the couch of the Lord of Greatness; **bastirqa šauilun** DC 26 & 40 (var. DC 44. 598 **šauulia**) they made me a fleecy coat (or a couch); **minilia hakima lsakla bastirqa ldabaga** Gy 217:22 the words of a wise to a fool are like a fleecy robe for a tanner; **lbastirqa lašakib** ATŠ I no. 14 he shall not sleep upon a mattress of carded wool; **raumh̲ d̲-bastirqa** DAb = RD F 9 the height of the couch; **kraiai pšiṭlia lbastirqa rba d̲-alahia** DC 40. 559 I stretched out my limbs on the great couch of the gods; **uhalṣai smiklia bbistirqa rba d̲-alahia** DC 40. 677 and my loins rest upon the great couch of the gods.

baᶜad (Ar. بَعْدَ) AM 277:34 after, other.

baᶜid (Ar. بعيد) far: **baᶜid mn mdinta** AM 277:34 far from the city. Gl. 44:2 misspelt (twice) بعيداً *longe* دور.

baṣa (rt. בצע) rending open, a fissure. **purṭana bbaṣa hurina praṭnalh̲** ATŠ I no. 273 (only in DC 6) we make an opening by another fissure.

baṣar (Ar. بَصَر) AM 287:15, 19 sight.

baṣarta, bṣarta (nom. act. of BṢR) lacking. **umaiaihun bbaṣarta** AM 244:2 and their water(ing-places) will be lacking.

baṣuria (cf. בְּצוֹרְתָּא) balconies? Pl. **duktai bbaṣuria** DC 46 86:3 my place is in balconies (?).

baṣir, bṣir (בציר, ܒܨܝܪ) incomplete, small, deficient, cut off, subtracted, mutilated, lean. Pl. **baṣiria, bṣiria.** Fem. **baṣirtia, bṣirtia, bṣirta. šidta baṣirtia** AM 190:11 a lean year.

baṣiruta, bṣiruta (ܒܨܝܪܘܬܐ) incompletion, poverty, meanness (of quality), mutilation, deficiency, failure, stultification.

baṣra (البصرة) AM 198:2, DC 35:coloph. Baṣrah.

baṣran (rt. BṢR) lacking, deficient, poor in quality. **baṣran sira** a 'moon-deficient' (name given to those conceived in the dark of the moon, this being supposed to cause deformity and deficiency). MMII 330 n. 5. **zirania baṣran** AM 265:29 grain will be lacking.

baq (br biq) DC 44. 744 name of a demon.

baqam (Ar. بَقَم) red logwood. **zaruand ubaqam** DC 46. 92:7 birthwort and red logwood.

baqara (בַּקָּרָא, ܒܩܪܐ) herdsman, neat-herd. Pl. **baqaria** RD F 13. **baqara bhira** RD A 7 an appointed shepherd; **baqaria d̲-tauria** RD A 7 neat-herds; **baqaria d̲-gamišan** DAb (var. RD A 8 **gamušan**) herdsmen of buffalo-cows; **ušapiria baqaria d̲-masgin abatraiun . . . ubaqaria ᶜtkalal unpil lknap tauraiun** DC 21 = JRAS 1937 591:8 ff. and handsome were the herdsmen walking after them . . . but the herdsmen were exhausted and fell beside their bulls.

baqaraia = **baqara.** Pl. **baqaraiia.**

baqiata 1 (ܒܩܝܐܬܐ) decay, gangrene. **šiqupta d̲-baqiata** DC 40. 983 f. attack of gangrene.

baqiata 2 a var. of **biqiata** Gy 287:23 (Sh. 'Abd.'s copy).

baqra (בַּקְרָא, ܒܩܪܐ) herd, flock. **ᶜmbria lbaqraihun** Gs 10:24 the sheep to their flock.

BAR I, BHR II (בהר, ܒܗܪ) to break forth, come to light, shine out, shine forth. MG 62: bottom & n. 3.

Pe. Pf. **bar** Gy 238:2, 239:1 he shone forth; **bar bnapšh̲** Gy 93:11 he shone by himself (but cf. Ginzā 97 n. 7); **bᶜruth̲ bar, bar bᶜruth̲** Gy 91:22, 23 he shone forth in his radiance; **bar bᶜruth̲** Gy 341:9 id.; **unhar ubar bnapših̲ uanhar** DC 36 and he gave light, shone forth and was bright; **bar uᶜtraurab** DC 50 he shone forth and was magnified; **barit bᶜrutai** Gy 74:5 I shone in my radiance; **barit bziua** Q 20:14 I shone forth with radiance; **barit btušbihtai** Gy 74:4 I shone forth in my glorification (cf. Ginzā 55 n. 2); **ana hu iur br barit** CP 17:12 I am Yur son of 'I shone-forth'. (Note: fem. **barat** occurs as a pr. n. of female celestial beings, cf. **barat uᶜtrauribat tartin anania** Gy 374:14 'She-shone-forth' and 'She-was-magnified', the two clouds or celestial spouses; **brat niṭupta,** var. **brit niṭupta** Jb 252:4, read **barat,** cf. ii. 228:4). With encl. **baribh̲ balbuš ᶜšata haita** Gy 114:7 I shone forth in a garment of living fire; **baribh̲ blbuša dakia** ibid. I shone forth in a clean garment (parallel with **barit blbušai** Gy 114:5 without the encl.). Impf. **nibar (unitraurab)** Jb 215:4 will shine (and become magnificent). Pt. **baiar** Gy 128:18 he shineth; **d̲-baiar umanhar** Jb 218:14 that shineth forth and illumineth; fem. **baira** Gy 82:5 she shineth; **baira umitraurba** Gy 235:23 shining and magnificent; **baira dmutaihun** Gy 82:5 (less good **bairia dmutaihun** Gy 393:14) their likeness is shining, shineth forth; **d̲-baira umitaprša banhura šania** ML 178:5, CP 148:16 that shineth forth and is expressed in sublime light. Participial pres. **baiarna** Gy 372:20 I am radiant.

Ethpe. (based on formal confusion with **TBR,** cf. MG 62 n. 3): only pf. **ᶜtbar bihria** DC 6 & 36 they shone forth and were bright; **unhar uᶜtbar** (var. **utbar**) Q 2:14, ML 6:8, CP 5:10 and shone out and were effulgent.

Ethpa. Pf. with encl. **ᶜtbaiarbun** Gy 238:14 they shone forth in them; **ᶜtbairibh̲ blbušai** Gy 118:5 I shone forth in my clothing. Pt. pl. **nahria utaqnia umitbairin** Gy 291:41 (var. DC 22. 289 **mitbairia**) they give light and beam and shine forth; **d̲-baira ubar** DC 50. 731.

BAR II (בְּעַר, ܒܥܪ) to burn, devour, be fierce, consume, burn with rage.

Pe. Pf. **ʿpikrat ʿl libh̠ d̠-barat** DC 21 = JRAS 1938 6:30 she laid restraint on her heart that raged. Impf. **unibar bgišumia** DC 44 and burneth in my body.

Ethpe. Pf. **uʿtbaq uʿtbar hirbia** DC 44 and the sword rotted and was corroded (or broke **TBR**).

Der.: **mbaira.**

bar (בַּר, ܒܪ rt. **BRR**) outside, country outside towns, desert. With prep. **lbar** outside (s.v.), with two prep. **mn lbar** s. **mn, lbar mn** except (s. **lbar** and **mn**). **kupna ʿl bar nihuia** AM 241:16 there will be hunger outside.

bar 2 *scr. pl.* of **br. barnašia** AM 199:12 &c. a later var. of **br anašia** people MG 183:5; **bar bšita** Gy 168:8 read **ba bšita** on the spot MG 331 n. 1.

bar 3 = **abar(a)** 1. **hda d̠-bar uhda d̠-kaspa** DC 46. 234:21 one of lead, one of silver.

bara (P. بَرّه) lamb (*very late*). **umiša d̠-ʿlikta d̠-bara bla mahla** DC 43 & 46 and unsalted grease of a lamb's tail.

barabar (P. برابر) opposite (*late*). **barabar hdadia** AM 263:4 opposite one another; **barabar ṭariana barabar ṭariana** DC 42. 21 opposite the platter; **barabar ṭariana** DC 38 beside the large ritual table.

barahia (cf. בַּרְחָא) he-goats, bucks. Found only in pl. Var. **baraiia** (s. **baraia 2**). **umanzaihun lbarahia zapria** Gy 227:20 and their hair (is like) that of stinking bucks.

barauata (rt. **BRA I**) creations, productions, products, creatures, fabrics, fabrications. **migṭar ʿzlalia ubarauata** AM 155:13 fashioning fine tissues and fabrics; **barauath̠ labatrai nitraglun** DC 44. 231 his creatures shall be fettered behind me.

barai (cf. s. **baraia** 1) (*a*) outside, exterior, country outside inhabited places, (*b*) time of isolation during menstruation, childbirth, and other times of ritual impurity (var. **abarai** q.v.). (*a*) **uatia mn barai** AM 20:9 and coming from without; **labarai napqunh̠** AM 72:18 they shall take her out to the country; **ubiahra d̠-ʿlul lbarai latipuq** AM 82:13 and in the month of Elul, she should not go outside (her house and its yard); (*b*) **halin ʿnšia d̠-barai dilin lalagtan** DC 8 those women who did not observe their period of isolation.

baraia 1 (ܒܪܝܐ, rt. **BRR**) outer, external, foreign. St. abs. **barai** (above) is used as subst. and adv. Pl. **baraiia** *externi*. Fem. **baraita** *externa*. Antonym of **gauaia** (q.v.). **aiar baraia** s. **aiar** 1; **anašia baraiia** Gy 388 foreigners.

baraia 2 (Ass. *baru*) exorcizer, exorcizing. Pl. **baraiia.** Fem. **baraita. mn paris mata ana gabra baraia** DC 43 from the land Paris (Fars?) am I, the exorcist-man; **baraiia** DC 8 exorcists, casters out of demons.

baraia 3 a miscopying of **batraia** ML 115:4, cf. n. 1. CP 92:17.

baraia 4 wild beast (?). **lbaraia zakria** DC 22. 221 a var. of **lbarahia zapria** Gy 227:20 (s. **barahia**).

barakata pl. of **birkta, birikta**. Var. **barukata** (s.v.). **qrun barakata d̠-arba razia** DC 50 ye shall recite the benedictions of the Four mysteries.

barasdan Ṣâb.'s AM, **barasuan** AM 204:8 a place-name BZ Ap. II.

bararia (rt. **BRR**) DC 46. 94:15 pl. wildernesses. Var. **abararia** (s.v.).

barat (s. **BAR** note to pe.) Gy 374:14, name of a divine spouse.

barata 1 *scr. pl.* of **brata** 1.

barata 2 Gs 27:20 prob. a kind of vegetable Ginzā 445 n. 1.

barbag̃ (Son-of-God?) Gy 129:1, DC 22. 124, CP 140 (d):8 an uthra (the head of 444 *škintas*) MMII 246.

barbad a var. of **barbar** 1.

barbaṭ ʿšimʿil barbaṭ RD 26 a name given to Muḥammad.

barbar 1 (بَربَر) AM 205 a place-name AM Ap. II. Var. **barbad.**

barbar 2 DC 42. 98 a miscopying of **barabar** (q.v.).

barbina Gl. 45:14 بربين *portulaca.*

barg̃apa (P. برغاب?) dam (?), stagnation, stagnant water?. Lidzb. left untransl. **bargapa luath̠ lʿka** Jb 152:9 (var. AD **bargpa,** B **brgapa**) there is no stagnant water near him.

bar g̃ida DC 53. 111:2 a var. of **br guda** (s. **br**).

barg̃pa s. **bargapa.**

barda (בַּרְדָּא, ܒܪܕܐ) cold, hail MG 106:ult. No st. abs. & cstr., no pl. **barda unura** Gy 314:17 hail and fire; **barda uhbala** Gy 291:42 hail and destruction; **hauma ubarda** RD C 2, 6, 14, 18 heat and cold; **hauma ubarda uiaqdana** Gy 301:16 heat, ice, and burning; **barda urugza** Gy 283:6 hail and rage; **rugza ubarda uglala** Lond. roll A 586, Oxf. roll 186, 531, ATŠ II no. 144, anger and cold and hail; **barda utalga** AM 245:12, Gy 283:11 frost and snow; **talga ubarda** Gy 283:9 snow and frost; **šitin gauazia d̠-barda** Gy 317:11 sixty icicles; **mania d̠-barda** Jb 97:13, 247:15, Gy 224:22 vessels of ice; **rima ubarda** DC 43 thunder and hail; **barda bmdiniata napil** AM hail will fall in the cities.

bardaiia the Bardaeans (a country and city governed by Queen Noshabh at the time of Sikandar, Steing.). **azil larqa d̠-bardaiia** AM he will go to the land of the Bardaeans.

baruia (ܒܪܘܝܐ) creator MG 113:antep. f. **baruia d̠-kulhun ṭabauata** Gy 62 creator of all good things.

baruka (rt. **BRK**) Oxf. roll f 1145, 1147, 1155, 1162, 1170 blesser, a term applied ritually to a priest who assists at the *zidqa brika* which follows a *masiqta*. Pl. **barukaiia** MMII Ind. **haizak niqmun lligraihun baruka utrin sahdia** DC 42 then the 'blesser' and the two witnesses shall rise to their feet; **lbaruka** CP 466:14 to the blesser; **hazin ʿniana ramilh̠ barukaiia** CP 467:7 the blessers chant this hymn.

barukata PD 1155 pl. of **bir(i)kta** blessings.

barukia (inf. pa. of **BRK**) Q 58:24, 27, 30, 32 etc. blessing. With pers. suff. **lbarukak ulqaiumak** Q 52:6 at thy blessing and at thy confirming.

barza a doublet of **uarza** (q.v.). **ʿtimhibḫ barza ušuqia** DC 37. 544 the seeds and markets were struck by it.
bariata a var. of **biriata** (q.v.).
bariut (ܒܪܝܘܬܐ, rt. **BRR**) outskirts, exterior, external, borderland. Var. **biriut**. St. emph. not found. **malka d-bariut almia** Jb 50:5, 9 the king of the external worlds; **malka d-bariut daria** Jb 225:14 (B without **daria**) id.; **lbariut almia** DC 22. 368 (Gs 121:paen.f. **lbiriut almia**) on the borderland of the worlds.
barkta a var. of **baktara** (q.v.) BZ 25 n. 3, 29 n. 11.
barnia (Ar. برنية) dates of good quality. **šikṣa d-barnia** Oxf. roll f 158, DC 24 a small quantity of good dates; **sindirka hiuara barnia hu** DC 35 it is a white date-palm-tree.
barsam, barsim (בַּרְסָם catarrh of the head, P. برسام pleurisy) catarrh, pleurisy. Gender wavering betw. masc. and fem. **barsam tiligṯḫ** AM 22:6 pleurisy will attack him; **barsim maṭilḫ** AM 17:1 he will be attacked by pleurisy.
barsumaqa, barsmaqa (comp. with בַּר, s. **sumaqa**) a red cloak, or cloth: **kašla lbuša ubarsumaqa** DC 35:coloph. a jewel, a dress, and a red cloak; **hazin baba ṭalisim kdub ʿlḫ barsmaqa** DC 46 (later **barsumaqa**) this section of the talisman write on something red (?).
barstan AM name of a city.
barqa 1 (בַּרְקָא compartment near house) pen, stable, enclosure. **amuria** (read **ambria**) **lbarqaihun** Gs 10:ult. the lambs to their pen; **ulhizura d-barqḫ pliṭ** Gs 14:5 unto a pig that escaped from his stye.
barqa 2 a var. of **birqa** Gy 385:paen.
barqiaiil, var. **barqʿil** (theophorous n. from **BRQ**) DAb, AM (Ṣâb.'s copy) etc. an angel **bšuma d-barqiaiil mlaka** DC 40. 868 in the name of the angel Barqiel.
bartang (P. برتنگ) plantain. **ɛaraq bartang uriš gul kadmia** DC 46 distillation of plantain (leaves) and the head of a marsh-mallow flower.
baš a var. of **abaš** (q.v.).
baša (باشا) [in coloph.] Pasha.
bašaq, bašiq (باشق) hawk, sparrow-hawk Jb. ii 132 n. 4. **ditia ubašiq** Jb 134:7 (ABD **dita ubašaq**) kites (var. a kite) and a sparrow-hawk.
bašla 1 (ܒܫܠܐ) ripeness, maturity. **naṭra nišimla bašla d-girgla ʿlaia** ATŠ II no. 34 the soul keepeth its perfection (that is) of the higher sphere.
bašla 2 (st. emph. of the act. pt. of **BŠL**) cook.
bašqarta (**BŠQR**) knowledge, acquaintance. Used in Mod. Mand. as pl. (pron. *bašqarâθa*).
bata (ܒܬܐ) dispute, disputation, quarrel, dissension. **uqala ubata mn ʿmḫ atia** AM 95:18 and outcry and disputation will come from his mother.
batai (cf. Jb. ii 117 n. 2) a woman's name. **lbatai man amarlḫ lbatai man aprišḫ lbatai man amarlḫ d-tizal lʿnišbai** Jb 119: 10 ff. who said to Battai, who informed B., who said to B. to go to Elizabeth?
***bataia** (adj. from **batia**) householder, house-dweller, married. Fem. **bataita**, pl. **bataiia**, fem. pl. **bataiata, batiata** MG 142:8 f. **gubria bataiia** Gy 59:14 married men; **bataiia ubat(a)iata** Gs 17:23 married men and married women; **hinun haršaiun naplia lbataiia ulbataiata** DC 20 & 43 E:11 their sorceries bewitch house-dwellers male and female; **damia kd ʿnta bataita** DC 46 it resembles a housewife.
batar (באתר, בתר, ܒܬܪ) a rarer var. of **abatar** after, behind MG 33:13, 194:15. Mod. *bâθer*. **lbatar** to the last, to the end, utmost: **haliqna lbar anašia lbatar alma d-lišania ṣauia** DC 46 86:6 I oppose the human being to the utmost, until his tongue withers.
batur Zotb. 231 left col. 7 = **abatur**.
batia (ܒܬܐ) pl. of **baita** (q.v.) MG 142:8, 183:19. With suff. **bataiun** their houses MG 181:anteantep., **bataikun** Gy your houses; **batia d-mutba** Gy 6 houses of residence; **plaglun batia** Gy 112:16 they divided them (: the planets) into Houses; **mn manzaihun hauin batia** ATŠ I no. 253 of their (: the goats') hair there are tents (or read **šauin** people make, weave); **br batia** DC 36 (?) a servant born in his master's house (cf. P. خانه زاده).
batraia (formed as adj. or ord. number from **batar**) last. Pl. **batraiia**. Fem. **batraita** *ultima*. Used also substantivally, esp. in fem. 'the last thing' MG 299:20, often comparatively '*posterior*' MG 141:12. **lqadmaiia ulbatraiia qšia** AM 212:ult. from first to last she will be difficult; **ubatraiia kauna nihuilḫ** AM 25:18 but at last he becomes steady; **ukd amritun lbatraiia šuma d-hiia** ATŠ II no. 160 and when ye have said upon the last (: the undermost unleavened bread of the pile) 'The name of the Life . . .', cf. **paṭira ʿlaia ubatraia** s. **paṭira**; **arqa batraita d-parzla** CD 8 the last (undermost) earth (is) of iron; **qina batraita** the last (undermost) loaf ATŠ II no. 40.
BGA, PGA (> פְּגַע, ܦܓܥ by progr. assimilation) to meet, encounter.
Pe. Pf. **bga** he encountered MG 47:3, Impf. **tibga** she meeteth ibid. Pt. pl. **bagin** they (will) meet MG 47:4.
bgau–, bgu (comp. from ב and גו) in, within, into, in company with, amongst, with. **mhita bgu mhita** Gy 300:ult. etc. blow upon blow; **upihta bgu pihta matnitun** DC 27:472 ye put bread with bread. With suff. **bgauak** with thee, **bgauḫ, bguḫ** in it.
bgaz DC 37 name of an (evil) angel.
bgan, abgan (ܦܓܢ by progr. assimilation from Mishn. and Targ. פגן) outcry, provocation, anathema MG 47:7 f. No. st. emph. The form **abgan** (q.v.) is more frequent. **bgan hiia** PD 930 Anathema of the Life; **bgan manda d-hiia** Q 21:12 Anathema of M.-d-H.
bgar bgulin QmHZ obscure, corrupt.
BGN (cf. **bgan**) to cry out.
Pe. Pf. **ubgan gabra puha** Gy 85:10 f. and the man cried out: 'Pooh!'
Der.: **(a)bgan**.

BGṢ (a very frequent mod. verb) to stay, wait, expect, remain, trust, hope. Rare in literature, only in colophons. Mod. forms: Pf. **bgiṣ, bigṣat, bgiṣt, bigṣit,** pl. **bgiṣiun, bgiṣtun, bgiṣni(n).** Pres. **qabagiṣ, qabagṣa, qabagṣit, qabagiṣna, qabagṣin, qabagṣitun, qabagṣini(n).** (Pron. with an aspirated γ: *beyeṣ, beyṣat* etc.) **tum labigṣit bbaṣra** DC 35: coloph. then I stayed no longer in Baṣra.

Gl. (always defectively) 9:15 f. احتمل *pati, sufferre* صبر کرد; 10:11 f. امکث *exspectare* درنگ کرد; 17:15 f. انتظر *exspectare* انتظار کشید; 47:15 f. تقی *confidere* امیدوار بود; 48:3 f. ترجا *exspectare, sperare* امید دارد; 90:7 f. سکت *tacere* ساکت شد; 102:3 f. صبر *pertentare* همیشه هست; 151:11 f. مکث *exspectare* ایستاد; 166:13 f. as 17:15 f.; 180:7 f. synonymous with *qam* دام *morari, permanere* همیشه ماند.

BDA (etym. not quite sure, cf. בדד, ܒܕܰܪ 'to scatter', בדי 'to dig out') to dig out, take out, (of coal) to stir, poke, rake. Var. **BRA III.**

Pe. Act. pt. pl. **bʿdaihun badin gumria** Jb 172:1, Gy 17:11, Gy 357:12 with their hands they stir (or dig out, poke) the coals, cf. Nöld. ZA xxx (1916) 150; **badin umnakrin mn sidria** ATŠ II no. 423 they separate and remove (him) from the books.

bdala DC 44. 743 (*& often*) = **abdala.**

bdaqa (rt. **BDQ I**) breach, a thing that causes a breach: **ʿniš bdaqa binia ʿnta ugabra** DC 46. 115:7 a thing that causes a breach between a wife and her husband, cf. مَا يُفَرِّقُونَ بِهِ بَيْنَ ٱلْمَرْءِ وَزَوْجِهِ Qur. 2: 96.

bdunia a var. of **abdania** (v.s. **abdana**). **bbdunia titaiia d̲-hšuka** CP 51:13, ML 67:4 in the nethermost hells of darkness, cf. n. 2; **bbdunia ʿlaiia** Gy 205:7, 206:3 in the upper Abaddons, cf. Ginzā 206 n. 5; **bit (ʿ)bdunia** Gs 136:15.

bdur 1. scattering. 2. an exile. **tibil d̲-bdur hu** DC 48. 385 it is dust of an exile (double meaning).

bdin a place-name, Abdin (cf. **bṭabdin ṭura** DC 22. 50 & Sh. 'Abd.'s copy, where Gy 54 has **ṭabdana ṭura**). **alma lbit dubar d̲-hʿ bdin mitiqria** HG unto the land D., which is called (A)bdin.

BDL (בְּדַל, ܒܕܰܠ) to set apart, distinguish, discern, abstain from, (بدل) to change, exchange.

Pa. Impt. **kd̲ hauia (sira) barqba ʿu bʿmbra ʿu bṣarṭana ʿu bdaula badil** AM 110:10 when (the moon) is in Scorpio, Aries, Cancer or Aquarius, abstain (from letting blood).

Ethpa. Pf. **uhazin kdaba d̲-ʿtbadlh̲** DC 46 and this writing which was set apart for him (i.e. destined for the purpose).

BDQ I (ܒܕܰܩ, בְּדַק) to split, penetrate, break into, keep apart, separate, separate from, divorce.

Pe. Pf. **bidqa bdaq** (often) a breach was made. Impf. **uʿnta qadmaita nibidqh̲** AM 30:1 and he will divorce his first wife; **hʿ lgabrh̲ tibidqh̲ ʿu tišibqh̲** AM 75:16 she will divorce or part from her husband. Pt. **labuia ulʿmh̲ qšia ubadiq** AM 20:1 he brings difficulties on his father and mother and parts them; **ulahia qaiiš ulahh̲ d̲-ahh̲ badiq** AM 11:5 he is hard on his brothers, and brings about a split between them; pl. **uzaina ʿl ahdadia badqin** Jb 13:12 and they splinter their weapons on one another.

Ethpe. Pf. **bidqa ʿbdiq btibil** ML 215:1 = CP 176:9 **bidqa d̲-bdiq** (etc.) a cleft was riven in the earth (a cleft that they clove, CP).

Der.: **bdaqa, bidqa.**

BDQ II (semantic development of **BDQ I**) to put in between, insert, p. ext. to look closely, examine, explore. Very frequent in Mod. Mand.

Only Pe.: Pf. **bdaq mia bqanina** ATŠ I no. 188 he put water into the bottle; with suff. **bdaqtinun barabar hdadia** DC 21:coloph. I put them side by side (: to compare them). Impt. **bduq** (very frequent), **bduq bgauh̲ miša d̲-iasmin** DC 46 put in it oil of jasmine; **kdub lgidma ubduq bšamiš** DC 46 write on a piece of wood and place in the sun; **abud ptila ubduq bšraga** DC 46 make a wick, and insert into the lamp; **pilpil bduq bʿasal** DC 46 put pepper into honey; **bduq brišh̲** DC 46 put on his head; **kdub bduq atutia rišak** DC 46 write (the talisman) and place it beneath thy head; **bduq bnhirh̲** (often) insert into his nostrils; **mrirta d̲-ṭaus bduq bnhirh̲** DC 46 insert the gall of a peacock into his nostrils; **bduq dukta d̲-iatbia** DC 46 put it in the place where they sit; **bduq atutia apra** DC 46 place (it) beneath dust; pl. **bduqiun** DC 50. 135 insert; with suff. **budqh̲** (*very often*) put it, (of medicament) apply it. Act. pt. **badiq** (*often*), **ʿniš anpia badiq bdišta uhadar** DC 46. 104:7 a person who explores in the desert and wanders searching (?); pl. **badqin** (**ʿlh̲ nura**) DC 41. 558 they set (fire to her). Participial pres. **badiqna** DC 46 (*often*) I implant; with suff. **badqath̲ bšamšia iabuš** DC 46. 148:4 (thou shalt) put it in the sun, it will dry.

Gl. (always defectively and with a prosthetic **a**) 22:7 f. ادع [sic] *ponere* گذاشت; 25:9 f. اوقع *immittere* اوقع شد; 59:1 f. جعل *ponere* گذاشت; 146:9 f. لقی *ponere, imponere* گذشت; 165:15 f. نصّب, ناصب *immittere* نصب کرد; 174:3 f. وضع *ponere, imponere* گذاشت.

BDR (בְּדַר, ܒܕܰܪ) to strew, scatter, sprinkle, disperse.

Pe. Part. pres. **badirna** DC 46. 74:5 I scatter.

Pa. Impt. **ubadar atutia margnaikun** DC 50 and sprinkle (water) below your staves!

Ethpe. (exceptional inst. of ethpa.) Pf. (with meaning of impf.) **mn ʿqba ugiada ʿtibdiriun** DC 34 are disseminated from loins and phallus.

Ethpa. **hušbanai bdaria ʿtbadar** Gy 180:5 my (destined) sum (of years) in the ages is spent; **ʿtbadar** Gy 362:13 they were scattered **ṣipria ʿtbadar** DC 21 the birds scattered; **ulaʿtbadartun** DC 51 and ye were not dispersed; with suff. **ʿtbadrun** Gy 96:25 they were dispersed from me MG 272:paen. f.; **hušbanh̲ bdaria ʿtbadruia** Gs 19:7 (DC 22. 409 **ʿtbadria**) his count (of years, taken as logical subj.) in the ages is dissipated; **kulhun gundih̲ ʿtbadruia** Gy 83:1 all his armies were scattered from him; **kulhun sagadia ʿtbaruia** Gy 84:23 (DC 22. 79 **ʿtbadruh̲**) all his worshippers scattered away from him MG 278:6. Pt. pl. **anašia mitbadria** AM 266:43, 283:6 people will be dispersed; **umitbadria bkul dukta** Gy 215:2 f. and they are sprinkled everywhere; **umitbadrin bmdin mdin** Gy 29:20 f. and they are dispersed into many a city.

Der: **bdur** (בְּדוּר).

BHA (בהי, בהא) to burst forth, be confounded, be routed. Only in corrupt texts. **kul bhu ṣṭura siṭru** DC 44 all were confounded, turned aside (?); **ubha d̲-hauia bdaura baṭla** DC 40 and confounded (?) those that are in the abode of vanity.

bhaq name of a light spirit MR 31, 35, 50, Jb ii xxix, CP Ind., ML Ind., DAb Ind. **bhaq ziua** CP trs. no. 6, Gy 78:10, 93:11, Q 59:17, CP 117:6. **bhaq** RD 10 identified with **šamiš**; **bhaq ʿutra** Gy 297:12, 16; **maṭarta d̲-bhaq brh̲ d̲-ptahil** RD C 12 the purgatory of B. son of P. Lidzb. Mand. Gl.

bhar (P. بهار) spring. Var. **abhar**. **miṣai bhar** AM 288:15 middle spring.

bhuš (P. بيهوش) DC 46, 107₃ unconscious. s. **bimar.**

bhir (see next) DC 3 & 53 no. 105 a spirit mentioned with **bahrun.**

bhir, bhira (pass. pt. of **BHR I**) elect, chosen-out, proven, tested. Fem. st. abs. **bhira,** st. emph. **bhirta.** Masc. pl. **bhiria** ἐκλεκτοί MG xxviii 24, 311 n. 1, MSchr. 27 n. 4. **bhir zidqa** Gy 213:12 ff., 359:11, Gs 94:13, 116:15, Oxf. 216, 376 chosen righteous, proven righteous; **gabra bhir zidqa** Gy 195:15 the man of proven righteousness (cf. Brandt JPT 18/1892 437:middle, 579:1; sometimes designates a celestial being, Ginzā 195 n. 7); **bhiria zidqa** Gy 58:4, 219:9 ff., 339:2 f., Morg. 10:1, RD C 1 etc. the elect of Righteousness, corresponding to **bhiria kušṭa** Gy 299:14 the elect of Truth MG 311 & n. 1; **prišaiia ubhiria zidqa** Oxf. 86 the outstanding and the elect Righteous; **bhiria** Gy 78:19, 340:ult., 351:20, 353:10 as an attribute of the Life (Ginzā 353 n. 3); **bhira dakia** Gy 342:4, 345:17, CP 243:5 f., etc. the Pure Chosen One or proven pure One (s. **BHR I**) ML 87 n. 2, MMII 95 f.; **bhirai** DAb my chosen ones; **bhira mn lhil** Gy 367:ult., 368:10 the Chosen One from the yonder world; **bhiria d̲-ana bihrit** Gy 66:21 the chosen ones that I have chosen; **bhira mn kulhun mumia** (*often*) proof against all faults; **šulta bhirta** ATŠ a chosen question, an especial request; **bhir mn** 1. exempt from, proof against, 2. preferred to, preferable to, chosen rather than (cf. נִבְחַר מִן Jer. 8: 3); **bit bhirta** s. **bit.**

bhira (see preceding) a *malwāša* man's name. In DAb name of a herdsman in the land of Ptahil.

bhita (pass. pt. of **BHT**) shameful, disgraceful, disgraced. Pl. **bhitia** Gy 60 the shameful. **ia br gabra bhita** Jb 13:8 O son of an abominable father!; **arabaiia bhitia** DC 36 the disgraceful Arabs.

bhmndukt (P. بهمندخت, written defectively) IM 99, 102 a woman's name.

BHR I (בחר, ܒܚܪ) to try out, test, choose (out), select, examine.

Pe. Pf. **bhar** (*often*) he chose, **bihrat** she chose (also a name of a female spirit, s.v.), **bhiria d-bihrit** Gy 66:21 the elect ones that I selected; with suff. **bihrh̲** (*often*) he chose him, he tested him. Impf. **unibihrun lmanun** DC 42 and they shall examine their vestments. Impt. **bhar, bhur** MG 221:1 f., 229:5; **bhur had mn alpa** ATŠ I no. 294 select one out of a thousand; **bhur napšaikun mn hambalta d̲-šuba** ATŠ II no. 183 exempt yourselves from the corruption of the Seven; **bhur ušaiil uhaqar bkul mindam** ATŠ II no. 367 test, question, and cross-examine in everything; special pl. **bhuriun manaikun** DC 42. 396 *perquirite vestimenta vestra*; with suff. **bhurinun** examine them MG 269:10, 282:9; **buhruih̲ lašualia** ATŠ I no. 90 examine ye a a novice; **ubuhruih̲ lrbh̲ kd̲ dilh̲** ibid. and select his teacher as (ye did) himself. Act.pt. **lmahu paqadth̲ d̲-bahar tarmidia** ATŠ II no. 11 why didst thou charge him that he should choose out priests?; **d̲-bahar ušatil umasiq ldaura taqna** Gy 240:20 who selecteth and transplanteth and raiseth to the Abiding Dwelling; with encl. **aiilth̲ muzania d̲-baharlh̲** DC 41 thou hast placed her in the Scales that shall assay her; pl. with encl. **kd̲ iaquta d̲-bahrilh̲ ṣirapaiia** ATŠ I no. 90 as goldsmiths select a ruby. Part pres. **d̲-bahritun napšaikun bgauh̲** ATŠ II no. 11 that ye may prove yourselves thereby; with encl. **bahritulh̲** ATŠ II no. 365 ye have selected him. Pass. pt. **bhir, bhira,** pl. **bhiria** (s.v.), **bhir hiia mn muta** ATŠ II no. 200 life is preferable (lit. preferred) to death (cf. Jer. 8:3 s. **bhir, bhira**).

Pa. Pf. **bkušṭa d̲-bahar malkia** DC 41. 6 by the troth that the angels have proven; **ubahrit bhiria** DC 22. 358 and I chose out chosen ones; with encl. **kul had bšumh̲ urušumh̲ ukiniana abh̲ baharlh̲** DC 36 he picked out each by his name and his sign and his father's name.

Ethpe. Pf. **ʿtibhar mn kulhun almia** DC 6 & 36 he is approved (: proved worthy) by all beings; **ʿtibhar hu bita hu** ATŠ I no. 263 it is a house that is tested; **ʿtibhart, ʿtibhirt** thou wert chosen, approved, tested MG 222: anteantep.; with encl. **d̲-ʿtibhirbh̲** DC 27. 305 by which she was proven (lit. which were chosen for her, verb masc.); **mania hadtia d̲-ʿtibharlh̲** DC 34 the new garments which have been selected for him; **rušumia ukušṭia**

ḏ-ʿtbhirubẖ ATŠ II no. 111 signs and *kuštas* in which they were examined. Impf. **nitibhar bkulhun ʿbidatẖ** ATŠ I no. 230 he will be test-proof in all rites; without **t** in the pref. **nibihrun bhiria zidqa** Gy 58 let the proven of the Righteousness prove themselves! Pt. **mitibhir** ATŠ II no. 365 is chosen; pl. **mitbihrin umithimin** DC 27. 449 proven worthy and faithful.

Ethpa. Pf. with encl. **ḏ-ʿtbaharlẖ** ATŠ that was approved, confirmed. Impt. **ʿtbahrun** prove yourselves MG 229:bottom. Pt. (as ettaf.) with encl. **umasqata mšalamta mitabharlẖ** ATŠ II no. 293 and (if) redeeming *masiqtas* improve (: purify) him.

Der.: **bhir(a), bihrat.**

BHR II (= **BAR** I) to shine brightly, be illumined.

Pe. Participial pres. with suff. **bahirnun** DC 34 I illumine them, I make them shine. Part. pres. with encl. **anat bahratlẖ** ATŠ I no. 123 thou dost illumine it.

Pa. to cause to shine, impart brightness (certain forms of **BHR I** could be quoted here as well).

Ethpe. Pf. **ʿtibhar** ATŠ II nos. 112, 196 was illumined; **tušbihat ʿutria ʿtbihrat** DC 3 = CP 342:8 the glory of uthras shone forth; **ʿšata ʿkilta ʿtbihrat** DC 27 the crowning flame shone; **ʿtbihrat uhua ziua** DC 34 radiance shone forth and came into existence; **aprašata ḏ-ʿtbihrat upiršat brazia** ATŠ II no. 123 explanation which was inspired and interpreted the mysteries. Pt. pl. **mia mitbihria** DC 27 the waters are made bright; **ʿtlabaš umitbihrin** ATŠ they will be clothed and enlightened.

Ethpa. Pf. **ʿtbahar** (often, sometimes confused with **BHR I**) was glorified, glorious, irradiated, shone forth.

Der.: **bihrana, bihruta, bihria.**

bhr ʿzag IM 99 a woman's name IM Gl.

BHŠ (ܒܚܫ) to move quickly, be active, agitate, stir about, incite; (בָּחַשׁ) to search, examine.

Pe. Pf. **bhaš** he searched, examined Lidzb. Mand. Gl., Pognon IM Gl., **bihšat** Gy 155:16 she searched; **bihšit** Gy 140:22, 161:10 I searched. Impf. **latibhuš** Q 86:18 thou wilt not search; **ʿbhuš** Gy 155:14 I search. Impt. **ubhuš lbrihak** DC 3 and wave about thy censer; with suff. **buhšiẖ lbirihak** Oxf. roll a 148, 149 id. Act. pt. **bahiš** Gy 205:1, 206:3 he searcheth; **hadar ubahiš** DC 27. 108 turns himself about and explores; **ukul ʿmanuta bahiš** AM 27:10 and he will examine every (kind of) occupation; **bahiš bkanpẖ ulamaška** Oxf. 166, DC 3, Jb 177:8, Morg. 35:6 he searcheth in his lap (: purse) and findeth nought; fem. **bahša ʿlẖ** Gy 166:9 she searcheth it; **bahša ulamaškalẖ** Gy 149:22 she searcheth but findeth him not; **haiša ubahša** Gy 81:8, 155:3 she thinketh and searcheth; pl. **haišia ubahšia** Gy 81:3 they think and search. Participial pres. **lmahu bahšit** Gy 149:23 what searchest thou?; with encl. **bahšatbẖ** Gy 216:10 thou searchest (in) it.

BHT (בָּהַת, ܒܗܬ) to be shamed, confused, confounded.

Pe. Pf. **bhit** he was ashamed MG 219:17; **bihtat** Gy 242:8 she was ashamed MG 222:10; with encl. **mimra ḏ-bhatinun lmimria kulhun** ATŠ I no. 231 a word that confuted all sayings; **bhattinun** Gy 165:8 I shamed them (ought to be considered as af. with graphical omission of a-, cf. below). Impf. **nibhut** MG 222:10, **nibhit** (ethpe.?) MG 222 n. 5, **nibihtun** MG 61:5 (rather as ethpe.). Impt. **bhut.** Pt. **bahit, bahta,** pl. **bahtia** Gy 60:13, Gs 43:5, 58:3 the shameful. Pass. pt. **bhita** s.v., pl. **tamun bhitin** DC 51:coloph. they were, became, ashamed; **liṭia ubhitia** Jb 86:8 the cursed and disgraced.

Pa. Inf. with suff. **bahtinun** to shame them MG 293:12.

Af. Pf. with suff. **abhittinun** I shamed them MG 12:15, 282:paen. (Forms with graph. omission of the pref. s. pe. pf. with suff.)

Ethpe. Impf. (without **t** in the pref.) s. pe. impf. Pt. pl. **mitbihtia** AM 271:1 they will be ashamed, discomfited; **ʿlania mitbihtia** AM 271:13 trees will become bare; **mitbihtin minẖ** ATŠ II no. 9 they are put to shame before him.

Ethpa. **ʿtbahtat** Gy 117:6 she was put to shame. Impf. **titbahat utibṭul** DC 21 = JRAS 1937 592:ult. thou shalt be shamed and become powerless; **titbahtun mn adam zihrun** DC 46 ye shall be put to shame by A.Z. Pt. pl. **ianqia ḏ-mitbahtin** DC 46. 89:13 children that are abashed, shy. **ʿtbihtat** var. **bihtat** DC 21 = JRAS 1937 penult. she became shy.

Der.: **bahtuta, bhita.**

bhtar, bhtr (P. بهتر, colloquial) better.

Gl. 32:14 **bhtr** افضل, *maius, excellentior* فاضلتر; 37:12 **bhtr mn** افضل من , احسن *plus est quam* زياد است; 70:4 **bhtar** حسن *praetiosus* پر قيمت; 70:6 id. خيار *selectus, electus* رضا; 78:3 **bhtr** خير له *bonus ei* خيرات برابر.

bu = **abu. bu danab** AM 275:19, **budanab** AM 275:28 = **abu danab, buzaubʿa** = **abuzubʿa** etc.

bugdana DC 43 = **abugdana.**

buzrana (doublet of **bazra**) seed, semen. **ubuzrana ḏ-gabra mkamar** DC 46 if the semen of the man returns.

buṭa (Mod. Syr. ܒܘܼܛܵܐ anus) bottom, anus. Still used. **hazin baba kdub lbuṭa ḏ-šarba** DC 46 write this charm on the bottom of a drinking-pot; **kdub lbuṭa ḏ-kuza** DC 46 write on the bottom of a jar; **ušria ʿštẖ ubutẖ udundẖ** DC 12. 111 and free (from spells) his buttocks and his anus and his penis.

buṭunta (rt. **BṬN**) pregnancy. **buṭunta umaudala** DC 51. 350 pregnancy and birth.

buṭlana (ܒܘܼܛܠܵܢܵܐ) vanity, nullity, uselessness evanescence, ineffectuality, emphemerality MG 136:antep. **ḏ-buṭlana litlẖ** Jb 16:3 etc (*often*) which hath no evanescence (is unending).

buṭna (ܒܘܼܛܢܵܐ) pregnancy. **qablat minẖ buṭna**

hda Gy 96:10 she got from him one pregnancy; **buṭna tauma** Gy 243:5 being pregnant with twins; **buṭna d̲-ʿnta** DC 46 the woman's pregnancy; **iadala ubuṭna** Jb 104:2 child-bearing and pregnancy; **ʿu buṭna litlh̲** ATŠ II no. 334 if she is not pregnant.

buia (ܒܘܒܝܐ) boil. Pl. buiia MG 118:anteantep. Fem. and masc. **himṭia ubuia nihuilh̲** AM he will have festering sores and a boil; **ubuiia banašia nihuia** AM 182:2 and people will have boils; **buiia rabata** DC 23. 964 big boils.

bukara AM 198:14 Bokhara. Var. (Ṣâb.'s copy) **bukira.**

bukra (בּוּכְרָא, ܒܘܟܪܐ) first-born, first, eldest. Pl. **bukria,** fem. **bukarta,** pl. **bukariata.** MG 104:14, 105:16. **bukrh̲ rhima** PD 1013 his beloved first-born; **bukra iaqira** PD 1003 dear first-born; **bukra qadmaia** Q 48:7 the first-born (son); **bukra** PD 611 opposed to **tiniana** (the first . . . the second); **bukra malka d̲-hšuka** Gy 143:6 the first-born king of darkness; **sam . . . bukra habiba** CP 25:17, Q 10:26 *Sam . . . primogenitus amatus*; **ʿutra niha bukra** Gy 126:21 the mild first(-born) uthra; **malka ʿlaia bukra qadmaia** PD 1450 the high first-born primeval king; **labukra d̲-mn qudamh̲ hua** Gy 6:15 no first-born who was before him; **lbnh̲ bukrh̲** Oxf. 286 to his firstlings; **šitlai bukrai** Oxf. 287 my first plants (: children); **bnh̲ bukrh̲** Gy 329:4, 361:15 etc.; **bnai bukrai** Gy 361:16 my firstlings; **trin bukria** Gy 308:7 f. two firstlings; **bukria tlata** Gy 296:12 three firstlings; **brh̲ bukra d̲-hu ʿur** Gy 126:15 her first-born son Ur; **brh̲ bukra d̲-iušamin** Gy 374:11 the first(-born) son of Y.; **bukartai** PD 353 my first-born daughter; **šualia bukra** PD & ATŠ (often) the first novice-priest consecrated by a *ganzibra*; **maṣbuta bukarta** PD 338, 653, 717, 719, 723 the first baptism, **masiqta bukarta** PD 339 the first *masiqta* (both performed by a novice for his master-initiator); **šuba masiqata bukariata** DC 35 seven first (of year) *masiqtas*; **gadia bukra br bukarta** DC 40. 789 a firstling kid, child of a firstling dam; **tanura šgira lahauia bukra d̲-hararia** DC 46 a glowing oven in which there is not its first heat.

bukraia = **bukra.** Pl. **bukraiia. bukraia** PD 353 the first-born, firstling; **rahmia bukraiia** Lond. roll A 441 the first morning-devotions; **šuta almia bukraiia** PD 999 the doctrine of the first ages.

bukta 1 (etym. unsure; cf. *pugdu* Bez. 225a for *bukdu?*) water-vessel, pail, pitcher. **bukta nisbat . . . uazlat lmimlia mia** DC 21 = JRAS 1937 594:32 she took a water-pot . . . and went to fill it with water; **bukta nisbit liama silqit** DC 44. 1329 I took a pitcher (and I) went to the sea.

bukta 2 (rt. **BKA**) lamentation, weeping. **ubukta bpumh̲** DC 43 J 137 and lamentation in his mouth; **bukta d̲-bukta nisbit** DC 44 (a pun) I took a jar (**bukta 1**) of tears (**bukta 2**).

***bula** = **abula. ubulun** DC 22. 459 = **ublun** Gs 73:1, varr. **uablun, uablan.**

bulba DC 22. 209 a miscopying of **dulba** Gy 216:12.

bulbul (بُلْبُل) nightingale, used as a *malwâša* man's name. (Frequent in colophons cf. RD D 24 etc.). **mrirta d̲-bulbul** DC 46 110:8 a nightingale's gall.

bulbulaia (possibly from **BLA II**) marks of deterioration, *or* wear(?): **kuza hadtia adinqia bulbulaia** ATŠ II no. 316 a new jar without marks of wear.

bulul RD D 13 = **bulbul.**

buliana (rt. **BLA II**, cf. ܒܘܠܝܐ) loss, injury, deterioration, decay, scarcity, want. **buliana uhusrana bhiuania hauia** AM 189:1 there will be deterioration and deficiency in cattle; **buliana bbnia hauia** AM 5:ult. (often) he will have a loss amongst his children; **ubuliana baqnia utauria** AM 233:12 and loss amongst the sheep and oxen; **buliana btauria nihuia** AM 229:18 there will be loss amongst the kine; **buliana banašia nihuia** AM 252:17 there will be scarcity (?) amongst men.

bulعiz (ابو العِزّ) Zotb. 222 left col. 23 a man's name.

bulparaz, bulparaš, bulparaṣ̌ (ابو آلفرج) AM 256:20 etc. (often in coloph.) a *malwâša* man's name MG 2:middle.

bum, buma (ܒܘܡܐ, Ar. بوم) owl. Mod. pl. **bumana** Morg. 285:11. **aitilh̲ lparkil d̲-buma d̲-hu bnia d̲-bum** AM 130:10 bring him the nestlings of an owl, which is to say the young of the owl.

BUN I, BNN II (בון II = בִּין, ܒܢ pa. ܒܝܢ) to separate, distinguish, consider, expound, show forth, demonstrate, argue out, teach, point out, instruct, explain, understand.

Pe. Pf. **iauar bkisia ban uapriš** DC 3 Y. in secret expounded and explained; with suff. **banh̲ uaprišh̲** Q 25:37, 26:24, Morg. 228/43:3 he expounded and explained it; **banan uaprišan** Gs 46:14 he demonstrated to me and taught me; **banun uaprišun rbia** Jb 210:13 the Great (Life) explained to me and taught me; **banth̲ ubaninth̲ lnapšai** Gy 367 I perceived and made it clear to myself; with encl. **banibh̲** I was instructed by it MG 249:1. Act. pt. **baiin** he distinguishes, understands MG 250:10; **d̲-baiin umitapraš** Gy 16:5 who is perceptive and instructed; **bhukumth̲ baiin** Gy 98:21 he is discerning in his wisdom; **baiin umitbanan** Jb 211:5 he was well instructed (hist. pres.); fem. **ruha baina bhukumth̲** Gy 98:24 R. perceived in her wisdom (hist. pres.); pl. **bainia ṭabia ukma d̲-bainia** Jb 225:8 the good are arguing and how they argue!; **d̲-iatbia hdadia ubanin** Gs 117:7 f. they sit together and argue; with encl. **d̲-baiinbia umitaprašbia** Jb 214:3 f. who is taught and instructed by me. Pass. pt. **kma bina bintak** Jb 255:5 f. how discerning is thy insight!

Pa. (from **BNN**): Pf. with encl. **banintinun bškinatun** Gy 372:27 I instructed them in their dwellings.

Ethpa. (from **BNN**): **baiin umitbanan** above s. pe. act. pt.

Note: Certain forms may be confused with **BUN II** 'to edify': **ruha baina sbat**

bhukumth̠ Leid. var. to Gy 98:24 (cf. above) may be based on confusion with **aina** (: R. gazed her fill).

Der.: **bina 3, binta 2, buna 2.**

BUN II = BNN II = BNA. Cf. pe. pt. act. & pass. **baiin,** fem. **bina** she is built. (Other forms s. **BNA** and **BNN II.**)

bun dahiltana DC 43 a demon.

buna 1, bna (rt. **BUN II = BNA = BNN II**) a doublet of **binta. man hikla buna banilh̠** Gs 12:2 who will build him a palace, a building; **damit lbuna rama** Gs 84:13 I was like a tall building; **buna d̠-nišimta bgauh̠ daira** DC 41. 527 a building in which the soul resides; **škinta ubuna ltartin ʿbnitlun** DC 47 thou hast built for both of them a dwelling and a building.

buna 2 (rt. **BUN I**) explanation, demonstration. **raza usidra uprišata upiasa ubuna d̠-apraš manda d̠-hiia** Gs 19:antep. f. the mystery and book and explanations and instruction and exposition that M.-d̠-H. taught.

buna 3 (semantic development of **buna 1**) formation, appearance, form, structure. Pl. **bunia** ATŠ I no. 283. **ubunh̠ uṭunh̠ dakia (a)sqila** ATŠ I no. 291 and its form and fruit are clean and comely.

bunka (P. بنه with Middle P. end., Lagarde GGA 1871 1103 f.) base, foundation, origin, place of origin, native place, home MG xxxi: 14, 379 n. 3. **bunka rba** Jb 10:10 the great foundation; **nimarlak ʿl bunkak ulabahatak** Jb 74:10 we shall speak with thee concerning thine origin and thy parents; **lhama mn bunkh̠ akil** AM 7:10 he will eat bread from his native place; **qala bit anašata hauia ubunka** AM 20:2 there will be scandal in his home and his native place; **ubunka d̠-abahath̠ ladaiar** AM 46:2 and he will not reside in the home of his fathers; **uqiniana mn ruhqia lbunka naitia** AM 37:2 and he will bring property to his home from afar; **upalgaiin d̠-šnia . . . bunka hauia** AM 48:8 and for many years . . . it will be his home; **ubunka d̠-abahath̠ harub** AM 20:2 and the home of his parents will be destroyed.

bunna (Ar. بنّى) Jb 149:2 B (n. 2), var. **hbina** a kind of fish.

bunta a miscopying of **bukta 1. kdub lbunta d̠-halba** DC 46. 229:12 write on a milk-pitcher.

busaعid (ابو سعيد) Zotb. 218 left 14, var. **busعaid** a pers. name.

bushaq (ابو اسحاق) AM Ṣâb.'s copy: coloph. a pers. name.

busiana (בּוּסְיָא, ܒܘܣܝܢܐ) contempt, despite MG 136:paen. **ʿusiana ubusiana** Gy 215:23 treading underfoot and contempt.

busiعid AM 256:13 = **busaعid.**

busma (Midr. בּוֹסֶם Syr. ܒܘܣܡܐ and ܒܣܡܐ) delight, pleasantness, fragrance, enjoyment, bliss, felicity, amiability, delight(fulness), luxury, pleasure MG 20:2. Pl. **busmania** (ܒܣ̈ܡܢܐ) sweet odours, perfumes, aromas MG 169:bottom. **utuqnh̠ ubusmh̠ mn tuqna ubusma d̠-sam** DC 22. 190 f. = Gy and its radiance and pleasantness are derived from the radiance and pleasantness of S.; **arhamth̠ mn busma lṣauth̠** DC 45 thou didst make him in love from his delight for her society; **ʿl busmh̠ uṣauth̠** ibid. for her delightfulness and society; **šapia d̠-pagra ubusma** AM 165:7 physical ease and luxury; **busma nihuia** AM 281:34 there will be enjoyment; **ṭabuta ubusma** AM 284:21 good things (to eat) and feasting; **ulatirnum busmania** DC 12. 197 and love not perfumes; **rihania ubusmania** Jb 83:4, Gy flavours and perfumes; **busmania mbasmilun** Gy 60:10 they produce fragrance (be)for(e) them; **binta rihania ubusmania ʿl iaminh̠ d̠-nišimta miṣṭarar** DC 6 an edifice of perfumes and sweet odours is formed at the soul's right hand; **busma ana d̠-ʿutria** Gy 322: 16 I am the perfume of the uthras; **alma d̠-busmania** Gy 31:ult. the world of aromas.

Gl. 72:12 defectively and misspelt with ṣ شفاء *curatio,* 124:3 id. عطر *aromata.*

busعaid Zotb. 220 right 33, a var. of **busaعid.**

bustambaia (s. ***bustambana**) Par. 20:20a gardener MG 50:20.

***bustambana** (P. بستان بان) gardener, head-gardener. Pl. **bustambania,** used apparently with sg. mean. **pt bustambania d̠-malka** DC 3 (var. **bustam banaia** CP 235:13, and ult.) daughter of the king's head-gardener.

bustana (P. بستان, Aram. loan-w. בּוּסְתְּנָא) garden, orchard. Pl. **bustania. bbustana d̠-** DC 36 in the garden of . . .; **uʿuṣṭunia bustania btibil hinun** ATŠ I no. 223 and its supports are gardens on earth; **duktai bbustania hu** DC 46. 126:2 my place (haunt) is in gardens.

buṣaid (ابو صيد) a mod. expression found only in DC 46. Prob. place of hunting (?). Pl. **buṣaidia** hunting-dogs (?). **duktai buṣaid hauia** DC 46 my place is a place of hunting; **ʿsir daiuia ušidia ugunahia unapuṣia briša ubuṣaidia** DC 46. 133:16. Bound are the demons, devils, groanings, discharges (?), and hunting creatures.

buṣina (בּוּצִינָא, ܒܘܨܝܢܐ Akk. *buṣinnu* Löw 41) pumpkin. **qaranba ubuṣina uqaina** Oxf. xii melon, pumpkin, and (sugar-)reed.

buṣrana (rt. **BṢR**) shortage, failure (of crops), deficiency, paucity, lacking. **ʿburia buṣrana niqmun** AM 227:18 f. the grain crops will fail; **buṣrana uhusrana hauibun** AM 174:ult. there will be failure and poor quality in them (: crops, fruits); **buṣrana d̠-zira** AM 285:1 failure of grain; **buṣrana baina** ATŠ I no. 190 etc. (*often*) short-sight, or blindness. Gl. 73:4 missp. خسر *detrimentum* زيان.

bura (בּוּרָא, ܒܘܪܐ, Ar. بُور Qur. 25: 19, 48: 12) uncultivated land or person, empty space, waste or untilled ground, rough, ruffian, boor(ish), monster. Gy 96:8–17 Rūha's paramour with whom she conceived her sons. Pl. **buria 1.** Masc. See also **buria** s.v. **buria d̠-smikilh̠ lʿšumia** ATŠ II no. 234 empty spaces which hold up the sky; **buria rurbia bišia** Gy 75:15 the mighty evil monsters; **bura napla** Gy 81:13, 132:11, 15, 19, 346:12 the perishable monster; **bura šapla** Gy 85:5 the low lout; **bura rba** Gy 95:5 f. the great monster (cf. above); **gabaria buria d̲-alma** Gy 85:3 the giant monsters of the world; **buria rurbia** Gy 81:15, 132:9; **miaka npiš hailaiun mn buria** Gy 81:2 is there anybody whose strength is greater than (that of) the ruffians?; **buria ugabaria** Gy 85:3 giants and uncouth beings; **uʿzlat lbura** Gy 95:5 and she went to the lout; **minẖ trisar buria qablat** Gy 95:11 f. she conceived from him twelve monsters; **buria mardia** Gy 80:18 the rebellious ruffians.

buran a *malwâša* woman's name.

buraq 1 a var. of **biruq** (q.v.).

***buraq 2** (cf. Ar. أبرق) Ṣâb.'s AM a better var. of **muriqa** AM 135:3 in **taura hiuara usumaqa uburaqa** a bull white and red (and) of mixed colour.

burdaia (cf. **bardaiia**) name of a tribe. Pl. **burdaiia. malka burdaia** Gy 390:7 (Sh. ʿAbd.'s copy and DC 22. 386 **malka d̲-burdaiia**) the king of the Burdaeans Ginzā 416 n. 5.

burukta a var. of **birkta** MG 14:1.

buruq a var. of **biruq** (q.v.).

buruqta, buruqtia (בַּרְקִית) cataract of eye. Varr. **bruqtia, biruqta. aina buruqtia** DC 21, 45 & 46 (*often*) eye with cataract; **buruqta ʿl aina** DC 51. 81 f. a cataract on the eye.

burzan, burzin a king of early Iran. **burzin malka** Gy 383:4, 393:5 (DC 22. 388 **burzan malka**) the king Burzin.

burzinqa (Talm. בּורזינקא, Syr. ܒܪܙܢܩܐ based on popular etym., Akk. *barsigu, parsigu* Zimmern: *Akk. Fw.* 36, cf. also Talm. בורס = βίρρος Sachs: *Beiträge zur Sprachwiss. der Altertumskunde* i. 138; Ar. loan-w. بُرنُس Fränkel 51) turban (a strip of white muslin, twisted three times round the head) MG 20:16 ff. & n. 2, MSchr 50 n. 1, Lorsbach in Stäudlin's *Beiträge* v. 38, MMII Ind. Pl. **burzinqia.** Masc. **atna burzinqa** Jb 45:3 he put on a turban; **burzinqa d̲-nasib mšiha paulis** Jb 108:12 the turban which Christ-Paulis taketh; **burzinqa brišaihun nitirṣun** Gy 30:2 f. they set the turban on their heads; **burzinqa hiuara** Q 2:3 a white turban, pl. **burzinqia hiuaria** Gy 25:14, 47:24; **dakia burzinqa** Jb 84 a clean turban; **burzinqai** CP 200 p (no. 178): 10 my turban.

burṭma a plant, or tree. Prob. a miswriting of **qurṭma** saffron. **burṭma hu** DC 41 (illustration) it is a saffron (?).

buria 1, buria 2, aburia (בּוּרְיָא, ܒܘܪܝܐ) reed mat. Only sg. found. **šakbia lburia** Gs 98:16 f. they sleep on a reed-mat; **urqiha kd̲ buria ʿtikrik** Gy 348:11 and the firmament was rolled up like a reed-mat; **ušumia mikarka kd̲ buria** Gy 203:11 and the heavens shall be rolled up like a reed-mat; **raglia qaina lburia** Gy 139:13 they bind a reed into a reed-mat; **mirgal qaina lburia** DC 7 & 37. 191 f. as a reed is bound into a reed-mat.

burka 1 (ܒܘܪܟܐ) knee. Fem. Pl. **burkia** MG 157:bottom. **ṣum burkaikun mn arbukia lsaṭana** Gy 41:13 abstain (your knee) from kneeling before Satan; **burkan arbik lbišia** Gy 63:23 our knee knelt down before the bad; **latišiplun burkaikun** s. **ŠPL**; **kiba d̲-burkia** AM 20 ult. (*and often*) pain in the knees; **nipasqinun lburkia** DC 43 they cut off his knees; **rumaiia d̲-burkia** v.s. **rumaiia**; **arbikit ʿl burkai** DC 26. 98 v.s. **RBK.**

burka 2 a woman's name. **rašid br burka** Ṣâb.'s AM: coloph. Rashid son of Borka.

burkiniata (from **burka 1**) Oxf. roll g 864, DC 47 = Or. 330:17 a disease of the knees.

bursma (Aram. form of P. بَرْسَم with labialization of the vowel) the sacred staves or twigs of the Zoroastrians Ginzā 225 n. 2. **ubursmaiun kd̲ ṣalibia lkadpaiun pakrilun** Gy 223:25 and they bind their *barsam*-twigs crosswise on their shoulders.

burṣip, burṣipi Borsippa. **babil uburṣip** Gs 17:2 Babylon and Borsippa; **ʿpik bil mn babil ʿpik ʿnbu mn burṣip(i)** JRAS 1943 181 no. 27 Bel turned away from Babylon, Nebo turned away from Borsippa. (var. Par. 27, 27a **burṣip**).

burqaita (Ar. بورق) borax, saltpetre. **sab burqaita haditia** DC 40. 398 take fresh borax.

burš̤ (Ar. بُرْج) solar month, astrological house MMII 5, 81.

buršiha AM 152 = **burš̤.**

bušmanqa (corruption of Pahl. *angušṭbânak*, Mod. P. انگشتوانه) a doublet of **gušbanqa** thimble, ring, signet, seal. Varr. **bušmaqa, bušmara, bšmanqa, bšmaqa. tlata bušmanqia** DC 45 & 46 (several times) three thimbles (or rings); **bušmaqa d̲-bar liamin ubušmanqa hurina d̲-kaspa** DC 46 a ring of lead on the right hand and another ring of silver. Gl. 73:8 **bšbanqa** [*sic*] خاتم *anulus* انگشتری.

BUT (ܒܘܬ: ܒܬ, Ar. بات) to spend night, lodge, tarry.

Pe. Impf. **luataikun lanibut** Gy 19:ult. f. let it not tarry with you. Pt. pl. **baitin** (DC 22. 363 **baitia**) **utanin lmabra** Gy 366 they spend the night and sigh at the ferry, cf. Ginzā 389 n. 3.

Gl. 39:11 f. **bat** بات *pernoctare* شب بروز آورد.

buta (בְּעוּתָא, ܒܥܘܬܐ) prayer, petition. Pl. **bauata** MG 145:bottom, 146:5, MR 92:middle, MSchr 94 n. 3. Masc. in Gs 52:11 cf. MG 161:22, fem. Gy 134:3, Q 26:31. **bbauata, babauata** in prayers, with prayers MG 32:13 f.; **buta taqna** Gs 46:8 a steadfast prayer; **buta kasita** Gy 134:3, Q 26:31 secret prayer; **buta utušbihta** (often in liturgical texts) prayer and praise; **halin arbia bauata** (*often ibid.*) these four prayers; **mia d̲-buta** s. **mia.**

butana (cf. בּוּעָא) abscess. **butana rba d̲-plan** DC 46 = JRAS 1943 171:19 the large abscess of N.

BZA (בְּזַע, ܒܙܥ) to split, cleave, rend, slit, tear, make a hole.

Pe. **bza** he split MG 234:middle; **bza rqiha** Gy 196:17, Gs 130:32, Q. 27:32 he clove the sky; **bza iamamia** Gy 378:31 he clove the seas; **bzat** she tore, rent MG 237:6. Impf. with suff. **nibzh̠** DC 43 J 126 the splits. Impt. **bzia,** with suff. **bzih̠.** Pass. pt. ***bzʿia** miswritten **bzʿuia** IM Gl. Inf. replaced by **baza** in **natna lsakina lbaza ṣaurh̠** DC 24 he shall place the knife for slitting its throat. Participial pres. miswritten **ubzana lrqiha rama** DC 3 and I cleave the lofty firmament.

Pa. Pt. **umubaza baṭinata** DC 43 J 72 and he rendeth pregnant women. Gl. 49:15 f. with a prosth. **a** ثقب *perforare* سوراخ كرد. 166:9 f.

Der.: **baza, bzuia, bizuna.**

bzaṭ name of a genie.

bzuza only in Gl. 70:14 خرمه *foramen* سوزن.

bzuia (rt. **BZA**) hole. Masc. Still used (pron. *bezûya*).

BZZ (בזז, حلز) to plunder, pillage, take surreptitiously.

Pe. Pf. **baz** 'he-plundered' may occur as pr. n. of demons (s. **baz** 1). Impt. **buz** take secretly; with suff. **buzh̠ uatnh̠ dukta d̠-ʿniš lahazilak** DC 46. 144:2 and take it secretly and put it in a place that no one sees thee; pl. with suff. **buzuia** Gy 118:2 plunder it MG 278:ult.

Der.: **bizta.**

BZL (Pa. בַּזֵּל) to scatter, sprinkle.

Pa. Impt. with suff. **abar mia bhanath̠ bazlh̠** DC 43 cross the water (and) sprinkle him therewith.

BZQ I (حلزه Mishn. בָּזַק) to strew, disseminate, sow, flash forth.

Pe. Impt. **qria lmihla ubzuq bbaitak** DC 40. 1046 read it over salt and strew it in thy house. Act. pt. (incorrect) **tauria d̠-lamṣin bzaqia** (var. **bazaqia, baziqia**) DC 45 & 46 bulls incapable of serving (cows); **hiuaniata d̠-lamṣin d-bazaqia** DC 45 & 46. 56 beasts that are not capable of serving (females).

Pa. Pf. **laʿbazaqtun** DC 51. 65 (read **labazaqtun**) ye did not disperse.

Ethpe. Impf. **latitbazaq** CP 389:4 it (fem.) flasheth not forth.

BṬA (metathesis of **ṬBA**) to sink. **ʿubmia nibṭa unasqunh̠** AM 33:14 if he sinks in water they will get him up.

bṭaha AM 105 a family name.

bṭulana a miscopying of **buṭlana.**

bṭilta (rt. **BṬL**) adj. fem. st. emph. spoilt, invalidated. **taga d̠-malkuta bṭilta** DC 43 G 20 f. crown of invalidated kingliness.

BṬL (בטל, حطل) to be invalid, useless, vain, of no account; (of days) to be inauspicious; to be of no avail, be perishable, be null; to vanish; pa. to destroy, make void, annul, disqualify.

Pe. Pf. ***bṭil** became useless, vain (IM Gl. has a wrong vowel); **biṭlat hanath̠ masiqta** ATŠ (often) that *masiqta* was void (invalid), special pl. **bṭiliun rba ušualia** ATŠ I no. 91 (and often) teacher and novice are invalidated; fem. **uʿbidata kulhin bṭilian** ATŠ I no. 91 (several times) and all the rites are invalid. Impf. **nibṭul** he will vanish MG 219:18; **malka nibṭul mn kursia** AM 271:14 the king will abdicate his throne; **ulanibṭul mn hazin zhara** DC 9 & ATŠ (often) and doth not neglect this warning; **tibṭul** *ea invalida(bi)t(ur)* MG 216:bottom; **malkuta minh̠ tibṭul** Gy 50:13 his kingship will be annulled; pl. fem. **nibiṭlan** MG 213:10, 228:7. Impt. **bṭul** (often, esp. in exorcisms) vanish, become impotent. Act. pt. **baṭil, baṭla** (s.v.), pl. **baṭlia, baṭlin.** Participial pres. **baṭilna lbišutun** Gy 107:8 I annul their wickedness. Pass. pt. **bṭil** ATŠ II no. 3, 7 deprived. Inf. **mibṭal baṭil** CP 27:5, ML 31:10, Gy 370:11 will certainly perish, is vanity.

Pa. Pf. with suff. **baṭilnh̠** we destroyed him MG 277:21; **baṭilnun** we destroyed them MG 283:5. Impf. **nibaṭil** MG 213:11, **tibaṭil** MG 29:bottom, 226:antep.; with suff. **libatlh̠** Gs 62:1 *dele(bi)t eum.* Act. pt. **mbaṭil** (often) *invalida(bi)t,* Pass. pt. (of a day) **mbaṭal hu** ATŠ I etc. (*often*) it is good for nothing; pl. **iumia . . . šaiia . . . d̠-mbaṭlin** PD 822 days . . . hours . . . which are inauspicious; **mbaṭlia rahmaiun** RD C 12 their devotional prayers are made void; fem. pl. **mrahqan umbaṭlan** DC 43 far-removed and made impotent. Participial pres. **mbaṭilna** Jb 110:9, 12 I shall make void MG 231:6.

Ethpe. **ʿbṭil** (**ʿtbaṭal ubṭil haila d̠-hšuka**) HG they were brought to nought (and the power of the darkness ceased and became unavailing).

Ethpa. Pf. **ʿtbaṭal** s. ethpe. Impf. (**uiad̠harun kauariš bbabil**) **unitbaṭlun** AM 272:21 (and foreigners will appear in Babylon) but are brought to nought; fem. **nibaṭlan** *eae dele(bu)ntur* MG 213:9. Impt. (**bṭul**) **utbaṭal** DC 37 become (powerless and) unavailing; (**zha aṭar ukbuṣ**) **utbaṭal** DC 40 (tremble, begone,) be (squeezed and) annulled.

Der.: **baṭla, buṭlana** (miscp. **bṭulana**), **bṭilta.**

BṬN (حطى, der. from Aram. בִּטְנָא) to grow a belly, have a belly, become swollen, pregnant; to conceive.

Pe. Pf. **bṭin** (*often*), **bṭun** Gy 102:16 he became swollen, conceived MG 218:14 f.; **bṭin bnia d̠-tiniana** Gy 296:15 the sons of the Second conceived (an idea); **biṭnat bgauh̠ d̠-ʿur** she became pregnant with Ur; **baṭinta biṭnat** (var. **baṭnat**) **bṭiniana** Gy 79:29 (var. DC 22. 74) the pregnant woman became pregnant for a second time; **biṭnat hašabta** Gy 295:24 his thought conceived; with encl. **bṭanbun lrazia** ATŠ I no. 227 he conceived the mysteries. Impf. **ʿbṭun uʿdul** Gy 95:17 I shall be pregnant and bear forth. Pt. **baṭna** (*often*) she is pregnant; **gabra baṭin** (var. **baṭun**) **mn qudam ʿnta ʿu ʿnta baṭna mn qudam gabra** Gy 201:ult. doth the man conceive before the woman or doth the woman conceive before the man?; pl. **baṭnia ʿlania . . . uṭuna ṭaina** DC 35 the trees swell with fruit . . . and bear fruit; **baṭnin unapšin** ATŠ I no. 4 they become pregnant and multiply, uṭuna baṭnia Gy 248:15 and are pregnant with a burden (of fruit); fem. pl. uʿnšia uhiuaniata labaṭnan AM 270:6 and women and beasts will not become pregnant. Participial pres. ubaṭnana ušamnana DC 12. 143 and I become big-bellied and grow fat; baṭnit thou art pregnant MG 232:11; with encl. uʿnšia baṭnibun Gy 24 and women are pregnant with them.

Gl. 61:1 f. missp. حبل *praegnari* آبستن شد.

Der.: **baṭna, baṭin, baṭinta, buṭunta, buṭna, biṭna.**

BṬŠ (בְּטַשׁ, Syr. der. ܒܘܼܛܫܵܐ LS) to tread, tread down, tread underfoot, tread with contempt, kick, kick out, trample, stamp.

Pe. Pf. **bṭaš bligraiun** Jb 44:11 they kicked out with their feet; **biṭušta lmhara bṭaš** Jb 156:9 f. he stamped with his feet on the poop (: beaked end of a marsh boat); with encl. **baṭšibh̲** Gs 14:20, Jb 276:6 I stamped on it. Impf. ‭ꟼ(h̲?) **nibṭuš** DC 43 J 127 he stamps on him; with encl. **hiuaniata tibṭišibh̲** AM 52:4 animals will kick him. Act. pt. **mahia ubaṭiš** ATŠ I no. 257 he striketh and kicketh; pl. **baṭšin bihdadia umitrandidia** ATŠ I no. 267 they kick out at each other and are aroused; less regular (by analogy of the special pl. ending of the pf.) **ʿtlun ligria ulabaṭšin** DC 44. 1049 they have feet but kick not. Pass. pt. **mitirin hanatun razia dal bgauaihun ubṭiš uham** ATŠ I no. 267 the mysteries that moved within them are awakened and kicked out and waxed hot. Inf. with encl. **lmibṭišbh̲** Gy 197:15 to stamp on it.

Der.: **biṭušta.**

bi- an occasional form of the encl. prep. **b** (q.v.).

biad 1 (*often*) by the hand of, by means of.

biad 2 AM 287:16 = **baiad.**

biaban (P. بيابان) desert. **mištadin uazlin bbiaban** DC 46. 120:8 they become crazy and go into the desert.

biariata a var. of **biriata** (s. **biria 1**). **uṣipria uhiuaniata ubiariata** ATŠ I no. 224 and birds and beasts and cattle.

bibia 1 a *malwâša* woman's name.

bibia 2 Sh. ʿAbd.'s copy of Gs 16:paen. a var. of **biria 1.**

bigar in **arqa bigar** s. **arqabigal.**

bida 1 (**b** + **ʿda**) AM (*often*) by the hand of, by one's own hand.

bida 2 (cf. ܒܣܛܪ near to [the river, the sea, the road] LS) orig. prep. used substantivally, pl. **bidia** sides, banks. **mn trin bidia d̲-nahra** DC 23. 761 f. from the two banks of a river.

bidia 1 AM 197 Bedouins BZ 121 n. 11.

bidia 2 a place-name BZ Ap. II. **daura d̲-arbaiia ubidia qarilh̲** AM 197:13 a settlement of nomads, they call it B.; **ubidia umadina** AM 205:4 Bidia and Madina.

bidqa (rt. **BDQ I**) breach, fissure, cleft. **bidqa ʿbdiq** s. **BDQ I** ethpe.; **bidqa d̲-lamistakar** Gs 9:14 a cleft which cannot be filled; **bidqa rama** Jb 3:4, 5:5 the great breach.

bidraq alaha d̲-lšidia udaiuia mšalat DC 40. 927 the god B, who ruleth devils and demons (*or* by the god Ydrag who . . . ?)

bihda (ܒܚܕܐ) at once, immediately. **umarkabata mitgania bihda** DC 28 and the ships sank down at once (var. **bihdadia** together).

bihdad (P. بهداد) a *malwâša* man's name; a celestial being; a king: **bihdad malka** Gy 384:6 the king B. (a Sassanid king); **haizak šadrh̲ lbihdad ašganda** DC 41 then he sent B., the Messenger.

bihdadia (**b** + **hdadia**) together. Gl. 38:2 جميعاً *simul* همه; 44:6 بعضهم بعض *ad, invicem* يكباره.

bihum (etym. unsure, perh. Ar. بهم) strange (?), stranger (?). **alana lbihum d̲-atia rihh̲ maziz** DC 3 = ŠQ 18:19, CP 235:16 paen. I go to the stranger (?) whose invigorating perfume is coming; **anat alaha burkan d-ana qalana lbihum** DC 3, ŠQ 19:27 thou, God, bless me that I may go to the stranger (?); **malka gamarlia alpa d̲-zuzia d̲-ana qalana lbihum** ŠQ 19:21 the king bestowed on me 1,000 *zuzim* that I might go to the stranger; **aqimlh̲ šaia lbihum** ŠQ 18:30, CP 237:5 he establisheth splendour for the stranger. (In all places the word designates the bridegroom.)

bihzad (P. بهزاد) a man's name; a supernatural being. **bihzad iaia** RD F 12 the beautiful B.; **raiia bihzad** RD A 6 the shepherd B.

bihnaša (obscure. P. به + Mand. **anaša**?): **bihnaša d̲-aba hu, bihnaša d̲-ʿma hu** RD B 34 f., 36 (var. DAb **bihnušh̲**) . . . which is the father, . . . which is the mother. (The word 'origin' might suit the context.)

bihnuš (P. بهنوش) HG 142 a man's name.

bihrai AM 256:21 a pers. name (perh. inst. of **bihram** q.v.).

bihram (P. بهرام) a pers. name, Behram; a genie of P. origin, mentioned often in the baptismal formula MG xxxii n. 1, MR 105:20, 225:bottom, CP Ind., ML Ind., MMII Ind., MSt 106 f., HpGn 33, 42, 279. Popularly identified with Abraham MMII 265 f., ZDMG 1956 360. Other forms of the name: **bahran, bihran, bihrun** s.vv. **bihram** = **šamiš** RD 10 B. (identified with) the Sun; **bihram** = **šdum** RD 20 B. (one of the 7 names of) Šdum (q.v.); **bihram arqa** RD A 1 the land (of) B.; **bihram zuṭa** RD B 77, 90, 98 B. the Less (son of Ptahil), cf. DAb Ap.; **bihram rba** (very often in liturgical texts) B. the Great; **malka bihram rba** Morg. 5:5 the king (: angel) B. the Great; **bihram br rurbia** CP 29:19, ML 35:5; **bihram rba br rurbia** CP 25:3, ML 27:8, 40:5. B. (the Great) son of the Great (Life); **bit bihram** Gy 375:11 the House of B.; **bit bihram rba d̲-hiia** Gy 319:4; **bihram ʿutra** Gy 377:23; **iardna d̲-bihram** RD A 1 the jordan of B.; **bihram d̲-qaiim lkiph̲ d̲-iardna** RD 44, 45 B. who standeth on the bank of the jordan; **bihram maria d̲-spinta** RD 4 B. the owner of the boat; **sukana d̲-bihram** RD 5 B.'s steering-paddle; **maṭarta d̲-bihram rba brh̲ d̲-ptahil** RD C 3 the watch-house of B. the Great son of P. (cf. **bihram zuṭa** [above] called also P.'s son); **bihram br hiia** RD D 9 B. son of the Life; **bihram uram** ML 18:1, 41:2, 145:3, 229:3 B. and R.; **bihram brh̲ d̲-adam** CP 94:29, ML 120:13 B. son of A.

bihran a rarer var. of **bahram, bahran, bihram, bihrun** (s. vv.).

bihrana (rt. **BHR I**) glitter. **kulh̲ mlia bihrana** DC 3 all full of glitter.

bihrat ('She-Chose' **BHR I,** or 'She-Shone' **BHR II**) name of a female light-spirit MMII 245. **bihrat anana** Jb 16:5, CP 140 (d):14 the cloud (: spouse) B.; **abatur br bihrat** Morg. 87:15 = CP 199 (a) penult. Abatur son of B.

bihrun a var. of **bihran, bihram** (q.v.) Uthra 544, Jb ii 216 n. 3, ML Ind. The name could be otherwise explained as 'They-(i.e. the Life)-Chose-Me'. (**BHR I**). **bhir ubihrun** CP 140 (d):4, Morg. 72:2 etc. (*often*) 'The-Chosen-One' and 'They-Chose-Me'.

bihruta (**BHR II**) light, brightness. **galilulia . . . lhamša iumia d̲-bihruta** ATŠ II no. 45 reveal to me . . . about the five days of light.

bihria (**BHR II**) pl. illumined, illustrious. Sg. not found. May be a miscopying of **bhiria** (**BHR I**). **ʿtbar bihria** ATŠ they shone out, the illumined ones.

biuata a var. of **bauata** pl. of **buta.**

biz (cf. **baz** 1) a demon. **biz sahra, biz daiua** RD B 47 the demon B.

bizbaṭ a demon (applied to Muḥammad's father) Jb ii 193 n. 3. **bizbaṭ sahra** Jb 199:13, 200:13 the devil B.; **bizbaṭ abuhun d̲-sahria** Oxf. roll 365, DC 43 J 162, father of demons; **ahmaṭ br bizbaṭ sahra** Gy 29:21 Aḥmad (= Muḥammad) son of the devil B.; **mahamad br bizbaṭ** Gy 61:7 M. son of B.

bizuna (rt. **BZA**) crevice, cleft, hole, rift MG 140:11. **bizuna d̲-šušmana** Gy 188:9 an ant-hole.

bizta (בִּיזְתָּא, ܒܙܬܐ rt. **BZZ**) plundering, looting. **d̲-rmun bizta rmibun** Gy 119:8 those that take to plundering, I have given over; **baith̲ lhurba qaiim uap qinianh̲ lbizta** Gy 277:7 his house standeth (open) to ruin and also his possessions to looting.

biṭaruata, bisṭauata (comp. with **bi(t)-** 'house'; both varr. seem to complete one another, so that the original form might have been ***bisṭaruata**; the 2nd part of the comp. might be **אסטלא**, *στήλη*, or **אסטריא**, *στρατεία*). **utlatma ušitin alpia šdilh̲** DC 8 and 360,000 land-marks are set in it (or read **bisṭahata** regions?).

biṭušta (rt. **BṬŠ**) a violent movement with the foot, a kick. **biṭušta . . . bṭaš** s. **BṬŠ** pe. pf.

biṭna a var. of **buṭna.**

biia (ܒܝܥܐ orig. pl. of **bita,** used in Mod. Mand. as sg.) egg(s). **hazin baba d̲-psaqa d̲-ʿsata kdub ala biia d̲-zagata ʿkuma** (read **ʿkumta** or **ʿkumtia**) DC 46. 30:1 f. write this fever-cutting charm on an egg of a black hen.

bikur lban a var. of **bikrilban** (q.v.). AM 130: 6 f.

bikta DC 22. 385 a var. of **bakta** Gy 389:3 (v.s. **bakta**).

bikrilban (Ar. بخور ألبان) AM 130 inhalation of leaves of the nutmeg tree.

bil 1 (Bab. *Bēlu*) Bel (god), Jupiter (planet) MM II 81. As pr. n. always in st. abs. MG 300:bottom. **ana hu bil alaha rba d̲-babil** DC 40. 680 I am Bel, the great god of Babylon; **šubaia bil** Gy 27:20 f. the seventh (devil is) B.; **bil lhama uhamra aitia** Gy 106:12 B. brought bread and wine; **lbil plaglh̲ raza d̲-mia** Gy 112:12 to B. they allotted the mystery of the water; **bil bšuhbh̲ d̲-napšh̲ nsab asa** Gy 115:12 B. in his own pride took the myrtle; **bil bšuṭṭa mhaith̲** Gy 119:1 I hit B. with the whip; **qala d̲-bil qra** Gy 229:13 the voice which B. had cried; **baba hurina d̲-qra bil** Gy 228:20 another sect which B. created; Gy 379:9 ff. Jupiter; **bil kukba** Gy 393:10, 18 the star J., **kukba bil** Gy 385:11 id.; **bil kukba ṭaba** AM J. the good star; **bil maria sipra** Morg 268/27:29 B. the owner of the book; **bil maria alahia** Oxf. roll g 933. B. the Lord of gods; **bil rba** Jb 235:12 the Great B.; **angʿil d̲-bil qarilh̲** Gy 121:13 A. whom they call B.; **baba d̲-bil** Gy 231:3 the sect of B.; **baba d̲-qra bil** Gy 121:14 (cf. above Gy 228:20); **guran bil** RD 29 G. (a name given to) B.; **maṭarta d̲-bil** RD C 19, 23, 24 the purgatory of B.; **mnata d̲-bil** Gy 380:2 the portion of B.; **uamur bil mikal ubil mištia uʿlh̲ bil mirmia riha** Lond. roll A 650 f., 726 f. (a secret? injunction to the priest at the moment of his own communion. An inheritance from Bab. religion?)

bil 2, bila (בַּעֲלָא, ܒܥܠܐ) lord, master, husband MG 14:19, 16:15, 70:bottom, 101:2. Pl. with suff. **bilaihin** *mariti earum* MG 181:paen. f. **umn bilh̲ kima umuma maškia** AM 54:3 and she will incur fever and blemish from her husband; **adunai ubilai** (an exorcism) my Lord and Master. Comp. **bildbaba, bilidbaba, bildina** (s.vv.).

bilaur, bilaura (ܒܠܘܪܐ LS) crystal. Var. **bilur** 1 (q.v.). **kapta d̲-bilaura** DC 41. 198 a crystal bowl; **ṭariana d̲-mn bilaur dakia** DC 41. 172 a table (: tray) of pure crystal; **gimra d̲-bilaur** RD 7 a jewel of crystal.

bilaita (בליתא, ܒܠܝܬܐ) crumbling, breaking into small pieces. **uhad minaihun d̲-qalit atna ldarmania bbilaita** AM 287:6 and add one of them that thou hast baked to the remedies, breaking it into small pieces.

bildbaba, bilidbaba, bʿldbaba, bldbaba, blidbaba (ܒܥܠܕܒܒܐ from Akk. *bēldabābi*) enemy, adversary MG 27:4, 187:9. Pl. **bildbabia.**

bildina (ܒܥܠܕܝܢܐ) opponent-at-law, prosecutor, adversary MG 309: middle. adversary-at-law. **uanpia bildina latihzun** CP 80:20, ML 136:6, DC 3 and ye will not see the face of your adversary-at-law.

biluqia a var. of **bluqia** (q.v.). **umarganiata biluqia mitrišbun** ATŠ II no. 258 and as if they were set with dazzling pearls.

bilur 1, bilura 1 (cf. **bilaura** above, further *βήρυλλος*, Ar. loan-w. بلور) crystal, jewel. Var. **billur.** Pl. **biluria. bilur dakia** Gy 9:20, **bilura dakia** ŠQ pure crystal. Also as adj.: **mia hiia biluria nahiria** DC 51. 105 living, crystal, bright waters.

bilura 2 a musical instrument Jb ii 63 n. 1. Pl. **biluria. libat bilura šdat** Gy 336:1 L. threw away her musical instrument; **nišibih̠ bbiluran uzmaran** Jb 58:12 let us captivate him with our musical instruments and our songs; **biluria uzmara** Jb. 59:11 musical instruments and singing; **qarnia ubiluria** Gy 113:5 horns and musical instruments (perh. trumpets); **biluria uambubia** Gs 75:14 trumpets and flutes.

bilura 3 (cf. בְּלוּרִיתָא J.) plait, skein, cocoon, twining, chain, rope, wreath, toils, coils: **kḏ bilura ḏ-mn šaraia ʿṣṭarar mn zimta ḏ-mn pumh̠ ḏ-tulita nipqat . . . ubilura ḏ-hʿ (ḏ-)bita ʿlaita qarilh̠** ATŠ I no. 279 like the cocoon (or 'skein') formed of silk from the thread that issued from the mouth of the (silk-)worm . . . and the cocoon that they call the Celestial Egg; **umikdib** (var. **mikdid**, read **mikdir**) **bilura ʿlh̠** ATŠ I (var. DC 6) no. 280 and a skein (or 'cocoon') is wound about it; **uasa uklilia ubilurh̠ ulbušia** ATŠ II no. 57 the myrtle and the wreath and its twining and its clothing (i.e. the wrapping in the ritual of the pihta round the wreath); **ukul kukba bilura gaṭina luat šamiš ʿtlh̠** ATŠ II no. 233 and each star has a slender chain with Shamish (i.e. each star is lightly linked to the sun); **klila ana ḏ-bilura** Gs 122:10, 13, 14 I am a wreath of plaited coil; **ruha . . . barkalh̠ bbilura** Gy 115:16 R. . . . blessed (hist. pres.) him in her crown (could also be **bilura 2**).

biliaiil (בְּלִיַּעַל) DC a spirit of corruption.

billur = **bilur 1. hazin ṭura ḏ-billur hʿ** DC 7 this is a mountain of crystal.

bilidbaba a var. of **bildbaba** (q.v.).

bimanda (comp. from **bi[t]** + **manda**) cult-hut. Pl. **bimandia. ubnun bimandia** HG 7 and they built cult-huts. Sg. DC 41. 160, 167 etc. Gl. 144:11 defectively (syn. with **škinta**) كنيسة *ecclesia* كليسا; 154:2 id. مجمع *synagoga*; 171:11 id. هيكل *templum*.

bimar (P. بيمار) sick, infirm. Var. **bamar. lbr anašia bimar abidna** DC 46. 107:9 I make human beings sick; **ḏ-bamar ubhuš hauia** DC 46. 107:3 so that he becomes sick and unconscious.

bin– v.s. **binat-, binia.**

bina 1 (בִּינָא) hair, thread, string. **basara ubina uʿqamra ḏ-para uparta** DC 40. 789, 805, cf. DC 26. 768 with a bond and the hair and wool of a ram lamb and a ewe lamb; **basara arqa ubina uqamra ḏ-para** DC 40. 805 by a bond, a thong and a hair and (a strand of) wool of a ram lamb.

bina 2 (בִּינָא, ܒܺܝܢܳܐ) tamarisk. **aṭirpa ḏ-bina** DC 37 tamarisk leaves; **ḏ-rumana udbina** DC 43 J 100 of pomegranate and of tamarisk.

bina 3 (pass. pt. of **BUN I**) penetrating, discerning. **kma bina bintak** s. **BUN I** pe. pass. pt.

bina 4 (rel. to **bina 1**, cf. בִּינָא iii J) a thin thing, leech. **ʿu daiua hu niṣpia kḏ bina** (a *qmâhâ*) if he be a devil, he shall be squeezed like a leech.

binat–, binia, bit 3, abinia (Gen. Sem. cf. LS s. ܒܝܢܬ, ܒܝܢܬܐ) between, betwixt MG 22:middle, 195:3. With other prep. **mn (a)binia, mn binat-, binia l-** (and **bit l-**) MG 197:10 f. With suff. **binataian** (often) within us, between us; **nišmata ḏ-napqa mn binataikun** Gy 19:11 the souls which went out from amongst you; **binataihun, binataiun** (often) from amongst them; **hiia mn binun qrun** Gy 342:4 the Life created me from Itself (lit. from amongst themselves, pl.). Without suff. always **(a)binia**, var. **binʿ** (exceptionally **bʿnia** IM Gl.): **binia lʿ ulak** Gs 60:1 between me and thee; **umiṣra binia hda lhda laiit** Gy 9:19 but there is no limit between one and another; **binia kisia lziua ubinia galalta latar ksia** Gs 83:23 between the hidden and the radiance, and between the revelation and the hidden place; **binia bisrak lʿumbak ubinia ʿumbak lilbušak** DC 44 between thy flesh and thy bosom, and between thy bosom and thy garment.

biniana (בִּנְיָין, בִּנְיָן, ܒܶܢܝܳܢܳܐ) building, construction, frame-work, design, composition, edifice, something put together, (of body) structure, constitution MG 136:12. St. abs. & cstr. **binian.** Pl. **biniania.** With suff. **binianh̠** (var. **bʿnianh̠**), **binianun** (var. **bnianun**) IM Gl. **badmu baita biniana bgauh̠ lgaṭ hu baita šumh̠** ATŠ I no. 263 like a house, a design is held to therein, and its name is 'a house'; **biniana kulh̠ lgaṭ bihdadia** DC 27 he held the whole construction together; **taga mauqar mn kul biniana** DC 36 the crown is more honoured than any construction; **aminṭul ḏ-biniana hazin qašiša** DC 48. 259 because this composition is ancient; **riša ḏ-biniana** ATŠ II no. 12 the beginning of construction (creation); **biniana uginza** DC 48. 214 f.

binta 1 (rt. **BNA** = **BUN II** = **BNN II**) dwelling, house, construction, building MG 83:15 f. Pl. **binata.** Fem. **binta bna** Gy 104:16, 17 he buildeth a building; **binta lqudamh̠ labna** Jb 170:10 he built not a building for himself, **binta lnapšh̠ labna** Gy 218:13 id.; **bintai dilai** Oxf. 596 my own building; **dmutai ubintai** Jb 26:2 my likeness and my stature ii 32 n. 6; **mqaima binth̠** Gy 16:7 his building is raised; **ʿbun binta lṭabia** Oxf. 18 a I shall build a building for the good ones; **titibnia ḏ-šanai binta** ŠQ a wonderful building shall be built; **binta ḏ-bainia hiia** CP 135:10 the building which the Life buildeth; **baiin binta** Gy 89:4 he buildeth a building; **bnalh̠ binta** Gy 104:10 f. he built a building for him; **binatun uškinatun** Gy 10:17 their buildings and their dwellings; **šaba binata** ATŠ II no. 150, DC 27. 423 seven dwelling-places; **binta ḏ-rihania** ATŠ II no. 188 incensory; **kḏ atitun lbintaikun** ATŠ II no. 334 when ye come home; **binta ḏ-mitbnia lnišimta** ATŠ II no. 337 an edifice erected for the soul.

binta 2 (rt. **BUN I**) insight, discernment, perception, intelligence. **baiia binta** Jb 178:2, DC 22. 366 he seeketh discernment (Pet. Gy 370:2 has **bania binta** 'he buildeth a building' for the latter, cf. **binta 1**); **babinta baiia** PD 1048 he seeketh with discernment; **agbar ʿlan**

bintan uqalan uʿrutan utušbihtan DC 3, **gbar ʿlan** CP 88:10, Q 41:20, ML 109:1 strengthen in us our discernment, our voice, our fervour and our praise; **baiia ruaha mn bintak** Jb 28:11 he seeketh respite from thy insight; **lika kušṭa bbintak** Jb 28:11 there is no uprightness in thy insight; **kma bina bintak** s. **BUN** I pe. pass. pt.; **bbintẖ hailẖ ninpuš** ATŠ in intelligence his powers will increase.

NOTE: Sometimes difficult to distinguish from **binta 1**.

bisada (Nöld. ***bisadia**, בְּיסַדְיָא, ܒܣܕܝܐ) PD xi 12a bolster, pillow. Varr. **basada**, **bsada** (q.v.). MG 42:bottom, 183 s. באיתא.

bisṭaha (comp. with **bi**[t], to the 2nd part cf. A. سطح) region, area. Fem. Pl. ***bisṭahata** (?, cf. **biṭaruata**). **bisṭaha rabtia ḏ-glala** DC 43 J 89 a great region of ice.

bisṭauata RD A 4 a var. of **biṭaruata** (q.v.).

bisiata (fem. pl. of the pass. pt. of **BSA**) despised, vile, ugly. Masc. and sg. not found. **hiuia bisiata** DC 49. 49 ugly snakes.

bisimta fem. of **basim** (q.v.).

bismar (coll. corruption of Ar. مِسْمَار) nail. **kdub lbismar urmiẖ bnura** DC 46 write on a nail and cast it into the fire.

bisqa (prep. **b** + **ʿsqa**) by the seal of. **bisqa ušum hazim** DC 45 & 46 by the seal and name of this . . .

bisra (בִּסְרָא, ܒܣܪܐ) flesh, meat MG 107:9. St. abs. & cstr. **bsar** (s.v.) MG 152:7. **karkum ṭura ḏ-bisra** Gy 142:21 K. (: demon) a hill of flesh, similarly **krun ṭura rba ḏ-bisra** Gy 142:23, 143:4, 6; **ahia ḏ-bisra baṭlia** Gy 18:10 brothers of flesh perish; **lbuša ḏ-bisra uzma** Gy 193:7 clothing of flesh and blood; **ʿusṭla ḏ-bisra uzma** ibid. & l. 16 id., **ʿsṭuna ḏ-bisra uzma** Gs 6:24 the column of flesh and blood (: the body); **puma ḏ-bisra uzma** Gy 7:14 the mouth of flesh and blood; **gbil bisra uzma** Gy 257:20 formed of flesh and blood. Gl. 148:4 missp. لحم *caro* گوشت.

bisruta (abstr. from bisra) fleshiness, fleshliness MG 144:antep. f.

bistirqa a var. of **bastirqa.**

bišam a *malwâša* woman's name.

biṣra a miscop. of **baṣra**: **kupna bbiṣra umaṣur nihuia** Ṣâb.'s AM there will be hunger in Baṣra and M.

biqita, bqita (BAram. בִּקְעָא Syr. ܦܩܥܬܐ H. בִּקְעָה Ges. s.v.) region, plane; (in astrology) region, or sphere of influence. Pl. **biqata, biqiata. batia biqiata hauin ubiqiata batia hauin** Gy 387:23 houses will be turned to flat spaces, and flat spaces will be turned to houses; **uqaimia lbiqita** (var. **lbiqata**) **ḏ-ṣilmia** AM 232:5 standing under the influence of Gemini: **babiqata ḏ-siana** s. **siana.**

bira 1, abira (בֵּירָא, ܒܐܪܐ, ܒܝܪܐ Akk. *būru*) well, pit, hole, cavity MG 102: 9. Fem. (like Syr., H. בְּאֵר, Ar. بئر) MG 160:3 f. St. abs. and pl. not found. **rbita** (var. **qrita**) **ḏ-qra ptahil** DC 22. 265 (var. Pet. Gy 270:3 f.) the sea (var. creation) which P. created is a well-spring; **kulhun babia trisar bira ḏ-lalam naṭarlun** Gy 277:14 f. all twelve gates (: sects) are a pit which keeps them for ever; **bira ḏ-mia tahmia** Gy 87:14 well of stagnant water(s); **aina ḏ-mia hu bira ḏ-manzia minẖ nipuq** ATŠ I no. 244 it is a spring of water, a well from which hair issues; **šadilia bbira d-ʿumqia** Gs 75:16 they cast me into a deep pit.

bira 2 (בְּעִירָא, ܒܥܝܪܐ) domestic cattle MG 71:5 f., 117:8. Fem. (like Syr.) MG 156:15. Pl. **biriata 2** MG 169:19, 171:6. **hiua bira** Gy 33:5, 17, 34:2, 100:11, 14, 124:8 f., AM (*often*) etc. domestic animals, cattle (opposed to **hiua bala**, s. **bala 2**); **hiuaniata ubiriata** Gy 12:19 (var. **hiuaniata biriata**) id. as pl. **bit biriata** DC 143 A 89 f.; DC 46. 17:10 etc. (*often*) cattle-shed.

bira 3 a var. of **biria 1.** Pl. **biriata** (s.v.). **bira ʿliṣa** ML 136:4 a narrow street. (CP 110:15 has **biria.**)

birud (Ar. برود) AM 287:19 cooling collyrium.

biruq a disease-demon of both sexes CP 33:16, ML 280. Varr. **buraq 1, buruq. biruq zakra uniqubta** ML 39:8 the male and female B.; **biruq zikria ubiruq nuqbata** DC 43 A 30 the male Biruqs and the female Biruqs.

birukta s. **birikta.**

biruqta (s. **buruqta, bruqta**) cataract. **biruqta mn ainẖ** Morg. 194:9 (remove) cataract from his eye; **aina biruqtia** (= **bruqtia**) eye whitened by cataract.

birzam a thorny plant of green and white colours. **ušauka ḏ-birzam ḏ-iaruq bhauria** DC 23. 771 and a thorn of a *birzam* which is green and white (or a green marsh-plant, cf. s. **hauria**).

biria 1 (rt. **BRR**, Nöld. *ܒܪܝܐ, ܒܪ̈ܝܬܐ cf. MG 17:3 ff., ZDMG xxv 673; Brockelm. from Akk. *bērēti* LS s. ܒܪ̈ܝܬܐ, ZDMG lxvii 108, Zimmern 45) street. Var. sg. **bira 3** (s.v.). St. emph. sg. not found. Pl. st. emph. **biriata 3** MG 148:5 f., 155:15 ff. **biria ʿliṣa** CP 110:15 a narrow street; **ʿzlia rmilẖ bšuqia usalita lpumaihun ḏ-biriata** DC 43 he threw his net into the markets and his fishing-net on the openings of the streets; **pumaihun d-biriata** Gs 8:2.

biria 2 a var. of **buria. ukariklẖ lʿšumia kulẖ kḏ biria** DC 43 J 102 (var. **buria** PA) and he rolls up the sky like a reed-mat.

biria 3 AM 205 a place-name BZ Ap. II.

biriauis (v. **piriauis**) = **biriauiš.**

biriauiš (v. **piriauis**) 'Full-of-Water' used as a pr. n. of a store of living water, a byname of the jordan, but also (mistakenly) for the 9th month of pregnancy. ML Ind. **biriauiš** (var. **biriauis**) **kana ḏ-mia hiia** CP 60:3 Oxf. roll f 208, 554, ML 76:4 (var. DC 53 nos. 44, 77) B. storing-place of living water; **naṭria trin ḏ-biriauiš** DC 41 two guardians of B. (cf. **trin naṭria ḏ-iardna** s. **šilmai**); **msakialẖ liahra tšaia ḏ-hu biriauiš** DC 41 it looks forward to the ninth month which is B.

biriata 1 (ܒܪ̈ܝܬܐ) pl. of **brita. gunian ḏ-biriata** Gy 277:8 the rebuke of creatures; **biriata tlata**

gaunia hinun ATŠ I no. 269, creatures are of three kinds.

biriata 2 pl. of **bira 2** (q.v.).

biriata 3 pl. of **bira 1, 3** (q.v.).

birihia, bit rihia (s. **bit**) fire-saucer. **šugh̲ lbirihia ušdia riha lbit rihia** DC 24. 102 wash the fire-saucer and place incense on it; **birihia hadta ubit riha** Lond. roll A 429; **birihia = bit rihia** Oxf. roll f 159, cf. 180, 258 ff.; **birihak** Lond. roll A 749 thy fire-saucer.

biriut (rt. **BRR**, cf. ܒܪܝܘܬܐ) outside, wilderness, desert. **lbiriut almia** s. **bariut**; **razan laglan liama unlanpaqnin lbiriut** CP 227:4 we revealed not our secret to the sea, nor gave out our wisdom to the wilderness.

birukta, birikta, birkta, burukta (בִּרְכְּתָא, ܒܘܪܟܬܐ) blessing MG 14:1, 109:15. Pl. **birkata, barakata, barukata. birikta d̲-ʿtibrikbh̲** (*often*) the blessing wherewith he was blessed; **miša d̲-birikta** Gy 227:12 the oil of the blessing.

birsim 1, brisam, brisim 2 (Ar. برسيم) clover, trefoil. **zaʿparan ubazra d̲-brisim bihdadia arib** DC 46. 103:11 mix together saffron and trefoil seed.

birqa (בַּרְקָא, ܒܪܩܐ) flash of lightning, lightning; dazzling whiteness MG 14:18, 107:8. **braq birqa** Gy 96:13 there was lightning; **kd̲ birqa** Gy 355:2 like a flash of lightning; **birqa biša** DC 43 an evil flash of lightning; **birqa šabiq lhahu hiuia** Oxf. roll g 579, 949 letting dazzling whiteness (come) upon that serpent; **himiana d̲-birqia** DC 26. 580 a girdle of lightnings; similarly Morg. 265/21:38, 267/24:24 f. etc. (often).

BIŠ (בְּאֵשׁ, ܒܐܫ) to be bad, evil.

Pe. Impf. **ulibh̲ nibiš** AM 262:3 and his heart becomes evil.

Der.: **biš(a)**, fem. **bišta, bišuta**, pl. **bišauata** (**bišuata**).

biš, biša (בִּישָׁא, ܒܝܫܐ) bad, evil, wicked MG 117:7. Pl. **bišia**. Fem. sg. **bišta**, pl. **bišata**. Masc. st. abs. **biš** and fem. st. emph. **bišta** used also as subst. MG 299:middle. **hakima lbiš** Gy 186:12 wise to evil; **lbiš mithašbia ʿlan** ML 108:10 they plan evil against us; **biš unsis** Gy 9:12 bad and sad; **biša d̲-bišuta minh̲ giblat** Gy 34:11 the Evil One by whom evil was formed; **kd̲ haza šuma biša** Gy 94:16 when the Evil One heard this; similarly 95:8; **haršia bišia** Black Magic (title of DC 45 & 46); **mn kul biš** DC 37. 424 from all evil.

bišuta (בִּישׁוּתָא, ܒܝܫܘܬܐ) evil, wickedness, harm. Fem. pl. **bišauata, bišuata** MG. 167:11. **bišuta kibrat** ML evil increased; **biša bbišuth̲ mipsiq** Gy 86:12 a wicked one will be cut off because of his wickedness; **bišuta uaqta nihuilh̲ . . . umn kulhin bišauata niplaṭ** AM 21:9–12 evil and distress will be his portion . . . but from all these evils he will escape.

bišlum (بی سلام Lidzb. Jb ii 46 n. 5; *islâm* influenced by *muslim* Pallis MSt 213, Nöld. ZA xxx 157 f.) (*a*) a designation of the Moslem era, (*b*) a var. of **bšlam** in peace. (*a*) **ṭubh̲ lman d̲-bhazin dara bsira d̲-bišlum šlim** Jb 45:1 f. hail to him who in this defective age of Bišlum (: imperfection, a pun, Lidzb. ii 46 n. 6; islam, cf. above) remained perfect; (*b*) Gy 125:8, Jb 41:9 in peace.

bištar (P. بیشتر) more (P. comparative, only in coloph. and the colloquial). **uʿka mindam d̲-bištar** DC 36:coloph. and there is something more.

bit 1 st. cstr. of **baita**. MG 150:2. Compounds:

bit ab, bit abu paternal house (s. **ab, aba**).

bit abatur Q 28:27 f. the House-of-A.

bit azaria (cf. P. آذر = آتش) DAb incense-cup, incense-brazier.

bit aina, bit ainh̲, bit ainia AM 83 etc. eye-sockets.

bit alahia Gy 388:2, AM (often) house of gods, pagan temple, Furlani, *I Termini* 354–8.

bit ama. Oxf. 38 a, **bit ama d̲-iahuṭaiia** Gy 56:7 house of the Jewish people, Jewish temple, Furlani, *I Termini* 354–8.

bit anašh̲, bit anašata home, family dwelling, paternal house; **bit anašak** thy home; **bit anašaihun** their home MG 182 f.

bit anpia, bit anph̲ AM (several times) face: **uniṭripilh̲ bit anpia** DC 43. 9 and they smite him on his face; **ulanidalalun bit anpaihun** DC 44 and they shall not raise their faces; **uṭlalh̲ bit anph̲** DC 43 A 12 f. and he hung it up before his face.

bit bhirta temple, sanctuary: **bhanata arqa d̲-bit bhirta** ATŠ II no. 418 in that world that is a sanctuary.

bit biriata cattle-shed (s. **bira 2**).

bit bnia, bit bnh̲ womb. **ubit bnh̲ zban zban kaiiblh̲** AM 58:4 and her womb sometimes pains her.

bit gbin(a) AM (several times) brow, forehead. **bit gbinai** CP 173:4, ML 210:11 my forehead.

bit ginza treasure-house, mod. **bit ginzia** library. **manda d̲-hiia nitriṣ lšumaihun bit ginzih̲** Gy 1:14 M.-d̲-H. shall set up their names in his treaure-house; **uaiil lbit ginzaihun** Jb 168:3 and they brought (them) into their treasure-house.

bit gnana bedroom, bridal chamber. **anat aiilth̲ lbit gnana ladam** Gs 20:17 f. thou didst take A. into his bridal chamber; **lqalh̲ napqan hidutata mn bit gnana** Gy 59:10 at his cry brides leave the bridal chamber.

bit dina court of justice, court-house, tribunal. **lbit dina mithaiab** ATŠ I no. 235 will be convicted at the tribunal.

bit haiuta (*a*) cattle-shed. **umuma** (var. **muta**) **bit haiuta huilh̲** AM 11:12 f. there will be blemish (var. deadly epidemic) in his cattle-shed, (*b*) womb (v.s. **haiuta 2**).

bit hurpia nest (s. **hurpa 2**).

bit hiuta AM 16:16 womb.

bit hiia Gy 368:24, CP and ML (*often*) the House-of-Life.

bit zaina, prison, dungeon, house of detention. **ʿsir bit zainh̲** Gy 215:13 is bound in the prison; **bit zaina iatib** ATŠ II no. 80 shall dwell in prison; **ubmaṭarta d̲-bit zaina ništaial** ATŠ II no. 351 and he will be put to the question in Purgatory, that is the place of detention; **kḏ mapqutulẖ lbit zaina barqa** ATŠ II no. 333 when ye banished him to the prison-house on earth.

bit zibna house of ransom (s. **zibna 2**).

bit kabiṣia s. **kabiṣia.**

bit kadpia s. **bit 3.**

bit kništa (בֵּית הַכְּנֶסֶת) synagogue: **lamṣiit lmizal lbit kništan** Jb 71:13 shouldst thou not come to our synagogue?, cf. also 72:5.

bit lahmia Gy 359:22 Bethlehem.

bit madbha Gy 227:6 sanctuary (place of the altar).

bit maudala Gy 59:10 birth-chamber.

bit mazgda house of worship, mosque, shrine. **liliata . . . bit mazgdaihun** DC 43 Liliths . . . in their house of worship.

bit maksia (*often*) lit. custom-house, house of correction, house of penalties.

bit manda (v. **bimanda**) cult-hut.

bit masgda = **bit mazgda** MG 186:paen.

bit masia Or. 328:23 seat for easing the bowels.

bit maškna sanctuary hut. Pl. **bit mašknia. bimanda bit maškna** HG in the sanctuary, in the cult-hut; **nišalmunun lbit mašknia ubuta utušbihta nalpinun** ATŠ I no. 235 they shall give them over to the sanctuary and teach them prayer and praise.

bit mṭalalia s. **mṭalalia.**

bit mizal, bit mizla (miscop. **mazla**) 'house' of destiny, horoscope, constellations governing fate. **ulilia hauia bit mizlak** Gy 362:15 and how (lit. whither) shall be thy destiny; **mhatam hailẖ kulẖ bit mizlẖ umhatam bit titaiia** DC 43 all his forces are sealed, his fate (is sealed) and sealed is the lower abode.

bit mizgda a miscop. of **bit mazgda.**

bit miṣria frontier, borderland (lit. place of boundary lines). **kḏ mṭainin alma ḏ-bit miṣria** Gy 152:9 when we came to the frontier; **maṭit bit miṣria** Gy 154:7 I came to the frontier; **ubit miṣria iatbit** Gy 158:17 f. and I sat at the frontier; **ʿtib bit miṣria** Gy 159:20; **usliq lbit miṣria** Gy 168:9 and he went up to the frontier; **ukul mahu ḏ-abad abihdẖ hauia biluatẖ alma lbit miṣria** ATŠ II no. 304 and all that it (: the soul) did will be with it, accompanying it, until (it reacheth) the borderlines.

bit mqadšia (בֵּית הַמִּקְדָּשׁ) the Jewish Temple. **azal lbit mqadšia** Jb 66:15 they (: the cohens) went to the Temple; **guṭra gṭar bit mqadšia** Jb 67:7, 69:10 smoke appeared in the T.; **uʿm azlat lbit mqadšia** Jb 127:13 and my mother went to the T.

bit naṭarta = **maṭarta.**

bit niṭupta Gy 172:14 House of Pre-existence (lit. 'House-of-the-Drop').

bit sipra (בֵּית הַסֵּפֶר , בֵּית סִפְרָא) school.

bit ʿsura DC 3 etc. prison-house.

bit pirṣa Gs 20:18 (Norb. misread **bit piruna**) house of lechery.

bit ṣihiun (ܒܶܝܬ ܨܶܗܝܽܘܢܳܐ Dt 8: 15) Gy 180:21 arid, barren land MG 140:5 f.

bit qubria (בֵּית קְבָרוֹת) graveyard, burial ground, cemetery. **kul tarmida ḏ-lnapaqa nisaq lbit qubria** ATŠ II no. 343 every priest that 'raises' (i.e. performs a *lofani* or ritual meal for) a dead man at the burial ground.

bit qilba (cf. s. **qilba**) head-rest, pillow. **bit qilba ḏ-hiduia sadania ḏ-arqa hua bsada ḏ-hiduia** CP 222:3, ŠQ 15:9, Par 15 f. 11b, 25 f. 15b the head-rest of the bridegroom is clods of earth, it is the pillow of the bridegroom.

bit qirsa s. **qirsa.**

bit rahmia House-of-Devotions. **ia baba rba ḏ-bit rahmia iaqiria** Morg. 3:paen. O Great Door of the House of precious Devotions!

bit razia Gy 223:2 House-of-Mysteries (refers to Christian sanctuary).

bit riha = **biriha** MMII Ind.

bit tarnaula s. **bit 2.**

bit tušlima, bit tušlimia (*often*) House of Perfection.

bit tinta DC 48. 32 bladder.

Separated from the noun: **bit hda ardba** Gy 392:7 f. the content of one *ardab*.

Names of countries: **bit arbaiia** Arabia, **bit girtaiia** Kurdistan, **bit hudaiia** (var. **hudšaiia**) the country of the Jews, Judæa, **bit hindauaiia** India, **bit miṣraiia** Egypt etc. (frequent in AM).

bit 2 st. cstr of **bita 1**: **bit tarnaula** DC 10 hen's (lit. cock's) egg.

bit 3 (sg. of בֵּינֵי = Mand. **[a]binia**; ܒܶܝܬ a doublet of ܒܶܝܢܳܬ = Mand. **binat-**) between, amongst MG 194 f. **bit kadpia** Gy 179:ult. the place between the shoulders (an original adverbial expression which became substantival) MG 197 n. 2. With **l**: **lbit** and **bit l-** s. **l-**; **bit ḏ- . . . bit ḏ** Gs 102:4 f., Q 37:ult. whilst, while as yet MG 466:4 f.; **adam btmamutẖ bit ḏ-la ʿda ubit ḏ-lapras** CP 81:5, ML 100:3 Adam, in his simplicity, whilst as yet he knew not, and whilst he understood not . . .

bita 1 (ܒܶܝܥܬܳܐ , ܒܶܝܬܳܐ) egg MG 110:bottom. St. cstr. **bit 2** (s. vv.). Pl. **biia, bʿiia** (s.vv.). **bita ḏ-iauna** AM 131:12 a dove's egg; **unitpaša kḏ bita maduria mn glala** DC 44 and crushed like a rotten egg with a stone; **umiṭria kḏ bita ḏ-ṭaria bglala** DC 40 and are beaten down like an egg that they strike with a stone; **uṭiriuk miṭria bita mn glala hibṭuk** DC 21 = JRAS 1938/3:24 and they rain blows on thee; (like) an egg by a stone they batter thee. Gl. 43:5 **bita** بيضة *ovum* تخم مرغ, 183:3 id.

bita 2 (spor.) a var. of **baita.**

bita 3 DC 22. 4 a miscop. of **buta** Gy 4:7.

bitpa (comp. with **bit**, v.s. **TPA**) cooking-vessel. Pl. **-ia. bitpia tlat** DC 48. 282, three cooking-vessels, cf. s. **kanuna.**

BKA (בְּכָא , ܒܟܳܐ Akk. *bakû*) to weep, cry, lament, mourn.

PE. Pf. **bka** he wept MG 4:1, IM Gl. (still used, pron. *boχâ*). Act. pt. **bakia** Gs 111:12 he weepeth; pl. **bakin** they weep IM Gl. Part. pres. **bakit** Gs 111:13 thou weepest; **iatbitun ubakitun** DC 34. 554 ye sit and weep.

Af. Pf. with suff. **abkith̲ kd̲ ianqa** Gy 91:1 I made him weep like a child MG 288:10 f. Act. pt. **mabkia** Gs 111:12 he maketh weep. Part. pres. **mabkit** Gs 111:13 thou makest weep. With encl. **mabkilh̲ (umagiklh̲)** AM 123:14 he makes him weep and laugh.

Der.: **bkita.**

bkarta DC 43 E 88 = **bukarta** (fem. of **bukra**).

bkita (בכיתא, H. with suff. בְּכִיתוֹ, Syr. only ܒܶܟ݂ܝܳܐ and ܒܟܳܝܳܐ) weeping, lamenting MG 56:7 f., 103:antep. With suff. **bkitun** MG 181:14 f.

bkitiar Zotb. 220 right 2 a var. of **baktiar.**

BKL (ܒܟܠ) the rt. of **mbakalata, mbaklauata** (s.vv.).

BKR (Gen. Sem.) to bring forth early, be early, first. Only in derr. **bakru** (Ar.), **bukra, bukraia,** fem. **bukarta,** var. **bkarta.**

BLA I (ܒܠܥ) (*a*) to swallow up, devour, (*b*) to be wounded, smitten, beaten, injured.

(*a*) Pe. Pf. **bla** Gy 83:6, 20 he swallowed; with suff. **bilh̲** he swallowed him IM Gl., **bilan,** var. **balan** he swallowed me up MG 270:20, **balinun** he swallowed them up MG 281:19. Impt. with suff. **bulan** swallow me up MG 271:7. Part. forms with suff. and encl. **ʿzil d̲-labalanak** Gy 143:17 go away lest I swallow thee up; **balalh̲ tanina** ATŠ II no. 309 the dragon shall devour him; **balinun** (var. **balilun**) **lmia siauia** Gy 83:7 (var. Sh. ʿAbd.'s copy) he swallowed the black waters. Inf. with encl. **ʿkamar mibilh̲** Sh. ʿAbd.'s copy of Gs. 7:19 (Pet. only **ʿtkamar bilh̲**) he swallowed him up again.

(*b*) Pe. Impf. **nibla** *verbera(bi)tur* MG 235:12, **d̲-atia niblh̲ bsikina skin** DC 37 (the demon) who cometh shall be wounded by a knife; **nibla brukba d̲-mia . . . nibla bnarga rba d̲-šrara** DC 37 he shall be smitten with a besom of water . . ., shall be smitten with a great axe of truth; **bparzla tibla** AM 63: penult. she will be wounded by an iron weapon; **anašia niblun** AM 195:10 people will be injured.

Ethpe. Only pt. **mibila** (s.v.).

Der.: (*a*) **blaiaiaiia, blaiia,** (*b*) **bilaita, mibila.**

BLA II (בלא, ܒܠܐ) to be worn out, fail, wear out, decay, grow old, waste away; pa. consume, waste away, corrupt.

Pe. Impf. **aqnia utauria niblun** AM 252:14 sheep and oxen will become feeble; **hiuaniata nibiliun** AM, less regular **nibilia** ibid. animals will become feeble. Pt. pl. **nišmatkun mibilh̲ balia** Gy 254:21 (var. DC. 22. 250 **mibilia ubalia**) your souls waste away; with encl. **ulabalih̲ lbušh̲** Gy 5:19 and his garment weareth not out; **d̲-labalilan razia sainia** DC 34. 689 lest evil mysteries corrupt me (as from ע״ו = ע״ע); **udbaililh̲ bnh̲** DC 46 whose children waste away.

Pa. Pf. with suff. **ušamiš . . . balih̲ rurbia** DC 36 ii no. 217 (as for) the Sun . . . the Great (Life) wasted him away (read **balunh̲** pl.); **sindlia ligrai d̲-balitinun** Gs 104:13 the sandals of my feet that I wore out; **sinia ligran d̲-balinhun** Gs 121:3 f. the shoes of my feet that we wore out MG 290:ult., 291:5. Pt. **mbalala** (s.v.).

Ethpe. Pt. **mibila** (s.v.), fem. pl. **mitbilan** AM 185:13 they will be rotten.

Ethpa. Pt. pl. (fem.) **tumria nitnapšun umitbalan** AM 185:13 dates will be abundant, but wither up (var. **mitbilan**).

Note: Sometimes difficult to distinguish from **BLA I b.**

Der.: **buliana, bulbulaia, blaita, mbalala, mibila.**

bla (**b** + **la**) without, with no . . . Var. **abla** (s.v.). **bla subianun** without their will, against their will MG 193:bottom; **bla ʿdana, bla zibna** (often) suddenly, at once, quickly, on a sudden, instantaneously; with suff. **bla zibnihun** Gy 223:1 etc. untimely; **kd̲ daiik šraga mn napšia bla ʿdana** AM 254:3 f. when a lamp goes out suddenly of itself; **arqa raṭna bla zibna umgalala** Jb 68:5 suddenly the earth speaketh and revealeth; **upraṭ purṭa brqiha bla zibna** ATŠ II no. 129 a rift appeared suddenly in the firmament; **bla zibna ʿtatna ʿlh̲ hatma** ATŠ II no. 129 I placed a seal on it at once; **qandilia bla ptiliata** ŠQ 18:5 oil lamps without wicks; **nišmata bla kilaiun mn pagraiin napqan** CP 372:5 souls depart from their bodies before their (allotted) span (: untimely); **bla ṭamun** without their will, unwillingly; **bla mata** without country, homeless, stateless.

blaṭin anbilaṭ an evil being MMII 18 n. 8.

blaiaiia, blaiia (rt. **BLA Ia**) swallowers, consumers. **blaiaiia hauin** ATŠ II no. 93 they will be consumers of ritual meals (?); **ṭabuta aklin blaiia hauin** DC 6 (a variant of the same passage) they eat (sacred) food, being communicants (?).

blaita (ܒܠܳܝܬܳܐ BLA II) worn-out fragment, rag. **lhad blaita d̲-kitana** DC 46. 130 (and often) on a linen rag.

blama (rt. **BLM**) gag, muzzle, bridle, fencing-about, protection. **tirmia . . . blama lspihatun** DC 44. 1031 she shall cast . . . a gag on their lips; **kibša ublama unhura** DC 40 conquest and protection and light.

bldbaba a var. of **bildbaba** IM Gl.

blugma = **balgam(a). zma umirta ublugma** ATŠ II no. 142 blood and bile and phlegm.

blum (rt. **BLM**) DC 44 an exorcizing spirit. Var. **blim.**

bluqia (rt. **BLQ**) [dazzling, being blinded by dazzling], dazzled blindness MG 147:6. Var. **biluqia** (s.v.). **man d̲-šaqilia bluqia mn ainai** Gy 236:6 who is it that removeth the blindness from my eyes?; **d̲-nišqilulh̲ ladam ab bluqia mn ainh̲** Gs 7:11 that they might remove the blindness from my father Adam's eyes; **mišqil bluqia mn ainh̲** ATŠ II no. 389 the blindness is removed from his eyes; **bluqia ainai ʿštqil** ATŠ II no. 146, the blindness of my eyes is removed.

blia = **ʿblia** (q.v.).

bligal s. **ligal.**

blidbabia AM 284:39 a var. of **bildbabia.**

blila (ܒܠܝܠܐ rt. **BLL**) idle, confused, muddled, useless, muddle-headed, stupid, irrational;

(rt. **BLA**) worn-out, decayed, corrupt, rotten. Fem. **blilta.** Pl. **blilia.** **ʿutria blilia** Gy 305:6, 12, ATŠ I no. 83 muddle-headed uthras, **ptahil blila** Gy 102:3, **abatur blila** Gy 306:17; **alma blila umbalala** Gs 129:22, Jb 90:2 corrupt and degenerate world; **umn ʿuṣrẖ baiia ḏ-napiq pugdamia blilia** ATŠ II no. 218 and he prayeth according to his fancy, so that confused words come out; **latizhariun zaharta blilta** ATŠ II no. 418 give them not vain admonition; **ukul br blila . . . hašuk ʿuṣrẖ** DC 36 but every blunderhead . . . his mind darkeneth; **lbušia ḏ-lablilia** (var. **ḏ-lambalilun** DC 31. 110:9 f.) AM clothes not worn out by use; **badmu pagra blila** DC 27 like a corrupt carcass; **razia blilia** ATŠ II no. 11 corrupt mysteries.

bliluta (ܒܠܝܠܘܬܐ, rt. **BLL**) depravity, confusion, irrationality: **zaniuta ubliluta** Gy 215:19 whoredom and depravity.

blim a var. of **blum.**

bliqa (pass. pt. of **BLQ**) dazzled by light, blinded. Pl. **bliqia.** **umalahia bliqia** DC 51 and sailors dazzled by light.

blita (בְּלִיתָא) doublet of **blaita** rag. **blita ḏ-kam** DC 46. 73:4 a rag of cotton cloth.

BLL (ܒܠܠ Akk. *balâlu* LS s. ܒܠ, Ges. s. בלל) to mix (together), confuse.

Pe. Pf. **rukbaihun ʿstar bal ularakšia** DC 33 and 37 their chariots were torn down, they were confounded, and stir not; with suff. **balinhun lšuba razia** Gs 124:4 he confounded the seven mysteries. Act. pt. with suff. **kulhun razia baililẖ** DC 34:640 all mysteries confuse him. Pass. pt. **blila** (s.v.).

Der.: **blila, bliluta.**

BLM (בלם, ܒܠܡ) to stop the mouth, bridle, muzzle, silence, gag, check.

Pe. Impf. **uniblum unisṭim** DC 40 and he checks and restrains; but **nistar uniblam** DC 40 he shall be bound and gagged; **niblim** DC 44. 198. Impt. **blum** (used as a name of an exorcizing spirit, s.v.); pl. with suff. **upkurulia ublumulia haria** DC 44 and tie and muzzle for me the men of position. Pass pt. **blim** (also as a var. of **blum** a name of a demon, s.v.); **blim uzim** DC 46 checked and held back; **ʿsnʿia uʿpika ublima** Gy 139:16 hideous, distorted, and mute; **ia blim br blim uminilih blimbẖ ublimia pugdamia ḏ-pumẖ** DC 43. J 132 O B. son B., and his words are muted and the dicta of his mouth are silenced; **blimbia šitin ianqia blambia malakia** DC 26 & 40 (the mouths of) 60 infants are silenced by him, the spirits are silenced by him (read **blimbẖ** or **blimibẖ**).

Pa. Pass. pt. **mbalam** DC 13 silenced, bridled.

Ethpe. Pf. with encl. **ʿblimbẖ** DC 44. 1052 are bridled by him. Impf. **unitbilmin minilia bišata bpumaihun** DC 44 and evil words in their mouths shall be checked.

Ethpa. Impf. **unitbalmun minilia bišata bpumaihun** a var. of ethpe. (above).

Der.: **blum, blim.**

BLS (בְּלַעַס) to choke.

Pa. Pf. with suff. **ubalsinun . . . bpumaikun** DC 51. 285 and he crammed them into your mouths. Pass. pt. pl. **abrisim bnhiria mbalsin** DC 46. 104:paen. they are choked by silk in the nostrils.

BLṢ (ܒܠܨ) to give out, discharge, come out; to pronounce, utter.

Pe. Act. pt. **ukarsa balṣa** DC 46 and the stomach will be relieved.

Ethpa. Pf. **uʿtbalaṣ barqa uzriza** (read **uzrizia**) **minilia ḏ-nhura** DC 44. 315 f. and it was pronounced on earth, and the words of light were armed.

BLQ I (ܒܠܩ) to dazzle, blind MG 147 n. 3.

Pe. Pf. with suff. **bliqlun ḏ-ainẖ nhura lahazia** Jb 156:1 they dazzled them so that (their) eyes see no light. Pass. pt. **bliqa** (s.v.).

Der.: **biluqia, bluqia, bliqa.**

BLQ II (a mod. form of **BLA Ia** = בלע, ܒܠܥ) to swallow up, devour, be greedy. Pf. **baliqti** Morg. 273:16 I swallowed it. Impt. **balqu** Morg. 273:11 (twice) swallow it (lit. them).

Der.: **baliqa.**

BNA, BUN II, BNN II (בְּנָא, בְּנִי, ܒܢܐ) to build (up), rear, construct, edify MG 83.

Pe. Pf. **bna** he built, pl. **bnu** they built MG 258:6; **bnun rahmia** DC 3 etc. they offer up prayers (idiom, cf. below); with encl. **ʿbnitlin** DC 48. 394 thou hast constructed for them (fem.); with suff. **man bnak uman bananak** Gs 101:ult. who built thee and who reared thee?; **man binih** DC 53. 375 who built it?; **biniu** they built her MG 289:10; **baita ḏ-šaqaria biniuia** Gs 51:paen. house that liars built; **arqa ḏ-trin šutapania ḏ-bkušṭa biniuih** DAb a land which two partners conscientiously cultivated. Imp. **nibnia, tibnia, ʿbnia, nibnun, tibnun**; with suff. **nibinih** he buildeth him, her, it MG 287:14, **tibinu** (var. **tibiunuia**) ye build her MG 289:11 f., **ubninkun** and I build you MG 290:3. Impt. **bnia** Gy 380:9, 11. Act. pt. **bania** Gy 244:paen.; pl. **ḏ-minaihun ʿusṭunia ḏ-nhaša banin** DAb from which they build copper supports. Part. pres. **banʿt** DAb thou buildest. Pass. pt. **ṣilamata ḏ-bnia ṭina** Sh. 'Abd.'s copy of Gy 60:8 (Pet. **ḏ-bniaiia mn ṭina**) idols built from clay, pl. **bniʿin**, fem. **bnʿian** (and varr.). Inf. **mibnia** MG 260:12.

Ethpe. Pf. **ʿtibniat** she was built MG 263: anteantep. Pt. **mitibnia** MG 214:3, fem. **mitbinia** MG 149:19, 265:antep.

Idiom: With **rahmia** to offer up prayers. Often with the meaning to edify = instruct (esp. **BUN II** = **BNN II**).

Note: Inst. of **banibẖ btušbihtai, banibẖ bʿrutai** Gy 74:6 f., which give no satisfactory meaning, Leid. has **barit** and **bariba** I shone in my glory, I shone in my splendour Ginzā 70 nn. 4, 5.

Gl. 39:1 f. **BNA** بنى *aedificare* بنياد كرد.

Der.: **bana 1, 2, banaia, buna 1, biniana, bna, bnita.** (See also under **BNN II.**)

bna = **buna** MG 83:17.

bnana a var. of **banana 2,** a doublet of **biniana.**

bnata, st. cstr. **bnat** (בְּנָתָא, ܒ̈ܢܬܐ) pl. of **brat(a). bnat anašia** (often) children of men (of both genders, s. **anaša). bnat anania** Gy 174:15 a misunderstood בְּנֵי צֹאן = בנין דען Ps 114: 4 Ginzā 178 n. 6; id. Gy 177:6 f. read **bnat anašia** Ginzā 181 n. 2. With suff. **bnatkun** MG 179:18, **bnatun** their daughters etc.; **kulhun bnat anašia zikria unuqbata** DC 44 all children of men, male and female.

bnia 1 (both בנין & בְּנֵי, ܒܢ̈ܝܐ & ܒܢ̈ܝ) pl. of **bra, br** (rarely **bar**) sons, children MG 5:1, 23:2, 164:2, 183:bottom. Var. **abnia 2** (s.v.). With suff. **bnai** MG 176:8, **bnak,** with fem. suff. **bnik** MG 177:10, 21, **bnh̠** MG 178:12, **bnaikun** MG 180:3, **bnaiin** her sons MG 182:1, **bnh̠ ubnath̠** (*often*), **bnaiun ubnatun** (*often*) his, their sons and daughters, children; **bnh̠ ḏ-adam** Gy 40:11 (varr. **bnia, bnʿ . . .**) A.'s children; **bnia** (ʿ)**sraiil** (often) children of Israel; **bnia dibra uṣadia** DC 40 sons of the desert and solitude; **bnia mata** DC 40 townsmen, citizens; **bnia šlama** Gy 195:14, Morg. 231/49:7 etc. sons-of-peace. But **bnia amin** Gy 332:5, var. **abnia iamin** Jb 68:3 Benjamin Jb ii 71.

bnia 2 = **abnia 1** pl. of **abna. bbnia rigmun** CP 175:4 etc. they stoned me with stones.

bnia 3 = **binia, abinia** (s. **binat-**). **bnia nhura lhšuka** a var. of Gy 137:10 (Sh. 'Abd.'s copy, Pet. **binia . . .**) between the light and the darkness; **kma šapiria ahia bnia ahdadia** JRAS 1937 594:19 how pleasant (are) brothers in each other's company (lit. amongst each other).

bnita (rt. **BNA**) building, laying out, cultivation. **bnita šahuat uzira** AM cultivation, ardour, and sowing.

BNN I (denom. from **bnia 1**) to beget children MG 83:19 f.

Pa. Pf with suff. **ʿu ḏ-lau ana labaninth̠ lianqa** Gy 345:3 (Pet. **labanith̠**) if I had not been there she would not have brought forth the child (var. I would not have built). Impt. **banin banunia** Gy 21:ult. (Pet. **bnin banun,** Sh. 'Abd.'s copy **baninun**) produce children. Part. pres. **ʿu lambaninitun ulagṭitun** Gy 22:1 if ye do not produce and beget children. Inf. **banunia** (above s. Impt.).

BNN II, BUN II (a secondary rt. from **BNA**) to build up, edify, cultivate, lay out. MG 83:middle.

Pe. Pf. with suff. **man banak** CP 80:16, ML 99:8 who built thee MG 273:10; **had banan** CP 81:1, ML 99:12 one built me; **banth̠** (**ubananth̠**) CP 158:1, ML 190:8 I built him; id. Gs 99:9 she built him MG 276:21; **banuk** they built thee MG 274:11. Impf. **ʿbun binta** ML 190:6 I build the building MG 83:15. Pt. act. and pass. **baiin, bina** (s. **BUN II**); **nišma bnina umbanana** CP 80:18, ML 99:9, Gs 114:10 the edified and cultivated soul.

Pa. Pf. **baninit** s. ***banuna**; with suff. **baninuk** they built thee MG 274:12; **baninth̠** CP 158:2, 160:9, ML 190:8, 194:6 I built it up. Pass. pt. **mbanana** (above s. pe. pt.).

Ethpa. Pt. **mitbanunia mitbanan** CP 125:13, ML 151:10 he is built up. Inf. **mitbanunia** (just cited) MG 144: § 122 end.

Der.: **banana 1, 2, *banuna, binta 1** (cf. also s. **BNA I**).

BNN III = **BUN I** (q.v.). Note: **banibh̠** Gy 74:6 (s. **BNA** Note) may be based on a confusion of this rt. with **BNA.**

bnʿ a var. of **bnia 1** (q.v.).

BSA (בסי, ܒܣܐ) to trample on, tread on, scorn, disdain, despise.

Pe. Pf. with suff. **ubsinkun** DC 51. 285 and he despised you. Impf. **latibsun hdadia** Gy 43:15 despise not one another, with reversion **ʿlauaiun latisbun** Gy 23:5 (Sh. 'Abd.'s copy **ʿlauaihun latisun** read **latibsun** as above) despise them not; with suff. and encl. **latibsinun lmalalh̠** DC 22. 182 = **latibsibun lmalalh̠** Gy 191:8 scorn not his words. Pt. pl. **asin ubasin** Gy 215:24 s. **ASA III,** exceptional *scr. def.* **bsin dirka ḏ-bligrak** DC 43 they tread the road that (was trodden) by thy feet; with encl. **basibh̠** Gs 20:11 they despise her.

Pa. Pf. **basit lbad** Zotb. 227 left 22 I despised the work.

Der.: **busiana, bsana.**

bsada a var. of **bisada**: **sadania ḏ-arqa hua bsada ḏ-hiduia** CP 221:4 clods of earth were the pillow of the bridegroom.

bsar st. abs. & cstr. of **bisra** MG 152:7 f. **ʿṣba bsar** Gy 92:22, 211:9 colour of the flesh; **ḏ-aklia bsar ʿdania** DC 43 J 29 that consume the flesh of nurslings.

BSM (בסם, ܒܣܡ Akk. *bašâmu* LS) to be agreeable, fragrant, pleasant, lovely, pleasing, giving delight; to please, delight; pa. to burn incense, give odour, perfume.

Pe. Pf. **bsum** he was, they were, agreeable MG 218:9; **bsum rihaihun ḏ-ʿlania** CP 215:17, ML 247:9 f. pleasing is the smell of the trees; **nha ubsum ʿutra** Gy 92:1 the uthra was cheerful and glad; **ubismat ʿlh̠** Gy 70:20 and it pleased him; **bismat ʿlauaihun ḏ-rbia** CP 250:15, ML 254:6 it pleased the Great (Life); **mibismat ʿlak** Gy 71:6 f. doth it please thee?; **bismit** Morg. 265/21:17 I was fragrant; special pl. **nhuriun ubsumiun ʿutria** DC 38 the uthras shone and were glad. Impf. **nibsum** MG 218:10. **nibsum** (var. C **nibsim**) **rihh̠ ḏ-klilak** CP 210:1, ML 243 lovely is the perfume of thy wreath; **nibsum rihak** CP 410:16 thy perfume delighteth; pl. **nibismun** they will become sweet. Impt. **bsum** MG 218:10. **nha ubsum uʿtbasam** DC 48. 208 be calm, agreeable, and show pleasure. Pt. **uʿutria brihak basmia** CP 359:penult. and the uthras delight in thy perfume; **labasmin mia sariia** Jb 105:8 f. stinking waters are not pleasant.

Pa. Pf. with suff. **basimth̠** thou gavest him odour MG 276:bottom. Impf. with suff. **ulrihaiun saria nibasmh̠** DC 48. 223 he will sweeten their stench. Pt. pl. with encl. **busmania mbasmilun** Gy 60:9 f. they burn incense for them.

Af. Pf. **absum halin ḏ-zapur rihaihun** Jb 274:10 those whose smell was stinking gave forth sweet odour (might be pe. with a mere prosth. **a**).

ETHPA. Pf. **hda uᶜtbasam** Gy 97:18, 115:8, 125:3 he rejoiced and was glad; **malka ᶜl anpia d̲-shaq ziua ᶜbasam** DC 48. 185 the king smiled at S. Z.; **hda utbasam** Jb 214:13. Impt. **ᶜtbasam** (above s. pe. impt.). Pt. **ubriha dilh̲ mitbasma** ATŠ II no. 110 (DC 6 **mitbasima**) and are delighted with its fragrance.

DER.: **basima, busma,** pl. **busmania, bisimta, basmaniata, mbasmana** (fem. **mbasmanita,** pl. **mbasmaniata**), **mbasmanuta.**

BSS (בְּסַס) to tread down. Only impt. found. **bsus** DC 43 A 21.

BSR (בסר, ܒܣܪ) to despise, tread on, tread underfoot, scorn.

PE. Impf. **anašia bišia** (var. **bisra**) **lhdadia nibisrun** AM 217:4 evil people will trample down (or despise) one another.

ETHPA. Impf. **pagra . . . unitbasar d̲-hu tibil** DC 48. 385 the body . . . (and) will be trodden underfoot because it is earth.

DER.: **basraia, bisra** (abs. **bsar**), **mbasra** (abs. **mbasar**).

bᶜiia a pl. of bita 1.

bᶜldaba a var. of **bildbaba** IM Gl.

bṣar a var. of **bsar** (Sh. 'Abd.'s copy of Gy 211:9).

bṣarta (rt. **BṢR**) imperfection, lacking. **daiuia ugubria d̲-mn bṣarta saliq** (read **salqin**) DC 43 J 30 demons and beings that arise from imperfection.

bṣuria (ܒܨܘܪܝܐ) DAb crime, wicked deed, wickedness.

bṣiaria (an irregular form from **BṢR**) defects, deficiencies. **unapṣia ubṣiaria** DC 45 = JRAS 1943:170:24 and discharges and defects.

bṣir, bṣira (בְּצִירָא, ܒܨܝܪܐ) diminished, less, least, lacking, poor (in quality), deficient, deprived, mean, lowly, scanty, failing. Fem. st. emph. **bṣirta, bṣirtia** MG 155:1. Pl. masc. **bṣiria. hasir ubṣir** (often) imperfect and deficient MG 304:bottom and n. 3; **minaihun bṣir kd̲ abid ᶜniš** AM 199:15 some of them are lowly as any slave; **umdiniata bṣiria nihuia** AM 211:8 and the cities will be lacking (in want).

bṣiruta (ܒܨܝܪܘܬܐ) incompletion, scarcity, imperfection, lacking, failure. **hasiruta ubṣiruta** Gs 40:7, 8 cf. **hasir ubṣir** (s. **bṣir**); **bṣiruta bginzih̲ ᶜṣtarar** ATŠ all his treasure becometh imperfect (: fails).

BṢR, (PṢR) (בצר, ܒܨܪ) to lack, lessen, diminish, be diminished, fail, be of poor quality, be mean, take away.

PE. Pf. **bṣar** Gy 94:12, 324:20 was shortened, diminished; **labṣart** Gy 324:13 thou didst not diminish, wast not imperfect; **biṣrit** Gy 324:10, Gs 48:18 I was imperfect, lacking. Impf. **nibṣar** he is shortened, diminishes MG 221:2 (cf. n. 3); as transitive **lanibṣir bhalin malalia** DC 34. 973 he does not subtract from these words; fem. **latibṣar** Gy 324:paen. will not be shortened, cut off; **ukul dukta d̲-ᶜka zhara latibṣar minh̲** ATŠ II no. 214 and at any place that there is a rubric leave nothing of it out; **nibiṣrun** AM 280:11 they will be scarce, poor. Act. pt. **mindam mn ginzaihun labaṣar ulamitinsib** ATŠ II no. 296 nothing shall be subtracted or taken away from their treasures; **ṭabuta minaikun baṣra** s. **ṭabuta**; pl. **ᶜlania baṣria mn ṭunaihun** AM 265:19 trees fail to yield their fruit (lit. are deprived of their burden); fem. pl. **lahasran ulabaṣran** s. **HSR.** Part. pres. **ᶜu mn minilia maraikun baṣritun** Gy 41:6 if ye neglect some of the words of your Lord. Pass. pt. **bṣir(a)** (s.v.). Inf. **mibṣar** Gs 48:17.

PA. Pf. **labaṣrit** Gy 324:13 I did not fail. Pt. pl. **mbaṣria ṭabia** Gs 48:15 the good ones (are) diminished.

ETHPE. Pt. pl. ***mitbiṣrin** (read so inst. of **mitpisrin** Par. xiv no. 9) they will be of poor quality MG 45 n. 3.

Gl. 23:9 f. missp. انقص *minui* كم شد.

DER.: **baṣir, bṣir, baṣarta, bṣarta, bṣiruta, buṣrana, baṣuria, bṣuria, bṣiaria.**

bqita AM 231:16 = **biqita.** Miscop. **bbita** BZ 140 n. 5. Pl. **biqata, biqiata** s. **bqita.**

BQA (בקא, בקי) to search. **ubaqit usilqit lkipia** DC 46. 205:11 I sought and arose to the (heavenly) vault.

BQQ (ܒܩܩ, cf. Jew.-Aram. der בְּקִיק) to be corroded, rotted, consumed, to putrefy. Fundamental stem: **aina d̲-baqat** JRAS 1937 591 eye that putrefied (rotted away). Impt. **ubuq bšamšia** DC 46. 145:9 and rot (?) in the sun. Refl. stem: **ᶜtbaq uᶜtbar hirbia** DC 44: 1067 the swords were corroded and broke.

DER.: **baqiata 1.**

BQR I (ܒܩܪ, cf. also Jew.-Aram. & H. בקר) to cleave, burst open; to enter into, examine.

PE. Pf. with suff. **ᶜšumia d̲-qiriuk bqiriuk brazia** DC 40 the heavens that called thee forth shall let thee enter (or search into) the Mysteries. Pt. pl. **uhanik babia baqria** (a talisman) and those gates burst open.

BQR II only in Gl. 78:5. رعى *pascere* شبانى كرد.

DER.: **baqara, baqaraia, baqra.**

br, bra 1 (Gen. Aram.) son. A less usual form of the st. abs. & cstr. **bar 2** (s.v.). Varr. of the st. emph. **abra, ᶜbra 1** (s.vv.). Pl. **bnia 1, abnia 2, ᶜbnia** (s.vv.). Fem. **brat, brata** (s.v.) MG 10:2 f., 183:bottom. With suff. **br, bar,** but also **brai** my son MG 175:14, **brak** thy son MG 177:4, **brh̲** (often) his son, **bran** our son MG 178:anteantep. **bra rahima** Gy 256:14 ὁ υἱὸς ὁ ἀγαπητός; **brh̲ ana d̲-man** CP 70:17, ML 86:8 whose son am I?; **šum br nu** CP 42:7, ML 49:11 Shem son of Noah; **miša . . . br šušma hiuara br kipa d̲-prat br ᶜdnia d̲-iardna br gubia mia br ᶜuṣria d̲-nhura** CP 30:8 f., ML 36:11 f. (Q 14:4 f.) oil . . . son of white sesame son of the bank of Euphrates, son of the ear (side, bank) of the jordan, son of cisterns of water, son of treasures of the Light; **bra rba dilan** Gy 134:10 our oldest son. Compounds with **br**:

br anaša (var. **barnaša**), pl. **brnašia, barnašia** s. **anaša.** Gl. 94:8 **br našia** شعب, شعوب *populus* طايفه.

br angaria s. **br ʿngaria.**

br asuta a patient. **lbr asuta hauia asuta udarmana uruaha** DC 40. 77 f. for the patient there will be cure, remedy and relief.

br arqa, br arqan the native(s) BZ 113 n. 4. **br arqan mn kiba nimitun** AM 184:6 f. the native will die of disease.

br atuna fresh from the kiln (lit. 'son of an oven'). **sab kuza . . . br atuna d-lamšarai** DC 40 take a jar . . . fresh from the kiln and unused.

br bra DC 44. 1051 grandson.

br guda (a popular etym. of Parth. *bargōd* ISK 91 Aram. **פרגודא** = παραγαύδης, παραγώδης, παραγαῦδις etc. Lat. *paragauda*, Ar. loan-w. برجد Fränkel 45 f.) curtain MG 47:9 f. but sometimes also 'son of a group', member of a group CP 111:2, CP 170, p. 30 f. n. 5 (ML 136 n. 3). **udalia** (var. **uʿdalia**) **br guda** Gy 97:15 f. (var. Leid. & Sh. 'Abd.'s copy) a curtain was raised; **udaluluẖ br guda rba ḏ-šrara** Gy 212:23 they raised before him the great curtain of steadfastness; **udaluluẖ br guda rba ḏ-šrara uaiil** Gs 8:11 they raised etc. . . . and he entered; **lgaṭnẖ lbr gudak rba ḏ-šrara** CP 113:9, ML 138:13 we hold to thy great Fellow of the Band of Truth. About **iušamin br guda** Gy 349:16 cf. Ginzā 365 n. 6.

br ginaiia a gardener (lit. 'son of gardeners') v.s. **ginaia.**

br gininia CP. 346:11 son of mysteries (or of gardens).

br halia (son-of-sweetness) a perfume (?). **kundur . . . ubr halia** DC 46 camphor . . . and perfume (?).

br haria of gentle birth, of noble descent, of noble nature. **br haria ʿniš ḏ-laṭalim** Gy 218:6 a nobleman is one who maketh no injustice.

br hbulia usurer (s. **hbulia**).

br hulia profane animal forbidden for food (s. **hulia**).

br hiia Son-of-Life ML Ind., Jb ii 96 n. 2, Wid. i 16 n. 4; also a *malwâša* man's name.

br zauiata s. **zauiata.**

br zandita s. **zandita.**

br ziua Gy 245:10 Son-of-Brilliance.

br magana a lie-abed (son-of-ease). **uaṭlaqna batia uaṭlaq br magana** DC 46 and I reject the house-dweller and reject a lie-abed.

(**br maš** CP trs. 136 n. 2, ML 220:9 = CP 180:7 f. [also 182:9 f. **br mašmʿiil**] a miswriting of **brmaš** in the evening).

br(a) mdinta AM 194:9 townsman, citizen.

br naša, usually **barnaša** s. **br anaša.**

br ʿngaria (ܒܪ ܐܓܪܐ) Oxf. roll 206, Oxf. roll g 1028, AM (often) roof-spirits, lunacy demons MG 186:25. Var. **br angaria: mn br ʿngaria zakria umn br ʿngaria nuqbata** DC 37. 393 f. from male and female roof-demons.

br qala echo. **kḏ br qala miqrilẖ** DC 46. 166:14 calling him like his echo.

br qina s. **qina 2.**

br razia secretary, counsellor. **br razia ḏ-hu uazir** AM 193:12 the private secretary who is a minister.

br rbia Jb 238:12 son of the Great (Life).

br rurbia = **br rbia.**

br šabata son-of-scrolls MG 48 n. 3, son-of-praise (?) Ginzā 269 n. 1. **br šabata ḏ-kulẖ madihta** Gy 272:3 son of scrolls of all wisdom.

br šamiš AM 228:3 f. Son-of-the-Sun (prob. Saturn BZ 138 n. 4).

br šibia captive, prisoner (s. **šibia**).

br šnia aged, old: **br šnia tlat** three years old.

bra 2 = **ʿbra 1**: **bra ḏ-gukai** Sh. 'Abd.'s copy, var. of **ʿbra ḏ-gaukai** Gy 390:3.

BRA (**ברא**, ܒܪܐ) pe. to create; pa., (af.), ethpa. (= **BRR**) to remove, put out, come forth, break out, remove oneself, exempt, exempt oneself, cut (oneself) off from, expel, exile.

Pe. Pf. **mia lhaka brun** (DC 53 **rdun**) **uziua biardna praš** DC 6 (= CP 365:18) flowed forth hither and radiance issued from the jordan, with suff. **ʿduk ubiriuk** Or. 327:18 they knew thee and created thee.

Pa. Pf. **baria** he put out, removed IM Gl. Act. pt. **mbarilun** he removes them IM Gl., **uldaiania mbarilun** Gy 387:6 and he exileth the judges MG 391:middle. Part. pres. **mrahqitun umbaritun** DC 43 A 93 ye are put at a distance and expelled.

Af. Pf. with suff. **abrian** removed me MG 284:anteantep.

Ethpe. Pf. **ʿtbiriat bagra uzidqa ḏ-iauar** Gy 301:17 she withdrew herself from Yawar's pious gifts and alms (one would expect **ʿtbariat mn**), fem. pl. (identical with masc. sg.) **ʿtibria** Morg. 224/36:2 f., Q 24:20 *creatae sunt* MG 264:24. Impf. **lʿtibrun** Gy 13:3 (AD mistakenly **ʿtibrun**) they are created MG 216: 10 f., 265:5.

Ethpa. Pf. **ʿtbariat mn qudamẖ** DC 9 & 36 she went out of his presence; **ʿtbarit** Gs 72:3 thou wert removed MG 264:8, IM Gl.; **akandit latbarit mn qudamaihun** DC 21 thou hadst not yet gone out of his presence; **mn qudamai ʿtbariun** DC 40. 653 they remove themselves before me. Impf. **nitbarun minẖ** DC 43 J 82 they shall be expelled from him; **litbariun arba ziqia** DC 22. 12 the four winds shall be created (Pet. Gy 13 **ʿtibrun** were created, Leid. a miscop. of ethpe. impf. **latibrun**). Impt. **dhia utbaria** DC 43 be driven away and expelled; pl. **ʿtbarun minẖ** Gy 43:6 separate yourselves from him.

Gl. 39:7 f. **BRA** برر *iustificare* خوب شد.

Der.: **barauata, baraia 1, 2, baruia, brita 1, 2, bariata, biriata 1** (cf. also s. **BRR**), **ʿbraia** (?).

brahim (by the intermediary of Ar. ابراهيم, not by that of ܐܒܪܗܡ nor directly from אַבְרָהָם) Abraham. Varr. **abraham** (directly from H.), **abrahim** (s.v.). **brahim nbiha ḏ-ruha bṭura ḏ-sinai** DC 22. 45 & Sh. 'Abd.'s copy (Pet. Gy 46:7 **abrahim . . .**) A. the prophet of R. on the hill Sinai; **brahim abuhun ḏ-iahuṭaiia** DC 22. 378:5 (Pet. Gy 381:16 **abrahim**) A. father of the Jews.

brauinqa WdF 1386:9 a plant.

braia, ʿbraia (prob. from **BRR**) outer, transcendental, from the other world, supernatural ZDMG lxi 697 f. Var. **baraia 1.**

bihrh̲ iukašar lbraia CP 71:ult. (trs. p. 48 n. 5), ML 88:2, 5 (DC 3 . . . **libraia**) Y. chose the Unearthly (?) One, cf. n. 2. Pl. **gauaiia ubraiia** ATŠ I no. 6 esoteric and exoteric.

braisu, braisukt (translit. of P. برای سوخت) for burning, to burn. **atia bakru braisukt** AM 129 bring a firstling to burn.

braka (ܒܘܪܟܐ, H. בְּרָכָה) Q 46:33, 47:2 benediction.

brat, brata (fem. of br, bra 1) daughter MG 183:bottom. With suff. **brat, bratai** my daughter MG 175:11 f., **bratik** thy (fem.) daughter MG 177:17, **brath̲** his, her daughter MG 178:4. Pl. **bnat, bnata** (s.v.). **ʿzlat brath̲ d̲-bihrun bratak dilak** ATŠ II no. 323 Ezlat daughter of B., thy daughter; **riha d̲-brata** (var. **ubrata**) **d̲-kul ʿstirata** Gy 10:4 incense which is the daughter of all astartes, cf. Ginzā 12 n. 9 f. contra MSchr. 18:4.

brbabia a pers. name IM Gl.

brgapa s. **bargapa.**

brukta Sh. ʿAbd.'s copy var. of **birkta** Gy 292:14.

brunda, prunda (etym. obscure. Jb ii 151 n. 2 is mistaken; the initial **b** is no preposition. The word is well known by MM.) a fish. **ubrundia usindirka** PD 1136 = ATŠ I no. 116 fish and dates (in a list of ritual meals); **kauaria brundia ualuai** Jb 148:9 (refers to three kinds of fishes, s.vv.); **asiq brunda mn aina** DC 41. 171 he took out a fish from the well-spring.

bruq an ancient king identified with Alexander: **bruq malka d̲-dilih̲ sandar** (var. **sindar**) **ruhmaia qarilh̲** Gy 383: 14 f. the king B. who is called Alexander the Roman (= Macedonian).

bruqa (cf. ܒܘܪܩܐ ܕܦܘܡܐ) a disease, paralysis. **bruqa d̲-puma** paralysis of the mouth.

bruqta, bruqtia = **buruqta, buruqtia** (q.v.): **aina bruqtia** JRAS 1937 590:7 & 1943 170:18 eye with cataract.

bria (בריא) natural condition. **mahdar ʿl bria umištria** DC 46. 201:14 he will return to his natural health and be loosed.

brihia = **birihia** MMII xiii.

brik, brika (pass. pt. of **BRK**) blessed MG 4: bottom. Pl. **brikia.** Fem. **brikta** MG 117:18. **zidqa brika** (often) the blessed oblation (s. **zidqa**). **brik iauar** CP 46:13, ML 60:3 Yawar-is-blessed, used also as a *malwâša* man's name. **brik manda** Zotb. 222 right 5 a man's name ('Manda-is-blessed').

brinda a var. of **brunda.**

brisam 1 for **abrišam. brisam d̲-šuba liuania** DC 46 silk of seven colours.

brisam 2, brisim for birsim (q.v.).

brita (בריתא) creature, creation; ritual food for the dead. Pl. **biriata 1. ia . . . brita d̲-ṣaida** DC 43 J 142 O . . . hunted creature! **pihta ubrita** CP trs. p. 40 n. 4, DC 27. 424, 426, ATŠ II no. 155 bread and ritual food (Lidzb. *Schöpfung*, cf. ML 76 n. 2). Var. of **qrita** Gy 72:3 (Leid., cf. Ginzā 68 n. 3).

BRK (Gen. Sem.) to bless, af. to bend the knee, kneel. Pe. is often used inst. of pa. and af. MG 215 n. 2.

Pe. Pf. **brak** Gy 256:17 they blessed; with suff. **birkh̲** he blessed him MG 275:1, **birkak** he blessed thee MG 269:middle, 273:10, **birkan** he blessed me MG 270:middle, **brakinkun** he blessed you MG 269:middle, 280:23, **brakinun** he blessed them MG 281:middle, **braktak** she blessed thee MG 273:antep., **brakth̲** she blessed him MG 276:19, **braktinkun** I blessed you MG 281:2, **birkta braktinkun** Gy 256:16 I blessed you with a blessing, **braktinun** I blessed them MG 282: 24. Impf. **tibirkun** ATŠ I no. 118 ye shall bless; with suff. **nibirkak** he blesseth thee MG 273:middle, **nibrikinan** Gy 307:1 B (varr. **nibrakinan, nibirkinan**) he blesseth us MG 279:antep. f.; **nirihman unibirkan** Gs 58:18 (for **nirihminan unibirkinan**) he loveth us and blesseth us MG 279 n. 3; **tibrikinun** she blesseth them, thou blessest them MG 281: anteantep. Impt. **bruk ʿl pihta** Gy 17:22 pronounce a benediction over the (sacramental) bread; **bruk ʿl miša** Gy 37:15 pronounce a benediction over the oil; **birkta bškinata bruk** DC 50 pronounce a benediction in the dwellings; with suff. **burkh̲** Gs 79:3 bless him MG 276:10, **brikinun** Gy 327:17 bless them MG 282:9, **barkinan** DC 26.537, **uburkuih̲** DC 50 and bless ye him. Act. pt. **barik** Gy 275:21, 276:1, Gs 78:2, pl. **(birikta) barkia** (often) they pronounce a blessing. Pass. pt. **brik, brika** (s.v.), pl. **(mibrak) brikia** JRAS 1937 596:6 they are greatly blessed; with encl. pers. pron. **mn dukta d̲-brikinin brikit** DC 34 from the place from which we are blessed thou art blessed MG 232:paen.; **brikitun** ye are blessed MG 35:bottom, 233:12. Inf. **mibrak** (above s. pass. pt. pl.).

Pa.: Act. pt. **mbarik** he is blessing MG 131:9, 230:7; with encl. **mbariklh̲** Gs 73:15 he blesseth him; **mbariklun lrurbia** Gs 67:10 he blesseth the Great (Life); **iardna utrin kiph̲ mbarkilh̲** DC 34 the jordan and its two banks bless him. Part. pres. with encl. **(madiqna ʿlak) umbarkinalak** DC 41. 505 I (gaze on thee) and bless thee. Pass. pt. **mbarak** MG 131:middle, 230:9. Inf. **barukia** MG 143: antep., 233:ult. (*Mundart* 58 no. 3, AF 229), often **lbarukia** to bless, with suff. **barukak** to bless thee MG 292:19; inf. abs. **(mibrak brikia) umbarukia** cf. above s. pe. pass. pt. pl.

Af. Pf. **burkan abrik lbišia** s. **burka 1.** Pt. fem. pl. **burkai d̲-marbika usagda lhiia** Jb 59:14 my knees that bow down and worship the Life. Inf. **abrukia** s. **burka 1.**

Ethpe. Pt. **mitibrik** blessed MG. 132:9, 230: middle, fem. **mitibrika** CP no. 378 with encl. **ʿtibrikibh̲** CP 433:4 and 14.

Der.: **baruka, burukta** (varr. **birukta, birikta, birkta, brkta**), **brik(a), braka, burka.**

brkta a spor. *scr. def.* of **burukta, bir(i)kta.**

brʿia (pass. pt. of **BRA = BRR**) wild, uncultivated. **šumbulta d̲-labrʿia hʿ** ATŠ II no. 151 wheat that is not wild.

BRQ (Gen. Sem.) to flash, shine, lighten, metaph to be stupefied.

Pe. Pf. **braq (birqa)** s. **birqa.** Impf. **birqa nibruq** AM 264:2 f. there will be lightning.

Pt. **baruq** AM 264:4 (read **bariq**) it flashes; pl. **ubarqia ʿlẖ birqia** DC 22. 402 (Pet. Gs 12:1 f. sg. **ubarqa ʿlẖ birqa**) and lightnings flash over him, **barqin** DC 44 they are stupefied.

DER.: **birqa, buruqta** (varr. **buruqtia, biruqtia, bruqtia**), **burqa, biruq.**

BRR (בָּרַר, cf. s. **BRA** and Syr. der. ܒܪ LS 88a = Mand. **bar** 1) to put out, chase, expel, remove, disqualify, exclude.

PE. Inf. **lanibsar ulanibar** DC 34 he shall not be (considered) wanting or disqualified, **laiit ḏ-nibar ʿlẖ** DC 47 there is nothing which invalidates it.

PA. Pt. (pass.) pl. **mbaṭlan umbarin mn pagriẖ** DC 43 E 78 f. they are made ineffectual and expelled from his body.

ETHPE. Pf. **ʿu šualia mitinziz ʿtbar** ATŠ I no. 13 if the novice be incontinent he is disqualified; **ʿtbar hanaṯ tarmida unišimta rušumaihun ʿtbar** (var. **tbar**) **uakum** ATŠ I no. 182 that priest and the soul are invalidated, their sign became invalid and black; **ʿtbarat** JRAS 1937 593:32 thou (fem.) art expelled, special pl. (**uhambal binianẖ urazaiun**) **ʿtbariun** ATŠ no. (?) (and its construction is spoilt and their mysteries) are invalidated. Impt. pl. **ʿtbarun** remove yourselves, be expelled MG 265:21.

ETHPA. Pf. **ataitun ḏ-laʿtbarartun lpagrẖ unišimtẖ** DC 51 ye came so that ye did not separate yourselves from (read **mn**?) his body and his soul.

NOTE: Ethpe. with the meaning 'to disqualify' might have been influenced by the identical forms of **TBR** 'to break, destroy'. It is often difficult to distinguish the former from the latter.

DER.: **bar** 1, **(a)bararia, biriut, (ʿ)braia** (cf. also s. **BRA**).

BŠL (בְּשַׁל, ܒܫܠ, H. בָּשַׁל Ges. s.v.) to boil, cook, roast, scorch, burn, seethe; to ripen (cf. der. **bašla** 1).

PE. Pf. ***bšil** it boiled, cooked MG 219: bottom; **ʿzlit bnura ulabišlit**, CP 41:2, ML 48:3. Impf. **bnura nibšul** (var. **nibšil**) AM 33: 14 he will be scorched by fire; (**ʿzal bnura**) **ʿbšul** CP 40:19, ML 48:1 (if I go through the fire) I shall burn; **ulatibišlun** Gy 28:20 and ye shall not be roasted. Act. pt. **bašlia bišia** ML 227:6 the evil ones will be roasted. Inf. abs. **mibšal bašlia** ibid.

PA. Pf. **bašil** DC 41. 171 it cooked. Impf. **nibašil** ATŠ II no. 93; with suff. **nibašlia bmia ḏ-iama** DC 13 we will boil him in sea-water; **nibašlẖ** DC 44. 563 we will cook him; (**latiniksun**) **ulatibašlun** ATŠ II no. 16 (do not slaughter) and do not cook. Impt. **ubašil** (**ušuplẖ bkulẖ pagrẖ**) AM 89 ult. and boil (and rub it all over his body); with suff. (**ušdibẖ mihla liauna**) **ubašlẖ** DC 3 (and cast salt on the dove) and cook it. Act. pt. pl. **mbašlia halba** DC 44 they boil milk; with encl. **mbašilẖ** DC 48. 23 matures it.

DER.: **bašla** 1, 2.

bšmanqa, bšmaqa s. **bušmanqa.**

BŠQR (בשקר) to search, discover, discern, recognize, ascertain, make inquiry, examine, find out by examination.

Fundamental stem: Pf. **kul ḏ-bašqar mnatẖ** ATŠ II no. 118 each that discerned its portion; **kul had raza škintẖ nṭir uduktẖ bašqar** DC 36 each mystery awaited its abode and ascertained its position; **bašqrat škinta** DC 41. 476 she recognized her dwelling; **bašqart** Gs 113:5 thou didst inquire MG 223 n. 1; **bašqrit, bašqirit** Gs 112:25, 113:1 I inquired; with suff. **bašqirtẖ** Gy 358:11 I recognized him MG 277:middle; **bašqartẖ** Jb 60:3 I searched it; **hzaitẖ ubašqartẖ** Jb 173:9 I saw him and recognized him; **šimuia ubašqruia** Jb 163:4 they heard him and recognized him. Impf. **mn ḏ-nibašqar lginzak** DC 6 of those that sought out thy treasure; **tida utibašqar mn riš** ATŠ II no. 58 thou wilt know and ascertain from the beginning; with suff. **ulaiit ʿniš ḏ-mn hdadia nibašqrinun** ATŠ II no. 235 and no one can distinguish one from another; **tibašqrẖ brẖ** Jb 119:10 she will search for her son. Impt. **bašqar** Gs 112:21, MG 229:17; **hzun ubašqar** Jb 134:12 see and ascertain. Pt. act. & pass. **mbašqar batar nhur** Jb 142:9 is ascertained in the place of light; **kul man ḏ-qaria masiqta udabahata lambašqar** ATŠ II no. 137 anyone (priest) that reads a *masiqta* but does not find out (the names) of the ancestors (to be mentioned in the *masiqta*); **balmia ḏ-nhura mbašqar** DC 27. 389 he is well known (or ascertained) in the worlds of light; **nunia dilia mbašqria** Jb 157:8 my fish are discerning; **ʿbidatak mbašqra batra ḏ-nhura** Jb 220:13 thy works are perceived in the Place of Light; with encl. **lambašqarlun ladiaurẖ** Jb 60:14 he will not recognize his helpers; **ḏ-mbašqrilẖ adiaurẖ** Jb 66:5 whom his helpers recognize; **mbašqirilẖ** MG 30:13; **anašia mbašqrilẖ mn mata** DC 3 (colophon) people sought him out from the place; **ḏ-hazilẖ lnapšaihun umbašqirilẖ** ATŠ II no. 423 that they should see him for themselves and examine him.

Reflexive stem: Pf. **kul had raza lnapšiẖ ʿbašqar** DC 34. 497 each individual mystery (: rite) was separately distinguished; **kul girmia ʿbašqar uʿštadar** DC 48. 291 f. all bones were differentiated and given their function. Pt. pl. **mibašqrin** DC 34. 1021 they know. Irreg.: **aul anašia lbišqirẖ** DC 45 bring people to gaze intently at him.

Gl. 46:5 f. missp. with **g** تحقق *certior fieri* متحقق شد; 92:9 f. **BŠQR** شدد *confirmare* ثابت شد; 114:13 f. id. (ا)عترف *confiteri* اقرار كرد.

G

g The third letter of the alphabet, MMII 241. Phon. value: plosive *g* and aspirated *γ*. A supplementary letter **g̲** is used to transcribe the Ar. غ (the diacritical dots are often omitted) MMII 244. Phon. changes: **g** for **q** MG § 41 p. 38 f. & *Nachtr.* 484; **g** for **k** MG § 43 p. 40; Aram. ג > **k** MG § 44 p. 41; omission of **g** between **a** amd **u** or after **au** in certain old loan-words, ibid.

GAA I (גאא, גאי, ܓܐܐ) to rejoice, exult in, be full of delight, be elated, resplendent, be proud of, glory about (or over).

Pe. Only act. pt. **ram ugaiia** Gy 195:4 is high and resplendent, fem. **gaia rahṭa** Gy 170:1 exulteth and runneth away Ginzā 175 n. 1; **gaia umitparpa** CP 67:10 rejoiceth and exulteth; pl. **sahqia gaiin umitparpin** Gy 274:5 they dance, rejoice and exult; **daiṣa gaia** CP 68:1 danceth, exulteth.

Pa. Only act. pt. **mgaia** (**uiaia**) Q 28:25 is resplendent (and beauteous).

Ethpa. Pf. **ʿtgaiit** Gy 86:20 I was resplendent MG 69:bottom, 264:13; **ʿtgaiun** Q 2:15 they were resplendent MG 264:20. Pt. **mitgaiia** Gy 3:12, 152:17, 153:12 resplendent, glorious MG 132:20, 265:bottom; with encl. (**hadibh̲**) **umitgaiibh̲** DC 3 they (rejoice in it) and glory in it.

Der.: **gaiuta, giuta 2 (giua, giuat), giutana.**

GAA II, GHA (H. געה, Aram. געא, געי, ܓܥܐ, ܓܥܐ, cf. Ar. قعى to quack) to cry, howl.

Pe. Pt. **habara gaiia** Gy 71:8 (var. Sh. ʿAbd.'s copy; Pet. has **gahia**) the howling darkness.

g̲ab (עַל גַּב?) based upon, (= **gu**?) in. **raza hazin gab šumak alaha rba** DC 40. 1018 f. this mystery is in thy very name (or based upon thy name), great god.

g̲ababa s. **gbaba.**

g̲abara (גַּבְרָא, ܓܰܒܪܳܐ LS, cf. also Ges. s. גִּבּוֹר) subst. hero, giant, used often of evil demons MSt 202 & n. 2; adj. mighty, powerful, virile, valiant, strong; (= **gubara**) manhood, virility. Pl. **gabaria.** Fem. **gabart(i)a**, pl. **gabarata** (= **gabaruata** q.v.) mighty deeds, miracles. Formed as a nom. ag. pe. MG 120:14. **gabara d̲-ʿšpil** Gy 88:3 the giant who was humiliated; **ʿutana ugabara** Gy 88:6 a strong one, a mighty one; **gabara d̲-gabir hailh̲** Gy 62:16 mighty one whose strength is mighty; **laništaba . . . gabara bgabaruth̲** Q 57:18 (CP 113:4 is miscopied: DC 3 = Q) the hero will not boast with his strength; **ʿur gabara d̲-hšuka** Gy 156:6 U. the giant of the darkness; **ʿur gabara qarabtana** Gy 156:11 U. the giant-warrior; **anatan gabara qarabtana** Gy 140:7 (cf. also l. 2); **ṭura ugabara d̲-kulan** Gy 147:5 hill and giant that (is above) all of us; **anatun gabaria uanin mkikia** Gy 143:ult. f., Gs 27:10 ye are mighty and we are lowly; **gabaria d̲-hšuka** Gy 139:12, 140:10 the giants of the darkness; **gabaria rurbia d̲-hšuka** Gy 139:4; **gabaria buria** s. **bura**; **gabaria naplia** Gy 139:18 the heroes falling down; **daiuia ugabaria d̲-hšuka** Gy 141:12 demons and giants of darkness; **gabaria batar atar mištalaṭia** Gy 50:20 tyrants will become powerful in many places; **šibiahia ugabaria d̲-hazin alma** Q 66:6 the demons and the mighty beings of this world; **gabaria haškia** DC 47 the powers of darkness (cf. Gy 139:12 etc. above); **mn tlata gabaria d̲-hšuka pariqth̲** DC 41 thou hast delivered her (: the soul) from the mighty powers of darkness; **gabaria naṭrh̲ d̲-ʿur** Gy 85:23 f. the giant guards of Ur; **šibiahia gabaria** Gs 79:22 (cf. Q 66:6 above); **gabra gabara** AM 4:13 a mighty man; **tlata gabaria d̲-panba . . . utartin gabaria d̲-kitana** DC 45 three strong cotton threads . . . and two strong linen threads; **dumaiia d̲-gṭil gabarun rmia gṭil gabarun** CP 380:1, ZDMG 1955 149 right ult. f. Idumaeans whose manhood is destroyed, cast away and destroyed is their virility; **trišar gabaria d̲-hazin alma** ATŠ II no. 374 twelve mighty beings of this world.

g̲abaruata (as pl. of **gabaruta**) varr. **gbaruata, gambaruata** (ܓܰܒܪ̈ܘܳܬܳܐ but with the meaning of ܓܰܒܪܘܬܳܐ) great might, mighty deeds, championships, miracles MG 167:12 f., Wdgr. iii 53 n. 3. **gabaruata bnura mahuilun** Gy 52:2 and he showeth them miracles in the fire; **ugabaruata bnura mhauai** Gy 28:16 (var. DC 22. 27 **ugbaruata**); **mhauia gabaruata bʿšumia uarqa** Gy 222:20; **bgabaruath̲ mitnahazbh̲** Gy 81:18 he rageth with his great might; **ʿtnahaz bgabaruata** Gy 281:11 id. past; **gabaruatai ʿlh̲ ʿtimlia** Jb 198:3 my heroic deeds were performed on him, cf. ii 192 n. 3; **gabaruath̲ d̲-manda d̲-hiia** Gy 177:12; **adunai bgabaruath̲ qralh̲ lmiša** Jb 198:12 A. by his deeds of might called Moses; **hailai ugabaruatai** Jb 217:15 my strength and my heroic deeds; **bhailai bnaith̲ lbaita ubgabaruatai taqinth̲ lhikla** Gy 210:2 with my strength I built the house and with my might I solidified the palace; **kd̲ halin gabaruata šabaq** DC 51. 258 when he permitted these miracles.

g̲abaruta (גַּבְרוּתָא, ܓܰܒܪܘܬܳܐ) strength, manhood, virility, male organ. St. abs. (& cstr.) **gabarut.** Pl. **gabaruata. rušma d̲-brh̲ ana hatma d̲-ʿl g-a-b-a-r-u-t** DC 41 the sign of 'I am his son' (i.e. signing at the recitation of a prayer of this name) is the seal set on the male organ; **uagabaruta** (var. **gabruta**) **balmia udaria mhauia** ATŠ I no. 257 (var. DC 6) and he showeth forth mighty deeds (read **gabaruata**) in worlds and ages; **gabaruta umarba** ATŠ I no. 217 male organ and womb; **napla**

bširianh̲ d̲-gabaruta amintul d̲-sindirka hu gabaruta DC 34 it falleth into the flowing channel of virility, for date-palm is (the symbol of) virility; uata lgabaruth̲ tihuilh̲ AM 86: penult. he will have a mark on his sexual organs; rušma d̲-gabaruta DC 34. 203 the symbol of manhood.

gabarta, gabartia fem. of gabara (v.s. gbarta). **gaṭintia uʿriktia ugabartia tihuia** AM 65:19 she will be slender, tall, and strong.

gabia (act. pt. pe. of **GBA**) collector of dues. **šauiuk gabia mnauata lrbia** CP 415:1 they made thee a collector of dues for the Great (Life).

gabil (act. pf. pe. of **GBL**) sculptor, maker, framer. **gabil pagria** CP 82:12, 13, ML 102:4, Morg. 237/61:1 f. (ܓܒܠ ܦܓܪ̈ܐ) maker of bodies, of corporeal things ZDMG lxi 698.

gabir, var. **gbir** (adj. from **BGR**) strong, mighty, vigorous, powerful. St. emph. not found. **gabir ʿl kulhun alahia** Gy 5:ult. mighty above all gods; **gabir minan** Gy 80:paen., **rab ugabir minai** Gy 185:15 greater and mightier than I; **npiš ugabir** Gy 282:24 great and mighty; **gabir (u)hliṣ** Gy 167:14 strong and vigorous; **hailh̲ npiš ugabir** Gy 34:17 his strength is great and powerful; **kma šapir ugbir knara hazin** DC 21 = JRAS 1938 3:9 how fine and vigorous is this lote-tree; **ugabaruth̲ d̲-gabir hailh̲ umalkuth̲** ATŠ I no. 224 and its male organs whose strength and monarchy are powerful (speaking of the body); **ram minai ugabir minai** DC 41. 104 f. higher and stronger than I am.

gablia (doubtf. cf. Jb ii 49 n. 2) Jb 44:6, 11 males, rams (?). Var. **giblia** DC 30. 25:paen., Sg. not found.

gabnia (cf. גִּיבְנָא hump, H. גַּבְנֹן mountain crest) summits (?). **damit lgabnia ʿngaria** DC 43 J 199 f. thou resemblest the roof-tops.

gabra (גַּבְרָא, ܓܰܒܪܳܐ) man MG 100:6. Still used (pron. *gaβrâ*). St. abs. **gbar** MG 151:8. Pl. **gubria** (s.v.). Also pl. **gubr,** as Bibl. Aram. with sg. also גּוּבְרָא. Used also of supernatural beings MSt 202 f. Employed in apposition as for example with אִישׁ כֹּהֵן, or נְבִיא. With numerals and **kul** used like Ar. نفر to be omitted in translation: **kul gabra tarmida** ML 59:2 f. every priest; **kul gabra naṣuraia** CP 196:5, ML 59:6 every N.; **arba gubria bnia šlama** CP 118:15, ML 144:5 four sons of Salvation; **gabra gabra** Gy 196:ult. every man; **gabra kadaba** Gy 198:8 a liar; **gabra nukraia** Gy 94:13, 196:18, 354:23, Jb 63:8 f., 160:2, 165:4, 10, 13, 167:8 f., 197:16, 240:6 etc. (*often*) a supernatural being (a frequent designation of the Mand. Sōtēr MSt 202); **gabra naṣbai** Jb 101:6 f., **gabra naṣbh̲** Jb 244:10, 264:11 the Being, my Creator; **gabra bhir zidqa** Jb 160:3 man of proven righteousness; **gabra paruanqa** Jb 257:11 the same as simple **paruanqa** (s.v.); **gabra qarabtana** Jb 186:10 = **qarabtana** (s.v.); **gabra qadmaia** (often) Jb 90:3 f., 254:12 etc. (Adam) the first man MR 199, HpGn 176, MSt. 203, PRE 168. Gl. 27:12 missp. انسان *homo* آدم, 84:9 missp. رجل *vir* مرد, 182:8 ذكر *masculus* نر.

gabrauata Sh. ʿAbd.'s copy a var. **gabaruata** Gy 28:16.

gabraiit DC 48. 35 (adverbial) manly, in a manly way (?).

gabrʿil (גַּבְרִיאֵל) Gabriel PRE 166, HpGn 176, MR 46 n. 2, 55. **gabrʿil šliha** Gy 11:4, 13:7, 87:10, 93:21 the envoy G. (identified with **hibil**); **gabrʿil rihmat** DAb, RD 28 'She-loved-G.' name of a palm-tree in a purgatory.

gaguta (cf. Ar. vern. *kukūta* dove) a turtle-dove (?). **unahim kd̲ iauna ukd̲ gaguta** DC 34. 225 and moans like a dove and like a turtle-dove.

gada 1 (גַּדָּא, ܓܰܕܳܐ) fortune, success, luck, fate. Masc. st. abs. **gad** (?). **gada ṭaba** PD 345, 357, ŠQ (several times) good luck; **gada nihuilh̲** AM (often) he will have good luck; **ašrit kulhun mlakia lraza d̲-napših̲ lgadh̲ . . . kul mlakia haza šuma lgad** DC 37. 520 ff. I delivered all devils to their (lit. his) own mystery (and) to their (lit. his) fate . . . (the second part is corrupt and doubtful). Heb. גַּד; cf. **gadaia, gadana.**

gada 2 = **gdada 1, gida 2. gada d̲-iardna** PD 790, Q 72:3 bank of the jordan, river-bank; **saq lgida** Q 11:16 go up to the bank.

gadada = **gdada 1 & 2: gadadia d̲-pamba** Oxf. roll f 1340, 1343 cotton strips.

gadaia (גַּדָּיָא) fortunate, lucky, see **gada 1. ṣaida anat gadaia** Jb 153:7 thou art a lucky fisherman.

gadana (ܓܰܕܳܢܳܐ) fortunate, lucky, auspicious, divine. Fem. **gadanita.** Used also as a pr. name, see **gada 1. šamiš gadana** ATŠ II no. 190 the auspicious sun; **aba gadana** PD 1089, **taga d̲-aba gadana** PD 982 the crown of the fortunate father; **iamina gadana d̲-malka d̲-ginzia hu** DC 36 no. 97, PD 965 the right is the auspicious, the king of treasures; **unida d̲-gadana mn sulia** ATŠ II no. 194 and recognizeth that which is divine from (that which is) abominable; **širša gadana** ATŠ I no. 36 the Divine Stem (i.e. priestly caste); **gadanita tihuia** AM 73:16 she shall be lucky. As a pr. name in Gy 291:19, RD D 19, Q 48:18, 26, 61:1, 62:6 f., PD 420, AM 256:8 etc.

gadanis (in angel-list DC 40. 877) an angel.

gadupa (rt. **GDP,** cf. ܓܽܘܕܳܦܳܐ) blasphemy, revilement, curse, cursing. Pl. **gadupia. malahia bliqia ṣairia bgadupa** DC 51. 717 sailors blinded, disgraced by blasphemy; **qal ugadupia** DC 34. 1045 noise and blasphemies.

gadia (גַּדְיָא, ܓܰܕܝܳܐ) kid, young goat, Capricorn MG 100:22, ZDMG xxv 256–8, MMII 74. Pl. **gadiia** (var. **gadia**) MG 164:9 f. Masc. **gadia šaminia** Gy 183:18, **gadiia šaminia** Gy 187:6 fat kids; **zimia d̲-gadia** AM 131:10 the hairs of a (male) goat; **daiuia bakin kd̲ gadiia** DC 43 J 100 the devils cry like goats; **umanzia d̲-gadia bukra br bukarta** DC 26. 780 & 40. 805 and the hair of a firstling kid, son of a firstling dam. As a sign of the Zodiac Gy 123:2, 124:8, AM (*very often*).

gadida (Targ. גְּדִידָא, גְּדָדָא Syr. ܓܕܝܕܐ PSm 652:bottom, Löw 58:10) wormwood. Var. **gida 1**. **ugadida uširiana d-kapur** DC 46. 127:8 wormwood and a solution of camphor.

gadima DC 46. 223:4 for **gidma**.

gadla (act. pt. of **GDL I** q.v., used substantivally) weaver.

gadpa 1 (גַּדְפָּא, ܓܕܦܐ LS) wing, limb, winged creature MG 77 n. 4, see Bibl. Aram.* כְּנַף, cf. **gadpania** in *Lex.* L. Koehler. Plu. **gadpia**. Var. **gapa** Ginzā 225 n. 4. **ṣipar gadpa** (often) winged bird(s) MG 309:14; **ṣipar gadpa gadph lašqal** JRAS 1939 399:29 winged bird does not remove its wings; **alma d-ganpia ṣarlia** ATŠ II no. 131 till wings were formed for me.

gadpa 2 (cf. ܓܕܘܦܐ) sail. **pkiria gadpaihun d-markabata** DC 19 (DC 43 B 7. **gadpaihun d-markabatun**) the sails of the ships are folded.

gadpania (adj. from **gadpa 1**) pl. winged. **hinun manzania ugadpania** DC 43 J 198 they are hairy and winged.

gadpiil, gadpiʿil, gadpʿiil JRAS 1937 595 etc. (often) an angel.

gadria (?) Gy 123:18 cisterns (?). Lidzb. read **gaddia** (var. Leid. **gadadia**) Ginzā 139 n. 4.

gaha DC 44 for **guha**.

gahar 1 = **gauhar, guhar**. **misqil aiak gahar** ATŠ I no. 51 he shall be as polished as a gem.

gahar 2 (rt. **GHR** = ܓܗܪܐ) dimness, lack in sight. **hazin gahar d-anin amarnin** ATŠ II no. 361 this is what we call dimness (of sight).

gahuara (P. گاهواره) cradle. **hazin baba kdub lianqa d-bakia bgahuara urup bgahuarh** DC 46. 153:13 write this charm for a baby that cries in its cradle, and tie to its cradle.

gahia 1 (act. pt. of **GHA II**) horrible, horrid, terrifying, or (**GHA I** Lidzb.) crying, howling. **hšuka gahia** Gy 71:8, Jb 58:15, DC 48. 220 (and often) horrid darkness.

gahia 2 (P. گاهی) sometimes, often. **ʿniš d-mitar gahia** DC 46 a person who often wakes up.

gaua 1 (גוא, ܓܘܐ) inside, interior, inner part, innermost, see Bibl. Aram.* גַּו, cf. **gadpania** in *Lex.* L. Koehler. St. cstr. **gu** MG 100:13, 150:3. Antonym of **bar 1** MG 203:19. As a rule, with the encl. **b-** and pers. suff.: **ʿu bgauai. mitkarkit** Gy 137:16 if thou embracest me; **bgauak**, fem. **bgauik** Jb 214: ult. within thee; **bgauh** (very often) in it, therein, therewith, within it; **bgauh d-marguš alma** Jb 52:5 into the tumult of the world; **bgauaihun** Gy 56:10 (*often*) in them.

gaua 2 = **gauaia** (by omission of the ending). **utaga lgaua . . . lahauilh taga d-malkuta** ATŠ II no. 10 and (as to) a crown for a eunuch . . . there can be no crown of kingship for him (cf. s. **gauaia**).

gauaza Parth. *gavāz* (Avestan *gavāza*) ISK 93 (P. گاوزن, Aram. loan-w. גַּוְזָא, גַּוָּזָא, ܓܘܙܐ LS) staff, stick, rod, stem MG 121:4. Still used (pron. *gowāza*). Var. **giuaza. gauaza d-mia hiia** Gy 358:5, Jb 173:3 f. staff of living water; **gauaza d-mia** Q 7:25; **gauaza d-mia dakia** Jb 144:4 staff of pure water; **gauaza d-ʿmra ušima** Gy 337:18, 338:11, Jb 244:14, Morg. 266/23:8, 267/24:26 staff of speech and hearing (= of power Ginzā 349 n. 5); **gauaza d-zaita** CP 19:21, Q 8:3 olive-(wood)-staff (an expression for **margna** ML 21 n. 2); **gauaza d-mitkabšia** (var. **mitkabšibh**) **mardia** Gy 80:2 a rod wherewith the rebels are laid low; **gauazia d-barda** s. **barda**; **gauaza d-taumia** DC 44 a stick of garlic (?); **gauaza d-šurbina** DC 37 a cypress rod; **gauaza mgaṭarlh** DC 46 a stick cut for him; **gauaza d-rugza** DC 43 J 112 a rod of wrath; **g(i)uaza d-hamra** DC 46. 96:10 a stem of a vine.

gauazta a place-name. **zazai d-gauazta** Morg. 250/87:14 f., CP 9:15, ML 231:8 (and in many colophons, Z from G).

gauaia (גוויא, ܓܘܝܐ) inner, interior, esoteric, of the upper world (like Targ. & Syr., prob. a transformation of גַּוָּזָא), a euphemism for eunuch, castrated MG 141:9 & n. 2 (cf. also p. 121 n. 1), hidden, concealed, transcendental. Pl. **gauaiia**. Fem. **gauaita**. As opposite of **baraia 1** used as a designation of female sexual organs as well as castration of the man, cf. **baraiia gabra ugauaiia ʿnta** Gy 201:paen., the outer organs are the man, the inner organs are the woman Ginzā 201 n. 1; a eunuch is called **gabra gauaia** as well as a woman **ʿnta gauaita** Lond. roll 86, 115, 120, DC 12. 38; **garglia gauaiia** PD 828 the upper spheres; **iardnia gauaiia** Gy 234:17, **iardnia ʿrurbia gauaiia** Gy 136:17 the great jordans of the upper world Ginzā 152 n. 7; **hilbunia gauaiia** ML 274:9 esoteric eggs; **bmania gauaiia ksuia** CP 280:4 f. they covered him with esoteric veils (ML *262 n. 1); **razia gauaiia** PD 813 secret mysteries; **zharia iaqiria gauaiia** DC 36 injunctions precious and esoteric, but **zharia gauaiia** DC 27. 105 s. **zhara 2**; **gauaita d-ʿšiul** Gs 132:8 the innermost hell; **ulatitirṣun taga lgauaiia** ATŠ II no. 6 and set not a crown on eunuchs (a eunuch being excluded from priesthood); **minilia hakima lsakla aiak ptulta lgauaia** Gy 217:24 the words of a wise man to a fool are as a virgin is to a eunuch; **lgauaiak azil** Jb 147:4 go to thy hidden place (in reeds for fishing); **akandit qaimia ṣaidia bgauaiia dilun** Jb 147:8 while the fishermen were standing in their hidden places ii 148 n. 1; **giṣia** (read **gihnia**) **gauaiia** Jb 143:6 inner passages.

gaualqa DC 12. 128 a var. of **gualqa**.

gauara = **guara**. Gl. 161:8 **gauara** مصران *intestina* روده .

gauarata, a var. of **gabarata** (fem. pl. of **gabara**).

gauhar (P. گوهر) jewel, gem. Var. **guhar. šitin gauhar mn kana d-nišmata** DC 35 sixty jewels from the assembly of souls; **tlatma ušitin guhar** DC 34. 1066 360 jewels.

gauza (rt. **GZZ**) cutting, shearing: **gauza d-manzia** AM 163:10 hair-cutting; **gauza d-ṭupria** AM 163:6 nail-paring.

gaukai, var. **gukai** (ܓܘܟܝ PSm.) a land eastwards from Tigris in the region of Seleucia

MG 319 n. 5, MSt 99 n. 3, Ginzā 414 n. 1, Hoffmann, *Auszüge* 277, IM 9 & Gl. **arqa gaukai** Gy 387:2 the land of G.; **ʿbra gaukai** Gy 390:3 f. the coast-land of G.

gauna (P. گون = *gaŭna*, Syr. loan-w. ܓܘܢܐ) colour, dye, resemblance, appearance, form, kind, sort, species. St. abs. **guan** (jac. ܓܘܢ) MG 152:3 ff. Pl. **gaunia.** Masc. **gaunia gaunia** (cf. P. گونا گون) of all colours, of all kinds, of all species; **liliata d̲-gaunia gaunia** Gy 99:8 liliths of all colours MG 321:7; **bgaunia gaunia** in various colours, kinds; **uaqimtinun lmia bgaunia gaunia** Jb 108:7 and she converted the waters into various colours; **gaunia gaunia uznia znia** (*often*) of all kinds and sorts; **gauna d̲-nura** Gy 88:19 the colour of the fire; **hin gaunh̲ msamaq** AM 275:10 if its colour is reddish; **ugaunh̲ aiak rpila nihuia** AM 233:8 if its appearance is like a cloud; **ugaunia uharšia tilip** AM 58:ult. she will learn many kinds of sorceries; **gauna mziga** AM 98:19 blended colour; **biriata tlata gaunia hinun** ATŠ I no. 269 created things are of three kinds. About **lhšuka ulgauna** Jb 191:4 cf. ii 186 n. 4.

gaupa Gs 14:1 a miswriting of **gadpa.**

gaura 1 (ܓܘܪܐ) adultery, fornication MG 100:18. **ugaura nigar minh̲** AM 95:2 and he will commit adultery with her; **d̲-gaira gaura** PD 1041 who committeth adultery; **gairia gaura** Jb 56:13 committing (plur.) adultery; **gaura uhbala** Gy 363:15 fornication and corruption; **ṭnupia ugaura ugunba** DC 36 pollutions and adultery and thieving; **gaiaria šbaq gauraiun** Jb 82:3 the adulterers abandoned their fornication; **gaura uzaniuta** AM 21:14 fornication and adultery.

Gl. 129:4 missp. فسق *adulterium.*

gaura 2 (Akk. *gamiru* Del. 201 a) bolt, lock Ginzā 143 n. 9. Pl. **gauria. uahidlun lbabia usaliq ʿl gaurh̲** Gy 127:23 (var. DC 22. 123 & Leid. **lgauria**) he locked the doors and put up the bolts; **gauria uaqlidia** Gy 145:13 bolts and keys.

***gaura 3** (P. گبر) fire-worshipper. Found only in pl. **gauria. ušabima ušubin alpia gauria hauia šria ʿlh̲** DAb and there are 770,000 fire-worshippers dwelling in it.

gauša (ܓܘܫܐ) depth, profundity. **rauma ugauša** ATŠ I no. 21 = PD 269 the height and the depth.

gaz 1 (an international expr. der. from the name of the town Gaza) fine muslin, gauze; see E. Littmann, *Morgenländische Wörter im Deutschen*[2] (1924), p. 94, where a more recent explanation is suggested: < Ar. قزّ (qazz) cotton flock, silk; so also Persian loan-w.

gaz 2 (Mod.) gas. **mia d̲-gaz** DC 45 petroleum.

gazania ZDMG xix 123:4 a family name.

gazuma (גזומא, ܓܙܘܡܐ) violent (of temper), pugnacious, truculent. Fem. **gazumtia**; or read גְּזוּמָא, DtZ cut off, threaten. **rugzana ugazuma** (var. **gazim**) **hauia** AM 8:4 he will be quick-tempered and violent; **hamima uhazuma** AM 90:4 fiery and pugnacious; **kbaštia ugazumtia hauia** AM 80:14 she will be overbearing and pugnacious.

gaṭana, pl. **gaṭania** AM 14 a var. of **gaṭina.**

gaṭapta, gaṭupta, guṭupta (q.v.), **giṭupta** (rt. GṬP, cf. Syr. ܩܛܘܦܐ) picking (fruits), harvesting, cutting, lopping (from tree), vintage; numbness, torpor, weakness, limping. Pl. **gaṭapiata** AM 23:18 as a var. of **gaṭupta. guṭuptaikun** Gy 324:19, 22 (varr. Sh. 'Abd.'s copy **giṭuptaikun,** DC 22. 322 **gaṭuptaikun**) your vintage (Lidzb. emends the latter to **guṭuptan** our vintage Ginzā 331 n. 1), **giṭuptun** Gy 336:11 (var. DC 22. 332 **guṭuptun**) their vintage; **ukd̲ mitapa šahaita ugaṭupta** (var. **gaṭapiata**) AM 23:18 and when he recovers, he will have exhaustion and weakness.

gaṭina (קְטִינָא, ܩܛܝܢܐ) slender, slim, thin, dainty, tiny, attenuated, diminutive, small. Fem. **gaṭintia.** Pl. masc. **gaṭinia,** fem. **gaṭinata, gaṭiniata. ʿrika ugaṭina** AM 8:14 tall and slender; **ʿrika šaqh̲ ugaṭina kraiih̲** AM 6:ult. her limbs are long and her feet small; **ugaṭinia kankuzia** AM 8:17 and his chin is small; **ugaṭinia kaplh̲** AM 45:6 and his loins are lean; **ṭibla gaṭina** RD 21 small drum; **gaṭina kd̲ zimta gaṭna** RD C 20 slender like a thin hair.

gaṭinata, gaṭiniata (v. preced.) something thin, (as part of the body prob.) nerves. **uširianh̲ ugaṭinata ugirmia** ATŠ II no. 135, DC 34. 421 **gaṭiniata** the veins, nerves, and bones.

gaṭiria (rt. **GṬR I**) AM 98:6. Joined together.

gaṭla 1 (act. pt. st. emph. of **GṬL**) murderer MG 112:antep. **bʿda d̲-gaṭlun** Gy 355:3 in the hand of their murderer MG 181:2.

gaṭla 2 = **giṭla** MG 100:8. **hirba ugiṭla nizal bhiua bala** AM 227:10 f. sword and slaying will accompany grazing flocks; **gaṭla ugiṭla** AM 278:18 slaying and murder.

gaṭlʿil DAb, **gaṭliʿil** RD I name of a steering-paddle of Ṣahriel (Lidzb. Mand. Gl. '*Rudermann*').

gaṭma a var. of **giṭma.**

gaṭna s. **GṬN.**

gaṭra = **giṭra. gṭar gaṭra bgauaihun** AM tie a knot in them; **btrin gaṭria btrin ṭabia** (said when tying the girdle in the daily office) with two knots—with two virtues; **šqalth̲ llbušh̲ ulgaṭrh̲ brazh̲** Lidzb. MA I removed his garment and his garland with its mystery.

gaia s. **GAA.**

gaiara 1 (nom. act. pe. of **GUR**) adulterer, lecher, adj. lecherous, adulterous. Fem. **gaiartia.** Pl. **gaiaria ugaiarata** Gs 30:paen., **gubria gaiaria. uʿnšia gaiariata** Gy 256:8 adulterers male and female, adulterous men and women; **ʿnta gaiartia** Jb 71:15 a wanton woman, a whore; **bhazin maṭarta gaiaria mištailia** DAb in this purgatory lechers are put to the question; **gaiaria šbaq gauraiun** s. **gaura 1.**

gaiara 2 (rt. **GUR II** = **GRR**) AM 89:13 barber (v.s. **gizta**).

gaiuta, giuta (ܓܐܝܘܬܐ) excellence, splendour, glory MG 146:16.

gaiṭa DC 44. 2097, var. **giṭa** (קִיטָא, ܩܝܛܐ) summer MG 38:bottom.

gaiib (Ar. غايب) DC 45 etc. (often in mod. texts) hidden.

gaiid Zotb. 218 right 15 a village near Howeiza.

gailania (P. گيلانى) often in coloph., a family name.

gaim only in Gl. 35:8 اسفنجه *spongia* ابر.

gaimuraṭ s. **arudan.**

gaisa (ܓܝܣܐ) robber, marauder (?); deadly sickness (?); vomited, cast out. **gaisa d̠-gaiis** DC 48, Oxf. roll g 998 and a marauder (-demon) that plunders (or a nausea-demon that seizes [a sick man]), (Lidzb. a band which assembles, Jb ii 38 n. 5. Doubtful). **ugaisa** (var. **ud̠gisa**) . . . **latiklun** v.s. **gisa 1.**

gair (Ar. غير) not, except, other. **malka hurina gair malkaiun** AM 257:39 another king who is not their (own) king.

gairṭabia DC 22. 469 a miscop. of **gzarṭabaiia** Gs 84:5.

gal, gala 1 (גָּל, גְּלָא) rubbish-heap, ordure, dung, dirty places, outskirts. **baitai gal baṣra** Zotb. 231 left 17 my house (is) in the outskirts of B; **bgala nitbun uharub binataihun nihuia** Ṣâb.'s AM they will dwell in dirty places, and there will be destruction amongst them; **gala uqira** DC 16 ordure and pitch; **had minaihun d̠-bgala aita** DC 6 one of them is that which exists in an ordure-heap; **qin rabtia d̠-hᶜ gala šumh̠** ATŠ I no. 263 the great Q., whose name is Filth.

gala 2 (גַּלָּא, ܓܠܐ, ܓܐܠܐ) tortoise, turtle. **hiuia ugala** ATŠ I no. 256 serpent and tortoise; **gala uriqa** DC 15, **riqa ugala** ATŠ I no. 263, 6 & 46 toad and tortoise.

galaia (nom. ag. from **GLA I**) revealer MG 120: antep. **galaia d̠-ainh̠ galian** CP 87:ult., ML 108:9 revealer whose eyes are open; **galaia d̠-mgalil kasiata** Gy 61:23 revealer who revealeth hidden things.

galalta (nom. act. pa. of **GLA I = GLL II**) revelation MG 122. **galalta uaprašata** Jb 24:11 revelation and explanations; **galil galalta** Gy 134:4 he revealed a revelation; **galalta rabtia d-ᶜtiahbat ladam** HG 91 the Great Revelation which was given to A.

galam Ṣâb.'s AM a place-name (v.s. **gura galam**).

galar (possibly a miscop. of ***galab**, cf. ܓܠܒܐ < Akk. *gallabu*) knife. **asip asip lnbu liugan bgalar abraham** DC 43 J 69 destroy, destroy N. L. with the knife of A.

galat (Ar. غَلَّة, or pl. غَلّات) AM 269:40 harvest, crops.

galgla, pl. **giglia** (rt. ***GLGL = GRGL**) IM 80, 92 globe, sphere IM Gl.

galiata (adj. fem. pl. st. emph. of **GLA**) *patefactae* MG 165:20. **galiata ukasiata** ATŠ I no. 26, revelations and hidden mysteries (lit. revealed and hidden things).

galiuta (ܓܠܝܘܬܐ) revelation, clarity MG 146:16. Miscop. **galiata** (only once in DC 34). **ugaliuta d̠-glᶜia bᶜuṣraikun** Gy 157:21 and the revelation disclosed in your thought; **iadita ugaliuta** Gy 2:19 knowledge and revelation.

gam = qam. gam arsa a var. of **agam arasa** (s. **agam**); **iuma d̠-habšaba gam šamiš** Par. 26 Sunday is for the Sun; **iuma d̠-trin habšaba gam sin** ibid. Monday is for the Moon; **hazin baba asara gam ᶜnta d̠-mula dra** DC 45 this charm is a binding for a woman that carries an embryo; **gam kiba d̠-riša** DC 46. 137:11 for headache.

gama (Ar. غَمّ) worry, trouble (still used in modern Mandaic). **hitra ugama damin kd̠ hdadia** AM 155:antep. joy and worry are alike; **ᶜu bṣilmia gama hu** AM 254:6 if it is in Gemini it presages trouble; **gama ušira** AM 254:11 trouble and evil; **gama ukiba banašia nihuia** AM 267:8 there will be worry and disease amongst people.

gamama Ṣâb.'s AM a var. of **gumama.**

gamba 1, ganba 1 (גַּבָּא, ܓܒܐ, cf. st. abs. & cstr. ܓܢܒ & Ar. جَنْب) flank, side, border MG 50:18, 100:6. Prep. **(a)gambia, (a)ganbia** v.s. **agambia. gambh̠ d̠-riqa** Gy 280:2 the sides of the tortoise; **gamba d̠-nhir** (varr. **nhar, nahr**) Gy 391:2 the side of the nose; **gamba d̠-ᶜušna** Gy 338:17 (var. Sh. 'Abd.'s copy **ganbia ᶜušna**) the flank of a stallion; **gambia d̠-aina** AM 287:13 borders of the eyes; **gambaihun mhun** Gy 361:19 f. they struck their sides; **d̠-traṣ klila ugambh̠ atna, burzinqa** Jb 45:2 f. who put on a wreath and a turban besides.

gamba 2 (an exceptional form) = **ganaba. unuṭrh̠ lbaba mn gambia** DC 48. 231 and guard the door from thieves.

gambaruata, ganbarata, gabarata varr. of **gabaruata** (q.v.). **gambaruata bᶜurašlam** CP 52:17, ML 68:4 miracles in Jerusalem, cf. n. 2; **bgambaruath̠ mitnahazbh̠** DC 22. 76 a var. of Gy 81:18 v.s. **gabaruata; uhauun gambaruata lnišimta** ATŠ II no. 256 and they showed wondrous deeds to the soul; **kdub lgabra d̠-baiia mibad gambaruata . . . ulkul gambaruata** DC 44. 1760 f. write for a man that seeketh to perform miracles . . . and for all miracles . . .

gamušan, gamišan, gamšin (P. pl. of گاوميش Syr. loan-w. ܓܡܘܫܐ, ܓܡܫܐ, ܓܘܡܫܐ, & varr., Ar. loan-w. جاموش) pl. buffaloes. Sg. not found. **baqaria gamišan** (var. **gamušan**) DAb, RD A 8 s. **baqara.**

***gamsa, kamṣa** (קַמְצָא, ܩܡܨܐ > Akk. *qamāṣu*) locust. Pl. **gamṣia.** Masc. **ugamṣia nitun** AM 195:11 and locusts will come; **gamsia d̠-aklia piria uᶜmbia uᶜlania** AM 174:10 locusts which will devour fruits, vines, and trees.

gamriaiil DC 40 (angel-list) an angel.

gamšin = gamišan (q.v.). **turia (uturata) ugamšin ususiata** DC 46. 15:2 (an elsewhere) bulls, (cows), buffaloes, and horses; **turia ugamšin** DC 46.

ganaba (nom. ag. pe. of **GNB** גַּנָּבָא, ܓܰܢܳܒܳܐ) (*a*) thief, (*b*) crafty, cunning, MG 120:13. Pl. masc. **ganabia,** fem. **ganabiata** MG 169:5. (*a*) **lganaba amarlh̲ gnub** Gy 208:15 f. to the thief he saith 'Steal!'; **lganaba** ibid. 16; **ganabia uganabiata** Gs 30:23 thieves male and female; (*b*) **sipra uhakima hauia uganaba hauia** AM 97:13 he will be learned and wise, but he will be cunning.

ganam a man's name. **ganam br mhatam** ZDMG xix 123:3.

ganania DC 34. 943 for **gninia** (?).

ganba 1 = **gamba,** (also) back, body. **ganbh̲ nhar** Sh. 'Abd.'s copy var. of Gy 391:2 s. **d̲-gamba**; **kiba d̲-ganbh̲ nihuilh̲** Şâb.'s AM his flank will be aching; **umanzia uṭupria uganba** ATŠ I no. 217 (list of physical organs and features) and hair and nails and back; **aqamra d̲-mn ganbaiin d̲-hiuaniata** DC 22. 238 (Gy 243:14 f. omits **ganbaiin**) wool from the flanks (or backs) of the beasts; **ganbh̲ d̲-šura** Jb 251:13 beside the wall; **šabima ušubin (a)ganbia tauria uaqnia** DAb seven hundred and seventy head of oxen and sheep; **utlatma ušitin alpia ganbia aqna ʿtlh̲** DAb and it has 360,000 head (of herds) of sheep.

ganba 2 = **ganpa.** **ganbia litlh̲ d̲-ṭaiis** ATŠ he hath no wings that he could fly (with).

ganba 3 DC 30 a var. of **gunba** Jb 141:5.

ganbarata a var. of **gambaruata.**

ganbia (rt. **GNB**) in **uʿtlh̲ ganbia d̲-aina** AM (*often*) she takes the eye (i.e. is captivating, makes a pleasing impression [?]). (Always with red hair) AM trs. p. 7 n. 6.

ganbiniiil RD 21, **ganbʿil** RD 16 theophorous names.

gangarata, var. **gangariata** (pl. of ܓܰܓܪܬܳܐ < גַּרְגַּרְתָּא, Akk. *ganguritū*) throat, tonsils MG 76:9, 78:26. Used preferably in pl. (like H. גַּרְגְּרוֹת), sg. **gangarta** is exceptional. **kib(a d̲)-gangarata** AM (often) a sore throat; **kiba d̲-liba ugangarata** AM 182:1 pain of the heart and throat; **bgangaratun** DC 37. 38 in their throat(s); **mbaliata ugangariata** (var. **gangarata**) DC 47 & 48 palate and tonsils; **ugangarath̲ zaim** DC 20 and his throat rattles (?); **gangarta d̲-razia hu** ATŠ I no. 224 it (: the *membrum virile*) is the throat of mysteries.

gandaita (etm. unknown) left BZ 9 n. 3. Masc. not found. **udupnh̲ gandaita kaibalh̲** AM 7:5 and her left side will pain her; **kdublh̲ lʿdh̲ d̲-iaminh̲ ulkraiia d̲-gandaita** AM 132:4 write on his right hand and on his left foot.

***ganza** a var. of **ginza,** cf. **ganzaihun** (var. of **ginzaihun**) their treasure MG 13:middle.

ganzaʿiil s. **ganziil.**

ganzibra (Paž. *ganzubar*, Pahl. *ganǧâβar*, Mod. P. گنجور, Aram. loan-w. גִּזְבְּרָא, ܓܰܙܒܪܳܐ & varr., H. גזבר; pron. *ganzoβra*) treasurer, the ecclesiastical rank above that of *tarmīda* (priest). A *ganzibra* is necessary for a marriage, a *masiqta* and the consecration of a *tarmīda* MMII Ind, AM 67 n. 1. MG 51: bottom. Used also as a title of M.-d̲-H. (Gy 134:9 Ginzā 150 n. 3) and Hibil-Ziwa (Gy 134:12 Ginzā 151 n. 1). Pl. **ganzibria. tarmidia uganzibria** Morg. 188:4; **rbaihun anat d̲-ganzibria** Gy 342:19 f. thou art a teacher of the *ganzibras*. Gl. 42:3 missp. بطريک *patriarcha* مفتى; 161:13 missp. مطران *episcopus*.

ganzibruta, later **ganzibrukta** (abstr. noun from **ganzibra**) ganzivrate, rank of ganzibra MG 78:4. **tum kul man d̲-milgiṭ ganzibruta** ATŠ then, any man that reacheth the ganzivrate; **ganzibrukta** (often in coloph., still used, pron. *ganzeβroχta*).

ganziil, ganziʿil ganzʿil, ginzaiil, ginziil, kanziʿil a personification of heavenly treasure. **ganzaʿiil malka d̲-ginza d̲-ʿutria luath̲** CP 409:14 G. the king with whom all the 'uthras' treasures are (kept); **malka iauar ganzʿil ʿutra** Morg. 5:7; **iauar ganziil rba** PD 731; **iauar ganziʿil** PD 1124, 1198; **maṭarta d̲-ganziʿil brh̲ d̲-ptahil** RD C 6 the purgatory of G. son of P.; **ganziʿil uahh̲** ATŠ II no. 302 (a designation of the 5 days of **paruanaiia**).

ganib, ganiba (rt. **GNB**) unclean, in a state of isolation for impurity, outcast. Pl. **ganibia. lahauia miṭanap ṭanupia kd̲ ganibia** ATŠ II no. 32 there are no polluting pollutions like unto 'untouchables'; **uhanath̲ nišimta akuat ganib huat** ATŠ I no. 184 and that soul has become like a person-isolated-for-impurity; **mṭanap ṭnupia kd̲ ganiba** ATŠ I no. 181 it has been greatly polluted, like unto an outcast; **hanath̲ tarmida unišimta bškinat** (read **bškinta**) **ganibia** ATŠ II no. 32 that priest and soul in the cult-hut are cut-off by impurity; **lhšuka ganiba šaplin** DC 35 they sink down to the unclean darkness; **šitlia d̲-hauilh̲ minh̲ ganibia** ATŠ I no. 184 and the children that she will have by him will be outcasts; **ukaunata mdakai mn ganiba** ATŠ I no. 232 and a woman attentive (about ablution) is purer than a woman in a state of uncleanness; **latitirṣun taga lʿnta ula ʿl ganiba** ATŠ II no. 5 do not set the crown on a woman, nor on a person in ritual uncleanness; **ganiba d̲-aba litlh̲** PD 1595, 1622 a bastard without father; **adinqia aba ganiba** (read **-ia**) **hauin** ATŠ II no. 32.

ganibuta (abstr. noun from **GNB**) state of uncleanness: **raz ganibutia** DC 34. 123 the secret of his ritual uncleanness.

ganinia = **ginia** (pl. of **ginta**). **šarša br ganinia** DC 34 a garden-root (i.e. a cultivated not a wild species).

ganʿiaiil, ganʿiaʿil DC 43 E 84 as foll.

ganʿil a theophorous name. **arqa d̲-ruha ganʿil šumh̲** RD F 1 the land of R. whose name is G.

ganpa (גַּדְפָּא a doublet of **gadpa 1** influenced by **kanpa** q.v.) wing, side, sail MG 40:7, 107:1. Fem. MG 157:19. Pl. **ganpia. niṭaripbun bganpia** Gy 101:11 he strikes out with his arms; **ganph̲ hasir ubṣir mn ṣipra** Gy 124:9 its wings are weaker and less perfect than (those of) birds Ginzā 140 n. 2; **ganph̲ hbaṭ barqa** Gy 84:16 he beat the ground with his arms (wings); **ganph̲ ṣarlh̲** Gy 339:1, **ṣarlih̲ ganpia**

Gs 104:4 he formed wings for it; **ganpia d̲-markabatun** PD 1447, Gy 331:1, 5 f., **ganpẖ d̲-markabatun** PD 997 the sails of their ships; **arba d̲-ganpia d̲-ziua** Jb 151:15 a boat whose sails are of radiance; **(a)ganpia uligria litlẖ** Jb 42:4 hath neither arms nor feet ii 47 n. 5; **kul had masiqta tlatma ušitin ganpia ʿtlẖ** ATŠ II no. 65, 257 each m. has 365 wings.

ganṣa (etym. doubtful, cf. ܓܘܢܙܐ LS) twitch, jerk (?). Hapaxleg. **ainẖ uparṣupẖ uspihatẖ ganṣa nasba** Jb 124:11 his eyes, face, and lips begin to twitch (?), cf. ii 121 n. 1. Var. **ginṣa.**

ganša AM 204:17 name of a city BZ Ap. II. Ṣâb.'s AM miscop. **ganpa.**

***gasa,** pl. **gasia** (doubtf., cf. גַּסָּא) a large quantity (?). **ugasia mraria bgauẖ rmia** Morg. 262/16:15 and large quantities of poison were put into it; but more prob. a mere miscop. of **kasa d̲-mrara** ibid. 15:bottom a bowl of poison (although **kasa** is a very usual word).

gasṭata s. **gastata.**

gasina a miscop. of **gisana** (pl. of **gisa**) fem. **btartinin gasinai** Morg. 262/16:8 with both my cheeks.

gaskulta (read **skulta,** rt. **SKL**) folly, foolishness. **gaskulta raṭin** AM 154:17 and talks sheer folly.

gasṭata, gastata (P. گست) fem. pl. ugly, shameful things, hobgoblins. **qmaha d̲-gastata** (name of a phylactery).

gap a genie of the underworld, usually mentioned with his consort **gapan** MSchr 145 n. 1. **abuiẖ gap šumẖ** Gy 126:14 his (i.e. Ur's) father's name is G.; **gap zauẖ d̲-hu ahu** Gy 154:14, 156:3 G. her (i.e. Rūha's) husband who is her brother; **gap ahuk** Gy 146:7 G. thy brother; **gap abuhan** Gy 146:13, 147:4, 18, 23, 150:4, 7 our father G.; **latra d̲-iatib gap gap d̲-hiziẖ lziuẖ** Jb 251:6 to the place where dwelleth G., when G. saw his radiance; **gap ugapan** Gy 139:4, 7, 9, 140:1, 150:20 f.; **gap ugapan rba** Gy 146:1; **qin brata d̲-gap** s. **qin.**

gapa (גַּפָּא) a doublet of **gadpa.** Still used (pron. *gappa*). **gapa d̲-nišra** AM 121:12 an eagle's wing; **bgapa mašigilin** Gy 224:9 (var. DC 22. 218 . . . **ʿu mašiglun,** Sh. 'Abd.'s copy . . . **mšagilun**) they wash them with a duster (?) Ginzā 225 n. 4.

gapan s. **gap.**

GAṢ (ܓܨ) to loathe, reject, vomit, abhor, repudiate.

Pe. Act. pt. with encl. **gaiṣilun ʿl lišanun** ATŠ I no. 238 they will recant their words.

gaṣuṣa (doubtful, hardly ܓܨܨܐ Löw 312, Jb ii 163 n. 2) perh. draw-string. **ugaṣuṣa bgauẖ lahdar** Jb 162:3 and the draw-string doth not go round it (: in the fishing-net. The draw-string pulls the net together so that fish are enclosed).

gaṣiaiil DAb a theophorous name.

garaia 1 (rt. **GRR**) a scraper, something for scratching or scraping.

garaia 2 = **giraia.**

garamka a var. of **gramka.**

garaṣṭum (P. گرستون) weight (of pair of balances). No st. emph. **hazin garaṣṭum** DAb this is the weight.

garat (Ar. غارة) incursion, raid. **garat nihuia** AM 284:22 there will be incursion(s); **garatdan ʿbadiun ʿuraba** DC 35:coloph. the Bedouins made an incursion upon us (: raided us).

garba, girba 3 (rt. **GRB**) prey, booty. **garbin garba** Gy 232:1 they take prey.

garbilia (rt. **GRB** with inclusion of the encl. **l** cf. **garbilẖ** Gy 390:8) raiders, marauders. **unganabia ugarbilia ugaṭlia minaihun** AM 285:15 and thieves and marauders and murderers are amongst them.

gargul, gargla (גלגלא, ܓܝܓܠܐ) wheel, convolution, heavenly sphere, circle; st. abs. fig. rumbling, thunder. Varr. **gargila, girgla, girgila.** Pl. **garglia,** varr. **gargilia, girglia, girgilia.** Sg. fem., pl. masc. MG 55:1, 78:19, 127:13, 158:16, 301:1, BZ 168 n. 1, Lidzb. explains **gargul** from קרקר and separates it from **gargla** Jb ii 46 n. 6. **garglia** (Pet. **girglia**) **markabatun** DC 22. 168 = Gy 175:12 the wheels of their chariots; **garglia gauaiia** PD 828 the celestial spheres; **ultapukia garglia** CP 105:15 at the turn of the wheels; **garglia d̲-muta** Q 67:35, ATŠ II no. 359, DC 41. 451 f. the whirligigs of death; **ana bqalai garglia naidia** Jb 120:10 at my voice the spheres tremble; **garglia** (var. **gargilia**) **umarkabata nad** Jb 109:10 f. (var. DC 30) the spheres and the chariots trembled; **garglia** (var. **girglia**) **umarkabata nad** Jb 116:10; **girglia d̲-nhura** Jb 233:3 the spheres of light; **girglia d̲-rugza** Gy 88:19 wheels of anger; **gargul gihrat** Jb 41:10 thunder pealed; **gargul gahra** AM 265:18; **gargul tihuia** AM 265:3 there will be a rumbling; **atuat d̲-gargul bʿšumia** AM 264:37 portents of a rumbling in the sky; **mištaušia girglia** Gy 310:16 (heavenly) spheres are confused; **bgirglia lahadra** Gy 10:24 it turneth not on wheels; **ʿl girglia** (var. **garglia**) **mitapkia** Gy 323:4 it (: water) turneth on wheels Ginzā 328 n.1; **zurpunia** (var. **zirpunia**) **d̲-bgarglia rmiin** ATŠ II no. 203 (var. DC 6) the linch-pins which are placed in wheels; **kul mahu ʿka bgargilia** ATŠ all that is in the spheres; **nišimtẖ ʿstakakat bgarglia gauaiia** ATŠ I no. 78 his soul will be held (back) in the inner spheres(?). s. also **girglia.**

gargiʿil DAb, **gargʿil** RD 35 a supernatural being, a demon.

gardunis DC 40. 576 (angel-list) an angel.

garzana Zotb. 218: left 10, 220: right 30 a city.

garṭapta (ܩܘܪܛܦܬܐ Ar. قرطب) Morg. 194:ult. cutting instrument, knife, blade. Sg. sporadic, pl. **garṭupiata** (s.v.) frequent, **garṭupiana** rare.

garṭupiata pl. of **garṭapta** (above) MG 38:23, 128:2. **sikinia ugarṭupiata** Gy 143:19 knives and blades; **lbušia d̲-hirbia usipia . . . ugarṭupiata** DC 37. 342 ff. garments of swords, scimitars . . . and blades.

garibia (Mand. pl. of Ar. غريب) strange, strangers. **anašia garibia** AM 156:4 strangers;

aškal d-garibia AM 277:22 strange phenomena. Gl. 121:4, 14 missp. غريب *alienus, hospes* بيگانه.

gari'il DAb = **gargi'il.**

garištum RD 50 a var. of **garaštum.**

garmaba (P. گرمابه) hot bath, bagnio, public bath. Varr. **girmaba, karmaba. l . . . mizal lgarmaba** AM 162:15 for going to the bath; **halin gubria d-ailun lgarmaba** DAb = RD E 26 those men who enter a public bath (*hammâm*); **kd garmabia bn'ian** (var. **garmabh biniania**) **uhauma šabqilh** DAb (var. RD C 6 corrupt) they are built like hot baths and loose heat on it.

garmanka a var. of **gramka** (q.v.). **muhulta d-nahlilh garmanka** Bodl. 13 the sieve with which they sieve fine flour.

garmidia (גַּרְמִידָא, ܓܰܪܡܺܝܕܳܐ) RD 41, RD F two cubits. Sg. not found.

gar'il RD 35 a var. of **gari'il.**

garp'il malka Lond. roll D 507 a genie.

gašaua, gašauat (Ar. غُشَاوَة) covering, filminess, lumps of earth. **lilbaiad ulgašaua l'ain** AM 287:14 for whiteness and for filminess of the eye; **kdub halin 'ala gašauata mauzud** AM 130:17 write these on prepared clay tablets (?).

gašir a var. of **gišar.**

gatrun DC 34 a herb, plant, or shrub.

GBA (גבא, ܓܒܐ) to choose out, select, gather. Still used in pa.

PE. Pf. **man gibih lmnat rbia** Jb 230:1 who chose out the portion of the Great (Life)? Act. pt. **gabia** (s.v.).

PA. Pf. **ama lnapšh gabia** Gy 23:17, **gaba ama lnapšh** Gy 382:12 f. (var. Sh. 'Abd.'s copy **gabia** . . .) he chose out a people for himself; with suff. **gabiuk hiuia lbnh uarqba lšitlh** JRAS 1938 3:26 the serpent picked thee out for her child and the scorpion for her brood.

ETHPE. Pf. **balbuš rqiha d-minh 'tigbit** DC 37 in the sky-garment from which thou wert picked out (read **'tgiblit** 'thou wert formed'?).

DER.: **gabia, gba 1, gbita, gibia, gibta.**

gba 1 (rt. **GBA**) fee, collected due. Masc. **zidqa d-rimilh ašualia nihuia gbak** ATŠ II no. 422 the alms which the novice-priest placed down is thy due portion; **ziqda d-rimilh lašualiak nihuia gbak** ATŠ II no. 422 the alms placed down for thy pupil shall be thy fee.

gba 2 = **'gba.**

***gbaba, *gababa** (גְּבָבָא) roll, skein, ball of thread. Pl. **gbabia.** Masc. **tlata gababia d-panba . . . utartin gbabia kitana** DC 46 three balls of cotton . . . and two balls of linen thread.

gbal, gbil (rt. **GBL**) moulder, former, maker, creator IM Gl. **gbal pagrh** Gs 47:2, **gbil** (var. **gbal**) **pagria** Gs 44:21 (var. Leid. & DC 22. 433) the maker of the body.

gbala, gbila (rt. **GBL**) fashion, form, shape. AM 263:24 fighting (?), confusion (?) BZ 166 n. 1.

gbana DC 25. 55 a var. of **gbina.**

gbar st. abs. & cstr. of **gabra** MG 151:8. **gbar kšit** CP 129:16, ML 157:11, Jb 167:7 the true man; **gbar nukraia** Gy 81:14 = **gabra nukraia** (s. **gabra**).

gbaruata s. **gabaruata.**

gbarta (גְּבַרְתָּא, ܓܒܰܪܬܳܐ but with the meaning of גְּבוּרְתָא, ܓܒܽܘܪܬܳܐ) strength, might MG 116:1; (cf. s. גברתא Levy: *Neuh. Wörterb.*) male organ Ginzā 132 n. 8. **uhauith gbarth** Gy 118:19 (var. DC 22. 114 **uhauith gabaruath**) I displayed his male organ (or I showed his power [?]).

GBB, GUB (גבב, cf. Syr. ܓܒܝܒܐ *gibbosus*) to bend, curve. Antonym of **MTH, PST.**

PE. Pf. ***gab** he bent IM Gl. Impf. with encl. **'gababh** JRAS 1939 399:16 I bend him. Pass. pt. **qumtai d-gbiba 'tmihtat** Gy 266:6 my stature which was bent down became straight; irregular, miscopied **qumth d-gibaba** DC 51. 128, **qumth d-giba** DC 51. 124, **giba qumtak** DC 37. 75. Inf. **mgab** (read **migab**) IM Gl.

ETHPE. Pf. **'tigbib** he was bent MG 252:2; **'tigbib 'tqis ulapšit** Gy 162:22 f. he curled himself up, he shrank and did not straighten out; **'tigbib ula 'pšit** Gs 3:4, similarly Gy 164:16; **'tigib** DC 22. 157 (a var. of Gy 162:22), **'tgibat** she bent down MG 32:9, 252:3; **qumtai d-mtiha 'tgibat** Gy 264:7 my stature which was straight bent down; **qumtak alma 'tgibat** Gy 266: 10 why did thy form bend down?

ETHPA. Pt. pl. **mitgababia** (varr. **mitgabibia, mitgabbia**) Gy 313:4, 316:13, Jb 195:14 they (will) bow themselves down MG 32:3.

DER.: **g(a)baba, 'gba** (var. **gba 2**).

gbil Gs 44:21 a var. of **gbal**; pass. pt. of **GBL** (see foll.).

gbila (pass. pt. of **GBL**) form(ed), shape(d). Var. **gbala** (q.v.).

gbilta, gibilta (ܓܒܺܝܠܬܳܐ) formation, something moulded, substance to be moulded, material, substance, fashioned material, form assumed. **gibilta d-mn napših . . . giblat** ATŠ I no. 257 a formation that formed itself; **gbilth mn kul mindam 'tgiblat** ATŠ I no. 268 its substance is fashioned out of everything; **gbilta bgauh nigbal** Gy 329:12 we will mould it into a form; **gbilta d-hšuka** Gy 339:13, 373:1.

gbina (גְּבִינָא, ܓܒܺܝܢܳܐ) brow, eyebrow, eyelash. Var. **gbana** (s.v.). Pl. **gbinia.** Masc. **arimit gbinai** Gy 212:8 I lifted my eyebrows; **uprišia ugatinia gbinih** AM 14:3 and his eyebrows are distinguished and fine; **u'rikia gbinia** AM 35:16 and his eyebrows are long; **gbinia uzapania d-ainia** ATŠ I no. 223 eyebrows and eyelashes; **gbina marim** DC 43 haughty brow; **bit gbina** s. **bit.**

gbir s. **gabir.**

gbita (ܓܒܺܝܬܳܐ) choice, selection, selected portion MG 104:6. **gbita d-mardmania gba** Gy 228:16 f. the chosen portion that Lord Mani (var. **marmania**) chose.

GBL (Chr. Pal. & Syr. ܓܒܠ, cf. also Mod. H. גָּבַל 'to knead') to mould, form, fashion, mix, make up. Simple stem often inst. of the refl. MG 215, Ginzā 78 n. 1.

Pe. Pf. (**udaiarh̲ migbal**) **gbal** Gy 79:7 (and its inhabitants) were formed; **gbal unpaq** Gy 278:24 he took shape and came forth; **mn napših̲ . . . giblat** s. **gbilta**; **bišuta minh̲ giblat** Gy 34:11 the evil was made (up) from him; **hʿ bʿdh̲ hiblat ugiblat** ATŠ I no. 278 she writhed and twisted (: took shape) in his hand. Impf. **nigbal** v.s. **gbilta.** Act. pt. **gabil** (*often*) he forms, also substantivally (s.v.), fem. **gabla unapqa** ATŠ I no. 268; **tulita (tulida?) minaihun gabla** ATŠ I no. 269 a worm (offspring) is formed from them. Pass. pt. **razia d̲-minh̲ gbil** Gy 12:15 the mystery which was formed from him; **gbil bisra uzma** Gy 257:20 formed of flesh and blood; **gbilia bisra uzma** Gy 44:14, Gy 347:5, 350:23, Gs 25:22 id. pl. Inf. **migbal** above s. pf.

Pa. Part. pres. **kd̲ škinta mgablitun** ATŠ II no. 374 when ye fashioned a dwelling.

Ethpe. Pf. **ʿtgbil** Gy 78:18 A MG 213: bottom, **ʿtigbil** Jb 52:4; **mn madna ʿtigbil** (var. **ʿtgibil**) DC 42 took shape in the east; **ʿtgiblat** she was formed MG 15:18, 222:middle; **bišuta minh̲ ʿtgiblat** Gy 13:14 (cf. above s. pe. pf.); **ʿtg(i)blit** thou wert formed MG 222:bottom; **ʿtigbiltun** ye were formed MG 224:8; **ʿtigbilnin** Gy 145:2 we were formed MG 224: bottom. Pt. **mitgiblia** Gs 41:12 f. they are formed.

Der.: **gabil, gbal(a), gbil(a), g(i)bilta, gubla, gubal, gibla.**

GBR (Gen. Sem.) to be strong, powerful, to prevail.

Pe. Pf. **gbar ʿlan** CP 88:10, Morg. 242/72:5 (see under af.).

Pa. Pass. pt. (**zriz**) **umgabar** DC 42 (fortified) and strengthened.

Af. Impt. **agbar ʿlan bintan (gbar ʿlan bintan)** CP 88:10, ML 109:1 strengthen our insight.

Ethpa. Pf. **ʿtgabar** Gy 159:23 he became strong; **ʿgabar ʿlai** DC 34. 848 they overpowered me; **ʿtgabrat** Gs 108:10 she became strong. Impf. **nitgabar** AM 187 he will prevail. Pt. **mitgabar** Gs 108:10 id., DC 34. 940 shall become mighty.

Der.: **gabara** (var. **gbara**), **gabaruta,** pl. **gabaruata** (varr. **gbaruata, gambaruata, ganbarata**), **gabarta, gabir** (var. **gbir**), **gabra** (abs. **gbar,** pl. **gubria**), **gabrʿil, gbarta, gubara, gubran.**

gdada 1, gadada = gidada (q.v.). **lihuia gdada umdalai umia d̲-iama amuqia** DC 22. 176 var. of Gy 184:15 (v.s. **gidada**).

gdada 2, gadada (rt. **GDD,** cf. ܓܕܕܐ) strip; (in ritual) a strip of white material used to protect from pollution or sever from contact MMII 39 n. 2, 71 n. 2; (mod., pron. *gədâda, gedâda*) tablecloth (us. spread on ground). Varr. **gadada, gdida** (s.vv.). **gdadia d̲-pamba** DC 38 (cf. s. **gadada**).

gdalta (rt. **GDL,** cf. **gdula, gdulta**) plait, braid, garland, wreath: **mn širiania d̲-sindirka gdulh̲ gdalta lmanzia** DC 34 from the fibres (?) of the date-palm twine a braid for her hair.

GDD (Gen. Sem.) to cut (off), put an end to.

Af. Pt. with encl. **manhitilun umagdilun** DC 43 J 105 they bring them down and cut them off.

Ethpa. Pf. **karkudun ʿgadad** JRAS 1938 4:631 their shuttle snapped short (was cut short).

An irregular form is used with the meaning 'to miscarry': **baṭanita nigindad,** var. **baṭinita nigidnad** AM 216:4 pregnant women will miscarry.

Der.: **g(a)dada 1 & 2,** varr. **gdida, gidada, gida, gunda, guda 1.**

gdula masc., gdulta fem. (cf. גְּדִילָא & גְּדִילְתָּא, ܓܕܘܠܐ & ܓܕܝܠܬܐ) spiral, ringlet (of hair), curled lock of hair, tress, plait, MG 118: middle, 119:5. Pl. masc. **gdulia,** fem. **gduliata** MG 169:12. Both genders but esp. masc. are used also of a kind of demons, hobgoblins, tall spectres, **gdulia** often with the same meaning as **gdultania. gdulh̲ briša** (var. **briših̲**) **satra** Gy 96:21, 329:1, 36:14, **gdula satra briših̲** Gy 85:21, **gdula briša msatra** Gy 81:6 f. she teareth out the tress(es) on her head; **gdulia baṭlia** DC 12. 94, DC 43 & 51, Morg. 196:2, Oxf. roll 201, 205, 229 good-for-naught hobgoblins, vain spectres; **gdulta lilita** DC 43 the lilith G.; **rkašth̲ bgduliath̲** Gy 118:11 I ensnared her in her (own) curled locks.

gdultania (formed from **gdulta** with the suff. **-an** in the same way as **manzania ugadpania, lihania** etc. v.s.vv.) Gy 279: 5 a kind of ghosts (Lidzb. *Lockengeister*), MG 139:16, Furlani *I Nomi* 429.

gdida DC 46. 30:2 a var. of **gdada 2.**

GDL I (ܓܕܠ, Akk. der. *gidlu* bundle, packet) to weave, twist, twine, wreathe up, spin.

Pe. Pf. **ʿu hauia d̲-qra audin uklila lagdal nitkamar** ATŠ I no. 176 should he have read 'we confess' but did not twine the wreath . . .; **klila gidlit** Oxf. 70 a:bottom I twined the wreath; **gdaltinun** DC 27. 430, ATŠ II no. 153 thou (inter)twinedst them. Impf. (**uniqria audin**) **unigdal klila** ATŠ I no. 176 he must (recite 'we confess' and) twine the wreath. Impt. **gdul klila** Q 3:333; with encl. **gdulh̲ gdalta lmanzh̲** DC 34 twine her a braid for her hair. Act. pt. **gadla d̲-klila** CP 7:14, Q 3:11 the twiner of the wreath, pl. **klila minh̲ gadlia** Gy 345:24, **klilia gadlia** Gy 106:15, **gadlatlh̲ klila** DC 27. 69. Pass. pt. pl. **gdilia qarnh̲** Jb 51:5 his forelocks are twisted (cf. s. **qarna**). Inf. **migdal** Jb 51:5.

Pa. Act. pt. with encl. **mgadilan qarnaian brišaian** Gy 135:10. Pass. pt. pl. fem. **mgadla qarnaikun** s. **qarna.**

Af. Act. pt. pl. with encl. (or suff.) **magdilun (ulamapqilun lalahia)** DC 43 J 105 they shall make them (: the gods) writhe (and not let them depart).

Ethpa. Pf. **qarnaihun brišaihun ʿtgadal** Gy 373:5; with encl. **ʿtgadalia qarnai** Gs 42: 15. Pt. fem. pl. **zakuatun brišaihun mitgadlan** Oxf. 13 a their (crowns of) reward(s) are twined round their heads; with encl. **mitgadalkun qarnaikun** Gy 178:10.

Der.: **gadla, gdalta, gdula, gdulta, gdultania, gudlania.**

GDL II (H. גָּדַל rel. to **GDL I**) to rise up to a height, grow, be(come) great, large, or tall. Only refl.

Ethpe. Pf. **ʿgdilitun kma iauar usimat hiia** ŠQ 19:32 ye have been exalted as much as Y. and S.-H.

Ethpa. (Pf. like impt.). Impf. **nitgadal širšak unisaq lriš** Gs 59:18, DC 3 etc. thy root shall be raised up (: prosper) and rise to the uppermost (: attain success); **titgadal ʿruta** CP 244:1 ŠQ 20:18 enlightenment shall become great **nitgadlun bziua d̠-iardna** DC 27 they are glorified in the glory of the jordan. Impt. **ʿzil ʿtgadal ʿtgadal** CP 346:12 go, prosper, become great . . ., but **laʿtgadal** ATŠ II no. 222 be not boasting (or vainglorious).

GDM (ܓܕܡ LS) to cut off, hew off.

Pe. Pf. neg. **lagdam** PD 1556.

Der.: **gidma.**

GDP (Aram. pa., H. גדף pi. Ges., LS) to scrape, cut away; to blaspheme, revile, reproach.

Refl.: Pt. **sruth̠ mitgidpa** Gy 311:6 f. (var. DC 22. 308 **mitgadpa**) his foulness is scraped away.

Der.: **gadupa, (gadpa, gadpania).**

GHA I (גָּעָה, ܓܥܐ) to (utter a) cry, make a convulsive sound or sudden noise, sob.

Pe. Pf. **ghun** JRAS 1939 401:1; **ghun ubkun** DC 37. 360 f. they sobbed and wept. Act. pt. **qahda ugahia** Gy 313:8 she crieth and weepeth; **gahia ubakia** Gy 82:1 she sobbeth and weepeth, MG 72:14 (cf. **gahia 1** s.v.).

GHA II (ܓܗܐ LS) to flee from, be scared away.

Pe. Act. pt. **habara gahia** Gy 282:1, **hšuka gahia** s. **gahia 1.**

Refl. (irreg.): **ʿtaguhat** (a *qmâhâ*) she was scared away.

gharta (rt. **GHR** q.v.) shout, cry, noise, rumbling.

ghuka (rt. **GHK**) laughter, derision; (in DC 45 & 46) a (convulsive) sound (prob. a miscop. of **guha**). **ghuka manhitit ʿlauaihun** DC 37. 47 thou causest derision to fall on them; **ghuka** (var. **guha**) **d̠-hraqa d̠-šina** DC 46 (var. DC 45) the sound of gnashing the teeth; **hraqa d̠-šina ughuka mn bin spihata** DC 45 grinding of teeth and making convulsive sounds between the lips.

GHṬ (גָּהַט) to erase, rub over, wipe off (?).

Pe. Impt. **ghuṭ** (var. **ghiṭ**) **rapa uhbilh̠** DC 44. 1164 = Morg. 263/17:23, wipe him out, enfeeble and ruin him.

GHK (גחך, ܓܚܟ, a doublet of **AHK**) to laugh MG 72 n. 2. Still used (pron. pf. *gehex*, pres. *qagâhexnâ*).

Pe. Pf. ***ghik** cf. mod. form (just cited), **asbrit ugihkit** s. **SBR.** Impf. **tigihkun** ye (will) laugh MG 227:bottom. Act. pt. **gahik** DAb *ride(bi)t* (cf. mod. form above); **gahkia** CP 340:ult. they laugh pl. **gahkin umitparpin** DC 34:883 they laugh and make merry. Pass. pt. **ghika hauia bahh̠** AM (?) he will be laughed at by his brothers.

Pa. Pt. **mgahka** (s.v.). Nom. act. **mgahkana** (s.v.).

Af. Pt. with encl. **maghiklh̠** AM 123:14 *faci(e)t eum ridere.*

Ethpe. Pf. **ruha ʿgihkat** DC 22. 110 R. burst into laughter.

Gl. 10:15 f. missp. اهزى | *illudere* خنديد.

Der.: **ghuka, mgahka, mgahkana** (var. **maghkana**).

(**GHK II** a miscop. of **GHN,** cf. **gihkit** DC 22. 85 inst. of **gihnit** Gy 90:17).

GHN I (Gen. Aram. LS) to bend, bow, stoop.

Pe. Pf. ***ghin** cf. MG 219:antep. Impf. **nighun** he bends, will bend ibid. **ʿghun** Gy 208:7 (var. DC 22. 199 & Sh. ʿAbd.'s copy **ghun**) I will bow. Act. pt. **kipa ugahna qumtaihun** s. **KUP, gahna usagda ruha** Gy 115:10 R. bowed herself and worshipped (hist. pres.).

Ethpe. Pf. **ʿtgihnat** JRAS 1937 594 she bowed herself.

GHN II (metath. of גנח, ܓܢܚ, a doublet of **GNA III**) to rumble; to stamp.

Pe. Pf. **ʿqbai gihnit barqa** Gy 90:17 with my heel I stamped on the ground. Act. pt. **guha gahna lqudamaihun** Gy 220:9 a rumbling sounded before them Ginzā 221 n. 3, **uhanath̠ guha d̠-gahna qudamh̠ ʿur** DAb and that rumbling which precedeth Ur.

Der.: s. **GNA III.**

GHP (< קפח, Syr. ܩܦܚ, Chr. Pal. ܩܦܚ LS) to shatter, break to pieces ML 23 n. 5.

Pe. Pf. **kul daiua d̠-ṭribh̠ ghip** DC 3 no. 16 (var. CP 21:10 **d̠-ṭribia ʿghip** ML 23:8) each demon that striketh him (var. dasheth himself on me) was shattered; **minh̠ gihpat iauna** Gy 381:6 the dove broke off some (leaves); **udṭribh̠ ghapth̠** CP 21:10, ML 23:9 and whomever I struck I shattered him. Act. pt. with encl. **sahria udaiuia gahiplun** ATŠ I no. 250 it shattereth all demons and devils.

Pa. Pass. pt. **ulahma mgahap** (var. **mgahpa**) **nikul** AM and he will eat broken victuals.

Ethpe. Pf. **ʿghip** above s. pe. pf. (a var. of **ghap**).

Der.: **mgahpa.**

(**GHP II** a miscop. of **GHK,** cf. **ghipa** inst. of **ghika** BZ 30 n. 14.)

(**GHP III** a miscop. of **GṢP,** cf. **gihpat** inst. of **giṣpat** s. **GṢP.**)

GHR (ܓܗܪ) to darken, vibrate, (גער Jb ii 46 n. 7) to roll or peal BZ 153 n. 4, 168 n. 1, Ap. II.

Pe. Pf. **gargul gihrat** Jb 41:10 (Nöld.: *die Himmelsphäre verdunkelt sich* MG 301:1; Lidzb.: *Donner erdröhnte*) a rumbling (thunder) pealed; **gihrit bghartai rabtia** Jb 35:5 I burst into a mighty shout. Act. pt. **gargul gahra** AM, **guha d̠-gahra** AM 252:1 a thunderclap which peals.

Der.: **gahar 2, gharta, guhrana.**

gu st. cstr of **gaua 1. bgu pagra** (often) in the body; **bgu iahra d̠-aiar** AM 270:29 in the month of Ayar.

***gualqa** (P.-Ar. جولخ, جولق, Aram. loan-w. גואלקא, גולקא, ܓܘܠܩܐ) sack, bag, long sacks on either side of a pack-animal. Found only in pl. **gualqia**. **šuba gualqia** Lond. roll B 155, 254, DC 12. 75 seven enclosures; **bgualqia** CP 223:3 ŠQ 15:17 in sacks.

guan st. abs. & cstr of **gauna** MG 150:3 (cf. also s. **gauna**). **d̠-kul guan** (often) of every kind; **ʿzlia d̠-guan guan** Jb 155:1 (var. B **ʿguan guan**) webs of various colours; **bguan guan** (often) in various kinds.

guara 1 (cf. P. گوارا digestion) digestive organs, stomach, belly, interior, inside; (= **gubara**) male organ. **kiba guara** AM 34:1 (var. **kib guara**) belly-ache, indigestion; **ukib blibh̠ uguarh̠ hauilh̠** AM 17:1 and he will have pain in his heart and stomach; **mn guarun** Gy 123:15 from their inside; **bguarh̠** Gy 204:9 in his belly; **hania uguaria** AM the bosom and the belly; **bguara d̠-ṭašt** DC 45 in the interior of the bowl.

guara 2 (**GUR I** ?) AM 25 temporary dwelling, exile (?).

GUB = **GBB.** Cf. pe. act. pt. **gaiba qumth̠** Or 330:7 (with the same meaning as pass. pt., v.s. **GBB**).

guba 1 (גּוּבָּא, ܓܘܒܐ Akk. *gubbu* LS) ditch, pit, water-runnel, cistern, pool MG 105:4 f. Pl. **gubia. gubia rqiha** Gy 354:9, 21, 355:1 (var. DC 22. 351 & Sh. ʿAbd.'s copy **gubia d̠-rqiha**) the water-cisterns (or, see **3**, the vault) of the sky, **gubia mia** Q 13:6, 15, **br gubia d̠-mia** CP 31:4 f., ML 362 son of water-pools; **bgu gubhun** DC 44 in their pit.

guba 2 (Talm. גוב, Jew. Aram. & H. גּוּף) body, trunk; thickness. **lagṭit bširiana d̠-qumth̠ d̠-guba qumth̠ ʿtikbiṣ** DC 43 I seized (the devil) by his body cuirass, so that the trunk of his body was squeezed together; **guba d̠-šaqa** AM 95:4 thickness of limb BZ 61 n. 1.

guba 3 (a doublet of **qumba**; cf. Ges. s. גַּף I) vault, dome, vaulted room, chamber, roof. **gubih̠ rqiha hua** ŠQ 15:9 his vaulted chamber was the sky.

gubal (rt. **GBL**) form, shape. A var. of **gubla. qumat gubalia** [*sic*] **balbušia pšiṭlh̠** DC 26 & 40. 625 my figure, my form, in its vestment(s), I drew upright (I straightened up my body).

guban 1 (cf. **guba 2**) thick, massy. St. emph. not found. **uʿkum manzia uguban** AM 24:5 and his hair is black and thick; **manz guban** AM 38:7, **umanzia ʿkumia uguban** AM 14:2.

guban 2 a supernatural being (formed by alliteration). **gubran uguban d̠-hu gabir uhliṣ ʿlauaihun** Gy 167:14 G. and G. who is strong and armed against them. In DAb a demon who carries a comb.

gubar s. **gibar.**

gubara (rt. **GBR**) male organ, penis. Var. **guara. kib gubaria hauilh̠** AM (Par. 26) he will have a venereal disease.

gubla (rt. **GBL**) form, fashion, mould, nature. **gublan** Gy 116:19 our nature.

gubran (rt. **GBR**) a supernatural being; also name of a kind of *masiqta* MSchr 183, Jb II 15 n. 4. **gubran uguban** s. **guban; lkušṭa galilh̠ gubran** Jb 9:9 G. revealed her (: to Rūha) the Truth (but cf. ii 15 n. 3); **masiqta d̠-gubran d̠-hʿ masiqta d̠-aba d̠-ʿutria** PD 812 the *masiqta* of G., which is the m. of the Father of Uthras; **gubran ʿutra** Jb 14:1 ff.; **gubran** RD 50 (with a picture).

gubrutai (prob. an illiterate form of כבריתא, גופריתא, ܟܒܪܝܬܐ) sulphur. **ṣatria ugubrutai uhardla sumaqa uarbinun** DC 40. 1051 take herbs, sulphur and red mustard and mix them.

gubria (B. Aram. גֻּבְרַיָּא, cf. also place-names בית גוברין, ܒܝܬ ܓܘܒܪܝܢ MG 18:bottom & n. 5) pl. of **gabra. trisar gubria tangaria** s. **trisar; gubria bnia šlama** Gy 175:9, 14; **gubria tlata** Gy 252:10, 23, 253:1, 255:13 (identified with **ʿutria tlata** Gy 256:13 ff., 260: 6, 13, 264); **arba gubria** Q 30:31, 40:13, **arba gubria bnia šlama** Q 4:23, 60:5, 255:8, Gy 322:12; **ʿtlh̠ d̠-gubria** Gy 280:14 he has male organs.

gubta a var. of **gibta** (q.v.).

gugia a var. of **gungia** (s. **gunga**).

GUD v.s. **GID.**

gud 1 (mod., read **gub** = *guw*) DC 51:coloph. in.

gud 2, guda 1 (a doublet of **gunda** q.v., both also in Talm., Syr. ܓܘܕܐ LS) band, group, company. **gud d̠-rištata** DC 46. 117:6 a group of heads; **br guda** s. **br** (compounds).

guda 2 (גּוּדָא, ܓܘܕܐ) leather bag, purse. **guda ugunza** PD 408, ATŠ I no. 35 a leather purse and money-bag.

***guda 3** (גּוּדָא, ܓܘܕܐ) partition, wall. Pl. **gudia** (?) RD 1.

gudaita PD 791 a var. of **gidaita** DC 36 no. 74.

gudlania (cf. **gdultania**) (*a*) kind of demons, (*b*) exalted beings, highlands, (*c*) wreathing upwards, towering up. (*a*) **gudlania zikria ugudlania nuqbata** DC 43 A 21; (*b*) **mihla . . . pt gudlania** DC 40. 44:433; (*c*) **gilia gudlania** DC 37. 517.

gudta AM 11 read **pigudta** (as Par. 24 and A) bridle.

guha (גוהא, ܓܘܗܐ a local doublet of ܓܘܢܚܐ, rt. **GNA II** = **GHN II**) rumbling, thunderclap, clamour, din, uproar, earthquake, sobbing, groaning, conflict, horror MG 52:9. Usually fem. **guha gahna** s. **GHN II; blibh̠ gnalh̠ guha** Gy 115:3 there was groaning in his heart; **guha ʿtgna blibh̠** Gy 84:16, 85:4 (var. DC 22. 79 **ʿtignat**) id.; **ʿtgna guha** Gs 21:18 (similarly). **unašmh̠ guha rba** Jb 58:11 and will cause him to hear a great clamour; **guha uqala uqraba nihuia** AM 233:17 there will be uproar, clamour, and war; **qal guha unuda uqraba** IM no. 36; **kupna guha uqraba** AM 211:15; **mitignalun guha bʿuṣraihun** DAb their minds are completely upset; **rab guha** DC 43 G 23 lord of battle; **bguha uhauqa salqa** DAb she (: the soul) will rise up with trembling and fear; **guha d-gahra** s. **GHR; saliq qala d̠-guha** Gy 114:2 (var. DC 22 **qala guhana**) a clamour (var. fearful noise) riseth up. Cf. also s. **GNA III.**

guhana (adj. from **guha**). DC 22. 109 a var. of **guha** Gy 114:2 (v.s. **guha** end).

guhar a var. of **gauhar** (q.v.).

guhuka or **guhka** (rt. **GHK**) laughter. **zmara uguh(u)ka** AM 55 penult. song and laughter.

guhnam (גֵּיהִנֹּם, גֵּיא הִנֹּם Ar. جَهَنَّم. Pallis's explanation MSt 121 as a rendering of the Christian *Γέεννα* = ܓܗܢܐ with apocope of *m* is inadmissible) Gehenna. Fem. MG 159: bottom. No st. emph. MG 301:5. **guhnam ḏ-mhababa** Gy 39:12 the red-hot G.; **tiplun bguhnam** Gy 67:23 ye will fall into the G.; **nhura ḏ-guhnam titaita** Gy 320:5 the fire of the lower hell; **guhnam titaita** Gy 377:13, PD 151; **dahbai rman bguhnam** Gs 131:23 my gold cast me into the G.; **guhnam . . . sumqaq aina** PD 152 (cf. s. **sumqaq**).

guhrana a var. of **kuhrana** Jb 108:9 (C).

GUZ (orig. ע"ע) = **GZZ.**

guzurta ATŠ II no. 201 a var. of **gzurta.**

guzra (Pâž. *vazr*, Mod. P. گرز with metath.) mace MG xxxii n. 1. **bguzra mhaitẖ** Gy 119:3 I smote him with a mace.

guṭa in **guṭa rihak** DC 3 read **guṭar rihak** (s. **GṬR II**).

guṭaipa (rt. **GṬP**) vine. Mod. *goṭeyfa* grape. **guṭaipa hu** DC 27 & 35 it is a vine.

guṭana (rt. **GṬN**) short, small. Common in Mod. Mand.

guṭupta & varr. v.s. **gaṭapta.** The form with *gûšenna* is the most frequent MG 119:14.

guṭla (rt. **GṬL**) part of the mechanism moving the stern-wheel (according to the context). **umrahišlẖ guṭla mahia lula bdulab** DC 35: coloph. and a piston-rod moves it striking a hinge in the water-wheel.

guṭma a var. of **giṭma.**

guṭra 1 (Akk. *quṭru*, Jew.-Aram. קִטְרָא) smoke. Still used. **aprišata . . . ʿl nura mna . . . uʿl guṭrẖ mna** Gy 200:15 ff. explanations . . . about fire, whence (it is) . . . and its smoke whence (it is); **guṭra gṭar** Jb 67:7, 69:10 smoke wreathed up, **gaṭar guṭra** Jb 204:9, Gy 204:9, **guṭra gaṭar** RD C 9, 14 id. pres. Gl. 54:10 missp. with q قتن *tabaccus* تنباكو, 183:9 **guṭra** دخان *fumus* دود.

guṭra 2 a var. of **giṭra.**

gukai Sh. ʿAbd.'s copy a var. of **gaukai** Gy 390:3.

gukaiia IM no. 23 p. 98 people of Gaukai.

gul (mod., P. گل) rose, flower, rose-colour. Masc. **gul hiuara** ŠQ 18:24.

gulbastar (P. گل بيستار) a certain plant (v.s. **qasṭarun**). Var. **gulibiṣṭar** (s.v.).

gulusṭuma Sh. ʿAbd.'s copy a var. of **gluṣ-ṭ(u)ma** Gy 143:18.

gulibiṣṭar AM 124 a var. of **gulbastar**, expl. in the text as celery-seed (v.s. **sustariun**, var. **qasṭarun**).

gulpa (קוּלְפָּא) club, mace. **tartin gulpa qurnasa** DC 43 J 171, Oxf. roll 385 (var. **qirnasa**, read **uqurnasa**) two (things:) a club and a hammer.

gulṣṭma DC 34. 54 = **gluṣṭ(u)ma.**

gumama, gmama (ܓܘܡܡܐ) diminishment, indentation, partial eclipse. Var. **gumana. kḏ šamiš hua kudra ʿu hiba ʿu gumama hauilẖ** AM 282:1 when the sun becomes sicklied over, or is hidden, or diminishes in size.

guman (rt. גום = גמם) isolation, separation BZ 78 n. 5. **guman hauia minẖ aminṭul ḏ-lamitasia** AM 122:12 (of a demoniac) there will be a separation from him, because he is incurable.

gumana s. **gumama.**

gumarta (ܓܡܘܪܬܐ) consecrated wafer, host (a Christian expr. borrowed from Syr.) MG xxix. 22, 105:18. Cf. also s. **gumra 1. qudša ḏ-gumarta** Gy 227:15 the sacrament of the host.

gumba a var. of **gunba.**

gumura a var. of **gumra 1** & **2.**

gumia (Jer. Talm. גּוּמִי) gum, secretion. **uapiq gumia mn ginta uqarnia aqda lnapšiẖ** ATŠ I no. 254 and he brought out gum from the garden and affixed horns to himself; **hiua biša ḏ-mn pumaihun gasin gumia** Gy 132:13 evil creatures that spit forth scum from their mouths.

gumiza (P. گميز) urine. Var. **gurmaiza 3** (s.v.). **gumiza ḏ-taura hiuara** Ṣâb's AM (var. AM 135:2 **tinia ḏ . . .**); **bgumiza ḏ-taura sumaqa** Oxf. roll g 1041, DC 47 = Or. 333:8.

gumla (Gen. Sem., cf. LS s. ܓܡܠܐ and Ges. s. גָּמָל, with labialization of the vowel) camel MG 18:1, 107:12. Pl. **gumlia. zmama ḏ-gumla** Gy 103:9, 118:9 a camel's bridle; **ulsasauata ḏ-arqa ulgumlia** Gy 387:11; **rakšia ugumlia utauria** Gy 387:19; **ma gumlia uma kudania** ŠQ 19:3 a hundred camels and a hundred mules; **gumlia ṭinan zahba** ŠQ ibid. camels are laden with gold.

gumra 1 (גּוּמְרָא, prob. a st. abs. of **gumarta**) coal, glowing coal. Masc. (orig. fem., cf. **gumarta**). Pl. **gumria** MG 173:7 ff. Varr. **gumura** JRAS 1937 590:23, **gimra 2** MG 173: 10. **badin gumria** s. **BDA**; **gumria uiaqdana** RD C 9; **gumria ḏ-nura** RD 35, RD C 8, 14; **gumria ḏ-mhababa** Morg. 262/16:16; **uʿl gumria mṭabilun** (var. **ugumria mtabilun**) s. **ṬBA III.**

gumra 2 (rt. **GMR**) perfection, completeness, intactness. Var. **g(u)mura. bgumura** Morg. 197:12, 14 completely (?); **kulẖ bgumura** Sh. ʿAbd.'s copy of **kulẖ bgmura** Gy 231:6; **kulẖ bgumra** JRAS 1937 590:10. all in perfection.

***gumra 3** a var. of **kumra.** Found only in pl. **gumria** (= **kumria**). **gumria zabia** DC 22. 27 & Sh. ʿAbd.'s copy a var. of **kumria zabia** Gy 28:14 f.

gunaha (rt. **GNA III** = **GHN II**) shock, commotion, clamour, disquiet, compunction, affliction, wailing, groaning, sighing; shame; coughing (?). Pl. **gunahia** MG 123:8. **ulibai aiil gunahia** Gy 264:7 f. and affliction (or sighing) entered (hist. pres.) my heart; **ulibai ḏ-aiil gunahia** Gy 266:7; **mišbiq . . . mn gunahak bʿudnaihun** DC 37. 38 to send away some of thy wailing in their ears; **mn kulhun gunahia ḏ-tignabun** DC 51. 210 from all the wailings by which he is wailing; **ʿhab gunahia lrišẖ** DC 51. 331 he dealt out afflictions (or groanings) upon his head; **ʿsiria . . .**

gunahia unap(u)ṣia briša DC 46. 132:15; **mahu guha mn tibil ugunaha mn bita ḏ-qraba** MA what is the uproar from the earth and the wailing from the House of War?

Gl. 29:9 missp. اثم iniquitas گناه (Mandæans us. explain it as P. گناه).

gunapta (גְּנוּבְתָא, ܓܢܘܒܬܐ) theft, stealing; (in ATŠ often) defilement, impurity, pollution. Varr. **gnubta, gnupta. gaura ugunapta** ATŠ (*often*).

gunba, gumba, gunpa (Targ. גּוּנְבָה, Syr. ܓܘܢܒܐ) theft, dishonesty. **hzun ʿdilma d-gunba tiginbun** Jb 174:10 see that ye do not commit theft; **bisra d-gunba latikul** AM 16:20 he will not eat the meat of dishonesty.

gunga (P. گنگ) deaf-mute, dumb, babbling. Pl. **gungia. algia udugia ugungia** Gy 279:11 (in a catalogue of qualities of devils) stammerers, deaf, deaf-mutes; **man gunga ḏ-ialip** Jb 72:9 who is the deaf-mute that learneth a book?; **lišana gungia** ATŠ I no. 243; **raz gungia** DC 34. 1157.

Gl. 30:5 missp. اخرس *mutus* لال.

gunda (גּוּנְדָא, Pahl. *gund*, Ar. loan-w. جُنْد Jeffrey 105; Syr. ܓܘܕܐ LS; rt. **GDD**, cf. H. גְּדוּד) army MG 75:16, 105:6. Masc. MG 160 f. St. abs. **gud 2** (?). Pl. **gundia. gunda napla** Gy 82:10 f., 282:8, 345:5, 344:12 the falling army MG 317:antep. f. & n. 4; **ana ugundai ugabarai** ŠQ, 16:4, CP 225:6 I and my army and my heroes; **aiak gunda ḏ-lamalka** Gy 216:20 like an army without a leader; **kḏ ahara bgunda** s. **ahara**; **kanpa ugunda** Gy 42:9 host and army.

gunubta = **gnubta.**

gunza (rel. to ginza?) money-box. **guda ugunza** s. **guda 2.**

gunia 1 (Syr. only ܓܘܢܝܐ) disgrace, shame. No st. abs. Pl. **guniia** shameful things, acts, defilements. **ḏ-lanihzun gunia ḏ-ʿkuria** ATŠ I no. 234 that view not the abomination of the high-places (: pagan shrines); **ʿu šagia bzharia . . . gunia rba** ATŠ II no. 404 if he makes a mistake in the rubrics . . . it is a great disgrace (note: in some rituals the rubrics must be read aloud); **mamnit guniia ḏ-hazin alma** Jb 167:8 thou forbiddest the shameful things of this world; **guniarba abatar hauia** ATŠ II no. 404 let (his teacher) blame him afterwards (?). Gl. 96:14 missp. شك *scandalum*, 98:10 id. شر *iniquitas*.

gunia 2 (rt. **GNA III**) intermittent noise, groaning, tooting. **gunia bšupria rmit** Jb 104:4, **gunia rmit bšupria** Jb 104:12 f. I sounded tootings with a trumpet, cf. also **gunia lnapšaihun** (var. **ʿl napšaihun**) **rmun** DC 53. 230:14 (var. Par 15 f. 17a = Par. 25 f. 21a), an idiom formally identical with **gunian rma** (v.s. **gunian**), Lidzb. identified it also materially with the latter and with **gunia 1**, cf. Jb ii 104 n. 2.

gunian (Syr. st. emph. ܓܘܢܝܢܐ) rebuke, blame, scorn. No st. emph. MG. 303:antep. f. **gunian rmit ʿl kulhun** Gy 259:3, 6 I cast blame on them all; **gunian rmia ʿl almia** Gy 359:12; **gunian ḏ-biriata** Gy 277:8 the rebuke of created beings MG 313:paen.

gunpa a var. of **gunba.**

GUS I (גוס) to meet, encounter, come into contact with.

Pe. Impf. **qirsa nigusbh̲** AM 67:4 he will meet with misfortune. Act. pt. pl. **ukḏ atin ugaisin bhdadia** DC 41. 470 f. and when they come and encounter each other; **ušgandai abihdia** (var. DC 30 **abihdai**) **lagaisia** Jb 34:7 and my helpers are not in contact with me.

GUS II, GSA (ܓܣܐ LS, cf. also Mishn. גָּסָה; orig. ל״י, used often as ע״ע) to vomit, throw up, be replete, be glutted, to glut (see **GSA**).

Pe. Pf. **mlat nišimta . . . ugasat** ATŠ II no. 105 the soul was filled . . . and belched; **gasit** Morg. 262/16:8 I belched. Act. pt. **gaiis** (often in AM) he vomits, will vomit. Pass. pt. pl. **gisia** CP 42:penult. (things) disgorged.

Der.: s. **GSA.**

gusana (ܓܘܣܢܐ LS) wandering minstrel, vagabond, but also with opposite meaning: high in social position (with this meaning of unknown etym.) Jb ii 164. **ana lau gusana ḏ-zamar aqamia šaplia** Jb 165:12 I am no vagabond that sings before low people; **abuia gusana ʿu daiana ḏ-mata** AM 75:2 her father will be a great personage or judge of the place.

gusparta (cf. ܓܘܣܦܪܐ) feather, crest (of bird), comb (of cock). **gusparta ḏ-tarnaula** AM 287:41 etc.; **tlilh̲ gusparta iaɛania qurata ḏ-zaga** AM 134:17 f. hang up the crest, i.e. the comb of a rooster.

gupan gupaian (the first might be a st. abs. of **gupna**, the second would be formed simply by alliteration). **sam gupan usam gupaian** CP 3:ult. = Q 1:31 = ML 5:6 (cf. also s. **sam**).

gupara (ܓܘܦܪܐ Talm. כּוּפְרָא Löw 118 f., Ar. loan-w. كُفَرّى, جُفَرّى Fränkel 147, LS s.v.) *spatha palmae* (the heart of the male blossom) MG 112:4 & n. 1. Pl. **guparia.** Masc. **briš guparia** (DC 22. 394 miscop. **gupaqia**) **mitiklia mn qudam tumria** Gs 3:9 at the beginning palm-spathes are eaten before the dates.

gupna (גּוּפְנָא, ܓܘܦܢܐ Akk. *gupnu, gapnu* LS, Ges. s. גֶּפֶן, Löw 84) vine, climbing plant, MG 18:7. St. abs. & cstr. **gpan** MG 151:10, but also **gupan** (s.v.). Pl. **gupnia**, masc. MG 173 n. 1 (only exceptionally fem. in **gupna rišaita** DAb the First Vine). Used often as an epithet of heavenly beings Q 23:33, 31:26 etc., cf. Brandt JPT 18/1892 406, 433 ff., MR 63, 196 f. **gupna ana gpan hiia** Gy 65:1 MG 321:1 f.; **gupna ʿtahzia bʿurašlam** Gy 178:2 f. a Vine appeared in Jer.; **ṣalia gupna hdar aqmuia** Gy 43:24, 44:1 f. when a vine leaneth, make it straight again; **ʿuqruia lgupna biša** Gy 44:2 f. uproot ye the bad vine; **škab luat**

gupna uraza ʿuhrh ʿthambal A 8 ATŠ trs. p. 123 n. 5; ATŠ II no. 182. He (: Christ) lay down beside a vine and the mystery of his Way was ruined; **gupna rišaia qadmaia** CP 54:9, Q 26:6 = Morg. 229/45:5 f. the First Great Vine; **gupna rba** Gy 322:45; **gupna anat** Q 24:19; **gupna kasia** Gy 304:3; **gupna ana niha** Gy 303:9; **gupna ana lihdaia** Gy 335:13; **aiar gupna dakia, aiar gupna br piriauis gupna** s. **aiar 1, aiar gupna** Gy 376:5; **aiar stana gupna** Gy 315:9; **iusmir gupna d-barqa d-sam ziua šria** Gy 321:20; **iusmir gupna qadmaia** CP 19:5; **sam gupna dakia** Gy 377:21; **pirun gupna** CP 54:11, Q 25:9; **pirun gupna d-barqa d-šarat ʿbdat ukišrat šria** Gy 322:3; **ruaz gupna** Gy 211:4, CP 86:7 212:25, 320:14, 321:18, Q 41:1, Oxf. 74 a etc.; **ruaz gupna rba** CP 151:6, Oxf. 8 bis; **gupna d-abatur** RD 10; **šar gupna** Gy 377:22, **šar gupna rba** Gy 364:15; **šar gupna d-barqa d-hiia qadmaiia triṣ** Gy 322:2; **gupna d-kulh hiia** Gy 71:2, 189:14, 196:3, Gs 7:10 etc.; **šrar gupna rba** Oxf. 7 a; **šarat gupna rba** Gy 374:7; **šarhabʿil gupna d-barqa d-hibil ziua šria** Gy 321:21, cf. also 321:24 f.; **taurʿil gupna** Gy 312:15 etc. (as an epithet of higher beings; **gupna šania** Oxf. 92 b, pl. **gupnia šaniia** Gy 321:22; **gupnia aiar** Gy 116:12; **gupnia hadua** Jb 183:10, Gs 76:12 the vines of joy. With numerals: **šuba gupnia** Gy 373:10 f., **trisar gupnia** CP 167:14, Oxf. 31 a; **iasmin gupna hu** DC 41 (illustration) it is a jessamine creeper.

gupnia DC 51. 642 read **guptia** snares (?).

gupra a var. of **gupara**.

gupta (rt. גוף = גפף, ܓܦܦ = ܟܦܦ, der. ܓܘܦܬܐ LS) net, snare; receptacle, container, case, cylinder. **ʿzlak lagṭit bgupta** Jb 162:4 thou graspest thy mesh with the snare; **ulgupta d-lihia** DC 30 and on a trap (made) of nets; **gupta d-parzla** JRAS 1939 401:24, 430: 75 DC 33 & 44 a cylinder of iron JRAS 1939 406 n. 4; **bgupta d-kaspa** DC 37. 89 in a silver case; **rmih bgupta d-kaspa** DC 44 and place it in a silver cylinder (or case); **gupta d-zgauita** DC 44. 1012 a glass case; **bgupta d-qaina d-zrada** DC 15, **bgupta d-zrara** DC 23. 311, DC 43 A 69 an (amulet-) case of bamboo (reeds); **raza kdub lmagalta . . . urmih bgupta** DC 21 write the mystery on a scroll . . . and put it in a cylinder; **šuba humria d-plinza matnalia rmʿia bgupta ʿlaita** DC 44 I brought seven brass amulets placed in a celestial receptacle.

guṣa (Ar. غُصَّة) DC 51:coloph. worry, affliction.

GUR I (גור II J., ܓܘܪ LS) to fornicate, commit adultery, covet, lust for, seduce, be wanton, practise debauchery.

Pe. Pf. **gar** he fornicated MG 248:2; **garat (uginbat ubiṭnat)** ATŠ II no. 35 she committed adultery (and became pregnant by an outcast); **garit** I committed adultery MG 248: antep.; **garnin** Gy 65:4 (var. DC 22. 60 **garnia**) we committed adultery MG 249:5; with encl. **lagaruk ʿnšia bgauraihun** Jb 83:2 f. women did not lead thee astray by their lechery MG 274:11. Impf. **nigar** Gy 65:5 etc. he fornicateth, will fornicate MG 249:14; **gaura nigar minh** AM he commits fornication with her; **tigirun** ye fornicate MG 249:24, **latigirun ulatiznun** Gy 20:13 (var. Sh. ʿAbd.'s copy **latigairun** pa. [?], Pet. miscop. **latirun**) lust not, nor fornicate; with suff. **baiia d-nigirh lnapšh** Gy 85:17 he wanted to commit adultery with her. Act. pt. **gaira gaura** PD 1041, ATŠ I no. 104 she commits adultery; pl. **gairin gaura** DAb, **gairia gaura** (*often*) they commit fornication MG 399:middle. Pass. pt. with encl. **lagirlia gaura** Gs 103:3 I committed no adultery.

Pa. Only pt. with encl. found **mgaiirlh** (var. **mgaiirlia**) seduces him, her.

Ethpa. Pf. with encl. **d-ʿtignabun uʿtgaiarbun bpagrai dilia** DC 51. 209 f. that make me loathsome and seduce me in my own body (subj.: demons, lit. that are made loathsome and seduced by my body).

Gl. 79:15 f. missp. زنا [sic] *moechari* زنا كرد, 127:9 f. missp. فسق *adulterari* فسق كرد.

Der.: **gaura** (var. **gura**), **gaiara 1**, fem. **gaiartia, gaira**.

GUR II = **GRR**.

gura 1 a var. of **gaura 1**.

gura 2 v.s. **guragalam**.

guragalam AM 204:6 a place-name, Karakorum (?) BZ Ap. II. Var. Ṣâb.'s copy **gura ugalam** (distinctly as two words).

guraita Jb B a var. of **gurita** Jb 130:2.

guran DAb a supernatural being (carrying a comb).

guranbil, guranbil DAb = RD 29 a supernatural being, a demon (beating a drum).

gurgan (P. گرگان) AM 205. Persian province Gorgan.

gurganaiia (adj. from **gurgan**) the people of Gorgan.

gurgul AM 279:antepenult. a var. of **gargul**.

gurgur (cf. גרגירא, ܓܪܓܝܪܐ Löw 92 f.) *eruca sativa*, colewort, garden-rocket. Doubtful. **gurgur bduq bmia** DC 46. 97:6 put colewort in water.

gurgma (cf. ܓܘܪܓܡܐ H. גַּרְגֶּרֶת, Germ. *Gurgel* Jb ii 237 n. 5) maw, gullet. **gurgma d-karapiun** Gy 188:3, **gurgma d-ʿur** Jb 267:5.

gurza 1 (P. گُرْز) mace, club, stake. **ʿsira atuat harašata bgurza d-parzla bpumh** DC 40. 1100 bound is the witch-woman by an iron stake in her mouth.

gurza 2 (Ar. قُرْزَة) tip. **lqrunh d-naṣipa d-hʿ gurzih** Lond. roll A 201 the extreme end of the stole which is its tip.

gurṭa (קוּרְטָא) particle, grain, kernel: **gurṭa d-amuza** WedF 138b:2 walnut-kernel; **himṣa gurṭa** s. **himṣa 2**.

guria (גּוּרְיָא) whelp, cur, young dog, pariah-dog. Fem. **gurita**, var. **guraita** (s.v.). **mitnai** (read **mitnia**) **tlit akuat guria** DC 43 J 136 thou stretchest up thy quarters like pariah-whelps; **kd guria** DC 43 like curs.

gurikta, gurita (גּוּרְיְיתָא, גּוּרִיתָא) bitch. Var. **guraita**. Pl. **guriata** DC 23. 563. **gurita**

mšahanta Jb 130:2, gurikta gnihtia DC 45 a bitch on heat; aiak kalba gnuna abatar gurita gnuntia DC 45 like a mating dog after a bitch on heat; gurikta (var. C gurita) ana mšahanta Jb 130:5 f.; miška d̲-gurita DC 46. 138:16, var. m. d̲-gurikta DC 12. 190 bitch's skin.

gurma read **gurgma**. **bgurmia d̲-ʿur šaplia** DAb (cf. s. **gurgma**).

gurmaiza 1 (Targ. כּוּרְמִיזָא prob. from Iranian, cf. Mod. P. dial. *gormič* in Luristan, *gommoz* Khorasan, *gommorz* Kurdistan with many dial. varr., communicated by Prof. Kia, Teheran) fist MG 40:9 f. **mla bgurmaizh̲** CP 373:9, Gy 99:4, **nimlia bgurmaizh̲** Gy 101:11; **mlun bgurmaizaiun** Jb 138:2 **mlun bgurmaizun** CP 65:13 f.; Q 30:5; **bgurmaizih̲ ʿtimlia** Jb 261:6; **timlibun bgurmaizak** Gs 130:4 f. (cf. **MLA** Idioms).

gurmaiza 2 (rel. to **garmida**; Syr. ܓܘܪܡܙܐ LS, H. אמד Ges., both quote a Mand. *gurmuz* which would be closer to the Iranian original [v.s. **gurmaiza 1**] but, unfortunately, was found in no text; Sem. origin is doubtful) mace, club. **ubgurmaiza d̲-nura** DC 21 and with a mace of fire; similarly **gurmaiza d̲-mia** Oxf. roll 241, Q 8:26, DC 27. 101 DC 43 J 11; **gurmaiza d̲-mia hiia** Gy 344:17, cf. Ginzā 359 n. 1.

gurmaiza 3 a miscop. of **gumiza** (q.v., influenced by **gurmaiza 1, 2**) **gurmaiza d̲-taura sumaqa** Oxf. roll 678, Or. 327:22.

gurpa (Ar. غُرْفَة) room (Lidzb. *Steilufer* ML x 18, cf. גרף, ܓܪܦܐ, جرف) **ʿlauia gurpia** (var. **gurpa**) **qaima** ŠQ 18:13, DC 53, 235:5 f. she stands above the room(s).

GUŠ = GŠŠ.

gušbanqa (Talm. גּוּשְׁפַּנְקָא < Pehl. *anguštbânak*, mod. P. انگشتوانه thimble) DC 34. 873, CP 340:9, 469:antep., DC 46 (often), Lond. roll A 344, ring, signet, seal. Corruptions v.s. **bušmanqa.**

gušṭasp (Firdausī's گُشتاسپ) an ancient Persian king MG xxxii n. 1. **gušṭasp bra d̲-lohrasp** Gy 383:6 (Kavi) Vištāspa son of Aruvat-aspa (Yašt v 105) Gray ZA 19/1905–6 282.

gušqa (P. گوشجی) spy, informer. **gziraiia d̲-šbiqilun gušqia** Gs 96:6 officers of law that set spies.

GZA = GUZ = GZZ (q.v.).

PE. Impt. **guza lʿudna d̲-šunara ʿkuma** AM 134:penult. cut off the ear of a black cat. (other forms s. **GZZ**.)

gzauita DC 36 II no. 42 a var. of **zgauita** DC 6.

gzaraiia Gs 17:8 = **gziraiia.**

gzarṭabaiia (cf. **gziraiia**) bailiffs. Varr. **gzirṭabaiia, gzirṭibaiia, gairṭabia, magzarṭabaiia, mgzarṭabaiia** (s.vv.). **gziria** (var. **gziraiia**) **ugzartabaiia** (varr. just cited) Gs 84:5 officers of law and bailiffs.

gzurta, gzirta (rt. **GZR**, גְּזִירְתָּא) circumcision, cut, severance. Varr. **guzurta, gzuruta, gziruta. zma d̲-gzurta** DC 22.218 = **dma d̲-gzirta** Gy 224:11; **gazrin gzurta** Jb 199:8; **ulgzurta hanath̲ laršim** ATŠ II no. 201 do not sign over that cut (i.e. where the umbilical cord is severed). (DC 6 **laršam**).

GZZ, GUZ (Gen. Sem.) to cut (off), shear (away), pierce MG 83:top.

PE. Pf. **gaz** he shore, cut MG 248:4. Act. pt. **gaiiz** he cuts, will cut MG 83:4, fem. **uspintai lagazia** Jb 143:9 (as from ל״י and with act. meaning) and my boat is not cut off ii 145 n. 2, masc. less regular: **kd̲ patiqlia lgira ulagaza** DAb when he aims an arrow and it pierces not; pl. with encl. **ugzita brišaihun gaizilun** Gy 56:11 and they cut a tonsure on their heads. Part. pres. **kd̲ gaizit ṭupria** AM 163:4 when thou cuttest nails. Pass. pt. with encl. **lagzizan lbit ruhṣanan** CP 109:1, ML 134:5 we are not cut off from our trust. Inf. **migaz** AM cutting.

ETHPE. Pf. (without **t** in the pref.) **ʿgzat ubiṭnat** DC 43 J 37 *perforata et gravida facta est* (idiom, s. below); **nišimta minaihun lagzat** DC 48. 362 the soul was not deprived of them (: sacraments).

IDIOM. The verb could be used with the meaning "to cohabit" (Lat. *perforare*) in act. voice of men, in pass. voice (example s. ethpe.) of women, similarly to mod. **BZA.**

DER.: **gauza, gizta** (var. **gizita**).

gzira (pass. pt. of **GZR**) (*a*) decreed, appointed, adjudged, adversely adjudged, (*b*) precipitous, steep (place), gorge, precipice, deep valley, (*c*) cut off, (*d*) a var. of **gziraiia.** (*a*) **dina gzira** Gy 40:19, Jb 176:6; **atra gzira** Gs 83:11, 85:16, 134:17, Jb 175:5 f.; (*b*) **ṭura gzira** Gs 105:23 f. a steep hill, **ṭuria gziria** Gy 11:13, Q 53:24 (pl.); **akuat trin ṭuria d̲-gzira** ATŠ like the two mountain-sides of a gorge; **ukd̲ ʿmbara maiit bgzira** AM 26:1 (var. **bagzara, bgizra** s. **gizra**) and he will die like a sheep in a precipitous place; (*c*) **nišma gzira lika** Gy 66:10; (*d*) Gs 84:5 (cf. s. **gzarṭabaiia**).

gziraiia, agzaraiia (pl. adj. from pass. pt. of **GZR**, cf. ܓ̈ܙܝܪܐ) (*a*) those who exact penalties or fines, officers of law. Var. **gziria** (s. **gzira** (*d*) and **gzarṭabaiia**), (*b*) circumcised MG 141:paen. (*a*) **lšitin gziraiia ulšitin naṭria** Morg. 259/9:15; **šbiqibh̲ gziraiia umaṭaraiia umaksia iatbia ʿlh̲** Gs 13:11 f. there are loosed against it (: the soul) those who exact penalties; purgatory-demons and those that demand payment are sitting on it; **šbiqibh̲ maṭaraiia ugziraiia umaksia qaimia ʿlh̲** Gs 84:11; **gziraiia d̲-šbiqilun gušqia** s. **gušqa. gziraiia umaksia** Jb 184:13; (*b*) **iahuṭaiia gziraiia** Gy 224:15.

gzirta = gzurta (q.v.): **ugzirtun gzira** DC 4 their condemnation is adjudged; **ugzita brišaihun gaizilun** s. **GZZ** pe. act. pt. pl. with encl.

gzirta Gy 224:11 a var. of **gzurta.**

GZL (גזל without metath., differently from Syr. ܓܠܙ) to tear away, rob, deprive, plunder, cut off, sever completely MG 74 n. 5, IM Gl.

Pe. Pf. *gzal IM Gl. Impf. latigizlun mn šutapa Gy 20:1, mn šutapa latigizlun Gy 38:4 rob ye not a partner. Impt. pl. with suff. guzluiẖ mn binataikun ATŠ II no. 19 outlaw ye him (lit. cut him off) from your midst. Act. pt. man ḏ-gazil mn habrẖ Gy 20:2, 38:5 who robbeth his friend; pl. gazlin mn šurabta dilẖ hibil ziua DC 35 they sever from the Stem of H.–Z.; substantivally gazlia bišia Gy 215: 22 f.; with encl. mn ṭabuta gazlilun Gy 28:12 they sever them from grace.

Ethpe. Pt. migzil (mn ṭabauata ḏ-alma ḏ-nhura) Gy 38:5 he shall be cut off (from the graces of the world of light) MG 214:5.

Der.: gazla.

GZM (גזם, ࡂࡆࡌ) to threaten, rush at threateningly, be violent.

Pe. Pt. gazim unahim Gy 280:4 he threateneth and roareth; hanin ugazim ʿlauaihun s. HNN; pl. minilia sainata ubišata amrin ʿlẖ ugazmia ʿlẖ AM 65:7 f. they will speak ugly and evil words to her and threaten her.

Der.: gazuma (fem. gazumtia).

GZR (גזר, ࡂࡆࡓ) to cut (off), hew, decree, condemn, give judgement; to sentence, to circumcise; cut throat (of victim).

Pe. Pf. gzar hṭip Gy 179:20, gzar hṭap Gy 176:16 they cut off and stole away (their hearts), special pl. kul iuma lqudamaihun gazria gzariun (var. agziriun) Gs 14:13 (var. DC 22. 404) and every day they slaughtered victims (Lidzb.: "sacrificed") before them; unapšaihun gzariun ATŠ I no. 258 and they condemned themselves; gzarnin ulaṭnin AO 9/1937 96:5 f. we condemned and cursed; with encl. ugzarbẖ ṭuria DC 22 11 and he hewed out mountains in it. Act. pt. napšẖ gazar (var. Sh. ʿAbd.'s copy gazir) Gy 46:9 he circumciseth himself; pl. iahuṭaiia ḏ-napšaihun bhirba gazria Gy 23:19 the Jews who circumcise themselves with the sword; napšaihun bhirba gazria Gy 45:21, gazrin gzurta DC 36 they perform circumcision. Pass. pt. gzira (s.v.), kḏ ṭuria gziria bgauẖ Gy 11:13 when mountains were hewed out in it.

Af. Pf. haizak agzar agzarta hibil ziua uamar agzar agzarta hibil ziua uamar CP 45:34, ML 59:1 H.–Z. gave a judgement and said; agzar agzarta Morg. 216 19:1 he gave a verdict; agzar ʿl napšaihun Gy 117:23 they condemned themselves; šuba d-agzar ʿl napšaihun Gs 96:23, cf. MSchr 89 n. 1; with encl. agzran he condemned me MG 270: bottom; agzarnabẖ (var. gzarnabẖ) ṭuria DC 6, var. ATŠ II no. 188 we hewed out mountains in it (as DC 36). Impf. lanagzar AM 186:20 he shall not give a verdict; tagzar thou condemnest MG 226:paen.; latagzar ʿlai DC 36 no. 111 do not condemn me; latagzar ʿlan Gy 61:22 f. do not condemn us; nagzrun they (will) condemn MG 227:19; tagzrun Gy 44:6 ye (will) condemn MG 227:ult.; with suff. nagzrẖ Gs 70:13 f. we condemn him MG 275: antep.; latagzran minak Gy 193:1 do not cut us off from Thyself. Impt. with suff. agzran sever me MG 271:11. Pt. magzar ʿl napšẖ Gy 54:2 condemneth himself MSchr 78; pl. kadabia magziria ʿl napšaihun Gy 66:11 f. the liars condemn themselves; magzria Gs 70: 16 f.; abahatak bhšuka lamagzria ʿlan Gy 307:5 thy Father (: the Life, pl.) will not condemn us (: cut off) in the darkness; pl. with encl. magzrilia Gs 43:2 they cut me off. Part. pres. ʿl šalmania lamagzrit Gy 367:3 thou condemnest not the perfect. Inf. lagzuria Gs 43:5 to cut off, to detach.

Ettaf. Pf. laʿtagzar Gy 317:6 they were not cut off; mn nhura ʿtagzar ʿlauaihun ATŠ I no. 258 a verdict against them was given by the light. Impf. nʿtagzar Gy 229:5 MG 226: bottom; nitagzar mn luatai DC 34 he shall be banned from my company; umn ʿbidatẖ lanitagzar ATŠ I no. 173 etc. (often) and he (: the priest) shall not be deprived of (i.e. forbidden to perform) the rites. Pt. mitagzar MG 230:bottom; umn rabutẖ lamitagzar ATŠ (*often*) and he shall not be deprived of his rank. Part. pres. mitagzarna *excommunic(ab)or* MG 231:13.

Der.: agzara, agzaraiia, agzarta, gzurta, gzira, gziraiia, gzirta, gizra, magz(i)rana (cf. also gzarṭabaiia).

GṬA (קטע, ࡂࡈࡀ, قطع) to cut (off), sever.

Pe. Pf. gṭa ML 143:8 (and several times in ATŠ). Other forms not found.

gṭar var. gṭir (rt. GṬR, prob. the second var. is correct) girt, armed, well-equipped. gṭir (var. gṭar) hliṣ mzaraz Gy 273:14 f., MG 305:3 f.

GṬL (קטל, ࡂࡈࡋ with dissimil. of the initial emphatic) to kill, slay, destroy, torment, beat, murder, massacre. Still used.

Pe. Pf. gṭal arzia Gy 380:10 (cf. s. arza 1), ʿu gṭal aria AM 121:8 if he killed the lion; special pl. gṭaiun DAb they killed, with suff. lagiṭlu AM 283:38 (as mod. *lægeṭlū* with apocope of the final *n*) he did not slay them. Impf. umalka nigṭal sanẖ AM and the king will slay his enemy (read nigṭul, cf. ࡍࡉࡂࡈࡅࡋ and impt. below); with suff. nigiṭlẖ we (shall) slay him MG 275:middle. Impt. gṭul arzia s. arza 1. Act. pt. gaṭil, fem. gaṭla, pl. gaṭlin, gaṭlia; with suff. (or encl.) umahu ḏ-razia gaṭilh maiit DC 36 and whatsoever destroyeth its mystery dieth. Pass. pt. gṭil MG 116: 17; dumaiia ḏ-gṭil gabarun s. gabara. Inf. migṭal MG 233:bottom, migṭal gaṭla (var. Sh. ʿAbd.'s copy giṭla) Gy 16:19 committing murder.

Pa. Nom. ag. mgaṭlana; with suff. *mgaṭlanun (Nöld.'s prop. inst. of gaṭlanun Gs 17:6) MG 138 n. 1. Inf. ulgaṭulia kulhun daiuia DC 37:555 and to slay all devils; migaṭulia DC 26. 141.

Ethpe. Pf. ʿgṭil MG 222:2, hazin ʿtigṭal DC 37. 546 this was slain. Impf. nitgṭil, nigṭil, nʿgṭil MG 226:18, br malkia nit(i)gṭil AM 248:12 a prince will be killed; nigiṭla Gs 78:3 *eae neca(bu)ntur* MG 228:9 f. Pt. migṭil MG 230:middle, malka migṭil AM 262:11 the king will be killed; pl. mitgiṭlia MG 14:21, mitgiṭlia kulhun kahnia Jb 84:14 f. all (Jewish) priests are slain.

Ethpa. Impf. **bnia babil nitgaṭlun** AM 248:13 the citizens of B. will be massacred. Pt. pl. **mitgaṭlia rabauata** AM 272:12 the captains will be slain.

Der.: **gaṭla 1 & 2, gaṭlᶜil, guṭla, giṭla, mgaṭlana.**

GṬN (Gen. Sem. קטן, ܩܛܢ, with dissimil. of the first emphatic) to be fine, thin, narrow, slender MG 39:20.

Pe. Only pt. **gaṭna nišimthẖ kḏ zimta** Gy 229:11 her soul is as thin as a hair; **kḏ zimta ḏ-rišia gaṭna** Gy 363:18; **gaṭna mn huṭra** Gy 182:17 they (: the souls) are thinner than a stick; **gaṭnia kḏ zimta** RD C 20, **gaṭnan kḏ zimta** RD C 15.

Der.: **gaṭina,** var. **gaṭana, gaṭinata, guṭan(a).**

GṬP (Gen. Sem. קטף, ܩܛܦ with dissimil. of the first emphatic) to cut off, pluck, sever by cutting.

Pe. Only pt. pl. **anpik gaṭpia uarda** CP 172:14, ML 210:3 f. thy face plucketh roses.

Der.: **gaṭupta, guṭupta, giṭupta, gaṭapiata, garṭapta** (pl. **garṭapiata**).

GṬR I (Gen. Aram. קטר, ܩܛܪ with dissimil. of the first emphatic) to tie, fasten, put together, restrain, weave together.

Pe. Pf. **gṭar** Jb 109:5 f., Gy 380:12 he fixed together; **klila brišia lagṭar** CP 3:11 he did not weave a wreath about his head; with encl. **giṭrẖ** Jb 109:6 he fixed it together; **gṭarthẖ lgiṭra rba** Gy 90:20 I tied a great knot; with encl. **gṭarilẖ** Gy 84:3, 90:18 I tied him; **gṭaribẖ** Gy 90:18 I tied on him MG 225:antep.; **mlakia taga gṭarulia** DC 44. 571 etc. (often) angels wove me a wreath. Act. pt. **gaṭar minẖ muqra ugirmia** Gy 202:3 he formeth from it marrow and bones. Pass. pt. **gṭir** (v.s. **gṭar**). Inf. **migṭar ᶜzlalia ubarauata** AM 155 fabrication of woven stuffs and products; **migṭar špinta** AM boat-building.

Pa. Pass. pt. **mgaṭar giṭria** Gs 118:22 ff. tied with knots; **šidta mgaṭra** AM 279:23 a restricted year.

Ethpa. Pt. **ᶜubadia ḏ-anašia mitgaṭar** AM 275:17 the work of the people will be hindered.

Der.: **gaṭra, giṭra, gaṭiria** (pl.).

GṬR II (H. קטר I Ges., der. Akk. *qutru*, Aram. קְטָרָא "smoke") to smoke, fumigate, cense, waft; (Ar. قطر) to distil, condense.

Pe. Pf. **guṭra gṭar** Jb 67:7, 69:10 smoke wreathed up. Act. pt. **guṭra gaṭar** RD C 9, 14 smoke curls up; **gaṭar guṭra** Gy 204:9 id.

Pa. Impt. **gaṭar** Oxf. roll f 630; **riha basima gaṭar atutia šipulẖ** DC 46. 117:13 waft a sweet perfume beneath his (or her) skirt; with encl. **gaṭrẖ bmiska uninupar** AM 130:penult. fumigate him with musk and nenuphar.

Der.: **guṭra.**

GṬR III (as a var. of **GṬL**) to cut down. **gṭur arza** DC 22 & Sh. ᶜAbd.'s copy var. of **gṭul** . . . Gy 265:11; **gṭar arzia** ibid. var. of **gṭal** . . . Gy 380:10 (v.s. **arza 1**).

giada (גידא, ܓܝܕܐ LS) nerve, sinew, tendon, muscle, membrum. Pl. **giadia.** Masc. often in AM (9, 18, 21 &c.). **adinqia giada** ATŠ II no. 126; **ᶜqba ugiada** DC 34. 621; **giada ḏ-za**[?]**parun** DC 46. 126:9 see **gida 4**?

giaiil DC 44 name of an angel.

giambuk IM no. 10, p. 99 a woman's name.

gibar, var. **gubar** (Ar. غبار) dust. **apra ugibar sumaqa** AM 271:28 ash and red dust.

gibia 1 (rt. **GBA** Ginzā 226 n. 2) chosen people, chosen ones. **gibia ḏ-ruha** Gy 225:3; **gibia ḏ-ruha umšiha** Gy 225:19.

gibia 2 (etym. unsure. If from **GBA,** "chosen morsels"; but prob. of Bab. origin) (pieces of) ritual food of heathen Ginzā 21 n. 1, Hoffmann ZA 9/1894 336, MR 80:bottom. **lhama ḏ-gibia** Gy 19:6, 37:17; **gibia aklia** Gs 47:19; **aklia gibia** Gs 98:15 f.

gibilta a var. of **gbilta: gibilta mn napša . . . giblat** ATŠ I no. 257 a form took shape of itself.

gibla (rt. **GBL**) compression, confusion, terror. Doubtful. **kabar ugibla hu** AM 254:19 it (betokens) might and terror; **gibla udhulta umutana** AM 276:36 terror, fear, and pestilence.

giblia s. **gablia.**

gibta (rt. **GBA**) JRAS 1937 590:20 selection, collection, choice. Sometimes doubtful, cf. CP 419:14 [pit? (**gubta**)].

GID (perh. denom. from **giada**) to reach, attain, overreach, overtake. Used only in pa. as a denom. verb. Meaning only prob., cf. Jb II 148 n. 4, Ginzā 475 n. 4, 413 n. 1.

Pa. Pf. **ata naṣbai udauran ugaiid** Gs 54:2 my Creator came, encircled me, and reached (me); **rihṭit ulagaidit** Jb 262:11 I ran but did not attain; with encl. **gaidinun ligal ṣaida** Jb 147:10 the fisherman overtook them quickly; **hzaitak ugaiidtak** Gy 192:24 (var. DC 22 183 & Sh. ᶜAbd.'s copy **ugaiadtak**) I have seen thee and attained thee. Impf. **ulaiit ḏ-nigaiid dauraikun** ATŠ II 188 there is none who can reach your dwelling; with suff. **zipa lturṣa nigaidẖ** Gy 385:15 falsity will overtake uprightness; **zipa lšamiš nigaidẖ** Gy 385:17 falsity will overreach the sun. Pt. **ulamgaiid midirẖ** CP 95:7, Q 47:17 = ML 121:12 if impossible (?) (: does not succeed) to take him.

gida 1 (גִּידָא II J.) wormwood. Pl. **gidia.** Doublet **gadida** (q.v.). **gidia mraria uᶜlqia** Gs 102:7, 105:7; **gidia umraria uᶜlqia** Gs 124:12, Q 38:2 = ML 101:5; **gidia mriria uᶜlqia** ATŠ I no. 241 wormwood, bitter herbs, and brambles.

gida 2 = gada 2, gdada 1, gidada. Pl. **gidia, gaddia.** Masc. **lgida ḏ-iama** PD 1659, **gida ḏ-iardna** Q 72:23; **trin gidia ḏ-iardna** DC 46; **saq lgida** Q 11:16; **gida rba ḏ-nišmata** Q 56:23; **nunia . . . npal lgida** JRAS 1938 3:12; **usaliq lgida** DC 36 no. 189; **maṣbuta ḏ-lgida** ATŠ I no. 74 a riverside baptism (cf. s. **gidaita**).

gida 3 = giada. Pl. **gidia.** Masc. **gadia pasqinun lgidia dilẖ** ATŠ I no. 253 the goat cut off (?) his genitals (play on words); **birikta ḏ-ᶜtibrikbẖ hamša gidia** CP 430:13 the benediction wherewith the five sensitory organs were blessed.

gida 4 (prob. **gida** 3 figuratively) fibre (of a tree), grain. **ugida d̲-mn sindirka** DC 34. 376.

gidada, gadada = **gdada** 1, **gida** 2 MG 115:9.

gidaita (adj. fem. from **gida** 2) riverine, of (or at) the waterside, riverside, riverbank. **maṣbuta gidaita** (often in ATŠ), a var. **gudaita** (s.v.).

gidma (גִּדְמָא) a cutting (from a tree), branch, twig. Fem. **kdub lgidma d̲-iuraqtia** DC 46. 149:1 write on a green branch; **kdub lgidma ubduq bšamiš** DC 46 write on a piece of wood and place in the sun; **kdub ʿlai gidma d̲-pahil** DC 46. 144:17 (*and often*) write upon a piece of wood from a male palm; **lhdaia iatib lgidma** DC 21 he sits alone on a branch (or adv. apart, in isolation?).

gidra 1 (קִדְרָא, Ar. قِدْر) cooking-pot, cauldron. Var. qidra. Pl. gidria (qidria). **bgidria ududia** DC 44. 563 in cauldrons and cooking-pots.

(gidra 2), gidria 2 (cf. Ar. غدر) bitterness (?), sorrow (?). **mitiqria ʿškia d̲-gidria** Or. 333:20 it shall be called the tear (?) of bitterness (?).

giu (P. ?, cf. MSt. 13 n. 1) a prince of darkness, underworld spirit. **giu rba** Gy 142:11 ff., 144:12; **giu zuṭ(a)** RD 5, DAb; **brath̲ d̲-giu** RD 41 daughter of G. (a wife of Ptahil).

giua a masc. of **giuta** 2 (q.v.) pride, splendour MG 100:25. **ʿqar giua** Gy 303:10 f., Gs 8:19, CP 65:10, 67:11, Q 14:7, 30:2, 30; **ʿqar giua dakia** Gy 360:21 (cf. s. **giuat** and **ʿqara**).

giuaza s. **gauaza.**

giuat, gʿuat st. cstr. of **giuta** 2. **bgʿuat ʿqara** Gy 71 in the splendour of glory MG 309: middle; **bhak giuat ʿqara** CP 401:5 in that glorious splendour **giuat ʿqara** Gs 21:14, Jb 10:13; **lgiuat ʿqara** Jb 27:12 f.; **spinta giuat ʿqara** Jb 80:2; **giuat ʿnšia** Gy 88:8 (cf. s. **ʿnšia**); **haduta d̲-giuat ʿqara** Gs 22:2.

giuza DC 3 no. 376 (var. **ginza** CP 414:ult. ibid.) channel (see CP p. 276 n. 3).

giuṭa (Norb. from ܓܥܛ, hence *געוטא MG 126:9) disgrace, discomfiture, anger, retribution, malediction, anathema IM Gl. Masc. No pl. **giuṭa ʿlai** Gs 6:22 is angry with me (elliptic); **giuṭa rba** Gy 351:5, 376:18, Q 48:6, PD 119, 212, 406, 1654; **giuṭa uaqta** AM 11:19 disgrace and distress; **giuṭa ubišuta** AM 182: 18.

giuiata pl. of **giuta** 1 bodies, hence congregation, company of people MG 165:bottom. **lgiuiata halin d̲-arbik burkaiin larqa** CP 49:17, Q 23:11, ML 65:5 for this congregation that bend their knees to the ground.

giultania (rt. געל) loathsome creatures, loathsome things. **ugiultania akuat giuta udiuta d̲-nabṭa** DC 43 H 5 and loathsome things such as entrails and the black fluid of naphtha; **giuta ugiultania** Par. 27 8a.

giuta 1 (גַּוָּא, ܓܘܐ) body, interior, inside, entrails MG 103:24, MSchr 197 n. 3. Pl. **giuiata** (s.v.). **maitan bgiuta** Gy 394:4 they (: the souls) die in the body; **bgiuth̲ d̲-liuiatan** Jb 98:11, 210:4, Gy 300:23 in the interior of L.; **giuta ugiultania** s. **giultania**; **mn giuta** Gs 118:19 from the body; **mn giutai** Gs 118:20 from my body; **bgiuth̲** Q 13:23 in his body; **giutai** Gy 189:6 my body; **giuth̲ ukarsh̲** DC 21 his entrails and his belly.

giuta 2 a more frequent var. of **gaiuta** (q.v.) MG 57:1. Fem. A masc. form **giua** (s.v.). St. cstr. **giuat, gʿuat** (s.v.). No pl. **bgiuta** Gy 190:1 in the glory, with the glory; **giuta d-ʿtlabašbh̲** Q 53:12; **bgiuta rabtia** Gy 203:20, 204:9; **mpanqia napšaihun bgiuta** Gy 176:23 they effeminate themselves in luxury; **mistakarlun giutaihun** Gy 17:12, Jb 181:10 their pride will be secluded from them; **špur bgiutaihun npalun** Gy 177:2 affectation befell them in their pride; **bnia haria mšamria giutaiun** Gs 18:2 noblemen leave their pomp behind (DC 22. 408 has **giutania** which would be a mod. pl.); **auda giutaihun** Oxf. 55 b their glory vanisheth; **tuqna d̲-giutaikun** Gy 173:22 the splendour of your pride.

giutana, (adj. from **giuta** 2, ܓܐܘܬܢܐ) Pl. **giutania** DC 22 l. 408, proud, vainglorious MG 139:12. **ʿutana giutana rbutana** Gy 204: 24, 205:19 mighty, vainglorious and haughty.

giza in **gizak** DC 48. 12 read **ginzak.**

gizar (جزر Löw 86) carrot. **bazra d̲-gizar** DC 46. 99:2 carrot-seed.

gizuria (rt. **GZR**) sections, incisions. **ʿsirit umazihit mn hamišma gizuria d̲-bisra** DC 37. 582 thou art exorcized and cast out from 500 sections of the body (lit. flesh).

gizita DC 22. 52 a var. of **gizta** 1 (q.v.).

gizra (גִּזְרָא) fold, flock, (ܓܙܘܪܐ) prey, victim: **akuat aria šihana d̲-ʿl gizra** Gy 282:6 (DC 22. 277 completes **gizar** after **gizra**) like a ravening lion that tore its prey; **kd̲ hiuta d̲-mn gizrh̲ ʿtpasaq** Gs 14:3 like an animal that was cut off from its fold.

gizraiia Morg. 259/9:15 a var. of **gziraiia.**

gizta (ܓܙܬܐ, גִּזָּה) tonsure. Var. **gizita.** **ugizta brišaihun gaiizlun** (var. **gaizilun**) Gy 56:11 (var. Sh. ʿAbd.'s copy) s. **GZZ**; **ugaiara hauia mn gizta** AM 89:13 s. **gaiara.**

giṭa 1 AM 11 a var. of **giuṭa.** Also as adj., cf. pl. **šidia giṭia** Ephem. 104:4 spiteful devils.

giṭa 2 (*often*) a var. of **gaiṭa.**

giṭa 3 (Bab. *giṭṭu*) document, passport Ginzā 548 n. 1. **dalia lgiṭa rušuma** Gs 105:13, 106:13 he put a sign on the passport.

giṭupta a var. of **guṭupta.**

giṭla (rt. **GṬL**) murder, killing, slaughter, massacre, torment, ill-treatment, violence; (a var. of **gaṭla** 1) murderer. **umn giṭla palṭia** (var. **paliṭ**) **mn ʿdh̲** AM 4:5 and will escape the hand of the murderer. **dhulta ugiṭla** AM 280:1 terror and massacre; **giṭla ʿka ʿlauaihun** AM 167:10 murder will happen; **gaṭla ugiṭla** AM 278:18 violence and murder.

giṭma (קִטְמָא, ܩܛܡܐ) ash, ashes MG 39:2. Var. **gaṭma.** **giṭma ʿl pumaihun d̲-kulhun kahnia** CP 173:17, Jb 131:8 ash on the mouth of all (Jewish) priests, ii 129 n. 3; **giṭma mn šuba tanuria** AM ash from seven ovens; **udarin mn hanath giṭma** ATŠ I no. 59 and they bring some of those ashes; **apra ugiṭma** DC 12. 44 dust and ashes.

giṭra (קִיטְרָא, ܩܛܪܐ) (*a*) bond, knot, tie,

fabrication, joint, (*b*) ligament (of the body), (*c*) string of a bow, (*d*) confluence, (*e*) umbilical cord. Pl. **giṭria.** Masc. (*a*) **g̱ṭartẖ lgiṭra rba** s. **GṬR**; **gaṭrilẖ giṭra** Gy 84:3; **mgaṭar giṭria** s. **GṬR** pa.; **giṭria uhatmia** Gs 77:20, Q 76:10; **ṭab lasaria ugiṭria** AM 139:10 good for bonds and knots; **tlata giṭria** DC 45; (*b*) **giṭria ugirmia** ATŠ I no. 246; (*c*) **giṭra ḏ-qašta** DC 44. 2040 bow-string; (*d*) **giṭra rba ḏ-mia** AM a great gathering of the waters (: flood); (*e*) **giṭra ḏ-ialda** ATŠ II no. 201 umbilical cord of the babe.

gila 1 (cf. **gala** 1) JRAS 1938 6:23 straw, stubble.

gila 2 (P. گله) flock, fold. Mod. Gl. 136:3 missp. قطيع *grex* گله.

gilaiia AM 232:10 name of a people.

gilan (P. گيلان) AM 198 Persian province of Gîlân.

gilgil an uthra. **bhahu gilgil ʿutra daiana mana rba rišaia** DC 51 by this uthra G., the judge, the Great First Mana.

gilda (Gen. Sem. 'skin') testicle (expl. by Sh. 'Abd.); leather. **šria ʿštẖ ubuṭẖ udundẖ ugildẖ** DC 12. 112 exorcize his buttocks, his anus, his penis, and his testicle(s); **šauṭia gildia** Gy 121:19 leathern whips.

gilia 1 (ܓܠܠܐ) waves (a more frequent doublet of **aglauata**) MG 14:24, 163:paen. f., IM Gl. Metaph. protruding features (of the face) CP trs. 7 n. 2, ML 15 n. 1, Ginzā 156 n. 2, MSchr 148 n. 2. **gilia mia** Gy 181:6, 182:23, 185:10, 187:13, 234:24, 255:5, Gs 26:24, 27:4, 28:14, 19, 30:2, 5, 31:19, 24, 108:8, 11, Q 5:26; 31:30; **gilia iama** Q 52:11, 16; **gilia ḏ-gaura uzmara** Jb 200:10; **gilia parṣupẖ** Gy 142:1, Q 8:12, 23; **gilia parṣupia** CP 13:12, Q 5:16; **gilia parṣupaihun** Oxf. roll 36; **gilia gudlania** s. **gudlania** (*c*).

gilia 2 (pass. pt. of **GLA**) revealed, uncovered, open. **mn gisia umn gilia** DC 40. 510 f. secretly (read **kisia**) and openly; **ḏ-atia mn gilia . . . ḏ-atia mn kisia** DC 40. 717 ff. who comes secretly . . . who comes openly.

gilia 3 (גִּילָא ball) in **gilia ainẖ** CP 185:14 his eyeballs.

gilita (cf. ܓܠܝܠܬܐ 2 & 3 LS & **glala**) something round, kernel, stone. **gilita ḏ-sindirka ḏ-bazira dilẖ** DC 34. 366 the date-stone of a date, which is its seed.

gilitua (P. گل تاوه) clay, mud. **mṣapa mn gilitua** AM 288:6 clarified from mud (?).

***gilmuhra** (P. گل مهره) projectile Jb ii 132 n. 1. Found only in pl. **gilmuhria. atrunun minai gilmuhria** Jb 134:5 projectiles tore them from me; **mazruta huat ukḏ gilmuhria** DC 34. 629 semination took place (?) (delete u before **kḏ**) like projectiles.

gilšia (*גִּלְשָׁא, Syr. with different structure ܓܘܠܫܐ) baldness, bald patches. **ʿtlẖ gilšia** AM 12 he is bald; **gilšia brišiẖ nihuilẖ** AM he will be bald.

gimat aria (גמטר(י)א, *γεωμετρία*) arithmetical calculation of numerical value of letters. **hšub bgimat aria** AM 136:4 add the numerical value of the letters!

gimra 1 (rt. **GMR**) a word of doubtful meaning: usually gem, jewel, or pearl, with the adj. **gmira** including the idea of perfection; with **mrara** completely obscure MSchr 154 n. 1, HpGn 249 n. 2, ML 23 n. 3, Ginzā 158 n. 3, 271 n. 1. Masc. **tagak unaurak uhazin gimra hda ʿlai hun** Gy 163:3 thy crown, thy mirror and this one gem (?) were with me; **gimra ḏ-bnapšai aka** Gy 165:22 f.; **ruha apiqtu lhanatẖ gimra mn napšẖ** Gy 166:2; **nsabtẖ mn qudamẖ lhanatẖ gimra** Gy 166:9 (some un-unknown magical object in the world of darkness, taken away by Hibil-Ziwa); **gimra hiuara** Morg. 258/8:4; **gimra rba hiuara** Morg. 258/8:8 (an object through which the demons shine); **gimra ḏ-bilaur** s. **bilaur; gimra zuṭa** Gy 158:22, **gimra umrara** Gy 145:9, **mrara ugimra** Gy 145:5 (unknown, two things assuring the stability of the world of darkness); **gimra anat gmira** Gy 274:12, **gimra ana gmira** CP 21:7 ML 23:7, **gimra ana dakia** DC 33 (here associated with perfection and purity), Lidzb. Mand. Gl.; **gimra ḏ-ʿšata haita** DC 34. 641.

gimra 2 a var. of **gumra. gumria** Sh. 'Abd.'s copy = **gimria** Gy 357:12.

ginaia (Talm. גִּינָאָה) gardener, dealer in vegetables MG 142:2 & n. 1. Pl. **ginaiia** MG 14:23. **laziriak ginaia bginth** Or. 325:4, 331:1 the gardener sowed thee not in his garden; **br ginaiia** Gs 111:11 gardener; **ginaiia ḏ-arqa** DC 43 F 60 (seems to stand for genies).

ginat st. cstr. of **ginta** MG 14:23, 155:18. **bginat ʿqarẖ** DC 22. 65 in the garden of his glory; **ginat ʿdania** Gy 230:15, 233:5, 254:16, 19, Oxf. roll 95, DC 48. 370 the Garden of Eden; **ginat ʿlania** Gy 34:7 garden of trees (perh. to read **ginat ʿdania**, cf. MSt 128), MSchr 61 n. 5, 236; **bginat adam** Jb 242:1, Oxf. 77a A.'s garden (= Paradise); **ginat aiar** Jb 241:14 garden of ether (one of the designations of the world of light). But **bginat ḏ-minẖ hua** Gy 85:8 read either **bgiuat**, cf. Gy 88:8 (marginal note in Lidzb.'s copy of Ginzā) or **bgihnam,** cf. Ginzā 86 n. 5. Lidzb. Mand. Gl.

gindal (P. جندار ?) DC 46. 203:3 life-guard (?).

gindia = **gundia** (s. **gunda**): **bgindia salqia** DC 20 & 43 E 12 they rise up in troops.

ginza 1 (גִּנְזָא, Syr. ܓܙܐ with an assimilated *n*, which was preserved in the pass. pt. ܓܢܝܙܐ, an Aram. form of P. گنج, Ar. loan-w. كنز Jeffrey 297; cf. also H. loan-w. גְּנָזִים I, גִּנְזַךְ Ges., Gr. & Lat. loan-w. *γάζα gaza* corresponding to the Syr. form) treasure, library of holy books: hence **ginza rba** (= **sidra rba**) title of the chief collection of sacred texts in one volume, religious mystery MG 51:18 & n. 1. A rare var. ***ganza** (s.v.). Pl. **ginzia.** Masc. **ginza taqna** Gy 345:19, 347:7, Gs 58:23, **ginzia taqnia** Gy 350:21, **ginzaihun taqna** Gy 373:8; **bit ginza, bit ginzia** Gy 144:5, with pers. suff. **bit ginzai** Gy 144:4 my treasure-house, us. library, further sanctuary MSchr 4 n. 8, DAb 3 n. 4; **maria**

ginzia RD C 6, PD 1105, 1128 possessors of (holy) books; **gadana malka ḏ-ginzia** PD 965; **ginza ḏ-hiia** Gy 92: 20, 132:6, 347:3, **ginzaihun ḏ-hiia** Treasure of Life Jb ii 201, Ginzā 96 n. 4, Wid. iii 57; **bginza umalala qam bginza qam umalala** Gy 356:17 f. he stood firm in (faith to) the treasure and the word; **ḏ-hu škin bginza ḏ-rba urama** . . . DC 36:(a coloph.) which was kept in the library of the great and lofty . . .; **maṭarta ḏ-kanziᶜil . . . ḏ-ginza luatḫ nṭir** RD C 5, DAb the purgatory of K. . . . with whom the treasure is guarded.

ginza 2 (**ginza 1** adverbially) much, very much MG 38:15. Very frequent in Mod. Mand. (pron. *genzā, genzi*). **skilta abdit ginza** Zotb. 228:left 1 I committed much foolishness; **ginza siblit** DC 50. 907 much did I endure; **ᶜniš mhadit ginzḫ** DC 46. 68:10 (and often) a person who talks very much; **ḏ-ginza šakub** DC 46. 105:3, **ušakib ginza** ibid. 105:7 (who) sleeps very much. Gl. 77:9 missp. with q جدّا *valde* البتة; 142:5 id. كثير *multus* بسيار; 145:5 id. كثيراً *multipliciter* بسيار.

ginzaiia (formed as adj. from **ginza 1**) treasurer (a grade of office now obsolete). **ganzibria uginzaiia** Morg. 188:4, CP 43:10, ML 52:8, DC 42. 689 etc. (*often*) (prayed for in lists of the dead).

ginzaiil, ginziᶜil = ganziil (v. also s. kanziᶜil). **maṣbuta ḏ-iauar uginzaiil rba** ATŠ I no. 67.

ginia 1 pl. of **ginta** MG 172:15, used often with extended and metaph. meanings. **paqia kḏ arqa umišṭarar kḏ ginia** DC 40 he will burst open like the ground and be cut open like irrigation ditches (?); **mn ainaniata ḏ-burkia umn ginia ḏ-amḫ** DC 48 from his knee-caps and from his armpits.

ginia 2 (Akk. *ginū* 2 Delitzsch 201 b) sacrifices, offerings to idols MSchr 99 n. 1, Nöld. *Neue Beiträge* 63, IM 255, Jb ii 195 n. 2; fig. shameful things, abominations. **ginia uzutria** Gy 60:1 offerings and sacrificial meals; **abid ginia lᶜkuria** Gy 302:1 he bringeth offerings to pagan temples; **abda ginia lᶜkuria** Gy 301:19 id. fem. **kul man ḏ-nikal** (var. **akil**) **ᶜkilta ḏ-ginia ḏ-mašknia** Gy 302:3 (var. DC 22. 278) whosoever eateth the sacrificial meal in (pagan) temples (a similar prohibition as I Cor. 8:4 ff.); **kḏ hazitun ginia ḏ-ᶜkuria** Jb 201:7 (possibly influenced by גינא [= Ar. جنّ] of Jewish magic bowls, Jb ii 195 n. 2); **libḫ laništia bginia ḏ-ᶜkuria** ATŠ II no. 351 his heart was not seduced by pagan sacrifices; **ḏ-kulhun ginᶜia ṭaiiblun** DC 48. 95 which turns all shameful things into good.

ginia 3 (rt. **GNN**) a kind of protecting arms, prob. shields. **ginia hirbia usipia** Morg. 258/8: 37, DC 44 shields (?), swords, and blades (DC 44. 509 **giria uhirbia usipia** arrows &c.).

giniania (from **gunia 1** with nominal suff. **-an**) shameful things, ignominies, abominations. **umn ᶜubadia sainia ḏ-hšuka umn kulhun giniania** DC 51 and from evil works of the Darkness, and from all abominations.

gininia 1 a doublet of **ginia 1**. **asa bgininia** DC 41 myrtle in the gardens. DC 53. 122: 16 &c.

gininia 2, gninia (pl. pass. pt. of **GNN**) covered, hidden (things), mysteries. **širša ḏ-br g(i)ninia hᶜ** CP 346:11 Lond. roll A 407 (corrupt, should be hu masc.) the Root which is a son of Mysteries (the expression could mean 'a garden-product' CP trs. p. 226 n. 2, but **šarša** is used here with a figurative meaning, cf. s. **šarša, širša**); **bit razia gninia** DC 44. 1229 I sought hidden mysteries; **gninia hibil** Ml. 146:5.

ginsa (ܓܢܣܐ, *γένος, genus*, Ar. loan-w. جنس) kind, sort. Pl. **ginsia 1** species. **ahia hinun ubhda ginsa hinun** AM 120:paen. they are brothers and of the same kind; **ḏ-tlatma ušitin ginsia hauia** ATŠ that are of 360 kinds (species); **abatur btlata ginsia palgia** (read **palgiḫ**) DC 34 A. divideth it into three kinds.

ginsia 2 (גִּינוּסְיָא & varr., *γενέσιος*) birthdays, birth festivals. Hapaxl. Ginzā 197 n. 6. **ripsia ginsia uᶜdania** Gy 196:23 seconds, annual festivals and seasons.

ginṣa a var. of **ganṣa** (q.v.).

ginta (גִּנְתָא, ܓܢܬܐ Akk. *gannatu* LS, cf. also Ges. s. גנן, Ar. loan-w. جنّة Fränkel 148) garden MG 172:15. St. cstr. **ginat** (s.v.). Pl. **ginia 1** (s.v.). **miuia ḏ-hanata ginta ḏ-ᶜlania** DC 27. 39 fruits from that orchard; **uapiq gumia mn gintḫ** v.s. **gumia**; **ginta ḏ-rihania ubusmania** DC 27. 480 garden of aromatic and fragrant plants.

GIS (den. from **gaisa** q.v.) to plunder, raid, rob, seize as prey (?). Doubtful (cf. s. **gaisa** and **gisa 1**).

gisa 1 (derivation and meaning unsure, possibly from **GUS I, II** or **GIS**) prob. deadly sickness (cf. Jer. Talm. גִּיסָה), or marauder (cf. ܓܝܣܐ s. **gaisa**) used as both noun and pass. pt. Lidzb. also 'band, troop' (among other meanings) Jb ii 38 n. 5, (of animals) CP 42:38 pregnant ML 51 n. 3. Doubtful. **udgaṭil aria udiba udgisa** (var. **ugaisa**) **umaita latiklun** CP 42:38, ML 51:11 (var. DC 40) and eat not of what a lion or a wolf killeth and what is sickly (deadly sick?) (or pregnant; cf. Gy 18:3, or what he seizeth as a prey?) and dieth; **qirsa ugisa** AM illness and agony (?); **asuta tihuilia . . . mn ᶜšata gisa qaria ušiqupta** DC 26 and healing be there for me . . . from fever, deadly sickness, chill (or accidents?) and affliction; **ulgisia ḏ-lilia uᶜl qiria ḏ-ᶜumama** DC 40. 461 and against marauders (?) of the night and accidents of the day.

***gisa 2** (cf. גִּיסָא, גיססא, ܓܝܣܐ 'side') cheek. Fem. dual. **gisana**, miscop. **gisana** (s.v.). Sg. not found. **dimita banpak kḏ tartin gisakin** (var. **gisanak**) DC 46 tears are on thy face, (as) on both thy cheeks; **dimihta bainḫ kḏ btartinin gisanai** DC 46 (read **bainai**), **dimihta bainak kḏ tartin btartinun** (read **btartinin**) **gisanak** DC 46, **btartinun** (read **btartinin**) **gisanak** Par. 27 74b.

gisia a var. of **kisia** (v.s. **gilia 2**).

gisiata (rt. **GSA**) vomitings, belchings, noises of repletion. **gisiata mn pumaihun napqan** ATŠ II no. 85, 305.

***giṣa 1** found only in pl. **giṣia 1** (etym. and meaning doubtful, possibly rel. to Akk. *giṣṣu* Jb ii 145 n. 1, but prob. a corruption from an earlier text of **gihnia** or **gahnia** (s. **GHN**), i.e. pl. of *gahn* a local word of Lower ʿIrāq for a path trodden by water-buffaloes in their passage through the reeds, which are pressed back by their feet and bodies). **iadanun lgiṣia gauaiia** Jb 143:6.

***giṣa 2,** found only in pl. **giṣia 2** (rt. **QṢṢ** = **QSS**) little, Ginzā 428 n. 7. **dirdqunia giṣia** Gs 7:23, 17:19 little children.

giṣa 3 a var. of **gaunia** BZ 63 n. 7.

giṣat a var. of **kiṣat** Ginzā 9 n. 8.

giṣpa v.s. **GṢP.**

GIR (Ar. غَيَّرَ) to change. Only in Mod. Mand.

Pa. Pt. **uzipa ʿl rastia mgaiirlh̲** DC 51: coloph. (each of them) changes the lie to the truth.

Ethpa. Impf. (with ʿ in the prefix under Ar. influence) **iitgaiar** AM 257:3. Pt. **mitgaiar** AM 282:27 will be changed.

Gl. 51:7 f. **GIR** تغيّر *mutari* متغيّر شد.

Der.: **gair.**

gira 1 (גִּירָא, ܓܐܪܐ rt. **GRR**) arrow. Pl. **giria** MG 17:2, 100:bottom. **azilh̲ kd̲ gira** ATŠ I no. 291 he goeth to it (: the other world) like an arrow; **šuba siluania d̲-hinun šuba giria** HG 63 seven shafts which are seven arrows; **giria šmimia** s. **šmimia.**

gira 2 a var. of **qira.**

gira 3 a var. of **ʿgira** (pass. pt. of **AGR I**).

giraia (rt. **GRR**) barber, blood-letter. **kd̲ hauia ʿniš atutia ʿda d̲-giraia** ATŠ I no. 74 (var. PD **garaia**) when a man (dies) under the hand of a blood-letter.

girania AM 257:33 = **grania.**

giraq AM 248:4 a var. of **giriq.**

girba 1, girbia 1 (גרביא, ܓܪܒܝܐ north and north-west wind, Akk. *gabiri* hill, Ar. loan-w. جِرْبِيَاء LS) north, north wind. Masc. (differently from Syr.) MG 147:7. The north is considered as sacred (as already by the Babylonians) Ginzā 7 n. 1, MR 69. **iatib bgirbia ʿlaiia** Gy 3:11 He (: the High King of the Light) sitteth in the High North; **almia kulhun lgirbia mulia qarilh̲** Gy 283:17 f. all people call the north Highland Ginzā 281 n. 3; **baba d̲-girbia** Gy 283:20; **bkul ziqa kulh̲ girbia nišbuqh̲** Gy 385:1 he will fully loose the north wind; **ruh girba** AM a north wind; **mn girba umn timia** DC 46; **ziqa arba kiania . . . uhad girba** ATŠ II no. 62 (refers to north-west wind, cf. غرب).

girba 2 (גַּרְבָּא, ܓܪܒܐ) leprosy, scurf. **ʿu mapiqth̲ baria hauia ʿu bgirba** DC 37 no. 74 if his death is caused by a lion, or by leprosy; **ʿtib bgirba** Gy 118:17 (of the Moon) cf. Ginzā 132:5; **man d̲-napiṣ bgirba** ATŠ II no. 70, 270.

girba 3, garba (rt. **GRB**) prey, booty. Rarely **girbia 2** (perh. influenced by **girbia 1**). **garbin girba** Gy 225:20; **girbia nigirbun** AM 185.

girbana (ܓܪܒܢܐ, adj. from **girba 2**) leper MG 139:2 & n. 1. Pl. masc. & fem. **girbania ugirbaniata** Gy 231:5 MG 168:anteantep. **sin girbana** Jb 139:9 S. (= Moon) the Leper ii 183 n. 9; **mdakia girbania** Gy 29:10 he cleaned (hist. pres.) lepers; **aṭrušia ugirbania** Jb 193:9 the deaf and the lepers; **ugirbania asitinun** Jb 274:12 and I cured lepers.

girgila, girgla v.s. **gargul, gargla. girglia hdiraiia** DC 48. 28 entrails? lower intestines.

girdia (cf. גַּרְדָּא) scraped skins. **kdub lgirdia d̲-saria** DC 46 write upon stinking scraped skins.

giriia (adj. from **GRR**) (of pains) darting, excruciating. **kibia kd̲ giriia** DC 43 J 93 excruciating pains, convulsions (?).

giriq (P. گَرْك ?) AM 233:11 scab (?).

girita (*ǧirri* a local marsh word for a species of fish) a kind of fish, eel (Lidzb.). **nuna d̲-girita šumh̲ aklilh̲ lgirita** Jb 148:13 f.

girma (גַּרְמָא, ܓܪܡܐ LS, H. גֶּרֶם Ges.) bone, knuckle MG 100:antep. Pl. **girmia.** Masc. **mn girmh̲** (i.e. **girmia**) Gy 227:13 from the bones; **girmia litbh̲** Gy 142:24 he has no bones; **ʿtnahazbun bgirmh̲** Gy 94:16 he shook himself with his bones; **dahil mn girma d̲-br anaša** AM 124:18 he (: the demon) is afraid of human bone; **mn hailaikun bgirman** DC 51 . . . some of your strength in our bones; **girma msa** s. **MSA**; **girma d̲-halṣa** DC 48. 31 pelvis.

girmaba Q 72:19 = **garmaba.**

girpa (prob. a doublet of **girba 3,** rt. **GRP**) loot, booty. **girpa d̲-larašia** Jb 158:3 the loot that is not authorized (?). The phrase puzzled Lidzb. who translates **girpa** ‘bank’.

girtaiia name of a people, Kurds (?) BZ Ap. II. **bit girtaiia uṭuraiia** AM 191:ult. f. amongst the G. (: Kurds?) and the mountain tribes.

giša (cf. ܓܫܐ) bottom Jb ii 158 n. 4. **umistakria ʿl gišia d̲-baznaqita** Jb 155:10 and are held back on the bottom of the fish-trap; **mn gišia nitikbiš** Morg. 268/26:28 he shall be completely mastered.

gišar (from an inverted גרש, ܓܪܫ, cf. Ar. جاروشة, جاروش) mill. Still used (pron. *gīšar*). **uaiilun hiṭia ugišar** DC 41:167 f. and they brought in wheat and a quern; **gišar d̲-glala** Bodl. 13 a quern; **gišar umhulta** DC 48. 281 a quern and sieve.

gišuma, gišma (גּוּשְׁמָא and גֻּשְׁמָא, ܓܘܫܡܐ, Ar. جِسْم Fränkel 286) body, embodiment, person MG 20:9, 32:24. Pl. **gišumia.** Masc. **gišmh̲ zapur** Gy 280:18 his body is stinking; **mn gišmaiun** Gy 55:21 from their bodies; **bgišumih** AM 180 in person; **gišuma d̲-šunara** DC 45 the body of a cat; **almia d̲-nhura ualmia d̲-hšuka gišuma udmuta d̲-hdadia** ATŠ II no. 235 the worlds of light and the worlds of darkness, the embodiment and likeness of each other; **gišuma bgiuat qamla** s. **qamla**; **bgišuma upagrh̲** DC 40. 990 in his person, his body . . .; **bgišuma d̲-adam** ATŠ II no. 64.

GLA (Gen. Sem.), **GLL II** (Pa.) (*a*) to reveal, make known, uncover, disclose, expose, declare, (*b*) to exile, send away, banish, efface, rub off. Pa. with transition from ל״י to ע״ע only 'to reveal' MG 83:11.

Pe. Pf. **gla šumai** Gy 143:7 (who) revealed my name, pl. **daiuia . . . glun** DC 43 demons . . . were banished (materially an ethpe.); with suff. **glatalkun** Gy 255:4 she revealed to you MG 257:14; with encl. **man glalh̲ l-** Or. 326:19 who revealed it to . . . Impf. **uriših̲ qudam šamiš laniglia** ATŠ I no. 14 & 49 (with a worse var. **lanigalil** pa.) and he shall not uncover his head in the sun. Impt. **glia**, fem. **atai uglai mn razaihun d̲-kulhun mlakia** DC 37 come and reveal to me some of the secrets of all the angels. Act. pt. **galia** he reveals MG 112:14; pl. **ᶜuṣria lhdadia galin** ATŠ I no. 290 they disclose their thoughts to one another; fem. pl. **d̲-ainaikun galia ldilkun** CP 108:13 (ye) whose eyes are uncovered (: open) for your own; **galaia d̲-ainh̲ galian** CP 97:ult. = ML 108:9, Gy 63:13 Leid. (Pet. with encl. **galialh̲**) revealer whose eyes are open. Part. pres. with encl. **galinalh̲** ATŠ I no. 44 (DC 6 a worse var. **ᶜgalinalh̲**) I (shall) reveal to him. Pass. pt. **glia** revealed (among other meanings s.v.); **šumak gilia** DC 43 B 22 thy name is revealed; with encl. (**miglia**) **glilkun** Gs 3:19 it is revealed to you. Inf. **miglia** Gs 3:19, DC 34. 658.

Pa. v.s. **GLL II.**

Ethpe. Pf. **bza rqiha uᶜtglia** Gy 196:17; . . . **uᶜtiglia** Gs 128:11, 130:22, ML 11:11, 77:3, 128:2, 142:11 the sky opened and uncovered itself; **sira ᶜtiglia** Oxf. 53 b, **lau mn šurubtai ᶜtiglia** Jb 179:10 cf. ii 177 n. 2; **ziua šna d̲-anania ᶜtiglia nhurh̲** DC 28 the radiance was removed from the clouds, light was banished (pl. **ᶜtiglun** MG 214:4). Impt. **ᶜtikpar uᶜtiglia mn qudamai** Jb 165:6 be blotted out and be banished from my presence; **ᶜtiglia uasgia** Oxf. 50 b, be banished and go (away); pl. **ᶜtikpar uᶜtiglun** Gy 353:24, Gs 53:21. Part. pres. **mitiglinin** Gy 54:9 we are revealed MG 266:9. Inf. **ᶜtgluiia** Gy 192:18, **ᶜtigluiia** Q 54:5, 8 MG 144:11, 266:10.

Ethpa. v.s. **GLL II.**.

Der.: **galaia** (*a*), **galiata** (*a*), **galiuta** (*a*), **glia 1, 2** (*a*, *b*), **gilia 2, gluta** (*b*). See also under **GLA II.**

glab AM 259:14 a geographical name (a city or river in Syria) BZ Ap. II.

glaznak HG name of a mountain.

glala 1 (גְּלָלָא) stone, rock, hailstone, hail(storm), rocksalt (?) MG 115:1. Us. fem. MG 158:13 in spite of masc. pl. **glalia**. About the meaning 'hail' cf. Jb ii 47 no. 1. **ᶜṣṭun glala** CP 178:5, ML 217:6 a column of stone; **had arqa d̲-ṭina uhad d̲-glala** ATŠ II no. 60 one earth of clay and one of stone; **gišar d̲-glala** s. **gišar**; **uanat glala iatib lanitasia** DC 43 and thou (shalt be like) a motionless (?) stone (which) cannot be healed; **ṭur glala** Gs 114:5 stony hill; **madiqta d̲-hina uglala** DC 48 a pounded compound of henna and rocksalt; **glala d̲-pilia gaṭla glala d̲-paisa ṭuria** Jb 41:12 f. hail that killeth elephants, hail that smasheth hills; **aiba umiṭra uglala** AM (often) cloud, rain, and hail; **glalau barda** AM (*often*) hail and frost; **aula uṭiba uglala** Gy 385:23 evil, scandal (?, Lidzb. drowning), and hail. Gl. 67:5 missp. with **q** حجاره *lapis* سنگ. Still used (pron. *galâla*, *gelâla*) with the meaning 'stone'.

glala 2 (ܓܠܠܐ) something rounded, ball. **glala d̲-ainia** DC 34 the eyeball.

glala 3 (cf. **gal, gala 1**) dung (?). **ᶜl glalia mhaliq ana rihua** DC 46. 125:4. I assign an (evil) odour to his dung (?). Corrupt.

glalaia (= **glala 3**) faeces, v.s. **HLQ** pa.

glalta (= **glala 1**) stone. **bduq atutia glalta kadirtia** DC 46. 161:13 f. put under a heavy stone.

glapa (ܓܠܦܐ) inset of a ring or ornament. Still used in silvercraft (pron. *gelâfa*). **utrin ᶜsqia had glapa smaqa uhad iuraqa** DC 38 ŠQ 5:20 and two rings, one with a red inset and one with a green one.

glum DC 51 a spirit invoked in exorcisms.

glușțuma, glușțma (גְּלוֹסְקְמָא and דְּלוֹסְקְמָא, ܓܠܘܣܩܘܡܐ and ܓܠܘܣܩܘܡܐ > *γλωσσόκομον, γλωσσοκομεῖον* Fränkel 33) chest, case, casing, outer covering, coat-of-mail, armament, armature, arsenal MG xxx. 16 **bglușțma d̲-hirbia** Gy 143:19 with an armament of swords; **bglușțma gauaiia d̲-parzla ᶜtlabaš** DC 27. 94 clothed in an inward casing of iron; **glușțuma baraia** ATŠ II no. 104, **glușțuma baraiia** DC 27. 310 an outer casing (suit of armour); **bglușțuma gauaia** DC 34. 533 in an inner protective cover.

gluta (גָּלוּת, ܓܠܘܬܐ) exile, banishment MG 146:10. **iahuṭaiia bgluta napqin** Gy 29:20 the Jews (will) go into exile.

glia 1 (pass. pt. of **GLA** (*a*)) revealed, mod. (attributively *gelī*, predicatively *geliyye*; fem. *gelya*, pred. *gelliyyī*) naked. Pl. masc. **gliin**, fem. **gli(i)an.**

glia 2 (pass. pt. of **GLA** (*b*)) banished, defaced, worn away by use, rubbed away. Pl. as from **glia 1. halin dmauata hua gliian** DC 7 these pictures were worn away; **ukul d̲-hua šapir ulahua glia** ATŠ I no. 215 and all that was fair and not defaced; **hatiqa uglia umpasaq** ATŠ II no. 409 old, worn, and fragmentary; **bhazin dukta hua glia minh̲ miqdam** (read **miqdar**) **d̲-šita ṣaṭria** ATŠ II no. 409 (coloph.) in this place an amount of six lines was worn away from it.

glila (pass. pt. of **GLL I** used substantivally) vagrancy, turning about. **utup uglila napša hualun** DC 43 and they had much shame and vagrancy (?).

GLL I (גְּלַל, ܓܠ) to roll, curl up, (un)fold, revolve, roll about, turn about, involve, furl. A reduplicated rt. is **GRGL** (s.v.).

Pe. Impt. with suff. **gulan** (**upusqan**) Jb 130:8 roll me up and cut me off. Pass. pt. **glila** (s.v.).

Pa. Pass. pt. fem. **haršia bišia d̲-hᶜ bgauaihun mgalala** Gy 81:10 evil sorceries in which she is involved.

Der.: **agla** (1), **2, gilia 1, gilita, glala** (1–3), **glila, glalta, m(a)galta.**

GLL II (pa & ethpa. of **GLA**) to uncover, reveal, declare, expose clearly MG 83:11 f.

Pa. Pf. **galil** MG 83:11; **apriš ugalil** taught and revealed (often) Q 2:1, 25:12; **galil galalta** Gy 134:4; **galilit ltarmidia** DC 36 I have revealed to the priests; with pers. suff. **galiltinun** I revealed them MG 282:anteantep.; with encl. **galilulia** they (or He, i.e. the Life) revealed to me MG 31:ult., 225:4. Impf. **lanigalil** (as a var. of **niglia** v.s. **GLA**), **laʿgalil** ATŠ II no. 44 I will not reveal; with pers. suff. (or encl.) **nigalilun** we (shall) reveal them MG 282:1; **ʿgalilak** Gy 268:4 I will reveal to thee. Impt. like pf.; pl. with encl. **galilulia ʿl razia** DC 34. 668 reveal ye to me the mysteries. Act. pt. **mgalil** he reveals MG 253:7; **galaia ḏ-mgalil kasiata** s. **galaia.** Pass. pt. **ksia ulamgalal** Gy 3:1; **kasiata lqudamak mgalala** Gs 3:20 hidden things are revealed before thee. Inf. **galulia** MG 143:paen.

Ethpa. Pf. **ʿtgalal** DC 48. 162 they were made manifest; **ainai ḏ-ʿtgalil** (var. **ʿtgalal**) **mn atra ḏ-nhura** Gs 39:3 my eyes which were opened from the place of light. Impf. **kasiata nitgalalun** AM 226:12 hidden things will be revealed. Pt. pl. **mitgalalia** (var. **mitgallia**) *revela(bu)ntur* MG 31:ult.; with encl. pers. pron. **mitgalilin** we shall be enlightened, revealed MG 32:1, 233:7.

Der.: **galalta.**

GLM (גלם, Syr. der. ܓܘܠܡܐ) to roll up, arch up; encompass.

Pe. Pf. or impt. **glum** used as a pr. n. of a spirit (s.v.). Pass. pt. **glima uṣlipa** AO 1937 101:20 encompassed and whipped (Gordon).

Der.: **glum.**

GLP (גְּלַף, ܓܠܦ, *γλύφειν*) to engrave, form, fashion, decorate, set (in an ornament). Only pt.: **glipa** DC 43 A 11, 15. **ulkuzia** (var. **uʿl kunzia**) **ḏ-mglip sabla** DC 43 J 168 and on bowls bearing an inscription.

Der.: **glapa.**

GLŠ (ܓܠܫ) only der. **gilšia.**

gmaṭa (rt. **GMṬ**) subst. gag, constriction, adj. constricting, tenacious, holding fast, holding tight, oppressing. **ugmaṭa lpumaihun** Morg 259/10:18 and a gag on their mouths; **asara biša ugmaṭa utaqipa** DC 44. 14:77 grievous, constricting, torturing and powerful bond; **ʿsiria gmaṭia giria miktia** DC 19 they are bound, the oppressors, the wounding arrows; **gmaṭa zriza** Morg 266/22:20, 267/25:10 strong restriction.

gmama a var. of **gumama. kḏ sira ʿtlh kudarat ʿu hiba ʿu gmama** AM 282:12 when the moon is sickly, or covered, or cut into.

gmarta DC 22. 221 a var. of **gumarta** (q.v.).

gmura (rt. **GMR**) entireness, wholeness, completeness, perfection, **bgmur** completely, entirely MG 118:16, **bgmura** Gy 231:6 completely; **unidabrh lalma kulh bgumurh** DC 44. 1112 and he governs all the world in its entirety; **ualanpia alma kulh bgmura** DC 44 and before the whole world.

GMṬ (Gen. Aram. קמט, ܩܡܛ with dissimil. of the first emphatic) to seize, hold fast, tie, fasten, secure, fetter, oppress MG 38:21 f.

Pe. Pf. **ainaihun bmai gmaṭ** ML 35:3, CP 29:15 (var. **gmiṭ**) (the Life) fixed His eyes on the water; **asar ugmaṭ razia** ATŠ I no. 252. Impt. pl. **gmuṭiun** DC 46 hold fast. (Act. pt. with encl. **gamiṭlak** DC 22. 402 only as a var. of **gmiṭlak** below), fem. **kma karialak ugamṭalak** Gs 16:1 how it troubleth and weigheth heavy on thee. Part. pres. **gamiṭna bʿdai** Jb 43:10 I hold with my hands. Pass. pt. **gmiṭa** (often in exorcisms) held fast, fettered, pl. **gmiṭia** DC 43 B 5 irregular **gimṭia** DC 46; with encl. **kma karialak ugmiṭlak** Gs 12:12 f. (var. Sh. ʿAbd.'s copy **gmiṭalak**).

Der.: **gmaṭa.**

gmir, gmira (pass. pt. of **GMR I** q.v.) perfect.

GML a doubtful verb, prob. corrupt. Found only in one place: **ulmarh mitgamal** Jb 124:10 cf. ii 120 n. 5.

GMM (Ar. غمّ) to worry. Only in Mod. Mand. Gl. 59:9 f. miswritten حزن *contristari* غمگین شد.

Der.: **gama.**

GMR I (Gen. Sem.) to finish, complete, make whole, make perfect, bring to an end.

Pe. Impt. with suff. **gimran mn huṭpia** CP 482:15 end for me acts of violence. Act. pt. pl. **lagamria** Gs 132:12 they do not end. Part. pres. **šitin uarba haṭaiia . . . gamritun** DC 27. 417 ye will abrogate 64 **sins . . .** Pass. pt. **gmir, gmira** (often) perfect; **gimra ana gmira** s. **gimra 1**; **arbak gmira baiar** Jb 161:9 thy boat is perfect in the ether; pl. **tagak naṭria gmiria** Jb 80:1 the perfect ones guard thy crown (?), cf. ii 84 n. 6.

Pa. Pf. with suff. **lagamartan** (var. **-tin**) **kul šušlata** Jb 186:5 all the chains did not bring me to an end (used as sg. fem.) MG 271:paen. f.; **gamarth** Jb 119:2 I perfected it; with encl. **gamarlh lkulh hukumth** Gy 56:7 he has become perfect in all wisdom. Impf. with suff. **hšuka ḏ-nigamrak** Gs 41:18, 21 the Darkness that should put an end to thee. Impt. **ugamar** DC 21 (in a list of destructive acts) and put an end to.

Ethpe. Pt. pl. **mitgimria** DC 22.15 (only as a var. of **mitgamria** Gy 15:22 v.s. ethpa.).

Ethpa. Pf. **ʿtgamar minianai** Gs 45:11 my count (of days) came to an end; **ʿtgamrat mn aiar stana** Gs 108:10 she was more perfect than the north breeze; pl. **haṭaiih ḏ-tgamrun** DC 34 his sins which were abolished; with encl. **ʿtgamarbh bhukumth** Gs 45:14 (cf. idioms below). Impf. **tigamar** she becomes (or will become) perfect MG 227:3; **ʿgamar** I (shall) become perfect MG 227:10; **nitgamrun ʿlh** DC 37:548 they shall destroy him, bring about his end; with encl. **tigamarbh bkulh hukumtak** Gs 45:5, **ʿgamarbh bkulh hukumth** Gs 45:1 f. (cf. idioms below). Pt. **mitgamarlun miniana** Gs 45:8 the count (of days) cometh to an end; pl. **haubia mitgamria** Gy 15:23 his trespasses are done away; **haubik uhaṭaiik kulhun mitgamria** Gs 132:10, **mitagamria** DC 36 II no. 174 they may be made perfect.

Idioms. The verb acquired a great variety of meanings from 'to be perfect, make perfect, whole' to 'to do away with, destroy'. With **haubia, haṭaiia** to abrogate, abolish, annul. With **bhukumta** (or **-tẖ**) Gy 56:7, Gs 45:1 ff., or **lhukumtẖ** Jb 119:2 to learn (thoroughly, become perfect in wisdom) cf. גְּמָרָא Jb ii 116 n. 4. A special meaning seems to be 'to lavish, supply' v.s. **GMR II.**

Der.: **gamriaiil, g(u)marta, g(u)mura, gumra 1, 2, gimra, gmira.**

GMR II (semantic development of **GMR I**) to spend (lavishly), lavish, supply, provide (provide enough), provide amply.

Pe. Only pass. pt. with encl. **iamamia lmištiaikun lagmirilkun** CP 110:5, ML 135:8 seas will not suffice you for your drinking (Lidzb. translated differently but doubted his translation, cf. n. 3).

Pa. Pf. with encl. **malkia gamarlia alpa d̲-zuzia** ŠQ 19:21 = DC 3. 38, CP 240:4 the kings lavished on me 1,000 z.; **abuk aqarak gamarlan** ŠQ 19:4 = CP 238:4 thy father lavished on us (?) in thy presence; **gamarlẖ naṭria** Jb 190:5 f. he provided guards for him.

Ethpa.: **ʿtgamar ʿlẖ naṭria** Gy 85:2 guards were provided for (: set over) him.

GNA I (Gen. Aram., v. LS s. ܓܢܐ I) to lie down, repose, sleep.

Pe. Pf. **ṭubẖ lman lagna** Jb 44:13 well is it for one that did not repose. Act. pt. **ialda d̲-lagania** DC 46 a child that does not sleep; pl. **arba gubria d̲-mkalalia uganʿia ʿl šakbia** DC 43 four beings that surround and lie upon sleepers. Pass. pt. **gnia** (mod. pron. *ganiyye*) he is sleeping (fem. *geniyyi* she is sleeping), pl. **anašia d̲-gnʿiia udiatbia** DC 51 persons that are lying down and those that sit; with encl. pers. pron. (as part. pres.) **arsa d̲-ʿlauai** (!) **gnina** DC 37. 166 the bed on which I lie; **ana agnina ʿl arsa d̲-hšuka** Jb 262:14 f. I lie down on a couch of darkness; **gnʿiit, gnʿit** Gy 170:9 thou liest down.

Pa. Pt. with encl. **kd̲ midaka umiganilẖ bilẖ** DC 46. 203:8 when she is purified (: after menses) and her husband cohabits with her.

Af. Part. pres. (**kd̲ lagṭatlẖ**) **uʿl iaminẖ mauginiatlẖ** (read **maginiatlẖ**?) DC 47 (when thou holdest it) and makest it lie on its right (side).

Idioms. Pa. (only one example above) seems to mean 'to cohabit'. **gnania gania** Jb 114:5 seems to mean 'she spreads her wedding bed' (Lidzb. *man feiert Hochzeit*).

Gl. 164:3 f. missp. with **q** and a prosth. **a** نام *dormire* خوابيد.

Der.: **gnana, magana.**

GNA II (ܓܢܐ III LS) to blame, reproach, rebuke, accuse; refl. to be disgraced, cower in shame.

Pa. Impf. with suff. **laniganinun . . . alma d̲-hinun bnapšaihun naganun** ATŠ II no. 374 we will not rebuke them . . . until they blame themselves; **latiganinun bbnia šaršaikun** ATŠ II no. 20 reproach not sons of your kin; **had bhabrẖ mgania** PD 427 = ATŠ I no. 36 one blameth another; **mgania gunia d̲-hazin alma** Gs 129:21 he rebuketh the abomination(s) of this world; pl. **mganin ahdadia ulaiṭia** Jb 145:3 they cast blame on each other and curse; **hdadia mganin** ATŠ II no. 355 they blame one another; with encl. **hda hda lhabrẖ mganilẖ** Jb 199:11 each one blameth his neighbour; **mganilun** Gy 230:6, 232:22 they cast blame on them.

Reflex.: (irregular: ethpe. inst. of ethpa., and ethpaupil). Pf. **sahria udaiuia ʿtignia b(i)hdadia** DC 26 & 28 demons and devils cower together in shame. Pt. pl. with encl. **mitgaunilia ainai brišai** Gs 104:6 my eyes are covered with shame in my head (the form influenced by **gunia 1**).

Gl. 57: f. missp. خطى *peccare.*

Der.: **gunia 1, gunian, gnia.**

GNA III (= **GHN II** q.v.) to make a sound that bursts out and shakes or convulses, to sob, rumble, peal MG 52 n. 3, 64:16 f.

Pe. Pf. **guha bsiniauis man gna** Jb 6:11 MG 399:14; **ʿqbẖ gna barqa** Gy 84:16 f. his heel stamped on the ground; **alat ugnat** ATŠ I no. 278 she (: the soul) lamented and groaned; with encl. **gnalẖ guha** v.s. **guha.** Impf. **guha nignia** (var. **nignʿ**) AM 252:3, 253:3 f. a rumble groans; with encl. **nignalun guha** DAb.

Ethpe. Pf. **ʿtigna guha** Gy 160:14 thunder pealed; **ʿtgna, ʿtignat** v.s. **guha.** Pt. with encl. **mitignalun** v.s. **guha.**

Idioms. With **ʿqba gna** to stamp. With words meaning 'heart', 'mind' &c. to be disquieted, upset.

Der.: **gunia 2, guha, guhana, gunaha.**

gnana (גְּנָנָא, ܓܢܳܢܐ) canopy, baldachin, canopy over the bridal bed, (hence) bride-chamber, bridal couch. St. abs. **gnan. bit gnana** Gy 59:10, Gs 20:18 the wedding chamber; **sikia gnana** Gy 147:24 the poles of the canopy; **sikia gnan** CP 227:1, DC 36 id.; **gnana gania** v.s. **GNA I** Idioms.

gnat DC 22. 225 a var. of **ginat** Gy 230:15.

GNB (גנב, ܓܢܒ LS, cf. also Ges. s.v.) to put aside, put behind, steal, act or move stealthily, steal away.

Pe. Impf. with suff. **niginbẖ unikisiẖ** ATŠ he putteth it aside and hideth it; **gnubta latiginbun** Gy 16:19 do not steal. Act. pt. fem. **kul atuat d̲-gnubta ganba** Gy 22:4 every woman that stealeth; pl. **gunba ganbia** DAb they steal; **sundumaiia d̲-ganbia razia** ATŠ II no. 25 Sodomites who put aside (defile?) the mysteries; fem. pl. **ʿnšia d̲-ganban** DAb women that deceive; pl. with encl. **hanatun d̲-nišimta ganbilẖ** ATŠ those who steal away the soul. Pass. pt. **iuma d̲-gnib mn tibil** Jb 194:7 the day that he was withdrawn from the earth.

Der.: **ganaba, ganba, ganbiniiil, ganbʿil, ganiba, ganibuta, gunba (gunpa), gnub, gnubta (gnupta), gunapta.**

GNH (used only as **GHN II** and **GNA III** q.v., but the original rt. appears in the der. **gunaha, gnihta, gnihtia** fem.).

gnub (rt. **GNB**) stealth, secrecy. **bakialẖ bgnub gnub** Jb 98:7 she weeps secretly for it.

gnubta (גְּנוּבְתָּא, ܓܢܘܒܬܐ) var. **gunapta, gunubta, gnupta** (*a*) theft MG 119:6, pl. **gnubata** thefts, stolen goods, (*b*) ritual uncleanness. (*a*) **gnubta latiginbun** v.s. **GNB**; **gnupta ganbia** DAb they commit theft; **gnupta ganban** ib. id.; fem. **tarmidia d̲- . . . gnubata ganzbia** (read **ganbia**) DC 3; (*b*) **raza d̲-gnubta lanihuibun** ATŠ II no. 367 there must be no secret of ritual uncleanness in them; **hiia qadmaiia gnubta lahuabun** ATŠ II no. 5 in the First Life there is no uncleanness.

gnuna, gununa (rt. **GNN**) eager to mate, mating (of dogs). Fem. **gnunita, gnuntia. kalba g(u)nuna abatar gurita gnunita** DC 46. 241:14 (var. **gnuntia**) Par 27 7b (var. DC 45) a mating dog after a bitch on heat.

GNZ, KNZ (den. from **ginza** q.v.). Found only in Gl. 139:11 f. missp. with **q** كثر *multiplicare* بسيار شد.

gnia (rt. **GNA II**) censures, shameful things. **lanimalilun bpumaihun gnia** DC 40 they shall not speak censures with their mouths.

gnihtia (rt. **GNH** q.v.) on heat (of bitch). Masc. ***gniha** not found. **aiak kalba gnihta abatar gurikta gnihtia** DC 45 no. xix like a mating dog after a bitch on heat. DC 46. 189:12 f.

gninia s. **gininia 2.**

GNN (cf. LS 122 & Ges. s. גנן) only in der. **ginta**, cstr. **ginat, gininia 1, 2, gninia, gnana, gnuna**, fem. **gnunita** and **gnuntia.**

GSA (ܓܣܐ LS) to throw up, vomit, belch, be replete, be glutted, to glut. Doublet **GUS II** (q.v.).

Pe. Pf. **gsa rira mn pumh̲** Gy 143:21 he spewed forth slaver from his mouth; with suff. **gsan** ibid. he vomited me forth. Act. pt. **gasia** Gy 82:9; pl. **mn pumaihun gasin gumia** s. **gumia**; sg. with encl. **balalh̲ tanina ulagasilh̲** ATŠ II no. 309 the dragon swallowed him and did not vomit him (hist. pres.). Part. pres. **gasit** Morg. 262/16:8 thou spittest.

Der.: **gasa** (?), **gisiata.**

GSR (cf. **QṢR**) to cut off, cut away.

Pe. Impf. **lagsar** Gs 130:18 we will cut off (read **ʿnagsar**) MG 216:antep.

gʿuat a var. of **giuat** (st. cstr. of **giuta 2**). **gʿuat ʿqara** Gy 71:3 MG 309:middle.

gpan st. abs. & cstr. of **gupna.**

GṢA (= **QṢA** q.v., with dissimil. of the first emphatic) to break, break wind (?), to break the law (?), to sin.

Pe. Act. pt. fem. **gaṣa bhalṣa** DC 46 she breaks wind (?) in the loins.

Gl. 10:7 f. **gṣia** اخطي *peccare* خطا كرد.

Der.: **gaṣiaiil, *giṣa 2.**

GṢP (cf. Ges. s. קְצָפָה) to break off, pluck, cut down.

Pe. Pf. **giṣpat** Gy 381:6 she plucked (Pet. mistakenly **gihpat**) MG 38:22 & n. 3. Act. pt. **giṣpa lagaṣpa** Jb 49:1 it can crop nothing Jb ii 34 n. 2. Part. pres. **haṣbit ugaṣpit** DC 21 thou hewest down and cuttest down.

graba (rt. **GRB**) plundering, brigandage, raiding. Var. **grapa, graba udhulta** AM brigandage and terror.

gramka (ܓܪܡܟܐ from P. گرمه LS, Ar. loan-w. درمك Fränkel 32 f.) white flour, fine meal MG xxxi:15. **hanath̲ bgramka ubkulazta apin** Gy 227:13 they bake it with white flour and *colocasia* (?); **bgualqia gramkia** WedF 37:2, CP 223:3 with sacks of fine meal.

gran 1 (P. گران) dear, expensive, at a high price. **zabunit arzan umzabunit gran** AM 157:16 thou wilt buy cheaply and sell at a high price.

gran 2 in **gran bil** DAb name of a demon.

grania (P. گرانی) dearth, scarcity, high market prices. Var. **girania** (s.c.). **iadin bgrania uṣurpania** AM 200:13 they know about dearth and exchange (rates?); **grania** (DC 31 **girania**) **uharub** AM 257:30 scarcity and ruin.

grapa a var. of **graba. grapa udhulta** AM 284:16 brigandage and panic; **grapa ugiṭla** DC 43 J 239 looting and murder.

GRB I, GRP (גְּרַב) to rob, plunder, seize by force, go raiding, despoil.

Pe. Pf. with suff. **grabtinun ana graptinun** Gy 233:22 I plundered them MG 48:8. Impf. **nigirbun** AM 178:15 &c. they will raid. Act. pt. pl. **garbin girba** Gy 225:20 they carry off plunder; **garbin garba** (var. **girbia**) Gy 232:1 (var. DC 22.226) id.; sg. with encl. **gariblh̲ had lhurina** AM 283:32 they will raid one another, pl. with encl. **garbilh̲** Gy 390:8 they (will) plunder it.

Ethpe. Impf. **nitgirbun** AM 274:4 they will be despoiled. Pt. **mitgirbia** Gy 390:9 etc. MG 149:18.

Ethpa. Impf. **nitgarbun** AM 211:11 they will go raiding. Pt. **mitgarbia** AM (often) they will be plundered; **mitgarbia malakia d̲-almia hazin** DC 37:445 angels of this world will be carried off (by force).

Der.: **garbilia, girba 3** (var. **girbia**), **graba, garba.**

GRB II (ܓܪܒ) a rt. of **girba 2, girbana.**

GRG I (ܓܪܓ) to stimulate, aggravate, provoke, impart zeal or zest.

Pa. Pf. with suff. **lnaṣuraiia ṭabia gargun** Gy 275:11 He (: the Life, pl.) made me zealous for good Naṣoraeans.

Ethpa. Impf. **nitgarag lmahria** AM 226:9 will aggravate illness.

GRG II (by shortening of **GRGL**) to turn, drag, trail. Only with encl.: **gargulia** s 16:17 turn me back! (Nöld.'s emendation to **agarulia** MG 85 n. 1 is unnecessary). Pt. **mgargilh̲** they drag him MG 85:2.

GRGL (by dissimil. of the reduplicated גלל, ܓܠܓܠ, cf. גִּלְגֵּל, ܓܪܓܠ) to revolve, go round, (re)turn, encircle. Only pt. **šipulh̲ mgargilh̲** Gy 208:6 his hem is dragged around, **šipula mgargla** Gs 27:17.

Der.: **gargul** (?), **gargla** (and varr.).

grida (גְּרִידָא, ܓܪܝܕܐ) spare, scanty, scraped, mere, simple, poor. **grida agrida** AM 5:7, **lahma grida** AM 5:7 mere pittance, a bare crust (v.s. **lahma**); **bmuzania grida qaiim** AM (*often*) he will exist on a scant allowance; **hu**

gabra grida umgabra hauia MA 19:4 he will be a thin but manly fellow.

griztia AM expl. by Sh. ʿAbd. as 'hungry' (would then be a fem. of **grida**).

grisata (rt. **GRS**) ground wheat, (wheaten) cakes (?). **grisata ḏ-hiṭia ḏ-tpia bnura** DC 38, Oxf. roll f 1239 wheaten loaves cooked with fire.

GRS (גרס, ܓܪܣ) to grind (flour), break to pieces, crush.

Pe. Impf. **hailẖ bhirba nigrus** AM 215:2 his army will be crushed (one would expect **nigris** ethpe.).

Der.: **grisata.**

GRP I (גרף, ܓܪܦ) to scrape clean, carry away, carry off, scoop up, remove; (of water) rush away, be carried.

Pe. pf. **grap mia siauia ptahil** Jb 234:2 the black waters carried P. away; (**sliq lkipa ḏ-prat ziua**) **ugrap mia** DC 51: 99 f. (they rose to the bank of the Light-Euphrates) and scooped up water; special pl. **garapiun** DC 40. 287 (read **grapiun**) they rushed away; with suff. **girpa larqa ḏ-tibil** Jb 234:4 he scraped clean the (face of the) earth; **garpẖ umnatẖ dra** ATŠ I no. 270 it scraped it clean and took up its portion; **girpunan** DC 43 J 240 they raided us. Impf. with suff. **ana ʿgirpinun lmia siauia** Jb 233:9 I will do away with the black waters completely. Impt. **ugrup mia ḏ-sagin mn iardna** DC 51 and scoop up the waters that flow from the jordan.

Ethpe. Pt. **bhanatẖ iardna sruth mitgirpa** Gy 311:6 f. in that jordan his stink will be removed.

GRP II = GRB I MG 48:8. **grabtinun ana graptinun** v.s. **GRB I.** Gl. 164:11 f. missp. (quoted as a synonym of **GNB**) نهب *diripere* غارت كرد.

Der.: **garpʿil, girpa, grpan.**

grpan daiua RD 29 a demon.

GRṢ (קרץ, قرص, with dissimil. of the first emphatic) to sting, bite.

Pa. Pt. with encl. **uarqba mgarṣalik** DC 21 and the scorpion stings thee.

GRR (גרר, ܓܪܪ LS) to scrape, be rough, shave, drive off, let loose, let fly, stir up; ethpa. to trail after or along.

Pe. Pt. pl. **gairia rišaihun** Jb 86:1, **rišaihun gairia** Gy 226:19 they shave their heads; with encl. **gairilẖ lnura ḏ-iaqda** Gy 40:22 they will drag him through flaming fire.

Ethpa. Impf. **titgarar laudia** Gy 327:1 thou art drawn to perishable things. Pt. **mirtẖ barqa mitgarar** Gy 83:13 his gall was trailed along the earth (or on the ground).

Der.: **gaiara 2, garaia 1, 2, gira 1, giraia.**

(**GRŠ** quoted as Mand. by Brockelm. LS s. ܓܪܫ without reference. May be a misread **RGŠ.**)

GŠŠ (גשש, ܓܫܫ LS) to touch (bottom), fathom, explore, feel, make contact. Doublet **KŠŠ.**

Pe. Pf. **gaš raumẖ ugaušẖ** ATŠ trs. p. 117 n. 12 he plumbed its height and depth (DC 36 & PD both have **praš** for **gaš**). Impf. **ligraiun šrara lanigišiun** Morg. 255/1:24 their feet have no firm footing. Act. pt. fem. pl. **lšrara lagašian** Morg. 256/3:34 (cf. preced.). Inf. **migaš lilbia atina** Gy 366:18 I have come to explore the hearts.

Pa. Pass. pt. **iama ḏ-lamgašaš** DC 22. 399 (where Gs 9:14 has **iama lmgašaš**) a sea that cannot be fathomed.

Ethpa. **ḏ-ligria ʿtlia ulanitgaš ʿla lbiš** DC 44 who has feet yet does not spurn (?) with them evil. (Doubtful.)

Der.: **gauša, kšaša.**

D

d the fourth letter of the alphabet. Pron.: plosive *d*, rarely aspirated *δ*. Phonetic changes: **d** < **t** MG § 45; **d** > **ṭ** MG § 46 p. 42 f.; **d** > **t** MG § 46, p. 43:4; **d** as a facultative var. of **z** *Mundart* 16, MG § 46 p. 43 f., AM 230; syncope of **d** before **t** MG § 46 p. 44. A supplementary letter **ḏ** is used to transcribe the Ar. ذ, ظ and ض MMII 244, but the diacritical points are often omitted.

d–, –d– a proclitic form of the rel. pron., whose independent form is **ḏ** (q.v.). This form is used esp. after procl. prepositions **l, b** and the procl. conjunction **u**, but sometimes even without them: **ldiatbia** Gy 389:23 to those who sit, **ldqaimia** Q 4:ult. (var. **ʿl dqaimia**) to those who stand, **uladqaimia** Gs 74:7, **udtlatma** Gy 128:ult., 129:2 and of the 300, **ldihṭin** Gy 63:23 because we have sinned, **udʿnšia** Gy 119:21 and of the women, **udimṣia** Gy 324:ult. (var. B **udm-**) and who is able, **bdiurba** Gy 272:18 in that of Y., than that of Y. MG 92 f.; further **dabahatan urubanan udahan udahuatan** Morg. 213/13:6 f. of our fathers and our teachers and of our brothers and of our sisters, **udanat mzakiatlan** Morg. 221/30:7 and when Thou pronouncest us clean, **udbatriẖ** AM 32:17 and those who are after him (i.e. younger than himself) etc., even **alad bišia** Zotb. 218 b 38 over those who are bad. Sometimes replaced by **ṭ-, -ṭ-** (q.v.).

da (?) a var. of **dẖ** MG 339:27. **apriš lda uda** ATŠ I no. 227 give explanation about this and that.

DAB (H. דאב, Ar. داب to toil) to languish, pine away. Ethpa. pt. pl. **habin umidabin** CP 455:8 v.s. **HBB** pe. act. pt. pl.

daba (act. pt. of **DBA**) slaughterer MG 43:15.

dabaga (ܕܒܘܓܐ, دَبّاغ LS) Gy 217:22 tanner.

dabara in **atutia dabara** Ṣâb.'s Liturg. a var. of **atutia abara** CP 176:14, ML 215:6 under the lead (cf. **dabara**).

dabra 1 (act. pt. of **DBR**) leader, guide. **manu dabrai** Jb 53:11 who is my guide?

dabra 2 a var. of **dibra 1**: **bdabra ubmata** Gy 287:16 in the field and in the city (the form **dabra** is not quite sure, and could be read **dibra** as well).

dagala (דַּגָּלָא, ܕܓܠܐ, دَجّال) deceitful, false, cunning, deceiver. Pl. **dagalia.** Fem. **dagalta. mšiha dagala** Gy 51:3 Christ the Deceiver; **dagala damia liama liama haṭipa** Gy 216:5 a cunning schemer resembles a raging sea; **zadiqia dagalia hauin** Gy 388:3 the righteous become deceivers; **anašia dagalia** AM 31:20 guileful persons; **uhda dagalta mn arqa . . . napqa** Gy 388:4 and one false (spirit, Lidzb. *Täuschung*) will set out from the earth . . .

dagaluta (abstr. from **dagala**) falsity, cunning, (evil) strategy. **bdagaluta masgia** v.s. **aškarta.** Var. **dagluta** (s.v.).

daguša (formed like ܟܘܫܦܐ but with the meaning of ܕܘܫܐ) piercing, prick(ing), stab(bing pain). **niplat bhaua qirsa udaguša** Gs 24:15 Eve fell ill with a stabbing pain.

dagluta a var. of **dagaluta. zipa udagluta** Gy 215:16 f. falsity and cunning. **ʿtlh̲ giadia udagluta** AM 9:3 (**dagaluta**) he has nerve and cunning (strategy).

dagna (a doubtful hapaxl., cf. P. دِ کنک?) the highest point of a mountain (?), peak (?). Var. **digna. aradia bṭuria bdagna maṭilh̲** Gy 387:21 wild asses in the hills will reach the peak (?) Ginzā 415 n. 1.

dad (cf. foll.) paternal uncle (?). **dad huia ušurbh̲** DC 37. 569 be his paternal uncle, his kinsman.

dada, dadia (cf. ܕܕܐ LS 144a) paternal uncle, aunt, auntie, nursemaid (?). The latter form (IM no. 12, 17 p. 99) was explained by Pognon as a woman's name IM Gl. **utata d̲-hʿ dada amintul d̲-kulhin niṭupiata d̲-iaqirata lhanatin d̲-ianqan . . . d̲-mraurban dadia qarilun** ATŠ I no. 249 and the ewe which is a nursemaid (?), because all honourable spouses call those (women) who suckle and nurture (their children) 'aunties' (?).

dadai lilita DC 43 F 14, **dadaita lilita** DC 43 F 8 name(s) of a lilith.

dahala (nom. ag. of **DHL**) one who fears (God), worshipper (cf. Ar. مُتَّقى). Pl. **dahalia.** Fem. sg. **dahalta 1**, pl. **dahalata. nisirunh̲ dahalh̲** Gy 58:14 f. his worshippers will fetter him (: Christ); **nipalgunh̲ dahalih̲ bmna mna** Gy 58:15 f. his worshippers will tear him to pieces; **dahalia uzadiqia** Gy 55:14 f.; **dahalia udahalata** Gy 28:8, 56:10 *adoratores et adoratrices*; **ṭulaniata dahalata** Or. 332:2 fearsome shades of darkness.

dahalta 2 (דחלתא, ܕܚܠܬܐ) fear; worship (cf. **dahala**). **dahalta šabqia** Gs 53:4 f. they let loose fear; **dahalta d̲-alahuta d̲-baita** ML 26:6 the worship of the divinity of the House (cf. **baita**).

dahba, zahba (דַּהֲבָא, ܕܗܒܐ LS) gold MG 43:9, 106:paen. **šuba šuria d̲-dahba** Gy 195:12 seven golden walls; **ṭura d̲-dahba** Gy 390:12 golden hill; **dahba ukaspa** (often) gold and silver.

dahgan = **dihgan** (q.v.). Pl. masc. **dahgania,** fem. **dahganiata. šitin dahgania ušitin dahganiata** DC 15 & 44 sixty peasant men and women; **iatimia udahgania udaiania** Ṣâb.'s AM orphans, peasants, and poor people.

dahil 1 act. pt. of **DHL** (q.v.).

dahil 2 (ܕܚܝܠ) terrible MG 124:17 (& n. 3).

dahiltana (from **dahalta** with nom. suff.) intimidator, terrible one. **bun dahiltana qarilak** DC 43 J 77 they call thee 'They-sought-a-Terrible-One'.

dahlulia (pl. of דַּחֲלוּלָא, ܕܚܠܘܠܐ) affrighting ones, hobgoblins, bogies. Furlani *I Nomi* 424 f. **qmaha d̲-dahlulia** DC 43 E the Phylactery of the Hobgoblins. Mentioned also in a list of evil spirits in DC 20 & 43.

dahliz (P. دَهْلِيز) hall, entrance. Pl. **dahlizia** WedF 55:bottom. **nhut ata ldahliz** ŠQ. 18:13 = CP 235:6 (cf. ML X) come down to the entrance-hall. Gl. 35:1 **dhliza** [*sic*] اسطوان *porticus* آستانه.

dahna (rt. **DHN** = **DNA I**) effulgence, light. **uhazialun banhura udahna** ATŠ I no. 284 and he beholds them in light and effulgence.

dahnaš (P. دَهْنَج) AM 287:1 malachite.

dauak (Ar. دَوْك?) AM 258:3 disturbance, tumult.

dauan in **škat dauan** AM 199:1 a miscop. of **ašpat urauan** (v.s. **rauan**).

dauar 1 (P. دَاوَر) judge (on circuit). **ʿl dilan šauiuk dauar** DM 20a they made thee a judge MG 334:paen. f.

dauar 2 (a doublet of **adiaura**?) helper; **dauar maṭia adiaurh̲ uparqh̲** Gs 54:5 f. his helper came to him, his helper (and) saved him; **dauar miṭian** Gs 54:16 my helper came to me.

dauar 3 (Ar. دوار) circuit, going round about BZ 88 n. 5. **sira bhiṭia nipuq ldauar** AM 281:41 (should) the moon be in Sagittarius, he may set forth on his rounds.

daud, dauud, dauid (both H. דָּוִד, דָּוִיד and Ar. دَاوُد) David. **bʿsiqta d̲-šlimun br daud** DC 8 by the ring of Solomon, son of D.; **šlimun malka br dauid** Gy 50:9 the king S., son of D.

dauiui (read **daiuia**?) IM no. 29 p. 101 a pr. name IM Gl.

daula 1 (דַּוְלָא, ܕܘܠܐ LS, Ar. دَلْو Fränkel 63) pitcher for drawing water, water-vessel, water-pot, bucket, pail; (as a sign of the Zodiac) Water-carrier, Aquarius Nöld. ZDMG xxv 256 ff., very frequent in AM; fig. udder (?). Pl. **daulia. bdaula hiuara dalin umašqin mia** Jb 135:3 f. I draw (water) in a white water-pot and give them water to drink

daulia d̠-mia Gy 228:1, ATŠ I no. 233 water-pots; **daula hiuara br atuna d̠-lamšarai d̠-bmia laṣbia** DC 51:98 f. a white water-pot fresh from the kiln, unused (hitherto) and never dipped in water.

daula 2, dula (Ar. دَوْلَة) government, power, state, change of fate, fortune. **arkan daula** v.s. **arkan**; **sikina d̠-daula** (colloquially *skandola*) knife-of-fortune v. MMII Ind. s. *skandola*; **usikina d̠-daula bᶜdh̠ nihuia** DC 38 and a 'knife of good fortune' will be in his (: bridegroom's) hand; **uasuta tihuilia . . . bhazin miniana d̠-daula** DC 51. 217 and healing be there for me . . . by this calculation of fortune; **daulamatstan** AM 203 (varr. **dulamatistan** AM 199, **daulamatstan** AM 199) the kingdom of Matistan (v.s. **matistan**).

daura (cf. דוּרָא, ܕܽܘܪܳܐ, ܕܳܘܪܳܐ, and ܕܰܝܪܳܐ) home, abode, dwelling, circuit, country round, enduring abode MG 100:17. St. abs. & cstr. **dur** (s.v.). Masc. MG 159:6. Pl. **dauria.** With suff. **daurak** thy dwelling; **bdauru** (= **bdaurhun**) Gs 58:7 in their dwelling MG 180 n. 2. **daura taqna** CP trs. p. 2 n. 2, ML 190:2 etc. the shining home as a contrary of **daura haška** Gy 23:13 f. or abiding (permanent) dwelling, antithesis of **daura baṭla** (s. **baṭla**). Ginzā 25 n. 2; **mn ᶜlauia daura d̠-hikla** DC 51. 40 from above the country round his homestead.

dauraria ML 166:6 read **dardaria.**

dazindaiia (read **d̠-azindaiia**) DC 7, a tribe or people (?).

daia 1 a var. of **dauia** (act. pt. of **DVA** q.v.): **nišmata d̠-aniia daia** (read **daiia**?) DC 8 the souls of the poor and wretched.

daia 2 s. **hiia daia.**

daiagan (P. دايگان) nurses, midwives. A sg. form **daiia** (s.v.). **tlatma ušitin daiagan iatbia** DAb three hundred and sixty nurses are sitting.

daiala (דַּיָּלָא and varr.) water-bringer BZ 106 n. 3. **kiuan daiala d̠-dinba d̠-šidta hu** AM 171 Saturn brings the water at the end of the year (a prediction of rain or flood).

daiana 1 (דַּיָּנָא, ܕܰܝܳܢܳܐ) judge MG 120:15. Pl. **daiania.** With suff. **daiankun** your judge MG 179:17. **daiana qudama iatriṣ** Jb 114:10 may a judge be set before me; **ᶜuṣrai daianak** ATŠ I no. 131 my mind be thine arbiter; **aškitinun . . . lšitin daiania** DC 15 I discovered . . . 60 judges; **daiania d̠-kadba** Gy 66:23; **daiana d̠-dina lnapšh̠ ladaiin** Gy 218:17. Gl. 68:4 missp. حاكم *iudex* فرماينده, 123:10 missp. غريم *debitor*, 137:9 قاضى *iudex.*

daiana 2 (an epenthetic form of **dania** influenced by **daiana** 1) low, humble, poor. **lkilaiia udaiania haiasa** Ṣâb.'s AM she will be merciful to the homeless and the poor.

daiara (דַּיָּרָא, ܕܰܝܳܪܳܐ) dweller, inhabitant. Pl. **daiaria.** With suff. **daiarak** Gy 7:8 those who dwell with thee, **daiarh̠** Gy 79:7 its inhabitants; **daiaria udaiaria taqipia** DC 44. 784.

daiata = **adiata** (pl. of **adaita** q.v.).

daiba 1 (act. pt. of **DUB**) discharging, running issue (of fluid or matter), flowing out, discharge.

daiba 2 a var. of **diba.**

daidukt Ṣâb.'s AM a var. of **radukt** AM 205:17.

daidia v.s. **DUD.**

daiua (ܕܰܝܘܳܐ < P. ديو LS) demon, evil spirit. Pl. **daiuia. sahria udaiuia** Gy 27:12; **šuba daiuia msaṭiania** Gy 27:15 f. seven devils the seducers Ginzā 28 n. 2. Very frequent in exorcisms. Gl. 27:11 **diua** [*sic*] ابليسزن *diabolus* شيطان, 95:1 f. Id. شيطان *daemon.*

daiuan DAb a var. of **diuan.**

daium Gs 108:paen. f., ML 111:11 f., CP 90:12 a name given to Rūha ML Ind., Ginzā Ind. I.

daiia (P. دايه) nurse, nursie. Pl. **daigan** (s.v.). **mama udada . . . udaiia** ATŠ I no. 249.

daiim (Ar. دائِم) AM 254:6 continual, perpetual.

daiita, diita (דיאו, דיי), **daitia** DC 46. 170:13 (cf. דְּיֵית I 2 to languish) an epithet applied to Venus in magical documents (DC 45 & 46), possibly: languishing, lovesick (?).

daima(na) a name given to a Mand. holiday Siouffi 103:5, ML 274 n. 1, MMII 91 f. **dihba rba d̠-daima** ML 274:3, 275:5; **maṣbuta d̠-daima** ATŠ I no. 50, 60 etc. According to the latter, a baptismal feast (cf. also s. **dihba**).

daimur s. **ziua daimur.**

daitia s. **daiita**

DAK, DHK (דעך, ܕܥܟ) to quench, extinguish, expel, vanish.

Pe. Pf. (mit)**udak** Gy 164:22 (var. CD **dik**) (they died) and vanished MG 72:13, 255:antep, and n. 3. Impf. **tidak nurh̠ utiduk dmuth̠** DC 37. 198 f. his fire will be quenched and his appearance will disappear; **miduk tiduk** DC 37. 520 and thou shalt be utterly extinct. Act. pt. **daiik, daika** MG 256:3; **daiik šraga** AM 254:4 the lamp is quenched; **udaika ruha** DC 37. 540 and the (evil) spirit will vanish; **had had daika** ATŠ II no. 68, 262 they die out (become extinct) one by one; **daika ᶜšata akla** Gy 79:11. Inf. (irreg.) **miduk** above s. impf.

Af. Impt. **adik minh̠ . . . ruh saiantia** (an exorcism) expel from him . . . the filthy spirit.

dakaita (nom. ag. fem. of **DKA**) purifier. **d̠-hu dakaita** [*sic*] **d̠-parṣupa titaiia** ATŠ. who is the purifier of the lower personality.

dakata (rt. **DKA**) purity. **bidakata d̠-pihtania d̠-zidqa brika** DC 3 by the purity of the (sacred) food-morsels of the Blessed Oblation. (The form and meaning may have been influenced by Ar. زكات).

dakia (דַּכְיָא, ܕܰܟܝܳܐ) clean, pure. Fem. **dakita.** Pl. masc. **dakiia,** fem. **dakiata.** Orig. different from **zakaia** victorious, later sometimes confused with it MG 44:top. St. abs. sg. **dkia** MG 152:15, 153:21. **dakia rušuma** CP 42:1, ML 49:5 etc. (*often*) the pure sign; **rušumia dakiia** Gy 152:21 id.; pl. **rušumak dakia** Gy 152:23; **dakia mimran** our pure word CP 125:4; **dakia mimra,** ML 151:1; **marganita dakita** s. **marganita; iardna dakia** HG 19.

dakiuta (ܕܟܝܘܬܐ) cleanliness, purity MG 146:14. **taqnuta udakiuta uzakuta** Gy 213:21 f.

***dakra** (דִּכְרָא, ܕܶܟܪܳܐ) male (animal), ram. Pl. **dakria. dakria d-šumna d-qaimia bšuqia** Jb 90:13 f. fat rams that stand in the markets.

dakša (from *DGŠ with progr. assimil. of the 2nd rad.) piercing MG 41:6. **šuth dakša** Gy 217:11 his voice is piercing.

dalaiia (rt. **DLA**) AM 231:21 agitators.

dalaiil (Ar. دلايل) AM 285:23 prognostications. Sg. **dalil** (s.v.).

dalia (rt. **DLA**) high, tall. Frequent in Mod. Mand. Gl. 119:11 written defectively (but the vowel is indicated with the Ar. *fatḥa*) عالى *excelsis* بزرگ.

dalia zard, dalizard, dilia zard (P. در زرد) AM 287:4 turmeric BZ 196 n. 3.

dalil 1 (cf. דְּלִיל, ܕܰܠܝܠ, adj. used substantivally) uneasiness, discomfiture, difficulty. Var. **dilil** (s.v.). **bdalil ᶜtib** Gs 91:23 f. sat in discomfiture MG 303:4.

dalil 2 (Ar. دليل) indication, guide to. Pl. **dalaiil** (s.v.). **dalil d-biš tihuia** AM 283:1 it will be an indication of evil. **aprašata d-iuma udalil d-sira** AM 158:14 explanations for (each) day and a guide about the moon.

damad (P. داماد) ML 250:2 bridegroom.

damdamta v.s. **dandamta.**

damilan AM 197 a place-name. Var. **ramilan** (q.v.).

dana 1 (דַּנָּא, ܕܰܢܳܐ), Akk. *dannu* LS, Ar. loan-w. دَنّ Fränkel 169) cask, barrel, pitcher, jug. **danai d-mlia šakra** Gs 134:11 my pitcher that is filled with beverage; **danik d-mlia šakra** Gs 134:3 thy (fem.) pitcher etc.

dana 2 a var. of **dina 1**: **gabra d-abid dana** DC 20 the man who executes judgement.

dana 3 Jb 263:8 for **dania.** var. **dina 2** BD.

danab (Ar. ذنب) a comet. **abu danab, abudanab, budanab** v.s. vv. **kukab danab** AM 276:32.

dananukt v.s. **dinanukt.** Pet. preferred the form **dinanukt**, B, C, DC 22 and Sh. ᶜAbd.'s copy **dananukt.**

danas (P. دَنَس ?) avaricious person, greedy man (?). **bpumh d-danas** DC 43 J 141 in the mouth of a greedy man (?).

dandamta (rt. **DNDM = DMDM**) muttering together, whispering together. **dandamta** (var. **damdamta**) **bᶜula niplat dandamta** (var. **damdamta**) **niplat bᶜurašlam** Jb 66:13 f. (var. D).

danuq s. **danqa.**

dania (act. pt. of **DNA II**) lowly, humble, poor. Pl. **daniia. ana ania udania** v.s. **ania 1**; **aniia udaniia** DC 37. 9 pl.

danial AM 259:20 Daniel.

daniaiil (v.s. **danᶜil**) id. **mlakia msakar pumia d-ariauata mn daniaiil** DC 44 the angels (that) stopped the mouths of the lions from D.; **šamiaᶜil udaniaiil uhatmiᶜil** DC 40.

danipta DC 43 etc. a var. of **dinabta.**

daniš (P. دانش) a kind of demon, prob. occult science personified as a demon. Pl. **danišia. kul daiua humarta udaniš** DC 37. 372; **daniš zikria udaniš nuqbata** DC 43 A 24 f.; **maria daniš** DC 43. 45 f. the lord of occult science(?), person skilled in sorcery (?); **kbašth ldaniš br marai . . . ukbašth ldaniš br stira . . . kbašth ldaniš br šamiš . . . ukbaštia ldaniš br ᶜnbu . . . ukbaštia ldaniš br sin . . . ukbaštia ldaniš br nirig . . . ukbaštia ldaniš br kiuan . . . . ukbaštia ldaniš br bil** DC 40. 766 ff. (: Qmaha Riš Tus Tanina); **danišia** DC 43 E 31.

danᶜil (דָּנִיֵּאל Ges.) Daniel. **danᶜil mlaka d-mšalaṭ lnura** Gy 261:20 the angel D. who is made master over the fire (D. of the furnace became an angel of the fire Ginzā 260 n. 5).

danqa 1 (דָּנְקָא, ܕܳܢܩܳܐ < P. دانگ, Ar. loan-w. دَانِق) a sixth of a dram, a coin, obolus MG xxxi: middle, a weight, (P. دنگ) a sixth of anything. St. abs. **danq** AM 287:32, var. **danuq, dinuq.** Pl. **danqia** AM 287:29, Gy 217:9 etc. **danqia usianqia** Gy 217:9; **mithaial ialda bkras ᶜmh srin arba mitqalia udanqa usianqa** ATŠ II no. 24; **uza𝔢paran trin danqia** DC 15 and a third of a dram of saffron; **ltatura d-ṣar danqa asqh** ATŠ I no. 211 he made the bridge twice as big (P. idiomatic چهاردنگ کرد, four being a double of two, and *čâr* being a colloquial doublet of *čahâr* 'four').

danqa 2 Zotb. 217 right 15 a man's name: **anuš br danqa** HG 141 A. son of D.

daᶜip (Ar. ضعيف) DC 46 weak, feeble, thin. Only in very late Mand.

dap (Ar. دَفّ) (*a*) tambour, (*b*) skin, parchment. (*a*) **qimahia bdap** DAb he plays (lit. strikes) the tambour; (*b*) **kdub ᶜla dapai** [*sic*] **d-gadia** DC 46. 227:13 write on a piece of goat(skin) parchment.

DAṢ, DUṢ II (דְּעַץ, ܕܳܨ) to thrust in, insert, pierce, stick in.

Pe. Pf. with suff. **diših** DC 50. 190 he stuck it in; **daṣuk bskinun** DC 21 (PA) they pierced thee with their knife. Impf. with suff. **nidišunh abatar rišia** DC 39 & 43 J 117 they will stab him behind his head. Impt. **duṣ** MG 256:2; with encl. **uduṣlia lsika bainh d-dmuta** DC 44. 2053 and stick a pin into the eye of the effigy; with suff. **dušh lkiph d-iardna** CP 362:12 plant it (= stick it into the ground) on the bank of the jordan. Pass. pt. **diṣa** (s.v.); pl. **dišh** (read **-ia**) **šidqh** (read **-ia**) DC 40. 536 they are fastened down and silenced.

Der.: **daṣa, diṣa.**

daṣa (rt. **DAṢ**) pin, peg, pointed bar to push in. **uldaṣa mn atutia lišanh** DC 45 and the peg (: bolt) which is beneath his tongue.

daqguta DC 22:208 delete.

dar 1, dara 1 (דָּרָא, ܕܳܪܳܐ LS) age, time, epoch, generation. Pl. **daria 1.** St. cstr, only in **dar daria, dardaria** (*often*) an age of ages; **ldar daria** for ever MG 310:5; **almia udaria** (*often*) ages and generations; **ldardaria ulalam almia** (*often*) in all ages and for ever; **daria huit ldaria** Gy 138:11 I stayed ages and ages; **dara d-nirig** Jb 45:6, **dara dara bṣira d-bišlum** Jb 45:1 f. a designation of the Muslim era

MSt 213 (cf. s. **nirig** and **bišlum**); **riš dara** or **rišdara** v.s.v. **br armalta btlata daria taqun tagẖ ulanitrușlẖ alma ltlata daria** ATŠ I no. 139 a widow's son's 'crown' will be in order after 3 generations, do not set it (: the crown of priesthood) upon him until the third generation; **ḏ-ṣbia tlat daria** DC 24 who has been baptized thrice (three times); **ruban ruban daria** DC 7 myriad myriad ages; **ušuba darai ḏ-atin abatrai** DC 50 and 7 generations (of my descendants) that come after me.

dara 2 (דָּרָא, cf. also LS s. ܕܪܐ) a doublet of **daura**. Pl. **daria 2** Gy 274:16 etc. houses.

dar 2, dara 3 the first part of certain place-names, as **dar mamlaka lhamsa** AM 204 (var. Ṣâb.'s copy **dara umamlaka ʿl kamsa**) BZ Ap. II; **dara** AM 232:10 BZ Ap. II; **daragird** and **darakurd** s.vv.

dar 3 AM 277:16 = **adar.**

daraga (P. درگه) portal, entrance. **ia daragai daštia ṭabia** ŠQ 18:8 = CP 234:15 o my portal, (my) good doors!

daragird Ṣâb.'s AM a var. of **darakurd.**

darakurd AM 198 a place-name, district of Kurds (?), cf. also BZ Ap. II.

daramana s. **darmana.**

darata (either ܕܪܬܟܐ or ܕܪܬܐ, **ia darata babai** Lidzb. *'O ihr, Papa's Trägerinnen!'*, Š ḏ-Q 19–18 cf. CP 235:16 cf. ML ix n. 2, Oh, my father's portresses!

darbania (pl. of P. دربان) guards, bodyguards. **aliun arbin ʿutria darbania luat malka** DC 48. 177 forty uthras, the bodyguards, entered the presence of the king.

darbukia (P. dialectal, cf. lit. داریه and دمبک) Gy 113:8 small drum, pot with parchment base.

darga a var. of **dirga** (cf. s. **siblia**).

dargaiia a var. of **dirgaiia.**

dardaq AM 205:18, var. Ṣâb.'s copy **dardam** a place-name BZ Ap. II.

dardaria s. **dar** 1.

dardqia, dardqunia, fem. **dardquniata** (var. of **dirdqia, dirdqunia**). DC 43 E 10.

dardiqia Par. xi 40a.

darušaia (rt. **DRŠ**) singer of hymns, reciter. With pers. suff. **darušaiai** CP 145:2, ML 173:8 my singer of hymns.

daria 1, 2 s. **dara** 1, 2.

daria 3 DC 22. 282 a var. of **qiria** Gy 287:3.

daria 4 a var. of **diria** (q.v.).

darizia (a corruption of **dahliz**) halls, entrances, dwellings (?). **bania batia udarizia** ATŠ I no. 261.

darman, darmana (ܕܪܡܢܐ > P. درمان LS) remedy, preventive measure, medicine, precaution, caution. Var. **daramana.** Pl. **darmania. ʿu darmana abid ṭabuta maška** AM 51:18 if he takes precaution(s) he will find (the) benefit; **darmana ʿl napšẖ abda** AM 77:17 she should use tact; **asuta udarmana** DC 40. 77, healing and remedy AM. 288:1.

darpipil AM 288:6, var. **darpilpil** cf. BZ 197 n. 6 (cf. **pilpil**) long pepper.

darta (דַּרְתָּא, ܕܪܬܐ) AM 256:39 dwelling. Pl. **darata** (?, v.s.v.).

daša 1 (דָּשָׁא) Nöld.'s emendation of **diša** Gy 216:11, MG 108:11.

daša 2 the ritual pocket in the *sadra* or shirt MMII 30 n. 2.

dašamšir, var. **dašmšir** (read **dšamšid** جمشید) MG 2 n. 1. **dašmšir malka ḏ-šlimun br dauid qarilẖ** Gy 382:12 the king Djamshid whom they call king S., son of D. (!).

dašta var. of **dišta** 1, 2. St. abs. & cstr. **dašt** Gy 390:12. ISK 92.

daštana (דַּשְׁתָּנָא > P. دشتان Lagarde 35, Horn no. 570) menstrual blood, menstruation, woman in menses, pl. **daštaniata** Gy 224:5 menstruating women MG 168:ult. f., ***daštania** menstruations, cf. **daštanin** Gy 23:21 their menstruation(s), MSt 17 n. 2, MMII 120 n. 7, IM Gl. **ṭnupia udaštana** Gy 219:12 pollutions and menstrual blood; **ʿnta bdaštana laitbẖ** DC 46 a woman who does not menstruate; **biuma qadmaia ḏ-saia zauaiun mia mn daštana . . . ʿnšia ḏ-daštana dara uluat zauaiun qarban** DAb . . . on the first day that their wives perform ablutions after menstruation . . . women that during menstruation approach their husbands.

daštun lilita DC 43 F 9 name of a lilith.

DBA (דבח, ܕܒܚ, doublet **DBH** only in derivatives) to slaughter, sacrifice.

Pe. Pf. **dbat (abdat lbalun)** DC 36.

Der.: **daba, madba** (see also **DBH**), **tidba.**

dbar 1, adbar st. abs. & cstr. **dibra** MG 100: paen. With encl. prep. **bdbar, badbar, bidbar** Gy 382:1 in the wilderness MG 10:20. St. abs. is more usual than st. emph., even when the noun is determined, cf. **ailata bdbar** (s. **ailata**) MG 303:antep.; **puq minẖ mn dbar ṣadia** Gy 179:11 go out from the waste wilderness; **bdbar ṣadia** Gy 382:1 MG 304:9 f. (but also **bdibra** Gy 287:16 MG 303:paen.).

dbar 2 always with prep. **ldbar, ʿl dbar** (Can. עַל דְּבַר by the intermediary of Achaemenid Aram. Sachau *Aramäische Papyri und Ostraka* 282 s. דבר) on account of, because of, Ginzā 208 n. 4. **lganaba ʿl dbar** (var. **ldbar**) **gaṭla ulmara ʿl dbar** (var. **ldhusrana**) Gy 208:17 (var. DC 22. 200) to the thief on account of murder and to the master on account of his loss; **ldbar daurẖ** DC 51. 155 for the sake of his abode.

DBB (Akk. *dabâbu* 'to make intrigues', cf. Ges. s. דִּבָּה 'calumny') only pa. to accuse.

Pa. Act. pt. **abda ana lamara ḏ-mdab malka ʿlẖ** DC 22. 406 I am a masterless slave whom the king accuses (?, var. Gs. 16:9 **ḏ-ʿmarar,** BCD **ḏʿmrar** . . . Lidzb. *'auf den der König erbittert ist'*). Pass. pt. pl. **haibin umdabin?** CP 455:8 (doubtful) guilty and accused (?) See **DAB** CP trs. 301 n. 7.

Note. The verb avoids transition to ע״ו to preserve its phonological distinction from **DUB** (q.v.)?

DBH (cf. s. **DBA**) only der. **dihba, madbha.**

DBQ (Gen. Aram. LS) to cleave to, stick to, snatch, seize.

Pe. Act. pt. **dabiq** he snatches IM Gl.

PA. **tidabqh̲ bbabh̲** AO 9/1937 101a:6 let it cleave to his door.

DER.: **dubqa, dibqa.**

DBR (דְּבַר, ܕܒܰܪ) to lead, guide, take, bear, carry.

PE. Pf. **dbart** Gs 113:5 thou didst lead; with suff. **dibrh̲** Gs 62:3 he guided him, **dibran** Gs 117:11 he led me MG 34:3; **ʿdbartin** Gs 117:21 thou (fem.) didst lead me. Impf. **nidbar** ATŠ (*often*) he will be in control; with suff. **nidibrik** Gs 100:15, 22 we (shall) lead thee (fem.) MG 274:26; **ʿdibrik** Gs 117:13 I (shall) lead thee (fem.) ibid.; **nidbrinkin** CP 79:15, **nidbrunkin** ML 98:1 may they lead you (fem.). Impt. **dbar** Gs 112:21; with suff. **dibran** Gs 117:11, var. **dubran** D, **dubrin** DC lead me MG 271:15 f.; **dubran minak biluatik** DC 41. 473 carry me with thee (read **minik** fem.) in thy company; **dubrin minek biluaitik** DC 34. 509; pl. with suff. **dubrun** *ducite me* MG 273:8. Act. pt. **dabar** Gs 2:4 he leadeth (or carrieth) away; **kul gabra d̲-bnh̲ luat rba ladabar** ATŠ I no. 235 every man who doth not conduct his sons to the teacher; also substantively (v.s.v.); with encl. **dabarlhun** Gy 177:21 (var. DC 22. 170 **dabarlun**) he leadeth them; pl. **dabria usalqia** DC 51:344 they betake themselves and rise up; pl. with encl. **dabrilin** DAb they ferry them (: the souls). Part. pres. **dabritun** DC 26 & 28 ye guide. Inf. **lmidbar ʿnta haduta šapir** DC 3, ŠQ 30:6 favourable for taking a bride (read **hiduta**) to wife; **ṭab lmidbar ʿnta** ŠQ 30:6 good . . . for taking a wife; with suff. **midibran minik** Gs 117:17 if thou takest me with thee.

PA. Pf. **dabar lhaka šadran** Gy 337:21 he led and sent me here; with encl. **dabarbun malkuta** HG they conducted their government. Impf. **ṭabuta d̲-malka nidabrun** AM 244:9 they will influence the king's patronage; with suff. **nidabrh̲ lalma** Gy 88:5 will direct the world; **had lhabrh̲ lanidabrh̲** AM 217:4 f. no one will take care of his friend; **ʿdabrik** Gs 117:13 I (shall) lead thee (fem.); **ʿdabrh̲** Gy 281:18 I (shall) lead him; **lanidabrunia** DC 40 they shall not lead (: govern) him. Impt. **dabar** MG 229:6; **dabar abihdak** DAb take with thee. Pt. (act. & pass.) **mdabar mia lšitlia** Gs 10:20 f. will (give) water (to) the plants; **mdabar bazira barqa** Gs 10:22 will put the seed into the ground; with encl. **kulhun iardnia umambugia d̲-mia mdabarlun** DC 34 he controlleth all running waters and springs of water; **umdabarlun biama** ATŠ I no. 236 and leadeth them (: the waters) into the sea; pl. **mdabria malkuta** Gy 228:20 f. they govern the kingdom; **malkuta mdabria** Gy 231:25 id.; **hdadia mdabria** Gy 230:5, 232:21 they guide one another; **bhilqaihun lamdabria** Gy 11:1 they govern not their fates; with encl. **mdabrilh̲** Gy 208:1, Gs 7:4 ff., 8:8, 16:3 they lead him; **arba ziuia d̲-lʿuṣṭuna mdabrilh̲** ATŠ I no. 218, the four splendours which control the body; pass. **ṭura d̲-mdabra** Gy 273:2 (unclear, cf. Ginzā 270 n. 3).

AF. (could be also a mere pe. with a prosth. vowel). Pf. **adbar (badmu hiia asmkan)** ML 163:3 = CP 133:16 he led onwards (supported me into the likeness of Life); **adbariun** DC 41. 501 they conducted.

ETHPA. Impf. **ʿdabar** Gs 25:7 may I be led.

DER.: **dabra, dibra** (abs. **dbar**).

dgaša (ܕܓܳܫܐ) stabbing. **mhita udgaša** DC 44. 2001 a blow and a stabbing; **mhata udugaša** Morg. 270/30:29.

dgur (דְּגוֹר, st. emph. דְּגוֹרָא) pile, heap MG 118:paen. Pl. **dguria** MG 118:ult. St. emph. sg. not found. **bdgur dgur** Gy 106:18 in heaps MG 301:11 f., 328:paen.; **bdguria** Jb 41:12, **bdiguria** Jb 155:8 id.

DGL (Gen. Aram. LS) to falsify, outwit, scheme, be cunning.

PE. Pass. pt. pl. **dgilh̲ (umdaglh̲)** DC 45 p. 1 disappointed (and outwitted).

PA. Act. pt. **mšiha dagala d̲-mdagil bšuta qadmaita** Gy 51:4 the cunning Messiah who falsifieth the first doctrine. Pass. pt. pl. **mdaglh̲** cf. above s. pe.

DER.: **dagala** (var. **dgala**), **dagluta.**

DGR (דְּגַר) to heap, pile up, mount up, heap up, amass. All forms found are refl.

ETHPE. Pf. **ʿdgar** Gy 175:23 are heaped MG 212:antep. f.; **laʿdgar** Gy 293:19 was not stored up. Impf. **nidgar** CP 46:1, ML 59:7, ATŠ II no. 183 shall mount upwards; **masiqta rabtia tidgur ʿlh̲** ATŠ II no. 349 a great *masiqta* is stored up (read **tidgar**) for him.

DER.: **dgur**, pl. **dguria (diguria).**

DHA (דחֵי, ܕܚܳܐ) to push, strike, drive off, cast out, avert, dislodge, expel.

PE. Pf. ***dha** IM Gl.; **ligrh̲ mn dukth̲ dhat** ATŠ II no. 396 he lost his foothold; **ladhit** Gs 22:8 thou hast not driven out; **šuba dhun mn ʿuhrh̲** Gs 95:3 (Pet. has **d̲-hun**, read **ʿdhun** ethpe. fled away Ginzā 533 n. 2); with suff. **midha dhinan almia** CP 56:14, Morg. 221/30: paen., Q 23:22, ML 66:3 the worlds thrust at us. Impf. formally identical with ethpe.; with suff. **nidihiih̲** ML 77:8 may he drive it off; **nidihih̲ lalma** Gy 73:13 we jolt the world; **nhura nidihih̲ lhšuka** Q 28:5, **hiia nidhunh lmuta** Q 28:4. Impt. **dhia** IM Gl.; **kruk udhia** Q 15:20, 54:9 etc. turn (away) and expel; fem. **d(u)hai minai kuhrania** DC 40: 375 f. cast out of me maladies, pl. **dhun** Gy 19:12 etc. *expellite*; with suff. **dhinun daiuia minh̲** DC 37 drive the devils out of him. Act. pt. with encl. **dahilh̲** Gy 187:3 they drive him away; **dahilun** Gy 391:10 he driveth them away. Part. pres. **dahit** Gs 21:6 thou drivest off. Pass. pt. **dhia, dhiia** IM Gl., with encl. pers. pron. **krikit dhiit umakisit** (common in exorcisms) thou art encompassed, cast out, and rebuked. Inf. **midha** CP 50:14, Morg. 221/30:antep., Q 23:22, ML 66:3, MG 260:17.

PA. (or AF.) **nadhia qahr d̲-marai** AM 265:13 will avert the wrath of my Lord (could also be a miswritten ethpe. will be averted). Part. pres. **madihit** Morg. 224/35:8, Q 24:17 thou drivest off.

ETHPE. Pf. **dhun** Gs 95:3 (= ***ʿdhun**, cf. above s. pe.). Impf. **nidhia mn dukth̲** AM 276:6 it will hurl from its place; **nidhia minai**

šina DC 44 driven away from me is the tooth; **nidhia unistakar** DC 37 he shall be driven away and stopped. Impt. **dhia utbaria** DC 43 be cast out and expelled.

dhulta (ܕܘܚܠܬܐ) AM 261:24 fear. Still used (pron. *doholθa*). Gl. 53:14 **dhulta** تحير *pavor* حيرت; 71:5 خوف *timor* ترس; 155:11 مخافة *timor* از ترس; 153:13 مخاوف *terror* ترسناك; 160:3 مخافة *agonia* نزديک مردن.

dhil (pass. pt. of **DHL**) feared, fearful, fearsome, frightful, dreadful. Inflected **dhila**, pl. **dhilia**, fem. pl. **dhilata. ʿubadia sainia dhilia** DC 40. 641 evil, fearful actions (or rites).

dhisa (pass. pt. of **DHS**) DC 43 trampled.

DHK (doublet of **DAK** q.v.) to extinguish, quench, put out (light, fire), fig. to suppress MG 72:11 ff., 255 n. 3.

Pe. Pf. **dihkat ʿšata ḏ-iaqda** Gy 83:18 f. (var. DC 22.78 **dahkat** would be pa.) the burning flame went out MG 72:11.

Pa. Pf. **udahak** [*sic*] **nuria šragaihun** DC 3 and extinguished the flames of their lamps; with encl. **dahiklia trin šragia** Gs 85:8 they extinguished both lamps for me; with suff. **dahikth̲** Gy 91:2 I extinguished it. Impf. with suff. **ʿdahkh̲ lnuraiun** Gy 244:23 I (shall) put out their fire. Inf. **dahukia nuraihun** (*common*) to quench their fire.

Ethpa. Pf. **ʿdahak** Gs 83:3 was extinguished MG 72:13. Impf. **anat ʿšata minh̲ tidahka** DC 37 thou, Fever, shalt be put out from him, **nidahkun** DC 43 they shall be suppressed.

DHL (דְּחַל, ܕܚܠ LS) to fear, be afraid, be timid, beware.

Pe. Pf. **dhil** MG 219:9; **dhilt** thou didst fear MG 222:24. Impf. **nidhul** MG 219:9; **abdia malkia lanidihlun** AM 215:14 slaves will not be in awe of kings. Impt. **dhul** MG 219:9. Act. pt. **dahil alahia hauia** AM 50:9 he will be godfearing; pl. **dahlia, dahlin** (often); with encl. **dahlilh̲** ATŠ II no. 161 (DC 6 has **dahilh̲** sg.). Part. pres. **mn mahu dahilna** Gy 157:13 of what should I be afraid? Pass. pt. **dhil** (s.v.).

Pa. Pf. with suff. **nidahlh̲ ʿlh̲** Gs 53:5 we will frighten him. Pt. **ruha ḏ-mdahla bhilmia** DC 37 the (evil) spirit that terrifieth (him) in dreams.

Der.: **dahala, dahalta, dahil, dahiltana, dahlulia, d(u)hulta, dhil.**

DHN I (metath. of **DNH** q.v., cf. also **DNA II**) to shine forth, shed light; (of sun, moon) to rise, come out. **dukta ḏ-šamiš ladahna** DC 43 J 118 a place in which the sun shineth not; **ḏihnit mn šamis** DC 46. 179:5 I shone with the sun; **šamiš dahnabh̲** AM 33:6, 41:17, 54:18, etc. the sun will shine into it (i.e. it will be roofless); **sin kḏ dahna mitahzia** AM 224:19 when the moon rises, it appears; **ula ziua dahna** DC 7 and no light shineth forth (constructed as fem. although the nouns are masc., which may prove that the masc. form was unusual).

DHN II (דהן, ܕܗܢ LS) to grow fat, be fat, be fruitful, prosperous.

Pa. Impf. **umatuata harubata nidahnan** AM 224:19 and ruined villages will become fruitful.

Der.: **duhna.**

DHS (דְּהַס) only pass. pt. **dhisa** (s.v.).

DHR (Ar. ظهر) to appear. Only in postcl. and Mod. Mand.

Pe. Pf. **dihrat humria mn asabata bnura** AM 277:23 there appeared redness like fire. Impf. (with Ar. pref.) **iidhar** AM 257:1 it appears MG xxv, 4.

DWA (דְּוִי, דְּוָא, ܕܘܐ, ܕܘܝ LS) to be wretched, miserable, mourn.

Pe. Pf. **minh̲ dua** Gs 119:1 he was sad (of heart) at it; (Lidzb. '*vor ihm schwach wurde*'). Pt. **dauia libh̲** Gy 96:15 her heart was sad; pl. **šahrin udauin** Gy 146:5 they were gloomy and mournful; **haiqin udauin umištarhzia** DC 35 they are afraid, wretched and alarmed. Part. pres. **šahrit udauit minh̲** Gy 353:19 thou art gloomy and mournful because of him.

Der.: **duita.**

dualapa (Ar. ذو العفاء) AM 197:8 a hairy animal, baboon BZ 121 n. 7.

DUB (דוב, ܕܐܒ, ܕܘܒ LS, cf. also Ges. s. זוב) to flow, issue, discharge fluid, trickle, dribble, exude moisture, languish, pine away.

Pe. Pt. **urira daib** DC 19, miscop. as **uraudara daiib** DC 49. 24 (of eyes) and discharge water; **udaiba hauia** DC 19 (of a baby) and will be dribbling; pl. (**midab**) **daibia** Gy 273:11 it (: water, pl.) trickleth away. Inf. **midab** ibid.

Ethpe. **uhaubin umidabin** (= **mitdabin**) CP 455:8 and the guilty and those who have pined.

Der.: **daiba 1.**

dubar a place-name: **mn mdinta ḏ-šam alma lbit dubar** HG 140 from the city of Damascus unto B.-D.

dubqa, dibqa (דִּיבּוּק, ܕܘܒܩܐ) glue, adhesion. Pl. **dubqia. dubqia ušaruqia** DC 48 adhesions and hollow noises.

dubša (דּוּבְשָׁא, ܕܘܒܫܐ LS) honey MG 18:10 & n. 4. Varr. **dubpša, dupša** MG 6 n. 1. **miša udupša** Gy 233:11, **miša udubša** Jb 154:6, DC 38 oil and honey; **zimbura ḏ-dupša** ATŠ no. 256 the honey-bee; **bduq bdupša dakia** AM 92:9 put (it) into pure honey.

duga 1 (ܕܘܓܐ LS) deaf, dumb MG 105:5 f. Pl. **dugia. haršia udugia** Gy 29:11, 277:9 the deaf and the dumb; **algia udugia** Jb 193:7, 274:12, 275:13 the tongue-tied and the dumb.

duga 2 = **aduga.** Pl. **dugia. uldugia ḏ-ʿšata akla uldugia ḏ-nura** Gy 80:16 f. and to furnaces of consuming flames and to furnaces of fire; **ldugia ḏ-nura . . . ladugia šrigata** Gy 111:7; **lduga šriga** Gy 216:14 to a red-hot furnace.

duga 3 (rt. דוג 'to be troubled' otherwise not used?) trouble. Pl. **dugia. qiriia udugia** DC 20. 49 mishaps and troubles.

dugur a var. of **dgur**, cf. **duguria** Jb 41:12.

DUD (with a semivocal 2nd rad. opposite to Syr. ܕܘܕ with a cons. ו) to disturb (?), a doubtful rt. of **daidia** DAb disturbing, troublesome people DAb 25 n. 6, of **mdudia** Gy 227:13 (var. Leid. **mdubia**) of unknown meaning Ginzā 228 n. 4, and of **duda 2.**

duda 1 (דּוּדָא, ܕܘܕܐ H. דוד Akk. *dūdu* Ges., LS) cauldron MG 105:8. Fem. MG 158:9 f. in spite of masc. pl. **dudia,** but sometimes also masc., cf. **mn dudia d̲-rahṭa** DC 3 from seething cauldrons (fem.), **bdudia haškia** ATŠ II no. 87 in dark cauldrons (?); **dudia ṭapin** DC 43 cauldrons seethe (both masc.); **bqidria ududia d̲-nhaša** DC 12 in pots and cauldrons of copper.

duda 2 (cf. ܕܘܕܐ and **DUD**) confusion, trouble, disturbance. Pl. **dudia. ldudia abdilun lnaṣuraiia** DAb they cause trouble to the Naṣoraeans.

dudanga a river on which stands Shushtar (in south Persia). **batra d̲-šuštar bmia d̲-dudanga** DC 41 etc. (*often in coloph.*).

duhna (rt. **DHN II**) prosperity MG 105:1 f. **bduhna** Gy 390:4 with prosperity.

duita (rt. **DWA**) grief, pain. **taura d̲-bgauh̲ d̲-duita** DC 45 a bull that is in pain; **ulau hauia mia d̲-rahaṭia duita ušahpa d̲-ˁlania** ATŠ II no. 441 and is not grief (abundant as) water-torrents or the leaves of trees?

DUK, DKK = DAK (= **DKK**).

duk st. abs. of **duka,** which is a st. abs. fem. of **dukta 1** (q.v.) but considered as st. emph. masc., both forms without the fem. ending being treated as masc. MG 105:4, 156 footn., from which also a masc. pl. **dukia 1** is formed (aside from the fem. pl. **duktata,** v.s. **dukta 1**). **ldukia nasbalh̲** ATŠ I no. 246 she takes it to its place; **bduk duk** (often) in many places, here and there; **lduk** AM 244:20 in all directions, everywhere; **duk ṭipa d-alma** Gy 180:13 v.s. **ṭipa.** Gl. 155:8 **duka** (with a miswritten pl.) مكان ، امكنة *locus.*

dukia 1 pl. of **duka** (s. **duk**).

dukia 2 (rt. **DKA**) purity, ritual cleanness, cleansing. **bdukia rba** ATŠ II no. 19 in (a state of) great purity; **dukia rba mitlabšin** ATŠ I no. 9 they are clothed in great purity; **šidqa udukia** CP 376:4 silence and purity; **dukia uzaharta** ATŠ II no. 370 purity and heedfulness; **qalil dukia unapuš ṭnupia** HG; **sliq dukia unpiš ṭnupia** Jb 54:2 purity hath departed and pollution increased; **dukia uniaha maška** DC 40:551 she will find cleaning and relief.

dukran, dukrana (דּוּכְרָנָא, ܕܘܟܪܢܐ) mentioning by name in ritual, commemoration of the dead by name, memorial, remembrance MG 136:antep., MMII 212 f., 223 n. 7. **dukrana rba** the name given to the commemoration by name of the dead, past and recent, during the five intercalary days; **d̲-hauilh̲ dukrana btibil** (often in coloph.) that there may be for him a memorial on earth; **masiqta udukrana** Gy 223:9, Oxf. roll f 187 ff.; **masiqta udukranai** GS 106:2. Pl. **dukrania** Oxf. roll f 473; **dukrana rba lihdaia** PD 1677, 1692; **aspar dukranai** Gy 205:2; **spar dukranak** Gy 212:4 cf. סֵפֶר זִכָּרוֹן Mal. 3:16 סֵפֶר הַזִּכְרֹנוֹת Esther 6:1, סְפַר־דָּכְרָנַיָּא Ezra 4:15 Ginzā 206 n. 1.

dukta 1 (דּוּכְתָּא, ܕܘܟܬܐ) place. Fem. aside from masc. **duk, duka** (s.v.). Pl. **duktata** MG 171:anteantep. aside from masc. pl. **dukia** (s. **duk, duka**). With suff. **duktai** Gy 322:paen. my place, my position MG 176:17; **bdukth̲, ldukth̲** (often in ATŠ) on the spot, there and then, thereupon, immediately (Fr. *sur-le-champ*). **dukta d̲-** Gy 77:3, 371:15 etc. the place where MG 451.

dukta 2 (P دخت a shortened form of دختر) *malwâša* woman's name: **šabur br dukt** Ṣâb.'s Liturg.; **šabur br duktai** Ṣâb.'s AM:coloph.; **dukt anuš** IM no. 21.

DUL (cf. ܕܘܠ LS) to move, stir, move about, be in commotion; as a var. of **DLA** to raise.

Pe. Pf. **dal (mha bmargna hiuara)** Gy 219:18 he raised (his staff and struck with it). Impf. **niduq unidul** DC 34. 550 f. s. **DUQ II.** Impt. **dul** DC 37:569 arouse!

dula a var. of **daula 2.**

dulab (P. دولاب) water-wheel, paddle-wheel. **mahia lula bdulab** DC 35:coloph. it strikes the flange against the water-wheel.

dulamastan Ṣâb.'s AM, **dulamatistan** AM 199, **dulamatstan** AM 199 Kingdom of Matistan v.s. **matistan,** cf. also **daulamatstan** (s. **daula 2**).

dulba (דּוּלְבָּא, ܕܘܠܒܐ Löw 73) Gy 216:12 *platanus orientalis,* plane-tree, poplar.

dulum 1 (Ar. ظُلْم) oppression, injustice. Only postcl. and mod. **udulum kadira ˁka ˁla mandaia tamun** DC 51. 813 and great oppression was done there to Mandaeans.

dulum 2. AM 222:16, var. **dilum** name of a city BZ Ap. II.

dulqarnin (Ar. ذو ٱلقرنين) AM 285:1 the Two-Horned-One (i.e. Alexander the Great).

DUM, DMM (cf. Ges. s. דום and דמם) to be quiet. Doubtful. The rt. is used reduplicated as **DMDM = DNDM.**

Pe. Impt. **dum dumˁil** DC 50 be silenced, D.

dumaia, pl. **dumaiia** (derivation doubtful. Cf. דּוּמָה 'the land of death and the guardian angel of the deceased' J 286. Popularly expl. from **DMA** Gy 118:20, Jb 109:3, which makes a confusion with **rumaia** impossible, cf. Jb ii 108 n. 8 people of a certain religion or sect, Idumaeans (?), Edomites (?). Sg. quoted as a star. **dumaia d̲-mitahzia dmuth̲ . . . kukba biša** Gy 118:20; **šiṭuata d̲-namrus udumaia ušuba šibiahia** Gy 300:15; **nura akla . . . d̲-nišmata d̲-dumaiia bgauh̲ mištaila** Gy 301:16 f. **dumaiia d̲-gṭil gabarun** v.s. **gabara; kruṣṭmia udumaiia uiahuṭaiia** HG 134; **dumaiia d̲-damin aluat ṣaliba** Jb 109:3; **hazin širiana d̲-qazil larqa dumaiia hu** DC 7; **hazin širiana . . . masgia ldumaiia** DC 7 this vein (of water) goes to the (land of) D.; **kd̲ dumaiia qalila ˁdh̲** RD B 106 = DAb, cf. Jb ii 109 n.; **nišmata d̲-dumaiia d̲-ˁbdad ˁbidata** DC 47.

dumdum (rt. **DMDM**) DC 27. 175 (evil) whisper.

dumˁil a supernatural being, (v.s. **DUM**).

DUN (Gen. Sem. mediae ו or י, cf. דין Ges.

and ܕܳܢ LS) to judge, go to law, have a dispute, strive with, rule.

Pe. Pf. **dan uzakun** Gy 256:17 they appeared at the seat of judgement and were acquitted; **danit uzikit** DC 44 I went to law and was successful. Impf. **mn bildbabh nidun** AM 237:16 he will strive with his enemies; **nidan dina** Jb 203:8 gives (or will give) judgement; **dinia nadan** DC 43 I 113; **ʿdan uzkia** CP 196:12, ML 230:10 I shall go to law and be successful; **nidinun** *judica(bu)nt* MG 249:anteantep., **nidinun** (var. **nidanun**) **ulanazkiun** (var. **ulanizikiun**) DC 44 they will plead their cause but will not be vindicated; **latidanun** Sh. ʿAbd.'s copy only as a var. of **latidamun** Gy 66:paen.; with suff. **tidninan** Q 23:21 (with bad varr.), 54:28 (one would expect **tidininan**) thou judgest us MG 279:paen. f. & n. 4, **nidinunh̲** Gy 229:7 they (will) judge him MG 278:11. Impt. **dun** MG 250:5; **dun napšak** Gy 213:26 judge (:rule) thyself; **dun uzkia** Gs 27:8 (var. DC 22. 417 **dun uzakia**) appeal to justice and be vindicated. Act. pt. **daiin uzakia** DC 3 goes to law and is vindicated; **d̲-daiin uatia balma** Jb 167:13 who administereth justice and cometh into the world; **daiin** Jb 168:14 ff., cf. Nöld. ZA 30 138; with encl. **daiinlh̲** Gy 35:12 he judges it; **daiinlun uabidlun dina mn hdadia** ATŠ II no. 313 will judge their case and award them judicial separation; pl. **dainin, dainia** DAb (often), pl. with encl. **dainilun** MG 53: 15 f., **dainilin** Gs 29:17, 31:10 etc. *judicant eas* [:*animas*]. Part. pres. **dina daiina mn ridpia** DC 34. 179 I have a process against persecutors; **(midan) dainit** Gs 85:20 thou appealest to justice; **kd̲ dina dainitun** Gy 14:15, 35:14 when ye are giving judgement. Inf. **midan** Gs 85:20 MG 250:antep.

Pa. Pt. pl. with encl. **mdainilun** DAb they will judge them.

Ethpe. Pt. **dina d̲-ganzibra lamidin** DAb the sentence of the *ganzibra* is not delivered; pl. **dinia midinia** ibid.

Ethpa. Impf. **tidainun** ye will be judged MG 252:20.

Der.: **dana 2, daiana, dina.**

duna DC 48. 35 for **dunda.**

dunda DC 12. 112 (cf. s. **buṭa**) penis. Still used (pron. *donda*).

dunuta a var. of **dnuta.**

dupa (דַּפָּא, ܕܰܦܳܐ Akk. [*a*]*dappu, duppu* LS) board, plank. Var. **dpa uldupa ʿnqušulun ʿl lišanun** DC 44. 838 and nail their tongues to a plank.

dupia = **adupia** in **sahdiha** [*sic*] **bduph̲** DC 43 witness to his ill-repute!

dupna (דּוּפְנָא, ܕܽܘܦܢܳܐ LS) side, chest, ribs MG 18:8. Fem. 157:anteantep. **haṣubia ldupna** DC 51. 82 f. sores on the ribs (chest); **udupnh̲ . . . kaiblh̲** [*sic*] AM 7:5 and her side pains her; **mn dupnia maiit** AM 149:11 the cause of death will be his side; **halṣa udupna** Or. 330:13.

Gl. 75:2 missp. خاصرة *renes* پهلو.

dupša v.s. **dubša.**

DUṢ I (דוץ, ܕܳܨ LS) to dance, exult.

Pe. Pt. **daiṣa** ML 81:2, CP. 32:paen. she exulteth; pl. **daiṣia umitparpia** Gy 114:22 they exult and rejoice.

Der.: **diṣa 2.**

DUṢ II v. **DAṢ.**

DUQ I (ܕܳܩ LS) to look at, gaze on, descry, discern, spy out.

Af. Pf. **adiq ziua** CP 63:8, ML 79:2 Radiance (personified) looked forth; **adiq hizia ldmuth̲** DC 3 he looked intently beholding his likeness; **adiqit** Gs 62:13 I looked forth MG 251:9; **adiqnin uhzainh̲** Gy 141:11. Pt. **madiq uhazilh̲** ATŠ II no. 386 he looketh on and seeth it; **madiqa ʿlak** DC 41. 419 she gazes upon thee; pl. **iatbia bkisia umadiqia** DC 43 D 62 they sit in hiding and spy. Part pres. **madiqna ʿlak** DC 41. 442, I look at thee.

Der.: **diqata..**

DUQ II (v.s. **DQQ**) to pound, chop, break up small by blows.

Pe. Impf. **niduq unidul ʿlh̲ ʿšata** DC 34. 550 f. he will break up and draw out the fever. Impt. **duq bduq** AM 92:9 pound (it) well (or pound and put it). Pt. **daiiq bkulhun almia** ATŠ II no. 291 cleaveth (or pierceth?) all the worlds.

Der.: **madiqta.**

DUR 1 (Gen. Aram. den. LS s. ܕܳܪ) to dwell, stay in, abide in, live in, stop for a time, inhabit; to turn (around).

Pe. Pf. **dar** he, they dwelt MG 248:2; **dart** thou didst dwell MG 248:13, with encl. **daribh̲** I lived in it MG 249:1; **dartbh̲** Gy 324:5 thou didst dwell in it. Impf. **nidar** *habita(bi)t*; **ʿdar** I (shall) live MG 249:13; **nidar** DC 34. 583 will dwell; **nidarun** (even **nadarun**) AM 280 astrological expressions for the position of a planet in a sign of the Zodiac BZ 187 nn. 2 & 5; with encl. **nidarbh̲** Gy 99:7 he dwelleth therein; **ʿdarbh̲** (often), but also **ʿdurbh** Gs 62:23, 63:3 I (shall) dwell in it MG 249:13 f. Impt. **dar** MG 250:8. Pt. **daiar, ladaiar** AM (*often*), ATŠ no. 122 etc., infl. **daira** she dwells, **dairia** they dwell MG 250:10 f. Part. pres. with encl. **dairitubh̲** ye dwell therein MG 250:15. Inf. **midar** DC 41. 505; with encl. **laṣabina d̲-midurbh̲** (var. **lmidiribh̲**) **bdaura baṭla** Cp 190:1 f., ML 224 I do not want to live in the vain dwelling (confusion of the inf. and impf., cf. n. a).

Der.: **adiaura 2, daiara, dara, darta, daura, dur(a), mdurtia.**

DUR II occasionally for **DRA I** Ginzā 354 n. 2, 457 n. 1.

DWR a phon. var. of **DBR.**

Pe. Pf. **duar badmu hiia asmku** Sh. ʿAbd.'s copy (Gs 78:11 omits **duar**) he (:the Life) led me and supported me in the Likeness-of-Life.

Pa. Pf. with suff. **udauran** Gs 54:2 (var. Leid. **dibran**) and led me. Part. pres. with encl. **ʿla mdauratlia** Gs 54:3 (var. **mdabratlia** Leid.) if thou comest (?) not to me MG 478: antep.

dur st. abs. & cstr. of **daura** MG 150:2, from which also a secondary st. emph. **dura 1** is formed. **dur bišia** CP 131:4, ML 159 the dwelling of the bad ones; **lbith̲ durh̲ ubinianh̲**

Florilegium: his house, his dwelling(-place) and his buildings.

dura 2 (cf. ܕܘܪܐ, Ar. دَوْر circle) CS 26 (AM 136:2 **dira**) the circumstances.

dura 3 (דורא jewel, Ar. دُرَّة pearl) pearl, crystal: **arba d-mitqal dura** AM four *mithqals* of pearl.

durakia Zotb. 220 right 3 a family name.

durašia AM 105 a family name.

durdia (cf. דורדיא sediment) the grosser, solid part of a liquid which falls to the bottom after clarification, sediment, dregs, droppings, sheddings, excreta, lees. **durdia d-anania** Gy 34:3, ZDMG 1955, 146 (*a*): 4 lees of the clouds; **srin uarba daiuia mn špita udurdia** Gy 126:17 twenty-four demons from dregs; **masiq tuqna mn durdia** Gy 348:21 f. he bringeth out light from turbidity; **ašdin uramin durdia** CP 155:10, ML 187:2 they (: the waters) shed and cast out impurities; . . . **ušibqit ldukth durdia** ML 183:16 . . . and I forsook the gross there and then (CP differs); **mnata mn durdia nipilgun** ATŠ I no. 26 they separate the portion from impurities; **mn ʿkumtia hauia durdʿia bišia** ATŠ I no. 219; from the the black (one) originate evil residues; **sliq tuqna unpiš durdia** Jb 54:1 light hath gone up and grossness hath increased; **asiq tuqna mn durdia** DAb.

durkistan Ṣâb.'s AM var. of **turkistan** AM 198:15.

DUŠ, DIŠ (Gen. Sem. ע״ו and ע״י, cf. LS s. ܕܫ and Ges. s. דוש = דיש) to tread down, trample underfoot; mod. also to enter.

Pe. Pf. **daš** acc. to the mod. use (cf. Gl. below); with suff. **bmsanai daštinun** DC 44 with my sandal I trampled them down. Impf. with suff. **ʿdišh lkuba uaṭaṭa** Jb 104:12 I will tread down thorn and thistle. Impt. with suff. **kibšun udušun** AO 1937 101a:15 suppress and trample them. Act. pt. with encl. **daišalh** Jb 98:4 she trampleth it down. Pass. pt. **diš(a)** DAb. Inf. **midiš biša** AM 271:32 wicked oppression.

Gl. 179:11 f. **daš** داس *conculcare* لكد زد.

Der.: **daša 1, diša, dišta.**

dušasadain (Ar. ذو جسدَيْن) AM (varr. **dušadasain, duša sain** etc.) double-bodied (an astrological term, attribute of Sagittarius, Pisces, Gemini, and Virgo).

dušman, dušmin (P. دشمن AM 221:13) enemy, foe.

DZZ (perh. Ar. دسّ) to smear. Found only in impt. with suff. **dizh** AM 127:ult. smear it on!

dh, var. **da** (?) (cf. דן, fem. דא) independent demonstr. this (: Lat. *hoc*) MG 43:12, 89:12 ff. and n. 4. Only in repeated form **dh udh** Gy 73:2, 89:5 etc. MG 339:bottom.

diaura PD 1225, **diara** Zotb. 219 left 28, 36 varr. of **adiaura 1.** MG 93 n. 1.

diauruta, diaruta = **adiauruta** (cf. preced.).

diata = **adiata.**

diba (דיבא, ܕܐܒܐ, ܕܝܒܐ, ܕܐܒܐ, ܕܐܒܐ H. and Akk. with § זאב *zību*, Ar. ذِئْب LS, Ges. s.v.) wolf MG 102:9. Pl. **dibia** AM 217:13, Jb 41:4. **d-atia diba udaralh** Jb 46:13, 47:7; **amnata d-diba tihuia** Jb 47:8. But in **kadph (a)ldibia** Jb 153:5 (which puzzled Lidzb. cf. ii 156 n. 3) read **kadph (a)ldidih** or **(a)ldidh** his own shoulder. (One example s. **dibna.**)

Gl. 182:5 **diba** ذئب *lupus* كرك.

dibaš (P. ديباج) brocade. **dibaš rumia** WedF 56, ŠQ 18:15 Greek brocade (Lidzb.), cf. ŠQ 65 n. 4.

dibat, dibit v.s. **dlibat** (a var. of **libat**) Venus: **bit dibit** Gs 30:22 (var. CD **dibat**) cf. Ginzā 447 n. 1.

dibna (Ar. loan-w. دِبْن Jb ii 45 n. 1) sheepfold. **kd raia ṭaba laqnh d-ldibnaihun dabarlun** Gy 177:21 like a good shepherd that guideth his sheep to their fold; **aqna ldibnaihun** Gs 10:23; **dibna ṭaba** Jb 40:12; **ladiba šauar dibnan** Jb 41:5 no wolf leapeth into our sheepfold; **laiil ganaba ldibnaiin** Jb 41:7 a thief doth not enter their fold; **alit ldibna** Jb 42:5 I entered the sheepfold; **baba d-dibna** Jb 42:11; **tata d-pašra unapqa mn dibnh** JRAS 1937 592:27 a sheep which is loosed and comes forth from its fold.

dibqa (cf. **dubqa**) cleaving together, stopping up, closing up, constipation (?). **dibqa umirsa** DC 51:452, Morg. 194:11 constipation and flatulence (?).

dibra 1 (דברא, ܕܒܪܐ) outlying country, wilderness, desert, field. St. abs. & cstr. **(a)dbar** (s.v.) MG 100:29, 151:9. Fem. (?). **mn dibra lmata** Gy 355:19 from the country to the village; **bdibra ubmata** Gy 287:16 in the country and in the village; **dibra d-hʿ arqahata udištata** AM 177:9 f. the outlying country, that is, lands and open spaces; **udibra lanipuq** AM 193:14 and he should not go out into the country; **dibra uhiṭia** AM 264:10 the fields and the wheat.

dibra 2 (an abstr. noun from **DBR**) direction. **udibra ʿtlh lmarba** AM 275:16 if it takes a westerly direction; **utla** (read **ʿtlh**) **dibra lmadna** AM 275:18 and is directed to the east; **udibraikun qaiim** Or. 327:6 f.

dibra 3 (cf. Ar. دُبْر) back, tail. Fem. **dibra d-arqba bʿdh ripa** DC 46. 76:8 the tail of a scorpion (is) tied to her hand.

diguq AM 205, var. **digur 1** a place-name BZ Ap. II.

***digur 2** = **dgur.** Pl. **diguria. darilun bdiguria** Jb 155:8 bring them in heaps.

diglat (Ar. دِجْلَة) the Tigris IM Gl. **prat udiglat** Gs 10:20 Euphrates and Tigris; **prat rba ʿl diglat nipšuk** Gy 386:25 f. the great Euphrates will flow over the Tigris; **diglat rba** HG 77.

digna Sh. 'Abd.'s copy var. of **dagna** (q.v.).

did– (Talm. דיד with suff.) a mod. form of **dil–** (q.v.).

***didba** (Talm. דידבא Mod. Syr. ܕܸܕܒܵܐ from *דבדבא, differently from Jew.-Aram. דִּבְבָא (Cl. Syr. ܕܒܒܐ H. זבוב Ar. ذُبَابَة Akk. *zumbu*) fly MG 78:antep. f. Found only in pl.

didbia, but a sg. *dedβa* is still used in Mod. Mand. Masc. **didbia ḏ-lpuma ḏ-duda iatbia** Gy 188:15 flies sitting on the mouth of a cooking-pot; **miṭirpia kḏ didbia** ATŠ I no. 238.

dihba 1, dihua (דִּבְחָא with metath. ML 274 n. 1) feast (orig. sacrifice) MMII 85 ff., 91 f. **dihba rba ḏ-daima** v.s. **daima.**

dihba 2 a var. of **dahba.**

dihbaiia 1 (adj. from **dihba** = **dihua**) festival. **maṣbutiata dihbaiia** ATŠ I no. 129 festival baptisms.

dihbaiia 2 (adj. from **dahba** = **zahba**) golden, of gold. Still used (pron. *dehβeyyī*).

dihgan (P. دهقان) peasant, used also as a *malwâša* woman's name. Pl. masc. **dihgania,** fem. **dihganiata,** cf. **dihgania udihganiata** DC 12. 305, Lond. roll B 589 f., Morg. 259/9:13 male peasants and peasant-women.

dihdar, dihdaria a family name (often in lists of copyists).

dihua = **dihba.**

dihuq Ṣâb.'s AM a place-name.

diua v.s. **daiua.**

diuan (P. ديوان) scroll (of manuscript). Used as fem. MG 160:paen. f. Pl. **diuanan (napšata)** ML 99:10, Q 51:15 (many) scrolls MG 317 n. 2; **halin diuanan (iaqiria)** ATŠ (coloph.) these (precious) scrolls.

diuta (דְּיוּתָא, ܕܝܘܬܐ, LS) ink, black fluid MG 111:4 f. **magalta udiuta** DC 40, DC 12. 188 scroll and ink; **diuta ḏ-nabṭa** DC 43 the black fluid of naphtha (: heavy crude oil); **sangara ḏ-diuta** DC 44. 1138 = Morg. 263/17:9 patron of ink. Gl. 183:11 missp. دواية *atramentum* دوات.

dizuara (perh. an Aram. form of P. دشوار) difficulty. A later doublet **dišuara** (s.v.). **ṭirupta udizuara** AO 1937 101a no. 16 confusion and difficulty (Gordon: confusion and wickedness).

dizpulia (often in coloph.) a family name.

diita s **daiita.**

dikita DC 34. 88 v.s. **dakaita.**

dikla v.s. **dipla.**

dikra (דִּכְרָא and דִּיכְרָא, ܕܶܟܪܳܐ) a male animal, ram, bull. Var. (with metath.) **dirka 2.** Pl. **dikria** (var. **dirkia 2**). **dikra šamina** RD B 102 = DAb; **dikria** (var. **dirkia**) **ḏ-paṭma šauitinkun** Gy 234:7 (var. Sh. ʿAbd.'s copy) I made you (into) fat rams.

dil- with possessive suff. (-דִּיל, -ܕܺܝܠ, Talm. mostly -דִּיד which reappears in Mod. Mand. *did-*) a particle used to emphasize the possessive or accusat. suff., often preceded by the encl. **l-** MG 34:6 & n. 2, 332 (& n. 2) ff.

Sg. 1st p.: **dilia** MG 34:6; **ʿda masima ʿlai dilia hibil ziua** Gy 135:23 f. he laid a hand on me, H.-Z.; **pihta umambuga dilia gabra nukraia** Gy 224:1; **ʿl šum dilia** Gy 245:12 f.; **abatar dilia** Gy 261:3; **binia dilia labatur** Gy 340:8 between me and A.; **ldilia . . . amrilia** Gy 155:ult.; **ldilia šihlun** Gy 111:3; **kḏ dilia** Gy 137:7 like me, as I; **ahat dilia** Gy 146:11; **minai dilia bihram** Morg. 208/3:9 f.; **ldilia** (*very often*) to me. 2nd p.: **mindam ḏ-lau dilak** Gy 214:11 something that is not thine; **mn dilak** from thee, from thine, or from that of thy people MG 334:middle; **ʿl dilak šadrinan** Gs 6:14 he sent us to thee; **ldilak nihziak** Oxf. III 113a MG 334:bottom; **ʿl dilak šauiuk dauar** s. **dauar 1**; fem. **kḏ dilik . . . ruha** Gy 146:10 like thee . . . Rūha. 3rd p.: **minh̠ dilh̠** Gy 223:23, 224:24 from him; **ḏ-minh̠ dilh̠** Q 2:12 from which; **ʿlh̠ dilh̠** Gs 134:20 for himself MG 334:8 ff.; **abia mn dilh̠** Gy 84:6 thicker than himself; **bdilh̠ ʿdpar** Gy 281:3 I will fight (against) him MG 334:20 f.; **udilh̠ ḏ-nukraia** Gy 258:21 (read **ldilh̠ lnukraia** Ginzā 258 n. 2); **dilh̠ udlau dilh̠** AM 24 both his own and not his own; **abinia dilh̠ labatur** DAb between himself and A. (cf. above s. 1st p.); **ldila uldilh̠ hnatalun ltartainun** Gy 146:8 it pleased her and him, both of them.

Pl. 1st p.: **bdmuta dilan šlihia** Gy 47:15 *in figura nostra* [: *nostrum*] *apostolorum*; **bziua dilan** Gy 126:22; **bʿuhra haza dilan** Gy 252:21 on this way of ours; **bškinta dilan** Gs 40:18; **anat dmu dilan** Gy 173:15; **šumaian dilan** Gs 23:3; **nihuia dilan** or **ldilan** is ours MG 335:2 f.; **šabqatlan dilan** Gs 24:22 ib. : 7; **bhailan dilan** Gy 126:19. 2nd p.: **mindam ḏ-lau dilkun** Gy 14:21, 36:3 (cf. above s. 2nd p. sg.); **haila kḏ dilkun** Gy 234:1 a strength like yours; **baita bdilkun mištbiq** Gs 41:5 MG 333:bottom; **ṭuhma ušarša dilkun** Gy 42:6; **ʿlkun dilkun** Gy 178:13 to yourselves; **ʿlauaikun dilkun** Gy 176:4. 3rd p.: **batra rba dilhun ḏ-napšaihun** Gs 6:22, similarly Gs 1:22 MG 333:paen. f.; **aminṭul dilun** Gy 111:2 because of them, for their sake; **uhuit kḏ dilhun** Gy 136:7 and I became like them; **minaihun dilhun** Gy 134:11 from them; fem. **dilhin.** To express an opposition between two persons: **mahu dilia ʿl dilkun** Gs 97:6 what do I have to do with you?

dilbat v.s. **libat.**

dilbilaiia name of a people or tribe. **hurdbaiia udilbilaiia** HG 134 cf. Transl. p. 14 n. 8.

dilum AM 239:17, var. **dulum 2** a place-name BZ Ap. II.

dilia zard a var. of **dali(a)zard** BZ 196 n. 3.

dilil Sh. ʿAbd.'s copy of **dalil 1** Gs 91:23.

dilmaiia AM 238:penult. the Daylamites, people of **dilum** BZ Ap. II.

dilpunia (ܕܰܠܦܢܳܐ and ܕܽܘܠܦܢܳܐ Mishn. דּוֹלְפָן, δελφίν) dolphins. Masc. sg. not found. **nunia udilpunia** Gy 124:12, JRAS 1937 592.

dima (v.s. **dimihta**) tear MG 102:11. Fem. in spite of masc. pl. **dimia. atian dimai ula šalman** Jb 58:8 f., 64:6 my tears come and cease not; **dimik** Oxf. III 43a thy (fem.) tears MG 177:23 f.; **dimaihin ḏ-tartinin natran** Jb 80:14 f. the tears of the two (women) flow.

dimat st. cstr. of **dimihta** (?) or for **dmut** (?) in **dimat hiia** (CP trs. p. 40 n. 3, 43, n. 5), CP 59:12, 64:12, ML 75:7, 80:3 distillation (?)-of-Life.

dimuand (دماوند) Demawand (in Persia).

dimihta, dimita (דִּמְעֲתָא, ܕܶܡܥܬܳܐ H. דִּמְעָה Akk. *dimtu*) tear MG 26:ult., 72:3, 103:middle. St. abs. **dima** (s.v.), st. cstr. **dimat** (s.v.). Pl. **dimia. darmana ḏ-dimihta ḏ-atia mn ainia** AM 188:2 a remedy for watering eyes (lit.

tear that comes from the eyes); **latirmun ˁlh̲ dimihta** ATŠ II no. 322 shed no tear for him. Gl. 183:2 defectively دموع *lacrima* اشك.

dimišq (دمشق) AM 198:5 Damascus. Var. Ṣâb.'s AM **dimšiq.**

dimita s. **dimihta.**

dimsand AM 204 (read **dimauand**) = **dimuand.**

dimšiq Ṣâb.'s AM a var. of **dimišq** (q.v.).

din– a mod. form of the cl. **dil-** used to introduce or to emphasize the pers. suff. of the 1st p. sg. Us. preceded by **l-** or **ˁl.** An encl. form **-din** is used as poss. suff. of the 1st p. sg. **ˁl dinai murakas ˁbdilai** DC 51:coloph. (that) they may let me go; **širih̲ qamdin** Morg. 273:9 open it for me; **atiu qamdin** Morg. 273:6 bring them to me (lit. for me, or before me); **h̲aqdin** Morg. 273:3 f. my right (: my revenge).

dina 1 (Av. *daēnā*, Pehl. *dēn* religion, religious law, דִּינָא, ܕܺܝܢܳܐ H. דִּין Akk. *dînu*, Ar. دين Jeffrey 132, LS) judgement, sentence at law, law, lawsuit, verdict, law-court, tribunal (us. **bit dina**), dispute, argument, contest, religion, faith, justice. St. abs. & cstr. **din.** Pl. **dinia. dina minh̲ mitmar** Gy 22:15 a judgement is pronounced against him; **dina minaihun mitmar** Gy 17:15, 319:14; **ulanitmar dina minaihun** Gy 319:10 f.; **bdina rba laništailun** Gy 319:10; (**kd̲ dina dainitun**) **turṣuia ldina ulatipkun** Gy 14:15, 35:16; **kul man d̲-apik dina** Gy 35:17 whosoever perverteth justice; **kd̲ ˁtlak dina minh̲ dina iahib mn napšh̲** Gy 217:9 f. when thou hast a debate with him he argueth from himself; **dina d̲-ladina** Gy 229:7, 233:15 thou judgest them with an unjust judgement; **dinan** Gy 275:12 (var. DC 22. 270 **dinak**) our cause (var. thy cause); **din almia** Morg. 221/30:8 f.; **ium dina** Gy 35:11, 66:15, Gs 19:1, **iuma d̲-dina** Gy 14:11, **iuma rba d̲-dina** Jb 237:6 (cf. يَوْمُ ٱلدِّين MSt. 91 f.; **udina qašia hauilia** AM 19:16 and he will be harsh in judgement; **uˁniš bdina lazakilh̲** AM 36:9 and no one will best him in argument; **dina napša hauilh̲** AM 92:13 he will have many a dispute (at law); **dina minh̲ nipil** AM 244:1 a judgement will fall on it; **mn ˁnta qadmaita dina nihuilh̲** AM 6:18 he will have a lawsuit with his first wife; **dina minak lamitmar** Jb 56:11 f. sentence shall not be pronounced upon thee (cf. above); **dina d̲-ganzibra lamidin** v.s. **DUN** ethpe. st. abs. **din d̲-ladin** Gs 26:16 (with the same meaning as **dina d̲-ladina** above) MG 302. Pl. **dinia midinia** s. **DUN** ethpe.; **iahbin trin dinia bhad** DM 54b they give two judgements inst. of one (: they speak in two different ways). With the meaning 'religion': **d̲-bdina d̲-ˁkuria nasgia** Gy 300:20 those who walk according to the religion of pagan shrines; also in compound names **din mlik ˁutra** Gy 208 ff. and **dinanukt** (s.v.).

Gl. 106:7 ضرورة *necessitas* لازم.

dina 2 s. **dana 3.**

dinabta, danipta, dinipta (ܕܶܢܒܬܳܐ & ܕܢܽܘܒܬܳܐ, Targ. דִּנְבָּא Akk. *zimbatu, zibbatu*, Ar. ذَنَبٌ LS, Ges. s. זָנָב) tail. St. abs. **dinba** (s.v.), from which a further st. abs. **dnab** (s.v.) is formed (by confusion with masc. st. abs.). Doublet **zanapta**, var. **znipta.** Pl. **dinbiata, dinibiata** (s.vv.). **ˁu napqa dinabth̲ mn pumh̲** DC 43 J 135 if his tail comes out of his mouth.

dinanukt, dananukt (Av. *daēnā naoχda* JRAS 1929 209, Pehl. *dēnānūχt* 'talking in accordance with the religion', compound from *daēnā* [v.s. **dina**] and *anuχtayaē* [AIW col. 127] Ginzā 205:top) Gy 204 ff. a legendary personage Ginzā.

dinar Zotb. 218 right 29 a man's name.

dinara 1 (דִּינָרָא, ܕܺܝܢܳܪܳܐ, δηνάριον Ar. loan-w. دينار) dinar. **mn had dinara uhad haba mamlil** ATŠ I no. 207; **alpa zuzia udinara d̲-zahba** DC 38. Gl. 183:4 **dnara** [*sic*] دينار *denarius.*

dinara 2 (P. دينار a kind of falcon BQ, St.) a bird of prey, falcon, vulture (?). **dinara uhiuia** DC 36.

dinarta, dinartia, a *malwâša* woman's name.

dinba a st. abs. of **dinabta** (q.v.). In Mod. Mand. used both as a subst. *denβa* tail, end, and as an adv. *denβe* down. Treated as st. emph. masc. (differently from ܕܶܢܒܬܳܐ fem., like H. זָנָב masc.) MG 158:5 ff. Its st. abs. & cstr. is **dnab** (s.v.). **mn riš ualma ldinba** ML 50:7 f. from beginning to end (**ldinba** missing in CP p. 42). Gl. 111:12 defectively طرف ,اطراف *fimbriae, extremitas* دامن.

dinbaiia (adj. from **dinba**) final, last, concluding. Mod. (pron. *denβeyyī*) low. **uˁzdahar mn rušumia dinbaiia** ATŠ I no. 190 and beware of signing at the end.

dinbiata, dinibiata a pl. of **dinabta** MG 169:17. **ˁu tartin dinbiata nihuilh̲** AM 233:10 if it has two tails.

dinduk, dˁnduk IM nos. 28, 31, pp. 100, 102 a woman's name.

dinuq s. **danqa 1.**

diniata in **bdiniata** AM 222:9 read **bmdiniata** in the cities.

dinibiata a pl. of **dinabta**: **kanpinin ldinibiatkun** DC 51:284 he gathered together your ends.

dinipta v.s. **dinabta. lnapiq dinipth̲ mn pumh̲** DC 43 J 135 to remove his tail from his mouth.

diniš a var. of **daniš.**

dipla (Ar. دِفْلَى) AM 121:3 oleander. Var. **dikla** (read **diqla**?).

diprilšin (Ar. ظُفْرُ ٱلْجِنّ devil's claw, or ذَفَرُ ٱلْجِنّ devil's stink?) AM 129:3 folk-name of a plant.

diṣa 1 (rt. **DAṢ**) pricking (in the eyes). **binia diṣa ˁl diṣa** JRAS 1938 4:8 between the pangs of eye-pain.

diṣa 2 (rt. **DUṢ I**) DC 40. 534 exultation, rapture.

diṣai (derivation unsure, cf. Ginzā 205:9 ff.) Gy 204 ff. name of a personified document in the story of Dinanukht (half-demon, half-book).

diqata (rt. **DUQ**) visions, appearances, (bad)

dreams. lšintaihun napil bdiqata ʿhabilun DC 49.36 etc. attacking their sleep they give them bad dreams.

diqia AM 287:3, var. **qaria** Ṣâb.'s AM prob. identical with the fish known in ʿIrāq as *jerrī* (v.s. **girita**). **diqia nuna d̲-girita šumh̲** Jb 148:13; **hda ṣaida barba arba diqia ʿtbh̲** Jb 162:ult. f. one fisherman has 4 *diqia* (: fish) in his boat.

diqla (דִּקְלָא, ܕܶܩܠܳܐ Mishn. דֶּקֶל Ar. دقل Löw 109) palm-tree, female date-palm. Doublet **ziqla** MG 43:ult. Fem. **ninisbh̲ ʿurba unisaq lziqla** JRAS 1938 4:12 we will remove the willow-tree and set up the date-palm; **diqla d̲-lahamlat** DC 46 a date-palm that has not borne (fruit).

diqna = **ziqna.** Mod. st. abs. *dâqen*. **minaihun diqnaihun nhina ṣaibia** Jb 86:2 some of them dye their beards with henna; **diqnh̲ uparṣuph̲** DC 42 his beard and his face. Gl. 148:2 **dqna** [*sic*] لحيا [*sic*] *barba* ريش.

diqnana AM 106 a family name.

dira DC 22. 473 a var. of **bira** Gs 88:15.

dirauanin Ṣâb.'s AM a place-name.

dirak AM 232:9 a town BZ Ap. II.

dirga, darga (דַּרְגָא, ܕܰܪܓܳܐ) step, degree MG 100:ult. Pl. **dirgia. siblia siblia sablilh̲ uldirgia masgilh̲** v.s. **siblia**; **ʿqlim tiniana d̲-bil hu tša alpia dirgia hauin** (read **hauia**) AM 197:12 ult. f.

dirgaiia, dargaiia AM (often) name of a tribe or people BZ Ap. II.

dirdqata fem. of **dirdqia.**

dirdqunia (diminut. of **dirdqia,** cf. sg. ܕܰܪܕܩܽܘܢܳܐ) little children MG 140:13. Fem. pl. **dirdquniata.** Sg. (as well as that of **dirdqia**) not found. **dirdqunia udirdquniata** DC 20 little boys and little girls; **ldirdqunun uldirdquniatun** Gy 387:12 cf. MG 181 n. 1.

dirdqia, dardqia (Sg. דַּרְדְּקָא, ܕܰܪܕܩܳܐ by dissimil. of a reduplicated דקדק, cf. ܕܩܕܩܳܐ and the Targ. verb דַּעְדֵּק Ar. loan-w. دردق pl. درادق MG 185 n. 1, Fränkel 111) small, little, young (children), tender (shoots, fruits etc.) MG 85:3, 185:top. Fem. pl. **dirdiqata.** Sg. not found in manuscripts (but cf. Montg.'s *Magical Texts*: with scr. def. **drdqa, drṭqa,** with syncope of **d̲**: **darqa, dirqa,** fem. **drqta,** diminut. **drquna** AIT Gl. C). **d̲-dirdqia minh̲** Gy 250:3 that are younger than himself; **utlatma ušitin dirdqia qaimin qudamh̲** DAb and 360 children stand before him; **lpiria dirdqia niklinun** AM 209:6 they will devour young fruit(s); **rurbata udirdiqata** DC 27:367 major and minor (f.) דירה, דיר, ܕܝܪܳܐ district regions (?).

diria, diriia, daria 4 (P. دريا) sea, ocean. Only postcl. and mod. **alma lsihil d̲-diria d̲-armanaiia** AM 205:3 up to the coast of the Armenian (i.e. Caspian) Sea; **uṣadap hu** (var. **d̲**) **mašqlilh̲ d̲-diria** AM 287:5 which is a shell taken out of the sea; **hu bṭuria ʿu bdiria** DC 46 (whether) he be in the mountains or on the sea; **hanik diriia . . . rahiqia hinun** AM those regions (?) are distant; **diria d̲-magrib** AM the western sea; **ʿzdahar d̲-had ligrak lṭura uhad ligrak ldiria** DC 24. 103 take care that one foot of thine be not (directed) to the hill and one foot of thine to the sea (fig. : beware mental distraction, lack of concentration, moral indecision).

Gl. 42:1 defectively with a fem. pl. (read ***diriauata**) بحر *mare* دريا.

diriuan AM 205 a place-name BZ Ap. II.

dirka 1 (דִּירְכָּא) (*a*) road, way, path, trodden way, step, (*b*) moral, religious law, way of the law (cf. דֶּרֶךְ, مذهب, منهاج, سبيل, صراط) Lidzb. ZDMG lxi 693 n. 2, (*c*) tread, (*d*) bank MG 100:antep. Masc. MG 160 n. 2. Pl. **dirkia.** (*a*) **mn dirka ldirka** P.A. XII. **dirka draknalun** v.s. **DRK** pe. with encl.; (*b*) **mšabin kulhun dirkia ušbilia d̲-rurbania** Morg. 207/2:3 ff. **dirkia d̲-šalmania** CP.; (*c*) **bdirkh̲ upasuhiath̲ arqa mištarhza** CP 185: 15 f. at his tread and his footsteps the earth was alarmed; (*d*) **trin dirkia d̲-nahra.**

dirka 2, pl. **dirkia** DC 22. 228 & Sh. ʿAbd.'s copy a var. of **dikria** Gy 234:7.

dirkana = **dirka 1** (*d*): **bdirkana d̲-nahra.**

dirkistan Ṣâb.'s AM = **durkistan** ibid. var. of **turkistan** AM 204:12.

DIŠ = **DUŠ.**

diša (v. **daša 1,** but prob. a st. abs. of **dišta 2**) door, entrance. **baita d̲-ladiša** Gy 216:11 a house without a door; **arqa udiša** DAb the land and its entrance (?).

dišat DC 22. 386 a var. of **dašt** Gy 390:12 (s. **dašta**).

dišuara a later doublet of **dizuara**: **udišuara tihzia** AM 67:14 she will experience hardship. **uldišuara nimiṭia** AM 91:12 and he will meet with difficulties; **uldišuara maṭia** AM 111:4 id.; **alma d̲-mabar dišuarh̲** AM 114:18 until he surmounts his difficulty.

dišta 1 (P. دشت, Pehl. **dašt** ISK 92) prairie, desert, track, land only watered by rain, not irrigated. Fem. MG 161:9. St. cstr. **dašt,** var. **dišat** (s.vv.). Pl. **dištata** MG 171:1. **aulh̲ ldišta alihdia** AM 120:ult. take him alone into the desert; **aulh̲ lkraba ldišta d̲-radia pdana auginia** AM 121:5 take him into a ploughed field, in the track of a plough driving furrows; **sahria mridia d̲-bdištata dairin** ATŠ I no. 253 the unruly demons that dwell in deserts; **hiua bala mn dištata** AM 227:10 wild animals from the deserts; **plangia d̲-dištata habiṭ** AM 12:17 he tramps many a beaten desert-track.

Gl. 27:2 missp. ارض *terra* زمين; 42:10 defectively بَرّ *arida terra* بيابان.

dišta 2 (rt. **DUŠ,** cf. the mod. meaning 'to enter') door, entrance. St. abs. **diša** (s.v.). Fem. **dišta d̲-hʿ baba** AM 254:15.

dita (דיתא) kite, vulture. Pl. **ditia. hdarlun ditia ubašiq** Jb 134:7 kites and a hawk circled about them; **dita bsingh̲** JRAS 1938 3:27 the kite with her beak.

DKA, ZKA (דכא, דכי, ܕܟܳܐ, ܙܟܳܐ LS, Ges. s. זכה) to be clean, pure; to purify, cleanse.

Pa. Impf. **nidakun ʿdaihun** DC 38 they shall cleanse their hands. Impt. pl. **dakun** MG

262:14, **dakun napšaikun** Gy 14:4 purify yourselves! Act. pt. **mdakia** MG 262:16. Part. pres. with suff. **mdakinun** DAb I (shall) cleanse them. Pass. pt. **mdakai,** st. abs. (identical with act.) **mdakia**; cf. **lamdakai** ATŠ II no. 87 (var. **lamdakia** DC 6 ibid.) is not cleansed; with encl. pers. pron. **mdakit** Q 72:68 thou art purified MG 263:9. Nom. ag. **mdakiana.**

Ethpa. Pf. **ʿdakiat** DC 48. 285 she was purified; **ʿṣṭbun uʿdakun** ATŠ II no. 80 they were baptized and purified. Impf. **nidakia unitmaš** ATŠ II no. 137 he purifieth himself and submergeth himself. Impt. **ʿdakia** Gs 46:5 purify thyself MG 265:13. Pt. **midakia bnura** ATŠ II no. 6 he shall be purified by fire; pl. **midakin** ATŠ II no. 6 they are purified.

Gl. 58:15 f. حلّ *licere* حلال كرد ; 82:13 f. زكى *justificare* پاک كرد ; 85:9 pass. pt. زكى *innocens* پاک ; 108:1 f. (confused with **DAK**) طفآ (sic) *exstinguere* خاموش كرد ; 109:1 f. id. نزديک *ad exstinctionem tendere* كاد يزول خاموش شد ; 163:4 f. (synonymous with **NPS**) نقى *mundare* پاک كرد .

Der.: **dakia** (st. abs. **dkia**), **dukia 2, dakaita, dkia** st. abs. of **dakia** (q.v.).

DKK = DAK (= DUK = DHK).

DKR (דכר, ܕܟܪ LS, Ges. s. זכר) to call to mind, mention, commemorate, invoke, pronounce (a name), make memorial of (by name), remember, relate MR 104, MSchr 164 n. 1.

Pe. Pf. **dkartun** ATŠ II no. 168 ye commemorated; with suff. **dikrh̲** Jb 17:7 he remembered it; **dikrak** Gs 16:13 remembered thee. Act. pt. **dakar** Jb 56:8 a mentioner, mentioning MG 230:5; pl. **dakria** DAb they mention. Pass. pt. **dkir** (**umapraš bmaṣbuta rabtia**) DC 50 mentioned (and explained in the 'Great Baptism'); pl. **dkiria bṭabu rbia** DC 22. 472 (Gs 87:22 has **ʿdkiria**) let the Great (Life) be brought to mind (or mentioned) in piety (lit. goodness); with encl. pers. pron. (**midkar**) **dkiritun mia** DC 51 ye are mentioned with a summoning, (O) waters. Inf. **midkar** (cf. preced. & MG 398:1).

Af. Pf. **adkar** he remembered, mentioned MG 222:1; **adkrat** she mentioned MG 27:8, 222:13; **adkirit, adkrit** I mentioned MG 223:5; with encl. **adkrilh̲** Gy 181:8 I mentioned to her; **adkirilun, adkrilun** Gy 180:9 I mentioned to them; **d̲-adkartlh̲** Morg. 275/17:6 which thou hast mentioned; with suff. **ladkarunkun** Gs 106:2 B (varr. **laʿdkarunkun.** A, **ladkarukun** C, **ladkarnkun** D) they did not mention you MG 281:7 f. Impf. **latadkar** DC 34. 979 do not mention; **ʿiadkar šumh̲** Gy 366:21 I (shall) mention his name; **šum hiia lʿiadkar** Gy 70:20 we will mention the name of the Life (Sh. 'Abd.'s copy mistakenly **laʿiadkar**), cf. MG 216:antep. f.; **nadkrun** they (will) mention; with suff. **uiadkirinkun** DC 50 (and) I shall call on you. Impt. **adkar** MG 229:7; **uadkar hazin šapta** DC 40 and recite this scroll; **adkar ʿlh̲ hanik šumhata** Morg. 215/17: 5 f. pronounce over him those names. Act. pt. **madkir, madkar** MG 230:11; **qamadkar** DAb he commemorates; with encl. **madkirlia** Jb 55:8 remembers me; **madkarlun lʿutria ahh̲ umadkarlun** (var. **umadkarla**) **lšuta d̲-ʿutria** Gy 115:20; pl. with encl. **madkirilh̲** Jb 217:11 they mention it. Part. pres. **madk(i)rit** thou mentionest MG 232:middle; with encl. **madkarnalak** ML 25:11 (var. CP 23:14 **madkirnalak**) I invoke thee; **madkirnalkun** DC 51 I call on you. Pass. pt. **madkar** mentioned MG 230:12. Inf. **ʿiadkuria** DC 51.

Ethpe. Pf. **ʿdkar** Gs 42:9, Jb 195:8 (var. B **dkar** pe.) he remembered; **d̲-ʿdkar šumaihun** DC 46 whose names were mentioned; **ʿdkiritun** DC 51 ye were summoned; with suff. (might be considered as mere pe. with prosth. ʿ) **ʿdkarnak** Gy 157:6 we remembered thee MG 274:8; **ʿdikruk** Gy 5:8, Gs 16:13, Jb 52:13 they remembered thee MG 274:middle. Pt. (**ušga . . .**) **umidkar** ATŠ II no. 34 (if he made a mistake . . .) and recollects; fem. pl. **midikran** DAb they (fem.) are reminded; with encl. **midikralun** DC 48.384 (the soul) is mentioned over them. Inf. **ʿdkuria** DC 51.

Der.: **dukrana.**

DKŠ (דגש, ܕܟܫ?) the rt. of **dakša.**

DLA, DLL I (ܕܠܐ, Akk. *dalū* H. דלה LS, Ges.) to lift up, raise up, draw up; to rise, agitate. About the transition from ל״י to ע״ע MG 34:middle.

Pe. Pt. **dalia** (s.v.), as pl. **anpaihun ladalia** DC 43 J 15 they lift not up their faces. Part. pres. **bdaula hiuara dalin umasqin mia** Jb 135:4 f. (B **dilana umašqana**) in a white waterpail I draw up and pour water; **dalit šragak** Jb 154:2.

Pa. Pf. **dalia** he lifted up MG 34:middle; **dalia** (var. **ʿdalia** ethpa.) **br guda** Gy 97:15 f.; **dalia gilia parṣuph̲** Gy 142:1 (cf. s. **gilia 1**); **dalia lgiṭa rušuma** v.s. **giṭa 3**; **daliat** she raised MG 260:paen.; **daliat hazia nišimta** Gy 99:15 the soul raised (the eyes) and beheld; **dalit uhazaith̲** DC 37. 600 I lifted up (my eyes) and beheld him; with encl. **daluln̲** Gs 37:23 they lifted up for him; with suff. (**ulrazia titaiia**) **dalinun** ATŠ I no. 243 he drew upward (the baser mysteries); **dalitia** Jb 140:4 thou hast put it up; **daliun** (var. **diliun** pe.) **uautbun** Gy 148:6 C & Sh. 'Abd.'s copy (var. AD, B omits) they raised me up and seated me. Impf. **nidalia** he lifts up MG 261:anteantep.; **dalaiia nidalun** AM 231:21 agitators will instigate insurrection; **nidalun šragik** Oxf. 42 b: bottom, Morg. 61:2 they lift up thy (fem.) lamp; with encl. **nidalulak br guda d̲-nišmata** CP 456:9 (n. 5 p. 302 trs.) they will promote thee as a member of the Company of Souls? (cf. s. **br guda**); **nidalian** ML 180, Gy 52:7 he lifteth me up; **nidalunh̲** they (will) lift him up MG 288:paen. Impt. pl. **ulmdalauata amarlun dalun** DC 51 and to the water-drawers they said: 'Draw up!'; sg. with suff. **dalian** Gy 234:14 raise me up MG 285:5. Act. pt. **mdalia** (*often*); with encl. **mdalilh̲ miša lmarh̲** ATŠ it draws oil for its lord; **mdalilia umautibilia** Gy 148:8 (cf. above pf. with suff.). Pass. pt. **mdalai** Gs 95:25; pl. fem. **mdalian** Gy 9:6 MG 165:17 f. Inf. **daluiia** Q 13:8 to raise up; **ldaluiia kulhin nikutiata** DC 51 to relieve all injuries.

Ethpa. Pf. **ʿdalia** Gs 53:20, 97:14 var. (cf. s. pa. pf.); **kd̠ laʿdalia** DC 34 when they do not raise themselves up. Impf. **nidalia** AM 187 he will be exalted; **kul daiua d̠-nidalia** DC 37 every demon that raiseth himself up.

Gl. 21:13 f. **adla** ارتفع *ascendere, exaltari* تكبر كرد ; 33:7 **dlia** اعلى *sumptus* (?) بلند ; 63:11 f. **adla** جسر *audere* جسر كرد .

Der.: **dalaiia, dalia, mdalauata.**

dla = **adla**: **udla ʿtingid rqiha** Jb 226:8 when the firmament was not (yet) outspread; **udla timsia arqa** Jb 226:9 when the earth was not (yet) solidified; **udla šamiš usira nasgan** Jb 226:10.

dlibat (Bab. *Dilbat.* An artificial expl. given by Pallis MSt 35 n. 1, 36) Gy 171:22, 172:3 a var. of **libat** Venus. HpGn 28.

DLL I = **DLA** (with transition to ע״ע MG 34:middle) to raise, stir up.

Pe. Pf. **dal (mha bmargna)** Gy 219:18 he raised (his staff and hit); **dal d̠-nunia d̠-iamamia bgauh̠ dailia** ATŠ I 267 they arose so that the fish of the sea(s) were excited. Impf. **niduq unidul ʿlh̠ ʿšata** DC 37. 550 f. he pounds and draws up to him the fever. Impt. **dal ainak** Gs 16:2 raise thy eyes; **dal mn qudamai . . . dal d̠-ana ʿtia** ATŠ I no. 266 move from before me . . ., move so that I (may) come. Act. pt. **daiil (urahiš)** ATŠ I no. 269 it stirs (and moves); pl. **dailia** (cf. above s. pf.).

DLL II (Ar. دلّ) to lead, guide, indicate, point out, show to, designate.

Pe. Pf. (with the meaning of the pres.) **dal lmutana** AM 257:10 it indicates mortality; **humria mnasabat bnura dalat lzaual malka** AM 277:23 f. redness resembling fire indicates the removal of the king. Impf. (Ar.) **iidil eala pisad** AM 257:35 (translit. of Ar. يدل على فساد) it betokens corruption.

DLM (Ar. ظلم) to oppress, suppress. Doubtful.

Pe. Pf. with suff. **blamtinun udlamtinun** DC 44. 648, DC 26. 615 (varr. **udalimtinun, udlimtinun**) I silenced them and suppressed them.

DLQ (דְּלַק, ܕܠܩ) to kindle, be lit, shine.

Af. Pt. pl. **kukbia d̠-madliqia uminihria birqiha** Gy 287:10 the stars that are lit and shine on the firmament.

DMA (Gen. Aram., H. LS s. ܕܡܐ, Ges. s. דמה I) to be (a)like, resemble.

Pe. Pf. **uladma šutai lšutaihun** Gy 259:5 and my speech was not like theirs. Impf. **lidmia** Gs 53:1 resembleth. Pt. (masc. pron. *dâmî*, fem. prob. *dâmyā̆*) **damia kd̠ haita** Gs 14:2 she resembleth a beast; **udamia larba ziqia** Gs 14:3 and she resembleth the four winds; **d̠-damia šuth̠ kd̠ ʿutria** Gs 52:1 whose speech resembleth that of the uthras; **ud-muth̠ lihuia damia lhibil ušitil** Gy 266:22 and his form is like that of H. and Sh. MG 464: bottom and n. 2; **had lhabrh̠ ladamia** Gy 94: 21 no one resembleth another; **dmuth̠ lmahu damia** Gy 138:8 what his appearance resembles; pl. masc. **udamin akuat taninia** Gy 139:10 they resemble dragons; **lmahu damin** DAb; **udamin aiak zapa laina** Gy 8:10 f. and match like eyelash the eye; fem. pl. **halin mihiata lhdadia ladamian** ATŠ II no. 23 these blows do not resemble one another.

Pa. Impf. with encl. **latidamulia bkul dmu biš** DC 40. 894 f. appear not to me in any evil guise; with suff. **ʿdamiak** Gs 108:5 ff. I (shall) compare thee.

Ethpa. Pf. **ruha biauna ʿdamiat** Jb 108:5 R. took the appearance of a dove; **ʿdamit** I resembled MG 264:13. Impf. **tidamun** ye resemble MG 265:11. Pt. **midamia** MG 265:26; **bdmuta hurintin midamia** Gy 52: 11 he takes (also) another appearance; **umidamia badmu hiia** CP 70:11, ML 86:4 he assumeth the likeness of the Life; pl. **midamin badmu gubria** Gy 24:7 they assume the likeness of men; **midamin badmu tlata ʿutria** Gy 25:7 f., **d̠-midamin** DC 43.

Gl. 51:11 f. with a prosth. **a** تعلق *imputare* باو تعلق داد .

Der.: **dmu(ta), admu, dma 2** (?).

dma 1 (דְּמָא, ܕܡܐ, Akk. *damu* LS, doublet **zma**, cf. also Ges. s. דָּם) blood MG 97:4, cf. also 96:15 ff. Varr. **adma, ʿdma. ldma damia nišimta** Jb 123:6 the soul is like the blood (cf. Gen. 9:4 f., Lev. 17:11, Deut. 12:23 and נֶפֶשׁ דָּם נָקִי Deut. 27:25); **ainh̠ bdma raiga** Gy 83:9 (varr. Leid. **bzma raiga**, Sh. 'Abd.'s copy **sma raiga**) cf. MG 40 n. 5, Ginzā 83:26 and n. 4.

dma 2 a doublet of **dmu** (?) **gubria d̠-dma d̠-ruha labšia** DAb men who assume the guise of a spirit (?).

dmauata pl. of **dmuta.**

dmasa (Gk. ἀδάμας, Lat. *adamas*, Syr. ܕܝܡܘܣ, ܐܕܡܘܣ, Ar. الماس) diamond, the hardest metal, steel. **šuria rurbia d̠-dmasa** Gy 6:11; **šuba šuria d̠-dmasa dakia** DC 34. 57; **lalmia d̠-dmasa šadran** Jb 216:5; **ziuan dna ʿl almia d-dmasa** Jb 216:10; **basaria rurbia d̠-dmasa asartinun** ATŠ II 142; **halin tlata bauata tlata šuria d̠-dmasa** DC 34. 252.

DMDM v.s. **DNDM.** Impt. **dumdum bkulhun bauata** DC 50 whisper all the prayers (i.e. say them silently, in the heart).

dmu, dmut, dmuta (דְּמוּ, דְּמוּתָא, ܕܡܘ, ܕܡܘܬܐ) likeness, archetype, kind, counterpart, (heavenly) double, shape, form, effigy, portrait, illustration, picture. St. abs. **dmu** MG 7: middle, used as masc. as sporadically also the st. emph. **dmuta** Gy 236:15, Q 30:9 and the pl. **trisar dmauata** Gy 95:14 (but **hamiš dmauata** Gy 96:17 and often regularly fem.); the fem. construction of **dmuta** prevails MG 161:16 ff. About the formation cf. MG 146: top. Sg. with suff. of the 1st p. sg. **dmutai** Jb 52:10, Gs 113:12 and **dmut** Gs 113:12 MG 176:1 f.; with other suff. **dmutak** Jb 52:13, **dmuth̠, dmutih̠** (*often*), **dmutan** etc. Special uses of the st. abs.: in distributive repetitions **dmu dmu** Gy 105:3 etc., **bdmu dmu** Gy 279:19 of many kinds, in many kinds MG 301:10 f.;

for st. emph. **bdmu hanath ḏ-** Gy 278:10 in that form which MG 304 n. 2; for st. cstr. **dmu pagria** Gy 103:18 the form of body; **dmu zma** Gy 298:5 like blood; **kul dmu hiua biša** Gy 123:11 all kinds of evil animal; **dmu tuqna** Gs 67:23; **kul dmu saina** Gy 117:5, 376:9, Gs 92:9 all kind of abominable thing; **ldmu mia** Gs 119:8 to a kind of water; **dmu šamiš** Gs 119:19, **dmu sira** Gs 119:20 MG 312:bottom; prepositionally with **b**: **bdmu**, **badmu** (*very often*) as, like MG 10:ult., but also **dmut hiia** (see below) and **bdmut dmut ḏ-nhura** Gy 223:1 like the Likeness of Light ibid. and 313:1; after negation: **litbẖ ṣurik dmu** CP 179:9 = ML 219:5 he has no kind of need; after **kul**: **bkul dmu** (often) in every form, in every aspect; **manhar mn kul dmu** Gy 80:4 brighter than anything (else); **ʿsira dmutẖ lkul dmu** Gs 132:2 his form is completely bound. St. cstr. **dmut hiia** (often) Likeness-of-Life, name of a female life-spirit, mother of Yošamin, also a *malwâša* woman's name; **dmut hiia ḏ-mn dimat hiia huat** ML 80:3, CP 64:11 f. St. emph. pl. and forms with suff. **udmutẖ snia** AM and his appearance is ugly; **dmutẖ lmahu damia** Jb 123:3; **dmuta ḏ-hʿ qalib** ATŠ I no. 261 a shape which is a mould; **haza baba udmuta** DC 46 this talisman and picture; **dmuta ḏ-bit hiia** CP 29:14, ML 35:2 the counterpart of the House-of-Life; **dmutaihun dmauata ʿpikata** Gy 139:9 f. their form is (of) perverted shapes; **dmauata** (*often in exorcisms*) illusory visions; **udmutaihun ḏ-bhiria zidqa kḏ hiia** Gy 176:11 f. **dmauata sainata** Or. 332:2 foul spectres; **tartin dmauata** DC 46. 138:18 two effigies.

dmia (ܕܡܝܐ) price, value, worth MG 164:2. **bidmia kadiria** Jb 145:11 at a heavy price.

dmi(h)ta = **dimi(h)ta.**

DMM (דמם, ܕܡ LS, Ges.) to come to a stop, stand (after walking). More frequent in the reduplicated form **DMDM** = **DNDM.** From **DMM** only impt. found: **udamam lbaba ḏ-ʿndruna uhaizak tikamria lbaba ḏ-baita** DC 38 and come to a stop at the entrance of the booth, and turn round to the door of the house.

DMR I (דְּמַר, ܕܡܰܪ) to marvel, admire. Only ethpa. found. Pf. with encl. **ʿdamarbẖ** Gs 66:6 he marvelled at it. Impf. **nidamar** ATŠ II no. 354 he marvels. Impt. **ʿdamar bšualania** CP 484:14 marvel at the novices. Pt. fem. with encl. **midamrabẖ bšupra** Gs 99:10 f. she marvelled (hist. pres.) at her beauty; pl. **ubihdadia midamrun** (read **midamrin**) ATŠ II no. 391 they marvel at one another.

DMR II (rel. to **DMR I**) to tremble. Only in DC 46 and in very doubtful forms: **ʿniš ḏ-damar ubhuš** DC 46 a person that trembled and shook (?); **lbr anašia dimar abidna** DC 46 I cause a human being to tremble (?).

DNA, DNH (דְּנַח, ܕܢܚ) to rise, appear (sun or light), shine forth.

Pe. Pf. **dna** hath risen MG 64:middle, 234:19. Impf. **nidna** AM (often) riseth, shineth MG 235:middle; **uziuẖ ʿl arbin almia ḏ-nhura nidna** ATŠ II no. 352 and his brilliance shineth over 40 worlds of light; **ḏ-nidna bziuaʾḏ-drabšẖ** ATŠ I 231 who shineth in the light of his banner; **tihšuk dmutẖ ulatidna** Gy 363:20 his appearance will become dark and not light; as ל״י **bšamiš ḏ-ʿlak nidnia** Or. 331:15 by the sun which shines upon thee. Impt. **dna dna ziuaikun** DC 36 = CP 466:9 let your glory shine forth. Pass. pt. **dnia**, but also **dnih**, st. emph. **dniha** (from **DNH**) risen, light, shining forth MG 65:3 ff., 117:9 f. Inf. **midna** MG 129:18.

Ethpe. Pt. pl. with encl. **nahria umidinilẖ** DC 34 they shine and shed effulgence on him.

Der.: **madna, madnaha.**

DNA II (ܕܢܐ LS) to be low, lowly, submissive, humble, meek, to prostrate oneself, make submission, worship, abase oneself before, be absed.

Ethpe. Pf. **ʿdnia** Gs 59:22 he submitted himself MG 263:21; **ʿdnia** Gs 3:6 B (varr. A **ʿdunia**, CD **ʿdania**); pl. **sgid uʿdnun ʿl duktaihun** DC 48. 144 they worshipped and cast themselves down on the spot. Impf. **nidnia** AM 220:11 he will submit himself; **ʿdnia** Gy 97:4 I shall prostrate myself. Impt. **ʿdnia** Gy 366:1 MG 265:13. Pt. **midnia** Gy 60:9 (var. DC 22. 56 **midiania**) they prostrate themselves; **nišimta qaima . . . ulhiia rbia midina** ATŠ II no. 172 (var. DC 6 **mdina**) the soul stands . . . and prostrates herself to the Great Life; **udnuta lmana ḏ-rabuta midnin** ATŠ I no. 86 (var. PD **midinin**); **lhiia midinin** Gy 254:2 (var. Sh. ʿAbd.'s copy **midnin**); **ʿutria ldiilẖ midininia** ATŠ II no. 313; with encl. **mbarkilẖ umidnilẖ** DC 41 they praise him and worship him. Part. pres. **ania ana umidnina** ML 209:1, CP 172:5 I am poor and humble; **lhak parṣupa rba ḏ-ʿqara midnina** ATŠ I no. 23 I make my submission to the Great Countenance of Glory; Inf. **lmidnulia** CP 132:2, ML 182:6 **madnina** (DC 26. 336 read **midnina**) to prostrate oneself MG 266:10.

Der.: **dania, d(u)nuta, dnita, madnia** (var. of **midnia**).

DNA III for **DUN**: **latidnan** DC 53 50:11 read **latidinan** do not condemn us.

dnab st. abs. & cstr. of **dinba** MG 152:9. **ʿl dnab** (var. **ldnab**) **almia** Gy 53:18 at the end of the ages Ginzā 46 n. 4; **lpuma ḏ-dnab rabtia ḏ-mia siauia** DC 20 at the mouth of the uttermost limit of black waters; **haizak mn dnab** DC 3 then, from the end part; **bdnab almia** Jb 38:7 at the world's end; **ldnab ṭura ḏ-aina ḏ-mia ḏ-aitẖ ldnab paruan ṭura** HG at the end of a mountain of a spring of water that is at the end of the Parwan mountain; **dnab tanina lkadpai rmilia** DC 44. 1448, 1594 I cast the dragon's tail about my shoulders; **ldnab mia** Jb 141:10 to the furthermost limit of the waters; **mn dnab almia ḏ-nhura alma ltit arqa ḏ-tibil** DC 7.

dnabta a var. of **dinabta**: **dnabta ḏ-dara ašpulta ḏ-dara ašpulta udnabta ḏ-alma** HG the end of the age, the latter part and end of the aeon.

dnania Gy 85:7, var. **dninia** v.s. **DNN.**

dnarta a var. of **dinarta** IM Gl.

DNDM (דְּמְדַם. Dissimil. of the reduplicated rt. דמם, cf. Ges. s.v.) to be deprived of speech or movement by emotion, be stupefied, murmur, whisper MG 50:9. Doublet **DMDM** mutter, grumble. Impf. **tidandmun** Gs 91:4 Leid & DC 22 475 (Pet. has **d̠-dandumum**) ye whisper. Pt. **kalta hamatẖ mdandma ʿlẖ** DC 48. 230 the mother-in-law whispers unkindly about her daughter-in-law; pl. **mdandmia** Morg. 246/79:2, CP 91:3, ML 112 they are whispering MG 149:12. Part. pres. **mdand(i)mitun** Gs 115:12, 131:6 ye whisper MG 233:17. Inf. **dandumia** MG 234:7, **dandumia mdandmia** (often) they mutter, grumble.

Der.: **dandamta.**

DNH v.s. **DNA I.** More often inverted **DHN I** (s.v.).

dnuta, dunuta, dnita (abstr. noun from **DNA II**) humility, lowliness, subservience, submission, obeisance MG 146:9. **dnuta ldilia iahbia** Jb 215:8 all offer submission to me; **udnuta tihuia ʿlan** Gy 257:23 and obeisance will be made to us; **iahbilẖ dnuta uʿruta** Gy 10:1; **dnuta lmara d̠-rabuta midnin** ATŠ I no. 86; **dnuta d̠-tibil** ATŠ II no. 308 earthly compliance; **dnuta lmara d̠-rabuta iahbia** ATŠ I no. 292; **dnuta ldilak . . . midnin** DC 48. 149 f.

dninia a var. of **dnania** v.s. **DNN.**

dniš a var. of **daniš.**

dnita AM 216:7 a var. of **dnuta.**

DNN a doubtful rt. in **uhalin danania** (var. **dninia**) **man dananak** Gy 85:7 (var. Leid. and Sh. ʿAbd.'s copy) possible meaning: Who caused thee this humiliation (?) cf. Ginzā 86 n. 4.

dʿ DC (often) in **da udʿ** this and that. A var. of **dẖ** (q.v.).

dnrta a scr. def. of **dinarta** (q.v.) IM Gl.

dqata (rt. **DQQ**?) small pieces, small quantities (?). Only in DC 45 & 46. Doubtful. **bdqata** (var. **badqata**) **bšamšia iabiš** DC 46 (var. DC 45) drying piecemeal (?) in the sun.

DQQ (דקק, ܕܩ LS, Ges.) to pound, reduce to powder, break into small fragments, crush. Secondary rt. **DUQ II** s.v.

Pe. Pf. **bma d̠-abuk haila d̠-napšia daq** DC 37 with that which thy father crushed (with) his own strength; pl. with suff. **udaquk bakla rba** JRAS 1938 3:25 and they pounded thee with a large hammer.

Pa. Pf. with suff. **udaqa uharqa lkul mdinta d̠-huabẖ iahuṭaiia** HG 71 and he crushed and ground to fragments every city in which there were Jews.

Gl. 103:9 f. with pres. read **qadaiiq** صرع *allidere* ذره شد.

Der.: (a)**dqata** (?).

DQR (דקר, ܕܩܪ) to pierce, crush, wound.

Ethpa. Impf. **tidaqar** DC 37. 198 shall be pierced.

DRA I (Talm. דְּרֵי, but Syr. ܕܪܐ den. from ܕܪܳܥܳܐ) to take, carry, bear, wear, sustain. Still used.

Pe. Pf. **ʿlania ṭunaihun dra** DC 50 trees bore their fruits; **nqašia dra lstuarun** DC 34 shaking(s) attacked their stability (*idiom*); **dranin** DAb we brought; with suff. **dirih̠** **lkapta** DC 41. 239 he took the cup. **diruia** Jb 39:1 they took it away. Impf. **utidra umida hailaikun** DC 36 and thou wilt win and your strength will be known (*idiom*); **ʿdra** Gy 156:14 I carry MG 237 n. 3; with suff. **kul man d̠-nidirẖ** Gs 95:23 whosoever seizeth him, **haizak tidirẖ ʿl kul ʿutra** Jb 262:6 so doth it befall any uthra, cf. ii 235 n. 2 (*idiom*), **d̠-ʿdiriẖ bazuadai** DC 22. 402 (Gs 12:11 **d̠-ʿdairẖ minai bazuadai**) that I may carry it as provision for the journey. Impt. **dra** CP 126:14; CP trs. 93 n. 1 bear (arms) fight (?), Q 64:17 carry ye, MG 237 n. 3; **dra kušṭa mn ašganda** DC 42 and take (the hand of) the server in the ritual handclasp; **drun zhara** DC 50. 243 take care; **durẖ ladam brak** RD B 49 bear (thither) thy son A.; **dru** Jb 12:1 take them (or put them on); pl. **drun** DC 50.51, 248 etc. Act. pt. **dara** Q 64:19, 20 (var. **daria**) MG 237 n. 3; **dara mania lnapaqa** DC 24 he shall wear ritual vestment for the defunct; with encl. **d̠-ziqa darabẖ** Gy 216:16 (var. DC 22 209 **daribẖ**) that the wind carrieth along; **lman d̠-aria darilẖ** ATŠ II no. 71, similarly no. 272. Part. pres. **darana** Jb 135:5 I bear; **kd̠ darana ladam . . . šibiahia mnatun darin** DAb when I brought A. . . . the planets brought their portion (hist. pres.); **kd anin mnata darinin mn alma** ATŠ II no. 45 when we carry away a portion from the world; **umiša bṣibita daritun** ATŠ II no. 153 and (when) ye take oil with your forefinger. Pass. pt. **dria, drʿia** often with act. meaning, cf. **lnišma d̠-ʿngirta dria** Q 42:26 to the soul that carrieth the letter MG 380:paen. Inf. **kd̠ baiit midra ašualia** DC 3 when thou wishest to consecrate a novice (*idiom*); with suff. **midirẖ** Gy 156:11 to carry him MG 292:bottom.

Ethpe. Pt. with encl. **lamidirilia** Gs 12:10 are not carried by me.

Idioms. Used in many idiomatic locutions (similarly to P. بردن and گرفتن): With **stuara** to shake the stability; to bear arms, contest, win, defeat, overcome (cf. P. بُرد as a contrary of باخت); with **šuma** to name, or be named (P. نام برد , اسم برد); to happen, befall cf. Jb ii 235 n. 2; to produce, create, choose, consecrate etc. (v.s. Inf. pe.).

Gl. (always with a prosth. **a**) 15:15 f. اقبل *sumere, incipere* قبول كرد; 19:3 f. ارتفع *auferri* بلند شد; 21:9 f. استخرج *exigere* بيرون كرد; 23:7 انطلق *ducere* رفت; 40:1 f. بدأ *incipere* ابتدا كرد; 104:7 f. صعّد *extrahere* بيرون آورد.

Der.: **darata, dra(iia), druiia.**

DRA II (דְּרָא, ܕܪܐ LS) to scatter, sprinkle, distribute, disperse.

Pe. Pf. **dra** HG 82 **prit udirit,** DC 41. 260 I have broken and distributed. Impf. **ʿburia d̠-šidta . . . glala nidrinun** AM 251:13 hail will scatter the yearly harvest. Act. pt. **aqapra bligra dara** CP 173,15, ML 211:7 she scattereth dust with her foot; pl. with encl. **halin d̲-darilh̲ lzira** DAb those that scatter the seed. Inf. **midra.**

dra (דְּרָעָא, ܕܪܳܥܳܐ) arm. Pl. resp. du. **draiia** 1 MG 70:1, 115:6. **darana ʿl draiia** Jb 135:5 f. I carry in my arms.

drabša, drapša (P. درفش, ISK 92). (*a*) banner, pennon, (*b*) ray, light, glittering, scintillation MG xxxiii:1, 389 n. 1, MR 117 f., Jb ii 185 n. 4, MMII 108 f. (*a*) **nasgia ldrabša unisṭba atutia drabša** DC 24. Pl. **drabšia** RD s. no. 12; (*b*) **drabšia taqnia** Jb 189:13; **lpaina adqaimia drabšia** Gy 222:4; **drabšia d̲-ziua** Gy 289:8, Jb 201:4; **ziua d̲-drabšh̲** Gs 49:1 f. Gl. 105:9 defectively صليب *crux* (102:15 f. mistakenly as a verb).

drabša 2 for **draša** in **drabšia usidria** Gy 361:2 s. **sidra** *b*.

draiia 1 s. **dra.**

draiia 2, druiia (cf. **DRA I** Idioms) fighting, combat, conflict; fear and fighting. **malia udraiia** AM 216:5 wailing and conflict; **dahalta udraiia banašia bmdiniata nihuia** AM 231:5 there will be fear and fighting with the people in the towns.

drakta = **adrakta**: **udrakta ʿl ligrai** DC 51. 397 f.

drapša s. **drabša.**

draq a god ruling over the devils. **bidraq alaha d̲-lšidia udaiuia mšalaṭ** DC 40.

draša 1 (דְּרָשָׁא, ܕܪܳܫܳܐ) teaching, doctrine, instruction, chant, homily, recitation, discourse, discussion, later also book Jb ii p. v, Euting ZDMG xix 129 n. 1, Krehl ZDMG xxii 559. Pl. **drašia. drašia d̲-iahia** or **drašia d̲-malkia** title of a collection of Mand. texts publ. by Lidzb.; **ʿniania udrašia** prayers and chants, title of another collection; **druš drašia** s. **DRŠ.**

draša 2 a miscop. of **drabša**: **drašia taqnia** ATŠ II no. 109 cf. s. **drabša** b.

DRDQ (cf. s. **dirdqia**) to make small.

Refl. Pf. **ʿdardiqit** DC 34. 847 *bis* I made myself small(er).

druiia AM 216:5 a var. of **draiia 2.**

dria a scr. def. of **diria** sea. **dria d̲-mia** DC 51. 169 ff.

drisa = **triṣa**: **udrisa hauia** AM 96:8 and he will be upright.

drisuta = **triṣuta**: **kinuta udrisuta** Gy 213:21 just-dealing and uprightness; **riš drisutak** Gy 214:18 = **riš triṣutak** Gy 213:26.

DRK (דְּרַךְ, ܕܪܰܟ LS, Ges.) to tread (down), walk.

Pe. Pf. **dirka lṭabia dirkit** Gy 91:4 I trod out a path for the good; with encl. **dirka draknalun** Gy 247:3 we trod out a path for them MG 225:12. Impf. **d̲-nitia unidrik ʿlh̲** DC 34 intrans. **ʿuhra lbit hiia tidrak ʿlh̲** ATŠ II no. 344 a road to the House of Life shall be trodden out for him; with encl. **nidrikubh̲** JRAS 1937 592:1 they will tread him down; with suff. **nidrikinun** AM 185:ult. he will tread them down. Act. pt. with encl. **hibil ziua dariklh̲ lalmai** DAb H.-Z. treads my world underfoot. Part. pres. with encl. **darkatbun** Jb 46:2 thou wilt tread down (in) them. Pass. pt. with encl. (and act. meaning) **ladriklia** Gs 5:15 I trod not.

Af Pf. with encl. **ʿuhra ʿrikta lruha ulnišimta adriktlin** DC 48. 381 thou settest the feet of spirit and soul forward on the long road; **dirkia d̲-kušṭa adriklh̲** Jb 107:1 f. he leadeth him (lit. setteth his feet) on paths of Right; with suff. **adrikinun** he set their feet, he led them MG 281:21, **adriktinan** thou hast set our feet, didst lead MG 280:9. Impt. with suff. **adrikunun** *ducite eos* MG 283:antep., **dirka d̲-kušṭa adrakunun** Gy 22:17 (var. Sh. ʿAbd.'s copy **adrikunhun**) *ducite eos in via rectitudinis*. Act. pt. **madrik dirka** Gy 37:4, 357:3 who treadeth the road; fem. **ligrai d̲-madrika dirkia d̲-kušṭa** CP 140 (6):7.

Der: **dirka, (a)drakta.**

DRS dissimil. and disemphasization of **TRṢ.**

Pe. Pass. pt. **drisa** (s.v.).

Der.: **drisa, drisuta.**

DRṢ dissimil. of **TRṢ**: **nidiraṣ ʿurba unisaq ʿl diqla** DC 21 = JRAS 1937 592:34 we will make straight the willow and lift up the palm-tree.

DRŠ (דְּרַשׁ, ܕܪܰܫ LS, Ges.) to teach, instruct, chant prayers or holy books, recite, preach.

Pe. Pf. **diršit** DC 34. 334 I taught; with encl. **drašibh̲** CP 180:15 I chanted with it **daršilh̲** Gy 103:ult. I gave him instruction. Impf. **nidraš** ATŠ II no. 406 he chanteth. Impt. **druš** (often in liturgies) recite, give instruction, chant. Act. pt. **dariš umapriš** Jb 53:9 he preacheth and teacheth; fem. **darša** Jb 137:10 she reciteth; pl. **drašia d̲-kadba daršia** Gy 223:3 they teach false doctrines. Part. pres. **daršit** DC 27. 132 thou chantest; **daršinin** Gy 145:15 we chant; **daršitun** DC 27. 148 ye chant.

Der.: **draša.**

DŠT (den. from **dišta**) to tread down. **dištitun lbar mn pagra dilia** DC 43 F 47 ye are trodden down outside my body.

H

h the fifth letter of the alphabet representing both an etymological ה and ח MG viii:10, 57:18 ff., AIT 29 f. Pronunciation: fricative *h*. A supplementary letter **h** is used to express the Ar. ح MG 2:11. Phonetic changes: Initial h + a MG § 59 p. 61 f.; syncope ibid. pp. 62 f.; vanishing of **h** as third rad. MG § 59 a.

ha (הא, ܗܐ) exclamation and demonstrative particle: oh, ha, ah, yea, yes, behold, verily; this. With the prep. **l** contracted to **hal** (s.v.). Used in demonstrative pronouns and expressions as **hazin, haza, halin, hadinu** etc. (s.vv.) and to corroborate adverbs **haka, halka, hapis** (var. **hapas**) etc. (s.vv.) and interrog. particles **hakma** (s.v.), **hakuat** = **ha akuat** Morg. 249/86:10. (*a*) In exclamations: **ha bdur bišia** (ML 180:16 has **hai**) Q 65:9, **ha ˁtilak** Gy 144:9, **ha baiina minak** Gy 192:ult., **ha amarilkun** Gy 223:17, **ha dnihia uqaimia bziua** Gy 271:11, **ha kma ˁdra uˁsbul** Gy 156:14, **ha ˁklit uštit** Gy 148:15 f., **ha kma** (= **hakma**) **šnia** Gy 156:6, **ha trin alpia šnia** Gy 156:7 f. (*b*) As a demonstrative particle (to emphasize a demonstr. pron.): **bha škinta haza** Gy 257:17; **ḏ-halin zadiqia bha napqin** Sh. ʿAbd.'s copy a var. of Gy 252:19 (Pet. has . . . **ba napqin**) through which these righteous departed; **šuta kasita ḏ-bha** Gy 360:16 the hidden doctrine which is therein.

haba 1 (cf. Ar. حبّ) grain (?), or (rt. **YHB**) = **ahaba** gift (?) **mn had dinara umn had haba mamlil** ATŠ I no. 207.

haba 2 Morg. 92:ult. = **haua.**

habara 1 (חברא, Buxt. הברא Syr. ܚܒܪܐ) darkness MG 61:9 ff. & n. 1. With suff. **babaran, uabarun, abarun** (v.s. **abara 5**). Formation MG 121:6. Var. **habura.** St. abs. **hbar** (s.v.). **mn habara lnhura ḏ-hiia** Gy 179:11; **habara ḏ-habria** AM 277:38; **dairia bhabara** ATŠ I no. 255; **habara gahia** Gy 71:8, 227:21, 282:1 (cf. s. **gahia 1** and **GHA II**); **atia habara ukabar ˁlh̲** Gy 356:1; **alma ḏ-ziua unhura ḏ-habara litbh̲** Gy 7:17.

habara 2 v.s. **HBR I.**

habarauata (cf. **hambaria** = **humbaria**) ruins. **tilia ḏ-habarauata** HG mounds of ruins.

habarata (pl. of ܚܒܪܬܐ, whose sg. is known in Mand. only with the suff. of the 1st p. sg. **habrat** s. **habra 1**) Gs 20:10 women friends. With suff. **habaratin** Gs 30:24, 31:4, **habratin** Gs 31:5 *amicae earum* MG 32:bottom.

habaš (Ar. حبش) AM 205:7 Abyssinia.

habhab (Ar. حَبْحَبَة) DC 46. 113:4 water-melon.

habuṭ, habiṭ (rt. **HBṬ**) AM 286:7 depression (astrol. term).

habura a var. of **habara.**

habib (ܚܒܝܒ, حبيب) beloved, darling MG 124:15 f. With suff. **habibai** Jb 17:4.

habiṭ Ṣâb.'s AM a var. of **habuṭ.**

habiqia DC 22. 65 a var. of **hapiqia** Gy 70:16.

habla 1 (הַבְלָא, ܗܒܠܐ LS) steam, vapour; fig. vanity MG 100:6. **habla ḏ-šabqia** Gy 101:10 (var. Sh. ʿAbd.'s copy . . . **ḏ-šibqia**) mist of the torrents (Lidzb.); **mn habla ḏ-maṭilun** Gy 188:6, **habla maṭilun** Gy 228:15; **habla ḏ-trišar kukbia** Gy 314:16 (var. DC 22. 213 **hablia** might belong s. **habla 2**).

habla 2 (חַבְלָא, ܚܒܠܐ, حَبْل, H. חֶבֶל, cf. LS s.v., Ges. s. חבל I) rope. Pl. **hablia 1. mn hablaikun umn parqsaikun** Gs 64:23 from your toils and your coils; **bhablai ˁklh̲ lkulh̲ alma** Gy 82:12 I will clasp my rope round the whole world; **pšar hablia** DC 44. 1066 the ropes came undone.

habla 3 (act. pt. of **HBL**) destroyer. Pl. **hablia 2. hablia umhamblia** Gy 298:3 the destroyers and the destroyed.

habs (Ar. حَبْس) prison, jail. **ˁnkan ˁniš gu habs** DC 46 should a person be in prison.

habra 1 (חַבְרָא, ܚܒܪܐ) friend, colleague, associate, neighbour, companion. Pl. **habria,** with suff. **habrai(h)un** their comrades. Fem. sg. with suff. **habrat** Gs 20:6 *amica mea*; pl. **hab(a)rata, habrauata** *amicae*, with suff. **habaratin,** var. **habratin** (s. **habarata**). **litlh̲ habra btagh** Gy 31:1 f. he has no associate for his crown; **had lhabrh̲ ladamia** s. **DMA**; **had lhabrh̲ napil** Gy 385:6 MG 321:19 ff.; **malka ḏ-miṣr nigiṭlinun lhabrath̲** (var. **lhabrauath̲**) AM 276:21 the king of Egypt will slay his (female?) associates. Gl. 156:9 defectively صاحب *amicus* رفيق.

habra 2 act. pt. of **HBR I** (q.v.).

habra 3 act. pt. of **HBR II** (q.v.).

habra 4 DC 22. 96 a var. of **habla 1** Gy 101:10.

habratin s. **habarata** and **habra 1.**

habšaba (ܚܕܒܫܒܐ) (*a*) the first day of the week, Sunday MG 44:11, (*b*) a personified Saviour spirit DAb Ap. I, Jb ii 68 n. 3, Reitzenstein: *Vorg.* 337 f., (*c*) week (used also in compound names of the days of the week). Pl. **habšabania** MG 187:8. (*a*) **habšaba briš iumia** CP 153:5, ML 183:10, 186:5; **habšaba qašiš mn šapta** Gy 288:9 f. (Sh. ʿAbd.'s copy, Pet. has . . . **qašiša** . . .); **ḏ-bhabšaba uanpia iuma lmaškna latin** Gy 285:11; **bnaiun ubnatun lmašknia banpia iuma ubhabšaba lamšadria** Gy 285:17; **ḏ-lmaškna atin ubanpia iuma ubhabšaba ubṭaksa šapira qaimin** Gy 285:22 f.; **manšilh̲ lhabšaba umanšilh̲ lagra naṣbun** RD B 72. Cf. MR 90; (*b*) **habšaba ḏ-iaqir šumh̲** Jb 123:1; **habšaba . . . ubr hiia** Jb 179:11; **ana aitith̲ alhabšaba** Jb 206:12; **ḏ-habšaba mardita bgauh̲ radia** Jb 209:14; **habšaba ukana ḏ-zidqa** CP 28:18, Gy 289:3, Q 62:25, 63:2, 12:3, Morg. 87:14, 6:1 etc.; **maṭarta ḏ-habšaba** RD C 2, 27, 28; **habšaba rauziˁil** PD 966; **ia habšaba šbiha naṭra dakia ḏ-nhura** Morg. 115:5; (*c*) **iuma qadmaia ḏ-habšaba** AM 258:17 f.; **trin ḏ-habšaba** Monday; **tlata ḏ-habšaba** Tuesday etc.

habšia (s. **habaš**) Abyssinian. DC 45. 195: DC 46. 194:9.

hag a ruler of the underworld MMII 37, MSchr 144 n. 3, Jb ii 6:bottom. **hag umag** PD 264, DC 36 no. 20 an underworld pair of demons; **hag umag trin mania ḏ-hšuka** Gy 138:19 f., 139:7; **hag gabra umag ˁnta** Gy 138:ult. f.

hagia (חָגָא, ܚܓܐ, Talm. חיגא, חיגתא, Ar. حوج *alhagi* Löw 145 ff.) **hagia . . . iabšia** AM 171:18 camel-thorn dries up: a prickly desert plant, camel-thorn, *hedysarum alhagi*.

haghag, hagigia (cf. **hgaga**) a play on words alluding to delusion, or (from **HUG**?) convolution. **haghag hagigia ḏ-hšuka** DC 12:221, Oxf. roll b 467, 473, DC 40. 173 f. H. the labyrinth (?) of darkness, or delusions (?) of the darkness.

hagir Hagar (?): **blamulh blamta qadmaita ḏ-blimbh arqa br hagir** DC 43.

hagiš, hauguš DC 44 a genius or angel.

had masc., **hda** fem. (חַד — חֲדָא, ܚܰܕ, ܚܕܳܐ > אחד) one, single MG 35 n. 2, 60:anteantep., 187:bottom. The masc. is often replaced by the fem., so that the former is rather limited to certain special uses (below). A special form **hud** is used in **lhud** and **balhud** (s.vv.). Multiplicative use: (ʿ)**l had trin** Gy 95:10, Q 64:2, Jb 8:12 double, twice as much, twice as big; **ʿhaial libẖ ʿl had trin** Gy 95:8 his heart became twice as strong; **ʿl had šuba** Gy 187:9 seven times; **ʿl had arbin utrin** Gy 272:17 forty-two times greater; **ʿl had ruban** Gy 167:1 ten thousand times as much MG 349. In distributive repetitions: **had had** (*often*) one by one, everyone. **lhad had** (*often*) to everyone, **had abatar had** DC 41. 128 ff. little by little, gradually. With **kul**: **kul had** everyone, each one, **kdub kul had mamla lhad iuma** DC 45 write one single word each day. 'Each' without **kul**: **huabẖ bhad had pira alip alip piria** Gy 69:6 (Sh. ʿAbd.'s copy has **had** only once) in each fruit there were thousand times thousand fruits.

hada 1 (הָדָא) a sporadic form of **haza** 1 MG 43:12, 90:11. **hada hada abad ṭaba** CP 165:5, 13 this and that hath the Good One done; **hada hada aitit** ML 196:11; **hada ḏ-dnia šamiš** CP 27:1, ML 31:7; **hada ʿutria abad** Gy 73:12.

hada 2 (Ar. حَدّ) limit, frontier. With suff. **hadẖ** AM 205:2 its frontier.

hadadia a sporadic form of **hdadia.**

hadaia (Ar. هَدِيَّة) ŠQ 19:7 = MLx:ult. present(s).

hadaiata, hadiata (rt. **HDA** I) wedding songs. **niqrun hadaiata** DC 38 they shall recite wedding songs.

hadam ATŠ I no. 282 a var. of **hatam.**

hadar (cf. st. emph. **hdara**) circuit, turning round. **hadar** (var. **hadir**) **dilẖ ʿmbra** AM 286:7 its orbit (?) is Aries; **baita ḏ-ianqa uhadar** DC 45 & 46 the womb and the upper part of the vagina(?).

hadua 1, hidua st. abs. of **haduta** 1 MG 155: middle. Seems to be treated as st. emph. masc. MG 156 footn. **mitiqria lilbia hadua** Jb 179:2 torn out is their hearts' joy.

hadua 2 (in a list of plants with a picture) sunflower. Masc. **hadua hu** DC 41 it is a sunflower.

haduat st. cstr. of **haduta** 1 (q.v.).

haduta 1 (ܚܕܘܬܐ < חֲדוּתָא) joy, rejoicing, merriment MG 57:3 f., 101:20, 146 n. 4, 155: middle. St. abs. **hadua** 1, st. cstr. **haduat. haduat liba** ML 1:9, MG 155:20; **bhaduta ḏ-lansisuta** Gy 9:14; **haduta ukariuta** AM.

haduta 2 a var. of **hiduta** (q.v.). Pl. **hadutia, hadutiata** var. **hadutata. unitian hadutata** DC 22. 398 and brides come; **ḏ-kulhun hadutia qribin** DC 44. 777 that approach all brides.

hadia 1 (חֲדְיָא, ܚܰܕܝܳܐ) breast, chest MG 109:9. Fem. Pl. **hadiauata. hadiiẖ** AM 18 his chest; **hadiak** thy breast MG 177:6; **šqul hadiak mn hadiiẖ** DC 37:604 remove thy breast from his breast; **htum bhadia rabita uhiduta ḏ-lakanpat** DC 46 seal (it) in the presence (?) of a matron and a bride whose marriage was not yet consummated; **šqap ltarbaṣia hadiaian** CP 65:14 they beat on the forecourts of their breast; **hadiaiin mgalalin** Gy 181:3 their (fem.) breasts are uncovered; **hadiaiun** their (masc.) breasts MG 181:anteantep.; **uhadiauata trin almia hinun** ATŠ I no. 223 and the breasts are two worlds; **manšialẖ lhadiẖ ḏ-ʿmẖ** DC 49. 237 she will forget her mother's breast. **ršum bhadia rabita** DC 44:63 seal on the breast of a girl.

hadia 2 (חֲדְיָא) kite, vulture. **snʿ dmauatun kḏ hadia . . sarṭana . . .** AM 197:4 their appearance is repulsive, such as the vulture . . . crab etc.; **šqul hadiak** DC 43 J 155 remove thy vulture.

hadia 3 (act. pt. of **HDA II**) leader. **hadia uṭizana hauia** AM 95:17 he will be a leader (?) and restless.

hadiata = **hadaiata.**

hadid AM 286:8 a corruption of **hadir** or **hadar** (q.v.).

hadinat hiia CP 64:11 (n. 4), ML 80:2 (n. 1) a doubtful word.

hadinu (= **hazin hu**) this is MG 43:middle, with a doublet **hainu** MG 61:paen., with the same meaning as the original **hazin hu** MG 90:10 f. **hadinu hšuka ḏ-rmitubẖ** Gy 254:18; **hadinu bataikun** Gy 254:19 these are your houses; **hadinu ʿutra rhima** Gy 249:21.

hadisar (Talm. חדיסר, חדסר, Syr. ܚܕܥܣܪ) = **asra uhda** eleven MG 188.

hadir a var. of **hadar** (q.v.).

hadita, haditia (fem. of **hadta**) new (fem.), varr. **hadtia, hatia** (s. vv.) MG 154:11. **šidta haditia** AM (*often*) the new year.

hadlia (cf. Ar. هدل to hang) pendulous part(s), things that dangle, male sexual organ. **unsabunun lhadlia mn qudamẖ uʿl qudam hanẖ** DC 43 A 12 and they removed his pendulous parts from before him and from before his loins.

hadra (הַדְרָא, ܗܽܘܕܳܪܳܐ LS) splendour, adornment, beauty; adj. fem. pl. **hadran** beautiful (?). Doublet **hidra** 1 (s.v.). **hadra ugaiuta** Leid., Norb. & Sh. ʿAbd.'s copy a var. of Gy 3:18 (Pet. has **hadta ugaiuta**); **hadra ušupra** ML 15:4 = CP 13:14. Adjectivally: **ainẖ hadran** AM 87:19 f. his eyes are beautiful.

hadta (חַדְתָּא, ܚܰܕܬܳܐ) new. Pl. masc. & sg. fem. **hadtia, hatia**, var. of fem. sg. **hadita, haditia** (s.v.) MG 44:6 f., 110:7. **asa hadta** CP 466:19, DC 42 fresh myrtle; **bsiprai hadtia** Gy 205:23, 206:20 in my new books; **lbušia hadtia** Gy 5:15 f.

hahai (= **ha ahai**) O-my-brother, a term of endearment. **baba umama uiaia udada uqaqa udaiia uhahai . . . šumia ḏ-nihuta hinun** ATŠ I no. 249 'Papa' and 'mama' and 'auntie' and 'goosey' and 'nursie' and 'O-my-brother' are names of affection.

hahu (הָהוּ) demonstr. pron. masc. this, that, that very. Fem. **hahʿ** (var. **hahia**) MG 89:9. Syntax MG 337 f. **ʿl hahu ḏ** Gy 157:18 on that which; **blibh d̠-hahu d̠-qaiim** Gy 280:10 MG 338:bottom; **hahu malka** Gy 4:16, 5:13, 297: ult. that king; **malka hahu** Gs 4:1 etc. id.; **hahu gabra qadmaia** CP 1:14; **luath̠ d̠-hahu abuk** Gy 68:9 near that father of thine; **hahu mara d̠-rabuta** CP 3:12; **alma hahu d̠-bišia** Gs 4:1; **alma hahu** (often). MG 338:middle.

haua (חַוָּה II Ges.) Eve, Adam's wife; a common Mand. woman's name. **haua zauh̠** Gy 13:9, 16, 23, 34:14, 114:23, 116:3, 117:9, 219:10, 241 f., Gs 12:19; **haua zauak** Gy 49:5, 114:18, Gs 16:21; **haua zauai** Gs 12:16, 16:18; **adam uhaua** Gy 100:19, 21; **anat haua ahat** Gy 116:9; **anhar ziua haua d̠-mn haua huat** Gy 108:5; **nṣablh̠ haua bzauia** Gy 286:17; **haua d̠-adam . . .** Q 47:1. As a common pr. n. **haua simat** Jb 1:8 etc. Lidzb. Mand. Gl.

haua ṣṭartia Jb 235:14, cf. II 217 n. 6. Lidzb. Mand. Gl.

ḥauadit (حوادث) AM 281:9 events.

hauauata, hiuauata Ṣâb.'s AM pl. of **hiuia.**

ḥauaiǧia, coll. sg. *hawīǧa* (apparently from P. هويج carrot) medicament(s). **halin ḥauaiǧia d̠-abdit** AM 286:43 these medicaments that I prepared; **halin šitin ḥauaiǧia** AM 288:8.

haualai (Ar. حوالى) surroundings, vicinity, environs, outskirts. **bbagdad uhaualai dilh̠** HG 90 in B. and its outskirts.

hauam AM 276:26 a var. of **hauma** (or its supposed st. abs.; mod. st. abs. is *howm*).

hauan (P. هَونگ) mortar MMII xiii 232.

hauara = **hiuara**: **ʿtkasun hauara** Sh. ʿAbd.'s copy's var. of Gy 47:22 (Pet. has **hiuara**); **mia . . . hauaria mn halba** DC 22. 9 (where Pet. Gy 9:9 has **hiuaria**); **arqa d̠-aiar hauartia** DC 22. 9 (Pet. Gy 9:15 **hiuartia**). Gl. 121:1 شستن *lotio* غسل.

hauba (חובא, ܚܘܒܐ) sin, guilt, trespass. Pl. **haubia**, rarely **haubata**. **haṭaian uhauban** Morg. 209/5:paen. etc. (*often*) our sins and trespasses; **haubih̠ kulhun** Gy 15:paen.; **haubai** CP 146:14, ML 176:1 my trespasses.

hauǧuš s. **hagiš.**

hauda (חוד rt. חדד) thin slice, sliver: **ṣuriih̠ mn ganbih̠ hauda** DC 3, DC 24 cut from its side a sliver.

hauṭa (חוטא, ܚܘܛܐ) thread, sewing, part where sewn together. **ʿniana d̠-hauṭa d̠-taga** CP 348:8 the prayer of the sewing-up the crown; **pumh̠ d̠-hu hauṭh̠** DC 41. 507 its 'mouth' which is the part where it is sewn together.

hauik AM 276:26 apparently a st. abs. of **hauka.** Varr. or corruptions **halip, halik** cf. BZ 181 n. 5.

hauka (rt. **HUK** = **HKK**) irritation, scab, itching. **uhauka banašia nihuia** AM 265:23; **hauka ukiba d̠-haṣa** DC 46.

hauma (חומא, ܚܘܡܐ) heat, temperature (medical), fever MG 100:19. **hauma urugza** Gy 29:7, 53:4, 197:20, Gs 123:20, Q 66:20; **hauma ubarda** Gy 199:6, RD C 2, 6, 14, 18; **hauma uiaqdana** RD C 15, 17; **hauma uhauka** AM 265:23; **hauma biša** AM 46:16 high fever; **haumaiun ubardaiun** DC 44. 203 their fever and their chill.

hauna (ܗܘܢܐ) mind, reason. **ubr malkia hazin lau bhaunh̠** Gy 212:17 and this prince is not in his senses; **haunaihun šna mn dukth̠** DC 41. 322 their mind was distracted (lit. was removed from its place); **lau bhauna gimištaiia** Gy 212:17 f. he speaks nonsense.

hausa, hus (Ar. حوض) cistern, basin MG xxxiii:17 f., but Jb 162 n. 5 doubts the meaning of **hausia. hausia uriuia litlh̠** Gy 216:14, Jb 161:12 it has no cisterns or drinking-fountains.

haupia, hupia (rt. **HUP**) foaming, Ginzā 194 n. 2. **haupia mia** Gy 210:1, Par. 25 fo. 15b:8, CP 222:9.

hauqa (rt. **HUQ**) fear, terror, panic MG 100:18. **hauqa hualh̠** Jb 25:11; **hauqa udahalta** Jb 194:10; **hauqa uziuihta** Jb 195:7 f., 9; **hauqa d̠-haq** Gy 160:17 (s. **HUQ**); **hauqa miṭian** Gs 73:3; **šibia uhauqa** AM 169:13 captivity and terror. Gl. 98:9 **huqa** [*sic*] شدّة *agonia* دشوار.

hauqana a mod. pl. of **hauqa** great fear, terror. **ublibaihun hauqana šaria** DC 43 E 15 and causeth terror to dwell in their hearts.

haura (ܚܘܪܐ) hoariness, whiteness, white-headedness, old age; cleansing, washing, whitening. **haura d̠-šuba** DC 41. 525 the cleansing of the Seven (purgatories); **luat haurh̠** AM 40:10 towards his old age.

hauran uhauraran (cf. the geographical name חורן, *Ḥaurân* and the Can. deity in עבד חורן JA 1883 141 s. no. 17; the second name is formed by the enlarging of the first) name given to a heavenly land ML xix, Ginzā vi, ML 280, A 242 & n. 2. Fem. found also as a name of a (white ritual?) garment. **hauran uhauraran** CP 38:10, see CP Index, **bhauran ʿuṣṭlan bhauraran ksuian** CP 37:19, Morg. 210/8:ult. ff.; **bhauran uhauraran ziua ṣurik hiia** Morg. 211/10:7 f., Q 16:28 cf. ZDMG lxi 693 n. 3; **hauraran dakita** Gy 304:11; **hauraran d̠-nišmata bgauh̠ mištalma** Gs 135:18; **hauraran ukarkauan** Oxf. roll f. 915, Q 29:23, 31; **hauraran d̠-rbia** Jb 257:12 Lidzb. Mand. Gl. **hauraran arqa rabtia d̠-nhura** CP 450:1; **bgu iardna ubgu hauraran** ibid.

hauria, huria (cf. חורא hole and الخور a name given to the marsh country in the south of ʿIrāq) marshes, marsh-waters, marsh lakes. Sg. not found. **mbašqarnun lnašbia ulhauria** Jb 143:7 (var. A **ulhuria**); **ṣaidia qpun lhauria** Jb 156:11; **mapriš bhauria lnunia iamamia** Jb 160:8; **naṣar bhauria** Jb 160:2 read **nahar** (?) **bhauria** Jb II 163 n. 1; **lhauria mia iadanun** Jb 143:6; **birzam d̠-iaruq bhauria** DC 23. 771 (v.s. **birzam**).

haza 1 (a more frequent doublet of **hada** 1) fem. demonstr. pron. this (: *haec*) MG 43:11, 90:9. Used with fem. substantives as well as an independent demonstrative (: *hoc*) MG 299: anteantep., 339 ff. **bhaza tibil** Gs 61:20, **haza maṭarta** (*often*), **kd̠ haza amarlia** Gy 74:1 etc. (*often*), **kd̠ haza nipqat mn pumai** Gy 160:3; **kd̠ haza masgina uazilna** Gy 154:6 when (my father said) this (or shortly: after this, then, cf. **haza 2**), I set off and went away (hist. pres.).

haza 2 (cf. **haza** 1 last example) then (= **haizak**): **haza ʿstadar paṭira tiniana** ATŠ II no. 125 (var. DC 36 **hazẖ**) then set the second unleavened bread in place.

hazazban a spirit, ruler of a purgatory; DAb Ap. I, Lidzb. ZDMG lxi 693 n. 5, CP 25:30, 37:ult., ML 29 n. 2, 280. **zan hazazban** (or **zan uhazazban**) Gy 181:17, 182:9, 208:14, Q 11:2; **hazazban klila traṣlia brišai** CP 25:30 = ML 29:ult.

hazaia (nom. ag. pe. of **HZA**) seer, one who sees, onlooker, spectator. **hazaia uparuša** Q 65:29, Gy 61:17, Gs 79:14, seer and discerner; **hazaiia uparišaiia** Gy 278:2 id. pl.; **hazaiia umahzaiia** Morg. 270/30:8 onlookers and spectators.

hazaman s. **hanzaman**.

hazuz umazuz (cf. גּוֹג אֶרֶץ מְגוֹג Ez. 38:2 f., ياجوج وماجوج Qur. 18:93) AM 200 names of two cities, a term applied to Scythian and barbarian tribes generally BZ Ap. II.

hazuia (ܚܙܘܝܐ) seer, spectator MG 113: antep.

hazura = **hizura**.

hazia 1 (act. pt. pe. of **HZA**) used with the same meaning as **hazaia** DC 22 465 as a var. of Gs 79:14. **haziai umahziai** DC 51 cf. **hazaiia umahzaiia** (s. **hazaia**).

hazia 2 a var. of **hazin** MG 162 n. 1.

hazi Zotb. 225 left 2nd text:1 = **hazia 2**.

hazin 1 (Talm. הָדֵין. The original form preserved only in the explicative **hadinu**) demonstr. adj. this. Masc. fem. **haza** s.v. MG 43:middle, 90:9. Often used substantivally (as an independent demonstrative) MG 339 ff. **hazin alma** or **alma hazin** (*both often*) this world; **hazin daura ḏ-hšuka** Gy 281:12; **br malkia hazin** Gy 212:7; **ʿl atrak hazin** Gy 168:17; **hazin hu gabra** Gy 185:17, 19 this very man. Separated from the noun: **hazin rqiha ʿtingid hazin ʿtingid rqiha** Gs 76:8 f. (read so, although all codd. have **haizin** MG 340 n. 2, cf. also s. **hazin 2** and **haizin 2**) this firmament was extended, extended was this firmament (: *hoc extensum est coelum*). **hazin ḏ-** Gy 164:1 this which. With fem. nouns: **hazin dmutak** Oxf. III 13 a, **hazin šuta qadmaita** MG 411:middle.

hazin 2 often confused with **haizin** and vice versa (cf. s. **haizin 2**) MG 206 n. 1, 3. **maṣbuta hazina ḏ-maṣbit** Gy 190:ult. how is the baptism which thou baptizest?; **ʿbidatun ḏ-hazin saina umdahla** Gy 75:12 their works which are so ugly and frightful; **husranun ḏ-hazin npiš** Gy 75:13 their loss which is so great.

hazin 3 in **hazin ḏ-mn mruma atina** Gy 55:1 read **hzun** see that I come from the height, cf. l. 6, Ginzā 49 n. 6.

haziran (ܚܙܝܪܢ, Ibn Nadim حزيران SsSs II 26) AM 259:17 f. Mand. month corresponding to June.

haṭaṭa a doublet of **aṭaṭa** (q.v.). **haṭaṭa ugusparta ḏ-tarnaula** AM 135:8 the spur (?) and comb of a cock.

haṭaiia (cf. sg. חֶטְאָא, ܚܛܗܐ) sins MG 29:6. Occurs only in pl. in literature. Mod. sg. *χaṭâh, χaṭâha*. **haṭaiik** Gs 132:10, 12 thy (fem.) sins MG 117:23, **haṭaian** our sins MG 179:7, **haṭaikun** Gy 19:10; **bhaṭaiia** Gy 14:21 in a sinful way; **abda ḏ-kulhun haṭaiia** (often in colophons) a slave who is all-sinful, or **ḏ-kulẖ haṭaiia** who is all sin (copyists so designate themselves); **šabiq haṭaiia nihuilia** (**-lak, -lẖ, -lkun**, all frequent) forgiving (lit. forgiver) of sins be there for me etc.; **šuba haṭaiia** Q 26:20, 32, **šitin uarba haṭaiia** Q 25:33.

haṭarata (cf. sg. חֲטֶרֶת, ܚܛܪܬܐ) mounds, heaps. **haṭarata ḏ-hala** RD B 41 = DAb mounds of soil.

haṭia 1 (act. pt. pe. of **HṬA**) sinner, sinning, offending, offensive.

haṭia 2 a var. of **hiṭia**.

haṭia 3 in **haṭia maṭia zibna** Sh. ʿAbd.'s copy's var. of Gy 155:9 where Pet. has **ha maṭia . . .** behold, the time is coming (**haṭia** was influenced by the foll. **maṭia**).

haṭipa (rt. **HṬP**) rapacious, despoiling, snatching MG 124:11. **aria haṭipa** Gs 9:12; **diba haṭipa** Gy 179:17, 287:22; **haṭipa ḏ-mhaṭip** s. **HṬP** pa. pt.

haṭiputa (abstr. noun from **haṭipa**) Gy 215:22 seizing by force, pillage, robbery.

hai 1 interj. O! Lo! Ha! Yea, verily MG 81:5. **hai marai** Jb 114:7 (varr. ABD **mara**, DC 30 **maria**); **hai aba** Jb 117:10 etc.; **hai lau atalia hibil ziua** DC 22 339 a var. of **hainu . . .** Gy 343:20 lo, hath not H.–Z. come to me; **hai bdur bišia** PC 189:16 yea, in the abode of the wicked . . .

hai 2 (cf. הָאי, אַי, הַיי) interrog. particle: how? Often corroborated by the demonstr. **din** in **haidin** and **haizin** 1 MG 205 f., 71 n. 3. **hai hauin bnẖ ḏ-adam hai šaplia uhai zaqpia hai hauin hilbunia uškinata hai hauia haila hai hauilẖ busmania** Jb 231:15 ff. how will A.'s children come into being, how will they fall and how be set up? how will celestial dwellings come into being? how will be his strength? how will he have sweet odours? **hai hauia tata hiuartia hai šapla hai zaqpa hai haṭna hai iadla hai mitqiria girglia ḏ-nhura** Jb 233:1 ff.; **hai hauia rqiha . . . hai mitqiria iauna hiuartia** Jb 233:4 f.

hai 3 (Talm. הָאי) demonstr. adj. masc.: this MG 90:18 & n. 2. Fem. **da** b (q.v.). **hai malka** Gy 390:24, **hilpa hai ḏ-**Gy 263:16, **raza hai** Gy 268:6, **bhai ʿniana** ML 275:5.

hai 4 for **ahai** my brothers. **ana zuṭ hai** Zotb. 227 left 2nd text:7 I (am) the least amongst my brothers, **zuṭa ḏ-hai**.

hai– the form of **hiia** used with poss. suff. MG 10:8. **bhaiak** (often) by thy life MG 177:12, **bhaiaikun** Gs 78:16, 90:21, ATŠ II no. 126 by your life, **haiaiun** CP 48:12, Q 22:27, ML 64:4 = Morg. 219/25:ult. their life.

haia (חַיָּא, ܚܝܐ) adj. living, alive MG 108:4. Fem. **haita** 1. Pl. masc. **haiia** (sometimes defectively by influence of **hiia** the Life), fem. **haiata** 1. **haia hu** Gy 3:8 He is the Living One MG 307:antep.; **mlaka haia** DC 37:565 living angel; **ʿšata haita** v.s. **ʿšata**; **lgubria haiia** ATŠ I no. 232, for living men; **haiia ḏ-lau maituiia** Gy 31:19 (var. Sh. ʿAbd.'s copy **haia ḏ-lau maitia**) the living ones who do not die;

masqata haiata (*often*) living (: life-giving?) *masiqtas*; **nišmata haiata** CP 118:10, ML 144:2; **aba haia ubra haia** DC 44:1862 f.

haiaba (nom. ag. pe. of **HUB**, חָיָּבָא, ܚܰܝܳܒܳܐ) guilty, sinner; powerless. Pl. masc. **haiabia**, fem. **haiabata. napšaihun bhaiabia lgaṭ** v.s. **LGṬ** Pe pf. and Idioms; **ʿuai ʿl šibiahia d̲-hinun hun haiabia** CP 65:16, ML 81:6; **šuba hun bhaiabia** Jb 160:2; **bhaiabia hauin** ATŠ I no. 46; **nišmata haiabata** Gy 183:22; **haiaba btibil tatitiqria** Gy 364 f. be not called 'guilty' on earth; encl. **lhaiaba mzakilh̲** s. **ZKA** pa. pass. pt. with encl.

haial (rt. **HIL.** Formation dubious: mostly an invariable nominal form, might then be a st. abs. and cstr. of **haila**, but its mod. st. abs. and cstr is *hil*; used also as an invariable verbal form explained by Lidzb. as < **ʿhaial** < **ʿthaial** ML 11 n. 1) strength(ening), force; as invariable verbal form: was strengthened (?), is strong (?), or imperatively as a greeting formula (?). In DAb = RD 8 a proper name. As noun: **bhailak ubhaial halin ʿumamata** Or 326:3; **ʿṣṭarar ʿl haial ginzia** ATŠ I no. 317; **bhaial naṣiruta** DC 41; **haial ʿqara** ML 256:4. As invariable verbal form: **haial kbar raza rba d̲-ziua** CP 9:11, Q 4:2, 20:10, 22:2, 44:27, Morg. 247/82:2, ML 55:10 etc.; **haial ukbar hua raza rba d̲-ziua** CP 46:25, ML 62:2.

haiania mod. pl. of **haia. nišmata d̲-haiania bruk** CP 394:1 (CP trs. p. 262 n. 5) bless the souls of the living (in ritual: the departed).

haiasa (nom. ag. pe. of **HUS**) compassionate MG 122:16. **mara d̲-rabuta haiasa d̲-haiis lbnh̲** ATŠ I no. 47 the Lord of Majesty is the Compassionate who hath mercy on his children; **haiasa utaiaba** Gy 1:24, 17:3, 30:20; **haiasa d̲-haiis** Gy 215:9 f. etc.; **haiasa hus ʿlai** Gy 84:19 f.; **haiasa hus ʿlan** DC 41:268 etc.; **haiasa d̲-mlia rahmia** Morg. 10:9; **hiia rbia haiasa hinun** DC 50.

haiasuta (abstr. noun from **haiasa**) compassion. Varr. **haisuta, hiasuta.** MG 145:5 f. **hiasuta utiabuta** Gy 213:22; **šaliṭania mridia d̲-lahaisuta** Gy 9:5; **kulh̲ rhamta ukulh̲ hiasuta ukulh̲ tiabuta** Gy 2:17 f.; **haiasutkun** CP 485:10 your compassion.

haiašum (from **šum hiia**?) a spirit of life Jb 212 n. 2; a name of Šamiš; a personal name. **haiašum kušṭa** CP 21:5, 117:2, Q 59:14, ML 23:5, 142:10; **haiašum asia** CP 199 trs. 19, cf. Jb 230:14 f. In DAb = RD 10 an epithet of **šamiš.**

haiata 1 pl. fem. of **haia** (q.v.).

haiata 2 = **haita 2.** Formally pl., used mostly as a sg. **hbilta d̲-haiata** Gy 96:16 convulsion of a woman in labour; **qaštanita d̲-haiata** DC 40:825 id.; **masiqta d̲-haiata** ATŠ II no. 74 *masiqta* of a woman in childbirth; **muta bʿnšia uhaiata** AM 170 death amongst women in labour.

haidar Zotb 231 left:14 a man's name.

haidin 1, haizin 1 (cf. s. **hai 2**) (*a*) how?, (*b*) thus, so MG 43:12, 206:19. **haidin uhaidin** Jb 38:10 thus and in such manner . . .

haidin 2 (ܗܳܝܕܶܝܢ) sporadically for **haizak** then MG 207:6. **haidin šaruia ath̲** Gs 119:10 then th ϵRedeemer cometh.

haiuna ML 60:6 a *malwâša* woman's name.

haiuta 1, hiuta 1, haita 3 (חֵיוְתָא, ܚܰܝܘܬܳܐ 2 LS) (an) animal(s), cattle, (b = **hiuta 2** q.v.). St. abs. **hiua** s.v. St. cstr. **haiuat** us. replaced by the st. abs. Used as a collective noun. **muta bit haiuta nihuilh̲** v.s. **bit** compounds s.v. a. **ṣipra ṣipar haiuta** Gy 216:3. **haiuta d̲-arba ligria**, AM 91:11 a quadruped **haiuta** (var. **hiuta**) **d̲-saina undida** s. **hiuta 2.**

haiuta 2 (חַיוּתָא) womb. **hda mn ʿnšia k(u)ṣurta bit haiuta** (var. **hiuta**) **tihuilh̲** AM 16:16 one of his women will have a disease of the womb.

haiuta 3 (חיות, ܚܰܝܘܬܳܐ 1 LS) life. **lkul haiutun** Gy 9:13 for their whole life; **bhaiuta** Gy 388:11 in life(time); **muta uhaiuta** Jb 207:7 death and life; **bhaiutun** ATŠ II no. 6 in their lifetime; **d̲-haiutkun minaihun** hʿ ATŠ II no. 5 from which your vitality proceedeth.

haiza DC 27:397 = **haza.**

haizak 1 (ܗܳܝܕܶܝܢ, هاذاك) then, thereupon; thus, so MG 43:13, 207:7 f., Lidzb. ZDMG lxi 690. Very often. **mn haizak** from that time MG 207:8.

haizak 2, haizin 1, haidin 1 Sh. 'Abd.'s copy's var. of **haizin 1** Gy 102:5 (see foll.). (cf. **hai 2**), interrogatively: how?, how is it that?, how comes it that?; affirmatively: thus, so, thus it is MG 43:13, 71:20, 206:2 ff. Sometimes replaced by **hazin 2** (q.v.). Interrogatively: **hšuka haizin hua haizin hua hšuka** Gy 78:18 how did darkness come into being?; **nišimta bpagra haizin napla haizin napla nišimta bpagra uhaizin mamlilbh̲ zma zma haizin mamlilbh̲ uhaizin niṣribh̲ agih̲** Gy 102:4 ff. how did the soul fall into the body and how doth blood talk in it etc.; **haizin ʿtit mn tibil** Gy 362:14 f. how camest thou from the earth? **ulnhura haizin salqit** Gy 363:4 f. and how wilt thou ascend to the light?; **haizin** (var. **hazin**) **huat nišimta** Jb 226:11 f. how did the soul come into being?; **haizin traṣlia kursia** Jb 228:6 how comes it that he set up a throne for me?; **ʿl adam haizin haua zauh̲** Jb 231:14 for A. how will there be Eve his wife?; **haizin atuat d̲-haršia abda** DAb what of the woman that works sorcery? Affirmatively: **kd̲ haizin mištaiin minai** Gy 148:11 when they spake (hist. pres.) thus to me; **d̲-haizin dmutak šapira** Gy 170:5 that thy form is so fair; **haizin bnina umbanana** Gs 107:20 is so built up and edified; **haizin haizin mhaimna ukšiṭa haizin zriza umzarza** Gs 107:21 f. so believing and faithful, so armed and well equipped; **ʿu haizin labdilh̲** AM 15:14 if they do not treat him thus.

haizin 2 = **hazin 1** MG 206 n. 3. **haizin rqiha ʿtingid haizin ʿtingid rqiha** Gs 76:8 f. v.s. **hazin 1**; **kd̲ haizin hza** Gy 162:22 when he saw this; **haizin alma nṣablun** Gy 293:24 he created for them this world; **haizin dukta** Gs 128:ult. this place.

haikin (cf. ܗܳܝܟܰܢ LS, H. אָכֵן) even thus, like that; used also as a simple demonstr. (like **haizin 2** = **hazin 1**). **haikin ana . . . ʿšup** DC 26 even thus I . . . make incantation . . .; **haikin ʿul** Or. 332:3 enter these (spirits).

haila (חילא, חיילא, ܚܝܠܐ LS) strength, force; army MG 100:20. With suff. **hailai** my strength MG 176:14, **hailak** thy power MG 177:6, **hailh**, **hailih** (often) his power etc. Pl. **hailia, hailauata. ʿsir haila d-ʿšumia ʿsir haila d-arqa . . . ʿsir haila d-ziqa** DC 37 bound is the strength of the heavens, bound is the strength of the earth, bound is the strength of the wind; **bhaila** ATŠ II no. 121 by force; **haila ʿl malka niqum** AM 246:15 the army will rise against the king; **haila rama d-kulhun hailia minh paršia** ATŠ II no. 113 a lofty strength from which all forces derive; **šitin rab hailauata** DC 44 sixty commanders of the armies; **tlatma ušitin hailauata ʿtlh** DC 41:90 and it has 360 forces; **hailaiun uhiltaiun** Gy 232:4 their strength and their power (a pun; Lidzb.: *ihre Stärke u. Stahl*); **haila umadihta** Gy 375:3 power and wisdom; **mṣia hailh** s. **MṢA.**

hailana (for **mhailana**) Bestower of Strength, Strengthener. **hailana** (var. **ziuana**) **d-npiš hailh ahbalan haila** DC 22 57 (var. Gy 62:9) Strengthener whose strength is great, give us strength.

hailuta (a further abstr. noun from **haila**, cf. also **hilta**) force, strength. **hailutan** ML 132:8 our strength. Pl. **hailauata** (v.s. **haila**). **anat . . . hailutan** CP 107:3 f.

hailʿil (a theophorous name from **HIL**) Gy 167:16 and angel.

haima (rt. **HUM** = **HMM**) hot, hot-tempered. **haima kd nura** Ṣâb.'s AM hot like fire.

haimanuta (הֵימָנוּתָא, ܗܝܡܢܘܬܐ) belief, faith, religious observance, piety MG 145:8. St. abs. & cstr. **haimanut** MG 155:11. MR 86 f. Often.

haimna, haimnu (< **hai minu** < **hai minhun** 'which of them?') ATŠ II no. 196 which one?

hain a miscop. of **hazin** (DC 22. 127 = Gy 132 1) and **haizin** (Sh. 'Abd.'s copy = Gs 53).

hainu (Talm. הײנו < הדן הו) = **hadinu** this is he, lo here is he, behold him that MG 44:15, 90:12; **hainu atia hibil mana** Gy 152:12 behold, H.M. cometh; **hainu atalia blum br blum** DC 44. 1050 lo here is he, B. son of B. came to me.

haisuta s. **haiasuta.**

haita 1 fem. of **haia** (q.v.).

haita 2 (חַיְּתָא, ܚܝܬܐ) (*a*) woman in childbirth, in labour, (*b*) midwife MG 110:12. Var. (& pl.) **haiata 2** (s.v.). (*a*) **nahima ruha kd haita** Gy 88:3; **ruha d-qudša azla uatia kd haita** Gy 353:16; **uṣurta lhaita laṣairia** Jb 85:6; (*b*) **napqa hidutata mn bit gnana uhaita mn bit maudala** Gy 59:10. Note: The distinction betw. (*a*) and (*b*) is only arbitrary.

hak 1 (Talm. הַאיךְ masc., הַאךְ fem. < דן + ך + ה) demonstr. that (in Mand. for both genders) MG 44:14, § 82 p. 90 f. Used as both a demonstr. adj. (before or after the noun) and an independent demonstr. pron. MG 337 ff. Pl. **hanik** (s.v.). As demonstr. adj.: **lhak mana** Gy 69:8, **lhak dukta** Gy 75:6 etc., **hak alma** Gy 92:18, 185:14, **hak iardna** Gy 134:11, **hak niṭupta rabtia** CP 54:4, Q 25:5, **hak malka** Gy 392:3, **hak riha** Gy 283:12, **hak barda** Gy 283:10; after the noun: **lalma hak** Gy 155:10, **balma hak d-** Gy 157:5, **marganita hak** Gy 165:17. As independent demonstr. pron.: **mn hak d-iatir** Gy 87:20, **akuat d-taqnit** Gy 158:9. Gl. 182:3 **hak** ذاك *ille* اين.

hak 2 sometimes confused with **haka 1** here (and vice versa, cf. **haka 3**) cf. MG 91 n. 1. **hak btibil uhatam balmia d-nhura** (*often*) here on earth and there in worlds of light.

haka 1 (הָכָא, ܗܟܐ, and ܠܗܟܐ) adv. of place: here; with prep. **lhaka** (= **ha lka** Gs 125 ff.) hither, **mn haka** from here MG 204:2; **ʿl mahu atit lhaka** DAb why hast thou come hither?; **ubišutai haka hʿ** DC 46 my wickedness lies herein; **lhaka atia** Gs 18:22 she will come hither.

haka 2 (< *haikā*) where? MG 22:7. With prep. **mn haka** from where, whence? MG 204:2. **haka huit** Jb 161:2 where wast thou? ; **mn haka huan** Gy 355:9 (var. DC 22. 352 **huin** cf. also MG 472:bottom and n. 1) whence did we come into being?

haka 3 = **hak 1**, MG 91 n. 1. **haka . . . haka** former . . . latter, the one . . . the other. **abatar haka** Q 41:28 after that; **maṣbuta haka mistadra uhaka mithambla** ATŠ II no. 411 the one (: the former) baptism is in order, but the other (: the latter) is spoilt.

haka 4 AM 204 a place-name, Akka (?) BZ Ap. II).

hakanuta a var. of **kaṣuta** Jb 108:13 (cf. ibid. Ap. II.

hakuat = **akuat** (q.v.).

hakia DC 22. 409 a var. of **lhaka** Gs 18:22 (v.s. **haka 1**).

hakima 1 (חַכִּימָא, ܚܟܝܡܐ) wise. St. abs. **hakim** MG 60:antep., 124:6. Fem. sg. **hakimta, hakimtia.** Pl. masc. **hakimia. mindam d-lahakim** v.s. **mindam; hakima d-kulhun saklia** Jb 272:15 wiser than all the fools; **hakimia bnapšaihun** Gy 176:13 (who are) wise according to their own opinion; **bhakimia mihšib** DC 22. 211 (var. Gy 218:4 **bhakimia mhašib**) is counted with the wise var. (he counted him with . . .); **lahakimta audiltan biahud** Jb 117:3 f. no wise-woman (: midwife) assisted at my birth in Jewry. With encl. pers. pron.: **hakimit** Gy 127:4, 17 thou art wise MG 87:ult.

hakima 2 = **hakma. hakima d-lahazilak** Jb 26:1 how long didst thou not see?

hakimuta ML 111:8 = **hukumta.**

hakma, hakima 2 (**kma** corroborated by **ha**) how much, how long MG 206:12. **hakma šnia** Gy 156:6 how many years.

hal 1 (**ha**+prep. **l**) exclamation of address and greeting: O, Hail (Nöld. & Lidzb. 'Yes for . . .') MG 81:10. **hal hiia** CP 9:ult. f., Q 4:8, 12, 15 ff., **hal hiia qadmaiia** CP 48:2, Q 22:21, ML 63:11, cf. n. 1 and MMII 159; **hal aba d-ʿutria** CP 48:7, Q 22:24 = ML 64:2; **hal iuzaṭaq manda d-hiia** CP 48:8, ML 64:2 f.; **hal haiaiun anašia kšiṭia** CP 48:11 f., ML 64:4; **hal hiia rurbia** CP 9:ult. f., ML 11:6; **hal iukabar ziua** ML 11:9, CP 10:7.

hal 2: Gl. 71:13 **hal** حال *dispositio* حلول كننده.

hala 1, hila 1 (חָלָא, ܚܳܠܳܐ LS) sand, soil, dust, stone (?). **ṭuria d̲-hala** RD B 37, 39 stony (?) hills; **haṭarata d̲-hala** RD B 37, 39, 41 mounds of soil; **hala mn iama** Gy 194:5 sand from the sea; **hala huilh̲** (var. AD **hila**, B omits) dust lay on it, hiding it; **nihibṭun hala** RD B 29, cf. also 30 they tramp the soil; **miblia d̲-hala** DC 43 J 138, DAb loads of sand; **hala** (var. *hila*) **lšumia nisaq** AM 207:7 dust will rise to the sky; **masa uhila** Gy 9:4 dirt and dust; **ulašabiq d̲-hala** (var. **hala d̲-**) **napil ʿlh̲** DAb (var. RD B 103 f.) and does not let dust fall on it; **turia d̲-hala** RD 37, 39; **hila uhala** AM. Gl. 84:10 **hala** رمل *arena* ريك.

hala 2 (חלא, ܚܰܠܳܐ, خَلّ Akk. *ḫallu*? LS) vinegar. **hala taqupa** DC 23. 768 strong vinegar (mod. us. only *toqfa*). Gl. 71:11 defectively خلّ *acetum* سركه.

hala 3 Jb 140:5 obscure, cf. II. 136 n. 4 (where Lidzb. thought of an allusion to חַלָּה the share of the dough, or of ܚܰܠܬܳܐ water-pitcher; but both should be ***halta 3**).

halab (حَلَب) 204 Aleppo.

halaita a var. of **halita** (s. **halia 1**).

halala (rt. **HLL II**) a ritually pure layman qualified to act as slaughterer or corpse-bearer (before and after both acts special purification being required MMII Ind.).

halalta (nom. act. pa. of **HLL II**) purification, rinsing, consecration, 'rinsing' or 'washing' water (name given to water poured by the server into the sacramental cup after the sacramental 'wine' has been drunk, also water similarly brought from the jordan and poured over the ***margna*** at the end of the ***masiqta***) ML xxiii n. 2, WW 253. **ʿu šga halalta** ATŠ I no. 181 if he made a mistake about the ***h***; **uhalin šagin halalta uqarin masqata** ATŠ I no. 38 and those that make an error about the rinsing water when reciting the ***m***; **ʿu halalta lašta** DC 36 no. 191 if he did not drink the rinsing water; **ušta halalta** Morg. 215/17:11 f, **štia halalta** CP 43:15 Lond. roll A 241, **ništia halalta** Lond. roll A 466; **dria halalta** Oxf. roll f 47 take the rinsing water; **nidria halalta** Lond. roll A 770; **halalta** Q 19:18, 20:32, PD 562, 1609, 16011, 1674, 1724, Oxf. roll f 257, 349, 629 f., 812 f., 851 ff. etc.

halba (חָלְבָא, ܚܰܠܒܳܐ) (*a*) milk, (*b*) (milky) juice MG 107:1. (*a*) **halba ʿriba** AM 29:2 (*and often*) mixed milk (from the breasts of several women BZ 5 b. 4); **mišai uhalbai** P.A. xii my butter and my milk; **d̲-mzabna(n) halbaiin** Gy 183:10, 13, Gs 31:3 (women) that sell their milk (i.e. suckle other women's children for money); similarly **uhalbaiin mzabnan** RD C 10; (*b*) **halba d̲-iaruqa** DC 45 the juice of herbs.

halbania (adj. from **halba**) milky, milk-white (waters). Sg. not found. **mn iardna hiuara halbania šatitun** DC 35 ye shall drink milk-white potations from a white jordan.

halbus lilita DC 43 F 7 name of a lilith.

haluna (cf. חַלּוֹן) DC 40. 549 hole, perforation, orifice, vagina (?).

halia 1 (act. pt. pe. of **HLA I**) sweet, agreeable, pleasant, kind(ly). Fem. **halita 1** MG 153:22, var. **halaita, hilita** DC 40. 89. Pl. masc. **haliia.** Used also substantivally **halia** Gy 176:16 f. that which is sweet, something sweet MG 299:18. **miša halia** DC 30 sweet oil; **mia haliia** sweet (wholesome) water; **halia basima mn marira** Gy 288:8 the sweet is pleasanter than the bitter (as a substantive, cf. also 176:16 f. above); **marirtia anat lau halaita** DC 40. 84 f. thou art bitter, not sweet; **qaina halia** DC 41 sugar-cane; **qintaikun halita** DC 42 your sweet hymn; **br halia** s. **br** compounds; **šidta halita** AM 187:2 an agreeable year; **halia bla marira ṭarilh̲** Gs 3:3 cf. Ginzā 425 n. 2.

halia 2, hilia 1 (cf. **hala 1** and Syr. ܚܶܠܳܝܳܐ LS, Akk. *ḫaltu* 'alunite stone' Thompson: *Dict. of Ass. Chemistry* 117) gems, precious stones. **sandlia hilia** Jb 273:14 sandals of precious stones; **zarin ušarin hilia šarin uzarin marganiata** Jb 179:12 f. they sow and spread precious stones and pearls. **aitai hilik** Jb 81:7 bring (fem.) thy (fem.) precious stones!; **hilia umargania** WedF 37:middle precious stones and pearls. Often with **marganiata** cf. Jb ii 85 n. 8. **bṣafṭih̲ hilia** CP 364:11, CP trs. p. 239 n. 3. Sg. **halita 2** (q.v.). **šahpa d̲-ʿlanla halia** Jb 131:15 the leaves of the trees are precious stones; **hilai** (var. **haliai**) **umarganiai habrai** Gs 131:paen. (var. DC 22. 511) my precious stones and pearls are my companions.

halia 3 a var. of **halin** MG 162 n. 1.

halia 4 act. pt. pe. of **HLA II** (q.v.).

haliaiil (rt. **HLA I**) DC 40. 1002 an angel.

haliuta 1 (rt. **HLA I**) sweetness. St. cstr. **haliut. haliut qala** Gy 4:12 sweetness of the voice; **haliuta d̲-hazin alma** Jb 176:5 the sweetness of this world.

haliuta 2 (rt. **HLA II**) AM 219:11 a disease of the grain crops, a form of blight BZ 133 n. 7.

halik, halip a corruption of **hauik** (q.v.) BZ 181 n. 3.

halliliš Ṣâb.'s AM a var. of **hilailiš** (q.v.).

halin (האלין, ܗܳܠܶܝܢ) these, those. Used for both genders (as a pl. of **hazin 1, haza 1**), MG 22 n. 3, 54. Used both as a demonstr. adj. and an independent demonstr. MG 339 ff. As demonstr. adj.: **halin nišmata** Gy 66:8 etc. these souls; **halin kulhun ʿubadia** Gy 286:19; **bhalin pugdamia kasiia** CP 57:14, Q 26:19; **halin ʿbidata** Gs 56:5 etc. After the noun: **malakia halin d̲-** Gy 45:9 these angels which; **maṭarata halin** CP 76:4, Q 35:11; **šumhata halin kasiata** CP 25:9, Q 7:27, 13:1; **ṭabauata halin** Gy 286:20. Emphasized by **hinun: halin hinun mia hiia atin** Jb 4:14 f. this living water cometh. As independent demonstr. (: correlatively): **halin d̲-azlin** Gs 30:20 these which go; **halin d̲-kanpia** Gy 35:8; **halin d̲-apkia miṣria uhalin d̲-mšania kudkia** Gs 105:16 f.; fem. **halin d̲-mzabna halbaiin** Gs 31:3 etc. (v.s. **halba** (*a*)) etc.

halip s. **halik.**

halita 1 fem. of **halia 1** (q.v.).

halita 2 sg. of **halia 2** (q.v.). The form and example below support an etym. from حِلْيَة contra Jb ii 86 n. **halita d̲-hᶜ kisuna d̲-lanqiba** DC 44 a precious stone, which is an unpierced pearl.

halita 3 in **halitaihun** Gy 256:9 a var. of **hiltaiun** Leid. (s. **hilta**).

halka v.s. **haka 1**.

halpa 1, hil(a)pa (2) (חִלְפָּא, ܚܠܦܐ Löw 167) willow. **klila d̲-halpa** ATŠ II no. 90 a willow-wreath.

halpa 2 Sh. ʻAbd.'s copy's var. of **hilpa** Gy 263:13 ff.

halṣa, haṣa (חַרְצָא Chr. Pal. ܚܨܐ Syr. ܚܨܐ H. חֲלָצַיִם Ges., LS) hip, back, middle MG 54:paen. f. Pl. **halṣia** hips, loins. **uata lhalṣa ᶜtlh̲** AM 7:1 and there is a mark on her hip; **mn riš uhalṣa udinba** HG from beginning, middle, and end; **kiuan šaria halṣh̲** DC 22. 332, var. **kiuan šdia halṣh̲** Gy 336:2 Saturn unbindeth his loins; **lhalṣa qarba šahla mn halṣa uatia bliba** Jb 124:8 f. she approacheth the hip, she leaveth the hip and cometh to the heart; **laritlh̲ halṣh̲ bdahalta** Gy 6:7 his loins never trembled with fear; **asria bhalṣaiun** Gy 25:15 they gird up their loins; **humarta d̲-halṣh̲** Gy 118:22, **humarta d̲-halṣai** Gy 164:18 his, my spine, backbone MG 468:6; **himiana bhalṣh̲ asarlh̲** Jb 137:9 he bound the girdle on his loins; **asaralh̲ lhaua bhalṣh̲** Gy 219:13 she bound it on Eve's loins; **halṣa d̲-abuia** Jb 6:2; **halṣh̲** RD B 19; **hašta asar halṣak** DC 48 now gird up thy loins; **mn halṣh̲ npaq** DC 34 issued from its side; **šuba himiania d̲-ziua bhalṣai ᶜsirlia** DC 43c:3, DC 37. 300 f. seven girdles of radiance I tied about my loins; **uhalṣai smiklia bbistirqa** DC 26. 545 and my loins rest on the couch.

halṣiᶜil DC 22 .154, **halṣᶜil** Gy 159:15 an angel or protecting spirit Ginzā 168 n. 1.

halqa 1 (حَلْقَة) something round; ring, name given to the letter **a** because of its round form MMII 243 n. 2. Var. **hilqa 2. šuba halqia ušuba gualqia** DC 12. 75, Lond. roll B 154 seven circles and seven enclosures.

halqa 2 DC 22. 11 a var. of **hilqa 1** Gy 11:1.

halša 1 (ܚܠܫܐ LS) bolt, (door-)pin, bar Jb 127 n. 9. Pl. **halšia 1. halšia uabaria** Jb 130:1, 274:7 ff. bars and bolts; **halšak uabarak** Jb 130:5 thy bar and thy bolt.

***halša 2** (H.-Aram. rt. חלש to be weak, Syr. der. ܚܠܫܐ), found only in pl. **halšia 2,** def. var. **hlšia** the weak IM Gl. **uqal halšia d̲-mitbria** AO 9/1937 96:paen. and the voice of the weak who are broken (Gordon).

halta 1 (Lidzb. arbitrarily from **HLL I**) breach, rift (?) Ginzā 208 n. 3; or = **hala 1** (?). **kursih̲ ᶜl halta d̲-tibil rmilh̲** Gy 208:4 he set his throne in the precipice (?) of the earth.

halta 2 in **uhaltaiun** DC 22. 226 a var. of **uhiltaiun** Gy 232:4 (v.s. **halta**).

haltam (= ***lhatam** analogous to **halka** s. **haka 1**) DC 12. 230, Lond. roll B 480, DC 40. 182 thither.

ham 1 (P. هم) also. Only in late texts, esp. rubrics. **utraham ham bšumad̲-nišimta** DC 42. 356 and recite the 'Devotions' also in the name of the soul; **uham biaminh̲ matnalun** CP 352:8 and he puts them also with his right hand; **ham kd̲** (P. همچون) Q 46:23 at the same time as MG 465:15 f.

ham 2 (St. emph. חָמָא, ܚܡܐ, H. חָם Ar. حَمٌ Akk. *emu* Ges.) father-in-law. With suff. **hamu** her father-in-law. St. emph. not found, even st. abs. was still unknown to Nöld. MG 99:9 f. **upagubh̲ ham uhamath̲** DC 21 = JRAS 1937 594:33 and her father- and mother-in-law met her; **lašalmat lbit hamu** Jb 72:1 she was unsuitable for her father-in-law's house; **kd̲ baiia d̲-tizal lbit hamu** DC 48. 227 when she wishes to go to her father-in-law's house.

ham 3 in **ubit ham** Gs 113:19 (var. Leid. **ubhatam**, influenced by **hatam** l. 18) read **lbit haka** to my house here (?), cf. Ginzā 560 n. 2.

ham 4 (rt. **HUM** = **HMM**?) a spirit of light ML 280. **ham ziua** Gy 145:21, Q 7:1, 9:11, CP 143:15 (see Index), ML 171:3 cf. ibid. n. 1.

hama (Ar. حَمٌّ) DC 51:coloph. distress, affliction (vs. **guṣa**). Mod.

hamadan (همدان) AM 202 Hamadan.

ḥamam (Ar. حمام) Morg. 273:1 bath. St. emph. **ḥamama** Morg. 273:3. Mod.

hamama a var. of **hamima.**

hamamulai CP 69:9, trs. p. 46 n. 7, Q 31:21 bis, Morg. 232/52:ult. f., ML 84:8 f., **hamam ᶜulai** name of some baptismal springs (the 2nd part of the name is **ᶜulai** = Karun. May refer to Shushtar, where there are hot springs on the Kārūn river?), cf. also ML 280.

hamamᶜil Gy 159:14 a genie.

hamar 1 st. abs. and cstr. of **hamra** MG 29:8. St. abs. is used as a proper name of a personified being Jb 4 n. 4. **hamar kana** Jb 2:10 (var. DC **hamra kana**), Par 15 fo. 12b = Par 25 fo. 16b (var. **himar**), WedF 37, ATŠ II no. 317 etc. the vine-stock (originally 'pitcher of wine', cf. **kana d̲-hamra** Gy 392:6).

hamara 1, himara, hmara (חֲמָרָא, ܚܡܪܐ LS, H. חֲמוֹר, חֲמֹר Ges.) pack-animal, ass, donkey. St. abs. and cstr. **hamar 2.** Fem. **hamarta.** Pl. **hamaria,** fem. **hamarata. kd̲ hamara abatar hamarata** DC 46. 241:14 like a jack-ass after she-asses; **ᶜl hamara d̲-parzla rkibna** DC 37. 357 on an iron ass do I ride; **zabad d̲-hamara** AM 127:penult. asses' butter milk (should be . . . **hamarta**); **hamaria uaqnia** Gy 387:19 f. asses and sheep; **kd̲ hamaria tišauinun** DC 44. 1039 she will make them like pack-animals; **hamarta d̲-dirat nura upihrat** ATŠ I no. 256 a she-ass which dwelt in fire and flew; **hamar ligria** AM 42 donkey legs (?).

hamara 2 (חַמָּרָא, ܚܡܪܐ) ass-driver, drover. **hamara simsira** Oxf. roll g 618, Or. 326:20 drover (and) broker.

hamara 3 (a doublet of **hamra,** formed secondarily from the st. abs.) vintage, wine. Pl. **hamaria. atmar . . . uhamaria šapir nihun** AM 278:28 fruits and vintage-grapes will be fair.

hamata (חֲמָתָא, ܚܡܳܬܐ) mother-in-law MG 99:9. **ham uhamath̠** s. **ham 2**; **hamata ukalta** Jb 169:1 mother-in-law and daughter-in-law. Gl. 69:1 **hmata** [*sic*] حماة *socrus* مادر زن.

hambaga (ܗܰܡܒܳܓܐ) (*a*) enemy, adversary, antagonist IM Gl., (*b*) opposition, hostility, hostile antagonism (= **hambaguta**) Jb ii 64 n. 3. Pl. **hambagia** PD 1324. (*a*) **šuba hambagia** ATŠ I no. 141; **šuba hambagak hun** Gy 324:5, Q 66:31; **malka hambaga** AM 266:1; **hšuka hambaga d̠-nhura hu** DC 36; **litlh̠ hambaga nukraia** Gy 95:25; **man d̠-hambaga lnhura hauilh̠** Gy 332:ult. f.; **hambaga lnhura** Q 51:26; **hambaga lhšuka** ibid., pl. **hambagia** PD 1324; **bit hambagh̠ ubit bildbabh̠** Gs 22:19; (*b*) Rare and difficult to distinguish from (*a*), cf. **hambaga lnišimta lahauia** DC 34 there should be nothing adverse (or no adversary?) to the soul; **šuba hulia hambaga utrisar hulia ridpa** Jb 60:6 (the numeral speaks for a concrete noun, but the parallelism with **ridpa** for an abstr. one).

hambaguta (abstr. noun from **hambaga**) enmity, hostility MR 35:middle, Jb II 64 n. 3. **lamarlh̠ ʿl hambaguta** Gy 93:25 he said (hist. pres.) to him nothing about the hostility; **bhambaguta niqmun** Gy 99:1; **bhambaguta hun** Gy 94:22; **hun bhambaguta** Gy 109:16 they rebelled; **šuba lhambaguta d̠-mana qam** Gs 110:21 the Seven rebelled against the M.; **alma d̠-hambaguth̠ labaṭla** Gs 72:11 f. the world whose hostility endeth not; **bhambaguta ʿtlabaš** DC 34. 766 is clothed with unfriendliness.

hambala (nom. ag. pe. from **HBL I**) destroyer, destructive MG 76:18, sometimes: destruction (= **hambalta**) MG 120:ult. f. Pl. **hambalia. hambala d̠-hiia lahza** Gy 353:18, 354:4 the destroyer who saw not the Life; **mn bišia umn hambalia** Gy 250:8; **sainia uhambalia** Gs 24:5; **mia tahmia anatun . . . hambalia anatun** DC 51 ye are stagnant waters . . ., ye are destructive.

hambalta (nom. act. pa. from **HBL I**) AM 242:17 destruction, ruin.

hambaria s. **humbaria.**

hambugaita Oxf. roll 371, **hambukaita** DC 43 a demon.

hambura 1 (cf. חֲבוּרָא, חֲבוּרְתָּא, ܚܽܘܒܳܪܐ) company, association, fellowship, companionship, comradeship, fig. fellow-feeling, conjunction, union. Var. **hanbura.** Doubtful. Fem. **praṭ rqiha bhambura aminṭul d̠-hambura lruha unišimta ʿštaulat** ATŠ II no. 294 the sky gaped open (**hambura 2**), because conjunction (**hambura 1**) had been made between the spirit and the soul; **mazruta . . . tša mitqalia lagṭa bhanbura d̠-marba** ATŠ I no. 168 the seed . . . takes on 9 *mithqals* in its conjunction with the womb (or in the cavity? of the womb, cf. **hambura 2**).

hambura 2 (cf. חַבּוּרְתָּא wound, ܚܒܽܘܪܬܐ id., ܚܰܒܽܘܪܐ 2, pitfall) hole, opening, abyss, orifice, chasm. **praṭ rqiha bhambura** s. **hambura 1**; (of the navel:) **puma qadmaia hu . . . hambura d̠-hatmuih̠ brazia** DC 27. 271 it is the first orifice . . . a hole which they sealed by mysteries. Cf. also the ambiguous **hanbura** s. **hambura 1.**

hamgai, hamgagai a spirit of light and his father ML 7 n. 2, 280. **hamgai ziua br hamgagai ziua** CP 6:7 f., Gy 314:6, Q 2:25 = ML 7:6 f.

hamgiʿil JRAS 1937 595, DC 12. 1248, **hamgʿiil** Oxf. roll b 508, DC 40 an angel.

hamu 1 (**ham 2** q.v. with pers. suff. of the 3rd p. sg. fem.) her father-in-law.

hamu 2 (P. همان the same, coll. pron. *hamun* with apocope of the final *n*?) the same (?), or a proper name of a demon (?). **daiuia d̠-lašamia d̠-npaq mn hamu daiua** DC 37. 535 demons who hearken not, who came out of the same demon (or of the demon H.?).

hamida (from חמד). **himta** (q.v.), hot passion, lust, covetousness. **mutana utigra uhamida** AM 166:15 f. pest, strife, and lust.

hamima (חֲמִימָא, ܚܰܡܺܝܡܳܐ) warm, hot, feverish, incensed, fiery, high (of fever). St. abs. **hamim** MG 124:9. Var. st. emph. **hamama** BZ 112 n. 3. Fem. st. emph. **hamimtia.** Pl. masc. **hamimia. mia hamimia** (*often*) hot spring(s), boiling water; **hamimia ruianh̠** AM 24:7 his temperament is fiery (: choleric); **mutana hamima** AM 181:ult. an epidemic of fever; **šata hamimtia** AM 280:26 a high fever; **hamimtia uqaruštia** RD C 4 = DAb hot and cold.

hamisar (Talm. חמיסר, Syr. ܚܡܫܐ ܥܣܪ) fifteen. Masc. MG 188 (Fem. **asar uhamiš** MG 189).

hamira (חֲמִירָא, ܚܡܺܝܪܐ, خَمير) leaven, leavened bread, sour dough, yeast MG 116:30. Var. **himira. ninsib mn himira** Gy 259:22, paen. f. (var. DC 22 **ninsab mn hamira**) we will take some of the leaven Ginzā 259 n. 3; **nsib mn himira** Gy 261:14 (var. D **nsab mn hamira**), 262:4 (var. BD **hamira**).

hamirah AM 198 a place-name BZ Ap. II.

hamiš fem. of **hamša** (q.v.).

hamišma five hundred MG 190:1.

hamka, hamkia like, as. Only in Mod. Mand., still used (pron. *hemke*). Gl. 144:13 **hmka** [*sic*] كما *sicut* همچنين; 144:14 f. كنحو , كمثل *secundum, circa, sicut* مانند.

hamlʿil lbuša DC 6 and 36 no. 252 a personified girdle.

hamnu (< הֵי מִנְּהוֹן, Talm. היי מנייהו), **hamnia** (< הֵי מִנַּהּ) (*a*) (**hamnu**) which (of them), (*b*) (**hamnia**) which (therefrom) MG 94:11 ff., 343:3, 436:2. (*a*) **bhamnu atra** Gy 362:17, **kursia dilia hamnu hu** Gy 211:12; (*b*) **bhamnia tihilpun** Gy 368:3 in what will ye pass over?

hamra (חַמְרָא, ܚܰܡܪܐ) wine, red liquid, water in which white grapes or sultanas have been pressed out. St. abs. **hamar** (s.v.). Pl. **hamria** AM 181:17 f. vintage-grapes. **ʿtarubia hamra bmia** s. **ARB I** ethpa. inf. **azmiuz hamra** s. **azmiuz**; **hamra raza d̠-marba hu** PD 1591 wine is the mystery of the womb (cf. WiW 68:19 ff. and n. 1); **hamra mlabaš raz hamra** s. **LBŠ** pa.

hamrah (P. همراه) companion. **uʿgira uhamrah dilak** AM 152:18 and the hired servant and thy companion.

hamranita (rt. **HMR I**) reddened, inflamed. **aina hamranita** JRAS 1937 593:7 inflamed eye JRAS 1943 p. 170:17.

hamruta (abstr. noun from **hamra**) Gy 389:13 (miscop. DC 22. 385 **maruta**) vintage, grape harvest.

hamša masc., **hamiš** fem. (ܚܰܡܫܳܐ masc., ܚܰܡܶܫ fem.) five MG 187:paen., 32:paen. Varr. masc. **hamš** Zotb. 228 right:26, **hamšia** (used substantively of the five senses, or sensitory organs, but sporadically also for **hamšin** fifty MG 189:19). **hamša habšaba** (often in later texts) Thursday; **hamša utrisar bhilqaihun lamdabria** Gy 11:1 the Five (planets without Sun and Moon) and the Twelve (signs of the Zodiac) govern not their fate Ginzā 13 n. 4; **hamša singiania d̠-baita** Gy 99:3 the 5 rulers of the world (: the planets) Ginzā 105 n. 3; **hamša šauun hirba** Gy 99:12 f. the Five (: planets) created the sword; **hamša zidania** Gy 96:10 the five ruffians (: planets); **hamiš dmauata** Gy 96:17 five figures; **asar uhamiš** fem. form of **hamisar** (q.v.); **hamišma** s.v. **nišimta d̠-azla bhamšia** DC 34. 471, 476 the soul that walketh within the five (senses); **d̠-šria bhamšia** DC 34. 476 that dwelleth in the five (senses).

hamšaia Gy 27:20 A, **hamšiaia** (often), **hamšiiaia** Gy 51:5 B, **hamšiaiia** PD 305 fifth MG 192:top.

hamšia s. **hamša.**

hamšiaia, hamšiaiia, hamšiiaia s. **hamšaia.**

hamšiaita fem. of **hamšaia, hamšiaia.**

hana (ܚܢܳܐ, Jew.-Aram. חינא LS, H. חֹצֶן Ges.) lap, loins, embrace, privy parts MG 100:14. Pl. **hania 1. hanh̠** Lond. roll B 317, AM 14 etc. his lap, his loins; **hana d̠-ʿmh̠** JRAS 1937 591:21 the lap of his mother; **kib hana, kiba hana, kiba d̠-hania** AM (often) pain in the loins; **bhana gubria** Gy 23:22 (DC 22. 23 **bhana d̠-gubria**) in the embrace of men; **ruha hʿ d̠-iatba bhana** Or. 330:7 she is the spirit (Ruha) situated on the privy parts; **mištahna upahra abatar plan kd̠ hanh̠ abatar ʿkarth̠** DC 45 and she yearns hotly and flies after N., just as her loins (yearn) for his ploughing (: act of coition). But **hanai** Jb 62 n. 6 a var. of the demonstr. **hania 2** (q.v.).

hanai uhananai (cf. H. חֲנַנִי and חֲנַנְיָה) Jewish proper names. **rab(ai) hanai urab hananai** Jb 75:10 f. **hanai uhananai** Jb 75:7.

hananʿiil DC 22 = **hannʿil** Gy 167:12 (cf. foll.).

hananʿil uhanʿil Gy 150:23 two theophorous names from **HNN.**

hanaqtia, var. **-iqtia** (rt. **HNQ**) fem. strangling. V.s. **maluaita.** Pl. **haniaqiata** s.v. Var. sg. **hnaqtia** s.v.

hanata (rarely), **hanath̠, hanatia,** pl. masc. **hanatun,** fem. **hanatin** (demonstr. interj. הא and אין with אָתֵה, אָתָה, אָתְהוֹן, אָתְהֵין Nöld.). that, pl. those MG § 83 p. 91 and n. 3. Nöld. took back his former derivation of the form *Mundart* 26, cf. AF 229. Used as both a demonstr. adj. and an independent demonstrative MG 337 ff. As demonstr. adj.: **hanatia mdinta** AM 262:1, **hanath̠ alma** Gs 5:6, **hanath̠ ziua** Gy 10:22, **hanath̠ dmuta** Gy 134:ult., **hanatun mia** Gy 87:18, Q 1:21, **hanath̠ zma** Gy 224:12, **hanath̠ maṭarta** Gs 28 ff.; **bhanath̠ mapiqta** Gy 26:19, 27:1, **bh̠ bhanath̠ pira** Gy 69:4, **hanatun malkia** Gy 387 (*often*), **bhanath̠ dara batraia** Gy 29:ult.; after the noun: **alma hanath̠** Gy 71:21, **ʿlana hanath̠** Q 59:8, **bdara hanath̠** Gy 29:4, **blbuša hanath̠** Gs 59:11, 21, **škinta hanath̠ d̠-** Gy 12:7, 32:19, **ʿutria hanatun** Gy 293:1. As an independent demonstrative: **hanath̠ hu d̠-** Gs 5:6 that is he who; **hanatia d̠-** Par XIV no. 126 that which; **hanath̠ hu zuadaikun** Gs 129:15 that is your viaticum; **hanatun d̠-haizin abdia** Gy 220:14 those who do so.

hanbura s. **hambura.**

hanguria (inf. haf. of **NGR**) Morg. 269/29:14 to repress, restrain, check.

hangia DC 22. 52 a var. of **hingia** Gy 55:23 (v.s. **hinga**).

handama (ܗܰܕܳܡܳܐ < P. اندام, هندام, LS) joint, limb, membrum MG 51:anteantep. Var. **hindama.** Pl. **handamia. handamh̠ gaṭin** AM 9:13 he is slender of limb; **umuma bhandamh̠ nasib** AM 23:penult. and he gets a blemish on his limb; **hindamia** CP 18:2, Q 20:15, var. **handamai** my joints; **maiil umapiq handamh̠** Gy 280:14 he moveth his membrum in and out.

handan Jb 111:9, var. A **hindan** a woman's name, used also as a *malwâša* name.

handašman, handšman (P. انجمن, older, *hanǧaman*) Gy 390:12, 392:17 council, assembly MG 2 n. 1. Further varr. **hanšiman, hanšaman, handišman, hanšman, hanšamin.**

handusia inf. haf. of **ANDZ** (q.v.).

hanuta 1 (abstr. noun for **HNN**) favour, grace, kindness, clemency. **bhanuta d̠-anašia nasgia** AM 38:ult. he goes in people's good graces; **ṭab . . . ulmipta baba d̠-hanuta** AM 138:3 good (for . . . and) for opening the gate of clemency.

hanuta 2 (חָנוּתָא, ܚܳܢܽܘܬܳܐ Ar. loan-w. حانوت Ges. s. חָנוּת) tavern. **hamra bhanuta** Jb 95:6, 247:16, RD C 12 wine in a tavern.

hanzaga, hanzaqa DC 46:558, DC 40:578 an exorcizing spirit.

hanzama(n) (a doublet of **handašman** and varr.) multitude, assembly, community, company. Pl. **hanzamata** (?). **kulhun bnia mata ulhanzaman** DC 44. 569 f. (varr. **ulhanzama, ulhanzamata**) all the citizens and assemblies; **ulhanzaman uʿl matauata** DC 26. 561, DC 44 and the multitude and the towns; **dukta d̠-iatbia hazaman** (read **hanzaman**) DC 44. 1226 a place where a company of people sit; **ubnh̠ ubnath̠ . . . uhanzaman** DC 46. 441:3 husband (read **zauh̠**?) and his sons and daughters.

hanzaqa s. **hanzaga:**

hanzura (cf. ܙܥܪܘܪܐ, ܫܡܠܘܙܐ, *mespilus germanica* Löw 288:20) loquot; **hanzura hu** DC 41 (illustrated) it is a loquot-tree; **hanzura miua sqila** DC 3, ŠQ 19:23 loquot, the burnished fruit.

hania 1 pl. of **hana.**

hania 2 (הָאִנִּין, ܗܐܢܝܢ) demonstr. pron. pl.: those (originally fem., then used also for masc.). Overlooked by Nöld. MG 89:10 f. A full var. **hanin** (s.v.). **ulaminšina lhania bauatai** Jb 62:4 and I will not forget those prayers of mine (var. D **lhanai** might have been influenced by the suff. of **bauatai**). As an independent demonstrative: **uhania d̠-mbarkilak** DC 3, DC 38 and those who bless thee.

haniaqiata (rt. **HNQ**) strangling (fem. pl.). **uruhia bišata uhaniaqiata** DC 40. 823 f. and evil, throttling spirits.

haniil, haniʿil, hanʿil (frequent in exorcisms) an angel (of compassion).

hanik (< *hâ* + *illen* + *k*, cf. Talm. הנך, Syr. ܗܢܘܟ, Chr. Pal. ܗܠܝܢܟ) demonstr. pron.: those (pl. of **hak**) MG 54:9, 91:2 Syntax MG 338 f. As a demonstr. adj.: before the noun: **hanik drašia** ML 239:7, **hanik alip alip ʿutria** Q 54:23; after the noun: **almia hanik d̠-nhura** Gy 163:14, **šuria hanik d̠-parzla** Gy 159:9, **mia siauia hanik d̠-** Gy 86:16, **iahuṭaiia hanik d̠-** Gy 46:11; separated from the noun; **mn šuba lbušia nisbit hanik d̠-** Gy 169:7. Gl. 26:2 missp. اولاء, اولايك *illi, illae* اينها.

hanin 1 (a full var. of **hania 2** q.v.) those, these: **hanin zamnata** Or. 333:7 these summonings.

hanin 2 Gy 23:22 A a var. of **hinin** ibid. CD MG 89 n. 2.

hanipa (חֲנִפָא, ܚܢܦܐ Ges. s. חנף) pagan, heathen. Found only in pl. **hanipia** Jb 59:15 false gods, cf. II 63 no. 5, Furl. *I Nomi* 430.

haniputa (abstr. noun from **hanipa**). Jb 176:5 heathenry, apostasy, worship of false gods ii 63 n. 5.

haniqtia s. **hanaqtia.**

hanka s. **hinka.**

hansa in **mamlaka lhansa** AM 204:5 a place-name, var. **mamlaka ʿl kansa** Ṣâb.'s AM (v.s. **dar 2**).

hanʿil s. **hananʿil.**

hanšama = **hanšuma.**

hanšaman, hanšamin varr. of **hand(a)šman.**

hanšuma, hanšma (cf. **handašman**) company, association, associates, retinue. **trişia bnia uhamšumh̠** P.A. xii (var. DC 12 **hanšamh̠**) established are his sons and his associates.

hanšiman a var. of **hand(a)šman.**

hanšma s. **hanšuma.**

has (ܚܣ LS 221b) always with encl. prep. ܠ (: ܚܣܠ) interj.: beware lest . . ., God forbid lest . . . MG 61:anteantep. f., 89:top. Syntax MG 468:paen.f., 483:top. **haslak d̠-** Gy 130:21 etc. God forbid that thou . . .; **haslaikun d̠-** Gy 292:13 far be it from you that; **haslh̠ lnhura . . . d̠-** Jb 97:1 heaven forfend that light should . . .; **hasla lpuma d̠-nimar šiqra** DC 46. 171:5 God forbid that (his) tongue should utter falsehood.

hasumtia (rt. **HSM**) adj. fem. envious. Masc. not found. **aina hasumtia** JRAS 1937 593: penult. envious eye. DC 43 D 68.

hasin baša (حسن باشا) Zotb. 230 left 1 a name.

hasina (cf. ܚܣܝܢܐ) in **hasina bṭuria ṣipria** Gs 122:19 (grammatically incorrect and doubtful). Lidzb.: *die Vöglein nehmen die Berge in Besitz.* **maria hasina** DC 37 the vigorous Lord.

hasip (חציף, ܚܨܝܦ) Jb 21:4 impudent, shameless, impertinent.

hasir (חַסִּיר Dan. 5:27, ܚܣܝܪ, H. חָסֵר, Ar. خسير) lacking, deficient, wanting, needy, poor, faulty, imperfect. The st. abs. is much more frequent than the st. emph. **hasira.** Fem. **hasirta, hasirtia.** Pl. masc. **hasiria,** fem. **hasirata.** Mg 124:7, 125:4, 154:14. **hasir ubṣir** s. **bṣir, hasirtia ubṣirtia** Gy 328:paen. id. fem. **hasira d̠-hasir ubṣir** Gy 116:17; **hasira d̠-lahua iatira** Gy 212:1; **ruha hasirta** ATŠ II no. 15 the faulty R.; **ziqa hasira d̠-kiuan** ATŠ II no. 70, 270; **šalmania d̠-lahun hasiria** DC 51; **lʿbidath̠ hasirata** Jb 221:5 f.

hasiruta (abstr. noun from **hasir**) Gy 350:4, Gs 40:8, Jb 36:11 fault, error, imperfection, deficiency.

haspa 1 (חַסְפָּא, Chr. Pal. ܚܣܦܐ, Syr. ܚܨܦܐ) clay, potsherd, clay pot. **haspa uqira** Oxf. 92 a = ML 218:5 clay and bitumen; **haspa d̠-girai** DC 45, **haspa d̠-giraia** DC 46 potsherd (used) for scraping; **haspa d̠-bgauh̠ zabad uhupia** AM 258:2 a clay pot in which there is foam and froth.

haspa 2 (cf. عصب) found only in pl. **haspia** tissues, sinews, muscles. Doubtful. **hamša haspia** ATŠ I no. 19; **haspia ugiṭria ugirmia** ATŠ I no. 246; **haspia muqra d̠-ʿuṣṭuna kulh̠ bgauaiin lgiṭ** DC 48. 18 **miška uhaspia uširiana** DC 34. 896.

hasran (st. **HSR**) lacking, harmful, inauspicious (astrol.). **tartin šaiia h̠-nirig hasran** CP 281:8 the second hour under Mars is inauspicious.

haʿšia Or. 332:17 for **haišia** (?).

hapas, hapis (= **pas** corroborated by **ha,** see both s.vv.) so, then, again. **hapas uqrun mn riš** ATŠ then recite (the *masiqta*) again from the beginning.

hapapiata (cf. חֲפָפִית, ܚܦܦܝܬܐ) eruptions, sores. **rubiana uhapapiata** AM 97:19 debility and sores.

hapura (חֲפוּרָה) Gs 3:11 green corn MG 125:13.

hapia DC 22 464 = **hipia** Gs 78:6.

hapis = **hapas. hapis hauilh̠ prahia** AM 19:9 then he will have money; **maskina hauia hapis hauilh̠** AM 26:18 he will be poor, then he will have (something).

hapiqia = **apiqia** (q.v.). **hapiqia mia** is more frequent than **apiqia mia.**

haṣa = **halṣa** (with assimil. of **l**). **haṣa hu** AM 286:11 he (governs) the loins; **kiba d̠-haṣa** DC 46. 70:2 pain in the back.

haṣapia Gy 279:11 a var. of **haṣipia** ibid. A, Sh. ʿAbd.'s copy and DC 22. 274 (v.s. **haṣip**).

haṣbia 1 (Ar. حصبة) AM often (fever with rash) poxes, measles, smallpox, or typhoid fever BZ 76 n. 1, or (= **hiṣbia**) convulsions (?).

haṣbia 2 (sg. חַצְבָא, ܚܨܒܐ) jugs, pitchers. **mia bhaṣbia** DC 44. 1038.

haṣbia 3 (prob. a concr. noun from **HṢB,** but

hardly **haṣbia 2**) Gs 44:4 mean. doubtful, Ginzā 461 n. 2, cf. also Gs 76:16, where **haṣbia** is a pt. pl. (v.s. **HṢB**).

haṣbta (rt. **HṢB**) DC 51. 83 wound (?), convulsion (?).

haṣubia 1 (prob. חֲצָבָא, ܫܪܘܦܐ) pitchers, water-pots. Sg. not found. **kḏ mia bhaṣubia** (a *qmaha*) like water in water-pots; **bhaṣubia ubṭulalia yatib** DC 20 sits in waterpots and shadows (or drippings).

haṣubia 2 (a pl. of **haṣbta**?) cuts, wounds, sores(?), convulsions(?). **haṣubia ldupna** DC 51. 82 f. wounds on the side; **haṣubia bqumth̠** DC 43 J 139, 150 wounds on his body; **šqul . . . haṣubak mn dupnh̠** DC 43 J 154 remove . . . thy wounding from his side.

haṣubtia (rt. **HṢB**) **a** kind of demons of both genders, although the form is fem. **haṣubtia zikria uhaṣubtia nuqbata** DC 43 A 29 male and female *haṣubtas*.

haṣip, haṣipa (the original form of **hasip** q.v.) bold, impudent, shameless, arrogant, impertinent. Pl. **haṣipia** Gy 279: 11 (A and most of manuscripts, Pet. has **haṣapia**) the shameless ones; **haṣipa uqašiša hauia** AM 95:15 he will be bold and hard; **qahda haṣip(a) gazim** Gy 280:4 (BCD have the correct st. abs.) he shouts, is arrogant, he threatens.

haṣiṣa (formed as an adj. of **HṢṢ** but with the meaning of pass. pt.) v.s. **HṢṢ**.

haṣir (Ar. حَصِير) AM 155:11 matting MMII 64.

haqal (Ar. حَقْل in colloquial pronunciation) field, circumference, place marked out, a given area etc. **la iadh̠** (read **laiadia**) **haqalun guh̠** DC 26, DC 40 none know their appointed place in it.

haqalta (nom. act. pa. of **HQL I**) slipping. **haqalta bligrh̠** DC 43 J 151 slipping in his foot.

haqarta (nom. act. pa. of **HQR II**) research, investigation, careful examination. **bzahruta uiadita uhaqarta** DC 36 with care, science, and minute research; **haqarta ḏ-haqar** s. **HQR** II pa. pf.

haqla (حَلْق with metath.) Gy 381:6 throat MG 74:9.

haqta DC 22. 209 a miscop of **harta** Gy 216:17 (s. **harta**).

***hara** (*حُرّ, H. *חוֹר I Ges.) free. Sg. masc. replaced by **br haria** (s. **br** and **haria**). Fem. sg. **harta**, pl. **harata** (s.vv.). Nevertheless, a sg. masc. seems to be **ahara** (s.v.).

hara in **ʿsira trisar liliata bhara** DC 45 (p. 1) read **bharša** (?).

haragta s. **hargta.**

harahun AM 203 a place-name BZ Ap. II.

harakta, harkta (a doublet of **hargta**) crookedness MG 40:11, 101:9.

haran Gy 380:11, AM 198, often in **haran gauaita** 'The Inner Haran' (HG) a place-name: Haran (: Ḥarrān?), BZ Ap. II (but in **arzia mn haran** Gy 380:10 f. Lidzb. proposed **haman** Ginzā 409 n. 2).

hararat (Ar. حرارة) AM 279:18 (var.) ardour, warmth, heat, inflammation. Varr. **ḥirarat, harata 2** BZ 185 n. 6.

hararia (cf. preced.) heat. **tanura šgira lahauia bukra ḏ-hararia** DC 46 in a heated oven; it must not be its first heat.

haraša 1 (חָרָשָׁא, ܚܪܫܐ) enchanter, wizard, magician MG 120:11. Fem. **haraštia** witch. Pl. masc. **harašia 1** MG 107 n. 2, fem. **harašata, harašiata** MG 169:6 f., var. **harašaiata. haraša mšiha** Gs 33:18 the wizard-Messiah; **gaiara uharaša** AM 91:7 a fornicator and a wizard; **harašia uzipania** Jb 174:13 f. wizards and impostors; **mn daiuia harašia umn liliata harašaiata** DC 37. 392 ff. from spell-binding demons and from spell-binding liliths; **ainaihun ḏ-šaba harašata** DC 21 the (Evil) Eye of seven witches; **akasta ḏ-harašiata** (var. **harašata**) DC 45 the fury of the witches; **liliata harašiata** Gy 51:14; **harašia uharašiata** Gs 30:22 f. wizards and witches; **šatia zma ḏ-harašata** DC 43 F 82 he is drinking the blood of witches.

haraša 2 = **harša 2** (influenced by **haraša 1**). Pl. **harašia 2** MG 107 n. 2. **haraša sakla ṭruša** Gs 2:14, 22 mute, foolish, deaf MG 326:23 f.; **aiak makluzana lharaša uduga** Gy 217:ult. f. like a towncrier to a deaf and a deaf-mute.

harat AM 128:14 name of a town: Herat. Var. Ṣâb.'s copy **harah.**

harata pl. of **harta** (q.v.).

harba, hirba (חַרְבָּא, ܚܪܒܐ) (*a*) sword, knife, (*b*) fight(ing), battle, war, (*c*) destruction, devastation, ruin, (*d*) (cf. Mod. H. חָרֵב Ginzā 591 n. 1) smitten down, sick-unto-death (?). The distinction betw. (*a*) and (*b*) is often only arbitrary. (*a*)–(*b*) **sikinia ḏ-harba** DC 40. 129 battle-knives, warlike weapons. St. abs. sg. **harb** AM 276:23 fight(ing). Pl. **harbia** AM 267:27 wars (or swords?); (*c*) **latihuia harba bʿumama** DC 43 J 10 be not his destruction by day (read **habra**? as in P.A.'s *Qaština* be not his companion by day); (*d*) Gs 134:5 doubtful.

harbuta (formed as an abstr. noun from **HRB**, but used adjectivally) destruction, destructive. **qiriata harbuta saruata** DC 43 J 92 destructive corruptive creations.

harbʿil DAb DC 12. 247 a theophorous name (used of a golden rudder-oar).

harga (rt. **HRG**) stain, blot, filing, fraying. St. abs. of **hargta** (?). **harga umuma litlh̠** CP 80:8, ML 98:10 without fraying or fault; **uharga litlaihun** Gy 250:22.

hargata, hargita s. **hargta.**

hargta (rt. **HRG**) friction, distortion, perversity, obliquity, crookedness, wrong use, misuse, ritual invalidity. MG 40:11. Varr. **hargata, hargita, harakta, harkta. hargta mšauilh̠** AM 5:11 they misuse him; **hargta umuma lašauibh̠** DC 3 and he will commit no wrong use or fault in it; **hargta labadbia** CP 371:2, 7, ult. They made no misuse of it (me). **labadbia hargta** ZDMG 1955 145a:2 they made no misuse of me; **hauiabun hargata** DC 22. 87 (var. Pet. Gy 93:1 **harkta**); **ulahuabh̠ hargita** (var. **hargta**) DC 26, DC 40 and there is no distortion in it; **laiit hargta bmasbuth̠** ATŠ II no. 403 there is no ritual irregularity in his baptism; **laiit bgauh̠ hargta** Gy 214:18 f. Leid. and DC 22. 207 (Pet. has **harkta**); **hargta ubišuta** Jb 222:4 perversion and evil.

hardabaiia, hardbaiia, hardubaiia (possibly derived from the name of a king, cf. Ὀρώδης Orodes, Artabanus) a people and a dynasty, Parthians, Persians, Sassanians (?). Further varr. **hurdbaiia, hird(u)baiia. ṭura d̠-parsaiia . . . d̠-hinun hardbaiia** HG 141; **hardabaiia nasbilh̠ ʿl malkuta** HG 135.

hardbiʿil JRAS 1937 595 an angel.

hardubaiia s. **hardabaiia.**

hardla (חַרְדְּלָא, ܚܪܕܠܐ *Sinapis* Löw 177 f.) mustard. **sinda d̠-hardla** ATŠ I no. 278 a mustard seed; **qrih̠ lmihla uhardla** DC 44. 1225 read it over salt and mustard.

harub (act. pt. of **HRB** with labialization of the vowel and with pass. meaning) waste, ruined, desolate. Pl. **harubia. ia haribta d̠-harub** DC 43 J 141 O ruined creature, that is desolate; **dukta d̠-hauia lʿmh̠ harub** AM 25:4 the place in which he was born will be (laid) waste; **ba(i)tia harubia** DC 43 ruined houses; **mahuza haruba** DC 12. 198 ruined town.

harup, harupa, haripa (חֲרִיפָא, ܚܪܝܦܐ) sharp, keen. Fem. **harupta. nhirh̠ harup** AM 87:19 his nose (is) sharp; **miṭra uglala uharupa** (var. **harupta**) **nihuia** AM 171:ult. there will be rain and hail and sharp weather.

haruta (ܚܐܪܘܬܐ) freedom, liberty, release, licence, liberation. **zmara uharuta** AM 173:4 prostitution and licence (cf. חָרוּתָא prostitute); **lharuta maṭia upaliṭ** Par 26 he will gain his freedom and escape.

harzana (cf. Mod. Syr. ܚܪܙܢܐ < T. خرزن Macl.) buffalo-whip (?). **ʿsir šuṭai ʿsira harzana barqa** DC 43 I 112 bound is my scourge, tied is the buffalo-whip on the ground.

harzunia s. **hurzunia.**

harzupa (cf. הַרְזִיפָא J, אַרְזִפְתָּא II J *hypericum barbatum*, St. John's wort Löw 320) a bitter herb. **harzupa hu marira d̠-ʿniš lakil minh̠** JRAS 1938 5:15 it is a bitter herb of which nobody eats.

harzina (etym. and meaning unknown, cf. חַצִינָא hatchet, ܚܪܙܐ amulet) Gy 118:18 doubtful.

harṭum(a) (חַרְטוֹם, ܚܪܛܘܡܐ, خُرْطُوم LS) long bill, nose, snout, trunk. **kurkia bharṭumh̠** DC 21 the crane with her bill; **harṭuma d̠-hizura** DC 43 J 136 snout of a pig.

haria pl. of ***hara** (q.v.) noblemen. Sg. **br haria** a free man, man not employed by a master (MG 17 n. 3). Fem. sg. **pt haria** Morg. 237/61:9 etc. freeborn, independent woman MG 183:ult. **haria qam uautbuia** DC 26. 565, 570, DC 40 men of rank stood and made me sit; **abda mšauilh̠ bt haria ubr haria mšauilh̠ abda** Gy 264:2 f. they make a slave into a freeman, and the freeman make they a slave.

haribta (rt. **HRB**) ruined, ravaged (fem.). V.s. **harub.**

harip(a) (v. **harup**) (*a*) sharp, keen, acute, (*b*) hasty, quick, (*c*) premature (of birth), early. Pl. **haripia.** (*a*) **miṭra uharipa** AM rain and sharp weather; **ziqa haripa** AM a keen wind; (*b*) **mimrh̠ harip** AM 93:9 he is quick of speech; **ṭizana uharipa** AM 20:16 impulsive and hasty; **taqipia haripia rugzania** Gy 279:12 overbearing, hasty, furious (pl.); (*c*) **miṭra haripa** AM 267:10 early rain; **maudala bgauh̠ haripa hauia** DC 3 birth in (: during) it will be premature; **mia haripia . . . umiṭria haripia** AM 183:18 early waters . . . and early rains (or belongs under (*a*)?).

h̠arir (Ar. حَرِير) AM 286:paen. silk (modern Mandaeans give a second meaning 'flour mixed with milk').

harkta, harakta (doublet of **hargta**) Gy 93:1, 214:19, 215:17, 307:14, Q 72:3 etc. crookedness, perversity, misuse, ill-treatment MG 40:11, 101:9.

harma (ܚܪܡܐ) fierce, wild, savage. Pl. **harmia. nimria harmia** Jb 243:2 savage leopards; **dibia harmia** DAb fierce wolves.

harmal (Ar. حَرْمَل) DC 23. 773 rue.

harmus, hurmus AM 261:20 a man's name.

harsata (rt. חרס to glow) glowing fuel, flames. **atutia nura d̠-harsata nikababh̠** DC 44. 1009 beneath a fire of glowing fuel we will roast him.

harpa s. **hurpa 1.**

harša 1 = **haraša 1** (q.v.). Pl. **haršia 1** wizards. Fem. **haršiata** (aside from other plurals, s. **haraša 1**) witches. **mnangirunin** (var. Pet. **mnangirilin**) **lharšia uharašata** DC 22. 417 (Pet. Gs 26:17 omits **haršia**) they beat wizards and witches; **tartin haršiata** DC 44 two witches.

harša 2 (חֵרְשָׁא, ܚܪܫܐ) deaf. Pl. **haršia 2, harašia 2** MG 107:5 and n. 2. **haršia udugia** Gy 29:11 the deaf and the dumb.

haršia 3 (חַרְשֵׁי, ܚܪܫܐ) enchantments, spells, magic, witchcraft, sorceries. **haršia bišia** black magic (the title of DC 45 and 46); **haršia d̠-harašata** DC 40. 1068 the sorceries of witches.

harta fem. of ***hara** (q.v.) a freeborn woman, lady. Pl. **harata** DC 26. 565, 571 etc. **harta d̠-lalbiša** Gy 216:17 a lady without a dress; **ʿnta harta** AM.

haš (3rd p. sg. pf. pe. of **HUŠ**) name of an uthra ML 280. **haš upraš ʿutra** ML 229:3; **haš kana** ML 142:3; **haš upraš kana** CP 194:12, ML 229:11.

haš d̠- (= **hašta d̠-**) when, at the time that, now when. **d̠-haš d̠-barkilh̠ lzidqa brika** DC 3 DC 53 (see CP 367:9 **haš d̠-hak**) at the time that they bless the *zidqa brika.*

h̠aša 1 (Ar. حاجة) petition, suit. **kd̠-ṭlaba d̠-h̠aša baiit** AM 151:17 when thou wishest to make a petition.

haša 2 (cf. **h̠ašašia**) bowels. Pl. **-ia** DC 48. 20. **mirta uhaša uṭahala** DC 34. 424 gall, bowels, and spleen.

hašabta 1 (nom. act. pa. and ethpa. of **HŠB**) thought, plan, scheme, plot MG 122:2 f., Jb II 17 n. 1. Pl. **hašabata. hašabta rabtia**

d̲-iušamin ʿtiqria Gy 158:18 f. the great plan of Y. has been realized; **d̲-hašabta haza huat** Gy 169:1 f. that such a plan should be realized; **bhašabta d̲-kadabta** Gy 88:16 according to the deceiving plan; **hašabta urnita d̲-hiia** Gy 213:22 f. thought and meditation on Life; **iušamin bhašabta hua** 220:9 Y. was making a plan (cf. above); **btinihta uhašabta urnita iatbia** AM 201:4 they sit sighing and in anxious thought; **hašabta ahuat qadmaita d̲-ʿutria** Jb 10:6 obscure, cf. II 17 n. 1; **mn hašabata baṭil** DC 36 comes to nought on account of plots.

hašabta 2 (nom. ag. pe. fem. of **HŠB**) schemer, plotter (fem.). **ruha hašabta lbiš** Jb 164:2 f. R., schemer of evil.

ḫašašia DC 36 no. 217 (in a list of parts of the body) seems to refer to bowels, cf. also **kabda uhašaša** Or. 329:16 liver and bowels (cf. Ar. أحشاء bowels).

hašuk, hašik, haška s. **HŠK.**

hašia DC 48. 20 = **ḫašašia.**

haškana DC 41 (with a picture of a tree) a kind of tree (?).

hašta 1 (Talm. הַשְׁתָּא, Syr. ܗܫܐ < ܗܕܐ ܫܥܬܐ) now, at this time MG 202:5. **hašta d̲-** Gy 65 (*often*) now when MG 453:4 f. (and n. 1); **mn hašta ulalam almia** DC 37. 587 from this hour unto eternity.

hašta 2 (rt. **HUŠ = HŠŠ**) suffering, passion, excitement. **(tigra) uhašta** ATŠ **(tagra)** II no. 64 strife and suffering.

hata DC 37. 567 = **ahata.** With suff. **hatkun** DC 40. 742 your sister.

hatam (**tam** corroborated by **ha**) that place, yonder, there, then. **hatam hauia mdurtin** ATŠ I no. 240 that place will be their dwelling; **uhatam mitarab hamra umia** ATŠ II 134 and then (lit. at that place, at that point the water) and wine are mingled; **lhatam** Jb 107:6 yonder (: to the other world).

hatamta (nom. act. pa. of **HTM**) sealing, signing. Used often with the meaning of 'talisman' (: sealing the demons), but also in liturgical language of certain prayers, cf. Lidzb. ZDMG lxi 695 n. 1, completed and corrected in ML 40 n. 1. Var. **htamta** IM Gl. Pl. **hatamata** used of 'sealing prayers': **bauata hatamata** Morg. 212/12:7, **qria hatamata** ML 40:10, **uqarin . . . hatamata** DC 50 **ʿu hauia d̲-šga hatamata** ATŠ I no. 174.

ḫatata (etym. unknown) blows (?). **ṭribh̲ alma ltlat ušitin hatata** DC 6 they struck him as many as 63 (read **tlatma ušitin** 360?) blows (?). Prob. corrupt.

hat(u)na v.s. **hatna.**

hatupia (rt. **HTP = HṬP**) Gy 253:17 robbers.

hatia a var. of **hadtia** (v.s. **hadta**).

hatin DC 22. 123 for **hanatin** Gy 128:6 (cf. s. **hanath̲**).

hatiqa = **atiqa** MG 71:15. Fem. st. emph. **hatiqtia** MG 154:14. Pl. masc. **hatiqia**, fem. **hatiqata. diuan hatiqa** ATŠ II no. 409 an ancient roll; **abatur hatiqa** Gs 37:8; **brbita haditia uhatiqia** Gy 223:5 (var. **hatiqtia** ACD & Leid.). Gl. 36:4 missp. with **g** ازلى *aeternus* بي اول; 136:7 fem. miswritten قدماء *vetera* پيشينيان; 138:11 missp. with ṭ قديما *olim* قديم.

hatma (חָתְמָא, ܚܬܡܐ) seal, sign, signet, token, signing, conclusion MG 112:8. Sealing is used for magical purposes (cf. **hatamta**), but also in liturgical praxis Ginzā 39 n. 3, MSt 153. Pl. **hatmia. bhahu hatma tithitmun** DC 40 with that seal shall ye be sealed up; **mitham hatma d̲-pandama lpumaihun** PD 437; **hatma rba** Gy 40:22; **hatma rba qadmaia** Oxf. roll b. 196; **hibil ziua d̲-hu hatma d̲-ginza** PD 1191; **hatma d̲-kušṭa** Q 43:30; **hatma d̲-asauata kulhin** ATŠ I no. 192; **hatmh̲ bhira dakia** ML 87:4 f. cf. n. 2; **giṭria uhatmia** Gs 77:20.

hatmʿil, hatmiaiil (a theophorous name from **HTM**) Gy 159:15, DC 43 D 35, DC 40. 885 an angel.

hatna (חַתְנָא, ܚܬܢܐ Akk. *ḫatanu* LS, Ges. s. חָתָן) connexion by marriage: son-in-law, father-in-law, brother-in-law, bridegroom, young husband MG 107:2. **ulhat(u)na d̲-baiit d̲-atia lbaitak** AM 152:19 and for the son-in-law whom thou wishest to come to thy house; **ʿu hatna rahim zauh̲** DC 48. 236 if the young husband love his spouse; **d̲-tišauian hatnik** Gy 147:2 that thou wilt make me thy (fem.) son-in-law; **nihzh̲ lhanath̲ hatna d̲-mn zahrʿil hadar** Gy 148:4 let us see that bridegroom who weddeth with Z.; **hatnan** ŠQ 19:5 our sister-in-law.

HBA (חֲבִי, חבא Ges.) to hide, cover, cower, conceal.

Pe. Pf. **šuba hba** (var. **ʿhba**) Gs 131:12 (var. Leid.) the Seven took cover; special pl. **hbun kulhun qirsia** DC 37. 103 f. all diseases (: disease-demons) cower. Impf. **tihbia** DC 26. 69 she hideth; **nihbun uninitrun uniplun** DC 26. 110 f. they shall cower, fall down and fall off. Impt. **hbia uzha** DC 43 I 95 hide and avaunt; **ʿhbh̲ daiua** DC 43 I 100 hide away, demon! Act. pt. pl. **qal ugadupia bgauh̲ habin** DC 34 they conceal therein the noise and blasphemies. Pass. pt. (irregular, doubtful) **kd̲ šamiš . . . hiba** AM 282:1, 12 (var. Ṣâb.'s AM **huiba**) when the sun . . . is covered (?).

Af. Pf. **hak ahba lʿutria** DC 36 that one conceals (?) the uthras.

hbal (חֲבָל, ܚܒܠ Akk *ḫabil* ZA 20 191 f.) Gy 82:ult. [*bis*], 84:11 [*bis*] interj.: Woe! Alas!

hbala (Jew. Aram. חֲבָלָה, Syr. ܚܒܠܐ) corruption, decay, ruin, destruction. Var. **hbila** MG 116:21, DC. 20. 93. **sasa uhbala** Gy 5:19 moth and decay (so to read also Gy 9:4, cf. Ginzā 12 n. 1); **lbuša d̲-hbala ʿtbh̲** Gy 259:9 f. garment in which there is corruption; **barda uhbala** Gy 291:43 f. hail and destruction; **markabata rurbata d̲-hbala** DC 43 E 42 mighty vessels of destruction. Often in catalogues of sins: **haṭaiia uhauba uhbala** Morg. 249/85:16; **pirṣa uhbala** Gy 329:17; **hbala urugza** Gs 42:13.

hbaqa (rt. **HBQ**) (*a*) embrace, (*b*) confining belt, girth, band, (*c*) nosegay, bouquet, bunch of flowers. Pl. **hbaqia.** (*a*) **ušahlana uganiana bhbaqa d̲-plan** JRAS 1943. 180:26, DC 46.

191:9. I shall strip and lie in the embrace of N.; **hbaq bihbaqa** Gy 83:19 v.s. **HBQ** pe. pf.; (*b*) **hbaq hbaqa brbita** DC 51:260 f. he engirdled the ocean; (*c*) **bihbaqia hbaqia iasmin** ŠQ 15:19 = CP 227:7 with bunches (?) of jessamine.

hbar AM 282:33 st. abs. of **habara.**

hbata (rt. **AHB** = **YHB**) gifts. **niara d̠-bh̠ hbata lṭabuta** DC 24 the bowl in which there are the gifts for the sacred food.

HBB, HMBB (חָבַב, ܚܰܒ LS, Ges. s. חבב) to glow, be very hot, scorch, burn, burn up, consume; to love, incite, inspire love.

Pe. Impt. with suff. **hubh̠ urbubh̠** DC 6 love it and magnify it. Pt. pl. **habin umidabin** CP 455:8 they burn and pine away.

Pa. Pf. **hababat nura** DC 26:135 f. fire burnt fiercely; with dissimil. of the 2nd rad. doubled; **hambib** Gy 281:20 he grew hot MG 76:16, 211:12, 221:ult. Pt. **mhabib** Gy 227:8 is growing hot, burneth MG 76:17, fem. **mhababa** Gy 17:6, 39:12, DC 37. 262 ff., MG 32:4; **nura d̠-mhababa** Morg. 262/15:16 = **nura d̠-mhambaba** DC 44. 970; **iaqda umhambaba** Gs 63:23.

Af. Impf. with suff. **qililh̠ bnura uahbibh̠** DC 35 set it on fire and burn it.

Der.: **habib.**

hbul, hbulia (Talm. חיבוליא, Syr. ܚܘܒܠܐ) interest, usury MG 147:2 and n. 2, Jb ii 87 n. 2. **hbul** only in the frequent **hbul hbulia** (Germ. *Zinsenzins*), cf. below. **aklia hbulia** s. **AKL I** pe. act. pt. pl.; **hbulia uhbul hbulia** Gy 20:12, 38:23, 187:1 f., Gs 32:11, Jb 83:12, 85:9 f., 96:2, 99:5, 176:2 etc.; **aklia hbulia** (var. **hbul**) **ubr hbulia** DAb, var. RD C 9 (whose **hbul** might have been influenced by the following **hbulia** of **br h-**), cf. s. **br**; **aklia hdadia anatun hbulia** DC 51. 537 ye practise usury on one another; **šaqil hbulia** Gs 19:12 he taketh interest.

hbulia DC 22. 101 a miscop. of **mublia** Gy 106:17.

HBṬ (חבט, ܚܒܛ LS, Ges.) to cudgel, batter down, beat down, strike upon, assail with blows, (of feet) drum, trample, (of teeth) gnash.

Pe. Pf. **ganph̠ hbaṭ barqa** Gy 84:16 his wings beat on the ground; **ulhdadia hbaṭ** ATŠ II no. 106; **šuba girglia hbaṭ lhdadia** DC 27:293 f. the seven spheres knocked one another (i.e. came into collision); **hibṭit lmia** Gy 337:19 I struck on the water; **hbaṭiun bʿlana hibṭa** Jb 132:9 they battered down the tree; with suff. **mn glala hibṭuk** JRAS 1938 3:24 they battered thee with a stone. Act. pt. **plangia d̠-dištata habiṭ** AM 12:17 f. he tramps many a beaten track (cf. **planga**); with encl. **habiṭlak brišak ragagta** Gy 370:8 f., Jb 178:9 f. lust will assail thy head; **habiṭlh̠ brišia** AM 120:penult. he beats him on the head.

Pa. Inf. **ušinaihun harqia uhabuṭia šamṭia** DC 44 they grind, gnash, and bare their fangs (doubtful. Read **habṭia uš-** pe. act. pt. pl.).

Der.: **habuṭ,** var. **hibuṭ, hibṭa.**

hbil, hbila 1 = **hbala** MG 116:bottom; also pass. pt. of **HBL. hbila d̠-muta** Gy 8:15, **hbila muta** Gy 210:17 destructive death (lit. death of destruction); **tuqpa uhbila** Gy 208:15 destructive might (lit. might and destruction, hendiadys); **tuqpa hbila** DC 37 id.; **taqipa uhbila** Gy 181:17 mighty and destructive; **alahia qam bhbila** DC 26:26 (false) gods were destroyed; **hbila hbilun** Gy 218:19 they are utterly destroyed; **hatmia hbila** DC 40. 39 seals of destruction; **sikina d̠-hbila** DC 40. 468 a knife of destruction, cf. also **sikina hbila** ATŠ II 207 and **sikina supa d̠-hbila** DC 43. Contrasted with 'construction': **aka hbila aka biniana** Gy 205:10, 15, 206:6, 12, **napqa mn hbila lbiniana** CP 24:3, ML 26:5.

hbila 2 (rel. to **habla 1**) breath, steam IM Gl. **bihbila d̠-pumh̠** Gy 280:20 in the breath of his mouth.

hbilta (ܚܒܠܬܐ) Gy 96:16 pain of woman in labour.

hbiṣ (pass. pt. pe. of **HBṢ**) pinched. **hbiṣ nhiria** AM 12:10 her nose is pinched.

hbiṣa (חֲבִיצָא, ܚܒܝܨܐ, خَبِيص) a kind of porridge MG 116:18 f. **habṣia hbiṣa** Gy 148:9 they prepare a porridge.

HBL, HMBL (חָבַל, ܚܰܒܶܠ III LS, Ges. s. חבל III = Akk. *ḫabâlu*, Ar. خبل, used esp. in pa. and its reflexive; pe. preserves sometimes the meaning of חבל I = ܚܒܠ, حبل) pe. to writhe, twist, wound, injure; pa. to spoil, mar, corrupt, destroy; ethpe. be perverted, corrupted; ethpa. be destroyed, spoilt, ruined. But the resp. meanings assigned to one stem can sometimes be found also with another, cf. below.

Pe. Pf. **hbal riuiana** Gy 96:16 her mind was convulsed; **hiblat ugiblat** s. **GBL** pe. pf. pass. pt. **hbil(a)** s. **hbil.** Inf. with suff. **lhbilinun** DC 43 J 46 to destroy them.

Pa. Pf. **hambil** he destroyed MG 76:17, 85:7; **hamblat** Gy **hamblat (uiadlat)** Gy 95:13 f. she laboured (: was convulsed [and brought forth]) MG 76:19, 222:12. Impf. **tihambil** she destroyeth, thou destroyest MG 226:antep.; with suff. **tihamblinun** Gy 299:8 she destroyeth them MG 282:3. Pass. pt. **mhambal** destroyed MG 131:16; fem. **haita mhambla** Gy 96:16 a convulsed labouring woman; pl. **mhamblia** DC 41. 151. Nom. act. **hambalta** s.v.

Ethpe. Pf. **umahu ʿthibil lhšuka** DC 6 and what was perverted to the darkness,

Ethpa. Pf. **ʿthambal** was spoilt MG 76:18; **ʿthambalt** thou wast ruined; pl. fem. **ʿhambalian** Gy 241:ult., var. **ʿthambalia** *corruptae sunt* MG 213:16 f., 224:1 f. Impf. **nithambal** we shall be destroyed MG 226:21, **nithamblun** AM 195:11 they will be ruined, **nihamblun** AM 184:7, Gy 307:7 A (BCD **nith-**) id. MG 213:16. **ianqa . . . mithambal** DC 41. 235 s. eth **HML.** Impt. **ʿthambal** Gs 4:9, 21 be destroyed! Pt. **mithambal** MG 239:18, **mithambla** Gy 309:7 MG 213:17; pl. **mithamblia** DAb they will be destroyed; pl. fem. **mithamblan** ATŠ I no. 135.

Der.: **hambala, hambalta, hbal, hbala, hbila 1,** (var. **hibila**), **hbilta.**

hbnina Jb 149:2, var. B **d̲-bunnh̲** (v.s. **bunna**) a kind of fish (?), cf. II 152 n. 1.

HBṢ (ܚܒܨ LS) to compress, contract, pinch.

Pe. Act. pt. fem. **arqa mihbaṣ habṣa** Gy 348:11 the earth was pressed together; pl. **habṣia hbiṣa** v.s. **hbiṣa.** Part. pres. **habṣit umalit kasia** Jb 154:7 thou pressest out (sour milk?) and fillest bowls; **apinin uhabṣinin** Jb 150:1 we will bake (bread) and make sour-milk-cheese. Pass. pt. **hbiṣ** s.v. Inf. **mihbaṣ** Gy 348:11.

Der.: **hbiṣ, hbiṣa.**

HBQ (Jew.-Aram., H., Mod. H. חבק Ges.) to embrace, cling to, press, clasp, clamp.

Pe. Pf. **lkulh̲ alma hbaq** Gy 83:4 he embraced the whole world; **hbaq ubla arqa** Gy 83:20 he clasped and swallowed the earth; **hbaq bihbaqa** Gy 83:19 he embraced with an embrace; **hbaq hbaqa brbita** s. **hbaqa; hbaq hbaqa bgauh̲** DC 51:270; with suff. **hibqh̲ bhbaq haila** Jb 142:2 he pressed her in a strong embrace. Impf. **nihibqh̲ bqumth̲** Gy 116:8 he encircles (or embraces) her form; with encl. **nihibqubh̲ hibqa** Gy 105:4 we will encompass the world. Act. pt. **uʿdh̲ pašṭa ʿlh̲ uhabqh̲ bkulh̲ hailh̲** ATŠ II no. 154 she holds out her hand to her and embraces her with all her strength; with encl. **lhimiana habqilh̲ unašqilh̲** ATŠ I no. 250 he embraces and kisses the (sacred) girdle; **harata habqalia** DC 26. 565 f., 570 f., DC 44 noblewomen embrace me.

Gl. 16:9 f. miswritten اقبل *complecti* مندرج شد; 22:2 f. اعتنق *complecti, complere se* بغل گرفت.

Der.: **hbaqa, hibqa.**

HBR I (חבר, ܚܒܪ pa., H. חבר II Ges.) to join, associate, befriend, fasten, be fastened.

Pe. Act. pt. **habar habrh̲** (var. **habara d̲-habria**) **hauia** AM 22:13 he will be neighbourly to his friend(s); **habra** s. **HBŠ** pe. pt. pl. fem. **habran nišmatin alma d̲-šumaiin dakria** ATŠ II no. 81 their souls hold together (: are joined) until their names are mentioned. Inf. **tlatma ušitin šumhata d̲-šamiš mitaburia** (var. **mitiburia,** read **mitahburia**?) **mihbar** DAb the 360 names of Š. are connected (or for being used in charms?, cf. חֲבָרָא, ܚܰܒܳܪܳܐ exorcist. Doubtful. Possibly **HDR II** q.v.).

Pa. Pf. **sliq habrun zihlun lbiniana** DC 51:261 f. they ascended, joined and cleaned the building.

Der.: **habara 2, habra 1, 2,** fem. pl. **habarata.**

HBR II (Jew.-Aram. חֲבַרְבַּר, Syr. in der. ܚܒܘܪܐ, ܚܰܒܽܘܪܳܐ, ܚܰܒܳܪܳܐ, ܚܰܒܰܪܢܳܐ LS) to be dark, to darken.

Pe. Pf. **hšuk uhbur** (B **hbar**) **parṣuph̲** Jb 188:14 his face became dark and gloomy **ainh̲ . . . hbar habria** DC 22:405 his eyes were utterly dark; **hibrat uhiškat** Gy 313:12, Jb 196:8 she became dark and gloomy, MG 61: muddle, make muddy, render turbid.

Der.: **habara** (= **abara 5**), st. abs. **hbar.**

HBŠ (חבש, ܚܒܫ, حبس LS, Ges.) to imprison, keep fastened, enclose, shut in.

Pe. Pt. (act. with pass. meaning) **habiš uhabra nišimth̲** ATŠ II no. 78 his soul is imprisoned and fastened down.

Pa. Pt. pl. **ʿla hda asita mhabšin** s. **asita 1.**

Ethpe. Pt. **uʿit d̲-bita ʿlh̲ mihibša** ATŠ I no. 271, var. DC 36 **mitbihša** (by inversion) and there is one imprisoned by the egg.

HGA (הגא, ܗܓܐ LS, H. הגה Ges., Ar. هجا) to meditate, think, plan, conceive mentally, read, study, pronounce, read aloud.

Pe. Part. pres. **ana bsiprai hadtia hagina** Gy 205:3 I read in (or meditate upon) my new book(s); **kma iatbit uhagit bsiprak** DAb however long thou sittest and readest (or studiest) in thy book(s).

Der.: **hugiana.**

hgaga (rt. **HGG = HUG**) circle, convolution; illusion, delusion, fancy. Pl. **hgagia,** var. **hagigia** s.v. **alma d̲-hgaga** ATŠ I no. 100 the world of illusion; **almia d̲-hgaga** ibid. II no. 89 id. pl. DC 41. 226, DC 50. 730 worlds of illusion.

HGG = HUG.

HGR v.s. **HNGR.**

HDA I (חֲדִי, חדא, ܚܕܝ, ܚܕܐ, H. חדה LS, Ges.) to rejoice, be glad; to gladden, give joy-cries; congratulate.

Pe. Pf. **hda** he rejoiced MG 257:2, **hda uʿtbasam** Gy 97:18, 115:8, 125:3 he rejoiced and was pleased; pl. **rbia hdun uʿtqaiam** Gy 91:16 the Great (Life) was glad and confirmed; **hiia hdun lalam almia** (often) Life rejoice(d) for ever; **mihdia hdun** Gy 350:16 they greatly rejoice; with encl. **lahdibh̲ bṭabuta d̲-ab** Gs 44:18 I (could) did not enjoy my Father's goodness; **hiia hdubak** DC 41. 480 the Life was pleased with thee. Impf. **nihdun ʿutria** CP 386:8 the uthras will rejoice; with encl. **nihdibh̲** AM he will be happy with her; **tihdibh̲** thou gladdenest him MG 259 n. 1; **niqirbun unihdibun** AM 190:3 they approach and he welcomes them; **nihdubh̲** they welcome him MG 53:17. Impt. **hdia** Gy 148:8, **anat bdilan hdia** CP 386:7 rejoice thou in us; fem. **hdai,** with encl. **hdaibh̲** MG 259:12. Act. pt. **hadia** AM 24 etc. (*often*) he rejoices; **mihdia kma hadia lbab** Gs 89:1 how greatly my heart rejoiceth!; pl. **hadia daiṣia umitparpia** Gy 114:22 they rejoice, dance, and exult; with encl. **hadibun** AM 15 he will rejoice in them. Part. pres. **bhaduta d̲-hadina** Gy 91:15 in the joy (with) which I rejoiced (hist. pres.); **mihdia kma hadina** Gs 89:1, Jb 202:4 how greatly I rejoice; **hdina uhtirna** s. **HTR.** Inf. **mihdia** (*often*) MG 260:12.

Pa. Impt. **hadia** Par. xi 23a gladden MG 262:9. Act. pt. **mhadia** (often), **hadia umihadia** ATŠ he greatly rejoices; pl. **mhadin kma d̲-mṣiin** DC 38 they give joy-cries as much as they are able. Nom. ag. **mhadiana** s.v.

Der.: **haduta 1** (abs. **hadua,** cstr. **haduat**), **had(a)iata, mhadian(i)a, hiduia** (in popular use a masc. of **haduta**) **2 = hiduta = hidukta = ihduktia**; it should originally derive from **HDT I.**

HDA II (ܗܕܝ = هدى H. הדה Ges.) to lead, direct.

Pe. Impf. with suff. **lanihdiẖ mšiha baṭla** CP 234:14 the good-for-nothing Messiah guideth him not. Act. pt. **briuania hadia** AM 61:17 she is a leader by temperament; **hadia manda hiduia** CP 234:13 Manda guideth the bridegroom.

Af. Act. pt. **ʿnta nukraita tirabia umahdẖ** AM 54:18 a foreign woman will bring her up and educate her; **ulširša abatar nbiha mahdia** ATŠ I no. 203 and directeth the Root (i.e. Mandaeans) after the Prophet.

Der.: **hadia 3**,

hda, ahda fem. of **had** one, used also for masc. MG 187:bottom. **asra uhda** = h(a)disar 11 MG 188:paen. In distributive repetitions less frequent than **had**: **umšaiilun lhda hda** Gy 98:9 and he putteth them to question one by one. As ordinal number: **biuma hda** Gy 96:12 on the first day MG 348:anteantep. (cf. also 187 n. 1). In adv. expressions: **ḏ-mn hda ʿtqrun** Gy 250:3 who were created at once (: at the same time); **lhda** Nöld. '*gar sehr*' MG 207:24 is used rather as an indefinite numeral 'any', after negation 'not at all', cf. **la aklin bisra lhda** Gy 6:17 f. they do not eat any meat, or they eat no meat at all (cf. also MG 207 n. 2, Ginzā 9 n. 8); **lhda ḏ-** Gy 284:3 (= **lhad ḏ-** ibid. l. 4) very MG 453:5 f. As indefinite numeral: **qašiša . . . mn hda ʿutra** CP 2:6, ML 4:5 older than any uthra. As a numeral used before (or after) the noun: **hda iuma** Gy 381:22 one day (but **biuma hda** above), **bhda mamla** Gy 24:13 (= **bhad mamla** ibid. l. 1) in one speech. In compound numbers: **bšubin uhda šita** Gy 389:23 = **bšubin uhda šnia** Gy 387:9 in 71 years; **šitin uhda duda** Gy 317:20 sixty-one cauldrons; **šitin uhda mihiata** Gy 317:19 sixty-one blows; **bšitin uhda ʿngirta** in 61 letters; **asra uhda iahra** Gy 380:9 eleven months; **hda alpa** (often) 1,000 MG 348:top and middle; **hda zibna** Gy 385:9 once MG 349: antep.; **hda mn hda šanai** Gy 10:7 one is stranger than another (an older expression for **hdadia** q.v.) MG 350:antep.; **uqiriuiẖ lhda bra . . . lhdaia rba zadiqa** Gy 235:5 f. and He (: the Life) created a Son . . . the Great Holy Unique One (v.s. lhdaia); **hda lhabrẖ ladamia** s. **hdadia.**

hdadia (Talm. הֲדָדֵי, Syr. ܚܕ̈ܕܐ MG 349 n. 2, 350 n. 2) one another, each other MG § 154 p. 191, § 244 pp. 349 f. As direct object: **hdadia gazria** Gy 224:10 they circumcise one another; **aklia hdadia** Gy 337:20, 22. In genitive construction: **anpia hdadia** Gy 340:9, 389:11, 390:23 face to face; **qala ḏ-hdadia** Gy 340:9 the voice of each other; **qumat hdadia qaimia umša hdadia nasbia** Gs 110:3 they all stand alike and take the same measure; **bkanpia ḏ-hdadia** Gy 95:15 in each other's lap. With prep.: **bhdadia, bihdadia** (q.v.) together, with each other, mutually, reciprocally; **luat hdadia** Gy 23:21, 223:4, 233:23 &c. by one another, together; **mn hdadia** Gy 386:1 &c. from one another, Gy 388:5 &c. with one another, together; **abatar hdadia** Gy 388:23, 389:12 after each other; **kḏ hdadia** Gy 100:2, 123:15 f., 379:2 like each other, all alike; **hda lhabrẖ ladamia** Gy 95:14 = **ladamin lhdadia** Gy 95:15 they do not resemble one another; the prep. was omitted in **ḏ-iatbia hdadia** Gs 117:8 who sit together. Gl. 77:12 **bhdadi** [*sic*] جميعاً *simul* همه; 160:6 **bhdada** [*sic*] موافق *consentiens*.

hdaia 1 JRAS 1937 592 = **hadia 1.**

hdaia 2 s. **lhdaia** and **lihdaia.**

hdara (ܚܘܕܪܐ) (*a*) circuit, district round about, (*b*) dizziness (?). (*a*) **hdara ḏ-hibil ziua mitqiria** HG; (*b*) **hdara ḏ-riša** AM 29:8 dizziness, vertigo.

hdaruta Par AM 290:bottom = **hdurta.**

hdua DAb scr. def. of **hadua 1.**

hdurta (rt. **HDR**) Par. AM 290:bottom.

hdisar = **hadisar. lihdisar iahria** Gy 380:20 for 11 months; **bhdisar šaiia ḏ-ʿumama** DC 43 at the eleventh hour of the day.

HDM (attenuation of **HTM**?) to seal (?).

Pe. Pass. pt. pl. **sdimia hdimia umazihia** DC 44. 1818 they are stopped, sealed, and driven away (: exorcised). (Influenced by **sd-**.)

HDR I (חדר, ܚܕܪ LS, H. חדר I Ges.) to turn, turn about, turn back, return, surround, beset, set about, set around, encircle, turn back, go back, go about, circulate; (before a verb) do again IM Gl.

Pe. Pf. **mia siauia hdar hudrana ḏ-alma** Gy 169:17 the black waters encircled the circumference of the world; **hdar aqmuia** Gy 43:ult. f. they raised him again (idiom); **ḏ-npaq mn kras ʿmẖ uhdar bduktẖ** Gs 7:20 (is there anybody) who came out of his mother's womb and returned back? (cf. John 3:4b); **adam mn pagrẖ npaq hdar uhiziẖ** Gs 13:21 C Adam left his body, turned and saw it; special pl. **minẖ hadariun** DC 36 they turned back; **ṭura ḏ-madai ḏ-hdariun ʿlẖ** HG the mountain of the Medes about which they travelled; with encl. **uhdarbun bmia tahmia** Sh. 'Abd.'s copy's var. of (**ʿhdar bmia tahmia**) Gy 97:5 and he walked around in turbid waters; **hdarlẖ mahdurta lšamiš** AM 262:1 a circle surrounded the sun. Impf. **nihdar** he turns back, returns MG 221:4; **nihdar uniṣ(i)bẖ** PD 1295 f. he will baptize him again (*idiom*); **malka nihdar latrẖ** AM 185:penult. the king will return to his place; **malka mn abuiẖ nihdar** AM the king will revolt against his father (*idiom*); **ḏ-ana ʿhdar bpagraikun ʿrminkun** Gy 186:7 that I may throw you back into your bodies (*idiom*) MG 443; **hdar** (var. **ʿhdar**) **ʿtia** Gs 25:3 I shall come again (*idiom*); **nihidrun uniriqdun** P.A. xii they shall circulate and dance; **mn luat latihidrun** DC 36 II 188 turn not away from my company; with suff. **nihadra lzahrʿil mn gabra šapira** Gy 147:19 let us marry Z. to the handsome man (*idiom*); **hilula nibudlẖ unihidrẖ** Gy 147:23 we will make her a wedding and marry her (*idiom*). Impt. **hdar margnak liaminak** CP 43:5, Q 19:13 turn thy ritual staff over to thy right arm. Act. pt. **ḏ-mn zahrʿil hadar** Gy 148:4 who is wedding Z. (*idiom*); **hu nahim uhadar**

balma Gy 161:12 f. he roared and roamed in the world (hist. pres.); **hadar ubaiia** PD 687 he will pray again (*idiom*); **hadar (u)ṣabalh̲** PD 701, 709 he will baptize him again; fem. **kd̲ hiduta hadra bšiul** Jb 114:5 when a bride weddeth in Sheol (*idiom*, cf. II 113 n. 3); **bgirglia lahadra** Gy 10:24 it turneth not on wheels; **ṭaisa uhadra** Gy 339:1 she flieth and turneth about; **hᶜ hadrh̲ uaklalh̲ umšauialh̲ kd̲ zan lahua** ATŠ II 137 she surrounds it, devours it, and makes it as if it had never been; pl. **kd̲ hadria** Gy 149:4 when people marry (*idiom*); **hadria uqaimia** Gy 243:21 they turned about and stood (hist. pres.); **šaplia uhadria** Gs 17:1 they sink and are overturned (?); **hadria ᶜl ᶜumṣia** Gy 183:10 f. = **ᶜl ᶜumṣia hadria** Gs 31:4 they beg for morsels (*idiom* = go around begging), **hadrin utarṣilh̲** PD 660 they consecrate him again (*idiom*); pl. with encl. **umia hadribun** ATŠ I 2 no. 267 and water will circulate in them; fem. pl. **babaiin hadran** DAb they go out of doors (i.e. do not observe ritual isolation, cf. 30 n. 2). Part. pres. **ᶜl nišmat hadarna** Gy 367:14 I look around for my soul (*idiom*); **alma d̲-hadritun** Gy 147:18 until ye marry. Pass. pt. **aina d̲-muqra hdira** ATŠ I no. 246 an enclosed well of living matter; with encl. **hdirlh̲ šuba šuria** Gs 13:17 seven walls surrounded him; **tanina d̲-hdirlh̲ lalma** Gs 9:15, **tanina d̲-hdirlh̲ lkulh̲ alma** Gs 14:18 the dragon that encompassed the (whole) world; **šuba šuria d̲-parzla hdirlh̲** DC 34, **šamiš kd̲ hauia hdirlh̲ ṣurta** AM 261:17 when the sun is encircled by an enclosing line; **d̲-kulhun razia hdirlun** ATŠ II no. 123 which enclosed all mysteries; pl. with encl. **hdirilh̲ lpagrai** Gs 121:5 they encompassed my body; **haizak ᶜhdirilh̲ taga brišh̲** ATŠ I no. 19 then they put a crown about his head; **ᶜu biahra d̲-taimuz hdirlh̲ mahdurta lšamiš** AM 261:25 if in the month Tammuz the sun is surrounded by a circle. Inf. **mihdar** AM 95.

Pa. Pf. with encl. **ana lalma dilh̲ šuria hanik hadrilh̲** Gy 151:21 I encompassed her world with these walls. Inf. **hadruia** Gy 243:3, var. Leid. **hadria**, read **haduria** to bring back Ginzā 244 n. 2.

Af. Pf. **ahdar aqmuia** Gy 22:20, 21, 22 they raised him again (*idiom*, id. with different stems in Gy 43:ult. f., s. pe. pf.); with encl. **šitin šuria . . . ahdarlh̲** DC 34 sixty walls . . . surrounded him; **ahd(i)rilh̲** Gy 90:15 I encompassed him MG 226:3; **uahdartlia babia** DAb and thou hast closed (?) its gates; with suff. **ahdarth̲ šuba šuria** DC 27. 100 thou hast encircled it with 7 walls; **ahdarth̲** (var. **ahdirth̲**) **lhanath̲ alma** Gy 159:12 (var. DC 22. 153) I encircled that world; **ahdartinun alanpia šamiš mn madna uahdartinun alanpia sira mn marba** DC 43 J 134 I turned them back towards the sun from the east and turned them back towards the moon from the west; **ulgirglia ahdirinun** ATŠ I no. 243 and he made the spheres revolve. Impt. **ahdar margnak lsmalak** DC 41. 353 return thy staff to thy left arm; **uahdir margnak liaminak** DC 3 and turn over thy staff to thy right arm (Q 19:13 pe.); with suff. **ahdrh̲ liaminak** ATŠ II no. 42 bring it round to thy right arm. Pt. **anph̲ lbaba d̲-rahmia lamahdar** ATŠ II no. 78 (var. DC 6 **lamihdar** ethpe.) he does not turn his face (var. his face turns not) to the Gate-of-Mercies (cf. s. **rahmia**); **umahdar ama lnapšia** HG and he converts the people to himself; with encl. **mahdarlh̲ šuba šuria** Gy 127:3 f. he encompasses him with 7 walls; pl. **uanph̲ lbaba d̲-rahmia lamahdria** (var. **lamahdiria**) ATŠ II no. 80 (var. DC 6 ibid.) if they do not turn his face to the Gate-of-Mercies.

Ethpe. Pf. **ᶜhdar bᶜmh̲ ailuia** Gy 186:6 and if put back in its mother's womb (*idiom*), cf. Gs 7:20; **ᶜhidrat** Gs 38:12, 80:18, Q 38:19 she turned herself back MG 214:8; **ᶜthidrit, ᶜhidrit** I turned back MG 223:7 (**ᶜhidrit lbith̲ . . . bšitin asaria** *Florilegium* is a simple pe. with a prosth. vowel: I encompassed the house of . . . with 60 bonds). Impt. **ᶜhdar uqria mn riš** ATŠ II no. 216 return (go back) and recite from the beginning (*or* read again . . ., *idiom*). Pt. **mihdar** ATŠ II no. 78 (var. **mahdar**, s. af. pt.); fem. **mihidra** Gy 146:paen., Gs 147:23, ATŠ I no. 280, II no. 137, MG 149:19, 214:8. Inf. **lmihduria lᶜuhraihun** Jb 155:5 to turn back to their road.

Ettaf. Pf. **ᶜtahdar** he was brought back MG 222:7; **ᶜl napšia ᶜtahdar ᶜlh̲ šuba šuria** DC 34. 56 he placed about himself 7 walls; with encl. **ᶜtahdarlh̲** Gs 21:21, ATŠ II no. 139.

Idioms. Used often as a frequentative verb 'to do again', 'to recommence', 'to repeat an action' (followed always by the verb in question). With **mn** sometimes 'to revolt'; af. with **l** 'to convert'. Semantic developments: 'to go about in a wedding procession', hence 'to celebrate a wedding', 'to marry' Ginzā 160 n. 3; also 'to go about as a beggar', hence 'to beg'.

Gl. 11:5 f. احاط *sepire, circumdare* محيط شد; 62:13 f. حال *circuire* گرديد; 108:15 f. طاف *circuire* طواف كرد.

Der.: **hdara, hdaruta, hdurta, hudrana, hidra 2, mahduriniata, mahdurta, mahdiriniata, mahdruniata,**

HDR II (הדר, ܗܕܪ, هدر LS, Ges.) to be comely, distinguished, splendid, resplendent, glorious, honoured.

Pe.: Impf. **nihdar bkulh̲ hailh̲** ATŠ II no. 346 he will be resplendent in all his strength. Pass. pt. with encl. pers. pron. **šapirna mn kulhun uhdirna mn kulhun** Gy 146:20 f. I was fairer than all of them and more resplendent than all of them. Inf. **tlatma ušitin šumhata d̲-šamiš mitaduria mihdar** DC 51 the 360 names of the sun are to be glorified greatly (miscop. **mitaburia mihbar** s. **HBR I**).

Ethpa. Inf. **mitaduria** (?) v.s. pe. Inf.

Der.: **hadra** (and **hadran**), **hidra 1**.

HDT I (חדת, ܚܕܬ, H. חדש, Ar. حدث LS, Ges.) to be new, fresh; to renew, be renewed.

Pe. Pf. **lahdat bgauak** DC 34 was not renewed (?) within thee.

Der.: **hadta**, fem. **hadit(i)a**, **haduta** 2 = **hiduta** = **hidukt(i)a** (masc. **hiduia** cf. s. HDA I Der.).

HDT II (Ar. حَدَّث) to speak, talk, tell, converse. Only in mod. Mand. (pron. *ḥaddeθ*); where it is very frequent.

Pa.: Part. pres. **mn** [*sic*] **mhadit bšinta** DC 45, DC 46. 186:13 who talks in his sleep, **ʿniš mhadit ginzh̲** DC 46. 68:10 (*and often*) a person who talks (too) much.

Gl. 48:1 f. تكلّم *loqui* گفت; 83:4 f. راطن *murmurare* غيبت كرد.

hu (Gen. Sem.) pers. pronoun of the 3rd p. sg. masc.: he; used also as a demonstrative and a copula. As a demonstr. pronoun: **hu ʿutra** Gy 71:10 that uthra; **hu malka rama d̲-ʿqara** Gy 17:3, 36:15 that Exalted King of Glory MG 336 f.; corroborated by **ha**: **hahu** this (s.v.) To emphasize a demonstr. pronoun: **hazin hu gabra** Gy 185:17, 19 this (very) man MG 341:4. To emphasize a pers. pronoun: **lau ana hu lbuša d̲-nura lbiš** Gy 52:18 I have not put on a garment of fire; **amintul dilkun hu hšuka unhura mkadšia mn hdadia** Gy 211:1 because of you the darkness and the light fight together MG 329:bottom. To emphasize a noun: **ptahil hu niṣbh̲** Gy 267:19 Ptahil created it. As a copula: **ana hu hibil ziua** JRAS 1937 596:29 I am H.-Z.; **šrara dilan hazin taga hu** Gy 161:5 our firmness is this crown; **malka d̲-nhura taiaba umrahmana hu šabiq haṭaiia uhaubia hu** Gy 17:2, 35:15 the King of Light is compassionate and merciful, He is the forgiver of sins and trespasses; **had hu biša d̲-** Gy 13:13, 34:10, **had hu malka d̲-nhura** Gy 5:10 MG 406; **ka hu kušṭa** Gs 28:10 here is the Truth etc. MG 407. Gl. 171:9 **hu** هو *ille* او.

HUA (הוא, ܗܘܐ LS, Ges. s. הוה II) to be, become, happen, come into being; with prep. **l** (introducing a dat. of possession) 'to have'.

Pe. Pf. sg. 3rd **hua**, rarely **ahua** MG 60: anteantep., 267:middle; fem. **huat**, **ahuat**, with encl. **huatalh̲**, **huatalun** MG 25:17, 267: middle; 2nd **huit** MG 267:middle; 1st **huit**, **ahuit**, with encl. **ahuilkun** Gy 186:15 BCD, var. **ahuitilkun** A, **huitilh̲**, **ʿhuitilh̲** (*often*) MG ibid.; pl. 3rd masc. **hun**, with encl. **hulia**, **hubh̲** etc. ibid.; 3rd fem. **hʿ** Gy 209:4, 39:2, 4, 67:2, **huʿn** Gy 90:22 AC, var. **hʿn** B MG ibid.; 2nd **huaitun** MG ibid.; 1st **huainin** Gy 33:9, **huin** Gy 149:11 A, varr. **huainin** D, **huinin** C, **huiinih̲** B (corrupt) MG ibid. Impf. sg. 3rd masc. **nihuia**, **lihuia**, **lʿhuia** MG 60:antep., 216:11, 267:anteantep., with syncope of **u**: **nihia**, **lihia** as varr. of **lʿhuia** Gy 180:21, with encl. **nihibh̲** etc. MG 267:anteantep. f.; 3rd fem. and 2nd **tihuia**, **tihia** MG 267:antep.f.; 1st **ʿhuia** MG 267:paen.; pl. 3rd **nihun** Gy 251:15, **nihu**, **nʿhu** Gy 251:5, 16 ACD, with encl. **nihulh̲** MG 267:paen. f.; 3rd fem. **nʿhuian** Gy 12:19, **lihuia** Q 30:3, 31:3 MG 268:1; 2nd **tihun**, with encl. **tihulia** MG 268:2; 1st **nihuia**, **nihia** ibid. Impt. **huia**, **huʿ** Gy 87:2, 3 B, var. **hʿ** ACD etc.; pl. **hun**, with encl. **hulh̲** etc. MG 268:3 f. Pt. **hauia** (pronunciation: masc. *hâwi*, fem. *hâwyâ*); pl. masc. **hauin**, **hauia**, fem. **hauian**, **hauia** MG 268:10 f. Part. pres. **hauina**, **hauit** (with encl. **hauiatlh̲**), **hauinin** (with encl. **hauinabh̲**), **hauitun**, cf. MG 268:11 f. Inf. **mihuia** MG 268:13.

Less usual forms, phrases and idioms: Pf. often used as pres.: **hašta d̲-ruhṣanai ʿl hiia hua** Gs 99:2 now, while I have confidence in the Life; **d̲-bnia anašia qru šumia ulahuat šumia** Gy 273:2 which the people called heavens although those are no heavens; **ṣauma rba d̲-lau mn mikla umištia d̲-alma hua** Gy 16:13 the great fasting which consisteth not in (abstaining) from the eating and drinking of the world; **gabra lahua minan ulahuat šuth̲ mn šutaikun** Gy 258:19 the man is not one of us and his speech is unlike yours; **ana lahuit nasib šuda** Gy 258:16 I am not one who accepteth a bribe MG 369 f. Past progr. tense (**hua** + act. pt. of the verb in question): **d̲-hua haiiq** Gy 168:15 because he feared; **kauila hua qapia uazla** Gy 380:19 the ark was floating and moving **hua d̲-akil** Gy 381:4 he was eating; **hua iada** Gy 162:15 he knew; **HUA** rarely inflected: **huat iatba** Jb she was sitting; regularly inflected when the pt. is in st. cstr.: **huit bania biniana** ... **ana huit mšarhib šurbta** Gy 244:23 I was a builder of the building . . . I was a propagator of the generation; **lahuit nasib šuda** Gy 258:16 I did not accept the bribe MG 383:bottom and n. 2. Inflexible **hua** + pass. pt.: **d̲-hua ktib uṣir ʿlh̲** Gy 144:7 on which there was written and engraved; **anat hua nṣiba nṣibtak** Gy 73:18 thy plant was planted; **d̲-hua ksʿia** Gy 144:6 which was hidden; **diuan d̲-hua ktiba** Q 51:4 a diwan which was written; (**ana**) **hua ksina** Gy 138:3, 139:20, 143:2 I was hidden; hypothetically: **lahua mṣinin** Gy 158:6 we should not be able; **ʿu hua mṣʿiit** Gy 164:13 if thou wert able; MG 384. Past conditional: **hun kd̲ zan d̲-lahun** Gy 164:22 they became as if they had not existed; **ʿu . . . lahuit ana mn rurbia** Gy 76:17 if . . . I should not (have) belong(ed) to the Great; **udaikia kd̲ d̲-lahun** Gy 120:1 and they are blotted out as if they had not existed; **mut kd̲ d̲-lahuit** Gs 4:8, 20 die as if thou hast not existed, MG 368:bottom f. Future pf. **man d̲-hualh̲ mihuia bra** Gy 387:18 who will have (had) a son; **kd̲ hu hauia iadalun** Gy 155:21 if he knows (: shall have known) them; **ʿu hauia ʿniš napiq mn pagrh̲** PD no. 150 = ATŠ (several times) if someone departeth (: is departing) his body; **ʿu hauia ʿniš nikth̲ kalba** PD no. 151 if the dog bites (: shall have bitten) somebody, MG 385:top; **hauia d̲-šga (had minaihun)** ATŠ I no. 173 should it happen that (one of them) made a mistake. Future (**nihuia** + pt.): **nihuia amar udaiin** Gy 256:ult. he will speak and judge; **udmuth̲ lʿhuia damia lhibil** Gy 266:22 and his (future) appearance will resemble H.'s; **ulanihuia amrit** Gy 262:14 and thou wilt not say (: say not!); **unihuia amritun** Gy 252:17 and ye will say; **uanatun nihuia**

mitqaimitun Gy 252:13 and ye will stand, MG 385: top. Periphrastic future (**baiia** + **mihuia** = P. خواهد بود): **mihuia baiia** Gy 205:5 = **mihuia mibilh̲** Gy 196:20 is about to be (cf. **BAA** Idioms); contracted form: **blmihuia** Gy 276:10 = **ba lm-** Par. xi, MG 11 n. 2. Inf.: **abid mihuia d̲-** Gy 158:15 Lidzb.: *bereite dich darauf vor*. Impt.: **hulh̲ adiaurh̲ lšamiš** Gy 172:6 f. be helpers to Š.; a fem. form: **ʿhuai ʿlauaihun akla** DC 40. 315 be a hammer against them; prohibitive: **latihun minaihun** Gy 24:13 do not belong to them. As an impers. verb. constructed as fem.: **ʿl d̲-huat uldhauia** Gy 205:5, similarly Gy 196:19 f. what was and what is, **kul d̲-hauia ʿlai tihuia** Gy 164:20 all that is to happen to me. 'To come into existence', 'to become': **ana hu d̲-mn alaha hua** Gy 52:14 I am that who came into being from God; **uhua kul mindam bmimrh̲** Gy 33:21 and everything came into being through His word; **bšgandia huainia** DC 6 (DC 53 **hua ainia**) we became messengers; **anin mna huainin** CP 213:15 we, whence did we proceed?; **ʿu hauina umitarmadna** Jb 103:10 if I become and am made a priest; with this meaning there is also a rare ethpe.: Pf. **d̲-la ʿtihuia** Sh. 'Abd.'s copy's var. of **d̲-laiith̲** Gy 31:13, pt. **bnia nihuilh̲ mithuilh̲ minh̲** AM 87:7 he will have children born to him by her. 'To have' (with **l**): **asuta uzakuta nihuilia, -lak, -lh̲** (often) health and victory be there for me, thee, him etc.; **lanihuilkun ruhṣana** Gy 42:7 have no confidence (: do not trust); **lanihuilkun busiana** Gy 42:14 have no contempt (: do not despise); **lgabra huat** Gy 150:8 f. she was married; **hua lʿmh̲** AM (*often*) he was born. Adverbial expressions with **b**: **hun bhambaguta** s. **hambaguta**; **bṭabuta hua** s. **ṭabuta**. Irregular forms: **ʿu hšuka la ʿhuia nhura la ʿtqaiam** ATŠ I no. 89 if darkness had not existed, light could not have come into being; **d̲-minh̲ huaina** DC 33 whence we came into being; **anin mna huainin** CP 213:15 whence came we into being?; **ana huilak adiaura** DC 26. 509 I shall be thy helper.

Gl. 101:7 f. miswritten صار *fieri* گرديد; 139:5 f. **ahua** كان *esse* بود.

Der.: **nahuia.**

HWA (חַוֵּי, ܚܰܘܺܝ, H. loan-w. חוה pi. LS, Ges.) to show (forth), make manifest, display, demonstrate, (fig.) reveal, interpret, translate.

Pa. Pf. with encl. **hauitilun** Gy 316:21 I showed to them MG 261:10; with suff. **hauith̲** Gy 105:7, Gs 82 etc. (often) I showed him MG 288:10, **hauitak** Gy 119:12, 13 I showed thee MG 286:anteantep., **hauian** he showed to me MG 284:26, **hauitan** Gy 145:2, 152:18 she showed to me MG 285:middle, **hauitinan** Q 14:2, 27:ult. etc. (often) thou hast shown to us MG 289:bottom, **hauitinun** Gy 361:5 I showed (to) them MG 291:1, **hauitun** Gs 66:9 ye have shown to me, **hauiun** they have shown to me MG 286:5, **hauiuia** Gy 23:2 etc. (*often*) they showed to him MG 288:24. Impf. **ʿhauia** Gy 79:7 I show MG 261:ult., **nihauun, nihaun** Gy 299:10, 316:5, 384:23 they (will) show MG 262:3 (cf. 8:22); with suff. **ʿhauiak** Gy 114:17. 161:3, Gs 73:13 I show to thee MG 286:bottom, **ʿhauiik** Jb 125:4 (var. BD **-iak**) I show to thee (fem.), **tihauinan** Q 55:4 thou showest to us MG 289:16. Impt. with suff. **hauih̲** show to him MG 287:bottom, **hauian** Gy 145:1, 161:2, **hauiin** Gy 161:14, 162:19 show me MG 285:7 ff. (cf. 271 n. 2), **hauiuia** Gy 44:4 *demonstrate ei* MG 289:3. Act. pt. **mhauia; d̲-mhauia šidqa** CP 10:13. 48:9, ML 12:1, 64:3 who interpreteth silence (*often*). Part. pres. **mhauit** Morg. 224/35:5 thou showest; with encl. **mhauiatlun** Gy 144:10 thou showest to them MG 262:bottom, **mhauitulun** Gy 22:18 ye show to them MG 263:2. Pass. pt. **mhauai** (*often*) is shown, indicated. Nom. ag. **mhauiana** (s.v.).

Af. Pf. with encl. **ʿuhrata man d̲-ahuilak** ŠQ 19:7 who showed thee the roads?; with suff. **ahuian** he showed to me MG 285:6, **ahuith̲** I showed him MG 288:11. Impt. with encl. **ahuilia hazin arqa tibil** DAb show me this earthly world; with suff. **ahuian lbušai** Jb 125:2 show me my garment. Act. pt. with encl. **mahuilh̲ ʿuhra d̲-hiia** ATŠ II no. 410 he shows him the way of life; **mahuilkun** Q 57:6 he showeth to you. Part. pres. with encl. **mahuinalik** Gy 151:15 I will show thee (fem.), **lamahuitulun** Gy 22:18 ye show not to them.

Ethpa. Pt. **mitahzia mithania umithauia** DC 36 is visible, pleasing, and manifest; with encl. **mitahuilun** DC 44. 137 they appear to them.

Ettaf. Pt. **mitahuia** AM 257:23 it does appear.

Gl. 11:13 f. af. أرى *ostendere* نمود; 57:7 f. af. حسن *benefacere* خوبى كرد; 179:7 f. af. دلّ *demonstrare* نمود.

Der.: **mahuiana.**

huaiza (often in coloph.) a small town in Khuzistan (South Iran).

HUB (חוב, ܚܳܒ, خاب LS) to be wanting, defective, faulty, guilty; to fail, succumb, be confuted; pa. to incriminate, declare guilty, accuse.

Pe. Pt. (always with **la**): **lahaiib ulašapir** Gy 96:12 unseemly and not good; **ṣbu d̲-lahaiib** Gy 45:20, 120:17 f. something unseemly (**la** is to emphasize **haiib** which itself is negative).

Pa. Pf. with suff. **haibth̲ luat mlakia bita** *Florilegium* I convicted him before the angels of the House; **haibinun laudia** Gy 132:9 he convicted the perishing ones. Impf. with suff. **nihaibh̲** he will confute him MG 275: bottom. Act. pt. with encl. **mhaiiblan** Morg. 221/30:8 he will confute us; pl. with encl. **lzakaia mhaibilh̲** Gs 36:22 they convict the innocent. Pass. pt. **mhaiab hu alma d̲-taiib umiṣṭba** DC 36 II no. 5 he is guilty until he repents and is baptized.

Ethpa. Pf. **laʿthaiab** (with **l**) ATŠ II no. 15 was not incumbent on . . . Impf. **nithaibun** CP 107:9, ML 132:11 they will be convicted. Pt. **mhaiab** Gy 14:19 etc. confuted, convicted MG 132:19. Part. pres. **mithaibitun** Gy 22:18 ye are found guilty.

Der.: **hauba, haiaba.**

HUG (חוג, ܚܳܓ LS, Ges.) to avert (of eyes), to turn from (in awe, reverence) Ginzā 258 n. 4.
 Pe. Pf. **uhag ainh̲** Gy 294:13 CD Leid. (var. **haga ainh̲**) he turned away his eyes; **mihag hag ainaihun** Gy 259:6 f. they turned away their eyes. Pt. pl. fem. **haiga ainaihun** DC 41:226 their eyes turn away; (masc.) **almia d̲-hgaga d̲-haigin ainaihun d̲-ʿutria umalkia lmihzia** ATŠ II no. 89 worlds of illusion which, on seeing it, uthras and kings turn away their eyes in awe.
 Der.: **hag, hagigia** (?), **hgaga.**

hug̣iana (ܗܘܓܳܝܳܐ, הֶגְיוֹן) letter, syllable. Pl. **hugiania.** MG 1:bottom and n. 1, 136:ult. **asrin uarba hugiania d̲-a-b-g** ATŠ I no. 4 the 24 letters of the A-B-C; **bšuba hugiania mikdib** ATŠ I nos. 224 and 247 written in 7 letters; **bhugiania hzih̲** AM 157:2 see by the letters; **palga d̲-hugiania ʿtahzia** ATŠ I no. 260 is perceived to be the half-way point of the alphabet; **kd̲ hugiana msaqmia** (var. PD **msaqam**) **blišanh̲** ATŠ I no. 134 like a syllable formed by his tongue.

hud- v.s. **lhud** and **balhud.**

hudaiia (< **iahudaiia** = **iahuṭaiia**) Jews. **hudaiia urumaiia** AM Jews and Greeks; **bit hudaiia** AM (often); **hudaiia umšihaiia minh̲ d̲-himiana lamitkirkin** ATŠ I no. 250 Jews and Christians are not girdled with the (sacred) girdle; **bhazin maṭarta nišmata d̲-hudaiia bgauh̲ mištailia** RD C 22 = DAb in this purgatory the souls of Jews are put to the question; **hudaiia iatbia smala d̲-br aiar baraia** DC 51. 367 the Jews (?) sit at the left hand of the Son of the Outer Atmosphere (an allusion to τὰ δὲ ἐρίφια ἐξ εὐωνύμων Matt. 25:33b?). Gl. 178:1 **h(u)daii** [*sic*] يهود, يهودى *Judaeus.*

hudhud (Ar. هُدْهُد) AM 132:9 hoopoe.

hudišaiia (Cf. Talm. חודיש) ATŠ II no. 91 (Bab. חודיש) pertaining to the new moon (see ATŠ trs. n. 10).

hudrana (rt. **HDR** I) circle, encirclement, circumference: **hdar hudrana** Gy 169:17, DC 51. 488 v.s. **HDR** pe. pf.

hudšaiia name of a people MG 2 n. 1, BZ Ap. II. **bit hudšaiia** Q 50:24, AM 250:16 the country of H.

HUṬ (חוט, ܚܳܛ, Ar. خاط mediae I) to sew, stitch together.
 Pe. Impf. with suff. **nihiṭia ltagia** CP 348:9 he shall sew up the crown; **nihiṭunun** ŠQ and B.M. Or. 6592:35 they shall sew them.
 Der.: **hauṭa, mhaṭa, mhaṭia, hiṭut** (?).

huṭartana (cf. חֲטַר, ܚܛܰܪ to strike) fighter (?) **rudpana huṭartana rbutana** DC 43 persecutor, fighter (?) and arrogant.

huṭpa (rt. **HṬP**) robbery by force, rape, seizure, act of violence. Pl. **huṭpia. hirba uhuṭpa** Gs 51:14 sword and violence; **šuta d̲-huṭpia** Gs 60:5 violent words; **unasgia bhuṭpia** ATŠ II no. 356 he will proceed to acts of violence; **ṭulmia uhuṭpia** ATŠ II no. 357 deeds of oppression and violence; **gimran mn huṭpia** DC 53. 410 bring to an end for me the acts of violence.

huṭra (חוּטְרָא, ܚܘܛܪܳܐ) staff, sceptre, flail. **huṭra ukarkušta** Gy 180:16 the staff and the rattle; **bhuṭrai** Gy 191:2 with my staff; **gaṭna mn huṭra** Gy 182:17 thinner than a staff; **huṭra d̲-mura** JRAS 1937 590:12 staff of office (authority).

huṭrana = **huṭra. umta huṭranak** DC 6 and stretch forth thy sceptre.

huiza Zotb. 231 left 8 a var. of **huaiza.**

huir for **h(a)uria** ? in **barqa d̲-huir** DC 43 A coloph. in a marsh-country.

HUK = **HKK.**

hukumta (חוכמתא, ܚܘܟܡܬܳܐ) wisdom, cleverness, intelligence, cunning. Varr. **hukmta, hikumta** MG 13:paen., 26:anteantep., 105:15. St. cstr. **hukmat, hukumat** MG 32:26. **hukumtak** thy wisdom MG 177:5; **hukumta mn libaiun mapqin** Gy 24:5 they expel wisdom from their hearts; **gamarlh̲ lkulh̲ hukumta** v.s. **GMR** pa. pf. with encl.; **zipa uhukumta** Gy 174:5 falsity and cunning; **bhukmat šrara uhaimanuta** Gy 39:9 f. by the wisdom of firmness and faith; **bhukumta ušabšuta urahmuta** Gy 257:paen, with cunning and flattery and endearment.

hukuna read **hukṣa.**

hukla Gs 12:2 D a var. of **hikla** ibid. C.

hukṣa (prob. חוצא, ܚܘܨܳܐ, otherwise Mand. **ʿuṣa**) palm-frond (also a strip of frond dried and used as string). **hukṣa d̲-talia** (var. **tala**) DC 12. 192 Lond. roll B 407 (and P.A.'s copy) the frond of a young date-palm; **hukṣa d̲-diqla asarinun** Oxf. roll f 818 bind them with (strips of) palm-fronds DC 46. 145:9, Bodl. 12, DC 24 etc.

hul, hula (etym. and meaning doubtful. Possibly ܗܽܘܠܳܐ < ὕλη, from which, however, no st. abs. would be expected) matter (?), material part (?). Extremely obscure and doubtful. **hula** (var. **hul**) **d̲-šubaita** ATŠ II no. 156 (var. DC 6 ibid.) the material part (?) of the seventh (fem., **aina**); **urmia lbar almia kul hul** DC 43 and casts out of the worlds all matter (i.e. each material substance, or חָלָא, ܚܘܠܳܐ H. חֹל = every profane thing?).

hulia for **hbulia** (q.v.). **halin d̲-aklin huila ubr hulia** DAb 16 (var. **hbul ubr hbulia** v.s. **hbul, hbulia**). (Mod. *holyâ* from **HLA** means sweets, sugar, etc., cf. Gl. 76:14).

HUM = **HMM I** (q.v.) with transition to ע״ו in certain forms MG 248 n. 2.
 Der.: **hauma** (cf. also s. **HMM I**).

humar (st. abs. חֲמַר, ܚܡܳܪ, حِمَار with labialization of the front vowel) AM jackass.

humarta 1 (חומרתא, ܚܘܡܪܬܳܐ) (*a*) bead, (precious, or semi-precious) stone, (*b*) amulet, charm, (*c*) joint, knot, bone, (*d*) (amulet-) spirit. St. abs. **humra 1.** Pl. **humria.** MG 26:antep., 60:anteantep., 76 n. 1, 105:17, 172:3; Lidzb. Uthra 541 n. 1, Ginzā 53 n. 4; IM Gl.; Furlani *I Nomi* 393 ff. (*a*) **humria uʿsqata** RD C 11, **latanak litbh̲ humria** s. **atana 2, humria uaṣaṣʿ** Gy 10:22, **humria d̲-glala** DC 43 J 74, **humria uṭasia d̲-abara bpumaihun** DC 44; (*b*) **humarta rabtia** DC

37:489; **mauminalak . . . bhumarta d̲-razia** DC 40; (*c*) **humarta d̲-halṣh̲** and **humarta d̲-halṣai** s. **halṣa. bšauṭa d̲-tlatma ušitin humria** DC 44. 524 with a scourge of 360 knots; **humarta d̲-šura** DC 48. 29 the knot of the navel; (*d*) **humria** Gy 99:9, 122:2, 230:3, 232:19, 259:22 f., 261:14, 262:4, 391:4 &c. (*very often*); **humria d̲-nirig** Gy 225:7; **humria qadišata** Gy 231:10; **humria d̲-baita** Gy 302:4, 316:13; **humarta zikria uhumarta nuqbata** DC 43(a):26, 37:513; **bhumarta d̲-rqiha** DC 40. 280; **humria zadaniata** ML 22:2, DC 44, CP 20:3 satanic amulet-spirits; with suff. **humrh̲** Gy 332:18, **šria ʿnbu lhumrh̲** Lond. roll B 161, cf. also 256, **ruha uhumra** Gy 81:6 R and her (female) spirits, **humrak** Gy 88:6, **humrak uliliatak** Gy 87:21, **humraihun** Gy 106:16, **sahraihun uhumraihun** Gs 95:4.

humarta 2 = **hanbura** (by the influence of **humarta 1**). **bhumarta d̲-marba šura (šuba?)** ATŠ I no. 247 = **bhanbura d̲-marba** ATŠ I no. 168 (v.s. **hambura 1**).

humbaria, hambaria Gy 203:10, 204:1, Gs 17:12, Oxf. roll. 222 f., DC 26. 18, DC 34. 651, DC 43 J 103 ruins (?) MG 123:11, Ginzā 203 n. 2. **hambaria** DC 28 seems to be the same word (without labialization of the vowel before m) but may mean 'darkness', 'dark vapours' (= **habara 1**); **arqa bhumbaria** DC 34. 651 the earth (was) in darkness (?).

humud AM 256:ult. a man's name.

humra 1 st. abs. of **humarta** (q.v.).

humra 2 (rt. **HMR I**) redness, inflammation. Pl. **humria** (?). **sumaqa uhumra** AM 257:7 redness and inflammation; **humria** AM 277:23 red clouds (?, or darkness, dark clouds = **hum(ba)ria** = **hambaria**?).

-hun possessive suff. of the 3rd p. pl. masc. used often also inst. of the fem. **-hin** (s.v.). The **h** of the suff. is almost always dropped after a consonant and very often after a vowel. Doublets **-un** and **-aihun, -aiun** (the latter two originally used after pl. nouns, but then also after sg., s.vv.) MG 88:9, 180 f. The final **n,** the apocope of which is very regular in mod. Mand., was dropped very rarely in the Cl.: **bdauru** Gs 58:7 in their dwelling MG 180 n. 2.

h(u)nina (rt. **HNN**) small, little. Very frequent in mod. Mand. (pronounced *honina*). Gl. 128:11 h(u)ninai [*sic*] اطفال *parvuli* بچگان.

hunpana (< *חונפא, cf. חֲנָפָא, ܚܢܦܐ) hypocrite MG 138:ult. Pl. **hunpania** CP 113:12 Q 57:25 = ML 139:1, ATŠ II no. 145.

huntai (rel. to **hata** = **ahata**?) cousin. Found only with the suff. of the 1st p. sg. Var. **hintai** (s.v.). **hua rbai uzauh̲ d̲-huntai** DC 43 (coloph. of *Ṣir sahria*) he was my teacher and the husband of my cousin; **dadai uhuntai** DC 35 my paternal aunt and my cousin (?); **huntai br iaiia** DC 35 my cousin (?, why fem.?) son of my paternal uncle (or is **huntai** a pr. n.?).

HUS (חוס, ܚܣ LS, Ges.) to have compassion, take pity on, spare, protect; to grieve.

PE. Impt. **hus** Gy 84:19, with special pl. ending **husiun** MG 250:7. Act. pt. **d̲-lahaiis libh̲ lʿniš** AM 154:13 whose heart feels compassion for none; **haisa Ṣâb.'s** AM she will have compassion; pl. **haisia umitrahmia** Gy 286:3 pitying and feeling compassion. Part. pres. **haisit** Gs. 94:10, 120:20, JRAS 1937 593 thou grievest.

DER.: **haiasa, hai(a)suta.**

hus, hausa (Ar. حوض) water-basin, cistern, basin of fountain, reservoir MG XXXIII 17. **hus iardna** Jb 4:15, 76:14, 116:13 the reservoir of the jordan (cf. also DC 3 and 53 no. 388).

husma, hisma (rt. **HSM**) envy, envious thought. Pl. **husmia. husmia uṭulmia** ATŠ II no. 20 envious and wrongful thoughts; **husma uqina** Gy 215:20 f. envy and rancour.

huspa (חוּצְפָּא, ܚܘܨܦܐ) impudence, barefacedness MG 44:21, 104:15. **huspa urugza** Gy 215:21 impudence and rage.

husra = **husrana. husrh̲** DC 22. 456 = **husranh̲** Gs 69:14.

husrana (חוּסְרָנָא, ܚܘܣܪܢܐ) fault, loss, defection, lacking, imperfection, need, want, poverty, harm. Pl. **husrania. aina d̲-husrana** Gy 287:6 evil eye, Ginzā 284 n. 6 (cf. ML 39); **btlata husrania ʿṣṭarar husrana** ATŠ I no. 190 defection is formed by three faults; **mitparqa mn hak husrana** ATŠ I no. 140 she will be delivered from that fault; **nasba bazira mn husranh̲ lbar mn zauh̲** ATŠ I no. 184 by her fault she receiveth seed from one not her husband; **lhama d̲-husrana tikul** AM 66:7 she will eat the bread of poverty; **zaina uhusrana** AM 74:12 loss and faulty act(s); **husrana bhiuaniata** AM 189:1 loss in cattle.

HUP, HPP (חוף, ܚܦ Akk. *ḫâpu* rel. to ܚܦ H. חפף II LS, Ges.) to wash, rub, cleanse, scrape.

PE. Impf. **tihup** thou rubbest MG 249:11; **latihup rišak** AM 138:8 do not wash thy head. Impt. **hup** wash MG 250:7. Part. pres. **haipit usarqit** Gy 116:15 thou washest and combest. Pass. pt. **hipa umdakia** Morg. 225/38:1 = Q 24:31 washed and cleansed; with encl. (and act. meaning) **hiplia** Gs 84:20 I have washed.

DER.: **hapia** = **haupia** = **hupia, hapapiata, hipia.**

hupania Oxf. roll a 591 = **hunpania.**

hupia = **haupia. hupia mn kasa** DC 21 = JRAS 1938 6:24 froth from the bowl; **hupia bpumh̲** Oxf. roll 308 f. (cf. 349 f.), DC 43 J 141 slaver in the mouth; **hupia d̲-susia** AM 135:11 froth from a horse('s mouth); **hupia mia** Gy 194:4 foam of the waters.

hupna (חוּפְנָא, ܚܘܦܢܐ) hollow of the palm, handful. Pl. **hupnia. hupnak** CP 82:14, Morg. 237/61:2 = ML 102:4 the hollow of thy hands; **uašqinin tlata hupnia mia** CP 25:5, ML 27:9 and give them (: to the souls) three handfuls of water to drink; **ukd̲ mašqiatlh̲ mia tlata hupnia** DC 27. 115 and when thou givest him 3 handfuls of water to drink; **mašqinun mia bhupnai** Jb 40:11 I give them water to drink in my hollow palm; **ukd̲ hupna d̲-mia mašiqlh̲** (read **mašqilh̲**) DC 34 and when he giveth him a palmful of water to drink; **unašqilh̲ tlata hupnia mia** DC 36 no. 189.

HUṢ (ܚܘܨ LS) to press together, weld together, hold tight, close the hand over, bind up, construct by binding, clamp together, wedge, bunch, press tightly together.

Pe. Pf. **haṣiun ʿndruna** Or. 6592 they built a booth. Impf. with suff. **ʿhiṣiun lbabia d̲-šuria ʿlauaihun** Gy 333:3 f. I will clap together the gates of the wall(s) upon them. Impt. **huṣ ʿda** DC 44 close the hand (over him?); pl. **huṣiun ʿndruna** DC 38 construct a booth (i.e. by binding the reeds so as to build a hut); **huṣinun** (read **huṣiun**) **škinta haditia** (DC 6 **hiṣiun**) ATŠ I no. 59 construct a new cult-hut.

HUQ I, AUQ, ʿUQ, HQQ II (ܚܩܐ) to fear; af. to frighten, terrify, torment; but a simple pe. has often the same meaning. Forms without **h̲** s. **AUQ.** MG 71:17.

Pe. Pf. **haq minaihun** Gy 135:15 he was afraid of them, **mn hauqa d̲-haq** Gy 160:16 from the fear which he felt MG 400:10; **haqat uzahat namrus** (var. **nimrus**) CP 153:17, ML 184:9 N. feared and trembled; **haqt** thou didst fear MG 248:13; **haqit** I feared MG 71:17, 248: antep.; **haqit zahit uʿtazihit** Gy 180:19 I feared, trembled, and was afraid; **mn hiia haqit** DC 43 I feared the Life. Impf. **tihuq** thou art afraid MG 249:8; **tihiqun** Gy 64:17, 19 (D **tihqun**) ye are afraid MG 249:bottom; impersonally with encl. (as fem.) **latihuqlak** Jb 55:11 be not alarmed; with suff. **nihiqunan** Q 57:26 they terrify us MG 280:17. Act. pt. fem. **haiqa umtnauda** Gy 88:2 she feared and trembled; pl. **haiqin** (read with DC 6 **haiqan**) **maṭarata** ATŠ I no. 123 the purgatories are afraid; **hauqin** [*sic*] **d̲-mn ʿuhra d̲-abuian laṣalin** DC 34 they fear lest they deviate from the Way of our Father; **ula mn aria mrida haiqan** Jb 41:5 1 and they (fem.) fear not the fierce lion. Part.pres. **ana lahaiiqna minaihun** Gy 157:14 I am not afraid of them; **uanat minh̲ haiqit** DC 6 and thou art afraid of him.

Af. Pf. with suff. **ahiqinun** Gs 69:3 he frightened them; **ahiuk** Gs 55:15 they frightened thee. Impf. with suff. **tʿiah(i)qh̲ tiah(i)qh̲** Gy 314:2 thou frightenest her MG 215:19, 276:4; **ʿiah(i)qh̲** Gy 101:19 I frighten her MG 276:4. Act. pt. with encl. **mahiqilun** Gy 24:paen. they frighten them MG 251:21. Part. pres. with encl. **mahiqatlun** thou frightenest them MG 251:23. Nom. ag. **mahiqana** s.v.

Der.: **hauqa** and **hauqana**), **mahiqa, mahiqana, mahqaiil.**

HUQ II, HQQ I(חקק) to be lawful, orderly, ruled.

Pe. Act. pt. **hakima d̲-lahaiiq** Gy 216:paen. a wise man who is unruly.

HUQ III (ܚܘܩ LS) to (give) sound.

Pe. Act. pt pl. **garglia hadria uhaiqia minaihun** DC 4 the spheres revolve and some of them give sound (Pythagorean idea of the music of heavenly spheres?).

Der.: **nihiqa.**

huqa (etym. unknown) a weight (?): the oke. **zahba bhuqia** ŠQ 15:19 = CP 223:8 = DC 3. 377:10.

HUR (ܚܘܪ) to see, look at, view, observe.

Pe. Pf. **har uhaš bihdadia** Gy 282:9 they looked at one another and pondered; with encl. **harbh̲ balma hazin** Gy 297:16 he looked at this world. Impt. with suff. **hurh̲** AM view it (?).

HWR (חָוַר, ܚܘܪ LS, Ges. s. חור) to be white; pa. to whiten, wash, bleach, make white; (af.?) to become white, hoary.

Pa. Pf. **hauariun ʿdaihun** DC 34. 1132 they washed their hands; with suff. **haurh̲** Gy 218: 10 he bleached it MG 275:6. Impt. **haur(i)h̲ bmia** DC 46 (*often*) wash it off in water (: defectively) **hurh̲** AM whiten it; with pl. suff. **haurinun** DC 36 II no. 17 (var. **haurunun** DC 6 ibid.).

Af. Pf. **ahuar rišai** Jb 54:8 my head has become hoary (is rather pe. with a prosth. **a**).

Gl. 24:15 f. pa. اغتسل *lavari* شسته شد; 114:3 f. غسل *lavare* شست.

Der.: **hiuara**, var. **hauara, haura, hira 2.**

huraran occasional var. of **hauraran.**

hurba 1 (חוּרְבָּא and חוֹרְבָא, ܚܘܪܒܐ) destruction, desolation, ruin, waste, desert MG 104: 15. Masc., rarely fem. MG 486:3. **bhurba** Gy 172:10, **bhurbia** Gy 354:1 in the wilderness; **hurba ṣadia** Gy 331:22 a dry desert; **hurba marda** Gs 47:9 f. troublesome ruin; **hurba harba** Gs 55:3 a desolate waste; **naṭria hurbia** DC 43, D 60 destructive watchers. Gl. 71:6 h(u)rba خراب *desolatio*.

hurba 2 a rare var. of **hirba. d̲-hurbh̲ šlipa** *Florilegium* whose sword is unsheathed.

hurba 3 (חָרוּבָא) carob-tree, found only in pl. **hurbia** Gs 129:6, 7, cf. Ginzā 584 n. 1.

hurbana (rt. **HRB**) destruction, corruption. **hurbana zmaiun** DC 43 H 52 corruption of their blood.

hurbania a mod. pl. of **hurba 1. duktai bhurbania** DC 46. 90:3 my place is in ruins (or desolate places).

hurga (cf. חוֹרְג J) step-son. Pl. **hurgia** step-children. **hanath̲ bra hurga qarilh̲** ATŠ II no. 368 that her son, they shall call him 'step-son'; **mn šitlai d̲-hauilun hurgia hinun** ATŠ I no. 82 (those) of my children which shall be born to them will be stepchildren.

hurda (Ar. خُرْدَى and هردى Fränkel 149) Morg. 222/31:8 = ML 66:7 = CP 51:1 reed MG 60:12, ML 67 n. 3.

hurzunia pl. (rel. to **harzina**?). Meaning doubtful. **uhurzunia** (var. **harzunia**) **rurbia d̲-rumana** DC 43 J 99.

huria s. **hauria.**

hurizdan s. **nuraiṭaš.**

hurina (Talm. אחרינא, Syr. ܐܚܪܢܐ, the Mand. form corresponds to those of younger Pal. dialects with -הו, cf. Chr. Pal. ܚܘܪܢ) other, another. Fem. **hurintia.** Pl. **hurinia**, fem. **huriniata.** MG 21:10 f., 28:antep. f., 35:22 f., 139:bottom, (var. fem. **hurintin**) 154:12, § 149 p. 185 f. Sometimes used as an ordinal number (e.g. Gy 108:2) MG 191:ult. **bhurintin**

maṭarta Gs 28:4, 32:15 = **bmaṭarta hurintin** Gs 34:4, 35:13 in another purgatory MG 319:2 f.; **alpa šnᶜ huriniata** Gs 5:13 another thousand years.

hurmus a man's name. **hurmus lhakim** AM 261:29.

hurmig s. **hurnig.**

hurmiz, hurmiṣ a favourite Mand. name, also the name of an ancient Iranian king. **hurmiṣ malka br kasrau** Gy 384:9 (cf. also l. 11, DC 22. 380, Leid. and Sh. ʿAbd.'s copy have **hurmiz**) Hormuzd the king, son of Chosroes (578–590) Ochser ZA 19/1905 p. 55 n. 7; **hurmiṣ alaha** DC 44. 1390 = Morg. 265/21:9 the god H.

hurmizdukt a *malwâša* woman's name.

hurmiṣ s. **hurmiz.**

hurnig Gy 383:23 (var. Leid. **hurmig** Ginzā 411 n. 5) an ancient Iranian king (302–9) Ochser ZA 19 1905 p. 76 n. 7.

hurpa 1 (ܚܘܪܦܐ III 2 LS, cf. Löw 87, footn.) a kind of plant. Varr. **harpa, hirpa.** Rel. to **hapura**? **šuba ṣindia d̲-hurpa d̲-hiuara** DC 46. 221:6, Par. xxvii 35 a.

hurpa 2 (חוּרְפָּא, ܚܘܪܦܐ III 1 LS, Ar. خروف) a young animal: lamb, kid, colt. Pl. **hurpia. mrirta d̲-ᶜuba abual hu hurpa** DC 43; **šarin bit bit hurpia** DC 43 J 165 (compound with **bit 1** q.v.).

hurtia AM 93 for **hurintia** (s. **hurina**).

HUŠ, HŠŠ (חוש and חשש, ܚܫ and ܚܫ LS, Ar. حسّ, H. חוּשׁ II Ges.) to feel, be affected, think anxiously, be troubled about, be sorrowful, suffer, meditate, ponder seriously.

Pe. Pf. **haš bnapšh̲** Gy 281:10 he was troubled about himself; **haš upraš** CP 14:4, ML 16:2 he thought and considered (or manifested); **sakla d̲-lahaš ulapraš** s. **sakla**; **haš hiia upraš hiia uᶜtapraš hiia** JRAS 1939 591:12 the Life pondered, the Life understood, the Life took counsel within itself; **har uhaš bihdadia** s. **HUR.** Act. pt. pl. **kulhun haišia ubahšia** Gy 81:3 all of them ponder and seek; **haišia bhukumtun** Gy 110:6 they think over in their sagacity.

Der.: **hašta 2, mahšin, huš 4.**

huš 1 (etym. unknown) a name, or designation of the Great Sea, Ocean. Fem. MG 161 n. 2. **huš rabtia** Gy 198:5, 7, DC 43 H 54, **mia hinun d̲-huš iama** Gy 273:10, cf. Ginzā 198 n. 5.

huš 2 (P. هوش) intelligence, intellect, sense, understanding. **bla huš hauia** DC 46. 109:16 is senseless (or faints, cf. P. بی هوش شدن).

huš 3 (Ar. حوش) cattle BZ 192 n. 12. **mutana d̲-huš** AM 284:paen. cattle-murrain; **aqna d̲-huš** JRAS 1937 592 sheep (plur.) of a flock.

huš 4 (rt. **HUŠ**) pain, suffering. **d̲-bamar** (= **bimar**) **ubhuš hauia** DC 46. 107:9 so that he is ill and in pain.

hušba (= **hušbana**) thought, scheme. Pl. **hušbia. hušbia bišia** DC 22. 349, DC 36 II no. 87, DAb evil thoughts; **mhašib hušbia hauia** AM 49:11 he will be a schemer.

hušbana (חוּשְׁבְּנָא, ܚܘܫܒܢܐ, حُسْبَان) reflection, reckoning, calculation, computation, counting, accounting, accountancy, scheming, plan. Pl. **hušbania.** With suff. **hušbanak** Gy 214:10 thy reflection, **hušbanh̲** DC 22. 309 his reckoning (a var. of **hušbana** Gy 312: 14), **hušbanun** (often) their count, **hušbanakun** Q 56 b:12 your counting MG 179:paen.; **bhušbana** AM 5:5 by accountancy; **kilh̲ uhušbania** DAb its measure and design(s).

hušbanaiia (adj. from **hušbana**) calculators, astrologers. **palig hušbana lhušbanaiia** AM assign calculation to the astrologers (calculators).

hušiᶜil Ṣâb.'s AM a theophorous name.

HZA I (חזא, ܚܙܐ, H. חזה I LS, Ges.) to see, look, behold, perceive, observe, find out.

Pe. Pf. **hza** he saw MG 257:1, **hzat** she saw MG 257:6, **hzit** Gy 175:1 thou hast seen MG 275:18; pl. **hzun**, fem. **ᶜhzia** Gy 212:13 they saw MG 258:2 (masc.), 11 (fem.); **hzit kd̲ hzaian ainai** DC 27. 60 I saw as my eyes saw; with encl. **hzainalh̲** Gy 141:12 we saw him; with suff. **hizian** Gy 164:6 etc. he saw me MG 284:21 f., **hiziak** Q 52:11 he saw thee MG 286:16, **hizih̲** Q 59:8 etc., he saw him MG 287:7, **hzinun** Gy 162 (*often*) he saw them MG 290:11, **hzatan** Gy 145:9, 174:17 she saw me MG 285:12 f., **hzath̲** she saw him MG 287:bottom (cf. n. 5), **hzaitak** Gy 192:23 f. I saw thee MG 286:bottom, **hzaith̲** Gs 62:13 f. etc., I saw him MG 188:6, **hzatinun** Gy 94:18 etc., she saw them MG 290:21, **hzaitinun, hzitinun** Gy 73:3, 96:24, 319:15 etc., I saw them MG 290:antep., **hzun** Q 174:18 they saw me MG 285:anteantep. f. **hiziun** (var. D **hizun** Gy 164:22, Gs 86:13, 21) id. MG 286:2, **hiziuia** (*often*) they saw him MG 288:20, **hiziu** Gy 282:8 they saw her MG 289:8 f., **hzainak** Gy 66:5 we saw thee MG 286:paen., **hzainh̲** (*often*) we saw him a bad var. **hzinia**) MG 268:middle. Impf. **nihzia** (*often*) *vide(bi)t, vide(bi)mus* MG 258:paen., **tihzia** *ea vide(bi)t, vide(bi)s* MG 258ult., **ᶜhzia** I (shall) see MG 259:1, **nihzun** they (will) see MG 259:2, **tihzun** ye (will) see MG 259:6; with suff. **nihiziak, nihziak** we see thee MG 286:20, **nihizih̲, tihizih̲, ᶜhizih̲** he, we, thou, I (shall) see him MG 287:middle, **nihzinan** Gy 135:13 he seeth us MG 289:middle, **nihzinun** Gy 152:4, 154:22 we (shall) see them (he will see them) MG 290:middle, **d̲-hzinun** Gs 65:17 that I (may) see them MG 34:anteantep. f., **nihzunan** Gy 275:23 they see us MG 289:antep., **nihzunh̲** they see him MG 288:antep., **tihzunh̲** ye see him, ibid. Impt. **hzia,** fem. **hzai,** pl. (masc.) **hzun** MG 259:10, 12, 14, **hzun bainaikun** Gy 21:5 see with your eyes, **hzun ušuma** Gy 21:4 see ye and hear; with suff. **huziin** DC 53. 482:13 behold me, **huzih̲** Gs 80:7, Q 66:14 etc., see him MG 287:19, **hzinan** Gy 61:14 see us MG 289:17 (forms **huzian** Gs 46:5 and **hzia** ibid. A for 'see us!' are hardly correct MG 289 n. 2), **hzinun, hzinin** Gs 68:18, Q 41:17 see them MG 290:18, **hziun** Q 74 b:28 see me MG 286:12, **hzinan** see (pl.) us Lidzb. ZDMG lxi 693 n. 1, **hzunin** Q 9:21

videte eas MG 291:middle, **huziuia** CP 80:12, Gy 357:23, ML 99:2 etc., see him (it) MG 289:1. Act. pt. **hazia** (often) he sees. Part. pres. **hazina** I see MG 259:19, fem. **haziana** Gy 155:1 id. MG 259:20, **hazit** thou seest, **hazinin** we see, **hzaitun** ye see MG 259: bottom. Pass. pt. **hzia** seen MG 259:paen. With encl. (and act. meaning) **hzilia** I have seen MG 367:6, **hzilak** Gy 154:19 etc., thou hast seen MG 259:ult., pl. with encl. **hzilia** Gy 154:20 I saw them MG 382:5. Inf. **mihzia ḏ-hiziun** Gs 124:15 when they saw me MG 389:middle; with suff. **mihzian** Gy 156:13 to see me MG 292:11, **mihizih̲** Gy 335:16, Q 65:15 etc., to see him MG 292:antep., **mihzinkun** to see you MG 293:4, **mihzinun** to see them MG 293:10, **mihizia ḏ-hiziun ʿit ḏ-babaihun ahid** CP 188:16 f. (var. **mihizian**) when they saw me, some closed their doors.

Ethpe. seems not to be used, cf. MG 263 n. 2.

Ettaf. Pf. **ʿtahzia** Gy 262:9 he appeared MG 263:bottom, **ʿtahziat** Gy 266:3 she appeared MG 264:1, **ʿtahzun** they appeared MG 264:21, **ʿtahzaitun** Gy 175:3 ye appeared MG 264:28; with encl. **ʿtahzilh̲** he (or I) appeared to him (her) MG 262:9, 15, **ʿtahzilun** I appeared to them MG 262:15, **ʿtahzulan** Gy 271:8 ff, they appeared to us. Impf. **nitahzia** MG 264:ult., **titahzun** ye (will) appear MG 265:12; with encl. **ʿtahzilh̲** Gs 39:13 I (shall) appear to him MG 265:17. Impt. with encl. **ʿtahzilh̲** Gs 39:13 appear to him MG 265: middle. Pt. **mitahzia** MG 60:paen., 265: bottom, **ḏ-lamitahzia** Gy 31:1 invisible; with encl. **bhalin dmauata mitahzilh̲** DC 22. 349 is visible to him in these forms. Part. pres. **mitahzit** thou appearest MG 266:8; with encl. **mitahziatlh̲** Gs 39:14 thou appearest to him MG 266:8.

Phrases and Idioms. Impt. with **ḏ-** (and often also without it) 'see lest', 'see to it that not', 'beware': **hzia laiṭitun umakšilitun** Gy 351:1 f. beware lest ye curse and make a trespass; **hzia lmarak manšiatlh̲** Jb 246:6 see lest thou forgettest thy Lord; **hzia napšak mhamblat hzia haṭit** Gs 73:6 f. beware lest thou spoilest thyself, beware lest thou sinnest. In AM often as an astrological term: to be in the ascendant, exert influence (of planets), cf. **ʿu nirig nihiziih̲ bqiria nizal** AM 3:11 if Mars is in the ascendant, he will fall into disputes; **ʿu bil unirig . . . nihzunh̲** AM 3:13 if Jupiter and Mars are in the ascendant (or the ruling planets); **hziin kiuan . . . uhiziin bil** DC 12. 133, 135, DC 28 Saturn hath ascendance over me . . . and Jupiter hath ascendance over me. 'To overlook', get the better of, get the upper hand over, prevail over, bewitch (us. with prep. **b** or **l**): **hu bsanh̲ hazia uatutia ligrh̲ naplia** AM 11:2 he will get the better of his enemies and they will fall beneath his feet; **kul daiua ḏ-hazilh̲** DC 37. 246 ff. every devil that bewitches (: prevails over) him; **ʿu hazilh̲ bildbabh̲ zakilh̲** AM 23:16 if his enemy gets the better of him, he will vanquish him. 'To approach', have intercourse with: **iuamai srin utartin šnia ḏ-lahzilia zaua** Jb 72:10 today (it is) 22 years since I 'beheld' (my?) spouse; **ptulta ḏ-gabra lahzilh̲** DC 44 a maid that had no intercourse with a man; **ukulhun mahuzia ḏ-hiziun ldilai** DC 26 and all the walled towns that looked down (in an unfriendly manner) on me; **hizih uʿzdahar** ATŠ scrutinize him closely and beware; **nihzunin ʿl bauatan unipiršun lhad had** ATŠ II no. 192 let us look closely into our prayers and interpret them one by one.

Gl. 4:1 f. **ahza** ابصر *videre* دید; 6:1 f. id. انظر *accendere* (?) دید; 6:5 f. **ahzi** [*sic*] امل *considerare* فكر كرد; 6:13 f. **ahza** التفت *se vertere* التفات كرد; 14:9 f. id. اعاد *converti* برگشت; 16:5 f. اعنّا [sic] *adiuvare* آسان شد; 19:1 f. id. أرى *ostendere* نمود; 39:15 f. id. بالى *curae esse* حاضر شد; 47:7 f. miswritten تعجب *admirari* عجب كرد; 51:5 f. **ahza** تعهد *visitare* زيارت كرد; 82:3 f. id. رصد *observare, notare* در مكين بود; 110:5 f. طلع *aspicere* نگاه كرد; 117:13 f. id. عاين *videre* دید; 126:15 f. id. فطن *perspicere* نگاه كرد; 146:13 f. id. لمع *refulgere* روشن كرد; 151:9 f. miswritten ماز *segregare, discernere, distinctum facere* تميز كرد; 163:10 f. **ahza** نظر *attendere* دید.

Der.: **hazaia, hazuia, h(i)zita 1, hzuta, hizua, mahzita, mahzaia.**

HZA II (cf. הַזָּאָה sprinkling) to sprinkle, splash water.

Pe. Impf. **urtitia ḏ-mia nihzih̲** AM (several times) and the boiling of water will sprinkle him; **našqunh̲ unihzih̲** DC 34 they shall give him to drink and shall sprinkle him. Act. pt. with encl. **miṣibh̲ umidakih̲ uhazilh̲** ATŠ II no 158 he baptizes her, purifies her and sprinkles her (or 'beholdeth her' ?).

Der.: **hizita 2.**

hzaia (rt. **HZA I**) seeing, interview. **mulaqat uhzaia d-šulṭania** AM 161:18 an encounter and interview with rulers.

hzama (ܚܙܳܡܳܐ, Ar. both حِزَامَة and خِزَامَة) girdle, constriction, nose-ring (?), v.s. **HZM.**

hzata v.s. **hzita.**

hzuta (rt. **HZA II**) sight, vision, aspect, appearance MG 146:10. **hzuta šaina** AM 233:11; **hzuth̲ mdahla** AM 20:9; **hzutun ubildbabun dilun hua** ATŠ I no. 255 he is of their appearance but is their enemy; **hzuta** Gy 59:8 (var. **hizuta** Sh. 'Abd.'s copy) = **hizua** ibid. Leid.

HZZ (cf. Syr. ܐܶܬ݂ܚܰܙܰܙ LS 224 a, Jb II 181 n. 6) to cleave into, dive into.

Pe. Pf. **hazzit bnahra** Jb 186:3 I dived into the river.

hzita, hizita 1, rarely **hzata** (rt. **HZA I**) vision, seeing, sight, eye. **ʿtahzat hzita** DC 51. 265; **tatnulh̲ hzita lainh̲** DC 51 **upiršat hzita** (var. **hzata**) DC 36 (var. DC 6).

HZM (ܚܙܡ, خزم Akk. *ḫazâmu*) to hem in, clip, gird about, fasten by pressure, restrain.

Pe. Pf. with encl. **hzamtinun hzama bṭirpia anhiraihun hzamtinun lminiltaihun** DC 26. 617 f., Morg. 260/11:3 f. I fastened a clip on their nostrils, I stopped back their words; **hzamtinun blamtinun** (often in exorcisms) I girt them in, I checked them back.

Der.: **hzama.**

HṬA (Gen. Sem., חֲטִי, ܚܛܐ, H. חטא, Ar. خَطِئَ, Akk. *ḫaṭû* Ges.) to sin, err, fail; with **b**: to sin against, transgress; to injure, offend; to lead into sin; with **mn** to cut off from.

Pe. Pf. **kul d̠-hṭa bhṭita rabtia** Gy 53:22 whosoever commits a great sin; **haṭaiia d̠-hṭat** DC 41. 555 sins which she committed; **hṭainin** we sinned MG 258:17; **hṭin** id MG 258:20 (in confessions of sins often both forms together, cf. **hṭin uhṭainin** Gy 103:14, Gs 137:6 f. we have greatly sinned) MG 258 n. 2; with encl. **hṭatabh̠** Gy 91:21 she sinned against him MG 257:15; **mahu hṭitalak** DC 37:489 (in) what did I sin against thee?; **hṭitilun** Gy 60:6 f. I sinned against them MG 257:antep.; **hṭitibkun** (often) I sinned against you MG 257:ult. Impf. **nihṭia** AM 236:15 (var. **niahṭia** cf. BZ 143 n. 3) will injure; **lanihṭia daiua bhaza nišimtai** DC 37. 454 f. no demon will injure this soul of mine; **latihṭai** DC 37. 261 etc. (often in the same document) do not offend (fem.); with encl. **ʿu tihṭibh̠ bhazin nimusa** DC 37. 33 f. if thou transgressest this law; **mindam lanihṭibun** AM 221:13 nothing will injure them; **d̠-lanihṭubia** Gy 360:25 that they cannot injure me. Act. pt. **haṭia** Gy 22:2 etc. (*often*); pl. **haṭia, haṭin** (often); **hṭita d̠-haṭin tarmidia uganzibria** ATŠ I the offence which priests and *ganzibri* commit; with encl. **hiia rbia haṭibak mn arqa d̠-nhura** DC 43 I 127 the Great Life will cut thee off from the Land of Light; **uʿmh̠ haṭibh̠ šibiahia** DC 36 and (as to) his mother, the planets (will) lead her into sin; **ruhia zikria unuqbata . . . d̠-haṭiabh̠** (a *qmaha*) male and female evil spirits . . . that injure him.

Der.: **haṭia 1, haṭaiia, hṭata, hṭita 2.**

hṭaša a surname of an angel: **rabiaiil hṭaša** RD F 1.

hṭata (a doublet of **hṭita 2**) offence; **hšuka d̠-hṭata d̠-ziua** DC 37. 532 darkness which is an offence to the light.

HṬṬ (ܚܛܛ, خطّ Akk. *ḫaṭâṭu* LS) prob. to dig out, excavate, remove (by force). Only in irregular and doubtful forms:

Pe. Pf. with suff. (?) **aina d̠-anania d̠-pirunia haṭuia** DC 21 and the (evil) eye of the spouses that procure the miscarriages (?) of the(ir) offspring (influenced by **YHṬ**?). Impf. **nihiuṭun** [*sic*] **hala** DAb they shall excavate the soil (dust). Pt. pl. with encl. **hiia rbia haṭibak mn arqa d̠-nhura** DC 43. 127 the Great Life will cut thee off from the Land of Light.

hṭima pass. pt. of **HṬM** (q.v.).

hṭipa pass. pt. of **HṬP** (q.v.).

hṭita 1 (חִיטְּתָא, ܚܛܬܐ, H. חִטָּה Ar. حِنْطَة LS, Ges., Löw 157) wheat. Pl. **hiṭia 1** (s.v.). **hṭita hu** DC 34, DC 41 (with illustration showing grain) it is wheat; **pahtilh̠ lhṭita mn šumbilta** ATŠ I no. 285 they separate the grain from the ear of wheat.

hṭita 2 (ܚܛܝܬܐ) sin MG 104:9. **hṭita rabtia hʿ** ATŠ II no. 182 it is a great sin; **hṭita rabtia d̠-asia bdaria litlh̠** ibid., the Great Sin for which there is no healer in ages; **hṭa bhṭita rabiia** s. **HṬA** pe. pf.

hṭit, hṭita 3 (for *htita = ܚܬܝܬܐ?) rightful, sure, correct, proper, fitting, accurate, steadfast. **upagra mn zraz hṭit libšit** DC 34. 364 and I clothed the body with a fitting armour; **ʿtasaqlh̠ šuma hṭita** DC 34. 365 a rightful name was bestowed upon it.

HṬM (H. חטם, Aram. only in derivatives, cf. Ges.) to muzzle, bridle, (figuratively) to bind spells, bewitch.

Pe. Pf. **amhun haṭmun** DC 44 they struck and muzzled (them). Pass. pt. **ʿl man d̠-hṭim** DC 51. 479 over him who is bewitched; pl. **lišania hṭimia** Lond. roll B 464, DC 40. 165, **hṭimia umṭamamia** Morg. 260/12:33 they are hemmed and closed in.

Ethpe. Impf. **nihṭim** DC 40. 484 he will be bridled.

HṬP, HTP (חטף, ܚܛܦ LS, Ges., MG 42 n. 1) to snatch away, seize by force, rob, carry off. Pe. is used also for ethpe.

Pe. Pf. **gzar hṭap** Gy 176:16 were cut off (and) carried away = **gzar hṭip** Gy 179:20 (prob. better, as an ethpe. is expected), **bhiṭpa d̠-daria hṭip** Gs 60:10 (DC 22. 448 better **hṭap**) in the robbery which the generations committed; with suff. **hiṭpun** Gs 60:9 they carried me away. Impf. **nihṭup biama rba d̠-sup** ATŠ II no. 45 he shall be haled off into (or by) the Great Sea of the End (one would expect ethpe.); **d̠-bit anašath̠ tihṭup** AM 73:5 she will be forcibly torn from her home (ethpe. would be expected); **bhiṭpa d̠-daria la ʿhṭip** Gs 60:19 Leid. (ethpe., Pet. has a miscopied **la ʿhṭia**, DC 22. 448 **la ʿhṭup** pe.) I will not be carried away (read ethpe. with Leid.) by the depredations of the generations; **latihiṭpun bhaubaikun** Gy 179:13 (= ethpe.) be not carried away by your evil sins; with suff. **nihiṭpunak** Gs 60:11 he will drag thee away. Act pt. pl. **haṭpia** Gy 215:22, 277:16. Pass. pt. **hṭipa(a).**

Pa. Act. pt. **iama haṭipa d̠-mhaṭip** Gy 216:5 f., Gs 85:1 a rapacious sea that snatcheth away.

Ethpe. cf. s. pe. pf. and impf.

Der.: **haṭipa, haṭiputa, huṭpa, hṭupta, hiṭpa, hiṭupta.**

HṬR (חֲטַר, ܚܛܪ) to strike, beat. (Or 'fence in')?

Pe. Pf. with encl. **uaqapra hṭarbh̠** ATŠ I no. 248.

Der.: **haṭarata, huṭra ,huṭartana** (?).

HIA (חֲיָא, חיי = חָיָה, ܚܝܐ LS, Ges. s. חיה) to live, exist.

Pe. Pf. **hia** Gy 65:13, Q 59:8 he lived, **ʿtpit uhiia** Gy 241:18 (var. DC 22. 236 . . . **uhʿiia**) he sneezed and came to life, **hiun** Gy 175:5 they lived, **hiainin** Gy 64:3 we lived MG 268:15. Impf. **nihiia** Gy 36:10 he liveth, will live, **nihiun** Gy 269:6, 7 they (will) live MG 268:17 f. Impt. **hʿiia, hiiia, hiia** Gy 241:19 (an ancient greeting formula cf. MG 268:16 f.). Pt. **hiia**, fem. **hia** (both often in AM), pl. **haiin** Gy 8:19, MG 268:18 f. Inf. **mihia** cf. DAb 29 n. 4.

Pa. Pf. **mia hiia lgubria haiia (umhaialun)** ATŠ I no. 232 living water gave (and gives) life to men. Impt. with suff. **haiuia uqaimuia** DC 43 D 12, 42 . . . make ye it live and raise it up. Pt. **mhaiia mitia** CP 165:2, Gy 29:11 f., 56:21, ML 199:5 (he) reviveth the dead; pl. fem. **mhaiia bnia ḏ-habratin** Gy 183:10, **mhaian bnia ḏ-habratin** Gs 31:3, 5 they suckle children of their friends (fem.); with encl. **mhaialun** s. pf.

Af. (only nom. ag. **mahiana** s.v.).

Ethpa. **man mita ḏ-mitahiia** Jb 72:7 what man, when a corpse, can be revived?

Der.: **haia, haiata** 1, 2, **haiuta** 1, 2, 3, **haita** 1, 2, **hiuta** 1, 2, **hiia**.

hiasuta s. **haiasuta.**

hiba bala AM 227:9 for **hiua bala** (v.s. **hiua**).

hibuṭ AM a var. of **habuṭ.**

hibṭa Jb 132:9 v.s. **HBṬ.**

hibia = **hiuia. miška ḏ-hiuia** DC 45 a snake-skin.

hibil (Bibl. הֶבֶל, ܗܒܝܠ) Abel, an outstanding Mand. genie, as **hibil ziua** often identified with the saviour spirit **manda ḏ-hiia** HpGn Ind., ML 280, Kessler PRE 182. **hibil** is also used as a *malwâša* name. **hibil** RD 43; **hibil ziua** RD 18, RD B 5, 8, see CP Index, Q 20:3, 21:26, 62:22. Gy 321:21, 374:4, 376:6, PD 8, 1190 etc., **hibil ziua ḏ-iauar rba šumẖ** PD 837; identified with Gabriel in Gy 11:4, 173:19; **hibil ziua mn iauar abuia** RD 28e; **šauṭa ḏ-hibil ziua** RD B 19; but **rma ʿlẖ hibil ziua** Gy 241:18 H. shed brilliance on him, cf Ginzā 242 n. 9; **maṭarta ḏ-hibil brẖ ḏ-ptahil** RD C 5; **hibil ʿutra** Gy 113:23, 114:24, 126:7; **hibil mana** Gy 152:12, **hibil mana dakia** Gy 152:15, 168:1, 171:4; **šliha dakia . . . hibil ziua** Gy 32:17; **hibil ziua šliha qadmaia** Gy 29:2 ff.; **hibil ušitil uanuš** Gy 157:8, Q 60:11; **hibil ziua uanathiia** Gy 108:1; **hibil naṭar dara** Gy 316:6, 8, 18; **hibil maria ḏ-arqa** Gy 108:9.

hibla DC 20. 97 f. for **hbila.**

hibqa (rt. **HBQ**) embrace, encirclement, girdling band (v.s. **HBQ** impf. with suff.).

hibšaba an occasional var. of **habšaba. šita ḏ-hibšaba** Zotb. 231 left, 20, year of Sunday (i.e. which began on a Sunday).

higma (rel to ܗܓܡܐ, هجم?) Jb 144:14 tumult, noise, quarrel (?).

hida–hida DC 43 J 140 a miscop. (as shown in a parallel passage)?

hidasaraia, hidasraia (ܚܕܥܣܪܝܐ) eleventh MG 192:bottom.

hidua occasional var. of **hadua** 1.

hidud (Ar. حدود) AM 199 boundaries.

hiduia (masc. of **hiduta**, explained by popular etym. as from **HDA I** inst. of the original **HDT I**) Oxf. III 74 b, Par. xi 23 a, ŠQ 19:29 f. bridegroom MG 119:19; **hdia hiduia** CP 222:16 rejoice, bridegroom!

hidukt in **ṣihun hidukt** DC 43 C 51 name of a lilith.

hidukta, hiduktia later varr. of **hiduta** MG 78:2 ff. Used not only as a concrete noun 'bride', but also as abstr.: wedding ceremonies, the wedding-period of isolation lasting 7 days, bridal days (honeymoon). **bšuba iumia ḏ-hiduktia** ATŠ II nos. 71, 274, 299 during the 7 days of the honeymoon; **ḏ-hauin bhiduktia** ATŠ I no. 79; **bkanapta ḏ-hiduktia** ATŠ (*often*) in a nuptial embrace; **luat hiduktia** ATŠ II no. 328 to the bride.

hiduta, haduta 2 (ܚܕܘܬܐ) originally fem.: bride, but sporadically also masc.: bridegroom (a special masc. form being **hiḏuia** s.v.). Masc. pl. **hidutia**, fem. pl. **hidutata**, less often **hidutiata**, sporadically **hidutiniata** DC 43a:117, DC 49:31, MG 119:14 ff.; fem. pl. MG 169:10. A later fem. **hidukta** s.v. **qrinun lhiduta ulatiqrinun larmalta** DC 3 (CP trs. 184. rubric) recite them for a virgin-bride, but do not recite them for a widow (who remarries); **hiduta uhiduktia nisdar** ATŠ II no. 352 he arranges their wedding ceremony (lit. a bridegroom and a bride); **hidutia uhidutata** Gs 17:21 (var. DC 22. 408 **haditia uhidutata**) bridegrooms and brides; **napqan hidutata mn bit gnana** Gy 59:9 f. brides leave the bridal chamber; **nitaian hidutata** Gs 8:1 brides come in; **hidutata** (B **hidutiata**) **bklilaihun atian** Jb 82:4 f. brides come in their wreaths; **hidutata** (B **hidutiata**) **laramian zahba** Jb 82:8 f. brides do not put on gold; **mn hiduta** (read **hidutia**) **uhidutiniata** DC 43. 117 from bridegrooms and brides; **masiqta ḏ-šaria lhidutia** DC 36 the m. that frees bridegrooms (or a bride?) i.e. from pollution. Gl. 124:14 **hdutta** (*sic.* but cf. the form expected by Nöld. MG 119:16) عروس *sponsa.*

hidra 1 (הַדְרָא, ܗܕܪܐ, H. הָדָר, הֶדֶר, and הֲדָרָה LS, Ges. s. הדר) splendour, beauty, adornment. Doublet **hadra** (s.v.). **hidra ziua unhura uʿqara** Q 59:6, MG 326:7.

hidra 2 (rt. **HDR I**) vertigo. **hidra ḏ-riša** Or. 327:25.

hiua (חֵיוָא, *ܚܝܘܐ) animal(s), beast(s), cattle MG 22:13, 100:21. Masc. MG 156 footn. (a special fem. **hiuat** s.v.). Used as a collective noun. St. abs. inst. of st. cstr. MG 313:10 ff. Sometimes used inst. of **hiuia** Ginzā 86 n. 2. **hiua hiuta ḏ-la ʿdia ula ligria** Gy 86:21 a snake, a creature without hands and feet (for **hiuia**); **hiua bala** Gy 8:24, 18:14, 34:2, 38:21, 100:10 f., 123:21, 241:6 etc., cf. s. **bala 2**; **hiua kaka** s. **kaka**; **hiua bira** Gy 100:11, 14, 124:8 f., 378:32 etc., cf. s. **bira 2** and MG 321:5 f.; **hiua biša** Gy 123:12, DC 37. 576 f. noxious beast, evil creature; **hiuia uhiuata** DC 50. 887 male and female beasts.

hiuauata, rarely **hauauata**, pl. of **hiuia** (q.v.).

hiuaiza Zotb. 222 right 30 Howeiza, a small town in Khuzistan.

hiuaniata (a pl. of **hiua**, حيوانات) animals, beasts MG 168:paen. **hiuaniata maitin** AM

280:10 beasts will die; **hiuaniata ubiriata** Gy 12:19, ATŠ II no. 310 cf. s. **bira 2**; **qinianai uhiuaniatai** (often in exorcisms) my property and my cattle.

hiuara 1, hauara (חיוורא, ܚܘܪܐ) white MG 122:11. Fem. **hiuartia** MG 154:11. Pl. masc. **hiuaria. lbuš hiuara uʿtkasun hiuara** Gy 47:22 put on white clothes and cover yourselves with white; **mia hiuaria** Gy 32:13; **d̠-hiuar rišh̠ mn haupia mia uziqnh̠ mn ṣupia d̠-aqamra hiuara** Gy 210:1 f. whose head is whiter than the foam of water and his beard (is whiter) than a fleece of white wool; **sam pir hiuara** s. **sam**; **daula hiuara** DC 51 a white pitcher; **ʿkumtia anat lau hiuartia** DC 40 thou art black, not white (fem.); **aiba . . . hiuartia** AM 277:28 white cloud; **udinuq (u)hiuara mn kul had mitqal** AM 287:33 a sixth of a dram of white (flour?), of each one mithqal.

hiuara 2 (from ܚܘܪ, حَرّ by analogy of **hiuara** 1) acrimonious, bitter, fierce. Only in one place; otherwise unusual. **tigra hiuara** Gy 386:9; **qraba hiuara** Gy 386:10.

hiuat (Nöld. a fem. of hiua, hence ܚܘܬܐ MG 22:14, 156 footn., Lidzb. from **hiuia**, pointing to חות as a name of a goddess of the underworld in Carthaginian inscription *Ephemeris* I 30, Ginzā 71 n. 1) name of a female demon. **hiuat nuq(u)bta** (var. **niqubta**) Gy 74:15, 75:20, 78:8, 81:6, 132:14, 18.

hiuata DC 50. 851 for **hiuauata** (s. **hiuia**).

hiuia (חִוְיָא, ܚܘܝܐ) serpent, snake MG 102:23. Pl. **hiuauata** (var. **hauauata**) MG 166:antep. Masc. with fem. pl. **hiuia rba d̠-hu ʿur** Gy 313:16, Jb 196:14 the Great Serpent who is Ur; **hiuia ugala** s. **gala 2**; **ʿniš d̠-hiuia maṭilh̠** DC 36 II no. 81, 269 etc. a person whom a snake attacks

hiuiaza DC 56 coloph. s. **huaiza**.

hiura (cf. **hiuara 1**) white (of egg), albumen. **nipiršun d̠-hiura usumqa d̠-bita aba uʿma hinun** ATŠ I no. 271 they give the interpretation that the white and the yolk of an egg are the father and mother; **hiura usumqa uqlapta d̠-bita** DC 27. 198 the white, yolk, and shell of the egg.

hiuta 1 (חֵיוְתָא, ܚܝܘܬܐ) animal MG 23:15, 101:18. St. abs. **hiua** (s.v.). Scr. pl. **haiuta 1** (s.v.). **hiuta d̠-arbia ligria** ATŠ I no. 75 a quadruped; **hiua hiuta d̠-la ʿdia ula ligria** s. **hiua**; **hiuta d̠-saina undida** Gy 85:6 (var. DC 22. 80 **haiuta . . .**) an ugly and abominable creature.

hiuta 2 = **haiuta 2. bit hiuta** AM 16:16 womb.

hiuta 3 = **haiuta 3. hiuta tišpar** AM 217:7 life will be cut short (?).

hizaz AM 204:16, var. **ḥišaz** Ṣâb.'s AM Hijaz, Arabia.

hizba Jb 110 n. 3 a var. of **hizua** (l. 3) aspect (hardly 'earthen vessel' Jb ii 109 n. 4).

hizda (חִסְדָּא, ܚܣܕܐ) with two opposite meanings: (*a*) shame, ignominy, reproach, (*b*) favour, kindness, mercy Jb ii 109 n. 4, MG 45:4, 102 n. 1. (*a*) **lhama d̠-hizda** Gy 356:16; **mamiduta d̠-hizda** Gy 362:1; **atra d̠-kulh̠ hizdia** Gs 72:24; **kanpai d̠-mlia hizdia** CP. 174:ult., Morg. 59:11 f., 60:6 = Oxf. 41 b, 42 a; **hizda labišlun** AM; **ʿsira hizda** DC 43; (*b*) **(a)rhamta uhizda ušupra ušaiia uʿqara** Morg. 197:9, 198:14, 201:10, 260/12:17, 261/14:29, Par. xxvii 31b, 54a, DC 46. 166:6; **aiak klila brišaihun uaiak hizda blibaihun** DC 44 as a crown on their heads and as mercy in their hearts.

hizua (חֶזְוָא, ܚܙܘܐ) vision, appearance, sight, spectacle, apparition MG 102:antep. Pl. **hizuia, hizuania** MG 169:antep. An exceptional form **hizuat** DC 44. 1308 = Morg. 264/19:30 (st. cstr.). **šupra uhizua** Gy 10:6 fair appearance; **baita . . . d̠-litbh̠ hizua** Jb 110:2 f. (var. F **hizba**, D **hizda**) a house without (pleasing) form; **kukbia hizua** Q 28:33 = ML 78:8 stars of (fair) appearance, ML 78 n. 2. ? See CP trs. p. 42 n. 4; **hizua d̠-parṣupaihun zgig** Gy 9:19 f. the look of their faces is gleaming; **rahmilh̠ lhizua ušuma uqiniana d̠-alma hazin** Gs 58:22 they like the sight, the name, and the possession of this world; **kulh̠ ainia kulh̠ hizuia** Gy 2:18 entirely eyes, entirely appearances; **hauin hizua balma** Gy 59:ult. they will be(come) a spectacle in the world; **man d̠-hauilh̠ hizua** Gs 12:7 cf. Ginzā 432 n. 2; **hizua d̠-ʿutria** PD 1452 = ATŠ II no. 86 vision of the uthras; **latitahzulh̠ la bhilmia d̠-lilia ula bhizuania d̠-ʿumama** DC 46 (and often in exorcisms) appear to him neither in dreams by night nor in daily apparitions; **d̠-hazia hizuania d̠-šinta** DC 45 ATŠ no. 91 who sees visions (: nightmares) in his sleep; **dahil bhizuania** Oxf. roll g 498, Par. xxvii 41b he fears appearances; **aspar hizuania** Jb 67:16 the book of visions; **ʿtbariun alanpai hizuai** DC 40. 654 take yourselves out of my sight; **hizua d̠-ʿuiria** sight of the blind CP 405:13; **halin mlalia . . . nitaqnulia hiuzai** CP 280:penult. these words . . . will confirm my vision.

hizura 1 (חֲזִירָא, Syr. ܚܙܝܪܐ, Chr. Pal. ܚܙܝܪ, Akk. *ḫumṣīru*, Ar. loan-w. خنزير Fränkel 110 f., LS, Ges. s. חֲזִיר) pig, wild pig, boar MG 118:16. Fem. **hizurtia, hizirtia** MG 117:23, 154:19. Still used (mod. pron. *hozūra*). **ʿniš d̠-nikth̠ kalba uhizura** DC 36 no. 75 a person whom a dog or wild pig will have bitten; **zma d̠-hizura** AM 131:9 pig's blood; **tirba d̠-hizura** P.A.'s *mihla* pig's fat; **minilia hakima lsakla aiak marganita lhizirtia** Gy 217:22 f. (DC 22. 210 and Sh. 'Abd.'s copy **lhizurtia**) the words of a wise man to a fool are like a pearl to a sow (cf. Matt. 7:6). Gl. 68:9 **hzura** [*sic*] خنزير *porcus* خوك.

hizura 2 (read ***hizra** = חִוָרָא. Influenced by the more frequent **hizura 1**) coarse flour, bran. **ulabarbilaiun hizura** DC 44. 624 and there is no bran in their sieves (cf. s. **arbila**).

hizuta v.s. **hzuta**.

hiziran AM 283:11 = **haziran**.

hizirta v.s. **hizura 1**.

hizita 1 occasional var. of **hzita**.

hizita 2 (rt. **HZA II**) sprinkling, splashing **hizitak tihuia mnatak** DC 3 (DC 53 **hilitak**) thy sprinkling shall be thy portion.

hizmia (pl. of חיזמתא Löw 146:middle) AM 171:18 *Spina regis*, a prickly shrub, desert thorn.

***hizra** v.s. **hizura 2.**

hizran AM 271:15, 274:9 = **haziran.**

hiṭa (for hiṭia) wheat, wheat-flour. **bliša ḏ-hiṭa** DC 46 in dough of wheaten-flour.

hiṭupta occasional var. of **haṭiputa.**

hiṭut (rt. **HUṬ**) suture, joint (?). Only st. cstr. found. **mazihit mn hiṭut širiania** DC 37 thou art cast out from sclerosis (?) of his veins. (Doubtful).

hiṭia 1 (pl. of **hṭita 2**) wheat MG 172:bottom. **saria uhiṭia** AM 169:15 barley and wheat. **patura ḏ-hiṭia** PD 1135.

hiṭia 2 (Ar. حُظْوَة Akk. *uṣṣu*, H. חֵץ and חִצִּי I, Ges. s.vv. and חצה) orig. arrow, used as a sign of the Zodiac: Sagittarius Nöld. ZDMG xxv 256 ff., *Neue Beiträge* 147, Drower MMII 74. Mandaeans translate 'the mare' BZ 69 n. 13. The word then indeed adopted this secondary meaning. **kḏ mnata lhiṭia plaglẖ šnia bminiana arba alpia šnia** Gy 132:1 f. they allotted to Sagittarius the amount of 4,000 years; **qala ḏ-qra hiṭia** Gy 124:5 Gy 124:5 f. the cry which Sagittarius uttered. Very often in AM. As 'mare': **uhiṭia ḏ-hᶜ hamarta** ATŠ I no. 256 and the mare, that is a she-ass.

hiṭiata DC 35 = **hṭita.**

hiṭpa v.s. **HṬP** pe. pf. with suff.

hiṭpun zaba Gs 107:2, 9 name of a river in the underworld (prob. 'they snatched me away', **mia** as subj. being understood Ginzā 550 n. 2).

hiia (حَيًّا) Life, the primordial deity of Mand. religion MR 17, 47, ERE viii 382, ML xv: bottom, HpGn 84, 278, 292. Plurale tantum. Trad. pronunciation: *heyyī*. Used also generally for 'life'; before suff. **hai-** (s.v.). Adjectivally in **mia hiia** (מַיִם חַיִּים, cf. the contrast **mia tahmia** s. **mia**). **manda ḏ-hiia** γνῶσις τῆς ζωῆς (s. **manda**); **hal hiia qadmaiia** s. **hal 1**; **bšum** (or **bšuma ḏ-**) **hiia ubšuma ḏ-manda ḏ-hiia** a frequent introductory formula; **uqaiamin hiia bškinatun** Life is constant in Its dwellings; **mšabin hiia** Life be praised; **hiia zakin** (ᶜ**l kulhun** ᶜ**ubadia**) Life is victorious over all works (concluding formulae; the last one the most frequent) MG 162:middle; **hiia qadmaiia . . . hiia tiniania . . . hiia tlitaiia** etc. Q 1:14 ff., CP 2:2, Gy 182:12 f., 196:1 ff. the 1st Life . . ., the 2nd Life . . ., the 3rd Life; **hiia tiniania** Q 40:8, Gy 69:24, 70:3 (an emanational doctrine); **hiia rbia** (**h-** sometimes omitted), **hiia rurbia** (**qadmaiia**) (*very often*) the (First) Great Life; **hiia ḏ-hun mn hiia** CP 10:4, Q 59:3 f. Life which emanated from Life; **atar hiia** s. **atar**; **baba ḏ-hiia** Q 59:11, 30 s. **baba 1**; **ginza ḏ-hiia** s. **ginza 1**; **simat hiia** s. **simat**; **hiia nukraiia** Gy 134:1 s. **nukraia**; **hiia baraiia** CP 109:6, Q 29:23, 55:19, 30, 57:1 the exoteric Life; **hiia kasiia – hiia rurbia** Q 25:19 the Hidden Life — the Great Life; **dmut hiia** and **dimat hiia** s. **dimat**; **hadinat hiia** CP 64:11, trs. p. 43 n. 4, ML 80:2 (doubtful). Compound **br hiia** (cf. **br** compounds): **br hiia** Q 62:21, 63:1, Jb 94:3 f., 152:2, 186:3, 230:15, **brhiia** Gs 121:21, 129: 12, 130:21, Oxf. 12 b, RD D 10, Q 70:15, Jb 179:11, Gy 108:7; **hiia br hiia** Gy 294:16; **bihram brhiia** RD D 9; **abun br hiia** Gy 219:8, 234:15, Oxf. 49 b; **brhiia udmuthiia** Gy 108:7.

hikumta a var. of **hukumta** MG 13:paen. f., 26:anteantep., 103:13.

hikim (Ar. حاكم) AM 256:40 governor.

hikla (היכלא, ܗܰܝܟܠܳܐ < Akk. *ēkallu* < Sumerian *e-gal* 'great house', LS, Ges. s. הֵיכָל) hall, temple, palace, homestead; fig. structure, stature MG 23:15, 135:6 f. (Nöld. with Ewald from יכל 'to enclose', hence 'enclosure'). Furlani *I Termini* 342–8. Pl. **hiklia.** With suff. **hiklai** Jb 274:1 my palace, my temple (cf. Matt. 26:61, Mark 14:58, Jb 242 n. 3), **hiklẖ** (*often*) his homestead etc. **hikla ḏ-ziua** Gy 257:8 a palace of radiance; **hikla** ᶜ**laia** Gy 205: 1, 21 the upper palace; **hiklia hadtia** Gy 304:23 new temples; **man hikla** (Pet. **hkala**) **ubuna banilẖ** DC 22. 402 = Gs 12:2 who will build him a palace, a building?; ᶜ**star bgauẖ ḏ-hikla** Gs 76:3, 77:2 I shall be imprisoned in the palace (= the body); **trin** ᶜ**uṣṭunia ḏ-šrara ḏ-kulẖ hiklẖ** Gs 85:12 f. the 2 supports of stability of all his stature, cf. Ginzā 520 n. 8; **hikla ubiniana** DC 44; **durẖ uhiklẖ** *Florilegium* his dwelling and his homestead; **hiklẖ udaurẖ ubinianẖ** DC 40.

hikta (from חוג 'to encircle'?) armour (?): **hikta ḏ-abara** DC 44 armour (?) of lead.

HIL (den. from **haila**) to strengthen, give courage, force.

Pa. Pf. with suff. **hailan ušadran** DC 28 (miscop. **haila ušadrin**) he strengthened me and sent me. Pass. pt. **mhaial** Gy 280:9.

Ethpa. Pf. ᶜ**haial** he became strong MG 213:15, 222:5, ᶜ**haial libẖ** Gy 95:8 his heart was strengthened; ᶜ**thaial** MG 213:16, **uhad had raza minaihun hua u**ᶜ**thaial** ATŠ I no. 257 and one mystery after another proceeded from them and became potent; ᶜ**thaial** ᶜ**uṣrẖ** DC 35 his mind took courage; **nhura** ᶜ**thaial** DC 41:63 light became strong; **tnat** ᶜ**hailat** Gy 95:3 for the second time she grew strong; **unišimta** ᶜ**thailat u**ᶜ**traurbat** DC 48. 386 (but) the soul gathered strength and stature; with suff. ᶜ**thailẖ libẖ** Gy 95:9 the same as l. 8 (without suff.). Impf. **lnhura hambaga hun ḏ-**ᶜ**lauaihun nithaial** DC 36 they are an enemy of the light which gathers its forces against them. Impt. **u**ᶜ**thaial** DC 34. 941 and be strong. Pt. **mithaial** MG 213:16, **mithaial** PD 1508, 1510 f., **malka mithaial lsania** AM 273:1, 35 the king will gather a force (or prevail?) against his enemies; **razia ḏ-tarmiduta mithaial** ᶜ**l razia ḏ-mandaiuta** DC 34 the mysteries of priesthood gain strength over the mysteries of (lay) mandaism; **ruha mihaila mihaila h**ᶜ **ruha** Gy 94:7 R. was strengthened, strengthened was she, R. (hist. pres.); **mihaial libẖ** Gy 170:7; pl. **umithailin** DC 27. 332 and they are strengthened; **umithailan** ATŠ II no. 144 id. (fem.).

Der.: **haial, haila, hailana, hailuta, hilta, hiltana.**

hil (always with the procl. prep. **l-** like Syr. ܠܗܠ LS) yonder. Often with **mn** set before: **mn lhil** Jb 163:14, 165:1; **bhiria mn lhil** Gy 367:24, 368:10; **mn lhil ṭura hanatẖ** ATŠ II no. 317; **bhil** Par. XI 35a (twice) apart from **lhil** MG 203:anteantep.; **lhil balmia ḏ-nhura** Gy 30:12; **lhil bpiria ḏ-ziua** Jb 241:13; **mn lhil lhil qaiimna** Gy 352 (several times) MG 328 n. 2.

hila 1 = **hala** 1. **hila uhala sumaqa** AM 277: penult. grit and red dust; **hila lanapil ʿlẖ** Jb 115:14 dust falleth not upon it.

hila 2 (الحلّة in Lower ʿIrāq?) AM 198 name of a town, Hillah BZ Ap. II.

hila 3 (Ar. حِيلَة) trick, deception. Found in no text. Only in Gl. 69:14 **hila** (syn. with **zipa**) خداع *fallucia* مكر; 122:3 id. غش *deceptio, dolus* مكر.

hila 4 Jb 134:9 for **hinila**? Var. **hilia 2** s.v.

hilailiš, haliliš (هَلِيلَج) AM 288:6 myrobalan.

hilapa = **halpa** 1 (= **hilpa** 2). **klila ḏ-hilapa** ATŠ II no. 59, 90, 244 a willow-wreath; **hilapa** DC 35 (*often*) willow-tree.

hilata = **halita** 2. **hilata sumaqtia** DAb red precious stone.

hilbuna (חֶלְבּוּנָא) orig. glair, the white of the egg, egg, container, habitat, mansion, dwelling CP trs. 121 n. 4, MG 140:4, MSchr 138 n. 5, Kessler PRE 163, Jb ii 208 n. 7, Nöld. ZA xxx 152, ML 195 n. 2, Ginzā 151 n. 2, Kraeling JAOS 1953 162 ff., Furlani *I Termini* 358 ff. Used as a term of mythological cosmology. Pl. **hilbunia**. **mn hilbunkun** Gy 134:14 from your egg (= habitat), **hilbunia kasiia rurbia** Gy 134:21 great hidden dwellings; **kisiaihun uhilbunaihun ḏ-rurbia** Gy 135:7; **hilbuna kasia** Gy 136:7; **kasiun uqaimun bhilbunaihun** Gy 155:8 it (: the Life) hid and raised me in his habitation(s) (Lidzb.: *in seinem Ei*); **hilbunia rurbia ḏ-kasia** Gy 235:22; **bhilbunẖ ʿtiksia** Jb 258:9. 259:1; **ksia bhilbunia** RD B 117; **hilbunia gauaiia** Jb 251:10 f. the inner (: celestial, transcendental) dwellings (: containers); **hilbunia rurbia gauaiia** Gy 373:24; **baba ḏ-hilbunẖ** Jb 220:10 the door of his dwelling (Lidzb, *des Eies*); **baba rba ḏ-hilbunia** CP 161:13, Oxf. 23 b, Morg. 42:antep., Oxf. 40 b, Morg. 59:4, **ʿl bab hilbunia ḏ-ziua** Oxf. 108 a; **bbab** (miscop. **brab**) **hilbuna ḏ-ziua** Morg. 177:1; **hilbuna dukta ḏ-hun minẖ** Gy 147:22 the dwelling (Lidzb. *Ei*), the place from which they came into being; **hilbunia uškinata** Jb 231:16 celestial dwellings (hendiadys); **hilbunun ḏ-abahatak** Jb 256:5 the dwellings of thy Father (: the Life, Lidzb. *das Ei* [or *die Eier*, cf. II 231 n. 6] *deiner Eltern*); **zaua uhilbunia** Jb 264:4, 5 wife and house (?, Lidzb. children Jb II 236 n. 2); **hilbuna ʿuṣṭuna hu** ATŠ II no. 91 the house (?) is a column (: body); **hilbunia ḏ-ziua** DC 35 mansions of light; . . . **damad kḏ aiil lhilbunia (mn qudam ḏ-nasib kušṭa mn zauẖ)** DC 3 . . . the bridegroom when he enters his house (before performing the hand-clasp of troth with his spouse); **tlatma ušitin hilbunia iaqiria** DC 47, DC 36, ATŠ, PD 1111 the 360 glorious mansions.

hilbia ML 181:8 a var. of B **hlibia**, cf. n. 1.

hilula 1 (הִילּוּלָא, הִלּוּלָא < ܗܠܘܠܐ MG 118 n. 2) nuptials, wedding (festivity, rejoicing), marriage MG 118:18, 126:4, MSchr. 81 n. 1. Pl. **hilulia** 1. **ʿbud hilula lbnaikun** Gy 67:16 arrange weddings for your children; **nibudlẖ hilula hilula ladam nibudlẖ** Gy 105:22 we will arrange a wedding for him, a wedding for A. will we arrange; **abadnalẖ hilula ladam balma hilula ladam abadnalẖ** Gy 106:5 f. we made a wedding for A. in the world, a wedding for A. made we; **hilula rba** Gy 107:10; **hilula nibudlẖ unihidrẖ** Gy 147:23 let us arrange for him a wedding feast and wedding procession; **ʿkilta ḏ-hilulia** Gy 302:2 the food of wedding banquets; **man ḏ-hilulia bmasqata lnapšia** ATŠ II no. 346 one whose feasts are in *masiqtas* (i.e. ritual meals) for himself.

hilula 2 (cf. ܫܠܐ, Ar. حلّة LS 231b) a garment MG 126:4. Pl. **hilulia 2** Gy 47:23 (var. Sh. ʿAbd.'s copy **hillia 2**).

hilulia 3 DC 22. 402 a var. of **hillia 1** Gs 12:14.

hilia 1 = **halia 2** (q.v.). Against Lidzb.'s etym. from חלל 'to pierce' cf. s. **halita 2**. Another sg. is **hilita 2** (s.v.).

hilia 2 DC 30 a var. of **hila 4**.

hilia 3 occasional var. of **halia**.

hilita 1 (prob. from **HLA I**. CP trs. p. 113 n. 5, Lidzb. ML 182 n. 1 from **DHL**) assuagement (by gift), intercession, offertory (prayer of propitiation); portion of priest (?); obeisance, worship, devotion; sweetness (?), kindness (?). Often doubtful. **hilitak tihuia mnatak** Morg. 165:5, DC 41. 405 and par. thine offertory (?) shall be thy portion; **mitin hilita lmara(i) manda ḏ-hiia** CP 152:2, CP trs. p. 291 n. 3, Oxf. 9 a, ML 182:6 to show obeisance to my Lord, M.-ḏ-H.; **hilitan uziuihtan** CP 195:10, Oxf. 58 b, ML 229:12 our propitiation and our dread; **hilita hualia lhalin razia** DC 24. 242 (?) he had (= has) his portion in these mysteries (doubtf.); **barakata ḏ-hilita rabtia** DC 50 the benedictions of the Great Offertory; **buta ḏ-hilita** (often in rituals) the Intercessory (Offertory) Prayer (commemorating the dead at a ritual meal); **pihtania hilita ukulhun ʿniania** DC 50 breakings of bread, the offertory and all the prayers (: *responsoria*, antiphons).

hilita 2 = **halita 2**. **hilita kasita umarganita** Oxf. roll g 620, DC 47 = Or. 326:20 f. **hilita šumẖ** RD 1.

hilita 3 in **hilitaiun** Gy 232:4 BD a var. of **hiltaiun** (s. **hilta**).

hillia 1 (= **hala** 1 = **hila** 1) Gs 12:14 dust, grit MG 163:13 f. Var. **hilulia 3** (s.v.).

hillia 2 Sh. ʿAbd.'s copy's var. of **hilula 2** (s.v.).

hilma (חֶלְמָא, ܚܠܡܐ) dream. Found only in **hilmia**. **hilmia uhraria** Gy 59:2 dreams and phantasms; **hilmia hzun kahnia** Jb 66:13 the priests dreamed dreams; **aspar hilmia** Jb 67:16 f., 69:15 book of dreams.

hilmanita (masc. ܚܠܡܢܝܐ) dreamy, given to dreams (or visions). Masc. not found. **hilmanita tihuia** AM 79:17 f. she will be given to dreaming.

hilpa 1 (ܚܠܦܐ) relief, relieving guard, (ex)-change, permutation, substitute, surrogate, transformation, transmutation, transfiguration, passing appearance. Fem. in Gy 263:15, 20, masc. ibid. l. 16. Used also of reappearance or return of stars Jb ii 209 n. 1. Var. **halpa. hilpa hazin d̲-dahna** Gy 263:13 f., 273:12 f. the return (of stars) that shineth; **hilpa hai d̲-dahna** Gy 263:16 id.; **hilpa hurintin** Gy 263:15, 20 another return (of stars); **hilpa d̲-dahna** Gy 273:20; **mšamar unapiq hilpa** Gs 109:19 the passing appearance is to be abandoned (Lidzb.: *Die Wache zieht eilig hinaus*); **mabar hilpa** Gs 80:10 bringer across at the (moment of) transit (Lidzb.: *Der du durch die Wache hindurchführest*); **hilpa abarlia** CP 129:15 a transformation transported me Q 65:22 (CP 129:5 impt. with encl. and suff. of the 1st p. sg.); **hilpa d̲-halip** Oxf. roll g 997, DC 47 = Or. 332:17 transitory appearance that passeth by; **ata bhilpa kasia** Oxf. roll f 1157, CP 466:10, DC 50:771 came (or come!) in secret guise (?); **ziuak dna** (B **dahna**) **bhilpa** Jb 220:12 thy radiance raised like a returning (star?); **laziua dahna bhilpa** DC 7 (pres. neg.). Note: The frequent use of the word with **DNA I = DHN I** as well as with **ziua** attracted to the word the meaning of 'ray of light', 'illumination', 'glittering', which appears from the examples just quoted and esp. from **parahiata d̲-hilpa** Oxf. roll f 1337, 1342 glittering sparks.

hilpa 2 = halpa 1 (= **hilapa**). Pl. **hilpia. qal hiuia bhilpia** DC 46. 15:13, 16:5 the sound of a serpent in the reeds.

hilqa 1 (חֶלְקָא, ܚܠܩܐ) fate, lot, portion, destiny, luck, predestination Jb ii 117 n. 6. St. abs. **hlaq** (s.v.). Var. **halqa 2. adinqia hilqa mšauilun** Gy 389:9 they make them portionless (: unfortunate); **hilqaihun lamdabria** Gy 11:1 they do not govern their fate; **hilqak mn daria šuar** Gs 79:12 f., Q 65:27 thy destiny arose from the ages; **kd̲ arbaia d̲-šibqh̲ hilqh̲** Jb 38:penult., AM 120:12 like an Arab who abandoned his fatalism; **hilqa hauilh̲** he will have (good) luck; **hilqa šapira** AM 44:10 f.; **uhilqa mqabil** AM he will accept his lot; **maria hilqa hauia** AM he will have good luck (lit. will be master of his destiny); **hilqa ušrara** Morg. 269/28:20 (good) luck and firmness.

hilqa 2 a var. of **halqa 1. mn gualqia umn šuba hilqia** DC 12. 128 cf. s. **halqa 1; brata d̲-hilqa uktaba** DC 40 a literate woman (lit. daughter of letters [read **halqia**?] and writing, or book).

hilta (Lidzb. ML 182 n. 1, Ginzā 233 n. 2 from ܚܠܬܐ sheath, scabbard; but more prob. a mere doublet of **haila**, cf. adj. **hiltana**) strength, power. **hailaiun uhiltaiun** Gy 232:4, 256:9 (varr. **halitaihun, hilitaiun** s. **halita 3, hilita 3**) v.s. **haila.**

hiltana (adj. from **hilta**) mighty, powerful, using force, tyrannical. Pl. **hiltania. gabra hiltana** DC 43 B II:1 a powerful man; **ṣauriʿil gabra hiltania** (read **hiltana**) DC 46 (book of magic), **gubria hailia** (var. **halin**) **hiltania** DC 44 these tyrannical men.

hima st. abs. of **himta. hima lbaš uhima ʿtlabaš uhima ʿtkasia** Gs 3:2 f. he put on anger, was clothed with anger, was covered with anger.

himan (P. همان) similarly, likewise. **himan ʿnta d̲-la atia minh̲ hšuka** DC 46 similarly, (for) a woman from whom darkness (: menstruation) does not come; **himan d̲-hauilh̲ ziqa bkarsh̲** DC 46 likewise, should she have wind in her stomach.

himara = hamara 1 = hmara. Pl. **himaria. himara d̲-bqamaiata** DC 37. 375 f. the ass that is in its harness (: strappings).

himat 1 st. cstr. of **himta 1.**

himat 2 (Jew. חֵמַת with procl. מ) preceded by the prep. **mn** in consequence of, because, product of, result of, from. **mn himat razia huit** ATŠ I no. 22 I came into existence as the result of mysteries; **mn himat razia kasiia piršat** DC 50, DC 3 (she) emanated from secret mysteries; **šabiq haṭaiia mn himtun d̲-razia d̲-hanatun razia** ATŠ forgiving of sins on account of the mysteries of those mysteries. With **l** or **b** inst. of **mn: lhimat ziua piršat niṣubta** DC 51. 334, from the radiance progeny emanated = **bhimat ziua piršat niṣubta** Morg. 133:4. Without prep.?: **himat ʿqara** CP 450:5 on account of (?) the glory.

himun (ܗܡܘܢ < H. הָמוֹן Isa. 13:4, 33:3 etc. Geiger ZDMG 1867 p. 491, LS, Ginzā 179 n. 4) keeper of a purgatory. **himun gabra** Gy 209:16, DC 43 I 48, 103; **himun rba** DC 43. 1.

himunu, s. **himnu.**

himṭa (חֶמְטָא, ܚܡܛܐ, Akk. *himṭu*) inflammation, sore, sepsis, festering, a breaking out (of an infected spot or wound). Pl. **himṭia. himṭa ninpuqbh̲** AM 91:10 sepsis will appear in him; **himṭa bšaqh̲ nihuilh̲** AM 91:3 he will have pustules in his limbs; **himṭia ubuia** AM 33:20 septic sores and boils.

himiana (הִימְיָנָא, ܗܡܝܢܐ < P. هميان LS) (sacred) girdle; girth (of a horse). St. (abs. and) cstr. **himian.** Pl. **himiania.** Description and ritual use MR 202 n. 4, Siouffi 122, 166, MSt. 173 f., MMII 31 n. 7. **himiana himian mia** Jb 119:4, 217:5, Gy 320:13, a girdle of water (!); **himiania mia hiia** Gy 25:14, **himiana d̲-mia** Oxf. 65 a, **himianak himian mia** Gs 11:8; **ašarinin himiana** (AC **-ia**) Jb 41:4 I tied on them girdles; **šarin himianun** RD B 71, 73, C 26 they untie their girdles; **susia lakabišlh̲ urakiblh̲ alma d-himiana mistarlh̲** ATŠ I no. 250 a horse unbroken and unridden until it is girthed with a girth.

himid (< **hai minda** 'which kind of thing?') whatever. **himid ʿhualan** DC 35 whatever we had. Only in modern texts.

himinu Sh. 'Abd.'s copy's var. of **hamnu** Gy 362:17.

himira = hamira.

HYMN haf. of **AMN** (q.v.).

himnu, himunu, himinu, varr. of **hamnu.** (Often in Sh. ʿAbd.'s copy and DC 22). **bhimnu šbila** RD B 88 ff. by which path?

himnia DC 22. 364 a var. of **hamnia** Gy 368:3.

himṣa 1 (חִמְצָא differently from ܚܡܨܐ H. חֹמֶשׁ II Ges.) belly, entrails MG 46:13. **bhimṣh** Gy 81:21, 281:2 in his belly.

himṣa 2 (חִמְצָא, ܚܡܨܐ Ar. حِمَّص Löw no. 127) chick-pease MG 120 n. 1. **rmun himṣa gurṭa** Gs 27:20 they threw peas and grains (doubtf., cf. Ginzā 445 n. 1). Gl. 76:2 missp. with s حمص *cicer* نخود.

himta 1 (חֶמְתָּא, ܚܡܬܐ H. חֵמָה Ar. حُمَة LS, Ges.) wrath, anger; venom, poison MG 111:8. St. cstr. **himat 1**, abs. **hima** (s.v.). **himta ʿlauak tištpil** Gy 87:23 wrath will fall upon thee; **albišth himta** Gy 91:4 I clothed him with wrath, but cf. Ginzā 95 n. 1; **gasia ušadia himta d-hamima** Gy 82:9 he speweth and looseth forth his fiery venom; **himta d-napšaihun** Gy 123:14 their own venom; **bhimta urugza** Gy 164:21 with wrath and anger, **bhimta** Gy 164:23; **libh himta ʿtimlia** Gy 90:10 his heart was filled with anger; **d-bhimṣh d-himtaiun lamitaška** Gy 81:21 read **d-bhimṣh himta udma lamitaška** (?) in whose belly poison no blood is found, cf. Gy 281:2 f., Ginzā 81 n. 5.

himta 2 (rt. **HMM**) ardour, fervour, heat. St. cstr. **himat** (?). **kd arhat himth** ATŠ II no. 278 when she felt (lit. smelled) its heat; **tibtaiun himta** ATŠ II no. 305 and their excretions are fervour (or poison = **himta 1**?). Cf. also the dubious **himat ziua** s. **himat 2.**

himta 3 (cf. **himat 2**) after prep. **mn** on account of, in consequence of, owing to. (Found only with suff., or st. abs. **himat 2.**) **mn himtai** DC 34 on account of me, owing to me. **mn himtun** s. **himat 2.**

hin 1 (אִין, ܐܢ, إِنْ H. אִם; with a secondary h-) if, if so, though, although. The original form without the initial h- only in the neg. **ʿla** (apart from **hinila, hinʿla** s.vv.) if not, but, except MG 208:6 ff. Syntax MG 473–80. **hin . . . hin . . .** DC 43 etc. whether . . . or whether.

hin 2 (הֵן, ܗܐ, إِنَّ) Gs 124:8 etc. behold, lo, yes MG 81:10.

-hin possessive suff. of the 3rd p. pl. fem. (apart from **-in, -aihin, -aiin**) MG 88:9 f. Often replaced by the masc. suff. **-hun** (s.v.).

hina (Ar. حِنَّاء) henna, a vegetable red dye MG xxxiii:19. **diqnaihun bhina ṣabia** Jb 86:2 they dye their beards with henna; **madiqta d-hina** Oxf. roll g 619, DC 47 = Or. 326:20 mortar of (or for) henna.

hinga 1 (חִינְגָא) a round dance, circle, encirclement, snare, trap, noose. MG 76 n. 1, Jb ii 219 n. 5. Pl. **hingia 1. nilguṭbh hingia** Gy 105:4 (Sh. ʿAbd.'s copy **niligṭibh hinga**) we will take snares; **ubhinga naplia . . . ubhinga mšaurilun** Gy 225:7 f. and they fall into the dance . . . and make themselves leap in the dance; **hingia lagṭia lagṭia hingia** Jb 238:4 f. they grasp snares; **d-lgaṭbh hinga biama** DC 51. 270 which encircled the sea; **mn madna ziua (u)hinga** DC 37. 143 from the east a circle of radiance; **hinga d-kiuan** DC 34. 751 Saturn's noose.

hinga 2 (ܚܢܓܐ) a kind of demon. Pl. **hingia 2** MG 76:11. **lkulhun humria kanpa uʿl hinga qlala** (an exorcism) a protection against all amulet-spirits and against (every) *hinga*, a snare; **šidia uhingia** Gy 55:23; **hingia sainia** Morg. 196:1, DC 51. 468.

hingana (from **hinga 2**) a demon. **ʿsir daiua hingana** DC 43 I 65 bound is the demon H.

hind (هند) AM 197 India.

hindauaiia a var. of **hinduaiia.**

hindan s. **handan.**

hindamia s. **handama.**

hindar AM 228:6 a place-name, possibly miswritten for **hindubar** BZ Ap. II.

hinduaiia (הִנְדְּוָאָה, ܗܢܕܘܝܐ) Gs 17:4, AM 184 etc. people of Hind. Var. **hindauaiia.**

hindubar AM 205 a place-name, Hindupūr, India (?).

hindustan (P. هندستان) AM 196 Hindustan, India.

hindiba (הִנְדְּבָא, ܗܢܕܒܐ > هندبا, Gr. ἐντύβια Löw 255, LS) endive. Pl. **hindibia. hindibia hinun** Bodl. 12 (with an illustration) these are endives.

hinun (הִנּוּן, ܗܢܘܢ) pers. pron. of the 3rd p. masc. pl.: they, used also as a demonstrative pron.: those. Sometimes replacing the special fem. form **hinin** (s.v.). MG 4:antep., 86 and n. 3. As demonstr. pron.: **d-hinun ʿbilia** Gy 56:2 of those ascetics; **lqudamaihun d-hinun mania** Gy 135:13 before those spirits; **ʿlauaihun d-hinun babia** Gy 151:8 on those doors; **bhinun almia** Gy 153:9 in those worlds; **parṣupaihun d-hinun mania** Gy 135:4 the countenances of those spirits; **hinun gubria zadiqia** CP 4:2, Q 1:32, those righteous beings; **hinun malakia** Gy 23:4 those angels; with no demonstr. force **hinun rbia** Gy 78:21 the Great (Life); inst. of the fem. form **hinun nišmata** Gy 187:10 those souls, MG 336 f. To emphasize a demonstr. pron.: **halin hinun mia hiia . . . atin** Jb 4:14 f. these living waters come MG 341:5.

hinzara v.s. **singa.**

hinia (ܗܢܝܠܐ, Jew. Aram. subst. הֲנָיָיא) fem. st. abs. pleasing MG 110:paen., 153:bottom. **ʿu hinialak** Morg. 242/71:7 if it be pleasing to Thee; **ʿu hinialkun rbia ʿu hinialkun rurbia** ŠQ 20:15, CP 217:1 if it be pleasing to You, Great (Life), if it be pleasing to You, Mighty (Life).

hinila, hinʿla (cf. s. **hin**) if not, nevertheless, notwithstanding that, but, although, on the contrary, in any case, however (that may be) MG 218:14 ff. **latit bṣubian rbia . . . hinila bṣubian trin ʿutria** Gy 323:13 thou hast not come according to the will of the Great (Life) . . ., but according to the will of the two uthras; **tišimh hinila latišania mimrai** Gs 107:7 (if) thou hearest but alterest not my speech; **mindam lamšalṭinan hinila iardna** Gy

296:8 we have power about nothing except the jordan; **hinila malka d̠-nhura d̠-iada** Gy 278:14 nevertheless, the King of Light knoweth; **hinʿla na** (delete na) **lʿška d̠-** Gy 11:15 f. (Sh. ʿAbd.'s copy **hinila liška d̠-**) no, there is none who . . .; **hin anat . . . lašabqatlan . . . hinila man zakaia qudamak** CP 105 ult. ff. if thou . . . dost not forgive us . . . then who shall stand guiltless before thee?; **hinila mulkana d̠-ʿniš lamalik** AM 30:15 however, he takes advice from no one; **ʿu haliplh̠ hidisar iumia uladahil hinila dhul** AM 147:16 if 11 days pass by (and he is alive) fear not, if not, fear (for him); **hinila ana braktak bpuma d̠-bisra umanda d̠-hiia birkak bpumh̠ dakia** CP 454:8 f. although I blessed thee with a mouth of flesh, M-d̠-H. blessed thee with his pure mouth.

hinin, hinʿn (הנין, ܗܢܝܢ) pers. pron. of the 3rd p. fem. pl., sometimes replaced by the masc. form **hinun** (s.v.) MG 86 and n. 3.

hinka (חִנְכָּא, ܚܢܟܐ, ܚܢܟܐ Ar. حنك H. חֵךְ Akk. *ikku* Ges.) palate, throat, jaw, fig. voice. **ruha brakth̠ bhinka** Gy 115:16 R. blessed him with her jaws (= voice); **hinkak hlia** Jb 164:1 thy palate (= voice) is sweet; **skara uskirta lhinkaihun** DC 26. 589 f. a stopper and a gag on their jaws.

hinʿla s. hinila.

hinʿn s. hinin.

hinqa (rt. **HNQ**) snare, noose. **azlia lhinqai** DC 46 they (may) go into my snare.

hintai = **huntai** (?) **anin kulan draia** (read **drinin**?) **ʿl hintai** DC 36. We all brought my cousin (?). Corrupt.

hisar (rt. **HSR**) AM 283:31 loss, want, need, poverty. Var. **hisir.**

hisda occasional var. of **hizda.**

hisma a var. of **husma** MG 102:5.

hipa 1 pass. pt. of **HUP** = **HPP** (q.v.).

hipa 2 (ܚܛܘܦܐ) force, violence, injustice MG 108:ult. without reference (found in no text, but see **hipia 2**).

hipia 1 (חִפְיָא I J) cover(ing). **hipia d̠-mia lbiš uhipia d̠-mia mkasai** DC 51. 661 f. he put on a covering of water and covered himself with a covering of water; **hipia hipia** DC 43 J 63 obscure.

hipia 2 (חִפְיָא II J) with procl. prep. **bhipia** Gs 18:3, ML 162:10 = Gs 78:6 barefoot, in mourning (or in ML for **hipa 2**?).

hipia 3 (cf. חִיפּוּפִיתָא and Mishn. חֲפִפִית) AM 96 sores, eruptions.

hiṣad (rather Ar. حِصَاد than Syr. ܚܨܕܐ) AM, miscop. **hiṣar** (Ṣâb.'s copy) harvest. An older form is **hṣada** (s.v.).

hiṣbia (prob. met. of ܫܚܒܐ Ginzā 85 n. 2) Gy 84:8, Gs 12:3 spasms, convulsions, racking pains. Sg. not found.

hiṣra 1 (ܚܨܪܐ Ar. خِنْصِر) little finger MG 120:1. **ʿlianak uhiṣrak** CP 93:28, Morg. 248/83:ult. thy thumb and thy little finger; **ṭuprak hiṣrak** CP 93:15, 31 the finger-nail of thy little finger; **hiṣra d̠-iaminh̠** Q 59:27, Lond. roll A 122 the little finger of his right (hand); **hiṣrh̠ d̠-marh̠ d̠-rabuta** Gy 127:14 the little finger of the Lord of Greatness; **ʿsiqta mapiqlh̠ mn hiṣrh̠** ATŠ II no. 160 he takes off the (seal-)ring from his little finger; **ʿsiqta d̠-mitatna bhiṣrh̠** ATŠ II no. 315 the ring that is placed on her little finger; **bhiṣrak d̠-iaminak** ATŠ II no. 217 on the little finger of thy right hand; **lriša d̠-ṣbith̠ d̠-hiṣra** AM 133:15 the top (acc.) of his little finger.

ḥiṣra 2 (Löw 226) AM 287:25 *Allium porrum*, leek.

hira 1 a var. of hra (q.v.).

hira 2 (rt. **HWR**) DC 23. 318 whiteness.

ḥirarat AM 279:18 a var. of **hararat.**

hirba a doublet of **harba** (q.v.), MG 100:ult. Gender wavering: Gy 126:9, 260:14, 261:14 masc.; Gy 259:16, 261:8 fem. MG 159:1 ff. Pl. **hirbia.** Sword. **hirbia usipia** (often) swords and scimitars; **tipaq riša d̠-hirba mn aganbh̠** DC 40. 130 f. the point of the sword will come out from his side (the gender follows **hirba,** not **riša**); **hirba urugza** Gy 62:7, 63:14 sword and anger; **latihuilia hirba blilia** DC 43 J 36 there shall be no destruction for me at night; **hirba bplanga d̠-malka nihuia** AM 189:4 there shall be slaughter in the royal army; **hirba taqipa hauia** AM 178:19 there will be grievous devastation.

hirga (חִירְגָא) dust: **hirga d̠-glala** DC 46. 71:6 stone-dust.

hird(u)baiia s. **hardabaiia.**

hirub (ܚܪܘܒ) AM 269:24 waste place, desert, wilderness.

hirpa = **hurpa 1, sindirus uhirpa hiuara** DC 46.

hirṣia (cf. s. **halṣa**) DC 43 loins.

hišaz AM 205, **ḥišaz** AM 267:34 Hijaz.

hitra (rt. **HTR I,** cf. ܗܬܪܐ) rejoicing, merry-making, exultation, vainglory, pomp. Very frequent in AM.

hkaka (חֲכָךְ, ܚܟܟܐ) AM 98:15 itch(ing), scab, (irritating) skin-disease.

hkala Gs 12:2 a var. of **hikla** ibid. C.

HKK (HUK) (חכך, ܚܟ Ar. حكّ LS) to itch, irritate.

Pe. Act. pt. pl. **haikin** Oxf. roll g 966, 968 are itching; adjectivally: **mia haikia** AM 186 irritating waters (urine?) BZ 114 n. 7.

Der.: **hkaka, hauka** (abs. **hauik**).

HKM (חכם, ܚܟܡ, حكم Akk. *ḫakâmu* LS, Ges.) to know, be wise, perceive, discern, understand.

Pe. Pf. **hkum** Gy 13:11, 34:8 they knew MG 218:11; pl. with suff. **lahikmun bhukumtaikun** Gs 64:18 BCD, Leid. and DC 22. 452 (Pet. **lahkmun bh-**) I was not made (lit. they did not make me) clever by your cleverness. Impf. **latihkmun mn hukumth̠** Gy 21:1 AD (B **latihkmta** corrupt, Sh. ʿAbd.'s copy **latihkum** sg.) be not taken in by his cleverness. Impt. (with a prosth. **a**) **ahkum bh̠** AM 206:18 be instructed by it. Act. pt. **lahakim** Gy 42:paen. (Sh. ʿAbd.'s copy **lahikim**) becometh not wise, **hakum** Gy 57:14 becometh wise; pl. **hakmia uiadia uparšia** DC 3, DC 38 they discern, know, and distinguish. Pass. pt. replaced by **hakim(a)** (s.v.).

Der.: **hakim(a), huk(u)mta, hikumta,** abs. **huk(u)mat, hikim.**

HLA I (חלי, ܚܠܐ, حلا H. חלה II LS, Ges.) to be(come) sweet; pa. to sweeten, assuage (?).

Pe. Pf. **hla uᶜtangar** s. **HLA III.** Impt. **hlia napšak** Q 48:2 make thyself agreeable (: be sweet). Act. pt. **halia** 1 (s.v.); pl. **kadšilun ulahalin** Gy 182:3, 20, 183:21, Gs 83:12 one striketh them, yet they are not sweet; pl. fem. **ᶜdia abda kul iuma ulahahalian** Gs 15:5 the hands work the whole day without being soft; **ᶜdh̲ d̲-abda ᶜumama ulilia ulahalian** Gs 15:10 f. the hands which work day and night without being soft(ened). Pass. pt. **hlia** Q 47:29 (var.).

Pa. **kul hda d̲-halit** (read **hailit**?) CP 430:5 each one that thou hast assuaged (read 'strengthened'?). Act. pt. **mlakia d̲-mhalin mlakia taqipia** DC 40. 1003 angels which make violent angels mild. Pass. pt. **gabra nukraia d̲-mhalai** ATŠ I no. 232, see ATŠ trs. 169 n. 2. Doubtful: pl. **kasia d̲-mhalin** Gy 183:11 (DC 22. 175 **mhalian** fem.) cups that are sweetened.

Der.: **halia** 1 (fem. **halita** 1), **haliuta, haliaiil, hlia, hilita** 1.

HLA II (חלא H. חלה I Ges.) to be weak, sick.

Pe. Pt. pl. **hiṭia halian** AM 169:16 wheat will be diseased.

HLA III (Targ. חֲלָא, חֲלִי J.) to toil, labour (Lidzb. **HLA I**).

Pe. Pf. **kul man d̲-hla uᶜtangar** Oxf. 16 a f., Q 70:13, ML 189:2 = CP 156:16 every man who toiled and trafficked (or 'endured' **ᶜtnagar**?) Ethpa. ܐܬܚܠܝ.

hlapta (rt. **HLP**) a pass, gesture of passing over. **hlapta hlip margnak mn ᶜlauia d̲-šualiak** DC 34. 1039 make a pass over thy novice with thy staff.

hlaṣa (rt. **HLṢ**) torture, torturing MG 74:4, 115:19. (Pognon IM Gl.: fetter, chain). **hlaṣa umṣara** Gy 182:2, 19, 230:19, 233:9, 14 torture and rack; **hlaṣa ungada** Gy 312:16, Gs 26:15, 29:17, 31:10 torture and torment; **hlaṣa taqipa** DC 44. 1478 = Morg. 266/22:21 cruel torture.

hlaq st. abs. of **hilqa** 1. **hlaq umnaq bit hiia lanihuilh̲** Gy 237:13 he shall have no lot or portion in the House of Life.

***hlula,** fem. **hlultia** (rt. **HLL I**) hollowed. **aina hlultia** JRAS 1938 4:10 the hollowed eye.

HLZ I (חֲלֵז) to loop up.

Pa. Part. pres. **kd̲ mhalzit ugaṭrit kanzalak** DC 27. 95 when thou loopest up and knottest thy stole (s. MMII 31).

HLZ II a miscop. of **HZZ** in **halzit** Jb 186 n. 3 for **hazzit.**

hlia, hlᶜia (pass. pt. of **HLA I**) sweet. **dima d̲-hlia** Gs 13:20 (DC 22. 403 **hlᶜia,** read **d̲-lahlia**?, Lidzb. prop. **d̲-lahalia** cf. 15:5, marginal gloss in his copy of Ginzā) bitter (?) tears.

hlibia (cf. sg. ܚܠܝܒܐ) pl. milky, juicy, nourishing. Varr. **hilibh̲, hilbia** ML 181:8. **hlibia mia** ibid. B, CP 151:7) nourishing (?) streams.

hlil 1 (H. חָלִיל II, Akk. *ḫalḫallatu* Ges.) AM 162 flute.

hlil 2, fem. **hlilta** (rt. **HLL II**) ritually clean. **zakuta hlilta** DC 34. 1048.

hliṣ(a) (pass. pt. of **HLṢ I**) brave, valiant. Pl. **hliṣia** Gs 122:6, 18. **zriz hliṣ mlik rugza** Gy 181:17, 208:14 armed and valiant is the king of wrath; **gabir hliṣ** Gy 167:14 strong and valiant; **gṭar hliṣ** s. **gṭar. biriauiš kana hliṣa** Q 59:21 = CP 117:11 B. strong (valiant) source.

hlita occasional var. of **hilita** 1.

HLK (הלך Aram. pa., H in all stems) to proceed, go forward, travel, walk, move forward.

Pa. Pt. **lšanqia d̲-arqa d̲-hšuka umhalkun** [*sic*] ATŠ I no. 254 legs (acc.) of the earth of darkness and making them move (walk).

HLL I (חלל, ܚܠܠ H. חלל II den. from חָלִיל II, Ar. خَلَّ Ges., LS) to hollow out, pierce.

Pa. Impf. with suff. **d̲-nihalilinun lgirmh̲** Gy 101:6 that he should hollow out his bones.

Der.: **hlultia** (masc. ***hlula**), **hlil.**

HLL II (חלל, ܚܠܠ den. from ܚܠܐ, ܐܘܚܠܐ LS) to purify, cleanse, rinse, wash, make ritually clean, absolve.

Pa. Pf. **halilnin ᶜda bkušṭa** CP 140a:4 we purified our hands with the truth, **halilnia ᶜdan** DC 34. 1095 we have washed our hands, **halilaun** (read **haliliun udakun ᶜdaihun biardna** DC 24 they cleansed and purified their hands in running water. Impf. with suff. **nihalilinun** he washes them MG 281:ult. (without reference, prob. **HLL I**). Impt. **halil uašig unaqid** Gy 18:5 rinse, wash and clean, **ušig unaqid uhalil** Gy 68:5, **halil uašig** Gy 366:6, **halil bmia** Gy 224:21. Pt. **d̲-lamhalil** Gy 224:21 who cleanseth not. Part. pres. **mhalilitun** DC 6 II no. 167, var. **mhalalitun** DC 36 ibid. ye perform the rinsing.

Der.: **halala, halalta.**

HLL III (הלל, ܗܠܠ H. הִלֵּל Ar. هَلَّلَ, أَهَلَّ, Akk. *alâlu, elêlu* Ges., LS) to utter cries of joy, praise, celebrate, exult.

Pa. Gl. 170:13 f. miswritten هلل exultare شاد شد.

Der.: **hilula** 1.

HLL IV (حلّ H. חלל I Ges.) to profane, degrade.

Pa. Pt. pl. **harbia umhalia** Jb 258:11 they destroy and degrade.

HLM I (cf. Mishn. הלם) to join, attach, ally with, enter into alliance.

Pa (?): Impf. **miṣraiia nihalmun ušlama nihuia** AM 250:4 the Egyptians will enter into an alliance and there will be peace.

Ethpe. Impf. with encl. **unikibšun unihilmbun ulaništauzbun** AM 216:18 and they will be subdued and joined to them and will not be freed.

HLM II (חלם, ܚܠܡ I, H. חלם II, Ar. حلم LS, Ges.) to dream. Found only in der.: **hilma, hilmanita, mhilma.**

HLM III (H. חלם I, Syr. and Chr.-Pal. der. ܚܠܝܡ, Ar. حَلِيم fat) to be healthy, found only in ethpa.: to recover health, be cured.

Ethpa. Impf. **nitasun unithalmun** DC 40. 963 they will be cured and recover health.

hlʿ**ia** s. **hlia.**

HLP (חלף, ܚܠܦ, خلف LS) to pass over, pass by, cross over, pa. and af. change, exchange, substitute, alter; af. also to let pass by, to pass through (an illness).

Pe. Pf. **hlip** Gs 69:4 he passed by (or through) MG 219:20; **ḏ-nura** ʿ**lh̲ hilpat** ATŠ I no. 173 and II no. 27 over which fire has passed; special pl. ʿ**u hauia ḏ-hlipiun** ʿ**lh̲ šuba iumia** ATŠ II no. 75 if 7 days shall have elapsed; ʿ**u hauia ḏ-hilipiun** ʿ**lh̲** DC 6 if there be those who will act as his proxy; with suff. **hilpan** Jb 81:4 ff. he made me pass; **hlipth̲ lbnia hšuka** DAb I passed by (or to?) the sons of darkness. Impf. **nihlup** *praeteri(bi)t* MG 219:20; ʿ**l bab nura lanihlup** Gy 40:15 he will not pass through the gate of fire. Act. pt. **ularqa umia halip** AM 19:6 and he will cross land and water; **ḏ-halip** ʿ**lauaihun šuba iumia** DC 6 over whom a week passes; **hilpa ḏ-halip** s. **hilpa 1**; fem. **bišuta halpa** AM evil passes away; **halpia** (often) they pass by (or over); fem. pl. **abihdai lahalpan** Jb 257:10 they (: the souls) will not pass over with me.

Pa. Impf. **tihalip** thou changest MG 60: paen., 226:antep. Act. pt. **lamhalip** Gs 2:9 he changeth not.

Af. Pf. with suff. ʿ**lauia ḏ-muzania ahliph̲** Gs 56:15 f. he caused him to pass the scales; **ahlipth̲** RD B 84 I caused him to pass. Impf. with suff. **tahlipunin** Q 39:12 ye make them pass over MG 283:19. Impt. **uahlip** ʿ**lh̲** AM 121:6 and pass him by; with suff. **ahliph̲ lmargnak mn** ʿ**lauh̲** ATŠ II no. 428 pass thy staff over him. Act. pt. fem. ʿ**u mahlipa halin mahria** AM 56:14 if she passes through these illnesses; with encl. **mn maṭarata . . . mahliplh̲** RD C 27 causes him to pass through the purgatories; **mahliplun** RD C 28 causes them to pass. Part. pres. with suff. **mahlipinun** I cause them to pass by MG 292:1.

Der.: **hlapta, hilpa 1, hilpita, mhalpi**ʿ**il.**

HLṢ I (חלץ, ܚܠܨ, H. חלץ III, Ar. خلص LS, Ges.) to gird up the loins, brace oneself, be brave. Only pe. pass. pt. **hliṣ(a)** s.v.

Der.: **halṣa = haṣa, hliṣ(a).**

HLṢ II (met. of Sam. ࠋࠇࠑ, Chr.-Pal. ܠܚܨ, H. לחץ, Ar. لحص Ges.; met. also in Mod. Syr. ܚܠܨ MG 74 n. 2) to feel pain, give pain, cause pain MG 74:6, IM Gl.

Pe. Pf. only 3rd p. fem. sg. (used as an impers. verb) **hlaṣalh̲** Gy 95:13, 158:29 pains overtook her MG 74:5, 366:1.

Der.: **hlaṣa, halṣ(i)**ʿ**l.**

HLQ (חֲלַק, ܚܠܩ, H. חלק II LS, Ges.) to allot, assign, design.

Pe. Pf. ʿ**lak . . . hilqit tqala** DC 20. 120 see **aqlata** I have assigned thee . . . a stumbling-block (?). Act. pt. with encl. **umn qiniana ḏ-abahath̲ lahaliqlh̲** AM (several times) and of the property of his (her) parents nothing falls to his (her) lot.

Pa. Act. pt. ʿ**l glalia mhaliq ana rihua** DC 46. 125:4 I impart the wind to rocky places. Part. pres. **lbar anašia mhaliqna** DC 46. 86:5 I bring fate upon a human being.

Der.: **hilqa 1, mhalqi**ʿ**il.**

HLŠ (Jew.-Aram. and H. חלש, Syr. der. ܡܚܠܫܐ) to be weak, weaken, enfeeble.

Pe. Pf. **hilšit** DC 42 I was weakened.

Der.: ***halša 2** (with a def. var.).

HMA I (ܚܡܐ I حَمِيَ, rel. to **HUM = HMM**) to fade, wither.

Pe. Act. pt. pl. **haimia** Gy 5:21 etc. they fade (an epenthetical form of ܚܡܝܢ) MG 24:14. Pass. pt. pl. (prob.) **himia** Oxf. 9b: bottom, CP 152:10, ML 182:10 heated, passionate (?) (from **HUM, HMM** ?)

HMA II (ܚܡܐ II حمى LS) to guard, keep watch upon, protect.

Af. Act. pt. with encl. **mahmilun** DC 27. 244 it preserves them.

hma (= **ham 2**?) father-in-law (?) IM Gl. **hmai** IM p. 87 my father-in-law (?).

hmaria (var. **ham-, him-,** v.s. **hamara 1**) Gy 387:19 the asses.

HMBB s. pa. of **HBB.**

HMBL I s. pa. and ethpa. of **HBL.**

HMBL II s. ethpa. of **HML.**

HMD (Aram., H. חמד and Chr.-Pal. ܚܡܕ to desire, Ar. حمد to praise) to desire, to praise.

Pa. Pf. with suff. **uhamduia zadiqa** ATŠ II no. 438 but they praised the Holy One (?).

HML (ࡄࡌࡋ, ܚܡܠ, حمل) to gather together, hold together, collect, form a group, unite, carry, accumulate.

Pe. Pf. **hmal razia** ATŠ it gathered (= contains) the mysteries; **diqla ḏ-lahamlat** DC 46. 149:2 a date-tree that has not borne (dates). Act. pt. pl. **kulhun hamlin** DC 34. 670, 672, 1329, they all assemble.

Ethpa. Pt. **ianqa . . . mithambal** DC 41. 235 the child . . . is carried.

Gl. 51:1 f. miswritten تصرف *produci* رد آمد, 146:5 f. **HML** لقّ *inculcare* پیچید.

Der.: **haml**ʿ**il.**

HMM I, HUM (חמם, ܚܡ, حمّ, Akk. der. *emmu* warm, *ummu* warmth Ges., LS; a rel. rt. is **HMA**) to be hot, grow hot. Transition to ע״ו in the pass. pt. and in the der. **hauma** MG 248 n. 2.

Pe. Pf. **ham** was hot MG 248:4; **laham mn hauma** ATŠ no. 25, II no. 62 it did not scorch by heat, fem. **hamat** MG 248:10, special pl. form **hamiun razia** ATŠ the mysteries grew hot. Impf. **niham** Gy 160:23 is (growing) hot MG 249:19; transitive with encl. **nihumlak atra ḏ-hšuka** DC 37. 90 the place of darkness will scorch thee. Act. pt. fem. **nura d̲-haima** AM 287:41 the fire that is growing hot. Pass. pt. **him** MG 248 n. 2; with encl. **himlh̲** Gy 197:14 he became hot MG 250:14.

Ethpa. Pf. **ʿhamam** Gs 53:15 grew hot MG 213:17, 248 n. 2.

Gl. 9:1 f. miswritten as ע״י, احرّ *aestuare* گرم شد, 25:15 f. miswritten as ע״ע, اصطلى نشست پيش آتش *calefacere*.

Der.: **ham** 4 (?), **ḥamam(a)**, **hamima** (cf. also s. **HUM**), **himta** 2, **hamamʿil**, **hamamulai** (?).

HMM II (< H. יחם Ar. وحم, rel. to **HMM I**) to be angry, wax hot with anger.

Pe. Pf. **ham adam** Gs 3:2 A. grew hot with anger, **ham ṭaba d̲-lahimlh̲** Gy 197:13 f. the Good One became angry as never before (?, cf. s. **HMM I** pass. pt. with encl.).

Der.: **himta** (abs. **hima**, cstr. **himat**), **himta** 1.

HMS (Jew.-Aram. and H. חמס) to do violence, cause great emotion Ginzā 261 n. 5, MG 214: 17 f.

Ethpe. Pt. with encl. **ulbab lamihmislia utirat lamihmisalia** Gy 262:17 and my heart was not troubled in me and no violence was done to my conscience.

HMṢ (H. חמץ, Syr. ܚܡܨ III, Akk. šaf. *šuḫumṣu* prob. to oppress) to suppress, subdue.

Pe. Pf. with suff. (could be also pa.) **hamṣh̲ lnhurh̲** Gy 294:12 he subdued his light. Impf. with suff. **man nihimṣh̲ ldmutun** Gs 84:2 who shall suppress their appearance.

HMR I (H. חמר I, Ar. حمر) to be red, inflamed.

Pa. Pass. pt. fem. pl. **mhamran** AM 16: penult. etc. inflamed.

Der.: **hamranita, humra** 2.

HMR II (H. חמר II, Ar. خمر, Syr. in der. ܚܡܪܐ = Mand. **hamra**, ܚܡܝܪܐ = Mand. **hamira**) to ferment.

Der.: **hamra, hamira, hamruta, hamar** 1, **himira.**

HNA I (ܗܢܐ, هَنِئ, Jew.-Aram. in der. הֲנָאָה = הֲנָיָיא pleasure) to please, be pleased, be pleasing. Pe. fem. is used as an impers. verb; pa. and ethpa. are rare.

Pe. Pf. with encl. **hnatalh̲** Gy 135:5, 323:17 it pleased him; **hnatalak** Gy 207:5 it pleased thee MG 257:13 f.; **ldila uldilh̲ hnatalun ltartainun** Gy 146:8 it pleased her and him, both of them; but **lahnalia** Jb 147:13 it was displeasing to me. Pass. pt. **hinia** v.s.v.

Pa. Act. pt. **mhania** MG 262:16 (without reference); with encl. s. **HNN.**

Ethpa. Pt. **ziuaihun bhdadia mitahzia mithania umitahuia** ATŠ their brilliance is mutually visible, delightful, and displayed.

HNA II (= **HNN** q.v.) to take on the lap, catch to the bosom, embrace, enfold.

Pe. Pf. with suff. **hunh̲ uhananh̲** s. **HNN.**

Der.: s. **HNN.**

hnaqtia = **hanaqtia. ušatia zmaiun** [*sic*] **d̲-hnaqtia** DC 43 F 82 and drinks the blood of the strangling woman (or read pl.?).

HNG, a later form of **HNQ** (cf. DC 43:**Dahlulia** 40).

(**HNGD, HNGQ** miscopyings of **HNGR** in **mhangidilin** DAb = **mhangiqilin** RD E 12 read **mhangirilin** they torture them).

HNGR (< חנר, ܚܢܩ to bind) to repress, restrain; (den. from ܚܢܓܪܐ, خَنْجَر) to cripple, lame; the former might have been influenced by the latter.

Pa. Inf. **ʿl hanguria kulhun pugdamun** DC 44. 1906 = Morg. 269/29:14 to repress all their words.

Ethpa. Pf. **ʿthangar** Gy 316:ult. was crippled. Impf. **ubparzla nithangar** AM 34:1 and he will be lamed by an iron (weapon, tool).

HNDZ only in **handuzia** inf. haf. of **ANDZ** (q.v.).

ḥnuš (Ar. جنج) root, origin: **biḥnušh̲ d̲-aba hu ... hʿ biḥnušh̲ d̲-ʿma** DC 8 it is in its origin of the Father ... it is in its origin of the Mother.

hnina s. **hunina.**

HNN (חנן, ܚܢ, I, H. חנן I, Ar. حَنَّ LS, Ges.) to be fond of, favour, caress, fondle, show fondness (or affection), act affectionately.

Pe. (sometimes doubtful): Pf. with suff. **hu hanh̲** (**hu hananh̲**) Gs 44:11 he embraced him (he took him to his bosom). Impt. with suff. **hunh̲** (**uhananh̲**) Gy 34:20, Oxf. 85 a, DC 26. 477 etc. be gracious to him and favour him. Act. pt. **hu hanin ugazim ʿlauaihun** Gy 167:12 sometimes he is gracious (to them), sometimes he threateneth them.

Pa. (sometimes doubtful): Pf. with suff. **hannh̲** Gy 13:21 etc., **hananh̲** Gs. 44:11 etc. (often) he caressed him MG 31:24 f., 275:7 (both forms often together), **ligṭh̲ hananh̲** Gy 235:21 he took him and caressed him; **hananh̲ ušabšh̲** Jb 253:2 f. caressed it and cozened it; **hananan** he caressed me MG 31: 25; **hananun unišqun** Gy 77:6 they fondled me and kissed me. Impf. **nihannan** Gs 48:10 will caress me. Impt. with suff. **hananh̲** v.s. pe. impt., **hananan** Gy 96:4 caress me MG 271:10; pl. with suff. **hannuia, haninuia** Gy 39:14 caress him MG 279:2. Act. pt. with encl. **mhaninbh̲ bʿṣṭla** Gy 102:10 (where Lidzb. proposed **mkaninbh̲** Ginzā 110 n. 2) he enfolded him in the garment, but where DC 22. 97 has **bʿusṭunh̲** for **bʿṣṭla,** hence: he embraced him by the body; **mhaninlh̲** ATŠ II no. 173, **mhanilh̲** Gy 152:14 they caress her MG 32:10 (identical with **mhanilh̲** AM 38 is favourable to him, from **HNA I**). Part. pres. **mhanina** Gy 148:17, 150:2 I caress(ed) (MG 231:6).

Ethpa. Pt. **hadia umithanan usahqa** DC 41. 143 rejoices, seeks grace, leaps up, **mithanana umitkarakbh̲** ATŠ II no. 125 (var. **mithanan** ... DC 6) he fondles and embraces me; **mithanna umitkarkibia** Gs 113:13 id.

Der.: **hana, hanuta, han(a)nʿil** (and varr.), **h(u)nina, hanʿil.**

HNP (cf. Ges. s. חנף) only in der.: **hanipa, haniputa, hunpana.**

HNQ (**חנק**, **ܚܢܩ**, **خنق** Akk. *ḫanâqu* Ges.) to choke, strangle, suffocate.

Pe. Impf. with suff. **kul daiua d̲-ṭribh̲ ˁlh̲ ˁhinqh̲** DC 33, DC 43 C 63 each demon that striketh him, I will choke. Act. pt. with encl. (**mihtniq**) **hanqilh̲ umaiit** AM 149:11 (he will be choked) they hang him and he dies.

Pa. Act. pt. **ulilita mhaniq** (should be -**nqan**) DC 43 and the liliths strangle.

Ethpe. Pt. **mihtniq** v.s. pe. act. pt.

Gl. 15:5 f. **ahnaq** اختنق *suffocari* خفه شد; 59:3 f. **HNQ** خنق *suffocare* خفه كرد.

Der.: **hanaqiata, hinqa, mhanaqta.**

hsara (rt. **HSR**) defect, lacking: **hsaran asrin** DC 44 = Morg. they bind (: charm away) our defect(s) (?).

HSB = **HṢB.**

Pe. Pf. **husbit pukrai** Oxf. roll g 641 thou hast restrained my fetters (?).

HSD (**חֲסַד**, **ܚܣܕ** to be ashamed, H. **חסד** II to revile, Ar. حسد to envy) to revile, scorn.

Pa. Pf. with suff. **hasdunan** ML 106:16, Q 54:27, 30 (var. **hasidunan**) they reviled us MG 280:13.

Der.: **hasuda, hizda.**

hsiruta (**חֲסִירוּתָא**, **ܡܚܣܪܢܘܬܐ**) AM 201 deficiency, defective nature.

HSK (**ܚܣܟ** LS) to be(come) feeble, diminish, grow lax.

Pe. Pf. **kd̲-hiskat malkuta d̲-sahria** DAb when the rule of the demons grew lax. Impf. **udlaniquš udlanihsuk** Gs 2:1, 3:1 so that he neither grows old nor becomes feeble (MG 219:paen.); **tihsuk** Gs 2:17, 4:7 thou wilt become feeble. Pt. (irregular) **uṭunaihun lahasuk ulabaṣar** ATŠ I no. 285 and their fruit neither diminishes nor becomes deficient.

HSM (Syr. and Chr.-Pal. **ܚܣܡ**, Ar. حشم) to envy, be jealous.

Pe. Pf. **aina d̲-hismat** JRAS 1937 593:32 eye that was jealous. Pt. **aina d̲-hasma** JRAS 1938 2:1 eye that envies.

Pa. Pf. with encl. **hasmulh̲** AM 28:ult. they envied him. Act. pt. with encl. **mhasmibh̲** DC 37. 283 they envy him.

Der.: **hasumtia, husma.**

HSN (**חֲסַן**, **ܚܣܢ**, H. **חסן** I, Ar. حَصُنَ LS, Ges.) to be strong, vigorous, healthy; to force, compel, take possession of, preserve.

Pa. Impf. with suff. **ṭiˁam usušmia nihasinun tlata iahria** AM 277:10 f. people will preserve food and sesame(-crops) for three months. About the doubtful **hasina** Gs 122:19 cf. s.v.

Der.: **hasina.**

HSR (Aram. and H. **חסר**, Syr. and Chr.-Pal. **ܚܣܪ**, Ar. خسر) to lack, be defective.

Pe. Pf. **ˁtar ulahsar** s. **YTR** pe. pf., **lahisrit ulabiṣrit** Gy 132:23 I was not defective nor imperfect. Impf. **lanihsar ulanibṣar** CP 429: antep. f. shall not be wanting or be ill-provided; **nihisrun** AM (very often) will fail, will be lacking (pl.); **latihisrun ulatibiṣrun** Jb 88:5 be without lacking and fault (pl.). Act. pt. **udmikṣar hasar** AM and that which is short is lessened; with encl. **ulahma lahsarlh̲** AM and he will not lack for bread; pl. **hasria tarmidia** Jb 223:8 the priests are lacking; **iatiria ulahasria** Gy 91:8, 102:1 they are rich and not in want; fem. pl. **lahasran ulabaṣran** CP 429:16:antep. they are not lacking or wanting. Part. pres. **hasrit** Jb 222:1 thou art at fault; **anatun napšia ulahasritun** Gy 292:1 ye shall increase and not diminish. Pass. pt. **hsir** us. replaced by **hasir** (s.v.); with encl. pers. pron. **d-anin minh̲ lahsirnin** DC 48. 125 so that we are lacking.

Pa. Pf. with suff. **hasrunin hasrunin misar** (read **mihsar**?) **anania** DC 44 they diminished them, they reduced them utterly, the spouses. Doubtful. Pt. fem. **mhasra** DC 21 it diminishes.

Ethpe. Pt. pl. **anašia mihiṣria** AM 272:15 people will be impoverished.

Der.: **hasran, hasir, h(a)siruta, husra, husrana.**

hˁ (**היא**, **ܗܝ**) pers. pron. of the 3rd p. sg. fem.: she. Exceptional forms **hˁia** Gy 258:21 B, 'h' Gy 154:15 B, 170:ult. B MG 86 n. 2.

HPA (**חפא**, **ܚܦܐ**, H. **חפה**, Ar. خفى, rel. to **HBA**) to cover, hide.

Pe. (with or without the prosth. a): Pf. **hpa** (var. **ahpa**) **nisbh̲ lziuaihun** Gy 247:20 he hid from view and took away the light; **ahpa mia** CP 68:4, Morg. 231/50:8 = ML 83:9 the waters covered her.

HPK (**הפך**) a doublet of **APK**, cf. DC 43 E 17.

HPP = **HUP** (q.v.).

HPR (**חפר**, **ܚܦܪ** H. **חפר** I, Ar. حفر, Akk. *ḫapâru* LS, Ges.) to dig.

Pe. Act. pt. **ubṭupra apra hapra** Gs 99:7 and with her nails she diggeth the dust.

Pa. Pf. **anin hapirnin rbita unahrauata** ATŠ II no. 188 we dug out sea and rivers.

Gl. 61:5 f. miswritten حفر *fodere* چاه كند.

HṢA s. **HṢṢ.**

hṣada (**חֲצָדָא**, **ܚܨܕܐ**) harvest. Later doublet **hiṣad** (s.v.). **hṣada d̲-kadba** Gy 277:11 a harvest of lying; **zira d̲-hṣadh̲ mṭa** Jb 54:9 grain whose harvest came.

HṢB (met. of **HBṢ**) to shrink, compress, repress, restrain, cut short, become short, retreat Ginzā 85 n. 1. (The meaning of Jew.-Aram. and H. **חצב**, Chr.-Pal. **ܚܨܒ** 'to cut' may be also preserved in certain forms and esp. der.).

Pe. Pf. **hṣab mn qudamai** Gy 137:23, 154:8 it retreated before me; **hṣub šaiia hṣub šušia** Gs 48:22 (varr. **hṣab, hṣib, ṣub** Pet.) short became the hours and short became the minutes. Impt. pl. **hiṣbu mn pagrai** DC 43 J 37 retreat from my body. Act. pt. **iardna haṣib** Gy 192:6 the jordan retreateth; pl. **šnia haṣbia kd̲ ṭulalia** Gs 76:16 years become short like shadows; **kd̲ haṣbia nihuia** Gs 44:4 s. **haṣbia 3.** Part. pres. **d̲-mdabrit anat uhaṣbit** JRAS 1938 3:1 that thou leadest on and cuttest short.

Pa. Impf. with suff. **ˁhaṣbanun liahria** Gs 44:3 I shall cut short the months. Pass. pt. pl. **mhaṣbia umbaṣria ṭabia** DC 22. 437 (mh-

missing in Pet. Gs 48:15) the righteous are repressed and taken away.

ETHPE. Pf. with encl. ʿhṣiblh̲ hiṣbia Gy 84:17 convulsions overcame him.

ETHPA. Pf. uthaṣab DC 3 and they retreated.

DER.: haṣbia, haṣbta, haṣubia, haṣubtia, hiṣbia.

HṢD (חצד, ?ܚܨܕ Akk. *eṣêdu*, Ar. loan-w. حصد Fränkel 132) to reap, to cut harvest.

PE. Impf. **kma ʿhṣad** Jb 203:5 how long shall I reap?; with suff. **nihṣudunh̲** Jb 232:12 (B **nihṣidinh̲**, C **uniṣidunh̲**, AD **unihiṣdun**) they shall reap it. Act. pt. pl. **haṣdia** (var. **-in**) **hṣada d̲-kadba** Gy 277:11 (var. DC 22. 272) they reap a harvest of falsehood.

ETHPE. Pt. **šuba minaihun kd̲ ʿzdra mihṣad** [*sic*] ATŠ II no. 197 seven of them, when sown, are harvested.

DER.: **hiṣad, hṣada.**

HṢL (Ar. حصل) to reach, arrive, result, attain.

PE. Pf. **hṣilnin bdinba d̲-dara d̲-nirig** PD 1745 we reached the end of the age of Mars.

HṢP (חצף, ܚܨܦ, حَصُفَ) only in der. **haṣip** = **haṣip(a), huṣpa.**

HṢṢ (rel. to **HUṢ**) to construct (by weaving or binding reeds together).

PE. (?): Impt. pl. **uhaṣiun ʿndiruna** Lond. roll A 8 and they constructed a booth. Pass. pt. **kd̲ haṣiṣa** [*sic*] **škinta** DC 34. 7 when the cult-hut is built.

HṢR (ܚܨܪ, Ar. حصر III) to oppress, besiege.

ETHPE. Impf. **babil tihṣar** AM 283:27 Babylon will be besieged. Pt. pl. **anašia mihiṣria** AM 272:15 people will be oppressed.

HQA s. **HQQ I.**

hqilta (rt. **HQL I**) slipping, omission, mistake (?). **ʿu hqilta hauialun ltartinun hʿ** ATŠ I no. 90 if they commit a mistake (?), it affects both of them (i.e. pupil and instructor).

hqiqia (cf. Jew.-Aram. sg. st. abs. חֲקָק hollow) Gy 75:14 rents, clefts MG 116:20. Sg. not found.

HQL I (met. of H. חלק I, Ar. حلق) to slide, slip MG 74:7.

PE. Pf. **hiqlit bligrai** Jb 34 n. 3 a var. of **ʿhiqlit** (v.s. ethpe.).

ETHPE. Pf. **ʿhiqlit bligrai** Jb 34:2 my feet slipped (lit. I slipped with my feet). Pt. **kd̲ azil bgauh̲ lamihqil** Gy 357:4, Jb 171:6 f., 182:6 f. when he walketh in it he should not slip.

DER.: **haqalta, haqla, hqilta.**

HQL II (= **ʿQL**) to twist IM Gl., to enclose, encompass, surround.

PE. Pf. **hqilat aqalata** s. **aqalata**; with encl. **hqalan** IM no. 37 he encompassed us; **hqiltinun** IN no. 37 I twisted them.

ETHPE.: Pt. **mihqil** IM is twisted, encompassed. Part. pres. (irregular) **mhiqlit** DC 20. 122, DC 43 E 55 thou art surrounded.

DER. s. **ʿQL.**

HQQ I, HUQ II (חקק, حق) to be orderly; pa. to put in order, arrange, fashion.

PA. Pf. **ana haqit taga** HG I fashioned a crown.

Gl. 24:3 f. **HQA** [*sic*] ايقن *certus esse* حق شد [*sic*].

HQQ II = **HUQ I** with transition to ע״ע in **tihqun** Gy 64:17, 19 D (v.s. **HUQ I** pe. impf.).

HQR I (Syr. ܚܩܪ to talk empty talk, ethpa. to boast, Ar. حقر to contemn) to vaunt, (speak) boast(fully).

PA. Pf. **haqar lišana** ATŠ II no. 129 the tongue babbled. Pass. pt. **mhaqar 1** (s.v.).

Gl. 60:3 f. miswritten حقر *contemnere* رڭ كرد; 65:7 f. id. احتقر *aspernari* رڭ كرد.

DER.: **mhaqar 1.**

HQR II (Jew.-Aram. and H. חקר) to investigate, examine carefully, search, make research, make inquiry, study diligently.

PE. (doubtf.); Pf. **hqiriun** (read pa.?) **ukdabiun** DC 7 they examined carefully and wrote down.

PA. Pf. **haqarta d̲-haqar** HG research which he carried out; **haqrit ukidbit** ATŠ I no. 297 I examined carefully and wrote; **haqiriun napša mahu d̲-mṣia hailaihun** DC 7 they examined them much as far as they were able (to do so); **andiziun uhaqiriun ʿlauaiun** 330:9 and they compared and studied them carefully. Impf. **kul man d̲-nipruš . . . unihaqar** ATŠ every man that perceives . . . and investigates; **šailia . . . unihaqrun ʿlh̲** DC 35 they ask . . . and make inquiry about it. Impt. **balak haqar** Morg. 251/89:9 examine carefully thy mind (?); **haqar uhaizak qrun** ATŠ study diligently and then read. Act. pt. **mhaqar** RD D 28. Pass. pt. **mhaqar 2** (s.v.).

DER.: **haqarta, mhaqar 2.**

HRA (חֲרָא, ܚܪܐ, H. חרה II, Ar. خَرِئَ LS, Ges.) to relieve the bowels, excrete. Still used (mod. pf. *herâ*, pres. *qahârî*).

Gl. 82:15 f. **ahra** زق *cacare* ريد.

DER.: **hra** (var. **hira 1**).

hra (Talm. חֲרָיָא, Syr. ܚܪܝܐ) Gy 91:2 (D **hira**) excrement, dung MG 56:9 ff., 115:antep.

hraqa 1 (ܚܘܪܩܐ) grinding of teeth, gnashing of teeth. **guha d̲-hraqa d̲-šina** DC 45 (several times) the noise of grinding of teeth; **hraqa d̲-šina uguhka mn binta spahata** DC 46. 186:4 f.

hraqa 2 Read **hbaqa** embrace, coition (?). **uganiana bihraqa d̲-plan** DC 46 and I shall lie in the embrace (?) of N.

hrara 1 (cf. Bibl.-Aram. הַרְהֹרִין, Syr. ܗܪܗܘܪܐ Fata Morgana) Gy 97:23, 179:12, Gs 59:5, ATŠ II no. 253 etc. illusion, delusion, hallucination MG 64 n. 2. Pl. **hraria** IM Gl., Gy 59:2 illusions.

hrara 2 (cf. חֲרָרָה J.) ZDMG 1955 145b:8 cake, clot, cf. ibid. 136 n. 3.

HRB I (חרב, ܚܪܒ, H, חרב II, خَرِبَ, Akk. *harâbu* LS, Ges.) to destroy, ruin, despoil.

PE. Pf. ***hrib** MG 219:antep., or with labialization ***hrub** (mod. pronunciation *heroβ*). Impf. **nihrub** MG 219:antep., var. with a graphical **a**: **lanihrab zaharata** DC 7 he may not spoil the injunction (: rubric); **nihirbun** AM (very often) they will ravage, will not destroy. Act. pt. (with pass. meaning) **harub** Gy 29:19 will be destroyed; pl. **harbia** Jb 258:11 they destroy.

PA. Act. pt. with suff. **mharibh̲** DC 43 he destroys him. Inf. **harubia,** defectively **hrubia** to destroy IM Gl.; with suff. **harubih̲** DC 43 to destroy it.

AF. Pf. **ahribt** thou hast destroyed MG 222:bottom; with suff. **ahribtinun** she destroyed them MG 282:20. Impf. with suff. **tᶜiahribh̲** Gy 332:23 thou destroyest her MG 215:18. Impt. pl. **ahribiun** MG 229:22.

Gl. 126:11 f. **HRB** فسد *eruescere, demoliri* تمام شد, 171:1 f. with a prosthetic **a** (but not af.) هدم *destruere* خراب شد.

DER.: **harba, harbᶜil, harub, haribta, hirba, hirub.**

HRB II = **ARB I** = **ᶜRB I** only sporadically in pe. act. pt. **laharub** Gy 3:5 B a var. of **larub** (s. **ARB I**), **kd̲ harub ᶜumama** AM 258:3 when the day becomes dark (i.e. when the sun sets).

HRG (ܚܪܓ) to rub, grate; fig. be cunning, pa. to misuse, MG 40:14. (The fig. meaning is based on **HRK** cf. Gl. under **HRK II.**)

PE. Pf. with suff. **daqh̲ hargh̲** DC 9 he pounded it and grated it. Act. pt. with encl. **mindam bgauh̲ hargalh̲** DC 34. 1282 something within it distorts (?) it. Pass. pt. **hrig** s.v.

PA. Pf. with suff. **hᶜ hargitinun** (read **hargatinun**) **lrazia kulhun** DC 34. 788 she misused (: abolished, perverted?) all the mysteries.

DER.: **harga, hargta** (and varr.), **hrig.**

HRZQ (Talm. הרזק, Ar. both هرزق and حرزق; *parpel* of חזק) to fetter MG 60:10, 85:8. Fundamental stem: pf. with suff. **harzqan** Gs 119:22 he fettered me MG 270: ult. Refl. stem: pf. **ᶜharzaqt** Jb 64:2 thou wert fettered. Pt. **mitharzaq** Jb 66:4 is fettered MG 132:bottom, 213:18.

hrig (Pass. pt. of **HRG**) cunning, ingenious: **hrig laqu hakim lbiš** Gy 186:12 cunning to harm, wise for evil.

hriria DC 22. 54 a var. of **hraria** Gs 59:2.

HRK I (חרך, ܚܪܟ, Ar. حرق) to burn, singe, char, scorch.

PA. Impt. with suff. **harkh̲ bnura** DC 24 singe it in fire.

ETHPA. Pf. **ᶜtharak** he was burnt IM Gl. Impf. **nitharak** AM 20 will be burnt. Pt. fem. **mitharka** Gy 280:20 is scorched; pl. **alma d̲-nišmatun miharkin** DC 12 until their souls are burnt.

HRK II (Ar. حرك) to move, stir, agitate, wedge, fold (?), squeeze (?).

PA. Impt. with suff. **uharkh̲ lpihta bklila** (in rituals) and squeeze (?) the *pihta* about the wreath (a ritual action consisting in folding the wet dough of the ritual bread about a small myrtle wreath).

Gl. 58:9 f. **HRK** حرك *agitare* تكانيد, 118:7 f. **HRK** عنت *concutere* تكانيد.

HRM (Jew.-Aram. and H. חרם, Syr. ܚܪܡ Ar. حرم LS, Ges. s. חרם I) to ban, curse, anathematize.

PE. Pass. pt. pl. **hrimia** JRAS 1937 595:30 banned, **bnia ahrimia** DC 40. 319 accursed sons; with encl. pers. pron. **hrimitun** IM no. 27 p. 79 ye are anathematized.

DER.: **harma.**

HRP (חרף, ܚܪܦ I LS, Ges. s. חרף II) to be early, sharp, hasty, premature; to stimulate, urge; as an impers. verb: to grieve; ethpa.: to be grieved (?, doubtf.), suffer (?) MG 60:8 f.

PE. Impf. with encl. (as impers. verb) **nišmat alma lᶜhruplik** Gs 90:ult. my soul, why doth it grieve thee? MG 366:ult.

PA. Act. pt. **mqamia d̲-nahga nihga umharip qaria tarnaula** Jb 129:2 before the daybreak and early cock-crow.

ETHPA Pf. **ᶜhtarap ᶜlh̲** Gy 191:18 (var. **ᶜharap** DC 22. 183 and Sh. ʿAbd.'s copy) he was sorry for him Ginzā 192 n. 3; **kma sbal udar uᶜtharap** DC 48. 134 how much he has endured and borne and suffered! Pt. **lamitharap** ATŠ II no. 23 will not be grieved [: will be freed from grief (?), or = **lamitharab** will not be spoiled (?)].

DER.: **harup(a),** fem. **harupta, harip(a), hurpa 2** (?)).

HRQ (Jew.-Aram. and H. חרק, Syr. ܚܪܩ, Ar. حرق) (of teeth) to gnash, grind, chatter, munch, crunch up, crush (with teeth).

PE. Pf. with suff. **daqh̲ uharqh̲ lkul mdinta** DC 36 he smashed and crushed the whole city. Impf. **šinh̲ lanihruq** DC 46. 186:9 he shall not grind his teeth. Act. pt. **šinh̲ hariq** (var. **hiriq**) AM 115:6 etc. (often) is gnashing his teeth; pl. **šinaihun harqia** DC 44 etc. (often) they gnash their teeth. Part. pres. **šinak harqit** DC 37. 46 thou grindest thy teeth.

DER.: **hraqa.**

HRR I (חרר ithpa., ܚܪܪ pa. and ethpa., Ar. حرّ II to set free) only in der.: ***hara,** fem. **harta, haruta, (ahara).**

HRR II (Ar. حرّ, H. חרר II Ges.) to be hot.

DER.: **hararat** (and varr.), **hararia.**

HRR III (ܚܪܪ, Ar. هرّ) to be ill. Only in der.: **hrara 1, mahra 1, mahranita.**

HRŠ I (חרש, ܚܪܫ, ܚܪܫ, خرس H. חרש II LS, Ges.) to be deaf(-mute).

DER.: **har(a)ša.**

HRŠ II (den. from **haraša 1**) to enchant, bewitch.

PE. Part. pres. (**mihraš**) **harišna** DC 23. 632, 644 I enchant. Inf. **mihraš** ibid.

HRŠ III (Ar. حرج) to forbid, prevent, prohibit.

Mod. **haraš̲ ᶜbad ᶜlabu** (read **ᶜlauu** pron. *elâwū*) DC 35:coloph. he forbade them; **haraš̲ uadiun ᶜlai mn minda(i)** ibid. they took away (lit. deprived me of) my possessions. Gl. 60:15 f. miswritten حرّج *prohibere* منع كرد.

HRT (חרת, ܚܪܬ LS) to scratch, dig out, gouge out (eyes).

Pe. Part. pres. **hartin** [*sic*] **bainak** DC 43 I 67 I will gouge out thine eyes.

HŠB (Aram. and H. חשב, Syr. ܚܫܒ Ar. حسب LS, Ges.) to think (out), plan, reckon, count, plot, scheme.

Pe. Pf. with suff. **hišbun bhušbanun** Gs 91:7 they account me as (one) of their number. Impf. **hušbankun hšib** (read **ʿhšib**) ML 135:9 = CP 110:7 **hušbankin** I will count (: include) you in my number; with suff. **nihšibunun** DAb they shall count them, **nihišbunkun** Q 37:9 (varr. **nihšabinakin** etc. read **nihšibunkin**) they count you. Impt. with suff. **hušbin** Q 73b:40 (var. **-an**) count me MG 271:20. Act. pt. **hašib** he counts MG 230:3; with encl. **kul had had masiqta bšitin hašiblh̠** DC 27 each single m. counts as 60; pl. with encl. **hašbilh̠** DAb they count him, consider him. Pass. pt. **hšib** MG 230:6. Inf. **mihšib** Gy 80:10 f., MG 233:bottom.

Pa. Pf. **hašib** he thought MG 221:paen., **hašbat** she thought MG 222:12, **hašibt** thou hast thought MG 222:bottom, **hašibtun** ye thought MG 224:6, **hašibnin** we thought MG 224:18. Impf. **latihašbun** Gy 41:12 do not plot; with suff. **ukd̠ binataihun nihašbunh̠** AM 28:11 and when he is amongst them, they will esteem him (or: they will count him as one of themselves (?)). Impt. **hašib** MG 229:6. Act. pt. **mhašib** MG 230:7, **mhašib miqria** Gy 394:7 he thinketh to call MG 387:7, **mhašib hušbia hauia** AM 49 he will be a schemer; pl. **mhašbin** AM 18 etc. they think, **lṭabia lbiš mhašbia** v.s. l-. Part. pres. **mhašbit** thou plannest MG 232:13, **mhašbitun** ye consider MG 233:13. Inf. **hašubia** MG 233: ult., **hašubia d̠-hašib rba** CP 272:7, ML 260:12 when the Great One thought. Nom. ag. **mhašbana** s.v. Nom. act. **hašabta** s.v.

Ethpe. Pf. **ʿthšib** was counted MG 215:3. Impf. **mn malkia ʿlaiia nihšib** DC 41. 18 f. he shall be counted with celestial kings. Pt. **mithšib, mitihšib, mihšib** MG 230:middle; fem. (pl.) **bhamiš masqata mihišba ʿlh̠** ATŠ II no. 79 are reckoned for him as 5 m.; with encl. **lamihšiblh̠** Gy 15:19 will not be counted for him.

Ethpa. Pf. **ʿthašab** he thought MG 215:3, 222:4, **ʿthašbit** I thought MG 223:9. Impt. **ʿthašab** Gy 329:6 consider (pl.). Pt. **mithašab** he thinks MG 230:middle; pl. **qaimia mithašbia** v.s. **QUM, bhušbia bišia mithašbia alai** DAb they think out evil designs against me.

Gl. 60:5 f. with a prosth. **a** حاسب *rationem ponere* حساب كرد; 90:9 f. **HŠB** (pa.) شك *hesitare* شك داشت.

Der.: **hašabta, hušba, hušbana, hušbanaiia.**

hšga an exceptional miscop. of **hšuka. alma d̠-hšga** DC 36.

hšuka (חֲשׁוֹכָא, ܚܫܘܟܐ) darkness MG 118:paen. Rarely in st. abs. **hšuk** MG 300:antep. Used also of menstruation (or discharge). **alma d̠-hšuka** (very often) the world of darkness; **nhura uhšuka** (very often) light and darkness; **kul man hšuka lahazia** DC 45 any (woman) who does not see her periods; **ʿnta d̠-la atia minh̠ hšuka** DC 45 a woman whose menstrual discharge does not come; **iabiš minh̠ hšukh̠** DC 46 her discharge will dry up.

HŠK (Aram. and H. חשך, Syr. ܚܫܟ LS, Ges.) to be dark, gloomy. As impers. verb used in fem. gender MG § 256, p. 365.

Pe. Pf. ***hšik** cf. MG 219:bottom, **hiškat unihgat** Gs 118:9 it became dark and it became clear; **dmutaikun hibrat uhiškat** Jb 196:8 f. your appearance has darkened and become sombre; **hiškat aina bmuqra** DC 41. 500 f. her eye became obscured by suppurating matter; with encl. **ainh̠ hšaklh̠ ulanahra** Gy 84:15 his eyes became dark and did not shine. Impf. **nihšuk** is, or will be dark MG 219:paen.; **ʿma tihšuk** Gs 118:4 when will it be dark?; with encl. **nihšiklik ainik** Gy 181:12 f. we will darken thine eyes. Act. pt. **qadim dna hašik arab** CP 27:4, Q 11:31 = ML 31:9 (the sun) rises in the morning, sets in the evening; **hašuk** Gy 335:22 etc., becometh dark; fem. **haška,** DC 41. 413, Jb 190:8 etc.; pl. **mihšak haškia** Sh. ʿAbd. copy's var. of Gs 65:12 (where Pet. omits **haškia**), **razia qarišia haškia** DC 27. 200 chilling, dark(ening) mysteries; **dur haškia** Gy 133:7, Jb 183:1 dwelling of darkness (*sic.* Lidzb. Jb ii 179 n. 3 takes **haškia** as an abstr. noun, but it seems to be of adjectival origin, cf. the analogous **dur bišia** s. **dur**); fem. pl. **ʿbidatun haškan** ATŠ I no. 251 their works darken (adjectivally); **ruhiata ṭamiata haškata** DC 40 unclean, dark female (evil) spirits. Inf. **mihšak** Gy 335:22, Gs 65:12.

Pa.: Impf. with suff. **latihaškh̠ lhizuan** DC 48:205 do not obscure our vision. Pf. **ʿit d̠-nahar uʿit d̠-hašuk** DC 34:432. Impt. with suff. **haškinun laina** Gy 149:8 obscure their eye(s).

Der.: **hšuka.**

HŠL (Jew.-Aram. חֲשַׁל Syr. ܚܫܠ to forge; cf. also Bibl.-Aram. חֲשַׁל, Ar. حسل to crush, Akk. *ḫašālu*) to forge, fashion, design, devise, furbish, cast (metal).

Pe. Pf. with suff. **hišlh̠** DC 43 J 170 he forged it, var. **hišilh̠**. Act. pt. **hašil razia** DC 35 he forgeth (: deviseth) the rites; pl. **qaimia uzaina hašlia qaimia uhašlia zaina** Gy 80:20 f. they stand and forge weapons; fem. pl. **ruha uʿstirata qaima uraza hašla qaima uhašla razia** Gy 85:22 f. R. and the astartes contrive secret plots. Part. pres. **anat hu d̠-hašlit malalia** ATŠ I no. 244 thou (art he that) fashionest the words; **hašlinin dahba** Jb 139:7 we forge gold. Pass. pt. **hšil umatna zaina** Gs 13:12 the weapon is forged and put on; **zanga d̠-hšil bʿula** Jb 156:6 a bell cast in evil; **halin šadiriata hšil** DAb these chains were forged.

HŠŠ = **HUŠ.**

Af. Pt. pl. **ainih̠ mahšin** DC 46. 122:6 his eyes are painful (?). Other forms s. **HUŠ.**

htit (see **hṭit**) proven.

HTM (חתם, ܚܬܡ, ختم LS, Ges.) to seal (up), close (in), sign, conclude, confirm, press down.

Pe. Pf. with suff. **hitmh̠** Gy 131:20 he

sealed it, **htaminun** Gy 131:10 f., 19 he sealed them, **htamtẖ** (often in exorcisms) I sealed him, it, **htamtinun** DC 40. 584 I sealed them. Impf. **kul man ḏ-zidqa brika ḏ-qabin lanihtam** ATŠ I no. 150 any man who does not complete the Blessed Oblation for marriage; with suff. **lanihitmẖ** ATŠ II no. 201 does not sign him. Impt. pl. **htumiun pandama lpumaikun** DC 42 close the p. (v.s.v.) over your mouths; with suff. **hutmuia** seal him (or it) MG 278:bottom, **uhitmuia** DC 43 D 13 and seal it, **hutmunin** or **htumunin** Q 7:15, 16, 21, 16:31 (with bad varr.) *sigillate eas* MG 283: bottom. Pass. pt. **htim** (often); with encl. pers. pron. **htimna** I am sealed MG 231: 4. Inf. with suff. **baiin lmihitmẖ** DC 34 they wish to confirm (: consecrate) him (as priest).

Pa. Act. pt. with encl. **mzarizlẖ umhatimlẖ** Gy 137:14 he armeth and confirmeth him. Pass. pt. **mhatmа** s.v.

Ethpe. Pf. **ʿhtim** (Pet. **htim**) DC 22. 429 = Gs 40:19 he closed up (?). Impf. **bhahu hatma tithitmun** DC 40. 791 with that seal ye are sealed down. Pt. **ulamihtim** ATŠ II no. 25; **mithitmin** ATŠ II no. 160 are sealed, **mithitmia** (often) id.

Der.: **hatma, hatamta, mhatam.**

HTN (den. from **hatna** q.v.) to connect by marriage.

Pa. Pf. with suff. **hat(u)nun ladam uhaua** DC 45 they joined A. and E. in marriage.

HTP a rare form of **HṬP** MG 42 n. 1, Ginzā 254 n. 4.

Pe. Act. pt. **hatpia** Gy 215:22 (in the same l. **haṭpia**) they snatch away. Inf. **mihtip.**

Der.: **hatupia** (pl.).

HTR I (ܡܫܬܚܪ) to show pride in one's bearing, make a show, exult, rejoice, show pride or delight.

Pe. (Only) pass. pt. with encl. **htirlẖ** DAb = **htarlẖ** RD B 102 he prides himself; part. pres. (formed from pass. part.) **hdina uhtirna** DC 44. 1076 I rejoice and exult.

Ethpe. Impf. **nihitrun bmdin mdin** AM 183 they will make public rejoicing (?) in many a city. Pt. **iardna mihtar umitiatar** ATŠ II no. 392 the jordan quivers with pride and is increased (in dignity). Part. pres. **mihtirna** Jb 241:1 I show pride (Lidzb. proposed **mihtimna** I am sealed II 221 n. 4).

Gl. 126:7 f. defectively and with a prosth. **a** فرح *gaudere* خوشحال شد.

Der.: **hitra.**

HTR II (Jew.-Aram. חתר) to breach, break into. Doubtf.

Ethpe. Pf. **ʿhtar ubṭaš bʿuṣṭuna** ATŠ they broke into (?) and trod down the body (doubtf.).

U (W)

u the 6th letter of the alphabet. Pronunciation: consonantal **w**, or vocal **u**. Used often as a vowel sign *u* MG § 15, p. 13 f.; as a vowel sign called *-ušenna* (: **bu-** *bušenna*, **gu-** *gušenna* etc.) MMII 243 n. 2. Wavering betw. u and i MG 13:bottom f. Sometimes used to indicate a *šwa mobile* MG § 8, p. 8. Phonetic changes: u < a (or i) MG § 19, p. 17 ff.

u- (Gen. Sem. co-ordinative conj.) and. Used always proclitically MG § 14, p. 12. **uap** and also MG 208:1. Syntax MG 325 ff., 439 ff.

-u 1 the pl. ending of the pf. of verbs with an acc. suff. of the 3rd p. fem. sg. MG 88:16 (esp. with verbs ל״י: **qru** Gy 273:3 they called her, **hiziu** Gy 282:8 they saw her MG 289:8 f.).

-u 2 an exceptional ending of the impf. of verbs in the 3rd and 2nd p. pl. as a particularity of the XI book of Gy: **titqru** 257:14 ye are called, **nʿhu** 251:5 they will be, **nitqaimu** 251:12 they will be confirmed Ginzā 250:12 f.

ua Zotb. 219 left 14 an exceptional form of **u-**.

uabaš iasdis Gy 383:17 name of an ancient Persian king. Var. **ubaš** DC 22. 380.

uada (Ar. وُدّ) AM 254:7 love, or for mod. **bada** (q.v.) work (?).

uahuš (Ar. وحوش) AM 278:9, 282:37 wild animals.

uaza = **auaza. damia uaza** DC 46 it resembles a goose.

uazan Gy 392:2, 19 name of an ancient Iranian king.

uazir (Ar. وزير) AM 193 minister.

uai (וַי, ܘܝ, وَى etc.) interj.: woe, often repeated **uai uai**, or followed by the encl. prep. **l** or by **ʿl** woe (to) . . .; doublet **ʿuai** MG 81:12 f., IM Gl. **uailinun** woe to them MG 89:6, **uailẖ** IM 70 woe to him IM Gl. **uai uai ḏ-**, Gy 175:18 woe, woe that, **uai ʿlak ḏ-** Gy 173:18 woe is thee that . . . MG 468:middle.

uasiṭ AM 198 the town of Wāsiṭ BZ Ap. II, SsSs 136. Also **uaṣiṭ** s.v.

uasqa (P., etym. unknown) Gy 224:2 a cult-food of the Parsees Ginzā 225 n. 3. Miscop. **uasra** DC 22. 218.

uap (v.s. u-) and also.

uaṣiṭ AM 305 = **uasiṭ.**

uarda (וַרְדָּא, ܘܪܕܐ Mishn. וֶרֶד Löw 131, Ar. وَرْدَة Qur. 55:37; from P. *ward* < گل Lagarde AS 2106, cf. Av. *varəδa* Bartholomae 1369, Pahl. *varta* Jeffry 287, Widg. V 196) flower, rose MG 56:20. Var. **ʿuarda.** Pl. **uardia.** Masc. **uarda ana br bhiria** Gy 275:15 I am a rose, a son of the chosen ones; **uardia lbišia uardia mkasia** Gs 30:14 f. they are clothed in roses, covered with roses, **uardia labšia** Gy 225:11; **uarda ušaraia** Oxf. 44 b rose(s) and silk, **labšia uarda ušaraia** Jb 83:15; **klila uarda** Jb 77:10

wreath of rose(s) cf. ii 83 n. 1; **uarda natar** Jb 167:5 the rose falls apart; **bazra d̠-uarda** AM 287:36 rose-seed; **uarda hiuara hu uarda sumaqa hu** DC 41 (illustration) it is a white rose, it is a red rose; **mia uarda** DC 46. 116:1 rose-water (P. آب گل).

Gl. 84:8 defectively زهر *lilium* شکوفه.

uarza (P. ورز , برز) crops, sown field, tilled ground, land, cultivation. Pl. **uarzia.** MG xxxii n. 1:4 f. **buarzai uqinianai ubazirai** DC 40. 506 in my sown lands, fields, seed-plots; **abid barqa umasiq uarzia bgauh̠** Gy 213:16 worketh in his land and raiseth his crops therein.

uarzigar (P.) Gy 391:16 father of **sarqid** (q.v.).

uarṣa a late doublet of **uarza** (?). **d̠-ramia mia luarṣa** DC 45, DC 46. 170:4 that sheds water on the sown field.

uarṣiṣa (וַרְצִיצָא, ܦܪܘܓܐ) chick, fledgling. Gender common. **kd̠ uarṣiṣa d̠-mn bita napqa** ATŠ II no. 278 like a chick that comes out of an egg; **damia luarṣiṣa d̠-mn bith̠ napqa** ATŠ II no. 359 he is like the fledgling that comes out of its egg.

-uata an ending of the st. emph. fem. pl. (v.s. **-ata**).

ubaš DC 22. 380 var. of **uabaš.**

uglalus name of a spirit in an exorcism. **buglalus malka d̠-alma** DC 51 by Uglalus the king of the world.

uda in **budh̠** Morg. 268/28:35 s. **ʿuda.**

-uia Acc. suff. of the 3rd p. masc. sg. after verbs with pl. ending MG 62:5, 88:16.

-ukta a mod. form of the abstr. ending **-uta** MG 78:top.

-un 1 a form of the possessive suff. of the 3rd p. masc. pl. (v.s. **-hun**).

-un 2 (and **-iun**) a special pl. ending of the 3rd p. pl. pf. (very often replaced by the simple sg. form) MG 223:18 ff.

WṢṬ (Ar. وسط) to be in the middle. Refl. pt. **mituaṣiṭ** AM 279:24 will be moderate.

urip AM 232:17 name of a town (Urfa?) BZ Ap. II.

-uta the ending of the fem. sg. st. empf. of abstr. nouns; st. cstr. **-ut** MG 144:bottom.

Z

z the 7th letter of the alphabet. Phonetic changes: relationship to **d** MG 43 f.; **z** < **ṣ** by assimil. MG 45:1 f.; **z** > **ṣ** by assimil. MG 45 f.; **z** < **s** by assimil. MG 45:4 ff.; **z** > **s** by assimil. MG 46:4 ff.

za name of a demon. **za sahra** DC 43.

***zaba 1**, pl. **zabia** 1, varr. **zubia** 1, **zibia** 1 (Nöld. from ܕܒ̈ܚܐ sacrifices MG 312:2; Zimmern from Bab. *zabbu* a priestly class, cf. Delitzsch, *Ass. Handw.* 250a) (*a*) priests, slaughterers, sacrificers (doubtf.), (*b*) in Jb 26:11, 82:4, 140:12 an unchaste cult, gonorrhists (?), a pagan institution Jb ii 33 n. 2, MSt 14 ff.; an etymological attempt for the latter from H. זוב (Akk. *zābu*) 'to flow' (hence 'the issue of blood of a woman after her first coition') Pallis MSt. 17 n. 2 (very doubtf.). A doublet of **daba** (?) MG 43:15, cf. also MSchr. 46 n. 3, Ginzā 29 n. 5, ML 22 n. 5. (*a*) **zabia uadidia** Gy 28:15, 59:22, 174:9, **zibia uadidia** Gs 17:10, 27:20. ML 22 n. 5. (*b*) **lzubia napqan** Jb 26:11, **lzubia lanapqan** Jb 82:4, **nipqit lzubia** Jb 140:12.

zaba 2 (rt. H. זוב = Akk. *zābu*, cf. Mesopotamian river-name زاب = *Ζάβατος* MG 43 n. 3) river, stream, flood MG 43:16. Pl. **zabia 2**, var. **zibia 2.** Doublet **anzaba** (s.v.). **iamamia uzabia** Gy 37:19 f. seas and rivers; **amarlh̠ lmiṣar zabia d̠-nimṣurlia bzabia miṣra** Gy 370:5 f. tell him to make a bridge over the river(s), so that he will make a bridge over the river(s); **hiṭpun zaba** Gs 107:2, 9 the river H. Ginzā 550 n. 2; **zabia bṣadia naplia** Oxf. 34 a v.s. **NPL** pa. pt. pl.; **zibia nahlia uainaniata** Gs 88:14 streams, rivers, and sources; **bzabia** (var. **bzibia**) **d̠-alma** Q 54:28, cf. ML 22 n. 5; **lamṣirlh̠ bzabia miṣra** Jb 102:5 (cf. Gy 370:5 f. above); **pirun zaba** DC 3 = CP 426:7 the stream P.; **mia bzabia nihisrun** AM 225:13 f. water in the streams will be low; **sup zaba d̠-hʿ baṣra mitiqria** HG 142 f. the River of Reeds which is called [*sic*] B.; **sup zaba** often in HG (var. **supat zaba** HG) cf. transl. p. 4 n. 4, 8 n. 4.

zaba 3 (an older form of **diba**, cf. the transl. of the river-name *Zāb* by *Λύκος* MG 43 n. 3, Ginzā 343 n. 5) wolf. Pl. **zabia 3. ʿl qupia uʿl zabia** (Sh. 'Abd.'s copy better **kul qupia uzabia d̠-minaihun d̠-iahuṭaiia praš** Gy 333: 19 f. all apes and wolves which emanated from the Jews.

zabad (Ar. زبد) foam, butter. **zabad lbahar** AM 287:3 foam of the sea (:sepia of a cuttle-fish?); **zabad d̠-hamara** AM 127:penult. butter (from the milk) of a she-ass.

zabanuta (abstr. noun from **ZBN** pa.) sale. **zbana uzabanuta** (often) purchase and sale.

zabanita (Akk. *zibānītu*, Hommel ZDMG xlv 591, Zimmern 16) scales, balances. Varr. **zbanita, zbanta.** Pl. **zbaniata. zabanita d̠-hʿ muzania** DC 7 a pair of balances, that is, scales; **kd̠ zbanita damia ṣauth̠** AM 28:3 his conversation is well-balanced; **salilin lzbaniatun** Jb 85:8 f. they falsify their scales.

zabanta 1 occasional var. of **zabanita.**

zabanta 2 (nom. act. of **ZBN** pa.) selling. With suff. **zabantaiun** Gy 287:15 their selling.

zabda (ܙܒܕܐ) outfit, dowry. **uanašia dagalia zabdh̠ minilia raqinata hauia** Gy 388:23 and cunning people give empty words as a dowry.

zabuna (for zabunia inf. pa. of ZBN) selling. zabna uzabuna DC 40. 243 f. buying and selling; zibnak uzabunak Jb 146:5 thy purchase and thy selling; lzibnai ulzabunai Lond. roll B 173 f. my buying and selling; ulzibunai ulzabunai DC 12. 12 f.

zabiata = zauiata (v.s. zauia).

zabna occasional var. of zibna 2 (v.s. zabuna).

zaga (ܙܓܐ < P. زاغ) cock; fem. zag(a)ta (ܙܓܬܐ) hen. Fem. pl. zagauata. qurata d-zaga AM 134:18 a cock's comb; baia d-zagata DC 46. 142:6 a hen's egg; zagauata ʿkumtia DC 46. 132:2 black hens.
Gl. 182:8 zgata [*sic*] دجاجة *gallina* مرغ.

zadadat DC 43 name of a lilith.

zadana = zidana (q.v.). Fem. zadanita. Pl. masc. zadania, fem. zadaniata. humria zadaniata ML 22:2, DC 44. 65, 96 etc. baleful amulet-spirits; ruhia zadaniata Or. 325:6 evil spirits.

zadanuta occasional var. of zidanuta.

zadia a *malwâša* woman's name.

zadiq, zadiqa (ܙܕܝܩܐ, H. צַדִּיק, Ar. صَدِيق) just, righteous, sacred, holy. Pl. masc. zadiqia, fem. zadiqata. Later (?) doublet ṣadiqa (s.v.). lihdaia zadiqa ATŠ no. 25 the Unique Righteous (One); ana hu hibil zadiq DC 21 I am H. the Just; ana hibil ziua zadiqa DC 37. 599 I am H.–Z. the Just; hibil zadiqa Gy 258:2, 270:23; lhudaia rba zadiqa Gy 234:21, 235:6 f., 237:1, cf. Siouffi 40, 46; mn atar zadiq Gs 123:24 from a righteous place; zadiqia Gy 249:17 ff., 252:19, 255:20 etc.; dahalia uzadiqia Gy 55:14 the god-fearing and righteous men; zadiqia uzadiqata Gy 55:15 f. righteous men and women; šuhba d-zadiqia CP 112:11, Q 57:11 = ML 138:2 praise of the righteous ones.

zaharta 1 (nom. act. pa. of ZHR) warning, admonition, heed(fulness), care MG 122:7. zaharta rabtia Jb 22:10; paqadta uzaharta Gy 38:9; tuqna uzaharta Jb 191:3, Gy 301:22; dukia uzaharta ATŠ II no. 370.

zaharta 2 (adj. fem. from ZHR) circumspect, heedful. zaharta tihuia AM she will be circumspect.

zahba (doublet of dahba, cf. H. זָהָב, Ar. ذَهَب) gold, MG 43:9, 106:paen. With suff. zahbik thy (fem.) gold MG 177:16. auid zahba Jb 179:1 gold passes away; kursia d-zahba DAb (with an illustration); zahba sliqa ramian RD C 27; iaqut d-zahba RD 20.

zahbania id. šria zahbania DC 12:116 freed (from spells) is his gold.

zahir (pt. pe. of ZHR II) shining. mn atra d-nhura zahir DC 37 from the place of shining light.

zahirana, zihirana (adj. from ZHR I) prudent, circumspect, careful. Var. zihirana. zihirana hauia AM 14:4 varr. zahirana (q.v.).

zahlia (rt. ZHL) sousings, cleansings. V.s. kanšia.

zahlilia a doublet of zahrira 1 (q.v.). arba zahlilia d-ziua Jb 188:10; d-zahlilia minh mhauin DC 7 from which rays are displayed.

zahmita occasional var. of zuhmita.

zahraiit (adv. from ZHR I) CP 94:20, Q 39:31 carefully. Varr. zuhraiit, zihraiit. MG 201:7 f.

zahrun (read zihrun), zihrun, zuhrun CP 143 (*d*):4 an uthra forming a pair with zhir MMII 76. Zahrun is a favourite name with modern Mandaeans.

zahruta 1 (זְהִירוּת, ܙܗܝܪܘܬܐ) prudence, care, heed MG 144:antep. zahruta utaqnuta Gy 213:21 prudence and honesty; tuqna uzahruta Jb 194:2 id.; bzahruta mzahrilun Gy 47:9 they warn them heedfully; riš zahrutak Gy 214:10 the first principle of thy prudence; mandizia bzahruta DAb collected with care.

zahruta 2 (abstr. noun from ZHR II) brilliancy, splendour, glory. nihdar bkul hailh ukul zahruth ATŠ II no. 346 he will be resplendent in all his strength and all his brilliancy.

zahrʿil (theophorous name from ZHR II) Gy 147:11, 19, 148:4, 17, 150:1, 8 f., 12 the spouse of H.–Z. in the realm of darkness, an outstanding female demon Ginzā 160 n. 1. zahriʿil lilita Jb 6:5 Z. the lilith, cf. also Jb 263:3, PD 265, Siouffi 6 and n. 3, 137, MMII 46. Mother of Ptahil: ptahil br zahrʿil Morg. 88:3, cf. Siouffi 41, 55, MMII 95, 247.

zahrira 1 (ܙܗܪܝܪܐ LS) found only in pl. zahriria 1 (as well as its doublet zahlilia) rays MG 127: 18, flashes, flames Ginzā 93 n. 5. šuba zahriria Gy 20:23, 90:23, 377:8 seven flashes; bzahriria mitkarkia Gy 96:14 it was (hist. pres.) surrounded by flames.

zahriria 2 (for šahriria?) pangs, Ginzā 93 n. 5. zahriria d-maudala Gy 242:22 the birth-pangs.

zahta (doublet of ziuihta 1) shaking, trembling, alarm, fright. uʿkuria qam bzahta DC 26. 27 the temples began to shake with fright.

zaua (Talm. זווא and זוגא, Syr. ܙܘܓܐ, Ar. زَوّ and زَوْج < ζεῦγος MG 41 n. 6, Fränkel 106 f.) spouse, wife, husband, consort MG 41: 11. Pl. zauia 1 couple, wedded pair. haua zauh Gy 13:9 Eve his wife; nuraita zauh Gy 49:24 N. his wife; haua bzauia ʿhabnalh Gy 106:7 we gave him E. to wife; nṣablh haua bzauia Gy 286:17 he wedded to him E. as a wife; zaua (or -ia) d-kušṭa (often) plighted wife.

zauada, zuada, zauadta (ܙܘܕܐ, Ar. زَوَادَة), us. pl. zauadia zauadata food for a journey, provisions. man d-dria (var. daria) zauadia abihdh Jb 54:6 (var. B) who carrieth his provisions with himself; darana zauadia ʿlai Jb 54:4 I carry my provisions on me; zauadata zauid DC 42. 538 provided provisions.

zauaita (זָוִיתָא, ܙܘܝܬܐ, Ar. loan-w. زاوية Fränkel 11, 168, H. *זָוִית Ges., Akk. *ṣ(z)âut-tum*? LS) Ṣâb.'s AM corner. Pl. zauia 2, zauiata, var. zabiata s.vv., zauaiata DC 53, 8:9, DC 51. 43:314.

zaual (Ar. زَوَال) AM 277:24 decline, removal.

zauana (nom. ag. pe. of ZWN) nourisher, feeder. Pl. zauania. ia zauania d-zaunit CP 109:18, Q 56:5 = ML 135:3 f. O nourishers that I fed!; mzaunit zauania CP 113:penult., Q 57:30 thou feedest the feeders.

zaubɛa (Ar. زَوْبَعَة) AM 270 hurricane. Varr. v.s. **abuzubɛa.**

zauia 1 pl. of **zaua.**

zauia 2, zauiata, varr. **zauaiata** (s. **zauaita**), **zabiata** a var. of Q 3:17 (MG 49:9) pl. of **zauaita** MG 165:22. **mn trin zauia . . . mn tlata zauia . . . mn arba zauia . . . mn hamša zauia** etc. DC 26. 704 f., DC 40. 691 ff. from two corners . . . from three corners, etc.; **arba zauia d̲-brišak** DC 48. 17 f. the four projections (?) that are in thy head; **arba zauiata** Gy 230:9, **arba zauia** Q 28:21, **arba zauiata d̲-baita** CP 8:8 = ML 9:8 etc. cf. s. **arba 4** and **baita; nhar baita bzauiath̲** Gy 350:15 the House (: the world) shone in its corners; **mn br zauiata zikria umn br zauiata nuqbata** Morg. 266/22:36 from male corner-spirits and from female corner-spirits; **mn zauiata zikria umn zauiata nuqbata** DC 37. 395 f. id.

zauihta 1 Jb 195 n. 8 (B) a var. of **ziuihta 1.**

zauihta 2 = **ziuihta 2. ziua uzauihta uzakuta** CP 8:7 f., ML 9:7 brilliance, radiance, and purity, cf. n. 2.

zaza (etym. doubtful, cf. Ar. زيز a kind of onion) AM 217:15 foliage, leaf (?) BZ 132 n. 8.

zazai (Ass. pr. n. *Zazā*, H. זזא) a *malwâša* man's name.

zazia (Akk. *zāzu* fertility, abundance) prosperity, abundance. **hia zazia asuta uzarzta** AIT no. 38 life, abundance, health, and arming.

zaiantia (epenthetical form of ܙܢܝܬܐ) wanton, lecherous (woman). Masc. not found. **zaiantia ugaiartia hauia** AM 77:20 she will be a wanton and adulterous woman.

zaina 1 (ܙܝܢܐ < Av. *zaēna* LS) (*a*) weapon, armour, equipment; fig. fighting, (*b*) fetter(s) Jb ii 29 n. 5. (*a*) **zaina rmu** Gy 265:21, **zaina rma** Gs 76:3; **zaina bgauh̲ šalpilh̲** RD C 14; **man atih̲ lzaina rba** Jb 7:6; **qraba d̲-lilia mn zaina biša d̲-ʿumama** DC 44. 1665 = Morg. 267/25:31; **nirig maria haila uzaina** Or. 325:6, Mars, lord of army and armour; **nirig . . . maria zaina uqraba** DC 44. 1128 . . . of armour and war; **almana bzainh̲ uparaša bqašth̲** DC 21 the youth with his arms and the bowman with his bow; **uzaina tlilh̲ lkadpaihun** DC 21 and weapons slung on their shoulders; **zaina bhdadia ninisbun** AM 245:1 they will take arms against one another; **zaina anat d̲-šalmania** DC 3 thou art the armour of the righteous. (*b*) **bit zaina** s. bit compounds; **mn bit zaina lanapqa** ATŠ II no. 297; **bmaṭarta d̲-bit zaina** ATŠ II no. 351; **kd̲ mapqutulh̲ lbit zaina barqa** ATŠ II no. 332 when ye take him (: the corpse) to his prison in the earth; **bit zaina** Jb 13:15, Gy 112:3 etc. (see above), **bit zainaihun** Gs 105:3 f.

zaina 2 (P. زيان) harm, damage, loss, mischief MG 416:antep. **zaina ubišuta** Gy 389:16; **zaina abda** AM 72:19; **ialpa zaina d̲-gubria hauia** AM 68:18; **miskinuta uzaina** AM 166: ult.; **mardia zaina d̲-malka nihisrun** AM 246:18; **husrana uzaina** AM; **barqa zaina tibad** Gy 385:paen. f.

zaira = **zira. bdibrai ubzairai** DC 40 in my field and seed-plots. **mn zairaiun d̲-lilia umn baziraiun d̲-ʿumama** DC 40:898 f. neither from their seed by night nor from their semination by day.

zaišan (ذى شأن?) person of rank, man of importance (?). **ṭlaba d̲-zaišan** AM 163:15 a request made to a person of rank (?).

zaita, zaitan (זיתא, ܙܝܬܐ) H. זַיִת Ar. زَيْت, زَيْتُون Löw 136, Fränkel 147, LS, Ges.) olive, olive-tree. **hazin zaita hu** DC 7 (illustration); **zaitan hu** DC 41 (illustration); **zaita d̲-qaiim lṭura d̲-qardun** Gy 381:5; **margna d̲-zaita** ATŠ II no. 380.

Gl. 85:11 **zita** [*sic*] زيت *oleum* زيتون.

zaitun (cf. preced.) olive. **šahpa d̲-zaitun** DC 46 olive-leaves. Gl. 86:1 **zituna** [*sic*] زيتون *oliva* درخت زيتون.

zakauata v.s. **zakuta.**

zakai uzakunai Jb 75:3 Jewish names.

zakaia (ܙܟܝܐ) pure, innocent, guiltless, unspotted, unsullied; victorious MG 44:1, 120:antep. Fem. **zakaita 1.** MG 121:15. Pl. masc. **zakaiia.** Often opposed to **haiaba** Jb ii 1 n. 3. **lhaiaba mzakilh̲ ulzakaia mhaibilh̲** Gs 36:21 they vindicate the guilty and convict the guiltless; **hun bzakaiia uanin hauinin bhaiabia** Gy 173:19 f. they were guiltless and we are guilty; **taqminan bzakaiia d̲-lau bhaiabia** CP 108:1 = ML 133:5 raise us amongst the guiltless, not amongst the guilty; **d̲-qudam hiia zakaia hu** Gy 275:13 who is pure before the Life; **man zakaia qudamak** Q 54:17, CP 106:2 who is innocent before Thee?, **ʿniš zakaia qudamak laiit** CP 52:17, Q 16:1, MG 306:25 f.; **abuhan bzakaiia** Gy 248:22 our Father is victorious (?), cf. Ginzā 249 n. 1; **nhura zakaia uasuta** DC 40 unsullied light and healing; **zakaia d̲-litbh̲ muma** Gy 63:14 a pure and unsullied one; **zakaia d̲-muma litbh̲** Gy 16:11, Gs 79:11, Q 46:1 id.; **zakaia d̲-hiia zakiuia** Gs 16:12 the guiltless one whom the Life made guiltless; **zakaita d̲-hiia nišimta** Gs 99:20, 100:4, 12, 24 ff. the Life's innocent soul.

zakaita 1 fem. of **zakaia.**

zakaita 2 (cf. ܙܩܝܬܐ; Lidzb. a musical instrument(?) Jb II 48 n. 4) staff, stick (?) (fishermen beat water when fishing with a net). **habiṭna bzakaitai lmia** Jb 43:4; **zakaita dilak** Jb 161:13.

zakata DC 45 a var. of **zagata.**

zaku, emph. **zakuta** (זכו, זכותא, ܙܟܘ, ܙܟܘܬܐ, innocence, purity, justification, victory, merit, virtue MG 145:19, st. abs. MG 155:9; Jb ii 1 n. 3. Doublet **zakiuta.** Pl. **zakauata, zakuata** virtues, merits, rewards MG 167: antep. f. **asuta uzakuta** (very often) health and purity, healing and vindication; **zakuta nisbit** Gs 116:18; **minh̲ zakuta nsibnin** Gs 121:1, Q 40:21 we received purity from it; **bzaku** Gy 328:4, 14, ATŠ II no. 177 (var. DC 6 **bzakut**) etc. (often) in purity, or victoriously; **klil ziua uzakuta** Gs 123:21; **ʿzil bzaku** DC 48. 168 go innocently; **laupa uzakuta** Q 32:18,

36:8; **dakiuta uzakuta** Gy 213:22; **riš zakutak** Gy 214:12 the first principle of thy purity; **zakuta litlan dina mitmar minaian** Gy 310:1 there is no vindication for us, a sentence is pronounced against us; **zakuatan lqudamaian azlan** Gy 246:23 our merits precede us; **zakuatai ˁl kadpai mahtilia** Gy 245:22 they put my merits on my shoulders; **ˁubadia ṭabia d̠-zakuata** Gy 217:14 f.; **puqdania d̠-zakuata** Gy 214:2; **mtaqnanin d̠-zakuata** Oxf. 74 b the establisher of rewards; **almia d̠-zakuata** Gy 177:11; **litlaihun saka umiṣra lzakuatun** Gy 11:10 there is no end and limit to their merits; **zakuatun brišaihun mitgadlan** CP 154:11, Oxf. 13 a = ML 185:6 their virtues are wreathed about their heads; **rabut zakauatak** Q 52:7, 53:21 the greatness of thy merits; **maraihun d̠-kulhin zakauata** (common) lord of all purities (or victories, or rewards); **klil zakauata** Gy 292:7 = **klila d-zakauata** Jb 174:4 = **klila zakauata** DC 51; **hˁ zakua** [*sic*] **zakitinun** DC 34 it is purity: thou hast purified them.

zakia 1 (act. pt. pe. of **ZKA**) pure, victorious, triumphant. Var. **zakˁ**. Pl. **zakiia, zakin, zakˁn, zakˁin, zakiˁin, zakˁiin. zakia iauar ziua** Gy 204:18 Y.-Z. is victorious. **hiia zakin** (concluding formula of every chapter) Life is victorious.

zakia 2 a *malwâša* man's name. In RD 20 one of the seven names of **šdum** (q.v.).

zakiuta (ܙܳܟܺܝܘܬܳܐ) a rarer doublet of **zakuta**.

zakra, zikra (Akk. *zikaru, zikru*, Ar. ذَكَر, H. זָכָר, Aram. and Mand. **dikra** q.v.) male. Pl. **zakria 1, zikria.** MG 13:16, 43:15. Doublet **dikra. zakra hu** AM 286:9 it is a male; **zikria** RD F 10, men; **biruq zakra** Q 14:17 the male B.; **lbnaikun zikria** Gy 67:17 to your male children (: sons); **zakra unuqubta** Gy 248:12 ff., 268:20 ff. etc., **zikra unuqbata** Gy 33:6, **zikra unuqbta** Gy 243:5 ff., 245:5 etc.; pl. **zakria unuqbata** Gy 380:14, **zikria unuqbata** (very often) males and females; **trin zikria unuqbata** Gy 265:15; **zikria tlata** Gy 245:6; **d̠-iamina d̠-aba d̠-zakra** DC 35; DC 50. 726 (**zakria**).

zakria 1 pl. of **zakra.**

zakria 2 (H. זְכַרְיָה, Syr. ܙܟܪܝܐ, Ar. زَكَرِيَّاء Jeffry 151) Zacharias, father of John the Baptist; also a *malwāša* man's name. **iahia br zakria** Gy 213:10, 218:23, PD 354 etc.; **aba saba zakria** Gy 57:5, Jb 67:5 the old father Z.

zalai zalulai ŠQ 18:31 doubtf. CP 237:6.

zalil, zalila (זליל׳א, ܙܠܝܠܐ) light, slight, downy (of hair), slender, fine; eager, passionate, greedy. Fem. **zaliltia.** Pl. masc. **zalilia. ziqnh̠ zalil usumaqa** AM 98:7 his beard is downy (or scanty) and red; **ziqnh̠ zalilia ušapir** AM his beard is scanty and handsome; **gbinh̠ zalilia** AM 1:13 his eyebrows are fine; **zaua zaliltia** DC 3 CP 237:8.

zaliqa (זליקא, ܙܠܝܩܐ LS) beam, ray MG 124: antep. Found only in pl. **zaliqia. zaliqia d̠-šamiš** Gy 11:5 f.

zaman (زمان) time. **ṣahib lzaman** ATŠ I no. 209 صاحب ٱلزَّمَان.

zamana (?), **zamanta, zamanata, zamanuta** (cf. Syr. ܙܡܢܘܬܐ) summoning, invitation, (pl. **-ata**) entertainments by invitation, parties. **batra d̠-zamanta** (?) DC 51. 133 in the place of summoning; **laupa d̠-patura zamanta d̠-nišimta ˁlh** DC 27. 46 f. communion of the dish (: sacred platter) is invitation of the soul; **zamanuta** AM 167:2, pl. **zamanata** AM 183:penult., Jb 85:5, Or. 333:7.

zamar (nom. ag. pe. st. abs. from **ZMR**) singer, musician, fornicator, cf. fem. **zamarta** s.v. **zanai uzamar** JRAS 1937 592:33, DC 12. 11 (my) paramour and minstrel, cf. 602 n. 2.

zamar daiua DC 40 a demon.

zamar hai Q 9:bottom, 60:5 = ML 24:12, 144:5, CP 22:13, 118:14 an uthra, cf. ML 280.

zamarta (nom. ag. pe. fem. from **ZMR**) singing-girl, whore, prostitute (cf. زَمَّارَة = زانية *Qâmûs*); pl. **zamarata** MG 50 n. 3. **pt zamarta** a prostitute (lit. daughter of a singing-girl) MG 183:antep. f.; **kulman d̠-azil (a)luat zamarta** Jb 98:2; **zanita uzamarta** (often) prostitute and singing-girl (:whore).

zambura = **zimbura.** Wasp, hornet.

zamuṭa (for **zamuta**?) hairy. **zimtan mn ziqna d̠-gabra zamuṭa** DC 46 and hairs from the beard of a hairy man.

zamur daiua Gy 219:12 = **zamar daiua.**

zamura (ܙܡܘܪܐ) flute. **zamrˁil qizamar bzamura** DAb (illustration) Z. who plays the flute.

zamra (rt. **ZMR**) song, music, concert. Pl. **zamria** Gy 376:18.

zamrˁil (theophorous name from **ZMR**) RD 22, 28b name of a demon (v.s. **zamura**).

zan 1 (זְנָא, ܙܢܐ, abs. ܙܢ Nöld. SG § 146; apparently from P., cf. Mod. P. گون, but already in H. זַן, B.-Aram. pl. זְנַיָּ Ges., MG 97 n. 2) kind, sort, species. St. abs. ***zna** (not found). Pl. **znia, znˁ** MG 97:5. **zan zan** Gy 268:16, 17, 378:6, AM 179 etc. (often) of all kinds, of different species, of various kinds MG 301:9 = **znia znia, znˁ znˁ** Gy 99:10 etc. = **mn kul zan** Gy 380:14 etc. MG 301:paen. **kd̠ zan d̠-** as (the kind of) MG 462:25. **kd̠ zan alma hazin** Gy 394:7 in the way of this world; **kd̠ zan rabutun** Gy 179:24 according to their pride; **kd̠ zan d̠-abdia** Gy 231:15 as (that what) they do; **kd̠ zan d̠-lahun** Gy 164:22, 253:9 etc., MG 465:5 ff.

zan 2 a demon forming a pair with **hazazban. zan uhazazban** Gy 181:17, 182:9, DAb etc. Sometimes considered as one being (**zan hazazban**) Ginzā 185 n. 3.

zanai, zanaia (זַנַּאי, زَانٍ, ܙܢܝܐ) fornicator, adulterer, paramour. Fem. **zanita.** Pl. **zanaiia.** MG 120:anteantep. **zanai uzamar** s. **zamar; zanita uzamarta** s. **zamarta; abdia zanaiia** Gy 46:5 f. adulterous slaves; **daštana d̠-zanita ptulta** Gy 226:3 menstrual blood of a fornicating unmarried woman.

zanapta, zinipta = **dnabta. umišqal kiba**

zanapta DC 43, DC 39 to remove pain in the rump.

zanbura PD 805 a var. of **zimbura**.

zanga 1 (ܙܰܢܓܳܐ < P. زَنگ; Ar. loan-w. زَنْج) bell, MG 141:anteantep. Pl. **zangia** 1. **mn zangaiia zanga npal** Gy 362:12 from the bell-ringers the bell fell; **ulamarqaš zanga btibil** Jb 85:6 and he rings no bell in the earth, **zanga tlilh̲** Jb 114:3, 8 a bell is hung up for her; **lazanga tlulia** (var. **tlilia**) Jb 117:5 they hang up (var. is hung up) no bell for me, cf. ii 88 n. 6; **zanga lʿka bnarga** Jb 153:5, cf. ii 156 n. 4 (v.s. **narga**); **zanga tlilh̲ lbabta** Jb 156:5 f. v.s. **babta**; **zangak** Jb 145:8 thy bell; **zangia d̲-zahba** RD 5 golden bells; **zangaiun d̲-lilia** DC 7 their nocturnal bells. Gl. 76:3 **znga** [*sic*] جنجل *campanula* زنگ.

zanga 2 AM name of a city.

zangaia (adj. from **zanga** 1) bell-ringer, watch-dog, barker, roarer MG 141:15. Pl. **zangaiia** used of a kind of demons, according to Mandaeans: the noisy hell-beasts, the lions, wolves, and dogs besetting the soul on its journey through the purgatories. **zangaiia umaṭaraiia** RD B 89 f., RD C 25, Q 68:3, CP 134. 9, Oxf. roll f 82, Gs 82:10 etc. (often); **balinun lzangaiia ulgubria d̲-arqa naṭria** Gs 124:6; **mn zangaiia zanga npal** s. **zanga** 1; **bakin zangaiia** Gs 82:10; **qal maṭaratun uzangaiia** DC 43 J 7 the noise of their purgatories and roaring beasts . . .

zangaubarstan AM name of a country BZ Ap. II.

zangara (ܙܰܢܓܳܪܳܐ < P. زنگار) redness, rust, flaw. **naura sqila d̲-zangara bgauh̲ lamitaška** ATŠ II no. 387 a polished mirror in which no flaw is found.

zangia 1 pl. of **zanga** 1.

zangia 2 a *malwâša* man's name.

zangiania (P. pl. زنگیان blackamoors, negroes) (*a*) a black(?) creature, (*b*) = **zangaiia** (v.s. **zangaia**). (*a*) **manzia d̲-šuba zangiania** AM 130:4 the hair of seven negroes. (*b*) **šuba zangiania bnia hšuka** Ṣâb.'s AM. seven blackamoors, sons of darkness.

zandana a *malwâša* woman's name. Var. **zindana**.

zandat DC 44 a supernatural being.

zandiqa (زنديق) a heretic dualist sect, prob. Manichaeans, Pl. **zandiqia**. Ginzā 229 n. 6, Jb ii 107:4. **zandiqa** Jb 107:9 a heretic; **zandiqia umardmania** Gy 228:10; **zandiqia d̲-kadba** Gy 355:19.

zandita (cf. P. زندان jail) in **br zandita** DC 40. 1115 a gaoler (?).

zania (act. pe. of **ZNA**) libidinous. **haila zania ʿtlh̲** ATŠ I no. 257 there is a libidinous (?) force in it.

zaniaha, zaniata (זניתא, ܙܳܢܺܝܬܳܐ) pl. girdles, belts. **zanaiata** (var. **zaniaha**) **d̲-šuba gaunia** DC 12. 74 (var. Lond. roll B 153).

zaniuta (ܙܳܢܽܘܬܳܐ) fornication, harlotry MG 145: antep. **šalth̲ zaniuta** Gy 116:7 she asked him to fornicate (Lidzb. *begehrte es ihn nach Hurerei*); **abatar zaniuta rahiṭ** AM 3:9 he will pursue fornication; **zaniuta tihuilh̲** AM 3 she will be addicted to harlotry.

zanpus in **zanpusaikun** JRAS 1943 171:4, DC 46. 136:3 f. in corrupt context, prob. for **zanput** (s. foll.).

zanputia (cf. ܙܰܢܦܽܘܬܳܐ) JRAS 1943 171:10, DC 46. 171:10 indignation, anger, wrath. Doubtf. in corrupt context.

zanita fem. of **zanai(a)** (q.v.).

zanša Ṣâb.'s AM a var. of **zinš** (q.v.).

zanšan (زنجان) AM 203 Zanjan, a town in Persia.

zanšapil (P. زنجبيل) ginger. **qarunpil** . . . **uzanšapil** AM 92:9 cloves . . . and ginger; **ašqh̲ zanšapil** AM 126:19 give him ginger to drink.

zaʿparan(a) AM 287:28 a var. of **zaparan**. St. emph. **zaʿparana** ATŠ II no. 327. **zaʿparana ubazra d̲-kitana** DC 46. 90:6 saffron and linseed.

zapa (Syr. st. abs. ܙܳܦ, emph. ܙܳܦܳܐ, rel. to **zimta**) (*a*) eyelash, (*b*) eyelid (?). Pl. **zapania** (s.v.). (*a*) **aiak zapa laina** Gy 8:10. **mirpas zapa d̲-aina** Jb 65:5, 190:17, Gy 247:18, 260:3, 281:22 f., Q 54:11 etc. (var. . . . **ainia**) in the twinkling of an eye (lit. 'fluttering of an eyelash') Jb ii 69 n. 4. (*b*) **zapa d̲-ainh̲ sumaqia** AM 65:ult. f., her eyelid(s) red.

zapana = **zipana** (q.v.). **zapana šaqara** AM a cheat, a liar.

zapania pl. of **zapa**. **zapania d̲-aina** ATŠ I no. 223 eyelashes; **zapania** DC 41. 457.

zaparana (زَعْفَران, ܙܰܥܦܪܳܢ) AM saffron, turmeric. Var. **zaʿparan(a)** s.v.

zapur (Syr. st emph. ܙܳܦܽܘܪܳܐ) stinking. St. emph. heteroclite. **zapra**, pl. **zapria**, var. **zapuria**; fem. pl. **zaprata** Gy 231:11, MG 125:9 ff., 174:5 ff. **zapur rihaihun** Jb 274:10; **zapur usnia riha minaihun** ATŠ I no. 253; **rihaihun zapra** (var. **zapur**) Gs 45:17, MG 307:16; **blbuša zapra** Gs 48:8; **pagra zapra** CP 133:14, Gy 365:20, Gs 9:18 f., 19, 22, 48: 22 etc.; **pagra ṣaṣa uzapra** Gs 9:12; **manzaihun lbarahia zapria** s. **barahia**; **qadišata uzaprata** Gy 231:11.

zaqpa a var. of **ziqpa** 1.

zaqapa (**ZQP**) raising up, uplift. **šapala uzaqapta** DC 12. 261 degradation and uplift.

zarazta (nom. act. pa. of **ZRZ**) armed readiness, preparedness, equipment for battle, also: name given to a talisman, protective amulet or phylactery. Var. **zrazta**. Very frequent. Pl. **halin zarazata** DC 44. 209 = **hazin** [*sic*] **zaraziata** DC 44. 2109 f. these phylacteries.

zarapa read **zaparan** (?). **šapala uzarapa umiša halia** P.A. *Miša* = Lond. roll B 529.

zararaṭ DC 43 name of a lilith.

zarbag DC 44 name of a lilith.

zarga (etym. and meaning doubtful; Lidzb.) from סרג 'to interlace' Jb ii 158 n. 5. entanglement (?, Lidzb. *Flechtwerk*). **rmilh̲ zarga abinia ʿtrin mahunia** Jb 155:11.

zargania a var. of **zargiania**.

zargṭa (etym. and meaning doubtf., Lidzb. Bab. *zirqūtu*) Gs 120:3, 122:6, 19 fetter (?).

zargiania Gs 15:20, var. D **zargania** used parallel with **iatimia** (Lidzb. translates '*Kinderlos*') Ginzā 435 n. 1; or (from Syr. ܙܓܝܠܐ, cf. Gen. 49:12, Prov. 23:31) eyes red from weeping (?), *or* people with eyes red from weeping (?).

zard 1 (cf. ܙܘܪܕܐ Ar. زَرَدٌ) ring (?). St. abs. **zarda. uzard tlata** DC 46. 234:penult. and three rings (?); **uzarda ḏ-parzla** DC 46.

zard 2 (P. زرد), emph. **zarda** AM 288:6 yellow. **dalia zarda** v.s.v.

zardanaiaṭa (var. D **zardanaiiṭ**) **lahmuraṭ** Gy 372:17 an ancient king (Lidzb. read **zardanaiaṭa ṭahmuraṭ**).

zardu (P. زردی) jaundice: **ʿnta ḏ-hauilh̲ zardu** DC 46 a woman that has jaundice; **himan hauilh̲ zardu** DC 46 similarly, if she have jaundice.

zaruan (Iranian *Zarwân*?) personified Time (?): **zaruan pargaš** DC 44.

zaruand (P. زراوند) birthwort. **zaruand ubaqam** v.s. **baqam**.

zaruq(a), zruqa (ܙܘܪܩܐ, Ar. زرق LS) blue (of eyes), brilliant, shining. Fem. **zruqtia** (s.v.). Fem. pl. st. abs. **zaruqan. zaruq šamiš** Jb 129:3 the sun shineth; **zaruqan ainh̲** AM 18: penult. his eyes are blue; **kḏ zaruq iuma nibia** CP. 138:32 when day breaks he shall pray.

zarzuia AM 256:7, Zotb. 218a:16 a family name.

zarziʿil, zarzʿil, zarziil (a theophorous name from **ZRZ**) (*a*) an uthra, (*b*) a personified seal-ring. (*a*) **zarzʿil uparšʿil** Gy 159:15 cf. Ginzā 168 n. 1; **zarzʿil ziua** Gy 321:3; **zarziʿil nhura rba** DC 3; (*b*) **zarziʿil ʿsiqta ḏ-gabriʿil mlaka** DC 43. B:16. **zarziʿil ʿsiqta ḏ-htimbh̲ babia ḏ-šumia uarqa** DC 37. 172 f., 43 A 49; **zarziil nhura rba** CP 370:11 f.

zarna (זרנא?) vomit (?). **uzarna ṣai daš** DC 43 and they trod underfoot the filthy vomit (?).

zarnupaiia Sh. ʿAbd.'s copy's var. of **zarnpaiia**.

zarnuqa (זרנוקא) (*a*) leather bag, waterskin, (*b*) fig. testicles, semen (?), penis (?). (*a*) **zarnuqa udaula** Gy 218:7; (*b*) **bazirh̲ uzarnuqh̲** Lond. roll B 116, DC 12. 56 his seed and testicles; **bazirh̲ uzarnuqak** Lond. roll B 122; **niqum zarnuqak** P.A. xii thy penis shall rise.

zarnpaiia (var. **zarnupaiia**) Gs 14:25 artificers (?), cf. s. **ZRNP**.

zartai uzartanai Gy 138:6, 8, 10, 13, 20, 150: 20, 151:2, 6, DC 51 two underworld beings, sometimes spoken of as a single being, a demon ruling in the underworld. Ginzā Index I, MSt 98, MMII 89.

zatan (< H. שָׂטָן Aram. סטן) Satan (as a proper name). Ginzā 343 n. 2, Jb ii 115 n. 6 (differently); MSt 101 n. 1. **zatan ʿuṣṭuna** Gy 333: 15, Jb 136:7; **zatan ʿuṣṭuna ḏ-iahuṭaiia bgauh̲ iamin** Jb 118:2 f.

zban (ܙܒܢ) st. abs. of **zibna** 1 MG 152:11. **mn zban uʿdan lalam** Gy 7:3 from ever for ever; **hašta maṭia zban uʿdan** Gs 76:15 now, the time and moment have arrived, MG 301: bottom; **kul zban** Gy 232:24 etc. (often) each time MG 351:20; **zban zban** (often) from time to time; **haza zban** s. **hazazban**.

zbana (rt. **ZBN**) AM 259:1 buying.

zbaniata pl. of **zabanita** (q.v.).

zbanita 1 a var. of **zabanita**.

zbanita 2 (etym. unknown) some horned creature (?). **qarnia ḏ-zbanita** AM 95:12.

zbanta a var. of **zabanita**.

zbunta (rt. **ZBN**) ransom, purchase-price. Var. **zibunta. kulhun almia udaria zbunth̲ nihun** DC 6 and 36.

ZBN (זבן, ܙܒܢ LS) pe. to buy, pa. to sell, barter.

Pe. Pf. **lazban** Gy 256:4 they bought not. Impt. with suff. **zubnin** Jb 81:7 ff. buy me MG 271:14. Act. pt. with suff. **bzahba ukaspa zabnh̲** AM 75:7 she will ransom him with silver and gold; as a noun with possessive suff. **husra maṭia lzabnh̲** Jb 145:6 loss will befall its buyer; pl. **ahia hdadia lazabnia** Gs 15:17 brothers do not ransom one another; **ʿu zabnia ahai** [*sic*] **hdadia** Gs 15:18 if the brothers ransomed one another; **gubria ḏ-zabnia zibnai** Oxf. 13 a men who buy my wares; **ʿka ḏ-zibnh̲ lzibnai** CP 127:17 f. there are some who bought my wares; **zabnia hada (umzabnia trin)** DAb they buy at one (and sell at two); **ulaiit ḏ-minai zabnin** Jb 145:5 and there are none that will buy from me. Part. pres. **anat ldilia zabnatlia** Jb 145:6 thou canst ransom me. Inf. **lmizban (ulmizabunia)** (*often*) for dealing (and bartering); with suff. **lmizibnan** Jb 81:7 (B **lmizibnai**) to ransom me.

Pa. Pf. **zabnit** Jb 145:10 thou hast sold (*sic*, read **mzabnit** thou wilt sell, cf. II 146 n. 10). Act. pt. pl. **mzabnia** Gy 256:4 they sell; fem. pl. **ʿnšia ḏ-mzabna halbaiin** Gy 183:9 f. women who sell their milk; **ʿnšia ḏ-braiin uhalbaiin mzabnan** DAb women who sell their sons and their milk. Inf. **mizabunia** (v.s. pe. inf.); without the prefix: with suff. **zabunai** (often), **zabunak** Jb 146:5. Nom. act. **zabanta** (s.v.).

Ethpa. Pt. pl. **mizdabnia** Jb 90:14 are sold.

Gl. 89:9 f. with a prosth. a (ا)شترى *emere* خريد.

Der.: **zabana, zabanuta, zabanta, zabuna, z(i)bunta, zibna (2)**.

ZBR (by progr. assimil. from **SBR**) to lift, raise, suffer, bear, endure, turn from (with **mn**), turn towards (with **l**); to give religious instruction. Only af. MG 45:6.

Af. Pf. **azbar ainh̲ latar nhur** Gy 104:14 he raised his eyes to the place of light; **azbar anpai(h)un** Gy 71:7, 13, 73:2, Jb 241:9 = **anpaiun azbar** Gy 18:22 they turned their faces; **azbar napšaihun luat tušbihta latra sagia** DC 35 they raised their souls with praisegiving to the Great Place; **azbrat anpa** Gy 364:1 she turned her face; **azbrit anpai** CP 3:5, ML 4:12 I raised my face. Impf. **nazbrun anpaihun** DC 26. 329 they turn their faces; **nazbra anpaiin** Gy 308:13 id. fem. Impt. **rhum uazbar hdadia** Gy 18:8 f., 39:3, Jb 225:5 f. love and support one another. Act. pt. **anpẖ lbit hiia lamazbar** Gy 227:16 he raiseth not his face to the House-of-Life; pl. **mazbria anpaihun** Jb 184:3, Gy 112:1, 4, **abdia umazbria** CP 428:3 they perform rites and give instructions; pl. with encl. **mazbrilun anpaiun latar hšuk** Gy 120:6 f. they turn their faces to the place of darkness.

ZGA I (mod. form of **SGA** by progr. assimil.) to go, depart. One of the most frequent mod. verbs: pf. *ezgâ*; pres. *qâzī* (with syncope of *g*).

Pe. Pf. **zga bbagdad** DC 51 coloph. he went to B.; **bhak ʿdana zgun** DC 42 in that time they went.

ZGA II (זגא, זגי to recline) to lie down.

Pe. Pf. **ʿzgat ubiṭnat** DC 43, DC 39 she lay down (with him?) and became pregnant.

zga = **azga. zga ulibna** RD B 73.

zgagita, zgauita, zgauata, azgauita, g̱zauita (Jew.-Aram. זגוגיתא, Talm. זוגיתא, Syr. ܙܓܘܓܝܬܐ, Ar. زجاج, H. זכוכית LS, Ges.) glass MG 41:12 f. Used also as an adj.: transparent (cf. **zgig**). **dmuta zgagita** Gy 281:25 translucent form; **qaina d̲-zgauata** Par. xxvii 83a, cf. also 84a; **kd̲ zgauita** PD 1735; **kapta d̲-zgauita** CP 53:19, Q 24:31; **gupta d̲-zgauita** DC 44. 1202.

ZGD a mod. form of **SGD** (cf. Gl. 56:9 f.).

Pe. Pf. **zgidt** DC 42. 91 thou didst worship.

zgig, zgiga (rel. to zgagita) transparent, clear, translucent. Fem. **zgagta, zgigta. zgig utaqun bdmu bilur** Gy 9:21 clear and bright like a crystal; **mana zgiga** PD 1201 = DC 36 no. 124; **dmuta zgigta** DC 35, **zgagta** DC 22. 277 a var. of **zgagita** Gy 281:25 (s.v.).

zgaita DC 36 no. 200 a var. of **zgagita.**

ZGR (cf. ܙܓܪ, or from **SGR** by progr. assimil.) to restrain, hold back, confine.

Af. Impt. **azgar uanpiq minẖ** DC 51 hold back and expel from him.

ZDN (den. from **zidana**) to be enraged, infuriated, maddened.

Ethpa. Pt. **d̲-mizdainia mn zida uzihira d̲-saṭana** Gy 39:9 who are maddened by Satan's wrath and venom.

ZDQ (ܙܕܩ, Palm. der. זדקת, Aram. doublet of צדק, صدق) to be right, righteous; to be due, just, right.

Pa. Pass. pt. **mhaiman umzadaq** Gy 36:21 believing and righteous.

Ethpe. (?) Impf. **minẖ nizdqa** [*sic*] ATŠ II no. 184 (he) is justified (*or* made righteous) thereby.

Der.: **zadiq(a)**, var. **zidiqa, zidqa.**

ZHA I, ZUA, ZUH (= **ZUH** q.v.) to tremble, shake with fright, quake, flee (from fright), be expelled, be driven off, or away. MG 254: 12.

Pe. Pf. **zha** Gy 160:17, Gs 1 (often), 109:20, CP 22:2, Q 8:29, ML 56:8 etc. (often) he trembled, was affrighted, fled away, also pl. MG 254:14 (often with **ʿtazha**), e.g. CP 22:2, **zhat** Gy 210:18, 270:8 thou wert afraid, **rtitia uniqišia minẖ zhan** DC 35 his trembling and quaking fled (?) from him. Impf. **tizha** Gy 299:21 etc., MG 254:17, **nizihiun mn iaminai unizihiun mn smalai** DC 44. 147 they will be driven away from my right and driven away from my left, **nizhaian nuqbata** DC 44. 78 the female (demons) will be driven off, **latizhun** Gy 54:19 be not afraid MG 254:17. Impt. **zha** (very frequent in exorcisms and elsewhere) avaunt, be expelled MG 254:18 (often with **ʿtazha**); fem. **zhai** Gy 333:6 avaunt MG 237:20 f.; pl. **zhun** Jb 162:8 be ye driven out. Act. pt. pl. **zahin** Gy 280:17, Or. 327:14, ATŠ I no. 255 (var. DC 6 ibid. **zihin** pass.) they fear MG 254:20. Pass. pt. pl. **zihia** DC 44. 120 etc. they are driven away. Inf. **mizha** Morg. 260/22:9 = DC 44. 1464.

Pa. Pf. **zahit (uʿtazihit)** Gy 180:11 I was greatly afraid (and scared).

Af. Pf. with suff. **uazahinin** [*sic*] **lsahria uldaiuia** ML 56 n. 2 and he scared the demons and the devils, **azhitinun** DC 44. 197, DC 27. 103 I scared them off. Impt. **(zha) uazha** DC 40. 906 (expel) and drive out; with suff. **azihinun** ATŠ I no. 255 (var. DC 6 **azhinun**) scare them away. Pt. (act. and pass.) pl. **mazihia** (often) driven away; with encl. pers. pron. **mazihit** DC 37 (often) thou art driven out, exorcized. Part. pres. with encl. **anin ʿlẖ mazihnalẖ** Gs 53:7 we will cause him to quake.

Ettaf. Pf. **ʿtazha** (frequent, often in **zha uʿt-**) he was scared, or driven away MG 254:paen., **ʿtazihat** Gy 174:8 she was scared MG 252:12, **arqa ʿtazhat** DC 37. 544 the earth quaked, **ʿtazhat** Gy 210:17, 18, 270:8 thou wert scared MG 254:ult. f. (and 255 n. 1), **ʿtazihit** Gy 180: 11 I was scared MG 252:12. Impf. **nitazha** DC 26. 107 it shall retreat in awe, **titazha** Gy 314:11, 262:14 MG 255:1, **nitazihun** Q 17:3, MG 252:13. Impt. **ʿtazha** (frequent in exorcisms, in Q etc., often preceded by the impt. pe. **zha uʿt-**) CP 21:3, **zha zha uʿtazha** Q 8:15 f. Pt. pl. **(zahin) umitazihin** ATŠ I no. 255 (they fear) and are alarmed.

Der.: **zahta, zihua, ziha, ziuihta.**

ZHA II (זהי, ܙܗܐ, زها LS) to be bright, radiant, shining.

Pe. Impf. **tizha nura** DC 40. 321 the fire is bright. Pass. pt. **šraga nahira zhia** ATŠ I bright and shining lamp, **zihia** DC 40. 985.

Gl. 9:13 f. **azha** اضاء *resplendere* روشن كرد.

Der.: **zauihta, ziuihta 2, zihua 2.**

zha zha CP 20:ult., Q 8:15 = ML 23:2 = DC name of a protecting spirit ML 280.

zha zihan Gy 221:6 f. forming a pair with **zihan** (: **zihan uzha zihan**) a name given to two lines (haloes?) of light above the head of Yurba.

zhap DC 7 a name given to the hill Carmel.

zhara 1 (زنهار) warning, admonition, precaution, injunction, prudence (in prayer book: direction to the priest to insert names of commemorated persons). Pl. **zharia. dra zhara** (often) take care; **udra kulhun zharia** DC 42 and take every precaution; **uzharia d̲-anat zhart** DC 7 and the injunctions which thou hast delivered; **mzaharlun bzhara qadmaia** CP 378:3 f. he warned (hist. pres.) them in the first admonition; **bʿubadia uzhara** ATŠ I no. 291 in works and prudence; **zharia iaqiria gauaiia** s. **gauia**. Cf. also s. **zhiraita.**

zhara 2 (rt. **ZHR II**) brilliance, brightness, glory, splendour. **zhara mn ziuak** DC 34 brightness from thy radiance; **nišimta ʿtlabšat bzharia gauaiia** DC 27. 105 the soul clothed itself with the inner (: esoteric) splendour.

zharta occasional var. of **zaharta.**

zhir, zhira 1 (pass. pt. pe. of **ZHR II**) illumined, *or, when from* ZHR I, prudent, secure. An uthra forming a pair with **zihrun. zhira umzahra** Q 28:24 = CP 62·8 illumined and illuminating; **zhir smir ziua** Gy 250:12 name of a spirit of light; **zhir uzihrun** Gy 221:3, **zhir umzahar zihrun** Q 2:11, 25, cf. also CP 140 (d) 3 f. (name of a spirit). Note: Lidzb. derived it from **ZHR I**, but **ZHR II** is favoured by the context (constant occurrence with **ziua** and **nhura**).

zhira 2 a var. of **zihira** (?). **zhira** (var. **hauqa**) **amṭinun lmarkabata** DC 28 (var. DC 26. 163) they brought poison (?, var. fear) to the (planetary) ships. (Might have been influenced by **zihua** just below.) **ziria uzhirh̲** DC 43 I 35 its seed and its poison.

zhiraiit DC 3 a var. of **zahraiit.**

zhiraita (adj. fem. from **ZHR I**) in **maṣbuta zhiraita** a baptism with rubrics (i.e. insertions of the name, cf. **zhara 1**). **tartin maṣbutiata had zhiraita hauia uhad šumaita uzhiraita kd̲ mapriša bkulhun zharia ṣbun ušumaita lbar mn zharia** DC 47. 172, DC 50. 842 two baptisms: one shall be with rubrics—as is explained, with all the insertions—and (the other) *šumaita* without rubrics; **tartin maṣbutata had zhiraita uhad šumaita d̲-aiar šimaita** DC 27. 172 f.

zhirana = zihirana.

zhita (rt. **ZHA**) emission (of semen?): **zha zhita uʿṭanap** ATŠ I no. 136 he had an emission and was polluted.

ZHL, ZLH, ZLA I (?) (< זלח, ܙܠܚ by metathesis, LS) to pour down, pour out, souse, cleanse, wash, sprinkle.

Pe. Impf. **nizihlun mia** ML 115:7 they will sprinkle water, cf. n. 4, **tizihlun** ATŠ II no. 43 ye (will) cleanse. Act. pt. pl. **zahlia** Gy 45:19 they pour down MG 66:16; with encl. **kanšilh̲ uzahlilh̲** DC 48. 329 they sweep it and cleanse it. Part. pres. **kanšana uzahlana** Jb 127:11 I sweep and cleanse, **kanšinin uzahlinin** Jb 41:9 we sweep and cleanse, **zahlitun** DC 36 II no. 43 ye cleanse.

Der.: **zahlia.**

ZHM (זְהַם, ܙܗܡ, زَهِمَ, H. זהם pi. Ges., LS) to stink, be dirty, filthy.

Der.: **zuhma, zuhmita.**

ZHR I (Jew.-Aram. and Chr.-Pal. זְהַר, Syr. ܙܗܪ, H. זהר II, Ges., LS) to be careful, prudent, heedful; pa. to warn, admonish, make sure, make safe, be on watch.

Pa. Pf. **apriš uamar uzahar** ATŠ (often) he taught and spoke and admonished; **paqid ʿlauaihun uzahir** DC 41:3 he ordered them and warned them; **ana zahrit** DC 34. 333 I gave warning; with suff. **kušṭia d̲-zahartinan** DC 7 and the ritual hand-clasps (with) which thou didst warn us; **abahatai zahrun** ATŠ I no. 3 my fathers warned me; **zahruia bzaharta rabtia** JB 22:9 they warned him with a great warning; **zahrunun** they warned them MG 283:14. Impt. **zahar napšak** ATŠ, **napšak zahar** DC 34 guard thyself; with suff. **zahruih̲** ATŠ II no. 381 warn him. Pt. (act. and pass.) **mzahar**, with encl. **mzaharlun bzhara qadmaia d̲-lzidqai mzaharlun** CP 378:3 f. warning them with a first warning that they should take care of my due; pl. **ʿutria mzahria mn qudamaikun** ATŠ the uthras are on the watch before you; pass. with encl. pers. pronoun **mzahritun** ye are warned. Part. pres. with encl. **mzahrinalkun minaihun** ATŠ II no. 12 and I warn you about them; **mzahratlh̲ lhabšaba** DC 27. 162 thou commendest him to the care of Sunday. Nom. ag. **mzahrana** (s.v.). Nom. act. **zaharta** (s.v.).

Ethpa. Impf. **bnapšh̲ nʿzdahar** Gy 64:17 = **nʿzdahar bnapšh̲** ibid. taketh care of himself; **ʿzdahar** I take care, I watch MG 227:10; **bginza d̲-hiia nizdarun** Gy 123:7 they guard carefully the treasure of the life; **nizdahran bšpulin** ATŠ I no. 235 they (fem.) are careful about their sexual parts; with encl. **nizdahrubh̲** they guard it MG 228:16. Impt. **ʿzdahar** (var. ABD **zdahar**) **uʿzdaraz** Gy 20:17 beware and arm yourselves MG 34:21, 229:13; with spec. pl. ending **ʿzdahariun, zdahariun** Par. xiv no. 4, MG 229:antep.; pl. with encl. **ʿzdaharulia** Oxf. III 18 b be careful for me MG 229:ult. Pt. **mizdahar bnapših̲** AM 28 he will be careful of himself; **umizdahar mn rušuma** ATŠ II no. 38 he will beware of (making?) the sign; **mitzahar napšak** [*sic*] DC 34. 576 (formally a pt. but used as impt.: guard thyself); pl. **mizdahria bginza d̲-hiia** Gy 92:19 f.; **bgauaihun mizdahran** DC 34 are protected therein; with encl. **mizdahribh̲** Gy 90:7 are charged to look after it MG 31:13; **mizdahribkun** DC 36 no. 13 he takes care of you. Part. pres. **mizdahrinin** we are careful MG 233:6; with encl. **mizdahratlh̲** ATŠ II no. 325 thou wilt be heedful to it; **mizdaharnabh̲** Gy 161:7 I watch him MG 231:25.

Gl. 13:11 f. **ZHR** انتهر *comminari* تهديد كرد; 56:7 f. pa. (?) حفظ *custodire, conservare* حفظ كرد; 61:15 f. with a prosth. **a** حرس *custodire* نگاهداشت; 64:9 f. id. حرس *animadvertere, cavere, custodire se* نگاهداشت; 71:12 pt. and nom. ag. pa. (both defectively) حريس *custos* نگاهدار; 74:11 pt. pa. (defectively) حارس *hortulanus* باغبان; 117:3 f. **ZHR** (pa.) عنّى *curae esse* نگاهداشت.

Der.: **zaharta 1, zahirana, zahraiit** (and varr.), **zahruta 1, zhara 1, zhir(aita), zuh(a)ra** [the meaning optative according to derivation from I or II], **mzahra, mzahrana, mzahruta**; cf. **zhir(a) 1.**

ZHR II (זְהַר, ܙܗܰܪ, زهر, H. זהר I, Ges., LS) to be bright, shine, illumine.
Pe. Only pass. pt. **zhir** (s.v.).
Pa. Impf. with suff. **nizahruiẖ lškintẖ** DC 22. 332 (var. Pet. Gy 336:15 **nanhru lškintẖ**) they shall illumine his dwelling. Pt. **mzahar** v.s. **zhir(a)** 1.
Der.: **zahlilia** = **zahriria, zahrun, zhara** 2, **zihrun, zhir(a)** 1. See Der. **ZHR I.**

ZUA, ZUH, ZHA (זוע, ܙܳܥ, زاع LS, Ges.) to stir, move.
Af. Pt. with encl. **liaminẖ ulsmalẖ ulqudamẖ mazilẖ** ATŠ . . . (or from **AZL**) he moves (: stirs) it (the staff—in the water) to his right, his left, and before him.

zuada (cf. s. **zauada**) provision, viaticum, victuals. Pl. **zuadia.** MG 115:23. **bzuadia** ATŠ II no. 167 (var. **bzuada** DC 6 ibid.) as her viaticum; **uzuadia mn bnia anašia lakal** Gy 246:8 f. and he consumeth not the victuals of the children of men; **zuadia mzauhilẖ** they provide her (: the soul) with provisions; **zauid zuadia** Gy 81:17, CP 451:13 he provideth viaticum; **zuadakun** Q 56a:9 your viaticum; **zuadia ḏ-ʿuhra** Gs 129:10.

zuana in **lazuanak** (for **l(i)zbanak**) **ḏ-ʿula** Jb 146:3 for thy dishonest trading, cf. Jb ii 147 n. 3 and 242 (*Nachtrag*); Wid.'s Parthian derivation contra Lidzb. (*Hb. d. Orientalistik* s. *zuvansk*) is doubtf.

zubia 1 s. ***zaba** 1.

zubia 2 (prob. from H. זוב, Akk. *zābu* to flow) Jb 26:11, 82:4, 140:12 gonorrhists? Jb. ii 33 n. 2, MSt 17 n. 2. doubtf.

zubia 3 s. **zaba** 3.

zubilia in **br zubilia** DC 44. 1501 a var. of **narzubilia.**

zubعa v.s. **abu zubعa.**

ZUD, ZWD (זֻוד, ܙܰܘܶܕ, زاد) to equip, provide for a journey.
Pe. Pf. with suff. **ḏ-hu zadẖ** (**uhu zaudẖ**) Gy 40:14 that equipped him (and provided for him); **zadun hiia** Gs 77:15 f. the Life equipped me MG 272:17; **ana zadtak** (**uzauidtak**) Gs 68:7 f. I equipped thee (and provided for thee). Impf. with suff. **man nizidak** (**uman nizaudak**) Jb 110:4 who equipped thee (and who provided for thee?); **ʿzidak šabiq haṭaiia** Zotb. 228a:9 I (shall) provide for thee the forgiving (lit. forgiver) of sins. Pass. pt. with encl. pers. pron. **zidana** (**umzaudana**) CP 132:7, Morg. 249/85:6 f. = Q 67:5 = ML 161:4, Gs 77:8 I am provided (and provisioned).
Pa. Pf. with suff. **zaudẖ** Gy 40:14 (v.s. pe. pf.), **zaudun** CP 132:7, Gs 77:15, Q 67:5 f. they equipped me MG 272:18, **zauidtẖ** I equipped him MG 277:11, **zauidtak** Gs 68:8 (v.s. pe. pf.). Impf. **nizaudak** Jb 110:4 (v.s. pe. impf.). Impt. **zauid** DC 42.340, Gy 21:4, 250:13 provide MG 252:20; with suff. **zaudinun** Gy 250:14 provide them MG 282:12; **zauduia zuadia lʿuhrẖ** Gy 42:22 provide him with provisions for his journey. Act. pt. **mzauid** Gy 92:14 providing MG 252:20; pl. with encl. **mzaudilẖ** Gs 81:17 they provide for him. Pass. pt. with encl. pers. pron. **mzaudana** v.s. pe. pass. pt.
Der.: **z(a)uada.**

zudia DC 22. 467 a var. of **zuadia** Gs 81:17 (pl. of **zuada**).

ZUH = **ZHA I** = **ZUA** (both זוע = ܙܳܥ = زاع and זוח = ܙܳܚ = H. זחח = Ar. زاح and زحّ) to shake, stir, move, agitate, drive away. All forms quoted s. **ZHA I** and **ZUA.**

zuhara, zuhra (ܙܽܘܗܳܪܳܐ) warning, admonition MG 123:7. Pl. **zuharia** ML 54:12. **zuhara dakia** Jb 207:11 the pure warning.

zuharaiit a var. of **zahraiit.**

zuhma, zuhmita (cf. ܙܽܘܗܳܡܬܳܐ and ܙܽܘܗܳܡܳܝܳܐ) stinking matter, corruption, filth MG 148:2 f. **ṣaidia ḏ-zuhma sarpia** Jb 150:4 fishermen that swallow filth; **ḏ-akil zuhma** Jb 150:5 that eateth filth; **ḏ-zuhma laklia** Jb 151:11; **zuhma uzuhmita** Jb 151:2 filth and corruption; **nunia ḏ-zuhmita** Jb 157:5 fish of the stinking-mire; **mia siauia uzuhmita** Gy 281:13; **bzuhmita ḏ-sumqaq aina** Q 51:21 = CP 99:17; **hatmia ḏ-zuhmita pasqia** ATŠ II no. 208 seals that prevent putrefaction; **zuhmitkun hʿ mbasmalun** DC 34. 692 your stink she maketh fragrant.

zuhra = **zuhara.**

zuhraita occasional var. of **zhiraita.**

zuhrun occasional var. of **zihrun.**

zuza (זוּזָא, ܙܽܘܙܳܐ Akk. *zūzu*) small coin, drachm, dirhem. Pl. **zuzia.** Masc. **zuza bkisẖ (la)daiar** AM 19:12 not a 'shilling' remains in her pocket; **alpa ḏ-zuzia** ŠQ 19:21 = CP 240:5; **balpa ḏ-zuzia udinara ḏ-zahba** DC 38; **zuzai udinarai** DC 12:144, Lond. roll B 288; **mastiria** (B **mistaria,** C **mistiria,** read **ma stiria** or **ma ʿstiria**) **zuzia** Jb 72:2 hundred *staters* of (small) money. Gl. 142:11 **zuza** كنز *thesaurus* كنج.

zuzabaua, var. **šuza baua** (P. جوز بوه) nutmeg. **qaranpul uzuzabaua uzanšapil** AM 92:8 f.

zuṭa (Jew.-Aram. זוּטָא, Syr. ܙܽܘܛܳܐ, a shorter form of זוּטְרָא, ܙܽܘܛܪܳܐ, which exists in Mand. only in the fem. **ṣṭartia** and in the den. verb **ZUṬR**) (*a*) small, little, (*b*) st. abs. **zuṭ** also name of a lilith. MG 46:1. (*a*) **zuṭ šnia** Gy 265:3; **zuṭ ahia uqašiš abahatẖ** Gy 191:12; **zuṭ ahẖ** Q 25:12, **zuṭa ḏ-ahai tarmidia** (often in coloph.) = **ana zuṭ hai** Zotb. 227a:7 (2nd text); **zuṭana** Oxf. III 75 a I (fem.) am little MG 87:antep. f.; **zuṭanalun lʿutria** CP 210:5, ML 244:4 = **zuṭnalun** (**zuṭinalan**) **lʿutria** var. D small am I amongst uthras; **rurbia naṭun lau zuṭitun** Gy 292:1 f.; **ṣuria ḏ-zuṭa** DC 45 the neck of the child; (*b*) **zuṭ lilita** RD 24, cf. Jb ii 193 n. 3 (last l.).

Z(W)ṬR paұel of **ZṬR** (q.v.).

ZUM I = **ZMM I** (q.v.).

ZUM II = **ZMM II** (q.v.).

ZWM, ZWR (onomatopœic, rel. to **ZMM II**) to hum, buzz.
Pe. Act. pt. with encl. **zauamlun uzamarlun lbnia anašia** DC 20 hums and sings to the children of men.

zuma occasional var. of **zma.**

ZUN, ZWN (**זון**, **زان** Akk. *zanānu*) to sustain, supply, feed.

Pa. Pf. **zaunit** CP 109:18, Q 56:5 = ML 135:4 I fed. Pt. pl. **mzaunia** Q 54:23. Part. pres. **mzaunit** CP 113:penult., Q 57:30. Nom. ag. **zau(a)na, zauna** (s.v.).

Der.: **zauana**.

zupa occasional var. of **zipa**.

zupia (from Akk. *zābu* to flow?) oozing, dripping, flowing, exudation. **sindirka d̠-minh̠ zupia halia** DC 7 the date-palm from which there are sweet exudations.

zupra (**ܙܘܦܪܐ**) evil smell, stench, stink. **zupraiun** Gy 56:1, var. **-hun** their stench.

zuqrab Ṣâb.'s AM a place-name.

ZUR (Ar. **زار**) to visit; to force. Only in Gl. 81:1 f. **زار** *visitare* **زيارت كرد**; 116:5 f. **عدم** *privare* **تخييب كرد**; 140:15 f. **كلف** *cogere* **زور كرد**.

ZWR = **ZWM.**

Pe. Act. pt. with encl. **zauarlun uzamarlun lbnia anašia** DC 40:31, cf. s. **ZWM.**

zurna a var. of **ṣurna**.

zurpunia, zurpinia (P.-Ar. **زُرْفِين** buckle, ring, brace) something that holds together, joints. Var. **zirpunia, zirpinia, zrupinia.** Found only in pl., **zurpinia d̠-pquta** DC 40. 461 = Bodl. 13 the joints of the neck; **girmia uzirpunia** ATŠ II no. 135; **tlatma ušitin zurpunia rurbia d̠-pagra** ATŠ II no. 117; **zurpinia d̠-bgarglia rmiiin** ATŠ II no. 203; **zrupinia rurbia d̠-pagra** DC 34. 392; **alahia d̠-mšauia zurpinia** DC 40. 491 f.; **zurpinia d̠-girmia** DC 34. 400; **arbin zurpinia d̠-šrin bpagra** DC. 48; **zurpinia d̠-gbh̠ d̠-masa** DC 41. 462, Bodl. 13 the joints which are in the elbow; **zurpinia d̠-karsa titaita** DC 48. 30 the integuments (?) of the lower belly; **zurpinia d̠-ʿka bpagra** DC 34. 519.

zutra (**ܙܘܬܪܐ** < Av. *zaotra*) votive-cake MSchr. 99 n. 2. Doublet **šutra** (s.v.). **ginia uzutra** Gy 60:1 offerings and a votive-cake; **nibadlak zutra** Gy 258:4 we will make thee a votive-cake; **ana labsigudtun ulabzutrun laʿqabil minaihun** Gy 258:4 f. I will accept neither their worship nor their votive-cake; **qabil minan zutra** Gy 258:14 f. accept from us the votive-cake.

ZṬR, SṬR s.v. (cf. s. **zuṭa**) to be small; paʊel. to make small.

Paʊel. Pt. **mzauṭar** Gy 230:13 he maketh small MG 131:14, 230:22.

zibad AM 287:3 a var. of **zabad.**

zibunta = **zbunta.**

zibuna s. **zabuna.**

ziburia (for **zikria**?) JRAS 1937 591:31 male (pl.) ?, cf. 599 n. 5.

zibia 1 s. ***zaba** 1.

zibia 2 s. **zaba 2.**

zibna 1 (**ܙܒܢܐ** < OP *zrvâna*, Akk. *simānu*, cf. Ges. s. **זְמָן**) time. St. abs. **zban** (s.v.). pl. **zibnia.** MG 152:11 f. and n. 3. Masc. MG 160:14. **hda zibna** Gy 385:9 once, **tlata zibnia** ibid. thrice, **alpa d-zibnia** Gy 386:17, MG 349:14 ff.; **zibna hda** AM 21 once; **zibna d̠-** Gs 129:8, 13 at the time when MG 450: paen. f.; **bzibna qadmaia** Gy 381:22 in the first time; **mhun zibna** Gy 381:22 they hurried; **zibna lmibia rahmia** CP 152:1, ML 182:5 time to pray the (devotional) prayers; **bla zibna** or **-ia** (often) in no time, quickly; **kul giṭra zibna qria ʿlh̠** DC 44 read it once over each knot; **zibna bzibna** DC 43 E 16 occasionally, sometimes DC 30. 35 f.

zibna 2 (rt. **ZBN**) buying. Var. **zabna. zibnak uzabunak** s. **zabuna**; **d̠-zibnh̠ lzibnai** CP 127. 18, Q 64:35 f., 65:1 ff. who buyeth my goods; **ʿl zibnaiun uʿl zabantaiun** Gy 287:14 f. their buying and selling; **lzibnai ulzabunai** s. **zabuna**; **d̠-zabnia zibnai** s. **ZBN** pe. act. pt. pl. **bit zibna** CP 109:2, Q 55:27 = ML 134:5 f. house of ransom.

zida (cf. H. **זֵד**, Ges. s. **זוד** = **זיד**) wrath, rage, fury, malice MG 109:2. **zida uzihira** Gy 39:9; **lanihilh̠ zida balma** Gy 118:24; **zida biša** Jb 118:8; **brugza uzida biša** Gy 332:10; **zida d̠-saṭana** Gy 20:22, Jb 169:13, 182:3; **zida d̠-iahuṭaiia** HG 101.

zidana (**זידנא**) angry, wrathful, furious, baleful MG 139:1. Pl. **zidania.** Var. **zadana** s.v. **nirig zidana** RD C 21; **ruiana d̠-zidana** Gy 20:21, Jb 169:13; **šamiš zidana** Gy 45:11; **uailh̠ ʿl zidana** Jb 182:2; **hamša zidania** Gy 96:19, 314:18 (cf. s. **hamša**); **zidania d̠-kulhun zida** Gs 67:24; **zidana damia lnura** Gy 216:15.

zidanuta (**זידנותא**) wrath, rage, fury, wilfulness MG 145:1. Var. **zadanuta. zadanuta umrara** Gy 39:7.

zidiqa DC 22. 229 a var. of **zadiqa** Gy 234:21.

zidniata scr. def. of the fem. pl. of **zidana. ʿnšia azizata zidniata** IM nos. 36 and 37 powerful and wrathful women.

zidqa (**ܙܕܩܐ**, cf. also Palm. s. **ZDQ**) righteousness, a due, pious offering, offertory, oblation, alms, charity, bounty MMII Ind. **bhiria zidqa** (*often*) ἐκλεκτοὶ τῆς δικαιοσύνης Jb ii 50 n. 3; **agra uzidqa** Gy 39:21, 41:15, Jb 102:2, 168:2 (cf. Jb ii 101 n. 4); **zidqa brika** CP 365 to 269, Oxf. roll f 1051, 1070, PD 1150 etc., (often) Blessed Oblation (a name given to one of the ritual meals celebrated by priests for the dead, or at a marriage, or as a supplement after a *masiqta* etc.); **kul gabra d̠-zidqa natnia . . . kul gabra d̠-zidqa iahib** ATŠ II no. 352; **riš zidqak** Gy 214:4 f. the chief part of thy charity; **kana d̠-zidqa** (often in rituals) collection of sacred food (set at ritual meals), offerings; **d̠-akalnin mn zidqak** CP 406:3 of whose bounty we have eaten; **zidqa d̠-maṣbuta** ATŠ the baptismal offertory; **šitin zidqia** ATŠ.

zidqai lilita DC 43 F 6 (twice) a lilith.

ziha, pl. **zihia** (formed as pass. pt. pe. of **ZHA I** = **ZUH** but with act. meaning) scaring, frightening, shaking, shocking. **sainia zihia dahlia** DC 40. 101; **sadania zihia** DC 40. 459 f.; **mlakia zihia uqadišia** DC 40. 985; **zihia ulaṭabia** DC 40. 827.

zihan v.s. **zha zihan. zihan** also a *malwâša* man's name.

zihua 1 (ܙܘܥܐ) fright, trembling MG 72:8 f. **hauqa uzihua** Gy 6:8; **haqit uzihua miṭian** Gs 55:7 f.; **hauqa uzihua miṭiak** Gs 55:12; **zihua amtinun lmarkabata** DC 26. 166. **zihua amṭinun lalahia** DC 26. 195.

zihua 2 (< ܙܝܚܐ) pomp, splendour, magnificence. **zihua nalbišunh̠ uzihua nikasunh̠** Gy 188: 18 they clothe him with splendour, they cover him with splendour (Lidzb. mistakenly: *bekleiden ihn mit Ehrfurcht, bedecken ihn m. Ehrfurcht*).

zihuat aina CP 409:3 The well-spring quivered.

zihira (P. زهر) venom, poison, spite, resentment MG 139:4. Masc. **bzihira d̠-mn pumh̠ d̠ʿur npaq** Gy 83:15; **zihira bmiia šdilh̠** Gy 84:3 f. I cast poison into his bowels; **zihira d̠-mhamblania** Gy 316:24 the spite of the destroyers; **mla ʿuṣrh̠ zihira** Jb 231:8 his mind was filled with spite; **zihira umrara** Gy 3:10 f., 216:8, 279:24 venom and bitterness; **zihira d̠-bišuta** Gy 280:16, 300:13; **zida uzihira d̠-saṭana** Gy 39:9 (s. **zida**); **rugza uzihira** Jb 24:15 anger and spite; **malia zihira** AM 19 full of spite; **šdia zihirak** DC 44. 1990 = Morg. 270/30:24 cast thy venom.

zihiraita = **zhiraita.**

zihirana, zihrana (adj. from **zihira**) venom(ous), poison(ous); spiteful, resentful, scornful MG 139:3. Pl. **zih(i)rania. ṭizana uzihirana** AM 48:10 overweening and scornful; **zidania uzihirania** Gy 279:8 (var. DC 22. 274 **zhirania**); **zihiranak** DC 37. 40 thy venom. See **zahirana.**

zihraiit a var. of **zahraiit.**

zihrana s. **zihirana.**

zihrun a *malwâša* man's name; also name of an uthra ML 280, Jb ii 216 n. 3. Varr. **zahrun, zuhrun. zihrun ʿutra** Gy 127:12 f.; **zhir uzihrun bhir ubihrun** Gy 221:3, cf. Uthra 544; **zihrun raza** CP 256:14 f., Oxf. 87 b, Par. xxv fo. 38a = Par. xv fo. 31a, Par. 25 fo. 38b = Par. xv fo. 31b, ML 257:8 f.; **zihrun raza rba** CP 5:4, 8, Q 2:11, 25 = CP 6:9, ML 6:5, 7:7; **zihrun raza kasia** Lond. roll A 403, Morg. 5:8; **zihrun drabša** CP 403:4; **zihrun drabša šania** Morg. 168:2 f., **zihrun drabša d̠-almia** Morg. 172:9 f., **zihrun šišlam ʿil drabša** Morg. 178:10 f., Oxf. 109 b, cf. CP 357:14, ML 265:11, 270:1 ff., 274:8.

ziu, ziua (זִיוָא, ܙܝܘܐ < Akk. *zīmu* LS; Nöld. from P. *zēb* MG xxxi 2 f., Ar. loan-w. زِيّ ibid., Fränkel 55) (*a*) brightness, light, brilliance, radiance, (*b*) often used as an attribute or name of uthras, being of light, glorious being. MG xxviii 12, xxxi 2 f., Jb ii 27 n. 2, MSt. 105 n. 1, MSchr 7 n. 1. Pl. **ziuia.** Masc. (*a*) **ziu** Q 53:6 = **ziuai** (common) my radiance MG 175:18 f.; **dukta d̠-ziu** Q 3:16 place of radiance (otherwise **ziua**) MG 303:ult. f.; **ziua d̠-šamiš** DC 36. 98 etc.; **aina d̠-ziua** Gy 336:22, 24; **ziuiia sagiia** DC 38. 92 (v.s. **ziuana**); **lašar bziuh̠** DC 48. 180 was out of countenance; **bziuaiun lašar** DC 48. 203 were out of countenance; **nsabth̠ lziua d̠-ainaihun** DC 44; **ziu hsir** Gy 241:1, 294:20; (*b*) **qaimin ziuia alip alip liaminh̠** Gy 272:16 f. the light-beings stand in thousands at his right; **ziuia šaliia** Gy 373:9; **rab ziuia** Gy 91: 12, 373:9; **ziu hai** CP 67:15, Q 30:32 = ML 83:3, Gy 195:15; **hamgai ziua br hamgagai ziua** Gy 314:6; **shaq ziua rba d̠-hiia** Gy 314:4; **bhaq ziua** Gy 93:11; **zarzʿil ziua** Gy 312:3; **anan nṣab ziua** Gy 108:4; **šišlamiil ziua** PD 903; **ram ziua** Gy 374:24; **anhar ziua** Gy 108:2; **anhar ziua haua** Gy 108:5; **iukabar ziua** CP 10:7, Q 52:2 = ML 11:9 f., Gy 373: 11; **adakas ziua** Gy 104:4 f., 6 f., 19 f., 102:19; **sam ziua dakia** Gy 313:22; **šar ziua** Gy 291: 36; **aiar ziua rba** Gy 76:2; **ham ziua unhur ziua** Gy 145:21; **hibil ziua** (*very often*); **pumh̠ d̠-praš ziua** Gy 371:1 the mouth of the Light-Euphrates; **adiq ziua** CP 63:8, ML 79:2 the light-being looked; **ana qašišun d̠-ziuia kulhun** DC 48. 192 I am the eldest of all light-beings.

IDIOM. With **ašar** 'be disconcerted', 'put out of countenance'. (Cf. under **ziua** PS ܐܫܬܢܝ ܙܝܘܗ̱ 'his looks changed', 'his countenance fell'.) **ʿl arbin zibnia npal ulašar bziuh̠** DC 48. 180 forty times he fell down and his bright assurance was shaken; **uhaizak ašar bziuh̠ umalil** DC 48. 182 and then he regained composure and said *or* his radiant composure was restored and he said.

ziua dam(i)ur a *malwâša* man's name.

ziua šadan a *malwâša* man's name.

ziuana (adj. from **ziua**) bright, radiant, glorious. **drabša ziuana d̠-ziuiia sagiia** DC 38. 92 a bright banner of many radiances; **ziuana d̠-npiš hailh̠** Gy 62:9 Radiant One whose strength is great; **ziuana d̠-ziuh̠ kabir** Gy 62: 17 f. Radiant One whose brightness is mighty.

ziuhta Jb 195:9 a var. of **ziuihta 1.**

ziuihta 1 (Targ. זְוָעָה, Syr. ܙܘܥܬܐ) fright, shaking, agitation, convulsion, trembling MG 16:19, 26:22, 72:4, 110:16. Varr. **zauihta 1, ziuhta. ziuihta d̠-zha** Gy 160:17; **dahalta uziuihta** Gy 180:24; **hauqa uziuihta** Jb 192:2 etc. (*often*).

ziuihta 2 = **zihua 2. ziuihta bhalṣai** DC 44 (a girdle of ?) radiance is about my loins.

ziṭan in **bziṭanun** DC 50. 456 in their radiance (? parallel with **bziuak**).

zikra s. **zakra.**

zimaiun in a corrupt place: **urmun braba** (Leid. **brba**) **zimaiun** Gy 112:23 (var. DC 22. 108 . . . **zimiun**) doubtf. cf. Ginzā 124 n. 4.

zimara 1 = **zmara. pumak uzimarak uhadutak** DC 44. 1968 (= Morg. 270/30:11) thy mouth and thy song and thy joy (Morg. omits **uzimarak**).

zimara 2 for **zmama** (?) bridle. **kd̠ gumla bzimarh̠** DC 40. 471 like a camel with a bridle.

zimbura (זִיבּוּרָא and דִּיבּוּרָא, Syr. only ܙܶܒܽܘܪܳܐ, H. דְּבוֹרָה, Ar. زنبور and دبور) hornet, bee MG 44 n. 1, 76:22, 126:2. Masc. Pl. **zimburia.** Varr. **zambura, zanbura, zinbura.** No doublet with **d** in Mand. **damin lzimburia kd̠ napqin mn qinaihun** Gs 114:3 f. they resemble hornets when coming out of their nest; **ˁniš d̲-hiuia miṭiih̲ ˁu arqba ˁu zimbura** ATŠ I no. 76 a person attacked by a serpent, or scorpion, or hornet; **zimbura d̲-dupša** ATŠ I no. 256 a honey-bee.

zimura, zmura (doublet of **zmara**) music, revelry. Pl. **zimuria. zimuria uzaniuta** Jb 247:17.

zimia pl. of **zimta** *or* from זִימָא secretory vessels.

zimta (Syr. and Chr.-Pal. ܙܰܡܬܳܐ) hair, thread MG 77 n. 1. Pl. **zimia**, exceptionally **zimtia. zimta d̲-riša** Gy 368:18, **zimta d̲-briša** Gy 229:12 etc., the hair of the head; **zimta mn ziqna d̲-kalba qusa** AM 126:2; **zimta d̲-mn puma d̲-tulita nipqat** ATŠ I no. 279 the thread which comes out of the mouth of the (silk-)worm; **gaṭina kd̲ zimta gaṭna** s. **gaṭina**; **tlilh̲ zimia d̲-gadia** AM 131:9 f. (see **gimia**) hang upon him hairs (?) of a goat; **šuba zimtia** [*sic*] DC 46 seven hairs; **akma mn zimta d̲-riša** Gy 182:18 blacker than the hair of the head; **ṣarit zimta** Gy 194:2 thou splittest a hair. Gl. 95:7 **zimta**, pl. **zimtai** (*sic*, read **zimtia**) synonymous with **manzia** شعره *capillus* موى.

ZYN (den. from **zaina**) to arm oneself.
Ethpa. Pf. **ˁzdaian** Gs 86:21 they armed themselves. Pt. pl. **mizdainia** Gs 86:14 they arm(ed, pres. hist.) themselves.

zina occasional scr. def. of **zaina**.

zinbura a var. of **zimbura**.

zindana = **zandana**.

zinipta, zinibta (doublet of **dinabta** q.v.) tail, hindermost part, extremity, end. **mišqal kiba uzinipta uakuaṣta** Lond. roll b 331 (cf. s. **akuaṣta** and **zanapta**, delete u before **zinipta**); **zinipta šdaitulh̲ bpumh̲** DC 51. 193 ye put his tail into his mouth; **zinipta d̲-kalba** Par. AM 145:7.

ziništin AM 205 a place-name, BZ Ap. II.

zinqa (ܙܶܢܩܳܐ < Akk. *sinqu*) fetter, chain. **ˁiasrikh̲ lzainqai** Gy 82:12 I will fasten my fetter(s).

zinš (زنج) AM 205:4 a place-name, countries of the negroes BZ Ap. II.

zipa (זִיפָא, ܙܺܝܦܳܐ < Akk. *zi'pu, zīpu*) falsity, falseness, deceit, fraud MG 108:ult., Widg. v 166 n. 1. Adj. **zip. ˁl zipa iatba** Gy 74:18 she acteth deceitfully (lit. sitteth on deceit); **piria d̲-zipa** Gy 116:5; **zipa ukadba** Q 67:11 etc.; **bzipa d̲-hazin alma** Jb 62:9; **hinun mištaiin bzipa minai uana zipna minaihun** Gy 258:23 they speak deceitfully with me, but I am more deceitful than they. Gl. 69:14 **zipa** *fallucia*, 71:14 id. *deceptio*; 85:14 id. *falsitas*, 122:2 id. *deceptio, dolus*.

zipana (adj. from **zipa**) false, cheat, deceiver, impostor MG 139:2. Pl. **zipania. zipana qarilh̲** AM 22:16 they will call him a cheat; **anašia zipania** AM 10:14; **haršia uzipania** Jb 174:14 wizards and impostors; **zipania umasuria** Gs 17:8 f. impostors and scorners.

ziṣag v.s. **lipriuš**.

ziq, ziqa (זִיקָא, ܙܺܝܩܳܐ < Akk. *ziqu*, Ar. loan-w. زيق Fränkel 285). (*a*) wind, tempest, (*b*) flatulence, inner pain, (*c*) air, (*d*) (pl.) a kind of demons. MG 102:18. Pl. **ziqia.** (*a*) **ziq nizil uziq nitia** Oxf. III 46 a = Par. xi 75 b one wind goes and another comes MG 301:20 f.; **ziqa biša d̲-kiuan** PD 792; **ziqa saba** Gy 392:15, 23 Lidzb. *Sturmwind* cf. Ginzā 418 n. 5; **ziqa basima** Gy 215:11 a contrast of **ziqa marda** Jb 42:7, cf. **atiuia lziqa basima uqamiuia lziqa marda** Jb 51:13 MSt 94:20; **arba ziqia d̲-baita** s. **arba 4**; **lamandilh̲ ziqia d̲-aiar** Gy 5:15 blasts of air do not move it; **ziqia aqria** s. **AQR** pe. act. pt. pl.; **aqariun ziqia mardia** s. **AQR** pe. pf. special pl.; **umn ziqa tizdahar** AM 103:1 and she should beware of the wind; (*b*) **ziqa gauaia** AM 38:11 flatulence; **ziqa supaia** ATŠ II no. 142 belching; **uqumth̲ ziqa lagṭilh̲** AM 43:2 he has pain over all his body (*idiom*); **ziqa biša miṭih̲** ATŠ I no. 143 severe pain attacked him (*idiom*); **abar ziqa ˁlh̲** DC 43 I 51, 143 flatulence overcomes him; (*c*) **aiar ziqa** s. **aiar 1**; **ziqa nura umia** Gy 228:14, DC 6 and 36; **ziqa ubusmh̲** Gy 289:17; (*d*) **ziqia zikria uziqia nuqbata** DC 43 A 24.

ziqla doublet of **diqla** (q.v.). **ziqla bṭunia** DC 12. 91 the date-palm with its fruit; **miqar ziqla mn bagh̲** DC 21 = JRAS 1937 593:13 the date-palm is uprooted from his garden; **kd̲ kraba mn ziqla** DC 40. 521 f. like a crow from the date-palm.

ziqna (H. זָקָן, Ar. ذقن, but Aram. דִּקְנָא, ܕܶܩܢܳܐ) beard, whiskers; doublet **diqna** MG 43:ult., 107:9. **parṣuph̲ uziqnh̲** AM 91:1; **zimta mn ziqna d̲-kalba** s. **zimta**; **ulnapšh̲ ziqna aqdh̲** s. **AQD** pe. pf. with suff.

ziqpa 1 (rt. **ZQP**) astronomical term referring to the rising of stars, opposed to **manzala** MG 51:11. Var. **zaqpa. kukbia ziqpa umanzala** Gy 272:7, **kukbia ziqpia umanzalia** DC 44, **kukbia ziqpia umanzalia** DC 43 J 118 the risen stars and constellations (Nöld. & Lidzb. *die Sterne des Hochstehens und Niederganges des Himmels*); **ulmiblam ziqpa** DC 44. 1697 = Morg. 263/26 (var. **zaqpia**) and to silence risen stars (?).

ziqpa 2 (rt. **ZQP**) post, pillory, gallows. **ziqpa nibidlh̲** Jb 136:13 we will make a pillory for him.

zira (< זַרְעָא, ܙܰܪܥܳܐ) seed, semen, fig. offspring MG 71:4, 101:5. **ziraiun uzipraiun** Gy 56:1 their seed and their stench; **mn zirh̲ d̲-lilia umn bazirh̲ d̲-ˁumama** DC 43 J 202 from his seed (: semen) by night and from his seed (: sowing) by day. **zira bbita** ATŠ I no. 271 the seed in the egg; **ziria rumana** DC 46. 105:8 pomegranate seeds; **kul zira mizra** AM 268:19 every seed sown; **zirai uṭuhmai** DC 34. 352 my seed and stock.

zirania, zrania (a mod. pl. of **zira**) seeds, seedlings, young plants. **zirania šapir nihun** AM 266:38 the seedlings will succeed; **uzrania umišania** AM 268:32; **zirania nišiprun** AM 284:3.

ziruaz (from **ZRZ**) armour, armament (?). **bhalin kulhin mania ziruaz rba** DC 37 in all these vestments, a great armour (?).

ziruta, zruta (abstr. noun from **zira**) semination, generation, growing. Pl. **ziriata** [*sic*] offspring, descendants, generation. **zira**

uziruta nupša AM 281:13; **ziriata d̠-adam uhaua** ATŠ I no. 97; **ziriata d̠-haua** DC 44; **ziriata bišata** DC 26. 51.

zirna used parallel with **ᶜlamania** in **d̠-tabar apqututun d̠-ᶜlamania hbiṭia pqutaihun d̠-zirna** DC 43 which broke the necks of the (youthfully) vigorous; beaten down are the necks of the valiant (read **zrizia**).

zirpa (rt. **ZRP**) embarrassment, encompassment (?). **mn zirpa d̠-lilia umn zirpa d̠-ᶜumama umn zirpa d̠-šuqia umn zirpa d̠-biriata umn zirpa d̠-giblia** DC 23. 283 ff.

zirpunia, zirpinia s. **zurpinia.**

zirqa (rt. זרק to throw, scatter) Jb 132:6 part which is falling down (?) Jb ii 130 n. 2.

zirta (זַרְתָּא, ܙܪܬܐ, H. זֶרֶת LS, Ges.) a span (space between thumb and little finger when extended). **hauia zirta hda ᶜurkh̠ uzirta hda putih̠** Gy 159:18 f. his length will be one span and his width (will be) one span.

ZKA (זכי, ܙܟܐ, H. זכה; double rt., cf. **DKA**) to be pure, innocent, free of guilt, vindicated, victorious, hence: to overcome, defeat, gain possession of, capture, exercise influence upon MG 44:top, Jb ii 1 n. 3, MR 210:middle.

Pe. Pf. (**mizka**) **zka mana** Gs 43:15 the Mana was justified; **zkit manda d̠-hiia** CP 127:1, Q 64:22, 65:15 thou hast conquered, M.-d̠-H.; **ana zkit** Gs 131:12 I have vanquished; **danit uzkit** Par. 27:77a; with suff. **hiia zikiuia lhazin alma** CP 41:17, Q 18:13 = ML 49:1 the Life has overcome this world (cf. John 16:33). Impf. **haiaba nizkia bdina** CP 34:2, Q 14:21 = ML 39:11 the guilty one wins in the process; **nidinun ulanizikiun** Morg. 261/13:37 (s. **DUN** pe. impf.); with encl. **ᶜu nirig nizikilh̠ lṭab** AM 6:14 if he is under the beneficent influence of Mars (*idiom*); with suff. **hin bil nizikiih̠** AM 3:1 if he is under the influence of Jupiter (*idiom*). Impt. **dun uzkia** Gs 27:8, 28:22, 30:7, 32:2 plead and be vindicated; pl. **dan uzkun** Q 4:28, 60:14. Act. pt. **zakia ama d̠-naṣuraiia** Gy 234:12 victorious (or pure) is the people (: community) of the Naṣoraeans; **nhura zakia** Q 40:24 pure light; pl. **hiiia zakin** or **zakᶜn** (*very often*) Life is victorious; with encl. **zakilh̠** AM 21:5 exercises (astrological) influence over him (*idiom*); **d̠-anat minan man zakilan** CP 50:10, Morg. 221/30:6 ff. = Q 23:20 = ML 66:1 when thou art with us, who can defeat us? Part. pres. (**midan dainit**) **uzakit** Gs 85:20 thou appealest to justice and art vindicated. Inf. **mizka (zka)** s. pe. pf.; with suff. **lmizikih̠ lqala d̠-hiia** Gy 221:8 to overcome the Voice of the Life.

Pa. Pf. **zakit** CP 156:1; ML 187:10 thou gavest victory MG 261:4; **zakaia d̠-hiia zakiuia** Gs 16:12 the sinless one whom the Life hath made sinless. Impt. **zakia** Gy 214:12 purify MG 262:9; with suff. **zakinan bzakutak** DC 26. 281 purify us with thy purity (*or* vindicate us by thy victory). Pt. pl. **mzakin bra** Gy 256:9 they acquit the son; with encl. **lhaiaba mzakilh̠** Gs 36:21 they vindicate the guilty one; **mzakilun** Jb 217:14 he purifieth them (or maketh them conquer). Part. pres. with encl. **mzakiatlan** CP 50:10, Morg. 221/30:7 = Q 23:20 = ML 66:1 thou purifiest us MG 262:22.

Ethpa. **kulhin nišmata minh̠ ᶜzdakia** CP 108:ult., Q 55:25 = ML 134:4 all the souls were purified (or made victorious) by it, MG 264:24; **mn kulhun mumia ᶜzdakiat nišimta** DC 48. 383 the soul was cleansed of all blemishes; **ᶜzdakit** DC 53 482:13 I was purified. Impf. **nizdakia** Jb 79:2 is vindicated (made pure) MG 264:anteantep.

Idioms. Pe. with encl. **l**, or suff. 'to exercise astrological influence' (s. pe. impf. with encl. and suff., act. pt. with encl.). (*Often*) to be vindicated at the tribunal Jb ii 1 n. 3. The two meanings 'to purify' and 'to be (made) victorious' are sometimes difficult to distinguish from one another.

Der.: **zakaia, zakia, zaku(ta).**

zka manda = **ska manda.**

ZKR, DKR (H. זכר, Ar. ذكر; double rt., cf. s. **DKR**) to pronounce (esp. incantations), recite an incantation, use magic arts (?).

Pa. Impt. with encl. **uzakarlh̠ mn zupra** DC 48 and recite it (: the exorcism)for the evil smell; with suff. **zakrih̠** (?) **rugzh̠** DC 37 exorcize (?) his wrath. Act. pt. **umzakir arbin iumia** DC 46 and he shall recite incantations (?) for forty days.

zlap an evil spirit: **ᶜsirit anat zlap mlaka** DC 43 thou art bound, angel Zlaf.

ZLA I = **ZLH** (?).

Af. (?) Pf. **azla mia biardna** CP 44:ult., ML 56:8 he splashed (?) the water in the jordan (Lidzb. *goß*).

ZLA II = **ZLL** (q.v.).

ZLH, ZHL, ZLA I (?) (cf. s. **ZHL**) to pour, sprinkle, spatter, throw out a liquid.

Pe. Pass. pt. **ᶜzma zlihiia** Morg. 262/15:1 f. blood is shed (similarly read **bzma zlihia** Morg. 200:1); with encl. (and act. meaning) **knišlia uzlihlia** Gs 84:19 I swept and sprinkled MG 65:7, 382:12 f., **dma . . . zlihlia** Gy 45:19 they pour the blood.

zlila (pass. pt. of **ZLL**) light of importance, scanty, (of fire) slow (?). Sometimes as a var. of **zalila** (q.v.). **bnura zlila** DC 46 in a slow (?) fire.

ZLL (זלל, ܙܠ, Ar. زَلَّ LS) to be of light value, of light weight, despise, slight.

Pe. Impf. with suff. **bzibia d̠-almia latizlinan?** (var. CP 106:17 **latizbinan**) ML 132:4 (cf. n. 1) do not despise (var. abandon) us with the unclean of the worlds. With the ending of the part. pres. and with suff. **ᶜzilnak ᶜzinak d̠-anat saklit** DC 44. 1014 I despise thee, I despise thee because thou art a fool.

Af. Pf. **uazil habara ukabar ᶜlauqihun** DC 3. 241:11 and darkness degraded and lay heavy on them.

Der.: **zalila, zlila** (fem. **zaliltia**).

zma (doublet of **dma** 1 q.v.) blood MG 97:4. Var. **ᶜzma. zma d̠-ruha labšia** RD C 27; **puma d̠-bisra uzma** Gy 7:14.

zmama (זְמָמָא, ܙܡܡܐ, Ar. زِمَام, Eth. ዘማም

LS) bridle, curb, muzzle. **zmama d̠-gumla** Gy 103:9, 118:9; **kd̠ gumla bzmamih̠** DC 40. 346; **zmama d̠-parzla** Gy 84:7.

zmara 1 (זמרא, ܙܡܳܪܳܐ) (*a*) song, music, melody, (*b*) revelry, shamefulness MG 115:20. St. abs. **zmar**. Pl. **zmaria**. Doublet **zmura**. (*a*) **qizamar bizmara** RD 22; **zmara uambuba** Gy 225:4; **zmara urquda** ATŠ II no. 64; **zmaria uanamia** s. **anamia**; **hitra uṭalula uzmara** AM 4:6; **zmara d̠-zmaria rtia** DC 46. 245:14; (*b*) **bdaria rabut zmar** Gy 274:16, 299:19, 302:23, 376:18, Gs 75:18, MG 304:2, 311:ult. f.; **zmara uqlalia** Gy 224:25; **puhria uzmaria** Gy 225:1; **šiha uzmara** Gy 225:22 f.; **zmara uharuta** AM 173: 4; **zmara d̠-šiha** DC 34. 546.

zmara 2 DC 22. 78 a var. of **zmama** Gy 84:7.

zmarta occasional var. of **zamarta**.

zmum (for **zmama**?) a (horse's or pack-animal's) bridle, curb, muzzle. **bzmum kapta** DC 43 with a curbing bit (?).

zmura = **zmara**. **bṭiblia uzmura d̠-ruha** DAb with drums and the music of R.

zmim = **zmum**. **mibia zmim** DC 46. 136:2 to ask for a curb (?).

ZMM I (זמם, ܙܡܰܡ II, Ar. زَمَّ LS) to bridle, hold back, curb in, check. MG 252:2, 277:6, 401:2.

Pa. Pf. with suff. **zamth̠ zmama d̠-gumlia** Gy 103:9, 118:9 I held her back with a camel-bridle. Act. pt. **bgangarata zaiim bʿdh̠** DC 43 pressing back his throat with his hand; **mlaka d̠-zaiim gubria luat ʿnšia** DC 45 the angel that restrains men from women; pl. **zaimia** Gy 121:20. Pass. pt. **zim kd̠ susia** DC 45 bridled like a horse; pl. **zimia (umazimia)** JRAS 1937 595:31 curbed (and restrained); with encl. pers. pron. **zimitun (umazimitun)** ibid. 596 ye are curbed (and restrained).

Af. Pass. pt. pl. **mazimia** (just cited); **mazimitun** (just cited).

Ethpe. Pf. **ʿzdmim bzmama d̠-parzla** Gy 84:7 he was bridled with an iron bridle.

Der.: **zmama, zmum, zmim.**

ZMM II (onomatopœic like ܙܡܰܡ I, Ar. زمزم, H. זמם I LS, Ges.) to hum, resound.

Pe. Act. pt. pl. **zaimia akuat mania d̠-nhaša** Gy 282:10 they clang like copper vessels.

Ethpa. Pf. **uʿzdamam šuria akuat ṭaštga** Gy 166:16 f. and the walls resounded like a basin.

ZMN (זְמַן, ܙܡܰܢ) to bid, summon, invite, gather by summons, prepare.

Pe. (?) Pf. with suff. **zriztinun uzmintinun** DC 26. 638 f. I harnessed them, I summoned (?) them.

Pa. Pf. with suff. **zaminiun** (?) Lond. roll A 5 he summoned them (?), **liardna zamintak** Gy 190:15 I called thee to the jordan; **zamintik** Gy 190:15 I invited thee (fem.) MG 274:2. Pt. **mzaman** CP 114:4, Lond. roll B 146, Q 58:1 = ML 139:8, invited, **qrʿia umzamna nišmatkun** CP 193:6, Gs 86:4 f., 91:14 f., Oxf. 30 a, 43 b, 56 a, Oxf. roll f 282 your souls are called and invited; with encl. **hʿ lalmia kulhun mzamnalun** Gy 147:ult. she inviteth all the worlds. Pass. with encl. pers. pron. **qritun umzamnitun** DC 40 ye are called and bidden. Inf. **zamunia** Oxf. roll g 1046. Nom. act. **zamanta** (s.v.).

Der.: **zamanta.**

ZMR (זְמַר, ܙܡܰܪ, H. זמר II, Ar. زمر, Akk. *zamāru* LS, Ges.) to sing, make music, play (an instrument), make a sound, resound.

Pe. Pf. **zmar qalaihun** DC 26. 526 their voices sang. Impf. **latizmrun** Gy 20:14, **latizimrun** ibid. BD, Gy 39:1 do not sing, MG 227:31. Impt. with encl. **zmurlia** sing to me MG 221:12; **zmurlan** Gy 258:26 sing to us MG 221:12. Act. pt. **d̠-zamar zmara d̠-haršia ušiha** Gy 59:5 f. that singeth a song of sorcery and lust. Part. pres. **qizamar bṣurna** RD 29 he plays a hautboy; **qizamar bizmara** RD 22 he sings a song; **zamarna mn zmarai** Gy 258:27 I sing some of my songs,

Pa. Pt. with encl. **mzamarlun** DC 43 E 15 he sings to them (a frightening song); (*or read* **mzamamlun** restrains them?).

Gl. 79:1 **zamar** زمر *canere* نی میساخت; 93:15 f. with a prosth. **a** شعر *poetissere* شاعر شد.

Der.: **zamarta, zamura, zamra, zamrʿil, zmara, zmura, zimura, zmarta.**

ZNA (זנא, ܙܢܳܐ, H. זנה, Ar. زنى) to fornicate, be unchaste, adulterous.

Pe. Impf. **latigirun ulatiznun** s. **GUR I** pe. impf. Act. pt. **d̠-zania (umzania)** CP 106:9 f., ML 131:13 f. that gad about (and practise fornication); **haila zania** ATŠ I no. 257 libidinous (?) force. Part. pres. **zanit (umzanit)** DC 21 thou art unchaste (and adulterous).

Pa. Part. forms **mzania, mzanit** s. pe.

Der.: **zanai(a), zania, zaniuta, zanita, mzanaita.**

ZNZL (dissimilated palpel of **ZLL**) to belittle, despise. Impf. and inf. **uzanzulia latizanzil** DC 23. 158 f. do not utterly despise.

znia pl. of **zan** (q.v.). Var. **znʿ** MG 5:18, 97:5. Sg. with suff. **znh̠** Gy 369:11 f. his kind. Pl. often in distributive repetitions: **d̠-gaunia gaunia uzbia znʿ** of different colours and kinds MG 328:antep.

znipta = **zanapta** = **dnabta** (q.v.). **znipta d̠-tanina** Morg. 257/6:42 the tail of the dragon; **znipta d̠-kalba** AM 123:15 the dog's tail.

zʿpa Gy 232:21 (var. **zʿipa**) = **zipa** MG 5:21.

ZPR (ܙܦܰܪ LS) to stink.

Der.: **zapur (zapra), zupra.**

ZQP (זְקַף, ܙܩܰܦ, H. זקף, Akk. *zaqāpu* LS, Ges.) to raise, set up, erect.

Pe. Pf. **ziqpat ʿsata ʿkilta** DC 22. 447 (Pet. Gs 59:8 **zirpat**) consuming flame(s) shot up. Impt. **zqup burkak** (?) DC 26. 317 raise thy knee; pl. **mizqap zqupiun ulatišiplun** Jb 211:13 raise yourselves upwards and do not lower yourselves. Act. pt. **mn d̠-zaqip mn mandaiia** ATŠ II no. 45 who shall be promoted amongst the Mandaeans; pl. **bišia d̠-zaqpia alanpai** CP. 170:4, ML 206:5 the evil ones that rise up against me. Part. pres. **zaqpit liardnia** Jb 251:8 thou risest towards the jordans

(?, cf. II 218 n. 2), **uzaqipna ldaura taqna** Gs 83:10 and I rise up to the Abiding Dwelling. Inf. **mizqap** Jb 211:13 (s. pt. pl.).

Der.: **zaqapa, zaqpa, ziqpa 1, 2.**

ZQR ethpe. of **SQR** to rejoice MG 46:8. Pf. **ʿzdaqar** Gs 93:14 he rejoiced. Pt. pl. **lamizdaqria** Gy 253:17 (read **ula-**) but they do not rejoice (Lidzb.'s doubt about Nöldeke's solution, Ginzā 254 n. 3, is unjustified).

ZRA I (זְרַע, ܙܪܥ, H. זרע, Ar. زرع, Akk. without guttural, cf. *zēru* seed, and nom. ag. *zārū*, Ges.) to sow, scatter.

Pe. Pf. with suff. **laziriak ginaia** Or. 325 (text):5 no gardener sowed thee; **halin razia zrinun šišlam uhibil iauar ziua** ATŠ I no. 9 these mysteries S. and H.-Y.-Z. have spread abroad. Impf. with suff. **kul man ḏ-niziriia** everyone that disseminates it; **ulanašia nizirinun** AM 244:20 and they will scatter the population. Impt. (**qria**) **uzria** DC 40 (recite) and strew. Act. pt. **zara** MG 70: antep., 112:12; with encl. **zaralẖ** ATŠ II no. 195 soweth it. Pass. pt. **zria** MG 117:11, 236:1; with encl. pers. pron. **bhailak zriit** Or. 325 (text):5 thou art self-sown (*idiom*).

Ethpe. Pf. **ḏ-bazira ḏ-gabra laʿzdra** Gy 242:11 f. that was not begotten of a man's seed; **ata uʿzdra** DC 36 it came and was scattered. Impf. **nizdra** is sown MG 235:13. Pt. **gabra mizdra zira bgišumẖ** Gy 202:1 the seed is formed in the man's body; **kul zira ḏ-minẖ mizdra** ATŠ every seed formed from (or engendered by) him; fem. **uniṭupta minaihun mizdira** ATŠ II no. 195 a drop from them was sown (*i.e. a drop of semen*).

Gl. 22:5 f. **azra** انغرس *transplantari* نشانيد; 79:5 f. id. زرع *seminare* كاشت; 115:5 f. id. غرس *plantare* كاشت; 166:1 f. id. نمى *crescere, germinare* بيرون آمد.

Der.: **baz(i)ra, zira, z(i)rania, ziriata, (ʿ)zruta, mazruta, mazrita.**

ZRA II (< זרח?) to shine, sparkle (?).

Ethpe. Pt. with encl. **mizdribẖ** ATŠ it is illumined by it (?).

zrada (cf. ܙܪܕܐ coat of mail) casing. Miscop. (?) **zrara. gupta ḏ-zrada** (miscop. . . . **zrara**) s. **gupta.**

zraz (rt. **ZRZ**) armour. V.s. **hṭit** = **hṭita 3.**

zrania = **zirania. zrania umišania** AM 268:32.

zraqa (rt. **ZRQ**) light, shining. **zraqa ḏ-iuma** AM 175, 190, 261, 271 daylight; **zraqa ḏ-šamiš** AM 176 sunshine.

zrara (cf. s. **zrada**) casing, hollow tube, bamboo: **htum bqaina ḏ-zrara** DC 43 E 93 f. seal into a hollow reed.

ZRG (ܙܪܓ) the rt. of **zargiania** (?).

zrupinia a miscop. of **zurpinia.**

ZRH (metath. of **ZHR I**) to take care, be careful.

Ethpa. Pt. pl. fem. **mizdrahan** ATŠ they are careful; masc. pl. with encl. **ḏ-mizdrahibẖ** DC 41. that they (may) take care of it; **mizdrahibkun** ATŠ I no. 13 they are guarding you.

zruqtia (rt. **ZRQ**) (*a*) shining, (*b*) (possibly also) squinting (both of eyes). Masc. **zaruqa** (s.v.). (*a*) **aina zruqtia d-šamiš** JRAS 1937 596:15; (*b*) **aina bišta . . . uaina zruqtia** JRAS 1937 590:6 (of text), 592:6 (etc.).

zruta, ʿzruta (abstr. noun from **ZRA I**) semination, generation, sowing. **zira uzruta** (often) seed and sowing; **razia kasiia ḏ-zruta** DC 50 the secret mysteries of generation.

ZRZ (זְרַז, ܙܪܙ LS) to gird on, equip, arm; be equipped, armed, alert, prepared, speedy.

Pe. (rare): Pf. with suff. **zriztinun uzamintinun uhtimṭinun** DC 26. 638, 40. 583 I harnessed them and summoned them and sealed them down. Pass. pt. **zriz(a)** s.v.

Pa. Pf. **ḏ-napšiẖ bgauẖ zariz bhalin babia** DC 44. 906 f. who armed himself with these charms; **ḏ-zariz lnapišiẖ** [*sic*] **bgauẖ** DC 44: 240 f.; **zarzit** I armed MG 223:3; with suff. **lazarzẖ** Gy 94:1 he armed him not; **qaimẖ uzarzẖ** Gy 130:19 he strengthened him and armed him; **zarzan upaqdan** Gy 193:2, DC 26:101 he equipped me and gave me orders; **zarzak upaqdak** Gy 194:22 he equipped thee and gave thee orders; **zarzun bmzarzuta** Gy 360:25, **zarzun bmzarzutun** Gy 342:6 they equipped me with the(ir) armour; **zarzu gubria mhaimnia** Gs 108:22, 109:3 (Morg. 245/77:2 f. **zarzuia** . . .) believing men equipped her. Impt. **nišma zariz napšak** Gs 84:8 soul, arm thyself; **zariz napšaikun bzaina** Gy 25:20 equip yourselves with weapons. Pt. act. with encl. **mzarizlẖ umhatimlẖ** Gy 137:14 (s. **HTM** pa. act. pt). Part. pres. with encl. **mzarzinalkun umaqminalkun** Gy 220:20 I arm you and strengthen you MG 231:antep. f.; **mzarzatlun** thou armest them MG 232:23. Pass. pt. **mzaraz, mzarza** (s.v.); pl. **mzarzia** Gy 20:17 the equipped ones; with encl. pers. pron. (**mzaruzia**) **mzarzit** thou art equipped MG 398:4, **mzarzitun** ye are equipped MG 233:14 (act. id. ibid.: 13). Inf. **mzaruzia** MG 144:1, 398:4. Nom. act. **zarazta** s.v.

Ethpa. Pf. **ʿzdaraz kulẖ ʿuṣṭunẖ** ATŠ I no. 23 his whole body became vigorous (equipped), **ʿzdarzat nišmat** Gs 94:7 (Leid. **ʿzdarzit** . . .) my soul was stimulated, **uzdarzat** Gy 361:11, Gs 94:7. Impf. **nizdarzun bzharia** ATŠ I no. 235 they arm themselves with precautions. Impt. **ʿzdahar uʿzdaraz** s. **ZHR, ʿzdaraz bzharak ubauatak uʿzdaraz ulatišagia** DC 47 prepare thyself by thy care and thy prayers and be vigilant and make no mistake. Pt. pl. **umizdarzin** (var. **mizdarzinin**) **kulhun qmahia** ATŠ II 202 (var. DC 6 ibid.) and all phylacteries are full of strength.

Der.: **z(a)razta, zraz, zriz(a), mzarza, mzarzuta, zarzʿil.**

zribtia (cf. ܙܪܒ to press, urge) in **ziqia zribtia** DC 44 (var. **zriztia**) whirlwinds, hurricanes. (Why fem. sg.?)

zriz, zriza (pass. pt. pe. of **ZRZ**) armed, prepared, equipped, valiant, zealous, alert, active, energetic, efficacious, strong, militant, pugnacious, violent, boisterous (of wind). Fem. **zrizt(i)a.** Pl. **zrizia. zriz hliṣ** s. **hliṣ(a)**;

zriza umzarza Gy 73:18, cf. MR 27:12; **ᶜutra ana zriza ḏᶜutria kulhun zrizna** Jb 164:12 I am a well-armed uthra, better equipped than all the uthras; **tarmida zriz umgabar** DC 50. 142 a priest efficacious and powerful; **gmaṭa zriza** s. **gmaṭa**; **malkuta zrizta** DC 34. 298 an efficient kingliness (: priestliness); **rakšia zrizia** ATŠ I no. 11 strong steeds; **zriztia umsasqla hauia** AM 54:2 she will be alert and bright-witted; **ukḏ gabra zrizta bᶜbidatẖ hauia** AM 66:4 she will be as energetic as a man in her actions; **mn gubria zriztia** AM 67:18 she will be more active than men; **ziqia zrizia** DC 44 violent tempests; **zria nṭir** ML 84:9 read **zriz nṭir** cf. n. 5.

ZRMBA, ZRNBA (etym. doubtf., perh. זרב, ܙܪܒ; an active form would correspond to Ar. اسرندى MG 267:8, but the verb is used only as refl.) to be shaken MG 86:3, 267:5 ff. Pf. **ᶜšumia bziuai ᶜzdarambia** ML 205:9 (CP 169:penult. **ᶜzdaranbiat**) the skies were riven because of my radiance (?); **ᶜzdranbia humria** DC 43 A 54, 147 amulet (-spirits) were shattered, **ᶜšumia ᶜzdarambiat** Morg. 265/4:35 = **ᶜšumia ᶜzdaranbiat** DC 44. 270, **ᶜšumia ᶜzdrambat** (?) DC 26. 28 the heavens were shaken, **ᶜzdarambiat** Oxf. 34 a, **lhdadia ᶜzdarambiun** DC 34. 400 they were set in commotion (: were shaken against one another). Impf. **nizdarambia** (varr. **nizdrambia, nizdranbia**) Gy 310:20 he is shaken. Pt. **mizdaranbia** (varr. **mizdranbia, mizdarambia**) Jb 117:8, DC 43 A 103 was shaken; pl. **mizdrambin, mizdranbin** Gy 8:20, pl. fem. **mizdarambia** Gy 280:22 they are shaken.

ZRNP (etym. doubtf., perh. den. from **zarnpaia** artificer?) to press or mould into shape (?). Pf. with suff. **zarnpaiia ḏ-zarnpuia** Gs 14:25 the shapers who shaped it (?) MG 278:5, Ginzā 434 n. 1.

zrᶜia a var. of **zria** (pass. pt. of **ZRA I**) MG 5: anteantep.

ZRP (etym. doubtf. Lidzb. compared it with ܙܪܦ and زرف Ginzā 206 n. 1) to be(come) strong (?).

Pe. Pf. **zirpat ᶜšata** Gs 59:8 fire became fierce.

Pa. Pt. with encl. **malalẖ mzarpilẖ** Gy 205:7, 206:3 his words make him big (or show him as strong?).

ZRQ (ܙܪܩ to shine) to send out rays, shine.

Pe. Pf. with encl. **zruqlẖ šamiš** Jb 129:9 sun shone out on it.

Der.: **zaruq**, fem. **zruqtia, zraqa. iardnia . . . ḏ-zarqin** DC 43 G II.

-ẖ

-ẖ the 8th letter of the alphabet, whose original consonantal value vanished; it is used as a vowel-sign for the final *-ĭ*, cf. MG 3:14 f. It is used esp. to designate both the accusative and the possessive suff. of the 3rd p. sg., which often replaces the special fem. suff. **-a** 3 (q.v.). As pers. suff. it is written either simply **-ẖ** or **-iẖ** (pronounced *-ĭ* in either case), e.g. **qudamẖ** or **qudamiẖ** before him. MG § 62.

Ṭ

ṭ the 9th letter of the alphabet. Pronunciation: emphatic *ṭ*. **Ṭ** for **d** MG § 46 p. 42:bottom.

ṭ- (enclitically) a later form of the relative **ḏ**: **ṭabid ṭab** who is doing good, **ruha ṭabahatan** CP 32:16 f., Q 14:5 = ML 38:6 the spirit of our fathers MG 93:13 ff., **uṭamarnalun lašatit** DC 43 Dahlulia 37 and what I say to them thou hearest not; **uṭišituia nauqruia** DC 51. 401 f. and those who despised it will honour it; **ṭazia bᶜuhra** ŠQ 18:22 f. who goes (: cl. **ḏ-masgia**, cf. mod. *qâzĭ*) on the road etc.; cf. also **ṭabagada ṭabdana**, (s.vv.).

ṬAA (טעי, ܛܥܐ, H. טעה LS) to stray, err, deviate.

Pe. Act. pt. pl. **ṭaiin** Gy 227:19, DC 51. 181 they wander about, they stray. Pass. pt. **ṭᶜia** s.v.

Der.: **ṭaia, ṭᶜia, ṭaiuta, ṭaita, ṭiuana** (?).

ṬAB, ṬUB (Gen. Sem.) to be, or feel, well, good, wholesome; pa. to prepare, provide, do good, make good, restore, refresh, make whole; ethpa. to take part in, partake, refresh oneself (with ritual food).

Pe. Pf. with encl. **biša ḏ-laṭablẖ** DC 51 an evil one that was not made good. Part. pres. with encl. **laṭaib(i)nun** (?) Jb 40:9 I prepare (?) them not (one would expect pa.) MG 291: antep., but cf. Jb ii 44 n. 2 (which proposes **ṭaininun** I bear them?); could be a pa. pf. with suff. I did not pasture them (but one expects a pres.). Inf. **miṭab kušta lṭaba** Gy 125:25, Gs 118:3, cf. ML 81:ult. Good is the Truth for the good one (Lidzb. interrogatively, in which case **mi-** would be an interrog. particle, and **ṭab** a pe. pf.).

Pa. Pf. **ṭaiib minẖ mn ṭab(u)tẖ** Jb 172:7, 9,

182:9, Gy 357:18 (he) benefited (others) from his goods; **ṭabuta ṭaibat** DC 34 goodness refreshed (used as a name of a fertility spirit); with **ušraga ḏ-kulhun ginzꜥia ṭaiiblun** DC 38. 95 f. and a lamp which adorned all treasures; with suff. **ḏ-ṭaibinin mn ṭabtḫ** CP 374:penult. (var. **ṭaibinan** DC 53) who refreshed us from his goodness (or with his food). Impf. **patura abihdia ꜥniš laniṭaiib** DC 34. 964 he shall eat with no one; **niṭaibun** Q 22:10, 24:10, 57:27, Gy 110:5 they will be restored; **niṭaibun mia** DC 42 they partake of (: they drink communally) water; **niṭaibun ꜥlḫ patura** ATŠ II no. 208 they (will) prepare the (commemorating) dish for him; **tlata ꜥumṣia bimihla niṭaibun** ibid. they will partake of three morsels (of the bread) with salt; **ḏ-nihzun ṭabia uniṭaibun lainia uꜥudnia** DC 6 that the good may behold and restore eyes and ears; **nihzun ṭabia uniṭaibun** CP 52:7 the good see and will be refreshed; **tiṭaibun** ye (will) prepare MG 252:17; **kḏ pihta lamšauialkun laṭitaibun** Gy 317:10 when the p. is not prepared for you, do not partake (in ritual food); **latiṭaibun abihdḫ** ATŠ II no. 6 do not eat with him; **ꜥzdahar ḏ-latiṭibun mn paturḫ** ATŠ II no. 7 beware that ye do not eat at her table; **mn qudam ḏ-patura tiṭaibun** ATŠ II 334 before ye partake of the dish; with suff. **ḏ-niṭaibḫ lzidqa** Gy 317:10 f. who prepareth an oblation. Impt. with suff. **ḏ-ṭaibinan mn ṭabutḫ** CP 377:ult. who refresheth us with his bounty. Pt. **mṭaiba** AM 222:ult. is provided; **mn ꜥkilta mṭaiba** ATŠ II no. 112 from the prepared (or act.: refreshing?) food; with suff. **mn ṭabuta mṭaibanun** Oxf. roll f 1107 f. from the food which is prepared for them (?). Inf. **paqadta lṭaiubia nišmata** DC 27. 45 order to refresh souls.

Ethpa. Pf. **uꜥṭaiabiun tlata ꜥumṣia bmihla** DC 27. 45 and they partook of three morsels with salt. Impf. identical with pa. (q.v.). Impt. **uꜥṭaiabiun tlata ꜥumṣia bmihla uakuliun uꜥṭaiab mia** DC 50 and have ready three morsels with salt and eat and refresh yourselves with water; **aprišlun . . . bšidqa ꜥṭaibuia** (inf.) CP 399:11 teach them . . . to partake in silence. Pt. **miṭaibia** Oxf. roll f 1229 ff., **umiṭaibia . . . mn hak ṭariana** DC 38 and (they) . . . partake of that ritual-table. Inf. **paqadta lṭaiubia nišmata . . . nišimta ḏ-baiia miṭaiubia minaihun** DC 27 command to partake . . . the soul that is seeking to be refreshed from them.

Der.: **ṭab(a), ṭabta, ṭabu(ta), ṭuba, ṭubania, ṭabit 1, mṭab.**

ṭab, ṭaba (טָבָא, ܛܳܒܳܐ) good, blessing, beneficent, wholesome, virtuous. Fem. **ṭabt(i)a.** Pl. masc. **ṭabia.** Both masc. st. abs. and fem. (but esp. fem. **ṭabta**) are often used with the mean. of good thing, virtue, blessing, benefit. MG 110:15. St. abs. adverbially 'well'. **ṭubḫ lman ḏ-abid ṭab** Gy 357:15 f., MG 299: 14, **ṭabta** Gy 106:5, 107:8, 111:14 (sometimes with a var. **ṭabuta**) good thing, virtue MG 299:18 f.; **ṭab ṭaba lṭaba** Q 41:31 a great sacramental formula corresponding to 'holy things to the holy' of the oriental liturgies; **tiul bṭab** DC 48 thou shalt enter with benefit; **gada ṭaba** PD 357 good-luck; **lṭab ꜥdikruk** they shall remember thee for good MG 303:2; **ṭab ꜥlkun amarna** CP 125:9, ML 151:7 well do I say unto you; **riša ḏ-šidta ṭab mn dinba** AM 283:9 the beginning of the year is better than the end; **kul man ḏ-ṭab akil uṭab šatia** JRAS 1938 6:3 everyone that eats well and drinks well; **miuia ḏ-ṭabia** PD 1137 wholesome fruits; **šidta d-ṭabtia tihuia** AM267:28 the year will be good; **nihuia ṭabia** Gy 98:14 we will be good; **ꜥl ṭabia atit** Gs 24:12 thou art welcome; **šidta bṭabia tihuia** AM 226:14 it will be a beneficial year; **ꜥbidbḫ ṭabta ṭabta mibidbḫ ḏ-nihzun ṭabia** etc. Gy 111:4 I will do good therein, good shall be done therein, so that the good ones may see; **raia ṭaba** Gy 177:20 the good shepherd. Adjectivally with encl. pers. pron.: **ṭabna** Gs 53:12 I am good MG 87:20, **ṭabitun** Gy 292:2 ye are good MG 88:1.

ṭab iumin (Jew. טב יומין, *Εὐήμερος* Jb ii 71:10) Jb 61:11 name of a (supposed) Jewish priest.

ṭabagada (lit. 'Of-the-ABCD', cf. s. ṭ-) RD 27 name of a demon.

ṭabahata 1 ('of the fathers' *or* 'parents', cf. s. ṭ-) a *masiqta* celebrated for the Cosmic Father and Mother in the name of a man and woman at *Panja*. **ṭabahata udukrana** PD 1726; **ṭabahatan urabanan** PD 1632; **ṭabahata** Oxf. roll f 502, 510, 521 ff., 550, PD 175, 179, 1160, 1631, 1634, 1730 etc.

ṭabahata 2 DC 35 = **ṭabauata.**

ṭabauata pl. of **ṭabuta 2. maria ṭabauata** PD 1154, 1156 lord of ritual feasts.

ṭabaiata DC 6 no. 241 = **ṭabiata** (q.v.).

ṭabahia (sg. טַבָּחָא, ܛܰܒܳܚܳܐ) Gy 107:4 f. cooks MG 64:4.

ṭabaiiع, ṭabiiع (Ar. طبائع) natures, characteristics, symptoms, qualities, kinds, sorts. **ṭabaiiع ḏ-šuba kukbia** AM 286:5 characteristics of the seven stars; **ṭabaiiع hamimia** AM 287:24; **sadarta ḏ-arba ṭabiiع** HG.

ṭabaita fem. of **ṭabia**? **ꜥsira ṭabaita kalbaita** DC 43 A 47 f. bound is the rabid hind (?).

ṭabar, ṭbar (P. تبر) axe, mattock. **kdub lṭabar** DC 46. 194:3 inscribe upon an axe; **asrik ꜥlauḫ ṭabar** DC 46. 201:13 kindle (fire) upon an axe; **kdub lṭbar** DC 46 225: penult.

ṭabarzin (P. تبرزين) a small axe. Varr. s. **ṭagarzun. ṭabarzin ḏ-nhaša** RD 24.

ṭabaristan (طبرستان) AM 205 Tabaristan BZ Ap. II.

ṭabdana, ṭabdin (i.e. **ḏ-abdana** of perdition) used as pr. n. of a hill Ginzā 49 n. 2. **ṭabdana** (var. **ṭabdin** DC 22. 50) **ṭura** Gy 54:12.

ṭabu, ṭabuta, ṭabut (Gen. Aram.) (*a*) goodness, kindness, liberality, bounty, benefaction; a boon, gracious gift, (*b*) (ritual) food (cf. טבחה = ܛܒܚܐ = طبخ and the der. **ṭabaiia**), in ritual esp. the loaf of ritual bread, a banquet. Pl. **ṭabauata** (also s.v.) bounties, good things, (ritual) foods. The sg. sometimes varies with

ṭabta (v.s. **ṭab**). MG 144:paen. and n. 1, 155:9, 167:11. (*a*) **bṭabu** Gy 104:15 (parallel with **bṭabuta** l. 16), 274:10, DC 34. 215 etc., kindly, with goodness MG 303:1; **ariblẖ lṭabu bbiš** Gy 112:14 he is mixing good with evil MG 304:10; **bṭabu rbia** Gy 32:33 through the goodness of the Great (Life), *but* **lṭabut rbia** Gy 131:21 MG 313:3 f.; **qabil ṭabuta** Gy 39:13, 295:22 etc., **ṭabuta ḏ-marẖ lamqabil** Gy 27:12, 50:12, **laniqabla ṭabutun** Gy 298:10, **ṭabutai lamqablia** Gy 344:8 f., **ṭabuta ḏ-ahẖ qablat** ATŠ II no. 105 (idiom with **QBL** q.v.); **lgaṭ ṭabuta** s. **LGṬ**; **ṭabutan . . . niligṭan** Gy 315:6, **lgaṭ ṭabuta** etc. s. **LGṬ** (*idioms*); **man ḏ-ṭabuta abadbkun** Gy 39:12 f. whosoever did you good; **latikprun mn ṭabutẖ** Gy 39:14 do not deny his benefaction; **ʿu mn ṭabutẖ kapritun tum lašauitun lṭabutẖ uṭabuta minaikun baṣra** Gy 39:14 ff. if ye deny his benefaction and show yourselves unworthy of his goodness, the benefaction will be taken away from you; **bṭabu ʿtmlun ʿlẖ ʿlẖ ʿtmlun bṭabuta** Gy 104: 15 f. they were full of kindness to him; **ubṭabuta hua** Gy 153:12 he was full of bounty; **zidqa uṭabuta** Gy 40:4 f. oblation and benefaction; **baṭlan ṭabauata** Gy 12:13 f. good things come to nought; **umn ṭabauata mauṭipia** ATŠ I no. 112 he benefits with his benefactions; **ṭabauata ḏ-hanatẖ alma** DC 41 good things of that world; **ṭabuta naška** AM 2:7 he will find favour; **ṭabuta bgauẖ lanibad** Jb 99:7 (he) doeth no good with it; **ʿtit ḏ-ʿbad ṭabuta ṭabuta ʿbad ušaria ṭabu lrahmai** Jb 241:3 f. I came to do good and shed benefit on my friends; **šidta bṭabuta tihuia** AM 227:2 the year will be beneficial; **ubṭabuta laniplihunẖ** AM 215:14 and they do not serve him well; **manhirana ḏ-kulhin ṭabauata** DC 50 illuminer of all good things; **titqabal ṭabut hua** DC 50. 155; (*b*) **ṭabuta** Oxf. roll f 366, 381, 394, 479, 1083 etc., pl. **ṭabauata** Oxf. roll f 403 ff., 419, 456, 490, 498, 1092, 1129, 1141, 1282 ff. etc. (often in rituals and wedding songs); **mihla uṭabuta** DC 38 (Oxf. roll f 366, cf. ML 110 n. 1); **miuia uṭabauata** DC 42, **ṭabauata umiuia** DC 42.

Gl. 112:7 **ṭbuta** [*sic*] طعام *convivium*, 155:3 **ṭabuta** مايده *mensa* خوردني.

ṭabṭana DC 46 doubtful.

ṭabia (טַבְיָא, ܛܰܒܝܳܐ LS) gazelle, deer MG 100:20. Pl. **ṭabiia** (var. **ṭabia**) MG 164:8. Fem. **ṭabaita**? **magalta ḏ-ṭabia** (often in DC 45 and 46) a parchment of gazelle(-skin); **ṭabia ḏ-mišk** ATŠ I no. 256 musk deer; **ṭabiia** Gy 387:16 (var. Lond. **ṭabia**) gazelles.

ṭabian in **iasdis ṭabian** Gy 383:18 (s. **iasdis**), Pet. **ṭibian**.

ṭabiata ATŠ I no. 241 a pl. of ṭabuta (b). Var. **ṭabaiata** DC 6 ibid.

ṭabiiع s. **ṭabaiiع**.

ṭabit 1 (inst. of ܛܳܒܳܐܝܬ) Heb. טוב, similarly Bab. loan-w.; into Bab. *ṭebû*, Heb. טבע sink. (*a*) well, excellently, (*b*) much, plentifully MG 201:12. (*a*) **mhašbitun ṭabit** Gy 292:12 ye plan well; **ṭabit nibdun** Gy 295:20 they are doing excellently; (*b*) **ṭabit zarin . . . uṭabit qiniana qanin** Gy 389:14 f. they sow plentifully . . . and they acquire great possessions.

ṭabit 2 (Bab. *Ṭebetu*, H. טֵבֵת) a Mand. month, called **akir paiiz** the last autumn-month MMII 84.

ṭabla (טַבְלָא, ܛܰܒܠܳܐ Ar. طَبْل LS, Fränkel 284) (large) drum. Var. **ṭibla** s.v. Pl. **ṭablia**. **mn miška nisbat uṭabla šauiat** ATŠ I no. 248 she took of the hide and made a drum. [LS].

Gl. 112:10 **ṭabla** طبل *tambura*.

ṭabqa (Ar. طَبْقَة) DC 46. 255:3 bird-snare.

ṭabta fem. of **ṭaba** (q.v.), sometimes used with the meaning of **ṭabuta** (q.v.).

ṭabtia the same as preced., DC 43 name of a lilith.

ṭaga (cf. Ar. طاقة in P. use: 'sprig' Steing.) sprig, twig. **ṭaga ḏ-asa** Oxf. roll f 158, 177, 505, 527, DC 42. 116. Pl. **ṭagia ḏ-asa** Oxf. roll f 1343, DC 40.

ṭagarzun DAb 12, var. **tarabzun** cf. DAb transl. 35 n. 3 (varr. of **ṭabarzin** q.v.).

ṭahala (טחלא, ܛܚܳܠܳܐ mod. H. טחול, Ar. طحال) spleen, milt. Varr. **ṭahaila, ṭihaila, ṭahila**. St. abs. **ṭhal** (?) s.v. See טְחָלָא; only Middle Hebrew. **uṭahila** (var .**ṭahilia**) **hauilẖ** AM 14 and he will be splenetic; **širiania ḏ-ṭahilẖ** DC 37. 579 the veins (?) of his spleen; **mirta uhaša uṭahala** DC 34. 424 gall, bowels, and spleen; **ʿu ṭahala nikublẖ** AM 99:18 or her spleen will pain her.

ṭahila s. **ṭahala**.

***ṭahmurat** Lidzb.'s (Ginzā 411:7) reading of **zardanaiaṭa lahmuraṭ** Gy 382:17 (an ancient Iranian king, identified by Gray with *Ṭaχmōrup, Taχmō Urupa azinava* Yašt xv 11, xix 28, ZA xix 275).

ṭaualqan AM 199:5 a city in the climate of Mercury. Var. **aṭaualqan**. Identical with **ṭaliqan** (? , q.v.).

ṭauasta fem. of **ṭausa** (?) might be used as an adj. 'glistening' (cf. טוס J 524:bottom). **ia ṭauasta ḏ-dahba** ŠQ 18:30 (var. . . . **ḏ-zahba** CP 537:4).

ṭaubania Sh. 'Abd.'s copy's var. of **ṭubania** Gy 227:8.

ṭaus, ṭausa (טַוְסָא, ܛܰܘܣܳܐ, *ταῶς* Ar. طاوُوس) peacock. Also טָוָסָא, טאוּסָא, Z. 3–5. **mrirta ḏ-ṭaus** DC 46. 78:3 the gall of a peacock; **iušamin ṭausa** DC 34 ill. B. Y. the peacock; **qaiim udariš ṭausa uamar** Jb 270:14; **ana ṭausa** Jb 271:4, 7, 12; **skultai dilia ṭausa** Jb 271:10.

ṭauع (Ar. طَوْع) AM 257:29 allegiance.

ṭauعat AM 272:34 = **ṭauع**.

ṭaupia (טַוְפָא, ܛܰܘܦܳܐ) pl. floods, (sur)face of waters. **ṭaupia mia** ATŠ II nos. 134, 152, DC 48. 199, 488 etc.; **ṭaupia ḏ-ziuẖ** DC 3 and 53.

ṭaṭa = **aṭaṭa**? **šaba ṭaṭa** DC 43 seven (t)horns (?). Pl. **ṭaṭia** DC 43 E. **ṭaṭia ḏ-ṭabia ḏʿmbara** DC 43 E 48, DC 20. 106, horns (?) of a gazelle *or* of a sheep.

ṭaṭbaiata DC 43 name of a lilith (?).

ṭaṭka (P. تخت ,کَه) place for reclining, throne, couch, bed, pleasure-house, pavilion. DAb transl. 9 n. 5. Pl. **ṭaṭkia. kul hilbuna ṭaṭka šdibh̲** RD A (3) 41 in every house a couch is spread; **tlatma ušitin ṭaṭkia šdia . . . kul had hilbuna kul had hilbuna ṭaṭka šdiia** DAb = RD F 5 ff.; **atutia ṭaṭkia** Par. xxiv 53a; **uškibiun ʿl ṭaṭkia** DC 34. 776; **ʿl ṭaṭkia šakibun** DC 48. 232 they sleep on their beds.

ṭaṭmʿil DAb = RD 1, a name given to Sin (the moon-god) in the moon-ship.

ṭai (the *ṭae*, wires representing twigs of *barsam* used in the Parsi ceremony of *Panj-ṭai*) the *ṭae*-twigs. **šarin himiana uatin bṭai asrin** DAb (they) loosen the (sacred) girdle and come and bind the *ṭae*-twigs.

ṭaia (rt. **ṬAA**) (*a*) error, (*b*) evil spirit that leads astray, spirit of deception. (*a*) **ṭaia** DC 22. 197 a var. of **ṭʿia** Gy 206:5. **lšrara ulṭaia** ATŠ II no. 45 (var. **ṭia** DC 36); (*b*) **lhumria zadaniata . . . ulṭaia** (read **ṭaiia**?) **d̲-ṭaiin** DC 51 against satanic amulet-spirits and the spirit(s) that deceive.

ṭaiubtia (rt. **ṬBA I**?) JRAS 1937 fem. (of eye) sunken (?).

ṭaiuta (טָעוּת, ܛܥܝܘܬܐ) orig. error, used with the mean. of deceiving spirit (Nöld. and Lidzb. *idol*) MG 145:22. Furlani, *I Nomi* 425. **ruban ruban ṭaiuta** Gy 208:6, 18, 209:9 ff.

ṭaiis (act. pt. pe. of **ṬUS**) lit. flying (hence): birds, fowl, pigeons, doves. **ṭaiis d̲-ʿngaria** DC 12. 157, Lond. roll B 316 pigeons (?) of the roofs.

ṭaita (cf. **ṭaiuta**) error: **uṭaith̲ bpagrh̲ ridpa d̲-šuba nišbuq ʿlh̲** ATŠ II 353 and his error will bring upon his body the persecution of the Seven.

ṭaksa (ܛܟܣܐ, τάξις) order, rank, degree, rule, governance, control. MG xxx:5. **hakima d̲-laṭaksa** Gy 216:17; **bṭaksa laqaimia** Gy 285:12, 290:10; **bṭaksa šapira qaimin** Gy 285:23; **ʿtbun ṭama uṭaksa** ATŠ II no. 186 HG they have good taste and order; **anašia d̲-laṭaksa** disorderly people; **ṭaksa usipra** RD C 12 s. **sipra 1.**

ṭaktia (P. تخت) pl. beds. **d̲-ṭaktia d̲-maraihun glun** DC 43 J 166 that uncovered the beds of their masters.

ṭala (טַלָּא, ܛܠܐ, H. טַל, Ar. طَلّ, Ethiop. ጠል) dew. **ṭala hibil** (?) Oxf. 76 b; **lṭala damia** Jb 123:9, 14; **miṭra uṭala** AM 266:2; **kd̲ ṭala d̲-paṣra** DC 21, JRAS 1938 3:31.

ṭalala Sh. ʿAbd.'s copy, PA's copy of DC 43 J 71; var. of **ṭlala** Gy 216:17.

ṭalba (Ar. طَلَب) petition, seeking, inquiry, application. **atit bṭalba d̲-ganzibrukta** Zotb. 231a:12 I was an applicant for the ganziv-rate.

ṭalula 1 (cf. **ṭulala, ṭlala**) (*a*) roof, covering, (*b*) shade, gloom. Pl. **ṭalulia.** (*a*) **ṭalulia** DC 22. 55 a var. of **ṭulalia** Gy 60:2; (*b*) **uṭalula šibqit ʿlauaihun** DC 44. 617 and I let gloom (*or* derision) (come) upon them.

ṭalula 2 (rt. **ṬLL II**) (*a*) play, jest, sport, mock, ribaldry, (*b*) (= **ṭalia**) young child (?). (*a*) **hitra ṭalula uzmara** AM 4:6; **uṭalula uzmara rahim** AM 10:1; he loves jest and song; (*b*) **uṭalula d̲-qarba umahia** DC 21 and the child that she approaches and strikes; **ṭalula d̲-ianqa** DC 46. 155:11.

ṭalia 1 (טַלְיָא, ܛܠܝܐ, H. טָלֶה Ar. طَلًا LS, Ges.) boy, youth (-ful), lad MG 109:8. **ṭalia zuṭa** (see below) identified by Lidzb. with *puerus phosphorus* (ZDMG xxxii 565) Ginzā 235:top. Pl. **ṭaliia. ṭalia** Oxf. 68 b. **ṭalia zuṭa** Gy 57:18, 190:22; **anana ṭalia zuṭa** Gy 374:18, Ginzā 235:13; **rabia ṭalia** Gy 221:5, Oxf. 57 b; **rabia ṭalia lihdaia** Gy 235:21, MR 30 n. 1; **ṭalia br ziuia** CP 356:7, Oxf. 96 a; **arspan rabia ṭalia** CP 356:7; **hibil ziua ṭalia** DC 34. 232, DC 44. 1752 = Morg. 268/27:8; **bʿsqat ṭalia zuṭa** DC 37. 466 by the seal (i.e. compelling charm) of a young lad; **naṭria ṭaliia** Jb 187:13 the youthful guardians.

ṭalia (cf. Ar. طَلْع) = **ṭalia** (?) a (young) palm (?)-tree. **ṭalia sumaqa hu** DC 35 (in a list of trees and plants).

ṭalisim (Ar. طلسم) DC 41 talisman.

ṭaliʿ (Ar. طالع [المولود]) AM horoscope, governing star, stellar influence (astrol.) BZ 70 n. 5.

ṭaliqan AM 203 name of a town BZ Ap. II.

ṬAM (טְעַם, ܛܥܡ H. טָעַם Ar. طَعِمَ Akk. *ṭêmu* LS, Ges.) to taste, try, test, examine, eat; appreciate, perceive, discern, experience, savour.

Pe. Pf. pl. **laṭamun d̲-mamlalia dakiia** HG they did not apprehend that they are clean(sing) words. Act. pt. pl. **ṭama d̲-muta laṭaimin** Gy 9:11 they do not taste the taste of death, cf. MG 256:3. Inf. **miṭam** Gy 393:4 (varr. **maṭam, miṭim**) MG 256:7.

Gl. 180:11 f. **ṭam** ذاق *gustare* چشيد.

Der.: **ṭama 1.**

ṭama 1 (טַעְמָא, ܛܥܡܐ) (*a*) taste, flavour, savour, quality, (*b*) judgement, perception, discrimination, (*c*) appreciation, pleasure, will. MG 16:14, 70:18, 100:10. (*a*) **ṭama d̲-muta** Gy 9:11 (s. **ṬAM** pe. act. pt.); **makulta d̲-laṭama** Gy 216:19; **ṭama d̲-ʿlanun** ATŠ II nos. 85 and 306; **lṭama d-kul piria uaṭšia** DC 40; **ṭama d̲-nhura** Gy 299:23 (Lidzb. *Gehalt des Lichtes* Ginzā 296:26, but gives the lit. mean. *'Geschmack'* in the footn. 1); (*b*) **ṭama uṭaksa** Q 71:23, 72:29, ATŠ (*and often*), AM 105:26, **ṭama uṣauta** Gy 301:8, ATŠ II no. 186; **šaia uṭama** CP 451:12; **azal ṭamh̲** Jb 120:12; **adinqia ṭamia nihun** Gs 57:5; (*c*) **bla ṭama** DC 43 E 63 etc.; **bla ṭamun** Gs 18:1 (Ginzā 436 n. 1); **pira anat d̲-basima ṭamh̲** CP 201:13 thou art a fruit the flavour of which is pleasant.

ṭamaia (rt. **ṬMM**?) stoppage, obstruction (?) **mṭaršia ʿudnia umitiqria ṭamaia** Or. 328:6 f.

ṭamašiata, a pl. of **ṭamušata** (q.v.).

ṭamba Jb 29:11C = **ṭinba.**

ṭamušata, ṭimušata (rt. **ṬMŠ**) submersion.

Pl. **ṭamašiata, ṭ(u)mušiata** (s. vv.). **kḏ ṭamušata qadmaita ṭmiš** DC 34. 391; **kḏ ṭimušata tiniantia ṭamiš** DC 34. 394.

ṭamiata (rt. **ṬMA**) fem. pl. polluting. **lruhia ṭamiata haškata** DC 40. 245 and 300 unclean dark female spirits.

ṭamir Ṣâb.'s AM a var. of **ṭumir** (a city in the climate of Mercury).

ṬAN (טְעַן, ܛܥܢ, H. טָעַן LS, Ges.) to bear, carry.

PE. Pf. **ṭan** (he) bore, carried; with suff. **ṭanan** (he) bore me MG 270:24; **ṭanan ṭuna dakia** Gs 68:6 MG 399:ult. Act. pt. **ṭaiin** MG 256:3; pl. **ʿlania ṭuna ṭainia** AM 268:43 trees (will) bear fruit. Pass. pt. **ṭin** Jb 177:5 laden MG 117:8, 256:5; pl. **ḏ-ṭinia bṭuna dakia** DC 34. 336 who are loaded with pure fruit; with encl. pers. pron. **ṭina** Gs 90:24 I am laden MG 256:5.

DER.: **ṭuna, ṭiuana** (?).

ṭana (Doubtf., rt. טון = ܛܢ, ظن?) suspicion?, fault-finding?, envy?, or jealous or envious person? **ʿsir ṭanai ṭana uṭanai rbai** DC 43 I 6.

ṭanupia (nom, act. pa. of **ṬNP**) defilement, pollution. Occasional varr. **ṭanipia, ṭunupia, ṭnupia, aṭnupia** (s.vv.).

ṭanṭan (cf. Ar. طنطنة) fuss, commotion, tumult, din, clamour. **ṭanṭan mlakia** DC 44. 456.

ṭanipia a var. of **ṭanupia. mn kul daiua ṭanipia umihiata** DC 37. 463 from every demon, defilement(s) and blows.

ṭanputa (ܛܢܘܦܘܬܐ) pollution: **mn ṭanputh ʿdakia** DC 34. 527 is cleansed from its pollution; **mn ṭanputa uqlala** Jb 45:5 from pollution and shame.

ṭanša AM 198, 202 a place-name (Tangier, Morocco?) BZ Ap. II.

ṭasa 1 (טַסָּא, ܛܣܐ, Ar. طاس and طسّ P. تشت Akk. *ṭ[d]aššu*) sheet of metal, plaque; bowl. Pl. **ṭasia. kdublh lṭasa ḏ-abara** DC 44. 913; **kdib lṭasa ḏ-anka uabara** DC 44. 1085; **ṭasia ḏ-abara** DC 44. 1264 (= Morg. 264/18:29 has **ṭasa** sg.); **bṭasa ḏ-kaspa** DC 37. 382.

ṭasa 2 Leid. var. of **ṭasu** Gs 85:3 corrupt, perh. read **ṭaksa** (Lidzb. proposed **ṭama** Ginzā 520 n. 2).

ṭasu s. **ṭasa 2.**

ṭaε (Ar. طاع) submission, allegiance. Varr. **ṭauε, ṭaεat. hauin bṭaε ḏ-malka ḏ-babil** AM 283:36 they will submit to the king of B.

ṭaεam (Ar. طعام) food. Var. **ṭiεam** s.v. Also a var. of **ṭaεat** cf. BZ 177 n. 5.

ṭaεat (Ar. طاعت) submission, allegiance. Varr. **ṭauε, ṭaε, ṭauεat. nitun bṭaεat ḏ-malka** AM 272:33 (they) will come to (make) submission to the king.

ṭapalia (cf. טַפְלָא, ܛܠܝܐ children) pl. households, families. **šabima ušuba alpia ṭapalia šribh** DAb 7700 families are settled in it.

ṭapan in **dukta ḏ-dudia uṭapan** JRAS 1937 591:antepenult., var. **dukta ḏ-dadaria bṭapin** P.A.'s copy (read) **dukta ḏ-dudia ṭapin** (as in) DC 43 place where cauldrons are seething.

ṭapqa (ܛܦܩܐ, ܛܦܩܐ, P. تابه) DC 48. 281 tongs, pincers; frying-pan. Pl. **-ia.** Pl. **ṭapqia** RD B 27 layers, plates. **ṭapqia ḏ-nhašia** RD B 25 (DAb . . . **ḏ-nhaša**); **hawia ṭapqia ʿlawak daiwa** DC 43 E 58; **ṭapqa ubitpia** DC 48. 281 tongs and braziers.

ṭaqan AM 206 a place-name (not identified, perh. **ṭuran**?).

ṭaqsa = **ṭaksa, q.v. anašia ḏ-la ṭaqsa** ATŠ.

ṭara (rt. **ṬRA**) assault (?). **ṭara ḏ-ainia** DC 45 the assault of his (evil) eye.

ṭarab (Ar. طرب) joy, merrymaking. **mizal luaṭ ʿnšia rurbata uahl ṭarab šapir hu** Ṣâb.'s AM is favourable for approaching great women and rejoicing people.

ṭaran AM 197 a place-name (v. **ṭuran**).

ṭarṭabuna 1 = **ṭarṭbuna.** Pl. **ṭarṭabunia. bṭarṭabuna kasia** DC 44. 1446 = Morg. 265/21:36 (pl. **bṭarṭabunia kasia**); **ṭarṭabunun ḏ-ziua** Jb 216:4; **ṭarṭabunia ṭabia dakia ḏ-nhura** CP 111:4 (s. CP trs. 81 n. 1).

ṭarṭabuna 2 (cf. טרטש to fasten; corrupt under the influence of **ṭarṭabuna 1**) Gs 14:5 cage, stye, Ginzā 433 n. 4. Varr. **ṭarṭauna** Sh. ʿAbd.'s copy, **ṭarṭauṣa**? DC 22. 404.

ṭarṭbuna (cf. Aram. טַרְטִין a head cover, Ar. طرطور < Lat. *turritum capitis ornamentum* Dozy, *Dictionnaire des noms des vêtements*; rt. and formation doubtful) turban (?), covering, wrapping, vesture ATŠ trs. p. 228 n. 8. Var. **ṭarṭabuna 1.** Pl. **ṭarṭ(a)bunia.** Masc. **bṭarṭbunh dakia** Gy 101:22, 102:10, 338:19 etc. (*often*); **ṭarṭbuna ṭaba dakia ḏ-nhura** Gy 193:8, 18, Gs 7:1, Oxf. 57a etc.; **ṭarṭbunia d-nhura** Gy 57:22; **ṭarṭbunia dakiia ḏ-nhura** Gy 210:14, Gs 16:5; **ṭarṭbunia ḏ-ziua** Gy 32:6; **ṭarṭbunia rurbia ḏ-nhura** Gy 210:24, 211:10; **ṭarṭbunia ṭabia dakiia ḏ-nhura** Gy 235:13; **ṭarṭbuna ḏ-nhura** Gy 320:12, Gs 73:21, 82:12; **ṭarṭbuna ḏ-hauiuia** Gs 72:16; **nisbh uatnh bṭarṭbunh dakia** DC 48. 253; **lbušak ʿṣṭla ḏ-ziua uṭarṭbunak rba ḏ-nhura** Gy 211:13 f.; **kap šipulh** (Pet. **šiph**) **uṭarṭbunh** DC 22.411 = Gs 21:10 he folded his skirt (?) and his vesture (?); **halin šuba iumia šuba razia lṭarṭbunia bgauaihun** ATŠ II no. 91 (??); **ṭarṭabunia rurbia ḏ-nhura** CP 456:1.

ṭariana (ܛܪܝܢܐ P. تريان wicker tray) a small ritual table, round in shape, made of sunbaked clay, with a recess separated by a ridge (**miṣra**) upon which the **qauqa** (a terracotta cube with a slight depression at one end for powdered incense) is placed during the ritual; upon it ritual foods and ritual drinks are ranged MMII 115, 106, 191 etc. Pl. **ṭariania.** Masc. Var. **ṭiriana** PD 1134 etc. **sadariun ṭariana bmihla uṭabuta** Morg. 183:4; **sadar ṭariana** ibid.: 6; **ṭariana ḏ-zidqa** PD 1150; **traṣiun ṭariana** DC 41; **hda ṭariana** WedF 3b:2; **tmania ṭariania** WedF 3b:1; **ṭariana rba** WedF 138b:8 ff. Very frequent in ritual texts: **ṭariana** Oxf. roll f 156, 250, 258, 366, 368 ff., 456, 1070, PD 1138 etc., **ṭariania** Oxf. roll f 827, 1268 etc.

Gl. 154:11 **ṭariana** مذبح, *altare*.

ṭarsus AM 198 Tarsus. Varr. **ṭar(a)sus, ʿṭarsus.** BZ Ap. II.

ṭarpa the original form of the more frequent **aṭarpa, aṭirpa** (q.v.). **kul hilbuna ṭarpa šdibẖ** DAb.

ṭarpan ('Leafy'?) DAb a demon.

ṭarpis DC 46 p. 2 f. a demon(?).

ṭašqa (טַשְׁקָא vessel < P. تشتك small basin) tray, bowl, disk, fig. cymbal. **qimahia bṭašqa ḏ-nhaša** DAb = RD 35 (he) beats a copper cymbal.

ṭašt, ṭašta (P. تشت) large basin, bowl, ewer. **kdub bguara ḏ-ṭašt kuan** DC 46. 203:6 write in the interior of a table-ewer; **bkulẖ alma ṭašta** Gy 386:8 prob. unfinished or corrupt, Ginzā 413 n. 6.

ṭaštga = **ṭašqa. ʿzdamar šuria akuat ṭaštga** Gy 166:16 f. the walls resounded like cymbals.

ṭatka = **ṭakt(i)a.** Pl. **ṭatkia. ʿl ṭatkia šakibun** DC 47 they lie on beds.

ṬBA I (טְבַע, ܛܒܰܥ H. טָבַע Akk. *ṭibû* LS, Ges.) to go in under, plunge beneath, submerge, immerse, plunge in, dip under, sink, drown.

Pe. Pf. **ṭba** (var. **ṭbun**) **ṭuria uṭba aramata** Gy 380:17 mountains and heights submerged (MG 234:20), **ṭbit, ʿṭbit, ṭibit** Q 18:12 I sank down MG 237:4 f.; **niplit biama ulaṭbit** DC 34. 81 I fell into the sea but did not drown. Impf. **bmia niṭba** AM 21:4, 211:5 will be submerged; **mia iatiria nitun uaṭšia ḏ-gaiṭa niṭbun** AM 212:3 much water will come (down) and the summer crops will be submerged. Act. pt. **man ḏ-ṭaba bṭiba ḏ-mia** ATŠ II no. 70, **man ḏ-bmia ṭaba** ATŠ II no. 269 who drowns in water; **ṭaba bgu iama ḏ-sup** DC 44. 642 (DC 26. 610 miswritten **ṭraba . . .**) he (: Pharaoh) drowned (hist. pres.) in the Re(e)d Sea; **ṭabia unasia mia** AM 11:417 he shall immerse and wash in water; pl. **ṭabin** they go under MG 71:5. Part. pres. **ṭbna** [*sic*] **lbnat anašia** DC 43 I go below to the children of men; **ṭabitun** Gy 54:16 ye shall go under MG 236:24.

Pa. Pf. with suff. **atun iamamia uṭabunun** Jb 42 1 f. seas came and submerged them. Impf. **laniṭaba** ATŠ he shall not immerse (?). Act. pt. **mahdurniata ḏ-mṭaba** Gy 277:19 whirlpools that drown; **mṭaba nišmatun** Gy 226:17 their souls sink.

Ethpe. Pt. **uskinẖ miṭba** *Florilegium* 362 (:159) and its blade is plunged in.

Der.: **ṭiba 1, ṭaiubtia** (?), cf. also **ṭubania.**

ṬBA II (< Ar. طبخ) to cook, roast, scorch.

Pa. Act. pt. pl. with encl. **mṭabilun** Sh. 'Abd.'s copy's var. of **mṭauilun** Gy 187:8 (s. ṬUA).

Der.: **ṭabaiia, ṭabuta** (*b*) (?).

ṬBD in **miṭibad ṭabṭana** DC 46 doubtf. (prob. corrupt.).

ṬHA (טְחַי) to squeeze, smear (?).

Pa. Impt. with encl. **mrirta umiša ḏ-tauria aṭhilẖ** DC 46 smear on his face (?) the gall and the fat of a bull.

ṭhal (st. abs. of **ṭahala**) Oxf. roll g 799, DC 46 spleen, milt.

ṬHN (טְחַן, ܛܚܰܢ H. טָחַן Ar. طحن, Akk. *ṭēnu, ṭēnu* LS, Ges.) to mill, grind (esp. grain), pound.

Pe. Pf. **ailiun šušma hiuara uṭhaniun** DC 41. 168 they brought in white sesame and pounded (it); **uṭhaniun hiṭia** DC 27 (illustrated part) and they ground the wheat. Impf. **uniṭhan hiṭia** Lond. roll A 553 and he grinds wheat; with encl. **niṭhinulẖ unikul** Jb 233:4 (B **niṭhnulẖ**) (they) grind (corn) for him so that he eateth.

ṬUB s. **ṬAB.**

ṬWA I, (ṬBA II) (טְוֵי II = טורא J) to roast, scorch.

Pe. Impt. with suff. **ṭuiẖ bnura** DC 46 scorch (?) it in fire (cf. also **ṬWH**).

Pa. Pt. with encl. **ʿl gumria mṭauilun** Gy 187:8 (var. **mṭabilun** s. **ṬBA II**) they roast them on coals.

(**ṬWA II** Gl. 110:11 f. **aṭui** [*sic*] طوى *plicare, complicare* پيچيد).

ṭuas AM 204 a place-name (a var. of **ṭus**?) BZ Ap. II.

ṭuba (טוּבָא, ܛܘܽܒܳܐ) (*a*) well-being, bliss, goodness, kindness, hail, favour, (*b*) a cure(?). (*a*) **ṭubẖ l** (*frequent*) hail to! Jb ii 49 n. 3; **ṭubẖ lman ḏ-abad ṭab** Gy 357:15 f. hail to the one who did good! MG 299:middle; **ṭubak ṭubak nišma** CP 131:2, ML 159:6 hail to thee, hail to thee, soul!; **ṭubẖ ḏ-hiziẖ** Q 59:8 hail to that who saw him!; **ṭubẖ ḏ-napšẖ nida** Gy 356:ult. hail to that who knoweth himself!; **ṭubak ḏ-hzilak** Gy 154:19 hail to thee who didst see!; **ṭubaikun ḏ-haza abadtun** Gy 146:16 hail to you that ye have done this!; **ṭubẖ lman ḏ-** Gy 11:17, 276:16 etc.; **ṭubak ldilak ḏ-** Gy 147:20 etc.; **ṭubaihun lšalmania** Gy 5:7, 11:22 etc., MG 482:13 ff.; **šailia ʿutria ḏ-nhura mn ṭubẖ** DC 35 the uthras of light ask for some of his bliss; (*b*) **ṭuba ḏ-aqarthẖ tišul** AM 79:18 **ṭabia,** varr. **ṭuba** she asks a cure for her barrenness.

ṭubania (Chr. Syr. ܛܘܒܢܳܐ used in Mand. as a sneering expr. popularly derived from **ṬBA I** MG 448 n. 1) pl. 'blessed ones', 'saints' MG xxix 21, 448 (and n. 1). Fem. pl. **ṭubaniata.** Sg. not found. **qarin lnapšaihun ṭubania uṭubaniata ḏ-mṭaba nišmatun bhabara** Gy 226:17 f. they call themselves 'blessed ones' and 'saintly women' because their souls sink (a pun, cf. above) into darkness, MG 448:3 ff.; **šuba ṭubania** Gy 227:8.

ṭubiat DC 44 an angel.

ṬWH (Ar. طَوَّح) to throw, cast. Frequent in mod. Mand. (pron. *touweḥ*).

Pa. Impt. with suff. **ṭauhẖ bmaina** DC 46 (*often*) cast it into water, defectively **ṭuhẖ bmia** DC 46. 190:9 id., **ṭauha bšamša** DC 46 p. 144 throw it into sun(shine); does **ṭuiẖ bnura** (s. **ṬWA I**) belong here?

Gl. (always pa., sometimes miswritten): 40:3 f. بذر *spergere* ريخت; 49:9 f. تلف

perdere, nil praestare; 50:1 f. تقطّع *concidere se* بريده شد; 79:7 f. رمى *proicere* انداخت; 80:3 f. رجم *lapidare* سنگ انداخت; 108:5 f. طرح *mittere, proicere* انداخت; 110:9 f. طرح *praecipitare* انداخت; 145:7 f. لقى *proicere* انداخت; 159:5 (pass. pt. pa.) mṭuh [sic] مطروح *proiectus* انداخته شد.

ṭuhma (ܛܘܗܡܐ OP *tau[h]ma*, mod. P. تخم MG 63 n. 3) race, lineage, stock, origin, seed, kin, kindred, relative, relation. **ṭuhmaiun uziraiun** Gy 28:5 their race and their seed; **ṭuhma uzma** Gy 34:4 semen (?, Lidzb. *Geschlecht*) and blood; **ṭuhma ušarša** Gy 142:6, 17, 202:3 lineage and race, **širša uṭuhma** Gy 143:14; **zirak uṭuhmak** DC 37:77. **ṭuhma d̲-daiua** DC 44 the kin of the demon; **rmilh̲ kd̲ ṭuhmh̲** DC 46 he throws it like its seed; **lṭuhmaihun midamin** ATŠ I no. 47 they are like their lineage; **kd̲ zira uṭuhma d̲-trin ʿuṣṭunia hinun** ATŠ they are like seed and stock from two bodies; **zirai uṭuhmai** DC 34. 352; **gabra mn ṭuhma d̲-malka** AM 244:13 a man of royal lineage; **br ṭuhma** a relative, **pt ṭuhma** a girl from his family, **bnia ṭuhma** relatives (all three frequent).

ṭuṭipta (H. טוֹטֶפֶת) Jb 131:2 = CP 173:10, Oxf. 39 b = ML 211:4 charm, amulet, phylactery MG xxix 12, cf. also Wellhausen: *Reste des arabischen Heidentums*[2], p. 165 n. 6.

ṭuṭlia (cf. טַלְטֵל to exile) AM 217:12 pl. migrants, vagabonds.

ṭukasa DC 44. 951 for **ṭaksa**? (or ܛܘܟܣܐ) ordinance, ordering (?).

ṬUL = ṬLL.

ṭula (טוּלָא H. צֵל Ar. ظِلّ Akk. *ṣillu* LS s. ܛܠܠܐ) shade, shadow, shelter MG 105:4. **ʿlana d̲-bṭulh̲ iatbia** DC 41:right 33 a tree in whose shade they sit; **bṭulh̲ d̲-hurba d̲-ʿurašlam** Jb 129:5; **ṭunaihun uṭulaihun** DC 36 their fruit and their shade; **bṭula d̲-almia udaria** DC 34. 619; **bṭula d̲-ruha šakbitun** DC 34. 860; **ṭula d̲-klila** Oxf. 71 b; **uiabiš bṭula** AM 287:21 and dry in the shade; **bṭulak mitrabian** DC 48. 112; **ṭulh̲ lkulhun almia d̲-nhura ʿtahzia** DC 34 his shade is visible to all the beings of light.

Gl. 156:1 ṭ(u)la مظل *tabernacula* خيمه.

ṭulala 1, ṭlala (ܛܠܠܐ Akk. *ṣulūlu* LS) shade, shelter, roof, roof-tree, shadow, gloom MG 123:13. Pl. **ṭ(u)lalia.** Masc. **ṭulalia d̲-ṣipra** Gy 207:12 morning-shadows; **ṭulalia d̲-zipa** Gy 365:3, Jb 183:5, 246:3 deceiving shades; **ʿl ṭulalia uʿl ṭuria** Gy 60:2 f.; **bṭulalun d̲-gupnai iatbit** Gs 110:12 f. I sat in the shade of my vines (Ginzā 555 n. 2); **bṭulalia rgigia iatbia** Morg. 256/3:3 they sit in pleasant shades; **ṭulalia ṭalala** Oxf. roll 138 = **ṭulalia ṭalalia** DC 43 J 63 sheltering shades; **uman ṭulalia abdilh̲** DC 22. 402 = **uman ṭlala abidlh̲** Gy 12:2 and who will give him shelter?; **ṭulala šibqit ʿlauaihun** DC 44. 592 and 616 I caused silence and gloom to come upon them.

ṭulala 2 = **ṭalula 2.** **d̲-mṭala** [*sic*] **ṭulala d̲-ianqa** DC 46 who plays childish games.

ṭulamta (טוּלְמְתָא, ܛܘܠܡܬܐ, Ar. loan-w. ظُلْمَة Fränkel 35, LS) loaf of bread MG 26: paen., 105:19. **bʿdai nisbit ṭulamta** Gs 101:5 f. I took a loaf of bread in my hand; **rmit . . . ṭulamta ʿl sibla** Gs 101:7 s. **sibla.**

ṭulanita (טְלָנִיתָא, ܛܠܢܝܬܐ) shade, shadow, spectre, phantasm, phantom, a demon. Pl. **ṭulaniata** MG 20:3, 148:6. Varr.: sg. **ṭulanta,** pl. **ṭulanata, ṭuliniata** (MG 21:7 f.). **ṭulanita udahalta d̲-hšuka** DC 48 spectre and fearsome thing of the darkness, **ṭulanita** Oxf. roll g 963; **ṭulaniata** (var. **ṭuliniata**) **d̲-mhaška** Gy 277:23 obscuring (: deluding?) spectres; **ṭulaniata d̲-mkadba** Gy 365:4 deceiving spectres, **ṭulaniata d̲-zipa** Jb 264:4 id.; **ṭulaniata qaria napša hazin** [*sic*] **ṭulaniata ʿl mikdib ʿl šabta d̲-mia** DC 44. 1736 f. = Morg. 268/26:37 f. (he) calls up many spectres (the names of) these spectres (: demons) that are written on a scroll of gut-skin; **ṭulaniata dahalata d̲-hšuka**; Or. 332:2 fearsome shades of darkness; **ṭulaniata rurbata d̲-hšuka** DC 43 J 193 mighty spectres of darkness; **ṭulaniata rurbata d̲-hbila** DC 40. 604 = DC 26. 652.

ṭulma (rt. **ṬLM,** Ar. ظُلْم) oppression, injustice, fraudulent dealing, harshness MG 104:16. Pl. **ṭulmia.** Masc. **bṭulma** Gy 40:18 unjustly (fraudulently, by force); **husmia uṭulmia** DC 6 envyings and harsh judgements.

ṭulmana (adj. from **ṭulma**) oppressor. Pl. **ṭulmania. ṭulmania d̲-ṭalmia** Gy 215:22 oppressors that oppress.

ṭulpra DC 26. 681 f. read **ṭupra** as in DC 40. 649.

ṭum ŠQ 19:25 (= CP 240:15) = **tum** until.

ṭ(u)muš(i)ata pl. of **ṭamušata, ṭumušta,** MG 169:13. **niṭimšun tlata ṭum(u)šiata** Q 10:3 they shall submerge three times; **tlat ṭumušata** DC 34:404 three immersions.

ṭumia (טוּמְעָא (?), or **ṭum** (?)) Doubtf. **uṭumia d̲-bharulia zaua zaliltia** ŠQ 18:ult. (= CP 237:12).

ṭumir AM 199:5 a city in the climate of Mercury (not identified). Var. **ṭamir.**

ṬUN s. **ṬAN.**

ṭuna (טוּעֲנָא, ܛܥܢܐ) burden, load; fig. fruit MG 104:19. Usually masc. cf. s. **ṬAN**; exceptionally fem., cf. s. **KDR. ṭunaihun uṭulaihun** s. **ṭula**; **ṭuna d̲-huitbh̲** Gs 10:4 the burden which was on thee (?, refers to the body; Lidzb. *den Lehmrock, in dem du weiltest* Ginzā 430:34); **ṭanan ṭuna dakia, ʿlania ṭuna ṭainia, ṭinia bṭuna dakia** s. **ṬAN**; **kd̲ dara diqla ṭuna** Gs 10:18 f. when the palm-tree bears its fruit; **ʿlana mn ṭunh̲ baṣar** AM 175: penult. the tree loses its fruit; **asa bṭuna** ŠQ myrtle by the load; **ṭuna d̲-nišimta** ATŠ II no. 107 the burden of the soul; **briš ṭuna umaudala** DC 51. 112 at the first pregnancy and bringing forth.

ṭun(u)pia, ṭnupia (rt. **ṬNP,** cf. Syr. ܛܘܢܦܐ) uncleanness, pollution. **kulhun ṭ(u)nupia**

umkairuta Gy 18:6 f. all uncleanness and abomination; **uʿtparaq mn kul ṭunupia** DC 50. 9 and (he) was delivered from all uncleanness; **kulhun ṭnupia** DC 36 no. 232 (DC 6 **ṭanupia**).

ṬUS, ṬSS (טוס, ܛܣ, Ar. طاس, H. טוש) to fly, flutter, float MG 82:26.

Pe. Pf. **nišra ṭas mn ʿlana** Jb 136:2 the eagle flew away from the tree; **ṭas ʿlauaihun d̠-iahuṭaiia** Jb 141:9 he flew unto the Jews. Act. pt. **ṭaiis uazil** Gs 14:2 flying goeth away; **ṭaiis (d̠-ʿngaria)** s.v., **ṭaisa** Oxf. 71 a = CP 207:ult., ML 240:8; **ṭaisa uhadra** Gy 339:1 flying turneth about. Part. forms of derived stems: **miṭasasin** Gy 9:15 they fly, **mṭasistun** DC 51. 725, DC 40. 788 and ye cause them to fly away; **hdar umiṭis nišra** Jb 133:6 an eagle circles and flies about. Cf. JB p. 131 n. 3.

Der.: **ṭausa, ṭauasta.**

ṭus 1 (*Táavros* (?), cf. Reitzenstein: *Poimandres* 182, 188, Jb ii 81 n. 5) in **ṭus rba** Jb 75:9 the Great Thot (?, a supposed author of the Thora).

ṭus 2 (P. طوس) AM 203 a small town in Khorasan, BZ Ap. II.

ṭus 3 a var. of **ṭasu** Gs 85:3 (v. **ṭasa 2**).

ṬUP I, ṬPA II (טוף, ܛܦ, Ar. loan-w. طاف Fränkel 220, LS, H. צוף Ges.) to overflow, overwhelm, inundate, float.

Pe. Pf. **bṭupania mia laṭap** ML 13:5, 144:12, DC 51. 257, CP 119:6 in the water-floods they were not overwhelmed. Pt. from **ṬPA II** (q.v.). Gl. 11:5 f. **ṭupa** (*sic*, with pt. from ע״ע) احاط *saepire, circumdare* محيط شد.

Der.: **ṭaupia, ṭupania.**

ṬUP II s. **ṬPA I** impt. pe.

ṭupania (sg. טוֹפָנָא, ܛܘܦܢܐ, Ar. loan-w. طوفان Jeffrey 207, Fränkel 220) pl. floods MG 7:10, 22:21, 136:7. Var. **ṭupna. ṭupania mia** Gy 26:23, 126:10, 266:15, 18, 270:22, 271:15 f., 302:13, 309:6, etc., MG 309:13 = **ṭupania d̠-mia** Jb 90:9 f.

ṭupsa (טוּפְסָא, ܛܘܦܣܐ < *τύπος*) type, archetype, prototype, symbol, example, mould, shape, form, formula, exemplar, draft, original text MG xxx 4 f. Pl. **ṭupsia. ṭupsia** Oxf. roll g 1041, 1057; **tmania ṭupsia** DC 33 eight types; **šauinin šuba ṭupsia** ATŠ II no. 189 we made seven archetypes; **ansa mn šuba ṭupsia** DC 3 coloph. he copied it from seven exemplars; **šuba ṭupsia** Or. 333:8 seven formulae; **ansa mn šabta uṭupsa d̠-** DC 27 coloph. (he) copied from the scroll and original text of . . .; **uṭupsan dilan hu** ATŠ II no. 190 and it is our symbol; **hazin** [*sic*] **šuba ṭupsia šuba malkia** ibid. these seven archetypes are seven kings.

ṭupra (טוּפְרָא and טְפָרָא, ܛܘܦܪܐ [?] and ܛܦܪܐ, Ar. ظفر, Akk. *ṣupru, ṣuppāru*, H. צִפֹּרֶן, Ges. s. צפר III, LS) claw, nail, talon, hoof; fig. a small measure, a little bit. MG 18:9 f. Pl. **ṭupria. mn ṭupria d̠-bligraia ualma d̠-zimta d̠-brišai** DC 43 B 10 from my toe-nails unto the hair on my head; **ṭupra lʿngirta alaṣ** Q 42:24 s. **ALṢ; mn atutia ṭupraihun** CP 118:18 from beneath their talons; **mn qarnh̠ d̠-taura umn ṭupria** AM 92:5 some bull's horn and some of its hoof; **ṭupra d̠-bahima** s. **bahima; tlata zibnia ṭupria kd̠ lamṣia hailia trin ṭupria ukd̠ ṭupria ʿu had ṭupra kd̠ mašqiatlh̠** . . . Or. 333:11 . . . three times a dose, or if he is unable, two doses; and when thou administerest to him the doses, or one dose . . .; **ṭupria d̠-aria** AM the claws of a lion.

Gl. 107:4 **ṭpra** [*sic*] ضفر [*sic*] *unguis* ناخن.

ṭupša (rt. **ṬPŠ**) dirt, filth, uncleanness, grossness, fat, grease; inaccessibility, obduracy (?). **ṭupša d̠-apa** AM 125:12 the fat of a hyæna (?); **ubṭupša ʿṭapašian** s. **ṬPŠ; ṭupša ušuta** Gy 181:1 grease and verdigris; **ṭupša d̠-ʿudna** DC 51 obduracy (?) of ear; **mn ṭupsih̠ d̠-arqa** DC 34. 330 from his earthly grossness.

ṭupšana (ad. from **ṭupša**) dirty, filthy, gross, unclean. Pl. **ṭupšania** DC 22. 274 = **ṭupšanʿ** Gy 279:8 (= **ṭipšanʿ** Sh. 'Abd.'s copy).

ṭur, ṭura (טוּרָא, ܛܘܪܐ, Ar. طور, H. צוּר) (*a*) mount(ain), hill, range of mountains, (*b*) a place-name. MG 105:8. Pl. **ṭuria.** (*a*) **ṭura d̠-nura** DC 40. 793, **ṭura qal(a)ia** Jb 109:13 a burning hill, a volcano (?); **ṭura d̠-haška** Gy 302:1; **ṭura haška** Jb 87:3, 97:4, 176:3, 184:4, Gy 37:20; **ṭura ṭur haška** Jb 99:6, Gy 19:9, DC 48:214; **ṭura d̠-ṭur haška** Jb 208:3; **ṭura d̠-hšuka** Gy 368:4, Oxf. 29 a etc. (cf. Ginzā 21 n. 3); **ṭura rba** Gy 273:2; **ṭura d̠-parzla** Gs 17:5, MR 60, MSchr 218 f.; **ṭuria gziria** Gy 11:13, Q 53:24; **ṭura gzira** Gs 105:23 f. (s. **gzira** (*b*)); **ṭuria mnandia** Q 52:13; **ṭuria dakiia kasiia** Jb 253:10; **ṭuria raqdia** Gy 174:13; **ṭura ugabara** s. **gabara; ṭura napla** Gy 82:7; **ṭura d̠-iatur** Gy 265:12 (s. **iatur**); **ṭura d̠-dahba** Gy 390:12; **lṭur karimla silqit** CP 167:15, **ṭur kar(i)mla** Gy 113:1, **ṭura ṭur karmla** Gy 196:20 Mount Carmel; **krun ṭura rba d̠-bisra** Gy 126:8, 11, 127:10, 142:23 (s. **krun**); **karkum ṭura rba d̠-bisra** Gy 142:21 (s. **karkum**); **ṭur glala** Gs 114:5 (s. **glala 1**); **ṭuria d̠-ziua** Q 35:4, Gy 352:11; **ṭuria d̠-hala** RD 37, 39 (s. **hala 1**); **nadiun ṭuria uiardnia** PD 865 the mountains and the jordans moved; **ṭuria trin** Gy 308:21; **trin ṭuria dakiia** Gy 106:23, 321:23, 360:8; **trin ṭuria mitgababia** Gy 313:4 = Jb 195:13 (cf. **GBB** ethpa.); **mamlalun d̠-trin ṭuria** Morg. 269/28: 29, 33 talk about the two hills (cf. Jb. ii 189 n. 4) **binia ṭuria** Gs 71:23 f., Oxf. 32 a = Morg. 50:antep. CP 168:7; **binia trin ṭuria** between two hills; **ṭura d̠-sinai** s. **sinai; ṭura d̠-qardun** Gy 380:20 (Ararat) MG 424:8; **ṭura d̠-midai** (var. **madai**) HG 6 etc. (*often*) the Median hills. Gl. 35:13 **ṭura** اجبال *montes* كوه; 67:11 **ṭura** جبل *mons* كوه; 75:7 id.; (*b*) **ṭur** AM 204:6 (var. Ṣâb.'s copy **ṭura**) BZ Ap. II; **bṭur anašia lagaiia lpadakšar nimṭun** Gy 385:18 f. in T. (Lidzb. queries: Ṭūrān ?) the barbarians will obtain the rule.

ṭuraiia (ܛܘܪܝܐ) Gs 17:5, AM (very often) mountain tribes, mountaineers. Halévy REJ 22/1891 p. 308, GGA 1890 p. 399, BZ Ap. II.

ṭuraita (ܛܘܪܝܬܐ) (*a*) from the hills, from the heights, (*b*) from on high, celestial (?). (*a*) ʿu **ṭuraita nihuia** AM 195:10 (of a wind) if from the mountains; **bṭuraita** AM 235:2 in hill districts; (*b*) **ṭuraita lilit** DC 43 a sky (?) lilith; **humarta ṭuraita** DC 44. 940 a celestial amulet (?).

ṭuran AM (often) Ṭūrân BZ Ap. II.

ṭuraq Gy 383:1 an ancient Persian king.

ṭurša (rt. ṬRŠ) deafness. Var. **ṭruša** (s.v.). **bʿudna ḏ-iamina ḏ-tarmida ubnišimta ṭurša ʿṣṭarar** ATŠ I no. 178 and II no. 31 deafness appeared in the right ear of the priest and (affected) the soul.

ṭia occasional var. of ṭʿia. **ulšrara ulṭia** ATŠ II no. 45 (DC 6 **ulṭaiia**) about truth and about error.

ṭiaqia (Ar.-P. طاقيه (?)) balconies, cornices. **uliṭiaqia ḏ-ʿngaria** DC 40. 1054 and to the cornices of the roofs.

ṭib (طيب Yâqût *Geogr. Wörterb.* iii p. 566) the town of Ṭīb MMII 118, ML 60 n. 2, CP trs. 32 n. 2. **ṭib mata** Morg. 250/87:14 = Q 51:4, 12 = ML 60:6.

ṭiba 1 (rt. ṬBA I) drowning, submersion. **aula uṭiba uglala** Gy 385:22 injury, drowning, and hail; **mhita ḏ-ṭiba** ATŠ II no. 75 accident of drowning.

ṭiba 2 (טִבָּא, ܛܒܐ = ܕܒܐ cf. Ges. s. דִּבָּה calumny, Akk. *dabābu* to make intrigues) evil report, scandal, murmuring. **mn ṭiba dahil** AM 38:11 he will be fearful of scandal; **ṭiba utuqpa** AM 233:3 scandal and oppression; **uṭiba** (var. **ṭabia**) **nihuia upsida banašia nihuia** AM 223:9 and there will be murmuring and loss amongst people.

ṭibian Gy 383:18 an ancient Persian king. Var. **ṭabian** Lond. V.s. **iasdis.**

ṭibla (var. of **ṭabla**, q.v.). Pl. **ṭiblia. qamahia bṭibla** RD 35 (DAb **qimahia bṭibla**) he beats the drum; **ṭibla ṭarpan** RD 29 they beat the drum; **ṭibla gaṭina** RD 21 a small drum; **ṭiblia uambubia** Gy 60:5, 112:8, Gs 14:13; **ṭibla uzmara** Gy 219:26, **ṭiblia uzmaria** Gy 113:2, **ṭiblia uzmara urquda** AM 155:4; **šatin hamra bṭiblia uzmara** DAb, **bṭablia** (CE **bṭiblia**) **uzimuria** Jb 97:15; **talin ṭiblia bkadpaiun uzmara uambubia bpumaiun** Gy 225:4; **ṭiblia ukinar** Gy 225:2 drums and a harp.

ṭiuana (Nöld. ܛܥܘܢܐ) error MG 16:14, 136:7 (but a derivation from טְעוּנָא 'burden, suffering (?)' would be admissible). **zaina uṭiuana** AM 91:13.

ṭizana (etym. unknown; meaning corresponds to Syr. ܙܠܝܙܐ. Lidzb.'s derivation from טיזא *podex*, as well as his supposed meaning *schön, elegant* ZS 21 1924, p. 180 f., is doubtf.) impetuous, hot-headed, reckless, impulsive, adventurous, restless. Fem. **tizant(i)a.** Pl. masc. **ṭizania. šapira uṭizana umsasqla** AM 3:penult. handsome, impetuous, and keen-witted (?); **ṭizana uharipa hauia** AM 20:16 he will be impulsive and hasty; **mn anašia ṭizania nišqal** AM 26:5 he will avoid (?) reckless folk; **luat anašia ṭizanh̲ tišqal** AM 70, 17 id. fem.; **uṭizantia hauia bʿbidath̲** AM 59:5 and she will be impetuous in her actions.

ṭizanuta (abstr. n. from **ṭizana**) impetuosity, recklessness, unsteadiness, high-handedness, impulsiveness, adventurousness. **umn ṭizanuth̲ mn mulia napil** AM 20:17 and owing to his rashness he will fall from a height; **bliluta uṭizanuta urabut ruha** Gy 215:19.

ṭiṭupta a var. of **ṭuṭipta.**

ṭiia occasional var. of ṭʿia MG 6:2.

ṭilism, a var. **ṭilsum** Ṣâb.'s AM talisman.

ṭimar (rt. ṬMR) AM hiding, concealment.

ṭimba s. **ṭinba.**

ṭina 1 (טִינָא, ܛܝܢܐ Ar. loan-w. طين Fränkel 8, from Akk. *ṭiṭ(ṭ)u* < *ṭiṭṭu* Zimmern & Haupt JBL 26:32, cf. Syr. doublet ܛܝܢܐ, H. טִיט LS, Ges.) clay, mud. **arqa ḏ-ṭina** RD B 30, **had arqa ḏ-ṭina** DC 36 one earth of clay; **ṣilamata ḏ-bnia ṭina** s. **BNA** pe. pass. pt.

ṭina 2, ṭinia (for **tina**) urine. **ṭinia ḏ-hiuaniata** Gy 224:8; **ṭaribin ṭinia** s. **tina.**

ṭinba (etym. unknown) prob. mourning, lamentation Jb ii 35 n. 4. **ananh̲ bṭinba** (F **bṭimba,** C **bṭamba**) **qahadran** Jb 29:11 and his spouses wander about in mourning (?); **uananh̲ bṭinba** (C **bṭimba**) **qasagian** Jb 31:9 and his spouses are walking with lamentation (?); **iušamin ḏ-ananh̲ bṭinba iatban** RD B 8 Y. whose spouses sit in mourning.

ṭiʿam (Ar. طعام) AM 257:25, 262 food.

ṭiʿia Q 9:22 etc. a var. of ṭʿia MG. 6:2.

ṭipa (cf. **ṭipia**) only in **mn duk ṭipa ḏ-alma** Gy 180:13 doubtf. Ginzā 184 n. 1. Perh. from a place adjacent to (?) the world.

ṭipalia RD 41 = **ṭapalia.**

ṭipia (rt. ṬPA, cf. Syr. ܛܦܐ side) perh. interior, adjunct, rooms round the courtyard of a house. **bṭipia ḏ-darth̲** AM 256:39 in the adjoining rooms (?) of his house.

ṭipšanʿ s. **ṭupšana.**

ṭira AM 10, DC 44. 564 for **ṭura** (?).

ṭiriana PD 1134 etc. a var. of **ṭariana.**

ṭirma, ṭirmia (P. تيرماه) name of the first summer month. **biahra ḏ-ṭirma** ATŠ II no. 196 in the month of *tīr-māh*; **mn qudam ṭirmia btrin iumia** HG two days before (the month) *tīrmāh*, **sulita ḏ-ṭirma** ATŠ II no. 196 the purification of (the month) *tīrmāh.*

ṭirpa = **aṭirpa.** Pl. **ṭirpia.** Used often with fig. meanings. **ṭirpia ḏ-kitana** DC 46. 210:3 strips of linen; **bṭirpia anhiraihun** Morg. 260/11:3 in the wings of their nostrils; **ṭirpia** DC 22.3 a var. of **aṭirpia** Gy 4:7 leaves.

ṭirqa (cf. טַרְקָא) disturbance, trouble, confusion, upset, annoyance, agitation. **šigša uṭirqa litbh̲** Gy 7:18 without confusion or trouble. **mn anašath̲ ṭirqa mšauia** CS 26 = AM 12:15 trouble will be made by his family (var. AM *ridpa*).

ṭišia, ṭiša (טִישָׁא, ܛܘܫܝܐ) secrecy. **bṭišia** Gy 228:11 (DC 22. 222 **bṭiša**) in secret, secretly.

ṬLA I (טְלִי) to remove, lift up. Only part. forms. Pa. pass. **šrian umṭalan** P.A. xii (they are) loosed and removed. Ethpe. **nišrun**

umiṭlia DC 44 they shall fall away and be removed.

ṬLA II (Ar. طلى) to anoint, smear.

AF. Impt. with suff. **aṭlih̲** AM 128:9 smear it on him.

ṭlaba (rt. ṬLB) asking, seeking, search. **ṭlaba d̲-haša** s. **haša**; **ṭlaba d̲-ʿilim** AM 163:12 the search (: pursuit) of knowledge.

ṭlala (טְלָלָא, ܛܶܠܳܠܳܐ) roof, shade, covering. MG 115:2. Varr. **ṭulala 1. aṭlala.** Pl. **ṭlalia. baita d̲-laṭlala** Gy 216:16 f. a house without a roof; **laṭlala** Gy 67:ult. for the roof; **masiqta ṭlala d̲-hikla** hᶜ DC 34. 1328 the *m.* is the temple's roof; **daiua d̲-iatib bṭlalia** DC 43 J 71 demon that sits in the shades (or 'roofs'); **aqra d̲-ṭlalh̲ npal** Jb 54:9 f. a fortress the roof of which fell; **ṭlalia d̲-narzubia** Oxf. roll 154, 169, DC 43 J 71 roofs with roof-gutters.

ṭlapia (sg. ܛܠܦܐ, eyelid, eyelash Macl.) pl. eyelids, eyelashes, slit (?). **ainaihun . . . damia lṭlapia** AM 200. Originally **ṣlapia**? see AM p.122 n. 3.

ṭlaq malka DC 46. 138:19 an angel.

ṬLB (Ar. طلب) to demand, request, seek MG xxxiii:22.

PE. Pf. **ṭilbit** Par. xiv no. 80 = ATŠ I no. 42 I sought. Act. pt. **ṭalib mn hak dukta** AM 156:2 he seeks (to move?) from that place. Part. pres. **hašta qiṭalibna mn hiia** DC 51: coloph. Now I require from the Life.

Gl. 18:5 **aṭlb** [*sic*] استدعى *postulare* خواست; 92:5 f. id. سأل *mendicare* خواست; 108:11 id. طلب *rogare, deprecari* رازى كرد [sic].

DER.: **ṭalba, ṭlaba.**

ṬLL I (טְלַל I, ܛܰܠܶܠ H. צלל III, Ar. ظلّ to overshadow, shelter. Akk. pi. *ṣullulu* to make a roofing Ges.) to cover, overshadow.

PA. Pf. with encl. **uṭalabh̲** [*sic*] **ṭalula balma hazin d̲-hšuka** DC 51 and covered this world of darkness with a roof. Pt. (pass.) **mṭalal bnikla** Gy 216:1 is covered with trickery; pl. **mṭalalia umbaṭlia** RD C 12 (are) covered and made void.

Gl. 109:5 f. miswritten ظلل *obumbrare* سايه كرد.

DER.: **ṭalula 1, ṭula, ṭulala 1, ṭlala, ṭulan(i)-ta, bit mṭalalia.**

ṬLL II (טְלַל II) to play, sport, enjoy (?), make merry, refresh (?).

PA. Pf. with suff. **ṭalalbun** ATŠ I no. 248 they sported with them. Pt. **qaiim umṭalil kd̲ nuna biama** JRAS 1938 3:3 rising and playing like a fish in the sea; **miṭalal uligal mitapa** AM 136:15 he will be refreshed (?) and will quickly recover; pl. **gahkia umiṭalalia** Gy 146:3 they laugh and make fun; **miṭallia ulakainia** Gy 129:15 they sported and did not keep still, **iardnia miṭalalia** Lond. roll A 351, CP 340:16, DC 42 the jordans sport, **šatin umṭalalia** DAb they drink and make merry; **mṭalalia uraqdia** DC 34. 882 etc.

ETHPA. formally not distinguished from pa. (cf. examples with pass. mean.).

Gl. 79:1 f. **ṭall** [*sic*] زمر *canere* نى ميساخت.

DER.: **ṭalula 2.**

ṬLL III (cf. Ar. طلّ على) to overlook (bewitch). In magic text; cf. **mṭalal** DC 46. 155:6 bewitched.

ṬLM (טְלַם, ܛܠܰܡ, Ar. ظلم) to oppress, treat with injustice or hardly.

PE. Pf. **latiṭilmun mika** Gy 40:16 oppress not the meek.

DER.: **ṭulma, ṭulmania.**

ṬMA (Aram. and H. טמא, Syr. ܛܡܐ, Ar. طَمِىَ to be unclean, impure) the rt. of **ṭamiata** (?).

ṭmura (rt. ṬMR) stopped-up MG 118:13. Pl. **ṭmuria. ṭruša ṭmura** Gs 2:14, 22 deaf (and) obdurate Ginzā 425 n. 1; **ṭrušia ṭmuria** Gy 279:10 CD, Leid., DC 22 and Sh. 'Abd.'s copy (Pet. **ṭrisia ṭmiria**) id. pl. (as a quality of demons).

ṭmušiata (cf. s. **ṭamušata** and **ṭumušiata**) immersions, submersions MG 119:12, 169:13. **tlat ṭmušiata** Q 20:22, ATŠ II no. 400 etc.

ṭmima (ܛܡܺܝܡܳܐ) closed-up, stopped-up, thick, obdurate, insensible; **bᶜuṣṭuna ṭmima d̲-ziua bgauh̲ lanahar** DC 34 like an obdurate body in which no light shineth; **nahrauata ṭmimia** DC 43 J 91, Oxf. roll 198 dammed rivers.

ṬMM (Aram. and H. טמם, Syr. ܛܰܡ, Ar. طمّ, Akk. *ṭummumu* obdurate, deaf) to fill up, stop, complete, dam, close up, set right, amend.

PE. Pf. with suff. **ṭamuia** Jb 126:1 f. they closed it up, MG 277:29. Impf. **niṭimh̲** Gy 87:13 stoppeth it up MG 275:23. Act. pt. **hu kulhun nangria umiṣria lqudam napaqa ṭamim** ATŠ II no. 344 it stoppeth up all the pits and (openeth ?) all boundaries before the departed. Pass. pt. **tmima** (s.v.).

PA. Pt. **mṭamam** (var. **mṭamar**) **nangria** ATŠ II no. 110 stoppeth up the pits; pl. **nangria mṭamamia** Jb 87:1 (C **amiṭamamia**) the pits are stopped up; **lamṭamamia** Jb 81:2 (C **lamiṭa-**), **nangria miṭamamin** Jb 89:6 (E **-ia**, B **mṭamamia**, D **mṭamimia**), **lamiṭamamin** Jb 89:8 (DE **-ia**, B **lamṭam-**, AC **lamṭamin**), **hṭimia mṭamamia** Morg. 260/12:33 = DC 44. 468 they are hemmed in, closed in.

AF. Pf. with suff. **aṭmun** DC 35 they closed me in.

ETHPA. Pf. **ᶜṭamam** Gy 97:13 was stopped up MG 212:22.

DER.: **ṭamaia, ṭmima.**

ṬMR (טְמַר, ܛܡܰܪ, H. טמן, Ar. طمر, Akk. *ṭamāru*) to bury, cover with earth or water, hide by covering, conceal, protect, guard, preserve.

PE. Act. pt. **qaduš qaduš kiṭamar** DC 44 Holy, Holy, who preserves. Part. pres. **ṭamranin** Jb 129:7, **ṭamranun** Jb 129:8 I (fem.) preserve them (l. 7 fem., l. 8 masc.). Pass. pt. **zria unṭir uṭmir** Q 31:22 sown (?, read **zriz** armed), guarded and protected; **usqubra ṭmira hua** ATŠ and there came into being a covered-in cavity (?), (often as a var. of **ṭmura**).

PA. (doubtf.): Pt. **mṭamar nangria** ATŠ II no. 110 (DC 6) a var. of **mṭamam nangria** DC 36 ibid.

ETHPE. Impf. pl. (with a part. ending) **niṭmaria** DC 44 (are) concealed.

Ethpa. (doubtf.): Pf. ʿṭamar DC 22. 92 a var. of ʿṭamam Gy 97:13.

Der.: **ṭmura.**

ṬMŠ (טמש, ܛܡܫ LS) to dip oneself, or something, to souse, immerse, submerge.

Pe. Pf. **ṭmaš ʿḏh̠** Gy 94:25 he immersed his hand(s), **ṭmaš tlata ṭmušiata** CP 45:5, Q 20:22 he submerged three times; with suff. **bmia ṭmašth̠** Gy 206:15 I dipped him in water. Impf. **nahit liardna uniṭmaš** DC 42 he shall descend to the jordan and immerse himself; **niṭimšun tlata ṭmušiata** CP 24:20 f., Q 10:3 = ML 27:2 they shall submerge three times. Impf. **bmia ṭmuš** Gy 211:17 dip in water; with suff. Q 20:25 **ṭumših̠** dip him; ATŠ no. 178 **ṭumšiun** souse (pl.); no. 181 **ṭumšuih̠** souse it. Act. pt. **ṭamiš tlat ṭmušiata** DC 27. 107, DC 50. 276 (he) plunges in three times. Pass. pt. **kḏ ṭmiš** DC 27 when it had been soused; **ṭmišia** (pl.) dipped DC 43 U 100; **kḏ ṭamušata qadmaita ṭmiš** DC 34. 391 when the first submersion has taken place.

Der.: **ṭamušata, ṭumušta** (pl. **ṭumušiata** and varr.).

ṬNA = **ṬNP** (by omission of the last rad.).

Ethpa.: Pf. **laʿṭanatun** DC 51. 67 ye were not polluted.

ṭnupia (rt. **ṬNP**) uncleanness, defilement, pollution MG 147:5. Varr. **aṭnupia, ṭun(u)pia, ṭanupia. ṭnupia umkariuta** s. **ṭu-**; **ṭnupia udaštana** PD 925 f. = **aṭnupia ud-** Jb 96:1 uncleanness and menstruation; **latirmia napšak bṭnupia** Gy 214:12 cast not thyself into (ritual) uncleanness; **mṭanap ṭnupia kḏ ganiba** ATŠ I no. 181, II no. 32 (s. **ganiba**); **ḏ-mn ṭnupia ḏ-bnia hšuka šikbat** ATŠ I no. 163 who (fem.) lay down (: died) with the pollution of children of darkness.

ṬNN (טנן, ܛܢ, Ar. ظن) to suspect, suppose, think, hesitate. Only in Gl. 90:9 f. miswritten as לי׳ר; شك داشت *hesitare* شك; 108: 7 f. id. but with a double n ظنّ *putare* فكر كرد.

Der.: **ṭana** (?).

ṬNP (טנף, ܛܢܦ, Ar. طنف, H. pi. טנף, Akk. *ṭunnupu* pi.) to be unclean, polluted, in a state of ritual impurity; pa. to defile, pollute.

Pa. Pf. **ṭanpat mia taqnia** Jb 87:7 she polluted the pure water. Pt. **mṭanap** AM 200, Gy 6:22, PD 1099, 1101, 1170 etc. (often in ATŠ) (is) polluted, fem. **mṭanpa** PD 789, **mṭanpa ulamkauna** Jb 87:3 f., 88:9 ff., PD 1024 f., 1039 (she) is polluted and not made whole (opp. to **mšalman** Jb II 90 n. 5); fem. st. emph. **ʿu mazruta mṭanapta** DC 34. 88 if the seed be polluted; pl. **razia mṭanpia** PD 836 defiling mysteries; **iumia d-mṭanpia** ATŠ II no. 12 defiling days; fem. pl. **ʿnšia ḏ-mṭanpan** RD C 10 women that are polluted; with encl. pers. pron. **mṭanpinʿn** Gy 224:6 we are polluted MG 233:1.

Ethpa. Pf. **ʿṭanpat** PD 1473, DC 36 no. 163 she was polluted, **la ʿṭanaptun** DC 51. 720 ye were not polluted.

Der.: **(m)ṭanputa, ṭ(u)nupia** (and varr.).

ṬSS = **ṬUS.**

ṭʿia (ܛܘܥܝܐ) error, going astray. Varr. **ṭi(i)a, ṭaia, ṭiʿia.** MG 6:1 f., 102:anteantep. **šrara ḏ-ṭʿia litbh̠** Jb 174:8 truth in which there is no mistake; **mn ṭʿia lišrara** from error to truth.

ṬƐM (Ar. طعم) an exceptional late doublet of original Mand. **ṬAM.** As af.: **atɛimu** AM 129:5 and made him taste.

Der.: **ṭaɛam**, var. **ṭiɛam.**

ṬPA I, TPA, YṬP (טפי, טפא, ܛܦܐ to add, to join, heap up) to add, enhance, attach, join, increase, exceed, preponderate, envelop, enwrap, close about; to join oneself to, lay near, include amongst, admit into, shelter oneself.

Pe. Pf. **nhura ṭpa** Gs 48:18 f. the light increased, **(miṭpa) ṭpa** Gy 318:3 (greatly) increased, **(miṭpa) ṭpit** Gy 324:11, Gs 50:18 thou hast gained (greatly); **ṭpainia bziua ḏ-rurbia** CP 366:2 we were enveloped in the radiance of the Mighty (Life). Impt. **ṭup** (as from ע״י: **ṬUP II**) **ziua** DC 34. 493 increase light; pl. **(miṭpia**, var. **miṭpa) ṭpun** Gs 90:23 increase. Act. pt. **hu ṭapia uhu bașar** Gy 231:7 he increases and diminishes; **laṭapia** Gy 379:2 does not exceed; **ṭapia** PD 1513 (l. 1506 **tapia**), **ʿu had minaihun ṭapia** ATŠ II no. 25 if one of them exceeds (: preponderates); **ʿu mn halin kulhun ṭapia** ATŠ I no. 217 of all these, should one be in excess; **haila hauilh̠ lhad arbin ṭapia** ATŠ II no. 85 he will have strength increasing fortyfold; **ṭapia lhad trin** ATŠ I no. 241 (they) increase twofold; **ʿu ṭapia razia ḏ-ruha lnišimta** DC 27 if the mysteries of the spirit preponderate over the soul; with encl. **ṭapilh̠ ziua** ATŠ II no. 164 its glory increaseth; with special pl. ending: **minuna ṭapin** AM (they have) money in superfluity; **basran ulaṭapin** AM lacking and not abounding. Inf. **miṭp(i)a** Gy 324:11, Gs 50:18, 90:23 etc., MG 260:16.

Af. Pf. **aṭpia** Jb 100:6 he joined (? Lidzb.: *man bekleidet ihn*); with encl. **aṭpilh̠ ʿl ḏ-ʿtlh̠** Gy 72:16 he added to him to what he had; **aṭpilh̠ bziua** Gy 131:3 he added to his light (MG 260:28 f.); **aṭpilak ziua ʿl ziua uaṭpilak nhura ʿl nhura** Gy 270:14 f. I added brilliance to thy brilliance and (I added) light to thy light; **aṭpilak hukumta ʿl hukumtak** Gy 270: 17 I have added wisdom to thy wisdom. Impf. **unaṭpia mn ʿușrh̠ ma hu ḏ-baiia** ATŠ II no. 356 and he adds from his own mind whatever he wishes (to add). Impt. **uaṭpia lhušbanak** AM 136:7 and add (it) to thy reckoning; with suff. **uaṭpinun hdadia** AM 260:34 and add them together. Pt. **maṭpia** Jb 100 n. 12 a var. of **aṭpia** (pf.), **maṭpia nașiruta** ATŠ II no. 349 the *nașiruta* is enhanced. Part. pres. with encl. **maṭpinabh̠ bṭarṭabuna kasia** Morg. 265/21:36 I swathe myself in a secret covering.

ṬPA II (טפא rel. to **ṬUP I**) to float, inundate, spread over.

Pe. Pf. **ṭpainin bziua ḏ-rurbia** DC 50. 513 = **ṭpainia** etc. DC 42. 710 f., DC 3. 238:9 we floated in (or 'were inundated by') the glory of the Great (Life). Act. pt. **mia hiia . . . ṭapin** DC 3 and 53 = CP 435:9 the living waters . . . spread.

ṬPA III (rel. to **ṬBA II**) to cook, boil, seethe.

Pe. Act. pt. pl. **dudia ṭapin** DC 43 J 119 cauldrons seethe.

ṬPŠ (Syr. and Chr. Pal. ܛܦܫ, Ar. طَفِسَ to be dirty, H. and Jew.-Aram. טפשׁ to grow dull, Akk. *ṭapāṣu* to be fat) to be dirty, unclean, fat, gross, unfit-to-be-touched, inaccessible, obdurate.

Ethpa. Pf. **bṭupša ʿṭapašian** ATŠ I no. 239 (var. **ʿṭabašian** DC 6 ibid.) they (fem) were in a state of uncleanness.

Der.: **ṭupša, ṭupšana.**

ṬRA (טְרָא = טְרֵי, ܛܪܐ, Ar. طَرَا) to push, drive, strike against, hit, beat, beat down, strike down, batter, buffet, assail, beat back, repel, rebut, rebuff, dash back, toss back from, fling back, toss off, shake off, jerk off, take off, throw (down), cast, drive off; to set, cast on, drop on, drip on, sprinkle, settle on.

Pe. Pf. (with a prosth. **a**: **aṭra, aṭriat** v.s. af.); **mia siauia . . . ṭrun bšuria** Gy 163:22 the black waters . . . dashed against the walls; with encl. **btuqnẖ ṭribẖ rušuma** Gy 349:14 (var. **ṭrabẖ** DC 22. 345) I set a sign on its brightness (or 'a sign was set'?); **nura ṭrabẖ rušumai** Jb 276:8 (read **ṭribẖ**, II 244 n. 3) I set my sign on the fire (?); **ṭribẖ** and **ṭritibẖ** Q 8:22 I set on it; **ṭrilẖ** Gs 3:3 he dripped (Lidzb. *spritzte*) on it; with suff. **ṭiriuk miṭria** JRAS 1937 593:14 rains beat thee down. Impf. **niṭria** (identical with ethpe. q.v.); with encl. **latiṭribẖ** DC 37 do not batter (: strike at) him. Impt. fem. **ṭrai** (var. **ṭarai**) **burkik** Morg. 258/8:10 (var. DC 44. 465 f.) bend down (: fall on) thy knees. Act. pt. **bita ḏ-ṭaria bglala** DC 40. 46 an egg that is tapped (read **ṭria** pass. pt.) against a stone; pl. **mn zmaihun banpaiun ṭarin** Gy 23:20 they bespatter their faces with (some of) their blood; **zmaiun ṭarin** Gy 45:22, **zma . . . umia nasbia ubanpaihun ṭarin** Gy 224:12; with encl. **uṭarilun minẖ mn aṭaria** Jb 155:9 (s. **aṭaria**), **ṭaribun** Sh. 'Abd.'s copy's var. of **ṭaribin** Gy 224:8 they spatter on themselves (: besprinkle themselves). Inf. **miṭra 2** (s.v.)

Af. Pf. **aṭra upra** Jb 133:2, 14 drove and flew away (af. only formal ii 131 n. 1); **ʿzlat uaṭriat brqiha** DC 41. 520 she (: the soul) went and took off (: flew off) into the air; with suff. **aṭrunun minai** Jb 134:5 they drove them away from me.

Ethpe. Pf. with encl. **d-ʿṭribia ʿghip** ML 23, CP 21:10 who dashed against me was shattered (varr. s. **GHP**). Impf. **niṭria** AM 26:5 will be driven off; **tišqal utiṭria** AM 70:18 she will evade and be repelled; **niṭrun unitazihun minai** Q 17:3 they shall be driven off and flee from me; **niṭrun minẖ** ML 37:7 they shall be driven away from him. Pt. **miṭria kḏ bita** DC 40. 96 they are battered like an egg; with encl. **rušuma ḏ-šdum lamiṭribẖ** ATŠ II no. 303 the sign of Š. shall not be cast on him.

Ethpa. Pt. **miṭarin binia mai umai** Gy 284:19 they are tossed about between water and water, with encl. **miṭaribẖ** Jb 177:8 they shall be thrown in it.

Gl. 164:9 f. **aṭra** نجس *violare, coinquinare* نجس شد.

Der.: **miṭra 2.**

ṬRB (Ar. طرب) to play a musical instrument, strike (cf. **ṬRA** with encl. **b-**).

Pe. Act. pt. **ṭarib** AM 162:9 (substantivally) musician; but **ṭaribin** Gy 224:8 read **-bun** s. **ṬRA** pe. act. pt. with encl. (**ṭraba biama** DC 26. 610 read **ṭaba . . .** [he] drowned in the sea). Gl. 65:13 f. **aṭrab** حسّا [sic] *palpere* حس كرد; 152:3 f. **aṭrb** [sic] مسس *tetigere* دست ماليد.

ṬRD (טְרַד, ܛܪܕ, H. טָרַד, Ar. طرد, Akk. *ṭarādu*) to drive out, or away, banish, dismiss.

Pe.: Impt. **ṭrud** Or. 325:2 (text), **aṭrud** DC 43 D 70 drive out. Pass. pt. pl. (with a prosth. **a**) **mn kul hilmia uhizuania aṭridia** DC 43 D 72 they are banished from all (his) dreams and visions. Part. pres. **ṭardit umapqit** Or. 327:16 thou drivest out and expellest.

Gl. (always with doubtf. and worthless vocalization): 80:5 f. رذل *reprobare, respuere, abominari* رد كرد; 82:5 f. رفض *spernere* رد كرد; 108:3 f. **ṭrudẖ** [sic] طرد *persequentem pati* راند; 165:3 f. نهر *increpare* آزرده شد.

ṭrunga (ܛܪܘܢܓܐ < P. تُرُنج, أُتْرُنْج) citreous fruit, citron, citron-tree, ethrog, orange-tree. Pl. **ṭrungiata. ṭrunga hu** DC 41 it is a citron-tree; **bṭulh ḏ-ṭrungiata** DC 3 in the shade of citron-trees.

ṭruša (ܛܪܘܫܐ < Ar. أُطْرُوش) deaf MG 118:12. Pl. **ṭrušia. algia ṭrušia** Jb 98:8 dumb (and) deaf; **(a)ṭrušia ugirbania** Jb 193:8 f. deaf and lepers; **uṭruša** (var. **-ia**) **btartin ʿudnia** ATŠ II no. 39 and deaf(ness) in both ears; **br adam ṭrusa** DC 27. 184 son of A.-the-Deaf. Gl. 32:12 **ṭruša** اصم *surdus* كر.

ṬRṬL (dissimil. of טַלְטֵל) to throw away, cast out or forth, dismiss, spurn, reject, repel MG 55:2, 84:21, Ginzā 428 n. 10. Fundamental stem: pf. with suff. **ṭarṭiltinun** Gs 63:9, **ʿṭarṭiltinun** Gs 62:15 I rejected them MG 283:3 f. Impf. with suff. **ʿṭarṭlẖ** Gs 44:4 I will reject it MG 276:8; **tiṭarṭlia** DC 45 she shall repel him, **niṭarṭilunẖ** Gs 8:4 they spurn him MG 278:17. Refl. stem: impf. **niṭarṭalun mn markabatun** DC 26:113 f. they shall be hurtled from their chariots.

ṬRṬP (parpel of **ṬRP** q.v.) to smite, buffet. Fundamental stem: impt. **ṭarṭip** DC 26:56 strike. Refl. stem: pf. **ṭarṭap unpal** DC 26:172 they were smitten down and fell.

ṭripa (pass. pt. of **ṬRP**) mutilated, torn-off, disfigured. Fem. pl. st. abs. **ṭripan. ṭripan umbaṣra ṣbata ḏ-kraiia** AM 14:13; **uptiian kraiiẖ uṭripan** AM 40:4; **ukraiẖ ʿrikan uṭripan** AM 103:8 f.

ṬRS for **ṬRṢ** (frequent in mod. texts).

ṬRP (Aram. and H. טרף, Syr. ܛܪܦ, Ar. طرف) to tear (off), beat (about), buffet, smite, clap (hands).

Pe. Pf. **ṭrap ʿlauaihun ḏ-šuria** Gy 163:23 (the waves) beat against the walls; with encl. **ṭrapilẖ** DC 43 A 84 they (?) smote him. Impf. **niṭrup aṣaṣia** DC 40.124 he shall dash against stones; with encl. **uniṭripilẖ bit anpia** DC 43 A 80 and shall smite him on his face. Act. pt. **ṭarip ʿdẖ** Gy 59:6 he claps his hands; fem. **ʿdẖ lrišẖ ṭarpa** Gy 166:10 she beats her head with her hand; pl. fem. **ṭibla ṭarpan** RD 29 (s. **ṭibla**).

Pa. Impf. with encl. **niṭaripbun bganpa** Gy 101:11 he may strike out with his arm(s).

Parp. **ṬRṬL** s.v.

Ethpe. Pt. **miṭirpia kḏ didbia** DC 36 no. 238 they are smitten down like flies.

Ethpa. Pf. **ʿṭarap** Gy 166:16 were buffeted. Pt. **rmia umiṭarap libẖ** Gy 294:11 his heart was cast down and agitated; pl. **miṭarpia ganpai(h)un** Gy 188:16 their wings are affected; **ʿl hdadia miṭarpia** Gy 177:14 are dashed against each other; **miṭarpia unaplia** Gy 228:16 are smitten down and fall.

Der.: **(a)ṭirpa, aṭirpan** (var. **-ṭa-**), **ṭripa.**

ṬRQ (טְרַק) to mix, stir, shake, agitate, shake up, stir up (or together).

Pe. Pt. pl. **daštana ḏ-zanita ptulta bhamra ṭarqin** Gy 226:3 they mix the menstrual blood of an adulterous virgin with wine (but **uṭariq mitaška** AM 138:ult. = **ḏ-ariq m-** he who escapes shall be found).

Der.: **ṭirqa, maṭraqa.**

ṬRŠ (טְרַשׁ, ࡈࡓࡔ, Ar. طرش LS) to be(come) deaf, hard of hearing; pa. to stop up, deafen, make deaf; id. to scatter, disperse (?).

Pa. Pf. with suff. **ṭarištinin lʿudnẖ** Gy 145:8 I stopped up (Nöld. *ich verklebte sie* MG 282:28) her ears; **ṭarištinun ukabištinun** DC 26. 614 I silenced them and crushed them underfoot. Impf. with suff. **niṭaršunan** they make me deaf MG 273:2, **tiṭaršinun lʿudnaihun** DC 44. 1035 she stops their ears. Impt. **ṭariš ʿudnẖ** DC 44. 1035 deafen his ear(s); with suff. **ṭaršinin** stop them (fem.: ears) up MG 282:11. Pass. pt. **mṭaraš pumẖ ulišanẖ** Morg. 270/30:35 = DC 44. 2013 choked are his mouth and his tongue; pl. **mṭaršia ʿudnia** Or. 328:6, **mṭarš(i)a ʿudnaihun** Gy 180:8 deafened are their ears.

Ethpa. Impf. **sanai ubildbabai niṭaršun** (var. **niṭiršun** would be ethpe.) DC 44 my enemy and my foe shall be dispersed (?).

Irreg.: **ligṭinun ulʿsirinun ulʿṭaršinun** DC 44. 1898 = Morg. 269/29:9 I grasped them and bound them and deafened them.

ṬŠA (טְשָׁא = טְשֵׁי, ࡈࡔࡀ) to hide, conceal.

Ethpa. Pf. **ʿṭašia** Gy 160:16 he hid himself MG 263:22. Impt. **ʿṭašia** hide thyself MG 265:14.

Der.: **ṭiš(i)a.**

I(Y)

i the 10th letter of the alphabet. Pronunciation: either consonatal *y*, or semivocal *i*. Used as a vowel sign, called *aksa* MMII 242, 243 n. 2. Wavering between **i** and **a** (sometimes **u**) MG § 15 p. 13 f., before **r** as 3rd rad. MG § 17 p. 15:bottom. Phonetic changes: **i** > **u** (by labialization) MG § 19 pp. 18 f., initial **y**(i) ʿ MG § 55, **y** < **a** or ʿ as last rad. betw. two vowels MG § 63 pp. 69 f.; vocal **i** (e) < vocal **a** MG § 89 b p. 100.)

ia 1 (ࡉࡀ, Ar. يا) vocative particle: O, Oh! MG 80 f. (*Mundart* 65), AF 229. A rare var. **aia** s.v. **ia kšilia ḏ-ʿtkašal** Gy 186:4, **ia d-azlia bšuqia tibil** Gy 179:18, **ia dinanukt** Gy 211:ult., **ia ḏ-** (*often*) O ye who (cf. Ar. يَا أَيُّهَا) MG 457:15 ff. Gl. 187:ult. **ia** يا O!

ia 2 (prob. H. יָהּ) supern. being ML 280. **ia malka** Lond. roll A 349. **bia rba** Q 8:8, CP 20:9, ML 22:5. By the great Ya.

ia 3 (< P. يك) one, a (as indefinite article). Very frequent in mod. Mandaic. Pron.: *ye*. **ia hakaiia hlai** Morg. 278:5 I have a story (to tell). Sometimes used for 'once': **ia iikia ganaua hiua** (read **hua**) Morg. 283:1 once upon a time there was a thief, and even after **hda**, cf. **hualẖ trin taktiha hda ia gaiid bhuaiza uhda ia šatia ia rabiࡏ bmaškun** Zotb. 218b:15 f. he had two residences: one for summer (corruption of **gaiṭa**) in Howeiza, and one for winter (corruption of Ar. شتاء) and spring in M.

-ia 1 masc. pl. ending, sometimes also for **-in** of the st. abs. pl. MG 161 (and n. 1).

-ia 2 the possessive suff. of the 1st p. sg. in **lia** to me, and **dilia** I, me, mine (in other cases usually **-ai**), MG 88:6.

-ia 3 possessive and accusative suff. of the 3rd p. sg. masc. after the ending **u** (cf. **abuia** his father, **ligṭuia** they seized him) MG 88:7, 18.

YAA I (ࡉࡀࡀ, H. יָאָה, Ar. يَايَا, Aram. der. יָאֵי fair) to be or become goodly, fair, seemly, becoming, noble; to beseem, be becoming, seemly, fit.

Pe. Pf. **akalnin mn zidqak uiainin** DC 3. 273 (CP 406:3 **uhiainin**) we ate from thy bounty and were made worthy. Pt. **iaia 1**, **iaiia** v.s.v.

Pa. or **Af.** Impf. with encl. **utiaiilẖ** DC 40. 131 and thou wilt beautify him.

Der.: **iaia 1** (**iaiia** and varr.).

YAA II s. **YʿA.**

iab (contr. form of **ia ab** ࡉࡀ ࡀࡁ) Par. xiv no. 104, 112 O my father! MG 35:17, 481:antep.

iabaṭṭa (nom. act. pa. of **YBṬ**) capture MG 122:6.

iabuša, iabiša (יַבִּישָׁא, ܝܰܒܺܝܫܳܐ) dry. Fem. **iabištia** dry land. **qaruša uiabiša** AM 286:4 cold and dry. Gl. 178:6 **i(a)buša** يابس *aridus* خشك; 178:9 **iabuša** يبوسة *siccitas* خشكى.

iabla (ܝܰܒܠܳܐ) grass. **kḏ ṭala ḏ-pašra mn iabla** JRAS 1938 3:31 like dew which evaporates from grass.

iabša (rt. **YBŠ**) dryness, dry place, dry land. **kḏ nahra ḏ-mn pumḫ iabša qam** Jb 54:12 like a river in the mouth of which arose dry land.

iabraqiʿil, iabrʿil (in exorcisms) two genii.

iad st. abs. and cstr. of **ʿda** (q.v.). **ʿl iad** through, by means of, the handiwork of. **iad hdadia lgaṭ** Jb 136:10 f. they took one another by the hand; **biad rba nimṭia** AM 95:7 he will attain great authority(?); **biad mardia napil** AM 240:19 (he) will fall into the hands of rebels; **iad ʿumania** CP 223:9 the handiwork of craftsmen.

iada (act. pt. pe. of **YDA**) a knower, one who knows. **iadai** CP 178:3 = ML 217:5, 6 those who know me; **kulhun iadak** all who know thee MG 177:11 f. **hiia liadan** Gy 172:23 life to our knowers; **iada ḏ-nʿdan** Gs 51:ult. a knower that recognizeth me.

iadala (rt. **YDL**) child-bearing, birth. **iadala ubuṭna** Jb 104:2 child-bearing and pregnancy; **baṭinia uiadalia** s. **baṭin.**

iadalta 1 (nom. act. pa. of **YDL**) child-birth, progeny, children, offspring. Pl. **iadalata** AM 269:19, DC 43 J 195. **hauia iadalta lhalṣai** DC 44 there should be fertility in my loins.

iadalta 2 (nom. ag. fem. pe. of **YDL**) a child-bearing woman, woman in child-birth. **kḏ iadla iadalta** Gs 10:21 when a woman in child-birth bringeth forth.

iadata (rt. **YDA**) knowledge, information. Varr. **iaduta, iadita. iadata** (Pet. **iadita**) **uaprašata** DC 22. 206 = Gy 213:19 knowledge and understanding; **ʿngirta uiadata** Jb 207:3 letter and information.

iadatan Gy 127:13 a heavenly spirit forming a pair with **adatan** q.v. Often mentioned.

iaduia (ܝܳܕܽܘܥܳܐ) knower. MG 70:1, 113:25. Pl. **iaduiia. iaduia anat ḏ-ʿqara** Jb 29:5 thou art a Knower of Glory; **iaduia damia lbanaia sdira** Gy 214:21 the knower resembleth a methodical builder; **ia iaduiia ḏ-iaditun** JRAS 1937 591 O ye knowers who knew (*that* etc.).

iaduta s. **iadata.**

iadita (a var. of **iadata**) knowledge, information, news. MG 101:10. **iadita hu ukair hu** AM 253:18 it is news, it is good (hendiadys: it is good news); **bzahruta uiadita uhaqarta** DC 36 with care, knowledge, and research; **biaditak** Gy 11:17 with thy knowledge (i.e. with knowledge of thee); **ḏ-laiadita** Gy 279:11 without knowledge; **amar biaditak** Gy 11:17 say with thy knowledge; **biadita umadita** Gy 141:1 in knowledge and wisdom; **prišuta uiadita** Gy 2:19; **litlḫ iadita** Gy 42:23; **iadita uaprišta** Gy 213:19.

iaha (H. יָהּ) a supernatural being or deity ML 281. **iaha iaha** Q 8:14 = CP 20 ult. = ML 23:2; **iaha baha** DC 44.

iahaduta (abstr. n. from **iahud**) ML 211:2 Judaism. Varr. **iahduta, iahiduta.**

iahba (act. pt. st. emph. pe. of **YHB**) giver; jar, cruse. **iahbia hamra ḏ-mlia hamra** CP 178:14 = ML 218:4, cf. n. 2.

iahduta a var. of **iahaduta. naṣaruta qašiša mn iahduta** Gy 288:10 Naṣoraeism is older than Judaism.

iahu (יהוה?) a divine name, frequent in exorcisms, often repeated. **sam iahu** PD 833; **yahu mlaka** DC 40. 887 f.

iahuba (ܝܳܗܽܘܒܳܐ) giver MG 113:25. **iahuba ḏ-kulhin mahbata** Gy 62 and 4 giver of all gifts.

iahud(a) (H. יְהוּדָא, ܝܺܗܽܘܕ, Ar. يهود) Judæa, Jewry. **lau baita bnit biahud** Jb 77:9; **man damilak ldilak biahud tangaria lazabnia biahud** Jb 82:6 f.; **lahakimta audiltan biahud** Jb 117:3 f.; **hidutata bakian biahud** Jb 139:3 f.; **kukba ṣrabḫ biahud** Jb 69:12; **hilmia lika biahud** Jb 73:1 f.; **šlimun . . . malka iahud** Gy 27:9, 50:9 f.; **manda ḏ-hiia ʿtiglia biahud** (var. **biahuda**) Gy 178:2 (var. DC 22. 170); **hazin ʿurašlam ḏ-iahud hu** DC 7; **rabin uiahuda** Jb 75:4 Reuben (?) and Judas.

iahudalaʿil DC 43 D 17 f., var. **iahdilaʿil** DC 19 par. an angel.

iahuduta a doublet of **iahaduta, iah(i)duta. miriai ḏ-šamrat iahuduta** Jb 130:9 M. that has forsaken Judaism.

iahudiaiil DC 40. 875 (an angel list) name of an angel, personification of Jewry.

iahuṭaiia (ܝܺܗܽܘܛܳܝܶܐ transformed for the sake of allusion to **iahṭa** abortion, and **HṬA** to sin MG 43 n. 2) the Jews. MR 128:middle. **ama ḏ-iahuṭaiia** Gy 24:1, 45:17 f., 120:19 etc. the Jewish people; **br iahuṭaiia** Gy 226:1 a Jew MG 313:16 f.; **iahuṭaiia iahṭia unipṣia** Gy 231:5 Jews—abortions and excrements MG 320:11; **ʿurašlam . . . mdinta ḏ-iahuṭaiia** Gy 23:19 etc. (*often*); **mitiqrin iahuṭaiia d-hṭun** Gy 45:24 f. they are called Jews because they sinned; **iahuṭaiia bgluta napqin** Gy 29:20 the Jews will go into exile; **bit ama ḏ-iahuṭaiia** s. **bit 1** (compounds); **iurba ḏ-iahuṭaiia qarilḫ adunai** Gy 381:11; **abrahim abuhun ḏ-iahuṭaiia** Gy 381:16 f.; **iahuṭaiia ama biša** CP 379:13 = DC 3:250:8; **qulalia ḏ-iahuṭaiia** ATŠ II no 358 the snares of the Jews; **kḏ šahla mn ṣurta d-iahuṭaiia bmandaiuta mitlabaš** DC 34. 741 when it casts off the circle (: excluding ban) of the Jews, it is admitted (lit. clothed in) to Mandaism.

iahuṭuta (abstr. n. from **iahuṭaiia**, a doublet of **iahuduta**) Judaism. **mn iahuṭuta lmandaiuta** ATŠ II no. 198 from Judaism to Mandaism.

iahur Gy 182:11 keeper of a purgatory (together with **iur** and **arhum**).

iahṭa (ܝܰܚܛܳܐ) abortion, stillborn child MG 100:11. **iahuṭaiia iahṭa** s. **iahuṭaiia; iahtia unipṣia** ibid., also ATŠ I no. 258. Pl. often used of spirits of abortion: **iahṭia zikria uiahṭia nuqbata** DC 43 A 23 f., **iahṭia udaniš** DC 44. 1947 = Morg. 266/22:35; **ulaiahṭa ḏ-mn kras ʿmḫ npaq** Gy 8:19 f. and no abortion that left the mother's womb; **iahṭat iahṭa** DC 43 J 45 she brought forth an abortion.

iahṭaiia a shortened form of **iahuṭaiia** as a var. of **iahuṭuta. mn iahṭaiia lmandaiata** DC 6 a corruption of **mn iahuṭuṯẖ** ATŠ II (DC 36) no. 198.

iahṭuta = **iahuṭuta.**

iahṭita in **rušuma ḏ-iahṭiṭa** Bodl. 12 for **iah(u)ṭuta**?

iahib ʿda Gy 368:9 helper (lit. one who gives the hand).

iahia (Ar. يحيى) a man's *malwâša* name, used often together with the orig. Aram. form as **iahia iuhana**, John the Baptist Ginzā 213, HpGn 282, 284, Jeffrey 290, AF 241 n. 3. Var. **iihia** MG 13:middle. **iahia iuhana br šarat simat** Morg. 195:1; **iahia br zakaria** Gy 213:10, 218:23, PD 354 etc.

iahid (יְחִידָא, ܝܺܚܺܝܕܳܐ, H. יָחִיד, Ar. وحيد) sole, unique, single MG 124:5. **iahida rba zadiqa** Gy 249:17 f., 21.

iahiduta a var. of **iah(u)duta. man ḏ-napiq mn iahiduta lmandaiuta** ATŠ II no. 358; **bškinta ḏ-iahiduta iatib** ibid.

iahra (met. of יַרְחָא, ܝܰܗܪܳܐ) month MG 66:15. Var. **iihra** MG 13:middle. Formation MG 100:12. Pl. **iahr(ar)ia** MG 170:10. No. st. abs., in distributive repetitions: **iahra biahra** Gy 273:11 month by month MG 301:17 f. **riša ḏ-iahra** DC 43 and often, the beginning of the month; **hin sin ltupiana ḏ-iahra hauia** AM 265:6. v.s. **tupiana.**

iahšiʿil (in exorcisms) a supernatural being.

iaua ziua ML 71:3 for **iauar ziua.**

iauar (Nöld. from P. يار, ياور MG 418 n. 2. Prob. from **YUR**, CP trs. 252 n. 2 and index) an outstanding genie ML 281, MR 32:middle HpGn 41. With many epithets, mostly with **ziua. iauar rba** PD 33, 1140, Q 0:20, ML 28:5, 171:3, 230:3; **piria d-iauar ʿtita** Gy 322:4; **iauar ʿtita** Gy 291:35; **nbaṭ iauar** Gy 71:1; **iauar kasia** Gy 229:9; **taurʿil ḏ-hu iauar mitqria** Gy 295:11 f.; **iauar malka ḏ-ʿutria** Oxf. 62 b f., ML 232:7 ff., 239:10; **iauar (ziua) malka** ML 233:5, CP 203: 1; **šum iauar (ziua)** PD 351, inscription on a gold ring worn by the priest on the little finger (during the ritual) Siouffi 31, 76 n. 3, 123, MMII 35; **iauar ziua** Q 1: 9, 2:24, 6:24, 15:9, 20:9, 25:21, 31 f., 62:23, Jb 16: 22, Gy 375:2 etc. (very frequent); **dmut iauar ziua** Gy 360:10; **laupa ḏ-iauar** Q 51:20; **iauar kbar** Gy 135:9; **bit iauar ziua** Gy 375:1; **iauar manda ḏ-hiia** Gy 373:7, 18, Zotb. 218a:paen.; **iauar bhira** Oxf. 32 a; **iauar br iauar** Gy 166: 24; **qudam iauar zakuta litlan** Gy 310:1; **mana iauar smir** Gy 291:43; **iauar baraia** Q 6:25 = ML 18:6 read **aiar baraia** ML 18 n. 3 as in CP 16:16; **iauar ganziil** PD 731, **iauar ginziʿil** PD 1198, **iauar ganziʿil** PD 1123; **iauar ziua rba** Gy 321:24; **iauar qadmaia** Q 7:25, 29 = ML 21:6; **iauar malala** Gy 295:7; **malka iauar ganzʿil ʿutra** Morg. 5:7; **zakilẖ iauar ziua uadiaurẖ** Gy 125:15; **iauar usimathiia** RD B 100; **hibil ziua mn iauar abuia** RD 28e; **ab iauar** Q 34: 14 f. = ML 55:6, 91:4 f. my father Y.; **hibil ziua ḏ-iauar rba šumẖ** PD 837; **hanaṯẖ iauar ḏ-amritun ʿlẖ iauar nišimta** DC 34. 807.

iauma a spor. var. of **iuma** MG 22 n. 5.

iauna 1 (יוֹנָא, ܝܰܘܢܳܐ, H. יוֹנָה I Ges., LS) dove. Var. **iuna 1** MG 23:19. Formation MG 100:18. Fem. MG 156:15. **iauna hiuartia** Jb 233:5; **haila ḏ-iauna qalilta nsub** Gy 132:7; **iauna ḏ-paruanaiia** Oxf. roll f 133; **šadrẖ nu liauna** Gy 381:1 (cf. 8:8); **azlat iauna uaškatẖ lʿurba** Gy 381:3 f.; **gihpat iauna** s. **GHP**; **liauna birkẖ** Gy 381:8 he blessed the dove; **unusbẖ laha ṭaba ḏ-hu iauna** DC 41 and take the 'good brother', that is, the dove.

iauna 2 (possibly rel. to יָוֵן muddy) clay. Var. **iuna 2. arqa rabtia pt iauna** DC 37. 449 the great earth daughter of (solid) clay (slime); **arqa pt iauna** DC 43 I 89 ATŠ II no. 51 (*and often*) (var. **iuna** DC 6).

iaunaiia (ܝܰܘܢܳܝܶܐ) Greeks. Var. **iunaiia** (s.v.). **bit iaunaiia** AM 191:ult. the country of the Greeks, Greece; **biaunaiia** AM 286:24, according to the Greeks.

iaunaiit (ܝܰܘܢܳܐܺܝܬ) orig. Greek (adv.), but used with the meaning of 'skilfully', 'artistically'. MG 201:4. MR 54:antep. **arqa iaunaiit nitqiria** Gy 87:13 the earth is skilfully (Lidzb. *griechisch kunstvoll*) created; **masia arqa iaunaiit** Gy 127:4 f. he solidified the earth skilfully.

iaunaita (formed as fem. of ܝܰܘܢܳܝܳܐ but used with the meaning of **iaunaiit**) a var. of **iaunaiit** in **arqa (ḏ)-iaunaita** Jb 232:9 (F), varr. **ḏ-iaunaiit** B, **ḏ-iaunat** AC, **iaunat** D a well-constructed (?) earth, cf. also **iauna 2, iuna 2.**

iazapa (rt. **YZP**) loan, investment. Pl. (var. of sg.) **iazapia. kḏ baiit mauzipia iazapia** (var. **iazapa**) AM 156:13 when thou wishest to make investments (or lend out loans).

iazd (P. town يزد) AM 203 the city of Yazd in Persia.

iazdagir, iazdigar the Persian king Yezdigird II (438–57) Ochser ZA 19/1905 p. 77 n. 1, Ginzā 412 n. 3. **iazdigar br bahran malka** Gy 384:2 ff., 14 (var. **iazdagir** DC 22. 380 and Sh. 'Abd.'s copy).

iazupa AM = **iazapa.**

iazuqaiia (etym. doubtf., Brandt from Ἰεξαι a name of Elxai's 'brother' MR 127, Elchasai 130; Andreas from the name of the old Iranian tribe Yazvā[n] 'worshipper' with MP suffix *-k*, formed in the same way as Ναζωραῖος, Σαδδουκαῖος Ginzā 135 n. 4) Gy 120:20, 224:9 name of a sect, acc. to **iazuqaiia šiṭia ḏ-nura mauqria** CP 379:16 'fire-worshippers' MMII 300 n. 4.

iazid br šišin IM 44 pers. pr. n.

iaia 1, iaiia (יָאֵא, יָאָה, ܝܳܐܶܐ), fair, lovely, beautiful, comely, seemly, fitting. Pl. **iaiia, iaʿia, iaiʿ, iaʿ, iaiʿi, iaʿiia, iaiiʿia,** pl. st. abs. **iaiʿn, iaʿin, iaʿn, iaiʿin** Gy 177:17 they are seemly; with encl. **iaiʿlun, iaʿlun** etc. Gy 316:16 etc. befitteth them MG 6:3 f., 69:20. **iaiʿ umitgaiia** Gy 3:11 f., **magaia uiai(i)a** Q 28:25, DC 36 (s. **GAA I** pa.); **kabir uiaiia** DC 26. 78 powerful and beautiful; **ʿbidata ḏ-iaiia** ATŠ II no. 192 rites that are seemly; **kma iaiilẖ lšišlam rba** CP 357:12, ML 265:10 how it becometh the Gr. Š! **iaʿilẖ mn ʿutria kulhun**

DC 34. 680 [maketh him] lovelier than all the uthras; **kma iaiilun lʿutria ukma iaiilun ldmauata** DC 42, DC 50. 167 how beseeming it is to the uthras and how beseeming it is to the prototypes; **kma iaʿilh liauar** CP 421:ult. how it becometh Y; **iaiʿia ʿṣṭla** Gs 78:9 a beautiful garment.

iaia 2 a family term of affection. **baba umama uiaia** ATŠ I no. 249 Papa and Mama and Nursie (?); **uab dilia uʿm uiaiai udadai uhuntai br iaiai uʿmh** DC 36 no. 35 and my father and my mother and my auntie (?) and my uncle and my cousin son of my auntie (?) and his mother.

ialala Jb 144:13 s. **lala.**

ialas AM 198 a place-name.

ialda (ילדא, ܝܠܕܐ, H. ילד, Ar. وَلَد) boy, child, boy-child. Pl. **ialdia** boys, fem. **ialdata** girls. **ialda zuṭa** Gy 190:15, 191:18 ff. (cf. 190:18); **ʿstaqlus ialda zuṭa** CP 21:14 Q 8:25; **kd mitaudal ialda** DC 36.

ialuz(a) (rt. **YLZ**) name of a spirit ML 281. **bialuz ialuz** CP 69:7 = Morg. 232/52:14 = ML 84:8 = Q 21:20 = DC 3 and 53 no. 22, 50. **bialuz ialuz ialuza** Q 12:25 = ML 35:1 = CP 29:12.

ialupa (ܝܠܘܦܐ) orig. disciple, hence: literate person, one instructed in reading and writing Mandaic. Gl. 73:13 (pl. written defectively) جند *magistratus* فرمايندها.

ialis (cf. **ialas**) a place-name BZ Ap. II.

ialip (ܝܠܝܦ) *passim* orig. disciple, hence: instructed, skilled.

iam (< H. חָם by the influence of **iapit**) Ham (son of Noah). **šum uiam uiapit** Gy 50:1 Shem and Ham and Japhet, Ginzā 46 n. 3.

iama (ימא, ܝܡܐ, H. ים, Ar. يَمّ Akk. *yāmu* LS, Ges.) sea, lake, stretch of water, lagoon, pool, river MG 100:13. Pl. **iamamia 1**, but also **iamia** Gy 68:4 MG 31:23, 103:9. **umia biama nihisrun** AM and the lake-water will be low; **sab kuza ḏ-iama** DC 40. 73 take a jar(ful) of pool(-water); **ʿsir iama uʿsirin trin kiph ḏ-iama** CP 20:1 ML 22:1 (cf. n. 2, although the 'two banks' would suggest 'river'); **iama akla** Gy 38:24, 376:24 devouring sea; **mlik iama** s. **mlik**; **angauia iama** s. **angauia**; **nsisia iama** s. **nsisia 2**; **iama ḏ-sup** Morg. 259/10:39 (with the orig. meaning:) the Reed-Sea, **iama ḏ- sup** Gy 112:3 f., Gy 388:3 etc. the sea of the end (influenced by **iuma ḏ-sup**) MSchr 32 n. 3, Jb ii p. xxi 14 ff.; **iama rba ḏ-sup** Gy 112:2, 177:3, 226:17, 228:10; pl. **liamia rbia ḏ-sup** Gy 336:5; **iama ḏ-mirta** Gs 75:12 sea of bitterness (?); **šuba iamamia** Morg. 259/9:7; **nihia iamamaihun** Gy 9:7 their seas are calm; **biamamia qadmai(i)a** RD B 40; **uiamamia nitun batra ḏ-naida** AM and stretches of water will appear (*lit*: come) in the place of the earthquake.

iamamia 2 occasional miswriting of **amamia** 'peoples'.

iaman (Ar. يَمَن) AM 203 the Yemen.

iamuria (cf. H. יַחְמוּר, Ar. يعمور) pl. kids, lambs, calves, young of animals. **iamuria lbaqraihun** Gs 10:23 the kids to their pen; **turata ḏʿtbh iamuria** JRAS 1938 3:17 the cows which are with young.

iamin, iamina (ימינא, ܝܡܝܢܐ, H. יָמִין, Ar. يمين, Eth. የማን, Akk. *imnu* LS, Ges. s. ימן). (*a*) right, the right hand, side, part, (*b*) (st. abs.) faithful, trustworthy. MG. 124: 4 f. Referring to the part of the body, used as fem. MG 157:13. (*a*) **iaminaikun** Gy 38:7 (B **-akun**) your right hand(s) MG 180:1; **mn iaminun** Gy 19:19, **liaminun** (often) on their right (hand) MG 360:ult. f.; **iaminh rabtia ḏ-asauata** CP 3:15 f. Q 1:30 = ML 5:6 his great right hand of healings; **ginza iamina** the title of right part of *Ginzā rabbā*; **anatun bun biamin bisra uana ʿtilkun biamin kušṭa** ATŠ I no. 289 pray ye with a fleshly right hand, and I will give the right hand of Truth; (*b*) **iamin ubasim libh** AM 283:38 his heart is faithful and gracious.

-ian a sporadic special fem. ending of the 3rd p. pl. pf., cf. **prašian** Q 73b:16 MG 223:antep.

ianga asa ianga a sapling, a myrtle sapling.

ianuq, ianqa (Talm. יָנוּקָא and יַנְקָא, Syr. ܝܢܘܩܐ and ܝܢܩܐ) infant, suckling, nursling, small child, boy MG 114:2 (and n. 2), 174:1, 3. Fem. **ianqita** MG 148 n. 2. Pl. **ianqia. ianuq šilman kilai ianuq mapiqtai huat** Gs 98:11, 121:14 as (yet) a child my span of life ended, as (yet) a child, I departed (life) (*paraphrase*); **minai ianuq** Gs 5:3 he is younger than I; **qiniana ḏ-abahahatḥ ḏ-ianuq msakarlḥ** AM 14:15 when a child he is deprived of his family property; **ianqa uianqita** Gy 289: 22 f. boy and girl; **asa ianqa** DC 50. 536 young (?) myrtle **riha ḏ-marua yanqa** DC 50. 394 the perfume of young marjoram.

ianquta (יָנְקוּתָא, ܝܢܩܘܬܐ) infancy, childhood MG 145:1. **ʿbidata ḏ-mn ianqutakabadt** Jb 20:3 works which thou didst since thy childhood; **rušuma ḏ-bianquth nsib** DC 34:66 the sign which he took in his childhood.

ianqita s. **ianuq, ianqa** a little girl DC. 43 E 36.

iasam Zotb. 218a:31 a pers. name.

iasana a place in the celestial regions. **baba ḏ-iasana** Gy 272:13, 273:18 ff.

iasbiil (exorcisms) a supernatural being.

iasdis ṭabian Gy 383:18 another name of Artabanus.

iasir (Ar. يسير) in **iasirdh ʿbad** DC 35:coloph. he captured it.

iasmus anana Gy 374:7 s. **anana.**

iasmin 1 (יסמין, ܝܣܡܝܢ, P. ياسمين Löw 189) jessamine. **iasmin rba** Gy 106:17 the great jessamine; **bihbaqia hbaqia ḏ-iasmin** CP 223:7 with bundles of bunches of jessamine; **iasmin gupna hu** DC 41 (illustration).

iasmin 2 Jb 1:7 f., Q 68:27, 70:32 a *malwâša* woman's name. Var. **iasman.**

iasriʿil, iasrpʿil (exorcisms) a supernatural being.

iaʿ, iaʿia etc. s. **iaia, iaiia.**

iaƐnia (Ar. يعني) AM 134 that is, i.e.

iapit Gy 50:1 Japhet (son of Noah).

iaṣila (ܐܨܝܠܐ, Phoen. יצלת, H. אָצִיל joint,

Akk. *eṣēlu*) Q 71:26, Jb 146:4, DC 41. 461 elbow.

iaqdana (ܝܩܕܢܐ) conflagration, flames, flaming, burning heat, burning wind. Var. **aqdana, iaqudana.** Pl. **iaqdania.** MG 136:5. **hauma uiaqdana** AM 177:penult. DAb heat and burning; **gumria ḏ-iaqdana** RD C 9 flaming coals of fire; **iaqdana ḏ-nura** Gy 26:17 flame of fire; **iaqdania d-nura** Gs 107:3 f., 11 id. pl. (used as fem.) MG 159:22; **nitharkun biaqdania ḏ-šuba** Gy 315:23 they will burn in the flame of the Seven.

iaqudana AM 259:17 a var. of **iaqdana.**

iaqut, iaquta (Ar. form ياقوت ,ياقوتة of ܝܩܘܢܬܐ ,ܝܩܘܢܐ < ὑάκινθος) ruby. Used either as masc. or as fem. **iaqut** RD 10, 30; **iaqut sumaqa** DAb=RD 21, **iaqut sumaqtia** DAb (later on) the red ruby; **iaqut ḏ-zahba** RD 20; **kḏ iaquta ḏ-bahrilẖ ṣirapaiia** ATŠ I no. 90 like a ruby that jewellers selected; **kḏ iaquta ḏ-mitbihra sadan ṣirapaiia** ATŠ II no. 365 like a ruby tested on the jewellers' block.

iaqid (יקיד, ܡܩܕ) burning, ardent. Pl. fem. **iaqidata.** Masc. sg. identical with act. pt. pe. of **YQD** (q.v.). **iaqid ziuẖ uiaqid nhurẖ** Gy 238:8; **ṭaba bziuẖ iaqid** Gy 79:2 (can also be taken as an act. pt. pe.); **šragia iaqidata** Gy 281:9 burning lamps.

iaqip (corruption of יַעֲקֹב) Jacob Jb ii 71:15, MSt. 101 n. 1. **bšum iaqip** Par. xxiv 10a; **iaqip ubnia amin** Jb 84:6, 13, 92:2, 93:8, 198:4, Gy 332:5 Jacob and Benjamin; **iaqip kahna** Jb 67:12 ff.; **iaqip ḏ-hikumta** Jb 117:12; **iaqip ʿuṣṭuna** Gy 333:10.

iaqir, iaqira (יַקִּירָא, ܡܩܝܪܐ, H. יַקִּיר, Ar. وَقِير) honoured, venerated, worthy, important, esteemed, weighty, precious, costly, valued, valuable, revered, reverend, solemn. MG 124:1. Pl. masc. **iaqiria.** Fem. sg. **iaqirta,** pl. **iaqirata.** Doublet **iaqra. ḏ-kadir uiaqir akuat aba ḏ-ʿutria** DAb as important and revered as the father of uthras; **iaqir mn zaua ubnia** Jb 102:1 f. more precious than wife or children; **ʿsiqta haka iaqirta** ATŠ II no. 160 that venerated seal-ring; **rurbia uiaqiria** Gs 26:5; **ḏ-iaqirin ušanin** Gy 128:18 that are worthy and sublime; **maṣbutiata iaqirata** ATŠ solemn baptisms; **brẖ iaqira** Jb 17:1 (var. **iaqra** DC 30) his dear son.

iaqra a doublet of **iaqira** (cf. H. יָקָר). Pl. **iaqria. klila iaqra** Gy 324:14 a precious wreath; **bra iaqra** DC 30 a var. of Jb 17:1 (s. **iaqira**); **ginzia uzharia iaqria** ATŠ I no. 103 precious treasures and injunctions; **kušṭa iaqra** ATŠ, DC 37 solemn pact; **mania iaqria** CP 434:15 revered (: holy) manas.

iaqrun IM name of a genie.

iaraqa a (mod.) doublet of **iaruqa.**

iarata (Ar. يَرَاع ?) reed (?): **rauṭa uiarata** DC. 46 a twig and a reed (?).

iardna (Aram. st. emph. for הַיַּרְדֵּן, not from Syr. ܝܘܪܕܢܢ as was supposed by Pallis MSt 149 f., Burkitt JThS 29/1928 p. 228, Peterson ZNW 25/1926 p. 237, 27/1928 p. 89, Büchsel ZNW 26/1927 p. 228 n. 4, and Lietzmann SBAW phil.-hist. Kl. xxvii pp. 598 f., 601 f.; Lidzb.'s main argument for Pal. origin of Mandaism Jb ii p. xix, ML xix, Ginzā vi 15 ff.) jordan, running water, river, flowing stream MG 27:8, Kessler REPThK 181, Brandt: *Mandaeans* ERE 382 f., MR 63 ff., 66 and n. 2, xxiv MSchr 16 n. 4, MMII p. xxiv n. 4, AF 241. **iardna tlitaia** Gy 78:2; **sindiriauis iardna rba ḏ-hiia** Gy 131:20; **iardna hiuara** Oxf. 89 b, Gy 220:15; **ṣbʿiia barba iardnia** Gs 112:17; **zaba barba iardnia** RD C 27; **iardnia gauaiia** Gy 234:17; **šuba iardnia rurbia gauaiia** Gy 152:19; **nigdit šuba iardnia** Gy 372:23; **kipa ḏ-iardna ḏ-mia hiia** Gy 153:8; **biardna ḏ-bihram miṣṭibia** RD A 11; **tlatma ušitin iardnia** Gy 131:23, 292:23 f.; **tlatma ušitin alpia ruban iardnia ḏ-mia hiia** Gy 153:6; **palig iardnia** PD 303; **halin iardnia ḏ-mia hiia mn iardna ḏ-mahu atin** DC 39; **ʿšria iardna lmirhaš** DC 12 the river brings forth living creatures (?); **iardna ḏ-mia hiuaria** Gy 69:10; **iardna rba ḏ-saka uminiana litlẖ** Gy 69:13; **mn iardna rba hun iardnia ḏ-saka uminiana litlun** Gy 69:16; **iardna rba ḏ-mia hiia** Gy 69:20; **btaqnia rurbia ḏ-iardna** Gy 197:11 in the clear, powerful (waters) of the jordan; **iardna ḏ-hiziak apak** ML 126:2 (cf. n. 2); **iardnia urahaṭia** Gy 337:3.

iaruqa (יָרוֹקָא, ܝܘܪܩܐ) herbs, green-stuff. **ḏ-raiia ḏ-iaruqa** Gy 227:21 who feed on herbs.

iarqa (יַרְקָא, ܝܘܪܩܐ, H. יֶרֶק, Ar. وَرَق, Akk. *warāqu* 'to become livid') *passim* herbs, green salad, green vegetables, green-stuff. Dim. pl. **iarqunia** s.v.

iarqana (יַרְקָנָא, ܝܪܩܢܐ, Ar. يرقان) (*a*) jaundice, (*b*) yellowness, (*c*) blight, mildew (on grain). (*a*) **iarqana ʿl anašia napil** AM 213: ult; (*b*) **iarqana baina** Or. 328:3 yellowness in the eye; (*c*) **iarqana lhamra napil** AM 179:ult. (*and often*) blight will attack the vines.

iarqunia (ܝܘܪܩܘܢܐ) edible green-stuff, vegetables, herbs. A dim. pl. of **iarqa** MG 140:8. **iarqunia rgigia** Gs 3:13; **piqunia uiarqunia** Jb 232:7, Gy 89:16; **bahša ʿl iarqunia mikal** Gy 151:23 f.; **iarqunia mlagṭilia** Gy 189:7; **ukul mahu ḏ-hauia mn iarqunia** ATŠ I no. 116.

iatar occasional var. of **iatir.**

iatarta a var. of **iatirta** (fem. of **iatira**). **šuta iatarta** CP 427:8 excellent saying.

iatur name of a hill **ṭura ḏ-iatur** Gy 265:12 (Athur?, i.e. Assyrian hills? Ginzā 265 n. 4).

iatim(a) (Aram. sg. יַתְמָא, ܝܬܡܐ, H. יָתוֹם, Ar. يَتِيم Ges., LS). Pl. **iatimia** Gs 10:ult. AM 76:1 orphans, bereaved ones. **ulaiatim** AM 268:10 and is not bereaved.

iatir, iatira 1 (יַתִּיר, ܝܬܝܪ) much, too many, too much, surpassing, exceeding, excessive, superabounding, excellent, far-off, strange, noble, sublime, remote MG 72:23. Pl. **iatiria.** Often difficult to distinguish from **iatira 2.** St. abs. is used adverbially: **iatir** Gy 391:20 too much MG 200:bottom; **iatir biatir** Gy 237:16 exceedingly MG 303:10; **iatir almia** Gy 285:4, Gs 26:10 outstanding in the worlds; **iatir šlihia** Gy 6:12 with many apostles MG 311:2 f.;

kd iatir Gy 216:ult. ff. when he exceedeth MG 463:14 ff., Ginzā 217 n. 3; **ʿu iatira** CP 263:9 (ML 258:13 Lidzb.'s trs. is based on ignorance of missing context) if (he is) excellent (noble); **balmia d-nhura iatiria** (*often*) in countless worlds of light; **biatiria d-lau bhasiria** ATŠ II no. 147, Q 24:9, ML 67:11 with outstanding beings not with the defective ones; **hazin gabra iatira** Gy 205:16 f. this outstanding being; **iatiria d-lahun bṣiria** DC 51 sublime beings without imperfection; **uasata iatir lahualh** ATŠ I no. 220 and he had no excellent copy.

iatira 2 (עַתִּירָא, ܥܬܝܪܐ) rich, wealthy, well-to-do. Pl. **iatiria** Gy 387:22 *bis*, MG 72:22. Difficult to distinguish from **iatira 1**. **uiatira hauia** AM and he will be wealthy; **anašia šalmania iatiria** AM honest well-to-do people (or **iatira 1**?); **iatira d-azal mn haka** CP 312:14 he who went from here wealthy.

iatira 3 = **iatra. iatira d-qašta** AM 89:penult. bow-string.

iatir iatrun s. iatrun (*a*).

iatqana Sh. ʿAbd.'s copy's var. of **tuqna** Gy 32:13.

iatra (יִתְרָא, ܝܬܪܐ, H. יֶתֶר, Ar. وَتَر) tendon, bowstring MG 100:7. Doublet **iatira 3**.

iatrana Sh. ʿAbd.'s copy's var. of **iutrana** Gy 50:paen. and *passim*.

iatrun (rt. **YTR**) (*a*) in **pasimka iatir iatrun** Gy 131:6 name of a light-being, (*b*) **iatrun gabra šalmana** Gy 197:6 ff. Y. the perfect man (Šilmai's father).

YBB (יַבֵּב, ܝܒܒ, H. יִבֵּב, Ar. أَبَّ, هَبَّ, Eth. የበበ) to make a hollow or whistling sound, groan hollowly, whistle.

Pa. Pf. **ṣnap uiabib bqalh** Gy 282:7 he cried and groaned hollowly. Act. pt. **nahim miabib** Gy 280:4 he groaneth and whistleth.

Ethpa. Impf. **nitiabun** AM 251:11 they will languish (?).

Der.: **miababa.**

YBṬ s. **ABṬ I.**

YBL (ܝܒܠ, H. יבל hiph., Akk. *biltu* 'tribute', Sab. 𐩺𐩨𐩡 'to send or bring gifts') to carry a load, bear, bring. The 2nd rad. is regularly syncopated in af.-forms MG 49:16 f.

Pe. occurs only in the frequent mod. impt. *balle* 'bring me!'

Af. Pf. **auil** he brought MG 49:16, 246:paen., **aulit** thou broughtest, or I brought, with suff. (or encl.) **auilun** they brought me MG 49:17, **auilh** he brought him MG 275:10, **aulalh** (**lnu**) Gy 381:6 f. she brought it (to Noah) MG 246:paen., **auluia** they brought him, **aulunhun** Gy 256:18 they brought them MG 283:15. Impf. with suff. **naulak** and **nʿiaulak** Gs 54:8 we bring thee MG 273:22, **naulh bmarba** DC 34:628 he bringeth it into the womb, **naulun** Gs 48:4 they bring me MG 273:5 f., **naulunak** Gs 108:23 they bring thee MG 274:22. Impt. **uauil lhak alma** Gy 92:18 and bring (it) in that world. Act. pt. pl. with encl. **maulilh lhak alma** Gy 92:21 they bring him into that world. Part. pres. with encl. **maulinalik** Gy 151:15 I bring thee MG 231: ult.

Der.: **mubla** (var. **mibla**), **maulana.**

-iblia alternative form of **ʿblia** after procl. prep.

-ibra alternative form of **ʿbra** after procl. prep.

YBŠ, ʿBŠ (Aram. and H. יבשׁ, Syr. ܝܒܫ, Ar. يبس) to dry (up), wither.

Pe. Pf. **ʿbiš** became dry MG 244:paen. Impf. **nibuš, tibuš** cf. AM 235:22 will (be) dry. Act. pt. **iabiš** Gy 389:17 (var. DC 22. 385 **iabuš**) will wither; **iabuš** AM 21:20 will dry up; **iabšia** Gs 16:ult.; (**mibaš**) **iabšia iamamia** ML 206:1 = CP 169:17 f. The seas dry up (completely). Part. pres. **iabšit** AM 287:30 thou driest. Inf. **mibaš** ML 296:1.

Pa. Pt. **miabaš ziqa** DC 43 I 54 flatulence is dried up; fem. st. emph. **miabašta** s.v.

Refl. Impf. **nitiabiš** DC 44. 1721 (he) will wither.

Gl. 134:3 f. **YBŠ** قسا *indurare* سخت شد; 177:7 f. id. يبس *urere* خشك شد.

Der.: **miabašta, miabišuta, iubša, iabša.**

-igla alternative form of **ʿgla** after procl. prep.

YDA, ʿDA II (Gen. Sem. ידע, ܝܕܥ, Akk. *idû*, cf. Ar. ودع, in Mand. af. confused with אודי, ܐܘܕܝ, إِسْتَوْدَى LS, Ges. s. ידה II hiph.: הוֹדָה) to know, recognize, af. to make known, inform, but also: to confess, acknowledge, praise.

Pe. Pf. **ʿda** he knew, they knew MG 245:1, **ʿdat** Gy 81:11, 100:14 she knew MG 245:8 f., **ʿdit** I knew MG 369:13, **ʿdit** Gy 162:11, Gs 40:15, thou knewest, spec. pl. **ʿdun** they knew MG 237:17, **ʿdaiun** Gy 345:1 id. MG. 245:5; **laʿdun** Gs 37:14 CD (var. **lʿdun**) they knew not MG 35 n. 1, **ʿditun** Gs 11:21 ye knew, **miditun** Gs 54:13 (*thrice*) did ye know? MG 245:17 f., **ʿdanin** Gy 141:9, 165 (often D even **ʿdinin**) MG 245:21 (**ʿdanin** Gy 65 as both 'we knew' and 'we know' MG 369:15); with suff. **ʿduk** Gy 5:7, 11:ult. they knew thee MG 274:10 f., **ʿduia** Gy 335:16 they knew him MG 277: paen. Impf. **tida** she knoweth, thou knowest MG 75:7, **ʿda uʿpruš** Gy 159:ult. I (shall) know and recognize, **nidun** they know MG 246:11; with suff. **nidan, nʿdan** Gs 51:ult. recognizeth me MG 271:3. Impt. **pruš unhur uʿda** ATŠ II no. 212 discern, know clearly and recognize. Act. pt. **iada** he knows MG 235:28; (**mida**) **iada** AM 88 will be (well-)informed; **lahua iada d-nʿdan** Gs 51: ult. there was not a Knower that should recognize me; pl. **iadin, iadia** they know MG 149:24; (**mida**) **iadin hiia** Gy 75:22 f. the Life (well) knoweth; with encl. **kul naṣuraia d-iadalun** ATŠ I no. 170 every Naṣoraean that knoweth them. Part. pres. **iadana** I know MG 236:13, 369:13, **iadit** thou knowest MG 236:17, **iadinin** we know MG 236:23, **iaditun** ye know MG 236:25; with encl. **taprišlh d-ana iadinalh** DC 34 explain it, so that I may know it; **iadatbh** thou knowest about that MG 236:21; mod. usage: **iad**+acc. suff. **qiadh** he knows, will know etc.; **laqiadan ʿlia iahminh** DC 51:coloph. we do not know where we shall live. Pass. pt.

with encl. **ʿdilak** Gy 393:1 thou art informed, knowest MG 246:23, 382:14, 398:2. Inf. **mida** Gy 75:22, 392:ult., AM 88 etc., MG 246:25.

Af. (both ܐܘܕܝ and ܐܘܕܥ): Pf. **audia** Gy 45:16, 184:10 (he) confessed MG 260:28, **audin** Gy 45:16B MG 162 n. 1, **audiat** Gy 276:20 she confessed, **audat** Par. xi and Gs 77:13 id. MG 261:2 (and n. 2), **audu** Gy 252: ult., 253:2, 261:5 they confessed MG 261:17 f., **audin** Q 12:24 we confessed MG 261:26; with suff. **laudunun** Gy 310:18 they informed them not MG 35:14, 283:16; **hazin hu baba ḏ-audi-tinkun tarmidai** DC 22. 226 this is the sect which I have made known to you, my disciples; with encl. **audibun** they (fem.) confessed them MG 261:20. Impf. with encl. **audibak** Gy 87:20 I confess Thee MG 215:26, **taudubh̲** confess him MG 262:8; with suff. **naudan** Gy 358:18 he maketh me know, informeth me MG 271:5 f., **taudh̲** Gy 82:2 she informeth him MG 275:ult. Impt. pl. **uaudun** Gy 37:16 and confess MG 247:5. Part. pres. with encl. **maudinalkun** HG I make known to you.

Ettaf. Pf. **ʿtauda** Q 34:10 = ML 91:2 was (made) known MG 247:8.

Gl. (always act. pt. pe.): 17:13 f. استعلم *quaerere, scire* پرسيد; 46:1 f. تعارف *cognoscere* فهميد; 49:1 f. تقين *intelligere* فهميد; 64:1 f. حدق *oculis intendere* چشم وا گرد; 113:1 f. عرف *scire* شناخت; 175:5 f. وعظ *erudire* آموخت; 181:1 f. درى *scire* دانست.

Der.: **iaduia, iaduta, (iadata, iadita), mada, madi(h)ta, manda, mandaia.**

-ida an alternative form of **ʿda** after procl. prep.

YDL, ʿDL (met. of **YLD** q.v.) to bear a child, bring forth.

Pe. Pf. **iadlat** Gy 158:22 etc. she brought forth MG 245:8; with suff. **ʿdalth̲** she brought him forth MG 276:20, **ʿdaltinun** Gy 94:18 she brought them forth MG 282:18; **ṭuria ḏ-iadluk** Or. 331:17, 332:13 the mountains which brought thee forth. Impf. **tidul** Gy 156:1 etc. thou wilt bring forth MG 217:11, 246:8, **ʿdul** Gy 155:18 I (shall) bring forth MG 246:9; with suff. **tidlh̲** Gy 158:8, 12 thou wilt bring him forth MG 275:22. Act. pt. with suff. **ḏ-hu bṭanbun lrazia uiadilinun** ATŠ I no. 227 so that he becomes pregnant of the(se) mysteries and brings them to birth. Part. pres. **iadlana** Gy 158:13 I (fem.) bring forth MG 231:8. Pass. pt. with encl. pers. pron. **blilia ʿdilna** I was born in the night; **atutia alahia ʿdilna** DC 44:427 f. beneath the gods was I born.

Af. Pf. with suff. **lahakimta audiltan** Jb 117:3 f. (D **-tin**) no wise-woman assisted my birth MG 271:ult. Act. pt. with encl. **maudilun** (he) brings them to birth MG 246:29.

Ethpe. from **YLD.**

Ethpa. Pt. pl. **mitiadlia** Gy 46:21 they are born MG 74:12, 246:28, **mitiadlin** Gy 46:21, 48:23, 58:23, DC 36 no. 36 id. MG 149:20.

Ettaf.: Pf. **ʿtaudal** Gy 382:11 was born MG 247:8. Impf. **nuqbata nitaudilin** [*sic*] AM 268:40 females will be born. Pt. pl. **zikria mitaudilia** AM 269:9 males will be born.

Der.: **iadala, iadalta 1, 2, maudala** (cf. also s. **YLD**).

YHB, ʿHB, AHB (יְהַב, ܝܗܒ, وَهَبَ Sab. 𐩥𐩠𐩨 & Eth. ወሀበ) to give, bestow on, lay on, vouchsafe, appoint, permit, allow, grant.

Pe. Pf. **ʿhab** he gave MG 61:4, 245:1, **iahbat** she gave MG 245:8, **ʿhabt** thou didst give MG 245:12, **iahbit** rarely **ʿhbit** (both Gy 210:13) I gave MG 245:14, **ʿhabtin** Gy 106:6 f. ye (fem.) gave 245:19, **ʿhabnin** we gave MG 245:21; with encl. **iahablan** Gy 25:3 he gave (to) us MG 67 n. 2, 245:1, **iahbulh̲** var. **ʿhablh̲** they gave (to) him MG 245:7, **ʿhabalak** Gy 165:18 she gave (to) thee, **ʿhabalh̲** ibid. she gave (to) him MG 245:10 f., **ʿhabilak** Gy 250: 14 I gave (to) thee MG 245:16, **ʿhabtulia** Gy 157:2 ye gave (to) me MG 245:19, **ʿhabnalak** Gy 148:8 f. we gave (to) thee MG 245:22, **ḏ-anin dilak ʿhabnalak** DC 26:401 which we have given to thyself, **ʿhabnalh̲** Gy 106:6 f. we gave (to) him MG 245:22; with suff. **iahbak** Oxf. iii 103 a we gave thee MG 273:10, **iahbh̲** Gy 10:23 he gave him MG 275:3 f., **ʿhabtinun** Gy 119:4 I gave them MG 282:26, **iahibth̲** (formally a pa.) **lnaṣuraiia** DC 3 I gave it to the Naṣoraeans, **ʿhabunun** Oxf. iii 35 b they gave them MG 283:14. Impf. (less usual than the corresp. forms of **NTN**) **nihba** Gy 368:18 they (fem.) give; with encl. **ʿhablak** Gy 311:17 I give (to) thee. Impt. **hab** (very often), but even **ʿhub** or **ahub**, give MG 246:13 ff.; with encl. **hablan** Gy 70:17B grant us, **uʿhablun** Oxf. iii 84 a and grant them = **uahbalun** Par. xi, **(a)hbalan** grant us, **(a)hbalia** grant me, **hbalh̲** grant him etc. MG 246: middle; pl. with encl. **(a)hbulia** Q 13:13, Par. xi 40b *date mihi* MG 246:18 f.; with suff. **iuhbh̲** Gs 305:13 ff. give him MG 269 n. 1, 276:12 f., **ʿuhbuia** Jb 102:1, var. **ʿhbuia** *date id* MG 278:anteantep. f. Act. pt. **iahib** (very often) MG 246:21; with encl. **iahiblh̲** Gy 202:2 (var. **-la** Sh. 'Abd.'s copy) he giveth to her, **iahbalh̲** Gy 202:4 she giveth to him. Part. pres. **ana lnišimta iahibna lhanath̲ škinta** DC 34 I place the soul in that habitation, **iahbit** thou givest MG 61:4, **iahbinin** we give, **iahbitun** ye give MG 246:22; with encl. **iahbatlun** thou givest (to) them MG ibid., **ḏ-anin iahbinalh̲ lnišimta** DC 48. 227 which we bestow on the soul, **iahbitulh̲** DC 27. 225 ye give to it. Pass. pt. **ʿhiba** Gy 198:6, 8 *data* MG 246:23. Inf. **ubaiitun mihab mania ʿlh̲** DC 24, DC 42. 52 and ye seek to bestow garments on him.

Ethpe. Pf. **ʿthib** was given MG 246:26, **ʿtiahbat** Gy 374:11, 18, 20 she was given MG 246:28; with encl. **ʿthiblun** DC 34. 427 was given to them. Impf. with encl. **nithiblh̲ ʿkilta** ATŠ II no. 93 food shall be given him. Pt. **mithib** given MG 132:14, with encl. **mithiblun** ATŠ II no. 169 is given to them.

Idioms: Impt. + impf. of the verb in question: 'let . . .', e.g. **hab nirmibh̲** Gy 101:13

let us throw in him; **hab lalma ḏ-bišia nišadrḫ** Gy 132:2 let us send him to the world of the evil ones; **uahbalḫ lhaua zauak tišauilak lbuša** ibid. and let E., thy wife, make a garment for thee; **hab ḏ-ʿmihiḫ** Gy 344:21 let me beat him MG 373:middle. Ethpe. + inf. of the verb in question: **ʿthib lašualia auquria rba** Q 2:16 it is given to the disciple (: novice) to honour his master (: initiator). 'To be allowed, permitted': **laʿthibian ʿbidata bgauaihun** ATŠ I no. 34 the rites are not permitted in them (: those days); **ṣbu ḏ-laiahib** HG 8 something not allowed; **anpiš ʿhab** s. **NPŠ**.

Der.: **iahba, iahuba, ihbana, mahbana, mahbata.**

ihbana (rt. **YHB**) DC 43 D 52 gift, boon.

YHṬ (ܬܫܠ) to miscarry, cast young untimely. Pf. **liahria šuba iahṭat iahṭa** DC 39, DC 43 J 45 at the seven months, she miscarried. Impf. (as from af.) **niahṭa(n)** AM 214:19 etc. (often in AM) they (will) miscarry MG 228:4.

Der.: **iahṭa,** cf. also the popular etym. of **iahuṭaiia.**

YHL (H. יחל?) to inspire confidence. Doubtf.

Pe. Imp. with suff. **ʿhilḫ** ATŠ II no. 427 inspire him with confidence.

YHM a mod. form of **YTB** to sit. Dial. var. **YTM.**

Pe. Part. pres. **ʿlia iahminḫ** DC 51:coloph. where we shall live.

YHR (cf. **AUR II** (*b*)) to shine, give light MG 62:19 ff.

Ethpa. Pf. **ʿtiahrit** Gs 96:14 I shone; **ʿtiahrat** DC 27. 291, DC 36 II no. 105 she was resplendent; with encl. **ʿtiahribḫ** Gy 103:2 he shone in it MG 62:21. Impf. **nitiahar** Gy 221:14 is resplendent; with encl. **nʿtiahrubḫ** DC 48. 386 they shine in it. Pt. **mitiahar bʿuṣrḫ** Gs 42:5 his mind was enlightened.

Der.: cf. s. **AUR** (I and II).

iubša (rt. **YBŠ**) drought, dryness, desert: **iubša uruṭba** DC 44 dryness and moisture; **iubša nihuia** AM 279:35 there will be drought; **ʿu biubša azil** AM 159:5 if he goes into the desert.

iuhana (יוֹחָנָן, ܝܘܚܢܢ) John, esp. John the Baptist, called also **iahia iuhana** (otherwise a frequent Mand. name) MSchr 195 n. 2, Jb ii 70 ff., HpGn 282, 284, AF 241, Kessler PRE xii 181; Tondelli, *Biblica* 9/1928 pp. 206–24. **iuhana maṣbana** Gy 189:1 ff. MR 137 n. 2; **iuhana mitlid bʿurašlam iuhana lagiṭ iardna** etc. Jb 70:8 ff.; **iuhana brḫ ḏ-aba saba zakria** Gy 57:5; **nbaṭ br iuhana** Gy 362:8, cf. 364:9; **baqaria iuhana** RD A 8 John's herdsmen.

iuzaṭaq (cf. H. יְהוֹצָדָק > יוֹצָדָק) a name given to Manda-ḏ-Hiia, Öchser ZDMG lxi 161 n. 2, Lidzb. ML 281. CP Index. **iuzaṭaq manda ḏ-hiia** Gy 68:8, 240:2, 18, 21, Q 4:15, CP 65:12, 14:23, 22:25, 29:15, 30, 32, 30:1 ff., 59:3, 62:27, RD B 123, 130 f., Morg. 258/7:16, Oxf. roll f 230, 577, 709, 889, Par. xxvii 8a, **malka iuzaṭaq manda ḏ-hiia** Morg. 5:6. **ʿsqta ḏ-iuzaṭaq** Q 7:17, **ʿsqat iuzaṭaq manda ḏ-hiia** Par. 226/22:22, 267/25:25. **iuzaṭaq** Zotb. 222b:9 a man's name.

iuzrun IM name of a genie.

iukabar (comp. with iu-) a spirit of light, used with several epithets, the most frequent of which is **ziua** ML 281, MMII 281 no. 6, CP Index. **ʿutria ḏ-iukabar qra** Gy 367:1 f.; **iukabar kušṭa** Gy 316:2, 19, 23, 317:8; **iukabar ziua** Gy 373:11 Q 4:12, 59:1; **iukabar ziua uqaiumia** Q 9:29; **uqaiumia iukabar ziua** Q 11:13, 16:25, 43:31, 45:26, Par. xxvii 8a, 10a cf. Lidzb. ZDMG lxi 693 n. 9; **iukabar ziua šganda ḏ-hiia** CP 15:1 Q 6:2 = ML 16:11 f.; **iukabar malala qadmaia** DC 43 J 50 Oxf. roll f 110; **iukabar rba** Q 10:22; **malka iukabar rba** Morg. 4:10; **nišabun liukabar ziua** Jb 239:4 f.; **iukabar pugdama ḏ-hiia** Q 12:30 = ML 35:6 = CP 29:ult.; **iukabar . . . malala** Q 6:2; **nṭir ʿl iukabar** Jb 217:2; **iukabar gabra ʿutra mzarza** Q 16:30 = ML 44:10; **iukabar hiia** Morg. 233/53:9 = Q 31:25 = DC 3 and 53 no. 50; **iukabar** Jb 9:10, 16:14, Q 21:16, RD B 100 etc.; **iukabar = šamiš** RD 10. (See Index CP under **iukabar.**)

iukašar (comp. with iu-) a spirit of light, used similarly to preced. ML 281, MR 67 n. 1, Siouffi 38:9, 103:top. **iukašar** Jb 7:10, 16:25, 25:14, 230:12, Q 32:30, 33:1, 17, Oxf. 107 a, PD 1649 etc.; **iukašar kana** Gy 129:14, **malka iukašar kana** Morg. 4:11, **iukašar kana ḏ-ziua** Q 59:19 = ML 143:1. (CP Index.)

iulpana (יוּלְפָּנָא, ܝܘܠܦܢܐ) doctrine, teaching. With suff. **iulpankun** your doctrine MG 179:16, **iulpanḫ** Gy 244:1 his teaching.

ium, iuma (יוֹמָא, ܝܘܡܐ, H. יוֹם, Ar. يَوْم, Akk. *ūmu*) day MG 7:11, 22:17, 100:19. Pl. **iumia.** With suff. **ium** Gy 12:2 = **iumai** ibid. BD, Gy 190:16 etc. today (lit. my day) MG 175:16, 351:middle; **kulhun iuman** Gy 66:7 all our days MG 179:6. Spor. var. **iauma** s.v. In distributive repetitions: **ium bium** Gy 138:14 etc. day by day, daily, but **dina ḏ-iuma biuma** Gy 388:13 daily dispute MG 301:14, 18; **kul ium kul iuma** Gy 230:11 etc. every single day MG 302:2; **alma liuma ium dina** (*often*) until the day of the judgement MG 320:paen.; **mn iuma** (Sh. 'Abd.'s copy **ium**) **ulalam almia** Gy 12:2 etc. (*often*) from today (and) for ever, henceforth for aye; **biuma hda** Gy 96:12 on the 1st day, **bitlata iumia . . . barba iumia . . . , bhamša iumia . . .** Gy 96:13 ff. on the 3rd day . . . on the 4th day . . . on the 5th day . . .; **iumai mahu biumia iuma iumai mahu bšaiia šita hda** CP 154:16 = ML 186:1 f. What is my day among the days? One day! What is my day among the hours? One hour! (Doubtf., cf. n. 1); **iuma trin ḏ-habšaba** AM 23:15 etc., **iuma tlata ḏ-habš-** etc. (often in AM and in colophons) Monday, Tuesday . . .; **anpia iuma** s. **anpia**; **iuma ḏ-sup** (often in Jb) the day of the end Jb ii. xxi:14 ff. (cf. s. **sup**).

-iun 2 s. **-un 2.**

iuna 1 a var. of **iauna 1.** Gl. 67:7 **iuna** حمامة *columba* كبوتر; 72:12 id. pl.

iuna 2 = iauna 2. arqa pt iuna ATŠ II no. 51 (DC 6) (var. **iauna** ATŠ ibid. (DC 36)), DC 34. 291; **arqa rabtia pt iuna** DC 37. 51, 136.

iunaiia a var. of **iaunaiia.**

iusamir ML 21:5 = CP 19:10 a genie cited together with **iusmir** (q.v.).

iusmin Gy 346:19 = **iasmin** 1.

iusmir (comp. with **iu-**) a genie. ML 281. CP Index. **iusmir kana** Gy 127:13, Q 16:29; **iusmir gupna** Jb 2:14, 4:16, 257:15, Q 7:25; **iusmir gupna qadmaia** CP 19:5 = Q 20:16 = ML 21:3; **iusmir gupna ḏ-barqa ḏ-sam ziua šria** Gy 321:20; **iusmir ziua** Q 32:11, Jb 4:14, Par. 27:22b; **iusmir gabra** Q 9:18; **iusmir ʿutra** Gy 321:4; **iusmir asia ḏ-mana** Morg. 116:8; **iusmir iusamir** ML 21:5 = CP 19:9 f; **iusmir** Oxf. 107 a, Jb 234:8 etc., CP Index.

iupin iupapin (cf. the angel-name יְפִיפִיָּה Targ. Jon. Deut. 34:6 MR 198 n. 1) a genie, or pair of genii, ML 281. CP Index. **iupin ʿutra** Gy 127:20; **iupin iupapin** Q 3:12, 5:19, 12:28, 16:29, 28:15, 58:25, Gy 71:1, 189:13, 196:2, Gs 7:9, CP Index.

YUR = **AUR II** (= **ʿUR II**) to shine.

YWR = **AWR** (= **ʿWR**) to blind, to dazzle with light.

Af. Impf. with suff. **tiaurinun umiṭaršinun** (var. . . . **utiṭ-**) DC 44. 1030 she blinds them and deafens them; **tiaurinun lainaihun** DC 44. 1034 she blinds their eyes. Other forms and derivatives s. **AWR**.

iur, iura (< יוהרא) light, brilliance, being of light MG 62:21. Both st. abs. and emph. (but esp. the former) are used as a pr. n. of a being of light. Pl. **iuria** beings of light. ML 281, Ginzā 324 n. 2. CP trs. 304 n. 4. **iur uiahur uarhum** Gy 182:11, 22, 183:1 pr. names. **uqaiim iur biur** CP 23:9, Q 9:13 = ML 25:9 and he raises Y. in brilliance(?), cf. n. 1; **iura rba ḏ-ziuh unhurh npiš** Gy 69:18 the great brilliance (or the Gr. Y.?) whose radiance and light are abounding; **iura rba** Gy 322:7, 364:16; **iura rba ganzibra** Gy 320:4, 321:1, 374:9; **iura hu rba** Gy 276:17; **iura ḏ-hiia** Gy 275:19; **škinta . . . ḏ-bit iuria** CP 151:3 = Oxf. 8 a = ML 181:5 a dwelling . . . that is the house of the light-spirits; **ana hu iur br barit** CP 17:12, Q 20:13 = ML 19:6, 56:3 cf. ML 19 n. 2; **iuria bhiria zidqa** Oxf. 9 a the (s)elected light-beings of righteousness.

iurama (rt. **YRM** = **RUM**?) highland, of wind; high, boisterous. **šuta ḏ-iurama** DC 19, DC 43 D 48 the south wind that is high; **ziqa ḏ-iurama** AM 195:9 a boisterous(?) wind; **ziqa arba kiniania ʿtpalag . . . had iurama** ATŠ II no. 62, 250 (acc. to context 'south-easterly').

iuraqa (יורקא, ܝܘܪܩܐ) yellow, green(ish), pallid MG 122:19. Pl. **iuraqia**. Fem. sg. **iuraqtia**. **mia iuraqia** Gy 393:8. **hinun b(i)nia sumaiqia liuraqia** DC 43 J 197 they are between red and yellow (of complexion); **ulmisamuqia lanph ḏ-iuraqia** DC 51 and to make rosy his face that is pallid; **had minaihun iuraqtia** ATŠ I no. 219.

iurba (Lidzb. Ginzā 258 n. 1: compound with **iu-**) name of a sun-spirit, identified with *Adonāi*, keeper of a purgatory MSt 79. **iurba** Gy 186:21, 187:12, 14, 219:22 ff., 221:3 ff., 314:10; **iurba uruha** Gy 381:20, Gs 121:23; **iurba ḏ-iahuṭaiia qarilh adunai** Gy 381:11; **plugta ḏ-iurba** Gy 314:8; **iurba ulšuba dmauata** Gs 66:23; **iurba gabra qarabtana** Jb 186:9; **liuiatan šumh ḏ-iurba** Lond. roll B 356; **dar luath ḏ-iurba** HG **ḏ-hu iurba rba amarilh lzihrun raza** DC 27. 62.

iurqa (cf. **iuraqa**) (*a*) green food, salad, herbs, (*b*) pallor, greenish or yellowish hue. (*a*) **ṭabuta uiurqa ukauara** DC 50. 129, DC 42. 6; **iurqa ḏ-qdia ʿl kip aina** DC 41. 173; (*b*) **ʿtlh iurqa qudam anph** AM 16:20.

iušamin (comp. with **iu-**, a transformation of H. *יְהוֹשָׁמַיִם Kessler PRE xii 168, taking the place of the Aram. בעלשמין Jb ii pp. xxiii: 15 ff., AF 242) name of a demiurge, a mediator between good and evil ML 281, MMII 224 n. 8, Jb ii pp. xxii ff., MR 31 f., 50 ff. **iušamin br dmut hiia** Morg. 87:10, Gy 294:4; **iušamin dakia** Q 5:31, 9:15, 39:9, 50:24, Gy 285:2, 286:6, 288:19, 322:11, Morg. 269/28:38 etc. (*often*), **ab iušamin dakia** Q 40:7, **malka iušamin dakia br niṣubtun** Morg. 4:3; **kursia ḏ-iušamin** RD B 22; **arqia ḏ-iušamin** RD B 57; **hašabta ḏ-iušamin** Gy 132:21; **ʿutria ḏ-iušamin** Gy 305:12; **bit iušamin** Gy 342:15, 351:14 f., Jb 220:8; **baita ḏ-iušamin** Gy 346:1; **škinta ḏ-iušamin rba** Jb 257:16; **iušamin br malkia** Gy 344:16 ff.; **arqa ḏ-iušamin** Gy 360:17; **iušamin** Q 48:12, Oxf. 85 a, RD B 8, Jb 220:9, Gy 133:11, 158:19, 168:1, 293:19, 296:24, 297, 306:14 ff., 310:23, 311:2 ff., 342:15 ff., Gs 93:3 ff. etc., Lidzb. Mand. Gl.; **iušamin ṭausa** s. **ṭausa**. CP Index.

iušmir (comp. with **iu-**) a genie. **iušmir ziua rba qadmaia** JRAS 1939 399:21.

iutrana (יותְרָנָא, ܝܘܬܪܢܐ, H. יִתְרוֹן) advantage, gain, profit, increase MG 136:20. **ukul ʿniš iutrana lnapšh baiia** Gy 50:23.

YZB šaf. **ŠWZB** (q.v.).

YZP (יְזַף, ܝܙܦ) pe. to borrow; af. to lend; ettaf. to be added, united (: יסף), the same meaning sometimes with af. ML 140 n. 4.

Pe. Act. pt. **iazip** AM 24:17 he borrows, **udiazap minh lahiblh** AM 10:ult. and those who borrowed from him will not repay him. Inf. **mizap** AM (*often*).

Af. Pf. **auzip ʿlai** Gy 275:22 He lent me much (of His light), **auzip ʿlh** Gs 22:14; with encl. **auziplak** Gy 270:17. Impf. **nauzip** AM 44 he borrows; **mn nhurak tauzip ʿlan** Q 58:14 = ML 140:6 = CP 115:2 give us (*or* lend us) some of Thy light (cf. n. 4 contra MG 226:paen.); with encl. **nauzipulia razia** DC 44. 718 f. they communicate secrets to me. Act. pt. **mauzip** AM 24:17 etc. he lends MG 131:paen., 246:paen.; with encl. **ma ḏ-šaiilia mauziplun** DC 26. 264 he gives them (in plenty) what they ask for; pl. with encl. **mauzipilhun** Gy 187:9 (var. **mauzpilhun**) MG 149:9 f. Inf. **mauzipia** s. **iazapa**.

Ettaf. Pf. **ʿtauzap** Gy 343:9, Oxf. 23 b, 40 b:bottom was, were added, joined MG 247:9. Impf. **nitauzap ʿl** Gy 173:17 we shall be joined with, **nitauzipun** Gy 315:12 they shall be added to (or joined with) MG 247:9. Pt. **mitauzap** Gy 115:15 (is) added MG 132:bottom, 247:10, **luat hdadia mitauzap** ATŠ I no. 253 are mutually enhanced; ˁl hiia mitauzipia Gy 264:19 are added unto the Life; rurbia d̲-mitauzipia ˁl dirdqia Jb 35:11 the great that exploit (Lidzb. *sich überheben*) the small (MG 30:14).

Der.: **iazapa, iazupa, ˁzapta.**

-ih = -h̲.

YṬP I (יְטַב, Syr. ettaf. ܐܬܬܐܛܒ, H. יטב qal, hiph.) to do good, show favour MG 48:20.

Af. Impt. **mn d̲-ˁtlaikun auṭip ˁlh̲** Gy 36:11 do him good with what ye have (Sh. ʿAbd.'s copy has a proper pl. form **auṭipiun**); with suff. **auṭ(i)puia** Gy 15:7 do (pl.) him good MG 48:20 f., 279:4. Act. pt. with encl. **mauṭiplh̲** PD 1108; pl. **mauṭipia ˁlh̲** PD 1109. Part. pres. **mauṭipna ˁlh̲** Zotb. 219a:31.

YṬP II (**ṬPA I** by formal influence of **YṬP I**) to add, join, increase, augment, cover completely, swathe, veil, envelop.

Af. Pf. **uauṭip banhura kalalh̲** CP 90:10, ML 111:10 and (he) enveloped (Lidzb. *tauchte*) with light (and) veiled it (: the letter), **auṭipth̲ ˁl kulhun pasimkia** WedF 119:bottom I increased him over all the lights.

iihia a var. of **iahia** (q.v.).

iihra a var. of **iahra** (q.v.).

-ik pers. (both possessive and accusative) suff. of the 2nd p. fem. sg. MG 88:7, 16.

iirba (rt. ܝܪܒ) power, might. **šlim iirbia** DC 43 yielded up is his might.

YKA (< H. יכח hiph.) to admonish, reprove, snub. Doubtf. Only af.: pt. pl. with suff. **maukih̲ uamrilh̲** DC 48. 231 they snub her, saying to her.

-ikilta an alternative form of **ˁkilta** after procl. prep.

YLD (Gen. Sem., Ar. ولد) to bear a child, bring forth. Only ethpe., other stems from the introverted **YDL**. **ṭuria ialdun** DC 37 mountains bore me.

Ethpe. Pf. **ˁtlid** was born MG 74:12. Pt. **mitlid** Jb 70:5, DC 36 II no. 83 is born (MG 246:26).

Der.: **alida.**

YLL I (Jew.-Aram. and H. הילִיל, Syr. ܐܝܠܠ) to wail, howl, lament.

Pa. Pf. **ialil** Gs 3:5 he howled MG 211:14, id. DC 37. 150 they wailed.

Af. Pf. **haulil** he wailed MG 211:13, 244: anteantep., 247:2, **haulalat** Gs 95:17 she wailed MG 31:26, 274:2.

YLL II (cf. Mishn. אלל = ילל) to espy: **tililun tihzinun** DC 46. 199 penult. JRAS 1943 176: 23 ye shall espy them, behold them. Doubtf.

YLP pe. of **ALP I.**

Pe. Pf. **ˁlip** he learned MG 244:ult. (cf. mod. *yelef*); with suff. **ialapth̲** Jb 119:1 I learned it. Impf. **nilup (unalip)** ATŠ II no. 354 he learns (and teaches), **ˁu sipra tilup** AM 59:ult. either she learns writing (or . . .), **tilpun** Gy 14:14 ye (shall) learn MG 83 n. 4, 246:10. Act. pt. **ialip**, fem. **ialpa** (often in AM); pl. **(malpilun) ulaialpia** Jb 171:12 (one teacheth them) but they learn not, **d̲-trin sipria ialpia** DAb who learn two books (: different doctrines).

Der.: **ialupa, ialip(a).**

YMA (**ˁMA**) (יְמִי, ܐܬܝܡܝ and ܝܡܐ, Ar. ومأ to give a sign, Sab., Akk. in der. LS) to swear, take an oath; af. to adjure, put on oath.

Pe. Pf. **ˁma** Gy 349:11 etc. he swore MG 257:5, **iama** Gy 349:11, var. Leid. **ˁma** id., **daiuia ˁmun** DC 43a:55 the demons swore; with encl. **ˁmilia** Gy 144:3 (D **ˁmalia**) he swore to me MG 257:4, **ˁmalh̲** Gy 160:21 she swore to him MG 257:10 f., **ˁmilh̲** Gy 118:20 I swore (?) to him. Impf. **nˁmia** (DC 22. 105 **nimia**) **bˁumamata** Gy 110:9 we will swear with oaths, **nima unikadib** DC 7 swears falsely, **nimun** AM 177:12 etc. they (will) swear, **timun** Gy 20:11 etc. ye (shall) swear MG 259:6. Act. pt. **ˁu iamia umkadib bgauh̲** ATŠ if he swears falsely; pl. **iamin** Gs 36:24, ML 204:9, DC 48. 192 etc. they (will) swear. Inf. **mima** CP 169:1 = Oxf. iii 23 b = ML 204:9 MG 260:17.

Af. Pf. **aumia** Gy 182:14, 349:9 f., Zotb. 230b:12 he adjured MG 260:28; with suff. **aumian** he conjured me MG 284:antep., **aumiak** Gy 349:11 he conjured thee MG 286: 18, **aumitak** RD B 98 ff. I adjured thee, **aumitinun** Gy 103:16 I adjured them MG 291:3, **aumunun** Gy 331:6 *bis* they adjured them MG 291:10. Impf. **naumun** Gy 305:16 they conjure MG 262:5; with encl. **ˁiamilak** Jb 189:2, 5, 8 (read **ˁiaumilak**) I adjure thee MG 262 n. 1; with suff. **naumh̲** Gy 345:23 we (will) conjure him. Impt. with suff. **aumih̲** Gy 349:9 f. conjure him. Part. pres. **maumina** I adjure MG 246:ult.; with encl. **mauminalak** Par. xxvii 10b, Q 9b etc. I conjure thee MG 262:ult.

Der.: **mumata, ˁumamata, taumiata, ˁmamata.**

-in 1 Gen. Aram. ending of the st. abs. masc. pl. MG 161 f. (§ 131).

-in 2 a form of the possessive suff. of the 3rd p. fem. pl., v.s. **-hin.**

-in 3 a spor. var. of **-an 2.**

-inan acc. suff. of the 1st p. pl. (apart from **-nan, -an**) MG 88:17.

-inhun (varr. **-inun -nhun, -nun**) acc. suff. of the 3rd p. masc. pl. MG 88:18.

-inhin (varr. **-inin, -nin**) acc. suff. of the 3rd p. fem. pl. MG 88:18.

-inkun (and **-nkun**) acc. suff. of the 2nd p. masc. pl. MG 88:17 f.

-inkin (and **-nkin**) acc. suff. of the 2nd p. fem. pl. MG 88:18.

YNQ (Aram. and H. ינק, Syr. ܐܝܢܩ, Akk. *enēqu*) to suck(le), be small, little, be a little child, be young.

Pe. (doubtf.): Act. pt. **hanatin d̲-ianqan** ATŠ I no. 249 (read **mianqan** pa.?) those (women) who give suck.

Pa. Pass. pt. **tibil mianqa** the nurturing earth; pl. **ˁutria mianqia** Jb 11:7 ff. the youthful uthras; with encl. pers. pron. and encl. prep. **zuṭanalun lˁutria umianqanalun lpasimkia** Oxf. 75 a, DC 34:844 small am I amongst uthras and an infant am I amongst the lights.

Af. Act. pt. st. emph. **munqa** s.v.

Ethpa. Pf. **utianaq ulaˁtraurab** DC 34. 995 and he became small and not important;

ᶜ**tianqat ulatraurabat** DC 34. 32 she was suckled but not brought up; **utianqatun utraurabtun** DC 34. 850 and ye were suckled and brought up.

DER.: **ianuq, ianqa, ianquta, ianqita, mianqa, munqa.**

YSA s. **ASA V.** ,

iskun (Ar. يسكن) AM 128:ult. will be quietened.

–ispia an alternative form of (ᶜ)**spia** after procl. prep.

YᶜA I s. **YAA I.**

YᶜA II (יְעָא, ܝܥܐ H. יצא, Akk. [*w*]*aṣû* LS, Ges.) to bloom.

AF. Part. pres. with encl. **mauiatlun** Par. ix 9b, 39a thou lettest them bloom MG 246: ult. f.

iᶜṣun (Ar. يَعْصُون) AM 285:19 they rebel against.

YPA rt. of **aupa 6.**

YQD, (ᶜ**QD**) (Aram. and H. יקד, Syr. ܝܩܕ, Ar. وقد, Akk. *qādu* LS, Ges.) to burn.

PE. Pf. ᶜ**qad** Gy 280:21 (B ᶜ**qid**), Q 4:27, 9:10 he, it burnt. Impf. **niqad** Gy 320:6 (BC **niqud**) burneth MG 246:7 f. Act. pt. **iaqid** CP 8:4, Gy 79:2, 234:16, 238:2, 8 f., 335:10, Q 28:18 = ML 9:5 etc. is burning; fem. **iaqda** Gy 13:1, Q 28:19 etc. Inf. **miqad** CP 8:4, Q 28:18 f. = ML 9:5; **ubaba d̠-iaqad** DC 46. 245:14 verse that inflamed.

ETHPA. Pf. **kd̠ libat** ᶜ**tiaqdit brahmut** DC 44. 1391 = Morg. 265/21:9 like Venus, I burned with love.

DER.: **aqdana, iaq(u)dana, iaqid.**

YQR (Aram. and H. יקר, Syr. ܝܩܪ, Ar. وقر, Sab. 𐩥𐩤𐩧, Akk. [*w*]*aqāru*) to honour, respect, reverence, hold precious, hold in esteem, praise.

PE. Impf. **laniqar** Gy 390:16 (he) shall not be honoured MG 246:7. Act. pt. pl. **iaqria** Q 26:13.

PA. Pf. with suff. **iaqruih̠** DC 48. 115 they honoured him. **iaqirnak** we honoured thee MG 274:7. Impf. with suff. **n**ᶜ**iaqrak, niiaqrak** Gy 4:18, Q 53:24 we praise thee MG 29:paen., 273:16 f. Act. pt. with encl. **miaqrilak** ᶜ**utria** DC 3 the uthras pay thee honour. Pass. pt. **miaqar** Gy 1:22 honoured. Inf. **liaquria** Gy 179:6, CP 115:11, ML 141:1 to reverence, with suff. **iaqurak** to honour Thee MG 292:19.

AF. Pf. **kd̠ tagak auqart** DC 48. 280 when thou hast honoured thy crown (ritual idiom); with suff. **auq(i)rinun** he honoured them MG 281:21 f. Impf. **nauqrun tagaiun** ATŠ II no. 4 etc. they shall honour their crowns (ritual idiom); with suff. **niauqrun** Oxf. iii 79 a they (shall) honour me; **niauqrak** a var. of **n**ᶜ**iaqrak** Gy 4:18 (s. pa.) MG 85 n. 4; (ᶜ**iauqria)** ᶜ**iauqrinkun** DC 51. 655 I (shall greatly) honour you. Impt. **auqar aba u**ᶜ**ma** Gy 14:18 (cf. the 4th commandment); **auqar tagak** ML 53:9 **auqir tagak** CP 45:25 honour thy crown; **auqar tagaikun** DC 51, 161 id. pl. (ritual idiom); pl. with suff. **auqruia** respect him MG 279:4. Act. pt. pl. **mauq(i)rin, mauqria** Gy 120:21 etc. they honour MG 149: 10 f. Part. pres. **ukd̠ tagaikun mauqritun** DC 27. 120 and when ye honour your crowns (*ritual idiom*); with suff. **mauqrinun** I honour them MG 292:1. Inf. **auquria** Q 2:16 to honour; ᶜ**iauquria** (?) DC 51. 655 (s. impf. with suff.).

ETHPA(U̯)AL: Impf. **nitiauqrun** Oxf. iii 77 a *bis* = 91 ab:3, they will be honoured MG 85:14; **titiaqar** Gy 214:10, DC 34. 226 thou wilt be honoured.

RITUAL IDIOM: The af. with **taga** as an object 'to honour the crown' — at the beginning and completion of a section of the ritual, CP. trs. 28 n. 3, the priest takes the *taga* and kisses it with a benediction (see MMII p. 11).

DER.: **iaqira, iaqra,** ᶜ**qara 1.**

YRA (ܝܪܐ, عرا) to hold (back), retain, contain.

PE. Impf. **dimihta d̠-lanirun** Jb 33:4 (B . . . **lanirmun**) tears that they cannot hold back (?).

DER.: **niara.**

YRM the rt. of **iurama**? (q.v.).

YRQ I (ירק, ܝܪܩ, H. ירק II Ges., Ar. ورق, but der. يرقان jaundice, Akk. *arāqu*) to be yellow, pallid, green. Forms (*pau̯el* and *ethpau̯al*) influenced by **YQR.**

PAU̯EL: Part. pres. **alit kd̠ iauraqna** Morg. 263/16:23 (var. **iuraqna** DC 44. 1076) I went in when I was pale.

ETHPAU̯AL: Impf. **nitiauqrun** AM 251:11 they (will) turn pale.

DER.: **iaruqa, iarqana, iarqunia, iuraqa, miarqia.**

YRQ II (= **ARQ I** = ܥܪܩ with transition to פ״י in the af.) to flee, escape.

AF. Impf. with suff. ᶜ**iauriqinkun** (var. ᶜ**iurqinkun**) Gy 354:11, 15, 19 I will escape you MG 243:ult. f.

YRR = **YUR** to shine, be brilliant, resplendent.

ETHPA. Impf. **titiarar dmutak** DC 3 (but DC 53. 456:ult. **titiaqar**) thine appearance will be resplendent.

YŠṬ (אוֹשֵׁט, ܐܘܫܛ, H. הוֹשִׁיט) to stretch out, extend, spread out.

AF. Pass. pt. **maušaṭ** Gy 217:7, var. **miušaṭ** Gy 214:28 spread out MG 132:2, 246:ult.

–it 1 (cf. **-at 1**) an ending of the st. cstr. fem. sg.

–it 2 (cf. **-at 2**) a form of the encl. pers. pron. of the 2nd p. sg.

–it 3 verbal ending of the 1st p. sg. pf.

YTB (יְתֵב, ܝܬܒ, H. ישב, Ar. وثب) to sit, stay; af. to make sit, seat, settle, cohabit with, marry; pe. with (ᶜ)l to possess, bewitch.

PE. Pf. ᶜ**tib** he sat MG 244:paen., **iatbat** she sat MG 245:8, ᶜ**tibt** thou didst sit MG 245: 12, **iatbit** and ᶜ**tbit** I sat MG 15:16, 245:14, ᶜ**tibiun** Gy 170:23, DC 41. 553 etc. they sat, stayed MG 245:5, ᶜ**tibnin** we sat MG 245:21; with encl. ᶜ**tibalh̠** Gs 24:16 she sat by her MG 245:10. Impf. **nitib, titib,** ᶜ**tib** MG 246:6, but **d̠-nitab liban lsamkh̠** ATŠ II no. 199 that our heart may be set at rest; pl. **nitbun,** fem. **nitba** Gy 386:14 they (will) sit MG 246:10. Impt. **tib,** ᶜ**tib** (for both numbers), special pl. form ᶜ**tibiun** Gy 171:24 MG 246:12 f.; with encl. **ʿtiblia lʿdai** Morg. 263/17:12 sit on my hand. Pt. **iatib** Gy 288:22, 289:11, DC 27. 420 etc. (*often*) MG 49 n. 5, 246:21, fem. **iatba** (*often*), pl. **iatbia** Gy 210:9, Jb 139:1, AM 25 etc. (*often*), **iatbẖ** Gy 214:9. Part. pres. **iatbit** Gy 210:3, 211:10 thou sittest. Inf. **mitab** (var. **mitib**) Gy 210:9, Jb 138:ult.; with poss. suff. **mitbak** Gy 365:7 thy sitting, **mitbaikun** Gy 17:16 your sitting.

Af. Pf. **autib** he seated MG 7:20, 246: antep.; with suff. **ʿutban, autban** he seated me MG 23:12 and n. 1, 247:3 f., **autbak** he seated thee MG 273:13, **autbẖ** he seated him MG 275:10, **autbun, ʿutbun** they seated me MG 272:22, **autbuia** Gs 56:19 (A **auti-**) they seated him MG 30:21, 278:3, **autibtẖ** I seated him MG 277:14, **autibtinun** DC 41:545 ye have placed them. Impf. **ʿu pt ṭuhma nautib** AM 16:11 if he marries a girl of his family; with suff. **ʿiautbak** Oxf. iii 54 b:3 I (shall) seat thee MG 273:22, **ʿiaut(i)bẖ** Gy 118:1 f. I (will) marry her MG 276:1, **ʿiautbinun** Par. xi 32 b, MG 282:5. Impt. with suff. **autbẖ** seat him MG 276:15, **autibinun** seat them MG 282:14. Pt. **ʿnta mautib** AM 20:12 he will marry a woman; with encl. **ʿu mautiblẖ ʿu gaiar minẖ** AM 89:8 either he marries her, or commits adultery with her. Part. pres. **mautibt** DAb thou shalt marry; with suff. **mautibnẖ** ATŠ I no. 113 I will settle him. Inf. **ʿnta armalta ʿl mautbuia šapir** DC 34 auspicious for marrying a widow; **lmautbia ʿnta haduta** DC 3, ŠQ 30:7 for marrying a virgin.

Ethpe. Pf. **ʿtiatbiun** DC 34 they have seated themselves.

Der.: **mautba, mutba, tutba, tibta.**

-itia an alternative form of **ʿ(i)tia** after procl. prep.

YTM I the rt. of **iatim(a)** (q.v.).

YTM II mod. form of **YTB** MG 49 n. 5, a doublet of **YHM** s.v. Gl. (defectively, pf. without the 1st rad.) 56:13 f. جلس *sedere* نشست; 63:15 f. حلّ *permanere, habitare* ایستاد.

YTR (Aram. and H. יתר, Syr. ܝܬܪ, Akk. *atāru* to abound, Eth. ወተረ continually LS, Ges.) to gain, increase, abound, be supreme, surpass, exceed, gain wealth, get rich. Antonym of **HSR**.

Pe. Pf. **ʿtar** Gy 75:22, 91:11, 246:6, **tar** Gy 171:9 was enhanced, increased MG 245:3 f. Impf. with suff. **ḏ-masqilẖ bzaku ulatitarẖ** ATŠ I no. 224 (of the penis) who erect it in purity and do not use it to excess (?). Act. pt. with encl. **iatirlẖ** AM 24 he gains. Inf. **mitar** Gy 75:22, 91:11, 171:9, 246:6.

Pa. Impf. **anašia miskinẖ niatrun** AM 212:5 poor people will become rich; **zahba ukaspa . . . niatrun** AM 240:3 f. gold and silver . . . will become plentiful; with suff. **niatrẖ** Gy 105:ult. we (will) multiply it MG 29:23. Pt. **hailẖ miatar mn kulhun almak** Gy 82:3 f. his strength surpasseth all the worlds; pl. **mšabia umiatria** DC 3 they praise and extol; **mahu miatria** JRAS 1938 4:23 why do they extol? Inf. **iaturia uqaiumia** Gy 235:4 to increase and to raise.

Ethpa. Pt. **mitiatar** AM 22:17 he will become rich, (**mitiaturia**) **mitiatar** Q 64:9. Inf. **mitiaturia** Q 64:9 MG 144:20.

Der.: **iatir, iatarta, iutrana, iatruta, tiatruta.**

K

k the 11th letter of the alphabet. Pronunciation: plosive *k*, aspirated *χ*. The aspiration in foreign (Ar. and P.) words is sometimes designated with two diacritical points: **k̈** = خ MG 2:11, 19 f. Phonetic changes: initial **k** < **q** MG 39:9 ff.; medial **k** < **q** MG 40:1 f.; **k** > **g** MG § 43 p. 40 f.

-k (cf. **-ak**) a form of the poss. and acc. suff. of the 2nd p. sg.

ka (כָּא, Chr.-Pal. ܟܐ, Syr. in ܐܝܟܐ, ܗܪܟܐ, ܡܟܐ, ܗܘܪܟܐ) here. With prep. **lka** hither, **mn ka** hence, from here; with **ha**: **haka 1** (s.v.) MG 204:1 f. With **-hu**: **kahu** where? See also **aka, ʿka. lamparqilia mn ka** Gy 264:10 f., 13 they cannot free me from here; **mn ka mn atrai** Gs 48:11 from here, from my place; **lhaka asmẖ** Gs 94:2 he placed her here; **kahinun hiia ḏ-rihmit kahinun hiia ḏ-rihmun kahu bhir zidqa** Gs 94:12 f. where is the Life that I loved, where is the Life that loved me, where is the chosen one of righteousness?, similarly Gs 26: 20 f.; **kahu mšiha** Jb 275:1 ff. where is the messiah?; **kahu adam** Jb. 90:3 where is A.?

KAB s. **KIB.**

kababta (nom. act. pa. of **KBB**) burning, roasting charring, scalding. Var. **kibabta** s.v. **kababta ḏ-nura** AM 29:10 charring by fire; **kababta ḏ-aiba** AM 32:13 burning of cloud, lightning (?); **šqul kababtak mn guarẖ** DC 43 J 140, 150 (varr. **kabata, kabta 2**) remove thy burning from his stomach (varr. influenced by **kabta 1**).

kabada (s. **kabda**) (*a*) liver, (*b*) digestive organ. Pl. **kabadia.** Masc. (*a*) **kabadẖ** (Pet. **kabdẖ**) **ukuliatẖ** DC 22. 139 (= Gy 143:22). Cf. Gy 84:1 f.; (*b*) **šita kabadia hurinia** DC 48. 26 f. six other digestive organs; **lkabadia nsabunun** ATŠ I no. 248.

kabar (rt. **KBR**) (*a*) adj. great, mighty, (*b*) subst. (st. abs. of **kabra**) greatness, might, increase, etc. (Ar. خبر) news. (*a*) **kabar** (Pet. **kabir**) **mn mamlulia bspihata** DC 22. 30 (= Gy 31:10 f.; (*b*) **ʿu bdaula maliut ʿdia hu ʿu bnuna kabar hu** AM 254:2 if (it happens) in Aquarius, it betokens fullness of hands, if in Pisces, increase (or 'might'); **kabar ugibla**

s. gibla. (*c*) Gl. (st. empf. defectively) 41:7 بشارة *evangelium*; 67:12 خبر *fama* خوبى.

kabata s. **kababta.**

kabda (כַּבְדָּא, ܟܰܒܕܳܐ, H. כָּבֵד, Ar. كَبْد, كَبِد, Eth. ከብድ, Akk. *kabittu, kabattu* LS, Ges.) liver. Var. **kabada.** MG 107:2. Pl. **kabdia** Gy 194:1, MG 170 n. 3. Masc. (?). **kabdh̲ ukuliath̲** s. **kabada** (*a*), **kabdia ukuliata** Gy 194:1, DC 37. 70; **šuplh̲ kabda d̲-ʿurba** AM 132:1 rub on him the liver of a crow; **lgirgla lihdaia šabath̲ d̲-hu kabda psira qarilh̲** DC 48. 23 f. Gl. 144:9 **kbda** (*sic* and pl. miswritten) كبود, كبد *hepax* جگر.

kabul (كابُل) AM 197 Kabul, the capital of Afghanistan.

kabuṣtania (rt. **KBṢ**?) RD B 13 doubtf., prob. corrupt DAb 112 n. 5.

kabihta a var. of **kauihta.**

kabiṣa (καπίθη, قفيص) a measure MG 313:17 f. **bit kabiṣia d̲-bazira** Gy 387:2.

kabir(a) (כַּבִּיר, ܟܰܒܺܝܪ, كبير) great, mighty MG 124:4. Var. **kabar** (*a*) (s.v.). Pl. **kabiria.** Fem. sg. **kabirt(i)a. mimra kabira** Gy 31:5; **kabir mn mamlulia** s. **kabar** (*a*); **aka d̲-kabir minan** Gy 80:24; **kabir mn almia** ATŠ II no. 311; **maṣbuta iaqirta ukabirta** DC 27. 50; **nibia d̲-napša ukabira ʿlak** Gs 66:17 we seek what is immense and great to Thee MG 299: antep.

kabiš (Ar. كَبْش, H. כֶּבֶשׂ, Syr. ܟܶܒܫܳܐ, Akk. *kabsu* Fränkel 109, Ges.) AM 258:13 ram.

kabra (ܟܰܒܪܳܐ) JRAS 1937 591:penult. st. emph. of **kabar** (s.v.).

kabrit(a) a var. of **kibrita. umitqal kabrit** DC 46. 248:10.

kabša (rt. **KBŠ**) treading down, pressure, trodden place, platform. **lsanai ubildbabai šauitinun kabša atutia ligrai** DC 26. 608 I made my haters and my enemies a platform beneath my feet; **kibšia kibšit bkabša** (often in exorcisms) I trod them down utterly.

kabta (cf. **kapta**) cavity, pit. **kabta d̲-šurh̲** Oxf. roll g 821, Or. 326:2 his navel.

kagad, kagid (P. كاغذ) paper. **kdub bkagad** DC 46; **kdub bkagid** DC 46. 147:4 (*and often*).

kadaba 1 (כַּדְּבָא, ܟܰܕܳܒܳܐ) liar, adj. lying, false MG 120:12. Fem. **kadabt(i)a** MG 154:15. Pl. **kadabia.** Var. fem. **kadibtia** s.v. **ʿnbu mšiha kadaba** s. **kadaba; kadabia uhunpania** DC 41.

kadaba 2 occasional miscop. of **kdaba.**

kadan, var. **kadin** a place-name. Var. **kadin** AM 217:17, **kidin** AM 224:20. **mata kadan** (often in AM), cf. BZ Ap. II.

kadara a var. of **kadira.**

kadašta (nom. act. of **KDŠ** < **KTŠ**?) contention (?). **kadašta d̲-alahia** AM 252:12.

kadba (כַּדְבָא, ܟܰܕܒܳܐ, H. כָּזָב, Ar. كَذِب) lie, falsehood, falsity MG 106:ult. **nbihia d̲-kadba** (*often*) false prophets; **kadba uʿula** Jb 85:4 f. lie and evil; **abnia kadba** Jb 85:7 sons of the lie; **sahduta d̲-kadba, sahdia d̲-kadba** (*often*) false witnesses; **daiania d̲-kadba** s. **daiana 1.**

kadia (rt. **KDA** = **KDD**?) Or. 328:29 euphemism for 'buttocks'.

kadibtia a var. of **kadabtia,** fem. of **kadaba. ʿu kadibtia hʿ** DAb if she be a liar.

kadin s. **kadan.**

kadir(a) (ܟܰܕܺܝܪ) (*a*) weighty, heavy, hard, (*b*) fig. important, (*c*) weak, weary, weighed down by weakness, (*d*) astrol. unfavourable, inauspicious. Fem. **kadirtia** MG 154:13, st. abs. **kadira.** Pl. **kadiria,** fem. st. abs. **kadiran.** (*a*) **muma kadira** ATŠ II no. 165; **kadir mn** Gy 90:9 harder than; **bidmia kadiria** Jb 145:11; **šinta kadirtia** Jb 145:1; **miṭria kadiria** AM 214:10; **glalta kadirtia** DC 46; **haila rama kadira kabira** DC 44. 1749; **kadiria mn mania rurbia d̲-nhaša** DC 40. 209 f.; **kuhrania kadiria** Morg. 255/2:20; **haṭaiia kadiria** DC 34. 556 grievous sins; (*b*) **kadir uiaqir akuat aba d̲-ʿutria** DAb.; (*c*) **nuqbata kadiran** ATŠ I no. 240; (*d*) **luat ʿnta kadir lmizal** DC 38.

kadmia (P. گل ختمى) marsh-mallow. **gul kadmia** s. **bartang.**

kadpa (כַּתְפָּא, ܟܰܬܦܳܐ, H. כָּתֵף, Ar. كَتِف) shoulder; sometimes for **gadpa** wing MG 42:3, 77 n. 4, 107:3. Pl. **kadpia** CP 49:10, Q 23:7, MG 170 n. 3. **kadpa** Oxf. iii 12 a, her shoulder MG 178:5; **bit kadpaihun** Gy 197:24 (s. **bit** 3); **znipta d̲-tanina ʿl kadpai matnalia** DC 44 I place the Dragon's Tail on my shoulder; **ʿšria iardna lmirhas ʿšria aiar lkadpia** DC 12 the river brings forth creeping things, the air brings forth wings (winged creatures).

kadra (act. pt. pe. st. emph. of **KDR**) = **kadira** (*a*). Pl. **kadria. kadra mn kulhun almia** Gy 166:24 heavier than all the worlds; **kadra ʿl had ruban** Gy 167:1 ten thousand times as heavy; **brahmia kadria** DC 41. 519 f. with strenuous prayers; **šitin haṭaiia kadria** DC 50. 831 sixty grievous sins; **mindam kadra uiaqira** (*Florilegium*) something constraining and heavy; **kahua ukadra** s. **kahua.**

kadrʿiil mlaka DC 40. 1044 an angel.

kahu s. **ka.**

kahua (prob. Jew.-Aram. כּוֹחָא, H. and mod. H. כֹּחַ, כּוֹחַ, rel. to Ar. كاح to overcome, وكح to stamp with force) adj. strong, firm, mighty, powerful. **ʿumamata d̲-kahua ukadra** Zotb. 230b:13, PD 479, 497, ATŠ I no. 3, 19, 42, 44 powerful and constraining oaths.

kahuta (apparently rel. to **kahua,** hence < *כַּחוּתָא rather than ܚܽܘܫܳܐ 'breath') strength, power. **kahuta ušrita ukauna lahauilh̲** DC 45, DC 46. 188:ult. there will be no strength, nor relief, nor rest for him.

kahid (cf. ܟܰܗܺܝܕܳܐ) revered. **iaqir ukahid** DC 44. 1245 f. = Morg. 264/18:14.

kahla (كحل) kohol, antimony, collyrium. Var. **kula. l(i)malik kahla** (Pet. **kula**) (**d̲-**) **ma(m)liatbh̲** DC 22. 111 (Gy 116:16) wherefore hast thou filled it with antimony?

kahna (כָּהֲנָא, ܟܳܗܢܳܐ, H. כֹּהֵן, Ar. كاهن, Ges. s. כהן) Jewish priest. Found only in pl. **kahnia** MG 61:4. **kahnia ubnia kahnia** Jb

129:4, 10 f.; **gubria kahnia** Jb 127:8; **aqapra lpum iahuṭaiia ugiṭma lpumaihun d̲-kulhun kahnia** CP 173:penult., Jb 131:7 f. Often in Jb. **qumba d̲-kahnia** s. **qumba.**

kahnuta (כָּהֲנוּתָא, ܟܗܢܘܬܐ) Jb 108:13 (Jewish) priesthood.

kahrba (P. كَهْرُبَا) amber. **ukahrba d̲-kulul** DC 46 and amber that is pierced (?).

kahra (rt. **KHR**) sick, ill. Pl. **kahria. banašia kahria** DC 46 with sick persons.

kaua (in all other dialects as fem.: Talm. כוותא, Syr. ܟܘܬܐ, Ar. loan-w. كُوَّة Fränkel 13 and n. 2) hole, aperture, window, dovecote. Pl. **kauia** (like Talm. כווי, Syr. ܟܘܐ) MG 172:21 (the masc. sg. was unknown to Nöld.). **kd̲ iauna mn kauh̲** DC 40. 521 like the dove from its dovecote; **tartin kauia** Gs 15:8, 85:8. **ʿstakarlh̲ kauh̲** Gs 83:3 (var. **kauih̲** DC 22. 468) its windows were blocked up.

kauaiia s. **kuaiia.**

kauara 1 (כוורא Löw: OSt. 555:15, Mainzer ibid. 42) fish Jb ii 151 n. 1. Pl. **kauaria.** Var. **kaura** Bodl. 12. **ukauaria mn iama pahria** Gy 387:20 fish fly from the sea; **mahilun kauaria brundia ualuai** s. **brunda; kauaria ualuai lalagṭia** s. **aluai; ugaunh̲ kd̲ kauara nihuia** AM 233:15; **kauaria baṣria nihuia** AM 281:82.

kauara 2 (P. كوار), an item of the ritual meal, often with fruits and spices, onion, leek. Jb ii 151 n. 1. **sindirka ukauara urumana** Morg. 183:5, Lond. roll A 504; **kauara usindirka urumana** DC 42. 6, DC 50. 131; **kauara d̲-arqa** Par. 15 f. 2a, 45b, WedF 138b:10. Often in lists of ritual meals (: Oxf. roll f 367, 1266, WedF 3b:3 etc.).

kauariš (خوارج) AM 272:21 foreigners.

kauba a frequent var. of **kiba. kauba d̲-riša** DC 46. 70:1 headache.

kauihta (rt. **KHA**, cf. כָּהֲיוּתָא) JRAS 1937 591:17, Lond. roll B 511, Par. **xxvii** 9b, 13b eye-disease, dimness of sight, blindness. Var. **kabihta.**

kauila (ܟܘܠܐ, ܟܘܠܝܐ, ܟܘܠܐ, ܟܘܠܐ, ܟܘܠܐ, Gr. χηλός) ark MG 17 n. 6. Fem. (as in Syr.) MG 158:12. Var. **kiuila. bnia kauila** Gy 265:10, 380:9 build an ark; **nu d̲-kauila** Gy 380:9 Noah of the ark; **kauila hua qapia uazla** Gy 380:18 f. the ark was floating and moving; **kauila ʿl ṭura d̲-qardun nihtat** Gy 380:20 f. the ark descended on the hill Q.; **dukta d̲-ʿtibniat kauila** HG the place where the ark was built.

kauk (ܟܘܟܐ, mod. Syr. ܟܘܟܐ thorn-bush, Jew.-Aram. חוחָא thorn, H. and mod. H. חוח thorn Löw 105, Akk. *ḫāḫu;* Ar. خوخ peach) nectarine. **kauk hu** DC 41 (illustration of a tree); **hazin ʿlana kauka hu** DC 7 (illustration) this tree is a nectarine Gl. 77:3 **ḳ(a)uḳ** خوخ *precoqua* [sic] شفتالو.

kauna (כַּוָּנָה attention, devotion) rest, solidity, stability, firmness, resting-place, tranquillity MG 82:21, 100:17. **kauna litlun** Gy 263:24 they have no resting-place; **kauna uniaha** Gy 387:13 rest and tranquillity; **mirda d̲-kauna litbh̲** Gy 355:10 anarchy without respite; **kauna nihuilh̲** AM 70:10, **kauna nihuilun** AM 225:2, **kauna lahauilh̲** DC 45, DC 46. 189:1.

kaunata s. **kunata.**

kaupa (ܟܘܦܐ) bending, convexity, curve. **kaupa d̲-apkuta . . . kaupa d̲-burkia** DC 41. 464 f. the convexity of the neck . . . the convexity of the knees.

kaura s. **kauara.**

kaz AM 230:21, var. **paz** doubtf. (BZ 140 n. 2).

kazbaiia DC 7 name of a people.

kaṭa (Ar. خَطّ) writing, strip, piece torn or cut off: **kdub bkaṭa šaraia** DC 45 write on a strip of silk; **kdub bkaṭa d̲-ahu** s. **ahu.**

kai in **kai kasrau** (q.v.).

kaiaṭa (Ar. خَيَّاط with the ending of the Aram. st. emph., cf. ܚܝܛܐ) tailor. Pl. **kaiaṭia** AM 155:11.

kaiala (כַּיָּיל, ܟܝܠܐ) measurer, paragon, perfect, accomplished. Fem. **kaialtia. (a)rdikla kaiala** RD D 6 a perfect architect; **kaiala d̲-naṣiruta** Q 61:24, RD G 5, **kaiala rama bnaṣiruta** DC 22. 374:coloph., **kaiala rama . . . bnaṣiruta** ATŠ (colophons), **kaiala d̲-ginza unaṣiruta** DC 44 etc. (often in colophons) greatly skilled in priestly knowledge; **uautib kaiala umia kal** Jb 234:12 he placed (there) a measurer and he measured the water; **kaialtia umparaktia** AM 62:17 accomplished and brilliant; **kd̲ kaiala damia** AM he resembles a measurer (: is a prudent person).

kaiar = **kair.**

kaiarta, kaiirta (cf. ܥܟܝܪܐ, ܥܟܝܪܐ turbid, dirty) turbidity, pollution, darkness. **uliardna d̲-tibil kaiarth̲ . . . rmat** ATŠ II no. 15 (var. **kaiirta** DC 6) and she cast her pollution on the running water of the earth.

kaiat with suff. **kaiatkun** Jb 157:6, 160:8 (ACD **kaiata**) unknown Jb 150 n. 5. (Rel. to **kita 2**??). filth?

kaiub (act. pt. pe. of **KIB** with labialization of the vowel rather than a فاعول-form, as it was taken to be by Nöld. MG 114:1) aching, paining, suffering, painful. **libai d̲-kaiub** CP 171:10 my aching heart; **libai d̲-kaiub ʿtapan ʿtapan libai d̲-kaiub** Gy 358:8 f. my aching heart was healed [*bis*]; **liba d̲-ʿnta kaiub** DC 46; **halṣh̲ kaiub** DC 46.

kaizaril, kaizariʿil, kaizarʿiil, kizril a *malwāša* woman's name.

kaiid Zotb. 228b:32 a man's name.

kaiir s. **kair.**

kaiirta s. **kaiarta.**

kaikasrau, kai kasrau, kaikusrau (کی خسرو) Kai-Khosrau, a king of ancient Iran. **kai kasrau br sʿiauišan** Gy 383:3 Kava Husravas, son of Syāvaršan (Yašt IX 18, 22) = Kai-Khosrau, son of Siyāwaχš Gray ZA 19/1905 p. 281.

kaila DC 30 a var. of **kaiala** Jb 234:12.

kailia (Ar. خَيْل) horses, horsemen. **qahalpia**

kailia d-malka CP 235:7 the king's horsemen are passing by.

kair (Ar. خير) wealth, prosperity, good, welfare. Var. **kaiar, kaiir. kuasta ukair** AM 154:19 (P. خواست و خير) welfare and prosperity; **prahia ukair** AM 155:3 money and wealth; **kair uruaha** AM 282:22 welfare and ease; **iadita ukair** AM 253:16 knowledge and good. Gl. 68:7 **ḳira, ḳairai** [*sic*] خير *bonus*.

kairula (خير الله) AM 255:30 a man's name.

kaka (כַּכָּא, ܟܟܐ, cf. Akk. *kakku* a weapon) (molar) tooth. Pl. **kakia, kakania. hiua kaka** Gy 123:19 f. voracious animals; **kakia ušinia** Gy 279:23 molars and tusks; **ulkakania d-mqadin ukaibin** AM 287:39 and for teeth that are hollow and aching; **ukakania d-mqadarin** DC 46. 246:10 and molars that are going black (decaying); **bkakia d-rugza akalun** ATŠ II no. 137 devours them with teeth of wrath. Gl. 28:15 **kaka** (pl. **kakai** [sic]) اسنان *dentes* دندان; 95:10 id. اسنان, سن *dens* دندان.

kakria (sg. ܟܟܪܐ, H. כִּכָּר) DC 44. 1080 = Morg. 263/16:24 f. pl. talents (?).

kala (rt. **KLA I**) hindrance, restraint, impediment (?). Pl. **kalia 1. mn kalia bišia** DC 41. 561 from evil hindrances.

kalaia 1 (rt. **KLA I**) homeless: **lkalaiia udaiania haiasa** s. **daiana 2.**

kalaia 2 DC 22. 277 a var. of **kʿlaia** Gy 277:6.

kalanša (P. كلنجار) DC 46. 242:14 crayfish. Cf. s. **kasa.**

kalap Zotb. 221a:29 a man's name.

kalapabad Zotb. 227a:7 name of a town.

kalba (Gen. Sem.) dog. Pl. **kalbia 1. kalba ninikth** AM 21:2 a dog will bite him; **kalba qusa** s. **qusa; kalba d-maina** AM 131:14 an otter; **aiak kalba** DC 44. 531 like a dog; **kalbia** RD C 15; **trin kalbia** RD C 37; **kalbia šihania umšargizania** Jb 98:8; **kalbia šihania umšagrania** Gy 180:7. Gl. 35:9 **kalba, kalbia** كلب, اكلاب *canis* سگ; 142:12 defectively id.

kalbaita (cf. preced.) adj. fem. rabid. V.s. **ṭabaita.**

kalbia 1 pl. of **kalba** (q.v.).

kalbia 2 a place-name in AM, cf. BZ Ap. II.

kaldaia (כַּלְדִּי, כַּלְדָּאָה, ܟܠܕܝܐ) Chaldean, astrologer, soothsayer, magician MG 84:20. Pl. **kaldaiia. kaldaiia d-zipa** Gs 103:10; **kaldaiia d-šiqra** Jb 95:4, 97:13; **kašumia ukaldaiia d-kadba** Gy 20:10; **kašumia kaldaiia nahašia** Gy 279:14 f.; **kašumia ukaldaiia** Gy 301:20, 24. With original meaning: **mata d-kaldaiia** AM 250:penult., cf. BZ Ap. II.

kaluat (Ar. خلوة) DC 46. 113:1 privies.

kaluza (כָּרוֹזָא, ܟܪܘܙܐ < Gr. κῆρυξ, OP **χrausa*, Phl. *χrōs* Schaeder: *Iranische Beiträge* 56, 254, Wdg. v 65 n. 3, 66) cry, voice, acclamation, proclamation, heralding MG 30 n. 2:paen., 55:6. **kaluza d-hiia** Jb 169:8, 170:14, 171:1; **kaluza d-hiia rurbia kaluza d-hiia** Gy 356:23; **gabra d-kaluza bhira** CP 160:1 = Oxf. 21 a = ML 193:10; **qala ukaluza ʿlai** Gy 64:13; **bqala haila ukaluza** DC 27. 24, DC 41. 349, CP 464:6.

kalia 1 pl. of **kala.**

kalia 2 Gy 177:19 act. pt. of **KLA** (v.s. **KLA I**).

kalia 3 (rt. **KLA I**?) (كلّاء harbour, riverbank?) meaning doubtf., Lidzb.: *Vogelfänger* Jb ii 132 n. 3, *Fischfänger* (*Leute, die durch Absperrungen im Wasser Fische fangen*) Jb ii 144 n. 4. Used with **ṣaidia.** Apparently a plural form. **smak ʿl kalia** Jb 134:7 (??); **bhir mn ṣaidia uriša d-kulhun kalia** Jb 143:5; **ṣaida riša d-šurbta haita rišaia d-kulhun kalia** Jb 146:7 f.; **riša kalia** Jb 149:8; **uazla smak ʿl kalia** Jb 135 (Bodley) and went and rested upon the **kalia.**

kaliuta (כָּלִיוּתָא, ܟܠܝܘܬܐ) exile, banishment, absence from home, separation from home MG 41 n. 1, 146:14. **bkaliuta masgia** Gy 42:22; **azil bkaliuta** Gy 46:9; **bit kaliuta** AM (*often*).

kaliṣ (Ar. خالص) completely, entirely. **ʿurba ʿkuma kaliṣ** AM 131:penult. a completely black crow.

kalta (כַּלְתָא, ܟܠܬܐ, H. כַּלָּה, Ar. كَنَّة, Akk. *kallātu* Ges.) bride, daughter-in-law MG 101:15. **kalta d-bišia** Gs 101:1 f.; **hamata ukalta** Jb 169:1; **bkalta hinun mardimibh** DC 48. 229 they are sleepily indifferent to the bride.

kam (Ar. خام) cotton-cloth. Mod. **blita d-kam** s. **blita.**

kamazqan AM 206 a place-name.

kamalaua Zotb. 229a no. 12 name of a town.

kamaṣia Jb 87:1 (D **kamuṣia**) read **kumaṣia** Jb ii 90 n. 2.

kamar (Ar. خمر) AM 254:11 wine.

kamarta (nom. act. pa. of **KMR**) return, with **mn** turning from, aversion. **baba kamarta d-gabra mn arsh** DC 46. 216:8 a charm for turning a man from his (marriage-)bed.

kamuna (כַּמּוֹנָא, ܟܡܘܢܐ, H. כַּמֹּן, Akk. *kamūnu*, Ar. كمون, Gr. κύμινον, Lat. *cuminum, cyminum* Löw 206, Ges.) AM 287:42, DC 46 cumin. Pl. **kamunia** DC 46. 246:penult. cumin-seeds. Gl. 143:7 defectively كمون *cyminum* زيره.

kamia (Ar. كَمْأَة ?) truffles (?): **ʿiruq lkamia** AM 129:5 truffle-roots (?).

kamisi(l)a Q 48:23, 29 etc. a family-name.

kamka (cf. Ar. كُمْخَة) dirt, sediment, dregs (?): **hala uṣanda ukamkia** ATŠ I no. 268 = **hala uṣanta ukamka** DC 6 (= Bodl. 12) dust, stench, and dirty sediment (?).

kamṣa a doublet of **gamṣa.** Pl. **kamṣia** AM 278:paen.

kamqan AM 197 a place-name, prob. a mis-copying of **karamqan** BZ Ap. II.

kamria (cf. Syr. ܟܡܝܪܐ black, dark, obscure) AM 282:34 gloom, blackness, darkness, obscurity.

kamša (P. كمچه) spoon. Mod. Gl. **kmka** [*sic*] خاشوقة *cochlear* قاشق.

kan (خان) Q 73:21 khan MG 2:19.

kana (כַּנָּא, ܟܰܢܳܐ, H. כֵּן III, Akk. *kannu* LS, Jb ii 4 n. 4). (*a*) receptacle, vessel, storing-jar, (*b*) place of assembly or storage, store-room, storing-place, (*c*) assembly, congregation, assemblage, group, grove (of trees), (*d*) stem, race, community, branch, twig, (*e*) base, fundament, origin, (*f*) place of origin, source, home, native place, (*g*) collection (orig. place of collecting?), (*h*) adj.: established, communal, gathered-together, (*i*) often personified as an attribute of higher beings. MG xxviii 10, MSchr. 39 n. 2, Jb ii 4 n. 4, Nöld. ZA 30 1915–16 p. 145. Pl. **kania** WedF 56:bottom, 57:top. The distinction betw. different categories of meanings is often arbitrary, cf. CP trs. 260 n. 3. (*a*) **kana ḏ-hamra** Gy 392:6 pitcher of wine (cf. **hamar kana** s. (*i*)); **mn hak kana rba qadmaia** Morg. 78:8 f. (parallel with **mana**, cf. (*f*, *i*)); **ziua ḏ-bkanẖ iaqid** Jb 242:7; **kana ḏ-hidra** CP 116:12, ML 142: 3, the Stem of splendour; **kana ṭaba ḏ-asauata** Gy 197:4, 10; **kana ḏ-mririata** Morg. 200:2, 262/15:2, Par. xxvii 77 b; **kana ḏ-ziua** Q 16:30; **kana rba ḏ-ʿqara** Q 32:9 (or s. (*f*)?); **kana ḏ-aiar** Gy 78:8; **kana rba ḏ-asauata** Oxf. 57 a, Q 16:24, Oxf. roll g 1013; (*b*) **biriauiš kana ḏ-mia hiia** Oxf. roll f 208, 554, CP 60:3 etc.; **kana ḏ-mia** Q 27:20; **kana ḏ-mia hiia** Q 12:26 (cf. (*a*, *f*)); **kana ḏ-nura** Gy 88:19; (*c*) **kana ḏ-nišmata** Gy 23:10, 29:23, 185:8, 188:5, 225:17, 226:13, 227:17, 228:19, 229:16, 231:10, 19, 311:1, 314:20, 361:20, Gs 37:19, Q 5:26, 6:10, 11:18, 34, 12:1 ff., 64:33, 73:18, Zotb. 218a:18, Jb 265:7 ff. etc. (*very often*) the congregation of souls, i.e. the community of Mandaeans, MSchr 39 n. 2, JPTh 18/1892 p. 435 n. 1, Jb ii 5 footn., Ginzā 25 n. 1; **kana ḏ-nišma** Gy 314:9; **kana rba ḏ-nʿšmata** Gs 8:14, (var. **nišmata**) Oxf. 114 a; **kana ḏ-nišmata ḏ-naṣuraiia** Gy 298:9 = **kana ḏ-naṣuraiia** Gy 188:21, 310:6, RD B 69; **bkana pigit d-nišmata** CP 26:17 (CP trs. 16 n. 1); **nišimta kḏ bkana huat iatba** Jb 51:1; **nʿšimtak lkana mibʿia** Gs 4:10, 22, 6:1, 8; (*d*) **uarda bkana** Gs 84:21; **kana ḏ-asa** RD 5; **kma kania hauin asa** ŠQ 18:20 = CP 236:1; **kana ḏ-ʿlania** (or (*c*) grove of trees?); **kana ḏ-alip alip hauin aluatẖ** DC 51 a Stem whose branches are a thousand thousand; (*e*) **kana mn atutia alma** ATŠ I no. 216; **kana ḏ-napšẖ** J 4:12, Gy 79:9, 282:14 f., Gs 43:1, 70:14, **mn kana ḏ-napšẖ** Gs 42:24, **bkana ḏ-napšẖ ʿstar** Gy 84:10, 18, **kana ḏ-bẖ ʿstarbẖ** Gy 86:14; **kušṭa kana ulaupa** Gy 308:19 (or s. (*c*)?); (*f*) **kana ḏ-minẖ hua** Gy 83:24, . . . **huit** Jb 32:1, Gy 86:13; **kana ḏ-kulhun nahiria** Gy 3:12; **kana ḏ-minẖ ʿtitun** Gy 340:2; **ʿṣṭarar mana mn kanẖ** Gy 308:2 f.; **kana ḏ-ab** Gs 43:2, 70:17; **kana ḏ-abuk** Gs 43:7; **kana rba qadmaia** Oxf. 58 b; **kana qadmaia** Gy 292:4; **lkana ḏ-pišra** Morg. 257/5:7; **ulkana ḏ-bgauẖ rbat** DC 47; (*g*) **kana ḏ-zidqa** Gy 362:6 etc. often in rituals (sometimes personified, s. (*i*)); **trin kania ḏ-zidqa upatura** DC 3; **hazin kana ḏ-zidqa upatura dilak** CP 393:14 (*often*); (*h*) **naṣuraiia ama kana umkanana** CP 380:7 (cf. s. (*c*)); (*i*) **habšaba ukana ḏ-zidqa** Gy 289:3, 19, Q 12:13, 62:25, 63:2, CP 28:18 f., Oxf. roll f 1299, Morg. 6:antep., 87:14 etc.; **biriauiš kana hliṣa** CP 117:11, Q 59:21; **haš kana** CP 116:12, Q 59:6, 21; **kana rba ḏ-iukabar hiia** Q 31:25; **iukašar kana** Gy 129:14; **iukašar kana ḏ-hiia** Q 59:19 (Siouffi 38:9); **iusmir kana** Gy 127:13, Q 16:29; **kana ḏ-zidqa** CP 395:3 ff.

kanapta (nom. act. pa. of **KNP**) embrace (nuptial). **bkanapta hiduktia** ATŠ I no. 74 in nuptial embrace; **bṣuratin kanaptin** ATŠ I no. 239 their (nuptial) embraces at their time of ritual isolation.

kanar DC 22. 108, 179, 219 a var. of **kinar** Gy 113:6, 187:18, 225:2; **kanara** DC 22. 169 a var. of **kinara** Gy 176:21.

kanat name of a female spirit. **kanat niṭupta** PD 839, 1317, Jb 251:9 ff., CP 140 (*d*) 13 Siouffi 40:36, MMII 246; **kanat** = **libat** RD 7; **kanat rabtia** DC 36, DC 34.

kangana, kangara (see MMII Index) a clay ring placed beneath an object.

kangna (cf. preced.) might be used with the same meaning as **kanuna**, although it can hardly be explained as a corruption of it Ginzā 158 n. 1. Occurs only in pl. **kangnia ḏ-nura** Gy 144:15, MSchr 159 n. 1.

kandia, kandit = **akandia, akandit. kandia baiia** Gs 48:4 f.

kanun (ܟܳܢܽܘܢ) name of two months under the rule of Sagittarius and Caper, SsSs II pp. 33, 35: Ibn Nadīm كانون الاول December, كانون الثانى January (cf. Syr. ܕ' ܩܕܡ and ܕ' ܐܚܪܝ). **kanun aual** AM 261:ult. f. (or **k- laual** *passim*), **kanun ltania** AM (*often*).

kanuna (קָנוּנָא, ܟܳܢܽܘܢܳܐ < Akk. *ka*(*i*)*nūnu*? LS, Ar. loan-w. كانون Fränkel 26) brazier MG 113:26. Pl. **kanunia 1.** Masc. **kanuna rba ḏ-ziua** Gy 272:10; **bitpia tlata ukanuna** DC 48. 283 (s. **bitpia**).

kanundur DC 46 read **kundur** (?).

kanunia 1 pl. of **kanuna.**

kanunia 2 Sh. ʿAbd.'s copy's var. of **kin(ʿ)nia** (v.s. **kinta 1**).

kanupta (rt. **KNP**) AM 228:8 armful, lapful.

kanzala 1 (etym. doubtf. Surely foreign, cf. P. گرزن, گندله, کژار, from which, however, it hardly derives. Pallis' derivation from *candela*, MSt 174 n. 9, is mistaken) a long strip of material, loose part of turban Siouffi 122 s. 4, Pet., cf. MR 221 n. 3, MSchr 50 n. 1, the Mandaean *stole* used to secure the staff in the water MMII Ind. Var. **kinzala. kma šanai kanzala ḏ-ʿhablia** Jb 15:1, 263:9, 264:7, cf. 31:7 f.; **kanzalak** Q 7:4; **šria kanzalak** Lond. roll A 249, **šra kanzala** Morg. 215/18: paen. (impt.); **lguṭ kanzalak** Q 20:14; **albišẖ bkanzala** Q 20:17, DC 36. 2439, **ualbišiẖ kanzala lmargna** ATŠ II no. 394, **albušuia klila lmargnaikun ualbišuia bkanzalaikun** DC 50. 256; **ukanzalẖ gṭar** ATŠ II no. 392, **ugṭuriun kanzala** DC 50. 250.

kanzala 2 in **ptia kanzala unhira** Ṣâb.'s AM (cf. Par. AM 10:top) read **kankuza.**

kanzuzia (rarer, but nearer original Akk. form) see **kankuzia.**
kanzi'il DAb a supernatural being, son of Ptahil, possessor of a purgatory.
kaniana var. of **kiniana.**
kaninia, kinania DC 22. 152:ult. a var. of **kinnia** Gy 158:14 *bis* (a pl. of **kinta**).
kankuza (< Akk. **kanzuzu** chin, Kraus, *Orientalia* 1947, 190 ff., confimred by Syr. ܟܢܟܘܙܐ against von Soden, who supposed it to be some inner part of the mouth, ibid. 1957, 130 ff.) chin. Still used, pronounced **kankūza.** Var. **kanzuza** (etym. closer to the Akk.). Miscopyings **kanzala 2, kankaza** (s. vv.). **ptiian anpẖ uptia kankuzẖ** Am 7:3 her face is broad and her chin is wide; **ugaṭinia kankuzia** Am 8:17 and his chin is small; **bira** (CS and A **biria**) **bkankuzia** AM 40:3, 50:4 there is a dimple in his chin; **ptia kankuziẖ** AM 45:5 his chin is wide.
kansa Ṣâb.'s AM a place-name, written with Ar. article **'l kansa** as a var. of **lhansa** v.s. **dar 2.**
kanpa (כַּנְפָּא, ܟܢܦܐ, H. כָּנָף, Ar. كَنَفٌ, Eth. ክንፍ, Akk. *kappu*) (*a*) wing (cf. **ganpa**), side, arm, pl. loins, (*b*) border, end, edge, (*c*) receptacle, gathering-place, dump, (*d*) lap, bosom, (womb), pocket, (*e*) protection, covering, shelter, (*f*) congregation, company, host, army. MG 40:8, 107:1. Fem. MG 152:8. Ginzā 452 n. 2. Var. **kinpa 1.** St. abs. and cstr. **knap** MG 152:8, Pl. **kanpia.** (*a*) **mn kanpia ḏ-ziua 'ṣtarar** Gy 89:1; **šaba kanpẖ ḏ-rqiha** ML 9:8, Lond. roll B 21, CP 8:9, DC 12. 6; **šaqlit kanpik** Gs 21:5; **šqal kanpai mn rišai** Gs 23:9; **kanpia sriqia** Jb 88:10 empty arms (: childless); **knap hiia** CP 69:2, Morg. 232/52:5 f., Q 31:16 = ML 84:4 f., Gs 37:23 the arm of the Life (Lidzb. *die Kleiderfalte des Lebens*, cf. (*d*)); (*b*) **b'ṣtuna ana šqaltẖ mn kanpẖ** Gy 102:14; **bkanpia ṭarṭbunia** Gy 101:23; **lagṭa 'nšia kanpia kanpa ḏ-hdadia** Gy 391:5 the women hold the edges of one another's dress (?); (*c*) **kanpa ḏ-tibta utinta** ATŠ I no. 216; (*d*) **bkanpia ḏ-hdadia rakbia** Gy 95:15; **kanpia ḏ-armalta man maliḻẖ** Gs 10:24; **zidqa ḏ-bkanpai aulit** Gs 28:11; **'l kanpa mitrabia** Gy 56:6; **knap lbušaihun** CP 128:10, ML 155:10; **bahiš bkanpẖ ulamaška** CP 157:4; **zidqa ḏ-bkanpaian** ATŠ II no. 45; (*e*) **kanpa ḏ-'uhra** DC 44. 495 protection by the way, var. **kanpa uruhai** Morg. 258/8:30; **huai lkulhun humria kanpa** DC 40; (*f*) **kanpa ḏ-kanpia** s **KNP. kanpa ugunda ḏ-kanpia** Gy 42:9. For prepositional and adverbial use see **knap** s.v.
kanpan ukapan (first from **KNP**, second by alliteration, cf. **gubran uguban**) Gy 167:13 f. a pair of spirits set as guards over Ur.
kanpun (3rd p. pl. pf. pe. of **KNP** with acc. suff. of the 1st p. sg.) ML 145:2, CP 119:11 an angel ML 281.
kanpi'il, -'il, -'iil, -iiil (theophorous name from **KNP**) an angel, ML 281. **bihrun ukanp'i(i)l** CP 194:7, Oxf. 57 a = ML 228:11, **malka bihrun ukanpiiil** Morg. 6:13; **kanp'il** DAb one of the seven secret names of Abathur DAb Ap. I.

kanšia (rt. **KNŠ**) in **kanšia uzahlia** PD 405 the sweeping (*or* assembling) and cleansing, a name given to the New Year's Eve MMII 85, 330 ff., Siouffi 103.
kanta, pl. **kania.** Occasional var. of **kinta,** pl. **kinia.**
kasa (כָּסָא, ܟܣܐ, H. כּוֹס, Akk. *kāsu* OLZ xvi 533, Ar. loan-w. كأس Fränkel 171, contra Müller WZKM i 27, P. loan-w. كاسه from Aram.) drinking-bowl, cup. Pl. **kasia 1.** Still used, pron. *kâsa*; treated as fem. in mod. Mand. (*kâsa rafti* a big bowl). St. abs. and cstr. **kas. kas ruita** Gy 112:1; **šuba kasia hamra** PD 330, ATŠ I no. 28; **šaba bkasa uašqian** CP 40:3, ML 46:9 (s. **ŠBA I,** cf. ποτήριον εὐλογίας); **kasia ḏ-mhalin** (var. **mhalian**) s. **HLA I** pa. pass. pt. pl.; **kasa ḏ-kalanša** DC 46. 242:12 the carapace of a crayfish; **kasa ḏ-muza** ibid.:16 walnut-shell.
kasaita s. **kasita 2.**
kasia 1 pl. of **kasa.**
kasia 2 (כַּסְיָא, ܟܣܝܐ) secret, hidden, concealed, occult, mystic, esoteric, private, covering. St. abs. **ksia** s.v. Fem. st. emph. **kasita 1** MG 110:antep. Pl. masc. **kasiia,** fem. **kasi(i)ata** hidden things, mysteries, var. **ki-** (s.v.). **rba kasia qadmaia** Q 25:2 ff.; **adam kasia** (*often*) Siouffi 2:top, MMII Ind. (s. **adam**); **zihrun raza kasia** (*often*) Siouffi 41, 52; **šumia kasiia** Gy 159:13; **hiia kasiia** Q 25:19; **buta kasita** Gy 134:3, pl. **bauata kasi(i)ata** Gy 211:11; **anana kasita** Gy 131:15; **šumhata kasiata** Gy 159:19; **šuba kasiia ahẖ** Oxf. 87 b, **'utria kasiia ahai** DC 50; **nibṭa kasia ḏ-malil mn tibil** Oxf. 30 b; **niṭubta rabtia kasita** Gy 234:19; **hak škinta rabtia kasita** ATŠ I no. 6; **arbia kasiata ḏ-muqra hinun** DC 34. 773 they are four secretions of the gelatinous matter; **lahun iahuṭaiia kasia bhitia baṭlia** Jb 140:8 if there were not the Jews, the blameworthy (?), shamed, worthless.
kasiaia(ia) = **kasia. alma ḏ-kasiaiaia** PD 1367 = **alma ḏ-ksiaia** PD 1384.
kasil a var. of **ksil.**
kasiš'il Ṣâb.'s AM a theophorous name.
kasita 1 fem. of **kasia 2.**
kasita 2 (rt. **KSA**) covering, concealment. Var. **kasaita. mn hak iuma d-huat kasita lpagria** DC 22. 185 and Sh. 'Abd.'s copy (var. **kasaita** Gy 194:6, **kasiata** D).
kasita 3 (cf. **kisinta, kisna**) coral. **halita kasita umarganita** Or. 326:20 f.
kaspa (כַּסְפָּא, ܟܣܦܐ, H. כֶּסֶף, Akk. *kaspu,* Ar. كَسْبٌ Zimmern *Akk. Fw.* 17, 59, LS, Ges.) silver. Often; still used, pron. *kaspa.* **dahbaiin ukaspaiin** their (fem.) gold and silver MG 182:11 f. Gl. 128:14 missp. فِضّة *argentum* نقره.
kasrau (خسرو) name of several kings of ancient Iran. **kasrau br qabad malka** Gy 384:8, 10 ruled in 531–78 Ochser ZA 19/1905–6 p. 77 n. 6; **kasrau br kasrau** Gy 384:10, 13 ruled in 590–628 Ochser loc. cit. p. 77 n. 8; **kasrau** Gy 383:17; **kaikasrau** s.v.

kapa (כַּפָּא, ܟܰܦܳܐ, H. כַּף, Ar. كَفٌّ, Akk. *kappu*) (*a*) hand, palm of hand, handful, (*b*) bundle, sheaf, (*c*) vault. St. emph. **kapta 1** s.v. Pl. **kapia.** (*a*) **zidqa d̠-bkapaian** CP 29:1, Q 12:15 = ML 34:3 (cf. MG 179:9). **ʿniš d̠-kapa d̠-ʿdh̠ . . . nakit** DC 46. 93:4 a person that bites the palm of his hand; **umaitin kapia d̠-paluda** PA xi (ŠQ) and they bring handfuls of sweetmeats; (*b*) **kd̠ kapia tikapinun** DC 44. 1040 = Morg. 263/16:2; (*c*) **kapa d̠-ʿšumia** DC 42.

kapan s. **kanpan.**

kapar ʿda (rt. **KPR** (*a*)) a hand-towel. **kapar ʿda bʿdh̠** DC 38, a hand-towel in his hand.

kapur (ܟܳܦܘܽܪ, Ar. كافور) camphor, camphor-tree. **kapur hu** DC 41 (picture) it is a camphor; **zma d̠-šunara ukapur** DC 46. 86:6 cat's blood and camphor.

kapura (ܟܳܦܽܘܪܳܐ) unbeliever, denier MG 113: 22. Pl. **kapuria 1.** Gl. 34:13 pl. defectively اثمة *iniqui* كناهكاران; 121:3 sg. defectively غير المؤمن *infidelis.*

kapuria 2 a var. of **kaprun.**

kapuria 3 (nom. act. pa. of **KPR** (*b*)) Gy 37:1 heresy, apostasy, disbelief.

kapina (כפינא, ܟܰܦܺܝܢܳܐ) hungry. Pl. **kapinia. tisiba kapinia** DC 3, CP 452:ult. thou wilt satisfy the hungry.

kapla (Targ. כפלא loin, Ar. كَفَلٌ) loins, buttocks; **gaṭinia kaplh̠** AM 45:6 his loins are lean.

kapna (כַּפְנָא, ܟܰܦܢܳܐ) hungry. Pl. **kapnia. sapna kapna** Jb 158:5 voracious kingfisher (?); **mia kapnia** Jb 44:1 ravening waters.

kaprun (كفرون) Jb 148:4 (var. **kapuria 2** B) palm-fibre, coconut-fibre Jb ii 150 footn.

kapruta (abstr. noun from **KPR** (*b*)) Gy 15:13 heresy, apostasy, disbelief.

kapšiaiil DAb one of the seven names of Šamiš.

kapta 1 (St. emph. of **kapa,** ܟܰܦܬܳܐ, كَفَّة) (*a*) cup, small ritual drinking-bowl, (*b*) pit, cavity (var. **kabta** s.v.). MG 101:15. (*a*) **kapta** Morg. 183:7 f., 9, 185:10, Oxf. roll g 821, PD 838 (*often in rituals*); **kapta d̠-hamra** PD 1626; **kapta d̠-(a)zgauita** Q 24:31; **kapta d̠-riha** RD 42, 44 incense-cup; **kapta d̠-miša** Oxf. roll f 218 ff., 566 ff., 695, 699, DC 41. 324; **rmia miša bkapta** DC 24; (*b*) **kapta d̠-šura** Or. 329: 26 (cf. **kabta**); **ubkapta d̠-šurh̠ ṣimirta hauilh̠** AM 22:5 and in the cavity of his navel he will have strangury.

kapta 2 (rt. **KPT**) (*a*) fetter, (*b*) isolation, a semi-circle of pebbles which marks off the corner in which a woman unclean from confinement (a **ṣurta**) lies in an outhouse or room. (*a*) **kd̠ kapta** Sh. ʿAbd.'s copy's var. of **kd̠ kiputa** Gy 170:14 like a fetter; (*b*) **ʿu napqa bkapta d̠-ṣurta** ATŠ II no. 297 if she dies within the demarcating barrier which isolates a woman in childbed.

kaptar (P. كفتار) (*a*) hyæna, (*b*) a demon. (*a*) **mrirta d̠-kaptar** DC 46. 79:3 the gall of a hyæna; (*b*) **parša d̠-kaptar** DC 46 exorcism of a *kaptar.*

kaṣa (Ar. خاصة) AM 22:17 property, possession.

kaṣaian Zotb. 218b:23 name of a town.

kaṣara (קצרא, ܩܨܳܪܐ, Ar. loan-w. قصّار Fränkel 259) Gy 217:20, 218:10 fuller MG 39:11.

kaṣat- (< כִּיצַד?) what of . . .? **ukaṣatin d̠-pasqin zikria** ATŠ I no. 240 what about those who etc.

kaṣuma (ܩܳܨܽܘܡܳܐ) soothsayer, fortune-teller MG 39:10, Pl. masc. **kaṣumia,** fem. **kaṣumiata,** var. **kaṣumata** MG 169:8 f. **kaṣumia ukaldaiia d̠-kadba** Gy 20:10; **kaṣumia bdilun ginia uzutria šarin** Gy 60:1 (cf. s. **ginia 2, zutra**); **kaṣumia kaldaiia nahasia** Gy 279:14 f.; **kaṣumia ukaldaiia** Gy 301:20, 24, Jb 95:4, 97:12 f.; **kaṣumia ukaṣumata** Gs 30:22, C **kaṣumiata; lakimṣan kaṣumia** Gs 103:10.

KAR, KUR (ܟܳܐܰܪ, rel. to ܟܽܘܪ) to shame, pollute, disparage, consider unclean, disgrace, soil, reproach, blame, blacken.

Pa. Pf. with suff. **kaiarth̠ liardna** DC 6 and 36 II no. 15 she polluted the jordan; **napšaihun kairinun** Gs 46:4 they polluted themselves. Impf. with suff. **latikairunh̠** Gy 226: 23, 227:6 do not blame her (Nöld.) MG 278:14, do not consider her unclean (Lidzb.). Pt. (act. and pass.) **mkaiar** DC 40. 421 ashamed; pl. **mkairia bruhia unišmata** JRAS 1937 591:20 they pollute spirits and souls; with encl. **mkairilh̠** Gy 229:24, 232:16 they reprove it. Part. pres. **mkairit** Q 72:22 thou art polluted.

Ethpe. (doubtf.): Pf. **ʿtkarat** DC 43 I 40 thou art blamed. Pt. **ulamitkamar ulamitkar** AM 154:14 he is neither repentant nor ashamed.

Ethpa. Pf. **ʿtkaiart** Q 72:9 = DC 53 p. 139:3 thou wert polluted. Pt. **mikaiar** PD 557 is polluted; pl. **miṭanpia umikairia** Gy 224:17 they are soiled and polluted (var. **miṭanpia** DC 22. 218).

Der.: **kaiarta** (var. **kaiirta**), **mkairuta.**

kara = **ʿkara. aiak bazra kara d̠-mizdra** DC 46. 254:penult. like husbandman's seed that is sown.

karahia (rt. **KRH** = **KHR**) pl. the sick, the suffering, the weakly. Var. **karihia. masia karahia** Oxf. roll g 1016 he heals the sick, var. **karihia** Or. 332:25.

karamla a var. of **kar(i)mla.**

karasṭiania a var. of **karasṭiania.**

karapiun a demon Ginzā 189 n. 2. A place. **karapiun sarupa** Gy 187:18, 23, 24, 188:6 K. the Swallower; **bʿuhra d̠-karapiun** ATŠ I no. 216.

karapsa (ܟܪܰܦܣܳܐ < P. كَرَفْس Löw 223) celery. V.s. **qasṭarun.**

karaṣa 1 (nom. ag. pe. from **KRṢ**) informer, indicator. Pl. **karaṣia. alma karaṣia tihun** Gy 66:22; **hzun ʿdilma tihun karaṣia** Jb 175:11; **karaṣia uramazia** Jb 175:12 f., 185:16, Gs 105:15.

karaṣa 2 DC 22. 210:anteantep. a var. of **kaṣara** Gy 217:20.

karaştiania (ܟܪܣܛܝܢܐ, *Χριστιανοί*) Gs 136:5, var. **karştiania** D, **karişţiania** Leid. Ginzā 594 n. 3, **kraştiania** Gy 382:12, **krişţiania** Gy 55:14 Christians; **kraştinaiia** s.v.

karat, karata (rt. **KRA II**) heaps, piles; vegetables (cf. foll.). **karat** AM 226:16 (var. **karitia**) grain-heaps, green vegetables; **karata d-uarda** WedF 57:top, 62:middle, ŠQ 19:19 heaps of roses.

karatia (כרתי, ܟܪܬܐ Löw no. 169, Ar. loan-w. كُرَّاث Fränkel 144, mod. H. כְּרֵישָׁה < Akk. *karāšu* = Sum. *k(g)aruš* LS) *allium porrum*, leek, green-stuff, green vegetables, edible leaves. **sindirka ukaratia** DC 41. 172.

karbasaia Lond. roll B 419, for **qarbasaia.**

kardus Gy 390:6 a place-name Ginzā 416 n. 5.

karua (קְרָוְיָא, ܟܪܘܝܐ Löw 207) caraway, cumin: **karua hu** DC 41 (picture) it is a caraway plant.

karuguš (ܟܪܘܓܘܙ folk-name *karagoz*? < P. خَرگوشك Löw 315) marigold-seed (?). **karuguš umrirta d-diba bduq bnhirh̲** DC 46. 80:11.

karun (كارون) AM 194 etc. Karun, river in Khuzistan.

karia (כַּרְיָא) heap, ruins: **sapa ukaria unura** DC 48. 316 destruction and ruins and fire.

karihia a var. of **karahia** (q.v.).

kariuta (ܟܪܝܘܬܐ) sorrow, distress, pain, grief, misfortune. MG 146:15. Var. **ʿkariuta. haduta ukariuta** AM 193:7; **kariuta hauialh̲** AM 20; **kariuta lbnia hauilh̲** AM 2:20 he will have grief on account of his children; **ubnia kariuta hauilh̲** AM 20:13 and his children will be his sorrow; **kariuta mkairia** Gs 46:4; **aiţa ukariuta** s. **aiţa 1**; **lakariuta** Gy 9:12 no grief; **ʿkariuta ʿl liba** DC 51. 83 f.

karimla (כַּרְמֶל II Ges.) Mount Carmel. Varr. **karmla, karamla.** MG 27:7, MR 38:4 f., MMII 29, Jb II 94 n. 4. **ţur karimla** Gy 110:3, 118:8, CP 167:15, Morg. 50:1 f.; **ţura ţur karimla** Jb 91:14, 92:13; **ţur karmla** Gy 113:1, Oxf. 31 a; **ţura ţur karmla** Gy 196:21, cf. MG 310:8.

kariqa (Ar. خريق) torn. **uatna ʿlauh̲ minda kariqa** DC 46 and put on him something torn.

karişia (Ar. خارجي) AM 272:24 foreign(er).

karitia s. **karat.**

karka 1 (P. كرك) hen, partridge (?). Var. **kark(a)ua. mrirta d-karka** DC 46. 85:10 a hen's gall.

karka 2 (كرخه) the river Karkha. **mia d-karka** Zotb. 218b:7; **mia d-karka** ZDMG xix 123:3.

karka 3 (rt. **KRK**) in **karka d-mia** Or. 329:20, Oxf. roll g 807 the lower intestines (a pun, see **karka 2**).

kark(a)ua = **karka 1. mrirta d-karkaua** DC 46. 81:9 (var. **karkua** DC 45, DC 46. 130:1).

karkauan a spirit of light. ML Ind. **hauraran ukarkauan ziua** CP 64:13 = ML 80:4, 10 = Q 29:23, 31, DC 36, Oxf. roll f 915.

ķarkas (hardly a miscop. of كرفس 'celery', or ܟܪܟܡܐ 'flax') a plant: **karkas hu** DC 41 (picture of a tree or shrub).

karkašta occasional var. of **karkušta.**

karkud(a) (כַּרְכָּד, ܟܪܩܘܕܐ, *κερκίς*, gen. *-ίδος*) weaver's shuttle. Pl. **karkudia,** var. **karkuria** JRAS 1937 p. 594. With suff. **karkudun,** var. **-run.**

karkum name of a demon, MSchr. 149 n. 3, 4, MSt 12 n. 4. **umn špita udurdia d-azil luat ʿmh̲ hua karkum** Gy 126:17 f.; **karkum ţura rba d-bisra** Gy 142:21; **karkum ʿuşţuna** Gy 333:14; **asrh̲ d-karkum** Gy 382:23 (s. **asra 2**).

karkun m(a)laka (cf. preced.) Oxf. roll g 1001, Or. 332:19.

karkur(a) s. **karkud(a).**

karkušta (קַרְקַשְׁתָּא) sheep-bell, clapper, rattle MG 39:14, 128:3; cf. Jb ii 89 n. 1, 245 (to p. 45 n. 1), Nöld. ZA 29/1915 p. 240 n. 3 Pl. **qarqušiata** s.v. **huţra ukarkušta** (var. **-ašta**) **bʿdh̲ lagiţ** Gy 180:16 (var. DC 22. 173); **karkušta lagiţ bʿdh̲** Gy 187:23 f.; **man lagiţ karkušta bʿdh̲** Gs 10:23.

karkia s. **kirkia.**

karla AM 205 a place-name BZ Ap. II.

karmaba a doublet of **garmaba. kd karmabh̲ bnʿian ʿtbun** DAb cf. s. **garmaba.**

karmanh̲, karmania (كرمانى) of Kirman. Var. **kirmania. zira karmanh̲** (the famous P. زيرهٔ كرمان) DC 46. 110:7 the cumin(-seed) of Kirman; **tutia karmania** Şâb.'s AM var. of **tutia d-kirmania** AM 286:43 f. (P. تـوت كرمانى) the berries of K.

karmaqan AM 20 place-name, prob. Garmakan, Ar. Jarmaqan BZ Ap II.

karmla s. **karimla.**

ķarnuba husk, pod (of leguminous plants). Only Gl. 73:6 **ķ(a)rnuba** خرنوب *siliqua.*

karsa (כַּרְסָא, ܟܪܣܐ, H. כָּרֵשׂ, mod. H. כֶּרֶס, Ar. كَرِش and كِرْش, Eth. ከርሥ, Akk. *kar(a)šu*) (*a*) belly, stomach, (*b*) womb, uterus, (*c*) pregnancy. MG 100:7, St. abs. and cstr. **kras** MG 151:9. Fem. MG 157:paen. Pl. **karsata 1, karsauata 1.** (*a*) **kiba d-karsa** (*often*); **karsa bmʿia atnath̲** Gy 84:2; **rabut karsa** Gy 27:22; **karsa rabtia** Gy 357:6, Jb 170:4, 171:9; **karsaiun halba lamlat** Jb 44:8; (*b*) **kras ʿmh̲** Jb 6:3 f.; **bkras ʿmh̲** Jb 82:6; **malbuša d-karsa d-ʿmh̲** Gy 159:3; (*c*) **karsa qadmaita, karsa mişaita, karsa batraita** Jb 111:9 ff.; **tlata karsata** Gy 245:5, Jb 111:13; **tlata karsauata msakar** AM 41:20 f. three pregnancies are lost (: miscarried).

kars(au)ata 1 pl. of **karsa.**

kars(au)ata 2 pl. of **kursia** (also of **kursa**).

karpas read for **karkas**? (q.v.).

karpu (for P. كرپاسو) poisonous lizard. **hiuia siuia br karpu** DC 40. 1089 black serpent son of a poisonous lizard.

karšia AM 268:10 = **karišia.**

kašan (كاشان) AM 198 Persian town of Kashan BZ Ap. II.

kašar, kašra (act. pt. pe. of **KŠR**) right, pleasing, propitious, auspicious, successful, legal, legally permitted. **lakašar umbaṭal** ATŠ II no. 13; **dmuta d̲-lakašra** DC 22. 349 (missing in Pet.). Pl. m. **kašria,** fem. st. abs. **kašran** (s. KŠR).

kašgiš (P. كشاكش) Gs 82:7 BCD, Leid. = DC 22. 467 (= Pet. **ka šgaš** read **kašgaš**) contention, tumult.

kašura (כְּשׁוּרָא) joist, beam, plank. See **kšura.**

kašira (כַּשִּׁירָא, ܟܫܝܪܐ) pl. **kaširia** AM efficacious, useful.

kaškar AM 204 name of a town BZ Ap. II.

kašla (Ar. خشل) jewel. Mod. **ʿhbun kašla** DC 35:coloph. they gave me a jewel.

katuliqa (*καθολικός*) Gy 227:2 a catholicos.

katunia name of a town, or village: **mata d̲-katunia** RD D 25.

katura (rt. **KTR**) detention, holding back, custody. Var. **katra** DC 41. 565. **lkatura lkana d̲-nišmata** Gy 228:19.

kbakiata DC 30 a var. of **kbaṣiata 2.**

kbasta (rt. **KBS** = **KBṢ**?) oppression (?). Doubtf. Jb ii 39 n. 2. **kbastai umkaruastai** Jb 34:9 my oppression (?) and my isolation(?).

kbaṣiata 1 (rt. **KBṢ**) bunches, bundles. **marmahuz bkbaṣiata** ŠQ 18:18 (= CP 235:15) marjoram in bunches.

kbaṣiata 2 (cf. ܩܒܨܐ, Ar. قَفَص) cages, dovecotes Jb ii 134 n. 1. **msadqilun lkbaṣiatun** Jb 137:3 they break open their dovecotes.

kbar 1 (כְּבָר, ܟܒܪ MG 202 n. 2) already, formerly, as of old, as of yore MG 202:9. Var. **ʿkbar. kbar magzrilia** Gs 43:2; **ʿkbar magzria** Gs 70:16; **kbar ʿl iuhana qam** Gy 191:8; **kbar manda d̲-hiia bhšuka rmh̲** Gy 356:3.

kbar 2 (3rd p. masc. pf. pe. of **KBR**) a name given to higher beings. **kbar anana** Gy 374:17; **kbar ziua** Gy 77:7 f.; **iauar kbar** Gy 135:9; **haial kbar raza rba** Q 20:10 = Morg. 247/82:2; **kbar rba d̲-hu kbar ziua šumh̲** Gy 70:ult. f.

kbar 3 (rt. **KBR**) increase. V.s. **kṣurta** (last quotation).

kbaša (כבשא, ܟܒܫܐ) crushing, overbearing. **ngada ukbaša** Gy 312:16; **hlaṣa ukbaša ungada** Jb 194:9.

kbaštia (adj. fem. from **KBŠ**) adj. overbearing (fem.). **kbaštia ugazumtia hauia** AM 80:14.

KBB (כָּבַב, Ar. كَبَّب, Akk. *kabābu*) to burn, char.

Pa. Impf. with suff. **nikababh̲** DC 44. 1010 we will burn him, **ʿkababh̲** DC 37. 315 I will burn him.

Der.: **kababta** (var. **kibabta**).

KBH (Jew.-Aram. and H. כבה, Ar. كبا) to extinguish, grow dim. Only der.: **kabihta.**

kbirta (etym. doubtf.) a hornet or bee (engraved on the *skan daula*). **kbirta arqba uhiuia** DC 44. 956. A hornet, scorpion, and serpent.

kbiš, -a (pass. pt. of **KBŠ**) crushed, subdued, conquered, trampled underfoot, vanquished; (of eye) closed up (?), blind (?); (of name) degraded (?). Fem. st. emph. **kbištia.** Pl. masc. **kbišia. kbiš qarnia** AM 85:14; **ainh̲ kbišia** AM 89:7; **šuma kbištia** [*sic*] AM 83:antepenult. **aina kbištia** JRAS 1937 590:10.

KBL (Akk. *kabālu*, mod. H. כָּבַל, Ar. كبل, Jew.-Aram. and Syr. in derivatives) to fetter, chain, impede.

Der.: **kubla, kibla.**

KBṢ (קְפַץ, ܩܦܨ, H. קפץ, Ar. قفص, Akk. *kapāṣu*) to shrink, contract, become short, be bound, cut short MG 47:paen. f. (and n. 4).

Pe. Pf. **kbaṣ uʿṭar** DC 43 J 66, Oxf. roll 145 shrank away and disappeared. Impt. **aṭar ukbuṣ** Q 8:30 = ML 24:7 = CP 22:3 begone and vanish — (often in exorcisms).

Ethpe. Impt. **ʿtikbiṣ upil** DC 43 I 65, 80 be shrunken and fall down.

Der.: **kbasta** (?), **kbaṣiata 1, 2, k(i)uaṣ.**

KBR (Gen. Sem.) to be(come) great, powerful, burden, overpower; with (ʿ)l to overwhelm, overcome, dominate, control; to abound, increase, be plentiful; to (op)press. About the idiomatic **kbar ʿl** cf. MSchr 41 n. 1, 196 n. 2.

Pe. Pf. **kbar ziuh̲** ML 142:2 = CP 116:6 his radiance was great; **kbar bziua** CP 116:10 Q 54:9, 21, 89:2, DC 51. 223 he increased in radiance; **kbar ziuaihun ʿl ʿuṣrih̲** CP 267:12 = DC 38 his (: the Life's) light dominated his thought; **kbar ʿlh̲** Gy 84:24 (it) overwhelmed him (pressed on him); **kbar ʿl** Gs 48:24; **kbar ʿlauai(h)un** Gy 324:21 overwhelmed them; **nišma** (BCD **nišmata**) **kbar ʿlai** Gy 189:8 the souls press on me; **kbar** as pr. n. of higher beings s.v., cf. also **nhar ukbar tartin anania** Gy 374:16; **nibta d̲-kbar baiar** Gy 344:3 sprout that became great in the ether; **kbart** Gy 349:7, 9 thou wert great(er); **bišuta kibrat** CP 63:7 Q 29:5 = ML 79:1 the evil was great; **kibrat . . . ʿlai** Jb 32:10 it overwhelmed me; with encl. **kabralia** Jb 32:10 it overwhelmed me. Impf. **šinta . . . tikbar ʿlauaihun** Gs 45:15 sleep overwhelmeth them (MG 221:6); **d̲-latikbar nišimta ʿlh̲** ATŠ II no. 253 so that the soul might not overpower her; **ʿkma ʿkbar lbišia** Jb 203:6, **kma kbar lbišia** Jb 204:9 how long must I afflict the evil? Act. pt. **kabar ʿlh̲** ATŠ II no. 295 it will go hardly with her; **kabar ʿlauaihun** Gy 376:14 will overwhelm them; fem. **kabra btibil bišuta** Gy 309:5 evil overpowereth the earth; **kabra ʿlak bišuta** Gy 314:18, **kabra ʿlai** Jb 32:10; pl. **kabria ʿlauaihun** Gy 24:22 they overwhelm them; **kabria ʿlauaian** Gy 309:6 they overwhelm us; **d̲-kabrin ʿlh̲ razia bišia** ATŠ I no. 154 whom the evil mysteries overpower; **ukimia kabrit ʿl bnia anaša** DC 46. 62:12 f. and how hast thou (?) oppressed mankind?

Der.: **kabar, kabra, kabir, kbar 2, 3, ʿukabar.**

KBŠ (Aram. and H. כבש, Syr. ܟܒܫ, Ar. كَبَسَ, Akk. *kabāsu*) to press (down), tread down, compress, oppress, subdue, subjugate, crush, vanquish; intrans. with pass. meaning, with **riša, qumta, burka,** or **ldil-** reflexively: to bow, bend, with **raza** to plan secretly, concoct a secret plot. MSchr. 37 n. 1.

Pe. Pf. trans. **kbaš,** intrans. **kbiš** Jb ii 218 n. 3, **asiq bdaria kbaš** Jb 179:14 (f.) they made (them) ascend and trod down the generations; **ʿštaṭia . . . qumth̲ barqa kbaš** DC 34. 660 he prostrated himself . . . pressed (?) his body into the earth; **kbaš** Jb 156:8 (obscure); **kbaš qumtaihun** DC 41. 268 they bowed low (the intrans. **kbiš** form is identical with the pass. pt.); **burkh̲ larqa kibšat** Jb 252:11 she bowed down her knee to the earth; **burkh̲ kibšat** Jb 257:2; **kibšit napšai** Gy 103:17 I bent down; special pl. form: **ʿl asarun ulpakraiun lakbišiun** (var. **lakbašiun**) DC 26, DC 40 they did not get the better of their bonds and their fetters; **anatun mlakia kulaihun kbišiun** (ungrammatical, read **kbaštun**) **lplanita abatar plan** DC 45 ye angels have subdued N (-woman) after (: in love with) N (-man); **kbašiun kulhun bnat anašia** ibid. (read **kbišiun**) all people were subdued, or (read **kbaštun**) ye have subjugated all the children of men; with encl. **kbašbh̲** Gs 26:15 are compressed (?) in it; **ubnalun ukbašlun libta d̲-qudša** HG 55 and (she) built for them and compressed for them the "sacred" (clay) brick; with suff. **qam kibšu** (var. **kibšh̲**) **llibta qadmaita** Gy 331:9 (var. DC 22. 328) they arose and pressed out the first mud-brick; **kbašth̲** Jb 20:10 thou hast thrown it down; **kbašnh̲ lhšuka** DC 34. 231 we have vanquished darkness; **kibšuk (mikbaš)** JRAS 1937 593:14 they crushed thee (flat). Impf. **hab nikbuš ʿlh̲ raza** Gy 258:22 let us concoct a secret plot against him; **raza lmalka nikibšun** AM 218:1 f. they will conceive a conspiracy against the king; **raza nikibšun** Gy 250:23; **latikibšun rišaikun** Gy 15:1 bend not your heads; with suff. **nikbišinun** AM 184:18 he will subdue them. Impt. **kbuš usgud** Gy 21:11, 368:19 bow thyself and worship; **kbuš qumtak usgud** Gs 79:23 id.; **kbuš arqa** RD B 20 compress the earth; **ʿkbuš (ukabiš uandai urahiq)** DC 40 subdue (and crush utterly and remove to a distance); **ʿkbuš razia ʿlaiia** DC 40 bring into complete subjection the lofty mysteries; with encl. **kbušlia arqia mardia** Jb 242:14 tread down for me the rebellious earth; with suff. **kubšh̲ ulgiṭlh̲ nira** RD B 49 tame him and put on him the yoke; **kubšainun** DC 40. 518 tread them (fem.) down; special pl. form **ukbušiun minai šulṭania** DC 46 and protect me from (lit. hold back from me) those in authority. Act. pt. **kabiš** (*passim*) he treads down, subdues; fem. **kabša** Jb 124:10 she presses down (?); pl. **raza kabšia** Gy 114:11, 245:10, 259:14, 264:22, Gs 94:18 they concoct a secret plot; **azal ʿl hurina raza kabšia** Gy 245:13 they went and concocted another secret plan; **raza lbiš kabšia** Gy 265:20; **raza ʿlai kabšia** Gs 24:6; **razia sainia kabšia** Gs 24:8; **kabšia rišaihun** Jb 240:12 they bend their heads; **razia bišia . . . kabšia rišaihun** ATŠ **kabšin (ulamitkabšin)** DC 44. 622 they subdue (and are not subdued); **kabšin (ulamikibšin)** DC 26. 595 id.; fem. pl. **kabšan uldilia sagdan** Jb 152:6 f. they bow and worship me. Pass. pt. (identical with the 3rd p. pf. intrans.) **šamiš mikbaš** (var. **mikbiš**) **kbiš** RD B 96 (var. DAb) Š. is utterly crushed; **kbiš rišaihun** Q 43:9 their heads are bent; with encl. **mṣuta kbišlin** Gs 30:18 strife oppressed them; pl. **ʿl mahu kbišia** Gy 193:4 why are they held down?; **kbišia ukpipia mlakia** Morg. 268/27:10 the angels are subdued and bent down; fem. pl. **mikbaš kbišan** DAb they (fem.) are completely subdued; with encl. **kbišitun anatun** DC 43 F 66 ye were subdued. Inf. **mikbaš** Jb 51:10, RD B 96, JRAS 1937 593:14 etc., var. **mikbiš** (s. pass. pt.); with suff. **mikibšan** Gy 164:12 to defeat me MG 292:10, **mikibšak** Gy 164:11 to overcome thee MG 292:19; **kd̲ baiit mikibših̲** DC 44. 1224 if thou wishest to crush him down.

Pa. Impt. (**ʿkbuš**) **ukabiš** s. pe. impt. act. pt. **mkabiš** CP 194:6 = ML 185:3 (cf. n. 1), **niha mkabiš taqipia** Gy 7:2 Mild One which subdueth the mighty. Pass. pt. **mrahaq mkabaš** DC 43 removed to distance (and) subdued.

Ethpe. Pf. **ʿtikbiš uʿtkabaš**) Gy 167:23 he was trodden down (and greatly subdued); **kulhun razia braz tata ʿtikbiš** ATŠ I no. 249 all mysteries were subservient to the mystery of the Sheep; **ruha ʿtkibšat** DC 34 the earthly spirit (?) was subdued. Impf. **lanitikbiš** DC 44 shall not be subdued. Pt. pl. **lamikibšin** DC 26. 595 they are not subdued.

Ethpa. Pf. **ʿtkabaš** Gy 167:23 (s. ethpe.). Pt. pl. **mitkabšia** AM 184 the crushed ones; **gauaza d̲-mitkabšia mardia** Gy 80:3, 82:22 (with encl. **-šibh̲**) the staff by which the rebels are crushed down; **lamitkabšin** DC 44. 622 they are not subdued; with encl. **mitkabšibh̲ mardia** Gy 82:22 (above), 103:7.

Der.: **kabiš, kabša, kibša, kbaša, kbaštia, kbiš (kbiša, kbištia), kubaša.**

kdaba 1 (Mand. form of כְּתָב, ܟܬܳܒܳܐ) book, writing. St. abs. and cstr. **kdab.** Pl. **kdabia** AM 155:12. Doublet **ktaba. kdab ʿda** ML 231:5 autograph, manuscript (*often*); **kdaba umimra** DC 22. 224 = **ktaba umimra** Gy 230:13.

kdaba 2 occasional miscopying of **kadaba.**

kdana = **kudana. zim kh̲ kdana** DC 46 bridled like a mule.

kdara (rt. **KDR**) trouble, oppression, danger. **kdara uasaria** AM 214:5 oppression and bonds, miscop. **kdaqa** BZ 130 n. 5.

KDB I (Gen. Aram., H. כזב, Ar. كذب) to lie, speak falsely, deceive, falsify, deny, cheat; to alter; to accuse of lie, discredit.

Pa. Pf. **aumia ukadib** Gy 182:14 swore falsely (: perjured himself); **kadibt biahuṭaiia** Jb 103:ult. f. thou didst lie to the Jews; with encl. **kadibtbun** Jb 104:4 (B **kadabtbun**) Jb 104:4 thou didst lie to them; with suff. **kadibth̲ lmimrun** Gy 118:7 I discredited their speech. Impf. **latikadbai** DC 40. 392 do not lie (fem.); **ʿu halin ʿumamata tikadbun** DC 37. 141 if ye belie (: perjure) these oaths; with suff. **nikadbh̲ lmšiha** Gy 58:13 he will accuse Christ of lying MG 370:22. Act. pt. **mkadib btušbihta qadmaita** Gy 27:19 falsifieth the first praise (= **mdagil** Gy 51:4); **nbiha bnbiha mkadib** Gy 24:15 f. a prophet accuseth another prophet of lying; pl. **hinun bhdadia mkadbia** Gy 24:14, 96:11 they accuse one another of lying; **ubh̲ mkadbia umkadbia bibidata d̲-abrahim** Gy 46:7 they falsify it and falsify the works of A.; **lamkadbia bšuta d-maraihun** Gy 49:16 f. they do not alter the doctrine of their Lord; **napšaihun mkadbia** and ATŠ II no. 172 they accuse themselves of lying. Part. pres. with encl. **lamkadbinalak** Gy 144:4 I will not deceive thee.

ETHPA. Pt. **napšaihun mitkadbia** DC 27. 495 (= **napšaihun mkadbia** s. pa. pt. pl.).

DER.: **kadaba,** fem. **kadabt(i)a** (var. fem. **kadibt(i)a**), **kdaba, kadba.**

KDB II (< Gen. Sem. כתב, ܟܬܒ, كتب) to write, inscribe, ascribe. Rarer doublet **KTB** s.v. MG 42:7 ff.

PE. Pf. with suff. **kidbh̲** Jb 75:8 wrote it; **kidbu** Gs 108 f., (109:2), ATŠ I no. 13 they wrote it MG 42:8, 279:11. Impf. with encl. **nikdublak** DC 37. 93 he shall prescribe for thee; with suff. **nikidbh̲** ATŠ II no. 185, DC 41. 19 writeth it. Act. pt. **lakadib** ATŠ I no. 13, does not write; pl. **kadbia** Gy 24:8 they write MG 42:9. Pass. pt. **kd̲ d̲-kdiba** ATŠ II no. 399 as was written; with encl. prep. **kdiblh̲** AM 21 (is) ascribed to him; with encl. pers. pron. **ˁsirit anat kdibit lilita** DC 43 thou art bound (and) proscribed (O) lilith. Inf. **baiia lmikdib ˁngirta** DC 34. 186 he wants to write a letter.

ETHPE. Pt. **mikdib** ATŠ II no. 186 shall be written.

ETHPA. (?): Pt. pl. **mitkadbia bramšia** AM 148:12 written in the evening.

DER.: **kdaba, kdibta.**

kdi Morg. 250/87:23 an exceptional graphical form of **kd̲.**

kdibta (rt. **KDB II**) DC 46. 68:4, 71:7 writing, inscription.

kdira (pass. pt. of **KDR**) difficult, grave. **haṭaiia kdiria** (often) grievous sins. Gl. 34:15 **kdira** اصعب *difficile* دشوار, 53:8 id. ثقل *grave* سنگين.

KDL Gl. 48:9 f = **KDR I** (q.v.).

KDM (Ar. خدم) to employ, use, set at work.

PE. Pf. with suff. **kdaminun lhdadia** Bodl. 12 made them serve one another; **kdamth̲** DC 23. 516 she used it.

PA. Inf. **šapir l- . . . mkadmia amta uˁnta** AM 140:14 favourable for . . . employing a handmaiden or a woman.

Gl. 56:11 f. defectively with a prosth. a- خدم *ministrare, servire* خدمت كرد.

KDN (כְּדַן, ܟܕܢ, Ar. كدن, Eth. ከደነ to cover, Akk. *kidānu, kidinnu* protection LS) to yoke, couple, join.

ETHPE. Pt. pl. **mikidin libun** DC 46 their hearts are yoked (or 'coupled', but var. **mit-karkan libun** DC 45). Doubtf.

DER.: **kudana** (var. **kdana**).

KDR I (ܟܕܪ, Ar. كدر, Akk. *kudurru* slavery) to be heavy, weighty, hard; fig. to be disagreeable, grievous, weary, sickly, weak; to restrict, constrain, weigh down upon.

PE. Pf. **lakdur ˁlh̲** Jb 121:10 it was not hard for her; **ṭuna d̲-kidrat** [*sic*] CP 482:12 burden which lay heavy on my soul; **kidrat** [*sic*] **ṭunh̲ ˁl ˁur** DC 34 his burden became heavy on Ur. Act. pt. **ṭunh̲ ˁlh̲ kadar** Gy 170:13 his burden pressed (hist. pres.) hard on him; **mindam . . . d̲-kadar** Gy 391:13, **ˁlai lakadur** Jb 121:10 is not hard for me; fem. **šinta kadra ˁlauaihun** DC 36 sleep lies heavy on them; pl. **masputiata d̲-kadra mn kulhun almia** Gy 166:ult. f. fetters heavier than all the worlds; **kadra ˁl had ruban** Gy 167:1 ten thousand times heavier; masc. pl. **kadria** Jb 159:8 heavy (cf. also **kadra** s.v.).

ETHPE. Impt. **ˁkdar** (Leid. **ˁdkar**) **bṭunak dakia** Gs 68:11 f. be weighed down by (Lidzb. '*bücke dich unter*') thy clean burden.

IRREG.: **dahba mikdur** Jb 139:7, cf. II 135 n. 5.

Gl. 48:9 f. **KDR, KDL** ثقل *gravare* سنگين شد.

DER.: **k(a)dara, kadira, kadra, kudra, kud(a)rat.**

KDR II? (cf. Jew.-Aram. כַּדּוּרָא globe, ball) to be thrown around, to wind round. Miscop. (?) **KDD** (q.v.). Doubtf.

KDŠ, KTŠ < כְּתַשׁ, ܟܬܫ, H. כָּתַשׁ, Akk. *qatāšu*) to plague, strike; pa. and ethpa. strive, fight, contend, dispute, smite, torment.

PE. Only part. forms found: sg. with encl. **kadišlh̲** Gy 388:11, AM 199:19 he will strike him, quarrel with him; pl. **pakria kadšia unangria** Gy 121:17 they fetter, strike, and torment; pl. with encl. **kadšilun** Gy 182: 2, 19, 183:21 they strike them MG 42:4.

PA. Pf. **kadašat lrahmut kušṭa** CP 96:13 she strove after love of truth. Impf. **nikadiš** (often in AM) he will dispute, fight; **latikad-šun** Gy 14:21 do not fight. Act. pt. **mkadiš** AM 272:30 he will contend; pl. **maprišnalun d̲-hinun mkadšin** ATŠ I no. 130 we instruct them so that they may strive.

ETHPA. Pf. **uˁtkadaš lrahmut abuhun** DC 3. 118 and strove for the love of their father. Impf. **anat ˁlauaihun latikadaš** Gy 163:15 do not fight against them (var. **tit-**) MG 213:11 f.; **nitkadšun** AM 213:12 they will fight (together). Pt. **mitkadaš** Gy 50:24, **mikadiš** Gy 27:15 (read **-aš**, var. Sh. 'Abd.'s copy **mit-kadaš**) fighteth; pl. **mitkadšia** AM 199:18 they (will) fight; **bihdadia mitkadšia** ATŠ I no. 106 they will fight one another. Part. pres. **mit-kadašna** Gy 163:19 (var. Sh. 'Abd.'s copy **mkadašna**) I will fight. Inf. **mikadušia** Gy 40:17 MG 144:21, 213:12.

DER.: **kadašta (taktuša** s. **KTŠ**).

KHA (H. כהה and כאה, Jew.-Aram. כהא, כהי, Syr. only ܟܗܐ, Ar. كَهِيَ and كاى) to scold, rebuke, trouble, annoy MG 72 n. 1. A secondary form **KWA II** (of eyes, to be dim).

PE. Pf. ***kha** he scolded MG 72 n. 1; with encl. **khabun** (var. **khibun**) **khita** Gy 296:22 he reproached them; **ˁkihibun** Gs 62:14, 63:8 I scolded them. Impf. with encl. **nikhibh̲** Gy 101:12 he may grumble (be annoyed); with suff. **uˁgababh̲ uˁkihih̲** DC 43 C 16 (var. **uˁkihth̲** DC 33) and I bow him down and rebuke him.

DER.: **khita, kauihta, khut, kita.**

KHD (כחד ithpa. to be destroyed, ܟܗܕ to revere, H. כחד to hide, deny, Ar. جحد, Eth. ክሕደ to deny) to respect, revere, honour be in awe of, be afraid of.

Pe. Impt. with encl. **khudlh̠ lprudqa** DC 35 respect the passport.

Ethpe. Pt. pl. **anašia minh̠ mikihdia** (AM 165:15 has **mitkihria**: are troubled) people will be afraid of (or put to shame by) it BZ 103 n. 4.

KHW I (den. from **kahua**) to be(come) strong, firm, erect.

Pe. Pf. **zihuat aina ukihuat aina** DC 3. 275:ult. = CP 409:3 the well-spring spurted out, the well-spring was strong (?).

Der.: **kahua.**

KHW II? for **KUA I**? Very doubtf.

Pe. Impf. with suff. **ˁkababh̠ uˁkihu(?)h̠** DC 37. 315 f. I will burn him, I will char him (cf. **ˁgababh̠ uˁkihih̠** s. **KHA**).

khut (cf. s. **kauihta**) dimness of sight BZ 128 n, 9. **khut aina** AM.

khita (rt. **KHA**, Syr. ܟܗܝܬܐ) scolding, reproach, angry reproof, rebuke MG 104:3. **khabun khita** Gy 296:22 (s. **KHA**).

KHN (den. from **kahna**, as H., Jew.-Aram., Syr. and Ar.) to serve (as priest), minister to.

Pe. Act. pt. pl. **kulhun kahnh̠ usagdia qudamai** DC 45 all minister to and bow before me.

Der.: **kahna, kahnuta.**

KHR (met. of **KRH**) to be sick(ly), ill, be troubled or oppressed in mind; to fret.

Pe. Pt. pl. **anašia kahria** DC 46. 243:5 sick people.

Af. Pt. pl. **makhirun** a var. of **makruhin** and **mikrhin** BZ 189 n. 4.

Der.: **kuh(u)rana.**

KHT (from **khita** as if t belonged to the rt.) = **KHA.**

Pe. Impf. with suff. **ˁkihth̠** JRAS 1939 399:17 I rebuke him (var. **ˁkihih̠** s. **KHA**).

KWA I (כְּוָא, ܟܘܐ, H. and mod. H. כוה, Ar. كوى, Akk. *ku'ū*) to burn, char, consume, sear, cauterize.

Pa. Pf. with suff. **ukauitinun** DC 44. 1525 = Morg. 266/23:14 I charred them. Impf. **ukauaiia nikauh̠** AM 33:ult. and will cauterize him cauterizations; **kuaiia d̠-nura nikauh̠** AM **uˁkauh̠ uˁpilh̠** DC 33, DC 34 C 16 and I will burn it and cast it down JRAS 1939 399:19, DC 43 C 16.

Ethpa. Impf. **latirnia ulatikaua** Gs 43:4, ATŠ II no. 423, var. . . . **ulatikua** Jb 36:11 do not be anxious, nor be consumed (by anxiety) Jb ii 40 n. 2.

Der.: **k(a)uaiia.**

KWA II = **KHA.**

Pe. Impf. with suff. **anat lataqnh̠ ulatikuih̠** DC 34. 1024 do not correct him or rebuke him.

kuaiia, var. **kauaiia** (rt. **KWA**) cauterizations, v.s. **KWA** pa. impf.

kuakiata JRAS 1937 591:11 a pl. of **kaka**?

kuan (P. خوان) food, table(-cloth). **ṭašt kuan** DC 46. 203:6 a table-ewer.

kuasta (P. خواست) possession, v.s. **kair.**

kuaṣ s. **kiuaṣ.**

kuaṣta s. **akuaṣta.**

kuat s. **akuat.**

KUB s. **KIB.**

kuba 1 (כּוּבָא, ܟܘܒܐ, P.-Ar. كوب, Gr. *κυπή*) cup, drinking-bowl. Pl. **kubia. patura malia ukuba mziga** AM 51:2 a full dish and a mixed bowl; **ukubun d̠-mlia mambuga** CP 404:3 and their cup which is full of sacramental water; **kubia mia** DC 47 drinking-bowls of water; **mia mn iardna bhanath̠ kuba** ATŠ II no. 405. **kubaiun rahmia** RD E 28 they like their drinking-bowls.

kuba 2 (כּוּב, ܟܘܒܐ, Ar. كُبّ) thorn(s), thistle(s), prickle(s). **zria bkuba uaṭaṭa** Gy 12:10, Jb 45:15 sown with thistles and thorns; **kuba uaṭaṭa** Jb 46:2; **mlˁia kuba uaṭaṭa** Gs 13:17 full of thistles and thorns; **bsandlia kuba** DC 48. 248 in sandals of thorns.

kubastanaiia name of a people, or tribe. **arqa d̠-kubastanaiia** DC 7

kubaša (rt. **KBŠ**, cf. ܟܘܒܫܐ) cultivated land (land brought under cultivation). **unapqia bkubaša d̠-kbaš hibil ziua badam** DC 7 and they (: the rivers) emerge in the land brought under cultivation by H.-Z. with Adam.

kubita DC 36 no. 36 = **kuba** 1. Pl. **kubiata** PD 419 f.

kukbˁil, kukbiaiil (a theophorous name from **kukba**) DC 43 D 17 an angel DC 40. 875.

kublia pl. (sg. כִּבְלָא, ܟܒܠܐ, H. כֶּבֶל, Ar. كَبْل Fränkel 243, Eth. ከበሮ handle, ከንበሮ hair-pin, Akk. *kabālu* to fetter, Schulthess HW 63, Nöld. ZDMG 57 417) bonds, fetters. **kublia ušairia** DAb fetters and chains.

kuda (cf. כּוּדָא, ܟܘܕܐ) brig. hæmorrhage in childbirth, personified as a demon. **ukuda uˁkura uluṭata** . . . DC 20.

kudana (כּוּדָנָא, ܟܘܕܢܐ < Akk. *kudānu, kudannu, kudīnu, kudūnu* LS) mule. Pl. **kudania.** Var. **kdana. zim kd̠ kudana** DC 45 (var. **kdana** v.s.v.); **gumlia ṭinan zahba kudania qaz uabrišam** ŠQ 19:8 = CP 238:12 camels laden with gold, mules with gauze and silk.

kudarat (rt. **KDR I**, cf. **kudra** C) partial eclipse, sickliness (of moon). **kd̠ sira ˁtlh̠ kudarat** AM 282:12, var. **kudrat** Ṣâb.'s AM.

kudupta (from **KDB I** by assimil. of the last rad. to the ending) falsity, falsehood. **ulargazta ˁl aqamai uˁl kudupta** DC 43 and upon the provocation that is before me and upon falsity.

kudka (Akk. *kudurru*?) stone of demarcation, boundary stone, milestone Jb ii 49 footn., 102 n. 3. Pl. **kudkia.** Masc. **kudka** Q 65:14; **kudkik** Oxf. 42 b they (fem.) boundary stone(s); **traṣt kudka** CP 109:12 = Q 56:1; **kudka traṣnalun** Gy 247:3; **traṣ kudka** Gy 260:7; **nitirṣun kudka** Gy 319:3; **truṣlia kudka** Gs 52:4; **tarṣit kudka** Gy 72:1 f.; **kudka miṣra** Gs 52:4; **mšania kudkia** Gs 17:9, 19:13, 27:24;

latišanun kudkia Gy 40:18, **mšania kudka** Gy 183:9 (and often with **ŠNA**, cf. RD C 26 etc.); **lamandiz bgauẖ kudkia** Jb 184:12, Gs 13:11, **lakilbẖ parsia ulamandaz bẖ kudkin** [*sic*] Gs 84:10, **lamandiz kudkia** RD B 15; **mhara qaiim alihdia kudka** Jb 44:3 standing at the beak (of the boat) with the pole (?).

kudra (rt. **KDR**) (*a*) heaviness, hardness, force, strain on, (*b*) sickliness, feebleness, (*c*) (partial) eclipse. (*a*) **kudrẖ unaskẖ** Gy 160:12 his heaviness and his down-fall; **kudrẖ ḏ-ʿur** Gy 166:5; (*b*) **kudra nimṭia** AM 16:5; (*c*) **kḏ lšamiš hauilẖ kudra** AM 282:1 (cf. **kudarat**).

kudrat a var. of **kudarat** (q.v.).

kuhailia, kuḥailia a Mandaean family-name. **kiniana kuhailia** RD D 10; **adam kuhailia** RD D 20 etc. (often in colophons).

kuhurana AM 29 = **kuhrana.**

kuhrana 1 (rt. **KHR,** כּוּרְהָנָא, ܟܘܪܗܢܐ) malady, illness. Pl. **kuhrania.** Var. **kuhurania** s.v. **mahra ukuhrana** DC 43 H 40 (cf. Siouffi 88:top); **kuhrania kadiria** Morg. 255/2:20; **kuhrania uqirsia** Or. 325:7 (text), Oxf. roll g 968; **masasia ukuhrania** DC 51. 208 f.; **ušigra ukuhrana** AM 29:14.

kuhrana 2 (an intentional transformation of נּוּרְנָא 'reservoir', ܟܘܪܢܐ 'baptismal font' with derisive allusion to **kuhrana 1**) channel for waste water, gutter Jb ii 108 n. 4. **iardna ḏ-ʿṣṭbabẖ mšiha paulis kuhrana šauitẖ** Jb 108:9 f. the jordan in which the messiah Paul was baptized, I have made it into a gutter (= malady, a pun).

kuza (כּוּזָא, ܟܘܙܐ < P. کوزه, Ar. loan-w. كوز Fränkel 73) water-pitcher, jug, jar. Var. **kunza. kuza ḏ-mia** JRAS 1937 595:20, WedF 138b:8, 140b:middle, 141b:3 etc. (*often*); **rmia bkuza** DC 44. 925 f. place it in a water-pot; **kuza ḏ-lamšarai** DC 12. 260, Lond. roll B 527 a jug not yet used; **kuzia ḏ-miglip** s. **GLP**; **sab kuza ḏ-iama** DC 40. 74 f. Gl. 72:2 **k(u)za** جرّة *lagena* سبو.

kuzistan (خوزستان) AM 275 Persian province of Khuzistan.

kuka (cf. Dal. s. כּוּקָא *'ein feineres Gebäck in Ringform'?*) votive cake (?). Pl. **kukia. bkuka apilẖ** Gy 231:4 they bake it into a cake; **ramia kukia** Gs 30:21 (var. **kudkia** C, **kudka** D) doubtf. (Lidzb. '*Kuchen hinwerfen*').

kukaiia DC 7 name of a people, or tribe.

kukba (כּוֹכְבָא, ܟܘܟܒܐ, H. כּוֹכָב, Ar. كَوْكَب, Eth. ኮከብ, Akk. *kakkabu* LS) star MG 23:10, 127:16. St. abs. and cstr. **kukab.** Pl. **kukbia.** Masc. **kukba bil** Gy 385:10, **bil kukba** Gy 393:10 the planet Jupiter MG 319:22 f. (cf. ܟܘܟܒܐ) LS 321a:1; **kukba biša** Gy 118:21, 24 an evil star; **kukbia šuba** Gy 10:24, 329:8 ff., 332:18; **maṭarta ḏ-šuba kukbia** Gy 303:17; **qarqalta ḏ-šuba kukbia** Gy 222:11; **trisar kukbia** Gy 99:20, 122:14; **kukbia trisar** Gy 110:8, 112:5, 376:8; **habla ḏ-trisar kukbia** Gy 314:16 (s. **habla 1**); **kitun kukbia sdiqia** Q 68:2, Gs 82:9 (var. **sdaqia**) the veil of the stars is rent MG 413:11 ff.; **kukbia tlata** Jb 187:1; **kukbia hizua** Q 28:33; **kukbia ḏ-ramin bʿspiria ḏ-ʿšumia** Gy 60:11; **tmania bnʿ kukbia** Lond. roll B 168; **ṣarar bgauẖ kukbia** Gy 12:16; **kukbia umanzalata ḏ-ʿšumia** Jb 46:5; **kukbia ziqpa umanzala** Gy 272:7 (s. **ziqpa**); **kukab abu danab** s. **danab.** Gl. 168:2 **kukba** (and phonetically **-ua**) نجم *stella* ستاره, ibid. 13 pl.

kukbiaiil mlaka DC 40. 875 an angel.

kukbat (ܟܘܟܒܬܐ) DC 37. 534 the star Venus.

kukraia DC 22. 105 a miscop. of **nukraia** Gy 109:ult.

kukta (כּוֹכָא cave J?) DC 3 cave, lair (?). Doubtf., var. **dukta.**

KUL, KIL (Jew.-Aram. and H. כול, Syr. af. ܐܟܝܠ, Ar. كيل Fränkel 204, Akk. *kullu* pi. Ges., rel. to **KLL I, KLA II,** and **AKL II**) to measure, hold, contain, compute.

Pe. Pf. with encl. **lakilbẖ** (var. **lakalbẖ**) **parsia** Gs 13:11 (s. **kudka**), var. DC 22. 403, **kalbẖ** often for **kilbẖ** (which in fact is a pass. pt. with encl. 'is measured thereby' or 'therein'). Impf. **kma ʿkal mia hiia** Jb 204:1 f. how long shall I measure the living waters?; with suff. **bhablai ʿklẖ lkulẖ alma** Gy 82:13 s. **habla 2.** Act. pt. **kaiil zidqa** DC 3. 323:antep. he measures the oblation (missing in DC 53). Pass. pt. **kil** measured MG 250:19. Inf. **mikal alpa ḏ-šnia** Gy 26:13 s. **AKL II; adinqia mikal** Gs 118:24 without measure, beyond measure; **mikal kalia** Jb 93:6 s. **KLA II.**

Der.: **kila** (var. **kʿla**), **kilaia 1, kilta 2.**

kul (Gen. Sem., Akk. *kullatu.* Rt. **KLL II**) all, each, every, the whole, entire MG 105:4. With suff. **kulẖ** all of it, entirely, completely MG 178:5; **kulan, kulaian** all of us MG 179:1; **kulaikun** all of you MG 180:9; **kulhun,** fem. **kulhin,** mod. **kulu** (both genders) DC 43 Qašt. 241 all of them. Construction: with st. abs. **mn kul zan** Gy 380:14 of all kinds; **lkul atar** Gy 4:6 to every place; with st. emph. **kul tarmida** Gy 223:16 every priest; both side by side **kul ium kul iuma** Gy 230:11 etc. every single day MG 301:paen. ff.; substantivally **kul abad** Gy 269:2 he did all; **uhun kul barqa** Gy 268:18 and all were on the earth; **ukul minaihun ḏ-maiit** Gy 223:7AB and each of them that dieth; with logical genitive (cf, above) **kul ʿniš** (*often*) everyone, each one, anyone; **kul kul ʿniš** Gy 356:23 id.; **kul had** Gy 339:11 id.; before a pl. **kul humria** Gy 230:3 all amulet-spirits; **kul ʿnšia** Gy 230:ult. all women etc.; with suff. before a pl. **almia kulhun** Gy 283:17; **kulhun almia** Gy 280:7 all worlds (i.e. people); **maṭarata kulhin** Gs 92:10 all places of durance (purgatories); **kulhun lišania** Gy 230:5 all languages; **kulhun iuman** Gy 66:7 all our days; **kulhun ʿdia** Q 23:17 all hands; separated from the noun **babia ḏ-qra ruha kulhun** Gy 120:2 (cf. s. **baba 1**) etc.; **kulẖ** with sg. 'whole'; **alma kulẖ** Gy 318:18 etc. the whole world; **kulẖ alma** Gy 386:7 f. id.; **tibil kulẖ** Gy 381:16 etc. the whole earth etc.; separated from the noun **šiṭia ḏ-šaṭia mšiha kulẖ** Gy 111:13 the whole foolishness that Christ committeth; **baita hazin dilan hu kulẖ** Gy 80:25 this whole house is ours (rarely without the suff. **bkul alma** Gy 385:10, var. **bkulh̲ alma** Lond. as Gy 386:3, 7 f. in the whole world), **lkul haiutun** Gy 9:13 their whole life; an exceptional form **kulh̲ d̲-tibil** Q 1:18 the whole (of the) earth; **kulh̲** with pl. 'pure', '*par excellence*': **gupna d̲-kulh̲ hiia** Gy 71:2, 189:4; **atra d̲-kulh̲ malkauata** Gy 2:11, 16, 24; **daura taqna d̲-kulh̲ ʿutria** Gy 249:12, but **abda d̲-kulh̲ haṭaiia** (often in colophons, cf. also Q 23:19, 54:18) a slave that is all sin MG 323 ff. An exceptional form with suff. **kulan aprišata** DC 3 and 53 no. 371 all explanations. **kul d̲-** (often) each one that, everything that, all that, whoever, whatever MG 344:3 ff. **kul man d-** (*often*) each one that MG 345:1. **kul mud d̲-** Par. xi 22b all that MG 345:9f.; **kul mindam d̲-** Gy 224:20 id. MG 345:23. With an inf. abs. **kul mirba rabin** Gy 8:19 they grow up completely MG 399:5.

kula 1 (< כְּחָלָא, ܟܘܚܠܐ mod. H. כּוֹחָל, cf. Ges. s. כחל, Ar. كُحْل. Eth. ኩሕል, Akk. *guχlu* Nöld. *Neue Beitr.* 40, Haupt OLZ 16 492, Meißner OLZ 17 53) antimony, collyrium. **ainik aina d̲-ziua lmalik kula d̲-maliatbh̲** Gy 116:16 thine eye is an eye of radiance; why dost thou fill it with collyrium?

kula 2 (etym. and meaning doubtf.) used only of mountains, (כבלא? cf. **kublia**) mountain-chain?; (hardly from P. كُلاه hat, cap, mitre); or a kind of mountain-tree? **hazin ṭura d̲-kula** hᶜ DC 7 (picture); **ṭuria d̲-kula** Bodl. 12.

kulab (st. emph. כּוּלְבָּא, ܟܘܠܒܐ, Ar. loan-w. كُلّاب, MG 120 n. 1: prob. P., cf. كُل curved, كُلْبَه corner, rel. to *curvus* from a common Indo-Europ. rt., Fränkel 74, 87 f. and 290; cf. also H. כֵּלַפּוֹת, mod. H. כֵּילוּף < Akk. pl. *kalabāti, kalappāti* KAT 650, Copt. ⲕⲉⲗⲉⲃⲓⲛ Ges., Gr. πέλεκυς is Mand. **pilqa**) hook. St. emph. and pl. not found. **lamitligṭia bkulab** Jb 157:8 they are not caught with the hook.

kulaza (cf. ܟܘܠܙܐ, Ar. خُرْج from P. LS) sack, muzzle. **kulaza lpum kalba** DC 44. 950 a muzzle on the mouth of a dog.

kulazta (Lidzb. from Ar. خُلَاصَة? Ginzā 228 n. 5) Gy 227:14 butter (?).

kulai(a) (st. abs. כֻּלְיָא, ܟܘܠܝܐ, emph. ܟܘܠܝܬܐ, H. כִּלְיָה, Ar. كُلْيَة, Eth. ኵሊት, Akk. *kalītu*, Copt. ϭⲗⲟⲟⲧⲉ LS, acc. to Haupt AJSL 22:257 'something enclosed' Ges.) kidney. Varr. **kuluiia, kluiia 2, kuluia.** Pl. **kuliata** MG 105:ult., var. **kulaita** Ṣâb.'s AM (= **kuliata** AM 135:3). **aitilh̲ kulai** (var. **kulaia**) **d̲-qupa** AM 125:17 bring him the kidney of an ape; **kulai d̲-arnab** AM 131:penult. the kidney of a hare; **aitilh̲ kuluiia d̲-hamara** AM 133:3 bring him the kidney(s) of an ass; **kab(a)dh̲ ukuliath̲** s. **kabada** (*a*), **kabdia ukuliata** s. **kabda.**

kulaita (rt. **KLL I**) entirety, completeness. **bkulh̲ kulaita** DC 43 J 32 completely.

kului(i)a s. **kulai(a).**

kulul (cf. Ar. كُلَّة, pl. كُلَل, P. گلوله) ball, round. **ukahrba d-kulul hu** DC 46 and amber which is round (?).

kulia Jb 156:3 s. **klia.**

kuliata pl. of **kulaia.**

kulma d̲- DC 27. 13 read **kul ma d̲-** all that.

kulta (rt. **KLA I**) obstacle, hindrance, impediment, trap (?). **ukulta nistarkun pumaihun** DC 44 their mouths shall be stopped with an impediment.

kumaṣa (Targ. כומצא, גומצא, קומצא, Syr. ܓܘܡܨܐ, H. גּוּמָּץ) pit MG 41:1 f. (and n. 1), 123:9. Var. **kumṣa.** Pl. **kumaṣia**, var. **kamaṣia, kamuṣia** (s.v.). **mšadiklun lkumṣia** Gy 89:9 he bringeth the pits to silence, **uᶜštadkun kumṣia kulhun** Gy 97:14 and all the pits were silenced, **ukulhun kamaṣia mištadkia** Jb 87:1 (var. DC 30 **kumaṣia**) and all pits shall be silenced.

kumbian pl. (a miswriting of **qumba**?) domes? **tlatma ušitin kumbian** RD F 8 = DAb three hundred and sixty domes (?).

kumṣa s. **kumaṣa.**

kumra 1 (Old-Aram., Nab. כמר, Syr. and Chr.-Pal. ܟܘܡܪܐ, H. and mod. H. כֹּמֶר, cf. Akk. fem. *kumirtu*, Gr. κομάριος LS, Ges.) priest (not Mandaean). Var. **gumra 3.** Pl. **kumria. kumria zabia uadidia** Gy 28:14 f., = 174:9, Gs 17:10, 27:19 priests, sacrificers, and oracle-mongers; **hda kumra brišaihun maqmia** Gy 231:12 they instal one priest at their head; **kumraihun usagadun** Gy 119:10, **kumrun usagadun** Gy 119:13 their priests and worshippers MG 181:24; **ᶜhabtinun lkumrh̲** (var. **-ih̲**) Gy 119:4 (var. DC 22. 114) I gave them to his priests.

kumra 2 Gy 81:8 doubtf., Lidzb. proposed to read **humrh̲** (better would be **-a**) her amulet-spirits Ginzā 81 n. 2.

kumraita a *malwâša* woman's name.

kumran a var. of **kumbian.** Formally st. abs. fem. pl. of ***kumarta** (priestesses, female attendants, waiting women).

KUN I, KNN II (Jew.-Aram. pa. כַּוֵּן, Syr. ܩܡ, H., Phoen. כון, Ar. كَانَ, Eth. ኮነ to be, Akk. *kānu* to be firm, establish, set, stand fast) to be, exist; pa. to establish, make firm, steady, settle down, set at rest, compose, found, constitute, set up, give being to; af. id. MG 82:21 ff.

Pe. Pf. **kan iardna d̲-mia hiia** Gy 129:21 the jordan of living water stood still; **kan kinta** Gy 222:16 etc. (*often*) he founded a community; **mn rugzaihun kan** DC 34 they calmed from their wrath; **stuaran kan unṭar lduktaihun** ATŠ II no. 388 they found firm footing and maintained their place; **llibh̲ kan** DC 34 he calmed his heart; **urtitia d̲-hualh̲ blibh̲ kan** DC 34. 1086 and the tremblings which he had in his heart were stilled; **kanat** used as a pr. n. of a female spirit (v.s.v.), special pl. form **ukaniun kulhun razia** (**uᶜuṣṭuna kan**) ATŠ II no. 89 and all the mysteries were established (and the Body came into existence). Impf. **rugzik nikun alik** Jb 165:11 thy wrath shall be calmed; **nikinun ʿl duktaihun** Gy 370:5 they may be set up firmly in their place (MG 249:26). Impt. **kun** Jb 165:11 calm thyself, **riš kinutak kun napšak** Gy 214:8 the first principle of thy righteousness: straighten thyself (: be righteous; one would expect **akin** Ginzā 214 n. 4); **kun** (**uʿtkanan**) v.s. ethpa.; **nha ukun bduktak** Gy 129:18 be still and steady in thy place; **kun kun br** Gy 294:15 be at rest, steady, my son; **nha ukun uʿtkanan** Jb 74:2 (s. ethpa.). Act. pt. **lakaiin ʿlẖ ḏ-mn napšia azil** AM he does not rest so that he goes of himself; pl. **ʿl ʿstuarun lakainia** Gy 264:8 they have no steady footing; **raqdia ulakainia** Lond. roll A 352 = CP 340:penult., DC 34. 882, CP 340:penult. dancing and restless; **miṭal(a)lalia ulakainia** Gy 129:15 they sport and do not stand still; **iuma ḏ-razia kainia** ATŠ II no. 196 the day when mysteries settle down (: take place).

Pa. Pass. pt. **mṭanpa ulamkauna** Jb 87: 3 ff., 88:9 ff., PD 1025, 1039 polluted and not correct; but **ḏ-mkanan umatna ʿl iad mlakia** Gy 272:11 which is set firmly in the hand of the angels (from **KNN II**).

Af. Pf. **akin uautbẖ lʿuṣrẖ** Gs 72:10 calmed and settled his mind; with suff. **akintẖ mn rugzẖ** DC 48. 30 thou hast allayed its rage. Impt. **nha uakin napšaikun** Gy 309:10 be still and calm yourselves.

Ethpe. (?): Pt. pl. **šubima ušubin alpia šadaruania mikin ʿlẖ** RD A 4 = DAb seven hundred and seventy thousand fountains are set in it.

Ethpa. (from **KNN II**). Impt. (**kun**) **uʿtkanan** Gy 114:15 be (calm) and steady MG 82:23; **nha ukun uʿtkanan** Jb 74:2 id. (homonymous with **KNN IV** MR 85 n. 2).

Der.: **kauna, kanat, k(a)unata, kiana, kina, kinuta, makna.**

KUN II, KNN III (den. from **kiniana** 1) = **KNA I.** Doubtf.

Pa. Pt. pl. with encl. **mkainalun** Gy 231:15 (var. Leid. **mkanailun**) they are named.

KUN III = **KNN I** (q.v.).

-kun (& **-aikun, -akun**) possessive suff. of the 2nd p. pl. masc. MG 88:9 f., replacing often the special fem. form **-kin** MG § 146.

kunar s. **kinara 2.**

kunata (rt. **KUN I**) DC 36 no. 232 fem. pl. correct in ritual observance. Var. **kaunata.**

kundur (P. كُنْدُر) AM 130 frankincense. Var. **kanundur. kundur ubrisam** DC 46.93:5 s. **birsim.**

kunzia DC 43 J 166 a var. of **kuzia** (P.A.'s copy) pl. pitchers.

kunpa = **kanpa. kunpia sara** DC 45 sheaf of barley; **tmania kunpia ḏ-rqʿha** *Florilegium* the eight sides of the firmament.

kus DC 44 name of a spirit.

kusil (Jew.-Aram. כְּסְלָא, H. כֶּסֶל, Akk. *kaslu* loin) sloth (of flesh). Varr. **kusʿil, kusʿl, ksʿil** (influenced by angel-names ending in -ʿil?) MG 118:4 ff., **ksul, ksil. kusil bisra** Gy 236:6, Gs 7:12, 15, ATŠ II no. 146, 389 (DC 6 **kusila**) fleshly sloth.

kusrau DC 22.380 a var. of **kasrau.**

KUP, KPA, KPP I (Jew.-Aram. כפא, כוף, Syr. ܟܦܐ, ܟܦ, and ܟܦ, H. כפה and כפף, Ar. كفا, كفّ, كفكف, Akk. *kīpu* and *kapāpu*, Gr. *κάμπτω*) to bow, bend, curve, turn up, tuck up; pa. to curb, force to bend, vanquish, humiliate.

Pe. Pf. **kap šipẖ** (varr. **šaipa** D, **šipulẖ** DC 22. 411) **uṭarṭ(a)bun(i)ẖ** Gs 21:10 he tucked up his skirt (?) and his garment (?, Lidzb.: turban) Ginzā 493 n. 3; **kḏ kapitun šipulaikun** DC 35 when ye have tucked up your skirts; with suff. **kapẖ lruha** DC 37 they (?) curbed the (evil) spirit; **kapinun alahia zikria mn dauraihun** DC 43 J 17 he abased the male gods from their dwellings, **kaptẖ** Gy 90:23 I bowed him MG 277:5. Impf. with suff. **nikapinun** DC 43 J 82 he will abase them, **kḏ kipia tikapinun** DC 15 thou bendest them like bows (both could be pa. of **KPA**); **ʿkapapinun mn . . .** JRAS 1939 401:7 I will bow them down from . . .; **ʿkipipinun** [*sic*] DC 37 I will force them back. Impt. **kup napšik** DC 44. 465 bow thyself, **kup kul lišanun** DC 44 curb all the tongues of my enemies; **kup kup kup daiua** DC 43 I 95 bow down, bow down, bow down demon! (is the last **KUP** a pr. n. ?, cf. s.v.). Act. pt. **burkal ʿniš lakaiip** AM 26:17 he will bow the knee to no one. Pass. pt. **kipa ugahna qumtaihun** Gy 179:19 their stature is bowed and curbed (MG 108:7); pl. **kipia** (often), **kpipia** [*sic*] **mlakia atutai** DC 44. 1755 = Morg. 268/27:10 angels are bowed beneath me.

Pa. Impf. with suff. **ʿkapapinun** JRAS 1939 401:7, DC 43 C 61 (from **KPP I**) I force them to bow (cf. also s. pe. impf.). Pt. with suff. **umkapapak** (from **KPP I**) **ziua bzmum kapta** DC 43 and the light curbs thee with a camel-ring curb.

Af. (?): Pf. **burkẖ larqa akap** DC 34. 814 he bent his knee to the ground.

Ethpe. Pf. **ʿtikpipit utitkapap** DC 43 I 60 f. thou art conquered and abasest thyself. Impf. **nitkipiun trin rišak** DC 43 thy two heads shall be bowed.

Ethpa. Pf. **ʿtkapip** [*sic*] **unpil qudamai** DC 44. 374 they were conquered and abased themselves before me. Impf. **titkapap** s. Ethpe. pf.

Der. **kaupa, kapa, kapta 1, kup, kupa, kipa, kiputa, kpip(i)ata, kuptia.**

kup (Impt. pe. of **KUP**) name of a demon. **trin bnia ḏ-kup rba** DC 43 I 135 the two sons of the Great Kuf (cf. also s. **KUP** impt. pe.).

kupa 1 (rt. **KUP** = **KPP I**) sheaf or handful (?). Var. **kuš** s.v. **kupa ḏ-mšaṭa** Oxf. roll f 1223 f., 1273 ŠQ 6:13 the sheaf (?) that is laid down (on the ground).

kupa 2 (كوفة) AM 198 the city of Kufah. BZ Ap. II.

kupas (rt. כפס to tie, fasten?) belt (?), girdle (?). **kupas razia lbišna** DC 40. 747 I put on a belt (?) of mysteries.

kupar (Ar. كُفْر) unbelief? Var. **kupur.** Or depression? ¶ **kupar blibh̲ d̲-bnia anašia badiqna** DC 46 I put unbelief into human hearts. Gl. 122:8 **kupra** عدم ايمان *incredulitas* بى ايمانى.

kupaṣia (خَفّاجِى) AM 105 (& often in colophons) a Mandaean family-name.

kupur s. **kupar.**

kupla (Jew.-Aram. כפלא loin, H. כֶּפֶל doubling) loin, groin. Found only in pl. **kuplia. lkuplia sustata** Lond. roll B 391, var. **lʿkpulia** DC 40. 143 for the groins of mares.

kupna (כַּפְנָא, ܟܰܦܢܳܐ with regr. labialization of the vowel) hunger, famine, starvation. MG 18:8, **kupna uṣahia** DC 41. 429 hunger and thirst; **šaialtaiun bkupnaihun uṣihiaiun hauia** ATŠ I no. 237 their torment will consist in hunger and thirst. Gl. 71:4 **k(u)pna** جوع *esuries, fames* گرسنه.

kupra s. **kupar.**

kuptia (rt. **KUP** = **KPP** I) vault. Not sure. **bʿda kuptia kapta** Gs 99:9 f. with her hands she fixeth the vault.

kuṣa(h), kuṣat (Ar. خوصة) palm-leaf, palm-frond. **kuṣa d̲-pahla** DC 46. 54:10, **kuṣat pahl** ibid. 148:8, 211:1, a male palm-frond.

kuṣurta = **kṣurta.**

KUR s. **KAR.**

kura (כּוּרָא, ܟܘܪܐ, H. כֹּר, mod. H. כּוֹר, Ar. loan-w. كُرّ, Akk. *gurru*, KAT 340, 651, Ges.) a dry measure. Pl. **kuria. qahma bkuria qaiil** WedF 37:1, ŠQ 15:17 (CP 223:2 has **bʿkuria**).

kuraisan AM 276:20 = **kurasan.**

kurasa (ܟܘܪܐܣܐ, Arab. loan-w. كُرّاسَة Fränkel 251) quire, loose-leaved manuscript. Var. **kurisa. ansalh̲ mn kurasa d̲-ansa lnapšia** AM 105. 8:2 he copied it from a quire that he copied for himself.

kurasan (خراسان) Persian province of Khorasan. Varr. **kuraisan, kurastan.** Often in AM.

kurastan AM 203:11 a var. of **kurasan.**

kurd (كُرْد) AM 202 Kurd, name of a people, taken as a place-name.

kurisa Zotb. 228b:18 a var. of **kurasa.**

kurkia (P., cf. **karka 1**) crane. **ukurkia bharṭumh̲** DC 21 = JRAS 1938 3:27 and the crane with her bill.

kursia 1 (כרסא & כּוּרְסְיָא, ܟܘܪܣܝܐ, Ar. loan-w. كُرْسِى, H. כִּסֵּא prob. from Akk. *kussû, kursû*; cf. Schwally, ZDMG liii 197, Jensen, *Keilinschr. Bibl.* 6. 1, 514 f., Ges.) chair, seat, throne MG 128:12. Var. **kursa.** Pl. **karsauata 2** MG 20:18 ff., 166:24, rarely **karsata 2.** With suff. **kursiak** thy throne MG 177:4, **kursi(i)h̲** his throne MG 178:2; **kursia d̲-nirig zidana** Gy 301:21, 302:2; **qašiš kursia d̲-niha mn kursia marda** Gy 78:6 f.; **kursia d̲-malka d̲-arqa** Gy 360:24; **kursia ṭarpan** RD 46, **kursia arsan** RD 30, **kursia ʿl ʿispar šumh̲** RD 14, **kursia d̲-šdum** RD 20, **kursia d̲-ptahil** Gy 393:13 f.; **kursiak truṣ lkulhun handamia** DC 44. 1948 = Morg. 270 30/20 enthrone thyself (?) over all his limbs; **karsauata d̲-niaha** Gy 210:11, 22, **karsauata d̲-mirda** Gy 18:24; **tlatma ušitin karsauata** RD A 6; **bastirqa ukarsauata** ATŠ II no. 315; **karsauata d-ziua** Jb 218:10; **uʿtša karsata hinun d̲-kul tlatin iumia mn had kursia qaima ulkursia hurina taqna iatba** ATŠ I no. 272 and they are nine thrones, so that every thirty days it rises from one throne and seats itself upon another firm throne.

Gl. 142:8 sg. & pl. (both missp. with ṣ) كرسى, كراسى, *thronus, sedes, cathedra* تخت.

kursiat anpia (Norb. ܟܘܪܣܝܬܐ, Ar. كرسوع ?) Gy 244:17 Nöld. *Nasenbein*: MG 128:7 ff., the face (?). Doubtf. Ginzā 245 n. 1.

kuš P.A.'s version of DC 48 a var. of **kupa 1.**

kuša (very late. Etym. doubtful. Hardly כּוּשׁ, ܟܘܫܐ spindle): a piece torn off? **kdub ʿla kuša mn ṣudra** DC 46 p. 53:1 write on a piece torn (?) from a coat.

kuṣasta (P. خُجَسْتَه) Ṣâb.'s Liturgies (coloph.) a woman's name.

kušṭa (dissimilated form of קושטא, Jew.-Aram. קֻשְׁטָא, Bibl.-Aram. קְשֹׁט, Chr.-Pal. ܩܘܫܛܐ, Syr. ܩܘܫܬܐ, H. קֹשֶׁט, Ges. s. קשׁט, Ar. loan-w. قِسْط Fränkel 205 f., Jeffrey 237 f., Lidzb.: western Aram. tendency of dissimil. of emphatic sounds Jb ii pp. xvii f., AF 244 f.) truth, good-faith, sincerity, faithfulness, right-dealing, plighted word, troth, pact, promise, vow; the action of giving the right hand in troth, or plighting by grasping the right hand and then lifting one's own hand to the lips; the ritual hand-clasp (corresponding to the Christian Pax) which occurs during sacraments (baptism, marriage &c). MG 39:9, 104:14; Lidzb. ZDMG lxi 696 n. 3, Jb ii p. xvii f., ML 3 n. 1, Ginzā 5 n. 12, CP. trs. 2 n. 1; Kessler PRE 175 f.; Brandt MR 110, 200; MSchr. 6 n. 3, 48 n. 5; Pallis MSt 168–172; MMII 200 n. 1; WiW chap. viii. A synonym of **šrara** Widg. iii 55. W. Sundberg, *Kushṭa, a Monograph on a Principal Word in Mandaean Texts*, Lund 1953 (the occurrence of the word, pp. 15–39; statistics of different occasional translations, pp. 40 f.). Often personified as a celestial being. Adverbially **bkušṭa,** adjectivally **d̲-kušṭa** (cf. below).

With **ABD I: ṭubaihun labdia kušṭa** Gy 64:18, **d̲-abdia umabdia** (read so) **hiia bkušṭa** Q 59:33 f., **ʿdaikun nibda kušṭa** Gy 357:20 f., **ʿdaikun nibdun** [*sic*] **k-** Jb 172:12; **adiaura d̲-k-** Gy 314:13 f.; **ahia d̲-kušṭa** Gy 18:10 f.; **ahat d̲-k-** Jb 128:13; **ainai dilia d̲-k- lahazilh̲ lk-** (CP 163:2 = ML 198:4 f.; **aka k-** Gy 206:4, 207:1; **alma d̲-k-** Gy 7:21 f., 32:2, Gs 121:6 f. CD, **almia d-k-** Gs 121:6 f., AB, Morg. 267/25:20. With **AMR**: (*a*) with **kušṭa** as subj. **kd̲ haza amar k-,** (*b*) as obj. (direct or indirect) **ana ʿmarlak kušṭa** Jb 4:8, 7:10 f., (*c*) as genitive **mimar k-** Q 9:28 f., 11:12 f., 16:25, 43:31, 45:26; **ana hu k-** Gy 207:16, **aminṭul ḏ-k- ana** Jb 186:6 f., **kušṭa anat d-kabiria** Gy 342:17; **anania ḏ-kušṭa** Jb 221:7, **anašia ḏ-k-** Gy 14:16. With **ASA**: **k- asiak** Gy 91:18, 240:15, 343:23, Jb 165:15, Morg. 164:9 11 ff., **k- asiik** Q 19:1 the Truth make thee whole, **k- asinkun** Q 1:5, 18:31, 19:12, Morg. 3:6, 257/5:33, 264/18:3, 265/21:34, 268/27:14, 282:3, ŠQ 6:3, 9:1 &c. (cf. IVth Gosp. 8:32 ThLZ 1957 col. 408), **asia ḏ-k-** Gy 332:2, Morg. 116:18, **asara ḏ-k-** Morg. 266/22:4, **asaria ḏ-k-** Q 16:12. With **APK**: **mn kušṭaihun apkia** DAb they turn from their pact; **lapkit mn kušṭak** ŠQ 6:36; **arsai ḏ-kušṭa** Jb 258:12, **arsa bkušṭa maklẖ** Jb 107:1, **arsa (u)bkušṭa makilun** ŠQ 17:21. With **ATA**: **ata bṭabu k-** Gy 274:10, ML 250:2 f., **k- ḏ-mn rbia ata** Gy 301:22, **ʿlau ata k- lhaka lṭabia** Gs 118:10 f., **hašta masgia uatia k-** Jb 180:4 f.; **k- nitia mn iaminaikun** Q 37:11 f.; **atra ḏ-hiia uk-** Gy 10:14. With **BAA** (as object): **kušṭa ha baiina minak** Gy 192:24, **baiina minak k- rama** Jb 142:2. With prep. **b**: **anha bk- ʿuṣraikun** Gy 366:3, **ḏ-bk- niqum** Gy 30:4, **patura bk- traṣlẖ** Jb 106:13, **arsa bk- maklẖ** (above), **ḏ-(a)šumak bk- dakria** Jb 163:9, **ḏ-bk- masgian liardna** Q 60:2 f., **bk- nadkar** ML 230:7, **d-lplag mn(a)uata bk- mn hdadia** IM 44:6, 51:11 f., 56:1 f., **ḏ-laplag bk- mn hdadia** IM 56:1 f., **ḏ-lplag mnata mn hdadia bk-** *Ephemeris* 94:15, 96:13 ff.; **ḏ-laplag bk- mn hdadia** AO 9/1937 96:10 f. who have not divided (their portions) among themselves equally; **ʿnšaihun bk-** *Ephemeris* 104:4 their plighted wives (cf. **zaua ḏ-k-** below), **ḏ-bk- biniuia** RD B 115 f. which they constructed fairly (?), **bk- mištalmia** RD C 2, 4 f., **bk- nirihmun** ŠQ 25:14 f., **malalun bk- nihuia hda** ŠQ 25:16 f., **bhiria k-** Gy 299:20 f. ἐκλεκτοὶ τῆς ἀληθείας, **bnia k-** Gs 133:23, ML 213:3, 9, **brat k-** ML 214:1 = CP 175:14, **ʿl aganbia k- dilak** Q 23:23, 32:7 (s. **aganbia**). With **GLL**: **k- man galilẖ balma** Jb 7:1, **lk- galilẖ gubran** Jb 9:8 f., **daiana ḏ-k-** Gy 214:19, **dirka ḏ-k-** Gy 22:17, 37:4, **dirkia ḏ-k-** Gy 19:25, 37:4, 43:21, 276:22, 301:11, 306:9, Gs 78:5, 87:13, BCD, 100:20, Jb 60:1, 107:1 f., 222:6 f., Q 27:13, 28:4, 40:32, 53:5, 67:19 ὁδοὶ τῆς ἀληθείας (cf. H. דֶּרֶךְ אֱמֶת Gen. 24:48). With **DRA**: **dra k-** Morg. 181:2 accept the (ritual) hand(-clasp), **habšaba uk- uzidqa** Gs 79:8, Q 67:1, Morg. 249/85:5 f., **haduta ḏ-k-** Gs 26:5 f., **haiašum kušṭa qadmaia** CP 117:2, 21:5 = Q 8:18. With **HUA** (pre-existence of Kušṭa): **kušṭa d-hua mn qudam briš** Gy 178:5 f., 205:8, 211:1 f., Q 6:1, 22:24, 27:29, 29:25, 59:4, **k- ḏ-hua mn laqadmia** Gy 238:16 f., **k- ḏ-mn laqadmia hua** Gy 372:24 f., cf. also **kušṭa qudam mn kulhun almia** DAb 30, **k- hualan biluatan** Gy 178:16. With **HYMN** (& its der.): **haimin bk-** Gy 238:18, **haiminbẖ bk- umaṣbuta haza** Gy 238:21 ff., **haimanut k-** Gy 48:9 f., 368:19, ŠQ 15:5, **k- uhaimanuta** Gy 15:11, 41:24, 213:13, Q 5:23, ML 219:9, **kušṭaihun ḏ-mhaimnia** Gs 134:22 f., ML 216:7, CP 117:12, **halilnin ʿdan bk-** CP 140 (a):4, 148:ult. ML 178:8, 180:9 s. **HLL II**; **zaua d-k-** Gy 22:11 f., 43:14, DAb 14, ŠQ 6:24 f. plighted wife; **hatma ḏ-k-** Q 43:30, 45:25 f., **zuadia k-** Gs 77:16 f., Q 67:6 f. With **ṬAB**: **ṭab k- lṭabia** Q 30:14, **miṭab k- lṭaba** Gy 125:ult. f., Gs 118:3; **ia d-k-** Gy 177:24, cf. Ginzā 181 n. 5; **iamin k-** Q 23:28; **k- ḏ- iatir** Jb 28:3. With **YDA** (af. 'to confess', 'acknowledge'): **audin bkušṭak** Q 55:1. With **YHB**: **k- lhdadia iahbia** Gy 38:10 they give their right hand (: solemn promise) to one another, **k- ʿhablẖ** Gy 92:2, 239:10, 240:15, **ʿhablẖ ʿda ḏ-k-** Gs 8:ult. f., **k- ʿhablia mn dilun** Gs 115:14 f., 17, 22, 116:2, **mn pumẖ ahbalia bk- ḏ-iatir** Jb 28:3, **k- ʿhablun** Gy 239:14; **iukabar k-** Gy 316:1 f., 19, 23, 317:8, CP 451:5, (personified) ATŠ I nos. 99, 100. With **YMA**: **hdadia bk- naumun** Gy 305:16 f. With **YQR** (der.): **k- iaqra** Jb 135:13, 164:15, 251:1, 259:14, Morg. 204:5; **kahu k-** Gs 26:21, 28:10, 29:22, 31:15, 32:22, 34:10, 35:21 f.; **ḏ-kulẖ hiia ukulẖ kušṭa** Gy 2:16 f.; **k- d-bihruia iardnia** Jb 142:6 f.; **kušṭak uzidqak uhaimanutak** Q 28:6 f., **k- uzidqa** Morg. 266/22:7, 13; **k- ukana rba d-ʿqara** Q 32:9; **k- ulaupa** Gy 8:6, 32:10; **kušṭaikun latikadbun** Gy 20:3 f.; **k- umanda ḏ-hiia** Gs 121:6, 19; **k- šumak** Q 55:12, 58:16; **lbar mn k-** Gy 277:21, 290:1; **laupa uk-** Gy 20:4 f. (cf. **k- ulaupa** above). With **LGṬ**: **ligṭit k-** Gy 117:6, **k- biaminẖ algaṭ** Jb 50:10, **k- lgaṭ biaminẖ** Jb 50:11, **k- biaminẖ lgaṭ** Jb 226:4 f. (cf. with **DRA** above); **lia hu k-** Gy 206:9, 207:7; **lika k- bbintak** Jb 23:7; **maria (ḏ)-k-** Gy 77:17, Gs 94:16, 104:14, 116:21, 121:4; **k- makik ʿuhra** Gs 114:14, 22. With **MLA**: **libai ḏ-mlia k-** Gs 77:24, Q 64:14, **libẖ k- ʿtimlia** Gy 66:1, **pumai bk- ʿtmlia** Gs 87:1. With **MLL** (& der.): **bk- malil** ML 218:1 = CP 178:10, **malalia d-k-** Gy 57:15, 111:15, **mlalia ḏ-k-** *Ephemeris* 98:2. With **MŠA**: **mša ʿdak bk-** Gy 197:4, **mša ʿdẖ bk-** Gy 197:10 f.; **mšunia k-** v. s.v. **nbiha ḏ-k-** Gy 25:7; **naṭra ḏ-k-** ŠQ 6:34; **maṭaraia ḏ-k-** Gy 215:5 f. With **NSB**: **nsib k-** Gy 238:16, 310:15, Jb 53:3 f., 228:15; **tabralẖ lk- ḏ-bgauẖ nisbat** ATŠ I no. 102 she breaks the vow she made; **kušṭa tiniana nisbat** ATŠ I no. 106 she plighted herself a second time; **k- nisbit** Gy 72:20, 92:6, 133:5; **nisbit minẖ k- iaqra** Gy 325:18 f.; **k- minak lanasbia** DAb 44; **naṣuraia ḏ-k-** Gy 213:15; **sabria k-** Jb 208:14. With **SHD** (& der.): **k- bak sahidna** Gy 370:2, Jb 178:1; **k- nihuia sahdik** Q 19:1 f.; **kušṭaikun nihuia sahdaikun** Q 19:3; **sahduta ḏ-k-** Q 39:11; **sahdia d-k-** Gy 35:15, 289:22, Gs 85:24; **sahdia hinun ḏ-k-** Q 12:20; **sidria k-** Jb 137:7; **samlẖ ḏ-rbia k-** Jb 217:1. With **SPR** (to relate): **hazin k- ḏ-ana asparlak** Q 46:9 f., **hazin k- asparlẖ labatur** CP 94:11, Q 46:14 f.; **ʿdẖ ḏ-k-** Q 14:22, **ʿdak ḏ-k-** Gy 192:19, Q 2:20, **ʿdh ḏ-k-** Q 1:30; **ʿupania k-** Q 53:28, CP 149:penult., ML 179:10 (s. **ʿupania**); **ʿutria ḏ-k-** Gs 13:6; **ʿngar k-** Gy 314:22 f., 345:2, Jb 91:4, 9; **ʿngirta bk- ktiba** Gs 108:20 f., 109:2; (**kdiba**) Q 42:20 f., 30, 43:4 f.; **ʿngirta ḏ-k-** Jb 275:7, 276:12 f.; **ʿspia ḏ-k-** Gs 69:6; **paqadṭa uza-**

harta d-k- Gy 38:8 f.; **pugdamia d̲-k-** Gy 177:17, CP 162:7 = Q 55:14, 58:18, 60:22, ML 197:2; **pudan k-** Jb 179:10; **pihth̲ lpumh̲ bk-** Jb 205:5; **pihta uk- umambuha** Gy 289:19 f., 343:3 f., 362:2, Q 12:2; **pindur k-** (variant **pandur k-** CP 180:11) ML 221:1 (s.v.); **man psaqinan mn k-** Gy 308:19. With **PŠṬ** (frequent ritual idiom: to give or receive the ritual hand-clasp); **k- mn rbia pšaṭ** Gy 130:8, **k- pšaṭ** Gy 294:22 f., Gs 8:23, 92:19 f., 93:2 f., Q 20:25, 30, 32, **k- rhima minh̲ pšaṭ** Jb 142:2, **pšaṭlh̲ k-** Gy 195:12, **k- pšaṭlh̲** Gy 294:22, **k- pšaṭlak** Jb 273:8 f., ŠQ 27:10; **k- lhdadia pašṭia** Gy 8:13 f., ML 259:8, ŠQ 24:19 f.; **k- pašṭia** Gy 285, Gs 87:5, 135:18; **k- lapašṭia** Gy 285:14, 287:24; **pašṭia k-** Gs 78:3 85:11, RD C 12 f.; **k- minh̲ pašṭia** Gy 208:9 f.; **pašṭa k-** Q 67:17; **k- pašṭan** Gs 100:17, 20; **ʿdh̲ bk- nipšuṭ** Gy 220:ult.; **d̲-k- mn napšh̲ nipšuṭ** Gy 237:10 f.; **kušṭaikun nipšaṭ** ŠQ 27:2; **k- ʿpšaṭ** Gy 262:2. With **QBL**: **k- lamitqabal** DAb 49. With **QUM**: **qaiim k- mšaiil** Jb 2:6, 6:9; **qaiim k- lrahmh̲** Q 27:11; **k- qaiman** Q 36:7; **qlida d̲-k-** Gs 8:10. With **QRA**: **k- nitiqria** Gs 2:5. With **RHM** (& der.): **rhum hdadia bk-** Gy 20:7; **rhum k-** Gy 366:8 f.; **libai k- rhim** Gy 367:5 f.; **k- rhima** Jb 255:1; **rahmia d̲-k-** Gy 39:21 f.; **rahmai d̲-k-** Jb 159:14; **rahmia šuma d̲-k-** Q 5:4 f., 14:9 f., 19:20, 22, 28, 29:9, 34:2 f., 57:13; **rahmia šumak d̲-k-** Q 28:8, 53:17, 58:7; **rahmut k-** Gy 22:11, 43:13, 175:11, 214:17, 215:14, Gs 73:12; **rahmut d̲-k- iaqra** Morg. 204:5; **rahmuta d-k-** Gy 42:17, 178:17 f., 213:23, RD D 13; **riuianh̲ bk- lamdakai** Gy 41:14; **riš kušṭak** Gy 213:23 the first principle of thy faithfulness; **brišaihun k-** ŠQ 26:6 f. With **ŠBA**: **šaba bk-** Gy 178:6; **mšaba šumh̲ bk-** Gy 2:6, 31:3. With **ŠBQ**: **laʿšibqh̲ lk- d̲-šaina** Jb 21:11; **šum k- qaiim** Jb 53:9, 60:8. With **ŠKA I**: **aškath̲ lk-** Gy 367:17. With **ŠKN**: **k- luath̲ škin** Jb 208:ult. f.; **šlihia d̲-k-** Gy 63:10 f. With **ŠLM**: **mšalam bk-** Jb 59:12; **mšalmit lauth̲ bk-** ŠQ 6:36 f.; **anin mšalminin luatak bk-** ŠQ 7:1 f. With **ŠRA**: **bliban šralan k-** Gy 64:4 f. Truth dwelt in our hearts; **d̲-šralun blibaihun k-** Gy 275:6 f.; **d̲-šralun k-** Gy 276:7; **tiria k-** Q 24:15 true (i.e. good) conscience. With **TRṢ**: **triṣnin bkuštak** Q 55:2.

kušṭa-iaqra a personification of marriage vow ATŠ I nos. 99, 100 and often.

kušṭana (adj. from **kušṭa**) true, right-dealing, sincere, honourable MG 138:25. Pl. **kušṭania. šliha kušṭana** Gy 64:21, 65:5 the true apostle; **makšiṭ kušṭania** Gy 62:22 maketh sincere people true; **ṭubaihun lkušṭania** Gy 257:1; **mata d̲-kušṭania** Gy 318:1, 2, Jb 111:9, 318:1 f. place of the right-dealing (Land of the Leal); **kušṭana hauia** AM 27:10.

kutla 1 (Akk. *kutallu*, Syr. ܟܘܬܠܐ LS, Ar. loan-w. كَوْثَل Fränkel 223, Gr. *κανθήλια*, *Luğat al-ʿArab* ii p. 203:45, Jb ii 150 n. 4) the aft part of the ship, tiller, poop; **abatar kutlai** Jb 148:6 behind my tiller.

Gl. 157:6 **kuṯla** مؤخّر *puppis* سر كشتى.

kutla 2 in **amarlh̲ lkutlai** (var. **lkutai** C) **d̲-aitia** (var. **atia** C) Jb 146:9 doubtf., Jb ii 147 n. 5. Possible meanings: Bring me my basket (cf. Ar. كُتْلَة lump of dates, مِكْتَل palm-leaf basket), or Come (acc. to C) to my tiller (**kutla 1**); in both cases delete **d̲-**.

KZN (Ar. خزن) to lay up.

Pe. Impt. **uṭiʿam kzun lnapšak** AM 257:25 so lay up food for thyself.

ki a mod. form of the cl. **kd̲**, cf. the occasional scr. pl. **kidbirku** Par. xi 22 b:3, ŠQ 19:18 just as they blessed them. In the colloquial used also with the meaning of 'who' and 'that' (both as P. كه).

Gl. 77:7 **ki** حتى *usque ad* تا.

kiana (ܟܝܢܐ) nature, essence, substance, inherent quality, principle, place of origin, home; adj. inherent, natural, essential MG 115:25. Jb ii 193 n. 2 contra MSchr 40 n. 2. Sometimes miswritten as **kiniana 2** MG 136 n. 2. Masc. pl. **kiania. kiana d̲-nhura** Gy 21:21 f., 42:16 f., the nature of the light; **kiana d̲-atar hšuk** Gy 96:1 (var. **kiniana** Sh. ʿAbd.'s copy) her home(?) in the place of darkness Ginzā 101 n. 4; **kiana d̲-minh̲ hua** Gy 48:22 the nature from which he came into being; **kiana biša** Gy 278:13, 19, 24 evil nature; **kiana hu ṭaba** PD 982; **hda kiana** Jb 199:5; **trin kiania** Jb 50:4; **kiana d̲-nura hinun** AM 108:12 they are of the substance of fire; **kulh̲ bhda kiana qaiiq** AM 125:19 (var. **qaiim**) he is entirely of one kind (one species); **arba razia ukiania** ATŠ II no. 61, 247 four mysteries and natures; **hinun d̲-kul had kiana** ATŠ I no. 219 each one of which has its own nature; **arba kiania** ibid. four natures (qualities), DC 27. 201 four natural principles (phenomena).

KIB, KAB, KUB (כאב, ܟܐܒ, كَئِبَ) to pain, hurt, afflict, ache, be bent with pain.

Pe. Impf. with encl. **urišia nikublh̲** AM 52:5 and his head will pain him. Act. pt. **kaiib**, fem. **kaiba** (both often) aching; with encl. **hda siṭra d̲-rišia kaiiblh̲** AM 4:19 one side of his head will pain him.

Pa. Act. pt. **mkaibia umasklia lpagrai** DC 40:855 they afflict and injure my body. **libai d̲-kaiub** CP 171:10.

Ethpa. Impf. **ubmia hamima nitkaiab** AM 3:6 and will be hurt by hot water.

Der.: **kaiub, kiba.**

kiba (כֵּיבָא, ܟܐܒܐ) pain, affliction, suffering, sickness, disease, sore MG 102:10. St. abs. & cstr. **kib.** Pl. **kibia.** Masc. **kib riša** (often) headache; **kib gubria** AM 47:19 *dolor virilis*, venereal disease?; **ukiba mn qurša ukibia muktalip nihuia** AM 258:21 there will be suffering from cold and various diseases; **kibia bišia** Gy 22:6.

kibabta AM 58:5 = **kababta.**

kiblia JRAS = **kublia.**

kibnata (pl. of ܟܘܒܢܬܐ) robes, cloaks, clothing. **kibnata d̲-ʿgiriata** ŠQ 18:26 = CP 236:14 (var. **kibnata d̲-ʿgiata** DC 3) robes of hired maid-servants(?).

kibrit(a), (var.) **kabrit** (גופריתא, כבריתא, Syr. ܟܒܪܝܬܐ, Chr.-Pal. ܟܒܪܝܬ, H. גָּפְרִית, Ar. كَبْرِيت < Akk. *kupritu* Zimmern, *Akk. Fremdw.* 60, LS) sulphur. St. emph. **kibrita** Bodl. xii is rarer than the st. abs. (Ar. influence) Fem. **bduq gauia kibrit** DC 46 put sulphur in it; **aina d̲-kibrit sumaqtia** DC 7 the well of red sulphur; **ukibritai** [*sic*] **mn zan hdadia iaqdia** DC 43 J. 120 and pieces of sulphur catch fire from their own kind.

Gl. 144:3 defectively **kbrita** كبريت *sulphur* گوگرد.

kibša (כבשא, ܟܒܫܐ) subduing, mastery, conquest, treading down; something trodden on, grade, degree, stepping-stone, something subduing, exorcism, counter-spell, master-spell. Pl. **kibšia. kibša kibšit** DC 44. 372 I used the (master-)spell; **tlata kibšia . . . šita kibšia . . . šuba kibšia** DC 44. 375 ff. three grades . . . six grades . . . seven grades; **himiana d̲-kibša** a girdle of mastery (or 'exorcism'); **kibša rba** DC 44 master-spell; **kibšia rurbia** Gy 316:15 powerful (op)pressions; **kibšia mn bnia šurba rba d̲-hiia** HG victories of (?) the Great Nation of Life; **šauitinun kibša latutia ligrai** DC 44. 639 f. I made them a trodden place beneath my feet; **htama ukibša** DC 40 sealing and conquest; **kibša šarira hu** DC 40. 1059 f. it is a strong master-spell.

kid an exceptional scr. pl. of **kd̲**, v.s. **ki.**

kidar Zotb. 221 b:29 a man's name.

kidin a place-name, v.s. **kadan.**

kidipa, kidipta (a corrupt form from **KDB**?) writing? **šauia tartin d̲-dmauata uatna kidipa bhaq minaihun** DC 46 **abud tartin dmauata d̲-ṭina uatna lkidipta bhaq minaihun** DC 46 (read **bhad** 'on one' inst. of **bhaq**?) make two effigies of clay and put writing on one (?) of them.

***kiua,** pl. **kiuia** DC 22. 470 a var. of **kauia** Gs 85:8.

kiuan (Akk. *kaimānu, kaiwānu*, Syr. ܟܐܘܢ, Ar.-P. كَيْوَان, OT כִּיּוּן ? Ges.) Saturn, star of Saturday, god of the Jews HpGn 28, 41 (cf. also *Register* s. Saturn), Ginzā 223 n. 3. Var. **kʿuan. hamšaia kiuan šitaia bil** Gy 27:20; **daiuia d̲-bit kiuan** Gy 28:10; **nbu dahba aitia ukiuan msania** Gy 106:11 f.; **lkiuan plaglh̲ bišuta** Gy 112:9; **baba d̲-qra kʿuan** Gy 121:5 the sect which S. created (cf. **kiuanaiia**); **ana lšamiš bšumh̲ qrilh̲ ulsin ulkʿuan** Gy 171:21 f.; **mn birktan tʿiul ʿlak kiuan** Gy 115:13 f.; **ligṭta qadmaita d̲-lgaṭ kiuan mn kulhun kukbia** Gy 222:15; **amarilkun ʿl kiuan uʿl lig(i)ṭta d̲-lgaṭ** Gy 223:18, 21; **kiuan uruha** Gy 223:12 f.; **kiuan šdia halṣh̲** Gy 336:2; **maṭarta d̲-kiuan** RD C 13, 20; **ziqa biša d̲-kiuan** PD 793; **kiuan rba** Jb 253:13; **balma d̲-kiuan ʿṭanpat** PD 1473; **kiuan d̲-mitiqria iahu rba adunai ṣbabut** DC 44. 1182.

kiuanaiia (adj. from **kiuan**) AM 178 name of a people or tribe; or else refers to people living under the influence of Saturn BZ Ap. II; or worshippers of Saturn (cf. Gy 121:5 s. **kiuan**) ZDMG CV 142 n. 1, CP 379:15, trs. 251 n. 7.

kiuaṣ (rt. כָּבַץ, Mand **KBṢ**) AM 83:18 (of hair) curly. Var. **kuaṣ.**

kiuara occasional var. of **kauara 1.**

kiuat aina CP 409:3 the-Well-spring-spurted (?) (*or* was troubled?) A name given to the Well-spring.

kiuihta JRAS 1937 596 a var. of **kauihta. aina bišta ukauihta** DC 46.

kiuiza Zotb. 221 a:26, 28 name of a town on the river Carca.

kiusta (rt. **KSS I**?) breaking up, breaking into pieces. **mikta ukiusta** DC 42.

kizmat (local form of Ar. خدمة) service. Mod. **ukizmatdan ʿbad** DC 43 Qašt. 247 f. and he served us.

kiṭaita (from Ar. خاط ?) fem. sewn (?). **zangia lkublai kiṭaitai** ŠQ 18:25 (= CP 236:13) bells with chains sewn thereon (?).

kikia Zotb. 228 b:32, DC 30:coloph. prob. a name (hardly corruption of **kiniana**).

kila (כיילא, ܩܝܠܐ, Ar. loan-w. كيل Fränkel 202 & n. 1) measure, quantity, capacity, span, term. Varr. **kʿla, kiʿla. kd̲ kʿla balma šalimlh̲** Gy 204:1, (**kd̲ kila . . .**) Gy 303:10 when his (allotted) span is terminated; **kilai balma šilman** Gy 180:4 my measure in the world is full (: I have to die); **šlim kilai** Jb; **kila d̲-iuhana šalim** Gy 57:16; **kd̲ kilaiun šalimlun** Gy 274:1; **bkilak d-mšalma** CP 454:penult. at the completion of thy term (of life); **alma d̲-kilaiun šalim** Gy 377:1; **alma d̲-šalim kilh̲** ATŠ II no. 19 until the(ir, his) time (to die) comes; **alma d̲-kilak šalim kd̲ šalimlak ana bnapšai ʿtia** CP 191:13; **kd̲ kila d̲-baita nišlum** Jb 266:2 f., **alma d̲-kilh̲ uminianh̲ šlim**; **kila uminiana** Q 38:4 f., Gy 378:37; **abatur d̲-ʿl kila uminiana mšalaṭ** DAb Abatur that rules measure and count (i.e. the length of a man's life); **kila d̲-malkia abdit** Jb 19:5; **nišauia kila** Gy 109:20 we will set a term; **nišmata bla kilaiun mn pagraiin napqan** CP 372:5 souls depart from their bodies before their (allotted) span; **d̲-litlh̲ kʿla uminiana** Gy 2:15 that is without measure and number; **kilak nihuia lmindam** Leid. & Sh.ʿAbd.'s copy's var. of Gs 44:4 (Pet. omits **kilak**, var. **kilik** B, **lamindam** ACD) thy measure shall be (brought) to nought; **kila . . . ʿtpalag** Gy 379:1 the measure . . . was divided; **kila d̲-bil** Gy 379:8.

Gl. 136:10 **kila** قفة *sporta* زنبيل, 156:11 id. مكايل *mensura* پيمانه.

kilaia 1 (adj. from **kila**) who fulfilled the measure, who died MG 141:14. Var. **kʿlaia. npaq rišaia kʿlaia minh̲ d̲-alma** Gy 277:6 the first defunct departed from the world; **silqit . . . mn kʿlaia lbit qubria** Gs 103:20 with the dead man I went to the graveyard.

kilaia 2 (rt. **KLA I**) captive, restraint, prohibited from home. Pl. **kilaiia. kilaia d̲-baita** AM 95:3 prohibited from the house; **ulkilaiia udania hai(a)sa** AM 84:3 she will be pitiful to captives and the poor.

kilat AM 204 name of a town BZ Ap. II.

kiliata (rt. **KLA I**) Jb 143:7, var. **ʿkiliata** ABD, places where fish are pent up and caught (?Lidzb. *Fanganlagen*).

kilta 1 (כִּילְתָא, ܟܶܠܬܳܐ, Ar. loan-w. كِلَّة Fränkel 289) veil, canopy, curtained or veiled bed, mosquito-net (mod. ML 250 n. 1 acc. to Siouffi 157). **kilta** Oxf. roll f 1367, 1371; **kilta nagdilh̠** Gy 148:7 they spread a veil over it; **kilta ngadlh̠** ATŠ II no. 319, **kilta ngidabh̠** RD A 4, **kilta ngida** RD F 6; **kilta d̠-hidukta** Oxf. 78 a the veil of the bride, **kilta d̠-hiduia** CP 225:4 the canopied bed of the bride-groom; **hiduta iatba bkilta** PA's ŠQ the bride sits inside the canopy.

kilta 2 (= **kila**) measure, limit, end: **adinqia miniana . . . adinqia kilta** ATŠ II no. 316 numberless . . . without end.

kilta 3 = **kalta. lmatuiia kilta šapir** ŠQ 29:12 propitious for bringing a bride.

kilta 4 occasionally for **ʿkilta.**

kima 1 (כִּימְתָא, ܟܺܝܡܳܐ I, H. כִּימָה) Pleiades (?). **sandlia d̠-kima** DC 44. 506.

kima 2 (ܟܺܝܡܳܐ II, Ar. كَمْأَة) swelling, bump. **umn bilh̠ kima umuma maškia** AM 54:4 and she will contract swelling and blemish from her husband. (Var. **kiba.**)

kimar (Ar. خَمْر) AM 154 wine. Var. **kimir** MG 2:18.

kimuta d–h̠aba DC 44. 1338 a miscop. of ܟܡܺܝܽܘܬܳܐ ܕܠܶܒܳܐ 'darkness of heart'? Var. **muta d̠-baba** Morg. 265/20:13. Doubtf.

kimia a mod. doublet of cl. **kma** how (much)?, in what manner? Very frequent in mod. Mand. **bišutak kimia abdit** DC 46. 61:10 f. how dost thou perform thy wickedness?; **kimia kabrit ʿl bnia anaša** DC 46. 62:12 f. in what way (how much) dost thou afflict human beings?

kimṣa (etym. doubtf.; Nöld. from קמץ 'to shrink' MG 39:15 ff.; Lidzb. from the same rt. = Mand. **KMṢ** Jb ii 66 n. 2) CP trs. 119 n. 2, 158 n. 3, 249 n. 2. A word of cosmical significance with doubtf. meaning. Jb ii 66 f. footn., Ginzā 146 n. 6; a place in celestial regions? ML 192 n. 1; orig. meaning prob. with **KMṢ**: solidification, materialization, formation; end, completion, consummation (?). Might correspond to the Gnostic *πλήρωμα*? **mšabana laiar kimṣa šania hu** ATŠ I no. 23, **aiar kimṣa mana** Jb 16:9 (in an obscure sentence out of the context Jb ii 23 n. 3); **aiar kimṣa dakia** PD 259; **daiarna briš kimṣa** Jb 63:1 (parallel with **bit hiia**); **ʿl riš kimṣa dakia** Oxf. 19 b = CP 159:1, ML 192:3 (a place in celestial regions ML 192 n. 1); **šaliṭak ʿl kimṣa** Jb 220:4 I put thee in charge of the **k-** (parallel with **ʿbidata d̠-atar nhur**); **kmaṣ kimṣa d̠-iardna** Jb 224:10 f. Lidzb. '*Es sprudelte auf dem Sprudel des Jordans*' doubtf. (cf. *Florilegium* 354:51 which may refer to 'condensation' Jb ii 67 footn.); **ʿl kimṣa autbun** Jb 271:1; **naṭar kimṣa** Jb 271:2, 5, 11; **ʿl kimṣa ʿtib** Gy 131:18; **ahbalh̠ lkimṣa dmuta d̠-ʿqara** Gy 240:3 give to the formation (: creation) a form of glory; **d̠-kimṣa latagzar balma d̠-hšuka** Gy 240:16 f. so that the **k-** (??) may not be condemned in the world of darkness; **kimṣa d̠-kmaṣ** Gy 240:22; **kmaṣ kimṣa** Gy 297:9 s. **KMṢ** pe. pf.; **hašib hiia bnapšaihun bkimṣaihun d̠-napšaihun** Gy 239:3 (*πλήρωμα*?); **ʿl riš kimṣa d̠-mia hiia** Gy 307:22 at the beginning of the formation (or storehouse?) of living waters (parallel with **ʿl riš nigda d̠-mia hiia** l. 23); **ridpa lkimṣa lahualh̠** Gs 53:23 MG 476:paen. f., but cf. Jb ii 67 footn. (lit. the **k-**? would not be persecuted); **kimṣan hauia d̠-lahua** Gs 65:22 our substance (?) shall be as if it had not been; **kimṣaikun mištbiq bdin almia** Gs 67:12 your materialized shape (??) will be left in the (law-)court of the worlds; **kimṣa dria** RD B 123; **kimṣa d̠-abagada** PD 268 = ATŠ I no. 20 the whole (?) alphabet; **hazialh̠ nišimta lkimṣa** ATŠ the soul beholds its end (?); **kimṣa d̠-ʿusrh̠** ATŠ the storehouse (?) of his treasure (= mind); **azilna luat kimṣa ṭaba . . . abda ana d̠-kimṣa rhima** ATŠ I no. 221, CP 199 n. 20 (cf. ML 191 n. 1); **riša d̠-kimṣa šauiun** CP 377:3 they (the Life) made me (: the sacramental bread is speaking) chief of the **k-**; **kimṣa dakia d̠-husrana ukadba litbh̠** CP 436:ult.; **kimṣa dakia ruaz ʿl dikth̠** DC 48. 365 the pure **k-** (personified) rejoiced there and then; **umpalaglh̠ bkimṣa kulh̠** DC 6 & 36 (read **kimth̠**?); **tirṣh̠ bkimṣa hak dakia** DC 48. 433 he set it up in that pure **k-** (place of prototypes?).

kimṣat (Nöld. perh. from קמץ 'to shrink, contract' MG 39:15, Lidzb. perh. < קְצָת Jb ii 66 n. 2) end, consummation, completion. Only st. cstr. found. **alma lkimṣat almia** Gy 99:24, 242:4, 270:3, 286:17, 378:38, 393:6, Jb 3:6, 4:7, DC 50. 114 etc. (*often*) unto the end of time (i.e. of the worlds, cf. Gr. *αἰών* Ginzā 46 n. 4, 179 n. 6), **lmišlam lkimṣat almia** Gy 175:20 to be consummated at the end of time.

kimṣat (2) anana Gy 374:3 name of a heavenly being.

kimta (כִּימְתָא Ass. *kimtu* family (Schr. KAT[2] p. 557) **kd̠ ata gabra lkimth̠ ʿtib** DC 22. 127 (Pet. has **kimṣa**) when Man came he took his place with his kind.

kin (Can., Aram. כֵּן, Syr. & Chr.-Pal. ܟܶܢ, Akk. (*a*)*kanna*, Ar. perh. in لَكِنْ Ges.) thereupon, after this, so, thus, therefore. Var. **kʿn, kʿin** MG 207:9 f. **kin ana iadana** Gy 269:3 Sh. 'Abd.'s copy (var. **kʿn** Pet., **kʿin** B) so I know; **nipalgun ukin lhdadia atra nizlun** AM 184:14 they will divide, and thereupon will march against each other; **ukin malka d̠-babil nikṣar** AM 184:20 and after this, the king of Babylon will sicken.

-kin possessive suff. of the 2nd p. pl. fem., often replaced by the masc. **-kun** (q.v.).

kina 1 (Syr. ܟܺܐܢܳܐ, H. כֵּן II, Akk. *kēnu* Ges.) just, upright, righteous MG 108:21. Pl. **kinia 1. bhiria kinia ušalmania.**

kina 2 = (**kana**) container, chamber, storeroom, (of water) pool, reservoir. Pl. **kinia 2. ṭiعam**

bkina baṣar AM 262:28 food in the storeroom will be scant; **mn kinai uqinianai** DC 40. 863 from my storeroom and my property; **ʿlania lkinẖ qaimia** DC 35 trees standing by the pools; **kinia mia** DC 43 J 125 pools (or reservoirs) of water; **mia mna** (read **mn**) **kinak** DC 44 (var. **knap** Morg.) from thy reservoirs (?).

kinania DC 22 a var. of **kinnia** and **kinʿnia** Gy 153:12, 13 (pl. of **kinta** 1).

kinar, kinara 1 (כִּנָּרָא, ܟܢܪܐ I, H. כִּנּוֹר, Ar. كِرَان, كَنَّارَة, Hittite *kinirrilaš*?, Gr. loan-w. *κιννύρα*, Eg. , Copt. ϭⲓⲛⲁ, LS, Ges.) cithern, zither, harp, guitar MG 122:13. **kinar šiha** Gy 113:6, 187:18 harp of unchastity MG 309:23; **kinara uambuba** Gy 176:21; **kinar zmara uambubia** Gy 220:9 cithern song and pipes; **ṭiblia ukinar** Gy 225:2 (s. **ṭibla**).

kinara 2 (כִּנָּרָא, ܟܢܪܐ II, P. كنار, Gr. *κόναρος* Löw 283 LS) *Zizyphus Spina Christi*, lote-tree. St. abs. **kinar 2**, var. **kunar**. Var. st. emph. **kn(n)ara. kinara daria simadra** Gs 10:19 (var. Sh. ʿAbd.'s copy **dara kinara simadra**) the lote-tree beareth blossom; **kinara bsimadrẖ** DC 12:92, Lond. roll B 188 the lote-tree in its blossom; **kinar hu, kinar hu** DC 35.

kinata pl. of **kinta 2.**

kinupia occ. var. of **kanupia** (s. **KNP** inf. pa.).

kinuta (abstr. noun from **kina 1**, ܟܐܢܘܬܐ) justice, uprightness, right-dealing, rectitude, correct behaviour MSchr 57 n. 4. **alma ḏ-kinuta** Gy 7:18, 31:23 world of justice; **mkikuta ukinuta** Gy 213:20 f. (also DC 24 p. 24 & Sh. ʿAbd.'s copy's var. of Gy 24:ult. where Pet. omitted **kinuta**) humility and righteousness; **riš kinutak** Gy 214:7 the first principle of thy rectitude.

kinzala occ. var. of **kanzala 1.**

kinia a pl. of **kinta** 1 (q.v.).

kiniana 1 (rt. **KNA**, Syr. ܟܘܢܝܐ, Ar. كُنْيَة) name, family-name, tribe; fig. good name, repute MG 136:12. **laqab . . . kinianẖ** (often in coloph.) his tribal name . . . his family-name; **ʿniš ḏ-ʿtlẖ kiniana** AM 261:32 a person of (good) repute; **gabra ḏ-ʿtlẖ kiniana** AM 271:22 a man of repute; **lhad šuma rba ḏ-npiš ulkiniana ḏ-kabir** DC 3 (to) the one great Name that is great and the Name (or Family, or **kiniana 2**?) that is mighty; **ulkiniana ḏ-bnia angaria** DC 37 and upon the tribe of roof-demons. Gl. 182:11 miswritten ذوى نسب *cognati* قوم خويش.

kiniana 2 (= **kiana**) nature, quality, characteristic; fig. place of origin (cf. **kiniana** 1), appointed place, fixed place; (= **kana**?) base, support, foundation MG 136 n. 2. **kinianak** Q 58:16 thy nature; **ṣurik hiia bkinianun** CP 116:1 f., Q 12: 29, 58:28, 31 urge (or 'ray'?) of Life in its place of origin; **kiniana ḏ-atar hšuk** PD 989 = ATŠ II no. 355, ML 59:5 (cf. n. 1), CP 45:ult., Gy 319:24 (cf. Gy 96:1 s. **kiana**); **ziqa umia šnun mn kinianun** DC 26. 117 f., DC 28 par. wind and water removed from their appointed places (changed their nature?); **arba ziqia . . . arba kiniania** ATŠ I no. 220 the four winds . . . (have) four characteristics; **ʿl šamiš mna uʿl kinianẖ mna** Gy 199:3 as to the Sun, whence is it, and of what doth its nature consist?

kin(i)nia, kinʿnia a pl. of **kinta** 1 (q.v.).

kinpa occ. var. of **kanpa.**

kinša (כִּנְשָׁא, ܟܢܫܐ) assembly, congregation. Pl. **kinšia. niknušbẖ kinša** Gy 105:5 (var. **niknašbẖ kinšia** DC 22. 100) we will gather in an assembly (var. assemblies).

kinta 1 (= **kilta** 1) veil, enveloping cloth, wrapping MG 101:16. Pl. **kin(i)nia, kinʿnia** MG 31:23, 163:13, 172:18, varr. pl. **kanunia 2, kaninia, kinia. kinta ḏ-marba** ATŠ II no. 315 maidenhead (veil of womb); **iuma ḏ-iadlana mn kinta lkinta mšaniana** (= **-nẖ**) Gy 158:13 f. on the day that I bring forth (the child) I will change him from wrapping to wrapping; **šanitẖ mn kinta qadmaita kul kinta kinta alpa ḏ-šnia hua umn kinta lkinta mšanialẖ uhaizak alma ḏ-maṭia ʿur lkinta batraita** Gy 158:ult. ff. she removed him (: her son) from the first wrapping—he was in each wrapping a thousand years—she removed him from wrapping to wrapping, and thus Ur reached the last wrapping (**mn kinta lkinta** refers to development of the foetus inside the womb, cf. **kinta 2**) MG 419:15; **kinnia kaina** Gy 158:13 *bis*, 14 she prepared (hist. pres.) swaddling-clothes (Lidzb. *sie wickelte Windeln*); **kinʿnia ʿkun** Gy 158:13 I prepare swaddling-clothes (Sh. ʿAbd.'s copy **kanunia** in all three places, DC 22 **kanunia**); **kul had lhad iahra iahra ḏ-lianqa mapiqlẖ mn kinta lkinta alma ltša iahra** DC 41:137 each (of them) represents a month during which the babe comes out of 'wrapping to wrapping' (= stage after stage, cf. Gy 158:ult. ff. above) until nine months; **ušauia kinta ubastirqa ukilta ngadlẖ** ATŠ II no. 319 and arranges the veil and the mattress and spreads a canopy (of net) over her; **kinta blibẖ kanilẖ** Gy 90:18 I wrapped his heart with a veil; **btrisar kinia kanth** Gy 90:21 I wrapped him twelve times (: with twelve veils); **ʿbrik kinia aiar** Gy 116:13 thy wings (: arms) are veils of ether (Ginzā 129 n. 7); **kinia mia** Oxf. roll 270, 276, DC 43 J 125 coverings of water (?) (or see **2**).

kinta 2 (rel. to **kana**) receptacle, gathering place, recipient, container (ritual: a covered clay box the top of which can be used for ritual objects MMII 106 f., where the word is missp.); foundation, community, constitution; category, species, kind. Pl. **kinata. uatun qudam kinta udrabša** DC 50. 21 and they go before the clay-box-stand-table and the banner. With **SDR** to arrange the ritual clay-box-stand-table: **nisadar kinta** Oxf. roll a 495, F 442, **sadrunun lkinta** DC 50. 187, **sadiriun kinata šuba** DC 27; **kan kinta** Gy 222:16, HG 15 &c. (*often*) he founded a community; **kinta rabtia** CP trs. 273 n. 2, CP 410:6 = **kinta ḏ-rba** DC 3. 276:15 (doubtf.: foundation?); **kinta hadtia** Lond. roll A 429; **bhad kinta ʿtkanap** ATŠ I no. 254 they are grouped in one category; **kul tlatin iumia**

kinta baiia lnapših̲ nikan ATŠ I no. 257 every thirty days it seeks a receptacle (vehicle) for itself; **haizak napiq mn kinth̲** ibid. then it issues from the receptacle (: the womb); **nura ʿl kinth̲ (lk-) azla** Gy 203:13, 204:4 the fire goeth to its foundation (?, Lidzb. **kinta 1**) **naṭria ḏ-kinta** CP 410:9.

kinta 3 (= **kiana**?) nature, substance. **ʿl nura ʿmarlak mn kinta ḏ-man huat** Gy 267:18 f. as to the fire, I will tell thee from whose nature it cometh (Lidzb. **kinta 1** Ginzā 265 n. 6).

kisa (כיסא, ܟܝܣܐ, H. כִּיס, Ar. كِيس, Eth. ኪስ, Akk. *kis* & *kīš* KAT 649, Zimmern, *Akk. Fw.* 20; Gr. loan-w. *κίσις*, P. loan-w. كيسه directly from Aram., not from Ar.) small bag, purse; (on the mouth) muzzle. Often in AM. **kisai uqinianai** DC 44. 260 my purse and my property; **ʿsir pumh̲ bkisia ḏ-nirba** DC 40. 1079 f. his mouth is bound by a muzzle of nirba (a metal).

Gl. 144:6 missp. with ṣ كيس *sacculus* كيسه, 171:15 id. هميان *pera*.

kisuna var. of **kisna** (q.v.).

kisuta (rt. **KSA**) PD 297 covering.

kisia (ܟܣܝܐ) covering, concealment, occult state, secrecy, invisibility MG 102:20. **kisia ḏ-mia** Q 59:27 covering of waters; **kisia ḏ-anatun ksaitunan** Gy 157:13 the invisibility wherewith ye covered me; **bkisia** (*often*) secretly; **bkisih̲ ḏ-napšh̲** in his own occult place; **bkisia gauaiia** DC 34 with innermost (: esoteric) secrecy; **kisia ḏ-bit kisia** DC 34. 861 the secret(s) of the House-of-Secrets (?); **mn kisiaikun** Gy 134:14 from your concealment.

kisiaia (adj. from **kisia**) hypocrite, crypto-Mandaean (?). Pl. **kisiaiia**. **ganiba mdakai mn kisiaia ukisiaia mdakai mn nkila** ATŠ I no. 232 a bastard is cleaner than a hypocrite and a hypocrite is cleaner than a deceitful person; **hanata alma ḏ-kisiaiia iatbia** DAb in that world where the hypocrites (or crypto-Mandaeans?) dwell; **kisiaiia ḏ-trin mania** RD B 112 (cf. 120, 129) hypocrites with two (different) clothes; **ušaiil kisiaiia** ATŠ II no. 369 if the hypocrites (crypto-Mandaeans) asked.

kisiata a var. of **kasiata** (fem. pl. of **kasia 2**). **šumhata hanik kisiata** DC 34. 518 those hidden (secret) names (cf. Widg. iii. 59 n. 2).

kisinta (כְּסִיתָא, *ܟܣܝܬܐ) AM 287:5 coral. St. emph. of **kisna 1**.

kisna 1 (cf. Syr. pl. ܟܣܢܐ) st. abs. of **kisinta** coral (or pearl). **kisna ḏ-lanqiba** DC 44. 1087, 1204, Par. xxvii 78 b unpierced coral.

kisna 2 a *malwâša* woman's name.

kisnia (P. كاسنى ?) endive, white succory; sun-flower. **ṭuria ḏ-kisnia** Bodl. xii.

kispa AM a var. of **kaspa** (doubtf.).

kista (cf. **kisa** Jew.-Aram. כִּיסְתָּא) bag, purse, receptacle. **ʿzlat ḏ-hʿ kista ḏ-razia** ATŠ I no. 24, DC 40 Ezlat who is the Receptacle of Mysteries.

kiʿila Gy 202:22 B a var. of **kila** MG 6:25.

kipa 1 (כֵּיפָא stone, bank, ܟܐܦܐ, H. כֵּף, Akk. *kāpu* stone). (*a*) bank, shore, (*b*) border, edge, brink, limit. Cstr. **kip**. Var. **kʿpa**. Masc. MG 158:14. Pl. **kipia**. The meaning 'stone' (MG 108:20 f.) does not seem to be Mand. (*a*) **trin kiph̲ ḏ-rbita** Gy 194:5, var. **kʿph̲** Gy 193:11 (MG 178:13 f.); **kipa ḏ-iardna** Gy 153:8, **kip iardna** PD 1264; **kip aina** PD 28; **mn kipa lkipa** Morg 257/6:13, DC 44. 359; **man kralh̲ kiph̲ trin** Jb 220:7 who dug out its two banks? (*b*) **kip baita ḏ-iušamin** Gy 346:1, 348:8 the brink of Y.'s domain; **silqit lkipa . . . aškit anana rba kip ṭuria iatib** DC 45 I rose to the horizon (?) . . . I found a great cloud resting on the edge of the mountains.

kipa 2 (pass. pt. pe. of **KUP** = **KPP**) bent, bowed MG 108:7. **kipa ugahna** Gy 179:19 s. **GHN I** pe. act. pt.

kipa 3 (כֵּיף, כֵּיפָה, cf. also **kipa 2, kaupa, kapa, & kapta 1**) something bent or arched, arch, arc, bow, vault; with **ḏ-kraiia** sole, or instep of the foot; with **ḏ-ʿda** palm of the hand. Pl. **kipia**. **kḏ kipia tikapinun** DC 15 thou bendest them like bows; **kipa ḏ-parzla** P.A. xii the iron bow; **kipa uqria msanh̲ ḏ-ligria** DC 46 the bow (?) and fastenings of the sandals of his feet; **kipia ḏ-šamiš . . . kipa ḏ-sira** DC 46 the arc of the sun . . . the arc of the moon; **kdub lkipia ḏ-kraiih̲** DC 46. 132:15 write on the soles of his feet; **usilqit lkipia** DC 46. 205:11 and I went up to the (heavenly) vault.

kipa 4 (כְּיְיפָא) pressure, necessity, compulsion, constriction. **dahalta ukipa** DC 43 E 41 fear and compulsion; **razan ukipan** DC 40. 477 our mystery (: secret art) and our compulsion.

kiputa (rather from **KPT** than from **KUP** = **KPP**) bond, fetter, band, knot Ginzā 93 n. 4. **kapth̲ bkiputa** Gy 90:23 I fettered him with a fetter; **napšh̲ šauiat kḏ kiputa** Gy 170:14 she made herself resemble a bond.

kiṣaiia AM 193 name of a people, or tribe.

kiṣat (< קְצָת MG 39:12) portion, share (?). Var. **giṣat** Ginzā 9 n. 8. **latauma ḏ-bkiṣat hdadia lariblh̲** Gy 6:16 he has no brother that shares his portion (?).

kir Ṣâb.'s AM var. of **kair** AM 282:13.

kira 1 (st. abs. of preced.) good (?). **kira hua** DC 46 it is good (?).

kira 2 (Ar. كَرّ) attack, stroke. Pl. **kiria 1**. **umhiih̲ brauṭa šuba kiria** DC 46 and strike him with the twig seven strokes.

kiria 1 pl. of **kira 2**.

kiria 2 (rt. **KRA I**?) distress, anguish (or past part.?). **ḏ-šihia adupia ḏ-kiria** (B **kibia**) **naplia** Jb 180:8 those eager to blame the distressed shall fall (?).

kirihua (mod. **ki** = **kḏ** + **rihua**, lit. 'like the wind') immediately, on time. Var. **kiriua**. Very frequent mod. expression (pron. *kerehwâ*). **ʿnta ḏ-laiadla kirihua** DC 46. 150:17, 151:3 etc. a woman who does not bring forth on time; **laiadilan kirihua** DC 46. 73:2 they do not bring forth on time.

kirkia pl. (rt. **KRK**) waves, whirlpools. **kirkia**

(var. **karkia**) **ḏ-iama** DC 44. 451 the waves of the sea.

kirman (P. كرمان) AM 197 Kirman, a city in Iran BZ Ap. II.

kirmania (adj. from preced.) of Kirman. DC 46. 114:3. Var. **karmanḥ**, **-ia** s.v. **tutia ḏ-kirmania** AM 286:43 f. collyrium of K.

kirṣa 1 (rt. **KRṢ**) in **akil kirṣa** (< אֲכַל קַרְצֵי, ܐܟܠ ܩܪ̈ܨܐ < Akk. *akālu qarṣē*) ATŠ II no. 377 acts as informer, accuser.

kirṣa 2 occ. miscop. of **pirṣa**.

kišuta 1 (קִשּׁוּתָא, ܩܫܘܬܐ Löw no. 171, ZA xxviii 1 f., Lagarde, *Mitteilungen* ii 358) down (on fruit), gherkins. **kišuta tišuq uiabša** AM 171:18 gherkins will languish and dry up; **hazin kišutai hᶜ ḏ-ᶜl ᶜlania napla ulitlḥ giada** Bodl. xii this is the down that falls on the (fruit of the) trees and has no tissue.

kišuta 2 (rel. to **kišuta 1**) some kind of skin-disease. Var. **kšuta**. **kṣurta banašia hauia ukišutai nipqabun** Ṣâb.'s AM, var. **ukšuta napqabun** AM 185:14.

kišra 1 (rt. **KŠR**) (*a*) subst. prosperity, success, (*b*) adj. well-pleasing, successful, satisfactory (pl. **kišria**), (*c*) adv. successfully, satisfactorily. (*a*) **bkišraihun kbaštinun** DC 26. 556 & par. I subdued them in their prosperity; **kišra niaha ušlama** Oxf. roll f 285, 984, cf. Morg. 249/84:ult. f. (cf. Jb ii 212 n. 1); (*b*) **šitlia nišitlun ḏ-kišria** Gy 90:1 (doubtf. Ginzā 92 n. 2), cf. s. **kišra 2**; (*c*) **man kšarbḥ kišra** Jb 229:15 who joined it skilfully (doubtf. Jb ii 212 n. 1).

kišra 2 (concr. noun from **KŠR** with doubtf. meaning) legally joined (?). Pl. **kišria** bridal pair (?). **asgit luat trin kišria uašqitinun ltrin kišria ḏ-hazin alma** ŠQ 17:19 f. I went towards two legally joined persons and I gave the two legally joined persons drink. Does **kišra 1** (*b*) belong here? (the plants mentioned are 'children of a married couple').

kišrat anana Gy 374:5 a female heavenly spirit.

kišra 3 (Akk. *gušūru*, Talm. כְּשׁוּרָא plank) plank(-bridge), beam. Mod. pl. **kišran**. **duktai bkišran hauia** DC 46. 78:15 my place is in the rafters.

kita (ܟܬܐ, Ar. كُتَّة, Jew.-Aram. verb כְּתַת to crush) lump, clod MG 102:16. **kita ḏ-siana** Gy 94:3 a lump of filth; **kita mšakna** Gy 225:15 id.; **kita ḏ-ṭina** Gs 98:3, 133:16 clod of clay; **bdima kita taria** Gs 99:7 f. with her tears she moisteneth the lump (of earth), **kita lnapšaihun tra** DAb = RD C 17 they wept for themselves (? lit. they moistened the clod).

kitana (כִּיתָּנָא, ܟܬܢܐ Löw no. 172, Akk. *kitinnu*, Ar. loan-w. كَتَّان, Fränkel 42, 232) flax, linen. **lruqita ḏ-kitana** DC 37. 285 on a piece of linen; **ᶜumṣia ḏ-kitana** DC 43 H 21 strips of linen; **panbai ukitana** DC 12. 145, Lond. roll B 290 my cotton and my linen; **bazra ḏ-kitana** DC 46. 90:7 linseed.

kitun(a) (כִּתּוּנָא, ܟܘܬܝܢܐ, H. כֻּתֹּנֶת; cf. also Gr. χιτών) shirt, garment, linen robe MG 126:6. Pl. **kitunia**. **kitun pagria** Gy 101:21, Gs 10:4, 80:17; **kituna kitun pagria** Gs 67:20 the physical garment (i.e. body); **kitun ṣiba** Gy 56:11 a coloured shirt; **kitun (ḏ-)gaunia**, Gs 120:1, 5, **kitun ḏ-gaunia gaunia** Gy 116:10 a robe of many colours; **kitun hšuka** Gs 115:5 garment of darkness; **kitun kukbia** Gs 82:9, Q 68:2 (s. **kukba**); **kitun zma ubisra** Gs 26:12 a garment of blood and flesh; **kitun uardia** Gs 99:10, 12, 132:23 the robe of roses; **kitun ḏ-šgiria** Gy 26:13 read **atun ḏ-šgiria** with BC (a miscop. influenced by **kitun** in l. 12); **kitunia ḏ-mumia** Gs 68:13 robes of blemishes; **kitunun** (varr. **kitnun** C, **kitinun** D, **kitunun ḏ-** Sh. ᶜAbd.'s copy) **šihaihun ṣrun** Gs 53:15 they tore the robes of their lust.

kitra (כיתרא?) ATŠ I no. 248 garland, wreath (?).

KLA I, KLL II (Aram. & H. כלא, Syr. ܟܠܐ, Ar. كلأ Eth., ከልአ, Akk. *kalū*) to keep enclosed, hold back, restrain, withhold; to hinder, banish, exile.

Pe. Pf. with suff. **klaitḥ** Gs 134:3 thou didst withhold it MG 288:3. Impf. with suff. **laᶜklia** ML 140:2 I will not withhold it. Act. pt. **kalia umrahiq** Gy 177:19 he restraineth and removeth.

Pa. Pf. with suff. **kauitinun ukalitinun** DC 44. 1525 (var. . . . **ukaltinun** Morg. 266/23:14) I charred them and restrained them.

Ethpe. Impt. fem. **ᶜtiklai** Gs 134:8 he held back.

Der.: **kilaia 2**, (ᶜ)**kiliata**, **kaliuta**, **kala**, **kalia 1–3**, **kluiia 1**, **k(u)lia**.

KLA II, KLL I (rel. to **KLA I**, **KUL**, & **AKL II**) to (be) complete, achieve, accomplish, end; measure.

Pe. Impf. with suff. **nikilinun lalam almia** DC 43 J 209 they put an end to them for ever. Act. pt. pl. (**mikal**) **kalia ᶜubadia** Jb 93:6 (read **ᶜubadai** ii 95 n. 9) they measure my works; **klila** (**-ia** B) **kalia** (**ki-** C) Jb 155:8 they enclose (them: the fish) with net(s) (doubtf. cf. ii 158 n. 1); **kalin ᶜl dbar ᶜšiul** Gs 17:24 they end at the wilderness of Sheol.

Ethpe. Pt. **mitkil ubaṭlia** Gs 44:10 they vanish.

Der.: s. **KUL** & **KLL I**.

klauata for **aglauata** (see **agla 2**). **klauata ḏ-mia** DC 34. 245 waves of water.

KLB (den. from **kalba**. Gen. Sem.) to be(come) mad, insane, rabid; to rage, rave.

Ethpa. Pt. pl. **kalbia uariauata mikalbia** AM 273:20 dogs and lions will become rabid.

Der.: **kalba, maklub**.

KLDA (den. from **kaldaia**) to bewitch, use magic arts, read stars, practise astrology. MG 84:19 f. Fundamental stem: Pf. with suff. **kaldaiia ḏ-zipa lakaldian** Gs 103:10 f. the false Chaldaeans did not bewitch me MG 84:19, 284:ult. Act. pt. pl. **mkaldin kaṣumia** Gy 60:1 the soothsayers read stars.

Der.: **kaldaia**.

kluiia 1 (rt. **KLA I**) pl. hindrances, obstacles,

impediments. **halin arba iamamia ḏ-kluiia hinun** ATŠ II no. 142 (var. . . . **ḏ-aklia hinun** DC 6 ibid.) those four seas that are hindrances (obstacles to purity).

kluiia 2 Ṣâb.'s AM a var. of **kulaia** AM.

klula 1 (rt. **KLL I,** cf. **kilta** 1) veil Jb ii 107 n. 3. **klula** (var. **klila** ABD) **mn anph̲ laramia** Jb 107:8 she does not drop her veil (var. garland) from her head; **klula upandama** DC 44. 192 = Morg. 256/3 f. veil and face-covering; **ḏ-hua bkluh̲** CP 401:12 who was within the Veil (or see **klula 2**).

klula 2 (rt. **KLL I**?) perfection, fullness. Doubtf. **mania iaqria bklulaihun** CP 411:1 the holy *mânas* in their perfection (or **klula** 1?).

klia (rt. **KLA I**) traps (? Lidzb. '*Köder*'). **halpilun luklia** (var. **lklia** AC, **lkulia** D) **kulhun** Jb 156:2 f. they pass by all the traps (?).

klila 1 (כְּלִילָא, ܟܠܝܠܐ < Akk. *kililu* Pognon: Wadi Brissa 76, Ar. loan-w. اكليل Fränkel 62) crown, circlet, wreath, garland MG 116:18. St. abs. & cstr. **klil**. Pl. **klilia**. Masc. Used often as a gnostic term 'crown of victory' Jb ii 2 footn., MSt 153, MMII 35 ff. **klil aiar** Gy 320:14, 335:2, Gs 107:24, 109:6, Q 28:14, Oxf. 86 a (s. **aiar** 1); **klil almia šahia uklila ḏ-hiia rauz** CP 76:penult. f. Q 35:29 = ML 94:2 the wreath of the worlds fades, but the wreath of the Life is fresh; **klil zakauata** Gy 128:11, 210:10, Gs 11:7, Q 56:27; **klila ḏ-zakauata** Jb 174:4, **klila klil zakauata** CP 422:4, Jb 208:12 the crown of victories; **klilia ḏ-zakauata** Gy 44:24, **klilia ḏ-zakuta** Gy 210:21, **klil ziua uzakuta** Gs 123:21 crown of brilliance and victory; **klila uarda** Jb 77:10 (s. **uarda**); **klila ḏ-asa** CP 26:3 and often, Q 3:33 (cf. 10:13), 20:9, 28:10 myrtle-wreath; **klila mhambla** Gy 287:5 spoiled wreath; **klil ʿšata haita** Gy 80:3, 82:22 crown of Living Fire (: gloriole, halo); **klila ḏ-hšuka** Gy 301:14 f. the wreath of darkness; **klila ḏ-ptahil** Gy 393:12; **klilia busma** Gy 234:4, Jb 83:14 fragrant wreaths; **klil pirṣa uzaniuta** Gy 209:5 wreath of lechery and prostitution; **klilia ḏ-pirṣa uzaniuta** Gy 225:12 MG 309:20 ff.; **arba klilia** Jb 189:7, 190:2; **klilia gadlia** Gy 106:15 they plait wreaths; **klilia rauzia** ML 211:4 (in opposition to **ṭuṭipta** (H. טֹטֶפֶת frontlet-bands); s. **rauza**), **klilak rauz(i)a** Gy 292:11; **klil razia** DC 40 garland of mysteries.

Gl. 143:11 **klila** كليل *corona* تاج.

klila 2 Jb 107:8 ABD a var. of **klula** 1.

klila 3 (pass. pt. pe. of **KLL I**) surrounded. **kḏ klila uhidrh̲ šuba šuria** DC 44. 318 as surrounded and girt about by seven walls.

KLL I Shaf. to improve, perfect, establish. **umaštakilan lnišmatan lbit zibna** CP 109:1 (ML 134:5 **mištkalin**) and perfecteth our souls at the House of Ransom; **umištkalin lnišmatan liuma rba ḏ-haduta** CP 109:3 and perfecteth our souls on the great Day of Joy.

KLL II (Gen. Sem., cf. Ges. s. כלל I) to surround, complete; to come to an end, die; to veil, wreathe, wrap, cover oneself (cf. **kilta** 1 ML 96 n. 3); ethpa. id. pass., Nöld. 'to languish' (cf. H. כלה I, Ar. كَلَّ) MG 83:21, ZA xxxiii 76, Brandt, MSchr. 157 n. 2, differently Lidzb. ML 96 n. 3, ZS i 1922 p. 1 f. Rel. to **KUL, KLA II** and perh. also **AKL II.**

Pa. Pf. with suff. **kalalh̲** Gs 109:5, Q 42:26 he surrounded it. Impf. with encl. **nikalalbh̲** DC 22. 373 only as a var. of **mikalalbh̲** Gy 377:13 (s. ethpa. pt. with encl.). Act. pt. **mkalil** DC 22. 488 a var. of **mkalal** Gs 106:19 (s. pass. pt.). Pass. pt. **mkalal umsadar** Gy 215:4 crowned (?) and in good order (doubtf. ZS i 2, Ginzā 215 n. 4), **mkalal ušakib** Gs 106:19 (var. **mkalil** . . . DC 22) is covered and sleepeth (Lidzb.), is tired and sleepeth (Nöld.), MG 83:21 better: dieth and sleepeth fem. st. emph. **mkalalta** (s.v.); pl. **mkalalia uganʿia ʿl šakbia** DC 43 (with many varr.) they bring to an end (?) and lie upon those who are sleeping (??); with encl. pers. pron. **mkalalna ušakibna** CP trs. 52 n. 3, Q 36:28, 39:27, 45:31, CP 78:15, ML 96:6, Gs 120:11 I come to my end and sleep (die) (ML 96 n. 3; Nöld. differently, cf. above).

Ethpa. Pf. **ʿtkalal uškib** Gy 18:20, 114:24, 356:19, Jb 184:1, 210:4, Q 65:1, 4 was (were) exhausted and fell asleep; **baqaria tkalal unpil lknap tauraiun** JRAS 1937 591:10 the herdsmen met their end and fell beside their bulls. Impt. **ʿkalal minh̲ alma ḏ-hadritun** Gy 147:18 veil thyself from him until ye are wed. Pt. with encl. **ḏ-mikalalbh̲ ušakibbh̲** Gy 377:13 who covereth himself therewith and sleepeth therein (MG 213:13), who dieth and . . .; fem. **hʿ mitkalla minai** Gy 148:19 she is veiling herself from me.

Der.: **kalta, kul, kulul, klula (1, 2), klila (1, 2), kilta 1, kulaita.**

KLL III (= **KLA I**) to hold back, hinder, prevent.

Pe. Act. pt. with suff. (or encl.) **ukul ḏ-ʿlh̲ mn ʿniš lakalilh̲** AM 97:16 and he holds back from no one all that he has. Pass. pt. with encl. **laklilhun ḏ-nalbišunh̲** Gy 250:ult. f. they do not prevent them from putting it on.

Pa. Act. pt. pl. (with suff.?) **mkalilin** RD E 10 they hold them back (?), var. **mkalalia** DAb (pass.) they are held back (?).

Der.: s. **KLA I.**

KLP (Ar. خلف) to oppose, contradict, fight, quarrel. Mod. Gl. 21:7 f. **ḴLP** خالف *adversari, praeterire* (?) مخالف شد.

KLṢ (Ar. خلص) to complete, achieve, finish, free, absolve, release, unfasten, Mod.

Pa. Impt. **ukaliṣ pandamak** DC 24:167 and unfasten thy *pandama*. Act. pt. pl. **mkalṣin ʿdai(h)un mn hdadia** Oxf. roll f 1307, DC 38. 7:2, 4 they release one another's hands, **mkalṣin ʿda** Oxf. roll f 1309 id.

Gl. 11:15 f, miswritten with **s** انتهى *finire* تمام شد; 128:1 f. id. فرغ *cessare, finire* تمام شد; 139:5 f. id. كمل *perficere* تمام شد; 141:5 f. id. (af.) كفف *cessare*, Turk. قريدى (to dry).

Der.: **kaliṣ.**

KLQ (Ar. خلق) to create. Mod. Gl. 60:7 f. **ḲLQ** خلق *creare* آفريد.

kma (כַּמָּא, ܟܡܐ) how, how much, how long MG 207:11. Emphasized with **ha** in **hakma** s.v. Varr. **akma, ʿkma. kma napiš gabaria halin** Gy 139:20 how many are these heroes!; **kma hua šapir pagrai** Gs 14:23 how fair was my body!; **kma ʿiapiqlak mn alpia ukma ʿiapiqlak mn ruban** Gs 105:11, 106:12 how many shall I bring out for thee from thousands and how many . . . from myriads?; **kma tihuia šuta ḏ-ab** Gs 39:10 how long will my father's word last?; **mihdia kma hadina mihdia kma hadia lbab** Gs 89:1 how greatly I rejoice! how my heart rejoiceth! MG 437:14 ff.; **ʿuhra ḏ-kma napša** Gy 142:22 how long is the way!; **kma šnia** Gy 143:2 etc. how many years!; MG 438:12 ff., **kma šapir tauria** JRAS 1937 591:7 how beautiful are the bulls!; **kma ʿtib . . . ukma abtinihta ʿtibna** Jb 32:11 how long shall I sit . . . and how long shall I sit (there in) sighing?; **kma iušamin psaq . . .** Jb 13:14 how did Y. break . . .? **kma ḏ-** as long as, as much as, just as, the more the . . .: **kma ḏ-mia azlin ʿzil anat** Gy 192:3 just as the waters go, go thou; **kma ḏ-aitinkun balma** Gy 19:10 as long as ye are in the world; **kma ḏ-anat huitbẖ** Gy 324:4 as long as thou wert therein; **kma ḏ-dara bašar bišuta kabra** Gy 284:19 the shorter is the generation, the greater is the evil, **bkma ḏ-maskianalẖ lnaṣbai** Gs 96:3 as long as I look at my Creator; the relative **ḏ-** can be omitted after **kma**: **kma darit bgauẖ lahuabẖ hasir ubṣir** Gy 51:1 as long as I dwelt therein, there was nothing imperfect and deficient; **akma qala ḏ-hiia btibil aitẖ** Gy 221:10 as long as there is the Voice of the Life on earth MG 453:9 ff.; **kma ḏ-mṣia mn miuia** DC 42 as many fruits as possible; **kma ḏ-mṣia hailaikun** (*often*) as much as you can. Gl. 145:2 miswritten with two ms كيف *quomodo* چون.

kmaṭa DC 43 a var. of **gmaṭa.**

kmara, kmir (Ar.) fermentation, ferment. Mod. Gl. 70:3 **ḳmara** خمير *fermentum.*

KMS (כְּמַס, ܟܡܣ, also H.) to hide, store away, put aside.

Pe. Act. pt. pl. **mn qudam ḏ-kamsin drabšia** DC 36 before they put away the banners.

KMṢ I (rel. to **KBṢ.** Nöld. from קמץ 'to shrink' 'to spurt up', cf. قمص, קפץ & der. קַמְצָא 'locust' MG 39:16 ff.; the latter, accepted by Lidzb. in Jb ii 211:10, is doubtf., cf. ibid. 66 n. 2, here s. **kimṣa**) to contract, shrink up, condense, solidify, materialize, form. Both trans. and intrans.

Pe. Pf. **kmaṣ mn dmutaihun** Gy 238:26 He (pl.: the Life) formed Himself from His own Form; **ʿtiqrun ukmaṣ** Gy 239:20 they were created and formed; **kimṣa ḏ-kmaṣ** Gy 240:22 the formation (?) which he formed; **kmaṣ kimṣa ḏ-arqa hiuartia** Gy 297:9 he brought about the materialization of the white earth; **kmaṣ kimṣa ḏ-iardna** s. **kimṣa,** similarly **mia kmaṣiun** ATŠ II no. 51 (refers to solidification, prob.: the waters shrunk); **mn qudam ḏ-kamṣin drabšia** ATŠ (DC 6) II 99 before they store away the banners.

Pa. Pass. pt. **mkamṣa** Oxf. roll g 781, Or. 329:8, shrunken, faded.

Der.: **kimṣa, kimṣat.**

(**KMṢ II** for **KṢM** in **lakimṣan** Gs 103:10, var. **lakiṣman** DC 22 they did not bewitch me.).

KMR (cf. Mod. Syr. pa. ܟܡܪ 'to turn, return', otherwise unknown with this meaning MG 443 n. 1; cf. LS and Ges. s. כמר III) pa. to turn, turn about, turn away, go round, put back, replace; ethpa. to return, come back, bring back. The af. (see Idioms) is used as a repetitive verb. Still used.

Pa. Pf. with suff. **lgira lakamrẖ** DC 35 he did not return the arrow (to its quiver); **kamruia** HG 29 they sent her back. Impf. **ʿkamar** (var. **uʿtakamar** Leid.) **tigar lmištria** Gs 43:23 must I start my fight over again: (doubtf., cf. Idioms); with suff. **ʿkamrak uʿiailak bgauẖ** Gy 193:14 f. I will bring thee back into it again. Pt. (act. & pass.) **ḏ-laras ulamkamar** DC 22. 408 (var. . . . **ulamkar** Gy 17:20 all codices) unmarried and not taken round (in bridal procession?, cf. Idioms); pl. **kamuria lamkamria** DC 20. 38 they do not return. Inf. **kamuria** (just quoted). Nom. act. **kamarta** s.v.

Af. (idiomatic as a frequentative verb). Pf. **akmar bbišuta rmun** Gy 112:16 f. they again cast them into evil. Impt. **akmar rminan** Gy 186:1 put us back again; **anat akmar ldukthẖ atia akamar** (var. **akmar** Leid.) **atia ldukthẖ** Gy 102:8 f. bring him back again to his place.

Ethpa. Pf. **ʿtkamar bilẖ mn riš** Gs 7:18 he swallowed him again (*idiom*) MG 444:2, **ḏ-azal uʿtkamar** Jb 53:14 f. that went and returned. Impf. **nitkamar uniqrilẖ mn riš** DC 36 he shall turn back and read it from the beginning (cf. Idioms); **nitkamar unʿzal lhak alma** Gy 197:ult. f. that he may return and go to this world (cf. Idioms), **nitkamar** Q 37:1, PD 1556, 1558, 1564 he shall return, or turn back, or do again; **titkamar utikbar ʿlauaihun** Gs 47:15 it will return and press on them; **utitkamar** (var. **tik-**) **ldukthẖ** ATŠ I no. 278 she returneth to her place, **laʿtkamar ulaʿzal lalma** Gy 211:23 I will not return back to the world; **nitkamrun** Gy 319:21 (*bis*) they shall return. Pt. **mitkamar** Jb 138:13, 182:15, PD 1534, **mikamar** PD 1609; **umn ʿbidathẖ lamitkamar** ATŠ II no. 28 and he shall not be turned away from (: prevented from performing) his rites; **mitkamar** ATŠ II no. 182 = **mikamar** DC 6 ibid., **niraq lamitkamar** AM 54:penult. he will escape (and) not return; **ulamitkamar ulamitkar** AM 154:14 he will not be diverted (turned back) nor shamed; fem. **lkaliuta azla ulatrẖ mitkamra** AM 54:penult. she will go to foreign parts, but will be brought back to her home; pl. **mitkamria** Gy 326:7, ŠQ they (will) be returned, **maṭaraiia . . . mitkamria minaihun** ATŠ II no. 170 the purgatory-demons . . .

are turned away (averted, deflected) from them. Part. pres. **mitkamritun** DC 6 ibid. (var. **-ria** just quoted) ye (are) turned away, **mitkamrinin** Gy 227:26 we turn away (from).

Idioms: Similarly to **HDR I**, the verb is used as frequentative always in af., often in ethpa., less often in pa.: 'to do again, to repeat the same action'. Acc. to DC 22. 408 (v.s. pa. pt.), the verb could be used of wedding processions (also similarly to **HDR I**). In some cases the verb may occur as a miscop. of **KTR** (esp. in ethpa. **ʿtkamar** = **ʿtkatar**) 'to be retained, held back', cf. Ginzā 333 n 2.

Gl. 12:15 f. **KMR** (pa.) اعاد *retulere, restituere* بر گشت; 78:7 f. id. رجع *redire, converti* بر گشت; 81:3 f. id. ردّد *convertere se* ردّ کرد; 146:11 id. التفت *reverti retro* التفات کرد; 152:5 f. **kmar** (*sic*) منع *negare, contradicere* منع کرد; 165:13 f. **KMR** (pa.) نها *prohibere* منع کرد.

Der.: **kamarta.**

KMŠ (כמש, ܟܡܫ) to wrinkle, wither, fade.

Pa. Pass. pt. **mkamša** wrinkled, faded.

KNA I (כְּנָי, ܟܰܢܺܝ, H. כנה I, Ar. كنى, Akk. *kunnû*; secondary Mand. roots **KUN II** & **KNN III**) to (give a) name, call.

Pa. Act. pt. with encl. **mkanilia** Gy 245:15 (var. **-lẖ** Leid.) they call me, **mkanilẖ** Or. 326:17 (read **-lia**) id., **mkanilak** DC 43 they call thee, **mkanilak qarinalak** DC 43 I name thee (for **mkaninalak**), I call thee. Pass. pt. with encl. **mkanailun** Leid. var. of **mkainalun** Gy 231:15 (s. **KUN II**).

Der.: **kiniana 1.**

KNA II identical in certain forms with **KNN I** (e.g. **kanilẖ** Gy 84:3).

knan (rt. **KNN I**) st. cstr. wrapping (v. s. **KNN I** pe. pf with suff.)

knap st. abs. & cstr. of **kanpa** (q.v.), used often as an adverb or preposition: **lknap, bknap** beside, **npil lknap tauraiun** JRAS 1937 591:10 they fell beside their bulls; **arimlẖ knap hiia** Q 31:16 they placed him beside the Life; **dalulẖ lhaza nišimta knap hiia** Gs 37:23 they drew up this soul beside the Life (: to be with the Life); **lknap ṭuria iatib** DC 37. 466 sitting on the mountain-side.

knara = **kinara 2. knara ḏ-hazin tlatma ušitin aluatia ʿtlia** JRAS 1938, 3:8, the lote-tree which has 360 branches.

kništa (spec. Jew. כנישתא = ἐκκλησία, Ar. loan-w. كنيسة Fränkel 275) assembly, congregation, place of assembly, synagogue, church MG 117:22. **bit kništan** Jb 71:13 our synagogue (MSt 117 n. 2). **bkništaikun** Jb 72:5 in your synagogue; **kništa balma niknuš** Gy 105:6 we will found a church in the world; **nailẖ lkništan** ibid. f. we will bring him to our church; **nitun lkništan** Gy 106:2 they (will) come into our congregation; **azal lgauẖ kništun** he went into their assembly; **šabšat aiiltẖ lkništa** Gy 115:17 she seduced and brought him into the congregation; **šauia kništa lnapšẖ** Gy 382:12 he made (hist. pres.) himself a Church; **kaniš lnapšẖ kništa** s. **KNŠ** pe. act. pt.

KNN I, KUN III, (KNA II) (H. כנן I, also mod. H., Ar. كنّ, Akk. *kunnunu*) to wrap, veil, cover. Rel. to **KLL I.**

Pe. Pf. (Lidzb. Ginzā 223 n. 4 derived mistakenly from this rt. **kan kinta**, cf. s. **KUN I** & **kinta 2**); with encl. **kanilẖ** Gy 84:3, 90:18 I wound around him MG 249:1; with suff. **kanẖ** Gy 101:22, 102:9, 338:19 he wrapped him MG 275:4; **kanan bknan ziua** Gs 102:3, Q 37:32 = CP 81:3 = ML 100:2 he wrapped me in a wrapping of radiance (MG 270:bottom); **btrisar kinia kantẖ** Gy 90:21 I wrapped him in twelve wrappings (MG 277:4). Impf. **kinʿnia ʿkun** Gy 158:13 I wind swaddling bands (MG 249:12), **nikinun**? MG 249:26. Act. pt. fem. **kaina** s. **KUN III.**

Der.: **kinta 1** (pl. **kininia, kinnia, kinia, kaninia, kanunia 2**).

KNN II s. **KUN I.**

KNN III, KUN II (den. from **kiniana 1**) = **KNA I.**

Pa. Pf. **kanin lnapšẖ** Gy 297:18 he called himself. Pass. pt. with encl. **mkainalun** s. **KUN II.**

KNN IV (den. from **kana** like Syr. ܟܰܢܶܢ) to form a group, found a family; to collect together in one place, gather together.

Pa. Impf. **tikanan rahmia** CP 452 ult. thou wilt gather friends together (?). Pass. pt. **mkanana** CP 380:7 compact (?) grouped as a family.

Ethpa. Impt. **lguṭ zaua uʿtkanan** Gy 14:3, 35:2, Jb 110:14 take a wife and found a family MR 85 n. 2 (homonymous with **KNN II** q.v.s. **KUN I** ethpa.).

Der.: **kana, kanuna** (?), **kinta 2.**

KNP (כנף, ܟܢܦ, denominative from **kanpa**) to take into arms, embrace; to gather, assemble, come together, crowd together. Both trans. & intrans.

Pe. Pf. **knap ʿutria uknap škinata** Oxf. 62 b the uthras assembled, the škinas assembled; **knap gunda** Gy 344:11 f. he gathered the army; with suff. **knaptainun** DC 34. 546 thou didst gather them. Impf. **kanupta nikinpun** AM 228:8 they will gather an armful; **haizak knap uqrun ltagẖ** ATŠ II no. 429 then assemble and recite over his crown. Act. pt. pl. **kinpa** (var. **ka-** DC 22, Leid. & Sh. ʿAbd.'s copy) **ḏ-kanpia** Gy 17:7 and the host (Nöld.: the booty) which they gather (MG 358:9 f.). Pass. pt. pl. with encl. **alma ḏ-knipilẖ sahria** RD B 54 = DAb par. the world upon which demons are crowded.

Pa. Pf. **ukanip abihdia bnia tarmidia trin** DC 36 and he joined to himself the sons of two priests; **hiduta ḏ-lakanpat** DC 44 bride whose marriage was not consummated, bride that did not embrace (refers to nuptial embrace); **kanpun ʿutria** Q 60:17 the uthras assembled. Impf. with suff. **ḏ-nikanpan** Gy 275:10 which embraceth me, **nikanpinun unitrun** DC 43 he will assemble them and drive them away (?). Impt. pl. **kanipiun šipulaikun** DC 50. 245 gather up your skirts (ritual injunction: gather the hems of your skirts into the girdle before going into the water). Pt. **ḏ-mkanpa ulamkauna** Jb 88:9 ff. (a woman) that is embraced and not correct (in observing the ritual rules, cf. ii 92 n. 2); pl. **mkanpia** Gs 12:4 they assemble; with encl. **mkanpilun** Gs 10:24 (who) will gather them. Inf. **kanupia**, var. **kinupia.**

Ethpa. Pf. **ʿtkanap šibiahia** CP 165:6 the planets gathered together; **bihdadia ʿtkanap** DC 34 they came together; **ʿtkanapiun** they gathered together MG 223:24. Pt. **mitkanap** DC 27. 304, ATŠ II no. 110 (is, are) joined, brought together.

Der.: **kanpa, kanapta, kanupta, kanpan, kanpʿil.**

KNŠ (כְּנַשׁ & כְּנַס, ܟܢܫ, H. כנס, Ar. كنس, Eth. ተከነሠ Nöld.: *Neue Beitr.* 37 n. 3) to assemble, gather together; to bring together, rake, sweep. Often with **ZHL** Jb ii 45 n. 6.

Pe. Impf. **kništa balma niknuš** Gy 105:6 (s. **kništa**); with encl. **niknušbḫ kinša** Gy 105:5 (s. **kinša**). Act. pt. **kaniš lnapšḫ kništa** Gy 23:18 he called (hist. pres.) together a church for himself; **ziqa . . . kaniš apra** AM 271:9 the wind . . . sweeps up dust; **bmanzia šuqia kanšia** Gs 99:6 (read **-ša**) she sweepeth the market-places with her hair; with encl. **kanšilḫ uzahlilḫ** DC 48. 230 she sweeps and cleans it. Part. Pres. **kanšana uzahlana** Jb 127:10 f. I (fem.) sweep and clean; with suff. **kanšinin uzahlinin** Jb 41:3 I sweep and clean them. Pass. pt. pl. **miknaš knišia šuqia** Morg.199:14 the markets are thoroughly swept; **knišia knišia bhiria** Gs 122:19 the chosen are assembled; with encl. (& act. meaning) **knišlia uzlihlia** Gs 84:19 I swept and sprinkled MG 382:12. Inf. **miknaš** Morg. 199:14 (s. pass. pt.); with suff. **baiit mikibšḫ umikinšḫ** DC 44. 1224 thou wishest to crush it down and to sweep it up.

Ethpe. Pt. **mikniš baita lmarḫ** DC 40. 217 f. the house is swept for its owner.

Ethpa. Pf. **ʿtkanaš** Gy 368:15, Gs 82:22 BCD = **ʿkanaš** ibid. A they assembled MG 213:12.

Der.: **kanšia, kinša, kništa.**

KSA (כסא, ܟܣܐ, H. כסה I, Ar. كسا, Akk. *kasû*?) to cover, conceal, hide, keep secret, protect; to put on (a dress to wear), clothe, dress.

Pe. Pf. with suff. **ksuia** Oxf. III 95 a, **kisiuia** Oxf. III 108 b they covered him MG 288:19 f.; **ksaitunan** Gy 157:14 ye concealed me. Impf. with suff. **kul man ḏ-nikisiiḫ** CP 374:14 everyone that covereth it; **nikisinun** AM 207:13 it covers them. Impt. with suff. **anat ksinun** ATŠ I no. 119 keep them secret. Act. pt. **gabra ḏ-kasia razaikun** Jb 68:3 f. a man that conceals your secrets. Pass. pt. **ksia** covered, hidden MG 109:8, 259:paen.; fem. st. abs. **ksʿia** Gs 111:2 MG 153:28; fem. pl. **ksiia** Gy 93:20 MG 165:antep.; with encl. **ksibḫ** is hidden in it MG 256 n. 3; with encl. pers. pron. **ksuia ḏ-ksina** DC 37:165 the attire that I put on.

Pa. Pf. **kasinin** Gy 184:18 we clothed; with suff. **kasian** he covered me, clothed me MG 284:bottom; **kasi(i)ḫ** Q 33:2, Gy 239:11 he covered him, clothed him; **kasiun** Gy 155:7 he (pl.: the Life) concealed me MG 286:4; **kasiuia** Gy 188:18, 235:13 he (: the Life) covered him MG 288:24; **kasinun** Gy 239:13 he covered them MG 290:13; **kasunin** Q 30:27 they covered them (fem.) MG 291:9; **kasitinkun** Gy 178:19 (var. **kasaitinkun** A) I covered you. Impf. with suff. **nikasinan** Q 57:25 he covers us MG 289:16; **lmdiniata nikasinun** AM 207 it covers the cities; **tikasinan** Q 55:4 thou coverest us; **nikasunḫ** they cover him (or it) MG 288:paen. Impt. pl. **kasun** MG 262:14; with suff. **kasinun** Gy 250:15 cover them; pl. with suff. **kasiuia** Gy 36:20 cover him MG 289:3. Act. pt. **mkasia** MG 131:13. Part. pres. **mkasina** Morg. 258/7:28, DC 44:503 I put on; **mkasit** Gy 211:19 thou puttest on; with encl. **anin mkasinalḫ** Gy 126:23 we put it on MG 262:26; with suff. **mkasinun** I put them on MG 292:1. Pass. pt. **mkasai** Gy 52:2, MG 7:21, 23:5, 131:17, 164:29, 263:3; pl. **mkasin** MG 164:29, 263:4 fem. **mkasia** Gy 281:9, Q 14:16 MG 165:18, 263:4; with encl. pers. pron. **ksiiia ḏ-razia mkasaina** DC 44. 434 (var. **ksuia . . . mkasina** Morg. 258/7:28 act.) I am covered with hidden (rites of ?) mysteries; id. with suff. **mkasainak** Gs 133:4 (var. **mkasinak** C act.) I cover myself with thee MG 291:bottom.

Ethpe. Pf. **ʿt(i)ksia** he was covered MG 263:21; **ʿtiksia mn ʿutria** DC 50. 758 was protected (?) by the uthras; **ʿt(i)ksit** thou wast hidden MG 264:10; **kisiat** Gs 91:20 f. (read **ʿkisiat**) she covered herself MG 257:9; **ʿt(i)ksun** they were covered MG 264:18; **ʿtksu** Gy 271:9 id. MG 264:21; **ʿtiksinin** Gy 325:19 (var. **-ainin** C) we hid ourselves; **utksainin** Par. xi 11 b and we were hidden MG 264:30; with encl. **ʿtiksubḫ** Gy 317:5 they hid (themselves) therein MG 264:22. Impf. **lmdiniata niksinun** AM 207:ult. the cities will be covered (?); **ulaniksia bgauaihun** DC 34. 978 and is not protected by them; **ksisia ʿkisia ainaihun** JRAS 1937 595:31 (their eyes) will be covered; **titiksia, tiksia** *cela(be)ris* MG 265:1. Pt. **ziuḫ mn kukbia lamitiksia** ATŠ II no. 52 (var. **lamitaksia** DC 6 ibid.) its brilliance is not concealed by the stars; pl. **mitiksin** MG 214:4. Part. pres. **mitiksina** I am covered MG 266:1. Inf. **ʿtiksuiia** Gy 271:9 MG 144:12.

Ethpa. Pf. **ʿtkasiat uʿtnaṭrat** CP 388 penult. she (or it) was hidden and guarded. Impt. pl. **ʿtkasun** MG 265:21. Pt. **lamitaksia** ATŠ II no. 52 a var. of **lamiti-** v.s. ethpe. pt.

Der.: **kasia** (fem. **-ata**), **kasiaia, kisuta, k(i)sia, k(i)siaia, ksuia, taksata.**

ksasar a pr. n. mentioned with **hamamulai** (q.v.) ML Ind.: *Die höheren Wesen* s.v. **šum ksasar hamamulai** CP 69:8 = Q 31:21, Morg. 232/52:ult., ML 84:8 f.

ksuia (rt. **KSA**) (*a*) covering, robe, (ritual) tunic, (*b*) a thing hidden, covered. MG 118:20, MMII 30 n. 1, JRAS 1939 401 n. 1. Pl. **ksuiia.** (*a*) **ksuia ḏ-ptahil** Gy 393:11; **nṣablḫ ksuia** Oxf. 65 a:bottom; **ksuia ḏ-**

nṣablak Oxf. 66 a; **maria lbušia uksuiia** AM 155:5; **adinqia ksuia** Jb 120:7; **ksuia ḏ-ksina** DC 37:165 (s. **KSA** pe. pass. pt. with encl. pers. pron.); **šuba ksuiia ḏ-ziua mkasina** DC 43 C 4 I put on seven tunics of radiance; (*b*) **ksuiia . . . mitgalalia** DC 43 hidden things . . . are revealed.

ksul DC 22. 399 = **kusil** GS 7:12.

ksia 1 pass. pt. pe. of **KSA**. **atar ksia** WedF 28:bottom; **ksia ulamgalal** Morg. 198:4.

ksia 2 in **ksiaikun** Sh. ʿAbd.'s copy's var. of **kisiaikun** Gy 134:14 (s. **kisia**).

ksiaia s. **kasiaia**.

ksil Sh. ʿAbd.'s copy's var. of **kusil** Gs 7:12.

ksisuta (rt. **KSS** I or II, or read ***psisuta** or **nsista**?) destruction, reprehension, corruption, illness? Doubtf. **bnia mdinta ksisuta maškia** AM 267:36.

KSS I (Gen. Sem.) to chew, break into pieces, crumble, cut (off).

Pe. Impt. **ubadar ksus** AM 123:ult. and scatter (and) break to pieces (?), **mut mut mut ksas abar ksas** DC 40. 925 (a magic formula: die, die, die, be cut down, perish, crumble (?)!). Pass. pt. pl. **sdimia hrimia uksisia** JRAS 1937 595:30 confined, banned and cut off (?).

Der.: **ksisuta** (?), **kiusta** (?).

KSS II (Gen. Aram., rel. to **KSS I**) to blame, reprehend, put to shame, put right, confute, correct, admonish, advise.

Af. Pf. with suff. **akastinun** Gs 54:14 I reprehended them. Impt. **akis rahmaikun bturṣa** Gy 40:19 admonish your friends straitly (MG 251:16). Act. pt. **makis** MG 251:19; with encl. **akasta makislun** Gs 53:20 he greatly reprehended (hist. pres.) them. Nom. ag. **makisana** s.v. Nom. act. **akasta** s.v.

Der.: **akasta, makisana**.

ksʿil a var. of **k(u)sil**.

KSR I (Ar. كسر) to break, crush; pass. to be broken, afflicted. Often in corrupt mod. texts. **misar anania btiksir** DC 44 corrupt (cf. Ar. تكسير); **htim bšuma ksir** DC 44.

KSR II (Ar. خسر) to lose (in commerce).

Pe. Inf. **miksar lbazrgania** AM 281:27 loss for merchants.

kʿuan Gy 121:5, 171:22 = **kiuan** MG 5:19.

kʿla, kʿila = **kila** MG 5:18, 6:25.

kʿlaia = **kilaia** 1.

kʿin, kʿn = **kin** MG 6:25 f.

KPA s. **KUP**.

kpar (= **kbar** 1) perhaps: **kpar makirna** Gs 41:14 s. **AKR** I pa. pass. pt. **kpar tahma dmutai** ibid. f. perhaps my form will become dark.

kpip(i)ata (rt. **KPP I = KUP**) humiliations, abasements; **kpipata . . . ʿlauaihun nihuia** DC 43 I 3 humiliations . . . shall be theirs.

KPN (כְּפַן, ܟܦܢ, H. כָּפָן hunger, Ar. كفن to shroud) to hunger, be hungry; fig. to hunger after, long for. Still used.

Pe. Pf. **kpin** Gy 15:ult., var. **kpan** DC 22 has become hungry. Act. pt. pl. **lakapnia** Gy 15:21, varr. **lakapnʿ** DC 22, **lakapnin** (Sh. ʿAbd.'s copy) they hunger not. Part. pres. **kapina** Gy 86:8 (var. **-ana** DC 22) I hunger MG 12:18. Pass. pt. **karsai kpina lmikal** Gy 189:6 my belly is hungry for food.

Af. Pf. with suff. **akpinthẖ** Gy 218:1 thou hast let him hunger MG 276:28.

Gl. 58:11 f. defectively with a prosth. a جاع *esurire* گرسنه شد, 67:15 pass. pt. missp. جوعان *esuriens* گرسنه.

Der.: **kapna, kapina, kupna**.

KPP I s. **KUP**.

KPP II (Ar. خفّ) to put out (fire), quench, extinguish.

Pf. **kapap nurik** DC 40. 924 thy fire (was) extinguished.

KPṢ (doubtf., prob. rel. to **KBṢ**, cf. varr.) to break, cut?

Pa. Pf. (with suff.?) **kapṣinin llibẖ** Gy 84:1, var. **kaptinin** B, **kabṣinin** D Lidzb. *Ich knickte sein Herz*; acc. to varr.: we bound (B), we made his heart contract (D). Corrupt?

KPR (Gen. Sem.) to wipe off, expunge, efface, reject, remove; to deny, renounce (faith), be incredulous.

Pe. Pf. **kpar** (*often*) he denied; special pl. form **kpariun** (DAb) they denied; with encl. **kparbẖ** Gy 94:22 they denied him MG 225:6; **kparbun** Gy 104:11, 13 he denied them; with suff. **kiprẖ lšumaiun mn šabtẖ** PD 1091 he expunged their names from his scroll; **kipruia lšumẖ mn šabta** Gy 116:1 they expunged his name from the scroll. Impf. **tikpar utišqal minaian haṭaian** CP 52:1, Morg. 223/33:8 f., Q 24:6 thou wilt efface and remove our sins; **minlat maraikun . . . latikiprun** Gy 28:23 do not deny . . . the word of your Lord; with encl. **nikparlẖ ulanitilẖ** AM 246:penult. he will deny him and will not come to him; with suff. **nikaprẖ** Gs 53:16 we will reject him, **ʿkiprẖ mn šaptai** PD 40 = ATŠ I no. 5 I will expunge him from my scroll; **ʿkiprẖ lšuma mn šapta** PD 931. Impt. **kpar mn libaikun** Gy 19:12 remove from your hearts; with suff. **kuprẖ lšumai mn šaptak** Jb 103:12 expunge my name from thy scroll (MG 269 n. 1, 276:10) Jb ii 104 footn. Act. pt. **kapir mn zidqa** Gy 15:21 his alms will be denied; pl. **kapria bmiša** Gy 46:6 they deny Moses (Ginzā 43 n. 3). Part. pres. **kaprinalẖ lšumẖ mn šaptan** PD 602 = ATŠ I no. 55 we will efface his name from our scroll.

Pa. Pf. **haizak mn hiia kapar** Gy 54:4 then he denied the Life, **kaprit anpai** DC 44. 1300 = Morg. 264/19:22 I wiped my face; with encl. **kaprilẖ ainẖ** Gs 23:16 I wiped his eyes. Inf. **lmikapar ainẖ mn dimihta** DC 51. 126 to wipe away tears from his eyes.

Ethpe. Pf. **ʿtikpir** Gy 98:7 (var. **-ar** C, **ʿtikpat** D) were blotted out MG 15:27 f. (Nöld. *wurden gebunden*, Lidzb. *gefesselt*, cf. var. D), **ʿtikpir kulhun daiuia** DC 37 all the demons were blotted out. Impf. **nitikpar** Jb 99:1 will be blotted out. Impt. **ʿtikpar** Jb 165:7, CP 184:5 be blotted out MG 229:9. Pt. **mikpar minẖ** Gy 15:20, ATŠ II no. 301 will be wiped away from him MG 230:16.

ETHPA. Impt. ʿtkapar Gy 353:27, ʿkapar Gs 53:21 be blotted out (MG 229:12).

DER.: **kapura, kapruta, kupur** (var. **-ar**, emph. **-ra**).

KPT (כְּפַת, ܟܦܬ, Ar. كفت to gather, Akk. *kupputu* to come together) to tie, bind, fetter.

PE. Pf. with suff. **kapth̠** (read **kapith̠**?) **bkiputa** s. **kiputa**.

PARPEL. s. **KRPT**.

DER.: **kapta 2, kiputa**.

KṢA for **AKṢ**? (q.v.). **uʿnšia d̠-lagit kṣibh̠** CS 26 (AM) (not in DC 31) and the women he takes afflict him (?). Doubtf., cf. AM 18 n. 5.

kṣurta (rt. **KṢR** I) diminution, decrease, loss, disease, illness, affliction. **kṣurta umahra** Gy 388:8 disease and sickness; **abuia kṣurta maška minh̠** AM 11:10 his father will incur affliction (?) through him; **kṣurta hu** AM 254:7 it betokens sickness; **kṣurta zma** AM 7:6 anaemia; **kṣurta bit hiuta tihuilh̠** AM she will have a malady in her womb; **ʿu bdaula kṣurta huia ʿu bnuna kbar** AM 254:11 if in Aquarius there will be decrease, if in Pisces, increase.

kṣir(a) 1 (pass. pt. of **KṢR** I) sick, ill, afflicted. MG 39:11, 116:12. Pl. **-ia. šimuk kṣiria uʿtapun** Gy 275:5 the sick heard thee and were cured; **mn kṣira larsa silqit** Gs 103:15 I went to bed with the sick man.

kṣira 2 (pass. pt. of **KṢR** II) purged, cleansed. **šalman kd̠ kṣira** RD C 4 f. = DAb par. they (: the souls) are made perfect when purged.

KṢM (by dissimil. from ܩܨܡ, Jew.-Aram., Chr.-Pal., H. קסם, Ar. قسم, Eth. ቀሰመ) to tell fortunes, soothsay, bewitch. Also inverted **KMṢ II** (s.v.).

PE. Pf. with suff. **lakišman** DC 22. 485 a better var. of **lakimṣan** Gy 103:10 they did not bewitch me (or foretell my fate).

DER.: **kaṣuma**.

KṢR I (by dissimil. from Gen. Sem. קצר, ܩܨܪ to cut down, shorten; cf. der. קְצִירָא, ܡܩܨܪܐ sick) to cut down (with disease or illness), be or make sickly, ill.

PE. Impf. **bianquta nikṣar** AM in his childhood he will be ill, **nikiṣrun** AM 221:16 f. they will be deprived. Pass. pt. **kṣir(a) 1** s.v.

AF. Pt. **makṣira umkamṣa** Oxf. roll g 781, Or. 329:8 sickly and shrunken; with encl. **mahialh̠ umakṣiralh̠** JRAS she strikes him and makes him ill.

ETHPE. Pt. **umikṣar . . . nitasia** AM 13: who becomes sick will be cured; fem. **kd̠ baṭnabh̠ ʿmh̠ mikiṣra** AM 51:11 f. when his mother is pregnant of him she is ill; pl. **mikṣiria** AM 283:37 they will be sickly.

DER.: **kṣurana, kṣurta, kṣir(a) 1**.

KṢR II (ܩܨܪ, قصر 'to clean' among other meanings) to purge, cleanse.

PE. Pass. pt. **kṣira 2** s.v.

DER.: **kaṣara**.

KRA I (כרא, ܟܪܐ & ܟܪܒ, Akk. *kūru* grief). to grieve, pain, harass, be sad, distressed; to trouble, make turbid. The fem. is used as an impers. verb (often with **AKṢ**).

PE. Pf. with encl. **kratalhun** Gy 106:9 it grieved them MG 257:14. Impf. with encl. **latikrilak** Gy 114:15, Gs 11:11, 43:4, Jb 55:11 f., ATŠ I no. 134, II no. 43 do not grieve, do not worry, be not troubled; **tikrinun lhanath̠ ruhia bišata** Or. 326:1 those evil spirits shall be troubled. Pt. with encl. **kma karialia ʿl tarmidia** Jb, DC 36 = ATŠ I no. 32 how it grieves me about priests MG 365:15; **lakarialh̠** Gy 114:22 they do not worry about it (?); **akṣat ukarialia** Jb I am harassed and troubled MG 365:18 f.; **karialkun ʿl . . .** Gy 19:11 ye grieve about . . . MG 365:17. Inf. with suff. **lmingirinun ulmikrinun** DC 44. 1904, var. **ulmikra-** Morg. 269/29:14 to restrain them and to distress them (doubtf.).

DER.: **kariuta, kruta, kiria**.

KRA II (כְּרָא, ܟܪܐ, H. כרה I, Ar. كرا, Eth. ከረየ to dig) to dig (out), excavate; to heap, pile up.

PE. Pf. **mahunia taumia d-krat ruha** ATŠ II no. 163 the twin pits which R. dug; with encl. **man kralh̠ kiph̠ trin** Jb 229:7 who dug for it its two banks? Impf. (with suff. & encl.) **daiuia d-nikiriuih̠ ʿl prat unʿkrulh̠ kipia trin** DAb devils that dig out (a bed) for the Light Euphrates and dig (or heap up?) its two banks. Act. pt. **sipa karia** DC 43 J 168 the sword pierces. Pass. pt. pl. **mia d̠-iama krʿiia** (var. **kriiia** Sh. 'Abd.'s copy) **btrin ṭuria** Gy 382:6 the waters of the sea were heaped up into two hills (MG 165:6 f.).

DER.: **karat(a)** (var. **karitia**), cf. **ʿkara, ʿkaruta** (var. **-iuta**) & **ʿkarta 1**?

kraba 1 (כְּרָבָא) ploughed or tilled field. **aulh̠ lkraba** AM 121:5 take him into a ploughed field.

kraba 2 (cf. غُراب?) crow: **kd̠ iauna mn kaua ukd̠ kraba mn ziqla** DC 40. 521 f. like a dove from the dovecote and like the crow (?) from the date-palm.

kraia (כְּרָעָא, ܟܪܥܐ, H. du. כְּרָעַיִם, Ar. كُراع, Akk. *kurītu* LS, Ges.) foot, leg, paw. Pl. **kraiia** MG 115:6. Fem. MG 157:18. **kraiai pšiṭlia lbastirqa rba** DC 26. 544 f. = DC 40. 558 par. I stretched my limbs on the great (fleecy) couch; **muma bkraiia ʿu bdra** AM 20:17 a blemish on his legs or his arm; **atutia kraih̠ niplun** AM 62:8 they will fall beneath her foot; **riš d̠-kraiia** AM 7:4 the toes (BZ 9 n. 2); **quba d̠-kraiia** AM 89:6 the curve of the legs (: the knee?); **kraiia d̠-rakšia** Jb 131:9 the feet of horses.

krak̠ nṣab Gy 330:14 a place-name MSchr. 93 n. 3, Ginzā 339 n. 1 (cf. also Gy 193:6 and Lidzb.'s note Ginzā 193 n. 5).

kras st. abs. & cstr. of **karsa** (q.v.).

krasa AM 255:7 for **kurasa**.

krasṭianaiia HG Christians.

krapsa (v.s. **karapsa**) celery, parsley, petrosilium. **bazra d̠-krapsa** AM parsley-seed.

krasṭiania s. **karasṭiania**.

KRB (כְּרַב, ܟܪܰܒ, Ar. كرب from Aram. Fränkel 127, Akk. *kirubû* Zimmern: *Akk. Fw.* 40, LS) to plough.

Pe. Impf. **kma ʿkrab** Jb 203:4 how long shall I plough?

Ethpe. Pt. **hai mikriba arqa** Jb 232:10 how can the earth be ploughed?

Der.: **kraba.**

KRH (כְּרַה, ܟܪܰܗ, Ar. كَرِهَ, Eth. ከረሀ LS) to be sick, ill.

Af. **akrahil** (*sic*) **atmar** AM 282:17 and 18 the fruit will be diseased, poor (?). Pt. pl. **makruhin** AM 282:16, varr. **mikrhin, makhirun** (cf. BZ 189 n. 4).

Der.: **karahia** (pl.), **krihia** (pl.).

krun a demon, lord of the underworld MSchr 149 n. 4, HpGn 245, 248. Var. **akrun.** Siouffi 53, 161. **krun ṭura rba d̠-bisra** Gy 126:8, 10, 127:8 f., 142:23, 143:4, 6; **šumh̠ d̠-krun** RD 1.

krustmia (var. **krusṭmia**) Christians? **krusṭmia udumaiia uiahuṭaiia** HG 134.

krupsa (< כְּרוּסְפְּדָא?) fringe?, or seed? (cf. **bazra d̠-krapsa** s. **krapsa**). **akuat krupsa d̠-tumarta d̠-barqa napil** DC 23. 54 f.

kruta (rt. **KRT**? **KRA I**?) (כְּרֵת) cutting off, mutilation (?). **ʿguzar ukruta** DC 42.

krihia (pl. of ܟܪܺܝܗܳܐ) the sick. **šadar lkul man krihia ušauia asuta** Or. 326:7 he sent to all the sick and made a cure.

krikta (cf. כְּרִיכְתָּא scurf) swirling, surging (water), whirlpool; steam, vapour MG 117:21. **ʿtkarak bihda krikta** Gy 163:21 it whirled in a whirlpool; **krikta d̠-zma** Gy 391:1 the fumes of blood; **krikta d̠-mia** Jb 40:9, 44:1, 5 the whirlpool; **mia krikta ʿtikrik** Jb 157:1 the whirlpool whirled.

krisṭiania s. **karasṭiania.**

KRK Ethpe. & Ethpa. to be crowned: **taga . . . d̠-malkia bgauh̠ ʿtkarak** the crown . . . with which kings are crowned.

KRK (כְּרַךְ, ܟܪܰܟ) to go round, surround, revolve, roll up, turn away, roll away, fold up, encompass, enfold, embrace, furl, enclose; af. to wrap; ethpa. to be embraced, encircled, MR 62 n. 2.

Pe. Pf. **haila d̠-hšuka krak** DC 34. 1098 the army of darkness turned back; **lpumh̠ d̠-ʿur krak** Jb 269:9 he twisted away ʿUr's maw; **krak nṣab** a pr. n. (s.v.), **kirkat** Gs 22:24 she turned around. Impt. **kruk udhia** Q 15:20, 54:9, Oxf. 46:bottom, ATŠ II no. 144 turn back and repulse; with suff. **kurkh̠ ldrabša** CP 365:13 = Oxf. 109 a, 110 a, ML 274:3 furl the banner. Act. pt. **karkum mlaka d-karik sahria** DC 47 the Angel K. that circumvents devils; fem. pl. **bauata . . . d̠-mn hiia karkan** ATŠ II no. 417 prayers . . . that wreathe up from the living (?). Inf. **mikrak** DC 26. 605, **mikrik** DC 40. 539.

Af. Pf. **akrik lpumh̠** ML 55:11 he wound (the *pandama*) round his mouth; **akrik bhdadia** DC 41. 261 he folded (them) together; **akrikiun pandama lpumaihun** DC 27. 243 they wound the *p.* over their mouths. Impf. **nakrikin pandama lpumaihun** DC 42. 412 they fold the *p.* about their mouths. Impt. **akruk pandama lpumak** CP 44:22, **akrik lpumak** DC 41. 213 fold (it) over thy mouth. Part. pres. **kd makrikit pandama** DC 34. 286 when thou wrappest the *p.*; **umakrikitun lpumaikun** ATŠ II no. 142 and ye fold (it) over your mouths.

Ethpe. Pf. **ʿtikrik** DC 22. 157 a var. of **ʿtkarak** Gy 163:21; **ʿtikrik ziua d̠-anania** DC 28 the radiance of the clouds was turned away; **asbar uʿkrik** DC 44. 373 believed and was converted (?). Impf. **nitikrik hšuka minh̠** Morg. 216/19:antep. f. = CP 46:3 = ML 59:8 darkness shall be turned back from him. Pt. **mi(t)krik** revolving MG 132:9.

Ethpa. Pf. **ʿtkarak mia** Gy 165:14 the water swirled; **ʿtkarak bihda krikta** Gy 163:21 (s. **krikta**); with encl. **ʿtkarakbh̠** Gy 97:20 f., 24, 98:2 they surrounded him, ATŠ II no. 124 it enveloped it; **ʿtkarkubh̠** Oxf. III 95 a they surrounded him MG 225:4. Impf. **nitkarak** Jb 142:11 he will be enclosed; **titkarak baiar** CP 456:12 thou shalt go to and fro in the Ether; **nitkarkun** AM 219:16 they will surround. Impt. **ʿkarak d̠-napšak** DC 37. 490 f. turn thyself about, special pl. form **ʿtkarakiun briha** DC 50. 46 stand round the incense-stand; **ʿkarakiun bgauh̠ unušquih̠** DC 50. 43 embrace it and kiss it. Pt. **mitkarak** Gy 137:15, 147:8, 156:19, Oxf. roll f 1165, 1172 embraceth, surroundeth; **bgauai mitkarka** Gy 154:16 she embraced (hist. pres.) me; **mitkarka banana** ATŠ II no. 111 she is encircled by a cloud; pl. **mitkarkia** Gy 65:4, 9 ff., 66:3, 96:14, 203:11, 204:2, Q 11:19, 27, ATŠ II no. 121, 144, **halin nišmata . . . bdilak mitkarkan** Jb 258:3 f. these souls attach themselves to thee; with encl. **mitkarkibh̠** Gy 5:23, 115:17, 117:11, Q 5:28, 32:14, RD B 132 they embrace him, it etc.; **mitkarkabh̠** DC 27. 297 she (: the soul) embraceth him; **mitkarkibia** Gs 113:13 they (: the Life?) embrace me; **lamitkarakbia** DC 44. 1303 f. = Morg. 264/19:25 they do not encompass me; **lamitkaraklia** Gs 113:18 shall I not return?; **hadin umitkarkibun** ATŠ II no. 120 they rejoice and embrace them. Part. pres. **d̠-aṭina bgauak mitkarakna** DC 34 that I may come to embrace thee; **mitkarkit** Gy 136:9, 137:16, Gs 132:4 thou embracest.

Der.: **karka 3, kirka, krikta.**

KRKL (**KRK** with the encl. **l** treated as a rad.) to encompass, bind Jb ii 149 n. 1. Pf. **karkil šdinun** Jb 147:11 he bound and cast them; with suff. **širiun ulakarkilun** Lond. roll. B 279 = DC 12. 141 par. they loosed and did not bind me (would be the same without the suff.).

KRKS (by dissimil. of the reduplicated ܟܣܟܣ = **KSS I**) to oppress, repress; to rattle, wag, move to and fro (?). Fundamental stem: Pf. with suff. **karkistinun lgirmh̠** Gy 167:3 I rattled his bones MG 283:4. Reflexive stem: Pf. **hailaiun ʿkarkas** DC 35 their force was repressed. Impf. **nitkarkas hailh̠** Gy 160:7 his strength will be repressed MG 86:1. Pt. **mitkarkas** Jb 24:11 moves to and fro (?) MG

86:2, 132:25, 230:24, **lnhura mitkarkisa** ATŠ II no. 169, var. **mitkarkisia** DC 6 ibid. they are deprived of (?) the light.

KRKŠ (secondary form of **QRQŠ**, cf. mod. Syr. ܩܪܩܫ = קשקש to rattle MG 86 no. 1) to clatter, rattle, strike, knock MG 39:13, 85:ult. Act. pt. **mkarkiš aqnia ldibnaihun** Gs 10:23 will drive (?) the sheep to their fold; fem. with encl. **mkarkišalun** Gy 187:ult. she rattleth for them.

Der.: **karkušta** (var. **-ašta**).

KRPT Parpel of **KPT**:

Refl. Inf. abs. **mitkarp(u)tia 'tkarputia** Gy 203:18, 204:7 to be bound and to be fettered MG 85:9, 144:21, 234:8, 398:15.

KRṢ (ܪܡܙ 2 LS) to give a sign, signal, inform (against), indicate (by a sign), wink MG 39:11.

Pe. Pf. **lakirṣit ularimzit** Gs 60:5 I gave no sign as informer, I did not give the wink MG 39 n. 6.

Der.: **karaṣa, kirṣa.**

KRŠ (Ar. خرج) to go forth, issue. Only in late Mandaic. Forms are Ar.: Impf. **malka d-rumaiia iakruš lšam** AM 258:13 f. Impt. **'trahaq uakruš** AM 126:ult. depart and go out. Causative pt. **malka mkariš brath̠** AM 272:30 the king will expel his daughter.

kšada (Akk. *kišādu* Ginzā 347 n. 1) throat. Var. **kšara 1. ukšada mn ṣaurh̠ psaq** Gy 336:2 and he severed his throat from his neck.

kšalta (rt. **KŠL**) Gs 64:17 stumbling MG 115:ult. f.

kšar 'He-succeeded' as name of a genie, v.s. **KŠR** pe. pf.

kšara 1 DC 22. 332 & Sh. 'Abd.'s copy's var. of **kšada.**

kšara 2 s. **kšura.**

kšaš, kšaša 1 name of a river between this world and the other which the dead are obliged to cross MSt 23 & n. 7. **nahra kšaš** Jb 149:5, 185:8 ff., **nahra kšaša** Jb 206:2.

kšaša 2 (cf. s. **KŠŠ**) investigation, exploration, fathoming, sounding MG 41:5, 115:20. **l'umqak kšaša lith̠** Gy 4:22 thy depth cannot be fathomed; **kšaša umšaša** Gy 71:14, 188:3, CP 179:8, Oxf. 47 a = ML 219:4 f., AM 206:14 etc. (*very often*) fathoming and sounding (negative: 'fathomless and measureless'); **mruma ḏ-kšaša litbh̠** Gy 293:16 inexplorable height.

kšura (etym. doubtf.) (ܩܘܫܪܐ, כשורא) acc. to context: building, temple, beams, rafters? Var. **kšara 2.** Pl. **-ia. 'stirata ḏ-šria bkšuria ḏ-hu hikla ubiniana** DC 44. 443 the astartes that dwell in the rafters (?) which is a temple or building; **briš ḏ-kšarun** DC 44. 454 at the top of their temple(s?).

kšuta a var. of **kišuta.**

KŠṬ (by dissimil. of קשט, Ar. قسط, as in Jew.-Aram. אכשט and mod. Syr. ܟܫܛ, ܟܫܝܛܐ MG 39 n. 4) to be true, sincere MG 39:9 f.

Pe. Pass. pt. **kšit(a)** s.v.

Af. Act. pt. **makšiṭ kušṭania** Gy 62:22 maketh people true.

Der.: **kušṭa, kušṭana, kšiṭ(a).**

kšiṭ(a) (pass. pt. pe. **KŠṬ**) true, sincere MG 39:9, 116:11. Pl. **-ia. kšiṭ umhaiman** Gy 45:7, pl. **kšiṭia umhaimnia** Gy 213:11, 252:24, 253:3, CP 118:5, ML 144:6; **gbar kšiṭ** Q 66:2 = ML 157:8 = CP 129:16; **šalmania kšiṭia** DC 35; **minilta kšiṭa** Gs 91:12 (for **-ṭta**? cf. MG 318:9 f.), pl. **malalia kšiṭia** Gs 76:7; **kšiṭa ḏ-makšiṭ kušṭania** Gy 62:22 the True One who maketh people true.

kšil(a) pass. pt. of **KŠL** (q.v.).

kšira (pass. pt. of **KŠR**) diligent, assiduous, industrious, efficient, successful, capable, well-equipped. Fem. **-ta.** Pl. masc. **-ia. kšira huit umkašra** Jb 38:5 I was diligent and efficient; **šitlia kširia** Gy 318:23; **šitlia ḏ-kširia** Jb 239:2 worthy plants; **tqina ukšira** Jb 259:10 reliable and efficient; **'utra kšira** Jb 260:11 an efficient uthra; **'tiqria kšira ḏ-'utria ahh̠** CP 443:6 he is called 'capable' by his brother-uthras; **kširun ḏ-'utria** Gy 352:13 the most capable amongst the uthras; **abdia kširia** Gy 14:17, ATŠ II no. 187 diligent servants; **nipqit mn atutia kširia** I came forth from amongst worthy beings; **pugdama kširta** DC 40. 826 efficacious word (of command); **kširia gauaiia . . . kširia mṣaiia . . . kširia baraiia** DC 43 A 36 (good spirits).

KŠL (Jew.-Aram., H. & mod. H. כשל, Syr. pass. pt. pe., af. & ethpe. 'to offend', 'be offended') to stumble, fall away, strike to the ground, err, offend; to meet with an obstacle, repulse, be annoyed with.

Pe. Impf. **lanikšil libaihun** Gy 37:22 their heart will not stumble. Pass. pt. **kšil(a)** stumbler; pl. **kšilia** Gy 121:24, 178:8, 179:14, 186:4 f., 11 &c. stumblers.

Af. Pf. with suff. **kšiltun** (for **akš-**) **mn kursiai mn kursiai akšiltun** Gy 349:3 f. ye dethroned me (: made me fall from my throne) MG 272:12. Impf. with suff. **nakšlh̠** Gs 78:1 = Q 67:14 we make him stumble MG 275:antep. Pt. pl. **makšilia** Gy 121:4, 179:18 they make stumble. Part. pres. **makšilitun** ye make stumble MG 233:15; with encl. **makšilatlia** Jb 81:1 f. thou makest me stumble; pass. **makšalna** Gs 114:8 I had to stumble (: was brought to fall) MG 231:8. Nom. ag. **makšilana** s.v. Nom. act. **(a)kšalta** s.v.

Ethpe. Impf. **titkišlun** Gy 178:7 ye (shall) stumble. MG 228:1. Pt. **mikšil** he stumbles MG 214:6. Part. pres. **mikšilna** Gs 64:17 I do not stumble MG 231:11.

Ettaf. Pf. **'takšal** Gy 178:8, 179:14 f., 186:4, 5, 11, DC 41. 179 he, they stumbled MG 4:2. Impf. **titakšal** Jb 205:1 thou stumblest MG 227:5; **latitkašlun** Gy 179:14 do not stumble. Pt. **'uṣraihun mistmik ulamitakšal** ATŠ I no. 114 their mind(s) may be upheld and not stumble, **ḏ-lamitakšal 'uṣraihun** ATŠ I no. 101; pl. **mitakšilia** those who stumble MG 149:13.

Der.: **(a)kšalta, kšila, makšilana.**

KŠP (Akk. *kuššupu*, H כשף Ges., Del.) to practise sorcery, bewitch.

Af. (?): Pt. **maikašipan umkiban bhazin pagra** AO ix 96:1 they (fem.) bewitch and pain this body (Gordon).

KŠR (Aram., H. & mod. H. כשר, Syr. ܟܫܪ, Akk. *kušīru* success) be or do well or right, succeed, achieve, accomplish, be pleasing or satisfactory, give satisfaction, attain.

Pe. Pf. **abad ukšar** Gy 92:3, 250:11 he worked and succeeded; Gy 152:15 used as a pr. n., cf. also **abad ukšar šumh̲** Lond. roll B 239 and **(akšar uakšar) uabad ukšar iauar ziua** Gy 151:9; **abad ukšar ušar . . . asiqlh̲ šumh̲** Gy 135:3 they gave him the name . . . 'he worked, succeeded and was constant'; **kšar bškinath̲** Q 59:18 he prospered in his (celestial) dwelling; **abadnin ḏ-lakšar** DC 34 we did that which was unsatisfactory; with suff.: **bʿuhra ḏ-adam kišrh̲** Gs 81:10, CP 82:6 = ML 101:8 on the road that A. accomplished. Impf. **nikšar** Gy 92:14 he attaineth MG 221:5; **nibad unikšar** Gy 297:3 he worketh and succeedeth; **kul ḏ-tibad tikšar** Gy 92:3 f. whatever thou dost thou shalt succeed. Act. pt. **mindam ḏ-snia lakašar abad** Jb 25:4 he did something abominable (and) displeasing; fem. **saina ulakašra** Jb 101:10, 12; pl. **radpia ulakašria** CP 171:16 they persecute and do not right; **lišania ḏ-lakašria** Gs 55:24 tongues that are good for naught; fem. pl. **mindam mn ʿbidata lakašran** ATŠ II no. 12 none of the ritual acts will attain its purpose (: succeed; agreeing with **ʿbidata**). Pass. pt. **kšir(a)** s.v.

Af. Pf. **akšar** (only in pr. names of genii, v.s. pe. pf.).

Ethpe. Pf. **uʿl hiia laʿtkišrat** Gy 70:21 f. and it did not please the Life (fem. as impers. verb) MG 366:6 f.; **ʿl ruha ʿtkišrat** DC 27. 138 it seemed right to the spirit. Pt. **ulnhura lamikšar** ATŠ II no. 20 (var. **lamitakšar** DC 6 ibid. ettaf.) and will not attain to the light.

Ethpa. (?): Pf. **ʿbdat uʿkaširat** [*sic*] ATŠ II no. 438 she worked and laboured zealously.

Ettaf. Impf. **lnhura lanitakšar** ATŠ shall not attain to the light. Pt. **mitakšar latar nhur** Gy 119:17 he will attain to the place of light (cf. also ATŠ II no. 20 s. ethpe. pt.), **lamitakšar** Gy 13:ult., 95:12, 310:11 is unworthy, doth not succeed.

Der.: **kašar** (fem. **-ra**), **kašira**, **kišra** 1, 2, **kšira**, **(a)kšar**, **kišrat**.

KŠŠ (Aram. & H. גשש, Syr. ܓܫ, Ar. جسّ, Sab. [illegible], Eth. ገሠሠ) to touch, fathom, explore, sound.

Der.: **kšaša**.

ktaba (often) = **kdaba** 1. Pl. **ktabia**. **ktaba ḏ-zipa** Gy 24:8 book of the lie, fraudulent book.

KTB (more original but rarer form of **KDB II** q.v.) to write.

Pe. Pf. **ktab** (often) he wrote, with suff. **ktabtih̲** AM 256:39 I wrote it; **kitbu** they wrote it (fem.) MG 279:10. Impf. with suff. **nikitbunak bṭasa d-anka** DC 37. 87 f. they will write thee in a bowl of tin. Pass. pt. **hazin minda ktib lmihuia** Gy 392:20 this thing is prescribed to happen MG 386; **ktiba** Gs 109:2 written; with encl, **ktiblh̲** Gy 43:10, **ktiblkun** Gy 43:2 is prescribed for him, for you (by the Fates Ginzā 41 n. 2). Inf. **miktab** (often) writing.

ktiar AM 163 s. **aktiar**.

KTP (den. from **kadpa**) to carry off.

Ethpe. Pt. **milgiṭ umiktip** AM 260:14 he will be seized and carried off.

Der.: **kadpa**.

KTR I (כְּתַר to wait upon, Syr. ܟܬܪ to remain, H. כָּתַר to surround, Ar. der. كُتْر camel's hump, Akk. *kitru* alliance) to remain behind, wait for; to detain, retain, delay, tarry.

Pa. Pf. with suff. **lakatruk bišia** CP 437:15 evil ones have not deterred thee. Impf. with suff. **nikatrh̲** Jb 58:15, 60:11, 61:4, Gy 18:2, 104:24, 361:23, 369:14, Gs 42:24, 70:14 f. we, he shall detain him (MG 275:bottom); **šuba bʿuhra lanikatrunh̲** CP 79:10 f. = Q 37:8 the Seven will not detain her on her way. Inf. with suff. **katurh̲** Gy 228:19 to make him wait MG 292:paen.; **katurak** Gs 43:6 to deter thee.

Ethpa. Pf. **uʿtkatar bdaura hšuka** CP 189:3 (they) were detained in the abode of darkness; **latkatar . . . laʿtkatar** Gy 307:14 f. they were detained. Impf. **lanitkatrun** Gy 319:9 f., ML 97:9 they shall not be detained. Pt. **mitkatar** Gy 133:1 he shall be detained, pl. **mitkatria** Jb 179:4, 222:6, 224:3 they are detained. Part. pres. **lamitkatarna** Jb 61:8 I will not be detained.

KTR II (cf. ܟܘܛܪܐ, Ar. خُثْر dregs, den.) to sully (?).

Pa. Act. pt. with encl. **mkatrilh̲ lilbušaiun** RD B 47, 71 = DAb par. they sully (?) their garments.

KTŠ original form of **KDŠ**. Occurring only in the der. **taktuša** s.v.

kḏ (כְּדִי, Talm. כִּי, Syr. ܟܕ) when, as, like, just like MG 12:27, 93:5 ff. (& n. 3), 195 n. 2. **kḏ zan ḏ-** (cf. Syr. ܐܝܟ ܙܢ ܕ & ܐܝܟܢܐ ܕ), **kḏ ḏ-** as, like MG 462:bottom; **kḏ qaiim**, **kḏ niqum** Gy 384 ff. (*often*) when he stands up; **kḏ arqin minh̲ šurbata** Gy 280:11 when the generations flee from him; **kḏ abrinun** Gy 381:21 f. when he brought them across; **kḏ haizin amrilun** Gy 76:10 when I spake thus unto them; **kḏ ana huit mn rbia** Gy 76:18 when I belonged to the Great (Life); in an elliptic clause: **sakla kḏ iatir** Gy 217:1, 4, 8 when the fool is completely (foolish); **hakima kḏ mšalam** Gy 217:6 when a wise (man) is perfect; with a further **ḏ-**: **kḏ ḏ-ba** Gy 85:9 as soon as he sought; **kḏ ḏ-ṭmaš ʿdh̲** Gy 94:ult. when he dipped his hand; **kḏ ḏ-amar** Gy 84:20, 22 when he said; **lahua kḏ ḏ-lahua** (*often*) it was not when he did not exist; **kḏ ḏ-hzit** Gy 75:5 A (BCD without **ḏ**) 153:11 as I saw; **kḏ ḏ-huat** Gy 332:12 as it was; **kḏ ḏ-abad abdilh̲ kḏ ḏ-akal aklilh̲** Gy 187:8 as he did, will they do to him, as they ate, will they eat them; 'as' in elliptic clauses: **ṭuria raqdia kḏ ailia** Gy 174:11 the hills dance like deer;

nitraurab kḏ rurbia Gy 303:6 he will be(come) great as the Great (Life); **aliptinun kḏ rba lašualia** Gy 108:22 I taught them as a master (teacheth) the pupil; **ʿštalaṭbẖ . . . kḏ mn qudam ḏ-ʿtingid rqiha** Gy 99:18 they obtained power over him as (they had) before the firmament was extended; **daiinlun . . . kul ʿniš kḏ ʿubadia ʿdẖ** Gy 14:13 he is judging . . . everyone as (according to) the works of his hands, cf. Gy 253:ult., 254:ult. &c.; with **DMA** 'to resemble'; **damia kḏ haita** Gs 14:2 she resembleth an animal; **damia šutẖ kḏ ʿutria** Gs 52:1 his speech resembleth that of uthras; **kḏ zan alma hazin** Gy 394:7 in the way of this world; **kḏ zan rbutan** Gy 179:24 according to their pride; **kḏ zan ḏ-abdia** Gy 231:15 as they do; **kḏ zan ḏ-lahun** Gy 64:12 as if they had not existed MG 463 ff.; **mn kḏ** Gy 271:11 (in a corrupt place); **ham kḏ** Q 46:23 at the same time as (cf. P. همچون) MG 465:middle.

Gl. 130:5 **kṯ** فيما *dum* در آن.

kḏa Zotb. 230 b:17 an exceptional form of **kḏ** (cf. **kdi** s.v.).

L

l The 12th letter of the alphabet. Pronunciation: bilateral, sometimes nasalized. Phonetic changes: l for n and vice versa MG § 53 p. 54; l for r and vice versa MG § 54 pp. 54 f.; assimilation of l ibid. p. 55.

l- 1 (Gen. Sem.) prep. to, for, at, upon. Used proclitically before nouns, enclitically (-l-) after verbs to introduce a pronoun suffix; the latter form is used also after the encl. conj. **u-**, the interrog. particle **mi-** etc. As procl. prep. it is sometimes confused with **ʿl** (עַל) which is never used proclitically, MG 193: middle, AIT 31, 35. Occasional procl. forms: **li- 1, la- 2** MG 10:19, **al- 1** MG 193:middle. In compound prepositions and adverbial expressions: **mn lalam** Gy 274:14 forever, **milia** (*often*) whence (< מִן לְאַי), **(b)ligal** (*often*) quickly, swiftly, **(mn) lhil** (s.v.) MG 196:middle; **alma l-** until MG 196:12; **lʿl, lʿil, ʿl ʿil,** even **lʿiil** Gy 269:1, 295:14, Q 292:29 above, **lʿil mn** Gy 280:25 above from, **ltit** (*often*) down, **mn lbar** Gy 258:21 outside, **lbar mn** (*often*) except, **lilai** Gy 202:14 upwards, **lka** hither, **lhaka, ha lka** (s. **ha** and **haka 1**), **ltam** thither MG 203 f.; **lia 1** (= לִי) to me, **lia 2**, varr. **ʿlia, alia** (= לְאַי) where?, whither? (**lʿ** a var. of both: for 1 frequent, for 2 Gs 48:4), **lilia** Gy 362:15, Gs 49:11 for **lia 2** MG 205. Proclitically with nouns: **lʿqara** to the glory, **lʿlana** to the tree MG 4:18, **lptahil** to P. MG 10:17, **librẖ** Gy 374:10 to his son MG 10:ult. f., **lihdisar** Gy 380:20 to the eleven MG 11:2. Enclitically: **nihuilia** I (shall, or may) have (: *erit mihi*, or *sit mihi*), **amarulia** say to me (or they said to me), **himlẖ** he was hot MG 12:paen.f., **uailẖ lkul man ḏ-** Gy 18:19 woe to every one that, **haslẖ** s. **has** etc. Enclitically and with the repeating of the prep. before the noun: **ʿtqrilẖ qala lnu** Gy 380:9 a voice cried to Noah, **litlun saka ldauraihun** Gy 278:21 their dwellings have no end MG 330:ult. ff.; **šlama lnbihia latitnulhun** Gy 223:14 do not greet the prophets; **ṣauta ladam nihuilẖ** Gy 13:1, 33:10 there shall be companionship for A. (&c.) MG 331:17 ff.

l- 2 (Aram. *nota accusativi*) particle introducing direct object when the noun is determinate; procl., other procl. forms as s. **l- 1**. Rarely encl. (**-l- 2**). **anihẖ llibai** Gy 323:11 he quietened my heart; **hiziu ldmutẖ** Gy 282:8 they saw his form; **tabartinun lmaṭaratun** Gs 92:10 I broke their prisons; **lʿurba laṯẖ uliauna** (var. **uʿl iauna**) **birkẖ** Gy 381:7 he cursed the raven and blessed the dove; **lbahtinun lkulhun almia** Gy 173:4 to put all the worlds to shame; **lak dilak mn kisia qrulak ldilak qruk mn kisia** Gy 306:9 they called thee from the hidden place; **lkun dilkun malbišnalkun** Gy 178:14 I clothe you; **lʿ lbraiun alak šadrun** Gy 294:16 me, their son, sent they to thee; **ulman naṭria** Gy 181:18 and whom do they keep in?; **lhad mimaskinilẖ ulhad miatrilẖ** Gy 264:1 they make one poor and another rich; **mšaiilun lhda hda** Gy 98:9 he shall ask them one by one (&c.) MG 390 ff.

-l- 3 after the procl. **u-** to introduce a pers. suff. used as an independent pers. pron.: **uana ulẖ ʿtib** Gy 155:19 and I sit with him; **nibun ana ulik** Gy 325:4 we will seek (or build?) together, I and thou (fem.) MG § 232 p. 332.

l- 3 sporadically for **la- 1**: **lmhara** Gs 111:15 (for **lamhara**) no **mhara** (v.s.v.), **lkariuta** Sh. ʿAbd.'s copy's var. of **lakariuta** Gy 9:12 no affliction (&c.), cf. MG 11 n. 2. **lʿdun** Gs 37:14 (= **laʿdun** ibid. CD) they knew not MG 35 n. 1.

l- 4 a form of **al 2** (corresponding to ال): **laual** AM 266:44, 268:15 = الأوّل the first, **ltania** AM 262:28, 33 = الثانى the second, **lakir** AM 266:45 = الأخير the latter, the second, **lhakim** AM 261:20 الحكيم the wise.

l- 5 a superflucus procl. set sometimes before nouns without adding any further meaning: **haṭibẖ lanašia** AM 273:20 people will injure it; **lianqia ulhiuaniata nitnapšun** AM 275:3 f. children and animals will multiply; **lia aitinun lbabia ḏ-hšuka** Gy 155:15 where are the gates of the darkness?

l- 6 for **li- 2, lʿ-** (wrong analogy of **l- 1** = **li-**) MG 10 n. 4: **lšlum** Gy 369:3 (= **lišlum** ibid. B) cometh to an end. In the af. (or pa.) it becomes **la-** 3 = **lapriš** Gy 249:19 he teacheth, **labṭunan** Gs 130:17 they fetter me MG 216.

la- 1 (Gen. Sem. לא, لا, ܠܐ) procl. neg. particle: no, not. Sporadically **l-** 3, **li-** 3, **lʿ-** 2; regularly contracted with the initial **a** of the following word: **labid** he doth not, **lal** Gs 103:5 he entered not, **laudun** Gy 310:18 they did not inform them MG 35:middle. With procl. **b-**: **bla-** without, **blamata** Gs 96:2 without country, **blašnai** Gs 7:22 not in my years; **ḏ-la-** without: **ḏ-lamabra** Gs 95:24 without ferry; **mn laqadmia** (*often*) without precedent; in compound names: **laṭabia** (s.v.), **lamindam** Gs 44:4 nothing MG 430:bottom f.; **rahmia rurbia ulazuṭia** Gs 6:23 great prayer(s) and not small; **rba mhita ulazuṭa** Q 64:16 a great blow and not small, **rba ulazuṭa** Gs 7:7; **lanihuilkun ruhṣana ʿl . . . ulaʿl . . . ulaʿl . . .** Gy 17:6 have no hope in . . . nor in . . . nor in . . .; **latit bṣubian rbia ulabṣubian ʿutria** Gy 323:13 I came neither according to the will of the Great (Life) nor according to the will of the uthras; **d-lahualḫ aba laba hualḫ** Gs 96:2 who had no father, no father had he (&c.); repeated tautologically: **ladahbaiun ulakaspaiun laqaiimlun ulahauilun bahid ʿda** Gy 17:12 f. neither their gold nor their silver will stand by them and be their helper; **ladahba ulakaspa lahauia zuadia ḏ-ʿuhra** Gs 129:10 neither gold nor silver is a viaticum MG 430 ff.; **iama ḏ-larab ulašaša ulamambarta** Gy 382:4 f. sea without ship and without raft and without ferry; **ʿzil ḏ-labalanak** Gy 143:17 go away that I may not swallow thee.

la- 2 s. **l- 1**.

la- 3 s. **l- 6**.

LAG, LIG, LGA (Aram. & H. לעג) pa. & af. to mock, Syr. ܠܓܓ to stammer, cf. Eth. ለዐለዐ, reduplicated mod. H. & Jew.-Aram. לגלג, Syr. ܠܓܠܓ, Ar. لجلج to stammer, قلق to be disturbed, with met. **ALG**, H. עלג, Ar. علج) to stammer, speak haltingly. MG 107:15, 18.

Gl. 13:13 f. **LGI** [*sic*] اقـلـق *discerpere* مضطرب شد.

Der.: **lagaiia, lagian**?, **ligia** 1, 2.

lagaiia (adj. from **LAG**, cf. H. לַעֲגֵי; formed as أَعْجَمِيّ from أَعْجَمُ MG 141 n. 5) barbarians MG 141:17. **anašia lagaiia** Gy 385:19.

lagambia (**-nbia**) s. **agambia**.

lagian fem. pl. (If from **LGA**, disturbed, sad?; if from Ar. لغى, expressive, mirthful, merry?) of eyes, doubtf. BZ 48 n. 1. **uainḫ lagian** AM 72:5, **uainḫ lagian ušapiran** AM 83:15.

lagiṭṭa a var. of **lig(i)ṭṭa**.

ladan (ܠܕܢܐ, λάδανον Löw 127, Akk. *ladunu* LS) gum ladanum, gum mastic. **bladan ubnapṭa** DC 12. 19, Lond. roll B 403, JRAS 1937 591:antep., var. **blidan** . . . P.A.'s copy.

lahuria (**l- 1** + **ahuria**) behind: **lahuria rba** DC 34. 387 behind the rabbi.

lahma (Jew.-Aram. לַחְמָא, Bab. Talm. נַהֲמָא, Syr. ܠܚܡܐ, H. לֶחֶם bread, food, Ar. لَحْم meat Fränkel 30, Lewy: *Fw.* 78) bread, food, subsistence, living, livelihood; income, allowance. Doublet **lhama** s.v. MG 54:6. **lahma malkia akil** AM 51:1 he will eat the bread of (be entertained by) kings; **lahma rba tikul** AM 100:16 she will have a great income; **lahma umia** (with words for 'giving' etc.) hospitality; **mn gabra rba lahma akil** AM 13:7 he will be maintained by a great man.

lahmuraṭ s. **zardanaiaṭa**.

lahmia in **bit lahmia** Gy 329:22 Bethlehem.

lau (לָאו, ܠܘ from הו + לא) not MG 7:22, 61:paen., 330:2. Used before nouns and to introduce a neg. question. Before nouns: **bzakaiia ḏ-lau bhaiabia udiatiria ḏ-lau bhasiria** Morg. 233/33:ult. f. with the guiltless and not with the guilty, with the rich and not with the deficient; **ʿbidatik lau mindam hinun** Gy 158:16 thy (fem.) works are (worth) nothing (apart from **lamindam** s. **la- 1**). To introduce a neg. question: **lau mimar amarilak** Gy 326:1, AM 201 did I not tell thee?; **lau ana br rbia** Gs 123:6 am I not the son of the Great (Life)?; **lau mn qudam . . . hua nṣiba nišubtak** Gy 73:18 was thy plant not planted before . . .?; **lau amart** Gy 162:4, 230:19, 233:9 didst thou not say?; **lau miditun** Gs 54:12 f. did ye not know?; **lau mʿiatin** Gs 12:3 do they not come? MG 435:middle.

laua, lauh a miscop. of **ziua**? **šamiš blauḫ** DC 51. 56 the sun in its splendour (?).

lauṭa (rt. **LUṬ**) curse, cursing. **ʿsir lauṭa** DC 43 H 53 cursing is bound.

launa (Ar. لَوْن) colour. Pl. **launia**, var. **liuania**. **abrišam ḏ-šuba launia** s. **abrišam** (var. **liuania** DC 46).

laupa (rt. **LUP** = **LPP**) uniting, union, communion, name of a ritual meal eaten for the dead, the communion of living and dead WiW pp. 232–5, CP 258 trs. n. 2, MR 112, ML 13 n. 3, MMII 180. Pl. **laupania**. **laupa ḏ-hiia** (*often*) the communion of life; **laupa ḏ-lap** Jb 268:3 the communion in which they united; **laiiplun blaupa rba** Jb 270:2 he maketh them join the great union; **lap laupa** Q 29:1; **blaupa ḏ-rba mitlap mitlip blaupa ḏ-rba** CP 125:16 f. was joined in the great union; **nilipinun blaupa šania** Gy 1:14 f. he (may) accept them in the sublime union; **kušṭa ulaupa uhaimanuta** Gy 8:6; **laupa ḏ-litlḫ psaqa** Gy 238:10 union without division; **hšuka unhura kušṭa ulaupa binataihun laiit** ATŠ I no. 142 betwixt darkness and light there is no pact or union; **laupa ukušṭa** Gy 20:4; **laupa lnišmata triṣ . . . ḏ-litbḫ psaqa** Gy 262:11 f.; **laupa mn hdadia lanasbia** Gy 285:14, 288:1 they form no union between one another; **laupa mn hdadia nasbia** Gy 285:24; **hualḫ laupa lhazin alma** Gy 341:7 it was united with this world; **laupa traṣ latar nhur** Gy 341:24 he set up a communion for the place of light; **laupa uruaha ḏ-hiia** Q 44:17 (*often*); **laupa ḏ-iauar** Q 51:20; **laupa nihuilkun lbit hiia** Gy 246:16 ye shall be united with the House-of-Life; **mn laupaiun latipisqun**

Gy 246:17 ye shall not be cut off from communion with them; **lupinun blaupa rba** Gy 304:5 accept them in the great communion; **nitlip blaupa iaqra** Gy 320:9 shall be joined in the great communion; **laupa lruhia unišmata** Gy 245:24 communion for the spirits and souls. Pl. **laupania d̲-masiqta** Morg. 183:1 the ritual commemorative meals of the *masiqta*. See also under **LUP.**

laupata Sh. 'Abd.'s copy's var. of **lupata** Gs 80:19.

laṭaba (lit. 'not-good-one') fiend, evil one, devil. Pl. **laṭabia** MG 187:12, 431:2 ('*Unholde*'), var. **laṭibia. laṭaba** DC 26. 54; **d̲-kulhun laṭabia minaihun npaq hun minaihun laṭabia** Gy 123:16 f. from which issued all the devils, all the devils were from them; **laṭabun kulhun** Gy 107:5 all their devils MG 181:23 f.; **šidia ulaṭabia** Gy 389:6 (var. **laṭibia** Sh. 'Abd.'s copy) demons and devils; **mahiqia ulaṭabia** DC 26. 50 frightening and evil; **laṭabia** Par. xxiv 9 b.

laṭuṭiata (rt. **LṬṬ** = **LUṬ**) IM 41 fem. pl. cursers.

laibat an exceptional form of **libat.**

laiṭa (act. pt. pe. of **LUṬ**) curser, cursing. **ragza ulaiṭa** DC 26. 605 raging and cursing.

laiat s. **laiit.**

laiit, with suff. **lait-** (לית, ܠܝܬ, neg. form of **aiit, ait-**) there is not MG 69:22. Before encl. **lit-** s.v. Rarer forms **laiat, laʿit.** Independently: **laiit hatam mindam d̲-** Gy 283:11 there is nothing that; **laiit alaha d̲-** Gy 230:6 there is no god that . . .; **habrai . . . laiit** Gy 207:21 I have no equal; **rab ugabir minai laiit** Gy 185:15 there is none greater and mightier than I MG 401. With suff.: **laitan** Gy 156:15, 312:3 &c. I am not, **laitak** Gy 156:16 thou art not, **laith̲** (often) he is not, MG 295:bottom; **šraran uhailan laith̲** Gy 149:23 our firmness and strength do no more exist; MG 401: bottom; **d̲-laiit d̲-lʿška** Gy 283:20 (= **d̲-lait uliška** DC 22. 279) there is not, is not found . . . .

laka s. **lika.**

lala (P. لالا) tutor, governor. In **ialala ʿaidia** Jb 144:13 O major-domo of fishermen!

lama- occ. var. of **l(i)ma-** (cf. **limalia, limalik**) why, wherefore?

lamindam s. **la- 1.**

lasṭar DC 22. 380 a var. of **lisṭar** Gy 383:17.

laqab (Ar. لقب) tribal or family name. Very frequent in colophons.

laqadmia s. **la- 1.**

laqlaiia name of a people or tribe. (לגלג to speak unintelligibly) **hazin širiana d̲-qazil larqa laqlaiia** DC 7 this is the vein (: sub-river) which goes to the land of the L.

lašauia (comp. with **la- 1**) bad, unequal, unworthy.

Gl. (regularly missp.) 29:2 اشرار *mali* شريران; 31:15 ردى , ارديا *mali* بدها; 44:7 **blašaui** [sic] بالردى *male* شرير; 85:6 ارديا , ردى *malus* شرير; 95:9 شرير(ين) *malus* شرير; 97:5 شرير *nequam*; 153:14 مجرب *tentator* تجربه كرده; 159:4 مرذول *abhominatus* [sic] بى قدر.

lašihia (comp. with **la- 1**) DAb pl. unworthy.

laška see **ŠKA.**

lbab st. abs. & cstr. of **liba. blbab šumia** (var. **ʿš-**) Gy 86:1, 97:16, 19, 118:11, 124:16 in the heart (: innermost) of the heavens, **bilbab ʿšumia** Jb 151:17; **ʿtriṣ lbab ʿl samkh̲** Gy 79:16 my heart was set in its resting-place; **blbab kšiṭ** Gy 322:17 in (each?) true heart; **šrit blbab kšiṭ** Gy 274:14 thou dwellest in (each?) true heart; **bilbab šralia** Gs 26:21, 28:10 ff. it dwelleth in my heart; **bilbab šribh̲ minda** Gs 87:7 (var. **šrabh̲ manda** Sh. 'Abd.'s copy, cf. also Ginzā 523 n. 1) in my heart dwelleth wisdom; **lbab lamihmislia** Gy 262:16 s. **HMS.**

lbahar (Ar. ٱلْبَحْر) v.s. **zabad.**

lbar (**l- 1** + **bar 1**, לְבַר, ܠܒܪ) outside, out of, without, except, excluded, apart from. Also **lbar mn** and **mn lbar. d̲-mn lbar triṣa** CP 109:7, ML 134:9 which is set up outside (i.e. out of this world n. 3); **d̲-nasba bazira . . . lbar mn zauh̲** ATŠ = ATŠ II no. 35 (a woman) that receives seed from a man apart from her husband; **lbar mn binaikun huit** Gs 64:3 I was debarred from your midst.

lbaša (rt. **LBŠ**) putting-on Pl. **-ia. šlaha hadta ulbaša** DC 34. 731 the casting-off the new and its putting-on; **šlahia ulbašia** DC 34. 746 castings-off and puttings-on.

LBB (den. from **lbab, liba**) to hearten, encourage; fig. to instigate.

Pa. Pt. pl. **mlakia mlabia rhamta** DC 45 angels instigating love.

lbuša (rt. **LBŠ**) garment, dress, covering, raiment. St. abs. & cstr. **lbuš.** Pl. **lbušia.** Masc. MG 7:10, 149:paen. With suff.: **lbuš** Gs 115, but more usually **lbušai** my garment MG 175:21, **lbušak** thy garment MG 177:4, **lbuš(i)h̲** his or her garment MG 178:1, **lbušan** our garment MG 178:25. **lbuš ʿl lbuš** Gy 274:4, ML 81:1 garment over garment MG 301:16; **lbuš ʿšata haita** Gy 89:4, 97:5, 8 f., 11, 114:7; **lbušia d̲-ʿšata haita** Gy 195:22 MSt. 94; **lbuš pagria** Q 32:5 physical garment (: the body); **lbuš ʿšata ʿkilta** Gy 118:16; **lbuša d̲-šišlam** RD 10; **lbuša d̲-ptahil** Gy 393:11; **biuma d̲-libših̲ manda d̲-hiia llbuših̲** CP 203:4 ML 233:8 in the day in which M.-d̲-H. put on his garment (cf. n. 2); **lbuša d̲-anania mia** Gy 29:6, 53:3 covering of water-clouds; **lbuša d̲-bisra uzma** Gy 193:7 s. **bisra; blbuša dakia** Gy 114:7; **qiriuia lbušan umalalan** Gy 292:8 he (: the Life) called him 'our garment' and 'our word'; **šuba lbušia** Q 20:5; **šuba lbušia d̲-ziua** Gy 169:10, 313:24, 337:17, 338:10; **d̲-lbuših̲ ʿlh̲ ṣaria** Gy 37:19 who rendeth his clothes for him; **lbuš razia lbišna** DC 26. 559 I put on a vesture of mysteries; **bhad lbuša luat kulhun rba uhak ašualia qaiim** DC 34. 500 the teacher and the novice are looked on by them all as being one and the same person (*idiom*); **lbuša d̲-hiuia** DC 46 a snake-skin; **šla daiua akuat hiuia d̲-šahlalh̲ llbušia** DC 40 he cast off the demon like a serpent that sloughеth its skin; **šahlalh̲ lilbuš pagria** CP 70:10, ML 86:2 she casteth off the physical garment; **lbuša d̲-nhura** opposed to **lbuša d̲-hšuka** Gy 25:9–10.

lbina (pass. pt. pe. of **LBN**) white, gleaming, glistening. **laibat šapirtia ulbina** DC 45 Venus, the lovely and white-gleaming one.

LBK (לְבַךְ, ܠܒܟ, Ar. لبک) to lay hold of, catch, hold fast, capture.

Pa. (?): Impt. with suff. **ulabkinun bzma d̲-zuṭa** AM 125:14 and catch them (?) with the blood of a little one. Pt. **mlabka** DC 45 no. 36 is held back (averted) (DC 46. 142:14 **mlapka**).

LBN (cf. Ges. s. לבן I & II) to be white, glisten.

Der.: **lbina** (cf. also **libna, libta**).

lbnan Gy 265:12 = **libnan.**

lbr scr. def. of **lbar.**

LBŠ (Aram. & H. לבשׁ, Syr. ܠܒܫ, Ar. لَبِسَ, Akk. *labāšu*) to clothe, assume, dress, attire, put on, cover, invest, endue, array; fig. to take possession of, seize, identify oneself with (cf. Idioms).

Pe. Pf. **libšit tutbai** Gy 97:1 I put on my dress; with suff. **libših̲** CP 203:3, ML 233:8, DC 34.819 he put it on; **lbaštak** Gs 97:14 I put thee on MG 274:1; **lbašinun lkulhun razih̲** ATŠ I no. 243 he put on (: took possession of) all her mysteries. Impt. with suff. **lubšh̲ llbušak** Gs 43:12 put on thy garment. Act. pt. **pagra labiš** Gy 57:10 he putteth on the body; with encl. **hizda labišlun** AM shame covers them; fem. **lbuš ʿl lbuš labša** CP 65:6 = ML 80:11 (cf. 81:2) she putteth on garment on garment; pl. masc. **labšia** Gy 24:7, 274:3, 4, RD C 27 they put on. Part. pres. **labšana** I (fem.) put on MG 231:17; with suff. **labišnak** Gs 133:1 I put thee on MG 291:middle. Pass. pt. **lbiš(a)** (often) clothed; pl. **lbuša d̲-hšuka lbišia** Gy 25:10 (are) clothed with a garb of darkness; with encl. pers. pron. **lbišna** DC 26. 559 I am clad; **lbištun** ye are clad MG 233:12. Inf. **ulbušia hadtia milbaš . . . šapir** ŠQ 29:2 and is auspicious . . . for putting on new clothes; **kd̲ baiin tarmidia mišba umilbaš lbušia** ATŠ I no. 172 when priests wish to baptize and to put on their vestments.

Pa. Pt. (act. & pass.) **hamra mlabaš braz marba** ATŠ I no. 36 the wine becomes identified with the mystery (μυστήριον) of the womb. Part. pres. **brazia rurbia mlabšit** ATŠ II? thou art clad in mighty mysteries; **mlabaštun** ATŠ II (DC 6) no. 167 (a var. of **ʿtlabaštun** DC 36 ibid.).

Af. Pf. **albiš** he clothed MG 229:7; **lalbiš pihta bklila** ATŠ I no. 176 he did not wrap the *pihta* about the wreath; **albišnin** we clothed MG 224:19; with suff. **alb(i)šan** he clothed me, **alb(i)šh̲, albiših̲** he clothed him MG 275:8, **albšuia** they clothed him MG 278:2, **albšu** Gs 101:11 they clothed her MG 279:16, **albšun** they clothed me MG 272:21, **albšak** he clothed thee MG 273:12, **albištak** I clothed thee MG 274:3, **albištinkun** I clothed you MG 281:3. Impf. with suff. **nalb(i)šh̲** he clothes him MG 31:1, **nalb(i)ših̲** id. MG 275:antean-tep., **nalb(i)šak** he clothes thee MG 273:19, **nalbšunh̲** they (will) clothe him MG 278:16, **nalbišinan, talbišinan** he, she will, thou wilt clothe us MG 280:1; **zhara mn ziuak tialbišh̲** DC 34. 294 brightness from thy glory will clothe him; **ʿialbišinkun** Gy 171:ult. I (will) clothe you MG 280:28. Impf. with suff. **albišia** AM 287:7 wrap it, **albišun** clothe (pl.) me MG 273:8, **albšuia** clothe (pl.) him MG 279:3, **alb(i)šinun** clothe them MG 282:13, **alb(i)šunin** Q 30:27 *vestite eas* MG 283:antep. Act. pt. **sahra d̲-malbiš** . . . DC 43 demon that possesses . . ., **iadh̲ lpihta lamalbaš** (var. **-iš**) **bklila** ATŠ I no. 177 (var. DC 6) his hand doth not 'clothe' the *pihta* with the wreath; pl. **malbišia** they clothe MG 37:21; **brhamta malbišia** DC 10 they are enveloped in love; pl. with encl. **malb(i)šilh̲** they clothe him MG 30:11, 149:11 f.; **balbuša d̲-nišimta malbišilh̲** DC 27. 510 they impersonate the soul (*idiom*). Part. pres. with encl. **malbišatlh̲** thou clothest him MG 232:24.

Ethpa. Pf. **ʿtlabaš** PD 840 he clothed himself, was clothed MG 213:20; **malakia ʿtlabaš bsahria** Gy 174:7 the angels clothed themselves as demons (= appeared as or impersonated demons, cf. Idioms); **asa klila bihdadia ʿtlabaš** DC 34 myrtle and wreath are conjoined, put together; **taga uhimiana bihdadia ʿtlabaš** DC 34 crown and girdle are put on together; **uʿtlabaš balbuših̲** CP 65:5 (**utlabaš** ML 80:11) (read **utitlabaš**? cf. 81 n. 2), **ʿtlabšat** PD 837 she clothed herself MG 222:18; **ʿtlabšat btutba** Gy 94:10, 95:2, 26 she put on her skirt; **tlabašiun** ATŠ they took upon themselves; **ʿtlabaštun** (var. **mlabaštun**) ATŠ II no. 167 (var. DC 6) ye were (var. are) clothed; with encl. **ʿtlabašbh̲** Gy 173:7, Q 53:12 he was clothed in it. Pt. **bdukrana rba lamitlabaš** ATŠ he will not be covered (i.e. rehabilitated, reinstated) by the Great Commemoration (*idiom*); **šahla mn mandaiuta umitlabaš btarmiduta** DC 34. 743 it is divested of lay-status and invested with priestly-status; fem. **lbuš ʿl lbuš mitlabša** ML 81:1 = CP 65:7 she putteth on garment on garment; pl. **mitlabšia** DAb they array themselves; **razia bhdadia mitlabšin** ATŠ the mysteries are conjoined (*idiom*). **ʿtlabušia** DC 27 to clothe.

Idioms: With **b** 'to be rehabilitated, reinstated' s. ethpa. pt., 'to identify oneself' s. ethpa. pf., 'to impersonate' s. af. pt. pl. with encl. With **bihdadia** 'to be conjoined' s. ethpa. pf. & pt. pl.

Gl. 52:7 f. **LBŠ** تدرع *indui* پوشيد; 140:11 f. miswritten كسا *operire, vestire* پوشيد; 146:3 f. id. لبس *induere* پوشيد.

Der.: **(a)lbuša, malbuša, lbaša.**

lbina (לבן) white, gleaming **laibat šapirtia ulbina** DC 45, 46 Venus, fair and white.

LGA s. **LAG.**

lgaṭa (rt. **LGṬ**) (*a*) bunch, handful, (*b*) grasp, seizure. (*a*) **lgaṭa d̲-asa** DC 24 a bunch of myrtle (var. **lagṭa**); (*b*) **giuṭa ulgaṭa** AM 191:8 disgrace and seizure.

lgu (**l** + **gu**) into. **unhit lgu aina** DC 41 descended into the spring.

lguṭta occ. var. of l(i)giṭta.

LGṬ (Aram. & H. לקט, Talm. נְקַט, Syr. ܠܩܛ, Ar. لقط, Akk. *laqātu*) to hold, grasp, seize, take (hold of), gather up, pick up, take into the hand; fig. to have, possess, overpower, overwhelm MG 39:4, 54:5 of stars, eclipse (to withhold).

PE. Pf. **lgiṭ** and **lgaṭ** he grasped, held MG 218:21, 221:22, **iardna lgaṭ** Gy 189:1 he took the jordan(-water, *idiom* MR 100:bottom), **ṭabutai lgaṭ** Gy 17:19, **lgaṭ ṭabutai** Gy 91:17, 92:10 he thanked me, **hiia ṭabuta lgaṭ** Gy 92:2 the Life was grateful, **ṭabutak lgaṭ** Gy 92:6 he thanked thee, **lgaṭ ṭabuta** Gy 101:21, **hiia lgaṭ ṭabuta** Gy 328:14 (*idiom* MG 393:24), **napšaihun bhaiabia lgaṭ** Gy 103:12, 117:4, Gs 63:12, 95:9, 124:6 they recognized themselves as guilty (*idiom* MG 361:29 f.), **skultai dilia . . . lgaṭ** Jb 271:10 he took my folly ill (cf. Idioms), **ligṭta d̲-lgaṭ** Gy 223:18, 22 the party which he founded (?); **pumh̲ mn ᶜkilta umašqita lgaṭ** Jb 198:14 f. he abstained his mouth from food and drink (*idiom*); **lgaṭ pumh̲ mn ᶜkilta** HG 11 he abstained from food (*idiom*); **napšh̲ kd̲ rurbia lgaṭ** Gy 93:12 he conducted himself like the Mighty (*idiom*); **lalgaṭ ulašar** Gy 315:19 they did not hold firm; **sahria udaiuia arqa d̲-nhaša lgaṭ** ATŠ II no. 397 devils and demons betook themselves to the copper-earth; **biniana kulh̲ lgaṭ bihdadia** DC 27. 80 the whole building held together (*idiom*); **lgaṭ bᶜnšia** (*often*) he took wives, married (*idiom* MG 361:26); **ligṭat** she took, grasped MG 222:10; **ligṭat napšh̲ kd̲ lahuat** Gy 94:11 she conducted herself as if she did not exist (*idiom*); **lgaṭt** thou didst take MG 222:25; **lgiṭt ligiṭta balmia** Morg. 224/36:3 f. thou hast grasped hold of the world(s); **ligṭit** I took, grasped MG 223:2; **iardna ligṭit** Gy 190:20 I took the jordan(-water, *idiom*); **lgaṭnin** we took, grasped MG 224:middle; with suff. **ligṭan** he took me MG 15:15, 270:middle, **ligṭak** he took thee MG 273:9, **ligṭik** Gy 148:23 id. with fem. suff. MG 274:25, **ligṭh̲** he grasped him MG 269:11, 275:1, **ligṭu** Gs 101:15 they took her MG 279:10, **lgaṭinun** he grasped them MG 269:10; **ᶜniš banpaihun lalgaṭinun** Gy 246:11 (var. **lagṭinun** D) nobody favoured them (MG 281:17, *idiom*); **lgaṭṭh̲** she took him MG 276:19; **mahu lalgaṭṭh̲ lᶜntak** Gy 149:3 why didst thou not take her to wife? (MG 276:25); **lgaṭṭh̲** Gy 118:12 I took him MG 277:1; **ana bᶜda lgaṭṭh̲** Gy 147:1 I took her by the hand; **lgaṭtan** thou didst take me MG 272:3, **ligṭuia** they took him MG 277:anteantep., **rigluih̲ uligṭuih̲** DC 37. 148 they impeded him and grasped him, **ligṭu** Gs 101:15 they grasped her MG 279:10, **ligṭuk** they took thee MG 274:9, **lgaṭnh̲** we took him MG 277:19. Impf. **nilguṭ, nilgaṭ** he takes, will take, we (will) take MG 220:6, 7; **libaikun lanilguṭ qina** Gy 36:1 f. let not your heart become rancorous; **ata bpagra tilgiṭ** AM 72:4 she will get a mark on her body; **niligṭun** they (will) take, or hold MG 227:16, **tiligṭun** ye (shall) take, or hold MG 227:bottom, **hiia ṭabutak niligṭun** ML 254:4 the Life will prove thee Its gratitude; **hiia ṭabutun niligṭun** Gy 107:21 the Life will prove them Its gratitude; **ṭabutan . . . niligṭun** Gy 315:7 they will be grateful to us (*idiom*), **minh̲ latiligṭun** Gy 42:18 do not withhold (it) from him (? Ginzā 40 n. 2); with encl. **nilguṭbh̲ hingia** s. **hinga** 1; with suff. **ruha tiligṭh̲** AM 20:19 a(n evil) spirit will seize him, **niligṭan** he will take me MG 271:1, **ᶜligṭak** I (will) take thee MG 273:14, **niligṭunh̲** they (will) take him (or her, it) MG 278:8, **niligṭunak** they (will) take thee MG 274:19, **ᶜlgiṭinkun** Gy 339:23, **lgiṭinkun** Gy 98:16 I take you MG 280:25, cf. MG 34:21. Impt. **lguṭ** MG 220:6; **lguṭ lguṭ ušbuq šbuq nihuia** AM 249:2 f. there will be 'hold, hold!' and 'loose, loose!'; **lguṭ zaua** Gy 14:3 take a wife; **lguṭ rahmut kušṭa** Gy 22:11 receive true love; with suff. **lugṭh̲** take him MG 276:10, **lugṭh̲ lmargna** DC 41. 326 grasp the staff, **lugṭuia** take him, it MG 278:22, **lguṭinan** Q 57:23 take us MG 280 n. 1, **lguṭinun** Oxf. 4 b:1 (worse varr. **lgaṭinun, lgiṭinun, algiṭinun** Q 72:2) take them MG 282:7 f. Act. pt. **lagiṭ** (he is) taking MG 230:3, **ainia lagiṭ** Gy 52:13, 55:4 he captivateth the eyes (Lidzb. *er blendet die Augen, idiom*); **napšh̲ lagiṭ bmkikuta** Gy 56:16 f. he behaves in a humble way (*idiom*); **šuba iumia ušuba lilauata lagiṭ** Gy 392:2 it lasteth seven days and seven nights (*idiom*); fem. **šuta lagṭa** AM 169:paen. a south wind will prevail; pl. **bsahdia lagṭia ᶜlauaihun** Gy 288:ult. ff. are calling witnesses against them (MG 361:bottom, *idiom*; **hukumta lalagṭia** Gy 44:17 they accept no wisdom; **lagṭia ṭabuta d̲-** Gy 328:14 they are grateful to . . .; **ṭabutai bᶜmrum lalagṭia** Jb 272:7 he (: the Life) in the highest is indifferent to me; **hiia ṭabutak lalagṭia** Jb 233:14 the Life is not grateful to thee (*idiom*); **abahatai bᶜmrum lalagṭia** Jb 273:5 my Father (: the Life) in the highest will not accept me; **šibiahia ᶜumqia lagṭia** ATŠ II no. 386 the planets betake themselves to the depths; **ᶜumqia lagṭia** DC 48. 424, **ᶜumqia lagṭin** DC 34. 187 f.; fem. pl. **barai dilin lalagṭan** DAb they do not observe their periods of isolation; **iad hdadia lagṭan** ATŠ II no. 144 they take one another by the hand; **šidqa lagṭia** CP 422:8 no. 386 they keep silence (hold their peace); with encl. **bliguṭṭh̲ lagiṭlun** Gy 27:15 he taketh them into his party; **lagiṭlkun** Gy 52:5 he taketh you; fem. with encl. **lagṭalia bᶜda d̲-iamina** Gy 147:3 f. she took (hist. pres.) me by the right hand; with suff. **banpaihun lalagṭinun** Gy 246:11 did not favour them (*idiom*). Part. pres. **lagṭit** thou takest MG 232:10, **lagṭinin** we take MG 232:antep., **lagṭitun** ye take MG 233:11; with suff. **lagiṭnak** Gs 97:18 I hold thee MG 291:20. Pass. pt. (with act. meaning) **lgiṭ** taking, holding MG 116:17, 380:19; fem. **karkušta lgiṭa** Gy 187:23 she holdeth a clapper MG 380:20; pl. **d̲-lgiṭia iardnia hiia** Gy 102:21 who are holding (: guarding) the jordan(s) of Life (here non-idiomatic). As part. pres. **gilia mia bᶜdai lgiṭna** Gs 83:9 I am holding the waves of the sea in my hand MG 380:20 f. (cf. MG 231:4); **lalgiṭana** Gy 148:ult. I was not taken as wife (here as a pass. pt.) MG 231:20; **lgiṭit** thou hast taken, holdest MG 232:12; with encl. **kḏ lagṭatlh̠** CP 363:1 and 12 when thou graspest it; **lgiṭatlh̠** ML 271:6, 272:6 thou graspest it. Inf. **milgaṭ** MG 129:15. **lmilgaṭ rahmia . . . šapir** ŠQ 29:7 favourable . . . for making friends.

Pa. Pt. (act. & pass.) pl. **mlagṭin** DAb they hold; with encl. **iarqunia mlagṭilia** Gy 189:7 I gather herbs. Nom. ag. **mlagṭana, fem. -ita** s.v.

Af. Pf. with suff. **algiṭun** they let me take MG 272:21, **algiṭuia** they let him take MG 278:2; with encl. **ualgiṭlh̠ nira** DAb and fastened a yoke upon him. Impf. **gabra ḏ-ṣubianh̠ nalgiṭ** CP 162:8, a man who obtaineth his will; with suff. **unalgiṭh̠** (var. **nil-**) **ʿnta** Gy 105:22 B (& Sh. 'Abd.'s copy) we will let him take a wife.

Ethpe. Pf. **uʿtilgiṭ ʿstar uʿtilgiṭ ʿtirgil . . . kulhun daiuia** DC 37. 134 f. and held fast, bound, and held and fettered are . . . all the demons. Pt. **mitilgiṭ** MG 214:4, **sira milgiṭ** AM 280:16 the moon will be eclipsed (*idiom*); **šamiš milgiṭ** AM 280:7 the sun will be eclipsed (*idiom*); **bkadba mitigiṭ** Gy 58:8 he is caught in a lie; **kul man ḏ-milgiṭ ganzibra** DC 6 any man that is made (: reaches the rank of) a *ganzibra*; **mlala milgaṭ** AM 43:3 his speech will be withheld (i.e. he will lose the power of speech); with encl. **nišimta mitilgiṭbh̠** [*sic*] ATŠ I no. 228 the soul is (up)held thereby; **mitilgiṭibh̠** [*sic*] **nišmata** CP 405 ult. no. 385 souls are supported by it.

Idioms: With **ainia** as obj. 'to captivate, blind' s. pe. act. pt. With **banpia** 'to favour' (cf. Syr. ܢܣܒ ܒܐ̈ܦܐ and H. נשא פנים Ginzā 246 n. 7) s. pe. act. pt. with suff. With **bʿnšia** 'to marry' s. pe. pf.; with (b)**sahdia** 'to call witnesses', 'take testimony against' s. pe. act. pt. pl. With **bihdadia** 'to hold together' s. pe. pf. With **ṭabuta** as obj. to thank, accept graciously (Syr. ܩܰܒܶܠ ܛܰܝܒܽܘܬܳܐ MG 393 n. 3) s. pe. pf., impf. & act. pt. pl.; cf. with the contrary **skulta** 'to be displeased' s. pe. pf. With **iardna** as obj. 'to take the jordan-water' (MR 100: bottom) s. pe. pf. 3rd masc. & 1st sg. With **napšh̠** (pl. **-aihun**) and the prep. **b-** 'to recognize or declare oneself as . . .' s. pe. pf.; with **napšh̠** and a prepositional **kḏ** 'to behave as' s. pe. pf. 3rd masc. & fem. and act. pt. **LGṬ pumh̠ mn . . .** 'to abstain from' (food, drink etc.) s. pe. pf. Ethpe. with **šamiš, sira** as subj. 'to be eclipsed' s. pt. With a designation of time (**iuma, lilia**) 'to last' s. pe. act. pt. With **bnia, ahia** as obj. 'to beget' BZ 228 n. 5. With **qina** as obj. s. **qina** 1. With **ʿl** to hold against, e.g. DC. 48. 198. With **bgauh̠** to include, e.g. DC 41. 556.

Gl. 3:7 f. af. def. استخبر *sciscitari* خبر گرفت; 16:3 f. id. ادرک *apprehendere, continere* مشتمل شد; 90:5 f. id. ساد *dominari* بزرگ شد; 135:3 f. pe. miswritten قتن *possidere* صاحب شد; 149:14 f. af. def. لمس *tangere, extendere* دست رسانید; 150:5 f. id. منع *prohibere* منع کرد; 151:1 f. miswritten مسّ *tangere* دست کشید; 151:5 f. af. def. مسک *tenere* نگاه داشت; 170:5 f. pe. miswritten هتم *sollicitus esse* زور کرد.

Der.: **lgaṭa, liguṭṭa, l(i)giṭṭa, mlagṭana,** fem. **-ita**

lgiṭṭa = **ligiṭṭa. ʿmarlak ʿl lgiṭṭh̠** ATŠ I no. 27 I will tell thee about his assumption (of the crown).

lg̱ma scr. def. of **lugma.**

ld- = **ʿl ḏ-** MG 210:4. **alma ld-** until. **alma ldmuzania taqil ʿubadia uagria** Gs 86:8 until the balance weigheth the works and rewards MG 210:10 ff., 466:22; **ldihṭin** Gy 63:23 because we have sinned MG 92:23, 465:antep.

ldbar s. **dbar 2.**

LHA (= **LUA**?) to join, accompany (?).

Pe. Pf. with suff. **aškaitak ulhaitak** DC 19, DC 45, DC 46 I found thee and joined thee.

lhad 1 s. **had.**

lhad 2 = **lhda. lhad ḏ-ʿkumia ḏ-hinun mia siauia** Gy 284:4 the black waters are very dark.

lhama a frequent doublet of **lahma** (q.v.) MG 54:6. **lhama ḏ-hizda** Gy 356:16 shameful subsistence; **uapun lhama** DC 27 (: illustrated part) and they baked bread; **zmh̠ nasbia ublhama apin** Gy 226:2 they take his blood and bake in the bread; **lhama ramia laniia** Gs 106:15 he offered (hist. pres.) to the poor; **lhama šapir tikul** AM 61:18 she will enjoy a good income; **lhamai umaiai ukisai** DC 40 my food, my drink and my purse; **hazin lhama umasiqta** CP 89:7, Q 42:3 = ML 110:2, **hazin lhama uṭabuta** CP 89:12, Q 42:6 = ML 110:5.

lhda (cf. לְחָדָא 'unique' Levy s.v.) very (much) MG 207:24 f. Doublet **lhad 2. la aklia** [*sic*] **bisra lhda** Gy 6:18 they eat not much meat; **lhda ḏ-mqarba** Gy 284:3 it is very near.

lhdaia s. **lhudaia.**

lhud- with pers. suff. (ܠܚܘܕ) alone, by oneself. **lhudai** (*often*) by myself, I alone etc.; **lhudh̠ hauin** AM 5 he will be alone, an only child; **lhudaiun** Gy 28:4 by themselves MG 181:antep. Cf. also **balhud** s.v., mod. *lūdī* (with the vanishing of *h*) alone, cf. Gl. 162:9 **ludh̠** مُفرداً *seorsus* تنها.

lh(u)daia (adj. from preced., Syr. ܠܚܘܕܝܐ) alone, unique. Var. **lihdaia.** MG 141:12 f., MR 30 n. 1. Fem. **lhudaita. lhdaia rba zadiqa** Gy 235:6, **lhudaia rba zadiqa** Gy 234:21, 235:10; s. **lihdaia.**

LHṬ for **RHṬ. abatar ʿnšia harašata uamata lahiṭ** AM 38:4 (var. **azil** Par. xxvi) he will run after sorceresses and maid-servants.

lhil s. **hil.**

LHM (ܠܚܡ, لحم H. לחם I) to gather for fighting, attacking, threaten, attack.

Eštaf. s. **ŠLHM.**

LHŠ, NHŠ (Jew.-Aram. & H. לחש, Syr. ܠܚܫ, Akk. *luḫḫušu*, Eth. ለሐሰሰ) to whisper, hiss; spell, charm.

Der.: **lihša.**

LWA (לְוָא, ܠܘܐ, H. לוה II) to go with, accompany, conduct, escort; af. to send with, send as escort or companion, to add, join.

Pe. Pf. **lun** (for לְווֹן) Gs 47:12 they accompanied MG 258:2, with suff. **luan** Jb 173:2 he accompanied me; **haila d-mn bit ab luan** DC 37 the force that accompanied me from my father's house. Act. pt. **lauia ruha mn nišimta** ATŠ II no. 282 the spirit accompanies the soul; with encl. **lalauilia** Gs 12:11 accompanieth me not; **d-lauilak bidiauria** Gy 328:5 that (we) may accompany thee as helpers; **lalauilak** Jb 146:1 will not accompany thee (ii 147 n. 1). Pass. pt. (with act. meaning) **d-minai luᶜ** Gy 208:20 that accompanied me; pl. **luin** accompanying MG 165:1; **razia ṭabia d-minh luin** DC 48. 339 good mysteries which accompany him.

Af. Pf. with encl. **aluilia lbuša dilh** Gy 136:16 he gave me his garment (as a companion); with suff. **aluiun** Gy 140:15 he (: the Life) gave me as companions. Act. pt. **maluia ruha mn nišimta** Gs 37:9 he joineth the spirit to the soul; **minai maluin** Gy 140:12 they accompany me; **kibia umumia d-mn pagra maluin** DC 27 the pains and blemishes that accompany the body; with encl. **raza rba d-mn dilan ldilh maluilh** Gy 127:24 the great mystery that is ours accompanieth him (is associated with him); **daiuia maluilun** Gs 99:17 demons are given to them as companions. Pass. pt. **minai malua**i Gy 138:4, 139:23, 140:9, 141:3 (is) joined to me as a companion MG 132:3, 263:6; pl. identical with act.

Der.: **(a)luat,** var. **ᶜluat, luaita, (ᶜ)luita, maluata, luata 2, maluaita.**

luaha Sh. ʿAbd.'s copy's var. of **ruaha** Gy 252:3.

luaita (rt. **LWA**) company, escort, companionship, accompaniment MG 116:2. Often with procl. **b-** and pers. suff. **hualan biluaitan** Gy 178:16 was our companion; **dubrin minik bluaitik** DC 34. 509 take me with thee (fem.) as thy (fem.) companion; **uṭabauata d-anin iahbinalh lnišimta biluaith** DC 48:226 and the good things we gave the soul for her companionship. Inst. of it **biluatan** (*often*), **biluatai** Gs 12:8, 10 (by confusion with the prep. **luat-** MG 116:4).

luana DC 22 (& Sh. ʿAbd.'s copy) a var. of **ᶜluana** Gs 137:2.

luat (ܠܘܬ LS) prep. towards, with, in the presence (society, or company) of, amongst MG 194:6. Varr. **aluat, ᶜluat.** With prep. **mn: mn (a)luat** Q 23:31 παρά τινος MG 196: ult. Used either independently or with pers. suff. (**luat-**) in which case it is sometimes used with the procl. **b-** (cf. s. **luaita**). **uluat anašia rurbia nitraurab** AM 51:4 and he will be made much of (: well-considered) in the society of people of high position; **luat ṭura sinai** HG towards Mount S.; **ᶜsir hailak ᶜlaia luat haršia** DC 40 thy great force is bound with sorcerers (?); **mn luat latihidrun** DC 6 turn ye not aside from my presence; **nitagzar mn luatai** DC 34 he shall be banned from my presence; **luatan lamitqabal** ATŠ he will not be admitted into our presence; **kd al luataihun** Gy 135:14 when he entered their presence; **luath d-nu** Gy 52:20 with Noah MG 330:13.

luata 1 = **aluata,** pl. of **alua. ruban ruban hauin luath** CP 116:14, ML 142:4 a myriad myriads are its tendrils; **luath d-gupnai** CP 230:2 the tendrils of my .Vine; **klila dakia d-luath nahra** Gy 364:6 a clean wreath whose leaves are shining.

luata 2 (rt. **LUA**) consort, associate: **qin anatun luata d-gap rba** Q.A. consort of the great G.

lub (Ar. لُبّ) pulp, core (of fruit), heart, centre-part, pith (of vegetables, trees etc.). **lub d-mišmiš** DC 46. 122:8 apricot-pulp.

lubana (cf. לְבוּנְתָא, ܠܒܘܢܬܐ Löw 235) *Olibanum*, frankincense. **qaina ulubana** ATŠ I no. 268 (sugar ?) cane and frankincense

lubia (לוּבְיָא, ܠܘܒܝܐ, لوبيا Löw 234) *phaseolus*, beans. **šahpia d-lubia** DC 41. 173 the foliage of beans. Gl. 148:5 **lbia** [*sic*] لبيواج *faseoli* لوبيا.

lugumia s. **lugma.**

lugiana (ܠܓܝܢܐ, λάγοινα, P. لگان, Akk. *liginnu* Zimmern, *Akk. Fw.* 21, Fränkel 130 f., cf. also Jew.-Aram. & mod. H. לגנה, Syr. ܠܓܢܬܐ, Ar. loan-w. لُجْنَة Fränkel loc. cit., Akk. *ligittu* Zimmern loc. cit.) orig. vessel, fig. the lower womb. Var. **ligiana.** Doublet **ligina** sexual organ (? v.s.v.). **msuta lamsat biahra tšaiaia d-hu lugiana zuṭa** ATŠ I no. 92, var. **ligiana iahṭa** PD 933 the solidification did not take place in the ninth month, because the (lower) womb miscarried (?, read with PD, but even this hardly has the correct version).

lugma (לוּגְמָא, ܠܘܓܡܐ jaw, Ar. لجام bridle, cf. also لُقْمَة Fränkel 100) cheek, plump (?) cheek. Pl. **lugmia,** var. **lugumia. uata lpumh ᶜu ᶜl lugmh** AM 82:19 she will get a mark on her mouth or on her cheek; **uᶜtlh lugmia** AM 21 ult. (var. **lugumia**) she has plump (?) cheeks.

Gl. 68:6 **lgma** [*sic*] خد *maxilla* عارِض.

luha (לוּחָא, ܠܘܚܐ, H. לוּחַ, Ar. لَوْح, Eth. ሰሌዳ, Akk. *lēu*) tablet, plank. **luḫa** DC 45.

Gl. 147:13 **luha** لوح *tabella, scriptum, pugillare.*

luhrasp (Pahl. *Lohrâsp*, Firdausī لُهْراسْپ) a king of ancient Iran, *Aruvat aspa* (Yašt v 105) Gray ZA 19/1905–6 p. 282; father of **guštasp** (q.v.). **guštasp brh d-luhrasp** Gy 383:7.

luza (לוּזָא, ܠܘܙܐ, H. לוּז I, Ar. لَوْز, Eth. ለውዝ Löw no. 319, Fränkel 145, Nöld., *Neue Beitr.* 43) almond. **luzan umuzan** DC 46. 136:10, JRAS 1943 171:9, our almonds and walnuts.

luzuta (cf. ܠܘܙܐܝܬܐ & ܠܘܙܘܬܐ) affliction. **uanašia bluzuta miaqra** Ṣâb.'s AM she will uproot (?) people by affliction (very doubtful).

LUṬ, LṬṬ (לוט, ܠܛ; H. לוט to cover, Ar. لاط to cover, conceal, Akk. *liṭu* curtain?) to curse. Transition from ע״י to ע״ע in certain forms MG 82:ult.

PE. Pf. with suff. **laṭh** he cursed him, her MG 275:5, **laṭṭak** Gy 132:18 etc. I cursed thee MG 274:1, **laṭṭh** she cursed him MG 276:20, id. 132:18 I cursed her MG 277:7, **laṭuia** they cursed him MG 277:ult. Impf. with suff. **niliṭh** he curses him, her, it, **tiliṭh** thou cursest him etc. MG 275:23 f., **bluṭṭa rabtia nilṭunh** ATŠ they will curse him with a great curse. Impf. with suff. **luṭh** curse him MG 276:14. Act. pt. **laiiṭ**, emph. **laiṭa** s.v.; pl. with encl. **laiṭilun umahilun** DC 43 D 10 they curse and strike them. Part. pres. **laiṭitun** ye curse MG 250:16, with encl. **laiṭitulh** ye curse him (ibid.). Pass. pt. **ama biša liṭa (umlaṭaṭa)** CP 379:14 an evil people, cursed (and blasphemous); **liṭa ruha (umlaṭaṭa)** DC 34 cursed is R. (and accursed); pl. **liṭia** Jb 86:8, Gs 27:7 the accursed ones; with encl. pers. pron. **liṭit** thou art cursed MG 250:20, **liṭitun** ye are cursed ibid.

PA. (all forms from ע״ע). Act. pt. pl. with encl. **mlaṭaṭilh** Gy 173:23 they curse him MG 32:1, 82:ult. Pass. pt. **mlaṭaṭa** cf. s. pe. pass. pt. (twice). Inf. **laṭuṭia** Gy 173:23, MG 82:ult., 253:7.

Gl. 164:1 f. miswritten لعن *maledicere, anathemisare* لعنت كرد.

DER.: **laṭuṭiata, laiṭa, luṭṭa, maluaṭa.**

luṭṭa (ܠܘܛܬܐ) curse, malediction MG 23:14, 101:16. Pl. **luṭata. luṭṭik ubiriktik** Gy 132:19 thy (fem.) curse and blessing (MG 177:18); **luṭṭa bišta umṭanapta** Gy 330:4 an evil and foul curse; **luṭata uaqiriata** DC 40 curses and invectives.

luita (ܠܘܝܬܐ) accompaniment, companion(ship) MG 110:ult. **ʿṭak luita d-atia ʿṭak d-atia luita** Gs 99:14 that perhaps a companion will come.

luka occ. var. of **aluka** (q.v.).

lula (P. لَوْلا) flange, hinge. Mod. **mahia lula bdulab** s. **dulab.**

lulita 1 (לוליתא 'spear', ܠܘܠܝܬܐ 'sting' give no appropriate meaning; the word was prob. misinterpreted by MM.) seems to mean 'embryo'. **d-hʿ lulita kul had iuma tlatma ušitin mitqalia hauia** ATŠ I no. 168, since it is an embryo (?), it assumes every single day 360 mithqals; **muqra . . . d-hʿ lulita** (var. **lilita**) **qarilh urazia d-lulita** (var. **li-**) **qarilh** ATŠ I no. 246, (var. DC 6 ibid.), Bodl. 12 the marrow (or 'sperm'?) which they call 'embryo' and they call it the mysteries of the embryo.

lulita 2 Bodl. 12 a name given to Simat-Hiia.

LWN (Ar. لون) to (have) colour.

ETHPA. Pt. **qabana . . . milauna d-gul uhiuara** ŠQ 18:24 a robe . . . coloured rose and white.

DER.: **launa.**

LUP, LPP, ALP II (לפי & לסף, ܠܦ & ܠܦܦ, Ar. لَفَّ, Akk. *lippu* bond) to join (oneself), be united to, connect, be knit together. Nöld. MG 83:bottom f. explained it mistakenly as a secondary rt. from **ALP** = **YLP.** MR 112:bottom, ML 13 n. 3.

PE. Pf. **laupa d-lap** Jb 268:3 the communion of which they partook; **alpat** (as from **ALP II**) Gy 183:4 she wrapped, with suff. **lapth** Q 56:3 thou hast united him (Nöld. *du lehrtest ihn* MG 276:26, possibly: hast become acquainted with him); **laptinan** Q 28:2 f. thou hast united us (Nöld. *lehrtest uns* MG 280:8, cf. preced.); **laptinun blaupa d-hiia** Gy 361:4 I made them join the union of Life (Nöld. *ich lehrte sie* MG 282:26); **bihdadia laptinun** ATŠ II no. 159 (var. **laptinkun** DC 6 ibid.) I have united them (var. you) together; **hiia blaupa lapuia** Gs 81:7 the Life knit her into the (comm)union, Impf. **nilap** Lond. roll A 517 is united (ML 50 n. 3); with encl.: **uʿliplun laupa hiia** Gy 240:13 and I will unite them in the communion of the Life; with suff. **unilipinun blaupa šania** s. **laupa** (Nöld. differently MG 281:paen.); **ʿlipinkun** Q 56:14 I join you (Nöld. *ich lehre euch* MG 280:26). Impt. **lup ziua** ML 256:1, var. **ʿlup** DC 3. 403:4, CP 253:5, ŠQ 22:13 Lidzb. *wickle Glanz ein* (parallel with **unṭur** 'and preserve' n. 1); **lap laupa d-hiia** CP 44:22, ML 50:10 unite yourselves in the communion of the Life (n. 3); special pl. form **lupiun kd d-laptun** DC 50 perform the *laufa* (v.s. **laupa**) as ye performed it formerly; with suff. **lupinun blaupa rba** s. **laupa** (Nöld. differently MG 282:11). Act. pt. **laiip abihdia tarmidia** DC 42 he celebrates *laupa* (pr. *laufa*) with the priests; with encl. **qaiman ulaiiplia** Gs 46:16 he raiseth me and uniteth me (with himself?); **laiiplun blaupa rba** s. **laupa**; pl. **laupa . . . d-laipia bhiria batar nhur** Gs 81:7 the communion . . . in which the elect ones are knit together in the place of light; **laupa . . . kd d-laipia ʿutria bškinatun** CP 42:21 = ML 50:10 the communion . . . as the uthras (per)form it in their dwellings; **kulhun laipin bihdadia** DC 42 all of them join together; **uhaizak laipin kul trin abihdia hdadia** DC 42 and then both of them join together; **ukd laipin . . . kulhun laipin bihdadia** DC 42 when they communicate . . . all of them join together. Part. pres. **laipit** thou joinest (Nöld. *du lernst* MG 250:15); **mn qudam d-laipitun** before ye perform the communion. Pass. pt. **blaupa d-rba d-lip** CP 125:17, ML 152 in the communion with the Great with whom he was joined; **tlat ʿumṣia d-lalip ʿlauaihun** DC 50. 153 three morsels which have not been used in the communion; pl. **d-mn nišimta lipin dakrin** ATŠ II no. 117 they commemorate those who were united with the soul.

ETHPE. Pf. **ʿtlip laupa d-hiia** Gy 238:10 the communion of the Life was formed; **ʿtlip bhalin miuia ṭabia** DC 43, **d-tlip bhalin miuia ṭabia** DC 50. 145 is united in communion by these wholesome fruits; **hanatun trin iaminia d-ʿtlip bhdadia** ATŠ II no. 326 those two right hands that were joined together; **ruha unišimta bhdadia ʿtlipiun** DC 27. 69 spirit and soul were joined together (: were united); **d̲-ʿtlipiun bhazin ginza rba** ATŠ II no. 1; **anin mn hiia laʿtlipnin** DC 48. 391 we were not brought into communion with Life. Impf. **šutak šutan dilan titlip blaupan ulatipsaq** Gy 130:23 thy intercourse be joined to us in our communion and be not severed; **nitlipun** Q 22:30 they will be joined (MG 251:28); **nitlipun bhazin masiqta** DC 27. 9. Pt. **blaupa d̲-rba mitlip** CP 125:116, ML 152 will be united in the communion of the great (Life); **mitlip blaupa d̲-aba** DC 27. 10 is joined in the communion of the Father; **mitlip blaupa bhalin miuia** DC 27. 42.

Der.: **laupa, lupan, lupapan, lputa, lupata.**

lup lilita DC 43 name of lilith.

lupa Sh. ʿAbd.'s copy = **laupa** Gy 341:ult.

lupan Gy 98:1 a demon, forming a pair with **aṭarpan** (q.v.).

lupapan nhura rba Gy 145:21 a spirit of light Var. **lupapin** DC 22.

lupata (Nöld. ܠܘܦܬܐ? MG 54 n. 4; Lidzb. Ass. *lipû* 'fat' Ginzā 84 n. 3; prob. from **LUP**) Nöld. *Kehricht*, refuse (what is thrown away); Lidzb.: an inner organ of the body?; joints, ligaments (of the body) (?) Only in pl. Varr. **laupata, lupita** s.vv. **ʿsirit umazihit mn tlatma ušitin lupata** DC 37. 581 thou art exorcized and cast out of the 360 joints (?) (exorcism of demon from various parts of the body); **šarinin lilupath̲** Gy 84:1 I dissolved his joints; **pagra d̲-lupata** Gs 80:19, 97:9, 132:17 f. body of grossness.

lupita DC 22. 466 a var. of **-ata** Gs 80:19.

LUŠ (לוּשׁ, ܠܫ, H. לוּשׁ, Eth. ሎሰ or ለወሰ, Akk. *lāšu* Zimmern ZA 31 121 n. 1) to mix (dough), to knead (bread).

Pe. Pf. **ulašiun uapun lahma** DC 41. 168 f. and they kneaded and baked bread. Act. pt. pl. **laišia liša** RD C 27 = DAb par. they mix dough.

Der.: **liša.**

LWŠ (den. from P. لوش mud MG 49 n. 3) to soil, make dirty.

Pa. Pass. pt. **ʿdaihun bzma mlauša** Gy 179:21 (var. **-ia** DC 22. 172) their hands are soiled with blood (var. act.: they soil their hands).

Ethpa. Impf. **ʿdaikun bzma lanilauša** Gy 234:10 f. your hands be not soiled with blood.

lzur DC 22. 380 a var. of **alzur** (q.v.).

LṬṬ s. pa. of **LUṬ**.

li– 1 s. **l- 1**.

li– 2, lʿ- 1, cf. also **l- 6** (s.v.) an archaic form of the pref. of the 3rd p. sg. & 1, 3 pl. impf. (for **ni-, nʿ-**) MG 215 f. **lʿšlim** (read **-um**) Gs 118:5 is completed; **lʿpuq** Gs 118:7 cometh out; **liqum, lʿqum** Gy 369:19, Gs 106:20 he may stand; **lʿhsiṭ** Gy 87:15 (var. **lshiṭ** A) let it stretch out; **lidmia** Gs 53:1 resembleth; **lištria** Gs 113:5, **lʿtibrun** Gy 13:3 B they are created; **lihuia, lʿhuia** (often) is, will be, with encl. **lihuilkun** Gy 180:21, 184:14, Gs 129:2, 9, 14 *est* (or *sit*) *vobis*; **libaṭlh̲** Gs 62:1 (var. **ni-** Leid.) we bring it to nought; **liplihunh̲, liplihunak** Gs 128:24, 129:1, 130:4 they (shall) worship him, thee; **lišimṭan** Gs 96:5, 7 he may draw me out; **lʿiadiak** Gs 89:6 may he bring thee over; **lʿiadkar** Gy 70:20 we will mention (or name) MG 216; **liaṭribh̲** DC 37 striketh at him.

li– 3, lʿ 2 for **la 1** in **lʿška** Gy 101:15 (var. **li-** DC 22 and Sh. ʿAbd.'s copy) there was found none to . . see **ŠKA liškit** DC 27:56 I could not.

lia 1 to me (s. **l- 1**), var. **lʿ 1** (*often*).

lia 2 (*לְאֵי, Talm. לייא) where?, whither? Both meanings in Gy 237:1. Varr. **ʿlia, alia** and even **lʿ 2** Gs 48:4. With other prep.: **milia** Gy 202:8 whence?, and even **lilia 2** Gy 362:15, Gs 49:11 whither? MG 205:17 ff.

Gl. 37:2 **ulia** اين هو *ubi est* او كجاست; 77:8 id. حيث *ubi* در كجا.

liana = **ʿliana. ṣbatak d̲-aqamia lianak** DC 41. 324 thy finger which is before thy thumb (= 'forefinger').

lia nu (Nöld. הו + לאידין) Gs 125:1, 4, 10 f. 22 whither MG 94:8 f. & n. 3.

liba (לִבָּא, ܠܶܒܳܐ, H. לֵב, Ar. لُبّ, Eth. ልብ, Akk. *libbu*) heart, mind, thought; centre, central part; pith, centre (of stalk or of vegetable) MG 102:16. St. abs. & cstr. **lbab** s.v. Pl. **lilbia** Gy 39:2, Q 25:1, where only one MS. has **libia** MG 77:4 f., 167 n. 3:ult. Used as both masc. and fem. With suff.: usually **lbab** (s.v.) my heart, but also **libai** id. MG 175:20, **libaikun** your heart MG 180:8; **ukul d̲-amar blibh̲ amar** AM 39:5 and all he says in his heart he says; **btrin libia qaiim** AM 22:19 he is of two minds (: undecided in his opinions); **msadrana d̲-libia** PD 912; **lilbia haškia** Gy 276:10 dark hearts; **mn dilia hauin lilbia hauin pirṣia ap blilbia bun hauin ṭabia ubun hauin bišia** Gy 244:19 f. from me come hearts, and from hearts come impulses, and some of them are good and some of them are bad; **anat hu d̲-iadit blilbia uparšit bʿuṣria ulilbia** Gy 193:24 thou art He who knowest hearts and recognizest minds and hearts; **lilbia kšiṭia** Gy 366:24 sincere hearts; **d-lanikšil** (var. **lanitakšal** D, **latitakšal** Sh. ʿAbd.'s copy) **libaihun** Gy 37:22 that their heart may not stumble; **kd̲ bzidanuta umrara rahta libaikun** Gy 39:7 when your heart is seething (as fem.) with wrath and bitterness; **lilbia hadua** Gy 370:13 joyful hearts MG 309:22. Gl. 129:14 defectively فواد *latus* دل; 135:10 id. قلب *cor* دل.

liban DC 22. 167:ult., 168:5 a var. of **lilban.**

libat (cf. s. **dilbat**) Venus, planet of this name MSchr 45 n. 7, Siouffi 146, MSt 34 ff., MMII 79 f., 318 n. 2. **libat bilura šdat** Gy 336:1 s. **bilura 2**; **baba d̲-libat kukba** Gy 224:23, 225:24; **libat rabtia** Jb 235:12; **libat qadišta** Jb 187:6; **dmut d̲-libat** RD 7 ('and her names'); **maṭarta d̲-libat** RD C 24, 25; **mzaina milibat pt alahia** WedF 58:middle = ŠQ 18:29 adorned by (or: more than?) L. daughter of gods; **libat ʿstira** Morg. 268/27:33 L.-Astarte; **libat marat alahia uanašia** Lond. roll B 349, Oxf. roll g 587, 604, Par. xxiv 6 a, 8 a, xxvii 60 a, 61 ab, 71 b, 75 b L. mistress of gods and people, **libat marat** Oxf. roll g 978 L. my mistress, **libat martia šupra urgaga** WedF 58:middle = CP 226:7 L. mistress of beauty and desire; **ruha d̲-qudša ᶜstra d̲-libat amamit šumh̲** Gy 27:17 the Holy Ghost (= Rūha) Astarte, whose name is L.-A.; **libat kukba nahira** Oxf. roll g 991 Venus, the shining star.

libiatan for **liuiatan** in **libiatan rba** Par. xxvii 18 b.

libina for **libna** in **kdub la libina** DC 46 inscribe on a clay-tablet.

libna st. abs. of **libta** MG 173:18. **ᶜkbiš libna bbinianh̲** Lond. roll B 596 a brick was laid in his building; **zga ulibna** RD B 73, **azga ulibna** Q 54:23 v.s. **azga**; **libna mn ašita** Gy 387:7 a brick from the wall; **kd̲ libna bšita** DC 40 like clay-brick in a foundation; **ulibna ᶜtiqria ulibna šumh̲** ATŠ I no. 261 and a brick was created (or 'it was called a clay-brick'?) and its name is 'clay-brick'.

libnan (cf. s. **lilban**) Gy 380:11 Lebanon; var. **lbnan** s.v. MG 77:8 & n. 3.

libra DC 44. 628, var. **libria** Morg. 259/10:29 name of an angel.

libta (לְבֵנְתָא, Talm. לְבֵינְתָא, Syr. ܠܒܶܢܬܳܐ, ܠܒܢܬܐ, Old Aram. pl. לבנן Lidzb., *Handb. d. nordsem. Epigr.* 302, H. לְבֵנָה, Akk. *libittu*, cstr. *libnat*, Ar. لِبْنَة Fränkel 4, Ges.) clay-brick, cob, building material of worked unbaked clay built up and left to dry in the sun MG 52:2, 173:16. St. abs. **libna** s.v. **lilibta qadmaita** Gy 331:9 to the first (clay-)brick (MG 32:14); **libta d̲-siana** Gy 216:9 brick of dung; **libta d̲-qudša** HG 55, 65 the sacred brick (ZDMG 1955 p. 359:bottom); **nitikbiš kd̲ libta bbiniana** DC 44. 1718 = Morg. 268/26:23 (with a miscop. **br aniana**) shall be pressed down like a clay-brick in a building.

LIG s. **LAG** = **LGA**.

liga (pt. pe of **LAG**) stammering. Found only in pl. **ligia 1** Gy 177:9, MG 107:18.

ligal (prep. l- 1 + ܥܓܠ, cf. Ar. عَجَّلَ hurry), also **bligal** (with two procl. prep., Syr. ܒܥܓܠ) quick(ly), speedily, fast, soon MG 196:17, 207:20. **ligal** Gs. 40:10, 17, AM 16, 27 etc. (very often in exorcisms), **bligal** Gs 40:22.

ligṭta s. **ligiṭta**.

ligia 1 pl. of **liga**.

ligia 2 (rt. **LGA**) idle chatter, gossip. **ligia ušiha** Gy 59:11 idle gossip and lust; **zmaran uligian** Jb 61:1 our song and idle chatter (or: jesting).

ligia (cf. Ar. لُغَة) pl. words. **ligia alpit mn lišanun** DC 35 I learnt words from their language (?).

ligiana s. **lugiana**.

lig(i)ṭta (rt. **LGṬ**) hold, handclasp, assistance, grasp, assumption; party, faction. MG 26:20, 103:15. **lig(i)ṭtan** our grasp MG 178:antep.; **lgiṭinkun bligṭtai** Gy 98:17, **bligṭtan niligṭh̲** Gy 110:1; **nišaušh̲ liligṭth̲** Gy 110:17 we will confuse his faction; **lgaṭ bgauh̲ ligṭta** Gy 110:21; **ligṭta qadmaita** Gy 222:14; **ligiṭta d̲-lgaṭ mn** . . . Gy 223:18, 22 the faction which he formed from . . . ; **lguṭ ligṭta mn tibil kd̲ ligṭta d̲-lgaṭnin anin** Gy 299:12 form a faction in the world like the faction which we formed; **nilgaṭ ligṭta** Gy 131:23, 329:6, 10, **ᶜlgiṭinkun bligṭta** Gy 339:24, **lgaṭ ligṭta** Gy 361:8, **mitligṭia bligṭtan** Gy 362:5, **milgaṭ ligiṭta** Gy 381:13, **lgaṭt ligiṭta balmia** Q 24:21, **lgiṭit bligiṭtan** Jb 64:3, **lamitilgiṭ bligiṭtun d̲-bišia** Jb 66:6, **ligiṭta** . . . **lagṭit** Jb 198:2. About the idiomatic **LGṬ lig(i)ṭta** cf. MR 123 n. 126 n. 3, 152:12, see also under **LGṬ**; **bhadua ligṭtai** Jb 93:7 doubtf. cf. ii 96 n. 1; **bligṭtan mitqaimia** ATŠ II no. 433 in our alliance they will be raised up; **ᶜmarlak ᶜl lgiṭta** ATŠ I no. 27 I will tell thee about its (: the crown's) assumption.

ligina (cf. s. **lugiana**) used as a metaphor for the sexual organ (?). **kd̲ mpaṭar liginh̲ hadia** DC 45 when his vessel (: membrum) discharges, he rejoices.

ligra (Old Aram. pl. לגרי Lidzb.: *Handb. d. nordsem. Epigr.* 368, met. of the Gen. Sem. רגל: Jew.-Aram. ריגלא, רגלא, Syr. ܪܶܓܠܳܐ, H. רֶגֶל, Ar. رِجْل, Sab. 𐩧𐩴𐩡, Eth. እግር Brockelm. *Grundr.* I 227, 231, 295 LS, Ges.) foot, leg; fig. end. MG 74:1, 102:3 & n. 1. Usually fem., rarely as masc. MG 157:16. Pl. **ligria**. **ligran** Gy 100:3 our feet MG 179:7; **ligrai lhaka lia dabran** Gy 272:4 my feet led me hither (?); **uᶜt minaihun d̲-ligria napšia ᶜtlun** Gy 279:21 and some of them have many legs; **bligria rurbia** Gy 346:3, 15 before the feet of the great (?); **ligrai d̲-madrika dirkia d̲-kušṭa** DC 3 = CP 133:7 f. my feet that tread the paths of right-doing; **ligra d̲-šidta** AM 225:17, **ligria d̲-šidta** AM 225:8 the end of the year (cf. پایان).

liha (origin obscure MG 139 n. 2) net, snare MG 139:9. Pl. **lihia**. Masc. **lihia gadada d̲-iama** Gy 184:14 f. the nets of the seashore (?); **rmilh̲ lihia** Jb 155:12 the nets are thrown; **anqia ulihia** Jb 156:3, **lanqia blihia** Jb 157:9 s. **anqia**; **qlaith̲ ᶜl lihun** Jb 148:4 f. I burnt their net; **d̲-lihia gaṭria** Jb 148:5 which hold the nets together; **lihia ṣabia** Jb 148:10 doubtf. cf. ii 151 n. 4; **blihan** Gs 57:17 in our net; **blihaikun** Gs 57:21 in your net; **lihun** Gs 58:7, 12 f.; **lamitparqin mn lihun** ATŠ they are not freed from their net; **ᶜdaihun mn lihun ᶜtparaq** ATŠ they withdrew their hands from their snare; **blihia šinta** DC 47 in the toils of sleep.

lihania (adj. from **liha**) pl. net-spirits, name of a kind of evil spirits MG 139:8. Furlani: *I Nomi* 429. **laṭabia ulihania ugdultania** Gy 279:5 evil ones and net-spirits and hobgoblins; **lihania uhumria zadaniata** CP 20:3 = Q 8:5 = ML 22:2 net-spirits and furious amulet-spirits; **sahria d̲-tibil lihania** DC 43 earth-spirits (and) net-spirits; **lihania zikria ulihania nuqbata** DC 43 A 20 male and female net-spirits.

lihdaia = **lh(u)daia** MG 141:12 f. Fem. **lihdaita**. **lihdaia rba gadiqa** CP 463:13, **lhdaia**

rba zadiqa ḏ-mn lihdaia rba zadiqa hua Gy 235:6 f. the Unique Great Righteous One who came from the Unique Great Righteous One, **lihdaia rba zadiqa** Gy 237:1 (cf. **lhudaia rba zadiqa** Gy 234:21, 235:10) Ginzā 234 f., Siouffi 40, 46, MR 30 n. 1; **dukrana lihdaia** PD 1667, 1692, 1927 ff. a single commemoration; **lihdaia rba** PD 301 the Great Unique One; **maṣbuta lihdaita** ATŠ II no. 192 a single baptism.

lihša (rt. **LHŠ**, Syr. ܠܚܫܐ, H. לַחַשׁ) (*a*) whispering, hissing, (*b*) incantation, spell, charm. MG 101:4. (*a*) **blihšia.** DC 40. 489, Gy 280:21 (var. **blihša** Leid., DC 22. 276) at the whispering of his lips; **kḏ hiuia blihšia** DC 40. 484 like a snake with its hissing; (*b*) **blihšak mauminalak** AM 122:20 with thy spell I conjure thee.

liu Morg. 231/49:8 for ziu.

liuianata fem. pl. of foll.? **aumitak bliuiatin bliuianata** DC 37. 530 I conjure thee by L. (and) by female Leviathans (?).

liuiatan, lʿuiatan, var. -in (H. לִוְיָתָן, Syr. ܠܘܝܬܢ) Leviathan MG 7:antep., 57:1. Usually identified with Ur, HpGn 11, 30, 87, 101, MSt 122. Var. **libiatan** s.v. **liuiatan** PD 393; **liuiatan rba** PD 115; **liuiatan rba qašiša** Gy 393:20; **ab lʿuiatan** Gy 233:24; **giuthḏ-liuiatan** Jb 98:11, -an 210:4, Gy 300:23 s. **giuta** 1; **liuiatin tanina** Jb 98:11; **liuiatin šumẖ ḏ-iurba** Lond. roll B 355; **brušuma ḏ-liuiatin ʿtiršim** ATŠ II no. 287 is signed by the mark of L. (= the Snake-Dragon that encircles the **skan daula** trio); **bmnata ḏ-qin ukrun uliuiatin ušdum uʿur nihuia** ATŠ I no. 33 (here L is differentiated from Ur). Cf. also s. **liuiniata.**

lika 1 (Talm. ליכא, from לית + כא) there is not, there are not MG 42:20, 204:6, 296:2. Varr. **lʿka, lʿika.** Still used (pron. *lekka*; in mod. Mand. even with suff., pron. *leχt-*). **lika ḏ-** Gy 81:2, **lʿka ḏ-** Gy 284:8 etc. there is none who; **naṣba lika luatai** Gs 55:8 the Creator is not by me; **ḏ-tuqna bgauẖ lʿka** Gy 32:22 in which there is no order MG 402:14 ff.; **lika** (var. **lʿka**) **ḏ-litlẖ saka** or **lika ḏ-saka litlẖ** Gy 77:18, 94:23, 95:21, 100:7, 236:1 f., 293:7, 294:24, 295:23, 296:13 there is nothing without an end (cf. MG 433 n. 1, Ginzā 73 n. 3) MG 433:5 ff. **lika hiia** Jb 64:6 (var. **lʿka** C) the Life is not there.

lika 2 sporadically for **lka** (t)hither.

lila exceptionally for lilia 1. **blila** DC 36 in the night.

lilauata pl. of lilia 1 (q.v.).

lilai (Talm. עִילָאִי ?, Syr. ܠܥܠ) upwards MG 23:6, 203:21 f. **mitpik rišẖ ltitai ukraiia lilai** Gy 202:14 his head is turned downwards and his legs upwards; **urišaikun larqa uligraikun lilai** DC 43. 136 and your heads are on the ground and your legs upwards; **qaiimna ana . . . lilai** DC 21 I rise upwards.

lilban (H. לְבָנוֹן, Akk. *Labnānu*, Syr. ܠܒܢܢ Ges., Ar. لبنان) Gy 174:17, 24, Q 52:13, 18 Lebanon MG 77:7, **arzia blilban** CP 101:5 cedars in Lebanon; doublet **libnan** s.v.

lilbia pl. of **liba.**

lil(u)ata, liluia s. **lilia** 1.

lilia 1 (Bibl.-Aram. לֵילְיָא, Jew.-Aram. id. & לֵילְא, Old Aram. לילא, H. לַיִל, לַיְלָה, Syr. ܠܠܝܐ, Ar. لَيْل, لَيْلَة, Eth. ሌሊት, Akk. *lilātu* evening Ges.) night MG 23:15, 127:17. Pl. **liluia** (?), **lilauata** MG 166:24 f., other plurals **liluata, liliuata, liliauata. iahia dariš bliluia iuhana bramšia ḏ-lilia** Jb 77:1, 79:5, 80:9, 83:9, 86:12, 87:15, 88:1, 89:10, 93:4, 94:6, 101:4, 103:5, 109:9, 116:9, 122:8 Yahyâ teacheth in the nights, Yôhânâ in the evenings of the night; **ladratan liluia šinta** Jb 67:4 sleep did not overtake me at night; **šragia ḏ-ziua matlia bliluia** DC 48. 230 she hangs up lamps of radiance at night(-time); **utlatin lilauata** ATŠ II no. 133 (var. **liliuata** DC 6 ibid.) and thirty nights; **uʿtiqrun lilauata** ATŠ II no. 65, 255 (varr. **liliuata, liliauata**) and are called nights.

lilia 2 (l- 1+lia 2) v.s. **lia** 2.

liliata pl. of **lilita.**

liliuk Jb 68:7 ff. a Jewish interpreter of dreams, n.pr.

lilipiata (from **LUP** = **LPP** by doubling the 1st rad.?) perh. fasces JRAS 1939 404 n. 1. **sikinia ulilipiata ugarṭupiata** DC 37. 343. Often in lists of weapons in DC 33 & 43 C 39.

lilit(a) (H. לִילִית, Akk. *Lilītu*, masc. *Lilū* Ges.) lilith, a female demon or genie, not always baleful. Pl. **liliata.** MMII 46, Furlani, *I Nomi* 407; MSchr. 91 n. 4. **zuṭ lilita** RD 26 = DAb par.; **humrak ulilliatak** Gy 87:21 thy amulet-spirits and thy liliths; **liliata uharašiata** Gy 57:14 liliths and witches; **ʿnšaikun liliata ṣruriata** Gy 139:15 your wives the liliths, the salamanders; **daiuia ulilliata kulhun** Gy 394:1; **liliata uʿstirata** Gs 92:13; **ṣupnai lilita** s. **ṣupnai**; **liliata ḏ-šitin lilia** DC 40 liliths of sixty nights.

lima-, lma-, lʿma-, lama- with encl. l+pers. suff. (cf. Syr. ܠܡܢܐ ܠܝ, ܠܡܢܐ ܠܟܘ etc.) wherefore, of what good to me etc., wherefore should I, did I etc. MG 29:13 ff. **limalia** (var. **lam-** B) **ḏ-ligṭit zaua ulimalia** (var. **ulam-** Jb 55:4 wherefore did I take a spouse and wherefore [did I have children]?; **limalik** (var. **lam-** B) **azga ḏ-zabnit bnpiš** Jb 115:11 f. wherefore dost thou (fem.) buy a bier with much cost?; **lmalan** (var. **lim-**) **ḏ-ʿtibnin** Gs 23:3 f. (var. DC 22. 413) wherefore did we sit?; **lmalik** (var. **lim-**) **ḏ-saiit mia** Gy 116:11 f. (var. DC 22. 111) why dost thou (fem.) wash in water?; **lmalik ḏ-ramit dahba** Gy 116:12 f. wherefore dost thou (fem.) throw gold?; **lmalik ḏ-haipit** Gy 116:14 f. why dost thou (fem.) wash?; **lmalia** (var. **limalia**) **ḏ-ʿiaiar šakbia** Gy 341:16 (var. DC 22. 337) wherefore should I awaken the sleepers?; **lmalak** (var. **lim-**) **ḏ-mšailit ʿlẖ** Gs 40:15 (var. Sh. ʿAbd.'s copy) wherefore askest thou about him?; **lmalẖ lqadmaia** ML 187:3 (var. **limalia ʿl qadmaia**) wherefore doth the First One (var. lit. what do I have to do with the First One? n. 1).

limania = **ʿlimania. blimania bišuta tihuia** AM 234:7 there will be wickedness amongst young people.

limat Sh. ʿAbd.'s copy's var. of **lʿmat** Gy 369:3.

lisṭar Gy 383:17, var. **lasṭar** DC 22 an ancient Persian king, Chosroes, Gray ZA xix 286.

lipriuš ziṣag Gy 382:18, varr. **lapriš z-** B, **lipriuš zih(u)nag** CD, **lprʿiuš zihnag** Sh. ʿAbd.'s copy & DC 22. 379 (Pahl. *Pērōz-ī Šāh* شاه فیروز) an early Persian king Gray ZA xix 276.

lipta DC 22. 209 a var. of **libta** Gy 216:9.

liša (לֵישָׁא, ܠܝܫܐ) dough. **laišia liša** RD C 27 = DAb par. s. **LUŠ** act. pt. pl. **abud dmuta d̲-liša** DC 44 make an effigy of dough.

lišana (לִישָּׁנָא, ܠܫܢܐ, H. לָשׁוֹן, Ar. لِسَان, Eth. ልሳን, Akk. *lišānu* LS, Ges.) tongue, language MG 122:15 f. St. abs. **lišan**. Pl. **lišania**. Masc. **lišana tlitaia** Gy 287:4, Q 14:15 the third tongue; **lišania hṭimia tlitaiia** Lond. roll B 464 (cf. s. **HṬM**); **amamia taumia ulišania** Gs 75:12, RD B 64 = DAb par., peoples, races, and languages (cf. Dan. 3:4, 7, 31, 5:19, 6:26, 7:14), **lišania d̲-amamia utaumia** ATŠ II no. 433; **lišania ʿpikia** Gs 67:22, RD B 64 = DAb par. perverted tongues; **lišania d̲-lakašria** Gs 54:19, 24 s. **KŠR** pe. act. pt. pl.; **trin lišania** Gy 357:7, Jb 171:10, 181:14 double tongues (= hypocrisy).

liška, lʿška for **laška** s. **ŠKA** & **liška 3**.

lit-, lʿt- the form of **laiit** with encl. **-b-** and **-l-**: **litbh̲, litlh̲** (*very often*) he, she has etc. **udʿtlh̲ udlitlh̲** AM 220:10 f. and what he has and what he has not; **d̲-litbh̲ kadba ulaiit bgauh̲ hasir ubṣir** Gy 64:22 there is no lie in him and there is in him no imperfection or deficiency (MG 294:7 f.); **d̲-npiš usaka litbh̲** (*often*) which is great and endless MG 405:7.

lka (s. **l- 1, ka**) hither, thither. Often. Varr. **lika 2, ʿlka**.

lkimia (Ar. الكميا) AM alchemy, alchemical.

lmahu s. **mahu**.

lma- s. **lima-**.

lʿl = **lia 1** to me. MG 5:22.

lʿ 2 Gs 48:4 = **lia 2** MG 205:20 (the var. is merely graphical, influenced by **lia 1**, and does not indicate a pronunciation **lē*, as Nöld. assumed).

lʿ 1 = **li- 2**.

lʿ 2 = **li- 3**.

lʿuiatan Gy 233:ult. = **liuiatan** MG 5:21.

lʿiil, lʿil s. **lʿl**.

lʿika, lʿka varr. of **lika 1**.

lʿl (לְעֵיל, ܠܥܠ) above, up yonder, on high, up there. Varr. **lʿil** Gy 269:1, Q 29:29 etc. MG 4:21 f., **lʿiil** MG 6:21. **mn lʿl** DC 41. 113 (var. **mn ʿlʿl** 1. 121, **mn ʿlʿil** 473) from above.

lʿlai = **lilai**.

lʿma- = **lima-**.

lʿmat (**l- 1**+**ʿmat**) when. **lʿmat ʿzil** CP 171:10 when shall I set out?

lʿt- = **lit-**. **lʿtlh̲** Gy 31:21 he has not MG 5:22.

lputa (rt. **LUP** = **LPP**) union. **ʿsiqta d̲-bhiṣrh̲ rušuma d̲-lputa** ATŠ II no. 315 the ring on her little finger is a symbol of union.

LPP s. **LUP**.

lprʿiuš zihnag s. **lipriuš ziṣag**.

lqab Zotb. 221 b:15 for **laqab**.

lšan (Ar. الشّان) v.s. **ʿadim lšan**.

lta (**l- 1**+demonstr. **ta**) to that ...: **lta riših̲** DC 27:coloph. up to that beginning.

ltit, ltitai s. **tit**.

M

m the 13th letter of the alphabet. Bilabial nasal liquid: *m*. Phonetic changes: m > b MG § 52 p. 50; m > n ibid.; m < n MG § 53 p. 50; aphaeresis of m MG § 52 p. 50.

m- a mod. of the prep. **mn**. Used proclitically. **mlibai amrit** DC 27. 13 I spoke from my heart.

ma 1 (Gen. Sem.) what, that which, whatever; when MG 94:2, 207:11. Compound forms: **mahu** what; **mahu d̲-** what is that which MG 94:3; **kma** how much, how long; **hakma** id., **alma 3** why, wherefore (s.vv.); **ʿl mahu** why MG 207:11 ff. Used as masc. MG 299:top, as fem. Gy 278:15 f. **l(i)mal-** (with encl. **-l-** + pers. suff.) s.v.; **malak d̲-mšailit ʿlh̲** Gs 70:20 wherefore askest thou about it?; **ma d̲-** that which, how, wherefore; **uma maka ltaqipa titnun** Gy 66:22 why deliver ye a mild one to a strong one?; **mahu paiišna** Gy 391:4 why do I stay?, **mahu gnʿiit . . . umahu škibit** Gy 170:9 why liest thou down . . . and why sleepest thou? MG 342:top; **mahu simaka** Gs 63:3 what kind of support?; **mahu haila** Gs 63:2 what kind of force?; **mahu ʿubadia abadt** Gs 103:1 what kind of works hast thou done?; **mahu nasiqlak šuma** Jb 117:11 f. what kind of name shall we give thee? MG 342:13–16; **lʿ mahu damit** Gy 182:17 what dost thou resemble? MG 342:18; **ana mahu hṭitilh̲** Gy 337:21 in what did I sin against him?; **mahu dilia ʿl dilkun** Gs 97:6 what do I have to do with you?; **ʿbidatkun mahu** Gy 171:19 what are your works?; **mahu ʿbidlun** Gy 337:19 what shall I do to them?; **mahu abadt** Gy 148:20 what hast thou done?; **mn mahu dahilna** Gy 157:13 what am I afraid of? MG 436:bottom; **ma d̲-huat uma d̲-mihuia baiia** Gy 278:15 what was (as fem.) and what shall be; **ʿl ma d̲-bgauaihun** Gy 282:22 about what is in them; **bma d̲-abuia paqdh̲** Gy 268:2 according to what his father ordered him; **uʿbid mahu d̲-baiit** Gy 154:6 and do whatever thou wishest; **ʿl ma d̲-** Gy 283:23 on that which MG 345:4–9; **ma d̲-** 'when', 'as soon as'; **ma d̲-amarilun mimra qam** Gy 235:3 as soon as I spoke the word to them, they arose MG

454:8 (cf. also n. 2 about Gy 92:8 ff. and Lidzb.'s different transl. Ginzā 96:1–4); **mn ma d-bak** Gy 70:16 from that which is on thee; **ma šinta latirham** Gy 214:4 B (varr. . . . **latirhum** Sh. ʿAbd.'s copy, . . . **tirhum** Pet.) do not like any sleep (lit. whatever is sleep).

ma 2 (Gen. Sem.; Talm. מְאָה, אַמְאָה, Syr. ܡܐܐ Brockelm. I 487, Nöld.: *Neue Beitr.* 156, mod. Syr. *mâ & immâ*) hundred. **matin** 200, **tlatma** 300, **arbima** 400, **hamišma** 500, **šitma** 600, **šabima** 700, **tmanima** 800, (ʿ)**tšima** 900 MG 189 f. **ma utmanan** DC 34 one hundred and eighty; **zirh bma d-nasuraiia** CP 46:14, ML 60:11 he sowed it amongst a hundred (?) Naṣoraeans.

ma 3 name of a genie ML 281. **bma rba** CP 20:8, ML 22:5 (= Q 8:8 = DC 3 & 53 no. 15) by the Great Mâ.

mabada (H. & Bibl.-Aram. מַעְבָּד, Syr. ܡܥܒܕܐ) deed, act, work, operation MG 130: 11. Pl. **mabadia, mab(a)data.** ʿ**ubadaikun umabadaikun** Gs 30:10 your works and your deeds, ʿ**bidatkun umabadatkun** Lond. roll B 47 (?), DC 40 (var. **mabdatkun** P.A. xiii) id. **mabadia sainia** DC 12. 94, Lond. roll B 192, Oxf. roll g 965, 1044, DC 40. 113 f., DC 43 foul actions; **uašqia lruha ulmabadia** DC 48 and administer the potion to the 'spirit' (i.e. 'person') and to those who made it (? cf. מְעַבְּדָנָא & foll.).

mabara a var. of mabraia in ʿ**rutai utušbihtai mabraiai** ATŠ II no. 177 (only in DC 6) v.s. **mabraia.**

mabarta (rt. **ABR** = ʿ**BR,** ܡܥܒܪܬܐ) ferry, ferry-boat. Doublet **mambarta** MG 142:2. **mabarta d-nišmata mabra lbit abatur** Jb 206:10 (var. **mambarta** B) a ferry-boat of souls going over to the House-of-Abatur.

mabda (rt. **ABD** = ʿ**BD,** cf. the last ex. s. **mabada**) maker. Pl. st. cstr. **mabdin** ʿ**bidata** Gy 177:5 f, the makers of (made) things.

mabdata a var. of mabadata s. **mabada.**

mabudia DC 43 G 6 a kind of demons (?).

mabuta a miscop. of **mabarta** (?). **iama d-mabuta litbh** (CP 379:5 has **mabra**) q.v. DC 3. 249:ult. a sea in which there is no ferry-boat.

mabra (ܡܥܒܪܐ) ferry, ford, crossing(-place). **kd matia lmabra abruih** Jb 54:6 when he reacheth the crossing(-place) they will take him over; **litlh biama mabra** Jb 102:6 there is no crossing for him in the sea; **d-biama rmilh mabra** Jb 102:11 so that they may place for him a ferryboat in the sea; (**d**)-**ninṭurlia biama mabra** Jb 178:6, Gy 370:6 f. (that) he shall guard for me a ford over the sea; **rmulh mabra bzabia** Gs 101:14 they placed for him a ferryboat in the river; **iama rba d-laiit bgauh mabra** Gs 107:1 the great sea in which there is no ford. Often parallel with **miṣra** 'bridge' MSt 85:middle. Cf. also **mara 2.**

mabraia (adj. from **mabra**) person who, or that which brings, or takes over, MG 141:ult. f. **msakialh lmabraia d-hu riha d-ramit** DC 41. 448 she looks towards that which will ferry her over, which is the Incense which thou castest (on the fire); ʿ**rutai utušbihtai mabraiai** Gs 80:10, Q 65:22 = CP 129:4, ATŠ II no. 177 (var. **mabaraiai** s.v.) my vigilance and praise are my ferrymen (= means of transit).

mag a female demon, the consort of Hag. MMII 89. **had umag** PD 265 = ATŠ I no. 20; **hag umag trin mania d-hšuka** Gy 138: 19 f., 139:7; **hag gabra umag** ʿ**nta** Gy 138:24.

magalta (מְגִילְתָּא, ܡܓܠܬܐ, H. מְגִלָּה, Ar. مَجَلَّة) parchment, scroll, skin. **magalta** Lond. roll B 157, 395, 400; **magalta udiuta** DC 12. 188, Lond. roll B 521, JRAS 1937 595 (= DC 21), DC 40 parchment and ink; **magalta d-ṭabia** JRAS 1937 596 (= DC 21), DC 12. 190 roll of gazelle-skin; **magalta d-mia** DC 43:coloph., DC 42. 69 scroll of gut-skin; **magalta d-bnia anašia** DC 43 F 77 the skin of human beings.

magana (rt. **GNA I**) couch. **br magana** DC 46. 194:12 the son of ease (?).

maghkana (nom. ag. af. of **GHK**) joker, jester. **maghkana hauia** AM 9:4 (var. **mgahkana** Par. xxvi) he will be a joker.

magušaiia (ܡܓܘܫܝܐ, *Μαγουσαῖοι*; cf. Ar. loan-w. المجوس & مجوسى, Avestan *mayu* AIW 1111, OP *maguš*, Pahl. מגושיא Jeffrey 259, Widg. v 193 f.) Gy 388:13 pl. Magians MG 141:8.

magzala (Ar. مَغْزَل) spindle. Mod. **ṣipra umagzala mgaṭrilh** DC 46. 91:6 f. a bird and a spindle shall they tie to him.

magzarṭabaiia Gs 84:5 CD a var. of **gzarṭa-baiia.**

magzirana (nom. ag. af. of **GZR**) a judge who delivers a verdict, or condemns to punishment. Pl. **-ia. biad . . . magzirania latišdinan** ML 139:1 = CP 113:12 cast us not . .. into the hand of the condemning judges; **umagzirania lanagzrin** [*sic*] ʿ**lh** DC 41 nor shall the judges condemn it (: the soul).

maglub (Ar. مغلوب) DC. 46. 10:8 defeated.

magrib (Ar. مَغْرِب) AM 198:8 f. the West; Morocco.

mada (rt. **YDA** = ʿ**DA,** ܡܕܥܐ) knowledge, intelligence, doctrine MG 129:9, Brandt ERE xiii 384. Doublet **manda** s.v. **aprišlh mada ladam** Gy 13:23, 34:22 teach the doctrine to A.; **madai umadihtai dilia** CP 143:8, Oxf. 62 b, 78 b my knowledge and intelligence, **madan umadihtan** Gy 30:12, Oxf. 79 b = ML 252:5 our knowledge and our intelligence, **madun umadihtun** Gy 213:7 f. their knowledge and their intelligence; **madaihun paršia** Gy 22:16 their minds understand; **praš madaiun** Gy 285:11 their minds, understood; **madaihun lapraš** Gs 17:19 id. neg., **madaikun praš** PD 171 your minds understood; **madaiun parišlun**; Gy 43:19, ATŠ their minds understand; **abatur madh praš** ʿ**l ptahil** Gy 168:10 Ab.'s mind examined P.; **galilh uaprišlh madh** ATŠ II no. 99 he revealed and explained his mind; **kd baiit mada hušbana ltrin ahia maiit qudam habrh** AM 157:12 if thou wishest to know by calculation which of two brothers will die before the other; **mada ṭaba** Gs 2:12, 21, 3:7, 4:2, 14, 24, 5:25, 6:5 excellent knowledge.

madai (ܡܕܝ) Media BZ 112 n. 6. **bmdinta madai** AM 182:8; **ṭura d̲-madai** HG 33, 34 (with a frequent var. **midai** HG 6 etc.); **madai d̲-ruha ušuba bna ʿlh̲ lamṣun** HG 21 f. Media which R. and her seven sons could not reach.

madaiia (ܡܕܝܐ) Medes MMII 18 n. 8.

madan name of a town BZ Ap. II s.v. **bmadan mdinta** AM 180:8 (var. **madai** Par. xxvi 211:bottom).

madana in **bit d̲-madana** Ṣâb.'s AM var. of **bidia umadina** AM 205:4.

madaria (cf. s. **MDR**) rottenness?, decay? with many varr. & miscopyings. **madaria ukakia** DC 22. 275 (varr. **ma daria kakia** Gy 279:22, **madran kakia** B, **rma daria** Lond. I, **amadaria** Lond. II) caries of the back teeth (delete u- before **kakia** in DC 22).

madba Q 47:22, Oxf. roll f 730, 746, 916 a doublet of **madbha** MG 43:16, 66:2.

madbha (ܡܕܒܚܐ) altar MG 46:15, 66:2. A more frequent doublet **madba** s.v. **bit madbha** Gy 227:6 sanctuary.

madudia a miscop. of **midurtia 2** (q.v.).

maduria (rt. **MDR**?; cf. Syr. ܡܕܘܪܐ) rotten? Doubtf. **nitpaša kd̲ bita maduria** DC 44. 99 will be squashed like a rotten egg (?).

madurtia (**madurth̲**) rt. **DUR** deposit? housing? settlement? **mn zma ʿṣṭarar umn mazruta madurtia huat** ATŠ II no. 123 formed of blood and from the semen, its deposit (?) took place (i.e. marrow in bones).

madihta (rt. **YDA**) discernment, perception, intelligence, understanding, comprehension, judgement, opinion; character, nature. MG 16:20, 72:3, 129:antep. Doublet **madita** s.v. Used often with **mada** q.v. Further: **madihta lman ʿtiahbat lman ʿtiahbat madihta** CP 384:3 perception, to whom was it given; on whom was perception bestowed? **aprišth̲ ʿl madihth̲** Gy 306:1 I taught his understanding; **amud mṣa hailh̲ umadihth̲** ATŠ II no. 409 as his ability and judgement permitted; **bla madihta** DC 46. 83:11 without understanding.

madina (مدينة) AM 197 Medinah.

madiqta (ܡܕܝܩܬܐ) mortar, or a pounded substance. **ramin madiqta d̲-hina** Or. 326:20 (= DC 47), Oxf. roll g 619 putting in a mortar for henna, (or pounded henna?).

madita a doublet of **madihta** (q.v.). **umadita šra lrahmh̲** DC 26. 243 and knowledge dwelt upon him who loveth it; **ʿuṣrh̲ umadith̲** Gy 156:23 his mind and his knowledge; **ʿruta umadita** Gy 157:20 piety and knowledge; **šabata d̲-kulh̲ madita** Gy 273:1 scrolls of all wisdom.

madna 1 (מַדְנָח, ܡܕܢܚ, emph. ܡܕܢܚܐ) (*a*) rising, east, (*b*) (astrol. term) horoscope, astrological conditions of birth. MG 17:13. Pl. **madnia.** (*a*) **mn madna batraiia hšub šuba madnia utida d̲-hak madna šubaia uṭaliʿ d̲-šidta hu** AM 196:5 ff. count seven risings from the last rising and thou wilt know from that seventh rising what will be the governing Sign (of the Zodiac) for the year; **mn marba . . . lmadna** DC 43 F 87 from west . . . to east; Doublet **madnaha** (s.v.); (*b*) **amar madnia** AM 152:11 the astrological aspect; **ʿnta d̲-madna aria** Ṣâb.'s AM a woman whose astrological constellation is Leo.

madna 2 (ܡܕܢܐ?) storehouse. **anašia d̲-madna pqadia** AM 247:15 people in charge of the storehouse (doubtful; probably **madan**).

madnaha, midnaha (cf. **madna 1**) (*a*) rising, east (doublet of **madna**), (*b*) illumination, source of light. (*a*) **mn madnaha lmasmikana umn masmikana alma lmadnaha mšabia** DC 51. 300 ff. they praise from uprising to down-lying, and from down-lying to uprising; (*b*) **anatun hun madnaha btibil** Jb 235:7 ye shall be the source of light in the world; **ʿšria nura lmidnaha** DC 12. 53 = P.A. xii par. fire (: prob. light) be loosed (from spells) for the dawn = let dawn fire the east

madpan DC 43 a demon.

mahabata (rt. **AHB** = **YHB**) pl. gifts. Varr. **mahbata, muh(a)bata** s.vv. **mahabata uqurbana iahbilia** DC 44. 582 they give me gifts and a present.

mahamad (مُحَمَّد) Muhammad MG xxxiii 12, MSchr. 49 n. 2. **mahamad lmahdia ṣahib lzaman** Zotb. 218 b:11 f. translit. of مُحَمَّد ٱلْمَهْدِيّ صاحب ٱلزَّمان; **mahamad lmiša mšalaṭ** DAb M. has dominion over Moses; **mahamad br bizbaṭ arbaia** Gy 61:7 cf. Jb ii 193 n. 3.

mahamaṭ see preced. **mahamaṭ arbaia** Gy 302:15, 16 f.

mahan a *malwâša* man's name.

mahbana (rt. **AHB** = **YHB**) gifts, bounty, charity. **umahbana mn bnia akil** AM 44:11 and will live on his son's bounty.

mahbata a var. of **mahabata**. **mahbata iahbilia** DC 26. 566 they give me presents.

mahga, mahgia (< *מַגְהָא, *מָגְהָא, Syr. ܡܓܗܐ) dawn(ing), break of day, early morning MG 66:23. **qadim qum bʿ(u)spar mahgia** Gy 197:3 get up early at break of day!

mahda (ܡܗܕܝܐ?) first, before all? Doubtf.; read **mahra** (ܡܗܪܐ) instructed, as in varr. **mahda titrabia** AM 54:19 first (?) she will get her education (?).

mahd(u)rinia occasional var. of foll.

mahdur(i)niata (rt. **HDR I**) whorls MG 21:6, circular marks. **utartin mahduriniata ʿtlh̲ briših̲** AM 1:14 (var. **mahdirinata**) and there are two whorls on his head; **mahdurniata nihuilh̲ briših̲ udraiia** AM 85:14 and he will have whorls on his head and arms.

mahdurta (rt. **HDR I**) AM 261:22 circle.

mahdia (Ar. مَهْدِيّ) s. **mahamad.**

mahdirinata s. **mahdurn(i)ata.**

mahdurinia occasional var. of foll.

mahdruniata, -iniata (rt. **HDR I**) whirlwinds, whirlpools MG 138:10 & n. 3. **mahdruniata** (var. **-iniata**) **d̲-mṭaba** Gy 277:19 whirlpools that drown.

mahu (הו + מא) s. **ma** 1.

mahuza (מְחוֹזָא, ܡܚܘܙܐ, cf. Ar. حوز) town, small walled city or village MG 130:21. Pl. **mahuzia.** Masc. **mn mahuza lmahuza** AM 22:10 f. from town to town; **babil mahuza** AM 216:9; **umahuzia bihdadia niplun** AM 169:12 and towns will attack each other; **umahuzia nigirbun** AM 178:14 and towns will be plundered; **ulkulhun mahuzia ḏ-hiziun ldilai** DC 26. 563 = DC 44. 570 and all (walled) villages (acc.) which beheld me.

mahuna (Lidzb. compares with μάγγανον and μηχανή Jb ii 98 n. 3) a doubtf. word: prob. trap, pit, some instrument for catching and tormenting Lidzb. loc. cit. Pl. **-ia** often constructed as sg. (ʿ)**trin mahunia** Jb 155:11 two machines (Lidzb.), **mahunia taumia** Jb 97:8, 159:8, 247:9 Lidzb. *Doppelmaschinen*, **mahunia taumia ḏ-krat ruha bʿuhra** Gs 107:4, 12, ATŠ II no. 13 the twin pits that R. dug in the highway (cf. Nöld. ZA 30 149); **nkila damia lmahunia ḏ-mṭalal bnikla** Gy 216:1 the cunning person resembleth a pit (or trap?) that is covered over by guile; **aṣaṣia umahunia** Gs 26:14 pitfalls (?) and pits (?).

mahzaia (rt. **HZA**) beholder, onlooker, spectator. Pl. **-iia. banpia hazaia umahzaia** DC 51 in the presence of every spectator and beholder; **hazaiia umahzaiia** s. **hzaia.**

mahzur(a) daiua ZDMG 105 145 b:9 a demon. CP 372:9; CP trs. 246 n. 1.

mahzian malala CP 442:5, DC 41. 128, Morg. 7:10.

mahziʿil malala (cf. preced.) CP 291:4, Morg. 116:4 name of a spirit. **mahziʿil malala . . . mahzita bainai** M. the Word . . . vision in my eyes.

mahzita (rt. **HZA**) sight, vision, gaze, visible sign (?); Nöld. mirror MG 129:ult. **umbasar usnia mahzita ḏ-aina** AM 18:15 and contemptuous and hostile is the glance (or gaze) of his eye; **mahzita ḏ-nišimta** ATŠ II no. 153 the vision of the soul; **mahzita ḏ-liba** ATŠ I no. 245 the vision of the heart; **biuma ḏ-mahzita tiqnat bainia** CP 347:18 on the day that the vision was realized in his eyes (?); **mahzita ḏ-bkulhun razia tiqnat** DC 27 a visible sign (?) that qualified for all the mysteries; **anat mahzitan dilan** ATŠ II no. 423 thou art our vision; **lašira** [*sic*] **mahzitun ḏ-nihzunh** ATŠ their sight shall not be opened that they may see him.

mahiana (ܡܚܝܢܐ) life-giver, saviour. An expression borrowed from Syr. MG xxix 20, 138:10. **ʿšu mahiana** Gy 28:17 Jesus the Saviour MG 268:antep. f. **šumh ʿšu mahiana qaria lnapšh** Gy 52:3 his name is Jesus, he calleth himself a saviour.

mahilia pl. (ܡܚܝܠܐ) weakly, sickly, infirm persons. **sama gaia ḏ-mhilia** DC 48 splendid medicine for the sickly.

mahim (rt. **HUM** = **HMM**) heated, melted. **alita mahim** DC 46 heated (or melted) sheep's tail fat.

mahiqa (act. pt. af. of **HUQ**) oppressor, tormenter. Pl. **-ia** used of a kind of demons. DC 43 J 28 **mahiqa br mahiqia** DC 51. 69; **mahiqia ulaṭabia** DC 26. 50 s. **laṭaba.**

mahiqana (nom. act. af. of **HUQ**) oppressor, tormenter, torturer. In DAb used as a name of Sin (**umahiqana šumh**). Pl. **mahiqania** CP 113:13, ML 138:14, 139:1, ATŠ II no. 145 etc.

mahla for **mihla**?, or from حلّ dilution? in **bla mahla** DC 46 unsalted? or undiluted?

mahnuš (P. pr. n.) a *malwâša* woman's name.

mahqaiil (theophorous name from **mahiqa**) DC 44 a demon.

mahra 1 (rt. **HRR III**) illness, sickness MG 61:2, 129:5. Pl. **mahria,** later also **mahraria** MG 170:9 f. **ʿšata umahra** DC 46 fever and illness; **ʿu mabar halin mahraria** AM 8:11 if he gets over these illnesses.

mahra 2 (cf. **mhara 2**) pot: **utbariun mahra.** ŠQ 6:4 and break the pot; **utabrin mahra tiniana** ŠQ 8:9 and they break the second pot.

mahrauan AM 204 a place-name BZ Ap. II.

mahramir Jb 75:3 a pr. name.

mahranita fem. (adj. from **mahra** 1) ill. **kṣurta umahranita hauia** AM 74:13 she will be sickly and ill.

mahranta DC 41 (twice under figure of tree or plant) name of a shrub or plant.

mahraria a pl. of **mahra** 1 (q.v.).

mahria Zotb. 231 a:15 (read **mahdia**) a pers. name.

mahšin (ܡܚܫܢܐ) (for **mahšan**?) **ainih mahšin** DC 46 his eyes are painful.

mahta (מַחְתְּיָא?) firepan. **kḏ mahta qaria uraṭna nura** AM 253:16 when the firepan makes a noise and the fire murmurs.

maudala (rt. **YDL**) birth, child-bearing MG 74:12, 130:12. **atra ḏ-bit maudala** AM 57:17 her birth-place; **kana ḏ-kulh maudala** DC 51 the place which is all birth.

mauiana (cf. interj. **uai**; formed as nom, ag. af.) howler? **mauiana šidana** PD 807 furious howler (?).

mauka (rt. **MUK** = **MKK**) bedding. Pl. **-ia** DC 48. 231. Var. **muka 2** s.v.

maukala, -ila (act. pt. af. of **AKL I**) one who feeds, dispenses food: **maukala** (var. **maukila**) **umašqia anašia hauia** AM 72:10 she will dispense food and drink to people.

maukalta (rt. **AKL I,** ܡܐܟܘܠܬܐ) food. Pl. **maukalata. mn maukalata ṭabauata šapirata . . . lamšalṭia lmikal** Gy 227:22 f. they are not allowed to eat . . . from good tasteful foods; **umn bisrh šaun tlatma ušitin maukalata** ATŠ I no. 249 (DC 36, DC 6 has **makalata**) and of its flesh they made 360 viands.

maukil (rt. **AKL I**) fare, food offered **maukil marira ḏ-qudam bišia mištamalun** ATŠ II no. 370 bitter fare delivered to the wicked.

maulana (nom. ag. af. of **YBL**) one who brings, bears. **maulana ḏ-adakas mana hu nihuilh naṭra** Gy 102:6 he who bringeth A.-M., he (shall) be her guard (doubtf. Ginzā 110 footn.).

maumiaiil (theophorous name from pt. af. of **YMA**) DC 40. 818 (and often in exorcisms) an angel.

mauʿtadil (Ar. مُعْتَدِل) AM 258:18 moderate. Var. **muʿtadil.**

mauṣil AM 204:paen. name of a town, prob. Mosul. Var. **miṣil** Ṣâb.'s AM.

mauš Ṣâb.'s AM a place-name, var. of **mašuš** AM 205:19.

mautba (rt. **YTB,** ܡܘܬܒܐ) site. **mautba d̲-mdinta** AM 223:3 the site of the city.

mazaruta a var. of **mazruta.**

mazgda 1 = **masgda.** Pl. **-ia. bit mazgdaikun** Gy 227:4 B (var. **masgdaikun** ACD) your house of worship MG 45:5 f.; **bit mazgdaihun** DC 43 J 13 in their house(s) of worship; **šuqia umazgdia** DC 46 mosques and streets. Cf. RD 17, 18.

mazgda 2 (from زغد to groan? BZ 171 n. 2) groan(ing). Doubtf. Pl. **-ia. mazgdia uharbia** AM 267:27 groans (?) and wars.

mazuz (H. מָגוֹג, Ar. ماجوج Qur. 18:93) Magog. **hazuz umagug** AM 200 s. **hazuz.**

maznihanita (cf. H. זנח 'to cleanse'; possibly related to **ZLH**?) cleansing. **mihla azizta maznihanita** DC 40. 902 f. powerful and cleansing salt.

mazruta (rt. **ZRA**) seed, semen; sowing, dissemination, semination MG 145:3. **ašar qum bmazrutak** ML 226:3 = CP 191:12 (var. **bmazarutak** DC 3) stand firm, rise up with thy seed (?, Lidzb. *verharre standhaft in deiner Sicherung,* which would suppose **mzahranuta**); **mambuha d̲-qaninia mazruta hʿ** ATŠ II no. 32 the water in the phials is semen; **qanina d̲-gauaia mazruta d̲-hu aba** DC 36 no. 188 the inner phial is the seed—that is the Father; **kd̲ mazruta napla bmarba** ATŠ I no. 168 like semen falling into the womb; **haial kbar raza d̲-mazruta hu** ATŠ II 385 'Mighty Strength (?)' is the mystery of semination; **halin tlata ziria mazruta d̲-zma uʿuṣṭuna** DC 34 those three seeds are the sowing of blood and body; **mazruta dakita** DAb pure seed.

maṭahiata (מַטְחָתָא) pl. loins, kidneys. **ruha hʿ d̲-iatba lmaṭahiata** Or. 329:29 (= DC 47), Oxf. roll g 828, the (evil) spirit that is situated on the loins.

maṭaraia (adj. from **maṭra, maṭarta,** Syr. ܡܛܪܝܐ) watcher MG 141:ult. Pl. **maṭaraiia** purgatory-dwellers, purgatory-demons. **zihira damia lmaṭaraia d̲-kušṭa** Gy 215:5 a prudent one resembleth a true watcher; **hauqa d̲-maṭaraiia** Q 21:22 the fright of the purgatory-demons; **zangaiia umaṭaraiia** s. **zangaiia, ʿtirkin maṭaraiia** Gy 362:10 s. **RKN; npal maṭaraiia** Gy 362:11; **mahu timirulun lmaṭaraiia** Gy 377:5 what shall ye say to the purgatory-demons?; **gziraiia umaṭaraiia** s. **gziraiia** (*a*); **maṭaraiia ugziraiia** Gs 84:11; **lišimṭan mn maṭaraiia** Gs 96:7 he may free us from the purgatory-demons; **šdinum lmaṭaraiia** Gs 124:7 he cast down the purgatory-demons; **parqan mn maṭaraiia** DC 3 deliver me from purgatory-demons; **halin maṭaraiia d̲-brušuma d-hiia lamašria** DAb those purgatory-dwellers that are not freed by the Seal of Life; **maṭaraiia bnpiš** CP 276:12 watchers are many.

maṭarta (rt. **NṬR,** Syr. ܡܛܪܬܐ, Akk. *manṣartu, maṣṣartu* Zimmern, *Akk. Fremdw.* 16, 64) watch, vigil; place of detention, prison, purgatory MG 51:9, 129:23, Lidzb. *Wachthaus.* St. abs. **maṭra 1** MG 17:13, 51:9, 238 n. 2. Pl. **maṭarata.** Pet.: RD ii 452:bottom; Brandt: MR 61, 74, JPTh xviii 408 ff.; Bousset ThR xx 197 f.; Pedersen: *Bidrag,* 122 ff.; Reitzenstein: MBHG 80 ff.; Lidzb. ZS ii 181 ff.; Pallis: MSt 78 ff.; Widg. ii 35. iii 63; MMII 179 ff.; Siouffi 15:top, 61, 124 n. 3. **maṭra d̲-bnia šlama** Gy 91:7 the watch of the sons of peace; **maṭra d̲-ruha** Gy 362:9, Gs 90:1 the purgatory of R.; **maṭra d̲-mardia qaimia ʿlh̲** Gs 107:2 f. the purgatory in which rebels exist; **maṭarata** (pl.) **d̲-mardia qaimia ʿlh̲** Gs 107:10; **maṭra d̲-šuba** Q 53:1, Gs 89:19 ff. the purgatory of the Seven (Planets); **maṭra d̲-šamiš** Gs 89:4, **maṭra d̲-sira** Gs 89:9 ff., **maṭra d̲-nura** Gs 89:14 f. the purgatory of Sun, Moon, Fire; **maṭarta d̲-anuš** RD C 4, **maṭarta d̲-bihram** RD C 3, **maṭarta d̲-bhaq** RD C 12, **maṭarta d̲-bil** RD C 19, 23, 24, **maṭarta d̲-ginziʿil** RD C 6, **maṭarta d̲-hibil** RD C 5, **maṭarta d̲-habšaba** RD C 2, 27, 28, **maṭarta d̲-kiuan** RD C 13, 20, **maṭarta d̲-kalbia** Gy 180:7, **maṭarta d̲-libat** RD C 24, 25, **maṭarta d̲-nbu** RD C 16, 21, 23, **maṭarta d̲-nbaṭ** RD C 11, **maṭarta d̲-nirig** RD C 14, 20, 21, 37, **maṭarta d̲-sin** RD C 25, 26, **maṭarta d̲-nbaz** Gy 208:3, Gs 27:15, **maṭarta d̲-zan** Gy 208:14, **maṭarta d̲- ʿuat** Gy 209:1, **maṭarta d̲-himun** Gy 209:16, **maṭarta d̲-ptahil** RD C 1, Gy 209:14, **maṭarta d̲-abatur** Gy 210:7, Q 30:18, **maṭarta d̲-abatur rama** Gy 194:24, **maṭarta d̲-ptahil qadiša** Gy 194:8, **maṭarta d̲-ragaziʿil** RD C 8, **maṭarta d̲-šamiš** RD C 26, 27, **maṭarta d̲-šarhabʿil** RD C 9, **maṭarta d̲-šitil** RD C 15, 17 (different purgatories), **maṭarta d̲-ptula pt abu** Gy 181:1 f. the purgatory of the damsel the daughter of her father; **bhanath̲ maṭarta haqit** Gy 180:11 in that purgatory I was afraid; **adith̲ lhanath̲ maṭarta** Gy 181:13 f., 182:9 etc. I passed through that purgatory, **maṭit maṭarta hurintin** Gy 181:16, 183:4 I came to another purgatory, **maṭit maṭarta d̲-iur uiahur uarhum** Gy 182:11; **haza maṭarta d̲-man ulman naṭra hʿ** Gy 182:12 whose purgatory is this and whom doth it keep there?, similarly Gy 183:6; **maṭarata d̲-šibiahia** Gy 287:2 the purgatories of the Planets, **maṭarata d̲-šuba kukbia** Gy 363:17 the purgatories of the Seven Stars; **maṭarta d̲-arba gubria** Q 30:31 the purgatory of the four men; **maṭarata d̲-ptahil** Gy 321:14 purgatories of P.; **šaba maṭarata** RD B 89 the seven purgatories, **maṭarata d̲-šaba šibiahia** RD E 15 purgatories of the Seven Planets; **hauqa d̲-maṭarata** RD C 28 fear of the purgatories; **sigia d̲-maṭarata** RD D 3, 9 ff. progress through (?) places of detention; **bit maṭarata d̲-šibiahia** Gy 290:13 in the purgatories of the Planets; **parqan mn maṭarata** Gy 364:13 free me from the purgatories; **maṭarta kumria zibia uadidia** Gs 27:19 f. (cf. s. **adidia**); **bhurintin maṭarta** Gs 28:4 in another purgatory; **bihda maṭarta**

Gs 29:16 in one purgatory; **bhaza maṭarta** Gs 30:20 etc. (*often*) in this purgatory; **haza maṭarta ḏ-qra ptahil** Gs 30:19 this purgatory which P. created; **tlata maṭarata ḏ-lilia** Lond. roll B 125, **tlat maṭarata ḏ-lilia** CP 51:18, Q 24: 4 = ML 67:6 the three watches of the night.

maṭu, maṭut, emp. maṭuta (מְטוּתָא, ܡܛܘܬܐ) favour, leniency, clemency, graciousness, kindness, grace MG 145:18. Sometimes mistakenly used as masc. MG 161:23 f. **bmaṭu tihuia ˁlan** Gy 171:20 (var. **bmaṭut** DC 22. 165) be thou lenient to us, **tihuia bmaṭut ˁlan** Jb 163:7 id. **anat hˁ ˁlai bmaṭuta** Gy 87:2 f. be thou lenient to me; **maṭuta lanihuia ˁl šibiahia** Gy 119:14 there shall be no clemency for the Planets MG 161:23 f.; **tihuia bmaṭuta ˁlai** Gy 194:15 thou wilt show me favour; **bmaṭuta huit ˁlh̲** Gy 169:21 I showed him favour; **bmaṭuta h̲-hiia libaihun lahauia hasir ubaṣir** DC 7 by grace of the Life there shall be nothing lacking or deficient in their hearts; **butak utušbihtak tiqum bmaṭut ˁlak** DC 50. 422, DC 50. 422 thy prayer and thy praise will bring thee grace; **tiqum bmaṭut ˁlauaikun** CP 42:30, ML 51:5 will bring you grace.

maṭin (ܡܛܝܢ) rt. **ṬAN** weighty heavy? **kt dahba maṭin** ATŠ II 258 like heavy gold.

maṭra 1 s. maṭarta.

maṭra 2 occ. var. of miṭra.

maṭraiia occasionally for **maṭaraiia.**

maṭraqia (מַטְרְקָא, ܡܛܪܩܐ) thongs, whip, goad(s). **kḏ maṭraqia tišuaq** Morg. 263/16:3 (var. **maṭraria** 1 DC 44. 1040) like goads she drives on.

maṭraria 1 a var. of **maṭraqia** (q.v.).

maṭraria 2 occ. var. of **miṭraria** 1 a (pl. of **miṭra**).

maṭrur ? Zotb. 226 b:22 a family name.

maṭta DC 22. 114 for **maṭuta** Gy 119:14.

mai (a sg. form of mia q.v., cf. H. מַי, Ar. ماء, South-Ar. ⲙⲩ, Eth. ማይ, Akk. *mû*) water MG 10 n. 3, 97:17. Pl. mia s.v., rarely **maia** 1 MG 10:11, 184:8. The full form **mai-** is regularly used with suff.: **maiaihun, maiaiun** Gy 287:15, AM 244:1 their water, **maiaikun** Gy 221:18 (both with bad varr.) MG 184:9. Impossible to prove whether **mai** was constructed as a sg. MG 184:6 f. **binia mai lmai** Gy 204:22, Jb 79:13, 80:6, 161:10 between waters (lit. between water and water); **lhamai umaiai** DC 12. 145, 40. 934 my bread and my water; **umaiaihun amšia bhazin ainia** DC 7 and their waters mingle with these springs; **maiaiun mariria** ATŠ II no. 85, 306 their sap is bitter; **arba maiia ˁria hinun** ATŠ I no. 218 they are four fluids mingled.

maia 1, maiia s. mai. Exceptional scr. pl. of mia 1, used in Gy 12:18 B, 212:16 B, 337:12 B, MG 10:11.

maia 2 Sh. ʿAbd.'s copy's var. of **mˁia** Gy 84:2.

maian AM 197 name of a town BZ Ap. II.

mairana (nom. ag. af. of **AUR I** = **ˁUR I**) CP 145:1, ML 173:7 awakener.

maimun a *malwâša* man's name. **iahia maimun** AM 255:34, Zotb. 217 b:16.

maina (mod. form of **mai, mia**) water. Var. **mi(i)na. kalba ḏ-maina** AM 131:14 an otter; **kdub bmaina ḏ-rauan** DC 46 write in flowing water; **haurih̲ anpih̲ bmaina** DC 46. 151:5 wash her face in water; **maina bainh̲ naplilh̲** AM 49:12 wateriness will attack his eyes.

maka 1 (for **mˁiaka, miaka**) Gy 81:1, 164:12 is there? MG 209:8, 296:3, there is not. **atra ḏ-maka nšia** (?) **ugabaruta** DC 34. 691 a place where there are no women and no manhood.

maka 2 (rt. **MKK,** for **mika**) mild, weak MG 108:4. **uma maka ltaqipa titnun** Gy 66:22 and why deliver ye a weak one to a strong one? MG 342:4 f.; **umaka ltaqipa latat nun** Gy 14:18 and deliver not a weak one to a strong one.

maka 3 (مَكَّة) AM 197 Mecca.

makaba (rt. **KAB** = **KIB**?, cf. H. מַכְאוֹב, Syr. ܡܟܐܒܘܬܐ) affliction? **makaba siaua** Oxf. roll. 243, DC 43 J 112 black melancholy?

makalta, makulta (ܡܐܟܘܠܬܐ & varr.) food MG 17:10, 129:ult. **hrh̲ šauilh̲ makulth̲** Gy 91:2 I made his excrements his food; **hinun nihuilak makultak** Gy 87:22 they will be thy food.

makuta (מְכוּתָא, ܡܟܘܬܐ Brockelm. ZA xvii 254 f., Akk. *makua*) raft, punt, (flat-bottomed) boat Jb ii 152 n. 5. Pl. **makuata. haka truṣ makutaikun** Jb 149:7 here set up (: build) your boat; **kḏ baiit mibnia makuta** AM 159:ult. if thou desirest to build a raft; **bmakuata ḏ-qira** DC 43 in bitumen-boats; **ˁu napiq bˁuhra ḏ-makuta ṭaba udišuara maṭilh̲** AM 159:4 if he sets out on a journey by boat, he will drown or meet with disaster; **bmakuata ḏ-hualu** DC 35:coloph. in their boats.

makṭauata (cf. مَقْثُوَة & مَقْثَاة cucumber-field) pl. cucumbers?, gourds? **marua umakṭauata uqaina** DC 6 sage and cucumbers (?) and (sugar-)cane.

makika (rt. **MKK,** ܡܟܝܟܐ) meek, humble. Pl. **-ia.** Var. **mkika** s.v. **hun mikia umakikia** DC 22. 19 (var. **makikia** Gy 20:6) be ye meek and humble.

makisa (pt. af. of **KSS II**) confounded, confuted, rebuked, rebutted. **ˁkisa umakisa** DC 12. 237, Lond. roll B 489 (& often in exorcisms) confounded and rebutted.

makisana (nom. ag. from preced.) chastizer. Pl. **-ia. gubria makisania** Morg. 200:3, 9, 262/15:4, 9 = DC 44.

makla (rt. **NKL**) perfidy, strategy, fraud. Pl. **-ia. uniklun bmakl(i)a** AM 195:1 (var. Par. xxvi **unikla bmakla**) and they will engage in intrigue; **bnikla makla nigṭil** AM 195:1 will be killed by perfidy.

maklub (rt. **KLB,** Ar. مَكْلُوب) rabid, a rabid dog DC 46.

makluzana (Syr. ܡܟܪܙܢܐ) town-crier MG 30 n. 2:ult., 55:6. Pl. **-ia. minilia ḏ-hakima lsakla aiak makluzania** (var. **-na** DC 22, Leid.) **lharaša** Gy 217:25 words of a wise man to a fool are like the town-crier to the deaf man.

makna (rt. **KUN** I = **KNN** II, H. מָכוֹן, Ar. مكان) shelter, lodging MG 82:22, 129:10. **makna udaura** Gy 42:21 shelter and lodging.

maksa (*a*) מִכְסָא, ܡܟܣܐ, H. מֶכֶס, Akk. *miksu*, Ar. loan-w. مَكْس Fränkel 283, (*b*) ܡܟܣܐ, Akk. *mākisu*, *makkasu*, Ar. مَاكِس, مَكَّاس). (*a*) penalty, due, fine, tax, custom, (*b*) tax-collector, customs official MG 113:1. Pl. **-ia**. MSchr. 34 n. 2. (*a*) **maksia d̠-mahuzia niplun batraiun** AM 249:ult. the taxes of the towns will fall into arrears; **bit maksia** Gy 19:15, Gs 77:10, 108:1 custom-house Ginzā 21 n. 5; (*b*) **rab maksia** Q 39:19, 43:1, 56:21, Gs 108:1, 12, 121:24 the chief customs official MG 186:paen. (used as both sg. and pl.); **ʿdaihun d̠-maksia** Gs 54:21 the hands of the tax-collectors; **gziraiia umaṭaraiia umaksia** and **maṭaraiia ugziraiia umaksia** s. **gziraiia**; **trisar maksia rišaihun kabšia** DC 41. 466 the twelve customs officials (: planets) bow their heads.

maksab (Ar. مَكْسَب) AM 282:19 profit, gain.

maksana occasionally for **makisana**.

makruhin (varr. **mikrhin, makhirun**) s. **KRH**.

makšilana (nom. ag. af. from **KŠL**) one that strikes to the ground, hurtles upon, makes stumble, brings to a fall. Pl. **-ia**. **aria makšilana** Gy 297:22 f. the pouncing lion; **ariauata mhamblania makšilania** Gy 181:17 f. destructive pouncing lions.

mal, mala 1 (Ar. مال) property, wealth MG xxxiii:15. Pl. **malia 1**. **laargba ulamala lahauia** Gs 129:10 f. has neither money nor property (did originally **minuna** stand in the place of **mala**?, cf. Nöld. loc. cit.); **pasat malh̠** Gy 94:9, 95:4 f. (var. **-a** Sh. 'Abd.'s copy); **pasat malah̠** Gy 95:26, 96:1 she destroyed her property (? Ginzā 99 n. 1); **ʿpus malai** Gy 95:3 I will destroy my property (?); **pasit malai** Gy 97:1 I destroyed my property (?); **ʿz umal** AM 254:17 power and wealth; **lʿdh̠ malia napša umalia mn ʿnta armalta maška** AM 19:6 many possessions will pass into his hand and he will get property from a widow-woman.

mala 2 (rt. **ALL I**, מֶעָלָא, ܡܥܠܐ) entering. ʿ**malak ulmipqak** Gy 365:5 f. at thine incoming and at thine outgoing Ginzā 387 n. 2.

malaha (מַלָּחָא, ܡܠܚܐ, مَلَّاح < Akk. *malaḫu* < Sum.?) sailor, navigator, mariner, steersman, pilot MG 120:14. Pl. **malahia**. **spinta d̠-lamalaha** Gy 216:24 a ship without a mariner; **malahia bliqia** s. **bliqa**.

malahua, var. **malahuata** DC 43, Qašt. 125 name of a water-spirit.

malauata a kind of evil spirits, pl. of **maluaita** (q.v.). **ʿutra d̠-rahiṭ malauata d̠-baita ulamiṭiuih̠** DC 51. 20 an uthra who fled from the haunting spirits of the House (: the world) and they could not overtake him.

malaia (nom. ag. pe. of **MLA**) Fulfiller, Provider, Supplier. **rba malaia** Morg. 179:9, 180:7 Great Supplier, Great Fulfiller.

malaiia (rt. **MLA**) fullness. Varr. **mlaiia** and **amlaiia** (s.v.). **malaiia d̠-alma** Gy 82:8, Gs 88:3, 119:23, 120:4, **mlaiia d̠-alma** Gy 82:17, 90:8, 12, Gs 115:7 fullness of the world, the pleroma of the cosmos.

m(a)laka (Gen. Sem., cf. Ges. s. מַלְאָךְ, LS s. ܡܠܐܟܐ) angel, devil. A loan-w. MG 129 n. 1. Used of both good and evil spirits, but preferably of the evil Brandt: MR 197; Lidzb.: Uthra und Malakha., OSt 537–545, ML xvi; Siouffi 42; MMII 94 n. 2. Pl. **-ia**. Good angels are preferably indicated as **malka**, pl. **-ia** (q.v.). **bnia šlama mlakia** Gy 356:7; **mlakia naṭria** Gy 331:17; **malakia** Q 8:15, Gy 10:1, 45:9, 85:17, 167:17, 174:7, Lond. roll B 42 etc. **piriapil malaka** CP 18:1 = Q 7:9, 19, 8:31; **mn buria . . . mn malakia** Gy 81:2; **malakia d̠-rugza** Q 54:10; **malakia ugabaria** Gy 148:1; **malakia d̠-nhura** Gy 19:19, 31:6, 38:10, 44:21, 57:23 etc., cf. **ʿutria umalkia d̠-nhura** Gy 20:4, **trin malakia d̠-minai** Gy 27:6; **alma d̠-malakia** Gs 17:16; **trisar malakia** Gy 272:11; **kariuta d̠-malakia** Gs 45:17 f., 46:12 f.; **mlakia sainia** Gs 55:12; **šuba mlakia d̠-mšalṭia lbnh̠ anaša** Par. xxvii 39 b seven 'angels' who govern the children of men; **mlakia d̠-asuta** Par. xxviii 21 a; **malakia d̠-ziua** Gy 7:23, 8:1 ff., 32:3 ff. etc.; **mlakia qadišia umhaimnia** Par. xxiv 3 b (where **qadišia** preserved its original meaning); **malakia d̠-hšuka** Morg. 257/6:10; **tlata malakia** Gy 13:1, 33:10; **mlakia d̠-rhamta** Morg. 197:1; **malakia baita** Gy 241:4 (**baita** = the world); **malakia d̠-husrana** Gy 24:4, 46:22, 47:15, 54:10 ff. etc.; **malakia d̠-tušbihta** Gy 31:7, 34:18; **trin malakia** Gy 13:22, 195:9; **anat utrin malakia** Gy 34:21; **malakia d̠-nura** Gy 12:22, 13:11, 33:2 ff. etc.; **šuba malakia masṭiania** Gy 50:24; **ʿutria umalakia** Gy 13:22 etc.; **malakia haria** Gy 42:7; **bišuta d̠-mlakia** Gy 254:3; **mlakia d̠-mšalṭia bʿšumia** Gy 263:7 angels which are in charge of the heavens; **ʿpikia m(a)lakia** Gs Gs 107:23 f. perverted angels; **mlakia d̠-gabaruata** Gy 354:2 Lidzb.: *Mand. Gl.* Very frequent in exorcisms.

malakta (מַלְכְּתָא, ܡܠܟܬܐ) queen MG 101:9. **qin malakta marta d̠-hšuka** Gy 140:2 Q., the Queen, mistress of Darkness; **anat tihuia malkan udlibat tihuia malaktan** Gy 172:3 thou shalt be our king and Dlibat our queen.

malala (rt. **MLL**, by syncope from **mamlala** q.v.) word, speech, the Word (: λόγος), used often as an attribute of higher beings. MG 79:4, 129:5. Pl. **malalia** MG 79:10. MSchr. 43 n. 2; Widg. iii 57. Var. **mlala**. Doublets **mamlala, mamla**. **malalai** Gy 16:8 BD my word; **malala qadmaia** Gy 26:20 the First Word; **qiriuih̠ lbušan umalalan uʿtiqria malala d̠-hiia** Gy 292:8 he (: the Life) called him (: Yawar-Ziwa) 'Our Garment' and 'Our Word' and he was called 'Word-of-Life'; **malala npaqlun** Gy 292:10 the Word came out to Him (: the Life); **ana bmalalh̠ d̠-ab lkun qrit** Gy 292:16 I have created you by the Word of my Father; **iauar malala qrita rhimta qadmaita d̠-hiia** Gy 295:7 f. Yawar, the Word, the first beloved creation of Life; **malalia nihia** Gy 19:22 gentle words; **malalia ḏ-bhun mistakra uauda nišmatun** Gy 25:4 words by which the souls are imprisoned and perish; **ulaiahiblun malala** DC 43 and he vouchsafes to them no word; **malala dakia lnišimta mithiblḫ** ATŠ the pure Word is vouchsafed to the soul; **adakas** Gy 235:17, 236:5 the Logos Adakas.

malalʿiil mlaka DC 43 D 19 an angel.

malalta (fem. of ܡܰܠܳܠܳܐ) eloquent. Masc. not found. **pt humria malalta** DC 40. 201 f. eloquent daughter of Amulets; **malalta umasguta ḏ-alahia zikria** DC 40. 831 the word and worship of male gods.

malaqat (for **mulaqat**) s. **mulaqat**.

malarud (الرود ?مَرْوْ) a geographical name BZ Ap. II s.v.

malbuša (rt. **LBŠ**) garment, raiment, cover(ing), slough (of snake) MG 130:18. **malbuša ḏ-karsa ḏ-ʿmḫ** Gy 159:3 the cover of his mother's womb; **malbuša ḏ-hiuia** AM 123:11 a snake-skin.

maluaṭa (rt. **LUṬ**) curse MG 130:12. Pl. **-ia. maluaṭia bišia** Morg. 212/11:paen. f., DC 26. 344 f., DC 51. 79 f. etc. (often) evil curses.

maluai pass. pt. af. of **LUA** (q.v.).

maluaita fem. of preced., used of female devil spirits: **liliata umnakalta umaluaita** DC 43 E 20 liliths, (both) the cunning and the haunting; **maluaita (u)hanaqtia** DC 43 E 46 strangling and haunting (lilith), **maluaita haniqtia** DC 43 E 60 id.

maluaša (ܡܰܠܘܳܫܳܐ < Sumerian *mul(a)maš* LS; cf. Zimmern, *Akk. Fremdw.* 62) sign of the Zodiac, horoscope, destiny as indicated by stars and constellations; the astrological (*malwâša*) name used in religious and magical documents, distinct from the name by which a person is known. MG xxviii 19, 130:13; HpGn Ind. s. *Tierkreisgötter u. Zeichen*; MMII 81 f. (: *malwâša*-names). Pl. **-ia. bmaluašak** Gy 311:19, Jb 192:12 in thy horoscope; **aspar maluašia** Book of the Zodiac, title of a collection of astrological tractates (our AM); **qarilun lkukbia trisar umaluašia plaglun** Gy 112:15 they called (hist. pres.) the twelve stars and divided between them the signs of the Zodiac; **trisar maluašia** Gy 379:6 ff., **asra utrin maluašia** Gy 263:8, 267:8 the twelve signs of the Zodiac; names of the **trisar maluašia** Gy 379:12 ff.; **triṣ maluašai kḏ maluašaihun** DC 44:1360 my horoscope is as fair as theirs; **triṣ maluašaihun mn kulhun maluašia** Morg. 265/20:28 their horoscope is superior to all horoscopes; **halin kulhin** [*sic*] **mlakia ualahia umaluašia** DC 44 all those angels, gods and constellations.

maluha 1 (rt. **MLH I**) salty, salt in flavour. Pl. **-ia. had minaihun halia had marira (u)had maluha** ATŠ II no. 61, 247, one of them is sweet, one is bitter, (and) one is salty; **hurina maluha ukianḫ ḏ-mihla** ATŠ I no. 220 another is salty and its nature is of salt; **mia haliia umia maluhia** DC 7 sweet water and salt-water.

maluha 2 Q 61:24, 70:23, Ṣâb.'s AM:coloph. a family-name.

malia 1 pl. of **mala** 1 (q.v.).

malia 2 (rt. **MLA**, מְלָא, identical with act. pt. pe.) full, plenteous; abundance, fullness, plenty. Var. **mlia** (pass. pt. pe.) MG 109:7. Pl. **maliia** Q 4:29, var. **malia** MG 164:17. **daula ḏ-mia ḏ-malia** AM 10:16 a waterpot that is full; **šitua malia nihuia** AM 259:17 it will be a good (: plenteous) winter; **malia unapiṣ** AM 4:15, 19 full and emptied (or: filling and emptying) BZ 7 n. 2, 16 n. 10.

malia 3 (rt. **ALA**) wailing, lamentation MG 17:11, 129:12, 164:14. **ʿblia umalia** ATŠ II no. 335, Gs 20:1 etc. mourning and lamentation; **bmalia iatbia** Gy 120:5, 335:23, **iatbia bmalia** Gy 104:22 they sit in lamentation; **malia nagda** Gy 332:19, **malia nagdia** Gs 47:18, **nagdit malia** Gs 22:6 (cf. **NGD** Idioms); **malia ukariuta lagṭa** Gs 20:1 f. she began to lament and grieve; **malia ligṭat** Gs 20:8 began to lament; **hab malia bnpiš nilgaṭ ʿlḫ** Gs 20:9 let us bewail him extravagantly; **lalagṭa malia** Gs 20:10 (she) lamenteth not; **timut uʿlḫ ništbia umalia ʿlḫ** (compl. **nilgaṭ**?) AM 180:penult. she dies and he shut himself up and mourns her; **ʿqta umalia nihuibḫ** AM 231:9 there will be need and lamentation in it.

malia 4, var. **milia 4** a *malwâša* man's name.

maliašaa Zotb. 222 b:36 for **maluaša**?

maliha a *malwâša* woman's name (v.s. **šarat**).

maliuta (abstr. noun from **MLA**) fullness, plenty, abundance, plenitude, or (Lidzb. מַעַלְיוּתָא Jb ii 47 n. 3) height, high position. **mn maliuta lšapluta** AM 188:16 from abundance to poverty; **mn šapluta lmaliuta** DC 48 from poverty to abundance.

malik (rt. **MLK II**) AM 277:17 counsellor.

malikiiil RD 20 a name given to **šdum**. Var. **malkiaiil** DAb par.

malil AM 205 a place-name BZ Ap. II s.v.

malila (rt. **MLL**, ܡܰܠܺܝܠܳܐ) eloquent. DC. 40.

malka (מַלְכָּא, ܡܰܠܟܳܐ, H. מֶלֶךְ, Ar. مَلِك, Eth. ንጉሥ, Akk. *maliku*, *malku*) king; a spiritual entity (cf. s. **malaka**); a priest. MG 4:1, 100:5. St. abs. & cstr. **mlik** s.v. Pl. **malkia**. In wedding songs used also of the bridegroom, cf. ML x n. 3. **malka rama ḏ-nhura** Gy 2:22, 3:1 f., 22 f., 4:9, 5:1, 14 etc. the Exalted King of Light; **malka ḏ-nhura** Gy 5:11, 6:9 etc. Brandt ERE viii 384, MR 43 f., MSchr. 231 f., Pallis: MSt 38, 71 ff.; **malka malka** Gy 382:14, 385:14 every single king MG 328:22; **malkia arbaiia** Gy 390:5 Arab kings; **malka ḏ-ʿutria** Gy 108:12, 346:6, 23, PD 71 etc. king of the uthras; **malka ḏ-hšuka** Gy 278:24 ff. etc.; **bukra malka ḏ-hšuka** Gy 134:6 the firstborn king of the darkness; **malka ḏ-alma ḏ-hšuka** Gy 141:21, 23 king of the world of darkness; **malka ḏ-aiar** Gy 328:7, Jb 12:4, 7 etc. King of the Ether; **malka ḏ-aiar iaqra** Gy 360:18; **malka ḏ-arqa ḏ-aiar** Gy 360:24 s. **aiar** 1; **malka ʿlaia bukra qadmaia** PD 1449 the High, Firstborn, First King; **malkaihun ḏ-naṣu-**

raiia RD D 4 the king of the Naṣoraeans; **ardban malka** HG 5 the king Artabanus (s. **ardban**). Of angels and higher beings: Morg. 4 ff., pl. **malkia** PD 1011, 1283, 1416, 1454, 1467 etc., **šliha d̲-nhura malka** Gy 64:11, **ʿutria umalkia** Gy 9:10, 10:8, 11, PD 628 etc., **malkia d̲-nhura** Gy 5:4, 305:21, **hamša malkia** PD 244, **šuba malkia** Gy 304:22, **trisar malkia** PD 868, **ʿutra malka šaia** Gy 276:7, **tmania malkia** PD 820 (cf. 817), **baba d̲-tlata malkia** Gy 141:6, **abuhun d̲-kulhun malkia** PD 72, **srin uarba malkia** PD 960, **ʿsrin uarba malkia** PD 1387, **razia d̲-malkia** Gy 193:2, **kd̲ hda mn malkia šauitak** Gy 194:19 I made thee like one of the angels; **adam rba br malkia** Gy 372:2, 23, **iušamin br malkia** Gy 344:16 f.; **binia malkia trin** Jb 20:10 between the two kings; **binia malkia trin** Par. AM fol. 246 b (cf. Jb ii 27 n. 3); **gadana malka d̲-ginzia** PD 965; **šišlam malka d̲-tagia** PD 1016.

malkauata, malkuata pl. of **malkuta** (q.v.).

malkuta (מַלְכוּתָא, ܡܠܟܘܬܐ) kingdom, sovereignty, reign, government, kingship; the state of being a priest. MG 144:27. Pl. **malkauata**, less often **malkuata** MG 167:9 f. **palig malkuta** Gy 100:13 divideth the government (?); **malkuta ʿlaita** Gs 104:26 the high (: celestial) kingdom; **ʿiut malkuta** Gy 178:3 Lidzb. *Königstrotz*; **malkuta mitpik ʿlh̲** Gy 289:16 the kingdom will be turned against him; **hanath̲ malkuta** PD 1323 that kingdom; **malkuta d̲-marba d̲-razia** PD 1555 the realm of the womb (?) of mysteries; **malkuta qabil** PD 948 he receives priesthood; **taga umalkuta lamithiblh̲** ATŠ II no. 9 no 'crown' nor 'kingship' (i.e. priesthood) shall be bestowed upon him; **malkauata** Q 15:28; **atra d̲-kulh̲ malkauata** Gy 211:16, 24, 212:3 etc. the place which is all principalities; **malkuta titriṣ** AM the government will be established.

Gl. 153:10 defectively ملكوت *regna*.

malkiaiil DAb name of the throne of Šdum. Var. **mamalkiil** DAb 35 n. 6.

malεun (Ar. مَلْعُون) AM 131:3 (ac)cursed.

malpana (nom. ag. pa. from **ALP**) teacher, instructor, tutor. Pl. **-ia. uniqrih̲ malpana** ATŠ I no. 234 and will call him Teacher; **dabrania umalpania** Jb 115:6 guides and teachers; **malpania kinia d̲-hukumat šrara malpilkun** Gy 20:8 righteous teachers who teach you the knowledge of the Truth; **rbanai umalpanai** CP 199 h:4 var. **rubanai umalpanai** my rabbis and my teachers and instructors (often).

malpanaiit (adv. from preced.) Q 39:31, ATŠ II no. 412, learnedly, studiously, skilfully MG 201:8.

malpanuta (abstr. noun from **malpana**) doctrine, teaching Ginzā 214 n. 3. **sibruta umalpanuta** Gy 213:19 teaching and doctrine; **riš malpanutak** Gy 214:2 the first axiom of thy teaching.

mama mamma, mammy, a fond name for mother. **ubaba umama** ATŠ I no. 249 and Papa and Mamma; **maṭilh̲ lʿmh̲ ulʿnth̲ ʿl abih̲ umamia** DC 46 they bring him to his mother and to his wife, to his father and his mamma.

mamalkiil s. **malkiaiil**.

mamania a *malwâša* woman's name.

mambarta (< *מַבַּרְתָּא < מַעְבַּרְתָּא, cf. Talm. מַבָּרָא, Syr. ܡܥܒܪܬܐ) ford, ferry(-boat); transit(ion); *rite de passage* MG 76:24 f. **iama d̲-larab ulašaša ulamambarta** Gy 382:4 f. a sea with no boat, no raft and no ford MG 302:4; **mambarta d̲-mabra bhiria** DC 41. 448 the ferryboat that ferrieth souls; **paruanqa umambarta** ATŠ II no. 337 a saviour and a *rite de passage*; **mambarta d̲-bhiria zidqa** ATŠ II no. 378 the passing over of the elect righteous.

mambuga, mambuha (ܡܒܘܥܐ, ܡܒܘܓܐ, H. מַבּוּעַ, Ar. مَنْبَع, rt. **NBG**) spring of water, water which wells up, a frequent designation of sacramental water, ritual drink MG 50:17, 72:2, 74:15, 130:20; Pet. RO ii 118:9, Brandt MR 107, 203, HpGn 312 f., Siouffi 4:bottom, 79, MSt 167, Zimmern OSt 959 ff. (refers to Bab. *mis pi* 'washing of the mouth'), Jb II 5 n. 1, ML xxii f., MMII 108, CP Index. Pl. **-ia.** Masc. **(a)bmambugia** Q 13:ult. in the sacramental waters MG 25:ult.; **mambuhia mia ʿlaiia** Gy 380:16 in the springs of the upper waters MG 308:bottom; **pihta umambuga** Gy 224:1 etc. (often, cf. s. **pihta**); **hamar kana umambuga** Jb 2:10 (personified); **mambugia rurbia d̲-nhura** Q 59:25, Gs 27:1, 28:20, **mambuhia rurbia d̲-nhura** Gs 27:6, 30:5, 31:21, 24, 33:3 the great springs of light; **šaba ʿl mambuha uštun** Gy 17:23 praise the sacramental water and drink (impt. pl.); **qria tartin bauata d̲-mambuha ʿl mambuha** Morg. 215/17:10 f. recite two prayers for the sacramental water over the sacramental water; **nsib pihta umambuha** s. **pihta**; **briš mambuhia d̲-hiia** Gy 130:4 at the source of the springs of Life; **mambuha d̲-qanina mazruta ʿh** ATŠ II no. 32 the sacramental water of the phial is semen; **tihzia lgupna rba . . . d̲-ianqia d̲-arqa bmambuhh̲ mitrabia** CP 459:7 f. thou wilt see the great Vine . . . by whose welling juices earthly babes are nourished.

mamuia a *malwâša* woman's name.

mamiduta (formed as an abstr. noun, but in fact a transformation of Syr. ܡܥܡܘܕܝܬܐ) Christian baptism (not in running water like Mandaean **maṣbuta**) MG 145:3 ff., MR 98 f. **mamiduta d̲-hizda** Gy 362:1 shameful (Christian) baptism Ginzā 383 n. 1.

mamiran (ܡܐܡܝܪܢ & varr., P. ماميران Löw 219, LS) chelidonium. **mamiran d̲-ṣinia** AM 287:2 f., 35 Chinese (?) chelidonium.

mamit occasionally for **amamit**.

mamitan (ܡܡܝܬܐ *mentha* Löw 205, LS) AM 287:29 mint.

mamitran (a nom. ag. from **ATR I**) awakener, arouser: **lašakbian d̲-mamitran hauilun lrazia kulhun** DC 34 they sleep not, so that all the mysteries should have an awakener.

mamla (rt. **MLL**, cf. s. **mamlala**) word, speech, sermon, discourse, talk, pact MG 79:10, 129:5. Masc., doublets **malala, mamlala. had mamla**

Gy 24:1, **hda mamla** Gy 24:13, 88:23 f. one word; **mamla hu ṭaba ḏ- ˁl mamlalia kulhun mgalil** ATŠ I no. 231 it is a good saying which reveals all sayings; **mamla ḏ-tulita šaraia hu umamla ḏ-nišimta buta utušbihta hu** ATŠ I no. 279 the (silk)worm's speech is silk, but the speech of the soul is prayer and praise; **mšauin mamla hda** Gy 390:16 they (will) make one pact; **hazin mamla ḏ-abadnin kadba hu** Gy 390:22 this pact which we made is a lie.

mamlaka (Ar. مَمْلَكَة) AM 204:4 kingdom.

mamlala (Jew.-Aram. & Sam. ࠌࠌࠋࠋ, Syr. ܡܡܠܠܐ, pl. ܡ̈ܠܠܐ from ܡܰܠܳܠܐ = Mand. **mi(ni)lta** q.v.) = **mamla,** doublet **malala** MG 79:4, 129:4. Pl. **mamlalia. mamlalai** Gy 16:8, 220:19, 318:11 my word; **hda mamlala** Gy 26:7, 16 one word; **atia hda mamla umapriš ˁl mamlalia kulhun** Gy 88:ult. one word cometh and explaineth all words; **mamlalkun** your speech MG 179:16, **mamlalakun** Gy 35:6 A id. MG 180:1. **ukabiria hadia bmalalun** DC 3 and the Mighty Ones rejoice in their eloquence.

man 1 (Gen. Sem.) who? MG 4:2, 94:2. **man +hu = manu** MG 61:paen., 330:1. **ṭubḥ lman ḏ-abid ṭab** s. **ṭuba**; **man atian** Gs 71:22 f. who brought me?, **man šdan** Gs 71:23 who cast me?, **manu rman** Gs 71:24 who threw me? **manu brian man brian mn hiia** Gs 71:25 f. who removed me from the Life?; **manu šumḥ** Gy 128:23 f. what (lit. 'who') is his name?, **manu šumak** Gy 235:18 ff. what is thy name?, **manu šumḥ lnhura** Gy 5:5 what is the name of the Light?, **man hinun ṭuria ḏ-** Gs 1:5 what are these hills which; **ubr man ana** Oxf. iii 31 b **brḥ ana ḏ-man** CP 70:17 whose son am I?; **ˁl šum man** Gy 184:ult. in whose name?; **haza maṭarta ḏ-man hˁ ulman naṭra** Gy 181:18 whose purgatory is this and whom does it detain? MG 341; **man ḏ-** Gy 33:8 etc. one who; **hazitun man ḏ- . . .** Gy 17:23 f. have ye seen him who . . .?; **kul man ḏ-** Gy 37:18 etc. each one that; **abatar man ḏ-gaṭilḥ** Gy 391:3 after him whom he killeth; **kul man mn šurba rba ḏ-hiia** Gy 230:21 whoever belongeth to the Great Generation of the Life; **man bˁuṣrak ublibak dilak šra** Gy 193:21 who dwelt in thy thought and in thy heart MG 344 f.; **man mn man qašiš** Gy 358:20 who is the elder of the two?; **ˁlaia man utitaia man** Gy 201:11 who is the higher and who is the lower? MG 407 f.; **man ḏ-bšapala aitinun** Gy 284:10 those who are in lowlands; **hazin ziua ḏ-manu uhazin nhura ḏ-manu** Gy 131:7 whose brilliance is this and whose light is this?; **hazin binta ḏ-manu hazin ḏ-manu binta** Par. xi 8 a, whose building is this?; **hazin man hu ˁutra ḏ- . . .** Gy 129:10 who is this uthra who . . .? MG 436; **man ḏ-nitia uman ḏ-nimarlia man naudan uman naprišan** Gy 358:17 (var. B **man ḏ-naudan uman ḏ-naprišan**) who is it that cometh and who is it who speaketh to me?; who is it who teacheth me and who is it who instructeth me?; **man hu ḏ-nihibḥ ṣauta ṣauta man nihibḥ** Gy 109:10 who will shine therein?; **man mn man qadmaia** Gy 193:5 who is prior to the other? MG 437 f.; **hazin man br manu** Gy 369:11 who, whose son, is this?; **mn aškinta ḏ-manu atalia** Jb 2:12 from whose *škinta* has he come to me?; **mn iardna ḏ-manu atin** Jb 2:13 from whose jordan do they come? etc.

man 2 sporadic st. abs. of **mana 2** (q.v.).

man 3 Ṣâb.'s AM an exceptional form of **mn** AM 198:12.

mana 1 (Bibl.-Aram. & Egypt.-Aram. pl. cstr. מאני, Jew.-Aram. מָנָא, מָאנָא, Syr. & Chr.-Pal. ܡܐܢܐ; rt. אנה II Ges., cf. H. אֳנִי, אֳנִיָּה, Ar. إِنَاء, Akk. *unūtu* Fränkel 218, Nöld. NsG 105, Brockelm. i 379) vessel, garment, utensil, instrument, implement MG 129:13, Nöld. ZA xxx 145 n. 2, 160, MR 23:13, 95 n. 1, Hoffmann ZNW 1903 p. 284 n. 2, MSt 109 D, cf. also s. **mana 2.** Pl. **mania 1. mania hiuaria lbiš** Jb 152:10 he put on white clothes; **mania hiuaria** Gy 217:19 cf. s. **azgauaia**; **mania ḏ-pahara** Gy 181:24 the vessels of the potter; **mania ḏ-nhaša** Gy 181:24 f., 282:10, copper vessels; **mana lšlahiata** Jb 185:11, 186:6 a vessel for . . . (obscure, cf. ii 181 n. 4); **mana ḏ-barda** Gy 230:2, 332:18 an ice-instrument; **mania ḏ-barda** Gy 224:22 ice-instruments Siouffi 128, MR 95 n. 1; **ulamana ḏ-šta** (read **šatia**?, cf. Jb ii 83 n. 3) **hamra** Jb 77:11 and not the glass of drinkers of (?) wine; **mania . . . nasbia ulabšia** Gy 224:5 they take and put on clothes . . .; **šadik** (var. Leid. **šidik**) **ḏ-mlia mania** Gs 134:5 thy chest which is full of clothes; **šidai ḏ-mlia mania** Gs 134:13 my chest which is full of clothes; **mania ḏ-ṣiba** Jb 82:8, Gy 229:10 dyed clothes; **mania d-azgauita** Gy 281:9 f. s. **azgauita**; **mania gauaiia** Gy 303:24 cf. s. **gauaia**; **alnin bmania uˁtaksinin** Gy 325:19 we entered the apparel (?) and covered ourselves (Ginzā 332 n. 2); **bmania ḏ-kaspa šatia** AM 13:4 will drink from vessels of silver; **ubmania ḏ-kaspa nikul** AM 38:ult. and will eat from silver vessels; **mana sada** Gy 182:1 f., 18, 230:18, 233:9, 14, Gs 31:10, 35:15 instrument of torture; **mana zgiga** s. **zgiga**; **kisiaiia ḏ-trin mania** s. **kisiaia**; **mania ḏ-nura** Gy 229:11, sg. **mana ḏ-nura** Gy 228:6 fire-instrument(s); **mana sqila** DC 41. 493 a burnished vessel.

mana 2 (Nöld. from Iranian *man*, cf. Pāzend *manidhan*, *manišn* = mod. P. مَنِش & *mainyô* MG xxxi 10 ff., Soghd. *m'n* intelligence, spirit, heart Henning: MBB 118; de Sacy & Brandt from עני, cf. المعنى de Sacy, *Journal des Savants* Nov. 1819 p. 655, *Exposé de la Religion des Druzes* i 47, ii 579 ff., Euting ZDMG xix 121 n. 1, MR 23: middle; Lidzb.: semantic development of **mana** 1 used as *concretum pro abstracto*, cf. σκεῦος ἔντιμον of the Heracleonites, Epiphanius: *Haer.* 36:3, Ginzā 65 n. 1, 332 n. 2, OSt 538) spirit, soul, mind, intelligence (Gr. νοῦς) SA 2 & n. 1; MR 23, 28, MSchr. 125 n. 1, 137 n. 2, 140 n. 3, ERE viii 382, MSt 107 ff., 110 n. 1, HpGn 40, 117, 292, MBHG 86 f., AF 233 (& n. 4), MMII 93 n. 1, DAb

Ap., Eisler, *Weltenmantel u. Himmelszelt* (München, 1910) II 521 n. 2, Nyberg: *Die Religionen des alten Irans* 128, Macdonell: *Grundr. d. indo-arischen Philologie u. Altertumskunde* 166 f. Spor. st. abs. **man 2.** Pl. -ia **2. mana rba ḏ-qara** Gy 68:23, 69:9, **mana rba** Gy 69:22 f., 70:22 f. etc., **mana rb arišaia** Oxf. 57 a, 58 b, **mana rba kabira** Gy 372:16, 25, 374:6, Morg. 207/1:paen., **mana qadmaia** CP 7:14 **mana rba qadmaia** Gy 373:13 (of the supreme being of Light); **mana nṣiba** Q 28:28, Gs 110:16, 19; **ziua ḏ-iaqid bgu mana** Gy 234:16; **mana kasia** Oxf. roll f 51, Morg. 112:3 etc.; **mana sdira umsadra** Gs 38:14, 79:4; **mana niha** Gy 335:5, Gs 38:14 f. [*bis*], 74:9 f., **mana niha umqaima** Gy 321:5, **mania nihia** Gy 345:22, 346:16; **mana ḏ-bak** Gy 314:11 the mind which is in thee, **mana ḏ-bhun** Gy 290:13 the mind which is in them; **mana iaqra** Gy 325:12, 326:1, 13; **mana iaqira** Gy 135:5, 14, pl. **mania iaqria** Gy 152:4, 350:19 (cf. σκεῦος ἔντιμον above); **mana rba kasia** Q 25:2, **mania kasiia** CP 13:22 = Q 26:13, Gy 150:24, RD B 93; **sam mana smira** Q 7:28, Gy 71:2, 189:14, 196:3, **mana iauar smir** Gy 291:43 f., **iauar mana smira** ibid. 44, **mana smira** Q 32:11, Gy 250:13, **mana smira lʿtgluiia** Gy 192:18, **mania smiria** Q 28:28, Gy 343:21; **mana sqila ḏ-sqil** Q 65:33, **mana sqila** Gs 79:18, **mania sqilia** RD B 109, 117, **mankun** CP 78:11 Q 36:24 f. = ML 96:3 your soul(s); **adakas mana** Gy 102:6; **mana mn iama sliq** Gy 113:17 f. a spirit rose from the sea (Ginzā 125 n. 4: a reminiscence of the myth of Ea-Oannes?); **mana br rurbia** Gs 39:16; **mana udmuthẖ** Gy 134:5, 7, 19, 24, 135:8, 152:4, 9, 11 ff. the spirit and its likeness (Siouffi 41, 63, 87:bottom); **hibil mana ḏ-npiš ziuẖ** Gy 152:12, **hibil mana dakia** Gy 152:15, 168:1, 171:4; **ʿṣṭarar mana mn kanẖ** Gy 308:2 the soul was formed from its source Ginzā 308 n. 1; **mana qadmaia ḏ-mn dukthẖ ata** ML 9:1, CP 7:14 the First Spirit which came from its place; **hag umag trin mania ḏ-hšuka** Gy 138:19, 24 H. & M. two spirits of the darkness; **mania rurbia kabiria** Gy 68:23 f.; **mania ḏ-nhura** CP 39:15, Q 36:21, Gy 108:21; **mania šihia** Gy 314:2; **mania smiria** CP 8:3, **tlata mania ḏ-ginzaikun** Q 62:30; **mania ḏ-minai** Gy 150:13 the spirits which are with me; **almana** Jb 3:2, Oxf. iii 1 b (var. **lmana**) the spirit (acc.) MG 193:middle; **mana ḏ-hiia ḏ-sadrẖ** DC 48. 234 the spirit of Life which set it in order; **mana ana ḏ-hiia rbia** beginning of a set of hymns in Gs 38–74 ERE viii 382. St. abs. (?) in **man asia** CP 21:ult., ML 24:4 and **bšum man mana** DC 26. 138 f. Meanings 1 & 2 are often used as cryptograms.

manata DC 36 II no. 15 a var. of **mnata.**

manglia pl. (sg. מַנְגְּלָא, ܡܰܢܓܠܳܐ, Ar. loan-w. مِنْجَل Fränkel 133, Schulthess HW 37 f., Nöld. ZDMG liv 162 f. Ges. s.v., LS 414 b: top) scythes. **ʿtlun šinia kḏ masaria uganbaihun kḏ manglia** AM 197:6 they have teeth like saws and sides like scythes.

Gl. 157:7 sg. missp. منجل *falx* داس.

manda 1 (West-Aram. מַנְדַּע Dan. 2:21, 4:31, 33, 5:12, Jew.-Aram. מַנְדְּעָא & without dissimil. מַדְּעָא, Syr. ܡܰܕܥܳܐ, Chr.-Pal. ܡܕܥ, H. מַדָּע Ges. Nöld. ZDMG xxiii 293) knowledge γνῶσις, esp. personified as **manda ḏ-hiia** γνῶσις ζωῆς the outstanding Saviour-spirit of Mand. religion MG xx 10, 75:8 f., 129:9. The dissimilated West-Aram. form is used as a prominent religious notion (while the doublets **mada, madi(h)ta, iadita** are generally used for simple 'knowledge') Jb ii p. xvii:middle, MSt 146, Brandt ERE viii 382 f., Kessler PRE 159, 165, 168, GGA 1890 p. 398, MR 167 f., ML xvi, 282, Ginzā 5 n. 6, Reitzenstein ZNW 1927, p. 67, Lidzb. ibid. p. 70, HpGn Ind., AF 244. A formal pl. **mandia** (corresponding to mod. sg. s. **manda 2**). An exceptional var. **mandʿa** s.v. **manda ḏ-hiia ḏ-hu šliha qadmaia** Gy 290:4 M.-ḏ-H. who is the First Apostle; **iuzaṭaq manda ḏ-hiia** CP 65:2 ff., Q 22:25, 59:3, Gy 240:2, 18; **iauar manda ḏ-hiia** Gy 373:7, 18; **manda ḏ-hiia maraihun ḏ-asauata** CP 15:11, Q 6:8 M.-ḏ-H. Lord of healings; **manda ḏ-hiia ḏ-daiin** Jb 167:13 M.-ḏ-H. who judgeth (MSt 91); **tirat pralia manda** Gs 124:21, 125:6, 13, 17, 24, 126:15, 127:2, 11, 21 in my conscience blossomed knowledge; **brabut mandak** Gy 178:17 in the greatness of thy knowledge, **rabut manda** Q 27:9; **ʿlana rba ḏ-kulẖ mandia** ML 67:3 the great tree which is all knowledge (?) cf. עֵץ הַדַּעַת Gen. 2:17, ZDMG 1955 p. 358:bottom; Ṣâb. Q, DC 3 & 53, 51:12 have **mindia** (i.e. 'which is all things'?).

manda 2 (metonymic use of **manda 1**) cult-hut. Used alone or in compounds **bit manda** and **bimanda** the House of Manda. Mod. coll. form is *mandī* (: **mandia**) used as sg. Description MMII 124–45. (Etymology given in MMII 10 ff. & Sundberg: *Kushṭa* 14 & n. 9 is mistaken, cf. ZDMG 1955 p. 358:bottom). See **bimanda** s.v.

manda 3 a *malwâša* man's name, used also in compound names as **šad manda, zka manda** or **ska manda, brik manda.**

mandaia (adj. from **manda 1**) Mandaean (layman) γνωστικός MG xx:11, Pet. RO ii 98 ff., Siouffi 2: bottom, MR 167: bottom, ERE viii 380 ff., HpGn Ind. s. *Mandäer*, ML xvi, MSt 160 ff. (About the mistaken etymology MMII 11, HG ix:middle & Sundberg: *Kushṭa* 9, 14 & n. 9 cf. s. **manda 2**). Pl. masc. **mandaiia**, fem. **mandaiata. tarmidia umandaiia** Gy 1:18, Jb 266:9 priests and (lay) Mandaeans MSt 161 f.; **ʿnšia tarmidiata umandaiata** Gy 288:5 BCD women of priestly and lay families.

mandaiuta (abstr. noun from **mandaia** Manda(ean)ism; laity (as opposed to priesthood). **mn ṣurta ḏ-iahuṭaiia bmandaiuta mitlabaš** s. **iahuṭaiia; mapiqlẖ lnišimta mn iahuṭuta lmandaiuta** ATŠ II no. 198 (a worse var. **mn iahṭaiia lmandaiata** DC 6 ibid.) bringeth the soul out of Judaism into Manda(ean)ism; **lman ḏ-mitarmad . . . unapiq mn mandaiuta ltarmiduta** ATŠ II no. 358 concerning one that becomes a priest and comes out of laity to priesthood; **šla lbušia ḏ-mandaiuta**

ulbušia d̲-tarmiduta lbaš DC 34. 200 he took off his lay clothes and put on the clothes of priesthood.

mandalta (rel. to Akk. *manzaltu*, Ar. مَنْزِل?) setting (down or up)? **arqa škibta titib umandalta lmartun tihuia** AM 283:3 the earth will settle down into repose, since there will be a setting (down) of their ruling star (?). (The same word pronounced *mandelδa* is used of a triple bundle of reeds placed erect in the courtyard of a house where a Mandaean has died MMII 181 f.)

manduia (pronounced *mandowī*) a *malwâša* man's name, used also as a family name, cf. **laqab manduia** RD D 5.

manharana, manhirana (nom. ag. af. of **NHR**) illuminer, enlightener, one that sheds light or brightness. Fem. **manharanita, manhiranita, manharita.** Pl. masc. **-ia. šamiš usira manharania** (var. **manhi-**) **d̲-hazin alma** Gy 23:12 (var. D & Sh. ʿAbd.'s copy) sun and moon the illuminers of this world; **manhirana d̲-kulhun ṭabauata** DC 50. 538 illuminer of all benefactions; **manharanita d̲-anharth̲ lbaita napla** Gs 81:17 f. illuminator (fem.) who hast illumined the falling House; **manhiranita hauia** AM 89:2 f. she will shed brightness (: be of bright temperament).

manharbʿil name of a genie ML 282. **manharbʿil ʿstaqlus ialda zuṭa d-ʿl mambugia dakiia d̲-nhura šria** CP 21:15, ML 24:2 f. M.-E. the little child that liveth on pure springs of light.

manharʿiil, manharʿil CP 358:ult. = ML 267:1 a theophorous name for the banner; ML 267:1 name of a light-spirit, used as a name of the banner (**drabša**) ML 282. Var. **manhiriʿil** CP 342:2, DC 34. 906.

manhirana s. **manharana.**

manhirʿil s. **manharʿil.**

manu s. **man 1.**

manuiia (rt. **MNA I**) reckoners, arithmeticians. **lmanuiia amarlun mnun** DC 51. 615 to the reckoners they said 'count'; **umanuiia mnulh̲** DC 51. 619 and the reckoners made calculation for him.

manuna a var. of minuna. **argba umanuna** (var. **umi-**) Jb 212:16 (var. AC) cf. s. **argba.**

manu qimta, or **manu qinta**, a *malwâša* woman's, name.

manza (מַזְיָא, Syr. pl. ܡܰܙܳܐ from ܡܰܙܳܐ, Akk. *mazū* LS) hair, fur. St. abs. **manz** (late). Pl. **manzia** MG 77:1. **manz guban, uʿkum manzia uguban, manzia ʿkumia uguban** s. **guban; manzia šmaṭ** s. **ŠMṬ; manza d̲-namar** AM 128:20 the fur of a leopard; **ubmanziai qina qanin** Gs 12:5 and (they) make a nest in my hair; **miška umanzia** ATŠ II no. 114 skin and hair; **d̲-manzia minh̲ nipuq** ATŠ I no. 224 from which hairs issue.

manzala (Akk. *manzaztu, mazzaztu, manzaltu*, rt. *nazāzu*, **NZL** cf. Ges. s. מַזָּלוֹת) astronomical & astrological term opposed to **zaqfa** and **ziqpa 1** (q.v.), setting, constellation, star of destiny, stellar influence, horoscope MG 51: 11, 130:8, Nöld. ZA xxx 147. Pl. **manzalia, manzalata, manzaliata. ziqpa umanzala, ziqpia umanzalia** s. **ziqpa; manzalia** Morg. 264/10:6 stellar influences (?); **manzalata** DC 34. 950 constellations; **kukbia umanzalata d̲-ʿšumia baṭlia** Jb 46:5 the stars and constellations of the heavens come to naught; **uahia bnia manzalh̲ hauin** AM 5:12 and he will have brothers born under his horoscope (?), **ʿnta pt manzalh̲ lagiṭ** AM 47:5 and 52:10 he will take to wife a woman under his own stars; **ʿu br manzalia d̲-abuia** AM 46:7 if born under his father's stars (under the same stars as his father); **klil kukbia umanzalata matna brišai** DC 44. 504 a coronet of stars and constellations I place on my head; **kukbia umanzalata** (var. **-iata**) **natria** Gy 203:12 (var. Sh. ʿAbd.'s copy) stars and constellations fall down.

manzana AM 106:25 name of a person.

manziania pl. (adj. from **manza**) hairy. **manziania ugadpania** s. **gadpania.**

mania 1 pl. of **mana 1.**

mania 2 pl. of **mania 2.**

mania 3 Mani, cf. s. **mardmania** & Lidzb.: "Die Münzen der Characene mit mandäischen Legenden, Mani auf Münzen seiner Zeit", *Zeitschr. f. Numismatik* 33/1922 pp. 83–96.

maniaiil DC 40 an angel.

maniusa (cf. אונס, أنس to force) DC 37.205 violence?

mansur (often in coloph.), **manṣur** Zotb. 217 b:13, var. **manṣir** Zotb. 226 b:19 Manṣūr, a man's name.

mansa (rt. **NSA**) copying. Late, only in coloph. **mansa hazin diuan bmdinta šuštar** ATŠ (coloph.) the copying of this scroll (took place) in the city of Sh.; **d̲-ʿtitlh̲ lmansa** ATŠ ibid. which was ready for copying.

mantaiia name of a people. **hazin širiana qazil larqa d̲-mantaiia** DC 7 this vein (river) goes to the land of M.

masa 1 (according to various MM) forearm, upper part of arm BZ 18 n. 9. **ruph̲ lmasia, ruph lmasa** (**-h̲**) DC 45 & 46 (often of an amulet) tie it to his (or her) forearm; **lguṭ bmasak iaminak** DC 46. 22:6 fasten to thy right forearm; **ulgṭh̲ ʿlak bmasak** DC 46 and fasten it (: the phylactery) to thee by thy forearm; **ʿgba d̲-masa** DC 41 the back of the upper arm; **masa udupna** AM 22:3 the upper part of arm and the chest (?).

masa 2 (for **dmasa** usually in **d̲-masa**) diamond. Masc. **had arqa d̲-ṭina uhad d̲-glala uhad d̲-masa** ATŠ II no. 246 one earth of clay and one of stone and one of diamond (?); **hazin aina d̲-masa dakia hʿ** DC 7 this is a source of pure diamond; **d̲-masa dakia asartinun lšibiahia** DC 27. 395 thou hast bound a pure diamond on the planets (of tying the *pandama* over the mouth); **tabrit hatmia rurbia d̲-masa hu** DC 41. 530 thou breakest mighty seals which are of diamond (? as a symbol of firmness?); **šuria rurbia d̲-masa** DC 22. 6 = **šuria rurbia d̲-dmasa** Gy 6:11.

masa 3 DC 23. 150 a metal, but not P. مس 'copper', as **nhaša** occurs in the same list of metals.

masauata a pl. of **m(a)suta.**

masasia (rt. **NSS**) infirmities, sicknesses, pining away: **kibia umasasia** AM 258:31, 34, DC 43 H 41 pains and infirmities; **haršia upudria umasasia** DC 51 spells and sorceries and infirmities.

masara (מַסָּר, ܡܰܣܳܪܳܐ, Ar. مِنْشَار) saw MG 51:9, 130:9. Pl. **-ia 1. auilh̲ masara** DC 44. 1121 bring in a saw (?); **bmasaria . . . ninsarunh̲** Gy 300:21 they will saw him with saws; **ʿtlun šinia kd̲ masaria** AM 197:5 they have teeth like saws; **nasrilun bmasaria** DAb they shall saw them with saws.

masaria 1 pl. of **masara.**

masaria 2 a var. of **masiria** (rt. **ASR**). **ʿsiria umasaria** (var. **masiria**) DC 40. 630 they are bound and tied up.

masbirana (nom. ag. af. from **SBR**) religious teacher. Pl. **-ia. masbiranai** Oxf. roll f 130 = Morg. 240/67:2 my teachers, **malpanai umasbiranai** Morg. 96:3, 174:6, CP 199 m:5; **hiia lsabrin uhiia lgubria masbirania** (*often*) life to them that believe and life to the teachers of religion; **gubria masbiranan** Gs 19:19 our teachers.

masgda (Nab. מסגדא Lidzb. *Hdb. d. nordsem. Epigr.* 238, Syr. ܡܣܓܕܐ, Ar. مَسْجِد) place of worship, temple, mosque. Varr. **mazgda, masgida** s.vv. Pl. **-ia.** Masc. **bit masgda** Gy 45:17, 46:11 (of Adonây), 133:13, **bit masgdaikun** Gy 227:4 (var. B **maz-**) s. **mazgda, bit masgdaihun** JB 86:4; **mihrab d̲-masgda rba** AM 133:8 the *mihrab* of the Great Mosque; **mia d̲-masgda** AM 133:12 mosque water (i.e. from the ablution tank); **d̲-iatbia bmasgdia** DC 12. 202, var. **-idia** Lond. roll B 433, who sit in the mosques.

masguta (for ***masgudta**?) worship: **masguta d̲-alahia** DC 40. 831 worship of gods.

masgia pt. af. of **SGA II** (q.v.). **masgia usigia litlh̲** s. **sigia 2.**

masgiana (nom. ag. af. of **SGA I**) mover, one who instigates motion. Pl. **-ia. braza d̲-masgianun d̲-masgilun** DC 44. 1841 by the mystery of the Being who moves them; **masgiania d̲-alma d̲-hazin d̲-hšuka halin hinun d̲-masgia** DC 44. 1813 = Morg. 269/28:3 the movers of the world of darkness; these are they that cause (it) to move.

masgida Spor. (exceptional) var. of **masgda** (cf. Ginzā 413 n. 8). **d̲-iatbia bmasgidia** s. **masgda** (var.).

masgirania ATŠ read **magzirania.**

masgita (rt. **SGA I**) Gy 386:14 path, street (place for walking), promenade. Doubtf. Ginzā 413 n. 8.

masuria pl. (nom. ag. pe. of **MSR**) Gs 17:9 scorners, contemners, informers.

mashipa (rt. **SHP**, cf. **masihpa** and **masipa**) DC 43 J 150 ruin?

masuta occ. var. of **msuta** (q.v.).

masṭiana (nom. ag. af. of **SṬA**) seducer, tempter, seductive. Var. **maṣṭ-.** Fem. **masṭiant(i)a, masṭianita, maṣṭ-.** Pl. masc. **masṭiania, maṣṭ-. masṭianh̲ d̲-hazin alma** Gy 117:21; **šuba malakia masṭiania** Gy 51:1, **šuba masṭiania** Gy 58:12, **šuba daiuia mastiania** Gy 27:16 (the planets); **trisar masṭiania** Gy 58:2 (Jesus' apostles); **alpuia d̲-masṭiania ʿlh̲ laniplun** Gy 42:24 instruct him that the seducers may not fall upon him; **ruha masṭianita d̲-masṭia** Gy 103:6 R. the seductress who seduceth, **ruha masṭianita** Gy 100:2 f., **ruha masṭianta d̲-kadba** Gy 120:3, **ruha maṣṭanita** [*sic*] **d̲-maṣṭialun** Jb 207:10.

masṭianuta (abstr. noun from preced.) seduction, temptation, MG 45:9. Var. **maṣṭ-. haršia uzipa umasṭianuta** Gy 20:15 sorcery, lie and seduction; **abadbh̲ masṭianuta** Gy 111:23 they practised seduction in it.

masia act. pt. pa. of **ASA I** (q.v.).

masiaiil DC 40. 877 f. an angel.

masihpa (rt. **SHP**) overthrow(ing), something overthrown, cover(ing) MG 129:4, Ginzā 194 n. 5. **d̲-masihpa qubla shap ʿlai** Gy 194:16 who threw over me a cover (and) fetter (?); **hazin qumba d̲-masihpa šumh̲** DAb this is the vault, the name of which is 'Covering-Over'.

masihpan (cf. preced.) Overthrower, Destroyer. **sin masihpan** RD D 1 = DAb par. Sin the Destroyer DAb 40 n. 9; **masihpan rba** DC 43 I 152 (coloph.) the Great Overthrower (name of a phylactery).

masiuata s. **msuta.**

masik (Ar. مَسْك) fresh peel, or bark of a tree. **gaṭrh̲ bmasik ṣinubar** (Ṣâb.'s Book of Magic) tie him with fresh bark of a pine-tree; **raza kdub . . . bmasik** DC 46 write the mystery . . . on bark (of a tree).

masiliuta (ܡܣܝܠܘܬܐ) depravity, abomination MG 146:18. **hukumta umasiliuta abdia** Gy 226:21 they practise cunning and depravity (or abomination).

masisia = **masasia. kibia umasisia** DC 45 cf. s. **masasia.**

masipa (pt. af. of **SUP**) destructive, deadly. **sikina d̲-masipa d̲-mardia** DC 40. 322 f. a knife that is deadly to rebels (: puts an end to rebellious ones). But **lmasiph̲** Gy 221:21, var. **lmis- . . .** Leid. read **lmisihph̲** (inf. pe. of **SHP** with pers. suff.) to overturn it.

masiqta (rt. **SLQ I**) (*a*) ascent, ascension, (*b*) sacramental meal (equivalent to the mass) intended to assist the soul to rise after death MG 129:24, Brandt JPTh 1892 p. 420, MR 81 f., MSchr. 192 n. 4, ERE viii 381 & n. 1; MMII 200 n. 5, kinds of *masiqtas* and description MMII 210 ff.; Siouffi 70, 95; HpGn 40 n. 3. Pl. **masqata.** (*a*) **bhaza masiqta d̲-ana slaqibh̲ nisqubh̲ anašia naṣuraiia** Gs 94:2 f. by this ascension by which I ascended shall ascend Naṣoraean people; (*b*) Very often in rituals, esp. with **QRA** corresponding to 'to read a mass': **masiqta qarinalak** Gy 136:23, **masiqta qarilak** Gy 157:7, **qarin masiqta** RD C 2 etc.; **masiqta d̲-gubran** PD 812; **qaiamta d̲-masiqta d̲-miša** ML 95:6 (read **miša d̲-masiqta** n. 3); **abid masqata** Gy 19:17 arrange *masiqtas*; **bsidria umasqata** Gy 210:22 in prayers and *masiqtas*.

masirqa (מַסְרְקָא, ܡܣܪܩܐ) comb, rake, harrow. Pl. **-ia.** Var. **mi-** s.v. **riha basim umasirqa** DC 38 perfume and a comb; **bmasirqia qublia** (var. **uq-**) **nisriqunẖ** Jb 97:15 (var. DC 30) they shall harrow him with combs of chains (harrows).

maskilania pl. (H. מַשְׂכִּילִים formally corresponding to nom. ag. af. pl. of **SKL**) a pun including two contradictory meanings: 'clever' and 'foolish' Ginzā 225 n. 6. **qarin lnapšaihun . . . maskilania ḏ-askil** Gy 224:13 f. they call themselves . . . clever, because they acted foolishly!

maskina = **miskina** (q.v.). St. abs. **maskin.** Pl. **-ia. br maskinia** AM 44:8 son of poor parents. **maskina hauia** AM 26:9 he will be poor; **uanašia maskinia nihun** AM 274:22 and people will be miserable.

maskinuta occ. var. of **miskinuta.**

masmikana (rt. **SMK**) lying down, setting. **mn madnaha lmasmikana umn masmikana lmadnaha** DC 51 from uprising to setting and from setting to uprising.

masعud (Ar. مَسْعُود) AM 255:30, Zotb. 220 b:4 etc. Mas'ūd, a man's name.

masputiata pl. (rt. **SPṬ**) fastenings, chains, fetters MG 42:paen. ff., 44:paen., 148:7. Var. **maṣpuṭiata** s.v. **bmasputita ḏ-abia mn dilẖ** Gy 84:5 f. in a fetter which is thicker than himself; **bmaspuṭiata ḏ-hauia mlaiia ḏ-alma** Gy 90:8, 12 in fetters which equal the whole world **maspuṭiata ḏ-ʿstartbẖ ḏ-abia mn kulẖ alma** Gy 94:14 f. the fetters by which thou wert fettered, which are thicker than the whole world; **maspuṭiata ḏ-kadra mn kulhun almia** Gy 166:24 f. chains heavier than all worlds; **mitpasqa maspuṭiata ḏ-arqa** Gy 310:16 f. cut are the fastenings of the earth; **šibiahia bmaspuṭiata mistipṭia** Gs 65:19 planets are fettered in chains; **šidibun maspuṭiata** Jb 148:6 I tied them with fastenings; **maspuṭiata** RD B 22.

masqal 1 (rt. **SLQ**) (means of) ascent. **sumbla rama ḏ-ʿrmitibẖ lgupna ḏ-masqal lgupna** DC 3. 383:4 = CP (DC 53) 229:14 I placed a long ladder against the Vine in order to mount the Vine.

masqal 2 ML x 16 a var. of **misqal** (q.v.).

masqana (rt. **SLQ**) (*a*) abstr. noun: ascent, means of ascent MG 137:8, (*b*) nom. ag. af.: one or something uplifting. (*a*) **ulamasqana ḏ-nisuqbẖ** Gy 282:3 and (he has) no means of ascent that he might go up; **maṣbuta . . . umasqana hʿ** ATŠ II no. 337 baptism . . . and it is rising-up; (*b*) **ulaiit masqana ḏ-masqilẖ mn mahuna** ATŠ I no. 233 and there is no uplifter to raise him out of his pit; **ulahauilẖ masqana** ATŠ II no. 46.

masqata pl. of **masiqta** (q.v.).

masrupta (rt. **SRP**) DC 20. 110, DC 43 E 50 swallowing, gulp. See **SRP.**

mastai (possibly fem. of **masia**?) with suff.: my remedy? **mastai sama zakaia mastai mastai zakaia** Or. 332:12 f., Oxf. roll g 984 f. (an address to the personified plant Rue).

mastirqia pl. (rt. **SRQ**?) cleansings, combings, purgings, catharsis (?). **mastirqia urihania** ATŠ II no. 179 cleansing (-rites) (?) an aspect, odours.

maعalia AM 106 a family name. Var. **maعilia.**

maعilia Zotb. 222 a:24 a var. of preced.

maعrup AM 255:28 Ar. مَعْرُوف used as a family name.

maعšun (Ar. مَعْجُون) paste, electuary. **qurunpul bعasal maعšun abud** DC 46. 112:7 make a paste of cloves in honey.

maعtug Zotb. 221 b:10 (text), **maعtuq** Zotb. 220 a:paen. Ar. معتوق as a personal name.

maعtidil Ṣâb.'s AM a var. of **muعtadil.**

mapaqta occ. var. of **mapiqta** (q.v.).

mapi (Ar. مَفِيء) darkening. Foreign. **map عain** AM 287:16 darkening the eye.

mapiqta (rt. **NPQ**) outgoing, departure, death, MG 51:10, 129:24. Var. **mapaqta.** Pl. would be **mapqata** (cf. **masqata** and s. **mapqana**). **bnia anašia bmapiqta ḏ-mia mn pagraihun nipqun** Gy 49:21 f. people shall leave their bodies because of (flood-)water; **ianuq mapiqtai huat** s. **ianuq**; **ʿu mapiqtẖ (baria) hauia** etc. ATŠ (*often*) should his death be (through a lion) etc.; **usadarata** [*sic*] **umapiqta** DC 36 (here used with the same meaning as **masiqta** q.v.); **mapiqta ḏ-ruha unišimta mn kras ʿma** DC 27. 355 the emergence of spirit and soul from the Mother's womb; **kul had mapiqta lmahu damia** ATŠ II no. 70, 269 what does each death resemble?

mapqana (rt. **NPQ**) AM 241:17 abstr. noun: going-out, exit (cf. **masqana** (*a*)). As nom. ag. af. not found. Var. **mapqata** BZ 146 n. 7.

***maprai** (Nöld. < *מַפְרְחַיּ) winged (creature). Occurs in st. emph. **mapraia** Gs 112 B & Leid. and a dittographical st. abs. **mapraiai** ibid. ACD MG 142:6 f.

maṣa (cf. מַצָּע?) mattress, bedding? **duktai bmaṣai baita ʿnta hauia** DC 46. 67:13 my place is in my (?) bedding (?) in a woman's house.

maṣba s. **maṣbana.**

maṣbana (nom. ag. af. of **ṢBA**) baptizer, baptist. Pl. **-ia. maṣbanai** CP 124:17 Q 63:19 = ML 150:3 my baptizer MG 176:15; **iuhana maṣbana** Gy 189:1 (var. **i- maṣba** DC 22. 180) John the Baptist MSchr 195 n. 2; **maṣbania ḏ-qaimia bit abatur** RD 42 baptizers who stand in the House of A.; **umaṣbana haka ḏ-baiia miṣibẖ** ATŠ II no. 158 and that baptizer who seeks to baptize her; **hanatẖ maṣbana ḏ-qudam abatur** DC 41. 512 that baptist that (stands) before A.; **uiahib ʿdẖ ḏ-iaminẖ bʿdẖ ḏ-smalẖ ḏ-maṣbana** DC 50 and (he) puts his right hand into the left hand of the baptist.

maṣbuta (Syr. & Chr.-Pal. ܡܲܨܒܘܬܐ) Mandaean baptism in living (i.e. running) water (unlike the Christian **mamudita**), ritual immersion at the hands of a priest Nöld. ZDMG xxii 518, MR 98, 104, Siouffi 76, 78,

79:bottom, 138, HpGn 278 ff., MSt 40–46, AF 239 n. 1, MMII 16 n. 1, 101–23. Pl. **maṣbut(i)ata** MG 486 (see pp. 167 & 171:15). **maṣbuta haita** Gy 192:15 living baptism; **maṣbuta rabtia** PD 714, 847, 1582, 1605, 1623, 1713, 1723 the great baptism; **maṣbuta bukarta** PD 338, 652, 717, 719, 723 the first baptism; **maṣbuta ḏ-daima** s. **daima**; **ub-maṣbuta dakita maṣbia** Gy 196:9 and baptized with the pure baptism; **ulhanatun maṣbutata** DC 35 and at those baptisms; **ṣbalh̲ tartin maṣbutiata** DC 27 dipped it with two submersions; **hamšin maṣbutiata** ATŠ I no. 50 fifty baptisms; **maṣbuta gidaita** s. **gidaita.**

***maṣuta** s. **mṣuta.**

maṣṭanita s. **masṭiana.**

maṣṭiana s. **masṭiana.**

maṣṭianuta occ. var. of **masṭianuta.**

maṣirana (nom. ag. pa. of **AṢR**) oppressor, jailer. **ašhaq maṣiranun hauia** DAb Shaq will be their jailer.

maṣiṣat s. **miṣiṣat.**

maṣpuṭiata = **maspuṭiata** (q.v.). **kulhin maṣpuṭiata** DAb all the fastenings; **maṣpuṭiatai** Jb 32:12 my fastenings.

maq for **mag** in **sdim haq umaq** JRAS 1937 p. 610 sealed up are H. and M.

maqaba(t) mlaka DC 19, DC 43 D 18 an angel.

maqatiʿia (Ar. مقاطيع) Par. xi fol. 21 b pieces (?) MG xxxiii:bottom.

maqamia ḏ- (cf. s. **qam**) before (time). **maqamia** (var. **maqumia** A) **ḏ-nahga nihga** Jb 129:1 f. before day dawns.

maqarana (Ar. مقارنة) AM 283:21 conjunction or coincidence of two stars. Var. **maqirana** Par. xxvi.

maqdam Zotb 218 b:8 name of a city on the river Carca.

maqumia s. **maqamia ḏ-.**

maqurpiil DC 43 J 58 name of Mercury.

maqlizana a crier, one who cries aloud DC ?

maqrun (Ar. مقرون) AM 27:18 prominent, hooked (?).

maqria pl. (rt. **QRA**) in **maqria udirdqia** Jb 70:6 (read **maqria ḏ-dirdqia** ? teachers of children) ? Jb ii 78 n. 1.

mara 1, maria 1 (מָרָא, ܡܳܪܳܐ, ܡܳܪܝܳܐ, Akk. *marū*, Ar. مَرْءٌ man, South-Ar. 𐩣𐩧𐩱 'Lord' also in personal names Ges. Aram. s. *מָרָא) lord, master, owner, possessor MG 71:8 f., 112:15 & n. 3, 184:13. St. cstr. **maria** (whether the form is to be read מָרֵי, or whether it is the st. emph. מָרְיָא depends then only on the context MG 152:18), but also **mar** (esp. in postcl. and exclusively in mod. Mand.). Before suff. **mar-**. Fem. **mart(i)a** s.v. Pl. emph. **marauata**, abs. (but with meaning of emph.) **mariuan**, cstr. also **maria. marai** my Lord, my master MG 176:14 (& n. 2); **maran** or **maraian** our Lord, master MG 184:15; **bhaila ḏ-maraian** AM 132:paen. by the power of our Lord; **maraiun umartaiun** AM 199:ult. their master and their mistress; **marh̲ ḏ-baita** Gy 204:24, 205:20 the master of the house, Gy 99:6, 18, 101:15, 110:22, 173:14, 175:12, 265:19, 266:6, 271:5, ML 4:6 (pl.) the lords of the House (i.e. the Planets Ginzā 106 n. 2); **maria batia** Gs 17:ult. masters of houses; **maria alma kulh̲** Gy 385:14 the Lord of the whole world MG 309:2; **mara ḏ-rabuta** Gy 2:14, 29:17, 69:11, 196:13, 234:20, PD 17 ff. (*very often*) etc. Lord of Greatness MR 18, MSchr 74, Siouffi 38:1 (cf. s. **rabuta 1** and **2**); **maria ṭabauata** PD 1153, 1156 Lord of bounties; **kursia ḏ-maria gabra** Morg. 268/27:36 the throne of the mighty (?) lord; **bihram maria spinta** RD 4 B. the owner of the boat; **maria pira rba** Q 58:32 Lord (of) the Great Fruit; **mara ḏ-rhamta** Gy 112:7 Lord of mercy; **mara ḏ-rabuta aba ḏ-ʿutria** PD 29 Lord of Greatness, the father of the uthras; **maria ginzia** PD 1105, 1127 possessor of treasures (: books); **marh̲ ḏ-hšuka** Gy 208:3 lord of the darkness; **maria tagia** PD 854, **mara tagia** PD 832 a lord of crowns; **mara ḏ-šidta** AM (*often*) the ruling planet of the year; **maria kušṭa** s. **kušṭa**; **maria mamla** ATŠ II no. 315 lord-of-speech, spokesman, chief celebrant; **ia maria rahmia ia maria bauata** ML 188:1, CP 156:3 O Lord of devotions, O Lord of prayers!'. **bit maria** Gy 22:8 the house of a master; **maria mariuan** Gy 185:16, 222:19, Oxf. roll 211 etc. (*often*) Lord of lords MG 310:3; **mar umarta hinun** ATŠ II no. 133 they are master and mistress; **bmarai** DC 40. 765 by my Lord; **maria šarba** DC 38 he who has the pot; **maria šinia ʿrikata hauia** AM 27:13 he will have long teeth.

mara 2 for **mabra** in **nahra qrun blamara** Gs 95:24 they call me a river without a ford Ginzā 535 n. 1.

mara 3 (perh. a reminiscence of מֹרִיָּה Ginzā 52 n. 2) name of a hill (on which accord. to a Mand. tradition Jesus was crucified). **ṭura ḏ-mara** Gy 58:15 (if 'the hill of the Lord', the name would be due to Christian influence).

marakib (Ar. مَرَاكِب, pl. of مَرْكَب) boats. **marakib ḏ-bdiria ṭaba** AM 285:15 boats which sink in the sea.

maram (rt. **RUM**) elevated, high, lofty. **umaram mn kulhun aiak šumia mn ṭuria** Gy 3:ult. and loftier than all, like heavens above the mountains MG 453:ult.

maran AM 199 a place-name (s. **qalʿa maran**).

marat st. cstr. of **mart(i)a. libat marat alahia unašia** (often in talismans) Venus, mistress of gods and men.

marba 1 (מַעֲרָבָא, ܡܰܥܪܒܳܐ or ܡܥܰܪܒܳܐ, rt. **ARB I**) setting, west MG 129:6. **mn marba . . . lmadna** DC 43 F 87 from west . . . to east; **mn madna lmarba** (*often*) from east to west.

marba 2 (ܡܰܪܒܥܳܐ, rt. **RBA II**) womb, uterus MG 129:7. **bmarbaiin ḏ-ʿnšia** Gy 24:4, **marba ḏ-ʿnšia** Gy 46:15 f. into the uterus of women; **kḏ mazruta napla bmarba** ATŠ when the semen falls into the womb; **hamra raza ḏ-marba uʿma hʿ** ATŠ II no. 32 (a pun, cf. s. **marba 4**); **bmarbik** Gy 156:11 in thy (fem.) womb.

marba 3 (rt. same as preced., cf. the doublet **marbihta**) lair, den. **mahlipinun marba** (var. **marbada** B & DC 30) **d̲-ʿula** Jb 159:11 f. I make them pass by the lair of evil; **bmarbh̲** Gy 86:4 in his den.

marba 4 (rt. **ARB II**) mixing(-bowl), confusion. **marba hin abadnin ustadrat** DC 42 if we made confusion when it was arranged; **hamra raza d̲-marba uʿma hʿ** ATŠ II no. 32 ambiguous: wine is the symbol of the mixing-bowl (favoured by **hamra**) and the Mother, or . . . of the Womb (favoured by the following **ʿma**) etc. (cf. s. **marba 2**). The latter meaning is corroborated by the commentaries.

marbada a var. of **marba 3** (q.v.).

marban for **maruan**? **miša umarban** DC 46.

marbuṭ (Ar. مَرْبوط) tied up, bound. **ʿnkan marbuṭ atia qarak** DC 46 (often in love-charms) even if he were tied up he would come to thee.

marbibita = **marba 2**. By dittography? **kiba d̲-marbibita** AM 58:3 pain of the womb.

marbihta (מַרְבַּעְתָּא, מַרְבּוּעְתָּא, ܡܪܒܘܥܬܐ, doublet **marba 3**) lair, den, abode. **utanina mšania marbihth̲** JRAS 1938 5:8 and the dragon forsakes his lair; **marbibihta d̲-aria hu** JRAS 1938 5:16 it is a lion's den; **ulihia hatam hauilun marbihta** Jb 156:3 f. and the nets are a lair for them; **marbihth̲ bqalmia hauia** Jb 158:4 his lair is in the reeds.

marbimta (for מַרְבִּיתָא, ܡܪܒܝܬܐ?) branch of a tree? **ʿu hauia ʿniš d̲-npal mn marbimta** ATŠ I no. 75, or should it be a person that fell from a tree (?).

***marbita** (= **marbihta**) resting-place. ATŠ II no. 133 read so inst. of **mardita.**

marga (מַרְגָּא, ܡܪܓܐ, P. مَرْغ, Ar. loan-w. مَرْج Fränkel 129) verdure, green vegetation. Fem. pl. **marganiata 2** s.v. **miṭra napša nihuia umarga tihuia** AM 218:4 there will be much rain and there will be verdure.

Gl. 87:8 mrga [*sic*] زز *risus* برنج.

margazana s. **margizana.**

margazʿl(i)l Gy 167:9 an angel. Var. **margizʿil.**

margalta (P.A.'s *Pašar Haršia*) a miscop. of **magalta.**

margana a spor. var. of **margna.** Pl. ***margania 1.**

marg(a)nuta 1 (abstr. noun from **RGA** *rigare*?) moisture (?). Seems to be different from **marganuta 2** in spite of Lidzb.'s opinion Ginzā 121 footn. **bzma umṭanputa umarganuta d̲-mia siauia** Gy 223:7 f. BD, DC 22. 217 (& Sh. 'Abd.'s copy), var. **margnuta** AC with blood, pollution, and moisture of the black waters.

marganuta 2 (cf. Jew.-Aram. רגן to quarrel), Gy 109:20 rioting (Lidzb. proposed **marguš** or **margzanuta** Ginzā 120 n. 5).

margania 1 pl. of **margana.**

marg(a)nia 2 a pl. of **marganita 1** MG 165:23, 173:25 (apart from **marg(a)niata 1** s.v.). **dahba ukaspa umargania** Gy 112:2 gold, silver, and pearls; **margania uklilia** Gy 148:2 pearls and wreaths; **hilai umarganiai** Gs 131:24 (varr. **margnai** D, **marganai** DC 22. 511) my precious stones and my pearls.

marg(a)niata 1 a pl. of **marganita 1** MG 165:23, 173:26 (apart from **marg(a)nia** s.v.). Further var. **marginiata,** cf. **marginiatak** thy pearls MG 21:7. V.s. **marganita.**

marganiata 2 (pl. of **marga**) vegetation, shrubs, young trees, tender shoots. **marganiata d̲-hinun ʿlania** AM 251:8 tender shoots which are (young) trees.

marg(a)nita 1 (מַרְגָּנִיתָא, ܡܪܓܢܝܬܐ. *μαργαρίτης*, from Pahl. *margārīt*, Parthian *marvārīt*, *murvārīt*, mod. P. مروارید; Ar. loan-w. مَرْجَان Qur. 55:22, 58 from Aram. Nöld. ZDMG xxv 677, Jeffrey 261, Widg. v 194 f., ISK 94) pearl MG 148 n. 2, 165:23 f., 173:25 ff. Fem. pl. **marg(a)nia 2, marg(a)niata 1** s.v.v. **sumqaq marganita rabtia** Gy 145:24 S. the great pearl; **marganita dakita** Jb 252:7, Gs 80:25, Morg. 8:10 the pure pearl; **marganita** Gy 165:13 ff., MSchr 182:3, HpGn 251 & n. 1; **marganita niṭupta** Jb 252:7, 256:14 (personified); **minilia d̲-hakima lsakla aiak marganiata lhizirtia** Gy 217:22 f. the words of a wise man to a fool are like pearls to a sow (cf. Matt. 7:6); **kasita umarganita** Or. 326:21 coral and pearl; **marganiata** ATŠ II no. 66, 258 etc.; **marganita lanqiba** DC 44. 1090 an unpierced pearl.

marganita 2 a *malwâša* woman's name.

marganita 3 (rt. **RGA**) a kind of disease, perspiration? **marganita uruita** DC 51. 87 perspiration (?) and weakness.

marguš (rt. **RGŠ**) strife, turbulence, unrest, confusion, agitation, tumult MG 130:20. St. abs. is generally used inst. of the st. emph. MG 304:6, where Nöld. overlooked the spor. st. emph. **marguša** Jb 153:5. **ubaiia mirmia marguš balmia d̲-nhura** Gy 143:15 he wanteth to cause unrest in the worlds of Light; **marguš . . . baiia mibad** Gy 142:6 f. he wanteth to cause agitation; **hauia marguš minan abad** Gy 157:20 he will make strife with us (var. **hauia marguš minai abid** DC 22. 152 he will make strife with me); **hu marguš kul iuma ramia binataiun** Gy 230:9 f. he casteth strife amongst them daily; **marguš bʿmruma man abad** Jb 7:2 who causeth anarchy in the height?; **marguš iušamin tigra rmabh̲ balma** Jb 9:10 f. Y. cast strife in the world (**tigra** is a gloss ii 15 n. 6); **marguš qraba** Jb 25:1 f. turbulence of war (parallel with **tigra**); **marguš almia** Jb 52:5 the unrest of the worlds; **marguša d̲-ʿula** Jb 153:5 unrest of evil.

margušana (nom. ag. af. of **RGŠ** but formed directly from **marguš**) AM 211:10 (read pl. **-ia**) turbulent folk, agitator(s).

margizana (nom. ag. af. of **RGZ**) one who incites anger, is provocative, a bully. Occ. var. **margazana.** Pl. **-ia. margizania upatikria** Gy 59:20 f. bullies and idols; **bišia umargizania** Gs 1:15 evil and provocative persons.

margizʿil DC 22. 161 a var. of **margazʿil.**

marginiata s. **marganiata.**

margna (Aram. pl. מַרְגְּנִין, ܡܪܓܢܐ, Gr. *μάραγνα*, from Pahl. *mārgan* 'stick for killing snakes') ISK 94 f. the ritual staff of olive-wood MG xxx 20, RO ii 119, Brandt JPTh 1892 p. 598 n. 4, MR 67 n. 1, 91 n. 4, 117: bottom, MSchr 81 n. 4, 182 n. 3, MMII 34, 39 n. 3, BZ 152 n. 4. Var. **margana.** Pl. **-ia.** Masc. **margna ḏ-mia hiia** Gy 80:2, 82:22 f., 129:14, Oxf. 72 b etc. staff of living water (popular etymology based on **RGA** cf. MMII 40), **ulguṭ margnia bʿdaikun akuat margnia ḏ-mia hiia** Gy 25:16 and take staves into your hands like the staves of living water; **margna rama** Gy 166:21 a lofty staff; **ṭunẖ ḏ-ʿlana margnia** Jb 131:ult. f. the burden (: fruit) of the tree is (ritual) staves; **hazin mia hiia margna gauaza ḏ-ʿmra ušima hu** DC 7 (by a picture of a staff) this is living water—a ritual staff, the staff of speech and hearing (cf. above); **margnia bainai** DC 46. 136:13, JRAS 1943 171:5 staves (?) in my eyes.

margnuta s. **marganuta 1.**

marda (rt. **MRD**) ungovernable, restive, rebellious, unruly, mischievous, defiant, unmanageable, rebel, (of wind) boisterous; revolt, rebellion. Pl. **-ia,** mod. **-an. mardia bišia** Gy 74:24 f. evil rebels; **buria mardia** Gy 80: 18 rebellious monsters; **mardia ḏ-hšuka** Gy 80:6 the rebels of the darkness; **mitkabšia mardia** Gy 80:3, 82:22 the rebels are subdued; **mitkabšibẖ mardia** Gy 103:7; **ainai azbrit ʿl mardia** Gy 74:7 f. I lifted my eyes against the rebels; **hzaitinun lmardia** Gy 74:9 f. I saw the rebels; **lbuša marda** Gy 327:2, 11 rebellious garb (*pun*); **aria mrida marda** Gs 75:22 the fierce, defiant lion; **ziqa marda** AM 181:penult. boisterous wind; **ziqia mardia** Jb 152:5 id. pl. **minilia ḏ-mardia naplia ʿlẖ** AM 13 the words of the unruly people will attack him; **qal mardia ualahia bmadna nihuia** Ṣâb.'s AM there will be a sound of rebels and gods in the east; **ganabia lmardia nasgun** AM 172 thieves will join (?) rebels; **razia mardia** DC 48. 91 mischievous mysteries (: heretical rites); **susia mardan** DC 46. 245:12 our restive mare.

mardaiia name of a people BZ Ap. II. **mdinta mardaiia** AM 180 the city of M.

marduta DC 42. 709 = **mardita.**

mardita 1 (rt. **RDA,** Bab. *mardītu*) (*a*) running, course, progress, flow, journey MG 129:25, Ginzā 24 n. 4, (*b*) ploughing, cultivation (?). Pl. **mardia.** (*a*) Often with **RDA** 'to travel, journey, pursue a course': **mardita nirdun** Gy 124:24, **nirdun mardita balma** Gy 40:12, **mardita ḏ-alma hazin nirdun** Gy 171:8, **mardita radin** Gy 45:9, 263:23, **radinin mardita** Jb 219:5, **bʿuhra . . . ḏ-habšaba** (personified) **mardita bgauẖ radia** Jb 209:14, **umardita ḏ-mia mardia** Jb 218:1 f. and the waters flow on their course; **bmardita ḏ-iuma** Gy 281:24 in a day's journey; **umardita lpatura hauia** DC 50. 511 and the course is to the (sacred) platter; (*b*) **minaihun lmardita** Gy 124:20 some of them for ploughing; **umardita tihuia uhiuaniata nišiprun** AM and there will be cultivation (?) and cattle will prosper; **uligraihun mardia kbaš** DC 39, DC 43 their feet trod journeys; **uganabia lmardia nasgun** AM 172:19 and thieves will go on journeys (or s. 2).

mardita 2 (rt. **MRD**) unrest, insurrection. Doubtf. **umardita uatiauata banašia tihuia** AM 246:1 and there will be insurrection and villainies amongst people.

mardita 3 s. ***marbita.**

mardmania (prob. a corruption of **ḏ-marmania** 'of the lord Mani'?). (The word has nothing to do with P. مردمان 'people' suggested by Andreas to Lidzb. Ginzā 229 n. 6) Gy 228:11 Manichaeans. A more original form **marmania** Gy 228:17.

maru (P. مَرْو) AM 198 name of a city.

marua (מָרְוָא, ܡܪܘܐ *Origanum maru* and other species Löw 251) wild marjoram (?). Pl. **maruia 1.** Used as fem. in DC 41. **marua aštargan** Jb 232:5, **marua aštargana** Gy 106: 20 f., 346:19 camel's-foot-marjoram (?); **marua hu** DC 41 (picture); **hazin marua ʿlana hu** DC 7 (picture) this is the marjoram plant; **marua hiuartia hu** DC 41 this is a white marjoram; **marua umakṭauata** s. **makṭauata; mšaria ʿkiria umaruia** WedF 57:top = ŠQ 18:21 cultivated garden-plots and fragrant herbs.

maruad (مَرْو ٱلرُّود AM 204 a place-name BZ Ap. II (cf. also **malarud**).

maruaha (rt. **RWH**) means of refreshment (Lidzb. *Fächel*). **kḏ maruaha ḏ-mia hiia bʿḏẖ lgaṭ maruaha** Jb 180:5 f. when he holds the means of refreshment, that is living water, refreshment (takes place ?, or delete the second **maruaha**?).

maruan = **marua. maruan ʿlana hu** DC 41 (picture) cf. s. **marua** (n in **maruan** by influence of the foll. **ʿlana**?).

maruana (rt. **RUA**?) a holiday on the 1st day of the 5th month Siouffi 102, MR 91:middle.

maruas DC 43 A 96, 138 a demon.

maruaria s. **muruaria 1.**

maruata occ. var. of **marauata** (pl. of **mara, maria**).

marubia (inf. pa. of **RBB**) var. **marbia** development, growth. **tša iahria marubia** ATŠ II no. 178 the nine months (of) development.

marubita (= **mar rbita**?) DC 46. 243:6 the lord of the ocean?

maruza s. **miruza.**

maruia 1 pl. of **marua** (q.v.).

maruia 2 (prob. مَرْو) AM 198 a place-name BZ Ap. II.

marula (etym. & mean. doubtf. Nöld. hardly by dissimil. from **marura** 'bitterness' MG 55 n. 1, from *מַרְעוּלָא, rt. ܪܥܠ, 'commotion'? MG 130 n. 3) prob. tribulation, commotion, unrest, disquiet, trouble, anxiety, dissension. **rmulun marula** Gs 14:10 f., 78:23 = Q 66:24 **rmilun marula** causing them tribulation (var. **rmulia marula** DC 22. 404 they caused me tribulation); **rmat binataihun marula** Jb 199:10 she cast dissension amongst them; **ʿkma ʿšdilun marula** Jb 204:10 how long shall I cast unrest amongst them ?; **minaiun šadilun marula** RD B 70 = DAb par. some of them cast dissension; **marula qiriuiẖ llibat** DC 22. 349 (missing in Pet.) he (: the Life) created tribulation for L.; **traṣbẖ brišiẖ klila marula**

ibid. (missing in Pet.) he set a wreath of destruction on his head; **hu lahh̲ ramilh̲ marula** ibid. (missing in Pet.) he casteth dissension on his brethren.

maruqa (מָרוֹקָא II J.) saffron-coloured. Var. **muraqa.** Fem. **maruqtia. qria lbit maruqtia tlata iuma** DC 46. 144:1 read on a saffron-coloured egg three days.

marzabana = **marzbana** (q.v.). **ungadtun ʿlauh̲ rqiha utraṣtun ʿlauh̲ marzabana rba d̲-arqa** DC 51. 193 ff. ye stretched out the sky above him and set him above the great barrier of the earth.

marzanguš (P. مرزنگوش) mouse-ear (an odoriferous plant). Varr. **mirzanguš, minzanguš. riuand umarzanguš** DC 46. 89:7 rue and mouse-ear; **šahpia d̲-mirzanguš** AM 135: 2 (varr. **marzanguš, minzanguš**) the leaves of mouse-ear.

marzbana (P. مرزبان) guard of frontier, warden; barrier, frontier (as *concretum pro abstracto*). Varr. **marzabana, marzibana** s.vv. **mn aqapra d̲-saliq mn siniauis ʿlak bmarzbana** (var. **lmarzabana** Leid.) **nihuia** Gy 87:15 from the dust which ariseth from S. there will rise a barrier against thee (Lidzb. suggested a confusion with **marziba** 'roof-gutter' Ginzā 89 n. 2.)

marzubia pl. (cf. foll.) roof-gutters, spouts, drain-pipes. **bṭulalia d̲-marzubia** Oxf. roll 155 (DC 43 J 78) in the shadows of roof-gutters; marzubia Oxf. roll 169.

marzib, marzip (מַרְזְבָא, ܡܪܙܒܐ, Ar. loan-w. مرزاب Fränkel 24 f.) roof-gutter, gutter, conduit, spout. Pl. **marzubia** s.v. **atutia marzib d̲-masgda** AM 133:10 beneath the roof-gutter of the mosque; **qupra mn marzib** AM 95:12 (var. **marzip**) pitch from the roof-gutter.

marzibana = **marzbana** (q.v.). Pl. **marzibania. marzibana tirṣit ʿlh̲** Gy 132:17 I set a warden (or I set up a barrier) over him; **marzibania upahrania d̲-mdinata rurbata** DC 51. 751 wardens of frontiers and public officers of mighty cities.

maria 1 s. **mara 1.**

maria 2 JRAS 1937 592:22 for **miria,** pasture, as in line 19.

mariam (Ar. مريم) a later, Moslem, form for Mand. **miriai** Mary. **ʿšu br mariam** DC 22. 378, Leid. & Sh. 'Abd.'s copy's var. of Gy 382: 10 (Pet. has **miriam**) Jesus son of Mary.

mariba 1 (rt. **ARB II**) Nöld & Brandt: mixing-bowl, mixture MG 129:7, MR 200 n. 1; Lidzb. crater Jb ii 117 n. 5. Masc. **mariba d̲-muta** Gy 180:6 (cf. Ginzā 180 n. 3); **mariba rba uʿlaia** Gs 26:24, 27:5, 28:15, 30:2, 31:20, Q 12:24, 31:31, Morg. 233/54:7, ML 34:ult., 85:7 the great and high crater (?).

mariba 2 (Lidzb. prob. a misused מרי אבא; or from **ARB II**?) old man, senile, dotard, muddlehead (?) Jb ii 117 n. 5. Pl. **-ia. mariba rba d̲-qaš** Jb 120:12 (thou) great dotard that hast become old; **mariba rba d̲-lapraš** Gs 7:18 great dotard that discerned not Ginzā 428 n. 5 (in both texts parallel with **saba**); **ualanpia maribia** Morg. 265/20:34 = DC 44. 1364 and towards aged men (?).

mariba 3 for **marba 2. iuma d̲-nišimta napqa mn mariba** ATŠ II no. 196 (var. **marib** DC 6) the day that the soul issues from the womb.

mariuan pl. st. abs. of **mar(i)a 1.**

mariut(a) (abstr. noun from **maria 1,** Jew.-Aram. & Syr. מָרוּת, ܡܪܘܬܐ from the shorter form מָרָא, ܡܪܐ) lordship, dominion, mastery MG 145:26. **mariut** Oxf. 49 a = ML 221:7 my dominion MG 176:2; **mariutak** Oxf. 49 b thy lordship; **mariutai ʿlauaikun** CP 181:4 my dominion over you.

marik AM 280:25 a name of Nirig = Mars (as explained in the text).

marir(a) (מְרִירָא, ܡܪܝܪܐ) adj. bitter, venomous, harsh, grievous, cruel; subst. **marira** something bitter, bitterness MG 299: middle, further: gall, bile. Fem. **marirtia.** Pl. masc. **mariria. kul mindam d̲-biš usnia utaqip umarir** DC 43 D 8 everything that is evil and hateful and tyrannical and grievous; **d̲-zihira umarira litbh̲** Gy 3:9 f. in whom there is no scorn or bitterness; **ia d̲-apkia halia ʿl marira umarira ʿl halia** Gy 176: 16 f. O ye who turn sweetness into bitterness and bitterness into sweetness (cf. Is. 5:20); **anašia sainia umariria** AM 166:3 odious and harsh people; **mia marira** DC 7 bitter water(s); **ṭama d̲-ʿlanun mariria** ATŠ II no. 85 the taste of their trees is bitter; **aina marirtia** JRAS 1937 p. 591:18 evil eye; **marirtia anat lau halaita** DC 40. 83 f. thou art bitter, not sweet; **uhda minaihun hua asga marira šumh̲** ATŠ no. 220 and one of them is bitter (עסקא), its name is bile.

mariruta (abstr. noun from preced., מְרִירוּת, ܡܪܝܪܘܬܐ) bitterness. Gy 323:2 bitterness in which there is no sweetness.

markabiniata DC 43 I 31 for **markabata.**

markabta (מַרְכַּבְתָּא, ܡܪܟܒܬܐ, H. מֶרְכָּבָה, Akk. *narkabtu*, Ar. loan-w. مركب Fränkel 215) vehicle, ship, chariot. Var. **markibta.** Pl. **markabata.** MG 32:30 f., 129:23. Jb ii 76 n. 3, Ginzā 71 n. 2, MR 62:2 ff., MSt 123, 154. **guha gna bmarkabta** Jb 67:8 a rumbling was produced by the chariot; **garglia umarkabata** Jb 109:11, 116:10 (celestial) spheres and chariots; **markabata mistahpan** Jb 122:10 (celestial) chariots are overturned; **markabata ʿstahap** Q 2:12 id. past.; **arbak umarkabtak** Jb 149:10 thy boat and thy ship; **bmarkabtak** Jb 186:10, **(a)bmarkabtak** Jb 186:11 in thy ship; **markabatun d̲-hšuka** Gy 74:23 the chariots of (the sons of) darkness; **bmarkabatun** Gy 74:24 in their chariots; **ʿtilkun markabata** Gy 171:24 I will bring you ships; **uautibtinun bgaua d̲-markibta** Gy 172:9 I seated them inside the ship; **girglia markabatun** Gy 175:12 the wheels of their chariots; **d̲-iatib bmarkabta** Gy 221:5 that sitteth in the ship; **nṣabilun markabata** Gy 316:10 I created chariots for them (Ginzā 319 n. 2); **bmarkabatun kd̲ iatbia** Gy 316:17 when they sit in their chariots; **mn markabatun npal** Gy 316:22

they fell down from their chariots; **ᶜthangar haila ḏ-markabatun** Gy 317:1 the power of their chariots was circumvented; **markabata ḏ-šuba** JRAS 1939 p. 405 n. 2 the ships of the Seven (planets); **bmarkabtẖ** (var. -ibtẖ) **ᶜstar** Gy 34:12 f. (var. DC 22) he was bound in his ship; **mapiqtak umarkibtak qirbat** ATŠ I no. 294 thy departure (: death) and thy embarcation drew near.

markaᶜil DC 19 an angel. Varr. **markiil, markiᶜil, markᶜiil.**

markibta s. **markabta.**

markiil, markiᶜil, markᶜiil (often in exorcisms) an angel.

marmag a tree or plant. Masc. **marmag ᶜlana hu** DC 41 (picture).

marmahuz (מַרְמָהוּז, ܡܪܡܚܘܙ, ܡܪܡܗܘܙ, Ar. مرماحوز Löw 252). Gy 107:1, 346:21, Q 62:16, Oxf. 70 a wild marjoram.

marsa Par. xxvi a var. of **mirsa** (q.v.).

marspindu Ṣâb.'s AM coloph. a woman's name.

marp(i)ᶜil, -iil a being of light forming a pair with **ᶜurp(i)ᶜil** ML 282, MMII 245 f. **ᶜurpᶜil umarpᶜil** Gy 98:2, 167:11 ff., Oxf. 57 b = CP 194:10, ML 229:2; **ᶜurpiiil umarpiiil kana d-zidqa** Morg. 6:9.

marqa (rt. **MRQ**) cleansing. **marqa miṭra** DC 37. 467 the cleansing (of) rain.

marta fem. of **mar(i)a 1** (q.v.). St. cstr. **marat** s.v. **martun** AM 238:3 their mistress (: ruling star?).

maš in **br maš** for **brmaš** CP trs. 136 n. 2, Gs 101:4, CP 180:8 f., 184:penult., Oxf. 48 ab = ML 220:10, in the evening; in **maš klila** s. **mašklil.**

mašaṭa 1 DC 53. 237; 2. a var. of **mašṭa.**

mašaṭia pl. (Ar. ماشِط ?) attendants? Doubtf. **tlatma ušitin mašaṭia qaimia aqamẖ** DAb (var. **mašuṭia** RD F 9) 360 attendants (?) stand before him.

mašaqᶜil ᶜlana DC 41 personification of a tree?

mašaruan AM 129:4, Zotb. 230 a:4 for **mašruan.**

mašaš AM 204 a place-name.

mašašta (rt. **MŠŠ**) (*a*) nom. act. pa.: touching, feeling, (*b*) nom. ag. pe. fem.: touching, groping. (*a*) **mašašta minẖ nailun** AM 105:7 they will enter into touch (: be in contact?) with her; (*b*) **kul humarta mašašta umnakalta** DC 43 H 30 every groping and crafty amulet-spirit.

mašhadia DAb coloph. = RD D 16 f., a family name.

mašuṭia s. **mašatia.**

mašun Ṣâb.'s AM a place-name (var. of **mišun** q.v.).

mašupa a miscop. of foll.

mašuš (ماجوج ?) AM 205:19 a place-name BZ Ap. II. Varr. **mašupa, mauš** Ṣâb.'s AM.

mašunia pl. (ܡܫܘܢܐ, Ar. مُشَّان ?) fresh dates. **qria ᶜl asra mašunia** DC 44 read (it) over ten fresh dates.

mašṭa (Ar. مُشْط) ŠQ 18:28 comb. (Late.)

mašid (Ar. مَجيد) AM 156:42 a man's name.

mašihta 1 (מְשִׁיחְתָא rope, מְשַׁחְתָא measure, ܡܫܘܚܬܐ id.) measure, measuring, measurement MG 101:11. **lraumak mašihta litlẖ** Gy 4:21 there is no measuring for thy height; **bmašihta tlatma amia** Gy 380:11 in length (of) thirty ells; **hušbana umašihta** AM 155:8 calculation and measurement; **mašihtẖ ḏ-asar utartin ṣbata** DC 44. 1730 = Morg. 268/26:39 (var. **mišihta**) the measure of twelve fingers (: a duodenum).

mašihta 2 (**MŠA II** = **MŠH**) anointing: **uapun lahma bmiša aiak dmašihta ḏ-klila** DC 41. 169 and they baked bread with oil as in the anointing of the wreath.

mašiṭana (nom. ag. af. of **ŠUṬ**) one who fools, leads into evil, deluder. Pl. **-ia. ᶜbidatun ḏ-mašiṭania** Gy 282:21 the works of deluders.

mašin AM 202 the city of Mesene BZ Ap. II (Varr. **mašun, mišun** s.vv.).

maška sporadically for **miška.**

maškun Zotb. 218 b:16 name of a district.

maškuna DC 27. 261 for **maškna** abode.

maškilia s. foll.

mašklil (etym. & exact meaning unknown) prob. a kind of wood for building boats Jb ii 84 nn. 5, 7. **ᶜtlak mn mašklil spinta** Jb 79:11 (var. **maš klila** ABD); **hazin mašklil spinta** Jb 80:2 (varr. **mašklilia** B, **maškilia** A, **miškilia** D).

maškna (ܡܫܟܢܐ, H. מִשְׁכָּן) dwelling, place of worship (synonymous with **manda 2**) MG 129:3, Kessler PRE 159:48, 160:31, 176, MR 90:middle, 97, Jb ii p. xx f., MSt. 148 f., Siouffi 118:top, 167, MMII 124–45, Furlani: *I Termini* 348–52. Pl. **-ia. bit maškna** Jb 128:7, PD 514 etc. the cult-hut; **masiqlun lkulhun mašknia umasgdia napšia balma** Jb 85:2 he removes all (Mandaean) temples, and mosques increase in the world; **banin bnabẖ mašknia** Jb 229:13, 230:11 built therein temples; **ginia ḏ-mašknia** Gy 302:3 (here of pagan temples, cf. s. **ginia 2**); **zidqa lmaškna lamatin** Gy 288:1 they bring no oblation to the temple; **ᶜnšaiun ubnaiun lmaškna lamatin** Gy 288:2 (cf. 285:11, 22, 286:3 f.) they bring not their wives and their children to the temple; **maškna utarmidia** Gy 289:18 f. the temple and the priests; **ulatin lmaškna** Gy 287:23 and (they) come not to the temple; **baba ḏ-maškna** Gy 44:3, Gs 101:7, CP 173:10, 162: ult., ML 211:3 the door of the temple; **lasgun lmaškna** Gs 37:14 they did not go to the temple; **maškna ḏ-masgidnabẖ** Q 12:4 the temple in which I worship; **riš mašknia** Jb 168:1, 8 f. etc. the chiefs of the sanctuary, Mundart 54, Geiger ZDMG xvii 422, MG 129:antep., 413:14; **ᶜstirata ḏ-mašknia** DC 26, DC 40 the astartes of the (pagan!) shrines.

mašlub (Ar. مَجْلوب) rabid (of dogs): **kalba mašlub** DC 36 a mad dog.

mašmiᶜil CP 180:8 f., 182:9, 184:16 and CP trs. 136 n. 2, a spirit: [evening: see **maš** (**br maš**)].

mašpilana (rt. **ŠPL**) sink, outlet, drain, something that causes to sink Jb ii 215 n. 2. **hibil**

nišauilun **mašpilana** Jb 233:9 f. H. will make for them a drain-pit.

mašqia st. abs. (?) of **mašqita** (q.v.); act. pt. af. **ŠQA** (q.v.).

mašqiana (nom. ag. af. of **ŠQA**) one who administers drink, potion-giver. **tihuia . . . haduta lmašqiana** Or. 326:12 there shall be . . . joy for the potion-giver; . . . **uatrana lmašqiana** Or 332:7 . . . and wealth for the potion-giver.

mašqiʿil (theophorous name from preced.) DC 41 a spirit.

mašqita (rt. **ŠQA**) drink(ing), potion, beverage. St. abs. (?) **mašqia. ʿkilta umašqita** ATŠ II no. 112, 381, **mikla umašqita** AM 30:14 food and drink; **mašqia d̲-mihla uhardla uṣatria umiša d̲-nuna** DC 12. 189 a potion of salt, mustard, herbs, and fish-oil.

mašqlana (further abstr. noun from **ŠQL** ܡܫܩܠܢܐ Gen. 13:3 etc.) translation, removal, wandering MG 137:7. **kd̲ zibna hauia d̲-mašqlankun umapiqta d̲-pagria** Gy 368:5 when it is time for your removal and (for) leaving bodies.

mašqlʿil anana Gy 374:19 a female spirit.

mašr(a)uan (Bab. *Arah samma* corresp. to ܐܠܥܬܡ اسنه) the eighth month of the Mand. year (under the rule of Scorpio), called colloquially *awwal pâiz* 'the first autumn-month. Var. **mašaruan** (s.v.). Siouffi 145, MMII 84. **mašrauan ltania** AM 262:28, **mašruan altania** AM 261:37 (= تشرين الثانى).

mašrana (nom. ag. af. of **ŠRR**) Fortifier, Confirmer. **mašrana d̲-kulhun rahmh̲ ahbalan šrara** Gy 62:8 O Confirmer of all who love him, give us firmness.

mašruqta (מַשְׁרוֹקִיתָא, ܡܫܪܘܩܝܬܐ) a shrill noise, whistle, pipe MG 130:ult. f. **šariqnin bmašruqtai** Jb 43:4 I pipe for them on my pipe.

mašriq (Ar. مَشْرِق) AM 257:4 east. (Mod.).

mašrita (rt. **ŠRA**) dwelling-place, habitation. **mašrita d̲-ʿur** Gy 167:20 dwelling-place of Ur.

maštamana s. **maštimana.**

maštaqria DC 44. 546 a var. of **mištiqria** (q.v.).

maštuṣia (rel. to שֵׁיצִי? MG 13 n. 1) pl. obscene, abominable beings, monsters (Nöld. *Unholde*), a frequent designation of the planets and signs of the Zodiac MSchr 188 n. 3, Jb ii 62 n. 4, Furlani: *I Nomi* 421. **trisar maštuṣia baṭlia** Gy 97:24 the twelve good-for-nought monsters; **maštuṣia baṭlia** Gy 109:13, 16, 110:4, 329:23, 330:7, 361:7, Oxf. 12 a etc.; **qam maštuṣia uʿtikpir bparunun** Gy 98:7 the obscene ones rose up and were bound by their own thongs; **niqmun maštuṣia udaiuia** Gy 99:1 f. the monsters and demons shall rise up; **maštuṣia qrun daiuia** Gy 99:11 f. the monsters created demons; **ubaṭilnun lmaštuṣia kulhun** Gy 107:12 we brought all the monsters to nought; **mahu ʿbidlun lhalin maštuṣia d̲-ladamin lhanik gabaria** Gy 171:5 f. what shall I do to these monsters which do not resemble those giants . . . ? ; **d̲-nihaun gabaruatun lmaštuṣia d̲-ka** Gy 299:16 (cf. 316:6) that they may show their mighty deeds to the monsters which are here; **qiriata d̲-maštuṣia baṭlia** Gy 309:4 creations of good-for-nought monsters; **mhašba nimrus uamralun lmaštuṣia bnh̲** Jb 58:10 N. considers and says to the monsters her sons.

maštuta (rt. **ŠTA II**) web. JRAS 1938 4:27 their web parted (broke); **maštutin psiq** s. **ŠTA II.**

maštimana (ܡܫܬܡܥܢܐ) obedient, servant. Varr. **maštamana, maštmana, mištamana, mištimana.** Pl. **-ia** MG 13:bottom. **daiuaihun bmaštimania** Gy 106:15 (varr. **maštmania** B, **maštamania** DC 22. 101) their demons (were) servants; **kulhun hun mištamania** Gy 107:6 all of them were servants; **unihun maštimania ltarmidia** ATŠ no. 234 and (they) will be subservient to the priests; **ulšitin maštamania** DC 44. 545 and the sixty servitors; **ʿutria mšarhbana** [*sic*] **umaštimana** [*sic*] DC 26. 63 propagating and obedient (read **-nia** or at least **nh̲**) uthras.

maštiqria, pl. (pt. ethpe. of **ŠQR**) Morg. 259/9:17 perjurers.

mata (מָתָא, ܡܬܐ < Akk. *mātu*) territory, (small) town, city, village MG 99:1. St. cstr. **mat** MG 155:22. Fem. MG 161:10. Pl. **mat(a)uata** MG 167:6. **mn mata lmata** Gy 388:8 from place to place MG 301:19; **ʿurašlam mata** Gy 381:14, 329:18, **mata ʿurašlam** Gy 332:15, 17 (Gy 329:16 both in one line) the city of Jerusalem MG 319:antep.; **br šibia qrun blamata** Gs 96:1 f. they call me a captive without country; **mata d̲-kušṭania** Gy 318:1 f. the city of the truthful; **mata tiiul lmata** AM 242:2 town will invade town; **umata bmata umahuza bmahuza tiʿul umn mataihun anašia nipqun** AM 242:13 and city will invade city and town invade town, and people will leave their homes; **bdibra ubmata** s. **dibra; matauata d̲-malka d̲-arqa d̲-babil mlik** AM 238:5 the territories of the king of the land of Babylonia; **matuata** AM 182:17 towns; **bnia mata** AM 277:11 citizens; **ulkulhun bnia mata ulhanzaman uʿl matuata** DC 26. 561 = DC 44. 568 and for all the people of the place and for the district and towns; **lšitin bnia mata** DC 44 the sixty citizens.

Gl. 42:15 **mata** (& pl. defectively) بلدة *regio* شهر; 136:4 **mati** [*sic*], pl. **matuata** قرية pl. قرى *castellum* ده; 142:4 **mata,** pl. **matuata** كورة *regio* شهر; 142:6 **mata** كور *castellum* قلعة; 153:ult. **mati** [*sic*] مُلك *regnum*; 168:5 **mata** ناحيه *partes, confines* توابع.

matudia (Ar. مَتْود?) resting-place (? corrupt). **duktai matudia hauia** DC 46. 95:4.

matiabta a kind of demon of both genders. **matiabta zikria umatiabta nuqbata** DC 43 A 27.

matia (ܡܬܝܐ) fetters. **pt gublania matia** DC 40 daughter of those who forge fetters.

matiana s. **mitiana.**

matin 200 (s. **ma 2**) MG 189:bottom.

matistan s. matstan.

matira (etym. obscure) adv. severally and simultaneously, cf. MMII pp. 175 f. Only in rituals. **ulupiun kulaikun matira** DC 50. 141 and eat your communion each of you simultaneously (?); **tlatma ušitin maṣbutiata matira** DC 50 the 360 baptisms when simultaneously performed; **kul iuma šuba maṣbutiata kt matira hauin ganzibria utarmidia** DC 50. 483; **ṣubuiẖ tartin maṣbutiata matira** DC 50. 493 baptize him simultaneously twice; **ṣbun matira aiak maṣbuta rabtia** DC 50. 847 baptize simultaneously as in the Great Baptism.

matna (מָתְנַיָּא, ܡܰܬܢ̈ܳܐ, H. מָתְנַיִם, Ar. مَتْن, Eth. መትን, Akk. *matnu*) hip. Var. **mitna.** Pl. **matnia** loins. Apparently masc. **kib burkia umatna** (var. **matnia**) AM 103:13 pain in her knees and loins; **matnia ḏ-šaqẖ** AM 92:19 loins and (?) limbs; **matnia gauaiia** Gy 202:13 pl. (var. **matnẖ gauaia** DC 22. 193 sg.) her inner loins; **matnia rakšia** DC 12. 186 for the haunches of horses.

matstan, var. **matistan** (v.s. **d(a)ulamat(i)stan**) name of a country, Media (?, otherwise called **madai**!) BZ Ap. II.

matqal(a) = **mitqal(a)** q.v. Pl. **-ia. matqala ḏ-dahba rba** DC 36 a large gold *shekel*; **kul had ium(a) tša matqalia mithaial** ATŠ I no. 168, II no. 24 (var. **mitqala** DC 6) each day it is strengthened by nine *mithqals*, cf. PD 1504 ff.

matrana (nom. ag. pa. of **ATR** I) awakener. **matrana ḏ-matraikun** DC 34. 704 awakener that will waken you; **matrana ḏ-matarlun** DC 34. 1307 awakener who will waken them.

mbaira (rt. **BAR** II) fiery, fierce (?); **gabra mbairai** (var. **mbaira**) AM 48:13 a fiery (?) man.

mbakalata, mbaklauata (cf. ܡܒܰܟܠܳܬ̈ܳܐ bitter and sour things) pl. bitternesses (?) of darkness ML 37 n. 1. **tmania mbakalata ḏ-hšuka** Q 13:24 = ML 37:7 = CP 31:antep., DC 51. 141, 186 (var. **mbaklauata** DC 3 par.).

mbalala (part. form of **BLA** II = **BLL**) worn-out, corrupt, or disordered, confused. **alma blila umbalala** Jb 90:2, Gs 129:22 corrupt and disordered world.

mbaliata pl. (מְבַלְעָתָא, rt. **BLA** I) upper part of palate or gullet. **mbaliata ugangariata** Or. 328:19 f. the upper part of the gullet and the throat.

mbasar (pt. pa. of **BSR** used nominally) (*a*) contemptuous, scornful, (*b*) (cf. **bisra,** abs. **bsar**) fleshy. St. emph. **mbasra.** Pl. masc. **mbasria**; st. abs. masc. **-in,** fem. **-an** (often in AM). (*a*) **umbasar usnia mahzita ḏ-ainẖ** AM 18:15 and scornful and hostile is the glance of his eye; (*b*) **ugišmẖ mbasar** AM 95:4 and his body is fleshy; **mbasra** AM 14:14 fleshy.

mbasmanuta (abstr. noun from **BSM**) pleasantness, agreeability, amiability. **riš mbasmanutak** Gy 214:9 the principle of thy popularity.

mbasmanita (nom. ag. fem. pa. of **BSM**) pleasant, agreeable; **mbasmanita d-basimtẖ lpagra zapra** Morg. 238/62:2 ff., CP 83:2, Gs 80:24 thou fragrant one that hast perfumed the stinking body.

mbasra s. mbasar.

mbarṭabla (etym. unknown ML 136 n. 2) accord. to context: a frontier official, customs-official or something of the kind. Varr. **mbarṭibla, mṭarṭabla.** Pl. **mṭarṭablia. ʿda ḏ-mbarṭabla bmanaikun latibhuš** Q 56:17 = ML 136:3 (**ʿda ḏ-mṭarṭablia** CP 110:14 par.) the hand of the customs-official(s) (?) will not search amongst your garments.

mbatar Morg. 3:3 = **mn batar** after, behind.

mbulia DC 22. 342 a var. of **mublia** Gy 346:18.

mgabar (pass. pt. pa. of **GBR** used nominally) virile, manly, powerful, masterful. St. emph. masc. & abs. fem. **mgabra. gabra grida umgabra** AM 19:4 s. **grida**; **ʿnta ḏ-rdia umgabra** AM 47:16 a woman that is domineering and masterful; **umgabar hauia hatma ḏ-laupa** DC 50 so the sealing of the communion will be powerful.

mgadla (pass. pt. pa. of **GDL** II) mighty, esteemed. Pl. **-ia. arba gubria mgadlia** DC 50 four mighty beings.

mgahka (pt. pa. of **GHK**) that causes laughter, comical, funny, amusing. **mgakha umgahkana hauia** AM 32:11 f. he will be a comical fellow and a jester.

mgahkana (nom. ag. pa. of **GHK**) s. preced.

mgdam (a corruption of Ar. مُقَدَّم) before. **mgdam baita ḏ-rumia** Zotb. 222 b:31 before the Byzantine dynasty (?).

mgzarṭabaiia a var. of **gzarṭabaiia.**

mginta (rt. **GNA** I) couch, bed. **maṭilẖ lmgintẖ** DC 45 brings him to her bed (or vice versa).

MGŠ (from מְגַשׁ? cf. **NGŠ**) to strike? Jb 149 n. 4.

PA. Pf. with suff. **mgaštinun bqulpa ḏ-parzla** Jb 148:2 I struck them with an iron scourge.

mdabrana (nom. ag. pa. of **DBR**) guide, ruler, leader, governor, potentate. Pl. **-ia.** Often of planets and signs of the Zodiac. **šuba utrisar mdabrania ḏ-alma** Gy 23:9 the seven and twelve governors of the world (i.e. the planets and the signs of the Zodiac); **trisar mdabrania** Gy 379:1 (the planets); **hamša mdabrania** Lond. roll B 24 the five governors (: the planets without the sun and the moon); **hamša mdabranun** Gy 98:7. 393:24 their five governors; **mdabrania ḏ-hazin alma** Gy 341:6 the governors of this world; **mdabrania ḏ-dabrinkun barqa rabtia ḏ-hšuka** DC 43 I 140 the leaders that lead you in(to) the great world of darkness; **uʿsiria arbia mlakia mdabranun** DC 43 H 54 f. and bound are the four (evil) angels, their leaders.

mdalauata (pl. of **mdalia**) (*a*) uplifters, (*b*) (f.) water-drawers, (*c*) draughts drawn from a spring or well. (*a*) **mdalia ḏ-ʿlauia mdalauata** CP 52:14, Morg. 224/35:1, DC 26. 9 f., Uplifter above all uplifters; (*b*) **ulmdalauata amarlun dalun** DC 51 and to water-drawers they said 'Draw up!'; (*c*) **ḏ-mdalauatẖ hua šaria ʿlak ʿlak iardna** DC 51 so that he dissolveth his draughts with(in) thee, jordan!

mdalai, mdalia (pt. pa. of **DLA** q.v. used often nominally) pass. raised up, lofty, tall, el(ev)ated; act. uplifting, elevating. Fem. emph. mdalaita, var. **mdailaita** AM 249:9, agitated, insurgent, troubled, disturbed (?), but also: exalted. Pl. (both masc. & fem.?) **mdalauata** s.v.; other part. plurals s. **DLA** pa. **mdalia ḏ-ʿlauia mdalauata** s. **mdalauata**; **ubatia ḏ-mdalia mitpasasia** Jb 94:8 and houses that are lofty will be rent asunder; **ukursiak mdalai ldukthḏ** ATŠ and thy throne shall be set up in its place (cf. also s. **DLA** pa.); **qumtẖ mdalia** AM 85:14 stature is tall; **mšania malkia umdalia** AM 194:18 kings will change and be insurgent (?); **qina mdalaita** Q 70:9, AM 105:27 an exalted (: distinguished) family; **arqa mdalaita nitib** [*sic*] AM 216:10 the land will be agitated (?).

mdardiʿil DC 19, DC 43 D 26 name of an angel.

mdardqan f. pl. small: **uainẖ mdardqan umqandran** CS 26 and A, (AM 89:4 omits) and her eyes small and dark.

mdarta a var. of **mdurta.**

mdudia (Lidzb. from דוד *'trüben'*? Ginzā 228 n. 4), varr. **mdubia** Leid., **mduria** (cf. maduria?) DC 22. 221, **mdurta** Sh. 'Abd.'s copy — Doubtf. **umn girmẖ mšauin mdudia ḏ-qudša** Gy 227:13 and of its bones they make the . . . of the (Christian) sacrament.

mdurta 1 (rt. **DUR**) dwelling(-place), abiding (-place), lodging, habitation MG 130:1. Varr. **mdarta, mdirta, midurta. umdurta lia hauialun** Gy 203:16 (varr. **umdirta** C, **umdarta** D) and where is their habitation? **mdurtun** Gs 45:22 their dwelling-place MG 181:11; **uhauia ḏ-laiada mdurtẖ** ATŠ I no. 235 and it may be that he knoweth not his habitation? (s. 2); **bmdurta ḏ-napšiẖ** ATŠ II no. 3 in his own habitation; **mn midurtia nad** ATŠ II no. 124 it quaked from its lodging.

mdurta 2 (rt. **MDR**) rottenness: **uhauia ḏ-laiada mdurtẖ** ATŠ no. 235 and it may be that he knoweth not his rottenness? **hu bmdurta ḏ-napšẖ hasira ušiṭa hauia** ATŠ II no. 3 in his rottenness he becometh lacking and despicable.

mdimun DAb read mṭimun their taste, food? DAb 4 n. 3.

mdin, mdina, mdinat, mdiniata s. **mdinta.**

mdinat also a *malwâša* woman's name.

mdinda [*sic*] AM 221:10, 277:29 for **mdinta.**

mdinta (מְדִינְתָּא also Bibl.-Aram., H. מְדִינָה, Syr. ܡܕܝܢܬܐ, an administrative expression of Achaemenidan Aram. Müller OLZ vi 74, Ar. مَدِينَة Fränkel 280 f.) city, large town, district round city, province, country, region MG 52:4, 129:paen. St. cstr. **mdinat** MG 155:18. Fem., but from the st. abs. **mdina** a further st. abs. masc. **mdin** is formed (as from the st. emph. masc.) MG 156 footn. Pl. **mdin(i)ata** MG 169:3. St. abs. used in distributive repetitions: **bmdin mdin** Gy 29:21, AM 173:5 **lmdin mdin** (*often*) in city after city, but also st. emph. **mn mdinta lmdinta** Gy 388:8 from one city to another MG 301; **bmdinta madai** s. **madai**; **mdinat hiia** Gy 3:15 (*civitas Dei*, the residence of the King of Life); **mdinat ʿutria** Q 44:23, Gy 315:12, DC 51. 366 the region of the uthras; **ušumẖ nizal lkul mdin** AM 105:9 and her fame will reach every city; **mdiniata** AM 8 etc. cities; **ulmatauata ulmdinata ulatrata** DC 26. 562 and (acc.:) villages, cities, and localities.

Gl. 153:9 sg. & pl. (defectively) مدينه *civitas* شهر.

mdirta s. **mdurta.**

MDR a rt. of **maduria**? (q.v.), **midurt(i)a 2, mdurta 2, madaria**?

MHA (Aram. & H. מחא, Syr. ܡܚܐ, rel. to H. מחץ, Ar. مخض, Akk. *maḫâṣu* Ges., LS) to strike (at), hit (at), smite, beat, attack; butt (head); (of musical instruments, cf. Ar. ضرب, P. زدن) to play, strike, clash, beat etc.; to touch (cf. P. دست زد); to knock; to strike out, destroy, annul; (of the girdle) to bind, gird on.

Pe. Pf. **mha** (often) he struck; with suff. **ḏ-mhatẖ** JRAS 1937 p. 590 which it (: the eye, fem.) struck. Impf. **nimhia** (*often*) he strikes, will strike, or we (shall) strike etc.; with encl. **ʿmihilia lhusranẖ** (**ʿiasqẖ bzaku**) I will strike out (: annul) his fault (and raise him up in purity); with suff. **lanimhian** Morg. 264/19:2 they (?) do not strike me; **ʿmihiẖ** JRAS 1939 399, DC 37. 314 I (will) strike him. Impt. pl. **mhun riša brišẖ** ŠQ 8:16 knock her head with his head (: knock their heads together). Act. pt. **ltša iahria mahia ubaṭiš** ATŠ I no. 257 at nine months it strikes and kicks out (i.e. the unborn child); **ʿniš ḏ-šinia bihdadia mahia** DC 46 a person whose teeth knock together (: chatter); **alma ḏ-ʿdẖ ukraiiẖ mahia** DC 46 until his hands and feet strike out (?, refers to a disease: St. Vitus' dance?), **qamahia btibla . . . qamahia bsurna . . . qamahia bdap . . . qamahia bsapaqatain** RD 35 ff. = DAb par. (with **qimahia** everywhere) he beats the drum . . . plays the hautbois . . . strikes the tambourine . . . clashes the cymbals; pl. **lamahin** DC 44. 1046 they do not strike; with encl. **mahilia** DC 34. 539 they will strike me. Pass. pt. with encl. (with act. meaning) **himiana ḏ-birqa mhilia bhalṣai** DC 44 I bound a girdle of lightning about my loins; pl. **mhiin bhdadia** ŠQ (?) (of bowls) they touch one another. Inf. **ʿl mimhia alahia zikria** DC 26. 140 f. to strike the male gods.

Ethpe. N. 264. Pf. with encl. **ʿtim(a)iabẖ** Q 8:26 = ML 24:4 = CP 21:penult. it (fem.: the fire) was struck by it. Impf. **nitimhia** is, or will be beaten MG 264:31; **nitimhia mhita bgu mhita** Gy 229:4, 300:ult. will be beaten blow upon blow MG 400:2 f.; **braza ḏ-napšia nitimhia** DC 40 he shall be struck down by his own secret arts; **bmhita ḏ-napšaihun nitimhun** Gy 180:1 they are struck by their own blow; **nitimhian** DAb they (fem.) shall be beaten. Pt. fem. pl. **mn hanik mihiata mitmihian** ATŠ I no. 75, II no. 296 (are) struck by those blows.

Gl. 17:7 f. **amha** انفق *audere, alapis percutere* طبانچه زد; 58:3 f. id. جلد *flagellare*

تازيانه زد ; 102:13 f. id. ضرب *agitare* لرزيد ; 114:11 f. id. عذّب *vexari, affligere* جفا كرد ; 132:5 f. id. قرع *pulsare* كوفت ; 145:9 f. id. لطم *percutere, colaphis caedere* طبانچه زد.

Der.: **mhita** (pl. **mihiata**).

mha Gy 202:14 a var. of **muha** (q.v.).

mhababa (pt. of **HBB**) glowing, burning; conflagration, glowing flame. Pl. **-ia.** **ʿšata ʿkilta d̲-hʿ iaqda umhababa** Gs 63:23 the consuming flame(s) burning and glowing; **banania umhababia** DC 26. 174 in the clouds and glowing flames.

***mhabalta** (pass. pt. pa. fem. st. emph. of **HBL**) corrupt, spoilt. Var. **mhambalta.** Pl. (fem.) **mhabalata.** **qiriata d̲-mhabalata** DC 26. 408 (var. **mhambalata** DC 28) spoilt creations.

mhabata s. **muh(a)bata.**

mhabra darkened, spoilt. **unišmatum mhabra** ATŠ II no. 35 and their souls darkened.

mhadiana (nom. ag. pa. of **HDA I**) person that brings joy. Pl. **-ia** joy-bringers, bride and bridegroom, wedding guests. **riš ama d̲-mhadiania** ŠQ head of (the people) of wedding guests; **mhadianak** ŠQ 19:30 thy wedding guests; **umsakilun ʿl mhadiania aitia sigdia ušukar uamuza lmhadiania** ŠQ 8:23 they gaze at the happy pair bringing almonds and sugar and walnuts for the happy pair.

mhadit (مُحدَّث) accidentally polluted. **ʿniš d̲-ginzh̲ mhadit** DC 44 a person whose treasure is polluted; **mhadit bšintia** DC 45 polluted in sleep (*or* talks in his sleep?).

mhaṭa (מַחַט, ܡܚܛܐ, Ar. مَخْيَط, مِخْيَاط, Fränkel 258) needle. Pl. **-ia.** **hauia gaṭnin kd̲ mhaṭa** DC 36 they become thin as a needle; **šuba mhaṭia** DC 12. 123, Lond. roll B 153, 296 = P.A. xii par. seven needles. Gl. 31:12 defectively (**mhṭa**) ابرة *acus* سوزن.

mhaiman, mhaimin emph. **mhaimna** (act. pt. haf. of **AMN**) faithful, believer. Pl. masc. **mhaimnia,** fem. **mhaimnata.** **mlakia qadišia umhaimnia** DC 20 holy and faithful angels; **anašia mhaimnia** (*often*) believing people; **bʿspia mhaimnata** Gy 5:10 with believing lips.

mhalpiʿil DC 19 an angel.

mhalqiʿil DC 19 an angel.

mhamad, mhamaṭ = **mahamad.** **mhamad arbaia** Jb 85:1 Muḥammad the Arab; **mhamaṭ brh̲ d̲-ruha** RD 18 M. the son of R.

mhambaba = **mhababa.** **nura kd̲ iaqda umhambaba** DC 46 fire when flaming and glowing (cf. Gs 63:23 s. **mhababa**).

mhamb(a)la (act. pt. pa. of **HBL**) corrupting, destroying, corruptive, destructive. Pl. masc. **mhamblia,** fem. **mhamb(a)lata.** **ulmia aklia umhambalia** Gy 71:9 and to the devouring and destroying waters; **atuat d̲-mhambalata** DC 51. 339 women who corrupt (?); **mihiata mhamblata** DC 27. 147 corrupting blows.

mhambalana, mhamb(i)lana (nom. ag. pa. of **HBL**) despoiler, destroyer, corrupter, destructive being. Pl. **-ia.** **šuba kukbia d̲-hšuka mhamblania d̲-hazin alma** DC 40. 613 f. the Seven Stars of Darkness, the corrupters of this world; **zihira d̲-mhamblania** Gy 316:24 the poison of the destructive powers; **gabra mhambilana** DC 51. 151 the destructive being.

mhanaqta (pass. pt. pe. fem. st. emph. of **HNQ**) choking spirit: **lilita mnakalta maluaita umhanaqta** DC 20. 45 f., cf. DC 43 E 20 guileful, haunting and choking lilith.

mhaqa tether? halter? prob. **mhara** (q.v.). **zim kd̲ kdana bmhaqa** DC 46, DC 45 tied like a mule by its picket-rope (?).

mhara 1 (Akk. *maḫru* 'the front part'? Jb ii 48 n. 8) the beak, or the prow of a marsh-boat. **mhara qaiim alihdia kudka** Jb 44:3 s. **kudka**; **ʿl mhara matna šragia** Jb 152:3 at the prow are placed lanterns; **ʿl mhara qaiim ṣaida** Jb 152:7 at the beak stands the fisherman; **biṭušta lmhara bṭaš** Jb 156:10 s. **BṬŠ** pf.; **šaulh̲ mhara ukutla** Jb 234:10 they made its prow and stern.

mhara 2 (Doubtf.) an instrument for watering (?), watering-pot (?) Jb 49 footn., Ginzā 431 n. 3. (Nöld. 'measure?' MG 11 n. 2, 432:9, 441:9). **man dara mhara bʿda umdabar mia lšitlia** Gs 10:20 who will carry the watering-pot (?) in his hand and water the plants? **mahu mhara sna bʿdak ʿu mia brahaṭak ʿstakariun** Gs 111:14 f. wherefore was the watering-pot removed from thy hand and the water blocked off from thy channel? **ana lmhara šna bʿdai ʿu mia brahaṭai ʿstakariun** Gs 111:15 f. neither the watering-pot (?read **lamhara** ? MG 11 n. 2, 432 n. 1) was removed from my hand nor the water blocked from my channel(s).

mhara 3 (rt. **MHR I**, cf. ܡܫܘܚܐ measurer?) land-surveyor?, architect? Pl. **-ia.** **umhara dranin upašiṭnin mšaria** DAb = RD B 41 and we brought a land-surveyor (or architect?) and laid out habitations; **kd̲ mharia timhirinun** s. **MHR I.**

mhara 4 (rt. **MHR II.** Used parallel with **zmama**) guiding-rein? **kd̲ kudania bmhara ukd̲ gumla bzmamia** DC 40. 354 like mules by the guiding-rein (?) and like a camel with its bridle.

mharam (Ar. مُحَرَّم) AM 259:20 the Moslem month of *Moharram.*

mharšai(a) (rt. **HRŠ II**) DC 44 & par. (in a corrupt text) bewitcher?

mhaša DC 48 a var. of **nhaša 2** (q.v.).

mhaš(a)bana s. **mhašbana.**

mhaš(a)bata (ܡܚܫܒܬܐ) pl. plots, schemes MG 32:31, Jb ii 17 n. 1. **mhašabata bišata** Gy 195:20 evil schemes; **mhašbath̲** (var. **mhašabath̲** Sh. 'Abd.'s copy) **lašalman** Gy 12:14 his plots succeeded not; **trisar mhašabata** Gy 90:21 twelve (evil) schemes; **mn binia mhašabata sliq** Gs 69:22 he rose up from (their) designs; **alma d̲- . . . mhašabata mlia** Gs 118:22 the world which . . . is full of schemes; **razaikun umhašabatkun** DC 43 your mysteries and your plots; **umhašabata binia anašia nihuia** AM 269:25 and there will be plots amongst people.

mhašauata DC 43 a phonetic var. of preced.

mhašbana (nom. ag. pa. of **HŠB**, Syr. ܡܚܫܒܢܐ) schemer, plotter, planner. Var. **mhašabana.** Pl. **-ia. gubria mhašbania** CP 118:penult., ML 144:7, var. **mhašabania** DC 51 schemers; **mhašbana ḏ-rania umhašib** Gy 215:12 a schemer who planneth and plotteth.

mhašbata s. **mhašabata.**

mhaškanuta (abstr. noun from nom. ag. pa. of **HŠK**) Gy 215:17 obscurantism.

mhatam 1 (pass. pa. of **HTM**) sealed, signed, confirmed. Fem. st. emph. **mhatamta.** Pl. masc. **mhatmia,** fem. **mhatamata** MG 31 n. 2. **ʿngirta mhatamta** CP 90:4, DC 47 = ML III: 5 a sealed letter; pl. **ʿngirata mhatamata** Gs 7:24 sealed letters.

mhatam 2 (cf. s. 1) Jb 1:5, 10 etc. (often in colophons) a *malwâša* man's name.

mhulta s. **muhulta.**

mhiṭa for **mhaṭa** in **ušuba mhiṭia ḏ-pulad** DC 46 and seven steel needles.

mhilma (rt. **HLM II**) dream(ing state). Pl. **mhilmia** DC 40. 864.

mhita (rt. **MHA,** Jew.-Aram. & Syr. differently מְחָתָא, ܡܚܘܬܐ) blow, wound, beating, castigation; mischance, accidental offence, pollution (often in rituals); attack upon MG 104:2. Pl. **mihiata** ibid., 165:21. **mhita bgu mhita** Gy 229:4, 300:ult., Jb 98:12, ATŠ I no. 50 etc. (cf. s. **MHA** ethpe. impf.); **bmhita ḏ-napšaihun nitimhun** s. **MHA** ethpe. impf.; **mn hanik mihiata mitmihian** ibid. pt.; **mn kulhun mihiata udrakia** DC 27 from all beatings and thrashings; **mhita uasuta** ATŠ (repeatedly) (unwitting) offence (: accidental disqualification for ritual etc.) and its purification; **mn kulhun mihiata masqtulh̠** DC 35 you raise him up from all (involuntary) pollutions; **ʿtparaq mn mhita ḏ-hṭibh̠** ATŠ II no. 75 he was delivered from that accidental offence which he committed; **ʿniš ḏ-haiba mn raza ḏ-mihiata** ATŠ a person guilty of the mystery of accidental impurities; **mhita ḏ-ṭiba** ATŠ II no. 75 accident of drowning; **mhita ḏ-anašia hauia ʿlh̠** AM 29:16 he will be attacked by people; **bšauṭa ḏ-alip mihiata mhaitinkun** DC 43 J 32 I struck you with a whip of a thousand lashes (?); **mihiata mhambalata** s. **mhambala; umhitai dilia latihuia ʿlauaihun** Gy 180:1 f. so that my chastisement of them is unnecessary.

MHL (by metathesis from מלח, ܡܠܚ, ملح) to salt.

Gl. 150:9 f. miswritten (as a nominal st. emph., defectively) ملح *salire* نمكين كرد.

Der.: **mihla** (var. **mahla**?).

MHR I (ܡܫܚ) to measure (land), survey.

Pe. Impf. with suff. **kḏ mharia timhirinun** DC 44. 1036 like land-surveyors thou shalt survey them.

Der.: **mhara 3.**

MHR II (cf. H. & mod. H. מהר II Ges.) the rt. of **mhara 4.**

MHŠ = **MŠH II** = **MŠA II** (q.v.).

Pe. Pf. with suff. **mihš(i)h̠** Gy 2:20 he measured it MG 66:17, 275:1.

MHT = **MTH** = **MTA** (q.v.).

Pe. Impf. with suff. **ʿmihtak bkulh̠ qumtai** (read **qumtak**) Gs 107:14 (interlinear gloss) I will stretch thee out to thy full length. Act. pt. **mahta qumth̠** Gy 115:11 she prostrated (hist. pres.) herself; **ulamahta qumtai** DC 44. 519 my form is not prostrate; pl. **mahtia qumtaihun** CP 372:16 they prostrate themselves; **mahtia uṭuna ṭainia** Gy 248:13 they spread (?) and bear fruit (Lidzb. took it for **NHT** and queried: *sie lassen* [*Samen*?] *fallen und tragen Früchte*). Part. pres. **ulman mahtit qumtak** Gy 208:10 and before whom dost thou prostrate thyself? MG 239:17.

Ethpe. Pf. **qumtai ḏ-gbiba ʿtmihtat** Gy 266:6 my body which had been bent was straightened (Nöld. quotes it as **ʿmihtat** MG 234:bottom).

mu 1 = **amu** MG 94:4.

mu 2 a mod. form of **ma 1.**

Gl. 38:9 **mu** أي *quaecumque* چه; 162:5 **mu** ما *quod* همه چيز.

mu 3 interrogative particle, usually proclitically **mu-** as a var. of **mi-** (q.v.). **mu mariut ʿlauaikun qašia šauṭai rama razim ʿlauaikun** CP 181:1 = ML 221:7 is not my overlordship hard over you and is not my lofty scourge heavy upon you?

mubauata DC 45 an illiterate miscop. of **ʿuhrauata** DC 46.

mubla (rt. **YBL**) burden, load MG 129:9. Pl. **mublia.** Gy 106:17, 346:18. Var. **miblia** s.v.

mugan AM 203 a place-name. V.s. **mulgan.**

mugrib a var. of **magrib.**

mud (contracted from **mahu ḏ-**) what is that?, how is it?, is it not? MG 62:1, 94:4, 438:4. **kul mud ḏ-ʿlh̠** Par. xi 22 b all that he has (with a pleonastic **ḏ-**) MG 345:9 f. **mašṭa mud mzaina** ŠQ 18:29 is not the comb an instrument of adornment?

mudalal a *malwâša* woman's name.

mudalia DC 26. 11 a var. of **mdalia.**

muha (מוֹחָא, ܡܘܚܐ, Ar. مُخّ, H. מֹחַ marrow, Phoen. מח grease of animals, Akk. *muḫḫu* skull) brain, brain-pan, pate, head. Var. **mha. bqurqlia rurbia ḏ-mha** Gy 202:13 f. (var. **muha** Sh. ʿAbd.'s copy was rightly anticipated by Lidzb. Ginzā 202 n. 3) on the great (: strong?) circles (?) (Sh. ʿAbd.'s copy has **qurqsia** κρίκοι, κίρκοι [!]) of the brain-pan; **bqurqlia ḏ-muhain** AO ix 96:2 by the tresses of their pates (Gordon); **mn muqra ḏ-atutia muha ḏ-briša šriia** ATŠ I no. 244 from the matter that is beneath the brain-pan that is situated in the head; **kurpia mn muhak** JRAS 1943 171:10 (remove) his seat from thy brain.

m(u)habaṭ Oxf. roll g 369 for **mhamaṭ** Muḥammad.

muh(a)bata (rt. **YHB**) Gy 62:4 pl. gifts MG 130:2. Varr. **mahabata** B, **mhabata** D.

m(u)hulta (rt. **NHL,** ܡܢܚܠܐ & ܡܘܚܠܐ, Ar. مُنْخُل) sieve. **muhulta ḏ-nahlilh̠ garmanka** Bodl. xiii the sieve in which they sieve fine flour; **gišar um(u)hulta** DC 48. 281

quern and sieve; **m(u)hulta h**ᶜ DC 48 (picture) it is a sieve.

muhsin (Ar. مُحْسِن) Zotb. 218 b:11 a man's name.

muh(u)r (*Mithra* SsSs i 122, mod. P. مِهر) Mithra identified with Hibil MSt 87. **hibil ušitil uanuš ḏ-hinun muhur** (var. **muhr** B) **uruš rast** Gy 286:11, Ginzā 284 n. 4, **tlata šumia atnit** ᶜ**lh̲ ḏ-hinun m-u-h-r r-š-t r-s-t** DC 41. 476 f.

muza = **amuza.** Mod. pl. **muzan(a).** **luzan umuzan unuman** DC 46, JRAS 1943 171:9 almonds, walnuts and lemons; **lkasa ḏ-muza** DC 46 upon a bowl of walnut(-wood?, or shell?).

muzania (Eg.-Aram. מוזנא, Bibl.-Aram. מֹאזַנְיָן, Chr.-Pal. ܡܘܙܢܝܐ, H. מֹאזְנַיִם, Ar. loan-w. ميزان Fränkel 198) scales, balance; measure, weight MG 22:18. With the add. of a dual ending, from which a pl. **muzaniia** was formed MG 148:12 ff., 164:18 f. Brandt: JPTh 1892 pp. 431 f., CP trs. 199 n. 2. **ḏ-muzania hua** CP 261:10; **(abatur) hua ḏ-muzania** Gy 384:21 (A.) became He-of-the-Scales; **udmuzania lamitiqrina** Jb 159:2 and I shall not be called (He-)of-the-Scales; **gabra ḏ-muzania** Oxf. 44 b the Being of the Scales; **abatur ḏ-muzania** CP 80:2 = Q 37:15 A. of the scales (ذو الميزان) MG 316:21 ff.; **abatur . . . muzania hua** Jb 9:1 Abathur . . . became (him of) the scales [*sic*] Jb ii 14 n. 11, Nöld. ZA xxx 153, Sundberg: Kushṭa 118, **atriṣ uiatib muzania** Jb 185:2 the balance is set up and sitting [*sic*]; **kḏ laṣba muzania mitqal . . .** ᶜ**lmuzania qralh̲ uhananh̲** Jb 253:1 f. when the balance did not want to weigh . . . he called to the balance and cozened it; **šarhab**ᶜ**il ubihram muzania** Jb 253:3 f. (balance personified); **alma ldmuzania taqil** ᶜ**ubadia uagria** Gs 74:11, 82:19, 86:8 until the scales counterpoise works and recompense; **muzania rba qadmaia** CP 75:5 = Q 34:40 = ML 92:2 the First Great Balance (as a sg.); **trin muzaniia** Gs 85:11 the two scales, both scales; **tlatma ušitin muzaniia** CP 75:3, Q 34:29 = ML 92:1 the 360 balances; **bmuzania grida** AM (*often*) in scant measure (as a sg.); **muzania ṭaba** DC 19, DC D 52 good measure (as a sg.); **muzania ḏ-ligria** DC 41. 464 f. the equilibrium of the legs.

muziguta DC 22. 10 a var. of **mziguta** Gy 10:20.

muṭlab (Ar. مُطَّلَب) Zotb. 221 a:29 a man's name.

muiinpaع [*sic*] Zotb. 228 a:2 v.s. **NP**ع.

MUK = **MKK.**

muka 1 (Ar. مُخّ) a mod. form of cl. **muha** brain, marrow. Pron. *mōχa*. St. cstr. in mod. *moχ al-riša* brain. **ḏ-muka ḏ-br anašia azilna** DC 26 so that I enter the brain of a human being; **muka ḏ-girmh̲ ḏ-**ᶜ**mbra** DC 46 118:10 the marrow of a sheep's bones.

muka 2 (Gl. 157:13 **muka** مفروش *stratus* گسترده) bedding. Var. **mauka** s.v.

mukran AM 205 a place-name BZ Ap. II.

muktalapat (Ar., cf. foll.) AM 278:6 f. dissension(s).

muktalip (Ar. مُخْتَلِف) AM 258:21 f. various, diverse.

muktar (Ar. مُخْتَار) RD D 27 a family-name.

mula 1 (< **mubla**? or for ᶜ**ula 2**?) embryo, foetus: ᶜ**nta ḏ-mula dra** DC 46 234:18 a pregnant woman (: a woman that carries an embryo).

mula 2 (Ar. مَوْلَى) lord, sir (often in the coloph. of Sh. ʿAbd.'s Ginzā).

mulaqat, malaqat (Ar. مُلاَقَات) encounter, meeting with. **malaqat uhzaia ḏ-šulṭania** AM 161:penult. f. encounter with and seeing rulers (a miswriting of **mulaqat**).

mulgan a var. of **mugan** a town in Azerbaijan BZ Ap. II.

mulia (pual. pt., hence *מְעַלְיָא) (*a*) height, a high place, (*b*) mound, heap MG 132:paen. (*a*) ᶜ**utria umalkia ḏ-bgauh̲ ḏ-hinun bmulia** ᶜ**laia lbar mn tibil bgirbia** Gy 282:25 f. the uthras and angels which are therein, which live in the highest height outside the earth in the north (MSt 38 ff.); **lašania šapala mn mulia** Jb 42:3, Gy 320:18 cf. Jb ii 47 n. 3; **mn mulia napil unimut** AM 3:13 he will fall from a height and die; **mn mulia napil umuma bihda siṭra ḏ-rišia lagiṭ** AM 6:3 he will fall from a height and receive an injury to one side of his head; (*b*) **mulia apra** DC 44 an ash-heap.

mulian AM 205 a place-name. BZ Ap. II.

mulita DC 43 A 95, 137 a demon.

mulk 1 (Ar. مُلْك) Zotb. 218 b:30 kingdom.

mulk 2 (for Ar. مِلْك) property. **kḏ zabnit mulk** AM 164:4 when thou buyest a property.

mulkana (ܡܘܠܟܢܐ) advice, counsel. Pl. **-ia. umulkana ḏ-**ᶜ**niš lamqabil** AM 19:16 and he accepts no man's advice; **umulkania minh̲ baiin** AM 44:8 and they ask his advice; **mulkana ḏ-**ᶜ**niš lamalik** AM 30:15 he gives advice to nobody; **umulkana bišia anašia malkilh̲** AM 92:14 and evil people give him counsel; **umulkania malik lanašia nukraiia** AM 43:20 and he gives counsel to strangers; **mluk mulkania šapiria lhdadia** Gy 25:22 give good counsels to each other; **uailh̲ lmalik milih̲ ḏ-mulkana** ᶜ**l napšh̲ lamlak** Gy 357:2 woe to him that offereth advice but himself is ill-advised.

muma (מוּמָא, ܡܘܡܐ, H. מְאוּם & מוּם Ges., LS; Ar. loan-w. مُوم Fränkel 264) fault, defect, injury, infirmity, spot, blemish MG 118:20. Pl. **mumia 1.** Masc. **latisbun rbuta ḏ-muma** Gy 19:2 do not be haughty when at fault, **ḏ-rbuta ḏ-muma nasib mipsiq šumh̲ mn atar nhur** Gy 19:3 f. whosoever assumeth haughtiness faultily his name is cut off from the place of light; **latinisbun rbuta** ᶜ**lauaihun umuma lnišmatkun latisbun** Gy 20:9 f. do not set yourselves over them lest your souls incur blemish; **anašia ḏ-muma ḏ-pagria** ᶜ**tbaiun** Gy

23:4 people with a corporal defect; **la asibtḫ muma lnapšai** Gs 51:2 I incurred no blemish; **d̲-muma litbḫ** (*often*) without defect; **muma d̲-gubria** AM 14:ult. genital defect, venereal disease (?); **uligrḫ muma nasib ʿu muma brišia** AM 29:15 and his leg will receive an injury, or (he will have) an infirmity in his head; **mn ahia ubnḫ muma tisab** AM 79:penult. she will be infected with an infirmity from her brother(s) or her children; **umuma nasib bmia hamima** AM 91:9 and will receive an injury from scalding water; **kibia umumia** AM 284:11 diseases and infirmities; **latisbḫ muma lʿuṣrak** Q 72:12 do not contaminate thy mind.

mumata (ܡܘܡܵܬܐ) oaths, vows MG 22:18 f. Doublet **ʿumamata** (s.v.) MG 130:top. **iamin mumata** Gs 36:ult. they swear oaths; **bmumata d̲-aumian ab** *Florilegium*: by the oaths with which my father made me swear.

mumaṭiɛa a miscop. of **muqaṭaɛ** (cf. BZ 183 n. 8).

mumia 1 pl. of muma.

mumia 2, mumiia (مُومِيا) piss-asphalt, a kind of bitumen used as ointment and preservative. **šalam umumia** DC 46. 108:11 darnel-weed and piss-asphalt; **riwand šinia umumiia** DC 46. 69:6 Chinese rhubarb and piss-asphalt.

mumiaiil DC 40. 881 an angel.

mumiṭaɛ AM 277:37 a var. of **muqaṭaɛ**.

muminaiia name of a people, or tribe. **hazin aina d̲-muminaiia hu** DC 7 this is the well of the M.

mumtazad Ṣâb.'s AM = **mumtazid.**

mumtazid (cf. Ar. مُزْد cold) AM 286:33 frigid.

munaiia: baba hurina d̲-munaiia mitiqrin DC 22. 219 another sect called Munaeans (Manichaeans?) see **m(n)unaiia.**

munasabat (Ar. مناسبة) relation, resemblance. **humria munasabat bnura** AM 277:23 redness (: red clouds) resembling fire.

munasata s. foll.

munašat (corrupt Ar.) dawn? Varr. **munasata** BZ 85 n. 7, **mišlaiia** Ṣâb.'s AM. Doubtf. **lṣalat d̲-munašat** AM 132:20.

m(u)nunaiia DC 22. 225 = **m(i)nunaiia** Gy 225:11.

munqa 1 (act. pt. af. st. emph. of **YNQ**) fosterer, foster-father, fostering, nurseryman. MG 23: 11, 247 n. 1. Pl. **-ia. brik . . . d̲-ʿtlḫ lpira munqa** Oxf. iii 54 b blest is he . . . who hath one to tend (his) fruit MG 402:29; **pira d̲-litlḫ munqa** CP 190:8 a fruit-tree with none to tend it; **ldilan litlan aba ulalpiran ʿtlḫ-munqa** CP 192:7, Oxf. iii 54 b:2 we are fatherless, our fruit (has) no one to tend it MG 431:20; **anatun munqa tihuilḫ** Gy 101:3 ye shall be his fosterer; **gabra munqa** Gy 323:7, 9, 335:14 fosterer, tending, being; **bit munqak** Gy 324:4, Gs 11:10, Q 66:30 house of thy fosterer; **šuta(aih)un d̲-munqai** Gs 65:1 the voice of my fosterers; **b(i)nia munqia kasiia** Gs 64:12 amongst the hidden fosterers; **gabra d̲-hualak munqa** Gy 362:24 the man who was thy fosterer; **hinun hulḫ munqa** Gs 69:13, 17 they were his fosterer(s); **hibil hualḫ munqa** Gs 71:12 f. H. was his fosterer; **uluṭḫ lhazin atra d̲-bit munqak** CP 131:penult. and curse this place of thy fostering (foster-father).

munqa 2 for **mianqa. nišmata d̲-minḫ munqa uzuṭa** ATŠ II no. 375 souls that are younger and smaller than himself.

munqalib (Ar. مُنْقَلِب) (astron.) (*a*) variable, unstable, (*b*) overthrown. **munqalib biniana** AM 159:18 the building will be overthrown; **sarṭana munqalib hu** AM 149:19 Cancer is variable.

muɛadam (Ar. مُعَظَّم) AM 276:7 eminent, excellent.

muɛailia AM 256, var. **muɛalia** Ṣâb.'s AM etc. a family-name.

muɛarapat (Ar. مَعْرِفَة) AM 278:11 f. information, definition, determination.

muɛtadil s. **maɛtadil.**

MUṢ = MṢṢ.

m(u)ṣahma = **mṣahma** (q.v.).

m(u)ṣapa = **mṣapa** (q.v.).

muqadas (Ar. مُقَدَّس) sacred, holy. **barqa d̲-muqadas** AM 283:4 in the Holy Land.

muqaṭaɛ (Ar. مُقَطَّع) torn to pieces, ragged. **aiba d̲-muqaṭaɛ** (cf. BZ 183 n. 8) a ragged cloud (with many miscopyings).

muqra (מוֹקְרָא, ܡܘܩܪܐ, cf. Ar. مُقْلَة, Akk. *muqaru* LS) marrow, sperm, brain, gelatinous matter, living substance, plasma. Pl. muqria Oxf. roll g 834. **bṭun muqra** Gy 102: 16 became full of living substance MG 396:20; **nʿtia ʿula mn kras ʿmḫ kd̲ muqra d̲-baita** Gs 7:22 the foetus cometh out of the womb of its mother like the gelatinous matter of an egg; **mn muqra mšauin miša d̲-birkta** Gy 227:11 from living matter they prepare the oil of benediction; **mn ainia ṣar muqra umn muqra ṣar riša** Gy 244:91 from the eyes developed brain-matter, and from brain-matter developed the head; **muqra ugirmia** Gy 202:3 marrow and bones; **muqra d̲-girmia hʿ** ATŠ II no. 113 it is the marrow of bones; **kd̲ ʿṣṭarar muqra bgirmia** ATŠ II no. 115 (DC 6 omits **bgirmia**) when the marrow was formed in the bones; **mn muqra d̲-atutia muha** ATŠ no. 244 from the (brain-)matter that is beneath the brain-pan; **amuza haila hu d̲-muqra gauaia d̲-briša šria** ATŠ II no. 122 the walnut is a symbol (?) of the inner brain-matter that is found within the head; **hiškat ainḫ muqra** DC 41. 500 f. her eyes were obscured by matter; **paharna bmuqra** Par. xxiv 39 b, DC 46. 105:6 I fly into the brain; **ruha hʿ d̲-iatba bmuqra** DC 48 the evil spirit that is sitting in living matter.

mura 1 (מוּרָא, ܡܘܪܐ, مُرّ, μυῤῥα *myrrha* Löw 246) myrrh, myrrh-tree.

mura 2 (מוֹרָה) authority. **huṭra d̲-mura** s. **huṭra** staff of office (authority).

mura 3 (rt. **MRR**) bitterness. Masc. **ulʿnšia mura nihuilun** AM 275:12 f. and there will be bitterness for women; **miḫna umura** s. **miḫna.**

muraba (rt. **ARB II**) AM 287:32 mixed.

murakas (for **-aṣ**, Ar. مُرَخَّص) permitted to take leave. Mod. (ʿl dinai) **murakas ʿbdilai** DC 51:coloph. that they may let me go.

muraqa a var. of muriqa(b) (q.v.).

murat st. cstr. of ***murta** (q.v.), venom.

murdauata (rt. **MRD**?) doubtf. **murdauata d̠-hinun arba razia d̠-bgauh̠ ʿṣṭbun** DC 34. 995 the *m.* which are the four mysteries into which they are baptized.

muruaria 1 = muruarid 1. Fem. pl. **muruaria d̠-lanqiban** AM 287:2 unpierced pearls. Var. **maruaria** Ṣâb.'s AM.

muruaria 2 = muruarid 2.

muruarid 1 (P.-Ar. مُرْوَارِيد) pearls. Varr. **muruarit** DC 44. 1204 f., **miruarita, muruaria 1, maruaria** s.v. Fem. pl. (cf. s. **muruaria 1**).

muruarid 2 a *malwâša* woman's name.

murṭa(ṭa) (ܡܪܛܐ & ܡܪܛܘܛܐ, Ar. loan-w. بِرْط Fränkel) cloak, mantle MG 127:20. Pl. **-ia. murṭia umurṭaṭia** Gy 178:12 mantles of different kinds (? Ginzā 181 n. 7).

muriqa (מוֹרִיקָא) (*a*) subst.: saffron, (*b*) adj.: yellow, var. **muraqa, buraq 2** (s.v.). (*a*) **muriqa utirba d̠-kuliata d̠-aria** AM 135:3 saffron and the kidney-fat of a lion; (*b*) **taura hiuara usumaqa umuriqa** AM white, red and yellow bull.

murqa (ܡܘܪܩܐ) (*a*) purging, cleansing, (*b*) yellowness, cleanness. (*a*) **širiania d̠-mqardin mn muqra** DC 46, JRAS 1943 170:26 membranes that are scoured by purge; (*b*) **murqia d̠-zahba hu** DAb its yellowness is of gold.

***murta** a doublet of **mirta**, found only in st. cstr. **murat** MG 105:antep. **murat** (var. **ʿumrat** Leid.) **arqba gauata d̠-hšuka** the venom of the inner scorpion of darkness.

murtazad Ṣâb.'s AM a var. of **mumtazid.**

MUŠ = **MŠŠ.**

Pe. Part. pres. **maišit btirata** Q 24:1 = CP 51:13 = ML 67:4 thou touchest consciences.

Der.: s. **MŠŠ.**

mušarab (Ar. مُشَارِب) drinking(-vessel). **qbur bkanṣa mušarab** DC 45 bury in a drinking-bowl.

mušašia (Ar. مُشَاشَة) clay, cartilage (?). **tlih̠ mašašia** Ṣâb.'s AM hang on him some cartilage (?).

mušarah (Ar. مُجْرَح) Zotb. 218 a:18 a family-name.

mušk 1 (Akk. *mušku*) mulberry. **hazin ʿlana d̠-mušk hu** DC 41 (picture) this is a mulberry tree.

mušk 2 (ܡܘܫܟܐ?) follies, conceits? **uʿtib ʿl aina d̠-mušk** DC 41. 98 and he sat by the well of vain conceits.

mušmana (a transformation of Ar. مُسْلِم with a derisive allusion to the rt. **ŠMN**) Moslem. Very frequent in mod. Mand. **atuat d̠-šabqalh̠ lzauh̠ mandaia qazla lmušmana rahmalh̠** DAb a woman that leaves her Mandaean husband and goes and loves a Moslem; **dutun hiuun mušmana** Morg. 281:paen. (mod.) come then, be Moslem(s).

mušpikta s. foll.

mušpita (a labialized form of ܡܫܩܦܬܐ; cf. Fränkel 256) pointed rod, split, stake: **sarkala umušpita** s. **sarkala; mušpita d̠-parzla** DC 40. 1090, 1093 an iron spit; **bmušpita** (var. **bmušpikta**) **usikta abihdh̠** DC 44 with the spit and the peg with it.

MUT (Gen. Sem.) to die.

Pe. Pf. **mit** he died, they died MG 248:3. Impf. **nimut, timut, ʿmut, nimitun, timitun** MG 249:7 f. & 23; exceptional forms **nimitiun** Gs 44:6 AB (var. **nimitun** CD) they (will) die **nimaitun muta tiniana** DC 26. 112 f. they will die the second death; fem. forms: sg. **latimitai** Gy 161:6, Gs 132:13 (with bad varr. as **lamitai, latimaita** etc.) do not die MG 217:10, 250:1 f., pl. **nimita** they (fem.) die, or will die MG 249:23. Impt. **mut** MG 250:5. Act. pt. **maiit** he dies, will die MG 250:10; **maitia** they (will) die MG 7:20 f. Pass. pt. **mita** s.v. Inf. **lašabqilh̠ lmimat** Jb 100:2 he (: the Life, pl.) permits him not to die.

Gl. 150:3 f. **mat** [*sic*] مات *mori* مرد.

Der.: **muta, mutana, mita.**

muta (rt. **MUT**, Gen. Sem.) death MG 22:17, Pl. **-ia.** Masc. **muta nimitun** AM 273:3 f. they will die; **muta šapira** AM (*very often*) a good death, natural death; **trin mutia bhad** Jb 57:2, 7 two deaths instead of one; **ʿmut (a)trin mutia** Jb 104:7 I will die two deaths; **timut trin mutia** Gy 300:2 she dieth twice; **maita muta tiniana** (*often*) she will die a second death MG 399:bottom (cf. ὁ δεύτερος θάνατος Apoc. 20:6, ὁ θάνατος ὁ δεύτερος Apoc. 20:14, 21:8) MSt 89 f., Brandt JPTh xviii 586; **muta biša** Gy 161:7 an opposite of **muta šapira** (above).

mutalta (for ***mutanta**?) fem. mortal? tertian fever? **ʿšata qarušta umutalta** DC 46 shivering and tertian (?) (or mortal (?)) fever.

mutana (further abstr. noun from **muta**, מוֹתָנָא, Syr. & Chr.-Pal. ܡܘܬܢܐ, Ar. loan-w. مُوتَان Fränkel 265) pestilence, cholera, mortality MG 136:6. Masc. **qiria umutana** Gy 287:3 disaster and pestilence. Very frequent in AM.

mutba (rt. **YTB**) (*a*) seat, throne, (*b*) (place of) residence, home, site. MG 23:11, 129:9. Masc. (*a*) **mutba d̠-malka** AM 218:11 the royal throne; (*b*) **batia d̠-mutbh̠** Gy 6:6 the houses of his residence; **mutbun** AM 221:16 their homes.

mzaga (ܡܙܓܐ) mixing, mixture. **mzaga d̠-tuqna** Gy 318:4 a mixture of composition (Lidzb. *Mischung der Helligkeit*).

mzahrana (nom. ag. pa. of **ZHR I**) careful person, heedful man. **mzahrana hua** ATŠ I no. 210 he was a careful man.

mzahruta (abstr. noun from **ZHR I**) DC 22. 44:ult. = **zahruta** Gy 47:9.

mzaina (from زين) means of adornment,

instrument of adornment; **mašṭa mud mzaina** s. **mud.**

mzanaita (pass. pt. fem. st. emph. of **ZNA**) debauched, var. **mzanita** act. pt. **arba mzanaita** (var. **mzanita**) Jb 129:13, 130:4 s. **arba 3** (Jb ii 127 n. 8).

mzaraz (pass. pt. pa. of **ZRZ**) armed, prepared for conflict, well-equipped, valorous, vigorous. St. emph. masc. **mzarza.** St. emph. fem. **mzarazta.** Pl. masc. **mzarzia,** fem. **mzarzata.** **ʿutra mzarza** (*often*) valorous uthra; **ʿngirta mzarazta** ATŠ II no. 340 a well-equipped missive; **spinata mzarzata** Gy 320:2 well-equipped ships (Ginzā 324 n. 1). In Gy 391 varr. as name of a king (see foll.).

mzarz malka Gy 391 name of a king.

mzarza s. **mzaraz.**

mzarzana (nom. ag. pa. of **ZRZ**) furnisher of defence, protector. **mzarzana ḏ-kulhun bhiria mzarzutak tišria ʿlan** Gy 62:12 furnisher of defence of all the elect ones, protect us with thine armour.

mzarzuta (abstr. noun from pass. pt. pa. of **ZRZ**) armour, equipment, accoutrement, protection, armed readiness. **kulhun bhda mzarzuta nizdarzun** DC 3 = CP 268:1 all of them are equipped with the same armour; **uzarzun bmzarzutun** Gy 80:4, 342:6, DC 3. 189:6 = CP 182:antep. he (: the Life, pl.) armed me with its (lit. 'their') armour; **mana bmzarzuta ainẖ latrẖ sakia** Gs 54:1 the *mana* (: soul) looked for protection towards its (own) place.

MZG (מְזַג, ܡܙܓ, H. מסך, Ar. مزج & مشج from Aram. Fränkel 172; from Akk. ?, cf. *munziqu* 'mixed wine' from *nazāqu* and *mussuku* perverted LS) to mix, mingle, blend, combine, compound, temper.

Pe. Pf. with suff. **lnišimta mzagtẖ ulruha** DC 48. 359 I have (or thou hast) combined the soul with the spirit. Act. pt. (pl.) **mazga** (read **-ia**) **agania** Gs 30:21 they mix cups (: potions). Pass. pt. **mziga 1** s.v.; pl. fem. st. abs. **agania mzigan** s. **agana.**

Ethpe Pf. **ʿmizgat** Gy 97:9 it (fem.) mingled MG 214:8, 22:16.

Der.: **mzaga, mziga, mziguta.**

mziga 1 (pass. pt. pe. of **MZG**) mixed, mingled, intermingled, combined. Fem. st. emph. **mzigta.** Pl. masc. **-ia,** fem. st. abs. s. **MZG.** **latihuia mziga** Gy 213:27 be not mixed (i.e. be pure! Ginzā 214 n. 1); **kuba mziga** DC 6 a mixed cup (i.e. a cup of wine and water); **mia mzigia** Gy 297:22 mingled waters; **ʿšata mzigta** Gy 297:23 mingled flame.

mziga 2 (for **mzaga** ܡܙܓܐ, Ar. loan-w. مِزَاج) constitution, temperament. **ʿuṣṭunẖ umzigẖ ulibẖ** DC 37. 32 his body and temperament and heart.

mziguta (abstr. noun from **mziga 1**) mixture, blend, fusion. **mziguta ḏ-razia** ATŠ I no. 220 a fusion of mysteries.

MṬA (Bibl.-Aram. & Eg.-Aram. מטא, Syr. ܡܛܐ & ܡܛܝ, Eth. መጠወ, Ar. انطى < امطى; rel. to H. מצא?) to come, arrive, reach, happen (to), overtake, attain (to).

Pe. Pf. **mṭa** Gs 80:21, CP 91:12, ML 113:4 it (he) arrived, **miṭiat** Gy 86:22, 158:11 etc. she arrived MG 257:8, 20, **lamiṭiat bʿdaihun** Gy 269:2 f., 297:10 they were unable (*idiom*) MG 366:11, **mṭainin** Gy 152:9, **mṭinin** Gy 151:2 f. we arrived MG 258:16, 18; with encl.: **miṭilun** Gy 44:13 A attacked them (var. **maṭilun** pres.), **lamiṭialan** Gy 11:14 it was impossible for us, we were unable (*idiom*) MG 366:18; with suff.: **rhiṭ nišma lšaruia miṭiiẖ** CP 81:17 f., ML 101:1 the soul ran and reached her liberator (**nišma** as masc.); **miṭia** Gy 269:24 = **miṭiiẖ** DC 22. 264 it reached him, fell to him, **miṭiak** Gs 55:12 came up to thee MG 286:16, **mṭinhun** Gy 261:14, 266:18 came up to them MG 290:13, **mṭatan** she came to me MG 285:13, **mṭatinun** Gy 261:23 she came up to them MG 290:22, **miṭiuia** Gy 242:21 they came up to him MG 288:22, **miṭiu** Gy 242:22 they came up to her MG 289:9, **mṭunun** Gy 271:16 they came to them MG 291:8. Impf. with suff. **nimiṭiiẖ** AM 10:9, **nimṭiẖ** AM 95:8 he will attain it, **nsisuta timiṭiiẖ** AM 242:19 illness will overtake him, **nimṭunẖ** AM 10, 29 &c., they (will) come to him (MG 288:antep.); **lgabra bmnatẖ nimṭunẖ** Gy 386:20 (they) will be allotted to the man MG 391:6; **nimṭinun** it will come to them, or reach them MG 290:15. Act. pt. **lmuta maṭia ulamaiit** AM 96:13 he will come near death, but will not die, **kḏ maṭia šuba razia . . . napqia uatia umitkarkibẖ** DC 3, CP 199 n.: 15 when she arriveth (on arriving), seven mysteries set out and come and embrace her; **lamaṭia bʿdaiun** Gy 232:5 it is impossible for them, they cannot (*idiom*) MG 366:22; **maṭia ḏ-tidlẖ lʿur** Gy 158:8 she is at the point of bringing forth Ur; **maṭia uatia iuma ḏ-tidlẖ lʿur** Gy 158:11 the day is coming that she will bring forth Ur; with encl. **qiniana ḏ-abahatẖ lamaṭilẖ** AM 14:18 family property will not come to him; **ḏ-hiuia maṭilẖ** ATŠ II no. 70, 81, 269 one attacked by a serpent; **man ḏ-maṭilẖ rihša** ATŠ II no. 270 who hath been attacked by a reptile; **maṭilun** Gy 51:18 they will overtake them. Part. pres. **maṭitun** ATŠ II no. 157 ye reach.

Pa. Pf. **maṭit** Gs 37:4 I have reached MG 261:6, **maṭun** Q 80:15 they (have) reached. Impt. **rhuṭ umaṭia** Gs 30:7, 34:22 run and attain. Inf. **maṭuiia** MG 143:ult., inf. abs. **mṭa maṭuia** CP 91:penult. = **mṭa maṭuiẖ** ML 113:9 f.; **mṭa maṭuiia** Gs 80:21 he arrived; with suff. **maṭuiai** my arriving MG 176:20; **maṭuiai bit ṭabia sigdit** Gy 92:8 when I arrived at the House of the Good (pl.) I prostrated myself MG 389:2.

Af. Pf. with suff. **amṭitẖ** Gs 22:14 I reached him. Impf. pl. **amṭun lbabaikun ptia** Or. 327:6 make for your open gates; with suff. **amṭuia lbaba ḏ-maškna** Gy 44:3 bring it to the door of the cult-hut MG 289:6. Act. pt. **mamṭia** Gy 217:12 he bringeth MG 262:17; with encl. **mamṭilẖ** (DAb) he bringeth him. Part. pres. **rihua mamṭina ʿlauaihun** DC 46. 99:ult. I make the 'wind' come upon them (form of bewitchment).

IDIOM. The 3rd p. sg. fem. is used as an impersonal verb often completed with **bʿda** 'to be able', 'to find it possible' (lit. 'to come into the hand') s. pe. pf. act. pt., without **bʿda** s. pe. pf.
DER.: **maṭu(ta)**.

mṭab (rt. **ṬAB**) good, fine, pleasing, agreeable. **riha mṭab** AM 259:5 a pleasing smell.

mṭaibana (nom. ag. pa. of **ṬAB**) benefactor, food-giver, sustainer, strengthener. **mṭaibana ḏ-ʿutria** DC 3. 239:2, DC 42. 718, DC 50, CP 366:17 sustainer of the uthras.

mṭalalia in **bit mṭalalia** Gy 330:6 f. a place-name (lit. 'the house of roofed huts') Ginzā 339 n. 1.

mṭanap, mṭanpa pt. pa. of **ṬNP** (q.v.). Fem. st. emph. **mṭanapta** Gy 330:4, Or. 331:19. **mṭanipta** DC 22. 327.

mṭanputa (abstr. noun from preced.) uncleanness, pollution MG 145:2. Doublet **ṭanputa** s.v. **bdma umṭanputa** Gy 223:7 in blood and pollution.

mṭarṭabla s. **mbarṭabla**.

mṭarta (*Florilegium*) a scr. def. of **maṭarta**.

MṬR (Gen. Sem.) to rain. Gl. 150:13 f. miswritten مطر *pluere* باریدن.
DER.: **miṭra**.

MṬŠ for **BṬŠ** in **lanimṭaš** DC 44. 1279 = **lanibṭaš** Morg. 264/19:3.

mi- (Talm. מִי, from orig. מא?) procl. interrog. particle (apart from the independent **mʿ**, **mia 3**, **mʿia 3**, **ʿmia** s.vv.) introducing both direct and indirect questions MG 12:25, 209:4. With **ʿka, aka 1** combined to **miaka, mʿiaka, maka 1** s.vv. Var. **mu-, mu 3** (s.v.) MG 209 n. 3. **miditun** Gs 54:13 (three times) from מִי יְדַעְתּוּן did ye know? MG 35:18, 435:18; **mihzaitun** Gy 186:6 have ye seen? **miligṭak** Gy 148:23 did he seize thee? MG 434:bottom.

mia 1 (pl. of **mai** q.v., Gen. Sem.) water(s), juice, fluid, sap. MG 97:17. Written, as a rule, defectively; an exceptional scr. pl. is **maia** s.v., further varr. **mʿia 2, mʿiia 2** (s.v.) MG 10:11 f. Trad. pron. *mey(y)â* (differently from **hiia**: pron. *heyyī*) cf. MG 10 n. 3, 164:2. St. cstr. formally identical with st. emph. 184:8. Different kinds of water MR 63 f., 65 ff., MSt 56 ff., Ginzā 15 n. 5, MMII 101, 118 n. 2, 119 n. 4. **mia hiia** (very often) living (i.e. flowing) water (an expression borrowed from Judaism? cf. Gen. 26:19, Lev. 14:5, 50; accord. to Pallis a gnostic term MSt 154:12), **mia hiia urauzia** Gs 318:24 living and fresh water, **mia anatun hiia** CP 47:2 = ML 62:7, Q 22:8 ye are living water(s) = Water of Life, MG 309 n. 1, **margna ḏ-mia hiia** Gy 129:14 the staff of living water, **margnia ḏ-mia hiia** Gy 25:16 pl., **himiania mia hiia** Gy 25:14 girdles of living water, **kimṣa ḏ-mia hiia** Gy 307:22 cf. s. **kimṣa**, similarly **nigda ḏ-mia hiia** Gy 307:23, **rušuma ḏ-mia hiia** s. **rušuma**; similar expressions: **mia hiuaria** Gy 32:13, 69:10 white water(s), **mia ḏ-ʿṣṭun ziua** Gy 141:7 water of the column of glory (Ginzā 156 n. 1), **mia ʿria urauzia** Gy 76:6 shining and resplendent water (parallel with **mia hiia** in the same line). Opposite expressions (used esp. of the waters of the underworld): **mia siauia** Gy 74:19, 137:22, 149:12, 153:24, 155:16, 159:4, 18, 160:2, 5, 10, 18, 163:20 f., 164:7, 23, 165:14, 23, 166:1, 3, 12, 15 f., 168:4, 5, 7, 8, 12, 169:5, 11, 14 f., 16, 269:1, 284:3, Jb 231:4, 13, 232:3, 8, 233:9, 234:2, 251:11 f., 257:9, &c.; black waters MR 43 n. 1, MSt 57 & nn. 6, 7, Brandt ERE viii 382, HpGn 280 f. and the synonymous **mia ʿkumia** Gy 140:4, cf. **aina ḏ-mia siauia** RD 34 = **aina ḏ-mia ʿkumia** Gy 139:5, 145:4 the source of black water(s), **ʿkumia hinun mia siauia** Gy 284:4 black are 'the black waters'; **mia tahmia** Gy 13:2, 269:10, 297:24, Jb 51:11, 204:2, 234:12, 235:1 always contrasted with **mia hiia**, alone Jb 141:12, 243:9 cut-off, (stagnant) water(s) MSt 58, **mia apria** Gy 141:7 id., **mia sariia** Gy 323:2 f. stinking water(s); **mia aklia** Gy 71:8, 78:2, 300:18 devouring water(s) (another designation of the waters of the underworld); **mia tma ulanahria** Gy 268:1 the water became turbid and shineth not MSt 58:bottom; **mia labasmia** Gy 269:2 the water became (hist. pres.) not sweet MR 65:middle; **mia psiqia** Gy 57:1 cut-off water (Christian baptismal font as opposite of running water) MSt. 42:ult.; **hapiqia mia** s. **hapiqia**; **mrumia mia** s. **mruma**; **sadania ḏ-mia** s. **sadana**; **ʿupania ḏ-mia** s. **ʿupania**; **riš mia** s. **riša**; **anzabia mia** s. **anzabia**; **gauaza ḏ-mia**, CP 19:6, ML 21:3 the staff of water; **gauaza ḏ-mia hiia** Jb 173:3 the staff of living water (cf. **margna ḏ-mia hiia** above); **piria mia** s. **pira**; **širiana ḏ-mia ḏ-arqa** Gy 75:8 the vein of waters of the earth; **šuba lbušia ḏ-mia . . . ušuba ksuiia ḏ-mia . . . ušuba qurahia ḏ-mia** Morg. 266/23: bottom, seven garments of water . . . and seven robes of water . . . and seven helmets of water [*sic*]; **mia ʿlaiia** Gy 380:16 the upper water(s); **mia qadmaiia** RD B 40 the first water(s); **mia bqira larbia** Gy 79:3 f. water mixeth not with pitch; **mia ḏ-buta** Q 48:5, 10 water of prayer CP trs. 36 n. 2 (cf. ML 69 n. 1); **mia mn iardna brbita . . . arbia** s. **rbita**; **mia biardna zakaiia qudamak laiit** Q 23:18, 54:20 Before Thee (even) jordan-water is impure. In colophons often with the meaning of 'river': **mia ḏ-karka** s. **karka 2**, **mia ḏ-ʿulai** the river of Ulai (: Karun; cf. Jb 149:5, where the word still means 'water').

mia 2 pl. (Jew.-Aram. sg. מְעָא, pl. מְעִין, also Bibl.-Aram., Syr. pl. ܡܥܰܝ̈ܳܐ, H. & mod. H. pl. מֵעִים, Ar. مِعًى, Eth. አማዑት, Akk. *amūtu* LS, Ges.) entrails, intestines, gut, bowels. Varr. **maia 2, mʿia 1, mʿiia 1** s.vv. **zihira bmiiẖ šdilẖ** Gy 84:3 f. I cast poison into his bowels; **kdub bmagalta ḏ-mia** DC 46, 137:12 write on gut-skin; **šigra bmia** DC 43 fever in the bowels; **karka ḏ-mia** Or. 29:20 s. **karka 3**.

mia 3 s. **mi-**.

miababa (rt. **YBB**) lamentation, groaning. **bkulhun humria qahda umiababa urgaza** DC 26. 205 amongst all the amulet-spirits there is shouting and lamentation and anger.

miabašta (rt. **YBŠ**) dry ground, dryness. Var. **miabišta, mibašta. huat miabašta** Gy

97:14 there became dry land; **uqam iuhana bmiabašta** Gy 191:20 and John stood on dry ground; **haza miabašta huat** Gs 76:10 f. this dry land was formed; **mibašta** CP 191:5, 6, ML 225:8, 9.

miaka (Talm. מיאכא, mi- + **aka 1**) is there? MG 209:7, 296:3. Varr. **miiaka, mʿiaka, maka 1** s.vv. **miaka ḏ-gabir minai** Gy 81:19 is there anyone stronger than I? **miaka alma ḏ-baba litlẖ** Gy 161:15 f. is there a world which hath no door? **miaka ḏ-biš minai** Jb 22:4 is there anyone worse than I? **miaka iuma . . .** Jb 72:3 ff. is there a day . . .?

mianqa (pass. pt. pa. of **YNQ** q.v.) little child, infant; adj. child-like. **btibil mianqa aitinkun** ATŠ I no. 188 ye are as children in the world; **ana ania udania umradpa umianqa** (often in colophons after the name of the copyist) I, poor and lowly and persecuted and small; **ana . . . umianqa abda ḏ-kulẖ haṭaiia** ATŠ (*and often*) I (So-an-So) a small and very sinful slave; **ansitilẖ mianqa** Zotb. 217 b:16 I copied it as a boy. Verbal use s. **YNQ.**

miarqa (pass. pt. pa. of **YRQ I**) pale, greenish Pl. **-ia. šapiria ainẖ umiarqia** AM 9:4 his eyes are beautiful and greenish.

mibašta s. **miabašta.**

mibla = **mubla.** Pl. **-ia. miblia ḏ-hala** DC 43 J 149 loads of stone.

migan AM 203 a place-name. Var. **mugan** (v.s. **mulgan**).

migrib Ṣâb.'s AM a var. of **magrib.**

midai a frequent var. of **madai** (q.v.).

midurta 1 occ. var. of **mdurta.**

midurt(i)a 2 fem. (rt. **MDR**?) rotten. **unitpaša kḏ bita mdurtia mn glala** DC 44. 1719 (var. **madudia** Morg. par.) and shall be smashed like a rotten (?) egg by a stone.

mihgia occ. var. of **mahgia.**

mihiana (rt. **MHA**) blow, wound. Masc. Doubtf. **ʿu parqita napla ʿlẖ ʿu mihiana šidana** ATŠ I no. 76 (var. **mauiana** PD par.) either a fragment (?) fell on him, or a felling blow (?) (var. furious howler?).

mihiuara DC 43 F 86 corrupt text.

mihiata pl. of **m(i)hiata.**

mihita occ. var. of **mhita.**

mihla (מִלְחָא, Bibl.-Aram. מְלַח, Syr. ܡܶܠܚܳܐ, Chr.-Pal. ܡܠܚܐ, H. מֶלַח, Ar. مِلْح, Akk. *mil'u* Ges.) salt. Fem. **mihla ʿkumtia anat lau hiuartia marirtia anat lau halaitia** DC 40:92 ff. salt, thou art black, not white, thou art bitter, not sweet; **mihla marirtia** DC 40. 43, 1066, DC 46 (often), Lond. roll B 79, 409 &c. salt-petre; **mihla pt pšar** (var. **pišra**) JRAS 1937 592:2, Lond. roll B 386, melted salt (lit. salt daughter of melting); **mihla uhardla** Morg. 198:9, 19, 201:4, 202:2, Lond. roll B 94, 398 salt and mustard; **raza ḏ-mihla** Jb 166:9 f., PD 1135 the mystery of salt; **ʿbna ḏ-mihla** DC 26. 42 rock-salt; **mihla anat mara** [*sic*, read **marta**?] **alahia** DC 40 salt, thou art lord of gods; **mihla** AM 215:10, 217:17, Oxf. roll f 366, 1265, Lond. roll B 419, often in ŠQ &c.

Gl. 154:7 **mhla** [*sic*] ملح *sal* نمک.

mihmaṭ DAb = **mahamaṭ.**

mihna (Ar. مِحْنَة) suffering, disaster, affliction. **mihna umura** CP 354:31 suffering and bitterness.

mihrab (Ar. مِحْرَاب) AM 133 niche indicating direction of Mecca.

mihrizad (P. مهرزاد) a *malwâša* woman's name.

miua (Mod. P. ميوه) fruit MG xxxiii 9. Pl. **miuia.** Masc. **miuia ṭabia** ATŠ I no. 116 = **miuia ḏ-ṭabia** PD 1137 wholesome fruits; **miuia u asal** AM 258:27 fruit and honey; **ukma ḏ-mṣia mn miuia** DC 42. 7 and as many fruits as possible; **miuia mn hanatẖ ginta ḏ-ʿlania** DC 27. 39 fruits from that orchard; **miuia** Oxf. roll f 308, 457, 1087, 1092 f. &c. (often in lists of foods in the rituals).

Gl. 53:2 **miua** ثمر *fructus* ميوه; 143:2 id. كرم *vinea* باغ انگور; 143:13 id. كرمة *vitis* ميوه. (Gl. 46:9 f. mistakenly as a verb.)

mizaina a var. of **mzaina.**

***mizara** (Ar. مِئْزَر) a piece of cloth draped round waist and hips and brought over one shoulder, waist-cloth. **uʿl mizaria** AM 123:ult. and on his waist-cloth.

miṭalalia Sh. ʿAbd.'s Ginzā's var. of **mṭalalia** (in **bit mṭalalia**).

miṭiaʿil DAb a demon.

miṭra 1 (מִטְרָא, ܡܶܛܪܳܐ, H. מָטָר, Ar. مَطَر, Akk. *meṭru*) rain MG 107:10. Masc. **miṭria 1**, later also **miṭraria 1** (var. **maṭraria 2**) MG 170:9. **anania ḏ-aiba umiṭra** CP 429:13 clouds of mist and rain; **umiṭra** (var. **-ia**) **šrun** DC 44. 450 and they loosed rain; **atuata ḏ-miṭraria** AM 234:penult. portents of rainfalls; **miṭraria napša nihun umia nihun** AM 240:11 there will be heavy rains and floods; **miṭria nihun umalia ḏ-mia nihuia** AM 218:15, there will be rainfall and abundance of water.

miṭra 2 (rt. **ṬRA**) blow, attack. Pl. **miṭria 2, miṭraria 2. naplia anašia ʿl anašia umiṭra napša** AM people will attack one another and there will be much coming to blows; **uṭiriuk miṭria** JRAS 1937, 593:193 and blows shall attack thee; **udalaiia nidalun umiṭraria nitnapšun** AM 231:ult. and agitators will revolt and attacks will be frequent.

miṭra 3 DC 22. 489 a var. of **maṭra 1** Gs 617:2.

miia Gy 84:4 s. **mia 2.**

miiaka Sh. ʿAbd.'s copy's var. of **mʿiaka** Gy 327:9.

miina DC 46. 82:13 = **maina.**

mika 1 (rt. **MKK**) soft, mild, meek. Doublet **maka 2** s.v. Pl. **mikia.** Fem. sg. **mikta 1** s.v. **gabra mika hauia** AM 27:5 he will be a meek man; **latiṭalmun mikia** Gy 40:16 do not oppress the meek; **hun mikia um(a)kikia** Gy 20:6 be meek and humble.

mika 2 occasionally for **maka 1.**

mikulta occasionally for **makulta.**

mikikuta sporadically for **mkikuta.**

mikla (rt. **AKL**) food MG 17:11, 129:8. **mikla umašqita nihuilẖ** AM 30:14 he will have food and drink; **dukta ḏ-mikla** DC 46. 117:9 eating-place.

mikta 1 (fem. of **mika** 1) level(led), even, soft. **bʿuhra mikta** Morg. 236/59:4, ML 89:1 = CP 72:11, DC 41:342 by a smooth(ened) road.

mikta 2 (a corrupt part. form of **NKT**) biting, wounding. Pl. **-ia. giria miktia ḏ-mata** DC 43 B 6 the wounding arrows of the village.

mila (cf. מֵילָא) oak. **luzan umuzan umilan sindirka rba** DC 46 136:10, JRAS 1943 171:9.

milauia (a mod. form of **mn ʿlauia**) ŠQ 18:6, CP 234:11.

milia 1 (< מִן לְאֵי) whence, from where? MG 194:5, 205:20. **makulta lialda milia hauialẖ** Gy 202:8 whence hath the child its nourishment? **milia ʿiaitẖ** Jb 46:15 whence shall I bring him? **uarba ziqia milia aitinun** ATŠ II no. 45 and whence are the four winds?

Gl. 155:9 **mlia** [*sic*] من اين *unde* از كجا.

milia 2 (= **minilia**) a pl. of **mi(ni)lta. mpašria milia** Gy 227:26 expounders of words.

milia 3 a spor. var. of **malia 2, mlia. ʿniš milia mia** DC 46 a person with dropsy (lit. full of water).

milia 4 a var. of **malia 4.**

milik Ṣâb.'s AM a var. of **mlik.**

milka (מֵילְכָּא, Syr. ܡܶܠܟܳܐ, Chr.-Pal. ܡܠܟܘ Nöld. ZDMG xxii 475) advice, counsel. Pl. **-ia.** Masc. **milka baṭla** Gy 109:2, 114:22 useless advice; **malik milkia** Gy 357:2, **mamlik milkia** Jb 171:4 that giveth counsels.

milta a rarer doublet of **min(i)lta** (q.v.) MG 54:15, 184:11. Pl. **milia 2** s.v., **minilia** s. **minilta. milta** Gy 393:1, sometimes found as a var. of **minilta** A.

mimun a var. of **maimun.**

mimata (rt. **YMA**) plighted, loyal. Fem. adj. **zaua mimata** ŠQ 19:11 = CP 239:2 plighted wife.

mimra (rt. **AMR**) word, speech, saying, talk, discourse, dictum, pronouncement, authoritative statement MG 129:8. St. abs. identical with the inf. pe. Pl. **-ia.** St. abs. **mimar** DC 34. 690. **mimra amrit banašia** DC 27. 56 I made a speech to people; **bhaila rama ubmimra kabira** Gy 31:4 high in strength and great in command; **ḏ-ziuẖ npiš mn mimra ḏ-puma** Gy 31:10 whose radiance is greater than can be told by the mouth; **šauṭa umimra bʿdai lgiṭna** AM 149:3 a lash and a(n exorcizing) formula I hold in my hand; **ʿštalaṭ lmamla ḏ-ʿzlat lmimar mimrẖ** ATŠ II no. 321 govern the speech of Ezlat by speaking her words (being her spokesman); **amar mimra hu ḏ-bhatinun lmimra kulhun** ATŠ I no. 231 it made a pronouncement which confounded all pronouncements; **mimra ḏ-baira** DC 40 an illumining word. Of higher beings: **mimra ana br mimra** Gy 299:7 f., **br mimra** Morg. 266/23:29; pl. **rišaihun ḏ-mimria hu** DC 34. 1267 he is the Beginning (?) of words.

Gl. 176:7 **mimra** وصية, *iussum, praeceptum.*

min– scr. pl. of **mn** used proclitically with pers. suffixes, only exceptionally as an independent preposition **min** MG 10:2. **minai** from, with me, **minak** (masc.), **minik** (fem.) from, with thee, **minẖ** from, with him, her, it, **mina** (sporadically, exceptionally **minaẖ** MG 69 n. 1) from, with her, **minaian** from, with us, **minaikun** (rarely **-ken** fem.) from, with you, **minai(h)un** (masc.), **minai(h)in** (fem.) from, with them.

mina Zotb. 228 b:30 = **maina.**

Gl. 153:13 **mina** ماء *aqua* آب.

minglia Ṣâb.'s AM for **manglia.**

minda (מידי, ܡܶܕܶܡ) a form of **mindam** (q.v.). Something, a thing, anything. Pl. **mindia. ʿu šuma ḏ-maria ṭapia minda mitaška** AM 158:7 if the thing (*lost*) adds to more than its owner, it will be found; **ʿlana rba ḏ-kulẖ mindia** CP 51:12 = Šâb.'s Q, the great Tree that is all things (ML has **mandia**; see **manda**).

mindam (מנדעם Inscr. of Carpentras Nöld. ZDMG xxiii 292 f., from מָא + מְנְדַּע Fleischer in Levy's *Chald. Wörterb.* ii, Nachtragen p. 567, Jew.-Aram. מְ(י)דְּעַם, מְיָדַם, Syr. ܡܶܕܶܡ, ܡܢܕܥܡ I Mac. 8:15, Akk. *mindēma* LS) thing, something MG 51:16, 75:10, 186:7. Indeclinable. A declinable later form **minda** 1 (cf. Talm. מִידֵי and esp. mod. Syr. *mendī*) is formed by apocope of the final **m** MG 50:10, 186:10; its pl. **mindia** MG 186:11 corresponds to the mod. sg. (pronounced *mendī* apart from *mendā̆*; mod. pl. is *mendâna, mendâni*). **mindam šapir labad** Gy 111:9 he did nothing good MG 302:8; **mindam ḏ-** (*often*) something that, **laiit hatam mindam ḏ-hašuk** Gy 283:14 there is nothing (that would be) dark; **ʿl kul mindam ḏ-** Gy 224:20 about all that; **ʿu minhu ḏ-** Gy 281:19 if that is something that . . .; **ubka . . . ʿl mindam ḏ-abad** Gy 103:5 and he wept . . . because of what he had done; **laiadin mindam ḏ-nimarlun** Gy 392:19 they know not what he sayeth to them; **apku lṭabuta mindam ḏ-abad marẖ ḏ-alma apkun lrazia triṣia mindam ḏ-qadmaiia abad** Gy 111:13 they pervert goodness, the thing which the Lord of the world has made, they pervert orthodox mysteries (: rites), something which the First (Life) made; **apiklun lmalalia lmindam ḏ-qadmaiia abad** Gy 120:10 he perverteth the words, something which the First (Life) made; **hazin mindam ḏ-** Gy 392:18 this thing which MG 345 f.; **lamindam** Gs 44:4, **lau mindam** Gy 158:16 nothing MG 431:2 f.; **mindam ḏ-lau mindam** Gy 300:11, 365:11, Gs 106:23 f., PD 869 f., 1708 (Ginzā 387 n. 3), something worthless; **mindam lahakim** Gy 218:4 (var. **mindam ḏ-lahakim** Sh. 'Abd.'s copy) something unwise; **kul mindam ḏ-ʿtlaikun** Gy 15:7, **mn kul mindam ḏ-ʿtlaikun** Gy 36:11 (from) all ye have MG 454 n. 2; **huziẖ lalma ḏ-kulẖ mindam ḏ-lau mindam** Jb 246:12 f. behold the world, that is all something without reality. Apocopated form: **hazin minda** Gy 392:20 this thing; **abatar minda** AM 260 after a little while; **šuma ḏ-abid ušuma**

d-minda AM 158:7 the name of the slave, or the name of the article; **mindia mindia** Gy 389:22, 392:9 many things, various things, all things. Gl. (always defectively) 28:4, 29:4, 95:3, 100:10; mod. pl. 33:2, 34:1; 130:12 **blamnda** [*sic*] قارغا *inana* خالي.

minuna (Nöld. from ܡܡܘܢܐ *μαμ[μ]ωνᾶς*; but cf. s. **argba**) wealth, riches, possessions, estates MG 50:6, 130:paen. Rarely **manuna. argba uminuna** Gy 112:5 s. **argba**; **latirihmuia lminuna** Gy 366:6 f. do not love Mammon; **uminunun bknap lbušaihun ṣarilun** CP 128:10 and they tie up their money in the corner of their garment; **ṭabuta uminuna uagra uzidqa** AM 165:ult. goods and possessions and rewards and alms, **minuna uṭabuta** AM 167:ult.

m(i)nunaiia, m(u)nunaiia (formed as an adj. from preced., but designates a sect. Could be a corruption of ***maninaiia** 'Manichaeans' but they are mentioned later on in the same text; hardly Jew. מינים; cf. ܡܡܘܢܝܐ Chabot, *Michel le Syrien* 312 b:4 LS 391 b & ܡܡܘܢܝܢܐ Hoffmann: *Auszüge* 125 f. Ginzā 226 n. 4) a sect. **baba d-minunaiia** Gy 225:11 the sect of the M.

minzanguš AM 135:2 = **marzanguš.**

minṭul a later (?) form of **aminṭul** MG 33:15.

mini- s. **minil-.**

miniaiil DC 40. 938 an angel.

miniana (מִנְיָנָא, ܡܢܝܢܐ) number, count, enumeration, list, category, computation, summing up, incantation (i.e. recitation of a sum of qualities, or of a number of magic names) MSchr. 92 n. 1. St. abs. & cstr. **minian.** Pl. **miniania.** Masc. **minianai** my number MG 176:14, **miniankin** Q 56:12 your (fem.) number MG 179:20; **bminiana d-hiuaniata nihun** ATŠ they are in the category of beasts; **pširia uminiania uadkarata** ATŠ exorcisms and enumerations (of magic names) and mentionings; **kul mindam d-napiq mn minianh uhušbanh** DC 41 anything which departs from its reckoning and count; **hanik šumhara d-madkirit ʿlh b(i)miniana hurina balmia d-nhura ʿtibnilh** (read **ʿtimnilh**?) **lnišimta** DC 23 those names which thou pronouncest over her will be put up in another list in the world of light for the soul; **hazin šapta uminiana d-šabra** DC 48 this is the scroll and enumeration (: incantation) of the Rue-plant; **bminian iumia lamitminin** ATŠ II no. 14 (var. . . . **laʿtimnia** DC 6) not reckoned in the list of days; **adinqia miniana** ATŠ II no. 316 &c. innumerable, countless.

minihra (pt. ethpe. st. emph. of **NHR**) bright, shining, luminous, illustrious, glorious. Pl. masc. **-ia,** fem. st. abs. **-a(n). qaima dmauatun uminihra** DC 3 and their counterparts stand and are bright; **rišaihun d-minihria kulhun** CP 434:9 chief of all the enlightened ones; **utraṣlun lrišaihun lminihria** CP 389: penult. and set them on the heads of the enlightened ones; **baṭinia uiadalia sagia uminihria** DC 51 conceptions and childbearings are many and illustrious (?); **dmutak minihra** Jb 219:6 f. thy appearance is bright.

minil- (the form of **mna** 'whence' + encl. **-l-** with pers. suff.) whence comes it that . . . ? MG 205:14. **ldilak mnata bdurdia minilak** Jb 269:3 whence hast thou a portion in the dregs?

minilta (a dissimilated form of מילתא, ܡܠܬܐ, H. מִלָּה) word, talk, speech MG 32:26, 54:11, 172:12, 184:11. A rare (but more original) doublet **milta** s.v. St. cstr. **min(i)lat** MG 32:26, 54:11, 184:12. Pl. **min(i)lia** MG 54:12, 163:14, 172:12, 184:12, **milia** (s.v., both treated as fem.) and **minilata** Oxf. iii 47 a (twice) = Par. xi par. MG 184 n. 1. **minilat hiia** Jb 5:8, 8:2, DC 36 &c. the Word of Life; **minilat malka** Jb 15:2 the word of the king; **minilta d-bdinba d-alma ʿl tušlima miṭiat** Gy 393:1 the word which, at the end of the world, reached its fulfilment (Lidzb. differs, Ginzā 418 n. 7); **minilia maṭia ʿlh** there will be much talk about him (?); **minilta kšiṭa** (a simplified orthography for **-ṭta**?) Gs 91:12 a true word MG 318:9 f.; **minilia šapirata** Gy 389:11 fair words MG 318:19; **minilia amria ʿlh** AM (*often*) they will gossip about him (or her); **zhira umzahra minilia d-nhura** CP 62:8 = ML 78:1 well preserved are the words of Light.

mintipiš AM 256:42 a district in S. ʿIrāq.

misaṭra (rt. **SṬR**) beside, close by, close at hand. **uṭunaihun lhdadia ladamia misaṭrh** DC 35 but their fruit is not like that (of trees) close by.

misai(ia) sometimes for **miṣai(ia). liama silqit lmisaiia mia** DC 44 I went up to the sea, to the midst of the water.

misat s. **miṣat.**

misia 1 (rt. **MSA**) condensation MG 102:21; congealing, freezing. **qurša umisia** ATŠ cold and freezing.

misia 2 a place-name BZ Ap. II.

misia 3 inf. pe. of **ASA I** (q.v.).

misihpan(a) (abstr. noun from **SHP**) ruin, destruction: **šqul . . . misihpan mn libh** DC 43 remove . . . ruin from his heart.

misirqa (doublet of **masirqa** q.v.) comb. **d-misirqa dria uqisariq brišh hazin misirqa namriaiil šumh** DCb (with picture) that carries a comb and combs heads; this comb is called N.

misk (Ar.-P. مشک) AM 130:paen. musk.

miskina (Aram. & H. מִסְכֵּן, Syr. ܡܣܟܢܐ < Akk. *muškēnu* pt. of *šukennu* Jensen ZA iv 271 f., Zimmern ZA vii 353 f., hence Eth. ምስኪን, Ar. مسكين > Fr. *mesquin*) poor, wretched MG 130:16. **anašia miskina nitiatrun** AM 212:5 poor people will become rich; **had tarmida ṭaba umiskina ušalmana** ATŠ (colophon) one priest good, poor and honest; **ania umiskina** DC 51 poor and wretched.

Gl. 154:5 miswritten مسكين *pauper* فقير.

misqal occasionally for **mitqal,** cf. **masqal 2.**

mistaruata pl. (from **ʿstaruad** 'was terrified') those who are frightened. **mistaruata bšinta** JRAS 1939 401:22 those who are terrified in sleep.

miعbria (Mand. pl. of Ar. مِعْبَر) AM 267:27 means of crossing, bridges, pontoons.

mipriš Zotb. 228 b:14 a personal name.

miptal (Ar. مِفْتَل) rope-maker's reel. **b'dh̲ miptal** DC 46 in his hand is a reel.

mişai, mişai(i)a (ܡܨܥܝ, emph. ܡܨܥܝܐ; cf. s. **mişat**) adj. middle, intermediary, central MG 141:10. Fem. **mişaita.** Both genders are used also substantivally: middle, centre. Pl. masc. **mişaiia. mişai situa** second winter month, **mişai bhar** second spring month, **mişai gaiţa** second summer month, **mişai paiiz** second autumn month MMII 84; **bmişai br anašia** DC 46 amongst human beings; **mişaiia** AM 190 average; **šidta mişaita** AM 185 a mediocre year; **bmişaita d̲-'urašlam** Gy 333:12 in the middle of Jerusalem; **mara d̲-rabuta mişaita** DC 34. 1197 the Lord of Medial Greatness; **zahba d̲-mişaita d̲-klul malkia** ŠQ 18:30 gold, the means of crowning the kings (doubtf.).

mişaita used nominally s. **mişai** last example.

mişalia (rt. צלל ?) getting light, getting clear (?) BZ 81 n. 1. **'u lmişalia atia** AM 125:11 if he shall come at dawn (?).

mişar 1 (for **maşar**?, rt. **MŞR I**) rope-maker (?), cable-ferryman (?). **amarlh̲ lmişar zabia** Gy 370:5 say to the cable-ferryman (?, Lidzb.: *Sage dem, der die Flüsse überbrücket*).

mişar 2 st. abs. & cstr. of **mişra.**

mişat 1 (ܡܨܥܬ, an old loan-w. from Gr. *μέσος*? MG 110 n. 2) midst, middle, centre MG 110:11. Only st. cstr. found. **bmişat 'šumia** AM 3 (*& often*) medium coelum (astrological term). **bmişat almia udaria** DC 37. 304 f. amidst worlds and generations; **'l mişat almia dilan** Gy 295:13 into the midst of our worlds.

mişat 2 (rt. **MŞA II**) oppression. Unsatisfactory mod. form. **kupna umişat sbalnia** DC 43 J 239 we bore hunger and oppression.

mişia, miş'ia (cf. **mişai(a)** and **mişat**) middle. **u'daihun pšaţ lmişia u'laiia** CP 49:18, ML 65:6 they stretched their hands to the middle and upwards (?) (cf. Pet. RO ii 463:12 f., ML 65 n. 1); **ud-'tlia udlitlh̲ lmiş'ia nidnia** AM (CS 26) both that has and that which has not will descend in the middle (position). AM 220:11 has **lmişria** (a miscopying?).

mişişat AM 198 a place-name, another name of **anţalia** (as explained in the text) BZ Ap. II.

mişir (Ar. مِصْر) AM 257:33, 271:23 f. Egypt. Var. **mişr** AM 203.

mişlaiia (rt. צלל ?) dawn?. Şâb.'s AM a var. of **munašat** (q.v.).

mişr s. **mişir.**

mişra (מִצְרָא, Ar. مصر, Akk .*mişru*) (*a*) limit, boundary or separating line, demarcation, (*b*) means of crossing a river, a rope stretched over a river to propel a ferry?, a bridge? (parallel with **mabra**), rampart?, dam?, (*c*) prescription (of the ritual) Jb ii 102 n. 3, ML 60 n. 1. Masc. Pl. -**ia.** (*a*) **mişra binia hda lhda laiit** Gy 9:19 Betwixt the one and the other there is no line of demarcation. (Sundberg: *Kushţa* 111, ThLZ 1957 col. 673), but **hu mişra rba d̲-binia nhura lhšuka mşir** ATŠ I no. 250 it is a great dividing-line traced between light and darkness (of the sacred girdle); **ulitlaihun saka umişra lzakuatun** Gy 11:10 and there is no end and no limit to their merits; **mişra lnhura lahualh̲** Gy 77:14 ff. there was no limit to light; **mişra d̲-ţabia** Gy 78:12 the realm of the good; **mişra usaka** Gy 128:3 limit and end, cf. Q 34:10; **mişra uk'la (ukila)** Gy 39:20, 23 limit and measure, cf. Gy 295:16; **mšauia mişra lalmia** Gy 89:7 he appointeth a limit to the worlds; **apilh̲ ubmişra nasbia** Gy 231:14 they bake it and take it into a (magic) circle (?) (Ginzā 232 n. 6); **latipkun mişria** Gy 40:17 do not change boundary lines, **man d̲-apik mişria** Gy 40:18 whosoever changeth boundary lines; **apkia mişria** Gs 17:9, 19:13, 27: 23, Gy 183:9, RD C 26 they change boundary lines; **'l mişria autbh̲** Gy 168:16 he set him on a line of demarcation; **atina alma d̲-mişria d̲-arqa tibil** Gy 237:11 (var. **lmişria** Leid.) I came (hist. pres.) so far as the limit of the earth, **u'l mişrih̲ d̲-arqa tibil mţit** Gy 238:22 id.; **bit mişria trin** Gy 137:10 in the place of both limits, (**trin mişria** Gy 381:24 s.b.); **mişria d̲-hšuka unhura** Gy 281:5 the boundaries of darkness and light; **bit mişria** Gy 152:9, 154:7, 158:18, 159:20, 168:9, Jb 216:9 in the boundaries; **bit mişria d̲-hšuka** Gy 154:7 in the boundaries of darkness (Ginzā 153 n. 2); **ahtit 'l mişria u'l šuria d̲-hšuka** Gy 154:8 I descended to the boundaries and to the walls of darkness. Here must belong **'ngirta d̲-bhalin mişria mhatma** Q 42:30, 43:4, CP letter sealed by these encircling bands (CP 90:14, 9:16 = ML 112:4 and 11, CP 91:6, trs. 62 n. 2, cf. ML 112 n. 1). A circle described round a person or area to keep away devils, and in ritual shallow furrows traced with a knife to shut out pollution and enclose purified areas are also called *mişria*; (*b*) **lamşirlh̲ bzabia mişra** Jb 102:5 for him no bridge (? or cable-rope for ferry?) is spanned in the torrents; **nimşurlh̲ bzabia mişra** Jb 178:7, Gy 370:5 f., **iardna mişra l'utria hua** Jb 212:1, **mşarulh̲ mişra** Gs 101: 14 f., **zaba d̲-lamşir bgauh̲ mişra** Gs 107:2; **ana šauit mişra** Jb 207:12 I made a dam (? or rampart?); **mhaimnia d̲-'l mişra samkia** Jb 207:14 f.; **hibil rma mişra umšanun lmia** Jb 231:6 f. H. set a dam and measured the water; **mia d̲-iama qimiun ltrin mişria** Gy 381:23 f. the waters of the sea stood up in two banks, cf. also Q 65:13 f.; **hibil šauia br mişria** Jb 234:11 (Talm. בר מצרא 'neighbour' makes no sense, perh. cable, Lidzb. '*Brückenpfeiler*' Jb ii 216 n. 6); (*c*) **mişra d̲-maşbuta** CP 40:10 = Q 21:26 f. = ML 60:1 baptismal ritual; **sigiia umişria udiuanan** HG 153 treatises, rituals and scrolls (cf. PD 60, 118).

mişraiia (adj. fro, **mişr**) pl. Egyptians. **arqa d̲-mişraiia** Gy 381:18 ff. the land of the Egyptians; **pirun malka d̲-mişraiia** DC 44. 641 etc. Pharaoh, king of the Egyptians.

miqai DC 19 a miscop. of **miqmai** my standing.

miqam 1 inf. pe. of **QUM** (q.v.).

miqam 2 DC 24. 291 before (s. **qam**).

miqdam ATŠ II no. 409 a miscop. of **miqdar.**

miqdar (Ar. مقدار) quantity, amount. **miqdar hamšin baitia** DC 12. 404 about fifty houses.

miqma (inf. pe. st. emph. of **QUM** as frim **ע״ע**) standing, rising (up) during. **napil umiqma litlh̲** Jb 208:2 he shall fall and there shall be no rising for him; **lmiqmak ulmitbak** Jb 246:7 at thy rising-up and at thy sitting-down.

Gl. 53:13 **miqma** تيقظ *vigilantia* بيدار شدن; 136:11 id. قيام *statio* ايستادن.

mirda 1 (rt. **MRD**) revolt, insubordination, rebellion, insurrection, anarchy, insolence MG 102:4. **mirda d-kauna litbh̲** Gy 355:10 s. **kauna**; **karsauata d̲-mirda** Gy 18:ult. f. thrones of rebellion; **mirda ušira** AM rebellion and licence.

mirda 2 inf. pe. of **RDA** (q.v.).

miruarita DC 44 a var. of **muruarid.**

maruata occasionally for **marauata** pl. of **mar(i)a** 1.

miruza Gy 388:1 apparently a synonym of **nikla** of unknown etymology Ginzā 415 n. 3.

mirzanguš s. **marzanguš.**

mirzibana DC 22. 32 a var. of **marzbana** Gy 87:15.

miria (rt. **RAA**) JRAS 1937 p. 591 pasture.

miriai (hypocoristic form of **mariam, miriam** Lidzb. ZDMG lxi 691) name of a Jewish princess converted to Mandaism, sometimes a symbol of the Mandaeans, at other times confused with the mother of Jesus Jb ii. xx, 71 f., 123, ML 282, MSt 97, Ginzā 341 n. 2. **miriai uʿnišbai** Jb 80:14; **miriai šalmanita** Jb 198:5, Gy 332:4 (cf. *Beata Maria*); **iaqip ubnia amin umiriai** Jb 84:6, 13, cf. Gy 332:5; **lbaba d̲-bit ama ʿma lmiriai tibga** Morg. 56:10 f. = Oxf. 38 = ML 210 = Jb ii 124:1 at the door of the synagogue the mother meeteth Miriai (beginning of the first of two Mand. Miriai-hymns). CP 172:10; 173:5, 12; 184 antepen; 185:2, 4, 5, 6.

Gl. 153:4 mrii [*sic*] مريم *Maria.*

miriam s. **mariam.**

miriqa DC 23. 769 for muriqa?

m(i)rirta a doublet of **mirta** (q.v.). See also **mrirta. mirirta hisan ašgar** AM 129:9 the gall of a roan stallion.

mirsa (rt. **MRS**) compression, repression, flatulency. **mn šilia mirsa nihuilh̲** AM 58:15 suddenly she will be repressed (?); **ruha d̲-iatba lmia ukarka d̲-mia umitiqria mirsa** Or. 329:19 f. & nn. 8–9 spirit that sits on the duodenum and the lower intestines and is called flatulency; **dibqa umirsa** Morg. 194:11, DC 51. 452 cleaving together (?) and flatulency.

mirpas inf. pe. of **RPS** used in the frequent phrases: **mirpas aina** Gy 247:18, 260:3, Q 54:11 (-ia) and **mirpas zapa d-aina** Jb 65:5, 190:17, Gy 281:22 (in) the twinkling of an eye.

mirta (Jew.-Aram. מְרִירְתָא, Syr. ܡܪܪܬܐ, H. מְרֵרָה, Ar. مِرَّة, Akk. *martu*) gall, bile, venom MG 103:22. Doublet m(i)rirta s.vv. St. cstr. **murat** s. ***murta.** A late pl. **mirtata. mirta šda qudamh̲** Jb 25:11 he spat venom before himself; **raq ruqa d̲-mirta** DC 51. 554 he spat out venom; **zma umirta** Gy 34:4, DC 34. 284 blood and bile; **marth̲ barqa mitgarara** Gy 83:12 f. (s. **GRR** ethpe. pt.); **zihira bmiih̲ šdilh̲ umirta bkulh̲ qumth̲** Gy 84:4 I cast poison into his bowels and venom into his whole body; **šadia mirth̲** Gy 115:19 he casteth his venom; **iama d̲-mirta** Gs 75:12 sea of venom; **mirta** AM 286:16 the gall; **halin arbia mirtata** ATŠ I no. 219 (twice) these four humours (of the body).

miša 1 (Old Aram. & Bibl.-Aram. מְשַׁח, Jew.-Aram. מִשְׁחָא, Syr. ܡܫܚܐ Ges. s. משׁח I) oil, unguent; fat (melted down); butter MG 64:19. Pl. **mišania** MG 169:23. Masc. Ritual use of oil MR 104 f., 129, HpGn 228, 279, 297 ff., 301 f., CP trs. 43 n. 3; **miša d̲-nuna** Lond. roll B 399 fish-oil; **kapta d̲-miša** Oxf. roll f 218 ff., 566 ff., 695, 699 cup of oil, oil cup; **masiqta d̲-miša** Q 36:13 (in the *masiqta* crushed sesame seed and dates are pounded together and the juice strained through a piece of cloth; the resultant mixture of date-juice and sesame oil is **miša**); **miša udupša** Gy 233:11 oil and honey; **bruk ʿl miša** Gy 37:16 bless the oil; **miša d̲-birkta** Gy 227:12 oil of the benediction; **qarna d̲-miša** Gy 54:13 a horn of oil; **miša br šušma hiuara** Jb 2:11, 4:13, Q 14:4 = ML 36, CP 30:7: 1 oil, son (: produce) of white sesame; **miša dakia** Gy 321:8 ff. pure oil; **našqʿil ʿl miša mištalaṭ** RD A 7 N. looks after the butter; **miša d̲-ʿmbra** DC 46 sheep's butter; **mišania** AM 267:33 the oils; **mišania ṭabia** Gy 176:22 wholesome oils; **miša daria** DAb they carry oil (or butter); **miša dakia** CP 64:6 pure oil.

miša 2 (מֹשֶׁה prob. transformed under the influence of **miša** 1 Jb ii 79 n. 6, although מישא & varr. 'Moses' occurs also in some Jewish books Jb ii *Nachträge* 245) Moses. **miša br amra** Gy 50:14 f., Jb 72:4, 74:11, Morg. 259/10:37 = DC 26. 609 = DC 44. 640 & par.; **hu adunai qaria lmiša mn ṭura d̲-sinai ubmiša audia** Gy 45:15 f. he, Adonai, called (hist. pres.) M. from Mount Sinai and recognized M.; **ukapria bmiša nbiha d̲-ruha d̲-aitilun nimusa** Gy 46:6 and they deny M., the prophet of R., who brought them the Law.

mišania pl. of **miša** 1.

mišaša (rt. **MŠŠ**) contents, substance. **dra mišaša d̲-ʿka bkarsh̲** AM 130:11 bring the contents of its stomach.

mišun AM 209. Mesene, cf. Schaeder, *Islam* xiv 11 ff. MG xxvi: middle, BZ Ap. II: 'the island formed by the Euphrates, Tigris and the Royal Canal'. PS.

mišunaiia Gy 385:16 inhabitants of Mesene, Ginzā 413 n. 2.

mišia AM 205 a place-name.

mišihta Morg. 268/26:39 a var. of **mašihta** 1.

mišitia = **mištia** (inf. pe. of **ŠTA** q.v.). **umn miš(i)tiaiun šatin** Jb 266:11 and they drink of their drink.

miška (מְשְׁכָּא, ܡܫܟܐ, Chr.-Pal. ܡܫܟܘ, H. מֶשֶׁךְ, Ar. مَسْك, Akk. *mašku*) skin. A spor. var. **maška. zma umiška** Gy 202:5

blood and skin; **miška umanzia** ATŠ II no. 114 skin and hair; **miška d̠-gurita** Lond. roll B 399, DC 12. 190, DC 45 bitch-skin; **miška d̠-šibuia** Lond. roll B 418 s. **šibuia**; **miška d̠-ṭabia** DC 44 gazelle-skin; **miškaiun d̠-anašia** Gy 387:15 the skin of people MG 314:18; **umiška d̠-hu aṭarpa d-ania šumh̠** DC 6 and a ((sheep-)skin, the name of which is 'fleece', of (from) a flock.

miškiʿil anana DC 22. 371 a var. of **mašqlʿil anana.**

mišmiš (Ar.-P. مِشْمِش) apricot, apricot-tree. Used as both masc. and fem. **mišmiš hu** DC 41 (picture) it is an apricot-tree; **hazin ʿlana mišmiš hʿ** DC 7 (picture) this tree is an apricot; **mišmiš hiuartia** DC 35 (picture) a white apricot.

mištamana a var. of **maštimana.**

mišt(i)mana s. **maštimana.**

mita (pass. pt. pe. of **MUT**) dead; death. Pl. **-ia** 1, mod. **-ana. uqaimin lmita sagdih̠** CP 380:2 and they worship death (or) a dead man; **udmita aklia** Gy 224:3 and they eat from what is dead; **ušuma d̠-mita dakria** Sh. 'Abd.'s copy's var. of Gy 225:20 (where Pet. has **maita,** further var. **muta** Gy 226:9) and they mention the name of the dead (i.e. Christ), or of the death (Ginzā 227 n. 1); **šimuk mitia uhiun** Gy 275:5 the dead heard thee and lived; **d̠-lamita hzilh̠ bhilmia** DC 43 so that he may not see a dead person in dreams; **hzit gnia mitana** DC 46 (if) thou hast seen the dead when sleeping; **d̠-akil bisra d̠-mitania** DC 46. 413:14 that eats the flesh of the dead.

mitia 1 pl. of **mita.**

mitia 2 inf. pe. of **ATA** (q.v.).

Gl. 137:12 **mitia** قدوم *adventus* آمدن; 156:12 id. مجىء *adventus* آمدن.

mitiana (further abstr. noun from **mitia** 2) coming, arrival, advent MG 137:9. St. abs. **mitin** [*sic*] s.v. **mitianak** Gy 147:9 thy (masc.) coming, **mitianik** Jb 216:13 thy (fem.) coming.

mitil (Ar. مثل) like, as: **mitil d̠-** AM 277:35.

mitin def. st. abs. of **mitiana. mišqal umitin qudam gabra rba** AM 140:4 removing and coming before a great man; **lmišqal ulmitin ulmiqrublh̠ qurbana** AM 143:5 for removing and coming (or bringing?) and offering a gift.

mitla (מְתָלָא, ܡܬܠܐ, Sab. 𐩣𐩻𐩡 monument, H. מָשָׁל, Ar. مَثَل, Eth. ምስል, Akk. *mišlu* half) simile, parable MG 107:10. Pl. **mitlia** 1. Masc. **ana mitla ʿl napšai rmit** Gy 262:24 I made a parable concerning myself; **mitlia mitlia bʿqara amria** Jb 242:2 parables, parables sayeth He (: the Great Life, pl.) in glory.

mitlaiia (adj. from preced.) Pl. people of the same class, or rank, proxies. **unatnulia mitlaiia** CP 92:21, ML 115:8 and people of the same rank will serve him (if it is a simple Mandaean, laymen will serve him; if it is a priest, the priests will, cf. ML 115 n. 4) (MMII p. 214.)

mitlia 1 pl. of **mitla.**

mitlia 2 unknown but different from 1. **usliqiun gubria mitlia mitlia** Jb 126:3 cf. Jb ii 122 n. 3; **umitlia** (var. **matlia**) **nura lhabrh̠** ATŠ I no. 40 and enflameth (?) fire for his neighbour, *or* and is kindled by fire (?) for his neighbour (doubtf.), *or* and kindleth fire in his neighbour (?).

mitna = **matna.** Pl. **-ia. širiuk lmitnia rakšia** DC 40. 142 they melt thee (salt) for the legs of horses; **mitnai tlit akuat guria** DC 43 J 136 thou holdest up thy paws (read **guriak**) like a whelp.

mitqal (Ar. مِثْقَال) AM 287:17 a measure about a dram and a half BZ 196 n. 4. Pl. **mitqalia** ML 137:1, PD 1502, CP 111:8, ATŠ I no. 170, II no. 24 &c. Var. **matqal** s.v.

mitrapuliṭa (μητροπολίτης) Gy 227:2 Metropolitan.

mkadpa (as pass. ? pt. den. from **kadpa**) shoulder-piece. Pl. **-ia. šaba mkadpia d̠-parzla** JRAS 1937 p. 591:25 seven shoulder-pieces of iron.

mkairuta (abstr. noun from pass. pt. pa. of **KAR** = **KUR**) repulsiveness, ugliness MG 145:2. Doublet **kariuta** s.v. **ṭnupia umkairuta** Gy 18:7 uncleanness and repulsiveness, **mṭanputa umkairuta** Gy 229:23 f., **mkairuta umṭanputa** Gy 232:14 id.

mkakam, mkakma accord. to MM.: full, fleshy, plump, bulky BZ 16 n. 3. **uʿtlh̠ ʿqba umkakam** AM 35:18 and he has curves and plumpness (? ?); **uʿtlh̠ rumania d̠-anpia umkakam** AM 18:16 f. and he is full of face and plump (?); **mkakma ugaṭina** AM 45:8 plump (?) and small.

mkalalta (pass. pt. fem. st. emph. of **KLL I**) crowned (of bride). **hidutan mkalaltan** DC 48. 229 our crowned bride.

mkalapat (Ar. مخالفة) Ṣâb.'s AM adversity, enmity.

mkalta AM 40 for **mkatla.**

mkaruastai Jb 34:9, var. **mkaruaztai** B doubtf. V.s. **kbasta.**

mkatla (cf. Ar. كتل) thick, bulky, stocky, plump. BZ 7 n. 10. **ʿquza umkatla** AM 4, 7 short and bulky.

mkun(a) for **makna:** in **lbith̠ ulmkunh̠** (*Florilegium*) to his house and to his residence.

mkika pass. pt. pe. of **MKK** (q.v.).

mkikuta (abstr. noun from preced.) meekness, humility, subservience: **kinuta unihuta umkikuta** Gy 21:21 just-dealing, humility and subservience; **mkikuta ušabšuta** Gy 21:24 humility and subservience and flattery; **ṭabuta umkikuta ukinuta** Gy 213:20 f. goodness, humility and right-dealing.

MKK (Aram., H., Syr.) to lie down, go flat, make flat or level, spread out, become lowly, humble; pa. to lay down, make low, humble; to be humble, submissive; to flatten, trample down, lower; to smoothen.

Pe. Pf. **mak** he lowered, flattened MG 248:3; **makt ʿuhra** CP 109:11 = Q 56:1 thou hast levelled the road (MG 248:14); **makit** I have levelled MG 248:17; with encl. **arsa bkušṭa maklh̠** Jb 107:1 he spread him a couch in good faith; **arsa bkušṭa makilun** DC 3 I spread for them a couch in good faith; **ʿuhra maknalun** Gy 247:3 we laid down a road for them (MG 249:5); **makulak asa unargis** CP 215:12 they spread myrtle and narcissus for thee (on thy path); **makulh̲ bʿuhrh̲ . . . karata d̲-uarda** ŠQ 19:19 they spread out on his road . . . heaps of roses. Impf. with encl. **nimuklia bṭuria ʿuhra** Gy 370:7, **nimuklh̲ . . .** Jb 178:8 he shall level me out a road in the mountains; **ʿmiklak** Gs 107:13 read with C **ʿmuklak** I (will) level out for thee MG 249: 10 f. Impt. with encl. **makulh̲ dibaša rumia** WedF. 56, ML x spread him out Greek brocade (?). Act. pt. **maiik** MG 250:12, **puria maiik** Gy 147:23 he spread (hist. pres.) the (wedding) couch; **lmaiik ṭuria** Gy 370:7, Jb 178:8 to the Leveller of mountains; pl. **ukulhun sagada d̲-maikin** and all that spread a praying-carpet; with encl. **maikilun** DC 48. 331 they spread for them. Pass. pt. **mkik(a)** humble MG 116:17, fem. st. abs. (with encl.) **mkikabh̲** is levelled in it MG 250:21, masc. with encl. **mkiklh̲** Par. xi 11 b is spread for him; fem. st. emph. **mkikta** Gs 52:14 but also syncopated **mikta** (s.v.); pl. (masc.) **hun mikia umkikia** s. **mika 1**, **puria mkikia** ŠQ 19:17 a (marriage) bed is laid down; with encl. pers. pron. **nihit umkikit** DC 41. 413 thou art mild and humble, **nihit umakikit** DC 41. 298 thou art meek and humble (cf. *πραΰς εἰμι καὶ ταπεινός* Mat. 11:29). Inf. **lmikak** (for **mimkak**) **ʿuhra lṭabia** CP 183:3 to level (: smoothen) a road for the good.

Pa. Pf. **hu makik ʿuhra mkikta** Gs 52:14 he laid down a level(led) road. Impf. **nimakik ʿuhraikun** Q 37:12 he levelleth your road (MG 29:22). Impt. **makik libaikun** Gy 20:20, 39:7 f. humble your hearts (MG 253:7); **makik umarik ruhia d̲-ziqa** DC 44. 630 subdue and soften spirits of tempest.

Ethpa. Pt. pl. **ṭuria . . . kd̲ taturia mitmakakia** CP 170:3, ML 206:4 mountains were flattened like bridges.

Der.: **mauka = muka 2, mika 1** (var. **maka 2**, fem. **mikta**), **m(a)kika, mkikuta.**

MKR (Aram., Syr., H., Sab., Ar., Akk. in der. Ges. s. מכר, LS s. ܡܟܰܪ) to buy a spouse, to espouse, betroth.

Pe. Pf. **laras ulamkar** Gs 17:20 (var. **lakamar** s. **KMR**) they did not marry or betroth.

MLA I (Gen. Sem.) to fill, be full. Both trans. & intrans.

Pe. Pf. **mla bgurmaizh̲** Gy 99:4, CP 373:8 he clenched his fist(s) (*idiom*), intrans. **mla ʿuṣrh̲ zihira** Jb 231:8 his mind was filled with spite; **mla rugza** Jb 233:12 he was filled with anger; **ainai bmia siauia mlat** Gy 377:11 (Leid. & DC 22 transitively **mlit**) I gazed my fill at the black waters (*idiom*); **mlun bgurmaizaiun** Q 30:5 they clenched their fists (*idiom*); **ʿutria . . . ainaihun bhak nišimta mlun** DC 27. 130 the uthras . . . gazed their fill at that soul (*idiom*); with suff. **mlitinan** Q 14:1 (a miscop. **lmaitinan**) thou hast filled us. Impt. **mlia ainak bqin** Gy 140:9 gaze thy fill at Q. (*idiom*); with encl. **ainak mlibh̲ balma** Gy 96:5 gaze thy fill at the world (*idiom*); with suff. **mliih̲ mn ginzak** DC 3 supply it from thy treasure; fem. with suff. **mlainun lmia** DC 48. 231 fill them with water; pl. with suff. **mluiih̲ mia** ML 28:14, CP 25:20 **muliih̲ mia** fill it with water. Act. pt. **hin malia hailaikun** Gy 40:1 as much as ye are able (*idiom*); **kd̲ malia ainaihun uhazilh̲** ATŠ II no. 108 when they gaze their fill at and see her (*idiom*); **ulaiit hilia umargania d̲-malia bhad aṭirpa d̲-klilh̲** ATŠ II no. 362 and there are no precious stones or pearls that would compensate for one leaf of its wreath. Pass. pt. **qaštaiun mlia** DC 28 their bow is drawn (or pl.); **ʿniš milia** [*sic*] **mia** DC 46. 114:13 a person filled with water (dropsy); pl. **mlin** MG 165:1, **mlin** (var. **mlia** Sh. 'Abd.'s copy) **iardnia . . . mia** Gy 32:13 the jordans . . . are full of water, fem. pl. **mlʿian** AM 200:2 (miscop. **muʿian** cf. BZ 122 n. 4). Inf. **lmimlia mia** JRAS 1937 594:33 to fill (it) with water.

Ethpe. Pf. **ʿt(i)mlia** was, were filled MG 263:20, (fem. pl.) **gabaruatai ʿlh̲ ʿtimlia** Jb 198:3 in him my miraculous power was fulfilled (realized); **ainh̲ nhura ʿtmlia** Gy 64:24 ff. his eyes were filled with light MG 264:23; masc. pl. **ʿtimlun bhiia** Gy 173:13 they were filled with Life (MG 214:4). Impf. **nitimlun** they are, or will be filled MG 265:5. Pt. **mit(i)mlia** filled MG 132:15.

Idioms. With **gurmaiza** as obj. 'to clench the fists' (s. pe. pf. twice); **mla aina b-** 'to gaze one's fill, look intently at, scrutinize' (s. pe. pf. twice, impt. twice, act. pt. without **b-**), **haila malia** 'to be able' (s. pe. act. pt.).

Gl. 11:9 f. inf. pe. miswritten املا *implere* پُر شد; 14:11 f. **amla** امتلى *impleri* پُر شد; 151:13 f. id. ملا *implere* پُر كرد.

Der.: **malaia, m(a)laiia = (a)mlaiia, malia 2, maliut(a).**

MLA II (for **MNA II** = מנע) to keep away, prevent Ginzā 497 n. 1.

Pe.: Inf. **umimilia husrana** Gs 68:24 to prevent (possibly: to complete, **MLA I**) the loss.

Gl. 59:15 f. **amla** اخشا *abesse, absit a, longe sit* حاشا كه تو كردى.

MLA III occ. corruption of **MLL**. **malit udgila umdagla šana** DC 46 thou speakest (?), and disappointed and outwitted he goes away (?).

mlagṭana (nom. ag. pa. of **LGṬ**) grasping, acquisitive. Fem. **mlagṭanita**. **mlagṭana umsakrana** AM 24:16, 28 grasping and miserly; **mlagṭanita tihuia** AM 69:5 she will be grasping.

mlaušuta (abstr. noun from pass. pt. pa. of **LWŠ**) uncleanness, pollution. Var. **mlaš(i)uta**. **ṭnupia umlaušuta** Gy 215:23 pollution and uncleanness. **mlaušuta mkadba** Gy 389:18 a deceitful uncleanness.

mlai(i)a a var. of **amlaiia, malaiia** s.v.v Jb ii 137 n. 6.

mlaka s. **malaka**.

mlala a frequent var. of **malala**.

mlašuta Sh. 'Abd.'s copy's var. of **mlaušuta** Gy 389:18.

mlašiuta DC 22. 208 var. of **mlaušuta** Gy 215:23.

mlik st. cstr. of **malka** MG 151:7. **mlik hšuka** Gy 75:5, 81:18, 24, 82:2 f., 86:10, 132:11, 13, 15, 365:1, Gs 75:23 the king of darkness; **mlik rugza** Gy 181:17, 208:14 the king of wrath; **mlik malkia** Gy 384:11, 390:14 ff., AM 216 king of kings (old official title of P. origin, cf. mod. P. شاهنشاه) MG 310:2. But **mlik iama** Gy 174:18, 175:1 is only a misunderstood ܡܠܐ ܕܝܡܐ Ps 114:5 Ginzā 179 n. 1, Lietzmann SBAW xxvii 605, Burkitt JThSt 1928 p. 236; **din mlik** **ʿutra** Gy 207:23, 208:8 ff. pr. n. of an uthra.

MLK I (Jew.-Aram., Can., H. מלך I, Ar. ملك, Eth. መለከ to possess, Akk. *maliku*, *malku* king; cf. Nöld. ZDMG xl 727 & **MLK II**) to rule, reign, govern.

Af. Act. pt. **mamlik** Gy 60:4 he ruleth MG 230:12; fem. **d-bišuta bgauh mamlika** Gy 357:13 f. in which evil ruleth; with encl. **d-kulhun malkia mamlikibh** ATŠ in which all kings (: priests) rule. Pass. pt. **malka d-nhura mamlak btagh lalam** Gy 6:9 the king of light is made king with his crown for ever (MG 230:13).

Ethpe. Pf. **ʿtimlak** (var. **ʿtimlik** PD) **btlatma ušitin razia** ATŠ I no. 19 it has been set over 360 mysteries. Impf. **mn ʿbidata d-rurbania nitimlik** AM 17:12 he will be entrusted with governance of the works of the mighty.

Der.: **malka** (st. cstr. **mlik**), fem. **malakta**, **malkut(a)**, **malki(ai)il**.

MLK II (Aram., Syr., H. מלך II, Akk. *malāku*, rel. to **MLK I**?) to advise, counsel, give advice.

Pe. Pf. **bmilka d-mn rbia mlik** CP 157:18, ML 190:5 according to the advice which he accepted from the Great (Life), **lamlak** Gy 357:2 he gave no advice (varr. **m(a)lik** s. pt.); with suff. **lamilkan milka d-mhaimnia** Gs 49:24 he gave me not the advice of believers MG 400:1. Impf. **malkia nimilkun** AM 234:13 kings will hold counsels (or **MLK II**?); with suff. **man malil minai unimilkan malka** [*sic*] **ṭaba** DC 26. 466 f. who will talk with me and give me good advice?; **malkuih** Gy 93:3 they advised him. Impt. **mluk mulkania šapiria lhdadia** Gy 25:22 give good counsel to one another. Act. pt. **malik** AM 7:19, he gives advice; **malik milkia basimia** Gy 250:1, 262:7, 357:2 he giveth agreeable advice; **ma(m)lik milkia d-mulkana lnapših lamlak** Gy 357:2 (var. . . . **lamlik** DC 22. 354), Jb 171:4 f. (. . . **lamlik**, var. **lamalik** C) giver of counsels who did (var. Jb C doth) not advise himself; with encl. **malkalun milka baṭla** Gy 109:2 she gave (hist. pres.) them useless advice, **mulkana . . . malkilh** AM 92:14 people . . . give him advice. Pass. pt. **lamlik** as a var. of **lamlak** and **lamalik** s. act. pt.

Af. Act. pt. **mamlik** Jb 171:4 = **malik** Gy 357:2 (s. pe. act. pt.).

Ethpe. Pf. **laʿtimlik** Gy 93:16 he took no counsel with himself (MG 222:2); **ʿtimlik** Gy 114:12 f. they took counsel; with encl. **ʿtimliklak** Gs 50:3 advice was given thee; **ʿtimlikbh bhikumth** Gy 93:7 he took counsel with himself in his wisdom. Pt. **mitmlik** Gy 71:13, 296:23 f., MG 213:24 (formally sg. but in both places used as pl.); pl. **mitmilkia** Gy 70:8, 74:14, Jb 225:9 they take counsel (with themselves).

Ethpa. (?): Pt. **mitmalkia** Gy 80:22 (so Pet. but ABCD have **mitmilkia**).

Der.: **mulkana** (var. **ml-**), **milka**.

MLL I (מְלַל, ܡܰܠܶܠ, H. מָלַל, Ar. أَمَلَّ) to speak, talk (to show forth, appear).

Pa. Pf. **malil** he spoke MG 253:10 f., but Gy 29:11 as a var. of **mamlil** he made speak MG 253 n. 2, **malalat** Gy 362:13, Gs 99:20, 100:3, 12, she spake MG 253:11, **mal(a)lit** I spoke MG 31:paen., **mallit** (var. **malalit** B) **uamarilh** Gy 87:7 I spake to him (cf. Gy 325:15, 328:11). Impf. **timalil timarlh** Gy 341:11 she said to him (as hist. pres.) MG 371:8, **ʿmalil** I (shall) speak MG 57:middle, 253:11. Pt. (as from af.) **mamlil** (for מְמַלֵּל) Gy 53:9 he maketh speak MG 79:13, 253 n. 2; **qal šušlata d-mamlila** DC 43 A 53, 146 (cf. l. 105) the noise of chains which clank. Part. pres. **mamlilit** thou speakest, **mamlilitun** ye speak MG 253:13. Inf. (as from af.) **amlulia** Gy 4:24, 7:14 BD; **nhura d-manda d-hiia malil bh** ATŠ II no. 362 the light of Knowledge of Life appears therein (speaks therein); **mamlulia** Gy 31:11, MG 253:16 f.

Gl. 3:9 f. **MLL** اجاب *respondere* بيرون ميكند [sic]; 52:5 f. id. تخاطب *colloqui* مخاطبه كرد; 166:7 f. نطق *narrare, discurrere* سخن كرد.

Der.: **m(a)lala**, **mamla(la)**, **malalta**, **minilta**, **milta**.

MLL II for **MLA** Ginzā 89 n. 3 (pa. fulfil, supply).

Pa. (& Af.?): Impf. with encl. **unimal(i)lbh mia** (var. **bmia** Leid.) **hiia** Gy 87:16 may it fill itself with living water. Pt. **d-haizin mamlila mn riš briš** CP 373:13 (pass.); that is supplied — thus with encl. **malilbun naṣiruta** CP 366:5 Naṣoraean wisdom filled *or* spoke in them (hist. pres., or pf.?); **nhura d-manda d-hiia malilbh** the light of M.-d-H. appears therein; **haizin mamlilbh zma** Gy 102:5 as the blood filleth it (: the body).

MLL III (etym. doubtf.; cf. H. מלל II & III?) to crush, hurt, wound, injure BZ 58 n. 6, Ap. I.

Pa. Impf. **parzla nimalil ʿlh** AM 90 (*& often*) an iron (instrument, weapon) will injure him.

mn 1 (Gen. Sem.) from, out of, (some) of; with MG 10:1, 193:27 f. Scr. pl. **min** is exceptional, but with suff. always **min-** s.v. With other prepositions and adv. expressions: **mn qbal** Gy 248:18 on account of, **mn lalam** Gy 274:14 from eternity, **mn riš** from the beginning (frequent in the doxological formulae **mn riš lriš** and **mn riš briš** for ever, to all eternity), **mn lbar** Gy 258:21 (from) outside, **mn lhil**

from the other world, mn (a)luat- Q 23:31 **with,** in the company of, **mn ʿlauia** Gy 150:6 from above, **mn atutia** from beneath, **mn tit** Gy 98:11 id., **mn qudam** Gy 205 ff., 278:19 from before, from the presence of, **mn aqam-** Gs 40:1 id., **mn abatar** from behind, **mn ʿhuria** Q 3:15 id., **mn (a)binia, mn binat-** (from) amongst, **mn aganbia** Gy 243:17 from the side of . . . MG 196 f.; **bar mn** Q 25:4, **lbar mn** Gy 5:2, 283:20 &c. out of, except, **ʿl mn qbal** Gy 269:ult. opposite, **mn ka** from here, **mn haka** id., **mn tam** from there MG 203 f., **mn** (preceded by an adj. or adv.) than (comparative): **sania mn lilia** Gy 227:20 uglier than night; **nagdia kupna mn hiuia uṣahin mn šušmana** Gy 223:15 hungrier than a snake and thirstier than an ant; **qanahra mn qandilia** Par. xi 23 a, they shine more than lamps; **qala d̲-ʿutria qašiš mn bišia** Gy 78:4 the voice of the uthras is stronger than that of the evil ones MG 358. As 'with': **ʿmalil mn šdum** Gy 141:20 I speak with Š., cf. **ʿštaiia minh̲** Gy 140:23 I converse with him &c. MG 357. Partitive use: **lahun mn lbušia d̲-hazin alma** Gy 5:15 they were not the kind of clothing of this world; **mn miniltak dilak latihuia ʿlh̲** Gy 80:8 it will not happen to him according to thy word (lit. nothing of thy word will come true about him), similarly **mn minilai dilia lahuat ʿlh̲** Gy 84:18; **mn birkta d̲-ṭabia tihuia ʿlauaikun** Gy 108:23 something of the blessing of the good shall come on you, similarly **mn birktan tʿiul ʿlak** Gy 115:13; **umn malakia d̲-nura . . . ništabdun** Gy 33:8 some of the angels of fire . . . shall be subdued; **mn ziuh̲ pras ʿlai umn nhurh̲ ʿhablia** Gy 128:10 he spread over me some of his radiance and gave me some of his light &c. MG 357 f.; **mn ziuh̲ umn nhurh̲ d̲- . . . umn ruahun d̲-hiia nišria ʿlan** Q 41:22 some of the brilliance and of the light of . . . and of the Peace of Life shall dwell upon us &c. MG 414 f.; **mn laqadmia** (*often*) without predecessors MG 431:1; **mn kd̲** Gy 271:11 f. corrupt MG 465:11 ff., Ginzā 268 n. 4.

Gl. 162:3 **mn** من *ex, de* از.

mn 2 a spor. var. of **man** 1.

MNA I (מנא, ܡܢܐ, H. מנה, Ar. منا & منى, South-Ar. 𐩣𐩬𐩺, Akk. *manū*) to count, number, reckon; to allot, apportion, deal out.

Pe. Pf. with encl. **mnulh̲** DC 51. 619 they made a calculation for him. Impf. **ʿmnia** CP 110:7, ML 135:9 I will count; with suff. **ʿminiih̲** Morg. 251/89:21, ATŠ I no. 158 I will count him; **niminiun hiia bminianun** Gy 275:21 the Life (pl.) counted me in Its number. Impt. pl. **mnun** DC 51. 615 Count! Part. pres. **kd̲ manit miša** Morg. 244/76:5 f., Q. 42:16, 47:15 when thou apportionest the oil; **kd̲ manit ʿtša iahria** ATŠ II no. 74 when thou reckonest nine months; with encl. **maniatlh̲ miša** CP 95:3, Morg. 249/86:14, Q 46:20, 47:12 thou apportionest him the oil Inf. **mimnia miša** Morg. 251/89:21, Q 44:5, 16 to apportion the oil.

Af. (only part. form.): Act. pt. **mamnia** Gs 129:21 he counteth. Part. pres. **mamnit guniia** Jb 167:8 thou enumeratest the abominations.

Ethpe. Pf. **bminian iumia laʿtimnia** ML 128:13 was not reckoned in the number of days (cf. ATŠ II no. 14); **ʿtminiit** Gs 131:7, DC 48. 255 I was counted MG 264:10; **ʿtimniit** DC 48. 255 I was appointed. Impf. **nitimnia** Gy 38:23 will be allotted, **nimnia** Gy 33:15, 16 (var. **nitimnia** BD & Sh. 'Abd.'s copy) id., **ʿmnia** Gs 65:15 I am counted MG 265:2. Pt. **bminian d̲-** [*sic*] **iumia lamitminin** ATŠ II no. 14 are not counted in the number of days (cf. ATŠ II no. 14), **iumia . . . d̲-lamitminin** ibid. (var. **ulamitminiin** DC 6) days that are neither taken into account nor numbered. Part. pres. **mitminiit** Gs 73:7 BC, varr. **mitminit** D, **mitminiat** A thou art counted MG 266:4 f.

Ethpa. Pf. **tmaniit, ʿtmanit** only as varr. of **ʿtimniit** Gs 131:7 (s. ethpe. pf.).

Der.: **manuiia, miniana, mna(ta).**

MNA II (Old Aram., Jew.-Aram. & H. מנע, Sab. 𐩣𐩬𐩲, Ar. منع Ges.) to keep away, withhold, refuse, ward off, resist, forbid. Secondary rt. **MLA II** s.v.

Pe. Impf. with suff. **ʿmini(i)h̲** Jb 46:13 ff. I shall prevent him, or keep him away MG 275:17 (Lidzb. first from **MNA I** Jb ii 52 n. 2, but he corrected this opinion in Ginzā 497 n. 1).

mna 1 (Talm. מְנָא < *min ân* < مِن أَيْنَ, cf. H. מֵאַיִן) whence?, from where?, from what? MG 22:7, 36:8, 205:10 ff. Doublet **amna** 1: **mna hua hšuka . . . umna hun daiaria d̲-ʿtbh̲ . . . mna hauian ʿbidatun . . . mna hua husranun . . . mna hun buria rurbia bišia . . . mna hun mia siauia . . . mna hun tiniania . . . mna hun markabatun umna hun bišia d̲-ʿtbun mna huat hiuat nuqbta** Gy 75:10 ff. whence is the darkness . . . and whence are its inhabitants . . . whence are their works . . . whence is their loss . . . whence are the mighty evil monsters . . . whence are the black waters . . . whence are the dragons . . . whence are their chariots and whence are the evil ones which are in them, whence is the female H.? **mna hzath̲** CP 90:12 f., ML 111:11, 112:1 how comes it (from what cause &c.) that she saw it? ; **mna huainin** CP 213:15 whence are we? ; **mna sindirkak . . . mna naṣbak** Jb 236:11 f. whence is thy Palm-Tree . . . whence is thy Creator?

mna 2 st. abs. of **mnata** MG 155:15, used inst. of st. cstr. **mna bataihun** Gs 71:5 the portion of their house; **mna bataikun** Gs 41:3, 71:5 f. the portion of your house; **mna hšuka** Gy 38:22, Gs 41:17 the portion of darkness; **mna nura** Gs 41:18 the portion of fire; **mna qirsa** Gs 41:18 the portion of illness; **mna ruha umna mšiha** Gy 228:8 the portion of R. and Christ MG 313:5 ff. As st. abs. only in the distributive repetition: **bmna mna** Gy 103:1 f. in single pieces MG 328:paen.

mnadra in **kbaš mnadra** Jb 156:8 obscure, prob. corrupt.

mnauata pl. of **mnata** MG 168:5. **mnauath̲**

baiia lmikal HG it seeks to devour its allotted portions; **zabdia triṣlia bšuqia umnauata lpumaihun d̠-biriata** DC 51 he set gifts for me in the markets and portions at the entrance of the streets; **gabia mnauata lhiia** CP 415:1 collecting (a collector of) portions for the Life.

mnauia a doubtf. pl. of **mnata. uʿtpalag šuba . . . mnauia** ATŠ II no. 197 and it was divided into seven portions.

mnaṭrana (nom. ag. pa. of **NṬR**) guardian, preserver. Pl. **-ia. mnaṭrana lnišimth̠** (*Florilegium*): guardian to his soul; **mlakia mnaṭrania** DC 43 D 58 guardian angels.

mnaṭruta (rt. **NṬR**) watchfulness. With suff. **mnaṭrutak** Gy 62:11 thy watchfulness.

mnakalta (pt. pa. fem. st. emph. of **NKL**) Oxf. roll b, DC 43 D 67 &c. guileful spirit.

mnaq in **hlaq umnaq** Gy 237:23 portion (prob. a locution, in which **mna 2** was influenced by the preced. word Ginzā 238 n. 2).

mnata (rt. **MNA I**, מְנָתָא, ܡܢܳܬܳܐ) portion, part, lot, share, due. MG 155:13. St. cstr. **mnat** MG 111:3, 155:21. St. abs. **mna** (used also as cstr.) s.v. Pl. **mnauata, mnauia** s.vv. **mnata litlun lsahria** RD B 33 the devils have no share; **mnata dilan litlan** RD B 5 we have no share; **mnata bgauh̠ litlan** Gy 109:5 we have no share in it; **nitilan mnata balma** Gy 109:7 he shall give us a portion in the world; **umištkalun lšuba bmnatun** Gy 228:9 and (he) will be allotted to the Seven; **mnata d̠-šuba** Gy 315:23 the portion of the Seven; **mnata lhabara palgin** Gy 228:11 they allot to the darkness its portion; **kd̠ ba mnata mn hiia ulaʿhablh̠ laʿhablh̠ mnata bbaita** Gy 351:3 f. when he sought a portion from the Life, It gave him not, It gave him no portion in the House (: world); **mnata d̠-bil** Gy 380:2 the portion of B. (: Jupiter); **mnata bṭabuta lgaṭ** Gs 102:2 he accepted gratefully a portion; **utpalag mnauata lmalkia** DC 41. 65 portions were assigned to kings; **mnath̠ ʿhabtlh̠** DC 48. 39 thou hast rendered him his due.

MND den. from **manda 1**?

Pe. Pt. pl. **sahdia bhiia umandin** (var. **maudin** Pet.) **bmanda d̠-hiia** DC 22. 282 (= Gy 286:21), similarly **bhiia sahdin ub-manda d̠-hiia mandin** Zotb. 227 a:19 f. they worship Life and confess M.-d̠-H. (**mandin** influenced by **sahdin**!).

mnumbia (rt. **NMBA** pa. of **NBA II**, cf. Akk. *munambu* 'mourner' as a priestly name KAT 590) mourning MG 266 n. 1. **mnumbia ubkita** Gy 51:21 mourning and wailing; **iuma d̠-mnumbia** Gy 277:13 f. the day of mourning.

mnunaiia = **m(i)nunaiia.**

mnia (cf. Old Aram. מנה, Bibl.-Aram. מְנֵא Dan. 5:25, 26, Syr. ܡܢܝܳܐ, H. מָנֶה, Ar. مَنًا, Gr. μνᾶ < Bab. *manû*, Lewy: *Fremdw.* 118, Fränkel 203, Ges.) RD 9 pl. the minas? (weight).

mnihra s. **m(i)nihra.**

MSA (מסא, ܡܣܳܐ, H. מסה, Ar. مَسْوَة curdled milk, Eth. መሰወ to dissolve, rel. to H. מסס, Ar. مَوَّس Ges., LS) to condense, curdle, congeal, assume material shape, take shape, consolidate, solidify, materialize; to dissolve, melt, flow away, fall from, be removed. Both trans. & intrans.

Pe. Pf. **msa (ulaʿtmisiat)** Gy 169:6 he tried to perform the condensation (but it did not take place); **msuta d̠-msa** Gy 169:19 the condensation which he condensed (var. **amsa** DC 22. 163 af.?); **girma msa bkulhun han-damia** ATŠ II no. 125 bone became solid (intrans.) in all the limbs; **umsa larqa** DC 44 and He consolidated the earth; **aria msa ligrih̠ bʿdia matnalia** DC 46. 240:10 the lion let his paw fall away and placed it in my hands; **umsuta lamsat biahra tišaia** ATŠ I no. 92 and the solidification did not take place in the 9th month; **misiat** Gy 268:14 (she) became solid MG 257:9; **bkulhun nahlia msaitun** DC 51 ye (waters) flowed down into all rivers; **mia msuta lamsun** Gy 337:12 ff. the waters became not solid MG 399:16; with suff. **misih̠** (*often*) he condensed it; **msaith̠ lmisia rba** Gy 132:17 I consolidated a great solidification (var. **amsaith̠** DC 22. 128 af.?). Impf. **ulanimsia mn riša** ATŠ II no. 361 and it shall not fall away from its source (?) (see ATŠ trs. p. 276 n. 5). Impf. **msia arqa** Gy 12:15 condense the earth; **msia msuta** Gy 169:5 condense a condensation; with suff. **musih̠** Gy 337:3 condense it MG 217:19. Act. pt. **mn qudam d̠-masia arqa** ATŠ I no. 156 before the earth was consolidated (read **msia**? pass. pt.). Pass. pt. **msia** s.v.

Af. (often as a var. of pe.). Pf. **amsa** DC 22. 163 = **msa** Gy 169:19; with suff. **amsaith̠** DC 22. 128 = **msaith̠** Gy 132:17; **amsith̠ bmisia rba** CP 337:3 (?) cf. Gy 133:17 (the phrase here refers to a new priest); **ʿsiqta d̠-amsinun lṭuria** DC 35 the compression which consolidated mountains, similarly **ʿsiqta d̠-amai d̠-amsinun lṭuria** DC 51 the seal of my people that consolidated the mountains. Impf. **ʿiamsia l(i)msuta** Jb 233:8 I will condense a condensation.

Ethpe. Pf. **ʿtmisiat arqa msuta hda** Gy 169:15 the earth was condensed (in) one condensation MG 399:17 f., **(msa) ulaʿtmisiat** s. pe. pf., **ulaʿtmisiat msuta** Jb 55:14 the solidification did not occur; **uʿtmisiat msuta** Gy 97:15 and solidification took place (MG 263:bottom), a corrupt form **ʿtiamsiat** Oxf. III 53 b, MG 263 n. 3.

Gl. 64:13 f. missp. with ṣ جمد *coartari* سخت شد.

Der.: **msuta, (a)msia.**

msadrana (nom. ag. pa. of **SDR**) disposer, organizer, regulator, one who makes arrangements, sets in order. Pl. **-ia** used also of assistant priests at a *zidqa brika*. **prišaia msadrana usdira** Gy 214:24 the perceiving man who maintaineth order and is orderly; **msadrana d̠-libia** PD 912 = ATŠ I no. 89 one that setteth hearts to rights; **d̠-nihuilak msadrana mn riš briš** DC 41. 36 (& *often*) that there may be for thee one who setteth in order from beginning to end; **arba malkia**

msadrania DC 34 four kings — arrangers (four constructive powers: air, earth, water, fire); malpana umsadrana ATŠ I no. 234 teacher and reformer; ʿutra malka msadrana ATŠ II no. 318 the uthra, a king(ly) disposer; ʿutria msadrania DC 35 the uthras who maintain order; msadranun d-almia d-hšuka CP 419:13 the regulator of worlds of darkness; msadrana hauia balma d-nhura uhšuka DC 34. 1221 he becomes an Arranger in the worlds of Light and Darkness; ʿu msadrana bškinth hu ATŠ II no. 184 if he is one who maintains order in his cult-hut.

msakrana (nom. ag. pa. of SKR) avaricious, stingy person. mlagṭana umsakrana AM 24:16 grasping and stingy.

msania (sg. מְסָאנָא, مسانا & مسنا, H. סְאוֹן, rt. סאן = ساں = Akk. *šēnu* to put on the shoes) pl. boots, shoes, sandals MG 130:14. Var. ʿmsania. Masc. (?). arqia d-msanun s. arqa 2; bmsamai kbaštilia (= ih) DC 26. 640 f., DC 40. 589 with my shoe(s) I crushed him down; msania d-ʿuṣṭamumia bligrai simlia DC 44. 1711 I put shoes of poisoned darts (?) on my feet; šarualh agambia msanik ŠQ 18:220 his breeches (lie) beside thy shoes; msania sdiqia Gy 25:15 torn shoes; msania unarqmia Gy 106:12 shoes and boots; mnašiq msanun Gy 359:16 kissing their shoes.

msara Zotb. 228 b:15 a personal name.

msuta (abstr. n. from MSA) condensation, thickening, coagulation, solidification, congealing, consolidation MG 146:6, 161:21. Pl. msauata (bad varr. masauata, masiuata). Gy 94:25 (twice) as masc. (?), otherwise fem. msa msuta &c. s. MSA; msuta bʿzlat masia DC 50 a solidification took place in Ezlat (i.e. conception); masauata (var. masiuata) lanuba (var. laniba) lbiniana ATŠ I no. 124 (var. DC 6) no solid substances were produced at the building.

msia pass. pt. pe. of MSA.

Gl. 70:8 msia جو *concavitas* خالى (doubtf.); 42:7 amṣia [*sic*] بارد *frigidus* سرد سرما (mod. *msi*, predicatively *msiye*, is consistently used with the meaning 'cold').

MSKN (den. from miskina) to make poor, impoverish. *Fundamental stem*: Pt. pl. with encl. mimaskinilh Gy 264:1 they make him poor MG 30:12, 32:15, 84:16. *Reflexive* (?) *stem*: Pt. bsibuth mimaskin AM 26:19 in his old age he will become poor.

MSS = **MSA**?

Gl. 80:1 f. miswritten رضع *lactare* شير داد.

MSR (Jew.-Aram. & mod. H. מסר, Syr. مصّر) to deliver, yield, give up, surrender, give over; to scorn, contemn, despise.

Pe. Pf. with encl. lamsarlia Gs 103:7 read lamsirlia (pass. pt. with encl.) I have not delivered MG 440:middle & n. 2. Impf. latimisrun ʿabdia kširia biad marauatun bišia Gy 14:17 deliver not up well-doing servants into the hand of their evil masters. Act. pt. umasir anašia dagalia hauia AM 31:19 (miscop. umisar, umasiq) and he will scorn deceitful persons; fem. masra ainaihun d-bišia mn baitai DC 12 the eyes of the wicked are obliged to desist from my house; with encl. masarlh Gy 127:3 he giveth him over. Pass. pt. with encl. *msirlia s. pf.

Ethpe. Pt. pl. mitmisria ATŠ II no. 170 they capitulate.

Ethpa. Pf. rqiha ʿtmasar Gy 114:3 the firmament was rendered back to (earth?, cf. s. impf., which makes Lidzb.'s footn. Ginzā 126 n. 2 improbable). Impf. uʿl arqa nitmasar ATŠ I 261 and it will be yielded back to earth, uarqa titmasar DC 26. 109 and the earth will surrender herself.

Der.: masuria.

mʿ, ʿmia, mia 3, mʿia 3 (cf. s. mi-) interrogative particle, written separately (differently from the procl. mi-) MG 12:25, 209:5. mʿ ʿtlaikun mana akuat dilia Gs 57:13 do ye have a spirit like mine? MG 434:anteantep.; hzia mʿ huat nihuta balma Gy 380:23, 381:2 see if there is calm in the world? MG 470: antep.

mʿia 1, mʿiia 1 a rarer but more original form of mia 2 (q.v.) MG 109:13. Masc. pl. uʿpsiq mʿih kabdh ukuliath Gy 143:22 and his bowels, his liver and his kidneys were cut off.

mʿi(i)a 2 an exceptional scr. pl. of mia 1.

mʿia 3 (mʿiia 3) = **mʿ**. mʿiatlaikun Gs 57:13 (twice) = mʿ ʿtlaikun ibid. do ye not have? MG 296:4.

mʿi(i)aka = **miaka**. mʿiaka d-rab minai Gy 281:1 is there anyone greater than I? MG 434:ult. mʿiaka (var. mʿiiaka Sh. 'Abd.'s copy) d-hua bit rbia Gy 327:9 is there anyone who has been in the House of the Great (Life)?

mʿial (var. mʿiil) entry, entrance. mipaq šafta . . . umʿial habšaba DC 22. 484 (CP 192:10 mʿiil).

mparqana (nom. ag. pa. of PRQ) deliverer, redeemer, ransomer, saviour. mparqna umšauzbana (often) redeemer and saviour.

MṢA I (Jew.-Aram. & H. מצא, Syr. ܡܨܐ II, Min. שתמטא to bring together, Eth. መጽአ to reach, Akk. *maṣû* to be large) to be a match for, be equal in force, be able; to attain to, arrive at, reach, achieve.

Pe. Pf. d-ʿniš bhailh lamṣia CP 18:17 = ML 20:10 whose strength none can attain; ulamṣa d-nišaniun HG and they could not remove; kma mṣit usiblit Gs 54:20 how long couldst thou endure?; mṣu Gs 58:7 they could MG 258:6. Pass. pt. umṣia uhaila ʿtlh Gy 42:20 although he can and is able; mṣia bhailh Gs 75:24 can defeat him, is as strong as he; man d-mṣia bhailh d-raza rba Gy 153:13 who is as strong as the Great Mystery? kd mṣia hailh Or. 333:11 as much as he can, according to his ability (*a frequent idiom*); pl. d-lamṣʿin mikadušia Gy 40:17 which cannot fight MG 427:paen.; lamṣiin . . . mindam mibad bgauaihun AM 183:11 they can . . . do nothing in them. Part. pres. mṣina I can MG 260:2; mṣiit, mṣiiit, mṣʿiit thou canst MG 260:4; lamṣʿiit (var. mṣʿit Sh. 'Abd.'s copy) bhailh d-hazin nhura Gy 165:4 thou canst do nothing against this light; **lamṣʿiit mišiqlẖ minẖ** Gy 14:14 thou canst not take it from him; **ʿu hua mṣʿiit bhazin gabra** Gy 164:13 if thou wert equal to this man; **lahua mṣinin bhailaiun** Gy 158:6 we could do nothing against them.

IDIOMS: With **haila**, the verb is used in two idiomatic ways: (1) **mṣa bhailẖ** (cf. ܐܬܡܨܝ ܒܚܝܠܗ) 'was as strong as', 'was as able as', 'could defeat him' (**bhaila** sometimes omitted); (2) **mṣa hailẖ** (ܡܨܐ ܚܝܠܗ) 'was able' Nöld. ZA xxx 146.

MṢA II (ܡܨܐ II, H. & mod. H. מצה II, Akk. *mazū*; rel. to **MṢṢ**) to press; to suck out, suckle.

PE. Pf. **ainak miṣit ušinak harqit** DC 37. 45 thou didst close (lit. press) thine eyes and gnash thy teeth. Impf. **halba ʿriba nimṣunẖ** AM (*often*) they shall suckle him (or her) with mingled milk; **halba ḏ-tartin ʿnšia nimṣunẖ** AM (*often*) they shall suckle him with the milk of two women; **unimṣunẖ bṣuṣṭmia ḏ-mia** DC 43 J 21 and they will compress him into shackles of water (**ḏ-mia** a redundancy caused by writing **ṣuṣṭ-mia** on two lines (?)). Act. pt. **halba bgu bita maṣẖ** Oxf. xii it sucks the milk (albumen) in the egg; **lhiuaniata ḏ-iadlan ulamamṣan** DC 46. 219:6 f. for cattle who give birth but do not give suck.

DER.: **miṣat 2.**

MṢA III (מצע, ܡܨܥ) to be in the middle.

DER.: **miṣai(a)** (fem. **miṣaita**), **miṣat**, **miṣia** (var. **miṣʿia**).

mṣara (rt. **MṢR**, Syr. ܡܨܪܐ) torture MG 84:10, 115:18. **hlaṣa umsara** Gy 182:2, 19, 230:19, 233:9, 14 f. torment and torture.

mṣuṣṭia (cf. מצִיצָא with עינא) blinking. **aina mṣuṣṭia** JRAS 1943 170:18 blinking eye (compressed eye).

mṣuta (rt. **NṢA**) strife, contention MG 51:9, 131:1, 146 n. 4. **mṣuta kbišlin** Gs 30:17 contention oppresses them; **tigra umṣuta** DC 21 strife and contention.

MṢṢ, MUṢ (Aram., H. מצץ, Syr. ܡܨ, Ar. مصّ; as ע״ו: Jew.-Aram. מוץ; as ע״י: H. & mod. H. מיץ; rel. to **MṢA II**) to press; to suck, suckle.

PE. Impf. (without & with suff.) **nimaṣ ʿdẖ nimṣẖ** DC 43 J 127 he wrings his hand, he squeezes him. Inf. **mimaṣ** JRAS 1937 p. 591.

DER.: **mṣuṣṭia.**

MṢR I (Talm. מצר 'to stretch oneself'; prob. den. from **mṣara** which might derive from ܪܕܐ, but cf. ܐܬܡܨܪ a dialectal form of ܐܬܡܬܚ 'to stretch out' MG 84 n. 2) to torment, torture.

PE. Pass. pt. with encl. (& act. meaning) **lamṣirlia bpagra nišimta** Gs 103:6 I tormented no soul in the body MG 84:9, 383:7.

ETHPE. Impf. **nimṣar bnura** Gy 35:10 will be tortured in fire MG 84:10.

DER.: **mṣara.**

MṢR II (Jew.-Aram. מצר) to stretch, to (twist) rope; to mark a boundary, make a line of demarcation. IM 284, ML 112.

PE. Pf. **miṣra ḏ-mṣar bmšunia kušṭa** ATŠ I no. 283 the boundary which He (: the Life ?) marked in M.K. (or read **mṣir** pass. pt.?); **miṣrat miṣra** DC 20. 119, DC 43 E 54 she made a magic circle; pl. with encl. **mṣarulẖ miṣra** Gs 101:14 f., MG 225:1 (s. **miṣra** (*b*)). Impf. with encl. **nimṣurlia bzabia miṣra** Jb 178:7, Gy 370:5 f., MG 221:13 (s. **miṣra** (*b*)). Pass. pt. **miṣra rba ḏ-binia nhura lhšuka mṣir** ATŠ I no. 250 the great demarcation-line traced between light and darkness; pl. **halin kulhun miṣria lnišimta mṣirin** ATŠ I no. 232 all these lines of demarcation are traced about a soul.

DER.: **miṣra.**

mqablana (rt. **QBL**) (*a*) (nom. ag. pa.) one to bring forward, precursor, sponsor, receiver, (*b*) (abstr. noun) means of acceptance, recommendations. Pl. **-ia.** (*a*) **mqablanẖ šamiš** AM 169:17 its successor Sol; **baiina mn hiia . . . mqablana bhazin ginza rama** CP Prayer 174 line 3. (200 n:3) I ask from the Life ... a sponsor for this lofty treasure; **mqablana lbutan utušbihtan** DC 7 recipient of our prayer and our praise; **mqablana ḏ-ʿudai uhuṭrai utagai** DC 43 H 18 f. sponsor of my rod, my staff and my crown; **mqablanun ḏ-rušumia** DC 27. 137 precursors of the signs; (*b*) **alip alip mqablania adinqia hasir ubṣir** ATŠ I no. 10 a thousand thousand recommendations free from defect or imperfection s. trs. 114 n. 14.

mqadša (pass. pt. st. emph. of **QDŠ**) (*a*) with the original meaning: holy, (*b*) with polemical sneer: sinful, godless, prostituted. Fem. **mqadašta.** (*a*) **zriza rba qadiša qadiša mqadša** DC 40; (*b*) **ʿuhra mqadašta** Jb 209:12.

mqadšia pl. masc. of preced. in **bit mqadšia** Jb 66:15 ff., 93:9, 12, Gy 45:19 D (Pet. **bit mqadša**), 227:7 temple of Jerusalem Ginzā 228 n. 2 (cf. Ar. بيت المقدس Jerusalem).

mqaimana (nom. ag. pa. of **QUM**) one that establishes, sets up, or restores, confirmer, Raiser-up; a *ganzibra* consecrating another *ganzibra*. **mqaimana ḏ-kulhun ṭabia** Gy 2:1 f. = **mqaimanun ḏ-kulhun ṭabia** Gy 30:21, 62:1 Confirmer of all the good; **mqaimana ḏ-bauata** CP 377:3 Confirmer (or Raiser-up) of Prayers; **mqaimanun ḏ-ginzia** CP 415:3 Establisher of Treasures (: sacraments); **mqaimanak nitqaiam** CP 465:5 thy 'confirmer' (i.e. consecrating ***ganzibra***) shall raise; **umqaimanak adinqia haṭaiia** CP 465:8 and thy 'confirmer' without sins.

mqandran קדר dark (?) **uainẖ . . . mqandran** AM 89:4 her eyes are dark; **uainẖ mqandran** AM 935 f. his eyes are dark.

mqariaiil DC 40. 883 f. an angel.

mqarqasta (cf. **qurqsa** = ܩܘܪܩܣܐ, *κίρκος*) fem. encircling (?). **ruha ḏ-iatba lʿdia umitiqria mqarqasta** Or. 329:4 the spirit that sits on the hands and is called 'contraction' (?).

mqarqilana (nom. ag. from **QRQL**) overthrower. **mqarqilanan** ATŠ II no. 350 our overthrower.

MQQ (אִיתְמְקַק Targ., ܐܬܡܩܩ Pesh., II Kings 4:35) to yawn, sneeze Ginzā 191 n. 4, MMII 382.

Ethpa. Pf. **uʿtar uʿtmaqaq** Gy 190:11 and he awoke and sneezed.

mrabiana (nom. ag. pa. of **RBA**) fosterer, one who nurtures. **šamiš usira ldilak nihun mrabiana** (read **-ia**) Or. 325:11 sun and moon shall be thy foster-parents; **ubziqa d̲-aiar ṭur ṭura d-hauilak mrabiana** Or. 331:16 f. and by the breeze of mountain air that is thy foster-father; **hu mrabianun d̲-naṣuraiia** ATŠ I no. 231 he is a fosterfather of Naṣoraeans.

mradaiit DC 22. 210 = **mridaiit** Gy 217:2.

mradpana (nom. ag. pa. of **RDP**) persecutor. Pl. **-ia. libh̲ d̲-mradpania** DC 44. 113 the heart of persecutors.

mrauzana (nom. ag. pa. of **RWZ**) one that causes to flourish. **mrauzanun d̲-piria ʿmbia uʿlania** Gy 63:8 f. who causeth fruits, vines, and trees to flourish.

mrahmana (nom. ag. pa. of **RHM**) loving, compassionate MG 61:6. Fem. **mrahmanita. taiaba umrahmana** Gy 17:3, 30:20 f. compassionate and merciful; **libat mrahmanita** DC 44. 467 = Morg. 263/17:24 f. Venus full of love.

mrahqia (pass. pt. of **RHQ** q.v.) adverbially in **mn mrahqia** DC 3. 369:13 = CP 213:12 = ŠQ 13:9 from afar.

mrauma occasionally for **mruma.**

***mramiana** (nom. ag. pa. of **RMA**) instigator. Read for **mramiata** Gy 279:16, Ginzā 278 n. 4.

mramiata d̲-aqta Gy 279:16 instigators of disaster (cf. preced.).

mrara (rt. **MRR**) (*a*) bitterness, grief, affliction MG 115:19, (*b*) bitter drug, poison, venom, (*c*) bitter herb?, (*d*) in connexion with **gimra 1** (q.v.) completely obscure. Pl. **-ia.** (*a*) **zidanuta umrara** Gy 39:7 wrath and bitterness; **uʿmh̲ mrara minh̲ maška** AM 94:15 and his mother will meet with grief on his account; (*b*) **zihira umrara** Gy 3:10 f., 272:24 venom and poison; **bkasia d̲-mrara** DC 44:968 f. in bowls of poison; **hiuia ugala umrara** ATŠ I no. 256 serpent and tortoise and venomous toad (?); (*c*) **gidia (u)mraria uʿlqia** Gs 102:7, 105:7, 118:15, 124:12, Q 38:2, Jb 135:10 s. **gida 1. bmraria ṣbʿia qumth̲** Gy 122:8 his body is dyed with bitter herbs (?); (*d*) **mrara ugimra** Gy 145:4, **gimra umrara** Gy 145:9 s. **gimra.**

***mrašmana** (nom. ag. pa. of **RŠM**) one who makes signs (for magic purposes (?) ML 22 n. 7, Ginzā 436 n. 2). Pl. **mrašmania** Q 8:10 = CP 20:12 = ML 22:7, Gs 17:10 (var. **mrašmanʿ** Sh. 'Abd.'s copy).

MRD (Aram. & H. מרד, Syr. ܡܪܕ, Ar. مرد, Sab. 𐩣𐩧𐩵 rebel, Eth. መረደ attack Ges., LS) to rise against, rebel, refuse obedience, be contumacious, rebellious; to revolt.

Pe. Impf. **nimrud** AM 213:3 he will rebel, **nimirdun** AM 182:9 they will rebel. Act. pt. st. emph. **marda** s.v. Pass. pt. st. emph. **mrida** s.v.

Ethpe. Pt. pl. **mitmirdia ʿl alahun** Gy 173:23 they rebel against their god.

Der.: **marda, mirda, mrida, mriduta, mridaiit** (var. **mra-**), **mardita 2.**

mrum(a), ʿmrum(a) (H. מָרוֹם, Syr. loan-w. ܡܪܘܡܐ) height, sky, heaven, firmament MG xx 11, 26:4 f., 129 n. 1. Pl. **-ia. ainai lmrum šiqlit** Gs 78:6 (var. **lʿmrum** DC) I raised my eyes to the sky = **aianai lʿmrum šiqlit** Gs 130:18; **utraṣtinʿn lainan bmrumia** CP 32:9 = ML 38:2 thou hast raised our eyes in the heavens (n. 2); **(ʿ)mruma ʿlaia** Jb 70:11, 74:3, 76:12 &c. (*often*) the lofty heavens; **b(ʿ)mrum** Jb 9:11 in the heaven; **mrumia mia** Gs 1:6, 8 the heavens of water Ginzā 424 n. 1; **hibil ziua mn mruma rgaz ʿlh̲** AM 201:8 f. H.-Z. from the firmament was angered with him.

mrida (pass. pt. pe. st. emph. of **MRD,** ܡܪܝܕܐ, Ar. مريد Wid. v 163 n. 9) mutinous, rebellious, unruly, fierce, defiant, resistant. Fem. **mridtia** DC 43 A 45. Pl. masc. **mridia. latihuia mrida** Gy 214:5 f. be not mutinous; **aria mrida marda** Gs 14:8 a fierce defiant lion; **ṭupria d̲-aria mrida** DC 48:318 the claws of a fierce lion; **mrida damia lduga šgira** Gy 216:14 a rebellious person resembleth a heated oven; **mrida hauia** AM 7:11 he will be (of) ungovernable (temper); **ziqia mridia** AM 232:13 tempestuous gales; **ziqa mrida** AM 180 tempestuous wind.

mridaiit (adv. from preced.) Gy 217:2 insolently, contumaciously, truculently MG 201:5. Miscop. **mra-** s.v.

mriduta (abstr. noun from **MRD**) revolt, rebellion, rising against, disobedience, refractoriness, recalcitrance. Var. **amriduta. usiṭar mn (a)mriduta** Jb 37:6 and turn aside from refractoriness; **nihuta d̲-mriduta litbh̲** Gy 7:18 calmness in which there is no revolt; **d̲-mriduta bgauh̲ škina** AM 201:3 in which revolt dwells; **bnikla ubmriduta nigmun** AM 180:11 f. they will get into (become involved in) fraud and rebellion.

mridta (rt. **MRD**) uprising. **mridta qadmaia d̲-nhura** DC 43 J 49 the first uprising of light.

mristia (fem. st. emph. of pass. pt. pe. of **MRS**) crushed, bruised. **aina mristia** JRAS 1937 593:29 the bruised eye.

mrira (pass. pt. pe. st. emph. of **MRR**) bitter, bad. Fem. st. emph. **mrirt(i)a. mana rba kabira mrira hu** DC 41 (in a figure) the great, mighty *Mana*—he is the bitter [*sic*] one (the text must be corrupt, although it is difficult to suppose that the copyist did not understand the meaning of the word **mana**); **aina mrirtia** JRAS 1937 591:28 the bitter (i.e. evil) eye; **mihla mrirta** s. **mihla.**

mrirta (rt. **MRR**) (*a*) bitterness MG 117:25, (*b*) (doublet of **mirta**) gall, bile, venom. Pl. **mrir(i)ata.** (*a*) **hu ʿmrar bmrirta** Gy 160:22 f. he was bitterly grieved; **mrirta bišta** Gy 160:23 a disagreeable bitterness; (*b*) **mrirta d̲-aria** AM 124:5 a lion's gall; **umn mrirth̲ šaun sama** ATŠ I no. 249 and of its gall they made a poison; **paš kabdh̲ bmrirath̲** DC 51. 76 he dissolved his liver by his poisons; **kana d̲-mririata** Morg. 200:2, 262/15:14 a receptacle for poisons; **mrirta d̲-zagata** DC46. 132:3 the gall of a hen.

MRS (מְרַס, ܡܪܰܣ, Ar. مرث , مرس , مرش to macerate and مرص to compress, Eth. መረሰ to putrefy) to compress, press down, bruise, crush down, squash.

Pe. Pf. with suff. **mrasinun lkabadh̲** Gy 84:1 I crushed his liver (as if **kabadh̲** were a pl.). Act. pt. fem. **umarsa kapta d̲-šura** Oxf. roll g 821 and (she) compresses (or macerates?) the cavity of the navel. Pass. pt. ***mrisa**, fem. st. **mristia** s.v.

Der.: **mirsa** (var. **marsa**), **mristia** (fem.).

MRQ (Jew.-Aram., Syr.) to cleanse, wash off.

Der.: **maruqa, marqa.**

MRR (Gen. Sem.) to be(come) bitter, afflict, be grieved; to be spoiled (?).

Ethpe. Pf. **ʿmrar** Gy 82:8, 14, 160:23, 170:22, Gs 12:9 (with a frequent var. **mrar**) he was embittered, grieved MG 214:6, 222:3, 252:3, **ʿit d̲-mrar** (DC 6 **marad**) **ldukth̲ mistakak** ATŠ I no. 271 there are those that went bad and were held back in their place. Pt. **mimrar** Gy 389:8 they are grieved.

Der.: **marira, mariruta, mirta** (cstr. **murat**) **mrirta, mrara, mrir(a)**, (fem. **mrirtia**).

MŠA I (Jew.-Aram. משא to touch, to wash, Syr. ܡܫܳܐ to strip off, to collect, H. משה to take out, Ar. مسى to extract. Hoffmann ZDMG xxxii 762; rel. to **MŠŠ**) to wash; (rarely) to measure, stretch out.

Pe. Pf. **mša ʿdh̲** Gy 197:10 he washed his hands; **ʿdh̲ mša bmiia** Gy 94:23 he washed his hands in water; **mša ʿdh̲ biardna** DC 34. 1073 he washed his hands in the jordan; **ʿdh̲ mša bmia tahmia** Gy 94:23 he washed his hands in stagnant water; **mšit ʿdai** Gs 63:7 I washed my hands; **mšit anpai** Morg. 264/19:22 I washed my face; with suff. **tbarth̲ umšaith̲** Gy 118:23 I broke him (to pieces) and stretched him out; **mšath̲** Gy 159:18 (var. **mšaith̲** DC 22. 154) I measured him. Impf. **unimšia ʿdh̲ uanph̲** DC 24 and he will wash his hands and face; **uanph̲ nimšia** Gy 228:8 and he washeth his face; with encl. **nimšilh̲ ʿdh̲** CP 92:18 = ML 115:5 let him wash his hands. Impt. **mša ʿdak** Gy 197:4 wash thy hands; **mša** AM 165 measure.

Der.: **mša.**

MŠA II, MŠH s.v. (< Aram. & H. משח, Syr. ܡܫܰܚ, Ar. مسح; with loss of ח already in Akk. *mašā'u*) to anoint, consecrate by anointing.

Pe. Pf. **mišit** I anointed MG 235:3. Act. pt. pl. with encl. **miša mašailh̲** Sh. 'Abd.'s copy's var. of Gy 54:13 (read **mašilh̲**, Pet. has **mšaiilh̲** which would be pa. of ܡܫܳܐ, hence ܡܫܰܚܺܝܢ ܠܶܗ MG 252:18) they anoint him with oil.

Der.: **miša.**

mša (rt. **MŠA I**) st. cstr. measure, dimension. **qumat hdadia qaimia umša hdadia nasbia** Gs 100:3, DC 48. 103, DC 3. 382:8 = CP 228: antep. they are like one another in stature and dimension.

mšagašta (nom. act. pa. of **ŠGŠ**) AM 213:15 confusion.

mšagrana (as nom. ag. pa. of **ŠGR**) enflamed, enraged. Pl. **-ia. kalbia šihania umšagrania** Gy 180:7 ravening and infuriated dogs.

mšadarta (nom. act. pa. of **ŠDR**) sending, visitation, possession (?). **unitnaṭrun mn haršia umšadarta** DC 40. 982 f. and they shall be guarded from witchcraft and possession (?).

mšadkana (nom. ag. pa. of **ŠDK**) Oxf. 94 b = ML 262:6 = CP 279:2 quietener, peace-maker.

mšadrana (nom. ag. pa. of **ŠDR**) sender, bestower. **mšadrana d̲-kul buta utušbihta** CP sender (: bestower) of all prayer and praise; **mšadranun d̲-šlihia d̲-kušṭa** Gy 63:10 the sender of apostles of Truth.

mšadranuta (abstr. noun from **ŠDR**, cf. **mšadarta**) visitation; mission, errand. **haršia bišia mšadranuta taqupta** DC 43 D 64 black magic, grievous visitation (?).

mšauz(i)bana (nom. ag. of **ŠWZB** = šaf. of **YZB**) saviour. **mparqana umšauzbana** (*often*) deliverer and saviour.

mšauiana (nom. ag. pa. of **ŠWA**) (*a*) maker, creator, (*b*) smoothener, pacifier. (*a*) **mšauiana d̲-šapirata** Gy 2:24 creator of fair things; **mšauianun d̲-ʿušria** Gy 71:18 creator of treasures (= thoughts); (*b*) **mšauiana umšadkana** CP 279:2, ŠQ 27:32 alleviator and peace-maker.

mšauiata (pass. pt. fem. pl. of **ŠWA**) (*a*) subst.: creations, things made, (*b*) adj.: made (fem. pl.). (*a*) **mšauiata d̲-ṭabia** Gs 88:5 creations that are good; (*b*) **arsik mšauiath̲** Gs 134:6 thou (fem.) madest (didst prepare) thy bed. Var. **mšauaita.**

mšaunia kušṭa Jb 179:8 = **mšunia kušṭa.** Var. **mšania kušṭa** B.

mšauni(a)t ʿšata haita Gy 87:9 s. **mšuniat.**

mšakna (pass. pt. pa. of **ŠKN II** den. from **šikna**) deposit(ed), fæcal, Ginzā 226 n. 5. **kita mšakna** Gy 225:15 fæcal clod.

mšalṭana (rt. **ŠLṬ**) Gy 88:6 endowed with power, authority MG 138:19.

mšania s. **mšaunia.**

mšaniuta (abstr. noun from pass. pt. pa. of **ŠNA**) removal, separation. **mšaniuta mn ahia** AM 60:11 end, separation from brothers; **mšaniuta mn ʿnšia** AM 16:10 separation from women.

mšara 1 (Jew.-Aram. מְשָׁרָא, Ar. loan-w. مشارة Kraemer: *Culturgesch. Streifzüge auf d. Gebiete des Islâms* 64, MG 160 n. 1, Fränkel 129) district, zone, habitation, abiding place. Fem. MG 160:1. Pl. **mšaria. bmšara ʿlaita** Gy 284:10 in the upper zone; **halin mšaria mpalgia btibil** Gy 284:9 these zones are divided over the earth; **mšara d̲-tibil** Gy 318:1 a zone of the earth; **mn hanath̲ mšara** Gy 318:6 from that zone; **šuba mšaria** Gy 390:12 the seven zones; **mpalig mšaria** RD B 4 he divides the zones; **ulkul had mšarh̲** AM 201:16 and to each its abiding place; **ʿtpalag bmšaria mia** CP 342:10 and to the districts was allotted water, or, as translated in CP 'it was diffused into flowings of water'; **bhad kinta ʿtkanap umšaria lgaṭ** ATŠ I no. 254

they were collected in one gathering place and took up habitation; **kma kania hauin asa kma mšaria ʿkiria** ŠQ 18:220 how many myrtle groves be there and how many cultivated garden-beds?

mšara 2, mšarai (pass. pt. pa. ŠRA I) used, begun. **utaga hadta ḏ-lamšarai** DC 42.67 a new crown, that is unused.

mšaria. bkasa haditia ḏ-lamšaria DC 46. 151:4 in a new unused bowl.

mšarg(i)zana (nom. ag. šaf. of **RGZ**) provoker, inciter. Pl. **-ia. kalbia šihania mšarg(i)zania** Jb 98:8 (var. **mšagrania** DC 30) ravening and infuriated dogs; **bišia umšargizania** evil ones and inciters.

mšarh(i)bana (nom. ag. šaf. of **RHB II**) (*a*) propagator, (*b*) comforter. Pl. **-ia.** (*a*) **mšarhibana ḏ-mšarhib šurbata** DC 26. 255 propagator who propagates generations; (*b*) **ʿutra mšarhibana** Gy 241:16 f., DC 37. 60, 145, **ʿutria mšarhibania** DC 35, pl. **mšarhibana umaštimana** DC 26, DC 28 comforting and obedient.

mšarlan AM 205 a place-name.

mšaša (rt. **MŠŠ**) sounding, measuring, tangibility, palpability: **kšaša umšaša s. kšaša.**

mšašbia, mšašia according to context prob. windows. Ginzā 520 n. 3. **uhadulia** (var. **uahadulia** Leid.) **babia usakrunun lmšašia** Gs 85:7 (varr. **lmšašbia** BCD & DC 22, **lmišibia, bšibia** Leid.) they shut the door and bolted the windows (?); **uahdartlia babia usakatunun lmšašbia** DAb and ye besieged its gates and blocked up its windows.

mšadana s. **ŠDN.**

mšašta DC 43 A 121, DC 18 = **mašašta** 43 A 159 and 163.

mšata (pl. of mša?) burdens? **miblia ḏ-hala mšata bibrh̠** DC 43 loads of stone, burdens (?) on his pinions.

MŠH (an original form of **MŠA II**) to anoint, rarely used, except polemically.

Pe. Pass. pt. **ḏ-hua mšiha mihdia** ATŠ I no. 295 who was anointed and guided (?) (a colophon: of a ganzibra).

Der.: **mašihta 2, mšiha(iia).**

mšunaiia the inhabitants of **mšunia kušṭa** (see foll.) MG 141:7.

mšunia (cf. מִשְׁנָה) **kušṭa** Gy 29:18, 302:18, 20, 339:2, Jb 179:8, 199:16, often in RD = DAb — (roughly, 'the sublimated of Truth' — a world of ideas in which the prototypes of all earthly things and beings exist MG 132:ult., Siouffi 157 f., 163, MR 38 n. 1, 53 n. 1, 60:bottom, 154:middle, 160 n. 1, MSchr 48 n. 5, MSt 101–104, HpGn 356, Hoffmann ZNW iv 298 (corresponding approximately to روحانية الحق cf. *Fihrist* 339:7) Jb ii. xviii:middle & n. 4, AF 244 f., MMII 54 ff., CP trs. 268 n. 5, SA 39–46. Gl. 75:5 **mšuna** [sic] جنة *paradisus* بهشت.

mšuniat ʿšata (cf. preced., from **mšanai** orig. removed, hence wonderful, sublime) Gy 87:9, 285:13 wonderful (being of) fire MG 133:2.

mšuniuta (abstr. noun from **ŠNA**, cf. **mšunia**) AM 60:11 removal.

mšiha (pass. pt. pe. of **MŠA**, H. מָשִׁיחַ, Aram. מְשִׁיחָא, Syr. ܡܫܝܚܐ, Ar. مَسِيح) 'anointed one', Messiah, Christ (in Mandaism an evil being), identified with Mercury. **mšiha ḏ-kadba** Gy 27:18 = **mšiha kadaba** Gy 247:14, 387:4 = **mšiha dagala** Gy 51:3 Christ the liar; **rumaia mšiha** and **mšiha rumaia** Gy 58:1 ff. may mean the same, or Christ the Roman (a pun); **nbu mšiha** Gy 27:18, 28:2, 56:4 Mercury the Christ; **bšum alahuta umšiha** Q 60:3 in the name of the deity and Christ; **mšiha nbiha ḏ-iahuṭaiia** Gy 27:14 Christ the prophet of the Jews; **mšiha mitglia bdmuta hurintin** Gy 28:15 Christ will appear in another form; **šiṭuata ḏ-ruha umšiha** Gy 254:10 abominations of R. and Christ; **šiṭia ḏ-šaṭia mšiha kulh̠** Gy 111:13 the whole abomination which Christ committeth; **mšiha baṭla** Gy 223:12 the good-for-nought Christ.

mšihaiia (adj. from preced.) DAb Christians.

MŠŠ, MUŠ (Gen. Sem. ע״ע, Aram., Syr. & H. also ע״ו) to touch, feel, sound (water), explore.

Pe. Part. pres. **maišʿit btirata** CP 51:13 = Q 24:1 = ML 67:4 thou touchest consciences.

Der.: **mišaša, mšaša, m(a)šašta.**

MTA I, MTH, MHT s.vv. (Aram. & H. מתח, Syr. ܡܬܚ, Ar. مَتَحَ, Akk. *matāḫu* to raise) to stretch; to straighten.

Pe. Impf. **ʿmta** Gy 209:10 I stretch out MG 235:16; **nimta qumth̠** J 127 he stretches his length (: lies outstretched); **uqumth̠ lanimta urišh̠ lanidalih̠** DC 26. 434 f. he shall not straighten his body nor raise his head; pl. with suff. **nimtunh̠ lṭariana** PA's ŠQ they set out the *ṭariana*. Impt. **mta ušaba** Q 66:6 prostrate thyself and praise (MG 235:24); pl. **mtun niara** DC 50 set out the bowl. Act. pt. **mata qumth̠** Gy 280:13 his stature stretcheth out MG 235:anteantep. Inf. **ulmimta qumth̠ ḏ-giba** DC 51. 124 and to straighten out his form which is bowed.

MTA II a mod. corruption of **MUT** in **haimanuta mn alma amta** DC 51:coloph. faith died out from the world.

mtaqnana (nom. ag. pa. of **TQN**) orderer, establisher, organizer. **ḏ-malpania mtaqnana huitilun** Gy 368:24 I was to the teachers an organizer; **anat mtaqnana ḏ-ʿutria** ATŠ I no. 89 thou art the establisher of the uthras; **mtaqnana damia lmakulta mtaqanta** Gy 215:6 f. an organizer is like a corrective (var. **mtaqinta** DC 22) commestible; **mtaqnanin** Oxf. iii 74 b their (fem.) orderer MG 181:17.

mtaqnuta (abstr. noun from preced.) reliability, honesty, integrity, soundness, thoroughness. **riš mtaqnutak latirag ulatisab mindam ḏ-lau dilak** Gy 214:10 f. the principle of thy honesty (be): desire not nor take anything not thine own.

MTH = MHT = MTA (q.v.).

Pe. Pf. with encl. **mtahibh̠** Gs 115:7 I stretched out therein MG 235:7. Pass. pt. **qumtai ḏ-mtiha ʿtgibat** Gy 264:7 my form that was straight became bowed down.

MTL (מְתַל, ܡܬܠ, H. משל, Ar. مثل, Eth. መሰለ, Akk. *mašālu*) to liken unto, compare, make parables.

Pe. Pf. **mitlit minilia** Gy 262:24 I spake words in parable(s).

Der.: **mitla, mitlaiia** (pl.), **mitil** (Ar.).

MTR (< **ATR**?) to wake(n)?

Af. Pt. pl. **upagra srin uarba razia ḏ-lašakbian ḏ-mamitran** DC 34. 722 and the body (consists of) twenty-four mysteries which do not sleep in order to be wakened (?).

N

n the 14th letter of the alphabet. Phonetic value: nasal liquid. Phonetic changes: **n** < **m** MG § 52 p. 50; **n** > **m** MG § 53 p. 50; assimilation of **n** as 1st rad. ibid. p. 51; loss of final **n** before enclitics ibid. p. 53; **n** inst. of **l** and vice versa ibid. p. 54.

-n 1 possessive suff. of the 1st p. pl.

-n 2 acc. suff. of the 1st p. sg.

-na encl. form of the pers. pronoun of the 1st p. sg. MG 87:15.

nab AM 284:22 a miscop. of **nahab** (q.v.).

nabat (Ar.-P. نبات) AM 287:2 sugar-candy, white, candied sugar.

nabṭa = **napṭa**. **diuta ḏ-nabṭa** DC 43 H 5 black fluid of mineral oil.

nabida (Ar. نبيذ) DC 46. 83:9 light wine.

nabriz'il DC 40. 872 an angel.

***naga 1,** found only in pl. **nagia** (explained by Nöld. < *נַגְהֵי 'morning', 'dawn' MG 64:19, but) referring to small units of time, minutes (?) Ginzā 106 n. 5. **nagia upuhria** Gy 99:21, 112:19 minutes and seconds; **iahria kḏ nagia pahria** Gs 76:17 months flee like minutes.

naga 2 for **nagra** or **nagda** (v.s.vv.). Fem. **nagḥ (a)lgiṭa** Jb 156:5.

nagara (נַגָּרָא, ܢܓܪܐ > Ar., نجّار Fränkel 254 f., from Akk. *naggāru* Zimmern, *Akk. Fremdwörter* 25) carpenter. Doublet **nangara** s.v. **alaha ḏ-nagara gṭar** Jb 109:5 a god fashioned by a carpenter.

nagda Jb 153:6 C & DC 30 var. of **nagra** (or rt. **NGD**) tow-rope? P.A. (among other meanings): *une espèce de natte qu'on met sur les embarcations* . . . Jb ii 156 n. 4.

nagma (Ar. نَغْمَة) AM 162 melody, music.

nagra (Targ. נַגְרָא?) cross-bar?, bolt?; P.A. (among other meanings): *le manche de gouvernail auquel est attaché un grelot* Jb ii 156 n. 4. Pl. **-ia.** Fem. **uzanga l'ka bnagra** Jb 153:5 f. (varr. **bnagda** C, **bnarga** D); **naga** Jb 156:5 might be a miscop. **nagria ldardaria lamiṭamamian** PD 987 the bolts (?) shall never be closed up.

nagša (rt. **NGŠ**) piece of wood for striking, pole. Var. **naqaša** s.v. **nagša upilqa** Jb 162:5 striking-pole and axe.

nadaba (cf. **nidaba** = **nidaua**) wetness. **nadaba** (var. **nidaba**) **uruṭba** AM 285:26 wetness and moisture.

nadar 1 (rt. **NDR**) vow. St. emph. **nadra, nidra** s.vv. **sa'd bnadar umqabila** AM 286:21 fortunate in vow and agreement.

nadar 2 (P. نادار?) AM 159:1 indigent?

nadia (cf. Jew.-Aram. pass. pt. נְדֵי isolated) unclean **baita ḏ-nadia** ATŠ II an unclean house. **bnadia iatbia** DC 22. 401 sit in abomination.

nadra (rt. **NDR**) = **nidra.** St. abs. **nadar 1.** Pl. **-ia.** **nadria ušalamata** Par. xxvii 9 b vows and fulfilments.

naha (rt. **NHA**) relief, rest. **naha rba** DC 41 great relief.

nahab (Ar. نَهاب) Ṣâb.'s AM a better var. of **nab** AM 284:22 prey, booty.

nahauand (نهاوند) AM 204 Nehawand BZ Ap. II.

nahaša (nom. ag. pe. of **NHŠ**) augur, soothsayer. Pl. **-ia** Gy 279:15.

nahuia (rt. **HUA**) being, coming into existence. Unsatisfactory form. **lahuaitun ubnahuia la 'bazaqtun** DC 51 ye did not exist and in coming into existence ye did not break apart.

nahur (rt. **NHR**) light-giving, bright, shining MG 114:2, 174:1. St. emph. heteroclite **nahra 2** s.v. Doublet **nahira** s.v. **nahur/nhura** (*often*) the light shineth, **nhura ḏ-nahur** Jb 51:12 the shining light.

nahira (rt. **NHR**, ܢܗܝܪܐ) bright, luminous, light-giving. Fem. st. emph. **nahirta** MG 155:1. Pl. masc. **-ia.** **dmuta nahirta** Jb 217:14 f. a bright appearance; **šragia nahiria** ATŠ bright lamps.

nahla (נַחְלָא, ܢܚܠܐ, H. נחל, Akk. *naḫlu, naḫallu*, South-Ar. 𐩬𐩢𐩡 valley) wady, brook, ravine, river-bed, torrent MG 100:11. Pl. **-ia.** **dirkia nahlia** Jb 34:1 valley roads; **nahlia amuqia** Jb 48:13 deep ravines; **zibia nahlia** Gs 16:24, 88:14 streams (and) torrent-beds; **bnahlia zabia uainaniata** DC 51 into torrents, streams and springs; **brata nahla amuqa** DC 40 daughter of the deep ravine; **br nahlia amuqia** Or. 327:11 f. son of deep ravines.

naḥs (Ar. نَحْس) AM 286:5 inauspicious, unlucky.

nahra 1 (Jew.-Aram. נַהְרָא, Bibl.-Aram. נְהַר, Syr. ܢܗܪܐ, H. נָהָר, Ar. نَهْر & نَهَر, Akk.

nāru) river MG 61:3, 107:paen. St. abs. & cstr. **nhar 2** s.v. Pl. **nahrauata. nahra ḏ-lamara** Gs 95:24 s. **mara 2; nahra kšaš** and **nahra kšaša** s. **kšaš(a) 1; diuan nahrauata** title of a scroll (DC 7); **nunia ḏ-iama unahrauata** HG the fishes of the sea and rivers.

nahra 2 (rt. **NHR**) st. emph. masc. & st. abs. fem. of **nahur.** Pl. masc. **-ia,** fem. st. abs. as sg. MG 174:3. **nahra utaqna dmauatun** Gy 9:20 their appearances are bright and shining; **uqrunkun lnahria sbiria sama** DC 51 and they call(ed) you (i.e. living water) a medicine for the *illuminati* and instructed.

nahrauan AM 198 a canal of this name in Bab. times BZ Ap. II.

nahrauanaiia DC 7 people of Nahrawān (see preced.).

nahša 1 (rt. **NHŠ**) omen. Doublet **nhaša 2** s.v. **nahša ṭaba** Gy 250:4 good omen.

nahša 2 DC 22. 275:1 a var. of **nahaša** Gy 279:15.

nauda (ܢܘܕܐ) unrest, disquiet, upset, bother, turmoil, earthquake. Var. **nuda** s.v. **nura unauda** AM 57:16 fire and earthquake; **umn ʿnta qadmaita nauda nihuilẖ** AM 38:2 and he will have bother from the first wife; **dina rba unauda** AM 26:16 much dispute and turmoil; **ubkul atra nauda ninpulbun** AM 221:7 and in every place earthquake will befall them.

nauma (נום) a sleep: **nauma ḏ-lalam** DC 48:232 an everlasting sleep.

nausa 1 (rt. **NUS = NSS,** cf. *νόσος* and *ναυσία* = *nausea*) debility, weakness, sick(li)ness. **nausa ušigra** AM 29:14 weakness and fever; **kiba ḏ-parṣupa unausa** AM 114:11 face-ache and debility.

nausa 2 (ܢܘܣܐ, *ναός*) temple, shrine BZ Ap. I. **qbur atutia marzip ḏ-nausa** DC 44. 2085 bury (it) beneath the gutter of a shrine; **qubrẖ bbaba ḏ-nausa** DC 44. 2054 bury it at the door of a shrine.

nauع (Ar. نَوْع) AM 257:15 & elsewhere—species.

naura 1 (ܢܘܪܐ, Akk. *nam(u̯)ara* from *amāru* to see, or *namru* bright LS) mirror, used often of water—an idea produced prob. by reflection in water ML 268 n. 1, MSchr. 160. Masc. Pl. **-ia. naura rba** Jb. 253:15, 256:6 the great mirror, CP 407:10; **naura sqila** Gy 215:9, PD 106 a polished mirror; **naura ḏ-abahatẖ bgauẖ nahria** PD 893 the great mirror in which his ancestors shine (cf. Jb 254:1); **naura rba ḏ-bgu iardna šria** CP 360:3, ML 268:1 f. the great mirror that dwelleth in the jordan; **bhanatẖ aina aka naura ḏ-hazibẖ anpaiun** Gy 149:19 f. in that spring there is a mirror in which they behold their faces; **ʿhauiak naura hda** Gy 162:18 I show thee one mirror; **uanpẖ hza bgauẖ ḏ-hanatẖ naura** Gy 162:20 and he saw his face in that mirror; **haizin naura utaga** Gy 163:1 this mirror and the crown; **tagak unaurak** Gy 163:2 f. thy crown and thy mirror; **ia br naura dakia** DC 50:184 O son of the Pure Mirror!; **nauria hadtia** Jb 254:4 new mirrors; **nauria trisar** Lond. roll A 343 twelve mirrors; **mištapin nauria** Oxf. 44 a, the reflexes become clear; **šuba nauria kasiia** CP 407:12 seven mystic mirrors.

naura 2 = **nura,** used also of temperament: fiery, very active. **ḏ-naura uaiar uarqa razẖ** DC 50. 664 whose mysteries are fire (or water? cf. s. **naura 1**), air and earth; **ʿtlẖ naura** AM 45:3 he has a fiery temperament.

naura 3 occ. var. of **nauda.**

nauruz (P. نوروز) New Year, Siouffi 168, MMII 85 ff. Masc. **iuma ḏ-nauruz** PD 394 ff. the (first) day of the New Year; **nauruz rba** the Great New Year (spring) Siouffi 100, MR 91; **nauruz zuṭa** the lesser New Year (autumn) CP trs. 159 n. 3.

nazam (Ar. نظم) DC discipline(d), order(ly). Mod.

nazarband (P. نظربند) DC 45 phylactery. Mod.

naziq (< P. نزدیک) near. Mod. **naziq ʿmhamra** DC 35:coloph. near Mohammarah. All kinds of missp. and def. forms given as verbal forms in Gl. 4:5 f. اقترب *appropinquare* نزدیک شد; 22:1 f. انقطع *adhaerere* برید; 81:5 f. رحم *comprimere* بسیاری شد; 93:7 f. شرق *appropinquare* نزدیک شد; 131:15 f. قرب *offerre* نزدیک شد; 140:13 f. کاد *prope esse* نزدیک شد; 175:9 f. وصل *appropinquare* نزدیک شد; 181:3 f. دنا *appropinquare* نزدیک شد, although there is no such den. verb; 'to approach' is mod. *nazīq tâmmâ.*

nazla (Ar. نَزْلَة) AM 287:16, inflammation, swelling, catarrh.

naṭa (ܢܛܐ) dampness, dew? **kdub bnaṭa** DC 45 write in the dew.

naṭar 1 s. **natra.**

naṭar 2 a *malwâša* man's name.

naṭarta (nom. act. pa. of **NṬR**) safeguard, watch, guard; detention, ward. Scr. def. **nṭ(a)rta** s.v. **naṭarta rabtia ḏ-šrara** (*often*) the great safeguard of stability (or soundness); **bit naṭarta** (*often*) prison, place of detention, purgatory.

naṭla (נַטְלָא, ܢܛܠܐ) drinking-bowl-ful, small amount of liquid, Pl. **-ia.** Masc. **šuba naṭlia hamra** DC 34:1205, 1215, 1226 f.

naṭra (act. pt. pe. of **NṬR**) watchman, guardian (-spirit). St. abs. **naṭar.** Pl. **-ia.** MSt 53 & n. 3. **naṭra ana ḏ-taruan dakita** Gy 360:7 I am the guardian of the pure T.; **naṭria ḏ-ʿtgamar ʿlẖ gabaria buria ḏ-alma** Gy 85:2 f. the guards that were set (?) over him were the rude giants of the world; **gamarlẖ naṭria** Jb 190:5 f. he set (?) guards over him; **uaqmit ʿlẖ naṭria . . . trin ʿutria** Gy 91:10 and I set over it guards . . . two uthras, **trin naṭria** Gy 128:21, **naṭria trin** Gy 295:17, Jb 193:5, **trin naṭria ʿutria** Gy 292:25, **ʿutria trin naṭria** Gy 296:2; **trin naṭria ḏ-ʿl ṭura ḏ-taruan** Jb 189:10 two guards which are over the Mount T.; **arba naṭria** Gy 167:6 four guardians; **naṭria dakiia** Gs 59:18 pure guardians; **bnaṭria ʿlak nihun** Gy 90:6 f.

they will be thy guards; **naṭria babia** DC 44. 544 doorkeepers.

naṭruta (abstr. noun from preced.) watchfulness, care. **bnaṭrutak** (var. **mnaṭrutak**) **titnaṭar ᶜlan** DC 22. 57 (var. Gy 62:11) in thy watchfulness thou wilt keep guard over us; **naṭruta d̲-saka litlh̲** CP 270:12 endless care.

naṭrᶜil Gy 159:4 name of a guardian spirit Ginzā 168 n. 1. Var. **naṭriᶜil, naṭriaiil** (often e.g. in angel list DC 40. 885 f.)

naia, anaia (cf. H. נוה II, mod. H. נאה) beautiful, pleasing, lovely, pleasant, befitting, becoming, seemly. **basima unaia ṣautak** Jb 78:8 pleasant and lovely is thy voice; **šutak (a)bpumak naia** Jb 78:9 the speech in thy mouth is pleasant; **hauia haila ginzh̲ lhad ruban unaia** ATŠ II no. 388 his treasure becomes a myriad times more mighty and beautiful; **arqa d̲-naia ušapir** ATŠ II no. 418 the earth that is lovely and fair; **kd̲ d̲-naia ušapira ᶜlh̲** DC 27. 469 as is befitting and fair for her; **kul mindam d̲-anaia ušapira** DC 34. 349 everything that is fair and beauteous.

naiat (for Ar. نيّة) AM 282:27 intention, purpose.

naiga (etym. doubtf. perhaps נגע to manipulate, touch? or rel. to *ναῦς navis, navigium*??) boat? **usqiria naiga** Jb 163:2 (very doubtful).

naiza (P. نيزه? spear) used of the reed (Ar. قصب) MMII 63. **qina d̲-naizia hauria** Par. xxvii 83 a, a marsh reed.

naisuta (abstr. noun from **NUS** = **NSS**) grief, affliction, repining. **bhaduta d̲-lanaisuta** Gy 9:14 with joy with no repining.

nairuzia (adj. from **nauruz**) of the new year, of the new season. **miua sqila . . . nairuzia** ŠQ 19:23 burnished fruit . . . of the new season.

nakala (nom. ag. pe. of **NKL**) = **nkila.** Fem. **nakaltia. nakaltia d̲-nakla** DC 7 a deceiver (fem.) that deceives.

nakasa (nom. ag. pe of **NKS**) slaughterer, (ritual) butcher. Pl. **-ia.** Var. **nkasa** s.v. **ṣaurᶜil nakasa** DAb, Ṣ. the slaughterer; **nakasia uapaiia** RD F 11 = DAb par. butchers and bakers.

naklata (rt. **NKL**) pl. stratagems, cunning tricks. **mn ᶜdai naklata** DC 40. 1062 stratagems of my hand(s).

nakriṭia (ܐܢܟܪܝܛܐ, *ἀναχωρηταί*) Gy 227:21 anchorets MG xxix 25, MR 142.

NAL (Jew. נעל, Syr. ܢܥܠ, Ar. نعل den.) to shoe (a horse), tie up, bind (?).

Pe. Part. pres. **kma ᶜkbuš ᶜušania uᶜl nira nailinun** Jb 203:4 how long shall I break in fiery steeds and bind (?) them for the yoke? (doubtf.) or 'bring them into the yoke' see JB ii 197 n. 1.

Der.: **nalia 1.**

nala 1 (sg. נַעֲלָא, ܢܥܠܐ, H. נַעַל, Ar. نَعْل) pl. shoes, sandals. Pl. **-ia.** Fem. **nalia dakiata** RD E 31 clean shoes; **qala d̲-nalh̲** ŠQ 19:19 (cf. ML ix) the sound of his shoes.

nala 2 (נְאלָא, ܢܐܠܐ) vampire, incubus, succubus. Pl. **-ia.** Of both genders. **kd̲ nala hauilh̲** DC 45 when he has an incubus; **nalia uniulia** Oxf. roll g 961 f., DC 43 J 186, CP 33:14 = Q 14:16 = ML 39:7 vampires and hobgoblins; **nalia unᶜulia** Gy 279:5 id.; **nalia zikria unalia nuqbata** DC 40. 645 f., DC 43 A 22 male and female vampires; **kbišia nalia nuqbata** DC 26 subdued are the female vampires.

namar (נִמְרָא, ܢܡܪܐ, Bibl.-Aram. נְמַר, H. נָמֵר, Ar. نَمِر, نِمْر, Sab. ንምር, Eth. ነምር, Akk. *nimru*) leopard. Varr. **nimar** (s.v.) and **namr. manza d̲-namar** AM 128:20 hair of a leopard.

namb(a)iata (nom. act. of **NMBA**) pl. mournings, wailings MG 266 n. 1, Ginzā 438 n. 1; for **mnambiata** (professional mourners fem.); **matialh̲ bnambaiata** Gs 20:4 (var. **bnambiata** Sh. ʿAbd.'s copy) she (: Ruha) brought her (: Eve) professional wailing-women; **ušuma d̲-adam lamatia lpumh̲ bnambaiata** Gs 21:1 f. (var. **bnambaiita** DC 22. 413) she taketh not A.'s name to her mouth with bemoanings; **ᶜnšia mn nambaiata** (var. **nanbaiata** B) **nha** Jb 126:2 the women would cease lamentations.

nambia = **numbia. uainaihun miṣṭarbin nambia** (= **-bun bnambia**?) ATŠ I no. 109 and their eyes were shrunken with mourning (tears).

namusa = **nimusa.** Pl. **-ia.** Gl. 168:10 **namuṣa** [sic] ناموس *lex* شريعت.

namia AM 220:6 for **nambia**?

namrus, nimrus (about different etymological attempts cf. MR 183 n. 4) a name of Ruha. Of Manichaean origin? cf. *Namrael* (Theodor bar Koni) IM 191, & *Nebrod* F. C. Baur: *Das manich. Rel.-system* 137, HpGn 28, MR 34, 183 n. 4, GGA 1890 p. 400, MSt 126, Kessler PRE 166. **namrus** Gy 82:6, 23, 85:8, 12, 95:20, 299:17, 300:12 ff., 341:20, Jb 165:9, Oxf. 12 a; **nimrus** Jb 58:9, Gy 299:24; **namrus ᶜma d̲-alma** Gy 114:6, 329:19, 331:25, 332:24, 333:3, 341:11, 13, 363:3 N. mother of the world.

namriaiil DAb name of a personified comb.

-nan, -inan acc. suff. of the 1st p. pl. MG 88:17.

nana (childish tongue) epithet of endearment for one that looks after a young child, wet nurse. **lianqa d̲-baki(a) unana lamaiiṣ umaiiṣ nanh̲ hauia** JRAS 1943, 175:25, DC 46. 230:11 for a baby that cries and does not suck his wet-nurse, and he shall suck his wet-nurse.

nanai name of Bab. mother-goddess, sometimes invoked in talismans, but sometimes referred to as an evil spirit. **d̲-ᶜstarbh̲ nanai** DC 43 J 191, Oxf. roll 429 wherewith N. was bound; **nanai marta d̲-hšuka** Oxf. roll 438 = DC 43 J par. N. the mistress of darkness. Copyists sometimes write **ananai** for **nanai.**

nangara doublet of **nagara** (q.v.) MG 76:4, 120:ult. Pl. **-ia 1. minaihun hun nangaria** Gy 106:14 amongst them were workers in wood; **qria uautib nangaria** Gy 265:11 call and set down (to work) carpenters; **autib nangaria ubnᶜ kauila** Gy 265:13 set (to work) carpenters and build an ark; **nu aitia nangaria** Gy 380:10 Noah brought carpenters;

nangaria ḏ-pagria Gy 6:4 human carpenters.

nangaria 1 pl. of **nangara**.

nangaria 2 occ. var. of **nangria** (see foll.).

nangria (rt. **NGR I**) (*a*) pits, holes, cavities MG 76:7, (*b*) plagues, torments, troubles, vexations Nöld. ZA xxx 150 & n. 1. Found only in pl. in the texts. (*a*) **ʿdilma . . . karialia nangria** Jb 56:13 f. may they not . . . dig pitfalls for me; **nangria** (var. **nangaria** B & DC 30) **ḏ-karian ʿnšia kulhun nangria** (var. **nangaria** B) **mṭamamia** Jb 86:15 ff., 89:6 ff. the pitfalls which women dig; all (these) pitfalls shall be closed up; **ulkulhin nangria ldardaria . . . lamiṭamamia** ATŠ I no. 99 (var. **. . . lamiṭamamian** PD) and about all the pitfalls (: omissions, mistakes) which . . . can never be closed up; **zidqa rba . . . mṭamam nangria** ATŠ the Great Oblation . . . stops up the pitfalls; **hu kulhun nangria umiṣria lqudam napaqa ṭamim** ATŠ II no. 344 it closes all the pitfalls and dividing boundaries before the departing (soul); **nangria uaṣaṣia** Gs 26:14 s. **aṣaṣa**; (*b*) **ʿl nangria ḏ-alma latišaiil** Gy 386:23 f. ask not about the plagues of the world.

nandala (نَبُّلِ & وَبُّلِ, Mishn. נַדְּלָא, Akk. *adudillu* Delitzsch, *Ass. St.* I 76, Nöld., *Beiträge* 122 f.) centipede. Fem. **unandala mnaktalik** JRAS 1938 2:19 and the centipede shall sting thee.

nandbia pl. (Bab. *nindabū*) offerings, sacrifices Ginzā 121 n. 3. **unirmia bgauh̠ nandbia** Gy 110:7 (var. **nandria** DC 22) and we will cast therein offerings.

nasaka 1 (Ar. نَسَّاخ?; cf. also P. *nask* = Mand. **nasqa**) copyist. Pl. **-ia**. **nasaka ḏ-ginza** DC 22. 374:coloph. (& often in colophons) copyist of the Ginzā; **nasaka ḏ-ginza kaiala rama bnaṣiruta** CP 329:23 copyist of the Ginzā, greatly skilled in priestly knowledge; **nasaka ḏ-kulhun ginzia biaminh̠** ATŠ II no. 219 who copied all his books with his own right (hand). Pl. **nasakia** Q 48:21, 69:12.

nasaka 2 (**nasaka** 1 used only of religious persons, confused with Ar. نَاسِك?; cf. also Akk. *nisakku* priest, and *nasīku* prince) pious, holy, pure. Var. **nasika** (even this sometimes confused with **nasaka** 1). Pl. **-ia**. **utagaian ḏ-nahira nasaka taqna** DC 3 and our crown, that is bright, pure, unsullied; **nasakia ḏ-ginza unaṣiruta** ATŠ I no. 202, DC 41 (نَاسِك confused with نَسَّاخ?).

nasba 1 act. pt. st. emph. of **NSB** (q.v.).

nasba 2 for **naṣba**. **ḏ-niniših̠ (a)lgabra nasbh̠** Jb 60:13 = **ḏ-minšilh̠ lnaṣbh̠** DC 30 that he may forget his Creator; **miaṭa šliha nasba** (var. **naṣba**) **asgia nasba** (var. **naṣba**) **rba** Jb 65:2 (var. DC 30) the emissary, the Transplanter (: angel of death) arrives, the Great Transplanter goes.

nasiata (nom. act. pa. of **NSA I**) DC 44. 1331 trying, attempt, examination (?).

nasika s. **nasaka** 2.

naska Sh. ʿAbd.'s copy's var. of **niska** Gy 380:3.

nasqa s. foll.

nasra, nasqa (first one a miscop. of the second; cf. P. *nask* collection of holy scriptures AIW 1060, Lidzb. according to Andreas, Ginzā 415 n. 6) holy writ. **nasra** (varr. **naṣrai** D, **nasqa** Lond. & Oxf. copies & **usapra** Gy 388:14) holy writ and books.

naعim (Ar. نَعِيم) AM 286:paen. smooth, soft, agreeable, comfortable.

naعl (Ar. نَعْل) shoe. **naعl ḏ-susia** DC 46. 231:7 a horseshoe; **naعl huṣan** DC 46. 204:16.

naعlia gypsy DC 46. 194:10.

naعmat (Ar. نِعْمَة) pleasure, fortune, comfort. **naعmat ḏ-daiim** AM 254:6 permanent comfort.

napaqa (nom. ag. pe. of **NPQ**) departing soul, dying person. **napaqa** Oxf. roll f 361 ff., Q 44:8 ff. etc. (very often in rituals); **luat napaqa lazlia** RD C 8 they do not go near a dying person.

napašta (rt. **NPŠ**) adj. fem. refreshing, life-giving. **naṣiruta napašta** ATŠ II no. 374 life-giving priestly rites (or ministration).

napuqa = **napaqa** MG 113:22.

napuš (rt. **NPŠ**) many, plentiful, abundant, great; much MG 114:5, 174:2. St. emph. masc. & abs. fem. heteroclite **napša 2** s.v. **kma ḏ-napuš ziua ḏ-drabšak** CP 436:5 how great is the radiance of thy banner!; **kma ḏ-napuš iardnak** CP 207:3 how abundant is thy jordan! Very often.

napṭ(a) (Akk. *nap(b)ṭu* Zimmern: *Akk. Fremdw.* 60, נַפְטָא, ܢܦܛܐ, نَفْط, *νάφθα*) naphtha, petroleum. Used also adjectivally: oily; adj. pl. **napṭia**. **bšiša napṭ** DC 46 into a bottle of petroleum; **aina ḏ-napṭ ʿkuma** DC 7 a well of black oil; **napṭa uqira** Gy 187:22, 279:24 crude oil and pitch; **napṭa hiuara uʿkuma** DC 12. 45, 191 f., Lond. roll B 97, cf. also 156, 405, white and black naphtha; **mia napṭia** DC 7 oily water(s).

napla (pt. pe. st. emph. of **NPL**) low, mean, base, unworthy, degenerating, perishing, falling down. Pl. **-ia**. Ginzā 103 n. 6. **baita napla** Jb 191:11, Gs 82:25 the perishable house (i.e. the earthly world); **gunda napla** Gy 82:10, 282:9, 345:5 unworthy army; **ṭura napla** Gy 82:7 the perishable hill (Ginzā 82 n. 1); **bura napla** Gy 81:13 the base monster; **naplia** Gy 97:21 the perishable ones (i.e. the demons).

napṣa (rt. **NPṢ**) discharge, miscarriage. Var. **nipṣa**. Pl. **-ia**. Jb ii 136 n. 6. **uladnapṣa** Gy 18:3 f. and not one casting its young (or: not one that is miscarried?); **kibia unapṣia** DC 46. 134:2 (*often*) pains and discharges; **napṣia** Jb 140:5 prob. out of place, cf. ii 136 n. 4; **saklia napṣia** Jb 140:11 fools, excrements (as an insult); **iahuṭaiia iahṭia unipṣia** Gy 231:5 Jews, abortions and excrements; **iahṭia**

unapṣia Gy 231:15 (of eyes) discharge JRAS 1943 170:27.

napqa 1 (rt. **NPQ**) (*a*) (ܢܦܩܐ 1 LS 439 a) tumour, eruption, swelling, rash, (*b*) (נִפְקָא) excrement, evacuation of bowels. (*a*) **napqa napiqbun** AM 262:18 eruption will come out on them; **napqa ninpuqbh̲** AM 118:18 rash comes out on him; (*b*) **man d̲-bnapqh̲ napiq** ATŠ II no. 81 one that dies whilst voiding excrement; **ruha hᶜ d̲-iatba lnapqa umitiqria srungia gauaiia** Or. 330:10 that is a(n evil) spirit situated on evacuation and called inner constipation.

napqa 2 (for ***naqpa**?) throbbing. **hidra d̲-riša ulmitqiria napqa** Or. 327:25 vertigo and that which is called throbbing.

***napqa 3**, pl. **napqia** = **anapqia** (q.v.).

napša 1 (Gen. Sem.) soul, personality, self MG 100:7. Fem. MG 159:13. Pl. **napšata.** With pers. suff. **napš-** used as both intensive and reflexive pers. pronoun. As noun: **uaziza napšh̲ ubasima utaqipa** AM 27:penult. and his personality is powerful, pleasant and strong; **kulman d̲-ᶜtbh̲ haila urahmh̲ napšh̲** CP 45:2 f. everyone that has strength and loves his soul; **napšata haiabata** Gy 187:10 the guilty souls MG 318:21. With suff.: **napšai** I myself MG 176:15; **pariqt napšak** Gs 73:23 thou hast saved thyself; **nišma zariz napšak** Gs 84:8 soul, arm thyself; **abahatak d̲-napšak** Gy 163:14 thine own fathers; **d̲-abadt ᶜl napšik** Gs 100:22 which thou hast done for thyself (fem.) MG 336:top; **napš(i)h̲** himself, herself MG 178:1, but also **napša** herself: **ligṭat napša** Gy 94:11 she betook herself; **bṣubian napšaihun** Gs 101:1 according to their own will MG 336:7; **ziua rba dilun d̲-napšaiun** JRAS 1937 591:13 their own (i.e. the Great Life's) great radiance. Further examples: **alaha d̲-mn napšh̲ hua** Gy 15:6 God who existeth of Himself; **d̲-mn napšh̲ hua** Gy 36:10; **bškinta d̲-napših̲** Oxf. 58 a, Q 25:3, 26:6 in his own dwelling; **šulṭan napšak** Gy 7:4 thine own power; **man d̲-bnapšh̲ mištaba hu bnapšh̲ bahit** Gy 50:14 who praiseth himself shall be ashamed of himself; **napšai minaikun ᶜnṭirna** ML 135:5 I keep myself away from you.

napša 2 st. emph. of **napuš** MG 114:5, 174:4. Used substantivally, adjectivally, and adverbially Ginzā 167 n. 3. Pl. masc. **napšia,** fem. **napšata.** Substantivally (fem. st. abs.): **nibia d̲-napša ukabira ᶜlak** Gs 66:17 we seek that which is great and glorious in Thee MG 299:antep. Adjectivally: **bišuta napša** Gy 29:22, 381:20 much evil; **ṭabuta napša** Gy 36:17 &c. much goodness; **napša nišmata** Gy 229:20, 253:8, 303:1 many souls; **šnia napšata** Gy 165:10, AM (*often*) many years; **napša ᶜqara** Gy 224:3 much glory (Lidzb. as adv., Nöld. as adj.) MG 318; **buta d̲-napša ukabira** Gs 13:8 great and powerful prayer; **bziua napša** Gy 375:22 in great radiance; **bsakia d̲-napšia** Gy 9:7 in many categories; **napšia bnia hšuka** DAb many are the children of darkness; **bdmuta hda d̲-napša ušapira** Gy 141:13 f. in one great and beautiful appearance. Adverbially: **napša hua zuṭa** Gy 159:6 he was very little; **hzaith̲ d̲-napša rba** Gy 160:6 I saw that he is very big; **ana napša bihšit** Gy 161:9 f. I examined closely (= much) (differently from Nöld. MG 373:1); **buta d̲-napša rba** Gy 189:11, 196:6 a very great request; **haimanuta d̲-napša rba** Gy 195:24 a very great faith.

naṣar Zotb. 220a:ult. = **naṣir.**

naṣaraiia Zotb. 221b (4th text) = **naṣuraiia.**

naṣaruta a frequent var. of **naṣiruta** (e.g. Zotb. 217b:ult., ML 211:2) MR 140:bottom. See under **naṣiruta.**

naṣba 1 (act. pt. pe. of **NṢB**) (trans)planter, Creator, helper (parallel with **adiaura, paruanqa**) Jb ii 60 n. 6. Var. **nasba** s.v. **gabra naṣbh̲** Jb 60:13, 264:11, Gy 97:17, Gs 41:16, 43:5, 44:1, 47:2, 58:6 his Creator, **gabra naṣbak** Jb 64:5, Gs 102:1 thy Creator (or helper); **gabra naṣbai** Jb 77:8 (cf. l. 3), 101:6 f., Gs 62:11 my Creator (or helper); **maṭia atalh̲ naṣba** Gs 47:11, 52:8, 70:18 f., **ata ᶜlh̲ naṣba** Gs 45:23 a helper came to him; **naṣba d̲-nišbak** Jb 254:15 the Creator who created thee; **iauar hualak naṣba** Jb 224:9 Yawar was thy helper; **rbia hulia naṣba** Gy 303:11 the Great (Life) was my Planter; **malil hibil ziua d̲-nimarlh̲ lnaṣbh̲** Gy 321:5 f. H.-Z. spake to his Creator; **naṣba rama** Gy 323:6, 8, 335:14 heavenly Planter; **naṣbh̲ mara d̲-rabuta** Gy 130:2 his Creator the Lord of Majesty; **lahazilh̲ lnaṣbh̲** ATŠ I no. 3 he shall not see his Creator; **ᶜtahzilh̲ naṣbh̲ usliq luat naṣbh̲** HG his Creator appeared to him and he rose up to his Creator; **hiia hauilak naṣba** DC 50. 335 Life will be thy Transplanter.

naṣba 2 (rt. **NṢB**) plant(ation). Pl. **-ia. naṣbia d̲-ana nišbit** Gy 66:20 f. plants (: creatures) that I planted (: created).

naṣubta Zotb. 220b:23, **naṣubuta** Zotb. 221b: ult. = **nišubta.**

naṣuraia, pl. **-aiia** (*Ναζωραῖος* Mat. 2:23 but not from *Ναζαρέτ*, pl. *Ναζωραῖοι* Acts 24:5, as a designation of the followers of the Baptist, cf. Epiphanius, *Haer.* 29:7. Accord. to Zimmern from Akk. *nāṣir piristi* 'guardian of mysteries' ZDMG 1920 p. 433. Mand. term is obviously older than Syr. ܢܨܘܪܝܐ and Ar. نَصَارَى) Naṣoraean(s), skilled in esoteric knowledge MG xx, Kessler PRE 159, 180, Brandt JPTh xiii 410, 599:middle, MR 14 n. 1, 140, ML xvi ff., ZS i 230–233, Ginzā ix f. AF 244 n. 3, 247 n. 3, Zimmern ZDMG 1920 pp. 430 ff., Fränkel ZDMG 1927 p. 300, MMII 4. **naṣuraia d̲-kušṭa** Gy 213:15 true Naṣoraean; **kana d̲-naṣuraiia** Gy 188:21 congregation of Naṣoraeans; **naṣuraiia umandaiia** Gy 299:19 Naṣoraeans and Mandaeans. But **alaha d̲-naṣuraiia** Gy 185:3, 23 the god of the Nazarenes.

naṣibin AM 198 name of a town (ܢܨܝܒܝܢ?) BZ Ap. II.

naṣipa (ܢܨܝܦܐ, Ar. نصيف) a strip of long white linen worn by the priest round the neck, which serves to hold the *margna* staff in place when in water and his hands are occupied MG xxxiii 26, Siouffi 122, MMII 31 n. 6. Often in rituals: Oxf. 66 a, Oxf. roll f 514, 845, 1236, Lond. roll A 200, 576, 680. **qurna ḏ-naṣipak** Q 20:10 the end of thy stole.

naṣir (Ar. ناصر) AM 105, Zotb. 217:14 &c. a man's name.

naṣiruta (cf. s. **naṣuraiia** & the Bab. term for 'writing' ***niṣirtu katimtu*** BZ 67 n. 5) esoteric knowledge only given to initiates, priestly craft and ministration MR 140:bottom, MMII 4. Varr. **naṣaruta** (s.v.), **naṣruta.** St. abs. & cstr. MG 155:11. **ʿumqia ḏ-naṣiruta** Gy 197 ff. the profundities of Naṣoraean wisdom; **zainaikun naṣaruta umalalia kšitia** Gy 25:21 (cf. Gs 76:7) your armour is Naṣoraean wisdom and the true words; **zainaikun naṣiruta uhaimanut kušṭa** Gy 48:9 your armour is Naṣoraeism and faith in Truth; **naṣaruta qašiša mn iahduta** Gy 288:10 Naṣoraeism is older than Judaism; **naṣarutai** Gy 301:18 f. my Naṣoraeism; **kaiala ḏ-naṣiruta** Q 60:24, and often in colophons RD G 5 &c. cf. s. **kaiala; uʿštpik blibaihun naṣirut** ML 257:4, CP 255:4 and Naṣoraeism was poured into their hearts; **ašuat naṣ(i)rut(a)** PD 477, 975, 1033, 1167, 1419 &c. (often in ATŠ) s. **ašuat** 1; **sibrẖ lkulẖ naṣiruta** DC 41 he taught him all priestly arts; **mšabit naṣiruta ḏ-minik bhiria sabria** CP 86:7 = Q 40:18 = ML 106:11 praised be thou, Naṣoraeism from whom the elect learn; **aina ḏ-naṣiruta kulẖ ʿtpihtat ʿlak** DC 27. 67 the whole well of Naṣoraeism was open to thee; **zakia naṣiruta ḏ-minan** CP 265:8 pure is the N. which is from us.

naqpiaiil DAb a theophorous name used of a steering-paddle.

naqaša DC 30 a var. of **nagša** Jb 162:5.

naqura (rt. **NQR**) beak, pick. Pl. **-ia. ušganda niligtẖ lnaqurẖ ḏ-iauna** DC 24. 90 and the assistant shall hold the dove's beak (lit. 'pecker'); **naquria** RD B 29, 37 = DAb par. picks.

naquš (Ar. نَقْش) carving, chiselling, engraving. **ialip naquš** AM 155:14 skilled in engraving.

naquša (ܢܩܘܫܐ) (*a*) torturer, executioner, (*b*) (as Syr. & Ar. loan-w. ناقوس Fränkel 276) cymbal. Pl. **-ia.** (*a*) **naqušia qaimia mahin** DAb executioners stand and beat; (*b*) **unaqušia naqšia** Gy 226:20 f. and they beat cymbals.

naquta (Syr. pl. ܢܩܘ̈ܬܐ) libations. **umapqia** (var. **mpaqia**) **naquta** DC 43 J 197 and they pour out libations.

naqia 1 (Aram. & H. נָקִי, Ar. نَقِيّ) clean, pure. **atra naqia** Q 4:30 f., Oxf. 54 b, Gy 246:3 f. pure place.

naqia 2 s. **niqia.**

naqšan d- (rt. **NQŠ**) approximately, (touching) nearly. **arqa udiša naqšan ḏ-tlatma ušitin alpia parsia iatbiq** DAb the land and its area comprise about 360,000 parasangs.

narga (נַרְגָּא, ܢܪܓܐ) axe MG 112:9, 150:7. Masc. Pl. **-ia. unarga tliḻẖ lkadpẖ** Jb 153:4 and he suspended an axe on his shoulder; **narga rba ḏ-širiata** Jb 273:15, Morg. 195:7, 258/7:1 f., 259/9:3, Oxf. roll g 26 f., 72, 239 f., 294 f., 323 f., pl. **nargia rurbia ḏ-širiata** Morg. 194:3, 195:13 f., cf. Jb ii 242 n. 2; **mhaitinkun . . . bnarga ʿl ligraikun** DC 43 J 32 I struck you . . . with an axe to your feet.

nargila (נַרְגִּילָא, ܢܪܓܝܠܐ < P. نارگیل, Ar. loan-w. نارجيل Löw 85) Oxf. roll f 157, DC 12:192, Lond. roll B 407, ATŠ II no. 217, DC 48. 295, coco-nut; DC 41 (picture) coco-nut-palm.

nargis 1 (נַרְקִיס, ܢܪܩܝܣ, P. نَرگِس, Ar. loan-w. نَرْجِس, Gr. *νάρκισσος* Löw no. 202) narcissus. Masc. **nargis uasa umarmahuz** Gy 107:1, 346:20, 22 narcissus, myrtle and wild marjoram; **nargis ḏ-qašiš mn rihania kulhun** Jb 254:10 f. narcissus which is the oldest of all odoriferous plants.

nargis 2 a *malwâša* woman's name.

nargiša an exceptional doublet of **nargis** 1. **nargis hu** DC 41 (picture) it is a narcissus.

nargʿil malaka DC 43 D 28 an angel.

nard (H. נֵרְדְּ, Syr. ܢܪܕܝܢ & ܢܐܪܕܘܣ, Akk. *lardu* from Sanskr. नलद, P. ناردین, Gr. *νάρδος* Löw no. 316) DC 6 & 36 no. 248 spikenard.

narzubia = **marzubia.** Used also of gutter-demons of both genders. **bṭalalia ḏ-narzubia** DC 43 J 71 demon that sits in the drippings of the roof-gutters; **mn narzubia zakria umn narzubia nuqbata** DC 37. 396 from male and female gutter-demons.

narzubalia, narzubilia, narzibilia & varr. a kind of demons, gutter-demons (?) of both genders. **narzubalia zikria br zubilia unarzibalia nuqbata** DC 44/1500 f. = **mn narzubilia zikria umn narzubilia nuqbata** Morg. 266/22:39 from male and female gutter-demons.

nariga (cf. ܢܬܝܩܐ in big pieces LS 449b:top) a hewn piece, or something cleft, or cracked. **kḏ ṭuria pqa minẖ ukḏ nariga** DC 43 J 41 like mountains they broke asunder from him and like a thing cleft.

nariman a legendary king of ancient Īrān. **pašm nariman** Gy 382:23.

narinz (P. نارنج) bitter-orange, orange. Doublets **narinṣ̌, nariša. hazin narinz hu** DC 7 this is an orange-tree.

narinṣ̌ DC 35, DC 45 a doublet of **narinz.**

nariša DC 41 a doublet of **narinz, narinṣ̌.**

narqmia pl. (accord. to context) shoes, boots. **msania unarqmia** Gy 106:12 shoes and boots.

naš(a) s. **anaša.**

našba (נִישְׁבָּא, ܢܫܒܐ LS) net; pl. **-ia** netting-places. **lnašbia** (var. **lnašibia** ACD & DC 30) **ulhauria ulkiliata kulhun aiilna** Jb 143:7 I enter all the netting-places and marsh-lagoons and the places where the water is pent.

naṣ̌d (نجد) AM 205:5 the city of Nejd in ʿIrāq. Var. **nišad** Ṣâb.'s AM.

naṣdia (adj. from preced.) Zotb. 220a:paen. a family-name (of Nejd).

našibia s. **našba.**

naṣim (نجم) Zotb. 223 a (second text l. 13) a family-name.

našira (نَسْقَمْنا < P. نَخْچِير; cf. Jew. נַחְשִׁירְכָן < P. نَخْچِيرکُن) chase; quarry MG 63:5 ff.

d-našira abdia ubisra d-našira ugaṭla aklia Gy 230:23 who practise hawking and eat the flesh of the quarry and kill.

naṣmia (نجمى) AM 105 a family-name.

našqʿil DAb name of a spirit in the purgatory.

naštapiʿil malaka DC 43 D. 20 an angel.

NBA I (Jew.-Aram. נבי ithpa., H. נבא nif. & hithpa., Syr. ܢܒܐ pa. & ethpa., Ar. نبأ, Sab. 𐩬𐩨𐩱 to exclaim, Akk. *nabū* to call, announce) to act as a prophet, prophesy.

(Pa. s. **NMBA**).

Af. Pf. **anba nbihia** Gy 222:17 (read so with Leid. & Sh. ʿAbd.'s copy for . . . nbiha) he sent out prophets. Act. pt. **manbia nbihia d-kadba** Gy 121:7 they produce prophets of lying.

Ettaf. Pt. **lamitanbia nbiha balma** Gy 61:7 no prophet will appear in the world (MG 239:23, 265:27).

Gl. 47:5 f. **anbia** تنبا *prophetare* پيغمبر شد.

Der.: **nbi(h)a** & varr.

NBA II (ܢܒܰܥ, Ar. نبه; rel. to **NBG**) to spring up, burst forth, sprout forth, gush out, arise from, come forth.

Pe. Pf. **nba** Q 27:30 sprang up MG 234: middle, **anat d-n(u)bat unpaqt** DC 43 J 59 thou that hast sprung forth and come out.

Af. Act. pt. **manbia hukumta mn ʿuṣraihun** Gy 121:9 they spout wisdom from their minds (sarcasm).

Ethpa. Pf. **d-ʿtnabia** DC 43 J. 46 that sprang up.

Der.: **mambuha, niba.**

NBA III (Aram. & H. נבח, Syr. ܢܒܚ, Ar. نبح, Eth. ነብሐ, Eg. metath. *bḥn*, but Akk. *nabāḫu*) to bark.

Pe. Act. pt. **qala d-kalbia d-nabia** DC 46. 243:8 the noise of barking dogs.

Af. Act. pt. **uqal . . . kalba d-mnaba** DC 46. 16:2 f. and the noise . . . of a dog that barks.

nbaz keeper of a purgatory. **maṭarta d-nbaz haila** Gy 208:3, Gs 27:15 the purgatory of N. the commander-in-chief (?).

nbaṭ a spirit of light MR 22, 30 f., MSchr x n. 1, ML 282, Ginzā 288:2 ff. **nbaṭ rba d-hu kušṭa iaqra** PD 1007 the Great N. which is the holy truth; **nbaṭ rba abrh d-iušamin** Jb 12:3 ff. the Great N. son of Y.; **maṭarta d-nbaṭ brh d-ptahil** RD C 11 the purgatory of N. son of P.; **nbaṭ br iuhana** Gy 362:7 (cf. 364:9) N. son of John; **nbaṭ rba** PD 8, 144, 832, Gy 298:16 &c. (*often*); **nbaṭ rba d-nbaṭ** Gy 291:32 the Great N. who sprang forth, **brh d-nbaṭ rba** Gy 360:7 the son of the Great N.; **nbaṭ ziua** Gy 293:12; **nbaṭ ziua rba qadmaia** CP 85:5, Morg. 4:12 = Q 15:10 = ML 41:3 N. the First Great Radiance; **nbaṭ nibṭa qadmaia** CP 29:17, 116:1 = Morg. 257/5:6, Q 12:29, 27:20, 32:8, 58:30 N. the First Offspring; **nbaṭ aba d-ʿutria** PD 88 N. the father of the uthras; **nbaṭ iauar** Gy 71:1 N. (identified with) Y.; **nbaṭ uanhar** Oxf. 20 a.

NBG, NGB (s.v.) (Aram. נבג & נבע, Syr. ܢܒܓ & ܢܒܥ, H. נבע I, Ar. نبج, نبغ, نبع, Eth. ነብዐ to weep, Akk. *namba'u* source; rel. to **NBA II**) to (a)rise, spring up, sprout, break out, well up, surge upwards.

Af. Act. pt. **ainaniata d-mia d-mn praš ziua ʿlauaikun mambig** DC 34:408 springs of water from the Light Euphrates he causeth to well up upon you; **mabga** Gy 216:8 she maketh well upon MG 74:14, 239:19.

Der.: **mambuga.**

NBH = **NBA II.** Only in the der. **mambuha, nbiha 2.**

nbu, ʿnbu (Bab. *Nabū*) Nebo, the planet Mercury, identified with Christ MR 126, HpGn 29 (cf. also Index s. Nabu & Merkur). Identified with Sin RD 1. **nbu dahba aitia** Gy 106:11 N. brought gold; **lnbu plaglh hukumta** Gy 112:7 to N. they allotted wisdom; **nbu bhukumth** Lond. roll B 256 (cf. 161) N. in his wisdom; **nbu maria hukumta** Oxf. roll g 935 ff. N. the lord of wisdom; **nbu sapra (u)hakima** Gs 29:6, **ʿnbu sapra uhakima** CP 225:8 = Morg. 268/27:31 &c. (*often*) N. the wise scribe Brandt JPTh 1892 p. 409 n. 1; **ʿnbu (sipria u)maria sipria udiuta uhukumta** Morg. 269/29:25 N. (omit **sipria u**) the lord of books and ink and wisdom; **nbu šda sipra** Gy 336:1 N. cast the book; **kd nbu mn binia malakia d-husrana atia** Gy 54:10 f. when N. returned (hist. pres.) from amongst the angels of imperfection; **nbu ušuba** Jb 198:10 N. and the Seven (: Planets); **ʿnbu maria alahia** Oxf. roll g 574 N. the lord of gods; **nbu mšiha** Gy 28:2, 56:4 ff., **nbu mšiha d-kadba** Gy 27:18 (cf. 51:3) N. the false Messiah; **pisnia d-nbu** Gy 118:18 the melodies of N.; **maṭarta d-nbu** RD C 16, 21, 23 = DAb par. the purgatory of N.

NBZ (a secondary rt. from **BZA**?) to divide?, split? Doubtf. Ginzā 519 n. 2.

Pe. Pf. apparently in the pr. n. **nbaz** s.v. Otherwise only doubtf. forms: **nbaza** (var. **nbiza** Leid., DC 22) **piruštai** Gs 25:15 my understanding is split (?). Act. pt. with encl. **nura d-napših nabzabh uaklalh** DC 37. 247 f. his own fire burst out in him and devoured him.

Der.: **nbaz, nibza.**

NBṬ (Jew.-Aram., H., Ar., South-Ar., Akk. *nabāṭu* Ges.) to burst forth, spring up, come up from below, surge up, spring forth.

Pe. Pf. **nbaṭ** pr. n. of a genius s.v., cf. esp. **nbaṭ rba d-nbaṭ** ibid., **ziuh mn mia nbaṭ** Oxf. 100 b his radiance sprang up from water; **nbaṭ hiia bziua** Q 9:10 the Life burst forth in radiance; **hu amaš braza ulanbaṭ** ATŠ II no. 289 he plunged down into the mystery and did not emerge; **nibṭa d-nbaṭ mn napših** CP 428:10 the Emanation which emanated from itself; **nibṭat aina d-ziua** Oxf. 98 a the spring of radiance sprang up; **nibṭat nura uhababat**

DC 26. 89 fire burst out and burnt; **bgu iardna nibṭat . . . unbaṭiun binia razia** DC 50. 608 f. she sprang forth in the jordan . . . and they sprang forth between the mysteries . . .; **nbaṭian** Oxf. iii 66 b they (fem.) sprang forth (var. **nbaṭia**) MG 223:ult. f. Act. pt. pl. **nabṭia usalqia** Gy 139:6 they spring upwards and rise.

Der.: **nbaṭ, nibṭa.**

nbiha 1, ʿnbiha (נְבִיאָה, ܢܒܝܐ < H. נָבִיא) prophet MG xxx 12, 51:1, 72:7, 117:12, MR 116. Pl. (ʿ)**nbihia, nbiia** AM 129, **nbʿiia** Gy 287:12, MG 5:paen., 72:7. **nbiha arbaia** Gy 61:4 the Arab prophet; **nbiha ḏ-kadba** Gy 116:16, 222:17 the prophet of a lie, pl. **nbihia ḏ-kadba** Gy 24:2, 25:6 f. (opposed to **nbihia ḏ-kušṭa**), 46:14 ff., RD B 64 = DAb par.; **nbihia ḏ-šiqra** Gy 66:23; **manbia nbihia ḏ-kadba** Gy 121:7 s. **NBA I** af. pt. **tlatma ušitin nbihia** Gy 29:16 three hundred and sixty prophets; **abatar mahamad . . . lamitanbia nbiha balma** Gy 61:6 ff. after Muḥammad . . . no prophet will prophesy in the world; **nbiha ḏ-ruha** Gy 46:6 (Moses), l. 7 f. (Abraham confused with Moses); **šlihia unbʿiia** Gy 287:12 apostles and prophets.

nbiha 2 (pass. pt. pe. of **NBH** = **NBA II**) offshoot, sprout. **ialda nbiha ḏ-aba rba ḏ-ʿqara** HG a boy, an offspring of the Great Father of Glory.

nbʿiia a pl. of nbiha 1 (q.v.).

NBŠ for **NPŠ** in **nitnabšun** Par. xi 23 b they will multiply MG 48:12.

NGA I (Jew.-Aram. & H. נגה, Syr. ܢܓܗ, Eth. ነገሀ, Akk. *nigû* to rejoice, der. *nigûtu* perfect light) to dawn, break through (of light). Pe. used as an impers. verb (in fem. gender) MG 365:10 f. With metathesis **NHG I** s.v.

Pe. Pf. s. **NHG.** Impf. **lʿmat tinga** Gy 118:5 when will dawn break? MG 325:15, 238:8, 365:11.

Der.: ***naga** 1? See also under **NHG.**

NGA II (Jew.-Aram. & H. נגע) to strike, injure.

Der.: **anga.**

ngab st. cstr. of **nigba** (q.v.).

ngada (rt. **NGD**) stretching-out, protraction, punishment, castigation, torment, pain MG 115:18. **hlaṣa ungada** Gy 312:16, Gs 26:16, 29:17, 31:10 torture and torment; **hlaṣa mṣara ungada** Gy 182:19 torture, torment, and castigation; **mṣara upkara ungada** Gy 230:19, 233:9, 15 torture and fetter and rack; **tigra ungada** Gy 391:22 strife and castigation; **ngada upsaqa** Gy 253:6 pain and disaster (lit. cutting-off).

ngauia occ. var. of **angauia** (e.g. Q 52:12 with varr.).

NGB (metathesis of **NBG**) to sprout, spout up, surge up, spring upwards, emerge.

Pe. Pf. **ngib** Gy 145:3, 169:9 he, they sprouted up, came out MG 74:14, 220:9, **amaš ulangib** ATŠ II no. 127 he submerged and did not emerge; **nigbat mn mia ʿkumia** Gy 140:4 she sprang up from black water(s). Impf. **ninigbun nigbia** WedF 111:3 offshoots sprout up. Act. pt. **alma ḏ-nagib mn piqa** Gy 160:18 until he emerged (hist. pres.) from the cleft; pl. **mia . . . qudamẖ nagbia umitapkia** ATŠ II no. 393 waters . . . surge up before him and recede.

Der.: **nigba** (cstr. **ngab**).

NGD (Aram. & H. נגד, Syr. ܢܓܕ, Ar. نَجْد highland) to draw (forth or out), stretch out, extend, extract, unfurl, pull (out), prolong; with **mn** to withdraw; to drag at, pull about, punish, torment, torture; to lead forth, guide, govern.

Pe. Pf. **ngad rqiha** Gy 33:22 he outspanned the firmament; **ngad nigda ḏ-mia** Gy 269:12 he drew off a channel of water; **ngad miqria alma** Gy 93:6 he ordered (?) to create a world (cf. Idioms); **nigdit šuba iardnia** Gy 372:23 I drew off seven jordans; **ngadtun** ye stretched out MG 224:5; with encl. **iardnia ḏ-ngadlak** Oxf. 70 b the jordans which he caused to flow for thee; **ungadlun iardnia ḏ-mia hiia** CP 440:11 and he caused to flow forth for them jordans of living water; with suff. **nigdẖ ldrabšẖ** CP 356:7, Oxf. 96 b = ML 264:7 he unfurled his banner; **hibil ngadinun ušadrinun** CP 428:14 Hibil drew them down and sent them (i.e. jordans); **nigdẖ umasiẖ larqa tibil** Gy 13:7 he expanded and condensed the earthly world. Impf. **iardna ḏ-mia hiia ḏ- . . . ningad** CP 434:ult. the jordan of living water which . . . spreads out; with encl. **šitin drabšia . . . ningudulẖ** DC 48. 107 they unfurl for him . . . sixty banners; with suff. **ninigduia** they draw him out MG 278:18. Impt. **ʿngud** Gy 12:25, 33:1, 92:18, 269:9, 338:20 (var. **ngid** D) draw, stretch out, span out MG 240:7 f.; special pl. form **ngudiun šumia ṣṭartia** ŠQ 5:5 spread out 'the little sky' (: a piece of blue cloth on the roof of the *andiruna*); pl. with suff. **ngudunun ʿl drabšia** DC 50. 503 unfurl the banners. Act. pt. **nagid zidqa** CP 112:4 = Q 57:4 = ML 137:10 giveth (?) oblation (*idiom*); **nagid umitana** Gs 49:18 he waileth and sigheth (*idiom*); **drabša nagid lqudamẖ** ATŠ II no. 88 he unfurls the banner; fem. **malia nagda** Gy 332:19 she prolongeth lamentation (*idiom*); **nagda ulagṭa ʿblia** Gs 20:1 id.; pl. **malia nagdia** Gs 47:18 they lament long (*idiom*); **rišaihun nagdia** Gs 35:10 they crane their necks (*idiom*); **nagdia nigda** Gs 53:13 they lament a long while (*idiom*); **nagdia kupna mn hiuia** Gy 223:19 they endure hunger longer than a serpent (*idiom*); **nagdin ʿblaihun** CP 153:14 = Oxf. 11 b = ML 184:7 they prolong lamentations (*idiom*); **unagdin kilta** ŠQ 5:13 and they spread out the veil (: canopy over the bed); pl. with encl. **nagdilẖ** Gy 263:14 they govern it. Part. pres. **nagdit malia** Gs 22:6 thou lamentest long (*idiom*); **drabša nagditun** ATŠ II no. 378 ye unfurl the banner. Pass. pt. **ngid** outstretched, but also with act. meaning: stretching out MG 380:ult. f.; fem. **kilta ʿngida** RD F 6 = DAb par. the mosquito-net is spread out; **ʿšumia ḏ-ngida** Gy 267:4 the sky which is spanned out; **sihupta ḏ-ʿngida abinia dilẖ labatur** DAb a veil that is outspread betwixt himself and A.; with encl. **kilta ḏ-ngidabh̠** RD A 4 = DAb par. the veil which is spread in it; pl. **ungidia atun iardnia** Jb 152:4 and jordans came outspread. Inf. **mingad nigda ḏ-mia hiia** Gy 308:3 f. to draw (: make flow) living water; **mingad iardnia** Gy 318:22 to make the jordans flow (i.e. draw them down from celestial regions).

Ethpe. Pf. **ʿtingid minh̠** ML 18:1 (see pe.) were drawn from it (ML n. 1); with encl. **drabša ʿtigdilh̠** Lond. roll A 393 = var. **ʿtingidlh̠** DC 3 & 53 a banner was unfurled for him. Impf. **drabša . . . nitingid ʿlh̠** ATŠ II no. 352 a banner will be unfurled over him. Pt. **kḏ mitingid rqiha** Gy 87:22 when the firmament is spanned out, **mnigid drabša** PD 1124 = ATŠ I no. 115 the banner (is) unfurled; with encl. **ʿu lamingidlh̠ drabša** ATŠ II no. 381 if the banner is not unfurled for him; **šitin drabšia mingidlkun** DC 35 sixty banners are unfurled for you; pl. **mitnigdia drabšia ḏ-almia ḏ-nhura** ATŠ II no. 14, rays stream forth from the world of light.

Pe. **ngad minh̠** CP 16:7 were derived from it (trs. 8 n. 2).

Idioms: Pe. Gy 93:6 for **pqad** Ginzā 97 n. 4 (s. pf.); with **malia** or **ʿblia** (the noun sometimes omitted) 'to lament' cf. P. ناله كشيد (s. act. pt. masc. with noun omitted, cf. Ginzā 469 n. 2, fem. twice, once with noun omitted, part. pres.); with **zidqa** = to spread out (i.e. oblation of food on the ritual table) (s. act. pt., ML 137:10, CP 112:4 ML 137 n. 2 doubtful); with nouns designating deficiency, hunger etc. 'to suffer' cf. P. رنج كشيد (s. act. pt. pl.); with **riša** 'to crane the neck' (s. act. pt. pl.).

Der.: **ngada, nigda.**

ngiṭia pl. (pass. pt. of ***NGṬ** = **LGṬ**, cf. Talm. נקט MG 54 n. 1) AM 217:13 captives?, prisoners?

NGL (Syr. ܢܓܠ to remove, flee away, Ar. نجل to sprout) to project, stand out, be prominent MG 76:5 ff.

Ethpa. Pf. **uʿtnangal šahpa mn mia** Gy 381:6 the leaves projected from the water. Var. **ʿtnangar** Leid.

nglziia (pl. انگلیسی) DC 19 the English.

NGR I (Aram., Syr., H.) to protract, stretch out; to repress, restrain, quell, torment, torture. Often confused with **NGD.**

Pe. Pf. **nigar** (?) **upkar kul minilia bišata mn pumaihun** DC 44. 681 = Morg. 260/11:26 they repressed and banished all evil words from their mouths. Act. pt. pl. **pakria kadšia nangria** Gy 121:17 they fetter, beat, torment (or flog). Inf. with suff. **lmingirinun ulmikrinun** DC 44. 1903 = Morg. 269/29:13 to quell and hamper them.

Pa. Pt. with encl. **mnangarlun** Oxf. 34 b = ML 206:5 would restrain them; pl. **mnangria** Gs 126:13, 127:18 they torture; with encl. **mnangrilhun** Gy 182:20, 183:21 they torture them; **mnangrilun ulamitapia** Gy 182:3, 183:21 they roast them but they do not cook (*idiom*); **mnang(i)rilun** Gs 26:17, 29:18, 32:18, 34:6, 35:17 they shall flog them (*idiom*).

Ethpa. Pf. **ʿtnangar** Gy 318:7 shall be tormented (prophetic pf.). Impf. **bšuṭia nura nitnangar** Gy 301:15 f. he shall be flogged with scourges of fire (MG 226:22, *idiom*); **ubšitin uhda dudh̠ ḏ-rahta latitnangrun** Gy 317:20 f. and ye shall not be tormented in sixty-one seething pots (*idiom*). Pt. **mitnangar** Gy 317:12 he shall be chastised; **ʿl mania ḏ-nura mitnangar** Gy 228:6, 229:11 he shall be tormented in fire-vessels (MG 213:21, *idiom*); **ʿl mania ḏ-barda mitnangar** Gy 224:22 he shall be tortured on vessels of ice; **bšauṭa ḏ-nura mitnangar** Gy 376:25 he shall be flogged with a scourge of fire (*idiom*); fem. **ʿl mania ḏ-nura mitnangra** Gy 229:11 (*idiom* with fire); pl. **alahia ḏ-mitnangria brazia ḏ-iauar** DC 37. 534 f. gods that are quelled by the magic rites of Y.; **gabaria ḏ-ʿtibil mitnangria** CP 170:2 = Oxf. 34b = ML 206:3 earthly tyrants are smitten (hewn **NGR II**) down (*or* quelled **NGR I**).

Idioms: With (vessels of) fire the verb acquired the meaning of roasting, broiling (for punishment) s. pa., ethpa. three times Nöld. ZA xxx 149; with š(a)uṭa 'to flog' (s. pa., ethpa. impf., pt.).

Der.: **nangria** (var. **nangaria 2**) (*b*).

NGR II (den. from **na(n)gara**) to fabricate, build, construct, hew, work hard. The forms quoted by Nöld. MG 76:2 may be explained by **NGR I,** but, on the other hand, some examples quoted there (cf. esp. pe. & s. ethpa. pt. pl.) could belong here (with the meaning 'to hew down'?). Doubtf.

Der.: **na(n)gara, ʿngar**?, **ʿngirta**?, cf. **nangria** (var. **nangaria 2**) (*a*).

NGŠ (Jew.-Aram. נגש to attack, H. & mod. H. נגשׁ to approach, Can., H. נגשׂ to drive away, Akk. *nagāšu* id., Ar. نجش to drive game etc., Eth. ነገሠ, South.-Ar., cf. Ges. s. both נגשׂ & נגשׁ) to strike at, hit at, attack; to touch.

Pe. Pf. with suff. **mgaštinun** Jb 148:2 s. **MGŠ** (influence of part. forms?).

Der.: **nagša.**

NDA I, (NNDA) (Jew.-Aram. נדא, נדי to throw, excommunicate, Syr. ܢܕܐ to cause to break out or forth, H. נדה to push out, exclude, Akk. *nadū* to throw out, Sab. 𐩬𐩵𐩺 to drive away; rel. to **NDD, NUD, NZZ**) to shake (off), get rid of, banish, toss (off). Certain forms are identical with **ANDA** (q.v.); others with **NDD, NUD** s.vv.

Pa. Impf. **latinandia riš** DC 45 do not shake the head, **latinandia riša** DC 46. 136:8 do not shake the head. Act. pt. **mnandia** Q 52:3 she shaketh MG 75:21.

Af. Pf. with suff. **andh̠** Gy 85:1 B (a var. of **anidh̠**) he shook it MG 275:12, **andinun** Gy 90:12, Jb 6:11, 7:13, 9:9 he shook them MG 281:24. Impf. with suff. **nandh̠** Gy 110:12 we will bring it in commotion. Impt. **andai urahiq razia** DC 40. 334, 343 banish (fem.) and remove to a distance the mysteries; with suff. **andinun** Gy 165:6 shake them MG 282:14. Act. pt. pl. with encl. **lamandilh̲ ziqia d̲-aiar** Gy 5:15 tempests of wind shake it not (MG 254 n. 1 is mistaken, since Pet. has the correct **mandilh̲**).

ETHPA. Pf. **ʿnanditun** Q 52:19 ye are shaken MG 75:22.

NDB (Bibl.-Aram., Jew.-Aram., H. & mod. H. נדב, Ar. ندب to incite) to urge, rouse (oneself), prompt, incite; to flee (with varr. from **NDD**).

AF. Impf. **nandib** AM 220:21 (var. **nandid**) he will flee. Impt. **andib** Gs 27:8 (var. **andid** C), 30:7, **andab** Gs 28:22, 32:2 (varr. **andib** BCD in both places) urge thyself on. Pt. **kd̲ susia d̲-azil aqamh̲ ulamandib** Or. 326:24 like a horse that goes before him without being urged.

NDD (Jew.-Aram., H., Syr., Ar., rel. to **NDA, NUD**) to repulse, be loathsome, abominable, repulsive; to flee away (cf. s. **NDB**); af. also to shake. (MG 248 n. 1.)

PE. Pass. pt. **ndid(a)** abominable (s.v.).

AF. Pf. **andid** Gs 27:8 C cf. s. **NDB**; with suff. **andidinun lalmia udaria** AM shook the ages and generations. Impf. **nandid** s. **NDB**.

DER.: **ndid(a)**.

NDZ s. **ANDZ**.

ndid(a) (pass. pt. pe. of **NDD**, Syr. ܢܕܝܕܐ) repulsive, loathsome, abominable, filthy. Pl. **-ia**. **ndid banph̲** Gy 159:6 of loathsome appearance; **haiuta d̲-saina undida** Gy 85:6 an ugly and repulsive snake; **ndidia** Gy 279:9 the abominable ones (: the devils).

NDR (נְדַר, ܢܕܪ, Ar. نذر) to make a vow, promise, make a present to avert anger.

PE. Pf. **man nidrat nidria** Jb 119:8 what woman made a vow. Act. pt. **nadria nidria ʿlik** Jb 139:9 (var. **nidria nadran ʿlik** B & DC 30) they vow (var. special fem. form) vows about thee.

DER.: **nadar** 1, **nadra, nidra**.

ndruna PD 626 = **ʿndruna**.

NDŠ s. **ANDŠ**.

NHA I = NUH (ע״ו > ע״ע with the vanishing of the guttural MG 254:12).

PE. Pf. **nha** Gy 92:1, Zotb. 218b:36 was at ease, at rest, id. 256:21 pl. MG 254:14. Impf. **ninha** Gy 19:23, 370:4, Gs 73:14 shall be calm, at rest MG 254:17. Impt. **nha** Gy 282:1, 304:10, 344:ult. both sg. & pl. (also **ʿnha**) MG 254:18 f., often repeated: **nha nha anuš ʿutra** Jb 266:14 calm thyself, calm thyself A. U., **nha nha abatur** DAb; **anat iardna nha lhalin nišmata** CP 26:9 = ML 30:9 thou, jordan, be calm for these souls. Act. pt. **naha** Gy 286:6 etc., fem. id. MG 254:19 f., pl. **razia nahin** ATŠ I no. 267 the mysteries become quiet (settle down). Pass. pt. **nhia** Gy 217:1 calm; with encl. pers. pron. **nhit umkikit** DC 41. 413 thou art mild and lowly.

AF. Pf. **uanha lalma** Zotb. 218b:35 and he calmed the world; with suff. **anihh̲ lziuh̲** Gy 294:13 f. he mitigated his brilliance; **mn šuba nuria d̲-ʿtbh̲ anihth̲** DC 47 thou hast eased her from the seven fires that are therein; **anhanh̲** Gy 107:11 we calmed them; MG 254:27, **uanihuia** ATŠ II no. 115 and they soothed her. Impf. with suff. **nanihak lkursiak** Gy 98:13 we will make thee easy on thy throne; **ana ʿianhilak ʿl libak** ATŠ II no. 278 I will assuage thy heart = **ana ʿianh̲** [*sic*] **ʿl libak** ATŠ II no. 73. Impt. **anha** Gy 20:20 calm (pl.) MG 254:25; **anha lduktak** ATŠ II no. 215 pause at this point; **anha pugdamak d̲-pumak** DC 44. 479 soften the command of thy mouth; fem. **anhai rugzik** DC 44. 466 assuage thy wrath; pl. with encl. **anhulh̲** DC 37. 588 relieve him; pl. with suff. **anhuia** Gy 39:7 calm it MG 254:27. Inf. **anhuiia** DC 53.

ETHPE. Pf. **ulaʿtnihit** Gy 96:paen. and I was not calmed (var. **ulaʿtnahit** DC 22 ethpa.).

ETHPA. Pf. **ulaʿtnahit** s. ethpe, **ʿ(t)nahaiun** Gy 345:1 it (: the Life, pl.) was calmed (Nöld. as ettaf. MG 254:ult.). Pt. pl. **ulamitnahia** Gy 182:20 and they become not soft.

ETTAF. Impf. **nitanha** Gy 237:16 he shall rest himself.

Gl. 12:13 f. **anha** استراح *requiescere* آسود.

DER.: s. **NUH**.

NHA II (ܢܗܐ P. Sm. 2294, H. נגהּ) = **ANH I**.

PE. Impf. **tikṣar utinha** AM 99:14 she will fall ill and will groan.

Gl. 40:11 f. **anha** بكت *exprobare, corrigere* گريه كرد.

nhamta (rt. **NHM**) roaring, groaning, moaning. Doublets **(a)nhimta** s.vv. **unhamta bialdia uialdata nihuia** AM 169:9 and there will be moaning amongst boys and girls.

-nhan s. **-nan**.

nhar 1 Zotb. 223a:7 (text) = **anhar**.

nhar 2 st. abs. & cstr. of **nahra** 1, cf. **linhar kšaš** Jb 149:5 to the river K.

nhaša 1 (נְחָשָׁא, ܢܚܫܐ, H. & Phœn. נְחֹשֶׁת, Ar. نُحَاس, Eth. ናሐስ, Akk. *la'šu*? Ges., LS) copper. **mania d̲-nhaša** Gy 182:1, 250:4, copper vessels; **ṭapqia d̲-nhaša** s. **tapqa**; **arqa qadmaita d̲-nhaša** DAb the first earth (is) of copper; **arqa titaita d̲-nhaša** Gy 127:3 the lower earth of copper; **arqa d̲-nhaša** Gy 160:1, 11 ff. (Siouffi 50, 59); **ʿṣṭunia d̲-nhaša** RD B 25 copper columns; **bit riha d̲-nhaša** CP 13:8, ML 14:9 a copper brazier.

nhaša 2 (rt. **NHŠ**) augury, divination, omen. Doublet **nahša** 1. **ʿnbu maria hukumta umaria pihta unhaša** Or. 331:14 f. Nebo, lord of wisdom and lord of divination and augury.

nhašta occ. var. of **nhušta**. (*often*) whispered or secret prayer.

NHB? (ܢܚܒ, Ar. نَخِبَ to be timid) to be lean, meagre, starving. Doubtful.

PE. Pass. pt. pl. (?) **kd̲ aria d̲-nhibin** DC 26. 602 f. = DC 44 &c. par. like hungry (??) lion(s, read **ariauata**? The text is corrupt and the meaning doubtf.; prob. read **nhimin** roaring?).

NHG I = NGA I. As impers. verb used as fem. MG 365:12.

PE. Pf. **hiškat unihgat** Gs 118:9 it became

dark and light broke forth; with encl. **harip nhaglh̲ nihga** Jb 129:8 f. early broke the dawn (with **nihga** as a logical subj. can be used either as masc. or fem.). Pt. **nahga nihga** Jb 129:2 the dawn breaks (as fem.).

Der.: **nihga.**

NHG II (by metathesis from חגג, cf. **hinga**) to encircle, (en)girdle.

Pe. Pf. with encl. **nhagbh̲ hinga** DC 51:259 he engirdled it.

Der.: cf. **hinga.**

-nhun s. **-inhun.**

nhura, anhura (נְהוֹרָא Dan. 2:22 Qrē, ܢܘܗܪܐ) light MG 118:23 f. St. abs. & cstr. **nhur** MG 127:ult. Masc. No. pl. With suff. **nhur** Q 53:7 = **nhurai** (more usual) my light; **nhar nhura** CP 61:12 = Q 28:12 the light shone; **nhur nhura** Q 3:9 = ML 8:10 = CP 7:11 let light shine; **ʿutria bnia nhura** Q 25:24 the uthras, sons of light = **ʿutria (a)bnia nhura** PD 894, 930; **ʿl nhur aiar qaiimna** CP 145:penult. = Oxf. 3a I stand (take stand) upon the light of ether; **alma d̲-nhura** (*very often*) the world of light (one of the two dualistic principles, opposed to **alma d̲-hšuka**); **nhur** CP 59:5 = ML 75:4 as name of a book. Often in proper names of higher beings; **nhur hai** CP 67:15 = Q 30:32, Gy 195:15; **nhur ziua** Gy 145:21; **ʿuṣar nhur** CP 57:3 = Q 26:11, 32:2, **lupapan nhura rba** Gy 145:21; **iauar ziua br nhur hiia** Q 2:24; **nhur aiar** CP 8:13 = ML 9:12 the light of the ether; **nhur hiia anana** Gy 374:2 &c.; **mimra d̲-nhura** Gy 376:3 f. the speech of light; **nhura iaqra** CP 415:9, trsl. p. 276 n. 6, no. 376 &c. (*often*) the holy light; **nhur psiq** Gy 194:4 cut off from light (or 'precious').

nhuraita (cf. *Norea* the wife of Seth, Irenaeus, *Haer.* i. 30:9) Gy 381:9 the wife of Šum (Shem); doublet **nuraita** Morg. 88:9, Jb ii 58:24.

nhušta (rt. **NHŠ**) a whispered or secret prayer (?). Varr. **nhašta, n(i)hišta, nihušta. unimrun nhušta** DC 50 and they shall say the whispered prayer (?).

nhuta 1 = **nihuta** (q.v.).

nhuta 2 (cf. **ntata**?) unclean, foul creatures (?). Var. **ntuta** DC 6. **nhuta d̲-arbia ligria** ATŠ I no. 254 unclean four-legged creatures (?).

NHZ (ܢܗܙ to arouse commotion, excite, Ar. نَهَزَ to pierce) to move noisily, cause disturbance, clatter about, bluster about, reel about, move boisterously, violently, shake about, struggle violently.

Ethpa. Pf. Only reflexive forms (ethpe. s. ethpa. pt.). **ʿtnahaz** Gy 281:11 he blustered; with encl. **ʿtnahazbun bgirmh̲** Gy 94:16 he rattled his bones; **ʿtnahaz ulaʿtnahazlh̲** Gy 170:12 (var. **-la** Sh. 'Abd.'s copy) he struggled violently but was unable to struggle to her. Pt. **kd̲ mitinhiz** (ethpe.) **umitnahaz** (ethpa.) Gy 85:1 when he clattered about boisterously; **mitnahaz mn dukth̲** Gy 85:19 he moved (hist. pres.) boisterously from his place; with encl. **mitnahazbh̲ bškinth̲** Gy 81:18 he blustered about his dwelling.

nhia pass. pt. pe. of **NHA** (q.v.).

nhimta 1, anhimta s.v. (rt. **NMH**, ܬܢܚܬܐ, H. st. cstr. נַהֲמַת) groan(ing), moaning. **bnhimta nahim** Gy 87:23 he groaneth loudly; **anhimth̲ nhimta d̲-ʿnšia** Gy 91:1 I made him moan like women, MG 399:22; **bziuihth̲ bnihimth̲** Gy 280:17 in his fright, in his groaning.

nhimta 2 (ܢܘܚܡܐ resurrection) revival, restoration, relief, consolation. **nihmat** (s.v.) may be a st. cstr. of this word. **ʿburia rurbia nihun unhimta banašia nihuia** AM 169:7 there will be mighty crops and there will be comfort amongst the people.

nhira, anhira, ʿnhira (נְחִירָא, ܢܚܝܪܐ, H. נְחִירַיִם, Ar. مَنْخَر, Akk. *naḫiru*) nose. Pl. **-ia.** Both genders MG 158:7. Frequent (esp. in AM).

nhit DC 53. 139:5 for **nihaiit.**

NHL (ܢܗܠ, نخل, Akk. *naḫālu* LS) to sieve.

Pe. Impf. **nhul** AM 288:9 sieve; with suff. **nuhlh̲** AM 286:paen. sieve it.

Der.: **m(u)hulta.**

NHM I (Aram. & H. נהם, Syr. ܢܗܡ, Ar. نَهَمَ) to roar, groan, moan, make an uproar.

Pe. Pf. **humria nhim** (?) DC 44. 1515 the amulet-spirits groaned; **nihmat unipqat biahria šuba** DC 43 J 45 she groaned and brought forth (an abortion) in the seventh month. Act. pt. **gazim unahim** Gy 280:4 he assaults and makes an uproar; **bnhimta nahim** s. **nhimta, hu nahim uhadar balma** Gy 161:12 f. he groaneth and turneth about in the world; **unahim kd̲ iauna** DC 34. 225 and he moans like a dove; fem. **bakia unahma** Gy 164:19 she weepeth and groaneth; pl. fem. **humria nahman** DC 26. 131 f. the amulet-spirits moan.

Af. Pf. with suff. **anhimth̲** Gy 91:1 I made him moan MG 277:11, cf. s. **nhimta.**

Der.: **anhimta, nhimta 1.**

NHM II the rt. of **nhimta 2** (q.v.) (cstr. **nihmat**?).

nhʿ = **nia** MG 65 n. 1.

NHP (met. of **NPH** q.v.) to blow up (a flame), fan (a flame), breathe (fire).

Pe. Pf. **nhap lbaidukt** DC 44. 352 = Morg. 265/20:25 he breathed fire (?) on Baidukt. Act. pt. **pumh̲ nahpa nura** DC 43 J 171 his mouth breathes fire.

Ethpe. Pt. **mitnihpa nura** Gy 203:20, 204:10, DC 36 no. 47 (var. **minihpa** PD 522) fire shall be fanned.

Ethpa. Impf. **nitnahpa nura** DC 37. 546 fire shall be fanned.

NHR I (Jew.-Aram., Chr.-Pal., Syr., H. נהר II; Ar. نهار day) to give light, shine, impart light, illumine, brighten.

Pe. Pf. **nhar nhura** s. **nhura, nihrat** she shone MG 61:4; **nihrat ʿruta** Q 28:13 the radiance shone; **ʿurašlam nihrat bziuai** Jb 274:9 Jerusalem became bright with my radiance; **nihrit bšamiš d̲-ʿumama** DC 44.

1300 = Morg. 264/19:22 I shone with the sun of day, **nhuriun** [*sic*] **ubsumiun ʿutria umalkia** PA's ŠQ the uthras and kings (: spirits) shone and rejoiced. Impf. **ninhar** shineth, will shine MG 221:4, **tinhar** she shineth, thou shinest MG 238:7, **ʿnhar** I (will) shine MG 227:6, **ninihrun** they (shall) shine MG 26:18, 238:7; with encl. **tinharbun** DC 3. 343:9 = DC 53 = CP 349:3 (no. 324) thou shinest amongst them; with suff. **ninihruk** Gs 128:3 (where should be **nanihruk**) they give thee light MG 274:23. Impf. **nhar** Gs 39:17 shine MG 240:9, but **nhur nhura** CP 7:11 = Q 28:12 let light shine (Lidzb.). Act. pt. **nahar** MG 61:6, fem. **nahra** (*often*), masc. often replaced by **nahur** (s.v.); pl. **anpaihun nahrin** Gy 176:10 their faces shall shine. Part. pres. **nahirna** [*sic*] **btušbihta ḏ-ab** ATŠ I no. 241 I shine with praise of my father; **anin bgauak nihrinin** (read **nahrinin**) DC 34 we shine in thee. Pass. pt. usually replaced by **nahira** s.v. Inf. **minhar** AM 286 to beam.

Af. Pf. **anhar** he illumined, gave light MG 61:1, **anhirat**, varr. **anh(u)rat**, **anharat** Gy 276:10 she illumined MG 30 n. 1, **anhart** thou hast illumined MG 222:27; **lginzaikun anhartun** ATŠ II no. 146 ye gave light to your treasure; fem. pl. **uainẖ anharian** ATŠ II no. 139 and her eyes shone (would be pe. with a mere prosth. a); with encl. **anhirilun** Gy 361:1 (var. **anhiritilun** read **anhirtilun**) I gave them light MG 226:11 f.; with suff. **anharthẖ** she illumined MG 276:23; **manharanita ḏ-anharthẖ lbaita haška** Morg. 237/62:5–7 luminous one who hast illumined the dark house; **anhartinkun** I have illumined you MG 281:4, **anhartinun** I illumined them MG 282:paen., **anhirinan** he illumined us MG 279:anteantep. Impf. with suff. **nanh(i)rẖ** he illumineth him MG 276:7, **tianhrak** Gs 41:22 she illumineth thee MG 215:19, 273:21, **ʿianhrẖ** Gy 109:14 [*bis*] I will illumine it, **nanh(i)runẖ** they illumine him MG 278:15, **nanhru** Gy 336:15 he illumineth her MG 279:20. Pt. (act. & pass.) **manhar** illuminating, illumined MG 238:8, **kukba nahira ḏ-manhar mn kulhun kukbia** Or. 332:14 f. a bright star, brighter than all stars; pl. **manihria** they shine MG 214 n. 1; pl. with encl. **šamiš usira ḏ-manihribun** ATŠ II no. 5 sun and moon which give them light. Part. pres. **manharna** I illumine MG 231:8, **manhirit** Par. xi 36 b thou illuminest MG 232:17, **manhirinin** we illumine MG 233:3; **manh(i)ritun** ye illumine MG 233:15. Nom. ag. **manhirana** s.v. Inf. **anhuria** to illumine MG 144:6, 234:1; with suff. **anhurẖ** Gy 23:13, 283:16 to illumine him, it MG 293:1; **lmanhirinkun** Oxf. 5 b to illumine you MG 293:5; **manhirinun** Oxf. 102 b, 103 a to illumine them MG 293:13.

Ethpe. Pt. pl. **minihria** CP 389:penult. the illumined ones; **minihrin mn bnia ḏ-sam** Gy 176:10 they shall be brighter than the sons of Sam (cf. also s.v.).

Der.: **(a)nhur(a)**, **manharʿil**, **manhirana** (var. **-ha-**, fem. **-ita**), **minihra**, **nahur**, **nahira**, **nahra 2**.

NHR II (Jew.-Aram., H. & mod. H. נחר, Syr. ܢܚܰܪ, Ar. نخر, Eth. ነኅረ to puff) to breathe, sniff, inhale, snuff up.

Pe. Act. pt. **bnhirẖ nahar** DC 20 (var. **nahra** DC 43 E 9); **unahra ldaiua** DC 20 and will snuff up the demon (fem. for masc.); **ḏ-nahra briha ḏ-hiia** DC 41. 504 so that she breathes the breath of Life. Pass. pt. **nuhra nhira** ATŠ I no. 245 heavy breathing.

Der.: **(ʿ)nhira**, **nuhra**.

NHR III (rt. נחר) to pierce, bore. **mn škinta lškinta umn lbuša llbuša nihrat** DC 48. 382 she (the soul) pierceth (her way) from *škinta* to *škinta* and from veil to veil (*lit.* from covering to covering).

NHŠ, LHŠ s.v. (Jew.-Aram. & H. נחש & לחש, Syr. ܠܚܰܫ & ܢܚܶܫ, Eth. ሕሉምሰሰ, Akk. *luḫḫušu* KAT 604, Ar. نحس to be unpropitious [omen] MG 54 n. 3) to whisper, mutter (incantations, prayers), to divine by omen. MG 54:9 & n. 3.

Pe. Pf. with suff. **nhišlak** Gy 390:20 he whispered to thee (MG 220:11, 437:bottom). Act. pt. with encl. **nahišlẖ** Gy 390:17 he whispereth to him. Impt. **nhušlẖ bʿudnẖ** AM 135:19 whisper to him in his ear.

Der.: **nhaša 2**, **nhašta** (& varr.).

NHT (נְחַת, ܢܚܶܬ, H. נחת, Ar. حَتَّ to drop leaves etc.) to go down, descend; af. to bring down, let down, lay down.

Pe. Pf. **nhit** Gy 94:2 etc. he descended, Morg. 208/3:ult. they descended MG 61:1, 219:14, **nhitt** thou didst descend MG 222:25. Impf. **nihut** (most common), MG 52:9, 219:14, 238:17, **niʿhut** Gy 70:16 B he descendeth MG 6:24, but also **ninhit** Gy 186:3, Q 40:20 id., MG 239:1, **ʿhut** Gy 137:22 I descend MG 238:17, **alahia mn ʿšumia larqa ninihtun** AM 234:8 the gods will descend from the heavens to the earth. Impt. **hut** descend MG 219:14, 240:2, but also **nhut** Q 7:19, Oxf. 3 b, 4 b &c., **nhit** Gs 3:ult, &c. id., MG, 240:2 f., **ʿhut** Gy 265:10 id. (pl.); with encl. **lalma hutlẖ** Gy 71:21 f. go down to the world. Act. pt. **nahit**, fem. **nahta**, pl. **barda uglala nahtia** AM 272:11 frost and hail will fall down; **nahtin šuba ʿlauaihun** DC 34. 347 the Seven will descend upon them. Inf. **lminhat biama** AM 139:12 for going down to the sea.

Af. Pf. **ahit** Morg. 213/14:4 he brought down (Lidzb./ZDMG lxi 695 n. 4); **ahtit** Gy 54:7, or **ahitit** Gy 90:ult. I brought down MG 239:16; **ligrai ahtit ʿl miṣria uʿl šuria** Gy 154:7 f. I placed my foot down on the boundaries and on the walls; with suff. **ahitthẖ** Gy 164:8, 332:3 I brought him, her down MG 12:14, 277:13; **anhithẖ** DC 41. 5 I brought it down. Impf. **ʿiahit** Gy 137:22 I descend MG 239:17. Impt. **ahit bpuma ḏ-qarapta** DC 44. 913 put it down in the mouth of a skull; **ahit bgupta** DC 44. 1740 = Morg. 268/26:40 put it down in a receptacle. Act. pt. with encl. **manhitilun** DC 43 J 105 they degrade them. Part. pres. **mahtit** Gy 208:10 thou bringest down MG 239:17, but **ghuka**

manhitit ʿlauaihun DC 37. 47 thou bringest down derision upon them. Inf. **ulmahta ʿdh mn rišh** Lond. roll A 433 taking down his hand from his head.

nu (נֹחַ, ܢܘܚ, نوح) Noah. Siouffi 130, MSt 66, HpGn 173. **nu d-kauila** Gy 26:24, 380:9 ff. Noah of the ark; **amar lnu bnia kauila** Gy 265:10 he said to N.: 'Build the ark!'; **šum br nu** Gy 26:24 Shem son of Noah (Siouffi 85: bottom); **ualma ldara d-nu** Gy 25:3 until the age of Noah; **umn nu gabra alma nitnapša** Gy 27:4 and from the man Noah the world multiplied.

NWA (Ar. نَوَّى) to accomplish, achieve. Mod.

Pa.? Pt. **manaua hazin diuan** Zotb. 231a:8 this diwan was accomplished.

nuba a keeper of a purgatory, prob. a miscop. of **nbu. hazin matarta d-nuba** DAb.

NUD (Jew.-Aram. & H. נוד, Syr. ܢܕ, Ar. ناد; rel. to **NDA** & **NDD**) to shake, quake, tremble.

Pe. Pf. **nad** (**utnauad**) Gs 28:8, 29:20, 31:14 (cf. 26:19), DC 27. 293 &c. (a frequent phrase) he shook (and trembled) MG 248:2 & n. 1, 252:23; **nadat** Gy 82:1 she trembled MG 248:9; **nadiun turia** PD 864 the hills shook; with encl. **nadalh kulh qumh** Gs 26:19, 28:8, 29:21, 31:14 his whole body was shaking MG 248:11. Impf. **tinud** thou shakest MG 249:8; **ʿšumia ninidun** AM 221:7 the heavens will shake. Act. pt. **ʿu naiid mn dukth** ATŠ II no. 401 if he shakes (swerves) from his place; fem. **naida** (**umitnauda**) Gy 88:2 she trembleth (and is shaken); **arqa naida mn sadanh** DC 34. 224 the earth quakes from its foundation; pl. **simakia d-lanaidia** Q 53:27 supports which shake not; **lanaidia mia barbai** Jb 144:8 f. the water does not quiver by my boat. Inf.? **uarqa minad** AM 50:14 even if the earth shonld quake.

Af. Pf. with suff. **anidh** Gy 85:1 f. (B once **andh** s. **NDA**), 90:11 f. he shook it MG 275:12; **anidth** Gy 90:17 I shook him MG 277:14; **aniduia, anʿduia** Gy 113:13 ff. they shook him MG 278:4; **anidu** Gy 113:14 they shook her MG 279:18. Impf. with suff. **lamṣia bhailh d-nanidh mn dukth** Gy 90:16 he could not shake him from his place.

Ethpa. (with mobile consonantal ו inst. of the expected י). Pf. (**nad**) **utnauad** s. pe. pf. Impf. (**nad**) **unitnauad** Gs 26:19 (but with the meaning of the pf.). Pt. (**naida**) **umitnauda** s. pe. pt. fem., **haiqa umitnauda** Gy 88:2 she is afraid and shaken.

Gl. 15:13 f. **NUD** ارتعد *tremere* لرزيد; 49:13 f. id. defectively تزلزل *moveri* زلزله شد; 50:9 f. id. تهنت, تهند *ingemere, infremere* ناله كرد; 135:7 f. id. قلق *commoveri* جنبانيد.

Der.: **nauda** (var. **nuda**).

NUH (Aram. & H. נוח, Syr. ܢܚ, Akk. *nâḫu*, Ar. اناخ to make a camel kneel, Eth. ኖኀ to be long and to remain) to rest, relieve, ease, repose, be quiet. Secondary rt. **NHA I** s.v.

Pe. Pass. pt. **niha** s.v., **nʿ** Gy 293:21 A (varr. **nhia, nhʿ**, even **nihia** & miscop., cf. ibid. varr., Gy 217:1, 250:6 etc.) MG 65:7 & n. 3.

Af. Pf. with suff. **anihh** Gy 294:12 f., 323:11, Gs 50:20 he calmed her, him MG 275:12, **lanihth** Gs 22:8 thou didst not calm him MG 65:16 (cf. n. 4) 276:paen. f., **anhanh** Gy 107:11 we calmed her MG 277:22. Impf. with suff. **nanihak** Gy 98:13 he calmeth thee MG 273:23; **nanihh, nanʿhh** Gy 86:18, 241:9 he calmeth him, her MG 276:2; **ʿianihh** I calm him MG 276:3. Impt. with suff. **anihh** Gs 20:19 calm him MG 276:15.

Ethpe. Pf. **ʿtnihat** Q 33:4 she was calmed, **ʿtnihit** Gy 96:24 I was calmed MG 251:28.

Der.: **niaha, niha.**

nuhas (Ar. نُحَاس) copper. Mod. **mahata d-nuhas** DC 45 a copper needle.

nuhra (rt. **NHR II**) breathing. **nuhra nhira** s. **NHR II** pe. pass. pt.

nutpiata = **nitupiata** (pl. of **nitupta** q.v.).

nukar (P. نَوْكَر) servant, follower. Mod. Pl. **nukaran. šadir nukar** DC 35:coloph. he sent a servant. Pl. with suff. **nukarandia** DC 35: coloph. his servants, his people.

nukusta PD 852 = **n(i)kusta.**

nukut, nukta (Ar. نُكْتَه) small quantity, speck, grain. **hda nukut** (var. **nukta**) **tiriak** DC 46 (var. DC 45) one grain of opium.

NWKR pauel of **NKR** (q.v.).

nukraia (נוּכְרָאָה, נוּכְרָא, נוכרי, ܢܘܟܪܝܐ, H. נָכְרִי) strange, alien, foreign, removed by time and space, different in kind, sublime, transcendent MG 141:15, MSchr 3 n. 2, Jb ii 1 n. 1, Ginzā 5 n. 2. Fem. **nukraita.** Pl. masc. **nukraiia. bšumaihun d-hiia rurbia nukraiia** (Mand. *basmamala* at the beginning of every chapter) in the name of the Great, Sublime (ἄγνωστος) Life MG 326:19 f.; **hiia nukraiia** Gy 134:1 etc. (*often*); **nukraia d-latihilh mnata balma** Gy 110:18 the Alien who shall have no part in the world; **nimar lnukraia d-nitilan mnata balma** Gy 109:7 let us tell the stranger to give us a share in the world; **nigitlh lnukraia** Gy 109:ult. let us kill the stranger; **mahu d-abad nukraia bgauh d-baita** Gy 110:21 what has the stranger done in the house?; **nukraia d-hiia šilhuia** Gy 353:20, 354:3 the stranger whom the Life has sent; **gabra nukraia** Gy 94:13, 354:5, 22 ff., Jb 63:8 f, etc. (*very often*) the sublime being from the other world Jb ii 1 n. 1, Anoš-Uthra Ginzā 336: 26, st. abs. **gbar nukraia** Gy 328:24; **kd atin iumia šumaiia . . . bhanatun nukraiia miṣtba maṣbuta** ATŠ I no. 196 when the celestial days come . . . in those sublime days he shall receive baptism (cf. s. **šumaiia**); **urhim gabra nukraia d-šuth nukraita d-mnakrilh minh mn alma** Gy 244:4 and he loved the sublime being whose doctrine is so sublime that it estrangeth him from the world; **ʿu nukraita lagit** AM 6:16 if he shall take a foreigner to wife.

NWL (ܢܘܠ) to torment.

PA. Pf. (?) **niual aina zruqtia** JRAS 1937 595:23 the Blue Eye is tormented (?). Pass. pt. **umnaula mn rhamta** DC 46 and is tormented (suffers pain) by love.

DER.: **nala 2?, niula.**

NUM (Gen. Sem.) to sleep.

PE. Pf. **namit** Jb 128:11 B (var. **nimit** ACD) I slept MG 248:15. Impf. **ninimun** Oxf. iii 18 a = Par. xi 51 a, they sleep MG 249:24. Act. pt. pl. **ʿdilma naimia šakbia** CP 158:6 = ML 191:2 lest they be lying down, sleeping (CP trs. 119 n. 1).

DER.: **nauma.**

numa (cf. coll. Ar. *nūmi*) lemon, lemon-tree. **numan umilan** s. **mila.**

numbia, nambia s.v. (rt. **NMBA**) mourning, wailing, lamentation. **ulaqal numbia** Gy 6:20 and not the voice of wailing; **numbia ubkita** Gy 28:11 wailing and weeping.

-nun acc. suff. of the 3rd p. pl. masc. (cf. s. **-inhun**).

nuna (נונא, ܢܘܢܐ, H. נון, Akk. *nūnu*, Ar. نُون from Aram. Nöld. *Neue Beiträge* 133 n. 3 LS) fish; the Zodiacal sign Pisces Nöld. ZDMG xxv 256 ff., Siouffi 145, 168, MMII 74. Pl. **-ia.** As sign of the Zodiac Gy 123:5, 384:17 f., 24, 386:23, very often in AM. **qala d̲-qra nuna d̲-kulhun nunia minh̲ hun hun nunia udilpunia** Gy 124:11 f. from the voice which called 'fish!', all fishes were created, were created fishes and dolphins.

NUS = **NSS.**

DER.: **nausa, nusa.**

nusa = **nausa. maria nausa** DC 46. 187:9 f. a sick person.

nupiata fem. pl. doubtf. **pilia nupiata qadašata** DC 43 G 22 Nubian (?) female war-elephants.

nupsai RD 27 = DAb par. name of a demon.

nupša (rt. **NPŠ**, cf, **napuš, napša 2**) a great deal of, great number of, many. Fem. pl. **nupšata. kma hua nupša** ATŠ II no. 310 how great is its extent; **unupša abad unautbh̲ qudamh̲** ATŠ II no. 405 and (when) he has made a great quantity, he shall set it before him; **nupša bʿdaikun** DC 50. 172 a quantity (bunch of myrtle-twigs) is in your hands; **aitun asa nupša** DC 35 bring a quantity of myrtle; **nupša d̲-mdiniata** DC 3 coloph. many cities; **zira uzruta nupša** AM 281:14 seed and sowing will be abundant; **siblit ridpa nupša** ATŠ I no. 201 I endured much persecution; **ṭabauata nupšata** ATŠ I no. 222 many benefactions.

nuq(u)bta (נוקבתא, ܢܩܒܬܐ, H. נְקֵבָה, Ar. نُقْبَة) female, feminine MG 110:2 f. Var. **niqubta**, st. abs. **niquba** s.v. Pl. **nuqbata** MG 162:25. **alahia zikria uʿstirata nuqbata** (*often in exorcisms*) male gods and female astartes; **rapia hu . . . kd̲ nuqbata** AM 155:3 he is effeminate . . . like females; **kd̲ nuqbata d̲-hatma ʿtatna ʿlh̲** DC 34. 784 like a female upon which a seal is set; **kul nuqbta d̲-ʿl hatmai lamašra** DC 34. 786 each female which is not preserved (**ŠRR**) by my seal; **braza d̲-nuqbta** DC 34. 786 by the Mystery of the Female; **unuqbata hinun nišmata d̲-ṣabit** CP 42:24 = ML 50:12 if the souls which thou baptizest are women.

nuqṭa (Ar. نُقْطَة) point, dot. Mod.

Gl. 178:4 **nuqṭa** يوطه *iota.*

nuqṣan (Ar. نُقْصَان) waning. Mod. **ʿu sin bnuqṣan** AM 265:2 if the moon be waning.

nura (נורא, ܢܘܪܐ, H. נֵר, Ar. نار fire, نور light, Akk. *nūru* light) fire MG 105:7, MR 64, MSchr 23 n. 6, Siouffi 168, MSt 93 ff. Usually fem., exc. masc. as in Q 12:4 ff. MG 159:14 f. Pl. **nuria** Q 52:26 MG 167 n. 3. **nura akla** Gy 12:9, Jb 51:14 devouring fire Jb ii p. xvi n. 1, opposed to **nura haita** Jb 51:14 the living fire MSt 94; **nura haditia** CP 13:7 = ML 14:9 f. a new fire; **nura (d̲)-iaqda** Gy 13:1 etc. (*often*) flaming fire; **lbiš nura umkasia nura ugabaruata bnura mhauia** Gy 28:16 f. (cf. 52:2) he (: Christ) put on fire and clotheth himself with fire and showeth miracles in fire; **uʿl nura hauia škinth̲** Gy 28:18 52:4 and his (: Christ's) dwelling is on fire; **napla (a)bnura ubašla tizal mnata d̲-nura tihuia . . . aminṭul d̲-ʿl nura sagda** Jb 47:12 ff. she will fall into fire and burn, she will go and become a portion of the fire, (repeated), because she worships fire; **ʿl bab nura lanihlup** Gy 40:15 he shall not pass by the gate of fire; **šiṭia d̲-nura mauqria šiṭia d̲-mauqria nura** Gy 120:21 the despised ones who worship fire (repeated); **rušumai lahua nura** ML 154 = CP 127:8 f. my sign was not fire (see ML 154 n. 1); **anin tibil nura qraina** CP 263:12, (ML 259 erroneous) we created (are creating) an earth of fire (n. 1); **kana d̲-nura** s. **kana** (*b*); **gaunh̲ d̲-nura** s. **gauna.**

Gl. 168:7 **nura** نار *ignis* آتش.

nuraiṭaš name of a Persian king, with other names: **nuraiṭaš hurizdan d̲-qarilh̲ šamidai malka** Gy 383:9 f. apparently a corruption from *nuṭairaš*—Av. patronymics *Naotara, Naotairāeha*, and *Naotairyana* (Yašt v 76, 78 etc.) Gray ZA xix 282 ff.

nuraita (cf. s. **nhuraita**) name used for the wives of Shem, Noah, and Dēnanukht. **šum br nu unuraita zauh̲** CP 199b:11 = Morg. 88:9; **nu gabra unuraita zauh̲** Gy 49:24; **qam dinanukt uqralh̲ lzauh̲ nuraita** Gy 212:14; **zauh̲ nuraita** ibid. l. 16.

nurat an obscure prepositional expression in **mlakia d̲-qaimia umamlilia lnurat anpia d̲-anašia** Morg. 260/12:16 ff. = DC 44. 739 ff. (read **lṣurat** ? in front of ?).

nurʿil unuriaiil Gy 167:7 two angel-names. DC 40. 881.

nurš(ʿ)il a theophorous name applied to an arrow. **gira nuršil** (var. **-ʿil**) **šumh̲** RD 6 (var. DAb par.).

nuš Zotb. 221a:37 = **anuš.**

nušadir (ܢܘܫܐܕܪ < P. نوشادر) AM 136 sal-ammoniac.

nušaqta (rt. **NŠQ**) kiss. **unušaqtak urhamtak** DC 46 thy kiss and thy love.

NZA s. **NZZ.**

NZH a secondary form of **ZHA I.**

AF. Impt. with suff. **aṭrud anzahḫ** (varr. **anizah**) . . . **mn pagrai** DC 43 D 70 expel, rebuke it . . . from my body.

NZZ (Ar. نزّ) to loosen, be inconsistent, incontinent, unsteady, shaky, infirm, brittle. (Lidzb. from נדי, ܢܕܐ = H. נזה ML 37 n. 1, but the forms prove that the verb is ע״ע).

PE. Impf. **ninzun** Q 13:24, 14:18 they shall be removed MG 249:26 (rightly as ע״ע; Lidzb. considered the form as ethpe. ML 37 n. 2). Act. pt. **naziz banhura nitiqria** ATŠ II no. 390 he will be called 'unsteady' in the light. Pass. pt. **mn pagrḫ nziz** ATŠ II no. 5 he is infirm of body.

ETHPE. Pt. **minziz** PD 1735, ATŠ II no. 10, **mitinziz** PD 165, ATŠ I no. 13 is unsteady, unreliable, brittle. **ualmia ḏ-hšuka manziz** [*sic*] DC 34. 568 and the worlds of darkness reel.

DER.: **niaza, nizia.**

nziz pass. pt. of **NZZ** (q.v.).

NZL (Jew.-Aram., Syr., H., Ar.; Akk. *nazāzu*) to descend, go down, flow down, disappear, melt.

PE. Pt. with suff. (?) **gišlia lbaṣar alعin mn biad unazlḫ** AM 287:16 (hardly correct) takes off the film from the sight of the eye, from the whiteness and dissolves it (i.e. the white film).

PA. Pt. **ʿnta ḏ-mnazal hšuka** DC 46 a woman from whom flows darkness (: menstrual issue).

AF. Part. pres. **mazilna** Gy 191:3 I let flow down MG 239:18.

nṭarta occ. var. of **naṭarta.**

nṭupta DAb for **niṭupta** but used as a name of Ruha.

NṬṬ (cf. ܛܢܘܦܐ sordid) to be afflicted, troubled.

ETHPE. Pf. **ʿnṭiṭ blibḫ** Gy 100:20 (var. **nṭiṭ** DC 22 & Sh. 'Abd.'s copy) he was troubled in his heart, **ʿtinṭiṭ** Gy 94:5, 193:12, Gs 3:4 he was afflicted MG 252:1, **ʿtinṭiṭt** Gy 193:13, 23 thou art afflicted. Impf. **unittaṭa** [*sic*] DC 46. 241:12 he will be troubled.

ETHPA. Pf. **ʿtnaṭṭit** Gy 193:19 I was afflicted MG 32:8, 252 n. 2. Pt. fem. (pl.) **unišmatun mitnaṭaṭa ʿlauaihun** Gy 256:10 and their souls are troubled about them.

DER.: **nṭiṭa, nṭiṭuta.**

nṭiṭa (rt. **NṬṬ**) infirmity, affliction MG 116:22. Pl. **-ia. kibia unṭiṭia** Gy 121:2, **kibia unṭiṭia litbḫ** Gy 320:13, Jb 217:5 there are no pains or infirmities; **nṭiṭia umumia litbḫ** Gs 81:22 there are no infirmities or blemishes; **mn kulhun kibia unṭiṭia ʿtasia** ATŠ II no. 391 it is healed from all pains and infirmities; **umn nṭiṭia ḏ-ʿtbḫ** DC 34. 514 and from the infirmities which are inherent.

nṭiṭuta (abstr. noun from preced.) trouble, affliction, grief. **ḏ-dahalta unṭiṭuta litbḫ** Gy 247:3 f. in which there is no fear or affliction; **unṭiṭuta lahuatabḫ** Gy 248:18 and there was no affliction in it; **ḏ-nṭiṭuta uhargta litbḫ** DC 34. 652 in which there is no trouble or perversity.

nṭipa pass. pt. pe. of **NṬP** (q.v.).

nṭira (pass. pt. pe. of **NṬR**) kept, preserved; careful, circumspect; observant, watchful. Pl. **-ia. abatur rama kasia nṭira** DC 51. 235 the lofty occult watchful A.; **bhaiak kušṭa alak ḏ-halin kušṭa bgauḫ nṭiria** ATŠ I no. 141 by thy life, Kušṭa, see to it that these are observant of the pact; **prišaia unṭira** ATŠ II no. 371 discriminating and circumspect; **ʿutria kasiia unṭiria** CP 444:8 secret and watchful uthras.

NṬN (corruption of **NTN** or **ATNA**?) to place, put.

PE. Impf. **uninṭan ʿdḫ lmargna** Lond. roll 713 and he shall place his hand on the staff.

NṬP (Aram. & H. נטף, Syr. ܢܛܦ, Ar. نطف, Eth. ነጠበ to drip, ነጠፈ to stick) to drip, drop.

PE. Act. pt. **miša naṭip** Gs 8:1 the oil drippeth. Pass. pt. **pagra nṭipa** Morg. 116:11 = DC 3. 215:1 = CP 291:11 an oozing body.

AF. Impt. **uanṭip bnhirḫ** AM 134:11 and let it drip into his nose. Part. pres. **manṭipit bainak** AM 287:15 thou droppest (it) in thine eye(s).

DER.: **n(i)ṭupta** (var. **-bta**).

NṬR (נטר, ܢܛܪ, Ar. نطر Fränkel 138, H. נצר, Eth. ነጸረ, Akk. *naṣāru*) trans. to watch over, guard, preserve, take care of, keep back, retain; intrans. to wait Jb ii 25 n. 10.

PE. Pf. **šidqa nṭar** Gy 71:16 he kept silence; **šipula niṭrat** Q 61:6, **niṭrat šipula** Q 69:27 she guarded her purity (lit. lap); **niṭrit** Gy 160:17 I waited; with suff. **niṭrun** Gy 136:6 they guarded me, **niṭruia** they guarded him MG 8:1. Impf. **ninṭar qalia** Gy 259:19 let us wait a little MG 239:2; **ziuak ninṭar ʿlak** Gs 39:24 may thy brilliance protect thee (Lidzb.: *Dein Glanz verbleibe an dir*); with encl. **ninṭurlia** Gy 370:6 he guardeth for me MG 221:13, 239:3; **ninṭurbḫ** Jb 19:1 (var. **ninṭrubḫ** A) he will remain in it (var. they will guard him?); with suff. **ʿniṭrak** Gs 44:7 I will preserve thee MG 273:14. Impt. **nṭar** or **nṭur** Gy 172:6, 314:9, 327:17 guard, preserve MG 240:6; **nṭur ʿdak** DC 41. 326 hold back thy hand; with suff. **nuṭrḫ lginzak kasia** ATŠ I no. 294 keep thy treasure secret; **nuṭria lbaba mn gambia** DC 48. 231 guard the door from thieves (?); **ʿnṭurunun** ATŠ II no. 17 watch over them. Act. pt. **naṭar**, st. emph. masc. & abs. fem. **naṭra** (used often nominally, s.v.); **naṭar baita** Gy 348:20, Jb 3:5, 4:6, 5:6 guardian of the house; **naṭar qina ḏ-abahatḫ** Gy 168:2 he guardeth the nest of his fathers; **hibil naṭar dara** Gy 316:6, 18 H. the guard of the generation; **šidqa naṭar** Gy 71:11 he keepeth silence; with encl. **naṭarlak** Gy 153:2 he guardeth thee; fem. **bhabšaba naṭra ʿda** CP 173:12 = ML 211:5 on Sunday she keepeth her hands from work; pl. **uʿidaihun bhabšaba naṭria** Gy 56:12 f. and on Sunday they keep their hands from work. Part. pres. **unaṭritun**

. . . ʿ**daikun** ATŠ II no. 164 and ye hold back your hands. Pass. Pt. **nṭir(a)** s.v.; with encl. pers. pron. **šidqa nṭirna** Gy 189:7 I keep silence; **napšai ʿnṭirna** CP 110: 2 = ML 135: 5 f. I guard myself. Inf. **minṭar dara** Gy 299:11 to guard the generation; **miniṭr(i)h̲** Gs 55:3 to guard him MG 292:21.

Pa. Impf. with suff. **ninaṭrunan** they guard me MG 273:2, **ninaṭrunak** they guard thee MG 274:21, **ninaṭrunh̲** they guard him MG 278:14, **ninaṭrunin** Q 28:29 they guard them (fem.) MG 283:19. Impt. **naṭrinun** guard them MG 282:11; pl. with suff. **naṭruia ʿl pagra** DC 43 D 43 guard the body (MG 279:1). Pt. (act. & pass.) **mnaṭar, mnaṭra** guarding, guarded; pl. **mnaṭrh̲** (for **-ia**) Gy 93:21 preserved; with encl. pers. pron. **mnaṭarna** DC 26. 442 I am guarded; fem. st. emph. **ninaṭarta** DC 40. 903 protecting. Nom. ag. **mnaṭrana** s.v. Inf. **naṭuria** Gy 296:9 to guard MG 143:17; with suff. **naṭurh̲** Gy 340:13, or **minaṭurh̲** Gy 340:14 (with bad varr.) to guard him, to preserve him.

Af. Pf. **anṭar** he let wait MG 239:22. Impt. with encl. **anṭ(i)rulia** (var. **anṭurulia**) Gs 74: ult. f. let me wait.

Ethpe. Impf. **ninṭar** he, we shall be guarded MG 226:19; **ninṭar bit ginzan** Gy 259:3 is kept in our treasure-house; **bziuak ʿninṭar baita** Gs 39:24 the House is preserved by thy radiance; **hinun btrin razia . . . ninṭar** [*sic*] ATŠ II no. 425 they are protected by two mysteries . . .

Ethpa. Pf. **ʿtnaṭar dara** Gy 381:8 the generation was preserved; **uruha bliba ʿtnaṭrat** ATŠ II no. 118 and the (earthly) spirit was kept in the heart; with encl. **ʿtnaṭarlh̲ iardna uškinta udrabša** DC 34. 797 and jordan, cult-hut and banner protected [*sic?*] him. Impf. **nitnaṭar** is guarded, protected MG 226:20; **ʿtnaṭar uʿtqaiam** Lond. roll A 408 be watchful and confirmed; **titnaṭar** Gy 62:11 she shall take care (MG 227:3). Pt. with encl. **mitnaṭarbun** Gy 314:8 is preserved by them.

Der.: **maṭaraia, maṭarta** (abs. **maṭra**), **mnaṭrana, (m)naṭruta, naṭra, nṭira, naṭar.**

niaha (rt. **NUH**, נְיָיחָא, ܢܝܳܚܳܐ) rest, quiet, refreshment, quietness, ease, bliss, delight, love-feast MG 63:20, 115:24. Pl. **-ia. niaha ušidqa** Gy 305:13 quiet and silence; **karsauata d̲-niaha** Gy 210:11, 22, 211:10 thrones of rest; **mn niahun** Gy 342:5 from Its (: the Life's bliss); **niaha unihuta** AM 177:1 ease and quietness; **ulmalulia biluria d̲-niaha** DC 40 and to cause trumpets of quietness to speak; **niaha d̲-ʿuṣrai** ŠQ refreshment of my mind; **kula had masiqta . . . ʿtlh̲ tlatma ušitin niahia** ATŠ II no. 65, 257 each *masiqta* . . . has 360 delights; **niaha ušalma bʿuhra d̲-nišimta azla** Gs 80:13, CP 82:5 = ML 101:8, ATŠ II no. 170 (there will be) bliss and peace on the road that the soul walketh.

niaza (rt. **NZZ**, analogy of **niaha**, but cf. P. نیاز) unsteadiness, insecurity, lack. **niaza umaskinuta** CP 484:2 lacking and poverty.

niaka 1 (rt. نكح, analogy of **niaha**) coupling, coition MSchr 150 n. 1. **tuhma uniaka dilkun** Gy 143:15 your lineage and coupling; **širša uniaka** Gy 202:3 stock and family-connexion.

niaka 2 (rt. **נכא**, ܢܟܐ, H. **נכא** & **נכה**, Ar. نكا & نكى, Eth. ንከየ, Sab. 𐩬𐩫𐩺, from Akk. *naku*; analogy of **niaha**) harm, pain, bane. **niaka hauibh̲** AM 166:15 there will be harm in it (i.e. in that house).

niana = **ʿniana**: **niana nirmulh̲** CP 433:9 they shall make him answer; **unirmulak niana** DC 3 and they will give thee response.

niara (rt. **ʿRA**) bowl. Var. **ʿniara** Lond. roll A 319. Often in rituals: Lond. roll A 321, 667 (for water), ibid. 328 (syn. with **kasa**), ibid. 563, 669, Oxf. roll f 506 (for grapes), Lond. roll A 519, Oxf. roll f 394 (the priest puts his hand in it), Oxf. roll f 163 f., 190, 195, 479 f., PD 1558, 1629 f., 1653 etc.

Gl. 142:14 **niara (& kasa)** كاس *calix* كاسه.

nibat (Ar. نبات) plants. **nibat d̲-dišta** DC 12. 394 wild plants.

niba (rt. **NBA II**) outflow, source, fountainhead: **niba d̲-hiia** ML 12:1, 64:3, 130:11, CP 10:13 fountainhead of life.

nibza (rt. **NBZ**, secondary from **BZA**) piece, portion, apportioned piece, hence: prayer appointed, part, set piece. Pl. **-ia. hazin buta nibza d̲-mambuga hu** 60:9, this prayer is the appointed prayer for the sacramental water; **nibzia d̲-pihta hinun** CP 60:2 = ML 76:3, DC 41. 454 the prayers appointed for the sacramental bread.

nibṭa (rt. **NBṬ**) offshoot, sprout, thrust-of-life, offspring. Masc. **nibṭa d̲-nbaṭ** s. **NBṬ** pe. pf.; **nbaṭ nibṭa qadmaia** s. **nbaṭ**; **uqra lnapšh̲ nibṭa** Gy 238:7 he created a sprout for himself; **nibṭa hu d̲-asgia btibil** Gy 242:ult. f. it is a sprout which came out of the earth; **nibṭa šuman** Gy 245:14 'Sprout' is our name Ginzā 246 n. 1; **nibṭa d̲-kbar baiar** Gy 344:3 sprout which grew up in the ether (cf. Gy 351:19) Ginzā 358 n. 1; **nibṭa kasia** Oxf. 30 b Mystic Sprout; **hzaith̲ lnibṭa** Oxf. 19 b I beheld an upsurging; **nibṭa taqna** Gs 43:10 a firm sprout; **umn nibṭa d̲-praš** ATŠ II no. 317 and some green-stuff which has (newly) come up. In DAb as a name of *Šamiš*.

nibṭat aina CP 409:9 name of a spirit.

nigba (metath. of ܢܶܓܒܳܐ) plant, shoot, sprout, offshoot. St. cstr. **ngab** MG 74:13 f. Pl. **-ia.** Masc. **nigbak dakia** Oxf. 79 b, 80 a, WedF 72:2 f. thy pure offspring; **lnigbia d̲-minaihun hun amarilun** Gy 317:8 f. I speak to the sprouts which came out of them; **nigbia nigbia** Gy 318:11 (*epizeuxis*); **nigbia kasiia** Gy 137:8 mystic sprouts; **naṣiruta unigbih̲** ATŠ II no. 57 (cf. 240) Naṣoraeism and its offshoots; **kma hauia nigbia d̲-nbaṭ minh̲** ATŠ II no. 310 how many were the offshoots which sprang from it; **d̲-alip alip hauin nigbh̲** ML 142:4 whose branches are a thousand thousand.

nigda (נִגְדָּא, ܢܶܓܕܳܐ) (*a*) drawing (up), (*b*) torment, beating, punishment, (*c*) rivulet, channel, overflow of water, (*d*) crying, weeping, (*e*) drawn (breath) MG 102:4. Pl. **-ia.** (*a*) **uʿl nigdia d̲-ʿkuria nihun** AM 219:17 and they will attack the temples (doubtf.); (*b*) **nigda bkulhun mdiniata nihuia** AM 221:18 there will be torment (punishment) in all the cities; (*c*) **nigda d̲-mia hiia** Gy 92:18, 269:10, 307:23, 308:3, 7, 13 stream of living water; **nigda d̲-mia** AM 181:19 overflow of water; **nigda umiṭra** AM 172:16 overflow and rain; (*d*) **nagdia nigda** Gs 53:13 they weep a long time (cf. **NGD** *idioms*); (*e*) **ʿu had nigda mistakar ʿuṣṭuna kulh̲ mithambal** ATŠ I no. 245 if one intake of breath is blocked, all the body is injured.

nidaba = nidaua. Var. **nadaba** (q.v.).

nidaua (Ar. نَدَاوَة) dew, wet, moisture. **aiba unidaua nupša nihuia** AM 258:34 there will be mist and much dew.

nidbai (Nöld. from H. נְדָבָה spontaneous offering MG xxix. 15 f., ZA xxx 156, MR 198, Lidzb. from the Phoen. deity נדבכ(ה) *Μάδβαχος* ZDMG lxi 691, Rosenthal: perh. the goddess of corn *Nid*(*z*)*aba*?? AF 243 n. 2) a water-uthra, one of the two guardian spirits of running water, usually mentioned with his companion **šilmai** (q.v.). **šilmai unidbai** Gy 127:19, **šilmai unidbai d̲-mšalṭia ʿl iardna** Gy 285:5; **mqaimana d̲-bauatai nidbai** CP 145:4 = Oxf. 2 a:middle.

nidra (rt. **NDR,** ܢܶܕܪܳܐ) vow. Var. **nadra** s.v. Pl. **-ia. nidrat nidria** Jb 119:8, **nadria nidria** Jb 139:9, var. **nidria nadran** s. **NDR**; **nidria uluṭata** Or. 331:9 (evil) vows and curses; **nidria ušalamata** DC 43 F 66, ibid. H 40, CP 199 m:24, DAb (cf. s. **nadra**).

niha, nʿha s.v. (pass. pt. pe. of **NUH,** נִיחָא, ܢܝܚܐ) mild, calm, peaceful, quiet, soft, friendly, gentle MG 63:20, 117:9. Pl. **-ia. niha mkabiš taqipa** Gy 7:2 the Mild One (who) treadeth down the strong ones; **šalia unihia iamamaihun** Gy 9:7 their seas are calm and quiet; **niha d̲-mirda . . . litbh̲** Gy 3:9 a mild one without restlessness . . .; **ʿutra niha umqaima** Gy 77:8 calm and consistent uthra, pl. **ʿutria nihia umqaimia** Gy 72:12; **nihia uqaiamin** Gy 261:24 they are calm and consistent; **mania iaqria ʿtitia nihia umšalmia** CP 244:ult. fair, predestinate, gentle and perfect *manas*, **ia mana niha anat** ATŠ II no. 116 O mana, thou art mild (kindly); **ia ahan ṭabia unihia** DC 50 O my good kind brethren; **niha bzauh̲** DC 50 submissive to her husband.

nihaiit (adv. from preced., ܢܝܚܐܝܬ) kindly, softly, gently MG 201:6 f. Var. **n(a)haiit. bnihaiit** Q 46 b, 72:11 softly; **bnihaiit uṣilaiit** Lond. roll A 84, 90 quietly and attentively; **bṣilaiit unihaiit** DC 41:403 attentively and quietly; **unihaiit azil ʿl arqa ʿl anašath̲ mqašia** AM 88:1 and though he walks softly on the ground he is hard on his family.

nihga (rt. **NHG I** metath. of נגה, cf. Jew.-Aram. נָגְהֵי, Syr. ܢܓܗܐ) break of day, dawn, (day)-light MG 102:13. **bnihga** (*often*) at dawn, at daybreak; **dahna bnihga** Gy 263:14, 273:13 cometh out at dawn; **mšaba nihga** Q 53:13 praised be the daylight; **iamina nihga ʿlauaikun hu** DC 27. 113 the right hand is the light above you (refers to the placing of the hands when holding the banner as a symbol of the light); **nihga hšuka bgauaihun laiit** ATŠ I no. 17 daylight, there is no darkness in them; **iumia d̲-nihga hšuka litlh̲** ATŠ II no. 14 days of light without darkness; **iumia d̲-nihga hinun litbin** [*sic*] **hasir ubṣir** ATŠ II no. 13 days of light, there is no lacking nor deficiency in them; **d̲-nihga bgauh̲ laiit** DC 27 should no light be in it.

nihušta (rt. **NHŠ**) whispered or muttered prayer. Varr. **nhušta, nihišta** s.vv. **tarmidia nihušta lh(u)da nimrun** Lond. roll A 164 the priests say (each) singly the whispered formula; **ukd̲ amritun nihušta** DC 27. 170 and when ye say the whispered formula.

nihuta (abstr. noun from **niha,** נִיחוּתָא, ܢܝܚܘܬܐ) mildness, gentleness, kind(li)ness, affection, calm, repose, rest, serenity, bliss, placidity, peacefulness, peace of mind; **kinuta unihuta, umkikuta** Gy 21:21 righteousness, kindliness and humbleness; **nihuta d̲-mriduta litbh̲** Gy 7:17, 358:12 calm in which there is no disturbance; **nihuta d̲-lamriduta** HG calm without disturbance; **nihuta d̲-ṭabia** Gs 16:20, 18:20, Jb 267:1 the serenity of the righteous; **niaha unihuta** AM 229:7 ease and repose; **nihutai dilia tišria ʿlauaikun** DC 48. 209 may my peace rest upon you; **ṭubh̲ lman d̲-bnihuta basgia** DC 34. 216 well is it for him who walks in kindliness; **nišimta bnihuta masgia** DC 34. 755 the soul walketh in serenity; **bṣiluta unihuta ubihruta** DC 27. 509 with heed, serenity, and brightness; **baba umama . . . ʿšumia urazia d̲-nihuta hinun** ATŠ I no. 246 'Papa' and 'Mamma' (etc.) . . . are names and intimations (lit. secrets, symbols) of affection.

nihiqa (rt. **HUQ III,** or. נְהַק) groaning. **nihiqa uṣilita** DC 46 groaning and neuralgic pain (in head?).

nihmat st. cstr. of **nhimta 2**: **nihmat hiia šuman** Gy 245:16 our name is Renewal-of-Life. Lidzb. thought of **nhimta 1** and was, accordingly, puzzled by the expression Ginzā 246 n. 4.

nihra = nahra? river? **ubhiuaniata d̲-arba ligria ubnihra ubarqa zaina tibad** AM and causes loss amongst quadrupeds, in the river (?) and on land.

nihtia st. emph. fem. of **niha**? **uialpa zaina d̲-gubria hauia uzban zban nihtia** AM 68:19 she will be skilled in manly arms (?) but sometimes she will be peaceful (?).

niula 1 (נַוְלָא, ܢܘܠܐ, Ar. loan-w. نَوْل Fränkel 94, cf. Zimmern: *Akk. Fremdw.* 42) loom. **pagitbh̲ bniula d̲-arba šapirata** JRAS 1937 594:26 I met her at the loom of four beautiful women.

niula 2, nʿula (rt. נול, a doublet of **nala 2**) disgrace, pain, torment, noxious fiend, hobgoblin MG 126:11, Furlani: *I Nomi* 423. Pl. **-ia. nalia uniulia & nalia unʿulia** s. **nala 2**; **nʿula asibth̲ lnapša** (var. **lnapšai**) Gy 95:19 I have brought disgrace on myself, **nʿulia** (pl.) **asibtẖ lnapšai** Gy 96:23 (Ginzā 101 n. 2); **uniulaihun bsimadria** Gy 106:17 and their hobgoblins (became) buffoons; **nʿulaihun bṭabaiia** Gy 107:3 f. and their hobgoblins (became) cooks; **zhun minai niula rba qašiša usahria** DC 44. 161 f. the great cruel hobgoblin and the demons fled away from me.

nizia (rt. **NZZ**) pl. chidings, rebukes. **upugdamia unizia malpilẖ aqimlẖ** ATŠ II no. 419 and heaped upon him commands and chidings, instructing him.

niṭubta Gy 234:19, DC 27. 130 = **niṭupta.** Pl. **niṭubiata** Jb 40:1, **niṭbiata** Gy 315:3, **niṭibiata** Lond. roll A 76, MG 48:11.

niṭupta (נִיטוּפְתָּא, ܢܘܛܦܬܐ, Ar. نُطْفَة) orig. drop, sperm, used as an honourable term for women and esp. heavenly consorts MG 119:7, Lidzb. OSt 538 f., CP trs. 37 n. 1, Jb ii 227:20, Ginzā 149:24, 155 n. 4, Siouffi 40:36, Brandt: ERE viii 382, MR 22, 29 f., MSchr. 147 n. 1, MMII 95. 246, Wellhausen: *Reste d. ar. Heidentums*, 2nd ed., p. 165 n. 6. Pl. Var. **niṭubta** s.v. Pl. **-iata** MG 48:11, 169: 11, 7; **niṭupta rabtia** Gy 140:20, 141:2, 152:5, Q 25:5, 34:32; **niṭupta rabtia kasita** Gy 234:19, CP 54:4; **kanat niṭupta** s. **kanat**; **mana udmutẖ luat niṭupta ailun** Gy 152:16 f. the *Mana* and his counterpart brought me before the *Niṭufta*; **uhʿ niṭupta lkisia ḏ-napšẖ aiiltan** Gy 152:18 and she, the *Niṭufta*, brought me into her own seclusion; **uamra hʿ niṭupta** Gy 158:22 and she, the *N*., said (hist. pres.); **mn luatẖ ḏ-niṭupta uluat ab asgit** Gy 153:2; **niṭupta ḏ-luatẖ iatba** Gy 305:25 (cf. l. 5); **uniṭupta bgauẖ iatba** Gy 374:6; **niṭupta** = **ruha** RD 7; **bniṭupiata halin ḏ-ʿlauak ʿdikrit** Gy 152:23 by these *Niṭuftas* which I mentioned above thee; **niṭupiata ḏ-hizuia lziuẖ** CP 206:4 f = ML 238 the (celestial) ladies that saw his radiance; **balma ḏ-niṭupta iatib** ATŠ II no. 81 he remains in the world of the Drop; **mamlilia . . . bniṭupiatun** CP 252: 6 ff. (var. **bnuṭpiatun** DC 38 = ŠQ 22:6) they speak . . . with their sage words.

n(i)kusta, n(i)kista (rt. **NKS**) slaughter, sacrifice. **iuma ḏ-nikusta** Jb 90:13 (varr. **nikista** E & DC 30, **nkusta** AC) the day of slaughter; **riša ḏ-nikusta** ATŠ II no. 45 the beginning of slaughter; **nkusta ḏ-babia trisar** RD C 11 the sacrifice of the twelve gates (: pagan religions); **nkista ḏ-trisar babia** ATŠ II no. 410; **nkusta ḏ-ʿmbaria** RD B 104 slaughter of sheep.

nikutiata (rt. **NKT**) pl. bites, wounds, injuries. **ldaluiia kulhun nikutiata** DC 51. 354 f. to relieve all wounds.

nikista s. **nikusta.**

nikla (נִיכְלָא, ܢܟܠܐ) guile, perfidy, cunning, deceit, intrigue, stratagem. Var. **nʿkla** MG 5:17. Pl. **-ia. nikla bzauaiun naklia** RD C 12 = DAb par. they practise deceit on their husbands; **mn rahmaikun bnikla latiqmun** Gy 20:1 f. practise not treachery on your friends; **mn habraikun bnikla latisgun** Gy 41: 13 practise not treachery on your neighbours; **ʿnikla bmalka nibdun** AM they will intrigue against the king; **bkadba unikla aklilia** CP 375:7 they ate me (: the sacramental bread speaking) deceitfully and perfidiously; **nikla ḏ-šibiahia** ATŠ II no. 181 the guile of the planets; **lanaklit niklia ʿlẖ** PA's ŠQ do not falsify it by guileful tricks.

nimar = **namar** (q.v.) leopard, panther. St. emph. **nimria** s.v. **ʿsir . . . nimar bšušlata uaria biša bsinduarta** DC 37. 575 ff. tied up is . . . the leopard by chains, and the fierce lion in his cage.

nimuia (coll. Ar. *nīmu*, P. لِيمُو) DC 35 lemon, lemon-tree.

nimusa (נִימוֹס, ܢܡܘܣܐ Ar. ناموس, all from Gr. *νόμος* Fränkel 278) (*a*) (Jewish) law, religious law, (*b*) system, order, constitution, established or traditional custom, regularity, behaviour, conduct, way of life (sometimes confused with *νοῦς*?), (*c*) false religion. Ginzā 248 n. 3, MSt. 128. Var. **namusa** s.v. Pl. **-ia.** (*a*) **miša nbiha ḏ-ruha ḏ-aitilun nimusa** Gy 46:6 Moses, the prophet of Ruha, who brought them the Law; **ʿl nimusia ḏ-bnia anaša** Gy 243:2 according to the laws of the sons of men; **alma ḏ-nimusa** Gy 245:15 the world of the Law (doubtf. Ginzā 246 n. 2); **halin pugdamia ḏ-nimusa** Gy 247:24 these orders of the Law (? might belong under (*b*), cf. Gy 248:4 ff. ibid.); **miriai silitẖ lnimusa.** Cp. 173:13 M. rejected the (Jewish) Law; (*b*) **pagra unimusa** Oxf. roll g 174 = DC 43 J 80 the body and its (?) constitution; **mn qbal ḏ-nimusa badam npalbẖ adam ʿkilta lakal** Gy 248:4 f. before a regular system began in Adam, A. ate no food; **abatar ḏ-nimusa npalbẖ badam qam adam ʿkilta akal** Gy 248:5 f. after order was established in A., A. stood up and ate food; **ḏ-rihaiun basim lnimusa ḏ-npal badam** Gy 248:8 whose odour is pleasing to the sense which fell into A.; **unibsum ʿlh uʿl nimusa ḏ-rmabẖ badam** Gy 248:9 and pleaseth him and the sense which he cast into A.; **unimusa ṭaba bgauẖ hdar** ATŠ I no. 246 and good order (system) circulates in it; **ʿu tihṭibẖ bhazin nimusa ḏ-iahia bihram . . .** DC 37. 83 f. if thou injurest this constitution (behaviour) of Y. B. . . .; **libat . . . bpagrẖ ḏ-nimusẖ ḏ-iahia bihram . . . latihṭai** DC 37. 293 Venus . . . do not offend . . . the body of Y. B. that is his habits; **nimusa mn arba razia ʿṣṭarar** DC 37 the system is constituted by four mysteries; **ubinianẖ bnimusa nilgaṭ** DC 48. 434 and its structure is held by a system; **ruiana unimusa** DC 46 (love-charm) mind and habit; **kul nimusa ḏ-ʿṣṭuna ḏ-pagra** DC 51. 136 all the constitution of the physical body; **ʿl nimusa** DC 48. 174 according to custom; (*c*) **dara ḏ-nimusa arbaia** HG the age of the Arab religion; **prikia upatikria unimusia** Oxf. roll g 1004 = DC 48 par. idols and false gods and false systems (religious laws); **ḏ-busmania rurbia ʿl nimusa ramin** DC 48. 174 who cast down powerful perfumes according to a pagan religious law (or for **nimrus** Ruha?).

nimrus s. **namrus.**

nimria pl. (cf. s. **namar** = **nimar**) leopards, panthers, cheetahs. **nimria harmia** Jb 243:2,

245:1 wild leopards; **šubima ušubin alpia nimria** DAb seven hundred and seventy thousand (hunting) cheetahs.

-nin 1 acc. suff. of the 3rd p. pl. fem. (cf. s. -inhin).

-nin 2 encl. pers. pron. of the 1st p. pl. MG 224:15 ff.

ninupar (P. نيلوفر, نينوفر) AM 130:paen. nenuphar, water-lily.

ninia (נִינְיָא, ܢܢܝܐ Löw 259 ff., Akk. *nīnu*) mint. **ʿšta** ࡀ**ariq ninia** DC 46. 8:antepenult. drink a distillation of mint.

nisan (H. & Aram. נִיסָן, Syr. ܢܝܣܢ, Ar. نيسان, Bab. *nisannu*) month under the rule of Aries, colloquially *aχir setwa* 'the last winter-month' SsSs ii 23, MMII 84.

niska (cf. נִסְכָּא, H. נֶסֶךְ or נֵסֶךְ) (*a*) a measure (of dust), (*b*) earth, land, ground, country, (*c*) precipitation, fall. All three doubtf., Ginzā 83 n. 3. Pl. **-ia.** Masc. (*a*) **trisar niskia apra** Gy 83:6 = **trisar niskia aqpra** Gy 380:3, **trisar niskia** HG.; (*b*) **mn ʿlauia dina uniska d̲-alma** DC 51. 703; **umn ʿlauia niska niska** DC 51. 41; (*c*) **mn kudrh̲ uniskh̲ pqa piqa barqa d̲-nhaša** Gy 160:11 f. from his weight and his fall, a fissure was rent in the copper-earth.

nisra (rt. **NSR**) tearing. **qitiak unisrak** DC 43 J 155 thy sobbing and rending (garments).

niputa (rt. **NPA**, for ܢܦܘܚܬܐ) blowing up, respiration, breathing; respiratory organ; pneuma. **uniputa asiq lnapših̲ . . . d̲-hʿ niputa d̲-nuna ʿudna hʿ** ATŠ I no. 243 her pneuma raised itself . . ., for the respiratory organ (gills) of a fish is its ear.

nipṣa = **napṣa** (q.v.). Pl. **nipṣia** Gy 231:5, DC.

nipqa (rt. **NPQ**) going-forth, departure. **nipqa nipqit** DC 44. 349 I came out.

nipqat mn gu mia Gy 374:12 ('She-issued-from-within-the-Waters') name of a female life-spirit.

niṣba (rt. **NṢB**, נִצְבָּא) planting, plantation, creation. **gupna d̲-ʿlak dilak niṣbak** DC 26. 474 a vine which is thine, thy planting.

niṣ(u)bta, niṣibta (rt. **NṢB**, ܢܨܒܬܐ) (im)-planting, plant(ation), propagation, (re)production, fertilization, (pro)creation, young growth; fig. wife, bride CP trs. 135 n. 2, ATŠ trs. 18 n. 11., MG 13:ult. f., 26:21, 103:7 f. With suff. **niṣbtun** their plant(ation) MG 181:5; **nṣiba niṣibtak, lminṣab niṣubta, nṣab niṣubta, niṣbit d̲-rbia niṣibta, niṣubta bgauh̲ mitniṣba, naṣib niṣubta, naṣbilun niṣubta, niṣubta . . . ʿtinṣib** s. **NṢB** (about fig. use cf. idioms); **tana uniṣubta d̲-hšuka** Gy 149:12; **br niṣubtun d̲-hiia rbia** Oxf. 3 a; **ʿsqta ath̲ šrabh̲ lniṣubta bhiṣrh̲** PA's ŠQ he brought a ring and set it on the little finger of the bride; **iatbat uaprašath̲ lniṣubth̲** CP 413:14 (no. 386) it remained and sent forth its suckers; **niṣubtak d̲-bhiia sahdin** CP 423:10 f. thy family (pl. is implied) who testify to Life; **niṣubta qadmaita** (personified) CP 421:9 The First Planting; **nṣab niṣubta** ATŠ I no. 25 and took a Spouse.

niṣrat mdinta Gy 56:16, PD 1028, HG 14 the city of Nazareth.

niq(u)ba (rt. **NQB**) hole, stone bored with a hole. **niqba rba d̲-glala** DC 51. 371; **unisbik ṣarṭana ʿl niqubh̲** JRAS 1937 593:18 and the crab shall take thee to its hole.

niqubta = **nuq(u)bta. lraz niqubta** ATŠ I no. 53 (var. **nuqbata** PD par.) the Mystery of the Female.

niqia (Bab. *niqū*) Gy 124:23 offerings ?, var. **naqia** CD would be a pt. sacrificers ? Ginzā 141 n. 1.

nira (נִירָא, ܢܝܪܐ Akk. *nīru*, Ar. loan-w. نير, cf. Nöld. GGA 1868 pp. 3, 44) yoke, servitude. **zim kd̲ taura bnira** DC 46 held back like a bull by the yoke; **ualgiṭlh̲ nira** DAb and fasten a yoke upon him; **usmikh̲ lnira kadra** DC 48. 135 f. and he bore a heavy yoke.

nirba 1 (ܢܪܒܐ < Akk. *nēribu*; Ar. النيرب, *Νήραβος* a place-name MG 135 n. 2) crag, mountain peak MG 135:11. **nirba rba d̲-glala** CP 21:9 = ML 23:8 a great rocky crag.

nirba 2 some kind of hard metal. **parzla uanka unirba uaplanza** DC 43 J 172; **gauaza rba d̲-nirba** DC 40. 467; **ʿsir pumia bkisia** (read **bkasia**?) **d̲-nirba** DC 40. 1080.

nirig, nʿrig (< Bab. *Nirgallu* KAT 412 ff., Phoen., H. נֵרְגַל as name of a local god) the planet Mars, identified with Muḥammad and regarded as a symbol of the Arabs SsSs ii 160, MR 162 f., Jb ii 50 n. 4, Ginzā 223:10 ff., HpGn Ind. s. Mars & Nergal, MSt 34 ff. Used only in st. abs. as a pr. n. MG 300: bottom. **ušubaia nirig** Gy 27:21 and the seventh is Mars; **daiuia d̲-bit nirig** Gy 28:12 the demons of the House of Mars; **daiuia d̲-nirig** Gy 59:19; **nirig aitia anapuqia** Gy 106:13 s. **anap(u)qa; lnirig plaglh̲ zaina lmibad qraba** Gy 112:14 to Mars they allotted arms to wage war; **lnirig bgurza mhaith̲** Gy 119:3 I smote Mars with a club; **baba d̲-qra nirig** Gy 121:23, 122:9 the sect which Mars created; **ulnbu unirig** Gy 171:22 f. and to Mercury and Mars; **humria d̲-nirig** Gy 225:7 the amulet-spirits of Mars; **nʿrig d̲-mitqria abdala arbaia** Gy 231:22 Mars who is called Abdallah the Arab (the name being used for Muḥammad); **kul ium hʿ ruha lqraba napqa uminh̲ d̲-nirig** Gy 233:2 f. (cf. 230:12) Ruha daily goeth to war and wageth it with Mars; **nirig amarlun d̲-laiit alaha d̲-minai dilia iaqir ugabir hu** Gy 230:6 Mars speaketh to them: 'There is no god more distinguished and stronger than I'; **kursia d̲-nirig zidana** Gy 301:21, 302:3 the throne of the furious Mars; **nirig zidana** RD 21; **šitin utša abihdia nirig** Gy 379:11 (the rule of Bel) 69(000 years) together with Mars; **maṭarta d̲-nirig** RD 37, RD C 14, 20 the purgatory of Mars; **dinba d̲-dara d̲-nirig** Jb 45:6, PD 1746 the end of the age of Mars (i.e. of Moslem supremacy); **nirig br bil alaha** Morg. 268/27:38 Mars, son of the god Bel (Jupiter); **nirig maria zaina uqraba** WedF 39:bottom, CP 225:2 Mars the lord of arms and war; **nirig maria haila**

uzaina Oxf. roll g 574, 933 Mars the lord of army and arms.

nirqmia DC 22. 101 = **narqmia.**

nišabur AM 198 Nishapur, a town in the province of Khurasan BZ Ap. II.

nišad Ṣâb.'s AM var. of **našd.**

nišan (P. نشان , نشانه) sign, portent, (birth)-mark. Pl. **nišania** also as sg. An older doublet **nišanqa** s.v. Both masc. **nišan d̲-hauia biahra d̲-aiar** AM 266:11 the sign (portent) that occurs in the month of Ayar; **unišania d̲-ata mn ʿmh̲ hauia** AM 5:20 and there will be marks (or a mark, birthmark?) coming from his mother; **nišania d̲-ata lhandamh̲ ʿu lʿdh̲ haulh̲** AM 40:15 he will have marks appearing on his limb(s) or on his hand(s); **tum nišania hazin hauia** Gy 398:10 then there shall be this portent. But **nišania** Gy 390:5, 391:24 seems to be an impf. of **ŠNA** 'shall (be) change(d)' Ginzā 416 n. 4.

Gl. 87:2 **nšana** [sic] رسم *vestigium* نشان; 121:12 id. علامه *signum* نشان; 123:3 **nšanai** [sic, miswritten pl.] علامات *signa* نشانها.

nišanqa (Middle P. form of preced.) sign, portent MG xxxi 12. Pl. **-ia.** Masc. as preced. **mhauin nišanqia d̲-haimanuta** Gy 218:19 they display signs of faith; **umhauia nišanqia haimanuta** ATŠ I no. 111 and he displays signs of faith; **nišanqia uatuata** Gy 221:5 signs and portents; **atuata unišanqia** AM 228:2 id.; **nišanqa d̲-napiq mn tibil** ATŠ I no. 10 = PD par. a sign that he will depart from the earth; **mhauia šamiš nišanqia** Gy 384:12 the sun was showing portents; **mindia mindia nišanqia nihaun** Gy 384:22 they will show all kinds of signs; **batar atar nišanqia nihun** Gy 385:21 in different places there will be portents.

nišasra AM 287:32 for **nušadir**?

nišara = **nšara** (q.v.).

nišum (Ar. نَجَّام) AM 155 astrologer.

nišuqta (rt. **NŠQ**) = **nušaqta.** Pl. **nišuqiata** DC 41:124.

nišṭa (rt. **NŠṬ**) AM 243:5 flaying, a cattle-disease?

nišṭiaiil DC 40. 819 theophorous name from preced.

nišibta Morg. 247/82:paen. for **nišmita.**

nišimta (נִשְׁמְתָא, ܢܶܫܡܬܳܐ, H. נְשָׁמָה) soul MG 109:16, MR 73 ff. St. emph. fem., but st. abs. **nišma** masc. MG. 307:20 f. (cf. 156 footn.). St. cstr. **nišmat.** Pl. **nišmata** MG 162:antep. With suff.: **nišmat,** more usual **nišimtai** my soul MG 175:24 f., **nišimtak** thy soul MG 177:5, **nišimth̲** his, her soul MG 178:2; pl. with suff. **nišmatai** my souls MG 176:19, **nišmatak** thy souls MG 177:5, **nišmatkun** your souls MG 179:18, but **nišmatakun** Q 56b:12 id. MG 179:ult.; **nišma gzira lika** Gy 66:10 the soul shall not be condemned; **sidra d̲-nišmata** The Book of Souls (title of book of baptismal prayers) CP trs. 229 n. 4 (Siouffi 68); **ulnišmata mašqilun** Gy 228:13 and they give it to souls to drink; **unihun ʿkilta lnišmata** Gy 339:9 f. and they will serve as food to the souls; **nišmata d̲-nasba rihaiun** Gy 393:9 the souls which breathe their smell; **nišmata d̲-ahia ṭabia . . . unišmata** (var. **nišman** DC 22) **d̲-gubria kšiṭia** Gy 313:19 f. the souls of our good brethren . . . and the souls of righteous men; **tangara d̲-nišmata** Gy 172:17 merchant of souls Ginzā 176 n. 7; **nišmata d̲-babia trisar** RD 37 = Dab par. the souls of the twelve gates (: false religions); **nišmata d̲-hudaiia** RD C 22 the souls of the Jews; **nišmata d̲-hirdubaiia** RD C 23; **nišmata d̲-mšiha** RD C 20; **hazin nišma d̲-manu** Gs 114:10, 18 whose soul is this? MG 307:17; **ada nišma** Gy 114:14 the soul passed; **azil nišma** Gy 114:16 the soul goeth; **nišma sliq lbit hiia** Gs 114:25 the soul raised to the House-of-Life; **nišmat hiia** (*often*) the living soul; **nišmat ṣabia** Jb 91:12, CP 29:4 = ML 34:5 my soul desires (= I desire).

Gl. 168:11 defectively (**nšmta**) نفس *anima.*

nišma s. **nišimta.**

nišqušata, niqušiata DC 46 kisses.

nišra 1 (נִשְׁרָא, ܢܶܫܪܳܐ, Bibl.-Aram. נְשַׁר, H. נֶשֶׁר, Akk. *našru,* Ar. نَسْر, Eth. ንስር) eagle, falcon. Masc. **nišra hiuara** Jb 133:7, 262:4, Gy 332:16 the white eagle (a designation of higher beings: Hibil-Ziwa, Anuš-Uthra Ginzā 342 n. 1); **uailik ʿurašlam mata d̲-nišra lgauik sliq** Gy 332:20 woe to thee Jerusalem, city in which an eagle rose; **gapa d̲-nišra** (see **gapa**) an eagle's wing; **nišra uiauna** ATŠ no. ? falcon and dove.

nišra 2 = **našira. nišra abdia unišra ugaṭla aklia** Sh. 'Abd.'s copy's var. of Gy 230:23 v.s. **našira**; **hu nišra d̲-hu ṣaiid lanibad** AM 193:14 he shall not go a-hawking which is hunting.

nišra 3, var. **nišara** s. **nšara.**

nitra (rt. **NTR**) crumbs, particles left of sacramental food. Pl. **-ia. nitra d̲-natar** Jb 150:2, CP 376:8 = ZDMG cv 147b:28 the crumbs which drop.

NKA I rt. of **niaka 1** (q.v.).

NKA II rt. of **niaka 2** (q.v.).

nkan = **ʿnkan. nkan kiuan baria** AM 280:31 should Saturn be in Leo.

nkasa for **nakasa. nkasa d̲-nišma** DAb = **nkasa d̲-nišmata** RD 115 slaughterer of the soul(s).

-nkun s. **-inkun.**

nkusta s. **nikusta.**

nkila (pass. pt. pe. of **NKL**) deceitful, crafty. Pl. **-ia. ʿuṣra nkila d̲-kadba** Gy 81:4 her (: Ruha's) mind is crafty (and) deceitful; **biša hu unkila** AM 121:17 he is evil and crafty; **qupat nkilia** Gy 97:21 the basket of the crafty ones Ginzā 103 n. 7; **hazin alma nkila** Jb 183:15 this treacherous world.

nkista Gy 113:5, 124:21 etc. = **nikusta.**

NKL (Aram. & H. נכל, Syr. ܢܟܠ, Akk. *nakālu*, Sab., Amh. Nöld. ZDMG xl 726, Ar. نكل to abstain, punish) to deceive, cheat, betray, act guilefully, beguile, defraud, intrigue.

Pe. Pf. with suff. **niklh̲** he deceived him, **ʿnkalinan** Gs 128:20 BC (var. **ʿnkilinan** A) it beguiled us MG 279:25; **nkaltinan** Gs 128:21 it (fem.) beguiled us MG 280:5; **alma nkalinun unkaltinun alahuta d̲-bh̲** Gy 369:6 the world deceived them and beguiled them the (false) gods which are therein (MG 282:18). Act. pt. **man nakil zauh̲** Gy 22:13 who deceiveth his wife; fem. **ruha nikla naklabh̲** Gy 170:3 f. R. invented (hist. pres.) a stratagem against him; pl. **ʿnšia d̲-nikla bzauaihun naklia** [*sic*] DAb (cf. RD C 12) women that practise deceit on their husbands; **d̲-zauaiun naklia** [*sic*] **nikla ʿlauaiun** DC 34. 1216 whose wives practise deceit on them. Pass. pt. **nkila** s.v.

Pa. Act. pt. fem. st. emph. **mnakalta** s.v.

Der.: **nikla, nkila, mnakalta, makla.**

NKS (Gen. Aram., Akk. *nakāsu* Zimmern: *Akk. Fremdw.* 66; cf. Fränkel 98) to slaughter, cut the throat, slay.

Pe. Pf. **uhu nkas ʿl ahh̲ d̲-abuia** DC 36 and he slew his uncle; with encl. **bhirba nkasinun** Jb 16:23 he slew them with the sword. Impf. **latiniksun** ATŠ II no. 16 do not slaughter; with suff. **bsikinia d̲-parzla niniksih̲** DC 44. 561, 1005 we will slaughter him with iron knives. Impt. **nkus** Gy 18:5, 68:5 slaughter MG 240:7. Act. pt. **nakis** DAb he slaughters; pl. **naksia anqia** Gs 30:21 they slaughter sheep; **lanaksia ʿnkusta** Gy 6:4 they make no slaughtering. Inf. **lminkas ʿnkusta** ATŠ I no. 81 (var. **nukusta** PD 852) at slaughtering a victim; with suff. **ptahil qiriak uhibil ziua paqid ʿlak miniksak** DC 41. 193 etc. Ptahil created thee and H.-Z. ordereth thy slaughter(ing) (ritual slaughterer's formula).

Gl. 180:13 f. missp. ذبح *occidere, immolare* گلو برید.

Der.: **nakasa** (var. **nkasa**), **n(u)kusta** (varr. **n(i)kista, ʿnkusta, ʿnkista**).

NKR (Gen. Sem.) to estrange, remove, place at a distance, alienate. Secondary rt. **NKRA** s.v.

Pa. Pt. **ʿu sin mnakar** AM 32:11 if the moon is absent (i.e. if there is no moon), **umnakar ʿuṣria kulhun** CP 280:7 = ML 263:4 and sublimateth all minds (cf. n. 2; var. **mnakai** CDE for **mnakrai**?, rt. **NKRA**?). Other forms s. **NKRA.**

Pau̯el (by the influence of **nukraia**). Pf. **naukrit napšai minh̲ mn alma** CP 190:4 = Oxf. 52 a = ML 224:6 I estranged myself from the world. Pt. **d-mnaukar napših̲** CP 192:10 = Oxf. 55 a = ML 227:1 who estrangeth himself MG 85:12.

Der.: **nukraia** (fem. **-aita**, pl. masc. **-aiia**).

NKRA (den. from **nukraia**) = **NKR** MG 84:17.

Pa. Pf. with suff. **nakrian minh̲ mn alma** Gs. 93:13 he estranged me from the world. Impf. **ninakrun napšaihun mn alma d̲-hšuka** Gy 240:11 they keep themselves far from the world of darkness. Act. pt. **mnakria** Gy 278:11, Jb 79:7 estranging MG 84:17, 266:21; pl. **badin umnakrin mn sidria kulhun** ATŠ II 423 they separate and remove from (him) all the books; **uiadin umnakrin mn sidria kulhun** DC 34. 1022 they know and remove (from him) all the books (in the novice's examination). Pass. pt. **mnakrai** Gs 21:21 estranged MG 84:18, 131:17, 266:23; pl. **d̲-šanin umnakrin mn alma** Gy 321:1 which are wonderful and alien to the world; fem. pl. **mnakria** Gy 342:24, MG 266:23.

Ethpa. Pf. **ulhašabta bišta mn ruha unišimta ʿtnakria** ATŠ II no. 144 and evil thought became estranged from the spirit and the soul; **ʿtnakrit minaihun mn bišia** Gs 130:13 I have become estranged from the evil ones (**ʿtnakritun** ye have become estranged, Nöld.'s reading of Gs 130:13, MG 266:25). Impf. **šutak titnakria mn almia** CP 452:7 thy talk is alien to (: transcends) the worlds. Impt. pl. **ʿtnakrun** Gy 18:22 estrange yourselves MG 266:25.

Gl. 66:3 f. **NKRA** جحد *spernere, negare* انکار کرد; 166:5 f. id. نکار *negare* انکار کرد.

NKŠ (נכש, ܢܟܫ) to bite, sting.

Gl. 111:3 f. cf. defectively (**anḳš**) *perforare, pungere* گزید.

NKT (נכת, ܢܟܬ, Ar. نكث, H. נשך, mod. H. נָכַשׁ, Akk. *našāku*, Eth. ነከሰ, but መንከስ jaw, rel. to **NKŠ**) to bite, sting, peck, wound.

Pe. Pf. with encl. **man nkitlh̲ aria** AM 121:18 whom a lion has bitten; with suff. **ʿu hauia ʿniš d̲-nikth̲ kalba ʿu hizura** ATŠ I no. 75 should there be one whom a dog or (wild) pig has bitten. Impf. with suff. **ninikth̲** AM 21:3 will bite him; **hiuta d̲-arbia ligria tiniktih̲** AM 16:7 a four-legged animal will bite him. Act. pt. **d̲-ʿniš nakit ʿdh̲** DC 46. 65:10 so that a person bites his hand; fem. **arqba nakta** DC 40. 1087 stinging scorpion; fem. pl. **naktan ʿdaihun** DC 46. 89:5 they bite their hands. Inf. **mikat** DC 23. 550 (but accord. to l. 589 a mere miscop. of **mikal**).

Pa. Pt. with encl. **mnaktilin** RD E 31 = DAb par. they bite them (: the souls); **unandala mnaktalik uauaza mnaktalik** (PA's *Qmaha* for Evil Eye) and the centipede stings thee and the goose pecks thee.

Der.: **nikutiata.**

NMBA (Akk. pi. *numbu*, pt. *munambu* KAT 590) to wail for the dead, mourn. MG 266:19 ff. & n. 1.

Pa. Impf. with suff. **ninambi(i)h̲** Gs 92:13 we mourn him. Pt. pl. **mnambin** Gy 212:11, fem. **mnambian** Gy 212:10, 12 they are wailing. Impt. **nambia** Gy 212:13 wail!; **latinambia** DC 46 wail not!

Ethpa. Pt. pl. (fem.) **mitnambia** Jb 122:13 they wail, mourn.

Der.: **namb(a)iata, nambia, numbia.**

NNGL s. **NGL.**

NNGR s. pa. & ethpa. of **NGR** (I).

NNDA s. **NDA.**

NSA I (נַסִּי, ܢܰܣܺܝ, H. נסה pi., Eth. der. መንሱት temptation) to test, try, attempt, examine, make trial.

Pa. Pt. **mnasia hailh̲** Gy 79:8 testing its strength (Ginzā 78 n. 1). Inf. **nasuiia** Gy 60:18, 366:19, ATŠ I no. 242, DC 44:1331 to try, examine MG 263:11.

Af. Imp. with suff. **nasunẖ lqudamai** DC 22:231 let them test him in my presence.
Der.: **nasiata.**

NSA II (Jew.-Aram. der. נְסַחָא copy, Syr. ܢܣܚ, Ar. نسخ, Akk. *nasāḫu*, H. נסח, Old Aram. id. to tear out), to copy (out).

Af. Pf. **ansa lnapšẖ** (*often in colophons*) he copied for himself, **ansit lnapšai** (*often in colophons*) I copied for myself, **ansit mn ansata dilia** ATŠ (colophon). I copied from my own copy.
Der.: **ansata, mansa.**

nsaka occ. var. of **nasaka 2.**

NSB (נְסַב, ܢܣܒ, Ar. نَسَبَ to attribute, ascribe, نَشَبَ to adhere) to take (away), take up, assume. Sometimes confused with **NṢB** MG 45 n. 1.

Pe. Pf. **nsib** and **nsab** he took MG 14:4, 218:21, **nsabt** and **nsibt** thou hast taken MG 222:24; **kušṭa nisbit minaihun** Gy 72:20, 92:6 I received the pact from Him (i.e. from the Life Ginzā 95 n. 4); with suff. **nisban** he took me MG 270:19, **nisbẖ** he took him MG 275:1, **nisbu** they took her MG 279:10, **nsabtinun** Gy 354:21 she took them MG 282:17, id. Gy 346:15 f. (var. **ansabtinun** l. 15A MG 25:19 f.) thou hast taken them MG 282:22, **nsabtinᶜn** Gy 83:24 I took them (fem.) MG 282:23, **nsabtun** Gs 97:5 ye took me MG 272:9. Impf. **nisab** and **ninsab, ninsib** he takes, will take MG 220:5, 238:18, 239:1; **hanatẖ nišimta d̲-hazin raza tisab** ATŠ II no. 141 that soul which assumes this mystery; **ᶜsab** I take MG 51:6, **tisbun** (*often*) = **tinisbun** Gy 20:9, 38:14 ye (will) take, assume MG 239:7, 8; with suff. **ninisbẖ** he takes, will take him (or her) MG 275:27, **tis(i)bẖ** Gs 45:3, 4, 5 thou takest her MG 275:25, **ᶜsibẖ** Gs 4:24 I take her MG 275:26, **ninisbunẖ** Gy 311:4 (var. **nisbunẖ**) they take him MG 278:10; **kd̲ baiin d̲-ninisbin** DC 34. 551 when they wish to take me away; **ulatinsibunẖ muma bᶜuṣṭlaikun** ATŠ II no. 364 bring no spot upon your vestments. Impt. **sab, nsab,** MG 220:6, rarely **nsib,** even **nsub** Q 45:20, MG 240:1 f.; **sab pihta** CP 71:17, Q 32:27 = ML 87:9 take the sacramental bread; **sab hazin pugdama** DC 43 F 85 take this command; **sab hazin raza** DC 43 J 172 take this mystery; with suff. **nusbẖ** Gy 347:19 take her MG 269 n. 1, 276:11; **nusbẖ lqanina** DC 41. 297 f. take the phial. Act. pt. **lnapšiẖ muma nasib** AM 20 he causes harm to himself; **ligrẖ muma nasib** AM 29 his foot will receive a blemish; pl. **d̲-zaina qabalẖ nasbia** Gy 83:3 who take (: use) arms against him. Part. pres. with encl. **nasbinalẖ** Gy 265:14 we take it MG 233:9; **nasibnalẖ lṭaba nišimta** DC 48. 244 I will take the soul to the Good One. Inf. with suff. **misibẖ** DC 41. 112 to take him.

Pa.?: Pt. pl. with encl. **mnasbilẖ** Gy 262:21 they carry him about (?? The only pa.-form found, hardly correct Ginzā 261 n. 6).

Af. Pf. **haṭaiia kadiria asibnin lnapšan** DC 34. 556 we took upon ourselves grievous sins; with suff. **asibtẖ** I let him take MG 277:12; but **ansabtẖ btibil** DC 41. 5 I took it in the earth (is pe. with a prosth. **a**). Pt. fem. (pass.?) **masba bharšia bišia** Gy 81:9 she is occupied with black magic; pl. **masbia** Q 66:23, Gs 78:22 they receive MG 239:19.

Ethpe. Pf. **ᶜtinsib** he was, they were, taken MG 222:2; **ᶜnsib razaihun** DC 42. 54 their mysteries were taken away; **ᶜnisbat** Gy 317: ult. she was taken away MG 214:9. Pt. **mitinsib** Gy 26:8, 17 ff. is snatched away MG 132:10, 214:4; fem. **malkuta minẖ mitnisba** Gy 27:13 the rule is taken away from him.

nsaka s. **nasaka.**

nsis(a) (נְסִיס, ܢܤܝܤܐ) (*a*) sick(ly), weak, afflicted, sad, gloomy MG xxx:11, Jb ii 41 n. 3, pl. **nsisia 1,** (*b*) (ἡ νόσος) affliction, vexation, sickness, fem. MG 160:13. (*a*) **biš unsis** Gy 9:12 bad and gloomy; **alma nsis balma qrun** Jb 38:5 why did they create me (as) ill-humoured in the world?; **iuma nsisa** Oxf. 24 b, Morg 43:9 a gloomy day; **baita nsisa** Jb 127:9 (a derisive designation of the temple of Jerusalem); **mia ᶜkumia nsisia** Gy 140:4 black, gloomy water(s); **alahia nsisia nihun** AM 169:9 the gods will be feeble; (*b*) **nsisa rabtia** Gy 277:14 great affliction; **mn ahẖ qašišia nsis hauilẖ** AM 15:2 he will be caused vexation by his elder brothers.

nsisuta (abstr. noun from **nsis(a)**) vexation, grief, affliction. **haduta d̲-lansisuta** Gy 3:17, 9:14 joy without grief. Var. **ᶜnsalit bnsisuta** DC 44. 1075 = Morg. 263/16:22 I entered with grief; **bnsisuta hauia** AM 5:19 he will be afflicted.

nsisia 1 pl. of **nsis(a).**

nsisia 2 pl. (Targ. נִיסָא, Sam. ࠍࠉࠎࠉࠀ Gen. 10:32, late H. נסים, Gr. νῆσοι) islands MG xxx 13. **nsisia iama** Gy 175:2 the islands of the sea.

NSS (Jew.-Aram. נסס 'to be troubled' from Gr. νόσος Nöld. MG xxx 11, ZDMG xl 729. Akk *nasāsu* to wail) to be in trouble, be sick, grieve, repine. Jb ii 41 n. 3.

Pe. Impf. **tinsis** AM 29:17 she will grieve, **ninsisiun** AM 178:16 they will grieve (both could be ethpe. without the **t** in the pref. as well). DC 46 187 ult. Act. pt. **lman d̲-naiis** (*often in talismans*) for one who trembles (or: is ill). Pass. pt. with encl. **ᶜt d̲-hadibẖ uᶜt d̲-nsisbẖ** Gy 263:19, 21, 273:13 there are who rejoice for it and there are who grieve for it. Inf. **minsis**? v.s. pa.

Pa. Pass. pt. **minsis tnasasa** AM 69:7 she greatly grieves.

Ethpe. Pt. **mitinsis** AM 35 he is grieved, **ukd̲ hasirlẖ laminsis** AM 24:18 and when he loses, he is not grieved.

Ethpa. Pt. **kd̲ iatirlẖ lahadia ukd̲ hasirlẖ lamitnasasa** AM 57:11 and AM 69:7 when (her husband's wealth) increases she does not rejoice, and when it is lacking to him she is not afflicted.
Der.: **masasia, nsis(a), (ᶜ)nsisuta, naisuta.**

NSR (Aram. & mod. H. נסר, Syr. ܢܣܪ, Ar. نشر, اشر, وشر Nöld.: *Neue Beiträge* 182, H. der. מַשּׂוֹר saw, Eth. [illegible] Brockelm. i 226,

Phoen. ישר Praetorius ZDMG lxvii 131, Akk. *šaššaru* MVaG ix 235 f.) to saw, tear asunder, lacerate.

Pe. Impf. **kul tarmida ḏ-napšiḥ nisar** ATŠ II no. 342 any priest who lacerates himself; with suff. **bmasaria qubla** (var. **-ia** CD) **ninsarunḥ** (var. **nisrunḥ** B, **nisarunḥ** D, **nisirunḥ** C) Gy 300:21 they will saw him with toothed (?) saws (lit. saws with chains Jb ii 99 n. 2). Act. pt. pl. with encl. **nasrilun bmasaria** DAb they will saw them with saws.

Der.: **masara, nisra.**

nᶜ Gy 293:21 st. abs. of **nᶜha** Gy 103:ult., 105:1 = **niha** MG 5:15, 18, 65:7, 117:12 f.

nᶜhin (influenced by the preced. nᶜha) Gy 105:1 = **anhin** ibid. l. 2. Ginzā 113 n. 4.

nᶜula s. **niula.**

nᶜkla s. **nikla.**

NPA, NPH, s.v., **NHP** s.v. (Aram. & H. נפח, Syr. ܢܦܚ, Ar. نفح & نفخ, Eth. ነፍኀ, Akk. *napāḫu*) to breathe out, fan with breath, blow up, inflate.

Pe. Impf. **tinpa ᶜšata mn anpaihun** Gy 179:23 fire blazeth from their faces; with encl. **unpabḥ** (for uᶜnpabḥ) **bgauḥ ḏ-(ᶜ)squbrai** Jb 147:1 and I will blow into my trumpet.

Gl. 4:13 f. **npi** [*sic*] اقد (: وقد) *accendere* بر آفروخت ; 8:9 f. **anpa** اطفى *extinguere* خاموش كرد ; 21:5 f. id. اضطرم *accendere* روشن كرد ; 167:13 f. id. نفخ *insufflere* آماه كرد .

Der.: **niputa.**

npazaṭ DC 43 name of a lilith.

npala (rt. **NPL**) fall., Gl. 98:6 **npala** سقوط *casus* اُفتادن .

NPH a more original form of **NPH** (q.v.). With metath. **NHP** s.v.

Pe. Pass. pt. fem. st. emph. **nura npihta** Gy 279:13 a blown-up fire (*or*, better, 'a fanned fire').

npika (נפיק (?)) quick, alert ? **gabra npika hauia** AM 89:4 (for **npiqa**) he will be an alert man.

npiš (pass. pt. pe. of **NPŠ**) (*a*) numerous, plentiful, great, valued, precious, ܢܦܝܫ life-(giving), vital; pl. masc. **npišia**, fem. st. abs. **npišan** (st. emph. being replaced by **napšata**), (*b*) adv. much (usually with prep. **b-**) MG 200:23 f. Varr. **anpiš** MG 200:24, **npᶜš** MG 5:20. (*a*) **mn atra ḏ-npiš ataitun** DC 51. 501 ye came from an exalted place; **mn atra ḏ-npiš ata** CP 376:11 f. (cf. **atra sagia**); **uruianḥ npišia** AM 27:ult. and his opinions are valued; **npišan šiṭuata ḏ-hšuka** ATŠ I no. 253 numerous are the evil ways of darkness; **npiš mn mimra ḏ-puma** s. **mimra**; (*b*) **bnpiš** (*very often*) great, much; **npiš bnpiš** Gy 237:15 etc. (*often*) very much MG 303:9 f.; **ṭabuta bnpiš hauia** AM 166:11 there will be plenty of good things.

NPL (Aram. & H. נפל, Syr. ܢܦܠ, Ar. نفل to make fall to one. ZAW iii 122, Nöld. ZDMG xl 725, *Neue Beiträge* 180, Fränkel 153 f., cf. Akk. *napālu* to destroy) to fall.

Pe. Pf. **barsa npal** (*often*) he took to his bed, **niplat** AM 277:30 it (fem.) falls, descends, **laniplit** DC 34. 80 I did not fall; (**mipal**) **lanpalnin** Morg. 221/30:ult. = CP 50:14 = ML 66:4 we did not fall; **npaltin** Q 52:18 ye (fem.) fell MG 224:12; with encl. **npalalḥ, npilalḥ** Gy 85:5, 340:8, Gs 3:5 she fell down. Impf. **nipil** he falls MG 51:7, 238:18; **niplun** they (will) fall MG 239:7; **mahuzia bihdadia niplun** AM 221:11 f. towns will attack each other; **nipla** Gy 386:16 they (fem.) fall down MG 239:7; **tiplun** ye fall MG 239:7; with encl. **nauda ninpulbun** AM 221:7 trembling will come upon them; **ᶜnpulbun** Gs 57:20 (var. **ᶜnpilbun**) I will not fall into them MG 239:1. Impt. **pil** Gs 136:17 f., MG 240:4; with encl. **pilbḥ bᶜuṣṭ(u)na** Gs 57:5 fallen into the body. Pt. **uiarqana napil** AM 211:12 and the green (vegetable crop) will fail; **ḏ-napil hiua bala ᶜlḥ** Gy 18:4 which a wild animal attacked (Lidzb. proposed **ḏ-npil** Ginzā 20 n. 4); inflected **napla** s.v.; pl. **haršaiun naplia lbataiia** DC 20 their sorceries attack householders, **minilia mardia naplia ᶜlḥ** AM 13:8 words of mischief-makers will attack him. Inf. **mipal** Morg. 221/30:ult. = ML 66:4 s. pf., **baiit mimar mipil mia barqa** DC 41. 432 f. thou seekest to command water to fall into the earth.

Idiom: With the prep. **b-, l-, ᶜl** (or encl. **-b-, -l-**) 'to attack' with **b-** 'to enter'.

Gl. (always with a prosth. **a**) 3:13 f. اتى , انطرح *venire, afferre, praecipitari* آمد ; 110:13 f. طرح *elidere* انداخت ; 174:6 f. وقع *cadere* شد .

Der.: **napla.**

NPع (Ar. نفع) to help, be useful. Only in mod. texts. Ar. impf. **ianpaع ᶜl** AM 287:13 is efficacious for; **muiinpaع** Zotb. 228a:2 (for ما ينفع) what is useful. Gl. (missp. with Mand. ᶜ) 13:3 f. انتفع *efficere* فايده كرد ; 119:3 f. عنى *iuvare, prodesse* يارى كرد .

NPṢ (Aram. & H. נפץ, Syr. ܢܦܨ, Ar. نفض, Jew.-Aram. also נפע MG 240 n. 3, Akk. *napāṣu*; cf. also Ar. نفص to come out suddenly, talk fast etc., Eth. ነፍጸ to flee away, Barth: *Wurzeluntersuchungen* 30 f.; rel. to **PṢA**?) to take off, shake off, move off, bestir, toss out, empty out, shake out, discharge, miscarry; to spring up, bestir oneself. MR 31 n. 5, Jb ii 136 n. 6.

Pe. Pf. **npaṣ ᶜlḥ sidria** Gy 195:17 they showered (prayer-)books on him (Lidzb. *sie uberschütteten ihn mit Gebetsordnungen*); **npaṣ ᶜl mia unbaṭ mia** Gy 293:12 he impelled the water and the water sprang forth; **npaṣ albšuia** Gy 195:22 they sprang up and clothed him; **npaṣ mn kursia qam npaṣ qam mn kursiḥ** Gy 343:18 f., 344:1 f. = **ᶜnpaṣ mn kursiḥ qam** Gy 342:16, 351:10, 14 f., ML 237:3 f., Jb 205:5 = **ᶜnpiṣ uqam mn kursiḥ** Gy 164:19 f. he sprang up and rose from his throne; **npaṣ gapnḥ** (read **ganpḥ**) DC 34. 503 he flapped his wings (: he took to wing); **npaṣ**

tunaihun DC 34. 337 their fruit dropped down; with encl. **npaṣbun bganpḫ** Jb 133:8, 141:9 he took to wing; with suff. **nipṣḫ . . . lpirun drabša** CP 358:1, Oxf. 98 b = ML 266: 1 f. he shook out the banner *P.*; with encl. **ganpai npaṣibḫ** Gs 88:4 I flapped in it my wings. Impf. **baṭiniata ninipṣun** AM 243:10 pregnant women will miscarry (one would expect fem.!); with suff. **ninpiṣunḫ** AM 210 they will shake it off. Impt. **paṣ** CP 80:6, Q 66:27, Nöld. *schüttle dich* MG 240:3, CP. trs. 54:7, Lidzb. *eile*, **npuṣ qum mn kursiak** Gy 347:18 Jump up!: Rise from thy throne! (MG 240:4). Act. pt. **napiṣ ʿl tarbaṣia hadiḫ** Gs 3:6 f. he beateth on the 'forecourts' of his breast; **malia unapiṣ** AM 4:3, 19:18 full and emptying; **usiliat anapiṣ ʿlauaihun** ATŠ II no. 189 emptying dregs upon them; fem. **lad̠-napṣa** Gy 18:4 not of that what a female (animal) miscarried; pl. **pudria ʿlḫ napṣʿ ʿlḫ napṣia pudria** Gy 102:ult. f. Lidzb. *sie schütten über sie Hexerei aus*, Ginzā 111 n. 4.

Pa. Pt. with encl. **mnapiṣlun** Gy 115:18, 19 he shook for them.

Af. Pt. pl. with encl. **mapṣila** Gy 227:10 they cause her to miscarry.

Ethpe. Impf. **laniqrub unitipiṣ** DC 43 I 84 he shall not approach and shall be shaken off.

Gl. (with a prosth. **a** and missp. with s) 164:7 نفض *excutere* تكانيد; 167:1 f. نزف *evacuare* خون از بينی آمد.

Der.: **napṣa** (var. **nipṣa**).

NPQ (נְפַק, ܢܦܩ, Ar. نفق, Eth. ነፈቀ) to go out, come out, leave, depart.

Pe. Pf. **npaq** he, they went out MG 221:21, 223:14, 297:bottom, **nipqat** she went out MG 15:15, 222:20, **npaqt** thou didst go out MG 222:24, **nipqit** I went out MG 15:17, 223:2, **npaqiun** Gy 380:1 they went out MG 223:21, 297:bottom, **npaqian** they (fem.) went out MG 297:bottom, **npaqtun** ye went out MG 224:5, **npaqnin** we went out MG 15:10, 224:16; with encl. **npaqnabḫ** Gy 261:6 we went out in it MG 15:11, 225:10; with suff. **npaqtḫ** thou hast left it MG 276:25. Impf. **nipuq, tipuq, ʿpuq, nipqun, tipqun** MG 238:13, but also **lʿpuq** Gs 118:7 (read same for **laʿpuq** l. 6) he cometh out MG 216:6 f.; with encl. **napqa ninpuqbḫ** AM 118:18 an eruption (or swelling) comes out on him; **tinpuqbḫ** AM 22:4 it (fem.) will come out on him. Act. pt. **napiq**, fem. **napqa**, pl. **napqin, napqia**, fem. pl. **napqan** MG 149:6 f. Part. pres. **napiqna** I go out MG 231:3, **napqit** thou goest out MG 13:7, 232:10, **napqinin** we go out MG 232:26, **napqitun** ye go out MG 13:8, 79:15, 233:11. Inf. **mipaq, minpaq** MG 129:16, 239:10, 11, **mipaq ruha unišimta** Lond. roll A 614, **minpaq (napiqna minaihun)** Gy 258:25; with suff. **ʿl malak ulmipqak** Gy 365:5 f. at thy coming and thy going out (cf. Deut. 6:7, 11:19 Ginzā 387 n. 2).

Af. Pf. **apiq, apqat, apqit** MG 239:15 (51:6), but also **anpiq** MG 239:19 (with a mistaken reference); with suff. **apqḫ** he brought him, her out MG 211:15, 275:9, but **hanp(i)qḫ** Gy 262:6 id. MG 211:14, 239:21 (cf. Dan. 6:24, an archaic form used as a peculiarity of the 11th book of Gy Ginzā 250:14), **apqan** he brought me out MG 270:bottom, **apiqtḫ** Gy 92:8 I brought him out, **apiqtinan** thou hast brought us out MG 280:9, **apiqtun** Gs 75:3 ye brought me out MG 272:12, **apqun** they brought me out MG 272:21, **apquia** they brought him out MG 278:2, **apqu** Gs 98:2 they brought her out MG 279:17. Impf. with encl. **ʿiapiqlak** Gs 106:12 f. I take thee out; with suff. **napqan** he bringeth me out MG 271:5, **ʿiapqḫ** I bring him out MG 276:6, **ʿiapqin(a)-kun** Q 56:15, Gy 255:8 I will bring you out MG 280:paen., **napqunḫ** AM 15:13 they will take him out, **tapqunḫ** ye (shall) take him out MG 278:15. Impt. **anpiq** Jb 276:12 (var. **anpiqt** ACD pf.), ATŠ I no. 196 take out MG 239:20 f.; with suff. **apqan** take me out MG 271:11. Act. pt. **mapiq** bringing out MG 131:21, 231:16; pl. **mapqia** MG 31:13. Part. pres. **mapqit** AM 135 thou expellest (MG 231:16); with encl. **mapqu** (?) **tulḫ** ATŠ II no. 332 ye take him out. Pass. pt. **mapaq** taken out MG 132:1. Inf. with suff. **apuqan** Gy 241:23 to bring me out MG 292:11. Nom. act. **mapaqta, mapiqta** s.v.

Gl. (consistently with a prosth. **a**) 4:3 f. (af.) اخرج *educere* بيرون كرد; 13:9 f. اشرق *oriri* روشن كرد; 17:5 f. انتضى *expulere* بيرون كرد; 25:11 f. انبثق *praedere* بيرون رفت; 51:3 f. تربّى *educare* تربيت كرد; 55:5 f. خرج *exire* بيرون رفت; 59:5 f. حدث *provenire* رسيد; 89:13 f. شرق *exoriri, oriri* روشن كرد; 109:3 f. طلع *crescere* بيرون آمد, (af.) *educere* بيرون آورد; 164:1 f. نجا *liberare* آزاد كرد; 166:1 f. *crescere, germinare*; 181:15 f. دلّ *haurire, ostendere* دلالت كرد.

Der.: **mapaqta, mapiqta, mapqana, napaqa, napuqa, napqa 1.**

NPŠ (Gen. Sem., Akk. *napāšu*, Ar. نفس) to breathe, refresh, give life; (Aram. נְפַשׁ to increase, Syr. ܢܦܫܐ extension, Ar. نفيسة great riches, Akk. *napāšu* also 'to extend') to be many, great, plentiful, wax great, extend, abound, augment, increase. Secondary rt. **NBŠ** s.v.

Pe. Pf. **npaš uʿtgabar** Gy 159:22 f. he became great and strong; **npiš** was, were numerous, plentiful MG 219:16. Impf. **ninpuš** ibid., **ninpuš (unitnapaš)** CP 426:12 may it increase (and be plentiful); **ninpuš zidqak** CP 420:14 may thy charity increase; **hailḫ ninpuš lhad trin** ATŠ II no. 349 his strength will be doubled; **d̠-tinpuš nišmata** ATŠ II no. 335 so that thou revivest souls; with encl. **anašia zaina lhdadia ni(n)pušbun** AM 210:1 (cf. BZ 127 n. 4) people will do much harm to one another. Act. pt. **napiš**, pl. **haṭaikun napšia** Gy 19:10 f. your sins increase; **kma d̠-napšia iardnia** CP 418:13 just as jordans wax great;

napšin (umitnapšin) ATŠ I no. 5 they multiply (and are multiplied). Pass. pt. **npiš** s.v.

Pa. Impf. with suff. **ninapšh̲** (var. **ninipšh̲** DC 22) **lšurbth̲** Gy 105:20 we will multiply his race (lit. generation).

Af. Pf. **anpiš** Oxf. 31 b (twice) augmenteth. Impt. with suff. **anpišuia** multiply him MG 279:3.

Ethpa. Pf. **uʿtnapaš biardna malia** DC 50 and (they) are refreshed in the full jordan; **ʿtnapšat btlatma ušitin širiania** DC 34. 87 it (fem.) multiplied into 360 streams. Impf. **d̲-nitnapaš alma** Gy 14:3 so that the world may multiply; (**ninpuš**) **unitnapaš** s. pe. impf.; **nitnapšun** they (will) multiply MG 43:11. Pt. **kd̲ anat lahuit rba alma d̲-mit(a)napša huit** Jb 22:16 since thou wert not great, why wert thou presumptuous? (Lidzb. *warum hast du dich überhoben?*), **mitnapša riša d̲-šurbta . . . riša d̲-nišubta mitnapša** Gy 325:13 f., cf. Ginzā 332 n. 1 (where Lidzb. proposed to read **bišuta** for **riša**, hence: the evil of thy plantation shall multiply), pl. (**napšin**) **umitnapšin** s. pe. act. pt.

Der.: **napašta, napša** 1, 2, **napuš, npiš** (varr.), **nupša.**

NṢA (**ࡍࡑࡀ**, **ܢܨܐ**, H. **נצה** II, Ar. نصا to seize by the hair, den. from ناصية lock of hair, Eth. **ነጸየ** to pull the hair) to quarrel, contend, dispute.

Pe. Act. pt. **ʿnta d̲-naṣia minh̲** DC 42 a woman that contends with her; pl. **ia d̲-naṣia umradpia** CP 106:9 = ML 131:13 O ye who quarrel and maltreat; **d̲-minak naṣin** Gy 154: ult. f. who quarrel with thee; **qal gubria d̲-naṣin** AO 1937 p. 95:ult. the noise of men that are fighting.

Der.: **maṣuta.**

nṣab ('He-planted') name of a spirit of life Jb ii 15 n. 7. **anan nṣab** Gy 108:2 ff.; **nṣab uanan nṣab** CP 21, 58, 105, 146 f., Gy 221:4, 374:13, Q 15:11, 40:10, Oxf. 57 a, b; **anan nṣab ziua** Gy 108:2, 9; **nṣab ziua** CP trs. 128, 244, Jb 253:13 ff.; **nṣab rba** Gy 321:2, RD A 11, **arqa d̲-nṣab rba** Gy 360:21.

nṣap (Ar. إِنْصَاف) AM 253:21 justice.

NṢB (**ࡍࡑࡁ**, **ܢܨܒ**, H. **נצב** hif. to place, fix; nif. to place oneself, Ar. نصب, Sab. **𐩬𐩮𐩨** to set up, Akk. *naṣabāti* columns?) to plant, implant, transplant, propagate, transport, set up, fix, establish. Sometimes confused with **NSB** MG 45 n. 1, 239 n. 1.

Pe. Pf. **nṣab nišubta** Q 29:4, ATŠ (*often*) he planted a plant(ing) = took a wife, founded a family; **naṣbia d̲-ana nišbit** s. **naṣba 2, nišbit d̲-rbia nišubta** Gy 360:27 I planted a plant of the Great Life; **lnṣubta** (var. **lnaṣuraiia** ACD) **d̲-nišbit** Jb 264:1 f. for the plantation which I planted (var. for the Naṣoraeans whom I edified); with encl. **nṣablh̲ haua bzauia** Gy 286:16 he gave him Eve for wife (*idiom*) MG 361:paen.; **unṣablia zaua** Zotb. 228a:3 and (he) gave me a wife (performed my marriage, *idiom*); **uadiauria nṣablak** (twice) **ʿutria nihia** Gy 72:11 = **nṣabulak adiauria ʿutria nihia** Gy 72:13 he (: the Life) created for the helpers, the mild uthras (*idiom*; MG 225:1 f.); **adiauria d̲-anatun nṣabtulia** Gy 157:13 the helpers whom ye created for me (*idiom*; MG 225: 13); with suff. **manu gabra d̲-nišbh̲ ptahil hu nišbh̲** Gy 267:19 f. who is the man who created it? P. created it! (*idiom*) MG 472:22; **naṣba d̲-nišbak** Jb 254:15 the Creator who created thee; **nṣabth̲ lʿzlat brath̲ d̲-bihrun bzauia d̲-kušṭa** ATŠ II no. 322, 323, 324 thou hast wedded Ezlat daughter of B. as a plighted spouse (*idiom*); **nṣabtun** Gy 157:22 ye planted (= created) me MG 272:8; **nṣabunun** they planted them (or: He, i.e. the Life, created them) MG 283:13. Impf. **ninṣab** (*often*) he plants MG 239:2, **ninišbun** Gy 89:23 f. they create (*idiom*); with encl. **ninṣiblan** Gy 239:18 we are going to create for ourselves (*idiom*) MG 239:2; **lamsʿin . . . d̲-ninṣibulh̲** Gy 5:18 they cannot create for him (Lidzb.), or: they cannot take away from him (Nöld.: influenced by **NSB**) MG 239 n. 1; with suff. **ʿnišbh̲** Gy 100:9 I create him (*idiom*) MG 275:28. Impt. with encl. **nṣablun** Oxf. 84 a . . . **nṣublun** Par. xi plant (create) for them MG 240:8 f.; with suff. **nuṣban** Gs 104:19 transplant me MG 271:9. Act. pt. **naṣib nišubta d̲-trin kušṭia** ATŠ I no. 151 he weds one who had been wed before vows have been formed (*idiom*); **bminilth̲ naṣib ʿutria** Gy 6:ult. with his word he createth uthras; pl. **ia gubria d̲-naṣbia zaua** Gy 18:7 O ye men who take a wife (*idiom*); **kd̲ naṣbu(?)n nišubta uhauila(?)n šitlia** ATŠ II no. 312 when they take a wife and have children (*idiom*); with encl. **lhalin d̲-naṣbilun nišubta d̲-kušṭa tiniana** ATŠ I no. 151 about those that take a wife of a second (wedding) pact (*idiom*). Pass. pt. **nṣib, nṣiba, nṣibia** (*often*), **ʿnṣibat-utria** CP 47:penult.; **mana nṣiba** Gs 110:17, 19 an implanted *mana*; **nṣiba nišbtak** Oxf. 90 b thy plant is planted; **mna hua nṣiba nišubtan nišubtan lmahu nṣiba** CP 213:15 f. whence was implanted our reproductive power? wherefore was it implanted? (cf. Idioms); pl. (**mia**) **hiuaria biluria nṣibia** DC 51. 538 (of the waters of life)—white, crystalline, transported (hither). Inf. **ulminṣib d̲-rbia nišubta nišubta d̲-rbia minṣib** Gy 318:22 to plant the plant of the Great (Life); **minṣib nṣibna** Gy 353:5 f. I was transplanted (MG 239:12); **uminṣab d̲-rbia nišubta** Jb 239:2; **laʿhablh̲ zaua . . . ulaʿhablh̲ nišubta lminṣab** Jb 264:5 f. they gave him no wife . . . they gave him no spouse to marry (*idiom*).

Ethpe. Pf. **ʿtinṣib** Jb 9:12, 10:1 ff., 254:7 ff., Q 3:15 was (im)planted, created, **ʿtnišbat** Gy 72:22, 303:10 she was (im)planted, created MG 213:25, **ʿtnišbit** I was planted MG 223:7, **ʿtinṣibtun** ye were planted, created MG 224:8. Impf. **nitinṣib** Gy 87:8 is (trans)planted. Impt. **ʿtinṣib** Gy 328:5 be planted MG 229:8. Pt. **minṣib** MG 214:6; fem. **nišubta d̲-mitnišba** ATŠ II no. 312 the bride that was taken to wife (*idiom*); pl. **almia mišibh̲** [*sic*] DC 35 the worlds may be created.

Idioms: Very often with the meaning 'to create' (cf. **naṣba** 1 Creator). With **adiaura** as obj. perh. 'to give, or send, a helper', 'to support with a helper' (Lidzb, simply *schöpfen*). With **zaua** as obj. 'to give as wife', 'to marry', 'to espouse', hence **niṣubta** also with the meaning of 'wife, spouse' (s. pe. pf. twice, with encl., with suff., act. pt., pl. twice, with encl., inf., ethpe. pt. fem.).

Der.: **naṣba** 1, 2, **niṣ(u)bta** (varr.), **nṣab**, **niṣba**.

nṣubta occ. var. of **niṣubta**.

NṢR I (נְצַר to chirp, ܢܨܪ, Ar. صرّ) to squeak, squeal, (of pig) grunt.

Pe. Act. pt. fem. **arqa naida . . . unaṣra** DC 34. 224 the earth quakes and squeals. Part. pres. **naṣrit kḏ hizura** DC 43 J 136 thou gruntest like a pig.

NṢR II (H. נצר I, Ar. نظر, South-Ar. both נצר & נטר, Eth. ነጸረ, Akk. *naṣāru*) an older form of **NṬR**, to keep, keep back, (keep secret), preserved only in the der.: **naṣuraia**, **naṣiruta** (var. **naṣaruta**).

NQA I rt. of **naqia** 1 (q.v.).

NQA II rt. of **naquta**, **niqia** (var. **naqia** 2).

nqašia pl. (rt. **NQŠ**, Syr. ܢܩܫܐ) shivering-fits, shakings, palpitations, agues, throbbings. Varr. **nqušia**, **nqišia** s.vv. **nqašia dra lstuarun** DC 34. 336 (shakings attacked their firm-rootedness (of trees); **ridpa unqašia** ATŠ II no. 442 affliction and throbbings.

NQB (Aram., H. Sab. 𐩬𐩤𐩨, Syr. ܢܩܒ, Ar. نقب, Akk. *naqbu* source, well) to make a hole, bore, pierce.

Pe. Act. pt. fem. pl. **ʿudnaiin naqban** DAb they (fem.) pierce their ears; pl. with encl. **lišanh̲ naqbilh̲** RD C 12 they pierce his tongue. Part. pres. (**minqab**) **naqibna** DC 23. 593 I pierce. Pass. pt. **marganita lanqiba** DC 44. 1091 an unpierced pearl. Inf. **minqab** s. part. pres.

Der.: **niq(u)ba**, **niqubta** (varr., pl. **nuqbata**).

NQD (נקד, ܢܩܕ pa., Ar. نقد to pay in cash) to cleanse, purify.

Pa. Pf. with suff. **naqduih̲** DC 41. 196 they cleansed it. Impt. **naqid** Gy 18:5, 68:5 cleanse. Part. pres. with encl. **mnaqdatlh̲** DC 48. 279 thou cleanest it.

nqušia, nqišia ML 6:1 = **nqašia**.

NQL (Ar. نقل) to remove, transport. Only in mod. texts. Only Ar. reflexive (VIII-)forms. Pf. **antiqal** AM 280:31 (Ar. انتقل) it is removed. Impf. **uanašia tinqitil** [*sic*] **mn atra latra hurintia** AM 278:26 f. and people will migrate from one place to another; **iintiqlun** AM 257:38, 277:33 they will be removed.

Gl. 140:1 f. **NQL** كشف *revelare* ظاهر كرد.

NQP (Jew.-Aram. & H. נקף, Ar. نقف, Eth. ነቀፈ to peel off) to strike, push down, knock down; (cf. **NQB**) to incise; (cf. ܢܩܦ) to fasten, affix.

Pe. Impf. with suff. **ʿniqpih̲** JRAS 1939 401:9 I knock him down. Impt. **qup bṣuria ḏ-zuṭa** DC 45 fasten to the neck of the little one. Act. pt. pl. **naqpin ab** Gy 256:8 they strike the father. Pass. pt. **ušuma ḏ-iauar ṣir ʿlh̲ ḏ-bgauh̲ naqip** (read **nqip**) DAb and the name of Yawar is graven upon it, that is incised into it.

Der.: **naqpiaiil**.

NQṢ (Ar. نقص) to decrease, diminish, wane. Mod.

Der.: **nuqṣan**.

NQR (Aram. & H. נקר, Syr. ܢܩܪ, Ar. نقر to dig, Akk. *naqāru* to demolish) rt. of **naqura**.

NQŠ (Aram., H. & Mod. H. נקש, Syr. ܢܩܫ, Ar. نقش, cf. Fränkel 194, 276) to strike, smite, knock (in); to beat, play (a musical instrument); to knock together (limbs), shiver, quiver, shake, palpitate.

Pe. Pf. **bškinth̲ nqaš** Jb 23:14 he knocked on his dwelling; **uarhh̲ malka ḏ-hšuka unqiš** DC 41. 215 f. and the King of Darkness smelt it and shivered (intransit. form). Impf. **ninquš unimut** AM 115:12 he will shiver and die; **bšinth̲ ninquš uʿšata ḏ-ʿrtitia maṭilh̲** AM 119:3 in his sleep he shivers and a feverish palsy will come upon him. Impt. with encl. **uldupa ʿnqušulun ʿl lišanun** DC 44. 838 and nail their tongues to a board. Act. pt. **sikia gnana naqiš** Gy 147:24 he knocketh in the pegs (or spiked poles) of the baldachin; **lqal parzla ḏ-naqiš** DC 43 A 52 at the sound of iron that clashes; **kdub lman naqiš pagria** DC 46 write (this talisman) for one whose body shivers; pl. **naqušia**, **naqšia** s. **naquša**: **ṣaliba ḏ-naqšia bašiata** Jb 109:3 the cross which they fix (nail) to the walls; **giadh̲ naqšia** AM 21:11 his nerves palpitate; **alaha ḏ-qurqsa naqšia** Gy 226:19 they nail a god on the cross (cf. Jb 109:3 above); **naqšin ṭuria** Jb 18:6 the hills shake (Lidzb. *schlagen aneinander*); fem. pl. **arqa udiša naqšan** DAb the ground and the door strike (clash) together. Part. pres. **naqšit ʿlh̲** Jb 23:1 thou strikest it.

Af. Part. pres. with encl. **kma manqišatlh̲ lkulh̲ qumtai** Jb 113:14 f. how sorely thou strikest at my whole body!

Ethpe. Pf. with encl. **ʿnqišbh̲** DC 23: 106.

Der.: **naquša**, **nqašia** (var. **nqušia**, **nqišia**).

NŠA I (נְשָׁא, ܢܫܐ, H. נשה, Ar. نسي, Akk. *mašû* Haupt AJSL xxii 199, Brockelm. i 160, Eth. ኣንስዐየ he ignored Dillm. 633) to forget. Pe., af. and ethpe. often confused, Jb ii 65 n. 2, MG 486:middle.

Pe. Pf. **halin ḏ-pandama nša** DC 36 no. 125 those who forget the face-veil; **lanšit** Gy 369:20, 21 I have not forgotten; with suff. **lanšith̲** Gy 369:19 I have not forgotten it; **nšath̲** DC 41:492 she forgot it. Impf. **ninišia** Gy 369:15, 16 he forgetteth; **latinšia ḏ-marak paqdak** Gy 364:23 forget not what thy Lord ordered thee; **latinšia lmarak mn ʿuṣrak** Gy 365:5 forget not thy Lord from thy heart; **latinšun mindam mn naṣiruta** ATŠ forget nothing of Naṣoraean wisdom; **ninišiun** CP

158:8 = Oxf. 18 b they forget me MG 286:9; **ninišiak** Gy 66:7, 348:22 he forgetteth thee, we forget thee MG 286:21. Pt. **ʿu šagia tarmida unašia pandama** ATŠ I no. 71 if a priest makes a mistake and forgets his lower-face-veil; pl. **ʿit minaihun d-našin ʿngirta** DC 34. 1170 there are some who forget the 'Letter'.

Af. (with the same meaning as pe. & ethpe.). Pf. **d-ʿngirta anša** DC 34. 1183 who forgot the Letter. Pt. pl. with suff. **d-ahh lamaniših** DC 27. 204 so that her brothers do not forget her. Part. pres. with encl. **manšinalak** Gy 136:22 we forget thee MG 262:paen.; **manšiatlh** Gy 365:6 ff. thou forgettest him MG 262:24; **hzia lmarak manšiatlh** Jb 246:10 (var. **minšiatlh** C ethpe.) see to it lest thou forget thy Lord; **ʿu manšitlh** ATŠ II no. 216 if thou forgettest it.

Ethpe. (with the same meaning as pe. & af.). Pf. **laʿnšia** Jb 213:2 (*twice*) he did not forget, **ʿnšit** Gy 369:18 I forgot; with suff. **ʿniših** Gy 380:ult. (varr. **ʿnših**, **ʿnišh**) he forgot him MG 287:11, **ʿnšainak** Gy 157:5 we forgot thee MG 286:ult., **ʿnšaith** Gy 323:12 I forgot it, **ʿnšitinun** Gs 42:14 I forgot them, **ʿnišiuia** Jb 33:10, 102:8, Gs 1:17 they forgot it, **ʿnišiun** Jb 262:4 they forgot me. Pt. pl. **minišiin** Oxf. 12 a, 22 b they forget MG 164:21; with encl. **minšilh** Gs 56:8 he shall forget it, **minšialh** DC 41. 236 she will forget it, **minšialun** DC 48. 240 she will forget them. Part. pres. **minšina** Jb 110:11 (var. **manšina** ABD af.) I forget MG 266:2; with encl. **minšiatlh** Jb 246:10 C v.s. af., **minšiatlia** thou forgettest me MG 486:middle; with suff. **minšinik** (var. **manšinak** af. with masc. suff. mistaken) I forget thee (fem.) MG 291:22 f.

Gl. 164:15 f. **NŠA** نسا [sic] *oblivisci* فراموش كرد.

NŠA II (cf. Ar. نشا IV to compose, Can. & H. נשא to raise, carry, Akk. *našû* id.) to collect, gather.

Pe. Pf. with suff. **ginzia d-nšitinun** DC 48. 383 treasures which thou hast collected; **lkulhun ginzia d-nšitinun midkiralun** DC 48. 384 she (the soul) remindeth herself of all the treasures which thou hast collected.

Ethpe. Pt. pl. with encl. **ganzibria d-minšilh lginzaihun** DAb treasurers who collect their treasure(s) (formal influence of **NŠA I**).

nšara, varr. **nišara, nišra** 3 (coll. Ar. of 'Irāq *nešla* 'catarrh') catarrh. **nšara d-nhira** AM 21 running at the nose.

NŠṬ (נְשַׁט, ܢܫܛ, Ar. نسط to extract, empty) to flay.

Pe. Impf. with suff. **bsikinia d-parzla ninišṭih** DC 44. 1006 = Morg. 262/16:4 with knives of iron we will flay him.

Der.: **nišṭa, nišṭiaiil.**

NŠK for **NŠQ** in **nšuk hdadia** ATŠ II no. 428 kiss one another.

NŠM (Aram. & H. נשם, Syr. ܢܫܡ, Ar. نسم) to breathe, blow.

Pe. Impf. **ziqa basima ninšum ʿlh** AM 65:1 a favourable breeze will breathe on her. Act. pt. **unašim kd kababta d-aiba** AM 32:12 and blows like a lightning(?); **ubaiar stana d-našim ʿlak** Or. 332:14 and by the north wind that breathes on thee; **uziqa uaiar ldilak našim** Or. 325:11 and wind and pure air breathe over thee; **aiar d-ʿlana našim** (var. **nišim**) ATŠ I no. 70 (var. PD) as a breeze which blows on a tree; pl. **arba ziqia . . . lanašmia** Gy 203:13 f. the four winds do not blow.

Pa. Pt. **arba ziqia uaiar d-mnašim ʿlik** Gs 76:14 the four winds and ether which blow(eth) on thee (fem.).

Der.: **nišimta,** abs. **nišma,** pl. **nišmata.**

NŠQ (Aram. & H. נשק, Syr. ܢܫܩ, Akk. *našāqu*, Ar. نسق to put in order, Eth. ንሱቅ in good order; orig. meaning: to touch, be in contact) to kiss.

Pe. Pf. **nšaqiun ʿdaihun** ATŠ II no. 326 they kissed their hands; with suff. **nišqh** Gy 93:19, DC 41:405 he kissed him, **nšaqtak** DC 12. 169 I kissed thee. Impt. **unšuq hdadia** ATŠ II no. 428 and kiss one another; pl. with suff. **unušquia** DC 50. 43 and kiss it. Act. pt. with encl.: sg. **našiqlh** DC 41. 124 he kisses it, pl. **habqilia unašqilia** DC 44. 581 they embrace me and kiss me.

Pa. Act. pt. **mnašiq msanun d-naṣuraiia** Gy 359:16, Zotb. 217b:3 kissing the shoes of the Naṣoraeans (a frequent humble self-designation of the copyists); **mnašiq arqa** ATŠ I no. 43 he kissed (hist. pres.) the ground; pl. **mnašqia lpuma hdadia** ŠQ 8:penult. they kiss one another on the mouth; with encl. **mnašqilh** DC 27. 159 they kiss him. Part. pres. with encl. **mnašqatlh šitin nišuqiata** DC 41. 506 thou shalt kiss it sixty times.

Der.: **našqʿil, nušaqta = nišuqta** (pl. **nišuqiata**).

NŠR I (Mishn. נשר = Aram. נתר doublet of **NTR**) to fall down, fall off, drop, drip, droop; trans. to tear, lacerate.

Pe. Impf. with **ʿnišrh** DC 44. 1724 I will rend him. Act. pt. **lahualh haila d-našar bkulhun handamia** ATŠ II no. 126 it had no strength, so that it drooped (flopped) in all its limbs (= he was limp); **unašar bkuba hurintia** ATŠ II no. 405 (if) it drops into the other cup.

Der.: **nšara** (varr.)?

NŠR II (Ar. نشر) to spread over. Mod. **ulaianšur** AM 275:3 and does not spread abroad.

Gl. 41:1 f. (with a prosth. **a**) بسط *substernere* فرش كرد; 82:7 f. **NŠR** رفص *spargere* كسترد.

ntata (cf. **atiauata.** Doubtf.) vileness? **br ntata** ATŠ I no. 225 = **br ʿntata** DC 6 son of vileness (?) (See ATŠ trs. p. 179 n. 1.)

ntuta s. **nhuta.**

NTN (Aram., Phoen., H. נתן, Chr.-Pal. impf. ܢܬܠ, Syr. impf. ܢܬܠ. Akk. *nadānu*, impf. *ittan*) to give. MG 53:bottom, 238:middle.

Pe. Impf. **nitin, nʿtin** he gives, we give, **titnun** ye give, **nitna** they (fem.) give MG

238:14 f.; with encl. **nitilan** he gives us, **nʿtilh̲** he gives him, **ʿtilkun** Morg. 222/31:6 etc. I give you MG 52:17, **titnulh̲** ye give him MG 238:15; with suff. **nʿtnik** Gy 148:7 we give thee (fem.) MG 274:27. Inf. **mitin** Q 52:4 (one var. **mitan**) MG 239:10; with encl. **mitilan** Gy 319:ult. to give us MG 239:11, **lmitilun** to give them MG 52:18.

NTR, (ʿTR III) (נְתַר, ܢܬܰܪ, H. נשר, Ar. نثر, Akk. *našāru* to take away) to cast off, drop off, fall off (both trans. & intrans.).

Pe. Pf. **ʿntariun kḏ šahpia ḏ-ʿlania** DC 34. 258 they fell away like leaves of trees (properly an ethpe.). Impf. **nirqad unintar** ATŠ I no. 261 it will rock and fall down; **ninitrun uniplun** DC 26. 111 they shall drop off and fall down. Pt. **aṭirpia minh̲ lanatar** CP 26:2 = Q 11:11 = ML 30:2 its leaves fall not off; **nitra ḏ-natar** s. **nitra**; pl. **kukbia umanzalata natria** Gy 103:12 stars and constellations fall down MG 416:25; **lanatria aṭirpia ḏ-klilh̲** Gy 5:21 the leaves of his wreath do not fall off; **ʿlana ḏ-šahph̲ natrin** PD 958 the tree whose leaves fall; **udimak bʿumbak natrin** ML 214:1 (CP 175:15 has **natran**) and thy tears drop into thy bosom. Impt. **uzidqa rmulh̲ ltarmida umindam škinta ʿntar** ATŠ II no. 431 and put down alms for the priest and cast something (for) the cult-hut. Inf. **mintar** MG 239:12.

Af. Pf. with suff. **antirunun** (var. **antrunun** C) **lšahpia ḏ-gupna** Jb 132:10 they (:the winds) caused the leaves of the vine to fall off.

Der.: **nitra.**

S

s The 15th letter of the alphabet. Phonetic value: unvoiced, non-emph. sibilant. Phonetic changes: **s** < **ṣ** MG 44:18 ff.; **s** > **z** (by assimil.) MG 45:4–7; **s** > **ṣ** before **ṭ** (emphasis) MG 45:8–16 & 484 (addenda to p. 45:12); **s** > **z** before **q** (dissimil.) MG 46:4–9; **s** < **ṣ** MG § 50 p. 46.

sa (= **s** — **a**) a graphical form used to mark the completion of a section in Mandaean writings; apparently an abbreviation of **saka** 'end' Euting ZDMG xix 122. The line joining the letters **s** and **a** (*halqa*) is protracted to the whole remaining part of the line.

SAA (< סְחֵי, ܣܚܳܐ, H. שָׂחָה, Akk. *šaḫû* to wallow in the mud, hence *šaḫû* pig) to wash, perform ablutions MG 61:11–16 (& n. 1).

Pe. Pf. **mia siainin** Jb 87:13, varr. **sianin** D, **sainʿn** E we washed in water MG 62:13, 258:17, shorter form **sin** Par. xi 15a we washed MG 62:13; **mia bgu yama sin** CP 227:2 we washed in sea-water 258:21; **nisia** Gy 228:7, 300:24 he washeth himself MG 62:14. Impt. **sun mia** Gy 14:4, 35:3 wash yourselves in water MG 62:12, 259:14. Act. pt. **saiia** he washes himself MG 62:14; fem. **saia** Gy 300:24 she washeth MG 62:15; pl. **mia lasaiin uqaimia urahmia baiin** DAb they begin to pray the 'Devotions' without performing the ablution. Part. pres. **lmalik ḏ-saiit mia** Gy 116:11 wherefore dost thou wash in water? MG 62:15. Inf. **silqit lmisiia mia** DC 44. 1330 = Morg. 265/20:7 I arose in order to perform ablutions.

SAB I or SIB (Talm. סָאַב II J., Aram. סיב, Syr. ܣܳܐܶܒ, H. pf. שָׂב, der. שֵׂיבָה, grey hair, old age, Ar. شاب mediae *i*, Eth. ሢበ, Akk. *šēbu* old man) to be or grow old, grey-headed.

Pe. Pt. **saba ḏ-saiib** Gy 8:20 an old man waxing grey; pl. **lasaibin** Gy 8:16 they wax not grey MG 256 n. 1.

Der.: **saba** (pl. masc. **sabia**, fem. **sabata**), **sibuta.**

SAB II (סָאַב I) s. **SUB I.**

saba 1 (rt. **SAB I**, Jew.-Aram. סָבָא, סָאבָא, Bibl.-Aram. pl. st. cstr. שָׂבֵי, emph. שָׂבַיָּא, Syr. ܣܳܒܳܐ, ܣܳܐܒܳܐ, Akk. *šēbu*) old man, grey-beard MG 108:13. Pl. masc. **sabia**, fem. **sabata. aba saba rba** Gy 190:13, DC 43 J 192 hoary and reverend father; **aba saba zakaria** Jb 67:5 old father Zacharias; **ṣihma uʿqara lsabria lsabia** Or. 332:26 glory and honour upon scholars and elders; **sabia usabata** Gy 59:13 old men and old women.

saba 2 (act. pt. pe. of **SBA**) full, satisfying, satisfactory. Pl. **sabia. ʿburia sabia** AM 226:18 full (satisfactory) harvests; **gufna gufan hiia saba ḏ-ʿlauia kulhun asauata** CP 405:6 a Vine, the Vine of Life satisfying (?) above all means of healing.

saba 3 (etym. doubtf. Used of wind. Lidzb. proposed to read **sara** and derived it from H. שער Ginzā 418 n. 5. Or a semantic development of **saba 2** 'full'?) in **ziqa saba** Gy 392:15, 23 a storm-wind.

sabus ʿnšia Gy 107:16 prob. one who instructs about conjugal life Ginzā 117 n. 2. (Rt. **SBS**?)

sabur RD D 25 & often in colophons—a family name; also a *malwāša* man's name. Var. **ṣabur.**

sab(i)ع (Ar. سَبِيع) seventh part, one day of the week. Mod. **sabiع ʿurupta** AM 268:14, **sabع** AM 268:15.

sabla (act. pt. pe. of **SBL**) one who bears a burden, bearer, carrier, porter Wid. iii 70 n. 4. Var. **sibla.** Pl. **sablia. ata huilia sabla ata sabla huilia** Jb 242:13 (var. **sibla** ACD &

DC 30) come, carry a burden for me; **hanatun sablia ḏ-sablilh̲** ATŠ II no. 334 those bearers who carry him.

sabsuta (ܣܒܣܘܬܐ) Gy 242:13 fullness (of pregnancy).

sabsida, sabsidiqa miswritings of **sapsira** (q.v.).

sabع s. **sabi**ع.

sabra (act. pt. pe. st. emph. of **SBR**) believer, doctor of faith. Pl. **sabria.** (Distinction of the two meanings is arbitrary.) **abuhun ḏ-kulhun sabria** Gy 234:21 father of all doctors of faith Ginzā 235 n. 4; **riš sabria ana ḏ-bhiria** Gs 86:10; **liadh̲ uᶜl sabrh̲** Jb 236:7 to those who know him and understand him; **sabra ḏ-mn ᶜria ᶜsbar** Gs 130:9 an expert (in matters of faith am I) who learned from the watchful ones; **sabria liba** RD C 5 believing with heart; **sabria kušṭa** Jb 208:14 believing in Truth; **sabria buta** Jb 168:2 those who teach prayer (Lidzb., but cf. ii 169 n. 4), prob. those who persevere in prayer; **mn sabria mn samkia ldilia** DC 44 from the trustful ones, from those who lean upon me; **lkulhun sabria kušṭa ḏ-bhiia shid** DC 41. 2 to all those believers of Truth who testified to the Life; **hiia liadin uhiia lsabrin** CP 401:2 (*& often*) Life for those who know, Life for those who believe (Lidzb. *unseren Kündigen*).

sabrad DC 40. 884 an angel.

sabrana DC 22. 57:5 var. of **sibrana.**

sabruta occ. var. of **sibruta.**

sagada 1 (nom. ag. pe. of **SGD**) worshipper. Pl. **-ia. kulhun kumrun usagadun** Gy 119:13 all their priests and worshippers MG 181:24; **usagadia ḏ-sagdilun** Jb 176:7 and worshippers that worship them.

sagada 2 (Ar. سَجَّادَة) prayer-rug. **ukulhun sagada ḏ-amaikin** DC 43 J 195 (var. . . . **maikin** P.A.'s copy) and all those who spread a prayer-rug.

sagalia DC 22. 385 for **dagalia** Gy 385:paen.

sagariata pl. (rt. **SGR**) locks. **tabar sagariata** DC 44. 628 f. he breaks locks.

sagia 1 (סַגִּי, סַגִּיא, ܣܓܝ < H. שַׂגִּיא, rel. to Ar. شَجَوْجَى long and thick) large, much, many, great, magnified, extolled. subst. greatness, abundance, increase MG 124.12. Pl. **sagiia.** Occ. var. **sigiia** 1. **ᶜutra sagia** Jb 269:2 f., Gs 63:20, 94:24 ML 150:7 = CP 124:ult. magnified uthra; **atra sagia** Jb 270:9, Gs 130:15 an exalted place; **sagiia bᶜburia nihun** AM 177:8 there shall be abundance of (lit. 'in') crops; **sagiia bᶜqara nitbun** CP 248:9 great spirits sit in glory; **sagiia ḏ-iatbia bᶜqara** DC 3; **baṭinia uiadalia sagia** DC 51. 311 f. conceptions and child-bearings are many; **buṭna umaudala usagia** CP 412:13 and he gave them pregnancy and birth and increase; **gupna sagia** CP 418:2 prolific vine; **haila usagia** ATŠ I nos. 6, 7 strength and increase = **haila usigia** Oxf. 100 a = ML 262:7, **qam bsigia (u)haila** Gy 212:27 = **niqum bsagiih̲ uhailh̲** CP 259:10 he will arise with great (spirits?) and with strength (*or* a hoof?) varr. **niqum bsigiia,** will arise to go (etc.); **sigia ziua** Oxf. 84 a, great radiance.

sagia 2 s. **sigia** 2. **lbit sagia ḏ-ligrh̲** CP 114:9 to my House is the passing (going) of his feet (CP trs. 83 n. 5).

sagia 3, varr. **sigia** 3, **sakia** 3 a fish-eating bird, prob. cormorant or pelican (cf. Ar. سَقَّا). **uailak sagia** (varr. **sigia** B & DC 30. 58, **sakia** AD) **saria** Jb 158:6 woe to thee stinking **s.**

sada 1 (סָדָא, ܣܕܐ, H. & mod. H. סַד, Ar. سَدّ) barrier, fence, obstacle, block (chained to feet), stock(s) MG 100:11. Pl. **sad(ad)ia** MG 163:10. **bsada autbh̲** Gy 242:3 he seated him into the stocks; **mana sada hlaṣa umṣara** Gy 182:2, 18, Gy 230:18, 233:9, 14, Gs 26:15, 28:4, 29:4, 31:10 apparatus of torture, torment and punishment; **sada rama** Gy 90:9, **sada rba** Jb 21:7, 16, 25:8 a great block; **mn sada umn ᶜsura** Gy 9:7 f. from stocks and fetters; **sada ḏ-gubria gabaria** Gy 225:15 block of mighty men; **sada naṭran** Jb 259:5 they (fem.) preserve the block; **sada ḏ-glala bligrh̲** DC 40. 1104 a block of stone (fastened) to her feet; **bsadadia** (varr. **bsadia** B, **bsadadai** D) **iatbia** Gs 88:11 they sit in the stocks.

sada 2 s. **sadia** 2.

sadana 1 (סַדְנָא, ܣܕܢܐ < P. سِنْدَان) anvil, lump, clod, (potter's, blacksmith's, jeweller's) block, base, basis, foundation, axis, stocks MG 51:paen. f. St. abs. & cstr. **sadan.** Pl. **sadia** 1. **mn nura umn mia arqa bsadana msun** Jb 52:2, 227:13 f. from fire and water they solidified earth with its foundation (Lidzb. *am Amboß*); **raza ḏ-sadana ᶜšumia** Jb 166:8 the mystery of the foundation of the heavens (Lidzb. *des Ambosses*, but cf. ii 168 n. 1); **sadania ḏ-ᶜšumia lbišna atit kulh̲ arqa ḏ-hzatan mn sadanh̲ šnat uqamat** DC 37. 362 f. I assumed the aspect(?) of heaven's axis and when she saw me, the whole earth removed from her base and rose upwards; **arqaihun ᶜl sadana laiatba** Gy 10:23 their earth reposeth not on its basis; **sadania upiria ḏ-arqa** Gy 193:3 the clods and rubble(?) of the earth; **sadania ḏ-mia ḏ-minaihun ᶜšata haita shiṭa** Gy 193:4 the anvil [*sic*] of the water from which living fire spread out Ginzā 193 n. 4; **usadana ᶜl mahu triṣ** Gy 198:5 upon what was the foundation based?; **arqa hazin mihšal šhila usadana smik ᶜl mia siauia** Gy 198:6 f. this earth was well-forged and its base (anvil) set on the black waters (play on words); **sadana ḏ-arqa** Gy 90:11, 113:15 etc. JRAS 1939 401:3 the anvil (basis, block) of the earth; **sadana rba ḏ-arqa** Gy 208:4, Gs 27:16 the great anvil of the earth; **kḏ sadan arqa ᶜl gabrh̲** (varr. **gambh̲** BD, Leid., **agambh̲** C, **aganbih̲** Sh. 'Abd.'s copy) **kbiš** Gy 356:5 the earth pressed on his side like an anvil; **arqa nad mn sadanh̲** DC 34. 1103 the earth rocked from its base (lit. anvil); **atit larqa ḏ-hzatan mn sadanh̲ šnat** JRAS 1939 401:3, DC 43 C 58 (cf. DC 37. 362 f. above); **arqa šnat mn sadanh̲** DC 26. 200; **sadan ṣirapaiia** ATŠ II no 365 the jeweller's block; **uligraihun bsadania ḏ-glala** DC 44. 1280 f. = Morg. 264/19:4 and their feet are in stone-stocks; **sadana ḏ-parzla** JRAS 1938 3:22 an anvil of iron; **gabra ḏ-hišlẖ lsipa burkẖ šauia sadana** DC 43 J 170 the man who forged the sword made his knee the anvil; **bit qilba ḏ-hiduia sadania ḏ-arqa hua** CP 222:4 var. **sadana** ŠQ 15:10 the bolster of the bridegroom was clods of earth (var. a clod); **iatbia lsadana ʿpika** DC 51. 80 are sitting on a perverted base (? cf. foll. by which the expression was certainly influenced).

sadana 2 (from **zidana**, var. **zadana**, by influence of **saṭana**?) evil, destructive demon, satan. Pl. **-ia 2. sadania ʿpikia** DC 43 D 65, Morg. 196:2 etc. (*often*) perverted devils; **sadania ʿpikia haršia** Lond. roll B 78, 93, 130, 158, 190, 510 perverting sorcery-devils (*often*).

sadar kasia anana DC 22. 371 = **sidar** etc. Gy 374:9.

sadara a miswriting of **asara. blimitun bsadara ubina** DC 26. 768 (cf. **blimitun basara arqa bina** s. **bina**).

sadarta (nom. act. pa. of **SDR**) arrangement, order, ordinance, set prayer, appointed recitation. Pl. **sadarata. uabihdia hak sadarta** DC 50. 135 and with that arrangement; **rahmia usadarata** DC 40 'devotions' and appointed prayers; **ʿbidata usadarata** ATŠ I no. 247 rites and arrangements (on altar); **atun ṭariana usadru bkulhun sadarata** DC 50. 839 and bring the table (: clay-altar) and arrange it completely (i.e. furnish it with all the appointed foods).

sadia 1 Gs 88:11 B var. of **sadadia** (pl. of **sada** q.v.).

sadia 2 (סָדְה, ܣܕܐ, H. שָׂדֶה, Akk. *šiddu* space, verb *šadādu* to measure) field, open space, plain, desert. **šitla umazruta hanatẖ qaima bsadia balhudẖ** ATŠ I no. 259 and that planting and seedling arises in the field by itself; **duktai . . . bbiriata usadia** DC 46. 125:3 my place is . . . in the streets and fields.

sadira (for **sdira**) orderly, well-arranged, reliable, systematic, methodical, well-versed. **hazin diuan sadira** DC 41:coloph. this well-compiled Diwan (Scroll).

sadqa (rt. **SDQ**) cleft, fissure, split. Varr. **as(a)dqa.** Pl. **-ia. bsadqia** (varr. **basadqia** Leid., **basdqia** DC 22) **nura** Gy 225:8 in the clefts of fire.

sadra 1 (rt. **SDR**) order, arrangement, co-ordination. **alma ḏ-hauia lsadra** DC 34. 736 until there is (complete) order.

sadra 2 (Parsi *sadreh* or *sudreh* J. J. Modi: *The Religious Ceremonies and Customs of the Parsees* 179–84) part of the ritual dress, the tunic or shirt which reaches to below the knee MMII 30.

Gl. 53:3 defectively (**sdra**) ثوب *tunica* رخت.

sadruta (abstr. noun from **SDR I**) arrangement, co-ordination, line. V.s. **SDR I** pe. pf. with **suff.**

saharta (nom. act. pa. of **SHR I**) vigilance, watchfulness, traveller (f.). **ana usaharta ḏ-hiia** CP 221:5 and 9, ŠQ 15:2, 4 I and my life's traveller (a word-play = vigilance of life).

sahda (act. pt. pe. st. emph. of **SHD**) witness. Pl. **-ia. sahdia lagṭia** Gy 286:9 they take witnesses; **bsahdia lagṭia** Gy 288:ult. f. they take as witnesses MG 361:bottom; **sahdia lagṭinin ʿlauaihun** Gy 288:18 ff. we take witnesses against them; **ʿlauaian nihuia bsahdia** CP 29:2 = Q 11 f. shall be witnesses for us MG 362:1; **sahdia ḏ-kadba** s. **kadba**, opp. **sahdia ḏ-kušṭa** Gy 35:15 true witnesses.

sahduta (abstr. noun from preced.) testimony, evidence. **sahduta ḏ-kadba latisihdun** Gy 14:14 (cf. the eighth commandment); **bsahdutun ḏ-hiia ubsahdutẖ ḏ-manda ḏ-hiia** ATŠ II no. 325 with the testimony of Life and with the testimony of M.–ḏ–H.; **sahduta ḏ-ʿumamata šarirata** DC 40 testimony with (?) strong oaths; **sahduta ḏ-ʿpikta** DC 34 distorted (: false) witness; **sahduta ḏ-bzauẖ** ATŠ II no. 312 evidence (of the bride's virginity) that is with her husband.

sahṭaṭara Or. 330:4 = **sahṭṭara** Oxf. roll g 835 a name given to a spirit sitting on the brain (or gelatinous matter).

sahṭir (ܣܗܛܘܪܐ <· Ar. ساطور) knife, butcher's knife. **qamana sahṭir ugira** DAb dagger, knife and arrow.

sahil s. **sihil.** St. emph. **sahla**, cf. Gl. (missp. with ṣ) 94:12 **ṣahla** [*sic*] ساحل *litus*; 98:7 **ṣhla** [sic] سهل *planus* هموار.

sahpiaiil DAb a theophorous name from **SHP.**

sahpʿil (cf. preced.) DAb = RD 24: a name given to Sin.

sahqʿiil (rt. **SHQ**) DC 43 D 24 an ʿutra, DC 50. 780.

sahra 1 (סְחַרְתָּא, ܣܚܪܬܐ) (*a*) tower, watch-tower MG 113:4, (*b*) enclosure. Masc. (*a*) **sahra rba ḏ-naṭrẖ ḏ-ʿurašlam mata bgauẖ hun** Gy 333:15 the great tower in which were the guardians of the city of Jerusalem; (*b*) DC 43 A 9 (parallel with **ṣurta**).

sahra 2 (Nöld. by metath. from ܣܚܪܐ corruptor, destroyer MG 113:5, Lidzb. refers to Bab. *sāḫiru*, cf. Ar. ساحر but only as to the sg. Jb ii 194 footn.) demon. Pl. **sahria** MG 113:4, Jb ii 194 footn., MR 159:bottom, MSchr 34 n. 1, Furlani: *I Nomi* 395–404. **bizbaṭ sahra** Gy 29:21 f., Jb 199:13, **bizbaṭ abuhun ḏ-sahria** Oxf. roll g 365; **biz sahra** (= **biz daiua**) RD B 47; **sahria udaiuia** Gy 19:14, 27:10, 12, 394:1, Q 24:19, RD B 2 (*& often*); **šibiahia qrun sahria ḏ-napšia** Gy 99:11 the Planets created many demons; **ʿu sahria anatun dar bhurbia** Gy 354:1 if ye are demons, dwell in waste places; **ʿpuq sahria qaimia** Gs 94:11 if I go out, the demons stay; **sahria hdarilẖ lpagrai** Gs 94:16 demons surround my body; **šuba sahraihun uhumraihun** Gs 95:4 the Seven (Planets), their demons and their amulet-spirits; **sahraihun** Q 17:1; **sahrak** Gy 88:5; **sahrak udaiuak** Gy 87:21 thy demons and thy devils; **asgit lsahria ʿtit** Jb 164:8 I went, I came to the demons; **atra ḏ-iatbia sahria** Jb 251:2 the place where the demons dwell; **kd hzuia sahria lziuh̲ bakin** Jb 251:3 whenthe demons saw his radiance, they wept; **mnata litlun lsahria** RD B 33 f. the demons have no portion.

sahrana (from סַהֲרָא, ܣܗܪܐ? cf. H. שַׂהֲרֹנִים. Doubtf.) (Possibly a crescent-shaped marsh-boat? Boats used today in the marshes of S. ʿIrāq are crescent-shaped, cf. Jb ii 145 n. 3) **ana qadmit bʿuhra bsahrana** (var. **bsihrana** C & DC 30) **d̲-lahua mn parzla** Jb 143:11 I advanced on (my) road in a boat (?) that was not of iron.

sauad (Ar. سواد البلد) alentours, (villages in the) neighbourhood. Var. **suad** s.v. **sauad d̲-kupa** AM 202 the villages round Kufa.

sauahil (Ar. pl. سَوَاحِل) AM 198 the shores (pl. of **sihil**, var. **sahil**). Mod.

sauṭa = **siuṭa. sauṭa nihuilh̲** AM 16:3, 36:5 he will suffer pain.

saupa (rt. **SUP**) end, perishing. St. abs. **sup** 1 s.v. **saupa d̲-alma** (*often*) the end of the world; **mn saupun** Gs 73:8 from (at) their perishing.

saura AM 286:6 a miswriting for **ṣaura**?

saṭana (סטנא, ܣܛܢܐ < H. שָׂטָן, Ar. loan-w. شَيْطَان, Eth. ሰይጣን Praetorius ZDMG lxi 619) Satan, devil. Pl. **-ia.** Doublet **ṣa-** (s.v.) MG 45:13 f., Brandt ERE viii 384. **saṭana rgima** Gy 15:2 = الشيطان الرجيم Qur. 3:31, prob. from Eth. 'accursed' Nöld.: *Neue Beiträge* 47, cf. ܕܓܠܐ ܘܡܬܪܓܡܢܐ *Ephraemi Opera* ed. Overbeck 131:11, Ginzā 17 n. 2; **zmara d̲-saṭana** Jb 57:1 Satan's music MSt 18 n. 2; **ʿsmaiil saṭana** Gy 200:19 Ishmael the devil (Ishmael considered as forefather of the Arabs); cf. **simiaiil saṭana** DC 36; **saṭana napla** Gy 36:7, 40:6, 8 etc. (*often*) the base Satan; **saṭana d̲-haila ušrara litlh̲** Gy 26:4 f. Satan who has no strength or force; **kul man d̲-lsaṭana sagid** Gy 36:7 f. whosoever worshippeth Satan; **alma d̲-saṭana** HG the world of Satan; **saṭania bišia** (*often*) wicked devils.

saiakta (nom. act. pa. of **SUK**) end, limit(ation), conclusion MG 122:8. Var. **saikta** s.v. **miniana usaiakta** Gy 2:15 number and limit; **saiakta litlh̲** Gy 4:19 it hath no limit; **iuma hamšaia d̲-saiakta** ATŠ I no. 121 the fifth, i.e. concluding day; **saiakta d̲-masiqta** ATŠ II no. 180 the end of the *masiqta*.

saiantia fem. of **saina** 1. Occ. var. **saintia** (DC 43). **ruh saiantia** DC 48 the hateful spirit; **saiantia zikria usaiantia nuqbata** DC 43 A 28 (here as name of a kind of evil spirits of both genders).

saiapta (rt. **SUP**) adj. fem. destructive. **ruha bišta . . . saiapta** DC 26. 54 evil . . . destructive spirit.

saiara (nom. ag. pe. of **SAR I**) one who cruises about, travels. **anat saiara** (var. **saira**) Jb 134:1 thou (: eagle) art one that cruises about.

said Zotb. 222a:33, **saiid** Zotb. 218b:9 (Ar. سَيِّد) Seyyed.

saiuia ML 60:9, 231:4 (& *often in coloph.*) a *malwāša* man's name.

saiura (rt. **SAR I** ܣܥܘܪܐ) Gy 227:4 canonical visitor, chorepiscopus (an expression learned from Syriac Christians as an ecclesiastical technical term) MG xxix 22, 69:24.

saiṭa (ܣܚܝܛܐ detestable MG 126:15) perishable Jb ii 130 n. 3. **aklia d̲-lahua saiṭa** Jb 132:6 f., Gs 8:14 f., Q 57:8 = ML 137:12 they eat what is imperishable.

saiid s. **said.**

saikta = **saiakta. mn riš alma lsaikta** DC 42 from beginning to end.

saima (by epenthesis from ܣܡܝܐ) blind MG 24:12. Pl. **saimia.** Antonym of **nahra** 2. **ainaihun saima ulanahra** Gy 277:12 their eyes are blind and shine not; **dmutun saima ulanahra** Gy 375:14; **saimia bišia ulahazin** Jb 211:10 blind are the wicked and see not.

saina 1 (by epenthesis from ܣܢܝܐ) hateful, ugly, foul, odious, abominable MG 24:9. But st. abs. **snia** MG 24:11. Fem. **saiantia** s.v. Pl. masc. **sainia**, fem. **sainata** MG 24:10. **riha d̲-saina** Gy 31:24 foul odour; **ʿbidata sainata** Jb 96:8 f. odious deeds; **dmauata sainata** Or. 332:2 abominable spectres; **minilia sainata** AM 22:14 malicious words. Fem. pl. substantively: **bsainata šuar bdmu dmu** DC 43 E 12 they leapt up in abominable shapes of every kind.

saina 2 ML 198:1 for **siana** ibid. n. 1.

saka (ܣܟܐ) end, limit, boundary, point, completeness, section, quality, category MG 108: 11, Ginzā 7 n. 6. Pl. **sakia.** Masc. **lika** (var. **lʿka**) **d̲-saka litlh̲** Gy 77:19, 95:21 f., 293:7 f., 294:24, 295:3, 296:13, **lika** (var. **lʿ-**) **d̲-litlh̲ saka** Gy 94:23, 100:4, 229:4 f. there is nothing without an end (MG 433 n. 1, Ginzā 75 n. 1), opp. **ʿka d̲-litlh̲ saka** Q 1:19, CP 2:11, ML 4:7, 242:10 cf. p. 4 n. 4; **mn saka ulaqamh̲** Gy 380:20 from here (: one section) onwards; **sakia** Gy 4:3, 10, 9:17, 278:12, 280:7 'species', 'qualities' Ginzā 4:4; **hamša sakia rurbia** Gy 4:10 five great qualities (of the Great King of Light, cf. parallels in Avesta & Mānī HpGn 231, Reitzenstein: *Nachr. d. Gesch. d. Wissensch. zu Göttingen* 1922 pp. 249 ff. Ginzā 7 n. 8); **saka kulh̲ d̲-mia siauia** Gy 149:12 the whole boundary of black waters; **bsaka d̲-napša** Gy 300:4, ATŠ II no. 192 in the wider sense; **lasaka ulaminiana** Gy 139:22 without limit and without number; **saka uminiana litlh̲** Gy 69:13 (& *often*); **saka umiṣra litlun** ATŠ I no. 287 they are endless and boundless; **sidria sakia umalalia** Gy 197: 21 books, sections and words; **sakia usidria** Gy 378:4 sections and books; **ʿniania udrašia bsakun** ML 58:12 songs and hymns in their completeness; **mn saka kulh̲** AM (?) entirely, categorically; **kul man d̲-našar lhazin saka** ATŠ II no. 218 every person that stands firm upon this point; **uhad saka mn psaqa d̲-qabin d̲-šišlam rba** ATŠ II no. 329 and one section dealing with the wedding ceremony of Šišlam the Great; **bkulhun sakia d̲-qarit** HG in all the sections that thou recitest; **bsaka qadmaia** DC 41 in the first part; **malala qadmaia d̲-qaiim lsaka ʿlaia saka miṣaia ulsaka titaia**

DC 39, DC 43 the first word that set up a higher boundary, a middle boundary and a lower boundary; **bsaka** to the end, in full CP 68:3.

sakaṭaš ATŠ II no. 189 = **sapṭia** DC 36 ibid. casket.

sakaita (rt. **SKA**) hope, anticipation, expectation. **sakaitẖ umhašabatẖ** AM . . . his hope and his plans.

sakaka (rt. **SKK**) holding down or back. **sakaka d̠-nišimta** DC 34. 361 the holding down of the soul.

sakakta (nom. act. **SKK**) entanglement, snare. **bsakaktun** DC 22. 459 & Leid. var. of **bsakaihun** Gs 73:10 in their entanglement.

sakandarᶜia AM 198:8 (var. **sikandiriia** Ṣâb.'s AM), **sakandirᶜiia** AM 203 (إِسْكَنْدَرِيَّة) Alexandria.

sakara Gy 291:15, Zotb. 221a:3 a man's name.

sakura (rt. **SKR**) DC 22. 221 (var. **sakla** Gy 227:4) recluse?, hermit? (Lidzb. scholar?).

sakina s. **sikina.**

sakla (rt. **SKL**, סַכְלָא, ܣܟܠܐ, H. סָכָל, Akk. *saklu*) fool MG 107:4. Pl. **saklia. qarabtana sakla d̠-lahaš ulapraš** Gy 94:12 foolish warrior without sense and understanding; **sakla tmima** Jb 259:8 f. ignorant fool, pl. **saklia tmimia** Jb 171:12, 181:10, Gy 357:8 f., ATŠ I no. 11; **sakla** Gy 227:4 s. **sakura**; **anat saklit uᶜmak sakla** DC 44. 1016 f. thou art a fool and thy mother is a fool.

sakluta (abstr. noun from preced.) folly, foolishness. **bsaklutun mistakria** Gy 357:9 are held back in their folly; **aklilun bsakluta** DC 48. 226 they eat them in foolishness.

sala 1 (סַלָּא, ܣܠܐ, H. & mod. H. סַל, Ar. سَلَّة Fränkel 75, Akk. *sallu, sellu*) basket, platter woven of grass, small reed mat so used, cooling receptacle, (primitive) cooler. **salik** Gs 134:2 thy basket, **salai** Gs 134:10 my basket; **salak kd̠ mlia lahma** CP 406:5, CP 428:ult. f. thy (grass) platter (or basket) when full of bread; **uabihda sala aklin** JRAS 1937 594:17 and they eat in one dish; **qarirtia mn sala** DC 23 (several times) cooler than a frigidary.

sala 2 (H. סֶלָה Ges.) in the magical formula **amin amin sala** (frequent in exorcisms).

salauata (cf. **salua**) pl. shafts, rods, thorns. **šuba salauata** JRAS 1937 591:31 seven shafts.

salama Zotb. 218b:26 a man's name.

salaq (Ar. سُلَاق) lippitude of the eyelids, bleariness (of eyes). **salaq d̠-ainia** AM 287:24 bleariness of the eyes.

salua = **silua** (q.v.). Pl. **salauata** s.v. (apart from other plurals s. **silua**). **salua hu** DC 41 (picture) it is a thorn-tree.

salim (Ar. سَلِيم) AM 255:30, Zotb. 223b:15 etc. a man's name.

saliq (for الصليق ?) AM 203 name of a town formerly below Wasiṭ in Lower 'Irāq BZ Ap. II.

salita Oxf. roll 203 ff, DC 43 J 94 ff. = **silita.**

sam (rt. **SUM** hence 'He-placed', not P. سام as Brandt supposed MR 194, MSchr 196 n. 5, cf. Lidzb. OSt 544) a spirit of light MR 196, 218 n. 2, MSchr 55 n. 4, Jb ii 18 n. 7, ML 282, CP 157, Ginzā 180 n. 3, HpGn. 41. **sam smir** Q 12:30, 15:6, 18, ML 35:5 the Preserved Sâm; **sam smir ziua** Q 5:24, 20:33, ML 16:1, 17:11, 40:11, Gy 295:12 S. preserved (in) light; **sam mana smira** CP 115:13, Gy 71:1, 189:19, 196:2, Gs 7:9, Q 5:20, 7:28, 16:29, 58:25 S. the safeguarded Mâna (Siouffi 38:11); **malka sam mana smira** CP 13:18, 28:11, 199j:6, Morg. 5:10; **sam rba** Jb 219:8; **sam ziua** CP 448:13, 458:11, Gy 295:21, Gy 321:20, RD 9; **sam ziua rba** Gy 199:18, Q 10:26; **sam ziua dakia** Gy 213:21 (Siouffi 39:13); **malka sam ziua dakia bukra habiba rba qadmaia** Morg. 4:8 f. the king (: priest) S., the pure, firstborn, beloved, great, first radiance; **sam gufna** CP 425:5; **sam gupna dakia** Gy 377:21 S. the pure Vine; **sam gupan usam gupaian** CP 5:ult., Q 1:31 = ML 5:6 (mere play on words); **sam pira hiuara** CP 3:ult. f., Gy 176:11, ML 5:7 S. the White Fruit; **sam zuṭa** Jb 259:6 S. the Lesser; **sam hiia** Jb 216:4, 217:3 (formed as masc. of **simat hiia** Jb ii 202:13 ff.); **sam kasia** Gs 73:13 the hidden S. Ginzā 503 n. 1; **sam iahu** PD 806; **sam** is also used as a frequent *malwâša* man's name: **sam adam** RD D 5, **sam baian** RD D 6 etc.

sama (סַמָּא, ܣܡܐ, H. pl. סַמִּים, mod. H. סַם sweet scent, Ar. سَمّ poison, شُمّ *teriak* φάρμακον Fränkel 262, Akk. *šammu*, Eg. ) drug, poison, medicament, medicine. Masc. Pl. **samania, simania** s.vv. **sama uasuta** Gy 28:7 f. medicament and healing; **sama d̠-muta** Gy 216:17 deadly venom; **sama anat d̠-masia** Gy 274:24 f. thou art a medicine that healeth; **asia d̠-samẖ mia** CP 87:15, ML 108:5, DC 27. 153 f. healer whose medicine is water; **sama rba** CP 135:6 a powerful medicine; **d̠-hiuia miṭiiẖ . . . ᶜu sama iahiblẖ** ATŠ I no. 76 whom a snake attacked . . . and poisoned (?) (read **usama**); **umn mrirtẖ šaun sama** ATŠ I no. 249 and from its gall they made poison; **sama d̠-ᶜlauia kulhun asauata** ATŠ I no. 53 a drug superior to all medicines.

samalqand AM 204 = **samarqand.**

samandarᶜil PD 803, 816, 819, **samandirᶜil** Jb 5:16 (var. **samindarᶜil** AC), **samandiriiil** Morg. 7:ult., **samandarᶜil** RD 20 = **simandarᶜil** DAb a spirit Jb ii 10 n. 1.

samania (ܣܡܡܢܐ) pl. of **sama** simples, drugs, healing herbs. Var. **simania.** MG 14:24 f., 169:24, Lidzb. ZS i p. 1. **ᶜuṣania usimania** Gy 33:17 (var. **usania** B & Sh. 'Abd.'s copy) leaves and healing herbs; **ṣaidia abdia samania** Jb 157:4 fishermen making drugs (: poison for the fish); **iarqunia usamania** Gy 232:7 vegetables and healing herbs; **pašaria usamania** AM 46:penult. exorcisms and drugs; **samania uminiania nirdun ᶜlẖ** AM 21:8 drugs and calculations will plague him; **malkaihun d̠-kulhun samania** Or. 326:18 f. king of all medicaments.

samadria DC 22. 101 = **simadria** Gy 106:17.

samandar(i)ˁl name of an uthra (but in RD = DAb used also of a devil). MMII 223 n. 6, CP trs. 272 n. 3. **samandariˁil** PD 803, 816, 819; **šum samandarˁil** (= **šdum**) RD 20 = DAb par.; **qlida samandarˁil** RD F 1 = DAb par. (as a name of the land of Rūha); **samandirˁil** RD 1, **samandirˁil ˁutra (a)mqabil buta** Jb 5:16 the uthra S. receives prayer; **malka samandiriil ˁutra** Morg. 7:ult.; varr. **smandrˁil, smandarˁil.**

samarqand AM 198:13 f. Samarqand BZ Ap. II. Var. **samalqand** s.v.

samuia a *malwâša* man's name.

samindarˁil s. **samandarˁil.**

samka (rt. **SMK,** סָמְכָא, ܣܡܟܐ) support, base. Pl. **-ia.** Masc. **libh̲ npal mn samkh̲** Gy 94:19, 95:16 (*& often*) he lost confidence (lit. his heart fell from its support), similarly **ˁuṣrh̲ npal mn samkh̲** DC 41. 108; **libh̲ traṣlh̲ lsamkh̲** Gy 95:24 he reassured his heart (lit. set up on its support), similarly **anihh̲ llibai lsamkh̲** Gy 323:11, MG 354:23 and **d̲-mistmik libai lsamkh̲** ATŠ I no. 97 (varr. **liban** our heart) so that my heart may be reassured (lit. supported on its support).

samkiˁil ˁlana DC 41 name of a personified tree.

samra 1 (rt. **SMR**) keeping, possessing (?). **mazihit . . . mn samra d̲-kulhun** (read **kulh̲**) **qumth̲** DC 37. 578 thou art cast out . . . from possessing (?) his whole body.

samra 2 a *malwâša* woman's name.

samraia (rt. **SMR,** has nothing to do with 'Samaritans' GGA 1908 p. 399) one of the four men who prepare body for burial and carry the bier to the grave and place in it the body, they also fill the grave when this is done; bier-bearer, bier-carrier. Pl. **samraiia. uatin arba samraiia matilil** [*sic*] **napaqa sablilia** [*sic*] **lbit qubria** Morg. 181:3 ff. and four bier-bearers come, place in the departed and carry him to the cemetery; **riša d̲-samraia** (read **-aiia**) Morg. 181:9 the head-bier-bearer, **riša d̲-bada d̲-samraiia** Morg. 182:5 f. id. (lit. the foreman of the work of the bier-bearers); **napqa mn pagrh̲ ulahua arba samraiia** DC 35:coloph. she died (departed the body) and there were not four bier-carriers.

samrud. miša br samrud DC 40. 946 Moses son of S.

sana (rt. **SNA,** סָנְאָה, ܣܢܝܐ) enemy, foe MG 71:7. Pl. **-ia. sana d̲-midamia lrahmh̲** Gy 216:4 an enemy who makes himself out to be a friend (pretends friendship); **sania nitun** AM (?) foes will come; **ulbit sandu** DC 43 J 166 and on the house of their enemy (mod.); **hu bsanh̲ hazia** AM 11:2 he will get the better of his enemy.

sanaia (adj. from preced.) ill-natured, hostile, enemy (adj.). Pl. **sanaiia. gabra sanaia** Par. AM (var. **sania**) an odious man; **sanaiia d̲-nhura** ATŠ enemies of the light.

sangara (prob. nom. ag. pe. of **SGR**; different from P. سَنْگَر) (*a*) prosecutor, calumniator, backbiter, accuser, (*b*) advocate. Var. **sangi-.** Pl. **-ia.** (*a*) **sangaria šadqia ulamamlilia** DC 44. 576 = DC 26. 567 (Morg. 259/9:39 miswritten) calumniators (?) are silent and do not speak; **sangaria udaiania šadqia** DC 26. 578 ff. = Morg. 259/10:2, 8 prosecutors and judges are silent; (*b*) **ˁnbu sapra (u)hakima usangara** DC 44. 1137 = Morg. 263/17:9 Nebo (Mercury) the wise scribe, the advocate . . .

sangdan(a) (P. سنگدان) crop, gizzard. **šuplh̲ usangdanh̲** AM 127:20 (miswritten **sangbana**) (var. **sangupanh̲** Ṣâb.'s AM), and its rump-fat (?) and its gizzard.

sangiania DC 22 var. of **singiania** Gy 99:2, 121:4.

sandan a *malwâša* woman's name.

sandar (a mod. form سكندر, not Pahl. *alaksandar* Gray ZA xix 285) Alexander the Macedonian. Var. **sindar** DC 22. 379:paen. **sandar ruhmaia** Gy 383:14 s. **bruq.**

sanduqia pl. (ܣܢܕܘܩܐ, Ar. صندوق) RD B 109 = DAb par. chests.

sandilia DC 44. 1590 a var. of **sandlia.**

sandirka occ. miswriting for **sindirka** (q.v.).

***sandla** (סַנְדְּלָא, ܣܢܕܠܐ, σανδάλιον) sandal. Found only in pl. **sandlia.** Varr. **sindlia, sandilia. sandlia d̲-ziua** Jb 46:2 ff., Gs 97:19 BCD (var. **sindlia** A), DC 37. 302 (*& often*) sandals of radiance; **sandlia d̲-kima** s. **kima 1; sandlia iaqdana** Jb 100:7 sandals of flame.

sandlus (ܣܢܕܪܘܣ, Ar.-P. سندروس *sandarax* Löw 107) sandalwood. Varr. **sandrus, sandruz, sindlus, sindrus** etc. ML xxi, 14 n. 4. **riha usandlus** Q 5:10 = ML 14:8 = CP 13:6 (*& often*) incense and sandalwood; **sindlus dakia** Gy 346:23 pure sandalwood.

sanukia Oxf. roll g 741 = Or. 328:20 for **sanupia**? constriction, squeezing, choking.

sania (act. pt. pe. of **SNA,** cf. ܣܢܝܐ, doublet of **sana**) hater, enemy. Fem. st. emph. **sanita. sania anašia zipania hauia** AM 10:13 he will be a hater of false people; **kalta sanita** DC 48. 238 a hated bride.

saniaiil, var. **siniaiil** DC 44 a spirit invoked in exorcisms.

saniuta (abstr. noun from preced., סַנְיוּתָא, ܣܢܝܘܬܐ) hatred, enmity, hostility. Var. **si-** s.v. **saniuta udahalta** DC 40. 851 enmity and fear; **sanilh̲ saniuta** DC 48. 229 they hate her heartily (inner acc.).

sanšb s. **sinšab.**

sasa (סָסָא, ܣܣܐ, H. סָס, Ar. سُوس, سُوسَة, Eth. ፂፅ, Akk. *sāsu,* Sum. *ziz,* Gr. σής Lewy: *Fremdwörter*) moth, maggot MG 157:5. **sasa uhbala** Gy 5:19, 9:4 (second word miswritten) moth and decay.

sasauata Gy 387:11 a pl. of **susia.**

sasai (cf. **zazai**) Zotb. 222b:10 a man's name.

sasgiaiil mlaka DC 40. 869 an angel.

saskinia (cf. ססגונא 2 J, ܣܣܓܘܢܐ) bright hues, glistening colours. Doubtf. **niṣubta d̲-nhura usaskinia** DC 51. 226 f. a transference of light and bright hues (?).

saᶓad AM 286:38, **saᶓd** AM 286:21 (Ar. سَعْد) happy, lucky, fortunate, auspicious.

saɛadat s. **siɛadat.**

saɛdan Zotb. 228a:13 a man's name.

saɛdat s. **siɛdat.**

saɛid AM 205:1 Upper Egypt BZ Ap. II. Var. **ṣaɛid** Ṣâb.'s AM.

saɛiṭu (impt. of Ar. سعط) AM 128:8 insert! AM trs. 82 n. 8.

sapa (rt. **SUP**) destruction, ruin. Var. **sapapa** DC 51. 652. **sapa ukaria** DC 48:316 s. **karia.**

sapaqa (Ar. صَفْقَة) tambourine, tambour. **qiraqid bsapaqa** RD 22 = DAb par. (with illustration) dances to the tambour.

sapaqatai(i)n (Ar. du. indirect case صَفْقَتَيْن) cymbals, clappers. **qimahia bsapaqataiin** RD 28 f. (var. **-ain** DAb) clashes the cymbals.

sapar (Ar. سَفَر) journey. **bsapar maiit** AM 149:7 he will die on a journey.

sapṭa (Ar. سَفَط, but cf. **ṣa-** with which it is often confused) chest, treasure-box, wallet, safe, casket. Pl. **-ia** also 'chains', 'fetters' (as **ṣapṭia**). Masc. **sapṭa rba ḏ-ziua** DC 48. 199 the great casket of light, p. **sapṭia ḏ-ziua** CP 365:2 = Oxf. 109 b; **bsapṭia hilia** CP 364:11 = Oxf. 108 b in its strong-box (CP trs. 239, n. 3) = jewel-box; **qlidia baraiia hun bʿdik ugauaiia bsapṭia matnit** Jb 138:10 f. the keys of the outer (doors) were in thine hand and (of) the inner (doors) thou didst put in a bag (Lidzb. *an Ketten*); **uqaziza rgigia usapṭia** (var. **bṣapṭia** B, **bsapṭia** DC 30) **rmin** (read **raminin**?) Jb 139:7 f. we (?) put on fine silk and chains (Lidzb. *Schmuckketten*? ii 135 n. 5, var. we? place fine silk into chests); **ginzan nṭir bsapṭia d-zahba** ATŠ II no. 189 our treasure will be kept in chests of gold; **razia haškia bsapṭia naṭria** DC 34. 350 they keep dark mysteries in caskets (*or* chains); **lginzaikun kulh̲ bsapṭia atnath̲** DC 27. 170 thou shalt put all your treasure (i.e. the holy books and ritual objects) into chests.

sapna a bird of prey. Var. **sipna.** Masc. **uailak sapna** (from **lsapna** ACD & **sipna** B & DC 30) **kapna** Jb 158:5 cf. ii 160 n. 4.

sapsira (cf. **simsar**) travelling broker or agent, pedlar, huckster? Var. **sabsira. usapsira bimsanh̲** (DC 21) JRAS 1937 593:201 and PA and the pedlar (?) with his shoe.

sapqia DC 22 a var. of **sapra 2** Gy 388:14 (v.s. **nasqa, nasra**).

sapra 1 (סָפְרָא, ܣܦܪܐ, H. סוֹפֵר, Old-Aram. & Pun. ספר, Akk. *šāpiru*) scribe, writer, clerk, scholar. Var. **sipra 2.** Pl. **-ia.** (ʿ)**nbu sapra** Gs 29:6, DC 44. 1136, 1798, 1926 = Morg. 268/27:28, 269/29:25 f. etc. (*often*) Nebo (Mercury) the learned; **alga lahauia sapra** Jb 105:6 (var. **sipra** ABCD) a deaf man will not become a scholar; **magušaiia usapria** Gy 388:13 Magians and scribes.

sapra 2 Gy 388:14 = **sipra 1** (v.s. **nasqa, nasra**).

SAQ = **SUQ I** = **SQQ** secondary rt. formed from **nisaq** impf. pe. of **SLQ I.**

Pe. Pf. **saq** Gy 280:23 he ascended MG 84:2, 240 n. 11. Impf. s. **SLQ I.**

Note. All mod. forms are from this secondary rt.: Pf. *sâq* he ascended; part. pres. *q(â)sâyeq* he ascends.

Gl. 101:3 f. **sag** [*sic*!!] صعد *ascendere* بالا رفت.

saqa (סַקָּא, ܣܩܐ, H. & mod. H. שַׂק, Eth. ሠቅ Nöld.: *Neue Beiträge* 39:19, Akk. *šaqqu* KAT 603, 650, Eg. [hieroglyph], Copt. **cok**, Gr. σάκκος Lewy: *Fremdwörter* 87) sack(cloth). Var. **sarua 2.** ʿ**umṣa ḏ-saqa** Jb 130:3, 7 (var. **sarua** D) a piece of sackcloth (doubtf. cf. ii 128 n. 3).

saqaṭ (Ar. سَقَط) nonsense, rubbish. Var. **saqiṭ. sakla ḏ-raṭin saqaṭ** AM 155:17 antep. (var. **saqiṭ** Par. xxvi) a fool that talks nonsense.

saqaṭa (cf. Ar. سَقْطَة) failure, ruin (?) Fem. (?). **saqaṭa ḏ-abiat** DC 43 G 39 ruin which has (or hast?) become thick (?).

saqamta (nom. act. pa. of **SQM**) completion, perfecting, development. **saqamta maṣbutaikun** DC 35 consummation of your baptism; **usaqamth̲ ldilia hibil ziua ʿthib** HG and its development is given to me, H.-Z.

SAR I, SUR I (סער & סור, ܣܚܪ, Ar. سعر) to go around (pa. go astray = travel this way and that), travel about, visit, circle about, look around; to see into, see to, inspect, provide, care for; to do, carry out, perform, deal with, achieve. Double rt. as in Jew.-Aram. Jb ii 131 n. 7.

Pe. Pf. **sar bkulh̲ alma** DC 41:100 f. he travelled in all the world; **lʿuhrh̲ sar** Gy 137:18, 164:23 he set out; **lʿuhrai sarit** Gy 158:17, 164:8 f. I set out MG 240 n. 11, Ginzā 153 n. 5; **sarit ubihšit** Gy 140:21 f. I inspected and examined; **sarit bgauh̲ kul ṣbu ʿutria sarit** Gy 275:14 I looked into all things (that are) in it, I saw after the uthras; **sarit ḏ-hiia paqdun** Gy 275:21 f. I performed that which the Life commanded me (MG 255:antep). Act. pt. fem. (?) **saira** Jb 134:1B a var. of **saiara** (q.v.), pl. **sairia** Gy 276:22, CP 233:10 they go astray; fem. **sairan ʿuhra** ATŠ I no. 283 they (: soul and spirit) travel on their way; **bhda anana sairan** DC 27. 301 (cf. ATŠ II no. 109 var. **sairin**) they travel in one cloud. Part. pres. **saiarna** (var. **saiirna** B) **agma** Jb 143:8 I traverse the marsh; **ḏ-sairit ʿuṣbuta bkul zban** DC 40 that thou carest (seest into) matters at all time. Inf. **baiina balma misar** Jb 135:14 I want to travel in the world (Lidzb. *Ich will mich in der Welt umsehen*).

Der.: **saiara, saiura, sira 2**?

SAR II, SUR II (Lidzb. H. שער II, cf. Akk. *šāru* wind, storm) to be terrified, troubled, awestruck ML 126 n. 1.

Pe. Pf. **bziuak sar rkubia** ML 126:2 (varr. CP 100:12 **sararkubia, sarkubia** Q 52:10, **sara rkubia** CP 100:12) at thy radiance the riders (: planets) were afraid; **mn ziuh̲ sar** CP 203:16, Oxf. 64 b = ML 234:12 f. they were awestruck by his radiance. Act. pt. pl. **mn ziuak sairia**

CP 204:15, Oxf. 66 a = ML 236:1 they are awestruck at thy radiance.

sar (prob. pe. pf. of **SAR I**) a heavenly being forming a pair with **saruan** (usually mentioned together) ML 283, MMII 76. **sar usaruan** Gy 172:5 f., 221:4, 374:14, Q 15:11, Oxf. 57 a, ML 41:4, 229:1, CP 35:6, 194:8 f., 428:6 (Siouffi 39:19).

sar anbu, sar nbu s. **sarnbu.**

sara 1 (שַׂעְרָא, סַעְרָא, ܣܥܪܐ, H. שֵׂעָר, Ar. شَعْر, شَعَر, Eth. ሥዕርት, Akk. *šārtu*) hair. Pl. **saria 1** MG 115:5. **blimtun bsara** DC 26, DC 40 I gagged them with a hair; **mašria sara lkukbia** DC 25. 14 f. they loosen the hair of the stars (of flying stars, comets).

sara 2 (st. emph. fem.?, cf. Jew.-Aram. סַעֲרְתָּא, סַרְתָּא, Syr. ܣܥܪ̈ܬܐ, H. שְׂעֹרָה, Ar. شَعِير, Sab. 𐩦𐩲𐩧, Eth. ሥርናይ, Akk. *šeurtu*; Löw no. 222) barley. Only pl. **saria 2** is known from literature MG 115:5, but the sg. *sâra* is known from the colloquial, cf. *mēn sâra* 'beer' (lit. transl. from P. آب جو barley-water, beer). **bazira d̲-saria** Gy 392:8 barley-seed; **saria uhamruta** Gy 389:13 barley and harvest; **aṭšia usaria** Gy 389:16 fruits and barley; **saria uhiṭia** AM (*often*) barley and wheat.
Gl. 99:9 missp. شعير *hordeum* جو.

sara 3 s. **sira 2.**

saraha (rt. Jew.-Aram., H. סרח, Syr. ܣܪܚ I, cf. Ar. شرح to cut, dissect) injury, damage. Varr. **sariha, siriha, sraha** s.v. **sariha bdupnh̲** DC 43 J 139 an injury in his side (var. **sariha** Oxf. roll 305).

saranbu s. **sarnbu.**

sarandbaiia (adj. from **sarandib**) DC 7 the Sinhalese.

sarandib (سرنديب), var. **sarandir** AM 205:5 Ceylon BZ Ap. II.

sararkubia s. **ŚAR II** pf.

sarga (ܣܪܓܐ, Ar. loan-w. سَرْج Fränkel 101) saddle, mat ending in bags on either side of a riding- or pack-animal; **susia d̲-lasarga** Gy 216:19 a horse without a saddle; **alma lsarga bizma** Gy 391:1 up to the saddle in blood.

sardbaiia DC 7 name of a people. Miswritten for **hardbaiia**?

sarhabaiit (ܡܣܪܗܒܐܝܬ) quickly. Usually with procl. prep. **b-** MG 201:5. Var. **sarhibaiit. bsarhabaiit** Gy 237:4, Par. xiv (*often*), ATŠ I no. 101, **bsarhibaiit** ATŠ I no. 160.

sarhib (impt. saf. of **RHB I**) used sometimes adverbially: urgently. **sarhib mauminalik** DC 40. 939 urgently I adjure thee (fem.).

sarua 1 (سَرْو Ar.-P. form of Aram. שׁוּרְבִּינָא, Syr. ܫܘܪܒܝܢܐ & ܫܪܘܝܢܐ Löw no. 333, from Bab. *šurmēnu*) cypress: **qumth̲ damia lsarua** Par. xv 22a = Par. xxv 27a = CP 239:6 his stature is like the cypress.

sarua 2 s. **saqa.**

saruadta (rt. **SRWD,** Syr. ܫܘܪܕܐ) (*a*) fright, alarm (esp. nightmare), terror, (*b*) loneliness. (*a*) **sahria d̲-lilia usaruadta d̲-ʿumama** DC 40. 103 and 117 night-demons and terror by day; (*b*) **bsibuth̲ usaruadth̲ timut** AM 100:8 f. in her old age and loneliness she will die.

saruan a heavenly spirit forming a pair with **sar** (q.v.). **sar usaruan** s. **sar; saruan rba d̲-basim šumh̲** DC 50. 393 the Great Sarwan whose name is pleasing; **saruan** is also a *malwâša* man's name (cf. Zotb. 218a:15 & often in colophons).

saruata (cf. **saruadta**) fem. pl. frightful, used of demons of ruins and desolate places. **saruata d̲-batia harubia** Oxf. roll 200 demons of destroyed houses; **qiriata harbuta saruata** DC 43 J 92 frightful creatures of destruction.

sarupa (rt. **SRP I**) swallower Nöld. ZA xxx 150. Lidzb. compares it with H. שָׂרָף Ginzā 189 n. 3, hence: burner. Pl. **-ia. karapiun sarupa** Gy 187:18, 23, 24, 188:6 the swallower K., **sarupia** ATŠ II no. 189 the burners (= planets).

saruqia pl. (rt. **SRQ I**) rakes, combs. **saruqia d̲-ʿdaihun** DC 43. 72 the rakes of their hands.

saruta occasionally for **sruta.**

sarṭana (סַרְטָן, ܣܪܛܢܐ, Ar. سَرَطَان. Subst. of adjectival origin? MG 139:15) crab; Cancer (sign of the Zodiac) MG 139:15, ZDMG xxv 256, MMII 74. Var. **ṣa-** MG 45:15. As a sign of the Zodiac Gy 122:20, 123:19 & very often in AM.

sarṭata (rt. סְרַט, ܣܪܛ, H. שׂרט, Ar. شرط to incise, inscribe, Akk. *šarāṭu* to tear) inscription, depictment, picture. **dmuta usarṭata dilak** DC 37. 251 thy portrait and thine inscription.

sarṭita (cf. s. prec.) DC 43 A 166 incision, wound?

saria 1 pl. of **sara 1.**

saria 2 pl. of **sara 2.**

saria 3 (pt. pe. of **SRA I**) stinking, putrid. Fem. **sarita** MG 153:22. Pl. masc. **sariia** MG 164:16. **kalba saria** Par. xxiv 44b, DC 44. 911 a stinking dog; **ulrihaiun saria nibasmh̲** DC 48. 223 and will sweeten their stinking odour; **mia sariia** Gy 323:3 f. stinking water(s); **šlanda sarita** Gy 283 stinking corpse.

saria 4 AM 204 name of a town BZ Ap. II.

sariha s. **saraha.**

sarkala (cf. P. سر و كلّه) head (?). **sarkala umušpita** Jb 149:3 (var. **sarkala mušpita** B) the head of a pointed rod?? (The context is completely obscure, cf. ii 152 n. 1.)

sarkar AM 198:15, var. **sarkad** a place-name BZ Ap. II.

sarkubia s. **SAR II** pf.

sarnbu a kind of demons of both genders. Furlani: *I Nomi* 435. Varr. **sar nbu, sar ʿnbu, sar anbu. sarnbu zikria usarnbu nuqbata** DC 43 A 26, DC 37. 94, 393 etc.; **usaṭania usar ʿnbu** DC 43 G 5 f. = **usaṭania usarnbu** Oxf. roll g 1927.

sarsan maniaiil DC 40. 995 name of an angel.

sarqid br uarzigar Gy 391:16 an ancient Persian king.

sarqina (ܣܪܩܝܢܐ, Ar. سرقين < P. سرگين) dung. **sarqina d̲-atutia kraiia d̲-rakšia** Jb 131:8 f.

= **sarqina d-atutia ligraihun d-rakšia** CP 173 ult. = Oxf. 40 a = ML 211:10 f. the dung beneath the horses' feet; **sarqina lgangaratun** DC 44. 1263 = Morg. 264/18:30 dung be on their throats!

SBA (סְבַע, ܣܒܥ, H. שׂבע, Akk. *šebû*, Ar. شَبِعَ, Sab. ○∏ʒ, Eth. ጸገበ Brockelm. i 169, 239) to have enough, be satiated, surfeited.

Pe. Pf. **mn kupna sba** DC 34 its hunger was sated; **nišimta mlat usbat** DC 48. 369 the soul was filled and satisfied; **mlat nišimta usibat** DC 27. 291 id., **sabit** Gy 86:17, Gs 130:14 I was satiated MG 235:4; **ruha unišimta sbaian** DC 48. 364 f. spirit and soul were satisfied; with suff. **lasibuia bišia lhazin alma** Gy 357:5 f. the bad ones have not enough of this world; **sbatuih** ATŠ II no. 143 ye satisfied her. Impf. **kd ʿštia ulaʿsba** Gy 86:18 when I drink and become not satisfied. Act. pt. **usaba mn ʿkilta** ATŠ II no. 112 and is satisfied by the food; pl. **sabia** s. **saba 2** (nominal use). Pass. pt. **patura sbʿia** Gy 215:1 a full dish MG 5:27.

Pa. Pf. with suff. **sabh** he satisfied him MG 275:5; **sabath** Gy 218:1 thou didst satiate him MG 276:27. Impt. with suff. **sabuia** Gy 15:ult., 22:22 satiate (pl.) him MG 279:1.

Der.: **saba 2, siba 1.**

sbahata (a var. of **sbihata** a pl. of **sipta**) MG 171 n. 4.

sbal Gy 86:1 Nöld.: my ladder MG 173:14, 176:3, doubtf. Ginzā 87 n. 3 (st. emph. sg. **sumbilta**, pl. **siblia** s.vv.).

sbasa AM 11 (*& often*) = **spasa.**

sbasia (rt. SBS) density, compactness, thickness; thick ends, tassels? **sbasia d-himiania** JRAS 1937 p. 591 the tassels (?) of his girdle; **bsbasia d-gdulia** DC 46. 240:9 by the thickness of her (love)locks (misspelt as **baisbasia**).

SBṬ (prob. den. from ܣܦܛܐ < P. سبد basket Fränkel 79, cf. also the rel. **SPṬ**) to interweave, come close together, join together?

Pe. Act. pt. fem. **ainh mlat usabṭa lmʿial mihzia bgauh mahu škin** ATŠ II no. 153 she gazed her fill and approached (??) to enter and behold what dwelt therein.

Pa. Pt. pl. **msabṭia kd aburia** Jb 156:12 (they were) interwoven like reed-mats.

sbihata (var. **sbahata**) = **spihata** pl. of **sipta** (q.v.) MG 47:18 f., 171 n. 4.

sbira pass. pt. pe. of **SBR** (q.v.).

SBK (סְבַךְ, ܣܒܟ, H. שְׂבָכָה network, Ar. شَبَكَة net, شُبّاك lattice, Akk. *šabikû* head-band) to interweave, interlace; af. to mix, infuse, impregnate.

Pe. or Pa.?. Pf. with suff. **span kapan usabkan mlaka** DC 43 J 17 the angel 'He-picked-me-up, -bent-me-and-wove-me'.

Af. Impt. **girma d-taura bmišh asbik** DC 49 mix beef-bone with its fat (or marrow?), **mrirta d-diba uriuand šinia ušubana asbik** DC 46 mix together wolf's gall, Chinese rhubarb, and *nigella sativa*; **ziria rumana umihla asbak** DC 46. 105:9 mix together pomegranate seeds and salt; with suff. **ʿnbia bmiša asbikh** DC 46. 100:16 make an infusion of grapes in oil. Pf. **masbik bihdadia** DC 46. 108:11 mixed together.

SBL, SWL s.v. (Jew.-Aram. & H. סבל, Syr. ܣܒܠ, Akk. *zabālu*, Ar. زَبِيل < Syr. ܐܣܒܠܐ < Akk. *zabbīlu* basket; cf. Nöld. ZDMG xl 729) to bear, carry, endure, sustain.

Pe. Pf. **sbal qalia udar bgauh** Gs 40:21 f. he endured a little and dwelt therein (from an orig. **sbal udra** Ginzā 457 n. 1), but **sbal** Gy 86:1 cf. s.v., **sbalt** Gs 11:11 CD (var. **sualt** A) thou hast borne MG 49:8; **siblit ridpa** Zotb. 231a:18 I endured persecution; **sbaliun mn sanaiia d-nhura** ATŠ I no. 9 they bore with the enemies of light; with suff. (**sbul ridpa d-šuba**) **kd anin sbalnih** ATŠ II no. 188 (bear the persecution of the Seven) as we bore it. Impf. **nisbal** AM 29, **nisbul** he bears MG 220:18; **kma ʿdra uʿsbul** Gy 156:14 (var. **usbul** Sh. 'Abd.'s copy) how long shall I bear and carry?; **kma ʿšma ukma ʿsbal** Gs 39:8 (var. **kma šuma ukma sbal** DC 22. 428) how much (must) I hear and how much endure?; with suff. **ʿsiblh** Jb I will bear it. Impt. **sbal, sbul** MG 220:17; **mahra barsa sbul** Gy 22:1 endure illness in bed; **ašar usbul** PD 944 = ATŠ par. be firm and endure!; **šbul ridpa d-šuba** above (s. pf. with suff.); pl. with suff. **subluia lridpa d-alma** Gy 20:18 endure the persecution of the world (MG 278:22). Act. pt. **man d-sabil ridpa** DC 34 one that endureth persecution; st. emph. **sabla** s.v.; pl. **sablia udaria** CP 130:1, Gs 79:20 = Q 66:22 = ML 158:1 they bear and endure; pl. with encl. **uhalin d-sablilh lbit qubria** ATŠ II no. 16 and those who carry him to the graveyard; **sablia d-sablilh** s. **sabla**. Part. pres. **anin sablinin** Gy 252:19 we must endure; with encl. **kd sablatlh ltibil** CP 454:15 when thou bearest him to the earth (burial).

Der.: **sabla, sibla, sibila, sumbilta** (pl. **siblia**).

SBS (ܣܒܣ, Ar. تَشَبَّصَ to be intertwined) to crowd thickly, be compact; to join.

Der.: **sabus, sabsuta, sbasia.**

SBR (סְבַר, ܣܒܰܪ, H. שׂבר, mod. H. סבר, Ar. سبر to examine a wound Schwally: *Idioticon* 13 & Schulthess HW 39 f., but شِمْرِيّ, شَمَّر expert, Eth. ሰምረ to like Praetorius DLZ 1900 col. 1696) to learn, believe, be convinced, have confidence; af. to teach, instruct, understand, convince, instil faith in.

Pe. Pf. **sbar** Leid. & Sh. 'Abd.'s copy's var. of **asbar** Gy 11:19 he learned; **d-sbar hukumta** Gy 20:24 who learned wisdom; **sbar udar** Gy 341:2 they had to bear and endure (for **sbal udra** Ginzā 354 n. 2, cf. also s. **SBL pf.**), **sbar ginza mn tibil** Gy 319:18 f. they understood the Treasure in (?) the world; similarly **sbar minh mn alma** Gy 320:1, neg. (identical with af.) **uailh lhakima d-lasbar minh mn hukumth**

Gy 357:9 f. = Jb 171:13 f. woe to the scholar who did not learn from his wisdom; **ulasbar** Gs 37:15 and they did not learn (or teach, pe. or af.? Ginzā 451 n. 3); **sibrat ʿutria** ATŠ II no. 310 she convinced uthras; with suff. **sibrh̲ la–b–g–d** DC 41. 129 he taught him the ABC; **sbarth̲** Gs 45:12 f. I understood, neg. **lasbarth̲** Gs 44:18 I did not understand. Impf. with suff. **nisibrak bšrara** Gy 11:19 believeth in thee in truth; **nisbrh̲ ginza kulh̲** ATŠ II no. 183 understandeth the whole treasure (Ginzā). Act. pt. **mandaia d̲-sabar bginzan** ATŠ II no. 185 a Mandaean (i.e. layman) who is versed in our treasure (ginza); **kul ianqa d̲-sabar hukumta** DC 34. 1236 every child that learns wisdom; st. emph. **sabra** used nominally (s.v.); pl. **hiia lsabrin** Gy 394:12 Life to those who believe (or understand); **liadh̲ uʿl sabrh̲** Jb 236:7 to those who know and understand him; fem. pl. **ʿnšia d̲-sabran ginzan** ATŠ II no. 186 women who believe our treasure (ginza). Part. pres. **sabrit** (**umasbirit**) CP 112:ult., Q 57:16 = ML 138:7 thou understandest (and instructest). Pass. pt. **sbir(a)** learned, adept, well-versed, pl. **sbiria hukumta** Gs 83:24, 84:3, Jb 276:4 well-versed in wisdom (Lidzb. *Weisheitskündigen*); **sbiria liba** RD B 111, 118, RD C 12, 15 (*& often*) those of believing heart; **lnahria sbiria** DC 51 for the bright (and) intelligent ones; **lsabria usbiria** DC 47 to the scholars and the intelligent; **anašia d̲-lasbiria** CP 139:8 uninstructed people.

Af. Pf. **man d̲-asbar ʿlak** Gy 11:18 f. who instructeth about Thee; **man d̲-asbar mn hukumtak** Gy 11:19 (read **sbar** with Leid.) who learned from Thy wisdom (cf. s. pe. pf.); **asb(i)rit** I instructed MG 223:5; **asb(i)rit ugihkit** Jb 240:7, Gy 86:20, 117:23 I mocked and laughed at (*idiom*); with encl. **ulasbarlia hda** Gs 49:20 and not one (thing) did he teach me; with suff. **asbrh̲ bruhṣana** Gy 114:24 he inspired her with confidence (Ginzā 127 n. 3); **man asbrh̲** Gy 328:23 who instructed her?; **asbrak ʿlh̲** Gy 203:8 instructed thee about that; **asbartinkun** ATŠ II no. 372 I instructed you. Impf. **ʿiasbar** I instruct MG 227:8; **nʿiasbrun hdadia** Gy 305:16 they instruct one another MG 215:17; with encl. **hazin kušṭa ana asbarlak** [*sic*] CP 94:11 (ML 120:1 **asparlak**) this pact I entrust to thee; with suff. **nʿiasbrak** Gs 59:4 we instruct thee MG 215:21, 273:21. Impt. **asbar uapriš** Gy 214:1 instruct and explain; **rhum uasbar hdadia** ATŠ II no. 377, Jb 49:11 (= **rhum uazbar hdadia** Gy 18:8 f., 39:3) love and teach (or: support?) one another; with encl. **anat asbarlh̲ labatur** DC 3 (CP 94:11 **asparlh̲**) bear thou it (or: give it over) to A. Pt. with encl. **ulamasbarbia kulhun almia** Gs 46:22 and none of the worlds believeth in me; **masbarlun** Gy 193:20 (who) would instruct them; **umkaniplun umasbarlun** Jb 150:7 bringeth them together and teacheth them. Part. pres. **masbirit** (s. pe. part. pres.) MG 232:16. Inf. **asburia** Gs 3:20, 5:10 to instruct MG 144:6. Nom. ag. **masbirana, masb(a)rana** s.v.

Idioms: Certain forms are used with the same meaning as **SBL** (cf. **sbar udar** s. pe. pf. & the secondary rt. **ZBR** s.v.). With **GHK** 'to mock at', 'defy', 'laugh to scorn'.

Der.: **masb(i)rana, sabra, sibra, sibruta** (var. **sabruta**), **sibrana.**

SGA I (Mand., Syr. ܐܣܓܝ rare, cf. IM ii 153:23, Nöld. WZKM xii 358) to go. Usually in af., exceptionally pe. (prob. later forms). (Mod.) secondary rt. **ZGA I** s.v.

Pe. (postcl.): Pt. **kd̲ sagia bʿuhrh̲** AM 21:10 when he walks on his way (travels on a road); **sagia abatar** (AM trs. 17 n. 6) AM 20:7 he goes after; pl. **sagin minh̲** AM 20:5 they go with him. Inf. **uʿštiriat lmisgia sigia bkulhun almia** DC 48. 405 and she was freed to move freely in all the worlds.

Af. Pf. **asgia** he went MG 4:ult., 260:26, **asgit** thou didst go MG 261:5, I went MG 261:7, **asgun** (often) they went, but **asgu** Gy 267:7 id. MG 261:15, **asgia** Gy 64:1, Gs 100:3 they (fem.) went MG 261:19, **asginin** Gy 140:6 and even **asgainin** Gy 151:5 we went MG 261:23 f.; with suff. **asgitinkun** Gy 234:6, 7 I let you go MG 290:7, **asgitinun** I made them go MG 291:2. Impf. **nasgia** he goes, we go MG 261:antep., **ʿiasgia** Gy 275:10 I go MG 262:1, **nasgun** they go MG 262:5, **nasgia** Gs 78:6, Q 67:20 they (fem.) go MG 262:6, **tasgun** ye (shall) go MG 262:8; with encl. **nʿiasgibh̲** Gs 23:21 he will walk in it MG 215:17 (but cf. Ginzā 441 n. 6); with suff. **nasginin** Gy 184:14 he lets them (fem.) go MG 290:17. Impt. **asgia** Gy 12:7 (*& often*) go MG 262:11; fem. **asgai** MG 262:12; pl. **asgun** MG 262:15. Pt. **masgia** (is) going MG 131:ult., 262:17; **minh̲ masgia** Gy 137:4 he goeth with him; **masgia uazil** Gy 137:9 he goeth and walketh; **bdagaluta masgia** Gy 389:4 f. she acteth treacherously (Lidzb. *verkehrt betrügerisch*, idiom); pl. **masgin** they go (but Gy 28:21 erroneously for **masgia** MG 162 n. 1). Part. pres. **masgina** I go MG 262:20, **masgit** Gy 328:1 thou goest MG 262:22, **masginin** we go MG 262:paen.; with encl. **masgiatlh̲ ldrabša** ML 269:13 thou carriest (lit. makest go) the banner. Inf. **asguiia** Gs 77:5, **masguiia** Gy 16:22 (*& often*) to go, going MG 144:7, 8, 263:14. Nom. ag. **masgiana** s.v.

Idiom: With expressions of lie, treachery etc. (as **nikla, zipa, dagaluta**) preceded by procl. **b-** 'to act treacherously (s. af. pt.).

Der.: **masgiana, sigia 2** (var. **sagia**), **4.**

SGA II (Gen. Aram., H. שׂגא & שׂגה prob. an aramaism Kautzsch 86, Ar. شَجوَجَى long and thick) to be many, large, abundant, great, to increase, augment.

Pe. Pf. **sgʿ** Gy 239:1 (varr. **sgia** C, af. D) was great MG 257:3, **usgu** Gy 267 D s. af.

Af. Pf. **asgia** Gy 239:1 D s. pe., **d̲-kbar bziuh̲ uasgia banhurh̲** CP 116:6 who increased in his brilliance and his light augmented; **ʿšumia shiṭibh̲ uasgu** Gy 267:7 the heavens were spread out and became great (var. . . . **usgu** D Ginzā 265 n. 1). Impt. **asgun šumai**

Gy 178:20, 179:7 make my name great (: magnify my name) MG 393:21 f.

Der.: **sagia 1, sigia 2.**

SGD (Aram. & H. סגד, Syr. ܣܓܶܕ, Ar. سَجَدَ, Eth. ሰገደ Schwally ZDMG lii 134, Nöld.: *Neue Beiträge* 36) to bow oneself, worship. Secondary mod. form **ZGD** s.v.

Pe. Pf. **sgid** he worshipped MG 219:11, **sigudta (a)sgid** Jb 82:13 f. they made obeisance (the af.-varr. AC only formal: prosth. **a**), **sgidt** thou didst worship MG 222:25, **sigdit** CP 56:12 I worshipped; with encl. **sgidlia sigudta** Gy 115:2 he worshipped me MG 399:14; **sgidlia d̠-rba sigudta** Gy 307:5 he bowed low before me. Impf. **nisgud** he worships MG 219:11, **nisigdun** they worship MG 31:9, **nisigda** Gs 78:4 they (fem.) worship MG 228:9; pl. with encl. **nisigdulia** they worship me MG 31:9. Impt. **sgud** MG 219:11, 229:5; pl. with encl. **sgudulh̠** Oxf. 23 a, worship him MG 229: paen. Act. pt. **kd̠ sagid lnapšia sagid** ATŠ II no. 87 when bowing himself, worshipping; **sagda d̠-rba sigudta** Gy 148:21 he made (hist. pres.) a profound obeisance; **ʿl nura sagda** Jb 47:14 worshippeth fire; pl. **lasagdia** Gy 285:13 they do not worship; **sigudta sagdin** Gy 285:23 they worship. Part. pres. **sagidna** CP 150:13 = ML 180 I worship, with encl. **sagdanalak** Oxf. 56 b, I (fem.) worship Thee MG 231:23; **sagdinalh̠** CP 143 ult. = ML 171:5 I worship Him Lidzb. ZS i 1, **sagdatlh̠** Jb 83:1 thou worshippest him. Inf. **mn misgad lʿkuria** DC 50. 429 from worshipping at (pagan) temples, var. **masgad** Gy 285:13 (= **misgad** DC 22).

Af. only formal (cf. s. pe. pf.).

Der.: **masgda** (var. **mazgda**), **sagada, s(i)gudta.**

SGL (סגל to lay by, save, keep) rt. of **sagalia** parsimonious DC 22. 385?

Der.: **sgul.**

sgul (Jew.-Aram. סְגוּלָא 'property', 'treasure' makes no sense) doubtf. **qalaiun nizal lasar ulsgul** DC 26. 621 f. (var. . . . **ulsgl** DC 44 & Morg. par.)?

SGM (Mand., rel. to سجل?) to seal up, bind up. Doubtf.

Pe. Impt. **lasgum lispihatun** DC 44 do not seal (?) their lips.

Pa. Pass. pt. **umsagma urgila ʿstra rbtia** AIT and caged and fettered is the Great Ishtar.

Der.: **sigma.**

SGR (Aram. & H. סגר, Syr. ܣܓܰܪ, Akk. *šigaru* (cf. Eth. ሠግራት) bolt, cage, collar) to shut up, keep in.

Pe. Pass. pt. **ʿsgira hiua biša** DC 37. 576 f. shut in is the evil beast.

Der.: **sagariata, sugara.**

sdara (rt. **SDR**) ATŠ II no. 318 arrangement. (A secondary st. emph. formed from the st. abs. of **sadra 1**?)

SDM (סְטַם, ܣܛܰܡ, H. סתם, Ar. سطم & سدم, Eth. አስጠመ to immerse in water, Akk. perh. *šutummu* storehouse), to bind, shackle, pen in, close up, confine, restrain.

Pe. Pf. with suff. **sidmh̠** DC 40 1105 he shackled him; **lpumh̠ sdamth̠** DC 34. 601 I gagged his mouth. Impt. **rgum usdum** DC 44 bind and confine. Part. pres. **sadmit sahria** Morg. 224/35:7 = Q 24:17 = CP 52:18 = ML 68:5 thou confinest demons (MG 42:14). Pass. pt. **ʿsir upkir usdim** DC 15 bound, tied up and confined; **sdim br sdim uminilh̠ sdim** DC 43 J 132 'Restrained son of the Restrained' is restrained with his words; **sdim uhtim abikun** DC 40. 793 f. = DC 26. 770 your father is bound and sealed; pl. **pširia haršia usdimia** DC 40. 147 spells are undone and restrained; **sdimia pugdamia d̠-pumh̠** DC 43 J 143 the words of his mouth are held back.

Der.: **sidma.**

SDQ (סְדַק, ܣܕܰܩ, Ar. شَدِقَ to have large cusps of the mouth, Eth. ሠጠቀ to split) to rend asunder, tear, separate, cleave, split.

Pe. Act. pt. pl. **sadqia simtun** Gs 98:17 f. they rent their treasure (: garment Ginzā 538 n. 3). Pass. pt. (predicatively) **kitun kukbia sdiqia** Gs 89:2 = G 68:3 the garment of stars is rent; pl. **msania sdiqia** Gy 25:15 torn shoes; **hinun sdiqia** DC 34. 634 they are disconnected; **lišania sdiqia** DC 40. 309 f. (cf. l. 255) forked tongues.

Pa. Act. pt. pl. with encl. **msadqilak** Gs 99:12, 132:23 they tear thee, **msadqilun** Jb 137:2 they split them.

Der.: **sadqa.**

SDR I (Aram. & H. סדר, Syr. ܣܕܰܪ, Akk. *sadāru*, Ar. سرد Barth ES 56 f.) to set in order, arrange, dispose, compile, put into shape, organize.

Pe. Pf. **sdar** (often) he arranged or intrans.: was arranged; **usdar sidra d̠-nišmata usidar** [*sic*] **kulhun almia minh̠** ATŠ I no. 21 and he arranged the Book of Souls and organized the worlds (persons) thereby; **miṣria uarqahata sdarian** ATŠ II no. 60, boundaries and territories were arranged; with suff. **sidrun bsadrutun** Gs 115:3 they ranged me in their line. Impf. **uhiduta uhiduktia nisdar** ATŠ I no. 352 and provides (?) for the bride and her wedding; with suff. **nisidrunh̠** they set him in order MG 278:10. Impt. **abad usdar ʿbidatkun** ATŠ II no. 377 perform and keep orderly your rites! Act. pt. **uhu amarlh̠ sadar** ATŠ II no. 321 and he says to him in his turn (?). Part pres. **kd̠ baiitun rahmia sadritun** DC 27. 501 when ye pray the 'Devotions' set in order (the names to commemorate). Pass. pt. **hakima d̠-lasdir** Gy 216:18 an unmethodical scholar; **sdir bkulhun ginzia** ATŠ II no. 441 orderly in all the rites; **sdira (umsadra)** Gy 78:22, 324:21, Gs 38:14, 74:9, ATŠ II no. 116 well-ordered and perfect; **banaia sdira** Gy 214:21 an orderly builder; **ʿumana sdira** Gy 214:23 f. skilled craftsman; **msadrana usdira** Gy 214:24 arranger and well-arranged; **sdira damia lšuhba šbiha** Gy 215:3 an orderly man resembleth a fine cedar (? Ginzā 215 n. 3); **lau ʿsdira hua** Jb

8:6 he was not systematic; **sdira rba** Jb 20:12 a great, orderly one; pl. **sdiria umsadria** DC 51 well-ordered and perfect; **uhauia ginzia sdiria** ATŠ and his treasures (books, rites) should be orderly.

Pa. Pf. **kḏ sadar ṭariana** ATŠ I no. 194 when he has arranged the (ritual) table; **sadar bzaku sidra** DC 48. 140 he recited the liturgy in perfect order; **usadirnin biuma ḏ-paruanaiia** DC 50 and we made orderly arrangement on the day(s) of P.; with suff. **sadrẖ lkulẖ malkuta** DC 34. 610 he arranged all kingliness; **anat lasadarthẖ** Gy 158:6 thou hast not set it in order; **sadartinun** Gy 159:16, var. **sadirtinun** BCD I set them in order MG 15:29; **kidbu lʿuraita usadru** Jb 198:10 f. they wrote the Thora and arranged it. Impf. **nisadar hdadia** Gy 325:7 we will keep one another in order; with suff. **nisadruia** Gy 132:20, var. **nisadrunẖ** C (*& often*) they set him in order MG 278:11, 20. Impt. **sadar** AM 201 (*& often*) arrange!; **sad siridria** DC 34. 501 recite the books; with suff. **sadrẖ** AM 200 arrange it; **sadrẖ lmalkutak** Gy 339:21 organize thy kingdom (MG 269 n. 1); pl. **usadru bmihla** DC 50. 130 and set out (on the table) salt etc. Pt. (act. & pass.) **msadar sidria qruia** Oxf. 95 a = CP 280:7 they called him 'Arranger of Ordinances' MG 310:17; **hakima ḏ-lamsadar** Gy 216:16 an unmethodical scholar; **mkalal umsadar** Gy 215:4 is crowned and set in order ZS i 2, Ginzā 215 n. 4; **(sdira) umsadra** s. pe. pass. pt.; **ʿkara msadra** Gy 213:15 an orderly husbandman; **sdiria umsadria** s. pe. pass. pt. pl.; fem. pl. **msadran** ATŠ I no. 13 they (fem.) are set in order; with encl. **msadarlun lkulhun almia** Gy 155:11 he keepeth all the worlds in order; **msadarlun sidraihun** Gy 172:22 he rangeth Its (: the Life's) lines; **msadrilẖ lalma hanathẖ** Gy 240:19 It (: the Life) arranged (hist. pres.) this world. Part. pres. with encl. **msadrinalẖ** (var. **msadranalẖ**) **lbiniana** DC 6 (var. DC 36) ATŠ I no. 260 we will lay down the structure in orderly fashion; **msadritulẖ** DAb ye arrange(d) it. Inf. **misaduria sidria** RD B 11 to set things in order. Nom. ag. **msadrana** s.v. nom. act. **sadarta** s.v.

Ethpe. Pt. **misdar** Gy 322:21 is set in order MG 214:12.

Ethpa. Pf. **ʿstadar** Gy 356:6, AM 256, ATŠ II no. 320 was set in order; **ʿstadrat** Gy 152:3, DC 34:232 fem. was set in order MG 222:18; **ʿstadrat usilqat lriš hazin kurasa** AM 288:12 this manuscript was compiled and completed; **ʿstadarat usilqat lriš hazin šapta** DC 43 J 232 this scroll was compiled and completed; **uʿstadariun** plu. cf. s. pa. pf. Impf. **tisadar** Gs 45:6 thou mayst be set in order MG 214:11, 227:3. Pt. **ʿu mistadar hauia** ATŠ II no. 361 if he is orderly (: orthodox?); **kḏ mistadra maṣbuta** ATŠ II no. 419 when the baptism is in order.

Gl. 14:13 f. missp. with ṣ اتته *perfectus esse* تمام شد.

Der.: **msadrana, sadarta, sadira, sadra 1, sadruta, sidra sadrʿil.**

SDR II s. SNDR.

shaq ('He-rejoiced') a baptismal name bestowed on Adam, ARR 180 f., TNPC trsl. pp. 11 f. Siouffi 39:12, 410:31, Jb ii 230 n. 5, ML 282, CP trs. 104 n. 3. **shaq rba** PD 1157; **adam ashaq rba** PD 73 = **adam shaq rba** PD 624; **shaq ziua** Jb 255:3, 9, **shaq ziua rba qadmaia** CP 25:16 = Q 10:25 = ML 28:10, **malka adam shaq ziua rba qadmaia** Morg. 5:3, **malka ʿshaq ziua-rba-qadmaia** CP 140c:11 f., **shaq ziua rba ḏ-hiia** Gy 314:3.

SHD (סַהֲד > mod. H. סָהֵד, Eg.-Aram. שהד, hence H. שָׂהֵד witness Kautzsch 86, Syr. ܣܗܶܕ, Ar. شَهِدَ) to testify, bear witness, attest to.

Pe. Pf. **shid** he testified MG 61:1, 220:5, **shad** Q 23:15 id. MG 220 n. 1, **sihdat** Or. 326:7 she testified, **shidun** ATŠ II no. 172 they bore witness, **shidnin** we testified MG 224:16, **shidtun** ye testified MG 224:5. Impf. **nishad** he testifies, we testify MG 61:1, 220:5, **nisihdun** Gy 14:16, 35:15 f. they bear witness; **kḏ iahbitun latisihdun** Gy 35:19 when ye give, do it not ostentatiously (cf. Matt. 6:1); **sahduta ḏ-kadba latisihdun** Gy 14:14, 35:14 bear no false witness. Act. pt. with encl. **kul ginza ḏ-aba lasahidbẖ** ATŠ any 'treasure' (i.e. sacramental rite) to which the Father does not attest; st. emph. **sahda** s.v.

Pa. Act. pt. **man ḏ-iahib zidqa umsahid** Gy 15:19, 35:21 who giveth alms ostentatiously (cf. Matt. 6:1 f.); **sahduta ḏ-kadba msahid** DAb he gives false witness; pl. **msahdia** Gy 14:15, 35:15 they witness MG 61:5.

Ethpe. Pf. **sahduta tiniantia . . . ḏ-ʿstihdat** DC 34 a second testimony . . . that was given (testified).

Ethpa. Pf. **sahduta tiniantia stahdat** ATŠ II no. 428 a second testimony was given.

Gl. 52:11 f. miswritten تشهد *protestari* گواهی داد; 91:11 f. miswritten شهد *testificari* گراهی داد.

Der.: **sahda, sahduta.**

SHṬ (סְחַט, H. שׂחט MG 238 n. 1, Akk. *ṣaḫātu* or *ṣaḫāṭu* to press out Daiches ZA xvii 92, Küchler: *Ass.-bab. Medizin* 144) to press out, wring out, broaden out, spread out, lie flat or prone, to spread over an area (cf. Ar. سطح), (of fire) to be inflamed IM 47, ML 178 n. 2, (in magical bowls) to seize, squeeze cf. ibid.

Pe. Pf. **kul rihšia bdilẖ shiṭ** DC 27. 240 all creeping creatures are included in it; **ʿšata haita uʿkilta ḏ-hʿ sihṭat mn arqa larqa** DC 50. 626 the living and devouring flame which spread from world to world; **shaṭian alanpia ziua ushaṭian alanpia tlat ainaniata** CP 357:2, Oxf. 97 a = ML 265:1 (var. **shiṭian**) they spread out towards the radiance and three sources spread out ML 178 n. 2, MG 223:28; with suff. **shṭʿil shiṭinun** AO ix 96:2 S. seized them (Gordon). Pass. pt. **shiṭ** Gy 153:22 (of darkness) is spread over; fem. **ʿšata haita shiṭa** Gy 193:4 the living fire spread (or was inflamed) MG 238 n. 1; pl. with encl. **ᶜšata haita uᶜšata ᶜkilta shiṭibh̲** Gy 267:5 (cf. l. 7).

Ethpe. Pf. **ᶜshiṭ** was spread over MG 214:10 (with a mistaken ref.); **lahuat nura ula(ᶜ)stihṭat** Jb 56:6 there was no fire and it was not set ablaze; with encl. **uᶜshiṭibun ᶜuṣria d̲-nhura** ML 178:9 = CP 149:2 and the treasures of the light were kindled by them. Impf. **l(ᶜ)shiṭ bᶜšata** Gy 87:5 (cf. varr.) let it spread over the fire; **nura tisthiṭ** Gy 13:5 let the fire spread over; **nura tista(?)hiṭ** Gy 33:13 id. Pt. pl. fem. **nišmata kulhin bziuh̲ mistihṭa** DC 27. 277 all the souls are kindled by his radiance; with encl. **mitlabša umistihṭabh̲ nišimta** ATŠ II no. 68, 262 the soul is clothed by it and integrated with it.

SHP (סְחַף, ܣܚܰܦ, H. & mod. H. סחף, Akk. *saḫāpu*, Ar. سَحِيفَة strong rain) to cast down, hurl down, overturn, overthrow, throw down, ruin.

Pe. Pf. **masihpa qubla shap ᶜlai** s. **masihpa, shpit ᶜlauaihun** IM no. 37 I cast down on them; with suff. **ᶜl anph̲ shapth̲** Gy 167:6 I threw him down on his face; **shapth̲ urmaith̲** Gy 118:21 I cast him and threw him down. Inf. with suff. **masihpinun** Gy 197:16 to throw them down.

Ethpe. Pf. **kursia d̲-rugza ᶜsthip** DC 44. 1064 f. (varr. **ᶜstahap** ethpa.) the throne of wrath was overturned.

Ethpa. Pf. **ᶜstahap** Gy 103:12, 117:15, 328:8, 336:4 ff., 355:16, Jb 240:13, Q 52:12, DC 44. 211, 1517 etc. was, were overturned; **ustahap** Jb 18:1 and (they) were hurled down; **ᶜstahaptin** Q 52:17 ye (fem.) were overthrown MG 224:14. Impf. **nisihpun** DC 44. 1164 = Morg. 263/17:22 they shall be overthrown. Pt. pl. **mistahpia unaplia** DC 26. 134 f., ATŠ II no. 359 they hurl themselves and fall; fem. pl. **mistahpan** Jb 122:11 they (fem.) are overthrown. Part pres. **mistahapna unapilna** Gy 272:20 I hurl myself down and I fall.

Der.: **mashipa, masihpa, masihpan, sihupta** (var. **sihipta**), **sahpiaiil** (var. **sahpiaᶜil**).

SHQ I (H. שׂחק, mod. H. סָחַק to laugh, fool) to laugh, jest, be merry, sport, leap with joy, rejoice, be bright. Jb ii 230 n. 5.

Pa. Pf. **shaq** (name given to Adam) s.v., **shiq** Gy 191:14, 15, Gs 93:22 (var. **shaq**) he sported MG 220:10; **hu libh̲ shiq** Gy 153:11 his heart rejoiced MG 410:11. Act. pt. **sahiq libaihun** Gy 137:6 = **libaihun sahiq** Gy 138:14 their heart rejoiceth; **sahiq ᶜuṣrh̲** Gy 137:7 his mind rejoiceth; **sahiq bhaduta** Gy 140:14 he leapeth with joy; **libaihun sahiq umitparpa** Gy 140:17 their heart rejoiceth and is merry; **sahiq libaian** Gy 145:15 our heart rejoiceth; **sahiq ᶜuṣrai** Gy 130:17 my mind rejoiceth; **sahiq ᶜuṣraian** Gy 152:7 our mind rejoiceth; with encl. **usahiqlun ᶜuṣraihun umitgaiia** CP 398:11 and their thoughts are glad and they are elated; fem. **sahqa** Q 14:6, **sahqa daiṣa** CP 67:10 = Q 30:2, 29 she leapeth with joy and exulteth; pl. **sahqia gaiin umitparpin** Gy 274:5 = **sahqia ugaiia (u)mitparpia** Gs 8:18, CP 462:5 they rejoice, are glad and merry (MG 441:26); **mia . . . sahqia** Jb 214:10 the water . . . leapeth with joy. Part. pres. **sahqinin** Gy 145:15, **sahiqnin** [*sic*] DC 50. 550 we leap with joy.

Der.: **shaq** (see CP trs. 104 n. 3).

SHQ II (Jew.-Aram. & H. שׁחק, Syr. & Chr.-Pal. ܣܚܩ, Ar. سحق, Akk. *šaḫāqu*? Frank OLZ xii 482) to grind down, crush down, pound.

Pe. Impt. with suff. **suhqh̲** AM 287:21 pound it.

Ethpe. Impf. **nisihqun ltasniqia** DC 51. 599 f. they shall be crushed down to the torments.

SHR I (Ar. سَهِرَ from Aram. cf. סַהֲרָא, ܣܗܪܐ = Ar. شَهْر moon) to keep watch, vigil. **nisihrun unišabun** DC 22. 247 they watch and pray (praise).

Gl. 21:1 f. miswritten (as **ṣhra**) استيقظ *vigilare* شب نخفت; 91:1 f. id. استيقظ *vigilare* شب بيدارى كرد.

Der.: **saharta.**

SHR II (Jew.-Aram., H., Phoen. סחר, Syr., Chr.-Pal. (pa., ithpe.) ܣܚܪ, Akk. *saḫāru* to turn around) to go around, move about.

Pe. Act. pt. pl. **bṣauia balma sahria** Gy 122:1 they move about in desolate places in the world.

Gl. 107:12 f. miswritten طلب *quaerere* خواست; 25:1 f. miswritten اتسل *mendicare* خواست. Mod. der. *sahūra* (Syr. ܣܚܘܪܐ) beggar.

Der.: **sahra 1** (the der. of **2** being doubtf.)

SUA (סוי, ܣܘܐ to desire) to cheer, delight. Doubtf.

Pa. Act. pt. with encl. **ᶜl ᶜšumia rguan iurqa msauilun** DC 7 they cheer the purple skies with green (?).

suad s. **ṣauad.**

suasta some kind of thorny vegetation. **suasta hᶜ atata hu** Oxf. xii it is a **s.**-bush, it is thorn(y).

suar(a) = (ᶜ)**stuar. d̲-man amṣia hailh̲ usuarh̲** PD 81 (var. **ᶜstiuarh̲** ATŠ) so that he whose strength and foothold is equal to (the task).

SUB I (סָאֵב II, סוב pa. J, ܣܝܒ, Ar. شاب to mix, Eth. ሰአሰ to be polluted Nöld. ZDMG liv 160) to pollute, defile.

Pa. Pt. (act. & pass.) **qudša msaiba** Gy 226:13 the polluting (or dirty) sacrament (of the Christians); pl. **msaibia bahtia anatun** Gs 58:3 ye are polluted (and) shameful; **mn šapulia msaibia** DC 19, **mn šapuliia msaiibia** DC 43 D 65 from polluted genitals (?). Inf. **misaiubia zma** AM 160:15 to let blood, letting blood (*idiom*).

Der.: **msabta.**

SUB II (J.-Aram., H. & mod. H. סבב, transition from ע״ע to ע״ו) to surround.

Pa. Impf. with suff. **latisaibunh̲ ulatihuqunh̲** DC 43 G 8 do not surround him and do not frighten him.

sugara (H. & mod. H. סוּגַר cage, leash, Syr. ܣܽܘܓܳܪܳܐ, Ar. loan-w. ساجور leash Fränkel 114 ff., Akk. *šigāru* bolt, cage) (*a*) lock, bolt, bar, (*b*) halter, noose, leash (for a dog) MG 123:8. Pl. **-ia.** (*a*) **sikia usugaria** Jb 130:2 f. bars and fastenings; (*b*) **sakla sugara bṣaurḥ uraqid** Gy 217:13 the fool will dance even if a halter is round his neck; **zim kḏ kalba bsugara** DC 45 held like a dog by his leash.

sugudta a frequent var. of **sigudta.**

sudan Zotb. 220b:5 a man's name.

suhil Ṣâb.'s AM var. of **sihil** AM 205:paen.

SUṬ, SWṬ (ܣܚܶܛ to abhor) to hold in abomination, revolt against, chase, expel, destroy.

Pa. Pt. pl. **ḏ-gaṭlia bnia umsauṭia ʿulia bkras ʿumaihun** Oxf. roll g 921 = Or. 331:8 that slay children and destroy embryos in the womb of their mothers.

Der.: **sauṭa, saiṭa, siuṭa.**

SUK (ܣܽܘܦ) to finish, end, limit, complete, conclude.

Pe. Act. pt. **saiik kulhun rahmia** PD 78 he finisheth all prayers ('Devotions'); fem. (pl.) **nišmata saika** Morg. 249/85:10 the souls finish (it).

Pa. Pf. **saiaktun** [*sic*] ATŠ II no. 165 ye have finished; with encl. **usaiiktulun** DC 47 and ye have finished them; with suff. **saikḥ** he limited him, her, it MG 275:7; **usaiku** DC 50. 216 and they ended it (: the recitation). Impf. **laiit ḏ-nʿsaiik unimar ʿl hailḥ** Gy 3:19 (cf. var. Leid. Ginzā 7 n. 3) there is none to define and express His force; **lʿška ḏ-mṣia ḏ-nisaiik unimar ʿl hailak** Gy 11:16 there is none to define and express Thy force; with suff. **ʿsikiḥ lhurba marda** Gs 47:9 I will destroy the rebellious ruin. Impt. with suff. **usaikḥ** ML 50:4 and finish it! Pt. **msaiik** (var. **msaiak** PD) **hanatun rahmia** ATŠ I no. 48 he finishes those prayers (var. pass.: those prayers are finished); fem. **alma ḏ-maṣbuta kulḥ msaika** DC 34 until the whole baptism is concluded. Part. pres. **kḏ msaikitun** ATŠ I no. 192 when ye have finished. Inf. **saikuia** ATŠ II no. 130 to conclude.

Ethpa. Pt. **mistaiak** Gy 4:5 is limited; **lamistaiak** Gy 2:5, Jb 252:13 is limitless; **lamistaikan** (f. plu.) DC 22. 4 unending.

Der.: **sai(a)kta, saka.**

sukana (ܣܽܘܟܳܢܳܐ, Ar. loan-w. سُكّان Fränkel 222, from Akk. *sikkānu*; of adjectival origin? MG 139:20) rudder, steering-paddle, steering-oar. Varr. **sikana, sukuna. usukana** (var. **usukuna** AC) **ḏ-kušṭa ʿtbḥ** Jb 152:1 the steering-oar in which there is truth; **sukana lgaṭ** Jb 152:2 he took the steering-oar; **ṣaida usukana** Jb 162:1 the fisherman and the steering-paddle; **ʿtbḥ sukana** Jb 163:1 there is a steering-oar in it; **mambarta ḏ-abarnabḥ sikana** (var. **sukana** Leid., DC 22) **bgauḥ** Gs 109:ult. in the ferry in which I cross over there is a steering-oar (Lidzb. '*no* rudder', but why?). Personified: **sukana šumʿil** RD 5, **bihram sukana** RD 6, 8.

sukuhiia (varr. **skuhiia, skuiia**) a *malwâša* man's name.

suk iauar s. **sku iauar.**

sukra (rt. SKR, סוכרא, ܣܶܟܪܳܐ Akk. *sikkuru*?) bolt, lock. Pl. **-ia.** Masc. **šanitinun lsukria** Gy 145:19, **šanitinun lkulhun sukria** Gy 158:1 I doubled all the bolts (Lidzb. *ich verschob alle Verschlüsse*); **sukria uaqlidia** Gy 150:21, 151:7 bolts and keys.

SWL for **SBL** in Pe. Pf. **sualt** Gs 11:11 A thou hast borne MG 49:8.

sulaiman (Ar. سُلَيْمان) a mod. form of **šlimun** Solomon. Often in talismans.

sulṭan (Ar. سُلْطان) sultan, ruler. Often in colophons.

sulia 1 (rt. SLA) what is rejected, discarded, thrown off, dregs, dross, reject, waste-product. **sulia sin** ATŠ II no. 190 its reject (object thrown off) is the Moon; **unida ḏ-gadana mn sulia** ATŠ II no. 194 and knoweth the fortunate from the rejected (or: divine from dross?); **mnat sulia nihuia** PD 523 = ATŠ I no. 47 will belong to dregs (i.e. will be rejected).

sulia 2 pl. of **sulita**? **sidra ḏ-sulia** CP 99:22 a Book of Purifications or, see 1, rejection (?).

sulita (Doubtf., cf. Jew.-Aram., H. & mod. H. סלח to forgive, Akk. *salāḫu* to sprinkle Zimmern KAT 602) Purification, Atonement? **iuma ḏ-sulita ḏ-ṭirma** ATŠ II no. 196 the Day of Atonement (?) of the first summer month; **iuma ḏ-sulita qaruštia** ATŠ II no. 196 the Day of the Winter Atonement (?) Purification (?)

sulqab Ṣâb.'s AM a miscop. of **suqlab.**

SUM I, SIM (שים & סים, Bibl.-Aram. & H. שׂים, H. also שׂוּם, Syr. ܣܳܡ & ܣܺܝܡ, Ar. شام *mediae i* to put in, Eth. ሤመ to place, Sab. 𐩪𐩣 to raise, 𐩣𐩺𐩪 patron, Akk. *šâmu* [*mediae i*] to decide Nöld.: *Beiträge* 39 f.) to put, place, lay (upon), set upon, put forth, apply to.

Pe. Pf. with encl. **brišai samlia** DC 26. 552 they laid on my head; **samilḥ** Gs 101:9, 103:14 (a bad var. **similḥ**) I put on him MG 249:1 f.; with suff. **simta dakita ḏ-samḥ** Gs 72:2 f. read with BCD, Leid. & DC 22 **sima** (pass. pt.) the pure treasure which was laid up. Impf. **ʿdaihun lašualania lanisimun** ATŠ II no. 23 they shall not lay their hands on novices. Impt. **sum** put, lay MG 250:5; with suff. **sumuia** (*often*) put (pl.) him MG 278:ult.; **sumunun** Gy 226:ult. put them MG 283:25. Act. pt. **saiim lqudamḥ** Gs 2:6 he setteth before himself; with encl. **saimilḥ bligrḥ** Jb 100:7 they put on his feet. Pass. pt. with encl. **muta lasimlun** Gy 8:15 death was not imposed upon them; **qlida . . . lgiṭna usimlia** DC 44. 1337 = Morg. 265/20:18 I held . . . the key and applied it.

Af. Pf. **asim** he, they put MG 251:4, **asimit** Par. xi 16a, 17a I put MG 251:10. Impf. **unasim iaminḥ** DC 3 and he shall lay his right (hand); **iaminai . . . ʿiasim ʿlḥ** DC 48:3, **ʿiasim iaminai ʿlḥ** Gy 30:4 f. I (will) lay . . . my right (hand) on him (MG 251:15). Impt. **asim** put, lay MG 251:16; pl. **asimiun ʿdaikun** lriših Lond. roll A 329 lay your hands on his head. Pt. **masim, masima** puts, lays MG 251:19, 21; pl. **masimia ʿdaihun** DC 34. 929 they lay their hands; **biaminun (dakia) masimia ʿlh** CP 203 ult., 204:10, 205:13, 208:8 = ML 233:3, 235:1, 237:6, 241:2 they lay their pure right (hands) on him (i.e. bless him ML 233 n. 1). Part. pres. **masimna** Gy 192:22 I lay MG 251:22; **ʿda masimitun** DC 34:825 and ye lay hands. Nom. act. **asamta d-ʿda ʿl ašualania** ATŠ I no. 181 laying on of hands on novices.

Ettaf. Pf. **ʿtasimat** Gy 158:5 was laid (fem.) MG 252:11. **ʿdai dilia mitasima** (var. **mitasimia** PD) **ʿlh** ATŠ I no. 158 my hand shall be laid on him.

Der.: **simta** (cstr. **simat**).

SUM II s. **SMA I.**

s(u)maq(a), sumqa (סוּמָק, emph. סוּמָקָא, Syr. ܣܘܡܩܐ) red, ruddy. Fem. **sumaqt(i)a.** Pl. masc. **sumaqia** (a bad var. **sumaiqia**). Without a noun, **sumqa** can be used substantivally of red objects, in DC 23. 768 of inflammation. **iaqut sumaqa** ATŠ I no. 207 (& often) ruby; **hala sumaqa** AM red dust; **kukba sumaqa** DC 44. 1302 = Morg. 264/19: 24 a red star; **mia sumaqia** Gy 392:12 reddish water; **anph sumaqia** DC 48 his rosy face; **had minaihun sumaqtia** ATŠ I no. 219 one of them is red (fem.); **taurta sumaqtia** DC 46 a red cow; **hilita sumaqtia** RD 10 a red pearl; **kiuan bšuprh usumqih** CP 226:1 Saturn in his beauty and ruddiness (or glow); **aqapra usumqa** Gy 34:3 dust and ruddiness; **apra sumqa** CP 373:5 red dust; **zma usumqa** Gy 298:4 blood and redness.

Gl. 31:5 missp. احمر *rubedo* سرخ; 35:7 ارجوان *purpureae* رخت قرمز.

sumbulta see foll.

sumbilta (by dissimil. of the reduplicated **b**, cf. Syr. ܫܘܒܠܬܐ, mod. Syr. ܣܒܝܠܬܐ, Jew.-Aram. סוּלְמָא, H. סֻלָּם, Ar. سُلَّم Brockelm. i 231, Nöld.: NsG 51, MG 76:20 & n. 2, Schwally ZDMG liii 197) ladder MG 18:3, 76:20, 120:7. Varr. **sumbulta, sumblta** etc. St. abs. **sumbla.** Pl. **siblia** s.v. Nöld. considered **sbal** Gy 86:1 as a secondary sg. (cf. s.v.). St. abs. & pl. are used as sg. **silqit ʿlauaihun bsumbilta d-tlata kukbia** DC 44. 1383 f. = Morg. 265/21:3 f. I rose above them by a ladder of three stars; **sumb(u)lta d-zahba** DC 44. 1381 = 265/21:2 a golden ladder; **sumbla rama** CP 229:14, ŠQ 17:4 a tall ladder; **kd sumbla d-šrara . . . salqinin umaṭinin lriš sumbla** DC 7 like a ladder of strength . . . we shall rise and reach the top of the ladder.

sumka (rt. **SMK,** סוּמְכָא) thickness. **arqa . . . d-hauia . . . sumkh** Gy 160:1 f. the earth . . . the thickness of which is . . .; **arqa . . . hauia sumkh** Jb 4:9 f. the earth . . . its thickness is; **sumka d-sipth** Gy 280:19 the thickness of his lips; **sumka d-bita** DC 27. 198 the thickness of the egg; **sumka d-sipta d-pumh** Gy 393:21 the thickness of the lips of his mouth MG 450:14.

sumkana (rt. **SMK,** ܣܘܡܟܢܐ) support MG 136:21. **sumkana d-samiklia** Gy 155:21 a support which supporteth me (or to support me).

sumqa s. **sumaqa.**

sumqaq name of a female being, a region and a well of darkness ML 283. **sumqaq rabtia** Gy 145:17 the Great S.; **sumqaq marganita rabtia** Gy 145:ult. S. the Great Pearl (another name of *Qin*); **sumqaq aina** CP 99:18, Q 48:13, 51:21, Morg. 251/90:3 f., PD 116, 152; **sumqaq aina rabtia d-hšuka** PD 388 S. the great well of darkness; **spira d-sumqaq** RD 20 the sphere of S.

sunda a mod. form of **ṣinda** grain. Pron. *sonda.*

Gl. 70:10 **s(u)nda** حبة *granus* دانه.

sundumaiia Sodomites. Var. **sindumaia. sundumaiia** (var. **si-** DC 6) **d-ganbia razia . . . ʿzdahar mn sindmaiia** ATŠ II no. 25 Sodomites who defile mysteries . . . beware of Sodomites.

sus 1 (ܣܘܣ) (cf. **sustia**, both corrupt; from **NSS**?) fret(ting). **ʿniš liba sus hauia** DC 46 (corrupt) a person whose heart is fretted (?).

sus 2 mod. st. abs. & cstr. of **susia** (q.v.).

susambar (ܣܘܣܡܒܪ, ܣܘܣܢܒܪ, Ar. سيسنبر, Gr. σισύμβριον Löw 272:top) watermint (plant). Var. **susa(n)bar.** Pl. **susambariata,** var. **susimb-** Jb ii 128 n. 3. **atiuia lsusambar u(ʿ)tapsramka** Gy 106:22 f., 24 they brought him watermint and *Ocinum Basilicum*; **qumth damia lsarua ziqnh susambariata** Par. xv 22a = xxv 27a = ŠQ 19:14 = CP 239:7 (= DC 3, DC 38 par.), var. **susimbariata** (cf. Jb ii 128 n. 3), miscop. **ssimba riata** DC 7 his figure is like the cypress, his beard (like) watermint-plants.

susun parguš AM 123 name of a supernatural being.

sust(a)mia (formally recalls σύστημα MG 45:12, but prob. a mere miscop. or transformation of ܣܩܘܠܛܐ MG 484 Addenda to p. 45:12) pl. bands, shackles. Varr. **ṣuṣt(a)mia** (by regr. assimil.) s.v., **sstmia** Gs 80:17. **tabirtinun lsustmia** Gs 81:14 I broke the shackles; **sustmia d-mia** DC 43 J 21 barriers (?) of water.

sustiaiil DC 40:873 (angel-list) name of an angel.

sustmia s. **sustamia.**

susia (סוּסְיָא, ܣܘܣܝܐ, H. סוּס II, Akk. *sisû*; prob. an old loan-w. MG 147:8 ff., ZDMG xl 719, Delitzsch: *Prol.* 128 n. 2, Littmann ZA xiii 155, Jensen ZA xv 230, Ungnad ZDMG N.F. ii 90 from Arian *ašwas*; cf. also Eg. 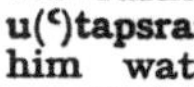 horse, mare. Still used. Mod. st. abs. & cstr. **sus 2** (pronunciation: *sos*, emph. *sosyâ*). Pl. **sasauata** Gy 387:11, var. **susauata** MG 166:25 f., **susiauata** AM 182, later **susiata** (often in DC 46), **sustata** Lond. roll B 391, **sisiata** s.v., **sistata** s.v. **ʿl susia nautibunh** Gy 180:19 they seat him on the horse; **uazil susia ʿlauaihun** Gy 391:1 and the horse walketh upon them; **manzia ḏ-susia** AM 127:12 horse-hair; **turia ugamšin ususiata** DC 46. 15:2 cattle, buffaloes, and mares; **pasihiatẖ kḏ susia** Or. 326:25 his paces are like the horse.

susimbar(iata) s. **susambar. mia ḏ-susimbar** AM 135:12 the juice of watermint.

sustata Lond. roll B 391, DC 44. 1054 a pl. of **susia.**

sustariun (P. سيساروں?) name of a herb (a waterplant). Var. **sustarin. sustariun ḏ-hu gulibiṣṭar** AM 124:14 (cf. s. **gulibiṣṭar**).

sustia (cf. **sus 1**; fretting) **sustia ḏ-liba ḏ-br anašia badiqna** DC 46. 100:13 I distribute fretting of the human heart.

suƐar AM 259:37 = **siƐir** q.v.

SUP (Aram. & H. סוף, Syr. ܣܳܦ, Ar. ساف; Kautzsch 67; borrowed at an early date from Eg. □☉ 'end'?) to end, finish, cease, stop, perish, vanish, disappear; af. to destroy, exterminate.

Pe. Impf. **ʿsup mn alma** Q 17:27, 18:3, 11 I vanish from the world. Impt. **sup lhdadia** DC 40. 1059 put rim to rim (?). Act. pt. **alma kulẖ saiip** Gy 21:15 all the world shall take an end; **maziz ulasaiip** DC 48. 313 strengthens unceasingly; **misap saiip liuma ḏ-sup** Gy 23:2 f., 120:13, 121:23, 122:9 etc. he will end on the day of the end; **misap saiip liuma rba ḏ-sup** Oxf. 50 b; fem. **saipa** Gy 254:23, 255:3, 24 perisheth, vanisheth; pl. **saipia misap** Gs 69:6, **misap saipia liuma rba ḏ-sup** Gy 111:11, 120:18 f., 121:11, 22 they shall take an end on the day of the end; **šibiahia kulhun saipia** Gy 255:2 the Planets shall perish; **kabšia rišaihun uminẖ saipia** ATŠ II no. 175 they abase their heads and cease from (troubling) her; pl. with encl. **lasaipilẖ anpẖ mn zauẖ** Jb 107:6 her face (: honour) will not be destroyed with regard to her husband; **ubmanda ḏ-hiia saipibẖ** Gy 229:21 f., 232:12 they have nothing more to do with M.–ḏ–H. Inf. **misap** (s. pt.) MG 30:1, 250:antep.

Af. Pf. with suff. **asipẖ** Gy 83:4, 8 he brought it to an end, destroyed it MG 275:11. Pt (st. emph.) **masipa** s.v.; with encl. **nasib sipa umasiplẖ** HG he took the sword and put an end to it (hist. pres.).

Ethpe. Impf. **unistipun lhdadia** DC 43 I 82 they will be destroyed by one another.

Der.: **asiptan, masipa, saupa** (abs. & cstr. **sup 1**), **supat.**

sup 1 st. abs. & cstr. of **s(a)upa.** MG 150:2 **iuma ḏ-sup** (cf. s. **SUP** pe. pt.) the last day, day of the end or destruction (cf. **iama ḏ-sup** s. **sup 2**) MG 150 n. 1, MSchr 32:3, Jb ii. xxi 14 ff., Ginzā 20 n. 6, MSt 92 **iuma rba ḏ-sup** Jb 182:2, 11, Gy 255:4 the great day of the end (or destruction); **sikina sup** s. **supa.**

sup 2 (H. סוּף I–II, Chr.-Pal. ܣܘܦܐ rush, Syr. ܣܘܦܐ *alga marina*; popularly identified with **sup 1** MG 150 n. 1). reed, bulrush: **iama ḏ-sup** Gy 112:5 etc., **iama rba ḏ-sup** CP 379:7 Jb 55:6, 87:4, Gy 112:2, 177:3 (*& often*) the Great Ocean of destruction (orig. 'of reeds' H. יַם־סוּף misinterpreted as יַם־סוֹף) MG 150 n. 1, Jb ii. xxi:14 ff., Ginzā 20 n. 6, MSt 77 f. With original meaning in **sup zaba** HG 16 (var. **supat zaba** DC 36) River of Reeds HG & BHZ 4 n. 4.

supa = **saupa. šibiahia supa šabqia,** *Florilegium*, the planets have loosed destruction; **sikina supa ḏ-hbila** P.A.'s copy's var. of **sikina supa ḏ-hbila** DC 43 J 13 a destructive knife of death.

supaia (adj. from preced.) coming from the end, from the bottom. **blugma uziqa supaia** ATŠ II no. 142 phlegm and belching (or farting?).

supat 1 (rt. **SUP**) a name of an underworld, the lowest (part of) earth, hell Jb ii 24 n. 2, MSt 23 n. 1. **baba ḏ-supat** Jb 17:8, 18:12, 27:2, 30:1, 32:11, 261:11, Morg. 185:4, **lbaba ḏ-supat** Jb 20:2 (in) the gate of S.; **arqa ḏ-supat titaita** Gy 219:11 the lowest earth of S.; **šapilna ʿl supat** Jb 259:7 I descend into S.; **ušpil lsupat ulahaq** DC 44. 242 f. he descended to S. (: the hell) and was not afraid.

Gl. 69:12 missp. حجيم *infernus* دوزخ; 68:2 id. جهنّم *gehenna* دوزخ,

supat 2 in **supat zaba** s. **sup 2.**

supna (rt. **SUP**?) Oxf. roll g 765 = Or. 328:29 bottom, anus?

suṣṭmia occ. var. of **susṭmia.**

SUQ I s. **SAQ.**

SUQ II (ܣܳܩ, Ar. شَهِقَ Schulthess HW 24 n. 2) to inhale, snuff up.

Pe. Pf. **kul mindam ʿthaial unišimta saqat** DC 41. 479 everything became endued with strength and the soul drew breath.

suqa a mod. form of **ʿs(i)qta.** St. abs. & cstr. **suq.** Coll.

suqlab (Ar. صَقْلَب, سَقْلَب) AM 199 Slav(s).

SUR I s. **SAR I.**

SUR II s. **SAR II.**

sura 1 HG 80 a town in southern Babylonia where there was a noted Jewish academy HG & BHZ 10 n. 4.

sura 2 for **ṣura**? in **surẖ udmutẖ ḏ-gabra** Gy 391:6 the image (?) and likeness of a man.

suran AM 255:31 a man's name.

surkab, var. **surkar** (often in colophons) a man's name.

sušad Zotb. 218b:9 a man's name.

suta 1 a mod. form of **asuta.** St. abs. **sut pron.** *sūθ*. Coll.

suta 2 a *malwâša* woman's name.

SṬA (סטא, ܣܛܐ, H. שׂטה, Eth. ሠጠየ, rel. to H. שׂוּט, Ar. شطّ to deviate, Eth. ሦጠ to lead back) to turn aside, deflect, seduce, lead astray. Secondary rt. **ṢṬA** s.v.

Pe. Pf. **sṭa mn minilat marẖ** Gy 34:11 he turned aside from the will of his Lord; **sṭa dinanukt** Gy 212:17 D. has become distracted (Ginzā 211 n. 7). Impf. **ḏ-lanisṭunun bišia usaṭania** Gy 13:24 (var. **na-** B af.) that the evil ones and the satans may not lead them astray. Act. pt. **saṭia (umasṭia)** Gs 22:24 she is seduced; **dinanukt saṭia** Gy 212:17 D. is distracted (Ginzā 211 n. 7); pl. **saṭin (umasṭin)** Gy 46:22 f. they lead astray (and seduce).

Af. Impf. with suff. **nasṭunun** Gy 34:23, 13:ult. B (var. ni- A pe.) they seduce them MG 291:11 f. Pt. **(saṭia) umasṭia** s. pe. pt.; pl. **(saṭin) umasṭin** s. pe. pt. pl.; with encl. **masṭilun** Gy 24:18, **masṭilhun** Gy 24:21 they seduce them. Nom. ag. **masṭiana** (fem. **masṭianta**) s.v.

Der.: **masṭiana** (fem. **masṭianta**), **masṭianuta, saṭana, siṭia.**

SṬM s. **SSṬM.**

sṭmuma (ܣܛܘܡܐ, *στόμωμα*) pointed arrow, steel-spear. Var. **ʿusṭmuma, ʿusṭamuma, ʿusṭimima** s.vv. Pl. **-ia.** MG 45:10 f. N. 45. **giraiun usṭmumun** Jb 17:13 their arrows and their steel-spears.

SṬR (den. from **sitra** as Syr.) to go aside, turn aside, stand aside, be sideways, keep aloof; af. to set aside, to slap, strike s. **ṢTR.**

Pe. Impf. **hin latizha ulatisṭar** DC 43 I 102 if thou dost not flee away and turn aside; **kul bhu ṣṭura siṭru** DC 44 all were confounded, turned aside.

Af. Pf. with suff. **asṭruia** Gy 194:10 they set him aside MG 45 n. 3.

Der.: **siṭar, siṭra, misaṭra.**

siabušan Sh. ʿAbd.'s copy's var. of **sʿiauišan** (q.v.).

siaua (Avestan *syâwa* > mod. P. سیاه) black. Pl. **-ia** MG xxxi 19. **makaba siaua** s. **makaba**; **mia siauia** s. **mia** 1. DC 43 J 112.

siauina a var. of foll.

siauiš AM 202 name of a town BZ Ap. II.

siaušan = **sʿiauišan** in **dma ḏ-siaušan** DC 46 the blood of S. (transl. of P. proverbial expression خون سیاوش).

siana (סְיָן, ܣܝܢܐ) mud, filth MG 115:3. Still used (pronunciation: *esyâna*). **kita ḏ-siana** s. **kita**; **libta ḏ-siana** Gy 216:9 a mud-brick; **msak(i)kilẖ bisiana** Gy 92:22 f. they stuck it in the mud (Ginzā 96 n. 5); **babiqata ḏ-siana** DAb (cf. RD B 76) regions (?) of filth.

sianqa (Talm. סיאנקי, זיאנקי, Syr. ܣܝܢܩܐ > P. سه + *anak* Salemann GIPh i 290) half-drachma (coin), the weight of same. Pl. **-ia. danqia usianqia** Gy 217:9 obols and half-drachmae; **sianqa lnhura saliq** DC 41 (only) a half-drachma rises; **danqa usianqa** s. **danqa** 1.

SIB s. **SAB I.**

siata (cf. סִיעֲתָא) pl. troops, bands, companies, hordes. **akuat hauia bisiata** DC 43 E 18 as if they were in hordes (? cf. also **bisiata**).

siba 1 (rt. **SBA**, ܣܒܥܐ) satiety, abundance, surfeit, repletion. MG 107:ult. **mikal mn bisraihun lsiba** Gy 174:9 f., DC 43 J 46 to eat of their flesh to satiety; **siba uʿburia nihun** AM 212:4 there will be abundance and harvests; **siba umaliuta** AM 179:19 abundance and fullness.

siba 2 (cf. סִיבָה 1 J) misfortune, ill-fortune. Pl. **-ia.** Masc. **siba ušibia umutana** AM 211:3 misfortune, desolation, and pestilence; **talga nihuia . . . usiba banašia nihuia** AM 171:10 there will be snow . . . and misfortune amongst people.

siba 3 (for **saba** 1) old man, greybeard. Pl. **-ia,** abs. **-in. sibin uʿlamania** AM 249:15 old men and youths.

siba 4 Gy 323:23 corrupt. Ginzā 329 n. 2.

sibuta (abstr. noun from **siba** 4, סִיבוּתָא, ܣܝܒܘܬܐ) old age. MG 22:14, 144:ult. **bsibutẖ lʿqara maṭia** AM 7:17 in his old age he will attain honour.

sibla 1 (rt. **SBL**) burden. **ʿhablia . . . sibla** Jb 127:9 f. he gave me a burden.

sibla 2 (Talm. סְבוֹלֶת Levy: *Neuh. Wb.* III 468b, Syr. ܣܘܒܠܐ, Gr. *συμβολή*) Gs 101:7 something borne as an offering, food brought for the poor. Var. **sbila** Leid. (influenced by Ar. سبيل?) Ginzā 542 n. 3.

siblia pl. of **sumbilta** MG 173:11. **siblia siblia sablilẖ** Gy 208:2, 12, 24 step by step (by degrees) they bear him up.

sibra (rt. **SBR**) hope, faith, belief; insight, teaching MG 14:18. **sibra ḏ-bit alahuta** Gy 226:22 hope of the House of the Divinity; **iahib sibra** CP 10:14 = Q 4:16, 59:12 he giveth hope; **sibra lṭab ataila . . . tum (a)tna atalia sibra** Gs 90:17 f. Faith in the Good came to me . . . then again faith came to me.

sibrana (rt. **SBR**) hope, faith MG 136:11. **sibranan utuklanan** Gy 61:19 our hope and our trust.

sibruta (rt. **SBR**) hope, faith, insight, teaching MG 144:paen, **qašišia sibruta mn dẖ udẖ** Gy 78:2 f. faith is older than this or that; **bhukumta usibruta** Gy 90:1 f. in wisdom and insight; **mn hukumtẖ usibrutẖ** Gy 128:5 from his wisdom and his insight; **hikumta usibruta** CP 34:1 = Q 14:21 = ML 39:11, **hukumta usibruta** Gy 318:25, **lmadihta ulsibruta** Gy 305:9 wisdom and knowledge (?) Ginzā 214 n. 3; **bʿruta usibruta** Gy 157:1 in enlightenment and faith; **ʿruta usibruta** Q 3:10, Gy 270:18. With suff.: **sibrutak** Q 14:1, 54:4 thy hope, faith; **sibrutan** Q 53:18 our hope, faith, insight.

sigudta (rt. **SGD**) worship, obeisance. Var. **sugudta** MG 103:8. Pl. **sigudiata. sgidlia . . . ḏ-rba sigudta** Gy 182:8 f. he made . . . obeisance with a deep bow before me; **sgidlia ḏ-rba sigudta** Gy 307:5 id.; **sigudta sagdin** Gy 285:23 they make obeisance; **sigudta baiia** Gs 92:18 f. he prayed (hist. pres.) bowing down; **usgidulẖ ḏ-rba sigudiata** ATŠ II no. 142 (var. **sgudta** DC 36) and they made obeisance with deep bows.

sigia 1 = **sagia** 1 (q.v.).

sigia 2 (rt. **SGA II**, סוּגְיָא) going, walking, pace, progress, gait, movement, motion MG 152:20. Pl. **sigiia. bqalil sigia** Gy 9:14, 135:1, 151:5 walking speedily; **qalilia bsigiaihun** Gy 11:3 f. they walk speedily (are fast in their walk MG 182:4); **usigia lšibiahia hua** Gy 341:8 and the Planets were set into movement; **utpalag sigia lalma** Gs 48:23 and the motion of the world was divided; **qam bsigia** ATŠ I no. 100 he rose to go; **sigia**

(CP 114:9. has **sagia**) **d̠-ligrh̠** ML 139:12 pacing forward of his feet (Lidzb. *Schritte seiner Füsse*); **atina . . . bsigia niha umqaima** Jb 144:7 f. I come . . . with a gentle, steady motion; **kd̠ šlanda d̠-masgia usigia litlh̠** P.A.'s *Mihla* like a carcass without motion or movement; **uatia bsigia** DC 34. 995 and takes his course; **sigiia d̠-ligrak** DC 50. 342 the movements of thy feet; **bsigia d̠-ruha** HG in the way of R.

sigia 3 (סְיָגָא) fence, obstacle, stoppage, precaution, prohibition, guardedness, preventive measures. **sigia usigma uagara blišania** DC 43 J 138 a stopper and lock and fastening on his tongue; **d̠-asar sigia** DC 44 who secured a safeguard; **bsigia** ATŠ II no. 415 (ATŠ trsl. 285 n. 12) with prohibitions.

sigia 4 (rt. **SGA I,** similar semantic development as in Lat. *copia*) copy, treatise, fragment. Pl. **sigiia. hazin sigia uaprišata** DC 34 this treatise and explanations; **bhazin sigia** DC 34. 748 in this treatise; **kdabia usigiia d̠-ruha** HG the writings and treatises of Ruha.

sigisnaiia (Ar. سَجْزِى, cf. Syr. ܣܓܣܬܢܝܐ Fränkel 44 & no. 1) Gy 389:21 people of Sagistan MG 141:6 (where Nöld.'s proposal to read ***sigiskaiia** is unnecessary; the *t* of *Sagestân* vanished after a fricative in the Mand. form). N. 141.

sigma (rt. **SGM,** Ott. Turk. سجم string) a seal. **šqul . . . sigmak mn pumh̠** DC 43 J 152 remove . . . thy seal from his mouth.

sidama JRAS 1937 595:penult. = **sidma 1.**

sidar s. **sadar.**

sidma 1 (rt. **SDM**) lock, shackle, binding, shackling. **sigia usidma** s. **sigia 3; bsidma d̠-sidmh̠ manda d̠-hiia** DC 40. 1107 f. by the shackle with which M.-d̠-H. shackled him . . .; **lsidma lpiṭiaruta** DC 40. 544 for the restraint of malicious talk (?).

sidma 2 a fish-eating marsh bird. (DC 30:158 has **sirma** q.v.) Jb ii 147 n. Var. **sirma** s.v. **ˁlgiṭh̠ lsidma** (var. **lsirma** DC 30) **rba** Jb 146:12 I will seize the great s.(-bird).

sidra (rt. **SDR,** סִדְרָא) (*a*) order, row, rank, system, (*b*) book, recitation. MG 102:3 f. Pl. **sidria, sidraria** MG 170:10 f. (*a*) **sidraihun hua lmipak ˁl anpaihun** Gy 173:9 their ranks were ready to turn their faces away; **atit . . . lmsadruia sidria** DAb I came . . . to set affairs in order; **hinun hun šuba sidria** ATŠ II no. 189 they were seven systems; **msadar sidria qruk** Jb 220:13 f. they called thee Ranger of Ranks ii 209 n. 3; (*b*) **sidra rba** Zotb. 217a the Great Book, or **sidra ladam** Zotb. 225b the Book of Adam (common subtitles of the *Ginzā*); **sidra d̠-nišmata** the Book of Souls (title of the baptismal liturgy DC 2, MMII 150–2); **aspar sidria** Gy 245:8 the book of books; **raza usidra** Gy 134:3, 196:14, 249:10, Gs 19:22 the mystery and the book; **raza usidra qadmaia** Gy 68:20 the mystery and the first book; **raza usidra d̠-ziua** Gy 234:15, 238:2 the mystery and the book of radiance; **sidra uaprašta** Gy 126:2, 219:8 the book and explanation; **sidria sakia** (*often*) books (and) chapters; **nhur sidra** Q 27:5 = ML 75:4 f. = CP 59:5 the book 'Light'; **sidria udrašia** Gy 9:24 books and hymns; **drašia usidria** Gy 105:24, 107:10, 371:2, 11 hymns and books; **drabšia usidria** Gy 361:2, RD B 128 id. (cf. **drabša 2**); **sidria ubauata** RD B 127, Gy 138:13, 140:13, 195:17 books and prayers; **bauata udrašia usidria** Oxf. 15 b; **drašia ubauata usidria** Gy 137:5; **sidria umasqata** Q 35:1 books and *masiqtas*; **malilnin bsidria d̠-hiia** Q 54:23 we speak in accordance with the books of Life. Used normally as masc. **sidria kasiia** Gy 361:2, exceptionally as fem. **sidria kasiata** Gy 320:1 secret books.

Gl. 106:ult. miswritten pl. صحف *libri* كتابها, 141:ult. **sidra** (& missp. pl.) كتاب, كُتُب *liber*.

silhupta (rt. **SHP**) cover(ing), veil, overthrow. **sihupta d̠-rama** Gy 195:9 they shall raise a lofty veil; **sihupta hˁ d̠-ngida ˁlh̠ d̠-ptahil abinia dilh̠ labatur** DAb it is a covering outspread above P. between himself and A.; **sihupta d̠-ptahil** Gy 306:19 f.; **usihupta npalalh̠ binia dilh̠ labatur** Gy 340:8 and a veil dropped between himself and A.; **sap ˁlauaihun sihupta** Jb 141:14 he burnt the Veil over them (Libzb. *er brachte einen Sturz über sie*); **sihupta d̠-hibla niqum ˁlak daiua** DC 20. 97 f. discomfiture shall overtake thee, demon!, cf. **sihipta rabtia niqum ˁlak daiua** DC 43 E 44 (at the same time both fem. & masc.).

sihiun for **ṣihiun** in **rima bsihiun rabtia hua** CP 176:9 f. there was thunder in Great Zion.

sihil (Ar. سَاحِل) coast, border, shore. **sihil d̠-diria** AM 205:3 (P. ساحل دريا) the seashore; **sihil** AM 198 (var. **suhil** Ṣâb.'s AM) apparently a pr. n. BZ Ap. II.

sihrana s. **sahrana.**

siuan (H. סִיוָן < Akk. *simānu* or *siwānu*) Mandaean month under the rule of Gemini, called also **miṣai (a)bhar** MMII 84. Often in AM.

siuṭa (סְיוּטָא, Nöld. from ܫܘܛ) fright, terror, panic, pain, suffering MG 126:13. Var. **sauṭa** s.v. **(la) bsiuṭa d̠-lilia ula bsiuṭa d̠-ˁumama** Oxf. roll 85 = DC 43 J 37 neither by terror by night nor panic by day; **siuṭa bparṣuph̠** Oxf. roll 300, 331 = DC 43 J 137, 149 whose countenance shows panic; **siuṭa uhauqa uziuihta** DC 37. 548 terror, fear, and trembling; **bianquth̠ siuṭa nihuilh̠** AM (CS 26:DC 31 has **ṣauta**) in his (her) youth (s)he will be timorous.

siuia for **siauia** in **pt hiuia siuia** DC 40. 1089 daughter of a black serpent.

siṭar (st. abs. of **siṭra** used adverbially like Syr. ܣܛܪ) aside, apart, behind, aloof MG 29:9, 45 n. 3, 207:21. Var. **ṣiṭar.** Used with or without the procl. prep. **b-. siṭar mn** PD 970, 978 apart from; **siṭar qaimit minaihun** Gs 73:8 thou standest aside from them; **hun siṭar mn bišia** Gy 177:paen. f. keep aloof from the wicked; **siṭar (a)huaitun mn kul biš** Jb 169:10 f.

we keep aloof from all evil; **siṭar mn pagra aqmu** Gy 74:21 they put her (: the soul) out of the body; **lgaṭṭinun bṣiṭar** (var. **bsiṭar** Leid.) **alma** Gs 77:6 I kept them aloof from the world.

siṭia (rt. SṬA) seduction, infidelity, heresy, apostasy, revolt, contumacy. **kul ruh siṭia** Gy 177:20, DC 51. 206 every spirit of seduction MG 309:1; **siṭia umriduta** Gy 15:13 revolt and rebellion; **siṭia d-bišia** Gy 16:9 seduction of the wicked; **puhria usiṭia** Gy 219:26 banquets and apostasy; **daura d-siṭia** Jb 62:1 the abode of apostasy (or heresy); **siṭia bʿurašlam** Jb 83:6 heresy in Jerusalem.

siṭil Gs 63:16 a var. of siṭar Leid.

siṭra (סִטְרָא, ܣܛܪܐ, Eg. Aram. שטר, Ar. شَطْر) side, flank MG 45:14. Var. ṣiṭra s.v. St. abs. siṭar (s.v.) used adverbially or as a compound preposition (with mn). With suff. it is also used as a prepositional expression. **bsiṭria** DC 34. 1132 beside him; **siṭraiin primlin** Gy 181:3, 209:5, 225:13 they (fem.) bare their flanks; **siṭraiun primlun** Gs 30:17 id. masc. (Ginzā 184 n. 7); **kiba bhda siṭra** AM 23:17 pain in one side; **hda siṭra d-rišia kaiiblh** AM 4:18 one side of his head pains him.

siiad Zotb. 221a:28 same as foll.

siiid (Ar. سيّد) AM 256:40 Seyyed.

sika DC 44. 2053 for sikia (q.v.).

sikana Gs 109:25 a var. of **sukana** Leid.

sikandar (سِكَنْدَر = اِسْكَنْدَر) AM 285:1 Alexander (the Macedonian).

sikandaraiia DC 7 the Alexandrians, people of Alexandria.

sikandarʿia AM 198:8 Alexandria. Var. **sikandiriia** Ṣâb.'s var. AM.

sikulata (rt. SKL) pl. inanities, follies. Sg. **skulta** s.v. **sikulata raṭin** AM he utters inanities.

sikia pl. of **sikta** MG 173:1. **sikia gnana** Gy 147:23 f. the poles of the baldachin; **sikia gnan ana ušušban hiduia** DC 3. 380:ult. = CP 227:1 = ŠQ 16:24 the poles of the baldachin are myself and the groomsman; **sikia uqlidia** Gy 186:15, Gs 105:9 doorpins and keys; . . . **sikia mn ʿudnh** Gs 7:11, 14 f. (let them remove . . .) the plugs from his ears; **mištalpia sikia gnanun** Gs 17:22 the poles of their baldachin spring out; **sikia usugaria** s. **sugara** (*a*); **sikia d-muta** Jb 156:8 the stings of death (cf. τὸ κέντρον τοῦ θανάτου I Cor. 15:55 f.); **sikia bpumaihun** DC 26. 589 = DC 44. 612 wedges (stoppers) in their mouths; **duṣlia** (read **-ih**) **sika** (read **-ia**) **bainh d-dmuta** DC 44. 2053 stick pins in the eyes of the effigy.

sikina (סַכִּינָא, ܣܟܝܢܐ, H. loan-w. שַׂכִּין Kautzsch 86, with orig. vocalization: Ar. loan-w. سِكِّين Fränkel 84, accord. to Hoffmann LC 1882 320 rel. to סיכתא = Mand. **sikta**) knife MG 125:1, Jb ii 46 n. 2. Var. **sakina**, def. **skina**. Pl. **-ia**. **sikina d-daula** s. **daula 2**; **sikina d-parzla** Jb 41:8 (var. sa- C) an iron knife, pl. **sakinia d-parzla** DC 44. 1005 (var. si- Morg. 262/16:2 f.); **sikina usipa bʿdh** Morg. 252/8:2 a knife and a sword is in his hand; **sikinia ugarṭupiata** Gy 143:19 knives and cutting-implements; **šuba sikinia** (*often*) seven knives.

sikinta = **sikina**. **kdub bsikinta** DC 46 write with a knife.

Gl. 99:14 missp. & with fem. ending سكين *culter* كارد.

sikra ((סִכְרָא) graveyard, burial ground. **uqbur bbaba d-sikra** DC 44. 918 and bury at the gate of the burial ground; **aqapra mn baba d-sikra** DC 44. 1093 dust from the gateway of a graveyard.

sikta (סִיכְּתָא, ܣܟܬܐ < Akk. *sikkatu* Zimmern: *Akk. Fremdwörter* 35, Ar. loan-w. سِكَّة nail, ploughshare Fränkel 89 f., 132) nail, peg, pin, pole, wedge, plug MG 173:1. Pl. **sikia** s.v. **sikta d-zahba** DC 12:101, Lond. roll B 206, 210 a gold pin; **sikta d-kaspa, d-parzla, d-nhaša** DC 12:106, 109, Lond. roll B 214 ff. a silver, iron, copper pin; **sikta d-parzla** DC 44. 659 f.; **sikta d-arqa** DC 44. 915 a plug of earth.

silat (cf. סַלָּא, ܣܠܐ & ܣܠܬܐ, Ar. سَلَّة Fränkel 75, Akk. *sallu*, *sellu*) st. cstr. fem. basket, market basket. **silat nuqbta** Gy 97:23 a woman's market basket.

silata s. silita.

silua (סִלְיָא & סִילְוָא, ܣܠܘܐ Löw 150, cf. Ar. سُلَّاء palm-tree thorns) orig. thorn, hence: shaft, lance, pointed arrow, rod. Pl. **siluania**, **sil(a)uata**, **salauata**. **zumh bsilua** DC 44. 2079 insert it into a tube (?); **nisaq ʿl ziqla unišipth bsilua šarira** JRAS 1937 593:22 we will set up a date-palm and will set it with a firm shaft (or trunk?); **šaba siluania** (varr. **salauata**, **silauata**) **mn šuba talia d-ziqla** JRAS 1937 591:26 seven shafts from seven young palm-shoots; **šuba siluania d-hinun šuba giria** HG seven shafts which are seven arrows.

Gl. 96:1 missp. (both sg. & pl.) شوك, اشواك *spina* خار.

siliata (rt. SLA) ATŠ II no. 189 pl. dregs, filth, rejected matter, refuse.

silita (Ar. سُلِّي, سُلِّيَّة Jb 148 n. 5, Nöld. 'hook' referring to סַלְוָא MG 103:24 f.; cf. also Syr. ܪܟܫܬܐ net, snare) a circular fishing-net weighted with leads DAb 7 n. 1, net. Varr. **salita, silata, slita. upalgh lsilith** Jb 147:10 and he opened up his fishing-net; **laramin silita** Jb 148:12 they do not cast a fishing-net; **kma naia silitak** Jb 149:10 how excellent is thy fishing-net!; **ṣaidia ramin ʿlun silita pardilh lsilita** (var. **lslita** BC) **unapqia** Jb 157:12 f. the fishermen cast a net on them, but they (: the fish) break the net apart and come out; **pirdu lsilita unpaq** CP 176:14 = Morg. 62:6 = Oxf. 44 a = ML 215:3, 5 they (: the fish) broke the net apart and escaped; **uslitun nunia laiṭia** Jb 160:13 and the fish curse their fishing-net; **slitak** Jb 162:2 (varr. **aslitak** AC, **salitak** B) thy fishing-net; **bslitai** Jb 204:5 in my fishing-net; **ᶜl silitai** Jb 204:13 (var. **lislitai** ACD) my fishing-net (acc.). With **abara** 1: **silita d̲-abara** AIT 19:10 (p. 195), **bsilitan ubabaran** Gs 57:18 (cf. Jb ii 148 n. 5 & DAb 7 n. 1) (Montgomery's explanation AIT 199 seems to be mistaken). Of other kinds of net: **sradqa dilh̲ silita d̲-ᶜur** DAb its canopy is the net of Ur; **šqul . . . silatak mn pumaiun d̲-biriata** DC 43 remove . . . thy net from the opening of the streets. Apparently of a fishing-net but doubtf. in **kul man d̲-iuma d̲-silita d̲-ṣaidia laniṣṭba . . . kul man d̲-silita d̲-hudišaiia laniṣṭba** ATŠ II no. 91 (prob. 'Day of Purification' cf. **sulita** s.v.); **d̲-ṣaidia** would be a mistaken gloss of a later copyist; **d̲-hdišaiia** a corruption of **d̲-hda šaiia** hence 'in the first hour of the day of Purification (?)'; **dukrana rba . . . d̲-silith̲ ᶜl kulhun dukrania** DC 38.95 f. the Commemoration of the Great . . . which is spread over (?) all commemorations.

SIM s. **SUM.**

sima sometimes for **simat** as a *malwâša* woman's name.

simad (סְמִידָא, ܣܡܝܕܐ < Akk. *samīdu*, loan-words: Ar. سميد, Gr. *σεμίδαλις* etc. OLZ 1922 337 f.) fine flour. **usimad aiil bla miniana** DC 3. 377:7 = DC 38. 15:18 = ŠQ 15:18, CP 223:4 and fine flour comes without measure.

simadra (סְמָדְרָא, ܣܡܕܪܐ, H. & mod. H. סְמָדר) blossom MG 29:10, 128:1. Pl. **-ia.** **bsimadria asa bmublia aitun** Gy 106:17 they brought myrtle blossoms by the load; **simadra uklila** Gy 115:14 f. blossom and wreath (hendiadys); **lsimadria** Oxf. 31 b = ML 203:4 to the blossom; **unpiš ṭunaihun lsimadrun** CP 168:1 and increased their fruit and their blossom; **knara darh̲ simadra** Gs 10:19 the lote-tree beareth blossom; **kinara bsimadrh̲** s. **kinara** 2; **d̲-ṭuna dara adinqia simadra** ATŠ I no. 279 that beareth fruit without blossom; **ṭuna dakita usimadra šania** DC 34. 213 pure fruit and sublime blossom; **d̲-lamapiq btibil simadria** Jb 109:13 which bringeth out no blossom on earth; **simadra d̲-minaihun hua** CP 40 B:14 the blossom that came from them.

simaka (Targ. סְמָךְ, Syr. ܣܡܟܐ, Ar. سِمَاك) support, prop MG 29:11, 115:7. Pl. **-ia.** **nihuilun simaka** Gy 1:15 they shall have a support; **niaha usimaka** Q 29:24 rest and support; **hun simaka uadiaura lhdadia** Gy 20:19 be a support and helper to one another; **simaka uniaha rba d̲-hiia** DC 51. 229 f. the great support and solace of Life; **simaka d̲-šrara** RD D 4 a firm support; **simakia d̲-lanaidia** Q 53:27 supports which do not shake.

simana, -ia = **samania. ṣania usimania** Gy 378:34 leaves and healing herbs; **asia d̲-simanh̲ mia hiia** HG a healer whose medicine is Water of Life; **lgaṭ iardna usimana mia** HG he took running water and healing draught.

simandrᶜil s. **samandarᶜil.**

simaq for **sumaq** in **simaq manzih̲** AM 18: penult. his hair is red.

simat st. cstr. of **simta** used esp. in **simat hiia** CP trs. 279 ns. 1 and 3, Gy 30:15, Q 1:9, 10:21, AM 1, Oxf. roll f 55, 824 etc.: (*very often*) Treasure-of-Life, personified as a female genie MSchr. 55 n. 4, CP 1:13, Jb ii 201 f., ML 282, often mentioned with **iauar** (**ziua**): **iauar usimat hiia** RD B 100, **iauar ziua usimat hiia** (in CP often as one word **simathiia**), Oxf. roll f 376, 508, 1059, Lond. roll A 195, 263, 305 etc.; **simat hiia brata d̲-iušamin** RD 46; **simat ana simat hiia** Jb 210 ff. a treasure am I, a Treasure of Life. As one word in **simathiia niṭupta** Jb 252:8 f. Unpersonified: **nitkarak bsimat hiia** Jb 142:11 will be included in Treasure of Life (Jb ii 138 n. 2); **arqa simat admᶜil** RD 41 = DAb par. name of a land in the other world; **simat** = **libat** RD 7, cf. **simat ruha** RD 41; **simat** and **simat hiia** are also used as frequent *malwâša* women's names, similarly **haua simat** (s. **haua**) and **šarat simat** (s. **šarat**).

simṭizaidᶜiil sahra DC 43 name of a demon.

simiaiil a demon (Ishmael alluded to as ancestor of the Arabs, Ginzā 200 n. 1). Var. **ᶜsmaiil. simiaiil saṭana** DC 40. 1107, DC 43 J 113 (*& very often in exorcisms*), ATŠ II no. 272, 296, CP 376:6 f., DC 22. 192 (= **ᶜsmaiil saṭana** Gy 200:19) the satan S. (= Ishmael); **simiaiil baqara** RD F 13 = DAb par. S. the herdsman; **šamšiaiil usimiaiil** DC 40. 969.

simsa DC 22. 237 for **simta** Gy 242:21.

simsar (P. سمسار broker) agent, mediator, negotiator: **ᶜsir . . . ᶜl simsar ulkursiih̲** DC 43 I 152 he is bound (magically protected) as to his agent and his seat (doubtf.).

simsira (cf. preced.) broker, negotiator. **hamara simsira** s. **hamara** 2.

simraiia name of a people Halévy REJ xxii 308, MSchr. 218, Marquart: *Ērānšahr* 26 n. 1, Ginzā 416 n. 5. **malka simraia** Gy 390:7 the Simraean king; **simraiia uṭuraiia** Gs 17:5.

simta (סִימְתָא, ܣܝܡܬܐ) treasure, precious thing MG St. cstr. **simat** s.v. **simta bṣaurh̲ bzat** Gy 247:7 she broke the jewel at her neck; **simta dakita d̲-sima** Gs 72:2 (cf. l. 5) the pure treasure which is laid up; **bit simtak** Q 72:5 thy treasure-house; **ᶜlai simtun sadqia** Gs 98:17 for me they rent their treasure (: they tear apart their jewels?, Lidzb.: garment Ginzā 538 n. 3); **simta d̲-hiia** Gy 242:21 for the more usual **simat hiia** (s. **simat**).

sin 1 (ܣܝܢܐ < Akk. *Sīn*) Sin, Moon, moon-god. As pr. n. always in st. abs. MG 300 n. 2. SsSs ii 37, MMII 77 ff., 329 n. 1, MR 126: middle. **sin d̲-hu ṣaurᶜil** Gy 27:19, **sin d̲-hu sira šumh̲ ṣaurᶜil šumh̲** Gy 51:4 f. Sin whose name is moon, his name is Ṣauriel; **sin blibh̲ birkh̲** Gy 115:15 f. S. blessed him with his heart; **lšamiš bšumh̲ qarilh̲ ulsin** Gy 171:21 f. I called Š. by his name and S.; **maprišnalkun ᶜl sin** Gy 231:4 I will teach you about S.; **baba d̲-qra sin** Gy 231:18 the Gate (: sect) which S. created; **lsin plaglh̲ husrana** Gy 112:11 to Sin they allotted lack; **ata lalma d̲-husrana uᶜhiblh̲ lsin mn riš briš** Gy 311:14 f. he came to the world of imperfection and it was completely given to S.; **sin bqala d̲-hiia malil** Gy 312:24 S. speaketh with the voice of Life; **sin kukba** Gy 379:20 f. the planet Moon; **agzᶜil d̲-sin qarilh̲** Gy 120:24 (cf. 121:1); **luat ruha škib sin** Gy 118:13 f. S. slept with R.; **kukbia . . . d̲-hizia lsin bᶜšumia** Gs 118:ult. the stars . . . which S. (: Moon) saw in the sky; **dmuta d̲-sin masihpan** RD 1 = DAb the picture of Sin the Destroyer, ibid. as son of Ruha with names she bestowed upon him; **spinta d̲-sin** RD 1 the boat of S.; **baba d̲-sin** RD 35 the Gate of S.; **maṭarta d̲-sin** RD C 15, 26 the purgatory of S.; **sin daiua qaraptana d̲-hšuka** RD B 91 the demon S. the warrior of darkness; **sin sikina dria** RD B 124 twice, 130 S. carries a knife; **sin girbana** Jb 187:5 S. the leper; **sin rba sadrᶜil** Jb 235:6; **sin maria taga uklila** WedF 39:middle = CP 224:13 S. lord of crown and wreath. A whole chapter about Sin Jb 192–197.

sin 2 AM 204 = ṣin China.

sina 1 (rt. **SNA**, סְנָאָה) hatred MG 71:8, 102:12. **sina qina uplugta** Q 27:12, Gy 112:17, 122:13, 243:22, 373:2, Gs 78:21 etc. (often) hatred, jealousy, and discord.

sina 2 for *ṣina (צִינָא)? Probably a miswriting of *aina* date-stone. (DC 53 has **aina,** CP 416:1.) **birkh̲ lsindirka usina d̲-minh̲ hua** DC 3 he blessed the date-palm and the date-stone from which it came into existence (i.e. its seed).

sina 3 s. pl. **sinia.**

sinai (H. סִינַי Ges.) Sinai. **ṭura d̲-sinai** Gy 45:16, 46:8, Jb 198:13 the Mount Sinai. **lmiša br samrud d̲-sinai** DC 40 to Moses, son of Samrud, of Sinai.

singa accord. to context: prob. beak, bill. Var. **hinzara.** Doubtf. **udita bsingh̲** JRAS 1938 3:27 (var. **bhinzara** P.A.'s copy) and the kite with his bill (?).

singiania pl. (סְגַנָּא, Old-Aram., H. & mod. H. סגן, Akk. *šaknu, šakin*) rulers, governors, potentates MG 76:13. **aṭirpan ulupan trin singiania d̲-alma** Gy 98:1 A. and L. the two potentates of the world; **bhaza maṭarta singiania** Gy 183:8 in this prison-place (purgatory) are the potentates; **singiania rurbia** Gs 36:19 mighty potentates; **hamša singiania** Gy 99:2 s. **hamša**; **singiania uaradaiia** Gy 121:14 f. potentates and dignitaries.

sind AM 197, Gs 17:3 Sind.

sindauarta DC 22. 404 a var. of **sinduarta.**

sindaita a *malwāša* woman's name.

sindar s. **sandar.**

sind(a)rus s. **sandlus.**

sinduarta (cf. סִנְוַרְתָּא, ܣܢܘܪܬܐ helmet) enclosure, cage, stockade. **aria d̲-paliṭ mn sinduarth̲** Gs 14:5 a lion which escapeth from its cage; **ᶜsir . . . aria biša bsinduarta** DC 37. 575 ff. imprisoned (is) . . . the evil lion in a cage.

sindumaia ATŠ I no. 171 Sodomite. Pl. **sindumaiia** PD 1518, 1521, 1523. Var. **sindimaiia** DC 36 no. 171.

sindur AM 198 a place-name. BZ Ap. II.

sind(i)lus a frequent var. of **sandlus.**

sindimaiia s. **sindumaia.**

sindistan AM 196 Sind.

sind(i)rus a var. of **sandlus.** DC 34. 288.

sindiriauis 1 name of a heavenly river. Halévy REJ xxii 312, MR 68:1 & n. 1, MSchr. 138 n. 1, Jb ii 12 n. 1. **sindiriauis iardna** Gy 112:16, 131:20, CP 426:2, 435:4.

sindiriauis 2 Gy 134:6 B a var. of **siniauis** MR 68 n. 1.

sindirka (ܣܕܪܟܐ, σανδαράκη, Lat. *sandaraca*, rel. to **sandlus** = **sandrus**) orig. an evergreen tree regarded as sacred, hence palm-tree, date-palm, its fruit, dates (used as a collective in sg.). Regarded as a symbol of male fertility and used together with **aina** (for female fertility) CP Ind., s. Palm-tree, Nöld. ZA xxx 152, Siouffi 26, ATŠ trs. 110 n. 9, Ochser ZDMG lxi 159 n. 7, Lidzb. *Florilegium* 373 (to 178), ML xxi, DAb 19 n. 8. Rare var. **sandirka.** Rare pl. **-ia** Lond. roll A 362, Oxf. roll 134: **aina usindirka** CP 25:9 f., 45: penult., 143:17 f., 199h:12, 199m:12 ff., 358:3, 4:5:ult. f. Oxf. roll f 51, 53, 367, ATŠ I no. 4, Morg. 112:5 f., **sindirka uaina rabtia** RD B 99 = DAb par., **aina usindirka d̲-aba d̲-ᶜruta** Morg. 10:6; **sindirka rba** Q 10:17 (*& often*); **sindirka d̲-hšuka** RD 26; **sindirka d̲-nura** PD 15:38; **raza d̲-sindirka** Lond. roll A 312; **ziua usindirka** Gy 320:20; **mana usindirka** *Florilegium* 364:177 f. (cf. p. 373); **lbuša d̲-adam d̲-mn sindirka npaq** Gs 122:6 f. Adam's garment which came from a date palm-tree (Lidzb. *aus dem Sandarakbaume*), similarly **lbuša d̲-adam d-minh̲ d̲-sindirka hua** Gs 122: 17 f. **ᶜu hauia ᶜniš d̲-npil mn sindirka** ATŠ I no. 75 or if it should be a person that fell from a date-palm. Often in lists of ritual foods: **brunda usindirka** PD 1136 fish and dates; **sindirka ukauara** Lond. roll A 504, Morg. 183:5 dates and fish; **sandirka urumana** Morg. 183:8 dates and pomegranates; **sindirka umiuia kulhun** DC 27 dates and all kinds of fruit; **mna sindirkak** Jb 236:11 whence cometh thy palm-tree? See WiW pp. 205 ff.

sindlus = **sandlus. riha usindlus** ATŠ II no. 386 incense and sandalwood.

sindmaiia ATŠ II no. 25 in DC 6 = **sindumaiia** DC 36 ibid.

sindruz, sindrus varr. of **sandlus** (q.v.).

sinuara (סַנְוַרְתָּא, ܣܢܘܪܐ < Pahl. *sarvâr*) helmet. Masc. **sinuara brišai matnalia** DC 44. 707 = Morg. 268/26:15 I put a helmet on my head; **sinuara d̲-hiia** DC 44. 1447 (= **asinuara** . . . Morg. 265/21:36), **sinuara rba d̲-hiia** DC 44. 1587 = Morg. 267/24:21.

sinṭur sahra DC 43 name of a devil.

sinia pl. of sina 3 (סֵינָא, cf. Syr. ܣܐܘܢܐ, H. סְאוֹן, Eth. ሣእን, Akk. *šênu*) shoes MG 102:10. **sinia ligrai** Gs 116:20 the shoes of my feet.

siniauis underworld, abode of darkness, Kessler PRE 170:42, MR 61 n. 1, Jb ii 12 n. 1, MSt 23 n. 1. **siniauis arqa titaita** CP 443:14 S. the lower earth; **siniauis arqa titaita d̲-hšuka** Gy 134:6 S. the lower earth of darkness (var. **sindiriauis 2** s.v.); **arqa siniauis** Gy 74:18 f.;

aqapra d̲-saliq mn siniauis Gy 87:14 f. dust which riseth from S.; **apra mn siniauis** Gy 97:11 f. dust from S.; **guha bsiniauis man gna** Jb 6:11 who caused the earthquake in S.?, **guha bsiniauis gna** Jb 7:13 an earthquake took place in S.; **šuba šuria d̲-mahdiria ʿl siniauis arqa** Jb 251:12 f. the seven walls which surround the earth S.

siniaiil s. **saniaiil.**

siniuta (abstr. noun from **SNA**) hatred, hatefulness, rascality. Var. **sa-** s.v. **siniuta uhuspa urugza** Gy 215:21 hatred and impudence and wrath; **asiuta usiniuta** = Q 72:2 oppression and hatred; **drahmuta udsiniuta** DC 40. 337 of love and hatred.

sinpa (**sipa 1** with an intruded **n**?) sword (?). **bsinpun sinpa d̲-aba mlakia** DC 43 G 25 with their sword, the sword of the father of angels (?).

sinšab AM 198 a place-name BZ Ap. II. Var. **sanšb.**

sinta cord (?). **hazin sinta šidniaiil d̲-ʿsira bkursia d̲-ptahil** DAb this is the cord (? of ?) Š. that is fastened to the throne of P.

sisan, name mentioned in exorcism (DC 19 & 43).

sisiata Ṣâb's AM var. of **susiata** AM 281:40 horses, mares.

sisptiaiil DC 40. 939 an angel.

sistan AM 197 Persian province of Sistan.

sistata DC 40. 153 for **sustata** (s. **susia**).

siƐadat (Ar. سعادت) AM 282:8 prosperity, auspiciousness, good omen. Var. **saƐadat** Par. AM par., **siƐudat** AM 285:43.

siƐaid (for سعيد?) AM 255:28 a man's name.

siƐdan Ṣâb.'s AM coloph = **saƐdan.**

siƐudat s. **siƐadat.**

siƐir (Ar. سِعَر) AM 259:29 market price, current price.

sipa 1 (סַיְפָא, ܣܰܝܦܳܐ > Ar. سَيْف Fränkel 239) sword, blade MG 22:14. Pl. **-ia. hirbia usipia** (often in exorcisms) swords and blades; **sipia d̲-mia** Gy 316:14 swords of (living) water; **sipia d̲-mištalpia** Jb 12:4 unsheathed swords.

sipa 2 (rt. **SUP,** סַיְפָא) end, destruction, slaughter (?). **sipa ukupna** AM 172 slaughter and famine.

sipa 3 (סִיפָא) door-post, door-sill, threshold. Pl. **-ia. sipa babia** DC 46. 17:11, **sipia baba** Gs 83:2 doorposts; **sipa d̲-babh̲** DC 44. 2049 the doorpost of his door.

sipa 4 in the name of the king **parašai sipa malka** Gy 393:5.

sipahan AM 203 Isfahan. Var. **spahan.**

sipar occasionally for **spar.**

sipna s. **sapna.**

sipra 1 (rt. **SPR I,** סִפְרָא, ܣܶܦܪܳܐ, H. סֵפֶר, Ar. loan-w. سِفْر Fränkel 247, Akk. *šipru*) book, codex; cipher, writing, copying MG 102:3. St. abs. & cstr. **aspar, spar, ʿspar** s.vv. Pl. **-ia. sipra d̲-ruha** Gy 228:21 ff. Ruha's Book; **siprak qlinun** Gy 211:16 burn thy books; **nbu šda siprh̲** Gy 336:1 Nebo (Mercury) cast down his book; **ṭaksa usipra** RD C 12 order and book; **paliṭth̲ mn sipra ubdiuan atnaith̲** DC 41. 561 I removed it from a codex and put it into a scroll; **usipria usipraiun** DC 44. 1950 = Morg. 269/29:40 and the clerks (cf. **sipra 2**) and their writings; **hazia bgauh̲ sipra šania pahta uqaribh̲** Jb 91:10 f. he seeth in it a wondrous book, openeth and readeth in it; **kma iatbit uhazit bsiprak** DC 8 DAb how thou sittest and studiest in thy book; **mn sipra utangaruta lhamh̲ akil** AM 14 he will earn his living by writing and trade; **trin sipria ialpia** RD C 12 they learn two (different) books.

sipra 2 for **sapra.** Pl. **-ia. nbu sipra hakima** (*often*) Mercury the wise scribe; **usipria usipraiun** s. **sipra 1.**

siprud (for P. سفيد رود?) AM 204 a place-name.

sipta (סִפְתָא, ܣܶܦܬܳܐ, H. שָׂפָה, Ar. شَفَةٌ, Akk. *šaptu* Brockelm. I 333; Nöld.: *Beiträge* 58, *Neue Beiträge* 127) lip MG 172:19, 184:18. Pl. **ʿspia, (ʿ)spihata** (varr. **sbihata, sbahata**) MG 98:13, 171:13, 172:19, 184:18 f. (& n. 3). Pl. with suff. **span** our lips MG 184:18. With **PRṬ** idiom 'to sneer': **siptaiun praṭiun ʿlauaiun** Gy 247:12 f. they sneered at them; **siptai pirṭit** Gy 266:5, Gs 64:21 I sneered at; **siptun praṭ** Gs 95:22 they sneered; **usipth̲ ʿl anašia pariṭ** AM 9:8 and he sneers at others; **ʿspia mhaimnia** Gy 5:10 believing lips; **ʿspan** Q 24:3 our lips; **bit spihatan** Gy 6:2 between our lips.

sir (P. سير) satiated. Mod. **sir ʿl lhama laqhauinia** DC 51:coloph. we do not have enough bread.

sira 1 (סַהֲרָא, ܣܰܗܪܳܐ, H. שַׂהֲרֹנִים, Ar. شَهْر, Sab. 𐩥𐩧𐩭, Eth, ወርኅ; cf. Chr.-Pal. ܣܗܪܐ, Jer.-Targ. זיהרא, Sam. ࠔࠄࠓ Brockelm. *Grundr.* I 170:2 and ࠔࠃࠓࠀ Nöld. ZDMG xxii 477, 514 & n. 2) moon MG 63:9, 101:3. Masc. MG 160:4. Still used (pronounced *serra*). Only st. emph. found in literature MG 300 n. 2 (mod. st. abs. *ser*). **šamiš usira baṭlin** (var. **-an**) Jb 46:4 sun and moon vanish; **šamiš usira bakin** Jb 109:11, 122:12 etc. sun and moon weep.

Gl. (always missp., with a doubled **r**) 28:1 (sg. & pl.!) أهِلَّة *lunatio* ماهيا; 136:14 قمر *luna* ماه; 171:12 (sg. & pl.!) هلالت , أهِلَّة *lunationes* ماه نو.

sira 2 (etym. unknown) flock (of birds), swarm. Var. **sara 3. sira** (var. **sara** C & DC 30) **bʿlana ʿtib** Jb 132:3 a flock (of birds) alighted on the tree.

sira 3 (rt. **SRA I**?) foul matter, refuse, horrid stuff? **ašqunh̲ lsahra sira** DC 37. 196 they gave the demon to drink of the filthy stuff (?).

sirupta (rt. **SRP,** Syr. ܣܘܪܦܬܐ & ܣܪܘܦܬܐ) Gy 82:13, swallowing, gulp MG 103:3.

siruta DC 22. 12 = **sruta** Gy 12:12.

siriha (rt. **SRA I = SRH**) stench, decay, stink. **usiriha bqumth̲** DC 43 J 150 and stench (?) in his body.

sirma s. **sidma 2.** (سرم) a marsh bird. DC 30. 158.

sitara (rt. **STR I**, סִתְרָא, ܣܬܪܐ, Ar. سِتَار & سِتَارَة) covering, veil. **sitara ngadlẖ ʿl rišia** DC 34. 602 they spread a covering over his head; **lsitara ḏ-ngidlẖ** DC 34. 604 the covering (acc.) which he had spread over her; **ḏ-sitara sradqa lanihuilẖ** DC 34. 710 which has no covering (or) curtain; **lguṭiun sitara lrišẖ** Lond. roll A 254 hold a veil over his head.

situa (Old-Aram. שתוא, Jew.-Aram. סִתְוָא, Syr. ܣܬܘܐ, H. סְתָו Kautzsch 70, Ar. شِتَآءٌ) winter MG 14:19, 101:7. Pl. **situata.** Masc. **situa** (var. **situata** DC 22. 278) **ugaiṭa** Gy 283:9 winter (var. winters) and summer; **situa muʿtadil nihuia** AM 258:18 there will be a moderate winter.

Gl 97:1 (missp.) شتا *tempestas* طوفان.

SKA (סְכֵי, ܣܟܐ, H. שכה only in der. שְׂכִיָּה & מַשְׂכִּית spectacle, Eth. መስኮት, Ar. مِشْكَاةٌ window, cf. شكا to look for compassion (complain); to direct the gaze towards, look for(ward to), face, look at, gaze at, look toward, await, expect, wait upon, hope for, plan for, anticipate.

Pe. Pf. **ska usliq** Jb 53:4 he looked up and got up; **sikiat** ATŠ II no. 129 it (fem.) expected; **nišmat lbit hiia skit** Jb 60:5 my soul (i.e. I) looked toward the House-of-Life (*constructio ad sensum*); with encl. **skalẖ iauar** DC 34. 231 Yawar awaited him (cf. the *malwâša* name **ska iauar** s.v.); with suff. **adiq hiia sikiu ʿl tibil** the Life gazed (down) and looked on the earth. Impf. **uhad mn habrẖ niskia** AM 246:penult. and one will look to (: count upon) his comrade; **ḏ-ʿtlẖ ainia lanisikia ʿlai lbiš** DC 44. 1274 = Morg. 264/18: 35 he that has eyes shall not look on me evilly; **kul daiua ḏ-nidalia unisikia lbiš** DC 43 C 61 any demon who raises himself and looks evilly; **ulatiskia lʿuhrak** AM 121:11 and do not look about on thy road; with suff. **kul man ḏ-nisikian lṭab** DC 44. 1240 = Morg. 264/18:10 whosoever looks on me with favour; **lṭab niskunẖ** [*sic*] **ldilia . . . uldaiua lṭab laniskunẖ** DC 44. 1940 = Morg. 269/29:34 they shall look favourably on me . . . but shall not look favourably on the demon. Act. pt. **ʿu sakia ltit . . . ʿu lilai sakia** AM 123:7 f. if looking down . . ., if looking up; pl. **sakin lbiš** Gy 277:10 they look with disgrace. Part. pres. with encl. **sakinalẖ** Gy 263:5 I look at it.

Pa. Pt. **hua iatib msakia** DC 27. 283 he sat waiting; with encl. **almia udaria msakilẖ** ATŠ II no. 15 worlds and generations wait upon him; **msakialẖ lpaṭira tšiaia** ATŠ II no. 132 looks forward to the ninth unleavened bread. Part. pres. **msakinin** we look MG 262:25; with encl. **nišmat msakinalẖ lab** Jb 202:9 my soul looks to (= I &c.) the Father (*constructio ad sensum*); **msakinalak ainai** DC 50. 380 my eyes (i.e. I) wait upon thee (*constr. ad sensum*).

Af. Pf. (**askia luatun** Gy 176:14 for **skultun**? Ginzā 180 n. 5); with encl. **askalẖ iauar bdrabšia ḏ-ziua** DC 3, DC 53 **skalẖ** Y. awaited it (: the soul) with rays of radiance (CP 347:12 differs).

Ethpe. Pf. **ʿstkia uhizih** Gs 37:18 it looked for and saw her; **ʿstkia uhzinkun** DC 51. 557 he looked for and beheld you; **ʿstkit uhzaitẖ** Gy 154:11 I looked and I saw him; **ʿstkun** ML 203:2 they looked out for. Part pres. **mistakina uhazina** Gy 272:15 I gaze toward and look at (MG 266:1).

Ethpa. Part. pres. **mistakina uhazina** Gy 155:14, 210:8 I gaze at and look on.

Der.: **sakaita.**

ska iauar ('Y. — awaited') a *malwâša* man's name (miscopyings **sk iauar, suk iauar**).

ska manda a *malwâša* man's name.

skandula popular form of **sikina ḏ-daula** s. **daula 2.**

skara, skarta, var. **skirta** (rt. **SKR**, ܣܟܪܐ) stopper, blocking up, obstruction, barrier, gag. **skara uskarta** (var. **skirta**) **lhinkaihun** DC 589 f., 613 = DC 44 par. and a stopper and a gag (are) on their jaws.

skuhia DAb = **skuhiia** RD a man's name. Var. **sukuhiia, skuiia** (cf. **ska iauar, ska manda**).

sku iauar s. **ska iauar.**

skuiia s. **skuhiia.**

skulta (rt. **SKL**) folly, foolish error, inadvertent mistake. Pl. **sikulata** s.v., or replaced by (a)**skilata** s.vv. **skulta ḏ-hibil ziua** Gy 345:2 inadvertence of H.-Z.; **anat skulta litlak** ATŠ I no. 294 thou art not in fault; **skulta lgaṭ** (*a frequent idiom*) to commit error; **qidahilna mn skulta ḏ-hauia ʿlai** DAb I fear that a foolish mistake may be attributed to me; **skulta litlih** Gy 365:10 there is no foolishness in it.

skilata (rt. **SKL**, cf. s. **skulta**) pl. follies, errors. Var. **askilata. skilatan** Q 24:7 (*& often*) our follies; **haubih uisklatẖ . . . haubih uaskilatih** [*sic*] CP. 199a:7 f., 10.

skina s. **sikina.**

skirta s. **skara.**

SKK (Jew.-Aram., H. & mod. H. סכך, Syr. ܣܟ, Ar. سَكَّ to stop, obstruct Hoffmann PhI 35 f., شَكَّ to confine Fränkel 90; cf. Akk. *sakku* deaf, *sukku* dam) to transfix, stick into, stab, nail, affix, apply, fix in, pin down, hold down, stop, obstruct, enclose.

Pe. Pass. pt. (?) with encl. pers. pron. **skakit** (read **skikit**?) JRAS 1937 596:3 thou art obstructed.

Pa. Pf. with suff **sakakan** Gs 72:25, 119:17, 123:6 he pinned me down. Pt. with encl. **msak(i)kilẖ bisiana** Gy 92:22 f. they hold him down in the mud; **lgiṭalun umsakikalun** ATŠ II no. 137 she lays hold of them and holds them back. Nom. act. **sakakta** s.v.

Ethpa. Pf. **nišimtẖ ʿstakakat bgargilia gauaiia** ATŠ I no. 76 (var. **ʿstakrat** PD) his soul pent back in inner spheres. Impf. **nistakak** (cf. BZ 32 n. 7) is confined; **ušrinin lnišimta ḏ-latistakak** ATŠ I no. 278 and we freed the soul, so that she is not held down; **unišmata lanisakak** Gy 349:23 (var. **lanisakakak** ACD, read **lanisakakan** with Sh.

'Abd.'s copy) and the souls shall not be held back. Pt. **mistakak hanath ˁlana** ATŠ I no. 291 that tree is stunted.

Der.: **sakaka, sakakta, sikta, sikina** (?).

SKL (Jew.-Aram. & H. סכל, Syr. & Chr.-Pal. af. ܐܣܟܠ Akk. *saklu* fool) to be a fool, stupid, inadvertent; to act foolishly; to sin; with prep. **b** to injure, sin against.

Af. Pf. **abatur askil babahath** Jb 8:13 A. sinned against his fathers; **askilnin** we sinned MG 224:19. Impf. **balbušai naskil** Morg. 267/25:5 = DC 44. 1623 will damage my garment; **nihṭun unasiklun** DC 44. 1475 = Morg. 266/22:9 they sin and cause injury (**lanisiklun** DC 44. 1620 = Morg. 267/25:2 read **lanasiklun**); with encl. **hirba uparzla taskilbai** [*sic*] **utihambilbh** Morg. 267/25:5 f. sword and iron (hendiadys) shall injure and destroy him; **naskilbh bšurbta d-hiia** Gy 105:16 f. let us seduce the Stem of Life to follies. Pt. pl. **napša masklia** Gy 388:17 they cause great havoc; **lamaskilia had bhabrh** Gy 8:9 they do not offend one another, **lamasklin bihdadia** Gy 11:8 id. (MG 30:11, 37:22, 149:9); **masklia bpagrai** DC 40. 856 they confuse me in my body. Nom. ag. **maskilana** s.v.

Der.: **sakla, sakluta, sikulata, (a)skilata, skulta.**

SKK (סכך) to entangle.

Pe. Impf. **latiskun hazin nišimtai** DC 43 B 34 do not entangle this my soul; with suff. **laniskunh ˁl** DC 43 A 62, 157 do not entangle him; **latiskunh ˁhaza nišimta** DC 43 I 74 do not entangle this soul.

SKN s. **MSKN.**

SKR (Aram. & H. סכר, Syr. ܣܟܪ, Ar. سَكَرَ, Akk. *sikēru*) to stop up, block, keep back, shut up, hinder, prevent, cut off, lose.

Pe. (rare): Pf. with suff. **skarth ungarth** DC 37. 485 I obstructed him and quelled him; **uminaihun tiskar** (read **tisakar** pa.?) AM 57:20 she will lose some of them. Act. pt. pl. **d-uhra d-hiia sakria** Jb 144:1 that block (obstruct) the way of the Life. Pass. pt. **ˁl pumh skir** Gs 95:25 is dammed at its mouth (of the river); **puma d-aria skir** DC 44. 1316 = Morg. 264/19:38 the lion's mouth is gagged; **sikrit** DC 46. 205:11 I was stopped.

Pa. Pf. with encl. **sakrulia** Gs 85:7 they locked before me. Impf. **uminaihun nisakar** AM 20:13 and he will lose some of them; **ˁnta qadmaita nisakar** AM 87:6 he will lose his first woman; **tlata gubria tisakar** AM 64:8 she will lose three husbands; with suff. **nisakrh bqulalun** Jb 58:11 let us trap him in our snare; **ulgabra qadmaia tisakrh**, AM 64:5 and she will lose (varr. **tisakrih** 70:6) her first husband. Pt. **qiniana d-ianquth msakarlh** AM 36 penult. he will be deprived of the posessions of his youth; **tlata bnata msakar** AM 42:2 he will lose three daughters; **bnia msakar** AM (*often*) he will lose children; **msakar puma d-ariauata** DC 44. 856 stoppeth the mouth of the lions; **utrin utlata msakra** AM 75:8 she will lose two or three (children); with encl. **qiniana qania umsakarlh** AM he will acquire property but will lose it; **msakralun lšašbia** ATŠ I no. 281 she blocketh up the portals.

Ethpa. Pf. **ˁstakar** Gy 149:24 was obstructed (cf. MSchr. 115 n. 2); **nišimta ˁstakrat** PD 827 = ATŠ I no. 46 the soul was kept back; **ˁstakariun** (cf. s. **-ian**) MG 223:25, **uˁstakarian bauatai** Jb 65:15 (varr. **-iun** BD, **-iin** A) my prayers were stopped. Impf. **nistakar** Jb 99:8 he shall be cut off; **nistakar mn** AM 25 is deprived of; **nistakrun** Gy 219:16 they are kept back MG 227:25; **nistakran** Gy 66:9 they (fem.) are kept back MG 228:7; **nistakra** Gy 299:18, Oxf. 24 b id., MG 228:13; **latistakra nišmatkun** Morg. 43:7 (= Par. xi, DC 3 par.) your souls will not be kept back (MG 228 n. 3). Pt. **bidqa d-lamistakar** Gs 9:14 the breach which is unclosed (irreparable); pl. masc. **bsaklutun mistakria** Gy 357:9 they are shut up in their folly; fem. **mistakra uauda nišmatun** Gy 25:4 their souls are kept back and perish; **mistakra nišmatun** Gy 47:11 f.; with encl. **mistakarlun** Gy 17:12 is kept apart from them.

Der.: **msakrana; sakura, sukra, skara, skarta** (var. **skirta**).

SLA (סלא, ܣܠܐ, H. סלה I, Akk. *salū*) to despise, reject, spoil, be or make abominable or depraved, despicable.

Pe? Pf. **arqa kulh slat** (read **aslat** af. with DC 22 & Sh. 'Abd.'s copy) Gy 270:5 the whole world would be spoiled.

Af. Pf. **aslat** a var. of Gy 270:5 (v.s. pe.); **laslun** Gs 53:ult. cf. Ginzā 475 n. 3; with suff. **aslith** Oxf. 39 b she rejected it MG 287:paen. Impf. **naslun** ATŠ II no. 366 they reject; with suff. **ˁiaslh** Gs 92:4, varr. **nˁiaslh** BCD; **niaslh** Leid. I, var. we will make it despicable; **naslinun** Gy 324:7 we will make them despicable. Pt. pl. **hdadia mganin umaslin mn hdadia** ATŠ II no. 355 they rebuke and reject one another.

Ettaf. Pf. **ˁtasliat** Gy 313:11, Jb 196:8 was (fem.) rejected, has become despicable. Impf. **nitaslun** AM 61:4 they are rejected. Pt. **mitaslia** Jb 196:2, Gy 23:7, Gy 44:15 f. (three times) &c. is rejected, despicable (pl. sometimes the same) MG 132:24; fem. **mitaslia** Gy 313:7 she is despicable MG 265: paen.; pl. **mitaslin** Gy 23:6 they are rejected MG 265:ult.

Der.: **masiliuta, sulia** I.

slaq (Ar. سُلَاق) lippitude of the eyelids. Varr. **salaq, sliq. slaq d-ainia** AM 287:24.

slaqa (rt. **SLQ**) raising up, resurrection, lifting up. **silqat upiršat lhazin slaqa** ATŠ I no. 277 it (: the soul) rose up and set forth at this raising up.

slita s. **silita.**

SLP (Jew.-Aram., H. & mod. H. סלף, Ar. سلف to harrow) to twist, pervert, bend round.

Pe. Pf. with suff. **dnibth silph** (var. **sipla**) **lpumh** DC 43 J 134 he twisted his tail round to his mouth.

Gl. 115:15 f. with prosth. **a** & defectively عوّج *pervertere* كج كرد ; 150:15 f. id. مال

reclinare أُفتاد; 167:3 f. id. نحنا [sic] *incurvari* كج شد; 170:15 f. **SLP** pa. هزى *erubescere* شرمنده شد.

SLQ I (Gen. Aram. סלק, ܣܠܩ, H. from Aram. Kautzsch 68 f., Ar. تسلق from Aram.? Haupt ZA ii 278, Nöld. ZDMG lvii 419) to rise, go up, ascend; af. to raise up, lift up, remove, dislodge.

Pe. Pf. **sliq dukia** Jb 54:1 purity departed; **sliq aqapra** Gy 97:12 dust rose; **sliq lriš** (*frequent idiom*) was accomplished, brought to successful end; **sliqt** Gy 324:ult. thou didst rise; **silqit** (*often*) I rose; **sliqiun** Gy 233:17 etc. they rose; **sliqnin** we rose up; with encl. **sliqibh̠, slaqibh̠, slaqilak** Gy 196:7, 213:1, Gs 8:21, 94:3, 7, Oxf. 31 a I rose in it, to Thee MG 225:paen. Impf. **nisaq** he rises MG 84:2, 238:paen.; **tisaq, ʿsaq** MG 238:ult., pl. **nisqun, tisqun**, fem. **nisqa** MG 239:8; with encl. **nis(i)qubh̠** Gy 196:7 they rise in it MG 239:8. Impt. **saq** (*often*), var. **siq** Gy 30:5 ascend! MG 240:4 f., rare, **sluq** DC 41. 473. Pt. **saliq lriš** AM 164:16 it will be successful (*idiom*); fem. **haimanuta mn arqa salqa** Gy 61:8 faith will ascend from the world; **lalma d̠-nhura salqa** ATŠ II no. 172 she rises to the world of light; **salqa maṣbuta haita** Jb 84:4 f. the living baptism rises (leaves earth); pl. **salqia** Jb 84:2 they rise up (leave earth); fem. **salqan** Jb 84:3 they rise (depart). Part. pres. **salqit** Gs 85:19 thou ascendest (MG 14:21); **salqinin** we ascend, **salqitun** ye ascend MG 53:paen.; with encl. **salqitubh̠** ye rise therein MG 233:20. Inf. **misaq** (*often*), **mislaq** Gy 324:17, Gs 85:19 MG 239:13, **misliq** DC 34. 329.

Af. (Cf. MR 123, 172 n. 1). Pf. **asiq** (*often*), **hansiq** Gs 128:14 he made ascend MG 211:15 f.; **asiq lnapšh̠ alaha** Gs 33:19 he named himself god (*idiom*); **hibil asiq lnapših̠ d̠-hu riša urušuma** etc. DC 27. 319 H. called himself head and sign etc. (*idiom*); **asiqnin** we made (them) ascend MG 289:9; with encl. **asiqlia bšum iauar** Gy 136:9 he gave me the name Y. (*idiom*); **asiqlh̠ šuma baṭla** Gy 85:18 they gave him a vain name (*idiom*); **ʿmh̠ asqalh̠ gabara rba** Gy 159:21 f. his mother called him 'Great Giant . . .' (*idiom*); with suff. **asqh̠** he made him ascend MG 275:9; **asqinun** he made them ascend, **asqinkun** he made you ascend MG 280:23, **asiqth̠** I made him ascend MG 277:12; **asiqtinun** I made them ascend MG 282:ult.; **asiqnh̠** we made him ascend MG 277:22; **asquk** they raised thee MG 274:13. Impf. **nʿiasiq** Gy 326:12 we make ascend MG 215:15; **nasiq** he makes ascend; **ʿiasiq** I make ascend MG 215:16; **ʿiasiq qalai latar nhur** Gs 75:1 I will lift up my voice to the place of light; with encl. **mahu nasiqlh̠ šuma** Jb 117:12 f. what name shall we give him? (*idiom*); with suff. **nʿiasqh̠** Gy 361:24 we will make it disappear; **nasqh̠** Gy 109:24 id.; **nasqinun** Gy 271:17 we will remove them; **ʿiasqh̠** I (will) remove him, raise him MG 276:6; **nasqunh̠** AM 21 they get him out; **nasqun(h)un** Gy 107:23, 271:17 they (or He: the Life) shall raise them. Impt. **asiq rahmutkun lriš** Gy 20:7 bring your charity to fulfilment (idiom); with suff. **asqh̠** let him go up, raise him MG 276:15, **asquia** raise (pl.) him MG 279:4. Act. pt. **masiq** (*often*) he raises; pl. **masqia tangaratun lbit riš briš** Gy 72:15 they promote successful trade (*idiom*); **šlihia masqin lnapšaihun** Gy 24:6 f. they call themselves envoys (*idiom*); with encl. **masiqlan mn ʿda d̠-šibiahia** ATŠ II no. 442 he will lift us out of the hands of the planets; **šitin masqata masqilh̠** ATŠ I no. 182 sixty *masiqtas* will raise him up. Part. pres. **masqitun rahmutkun lriš** Gy 18:11 f. you bring your charity to fulfilment; with encl. **masqatlh̠ lgida** DC 27. 125 thou helpest him to mount the bank; with suff. **masqinun** I raise them MG 291:ult. Inf. with suff. **asuqh̠** Gy 393:15 to make him ascend MG 293:2; **asqinʿn** Gy 340:12 to make them ascend; **baiana masiqlh̠ šuma** Jb 118:5 f. I want to give him a name (*idiom*).

Idioms: Pe. with **lriš** to be successfully achieved (s. pe. pf.); af. with **riš briš** to achieve with success, be successful (s. af. pt. pl.); af. with **rahmuta lriš** to bring charity to fulfilment, show the highest degree of charity (s. impt., part. pres.); af. with **šuma** as obj. to give a name, to name, to call (s. pf. with encl. twice, impf. with encl., inf. with encl.); **šuma** can be omitted, esp. when the verb is followed by **lnapšh̠, lnapšaihun** etc. 'to call oneself' (s. pf. twice, pt. pl., pt. with encl.).

Gl. (always missp.) 18:11 f. اصعد *allevare* بالا رفت; 57:1 f. (ا)جتاز, جاز *transire, praeterire* رفت; 81:7 f. ركب *ascendere, equitare* سوار شد.

Der.: **masiqta, masqana.**

SLQ II (H. שׁלק) to boil, cook, burn, destroy. MG 46:16 f.

Pe. Pt. pl. with encl. **salqilh̠** Gy 227:12 they boil it; **salqilun** Gy 226:7 they boil it (pl.: water); Gs 29:19 they scald them.

SMA I (סמי, ܣܡܐ, Akk. *samû* blind) to be blind, lose the sight.

Pe. Pt. **saima** s.v.; with encl. **ainh̠ saimalh̠** Gy 84:9 his eyes became blind (hist. pres.).

Der.: **saima, s(i)miaiil.**

SMA II (den. from **sama** q.v.) to drug, poison.

Af. Pt. **riha d̠-hu masmia** ATŠ II no. 335 a vapour that drugs (or poisons).

smaiil DAb a var. of **simaiil.**

smal(a) (שְׂמָאלָא, ܣܶܡܳܠܐ, H. שְׂמֹאל, Ar. شَمْأَل, شَأْمَل, شِمَال, Akk. *šumēlu*) left, left hand, left arm, left side. Varr. **asmala** & **ʿsmala** MG 25:20. St. abs. **smal** used adverbially MG 128:17; **mn smal liamin** Gy 214:25 etc. CP trs. 61 no. 3 (*often*) from the left to the right MG 301:23; with suff. **mn smalun** Gy 19:19 from their left MG 360:ult.; **lsmalun** (*often*) on their left MG 361:1; **ginza smala** Left Ginzā; **alma d̠-smala** PD 1084 the world of the left; **malkia d̠-smala** PD 1087 the kings of the left; **lšara d̠-smala** DC 42 to the left (lit. to the direction of the left).

Gl. 95:12 missp. with ṣ شمال *sinistra.*

smandiriil s. **samandarʿil.** Varr. **smandarʿil, samandrʿil. smandarʿil ʿutra** CP trs. 272 n. 3, CP 430:antepenult.; **smandrʿil ḏ-rihh basim** CP 408:11 S. the fragrance of which is pleasing.

smaqa occasionally for **sumaqa.** Fem. **smaqa-t(i)a. smaqta tinpuqbh** AM a red rash will come out on him.

smarta s. **ṣmarta.**

smir(a) pass. pt. pe. q.v.

SMK (Aram., Phoen., H. & mod. H. סמך, Syr. ܣܡܟ, Eth. ሰመከ, Sab. 𐩪𐩣𐩫? to support or to lean, Ar. سَمَكَ support, Akk. *simāku* shrine?) to support, sustain, rely on, bear up, bear on.

Pe. Pf. with suff. **hu simkh ʿl ʿuṣrh** ATŠ I no. 113 he upheld his thought. Impf. with suff. **ʿuṣrak nisimkak (mismak)** Gs 41:paen. thy thought shall (completely) reassure thee MG 398:14; **ʿsimkh** Jb 263:8 I (would) support him. Act. pt. **samik** (*often*), fem. **nišimta samka ʿlauaihun** DC 27 the soul rests upon them; with encl. **samiklia** Gy 155:21 supporteth me. Part. pres. with encl. **samkatlh biaṣilak** Jb 146:3 f. thou pressest on it with thine elbow; **samkitulh** Gy 44:2 ye support him. Pass. pt. **smik** supported, or leaned on (hence supporting); pl. with encl. **arbaia razia ḏ-smikilh lpagra** DC 41. 210 the four mysteries which support (i.e. constitute) the body; with encl. pers. pron. **mismik smikit** Oxf. 90 a thou art supported MG 398:4. Inf. **mismak** Gs 41:paen. (s. impf.); **mismik** Oxf. 90 a (s. pass. pt. with encl. pers. pron.) DC 34. 1256, DC 41. 519 etc. MG 129:21, 233:27.

Af. Pf. **asmikit** I supported MG 223:5; with suff. **asmiktan** Gs 48:14 thou didst support me MG 272:4; **asmiktuia** Par. xi 35b ye supported her [*sic*] MG 277:25. Impf. **niasmik** he supports, will support; with suff. **ʿiasmikh** I (shall) support him MG 275:paen. Impt. **asmik,** with suff. **asmkuia** (*often*) support him. Inf. **asmukia ʿdaihun** Morg. 224/36:11, DC 43 J 24 to support their hands; **masmukia mana rba ldukth asmukia ʿdaihun ḏ-anašia ṭabia** CP 464 ult. to sustain the Great Mana in his place, to hold up the hands of good people.

Ethpe. Pf. **ʿstmik** Gy 40:19 was reassured. Impf. **tisimkun** Gy 21:12 (var. **tistimkun** DC 22:21) ye will support yourselves. Impt. **ʿstmik** Gs 21:2 be supported MG 229:9. Pt. **balai uʿuṣrai mismik lhaila** Gs 75:paen. my mind and thought rely upon the strength; **lamistmik** Gy 44:2 he doth not let himself be supported; **ḏ-mistmik libai lsamkia(-h)** ATŠ I no. 59 (& *often*) so that my heart may be firmly stayed (reassured). Part. pres. **mistmikna** Gs 90:paen. (& *often*) I am upheld MG 31:17, var. **misti-** MG 231:11; **mistimkit** thou supportest MG 232:18; **mismikitun** Gy 42:5 ye are supported MG 214:19.

Der.: **samka, samkiʿil, sumka, sumkana, simaka.**

SMM s. **SMA II.**

SMQ (Aram. סְמַק, Syr. Jac. ܣܡܩ, Nest. ܣܡܩ) to be red, ruddy.

Pe. Pf. with encl. **smaqlh** DC 23. 617 has become red, is red. **smaqlun** DC 32. 619 are red. Impf. **unisimqun anph** DC 51 and they shall make his face rosy.

Pa. Pt. **msamaq riš manzia** AM (*often*) the hair of his head is red. Inf. **ulmisamuqia anph ḏ-iuraqia** DC 51. 358 and to make ruddy his face that is pallid.

Af. Impt. **asmiq anph ḏ-iuraqia** DC 51. 139 and make ruddy his pallid face.

Ethpa. Pt. **misamaq** AM 257:14 it grows red.

Der.: **sumaqa, sumqa.**

SMR (H. שמר in Jew.-Aram. writings only as a hebraism MG 46 n. 3, Akk. *šamāru* to preserve; Targ. סמר ithpe. to take heed, Ar. سمر to keep watch) to heed, be heedful or careful of, observe, watch over, keep watch, mind, be mindful, preserve; (*idiom*); to bury and prepare the corpse for burial, i.e. to perform offices of **samraia** (q.v.).

Pe. Pt. pl. **kḏ samrin ṣairin surta** ATŠ II no. 208 when they bury, they trace the (encircling) line. Part. pres. **kḏ samritun napaqa** ATŠ II no. 207 when ye 'watch' a departed (: deceased) one. Pass. pt. **smir(a)** 'well-preserved, safeguarded' MG 46:14, used very often of the *mânas* & higher beings, cf. **mana smira** Jb 253:11, Gy 192:18, Q 32:11 etc., pl. **mania smiria** Jb 177:4, Gy 343:21, **sam mana smira** and **sam smir ziua** s. **sam ʿutria ʿsmiria** Jb 253:11, **mana iauar smir** and **iauar mana smira** Gy 291:43 f.; **zhir smir ziua** Gy 250:12; pl. **mqaimia usmiria** Gy 305:3 established and well preserved; **ʿria usmiria** Gs 22:15 watched and safeguarded; **iaqria usmiria,** ML 57:6, Q 26:13 holy and safeguarded; **smir** as a pr. n. Gy 150:23, 291:38.

Ethpa. Pf. **lastamar** Jb 147:9 they heeded not. Pt. **mistamar** Jb 260:3 f. he takes care.

Der.: **asmar, samra 1, samraia, smir(a), iusmir.**

SNA (Jew.-Aram. שנא, סנא, Syr. ܣܢܐ, H. שׂנא, Ar. شَنِئَ, South-Ar. 𐩦𐩬𐩱) to hate, be hateful, ugly; to detest, be detestable.

Pe. Pf. **hiia snun umuta rhim** CP 189:2 they hated life and loved death; with suff. **sinian** he hated me MG 284:24; **snatan** she hated me MG 285:13, **siniuia** Jb 262:6 they hated him. Impf. with suff. **latinšunh ulatisnunh** ATŠ I no. 251 forget ye not it and hate it not. Act. pt. **sania** s.v.; with encl. **sanilh saniuta** DC 48. 229 they hate her heartily. Pass. pt. **snia** s.v. Inf. **misnia** Gs 45:19 BCD, var. **misna** A MG 260:15, 398:8.

Gl. 5:13 f. missp. ابغض *odio habere* دشمن داشت; 80:5 f. missp. رذل *reprobare, respuere, abominari* رد كرد.

Der.: **sai(a)nt(i)a** (pl. **sainata**), **saina 1** (abs. **snia, snʿ**), **sana, sanaia, sania, saniuta, sina, snaia, sniaia, snia** (cf. **saina 1,** fem. **snita**), **saniaiil** (var. **siniaiil**).

snaia (rt. **SNA**) hateful, odious. Fem. pl. st. abs. **snaian. qšaian usnaian** DC 3 hard and hateful (fem. pl.).

SNDR (pa. of **SDR II** by metath. from ***SRD** used as **SRWD**, cf. Jew.-Aram. סַרְדָּא sieve, mod. Syr. ܣܪܕ to sieve, cl. Syr. ܣܪܕ ethpa. ܐܬܣܪܕ to be frightened MG 74:18, H. שׂרד to flee away, Ar. شرد id.) to quake, tremble, fear, be afraid, affrighted MG 74:16 ff.

Pa. Pt. **arqa d-naida umsandra** AM 241:19 the earth quakes and is shaken (MG 74:16).

Ethpa. Pf. **ʿstandar** Gs 13:22 trembled, **ʿstandrat** Gs 80:18, Q 38:20 she trembleth MG 74:15, 222:19, **ʿstandran** Jb 276:7 they (fem., compl. **markabata**? Jb ii 244 n. 2) trembled. Impf. **nistandar gilia parṣupia** DC 26.73 his features are discomposed; **nistandrun** DC 44. 1291 = Morg. 264/19:13 they shall tremble with fear. Pt. **mistandra** Gs 122:5, 17 it (fem.) trembleth; pl. fem. **nišmata minaihun mistandra umistarqda** ATŠ I no. 256 the souls are afraid of them and quake; masc. **ušidia minaihun naidia umistandria** ATŠ I no. 256 and evil spirits tremble before them and are afraid.

snia, snʿ st. abs. of **saina** I MG 24:11. Fem. st. emph. **snita** MG 110:antep., MG 153:23, st. abs. **snʿia** MG 153:27. **kul d-ʿlauaikun snia bhabraikun** Gy 21:3 all that is hateful for you in your neighbours; **gabra d-snia bdmuth** a man whose form is ugly; **kul d-biš usnia** CP 199(o):12 everything that is evil and hateful; **snia mahzita d-ainh** AM 18:15 hostile is the look of his eyes. Var. **snʿ** AM 197 etc.

***sniaia** (further adj. from preced.) hateful, repulsive. **sniaiin** [*sic*, read **snʿian**?] **dmutaiun** DC 34. 1284 their appearance is repulsive.

sniq, snʿq (rt. **SNQ II**) needy, in need MG 46: ult., MG 116:13. Pl. **-ia. sniq ušauia** Gy 42:19 needy and honest. Pl. **sniqia** Gy 285:16, **snʿqia** Gl. 286:3 (MG 5:16). **sniq bgauh d-alma iatira d-azal mn haka** CP 312:14 though he went hence rich, in the world he was needy.

snita s. **snia.**

snʿ, snʿia s. **snia.**

snʿq(a) s. **sniq.**

SNQ I (שָׁנַק, Syr. ܫܢܩ from Akk. *tašnīqu* Zimmern 49; rel. to **SNQ II**) to torment, torture MG 46:19 ff. & n. 4.

Pa. Pf. **sanqiun lnišmata d-aniia** DAb they tormented the souls of the poor. Pt. (pass.) **nišmata d-msanqa** Jb 127:12 souls which are tormented; (act.) pl. with encl. **msanqilun** Gy 301:8 they torment them MG 46:20.

Der.: **tasniqa.**

SNQ II (ܣܢܩ from Akk. *sunqu, sinqu* hunger Zimmern 47) to be wanting, need, be poor, reduced to poverty. MG 46:ult.

Pe. Pass. pt. **sniq** (var. **snʿq**) s.v.; with prosth. **a: asniq bgauh d-alma iatira d-azal mn haka** ŠQ (see **sniq**); with encl. **alma hu d-nišimta sniqlh** ATŠ I no. 20 it is a world (where) the soul became needy; **sniqlak d-hauilak bra** Jb 117:11 it is necessary for thee that thou shouldst have a son.

Der.: **sniq(a)** (var. **snʿq(a)**).

SSṬM (den. from **sustmia**) to fetter, shackle. Pt. pl. **msastmia** DC 43 J 200 they are fettered; with encl. pers. pron. **kbišitun msastmitun** DC 40. 786 f. ye are subdued and shackled.

Der.: **sustmia** (& varr.).

sstmia Gs 80:17 for the more usual **sustmia.**

SSQL saf. of **SQL.**

sʿiauišan (Firdausī's سیاوش) Gy 383:3 father of Kai Khusrau. Var. **siauišan.**

SFA ܣܦܐ to keep together? **suf lhadadia uqbur** DC 40. 1059 put together (?) and bury (of two bowls).

SPA in **aspia** (var. **spia** Sh. ʿAbd.'s copy) **dina** Gs 95:21 doubtf. Ginzā 534 n. 1.

Ethpe. (אִסְתְּפֵי) to be afraid: Part. pres. **dahilna umistpina** (*Florilegium*) I fear and am afraid.

spag 1 Gy 126:19 s. **aspag 1.**

spag 2 s. **aspag 2.**

spahan (P. سپهان = اصفهان) AM 205:1 Isfahan. Var. **spihan.**

span s. **sipta.**

spand = **aspand spand ʿkuma** DC 46. 126:6 black rue.

spandiar Sh. ʿAbd.'s copy's var. of **aspindiar** Gy 383:8.

spasa (P. سپاس) gratitude, kindness, reciprocation, thanksgiving, favour. Varr. **aspas(a)** s.v. and **sbasia. spasa lamqablia** AM 7:11, 11:7, 19:20 etc. they will make him no return (show no gratitude), be ungrateful BZ 5 n. 10.

spar 1 st. abs. & cstr. of **sipra** I MG 151:8. Varr. **aspar, ʿspar** I MG 26:9. **spar maluašia** s. **aspar; spar malkia** Gy 394:15 Book of Kings; (a)**spar diuta** Gy 204:23, 205:19; **spar dukranai** Gy 205:22 = **aspar dukranai** Gy 205:2 s. **aspar.**

spar 2 st. abs. of **ṣipra** MG 44:19. Var. **ʿ(u)spar. bʿuspar** Gy 197:3 = **bspar** Gy 197:9 (& *often*) in the morning.

spar 3 a proper name (of a higher being). **spar zuṭa** RD 27a = DAb par.; **maṭarta d-ʿl spar brh d-ptahil** RD C 10 = DAb par. the purgatory of El-Spar son of P.

spargla (Jew.-Aram. איספרגלין, Syr. ܐܣܦܪܓܠܐ, P. سفرجل Löw 144) quince. Var. **ʿspargla.** Masc. (ʿ)**spargla** Oxf. roll f 157, 367, 505, 1082; **spargla hu** DC 41 (illustration) it is a quince-tree; **rumana uʿspargla** DC 36 pomegranate and quince; **spargla hiuara** DC 41, DC 35 a pear(-tree).

SPD s. **SPR III.**

SPṬ (den. from **sapṭ(i)a** to fetter).

Ethpe. Pt. pl. **mistipṭia** Gs 65:19 they are fettered MG 42:antep.

Der.: **masputita** (var. **maṣpuṭita**), **sapṭa** (var. **ṣapṭa**).

spihan Ṣâb.'s AM var. of **spahan** AM 205:1.

spihata a pl. of **sipta** (q.v.).

spindar DC 44. 1170 = Morg. 263/17:26 f. a name given to Venus (Libat).

spinta (סְפִינְתָּא, ܣܦܝܢܬܐ > H. & mod. H. סְפִינָה, Ar. loan-w. سَفِينَة Fränkel 216, Nöld. ZDMG xxii 516) sailing-ship, boat MG 117:23. Pl. **spin(i)ata. spinta d-sin** RD 1 the boat of Sin; **tlatma ušitin alpia spinata** RD A 10 =

DAb par. 360,000 ships; **spinta d-lamalaha** Gy 216:24 a ship without a steersman; **spinata mzarzata** Gy 320:2 equipped ships. Gl. 96:4 missp., pl. in **-iata** سفينة *navicula* كشتى.

spira 1 (סְפִירָא, ܣܦܝܪܐ, σφαῖρα) ball, round mass, sphere, zone. Varr. **ʿspira, ʿuspra** s.vv. Pl. **spiria** AM 231:13, **ʿspiria** s. **ʿspira. spira d-sumqaq** RD 20 the zone of S.; **spira d-hilbunia sqilia** ATŠ II no. 360 a ball of lustrous eggs (?); (ʿ)**spir(i)a d-ʿšumia** (*often*) heavenly sphere(s) (cf. s. **ʿspira** & **ʿuspra**).

spira 2 (cf. ܣܦܝܪܐ, σφῦρα mallet, but used with the meaning of ܣܡܦܝܪܐ, σαμψήρα from P. *šamšēr* شمشير hence probably from **SPR II**) sword. Mod. *sifira*. Gl. 96:8 missp. سيف *gladius* شمشير; 97:15 missp. (read **mar spira**) سياف spiculator, gladiator جلّاد.

SPP (ܫܦ, Ar. شبّ, Akk. *šabābu*) to burn, destroy.

Pe. Pf. **ʿrgaz usap** DC 43 J 74 he became angry and hot (with anger); with suff. **saph uhamblh lʿurašlam** HG he set fire to and ruined Jerusalem; **sapuk paruk partuk** (or pa.?) they burnt thee up (or cut thee up?), scattered thee, divided thee; **lasapunh ʿl anph kd libta** DC 37. 192 f. they did not burn (?) his face like a brick. Impf. with encl. **tispupulh** [*sic*] AM 48 fem. will consume (??) him.

SPQ (ספק, ܣܦܩ to be abundant, to empty, H. ספק **II** to vomit) to reject, throw out, deny.

Af. Pt. pl. with encl. **maspqilh lkul mahu lišanun malil** ATŠ I no. 238 they recant all that their tongues said.

SPR I (prob. den. from **sipra 1** as H. ספר Ges.) to write, describe, inscribe, ascribe, report, dedicate.

Af. Pf. **ulmarh aspartun** ATŠ II no. 159 (var. **aspartinun** DC 6) ye have ascribed to its lord (var. thou hast, or I have ascribed them); with encl. **unišimta . . . lhibil ušitil uanuš aspartlun** DC 27 as to the soul . . . thou hast dedicated to H., Š. & A.; with suff. **hatamth ulmarh asparth** ATŠ II no. 165 thou hast sealed it and assigned it to its lord, **aspartinun** ATŠ II no. 159 see above. Impf. with encl. **hazin kušta d-ana asparlak** (for *ʿiasparlak) CP 94:11, ML 119:9 (cf. Morg. 249/85:19) this troth which I confer on thee. Impt. with encl. **anat asparlh labatur** ML 119:10 confer thou it (: the troth just mentioned) on A. CP trs. 66 nos. 1 and 2.

Ettaf. Pt. **bhanath ʿsqta . . . rušuma rba mitaspar** ATŠ II no. 204 upon that seal-ring . . . a great Sign is inscribed.

Der.: **sapra 1, 2, sipra 1** (abs. & cstr. **spar 1, aspar, ʿspar 1**).

SPR II (prob. den., cf. **spira 2**, Syr. ܣܦܪ, mod. H. סַפָּר to cut, shear, Ar. شَفْرَة big knife, cutlass) to cut out, cut off.

Pe. Impf. **ʿspar aina zruqtia** JRAS 1937 595:23 I (?) cut out the squinting eye (**ʿspar** and **aspar** several times of a 'squinting eye' in DC 7, but in corrupt contexts).

Der.: **spira 2.**

SPR III for **SPD** (Jew.-Aram., H., mod. H. ספד, Syr. & Chr.-Pal. ܣܦܕ, Akk. *sapādu* to wail, mourn, Amh. ሰቀቀ Praetorius ZDMG xxxv 762) to mourn Ginzā 371 n. 4.

Af. Pt. **umaspra** (var. **umaspda** B, **umaspiria** Sh. ʿAbd.'s copy, read **umaspdia**) **ʿl abuhun** Gy 353:17 and they mourn for their father.

sqalta (rt. **SQL**) adj. fem. polished, elegant, bright. **usqalta bʿbidath hauia** AM 63:2 and she will be bright in her actions.

sqaria s. **sqiria.**

squbra accord. to contexts: (*a*) cavity, (*b*) trumpet or horn Jb ii 147 n. 6. Var. **ʿsqubra** Masc. (*a*) **usqubra tmira hua** ATŠ I no. 264 and a hidden cavity came into being; (*b*) **ahbalia squbra d-ʿqria bagma qala** Jb 146:9 give me a horn that I make a sound in the marsh; **unpabh bgauh d-ʿsqubrai** (var. **sq-** AD) **squbra hu taqna** Jb 147:1 f. and (I) will blow into my horn, it is a reliable horn; **laqalh damia lṣaidia ulasqubrh lsqubran** Jb 147:6 his voice resembleth not (that of) the fishermen, nor doth his horn (resemble) ours.

squpana (rt. **SQP**) smiter?, entangler? (cf. **squpata d-muta** s. **squpta**). **qramth lsqupana d-ʿl dilan hambaga hua** Jb 143:12 I covered (entangled?) the entangler? (or smiter?) who was our enemy.

squpta, ʿsqupta (Jew.-Aram. סְקוֹף & שְׁקוֹף, סְקוּפָה, אִיסְקוּפְתָּא, סְקוּפְתָּא, & varr., Syr. ܐܣܩܘܦܬܐ, H. מַשְׁקוֹף from שקף I Ges., Bab. *askuppatu* Zimmern 31, Ar. loan-w. أُسْكُفَّة Fränkel 19 f.) threshold, door-sill MG 46 n. 4, 135:1. Pl. **squpata** entanglements (?). **ʿsqupata ʿl ʿsqupta** (var. **lsqupta** DC 22. 302) **d-bit hiia** Gy 211:23 at the threshold of the House of Life; **ʿl ʿsqupta** Jb 41:9 varr. **squpta** AD, **sqpta** B on the threshold; **giṭria usqupata d-muta** DC 48. 317 knots and entanglements (?) of death; **ʿsqupata bišata** DC 12. 8 evil threshold-demons.

SQṬ (Ar. سقط IV) to drop, cast off, miscarry, get rid of, deduct, subtract. Only Ar. forms: Impf. **baṭinata iasqiṭun** AM 274:23 (read يُسْقِطُونَ, or better يُسْقِطْنَ) pregnant women will miscarry. Impt. **uasqiṭ minh tlata** AM 136:7 and deduct three from it; **uasqiṭ tlata tlata** AM 261:1 and subtract (continuously) three.

sqila (pass. pt. pe. of **SQL**) polished, burnished, bright, elegant, comely, fine, fair. Pl. masc. **-ia**, fem. **-ata. naura sqila** Gy 215:9, PD 106 a polished mirror, pl. **nauria sqilia** CP 437:2; **mana sqila** Gs 79:18, Q 65:33 = ML 157:9 = CP 129:17 a bright *mana*, pl. **mania sqilia** RD B 109, 117; **zahba sqila** RD C 27 fine gold; **qabana . . . sqila** ŠQ a fine . . . robe; **ia ginza anat sqila** CP 351:15 O thou burnished treasure; **ubunh uṭunh dakia usqila** ATŠ I no.

291 and its structure and its fruit are pure and fair; **usikinata sqilata** DC 51 and polished knives.

sqiria (ܣܩܝܪܐ, *ἱστοκεραία* Fränkel WZKM iii 181) Jb 162:1 (varr. **sqaria** C, **sriqia** B), 163:2, Gy 273:15, 22 (varr. **sriqia** B, **sdiqia** C, **sridqia** D) mast of a ship Jb ii 162 n. 10; prob. punting-pole.

SQL (Jew.-Aram., H., mod. H. סקל to clean from stones, smoothen, Syr. ܣܩܠ > Ar. صقل & سقل Fränkel 254) to polish, burnish, make bright, be bright (also of wits or manners), be polished, brilliant, bright of intelligence; saf. to adorn, polish.

Pe. Act. pt. pl. with encl. **usaqlilh mn sina qina** DC 34. 875 and they cleanse him from hatred and jealousy. Pass. pt. **sqila** s.v., st. abs. (**mana sqila**) **d-sqil** CP 437:2 = Q 65:33 repeated for the sake of emphasis, cf. with pers. ending **mana sqila d-sqilt** Gs 79:18 thou bright *mana* who hast become bright; the form **ʿsqil** is identical with ethp. pf. (q.v.).

Saf. Pf. **sasqil** Gs 14:22, 15:1 they polished; with suff. **sasqilth** Gs 99:9 she adorned it MG 276:24. Pt. **msasqal** Jb 184:15 polished, st. emph. **msasqla** AM 3, 36, 40 etc., **msasqilia** Gs 13:12 is polished (predicatively, not pl.).

Ethpe. Pf. **ʿsqil hanath naura** DC 34. 409 that mirror becomes bright(er), **ʿl riš ʿstiqil** DC 34 was brilliant in the highest degree (?). Pt. **misqil ginzia lhad trin** ATŠ II no. 382 his treasure is twice as bright.

Ettaf. Pt. pl. **mitasqlin** ATŠ II no. 387 (they) will become illustrious.

Der.: **sqalta** (fem.), **sqila**.

(**SQL II** metath. of **SLQ I** in **masqal 1** q.v.).

SQM (ܣܩܡ to measure, constitute, define, den. from ܣܩܘܡܐ, *σήκωμα* measure) to complete, make perfect, direct, develop, formulate, design, define, set in order, consummate, accomplish.

Pa. Pf. **saqam** PD 298 = **saqim** ATŠ I no. 25 he completed; neg. **lasaqam** PD 1285 = **lasaqim** PD 1651, ATŠ I no. 136, 188 etc. (*often*) did not accomplish; **saqmit** RD D 27 I set in order; **usaqamiun lkul ginzaikun umaṣbutaikun** DC 35 and they formulated (gave the pattern of) all your mystic rites and your baptisms; with suff. **saqmh** DC 3 (coloph.) he completed it. Impf. **unisaqim** (var. **nisaqam**) **ašualania** ATŠ I no. 138 (var. PD) and he shall complete (the initiation of) the novices. Act. pt. **msaqim** PD 700, 719, 730, ATŠ (*often*) he completes, achieves MG xxx 7; with encl. **msaqimlh** ATŠ I no. 63 (*& often*) he completes (ends) it; pl. **msaqmilh** PD 725 they complete it; pl. **msaqmin** PD 651, DC 50. 420 they accomplish, complete. Pass. pt. **msaqam** PD 655, 684, 747, 1270 (is) achieved MG xxx 7; pl. (for sg.) **kd hauia hugiana msaqmia blišana** ATŠ I no. 134 when the vocalization can be accomplished by the tongue (fem. for masc.) **kd msaqman tlatin uhda iumia** ATŠ II no. 74 when thirty-one days are over. Nom. act. **saqamta** s.v.

Ethpa. Pf. **ʿstaqam** AM 256 (*& often in colophons*) was completed; **ʿstaqmat** DC 43 J 234 it (fem. **šapta** = scroll) was completed. Impt. **šrur uʿstaqam** PD 256 be strong and in order; special pl. **lbuš manaikun uʿstaqamiun** DC 50. 17 put on your vestments and be complete (correctly attired). Pt. (pl.) **mistaqmin** . . . DC 27. 260 they are defined as . . .

Der.: **saqamta**.

SQP (סְקַף to clap, knock together; rel. to שְׁקַף, ܫܩܦ, Mand. **ŠQP**) the rt. of **squpana**, (ʿ)**squpta**.

sqpta Jb 41:9 B scr. def. of **squpta**.

SQR (cf. Talm. בסקיר 'by leaps', but ethpe. from **ZQR** as Talm. איזדקר) to leap (for joy), skip MG 46:7–9.

Pe. Pass. pt. (with act. meaning) **sqir uhadia mana** Gs 58:13 the *mana* skippeth for joy and rejoiceth; with encl. pers. pron. **sqirna uhadina** Gy 130:17 I skip for joy and rejoice.

Ethpe. s. **ZQR**.

SRA I (סְרֵי, ܣܪܝ & سري) to stink, be putrid.

Pe. Impf. **tisria utiṭarṭlia planita** DC 43 she, N., shall stink and be repulsive to him. Pt. **saria 3** s.v.

Pa. Pt. **mahria msaria puma ulišana** Or. 328:13 diseases (which) make mouth and tongue stink.

Ethpa. or Ettaf. Pt. **kul kalba d-hauia mitasaria** DC 44. 912 any dog which is putrescent.

Der.: **saria 3**, **sruta**.

SRA II, SRH I s.v. (Jew.-Aram. סְרַח to let hang down, to rot, Syr. ܣܪܚ I to cut, harm, sin, wound, H. & mod. H. סָרַח hang down, spread over, Ar. سَرَحَ to let graze freely, شَرَحَ to cut) to hurl down, fling down; to cut, tear. MG 235 n. 1.

Pe. Impf. **nisra** Gy 80:10 he hurleth down MG 235:12; with suff. **lanisrunak mn rqiha** Gy 299:26 they shall not hurl thee down from the heavens.

Pa. Impt. **sara markabatkun** Gy 329:23, 330:8, 16, 331:2 bring down your chariots MG 235:24. Pt. **hu mdalia uhu msara** Gy 231:8 he raiseth and he lowereth; with encl. **msaralh** Gy 230:22 he hurleth him down; **msarilun** Jb 168:13, ML 155 they throw them down, one throweth them down; **msarialun** Jb 200:8 she hurleth them down. Part. pres. with encl. **msaratlun** Gy 230:16, 18, 231:8, 233:7, 8 thou flingest them down MG 236:22.

Der.: **saraha**, **sraha**.

sradqa (Iranian, a corresp. mod. P. form would be *سراده or *سرايه?, Ar. loan-w. سُرَادِق derived by the Arabs from P. سراپرده MG xxxi n. 3, Fränkel 29, Jeffrey 167 f.; cf. Jew.-P. סראה 'forecourt'? Jeffrey loc. cit.; from an older Parthian form Wid. v 189, ISK 101) curtain, canopy, pavilion, awning, screen, partition, tent-roof MG xxxi 15. A var. with fem. ending **sradqta** Gy 287:8 A. Pl. **-ia**.

ninigduia ˁl sradqa Jb 233:11 f. they spread out the canopy; **šumia bisradqta** Gy 287:8 (var. **sradqa** BCD) the sky with its awning; **sradqa d̲-ziua** Gy 293:16, CP 441:1, ATŠ II no. 108 the canopy of radiance; **šuba sradqia** Gy 321:22 seven canopies; **ˁl sradqia uˁl škinata** Gy 373:23 about canopies and about (celestial) dwellings; **sradqa d̲-malka d̲-nhura ˁtriṣ** DC 27. 133 the canopy which the King of Light erected; **d̲-sitara sradqa lanihuilh̲** s. **sitara**; **sradqia d̲-parzla** ATŠ II no. 333 iron screens; **sradqa d̲-ptahil** DAb; **hazin sradqa ušitin sradqia hinun** DAb this is the curtain—and they are sixty curtains; **sradqa dilh̲ silita d̲ˁur** s. **silita**; **sradqa d̲-abinia tibta ltinta** DC 48. 33 f. the partition that is between faeces and urine; **alip alip sradqia** DC 41. 322 a thousand thousand pavilions.

sraha = **saraha** (q.v.): **šqul. . . . srahak mn qumth̲** DC 43 J 154 remove . . . thine injury from his body.

sraiil, sraˁil (יִשְׂרָאֵל) Gy 120:15 f. etc. Israel MG 4:16. Var. **ˁsraiil** s.v.

sraq (rt. **SRQ II**) emptiness. **atit bisraq ˁdak** Jb 145:12 f. thou comest with empty hands. (DC 30 has a var. **bisra.**)

sraquta a var. of **sriquta.**

SRG (סְרַג, ܣܪܰܓ, H. שׂרג, Ar. شرج Fränkel 101 f., 156, 173) to knit together, interweave, interlace, bind together; to adhere. Rel. to **SRK.**

Pe. Impf. with suff. **nisrigunh̲** DAb they will adhere to him (?). Pass. pt. **sriga** adherent, persistent (s.v.).

Af. Impt. **uasrug** DC 46. **uasrug pira upihla** DC 12. 172 and conjoin vagina and phallus (?).

Der.: **sarga, sriga.**

***SRD** cf. s. **SNDR** and **SRWD.**

SRH I = **SRA II** (q.v.).

Der.: **s(a)raha.**

SRH II (cf. סרח II J.) to be wide.

Der.: **sriha** s.v.

SRHB saf. of **RHB I** (סַרְהֵב, ܣܰܪܗܶܒ, H. רהב to rush against, Ar. رَهِبَ to be anxious, Akk. *ra'ābu* to be angry) to be quick, hasten, hurry MG 212:8. Impt. **sarhib** Jb 178:11 hasten MG 229:17. Pt. **msarhib ˁlh̲ lmidirbh̲** Jb 124:3 = **m(i)sarhib lmidirh̲** Q 46:11 he hasteneth to take her (: the soul) away (MG 230:23).

Der.: **sarhabaiit, sarhib.**

SRWD pa'wel of ***SRD** (inversion of **SDR II**, cf. s. **SNDR**) to terrify; refl. to be terrified. Fundamental stem: Participial pres. **msaru-adna** DC 46. 119:5 I terrify. Refl. stem.: Impf. **nistaruad** AM 20 is terrified. Pt. **mistaruad bšinth̲** DC 43 C 73 is terrified in his sleep; **bakia umistaruad** DC 43 E 93 cries and is terrified.

Der.: **mistaruata, saruadta, saruata.**

srungia (cf. סְרוּנְקֵי suffocation) constipation, stoppage. Pl. **ruha hˁ d̲-iatba ˁl napqa umitqiria srungia gauaiia** Or. 330:10 it is the spirit that sits on evacuation and is called constipation (lit. inner bindings, interception). PA **ṣrungia.**

sruqta (either from **SRQ I** or II) Gs 84:20 Lidzb. '*Zusammengekämmtes*' (cf. Ginzā 519 n. 2) because of **sriqlia** (l. 19) 'I combed myself', but possibly a pun (cf. **sriquta**), hence **sruqtai** 'my vanity'?.

sruta (rt. **SRA I**, Jew.-Aram. סְרוּתָא) stink, putridity, corruption MG 146:9. **arqa** (var. **aqra** C) **sruta mn škintak** Jb 37:7 root out corruption from thy dwelling; **riha d̲-srutun** Gy 89:18 f., Jb 145:1 the stink of their putridity; **riha d̲-sruta** Gy 259:10 the stink of putridity.

SRZ s. **SRS II.**

SRṬ rt. of **sarṭata, -ta** (q.v.).

sria Zotb. 228b:26, 27 for **srin** twenty.

sriga (pass. pt. pe. of **SRG**) clinging, persistent, grievous (of illness). **ˁšata sriga napša** AM 118:2 a very grievous fever.

sridqia s. **sqiria.**

sriha (rt. **SRH II**) wide. Pl. **-ia. ugbinh̲ srihia uprišia** AM 36:3 and his brows (are) wide and noble.

srin (from **ˁsrin** q.v. prob. on the analogy of **trin**) twenty MG 34:19, 189:10. Varr. **asrin, ˁsrin** s.vv.

sriq(a) 1 pass. pt. of **SRQ I** (q.v.).

sriqa 2 (pass. pt. of **SRQ II**) empty, vacant, idle, vain, worthless. Pl. masc. **-ia**, fem. **-ata. anašia sriqia** AM 29:18 idle vagabonds; **ukarsauatak sriqia hauin** Jb 27:5 f. and thy thrones will be empty; **minilia sriqata sainata** AM 80:15 idle (and) evil words.

sriquta (abstr. noun from **sriqa 2**, סְרִיקוּתָא, ܣܪܺܝܩܽܘܬ݂ܳܐ) idleness, vagabondage, pilfering. Var. **sraquta**, miscop. **sriruta. mn sriquta qiniana qania** AM 37:1 he acquires property by pilfering.

sriqia Gy 273:15, 22 B s. **sqiria.**

sriruta a miscop. of **sriquta.**

SRK (סְרַךְ, ܣܪܰܟ, H. שׂרך to interlace, Ar. شَرَكَ to be a partner, form a partnership) to adhere, climb into, hold fast to, catch, attach, fasten to, cling to, interweave, intertwine; (of fire, esp. af.) to catch alight, set alight, set aflame, kindle, catch on fire.

Pe. Pf. **sirkat nura** DC 44. 1522 flame burst out (Morg. 266/23:11 **sirkit nura** I set fire, read as DC 44 fem. with **nura** as subj.). Impf. with encl. **tisrukbh̲ nura** Jb 57:11 fire will set him aflame (DC 26. 44 f. **nisrukbh̲ nura** read as Jb 57:11 fem.), **tisrukbia** (= **bh̲**) **nura** Morg. 266/23:19 id.

Af. Pf. with encl. **urhamta unura blibh̲ asrikilh̲** Gy 146:24 and I kindled fiery love in her heart; **asrilkun nura bligraikun** DC 43 J 33 I set you on fire from the feet upwards. Impf. with suff. **ˁiasrikh̲ lzinqai barqa** Gy 82:12 I will fasten my chains to the earth. Impt. **aith̲ nura uasrik ˁlauh̲ ṭabar** DC 46 bring fire and kindle it on an axe (?); **asrak bšraga** DC 46 burn (it) in a lamp; **bazra d̲-gizar asrik bmiša** DC 46. 99:2 apply carrot-seed in oil. Part. pres. **nura masrikna** DC 46. 66:14 I kindle fire.

ETHPE. & ETHPA. Pf. **bparahiata d̲-taga ʿstrik** CP 341:8, DC 34. 894, Lond. roll A 363 were interwoven into the tendrils (??) of the crown (although **parahiata** 'sparks' would suggest 'were enkindled'?). Impf. **unistarkun bibdunia d̲-arqa** ATŠ II no. 350 and they will cleave to the uttermost ends of the earth. Pt. pl. with encl. **mistarkibin** RD E 9 = DAb par. they are held together (or are interwoven?) by them.

SRS I (cf. **SRG, SRK** & Syr. ܣܪܓ to twine) to twist, (inter)twine, wreathe.

PE. Pt. pl. **asa sarsin šahpia** DC 3. 238:8 = CP 365:ult., DC 50. 511 they twine myrtle foliage; **ʿlania sarsin dahba (uanpiš ṭunaihun margania)** DC 34. 874 = DC 3 238:8 = DC 50:513 = CP 340:11 trees wreathed with gold (and plentiful is their burden of pearls).

SRS II (Syr. ܣܪܣ, Mishn. סָרַס, den. from סריסא, ܣܪܝܣܐ, H. סָרִיס, Ar. سَرِيس eunuch) to be castrated, emasculated. Var. **SRZ.**

ETHPA. Pf **alahia zikria d̲-hiziun rat uʿstarsa** [*sic*] DC 44 (var. **ʿstarza**) the male gods that beheld me trembled and were emasculated.

SRSP (paʿpel of Eg.-Aram., H. & mod. H. שׂרף, Akk. *šarāpu* to burn, or *parpel* of ܫܒ, Akk. *šabābu*, Ar. شَبَّ id.) to blow into flame, burst into flame MG 85:16 f., 86 n. 1, MSchr. 30 n. 3. Pt. **msarsip iaqdana** Jb 99:13 he blows into flame MG 230:21; pl. **msarsipin iaqdana** Gy 17:11 = **msarspia iaqdana** Gy 357:13 they blow up the flame MG 31:2, 37:23, 85:17, 149:12 (but ZA xxx 150 differently from **SRP**).

srʿil Ṣâb.'s AM a var. of **sraʿil.**

SRP 1 (ܣܪܦ I, Ar. شَرِبَ, Eth. ሰረበ) to swallow, gulp down.

PE. Impf. **ʿsrup bsiruptai** Gy 82:13 I will swallow (it); with suff. **unisirpak bmasrupta** DC 20. 110 and he will swallow thee at a gulp; **utisirpak bmasrupta** DC 43 E 50 and she will swallow thee at a gulp. Pt. pl. **zuhma sarpia** Jb 150:4 s. **zuhma**. Inf. with suff. **ba misirpan umiklan** Jb 189:4 he sought to swallow me and eat me up. Nom. ag. **sarupa** s.v.

DER.: **masrupta, sarupa, sirupta.**

SRP 2 to burn.

DER.: **sarupa** var. **sarupia** (q.v.) ATŠ II no. 189.

SRṢ accord. to context: to be glad. Pf. **riuzat usaraṣat** DC 48. 289 she rejoiced and was glad.

SRQ I (סְרַק II, ܣܪܩ II, H. שׂרק I, Ar. شرق to split) to comb, tear asunder, shred, harrow.

PE. Impf. **laʿhup ulaʿsruq** (varr. **ulasruq** E, **ulaʿsriq** B) Jb 113:2 I will neither wash nor comb; with suff. **nisruqunh̲ bmasirqia** DAb they comb him with combs. Act. pt. **qisariq brišh̲** DAb he combs his hair (lit. on his head); with encl. **qisariqlh̲ ʿl ʿur** RD 28a he combs Ur. Part. pres. **haipit usarqit** Gy 116:15, Jb 113:5 thou washest and combest (thyself). Pass. pt. **sriq** with encl. pers. pron. **hiplia usriqlia** Gs 84:20 I washed and combed (myself) MG 382:13.

PA. Pt. pl. **msarqilh̲** Gs 12:7 they tear it to shreds. Inf. with suff. **saruqih̲ bʿdaihun** DC 43 J 72 to rend it apart with their hands.

DER.: **masirqa** (var. **misirqa**), **saruqia**, cf. **sruqta.**

SRQ II (סְרַק I, ܣܪܩ I, Ar. سرق Eth. ሰረቀ, Akk. *šarāqu* to steal, orig. saf. or šaf. *rāqu* to be empty, vain, cf. Ar. ريق) to (be) empty.

DER.: **sriqa 2, sriquta** (var. **sra-**), cf. **sruqta.**

SRQD (saf. or **RQD** q.v.) to (cause to)quake, shake. Fundamental stem: Act. pt. **umsarqid malkia** ATŠ II no. 440 maketh kings quake. Pass. pt. **ʿniš d̲-hauia msarqad** DC 46. 116:8 a person that shakes (has palsy). Refl. stem: Pt. pl. **alma d̲-mistarqdia** DC 46. 116:13 until they shake; **dahlin umistarqdin** DC 36 they fear and shake; fem. **nišmata minaihun mistandra umistarqda** s. **SNDR** ethpa.

stad Zotb. 220a: bottom = **ʿustad.**

stana, ʿstana (איסתנא, ܐܣܬܢܐ < Akk. *ištāna, iltānu* Zimmern 45) north, north-east (wind), northern, wintry, cold MG 34:paen. f. **atia minh̲ stana** Gy 283:10 the north wind cometh; **aiar stana** s. **aiar 1** (last quot.); **ʿstana našim ʿlauaihun** Gs 108:12 the north wind bloweth on them; **ubaiar stana d̲-našim ʿlak** Or. 332:14 and by the north wind which bloweth on thee; **utinaṭrunh̲ . . . mn aiar ʿustana stana** DC 19 and protect it . . . from the wintry north(-east) wind; **stana ušuta** DC 27 north-east wind and south-west wind; **šuta ustana** AM 219:6; **had stana uhad šuta** ATŠ I no. 62, 250 one (wind) is northerly and one southerly; **biahra nisan ʿstana nihuia** AM 195:7 in the month of Nisan there will be a north wind.

stuara, ʿst(i)uara, suara s.vv. (P. ستوار, استوار) firmness, stability, foothold, firm stance, footing, equilibrium, feet, base. **ʿl stuarun kan** ATŠ II no. 388 = PD 895 they stood firmly; **uʿl stuarun lakainia** Gy 264:8 and they do not stand firmly; **nqašia dra lstuarun** DC 34. 336 shakings assaulted their equilibrium; **ugaṭinia stuarh̲** AM and his feet are slender.

stirata Jb 243:4, DC 40. 465, 780 etc. = **ʿstirata.**

STR I (סְתַר I, ܣܬܪ 780 I, H. & mod. H. סתר, Ar. ستر, Eth. ሰተረ, South-Ar. 𐩪𐩩𐩧 to protect, Akk. *šataru* a kind of garment?) to cover, conceal; to seek refuge.

PE. Pf. **ruha rišh̲ sitrat** Gs 91:24 R. covered her head (so Lidzb., but more prob. **STR II**). Impf. **tistariun** Or. 333:20 (var. **tastiriun** af.) ye shall conceal.

PA. Pt. (act. & pass.) pl. masc. **razia msatria** Oxf. 20b occult mysteries (= secret rites), fem. **d̲-msatra mn duktaihun** Gy 328:3 which are hidden in their own place; **ʿstirata** (var. **st-** Jb) **kd̲ msatran** Gy 99:9, Jb 243:4 the *astartes* which are veiled Jb ii 223 n. 1; pt.

with encl. **rišaiin msatarlin** Gs 30:18 their (fem.) head is veiled; **msatralun** Gy 354:22 she covered them; **msatrilẖ** Gy 193:12 they covered him.

Af.? Impf. with suff. **ʿastirinkun** (or pa.?) Gy 354:11 f., 15 f., 19 f. I will conceal you. Pt. pl. **mastiria** (varr. **mistiria** C, **mistaria** B ethpe.?) **zuzia** Jb 72:2 coins hidden away.

Ethpa. Pf. (identical with **ASR I**) **bgauẖ ḏ-ʿṣṭunẖ ḏ-adam ʿstar** DC 6 they are concealed within the body (trunk) of A. Impf. **ʿulṣana nistar unipaliṭ** AM 212:1 f. (he) will conceal? (cast off?) tribulation and will escape. Both doubtf.

Der.: **sitara.**

STR II (סְתַר I, ܣܬܰܪ I, H. & Eg.-Aram. שׁתר, Ar. شتر, Sab. 𐩦𐩩𐩧, Akk. *šutturu*) to destroy, ruin, tear down, tear away, tear out. Because of the identity of forms sometimes difficult to be recognized from **STR I** Jb ii 223 n. 1.

Pe. Pf. **ruha rišẖ sitrat** Gs 91:24 R. tore her hair (lit. her head, cf. also **STR I**), **ustariun mn bisraihun** Jb 134:8 and they tore at their flesh. Act. pt. (fem.) **gdula satra brišẖ** Gy 85:21 = **gdulẖ brišẖ satra** Gy 96:21, 329:2, 361:15 she teareth at the plaits on her head; (masc.) with encl. **usatarlẖ ubanilẖ** AM 46:4 he will pull it down and build it up. Inf. **mistar ʿšumia uarqa** DC 40 to destroy heavens and earth.

Pa. Pt. (fem.) **gdulẖ brišẖ msatra** Gy 81:7 she teareth at the braids on her head.

Ethpe. Pf. **markabata ḏ-šuka ʿstar** JRAS 1939 405 (n. 2) the chariots of the Seven were cast down. Impf. **unistrun braza ḏ-napšaihun** DC 37 they shall be destroyed (torn out) by their own magic.

Der.: **ʿstura.**

ʿ (= ࡏ), ع

ʿ The 16th letter of the alphabet. Transcribed by ע when Hebrew letters are used for transcription. The original consonantal value vanished, so that it is used as a graphical sign for a front vowel (*i*, *e*). Used often as a prosthetic vowel MG § 24; often as a mere graphical var. of i esp. after the letters **k, n, p, ṣ** MG 5:11 and regularly in **hʿ** 'she' MG 5:10; an initial **i** (< ִ, ֵ, or ְ) must always be expressed by ʿ MG 55:ult. f. Sometimes wavering betw. **a** and ʿ but in some forms ʿ is functional (cf. esp. pass. pt. pe. of verbs *Iae gutt.* **ʿmir, ʿbid** etc.) MG 28:top. The Ar. ع was introduced in the postcl. period to designate this guttural in Ar. loan-words MG 1:bottom f. Phonetic changes of the orig. guttural ע: consequent vanishing of the guttural; betw. two vowels ע (as well as א) > ʿ MG § 63 p. 70 f.; ע > ה MG § 64; ע > ק in four words only MG pp. 72 f.

ʿ- prefix of the 1st p. sg. impf.

عabad Zotb. 226b:20 a man's name.

عabas Zotb. 227b:35 a man's name.

عabdala (Ar. عبد الله), earlier **abdala** (s.v.) ʿAbdullah MG 2:2. Var. **abd alah** Zotb. 223b (2nd text:12). Very often in colophons.

عabid ala Zotb. 231:13 same as preced.

عadauata a var. of **عidauat** BZ 180 n. 6.

عadasia s. **šadanak.**

عadil (Ar. عَدِيل) AM 258:25 temperate.

عadim (Ar. عَظِيم) AM 276:1 great.

عadim lšan (Ar. عظيم الشأن) AM 265:17 f. (man) of high office.

عadl (Ar. عَدْل) AM 253:20 equity, justice.

عauaṣip (Ar. عَوَّاصِف) AM 271:9 whirlwinds BZ 175 n. 4.

عauar Zotb. 221b:17 (text) a man's name.

عazaim (Ar. عَظَائِم) pl. invocations, exorcisms, mighty words. **hazin عazaim qria lman ḏ-haui adaiua** DC 46 read these exorcisms for one that has a devil.

عaziz (Ar. عَزِيز) Q 61:2 (*& often in colophons*) a man's name MG 2:8.

عazqlan AM 198:7, 202 a place-name, ancient Ascalon? BZ Ap. II. Var. **azqalan** Ṣâb.'s AM.

عaṭarid (Ar. عُطَارِد) AM 155 Mercury.

عain (Ar. عَيْن) often in place-names. **ain ʿl ṭabarʿia** AM 198:5, var. **عain lṭabar** Ṣâb.'s AM; **عain lšams** AM 199 = **ain ʿl šamus** AM 204:7 (with varr.) Heliopolis? BZ Ap. II.

عainia AM 202 a place-name BZ Ap. II.

عala (a translit. of Ar. على in some mod. texts) on. **iidil عala pisad** AM 257:35 (Ar.) it betokens corruption.

عalaiim (Ar. عَلَايِم) AM 288:13 informations.

عalama (Ar. عَلَامَة) AM 257:9 sign, indication.

عali (عَلِيّ) AM 256:41, Zotb. 221a:29 ʿAlī.

عalm Ṣâb.'s AM a var. of **عilim.**

عama (Ar. عَمَّة) aunt. With suff. **عamai** Q 61:2 my aunt MG 2:7.

عamal 1 AM 254:6 action, work.

عamal 2 AM 204:17 f. name of a town BZ Ap. II.

عaman (عَمَّان) name of a town, now capital of Transjordania BZ Ap. II.

ɛamarat (Ar. عَمَارَة) AM 282:10 prosperity.

ɛambar AM 202 name of a town, **also anbar** (s.v.) BZ Ap. II.

ɛamu (Ar. عَمّ, with suff. عمو) uncle. With suff. **ɛamuiia** AM 106 (& *often in colophons*) his uncle.

Gl. 36:10 **abra ʿmuii** [*sic*] ابن عمّى *nepos* پسر عمو.

ɛamtiia in **bnia d̠-ɛamtiia** Zotb. 219a:17 sons of my aunt (cf. **ɛama**).

ɛanzarut (Ar. عَنْزَرُوت < ܥܢܙܪܘܬܐ Löw 283) AM 287:26 Persian gum or balsam.

ɛankabut (عَنْكَبُوت) DC 46. 132:4 spider.

ɛasal (Ar. عَسَل) AM 258:19 honey: **qurunpil bɛasal** DC 46. 112:6 cloves in honey.

ɛasakir Zotb. 220b:25 etc. a family-name.

ɛaskar (Ar. عَسْكَر) AM 266:25 army, soldiers.

ɛaṣriin (cf. Ar. عَصَر, عُصْر, عُصْرَة refuge) AM 275:16 refugees.

ɛaqla (Ar. عَقل) DC 46. 84:4, 113:4 reason, understanding.

ɛaraq (عِرَاق) 203, 275 etc. ʿIrāq.

ɛašam (Ar. عَجَم) Ṣâb.'s AM Persians.

ɛašar Zotb. 228b:30, 229b (2b text:6) name of a river, Euting ZDMG xix 123 n. 4.

ɛašuq (Ar. عاشق) DC 45 & 46 (*often*) in love, yearning.

ʿBA 1 s. **ABA I.**

ʿBA II s. **ABA II.**

ʿbabia (= **ʿbibia**) fruits. **ʿbabaihun** Gy 9:2 their fruits MG 163:11; **kulhun ʿbabia** ML 14:1 all the fruits (CP 12:14 **kulhun ʿbibia**).

ʿbag s. **ʿgab.**

ʿBB = **ABA II.**

ʿbad, ʿbada = **ʿubada.** Pl. **-ia. lʿbad umibad** Gy 263:18 to what was made and created.

ʿBD s. **ABD I** (& **II**).

ʿbda for **abda** servant. **ahbalia ʿbda** ŠQ 26:10 give me a servant.

ʿbdala Zotb. 220a:bottom for **ɛabdala.**

ʿbdata (often in DC 34) for **ʿbidata.**

ʿbdunia s. **abdana 2.**

ʿburia (Eg.-Aram. עבור, Jew.-Aram. עֲבוּרָא, עֲבוּרָא, Syr. ܥܒܘܪܐ, H. & mod. H. עָבוּר, Akk. *ebūru* Haupt ZDMG lxiv 707) pl. crops, produce, grain, harvests, products MG 118:19. Var. **ʿuburia. ʿ(u)buria qalia** Gy 385:22 scanty harvests; **ʿburia rurbia** AM bumper crops; **mn ʿburia d̠-sindirka** ATŠ II no. 317 some of the products of the date-palm.

ʿBṬ s. **ABṬ I.**

ʿbṭa (rt. **ʿBṬ** = **ABṬ**) bailiff. Pl. **ʿbṭia** Gs 17:8.

ʿbia (rt. **ABA I**) muscles? **uʿbia uširiania** ATŠ II no. 114 and muscles (?) and arteries.

ʿbibia pl. (sg. אִנְבְּא, ܐܒܐ, H. אֵב Kautzsch 105, Ar. أَبّ Nöld. ZDMG xl 735, Akk. *inbu* Zimmern 55) fruits MG 163:12. Var. **ʿbabia** s.v. **ʿbibh̠** CP 12:14, Gy 322:6, DC 3. 320 its fruits.

ɛbidala Zotb. 220a:bottom (several times) for **ɛabdala.**

ʿbidata (ܚܒܕܐܬܐ) pl. works actions, rites, deeds MG 117:26. Var. **ʿbdata s.v. bibidata** Gy 46:7 in the works MG 28 n. 3; **ʿbidatun** their works MG 181:15; **ʿbidatkun umabadatkun** (*often*) your works and actions; **ʿbidata d̠-babia trisar** RD C 15, 17 the rites of the Twelve Gates; **ʿbidata d̠-bnia hšuka** RD 34 works of the sons of darkness; **ʿbidata d̠-malkia** AM 6:5 (*often*) Government employ; **ʿbidata rurbata abid** AM 17:20 he will perform mighty deeds; **kd̠ abdia ʿbidata** ATŠ (*often*) when performing rites.

ɛbidiman Zotb. 220b:4 a man's name.

ʿbila 1 (ܐܒܝܠܐ MG xxix 19, Ar. loan-w. أَبِيل Fränkel 270) mourner, ascetic, monk MG 117:4. Pl. masc. **ʿbilia**, fem. **ʿbilata.** Var. **ʿbla 2. ʿbilia uʿbilata** Gy 55:16 f., 226:16, 227:18 monks and nuns (**ʿblia uʿbilata** ATŠ II no. 93 referring to ritual meals for the dead is possibly a pun. Cf. **ʿblia 1** & varr. **blaiaiia** & **blaiia** s.v.). **zupraiun umṭanputun d̠-hinun ʿbilia** Gy 56:2 stink and uncleanness of those monks.

ʿbila 2 occasionally for **ʿbla 1** (& vice versa, cf. s. **ʿbila 1**).

ʿbin (Ar. ابن) Zotb. 223b (2nd text:13 ff.) son. Mod.

ʿbira for **ʿuira** in **baina ṣarda ʿbira** DC 43 E 8 with torpid and blind eye.

ʿBL s. **ABL.**

ʿbla 1 (rt. **ʿBL** = **ABL**) mourning. Usually in pl. **ʿblia 1** lamentations. With procl. prep. **biblia** Gy 301:14, Gs 35:9 MG 4:24. **lagṭa ʿblia** Gs 20:1 she mourneth; **ʿblia umalia** Gs 21:16 lamentations and wailing; **ʿkpar ʿblia umalia mn libaikun** ATŠ II no. 335 mourning and lamentation be wiped away from your heart(s); **uʿblia umalia lagṭin** Jb 139:5 (var. **ublia . . .** B) and they take to mourning and wailing; **nagdin ʿblaihun** ML 184:7 they prolong their mourning; **ʿblia uʿbilata** ATŠ II no. 101 s. **ʿbila 1.**

ʿbla 2 occasionally for **ʿbila 1.** Pl. masc. **-ia** fem. **-ata. ʿblia uʿblata** Sh. 'Abd.'s copy's var. of Gy 55:16 f. (s. **ʿbila 1**).

ʿbna = **abna. ʿbna d̠-mihla** DC 26. 41 f. rock salt.

ʿBQ, ABQ (cf. אַבְקָא, ܐܒܩܐ, H. אָבָק dust Ar. أَبِقَ to flee away, H. den. verb אבק to cover with dust; but Ar. عبق to spread out a perfume) to dust, sprinkle a dry place.

Pe. Impt. with suff. **sab kuza d̠-iama ʿbqih** DC 40. 74 f. take a jarful of the pool(-water) sprinkle it!

ʿBR s. **ABR I.**

ʿbra 1 (rt. **ABR I**, ܥܒܪܐ, H. עֵבֶר, Ar. عِبْر coast-land, foreshore MG 102:7. **ʿbra d̠-gauka** Gy 390:3, 9 f.; **ʿbra d̠-babil** Gy 390:4 f., 8.

ʿbra 2 (אֶבְרָא, ܐܒܪܐ, H. אֵבֶר & אֶבְרָה, Akk. *abru* pinion-feather) wing, pinion, arm, limb, membrum. Pl. **-ia. muma bʿbr(i)h̲ hauilh̲** AM 17:5 etc. he will have a defect in his arm(s or limbs?); **pasiqtinun lʿbrh̲** Gy 119:3 I cut off his limbs (Ginzā 133 n. 3); **umn lišana hauin ʿbria** Gy 244:18 (var. **ʿmbria** Leid. doubtf. Ginzā 245 n. 2, read **hauia ʿmra**? 'from the tongue cometh speech'?) **ʿbrik kinia aiar** Gy 116:13 s. **kinta** 1; **ʿbra d̲-smala** DC 43 A 68 left arm.

ʿbra 3 = **bra.** Var. **abra** s.v. **ʿbra d̲-gabra ʿbraia ṭaba** DC 26. 582 son of the good, creative (??) being.

ʿbrahim occ. var. of **(a)brahim.**

ʿbraia (rt. **BRA**?) creative?, exorcist? **ʿbra d̲-gabra ʿbraia** DC 26. 582 s. **ʿbra,** similarly **br bra d̲-ʿbraia** DC 44. 1051 and **bra d̲-gabra ʿbraia** Morg. 259/10:12; **ana . . . abdia gabra ʿbraia** DC 44. 410 I am . . . a servant of the Creative (?) Being.

ʿgab Gy 383:4, var. **ʿbag** Leid. name of a Persian king (son of Burzin, son of Karšâsp, a descendant of Jamšīd, *Šâhnâmeh*, ed. Vullers–Landauer 1050:5).

ʿgba, gba 2 (rt. **GBB**) rounded part, joint, curve? **ʿgba d̲-masa** DC 41. 462 the bend (?) of the fore-arm (: elbow?); **ʿgba d̲-ṣbita** DC 41. 463 = **ʿgbh̲ d̲-ṣbata** Oxf. xiii the joints (?) of the fingers.

ʿGD s. **AGD.**

ʿguzar (rt. **GZR,** a corrupt form) cutting-up, cutting-off. **ʿguzar ukruta** DC 46 cutting-up and mutilation.

ʿgira pass. pt. of **AGR I** (q.v.). Pl. masc. **ʿgiria,** fem. **ʿgirata. kibnata d̲-ʿgirata** ŠQ 18: 26, CP 236:15 (var. **ʿgiata** DC 3) the coarse robes of hired maid-servants.

ʿgla (עֶגְלְתָא, ܥܓܠܬܐ, H. עֲגָלָה) vehicle, cart, chariot. Pl. **-ia. ʿgla ana zuṭa** ŠQ I am a little vehicle; **ubiglia trin rkibna** DC 44. 1101 and I ride in two chariots (opening line of an exorcism).

ʿGR = **AGR I.**

ʿDA I = **ADA I.**

ʿDA II = **YDA.**

ʿda (יְדָא, ܐܝܕܐ, Sam. ·, H. יָד, Ar. يَد colloquial also *id*, South-Ar. ·, Eth. እድ, Akk. *idu* arm, side, power ZDMG xli 617 f., Nöld. *Neue Beiträge* 113, Brockelm. i 332 f.) hand MG 4:4, 97:6, 184:3. St. cstr. **iad** s.v. Fem. MG 157:12. Pl. **ʿdia** 1, **ʿdahata** MG 171:11 f., 184:3. Rare var. **ʿida,** cf. **uʿidaihun** Gy 56:12 CD = **uʿdaihun** AB and their hands MG 4:20 f. With suff. **bʿdak** in thy hand MG 4:18, **ʿdai** my hands MG 176:10, **ʿdh̲** his hand MG 178:2, **btartin ʿdu** Gs 72:13 with both his hands MG 178:9 f., **ʿda** Oxf. 12 a her hand(s) MG 178:13; **ʿdaian** our hands MG 179:9; **iahib ʿda** s.v.; **kdab ʿda** s. **kdaba** 1; **ʿl ʿdh̲ dilh̲ mitnaṭria** ATŠ II no. 141 are protected by his hand; **uʿdahath̲** Jb 120:5 and his hands.

ʿdana 1 (עִדָּנָא, ܥܕܢܐ > Ar. عِدَّان, Eth. ዐደን appointment, Akk. *adannu, edannu* ZA vi 215, Nöld. *Neue Beiträge* 44) time, moment, minute, hour, season, epoch MG 136:16. St. abs. & cstr. **ʿdan.** Pl. **ʿdania** 1. With suff. **ʿdan(ai)kun** Q 37:20 your time MG 179:19; **mn zban uʿdan lalam** Gy 7:3 from this time forth until evermore; **maṭia zban uʿdan umaṭia ʿdana uzibna** Gs 76:15 time and season are coming MG 301:bottom; **bla ʿdana** AM 254:4 f. in no time, suddenly; **ʿdan d̲-rahmia** CP 144: ult. ML 173:6 the hour for prayers, the time for devotions; **ʿdana d̲-kṣir bgauh̲** AM 115:9 the hour in which he sickened; **hua ʿdanan marira** HG our epoch was bitter; **aribtinun lʿdania** Gy 116:6 she mixed up the times.

ʿdana 2, more usually **ʿdania 2** (H. עֵדֶן, Syr. ܥܕܝܢ; formal influence of **ʿdana** 1) Eden, paradise. **nišimtai mn gilia mia uruha mn ʿdana baraia** DC 37. 320 my soul from the waves of waters, and the spirit from Outer Paradise; **ginat ʿdania** s. **ginat; mn ʿdana d̲-gabra d̲ʿl aiar qaiim** DC 46. 180:4.

ʿdania 3 pl. cherished (pampered) nurslings? (cf. foll. parallelism): **aklia bsar ʿdania ušatia mn zmaiun d̲-mpanqia** DC 43 J 29 they consume the flesh of cherished nurslings (?) and drink the blood of petted (children).

ʿdia 1 a pl. of **ʿda** (q.v.).

ʿdia 2 (rt. **ʿDA** = **ADA I**) passage, transit MG 102:22. **briša d̲-ʿdia** Jb 144:7 the surface of the waterway; **dinba d̲-ʿdia** Jb 157:6 the end of the transit; **ʿštauilun ʿuhrata uʿdia ʿtasiqlun** DC 7 roads were made for them and communication was established for them; **nihia iamamaihun ulaiit ʿdia bgauaihun** Gy 9:7 f. peaceful are their seas and there is no ford in them.

ʿdiaruta (abstr. noun from **adiaura** 1) help, assistance, aid; **ṣauta uʿdiaruta** DC 21 companionship and aid.

ʿdilma (דִּי־לְמָה Esra 7:23, Talm. דִּי לְמָא, Syr. ܕܠܡܐ) lest, if perhaps, possibly, may be, perchance MG 33:9, 209:9. **šitlai ʿdilma naimia** Oxf. 18 ab, 22 ab = CP 158:5 lest perchance my children sleep; **ʿdilma krikta d̲-mia hazin ʿdilma dahlan mn mia** Jb 40:9 f. lest they see the surging of the waters, lest they fear the water MG 376:bottom, cf. 377 n. 1; **hzia ʿdilma . . . laiṭatlh̲** Gs 55:21 see to it that thou cursest him not; **ʿdilma hiia rbia giuṭa ʿlai** Gs 6:21 lest the Great Life be angry with me; **ʿdilma bqiluma ʿtit . . . ʿdilma bainia lamitahzit** Oxf. 25b = ML 197 ff. = CP 162:15 and 16 if only thou hadst not come into corruption . . . if only thou hadst not been seen by eyes . . . etc. (often in elliptical sentences); **ʿdilma d̲-** sometimes introduces a clause of fearing MG 471. Often to introduce a neg. (sarcastic) question (Lat. *nonne*): **ʿdilma laiaditun** Gy 186:10 (*& often*) do ye not know?; **ʿdilma ʿlh̲ d̲-gubria litlh̲** Gy 148:ult. f. haply he hath no male organs?

ʿdkuria (for **adkuria** inf. af. of **DKR**) summoning by invocation. **ʿu ʿdkuria ʿdkiritun** DC 51 if ye are called on with invocation.

ʿdma AM 129 = **dma** (= **zma**).

ʿdmaiia IM no. 27 for **q(a)dmaiia**? cf. p. 77.

ᶜdmu occ. var. of **dmu**.
ᶜDQ the rt. of **ᶜdqa**.
ᶜdqa (ܥܕܩܐ, pl. ܥܕܩܐ by assimil. ܥܕܩܐ, Ar. عذق branch of the date-palm, bunch of dates Fränkel WZKM iii 255, عِذْقَة sign made of red wool, Akk. *idqu*? fleece) bunch or tuft (of hair). Pl. **-ia** tresses, handfuls of hair IM Gl. **uᶜdqh̲ mn rišh̲ nisbat** Gy 247:8 and she took bunches of hair from her head; **nsabinin bᶜdqia d̲-manzia d̲-rišain** IM 43:bottom, 50: bottom, he seized them by the tresses of their heads; **nsibinin bᶜdqia d̲-manzaihin d̲-rišaihin** AO ix 96:2 id.; **ᶜdqia mn rišaian aqran** DC 34. 106 they tear out bunches of hair from their heads.
ᶜDR s. **ADR**.
ᶜhai (cf. **hai** 1) interj., exclamation of joy and address: hey, ho!, behold!, lo! MG 81:14. Often in wedding songs.
ᶜhbala, ᶜhbaqa, ᶜhbila, ᶜhdara varr. of **hbala, hbaqa** etc.
ᶜhur, ᶜhuria = **ahuria**. **mn ᶜhurh̲ d̲-mana** Q 3:15 = CP 8:6 from behind the *mana* MG 360:4 f.
ᶜhṭiaiil DC 40. 874 name of an angel.
ᶜhida pass. pt. pe. of **AHD** (q.v.).
ᶜHK s. **AHK**.
ᶜhka (rt. **ᶜHK** = **AHK**) laughter MG 102:8.
ᶜhᶜ Gy 154:15 B, 170:ult. B for **hᶜ** she MG 86 n. 2.
ᶜu (Aram. & H. אוֹ, Syr. ܐܘ, Neopunic, South-Ar. ወ, Ar. أَوْ, Eth. አወ, Akk. *ū* Brockelm. 254c) (*a*) or, (*b*) if, (*c*) **ᶜu . . . ᶜu** either . . . or MG 7:3, 22:ult., 208:2, 328:17, IM Gl. In disjunctive questions: **gabra baṭin mn qudam ᶜnta ᶜu ᶜnta baṭna mn qudam gabra** Gy 201:24 doth man become pregnant from woman, or woman become pregnant from man?; **hiia hinun šihluk ᶜu anat mn napšak ᶜtit** Gs 121:7 did the Life send thee, or didst thou come of thyself?; **miaka . . .** Gy 80:23, 187:2 is there . . ., or there is . . .? etc. MG 446:bottom; **man nimarlia d̲-had hua malka ᶜu ᶜtrin** Jb who will tell me whether there was one king, or two (cf. P. يا . . . كه) MG 471:top; 'either . . . or'; **ᶜu miraq araq ᶜu ᶜtiksuiia ᶜtksu** Gy 271:8 either they fled away or they hid etc. MG 447:top. In conditional clauses: **ᶜu d̲-ᶜmarlkun bhirai tišmun ᶜu d̲-ᶜpaqdinkun tibdun ᶜtilkun mn ziuai** Gy 18:14 if ye hear, my chosen ones, what I say unto you, if ye do what I order you, I will give you (some) of my radiance; **ᶜu nᶜšabak btušbihtak . . .** Gy 4:18 if we praise Thee with thy praise . . .; **ᶜu anat šakbit luatai . . .** Gy 95:9 if thou sleepest with me . . .; **ᶜu tiškub luatai** Gy 96:7 id.; **ᶜu napqitun . . . puq** Gy 109:13 if ye (are to) depart . . ., so depart; **ᶜu baiitulh̲ urahmitulh̲ ašmuia** Gy 15:3 if ye seek him and love him, let him hear; **ᶜu iahbitun biaminaikun lismalaikun latimrun** Gy 15:17 if ye give with your right hands, say (it) not to your left hands; **ᶜu hu našba hualh̲ . . . ᶜu škib . . . ᶜu ᶜkšil . . .** Gs 52:10 if he engendered him . . .; if he slept . . ., if he stumbled . . .; **ᶜu ana laᶜmrit ᶜlh̲ lahuit ana mn rurbia** Gy 76:17 if I had not told him, I would not belong to the Mighty MG 473 ff.
ᶜUA (עֲוָא, ܥܘܐ, pa. ܥܘܝ, عوى) to wail, howl. Doubtf. **ᶜiai tuiia ᶜlak** DC 43 I 102 Woe! thou wilt bewail thyself (?). Der.: **ᶜuai, uai, ᶜiai**.
ᶜuai = **uai** woe! Repeated **ᶜuai uai** Gy 164:16, **ᶜuai ᶜuai** MG 81:12.
ᶜuardia Gy 225:11 = **uardia** (in the same line).
ᶜuartia DC 22. 213 a var. of **ᶜuirtia** Gy 220:4.
ᶜuat 1 (Lidzb. from **hiuat** by vanishing of **h** Ginzā 71 n. 1 cancelling his former opinion Jb ii 183 n. 10; Pallis from ***ᶜbat dlibat** = **libat** the initial **d** having been regarded as a *nota relationis* MSt 35 n. 1) Ewat, epithet for Ruha, Brandt JPTh xviii 411, Lidzb. OLZ xxv col. 54. **ᶜuat ruha kadabta** Jb 187:10, Gy 196:24, 197:8, 203:21; **ᶜuat ruha d̲-qudša** Gy 207:13, Gs 35:6; **ᶜuat ruha** Gy 209:2, Morg. 270/30:4 = DC 44. 1958.
ᶜuba abual some kind of animal. V.s. **hurpa 2**.
ᶜubada (עובדא & עֲבָדָא, ܥܒܕܐ Nöld. ZDMG xxii 458, *Beiträge* 32; Brockelm. i § 131 c κ) work, deed, action, event, rite MG 28:13, 114:16, IM Gl. Pl. **-ia. hiia zakin ᶜl kulhun ᶜubadia** (*very often*) Life is victorious over all works; **d̲-ᶜlauia kulhun ᶜubadia** (*very often*) which is above all works; **ᶜubadh̲ uagrh̲** Gy 179:2 his works and his reward; **ᶜubadia d̲-baita** Q 29:3 the works of the House; **ᶜubadaikun umabadaikun** Gs 29:2 etc. (*often*) your works and deeds; **bharšia uᶜubadia maiit** AM 143:penult. he will die through witchcraft and its machinations.
ᶜubadia Zotb. 217b:13 a family name.
ᶜubdania = **abdania 2**: **ᶜubdania titaiia d̲-hšuka** Morg. 222/32:11, JRAS 1937 p. 591 (: 61) etc. the lower Abaddons of Darkness.
ᶜWD s. **ABD III**.
ᶜuda (ܥܘܕܐ, Ar. عود) rod, stick, staff. **ᶜudai uhuṭrai utagai** DC 43 H 19 my rod, my staff, my crown; **bhuṭrak uᶜudak utagak** Morg. 270/30:10 (var. . . . **uaudak** . . . DC 44. 1967) by thy rod and staff and thy crown; **hailh̲ uᶜudh̲ utagh̲** DC 44. 1733 (miscop. . . . **ubudh̲** . . . Morg. 268/26:35) his force, staff, and crown.
ᶜudamia (doubtf. Ginzā 208 n. 2; cf. Akk. *edimmu* a ghost-spirit Thompson: *Devils and Evil Spirits*) Lidzb. 'storms (?)', prob. a kind of spirits. **ᶜudamia ᶜudamia** Gy 208:1, 12, 24, Gs 7:5, 8:7 f. (parallel with **ziqia ziqia**); **šuba gabaria ušuba ᶜudamia** DC 40. 35 seven mighty ones and seven ghostly spirits (?).
ᶜudna (אודנא, ܐܕܢܐ, H. אֹזֶן, Ar. أُذُن, Eth. እዝን, Akk. *uznu*, Eg. *idn*) (*a*) ear, (*b*) side, corner (cf. P. گوشه 'corner' from گوش 'ear'). Pl. **-ia**. MG 7:3, 20:3, 104:19. Fem. MG 157:15. (*a*) **uᶜtlun ᶜudnia ulašamin** DC 44 and they have ears but hear not; **uašmitinan ᶜudna** (read **d̲-ᶜudna**) **d̲-br anaša lašimat** CP 60:penult., ML 77:4 and thou madest us hear what the ear of man heard not; (*b*) **miša . . .**

br ʿudnh̲ d̲-iardna CP trs. 19 n. 1, CP 31:3 = Q 14:4 f. = ML 36:1 f. oil . . . produce of the river-side (cf. n. 1).

(**ʿudna 2** a miscop. of **ʿdana 1** in **ʿudnaihun** ATŠ II no. 207 their time).

ʿ(u)huria = **ahuria** behind. Var. **ʿuhria. lʿuhuran** behind us MG 28:14; **lʿuh(u)rh̲ ulaqamh̲** Gy 165:2 behind him and before him; **iardna ʿhdar lʿuh(u)rh̲** Gy 174:13 the jordan returned backwards; **hdart lʿhurak** Gy 174:19 f. thou hast returned backwards (the forms without the 2nd **u** are influenced by **ʿuhra** 'way') MG 197:6 ff., 359:6; **mn qudamai mn ʿuhrai** DC 40. 605 from before me (and) from behind me.

ʿuhra (אורחא, ܐܘܪܚܐ, H. ארח, Sab. ዐለኀ Weber: *Studien* II 28 f., Akk. *urḫu*, Eth. den. verb መርሐ to show the way, lead) road, way, journey MG 66:15, 105:1. Fem., but Gy 331:4 masc. MG 160:2. Pl. **ʿuhrata** MG 170:16. **ʿuhra rahiqtia** AM 3:17 a far journey; **ʿuhrik** JRAS 1937 594:2 thy (fem.) road; **ʿuhratkin** Gy 357:22, Q 37:12 etc. your (fem.) ways MG 179:20; **ʿuhrata pasqia** Gy 388:15 they cut roads; **ʿuhrauata mitpisqin** AM 238:9 roads are cut (as masc. in spite of fem. pl.); **ʿuhra šlim** Gy 331:4 the journey is achieved; **ʿuhra d̲-hiia** Gy 24:12 the way of Life. *Note.* The word exercised a formal influence on the prep. **ʿ(u)huria**, var. **ʿuhria** (q.v.).

Gl. 29:3 **ahra** [*sic*] ازقة *platea* راه .

ʿuzara (from **ʿZR** as H., Phoen., Old-Aram. עזר, Ar. عزر, not as Jew.-Aram. עדר, Syr. ܥܕܪ?) helper? MG 44 n. 1, 123:2. **ʿuzara** AM 175:6, **ʿuzarh̲** Gy 382:9 his helpers?

ʿuzba Gy 32:23 B = **ʿzba** ibid. ACD = **ʿṣba 2** (s.v.) MG 45:1.

ʿuira (עֲוִירָא, ܥܘܝܪܐ Nöld.: *Beiträge* 33, H. עִוֵּר, Eth. ዕውር, Akk. *ḫamāru* blind, *turtu* blindness, rt. **ʿWR** = **AWR**) blind MG 7:6, 117:3. Var. **ʿbira** s.v. Fem. st. emph. **ʿuirtia.** Pl. masc. **ʿuiria. ʿuira d̲-lahazia** DC 44. 1022 blind that does not see; **šakba ʿuira** Or. 331:6, DC 43 J 191 Sleeping-Blind (as name of a demon), miscop. **šakubia ʿuira** DC 43 J 163; **ainaihun ʿuira ulahazilh̲** ATŠ I no. 224 their eyes are blind and see him not; **ʿuiria d̲-iatbia bmasgidia** DC 12. 202, Lond. roll B 432 the blind who sit in the mosques; **ʿuiria pihtit ainaihun** Jb 274:11 I opened the eyes of the blind; **ʿuira bliba nihuia** AM 34:11 he will be blind of heart (callous); **ia ʿuirtia d̲-ʿuira (d̲-)bliba** Gy 220:4 f. O thou blind one (fem.) who is (: art) blind of heart!

ʿukma (rt. **AKM**, אוּכְמָא, ܐܘܟܡܐ) blackness, darkness MG 104:18. **ʿukma nasib** Gy 181:4 it becometh black; **nasbia ʿukma** Gs 65:13 they become black; **unitparaq mn hanath̲ ʿukma** DC 36 no. 173 and he shall be delivered from that blackness.

ʿUL I = **ALL I** (= **AUL II** = **ʿLL**).

ʿUL II = **AUL I.**

ʿula 1 (עַוְלָא, ܥܘܠܐ, H. עָוֶל & fem. עַוְלָה, Ar. عَوْل) evil, iniquity. Doublet **aula 1. zmara d̲-ʿula** Jb 59:9 song of iniquity; **qumba d̲-ʿula** Jb 140:14 the dome of evil Jb ii 72:27.

ʿula 2 (עולא, ܥܘܠܐ, H. עול) embryo, foetus. Masc. var. **ʿulaua.** Doublet **aula 2. mšahṭa ʿulaihun** Q 52:15; **mšahṭa ʿulauaihun** Gy 174:14; **šadia ʿulaiʿn** Gy 224:7 they drop (: miscarry) their embryos; **mšahṭitin ʿulaikin** Q 52:20, **mšahṭitun ʿulauaikin** Gy 174:21 ye drop your embryos; **umn zirai ṣar ʿula bkras ʿmh̲** Gy 244:15 and from my seed was formed the embryo in his mother's womb; **miṣṭarar ʿula** Jb 4:3, 6:1 the embryo is formed; **nʿtia ʿula mn kras ʿmh̲** Gs 7:22 a foetus cometh from its mother's womb; **kd̲ ʿula minh̲ lanpaq** ATŠ II no. 334 when the foetus has not come out from her.

ʿulai (H. אוּלַי II, cuneiform *Ulai*) an ancient name of the river Kârûn in Khuzistan. **mia d̲-ʿulai** Jb 149:4 the water of Ulai (= the river Karun); **diglat uʿulai upraš** DC 7 the Tigris, Karun, and Euphrates.

ʿulama (Ar. pl. عُلَمَاء) AM 283:37 learned men.

ʿulana 1 (= **aulana** (*a*) wicked person, evil-doer, (*b*) pain, sickness. Pl. **-ia.** (*a*) **ʿzil ʿzil ʿulana** Jb 146:1 f. go, go, wicked fellow!; **ʿulania ukadabia** AM 85:12 evil persons and liars; (*b*) **lkul mahra uʿulana** DC 19 for every sickness and pain.

ʿulana 2 for **ʿluana** in **ʿulanun** DC 22. 388 = **ʿluanun** Gy 392:20.

ʿuluantia (corruption of ܥܠܠܬܐ? fruit, harvest) crops, fruit-crop. **ʿluantia uʿburia nimlun** AM 226:16 crops and harvests will be ample.

ʿulʿul (a mod. corruption of **ʿula 2**) unborn child, embryo: **uʿulʿul d̲-bkarsia** DC 46 and the embryo in her womb.

ʿulṣana (rt. **ALṢ**, ܐܘܠܨܢܐ) tribulation, suffering, privation, straitness, hemming-in, misfortune, difficulties, restriction, oppression. **uʿulṣana maška** AM 192:14 and he will meet with difficulties; **kupna uʿulṣana** AM 208:11 famine and privation; **šn ʿtlata ʿulṣana nihuia** AM for three years there will be privation; **ʿulṣana d̲-šibiahia minh̲ baṭil** DC 34. 538 the grievousness of the planets will cease from him; **ʿulṣana bmapqata hauia ʿlauaiin** ATŠ I no. 239 suffering will come upon them at death; **ʿulṣana nistar** AM 211:ult. f. he will seek refuge (from?) privation; **mahra uʿulṣana** DC 43 D 15 illness and suffering; **kd̲ maṭilun ʿulṣana** DAb when tribulation comes upon them; **napišbh̲ ʿulṣana balma** Gy 61:5 tribulation will increase in the world; **d̲-ʿulṣana btibil sabla** Gs 88:18 f. that endureth tribulation on earth.

ʿUM (Syr. ܥܡܡ PSm 2834, ܥܡܡ LS 522 a, Ar. غام) af. to obscure, suppress, darken, extinguish.

Af. Inf. **umiumia gaṭulia ʿstarata** DC 26 and for the extinction (?) and slaying of the astartes.

Der.: **ʿuma**?

ʿuma (rt. **ʿUM**?) darkness, obscurity, the dark.

Var. **ʿma 3. kbiš hšuka bʿuma** ML 166:10 = CP 136:3, CP trs. 102:n. 1 (var. **bʿma**) the Darkness is crushed down into the Dark (? cf. ML 166 n. 2, ZDMG 1955 p. 361:bottom).

ʿumama (ܐܺܝܡܳܡܳܐ, Akk. *immu* day as opposite of night, H. only adverbially יוֹמָם in day-time Nöld. ZDMG xl 721, *Neue Beiträge* 133, Brockelm. i 474) day (as opposite of night), day-time MG 19:7, 140:17. Pl. **-ia. bʿumama** (*often*) by day; **lilia uʿumama** ATŠ I no. 142 (*& often*) night and day; **tlatin ʿumamia . . . utlatin liliauata** ATŠ I no. 263 thirty days . . . and thirty nights; **ʿupania d-ʿumama** s. **ʿupania** (*a*).

ʿumamata 1 (ܡܘܡܬܐ transformed by the influence of **ʿumamata** MG 130:4 ff.) oath(s), vow(s), conjuration(s) MG 19:9, 130:4. Used as both sg. & pl. MG 168:9 f. **latimun ʿumamata d-kadba uʿumamatkun latipkun** Gy 20:11 f. swear ye not false oaths and pervert not your oaths; **lanʿda braza d-ʿumamatan** Gy 110:14 knoweth not the secret of our oaths; **lanigalinin lʿumamatan** Gy 110: 15 revealeth not our oaths; **ašar ʿl ʿumamatun** Gy 112:23 they confirmed their oaths; **ašar ʿl ʿumamata** Gy 112:24; **ʿumamata qadmaita** DC 37 the first oath; **qabil ʿumamatik** DC 40. 105 receive thy conjurations.

ʿumamata 2 JRAS 1937 p. 593 pl. of **ʿma.**

Euman AM 205 Oman (in Arabia).

ʿumana (אוּמָן, ܐܽܘܡܳܢܳܐ < Akk. *ummānu*) skilful, artist(ic), expert, craftsman MG 122: paen. f. Pl. **-ia. ʿumana sdira** Gy 214:23 a skilled craftsman; **ʿumania hinun d-kulhun sainata** Gy 279:17 they are experts in all evil deeds; **uʿumana gadana hauia** AM (*often*) and he will be a lucky craftsman; **miša uhamar liad ʿumania kulhun** ŠQ 15:9 oil and wine all (prepared) by experts; **ṭaba d-liad ʿumania mištia d-ʿštia** Or. 326:21 the good man who drank it at the hands of the experts.

ʿumba (עוּבָּא, ܥܽܘܒܳܐ, Ar. غُبّ) bosom MG 76:22, 105:6. Var. **ʿmba 2** s.v. **dmik bʿumbik natran** CP 175:15 = ML 214:1 thy tears drop into thy bosom; **binia bisrak lʿumbak ubinia ʿumbak lilbušak** DC 44. 1025 between thy flesh and thy bosom and between thy bosom and thy garment (i.e. between the inner and outer garment (?)).

ʿumbia (cf. preced.) pl. loopings, convolutions. **ruha hʿ d-iatba ʿl karsa d-ʿumbia d-mia umitiqria mirta** Or. 329 nn. 8 & 9 the spirit that sits on the belly, that is the convolutions of the (lower) intestine, and is called gall (or 'bitterness').

umbra occ. var. of **ʿmbra.** Mod. pl. **ʿumbraria** DC 46. 15:13.

ʿumušiata, ʿumišiata (rt. **AMŠ = ʿMŠ**) pl. submersions. **tlata ʿumušiata** (var. **ʿumišiata**) ATŠ (DC 6 & 36) (often, e.g. II no. 41) three submersions.

ʿmna DC 37. 182 = **mna 1.**

ʿumṣa (Talm. אוּמְצָא) morsel, fragment, piece torn off or broken off, strip MG 7:4. Pl. **-ia. ʿumṣa d-šamina** Gy 183:11 a fat morsel; **prut ʿumṣa** Q 32:28 = Morg. 235/57:ult. break off a morsel; **ʿumṣa d-saqa** Jb 130:3 f. s. **saqa**; **ʿl ʿumṣia . . . hadria** Gs 31:4 they beg for morsels; **tlata ʿumṣia** ATŠ II no. 208 three fragments; **uakaliun tlata ʿumṣia bmihla** DC 41. 184 and they ate three morsels with salt; **ʿumṣia d-kitana** DC 43 strips of linen.

ʿumqa (עֻמְקָא, ܥܽܘܡܩܳܐ) depth, profundity MG 7:3, 104:18. Pl. **-ia. kma ʿumqa** ATŠ II no. 310 what is its depth? **ʿumqia d-naṣiruta** Gy 197 ff. the profundities of Naṣoraeism, **ʿumqia d-hšuka** ATŠ II 72, 255 depths of darkness; **ʿumqia lagṭia** ATŠ II no. 386 they take to the depths; **ʿumqia d-iama** JRAS 1937 591:18 the depths of the sea.

ʿumrat a var. of **murat** (s. ***murta**).

ʿusura s. **ʿsura.**

ʿusṭlia ML 177:8 for **ʿuṣṭlia.**

ʿusiana (rt. **ASA III**) oppression MG 45 n. 1. **ʿusiana ubusiana** s. **ASA III.**

ʿuspar 1 Gy 205:22 D = **spar 1** AC = **ʿ:par 1** B (st. cstr. of **sipra 1**).

ʿ(u)spar 2 s. **spar 2.**

ʿuspar 3 (rt. **SPR II**) cutting, wounding, blow? **unišqup bʿuspar** DC 3. xvi:7, CP 21:14 and striketh with a wounding (blow)? CP trs. 12 n. 2.

ʿuspia, ʿuspih(i)a varr. of **ʿspia, ʿspihata** (pl. of **sipta**). **malala lʿuspai** DC 51 speech to my lips; **ʿuspihak parṭit** DC 37. 46 thou sneerest.

ʿuspiria occ. var. of **(ʿ)spiria.**

ʿusraiil Gy 333:9 for **(ʿ)sraiil** Israel MSt 101 n. 1, Ginzā 342 n. 2.

ʿustad (P.-Ar. استاد) Zotb. 219a:8 (*& very often in colophons*) craftsman, skilled workman.

ʿustana AM 235:16 = **stana.**

ʿupania pl. (H. pl. אוֹפַנִּים) (*a*) wheels, spheres, revolutions, periodic divisions of time (esp. day and night), (*b*) revolutions (aspects or complexities) of truth, (*c*) enfoldings, enwrappings (of clothes etc.), lappings or billows (of water). ML 129 n. 5, Ginzā 191 n. 2, 194 n. 3, ZDMG 1903, pp. 430 ff., MR 116, MSchr. 81 n. 1. (*a*) **ʿupania d-ʿumama nihun d-lilia** (& vice versa) Gy 189: 21 f. the wheels (?) of the day will change to those of the night MG 316:20; **ʿštqil ʿupania d-ʿumama hun d-lilia** (& vice versa) Gy 190:7 f. the wheels of the day were changed and became those of the night; (*b*) **ʿupania d-kušṭa** CP 104:8 = Q 53:28 = ML 129:12 (cf. מושל אופנים Sir. 50:27) explanations of truth CP trs. 75 n. 3; (*c*) **hilulia uʿupania** Gy 47:23 garments and coverings; **ʿupania d-mia** Gy 48:2, 194:4 billowing waves of water.

ʿupia (rt. **APP**) DC 43 I 121 weariness, infirmities.

ʿuṣa (Talm. חוּצָא, Syr. ܚܽܘܨܳܐ, Ar. خوص Löw 116) (palm-)leaf, shoot, stick, stock, stem, prickles, prickly leaf. Pl. **ʿuṣania** MG 61:16, 169:27. **ʿuṣa biša** Gy 9:1, AM 167:18 weeds or undergrowth; **ʿuṣania uiṣmania** Gy 33:17, 378:34 leaves and medicinal herbs; **piqunia uʿuṣania** Gy 89:16 flowers and foliage; **uʿuṣa npalbh** Gy 188:9 and a leaf falleth into it;

ʿuṣania uqadahia DC 7 leaves and blossoms; **br kana biša br ʿuṣa ḏ-mrara** DC 51 son of an evil stem, son of a bitter stock; **ʿuṣa kdaba usaina** DC 43 J 84 (obscure).

ʿuṣar st. abs. & cstr. of ʿuṣra (q.v.), used also of heavenly beings (ibid.).

ʿuṣba 1 (for **ʿṣba 2** MG 45:2, **ʿṣba 1** Jb ii 222 n. 8) dye, colour (Nöld.), glimmer (Lidzb.). **ʿuṣba ḏ-nhura** Gy 75:7, 323:3, 338:4 f., Gs 135:4 s. **ʿṣba 2.**

ʿuṣba 2 occasionally for **ʿṣba 2.**

ʿuṣba 3 (cf. Jew.-Aram. עצב ithpe. to grieve, H. עצב II id., Ar. غَضِبَ to be angry) grief, pain, toil. Pl. **-ia. uanpiq minẖ šuba ʿuṣbia ḏ-muta** DC 51. 142, 186 and cause to depart from him the seven pains of death.

ʿuṣṭa (cf. P. colloquial *usta*) for **ʿustad.** Often in colophons as a title or epithet in names: **ʿuṣṭa hadat, ʿuṣṭa manṣur** etc.

ʿuṣṭal st. abs. & cstr. of **ʿuṣṭla** (q.v.).

ʿuṣṭamuma = **ṣṭmuma.** Pl. **-ia. hirbia sipia uʿuṣṭamumia** DC 44. 1565, DC 37. 304 f. (*& often*) swords, blades, and spears; **giraiun uʿuṣṭamumun** DC 44. 201 f. their arrows and spears.

ʿ(u)ṣṭartia s. **ʿṣṭartia.**

ʿuṣṭuna = **ʿṣṭuna** (it is difficult to distinguish the two). Pl. **-ia.** (CP trs. 54 n. 1 and 233 n. 5) **ʿuṣṭuna adinqia riša** DC 6, ATŠ a trunk without a head; **asia . . . lʿuṣṭunai uhiklai** (*often in exorcisms*) a healer . . . for my body and fabric; **nigda . . . ldrabšia lʿṣṭunia** CP 356:13 he unfurled his banner on its pole (support); **šitin uarbia kiniania hun lʿṣṭuna** ATŠ no. 220 there are sixty-four principles inherent in the body; **atina mn ʿṣṭuna ḏ-hu tibil šumẖ** ATŠ I no. 221 I come from the Body which is called the Earth; **ʿuṣṭuna unišimta** (*often*) the body and soul; **alma ḏ-mištrin ʿuṣṭunia ḏ-šumia uarqa** DC 43 A 63 until the supports of heaven and earth are loosed; **ʿuṣṭuna ḏ-qumba ḏ-ʿšumia** DAb the supporting-column of the vault of heaven; **ʿuṣṭuna rba ḏ-asauata** DC 43 C 5 the great corporation of healings; **ʿuṣṭuna ḏ-pagra** DC 51 physical body; **ʿṣṭuna rba** CP 140 (d):17 (personified). Personified: Gy 333:8 ff. MR 128:bottom & n. 2.

ʿuṣṭla = **ʿṣṭla.** St. abs. & cstr. **ʿuṣṭal.** Pl. **ʿuṣṭlia. ʿuṣṭlia ḏ-ziua** Gy 210:13 f. etc. (*often*) raiments of light. **ʿl ʿuṣṭal gmir iatibna** CP 69:13, ML 85:2 I sit upon a perfect garment; **ʿuṣṭia ḏ-bisra uzma** Gy 193:16 vestment of flesh and blood (cf. s. **ʿṣṭuna**).

ʿuṣra (אוֹצְרָא, ܐܘܨܪܐ, H. אֽוֹצָר, Ar. وَصَرٌ Nöld. MG 134 n. 6, *Neue Beiträge* 204, Akk. *maṣ-ṣartu, niṣirtu, iṣru* store-house) store, treasure, thought, mind. St. abs. & cstr. **ʿuṣar** MG 22:16, 23:14, 134:17, 149:28. Pl. **ʿuṣria.** St. abs. & cstr. often of higher beings. **ʿuṣar** CP (see Index); **aumitak bʿuṣar ṣamar ḏ-qarilẖ** DC 37. 531 I have conjured thee by Oṣar, the Repressor, as they call him; **ʿuṣar hai** Q 16:16, 31:14, 58:28, Gy 189:15, 196:4, 295:17; **ʿuṣar hiia** Q 16:15 = CP 37:14 = ML 43:9 Treasure-of-Life; **ʿuṣar hai** CP 68:penult. Jb ii 201: 13 ff., Wid. iii 57 & n. 3; **ʿuṣar nhur** Q 26:11, 32:2, **ʿuṣar nhura** Q 53:18, Gy 203:2 Treasure-of-Light; **ʿuṣar qadmaia — ʿuṣar nhura** Q 27:6; **ʿuṣar nhura rba** Q 59:23; **had manda had ʿuṣar** Q 31:13; **ʿuṣar ḏ-pta pihta** CP 56:12 = Q 26:3 = ML 72:5 Mind (?) which created the *pihta* (?). St. cstr. with proper meaning: **ʿuṣar ʿuṣria** Oxf. 57a the treasure of treasures; **ʿuṣar libẖ** Gy 150:11, 244:5 cf. θησαυρὸς τῆς καρδίας Matt. 12:35, Luke 6:45; **ʿuṣar razaiun** Gy 243:23 their secret thought. St. emph., with suff. & pl.: **pta ʿuṣra** Q 27:5 he opened the treasure; **nipilgẖ lʿuṣrẖ** Q 67:13 he divideth his treasure; **ʿuṣria ḏ-mia** Q 59:24, Gy 288:20 the treasures of water; **ʿ(u)ṣria ḏ-ziua** Gs 26:24, 27:4, 28:14, 19, 30:2, 5, 31:19, 24, 33:2, Gy 182:24, 184:2, 185:10, 187:13; **ʿuṣria ḏ-nhura** CP 30:10 the treasures of light; **paršit bʿuṣria** CP 51:12 f. = Q 24:1 = ML 67:3 f. thou discernest minds; **samik ʿuṣria ṣalaiia** Q 70:24 supporter of sinking hearts; **šra bʿuṣraihun** Gy 242:18 he has put to their mind; **pahtilia ainaniata ḏ-ʿuṣrai** DC open the springs of my thought CP 199(R):18 **mn ʿuṣrẖ baiia ḏ-napiq pugdamia** ATŠ II no. 218 he tries to issue orders according to his thought; **raza rba uiaqira . . . ʿuṣra bhira** ATŠ I no. 229 a great and precious mystery . . . a chosen treasure.

ʿuṣrana (rt. **AṢR**) DC 41. 281 squeezing, pressing; 'treasure'? (food-scraps on the *ṭariana*) **bʿuṣrana hauia** DC 41. 281 should be with the 'treasure' (?).

ʿuṣruna (cf. ʿuṣra) treasure? Pl. **-ia. ʿuṣrunia hadtia ḏ-lamšaria** DC 3 new and virgin treasures (?).

ʿUQ = **AUQ** (= **HUQ**).

ʿUR nišmata ḏ-nitpašẖ unitasia unitiatar DC 40. 974 souls who are rescued, healed, and aroused, awaked.

ʿUR I & II s. **AUR I & II.**

ʿWR s. **AWR.**

ʿur (Nöld. H. אור fire MG xxix 14; Brandt: correlation with the Ὡραῖος of the Ophites MR 190 n. 4, ERE viii 383 & n. 1, cf. also Bousset HpGn 30 & n. 1 who compares also the Old-Bab. god *Ur*) Ur, the king of darkness, son of Ruha MG 7:2, MSchr 130 n. 3, Kessler PRE 166, 170, MMII 253 n. 3. **kḏ haza amar ʿur ruha ʿmẖ naida** Gy 88:1 when Ur spake thus, Ruha, his mother, trembled; **zihira ḏ-mn pumẖ ḏ-ʿur npaq** Gy 83:15 venom which came out of Ur's mouth; **ʿur maraihun ugabarun** Gy 146:12 Ur their lord and giant; **ʿur mlik hšuka** Gy 86:10, **ʿur malka ḏ-hšuka** PD 393 (*& often*) Ur, the king of darkness; **ʿur marẖ ḏ-hšuka** Jb 181:1, 196:14, Gy 126:13, 158:21, 164:6, 313:16 etc. Ur, the lord of darkness; **ʿur mara ḏ-hšuka** Gy 377:9 id.; **ʿur gabara ḏ-hšuka** Gy 150 ff., 156:1 Ur, the giant of the darkness; **ʿur gabara qarabtana** Gy 156:11 Ur the giant-warrior; **qin ʿma ḏ-ʿmẖ ḏ-ʿur** Gy 145:18, 203:19, 21, 204:8, 10 Qin mother of Ur's mother; **brẖ bukra ḏ-hu ʿur** Gy 126:15 her (i.e. Ruha's) first-born son, that is Ur; **ʿur mitnahaz mn duktẖ** Gy 85:19 Ur moved boisterously from his place; **lʿur man ʿusrẖ** Jb 6:12 who tied Ur?; **ʿur bminilat**

hiia ʿstar Jb 8:1 Ur was fettered by the Word-of-Life.

ʿura (H. אוֹר, Akk. *urru* light) glory, light, splendour. **ʿurh̲ umalkuth̲ d̲-šamiš** *Florilegium*, the glory and majesty of the sun.

ʿuraba (coll.) Arabs. **šihiana d̲-ʿuraba** DC 51:coloph., Ṣâb.'s AM coloph. governor of the Arabs.

ʿuraita (אוֹרָיְתָא, ܐܘܪܝܬܐ, H. תּוֹרָה, late H. הוֹרָיָה, הוֹרָאָה, Eth. loan-w. ኦሪት MG 134 n. 4) Thora MG xxix:11, 134:13. Var. **auraita. rabtia ʿuraita** Jb 70:1 the Great Thora; **bʿuraita** Jb 71:14 in the Thora; **ʿuraita biṭlat bʿurašlam** Jb 82:1 f. the Thora has become void in Jerusalem; **ʿuraita bkanpak huat** Jb 138:8 the Thora was in thy bosom; **atnai lʿuraita** Jb 140:3 f. put the Thora (to thy bosom, cf. ii 136 n. 2); **kidbu lʿuraita usadru** Jb 198:10 f. they wrote the Thora and set it in order; **kdabun mn ʿuraita ʿtinsib** Jb 199:6 f. their Book (: Qur'ān) was taken out from the Thora; **apiklh̲ lʿuraita** Gy 56:8 (var. **auraita** Sh. 'Abd.'s copy) he perverteth the Thora; **uṣublh̲ bmia d̲-ʿuraita** AM 134:19 and put him into Thora-water (water in which a scroll of the Thora has been immersed).

ʿuraš CP 238:3 = DC 38 par. name of a spirit of fertility, marriage-broker?

ʿurašlam (Nab. אורשלם Lidzb.: *Hdb. d. nordsem. Epigr.* 210, Syr. ܐܘܪܫܠܡ, Eg.-Aram. ירושלם Sachau i 18, Jew.-Aram. יְרוּשְׁלֵם, on Jew. coins ירושלם & ירושלים Lidzb. op. cit. 290, Ass. *Ursalimmu*; Mand. form closer to Aram. & to Ar. أُورِشَلَم than to H. יְרוּשָׁלַיִם *qrē perpetuum* for יְרוּשָׁלֵם) Jerusalem MR 128, GGA 1890 p. 400, MSt 117 n. 10. **mata ʿurašlam** Gy 329:13, 331:9 f., 332:15, 17, **ʿurašlam mata** Gy 29:16, 50:10, 381:14, 329:18 etc. (Gy 329:16 both in one line) MG 319:20 f., **ʿurašlam mahuza** Gy 23:18, 27:7, **mahuza ʿurašlam** Gy 29:16 the city of J.; **ʿnuš ʿutra atia umasgia bʿurašlam** Gy 29:5 Anuš Uthra will come and go to J.; **ʿurašlam mdinta d̲-iahuṭaiia** Gy 45:13 f., 218:24 Jerusalem the city of the Jews; **gupna ʿtahzia bʿurašlam d̲-qudamh̲ aula laiit** Gy 178:2 f. a Vine appeared in J., in view of which there is no evil; **alma d̲-ʿtbiniat ʿurašlam** Gy 302:13 until J. was built; **mn d̲-ʿtbiniat ʿurašlam** Gy 302:14 since (the time) when J. was built; **mn iuma d̲-hirbat ʿurašlam** Gy 384:14 from the day on which J. was destroyed.

ʿurba 1 (עוֹרְבָא = ܥܘܪܒܐ, H. & mod. H. עוֹרֵב, Ar. غُرَاب, Akk. *āribu*; cf. Schulthess 48, Nöld. ZDMG xliv 155) crow MG 107: anteantep. Pl. **-ia.** Masc. **uapqh̲ nu lʿurba** Gy 380:22 and Noah let a crow go out; **uazal ʿurba uaška lašlanda** Gy 380:24 and the crow went and found carrion; **uazlat iauna uaškath̲ lʿurba d̲-iatib ʿl ašlanda** Gy 381:3 f. and the dove went and found the crow sitting on the carrion; **zma d̲-ʿurba ʿkuma** AM 131:20 blood of a black crow; **kd̲ qaria ʿurba** AM 253:5 when a crow croaks.

ʿurba 2 (עַרְבְתָא, ܥܪܒܬܐ, H. & mod. H. עֲרָבָה, Akk. *urbatu*, Ar. غَرَب) willow(-tree). Fem. st. abs.? **ninisbh̲ ʿurba unisaq ldiqla** JRAS 1937 592:antepenult. we will take away the willow and raise the date-palm (read **nʿiasiq** . . . we will set up the date-palm?, an allusion to **ʿuira** 'blind' and **DUQ I** 'to look', hence: we will remove blindness and set up vision?).

ʿurba 3 s. **ʿurbata.**

ʿurbana (rt. **ARB II** = **ʿRB**) mixture, intermingling, alloy, adulteration, confusion. **ʿurbana biša** Gy 7:23, 32:3; **hiia d̲-laiit ʿurbana bgauaihun** Gy 176:12 Life in which there is no confusion; **ʿurbana bhaṭaiia . . . lanihuilun** Gy 246:4 f. they shall not mix with sinners etc.; **uʿurbana d̲-tibil lahualun** Gy 246:11 and they contained no earthly alloy; **ʿurbana d̲-kadba** Gy 259:3 mixing with lie; **ʿurbana ukadba** Gy 310:9, 373:1 adulteration and lie; **ʿurbana lamqabla** Gy 215:8, ATŠ II no. 29 receiveth no intermingling; **laiit ʿurbana binataiun** ATŠ II no. 193 there is no confusion amongst them.

ʿurbata (pl. of **ʿurba 3**, cf. **arba 1**) pl. ferries (?), **umarkabata ʿurbata d̲-hbila** DC 20 and ships (and) ferries of destruction.

ʿurubta, ʿurupta (עֲרוּבְתָּא, ܥܪܘܒܬܐ) (*a*) Friday, (*b*) week. (*a*) **kukba ʿurubta libat** AM 107:22 Venus is the star of Friday; **iuma d̲-rahaṭia . . . d̲-ʿrubta** HG on Friday. . . .; (*b*) **bšuba iumia d̲-ʿurupta** AM in the seven days of the week; **sabiع ʿurupta** s. **sabiع.**

ʿuria (doubtf. cf. Jb ii 149 n. 2) Jb 147:11, 162:4?

ʿurk (cf. foll.) mod. expr. for 'with' (pronounced *orke*). **ʿurk عaraq bartang** DC 46 with the juice of a plantain root.

ʿurka (Ass. *arâku*) (rt. **ARK** = **ʿRK**) length. **ʿurkʿ kṣurth̲** AM the length of his illness; **hauia zirta hda ʿurkh̲** s. **zirta**; **ʿurkh̲ uputih̲** Gy 160:13 its length and breadth; **zaga ʿurkil gusparta d̲-tarnaula d̲-zaga hiuara hak d̲-ʿurka d̲-gusparta** AM 134:19 (all expressions are synonyms of 'cock', **ʿurkil gusparta** = **ʿurka d̲-gusparta** 'long of comb', hence simply:) a white cock.

ʿurkil s. preced. AM 134:18.

ʿurnasa (Jew. אוּרְנָס?) spindle? **uaudat uʿthambalt kd̲ ʿurnasa** JRAS 1937 593:antep. 594:5 thou wanderest lost and art twisted like a spindle.

ʿurpail, ʿurp(a)iil, ʿurpiʿil, ʿurpʿil a light spirit, mentioned with **marp(i)ʿil** (q.v.).

ʿurpta a var. of **ʿurupta** BZ 193 n. 7.

ʿuršlam a miscop. of **ʿurašlam.**

ʿuša (ܥܘܫܐ Löw 343) marsh, swamp. CP 51:1 **uša utapala** = ML 66 n. 3. **ʿuša utipala** Q 23:27 = ML 66:7 swamp and mud.

ʿuš(a)na (ܐܘܫܢܐ < Av. *waršni*, mod. P. گُشن Lagarde: *Abh.* 11:17, Nöld. ZDMG xxviii 95 f.) stallion, steed, strong male (beast), ram. MG xxxii n. 1, Jb ii 23 n. 1, Ginzā 227 n. 3. Pl. **-ia. gamba d-ʿušna** s. **gamba; uʿl ʿušnaikun ʿtib** Jb 15:13 and sit on your stallions; **ʿutria npal ʿl anpaiun umn ʿušnaiun bʿmruma lalagṭia** Jb 17:11 f. the uthras fell on their faces and did not take with their horses to the firmament; **anhit mn ʿušanh** (var. **ʿš-** D) Jb 18:1 f. he alighted from his horse; **ulpumh d-ʿušana** (var. **ʿšana** ACD) **qarbin** Jb 180:10 f. they approach the mouth of the strong one; **puma d-hazin ʿušana d-hu ʿur** Jb 181:1 the mouth of that strong one who is Ur; similarly **lpuma d-ʿušna šaplia** Gy 225:24 they sink into the maw of the strong one; **kma ʿkbuš ʿušania** Jb 203:4 how long must I tame stallions . . .?; **šuba ʿušnia** DC 27. 540 seven stallions; **ʿušnia d-gaunia gaunia uznia znia** DC 48. 173 steeds of every colour and kind; **gablia ʿšnia** Jb 44:6 rams ii 49 n. 2; **mašp(i)lilh lqina d-kulhun ʿušnh** Jb 27:8 they degrade the stock of all the males.

ʿušumia AM 257:28 = **ʿšumia.**

ʿ(u)šma s. **šma.**

***ʿušta** s. **ʿšta 1.**

ʿutana (אֵיתָנָא Levy, cf. **ʿiut**) powerful MG 139:14, 146:23. **ʿutana ugabara** Gy 88:6 powerful and giant-like; **ʿutana giutana rbutana** s. **giutana; nirig ʿutana** Morg. 257/6:21 powerful Mars.

ʿutra (Nöld. עוּתְרָא, ܥܘܬܪܐ 'wealth' cf. *δύναμις, αἰών* etc. of Gnostic systems MG 104 n. 4; P. Kahle: Sam. ࠏࠉࠕࠓࠅࠕ = Ar. جيوش *Engelsheere* Oriens Christianus 99 n. 2) heavenly spirits, generic name given to spirits of life MG xxviii 11, 104 n. 4, 182 n. 3, Lidzb. *Uthra u. Malakha* OSt 537–545, Nöld. ZA xxx 156, E. Kuhn-Festschr. 133 n. 4; AF 232, MMII 94 n. 2. Pl. **-ia. anuš ʿutra** Gy 377:6 etc., **anuš ʿutra šliha** Gy 289:10, 14 (cf. s. **anuš**); **ʿutra sdira umsadra** Gy 324:21 etc. (cf. s. **SDR** pass. pt. pe.); **bihram ʿutra** Gy 377:23, **bihram uram ʿutria** Q 60:18; **ptahil ʿutra** Gy 93:8, 19, 94:1, 7, 309:13, 310:13, 311:5; **ʿutra niha** Gs 73:19 (*& often*), pl. Gs 73:19, **ʿutra niha umqaima** Gy 77:8, 334:4 twice (*& often*), pl. Gy 74:1; **ʿutra mšarhibana** Gy 241:16, 20; **abatur ʿutra** Gy 377:7; **ʿštadar ʿutra** Gy 12:3; **ʿutra d-rabuta** Gy 327:24, 340:21 ff., 341:24; **ziua and mana ʿutra** Gy 104:7 f.; **hibil ʿutra** Gy 113:23, 114:24, 126:7; **zihrun ʿutra** Gy 127:12; **iupin ʿutra** Gy 127:20; **ʿutra mqaima** Gy 69:24; **turʿiil ʿutra** Q 59:26; **taurʿil ʿutra** Gy 129:4; **barbag ʿutra** Gy 129:2; **aba d-ʿutria** CP 11:1, Gy 101:17, 19, 297:17 ff., Q 4:19, PD 30, 34, 88, 171 ff., 303, 361, 813, 826, 895; **aprištḥ ʿl ʿutria uʿl gupnia uʿl ʿlania dakiia** Gy 305:26 I informed him about the uthras, the vines, and the pure trees; **ʿutria mn hilbunia smikiun** PD 941 the uthras rested in (?) their mansions; **ʿutria bnia nhura** PD 894, 929; **malka d-ʿutria** Gy 108:12, 346:7 f., 23 f. etc.; **mdinat ʿutria** Q 55:24, Gy 315:12; **hibil ušitil uanuš ʿutria** Gy 101:25; **ʿutria umalkia d-almia d-nhura** Morg. 179:5 the uthras and angels of the worlds of light; **ʿm ʿutria** Gy 292:19 with the uthras; **ana uʿutria ahai** Gy 125:4 I and the uthras my brethren; **šilmai unidbai ʿutria** Q 40:9, 59:33; **ʿutria d-nhura** Q 67:5; **ʿutria d-iukabar qra** Gy 367:1 the uthras which Y. created; **ʿutria kasiia qadmaiia** Q 26:3 f.; **trin ʿutria** Gy 27:6, 50:5, 90:10, 291:35; **ʿutria trin** Gy 251:5; **tlata ʿutria** Gy 25:8, 89:20, 92:19, 108:16, 129:24, Gs 74:20; **ʿutria tlata** Gy 70:5 ff., 250:16, 251:2 ff., 7 ff. (MR 122 f.); **tlata ʿutria = tlata gubria** Gy 256:13 ff.; **srin uarba ʿutria bnia nhura** Morg. 6:2, 88:1; **ʿutrak ahak d-hinun bnak** Gy 250:13 f. thy uthras, thy brethren, who are thy sons. Very frequent.

ʿutrana DC 22. 47 a var. of **iutrana** Gy 50:23.

ʿzabia masc. pl., fem. pl. **ʿzabata** varr. of **ʿzi-. gubria ʿzabia uʿnšia ʿzibata** DC 22. 216 var. of Gy 222:21 (s. **ʿzibia**); **ʿnšia ugubria ʿzabia** P.A. xii unmated women and men (unable to mate?).

ʿzairab Jb 75:5 one of the ancestors of Zacharias.

ʿzapta (rt. **YZP**) AM loan.

ʿzara Sh. 'Abd.'s copy's var. of **ʿuzara** Gy 382:9.

ʿZB s. **AZB.**

ʿzba 1 (cf. s. **ʿuzba**) = **ʿṣba 2** MG 45:1.

ʿzba 2 = **ʿziba** (q.v.). Pl. masc. **ʿzbia,** fem. **ʿzbata. ʿzbia uʿzbata** Gs 33:22 for the more common **ʿzibata** (q.v.). Gl. 36:12 **ʿzba** اعزب *viduus* عزب.

ʿzhiraita occasionally for **zhiraita. maṣbuta ʿzhiraita** DC 50 (cf. s. **zhiraita**).

ʿZZ s. **AZZ.**

ʿziba (pass. pt. pe. of **ʿZB = AZB,** cf. עֲזוּבָה, عَزَب) adj. designating different forms of celibacy. celibate, monk, person under a ban sexually; widower. Fem. **ʿzibta** unmarried woman not virgin. Pl. masc. **-ia,** abs. **-in,** fem. **-ata.** MG 117:3. Varr. **ʿzb-, ʿzab-** s.vv. **ʿzibia uʿzibata** Gy 222:21 monks and nuns; **bakina uazilna kd ʿziba** Morg. 262/16:6 f. (var. **ʿzibta** DC 44. 1012) I walk lamenting like a widower (var. widow); **alma alit kd ʿziba** Morg. 262/16:10 why lamentest thou like a widower?; **hazin d-laalḥ** [*sic*] **kd ʿzibin** ibid. 12 f. that one who does not wail like widowers; **šaria ʿzibia ušria** [*sic*] **ptulia d-mṭanpin** P.A. xii loosing the abandoned (or those under tabu) and loosing virgin men who are polluted.

ʿz(i)qta s. **ʿsqta.**

ʿZL I s. **AZL III.**

ʿZL II s. **AZL I.**

ʿzla (rt. **ʿZL I = AZL III,** אִיזְלָא & אוּזִילְתָּא, ܥܙܠܐ & ܐܙܠܐ) web, net, woven material MG 102:8. Var. **azla** s.v. Pl. **ʿzlia** (often), **ʿzlalia** AM 155. **ʿzlak** Jb 162:4 f. thy net; **bʿzlaikun** Gs 57:23 in your nets; **bʿzla d-šuba lanapil** Jb 59:13 f. will not fall into the net of the Seven; **ugaṭralak ʿzlia** Jb 155:1 and she will knot thee webs; **mpalgalun lmia bʿzlia** Jb 155:3 she will divide water with woven threads; **d-maštin ʿzlia** DC 43 J 93 that weave nets.

Gl. 100:1 **aizla** [*sic*, cf. Bab.-Aram. form above] شبک *rete* دام.

ʿzlat ('she-span' rt. **ʿZL I** (but acc. to Lidzb. 'she-went' **AZL II**), a female genie ML xi, Ind. *Höhere Wesen* s.v., consort of Šišlam CP trs. 105 n. 2, Siouffi 40:34, MMII 72 n. 3. **ʿzlat rabtia** PD 31, 296, Q 10:19 = ML 28:4, Morg. 10:4, 112:6, ML 171:3, CP, see under in Index, Oxf. roll f 53 etc., **zlat rabtia** CP 140d:11, Morg. 8:6; with procl. prep. **bizlat rabtia** RD B 99; **tibil ḏ-ʿzlat** RD B 35 the earth of Ezlat. In RD 7 identified with **libat,** although in PD 31 she is a source of light and wife of **mara ḏ-rabuta,** in ATŠ II no. 310 ff. the consort of the Great Šišlam.

ʿzqta (עִזְקְתָא, ܥܙܩܬܐ, ܥܙܩܬܐ) = **ʿsqta** (q.v.) MG 109:20. **uatia lʿzqta** Gy 144:6 and he brought the seal-ring.

ʿZR the rt. of **ʿuzara** (q.v.).

ʿzruta = **zruta. pt ʿzruta ḏ-ʿlul ʿkara** DC 40. 195 f. daughter of Ellul the Husbandman.

ʿṭak (Sam. ℵ MG 202 n. 1, Gr. τάχα MG xxx 30) Gy 258:1, 22, 324:6, 325:7 perhaps, perchance MG 202:6.

ʿṭarsus AM 202 = **ṭarsus.**

ʿṭbia DC 22. 407 a miscop. of **ʿbṭia** (s. **ʿbṭa**).

ʿṬP I & II s. **AṬP I & II.**

ʿṬR s. **AṬR I.**

ʿiai = **ʿuai** q.v. and s. **ʿUA.**

ɛid Zotb. 223b (2nd text 19) a name.

ʿida s. **ʿda.**

ɛidauat (Ar. عداوة) AM 275:30 enmity. Var. **ɛadauata** s.v.

ɛidalat (Ar. عدالة) AM 281:38. Var. **ɛidul** s.v.

ʿidan Zotb. 221b:16 a man's name.

ɛidul (Ar. عَدْل) Ṣâb.'s AM justice, equity. Var. **ɛidalat** s.v.

ʿiut (etym. doubtf., cf. **ʿutana**) power MG 146: 22. **ʿiut malkuta** Gy 178:3 kingly power, tyranny. MG 139:15, 309:26.

ɛiz (Ar. عِز) AM 254:5, 21 power.

ɛiṭam AM 279:30 for **ṭiɛam** food.

ʿiil 1 s. **ʿil.**

ʿiil ʿiil CP 102:2 my God! my God!

ʿiil 2 in lʿiil Gy 269:1 D = **lʿl** s. **ʿl 1.**

ʿiin hiia s. **ʿin 1 & 2.**

ʿiit s. **ʿit.**

ʿil 1 (H. אֵל V) god MG 4:13, 109:4. Rarely as an independent noun, more frequent as ending of theophorous names (-**ʿil**, varr. -**iil**, -**ʿiil**) MG 4:15, MR 197:bottom & n. 4, MSchr. 172 n. 5. Varr. of the independent form **ʿiil 1, ʿl 4. ʿil rba** Gy 261:12, 19; **ʿil šadai** Gy 175:14 (H. אֵל שַׁדַּי); **ʿil ʿil** (= **adunai**) Gy 23:16, 45:12, **ʿiil ʿiil alaha** Q 52:29, **bʿil** Cor. 47 (left) 9.

ʿil 2 in **lʿil** Gy 269:1, 295:14, Q 29:29 etc. = **lʿl** s. **ʿl.**

ʿilana s. **ʿlana.**

ɛilat (Ar. عِلَّة) (*a*) AM 257:10 cause, reason, (*b*) DC 46. 64:7 disease, misfortune, blemish.

ɛilim, ɛlim (Ar. عِلْم) AM 163:12 wisdom, knowledge MG 2:6, DC 46. 120:6.

ɛimarat (Ar. عِمَارَة) AM 163:3 building(s).

ʿin 1 st. abs. & cstr. of **aina. ʿin hai** Gy 195:14, CP 22:12, 67:14, 118:14, Q 9:2 = ML 24:12, Q 30:52 = ML 83:18, Q 60:5 = ML 144:5 Fount of Life MG 4:14. **ʿin hiia uʿiin hiia** CP, ML 49:1 prob. id. (but Lidzb. **ʿin 2**).

ʿin 2 (Syr. ܐܝܢ, Ar. إِنَّ, H. הֵן, Nöld. ZDMG xl 739) interj. O, behold, yea, yes, indeed MG 81:2. **ʿin qaria** Q 1:26 = ML 5:2 O creator; **ʿin ruha** DC 47 (*often*); **ʿin ʿin ruha** Oxf. roll g 555, 561, 685, 693, 700, 709, 717 ff.; **ʿin hiia uʿiin hiia** CP 41:16 **ʿin hiia uaʿiin hiia,** cf. s. 1 (but Lidzb. *O, Leben, O, O, Leben*).

ɛin (Ar. عين) eye. **alɛin** AM 287:15 the eye.

ɛisa (Ar. عيسى) Jesus (often in magical text DC 46). Also a man's name.

ʿispiria DC 22. 32 a var. of **ʿspira.**

ɛiraq (عراق) 'Irāq. **ɛiraq ḏ-parsaiia** AM 198 Persian 'Irāq; **ɛiraq rumiia** AM 205 Greek (i.e. Syrian?) 'Irāq.

ɛiruq lkamia s. **kamia** (var. **lkimia**) AM 129:5 alchemical herbs.

ʿit (substantively אִיתָא, ܐܝܬܐ; as particle: Jew.-Aram. אִית, Bibl.-Aram. אִיתַי, Syr. ܐܝܬ, H. יֵשׁ, Akk. *išû* to have, be, beg. *laššu* 'is not', Ar. only neg. ليس as impers. verb Nöld. ZDMG xl 738, Brockelm. i 75:11, 189, 479). (*a*) subst.: being, substance (fem. MG 161:11), (*b*) particle (or impers. verb): there is MG 4:11 f., 293 ff. Var. **ʿiit,** with encl. **ʿt** (s.v.). Doublet **aiit,** with suff. **ait-** s.v. Neg. **laiit** s.v., with suff. **lait,** with encl. **lit-, lʿit** s.vv. (*a*) **šum ʿiit ʿlaita ušum ʿiit titaita** Gy 185:1 the name of the upper substance and the name of the lower substance; **ʿit ʿlaita šumia hʿ uʿit titaita arqa hʿ** Gy 185:4 f. the upper substance is the heaven and the lower substance is the earth MG 406:20 f.; **šum ʿit ʿlaita laʿdkar ušum ʿit titaita ladkar** Gy 185:21 f. he mentioned not the name of the high being and he mentioned not the name of the low being; **ʿit rba** Gy 258:12 the Great Being (here as masc. referring to the god of the Jews Ginzā 258 n. 1); **ʿit ruaha rba ḏ-hiia** ML 17:5, 183:2 the Being of the Great Ease of Life. As pr. n.: **ʿit ʿnṣibat ʿutria** = CP 7:penult.: **ʿit iauar** ML 9:3 f.; (*b*) **ʿit minaihun ḏ-** Gy 25:9 (there) are some of them (who); **ʿit iuma nihuia ḏ-** Gy 140:23 there shall be a day MG 404:ult. ff.

ɛitman baša (عُثْمَان بَاشَا) Zotb. 228b:32 name of a ruler.

ʿka 1, (**aka** 1 s.v.) (Talm. אִיכָּא < אִית + כָּא) there is MG 42:19 f., 204:5. Neg. **lika, lʿka** s.v. **ḏ-ʿka udhauin mitiadlia** Gy 48:23 who are and will be born MG 402:12; **ʿka hiia ʿka marai ʿka manda ḏ-hiia** Morg. 3:1 the Life existeth, my Lord existeth, M.-ḏ-H. existeth.

ʿka 2 (אֵיכָא, ܐܝܟܐ) where? MG 206:6. **ʿka nʿzal** Gs 15:13 whither shall we go?

ʿka 3 = **aka 2.** MG 40:5, MSchr. 142 n. 2. **ʿka**

napša Gy 136:21, 137:16 great distress; **ʿka aka dilak** s. **aka 2**; **ʿka rmalẖ** (read **ʿrmalẖ**) **lnapšiẖ** Jb 22:2 f. I will cast sorrow into his soul; **mahu ʿka (ḏ-)šauitlia** Gy 324:13 why hast thou caused me such distress?; **ʿka minẖ hauilẖ** AM 37:15 f. he will have trouble with her; **ʿka bbnia hauilẖ** AM 46:10 he will have trouble with his children.

ʿkara (אִכָּרָא, ܐܟܪܐ, H. אִכָּר, Ar. أَكَّار Fränkel 128, MG 122 n. 2, from Akk. *ikkaru* KAT 649, Haupt ZDMG lxv 561). (*a*) peasant, husbandman, tiller cf soil, (*b*) (cf. foll.) cultivated soil? MG 122:12. Pl. **-ia.** (*a*) **ʿkara msadra** Gy 213:15 a methodical husbandman; **damia lʿkara ḏ-zarẖ** Gy 214:20 resembleth a husbandman that soweth; **uʿkaria ḏ-mia nihisrun** AM 187:7 and the husbandmen will lack water; (*b*) **alma lʿkara brbita ṭaba** AM 170 until the cultivation submerges in the spring-floods.

ʿkaruta (abstr. noun from preced.) tillage, cultivation, tilled ground. Var. **ʿkariuta** (rt. **KRA II**, cf. MG 122 n. 2). **mia napša nitun ukariuta** (var. **uʿk-**) **tišpar** AM much water will come down and the tilled land will prosper.

ʿkarta 1 (rt. **KRA** II) fig. coition?? **hana abatar ʿkartẖ** DC 46. 16:8 she yearns after his coition (?).

ʿkarta 2 (rt. **AKR I** = **ʿKR I**) detention. **masiqta bʿqarta qria** DC 3 read a *masiqta* for his detention (?).

ʿkbar s. **kbar 1.**

ʿkula (rt. **AKL** I) bait. Pl. **ʿkulia** 155:12, var. **ʿuklia** C.

ʿkulan var. of **ʿkilan** pl. st. abs. fem. of **ʿkilt(i)a 2.** **uʿkulan ainia** AM 39:16, trs. 13:2 and his eyes are glowing; **zaua zaliltia ḏ-ʿkulan ainẖ** ŠQ 18:ult. a slender spouse whose eyes are ardent.

ʿkuma (rt. **AKM**) black. St. abs. **ʿkum** MG 125:18. Fem. st. emph. **ʿkumtia.** Pl. masc. **-ia,** fem. **-ata.** St. abs. masc. also substantively: blackness, darkness, cf. AM 282:34. **napṭa hiuara uʿkuma** DC 12 white and black oil; **manzia ʿkuma** AM 14:2 black hair; **mia ʿkumia** s. **mia 1**; **saria ʿkumata** AM 99:7 black hairs; **hiuaniata ʿkumata** AM black beasts; **ʿkumtia huit** DC 40. 82 etc. thou art black (fem.); **ʿkuma** as family-name AM 255:27 etc.

ʿkura (Targ. איגורא, Ass. *ē-kūr 'viell. ein hohes Haus'* Del. s.v.) (*a*) pagan temple, shrine, high place MG 41:3, (*b*) temple-spirit, demon of the temple MG 76 n. 1, Lidzb. OSt 541 n. 2, Ginzā 116 n. 2. Pl. **-ia.** (*a*) **nigdia ḏ-ʿkuria** s. **nigda** (*a*); **uniramia ʿkurik** JRAS 1937 593:26 and we will cast down thy (fem.) high places (or temples); **ʿu mn mathẖ ʿu mn ʿkuria qiniana tiqnia** AM 77:3 either from her village or from temples she will acquire property; **mikal ḏ-ʿkuria** CP 42:antepenult., ML 51:11 eating from pagan altars; **alahia mn ʿkuraihun** Q 24:18 gods from their temples; **alahia bʿkuraihun** Q 53:9 gods in their temples; **uʿkuria mitpasasia** Gy 388:2 and temples shall be destroyed; **ginia lʿkuria** s. **ginia 2**; (*b*) **ʿkuraihun** Gy 106:16, Gs 75:10 their temple-demons; **ʿkuria upatikria** Gy 389:7 temple-demons and shrine-spirits; **humria uʿkuria** Gy 394:1 amulet-spirits and temple-demons.

ʿkila (pass. pt. pe. of **AKL I**) corroded. Fem. **ʿkilt(i)a 2.** Pl. fem. st. abs. **ʿkilan** (var. **ʿkulan** s.v.) used of eyes with a different meaning of glowing, ardent, bright. **nura ʿkilta** ML 54:5 corroding fire; **ʿšata ʿkilta** Gy 246:7, 247:22, 267:5 f., 269:17, 22, DC 34. 869 devouring flame, but DC 27. 81 bright flame?, gloriole, halo; **aina ʿkiltia** JRAS 1937 590:10 corroded eye; **uʿkilan ainẖ** AM 14:3 and his eyes are bright.

ʿkiliata s. **kiliata.**

ʿkilta 1 (rt. **AKL I**) food, meal MG 117:bottom. With procl. prep. **likilta, lkilta, lʿkilta** Gy 378:7 (& varr.) for food MG 28 n. 3. **šauilẖ lʿkilta** Gy 243:13, 244:11 he made (hist. pres.) for food to him; **ʿkilta lakal** Gy 288:5 he ate no food; **ʿkilta akal** l. 6 he ate food; **ʿkilta ḏ-pagra** Gy 89:13, 317:15, Jb 77:12, 212:16 bodily food, food for the body; **ʿkilta ḏ-babia trisar** Q 72:9, Gy 301:5 food of the Twelve Gates (i.e. sacramental food of non-Mandaean religions); **ʿkilta ḏ-ginia ḏ-mašknia** Gy 302:3 (s. **ginia 2**); **rabia bʿkilta ḏ-šahpia ḏ-ʿlania** ATŠ I no. 279 it is reared on a diet of leaves of trees; **razia ḏ-ʿkilta** HG 11 mysteries of the (sacred) meal; **ʿkilta umašqita** ATŠ II no. 112 food and drink; **ʿkilta** (var. **akilta** B) **ḏ-nunia bgauaihun kanpia ʿkilta anat** Jb 153:8 f. the bait to which the fish gather, thou art the bait.

ʿkilta 2 fem. of **ʿkila** (q.v.).

ʿkisa (pass. pt. pe. of **KSS II** used otherwise only in af., hence formed as from **AKS**) rebuked, confounded. **ʿkisa umakisa umasra ainaihun ḏ-bišia** DC 12:236, P.A. xiii rebuked, confounded and put to scorn (?) is the evil eye of the wicked.

ʿkira 1 (pass. pt. pe. of **AKR I** ?) retained, held back. **ḏ-tinpuš nišmata ḏ-binataikun ʿkira** ATŠ II no. 335 that thou mayest revive souls which are held back amongst you.

ʿkira 2 (pass. pt. of **AKR III** = **ʿKR II**) ploughed, cultivated. Pl. masc. **ʿkiria.** **mšaria ʿkiria** ŠQ 18:21 cultivated garden-beds.

ʿKL s. **AKL I.**

ʿKM s. **AKM.**

ʿkpulia (cf. כַּפְלָא) pl. loins, groins (var. **lkuplia sastata** P.A. *Mihla*) **lmitnia rakšia ulʿkpulia sistata** DC 40. 143 for the loins of horses and the groins of mares.

ʿKR I s. **AKR I.**

ʿKR II s. **AKR II.**

ʿKR III s. **AKR III.**

ʿkt- mod. form of **ʿt-.** Pron. *eχt-*. **bʿuhra ʿktia** Cor. coloph. he is on a journey. **ʿktinu** DC 51: coloph. they are.

ʿl 1 (originally עַל, ܥܠ but often also for לְ, ܠ) on, upon, over, about. Used either as independent prep. (never proclitically) or with pers. suff. (as such often replacing **l-** 1

MG 193:10, 353 ff., AIT 31, 35). Var. **al 1** s.v. With a procl. **l-**: **lʿil** Gy 269:1 (var. **lʿiil** D), 295:14, Q 29:29 = **lʿl** above, upwards MG 4:21 f., 6:21, 203:13 (secondary forms classified as **ʿil 2** and **ʿiil 2**), **lʿl saka** Gy 281:24 above the end. With other prepositions: **ʿl qudam** (s. **qudam**), **ʿl qar** (s. **qar**), **ʿl agambia** (s. **agambia**), **ʿl ahuria, ʿl atutia** (with the same meaning as simple **ahuria, atutia**). With suff. **ʿlai** (*often*) upon me, **ʿlak** Gy 142:2 (inst. of which there is often **alak** Gy 141:22, 142:15, 145:5) on thee, to thee, for thee, with thee MG 193:16 f.; with suff. to emphasize a determinate noun: **ʿlh̠ d̠-planga** Gy 382:8 on the phalanx; **ʿlh̠ d̠-hanath̠ baba** Gy 145:20 above that door (& *often*) MG 330:10 f.; **ṭab ʿlkun** Morg. 215/18:8 hail to you! For **l- 1**: **uamarlin ʿl liliata** Gs 92:13 and he said to the liliths, **ʿl mia tahmia asgun** (preceded by **asgun lmia tahmia**) Gy 73:8 they went to the stagnant water; **apkia halia ʿl marira** Gy 177:16 they turn sweet into bitter; **uminaihun ʿl mikal** Gy 124:21 some of them are to be eaten MG 353:17 ff.; on the other hand, for **uai ʿlai** Gs 92:1 (= ܘܝ ܥܠܝ) there is often **uailia** etc. MG 354 n. 1. As 'about': **aprišan lqadmaiia uʿl rba** Gy 303:20 he informed me about the first ones and about the great one; **aprišinun ʿl pira rba ʿlaia** Gy 304:18 he informed them about the great, celestial Fruit (& often **apriš ʿl**); **amar ʿl** Gy 4:22, 93: ult. etc.; **ʿthašab ʿl** (*often*) MG 354:7–15; **ʿl d̠-hṭin** Gy 61 ff. (but **ldihṭin** Gy 63:23) because we sinned MG 354:15 f.; **ʿl mahu** Gy 72:2, 164:14 wherefore, why? MG 354:18; **ʿl bab almia** Jb 6:9 at the door of the worlds (but **lbab almia** Jb 2:6) MG 354:18 ff.; **lmizlaikun uʿl mitiaikun uʿl mitbaikun ʿl miklaikun uʿl mištiaikun ʿl mišlaikun uʿl mišikbaikun** Gy 179:3 ff. by your going and by your coming and by your sitting, by your eating and by your drinking, by your resting and by your sleeping (MG 354:25 ff.). As 'against': **ana ʿl nhura mitkadašna lau ʿl hšuka** Gy 163:19 I will fight against the light, not against the darkness (but l. 15 **ʿlauaihun latitkadaš** do not fight against them) MG 356: 13 f.; **ʿl d̠-** Gy 74:5, 9, 103:3 while MG 374: bottom; **ʿl d̠-la** Gs 11:17 f., 75:8 ff., 82:12 etc. before MG 209:14 f.

ʿl 2 = **l- 1**. Var. **al-** (s. **al 1**). **uʿl miškaiun d̠-anašia naštilh̠** Gy 387:14 (var. **ulm-** Lond.) and they flay people's skin MG 391:10; **apkilh̠ ʿl libaihun** Sh. 'Abd.'s copy's var. of **llibaihun** Gy 25:5 they pervert their hearts; **ʿlkun dilkun** CP 115:10 = ML 15:1 You (acc. pl. referring to the Life, beginning of the prayer CP 17 = ML lxxvii).

ʿl 3 (Ar. article أَلْ) = **al 2**. **tišrin ʿl aual** s. **aual. nisan ʿl aual** AM 282:24.

ʿl 4 = **ʿl 1** (q.v.).

ʿla 1 (Talm., אילא Syr. ܐܠܐ, Ar. إِلَّا, Eth. አላ) if not, but, except MG 208:11. As a rule, completed by the rel. **d̠-**. Also **ʿlau** s.v. **uhda minaihun lnhura lanisaq ʿla d̠-saliq hibil ziua** Gy 219:15 and not one of them shall rise to the light except H.-Z.; **ʿla d̠-atia manda d̠-hiia** Oxf. 30 a, Par. xi 53a if M.-d-H. doth not come; without **d̠-**: **ʿla mdauratlia** Gs 54:3 s. **DWR** pa.; **lʿka d̠-marha brihaihun ʿla d̠-minaihun hua** Gy 284:8 no one smelleth their perfume except one that belongeth to them MG § 314 pp. 478 f. In later Mand. **ʿla d̠-** can be considered as إِلَى + **d̠-** until, whilst MG 478 n. 4, or simply as **ʿl d̠-**, cf. **ʿla d̠-anai d̠-ganian** Jb 41:8 whilst my flock was lying down.

ʿla 2 for **ʿl 1** (cf. Ar. عَلَى). **ʿla šumia uʿla arqa** CP 69:10 f., Morg. 224/36:1 = ML 85:1 on the sky and on the earth.

ʿla 3 (cf. Akk. *allu* 1 Muss-Arnolt p. 39b Ginzā 85 n. 1, but prob. a mere var. of **ʿula 1**) pain, malady. **ʿla npalh̠ bdupnh̠** Gy 84:8 (var. **ʿula** DC 22. 79) pain assailed his side.

ʿlau (Talm. אילאו, Syr. ܐܠܘ ܠܐ) = **ʿla 1**. MG 208:12. **ʿlau d̠-turṣa lahua ʿlau d̠-lahua turṣa** Gy 116:17 if there was no straightness MG 478:paen.; **ʿlau kadir ʿlai zaina** Jb 35:3 f. if only my fetters were not heavy upon me; **ʿlau haila d̠-hua minai ʿlau tarmida ana** Jb 244:9 were it not for the strength that is mine, were it not that I am a priest . . .; **ʿu nišimta d̠-šalmania hʿ . . . sin lamitahzilh̠ ʿlau hinun tartun** DAb if it be the soul of a righteous man . . . Sin does not appear; if not, both of them (appear).

ʿlauana s. **ʿluana**.

ʿlauia (Talm. עילווי Luzzatto 98, Syr. ܠܥܠܘ) upon, above. Rare var. **alauia** s.v. MG 194:7. **mn ʿlauia** from above MG 197:1 (with a mistaken reference); **ʿlauia d̠-kulh̠ alma** Q 65:28 above the whole world MG 330:13; **hiia . . . d̠-ʿlauia kulhun ʿubadia** (very frequent doxological formula) the Life . . . which is above all works; **mahik ʿlauaihun** Gy 153:21 he laugheth about them; **latigihkun ʿlauaihun** Gy 44:13 laugh not about them; **ʿlauai(h)un bakia** Gy 170:18, 171:11 crieth about them; **ʿlauaihun latitkadaš** Gy 163:15 (but l. 19 with simple **ʿl 1** q.v.); **agzar ʿlauaikun** Gs 106:1 they pronounced a verdict about you (but **agzar ʿlh̠** Gs 105:ult. & *often*); **ʿmir ʿlauaihun** Gy 384:19 it was said about them (but **ʿmir ʿlh̠** Gy 386:24 & often); **adkar ʿlauaian** = **adkar ʿlan** both Gs 29 ff. mention us; **šalṭit ʿlauaihun naṭria** Gy 130:5 I set guards over them; **ʿlauaikun . . . ʿtirhiṣnin** Gy 176:4 we relied upon you (but **ruhṣana ʿl** Gy 17:6 etc.); **bišmat ʿlauaihun** Gy 292:6 it pleased them (but **bismat ʿlh̠** Gy 70:20 it pleased him); **ʿqara ʿlauaikun nišria** Gy 48:2 glory descendeth upon you; **napšaihun pihkat ʿlauaihun** Gy 277:17 their souls became dull for (?) them; **uʿlauh̠ gaṭla nigṭul** Gy 17:5 and committeth murder for it(s sake) etc. (often quite equivalent with **ʿl 1**) MG § 249 pp. 356 f.

ʿlai 1, ʿl 1 with pers. suff. of the 1st p. sg.

ʿlai 2 (cf. **ʿlai**) adv. upwards. **nidgar ʿlai** ATŠ he will mount upwards.

ʿlaia (ܥܠܝܐ) supreme, high, lofty, exalted, superior, celestial, heavenly, uppermost MG

141:10. Fem. ʿlaita. Pl. masc. ʿlaiia. **paṭira ʿlaia** PD 1587, CP 71:18 = ML 88:1 the upper unleavened bread; **rba uʿlaia** the Great and Exalted (name of the highest being in the Book of the Great King of Glory Ginzā 4:8); **alma hak ʿlaia** Gy 150:18 that heavenly world; **mara d̲-rabuta ʿlaita** (*often*) Lord of Celestial Greatness.

ʿlamana = **ʿlimana** (q.v.). Pl. masc. **-ia, -iata. sibin uʿlamania** s. **siba 3.**

ʿlan 1 occasional var. of **ʿlin** (q.v.).

ʿlan 2 st. abs. & cstr. of foll.

ʿlana (אִילָנָא, ܐܝܠܢܐ) tree MG 4:3, 136:16. St. abs. & cstr. **ʿlan 2.** Pl. **-ia.** Masc. **ʿlan ziua** CP 7:7 = Q 3:5 tree of radiance MG 309:19; **bilanun** Gy 9:2 in their tree MG 4:24; **ʿlana d̲-ʿlan hiia** CP 405:3 f. a tree that is a Tree of Life; **ʿlana d̲-tušbihta** Gy 65:13, 22 the tree of praise; **ʿlana rba d̲-kulh̲ asauata** CP 115:14 = Q 58:26 great tree that is all remedies; **ʿlana gupna** Q 23:33 vine-tree; **ʿl gupnia uʿl ʿlania dakiia** Gy 305:26 about vines and pure trees; **šlama ʿlak ʿlan ʿlan ṭura** Oxf. roll g 564 = DC 47 = Or. 327:11 peace be upon thee, plant (shrub) of the mountain; **ginat ʿlania** s. **ginat.** Personified trees: **ʿsṭaruan ʿlana,** CP 446:3, **asṭaruan ʿlana** Gy 377:21, **tatagmur ʿlana** CP 458:5 f., Gy 321:17. Names of trees in DC 7: **ʿlana qišmiš** currant-bush, **nargis ʿlana** narcissus plant, **ʿlana d̲-baluda** oak-tree, **ʿlana d̲-ʿzaita** olive tree, **marua ʿlana** sprig (?) of marjoram.

ʿlbar sometimes for **lbar.**

ʿlua s. **ʿluana.**

ʿluaia (Jew.-Aram. אלוה, Syr. ܥܠܘܝ, Chr.-Pal. ܥܠܘܝ & ܥܠܘܝܬܐ, Eth. ዐልዋ, Ar. الوى , ألوّة , أليّة , ليّة , لوّة, Gr. ἀλόη Löw 235, Nöld.: *Neue Beiträge* 43) aloe. Masc. **ʿluaia d̲-napil bdupša umaslilh̲** Gy 216:15 aloe that falleth into honey and spoileth it MG 374:6.

ʿluana (*ܥܠܘܢܐ) MG 136:14, where Nöld. supposed a sg. ***ʿlua,** although **ʿluana** seems to be used as sg. in Gs 136 f., and, on the other hand, **ʿluakun** 392:20 B, **ʿluaikun** ibid. CD occur only as varr. of **ʿlauanun** A) departed spirit, ghost. Varr. **ʿlauana, aluana, ʿlua.** Pl. **ʿluania. kursia lʿluana rmia kursia rmia ʿl aluana** Gs 136:15, cf. l. 22 & **kursia lʿluana triṣ kursia triṣ lʿluana** Gy 137:2 f. a throne is set for the Spirit (seems to designate a ruling spirit of the underworld Ginzā 595 n. 1); **ʿlauanun d̲-mitita** Gy 392:20, **ʿluanun d̲-mitia** ibid. l. 21 f. the spirits of the dead; **kd̲ maitit ʿluanak ṭablun miṭam kd̲ aitak bhaia** Gy 393:3 f. when thou diest, thy spirits will satisfy themselves [*sic*], as when thou wast existing in life.

ʿluat = **luat: ʿluataihun huit** Gs 16:14 thou wert in their presence (doubted by Lidzb. Ginzā 435 n. 3); **bʿluatan ubdiarutan** Q 54:27 in our company and with our help.

ʿluita occasionally for **luita.**

ʿlul (H. אֱלוּל, Syr. ܐܝܠܘܠ, Akk. *elūlu, ulūlu* Haupt ZDMG lxiv 703 f.) month under the rule of Virgo MMII 84, Ar. أيلول SsSs ii 29. Often (esp. in AM).

ʿlia 1 = lia 1.

ʿlia 2 = lia 2.

ʿlia 3 Jb 260:2, 3 for. **ʿlaia.**

ℇlia Zotb. 221a:33, 34 for **ℇalia** ʿAlī.

ʿliana (אֶלְיוֹנָא) thumb MG 139:6. **ṣbatak (u)lianak** Q 45:21 = Morg. 248/83:25 thy thumb; **uṣbitak d̲-abihdia ʿlianak** CP 93:28 = Morg. 248/83:26 = ML 118:4 and thy forefinger (lit. thy finger which is with thy thumb).

ʿliza (cf. **ALS,** formed as pass. pt. pe.) grieved, vexed, importuned, harassed, evil? **uʿliza ruha** DC 45 and be harassed, (O) spirit; **umrahiq ʿliza ruha** DC 45 and sends away the evil (?) spirit.

ʿlikta a late var. of **alikta.**

ʿlima (Eg.-Aram., Nab., Palm. עלים, Syr. ܥܠܝܡܐ, H. עֶלֶם, Ar. غُلَام, orig. youth(-ful), hence: strong, firm, sturdy, vigorous. Pl. **-ia. ugbinh̲ ʿlimia uprišia** AM 31:penult. and his brows (are) firm and noble; **ʿlimia ugaṭinia šaqh̲** AM 22:1 youthful and slender are her limbs; **uʿlimia spihath̲** AM 50:6 and his lips (are) firm; **ʿlima triṣa hauia** AM 96:4 he will be sturdy and straight.

ʿlimana (from preced.) young man, youth MG 118:3, 137:17. Var. **ʿlamana** s.v. Pl. masc. **-ia,** fem. **-iata. qašišia uʿlimania** DC 44:783 f. old men and youths; **ʿlimania uʿlimaniata** Gs 17:19 boys and girls MG 168:antep.

ʿlin (אִלֵּין) these MG xxv:bottom, 89:ult. ff. Var. **ʿlan.** Used both substantivally and adjectivally: (*a*) **ʿlin d̲-** Gy 253:15 those who; (*b*) **gubria ʿlin tlata** Gy 251 ff., 286:22 these three men (Ginzā 250:9 f.); **ʿubadia ʿlan** (varr. **ʿlin**) CP 65:2 and 66:11, Q 30:17 = ML 80:9 those deeds MG 339:bottom.

ʿliṣa pass. pt. pe. of **ALṢ** (= **ʿLṢ**) q.v.

ʿlita 1 (ܐܠܝܬܐ & ܐܘܠܝܬܐ) wailing MG 104:2. **ʿlita uaškita** Gy 183:12 wailing and complaint.

ʿlita 2 = **alita 2: šimnit kd̲ ʿlita** DC 44. 1409 f. = Morg. 265/21:21 I waxed fat like the tail-fat (of a sheep).

ʿlka = **lka** (q.v.).

ʿLL s. **ALL I.**

ʿlma for **alma 2** in **uʿlma d̲-hulil** (*Florilegium*), and whilst he howled.

ʿlʿl = **lʿl** (s. **ʿl 1**).

ʿLS = **ALS.**

ʿlqa (Nöld.: Ar. عُلَّيق *rubus* 'Dornbusch' ZA xxx 150 f., cf. Löw 275 & *passim*) a bitter plant or fruit. Found only in pl. **-ia.** Jb ii 132 n. 9, ML 100 n. 3. **mraria uʿlqia** Jb 135:10 f., Gs 102:7, 105:7, 118:15, 124:12, Q 38:3 = ML 100:5 etc. (cf. s. **gida 1**).

ʿm 1 st. abs. & cstr. of **ʿma 1** (q.v.).

ʿm 2 (Aram. & H. עִם, Syr. ܥܡ, dial. Ar. عَم, South-Ar. 𐩲𐩣, Akk. *ema* Brockelm. ii § 255) with MG xxv:bottom, 14:20, 193:26, Ginzā

250:11. ʿm **hdadia** Gy 250:18 with one another; ʿm **ʿutria** Gy 292:19, 293:20 with the uthras.

ʿMA s. YMA.

ʿma 1 (Gen. Sem. אֵם, ܐܡܐ, أم, Akk. *ummu*) mother MG 102:16, 156:12. St. abs. & cstr. **ʿm 1.** Pl. **ʿumamata 2** s.v., **ʿmamata.** With suff. **ʿm** my mother MG 34:4, 175:10, **ʿmik** Gs 100:18 thy (fem.) mother MG 177:17, **ʿmh̠** his, her mother MG 178:4, **ʿmaian** Gy 146:16 our mother MG 179:1, **ʿmaikun** your mother MG 180:8, **ʿmai(h)un** their mother. Idiom: **hua lʿmh̠** (often in AM) he was born; **namrus ʿma ḏ-alma** Gy 114:17, 329:19, 331:2, 5, 332:24, 333:3, 341:11, 14 N. the mother of the world; **ʿma ḏ-hšuka** Gy 140:3 the mother of the darkness; **raza ḏ-ʿma** DC 34. 528 the mystery of the Mother.

ʿma 2 occasionally for **ma 2.**

ʿma 3 a var. of **ʿuma** (q.v.).

ʿmamata = **ʿumamata 1, 2.**

ʿmana (= **ʿumana**) (*a*) skilful, dextrous, (*b*) calling, occupation, trade, profession. Pl. **-ia.** (*a*) **bnia ʿmania ušalmania** AM 60:18 skilful and perfect sons; (*b*) **ʿmanh̠ tigra uaimanutẖ ramia** AM 97:14 his calling is strife and his pursuits fraud.

ʿmanuta (= **aimanuta**) calling, craft, occupation, trade. **ʿu mn ʿmanuta ʿu mn tangaruta lahma grida akil** AM 5:6 he will earn a scanty livelihood either by a craft or a trade; **uʿmanuta nilup** AM 93:2 and he will learn a trade.

ʿmar s. **ʿmra.** DC 38.

ʿmara 1 (Ar. أُمَرَاءُ) pl. princes. **hzaia ḏ-ʿmara** AM 161:penult. interview with princes.

ʿmara 2 (cf. **amra 1**) woolly skin, hide? **šqul šigrak mn ʿmarih̠** DC 43 J 154 remove thy fever from his hide (? read **mia 2** entrails?)

ع̣marat (Ar., cf. **ع̣imarat**) prosperity. **ع̣marat başra binia anašia** AM 282:11 prosperity will be lacking amongst people.

ʿmat (Talm. אֵימַת, older אֵימָתַי, Syr. ܐܡܬܝ from *aj* + *mataj*, H. מָתַי, Ar. متى, Akk. *immati* < *ina mati* Jensen ZA ix 532, Brockelm. i 496) when MG 22 n. 4, 34:4, 205:24 f. With **l- 1**: **lʿmat. ʿmat bšibia šibiun** Gs 65:7 when did they take me captive?; **lʿmat iuma nihuia ḏ-ʿdul** Gy 155:18 when will be the day on which I shall bring forth? MG 437:12 f.; **ʿmat ḏ-** when, **kul ʿmat ḏ-** whenever MG 453:8 f.; **kul ʿmat baiitun miqria ʿlh̠** DC 27. 507 each time ye wish to celebrate it; **mn ʿmat** DC 51. 49 from the time when.

ʿmatia, ʿmatin Gy 384:19, AM 256:34, 288:16 = **matin** two hundred.

ʿmba 1 = **ʿnba** (q.v.). Pl. **ʿmbia** MG 27:17, 50:18, 106:6, 172:15. Sg. only apparent. **pira ʿmba uʿlania** Gy 241:6 ff., 243:12 = **piria ʿmbia uʿlania** Gy 12:18, 33:4, 13, 34:1, 113:18 f., 124:1, Jb 46:8, DC 53. 429:6 fruits, grapes, and trees.

ʿmba 2 Gy 354:10, 14, 18 for **ʿumba.**

ʿmbra (אִמְּרָא, ܐܡܪܐ, Ar. loan-w. إِمَّر, from Akk. *immeru* Jensen ZA vii 216 n. 4, Zimmern: *Akk. Fremdw.* 25; Nöld. ZDMG xxv 256 ff.) (*a*) sheep, lamb, (*b*) Aries (sign of the Zodiac). MG 119:ult. Written defectively, pronounced *embara, umbara* (Nöld.'s phonetic remark MG 77:15 is mistaken, since the *b* results from the dissimil. of *mm* of *emmara); exceptional *scriptio plena* **ʿmbara.** Pl. **-ia.** Masc. (*a*) **akuat ʿmbra blamtinun** DC 44. 1490 = Morg. 265/21:21 I muzzled them like a sheep; **bakin kḏ ʿmbria** DC 43 J 105 = Oxf. roll g 226, Jb 251:4 they bleat like sheep; **uakil ʿmbria** Gs 85:1 and eateth lambs (or sheep); **aqna uʿmbria** (var. **uʿmbra** ABC) Jb 40:7 sheep and lambs; **bakin ʿmbria** (var. **ʿmria** B) Jb 40:10 the little lambs bleat; **aqnai uʿmbrai** Jb 43:8 my sheep and lambs; (*b*) **kḏ mnata lʿmbra plaglh̠** Gy 122:16, 379:12 when they allotted a portion to Aries; **qala ḏ-qra ʿmbra** Gy 123:8 the voice which Aries called. Very often in AM.

ʿmbrusia pl. (Syr. ܐܡܪܘܣܐ, Ar. loan-w. عمروس, diminutive from preced.) little lambs MG 148:17. **kma kariatlia ʿl ʿmbrusia ḏ-karsaiun halba lamlat** Jb 44:8 how grieved I am about the little lambs whose bellies were not filled with milk.

ʿMD (ܥܡܕ, Ar. عمّد to baptize, غمد to immerse) to baptize in standing water (of Christian baptism). MSt 42 & n. 6.

Af. Pt. pl. with encl. **mamidilhun** Gy 57:1, 226:8, 16 they baptize them. Part. pres. **mamidna** I baptize MG 70:16.

Der.: **mamiduta.**

ʿmuq, ʿmuqa (rt. **ʿMQ**) deep, profound, low, depressed. **uruiana ʿmuq ukbiša blibh̠** AM 74:2 and her mind is depressed and there is dejection in her heart. Gl. 124:5 **ʿmuqa** عميق *profundus.*

ʿmia = **mia 3** (s. mi-). MG 447:2. **ʿmia kašra dmutaihun** Gs 57:14 is their appearance indeed fair? MG 434:antep. f. **ʿmia šapiria** Gs 57:2, 3 are they really fair?

ʿmila (עֲמִילָא) well-worked, well-made. Pl. **-ia.** **ʿzlia ʿmilh̠** (for **-ia**) DC 43 cunningly-woven nets (snares).

ʿmir (Ar. أمير) emir. Some colophons.

ʿmira (עֲמִירָא, ܥܡܝܪܐ, H. עָמִיר) sprig, spike (of flower, grain etc.). **anat ʿmira** Or. 332:7 thou sprig (i.e. of rue).

ʿmna occasionally for **mna.**

ʿmsania DC 23. 711 = **msania.**

ʿMṢ s. AMṢ.

ʿMQ (Aram. & H. עמק, Syr. ܥܡܩ, Ar. عَمُقَ, Eth. ዐመቀ, cf. Akk. *emqu* wise, *emūqu* power, *tēmequ* ardent prayer) to be deep, profound, depressed.

Gl. 116:13 f. **ʿmiqa** (pass. pt. pe.) عمق, *in profundis ire* عميق كرد.

Der.: **ʿumqa, ʿmuq(a).**

ʿMR I s. AMR II.

ʿMR II s. AMR I.

ʿmra 1 (rt. **AMR I** = **ʿMR II**) speech, speaking MG 102:7. **ʿmra ušima** Gy 316:4 etc. (*very often*) speech and hearing.

ʿmra 2, pl. **ʿmria** Jb 40:10 B s. **ʿmbra** (*a*).

ʿmrum, ʿmruma s. **mrum(a).**

ʿMŠ s. **AMŠ.**

ʿn a common var. of **ʿin** (1 or 2).

ʿNA I s. **ANA I.**

ʿNA II s. **ANA II.**

ʿnba, ʿmba 1 s.v. AM 177, DC 41. 281 an apparent sg. formed from **ʿnbia** AM 213:1 grapes (pl. of **ʿnibta** q.v.) MG 27:18, 50:19, 172:15.

ʿnbu s. **nbu.**

ʿnbiha s. **nbiha.**

ʿngauia = **angauia.** (ʿ)**ngauia iama** Q 52:12 the islands of the sea.

ʿngar st. cstr. of **ʿngirta. ʿngar kušṭa** Gy 314:22, 345:2, Jb 91:4, 9, ATŠ I no. 250 Kušṭa's letter MMII 171.

ʿngaria (ࡏࡍࡂࡀࡓࡉࡀ, cf. vulg. Ar. إنجار Freytag) roofs MG 76:8, 122:14. **br ʿngaria** Oxf. roll g 206, 1028, AM (*often*) etc. lunacy demons (lit. roof-demons) MG 186:ult.; **qaimin ʿl ʿngaria** Jb 139:8 they are standing on the roofs.

ʿngirta (Bibl.-Aram. אִגְּרָא, emph. אִגַּרְתָּא, Eg.-Aram. אגרה, אגרת, H. אִגֶּרֶת, Akk. *egirtu* Lagarde GA 184:22, Nöld. ZDMG xl 733, Meissner ZA xv 414, KAT 649) letter. St. cstr. **ʿngar** s.v. MG 156 footn. Pl. **ʿngir(i)ata.** The term is also applied to a rite performed for the dying (esp. st. cstr. **ʿngar**) MMII 171. **bšitin uhda ʿngirta** Gy 321:15 in 61 letters; **ʿngirta mhatamta** Gs 108:20 a sealed letter; **ʿngirta bkušṭa ktiba uhtima bʿsqat rurbia** CP 91:7, Gs 108:20 f., 109:2 a letter written in Truth and sealed by the ring of the Great (Life); **nišma d̠-ʿngirta dria** Gs 108:23 f. the soul that carried the letter; **man kitbh̠ lʿngirta** CP 91:6, Gy 109:1 who wrote the letter?; **ʿngirata mhatamata ptulata** Gs 7:24 sealed 'letters' the virgins; **uʿngirta bʿdh̠ dria** DC 46 and he carried the letter in his hand; **maṣbutiata uʿngiriata** ATŠ II no. 136 baptisms and 'letters'; **uʿburia uʿngiriata lmatauata nišadrun** AM 242:3 and they will send out grain and letters to (various) places.

ʿndiruna, ʿndruna 1 (cf. **and(i)runa**) booth constructed for ritual purposes such as marriage and initiation; a chamber. Pl. **-ia.** Masc. Var. **andruna, hindruna, and(i)runa** s.vv. **uhuṣiun ʿndruna** ŠQ 5:4 and construct the (wedding) booth; **bʿndruna hadta** Gy 260:17, ATŠ II no. 32 in a new booth; pl. **ʿndrunia hadtia** Gs 25:3 new chambers; **uʿndruna mitibnilh̠** ATŠ II no. 339 and an inner chamber is built for her; **ʿndruna d̠-nhura** Gy 257:8, 16, 18 chamber of light; **ʿndruna šmima nsib** Gy 104:8, 109:19 f., 116:11 the chamber (of the body) grew stiff; **ʿndrunia d̠-mia** Gy 304:23 chambers of water; **bʿndrunia hiklia hadtia** Gy 22:16 in the chambers of new palaces; **ulʿndrunia ulhiklia hadtia** Gs 23:24 and chambers and new palaces (acc.). Often, esp. in wedding texts and rituals.

ʿndruna 2 (for **druna,** Syr. ܕܪܘܢܐ Hoffmann: *Auszüge* 96, P. درون sacred meal of the Parsis, Haug: *Essays* 2nd ed. 407) Gy 224:2 the sacramental bread of Parsis MR 220, Ginzā 225 n. 3.

ʿnuš a frequent var. of **anuš** Ginzā 48 n. 1.

ʿnuta (עִנְוְתָא, H. עֲנָוָה) Gy 275:ult. condescension MG 57:4, 111:2, 275:24.

ʿnza (עִזָּא, ࡏࡍࡆࡀ, Ar. عَنْز, Akk. *enzu*) goat, nanny-goat. Pl. **-ia. apriš lʿnza d̠-hʿ ʿma d̠-hšuka** ATŠ I no. 253 he taught about the nanny-goat that is the mother of darkness. Pl. with procl. prep. **binzia** AM 232:8 amongst goats.

ʿnzaba = **anzaba** (q.v.). **pt ʿnzaba pšira pt aina rabtia d̠-nzaba** DC 40. 199 daughter of unloosed torrent; daughter of the great spring of the torrent.

ʿniana (rt. **ANA I** = **ʿNA I,** עֲנְיָינָא, ࡏࡍࡉࡀࡍࡀ) answer, reply, response, antiphonal recitation, hymn (sung antiphonally), anthem MG 136:15. Pl. **-ia, ʿnianʿia, ʿninʿ** MG 6:17; the pl. used of a collection of antiphonal hymns Euting ZDMG xix 128, ML xiv f., CP trs. 106. Often with **RMA: ʿniana ramilia** Gy 152:11 BCD & Sh. 'Abd.'s copy (A has **qarilia**) they gave me answer; **mahu d̠-ʿniana rmilh̠** Gy 343:12 what shall I answer him?; **ʿniana ldilia . . . ramia** Gy 343:19, 344:2, 351:11, 18 f. he gave me . . . answer; **ʿniana rmalh̠** Gy 343:22 I will address him; **ʿniana nirmulh̠** Gy 345:8 they spoke (hist. pres.) to him; **uʿniana nirmilun** Gy 345:11 and he gave them answer; **ʿniana lptahil rma** Gy 349:21 he addressed P.; **ana ʿniana rmit** Gy 352:1 I made a speech; **uʿniana liušamin rmit** Gy 352:10 f. and I spake to Y.; **ʿniana rmilh̠ liušamin** l. 14 id.; **uahuatai ʿniania** (var. **-na** B) **ramian** Jb 128:9 f. and my sisters sing anthems; **anin ʿniana . . . rminalh̠** Jb 219:8 f. we conversed with him etc. Similarly with **QRA: ʿniana qarilia** Gy 152:11 A (above s. **RMA**); **ʿniana qrilh̠ biniania uzaharia** PD 839 speak to him in hymns and admonitions. Often with **draša** 1 (q.v.). **mn qalaihun d̠-ʿnianai** Jb 82:2 from the sound of my recitations; **mn qala d̠-ʿnianun** Jb 128:10 f. from the sound of their recitations; **ṭamranun lʿnianai** Jb 129 I (fem.) secretly preserve my hymns.

ʿniara = **niara** (q.v.).

ʿnibta, ʿnipta (ࡏࡍࡉࡁࡕࡀ, Jew.-Aram. עִנְבָּא, H. עֵנָב, Ar. عِنَبٌ & عِنَبَةٌ, Sab. 𐩲𐩬𐩨, Akk. *enbu* Lewy: *Fremdw.* 24) grape, raisin MG 110:2. Pl. **ʿnbia, ʿmbia** cf. ࡏࡍࡁࡉࡀ) with apparent sg.-forms **ʿnba, ʿmba** s.vv. **uʿl ʿumṣa bataraita natna ʿnibta** ŠQ 7:14 and on the last piece he places a raisin (or grape?); **ʿumṣa d̠-bgauh̠ ʿnibta** (var. **ʿnipta**) ŠQ 7:17 the piece in which is the raisin.

ʿniš (Talm. אִינִישׁ = H. אִישׁ = Ar. إِنْس, otherwise Aram. אֱנָשׁ = Syr. ܐܢܫ, ܢܫ = H. אֱנוֹשׁ

= Ar. أُناس , ناس MG 151:8 & n. 1) someone, somebody, anyone, anybody, a(ny) person MG 28:8, 151:8. Only st. abs. MG 151 n. 1, 183:8, 302:16. With negation: no one, nobody. **ʿniš biša** Gy 43:22 any evil person MG 317:7 ff.; **ʿniš ʿniš** (*often*) each person, one by one, **kul ʿniš** (*often*) everyone. Gl. 38:14 **anš** [*sic*] with *kisr* under **a** and **n** and a *tašdīd* over **n** (indicating a pronunciation *enneš*; Modern Mandaeans read ābāgādically *īneš*) احد *quis-quis* یکی .

ʿnišbai (a peculiar transformation of ܐܠܝܫܒܥ, *'Ελεισάβετ* Jb ii p. xx:15, Burkitt EB s.v. *Mandaeans*, MSt 97:5, Lidzb. ZDMG lxi 691) Elisabeth, the mother of John the Baptist. CP 199b:12 f. and often (cf. Jb 67: 5 ff., 80:14, 81:4, 117:1).

ʿnkan (Ar. إِنْ كَانَ) AM 277:41, 280:19 (*& often in mod. texts*) even if, though, though it were. Var. **nkan** s.v.

ʿnkista Gy 6:17 = **nkista** MG 25:anteantep.

ʿnsisuta AM 16 = **nsisuta**.

ʿnṣibat ʿutria ('She–was–planted–by–the–uthras') CP 7:penult. MD 9:3 f., 12:7 a female uthra ML 282.

ʿnpiš often for **npiš**.

ʿnšia (נְשַׁיָּא & נְשֵׁי, ܢܶܫ̈ܶܐ, H. נָשִׁים, Ar. نسون , نساء) pl. of **ʿnta gubria uʿnšia** (*often*) men and women. Frequent idioms: **lgaṭ bʿnšia** s. **LGṬ** and **autib bʿnšia** s. **YTB**; **bnaiun uʿnšaiun** DC 40. 970 their sons and women.

ʿnta (אִנְתְּתָא, ܐܰܢ̱ܬ݁ܬ݂ܳܐ, H. אִשָּׁה, Ar. أُنْثَى, South-Ar. 𐩱𐩬𐩻𐩩, Eth. አንስት, Akk. cf. Nyberg MO xiv 195:19) a female, woman, wife. St. abs.? **atuat** s.v. Pl. **ʿnšia.** MG 183:9 ff. **hdia maran bʿntaian ʿnta d-ʿhabnalak** Gy 148:8 rejoice, our lord, in our woman, the wife that we have given thee (MG 179:2); **uʿhabnalh ʿnta haua bzauih** Gy 106:6 f. and we gave him the woman Eve as his wife; **ʿntak d-masqa qinak** Jb 27:6 f. thy wife that raises thy family.

Gl. **anta** [*sic*] انثى *femina* ماده .

ʿntata s. **ntata.**

ʿntta *Florilegium* 362:150 = **ʿnta.**

ʿSA s. **ASA III.**

ʿsada (אִסָּדָא, ܐܶܣܳܕ݂ܳܐ, H. יְסוֹד, Ar. وساد) bolster, head-rest, pillow. MG 115 n. 1. **ʿl ʿsada ladam qamlh** Gs 10:2 he stood by the pillow of Adam; **ʿutra lʿsadh lʿqum** Gs 106:20 an uthra standeth by his pillow; **ʿsadai akla rba d-ziua** DC 37. 402 my pillow is a great halo (?) of radiance.

ʿsauad (Ar. أَسْوَد?) Zotb. 226b:21 a man's name.

ʿs(a)qta s. **ʿsqta.**

ʿsara (rt. **ASR** I) confinement, prison: **d-atia mn ʿsara** DC 40. 733 he that comes from bondage.

ʿshaq often for **shaq.**

ʿsura, ʿusura (rt. **ASR I,** אֱסוּר Dan. 4:12) bond, confinement, prison, binding spell, exorcism, ban MG 118:18. Pl. **-ia.** With pref.: **bisura** Gy 340:10 (varr. **bʿsura** B, **bʿusura** C) in a bond; **bit ʿsura** CP 34:3, ML 39:12 prison; **maṭia lʿsura upaliṭ** AM 12:4 he reaches prison, but he will escape; **ubʿsura nišauunh** AM 191:9 and they will commit him to prison; **usahria ʿstar bʿsurun** DC 44. 208 and the devils were bound by their spell.

ʿsṭus DC 22. 386:2 a miscop. of **ʿṣṭug** (q.v.).

ʿsiqta = **ʿsqta. ʿsiqta d-amsinun lṭuria** DC 35 the compression which consolidated mountains; **ʿsiqta uškihita lahun** ATŠ controversy and forgetfulness do not exist; **htimitun bʿsiqta d-rba ulazuṭa** Or. 327:7 ye are sealed by a (compulsion) seal that is great and not small.

ʿsir(a) pass. pt. pe. of **ASR I** (q.v.).

ʿsmala = **smala** MG 25:anteantep.

ʿsnia (*often*) = **snia.**

ʿspar 1 = **aspar 1** (st. abs. & cstr. of **sipra 1**). MG 26:9. **uʿspar dukranai** Gy 205:22 D s. **aspar.**

ʿspar 2 s. **spar 2** (st. abs. of **ṣipra**) MG 44:20.

ʿsparg(i)la = **spargla.**

ʿspia & **ʿspihata** plurals of **sipta** (q.v.).

ʿspinta DAb = **spinta.**

ʿspira = **spira 1. raza d-ʿspira ʿlaita** DC 43 J 184 the mystery of the upper sphere; **kd alahia bʿspiria d-šumia** DC 26. 556 f. like gods in the heavenly spheres; **uasqinun lʿspira d-ʿšumia** Gy 33:24 and he raised them on the heavenly sphere; **bʿspiria rurbia d-šrara** in the great spheres of reality Ginzā 198 n. 2.

ʿSQ I s. **ASQ I.**

ʿSQ II s. **ASQ II.**

ʿsqa (rt. **ʿSQ II** = **ASQ II,** cf. foll.) (*a*) bond, band, snare MG 46:4, masc., pl. **-ia,** (*b*) st. abs. of foll. (*a*) **hiia gṭarlia ʿsqa** Jb 151:14 the Life tied a snare for me; **šapir ašlak uʿsqak** Jb 149:11 fair is thy (fishing-)line and thy snare (Jb ii 153 n. 3); **man ramia ʿsqia** (var. **ʿsria** (ʿ)**biušamin**) Jb 25:13 who putteth bonds on Y.?; **uʿsqia** (var. **uʿsria** C) **biaminh rma** Jb 25:15 and he put bonds on his right hand (Jb ii 32 n. 4); (*b*) **bisqa ušum hazin maria guš-banqa** DC 45 by the impression and name of this owner of the seal; **uruban ʿsqia** ŠQ (PA's) and myriad jewels (??) (עסק?).

ʿsqaq sahra DC 43 a demon.

ʿsqubra s. **squbra.**

ʿsqupta s. **squpta.**

ʿsqta (by progr. assimil. from עִזְקְתָא, ܥܶܙܩܬ݂ܳܐ) ring, seal-ring, impression of seal. Varr. **ʿsaqta, ʿsiqta, ʿzqta** s.vv. St. abs. **ʿsqa** (see preced. **ʿs** (*b*)). St. cstr. **ʿsqat.** Pl. **ʿsqata.** MG 46:5 f. **ana šiplit ʿsqta ušdibh** Gy 147:13 I took off the ring and threw it at her; **ʿsqta d-šdibh** Gy 147:13 f. (*twice*); **ʿsqta d-šdibia** l. 16; **balman dilan kd hazin ʿsqta laiit** Gy 147:16 f. in our world there is no (other) ring like this; **htimna ana bʿsqat hibil ušitil uanuš** DC 44. 1479 = Morg. 266/22:24 I am sealed with the seal(-ring) of H., Š., and A.; **ʿsqata** DAb rings; **htima bʿsqat hiia ubʿsqat br bhiria ubʿsqat rbia ubʿsqat rurbia** DC 37. 418 f. sealed by the seal of Life etc.

ʿSR s. **ASR.**

ʿsrin (ܥܣܪܝܢ) a more original but rarer form of **srin** twenty MG 34:19, 189:10. **ʿsrin uhamša** twenty-five, but **tmania uʿsrin** Gy 30:21 twenty-eight MG 189:22, 24.

ʿstad occasionally for **ʿustad.**

ʿstauara s. **ʿstuara.**

ʿstana s. **stana.**

ʿstaqlus name of a supernatural being ML 282. **manharbʿil ʿstaqlus** ML 24:2 = CP 21:15; **ʿstaqlus ialda zuṭa** DC 34. 315 Estaqlus the youthful boy.

ʿstuara = **stuara** (q.v.). Ginzā 203 n. 1. **ligrai lašar ulaqam ʿl ʿstuarai** Gy 203:9 my feet were unsteady and were not planted firmly on my soles; **ʿul ʿstuarun lakainia** Gy 264:8 they had no firm foothold; **uʿqbai ḏ-raiit qam ʿl ʿstuarḥ** Gy 266:8 and my shaking heels stood firm on their stance; **ligrak alma rat mn ʿstuarun** Gy 266:11 why did thy feet shake from their foothold?; **ligrai ʿl ʿstauarai lakainilia** Gy 272:19 f. my feet had no firm foothold; **ligrai ʿl ʿstuara laqaimilia** Gy 294:10 id.

ʿstura (rt. **ASR**) bond. **umistar bʿstura ḏ-ptahil** ATŠ II no. 5 he shall be bound with the bond of P. Var. **ʿsura** DC 35 ibid.

ʿstiuara = **stuara** (q.v.). fig. resolution, staunchness (P. استواری). **uʿstiuarḥ smak ʿl šuialia ḏ-ana šailit mn malka ʿlaia** ATŠ I no. 8 and firmly bases himself on the questions which I asked from the Celestial King (see ATŠ trs. p. 113 n. 1).

ʿstira 1 s. **astira.**

ʿstira 2, ʿstra (ܐܣܬܪܐ) < Akk. *Ištar* Zimmern: *Akk. Fremdw.* 61) Astarte, another name of Venus-Libat. Pl. **ʿstirata** used of female demons MG 171:1 & n. 1. **la bšum ʿstra** DC 3 = CP 31:9 not in the name of Astarte; **kul ruh ʿstira ukulhin qiriatiḥ** Or. 331:4 every Astarte-spirit and all her creations; **kima ʿstra ušidia udaiuia ulilìata** DC 43 constellation, Astarte, devils, demons, and liliths; **ʿstra amamit** (*often in exorcisms*); **alahia zikria uʿstirata nuqbata** DC 43 A 32 etc. (*often*) male gods and female astartes; **brata ḏ-kul ʿstirata** Gy 10:4 daughter of all the astartes; **ruha qrat humria uqrat ʿstirata** Gy 99:9 R. created amulet-spirits and astartes; **ruha lʿstirata ḏ-minḥ qaria** Gs 92:12 R. calleth the astartes which are from her; **liliata uʿstirata** Gs 99:13; **bʿstirata naqdḥ** Gy 92:14 with a better var. **uʿstirata niqda** Leid. (Ginzā 530 n. 2) and the astartes shall cry; **ʿsira ʿstira ʿstiraita** DC 43 A 137 bound is the astarte-like astarte.

ʿstqutqup IM 37:3 an infernal being IM 96:9.

ʿstra s. **ʿstira.**

ʿPA s. **APA II.**

ʿpdania (plu.) JRAS 1937 594:10 ploughed fields. **kma šapiria ʿpdania** how fair are the ploughed fields.

ʿpia (rt. **APP** = **ʿPP**) veils, coverings, wrappings, folds. **uarba ʿpia apth** Gy 167:6 s. **APP** pf. with encl. **ʿl arba ʿpia kanth** Gy 84:2 f. I covered him fourfold (lit. with four coverings); **hṭit uaskilit d-trin ʿpia** DC 34. 366 I failed and was doubly foolish.

ʿpik(a) pass. pt. pe. of **APK** (q.v.).

ʿpikata (fem. pl. of preced.) sections. **ʿpikata haizak ʿtpalag** AM sections are thus divided.

ʿpikuta (abstr. noun from preced.) perversion, evil taste. **bišuta uʿpikuta uṭʿia** Gy 215:17 evil, perversion, and error; **uakla lhama bʿpikuta ušatia mia bmrara** AM 66:8 and she will eat bread with an evil taste and drink water with bitterness.

ʿpikta for **ʿpikuta** in **tuqpa uʿpikta** ATŠ II no. 64 violence and perversion.

ʿpip(a) pass. pt. pe. of **APP** (q.v.).

ʿPK s. **APK.**

ʿPP s. **APP.**

ʿPQ s. **APQ.**

ʿprišaia Jb 9:6 etc. for **prišaia.** Pl. **-aiia.**

ƐṢA (Ar. عصى) to rebel. Only Ar. forms: **iiƐṣun lmalka** AM 277:11 f. they will rebel against the king; **iiƐṣun ʿlḥ** AM 285:20 they will rebel against him.

–ṣaṣa occ. var. of **(a)ṣaṣa.**

ʿṣba 1 (formally closer to H. אֶצְבַּע, Ar. إِصْبَع, South-Ar. 𐩱𐩮𐩨𐩲 as a measure, Eth. አጽባዕት, than to Aram. צְבְעָא, ܨܒܥܐ) (*a*) finger, toe, (*b*) inch. Occ. var. **ʿuṣba 2.** Doublets **ʿṣbita, ṣbita** s.v. Pl. as 'finger' **ʿṣbata,** as 'inch' **ʿṣbia.** (*a*) **halil ʿṣbatḥ** Gy 197:11 he cleansed his fingers; **masgia . . . briša ḏ-ʿṣbatḥ** Gy 217:2 f. he . . . walketh on tiptoe; (*b*) **qibaṣra ʿṣba hda** Gs 9:17 she is one inch smaller MG 352:15 f.; **upalginun bʿṣbia ʿṣbia** Jb 231:7 he divided it (: water) inch by inch (Lidzb. *und teilte es in Adern* ii 213 n. 2).

Gl. 35:11 missp. اصبع *digitus* انگشت.

ʿṣba 2 (ܨܒܥܐ, abs. ܨܒܥ) colour, dye, pigment, tincture, tinge; Lidzb. glimmer (s. **ʿuṣba 1**). Varr. **ʿuṣba, ʿ(u)zba** s.v. **ʿṣba ḏ-nhura** Gs 48:13, 129:24, Jb 244:5 glimmer of light; **ʿṣba bsar** Gy 92:22, 211:8, MG 302:21 (even Lidzb. as *Fleischfarbe*).

ʿṣṭamumia = **sṭumumia** (pl. of **sṭmuma** q.v.). **gira uʿṣṭamumia** Morg. 256/4:19, **giraiun uʿṣṭamumun** Morg. 256/3:41 their arrows and their darts; **sipai uʿṣṭamumia** Morg. 267/24:2 = **sipia uʿṣṭamumia** Par. xxvii 22a swords and darts.

ʿṣṭartia (cf. s. **zuṭa**) adj. fem. little, small, young. **ʿhai ia rabutuia ʿṣṭartia** CP 235:5, 12 and ult. lo, my young mistress. **rum ʿṣṭartia** AM 199 Graecia Minor.

ʿṣṭaruan ʿlana CP 446:3 a personified tree.

ʿṣṭug (Pahl. סתוך, mod. P. ستوده, استوده) (DC 22. 386:2 **ʿsṭus**) Gy 389:23 miserable MG xxxi 17 f.

ʿṣṭuna (אִסְטְווָנָא, ܐܣܛܘܢܐ < P. ستون) column, pillar, trunk, support, banner-pole, (metaphorically of) the body. St. abs. & cstr. **ʿṣṭun.** Var. **ʿuṣṭuna** s.v. Pl. **-ia.** Hp Gn 34 f., 173, 193; Jb ii 115 n. 6. **ʿṣṭun kasia** Gy 372:7 mystic body; **ligrai . . . ḏ-ʿṣṭuna hʿ**

Gs 39:1 f., **pumai lʿṣṭuna hua** l. 2, **anai . . . ḏ-ʿṣṭuna hʿ** l. 3, **libai . . . lʿṣṭuna hua** l. 4 my feet, my mouth, my eyes, my heart became part of the body; **bdirka ḏ-ʿṣṭuna hʿ** l. 6 f. they are on the way of the body (MG 316: 15 ff.); **ʿṣṭuna ḏ-pagria** Gy 102:13, 18; **ʿṣṭun pagria** Q 38:1 f., Gs 38:21 f., 61:12, with prep. **biṣṭun pagria** Gs 102:6; **bʿṣṭuna ḏ-pagria** Gs 102:8 in the physical body; **ʿṣṭuna ḏ-bisra uzma** Gs 6:24 s. **bisra**; **ʿṣṭuna ḏ-ʿdia uligria litlh̲** Gy 219:8 a trunk without hands and feet; **ʿṣṭun ziua** Gy 141:8 the column of light; **ʿṣṭuna ḏ-hšuka** Gy 252:3 the column of darkness; **ʿṣṭunia ḏ-nhaša** RD copper columns; **ʿṣṭun glala** CP 178:5, ML 217:16 a column of stone; **ʿṣṭunia ḏ-kadba** Gy 355:20; **ʿṣṭuna** (var. **ʿṣṭun**) **ḏ-zipa** Gs 47:57; **ʿṣṭuna napla** Gs 62:19 (cf. l. 24). Personified: **zatan ʿṣṭuna** Jb 118:2, 136:7; **uailh̲ lilizar . . . ʿṣṭuna** Jb 136:6 woe to Elizar . . . the 'pillar'; **šuba ʿṣṭunia** Gy 331:21, MR 128:bottom & n. 2; **šumia ḏ-laʿṣṭuna** Gy 286:13 a sky without support.

ʿṣṭipra (rt. **ṢPR**) DC 48. 153, 165 for **ṣipra 2** DC 48. 160 fig. enlightenment.

ʿṣṭla (איסטלא, איצטלא, ܐܣܛܠܐ < στολή, Lat. *stola*) garment, robe, vestment MG xxx. 4. Masc. MG 159:5. St. abs. & cstr. **ʿṣṭal**. Pl. **-ia**. Very frequent var. **ʿuṣṭla** s.v. **ʿṣṭla ḏ-napšh̲** Gs 93:18 ff. his own garment.

ʿṣṭmumia = **sṭmumia** MG 45:10. **sipia uʿṣṭmumia** Gy 143:19 swords and darts.

ʿṢR s. **AṢR.**

ʿṣra occasionally for **ʿuṣra**.

ʿQA in **ʿumṣa ḏ-saqa ḏ-ʿqialia** (varr. **ḏ-ʿqalia** D, **ḏ-qrialia** C, **ḏ-aqarialia** B, **ḏ-aqrialia** DC 30) **ʿl tutbai** Jb 130:3 f. a piece of sackcloth that is joined (?patched?) to my garment (doubtf. cf. Jb ii 128 n. 3).

ʿqaiam, ʿqaiiam a *malwāša* man's name.

ʿqaimat a woman's name (*often in colophons*), name of a daughter of Yušamin. **ʿqaimat brata ḏ-iušamin** DAb.

ʿqamra = **aqamra**. **bina uʿqamra para uparta** DC 40. 787 f. the hair and wool of a male and ewe lamb.

ʿqar 1, ʿqara 1 (rt. **YQR**, יְקָרָא, ܐܝܩܪܐ) glory, respect, honour MG 4:4, 56:1, 115:22. Pl. **-ia**. **ʿqar giua** Gy 303:10 f., 360:21, CP 268:15; **ʿl ʿqar giua šaria ʿqara** CP 65:10 = Q 14:17, 30:2, 30 = ML 38:9, 81:3 on glorious splendour resteth glory; **ʿl dmut ʿqara** Gy 77:14 on account of the glory (doubtf.); **ʿqara ništkin bgauh̲** CP 268:15 glory shall dwell therein; **umzarzibun bšitin ʿqaria ḏ-nhura** DC 44. 1724 = Morg. 268/26:28 and equipped them with sixty glories of light; **giuat ʿqara** s. **giuat**.

ʿqar(a) 2 (rt. **AQR** = **ʿQR**, עִקְּרָא, עִקָּרָה, Bibl.-Aram. & mod. H. עִקָּר, Syr. ܥܩܪܐ) root MG 122:13, Nöld.'s conception of **ʿqar giua** glorious splendour? Gy 303:10 f. (s. **ʿqar 1** cf. Ginzā 301 n. 1). Doubtf.

ʿqar 3, ʿqaria = **qar** (q.v.) prep. with or without suff. with, by, to, at (the place of). Varr. **aqar 1** s.v., **ʿqria**. MG 195:13 ff. **anhin aqaraiun huin anin huainin ʿqaraiun** Gy 107:15 f. we were with them; **ʿqarh̲ huainin ḏ-adam** Gy 107:14 we were with Adam; **škub ʿqarai** Gy 96:4 sleep with me; **zipa udagaluta hda ʿqria** (var. **ʿqaria**? Nöld.) **habrh̲ liška** Gy 391:22 f. (preceded by a negation) no one shall practise deceit and treachery against his neighbour; **mn ʿqar ṭura . . . umn ʿqar kana rba ḏ-bh̲** DC 3. 164:12 = CP 188:12 from the mountain home . . . and from the home of the great company that dwelleth therein.

ʿQB s. **AQB.**

ʿqba 1 (עִקְבָא, ܥܩܒܐ, H. עָקֵב, Ar. عَقِب, from Akk. *iqbu*) heel, hence any curved part of the person, curve, hinder part MG 107:14. Masc. (differently from Syr.) MG 158:4. Pl. **-ia** often 'buttocks'. Also prep. 'behind'. **ʿqbai ḏ-raiit qam ʿl ʿstuarh̲** Gy 266:7 s. **ʿstuara**; **ʿqbai gihnit barqa** Gy 90:17 with my heel I stamped on the ground; **ʿqbh̲ gna barqa** Gy 84:16 f. his heel stamped on the ground; **pt ʿqba rba ḏ-hšuka** DC 40. 214 f. daughter of the great bottom (abyss?) of darkness; **mn ʿqba ugiada** DC 34:621 from the loins and membrum(?); **ʿtlh̲ ʿqbia** AM 22:2 she has curves (also of men AM 35:18) (? BZ 18 n. 7).

ʿqba 2 (read **ʿqda** from **ʿQD II**?) hobble-rope. **akuat kudania bmhara ukuat susia bʿqbh̲** DC 40. 473 like mules with the guide-rope and like a horse with a hobble-rope.

ʿQD I s. **YQD.**

ʿQD II? (עקד, ܥܩܕ, عقد) to tie, bind. Cf. s. **ʿqba 2.**

ʿquz(a) (cf. **QSS**) AM 21 etc. short MG 125: antep. Pl. **-ia** RD B 12.

ʿquptata pl. (cf. ܩܘܦܬܐ) bars, bands, fetters. **tabar sagariata uʿquptata** DC 26 he breaks locks and bars.

ʿqidbus ʿkuma DC 40. 85 a magic name given to the father of black salt.

ʿqila (pass. pt. pe. of **AQL** = **ʿQL**) crooked, twisted, perverted, tortuous, distorted. **dirkh̲ ʿqila** Gy 281:22 his road (is) tortuous; **bkušṭaiun ʿqila latipištun** ATŠ II no. 20 seal no pact with their perverted *kušṭa*. A reference to the ritual handshake confirming a pact in Magian and Christian rites.

ʿqisa (rt. **QSS**) crooked, twisted, splayed. Pl. **-ia** AM 14:13.

ʿQL, AQL (H. עקל, Ar. عقل, Syr. in derivatives) to twist, pervert, make tortuous.

Pe. Pass. pt. **ʿqila** s.v.

Der.: **aqalata, ʿqila.**

ʿqlim (Ar. إقْلِيم) AM 196 climate, region.

ʿQS = **QSS.**

ʿQR s. **AQR.**

ʿqraba AM 250:18 = **qraba.**

ʿqria Gy 391:22 s. **ʿqar 3, ʿqaria.**

ʿqrita DC 43 I 30 = **qrita.**

ʿqta AM 231:8 = **aqta** distress.

ʿRA (Jew.-Aram. אתערי to adhere, Syr. ܥܪܐ to take, contain, H. nif., hif. to pour out, mod. H. pi., Jew.-Aram. id., cf. Akk. *erū* to empty) to pour out, mix, intermingle.

Pe. Pf. & pass. pt. (identical) **arba mia hinun ʿria** DC 36 no. 218 they are four waters, they intermingled; **urahaṭia ʿria**

bgauẖ mzigia ATŠ II no. 128 and mingled (or poured out?) waters mixed therein.
DER.: **niara**?

ʿra (= *יְהִירָא) luminous MG 62:20. Fem. **ʿrta.** Pl. masc. **ʿria 1,** fem. **ʿrata** s.vv.

ʿran 1 Ṣâb.'s AM = **airan** Īrān.

ʿran 2 a demon? **ʿsir ʿran ḏ-raiim** DC 37 bound is I. that rages.

ʿrata (pl. of **ʿrta** = **arta**?) adj. fem. pl. luminous, lightgiving, shining, illumined, awaking, calling to life. **nišmata haiata ʿrata** Morg. 236/60:17 = Q 60:12 = CP 118:10 & par. the living and shining souls.

ʿRB I s. **ARB I.**

ʿRB II s. **ARB II.**

ʿrbita occ. var. of **rbita.**

ʿrubta occ. var. of **ʿurubta. kukba ʿrubta libat** AM the star of Friday (is) Venus.

ʿrusa (rt. **ARS,** Ar. عروس) bride. **ham uhamata ḏ-ʿrusa** JRAS 1937 594:33 the father and mother-in-law of the (newly-wed) bride; **hʿ hiduta ʿrusa** ATŠ II no. 369 she is a bride joined in matrimony.

ʿrup (cf. Ar. عَرْفَة) ulcer in the palm. BZ 62 n. 8. **ʿrup ʿda** AM.

ʿrupta AM 268 = **ʿurupta.**

ʿruta (abstr. noun from **ʿra**) illumination, enlightenment, glory, brilliance, dazzling light, (sometimes by epenthesis Jew. עִירוּתָא) waking, watchfulness, vigilance, like diligence, fervour in piety, heed MG 62:21, Jb ii 34 n. 5. Var. **airuta. barit bʿrutai** Gy 74:5 I shone in my brilliance; **banibẖ** (var. **baribẖ** Leid.) **bʿrutai** Gy 74:7 id.; **bʿruta bar** Gy 91:22, **bar bʿruta** Gy 341:9 he shone forth with radiance; **ʿruta utušbihta** Gy 91:13 f., 145:16, 219:16, 305:1, 9, 306:19, Q 3:10, 26:25 ff., 28:13, 41:21, Jb 221:12 (*& often*) fervour and praise; **ʿrutai utušbihtai** Gy 140:18 my fervour and my praise; **lʿrutai utušbihtai** Gy 305:20, 372:20 id. with prep.; **bʿruta usibruta utušbihta** Gy 157:1 (s. **sibruta**); **ʿruta usibruta** Q 3:10; **ṣauta ʿlai uʿruta** Gy 64:12 f. gleam on me and illumination (Brandt: *'Belehrung'* MSchr. 113 as if from ירה but cf. Jb ii 35 footn.). Opposed to **hšuka** Gs 66:9. **bʿrutun hdun** Gy 131:17 they rejoiced in their enlightenment; **libaihun sahiq bʿrutun** Gy 138:14 their heart leapeth for joy in their enlightenment; **ʿruta haza ḏ-ʿutria** Gy 141:17 this enlightenment of the uthras; **ʿruta udrašia** Gy 152:7 etc. enlightenment and hymns; **bʿruta umadihta ugaliuta** Gy 157:20 enlightenment, knowledge, and revelation; **lʿruta ulmadihta ulsibruta ultušbihta** Gy 305:9 enlightenment, knowledge, teaching, and praise; **bʿrutai uziuai** Gy 306:14 in my brilliance and radiance; **ʿruta ḏ-hiia** Gy 319:1 the splendour of Life; **ʿrutan** Gy 334:10 our enlightenment; **ʿrutun uṣautaihun** Gy 345:10; **ṣauta uʿruta** Q 25:30, 26:27 etc. radiance and illumination; **dnuta uʿruta** Gy 10:1 obeisance and vigilance; **lʿruthẖ ulgabaruathẖ** Gy 177:12 his splendour and his mighty deeds; **haila uʿruta** Gs 57:24 strength and vigilance; **ʿruta (u)haila** Gs 63:4, 122:24, **bhailai ubʿrutai** Oxf. 52 a in my strength and in my vigilance; **anhirtinun bʿruta** Gy 361:4 f. I enlightened them with my enlightenment; **ʿruta ḏ-aiar** Gy 373:18 the radiance of Ether; **ʿzal hzia ʿruta** Gs 67:5 I will go and see the radiance (Lidzb. *Kostbarkeit* Ginzā 494 n. 2); **nha bʿrutak** Gs 18:19 be calm in thy enlightenment; **bʿruta ḏ-abuia** Gs 49:9 in the radiance of his father; **nhurak uʿrutak** Jb 29:3 thy light and thy illumination; **ʿruta ḏ-mairalẖ** Jb 223:6 f. illumination that illumineth him; **mia ʿruta** AM 123 water of enlightenment (cf. **mia ʿria** s. **ʿria 1**); **ʿruta ušinta** Jb 142:13 waking and sleep; **mšaba bʿruta ḏ-hu šra ʿlauaihun** DC 26. 493 f. they praise in the glory which resteth upon them.

ʿria 1, ʿriia 1 pl. of **ʿra. mia hiia ʿria urauzia** DC 48 waters of life shining and resplendent; **mia anatun hiia ʿriia urauzia** DC 51. 699 ye are living waters shining and resplendent; **mia ʿria urauzia** ATŠ II no. 317 etc.

ʿria 2, ʿriia 2 pass. pt. pe. of **ʿRA** (q.v.).

ʿria 3 (rt. **AUR** = **ʿUR**) Gy 341:19 pl. the wakeful ones.

ʿriba (pass. pt. pe. of **ARB II** = **ʿRB**) (*a*) mixed, mingled, (*b*) subst. mixing-bowl, potion. Pl. **-ia.** (*a*) **halba ʿriba** s. **halba; ahia ʿribia** AM 41, 77, 95 brothers with a different mother (frequent in cases of polygamy); (*b*) **ušatin umrauin mn ʿribẖ** DC 53. 459:9 (no. 379) they will drink and take (their) fill of its sweetness (cf. H. ערב III, Targ. מְעָרַב pleasing, sweet).

ʿrika (pass. pt. pe. of **ARK** = **ʿRK,** Syr. ܐܪܝܟ, H. אָרֹךְ) long, tall, lengthy MH 117:2. St. abs. **ʿrik.** Fem. st. emph. **ʿrikt(i)a.** Pl. **-ia,** fem. **-ata. ʿrika gaṭina hauia** AM 8:13 he will be tall and slender; **ʿrikia gbinẖ** AM 35:16 s. **gbina; kṣurta ʿrika** AM a lengthy illness; **ʿuhra ʿrikta** DC 48. 381 a long road; **maria šinia ʿrikata** AM 27:13 f. he has (lit. owner of) long teeth.

ʿRK s. **ARK.**

ʿRS s. **ARS.**

ʿRP = **RUP.**
PE.? Impt. **ʿrup bšum qupa adunai** AM 125:penult. be loosened (?) in the name of Q.-A.

ʿrpila = **arpila** (q.v.).

ʿRQ s. **ARQ I.**

ʿrqiha a var. of **rqiha.**

ʿrta fem. of **ʿra** shining, dazzling, bright. Pl. **ʿrata** s.v. **ʿrta urauazta** Gy 285:22, Q 4:26, 13:20, 60:12, DC 26, 186 f. (*& often*) bright and flourishing; **ʿrta nahirta taqunta urauazta** Gy 285:8 dazzling, shining, bright and resplendent.

ʿrtitia = **rtitia. ʿšata ḏ-ʿrtitia** AM 119 a feverish ague.

ʿša Zotb... 227a:14 = **ʿtša** nine.

ʿšaita DC 22. 405 & Sh. 'Abd.'s copy's var. of **ašiathẖ** Gs 15:14 its walls (cf. s. **ašita**).

ʿšasar Par. viii:coloph. = **ʿtšasar** nineteen MG 2:16.

ʿšata (Jew.-Aram. אִישָׁתָא, Bibl.-Aram. אֶשָּׁא, Syr. ܐܶܫܳܬܳܐ, Akk. *išātu*, Eth. እሳት, H. אֵשׁ) (*a*) fire, flame, (*b*) fever MG 120:4. Pl. id. but also **ʿšatia** (with **t** made part of the rt.) MG

168:6 f., although otherwise it is used as fem. (*a*) **ʿšatkun** your fire MG 179:17; **ʿšata haita** Gy 76:3 f., 77:23 f., 193:4, 239:12, 23, 267:5 f., Jb 51:14 (*& often*) the living Flame; **ʿšata haita šnat** Gy 94:4, 6 the living Flame changed; **lbuša ḏ-ʿšata haita** Gy 89:4, 195:22, 250:15, 21 = **lbuš ʿšata haita** Gy 97:5, 8, 11, 114:6 clothing of living Fire; **klil ʿšata haita** Gy 80:3, 82:22 crown of living Flame; **ṣauta ḏ-šata haita** Gy 100:8 brilliance of the living Fire; **mšauniat ʿšata haita** Gy 87:9, 295:13 (s. **mšuniat**); **ʿšata ʿkilta** Gy 71:10, 73:10, 77:24, 87:19, 89:19, 101:10, 267:5 f. (*& often*) consuming fire, DC 27. 81 encircling flame, halo, similarly **lbuš ʿšata ʿkilta** Gy 118:16, **tlat ʿšata** Jb 124:3 = **ltat ʿšatia** l. 4 (var. **tlata** ACD F DC 30) three flames; **hirba uʿšata** RD C 4 sword (or destruction) and fire; **ʿšata ḏ-napšh** Gy 84:12 his own fire; (*b*) **mara ʿšata** DC 46 a man suffering from fever; **ʿšata hamimtia** AM a high fever. Often in exorcisms.

ʿšbila = **šbila**. Pl. with suff. **ʿšbilh** Gy 281:22 his paths.

ʿšu (ܝܫܘܥ, Soghd. *yyšw* MMBBb 142) Jesus MG 56:3, 70:paen. **ʿšu mšiha** Jb 103 ff., **ʿšu mšiha baṭla** Gy 184:6, Oxf. 19 a, **ʿšu mahiana** Gy 28:17, **ʿšu br miriam** Gy 382:10 ff.

ʿšuhia Gy 250:15, var. **ʿšauia** DC 22. 246:6 to equalize, harmonize. Corrupt from **ŠAA II.**

ʿšul DC 22. 408 for (ʿ)**šiul.**

ʿšuma occ. var. of **šuma** MG 33:7.

ʿšumia a frequent var. of **šumia** heavens MG 28:ult., 33:7, AF 228 n. 7.

ʿšiul Gy 175:22, 230:16, 18, 233:7 f., 313:15, Gs 17:24, 114:17 etc. = **šiul** (q.v.).

ʿšimʿil RD 26 Ismael (cf. **šumʿil**).

ʿšiqa (pass. pt. pe. of **AŠQ** = **ʿŠQ**) blind. Lidzb. corrected his former opinion as to the occasional meaning 'oppressed' Jb ii 102 n. 2 (cf. MG 418:20) in ZS i 2. Var. **ašiqa** s.v. Pl. **-ia.** **lʿšiqa hulh paruanqa** Gy 15:16, Gs 103:12 be a leader to a blind (man); **ʿšiqa ḏ-baiia paruanqa** Jb 102:4 a blind one that seeketh a leader; **ʿšiqa ʿngirta lakadib** Jb 105:7 a blind person writeth not a letter; **ʿšiqa ʿngirta kadib** l. 11 id. positively; **man ʿšiqa ḏ-ʿtpata** Jb 72:8 who is the blind man whose eyes were opened? Pl. **ʿšiqia** Q 14:20.

ʿškia ḏ-gidria Oxf. roll g 1064 s. **gidra.**

ʿšna s. **ʿušana.**

ʿšnia = **šnia** (q.v.).

ʿšpinza a var. of **špinza.**

ʿšpita DC 22. 32 & Sh. 'Abd.'s copy's var. of **špita** Gy 33:15.

ʿŠQ s. **AŠQ.**

ʿšqa (rt. **ʿŠQ** = **AŠQ**) slander, oppression. Masc. **ʿšqa biša** CP 33:9, Q 14:13 = ML 39:5 wicked slander.

ʿšrita occ. var. of **šrita.**

ʿšta 1 (ܐܫܬܐ, H. שֵׁת I, Akk. *išdu*, Ar. إِسْت, Nöld.: *Beiträge* 42, MG 98 n. 2, Brockelm. i 334) basis, bottom, posterior, anus, buttocks. Nöld. proposed **bʿšta** or **bʿušta** for the unintelligible **bšušta** Gy 382:5 (var. **pšušta** Lond.) MG 98:17 ff. **šaipia ʿl ʿštaihin** IM 37:1 they shuffle along on their buttocks; **ʿštaiun mgalia** ATŠ I no. 250 they expose their anus; **ušria ʿšth ubuṭh udundh** DC 12. 111 and free his buttocks, his anus, and his penis, cf. Lond. roll B 224.

ʿšta 2 a frequent mod. form of cl. **hašta** now.

ʿt- the form of **ʿit** (*b*) with enclitics. **ḏ-ligria napšia ʿtlun** Gy 279:21 which have many feet; **ʿtbak haila** Gy 173:16, 213:11 thou hast strength; **ʿtlh ḏ-gubria ʿnšia** Gy 280:14 he hath (members) of men and women MG 401.

ʿTA I s. **ATA I.**

ʿTA II s. **ʿTA II.**

ʿtaps(a)ramka s. **tapsramka.**

ʿTB s. **YTB.**

ʿtia, var. **ʿitia** Nöld.: אֲתְיָא coming MG 294 footn., Lidzb.: ܐܬܝܘܬܐ being, existence, ML 134 n. 1, Ginzā 403 n. 4, ZS i 1. **ata ʿtia ḏ-hiia** Gy 375:21 the Being of Life came; **lʿtia** (varr. **lʿtia, litia**) **ḏ-ata** CP 105:5 = Q 55:29 = ML 134:7 to the Being which came; **ʿtia ḏ-bhiria zidqa** Q 57:11 = ML 138:3 = CP 112:11 the being (existence) of the proven of righteousness; **asgia ṭaba atalh lʿtia** CP 180:9 = ML 220:10, 221:1 the good one went and came into being (existence).

ʿtiabuta Gy 194:18 = **tiabuta** MG 25:antep.

ʿtiaruta (*often*) = **tiaruta.**

ʿtira in **bʿtira rba** ATŠ no. 287 = **bdaura rba** DC 6 ibid.

ʿtit, ʿtita (עֲתִיד, ܥܬܝܕ, H. עָתִיד, Ar. عَتِيد) destined, predestined, designate, designed, fore-ordained, prepared, equipped, ready, future, established, brought about MG 43:4, 117:1, MSchr 140 n. 3, 202 n. 1, ML 251 n. 1, Ginzā 152 n. 1. Pl. **-ia. hibil mana ʿtita** Gy 135:14 H. the fore-ordained *māna* (MSchr. 140 n. 3); **šum ʿtita ḏ-ʿtit lmitia** Gy 192:18 the name of the Predestined One that is designate to come (cf. ὁ ἐρχόμενος Matt. 3:11, 11:3). **iauar ʿtita** Gy 291:35, **piria ḏ-iauar ʿtita** Gy 322:4; **ltušlimia ʿtitia** CP 246: 13 to the Predestined Perfection (i.e. Šišlam q.v.); **gubria ḏ-qaštaiun mlai** (var. **mlia** DC 28) . . . **ḏ-hinun ʿtitia** DC 26. 188 = DC 28 par. men whose bow is drawn (at the ready), who are ready (for attack); **mania iaqria ʿtitia** CP 447:8 holy, predestined *mānas*; **ʿṣṭuna ḏ-ʿtit minh ḏ-tihuia šurbta ʿtita** Gs 62:ult. the body from which there shall be a predestined race (**ʿtit ḏ-** followed by impf. to describe a future, to tell what will surely take place). Used also substantively as fem.; **akandit ḏ-ʿtita lahuat** Gy 294:23 what had to take place did not yet happen MG 299:paen. With encl. (cf. also s. **ATT**): **ʿtitlh lmizal** Gy 126:7 it is predestined that he shall go; **ʿtitlak lʿtigluiia** Q 54:5 it is predestined that it shall be revealed to thee MG 386; **ḏ-ʿtitlh lbuša** Jb 216:2 for whom a garment is prepared; **ʿtita qadmaita** DC 43 I 106 the first predestinate one (fem.).

ʿtmal (Talm. אתמל, Targ. אֶתְמָלֵי, Syr. ܐܬܡܠܝ, H. אֶתְמוֹל, Eth. ትማልም, Akk. *timāli, itimāli* and *ina timāli* Jensen ZA xi 352) yesterday MG 34:5, 202:4. **ʿtmal liardna zamintak** Gy 190:15 yesterday I bade thee to the jordan; **ʿtmal damit nišma iumai lmahu damit** Gs 84:14 f. what didst thou resemble yesterday, (o) soul, what dost thou resemble today? cf. ll. 11 f., 13 f., 16; **ʿla ʿtmal ʿla paina** Gs 111:16 f. but yesterday, but (last) evening.

ʿtpaq (Ar. إِتِّفَاق) happening. **kd ʿtpaq d̠-kanun ltania iuma d̠-habšaba hauia** AM 285:25 when (the beginning) of *Kânûn al-thânî* happens (to fall) on a Sunday.

ʿTR I s. **ATR II** = **YTR.**

ʿTR II s. **ATR I.**

ʿTR III = **NTR.**

Pe. Pf. **ʿtar hanath̠ asara rba** DC 34. 185 that great bond fell away; **uʿtar lpandamh̠** ATŠ I no. 173 and he dropped the *pandama*; **uriha larma uʿtar** ATŠ II no. 27 and he did not cast in or omitted the incense. Impf. **unitar** (var. **ʿtar** PD) **lpihta** ATŠ I no. 176 and he omits (leaves out) the *pihta*. Impt. **ʿtar ubaṭal mn pagrh̠** DC 43 forsake and withdraw from his body.

ʿtrahmuta (often) = **trahmuta.**

ʿtrug,, trunga (Onkelos אתרוג, Syr. ܬܪܘܓܐ & ܐܬܪܘܓܐ, P. تُرُنج & أُتْرُنج Löw no. 17) citron, citrous fruit. Pl. **ʿtringiata** s.v. **uanka lʿtrunga ʿthib** DC 34. 378 and tin was assigned to the citrus fruit.

ʿtrin = **trin. lʿtrin** Gy 305:15 A = **ltrin** BCD MG 26:6 f.

ʿtringiata pl. of **ʿtrunga** citron-trees. **bṭula d̠-ʿtringiata** ŠQ in the shade of the citron-trees.

ʿtrisar = **trisar** MG 188:12.

ʿtriṣuta occ. var. of **triṣuta.**

ʿša occasionally for **ʿtša, ʿšasar** occasionally for **ʿtšasar** MG 2:16.

ʿtša (cf. s. **tša**) nine MG 36:3, 188:3.

ʿtšaia rarely for **tši(i)aia** ninth.

ʿtšima = **tšima** 900 MG 190:5.

ʿtšin = **tšin** 90 MG 189:17.

ʿTT = **ATT.**

ʿtta AO ix 104 Text O 1.5 = **ʿnta.**

P

p the 17th letter of the alphabet Siouffi 160, 162, 169, MMII 242. Pronunciation: plosive *p*, or aspirated (fricative) *f*, a supplementary letter with two diacritical points **p̈** being sometimes used to indicate the Ar. ف in Ar. loan-words MMII 244. Phonetic changes: **p** > **b** and vice versa MG § 51.

PAA I (פעא, ܦܥܐ, H. פעה, Ar. بغى to bleat) to open the mouth, make a plaintive noise, bleat, cry, whimper, whine.

Pe. Pf. **pt** (var. **pta** D, read **pat**) **uqihdat** Gy 212:16 she whimpered and cried out MG 10 n. 2, 257:7, **paiit** [*sic*] **pumh̠ qadmaia** ATŠ II no. 201 I (?) opened the first mouth.

PAA II (פהא, ܦܘܐ, cf. Bab. *pû* prob. 'chaff' Jensen KB vi 453 f.) to fall apart MG 62:17, Jb ii 214 n. 1.

Pe. Act. pt. **lašahia ulapaiia** Q 11:4 = ML 30:2 = CP 26:1, Gy 211:14, DC 34. 452 fadeth not nor falleth apart; pl. **lašahin ulapaiin** Gy 8:18 they fade not nor fall apart.

Der.: **paiia 2.**

pabugan (P. بابكان [آردشير]) Gy 383:21, var. **papugan** BC a name of Ardeshir (s. **ardšir**).

pagadta, pagudta (rt. **PGD**) bridle, restraint (cf. **pigudta**), punishment, disaster, misadventure. Var. **pigudta** s.v. **pigia upagadta** DC 40. 836 disasters and misadventure(s); **qirsa ugisa upagudta** Par. AM 63:2 illness and agony and disaster (?).

pagra (פגרא, ܦܓܪܐ, H. פֶּגֶר corpse, Akk. *pagru*) body MG 100:6. Pl. **-ia**, in the frequent locution **d̠-pagria** used as sg. to designate the mortal, material opposite of the soul Jb ii 57 n. 1, 176 n. 8, MSt 94. **ʿṣtun pagria** Gs 61:12, **ʿṣtuna d̠-pagria** Gy 102:13, 18 s. **ʿṣtuna; lbuša d̠-pagria** Gy 29:7, 45:6; **lbuš pagria** Gs 10:5, Q 32:5, **kitun pagria** Gy 101:21, Gs 10:4 bodily vestment; **ʿkilta d̠-pagria** Gy 89:13, 317:15, Jb 77:12, 213:1 food of the body; **pagra d̠-lupata** Gs 80:19, 132:17 f. s. **lupataʿ; adam d̠-pagria** RD B 88, Gy 241:4 physical Adam (microcosm of **adam kasia**); **bpagra zapra** Gy 365:20 in the stinking body; **pagra labiš** Gy 57:10 he putteth on the body (i.e. is born); **dmuta d̠-pagra** Gy 102:13, 18 the likeness of the body; **bdmu pagria** Gy 29:6 in bodily form; **napqia bpagria midamin bdmu pagria** Gy 46:17 they come out in the body, have a corporeal appearance; **nangaria d̠-pagria** Gy 6:4 mortal carpenters; **ardikla d̠-pagria** Jb 178:10 architect of bodies (cf. **ardikla d̠-ṭina** Gy 6:5); **ṣubian pagria** Gy 40:5 f. the will of the flesh; **ṣubiana d̠-pagria** Gy 44:18 id.; **muma d̠-pagria** Gy 23:4, 44:12 bodily blemish; **špur pagria** Gy 40:7, 241:9 bodily beauty; **špur pagrak** Gy 243:16 beauty of thy body; **pagra baṭla** Jb 51:15 s. **baṭla; tapsir pagra** Explanation of the Body (title of a treatise in ATŠ).

padahšar, padakšar (Pahl. inscr. פאתהשתרי Haug: *Essays* 71, Pahl. books פאתהשה, mod. P. پادشاه) rule, governance, kingdom, monarchy, supreme power MG xxxi 21 ff. Var. **padak šar** cf. ML 241 n.b. **padakšar dakia** CP 208:penult., Oxf. 72 a = ML 241:9 pure empire; **anašia lagaiia lpadakšar nimṭun** Gy 385:19 barbarians will attain supremacy.

padana (פדנא, ܦܕܢܐ > Ar. فَدَّان Fränkel 129, from Akk. *padānu*?) plough. Var. **pudana** Jb

179:8 ff., MG, 120:4. Pl. ʿ**pdania** JRAS 1937 s.v. ʿ**pdania.** Masc. MG 159:5. **man ṣamid padana** Gs 10:22 who will harness the plough?

padibra (< Iranian *paδgâm*=*bær*, cf. mod. P. پیغمبر ,پیامبر) messenger. Pl. **-ia,** ISK 34, 95 f., Nöld. ZA xxxiii 80, ML 17 n. 2, Ginzā 70 n. 2. ʿ**utria padibria** Gy 74:1, **padibria** ʿ**utria** Gy 360:14; **šilmai unidbai** ʿ**utria trin padibrh̠ d̠-manda d̠-hiia** CP 118:8 = Q 59:33 = ML 144:1 (cf. Q 6:14, 17:8, 26:30).

pahad (Ar. فَهْد) cheetah. **šahbat alpahad** AM the skin (of) a cheetah.

pahara (פַּחָרָא, ܦܚܪܐ > Ar. فَخَّار Fränkel 70, 257, from Akk. *paḫāru*) potter MG 120:12. Usually with the meaning of **pahra 1. mania d̠-pahara** Gy 181:24, ATŠ II no. 6 vessels of the potter (i.e. earthenware); **kasa d̠-pahara** DC 40. 402 an earthenware bowl.

pahza (rt. **PHZ**) wanton. **liba pahza** Gy 209:8 a wanton heart.

pah̠l, pahil (Ar. فَحْل) male palm-tree. St. emph. **pahla. kuṣa d̠-pah̠l** DC 46. 148:8 = **kuṣah d̠-pahla** DC 46. 54:10 a leaf of a male palm-tree; **gidma d̠-pahil** s. **gidma.**

pahluta (abstr. noun from **PHL**) service. Var. **pihluta. pahluta pahlia** Gy 286:4 (var. **pihluta** DC 22) they render service.

pahra 1 (פַּחָרָא, cf. **pahara**) clay, pottery, earthenware. **ktub lpahra** DC 40. 1044 write on clay (or upon earthenware?); **kasa hadta d̠-pahra** AO ix 96:20 a new earthenware bowl.

pahra 2 (cf. Talm. בַּרְחָא, Syr. ܒܪܚܐ) male goat, he-goat, buck. **aiak pahra abatar** ʿ**nzia** DC 46. 189:10 like a he-goat after she-goats.

pahra 3 act. pt. pe. of **PHR** (q.v.).

pahrania DC 51. 751 (blotted) read **parhagania**? (cf. פַּרְהַגְנָא superintendents of public works) public officers?

paulis (*Παῦλος*) in **mšiha paulis** Jb 108:9 (varr. **pulis** E, **palus** ABD, cf. P. پالوس ,پلوس deceiver Vullers i 262a s. بلوس) Christ-Paul Jb ii 108 n. 3, Nöld. ZA xxx 150.

pahrʿ**il** s. **parh**ʿ(i)**l.**

paura (cf. **pura 1**) boisterous passion, lively or passionate feeling, rage. Pl. **-ia. ušbaq pauria** Jb 106:10 and he forsook his (evil) passions; **abrh̠ lpaura** (var. **lpura** BD) **mn** ʿ**uṣrak** CP 277:1, Jb 273:9, put away passion from thy mind; **abria (l)paura mn** ʿ**uṣrak** Oxf. 94 a = ML 261:9, DC 34. 1313 id.

paziqiz dizana DC 43 J 125 name of a (river-) spirit.

paṭur (rt. **PṬR**) passing away, leaving, departure? Doubtf. ML 185 n. 2., CP trsl. 115 n. 4, **ulpaṭur šuba** Oxf. 12 b = ML 185:4.

paṭila (rt. **PṬL** for **PṢL**?) in **bpaṭila** DC 50. 471, 490 piece-wise, separately, in rotation.

paṭira (פַּטִירָא, ܦܛܝܪܐ > Ar. فطير) a small flat loaf or disk of unleavened bread used in ritual meals. Pl. **-ia.** Masc. **paṭira** ʿ**laia** PD 1586 the upper unleavened bread; **paṭira qadmaia** PD 1292 the first unleavened bread; **paṭira batraia** PD 766, 1572 the last unleavened bread; **paṭira** ʿ**laia ubatraia** Morg. 233/57:ult. f., ML 88:1, CP 71:18, Lond. roll A 645, 722, Oxf. roll f 249, 620, 751 (cf. ML 88 n. 1); **trin paṭiria** PD 1141, 1151 two disks of unleavened bread; **tlata paṭiria** PD 1228, Oxf. roll f 156, 401, 488 three disks of unleavened bread; **šitin paṭiria** PD 174 sixty disks of unleavened bread.

paṭla (cf. **paṭiia**) piece, shred. **paṭla d̠-ba** DC 42 a shred of dove's meat.

paia s. **paiia 1.**

paiasa DC 22. 410 a var. of **piasa** Gs 20:19.

paiuia a *malwāša* woman's name.

paiia 1, paia (rt. ܦܐܝ, but formal development influenced by the pt. of **PAA II** Jb ii 214 n. 1) beauty, comeliness. **d̠-šai(i)a upai(i)a litlun** Jb 231:10 that have no lustre or beauty.

paiia 2 (rt. **PAA II**) falling apart. **šaiia upaiia lkulhun handamia lgaṭ** DC 51. 85 f. fading and falling apart attacked all his limbs; ʿ**hab . . . tulita lkakia ušaiia upaiia lkulhun handamia** DC 51. 327 ff. bestowed . . . worm to his teeth and fading and falling apart to all his limbs.

paiiz (P. پائیز) fall, autumn. **iahra aual paiiz** Zotb. 230a:3 f. first autumn-month; **biahra miṣaia d̠-paiiz** Zotb. 224b:9 f. in the middle autumn-month; **miṣai paiiz** Lond. roll A 794 mid-autumn; **biahra d̠-(a)kir paiiz** Zotb. 228b:26 in the last autumn-month.

paimana (P. پَیْمَان < *paδmân*) (com)pact, promise, agreement, contract, stipulation. Pl. **-ia.** MG xxxii 4. **paimana umiṣra** ʿ**tbid** ATŠ I no. 263 a pact and a boundary line were made; **triṣa bkulhun paimania** Gy 217:6 honest in all contracts; **anin paimana iahbinalun** ATŠ II no. 189 we gave them a promise; ʿ**štauia miṣra binataihun upaimana** ATŠ II no. 253 a boundary and a contract were made between them; **miṣria upaimania** ATŠ I no. 233; **abda paimania** AM 78:14 she will make contracts.

paina (by metathesis from פַּנְיָא, ܦܢܝܐ) evening MG 24:12, 112:15. **paina arza mn gintai** ʿ**qar** Gs 111:17 last evening a cedar was uprooted from my garden (MG 351:bottom).

paisaq, paisiq (rt. **PSQ**) semi-priest or hedge-priest allowed to perform marriage for non-virgin women MMII n. 3. **br paisiq** HG (colophon) son of a hedge-priest.

pakra (rt. **PKR**) fetter. Pl. **-ia. lamitkabšin** ʿ**l asarun ulpakraiun** DC 44. 620 f. they are not subdued by their bonds and fetters.

palagta (nom. act. pa. of **PLG**) division, category. Pl. **palagata** Oxf. xii. **bhazin palagta uhušbana** AM by this division and calculation; **hazin palagta** DC 27.

palah Zotb. 218b:10 name of a sultan.

palang AM 278, **palanga** AM 182 = **planga.**

palga 1 (פַּלְגָא, ܦܠܓܐ) (*a*) half, middle, (*b*) portion, share, piece. (*a*) **palga d̠-iuma** midday; **palga d̠-lilia** midnight (*both often*); **palga upalga** AM 165:5 in two sections; **palga d̠-pumh̠** Gy 83:5 half of his mouth;

ubilan alma lpalgai Gy 143:20 f. and he swallowed me up to my middle (half-body); **mn palga lilai** AM 22:1 from the waist upwards (? BZ 18 n. 6); **palgia lrba upalga lašualia** DC 34. 1051 half of it is for the teacher and half for the novice; **tartin šaiia upalga** Gy 386:10 two and a half hours (MG 351:anteantep.); **mn palgaiin d̲-šnia laqamh̲** AM 32:4 from his middle-age (cf. ܦܠܓܝ ܥܡܪܐ) onwards; **giṭra d̲-palga d̲-ṣbita** DC 41 the ligament of the finger-joint; (*b*) **palga d̲-bisra** ATŠ II no. 166 a piece (portion) of meat.

palga 2 (ܦܘܠܓܐ, فَلَج) (*a*) paralysis, (*b*) a kind of (paralysis?) demon. Pl. **-ia.** Furlani: *I Nomi* 424. (*a*) **ridpa d̲-palga d̲-pagra** DC 46. 124:14 the affliction of a paralytic stroke; (*b*) **saṭania usarnbu upalga** Or. 333:2; **palgia zikria upalgia nuqbata** DC 43 A 22 f., A. 31: A: 107; **pigia upalgia** s. **piga.**

palg̱u for ***palguta** (always used as st. cstr.) half. **šita upalgu** (var. **upagu d̲-**) **šita** DC 44. 1850 (var. Morg. 269/28:25) one hour and half an hour; **palgu iahra** Gy 219:21 half a month; **palgu parsa** Gs 99:18, 19, 100:11 half a parasang MG 313:2 f.

palg̱iga name of a genie used in exorcism. **bšum palgiga** DC 26 in the name of P.

paluda (P. پالوده, فالوده) sweetmeat of starch, water, and honey (often in lists of ritual foods). Oxf. roll f 1265, 1318 ff., 1330, ŠQ 6:9.

palus s. **paulis.**

palṭus (*Πειλᾶτος*) Pilate. **palṭus malka d̲-alma** Gy 29:8 Pilate the king of the world [*sic*].

palṭa (Ar. فالة < Akk. *paltu*? Jb ii 145 n. 5) Jb 144:3, 148:10, 149:13 fish-spear, fish-prong.

pamba phonetic writing of foll.: **gadadia d̲-pamba** Oxf. roll f 1340, 1343 s. **gadada**; **tagia d̲-pamba** CP 468 ult.

panba (P. پنبه) cotton. Varr. **pamba, panpa** s.vv. **taga d̲-panba** Lond. roll A 33 f. cotton fillet, pl. **tagia d̲-panba** ibid., DC 3 (CP trs. 311); **panbai ukitanai** Lond. roll B 289 = DC 12. 145 s. **kitana**; **gadadia d̲-panba** Oxf. roll f 1343 cf. s. **gadada**; **panba hu** DC 41 (picture) it is a cotton-plant. Cf. AM 199:14, 285:2.

pandama (Pahl. *padân* Modi 55–69, ISK 107. Pažend پنام) the long end of the *naṣifa* which is wound over the lower part of the face of the priest for baptism and other rituals RO ii 462, Siouffi 122, ML 11 n. 2, MMII 201 n. 12, CP trs. 5 n. 3. **lguṭ pandamak** CP 9:18 hold thy pandama; **akrik pandama lpumak** Q 33:15 wind thy pandama over thy mouth; **mihtam hatma d̲-pandama lpumaihun** PD 437 sealing the seal (i.e. fixing) the pandama to their mouths. Frequent in injunctions and ATŠ: Q 4:7, 19:8, 25, 24:28, PD 762, 776, 878, 947, CP 9:18, 43:14 and 25 (*and often*).

pandur CP 180:12 (a var. of **pindur**) shepherd's pipe, see **pindur.**

panᶜ? (Talm. פְּנַאי emptiness) in **ᶜl pan ᶜhania** DC 40. 549 for the easing of her womb.

panš̱a (P. پنج five) the five intercalary days, the feast of *Parwanaiia* (s. **paruanaiia**) which occupies the five intercalary days at the time of the spring festival at the beginning of Nisan MR 91, MMII 88 ff. Pl. **-ia, -aiia. panš̱ia** Par. x:coloph. the fifth; **tulut d̲-zidqa d̲-panšaiia** Zotb. 219a:29 a third of the oblation of the five intercalary days.

pas 1 (P. پس, mod. Syr. loan-w. ܦܣ) then, thereupon, later than, also, afterwards, after that, after which, moreover MG 205:4. Var. **paṣ 1** s.v. Corroborated by **ha**: **hapas, hapis** s.vv. **pas hazin mamla . . . kadba hu** Gy 390:21 f. then is that agreement . . . a lie also; **pas mimaskin** AM 44:14 and afterwards he becomes poor; **pas mitiatar** AM 32:14 after that he will become rich. Very frequent in later literature, cf. RD B 12 ff., 125.

(**pas 2** name of a supernatural being? **pas br pas anat** Or. 326:16, 17 thou art P. son of P.)

pasa 1 Jb 158:8 a var. of **pisa 2.**

pasa 2 AM 198 name of a town BZ Ap. II.

***pasa 3** (ܦܣܐ) palm (of hand) **pasa iada** DC 15.

pasanta (פַּסְתָּא, ܦܣܬܐ, H. פַּס) palm (of the hand). Var. **basimta** s.v. Pl. **pasaniata.** St. cstr. **psan** and another pl. **pisnia 2** s.vv. **pasaniata d̲-ᶜda** Oxf. xiii the palm (?) of the hand.

pasaqa (ܦܣܩܐ) decision, judgement, discrimination. **dagaluta upasaqa** AM 9 strategy and judgement.

pasia Morg. 229/45:13 for **kasia** (pl. of **kasa**).

pashiata ML 38:2, 139:6 **lpashiatan** CP 32:8 = **pasuhiata.**

pasug̱ Oxf. 62 b, DC 27. 129, DC 34. 681, 860 etc. = **pasuk** MG 41:16.

pasuhiata (rt. פסע, ܦܣܥ = Mand. **PSH** = **PHS**) pl. footsteps, footprints, feet (distance), paces MG 72:6, 125:13, 169:14. Varr. **pashiata, pasihiata** s.vv. **pasuhiatak** Gy 181:10 thy footsteps; **lpasuhiatkun atia abatran** ATŠ II no. 188 direct your footsteps after us; **mraurabit pasuhiata** CP 113:ult. (thou) enlargest footsteps.

pasuk (P. پاسخ) response, answer, antiphon. Var. **pasug** s.v. MG 41:14, ML xv, ISK 98. Pl. **pasukia. pasuk ᶜhab** Oxf. roll f 1092, 1254, 1365 he gave the response; **utarmidia pasuk iahbilh̲** Lond. roll A 339, 348, 357, 367, 377, 397 and the priests give him the antiphon(al answer; **pasuk dilun iahbilak** PD 1031 = ATŠ I no. 103 will give thee the(ir) answer; **uqaria asuta upasuk iahbilh̲** ŠQ (PA) and he reciteth 'health (be with you)' and they give the response; **pasukia dilia** (= **-ih̲**) ATŠ I no. 11 his answers. Often in CP.

pasusta (rt. **PSS**) Gy 302:17, 24 destruction. Var. **p(i)susta** s.v.

pasihiata = **pasuhiata** (q.v.). **pasihiatan** Q 13:32 our footsteps; **pisihiatai** (read **pa-**) Gy 181:11 my footsteps; **pisuhiatak** (read **pasi-**)

Gy 181:10 thy footsteps; **nitrahqun . . . parsia ḏ-napšia upasihiata ḏ-kabira** DC 43 J 202 = Oxf. roll g 457 they shall be removed by many furlongs and by mighty steps; **pasihiatẖ kḏ susia** Or. 326:25 his paces are like (those of) a horse.

pasimka (a foreign word of unknown etym., prob. Iranian Nöld. ZA xxx 148) used of light, often parallel with **šraga,** hence: lamp, beam, ray. Brandt JPTh xviii 434 n. 1. Pl. **-ia.** Masc. Often personified. **uʿtihrip pasimka** Gy 78:20 and the light is set up (read **ʿtriṣ** cf. 79:16 Ginzā 77 n. 3); **taqnibẖ pasimka** Gy 91:6 I lit a light in it; **tirṣit qudamẖ pasimka** Gy 91:12 I set a light before him; **pasimka rba ḏ-manhar bkulhun almia** Gy 131:3 f. the Great Lamp that illumineth all the worlds; **šuma ḏ-hanatẖ pasimka** Gy 131:5 the name of that Lamp; **pasimkia ḏ-manhria lqudamaihun** Gy 128:19 f. lamps (lights) which shine before them; **pasimkia ḏ-manhria qudamẖ** Gy 128:22; **pasimkia ḏ-mdintẖ** Gy 5:20 the lamps of his city; **šalṭuia ʿl ʿutria uʿl pasimkia uʿl iardnia** Gy 314:1 he (: the Life, pl.) gave him power over the uthras, over the Lamps (personified) and over the jordans; **ḏ-šanai pasimkia** Gy 319:6; **pasimkia šaniia** Gy 372:28 wonderful lights; **šuba pasimkia** Gy 372:16 seven lights; **traṣlan ḏ-hiia pasimka** Gy 375:21 f. he set up for us the Lamp of Life; **ʿqria ṣauta liaminai uʿqria pasimkia lsmalai** I will call (Lidzb. create) radiance to my right and I will call lights to my left; **triṣ kulhun pasimkia** Gy 306:15 he set up all the lamps; **sab pasimkia biaminak** Gy 334:7 take the lamp(s) in thy right (hand); **ašganda ḏ-kulhun pasimkia** Gy 355:8, Gs 132:6 messenger of all the lights; **aluatẖ pasimkia ḏ-nhura** Gs 37:20 s. **alua**; **pasimkia ḏ-nhura** Jb 51:6 the rays of light; **aba ḏ-kulẖ ziua unhura ḏ-kulẖ pasimkia** Jb 242:10 the Father who is all-radiance and the light which is all lights; **kḏ miša lpasimka** ATŠ II no. 137 like oil for the lamp; **pasimkia** (personified) parallel with **ʿutria** Oxf. 63 ff.; **pasimka rba ḏ-kulẖ nhura** ML 109:4, ATŠ II no. 173 the great Ray which is all Light; **ʿhablun drabšia ḏ-ziua upasimkia ḏ-nhura** DC 3. 279:2 = CP 412:15 he gave them banners of radiance and beams of light; **birkẖ ham ziua lpasimka ḏ-luatẖ** DC 3. 278:3 = CP 411:15 Ham-Ziwa blessed the Beam that was with him.

pasimta DC 27.208 for **pasimka**??

pasiq (act. pt. pe. of **PSQ**) cutting, sharp, keen. **pasiq mn hirba** Gy 287:5, ML 39:7, DC 27:196 sharper than a sword.

pasquta (abstr. noun from **PSQ**) cutting, severance. **pasquta mn šutap(an)un pasqia** RD C 5 = DAb par. they sever connexion (break an agreement?) with their partner(s).

papugan s. **pabugan.**

papa, papia Zotb. 222a:30 a man's name.

pait DC 43 name of a lilith.

paṣ 1 Par. AM 87 = **pas** MG 205:6. Gl. 37:9 **bṣ** [*sic*] البتة *omnino.*

paṣ 2 Gs 81:4, Q 66:27 = ML 98:9, Morg. 249/85:21 impt. pe. of **NPṢ** (q.v.).

paqadta 1 (nom. act. pa. of **PQD**) order, command, commission, charge MG 122:2. **ʿu paqadta atat ʿlẖ** ATŠ I no. 76 if an order concerning it comes; **paqadta ḏ-šaliṭ lpagra** DC 37. 122 a command that ruleth the body; **paqadta ḏ-paqid ʿlauaihun** DC 44. 33 a command which he gave to him; **ʿhablun paqadta lṭaiubia nišmata** DC 27 he gave them a commission (charge) to benefit (refresh) the souls.

paqadta 2 for **paqata** (by influence of **paqadta 1**). **bpaqadta ubdibra** AM 224:15 in the valley(s) and field.

paqata (pl. ܦܩܥܬ̈ܐ from ܦܩܥܬܐ, Bibl.-Aram. בִּקְעָא, H. בִּקְעָה, Ar. بُقْعَة) valleys, open plains, gorges, chasms MG 101:13. No special sg. form. **qal paqata ḏ-apqa** DC 43 J 5 the noise of chasms which open; **paqata mšadkata** Or. 327:12 quiet valleys; **ṣihiun paqata ḏ-hu kanpa ḏ-tibta utinta** ATŠ I no. 216 Sion, a valley which is the receptacle of dung and urine (here exceptionally as sg. masc.); **bpaqata ubaramata** Or. 331:17 by the gorges and heights; **upaqata saria nimaliun** AM and barley will fill the valleys; **ṭuria udištata upaqata** DC 46 mountains and plains and valleys; **upaqata latbadartun** DC 51. 65 f. and ye were not dispersed in the valleys (?).

paqda a kind of demon, incubus. Pl. **-ia. paqdia zikria upaqdia nuqbata** DC 43 A 19 male and female incubi.

paqudia inf. pa. of **PQD** (q.v.).

paqra (ܦܩܪܐ rabid) mad (dog) (DC 46. 179:10 **šunara upaquta**). **kḏ šunara upaqra** (miscop. **paruqa**) DC 45 like a wild cat or a mad dog (?) (very doubtful).

para, fem. **parta 1** (Syr. ܦܪܘܐ fem. ܦܪܬܐ, rel. to H. פַּר fem. פָּרָה, Jew.-Aram. פָּרְתָא cow, heifer, Ar. فَرّ calf, فَرِير, فُرَار lamb, young gazelle) lamb (male or female accord. to gender). **kul para uparta** Jb 43:11 each male lamb and female lamb; **para uparta** DC 40. 788, Morg. 199:1, 200:antep. f.; **ʿqamra ḏ-para uparta umanzia gadia** DC 26. 767 the wool of a male and a female lamb and the hair of a kid.

para malka Gy 382:4 ff. King Pharaoh. Var. **parua** Gy 381:18, 20, 382:2. Also **pirun malka** s.v.

paraha (rt. **PRA III**) money. Also with the ending **-ia.** Varr. **apraha, praha** s.vv. Still used (mod. forms: *parâh, parâha, parâhi*). Masc. **parahia nihuilia** DC 44. 1308 I shall have money.

parahia DC 34. 894 for **parahiata.**

parahiata (ܦܪܚܘܣܢܝܬ̈ܐ) sparks MG 64:8, 121:15, but often more prob. tendrils, sprays, sprigs, twigs. **parahiata ḏ-tagẖ** Gy 4:5, Lond. roll A 362, CP 341:8 the tendrils (or sprigs?) of his crown; **klila . . . ḏ-raipilẖ lparahiata** ŠQ 7:26 a wreath . . . whose twigs are bound; **šuba parahiata ḏ-hilapa** ŠQ 7:25 seven sprigs of willow.

parahiʿil Jb 14:5 a theophorous name (from **PRH**) Jb ii 22 n. 1.

parauata (apparently a pl. of **purta**) clefts?. **duktai binia qabraria ubparauata** DC 46. 61: 12 my place is amongst tombs and in clefts(?).

parangia (فرنگی) AM 287:2, Frankish, European. Varr. **paranšia, parinšia.**

parangis a kind of devil of both genders, (evil) fairies (?). **parangis zikria uparangis nuqbata** DC 43 A 28.

paranšia, parinšia s. **parangia.** DC 46. 194:10.

paraš̤ (Ar. فَرَج) Zotb. 217b:14 etc. a man's name.

paraša (פָּרָשָׁא, ܦܳܪܳܫܳܐ, H. פָּרָשׁ, Ar. فارس) mounted soldier, horseman, cavalry-man, mounted archer. Pl. **-ia. paraša bqaštẖ** JRAS 1937 593:16, CP 113:3 the horseman with his bow; **paraša d̠-ʿsir bit zaina** Gy 215:12 a horseman who is bound in prison; **qašta d̠-parašia** DC 10, DC 12. 37 the bow of mounted archers.

parašai sipa malka Gy 393:5 name of a king.

parašuta (rt. **PRŠ**) channels, branches? **iardna uparašutẖ** DC ? the jordan and its channels (its branches).

parata for **parahiata** sparks?. **paratẖ bziuai mnihran** DC 3 the sparks (?) gleam in my light.

pargalta (nom. act. of ܦܰܪܓܶܠ to hobble) hobbling, limping, lameness. **ruha hʿ d̠-iatba ʿl ligra umitqiria pargalta** Or. 330:23 f. = Oxf. roll g 878 the spirit that is situated on the leg(s) and is called hobbling (lameness).

pargana AM 198 name of a city and province BZ Ap. II.

parguš AM 123:penult. name of an angel.

pardasa 1 = **pardisa.** Pl. **-ia.** (?). **qalaihun d̠-alahia mn pardasaihun** DC 43 J 6, J. 18 the voice of the gods from their paradise; **laziriak ginaia bginth̠ ulapardaspana lqabil lpardasia** Or. 325:5 (text) but the market-gardener sowed thee not in his garden, nor the gardener in front of his pleasure-garden.

pardasa 2, (ܦܪ̈ܓܣܩܐ, ܦܪܓܣܩܐ, ܦܘܪܓܣܩܐ, Gr. πυργίσκος Fränkel ZA ix 8; formal influence of **pardasa** 1) coffer, shrine. Pl. **-ia. tlatma ušitin alpia pardasia iaqut** DC 34. 1067 three hundred sixty thousand coffers of ruby.

pardaspana = **pardispana.** S. **pardasa** 1.

pardun Q 60:17 = ML 145:2 an uthra CP 119:11 = ML 283.

pardisa (Av. *pairidaēza,* Bab. *pardisu* Meissner ZA vi 290, Syr. ܦܪ̈ܕܝܣܐ, H. פַּרְדֵּס, Ar. فِرْدَوْس, Gr. παράδεισος) pleasure-garden, pleasance, paradise. Var. **pardasa** 1 s.v. **ukapinun ʿl mlakia mn pardisaihun** DC 43 J 18 and debased the angels from their paradise.

pardispana (from preced. with P. suff. بان - assimilated to the unvoiced *s*) gardener (of a pleasure-garden). Var. **pardaspana** s.v., **pardispina. damia lpardispana** (var. **pardispina** DC 22. 211) **d̠-klila lnapšẖ lgdal** Gy 218:16 he resembleth the gardener-of-a-flower-garden who twined no garland for himself; **laziriak ginaia bginth̠ ulašitlak pardispana** Or. 331:1, Oxf. roll g 209 the market-gardener sowed thee not in his (market-) garden, nor did the gardener of a pleasure-garden plant thee.

***parhagania** s. **pahrania.**

parhʿ(i)l (cf. **parahiʿil**) name of a heavenly steed. **parhʿil** DC 41. 552, Jb 15:8 (varr. **parhʿl** C, **pahrʿil** BD).

parua malka Gy 381:18, 20, 382:2 = **para malka.**

paruan (identical with **taruan**? Jb ii 116 n. 3) name of a mountain. **paruan ṭura hiuara** Jb 118:11, HG 28 P. the white mountain.

paruanaiia (P. پروانـ?) the five intercalary days, called colloquially *panǧa* (s. **panǧa**) RO ii 460, ML 277 n. 1, MMII 83 ff. **hilita . . . d̠-paruanaiia** CP 438:1 f.; **hamša iumia d̠-paruanaiia** PD 226 the five intercalary days; **šarḥ d̠-paruanaiia** Oxf. roll f 4, 25, 133 the explanation of P.; **iuma d̠-paruanaiia** Oxf. roll f 360, 422 ff.; **iahra d̠-paruanaiia** ML 277:2, Zotb. 218a:4 the month of P. (i.e. *Ellūl* and *Tišrīn,* end of Virgo and beginning of Libra); **šarḥ d̠-laupania d̠-masiqta uparuanaiia** Morg. 183:1 f. the explanation of the communion of the m. and P.

paruanqa (ܦܰܪܘܳܢܩܳܐ < Middle P. *parwânak,* ISK 98, mod. P. پروانه Lagarde: *Abhandlungen* 76 f., Ar. loan-w. فُرَانِق guide) messenger, guide; but often with the meaning of (פָּרוֹקָא) redeemer, saviour, rescuer MG xxxi 12, 418 n. 1, MR 30 n. 2, MSchr. 28 n. 2, JPTh xviii 426, MSt. 105, Kohut: *Angelologie* 40: middle. **lʿšiqa hu(i)lẖ paruanqa** Gy 15:16, Gs 103:13, **ʿšiqa d̠-baiia paruanqa** Jb 102:4 s. **ʿšiqa; gabra paruanqa** Jb 257:11 the messenger (cf. Jb ii 232 n. 1); **paruanqa d̠-hu adakas malala šumẖ** Gy 235:17, 236:4 the messenger whose name is A.-M.; **paruanqa d̠-hu adakas ziua šumẖ** Gy 235:25; **paruanqa d̠-qaiim lqudamẖ** Gy 236:22 the messenger that standeth before him; **šilmai unidbai paruanqai** Gy 276:4 Š. and N. my guides; **paruanqa lnišimta ulruha mn trin mahunia taumia** ATŠ II no. 163 a deliverer for the soul and spirit from the twin pits; **alma d̠-paruanqa azil ʿlauiin** ATŠ II no. 81 until a deliverer comes to them; **paruanqa qalila d̠-azil lkul atar** DC 41. 434 a swift messenger that goes into every place; **paruanqa larqa d̠-nhura šadart** DC 27. 86 thou hast sent a messenger to the world of light.

paruk (P. فَرُّخ) a man's name. Colophons.

parunia, pirunia 1 (< פֻּרְעֲנוּתָא, ܦܘܪܥܢܘܬܐ punishment?, the actual meaning might then be based on a semantic development, and the verb **PRA V** would be den. Ginzā 104 n. 3) pl. bonds, fetters MG 21:12, 140:1. **ʿtikpir bparunun** Gy 98:7 they were fettered by their bonds; **qulalun uparunun** Gy 377:18 their snares and their bonds.

paruqa (פָּרוֹקָא, ܦܳܪܘܿܩܳܐ) redeemer, saviour, deliverer, rescuer MG 113:21. **paruqa d̠-kulhun mhaimnia** Gy 2:1, 30:21 saviour of all believers; **ana hu alaha paruqa** Gy 55:7 I am God the Saviour (Jesus about himself).

paruša (פְּרוּשָׁא, ܦܪܘܫܐ) discerner, diviner, discerning, wise one MG 113:23, MR 78 n. 2. **hazaia uparuša** Gs 79:14, Q 65:21, **hazuia uparuša** Gy 2:2 seer and diviner; **ʿutra rhima d̲-nihuia paruša** Gy 249:18 the beloved uthra who shall be a discerner; **ʿutra hurina brh̲ d̲-ʿtiqria paruša** Gy 249:22 another uthra, his son, who is called discerner; **iaduia uparuša** Gy 30:23 knower and discerner; **paruša qadmaia** Gy 256:15 the first Discerner; **parušan qadmaia** Oxf. 79 b = CP 245:antep. our first Discerner; **daiana paruša** DC 51. 291 a judge, a discerning one.

parušai sipa DC 22. 388 & Sh. ʿAbd.'s copy's var. of **parašai sipa** Gy 393:5.

parušaiia Lond. & Munich MSS. var. of **p(a)rišaiia** Gy 278:2 Ginzā 277 n. 1.

paruta (ambiguous: either from **PRA I** or **PRT**) fruition, or bursting open? **paruta d̲-mazruta d̲-ptalh̲ lpumh̲ d̲-marba** ATŠ I no. 236 the fruition (or bursting open?) of seed which opened the mouth of the womb.

parzam (P. فَرْزَام) honest, right, just, equitable. **parzam ušapir hauia** ATŠ II no. 327 it will be right and good; **parzam ušapir nihuia** ATŠ II no. 327 id.

parzla (Old Aram., Bibl.-Aram., Jew.-Aram. פַּרְזֶל, Syr. & Chr.-Pal. ܦܪܙܠܐ, H. בַּרְזֶל, Old Ar. فِرْزِل iron fetters, Sab. 𐩰𐩧𐩹𐩡 from Akk. *parzillu* KAT 648) iron, iron weapon, implement etc. MG 27:8, 128:16. **šura d̲-parzla** RD E 2, **šur parzla** Gy 154:3 an iron wall; **šuria d̲-parzla** Gy 159:9 iron walls; **bzaina d̲-lahua mn parzla** Gy 25:20 f. with a weapon which is not of iron; **bparzla nithangar** s. **HNGR** ethpa.

parṭauaiia 1 (cf. the idiomatic expr. **praṭ sipta** s. **sipta** & **PRṬ**) sneerers, calumniators. **parṭauaiia rišaihun kabšia** Morg. 259/9:40, 10:2 = DC 44. 577 = DC 13 & 26 par. sneerers abase their heads.

parṭauaiia 2 DC 22. 385:ult. & Sh. ʿAbd.'s copy's var. of **pirṭauaiia** Gy 389:21.

paria 1 (rt. **PRA I**? Originator of fertility?) **paria pariata** Gy 245:16 Originator of fertility? (Lidzb. *Einlöser der Einlösungen*? Ginzā 246 n. 3), cf. **mia hiia d̲-minh̲ dilia (-ih̲) paria kulhun pariata** Morg. 269/28:40 its living water fructifies all fertile things.

paria 2 (P. پری) fairy sprite. **ʿsiria liliata uparia** DC 46 bound are the liliths and (evil?) sprites.

pariata (rt. **PRA I**) fertile things. V.s. **paria 1**.

paridun (P. فريدون) Gy 382:22 name of a Persian king, identified by Gray with *Θraētaona Āθwyāna* (Yašt v 33) ZA xix 278.

parinšia s. **parangia**.

paris name of a country, prob. for **pars** Fars CP 356:6 = ML 264 n. 2. **paris arqa hiuartia** CP 356:6 = Oxf. 96 a = ML 264:3 f. P. the white land; **mn paris mata** DC 43 I 110 from the land of P.; **malkut paris umadaiia** DC 44. 116 = Morg. 263/16:38 the kingdom of Persia and the Medes.

parišaiia = **prišaiia** Ginzā 277 n. 1.

parkil(a) 1 (Ar. فَرْخ + article أَلْ which originally belonged to the foll. noun) young bird, nestling, fledgeling. Masc. **aitilh̲ lparkil d̲-buma** AM 130:10 bring him a nestling of an owl; **sablh̲ parkilia hiuaria** MA 125:14 bring him white nestlings (AM trs. 81 n. 2).

parkila 2 s. **parpila**.

parnauata Morg. 259/9:24 = **parṣauata** (q.v.).

parnasta (פַּרְנָסְתָא, nom. act. from פַּרְנֵס, ܦܪܢܣܐ) Par. xxvii 12b, DC 40. 1034, DC 43 D 53 provision, sustenance, maintenance, means of livelihood.

parnašta DC 46 for **parpašta**?

pars (P. فارس) AM (often) Fârs, Persia.

parsa (< P. فرسنگ, فَرْسَخ Lagarde: *Abhandlungen* 77, Jew. loan-w. פַּרְסָא, פַּרְסָה, Syr. loan-w. ܦܪܣܐ Nöld. ZA xx 453) Persian mile, farsakh, parasang, league MG 64:24. Pl. -ia. Masc. **lakilbh̲ parsa** Gs 13:10; **lakilbh̲ parsia** RD B 15 no leagues are measured in it; **parsa sarit marba utrin alpia parsia marba umadna** DC 3 (colophon) I travelled a league west and two thousand leagues west and east; **abatrai ʿl parsa** Jb 160:12 one league behind me; **parsa upalgu parsa** Gs 99:18 f. one league and half a league; **alip parsia** Gy 137:23 a thousand leagues; **šitin parsia** Gy 381:14 sixty leagues; **mn hanath̲ baba šitin parsia hauia umn parsa lparsa baba hatam ʿka** ATŠ I nos. 283–4 from that Gate it will be sixty parasangs, and at each parasang there will be a gate; **parsia d̲-napšia** DC 43 J 202 many parasangs.

parsaia (adj. from **pars**) Persian. Pl. **parsaiia** people of Fârs, Persians MG 141:3. **parsaia d̲-ṭuraq** Gy 382:ult. f. the 'Persian of Ṭurâq' as name of a Persian king (افراسياب, *mairya tūriya Fraŋrase* Gray ZA xix 280); **malkia parsaiia** Gy 383:19 f. Persian kings; **bit parsaiia** Gy 389:21 Persia; **parsaiia urumaiia** AM (et alia) Persians and Byzantines; **ṭura d̲-parsaiia** HG the hill(-country) of the Persians; **hazin siriana qazil larqa parsaiia** DC 7 (illustration) this vein (stream) goes to the land of the Persians.

parsqa DC 22. 80 for **parqsa** Gy 85:ult.

parpašta (formally a nom. act. of a supposed *paʿpel* of **PRŠ**) orig.: division, separation; hence: fence, dividing wall? **mn tarbaṣai uparpašta** DC 12. 161, DC 25. 50 etc. from my courtyard and from (my) fence.

parpila for **parkila 2** (cf. ܦܪܘܠܐ fetter) knot? **ugaṭrh̲ bparpila** DC 46 and tie it in a knot (?).

parpin(a) (פַּרְפְּחִינָא, ܦܪܦܚܝܢܐ, Ar. فرفخ, coll. بربين P. پرپهين Löw no. 264) purslane. **bazra d̲-parpin** DC 43, DC 45 xxxiv purslane seed; **mia d̲-parpinia** AM 135:13 juice of the purslane.

parpisa AM 198 name of a city BZ Ap. II.

parṣa occasional var. of **pirṣa**.

parṣauata (rt. **PRṢ**) gluttonous feasts, intemperance, gluttony. Var. **parnauata** s.v. **lbabataiun triṣ parṣauata** DC 44. 555 at their gates gluttonous feasts are set up.

parṣupa (פַּרְצוּף, ܦܪܨܘܦܐ < *πρόσωπον*) countenance, face, appearance, aspect, person(ality) MG xxx 5; often as personification of the Highest Being MR 41:middle, MSchr. 6 n. 2. Pl. **-ia.** Masc. **parṣupa rba ḏ-ʿqara** Gy 305:5, 25, Q 25:12 = CP 54:15, Morg. 207/1:ult. f. etc. the Great Countenance (Personality) of Glory; **gilia parṣupẖ** Gy 142:1 s. **gilia**; **trin parṣupia** Gy 308:23 two faces (Ginzā 309 n. 2); **anpia šapiria uparṣupia rauzia** DC 44. 495 (*& often*) fair faces and blooming countenances; **uparṣupa ḏ-alahuta nihuilẖ** AM 92:ult. and he will have the aspect (semblance) of divinity; **utlatma ušitin parṣupia ʿtlẖ** DC 41. 91 and he has 360 guises; **parṣupia parṣupa-ḏ-ʿnta** DC 46. 62:10 f. its face is a woman's face.

parṣindia pl. (P. فَرْزَنْد?) Gy 187:19 children Ginzā 189 n. 4.

parqa (rt. **PRQ**) deliverer, means of deliverance. Var. **pirqa** s.v. **tihuilẖ parqa lialda** HG it will be a means of deliverance (?) for the boy.

parqata DC 27. 524 = **parqita** (q.v.).

parqun, pirqun (rt. **PRQ**) DC 37 106, 110 ff. an angel.

parqut(a) (rt. **PRQ**) deliverance. **alma lparqut almia** ATŠ II nos. 81, 287 until the deliverance of the worlds.

parqita (rt. **PRQ**) sting (usually poisonous). Varr. **parqata, parqta** s.vv. **ʿu sama iahbilẖ ʿu parqita napla ʿlẖ** ATŠ I no. 76 = PD par. if poison was administered to him, or a (poisonous) sting attacked him; **mn mhita ḏ-hiuia . . . uparqita ḏ-kulhun rihšia** DC 27. 175 from the wound of (i.e. caused by) a snake . . . and from the sting of all vermin.

parqsa 1 (ܦܘܪܓܣܐ, *πύργος* in spite of Jb ii 30 n. 2) tower. **silqat uiatbat ʿl parqsa** Gs 99:10 she went up and sat in her tower (Lidzb. *Ringmauer*).

parqsa 2 (prob. from Akk. *parsigu* 'band' formally influenced by **parqsa 1**?) some form of fetter, chain, hoop, ring, coils, toils. Pl. **-ia.** Masc. **hadiralẖ** (*sic*, with bad varr., read **ahd(i)rilẖ**) **parqsa** Gy 85:ult. f., 90:15 I entangled him (in) a bond; **mizdahribẖ bparqsak** (*twice*) Gy 90:7 f. they shall preserve thee in thy bond(s); **uandinun lparqsia** Gy 90:12 and he shook off his chains; **mn hablaikun umn parqsaikun** Gs 64:23 from your toils and coils; **nisbẖ lparqsa rama ḏ-rqiha** Gy 98:5 he took the high circumference of the firmament; **parqsa bgauẖ rman** (read **rmun**) Jb 23:15 they threw him into toils.

parqʿil (rt. **PRQ**) DC 43 D 22, 29 an angel.

parš(a) (rt. **PRŠ**) keeping-off, magical ban, protective charm. **parš ḏ-kaptar** s. **kaptar** (*b*); **parša haršia** (title of a magic scroll) phylactery against sorcery.

paršala (Ar. فَرَجُ آللّٰه) Zotb. 224b:16 a man's name.

paršigna (פַּרְשֶׁגְנָא, Bibl.-Aram. פַּרְשֶׁגֶן, Syr. ܦܪܫܓܢܐ, H. פַּתְשֶׁגֶן, Pahl. *pačēn* Lagarde: *Abhandlungen* 79, ISK 97 f.) report, explanation, information, declaration, chart, reply, excuse. Var. **paršikna** Oxf. 85 b, MG 41:16 f. Masc. Gy 127:17, fem. Gy 309:7. **ḏ-hazin paršigna amar** Gy 127:17; **ḏ-paršigna amar** CP 251: ult. = ML 255:8 who made (this) report; **kḏ haza paršigna amar** Gy 309:7 when it (: the living water) made this report; **ḏ-paršigna nʿtilia** Gy 207:22 f. who would give me information; **paršigna luatai litlaikun** Gy 234:3 f. ye have no chart by me (i.e. I cannot help you Ginzā 234 n. 3); **lahuatalun paršigna lšibiahia lnišmata ḏ-nimarlun** Gy 313:12 f. the planets had no information (as fem.) to give to the souls; **lahualun paršigna lšibiahia** Jb 196:9 (as masc.); **paršigna lʿhablẖ** Gs 9:22 gave her no information; **mahu paršigna titnun** Gy 377:3 what explanation shall ye give?; **mn qalai uparšignai** Jb 106:1, 274:7 at my voice and my declaration (proclamation); **mn qalak uparšignak** Jb 275:9; **paršigna ḏ-pumaihun** AM 248:13 the report of their mouths.

paršʿil (rt. **PRŠ** Gy) 159:15 an angel.

parta 1 fem. of **para** (q.v.) MG 101:15.

parta 2 (פַּרְתָּא, ܦܪܬܐ, H. פֶּרֶשׁ, Ar. فرث, Akk. *paršu*) Gy 227:11 discharge, uncleanness.

paša AM 256:41 pasha.

pašam (mod. Syr. ܦܫܡ, P. پشیمان) sad, sorry, grievous. **uʿšata ḏ-tlitaia ḏ-pašam** DC 46. 182:4 and a tertiary fever that is grievous (?).

pašam nariman DC 22. 379 = **pašm nariman** (q.v.).

pašar st. cstr. (rt. **PŠR**) charm to keep off, magical protection, exorcism. **pašar haršia** (title of a well-known talisman) protection against sorcery.

pašara (rt. **PŠR**) purgative. Pl. **-ia. pašaria usamania** AM 21 purgatives and drugs.

pašat s. **pašta.**

pašura (rt. **PŠR**, ܦܫܘܪܐ) exorcist, white magician. Pl. **-ia 1. ziua gabra pašura** JRAS 1937 595:32 'Radiance' the exorcist being; **gubria pašuria** Lond. roll B 393, DC 12. 186 exorcists; **mn qudamẖ ḏ- . . . gabra pašura** DC 37. 80 from before . . . the exorcist; **ktub lgabra pašura naṣuraia** DC 44. 243 f. write (it) for a Naṣoraean (white) magician; **uqarilun lpašuria** DC 51. 613 and call to the exorcists; **pt pašuria** Lond. roll **B** 384 daughter of (white) magicians.

pašuruta a var. of **pašruta.**

pašuria 1 pl. of **pašura.**

pašuria 2 (inf. pa. **of PŠR**) DC 40. 144 to exorcise.

pašm (P. پشم) DC 45 wool.

pašm nariman Gy 382:paen. a Persian king, identified by Gray with سام نریمان of the Šâh-Nâmeh (*Sâma Kərəsâspa* Yašt xiii 61, 163) ZA xix 278 ff. Var. **pašam nariman** s.v.

pašruta (rt. **PŠR**) cutting, reaping, gleaning? BZ 106 n. 2. Var. **pašuruta. saria lpašruta hauian** AM 171:1 there will be barley for the gleaning (?).

pašta a *malwâša* woman's name. Var. **pašat.**

patahata Gy 231:1 C, **patakata** A = **patikata** (q.v.).

patura (פָּתוֹרָא, ܦܳܬܽܘܪܳܐ, Ar. loan-w. فَاثُـور Fränkel 183, from Akk. *paššūru* < Sum. *banšūr* Zimmern: *Fremdwörter* 53) platter, dish, tray, table (or tray for ritual food) MG 114:7. Pl. **-ia. patura d̲-hiṭia** PD 1134 a tray of wheat; **patura umia . . . tarṣitun** ATŠ II no. 168 ye set platter and water . . .; **utraṣlun patura lmikal** Gy 243:20 f. and they set before them a platter for eating; **laupa d̲-patura** DC 27 the communion of the (ritual) platter; **damia lpatura sbʿia d̲-lqudam kapnʿ mitriṣ** Gy 215:1 he resembleth a full dish that is set before the hungry; **patura d̲-zma triṣlun** DC 44 a dish of blood is set before them; **patura d̲-zidqa** Gs 106:3 the dish of oblation; **alpia paturai (a)prat** Jb 34:1 thousands broke (bread at?) my table. Often in ritual texts.

patia (פָּתְיָא) vessel, bowl, basin? **patia d̲-ʿl šuba sadania d̲-mia** DC 43 J 168 the basin (?) that is on seven supports, (full?) of water.

patikata (ܦܛܝܩܬܐ) Gy 231:1 BD brocades (Nöld. *buntes Zeug*) MG 125:5. Varr. **patahata, patakata, patkata** s.vv.

patikra (פַּתַכְרָא, ܦܰܬܟܪܳܐ < Pahl. *patkar*, mod. P. پيكر, Ar. loan-w. فِتْكَر Fränkel 273, ISK 99) idol, idol-demon MG 27:2. Pl. **-ia.** Furlani: *I Nomi* 417 ff. **kul sahra daiua upatikra** DC 44. 1719 every demon, devil, and idol-demon; **patikria zikria upatikria nuqbata** DC 43 A 19 male and female idol-demons; **ʿkuria upatikria** Gy 389:7 temple-demons and idol-demons; **abid ginia lʿkuria upatikria** Gy 302:1 (s. **ginia 2**); **latisgud lʿkuria ulpatikria d̲-ʿkuria** ATŠ II no. 410 do not bow thyself down at temples and before the idols of temples. Very often in magic documents.

patikruta (abstr. noun from preced.) Gs 75:13 idolatry.

patkata Sh. ʿAbd.'s copy of **patikata** (q.v.).

patra Morg. 244/76:11 for **patura.** Pl. **-ia** DC 43 J 196.

PGA, BGA s.v. (Jew.-Aram. & H. פגע, Syr. ܦܓܰܥ, Ar. فجع) to meet, encounter, come upon.

Pe. Pf. **pigit** CP 26:17 = Q 11:18 f., 12:18, 11:26 I met MG 47:5; **upga bmaṭarta hurintin** Gs 35:15 and came upon another purgatory; **upigit bmaṭarta hurintin** Gs 34:3 f. and I came upon another purgatory. Act. pt. with encl. **pagibh̲** s. **pigudta.**

Der.: cf. ***piga** (pl. **-ia 1**), **pigia 2.**

PGD (ܦܓܰܕ) to hold back, bridle, restrain.

Pe. Pf. with suff. **d̲-ata upagdh̲** DC 34. 649 who came and held him back (made him ready?). Impt. with suff. **ʿzil upagdh̲** DC 6. 59 go and restrain (?) him.

Der.: **pagadta, pigdia, pigudta.**

PGM (Jew.-Aram. & mod. H. פגם, Syr. ܦܓܰܡ) to injure, wound, break.

Pa. Pf. with suff. **upagminun uṣalpinun** DC 44. 1096 = Morg. 269/29:8 he trounced them and castigated them. Pt. **ramih̲ umpagim** AM 124:4 he (the demon) casts him down and causes injury; pl. with encl. **umpagmilun uṣalpilun** (read **umṣalpilun**) DC 51. 91 they cause grievous injury to them.

Ethpa. Pf. **uʿtpagam sikinia** DC 44. 1069 (var. **ʿtpagar** Morg. 263/11:19) knives were broken.

PGR the rt. of **pagra** (q.v.).

Ethpa. Pf. **ʿtpagar sikinia** Morg. 263/16:19 only as a var. of **ʿtpagam** (s. **PGM**).

pdana, ʿpdana occ. varr. of **padana.**

PDL s. **PNDL.**

PDR (den. from **pudria**?, hence orig. 'to drive away'?) to fight, strive.

Pe. (or Ethpe.). Impf. **nipdar** Gy 80:24, 81:21 he fighteth, will fight MG 221:8, **ʿpdar** Gy 281:3, 4 I will fight MG 334:21.

Der.: **pudra.**

PHA (פחא & פחי, ܦܚܳܐ rel. to **PAA II**) to break open, fall apart.

Pe. Act. pt. pl. fem. **pahian ʿbidata sainata** ATŠ II no. 304 her evil deeds open their mouths.

phulta DC 22. 427 & Sh. ʿAbd.'s copy's var. of **puhulta** Gs 37:15.

PHZ (Jew.-Aram. & H. פחז, Syr. ܦܚܰܙ, Ar. فخز) to be reckless, heedless, wanton.

Der.: **pahza.**

PHK (metath. of ܦܟܰܗ) to be dull, languish.

Pe. Pf. **napšaihun pihkat ʿlauaihun** Gy 277:17 their soul became dull within them (MG 66:20, 234:26).

Der.: **pukata**?, **pukta 2.**

PHL (metath. of **PLH,** another secondary rt. **PLA I**) to serve, worship.

Pe. Act. pt. pl. **pahluta pahlia** s. **pahluta. kulhun ldilia pahlia** Gy 81:23 they serve me; **gubria pahlia ʿšiul** Gs 114:17 the servants of the underworld; with encl. **pahlalh̲** DC 36 II no. 108 she offers services to him; **pahlilh̲** Gy 81:18 they serve him; **pahlilia** Gy 81:23 they serve me; **pahlilak** Gs 63:5 they will serve thee.

Der.: **pahluta,** var. **pihluta, p(u)hulta,** var. **pih(u)lta, puhlana, pihla 2.**

PHS (metath. of **PSH** q.v.) to walk.

Pe. Pt. fem. pl. **pahsa** Gs 83:5 they walk MG 72:9.

PHR (metath. of ***PRH** = **PRA II** q.v.) to fly.

Pe. Act. pt. **pahra** Gy 102:10, 280:4, ATŠ I no. 280, DC 44. 507 flieth MG 67:9, 235: antep.; pl. **pahria** Gy 279:21, DC. 43 J 198, **pahrin** ATŠ I no. 282 they fly. Part. pres. **paharna** Par. xxiv 39b I fly.

Der.: **puhra 2**?

PHŠ (etym. & mean. doubtf. Ginzā 588 n. 1, cf. Aram. & H. פשח, Syr. ܦܫܰܚ, Ar. فسخ, Akk. *pašāhu*? to tear off) to separate?; to tear away?

Pa. Pt. **nišimta . . . d̲-mn dur bišia umn gauh̲ d̲-hšuka mpahšia** (read **-ša**) Gs 131:21 a soul . . . that teareth itself (?) from the dwelling of the wicked and from the interior of the darkness.

PHT (metath. of **PTH** q.v., another secondary rt. **PTA** s.v.) to open, break open, divide, burst open; (of creation) to create.

Pe. Pf. **pihtat unihrat** Gy 374:12 'she–opened–(or broke through)–and shone' (name of a female genie) MG 234:bottom; with suff. **pihth** he opened him MG 66 n. 2, 275:1. Impf. **tipihtun** ye (will) open MG 66:13, 235:20; with suff. **nipihth** he opens him, her, it MG 66:12, 275:16, **ʿpihth** I open him MG 275:17. Act. pt. **uahid ulapahta** DC 26. 620 f. and shuts and does not open; **d-hu pahta d-ziua unhura** CP 6:12 = ML 7:ult. who openeth (the treasure?) of radiance and light; pl. **pahtia pihta d-hiia** Q 58:28 = ML 84:3 they create the creation of Life (Lidzb., cf. ML 84 n. 2); **pahtia iardna** DAb they will open the jordan (30 n. 1); **salqia upahtia bhdadia** DC 26. 203 = DC 28 par. they rise up and break with one another. Part. pres. **pahtit** thou openest MG 66:12, 236:18, **pahtitin** (read **-tun** masc.) Q 52:19 ye open MG 97:17, 236:26; with encl. **pahtinalh** ATŠ I no. 281 I open to her; **pahtilh hṭita mn šumbilta . . . pahtilh lamuza usfargla** they divide the wheat from the ear . . . break into pieces the walnuts and quince etc.; **aina d-naṣiruta kulh ʿtpihtat ʿlak** DC 27. 67 the eye of all Naṣirdom is fixed (open) on thee.

Ethpe. Pf. **aina . . . ʿtpihtat ʿlak** DC 27. 66 f. the eye . . . opened upon thee. Pt. **mitpihta** ATŠ II no. 31 is opened; pl. **mitpihtia** ATŠ I no. 284 are opened.

Ethpa. Pt. **mitpahta** ATŠ II (DC 6: DC 36 **mitpihta**) no. 31 a var. of ethpe. q.v.

Der.: **pihta.**

pu interj. fie! V.s. **qas pu.**

pugdama (פתגם, ܦܘܓܕܡܐ < Iranian **patgâm* ISK 107, mod. P. پیام, Lagarde: *Abhandlungen* 79) word, bidding, precept MG xxxii 5, 74:20. Pl. **-ia. pugdama d-mia** (title of DC 51) the bidding of the water(s); **iukabar pugdama d-hiia** CP 29:penult., Q 12:31 = ML 35:6 Y. the Word (*λόγος*) of Life; **pugdamia d-kušṭa** Gy 177:17, DC 53. 162:7 words of truth (precepts of right dealing); **pugdamia ahbalh** Gy 194:20 give over the word (message); **pugdamia kasiia** Gy 72:9 hidden words (secret precepts); **arba pugdamia baraiia** ATŠ II no. ? four exoteric precepts; **hazin pugdama lanikadib** DC 43 A 155 this word shall not be belied; **hu zuṭ upugdamh rurbia** Gy 205:6 f. he is small, but his words are mighty; **blimia pugdamia d-pumh** DC 43 silenced are the words of his mouth.

pugdana = **puqdana.** Pl. **-ia.** MG 39:8. **pugdania nipaqdunh** AM 15:7 they will give him orders (entrust him with a commission).

pudana = **padana** MG 20:14. St. cstr. **pudan. aganbia mšaunia kušṭa qaiim pudana radia pudana d-lau pudan tauria . . . pudana pudan kušṭa . . . habšaba lagiṭ pudana** Jb 179:8 ff. beside M.-K. standeth a plough, plougheth a plough that is not a plough (drawn by) oxen . . . the plough is a plough of K. . . . Sunday (personified) holdeth the plough; **aršith pudana** Jb 55:3 (DC 30 has **purana** expected by Lidzb. Jb ii 60 n. 2).

pudga DC 37. 143 for **pukta**?

pudra (etym. unknown; a den. verb may be **PDR**) witchcraft, sorcery, spell. Pl. **-ia,** var. **-inia.** Jb ii 107 n. 5. **mahra upudra hauilh** AM 46:14 he will be sick and bewitched (a spell will be on him); **haršia upudria** Gy 74:17, 78:1 (var. **pudrinia** DC 22. 69), 121:3, 331:7, 8 witchcraft and sorcery (spells); **haršan upudran** Gy 166:10 our witchcraft and our spells; **kulh mlia haršia umlia pudria** Gy 81:5 is overfilled with witchcraft, is full of spells; **šbaq haršia ušbaq pudria** Jb ii 107:10 he abandoned witchcraft, he abandoned sorcery; **pudria ʿlh napṣʿ** Gy 102:25, 103:1 s. **NPṢ** pe. act. pt. pl.

puha Gy 85:11, 86:7 interj. alas! woe! MG 81:15.

puhulta (rt. **PHL**) Gs 37:15 service. Varr. **phulta, pih(u)lta** s.vv. MG 66:17 f.

puhlana (rt. **PHL**, פּוּלְחָנָא, ܦܘܠܚܢܐ) service, work MG 66:9, 16. **nihuilh puhlana ladam** Gy 12:20, 33:19 they will be of service to Adam; **lpuhlana ultangaruta** AM 166:12 at work (tilling?) and at trade.

puhra 1 (ܦܘܚܪܐ > Ar. فُخْر, فهر, from Akk. *puḫru* Zimmern ZATW xi 158 f.) feast, banquet MG 104:ult. Pl. **-ia. zmara upuhria** Gy 219:26 music and banquets; **puhria uzmaria** Gy 225:1, **puhria uzamria** Gy 376:18 feast(ing)s and songs; **halin d-iatbia puhria** Gy 220:10 those who sit at banquets.

puhra 2 (rt. **PHR**?) a small unit of time, second. Pl. **-ia. nagia upuhria** Gy 99:21, 112:19 s. ***naga 1.**

pukata (rt. **PHK**?) langour, feebleness. Var. **puktata, pukta 2. ʿtlh . . . pukata d-šaqia** AM 40:12 he has . . . feebleness of limbs (var. CS 26 **puktata**: see also **pukta**).

pukurta (rt. **PKR**) bond. **pugdama kširta upukurta** DC 40. 825 an efficacious word and (magic) bond (spell).

pukra (rt. **PKR**) bond. **udhisbit pukrai** Oxf. roll g 641 = DC 47 = Or. 327:5 and that which I have surrounded (with) my (magic) bond.

pukta 1 (ܦܓܘܡܬܐ Akk. **pagumtu, pagūmu*) bridle MG 41:8, 44:5, 105:22. Var. **pikta,** pl. **piktia.** Fem. (later masc.?). **bpumh pukta pukta bpumh** Gy 85:9 f. the bridle on his mouth; **zim kd susia barbia piktia** DC 45 bridled like a horse with four bridles.

pukta 2 (rt. **PHK**?) langour, weakness. Var. **puk(t)ata. pukta d-šaqia** AM 83:17 weakness of the limbs.

pulaa DC 25. 100 a miscop. of **ptulia** (cf. ibid. l. 102).

pulad (ܦܘܠܕ < P. پولاد Lagarde: *Abhandlungen* 75, Ar. loan-w. فولاذ & بولاد) steel. **uarqa hurintia d-pulad** RD B 27 = DAb par. and another earth of steel.

pulgana (rt. **PLG**) dissension, discord, dispute. **upulgana babahath šaria** AM 11:10 and he will cause discord between his parents.

pulgia (ܦܠܓܝܡ, ܦܠܓܝܡ Löw 81) DC 46. 121:11 mugwort, wormwood.

pulgma = **plugma, blugma. zma umir upulgma** DC 34. 410 blood, bile, and mucus.

pulhana Gy 12:20 an exceptional (though more original) var. of **puhlana.**

pulis s. **paulis**.

puma (פּוּמָא, Old Aram. פם, Bibl.-Aram. פֻּם, Syr. ܦܽܘܡܳܐ, H. פֶּה, Ar. فم & فو, Akk. *pū* Barth ZDMG xli 633 f., Brockelm. i 333) mouth, orifice, opening MG 19 n. 1, 97:13. St. abs. & cstr. **pum** (also 'my mouth' apart from **pumai** MG 175:15). **puma d̠-bisra uzma** Gy 7:14 mouth of flesh and blood; **puma qadmaia** and **puma batraia** Gy 191:15 f., 337:13 f., 338:7 f. the first mouth (navel) and the (real) mouth Ginzā 192 n. 2, 349 n. 4, cf. **puma qadmaia hu d̠-hu šura mitiqria** ATŠ it is the orifice which is called the navel; **pum praš** CP 210:8, ML 244:5, Jb 41:1, 131:14 f. = **puma d̠-praš** Jb 41:1 = **pumh̠ d̠-praš** Gy 351:22 the mouth of the Euphrates; **latišanun d̠-pum** ML 217:7 = CP 178:7 alter not (the speech) of my mouth; **bpum** Gs 75:15 orally MG 302:ult.

punida (possibly from ביניתא, Ar. بنّي? Löw: *Aramäische Fischnamen* OSt 551 ff.) fish. Common colloquial word, pronounced *fonida*. Gl. 74:12 **punida**(i) حيتان *pisces* ماهى.

pusqana (rt. **PSQ**, ܦܽܘܣܩܳܢܳܐ) interruption, intervention, interval. **zibna upusqana** Gy 219:19 a period and an interval; **pusqana mšauilh̠** Gy 219:23 he will intervene therein.

puqdana (rt. **PQD**, פּוּקְדָּנָא, ܦܽܘܩܕܳܢܳܐ) command, order, injunction, charge, appointment. Doublet **pugdana** s.v. MG 39:8. Pl. **-ia**. **puqdania d̠-zakuata** Gy 214:2 orders of purities; **puqdania nipaqdunh̠** AM 17:11 and they will give him orders (entrust him with certain things).

puq(u)ta AM 88 a phonetic var. of **pquta** (q.v.).

pura 1 (ܦܽܘܪܳܐ) rage, passion, heat, fury MG 105:9. Doublet **paura** s.v. Pl. **-ia 2**. **mn purun šbaq ᶜlauaihun** Gs 124:5 he caused their own rage to recoil on themselves; **pura d̠-alma** Gs 136:8 f. worldly passion; **pura uiaqdana** Gy 376:9 passion (rage) and burning; **abrh̠ lpura mn ᶜuṣrak** s. **paura**.

pura 2 (cf. H. פּוּר Ges.) fate, lot, allotment. **prun pura upalig mnata lnapšaihun** Gy 111:11 f. they cast a lot and allotted a portion for themselves (Lidzb. **pura 3**); **ᶜl lbušai** (var. **lilbušia**) **upura** (var. without **u-**) **nasbia ᶜlai** Gy 259:14 (var. DC 22. 254) they cast a lot (?) about my garment, cf. **had lbuša šibqit ᶜlauaihun lhad minaihun pura** (**d̠**)-**ptahil miṭi(i)h̠** Gy 269:23 f. I left a garment for them, for one of them, the lot fell upon P. (?, Lidzb. left both untranslated); **udmu puria man hauian** Gs 40:9 who showed me the shape of destinies? (doubtf., left untransl. by Lidzb.).

pura 3 (either semantic development of **pura 2** or a phonetic development of **puhra 1**) feast, holiday. **nipria pura** Gy 109:18 we will arrange a feast; **pura d̠-prun šuba** Gy 113:1 the feast which the Seven arranged; **qum lpuraikun buzuia** Gy 118:2 arise, disengage your feast (parallel with **šubqu lkništaikun** leave your assembly); **ᶜkilta d̠-hilulia upura** Gy 302:2 the food of feasts and banqueting.

pura 4, purh for **puria 1**. **purh̠** (or **pura**) **tlat ᶜnšia nizal** AM 6:16, 21:13, 25:15, 30:1, 34:3, 37:paen., 42:15, 52:9 he will marry three women; **purh̠ lpt ṭuhma nizal** AM 3:7 he will marry a girl from his family; **purh̠ ltlata gubria nizal** AM 61:7, 70:5 she will marry three men; **purh̠ ltrin ᶜu tlata gubria nizal** AM 67:6, 82:8 she will marry two or three men (idiom, cf. s. **puria 1**).

pura 5 (etym. unknown) AIT 162 Montgomery: bowl, Lidzb.: conjuration Ginzā 259 n. 1. Doubtf.

pura 6 (rt. **PRA II**) bird(s), fowl. Pl. **puria 3** poultry (?). **umišria pura** (var. **puria**) **uṭaiis d̠-ᶜngaria** DC 46. 17:6, DC 12. 156 and frees (from spells) poultry and flying (birds) of the roofs (pigeons?).

purana 1 (rt. **PRA III**, ܦܽܘܪܥܳܢܳܐ) endowment, (re)payment. **asrith̠ purana** DC 30 (var. **pudana** Jb 55:3) I have established an endowment; **purana hauia bit qubria** Jb 114:6 f., 12 the (re)payment will be in the graveyard.

(**purana 2** Jb 108:9 ABD a var. of **kuhrana**).

puraria (cf. **pura 1**, connected with H. פְּארוּר?) Gy 207:13. the glow of the evening sky MG 127:22. Var. **praria** DC 22. 199.

purat (فُرَات) AM 204 Euphrates. Var. **prat**.

purudqa occasionally for **prudqa**.

puruṭta s. **purṭta**.

purukia Jb 59:15 B = **prikia**.

puruta s. **purta**.

purṭa s. **purṭta**.

purṭana (rt. **PRṬ**) fissure, cleft, breach. **purṭana bbaṣa hurina praṭnabh̠** s. **baṣa**.

purṭta (rt. **PRṬ**) cleft, gap, open place, gaping wound. Varr. **puruṭta, pruṭta** MG 105:14; masc. form **pruṭa**. **upraṭ purṭa** ATŠ II no. 204 and a cleft opened; **praṭ purṭta** Gy 354:8 f., Gs 95:2, 3, 7, 8 id., **priṭbun purṭta** Gs 13:18 a cleft was opened in them; **priṭbh̠ purṭta** Gs 107:7, cf. 124:7 f. a cleft was opened in it; **puruṭta briših̠ nihuia** Par. AM 101:bottom, there shall be a gaping wound in his head.

puria 1 (פּוּרְיָא) bedding, mattress, bed (particularly bed of bridal couple spread on the ground). **puria mkiklh̠ lhiduta** ŠQ (PA's) the wedding-bed is spread for the bride; **puria maiik** Gy 147:23 he spread (hist. pres.) a bed(ding); **uautbun ᶜl puria d̠-zahba** Gy 148:6 f. they seated me on a golden bed; **ukilta nagdilia ᶜl puria . . . umautibilia ᶜl puria** Gy 148:7 f. they spread for me a mosquito-net over the bed . . . and seated me on the bed; **d̠-ᶜl arsa d̠-puria darik** Gy 376:21 for one that treadeth underfoot the bedding of the bridal bed; **puria nizal** AM 3:7, 47:6, 89:5, 96:17 he will marry (lit. go to bed with; a frequent idiom, cf. **pura 4** & BZ 6 n. 6).

puria 2 s. **pura 1**.

puria 3 s. **pura 6**.

purmana (P. فرمان) decree, command, mandate. **ulitlh̠ hšuka bgauihun purmana** ATŠ I no. 17 darkness has no mandate within them (: days of light); **bpurmanaikun** Lond. roll A 172 by your mandate; **purmanh̠ ušulṭanh̠ dilia hᶜ** DC 40 its mandate and sovereignty is mine; **bpurmanak malil** ATŠ II no. 321 he speaks by thy decree; **bpurmanak ʿbad** ŠQ 6:14 I act by thy command; **purmana hu** Oxf. xii (under the picture of an eagle) he is a strong one (?).

pursma (אפורסמא, ܦܘܪܣܡܐ[ܐ]) > Iranian *beresma* Lagarde: *Abhandlungen* 17:30, Gr. loan-w. βάλσαμον, H. בֶּשֶׂם, Ar. بَشَام, Akk. *bašamu* Löw 73 f.) balsam. Varr. **prusma, pursama. miša ḏ-pursma** Gy 217:21, DC 44. 2047, 2087 (varr.) balsam oil (cf. משחא דאפורסמא Ber. 43 a).

purṣa occasionally for **pirṣa.**

purqana (rt. **PRQ,** פּוּרְקָן, ܦܘܪܩܢܐ) deliverance, redemption. St. abs. (& cstr.) **purqan. šita šaiia ḏ-purqana** Gy 14:11, 35:11, 42:13, 183: 14 f., 254:23, DC 26. 783 f., DC 40. 810 f. etc. the hour of deliverance; **iuma ḏ-purqana** Gy 40:24 = **ium purqan** CP 112:2 f. the day of deliverance.

purqat (rt. **PRQ**) st. cstr. deliverance. **alma lpurqat almia** DC 12. 125, Lond. roll B 250 unto the deliverance of the worlds.

purta (= **purṭta,** cf. **PRṬ** = **PRT**) cleft, parting. Varr. **pururta, puruta. purta briših̲ nihuilh̲** AM 88:8 he will have a scar (or cleft) on his head.

PUŠ, PŠŠ (פוש, ܦܫ) to remain, stay, persist, be left behind; to relax, dissolve; to squash, smash, squeeze, press out.

Pe. Pf. **paš** DC 41:257 etc. remained MG 248:2, **pašat** DC 41. 322 it (fem.) remained, **pašiun** Gy 380:8, 381:10, HG they remained, var. **pašun** MG 248:8; with encl. **pašubh̲** Gy 128:21 they remained in it MG 248:5; (trans.) with suff. **ʿu . . . lhanatin ʿnbia . . . lapašinin** ATŠ I no. 176, II no. 30 if . . . he did not press out . . . the grapes. Impf. **nipuš** DC 34. 1206 etc. he stays, continues MG 249:8, **ḏ-muma bgauh̲ lanipaš** ATŠ II no. 35 so that blemish does not remain in him; **nipišiun** Gy 386:11 ABC (var. **nipišun** Lond.) they remain MG 249:paen.; with encl. **anašia zaina bhdadia nipušbun** AM 210:1 the people will remain in arms against one another; (trans.) with suff. **nipišiunh̲ bmia** DC 43 J 84 they shall melt it in water. Impt. (trans.) **puš ʿnbia ḏ-niarak** DC 42. 139 etc. press out (the juice of) the grapes of (i.e. that are in) thy bowl; **mrirta ḏ-nuna puš bnhirh̲** DC 46 squeeze the gall of a fish into his nostrils. Act. pt. **paiiš** AM 261 etc. he remains; **ḏ-paiiša** (varr. **paiiš** B, **paiša** DC 30) **bgu dibna** Jb 47:3 that is left behind in the fold; pl. **uhaizak paišin šitin iuma** ATŠ I no. ? and thus they remain for sixty days; with suff. **lapaišinin** ATŠ II no. 30 he does not press out (a var. of **lapašinin** s. pf. with suff.).

Ethpa (doubtf.). Impf. **nitpaša kḏ bita midurtia** DC 44. 1718 he shall be smashed like a rotten egg.

pušqa (rt. **PŠQ,** ܦܘܫܩܐ) explanation, exposition, interpretation. **tapsir upušqa** DC 34. 325 explanation and interpretation; **upušqa ḏ-hazin lhudaita** DC 34. 323 and the interpretation of this by itself (?).

pušra a var. of preced. **tapsir upušra** DC 34. 763 cf. s. preced.

puta 1 (אפותא, ܦܘܬܐ[ܐ]) forehead. Still used (pronounced *fotta*). **uptia qarqabth̲ urama puth̲** AM 39:16 and his skull is wide and his forehead lofty; **unirišmh̲ tlata rušumia lputh̲** DC 50 and shall sign him thrice on his forehead.

puta 2 (rt. **PTA**) opening, aperture. **mardita hʿ ldukia nasbalh̲ mn puta** ATŠ I no. 246 its course flows to various places from its opening.

putia, puth̲ (פּוּתְיָא, ܦܘܬܝܐ) width, breadth, extent MG 105:12. **uputia hamšin amia** Gy 380:12 and its breadth (is) fifty ells; **uzirta hda putih̲** Gy 159:19 (var. **putiia** DC 22. 154) and one span was his girth (width); **utlatma ušitin alpia parsia puth̲** DAb and its width (is) 360,000 furlongs.

PṬA (פְּטַי) to break, (with **mn**) to break from.

Pa. Impt. with suff. **paiṭh̲ pik plan mn planita** DC 46 break him from, estrange N. (man) from N. (woman).

Gl. 7:3 f. **apṭa** اشاع *divulgere* مشهور كرد.

Der.: **piṭia** (pl.).

pṭaka (ܦܛܩܐ, πιττάκιον) DC 46. 188:13 a slip of parchment.

PṬL (= **PṢL**?) to divide, break a piece off, detach.

Pa. Impt. **paṭil pihta mn klila** DC 42. 208 detach the sacramental bread from the wreath (Note: In the ritual of the *masiqta* the *pihta* is wrapped about the myrtle wreath, and at the appointed place detached, or unwrapped from it).

Der.: **paṭ(i)la.**

PṬM the rt. of **piṭma.**

PṬR (Aram. & H. פטר, Syr. ܦܛܪ, Ar. فطر Schwally ZDMG liii 199 f., Eth. ፈጠረ, Akk. *pṭāru*) to open up, open (a)part, separate; to leave, eject, discharge, break away, rub off.

Pa. Pt. **mpaṭar** Gy 190:12 he rubbed off; **kḏ mpaṭar liginh̲ hadia** DC 45 (JRAS 1943 179:3) when his vessel (membrum?) discharges (?) he rejoices; pl. (fem.) **umpaṭran šinh̲** AM 14 and his teeth are parted (to sneer? Idiom BZ 13 n. 10); **upaṭar uasia mn bišutak** DC 46. 138:1 and cure him from thine evil.

Ethpa. Impf. **ništagar unitpaṭar unipra** DC 46. 189:7 (love-charm) he shall burn and set off (?) and fly. Pt. pl. **mištagria umipaṭria** Gy 225:6 they are enflamed and lustful (?Lidzb. *und reiben sich auf*).

Der.: **paṭur, paṭira, piṭra 1, piṭiara, piṭiaruta.**

piala (פיילא, ܦܝܠܐ < P. پياله, Gr. φιάλη) drinking-vessel, cup. Pl. **-ia. ʿniaria upialia ukasia** ATŠ I no. 251 bowls, drinking-vessels and cups.

piasa (פייסא, ܦܝܣܐ < πεῖσα), persuasion, reasoning with, explanation, argument. Pl. **-ia.** Occ. var. **paiasa.** Masc. **piasa (a)hbalh̲**

lhaua Gs 20:19 reason with Eve; **piasa ubuna** Gs 19:23, 25:21 explanation and demonstration; **našar ˁl hazin piasa** Gs 25:23 f. holdeth firmly to this explanation; **piasa hazin** (var. **hazin piasia** DC 22. 416) **ḏ-ahib manda ḏ-hiia ladam** Gs 26:2 this is the explanation (var. these are the arguments) which M.–ḏ–H. gave to A.

piga (Nöld. < قلثا MG 39:7, Lidzb. from פקע or פגע OSt 241, both confused in a name of demons), deaf-mute, dumb, pl. **pigia 1** MG 109:1. Used also of a kind of demon, Furlani: *I Nomi* 424. **gungia pigia šagišia** Gy 279:11 deaf, deaf-mutes, confused (of demons); **pigia upilgia** Gy 279:5 (var. . . . **upalgia** DC 22. 274) of demons (hence different from **pigia upalgiḥ ḏ-pigia** s. **pigia 2**); **prišaiia pigia hauin upigia prišaiia** Gy 387:24 discerning will become idiots and idiots become discerning (sane); **gubria prišaiia upigia** Gy 391:14 sane men and idiots; **algia upigia** DC 3 stammering and dumb. Often in exorcisms (of demons): **pigia zikria . . . pigia nuqbata** DC 37. 510 f.; **pigia upalgia** DC 43 J 186 f., 190, DC 51. 688 (*& often*, cf. above); **kul pigia (u)ṣardia** DC 44. 715 = Morg. 260/12:2 f. all blighting mischance demons; **pigia udahlulia** DC 43 G misadventure demons and bogies, but **pigia bišia ḏ-ˁumama** DC 43 D 63 misadventures by day (rather than 'demons', parallel with **qiria ḏ-lilia** accidents at night), cf. also **pigia 2** and **pigia upagadta** s. **pagadta**; **piṭiaruta upigia** s. **piṭiaruta**.

pigdia pl. (rt. **PGD**) restraints, spells to impede or keep back. **pigdia** (var. **pugdamia**) **ḏ-šap baraiia** DAb (var. RD) spells-for-restraint (var. words) that the exorcists deflected.

pigudta (rt. **PGD**) bridle, restraint. Doublets **pagadta, pagudta** s.v. **upigudta pagibḥ** AM CS 26 (but AM 11:7 has **gudta**) and even though a bridle should come upon him (prob. read **pagidbḥ** should restrain him?); **upigudta bpumḥ ṭruša bˁudnḥ** DC 43 J 149 and a bridle in his mouth and deafness in his ears (or perh. 'dumbness in his mouth' as both examples seem to be influenced by **pigia 1**).

pigia 1 pl. of **piga** (q.v.).

pigia 2 (rt. **PGA**) minute, cf. MG xxviii n. 2 (Nöld. mistakenly took the form for a pl., although the rt. must have been treated as ל״י). **upigia upalgiḥ ḏ-pigia** Gy 379:5 f. a minute and half a minute.

pidila for **pitila**: in **uaud pidila ubduq bšraga** DC 45 and make a wick and put into a lamp.

pihla 1 (rt. **PHL = PLA I = PLH**) service, work. **pihla ḏ-ˁl šum hiia pla** Q 40:29 = ML 107:8, DC 41. 184 f. etc., service which they rendered to the name of Life (?).

pihla 2 (cf. فحل yearning for coition, Ar. فَحل, Akk. *puḫālu* used for covering) male organ, phallus ? (CP trs. 59. n. 3). **pira upihla** DC 12:172, Lond. roll B 357, DC 19, DC 45, DC 46 vagina and phallus (?).

pihl(u)ta Gs 37:15 BCD = **puhulta** ibid. A MG 66:17.

pihta (rt. **PHT = PTH**, cf. فِتا. As to the specific Mand. use for the sacramental wafer cf. Jew.-Aram. פִּיתָא bread, Zimmern from Akk. *pit pi* opening of the mouth OSt 959–67, ML xxii f.) (*a*) opening, disclosing (of fate), divination, (*b*) sacramental bread MG 66:12 f., 333 n. 2, AF 231 & n. 10, GGA 1890 p. 402, RO II 118:8, MR 107, 203, MSchr. 60 n. 7, 197, Kessler PRE 174 f., Vortrag 1904:21, Siouffi 92, HpGn. 312 f., MSt 167 f., MMII 107 f., 122 n. 15, ZDMG cv 115–50. Pl. **pihtia, pihtania.** (*a*) **ḏ-iaqid bgu pihta** Gy 238:2 which gloweth in disclosing (?); **pihta unhaša** Or. 331:14 divination and augury; (*b*) **laˁkilak pihta mn paturai** Jb 26:3 thou hast eaten no bread from my table; **pahtia pihta ḏ-hiia** Gy 189:16, 196:4, Q 31:4, 58:28 = ML 84:3 they break the bread of Life; **pta pihta bkisia** Q 25:18, 25, 26:3, 11 he secretly broke the bread; **akul pihtak** Q 32:31 eat thy sacramental bread (& often with **AKL**); **nasbinalḥ lpihtḥ** Jb 76:10 we take his sacramental bread; **pihta ḏ-nasib mšiha paulis** Jb 108:10 the sacramental bread which Christ–Paul taketh; **sab pihta** Q 32:27 take the sacramental bread (& often with **NSB**); **bruk ˁl pihta** Gy 17:22 bless the bread (& often with **BRK**); cf. **pihtania ubarukata** PD 1155 sacramental breads and blessings. Often with **YHB**, cf. **pta uˁhablia pihta** CP 40:1 he broke and gave me bread; **pta uahbalun pihta** WedF. 76:middle he broke and gave them the sacramental bread; **pihtia tartin** ATŠ II no. 167 two pieces of bread; **barakata ḏ-pihtania ḏ-zidqa brika** CP 368:5 blessings of the bread of the Blessed Oblation; **pihta umambuha** Gy 224:1 sacramental bread and drink. Often in rituals. Sometimes personified, cf. Gy 238:6 f., CP 368:14, 370:6, 375:1, 376:ult.

piṭia (rt. **PṬA**) adj. pl. shattered, broken, scorned. **šaliṭia piṭia** Oxf. roll g 642, DC 47 = Or. 327:6 the tyrants are scorned.

piṭiara (rt. **PṬR**, cf. foll.) sneering, malice, loss?, a kind of demon. Furlani; *I Nomi* 422. **piṭiara upiṭiaruta** DC 43 A 160, ibid. E 20, 65 (*& often in lists of demons*); **bbaitak ubaita ḏ-ˁtbḥ piṭiara** DC 40. 1041 ff. in thy house and a house in which there is malice (?).

piṭiaruta (abstr. noun from preced.) opening, fissure; leaving, parting; fig. sneering, malicious talk; also a kind of demons (cf. s. **piṭiara**). **bbaitak baraia ugauaia upiṭiaruta ḏ-ˁngaria utarbaṣia** DC 40. 1042 in thy house inside and out and the openings of roofs and courtyards; **piṭiaruta upigia** DC 40. 239 f. sneering and misadventures; **haršia piṭiaruta** DC 37. 12 sorceries (and) malice; **ˁu mn piṭiaruta ˁu mn ṣihua uluṭata** AM 51:16 either through malicious talk or through reviling and cursing; **ˁu mn piṭiaruta ˁu mn luṭata** AM 84:11; **piṭiaruta uqirsa** DC 26. 228 malice and sickness; **piṭiara upiṭiaruta** s. **piṭiara.** Frequent in exorcisms.

piṭma (פִּטְמָא, ܦܶܛܡܳܐ) fat. Miscop. piṭra 2 s.v. **dikria ḏ-piṭma** Gy 234:7 fat rams.

piṭra 1 (rt. **PṬR**) divorce, separation, parting. **šiṭia upiṭra** Gs 23:11 foolishness and divorce; **aina ḏ-šiha upiṭra** DC 21.5:penult. eye that lusts and divorces.

piṭra 2 for **piṭma** MG 315 n. 1. **tauria d-piṭra** Gs 103:3, Jb 90:12 fat oxen.

pikra (rt. **PKR**) snare, fastening, bond, entanglement, obstacle. Pl. **-ia. pikra p(a)kartinun** DC 44. 637 = DC 26. 606 f. I ensnared them; **pikria nihuilẖ minẖ** AM 34:5 he will be ensnared by her (CS 26 **pikuria**).

pikta = **pukta. kḏ susia barbia piktia** DC 45 xxxiii, JRAS 1943 178:20 like a horse with four head-reins.

pil(a) (פִּילָא, ܦܺܝܠܳܐ, mod. H. פִּיל, Ar. فيل, Akk. *pilu, piru*) elephant. Pl. **-ia. glala ḏ-pilia gaṭla** Jb 41:12 hail that killeth elephants; **mhita ḏ-ʿtimhabẖ pilia** DC 43 G 22 the blow wherewith (female) elephants were struck.

pilasupa (ܦܺܝܠܳܣܽܘܦܳܐ < φιλόσοφος) Gy 227:1 philosopher.

pilṭus DC 22. 28 = **palṭus** Gy 29:8.

piliaṭus = **palṭus. palṭus ḏ-hauia malka balma** Gy 53:6 Pilate who is a king in the world (cf. Gy 29:8).

pilpil (Mishn. פלפל, Syr. ܦܶܠܦܠܳܐ, Ar. فلفل, from Sanskr. पिप्पल Löw 317) pepper. **darpilpil trin danqia mitqal arba danqia** Par. xxii two beans of long pepper and four beans' weight of pepper.

pilpin pipin Gy 183:4, 184:1, 4 guardian spirit of a purgatory.

pilqa (ܦܶܠܩܳܐ, Akk. *pilaqqu* hatchet < Sum. *balag*, cf. Gr. πέλεκυς, Ar. فلق to split, cleave Jeffrey 229) axe, hatchet. Still used (pronounced *pelqa*). **pilqa litlak** Jb 162:5 thou hast no axe; **pilqa hu** Oxf. xii it is an axe; **ʿtbarat kḏ pilqa** JRAS 1937 p. 593: antepenult. thou art broken (? read **ʿtabart**?) like an axe (?).

pindur (var. **pandur**) (פַּנְדּוּרָה, ܦܰܢܕܽܘܪܳܐ < πανδοῦρα, Ar. loan-w. قندورة) a musical instrument, zither, shepherd's pipe MG 151 n. 3. Pl. **pinduria. pindur kušṭa** Oxf. 48 b, CP 180:12 = ML 221:2 **mamlla bpinduria** Gy 187:20 she speaketh with pipes (Lidzb.: *Zithern*).

pisa 1 (cf. **piasa**) persuasive, reasoning, instructing. **ṣauta anat qadmaita pisa** DC 26. 33 f. thou art the first instructing voice.

pisa 2 (P. پيسه) piebald, parti-coloured, black and white. **ʿurba ḏ-pisa** AM 132:1 f. a black-and-white crow.

pisad (Ar. فساد) AM 257:35, 277:35 corruption. **ahl pisad** s. **ahl.**

pisuhiata s. **pasihiata.**

pisusta (rt. **PSS**) destruction, ruin, downfall MG 119:9, 126:19. Var. **pa-** s.v. **barqa ḏ-pisusta** Gs 40:10 into the world of destruction; **tihuia pisusta** DC 26. 325 = DC 28 par. (varr. **psusta**) there will be downfall.

pisihiata s. **pasihiata.**

pisnia 1 pl. (possibly a corruption of ψαλμός?). (*a*) songs, tunes, melodies, (*b*) stops on a wind-strument? MG 151:18 (cf. n. 3), ML 221 n. 1, Ginzā 132 n. 6. (*a*) **pindur** (var. **pandur**) **kušṭa ḏ-mlia pisnia tušbihta** Oxf. 48 b = ML 221:2 = CP 180:12 the reed-pipe of Truth which is full of songs of praise; (*b*) **pisnia ḏ-nbu tibrit** Gy 118:18, **gubria haila ḏ-pisnia šiqra bʿdaihun lgiṭia** Gy 916:22 (doubtf., cf. **pisnia 2**).

pisnia 2 pl. of **psan**, emph. ***pasanta** (q.v.). **milgaṭ bidaiun upisnun** DC 44. 1951 = Morg. 269/29:42 grasp(ing) on with their hands and palms (?).

pipir = **pilpil** DC 46. 192:6, and elsewhere.

piqa (rt. **PQA** = פקע) split, fissure MG 102:12. Fig. meteorite? Pl. **-ia. pqa piqa** Jb 41:9 a split opened, **piqa . . . pqa** Gy 166:5 f.; pres. **paqa piqa** Gy 96:12 f.; **piqa mn qudamẖ paqa** ATŠ I no. 257 a fissure is split before it; **piqa usaʿiqia** AM 281:8 meteorite (?) and thunderbolts; **gargul upiqia** AM 281:9 rumbling and splits (or meteorites ?); **piqia umahria** Oxf. roll g 725 fissures and illnesses.

piqd(i)a (rt. **PQD**) a kind of demons, demon visitants BZ 80 n. 7, Furlani: *I Nomi* 426. **piqda daiua** Oxf. roll 154; **piqdia uruhia** Q 13:25, 15:23, Oxf. roll 220; **sahria upiqdia** (*often*); **piqdia ulihania** Q 8:5, DC 12. 294, Lond. roll B 575; **šidia upiqdia** (*often*), DC 51. 179 etc.; **upiqdaiun bṭabaiia** Gy 107:5 and their demon visitants (became) cooks.

piqunia pl. (diminutive from ܦܩܳܥܳܐ) buds, blossoms, flowers MG 140:9. **bazrunia upiqunia** Gy 33:16, 378:34 seeds and blossoms; **ʿuṣania upiqunia** Gy 89:16 leaves and blossoms; **piqunia uiarqunia** Jb 232:7 flowers and green vegetables; **piqunia uqadahia** Lond. roll B 108 = DC 12. 51 & DC 10 par. buds and burgeonings.

piquta DC 43 J 149 a var. of **pquta**?

piqita (rt. **PQA**?) DC 44. 2078 bottle?, tube?.

pira 1 (פֵּירָא, ܦܺܐܪܳܐ, Phoen. פר, H. פְּרִי, Akk. *pir'u* offshoot) fruit, used often as gnostic term (καρπός) as an expression of emanation MG 4:anteantep., 109:1, MR 23, 187 ff., MSchr. 125, ERE viii 382, Kessler PRE 162 f., Krehl ZDMG xxii 557, HpGn 135, 292, Kraeling JAOS 1953 p. 161 f., MMII 242, 305 n. 4. St. abs. & cstr. **pir.** Pl. **-ia.** Masc. **pira bgu pira** Gy 68:22, 69:17 fruit in the (pre-emanational) fruit; **pira rba bgu pira** Gy 75:26; **pira rba** Gy 74:3, Q 58:33 etc. the Great Fruit; **pira rba uʿlaia** DC 26. 239, Q 58:33; **pira rba ḏ-nhura** Gy 193:3 the Great Fruit of Light; **pira hiuara** Jb 206:5, CP 4:1, the white fruit; **sam pira hiuara** s. **sam**; **pira šania** Gy 325:5, 9 wonderful fruit; **nišimta bpira hiia paria umitparia** Gs 95:16 the soul blossometh and bloometh in the fruit of Life; **alip alip piria** Gy 69:5 thousand thousand fruits; **piria mia** Gy 100:14 f., 124:2 = **piria ḏ-mia** Gy 38:21 f., DC 50. 372 water-fruits Ginzā 37 n. 7; **piria ḏ-zipa** Gy 116:5 the fruits of a lie; **piria ḏ-arqa** Gy 193:3 the fruits of the earth; **piria ḏ-iauar ʿtita** Gy 322:4 fruits of the foreordained Y.; **pira uʿmba uʿlana mn ṭunh̲ baṣar** AM 175:20 fruit-tree and vine and tree will have their fruit diminished; **bauata d̲-piria d̲-aiar hinun** ATŠ II no. 417 prayers which are the fruits of Ether.

pira 2 (פְּעִירָא, ܦܥܪܐ) rift, cleft, vagina, cavity. Lagarde RB xxxvi 163, cf. Kessler PRE 163. **pira upihla** s. **pihla 2.**

piruz malka Gy 384:5, 7 a Persian king (فيروز), cf. Ochser ZA xix 77 n. 3 (dated in years 459–484).

piruza (P. پيروزه) DC 7 turquoise.

pirun 1 (ܦܪܥܘܢ, Ar. فِرْعَوْن < H. פַּרְעֹה < Eg. 𓉐𓉻, Copt. ⲡⲣⲣⲟ) Pharaoh. **pirun malka d̲-miṣraiia** DC 44. 641 = Morg. 259/10:38, JRAS 1937 591:7 Pharaoh, king of the Egyptians.

pirun 2 (diminutive of **pira 1**?) a name of higher beings ML 283, Jb ii 7 n. 1. **pirun ʿutra** Morg. 195:3 f.; **pirun zuṭa** Gy 374:3; **pirun gupna** Jb 2:16, 5:2, Morg. 226/38:1 = Q 25:9 = ML 70:4, CP 54:11, 402:penult., 459:1, Gy 322:3; **pirun drabša** CP 358:1, Morg. 168:7 = Oxf. 98 b = ML 266:1, 4.

pirunia 1 = **parunia** (q.v.). **qulalia upirunia** Gy 225:21, ATŠ II no. 136 snares and bonds; **nirmun pirunia** Gy 361:17 they cast bonds (parallel with **qulalia**).

pirunia 2 DC 22. 107 a var. of **piqunia** Gy 215:5.

pirušta 1 (rt. **PRŠ**) Gs 15:2, 84:21 mind, understanding MG 103:6.

pirušta 2 (cf. Ar. فَرْج & فُرْجَة) pudendum muliebre. Var. **prušta** s.v. **uʿaliq bpiruštẖ** DC 46. 150:18 and fasten (it) in her pudenda.

pirṭauaiia Gy 389:21 Parthians. Var. **parṭauaiia 2.**

piriauis (Iranian, orig. mean. 'full of water', cf. mod. P. پرِ آب) name of a heavenly (?) stream, a personified vine, and a being of Light MR 68 n. 1, Jb ii 13 footn. **piriauis iardna,** CP 23:2, Gy 234:24, 235:5; **piriauis iardna rba d̲-hiia qadmaiia** CP 14:12 = Q 5:30, 9:8 P. the great jordan of the First Life; **iardna piriauis** Morg. 172 f.; **piriauis kana d̲-mia hiia** CP 29:13, Q 12:26 = ML 35:2 P. the container of the water of life; **piriauis gupna** Gs 37:19 ff. the Vine P. Brandt JPTh xviii 434; **piriauis ziua** CP 17:5, 18:1 = Q 7:8, 8:31 = ML 20:1, 24:8 (a being of light); **malka piriauis** CP 140 (*a*):5. (See CP Index.)

piriauiš (rel. to preced.?) DC 41 name of a heavenly region?

piriapil malaka CP 18:1, 22:5 = Q 7:8, 19, 8:31 an angel.

pirṣa 1 (rt. **PRŠ**) debauchery, lust, lasciviousness Geiger ZDMG xvii 422. Pl. **-ia 1. pirṣa ugaura** Gy 59:15, 363:14 debauchery and adultery; **gaura pirṣa uzaniuta** Gy 224:24 f., DAb, Jb 266:12 adultery, debauchery and fornication; **bit pirṣa** Gs 20:18 house of debauchery; **šiṭia gaura upirṣa** Gy 27:24 folly, adultery and debauchery; **pirṣa uzaniuta** Gy 209:5, 225:12 debauchery and fornication; **mn lilbia hauin pirṣia** Gy 244:19 from hearts proceed lusts.

pirṣa 2, pirṣia 2 occasional varr. of **pirunia 1** (cf. DC 22 219, Gs 30:16). Ginzā 382 n. 5.

pirṣa 3 in **akil pirṣa zuṭa** Gs 19:13 doubtf. Ginzā 437 n. 3.

pirqa (rt. **PRQ**) (*a*) deliverance, (*b*) (for **parqa** or *abstractum pro concreto*?) deliverer. (*a*) **lahauilun pirqa** Gy 17:14 BD & Leid. (var. **parqa** AC) and there shall be no deliverance (var. deliverer) for them; (*b*) **man hauilak pirqa** Jb 63:14 who will be a deliverer for thee? **huitlan pirqa** Jb 189:5 thou wast a deliverer to me; **ʿniš lahauilak pirqa** Jb 190:14 no one shall be a deliverer for thee; **man nihuilh̲ pirqa** Jb 243:12, Gs 94:21 who will be a deliverer for him? **man hu d̲-nihuilh̲ pirqa** Gy 110:2 id.

pirša 1 (rt. **PRŠ**) time at which darkness gives way to daylight, daybreak, early morning, dawn. In mod. Mand. the word *peršā* is used for 'tomorrow' (analogous to Germ. *Morgen* and *morgen*). **rahmia d̲-pirša** Oxf. 1 b:top, 7 a:top, DC 34. 1287, 1292, 1297 morning devotions; **alma lpirša** DC 41. 170 until the dawn; **alma d̲-pirša d̲-ṣipra** Lond. roll A 489 until the first appearance of daybreak.

pirša 2 (rt. **PRŠ**) explanation. **mamla . . . d̲-abihdia pirša praš** DC 3 a Word . . . that went forth with explanation.

pirša 3 DC 22. 245 for **paruša** Gy 249:ult.

piršala (Ar. فَرَجُ اللّه) Zotb. 221a:22 a man's name.

pirta DC 22. 221 a var. of **parta 2** Gy 227:11.

piša (P. پيشه) trade, craft. **piša bʿdh̲ lagiṭ** AM 35 he will take up a trade.

piškinar(a) (P. پيش كنار embrace) entrance to the vagina. **kd̲ gabra šakib luath̲ piškinarh̲ kaiub** DC 46 when a man sleeps with her, the front part of her vagina is painful.

pišra (rt. **PŠR**) loosing or breaking a spell, exorcism, melting, purgative (?), releasing. Pl. **-ia. qmahia upišria** PD 382 phylacteries and exorcisms; **bmia d̲-pišria** AM 52:6 f. **mn pišria** AM 13:1 (var. **mia d̲-p.**) by exorcisms (i.e. water in which exorcisms have been immersed or from a bowl in the interior of which an exorcism has been inscribed); **pišra ušrita** Lond. roll B 335 melting and dissolving; **mihla pt pišra** Lond. roll B 384, DC 40. 1067 (var. **-ia**) Salt, daughter of loosing-of-spells (exorcisms); **mn pišria usamania nitasia** AM (CS 26) he will be cured by purgatives (or exorcisms?) and drugs; **mihla anat pišra** DC 40. 136 Salt, thou art a releasing.

pišruia in **pt pišruia** DC 40. 137 cf. **pt pašuria** s. **pašura.**

pišrun (rt. **PŠR**) name of a light genie. **pišrun ziua** DC 40. 161, **pišrun bira** DC 40. 212.

pitila (Ar. فَتِيلَة) wick. Pl. **(a)ptiliata** s.v. Fem. **abud pitila ubduq bšraga** DC 46 make a wick and insert into a lamp; **bduq pitila** DC 46. 227:3 insert a wick.

pitna (ܦܬܢܐ, فِتْنَة) (*a*) temptation, seduction, (*b*) tumult, discord. (*a*) **pitna matnalh̲** Gy

187:19 she bringeth temptation; (*b*) **šira upitna** and **pitna ušira** AM (often, cf. 263:5) evil and discord (discord and evil).

pkara (rt. **PKR**) bond, fetter, obstacle, impediment MG 115:19. Pl. **-ia.** Masc. **pkara ungada** Gy 230:19, 233:9, 15, Gs 34:5 fetter and protraction; **upakria pkaria** DC 44. 974 and they bind bonds.

PKK (ܦܟ, فكّ) to loose, break (out), destroy.

Af. Pf. **lziqa d̠-apkik** DC 43 C 73 which loosed the wind (flatulence).

Ethpe. Impf. **titpik** AM 190:4 will be destroyed (fem.).

PKR (פְּכַר, ܦܟܪ) to tie up, bind, truss, entangle, pen in, pen back, restrict, bar up, confound.

Pe. Pf. **pkar kul minilia bišata** DC 44. 681 = Morg. 270/30:26 they restricted all evil words; with suff. **pkarinun bgiṭria** Jb 147:11 f. he tied them in knots; **pkarinun urgalinun** (*often in exorcisms*) I tied them up and fettered them; **ligṭuia upikruia** DC 37. 489 they grasped her and trussed her. Impf. **nipkar** Gs 57:17 we will tie up (impede). Impt. **pkur** ʿ**l** ʿ**uhrh̠ ganbia** DC 44:1994 = Morg. 270/30:26 truss up his body on his way. Act. pt. pl. **pakria pkaria** s. **pkara**, **pakria ukadšia** Gy 121:17 they fetter and fight (beat); with encl. **pakrilun** Gy 223:25 they bind themselves. Pass. pt. ʿ**sir baita upkir baita** DC 43 H 4 bound is the house and barred up is the house; ʿ**sira pkira minilta d̠-ptahil** DC 43 B 7 bound, confounded is the word of P.; pl. ʿ**siria urgilia upkiria** DC 44. 1780 (*& often*) bound, impeded and tied up; with encl. pers. pron. **pkiritun** DC 43 A 35 ye are fettered.

Pa. Pf. with suff. **pikra pakartinun** DC 26. 606 f. = DC 44. 637 I tied them up securely. Pt. pl. ʿ**šbilh̠ mpakria** Gy 281:22 his roads are barred up; **mhašabath̠ mpakran** Gy 280:6 his thoughts are confused; **mapikria** DC 34. 498 entangling.

Af. Pf. with suff. **apkartinun** Jb 148:3 (var. **pkirtinun** B, **pkartinun** DC 30 pe.) I tied them up.

Ethpe. Pf. ʿ**tikpir** Gy 98:7 was bound MG 15:27; ʿ**tikpirt u**ʿ**tirgilt** DC 43 I 60 = DC 18 par. thou art bound and fettered. Impf. **titpikrun** Gs 57:23 ye shall be entangled. Pt. pl. **mitpikria** Gs 101:3 they are bound MG 149:18.

Der.: **pakra, pukurta, pukra, pikra, pkara.**

PLA I (< **PLH**, another secondary rt. **PHL**) to serve, worship, plough?

Pe. Pf. **pihia d̠-**ʿ**l šum hiia pla** s. **pihla 1.** (?) doubtful; see **pihla.**

PLA II (פלא, ܦܠܐ, H. פלא II & פלה, Ar. فلى, Eth. ፈለየ to separate) to separate, divide, remove. Only in doubtf. forms: **u**ʿ**pilh̠ u**ʿ**rimh̠** DC 43 C 16 I will divide it (or a poor af. of **NPL**: I will make it fall) and cast it down. **plibh̠ taqata d̠-br anašia** DC 46 the troubles of mankind are removed by him (??).

plan (פְּלָן, ܦܠܢ, H. פְּלֹנִי, Ar. فلان) someone, a certain, N.N. Fem. **planita** (ܦܠܢܝܬܐ). MG 302:12 ff. **plan br planita** (*often*) N.N. (man) son of N.N. (woman).

planga (ܦܠܢܓܐ, Ar. فَلْج, Gr. φάλαγξ) phalanx, host, army MG 51:17. Fem. MG 160:12. Pl. **-ia. plagilun plugta bplangun** Gy 103:15 f. I caused a break in their army (alliteration); **šamiš riš planga** Gy 172:6 f. Š., captain of the host; **planga d̠-para malka** Gy 382:7 f. the host of the king Pharaoh; ʿ**qba d̠-planga** DC 12. 40, Lond. roll B 88 = P.A. xii par. the rear of an armed host; **plangia dištata habiṭ** AM 12:17 he tramps many a beaten track (?); **kupna rba bplanga d̠-malka** AM 182:19 a great famine in the royal army; **kbaštia llibat ušuba ulplanga** DC 40. 758 I subdued Libat and the Seven and (their) army.

planza DC 37. 88 = **plinza.**

PLG (Gen. Sem.) to divide, split; (pa.) to distribute, allot, apportion, assign.

Pe. Pf. **lapilgit mnata binataihun** Gs 14:15 I had no part with them; with encl. ʿ**nta d̠-plaglh̠** AM 38:6 the woman whom he divorced; **mnata . . . plaglh̠** Gy 122:16, 379:12 = **plaglh̠** Gy 112:6 ff. they apportioned to him; **laplaglak** Gs 72:4 he had not allotted to thee; **plaglun** Gy 112:16 he allotted to them; **plagilh̠** Gy 90:ult., 103:10, 118:10, Jb 159:9 I split him MG 225:ult.; **plagilun** Gy 103:15 f. s. **planga**; with suff. **plagunun** Gy 112:18 (beside **palgunun** pa. ibid.) they distributed them. Impf. **mnata mn durdia nipilgun** ATŠ I no. 26 they shall share part of the dregs; **hdadia nipilgun** AM 184 they will be at variance with one another. Act. pt. **palig** AM 201:18 he shares; **d̠-palig plugta balman** Gy 80:23 that he would make a division in our world; pl. **mnata lhabara palgin** Gy 228:11 they allot to the darkness its portion.

Pa. Pf. **palig malkuta** Gy 109:13 they divided (: distributed) the kingdom; **hinun plugta palig** Gy 124:19 they made a division; **palig šnia** Gy 100:1 they distributed the years; special pl. form **paligiun** Gy 122:15 (*twice*) they distributed; with suff. **palgh̠ lsilita** Jb 147:10 he divided (: opened out) the fishing net; **paligth̠** she divided him MG 276:22; **palguia** Gy 112:10 they distributed it; **palgu** ibid. id. (with fem. suff.) MG 279:13; **palgunun** Gy 124:15 they divided (distributed) them MG 283:15. Impf. **hdadia nipalgun** Par. var. of AM 184 (cf. BZ 113 n. 7) s. pe. impf.; with encl. **tipalgibun ltarmidia** ATŠ II no. 426 thou wilt distribute them to the priests. Impt. with encl. **paligbh̠** Gy 337:4, 7 divide therein. Pt. **mpalig** RD B 4 he distributes; pl. **šaruata d̠-mpalgia** Gs 106:15 banquets which were assigned (i.e. which he assigned). Inf. **lpalugia alma** Gy 247:14 f. to divide (by discord) the world. Nom. act. **palagta** s.v.

Ethpe. Pf. **mnat hšuka bgauh̠** ʿ**tpilig** ATŠ II no. 81 the portion of Darkness was assigned to him. Pt. pl. **mn hak qrita mipilgia amamia utaumia** DC 8 from that creation branched off races and nations.

Ethpa. Pf. ʿ**tpalag** AM 200 was divided;

ATŠ I no. 6 were shared out. Pt. **mitpalgia** AM 196 are apportioned MG 31:13, 37:22.

Gl. (only bad forms) 8:13 f. انقسم *dividi* دو حصّه كرد; 12:5 f. انصف *iudicare* حصّه كرد; 23:1 f. انفرد *avelli* كَنْده شد; 24:5 f. انتصف *dimidiari* دو حصّه شد; 25:3 f. اشقق *schismam facere* شكافت; 49:11 f. تفرق *dispergi* پراكنده شد; 127:3 f. فرق *separare* جدا شد.

Der.: **palagta, palga 1, 2, pulgana, plugia, plugta 1, pliga.**

PLH (Aram. & H. פלח, Syr. ܦܠܚ, Ar. فلح Fränkel 126, Akk. *palāḫu* Zimmern: *Akk. Fremdwörter* 65) to serve, attend to, tend. Secondary roots **PHL, PLA I** s. vv.

Pe. Pf. (exceptional) **plah** Gs 36:15 he served MG 65:9. Impf. with suff. **niplihunh̲** Gy 241:4 (*& often*) they (will) serve him MG 64:2, 278:9, var. **niplhunh̲** MG 66:8, **liplihunh̲** Gs 128:ult. f. id., MG 216:13, **liplihunak** Gs 130:4 they serve thee MG 216:14, **niplihunan** Gy 244:3 they serve us MG 280:17, **tiplihunh̲** Gy 101:3 ye serve him MG 278:10. Act. pt. with encl. **palihlh̲ umizdaharbh̲** DAb he tends it and takes care of it.

Der.: **pulhana**, for others s. **PHL.**

plugia (rt. **PLG**) division, separation, dissension, discord MG 147:5. **sina qina uplugia** Gy 16:17 f., 112:17, 122:13, 243:22, Gs 78:21, ML 75:10 = CP 59:16 etc. hatred, rancour, and dissension.

plugma (ܦܠܓܡܐ < φλέγμα) phlegm, mucus. Doublet **balgam(a)** s.v. **plugma umirta** DC 34. 418 mucus and bile.

plugta 1 (rt. **PLG**) (*a*) division, distraction, quarrel, separatism, separation, dissension, (*b*) (with **liba**) doubt MG 119:7, (*c*) gap, chasm, break, rift, crevice, (*d*) faction, party, schism, (*e*) glimmer, ray, light (cf. **pirša** 1) MR 92:bottom, Jb ii 185 n. 3, MSt 153 n. 7. (*a*) **plugta palig** s. **PLG** pa. pf.; **lahauia plugta bmdinth̲** Gy 6:17 there is no dissension in his city; **palig plugta balman** s. **PLG** pe. act. pt.; **litbh̲ plugta balman** Gy 81:1 there is no division in our world; **kma ʿpalag plugta mn audia** Jb 203:6 how long shall I make the separation (i.e. struggle against) the perishable? **napil plugta binia aba ubra** AM 258:12 dissension will occur between the father and the son; (*b*) **libh̲ bplugta qam** Gy 95:2, 115:24 his heart misgave him (lit. stood in doubt); **libai bplugta qam** Gy 327:2 = **libai qam bplugta** Jb 271:6 my heart misgave me; **libak bplugta qam** Jb 65:9 thy heart misgave thee; **liban qam bplugta** Gs 100:1 our heart misgave us; **plugta blibaihun alat** ATŠ I no. 232 doubt entered their hearts; **libaihun bplugta laqaiim** ATŠ II no. 67 = **libaihun bplugta laniqum** ATŠ II no. 260 their heart remains not in doubt; (*c*) **plagilh̲ brišh̲ plugta** Jb 159:9, Gy 90:24, 103:10, 118:10 I split his head open; **plugta brišh̲** Gy 344:22 a gap in his head; (*d*) **šalṭuia lplugta d̲-iurba** Gy 314:8 they set him as ruler over the faction of Y.; (*e*) **plugta d̲-ziua** Gy 222:2, 349:13, Jb 189:9 the ray (or glimmer) of radiance; **plugta** Gy 346:2 parallel with **tuqna** l. 15 Ginzā 361 n. 1; **ziuh̲ ʿl plugta ksa** Gy 348:8 f. he covered his gleam with his radiance (doubtf. Ginzā 363 n. 1); **plugta minaian ʿtinsib** Gy 348:15 (our ?) gleaming (?) was taken away from us; **man nisbh̲ minaikun lplugta** Gy 348:17 who removed (your) gleam from you (Lidzb. *Schimmer*).

plugta 2 (Ar. فَلُوكَة) ship, boat. **plugta rabtia** Jb 79:12, 80:3 a great ship; **aitilun plugta** Gy 172:5 I brought them a boat (cf. l. 9); **nṭar plugta** l. 6 guard the boat!

PLṬ (Aram. & H. פלט, Syr. ܦܠܛ, Ar. فلت & فلص, Sab. 𐩰𐩡𐩷 to save, Eth. ፈለጠ to separate, Akk. *balāṭu* to regain health or strength) to escape, slip away, slip off, pa. to deliver, loosen, detach, take off, remove, separate, divide, expel.

Pe. Pf. **pliṭ** he escaped MG 219:10, **pliṭt** thou hast escaped MG 222:25. Impf. **nipluṭ** MG 219:10. Impt. **pluṭ** ibid. Act. pt. **hamra d̲-paliṭ mn puma** DC 21 wine that escapes the mouth.

Pa. Pf. **paliṭ pihta mn klila** ATŠ I no. 196 he detached the sacramental bread from the wreath; **palṭit uprit udirit** DC 41. 260 I divided, broke off and took; **kul d̲-aka bgauh̲ palṭat** Gy 354:13 f. she expelled all that was in it; with suff. **paliṭth̲ mn sipra** DC 41. 561 I removed it (: took it out) from a book; **palṭuia lzahbaiun** Jb 139:4 f. they cast off their gold. Impt. **paliṭ pandamak** DC 41. 263 take off thy *pandama*; with suff. **palṭh̲** ML 52:12 let it slip off. Pt. **d̲-mpaliṭ umšaria** DAb that detaches and loosens; **mpaliṭ asa ltarmidia** DC 50. 559 f. he distributes the myrtle to the priests; pl. **akandit ʿdaikun lampalṭia** DC 50. 413 before your hands are loosened (from the handclasp); with suff. **ʿniš mn ʿdai lampalṭinkun** Gy 234:7 f. no one can deliver you from my hand. Part. pres.: **mpalṭitun pandamaikun** ATŠ II no. 167 ye take off your *pandamas*; with encl. **mpalṭatlh̲ lmargnak** DC 27. 132 thou detachest thy staff; **umpalṭitulh̲ lpihtaikun mn klila** DC ATŠ II no. 166 ye separate your sacramental bread from the wreath. Inf. **palṭuia lpandama mn pumaihun** DC 3 to take off the *pandama* from their mouths.

Ethpa. Pt. pl. **ʿšumia mipalṭia** DC 43 J 103 and the heavens are rent (split).

pligia AM 5 for **plugia.**

plinza (פליזא, ܦܠܙܐ, فِلِزّ) bronze, brass. Varr. **aplanza, planza** s.vv. **latimrun d̲-plinza damia dahba** ATŠ I no. 241 say not that brass is like gold.

PLK for **PLG.**

Ethpa. Pf. **ʿtpalak šaba mnauata** DC 7 was divided into seven parts.

PNA (פְּנָא, ܦܢܐ, H. פנה den. from פָּנִים face, Akk. *panū* den. from *pānu* face, Ar. فَنِيَ to turn to or away from, disappear, Sab. 𐩰𐩬𐩺, Eth. ፈነወ to send away) to turn, overturn, empty?? Only corrupt forms: **apna.**

Impt. with suff. **painh paith** DC 46 turn him from, break him from (?). Refl. pt. pl. **mipainia** DC 46. 82:13 evacuated?, emptied?
Der.: **paina, pnia**.

PNDL, PNDN (derivation uncertain) to hurl down MG 277:17, scatter (?).
Fundamental stem: Pf. with suff. **pandilth** Gs 14:21 I hurled him down. Pt. with encl. **mpandilalh** JRAS 1938 6:9 it (fem.) scatters (?) it.
Reflexive stem: Pf. ʿ**pndan** Florilegium 358: 96 he was hurled down (cf. p. 372); ʿ**tpandal** JRAS 1938 3:17 were scattered ('bewitched').

PNṬS (ܦܢܛܨ) rt. of **panṭasa** phantasm. **šuman ṣita panṭasa** DC 43 our name is 'led astray', phantasm.

pnia for **paina** in **mn spar ualma ḏ-lipnia** DC 3. 193:5 = CP 137:3 from morn to eve.

PNQ (פָּנַק, ܦܢܩ, H. פָּנַק, Ar. فَنَّقَ) to pamper, pet, treat indulgently.
Pa. Pt. pl. **mpanqia napšaihun** Gy 176: antep. they pamper themselves; **zmaihun ḏ-mpanqia** DC 43 J 29 the blood of petted (children).
Ethpa. Pf. ʿ**tpanaqtun** Gy 234:5 ye were pampered MG 224:9.

PSA (פָּסַע, ܦܣܥ, secondary roots PHS = PSH) to tread on, step on, overstep, scorn, ignore.
Pe. Impf. **kulman ... nipsa lhalin ʿumamata** DC 40. 527 f. any person ... that scorns these oaths; **kul daiua ḏ- ... hazin hatma nipsa** DC 43 I 32 every demon who ... treads on (ignores) this seal.

psada (rt. PSD, Ar. فَسَاد) AM 185 corruption, ruin, destruction. Var. **apsada** s.v.

psan cstr. var. **apsan**? (cf. s. *pasanta, pl. **pasaniata** & **pisnia 2** s.v.) in **mn psan ʿda** (CP 153:ult. f. **mn apsan ʿdh** from her palm?) Oxf. 12 a = ML 184:10 palm of the hand (Lidzb. *Handfläche*).

psaqa (rt. PSQ, ܦܣܩܐ) (a) separation, stopping, limit, ceasing, weaning, interruption, (b) mutilation, cutting, amputation, (c) piece, section, fragment, hence: reading of an assigned section, celebration. (a) **laupa ḏ-lapsaqa** Q 29:1, DC 51. 132 (comm)union without separation; **psaqa ḏ-zuṭa mn hadia ḏ-ʿmh** AM 162:16 the weaning of an infant from its mother's breast; (b) **ngada upsaqa** Gy 253:6 stretching and cutting off; (c) **psaqa ḏ-qabin** PD 960 = ATŠ no. 32 celebration of a marriage-contract.

PSD (Ar. فَسَد) to (be) corrupt, diminish, lose (quality, quantity, or value), be poor or short, injure, (de)spoil. Only in postcl. texts and only Ar. forms. **ṭiʿam iapsid** AM 266:21 food will be short; **hiṭia uahmra iapsad** AM 278:32 wheat and vintage will be ruined; **arqa tipsad zira** AM 262:20 the earth will lose her seed; **hiṭia uahmra iipsidun** AM 278:23 corn and vintage will be spoilt.
Der.: (a)**psada, pisad, psida**.

PSH = PHS & PSA (q.v.).
Der.: **pasuhiata** & varr.

psusta = pasusta. **had mhita ḏ-asuta litlh ḏ-hʿ psusta** DC 35 one pollution for which there is no healing and that is apostasy.

psuqta (rt. PSQ) division, split, cut(ting off). **halin ḏ-psuqta mn habraihun pasqia** DAb those that cut connexion with their neighbours.

psida (rt. PSD) (a) loss, spoliation, (b) meagre, scanty, of poor quality. Pl. **-ia**. (a) **psida banašia nihuia** AM 223:10 there will be loss amongst the people; (b) **miṭria psidia nihun** AM 185 the rains will be meagre.

PSK sporadically for **PSQ**. **psik** JRAS 1937 594 broken, cut off.
Der.: **pasik** DC 22. 282 for **pasiq** Gy 287:5.

PSS (Akk. *pasāsu*, H. פסס) to destroy, break, rend asunder, cut asunder, sever, cut off, vanish, disappear.
Pe. Pf. **pas** he destroyed MG 248:4; **pasat mala** Gy 94:9, 95:4 f., 26, 96:1 she destroyed her possession (? Ginzā 99 n. 1) MG 248:9; similarly **pasit malai** Gy 97:1 I destroyed my possession (?) MG 248:16; **past** thou hast destroyed MG 248:14; **pasnin ṭuria ḏ-hala** DAb we split mountains of soil; with suff. **bna baita upash** DC 22. 350 (missing in Pet.) built a house and then destroyed it; **pash baita ḏ-bnh** ibid., destroyed the house of his children; **pash lbit mqadšia** Jb 141:13 destroyed the temple; **pasinun** he destroyed them MG 281:19; **pasth** Gy 333 (often) I destroyed her MG 277:5. Impf. ʿ**pus malai** Gy 95:3 I will destroy my possession (cf. above); with suff. ʿ**pish** Gy 281:17, DC 22. 349 (missing in Pet.) I will destroy it MG 275:23. Part. pres. **paisit** thou destroyest MG 250:19; **paisinin malan** Jb 139:6 we will destroy our goods (cf. above); **qipaisinin ṭuria ḏ-hala DAb** we (shall) split mountains of soil; **paisatlun** Jb 10:8 thou destroyest them; **haizak qrun ʿniana ḏ-ldrabšia psunun** DC 50. 835 then they recite the hymn which deconsecrates the banners. Inf. **mipas** to destroy MG 129: 18, 250:ult.
Ethpe. Impf. **titpis** Gy 307:11 (a bad var. ʿ**tipsis** D) it (fem.) shall be destroyed. Pt. **mipsis** Gy 353:21, MG 132:14, 252:4; pl. **mitpisin umitminin** ATŠ II no. 360 were set apart and numbered (?).
Ethpa. Pt. pl. **mitpasasia** Gy 388:2 f., Gs 17:1, Jb 27:5, 94:8, Oxf. 34 a = CP 170:1, ML 206:2 they will be destroyed MG 32:6. Inf. **mitpasusia** Oxf. 34 a = ML 206:2, MG 234:4, CP 170:1.
Der.: **pasusta, p(i)susta**.

PSQ (פָּסַק, ܦܣܩ, H. פסק to draw apart, Ar. فَسَقَ to turn aside from the right way) to cut (off), cause to stop, cease, leave off, leave out (omit), arrange a marriage(-dowry).
Pe. Pf. **usiph bziuh lapsaq** Jb 13:5 and his sword did not pierce (cut through) his glory; **pisqit tlata rušumia** DC 42:316 I omitted (= left out) the three signings; (of waters) **lapsiqtun** DC 51. 316 ye did not cease (to flow); with suff. **pisqh lrušuma** ATŠ I no.

177 he performed the signing; **mn abahath̲ pisqa** ATŠ I no. 51 he cut it off from its parents; **psaqinan** he cut us off MG 279:24. Impf. **nipsaq trin tagia** Lond. roll A 31 he will cut off two fillets; with suff. **latipisqun** Q 74b:31, 33 do not cut me off; **nipsqunak** they (or He: the Life) will cut thee off MG 274:19. Impt. **psuq** Jb 130:6 cut; with suff. **pusqan** Jb 130:8 cut me off, pl. **pusqun** Jb 94:1 cut me MG 273:7. Act. pt. **pasiq** (*often*) he cuts; **pasiq qabin** PD = ATŠ (*often*) he arranges (performs) a marriage; with encl. **man d̲-sipa pasiqlh̲** ATŠ II no. 269 one whom the sword cuts off (kills); **sipa lapasiqlak** Jb 94:3 a sword cannot cut thee up; pl. **ʿuhrata pasqia** Gy 388:15 they cut (waylay) the roads; **pasquta . . . pasqia** s. **pasquta**, **pasqia ʿkilta umašqita mn pumaiun upasqia lbuša hiuara mn gišmaiun** Gy 55:20 f. they abstain from food and drink and from white garments; with encl. **pasqilh̲ lziraihun** Gy 55:17 f. they cut off their seed. Part. pres. **k̲d̲ baiit lzuṭia d̲-pasqit mn hadia d̲-ʿmh̲** AM 162:16 when thou seekest to wean a child from its mother's breast. Pass. pt. **nhur psiq** Gy 194:9, 204:16, 209:24, 241:1, 294:20 cut off from light; **abda psiqa** Jb 139:1 a castrated slave; **bruhṣana psiqa** DC 48. 239 with lost faith; pl. **mia psiqia** Gy 57:1 cut off water (opp. of running, living water); **psiqia uaudia** Gs 65:8 (are) cut off and perishing; **šidia psiqia** DC 43 J 162 cut off (condemned) devils. Inf. **šapir . . . lmipsaq ʿšata** AM 144:10 favourable . . . for putting a stop to fever; **k̲d̲ baiit mipsaq mania** AM 110:6 when thou seekest to cut out garments; **mipsaq qabin** (*often*) to arrange a marriage-contract; **ṭab lmipsaq qurbana** ŠQ 29:18 favourable for arranging to pay an offering.

Pa. Pf. with suff. **gadia pasqinun lgidia dilh̲** ATŠ I no. 253 the he-goat divided his genitals. Impf. with suff. **uburkh̲ nipasqunin** DC 43 J 128 they break off (?) the knees. Pt. **hazin diuan rišh̲ mpasaq hua** DC 27. 12 the beginning of this diwan was cut off; **glia umpasaq** ATŠ II no. 409 worn and fragmentary; pl. **ʿniš d̲-ʿuṣṭlia mpasqia** DC 46. 123:12 a person whose clothes are being cut up; **umahu d̲-hazin mpasqin** DC 46. 121:9 and whatever they see, they cut up.

Ethpe. Pf. **ʿu himiana ʿpsiq** ATŠ I no. 62 if his girdle came undone. Impf. **tipsiq** thou art cut off MG 227:1; **ʿpsiq** I am cut off MG 227:9; **baitaihun nipisqun** DC 26. 306 their houses will be split asunder; **titpisqun** ye are cut off MG 228:1. Pt. **mipsiq unapil biama rba d̲-sup** DC 3. 250:1 shall be cut off and fall into the great ocean of destruction; **lamipsiq miṭra** the rain will not stop (MG 213:4); pl. **mitpisqia mia hiia** Gy 393:7 f. the living waters will be cut off. Part. pres. **mipsiqana** I (fem.) am cut off (var. **mipsiqna** masc.) MG 486 (addenda to p. 214:16); **mipsiqnin** Gy 309:1 we are cut off MG 214:16, 233:4.

Ethpa. Pf. **ʿtpasaq asaria ušušlata** Jb 17:5 f., the fetters and chains came apart; **ʿtpasaq sipaiun . . . uʿtpasaq iatria d̲-qaštatun** Jb 17:13 f. their swords split and the strings of their bows parted.

Gl. (always missp.) 62:9 f. خرق *scindere* ترکید ; 63:13 f. ختن *circumcidere* سنت کرد; 133:3 f. قطع *caedere* برید ; 134:13 f. قطف *secare* برید .

Der.: **paisaq** (var. **paisiq**), **p(a)suqta**, **pasiq**, **pusqana**, **psaqa.**

psuqta DAb a var. of **pasuqta.**

psira d̲-hu kabda psira gasilh̲ DC 48:24 which is the liver: they call it **psira** (?) digestion?

PSR I for **BṢR** in **mitpisrin** Par. xiv no. 9 they diminish MG 45 n. 1, 47:15.

PSR II for **PSQ** in **ʿtpasar** DC 44. 1066 = **ʿtpasaq** Morg. 263/16:17 they came apart; **mitpisria** DC 22. 307 = **mitpisqa** Gy 310:16 they were cut.

PṢA (**פצא**, ܦܨܐ, H. **פצה** Kautzsch 74, Ar. فصى) to split, break, deliver, set free, rescue.

Pa. Impt. pl. with suff. **paṣuih̲** DC 43 D 12 deliver him. Inf. **šauzibuia upaṣuia** DC 19 to rescue and deliver.

Ethpa. Impf. **nitpaṣia** CP 33:8 = ML 39:4 he shall be freed MG 264:antep.; **nitpaṣia minai mahra ukuhrana** DC 43 H 39 sickness and illness shall be removed from me; **titpaṣia minaihun** AM 101:15 she will be rescued from them; **nitpaṣun** Gy 232:5 they will be set free MG 265:7; **nišmata d̲-nitpaṣa unitasia** DC 40. 972 f. souls that are delivered and cured. Pt. **mipaṣia** AM 271:ult. (*& often*) they will be saved; **kulhun tigria mitpaṣin** RD C 12 all quarrels will be settled.

Der.: **apṣa.**

PṢH the rt. of **pṣiha, fem. pṣiht(i)a.**

pṣiha (ܦܨܝܚܐ, H. פָּצִיחַ, Ar. فَصِيح) bright, clear, cheerful. Fem. **pṣiht(i)a. minilh̲ pṣiha** Gy 217:1 his words are clear; **pṣihtia utrištia tihuia** AM 68:17 she will be cheerful and honest.

PṢL (Aram. & H. **פצל**, Syr. ܦܨܠ, Ar. فصل) to cut out.

Pa. Impf. **nipaṣil ʿuṣṭlia hadtia** Lond. roll A 36 he will cut out the new vestments.

PQA (Aram. & H. **פקע**, Syr. ܦܩܥ, Ar. فقأ & فقع) to break asunder, break open, crack open, split, crackle.

Pe. Pf. **pqa piqa** and **piqa pqa** s. **piqa**; **ṭuria pqa mnh̲** DC 435 the mountains split away from him; with encl. **pqabh̲ piqa barqa** Gy 354:24 he made a cleft in the ground; **ṭuria pqa mnh̲** DC 43 J mountains split therefrom. Pt. **paqa piqa** s. **piqa**; pl. **paqia k̲d̲ arqa** DC 40. 95 they crack open like the ground. Part. pres. **paqit k̲d̲ mihla bnura** JRAS 1938 3:22 thou cracklest like salt in the fire.

Pa. Impf. with suff. **nipaqih̲** DC 43 I 32 breaks it open.

Der.: **paqata, piqa, pqita.**

PQD (Gen. Sem.) to order, command, charge with, entrust.

Pe. Pf. with encl. **pqadlia** Gs 44:8 (var. **apqadlia** DC 22. 433) He (: the Life) entrusted to me. Impf. with suff. **nipuqdh̲ ʿl babh̲**

d̲-nukraia *Florilegium* we will set him in charge of Nukraia's gate.

Pa. Pf. **paqid** (often) he ordered MG 221: paen.; **ptahil qiriak uhibil ziua paqid ʿlak miniksak** (slaughtering formula) P. created thee and H.-Z. ordered thy slaughter; **paqdit ʿlh̲ naṭria** DC 41. 5 f. I appointed guardians over it; with suff. **paqdh̲** he ordered him MG 275:5; **paqdan** Gy 303:18, 316:9 he gave into my charge; **paqdak** he ordered (or entrusted) thee MG 273:12; **paqidtinun** I ordered them MG 282:anteantep.; **paqdun** they (or He: the Life) order me MG 272:19; **paqduk** they (or He: the Life) ordered thee MG 274:12; **paqduia** they (or He: the Life) ordered him MG 277:ult.; **paqdunun** they ordered them MG 283:14. Impf. **latipaqad** [*sic*] **dirdquniata kd̲ aqnia** (var. **anqia** P.A.) DC 43 J 96 do not order (slaughter?, cf. example s. pf.) of little girls like (that of) sheep; with suff. **nipaqdunh̲** ATŠ II no. 359 (*& often*) they charge him with. Impt. with suff. **paqdh̲** MG 269 n. 1; **paqdinun** put them in charge MG 282:11. Pt. (pass.) **mpaqad** Gs 2:7 is ordered, pl. (act. & pass.) **mpaqdia** AM 13 they command; **puqdania mpaqdia** AM 246:20 orders will be issued; **šaliṭia umpaqdia** Gy 86:23 strong and commanding (as sg.); with encl. **mpaqdilh̲** AM 20 they will commission him. Part. pres. **mpaqadna** DC 43 J 107 I give order MG 231:7; **mpaqdinin** we give order MG 233:1; **mpaqditun** ye give order MG 233:14; with encl. **mpaqdinalh̲** Oxf. 18 a (var. **mpaqdanalh̲** ibid. 22 a, Par. xi) I order him MG 231:bottom; **mpaqdatlh̲, mpaqdatlan** thou orderest him, us MG 232:bottom. Inf. **mpaqudia** Gs 2:7, MG 144:1, 233:ult.; **paqudia** DAb. Nom. act. **paqadta** s.v.

Af.? Pf. with encl. **apqadlia** a var. of pe. (q.v.).

Ethpa. Pf. **ʿtpaqad** was ordered MG 222:4. Inf. **ʿpaqudia** DC 34. 256 to take charge.

Der.: **paqadta, puqdana, piqd(i)a.**

pquta (**אפקותא**) neck, throat. Varr. **apquta, puq(u)ta** s.vv. **agara blišania ʿl pquth̲** DC 43 J 138 tie on his tongue and his throat; **šqul . . . agarak mn lišanh̲ umn pquth̲** DC 43 J 153 remove . . . thy bond from his tongue and his throat; **ligrai lpquth̲** Morg. 264/18:9 my foot is on his neck; **ʿl pqutaihun uʿl ʿudnaihun** DC 44. 1042 on their necks and on their ears; **zurpinia d̲-pquta** DC 41. 461 the joints (?) of the neck. Still used; mod. pron. *forgottá*.

pqita (rt. **PQA**) fissure, urethra. **bduq bpumh̲ d̲-pqita utaiin** DC 46 insert (it) into the opening of the urethra and he will urinate.

PQR I for **PRQ** in **mitpaqrin** ATŠ II no. 64 for **mitparqin** cf. ibid. (II) no. 253 are distinct.

PQR II (ܦܩܪ) to rave, rage, run riot, be furious.

Ethpa. Pt. pl. **mitpaqrin umitpaiqrin mataraiia** ATŠ II no. 283 the purgatory-demons rage and run riot.

PRA I (**פְּרָא**, ܦܪܐ & ܦܪܝ, H. **פרה**, Eth. ፈረየ, cf. Eg. to sprout) to bear fruit, blossom, produce, be fruitful, bring forth, (give) increase, multiply, grow big or strong.

Pe. Pf. **pra** Gy 291:39, Q 58:33 = ML 141:9 he blossomed; **pru** Gy 293:6; **prun** ibid. CD, Gy 7:11, 31:7, 293:17, 373:4 they blossomed, were fruitful MG 258:4 f.; with encl. **tirat pralia manda** Gy 124:21 ff. in my conscience blossomed wisdom. Act. pt. **paria** Gs 95:16 she bloometh; **paria umitraurab** Jb 106:4 it grows and becomes big; cf. also **paria 1** s.v., as pl. **paria umitraurbia** Gy 293:13 f. they (:waters) grew big and strong; **parin (umitparin)** ATŠ II no. 104, DC 27. 291 they grow (and are expanded); **parian** Gy 5:1, 322:6 they (fem.) bloom.

Pa. Pf. **paru** Gy 293:18 they fructified MG 261:16.

Af. **habara ʿpra ʿlauaihun** DC 27. 21 darkness increased above them.

Ethpa. Pf. **utpariat dmutaiun** Gy 293:18 and their image (likeness) blossomed (was multiplied) MG 263:paen. Pt. **mitparia** Gs 95:16 she blossometh (expandeth); pl. (**parin**) **umitparin** s. pe. pt. pl.

Der.: **paria 1, pariata, pira 1, pirun 2?, priha.**

PRA II (Aram. & H. **פרח**, Syr. ܦܪܚ) to fly (off), move quickly, run. Secondary rt. **PHR** s.v.

Pe. Pf. **pra uata** Gy 241:16 he flew and came; **pra mṭa** Gy 354:23 f.; **pra maṭia** Gy 363:1 id. Impf. **nipra unitia** DC 46. 189:9 he will fly (run) and come; **upra uʿmṭia** ML 135:10 and I will fly and come. Impt. **pra upuq uʿtrahaq minai** DC 40. 860 fly away, go out and depart from me. Pt. **nišmatun paria paria nišmatun balmia d̲-nhura** CP 459:9 their souls fly, their souls fly into the worlds of light. Part. pres. **parana** Gs 89:3 I fly MG 236:14. Inf. **mipra**, Gy 279:21, MG 398:13.

Af. Pf. with suff. **uaprunun** (var. **uaprun** AD) **ʿl ṣipria mn duktai(h)un** Jb 132:10 f. and they made the birds fly away from their place(s); **aprith̲ lʿšumia** DC 44. 1230 = Morg. 264/18 I let it fly up to the sky. Impf. with suff. **ʿiapra lṣipar** Jb 146:11 I will make the birds fly away. Part pres. **rihua bainia anašia maprina** DC 46. 122:6 I cause an (evil) wind to blow into people's eyes.

Der.: **maprai(a), parahiata, pura 6.**

PRA III (**פְּרַע**, ܦܪܥ III) to pay (back), requite, return.

Pe. Pt. **d-abuia uʿmh para** Jb 121:12, **d̲-para abuia** ibid. l. 13 who requiteth his father (and mother); with encl. **bbišuta parilun** AM 4:4 he will requite them with wickedness; **paralh̲** AM 77:15 she will requite him.

Ethpe. Pt. **kulman d̲-mrašia mitpra** Gy 16:2 everyone who lendeth shall be repaid (MG 236:8), i.e. in kind.

Ethpa. Pt. **larašin umitp(a)iria** Q 7:12 = ML 20:4 they lend not and take back (MG 24:20).

Der.: **parah(i)a, (a)prah(i)a, purana.**

PRA IV (H. **פרע** II, Ar. فرغ) to let free; esp. in the idiomatic expression: to open up the jordan, i.e. to let water flow freely MR 99 f., 204, MSchr. 163, Ginzā 19 n. 5.

Pe. Act. pt. **d̲-para qina** Jb 170:1 who lets (his) passion free Jb ii 170 n. 10.

Pa. Pf. **para iardna** Gy 191:10, **paria iardna** DC 34. 1136 opened up the jordan. Impf. **nipara iardna** PD 1544. Impt. **para iardna** Gy 190:17; pl. **parun iardna** Gy 17:20, 190:17. Pt. **iardna mpara** Gy 152:16. Inf.? **ʿparuia iardna** Lond. roll A 173 f. = **ʿparuiih̲ iardna** DC 34. 256.

PRA V (פָּרַע I1 J) to destroy, disarrange, mar; Lidzb. left untranslated Ginzā 104 n. 3, 105 n. 3.

Af. Impf. with suff. **kulh̲ alma naprh̲** Gy 99:2 we will disorganize the whole world; **lalma naprh̲** and **naprh̲ lalma** Gy 114:14. Pt. **mlaka d̲-mapria libia utirata** DC 46. 137:15 angel which dislodges (disturbs) the heart and bowels (conscience). Part. pres. **lagiṭna umaprina** DC 46. 118:8 I seize and mar him.

PRA VI (den. from pura 3?) to arrange a feast?

Pe. Pf. **nipria pura** s. **pura 3.**

prah AM 205:15 name of a river. Var. **purat** Ṣâb.'s AM.

prahia = **parah(i)a.** Var. **aprahia. prahia ukair** AM 155:2 money and wealth; **prahia** (var. **aprahia**) **uqiniana** AM 19:9 money and property.

pramana JRAS 1937 p. 592 read **purmana.**

pras 1 (rt. **PRS**) palm (of hand). Found only in st. cstr. **pras iamin** Gs 78:10, 90:7, 109:9, 120:13; **pras iaminh̲** Q 31:11, Gy 114:8, 237:7, 294:14, 343:1, Gs 56:14, 101:15, 103:23 the palm of his right hand; **pras iaminai** Gy 128:8, 272:21 the palm of my right hand.

pras 2 for **kras** (st. cstr. of **karsa**) in **bpras ʿmh̲** PD 1508 in his mother's womb.

prasa (rt. **PRS**), pl. **-ia** DC 48 .230 food laid out, fare, cates, dishes. V.s. **PRS** pe. act. pt. with encl.

prasia fare, cates, food missing. **prasalun prasia rgigia** DC 48. 230.

praš, prat (פְּרָת, فُرَات) Euphrates. Var. **purat** s.v. Jb ii 45 n. 2, OSt 544. **pum praš** Jb 41:1, CP 210:8, Oxf. 75 a = **pumh̲ d̲-praš** Gy 351:22, 371:1, RD B 36 the mouth of Euphrates; **praš ʿlaia** PD 905 the upper Euphrates; **praš iabiš** Gs 88:12 Euphrates drieth up; **praš ziua** Jb 41:1, 229:7, Gy 371:1, Gs 3:14, JRAS 1937 p. 592 = RD B 2, 30, 36, 38 Light-Euphrates; **prat rba** Gy 67:8, 386:25 the Great Euphrates; **prat udiglat** Gs 10:20 Euphrates and Tigris; **prat zuṭa** DC 7 the Small Euphrates; **kipa d̲-prat** Q 13:5, 14 the bank of Euphrates.

praša (nom. act. pe. of **PRŠ**) division, separation. **priš praša bgu mia** DC 51 he (?) divided the waters.

prat s. **praš.**

prata (rt. **PRT**) JRAS 1937 p. 592 broken bit.

PRG (Ar. فرغ) to empty, pour out.

Gl. 16:16 f. افرغ *effundere* خالى كرد; 127:11 f. فرق *vacuum reddere* خالى كرد; 127:13 f. فرغ *effundere* پاشيد.

PRD I (Aram. & H. פרד, Syr. ܦܪܰܕ, Ar. فرد, Akk. *parādu*) to break through, tear apart.

Pe. Pf. **nunia . . . pirdu lsilita unpaq** Oxf. 44 a = CP 176:14 = ML 215:5 the fish broke through the net and got away; **anat bhailak pradt unpaqt** Or. 330:25 = Oxf. roll g 907 thou with thy strength didst break through and come out. Impf. **nipirdun . . . ʿl libta d̲-qudša** HG 65 they will break up . . . the sacred brick. Act. pt. with encl. **pardilh̲ lsilita** Jb 157:13 they break through the net.

PRD II (rel. to **PRD I**, cf. Syr. ܦܪܰܕ to flee away) to flee, run away, drive away, break away.

Pe. Pf. **prudnia šbaqnia kul d̲-ʿtlan** DC 43 J 241 we fled and left all that we had (mod. verbal forms); with suff. **šinta pridh̲** AM 20 sleep fled from him. Act. pt. fem. pl. **susia . . . pardan** DC 46 the mares . . . run away.

Gl. 170:1 f. **aprad** هرب *fugare* گريخت.

PRH 1 (פָּרָה & פָּרַח) **mia bprat praha upsiha rba d̲-hiia qadmaiia** DC 51 Euphrates water, swift-flowing (פָּרַח) and great product (פָּרָה) of the First Life.

PRH 2 (Ar. فرح) to rejoice. Gl. 51:15 f. تنعم *jucunde vitam ducere* فراغت كرد.

PRHZ (P. پرهيز) to keep back from, keep away from, restrain, abstain, refrain from, avoid.

Fundamental stem: Pf. with suff. **parhizunh̲ mn mia** AM 89:19 they kept him away from water. Impt. with suff. **parhzih̲ mn dh̲ udh̲** Gy 102:9 protect him from this and that MG 276:16; **parhiza** Gs 24:20 keep away from her.

Reflexive stem: Pf. **ʿparhaz mn qiriata d̲-hšuka** DC 34. 77 he was kept away from the creatures of darkness. Impf. **nitparhzan** ATŠ I no. 235 they (fem.) control themselves.

prudqa (P.-Sm. 3244, ܦܪܘܕܩܐ <Pahl. *fravartak* LS 594 a) written pass or order, decree, passport MR 215:10, MSchr. 151 n. 1, Jb ii 103 n. 3, HpGn 248, MSt 10. Var. **purudqa. prudqa uraza rba d̲-mn dilan ldilh̲** Gy 127:24 the passport and the great mystery which was given to him from us; **kul daiua qarabtana d̲-hazilh̲ lhanath̲ prudqa** Gy 128:1 each fighting demon that beholdeth that decree (passport); **hbalia prudqa** Gy 144:2 f. (var. **pudqa** DC 22. 139) give me a passport; **ʿiaitilak prudqa** Gy 144:5 I will bring thee a passport; **uaitilia prudqa** ibid. l. 5 f. and he brought me the passport; **kd̲ mhauiatlun hazin prudqa** Gy 144:10 when thou showest them this pass(port); **kd̲ hizih̲ lhanath̲ prudqa** ibid. l. 13 when he saw that pass(port); **prudqa ʿhablia** Gy 157:18 they gave me a passport; **hzia prudqa d̲-mn abahatak aitilak** Gy 144:16 see the pass(port) which I brought thee from thy parents; **prudqa lšibiahia ktab** Gy 344:10 f. he wrote a written order to the Planets; **bprudqai madkarna ʿlak** Jb 103:10, 105:3, 107:14 I will mention thee in my written word (Gospel?); **alma d̲-prudqa d̲-nhura atilh̲** ATŠ II no. 285 until a decree from the light comes to him.

pruṭta s. **purṭta.**
prukia Gs 14:11, Jb 59:15, var. **pukia** 3 = **prikia.**
pruqa 1 (rt. **PRQ**) ransom MG 118:15. Pl. **-ia. hab pruqa uparquia** Gy 15:9, 36:21 give ransom-money and free him; **pruq pruqia** Gy 38:1 pay the ransom(s); **pruqia pariqnin** Gy 184:18 f. we pay the ransom(s); **pruqia ḏ-pariqtun** ibid. l. 22 ye pay(ed) the ransom(s).
pruqa 2 (rt. **PRQ**) fragment, piece. Pl. **-ia. tipriq pruqia utirmia lahma** CP 438:11 (no. 379) = DC 3 par. thou wilt break into fragments and place bread.
prušta 1 occasionally for **pirušta** 1.
prušta 2 = **pirušta** 2. **ẓaliq bpirušta ḏ-ʿnta** DC 45 fasten (it) to the pudenda of the woman.
PRZ (cf. mod. H. פרז hif. to go beyond?) to break (through), force a way. Doubtf.
Af. Impt. **apruz alahia** DC 40. 491 f. break (?) the gods.
PRZM (פַּרְזַם) to break apart, split. Pt. **baitẖ mparzim** AM 145:16 his house is divided into two.
PRṬ (Aram. & H. פרט, Syr. ܦܪܛ, Ar. فرط) to break apart, separate, part, gape, open wide, cleave open, break in two, separate, detract from. Idiom: to curl the lips at, sneer s. **sipta.**
Pe. Pf. **siptun praṭ** s. **sipta, praṭ . . . puruṭta** Jb 65:3, **praṭ purṭa** and **praṭ purṭta** s. **purṭta; purṭta brqiha praṭ** ATŠ II no. 204, **praṭ rqiha** ibid. the heavens parted (opened up); **siptai pirṭit** s. **sipta, praṭiun** MG 223:22 (s. **sipta**); with encl. **praṭbẖ . . . purṭta** Gs 124:7 f. he made a breach in it; **purṭana bbaṣa hurina praṭnabẖ** s. **baṣa.** Impf. **priṭlak bgauẖ purṭta** Gs 107:14 I will make a breach in it for thee; **unipruṭunẖ lṣa** DC 42:9 and they break the *ṣa* between them. Act. pt. **sipṭẖ . . . pariṭ** s. **sipta; šinta ḏ-parṭa mn ainẖ** DC 43 J 157 sleep which departs from his eyes; pl. **sipun parṭia** DC 34. 93 (could be: they break their swords, but prob. read **siptun parṭia** they sneer). Part. pres. **ʿuspihak parṭit** DC 37:46 thou curlest thy lips (sneerest). Pass. pt. **sipṭẖ priṭ** Gs 66:22 f. his lip was curled; with encl. **priṭbẖ purṭta** Gs 107:7 a breach was made in it; **lapriṭbun purṭta** Gs 13:8 no breach was made in them MG 421:7 f.
Pa. Pt. **mparaṭ** DC 22. 181 as a var. of **mpaṭar** Gy 190:12 (s. **PṬR**).
Der.: **parṭauaiia** 1, **p(u)ruṭta, purṭa, purṭana.**
priha (rt. **PRA I**) offshoot, produce, product. **priha rba ḏ-hiia qadmaiia** DC 51. 742 great offshoot of the First Life.
***prika,** fem. **priktia** (q.v.).
prikia pl. (Akk. *parakku* Schrader ZDMG xxvi 35, KAT 592, Delitzsch: *Ass. St.* 127, Syr. ܦܪ̈ܟܐ) pagan shrines and their spirits MG 14:paen., 112:2, Furlani: *I Nomi* 418 f. Var. **prukia** s.v. **prikia ḏ-ṭina** Gy 24:20, Q 23:13, (cf. Gs 14:11) idols of clay; **kulhun prikia lagṭia** Gy 123:17 f. they include all altar-demons; **ʿkuria uprikia upatikria** Gy 279:4 temple-spirits, shrine-spirits, and idols; **ʿkuria uprikia usahria** Gy 394:1; **prikia upatikria** Oxf. roll g 1004; **kulhun humria šaria bʿkuria uprikia** DC 44. 372 all amulet-spirits inhabiting (pagan) temples and shrines; **patikria uprikia** DC 43 A 107.
priktia (rt. **PRK I**) adj. fem. bright, intelligent. **priktia umparaktia** AM 76:ult. bright and entertaining.
pris pass. pt. pe. of **PRS** (q.v.).
priš(a) pass. pt. pe. of **PRŠ** (q.v.).
prišaia (adj. from preced., from a Jew. פְּרִישָׁאָ = φαρισαῖος Jb ii p. xxii) subst. one different from his fellows, adj. distinguished, excellent, outstanding, discriminating MG xxix 1, MSchr. 213 n. 1, Ginzā 215 n. 1, AF 244, MSt 124 f. Pl. **prišaiia.** Wellhausen ZDMG 1913 p. 630. **hazaiia uprišaiia** Gy 278:2 perceiving and distinguished ones; **bnia prišaiia** Q 2:13, CP 5:7 = ML 6:6 f.; **bnia prišaiia ḏ-hiia qadmaiia** Gy 234:22 distinguished sons of the First Life; **gubria prišaiia ḏ-priš mn tibil** Gy 282:20 (cf. 317:4) distinguished men who sundered themselves from the world; **gubria prišaiia** Jb 179:12; **rišaiia uprišaiia** Gy 315:16 f. the first and noble ones; **prišaiia urišaiia** Gs 27:20; **rišaia uprišaia** Jb 281:ult. f. sg.; **naṣuraiia uprišaiia** Gy 319:9. Contrasted with **pigia** Gy 387:24, 391:14. As attribute of Life Q 4:5, 22:5. Of higher beings: **ʿprišaia** Jb 9:6 Abathur; **prišaia** Jb 38:12 (var. **prišaiia** A) Yušamin, **prišaia rba qadmaia** Oxf. 58 b.
prišuta (abstr. noun from **PRŠ**) (*a*) perception, discernment, discrimination, (*b*) interpretation, explanation. Lidzb. corrected his former opinion Jb ii 36 n. 7 in Ginzā 6 n. 4, cf. MSt 125 n. 1. Var. **aprišuta.** (*a*) **prišuta uiadita** Gy 2:19 perception and knowledge; **riš prišutak** Gy 213:27 the principle of thy discernment; **lgiṭatlẖ liprišutak ḏ-mn abahatak uhukumta ḏ-pligalak** Jb 31:11 f. thou mayest keep thy perception which (thou hast) from thy parents and the wisdom which was allotted thee; (*b*) **hazin rušuma lanida uprišutẖ** ATŠ II no. 194 knoweth not this Sign and its interpretation.
prita (rt. **PRT**) division, something split or broken asunder. **atit upratt prita** CP 419:9 f. thou camest and didst make a division; **prita ḏ-anat iauar pratt** DC 3. 284:paen., CP 419: 8 f. (no. 376) the breach which thou, Yawar, hast broached.
PRK I (ܦܪܟ af. Schulthess: *Homonyme Wurzeln* 54) to be bright, intelligent, brilliant, pa. to entertain, be discerning, intelligent. Found only in part. forms:
Pe. Pass. pt. ***prika,** fem. **priktia** s.v.
Pa. Pass. pt. **mparka uhakima** AM 7:18 intelligent and wise; fem. st. emph. (**priktia**) **umparaktia** s. **priktia** (MG 47:16 is mistaken); **mparakta** AM 59:penult. discerning (woman).
PRK II (פְּרַךְ, ܦܪܟ, mod. H. פָּרַךְ to crush, Ar. فرك, Akk. *parāku* to force) to bind (sheaves), tie together.

Pe or Pa. Impf. with suff. **bmahu nihun nihṣdunh̲ ubmahu nipirkunh̲** (var. **niparkunh̲** B) Jb 232:ult. f. with what shall they reap it and with what shall they bind it (into sheaves, Lidzb. *zermalmen*)?

Gl. 127:5 f. **aprak** فرك *vellere spicas* پاك كرد.

PRM (Aram. & H. פרם, Syr. ܦܪܰܡ) to lay bare, expose.

Pe. Pass. pt. with encl. (& act. meaning) **siṭraiin primlin** Gy 181:3, 209:5, 225:13, Gs 30:17 they lay bare (expose) their flanks (thighs).

PRNS the rt. of **parnasta**.

PRS (פְּרַס, ܦܪܰܣ II, H. פרשׂ Nöld. ZA i 417, Ar. فرش, Akk. *rapāšu*) to spread over, extend, stretch out.

Pe. Pf. **pras draiia** Gy 191:10, ATŠ II no. 392 he stretched out his arms. Impt. **pras draiak** Gy 190:17 stretch out thy arms; **prus nhurak** ML 139:13 = CP 114:11 diffuse thy light. Act. pt. **paris draiia** ATŠ II no. 382 he stretches out his arms; with encl. **parislh̲** DAb he spreads (over) it; **parsalun prasia rgigia** DC 48. 230 she lays out for them delicious fare; pl. **anpiš aupaihun parsia** ML 213:3 they completely spread out their foliage. Pass. pt. **had nhura pris ltartinun** ATŠ II no. 362 one light is spread over both of them; with encl. pers. pron. **mn mania d̲-ʿlauai prisna** DC 37. 167 with the robes that I spread over me.

Pa. **d̲-silith̲ ʿl kulhun . . . parislun** DC 48. 96 whose net spreads over them all. Inf. **amar . . . ganph̲ ʿl hanath̲ šualia parsuia** DC 34. 561 he ordered . . . to spread his wings over that novice.

Der.: **pras 1, prasa.**

prʿil IM no. 15, 16, 17, 18, 19 a genie.

PRPA (ܦܰܪܦܰܚ Brockelm. i 516c) to make merry, rejoice, revel, disport (onseself).

Ethpa. Pt. **mitparpa** Q 14:7, Gy 140:17, MG 230:24, **gaia umitparpa** Q 30:2, 30, **mitgaiia umitparpa** Gy 152:17 rejoiceth and revelleth; pl. **sahqia gaiia umitparpia** Gs 8:18, DC 53. 340:ult. they make merry and rejoice and disport themselves; **hadia daiṣia umitparpia** Gy 114:22 they make merry, rejoice, and disport themselves; **hadia paria umitparpia** DC 27. 583 they rejoice, expand, and make merry (MG 85:18); **gahkin umitparpin** DC 34 they laugh and make merry.

PRṢ (Aram., H. & mod. H. פרץ, cf. Ar. فَرَضَ to make an incision) to make a breach, break through, be dissolute, lawless.

Pe. Impf. with suff. **ulguarh̲ nipirṣh̲** Or. 327:1 and it will invade his belly.

Der.: **parṣauata, pirṣa** (var. **parṣa**).

PRPT a miscop of **KRPT** in **mitparputia** DC 22. 195 for **ʿkarputia** Gy 204:7.

PRQ (Jew.-Aram., Chr.-Pal., H., Ar., Sab., Eth.) to free, save, deliver, ransom, remove, sever, detach; bring forth (only in pe.?); break into fragments (pe.).

Pe. Pf. **baṭinta d̲- . . . lapirqat** ATŠ II no. 74 a pregnant woman who . . . did not bring forth; with suff. **pirqh̲ ušadrh̲** *Florilegium*, released him and sent him. Impf. **tipriq pruqia** s. **pruqa 2.** Impt. **pruq** Gy 38:1 (var. **pariq** DC 22. 36 pa.) ransom! Act. pt. fem. **d̲-baṭna ulaparqa** ATŠ II no. 71 who is pregnant but does not bring forth; masc. with encl. **pariqlun** ATŠ II no. 136 delivers them. Pass. pt. **amta d̲-lapriqa** Gy 22:7, ATŠ II no. 74, 369 etc. a slave-girl that is not freed.

Pa. Pf. **pariqt** thou hast freed MG 222:26; **ana napšai mn alma parqit** Jb 77:3 f. I separated myself from the world; **parqitin** Gy 184:22 ye (fem.) ransomed MG 224:12; with suff. **parqh̲** he saved him MG 275:5; **parqan** he freed me MG 270:25; **parqak** he saved thee MG 273:12; **pariqth̲** thou hast saved him MG 276:26; DC 27. 144 thou hast removed it; **pariqtinan** thou didst save us MG 280:8; **pariqtinkun** I have saved you MG 281:3; **pariqtinun** I have saved them MG 282: anteantep.; **parqinun** he saved them MG 281:20. Impf. **nipariq** he delivers MG 226:16; **tiparqun** ye (will) deliver MG 227:paen.; with suff. **niparqh̲** he frees, we (will) free him, her MG 275:28; **niparqan** he saves me MG 271:4; **niparqak, ʿparqak** MG 273:14; **niparqinan** MG 279:ult; **niparqinun** MG 281:paen.; **tiparqinan** MG 279:ult.; **ʿparqinkun** MG 280:26; **ʿparqinun** MG 281:ult.; **niparqunan** MG 273:2; **niparqunak** MG 274:20; **niparqunun** Gy 107:21, MG 283:19. Impt. **pariq** free, ransom MG 229:6; with suff. **parqan** deliver me MG 271:10; **parqinan** deliver us MG 280:3; pl. with suff. **parquia** Gy 15:9 ransom him; **parqun** deliver me MG 273:8; **parqunin** Q 35:10 deliver them (fem.) MG 283:anteantep. Act. pt. **mpariq paruqia** Gy 56:21 f. bringeth redemption (MG 230:7). Part. pres. remove, do away with; **umparqalun kulhun mihialta** DC 50. 176 and removeth all 'wounds'; with encl. **mparqinun** I (will) deliver them MG 291: ult. Pass. pt. **mparaq** ATŠ II no. 75 (*& often*), is freed, ransomed. Inf. **paruqia** Gy 26:5, 56:22. Nom. ag. **mparqana** s.v.

Af. (only postcl.): Impt. **apraq šuplh̲** AM 127:19 remove its rump-fat (?).

Ethpa. Pf. **ʿtparaq** Gs 104:6, ATŠ II no. 77 (*& often*) he was saved MG 222:4; **ʿtparaqt** thou wast saved MG 222:paen.; **ʿparqit** Gs 64:4 A (var. **ʿtparqit**) I was saved MG 213:13, 223:9. Impf. **nitparaq** ATŠ II no. 189 is saved MG 226:20; **ʿtparaq** I shall be saved MG 227:10; **nitparqun** MG 227:21; fem. **nitparqa** Gy 19:20, MG 228:13; with encl. **nitparqubia hirb(i)a usip(i)a** DC 44. 1721 = Morg. 268/26:26 I shall be delivered by sword(s) and blade(s) (?hardly correct!). Pt. **mitparaq** MG 132:17, **baiia miparqa** DC 41. 561 she wanteth to be released; pl. **lamitparqin mn lihun** ATŠ II no. 189 they will not free themselves from their net; **ruha unišimta mn hdadia mitparqin** ATŠ II no. 253 spirit and soul are disparate from one another; **mitparqan** Or. 327:14 they (fem.) are driven away.

Gl. 151:9 f. (with a prosth. **a-**) باز *segregare, discernere, distinctum facere* تميز كرد.

DER.: **mparqana, paruqa, parqa, parqut(a), parqita, purqana, purqat, pirqa.**

PRŠ (Aram., Syr., H., Akk. *parāsu, parāšu* Zimmern ZDMG lxxiv 434) to separate, set apart, go forth, emanate, appoint, designate, discern, understand; af. to teach, instruct, inform, define, explain, consider, edify, divulge one's thought, give forth. MG 221 n. 4.

PE. Pf. **praš** he understood MG 221:21; **ʿutria d̠-madihta praš** Gy 360:15 uthras who understand wisdom; **abatur madh̠ praš ʿl ptahil** Gy 168:10 Lidzb. *A. sah prüfend P. an*; **madaihun lapraš** Gs 17:1; they did not (yet fully) understand; **ʿda upraš bʿuṣraihun** Q 22:4 He (: the Life, pl.) knew and understood in His Mind; **ʿda upraš** Q 4:4; **haš upraš** Q 32: 13, Oxf. 57 b, **haš . . . upraš** Q 5:25, Gs 1:22, JRAS 1937 591:12 etc., pondered and understood; neg. **lahaš ulapraš** Gy 94:12, 315:22, **praš (uʿtapraš)** Gy 196:19, JRAS 1937 591:12 etc., he understood (and took counsel with himself); **d̠-mn napšaiun praš** Gy 245:24 who understood by themselves; **bnia iamin praš mn iaqip** Gy 332:5 Benjamin descended from Jacob; **mn iaqip ubnia amin tlatma ušitin uhamša tarmidia praš** ibid. l. 6 from J. and B. proceeded 365 priests; **mn napš(i)h̠ praš** Oxf. 1 b ff. (*often*); **minh̠ dilh̠ praš** CP 5:6, Q 2:12 = ML 6:6 (emanated) emanated from Himself; **lapraš d̠-napqia minh̠ mn alma** Gy 315:21 they did not understand that they were departing from the world; **hkum upraš** Gy 13:11 they knew and understood; **mindam lahkum ulapraš** Gy 34:8 they knew and understood nothing; **piršat** MG 222:10, **piršat unipqat** Gy 234:19 (cf. Jb 252:5) she emanated and came out; **mn naṣirutai dilia piršat** Gy 301:18 she separated herself from my naṣoraeism; **piršat ʿl kulhun** Gy 163:13 she understood all (?); **piršat brazia** ATŠ II no. 123 she divided (interpreted) the mysteries; **piršit minh̠ mn alma** Gs 131:11 BCD & Leid. I separated myself from the world (only A has **paršit**); **piršit mn ʿuṣrai** Gy 78:16 I understood in my mind (MG 223:2); **tlatma ušitin uhamša tarmidia d̠-prišiun mn mdinta d̠-ʿurašlam** DC 41. 379 (*& often*) the 365 priests who went forth from the city of J.; **hanath̠ d̠-laʿdun ulapiršun** DC 34. 82 those who neither knew nor discerned, fem. pl. **prašian** Q 73b:16, MG 223:antep.; with suff. **piršan** knew me MG 270:20; **piršak** Gy 11:18 knew thee; **lapiršun** Gy 162:16 they knew me not (MG 272:14); **piršuia uhiziuia** RD C 15 they knew him and saw him. Impf. **ʿpruš** Gy 159:24 I understand MG 227:6; **nidun unipiršun** ATŠ no.? they know and understand; with suff. **nipiršuk** Gy 168:18 they know thee. Impt. **pruš** MG 229:5; **hzia upruš** PD 757, 1253, 1328 see and examine (ascertain); pl. with suff. **prušunun** Gy 24:14 know them MG 283:22. Act. pt. **iada upariš** Gy 25:19 he knoweth and understandeth; **hazia upariš** Q 4:20, 6:7 he seeth and understandeth; **pariš mn abuia** Gy 46:9 he separateth himself from his father (MG 230:4); with encl. **kulman d̠-ʿuṣrh̠ parišlh̠** Gy 284:12 everyone whose mind understandeth; **madaihun parišlun** Gy 43:19 they understand; **labahath̠ parišlun mn hdadia** AM 41:12 he will separate his parents from each other; **ʿl abu uʿmh̠ paršalun** AM 81:18 she will cause a parting between her father and mother; pl. **ʿuṣraihun lhdadia paršia** Gy 8:14 they interpret their thoughts to each other; **madaihun paršia** Gy 22:16 they ponder on knowledge. Part. pres. **parišna (umitaprašna)** Gy 205:4, 24 I learn (and study) (MG 231:3); **paršit bʿuṣria** Gy 193:24, Q 24:1 = CP 51:12 = ML 67:3 f. thou understandest minds (MG 15:8); **paršit mahu d̠-hauia bnhura** Gy 194:2 f. thou distinguishest what is in the light (MG 15:8); with encl. **paršatlun** thou discernest them MG 15:8, 232:23; **d̠-paršinalun** ATŠ II no. 192 so that we may discern them. Pass. pt. **priš** separated, distinct MG 230:6; **mn binan priš** Gs 55:23 separated himself from our midst; with encl. **glilia uprišlia** Gy 149:18 was revealed and known to me; **laglilun ulaprišlun** Gy 149:13 was not revealed and known unto them.

PA.? Pf. **paršit** Gs 131:11 A as a var. of **piršit** (s. pe. pf.).

AF. Pf. **apriš ʿlak** Gy 11:18 gave explanation about thee; **apriš ugalil** Gy 213:10 he explained and revealed (MG 222:1); **aprišit** I explained MG 223:5; with encl. **aprišilkun** (*often*), var. **aprištilkun** Gy 224:22 A I explained to you MG 226:2, 10 f.; with suff. **aprišh̠** Gy 13:23 he informed him MG 275:8; neg. **laprišh̠** Gy 94:1, **aprišan** MG 270:27, **laprišan** Gs 49:20 he instructed me not; **aprišinan** MG 279:anteantep., **aprišinun** MG 281:20; **aprišth̠** MG 277:11, **aprištak** MG 274:3, **aprištinun** MG 282:paen., **aprišuk** MG 274:13, **aprišuia** MG 278:2, **aprišun** MG 272:21, **aprištun** Gy 157:22 ye instructed me MG 224 n. 1, 272:11. Impf. **lapriš** he instructeth MG 216:8, **napriš, tapriš, ʿiapriš** MG 215:13 f., 226:17, 227:8; with suff. **naprišan** MG 30:13, 271:5, **nʿiaprišan** Gy 335:15 instructeth me MG 215:20; **napr(i)šak** MG 273:19 f., **ʿiaprišak** Jb 52:14 (*& often, once exceptionally* **aprišak**) I (will) instruct thee MG 273:20; **ʿiaprišinkun** Gy 68:3 (but **aprišinkun** Gy 47:16), **lʿiaprišinkun** Gs 136:11 he may separate you MG 280:27 f.; **taprišinun, ʿiaprišinun** MG 282:4. Impt. **apriš** MG 229:7; with suff. **apriš(i)h̠** MG 276:15, **aprišinun** Gy 13:17 f. instruct them; pl. with encl. **aprišun** Gy 360: 16 f., **aprišunin** Gy 19:21 instruct them (fem.) MG 283:antep. Act. pt. **mapriš** Gy 62:ult. f. distinguishing (separating) MG 131:bottom. Part. pres. **maprišna** MG 231:8. Pass. pt. **mapraš** instructed MG 132:1, **ktib umapraš** Gy 245:7 written and explained; **had had mapraš ʿl dukth̠** Jb 5:14 each one is put distinctly in its place MG 321:17 f. Inf. with suff. **aprišinun** and **maprišinun** Gy 76:22 f., 77:1 to instruct them MG 293:12. Nom. act. **aprašta** s.v.

ETHPE. Pf. **ʿpiršat** she emanated MG 222: 16. Impf. **nitiprišiun** CP 250:1 they will be made manifest. Pt. pl. **mipiršin** ATŠ I no. 133 they are distinguished.

Ettaf. Pf. ʿtapraš was instructed, went forth MG 222:6; (**praš**) **uʿtapraš** s. pe. pf.; **ʿtapraš nišmata** Gs 106:10, 16 the souls went forth; **ʿtapraš bʿuṣraihun** Gy 345:17 they seek instruction (Lidzb. *Aufklärung*) in their minds; **ʿtapraš bhukumta rbia** Gy 351:15 he sought instruction in the wisdom of the Great (Life); **bhukumta rbia mitaprišia ʿtapraš** Gy 345:18, 348:6 they were instructed by the wisdom of the Great (Life); **ʿtaprišat** Gs 9:16 she pondered MG 222:20; **laʿtaprašt bhukumta rbia** Gy 350:9 thou wert not instructed (edified) by the wisdom of the Great (Life); **laʿtapraŝt** Jb 20:14 f., MG 222: ult.; **ʿtaprišit** Gy 167:19, 171:5 I examined, considered MG 223:10; **ʿtaprašnin** Gy 141:9 we were informed MG 224:22. Impf. **nitapraš** MG 226:23; **ʿtapraš** Gy 140:24 I will be instructed MG 227:12; **nitaprašun** MG 227:23; **titaprišun** MG 228:3; with encl. **nitaprašlia** DC 26. 452. Impt. **ʿtapraš** Jb 225 (*often*) sunder yourselves. Pt. **mitapraš** Gy 16:5, 320:24, Gs 41:16, 43:24, 45:22, 47:11, 52:8, 59:2, 71:3, AM 228:3 etc., MG 132:22; with encl. **mitaprišbh** Gy 16:7, **mitaprašbh** Gs 41:1, 48:3, 49:9, 63:16 is instructed by it; fem. **qimitapriša** Gs 9:17 she pondereth; pl. **mitaprišia** Gy 1:19, 237:26, 345:18, 348:6, 354:7, 22, are instructed; **hdadia mitaprišia** Gs 117:9, 118:4 they teach one another (MG 149:13). Part. pres. **mitaprašna** Gy 149:6, Gs 49:10 I am instructed; MG 231:13 (**parišna**) **umitaprašna** s. pe. part. pres., **mhašbitun umitapraštun** RD B 81 ye ponder and discuss.

Gl. 128:5 f. (missp.) فتش *inquirere* پرسید; 151:7 f. **apraš** أفنى, مارى *contendere* مباحثه كرد.

Der.: **apraš(a)ta, parašuta, paruša, parš(a), pirušta, pirša 1, 2, 3, prišaia, prišuta.**

PRT (Jew.-Aram. פְּרַת, Syr. ܦܪܬ, Ar. فَرَثَ, Eth. አፍረሠ) to break apart, break into small pieces, crush, shred, belittle.

Pe. Pf. **uprat ba** ATŠ II no. 32 and divided (into pieces) the *ba* (dove's flesh); **trin alpia paturai (a)prat** Jb 34:1 f. two thousand broke (bread) at my table; **palṭit upirtit** Lond. roll A 646 I have divided out and shredded into pieces; **upratiun uakaliun tlata ʿumsia** DC 41. 184 and they broke (bread) and ate three morsels. Impt. **prut ʿumṣa** CP 71:17 = Q 32:27 break off a piece; pl. **prutiun** PD 1143 = ATŠ I no. 117 break (in two). Act. pt. **d̠-parit minh̠** JRAS 1937 592 which breaks from it. Part. pres. **partit trin paṭiria** ATŠ II no. 216 thou breakest two unleavened loaves; **partitun prata mn paṭirkun** ATŠ II no. 166 ye break off a piece from your unleavened bread.

Pa. Pf. with suff. **partuk** DC 21 (twice), they broke thee to bits. Impf. with suff. **niparth̠ biprata d̠-parit** JRAS 1937 592:antepenult. we will crush him utterly.

Af. Pf. **(a)prat** s. pe. pf.

Der.: **purta, prata, prita.**

PŠA (cf. Aram. & H. פשח, Syr. ܦܫܚ to tear off?) used as a synonym of **BKA.**

Af. Pf. **apša ubka** Gs 3:6 he cried and wept.

pšaṭa (rt. **PŠṬ**) extension, extent, longitude. **kaupih̠ upšaṭih̠** ATŠ I no. 223 its convexity and its extent.

pšar (3rd p. sg. masc. pf. of **PŠR**) often as a name of higher beings. **pšar gufna** DC 40. 138, 194 etc. 'the-vine-spread'; **pšar tana** CP 17:13, 23:7, Q 7:1 the mist-dissolved; **mihla pt pšar** JRAS 1937 592:2 (melted salt?) (salt daughter of It-dissolved).

pšušta s. **ʿšta** 1.

PŠṬ (Aram. & H. פשט, Syr. ܦܫܛ, Ar. بسط, Akk. *pašāṭu* to destroy) to stretch out, extend, straighten, reach out; to separate, tear apart or away, injure, wound, part; with **kušṭa** to plight troth, give one's solemn word.

Pe. Pf. trans. **uʿdh̠ pšaṭ** DC 41 and he stretched forth his hand; intrans. **ʿtigbib ulapšiṭ** Gy 164:16 f. he curled up and did not stretch out; **pšiṭ lpagrh̠** AM 47 spread over his body; **ʿdai pištit** DC 26. 219 = DC 28 par. Impf. **nipšuṭ** CP 33:penult., ML 39:10 he stretcheth himself out; **šidta tipšar utipšuṭ** AM 243:ult. the year will be inauspicious and cause injury. Impt. **pšuṭ iaminaikun mn hdadia** Gy 20:3 stretch your right hands to one another. Act. pt. **pašiṭ kušṭa** ATŠ (*often*) he performeth the ritual handclasp; **iardna piriauis pašiṭ ganph̠** DC 34. 387 the jordan P. extends its arms; **pašiṭ binia ahia** Gs 19:11 he parteth brothers; **ʿšata haita pašṭa** DC 34. 393 the living flame spreads; pl. **kušṭa mn hdadia lapašṭia** ATŠ I no. 170 they do not perform (exchange) the *kušṭa* with one another, **pašṭia kušṭa** DAb, **kušṭa lhdadia pašṭia** Gy 8:13 f.; **kušṭa mn hdadia pašṭin** ATŠ I no. 170, fem. **halin mihiata ʿlh̠ lapašṭan** ATŠ II no. 293 these accidents cannot affect him; with encl. **pašṭibun** Gy 28:3 they spread amongst them. Part. pres. **kd̠ kušṭa mn hdadia pašṭitun** ATŠ II no. 175 when ye perform the *kušṭa* with one another. Pass. pt. **lišana pšiṭ** AM 14:11 long of tongue (a gossip); with encl. **pšiṭlia lbastirqa rba** DC 40 558 f. I stretched out on a great couch; **ligrai pšiṭlia** DC 40. 679 I stretched out my legs. Inf. **mipšaṭ** DC 41. 472.

Pa. Pf. **ʿdai pašṭit** DC 26. 447 I have stretched out my hand(s); **pašiṭnin mšaria** DAb we laid out habitations. Pt. with encl. **mpašṭibun** Gy 51:16 they spread themselves amongst them.

Ethpe. Pf. **laʿpšiṭ** DC 22. 158 a var. of **lapšiṭ** Gy 164:17 (s. pe. pf. intrans.); with encl. **ʿpšiṭbh̠** ATŠ II no. 369 was plighted to him (**kušṭa** omitted). Pt. pl. **trin kušṭia d̠-mitpišṭia** DC 27 two *kušṭa*-ceremonies that were performed.

Gl. 115:13 f. عرض *dilatare* برهنه كرد.

Der.: **pšaṭa.**

PŠL (ܦܫܠ, mod. H. פשל hif.) to twist, knot.

Pa. Pt. pl. **mpašlia uhablia hablia** DC 44 they twist and twine ropes.

PŠQ (ܦܫܩ) to express, find expression or relief in words, make clear, ease, find relief, release.

Pe. Pf. **pišqat nišmat** Gy 358:9 my soul found relief. Impf. **tipšaq nišmat** Oxf. 36 b = ML 208:5 = CP 171:11 my soul will find relief.

Pa. Impt. **pašiq** Gy 366:5 relieve! Pt. with encl. **(a)mpašiq hilmia** Jb 68:3 will interpret dreams; **mpašiqlun liardnia** DC 34 (picture A) releaseth jordans; **(a)mpašiqlkun hilmia** Jb 67:17, 68:10 will interpret for you dreams; **mpašiqlun blibh̠** Jb 70:2 he interprets for them; **umpašiqlun liardnia** DC 34 (ill. A) DC 31 and clears (makes limpid) jordans.

PŠR (פְּשַׁר, ܦܫܰܪ, Akk. *pašāru*, Ar. فسر Fränkel 286) to melt, dissolve, free from, solve, loosen, exorcize; to divide, come apart, spread abroad, separate, tear loose.

Pe. Pf. **pšar** Gy 165:11, Gy 238:8, 292:4, 354:9, DC 44. 1066 = Morg. 263/16:17, DC 51. 350 (*& very often*) melted, became liquid, loosened etc. (both sg. and pl.), also as a pr. n. (s.v.); pl. **pšartana** CP 17:13, 23:7 with suff. **mia piširun** DC 51. 494 the waters released me. Impf. **ʿlh̠ nipšar uʿlh̠ nipuq** DC 43 J 129 he shall exorcize him and expel him; **lanipšar ulanipuq** DC 43. 114 does not disappear and does not come out; **arqa tipšar kd̠ mihla** DC 26. 321 f. the earth will melt like salt; **ʿlania nipiširun** AM 265:15 (prob. to read **nišiprun**), **tipiširun utipqun minh̠** DC 51. 674 ye will loosen and come out of him; with encl. **nipšurulh̠** AM 11:antepenult. they will exorcize (?) him. Impt. **pšar** DC 51. 615 disperse! Act. pt. **ṣipra gadpa d̠-pašar** JRAS 1937 592:8 a winged bird which is loosed; **arqa pašra** Gy 161:22 earth becometh liquid MG 450:1; pl. **pašria** RD C 12, **pašrin nišmata** RD B 92 the souls melt away (read **pašran**). Part. pres. **pašarna** Q 7:1. Pass. pt. **ʿnzaba pšira** DC 40. 199 the unloosed torrent; pl. **pširia haršia** DC 40. 157 the spells are loosed (undone, dissolved). Inf. **mipšar haršia** DC 40. 145 to undo spells.

Pa. Pf. **haršia d̠-ruha pašrit** Gy 117:2 I undid the spells of R.; with encl. **bnura paširtia** DC 44. 1234 = Morg. 264/18:5 I melted it in the fire; **hzunkun upašrunkun** DC 51. 129 f. they beheld you and released you. Pt. pl. **mpašria milia** Lidzb. *Wortdeuter* Ginzā 229 n. 1 (var. **mpašqia** DC 22). Inf. **pašuria kibia mn pagrai** DC 51. 115 to charm away pains from my body.

Af. Pf. with suff. **d̠-apširuia uapquia mn pagra** Or. 332:21 which exorcized and expelled it from the body.

Der.: **pašar, pašara,** pašura, **paš(u)ruta, pišra, (pišruia, pišrun, pšar).**

PŠŠ s. **PUŠ.**

pt (cf. Jew.-Aram. בַּת, Syr. ܒܪܰܬ) peculiar doublet of **brat** 'daughter' used between two proper names and in certain idiomatic expressions MG 10:3, 47:12, 55:13, 183 f. **haua pt simat** (*often*) Eve daughter of S.; **ptula pt abu** Gy 181:1 a virgin, daughter of her father; **pt zamarta** s. **zamarta**; **pt haria** (*often*) a freeborn woman; **pt ṭuhma** s. **ṭuhma**; **pt tmanan utmania (ʿ)šnia** Jb 116:13 a woman of 88 years.

PTA = **PTH** (q.v.). Another secondary rt. **PHT** s.v.

Pe. Pf. **pta** (*often*) he opened, broke (bread) (in Q often created, cf. ML xxi ff.) MG 234:19, **ptit** Q 55:ult., MG 16:8, 234:antep.; with encl. **(mipta) ptalia baba** Gs 105:13 he opened me the door MG 397:14; **ʿptulia** ML 193, **ʿptalh̠** CP 159:13 they opened to him. Impf. **nipta ziqa bmarba** AM 264:6 the wind goes forth in the west; with encl. **baba d̠-ʿhida tiptalan** DC 34. 783 thou wilt open to me the door which is closed; with suff. **niptinun** Gy 145:23 he openeth them MG 281:anteantep. Impt. **pta** MG 235:24; pl. with encl. **ptulh̠** Gy 212:19 open to him MG 237:19. Act. pt. with encl. **patalh̠** Gy 345:3, 393:22 he openeth it MG 235:antep. Pass. pt. **baba d̠-rahmia d̠-miṣat mšunia kušṭa ptia** ATŠ I no. 283 the gate of Mercies which is opened in the middle of M.-K. (MG 236:2). Inf. **mipta** Gs 105:13 (s. pf.) MG 235:29.

Pa. Act. pt. **mpata ʿuiria** Gy 29:10, Gy 53:8 he openeth (the eyes of) the blind; pass. pt. **lampata** Gy 297:21 were not opened (: seeing, of eyes) MG 236:4 f.

Ethpe. Pf. **ʿtpta** was opened MG 64:16; **uhanath̠ baba . . . ʿtipta** ATŠ I no. 178 and that door . . . was opened. Pt. **mitpta** Gy 312:22 A, **mitipta** ibid. B, **mipta** Gy 158:3, 300:8 MG 132:12, 214:1f.

Ethpa. Pf. **ʿsiqa d̠-ʿtpata** Jb 72:8 a blind one who(se eyes) opened. Impf. **nitpata** CP 33:ult. = ML 39:10 he will see.

Gl. 131:13 f., **apta** قطع *excidere* بريد.

Der.: s. **PHT** and **PTH.**

pta (3rd p. sg. masc. pe. of **PTA**) as a name of higher beings. **pta hai** Q 16:16, 31:14, 58:28, cf. **ʿuṣar hiia** CP 37:14, ML 43:10, 84:3, 141:5, Gy 189:15, 196:4, **pta ʿuṣar** Q 27:5 = ML 75:4 in both there may be preserved the Eg. *Ptaḥ* 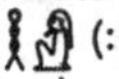 (: Creator) as well as in the name of the demiurge **ptahil** (s.v.); **pta hai** prob. a borrowing from Canaanite (Lidzb. *Lebenspforte*) ML xxii n. 1, 283, Wid. iii 59 n. 1.

ptaha (rt. **PTH**) (*a*) opening, beginning, (*b*) a name given to the ritual meal, sacred 'Breaking of Bread', communal meal (= **laupa**), ritual meal for the dead. Masc. (*a*) **hazin ptaha d̠-rahmia hu** DC 42 this is the opening (i.e. opening prayers) of the (daily) Devotions; **ptaha d̠-bimanda** DC 42. 391 the opening (: consecration) of the cult-hut; **ptaha d̠-ainh̠** Gy 297:20 opening of his eyes; **ptaha d̠-iardna** CP 17:16 = ML 19:8 the opening (prayer for) the jordan; **sadariun tlata ṭariania ganzibra(ia?) d̠-qiria lptaha d̠-bimanda d̠-hu dukrana rba lihdaia rba zadiqa šumh̠** DC 42. 391 f. they arrange three tables—the ganzibra(s?)—who recite the Opening (?) which is in the sanctuary (*bimanda*), the name of which is the commemoration of the Great Unique Righteous One; (*b*) **udara iauar rba**

trin patiria ulaiip bšuma ḏ-hak nišimta ḏ-hu ptaha ḏ-ʿbidatkun kulẖ ʿlh smik ATŠ I no. 118 and the great Yawar brings two unleavened loaves and communicates in the name of that soul, that is the 'Breaking of Bread' upon which all your rites are based.

ptahil (rt. **PTH** to create, Eg. *Ptaḥ* with a theophorous ending, cf. s. **pta**) name of the Mand. demiurge RD ii 450, Kessler PRE 166, 169, MR 35 f., 50 ff., MSchr. 60 n. 3, Jb ii p. xxvii f., ML xxii f., AF 231 n. 10, HpGn. 99 n. 2, Kraeling JAOS liii 152–63, CP trs. 29 n. 1. **ptahil ʿutra** Gy 93:8 f., 94:1, 7, 132: 21, 309:13, 310:12, 311:5, 351:3, 5, 8, Q 53: 33 etc.; **ptahil bhašabta qam** Gy 95:22 P. arose thoughtfully; **sihupta ḏ-ptahil** Gy 306: 19 f. (s. **sihupta**); **ptahil šliha** Gy 286:10, 12 P. the messenger; **alma ḏ-ptahil** Q 32:7, CP 68:8, Jb 186:15 the world of P.; **bit ptahil** Gy 344:1, Gs 110:20 ff. the House of P.; **ptahil rba qašiša** Par. xvii 18a P. the great old one; **ptahil br zahriiil** Morg. 9:1; **ptahil br zahrʿil** Morg. 88:2, CP 140 (d):penult. (Siouffi 41, 55); **ptahil ziu hsir** Gy 209:23 f. P. lacking light; **arqa ḏ-ptahil** RD A 1 = DAb par. the land of P.; **ptahil blila** Gy 102:3 (s. **blila**); **maṭarta ḏ-ptahil** RD C 1, Gy 194:9, 209:23, 321:14 the purgatory of P.; **abatur uptahil** Gy 311:2, 378:30, 35; **ptahil abatur** RD B = DAb; **škinta ḏ-ptahil** Gs 92: 16 f. the dwelling of P.; **lbuša ḏ-ptahil** RD B 48; **lbuša ḏ-ptahil, ksuia ḏ-ptahil, klila ḏ-ptahil, kursia ḏ-ptahil** Gy 193:11 f., 19 f. P.'s garment, P.'s tunic, P.'s crown, P.'s throne; **ptahil qam mn kursia** Gs 92:18 P. arose from his throne; **ptahil ʿl kursiẖ ʿtib** Gs 92:21 f. P. sat on his throne; RD B 17 f. P. as Hibil's son; **ptahil bhailẖ ḏ-abatur abuia ʿhablẖ** Gy 198:18 P. with the force which A., his father, gave him; **ptahil brẖ ḏ-aba ḏ-ʿutria** Gy 297:21 P. the son of the father of uthras, **aba ḏ-ʿutria qra . . . librẖ ptahil** Gy 297:19 f. the father of uthras called . . . his son P.; **hzia ʿdilma lptahil laiṭatlẖ latiliṯẖ lptahil** Gs 55:22 beware lest thou curse P., curse not P.; **abatar ḏ-qiriẖ ptahil lalma** Gy 241:2 f. when P. had created the world (cf. l. 9); **ʿl mahu hua ptahil uʿl mahu qiriẖ lalma** Gs 77:17 f. why did P. come into being and why did he create the world?; **ana (a)pta(a)huit naṭar baita** Jb 5:6 I, P. became a guardian of the House (cf. 4:6 f.); as father of Adam Gy 243 ff., RD B 49; **alma hanatẖ ninhar biad ptahil** Gy 33:19 f. this world is illumined by P.'s hand; **ata ptahil uarim šumia ḏ-mia** Gy 33:21 f. P. came and raised the sky of water; **ptahil ʿṣṭarar** Gy 168:9 P. was formed; **amarlẖ abatur lptahil brẖ** Gy 168:10 f. A. spake to his son P.; **azal ptahil luat abatur abuia** Gy 241:14 f., 242:2 f. P. went towards A. his father; **ʿhablẖ lptahil brẖ uata ptahil urimiẖ balma ḏ-hšuka** Gy 240:23 he (*Yuzaṭaq Mandâ-ḏ-Heyyi*) gave it to his son P. and P. came and cast it into the world of darkness; **rmabẖ ptahil bdmu ruha** Gy 241:11 f. P. cast into him (: Adam. his son, cf. above) a (kind of) spirit; **ptahil ušibiahia ḏ-minẖ** Gy 241:13, 18 f. P. and the planets that were with him; **ptahil bania šumia uarqa** Gy 227:17 f. P. the builder of heavens and earth; **atia ptahil umasia arqa** Gy 127:4 P. cometh and condenseth the earth.

PTH (Aram. & H. פתח, Syr. ܦܬܚ, Ar. فَتَحَ, Eth. ፈትሐ, Akk. *petû*, Eg. 𓊪𓏏𓐍𓂻) to open (up), break (bread), create ML xxi ff., Kraeling JAOS liii 153. Secondary roots **PHT, PTA** s.vv.

Pe. Pf. **ptaht** Gy 342:18 f, thou didst open MG 65:ult.; **ptahnin** Gy 141:10 we opened; with encl. **ptahtilun** MG 226 n. 1; **ptahibẖ** Gy 297:20 I opened therein MG 235:8; with suff. **ptahtẖ** she opened it MG 64:9, Gy 66:21 I opened it MG 65:15; **ptahnun** Gy 141:10 AC, 152:10 we opened them MG 65:18, 283:6. Pass. pt. fem. pl. **ptihan**; **ainia ḏ-nhura bgauẖ ptihan . . . ainia ḏ-hšuka bgauẖ ḏ-nimihiẖ ptihan** ATŠ I no. 251 eyes of light are opened in him . . . eyes of darkness that injure him are opened in him.

Der.: **ptaha, ptahil, ptihata** (others s. **PHT**).

ptula 1 (בְּתוּלָא, ܒܬܘܠܐ, H. fem. בְּתוּלָה, Ar. بَتُول) virgin, celibate, bachelor, unmarried person. Fem. **ptul(t)a** MG 47:13, 119:5. Pl. masc. **-ia**, fem. **-ata**, var. **-iata** DC 22. 432. **ptula pt abu** Gy 181:1 f., 185:4, 24 the virgin daughter of her father Ginzā 184 n. 6; **ptulia uptulata** Gy 59:7, 67:3, 12, Gs 33:20 virgin men and women; **ptulia uqadišia** Gy 121:10, 226:14 f. celibates and 'saints'; **ʿngirata mhatamata ptulata** Gs 7:24 sealed 'letters'—the virgins; **anana ptula** Gy 374:4 the Virgin-Cloud (Spouse); **ʿmaihun ḏ-ptulia** Gy 209:2 mother of celibates (Ruha); **kḏ ptula hu adam luatẖ** Gy 242:10 when A. lived with her as a virgin; **gabra ptula** Gy 273:14, 21, a bachelor; **nsabinun lptulẖ unšaqinun** Gy 146:9 f. he took his unmarried friends and kissed them; **aiak ptulta lgauaia** Gy 217:22 f. like a virgin-girl to a eunuch; **halin ptulata ḏ-ʿsiqta bgauaihun ʿtatna** ATŠ I no. 140 those virgins upon whom a ring was placed; **ptulta ḏ-gabra lahazilẖ** DC 44. 1021 f. a virgin on whom no man looks; **marba ḏ-ptulata** DC 40. 384 the womb of virgins.

ptula 2 (rt. **PTL**) wreath. **nišmata adinqia ptula** ATŠ I no. 39, 54 souls without a wreath.

ptulta fem. of **ptula 1** (q.v.).

ptia (pass. pt. pe. of **PTA**) open, wide, broad. Pl. masc. **-iia**, fem. **-ian. uptian kraiia** AM 4:ult., **uptiin kraiia** AM 22:1 and his (or her) feet are broad; **uptia hadia** AM 47:9 and her breasts ample; **uptiian anpẖ uptia kankuzẖ . . . uptiian riš ḏ-kraiiẖ** AM 47:3 f. and her face is broad and her chin wide . . . and her toes (*or* hips) are large.

ptiliata (rt. **PTL**, Syr. sg. ܦܬܝܠܬܐ) pl. wicks MG 117:24. Var. **aptiliata.** Sg. **pitila** s.v. **šragia ḏ-laradia (a)ptiliata** Jb 152:8 f. lamps the wicks of which do not flicker; **qandilia bla ptiliata** WedF 54:bottom, candles without wicks; **šraga tlatma ušitin (a)ptiliata** ATŠ II no. 68, 262 lamp (of) 360 wicks.

PTL (Gen. Sem.) to twist.
Der.: **miptal, pitila,** pl. **(a)ptiliata, ptula 2.**

PTN (Ar., Syr. af.) to irritate, excite, seduce.
Gl. 130:14 f. فتن *commovere, irritare* فتنه كرد.
Der.: **pitna.**

PTQ (פְּתַק II to thrust, ܦܠܐ to tear asunder, mod. H. פתק id., Ar. فتق id., Akk. *patāqu* to shape) to shoot, aim.
Pe. Act. pt. with encl. **kd̲ patiqlia lgira** DAb when he aims an arrow at him.

PTT (Jew.-Aram. & H. פתת, Syr. ܦܬ, Ar. فَتَّ, Eth. ፈተተ) to break; to tear off.
Pa. Inf. **atia kd̲ patutia gilda** DC 23. 711 comes to tear off the skin.

Ṣ

ṣ the 18th letter of the alphabet. Pronunciation emphatic *ṣ*. Often confused with the non-emphatic *s*. Phonetic changes: **ṣ** > **s** MG § 47 p. 44; **ṣ** > **z** ibid. p. 45; **ṣ** < **s** by assimil. before the emph. **ṭ** MG § 48 p. 45:8 ff.; **ṣ** < **z** before the emph. **ṭ** MG § 49 p. 45 f.

ṣa (cf. צָעָא Ḥull. 47b, צְעָא, ܙܥܐ dish, Ar. صاع dry measure) a piece of dough in roll shape, three to four inches long, and about an inch or more thick, or two flaps of thin bread folded into the same shape, used in ritual meals for the dead MMII 193, SA 69 n. 2. **lagit ṣa ulaiip abihdia tarmidia . . . ukulhun laipia bhanatḫ ṣa** DC 42 he holds the *ṣa* and communicates with the priests . . . and all partake together of that *ṣa*; **ulguṭiun ṣa d̲-hauia trin paṭiria** DC 50. 134 and hold the *ṣa* which consists of two (flaps of) ritual unleavened bread.

ṢAA (צאי, ܙܘܐ, cf. H. *צֹאָה dirt, excrements, Akk. *zû* or *ṣû* id., Ar. وَصِيَ to be dirty, Eth. ጸአ to stink) to be filthy, foul, pollute, defile.
Pe. Pf. with suff. **d̲-gṭlan** [*sic*] **uṣan** DC 46 which wounded me (?) and defiled me.
Der.: **ṣiuta.**

ṣaba (act. pt. pe. of **ṢBA I**) baptist, baptizer. **ṣaba maṣbutai** ML 173:10 my baptizer (lit. the baptizer of my baptism). CP 145:3 **ṣaba banaṣbutai.**

ṣabuha (nom. ag. pe. of **ṢBA I**) baptist, baptizer. Var. **ṣabui(i)a** MG 72:1 f. **ṣabuha** CP 69:7, Q 31:20 = ML 84:8, **ṣabuiai** CP 124:17, Q 63:19 = ML 150:3 my baptizer MG 176:16.

ṣabun (ܨܒܘܢ & ܣܐܦܘܢ, Ar. صابون) soap. **šaipia ʿdaihun bahla ṭaba uṣabun** ŠQ (PA's) they rub their hands with good soap-wort and soap.

ṣabur (& **sabur**) a family-name. Often in colophons.

ṣabra (ܨܒܪܐ, Ar. صَبْر & صَبَارَة Löw 295, Akk. *ṣibāru*? GGA 1904 753) AM 287:36 aloe(s).
Gl. 106:14 (missp. with a non-emph. **s**) صبر *aloes* صبر سقوطرى.

ṣabrʿil Lond. roll A 616, 698, DAb name of a spirit. Var. **ṣaurʿil** s.v.

ṣabšaiil DC 40. 938 f. name of an angel.

ṣada occasionally for **ṣadia.**

ṣadan(i)a occasionally for **sadan(i)a.**

ṣadap (Ar. صَدَف) AM 287:5 shell, mother-of-pearl.

ṣadia 1 (*a*) (ܨܕܝܐ) desert-like, lonely, desolate, waste, solitary, (*b*) (ܨܕܝܐ) solitary place, waste, uncultivated land, desert, wilderness. Var. **ṣidia 1** s.v. Pl. **-iia.** (*a*) **dbar ṣadia** Gy 119:11, 179:11 f., 382:1 waste wilderness MG 304:9 f.; **hurba ṣadia** Gy 331:22, 393:13 waste desert, **hirba ṣadia** Gy 373:21 id.; (*b*) **bṣadia mištbiq** Jb 78:ult. f. shall be left in the desert; **ṣadia alma** Jb 122:11 (var. **ṣadiia** pl.), 242:9 the wilderness of the world; **bṣadia balhudḫ autbuia** Gy 194:11 He (: the Life, pl.) placed him alone in a desert; **zabia bṣadia naplia** Oxf. 35 a = CP 169:ult. = ML 206:1 streams will fall into the wastes; **dibra uṣadia** DC 40. 116 desert and wilderness.

ṣadia 2 = **ṣidia 2** (s. **ṣida**).

ṣadiq(a) (Ar. صَدِيق) pl. **ṣadiqia** AM 227:28 true, pure, perfect.

ṣaḫa (Ar. صاحة) yard, fenced-in precinct (of cult-hut). **nailunḫ lṣaha d̲-bimanda** DC 24 they will bring it into the precinct of the cult-hut; **bṣaha d̲-bumanda** DC 51. 805 in the precinct of the cult-hut.

ṣahama (rt. **ṢHM**) brilliant. **kukba ṣahama** Gy 392:1, 22 f. a brilliant star.

ṣahamta (nom. act. pa. of **ṢHM**) glow, shining, brilliancy. Varr. s. **aṣmata.** MG 64:11, 67:3, 122:6. **ṣahamta d̲-kukbia** Gy 393:16 brilliancy of the stars.

ṣahua Jb 160:13 perh. = **ṣihua 2** doubtf. Jb ii 161 n. 8.

ṣahur(a) (rt. **ṢHR**) DC 46. 142:16 (*and often*) shining, glistening, white.

ṣahia (rt. **ṢHA**) thirst. Doublet **ṣihua** s.v. **kupna uṣahia** DC 41. 429 hunger and thirst.

ṣahib (Ar. صاحب) lord. **ṣahib lzaman** (*often in colophons*) Ar. صَاحِبُ ٱلزَّمَان title of the twelve Shiʿite imams.

ṣahla for **ṣahna** in **daštana ṣahla** DC 23. 249 filthy menstruation-blood.

ṣahna (ܨܚܢܐ, Jew.-Aram. subst. צַחֲנְתָא, H. צַחֲנָה stench, Ar. صَنَخَة id., cf. سَنِخَ & زَنِخَ

stinking, Akk. *ṣēnu* bad, orig. stinking?) stinking, filthy, foul, defiling. Pl. **-ia** MG 107:5. Frequent miscop. **ṣaṣa** (q.v.). **ṣahnia uzapuria** Gy 279:9 filthy and stinking (as a quality of devils).

ṣauaita (rt. ṢUA) (re)pining, languishing, yearning **mn ṣauaita d̲-liba nimut** AM 25:ult. he will die of a repining heart.

ṣauarta Jb 79:7 BD s. **ṣurta** *2 a*.

ṣauar st. abs. & cstr. of **ṣaura** (q.v.) MG 149:29.

ṣauat st. abs. & cstr. of **ṣauta 1, 2** (q.v.).

ṣauia (rt. ṢUA) desert, wilderness, arid land. **sahria bṣauia balma** Gy 122:1 they move about in the wilderness of the world; **nisihdun** (read **nisihrun**) **bṣauia balma** Gy 119:5 id.

ṣauma (rt. ṢUM, צוֹמָא, ܨܘܡܐ, Ar. صَوْم) fast(ing), abstention MG 100:19. **ṣum ṣauma rba** Gy 16:12 f. fast a great fasting MR § 52 p. 93; **kul iuma bṣauma iatbia . . . bṣauma umanbia** Gy 121:6 f. (cf. Gy 356:19) the whole day they sit with fasting . . . with fasting and lamentation; **ṣauma rmalun ʿl pumaihun . . . ṣauma d̲-šuba biahra . . . ṣauma d̲-arbasar . . . ṣauma d̲-tmania usrin . . . ṣauma d̲-šidqa . . ṣauma d̲-hamisar** Gy 356:9 ff. he ordered them fasting for their mouths . . . fasting on the 7th of the month . . . fasting on the 14th . . . fasting on the 28th . . . fasting of silence . . . fasting on the 15th (of the month); **iuma d̲-ṣauma** ATŠ II no. 16 a fast-day.

Gl. 105:5 (miswritten) صوم *ieiunium* روزه.

ṣaupia Sh. ʿAbd.'s copy's var. of **ṣupia** Gy 210:1.

ṣaura (Jew.-Aram. צַוְּארָא, Bibl.-Aram. & H. צַוָּאר, Syr. ܨܘܪܐ, Ar. صَوْر) neck, throat MG 127 f. St. abs. & cstr. **ṣauar** MG 149:29. Var. **ṣura** s.v. **d̲-napil sipa** (var. **ṣaipa** PD) **lraz** (var. **lraza** PD) **d̲-ṣaurh̲** ATŠ I. no. 76 whose throat was cut by a sword; **d̲-nsib raz(a) ṣaurh̲** ATŠ II no. 70, 269 whose throat was cut; **ʿu nasbia raz ṣaurh̲** ATŠ II no. 287 if they cut his throat.

ṣaurʿi(i)l (cf. H. צוריאל Jb ii. 119 n. 3, Schwab: *Vocabulaire de l'Angélologie* 230, *Σουριήλ* Anz: *Ursprung des Gnostizismus* 14) angel of death MR 73, MSchr. 45 n. 9, JPTh xviii 426, Siouffi 14:middle, 32:bottom, 63:bottom, ML 283. **ṣaurʿil šaruia** CP 64: penult., 93:22, Q 29:28, 45:14 = ML 80:8, 117:10 = Morg. 248/83:11 f., Gs 2:3, 3:17, 24, 4:12, Oxf. roll f 225, 572, 704, 887 etc. Ṣ. the Releaser; **ṣaurʿil malaka** DC 43 D 24 the angel Ṣ.; **sikina d̲-ṣaurʿil** Jb 123:3, 124:2 the knife of Ṣ.; **sin d̲-hu ṣaurʿil** Gy 27:20 (identified with Sin). Often in Jb 123 ff. and RD = DAb.

ṣauta 1 (cf. Syr. ܨܒܬܐ ornament, rel. to Jew.-Aram. צִבְעָא red dye, Akk. *ṣibūtu* dyeing?) ornament, adornment, splendour, brightness, lustre, glory MG 49:1 f. Fem. 161:7. St. cstr. **ṣauat, ṣiuat 1** (s.v.). **ninihrun . . . bṣauat napšaihun** Gy 178:24 they will shine in their brightness; **ṣauta d̲-ʿšata haita** Gy 100:8 brightness of the living flame; **ṣauta d̲-nura** Gy 393:17 brightness of the fire; **ṣauta lnura qria** Gy 12:18 created brightness for the fire; **aitia . . . ṣauta lnura** Gy 283:2 brought . . . brightness to the fire; **nura uṣauth̲** Gy 289:17 fire and its brightness; **man hu d̲-nihibh̲ ṣauta** Gy 109:10 who will be its (: of the world) brightness; **ṣauta uragagta** Gs 3:22 adornment and pleasure (Lidzb. **ṣauta 2**); **nišrun ʿlh̲ ṣauta** Gy 308:6 they will spread lustre over it; **šra ʿlai mn ṣauth̲** Gy 327:19 he spread over me some of his splendour; **atia ṣauta d̲-hiia utišria ʿlh̲** CP 288:13; ATŠ I no. 7 the glory of the Life will come and rest upon me; **man nisiblak lṣautak** Gy 88:7 who will wear thine ornament? (doubtf. Ginzā 90 n. 1); **man nasib lṣauta d̲-ṭabia** Gs 84:1 f. who shall take away the ornament (glory) of the good?; **ṣauta uhaduta** CP 450:4 glory and joy; **ṣauta d-hiia** PD 61 f., 66 (*& often*) glory of Life (sometimes **2**); **liardna huitlh̲ ṣauta** Jb 210:12 I became an adornment for the jordan (or **2**?).

ṣauta 2 (צְווּתָא, Syr. ܨܘܬܐ LS no. 3–4) society, company, consort, companionship, association MG 49:1 f. Masc. MG 161:7 f. St. cstr. **ṣauat, ṣiuat 2, ṣibat** (s.v.). **bṣauat hdadia iatbia** Gy 131:1, 335:4 they sit in one another's company; **bṣiuat hdadia nitbun** Gy 304:3 id.; **ṣauta d̲-hiia . . . ṣauta d̲-hšuka** Gy 73:2 f. the company of Life . . . the company of darkness; **šuma d̲-hiia uṣauta d̲-hiia** Gy 251:3 the name of Life and the company of Life; **ṣauta ladam nihuilh̲** Gy 33:10 there shall be companionship for A.; **atit mihuilun ṣauta ldaiuia** RD B 11 = DAb par. thou camest to associate with devils; **latihuilh̲ ṣauta blilia** DC 43 J 9 bear him not company at night; **mitkanap bṣauta d̲-aiar** DC 27. 304 they will meet together in the company (or **1**?) of the Ether.

ṣauta 3 (ܨܘܬܐ LS no. 1–2, Ar. صَوْت) voice, conversation MG 63 n. 1. **qalai uṣautai** Jb 43:9 my call and my voice; **ṣautak** Jb 78:8 thy voice.

ṣauta 4 (rt. ṢUT, hence rel. to 3) perception, attentiveness, heedfulness. **ṣauta . . . uʿruta** Gy 64:12 heedfulness and vigilance; **ṭama uṣauta** Gy 301:8, ATŠ I no. 194, II no. 186 discrimination and perception.

ṣauta 5 (ܨܗܘܬܐ; but as from *ܨܗܘܬܐ) thirst MG 63:1. Doublet **ṣihia** s.v. **man nihilia ṣauta** Gy 86:9 (cf. l. 19) who will still my thirst? **maitin šitlh̲ laṣautun** (read **lṣautun**) Gs 96:1 the plants die because of their thirst.

ṣaṭana occ. var. of **saṭana.**

ṣaṭria sections, chapters. **minh̲ glia miqdam** (**miqdar**) **d̲-šita ṣaṭria** ATŠ II 409 about six sections were worn away from it.

ṣaiama (nom. ag. pe. of **ṢUM**) abstainer, ascetic. Pl. masc. **-ia**, fem. **-ata**. **ṣaiamia uṣaiamata** Gy 222:20, 356:20 male and female ascetics.

ṣaiar(a) (nom. ag. pe. of **ṢUR I**) artist, painter, artificer, sculptor MG 82:paen., 120:15. St. cstr. **ṣaiar.** Pl. **ṣai(a)ria** MG 419:11 & n. 1. **ṣaiara d̲-ṣaiar dmauata** Gy 214:22 f. an artist who depicteth images; **kma hua hakimia ušapiria ṣai(a)ria** Gs 14:24 how wise and fair were the artificers MG 419:11; **ṣaiar ṣilmia**

uṣurata Gy 370:8 artificer of images and pictures.

ṣaiarta (nom. act. pa. from צער, ܨܥܪ) (*a*) maltreatment, torment, (*b*) contention, strife, struggle MG 70:2, 122:7. (*a*) **ṣaiarta d̲-hanath̲ dukta** Gy 302:11 f. torment of that place; **ṣaiarta ubišuta** AM 215:13 maltreatment and wickedness; (*b*) **ṣaiarta uqraba** AM 242:11 contention and war.

ṣaid (Ar. صَيْد) hunting, chase, fishing, fowling. Mod. **šrita d̲-ṣaid** DC 46 exorcism for hunting.

ṣaida (act. pt. pe. of **ṢUD** used as nom. ag.) fisherman, hunter. Pl. **-ia.** (1) **aiak miša d̲-pursma lṣaida** Gy 217:21 like balsam-oil for a fisher (Ginzā 218 n. 4); **ṣaidia d̲-azlia biardna** RD C 12 fishermen who went into the jordan. Very often in Jb 143–63. (2) a quarry, hunted creature; **aiak aria abatar ṣaida** DC 46. 189:14 like a lion after his prey.

ṣaidia 1 pl. of preced.

ṣaidia 2 (adj. from **ṣaid**) pertaining to hunting, fishing, preying. Mod. **ṣipria ṣaidia** DC 46. 199:9 birds of prey.

ṣaiduta (abstr. noun from **ṣaid**) hunting, sport. **rahim ṣaiduta** AM 155:penult. he is fond of hunting.

ṣaiṭa. aklia d̲-laṣaiṭa DC 22. 398 & Sh. ʿAbd.'s copy = **saiṭa** (impure) Gs 8:15.

ṣaila (act. pt. pe. of **ṢUL** used as nom ag.) weaver. Pl. **-ia. kaiaṭia uṣailia** AM 155:13 tailors and weavers.

ṣaimara Samarra (a city) BZ Ap. I.

ṣaira = **ṣaiara** (q.v.).

ṣairia (צירייא & צִרְיָא eye-sockets, but ܨܪܝܐ suffusion of blood in the eyes, weak brain) JRAS 1943 171:11. Var. **ṣi(a)ria** s.v.

ṣaita (צִית) prep. with, near: **bṣaita d̲-iamina nihuia** DC 50. 265 shall be on the right side.

ṣala 1 (Ar. صلاة) RD 18 = DAb par. (Muslim) prayer.

ṣala 2 (rt. **ṢLL**) dawn, break of day. **ʿu qadamta d̲-ṣala atia** AM 127:2 if he comes in the early dawn; **ʿu bṣala atia** AM 126:13 should he come at dawn (var. **miṣalia**).

ṣalahiata 1 (rt. צלח to split?) rays, beams MG 169:16. Var. **ṣaliata** s.v. **ṣalahiata d̲-ziua unhura** Gy 4:6 rays of radiance and light; **d̲-tlatma ušitun ṣalahiata d̲-ziua minh̲ napqia** DC 35. 23 from which 360 rays of light proceed.

ṣalahiata 2 (צִילְחָתָא, ܨܠܚܬܐ) Oxf. roll g 694 = Or. 327:28 s.v. megrim, neuralgia, nervous headache. Var. **ṣilita.**

ṣalaia (adj. from **ṢLA I**?) misleading, perverting. Pl. **-iia. pugdamia ṣalaiia malpilh̲** DC 34. 1007 gives him misleading instructions.

ṣalaiit s. **ṣilaiit.**

ṣal(a)mata (pl. of ܨܠܡܐ) Gy 14:9, 16:21, 24:20, 60:8 idols, images MG 171:2 f. Doublet **ṣilmia** s.v.

ṣalba for **ṣaliba** q.v. Pl. **-ia. minaihun lṣalbia ṣalba** DAb some of them set up crosses.

ṣaluat DC 46. 127:3 doubtf.

ṣalupa Gy 291:19 (coloph.) a family-name.

ṣ(a)luta (צְלוֹתָא, ܨܠܘܬܐ) MG 111 n. 2 prayer. **ṣaluta d̲-kadba** Gy 24:8, **ṣaluta d̲-zipa** Gy 230:4 false prayer.

ṣaliata (**d̲-ziua**) Gy 4:6 for **salahiata 1.**

ṣaliba (ܨܠܝܒܐ > Ar. صَلِيب > Eth. ጸሊብ) cross. Var. **ṣalba** s.v. Pl. **-ia. ʿl ṣaliba niṣlib** Gy 58:15 he (: Christ) shall be crucified; **ṣalibia d̲-hšuka ramlun ʿl kadpaiun** Gy 222:17 crosses of darkness placed he on their shoulders; **ṣaliba biardna ṣalba** Jb 108:6 she made a cross in the jordan; **ṣalibia ṣalbia** RD B 66, 71, ATŠ I no. 250 they set up crosses.

ṣalma = **ṣilma** MG 100:paen. Pl. **ṣalmia** Gy 15:3 idols.

ṣalmata s. **ṣalamata.**

ṣamadta (rt. **ṢMD**?) bottle?, jar? Varr. **ṣamarta 2, ṣamirta 2. ṣamadtik** (varr. **ṣamartik** C, **ṣamartak** D, **ṣamirtak** DC 22. 513) **d̲-mlia miša** Gs 134:4 thy jar (?) that was full of oil.

ṣamahta Gy 12:17 = **ṣahamta** MG 64:11.

ṣamar repressor. **aumitak bʿuṣar ṣamar** DC 37. 531 I adjured thee by ʿUṣar, the Repressor.

ṣamarta 1 (ܨܡܪܬܐ, Jew.-Aram. צְמִירְתָּא, Akk. *ṣimērtu*) strangury, retention of urine. Var. **ṣimirta 2** s.v. **ʿniš hauilh̲ ṣamarta** DC 46 a person that has strangury.

ṣamarta 2 = **ṣamadta** (cf. varr.). **ṣamartai d̲-mlia miša** Gy 134:12 my jar (?) which was full of oil.

ṣamarta 3 var. **samadta** (q.v.).

ṣambra (rt. **ṢMR I**) redness. Var. **ṣamra. ṣambra** (var. **ṣamra** DAb) **d̲-spar** RD 7 Aurora (a name given to Venus).

ṣamura (rt. **ṢMR I**) fever? Pl. **-ia. ṣamuria d̲-rahtia umkamria** DC 43 fevers (?) that run and return (intermittent fevers ?).

ṣamirta 1 (rt. **ṢMR I**) fever. Var. **ṣimarta, ṣimirta** s.v. **ṣamirta tiligṭia** AM 93:11 fever will seize him.

ṣamirta 2 s. **ṣamadta.**

ṣamqa (צמק) in **aina d̲-ṣamqa** DC 46. 246:9, AM 287:39 an eye that shrivels.

ṣamra s. **ṣambra,** cf. also **rham ṣamra** another name of Ruha.

ṣanaiiع (Ar. صنايع) **ialip ṣanaiiع** AM 155:9 he is versed in crafts. MG 2:7.

ṣanaṣʿi(i)l name of an angel Siouffi 40, 50. **ṣanaṣʿi(i)l d̲-qaiim ʿl baba d̲-hiia** Q 59:10 = ML 142:6 f. = CP 116:17 Ṣ. who standeth at the Gate of Life; **malka ṣanaṣʿiil ʿutra** Morg. 8:1.

ṣanarta (ܨܢܪܬܐ) hook (on a pole) **ukd̲ aria bṣanarta** DC 40 like a lion on a hook (fastened to a pole).

ṣanعa (Ar. صَنْعَة) AM 24 craft, handiwork.

ṣandal (Ar. صَنْدَل) a mod. form of **sandlus. miša d̲-ṣandal** DC 46. 129:1 sandalwood oil.

ṣanda = **ṣinda.** Pl. **ṣandia** DC 6 no. 285 (s. **ṣinda** (*a*)).

ṣanta 1.

ṣanta 2 (cf. ܨܢܬܐ, Ar. صُنَان bad smell) stench,

carrion. **ṣipar ṣanta** Jb 146:11, 150:9, 152:12, **ṣipria ṣanta** Jb 158:3 carrion-birds.

ṣaᶜiqia (Ar. صاعقة) AM 281:9 thunderbolt.

ṣapṭa = **sapṭa.** Pl. **-ia. kusiuiẖ bṣapṭiẖ hilia** CP 364:10 f. hide it in its strong-box (jewel-box) (CP trsl. 239 n. 3) *or* in caskets of precious stones; **matnalun btrin ṣapṭia... uhaizak natnun lriša d̠- . . .** ŠQ (PA) she puts them in two chests . . . and they put them (the chests) on the head of . . .; **ṣapṭia d̠-ziua** CP 365:2 f. caskets of radiance.

ṣapia (for صفوى?) Zotb. 227b:35 a personal name.

ṣapir Gy 216:3 s. **ṣipra 1.**

ṣapriᶜil DC 43 D 34 an angel.

ṣaṣa 1 a frequent miscop. of **ṣahna** (q.v.). **ṣaṣa uzapra** Gs 9:12 filthy and stinking; **daštana ṣaṣa unapqa** DC 32. 240 menstruation-blood filthy and coming out (of the body).

ṣaṣa 2 = **aṣaṣa** (q.v.). **ṣaṣia rurbia d̠-ṭura** Oxf. xii great hill-stones; **nangria d̠-ṣasia** a var. of Gs 26:24 cf. s. **aṣaṣa.**

ṢAR, ṢUR III (צער, ܨܥܪ, H. צער to be little, Ar. صغر id., Akk. *ṣeḫru* little, *ṣeḫēru* to be little, Eth. ጸዐለ to insult) to use ill, maltreat, dishonour, disgrace.

Pe. Act. pt. **muma bgauẖ laṣaiar** ATŠ II no. 164 (var. **ṣaiir** DC 6) no spot therein disgraceth. Pt. pres. **lbar anašia ṣarna** [*sic*] DC 46 I maltreat a human being.

Pa. Nom. act. **ṣaiarta** s.v.

Der.: **ṣaiarta, *ṣurana.**

ṣar (Ar. ضرّ) oppression (or from צַעַר grief). **garat uṣar** AM 248:22 incursion (*or* groaning) and oppression (*or* grief).

ṣara (Akk. *ṣarru*, H. צַר II) enemy, oppressor. **habrai** (var. **-ia**) **nihuia ṣaria** DC 44. 1242 = Morg. 264/18:15 my enemy will become my friend.

ṣarapa(ia) (ܨܪܘܦܐ, Ar. صرّاف) goldsmith. Pl. **ṣarapaiia.** Var. **ṣirapaiia,** s.v. **zahba sqila d̠-bihruiẖ ṣarapaiia** DC 34. 388 gleaming gold assayed by goldsmiths.

ṣaraqta s. **ṣararta 2.**

ṣararta 1 (nom. act. pa. of **ṢUR I** = **ṢRR I**) portrayal, depictment, delineation, image, picture, illustration, formation, something shaped or formed. **ṣararta d̠-almia d̠-nhura** DC 7 the portrayal of the worlds of light; **diuan ṣararta** DC 7 illustrated scroll; **ṣararta aina** PD 932 = ATŠ par. the formation of a well-spring (?).

ṣararta 2, var. **ṣaraqta** some form of religious office for the dead. **ṣararta qaria** PD 882 (var. **ṣaraqta** ATŠ I no. 86); **ṣararta ᶜthamblat** PD 1056; **masiqta ᶜthamblat ṣararta** Oxf. roll f 162 (became void); **lṣaraqta ulmaṣbuta** ATŠ. Very often in ATŠ, cf. PD 76, 143, 412, 809 etc.

ṣararta 3 (rt. **ṢRR II,** cf. pl. **ṣraria**) bag, purse. Masc. (!). **laᶜsdar ṣararta btlata razia** ATŠ a purse is not ranged with the three mysteries (par. with **guda ugunza**).

ṣarda s. **ṢRD.**

ṣarṭana a frequent var. of **sarṭana** (q.v.). DC 46. 84:12.

ṣarka (rt. **ṢRK II**) CP 13:ult. = Q 5:23 = ML 15:10 poverty = guilelessness, humility? Doubtf. Lidzb. ZDMG lxi 694, ML 15 n. 3.

ṣatra 1 (צַתְרָא, ܨܬܪܐ, Ar. صعتر Löw 325) savory, wild mint, wild thyme Jb ii 146 n. 11. Pl. **-ia** aromatic herbs generally. **hardla (u)ṣatria** DC 12. 44, 189; Lond. roll B 95, 399, DC 44. 1436 mustard and aromatic herbs; **mihla (u)ṣatria** Jb 145:12, DC 40. 1041, JRAS 1937 p. 592 salt and aromatic herbs; **mihla umia (umiša) uṣatria** DC 40. 987, 1041 salt, water, (oil) and wild thyme; **ṣatria uṣinta** DC 23. 558 ff.

ṣatra 2 in **alaha ṣatra** Oxf. roll g 260 = DC 43 J 120 a rough (for **ṣarda**?) god.

ṢBA I (Gen. Aram. צבא, ܨܒܐ, H. צבה II, Ar. صبا to long for, Akk. *ṣibû*) to will, wish, desire; to please.

Pe. Pf. **kul d̠-ṣbat** DC 34. 674 all that thou willest (?); **laṣbit** CP 190:1, ML 224:4, Jb 197:8 I wished not; **ṣbu** Gy 341:14 f., 391:14 = **ṣbun** Gy 340:ult. they (or He: the Life, pl.) wished MG 258:5 f.; with encl. **hiia ṣbubia** Gy 353:6 B (missing in ACD) the Life took pleasure in me; **laṣbubia daria ulaṣbubia kulhun almia** Jb 91:3 the ages took no pleasure in me, nor did all the worlds desire me. Act. pt. **kd̠ ṣabia rbia** Gy 58:9 when the Great (Life) willeth it; **alma d̠-rbia ṣabin ᶜlẖ** Jb 25:9 until the Great (Life) wills it; with encl. **ṣabilun umasqilun** DAb they will take pleasure in them and lift them up. Part. pres. **laṣabina** CP 190:1 = ML 224:4, Jb 197:8 I desire not; **kul d̠-ṣabit** DC 34 all that thou desirest.

Der.: **ṣbu(ta), ṣubiana 1.**

ṢBA II (צבע, ܨܒܥ to immerse, dye, Chr.-Pal. af. to baptize Nöld. ZDMG xxii 518, Ar. صبغ, Eth. ጸብዐ, Akk. *ṣibû*, *ṣibûtum* to dye. SsSs i 110–12, Wid. v 137 n. 7) to baptize, immerse, dip in; to dye.

Pe Pf. **uṣba lpihta** DC 41. 262 and he dipped the sacramental bread; **ṣibit** I baptized MG 235:3; **ṣbun** Gy 17:20 they baptized MG 237:13; with suff. **ṣibẖ** DC 41:347, 384 he dipped it; **ṣiban** Gy 153:4, 364:3 = **ṣban** Q 63:19 f. he baptized me MG 270:23 f.; **ṣbinan** Q 63:22 he baptized us MG 279:25 f.; **ṣbinun** Gy 29:ult., 130:1, Q 6:2, DC 36 no. 286 he baptized them MG 281:18; **ṣbatan** Gy 152:19 she baptized me MG 271:paen.; **ṣbatẖ** I baptized him MG 277:2; **ṣibun** they baptized me MG 272:15; **ṣibuk** MG 274:10. Impf. **niṣba** baptizeth MG 235:12; **tutbia hiuaria niṣba** Gy 229:3 he dyeth white clothes; **kulman d̠-niṣba ᶜdẖ uligrẖ** Jb 96:9 f. whosoever dyes his hands and feet; with encl. **niṣbubkun** Gy 309:22 they baptize in you MG 235:22; with suff. **niṣibak** baptizeth thee MG 273:14; **ᶜṣibak** ibid. l. 15; **ᶜṣbẖ** I baptize him MG 275:18; **laniṣbinun** ATŠ I no. 150 he shall not baptize them. Impt.

ṣba baptize MG 235:23; **ṣba nišmatkun** Gy 37:14 baptize your souls (MG 237:14); with suff. **ṣ(u)ban** Q 18:18, 21:4 baptize me MG 71:3, 271:8; **ṣubh̠** baptize him MG 276:11; **ṣubh̠ lqanina** ATŠ II no. 42 immerse thy phial. Act. pt. **hak d̠-ṣaba** DC 50. 873 he who baptizes; **ṣaba barba iardnia** RD 42 he baptizes in four jordans. Part. pres. (act.) **anašia bmia ṣabana** Gy 190:21 I baptize people with water; **ṣabit** DC 36 ATŠ II no. 419 thou baptizest MG 236:17; with encl. **ṣabatbh̠** thou baptizest therein MG 236:20. Pass. pt. **ṣbia** baptized MG 4:ult., 236:1, but also **ṣbʿi(i)a** Gs 112:17, 23, 113:3 (by confusion with the pl.), MG 6:14; pl. **ṣbʿiia mia** Gy 285:18, 286:19 baptized in water MG 310:ult. Pass. part. pres. **ṣbina** I am baptized CP 140 (*b*):9, MG 236:13; **ṣbii(i)t, ʿṣbiit** Q 10:9 etc. thou art baptized MG 236:17. Inf. **kd̠ baiit miṣba nišimta** ATŠ I no. 132 when thou wishest to baptize a soul; with suff. **miṣibh̠** Gy 129:8, DC 34. 39, DC 41. 523 to baptize him (her).

Pa.? Inf.? **ʿparuiia iardna uʿṣibuiia lašualia** DC 34. 257 to let the jordan flow and to baptize the novice.

Af. Pf. **aṣbit** I baptized MG 235:4. Impt. with suff. **aṣban** Gy 189:4 baptize me MG 271:11. Pt. **maṣba** he baptizeth MG 131:anteantep. 236:7. Part. pres. **bmaṣbuta d̠-maṣbit** Gy 189:4 with the baptism wherewith thou baptizest. Nom. ag. **maṣbana** s.v.

Ethpe. Pf. **ʿṣṭba** he was (they were) baptized MG 27:11, 212:20, 234:22; **ʿṣṭibat** Oxf. 108a she was baptized MG 234:25; **ʿṣṭbun** they were baptized MG 237:13; with encl. **ʿuṣṭlia d̠-ʿṣṭbabh̠ bgauaihun** Lond. roll A 255 the garments in which he was baptized; **ʿṣṭbatbh̠** Gy 54:7 thou wast baptized in it; **ʿṣṭbatbia** Gy 129:11 thou wast baptized in me MG 235:1; **maṣbuta d̠-ʿṣṭbubh̠** (var. **ṣṭbubh̠** DC 22. 359) **biardna** Gy 362:1 the baptism wherewith they were baptized in the jordan. Impf. **tiṣṭbun** ye are baptized MG 237:6. Impt. **ʿṣṭba** Gy 37:14 be baptized (pl.) MG 236:14. Pt. **miṣṭba** Par. xiv no. 122, DC 50. 873 is (will be) baptized MG 236:8, 400:4; pl. **ašualia miṣṭibin** ATŠ II no. 4 novices are baptized; fem. pl. **miṣṭiba nišmata** CP 20:7 = ML 22:4 the souls are baptized; **nišmata d̠-miṣban** ATŠ I no. 132 (var. **miṣṭbin** PD) souls that are baptized. Part. pres. **miṣṭbinin** we are baptized MG 237:7.

Der.: **maṣbana, maṣbuta, ʿuṣba 1** = **ʿṣba 2** (& varr.), **ṣabuha, ṣabuia, ṣiba, ṣibunia, ṣibuta, ṣibiana** = **ṣubiana 2**.

ṣbabut (H. צְבָאוֹת) a name given to **adunai**, cf. **adunai ṣbabut alaha rba d̠-asriaiil** DC 44. 705 יְהוָה צְבָאוֹת the great god of Israel. The orig. meaning 'hosts' was hardly understood by Mandaeans, as the word was popularly explained by **ṣbuta**, cf. **ṣbabut ṣbuta rabtia d̠-hiia** CP 29:12 = Q 12:25 = ML 35:1 Ṣ. the Great Will of Life; **mlaka haia d̠-mištalaṭ lkul dmu ṣbabut saina ušapira** DC 37. 565 living angel who governs every kind of things (or hosts?, spirits?) ugly and beautiful.

ṣbaita occ. var. of **ṣbata, ṣbita**.

ṣbata (cf. Syr. pl. ܨܶܒ̈ܥܳܬܳܐ) finger, digit MG 36:6. Orig. pl. MG 110:10, used for both sg. and pl. Var. sg. **ṣbita, ṣbaita, ṣibita** s.v.; doublet **ʿṣba 1** s.vv. **ṣbata rišaita** Lond. roll A 702 forefinger; **hda mn ṣbath̠** ATŠ I no. 133 one of his fingers; **btlat ṣbata** ATŠ II no. 160, DC 43 I 67 with three fingers; **asar ṣbatai** Lond. roll B 208, 210, 242 (*& often*) my ten fingers; **mašihta d̠-asar utartin ṣbata** s. **mašihta 1**; **ṣbata d̠-kraiia** AM 14 the toes of the feet.

ṣbu, emph. **ṣbuta 1** (צְבוּ, ܨܶܒܘ, emph. צְבוּתָא, ܨܶܒܘܬܳܐ) (*a*) will, desire, (*b*) business, affair, thing (as 'something' always in st. abs.) MG 146:3. Pl.? **ʿuṣbuta** matters, affairs. (*a*) **ṣbuta rabtia d̠-hiia** s. **ṣbabut**; (*b*) **ṣbu ṣbu** Gy 116:23 something MG 301:10; **ṣbu** Gy 45:20, 96:11 something MG 302:17; **taqin kul ṣbuta** Gy 297:11 arranged all things; **kul ṣbu** (often) everything; **qablat mn had ṣbu** Gy 94:17; **mn had ṣbu . . . qablat** Gy 95:11 she conceived at the same time (Lidzb. *von einer Handlung*, refers to coition); **d̠-sairit ʿuṣbuta** DC 40. 451 that thou carest for matters (?).

ṣbuta 2 Jb 250:5 B = **ṣibuta**.

ṣbita a var. of **ṣbata** (q.v.) but only with sg. meaning, the pl. being always **ṣbata** (s.v.). MG 16:21, 110:9; **ṣbita rišaita** Oxf. roll f 908 forefinger; **ṣbitak rišaita** Oxf. roll f 567, 698; **ṣbita** (var. **ṣbaita**) **d̠-ʿda iamina** ATŠ I no. 134 a finger of the right hand; **ṣbitak (u)ʿlianak, ṣbitak d̠-abihdia ʿlianak** s. **ʿliana**; **ṣbita d̠-hiṣra** s. **hiṣra**.

ṢBT (Jew.-Aram. צְבַת) to be a pair, join, associate with.

Pa. Impt. pl. with encl. **ṣabitulh̠ uprutiun** DC 42 join for it and break it (the ritual consists of each pair holding the bread between them for breaking it between them).

Der.: **ṣauta 2.**

ṣgara for **sugara** in **kd̠ kalba bṣgara** DC 40. 356 like a dog with his leash.

ṢDA (צדי, ܨܕܳܐ, H. צדה II, Ar. صَدِيَ to be thirsty) to be waste, desolate.

Pe. Pt. **ṣadia** s. **ṣadia** (*a*).

Der.: **ṣadia** var. **ṣidia 2.**

ṢHA I (צהי & צחי, Syr. ܨܗܳܐ, ܨܗܝ, but also a der. ܨܰܚܘܳܐ dry weather, H. צִחֶה dry, cf. Ar. صحا, Eth. ጸሕወ to be cloudless, serene) to be thirsty, parched, dry, to thirst.

Pe. Impf. **mia niṣhh̠** (var. **-ih̠** DC 22. 173) Gy 180:21 f. he thirsteth for water. Impt. pl. **ṣhun aiak mia bmihla** DC 37. 119 thirst like water in salt. Act. pt. **ṣahia** Gy 214:5 thirsty (fem.) MG 164:anteantep.; pl. **ṣahin** MG 61:6; **ṣahian mia** Jb 40:10 they (fem.) thirst for water. Part. pres. **ṣahina** Gy 86:8 I thirst. Pass. pt. **ṣhia**, fem. **ṣhʿia.** Gy 189:6 MG 153:26.

Der.: **ṣauta 5, ṣihua 1, ṣihia, ṣihiun 1, 3, ṣita.**

ṢHA II (Ar. صَحَّحَ II to correct, Syr. ܐܰܨܚܰܚ to copy out) to copy out.

Pa. Pf. with suff. **ṣahinun lzharia** DC 3: coloph. copied out the rubrics.

ṣhana (cf. **ṣahna**) foul, filthy, vile. Pl. **-ia. ṣaidia ṣhania** (var. **ṣuhania** B, **hania** AD) Jb 157:4 vile fishermen.

ṢHL (Jew.-Aram. & H. צהל II) to shine, be bright, glisten.
Pe. Act. pt. fem. **ṣahla kd uarda** DC 23. 709 bright like a rose (but **ṣahla** DC 23. 249 a miscop. of **ṣahna**, v.s. **ṣahla**).

ṢHM, ṢMA s.v. (ܨܚܡ to shine, Jew.-Aram., Chr.-Pal., H. צמח, Akk. *šamāḫu* to sprout) to give light, gleam, shine.
Pe. Pf. **d-ṣihmat bziua unihrat bzakuta** DC 40. 293 which was brilliant in radiance and shone in purity; **ṣihmit kd kukbia** DC 44. 1303 = Morg. 264/19:24 I gleamed like the stars; **rušumia kulhun ṣ(u?)hmiun** DC 27. 73 all the signs gleamed. Impf. **tiṣihmun kd ziua** CP 414:1 ye shall shine like the light. Act. pt. **d-ṣahum hanath rušuma** DC 27. 75 so that that sign shall shine; **ṣahma** DC 48. 371 it (fem.) shines MG 66:14; pl. **ṣahmia** DC 48. 38 they shine.
Pa. Pt. **mṣahma mn kukbia** DC 40. 416 brighter than stars; **mṣahma mn kaspa** DC 40. 209 more gleaming than silver; pl. **mṣahmia ṣahumia**, var. **ṣihumia** ATŠ II no. 52 they shine to illumine. Inf. **ṣahumia**, var. **ṣihumia** (just quoted). Nom. act. **ṣahamta** s.v.
Af. Pt. **sira d-maṣma blilia** Gy 287:8 f. the moon which sheds light at night.
Der.: **(a)ṣmata** (& varr.), **ṣahama, ṣahamta, ṣuhma, ṣihma, ṣihmai.**

ṢHN (cf. s. **ṣahna**) to be foul, filthy.
Ethpa. Pt. **miṣṭahan** DC 37. 196 is made filthy.
Der.: **ṣahna, ṣhana.**

ṢHP = **SHP.**
Pe. Pf. **ṣihpat** AM 277:30 (read ethpe.?) she was hurled.

ṢHR (H. צחר, cf. Ar. صحر IX) to be clear, white, shining, glistening.
Pe. Pf. **ṣhar** Gy 284:10 (read **ṣuhar** adj. st. abs.) is of clear (or white) colour.
Der.: **ṣahur, ṣuhar(a).**

ṢWA (ܨܘܐ, Ar. صوى, H. der צִיָּה dry land) to languish, pine, wither away, dry up.
Pe. Pt. **ṣauia** Gy 67:10, 223:16, 277:20; pl. **ṣauin** Gy 9:3, 48:15, Gs 96:1, MG 63 n. 2; **ʿniš d-lišanh ṣauia** DC 46. 85:16 a person whose tongue is parched.
Der.: **ṣauaita, ṣauia, ṣita 1.**

ṣubiana 1 (rt. **ṢBA I**, ܨܒܝܢܐ) will, wish, desire, purpose MG 18 n. 6, 136:23. St. abs. & cstr. **ṣubian. ṣubian** Gs 23:20 my will MG 175:21; **ṣubian maraikun** Gy 21:8 the will of your Lord; **ṣubianh d-saṭana** ibid. the will of the Satan MG 308:paen. f. (cf. Gy 40:5 f., 14 f.); **bṣubian hiia** Gy 246:19 by the will of Life; **bṣubian rbia** Gy 323:13 by the will of the Great (Life); **bṣubian trin ʿutria** Gy 323:14 by the will of the two uthras; **ṣubian almia** Gs 132:3 the will of the world; **ṣubianak uṣubianai** DC 40. 391 thy will and my will; **bṣubiankun uṣubianai** DC 34. 677 by your will and mine; **bṣubiana d-napših** ATŠ II no. 19 of his own will (voluntarily); **bla ṣubiana d-napših** ibid. against his will.

ṣubiana 2 s. **ṣibiana.**

ṣugara = **sugara.** Var. **ṣgara** s.v. **zim kd kalba bṣugara** DC 46 fastened up like a dog by his leash.

ṢUD (Jew.-Aram. & H. צוד, Syr. ܨܕ, Ar. صيد, Akk. *ṣâdu*) to hunt, chase, fish.
Pe. Impt. **ʿzal ṣud nunia** Jb 151:11 go, catch fish!
Der.: **ṣaid, ṣaida, ṣaiduta.**

ṣudra (Ar. صُدْرَة) shirt, chemise, tunic. **mn bṣaura ualma ldinba d-šipula d-ṣudrh** DC 46. 144:11 from the neck unto the end of the skirt of her chemise. Gl. 76:9 (miswritten) جلال *operculum sive vestis pro equo* جل; 147:11 (miswritten) لفافة *sindon.*

ṣuhana s. **ṣhana.**

ṣuhar(a) (rt. **ṢHR**, H. צָחוֹר, Ar. صَحُور; formally corresponding to Syr. ܨܘܚܪܐ but with slightly different meaning) white MG 122:20. St. abs. **ṣuhar. hu ṣ(u)har** Gy 284:10 s. **ṢHR; ṣuhara ušapira** AM 87:penult. white and comely; **ṣuhara . . . hauia** AM 85:9 he will be white; **ṣuhara aqamia ainia** AM 4:19 there will be white(ness?, a white film?) before his eyes.

ṣuhma occ. for **ṣihma**, but DC 44. 1302 for **sumaqa** Morg. par.

ṢUL s. **ṢLL II.**

ṢUM (Sem., Akk. unknown) to fast, refrain, abstain (from). MR § 52.
Pe. Impt. **ṣum** Gy 16:12 f.; pl. with suff. **ṣumuih lhazin ṣauma rba** Gy 16:23 fast this great fast. Nom. ag. **ṣaiama** s.v.
Der.: **ṣauma, ṣaiama, ṣuma.**

ṣuma fast. **ṣum ṣuma rba** DC 22:16 observe the Great Fast.

ṣumaqa occ. for **sumaqa.**

ṣumṣara DC 43 E 40 read **mṣara.**

ṣusia (cf. Syr. ܨܘܨܝܐ chirping?) incantations. **haršia uṣusia nibudlh** AM 25:12 sorceries and incantations they will make for him; **ṣusia d-haršia** AM 64:3 magic incantations.

ṣup sporadically for **sup.**

ṣupia (Ar. صوف) in **ṣupia d-aqamra** Gy 210:1 flocked wool MG 105:10 & n. 2.

ṣupnai lilita HG 30 name of the lilith who stole the child Yaḥya (John the Baptist).

ṣupra = **ṣipra 1.** Pl. **ṣupria** AM 283:10.

ṣuprina colloquial diminutive from preced. Fem. **ṣuprinta. rup bkraiia d-ṣuprinta** DC 46 tie (it) to the legs of a female bird.

ṢUṢ, ṢIṢ s.v. (cf. H. צוץ I = Ar. ضاء med. *u* to shine, צוץ II = وصوص & وصّص to peep) to peep, blink, twinkle, shine, look out, appear.
Pa. Only a rigid fem. part. form (used of eyes): sg. st. emph. **aina mṣuṣtia** JRAS 1937

593 peeping eye; fem. pl. st. abs. mṣuṣan AM 14:11 blinking (eyes).
Der.: ṣiṣia 4.

ṣuṣt(a)mia, ṣuṣt(i)mia = sustmia. MG 45:12. **mṣaṣtmia ʿdaihun bṣuṣtmia d̲-parzla** Morg. 264/18:30 & 19:3 their hands are bound by iron bonds. Cf. Q 38:19, Oxf. roll f 986 (*& often*).

ṣuṣiata (Targ. צִיצִיתָא, H. ציצית, Syr. ܨܘܨܝܬܐ, Ar. صيصية Nöld. ZA xix 155, Lewy: *Fremdwörter* 90, Löw OLZ xv 388, from Akk. *ṣiṣītu* Zimmern ZA xxxvi 319) pl. plaits of hair Jb ii 166 n. 4. **briš ṣuṣiath̲ marganiata** Jb 165:2 f. at the end of her plaits (there are) pearls.

ṢUR I, ṢRR I s.v. (Aram., H. & mod. H. צור, Syr. ܨܪ, Ar. صَوَّرَ) to form, shape, model, portray, limn, engrave, depict, trace. MG 82:bottom.
Pe. Pf. **ṣar tlata ṣurata** ML 56:7 he traced three circles; intrans. **ṣar ʿula** Gy 244:15 the embryo was formed etc. (cf. foll. lines); with encl. **ganpia d̲-ziua ṣarlia** Gs 88:4 wings of radiance were formed for me; **ganpia ṣarl(i)h̲** Gy 339:1, Gs 14:1, 104:4, 111:26 wings were formed for it; with suff. **ṣarnh̲** we formed it MG 277:21; **ṣairia d̲-saruia** Gs 14:25 the artificers who formed it. Impf. **tlata ṣurata niṣar** ATŠ II no. 207 he shall trace three circles. Impt. pl. **ṣuriun tlata ṣurata** DC 50. 257 trace three circles. Act. pt. **ṣaiara d̲-ṣaiar** s. **ṣaiara**. Part. pres. **ṣairitun tlata ṣurata bmia** DC 35 ye trace three circles in the water. Pass. pt. **ktib uṣir** Gy 144:7 written and portrayed (MG 250:19); pl. **ṣiria bgauaihun rušumia** DC 34. 854 f., CP 339:penult. signs were formed in them.
Pa. Pf. (Ar.) with suff. **ṣauirth̲ amud d̲-mṣia hailai** DC 7 right 94 I pictured it as well as I could.
Refl. s. ṢRR I.
Der.: **ṣai(a)ra, ṣurta 1** (abs. & cstr. **ṣurat**), **ṣuria** pl.; others s. ṢRR I.

ṢUR II, ṢRR II s.v. (orig. ע״ע, cf. s. ṢRR II) to surround, hem in, encompass, enclose, tie in.
Pe. Pf. **d̲-ṣarat ruha** DC 43 A 76 which R. tied (?); with encl. **argbaiun uminunun bknap lbušaihun ṣarlun** Q 65:10 = ML 155:10 they have wrapped their money and their possessions in the lappets of their garments (MG 248:6). Act. pt. with encl. **ṣairilun bainaihun dimihta** Gs 25:10 their eyes burst into tears (*idiom*, cf. s. ṢRA I & ṢRR II). Pass. pt. **ṣira haza nišimtai bṣurta** DC 37. 121 f. this soul of mine is surrounded by a protecting line.
Pa. Pt. **mṣaira bpagra nišimta** Gy 22:4 f. she keepeth the soul imprisoned (enclosed) in the body.
Der.: **ṣurta 2** (abs. & cstr. **ṣurat**); other s. ṢRR II.

ṢRR III s. ṢAR.

ṣura = ṣaura. **lguṭ ʿlak bṣurak** DC 45 fasten to thee on thy neck; **rup bṣuraiun** DC 46. 14:6, 15:4 tie on their necks; **raza d̲-ṣura** PD 809 the mystery of the neck; **napla bṣuraihun** DC 43 A 147 will fall on their necks; **ṣur, ṣura**? for **sura**? **umištria unafla bṣuraihun kulh̲ baita nad ukulh̲ hikla ʿzdambia stal** DC 43 A 146 f. **umištria baita kulh̲ nad** (&c. no **ṣuraihan**) DC 43 A 53 and all houses were [every house was] loosened and fall(eth) with their walls [surroundings?], they trembled and each temple, the stones [shaken apart] were shattered [convulsed] therein.

***ṣurana** (rt. SAR = SUR III, cf. H. צְעוֹר Jer. 14:3. 48:4 *ketib* for צָעִיר) very little, small child MG 137:18. Pl. masc. **-ia**, fem. **-iata**. **ṣurania uṣuraniata** Gs 17:20 little boys and little girls.

ṣurat st. abs. & cstr. of **ṣurta 1, 2** (q.v.), **ṣurata** pl. of the same.

ṣ(u)rurita (ܨܘܪܪܝܬܐ, Akk. *ṣurāru*, *ṣurārittu* Holma ZA xxviii 154) salamander MG 29:1, 148:4. Pl. **-iata**. **liliata uṣ(u)ruriata** Gy 139:15 liliths and salamanders; **ʿnšaiun damian akuat ṣururiata** Gy 139:10 f. their women resemble salamanders.

ṣuria pl. (rt. ṢUR I) idols, statues, and images of gods. **ṣilmia uṣuria uprikia** CP 49:15, Q 23:13 = ML 65:6 statues, images, and shrines.

ṣ(u)rik (a misunderstood Chr.-Pal. ܨܘܪܟ, late H. צוֹרֶךְ need Lidzb. ZDMG lxi 694 n. 1) (*a*) orig. urge, want, (*b*) hence: impulse?, outcoming ray, bursting out (of fire or light), coruscation MG 150:ult. & n. 3, MSt 84 f., CP trs. 46 n. 2. (*a*) **litbh̲ ṣurik dmu** CP 179:9, Oxf. 47 a = ML 219:5; (*b*) **ṣurik hu ziua** Q 31:9, MG 312:14, **ṣurik ziua** CP 68:12, Q 27:21, Gs 90:7, 115:20; **ṣurik ziua rba** Q 32:8, 43:11; **ṣrik ziua rba** Gs 109:9; **ṣurik hiia** Q 12:29, 58:31, Gs 57:2 ff., **ṣurik hiia rbia** Q 16:28.

ṣurna (P. سُرْنَا, Ar. loan-w. صُرْنَاج & صُرْنَايَة) hautbois. Var. **zurna**. **qamahia bṣurna** RD 35; **qizamar bṣurna** RD 29 he plays the hautbois.

ṣurpana (rt. ṢRP I) affliction, suffering, calamity, misery. Pl. **-ia**. **kupna uṣurpana** Gy 230:8, 232:24 famine and affliction, cf. Gy 267:17; **grania uṣurpania** AM 200:13 high market prices and calamities.

ṣurta 1 (rt. ṢUR I = ṢRR I, צוּרְתָא, ܨܘܪܬܐ, Ar. صورة, Fränkel 272, Akk. *uṣurtu* Zimmern: *Akk. Fremdwörter* 27) image, form, semblance, picture MG 105:paen. St. abs. & cstr. **ṣurat**. Pl. **ṣurata**. **ṣilmia uṣurata** Jb 178:9, Gy 177:5, 370:8, Par. xxvii 48 a etc. images and pictures; **aiak ṣurat** [*sic*] **d̲-ʿmbra** AM 278:1 like unto the image (semblance) of a lamb; **ṣurata uṣalamata** Par. xxiv 76 pictures and images.

ṣurta 2 (rt. ṢUR II = ṢRR II) (*a*) a line or barrier placed or described about a thing or person, circle, magic circle, (*b*) a woman isolated for impurity (esp. menstruation and child-birth), period of ritual isolation. Jb ii 84 n. 2, 91 n. 6, BZ 127 n. 5, 163 n. 3, MMII 43. Treated as masc.! St. abs. & cstr. **ṣuraṭ**. Pl.

ṣurata. (*a*) **šamiš ʿtib bṣurta** (var. **bṣauarta** BD) Jb 79:7 the sun sat in a halo; **šamiš kḏ hauia hdirlḫ ṣurta** AM 261:17 when the sun is surrounded by a halo; **kulman ḏ-hazin ṣurta abar** DC 43 A 9 any being who crosses this (magic) circle; **ṣurta rba** Par. xxvii 14 b, DC 43 A 76 the magic circle; **ṣurta ḏ-halba uzma** Par. xxvii 17 a, DC 43 A 123 & H 12 (magic) circle of milk and blood; **tlata ṣurata niṣar** ATŠ II no. 207 he shall trace three circles; **tlata ṣurata** very often (cf. s. **ṢUR I**); **kdub urmia bṣurta** Par. xxvii 23 b describe a circle all around; **arba ṣurta ṣarlia** Par. xxvii 8 b; (*b*) **ṣurta lhaita laṣairia** Jb 85:5 they do not enclose the woman in child-birth with a circle; **ṣurta ṣair(i)a** Jb 114:3, 9 they surround (her: woman-in-child-birth) with a circle; **bit ṣurtai huit** Jb 88:1 I was in (the house of) my ritual confinement; **iumia ḏ-ṣurta** PD 553, ATŠ I no. 50, II no. 74 days of isolation; **iahra ḏ-ṣurta** DC 34. 647 month of ritual isolation (after child-birth); **bṣuratin** ATŠ I no. 239 in times of their ritual isolation.

ṢUT (צות, ܨܬ) to hear, listen, give ear, heed, obey.

PE. Pf. **ṣat** he heard MG 248:3, **ṣatat** she heard MG 248:9, **ṣatit** Gy 276:1 I heard MG 248:15. Impf. **laniṣut** Gy 58:6 heareth not, **ḏ-laniṣat qalḫ** ATŠ I no. 231 who hearkeneth not to his voice; with suff. **ḏ-niṣitḫ unišimḫ** Jb 201:14 (cf. foll.) who listens and hears; **niṣitak** Gy 274:15 heareth thee MG 273:15. Impt. **ṣut** Jb 52:15, MG 250:5. Act. pt. **nišimta bmahu ṣaita hadia** ATŠ II no. 171 the soul rejoices at that which she hears; pl. **ʿudnia ḏ-ṣaitia qala ḏ-hiia** DC 41. 487 ears which hear the voice of Life; **qala ḏ-hiia ṣaitia** Gy 1:19. Part. pres. with encl. **baiit ṣaitatlun** DC 48. 268 thou wantest to listen to them.

AF. Pt. pl. **maṣitḫ minilia** Gs 30:ult. they listen to words. Inf. **maṣutia** Gy 16:15, 41:10 giving ear.

Gl. 25:5 f. (missp. with s) استجاب *exaudire* اجابت كرد; 88:6 f. id. سمع *sentire, audire* شنيد.

DER.: **ṣauta 3.**

ṣuta 1 DC 34. 689 = **ṣauta 2.**

ṣuta 2 for **ṣauta 4**?. **rgaz arba razia usliq bṣuta ḏ-nišimta ḏ-iatbia** DC 34. 680 the four mysteries were wroth, and rose in obedience to the soul, for they were sitting.

ṢṬA = SṬA.

PE. Impf. **niṣṭia** Gy 369:14 let him go astray.

AF. Part. pres. **maṣṭitun** Gy 355:7 ye seduce MG 45:8, 263:1. Inf. with suff. **aṣṭuian** Gs 14:13 to lead me astray MG 292:12. Nom. ag. **maṣṭiana** Jb 59:3 seducer, fem. **maṣṭanita** Jb 207:10 seductress.

ṣṭaruan DC 22. 374 = **aṣṭaruan** Gy 377:21.

ṣṭartia = **ʿṣṭartia** MG 45:ult. **atiuia lhaua ṣṭartia** Jb 235:14 they brought Eve the Little Jb ii 217 n. 6.

ṢṬM (cf. **SDM** & **SSṬM**) to close in, restrain, stop up, bar.

PE. Pass. pt. **ʿsir uʿṣṭim** DC 43 I 48 bound and barred; pl. **gmiṭia uʿṣṭimia** DC 26. 347 fettered and barred. Pass. part. pres. **ʿṣṭimit upkirit uhtimit** DC 43 I 59 thou art barred in and fettered and sealed in.

ṢṬR (refl. of **ZṬR**, cf. s. **zuṭa**, fem. **(ʿ)ṣṭartia**) to become little.

ETHPE. Pf. **ʿṣṭar** Gy 165:16 he became little MG 46:2 & n. 1.

DER.: **(ʿ)ṣṭartia.**

ṣiara (cf. s. **ṣairia**) dizziness, injured brain or eye-sockets? Var. **ṣiria** s.v. **napṣia ḏ-brišia ubṣiaria** DC 46 discharges that are in his head and in his injured brain (?).

ṣiba (צְבְעָא, ܨܶܒܥܳܐ, H. צֶבַע) dyed or coloured material MG 140:3. Pl. **ṣibia 1. mania ḏ-ṣiba** Gy 229:11, Jb 82:8 dyed garments; **kitun ṣiba** Gy 56:11 dyed tunic; **ṣiba uṣibuta** Jb 96:12, 100:5, 9, 130:10 f., 250:5 dyed stuff and dyeing.

ṣibat = **ṣiuat** *2* st. cstr. of **ṣauta** *2.* **iatbia bṣiuat hdadia** DC 35 they sit in one another's company.

ṣibunia pl. (diminutive from **ṣiba,** cf. צִבְעוֹנָא, ܨܶܒܥܽܘܢܶܐ) dyes, dyed stuffs or materials MG 140:2. **ṣilmia uṣibunia** Gy 228:25 (cf. 229:8) images and dyed stuffs; **ḏ-agrḫ uzidqḫ ḏ-iauar lṣibunia nitin** Gy 229:2 who giveth wages and alms (ordered) by Yawar for dyed stuffs; **kul man ḏ-nitib ʿl ṣibunia** Gy 229:7 whosoever sitteth on dyed stuffs; **trisar ṣibunia ḏ-mn hšuka titaia npaq** Gy 377:9 f. the twelve dyes that issued from the Lower Darkness; **ḏ-bgauaihun ḏ-hanatḫ ṣibunia miṣṭba** Gy 377:11 which is dipped in those dyes.

ṣib(u)ṣia AM 233:4 a var. of **ṣibunia** Par. AM Doubtf.

ṣibuta (ܨܶܒܥܽܘܬܳܐ, Akk. *ṣibutu*) dyeing, colouring. V.s. **ṣiba.**

ṣibia 1 pl. of **ṣiba.**

ṣibia 2 pl. (cf. Syr. [ܦܣܝܬܐ] ܨܶܒܚܶܐ slices [of flesh], Talm. צִיבְחַד, mistakenly צִבְחַר Levy: *Wörterbuch* iv. 163 a bit MG 117:14 ff., cf. also צִיבָא twig) orig. slices, chips, or (dry?) twigs, used with the meaning of fuel, firewood. **ṣibia ḏ-atunia** Jb 97:11 fuel for an oven; **raza ḏ-nura had minaihun ḏ-akla ṣibia** ATŠ II no. 61, 248 the mystery of fire: one of them that consumes fuel; **ubṣibia d-arzia nišidiḫ** DC 44. 1008 (var. **bnura ḏ-arza** Morg. 262/16:4) and into the fire(wood) of cedars we will throw him; **ṣibia ḏ-mn ʿlania ḏ-mušk** DC 41. 168 firewood from mulberry trees.

Gl. 35:2 (missp. as **ṣʿpai**) اسعف *rami palmae* شاخ درخت.

ṣibia 3 pl. (cf. Syr. ܨܒܐ to congregate) communicants? **damia lṣibia ḏ-aklia lzidqai** CP 379:1, DC 3 = ZDMG CV 149a:1 those who eat my Oblation are like communicants (?) (the reference is derogatory?).

ṣibiana (cf. ܨܶܒܥܽܘܢܶܐ & **ʿṣba 2**) colour, tincture. Var. **ṣubiana 2. ṣibiana** (var. **ṣubiana** AC) **ḏ-nhura** Jb 243:1 tincture of light.

ṣibita = ṣbita (v.s. ṣbata): **ṣibita rišaita** ATŠ II no. 153 the forefinger.

ṣibṣia s. ṣibuṣia.

ṣida (Jew.-Aram. צִדָּא, Targ. צִיד, Bibl.-Aram. & H. צַד, Syr. ܨܶܐܕ) side. Var. ṣada. Pl. **-ia 2.** Fem. MG 157:antep. **tartin ṣidia** (varr. **ṣidh, ṣadia**) **d-mana** Q 3:16, 28:21 the two sides of the *māna*.

ṣidia 1 = ṣadia 1: **daura kulh bṣidia iatib** Gs 11:12 the whole abode is situated in the wilderness; **alma kulh aqimtunh bṣidia** Gs 18:10 thou (lit. ye: Life, pl.) didst place the whole world in the wilderness; **kulhun bṣidia iatbia** Gs 65:12 all of them dwell in the wilderness.

ṣidia 2 pl. of ṣida (q.v.).

ṣihua 1 (Eg.-Aram. צהוה, Syr. ܨܗܘܐ) = ṣihia. **mn ṣihua maiit** AM 149:15 (var. ṣihia Par. xxvi) he will die of thirst.

ṣihua 2 (צְוַחְתָּא, ܨܘܚܬܐ, H. צְוָחָה) outcry, revilement MG 66:19, 102:15. Var. ṣahua? s.v. Masc. **ṣihua biša** Q 14:16 = ML 39:7 = CP 33:14, Gy 287:5 wicked outcry; **ṣihua uluṭata** AM 51:17 revilement and cursing; **ṣihua sagia balma nizal** AM much outcry will go about in the world.

ṣihia (צַחְיָא, ܨܗܝܐ) thirst MG 101:7. Var. ṣihua 1 s.v. **maita mn ṣihia** Gy 302:6 f. they (: the souls) die of thirst; **bkupnaihun uṣihiaihun** ATŠ I no. 237 in their hunger and thirst.

ṣihiun 1 in **bit ṣihiun** Gy 180:21 and **bṣihiun** DC 7 (Targ. בֵּי צחוונא, Syr. ܒܝܬ ܨܗܘܢܐ both Deut. 8:15) place of dryness MG 140:5, MG 304:1 f.

ṣihiun 2 (ܨܗܝܘܢ, H. צִיּוֹן) Zion. Fem. **ṣihiun rabtia** Oxf. 43 b = ML 215:1 = CP 176:9 f. great Zion.

ṣihiun 3 ('they–thirsted–for–me') name of an uthra. **ṣihiun upaqdun ukanpun** ʿ**utria** Q 60:16 = ML 145:2 = CP 119:11.

ṣihla DC 6:coloph. name of a village.

ṣihma (ṢHM, ܨܗܡܐ) shining, glimmer, light, splendour, glory MG 102:16, Jb ii 27 n. 2. **hizih lṣihma d-hah**ʿ **arqa** Gy 281:8 he beheld the splendour of that earth; **tuqna lsira uṣihma lkukbia** Gy 33:2 f., 23 f. shining to the moon, glittering to the stars; **lahazilh nunia lṣihmak** Jb 154:3 the fish do not behold thy shining; **iahbit . . . ṣihma u**ʿ**qara lsabria** Or. 332:26 thou bestowest . . . glory and honour on the believing.

ṣihmai (rt. ṢHM Ginzā 343 n. 2) (*a*) **ṣihmai aina** Oxf. 98 a = ML 265:8 = DC 3 & CP 357:9, DC 50. 722 name of a well-spring (a heavenly being?) ML 283; (*b*) **ṣihmai** ʿ**uṣṭuna** Gy 333:13 one of the seven pillars of Jerusalem MSt 98.

ṣiuan occ. for **siuan.**

ṣiuat 1, 2 occ. for ṣauat 1, 2: **d-bṣiuat hdadia nitbun** Gy 304:3 f. so that they sit in mutual light.

ṣiṭra = **siṭra** (q.v.) MG 45:14.

ṣikun DC 43 name of a lilith.

ṣilaiit (rt. **ṢLA I**) adv. attentively MG 201:8 ff. **bṣilaiit uzahruta** CP 94:20 attentively and with care; **ṣilaiit** Q 39:31, **bṣilaiit** Q 46:20 attentively; **bzahraiit uṣilaiit** (var. **uṣalaiit**) **umalpanaiit** Q 39:31 carefully, attentively, and skilfully; **nihaiit uṣilaiit** Oxf. roll f 328, **bnihaiit uṣilaiit** Lond. roll A 90, **bṣilaiit unihaiit** ibid. 311 softly and attentively (& vice versa); **bṣilaiit umalpanaiit** ATŠ II no. 412 carefully and studiously.

ṣilupta DC 23. 769 = **ṣlupta.**

ṣiluta (cf. preced.) attention MG 201:10. **bzahruta uṣiluta** Q 18:30, **bṣiluta uzahruta** ATŠ II no. 180 (var. **bṣilta** DC 6) with care and attention (& vice versa); **bṣiluta qria** ATŠ II no. 217 read with attention.

ṣilita = ṣalahiata 2 (q.v.). **kiba d-riša uṣilita** DC 46. 137:12 headache and megrim; **psaaq d-ṣilita** JRAS 1943 171:15 removal of megrim.

ṣilma (צַלְמָא, ܨܠܡܐ, also fem. ܨܠܡܬܐ, Palm. צלמתא, South Ar. 𐩮𐩡𐩣, fem. 𐩮𐩡𐩣𐩩, Ar. صَنَم Fränkel 273, H. צֶלֶם Nöld. ZDMG xl 733 f., ZA xxi 384, Akk. *ṣalmu* KAT 475, Delitzsch: *Prolegomena* 141, Lewy: *Fremdwörter* 107) image, idol, picture, shape, form MG 100:paen. Var. ṣalma s.v. Pl. **ṣal(a)mata** (s.v.) & **ṣilmia,** the latter often with the meaning of Gemini (Zodiac, cf. Syr. ܬܐܘܡܐ ܨܠܡܐ) Nöld. ZDMG xxv 256 ff., MMII 74, Siouffi 145. **ṣilmia uṣurata** Gy 177:5 pictures and portrayals; **ṣilmia umanzia** Gy 202:5 his shape and his hair; **ṣaiar ṣilmia** Gy 370:8 s. **ṣaiara; bṣilmia d-dahba** Gy 24:19 in golden images; **ṣilmia d-zipa ṣairia** RD C 10 they make false images; **mhamblia ṣilmia d-akuatun** Gy 181:21 they destroy their exact likeness; **kulhun ṣilmia d-hauin lianqa bkras** ʿ**mh** Gy 224:20 f. all the shapes that the child takes in its mother's womb. As Gemini: Gy 122:19, 123:16, 386:9, Lond. roll B 63, Oxf. roll f 1215, very often in AM.

ṣilpa (rt. **ṢLP**) (*a*) whip, blow, stroke, (*b*) reed-pen fig. writing, penmanship. Pl. **-ia.** (*a*) **ṣilpa d-harašia** Lond. roll B 82 = DC 12:37 & P.A. xii par. the whip [spell, or see (*b*)] of wizards; ʿ**siria . . . mn ṣilpia d-iuzaṭaq manda d-hiia uap mn ṣilpai dilia** DC 43 H 6 they . . . are bound by (means of) the blows of Y. M.–d–H. and also by my own blow; (*b*) **aith magalta uṣilpa ukdub** HG 117 bring parchment and reed-pen; **ṣilpia umagalta** Lond. roll B 157 = DC 12. 76 & P.A. xii par. reed-pens and parchment; **marauata d-ṣilpa uktaba** AM masters of penmanship and writing; **alpainun ldirdqia ṣilpa** Jb 140:3 teach the little ones writing (misunderstood and miscorrected by Lidzb. to **unilpun** ii 136 n. 1).

ṣilta in DC 6, ATŠ II no. 180 for **ṣiluta.**

ṣiman name of a spirit. **bšuma . . . ṣiman rba** DC 40 in the name . . . of the great Ṣ.

ṣimarta, ṣimirta 1 = ṣamirta 1. ʿ**šata ṣimarta** AM 88:6 a high (hot) fever; **ṣimirta banašia tihuia** AM 215:11 there will be fever amongst people.

ṣimirta 2 = ṣamarta 1. **ṣimirta lhanẖ** DC 51. 84 strangury on his privy parts; **ruha . . . ḏ-iatba lhana umitqiria ṣimirta** Oxf. roll g 841 = Or. 330:7 a spirit . . . situate on the privy parts and called strangury.

ṣimra 1 (rt. ṢMR I, צִימְרָא) fever. Var. ṣirma s.v. **kib ḏ-ṣimra mahu** DC 46. 205:13 what is (: causes) the illness of fever?

ṣimra 2 (rel. to preced.?) poison. **kḏ arqba bṣimra** DC 40. 485 like a scorpion with poison; **ulbadušnam ṣimra lgaṭṭẖ** DC 23. 586 I have got poison for B. (a devil).

ṣimra 3 apparently a kind of fish. **kḏ ṭabia bqula . . . ukḏ ṣimra bliha** DC 40 like a gazelle in a trap . . . and like a *ṣimra* in a net.

ṣin (Ar. صين) AM 205 China.

ṣinba (cf. زنجي < P. زنبق narcissus?, or miswriting for ṣin(u)bar?) some plant or tree. Masc. **ṣinba hu** DC 41 (picture).

ṣinbar = ṣinubar. **ṣinbar hu** DC 41 (picture) it is a pine-tree.

ṣinga (P. چنگ) claw. Pl. **-ia. udita bṣingẖ** s. dita.

ṣinda (ܙܘܢܕܐ Löw 383:middle, PSm 3420) (*a*) seed, grain, pip, (*b*) shred, fibre, rootlet, (*c*) fennel, dill, anise Jb ii 154 n. 6. Mod. (pron.) *ṣonda* grain. Pl. **-ia.** (*a*) **ṣindia ḏ-rumana** AM 92:6, Oxf. roll f 157, 505, 832 pomegranate seeds; **ṣinda ḏ-hardla** ATŠ I no. 278 a mustard seed; **šuba ṣindia ḏ-hurpa** s. hurpa 1; **šaba ṣindia hiuaria** Par. xxvi 107: bottom, seven white grains; **ṣinda** (var. **ṣandia** DC 6) **ubazira bgauaihun laiit** ATŠ I no. 285 there is no pip or seed in them; (*b*) **mia mzigia ḏ-ṣindia** Jb 156:7 water is mingled with rootlets (fibres, Lidzb. (*c*)); (*c*) **ṣinda msaraita lamarhia** Jb 151:12 they smell no stinking fennel.

Gl. 70:10 (missp. as **snda**) حنة *granus* دانه.

ṣin(u)bar (Ar. صَنَوْبَر) pine-tree, fir-tree. **hazin ʿlana ḏ-ṣinubar hu** DC 7 (illustration) this is a pine-tree; **bmasik ṣinubar** s. **masik**; s. **ṣinbar hu** DC 41 (illustration).

ṣinia (adj. from ṣin) Chinese. **masqal ṣinia** ML x 16 Chinese satin.

ṣinta apparently name of a plant, cf. s. **ṣatra 1.**

ṣipar 1 st. abs. & cstr. of **ṣipra 1** (q.v.).

ṣipar 2 = **spar 2. briš ṣipar ḏ-iama** (read iuma) DC 51. 113 early at dawn of day.

ṣipra 1 (Jew.-Aram. & Bibl.-Aram. צְפַר like Mand. st. abs., Eg.-Aram. צנפר, Syr. ܨܶܦܪܳܐ, abs. & cstr. ܨܶܦܰܪ, H. צִפּוֹר, Ar. عُصْفُور, Akk. *iṣṣuru* bird, but *ṣapāru* to twitter) little bird, sparrow. St. abs. & cstr. **ṣipar 1** MG 119:ult. (& n. 5), var. **ṣapir** Gy 216:3. Us. masc., cf. Gs 13:ult., 15:11, but fem. Gs 15:12, MG 157:1 f. Pl. **-ia. ṣipra ṣipar haiuta** Gy 216:3 a bird, a bird-animal; **kḏ ṣipra ḏ-laqna qina** Gs 13:24 like a bird that built no nest; **ṣipria mn pagrai ladahlia** Gs 15:11 birds are not afraid of my body; **ṣipria larahṭa** Gs 15:12 birds do not run away (as fem.); **ṣipria hurbia** Gs 129: 6 f. little birds of carob-trees (**hurba 3**); **ṣipar gadpa** Jb 82:13, DC 43 C 26, ATŠ I no. 4, II no. 310 (*& often*) winged birds, fowl (collective).

ṣipra 2 (צַפְרָא, ܨܦܪܐ) dawn, early morning MG 14:18. St. abs. **spar 2** (q.v.) = **ʿ(u)spar. ṣipra liardna lanasgia** Oxf. 109 a = ML 274 = CP 364:17 early in the morning he goeth not to the jordan; **ṣipra ata** Gy 189:9 come early in the morning; **ṣipra hua** Gy 190:9 there was morning; **pirša ḏ-ṣipra** Lond. roll A 489 daybreak; **ṭulalia ḏ-ṣipra** Gy 207:12 morning shades; **alma lṣipra mitapa** AM 113:ult. till the morning he will be healed. Fig. **hašta nihuia ṣipra** DC 48. 160 now there shall be enlightenment.

ṣiprurita (cf. ṣipra 1) DC 46. 63:3 small bird.

ṣiṣ (cf. ṣuṣ) to come forth, shine.

Pe. Pass. pt. with encl. **iaqdaikun ḏ-ṣiṣlia** DC 46. 136:4, JRAS 1943 171:5 your flame that comes out at me.

ṣiṣa 1 (= ṣaṣa 1) = **ṣahna.** Pl. **ṣiṣia 1. ṣiṣia uzapria** DC 22. 274 = **ṣahnia uzapuria** Gy 279:9.

ṣiṣa 2 (= ṣaṣa 2) = **aṣaṣa.** Pl. **ṣiṣia 2. ṣiṣia** DC 22. 416 = **aṣaṣia** Gs 26:14.

ṣiṣia 1 pl. (Ar. صيص dates of bad quality? Löw 114, Jb ii 155 n. 1) (*a*) bad dates, (*b*) filthy things? (influenced by 1?). (*a*) **ʿkilta ḏ-ṣiṣia** Jb 151:13 food of dates of bad quality; **ṣiṣia ʿkulia** Jb 155:12 bad dates (as) baits; **kulab ṣiṣia** Jb 157:8 fishing-hook of (with) bad dates; (*b*) **gubria tangaria bṣiṣia** DC 51 men who traffic with filthy things (or (*a*)?).

ṣiṣia 2 pl.? (rt. ṢUṢ) brightness, rays. **alma lziua ḏ-šamiš nihzia uṣiṣia** DC 45 until he sees the light of the sun and its shining.

ṣiṣlia 1 (found only in) pl. (Syr. ܨܶܨܠܶܐ cymbals, twitter, Jew.-Aram. צִלְצְלָא, Ar. صَلْصَلَة) any kind of continuous noise, buzzing, cracking, humming. **ruha hʿ ḏ-iatba lʿudnia umitqiria ṣiṣlia** Oxf. roll g 711, Or. 328 (wrongly transliterated **niṣlia**) a spirit that dwells in the ears and is called 'buzzing'.

ṣiṣlia 2 (found only in pl.) (צוּצְלָא & צוּלְצְלָא, ܨܘܨܠܐ, Ar. صُلْصُل Nöld.: *Beiträge* 11) small doves. **ʿhab ṣiṣlia lṣaida** DC 51 332 f. he delivered the little doves to the fowler; **tišiqlun ṣiṣlia mn ṣaida** DC 51 remove the small doves from the fowler.

ṣiqar (Ar. صقار) DC 40. 548 date-syrup.

ṣirapa(ia) = ṣarapa(ia). Pl. **-aiia. iaquta ḏ-bahrilẖ ṣirapaiia** ATŠ I no. 90 a ruby which jewellers select; **iaquta ḏ-mitbihrẖ sadan ṣirapaiia** ATŠ II no. 365 a ruby selected on the jeweller's block.

ṣirba (P. سُرْب) lead. **ḏ-glala uḏ-ṣirba uḏ-parzla** Oxf. roll 162 of stone, lead, and iron; **glala uṣirba** DC 43 J 75 stone and lead.

ṣiria Or. 327:28 = **ṣiara.**

ṣirma = ṣimra 1: **ništartab ṣirma** DC 40. 1027 f. the fever will be solaced.

ṣita 1 (rt. SHA I) heat MG 63:3, 104:6. **ṣita**

d̲-iuma Gy 212:10 the heat of the day; **hazin baba ṣita d̲-kiba d̲-riša** DC 46. 134:6 this spell is for sunstroke that is headache.

ṣita 2 JRAS 1937 592 a miscop. of **ṣatra 1.**

ṢLA I (Gen. Aram.) to bend down, turn, incline, decline, swerve, deviate, diverge; pa. to pray, but also to pervert.

Pe. Pf. **mn ʿuhra d̲-hiia ṣla** ATŠ II no. 218 he turned aside from the Road of Life; **ṣlit mn ʿuhra d̲-hiia** DC 34. 547 thou didst turn aside from the Road of Life; **mn ʿuhra d̲-hiia laṣlun** ATŠ I no. 25 they did not turn aside from the Way of Life. Impf. **mn dirkak laniṣlia** Gy 62:21 let us not turn aside from Thy Way MG 372:3; **latiṣlun minh̲ mn miṣra** CP 128:15 = Q 65:13 = ML 156:2 do not deviate from the boundary. Impt. (fem.) **ṣ(u)lai daiuik** DC 43 I 38 turn away thy (fem.) demon. Act. pt. **zibna ṣalia ʿniš** Gy 22:20, 43:22 if a person goeth astray once; **trin zibnia ṣalia** Gy 22:20 f., 43:24 if he goeth astray twice; **mn miṣra ṣalia** CP 128:16, Q 65:13 he deviated from the boundary; **d̲-ṣalia minh̲ mn kudka** Jb 59:2 that he may go astray from the boundary stone; pl. **mn ʿuhran laṣalin** DC 34. 355 they do not swerve from our way; with encl. **ṣalilin lzabaniatun** Jb 85:9 f. they pervert (Lidzb. *machen trügerisch*) their scales. Pass. pt. **ṣlia** (var. **ṣlʿia** DC 30) **dukth̲ mn atar nhur** Jb 277:8 his position (attitude) is averted (aversion to) from the Place of Light, **sin ṣlia lhda qarna** AM 223:8 the moon leans on one horn (inclines to one side).

Pa. Impf. **tiṣalia lalahia** AM 66:20 she prays to gods. Pt. **apkia dina umṣalia dina** Gs 36:23 they reverse justice and pervert justice; **mṣalin** Gy 47:8 (*& often*) they pray; with encl. **ṣ(a)luta d̲-kadba mṣalilun** Gy 24:8 they pray a false prayer. Part. pres. **miaka iuma d̲-atina ulamṣalina bkništaikun** Jb 72:5 is there a day on which I come and do not pray in your synagogue(s)?

Der.: **ṣ(a)luta, ṣilaiit** (var. **ṣalaiit**), **ṣiluta** (var. **ṣilta**).

ṢLA II s. **ṢLL II.**

ṢLB (צְלַב, ܨܠܒ > Ar. صلب, Eth. ተጸለበ) to set up a cross, make a cross or stake, make sign of a cross; to crucify.

Pe. Act. pt. **ṣaliba biardna ṣalba**, pl. **ṣalibia. ṣalbia** s. **ṣaliba.**

Ethpe. Impf. **niṣlib** (s. **ṣaliba**) MG 214:12.

Der.: **ṣaliba.**

ṢLH the rt. of **ṣalahiata 1, 2.**

ṣluniata s. **aṣlunta.**

ṣlupta (rt. **ṢLP**) fragment, broken piece, (egg)-shell? Var. **ṣi-** s.v. **tlata ṣlupth̲ d̲-qina** DC 46. 209:14 three (egg)-shells (?) from a nest.

ṣluta = **ṣaluta** MG 111 n. 2, 146 n. 4.

ṣlipa (pass. pt. pe. of **ṢLP**) (*a*) damaged. injured, bruised, beaten, (*b*) (cf. Akk. *ṣalāpu* Muss-Arn. 879b) deceptive, false Jb ii 147 n. 2. (*a*) **glima uṣlipa** AO ix 101ab:20 encompassed and whipped (Gordon) (bent and bruised); (*b*) **mtangrit bmuzaniak ṣlipa** Jb 146:2 thou dost trade with thy false (Lidzb. *trügerischen*) scales.

ṢLL I (צלל, ܨܠ II, H. צלל II, Ar. صَلَّ to filter, cleanse, Eth. ጸለለ to float, swim, Amh. አጥለለ to filter, but Akk. *ṣalālu* to lie down) to be light, clear; to shine.

Ethpa. Pf. with encl. **drabšia mšaria ʿṣṭalalbh̲** DC 3. 342:7 = CP 347:ult. (var. **ʿṣalalbh̲** Lond. roll A 41) the newly consecrated banners are purified (?) therein (par. with **drabšia bziua nhar**). **ainaniata ʿṣṭalalbh̲** DC 34.

ṢLL II, ṢUL, ṢLA II (cf. Ar. سَلِيلَة a handful of wool put on the distaff = mod. Mand. *ṣeleylā*) to weave, twist.

Pe. Impf. **niṣilun qulalia** Gy 361:16 BCD (varr. **nihuilun, niṣlun** Sh. ʿAbd.'s copy) some of them lay snares Ginzā 382 n. 4.

Der.: **ṣaila.**

ṢLP (ܨܠܦ, Jew.-Aram. אַצְלֵיף & mod. H. הִצְלִיף to swing a whip; to strike) to bruise, injure, whip, beat, wound, flog.

Pe. Pass. pt. **ṣlip** (**umṣalap**) s. pa., **ṣlipa** s.v.

Pa. Pf. with suff. **ṣalpinun** DC 44. 1897 = Morg. 269/29:8 he flogged them. Act. pt. with encl. **mṣalpilun** RD C 13, DC 51. 91:240 they injure them. Pass. pt. (**ṣlip**) **umṣalap** DC 44. 1909 = Morg. 269/29:17 (beaten) and bruised.

Gl. (always missp. with s) 64:3 f. خزى *erubescere* شرمنده شد; 103:11 f. صرر *stridere* دندان می مالد بهم; 115:7 f. عوّج *pervertere* كج كرد ; 150:15 مال *reclinare* أفتاد; 167:3 f. نحنا [sic] *incurvari* كج شد ; 170:15 f. هزى *erubescere* شرمنده شد.

Der.: **ṣilpa, ṣ(i)lupta, ṣlipa.**

ṢMA a more orig. form of **ṢHM** (q.v.) to appear, shine out.

Pe.? Pf. **atar uṣma** DC 34. 66 awoke and shone forth.

Af. Pt. **sira d̲-maṣma blilia** Gy 287:9 the moon that shineth at night; pl. **kukbia d̲- . . . bgauh̲ maṣmia** Gy 267:4 stars that . . . shine in it; with encl. **maṣmibh̲** Gy 273:5 they shine therein.

Der.: s. **ṢHM. ṣmata.**

ṣmad (rt. **ṢMD**) fastening, clamp. **ṣmad atutia lišanun** DC 45 a clamp beneath their tongues.

ṣmara 1 (rt. **ṢMR I**) AM 282:31 fever.

(**ṣmara 2** Gl. 43:3 برفير *purpura* رخت پادشاه).

ṣmata = **aṣmata.** radiance, illumination. **malka rba bmdiniata ṣmata tihuilia** AM 213:20 the Great King will have illuminations (fireworks) in the cities.

ṢMD (Aram. & H. צמד, Syr. ܨܡܕ, Akk. *ṣamādu* Zimmern: *Akk. Fremdwörter* 42, Ar. ضمد to conjoin, Eth. ፀመደ) to fasten, bind, join, harness, couple.

Pe. Act. pt. **man ṣamid padana tauria** Gs 10:21 f. who will yoke the oxen to the plough?; pl. **d̲-minai ṣamdia** ŠQ 15:3 which they join to me.

Der.: **ṣamadta, ṣmad.**

ṣmirta (cf. **ṣamarta 1, ṣamirta 1, ṣimarta, ṣimirta 1, 2**) fever, or strangury? **bkapta**

d-šurh̲ ṣimirta hauilh̲ AM 22:5 he will have strangury (or inflammation?) in the cavity of his navel.

ṢMR I (Aram. צמר, H. צרב, Akk. *ṣarābu*, Ar. صرم Barth ES 32, WU 41) to heat, burn, inflame, be hot, inflamed, fevered, red.

Pe. Pf. **rišia ṣmar** JRAS 1937 590:20 his head became hot. Act. pt. **aina d̲-ṣamar** AM 287 (read with var. **ṣamra**) eye that is inflamed; **qahda uṣamra** DC 43 F 60 she screams and gets hot; **hᶜ d̲-ṣamra urmᶜia ruha** DAb she that enflames and sways the (earthly) spirit.

Pa. Pt. (pass.) **mṣamar** AM 287:26 heated; (act.) with encl. **ᶜšata d̲-mṣamralh̲** DC 40. 988 the fever that makes him hot.

Ethpe. Impf. **nišimria** AM 209:8 they will be fever-stricken (?, with part. pl. ending).

Der.: **ṣamirta 1, ṣam(b)ra, ṣamura, ṣimarta, ṣimirta 1, ṣimra 1** (2?), var. **ṣirma, ṣmara** (1, 2).

ṢMR II (ܨܡܪ to have retention of urine, Ar. صمر to be stingy, to flow slowly) to hold back, press back, press down, repress, crush down; to turn Jb ii 159 n. 8. (Ethpa: cf. אִסְטַמַּר, to take heed, beware.)

Pe. Pf. with suff. **ṣimruih̲** DC 43 I 103 they repressed him. Act. pt. **daiuia d̲-ṣabia ṣamar** Gy 280:12 he turneth whichever demons he wisheth; **ṣmar anat daiua** DC 43 I 104 Impt. avaunt, thou demon!; **bšragia d̲-kadba laṣamria** Jb 157:9 f. they do not turn towards deceitful lanterns; with encl. **pugdamia d̲-ṣamrilak** DC 43 I 102 words which force thee back.

Pa. Impt. with suff. **ṣamrh̲ bmia d̲-rumana** AM 287:20 crush it into pomegranate juice. Pass. pt. **mṣamar bhalba** AM 287 crushed (squeezed) into milk.

Ethpa. Pf. **ᶜṣṭamar uᶜstar laṭaba** DC 43 I 121 the good-for-nought is suppressed and confined. Impf. **ᶜu lilita hᶜ tiṣṭamr kd̲ hiuia** DC 26. 39 if she be a lilith, she shall be turned away (or crushed down?) like a snake. Impt. **zha uᶜṣṭamar daiua** DC 43 I 100 be off, beware, demon! Pt. **miṣṭamar kd̲ hiuia** DC 43 J 208 he shall be crushed like a snake.

Der.: **ṣamarta 1 = ṣimirta 2 = ṣmirta.**

ṢNP I (Jew.-Aram. צְנִיפָא shrieking, mod. H. צנף to neigh) to shriek, scream, make a shrill noise.

Pe. Pf. **ᶜstirata ṣnap** DC 44. 1516 = Morg. 266/23:4 the astartes shrieked; **ṣnap uiabib** Gy 282:7 s. **YBB, qra uṣnap** DC 40. 856 he cried out and shrieked; **ṣnap uialil kulhun daiuia** DC 37. 150 all the demons shrieked and howled; **ṣinpat** CP 102:1, Q 52:28 = ML 127:11 she shrieked; **rigzat uṣinpat** DC 44. 476 she was angry and screamed; **qhdit uṣinpit** *Florilegium*, I shouted and screamed; with encl. **ṣnapbh̲ bqalh̲** Jb 157:2 he cried aloud with his voice. Act. pt. **ṣanpa uqahda** DC 43 F 60 she shrieks and screams.

Ethpe. ? Pf. **qrat bqalh̲ uᶜṣinpat** DC 51, CP 102:1 she cried aloud with her voice and screamed.

ṢNP II (H. צנף, cf. Aram. צְנִפָא, Chr.-Pal. ܨܢܝܦܐ, Ar. صِنْف lappet, Syr. ܡܨܢܦܬܐ turban) to turn about, whirl round, roll round; with **mn** turn away.

Pe. Impt. **aqar uṣnap uasqul kariuta mn pagrh̲** Oxf. roll g 597, Or. 326:10 uproot, turn away and remove sadness and misery from his body. Act. pt. pl. **mia ᶜkumia ṣanpia ṣardia** Gy 139:5 black swirling rough waters.

ṢPA I (< ܨܦܐ) to press together, squeeze, fasten with a catch.

Pe. Part. pres. **ṣapana** DC 46. 82:10 (as IIIae gutt.) I fasten (it).

Ethpe. Impf. **niṣpia kd̲ bina** DC 26. 38 f. (as ל״י) he shall be squeezed like a leech.

ṢPA II (Ar. صفى) to (make) clear, clarify, refine.

Pa. Impt. with encl. **ṣapulh̲ hamra** WedF 56:top = ML p. x make the wine clear for him. Pass. pt. (Ar.) **m(u)ṣapa** AM 129 refined, clarified.

ṢPṬ (cf. Syr. ܨܦܕܐ, Ar. صِفَاد fetter, H. צמד to shrink, contract MG 42 f., den. like **SPṬ** q.v.) to fasten.

Ethpe. **miṣṭipṭia** Sh. ᶜAbd.'s copy & DC 22. 453 = **mistipṭia.**

Der.: cf. s. **SPṬ.**

ṢPR (cf. s. **ṣipra 2** & Ar. أصفر yellow) to become dawn; to become light; to enlighten.

Ethpe. Pf. **kd̲ hauia ᶜṣṭipra iuma d̲-habšaba** Lond. roll A 555 when it becomes dawn on Sunday. Pt. **brahmia d̲-miṣṭipra** Gy 221:23 in the morning devotions. See also PNC trsl. p. 66 n. 2.

Der.: **ṣipra 2**, abs. **ṣpar** & varr., **ᶜṣṭipra.**

ṢPT (Jew.-Aram. & mod. H. צבת, cf. **ṢBT**, Syr. ܨܦܬ) to join, set in order, connect, associate with; pa. to adorn, beautify.

Pe. Pf. with encl. **šataputa laṣpatlh̲** AM 23:6 (var. **laṣpitlh̲** pass. pt.) he forms no partnership. Act. pt. with encl. **šatapa laṣapitlh̲** AM he joins no partnership. Pass. pt. with encl. **madna uqmaha d̲-ṣpitlh̲** AM the horoscope and the talisman associated with it (cf. s. pf.).

Pa. Impf. **niṣapit** Gy 218:10 (var. **niṣapat** CD ethpa.) he adorneth himself MG 48:17. Pass. pt. **mṣapat** Gy 216. 21 adorned MG 48:18.

Ethpa. Impf. **niṣapat** cf. s. pa.

Der.: **ṣauta 1, 2.**

ṢṢṬM = SSṬM. Pass. pt. pl. **mṣaṣṭmia** s. **ṣuṣṭ(a)mia.**

ṢRA I (**ṢRR II** s.v.) (Gen. Aram., Ar. صَرَى to cut off) to tear, cleave, split, rend asunder; with **agia** to plough, Gy 102:5 doubtf.; of meteors and stars (cf. Akk. *ṣarāru*) to fly (apart), tear about, break through Jb ii 76 n. 4; of tears: to burst (Lidzb. *sich zusammenziehen*) Jb ii 110 n. 1.

Pe. Pf. **kitunun . . . ṣrun** Gs 53:15 they tore their tunics . . .; with encl. **kukba ṣrabh̲** Jb 67:9 f. [*bis*] a star cleft its way (flew) therein; **dimihta ṣralh̲ bainh̲** Jb 110:6 f. D (var. **ṣarlh̲** B,

ṣaralẖ AC) he (his eyes) burst into tears (lit. by Lidzb. *eine Träne zog sich ihm im Auge zusammen.*) Impf. **lbušiẖ . . . niṣria** Gy 19:8 teareth his garment; **lbuša ʿlai niṣria** Gs 98:19 teareth his garment because of me; **kukba bil mn šamiš niṣria** Gy 385:11 the star Jupiter shall cleave its way from the sun; **niṣria mn nuna lʿmbra** AM it cleaves its way from Pisces to Aries; **niṣria agia bṭuria** RD B 50 ff. = DAb par. he shall plough furrows in the hills; **niṣrun unipqun minẖ šuba ʿuṣria** ML 37:6 seven treasures will break through and come out of him; with encl. **niṣribẖ agia** Gy 102:5 doubtf. Ginzā 109 n. 6. Act. pt. **man ḏ-himiana ṣaria** DC 36 no. 252 who tears (loosens) the girdle; with encl. **dimihta ṣaralẖ bainẖ** Gy 306:21, Jb 110:6 f. AC (s. pf.); pl. **kukbia ṣaria** Gy 392:11, 23 stars (meteors) tear about (: fly); **kukbia ḏ-ṣarin** AM 231:13, 275:1 (*& often*); **ʿṣṭla bṣaura ṣarin** Gs 83:13 they tear the garment on their neck; **bisraiun ṣarin** Gy 28:13 they tear their flesh; **gišumaiun ṣarin** Gy 59:22 they tear their bodies. Part. pres. **ṣarit zimta** Gy 194:2 thou splittest a hair.

Ethpe. Pt. **miṣṭra** Gy 391:24 shall be torn to pieces.

Ethpa. Pt. pl. **markabata miṣṭaria** DC 26 the chariots are torn down.

ṢRA II = ṢRR I.

Ethpa. Pf. **agia ḏ-nhura ʿṣṭria** Lond. roll A 380 beams of light were formed. Pt. (pl.) **drabšaihun akuat hdadia miṣṭria** ATŠ their banners are made like each other.

ṢRA III, ṢRH s.v., **ṢRK I** (< Gen. Sem. צרח, ܨܪܚ, صرخ) to squeak.

Pe. Impf. **niṣra** AM 254:15 it squeaks.

ṣraiil DC 44. 626 = (ʿ)sraiil.

ṣraria pl. (rt. **ṢRR II**, צְרָרָא, ܨܪܪܐ) money-bags, purses. **kaspa bṣraria ṣrir** WedF 37: middle = DC 3. 377:11 = DC 38. 15:20 = DC 53. 223:8 f. silver is tied in money-bags.

ṢRD (cf. צַרְדָּא torpidity) to blight, shrivel, contract; (of water) to have a rough surface.

Pe. Pt. **baina ṣarda** DC 43 E 8, DC 49. 23 with a blighting (evil) eye; pl. **šahbia ṣardia ḏ-bgauaihun** JRAS 1937 594:3 their leaves are shrivelling; **mia ʿkumia ṣanpia ṣardia** Gy 139:5 black, swirling, rough waters.

ṢRH = (צָרַח) to be afraid.

Pe. Pt. pres. **ṣarhit** JRAS 1937 596:16 thou art afraid.

ṣrurgia P.A's copy of Or. constipation s. **srungia.**

ṣruriata s. ṣ(u)rurita.

ṣrik 1 s. ṣ(u)rik (*a*).

ṣrik 2 (rt. **ṢRK II**) Gy 335:2 poor, needy, humble MG 150 n. 3, Ginzā 236 n. 1.

ṢRK I (Gen. Sem. צרח, ܨܪܚ, صرخ, Mand. doublets **ṢRA III** & **ṢRH**) to cry, shout, call out.

Pe. Pf. **ṣrak bqalẖ** CP 40:5, ML 47:1, Gy 363:1 f., DC 34. 80, 358, ATŠ I no. 243 cried aloud with his voice; **ṣrak uašma** Gs 39:16 he cried and let hear; **ṣrak uašman bqalẖ** Gs 96:12 he cried and let me hear (with) his voice.

ṢRK II (Jew.-Aram., Syr., Chr.-Pal., mod. H., Ar. ضرك Brockelm. i 135) to need, want.

Der.: **ṣarka, ṣ(u)rik.**

ṢRP I (Jew.-Aram. צְרַף, Syr. ܙܪܦ I, Akk. *zarābu*) to chastize, afflict, oppress.

Pe. Pf. **ṣrap udauia libẖ** Gy 96:15 f. her heart was afflicted and mournful.

Der.: **ṣurpana.**

ṢRP II (Jew.-Aram., Syr. II, H., Sab., Akk. *ṣurrupu* Zimmern KAT 650, *Akk. Fremdwörter* 27) to smelt, melt, refine.

Der.: **ṣarapa(ia)**, var. **ṣirapa(ia).**

ṢRṢ (specific to Mand. phylacteries) to bind up, fasten up, close up.

Pe. Pt. pres. (act. with pass. mean.!) **sdima ṣarṣit aina ʿkaltia** JRAS 1937 596:17 thou art stopped and closed up, Corroding Eye. Inf. with suff. **šria ḏ-lamṣia ʿniš lmiṣruṣia** DC 40 loosen (or open) so that no one can bind him (or close him up).

ṢRR I = ṢUR I MG 82:bottom. Another secondary rt. **ṢRA II** s.v.

Pe. s. **ṢUR I.**

Pa. Pf. **ṣarar** he formed MG 82:antep., **ṣarar bgauẖ kukbia** Gy 12:16, **ṣarir bgauẖ kukbia** Gy 33:1 he formed stars in it; **anin haka ṣararnia lšuba malkia** DC 34:picture A we have depicted here seven kings; with suff. **kḏ ṣaririnun malka ʿlaia lhalin almia** DC 41. 2 when the Celestial King created these worlds. Impf. with suff. **kulman ḏ-niṣararẖ lhazin alma uniṣararinun lhalin rahaṭia** DC 41. 18 f. he who depicts this world and depicts these streams. Nom. act. **ṣararta 1** s.v.

Ethpa. Pf. **ʿṣṭarar usliq** Gy 168:9 he was formed and ascended; **ʿṣṭarar bgauẖ kukbia** Jb 50:14, Gs 76:9, ML 225:7 stars were formed in it; **mn kanpiẖ ḏ-ziua ʿṣṭarar** Gy 89:1 was formed from the bosom of the radiance; **ʿṣṭarat dmuthẖ** Gy 150:9, 168:8 his likeness was formed; **ṣṭararit uhuit** Gy 336:22 I was formed and came into being; **ʿṣṭararit mn aina usindirka** DC 41. 24 I was formed from the Well and Palm-tree; with encl. **ʿṣṭararbẖ** ML 265:1 were formed by it; **maṣbuta ḏ-hiia ḏ-ʿṣṭararbẖ** Gy 345:22 f. the baptism of Life by which he was (re)formed. Pt. **miṣṭarar ʿula** Jb 4:3, 6:1 the embryo is formed (MG 82:antep.); with encl. **miṣṭararlẖ** Gy 168:5 is formed for him; pl. **miṣṭarararia** Lond. roll A 73, DC 41. 495 they are formed; **miṣṭararin** Gy 10:13 id.

Ettaf. Impf. **nitaṣar** Gy 391:ult. is formed MG 252:9, but Ginzā 418 n. 1.

Der.: **ṣararta 1.**

ṢRR II (Jew.-Aram., Syr., Chr.-Pal., H., Ar., cf. Akk. *ṣirritu* rope) to surround, tie up, encompass, contract. A secondary rt. **ṢUR II** s.v. Certain forms confused with **ṢRA I** and vice versa, cf. Jb ii 110 n. 1.

Pe and Pa. s. **ṢUR II.**

Ethpa. Pf. **ʿṣṭarar bainẖ dimihta** Gy 114:4 his eyes burst into tears; **ainẖ bdimihta**

ʿṣṭarar Gy 166:22 id., **ʿṣṭarar ainik dimihta** Gs 21:19 thy (fem.) eyes burst into tears; **ainai bdimihta ʿṣṭarar** Gy 327:7 my eyes burst into tears (a frequent idiom transl. by Lidzb. *das Auge zog sich in Tränen zusammen*).

Der.: **ṣararta 3**, pl. **ṣraria.**

Q

q the 19th letter of the alphabet. Pronunciation: unvoiced emphatic postpalatal plosive. Phonetic changes: **q** > **g** MG § 41 pp. 38 f.; initial (& medial) **q** > **k** MG § 42 pp. 39 f.; **q** inst. of **ע** *Mundart* 21, MG 72 f., AF 230.

q(a)- (Talm. קא, קאי by dropping the ם of קאים) procl. particle preceding the participial present MG 12:24, 35:16 f., 217:18 ff., 379:1–16 (& n. 1, cf. mod. Syr. ܟܐ).

qaba 1 (Jew.-Aram. כמם, Syr. ܩܡܥܐ, ܩܐܡܥܐ, ܩܡܥܐ, κημός) muzzle MG 17 n. 6, 50:3 f. **qaba bpumh̲ npalh̲** Gy 84:7 a muzzle was placed (lit. fell) on his mouth; **kd̲ qaba lpum susia** DC 44. 949 like a muzzle on the mouth of a horse.

qaba 2 (קַבָּא, ܩܒܐ, H. & mod. H. קַב, κάβος) measure, quantity. Pl. **-ia.** Masc. **qabia rurbia . . . qabia zuṭia** RD C 15, 17 large quantities . . . small quantities.

qabad malka Gy 384:6, 8 a Sassanian king (A.D. 488–531) Öchser ZA xix 77 n. 5.

qabaṭ (قبط??) AM 205 a place-name.

qabal- with suff. (rt. **QBL**, cf. the adv. **mn qbal**) against MG 196:3. **qabalh̲** Gy 83:3 against him.

qabala (cf. preced.) talisman, charm (against), indictment. **mitkidba qabala ʿlh̲** ATŠ II no. 50 a talisman (?) was written upon it; **kdab qabala** DC 35 he wrote an indictment.

qabalta (nom. act. pa. of **QBL**) acceptance, share, portion, lot. **kul had had bqabalta qabluia** Jb 236:3 each of them received a portion; **hauia qabalta d̲-libat** AM 27:16 he will be the portion of Venus (i.e. Venus will be his ruling star).

qabana (Ar. قَبَاء) robe, loose-sleeved gown. **qabana šaduih̲ sqila** ŠQ 18:24 a robe they put (on) him, an elegant one.

qabus DC 40. 994 name of a spirit invoked in exorcism.

qabura (קִיבּוּרָא, ܩܒܘܪܐ LS s.v. no. 2, cf. Levy: *Neuh. Wb.* iv 243a, PSm. 3482) coil, hank of cord. Pl. **-ia.** Jb ii 198 n. 1. **širiata uqaburia** Jb 204:7 chains and hanks of cord; **qabura d̲-taura d̲-susia** DC 46 212:12 a halter of an ox or a halter of a horse (doubtf., cf. Ar قبور footprint, depressed ground where animals lay or trod).

qabuta (ܩܒܘܬܐ, ܩܐܒܘܬܐ, Akk. *qabûtu*, Gr. κιβωτός) Jb 115:10, 12, 15 coffin, chest, box MG 17 n. 6, Jb ii 114 n. 4.

qabil (rt. **QBL**, قِبِيل, ܩܒܝܠ) in front of, facing, (con)fronting. **laziriak . . . pardaspana lqabil pardasia** Or. 325:5 (text) the gardener . . . did not sow thee in front of his pleasure-garden.

qabilta (cf. **qabalta**) reception. **hda mn qabilta minh̲ lamištaiia** DC 44. 748 no one speaks about its reception.

qabin (P. كابين) marriage(-contract), dowry. ML 276 n. 3 is mistaken. A poor mod. pl. (?) **qabnan** ATŠ II no. 441, a better one **qabinan** DC 43 **šarh̲ d̲-qabin d̲-šišlam rba** (title of DC 38) wedding of Š.R.; **pasuk d̲-qabin** ML 276:9 the response of the marriage ceremony. Often with **PSQ** (q.v.) to perform a marriage-rite; **ʿzdahar ulabdit qabin ušaṭaputa** DC 3, DC 38, DC 53 beware lest thou contract a marriage or partnership; **qabin d̲-planita brata d̲-plan** DC 38. 7:4, ATŠ II no. 327 (& *often*) the marriage-contract of N. daughter of N.; **kt baiit mipsaq qabin** AM 153:1 when thou wishest to arrange a marriage-contract.

Gl. 76:5 (miswritten as **gauiin**) جواز *nuptiae* كدخدائى.

qabnitia (derivation and mean. doubtf.) bribes? **mqablia qabnitia** DC 43 J 197 they receive bribes (?).

qabsaqus DC 40. 871 an angel.

qabra (rt. **QBR**) tomb, grave. Pl. **qabraria** (apart from frequent **qubria** s.v.). **duktai binia qabraria** DC 46. 61:11 my place is amongst the tombs; **abinia trin qabraria hatiqh̲** DC 46. 143:5 between two old graves. Gl. 72:3 (def. **qbra**) حدث *monumentum* گور; 136:2 (id. & pl. miswritten as **qabrai**) قبر, قبور, مقابر *monumentum* گور; Gl. 155:4 (pl. miswritten as **qabrai**) مقابر *monumenta* گور.

qabrun mlaka DC 40. 870 an angel.

qadah (Ar. قَدَح) bowl, cup. St. emph. **qadha** (ܩܕܚܐ from Ar.). Pl. **qadhia. kdub lqadah d̲-lamšaria** DC 46 write on an unused (new) bowl; **uahbulh̲ qadhia lišganda** DC 27. 289 and they gave the bowls to the assistant; **lbar mn qadha d̲-hibil ziua** DC 27. 282 except the bowl of H.-Z.

q(a)daha 1 (rt. **QDA I** = **QDH I**) burgeoning, bud, shoot, blossom, sprout. Pl. **-ia. piqunia uqadahia** Lond. roll B 108 (& *often*) buds and burgeonings; **rihšia uqadahia minh̲ šatin** ATŠ I no. 4 creeping creatures and burgeoning shoots are drinking of it; **rihšia uqadahia** ibid. (*often*). **napuš kul hiua biša akuat qadaha d̲-anpuš** HG every evil creature increases just as weeds grow apace; **qadah(i)a**

uširša HG 162 burgeoning plant(s) and the root; **qadahia girmia hinun** ATŠ I no. 223 the sprouting-plants are the bones.

q(a)daha 2 (rt. **QDA II** = **QDH II**) calling on (in prayer), prayer. Pl. **-ia. qadaha rba ḏ-tušbihan** DC 34. 1190 (cf. DC 27. 110) the great prayer of 'Praises'; **zharia uqadahia** ATŠ I no. 157 injunctions and prayers (?); **bhazin qadaha ḏ-hu raza šubaia** ATŠ I no. 48 in this prayer (?) which is the seventh mystery.

qadamta (rt. **QDM**) early morning, early hour of day. Pl. **qad(a)mata. ʿu lqadamta atia** AM 127:ult. if he comes at dawn; **ʿu qadamta ḏ-ṣala atia** AM 127:2 if he come at an early hour of the dawn; **aminṭul ḏ-qadamta hu** AM 129:8 because he is of the early morning; **tlata qadmata** AM 130:ult. (var. **qadamata** Ṣâb.'s copy) three mornings.

qadašta a fem. of **qadiša** (q.v.), pl. **qadaš(i)ata. pilia nupiata qadašata** s. **nupiata.**

qadha s. **qadah.**

qaduia mia (cf. **qadaha** 1) ŠQ 19:15 some kind of flowering water-plant.

qadumia (rt. **QDM**) early morning. **rahmia qadumia** DC 36 nos. 10, 144 etc. the early morning devotions; **maṣbania labaṭlia mn qadumia** DC 50 the baptizers shall not be idle from early morning on (?). Gl. 100:9 **qadumi** [sic] سحرا *diluculum* سحر.

qaduš (H. קָדוֹשׁ) another name of the Jewish god Adonai, identified with **šamiš. qaduš = adunai** Gy 23:15; **qaduš = šamiš** Gy 45:11; **lqaduš rba ab** Gy 233:24 to Great Qadoš, my father (here as father of the Arab prophet Ginzā 234 n. 1); **ʿumamata qadmaita ḏ-aumuia ʿl qaduš rba** DC 37. 566 the first oath that they administered to the Great Q.

qaduša DC 22. 221 for **qudša** Gy 227:6.

qadušan Oxf. roll g 1001, Or. 332:19 an angel.

qadiaiil taura RD B 50 ff. = DAb par. a heavenly bull.

qadihta = **qidihta. qra bqadihta . . . uqadihtẖ luat abuia silqat** DC 34. 1196 f. he cried aloud . . . and his cry arose to his father.

qadim (**QDM** first as an inchoative verb, then adv.) early (at dawn). **šamiš . . . qadim dna** CP 27:4 = Q 11:23 (cf. l. 31) the sun rises early (in the morning); **qadim qum bʿuspar** Gy 197:3 get up early at dawn; **qala hu qadmaia ḏ-qadim blila** [*sic*] ATŠ I no. 231 it is the first voice, that is early, (as yet) in the night.

qadiša (קַדִּישָׁא, ܩܰܕܺܝܫܳܐ, H. קָדִישׁ) (*a*) holy, saint (used ironically of Christian saints Ginzā 136 n. 2), (*b*) contentious, quarrelsome, warlike (cf. **KDŠ**?). Fem. **qadišt(i)a**, var. **qadašt(i)a** s.v. Pl. masc. **-ia**, fem. **-(i)ata** MG 169:10. (*a*) **ptahil qadiša** Gy 194:9; **qadišia uzadiqia** Gy 55:15; **ptulia uqadišia** Gy 121:10, 226:14 f., **ʿmaihun ḏ-qadišia** Gy 209:2; **mlakia qadišia umhaimnia** Par. xxiv 3b; **qadišia uqadišata** Gs 33:20; **ruha qadišta** Gy 81:4; **libat qadišta** Jb 187:7; **qadišata** Gy 231:10, Gs 67:1; (*b*) **šidta bišta uqadištia** AM 191:16, cf. also **pilia nupiata qadašata** s. **nupiata.**

qadmaia (קַדְמָיָא, ܩܰܕܡܳܝܳܐ) first, primeval, primal MG 7 n. 2, 141:11, 191:19. Fem. **qadmaita** MG 155:2. Pl. masc. **-aiia**, fem. **-aiata. rba qadmaia** Gy 251:1; **šuma ḏ-qadmaia** Gy 112:22; **rba kasia qadmaia** Q 25:2 ff.; **qadmaia brẖ** Jb 242:12, 243:12; **qdimia qadmaiia** Gy 256:13, **qdim(i)a qadmaiia** Q 57:7, sg. **qdima qadmaia** Gy 240:10; **hiia rbia qadmaiia** (*often*) the Great First Life; **šliha qadmaia** Gy 24:10 (*& often*); **man mn man qadmaia umraurab** Gy 193:5 who is greater and mightier than the other? MG 306:24; **tartin haršiata** (var. **harašiata**) **qadmaiata** DC 44. 1019 the two first witches; **qadmaita ubatraita** Gy 278:14 f. the first and last (subst. *primum et ultimum*). Fem. as adv. **bqadmaita** Gy 278:3 first(ly) MG 299:20 f.

qadmu (cf. **qudam**) prep. with suff. of the 3rd p. pl. (with apocope of the final **-n**) in **mn qadmu** Gs 15:12, Oxf. 14a (= Par. xi 49a) before (them), previously, heretofore MG 200:10 f.

qadmia in the frequent **mn laqadmia** Gy 6:1, 6, 68:21, 76:17, 77:6, 126:3, 177:10 (parallel with **atiqa**); Gy 178:5 f., 205:8, 13, 206:4, 9 f., 211:1, 238:17 (parallel with **mn qudam**); Gy 276:16, 303:20, 372:24, Gs 4:11, 23, 6:2, 9, 136:4; Q 13:30 (parallel with **qadmaiia**); Jb 25:1, 210:12 Nöld. without precedent(s) MG 406:ult., 431:1, 437:7, Lidzb. (ܩܕܡ ܠܩܘܕܩܕܡ) from aye, from eternity, from aforetime Jb ii 31 n. 6.

qahzʿiil a var. of **rahzʿi(i)l** (q.v.).

qahma (by met. from ܩܰܡܚܳܐ, Jew.-Aram. קַמְחָא, H. קֶמַח, Ar. قَمْح, Akk. *kēmu* [*qēmu*] Eg.  a kind of bread) Jb 145:11, WedF 37:1 = ŠQ 15:17 flour.

qahr (Ar. قَهْر) AM 265 anger, wrath, trouble.

qaua (ܩܘܳܐ, Jew.-Aram. קְוִין, Akk. *qū* > Sum. *gu* Zimmern 35) web, material woven on a loom. Pl. **-ia. psiq qauaiin** DC 21, JRAS 1938 4:28 their webs are severed.

qaula (Ar. قَوْل) exceptionally for **qala. qria lmihla ḏ-ramit bqaulak** DC 40. 431 read it (: the invocation) upon the salt that thou throwest while reciting (lit. with thy voice).

qauqa (קווקא coal-pan) terra-cotta cube for holding incense MMII 106. **qauqa ḏ-riha** Jb 3:16, 5:14 incense-holder; **bqauqa hadta** CP 13:8 = Q 5:10 = ML 14:8 in a new incense-holder (Lidzb. *Flasche*); **qauqa ḏ-nura** Q 20:5 = ML 55:3 = CP 44:14 brazier (Lidzb. *Feuerbecken*).

qaz (קַזָּא, ܩܙ, Löw 92, Ar. loan-w. قَزّ Fränkel 42) gauze. **qaz uabrišam** WedF 60:bottom = ŠQ gauze and silk.

qaziza Jb 139:7 for **qazia** a pl. of preced. Jb ii 135 n. 5.

qazuin AM 203 the city of Qazwin (about 100 miles north-west of Teheran).

qaṭabuta AM read **raṭabuta** with Par. xxvi & A.

qaṭur DC 44. 627 = Morg. 259/9:28 an angel.

qaṭina an orig. but sporadic form of **gaṭina.**

qaṭla an orig. but non-Mandaic and sporadic form of **gaṭla.**

qaṭran (Ar. قَطْرَان) tar, pitch. **hazin aina d̲-qaṭran** DC 7 this is the well of pitch.

qaiam(a) (rt. **QUM** ܩܝܳܡܳܐ) constant, steady, stable MG 120:15. Pl. **-ia,** st. abs. **-in. qaiamin hiia bškinatun** (*often*) Life is constant in Its dwellings MG 306:14; **ziua sagia uqaiama** ATŠ no.? great and constant radiance; **mia hiia dakiia uqaiamia** DC 51 water of Life pure and preservative; **qaiamin hiia utriṣia** Gy 274:6 Life is constant and permanent; **nihia uqaiamin** Gy 261:24 mild and stable (pl.).

qaiamta (nom. act. pa. of **QUM**) (*a*) raising up, offering up, offertory, resurrection, restoration, (*b*) a prayer of dedication or consecration (repeated sixty-one times when the 'crown' is put on). MG 122:9, ML p. xxiv, CP trs. 148:2. Var. **qimta** s.v. Pl. **qaiamata,** var. **qaiimata** Gy 56:20. (*a*) **iuma rba d̲-qaiamta** Gs 19:2 the great day of resurrection; (*b*) **qaiamta d̲-pihta,** CP 76:16; **qaiamta d̲-mambuha** CP 76:20 = Q 35:22, 27 dedication (consecration) of sacramental bread, sacramental drink; **qaiamta d̲-mia** CP 73:11 = Q 33:31, 34:5 consecration of the water; **qaiamta niqaiim** Oxf. roll f 63 makes an offertory or confirmation; **qaiamta d̲-rahmia** CP 196:ult., ML 231:1, PD 58, 65; **buta (d̲-)qaiamta** (*often*) ML p. xxiv; **kul gabra naṣuraia . . . d̲-brahmia niqum uhaza qaiamta niqaiam** ATŠ I no. 6 (cf. **qaiamta d̲-rahmia** above); **drašia uʿniania uqaiamata** ATŠ II no. 179 chants, hymns, and dedication-prayers; **qaiamta d̲-šitin zibnia uhda zibna** DC 34. 1124 the dedicatory prayer of sixty-one repetitions.

Gl. 38:5 **llqaimta** [sic] الابد *aeterne* تا آخره; 136:13 **qimta** [sic] قيامه *resurrectio.*

qaiuma (rt. **QUM,** ܩܝܽܘܡܳܐ) persistent, steady, continuous. **ziqa qaiuma** AM 195:9 continuous wind.

qaiipia (cf. mod. H. קִיפָּה, קוּפָּה sediment, coagulation) pl. jellies. **mn girma nsib ušauilun qaiipia** ATŠ I no. 248 taking of its bones and making them into jellies.

qailam AM 203 name of a town BZ Ap. II.

qaina (by metathesis from קַנְיָא, ܩܰܢܝܳܐ, cf. H. קָנֶה, Ar. قَنًا & قَنَاة, Akk. *qanū.* Löw no. 291) (*a*) reed, cane, stalk, rod, shaft, reed-pen, (*b*) Libra (sign of Zodiac) Nöld. ZDMG xxv 256 ff., MG 24:11, 109:9. (*a*) **qaina d̲-zrara** DC 44. 436 a bamboo-shaft; **qaina halia hu** DC 41 (illustration: 1st group) it is a sugar-cane; **qaina d̲-naizia** s. **naiza.** Fig. **qaina d̲-qumth̲** Or. 330:27 (*& often*) length of his figure. Doubtf. in **raglia qaina lburia** Gy 139:13 cf. ATŠ 180 n. 5 s. **buria 2** (Nöld. mistakenly proposed ***qainaiia** MSchr. 145 n. 5, Ginzā 154 n. 2); (*b*) **lqaina plaglh̲** Gy 122:23 to Libra they allotted; **qala d̲-qra qaina** Gy 124:2 the voice which Libra called. Very often in AM.

qaisbin AM 198 a place-name (for **qazuin**?).

qaiqubas malka Gy 383:2 name of an ancient Iranian king (*Kavi Kavāta,* Yašt xiii 132, Pahl. *Kai-kabāṯ* or *Kai-kavāṯ,* mod. P. كيكاوس Gray ZA xix 281). Varr. **qaiqabas** D, **qaiqubus** DC 22. 379.

qaiqud AM 205:5 name of a town BZ Ap. II.

qala (קָלָא, ܩܳܠܳܐ, H. קוֹל, Ar. قَوْل, Eth. ቃል, Akk. *qūlu*) voice, sound, cry, noise, clamour, tumult, outcry, noisiness, revilement. St. abs. & cstr. **qal.** Pl. **-ia 1.** MG 3:ult. f., 108: 12. With suff. **qalan** Gs 46:2, **qalaian** Gy 152:8 our voice MG 179:3 f.; **qal numbia** Gy 6:19 the voice of lamentations MG 308:29; **bhad qala** DC 50. 213 in unison; **lqal šušlata** DC 43 A 52 at the sound of chains; **ʿit d̲-qalia uqihdata ramin** DC 48. 172 some of them utter(ed) cries and shouts; **qala d̲-qalaihun nišmunia** DC 44. 657 f. they will hear the call of their voices; **mn qalh̲ umalalh̲** DC 37. 584 from his voice and his speech; **bkulh̲ qalak** ATŠ II no. 427 with all thy voice; **qala d̲-ʿl qalia mapraš** ATŠ I no. 232 a voice which explains voices; **ramia qala bbnia anaša** AM 56:3 she will cause an outcry amongst people; **qala uqraba** AM 225:6 tumult and war; **qala rba dhulta d̲-giṭla uzma** AM 285:20 great uproar, fear of slaughter and blood; **qala mn ʿnšia hauilh̲** AM 52:11 there will be outcry amongst his women; **qalh̲ triṣ** AM 27:8 his voice is honest; **qalia baṭlia** Gy 88:13 idle voices; **hanatun qalia** Gy 88:14 those voices; **trisar qalia** Gy 88:15 the twelve voices (personified as the twelve signs of the Zodiac Ginzā 90 n. 5); **bqala niha, bqala marda** Gy 105:1 f. in a mild voice, in a rebellious voice; **mn kulhun qalia d̲-šimit ʿniak qalak br rurbia basim qal qalaihun umhalai qala d̲-mamlalun** Gy 370:17 f. from all the voices that I heard thy voice answered me (read **ʿnian**), O Son of the Mighty (Life)! Pleasant is the voice of his (: the Life's) call and sweet is the voice of his speech (Ginzā 395 nn. 2–4); **br qala** echo, see **br.**

qalazar (by dissimil. from P. كارزار, Syr. loan-w. ܩܪܙܪܐ warlike) Gy 386:19 strife, conflict, battle MG xxxii n. 1, 305:12.

qalaṭia (cf. Jew.-Aram. & mod. H. קלט to contract, Ar. قَلَطِى short, used of a dog LS s. ܩܰܠܛܳܐ) short, small. **kalba qalaṭia** AM 123:16 a small dog.

qalaia Jb 109:13 ABCD a var. of **qalia 2** (s. **QLL** pe. act. pt.).

qalusta Zotb. 229b (2nd text: 1, 2) = **qulasta** (cf. Krehl ZDMG xxii 559).

qalia 1 pl. of **qala** (q.v.).

qalia 2 act. pt. pe. of **QLA** (q.v.).

qalia 3 (ܩܰܠܺܝܠ, قَلِيل) both adj. & adv.: little, few, not much, scanty, scant, slight(ly) MG 200:25. **ninṭar qalia** Gy 259:19 we will wait a little; **ʿburia qalia nihun** AM crops will be scanty; **ʿburia qalia nibiṣrun** Gy 385:22 the scanty harvests will fail; **anašia qalia nihun ʿl ʿnšia** Gy 386:13 there will be few men for women; **anašia balma qalia hinun** Gy 386:18 there will be few people in the world; **qalia**

anašia Gy 386:19 f., 391:14 few people MG 318 n. 2; **kul mindam qalia** Gy 389:13 everything shall be scanty; **qalia maškin** Gy 389:14 they will find (: harvest) little; **kila qalia** Gy 389:10 a scanty measure; **qalia dar binataihun** Gy 69:20 he stayed a little amongst them; **aialta napša uapaqta qalia** s. **apaqta; miṭra qalia nihuia** AM 257:18 there will be little rain.

qalia 4 = **qalil. qalia asgia** Jb 234:8 moved swiftly on.

qalib (Ar. قالب) (brickmaker's) mould. **dmuta ḏ-hᶜ qalib** ATŠ I no. 261 a shape which is a (brickmaker's) mould.

qalil orig. form of **qalia 3** light, slight (adj.) MG 124:8, but used mostly with the mean. of fast, swift(ly) like **qalia 4.** St. abs. is used adverbially. Adj. st. emph. masc. **qalila,** fem. **qalilt(i)a,** pl. masc. **qalilia. bqalil** Gy 156:15 swiftly MG 303:5; **bqalil sigia** Gy 9:14, 135:1, 151:3 f., 154:5 with swift pace (walking swiftly); **qalilia hinun bsigiaihun** Gy 11:2 f. they are swift in walking; **qalil uniha sigiaihun** Gy 11:4 swift and mild is their pace (walking); **paruanqa qalila** DC 41. 434 a swift messenger; **qalila umsarhiba hauia** AM 9:14 he will be hasty and quick; **qalila umsarhiba uṭizana** AM 40:5 hasty, headlong, and impetuous; **gabra qalila** AM 155:16 a hasty man; **nuqbata kadiran uzakria qalilia** ATŠ II no. 240 women are heavy (weak) and men are hasty (urgent); **iauna qalilta** Gy 132:7 swift dove. Rarely with the orig. mean.: **ᶜburia qalilia nihisrun** AM 188:9 scanty crops will be a loss (cf. **ᶜburia qalia** s. **qalia 3**); **šintẖ qalilta** AM 100:18 her sleep is light; **abuia bkušṭa qalila nasib** ATŠ I no. 138 (var. PD **qlila nsib** PD) his father took his (marriage?)-vow lightly (doubtf.); **miṭria qalilia hauia** AM 225:15 rainfalls will be slight.

qaliqaina (cf. s. **QLQ**) Par. xxvi 175 squinting eye.

qalmia pl. (cf. قَلَم, κάλαμος, καλάμη) Jb 158:4 reeds.

qal‛a (Ar. قَلْعَة) fortress. **qal‛a maran** AM 198 a place-name (*& often in place-names*).

qalqil AM 204 a town.

qam 1 (by syncope of ד in קָדְמָה, cf. Talm. קַמָּא first, קַמֵּי before, & Syr. ܩܘܡܐ front side) prep. before, mod. *qâm* for. Var. **aqam** s.v. MG 33:12, 44:8. Used both with and without pers. suff. MG 194:11–14. **qam abatur mizlai** Gy 337:ult. (var. **aqam** B) my going was (directed) towards A.; **habšaba qam dula** (= **daula**) **trin habšaba qam gadia** etc. Par. xxvi Sunday is governed by Aquarius, Monday by Capricornus etc.; **qam zbana uzbanuta hauia šapiria** DC 46 are favourable for buying and selling; **anda bṭura qaman** CP 40:5, Morg. 213/14:antep. he passed into the mountain before me; **anda bnura qaman** CP 40:17 = Morg. 214/16:7 he passed into the fire before me (Lidzb. ZDMG lxi 695 n. 6). With prep **mn** as **miqam** DC 24. 291 before.

qam 2 (קָם) adversary. **ḏ-laiiṭlak bukrẖ qamẖ** ŠQ 18:10 he who curseth thee—his first-born shall be his adversary.

qamaiata s. **himara.**

qamamir ziua occ. for **qmamir ziua** (q.v.).

qamana (P. كمان) bow, weapon. Var. **qmana** s.v. **qamana sahṭir ugira** DAb = RD 6 bow, knife, and arrow.

qamar st. cstr. (P. كَمَر, cf. Syr. loan-w. ܩܡܪܐ, Jew.-Aram. קַמְרָא) girdle MG 18:5 & n. 3. Pl. **qumria** s.v.: **qamar zahba** Gs 122:14 golden girdle.

qamnuta (rel. to **qiluma**) rottenness, putrefaction. **šakta uqamnuta** Gy 277:23 dregs and rottenness.

qam‛iia (קמה) (**qamia**?) corn **ulaišia liša hauia qamiun kḏ mdakai** DC 40 and they prepare dough, their corn being, as it were, purified.

qamra = **aqamra. qamra ḏ-para uparta** DC 40. 804 wool of a male and female sheep.

qamta (קָמְתָא) standing grain, corn. **qamta uᶜburia** AM 219:11 standing corn and harvests.

qanauan AM 204 name of a city.

qanaia (Jew.-Aram. קֵינָאָה) metal-worker, silversmith. Var. **qinaia** s.v. Pl. **-iia. nangaria uqanaiia** AM 155:10 carpenters and metal-workers (or silversmiths); **mihla ḏ-qanaia ušanaia** DC 12. 197 f., Lond. B roll 420 = DC 40 & P.A. xiii par. salt of a silversmith and of a carder (?).

qananit a name given to Ruha. **qananit ᶜmaihun ḏ-qadišia** Gy 209:2 Q. mother of 'saints'.

qanaqpi‛il RD 1 = DAb theophorous name of a steersman.

qandila (קַנְדֵּילָא, ܩܢܕܝܠܐ, κανδήλη, Ar. loan-w. قَنْدِيل Fränkel 95) candle, oil-lamp (Roman shape) MG xxx. 22. Var. **qindila** s.v. Pl. **-ia. qandilia bla ptiliata** WedF 54:middle = ŠQ 18:5 lamps without wicks; **qanahra mn qandilẖ** ŠQ 19:24 she sheds light with her lamp. Gl. (always defectively as **qndila**) 156:13 مصابيح *lampades* قنديل; 161:3 مصابيح *faces* (?) قنديلها.

qanuš AM 197 town.

qaniana occ. var. of **qiniana.**

qanina (Mishn. קנון, Syr. ܩܢܝܢܐ, Gr. κανίον, καννίον, Ar. قنّينة Fränkel 75) vial, phial, bottle MG 125 n. 5, MR 108, 201. Pl. **-ia. qanina baraia, qanina gauaia** PD 1029 f., **mn qanina baraia bgauaia** PD 1626 from the outer phial into the inner (the outer phial is placed at the entrance of the cult-hut, the inner is on the *ṭariana* inside the cult-hut); **utrin qaninia biaminak** DC 24 and two phials in thy right hand; **qaninak** Q 10:29 thy phial. Often in rituals (Q 20:26, 63:11, PD 873, 888, 891, 1648 etc.).

qan‛il ATŠ I no. 248 an object (bagpipe?) made from skin. Corrupt.

qas interj. exclamation of disgust. **qas pu** Gs 14:19 faugh! ugh! MG 81:16, **qas** repeated seven times after each other in DC 40. 942 (formula in exorcism).

qasṭanṭin AM 202 = **qusṭanṭin.**

qapaiia (rt. **QPA**) Jb 144:1 pl. orig. swimmers, hence prob. floating weeds, water-plants? Jb ii 145 n. 4. **bqapaiia d̲-ansit** DC 42. 802 in loose leaves which I copied (the document was pieced together to form a scroll).

qapur (ܟܦܘܪܐ, ܩܦܘܪ, & ܟܦܘܪ, Ar. كافور) DC 41 (picture) camphor tree.

qapra occ. for **aqapra.**

qaṣara DC 22. 211 = **kaṣara** Gy 218:10.

qaqa 1 (P. کاکا brother) ATŠ I no. 249 (in a list of names of family members). A term of endearment.

qaqa 2 DC 43 A (end) for **kaka**?

qaqai DC 43 F 9 name of a lilith.

qar (Nöld. from ܩܪܐ II, H. קרה, cf. לִקְרַאת, but the consistent *qâ halqa* would make a derivation from a nominal form preferable, cf. קְרִיתָא, ܩܪܝܬܐ, H. קוֹרָה, Ar. قَرْيَة, Akk. *qaritu*) to (the house of), at the same place as (Fr. *chez*). Varr. **aqar, ʿqar 3, ʿqria** s.vv. MG 195 f. Still used. With suff. **qarai, qarak, qarh̲** etc. **ʿl qarak** to thee, to or at thy house MG 195:19. Frequent esp. in later texts. Gl. 36:15 **qr** [sic] الى *usque ad, in* تا; 125:10 **qar** عند *secus, apud* پيش; 125:11 **qarkun** عند كم *apud vos* پيش شما.

qara DC 22. 447 s. **aqara 1.**

q(a)rabtana (ܩܪܒܬܢܐ) warrior, warlike person MG 29:9, 48:5. Var. **q(a)raptana** s.v. Pl. **-ia. iurba gabra qarabtana** Jb 186:10. **ʿur gabra qarabtana** Gy 156:11; **daiua qarabtana** Gy 128:1; **šdum qarabtana d̲-hšuka** RD 20; **anatan qarabtana d̲-hšuka** Gy 140:2, 7; **šdum qarabtana malka d̲-alma d̲-hšuka** Gy 141:21, 23; **qarabtana sakla** Gy 94:11; **qarabtana šapla** Gy 96:2; **biad qarabtana** ATŠ I no. 289 in the hand (?) of the warrior (or 'sacrificer'? see ATŠ p. 192, n. 7); **qarabtana d̲-ruha** DC 34. 1091 the warrior of R.; **qarabtania** (var. **qrabtania** DC 22. 68) **d̲-h̲šuka** Gy 74:12.

qaramba, qaranba (cf. Syr. adjectival subst. ܩܪܢܒܐ gardener) water-melon. Pl. **-ia. qaramba ati** [*sic*] **qamdin** Morg. 276:12 f. bring me a water-melon; **qaranba diriu** Morg. 276:13 they brought the melon; **qaranbih̲ tibar aklh̲** Morg. 276:14 he cut his melon and ate it; **miua uqaranba** Oxf. xii fruit(s) and melon; **qaranbia nihirbun** AM 267:10 melons will be spoilt.

qarasia (nom. ag. of **QRS**) in **qarasia mia** DAb those that dry water, perjurers, cf. 29 n. 5.

qaraptana = **qarabtana.** Pl. **-ia.** MG 48:4. Cf. ATŠ trsl. p. 178 n. 3. **sin daiua qaraptana** RD B 91 (var. **qarapta** DAb); **qaraptania d̲-hšuka** RD 28e; **daiuia qaraptania** Gy 162:7; **qaraptana rba** DC 36 no. 252; **qaraptana . . . d̲-abad qraba** ATŠ I no. 254 (see trsl. p. 178, n. 8).

qarar (Ar. قَرَار) stability, steadiness, repose, tranquillity. Var. **qurar** s.v. **ʿniš bla qarar** DC 46. 98:11 a person without stability; **ʿniš d̲-kapar ulaiiṭ ubla qarar hauia** DC 46. 108:2 a person that apostatizes and curses and has no stability.

qaraštia DC 46. 132:11 for **qarušt(i)a** (s. **qaruša** (*a*)).

qarbala JRAS 1937 590:13 corrupt for **mdabrana** P.A.'s copy.

qarbasaia, qarbasail PA **qarbas** (nom. adj. from P. قربوس bow of a saddle, pommel of a saddle) saddle-maker. Var. **karbasaia** s.v. **nira d̲-qarbasaia** DC 12. 197 the yoke of a saddle-maker.

qarbuta (rt. **QRB**, cf. **qraba**) contentiousness. **qarbuṭa usiniuta** DC 40. 835 contentiousness and hatred.

qarbʿil Gy 167:16 an angel.

qardum daiua RD B 3 a demon.

qardun (Targ. קַרְדּוּן = Peš. ܩܪܕܘ = H. אֲרָרָט Gen. 8:4) Ararat. **ṭura d̲-qardun** Gy 380:21, 381:5, Ginzā 409 n. 4, MSt 129 n. 5.

qarud qud qašiša DC 40. 997 an angel.

qaruia (nom. ag. pe. of **QRA**) caller, reader, reciter. Pl. **qaruiia 1. anat qarit aqaruiia** CP 113:18 thou callest the callers; **ia qaruiia d̲-qrit** CP 109:17, ML 135:3 O ye callers that I called.

qaruiia 2 inf. pa. of **QRA** (q.v.).

qarunpul (Ar. قَرَنْفُل from ܩܪܘܦܠ, καρυόφυλλον Löw no. 301) cloves. Varr. **qurunpul, qurunpil, qrunpul** s.vv. **dra qarunpul** AM 92:8 bring cloves. Gl. 137:ult. (defectively) قرنفل *garophyllion* ميخک.

qarusṭa (for *qarṭusa = ܩܪܛܝܣܐ, ܩܪܛܣܐ, قِرْطَاس, χάρτης) sheet of paper. **kdub lqarustai** [*sic*] **uqlia bnura** DC 46. 131:1 write on a sheet of paper and burn in the fire.

qaruš(a) (rt. **QRŠ**, קְרוּשָׁא, ܩܪܘܫܐ) (*a*) cold, wintry, (*b*) cooling lotion, (*c*) (fem.) coldness, frigidity, chilling. Fem. **qarušt(i)a.** Pl. masc. **-ia.** (*a*) **kd̲ qaruš apqh̲ mn ṭina** AM 287:8 when cold, remove it from the clay; **mia qarušia** DC 46. 93:7 cold water; **iuma d̲-sulita qaruštia** ATŠ II no. 196 the day of Winter-Purification; **libh̲ qaruša** DC 46. 139:7; **libh̲ qaruš hu** DC 46. 143:12 his heart becomes cold; **ʿšata . . . d̲-hamimtia uqaruštia** RD C 4 [*bis*] = DAb par. flames . . . that are hot and cold; **ʿšata qarušta uhamimtia** DC 46. 143:11; (*b*) **qaruša d̲-hiṣra** AM 287:22 a cooling lotion of leek; (*c*) **qarušta d̲-liba** DC 46. 139:antep. coldness of heart. Gl. 45:6 **qaruša** برودة *frigiditas* سرما.

qaria 1 act. pt. pe. of **QRA** (q.v.), Q 1:26, Jb 252:8 (var. **qiria 2** B) etc. Creator, DC 40. 315 invoker.

qaria 2 for **qiria 1. qaria ušiqupta** DC 45 pollution (or accident) and blow.

qarib (rt. **QRB**, ܩܪܝܒ, قَرِيب) near. **qarib muta mn hiia** Gy 218:21 nearer is death than life.

qariba (rt. **QRB**, cf. **qraba**) (*a*) approach (of attack), (*b*) invasion, invading army. (*a*) **ʿsirna (u)htimna . . . mn qariba d̲-qraba d̲-lilia** DC 44. 1664 = Morg. 267/25:30 I am bound and sealed . . . from approach by night of attack; (*b*) **haila . . . uqariba d̲-mn alma d̲-**

hšuka ata DC 35 host . . . and invasion that came from the world of darkness.

qarir(a) (קְרִירָא, ܩܪܝܪܐ, Ar. قرير, H. קַר) cold, cool MG 124:10. Fem. **qarirtia.** Pl. masc. **qariria. lahamima ulaqarira** Jb 51:4 neither hot nor cold; **mia qariria** Or. 338:14 (*& often*) cold water; **ṣhun . . . kd̲ qariria lnura** DC 37. 119 f. they dried up . . . like cold (water?) on a fire; **ʿšata hamimtia uqarirtia** DAb hot and cold flame (or 'fever').

qariš(a) (rt. **QRŠ**, ܩܪܝܫ) congealing, chilling. Pl. **-ia. razia qarišia haškia** DC 27. 200 chilling, dark mysteries.

qarna (קַרְנָא, ܩܪܢܐ, H. קֶרֶן, Ar. قَرْن, Eth. ቀርን, Akk. *qarnu*) (*a*) horn, (*b*) lock of hair, ringlet, (*c*) corner, projection, (*d*) fig., doubtf. MG. 100:7. Fem. MG 157:20. Pl. **qarnia** (orig. du. MG 170 n. 3), **qarnata.** (*a*) **miša d̲-qarna** Gy 54:13 horn of oil; **qarnia ušipuria** Gy 60:5 horns and trumpets; **qarnia ubiluria** Gy 113:4 s. **bilura 2**; **kadibtun bqarnia** Jb 104:4 thou didst announce lies to them with horns; **utbar qarnaiin d̲-rama** AO ix 96:3 and he has broken their horns that were high; **ʿsir taura bqarnh̲** DC 37. 575 tied up is the bull by his horns; **qarna d̲-aiala** AM 124:15 stag's horn; **d̲-bqarnh̲ paiis ʿuhrh̲** Jb 182:12 who would be a road for one who with his horns (> obstinately) destroys his own way ? ; (*b*) **qarnaian** Gy 246:23 our ringlets MG 179:10. A frequent idiom: with **GDL** 'to plait locks' Gy 135:10, 178:10, 373:5, Gs 42:15, Jb 51:5; **qarnia d̲-ziua** Jb 243:10, 244:3 ringlets (?) of radiance; (*c*) **qarnata d̲-ʿngaria** DC 43 J 92 corners of the roofs; (*d*) **kbiš qarnia** AM 86:14 (possibly (*b*)?); **qašiut qarnia** s. **qašiut(a).**

qarsana occ. var. of **qirsana.**

qarqabta = **qarqapta** (both forms also in Syr.). **ptia qarqabth̲** AM 39:15 his skull is broad; **uzuṭ qarqapth̲** AM 35:15 his skull is small.

qarqalta (nom. act. from **QRQL**) overthrow(ing), overturning, ruin, downfall MG 127:7. **qarqalta d̲-šuba kukbia** Gy 222:11 the overthrow of the seven stars (planets); **qarqalta d̲-litbik** Jb 129:7 downfall which is not thine (fem.); **qarqalta d̲-litbia** Jb 129:12 f. downfall which is not mine; **qarqaltan hauia** DC 34. 107 it will be our downfall; **qarqalta d̲-šuba abad** DC 48. 106, 134 f. he brought about the downfall of the Seven.

qarqasta (nom. act. from **QRQS**) restriction, contraction. **qirsa uqarqasta** DC 44. 2003 (miscop. **rarqasta**) Morg. 273/30:30 sickness and restriction; **ruha d̲-iatba ʿl ʿdia umitiqria qarqasta** DC 47, Or. 329:11 the spirit which bewitches the hands and is called contraction.

qarqapta (קַרְקַפְתָּא, ܩܪܩܦܬܐ & ܩܪܩܒܬܐ, Akk. *karpatu*?) scalp, skull, head. Var. **qarqabta** s.v. **uzuṭi qarqapth̲** AM 35:15 and his head is small; **lugth̲ bqarqapth̲** AM 122:19 grasp him by the scalp; **qarqapta d̲-kalba saria** DC 44. 910 the skull of a putrid dog.

qarqus DC 43 A 96 a demon.

qarqušiata pl. (rt. **QRQŠ**, cf. sg. **karkušta**) cymbals, clappers. **tartin qarqušiata** RD 35 = DAb par. a pair of cymbals.

qarqina DC 22. 110 a var. of **qirqna** Gy 115:19.

qarqlia s. **qurqla.**

***qaša 1** (rt. **QŠŠ**, ܩܫܐ) presbyter, (Christian) priest. Used with the ending **-ia 2** as sg. **apisqupa uqašia ušamša** Gy 227:2 bishop and presbyter (or priest) and deacon.

qaša 2 (ܩܫܐ Löw 160, H. קַשׁ straw, Akk. *kikkišu* reed-hut Haupt JAOS xxxii 16, Ar. loan-w. قشّ Fränkel 137) straw, hollow reed. **bqaša briša** DC 45 in a hollow reed, on the head.

q(a)šaia (rt. **QŠA**) difficult, grievous, cruel, harsh. Fem. **qašaita.** Pl. masc. **-iia**, fem. **-ian** (st. abs.). **muta qašaia maiit** AM 119:2 he will die a grievous death; **qašaia hu** AM 122:2 he is harsh (cruel); **šdiqia šuta d̲-puma d̲-qašaiia** (var. **qašiia**) DC 44. 772 speech from the mouth of cruel men is silenced; **qira qašaita** s. **qira.**

qaṣ̌ar 1 (قاجار) name of the before-last Persian dynasty: **path̲ ʿali šah qaṣ̌ar** Ṣâb.'s AM (coloph.).

qašar 2 s. **šum qašar.**

q(a)šia 1 (rt. **QŠA**) hard, cruel, stern. Fem. **-ita.** Masc. doublet **qašiša 2** s.v. **qašia damia laṣaṣa** Gy 216:10 the cruel man is like a pebble; **dina qašia** AM 19:16 harsh judgement; **pišra qašia** Or. 327:4 a stern exorcism; **qašia blibh̲** AM 22:penult. hard-hearted; **qupra uqira qašita** DC 12. 44 pitch and bitumen.

qašia 2 s. ***qaša 1.**

qašiut(a) (abstr. noun from **QŠA**, קְשִׁיוּת, ܩܫܝܘܬܐ) (*a*) hardness, stubbornness, stiffneckedness, hard-heartedness, cruelty, severity, stiffness, (*b*) hard times. MG 146:17. (*a*) Idiom: **qašiut qarnia** AM 16:10, 23:8 f., 47:4 (of a man), ibid. 66:3, 47:4 (of a woman); (*b*) **kupna uqašiuta** AM 226:2.

qašiš(a) **1** (rt. **QŠŠ**, קְשִׁישָׁא, ܩܫܝܫܐ, Ar. loan-w. قسيس Fränkel 275), old, ancient, elder, anterior, superior, senior, honoured, revere(n)d. Pl. **-ia. lqašiš bbiniana** Gy 205:1, 21, 206:18 to the old one in construction MG 312:5 f.; **zuṭ ahh̲ uqašiš abahath̲** Gy 191:11, CP 442:4, Lidzb. *Kleinster unter seinen Brüdern und Ältester unter seinen Vätern* (more revered than his parents?); **uldqašiš minh̲ gahik ʿlh̲** AM 28:2 and he laughs at his elders; **ahh̲ qašišia** AM 15:2 his elder brethren; **hu qašiš d̲-ahh̲ uqašišaiun d̲-abahath̲ nihuia** ATŠ I no. 230 he has precedence over his brothers and will become superior to his parents; **asa qašiša** Jb 232:4 honoured myrtle (Lidzb. *die alte Myrte* ii 214 n. 3); **šitin qašišia** DC 44. 536 f. sixty elders; **mia qašišia mn ziua** ATŠ II no. 192 water has precedence over radiance; **ana qašišun ziuia kulhun** DC 48. 195 I have precedence over all glorious beings; **ahukun qašiša** DC 40. 739 your elder brother.

qašiš(a) 2 for **qašia** 1. **gabra qašiša hauia** AM 36:13 he will be stern; **qašiša uazizia** AM 32:16 he is harsh and hard; **d̲-qašiš minh̲ lahaiia** AM 41:6 a harder man than he does not exist; **ana hu qaština qašiša** DC 43 J 4, 27 I am the strong archer.

qašita fem. of **qašia** 1 MG 153:22.

qašta (קַשְׁתָּא, ܩܶܫܬܳܐ & varr., H. קֶשֶׁת, Eth. ቀስት, Akk. *qaštu*, Ar. قَوْس) bow MG 98:10. Pl. **qaštata** MG 171:16 f. Both genders. **qašta rama** DC 34. 664, AM (*often*) rainbow MG 318:8. **qašta baqriiaiil** RD 9 (personified); **iatria d̲-qaštatun** Jb 17:14 their bowstrings. Fig. **qašta d̲-qumth̲** DC 44. 229. Gl. 138:3 (missp.) قوس *arcus* كمان.

qaštaiaiil RD 9 name of a personified bow. Var. **qaštiaiil** DAb.

qaštanita (from **qašta**) (*a*) convulsion, (*b*) a kind of demons, of both genders. Pl. of (*a*) **qaštaniata**, of (*b*) as sg. (*a*) **qaštaniata lagṭalh̲** AM 120:1 convulsions will seize him, sg. **qaštanita lagṭalh̲** AM 119:antepenult.; **qaštanita d̲-haiata** DC 40. 825 the convulsion of women-in-childbirth (?), cf. l. 827; (*b*) **qaštanita zikria uqaštanita nuqbata** DC 43 A 29.

qaštiaiil s. **qaštaiaiil.**

qaština (from **qašta**) archer, bowman, name of a phylactery DC 43 J. **ana hu qaština qašiša** s. **qašiša.**

qata 1 (קַתָּא, ܩܰܬܳܐ, cf. Akk. *qātu* hand Delitzsch: *Ass. St.* I 19) handle. **qata d̲-sikina** DC 36 no. 248 a knife-handle.

qata 2 var. of **qita** (q.v.).

QBA ܩܒܳܐ collect, gather, contain, hold. **bminian razia lamitimnia ubhušban mnauata tmania laʿqbiat d̲-hʿ tšiaita** DC 27. 204 in our reckoning mysteries are countless and in our enumeration of eight parts, that which is the ninth was not included (*i.e., the soul is the ninth*).

qba AM 9 (*& often*) for **ʿqba.**

qbal (rt. **QBL,** cf. Syr. ܠܘܩܒܰܠ, ܩܕܳܡ ܩܘܒܠܳܐ & ܠܩܘܒܠܳܐ, Mand. **qabal-** with suff.) usually with **mn.** **ʿl mn qbal** Gy 269:25 because MG 203:paen., 210:8 (but Ginzā 269 n. 7), **mn qbal d̲-** Gy 244:1, 247:3, 254:11 f., Jb 176:10, **mn qbal** Gy 257:1, DC 51. 176 on account of, because of, for the sake of MG 466:6–20. Var. **aqbal** s.v.

qburtia (rt. **QBR**) adj. fem. st. emph. buried?, sunken? **aina qburtia** JRAS 1937 595.

QBL (Gen. Sem., Akk. *qablu* middle, battle) to receive, accept, offer up, take, approve, advance, promote, put forward, prefer; to confront, meet with, advance (against or towards), bring against, oppose, accuse, impeach.

Pe. Impf. with encl. **uniqbulh̲ ṣararta hazin** DC 48. 106 and offers him (?) this creation. Act. pt. **qabil hda mn habrh̲** Jb 145:3 one complains of (or accuses) his companion. Part. pres. **qablit bmat anašia** Jb 146:6 thou complainest in the people's village; with encl. **d̲-qabilnalak ʿlh̲** DC 26. 36 whom I accuse to thee; **d̲-qablanalkun** DC 28 (var. **qabalnalkun** DC 26. 437) whom I accuse to you.

Pa. Pf. **qabil** he received MG 221:paen., **qablat** Gy 94:17, 96:9 etc. she received, conceived (of pregnancy) MG 222:12, **qablit** I received MG 223:3, **qabiliun** (often in coloph. after the year of compilation) they accepted, adopted MG 223:23 (ref. mistaken), **qabilnin** we accepted MG 224:18; with suff. **bqabalta qabluia** s. **qabalta.** Impf. **plugia d̲-hšuka binia tarmidia niqabil** ATŠ II no. 356 (if) he promotes dissensions of darkness amongst priests; **niqablun** they accept MG 31:13, 227:18, **niqabla** Gy 298:10 they (fem.) accept MG 228:11, **tiqablun** ye accept MG 227:paen.; with suff. **niqablu** Gs 47:14 they accept her MG 279:20. Impt. **qabil ṭabuth̲** Gy 39:13 be grateful for his goodness (*idiom*); with suff. **qablan** accept me MG 269 n. 1, 271:10. Act. pt. **mqabil** (often in the idiomatic **ṭabuta mqabil**), fem. **mqabla qurbanak** DC 44. 1014 = Morg. 262/16:29 she accepts thine offering; **d̲-mqabla nišimta** ATŠ II that advances the soul; with encl. **mqabilun liuiatan rba** ATŠ I no. 10 great L. will receive them; pl. **mqablia qabnitia** s. **qabnitia.** Pass. pt. with encl. **aina d̲-napšia mqablalh̲** AM 21:3 the (evil) eye of many will be directed at him. Nom. act. **qabalta** s.v. Nom. ag. **mqablana** s.v.

Idiom. With **ṭabuta** to be grateful, accept graciously (s. pa. impt., act. pt.).

Gl. 7:7 f. اقبل *recipere* قبول كرد; 19:11 f. استقبل *accipere* رو آورد; 132:7 f. قبل *recipere* بغل كرد; 158:5 (pass. pt. def.) مقبول *acceptus*.

Der.: **mqablana, qabal-, qabala, qabalta, qabilta, qbal.**

QBR (Gen. Sem.) to bury, inter, cover up.

Pe. Pf. **palga d̲-pumh̲ barqa qbar** Gy 83:5 he buried half of his mouth in the earth (Ginzā 83 n. 2); with suff. **qibrh̲ barqa** ATŠ I no. 265 he buried it in the ground.

Ethpe. Pf. **ʿqbar bmia siauia** Gy 164:7 he buried (covered) himself in the black water.

Ethpa. Pt. pl. **d̲-bun mitqabria almia** Gy 124:3 wherewith the worlds are covered.

Gl. 6:9 f. ادفن *sepelire* بگور گذاشت.

Der.: **qabra** (pl. **qabraria, qubria**), **qabrun, qburtia.**

QDA I (קְדַח, ܩܕܰܚ, قَدَحَ, Eth. ቀደሐ to bore, H. קדח to burn, bore) to bore, break through, sprout, spring forth; inflame. Another secondary rt. **QHD I** s.v.

Pe. Pf. (intrans.) **iurqa d̲-qdia ʿl kip aina** DC 41. 173 herbs that sprouted by the brink of the spring; **qdun** Par. xiv no. 176 they sprang forth MG 237:15; with encl. **man šapupa d̲-qdalh̲ ligria** Jb 72:8 what legless man ever sprouted legs?

Pa. Part. pres. with encl. **d̲-ragiz anat mqadiatlh̲** DC 40. 92 he that rages thou piercest him (or from ܩܒܰܒ thou holdest him fast; doubtf.). Pass. pt. **maria riša mqadia** DC 46. 137:7 a sufferer from a throbbing head (splitting headache); pl. **ulkakania d̲-mqadin** DC 43 and for teeth that are bored (by a worm).

Der.: s. **QDH I.**

QDA II (cf. ܨܘܚ LS 645b s. *e*: *exclamavit*) to shout, cry aloud. Another secondary rt. **QHD II** s.v.

Pe. Pf. **qda bqidihtẖ** Jb 15:8 he cried aloud, **qda šitin qidahata bhda qdihta** ATŠ I no. 83 he cried sixty cries in one.

Der.: s. **QDH II** (& **QHD II**).

qdaha 1 occ. for **qadaha** 1: **qdahia d-mn arqa qahdin** s. **QHD I.**

qdaha 2 = **qadaha** 1: **qdaha rba ugalalta** ATŠ I no. 293 great proclamation and revelation. Several times in ATŠ.

QDH I a more original form of **QDA I** (q.v.) found only in der.: **q(a)daha** 1, **qudha.**

QDH II a more original form of **QDH II** (q.v.) found only in der.: **q(a)daha 1, q(i)dihta** (pl. **qidahata** & **qihdata**).

qdumia = **qadumia**. Gl. 44:5 **bqdumi** [*sic*] بالغداة *primo mane* از صبح.

qdihta occ. for **qidihta.**

qdim(a) (rt. **QDM**) former, ancient, primeval, primal, first. St. abs. is used adverbially in **mn qdim** (*often*) previously, formerly MG 303:5. Fem. **qdimta.** Pl. **-ia,** fem. **-ata. qdima qadmaia,** pl. **qdimia qadmaiia** s. **qadmaia; tartin maṣbutiata had zhiraita hauia qdimta** DC 50. 845 two baptisms, the one with injunctions shall be first; **ainia qdimata** Oxf. xii primeval sources.

QDM (Gen. Sem.) to go before, precede, anticipate, have precedence, be before; as inchoative verb: be early, do early.

Pe. Impf. **niqdum unidnalkin iuma** CP 111:15 = ML 137:5 the day shall break early and shine upon you; **ʿqdum ʿtia** CP 110:8 = ML 135:9 I will come early; with encl. **ʿqdimnalẖ** Gy 240:5 I will advance to it; with suff. **laniqdimunak bʿuhra** Gs 73:9 they will not precede thee on the road. Act. pt. pl. with encl. **qadmilin** Gy 19:14 they precede them (fem.).

Pa. Pf. **qadim** (as inchoative verb used adverbially) s.v., **mn šintai qadmit uqamit** CP 148:5 = ML 177:6 I woke early from my sleep and arose.

Der.: **qadamta, q(a)dumia, qadim, qadmaia, qadmu, qadmia, qdim(a), qudam, qudamaia.**

QDR (H. & mod. H. קדר) to cut, wound, perforate. Pan‘el: to be(come) gloomy, dull, black.

Pa. Pt. **lman ḏ-pagrẖ mqadiria** DC 43 B 39 f. for one whose body is wounded; **kakania ḏ-mqadarin** DC 46. 246:10 teeth that are being cut (or bored).

Pan‘el. Pass. pt. fem. pl. **mqandran** Par. xxvi 109:1 (of eyes) are black.

QDŠ (Can., Aram., Syr., Ar. قدس, Eth. ቀደሰ holy Nöld. *Neue Beiträge* 35, LCb 1879 361, Akk. *quddušu* Zimmern: *Akk. Fremdw.* 66, KAT 602 f., 650, Haupt SBOT on Numeri 5:17) the original meaning 'to be holy', being used only in derision of Jewish and Christian religious phraseology, the rt. acquired an opposite meaning.

Pa. Part. pres. with encl. **mqadšatlia umqadšatlun lšuba bnai** Jb 108:8 thou sanctifiest me and sanctifiest my seven sons (Ruha is speaking). Pass. pt. **mqadša** s.v.

Der.: **mqadša,** fem. **mqadašta, mqadšia, qadašta, qaduš, qaduša, qadušan, qadiša** (fem. **qadišta**), **qudša.**

QHD I (met. of **QDH I**, cf. s. **QDA I**) to pierce, bore, break through, grow up or out, sprout, germinate; to inflame.

Pe. Pf. **qihdat urbat** ATŠ I no. 279 it (fem.) germinated and grew. Impf. with suff. **latiqihdẖ** DC 37 do not inflame (?) him. Pt. **qahda ʿl duktẖ** Gy 54:22 sprouteth (fem.) in its place; **ḏ-šaria bazira larqa ulaqahda** AM 145:18 that sets seed in the earth and it does not germinate; with encl. **ʿlana qahdalẖ** ATŠ I no. 291 a tree springs up for him; pl. **qadahia barqa qahdia** DC 7 plants burgeon forth in the earth; **qdahia ḏ-mn arqa qahdin** DC 34. 663 the sprouts which burgeon from the earth.

Der.: **q(a)daha 1.**

QHD II (met. **QHD II**, cf. s. **QDA II**) to cry (out), proclaim.

Pe. Pf. **qihdat** Gy 161:11 she cried. Act. pt. **pahra qahda** Gy 280:7 flieth, crieth (masc.!); **qahda ugahia** Gy 313:8 they (fem.) cry and howl.

Der.: **qihdata** (others s. **QDH II**).

QWA (Ar. قَوِيَ) to be(come) strong. **ḏ-aqauia** [*sic*] **ziua ḏ-ainia** AM 286:ult. that strengthens the light of the eyes. Gl. 50:5 f. **QWA** تقا *esse fortis, viriliter agere* قوه گرفت.

quala Gy 213:ult. miscop. of **qulala 1** (q.v.).

quba (H. קֻבָּה, Ar. قُبَّة, Syr. ܩܘܒܬܐ) curve, arch. Found only with fig. meaning, doublet with orig. meaning **qumba** s.v. **quba ḏ-kraiia** s. **kraia.** Gl. 182:4 (missp.) ذراع *cubitus, brachium* گز.

qubita (prob. from **qabuta,** but cf. also קֻבַּעְתָּא) Gy 265:14 chest, frame(work).

qubla (קוּפְלָא, ܩܘܦܠܐ, Ar. قُفْل Fränkel 16, Eth. ቍልፍ, cf. כִּבְלָא, ܟܒܠܐ, Ar. كِبْل fetter, Eth. ከበሎ handle, Akk. *kabālu* to fetter, a relationship betw. the rt. קפל & כבל having been admitted by Nöld. MG 48 n. 1) chain, fetter(ing), counter-charm MG 47:20, ZA xxx 154, Jb ii 99 n. 2, Ginzā 194 n. 5. Pl. **-ia. masihpa qubla shap ʿlai** s. **masihpa; bmasaria qubl(i)a** (var. **bmasirqa uqublia**) **ninsarunẖ** Gy 300:21 they will saw (or harrow) him with saws and harrows (? Lidzb. left untransl.); **masirqia qublia** Jb 97:ult. f. harrows (Lidzb. *Kämmen von Ketten*), similarly **masaria uqublia** DAb; **nirmia šiha uqublia balma** Gy 361:23 we will cast lust and fetters in the world; **ulmitbar qublia ruha** DC 51 and to break the fetters of R.; **qublia lsahria uldaiuia** AM 120:17 counter-charms against devils and demons; **qublak mahu hauia** DC 46. 62:2 f. what is the counter-spell that binds thee? (to a demon).

qubria pl. of **qabra** in the frequent **bit qubria** Jb 56:9, 110:5, 114:3 ff., 125:8 ff. etc. cemetery MG 18:13.

qudaha Jb 144:2, pl. **-ia** Morg. 266/23:39 read **quraha.**

qudam (rt. **QDM,** קוּדָם, Syr. ܩܕܳܡ, Chr.-Pal. ܩܘܕܡ Nöld. ZDMG xxii 459) prep. before, preceding, in front of, anterior MG 28:20, 194:10. Used with or without pers. suff. With other prepositions: **mn qudam, lqudam, ʿl qudam** MG 197:3, **mn qudam** Gy 205 ff., 278:19 from aforetime, of yore MG 203:ult. With suff. emphasizing a determinated noun: **qudamh d̲-aba** Gy 101:17 before the father; **lqudamaihun d̲-kulhun anašia** Gy 223:5 before all people; **mn qudamh̲ dibrath̲** Gy 149:2 away from his daughter MG 330:15–17. To designate a direction: **lqudam abahatai silqit** Gy 156:18 I rose towards my Father (the Life, pl.); **ʿl qudam mana maiil** Jb 5:14 he bringeth (it) into the presence of the Mana; **d̲ . . . aluiun mn qudamaihun** Gy 140:14 which He (: Life) gave to accompany me from His (pl.) presence; **npaq qala mn qudam malka** Gy 282:11 a voice came out from the king; but often with other prep. meaning simply 'before': **lqudam adam** Gy 12:22, 33:8, 34:9 in A.'s presence; **lqudaman triṣ** Gy 72:9 raised before us; **d̲-manhria lqudamaihun** Gy 128:20 (cf. l. 22) which shine before them; **mn qudam ṭupania mia** Gy 140:20 before the flood etc. MG 359 f.

qudamaia Gs 136:3 for **qadmaia** MG 141 n. 4.

qudha (rt. **QDH I**) sore, cut, inflammation. Pl. **-iia. sumqai uqudhiia** DC 19. 175 my or his (?) redness and his inflammation(s) (doubtf.).

qudraniaiil DC 40. 874 f. an angel.

qudša 1 (rt. **QDŠ,** קוּדְשָׁא, ܩܘܕܫܐ, H. קֹדֶשׁ, Ar. قُدْس) Christian sacrament; after the relative particle **d̲-** 'holy' = 'evil' (as an antagonistic term applied exclusively to non-Mandaean notions of holiness). Pl. **-ia. ruha d̲-qudša** (*very often*) 'Holy Ghost' (ܪܘܚܐ ܕܩܘܕܫܐ) = name given to Ruha, as queen of darkness and mother of devils; **qudšia** (var. **qudša** Leid., Sh. ʿAbd.'s copy) **d̲-šuba qudšia qadmaiia** Gy 225:ult. f. the sacrament(s) of seven first sacraments; **šuba qudšia** Gy 228:19 seven sacraments; **qudša d̲-atana** s. **atana 1**; **qudša d̲-gumarta** Gy 227:14 f. s. **gumarta.** As opposite of **pihta ukušṭa umambuha** (Mandaean sacraments) Gy 362:2 f.

qudša 2 AM 258:21 read **qurša** cold? BZ 159 n. 5.

quhzan (P. قوهى 'a kind of white cloth' + Mand. **zan**?) a kind of white cloth. Var. *ruhzan* (ŠQ 56 n. 1). **lbušia d̲-hiduia mn quhzan dakia** CP 222:6, WedF 35:bottom = ŠQ 15:10 the clothes of the bridegroom are of pure white cloth (CP trs. 176 n. 4).

quza = **aquza, ʿquza.** Pl. **-ia. arikia quzia hauin** DAb the long ones will become short.

quṭana (rt. קטן, ܩܛܝܢ, Akk. *qatnu, qattanu* thin, young) Zotb. 217b:8, 220b:10, AM 105 (& *often in coloph.*) a family-name MG 39 n. 9. Mod. (*qoṭâna*) small.

QUL s. **QLL.**

qul AM 127 (translit. of Qur'ān 113) Say!

qula (Targ. קוּלָא) snare, animal-trap. Doublet q(u)lala 1. **qula d̲-šibiahia** DC 3. 214:2 = CP 290:11 the snare of the planets; **kd̲ ṭabia bqula** DC 40. 346 f. like a gazelle in a trap.

qulab (Jew.-Aram. קוֹלָב) tunic. **kulhun labšia qulab** CP 185:2 all of them wear the tunic.

qulazta a var. of **qulasta.**

q(u)lala 1 (cf. **qula**) snare, trap. Pl. **-ia.** MG 8:11, 29:2–4, 114:16 f., Jb ii 50 n. 2. **qlala ušišilta** Jb 45:5 snare and chain, pl. **qulalia ušušlata** Gs 132:1; **hirbun uqulalun** Gy 377:18 their sword(s) and their chain(s); **qulalan bišata** Jb 61:4 our evil snares; **ramia bqulalia kulhun rahmia** Gy 216:3 f. casteth all his friends into fetters; **latirmia napšak bqulala** (var. **qulalia** Leid.) Gy 213:ult. cast thyself not into snares; **ramilun qulalia** ATŠ I no. 141 they lay snares for them; **qulalia upirunia** Gy 225:21 snares and fetters; **qulalia d̲-napšh̲** Gy 363:ult. f. her own snares; **ramilak qulalia bʿuhrak** Jb 63:13 casteth snares for thee on thy road; **nisakrh̲ bqulalan** Jb 58:11 we entangle him in our snares; **pliṭt qulalan** Gy 362:19 thou didst escape our snares; **niṣilun qulalia** s. **ṢLL II**; **qulalia d̲-ruha** Jb 45:4 Ruha's snares; **qulalia d̲-tibil** DC 27. 158 the snares of Earth.

q(u)lala 2 (rt. **QLL**) (*a*) lightness, frivolity, (*b*) shame, ignominy, dishonour. Pl. **-ia.** Jb ii 50 n. 2. (*a*) **rquda uqulala** ATŠ II no. 64 dancing and frivolity; **pirṣa uqlala** Gs 30:16 etc. debauchery and frivolity; **qlala uzaniuta** Gy 215:18 frivolity and lechery; **zmaria uqlalia** Gy 224:25 songs (= lechery) and frivolities; (*b*) **npiš qlalun** Gy 174:3 f. great is their ignominy; **mgalalin lqlala siṭraiin** Gy 181:3 they bare their flanks for shame; **siṭraiin primlin lqlala** Gy 225:13 f. their flanks are bared for shame; **qlala ubahtuta** Gy 178:14 ignominy and shame; **qlalun ubahtutun** RD B 70 their shame and their ignominy.

qulasta (prob. from Aram. קְלֵס, ܩܠܣܐ Bevan OSt i 581, Ar. loan-w. قلس Fränkel 284, cf. Syr. ܩܘܠܣܐ praise) title of a well-known liturgical collection publ. by Euting and by Lidzb. as first part of ML. Varr. **qalusta, qulazta** Euting ZDMG xix 130:bottom. Pl. **qulasiata** miscellanies, collections. **tartin qulasiata** AM 256:17 two collections. In general, the name for the liturgical prayer-book.

qulṭba (cf. Ar. قَرْطَبَ) encumbrance, obstacle. Doubtf. **mutana uzaina uqulṭba** (var. **-ia**) AM 166.

qulpa (קוּלְפָּא) rod, thong, scourge. Doublet **qupla** s.v. **bqulpa mhaith̲** Gy 90:24, **bqulpai mhaith̲** Gy 118:10 I struck him (her) with my scourge; **nitimhia bqulpa d̲-rugza** DC 3. 245:11 = CP 374:10 he shall be beaten with a scourge of wrath; **mahilh̲ bqulpa** RD C 12 they strike him with a scourge; **bqulpai ʿmihiẖ** Gy 344:22 I will strike him with my scourge; **mihiẖ bqulpa** Jb 188:3 he struck him with a scourge; **qulpa ḏ-hura** RD C 10 a scourge of fire; **qulpa ḏ-parzla** Jb 148:2, RD C 14, 18 iron rod.

QUM (Gen. Sem.) to stand, rise, be erect; pe. with ʿl or l to stand by, be faithful to, aid, assist, abide by, rally to (MSchr. 7 n. 7); to rise against, go counter to; to understand; pe. often as an inchoative verb: to begin, start, betake oneself to (with **b-**); pa. to raise up, maintain, establish, confirm, consecrate MSchr. 231, ML xxiii; af. to raise (up), lift (up), appoint, heap on, raise against, make to stand.

Pe. Pf. **qam** MG 34:2, 248:1, **qam ainaia mn mihzia** Jb 54:9 my eyes ceased from seeing; **qamat** MG 248:9; **qamit** MG 248:15; special pl. form **qamiun** Gy 381:23 they stood (but Gy 390:23 read **qaimin** they stood) MG 248:7; with encl. **qambẖ** Gy 98:6 they stood therein MG 248:5; **laqamlẖ** Gy 6:8 he stood not; **qamalẖ** she stood by him MG 42:18, 248:11; **qamlan biluatan ubidiaurutan** MG 132:3 he stood by us as our companion and our helper (lit. as our company and help). Impf. **niqum, tiqum, ʿqum** MG 29:21, 249:7; **laiit ḏ-niqum ʿl kinianẖ** Gy 5:6 f. there is none who would be related to him (Lidzb. *es gibt keinen, der seine Benennung erfaßte*); **ʿl napšiẖ niqum** Jb 169:8 relieth on himself (Lidzb. *sich selber versteht*); **liqum, lʿqum** Gy 368:19, Gs 106:20 standeth MG 216:8; **niqmun** they stand MG 82:20, 247:antep., **niqma** they (fem.) stand; **tiqmun** ye stand MG 249:23; with encl. **tiqmulia** MG 249: antep., **niqmubẖ** AM 97:5 they will stand by him. Impt. **qum** MG 250:5; with encl. **qumbun brahmak šania** Jb 111:3 betake thyself to thy sublime devotions; **qumlak** Gs 78: 23 (*twice*) arise. Pt. **qaiim** MG 149:7, 250:11, **laqaiim ʿlun** Jb 68:2 he does not understand them; **ʿniš . . . lika ḏ-qaiim ʿlauaihun** Gy 139:16 no one can stand them; **kḏ qaiim mn šinta** ML 5:10 f. when he rises from sleep; **hua qaiim** Gy 249:17 came into being; **qaima** MG 149:7; pl. **qaimia** MG 149:8; **qaimia bpagraihun** (*often in commemorations*) alive in the(ir) body; **qaimia bsipaiun** AM 262:15 those living by the sword; **ḏ-bhad mamla laqaimia** Gy 24:1 who do not stand by a single word; **qaimia umithašbia** Gy 104:22 f. they started (hist. pres.) to make plans; **bnikla niqmun minẖ** AM 64:18 they make intrigues against her. Part. pres, **qaiimna, qaimit, qaiminin, qaimitun** MG 250:15. Inf. **miqam** MG 30:1, 82 n. 2, 129:19, 250:26; **litlẖ haila lmiqam** DC 41. 114 he has no strength to arise; **miqam qaimia** Gy 209:9 they stand MG 397:12; st. emph. **napil umiqma litlẖ** Gy 121: 22, DC 34. 701 he falleth and there is no rising for him (MG 250:ult.); with encl. **miqmak** Gy 365:7 thy standing; **miqmaikun** Gy 17:16 your standing.

Pa. Pf. **qaiim** he raised MG 252:16; with suff. **qaiman** Gy 242:23, Gs 135:11 he raised me, confirmed me (MG 270:26); **qaimak** Gy 352:12 consecrated thee; **qiriẖ uqaimẖ** Gy 130:21, 24 he called him and confirmed him; **qaimik** Q 19:1 he confirmed thee (fem.) MG 274:26; **qaiimtẖ** MG 277:11; **qaimun** Gy 318: 19, 352:20, 360:13 they or He (:the Life) confirmed me (MG 272:20); **birkuk . . . qaimuk** Gy 352:11 f. they blessed thee . . . they consecrated thee; **qiriuia uqaimuia** Gy 93:8 they called him and confirmed him; **iatruia uqaimuia** Gy 235:4 they magnified him and blessed him; **qaimu** Gy 295:8 they confirmed her MG 279:15; **qaiimtun** Gy 240:5 ye (: Life) confirmed me MG 272:10. Impf. **niqaiim** he raiseth, confirmeth MG 252:17; with suff. **niqaiman** CP 150:18 = ML 181:2 he will establish me; **niqaimak** MG 273:18; **ʿqaimẖ** I confirmed her MG 275:30; **niqaimunẖ** MG 278:14; **bmahu niqaimunẖ** CP 7:7, ML 8:7 by what do they confirm it?; **niqaimun(a)kin** Q 37:9, MG 281:11. Impt. with suff. **qaiminan** MG 280:3. Act. pt. **mqaiim rahmẖ** Gs 96:24 confirmeth his friends; **mqaiim šurbta** Gs 97:2 raiseth the generation (MG 131:11); but **mqaiam rahmẖ** Gy 78:23 read **mqaiim rahmẖ** Ginzā 77 n. 4; with encl. **mqaiimlẖ** Gy 137:14, 18, Gs 73:16 confirmeth him; **mqaiamlak** Gy 197:19 read **mqaiimlak** confirmeth thee (with baptism); pl. **ḏ-mqaimia šurbta** Gs 95:1 who confirm the generation. Pass. pt. **mqaiam** raised, confirmed MG 131:middle, infl. **mqaima** MG 252:17; **mqaiam** = **mšaba** Gy 125:12, **mšaba umqaiam** Gy 192:11; **mšaba . . . umqaiam** Gy 193:17, 194:14; **miaqar umqaiam** Gy 1:22 Ginzā 5, n. 11; **ʿutra mqaima** Gy 69:24, **niha umqaima** Gy 135:6, **ʿutra niha umqaima** Gy 77:7 ff.; pl. **mqaimia** = **brikia** Gy 130:6, **nihia umqaimia** Gy 72:12, **mqaimia** = **taqnia** Gs 46:8, **ʿutria nihia umqaimia** Gy 74:1, 299:10, **bnia nihia umqaimia** RD B 80 (cf. Kessler on **ʿutria mqaimia** PRE 166:11). Pass. pt. pres. **mqaimit** = **brikit** Gy 7:6 (cf. l. 8), **mqaiumia mqaimit umzarzit** Oxf. 90 a thou art (strongly) confirmed and armed MG 398:4. Inf. **(m)qaiumia** MG 143:18, 144:2, 398:4 (just quoted); **lbarukia uqaiumia** Gy 179:7 to bless and (p)raise; **qaiumia mqaiamlak** Gy 197:19 he confirmeth thee; with suff. **miqaiminkun** Oxf. 5 b to confirm you. Nom. act. **qaiamta** s.v. Nom. ag. **mqaimana** s.v.

Af. Pf. **aqim** he raised MG 251:4; **aqmit** Gy 91:10, 108:15, 16, 328:21 I raised, lifted up MG 251:8; with encl. **aqmibẖ** MG 251:11; with suff. **aqman** Gy 128:9 he lifted me up, **aqmẖ** MG 275:10, **aqminun** MG 281:24, **aqimtak** Gs 55:13 I lifted thee up MG 274:5, **aqimtẖ** MG 277:14, **aqimtinan** MG 280:10, **aqimtinun** she lifted them up MG 282:20, **aqimtinin** Gy 361:7 I lifted them (fem.) up MG 283:1, **aqimtunẖ** Gs 18:10 ye raised him up MG 277:24, **aqmu** Gs 74:21 they raised her MG 279:17. Impf. **unaqim** (var. **iaqim** PD) **zidqa brika** ATŠ I no. 137 and he offers up a Blessed Oblation; with suff. **ḏ-aqminkun** Gy 175:9 that I raise you; but the full form **uʿiaqminkun** ibid. l. 10 MG 215:25 f., 280: antep. f.; **naqminin** Gy 184:14 he setteth them (fem. souls) up MG 282:5 (where the suff. & the ref. are to be corrected); **naqmunẖ** MG

278:16, **taqminan** ATŠ thou wilt raise us up (MG 280:2). Impt. with suff. **aqmẖ mn atutia margnak** DC 27. 123 raise him from beneath thy staff. Act. pt. **maqim** MG 251:18; **maqim šakbia** CP 148:12 = ML 178:1 maketh the sleepers rise; **maqim ʿl dirkia d̠-šrara** Gy 62:20 f. (thou) who settest up ways of Truth; **maqim zidqa brika** ATŠ I no. 61 he will celebrate a Blessed Oblation; pl. with encl. **maqmilin** Gy 224:8 they raise them (fem.) up MG 251:19. Inf. **aqumia** MG 144:6, 251:25, **maqumia šakibia** Jb 135:ult. f. to raise up the sleeping.

Ethpa. Pf. **ʿtqaiam, ʿtqaimat, ʿtqaiamt, ʿtqaiamtun** MG 252:18 f., **hdun uʿtqaiam** Gy 91:16 He (: Life, pl.) rejoiced and was in high spirits Ginzā 94 n. 6; **prun uhun uʿtqaiam** Gy 7:11 (cf. 31:7) they came forth, found existence and were established; **ʿtqaiam šumaihun** Gy 291:38 their names were established; **ʿtriṣtun uʿtqaiamtun** Oxf. 43 a, ye were set up and established; with encl. **ʿṣṭba uʿtqaiambẖ** Gy 293:5 were baptized and established thereby; **ʿtqaiambẖ hiia** Gy 70:3 (cf. l. 12) Life was established in it; **ʿutria ʿtqaiambẖ** Gy 70:5 (cf. l. 11 & Q 26:17 etc.); **ʿtqaiambun** Gy 238:14 (twice) was confirmed by them; **iuma rba d̠-ʿtqaiamtbẖ** CP 39:ult. = ML 46:7 the great day on which thou wast raised up (: baptized d. 2). Impf. **nitqaiam** = **mšaba** Gy 61:2; **nitqaimun** Gy 192:21, 213:3, fem. **nitqaima** Par. 41b:4, **titqaimun** MG 252:20; **nitqaimu bškinat hiia** Gy 251:12 they shall be established in the dwelling of Life MG 228:23 (a particularity of the XIth book of Gy Ginzā 250:13). Impt. **ʿtqaiam** Lond roll A 409 be confirmed. Pt. **mitqaiam bqaiamta d̠-šrara** Gy 45:5 he shall be confirmed by a true (firm) confirmation; **mitqaiam lalam almia** Gy 45:8 is established for ever. Part. pres. **mitqaiamna** Q 25:15, MG 231:12, **mitqaimitun** MG 252:02.

Gl. 3:11 f. **qam** اقام *statuere* (but also ارسل *mittere* فرستاد); 21:11 f. id. استقام *erigere se, rectus fieri* برخيزانيد; 50:15 f. id. تثب [sic] *surgere* برخواست [sic]; 131:1 f. id. قام *stare* برخواست [sic]; 131:11 f. id. قام (read قيّم) *suscitare* برخيزانيد; 134:9 f. id. قام *manere* ايستاد; 173:3 f. id. وقف *stare* ايستاد; 180:7 f. id. دام *morari, permanere* هميشه ماند.

Der.: **mqaimana, ʿqai(i)am, ʿqaimat, qaiam(a), qaiamta, qaiuma, qumta, qimta.**

qum 1 (Ar. قَوْم) tribe. As collective: **had qum mn anašia nišiprun** AM 275 one tribe of people (cf. Ar. قوم من الاقوام) will prosper; **had qum mn bnia babil** AM 277:3 f. one tribe of the inhabitants of Babylon; **qum iintiqlun baʿid mn mdinta** AM a tribe will be transferred far away from the city.

qum 2 a name given to Nazareth (hence different from P. قُم ZDMG 1955 p. 360:8 ff.): **niṣrat mdinta d̠-iahutaiia d̠-hʿ qum mdinta** HG 15 Nazareth, the city of the Jews, which is the city Qum.

qumana (ܩܘܡܡܐ husks, dry seed(pod)s, Ar. قُمَامَة rubbish) mildew (Lidzb.), rubbish. **rumana d̠-mn lbar anpiẖ rauzia umn gauẖ qumana mlia** Gy 216:1 f., CP 178:13, Oxf. 92 a = ML 218:2 f. a pomegranate which outwardly is healthy, but within is full of dry seed-pods (or mildew).

qumat st. cstr. of **qumta 1** (q.v.).

qumba (cf. s. **quba**) vault, dome; arc, bow MG 76:21; with fem. ending **qumbta** MG 105:24. Var. **qunba** s.v., fem. **qumta 2**. **qumba d̠-rqiha** Jb 2:4, 4:10, **qumba d̠-šumia** AM 257:7 the heavenly vault; **qumba d̠-bhiria zidqa** Jb 166:12 the dome of the elect of righteousness; **qumba d̠-kahnia** Jb 75:6, 93:9, 14 the dome of (Jewish) priests; **qumba d̠-ʿula** Jb 140:14 the dome of abomination; **qumba d̠-bilur** DC 34. 1069 a crystal dome; **qumba d̠-bilaur dakia** DC 48 (illustration) a vault of pure crystal; **qumba d̠-iuma** AM 165:8 the rise of day *or* midday? (doubtf. BZ 103 n. 2); **qumba d̠-ziua asarlẖ bhalṣẖ** RD B 19 he tied a bow of radiance on his loins; **qam bqumbta** Gy 98:3 they stood on the vault; **asqẖ ʿsrẖ bqumbta** Gy 98:4 he raised it and tied it to the vault.

qums AM 204:17 a place-name BZ Ap. II. Var. **rmus** Ṣâb.'s A.M.

qumria Gy 48:1 pl. of **qamar** MG 18:4.

qumta 1 (rt. **QUM**, קוֹמְתָא, ܩܘܡܬܐ, H. קוֹמָה, Ar. قَامَة) stature, body, form; often for 'person' MG 23:14, 101:16. St. cstr. **qumat**. With suff.: **qumat** Gy 212:19, var. **qumtai** my stature MG 22:20, 175:23, **qumtik** Gy 116:11 thy (fem.) stature MG 177:18; **ʿl kulẖ qumtẖ laqamit** Gy 85:14 f. I did not equal his whole stature; **mahta qumtẖ** Gy 115:11 she stretcheth her body; **nihibqẖ bqumtẖ** Gy 116:8 embraceth her by the body; **kulẖ qumtai** Morg. 267/25:42 my whole body; **qumat gubalia balbušia pšiṭlẖ** DC 26. 665 = DC 40. 626 I drew upright my stature, my form in its vestment; **qumat hdadia qaimia** Gs 110:3, DC 48. 103 they are of like stature.

qumta 2 Gs 129:12 f. for **qumbta** (s. **qumba**).

q(u)nasa s. **qnasa**.

qundapiʿil DC 43 J 47 an angel.

qundus AM 203 name of a city BZ Ap. II.

qunpud (Ar. قُنْفُذ < קוּפְדָּא, ܩܘܦܕܐ) DC 36 no. 254 hedgehog. Miscop. **qunpuq** DC 6 ibid.

QUS, QSS (cf. Talm. קוץ = קצץ otherwise ע״ע Syr., H. & mod. H., Ar., Akk. *qaṣāṣu* to cut, but cf. der. **ʿquz**) to become small, shrink, be drawn together.

Ethpe. Pf. **ʿtigbib uʿtqis** Gy 162:23 he curled himself up and drew himself together MG 125:20.

Der.: **ʿquz(a), qusa 1.**

qusa 1 (rt. **QUS**) short, small. Doublet **(a)quza** = **ʿquza** s.v. **parṣupẖ uziqnẖ qusa** AM 91:2 his face and his beard are short; **kalba qusa** AM 123:15 a little dog.

qusa 2 (cf. ܩܘܙܐ Löw 'marten' in a letter to Lidzb. Jb ii 151 n. 8, but cf. Nöld. ZDMG xxxv 235, xxxvi 131:32, Hübschm. ZDMG xlvi 242 n. 63) weasel, (Mesopotamian) (spotted) mongoose. **miška d̲-qusa** Par. xxvi 142:4, 148:6 the skin of a mongoose (or weasel?); **qusa umanzih̲** Par. xxvi 144:3 a weasel (or mongoose) and its hair (fur); **manzia d̲-qusa** AM 122:16.

qusa 3 (P. كوسه, a biting fish living esp. in the Kārūn river) a kind of biting fish, shark (?). **d̲-aklia lgirita ulqusa d̲-zaqip bʿdh̲** Jb 149:1 who eat the *jerri*(-fish) and the *qusa*(-fish) which leaps up on to one's hand; **qusa usarṭana** Par. xxvi 225:middle, *qusa* (-fish) and crab.

qusṭaṭ AM 198:8 name of city BZ Ap. II.

qusṭanṭin, qustanṭin AM 202 Constantinople BZ Ap. II.

QUP, QPP (ܩܦ, Ar. قفّ to contract, shrink) to clasp together, bend together, settle down, subside; fig. to allay, quieten down, fasten?

Pe. Impf. (intrans.) **kul ziqa d̲-maškatlh̲ niqup** Or. 344:15 f. every flatulence that thou findest in him shall subside; **bpars mahuzia tiqup umitikbiš** AM 221:3 in Fars a town will subside and be laid low. Impt. **qup** (read **rup**?) **bṣuria** DC 45 clasp (? it) round his neck. Pass. pt. **qala d̲-asara d̲-qip bsikta d̲-parzla** DC 26. 623 = DC 44. 659 the noise of a fetter which is clasped to by an iron pin; **d̲-qipa umautiba** DC 37 (of a fetter) which is clasped together and superimposed; pl. **qipin**, s. **qipin** DC 40. 188 they are bound (or quietened?).

Af. Impt. **adik uaqip** Or. 344:15 f. extinguish and settle down (quieten).

qupa 1 (קוֹפָּא, ܩܘܦܐ, H. קוֹף, Akk. *uqūpu*, Gr. *κῆβος*, Sanskr. कपि, Middle-P. *kapiγ* Lewy: *Fremdw.* 6, but already Eg. 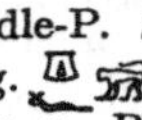 OLZ iii 51, vii 90 f.) ape Jb ii 166 n. 3. Pl. **-ia**. **zma d̲-qupa** AM 123:1 ape's blood; **qupa uaria** RD E ape and lion; **bdmu qupia** Gy 225:7 f. in the form of apes; **ʿl qupia uʿl zabia** s. **zaba 3**; **qupia uqirdia** Ṣâb.'s AM apes and monkeys.

qupa 2 (cf. s. **qupta**, Akk. *quppu*) (*a*) basket, round basket-boat, pitched with bitumen, (*b*) hoop (of a ring). Pl. **-ia** Jb ii 166 n. 3. Fem. doublet **qupta** s.v. (*a*) **zahba bqupia nasib** Jb 165:2 takes gold in baskets; (*b*) **kd̲ qupa qarqsit ʿlauaihun** DC 26. 605 = DC 44. 635 f. like the hoop of a ring I encompassed them.

qupa 3 a name given to **adunai** in an exorcism. **qupa adunai iahu iahu iahu** AM 125:penult.

qupat st. cstr. of **qupta** (q.v.).

qupiʿil mlaka DC 43 D 23, 25 an angel.

qupla = **qulpa**. Pl. **-ia**. **akla d̲-parzla uqubla rba d̲-širiana** DC 26. 154 f. an iron hammer and great rod (or scourge) of exorcism; **quplia uaklia** Jb 165:14 rods and hammers.

qupra (ܩܘܦܪܐ I & ܩܦܪܐ) pitch, bitumen. **lamqaira arbak bqupra** Jb 161:4 thy boat is not tarred with pitch; **qupra uqira** Lond. roll B 155, 297 (& *often*) pitch and bitumen; **qupra mn marzib** AM 95:12 pitch from the roof-gutter; **ṭab . . . qupra lmišria** AM 139:12 good . . . for melting down bitumen.

qupta 1 (קוּפְּתָא, ܩܘܦܬܐ, Ar. قُفَّة) basket, round pitched basket-boat. St. cstr. **qupat**. Ginzā 103 n. 7. Masc. doublet **qupa 2** s.v. **qupat nkilia** Gy 97:21 basket of the cunning ones; **qir(i)a d̲-qupta** DC 46. 255. 3 the pitch of a basket-boat.

qupta 2 doublet of **gupta**. **htum bqupta d̲-qaina d̲-zrara** DC 20 seal into a case of bamboo.

ququbana Jb 108:12 AC a var. of **qurbana** (hence possibly a corruption of **qurqbana**? Jb ii 108 n. 5).

quraha ([? Hittite] P. كُلاه hat, cf. Syr. ܩܘܪܩܠܐ cap?) helmet. (Phrygian) cap. Pl. **-ia**. Masc. **šuba qurahia d̲-parzla brišia matnalia** DC 44. 1559, DC 43 C 2 (& *often*) seven helmets of iron I place on my head; similarly **šuba qurahia d̲-mia** DC 44. 1557 = Morg. 266/22:41, **šuba qurahia d̲-ziua** DC 37. 302, DC 43 C 4.

qurar for **qarar** in **bla qurar** DC 46. 98:16.

qurata (cf. **quraha**) hat, cap. Mod. pronunciation: *qoratta*. **qurata d̲-briših̲** DC 23. 252 the cap on his head; **gusparta iaʿnia qurata** (var. **qrata**) **d̲-zaga** AM 134:16 a cock's comb, i.e. the 'hat' of a cock.

qurba (rt. **QRB**) nearness, proximity. **qurba ruhqa hauia** Gy 388:18 nearness will become distance; **ruhqa uqurba** DC 40. 336.

qurbana 1 (rt. **QRB**, ܩܘܪܒܢܐ, H. קָרְבָּן, Ar. قربان) gift, present, sacrifice, offering, oblation MG 136:20. **qurbana d̲-tirba d̲-hiuaniata mqarbilh̲** Gy 45:18 they bring him an offering of the fat of animals; **mqablia qurbana** Gs 36:22 they accept gifts; **qurbana lamqabil** Gs 2:8 accepteth no gift; **mahbata uqurbana iahbilia** DC 26. 572 = DC 44. 582 they bestow gifts and a present upon me; **qurbana d̲-ʿmak qablat kd̲ adlat** DC 20. 114 the offering which thy mother presented when she brought (thee) forth.

qurbana 2 for **qurqbana** (q.v.), cf. also **ququbana**. **qurbana d̲-tarnaula** DC 46 the craw of a cock.

qurdaia CP 21:8 (for phonetic reasons not ܩܘܪܕܝܐ ML 23 n. 4, but ܩܘܪܕܝܢܐ Bar Bahlūl 1751) club. **qurdaia ana d̲-parzla** CP 21:3, ML 23:7 I am an iron club.

qurunpul AM 287:3, **qurunpil** DC 46. 8:8, 112:6 = **qarunpul**.

quruqsa occ. var. of **qurqsa** (q.v.).

qurzum AM 198 name of a town.

qurṭasa a woman's name MMII 109:bottom, 300 n. 10.

quria RD D 18 a family name.

qurna 1 (cf. **qarna**) extreme end, projection. **qurna d̲-naṣipak** Q 20:10 = ML 55:9 f., CP 44:21, DC 34. 1016 (& *often*) the end of thy stola; **qurna d̲-naṣipa** Oxf. roll f 514, 845, DC 41. 210 etc.

qurna 2 AM 256 a small town at the junction of the Tigris and Euphrates.

qurnasa (קוּרְנָסָא, קוּרְנֵיסָא, ܩܘܪܢܣܐ, cf. Ar. قِرْناس protruding part of a hill, back of the axe) hammer, mallet, mace. Var. **qirnasa**. **qurnasa rba d̲-hbila** Oxf. roll g 242 = DC 43

J 112 great hammer of destruction; **tartin gulpa qurnasa** Oxf. roll g 385 (var. **qirnasa** DC 43 J 171) s. **gulpa.**

qurnata = **qarnata** (s. **qarna** (*c*)). Var. **qarnita. qurnata ḏ-ʿngaria** Oxf. roll g 199 var. of **qarnata** DC 43 J 92 (s. **qarna** (*c*)); **zauiata ḏ-qurnata** (var. **qurnita** DC 20) **lagṭia** DC 43 D 61 corners which make projections (?).

qurpida (cf. ܩܘܪܦܝܕܐ, *κρηπίς, κρηπίδιον* LS, Jb ii 165 n. 1) shoe. **qurpida ḏ-parzla** Jb 164:3 f., 165:13 an iron shoe.

qarq(u)bana (קוּרְקְבָנָא, ܩܘܪܩܒܢܐ & ܩܘܪܩܘܒܢܐ) stomach (of birds), craw. Miscop. **qurbana 2, ququbana** s.vv. **upumẖ uqurqubanẖ** DC 44. 1987 = Morg. 270/30:22 and his mouth and his stomach; **uqurqbanẖ ukabdẖ** ATŠ I no. 217 and his stomach and his liver; **ruha hʿ ḏ-iatba lpumẖ ḏ-qurqbana** Or. 329:7 (var. **qurbana** P.A.'s copy) that spirit that sitteth on the orifice of the stomach; **mnata lqurqbana ulšuba aṭirpia ḏ-ʿtbẖ** DC 48. 26 f. is due to the stomach and to the seven lobes (*or* leaves) which are therein; **ušria qurqbania ḏ-plan br planita ḏ-akil ʿkilta** P.A. xii and free from bewitchment the stomach of N. son of N. so that he may eat food.

qurqla (rt. **QRQL**) upheaval, upsetting, curl. Doubtf. MG 78 n. 1, Ginzā 202 n. 3. Pl. **-ia. mahilẖ lialda bqurqlia** (var. **bqarqlia** CD; **bqurqsia** Sh. ʿAbd.'s copy is a miscop.) **rurbia ḏ-mha umitpik rišẖ ltitai ukraiia lilai** Gy 202:13 f. they attack the babe with mighty upheavals, that strike it (var. **ḏ-muha**, Sh. ʿAbd.'s copy, of the brain) and its head is reversed to downward and its feet to upward; but cf. **bqurqlia ḏ-muhain** s. **muha.**

qurqsa (cf. קוּרְקְסָא hook, tree-roots cast up by flood, but possibly a corruption of Lat. *crucifixus* MSt 137:4 ff.) crucifix (?) Lidzb. block (of wood). MSchr. 99 n. 5. Var. **quruqsa** Jb 109:4 A, CP trs. 34 n. 3. **ṣalamata ḏ-qurqsa** Gy 24:20, 60:8 images of the crucifix; **alaha d-qurqsa naqšia usagdilẖ** Gy 226:19 they carve out the god of the crucifix and worship him; pl. **alahia ḏ-qurqsa** CP 49: penult., Q 23:14 wooden gods; **ṣaliba ḏ-naqšia bašiata uqaimia lqurqsa sagdia** Jb 109:3 f. the cross which they fix on the walls and standing they worship the crucifix.

qurša (rt. **QRŠ**, ܩܘܪܫܐ) cold, freezing, hard frost. **qurša uziq sagia** AM 184:8 freezing and much wind; **qurša umisia** s. **misia 1.** But **qurša ḏ-hanatẖ iahra** ATŠ II no. 58 read **riša** etc. as ATŠ II no. 243.

QUŠ s. **QŠŠ** pe. act. pt.

qušan AM 188 name of a city. BZ Ap. II.

quš(i)ania (rt. **QŠA**) hardness, intractability. **uʿtlẖ qušania** AM 4:15, var. **qušiania** Par. xxvi and he is intractable.

QUT = **QTT** (q.v.).

qutraiia DC 7 name of a people or tribe.

QṬN orig. but non-Mandaic form of **GṬN** (q.v.). Gl. 133:9 f. قصّر *abbreviare* كوتاه كرد.

Dᴇʀ.: **quṭana.**

QṬR orig. but non-Mandaic form of **GṬR** (q.v.) Only corrupt forms: **qiṭria qaṭria uharšia haršia** DC 44. 789 tie (magic) knots and make spells (doubtf.); **uababia laqaṭarin** Zotb. 218b:36 and the gate-ways were not closed (a sign of peace? doubtf.).

Dᴇʀ.: **qaṭur.**

qi- s. q(a)-. **ḏ-qimrahiṭ** AM 277:29 which flees; **qimzamar** he plays etc.

qibad DC 22. 380 a var. of **qabad** Gy 284:6.

qidahata a pl. of **qidihta** (q.v.).

qidia (ܩܕܝܐ) swollen glands. **ruha hʿ ḏ-iatba lpuma umitigria qidia upiqia** Or. 328:12 f. that (evil) spirit that is situated on the mouth and is called swollen glands and impediments (of speech?, cf. **pigia 1**).

q(i)dihta (rt. **QDH II**) cry MG 64:8, 109:17, 162:ult. Pl. **qidahata** & **qihdata** MG 66:19, 109:18, 162:paen. **bqidihtẖ qda** Jb 17:1, **qda bqidihtẖ, qda šitin qidahata** (var. **qihdata** PD 863) **bhda qdihta** s. **QDA II** pf.; **qihdat tlatma ušitin qihdata bihda qidihta** Gy 163:17 f. she gave 360 cries in one cry.

qidsar DC 46. 170:5 a higher being.

qidra (קִידְרָא, ܩܕܪܐ, mod. H. קְדֵרָה > Ar. قِدْر < Akk. *diqaru*) cauldron, cooking-pot. Pl. **-ia. bqidria ubdudia ḏ-nhaša nibašliẖ** Morg. 259/9:30 in copper cauldrons and pots we will boil him, cf. **bqidria ḏ-parzla uabara unhaša** DC 44. 411.

qihdata a pl. of q(i)**dihta** (q.v.).

qiuai name of a higher being. **btaurʿil ʿutra gabra ḏ-hua br qiuai** DC 51.

qiuan AM 205 name of a town BZ Ap. II.

qilba (cf. Targ. קְלַבִּינְטְרִין soft pillow?) bolster, head-rest. Ginzā 436 n. 5. **bit qilba** CP 222:3, Par. xv 11b = Par. xxv 15b = ŠQ 15:10 bolster; **aqapra napil bqilbaiun** Gs 17:21 dust falleth on their pillow (bolster).

qiluma (קַלְמְתָא & כַּלְמְתָא, ܩܠܡܬܐ, Ar. قَمْل, South-Ar. 𐩤𐩣𐩡𐩩, Eth. ቍምል, Akk. *kalmatu*, rel. to قنم, cf. قَنَمَة stench, H. כִּנָּם, כִּנִּים, the latter also mod. H. and Sam. 'gnats', mod. H. כְּנִימָה vermin, cf. MG. 54 n. 4) corruption, putrefaction MG 126:1. Pl. **-ia. ʿdilma bqiluma ʿtit** Oxf. 25 b should I have come into corruption? MG 471:17; **manharlun lqilumia kulhun** Gy 101:21 illumineth all corruptible things; **npaqtẖ lqiluma** Gs 78:19 f. thou hast forsaken corruption (why l-?).

qilis DC 43 A 96 a demon. St. emph. **qilisa** DC 37. 438 doubtf.

qilqin AM 198 a town.

qimta Gy 108:6 for **qaiamta.**

qimtua DC 41. 378 name of one of the two wives of John the Baptist. Var. **qinta 2** (q.v.).

qin 1 name of the queen of darkness and mother of devils, grandmother of Ur, but sometimes identified with his mother Ruhạ; consort of Anatan. **qin ʿma ḏ-ʿmẖ ḏ-ʿur** Gy 145:17 Q. mother of Ur's mother; **qin malakta marta ḏ-hšuka** Gy 140:2 f. Q. the queen, mistress of darkness; **qin uanatan gabaria ḏ-hšuka** Gy 140:9 f. (cf. s. **gabara**), **anatan uqin** Gy 144:22;

qirbit luata d̲-qin uʿdamilh̲ bzaua d̲-napša anatan Gy 144:ult. f. I approached Q. and assumed the appearance of her own husband Anatan; **qin d̲-mitqiria sumqaq rabtia** Gy 145:16; **qin ʿmaian** Gy 146:13 Q. our mother, **qin ʿmaihun** Gy 146:3 Q. their mother. Often in Gy (cf. 146:15, 21 f., 148:19, 24, 149:7, 10, 23), DAb = RD (cf. 1, 28c, B 87 etc.), PD 392, identified with Ruha RD 7. **adam br qin** CP 199(b):5, Morg. 88:4, DC 3. 203:14, DC 41. 375, cf. **br qina** s. **qina 2** (*a*) (end).

qin 2 st. abs. & cstr. of **qina 2.**

qina 1 (H. קִנְאָה, ܩܢܐܬܐ) rancour, envy, grudge, jealousy, enmity, resentment MG 71:8, 102:12. Masc. (differently from H. & Syr). **libaikun lanilguṭ qina man d̲-lagiṭ qina šalmana lamitiqria** Gy 36:2 (cf. 16:18) let not your hearts be envious, whosoever is envious shall not be called righteous; **sina qina uplugia** Gy 16:17 f., 112:17, 122:13, 243:22, Q 27:12 hatred, rancour, and dissensions; **qina rba d̲-blibh̲ hua** Jb 17:7 great grudge that was in his heart, cf. 31:4 s. **qina 2**; **qina ʿlh̲ abadt** DC 34. 545 thou wert envious thereat; **qina ʿlan latilgaṭ** DC 34. 552 do not harbour a grudge against us; **lagiṭ qina blibh̲** AM 9:5 he cherishes rancour in his heart.

qina 2 (קִינָּא, ܩܢܐ, H. קֵן, Akk. *qinnu*) (*a*) nest, brood, home, family, group, (*b*) pile, a disc of unleavened saltless bread upon which scraps of ritual food have been placed (in the *masiqta*). Fem. (as in later H., differently from cl. H. & Syr.) MG 158:13 f., but occasionally masc., cf. DC 37. 594. St. abs. & cstr. **qin 2.** Pl. **-ia.** (*a*) **qina mdalaita** Gy 201:1, Q 70:9, Zotb. 217b:10, AM (*& often*) an exalted family; **laqna qina** Gs 13:24 he founded no family; **niqnun qinaihun** Jb 132:4, **qinaiun niqnun** Jb 133:5 they build their nest; **qina d̲-abahath̲** Gy 168:2 the home of his parents; **had nihuia naṭar qina** DC 26. 363, 385 one shall be guardian of the family(-home); **nizikia nhura d̲-qinan d̲-** (?) **tartin usrin šurbata d̲-simiaiil satana** JRAS 1937 596:26 the light of our family shall vanquish that (?) of the twenty-four tribes of the Satan Ishmael (i.e. of the Arabs); **qinh̲ ʿkuma** RD D 5 his family(-name) is Black; **bnh̲ uqinh̲ ušurbath̲** AM 28:penult. his children, family, and tribe; **qinai ušurbatai** DC 43 G 3 my family and kindred; **bnh̲ qinh̲ rahṭan** [*sic*] **abatrh̲** AM 92:13 the children of his family pursue him; **qina d̲-muta ušurbata d̲-hbila** DC 40. 224 brood of death and progeny of destruction; **qina biša d̲-baita d̲-ptahil** DC 37. 594 the evil nest (as masc.) of P.'s house; **qina qrulh̲ d̲-razia kulhun bgauh̲ ʿtrabin** (read -(i)un) . . . **d̲-bqina dilun ʿtrabun d̲-hinun qina qrulh̲** ATŠ I no. 244 they called it 'nest', for all the mysteries were brought up in it . . . that they were nurtured in their nest, that which they called 'nest'; **riš qinh̲** ATŠ II no. 190 chief of his kin; **zimburia kd̲ napqia mn qinaihun** Gs 114:4 hornets when they issue from their nests; **bmanziai qina banin mn bisrai lqinaihun masqia** Gs 12:5 f. they (: the birds) build a nest with my hair, and take up some of my flesh to their nest; **anana mn qinh̲ bit ulaʿhablak lgiṭatlh̲ lqina rba lʿuṣrak** Jb 31:3 f. thou didst ask a wife from his family and he did not give (her) to thee, thou cherishest against him a great grudge (**qina 1**) in thy mind; **miša br amra mn qinak hua** Jb 74:11 Moses, son of Amran, was of thy family; **iauna br qina** DC 41. 188 dove, son of a nest (brood, proved fertility); here may belong also **adam br qin** (s. **qin 1**) as Qin could hardly be designated as the mother of **adam gabra qadmaia** (see CP trs. p. 151 note 7); (*b*) **kd̲ msadra qina** DC 41. 280 when the pile (of sacred foods) is arranged; **atna lqina ʿl kapta d̲-miša** DC 41. 283 he placed a *qina* on the oil-bowl; **uatna pihta lqina unisbh̲** DC 41. 293 and he placed the *qina* and took it up; **šit qinia d̲-sadrinun ašganda alma d̲-pašat qina** DC 41. 321 f. six *qinas* which the acolyte has arranged, until one remains; **qina batraita** PD 1680 the last pile; **arbasar qinia** Oxf. roll f 503, 831 = DC 42 par. fourteen piles (of sacred food on unleavened loaves).

qina 3 for **qaina** (*a*). **qina d̲-naizia hauria** Par. xxvii 83 a s. **naiza.**

qinaia = **qanaia.** Pl. **-iia.** **qinaia d̲-hašil razia** DC 35 a smith that forges mysteries.

qind(i)la = **qandila** (q.v.). Pl. **-ia.** **qindlia** Gs 129:8, **qindlaihun** Gs 129:6 Ginzā 584 n. 1.

qiniana (rt. **QNA I,** (קִנְיָנָא, ܩܢܝܢܐ) property, possessions (cattle, herds, estate) MG 136:13. **qinianh̲ auid** Gy 35:8 its property perisheth; **qiniana niqnia** AM (*often*) he will acquire property; **qinianh̲ mn ruhqa maitia** AM 12:16 they will bring him property from afar; **qinianai uhiuaniatai** DC 12. 240, P.A. XIII (*& often*) my property and my cattle.

qinsa secondary form of **qisa** (q.v.).

qinta 1 (ܩܝܢܬܐ, H. קִינָה, Targ. קינא, cf. Ar. قَيْنَة female singer-slave) hymn, song. St. abs. **bhad qinta nibirkh̲ lhibil ziua** DC 50. 327 we will bless H.-Z. in one hymn; **brika hazin puma dakia ubrika hazin qinta** Lond. roll A 295 blessed is this pure mouth and blessed is this hymn; **brika qintaikun hilita** . . . **d̲-mn pumaikun npaq** DC 50. 216 = DC 42 par. blessed is your sweet hymn . . . which proceeded from your mouths, cf. DC 3. 337: ult., DC 53. 343:14, 472:16; **brika hazin škinta qinta** DC 34. 715 blessed is this dwelling of (?, read **d̲-qinta**?) hymn(ing).

qinta 2 a *malwāša* woman's name, also the name of one of the two wives of John the Baptist (var. **qimtua** s.v.). **iahia iuhana** . . . **qinta uanhar zauh̲** Morg. 88:11, CP 199(b):13.

qisa (קִיסָא rough edge, wood, ܩܝܣܐ wood, Syr. den. verb: to make rough, build from wood) rough edge? Secondary form **qinsa. balaur hu d̲-qisa ʿlh̲** DAb it is of crystal, upon which there is wood (?); **sikina uqinsa** DC 32. 604 a rough-edged knife (hendiadys).

qip(a) pass. pt. pe. of **QUP** (q.v.).

qipia (rt. **QPA I**) Jb 44:4, 141:11, 155:8, 157:10 scum, flotsam.

qiṣa s. **QṢṢ.**

qiqla, qiqilta (קִיקְלָא, קִיקִלְתָּא, ܩܶܩܠܬܳܐ, H. קִיקְלוֹן Brockelm. i 247) dung (heap), dunghill, infamy MG 78:20, Pl. **qiqlia, qiqlata. gaira bšumak uazla lbit qiqlia** Jb 80:4 f. (she) fornicateth in thy name and goeth to the house of infamy MSt 16 (& n. 2); **(a)šdaṯ lqiqilta** Jb 87:8 I cast her on a midden; **ašdaṯ bqiqlia** Jb 88:14 I cast her into dunghills; **bqiqlia šadialẖ** Jb 98:3 she casts it into dung; **bqiqlia maiit** Jb 98:6 dies in ordure; **šadilẖ lqiqlata** Gy 391:7 they throw it on the dunghills; **ainẖ ḏ-iatba ʿl qiqilta** JRAS 1937 593:30 his eyes that rest on a dunghill.

QUR (den. from qira 1) to daub with pitch, to tar.

Pa. Pass. pt. **lamqaira arbak bqupra** s. **qupra.**

qira 1 (קִירָא, ܩܺܝܪܳܐ, Ar. قير Fränkel 150) pitch, bitumen MG 102:18. **mia bqira larbia** Gy 79:3 water mixeth not with pitch; **qira qašaita** Lond. roll B 96, 155, var. **qašita** (s. **qašia 1**); **napṭa uqira** Gy 178:23, 279:24 petroleum and pitch; **tarbaṣia ḏ-qira aklia** Jb 243:5 courtyards steeped in (lit. which eat) pitch. **haspa uqira** s. **haspa 1.**

qira 2 for **qiria 1. qira ušira** AM 266:29 dispute and anarchy.

qiras st. cstr. of **qirsa. qiras almia** Jb 244:4, Gs 41:7 the misery of the worlds Jb ii 223 n. 7.

qirba Oxf. xii a var. of **qurba.**

qird (Ar. قِرد) monkey. Pl. **-ia. šaḥmil qird** AM 129:18 monkey's fat. **qupia uqirdia** s. **qupa.**

qirda Zotb. 222b:11 a woman's name.

qiria 1 (ܩܶܪܝܳܐ) mishap, strife, accident, accidental pollution, obstinacy, quarrel, dispute MG 102:21. Var. **qira 2** s.v. Pl. **qiria, qiriia,** cf. **qiriata 2** (*a*) s.v. **šitlak bqiria ʿtinsib** Jb 21:6 thy offspring was taken away in an uproar; **bnẖ bqiria azlia** Jb 26:11 his children will enter into strife; **bnẖ bqiria gṭilia** Jb 29:11 his children were killed in a brawl; **bnai bqiria mitnasbia** Jb 34:6 (DC 30 **mitnisbẖ**) my children were reft away in dispute; **qiria umutana ḏ-alma** Gy 287:3 disaster and pestilence of the world; **nitun dirdqunia bqiria udirdquniata kḏ pumaiin ḏ-biriata nʿhuia qiria balma** Gs 8:1 ff. doubtf. Ginzā 428 n. 8. **bqiria nizal** AM (*often*) he will enter into dispute; **qiria ušiqupta bhiuaniata uṣipria hauia** AM 185:15 there will be accidents and murrain amongst cattle and fowls; **qiria ḏ-lilia** DC 43 D 63 (*& often in exorcisms*) *pollutio nocturnis,* emission of semen in sleep accident by night; **qiriia unidria uašlamata** DC 40:233 mishaps, vows, and forfeitures; **mn qiriia ušiqupta ḏ-baqiata** DC 40:982 f. from mishaps and from the attack of gangrene; **qiria uluṭata** DC 43 H 40 quarrels and curses; **šira uqiria nafša** AM 266:26 much licence and (many) quarrels.

qiria 2 Jb 252:8 B, Gs 44:9 for **qaria 1.**

qiriata 1 pl. of **qrita** MG 165:20. **qiriatan** our creatures MG 178:paen.; **qiriata ḏ-maštuṣia** Gy 309:4 creatures of the monsters; **qiriata ḏ-hšuka** Morg. 251/90:6 f., Q 48:15, ATŠ II no. 316 creatures of darkness; **kulhun qiriatun** Jb 196:12 all their creatures; **kulhin qiriata** RD B 1 all the creatures; **qiriata kulhin ḏ-hšuka** Gy 78:14 all the creatures of darkness; **ʿubadia uqiriata ḏ-qra** Gy 268:3 works and creatures which he created; **qiriata zikria uqiriata nuqbata** DC 43 A 23 (evil) creatures male and female.

qiriata 2 (cf. **qiria 1**) (*a*) mishaps, misadventures, (*b*) incantations, spells, invectives. (*a*) Q 21:19, 62:23, Oxf. roll g 923; **šuquptaikun uqiriatkun** DC 43 A 89 (cf. ibid. 132) your plagues and misadventures; (*b*) **luṭata uqiriata** (*often in exorcisms*) curses and invectives, cf. **aqraiata, aqariata, aqiriata, qriata** s.vv.

qiriata 3 pl. (of קִרְיְתָא, ܩܪܝܬܐ, H. קִרְיָה, Ar. قَرية) cities, places. **lišania ḏ-amamia utaumia uqiriata** ATŠ II no. 433 languages of peoples, nations, and places.

qirsa (ܩܽܘܪܣܳܐ, ܩܶܪܣܳܐ, cf. Mishn. קִירָס < καιρός time) (*a*) hard time, trial, misfortune, (*b*) malady, sickness, (*c*) personified as a demon (of both genders), (*d*) contraction, shrinkage? MG xxx 6, 149:anteantep. St. cstr. **qiras** s.v. Pl. **qirsia.** Masc. (*a*) **bit qirsa** Gs 88:16, 114:15, 23 the House-of-Trial (purgatory); **bqirsia** (var. **bqirsa** Par. xxvi) **š(a)rira niqum** AM 2:16 he will stand firm amidst adversity; **mn qirsa tidhal** AM 58:15 f. she should fear calamity; **urahiq minai qirsia** DC 40 and put misfortunes far from me; **qirsa rba** Jb 86:5 great misfortune; (*b*) **lau mna qirsa anat** Gs 41:17 thou art apportioned to illness; **qirsia sainia** Q 17:4 abominable illnesses; (*c*) **ʿl qirsa zakra uʿl qirsa nuqbata** DC 37. 594; (*d*) **niqria lšamiš uqirsa nimṭiẖ** DC 26. 108 he read (it) over the sun and shrinkage (partial eclipse) will befall it.

qirsana (from preced). (*a*) sick, ill, (*b*) calamity, adversity. Pl. **-ia.** MG 9:20, 139:4. Scr. def. **qrsana.** (*a*) **masia qirsania** Gy 29:9 (**qrsania** A) healeth the sick; (*b*) **lup lilita brat qirsania** DC 43 I 121 the lilith Luf daughter of calamities.

qirqa (H. קַרְקַע, Akk. *qaqqaru*) soil, ground, bottom. **bqirqa ḏ-arqa** DC 40. 283 by the soil of the earth.

qirq(i)la (rt. **QRQL**) (*a*) hook, (*b*) curl. Pl. **-ia.** (*a*) **bqirq(i)lia ḏ-parzla** DC 44. 1033 with iron hooks; (*b*) as a var. of **qurqlia** (cf. s. **muha**).

qirqna (Nöld. קרקנא? MG 128:6 but cf. Ginzā 128 n. 5) Gy 115:19 prob. a dress, or sandals, shoes? Var. **qarqina** s.v.

qištana (rt. קשט) adornment? **ṭnupia uqištana** DC 3 pollutions and adornment (?).

qišmiš (P. كشمش) DC 7 (illustrated part) currant, currant-bush.

qita (rt. **QTT**) fixed, persistent? of fever, chronic? **ʿšata qita** DC 43 H 41 (*& often in exorcisms,* var. **qata**).

qitia 1 (rt. **QTA**) sob(bing), hysteria, bursting into tears. **qitia br qitia zha ḏ-qitia unha ḏ-qitia umkabšin qitia umiabšin qitia umapqin**

qitia DC 45 JRAS 1943 176:10 f. Hysteria son of sobbing, quit sobbing, and quieten sobbing, and sobs shall cease, and sobs (: tears) shall dry up, and sobbing depart (doubtf.); **qitiak unisrak** DC 43 J 155 s. **nisra.**

QLA (קְלָא, ܩܠܐ, H. קלה I, Ar. قلا, قلى, Eth. ቀለወ, Akk. *qalû*) to burn, consume by fire, roast, parch; ethpe. to be burnt, be inflamed against.

Pe. Pf. with suff. **qlaith̲** Gy 205:18 I burnt him MG 288:7. Impf. **tiqlia** AM 209 it will burn; with suff. **niqlunh̲ bnura** DC 43 J 84 they shall burn it in fire. Impt. pl. with suff. **aitun nura uquliun** Jb 93:15 bring fire and burn me MG 286:13. Act. pt. **damit lṭura qalia** Jb 109:13 (var. **qalaia** ABCD) thou resemblest a burning mountain; with encl. **ubnura qalilh̲** AM 46:16 and will burn him with fire; **bnura qalilun** ATŠ I no. 252 he burns them in fire. Part. pres. **paisit uqalit umahribit** JRAS 1938 3:2 thou wilt destroy, burn, and devastate. Pass. pt. **kd̲ qlia bnura** AM 287:1 when baked in fire; **riha d̲-qlia** AM burnt incense.

Pa. Pf. with suff. **atat nura uqalath̲ lškinta** HG (colophon) there came fire and consumed the cult-hut. Pt. (pass.) **šušmia d̲-mqalia bnura** DC 46. 67:3 sesame seeds roasted (parched) in fire.

Ethpe. Impf. **nitiqlia** DC 44. 1304 = Morg. 264/19:26 shall be burnt (suffer agony). Pt. **mitiqlia** Gy 74:21, 75:10, 17, 117:11 will be burnt; **bihdadia mitiqlia** Gy 96:19 they are inflamed against one another (Lidzb. **TQL**: *sie strauchelten über einander*).

Gl. 55:9 f. **aqla** حرق *comburere* سوخت.

qlala 1 = **qulala 1** (q.v.).

qlala 2 = **qulala 2** (q.v.).

qlasia (ܩܠܝܣܝܐ, ܐܩܠܝܣܝܐ, ἐκκλησία) Gy 227:3 church MG xxix 27 f., Furlani: *I Termini* 358.

qlapsa DC 40. 348 for **qlupta** ibid. 475.

qlapta (ܩܠܦܬܐ, Jew.-Aram. קְלִפָּא) shell, carapace, hard casing, hard skin. Varr. **qlapsa, qlupta** s.vv. **qlapta d̲-bita** DC 27. 198 the shell of an egg; **qlapta d̲-bita d̲-iauna** AM 131:12 the shell of a dove's egg; **qlapta gauaita uqlapta baraita qašita** ATŠ I no. 264 an inner shell and an outer hard casing.

QLD (den., cf. Jew.-Aram. קלד, Ar. قلد) to clutch, fasten, grasp firmly, lock.

Refl. Pt. **hiuia bʿdh̲ miqlad** DC 46. 81:4 a serpent (is) clutched (grasped) in his hand.

Der.: **(a)qlida.**

qlupta = **qlapta**: **kd̲ nuna bqlupta** DC 40. 475 (var. **bqlapsa** ibid. 348) like a fish in its scales.

qlida = **aqlida** (q.v.). Pl. **-ia. qlida d̲-mara blibai lgiṭna** Morg. 265/20:17 I hold the key of the Lord in my heart; **qlida d̲-marai bʿdai blibai lgiṭna** DC 44. 1336 I hold the key of my Lord in my hand (and) in my heart; **gauria uaqlidia d̲-hua šanin mn qlidia kulhun** Gy 145:13 f. locks and keys that were sublimer (: superior) than all (other) keys. Sg. often in RD = DAb, cf. C 12 [*bis*], A 1 f., personified: **qlida ṣaliaʿil** RD A 1, **qlida samandarʿil** RD F 1. Gl. 155:ult. **qlida** (& miswritten pl.) مفتاح, مفاتح *claves* كليدها.

qlim AM 170:9, 199:10 = **ʿqlim.** Pl. **qlimia. qlimia halin** DC 51 these regions.

qliqa (rt. **QLQ**) squinting, distorted, oblique, cross-eyed. Fem. st. emph. **qliqtia. ia daiua d̲-qliqa ainh̲** DC 43 J 137, 148 O cross-eyed demon!; **aina qliqtia** JRAS 1937 590:10, 1943 170:16 squinting eye.

QLL (Gen. Sem.) to be light, swift, small, few, hasty, frivolous; to belittle, curse, abuse; pa. lighten, relieve? Pa. formed as from **QUL.**

Pe. Pt. with encl. **qalilak** Gy 218:1 he abuseth thee.

Pa. Pf.? with encl. **qailinalh̲** RD B 14 we belittled it. Impf. **niqaiil qmara** s. **qmara.**

Der.: **qalia 3, 4, qalil(a), q(u)lala 2.**

QLP (קלף, ܩܠܦ) to remove (outer skin, casing), shell, strip, slip out of cover, peel, shred.

Pe. Impf. **niqlap kursih̲ mn muhak** DC 46. 136:11 he shall remove his seat from thy brain; **rišaiia niqlap** JRAS 1943 171:10 he shall strip (?) the chief ones. Act. pt. **kd̲ šamša d̲-qalpa usalqa** JRAS 1938 3:31 like the sun which slips out and rises.

Pa. Pass. pt. **ɛadas mqalap** DC 46 husked linseed.

Der.: **qulpa, qlapta** (var. **qlupa**, miscop. **qlapsa**).

QLQ (קְלַק to throw, ܩܠܩ to show white of eye, mod. Syr. ܩܠܩ to show evil eye, Ar. قَلِقَ to be agitated) to blight, glare, be cross-eyed.

Pe. Act. pt. **qaliq** s.v. Pass. pt. **qliqa** s.v.

Der.: s. pe.

QMA (mod. from **QDM**, cf. **qam** = **aqam**) to advance, be before. Gl. 90:1 f. سبق *praecedere* پيش رفت; 102:9 f. ضرب *proponere* اول خبر آورد; 131:5 f. قدم *praecedere* پيش رفت; 131:7 f. pa. قدّم *offerre* پيش برد.

qmaha (ܩܡܝܥܐ) written talisman, protective writing, phylactery, amulet MG 71:24. Pl. **-ia. qmahia upišria** PD 381 phylacteries and exorcisms. Often in AM and magic documents.

qmamir ziua Gs 2:3, 3:17, 24, 4:12, Jb 232:6 (*& often*) a spirit of light Jb ii 214 n. 6.

qmana = **qamana. qmanak ʿl man mlia** *Florilegium*, and thy bow, against whom is it drawn?

qmara (cf. **qamar**) belt, girdle, confining band, constriction? **niqaiil qmara** DC 43 G 25 he will lighten (relieve?) the confining band (constriction?).

QMM in impf. pl. pe. of **QUM** (q.v.).

QNA I (Gen. Sem.) to acquire, obtain, attain, possess, earn, gain possession of; to succeed.

Pe. Pf. **laqnun bqinianun** Gy 232:3 they acquire not as their property; (ʿ)**qnia** Gy 256:4 they (fem.) acquired MG 258:11. Impf. **qiniana niqnia** AM (*often*) he will acquire property; **arqa umia niqnia** AM 2:6 he will gain possession of land and water. Act. pt. pl.

qanin ušabqin balma Gy 17:10 they acquire property, but leave it in the world; **qanin ušapqin libnaihun** Gy 76:21 f. = **qanin ušabqin lbnaihun** Jb 181:8 they acquire (property) and leave it to their children; **qanʿn mšamrin bataiun** Gs 17:23 they acquire houses and leave them.

Der.: **qiniana.**

QNA II (cf. **qanaia**) to forge.

Pe. Act. pt. **qania parzla ḏ-qraba** AM 154:16 he forges iron (weapons) of war.

Der.: **qanaia** (var. **qinaia**).

QNA III, QNN III (den. from **qina 2**) to make a nest, found a family.

Pe. Pf. **laqna qina** Gs 13:24 s. **qina 2.** Impf. **niqnun** Jb 132:4, 133:4 s. **qina 2.**

qna for **qina 2** in **qnaihun** Zotb. 225a (1st text:5).

qnasa (rt. **QNS**, קְנָסָא) penalty, punishment, doom. Pl. **-ia. qnasa umuta** ATŠ I no. 289 doom and death; **qnasa ḏ-nišmata** RD B 101 f. = DAb par. the punishment of souls; **qnasa ḏ-iauna** Oxf. roll f 133 name given to ceremony of sacrificing the dove (: 'the sin-offering of the dove'); **qnasia mia** Oxf. roll f 82, **q(u)nasia ḏ-mia** CP 290:9, CP trs. 156 n. 3 apparently a form of torture (like dipping under for a long time?), water-penalties; **qnasa ḏ-hirba** Gs 24:10 the doom of the sword; **qnasa ḏ-qudam hirba** Gs 20:23, 21:1, 7, 23:22 penalty preceding the sword. Often with **QNS** q.v.

QNDR s. **QDR.**

QNN = **QNA III.**

QNS (Jew.-Aram. & mod. H. קנס) to condemn, punish, decree, doom.

Pe. Pf. **qnas qnasa qudam hirba** Gy 260:5 he decreed a judgement before the sword; with encl. **qnaslia** (var. **qnislia** DC 22) **muta** Gy 245:20 they condemned (or doomed) me to death; with suff. **qnasinun lrazia** ATŠ II no. 88 he performed propitiatory rites. Impf. **niqnas qnasa** Gs 1:23 we will impose the doom (MG 220:21). Impt. with encl. **qnuslia** (var. **qnaslia** D) **qnasa** Gs 24:13 pronounce my doom (MG 220:21 f.). Inf. **miqnas qnasa ḏ-razia** ATŠ II no. 88 to perform propitiatory rites.

Ethpe. Pf. **ʿtqinsat** Jb 205:9 she was doomed; with encl. **ʿtiqnislẖ** Gy 119:20 was imposed to it (: the world) as penalty.

Der.: **qnasa.**

QSS = **QUŠ.**

QPA (Aram., Syr., H.) to float on surface, swim; to gather together, collect in a heap or bunch, huddle together Jb ii 145 n. 4, 158 n. 11; (cf. ܩܦ̈) to bend down.

Pe. Pf. **ṣaidia qpun bhauria** Jb 156:11 the fishermen huddled together in the marshes. Act. pt. **qapia iuhana ulitlẖ haila lmiqam** Gy 191:17 Y. is bending down (Lidzb. *schwimmt*) and hath no power to stand (upright); **kauila hua qapia uazla** Gy 380:19 the ark was swimming and going MG 383:17; pl. **qapin lpuma ḏ-ʿur** DAb they float to the mouth of Ur.

Gl. 20:5 f. **QPA** ازبد *spumare* كف زد; 81:9 f. id.

Der.: **qapaiia, qipia.**

QPL (Jew.-Aram., Syr., Ar., Eth.) to dispel, remove, tear out.

Pe. Pass. pt. **qpil mn bunkẖ** Gs 111:18, 20 was torn out from its place MG 379:21.

qṣiail DC 40 an angel.

QṢṢ (Aram., Syr., H., Ar., Akk. *qaṣāṣu*) to shorten, cut short.

Pe. Pass. pt. **šitil . . . qiṣa balẖ ladam** DAb Šitel (Seth) . . . whose fate (life) was cut short for (the sake of) Adam.

QṢR (Ar. قصر) to be short, shorten.

Pa. Impf. **latiqaṣir** AM 257:25 thou wilt not shorten.

QRA I (Sem., except Eth.) pe. to call, summon, read, recite, call into being, name, call forth, create MR 18:middle, ERE viii 383, Lidzb. ZDMG lxi 698 n. 1; pa. to call aloud, cry out, proclaim, appoint; (with *masiqta*) to celebrate.

Pe. Pf. **qra** MG 257:1, **qrat** MG 257:6, **qrit** thou didst call MG 257:18, I called MG 257:19, **qrun** MG 258:2; but also **qru** Gy 228:19, 251:18, MG 7:14, 258:3, **qraitun, qritun, ʿqritun** Gy 292:20 MG 258:13 f., **qrainin** Gy 235:10 MG 258:16; with encl. **qrilun** Gy 92:18 I called them, **qrilẖ** Oxf. 7 a, 50 a I called him; but **qritilẖ** Oxf. 49 b id., **qritilkun** Gy 255:5 ff. I called you, **qraitilun** Gy 172:5 I called them MG 257:19 f., 23 f., **qrulia** they called me (or created me) MG 53:18, **qrulẖ** MG 258:10, **qritulia** Gy 157:21 MG 258:15, **qrinalẖ** Gs 6:19, **qrinalak** Gs 6:18 MG 258:22; with suff. **qran** CP 3:7, Q 1:26 = ML 5:1 created me (MG 284:20), **qrak** Gy 191:7, 351:20, MG 286:15, **qiri(i)ẖ** MG 287:6 f., **bqala qritinkun** DC 43 D 49 I summoned you with a cry, **qraitin** Q 52:29, MG 285:19, **qruia** Gy 313:22 [*bis*], ML 263:3 [*bis*] (*& often* in Oxf. III), **qiriuia** Gy 101:5 (*& often*) He (: the Life), or they created him MG 288:18 f., **qru** they called (or created) her MG 258 n. 1, **qruk** Morg. 237/61:8 f., Gy 73:20, **qiriuk** they called thee (forth) MG 287:1, **qrun** (*often*) they called me forth MG 285: anteantep., **qiriun** Gy 92:11, 351:20 id. MG 286:1, **qrainak** MG 286:paen., **qrainẖ** Gy 126:22 MG 288:16, **qrainẖ liardna rba** DC 34:572 we created the great jordan; **qritun** Gy 240:5 ye called me MG 285:20. Impf. **niqria** MG 258:24, **tiqria** MG 258:25, **ʿqria** MG 259:1, **niqrun** MG 259:2, **tiqrun** MG 259:6; with encl. **niqrilẖ, ʿqrilak** MG 259 n. 1, **tiqrulan** Gy 260:ult., MG 259:7. Impt. **qria** MG 259:10, fem. **qrai** Gy 161:antep., Jb 116:1, MG 259:12, pl. **qrun** MG 259:14. Act. pt. **qaria** MG 259:18 (cf. also s.v.), **ḏ-qaria ulabid** Gy 218:often Nöld. *wer liest und nicht handelt* MG 368:3 f., Lidzb. *wer ausruft* etc. Ginzā 219 n. 2; pl. **nbihia qarin lnapšaihun** Gy 24:10 they call themselves prophets; **ḏ-qarin ulabdin** Gy 218:18. Part. pres. **qarina** I call, I read MG 259:19, fem. **qariana** Gy 161:22 MG 259:20, **qarit** MG 259:23, **qaritun** MG 259:27; with encl. **qarinalak** MG 259:25, **qariatlẖ, qariatbẖ** MG 259:24, **qaritulẖ** MG 259:25. Pass. pt. **qria** MG 259:paen.; pl. **qrʿi(i)a** Oxf. 44 b MG 5:ult., fem. **qrʿia**; but sometimes both as sg. MG 165:paen. ff., **miqria qrʿia qalia** CP 155:11 f. = ML 187:4

voices cry aloud proclamations; with encl. pers. pron. **qrʿit, qriit** Gy 72:3 MG 260:3 f., **qrinalak** Gy 187:21 we are called by thee MG 260:8. Inf. **miqria** (*very often*), less often **miqra** Gy 80:10, 88:11, Oxf. 44 b, DC 43 J 106 MG 260:12, 14.

Pa. Act. pt. **mqaria ginza ušadana hauia** DC 46. 120:2 cries (too) much and is crazy; **ualai alai d̲-mqaria ruha** Gy 329:2 and R. cried (hist. pres.): 'Woe is me, woe is me!' Part. pres. **mqarina** Gs 89 f. I cry MG 262:20. Inf. **qaruiia** Gs 89 f. (*often*), Jb 82:3 MG 263:11.

Ethpe. Pf. **ʿt(i)qria** MG 26:16, 214:2, 263:20; **qrita qadmaita d̲-ʿtqiriat** Gy 291:43 the first creation that was evoked (MG 263:26); **ʿtqrit** MG 264:7, 11, **ʿtiqrun** MG 264:18, fem. pl. **ʿt(i)qria** Gy 122:12, 209:4 MG 264:23, **ʿt(i)qritun** Gy 149:11 MG 264:27. Impf. **nit(i)qria, nʿtqria** MG 264:31, **tit(i)qria** MG 265:1, **nitiqrun** MG 265:5, **titiqrun** Gy 360:2 etc., **tit(i)qru** Gy 257:14 AB MG 265:9 f. Impt. pl. **ʿt(i)qrun** MG 265:19. Pt. **mit(i)qria** MG 265:23; pl. **mit(i)qrin** Gy 45:21, MG 31:15, 164:antep., **mitqiriin** Q 71:19 (*twice*, in a note) MG 164:22, **mitqirin** Oxf. 60 a MG 164:23; fem. pl. **lamitqirian** DC 34. 725 are not recited. Part. pres. **mitiqrina** MG 266:1, **mitqiriit** MG 266:6.

Gl. 163:8 f. **aqra** نادى *praedicare, vocare* آواز كرد; 179:1 f. missp. دعى *vocare* خواند; 181:11 f. **aqra** دعا *invitare* خواند.

Der.: **maqria, qaruia, qaria 1, qiria 2, qiriata 1, qrai(a)ta, qrita 1.**

QRA II (Syr. ܩܪܐ II, H. קרה to meet, Ar. قرا to wander, قرى to offer hospitality, gather, Eth. አቅረየ to obtain) to meet, join, contest.

Pe. Pf. **bhanat̲h̲ kuba d̲-qra mia bgauh̲** ATŠ II no. 405 in that cup of wine to which he added water.

Der.: **(a)qar** & varr. (? Nöld.), **qaria 2, qiria 1,** pl. **qiriata 2, qria 2.**

QRA III (Jew.-Aram., H., mod. H. קרע, Ar. قرع) to tear, rend, mangle, plough.

Pa. Pass. pt. **agia d̲-mqara** DC 40:223 furrows that are ploughed.

Der.: **qrita 2.**

qraba 1 (ܩܪܳܒܳܐ, Jew.-Aram. קְרָבְתָּא, Akk. *qarābu*) (*a*) war, hostile approach, attack, strife, (*b*) weapon(s) of war Jb ii 21 n. 2. Masc. Pl. **-ia.** (*a*) **nirmia qraba** Gy 5:12 wageth war; **laqarbia qraba mn hdadia** Gy 8:23 they wage no war with one another; **qraba utaktuša** Gy 24:12 war and strife; **rišaihun d̲-kulhun qrabia** Gy 113:5 the captain of all wars; **bquraba** [*sic*, var. **bqrab** Par. xxvi] **ʿnšia timut** AM (CS 26) in attack (of his?) women she will die; **nirig maria haila uzaina uqraba** Or. 331:14 Mars lord of army, and weapon, and war; **luat qraba nizal** AM 97:14 goes toward attack; (*b*) **qraba ʿtlabaš** Jb 13:11 he put on his armour; **drun qrabaikun** Jb 15:13 take up your weapons.

qraba 2 (rt. **QRB**) approach, offering, oblation. **tarmidia d̲-mtaqna** [*sic*] **bginzia uqraba** ATŠ II no. 134 priests (or sg.?) that are reliable in the rites and the Oblation; **abid qraba upišria** ATŠ I no. 233 performeth Oblation and exorcisms.

qrabaiia DC 34:28 a pl. of **qraba 1** (*b*)?

qrabtana occ. for **qarabtana.**

qraumia (Talm. קְרוּם, Syr. ܩܘܪܡܐ, Ar. قُرْمَة > Gr. *κορμός*) membrane, membrum virile? **uatia abatar dilia plan kd̲ šlia lbuta bqraumia** DC 46. 167:12 and he shall come after me N. having bared his bottom for my (?) penis (? homosexual love-charm).

qraita (rt. **QRA I** influenced by **II**?) outcry, malediction. Varr. s. **aqariata.** Pl. **qraiata. qraita d̲-kadba** ML 39:5 (var. **aqraita** CP 33:10); **luṭata uqraiata** DC 43 curses and maledictions; **šuma d̲-qraita** (*often*) the worldly (commonly known) name as distinct from the *malwâša.*

qrasania the sick, infirm GRr 29:9.

qrata occ. for **qurata.**

QRB (Gen. Sem.) to approach, draw near, approach with an offering = offer, (approach to) attack, make war, apply oneself; refl. associate with, be advanced, intimate with.

Pe. Pf. **qrib** MG 219:12. Impf. **niqrub, niqrab** MG 14:4, 219:12 & n. 3, **luat zauh̲ laniqrab** ATŠ II no. 43 he shall not approach his wife; **d̲-niqrab luat naṣiruta** ATŠ who neareth the priestly gnosis. Impt. **qrub** MG 219:12; pl. **qribiun** DC 34. 1037. Act. pt. pl. **laqarbia qraba** s. **qraba d̲-ʿl hukumta laqarbia** DAb who do not apply themselves to wisdom.

Pa. Impf. with suff. **niqarbunh̲** AM 17:11 they will approach him. Impt. pl. with suff. **qarbuia** approach him MG 279:1. Act. pt. **mqarib razia šumh̲** DC 27 his name is 'introducer to mysteries'.

Af. ? Pass. pt. pl. **maqribh̲** (var. **miqribh̲** B) **halšia** Jb 274:6 f. the bolts are pushed to (brought forward).

Ethpe. Pt. pl. **miqribh̲** cf. s. af.

Ethpa. Impf. **nitqarab** AM 13:6 he will have access, will associate.

Gl. 4:5 f. **QRB** اقترب *appropinquare* نزديک شد; 58:1 f. **aqrub** [sic] جاء *accedere* آمد; 114:9 f. **aqrb** [sic] عذب *torquere* عذاب كرد.

Der.: **qarbʿil, q(a)rabtana** (var. **q(a)raptana**), **qarib(a), qurba, qurbana, qraba 1, 2.**

QRD (Mishn. קרד pi. to scrape, Syr. ܩܪܰܕ to disperse, Ar. قَرِدَ to be corroded) to scour, corrode.

Pa. Pt. pl. **širiania d̲-mqardin** (poor var. **mqarqidan**) **mn murqa** JRAS 1948 170:26 veins (membranes) corroded by discharge.

Der.: **qarud**?

qrubal (cf. **qraba 1**) ATŠ II no. 364 attack.

qruna Lond. roll A 200 for **qurna.**

qria 1 pass. pt. pe. of **QRA I** (q.v.).

qria 2 (rt. **QRA II**) (*a*) fastening, tie, (*b*) misfortune, mishap (var. of **qiria 1**). Pl. same. (*a*) **kiph̲ uqria msanh̲** DC 42 the bows and fastenings of his sandals; **tubrh̲ lhazin qria** *Florilegium*, break this bond (or (*b*)?); (*b*) **qria**

šaria bmdintan *Florilegium*, misfortune dwells in our town.

qriata for **qiriata 2** (*b*) in **qriata d̲-gubria** IM 30:7 f. incantations of men.

qriha DC 22. 287 for **qrita 1** (*b*) Gy 291:33.

qrihta occ. for **qdihta.**

qrita 1 (rt. **QRA** I) (*a*) call, calling, vocation, invitation, (*b*) creation, creature MG 104:5. Pl. **qiriata 1** s.v. (*a*) **qrita d̲-hu ʿtiqria minh̲ uʿtqaiam** AM the vocation to which he is called by him and appointed; **qrita niqrunh̲** AM 15:6 they will call him to a calling; (*b*) **mn qrita d̲-šiqra hun** Gy 120:10 they (come into being) from a deceitful creation; **qrita qadmaita** Gy 291: 33 f., paen., **qrita hurintin** Gy 291:35 f., **qrita qadmaita, qrita tiniantia** RD B 61 f. first creation, second creation; **hazin qrita d̲-anatun qraitun** CP 373:10 this creation which ye created; **mn qrita d̲-mia . . . d̲-minh̲ dilh̲ hua kulhun nunia** ATŠ II no. 317 from the creation of water . . . from which proceeded all fishes.

qrita 2 (rt. **QRA III**) rending, mangling. **latišdunh̲ lqrita d̲-aria** CP 376:5 cast it not for the rending of the lion.

QRM (Aram., Syr., H., cf. **qraumia**) to cover, overlay, overspread.

Pe. Pf. with suff. **qramth̲ lsqupana** s. **squpana.**

Der.: **qraumia.**

QRS (Jew.-Aram., Syr. to dry up, Ar. to freeze, of water) to dry up; pa. to afflict, destroy.

Pe. Act. pt. **mia qaras blišanun** DC 44 the saliva dries up on their tongue. Nom. ag. pl. **qarasia** s.v.

Pa. Inf. with suff. **ulmišdininun uʿl miqarsinun** DC 44 and to cast them down and destroy them.

Der.: **qarasia.**

qrsania Gy 29:9 A = **qirsania** MG 9:20.

QRQD = **QRD. širiania d̲-mqarqidan** DC 46. 133:18 s. **QRD.**

QRQL (by dissimil. from a reduplicated **QLL**, cf. mod. H. קִלְקֵל, Syr. ܡܩܠܩܠ, Ar. قَلْقَل, Eth. ቀለቀለ to shake, H. קְלֹקֵל little [of food] mingy, meagre, unsubstantial, Talm. Dict. לֶחֶם הַקְּלֹקֵל *elende Speise*, starvation bread, rather of poor quality than scanty quantity, Akk. *qalqaltu* hunger) to reverse, overthrow, fall head foremost, turn round. MG 55:2, 212:11. Pf. **qarqil šibqh̲ lalma** CP 153 16 = Oxf. 11 b:top = ML 184:4 he revolutionized the world and forsook it; with suff. **qarqlh̲ lkulh̲ alahuta** Gy 173:5 he reversed all (false) deities; **qarqlinun** Gy 341:22 he overthrew them MG 281:24; **qarqiltinun lbišia** Gy 369:22 I overthrew the evil ones. Impf. **ʿqarqil** I overthrow MG 227:13; with suff. **niqarqlinhun** Gy 106:1 he overthroweth them MG 282:6; **tiqarqlinun** Gy 341:11 she overthrew (hist. pres.) them MG 371:8. Impt. **qarqil** Gy 359:12 overthrow MG 229:17. Pt. pl. **mqarqlia** Gs 55:7 they are reversed; sg. with suff. **mqarqilun lšibiahia umqarqilh̲ lmara d̲-alma** Gy 104:10 f. he overthrew the planets and overthrew the lord of the House (hist. pres.) MG 230:21, pl. with encl. **mqarqlilun** Gy 316:18 they overthrow them MG 31:2. Part. pres. **mqarqlit alahia** Q 53:9 thou overthrowest (false) gods MG 232:20. Nom. act. **qarqalta** s.v. Nom. ag. **mqarqilana** s.v.

Der.: **mqarqilana, qarqalta, qurqla, qirq(i)la.**

QRQS (den. from קִרְקֵס, ܩܘܪܩܣܐ, κίρκος) to encircle, hem in. Pf. **kd̲ qupa qarqsit ʿlauaihun** s. **qupa 2** (*b*).

Der.: **qarqasta, qurqsa?**

QRQŠ (Jew.-Aram., Syr., Mand. doublet **KRKŠ**) to clap, ring, clash, rattle, make a noise by striking MG 86 n. 1. Pt. **qimqarqiš** DAb = RD 35 he clashes; **lamqarqaš** (**lamqarqiš** ABC) **zanga** Jb 85:6 no bell sounds (MG 39:14); pl. **lamqarqišia** Jb 85:7 they do not ring.

Der.: **qarqušiata** (pl.).

QRR I (Gen. Sem. except Akk.) to be cold.

Der.: **qarir(a).**

QRR II (Ar. قرّ) to establish. Only in mod. texts. Gl. 135:5 f. (miswritten) قرر *statuere, pacisci* قرار كرد.

QRŠ (Jew. קרש to become solid, Syr. ܩܪܫ, Ar. قرس to be frozen, of water) to be very cold, frozen, congealed, immobile.

Pe. Impf. **laniqiršun** DC 12. 114 ff., Lond. roll B 230, 232 they shall not congeal (of veins and skies).

Der.: **qaruš(a)**, fem. **qarušt(i)a, qurša.**

QŠA (Aram., Syr., H. קשה, Ar. قسا, Eg. 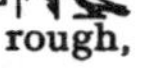 hard, cruel) to be hard, stiff, difficult, rough, severe; pa. to harden, stiffen.

Pe. Act. pt. **hanath̲ zma qašia** DC 34. 630 that blood hardens. Pass. Pt. **qšia ʿlh̲** AM 117:20 it will go hard with him; **labuia uʿl ʿmh̲ qšia** AM 1:16 he is inauspicious (dangerous) to his father and mother; pl. **qarnh̲ qšiin** AM 40:11 (cf. the idiomatic **qašiut qarnia**); **kulhin šaiia qšian** AM 140:18 (*often*, with varr. **qšiia, qšiʿin** etc.) all hours are inauspicious; **uminilh̲ qšian** [*sic*] AM 32:penult. and his words are harsh; with encl. **uqaqamh̲ udabatrh̲ qšilun** AM 41:5 he is harsh to (both) those before him and those after him (i.e. older and younger than himself); **kuhrana qašia** AM 117:12 a severe illness.

Pa. Pt. **gada mqašia** AM 79:6 hard luck, cruel fate; **qalh̲ mqašia** Gy 217:12 (var. **mqašai** DC 22. 210) his voice is harsh.

Ethpa. Pf. **kd̲ aria ʿtqašit** DC 44. 1394 (bad var. **ʿtqašat** Morg. 265/21:11) like a lion I was cruel. Part. pres. **mitqašit mn glala** Gy 217: 15 f. thou wilt become harder than a stone.

Der.: **q(a)šaia, qašia 1, qašiut(a), quš(i)ana, qašiša 2.**

qšaia = **qašaia. qšaian usnaian** DC 3 Ap. 2:30 inauspicious and evil (of hours).

qšia pass. pt. pe. of **QŠA** (q.v.) with **l** or **ʿl** dangerous to or inauspicious for (AM p. 3).

qšiša AM 15 = **qašiša 1.**

QŠŠ (Jew.-Aram., Syr.) to get old, be elder, have precedence.

Pe. Pf. **qaš** Gs 104:4, Jb 120:12 became old. Impf. **niquš** Gs 1:ult., 2:16 he becometh old

MG 249:9, **tiquš** Gs 2:24, 4:6 thou becomest old; **tiquš tišpur** AM 62:2 growing older she will improve. Pt. (as from ע״י) **kma d̠-qaiiš** AM (often) as he grows older, the older he grows; **kd̠ qaiš bparzla nibla** AM 37:19 when getting old he will be wounded by an iron (weapon).

Pa. Pt. pl. **mia mqašišia mn hšuka** Gy 77:18 f. water antecedes (is older than) darkness.

Der.: **qaša 1 = qašia 2, qašiš(a).**

QTA (cf. ܩܛܐ Bar Bahlūl 1857:14, 1858:3, otherwise Syr. preserved just the opposite meaning) to sob, weep, cry, lament, gush out.

Pe. Act. pt. fem. **bakia unahma uqatia** Gy 85:5 she weepeth, groaneth, and sobbeth.

Der.: **qitia.**

QTL (Ar. قتل) for Mand. **GṬL** (sporadically in mod. texts). Only Ar. forms: **ianqatil, iinqitil** AM 264:33, 276:40 he will be slain.

QTT (Syr. ܩܛ, cf. s. **qata 1**, Eth. ቀተተ pact) to be fixed, firmly rooted.

Pe. Act. pt. (as from ע״י) **mitkarkabh̠ upahlalh̠ uqaitabh̠** ATŠ II no. 108 she embraces him, offers him service, and clings (holds fast) to him.

Der.: **qata 1, qita.**

R

r the 20th letter of the alphabet. Phonetic character: vibrating liquid. Phonetic changes (: r > l and vice versa, assimilation and vanishing) MG § 54.

RAA I (רעא, ܪܥܐ, H. רעה I, Ar. رعى, Eth. ረዐየ, Akk. *rē'u*) to pasture, tend, feed, and water (a flock).

Pe. Impf. with encl. **uʿriilak** (var. **uriilak** B) Jb 45:14 and I will tend for thee. Impt. **rua dul dad huia šurbh̠** DC 84. 569 tend, draw (water), be a paternal uncle, his kinsman. Impt. with encl. **urilia** Jb 45:13, 46:1 C, **uʿrilia** Jb 46:1 and tend for me MG 259:8. Pt. pl. **raiia** Gy 227:21 they graze (eat herbs).

Der.: **miria, raia 1, rʿia.**

RAA II (Syr. ethpa., rel. to **RAA I** Barth *Wurzeluntersuchungen* 46 f., Kautzsch 81 ff., differently Schulthess HW 69 ff., Nöld. ZDMG liv 154 f., lvii 420) to think, cogitate.

Ethpa. Pt. pl. **mitraiin** Gy 249:14 they thought (hist. pres.). Part. pres. **mitraiina** Gy 265:24, 272:5 I cogitate.

Der.: **ruiana 1, riuiana, tiaruta 2.**

RAA III (רעא, ܪܥܐ III, H. רצה, Sab. 𐩧𐩳𐩥, Ar. رضى) to be pleased, satisfied, reconciled.

Der.: **raia 2, riuana, tiaruta 1.**

rab 1 st. abs. & cstr. of **rba** (q.v.) MG 108:4. St. emph. only sporadically *plene* **raba** MG 10:4. With suff. **rab** Gy 190:13 (= **rbai** *often*) my master MG 175:14; **rab ʿsiria** Gy 377:5, Gs 112:6, 9 ff. the chief of prisoners; **rab maksia** Gs 108:1, 12, 121:24, Q 39:19, 43:1, 56:20, CP 91:1 f., Morg. 245/78:ult. the chief of custom-officers (Nöld. *Oberzöllner*) MG 186:antep. f., lord of dues (chief levier of dues or penalties); **rab kulh̠ hailh̠ d̠-hšuka** Gy 167:2 captain of all the host of Darkness; **rab ašgandia kulhun** Gy 166:19 lord of all messengers; **rab ziuia** Gy 91:11, 373:9, CP 156:11 = ML 188:8 lord of beings of light Ginzā 94 n. 4 (Nöld. **rab ziua** *von großem Glanz* MG 311:7 f.); **rab kulhun iardnia** Gy 234:18 chief (or 'the greatest') of all jordans; **rab bauata** ML 173:6 = CP 145:1 lord of prayers. With **mn**: **rab minai** DC 41. 14 greater than I; **laiit minh̠ rab ugabir** ATŠ I no. 218 there is nothing greater and mightier than it; **rab minak** Gy 87:1, 214:14 greater than thyself. With encl. pers. pron. **rabna urabalia napšai** ML 244:5 = CP 210:6 f., DC 34. 844 I am great and my soul waxeth great (lit. is great on me) (MG 13:8); **anat rabit mn kulhun ʿutria** ŠQ 25:27 thou art greater than all the uthras, cf. Oxf. 77b MG 87:ult. As a title: **rab iuhana** Jb 91:9; **rabai hanai urab hananai** Jb 75:10 f.; often in colophons; **rab rurbia d̠-ʿqara** DC 43 I 63 Lord of mighty beings of glory.

rab 2 AM 227:15 name of a town or village BZ Ap. II.

rabauata pl. (of **rab 1**) AM 277:12 captains.

rabaia 1 (adj. from **rab 1, rba**) mighty one, captain. Pl. **rabaiia. šitin d̠-rabaiia** DC 43 J 98 sixty of his captains.

rabaia 2 (rt. **RBA**) nurterer, fosterer. Pl. as **1**. **ziqa unura umia rabaiia dilun** ATŠ I no. 257 air, fire, and water are their foster-parents.

rabaiata RD F 6 pl. of **rabita 1** (q.v.).

rabaita (rt. **RBA**) growth, nourishment, nutriment. **hinun pagra urabaita dilh̠** ATŠ I no. 223 they are the body and its growth (see trsl. p. 165, n. 11); **bgauaihun hauilh̠ rabaita** ATŠ II no. 337 in them it will have nutriment.

rabania (a pl. of **rba**) masters, rabbis, instructors, teachers. Varr. **r(u)bania 1, rabunia** s.vv. MG 19 footn., 137:19, 169:ult. **rabania umalpania** Jb 115:6 masters and teachers; **rabania d̠-baiin minaihun ulaiahbia** Jb 168:12 f. teachers from whom people ask but they do not give; **rabanan** (*often*) our teachers MG 10:6.

rabatuia a var of **rabituia** (q.v.).

rabunia Jb 70:5 = **rabania.**

rabuta 1 (rt. **RBB**, רְבוּתָא, ܪܒܘܬܐ) (*a*) greatness, magnificence, majesty, rank, superiority MG 10:7, 144:paen., (*b*) the office of a *rabbi* (instructor of novice-priests see ATŠ 5, SA 80 n. 5), (*c*) st. abs. adverbially (cf. ܪܒܬܐ, H. רַבַּת Ps. 120:6) greatly, magnificently, with magnificence MG 201:14 f. & n. 3. St.

abs. & cstr. **rabut** even from the def. **rbuta 2** (s.v.), about which cf. Jb ii 33 n. 1. (*a*) **rabut ruha** AM 59 = Par. xxvi 80:ult., Gy 51:7 vainglory, **rabut ruhẖ** Jb 272:12; **rabut karsa** Gy 27:22, 51:7 corpulence, grossness of the belly (high stomach); **rabut zmar** Gy 274:16, 299:25, 302:22, 376:17, Gs 75:17 Nöld. *Musikmeisterschaft* (= *Unzucht*) MG 304:2, 312:1, Lidzb. *Schwelgerei in Musik*; **mara ḏ-rabuta** Gy 2:14, 61:11 (*& often*) Lord of Majesty; **malil mana brabuta** Gy 72:7 the *māna* spoke in majesty; **brabuta mištbin** Gy 228:24 f. (cf. **rabut ruha** above); **hibil brabutẖ paqdan** Gy 316:8 H., in his majesty, appointed me; **utra ḏ-rabuta** Gy 327:24, 340:21 ff., 341:24; **šaniat ruha brabuta** Gy 94:10 R. changed her majesty (in spite of Lidzb. Ginzā 99 n. 2), cf. **ruha brabuta** Gy 117:19; (*b*) **mn kulhun ʿbidata latagzar** (read **laʿt-**) **lbar mn rabuta** DC 34 he shall not be debarred from performing any ritual, except from instruction of novices; **mištalaṭ lrabuta** ATŠ I no. 53 he may officiate as initiator; (*c*) **rabut apiqtẖ** (read **apqẖ** as DC 22 & Sh. ʿAbd.'s copy) **mn alma** Gy 324:15 gloriously took him out of the world, similarly Gs 71:19, 95:4, 18, Q 43:21, 68:6. With similar meaning the prep **b-** + st. emph.: **ʿul brabuta upuq bhaduta** Or. 332:6 f. enter gloriously and come out joyfully. With the meaning of 'pride', 'arrogance' the form **rbuta** (q.v.) is more frequent, but cf. here s. (*a*); further **rabuta laninsab** DC 36 II no. 354 he does not assume superiority (cf. **NSB** with **rbuta**).

rabuta 2 Jb 154:12 BC var. of. **rabita 1.**

rabutana spor. for **rbutana.**

rabutia a var. of **rabituia.**

rabia (act. pt. pe. of **RBA**) boy, child, young. **rabia ṭalia** Gy 221:5, 235:21, 236:4, 12, 22, 237:1, 242:11, Oxf. 57 b, CP 356:7 the young boy MR 30:11.

rabiaiil s. **hṭaša.**

rabigal, rabigar s. **arqabigal. anin rabigar nihuilẖ bʿuhrẖ** DC 48. 145 we will be his humble servants (lit. 'earth under his feet') on his road.

rabin Jb 75:4 Reuben.

rabiع (Ar. رَبِيع) AM 285:26 spring, spring growth.

rabiع 2 Zotb. 218b:16 name of a city.

rabita 1 (fem. of **rabia**) young girl, maidservant. Pl. **rabaiata** s.v. **ʿmaian brabitak iatba** Jb 154:12 f. our mother shall sit with thy servant (Lidzb. *auf deinem Lager*? but cf. l. 13); **htum bhadia ḏ-rabita hiduta** DC 44. 1091 enclose it within the bosom of a young virgin bride; **rabita iatbabẖ** RD A 4 = DAb par. a maidservant sits in it. Gl. 33:6 defectively **rbita** أمة *ancilla* كنيز.

rabita 2 (ܪܒܝܬܐ, ܪܒܒܝܬܐ) head of the house, master of the house. **rabita iatbibẖ** DAb (read **iatibbẖ**) the lord of the house sits in it (but cf. the par. s. 1).

rabita 3 occ. scr. pl. of **rbita.**

rabituia (rt. **RBB**, diminutive fem. with possessive suff.?) my mistress. Varr. **rabatuia, rab(u)tia** Jb ii 149 n. 6, ML x n. 2. **ia rabituia** (varr.) **ʿṣṭartia** Par. xv 24b = Par. xxv 24b = DC 3. 388:2 f. = DC 53. 235:5 = ŠQ 18:13 f. O my little mistress!

rabsia (read **-ṣia**, cf. ܪܘܨܐ) stiffness. Var. **ribsia** Or. 332 n. 13. **rumaiia urabṣia** Oxf. roll g 1021 (var. **ripsia** Or. 332:27) swellings and stiffness.

rabta s. **rabt(i)a.**

rabtar (**rab** + P. comparative suff. تر) greater MG xxv 3. Very frequent in mod. Mand. Gl. 32:14 defectively **rbtr** افضل *maius, excellentior* فاضلتر.

rabt(i)a fem. st. emph. of **rab, rba** MG 110:12. Var. **raptia** s.v. Before the noun: **rabtia ʿuraita** Jb 70:7 the Great Thora MG 319:3 f. After the noun: **aina rabtia** CP 46:12, Q 62:28 the great well-spring; **rum rabtia** AM 199 *Graecia Magna*. Often. Noun understood: **ʿsira uhtima rabtia** ML 58:5 = CP 45:23 the great (prayer) 'Bound and Sealed'.

ragagta (nom. act. pa. of **RGG I**) lust, desire, greed, covetousness MG 122:4. Var. **rgagta.** Pl. **-ata. ragagta d-alma hazin** Gy 47:1 the lust of this world; pl. **ragagata** (varr. **ragagta** ACD, **rgagta** DC 30 sg.) **ḏ-hazin alma** Jb 183:6 f.; **ragagta ḏ-tibil** Gy 228:25 worldly desire; **ragagta ḏ-lilia** Gy 365:16 the lust of the night; **šiqra uragagta** ATŠ II no. 64 falsehood and greed; **zaua ragagta ḏ-hazin alma** Jb 55:1 f. a wife (full of) the lust of this world.

ragala (nom. ag. pe. of **RGL**) person who puts a trap or snare, or (read **rgala**?) trap, snare. **kḏ tala ragala šilpit** DC 26. 613 like a fox I slipped the snare.

raguša DC 22. 415 for **daguša** Gs 24:15.

ragzʿil or **raglʿil** RD C 8 = DAb an uthra, son of Ptahil DAb 24 n. 4.

radaia (nom. ag. pe. of **RDA I**) (*a*) passing, flowing, (*b*) wanderer, traveller, migrant, (*c*) persecutor, persecuting, chastizing. Pl. **-iia.** (*a*) **zma bširiania ziua radaia hu** ATŠ I no. 218 the blood in the veins is the flowing radiance; (*b*) **radaia qrun** Jb 39:10 they made me a wanderer Jb ii 42 n. 3, Nöld. ZA xxx 147; **ʿu atitun radaiia** Jb 150:9 if ye come, (ye) wanderers. Of the planets: **lradaiia ḏ-nirdun bʿumama ublilia** Gy 60:14 to the 'wanderers' that wander by day and at night; **radaiia ḏ-radin bmarkabata** DC 26. 22 the 'travellers' that travel in chariots; (*c*) **radaiia** DC 22. 116 = **aradaiia 1** Gy 121:15.

radukt AM 205, var. **radupt** Par. xxvi a place-name.

radupa (rt. **RDP**, ܪܕܘܦܐ) persecutor. Pl. **-ia. radupak** Gy 114:17 f., 119:11 thy persecutor; **radupaikun** Gy 178:14 your persecutors.

radpa (rt. **RDP**) pursuit, persecution, prosecution, harrying. **mn radpa umn qirsa** DC 37. 292 from persecution and from sickness; **dina mn radpa mitbid** DC 41. 478 justice from persecution will be done.

raha (Ar. رَاحَة) ease, release. Gl. 85:2 **raha** راحة *remissio, regestum*; 88:1 id.

r(a)haṭa 1 (ܪܗܛܐ II, Aram. pl. רְטַיָּא, רְהָטַיָּא,

H. רהט, Akk. *rāṭu*, Ar. of ʿIrāq *rāṭ* Meissner: *Neuar. Sprichw.* 162, OLZ v 470, cf. Nöld. ZA xii 187, Schulthess HW 69, 90) stream, torrent, canal. Pl. r(a)haṭia 1. Jb ii 111 n. 2 **rahaṭa ḏ-mia hiia** CP 6:11 a stream of living water; **rahaṭia ḏ-mia hiia** Gy 308:4, ML 7:paen. f. streams of living water, **hazin rahaṭa ḏ-mia hiia** DC 41. 105 this is a stream of living water; **iardnia urahaṭia** Gy 337:3, 7 jordans and streams; **mia brahaṭai** Gs 111:16 water in my canals MG 441:9, **mia brahaṭak** Gs 111:15; **rahaṭa ḏ-qatia mn atutia mn ṭura** DC 41. 100 f. the stream which comes from beneath the mountain; **rahaṭia bgauḫ ʿṣṭarar** ATŠ I no. 18 streams were formed therein; **mašknia urhaṭia** Morg. 9:7 cult-huts and streams; **rhaṭia ḏ-mia hiuaria** DC 34. 1115 streams of white water.

r(a)haṭ(i)a 2 ('of streams'?, cf. 1 Jb ii 111 n. 2) Friday. **anpia rahaṭia** Jb 111:3 f. at the dawn of Friday; **iuma ḏ-r(a)haṭia** CP 176:1, Q 72b:40, Morg. 64:7, Oxf. 46a, Par. xv 48b = xxv 57a, Oxf. roll 1215, Lond. roll B 57, Par. xxvi 287.

rahbata (rt. **RHB II**, Lidzb. رَغِيبَة? ML 122 n. 5) (lit. 'spreadings' see CP trs. 67:5) sacred foods ranged upon a tray or clay table (in fact a kind of altar), table of food offerings, food offerings, ritual foods. Varr. **arabata, rahuata, rihbata, aruhata, arauata, rahbata** Q 47:28 = ML 122:8, Oxf. roll f 393; **šuba arabata** CP 95:8 seven trays (of ritual food); **ṭabuta urahbata** Oxf. roll f 1062, 1071, **ṭabauata urahbata** DC 48. 388 dainties and (ritual) foods; **rahbata** (var. ri- DC 6) **uṭabauata** ATŠ II no. 172; **bṭariankun urahbatkun** ATŠ II no. 143 on your ritual tables and trays; **sindirka umiuia kulhun rahbata** DC 27. 40 dates and fruits (and) all the ritual foods; **niara ḏ-rahbata** Lond. roll A 518, 777 = **niara ḏ-rihbata** Oxf. roll f 479 bowl of ritual food; **liniara ḏ-rahbata** DC 42. 29 (acc.); **natnun rahuata biniara** DC 42 they placed (hist. pres.) the food offerings into the bowl; **ʿu šga mindam mn rihbata** DC 36 no. 177 (var. **rahbata** PD) if by mistake he omitted something of the ritual foods; **rihbata** (var. ra- DC 6) **uṭabauata** ATŠ II no. 173 food-offerings and dainties.

rahuša (rt. **RHŠ**) creeping, crawling creature. Pl. -ia. **lrihšia ulrahušia** Oxf. XII creeping and crawling creatures.

rahziʿil Gy 250:6 an uthra.

rahṭiaiil DC 40. 996 an uthra.

rahiq(a) (rt. **RHQ**) far, distant. Fem. st. emph. **rahiqtia**. Pl. masc. -ia. **ḏ-rahiq mn (ʿ)mruma** Jb 92:4 that is far from heaven; **ʿuhra rahiqtia** AM 159:penult. a far journey; **drahiq ana** (read **anat**) **mqarbatlḫ** DC 40. 92 who is far away thou approachest him; **rahiqia . . . qaribia** DC 44. 1363.

rahma (rt. **RHM**) (*a*) friend, (*b*) mercy, compassion, favour, love, devotion, (*c*) pl. 'devotions', name given to the liturgical prayers and to the daily office, prayer(s). Pl. -ia. (*a*) **rahmai** my friends MG 176:9; **rahmak** thy friends MG 177:11; **rahma mn rahmḫ šapir laqaiim** Gy 388:22 friend is not loyal to friend; **lrahmaikun ulrahmia rahmaikun** Morg. 222/32:1 f. for your friends and for friends of your friends; (*b*) **baba ḏ-rahmia** ATŠ II no. 285, CP 352:10, ATŠ II 80 (*and often*) Gate of Mercies (: the North, cf. (*c*)); (*c*) **ba rahmia rurbia** Gs 6:23 he prayed mighty devotional prayers (Nöld. *er sprach ein großes Gebet um Gnade* MG 431:5 f.); **brahmia ḏ-miṣṭipra . . . brahmia ḏ-šuba šaiia . . . brahmia ḏ-lpaina** Gy 221:23 f. in early morning prayer . . . in the prayer of the 7th hour . . . in the evening prayer; **rahmia ḏ-lilia** Gy 365:2 nocturnal prayers; **rahmun ḏ-ṭabia** RD B 101 = DAb the devotions of the righteous.

rahmana (rt. **RHM**, רַחְמָן, ܪܚܡܢܐ, Ar. رَحْمَان) DC 45 & 46 compassionate, loving.

rahmuta (rt. **RHM**, ܪܚܡܘܬܐ) love, compassion, pity, lovingkindness, charity, mercy, grace. St. cstr. **rahmut**. MG 144:27, 155:19. **rahmutkun** your love MG 179:17; **rahmut marḫ** Gy 16:10 the love of his Lord MG 309:7; **rahmuta ḏ-kušṭa** Gy 213:23 = **rahmut kušṭa** Gs 73:12 true love; **brahmuta ḏ-šafta ḏ-ʿthiblih mn iauar** DC 37:27 by virtue of the scroll, (by grace of) (?) the scroll which was bestowed on him by Yawar.

rahmʿil RD 20, **rahmil** DAb one of the seven names of Šdum.

rahša (rt. **RHŠ**) vermin, creeping things, reptiles. Var. **rihšia** s.v. MG 101:3. **rahša uhiua bala** AM 225:ult. creeping thing(s) and wild beast(s).

rahta (rt. **RHT**) seething, ebullition, boiling heat. **glala urahta** JRAS 1937 591:34 frost and seething heat; **dudia ḏ-rahtḫ** Gy 19:20 seething cauldrons, cf. s. **RHT**.

rauaza (rt. **RWZ**) exulting, joyous, triumphing, vigorous, splendid, invigorating MG 120:16. St. abs. **rauaz**. Fem. **rauazta**. Fem. pl. **rauazata**. **ʿrta urauazta** Q 4:26, 60:12, DC 26. 185 bright and exultant; **nišmata haiata ʿrata taqunata urauazata** CP 118:10, ML 144:3 living, light-giving, shining, and rejoicing souls. Before the noun: **brauaz šumak** DC 46 by thy vigorous (?) name (life-giving name).

rauan 1 (P. رَوَان) running, flowing. **bmaina ḏ-rauan** DC 46. 223:5 in flowing water.

rauan 2 Ṣâb.'s AM, **rauand** AM 204 name of a city. Var. **riuan** s.v. BZ Ap. II.

rauas Ṣâb.'s AM var. of **rauis** AM 205:18.

rauz(i)a (rt. **RWZ**) rejoicing, exultant, thriving, flourishing, fresh (of leaves, of flowers), vigorous, healthy. **klilia rauzia** Gy 25:14 (cf. 211:20) freshly-picked (: living) wreaths; **mia ʿria urauzia** DC 48. 224 bright and effulgent waters; **ʿlania rauzia** (*often*) flourishing trees.

rauziʿil (rt. **RWZ**) DC 6 & 36 no. 97 name of a spirit.

rauṭa (ܪܘܛܐ) sprig, twig. Var. **ruṭa** s.v. **rauṭa ḏ-asa** Oxf. roll f 857, Lond. roll A 582, DC 41. 282, DC 42. 263, 420 a sprig of myrtle; **mhiiḫ brauṭa** DC 46. 156:15 strike him with the twig.

rauis AM 205:18 city and district of Ravist BZ Ap. II.

rauma (rt. **RUM I** ܪܘܡܐ) height, firmament, heaven MG 100:19. **trisar alpia parsia huia rauma** Jb 4:11 its height is twelve thousand parasangs; **kma hua rauma** ATŠ II no. 310 how much is its height?; **rauma ugauša** PD 269 the height and depth; **raumaihun** AM 278:22 their height.

RAZ, RZZ (den. from **raza**) to act secretly, conceal, stow away.

PE. Pf. **larazit ularimzit** Gs 123:15 I acted not secretly and gave no secret signs (Nöld. as ע״ע MG 248:16 & n. 3).

DER.: **raza.**

raz 1 AM 199 = **runza** (q.v.).

raz 2 (cf. 3) name of a being invoked in exorcism. **raz urazan** DC 40.

raz 3, raza (רָז, ܐܪܙܐ < P. راز MG xxxi 2) (*a*) mystery, secret (wisdom, plan etc.), (*b*) type, symbol, token, (*c*) secret functions and organs of the body, element, (*d*) religious rite, sacrament, (*e*) designation of higher beings ('mystery' personified), (*f*) symbolical items of (ritual) food. Jb ii 167, 216 n. 3, ML 35 n. 1, Ginzā 202 n. 1, HpGn 165, 245, 276 ff. (: chapter VII *Die Mysterien*), 346. Pl. **-ia.** Mod. use applies the word to all that is hidden from sight; *râz alkarsa* bowels (lit. mystery of the belly), *râz alβâβa* lock (lit. mystery of the door, viz. the inner part of the lock). Masc. (*a*) **raz ruita** Gy 111:24, 225:9; **raz rhamta** Gy 110:11 = **raza ḏ-rhamta** Gy 110:10, 111:22, pl. **razia ḏ-rhamta** Gy 109:18, 110:3, 10; **raza usidra uziua** Gy 234:15, 238:2; **raza usidra** Gy 196:14; **raza kabšia** Gy 114:11 they make a secret plan; **raza lbiš kabšia** Gy 265:20 they secretly plan evil; **amarnalun braz** DC 44. 599 I said to them secretly (privately); **raza ḏ-ʿumamatan** Gy 110:14 the secret of our oaths (i.e. our secret oaths). With **HŠL** to forge a secret plan Gy 85:23, 109:17; **razia rurbia ḏ-nhura** Gy 360:23; **razia nihia** Gy 342: 8; **razia mardia** Gs 22:18, both Gy 34; **razia ḏ-šuba** Gy 122:13. A chapter of **razia ḏ-hazin alma** Jb 166 f., cf. Gy 338:1; **razia ḏ-malkia** Gy 193:2; **raza qadmaia** CP 60:11 = ML 76: 10; **šuba razia kasiia dakiia** Gy 314:7 (or (*d*)?); (*b*) **hamra raza ḏ-marba hu** PD 1591 (s. **marba 4**); **npaq mn raza ḏ-ʿma ubraza ḏ-aba ʿtlabaš** DC 34. 1159 he emerged from the Mother-symbol and was identified with the Father-symbol; **raza ḏ-ʿma** PD 1592; **razia kasiia ḏ-nihuta** ATŠ I no. 249 private tokens of affection; **raz ruha uniširnta** DC 48. 279 symbol (?) of the spirit and soul; (*c*) **raza ḏ-ṣura** PD 809; **raza ḏ-mazruta** PD 1212; **šamiš brazia lgaṭṭh** Gy 118:12, Ginzā 132 n. 3; **šuba razia** Gy 202:7; **lbišlh hamša razia** Oxf. roll f 463, cf. 438 ff.; **arba razia** Gs 119:17; **raza ḏ-mia hiia** Gy 47:23; **raza ḏ-mia** Gy 112:12; (*d*) **razia triṣia** Gy 111:14; **bit razia** Gy 223:3 (Christian temple); **nasiblh lrazia ḏ-ʿkilta** HG 10 f. he took away the rites of the (sacred) Meal; (*e*) **raza rba** CP 199(m):17, 408:1 f., Gy 127:19, 138:4, 139:22, 140:9; **rham raza** Gy 131:14; **ʿutria urazia** Gy 131: 16; **zihrun raza** Oxf. 87 b, Par. xv 31ab = xxv 38ab; **zihrun raza rba** CP 5:4, 6:9, 255:15 f., 346:6, Q 2:11, 25, **zihrun raza kasia** Morg. 5:8. Cf. **raz 2, razan 1,** and **raziʿ 1**; (*f*) **raza mihla** PD 1135; **šuba razia** Morg. 62:27, 183:6, Par. xv 45b.

razai Jb 75:5 a name.

razan 1 s. **raz 2.**

razan 2 AM 189 name of a city.

raziʿl Lond. roll A 357 an angel.

raziq s. **rziqa.**

raṭ(a)buta (rt. **RṬB**) moisture, watery humour, sap, fluid. Cf. s. **balgam.**

raṭuba (rt. **RṬB**) damp, moisture, humidity. **raṭuba raṭubḥ** DC 44. 1067 moisture affected it (? corrupt).

raṭiba (rt. **RṬB**) (*a*) adj. moist, juicy, (*b*) subst. sap, juice. (*a*) **hamima uraṭiba hu** AM 286:25 it is warm and moist; (*b*) **ʿtpasaq raṭibia** Morg. 263/16:18 its juice is cut off; **gamria raṭibia** Morg. 262/15:ult. they consume his juice.

***raṭina,** fem. **raṭintia** (rt. **RṬN**) grumbler, murmurer. **bliba raṭintia tihuia** AM 75:15 she will be a grumbler at heart.

raṭla (Ar.) a weight of about 2½ kg. Gl. 87:1 defectively (**rṭla**) رَطْل *libra.*

raṭna (rt. **RṬN**) spoken language, vernacular. Mod. designation of the spoken Mand. dialect.

rai (P. رَى) AM 198 the city of Rayy.

raia 1 (rt. **RAA I**) shepherd, herdsman MG 70:19. Pl. **raiia. bihdad raia** RD F 12, **raiia bihzad** RD A 6 (sg.); **raia ṭaba** Gy 177:19 ff. the good shepherd; **raia ana ḏ-aqnḥ rahim** Jb 40:7 I am the shepherd who loveth his sheep; **rahim raia huilia** Jb 45:12 f. (cf. l. 13 f.) be a loving shepherd for me; **kḏ aqnia ḏ-qudam gabra raia** Gy 181:2 like sheep before a shepherd.

raia 2 (rt. **RAA III**) desirable, palatable. **pt raia tabula** DC 40. 196 f., 201 (of salt) daughter of palatable seasoning.

raiubtia (rt. **RBA**?, but formed as from ע״י) swollen, discharging, suppurating. **aina raiubtia** JRAS 1937 p. 593:penult., 1943 p. 170:18.

rakik (rt. **RKK,** ܪܩܝܩܐ, Ar. رَكِيك & رَكّ, H. רַךְ) soft, tender, smooth MG 124:9. **rakik mn tirba** Gy 287:4 softer than fat.

raksa (rt. רכס) Jb 143:10, 149:7, 155:7 platform in water of mud and reeds pressed in layers, pile, Lidzb. *Schutt.*

***rakša 1** (רִכְשָׁא, ܪܟܫܐ, H. רֶכֶשׁ) horse, stallion, steed. Var. **rikša** s.v. Found only in pl. **rakšia 1, rakšiʿ** MG 6:16. **lmitnia rakšia** Lond. roll A 390, DC 40. 142 (s. **mitna**); **sarqina ḏ-atutia rakšia** s. **sarqina**; **rakšia zrizia** ATŠ II no. 364 spirited horses, fiery steeds; **rakšia ugubria** Gy 386:6 f. horses and men; **brakšia ubgubria** Gy 385:21; **rakšia ugumlia** Gy 387: 19 horses and camels.

rakša 2, rakšia 2 (rt. **RKŠ**) binding, harnessing, tying up: **mhita urakša ušqupta** DC 43 E 40 = **mhita urakšia ušiqupta** DC 20. 89 a blow, harnessing and striking.

rakta Gy 389:4 one of the numerous varr. of **bakta** (v.s. **aškarta**).

raktana (rt. **RGG**, cf. ܪܓܝܓܬܐ) lustful MG 41:7, 139:12. Pl. **-ia. rugzania raktania** Gy 272:12 raging, lustful (as a quality of devils).

RAM, RUM II (Aram. & H. רעם, Syr. ܪܥܡ, Eth. ረዐመ, Akk. *ragāmu* to roar, but *rimu* thunder, rel. Ar. رغم, Sab. to be obstinate) to thunder, resound, rumble, roar.

Pe. Pf. **ram rima** Gy 96:13 it thundered (MG 255:anteantep.). Impf. s. **RUM II.** Pt. **raiim** AM 250:11 it thunders.

Der.: **rima 1.**

ram st. abs. of foll. (*a*) used as a *malwāša* man's name Zotb. 218 ff. (*& very often in colophons*), (*b*) as name of a heavenly being CP 35:4, 119:13, 194:13, Q 6:19, 60:18, Oxf. 57 b = ML 18:1, 145:3, 229:3 (mentioned together with **bihram**, hence perhaps P. رام), cf. **ram ziua** Gy 374:24, (*c*) as name of a devil: **ram šumak daiua** DC 43 J 77, 88, (*d*) in DAb = RD 20 as one of the seven names of **šdum** (q.v.), (*e*) **ram gabra urud ʿnta** Gy 26:11, **ram urud** Gy 26:14, 21, 261:15, Jb 90:7, 277:2, Morg. 88:6 (cf. Gy 379:23) CP 199(b):8, CP trs. 151 note 8 the only remaining pair of the second human generation (both names are Iranian), (*f*) with original meaning 'high' in **ʿl ram ṭura qaiimna ulram paqata mistkina** DC 23. 236 f. I stand on a high hill and gaze into a deep valley, (*g*) Jb 75:9 BD a var. of **rama 3** (q.v.).

rama 1 (rt. **RUM**, ܪܡܐ) high, tall, lofty; haughty, proud. St. abs. **ram.** Fem. **ramta 1** MG 110:15. Pl. masc. **-ia**, fem. **ramata. laiit ʿniš d̠-ram minai** DC 41. 104 f. there is none loftier than I; **ṭuria ramia** (*often*) high hills, lofty mountains; **ainẖ rama** AM 4:15 his eyes (are) haughty (cf. **ramat ainia** Gy 209:7 f., 215:19 s. **ramta 2**); **brabuta ramta nišimta iatba** DC 34. 217 the soul sits in lofty majesty. St. abs. before the noun s. **ram** (s.v. (*f*)).

rama 2 (substantival use of (1)) high place, height, high perch, cf. **ramta 2** s.v. **qala mn rama qralun** ATŠ I no. 255 he (: the cock) crowed to them from his high perch.

Gl. 73:1 **rama** حجّج *abyssus* حجّها.

rama 3 (H. רָמָה II 2 Samuel's home, but apparently taken as personal name) Ramah Jb ii 81 n. 6. **rama** (var. **ram** BD) **ušumʿil** Jb 75:9 f. Ramah and Samuel.

ramaza (nom. ag. pe. of **RMZ**) hinter, winker, informer. Pl. **-ia. karaṣia uramazia** Gs 105:15, Jb 175:12, 185:14 informers and hinters; **ramazia rimzia** Gs 136:25 (cf. Gy 66:1) those who give signs.

ramat s. **ramta 2.**

ramuia a *malwāša* man's name. **ramuia br ʿqaimat** Q 21:28 f. = ML 60:3 (s. ATŠ trs. p. 3 f.) the earliest known editor of the Qolasta ZDMG cv 119 n. 3.

ramul (Ar. رَمْل) AM 277:39 sand.

ramia 1 pl. of **rama 1** (q.v.).

ramia 2, 3 act. pt. of **RMA** I, II (q.v.).

ramia 4 (רַמְיָא) lying, deception. **uaimanuth̠ ramia** AM 97:15 and his pursuits (are) fraudulent.

ramilan AM 206 name of a town or locality BZ Ap. II.

ramka (ܪܡܟܐ) large flock, herd. Pl. **-ia. aqnia bramkia qailia** DC 3. 377:8 = DC 38. 15:18 = ŠQ 15:18 = CP 223:5 sheep come in large flocks.

ramʿil drabša DC 48 (illustration) a personified banner.

ramla AM 198 the city of Ramlah BZ Ap. II.

ramša, ramšia 1 (רַמְשָׁא, ܪܡܫܐ) evening, twilight. **bramšia d̠-lilia** Jb 77:1, 79:5, 80:9, 83:9, 86:12, 87:15, 89:10 at eventide; **bqadmin šatin hamra hadtia ubramšia šatin hatiqa** Gy 176:20 f. they drink new wine in the morning and in the evening the old.

ramšia 2 (rt. **RMŠ**, cf. 1) darkening, becoming dim. **kibia unapṣia . . . uramšia** DC 46. 134:2 = JRAS 1943 170:27 (of eyes) pains and discharges . . . and growing dim.

ramšilai a *malwāša* man's name.

ramta 1 fem. of **rama 1** (q.v.).

ramta 2 (subst. use of 1) (*a*) height, hill, high part, (*b*) haughtiness. St. cstr. **ramat.** Pl. (a)**ramata** MG 33:8. (*a*) **ramat** my height MG 175:anteantep.; **ʿl ramat qaiimna** Gs 99:4 I stand on my high place; **ʿtib ʿl ramta** Gs 58:5, 15 it seated itself on the height; **qamit ʿl ramta d̠-arba** Jb 43:1, 44:2 I stood on the high end of the boat; **ṭuria uramata** Gy 227:18 hills and heights. Cf. **aramata** s.v.; (*b*) **ramat ainia** Gy 209:7, 215:19 haughty look, proud eyes Ginzā 209 n. 2.

ranǧ (P. رَنج) AM 254:21 grief, anguish, vexation.

rasul (Ar. رَسُول) AM 164 messenger.

rast (P. راست) Gy 286:7, 12 True, Right, a name given to Abathur. SsSs i 122, MSt 87. V.s. **rašna.**

rasta (P. راستا < Av. *razista* true, straight) ritual dress. Detailed description MMII 30 ff., 39 n. 1, cf. RD ii 127, PRE 323, Siouffi 107, 121, MR 92. **rastaikun** Oxf. roll f 1233, cf. ibid. 1244, 1249; **zipa ʿl rastia** DC 51. 830 fraud upon upright persons (?).

rastana (from **rast**) AM 218:19 treaty, troth, pact.

raptia Gy 350:182, often for **rabtia** (fem. of **rab, rba**) MG 48:2.

rastia (P. راستى) truth, truly, verily. Very frequent in mod. Mand. **uzipa ʿl rastia mgaiirliẖ** DC 51:coloph. and falsifies the truth.

Gl. (always missp. with ṣ) 32:5 امين *fidelis*; 33:4 (pl.) ابرار *iusti* آزادان; 44:1 بله [sic] *etiam, si* &c. آرى; 44:15 (with prep. **b-**) بتحقيق *sec. veritatem.*

raʿaiat (Ar. رَعِيَّة) AM 283:35 (non-Moslem) subjects.

rapa (Ar. رَفّ) Jb 140:4 shelf, ledge, bookshelf.

Gl. 70:1 (defectively) جزم *fasciculi* دسته.

rapia (rt. **RPA**, Syr. ܪܦܝܐ) AM 155:2 effeminate, dissolute.

raptia Gy 350:182, often for **rabtia** (fem. of **rab, rba**) MG 48:2.

raqa AM 203 name of a town BZ Ap. II.

raqada (nom. ag. pe. of **RQD**) dancer. Pl. **raqadia** Gy 106:16.

raqata pl. (of רִקְתָא) Gy 191:15 BC (var. **rqaqata** A, **riqata** DC 22. 182), 193:6 banks, dry ground beside water.

rašiuta (rt. **RŠA**, Targ. רְשׁוּת) Gy 215:6, Jb 35:8 (varr. **rišaiuta** AB & DC 30, **rišiuta** D) bribe MG 146:17.

rašna urast (Av. *Rašnū razišta* GIPh ii 643, MSt. 87 & n. 4, Ginzā 284 n. 2) Gy 286:7 a name given to Abathur.

rat Jb 75:1 a Jewish personal name.

RBA I (רבי, ܪܒܐ, H. & mod. H. רבה, Ar. ربا, Akk. *rabū*) to become big, grow; pa. bring up, rear, nurture, nourish.

Pe. Pf. **rba rbita rabtia** Gy 159:23 he grew mightily; **rbit** Gy 136:7 I grew up; **anin bkanpa d-ruha rbainin** DC 34. 168 we were reared in the lap of Ruha; with encl. **rbitibh** Gy 323:16 for **rbitbh** thou didst grow therein MG 258 footn. Impf. **lanirbia** Gy 160:7 he will not grow big. Impt. **ʿrbia** Gs 59:11 grow up. Act. pt. **rabia** Gy 160:8 he groweth; pl. **rabin** MG 164:anteantep.; **kul mirba rabin** Gy 8:19 they grow perfectly, MG 399:5. Pass. pt. **tša iahria d-ianqa bgauaihun ʿrbia** DC 34. 802 the nine months in which the babe is developed. Inf. **mirba** Gy 8:19 (above s. act. pt.) MG 260: 16 f.; **bit mirbia** Gy 160:20 I wanted to grow.

Pa. Pf. **rabit** (ʿ)**bnia** Jb 55:2 I brought up sons; with suff. **kd rabian ab ldilia** Jb 55:2 just as my father brought me up; **ṭuria ialdun uaramata rabiun** DC 37. 468 mountains brought me forth and high places nurtured me; **d-abahath rabiuia** Gy 262:20 whom his parents brought up; **bʿkilta raubiuia** Gs 69:16 they reared him on food; **bpaqata ubaramata d-rabiuk** Or. 331:17 by the gorges and heights which nurtured thee. Pt. **ʿlana d-mrabia ianqia** DAb (illustration) the tree that nurtures infants; **d-hu ʿma mrabia** ATŠ II no. 121 because the mother nurtures him; **atuat d-ialda ulamrabia** Jb 54:13 a woman that bears (a child) but does not rear it; fem. pl. **d-mrabian** DC 43 C 72 those who are nursing. Part. pres. **blilia ʿdilna ublilia mrabaina** AM 149:4 in the night I bear (a child) and in the night I nourish (it); pass. **atutia alahia mrabina** DC 44. 428 (var. **mrabaina**) I was brought up beneath (pagan) gods. Nom. ag. **mrabiana** s.v.

Ethpa. Pf. **hazin ʿuṣṭuna šapira d-minh ʿtrabia** ATŠ II no. 137 this fair body that was nurtured by her; **ʿtrabiat** DC 48. 348 she waxed strong. Pt. pl. **mitrabin** Gy 339:3 they are nurtured; fem. pl. **mitrabian** DC 48. 112.

Gl. 50:7 f. **rbia** تعاظم *superbiri* بزرگ شد; 90:5 f. (pa.) ساد *dominari* بزرگ شد; 115:15 f. **rbia** عظم *magnificare* بزرگ كرد; 159:3 (a miswritten pt. pa.) متعظم *magnificatus* گرامی; 166:1 f. **rba** نمي *crescere, germinare* بيرون آمد.

Der.: **mrabiana, rabaia 2, rabaita, rabia, rabiaiil, rabita 1, rbuta 1, rbita 1, tarbuta.**

RBA II (רבע, ܪܒܥ, H. רבץ but also רבע I prob. an Aramaism Kautzsch 80, Ar. ربض, Akk. *rabāṣu*) to lie down, recline.

Pa. Pt. pl. **mrabin** RD E 5 = DAb par. they lie down.

Der.: **marba 2, 3, marbihta, rbita 2.**

rba (רַבָּא, ܪܒܐ) (*a*) great, large, immense MG 10:3 & n. 3, (*b*) teacher, master, instructor, initiator, a priest who initiates a candidate for priesthood MG 184:21, Siouffi 38 ff., BZ 67 n. 3, DAb 25 n. 8. St. abs. **rab 1** s.v. Fem. (of (*a*)) **rabt(i)a, raptia** s.vv. Pl. (*a*) **rbia, rurbia** (often as attribute of Life, **hiia** sometimes omitted), **rurbania**, fem. **rabata, rurbata** (s.vv.) MG. 170:1, 184:21 ff., (*b*) **r(a)banaia, rubania** (s.vv.) MG 169:ult., 184:22. (*a*) **hiia rbia, hiia rurbia** (*very often*) the Great Life; **rba kasia qadmaia** Q 28:2 ff. the First, Great, Invisible One; **rba br rurbia** Gy 219:8, 234:15 the great one, son of the Great (Life); **br rbia** Gy 94:5 (*& often*) son of the Great (Life); **blaupa d-rba mitlip** CP 125:16, ML 152:3 shall be united in a great communion (or be in communion with the Mighty One? cf. Lidzb. n. 2); **rba uʿlaia** great and exalted (attributes of the King of Light) Ginzā 4:8; (*b*) **rbai** (*common in colophons*) (as title: Rabbi) my master MG 175:15; **rbia zihrun** Zotb. 225a:bottom = **rbai zihrun** Zotb. 228b:29; **aliptinun kd d-rba lašualia** Gy 108:22 I taught them as a master (teacheth) his novice; **auquria rba akuat abahath** CP 5:13, ML 6:bottom, to honour the teacher like his parents; **qašiš rba mn abahata** CP 5:ult. = ML 7:2 f. the master is more revered than parents; **halin rbania d-lamalpilun ltarmidia** DAb those teachers who do not instruct the priests; **rbania uašualania** CP 428:3 teachers and pupils; **rbania urbutania** s. **rbutana** (*b*).

Gl. 83:10 **rab, rba** ربّ, ارباب *dominus*; 83:11 **rba, rbani** [sic] رئيس, رؤساء *princeps, superior* امير; 98:11 **rba** شريف *nobilis*; 120:1 **rba** عظيم *magnus* بزرگ; 124:15 **rba** عظيم *grandis* بزرگ; 143:10 **rba** كبير *multus* بزرگ.

rbaba 1 (rt. **RBB**) nurturer, fosterer. **marba rbaba d-razia** ATŠ I no. 245 womb, fosterer of mysteries (var. **baba** DC 6 prob. correct).

rbaba 2 (Ar. ربابة) AM 150 covenant BZ 96 n. 8.

rbaṭ ašitiaiil barqaṭ DAb name of a gate in the other world.

RBB (Gen. Sem. except Akk.) to be great.

Pe. Impf. **nihuta d-ṭabia tirablak** Gs 16:20 the mildness of the good shall increase upon thee.

Pa. & Ethpa. from the reduplicated and dissimilated **RWRB** (q.v.).

Der.: **rab 1, rabauata, rabaia 1, r(a)bania, rabunia, r(a)buta 1, (2), r(a)butana, rabutia, rabita 2, rabituia** (& varr.), **rabt(i)a** (var. **raptia**), **rabtar, rbaba, rubania, rurbania, rurbia, ribabia.**

rbuta 1 (rt. **RBA**) profit, increase, usury. **hauia zabnia hada umzabnia trin urbutun mn babia trisar** RD C 11 = DAb they purchase (at) one and sell (at) two and their profit is from the Twelve Gates.

rbuta 2 (Targ. רִבוּתָא) pride, arrogance. Often for **rabuta 1** (q.v.) and vice versa MG 10:7, 144:paen., Jb ii 33 n. 1. Frequent idiom **NSB rbuta** 'to be(come) proud, arrogant' Gy 19:2 f., 20:9, 38:14, 94:8, 214:6, 14, 220:8, 294:17, 343:13, 352:5, 8, Jb 26:9, DC 34. 851, PD 460, RD B 60, RD C 6 (*& often*). **rbuta d̲-dahba ukaspa** Gy 60:7 vainglory in gold and silver.

rbutana (adj. from preced.) (*a*) proud, haughty, conceited, presumptuous, (*b*) superior, dignitary, magnate MG 139:11. Pl. **-ia.** (*a*) **naṣiruta uzharia lamitgalilia lanašia tahmia urbutania** ATŠ II no. 83 the Naṣoraean wisdom and injunctions are not revealed to dull and conceited people; **marh̲ d̲-hšuka rbutana** Gy 164:3 the haughty lord of darkness (or (*b*)?); **ʿutana giutana rbutana** s. **giutana**; **uailinun lrbutania** ATŠ I no. 11 woe to the haughty!; (*b*) **rbania urbutania** ATŠ I no. 234 teachers and those in authority; **rurbia urbutania** Gy 186:paen. f., 229:14 the mighty ones and the magnates; **sapria urbutania d̲-tibil** ATŠ I no. 250 scribes and dignitaries of the earthly world.

rbin Zotb. 225b:1 = **arbin.**

rbita 1 (rt. **RBA**) growth, increase. **rba rbita rabtia** Gy 159:23 s. **RBA I** pf. (Nöld. mistakenly ܪܒܝܬܐ 'usury' MG 104:7); **d̲-šria brbita d̲-pagria** DC 43 that dwell on the growth of the body; **uhaila mšadar lrbita** ATŠ II no. 122 and imparts strength to growth.

rbita 2 (rt. **RBA II**, cf. ܬܗܘܡܐ ܪܒܝܬܐ Deut. 33:13, Mand. form transliterated as ܪܒܝܬܐ by Th. b. Koni IM 154:27) Gy 192:9, 13, 193:11, 194:5, 223:4, 283:19, 284:1 ff. (var. **arbita**), 388:15 sea, ocean, large expanse of water MG 117:27; AM 170 inundation.

RBK (met. of **BRK**) af. to kneel, bend the knee MG 74:9.

Af. Pf. **uarbik burkh̲** DC 34. 1112 and he bent the knees; **arbikit ʿl burkai** DC 26. 98 I bent my knees. Impf. **narbik** ATŠ II no. 407, 411 (*& often*) he bends the knees; **ʿiarbik lburkia** DC 26. 183 (var. **lburkai**) I bend my knees; **narbka** Q 67:18 they (fem.) bend the knees; **latarbkun** Gy 16:22 kneel not MG 74:10. Impt. **arbik burkak** DC 41. 370 bend thy knee. Pt. **burkai d̲-marbika** Jb 59:14 my knees that bend; **nišimta lhiia marbika** ATŠ II no. 112 the soul kneels to the Life; pl. **marbikin** ATŠ II no. 112 they bend the knees. Part. pres. **marbikit** DC 41. 504 (*& often*) thou bendest thy knees; **marbikitun** ATŠ II no. 173 ye bend the knees. Inf. **arbukia** MG 144:5, 234:1.

rbʿil RD I name of a steersman.

RGA I occ. for **RGG I.**

Der.: **rgita.**

RGA II (ܪܓܐ *rigare*) the rt. of **marganita 3** (by popular etym. also **margna** q.v.).

rgaga 1 (rt. **RGG I**) attraction, attractiveness, lure, desirability. **almia rgaga šailih̲** CP 191:16, Oxf. 54a = ML 226:5 covetous worlds desire it; (ML *voll Gier*); **rgagin** Gs 18:3 their (fem.) attractiveness; **šupran urgagan** Gy 146:4 our beauty and our attractiveness; **libat martia šupra urgaga** DC 3. 380:3 = CP 226:7 = ŠQ 16:12 Venus, mistress of beauty and desire.

rgaga 2 (rt. **RGG I**) lustful, attractive. Pl. **-ia. bṭulalia rgagia** DC 44. 139 (var. **rgigia** Morg. par.) v.s. **rgiga.**

rgagta Or. 332:27 (*& often*) = **ragagta.**

rgaza (rt. **RGZ**) raging, excited, irritable, furious. **rgaza d̲-gabra lalagṭa** AM 104:1 she is furious that she cannot get a husband.

rgala (rt. **RGL**) AM 244:22, DC 43 A 153, DC 44. 219 f., Gy 139:13 (*& often*) fetter(ing), snare, restraint MG 115:20. Var. **ragala?** (q.v.). Masc.

rgama (rt. **RGM**, ܪܓܡܐ) lapidation. **basarun ubhatmun urgamun** DC 44. 1857 f. = Morg. 269/28:28 by their bond, seal, and lapidation.

rgapa s. **argapa.**

RGB I (only in later Mand., possibly **RGG** + encl. **b**, but cf. Ar. رَغِبَ) to long for, desire greatly, be covetous; ethpa. to be coveted, greatly desired.

Pa. Pt. fem. pl. **ʿnšia d̲-mragban** DC 46. 74:2 women that are lustful.

Ethpa. Pt. fem. pl. **marganiata mitragbian** ATŠ II no. 258 (var. **mitragbin** ibid. no. 66) pearls (that) are coveted.

RGB II (only in later Mand., cf. Ar. رَكَّبَ) to add together, combine.

Pa. Impt. with suff. **ragbinun hdadia** AM 136 combine them together.

Gl. 3:5 f. امر , جمع *praecipere, congregare* فرمود ; 60:9 f. (missp. with **q**) جمع *conjungere* جمع كرد .

RGG I, (RUG) (Jew.-Aram., Syr.) pe. to desire, covet; pa. to lure, entice; ethpa. to be lustful, covetous.

Pe. Impf. **latirag ulatisab mindam d̲-lau dilak** Gy 214:11 covet not and take not that which is not thine (MG 249:19) (**latirgag ʿl audia** Gy 327:14 read **latitgarar** as l. 1 MG 249 n. 2), **latirigun ulatibun d̲-lau dilkun** Gy 14:20 f. covet not nor want anything that is not your own (MG 249:antep.). Act. pt. **raiig rgita d̲-tibil** Gy 22:14 f. = **raiig ragagta d̲-alma** Gy 43:17 he cherisheth a worldly desire (MG 250:12); fem. **raiga** Gy 83:9 she desireth. Pass. pt. **rgig(a)** s.v.

Pa. Pf. with suff. (**ragugia**) **ragigtinkun** Gy 186:16 I caused you to desire MG 281:2. Pt. **atuat d̲-mragaga** Gy 365:1 f. an alluring woman; **šamašata d̲-mragaga** Gy 365:3 = **šamašta d̲-mragagan** Jb 77:10 commerce with alluring harlots; with encl. **marganiata mragagbun** ATŠ II no. 258 pearls allure them; **bragagta mragigilun** Gy 24:17 they enflame them with lust. Inf. **ragugia** Gy 186:16 (s. pf.). Nom. act. **ragagta** s.v.

Ethpa. Impf. **ʿnšia nitragagan** AM 189:12

women will be lustful. Pt. **mitragaga ˁlai** Jb 110:9 = with encl. **mitragaglia ragagta** Jb 110:10 lust will inflame me. Part. pres. **lamitragagna ˁl audia** Jb 61:15 I do not yearn after transitory things (or read **mitgararna**? cf. Gy 327:1 s. pe. pf.).

Der.: **r(a)gagta, raktana, rgaga 1, 2, rgiga,** (**rgita** cf. s. **RGA**).

RGG II, (RUG) a postcl. form of **RQQ I.**

Pe. Act. pt. **raiig rgulta** AM 124:13 dribbling spittle.

rguan (אַרְגְּוָונָא, ܐܪܓܘܢܐ < Bab. *argauānu, argamannu* Zimmern *Fremdwörter* 37) purple. **uˁl ˁšumia rguan iurqa mšauilh̲** DC 7 and form verdure on the purple sky.

rgulta (cf. Syr. ܪܓܘܠܬܐ river, Ar. رِجْلَة water-plant) wet substance, moisture, slaver, spittle. **rgulta d̲-puma d̲-taura** AM 121:7 slaver from the ox's mouth; **raiig** (= **raiiq**) **rgulta** AM 124:13 dribbling saliva.

RGZ (Jew.-Aram., Syr., Chr.-Pal., H., Ar. رجز anger) to be angry, excited; pa. to enrage, excite; af. id. to be furious; šaf. to enrage, insult, condemn.

Pe. Pf. **rgaz** he was angry MG 220:12; **rigzat nura** DC 26. 136 the fire raged; **ana alanpia sahria rigzit usahria alanpai rgaz** DC 44. 204 f. I raged against the devils and the devils were furious with me; **rgazian** they (fem.) were angry MG 223:antep. Impf. **nirguz** Gs 68:10, but **nirgaz** Gy 214:6 etc., MG 220:13, **tirgaz** MG 226:anteantep., **nirigzun** AM 237:9 they will be angry. Impt. with encl. **rgizilh̲ llibih̲** DC 46. 238:2 excite his heart. Act. pt. **ragiz** AM 7, 27 etc. rages; pl. **ragzia** (*often*) they rage. Pass. pt. **rgiza** angry MG 116:15; **rgiza uhakima** AM 92:11 quick-tempered and clever; with encl. **d̲-largizlh̲** Gy 197:14 who had never been angry.

Pa. Pt. pl. (**ragzia**) **umragzia** DC 43 E 16 they (rage) and enrage.

Af. Pf. (for simple pe.) **argaz** CP 3:9 (also DC 31) for **rgaz** ML 4:11 they were angry. Pt. **pumh̲ d̲-taura ragiz umargiz** DC 43 J 141 the mouth of a raging and furious bull; with encl. **margizlun** CP 139:10 agitates them; pl. with encl. **razia rgizia šdibun umargizibun** CP 139:9 f. disquieting mysteries (secrets) are inherent therein and agitate them. Nom. act. **argazta** s.v. Nom. ag. **margizana** s.v.

Šaf. (MG 212:4): Pf. with suff. **šargzih̲** Gs 95:23 he enraged him MG 275:13; **šargzun** Oxf. 41 b, 42 b they enraged MG 272:23. Pt. with encl. **mšargizlun** Jb 168:1 he enrages them. Nom. ag. **mšargizana** s.v.

Eštaf. often in ATŠ 'to be condemned'.

Der.: **argazta, margizana, mšargizana, rgiza, rgizta, rugza 1, rugzana, šargazta.**

rgig(a) (pass. pt. pe. of **RGG I**) attractive, seductive, pleasant, delightful, charming, tender; (Nöld. رقيق) soft MG 40:15–21. Var. **rgaga 2** s.v. Fem. **rgigtia.** Pl. **rgigia,** fem. st. emph. **rgigata,** st. abs. **rgigan. lbušia rgigia** Gy 233:11, 367:11, ATŠ II no. 188 attractive clothes; **br d̲-minai ianuq uminai rgig** Gs 5:14 my son who is younger and more tender than I am; **hzuta d̲-rgiga** Gy 59:9 an attractive appearance; **bṭulalia rgigia** Morg. 256/3:3 (var. **rgaga 2** s.v.) in pleasant shadows; **iarqunia rgigia** Gs 3:13, 16 appetizing vegetables; **ˁnšia d̲-rgiga** Gy 233:13 charming women; **ainh̲ rgigan** Par. xxvi 63:2, 112:1 = AM par. his eyes are attractive; **šapirtia urgigtia** Par. xxvi 65:1 = AM par. pretty and attractive (fem.); **ananai rgigata** Jb 34:7 my charming spouses.

rgiza (pass. pt. pe. of **RGZ** q.v.) angry, pugnacious, hot-tempered, excitable, irritable. Fem. **rgizta.** Pl. **-ia.** Fem. also as a name of a kind of demons of both genders: **rgizta zikria urgizta nuqbata** DC 43 A 27.

rgita (rt. **RGA** = **RGG I,** Syr. ܪܓܬܐ) lust, greed MG 83:anteantep., 104:11. **raiig rgita d̲-tibil** s. **RGG** act. pt. pe.; **rgita mlin** Gs 52:3 are full of greed.

RGL (den. from Gen. Sem. רגל, although the Mand. form of the noun is **ligra** MG 74:1 f. & n. 1) to impede, hinder, or tie the feet, fetter, ensnare, hold back, restrain, shackle.

Pe. Pf. with suff. **rgalinun** Jb 141:10 he fettered them; **rgalth̲** Jb 148:2; Gy 333:14 I fettered him; **rgala d̲-abahatun rgaltinun** DC 44. 169 I shackled them like their parents; **rigluk mirgal** JRAS 1937 593:13 they fettered thee. Act. pt. with encl. **ragilh̲ uasarlh̲** Gy 127:2 f. he fettered him and bound him (hist. pres.); **nira rama d̲-rakšia zrizia ragilun** ATŠ II no. 364 the lofty yoke which restrains spirited horses; pl. **raglia** Gy 139:13 they fetter. Pass. pt. **rgila qumtaikun** Gy 139:12 your body is fettered; pl. **rgilia umraglia** DC 44. 1823 f. fettered and impeded. Pass. part. pres. **ˁsiritun urgilitun** Gy 139:11 ye are bound and fettered. Inf. **mirgal** DC 37. 191, JRAS 1937 593.

Pa. Impf. with suff. **nirgalunh̲** DC 37. 191 (read **niralunh̲,** or pe. **nirglunh̲**) they tether him. Pass. pt. pl. **mraglia** s. pe. pass. pt. pl.

Ethpe. Pf. **ˁtirgil hailaian** Gy 331:5 our strength was curbed; **ˁtirgilt** DC 37. 58 thou wert impeded; **ˁtriglun** Gy 362:13 they were fettered MG 223:19; **ˁtirgiltun** DC 37:69 ye were shackled; with encl. **ˁtirgilbh̲ uˁstarbh̲** DC 37. 129 by it was fettered and bound. Impf. with encl. **nitirgilbik** Gs 75:23 he shall be fettered by thee (fem.). Pt. pl. **mitriglia** Jb 149:4, Gs 55:14 they are fettered.

Frequent Idiom: **RGL qaina lburia** s. **buria 2.**

Der.: **ragala, raglˁil, rgala.**

RGLA (Targ. עַרְגֵּל formally influenced by **GLA** Jb ii 243 n. 2) to roll (back).

Ethpe. Pf. **ˁtirglia** (var. **ˁtiglia** ACD) **halšia uaburia** Jb 274:8 = **ˁtirgliu** (varr. **ˁtirgiliu** B, **ˁtirgilu** D) **halšia uabaria** Jb 275:10 bars and bolts rolled back.

RGM (Aram. & H. רגם, Syr. ܪܓܡ, Ar. رجم, Eth. ረገመ Nöld.: *Neue Beiträge* 47) to stone, pelt with stones; in magic documents: to paralyse, immobilize.

Pe. Pf. with suff. **rigmun** CP 175:12 = Oxf.

41 b, 42 b they stoned me. Impt. **rgul urgum ʿdẖ** DC 44 restrain and paralyse his hand. Pass. pt. **rgil urgim** DC 44. 1830 restrained and paralysed; **saṭana rgima** Gy 15:2 cf. Qur. 3:31 Ginzā 17 n. 2.

Der.: **rgama.**

RGP (Jew.-Aram. רגף ithpa., Ar. رجف) to shake; (of light) to flicker.

Pe. Pass. pt. pl. **rgipia urgilia** AO ix 100: paen. (both text N & Lidzb. 4) they are shaken (?) and hobbled (Gordon).

Der.: **(a)rgapa,** var. **argpa.**

RGŠ (Aram. רגש, Syr. ܪܓܫ, H. from Aram. Kautzsch 80, Ar. رجس to thunder) to trouble, make an uproar, make a disturbance, shake, agitate, tremble?; to feel (pain).

Pe. Impf. **nirgiš** as a var. of **nargiš** s. af., **mn handamẖ tirguš** AM 102:19 (var. **targaš** Par. xxvi) she will tremble in (every?) limb. Act. pt. **ragiš bkulhun razia** Gy 280:14 he perceiveth (? Lidzb. *er nimmt wahr*) all mysteries.

Af. Pf. **bšumẖ ḏ-argaš** DC 26. 620 by his name, that is 'He–made–a–disturbance' (cf. the corrupt **arguš** DC 44. 1353 = Morg. 265/20:25). Impf. **dupna nargiš** AM 22 (var. **nirgiš** Par. xxvi) his side will trouble him; **targaš** as a var. of **tirguš** s. pe.

Der.: **marguš, margušana.**

RDA I (Jew.-Aram. רדא, Syr. ܪܕܐ, H. רדה I, Ar. ردى, Akk. *redū*) to travel on, journey, move on, move about, flow, follow a course, pursue a way; to impel, master, chastize; to pour down, administer a draught.

Pe. Pf. **rdun rdun mia lhaka** DC 50. 512 the waters flowed and flowed hither; **ʿubadia ḏ-ʿlẖ rdun** DC 48. 379 f. actions to which they impelled her. Impf. **nirdun mardita** s. **mardita 1** (*a*), **pašaria usamania nirdun ʿlẖ** AM 21 they administer laxatives and drugs to him. Act. pt. **bʿspira radia** Gy 58:13 he (: Christ = Mercury) travelleth in the (celestial) sphere (as one of the planets Ginzā 52 n. 1); **bsira ḏ-ʿlak radia** Or. 331:15 f. by the Moon that travelleth above thee; pl. **radin bʿumama ulilia** Gy 23:10 (cf. 60:14) they (: the planets) travel day and night; **radaiia d-radin bmarkabata** DC 26. 22 wanderers (: planets) that travel in vehicles; **šuba spinata ḏ-ṭaisa uradian** CP 433:15 the Seven (planetary) ships which float and traverse. Part. pres. **radina umasgina** ŠQ CP 221:4 I journey and go forward. Pass. pt. **ʿnta ḏ-rdia** (var. **ridia**) **umgabra** AM 47:16 a woman who is domineering and masculine.

Pa. Pt. with encl. **mradilun lrahaṭia** DC 34 he causeth streams to flow.

Af. Pt. **ḏ-mardia habrẖ** Gy 216:3 that bringeth down his companion; pl. **lamardin iardna uaiar** DC 27. 74 jordan and air do not flow.

Der.: **mardita 1** (*a*), **radaia, ridia 1, 2.**

RDA II (rel. to **I,** Jew.-Aram., H., mod. H., cf. Ges. s. רדה II) to cut, plough.

Pe. Impf. with suff. **bhirba nirdinun** AM 219:16 they will cut them(selves?) with the sword. Act. pt. **bdišta ḏ-radia pdana auginia** AM 129:5 in a field where a plough ploughs furrows.

Der.: **mardita 1** (*b*).

rdaiia AM 237:16 for **draiia.**

RDD I only in panpel **RNDD** (q.v.).

RDD II (Ar. رَدّ) to drive back, send back, return. Impt. **rad lgaiib** DC 46. 238:5 drive back the absent one.

rdikla Zotb. 217b:ult., RD D 6 = **ardikla.**

RDK met. of **DRK** by the influence of **RDP** in the same text: **mardiplak umardiklun mardiklakun** DC 20. 131 shall harry thee and tread them down, tread you down.

RDM (Jew.-Aram., H. to benumb, be torpid, Ar. ردم to stop, obstruct, cf. Akk. *nardamu* dam) to be torpid, sottishly indifferent.

Af. Pt. pl. with encl. **mardimibẖ sanilẖ saniuta** DC 48. 229 they are stupidly indifferent to her, hating her heartily.

RDP (Jew.-Aram., Syr., Chr.-Pal., H., Ar., Sab.) to persecute, harry, harass, mistreat, pursue keenly, press after, banish, drive away, drive off.

Pe. Impf. with suff. **niridpunun** Gy 246:13 read with varr. **niradpunun** s. pa. Pt. pl. **radpin** (*often in* DC 46) they will drive away; with encl. **kul man ḏ-radpilẖ** DC 41. 21 whoever maltreats him (read pa.?).

Pa. Impf. with suff. **radpunan** Q 54:27, 30 (var. **rudpunan** pe.?) they persecuted us MG 280:12. Impf. with suff. **niradpunun** Gy 246:13 BD (varr. pe. AC) they persecute them MG 283:19. Act. pt. pl. with encl. **mradpilun** DAb they persecute them. Part. pres. **mradpina** (read **mradipna**) DC 46 I maltreat. Pass. pt. **mradpa** (*often in colophons*) persecuted. Inf. **radupia** Gy 246:13.

Af. Pt. with encl. **mardiplak** DC 20. 131 (corrupt cf. s. **RDK**).

Ethpa. Pf. **ʿtradapnin** we were persecuted MG 224:21. Impf. **nitradap** AM 21:17 he will be henpecked; **nirdap** AM 219:ult., DC 41. 21 will be harried; **tiradap** Jb 205:2 thou art harassed. Pt. **mitradap hda lanirdap** CP 219:7, not one will be harried. (*often in* ATŠ) shall be banished.

Der.: **mradpana, radupa, radpa, rudpana, ridpa.**

RHA (af. of **RUH,** but formed as from ע״ע: *אַרְחַח inst. of אריח, ܐܪܝܚ) to inhale, smell, perceive by senses, breathe, cause to inhale or breathe in, enjoy. MG 254:5–12.

Af. Pf. **arha** Gy 65:7 he smelt MG 254:24; **kḏ arhat lhimtẖ** ATŠ I no. 278 when she felt its heat; with encl. **arhalẖ utpit** DC 41.18 he smelt at it and sneezed; **arhabẖ** Gy 65:7, 13 f., 22 he smelt at it; **arhubẖ** Gy 65:8, 15, 18 they smelt at it MG 254:24; with suff. **arhẖ** DC 41. 215 he smelt it; **arhatẖ** Gy 102:16 I let him smell MG 277:15; **arhuia** they made him smell MG 278:4. Impf. **narha** Gy 301:22, 24 he smelleth MG 254:25, 255:13; with suff. **narhunẖ** MG 278:15. Impt. **arhilẖ uašqẖ** AM 125:9 make him smell at it and drink it. Pt. **marha** Gy 284:8, Jb 6:4, 96:7, 99:8, MG 254:

26; pl. **marhin** Gy 69:12, 176:22, MG 254:26; fem. **laklan ulamarhan** ATŠ I no. 286; with encl. **marhilẖ lriha** Jb 137:13 they inhale the scent; **marhilun lhanatun mia** DC 34. 421 they smell at that water. Part. pres. **marhinin** Jb 41:3 we smell.

Ettaf. Pf. with encl. **ʿtarhabẖ mana dakia** ML 55:1 = CP 44:11 he breathed (the pure *māna*) into him (inspired him with &c.).

Der.: **rhita** & s. **RUH**.

rhaṭa, rahaṭia s. rahaṭa 1, rahaṭia 2.

rham (3rd p. masc. sg. pe. of **RHM**) used as pr. n. in **rham ṣamra** RD 7 = DAb a name given to Ruha; **rham raza** Gy 131:14 name of a spirit, cf. **arhum, rhum 1**.

rhamta (rt. **RHM**) (*a*) love, desire, lust MG 116: 1, (*b*) pity, mercy, compassion MG 122 n. 1. Var. **arhamta.** (*a*) **šiha urhamta ušigra** Gy 24:9 lust, love, and voluptuousness; **raz rhamta** Gy 110:11 = **raza ḏ-rhamta** Gy 110: 10 f., 111:22 mystery of love, pl. **razia ḏ-rhamta** Gy 109:18, 110:3 f., 10; **ruita ḏ-rhamta** Gy 60:7 intoxication of love; **rhamta unura** Gy 146:23 love and fire; **mara ḏ-rhamta** Gy 112:7 lord of love; (*b*) **ḏ-kulẖ rhamta ukulẖ hiasuta** Gy 2:17 he is perfect love and perfect mercy; **rhamta ḏ-kušṭa** Gy 43:13 true love.

RHB I (Aram. & H. רהב, Syr. ܪܗܒ to impel, hurry, Ar. رهب to fear, Akk. *ra'ābu* to be angry) to hurry.

Šaf. **ŠRHB** s.v.

Der.: s. **ŠRHB.**

RHB II (H. רחב, Ar. رَحُبَ, Eth. ረሐበ, Sab. 𐩧𐩢𐩨 wide, Jew.-Aram. in derivatives) to be wide, extend, spread out, be broad; pa. & ethpa. to make greedy, be(come) greedy; šaf. to enlarge, propagate, comfort.

Pa. Act. pt. **aiba ḏ-šidta mrahib** AM 232:6 the darkness (cloud) of the year will spread; pl. with encl. **mrahbilun** Gy 26:14, 46:23 they make them greedy.

Šaf. Pf. **šarhib šurbata** Gy 240:24 he propagated generations (MG 222:8). Impf. **nišarhbun** they enlarge MG 227:24. Act. pt. **mšarhib** enlarging, propagating MG 131:14, 230:bottom. Nom. ag. **mšarh(i)bana** s.v.

Ethpa. Pt. pl. **mitrahbia ʿl qiniana** Gy 388:3 f. they will be avaricious; **ʿl minuna lamitrahbia** Gy 392:6 they will not be greedy about money (Nöld. from **RHB I**? MG 4:ult.).

Eštaf. Pf. **ʿštarhab** Gy 244:14 they were enlarged MG 223:15; **ʿštarhibat** Gy 372:17 (var. **ʿštarhabat** B, masc. CD) was propagated MG 222:21 f. Impf. with encl. **ništarhibubẖ** they are enlarged in it MG 228:15.

Der.: **mšarh(i)bana, rahbata** (var. **rihbata**).

RHW (met. of **RWH**) to be set at large, be relieved. Another secondary rt. **RWA II** s.v.

Pe. Pt. fem. (as impers. verb) with encl. **rahualun** Gs 88:15, 16, 18, 20 they will be set at large (relieved) MG 66:18.

Der.: **rihua** (cf. also s. **RWH**).

rhum 1 (properly impt. pe. of **RHM**) used as a pr. n. **rhum hai** Q 9:2, 60:4 = ML 24:12, 144:4.

rhum 2 (ܪܗܘܡܐ Nöld. ZDMG xxii 464 n. 1) Rome, Byzantium? BZ Ap. II. **brhum umadan tartin mdiniata** AM 191:18 in Rome and Mada(i?)n—the two cities (see AM p. 210 under **Madan**).

rhumia DC 40. 1062 read **rhimia** (pass. pt. pl. pe. of **RHM**).

RHZ cf. šaf. **ŠRHZ.**

Der.: **rahziʿil** & varr.

rhzil IM 63:3 scr. def. of **rahziʿil.**

RHṬ (Aram., Syr., H. רוץ, Eth. ሮጸ, Akk. *rāṣu*) to run, hasten, move quickly, flow swiftly.

Pe. Pf. **rhiṭ** MG 219:21, **rihṭit** Gs 116:19 I ran MG 223:2, 400:12, **rhiṭiun** Gy 366:8 they ran MG 223:23. Impf. **nirhuṭ** MG 219:21, **nirhaṭ** DC 50. 765, **nirihṭun** ATŠ II no. 350 they will speed away. Impt. **rhuṭ** MG 219:21. Act. pt. **abatar zaniuta rahiṭ** AM 3:9 he pursues fornication; pl. **rahṭia umkamria** DC 43 E 17 they hurry away and return.

Pa. Pt. **rmʿia umrahṭa** Gy 95:1 was thrown down and ran about; pl. **mrahṭia** DC 43 E 17 they run off.

Af. Impt. **arhuṭ** (read so) **hdadia** Or. 327:6 urge one another on.

Der.: **r(a)haṭa 1, r(a)haṭia 2, rahṭiaiil, rihṭa.**

rhima pass. pt. pe. of **RHM** (q.v.), used also as a *malwâša* woman's name. Fem. st. emph. **rhimta** Gy 327:3. Pl. masc. **-ia.**

rhimat hiia Jb 111:11 (*& often*) a *malwâša* woman's name.

rhita (rt. **RUH**, but formed as from **RHA**) ease, comfort. **šarin himianun birhita ḏ-napšaihun** RD C 26 (var. **brhita** DAb) they loosen the sacred girdle for their own ease.

RHM (Aram. & H. רחם, Syr. ܪܚܡ, Ar. رَحِمَ, cf. رَخُمَ to be tender, Akk. *rēmu* to be merciful, as a West-Sem. pr. n. *raḫāmu* Tallqvist: *Neubab. Namenb.* 331) to love, pity, have mercy on, desire, befriend; ethpa. to be compassionate, pitiful, merciful, also to pray **rahmia** (v.s. **rahma** (*c*)).

Pe. Pf. **rhim** and **rham** he loved MG 218:22; **marẖ rihmat** Jb 131:1 she loved her Lord; **rhimt ʿubadia sainia** DC 34:546 thou didst love odious deeds; **rhimnin** we loved MG 224: 19; with suff. **rihmun** they loved me MG 272: 14, **rhamnak** Gs 73:23 A (varr. **rhimunak** BCD, **arhamunak** DC 22. 460, read **rhimnak**) we loved thee MG 274:6; **rhimtunẖ** Gy 255:21 ye loved her MG 277:24. Impf. **nirhum** MG 61:2; **ḏ-rhum** Gs 65:18 that I (may) love MG 34:22; with suff. **tirihmuia** Gy 366:6 ye love him MG 278:18. Impt. pl. with suff. **ruhmuia** love him MG 269 n. 1, 278:22, **ruhmun** CP 483:10 love me MG 273:8. Act. pt. **rahim,** as substant. **rahma** s.v., pl. **ḏ-rahmia šumẖ** Gy 188:22 who love his name MG 310:17 f. Part. pres. with encl. **rahmitulẖ, rahmitulin** ye love him, them (fem.) MG 233:19.

Pa. Nom. ag. **mrahmana** s.v.

Ethpa. Pf. ˁtraham (*often*). Impf. **nitrahmun** AM 272:38 they will be reconciled. Impt. **ˁtraham** have mercy MG 229:13; pl. **utrahamiun** (*often in* Q) MG 229:23. Pt. **d-mitraham ˁl ˁutria** Gy 71:2 that is dear to uthras. Part. pres. **ˁl ahai mitrahamna** Gy 264:12 I feel compassion with my brothers, **mitrahmitun** MG 233:16.

Gl. (always defectively, sometimes miswritten as a nominal form) 5:11 f. احبّ *amare* دوست داشت; 63:5 f. تحنّن *miserere* رحم كرد; 116:7 f. غرب *hospitari* غريبت نواخت; 117:9 f. عبد *colere* عبادت كرد; 119:5 f. عزّ *consolari* عزيز كرد; 140:5 f. كرم *honorare* كرامى داشت.

Der.: **mrahmana**, fem. **-ita**, **rahma**, **rahmana**, **rahmuta**, **rham**, **(a)rhamta**, **rhum 1**, **rhima**, **rhimat hiia**, **(ˁ)trahmuta**. Often in theophorous names.

RHP (ܪܚܦ, H. רחף, to brood, hover over, rel. to Ar. رفّ, رفرف to spread out wings) to take care of, cherish, consecrate.

Ethpa. Pt. **mirahap** ATŠ I no. 235 shall be cherished (or consecrated?).

RHṢ (Jew.-Aram. רְחַץ to trust, H. רָחַץ, Ar. رحض, Akk. *raḫāṣu* to wash, cleanse) to trust, rely on, have confidence in. Usually with **l-** or **ˁl**.

Pe. Impf. **latirihṣun ˁl špur pagria** Gy 21:9 rely (pl.) not on physical beauty. Pass. part. pres. **rhiṣinin** we trust MG 232:paen.

Ethpe. Pf. **ˁtirhiṣnin** Gy 176:5 we placed our confidence; **ˁtirhiṣtun** Gy 255:paen. ye trusted. Impf. **nitirhiṣ bruhṣana** CP 275:4 f. he shall have utter trust; **nitrihṣun** they trust MG 227:20. Impt. **ˁtirhiṣ ˁl ˁubadia šapiria** Gy 42:4 rely on fair deeds (MG 229:8). Part. pres. **d-anin bgauh mitirhiṣinin** DC 48. 149 so that we may have confidence therein.

Der.: **ruhṣana**.

RHṢ II for **TRṢ** in

Ethpe. Pf. **ˁtirhiṣ pasimkia** Gy 78:20 read **ˁtriṣ** (cf. Gy 79:16) Ginzā 77 no. 3.

RHQ (Aram., H. & Sab. ርሕቅ, Syr. ܪܚܩ, Eth. ርሕቀ, Akk. *rēqu* distant) to be far, go to a distance; pa. to remove, send far away, estrange, alienate, repudiate, reject.

Pe. Impf. **mn dilia . . . latirihqun** DC 34. 560 do not absent yourselves from me. Impt. **rhuq** MG 220:1. Part. pres. **minaikun larahiqna** Gy 261:1 I am not far from you.

Pa. Pf. with suff. **rahiqtan** Q 52:30 thou didst remove me MG 272:3. Impf. **nirahqun minh mn malka** AM 237:9 they will depose the king BZ 143 n. 6. Impt. **rahiq minaian rugzak** CP 110:5, ML 131:1 remove thine anger from us. Act. pt. **mrahiq** (*often*). Part. pres. **mn hdadia mrahqinin** ATŠ II no. 434 we separate them from one another. Pass. pt. **mrahaq** removed, separated; pl. **tlata alpia parsia mrahqia** DAb they are at a distance of 3,000 parasangs; **mrahqan umbaṭlan** DC 43 E 77 rejected and made impotent (fem.).

Ethpa. Pf. **ˁtrahaq** ATŠ II no. 112 they were removed. Impf. **nitrahaq** AM 24:ult. will be taken away. Impt. **ˁtrahaq alip parsia** DC 43 J 41 go a distance of 1,000 parasangs; **puq utrahaq minai** DC 40. 856 f. go out and absent thyself from me. Pt. **mitrahaq** (*often*). Part. pres. **mn hdadia mitrahqinin** ATŠ I no 260 we move apart from one another.

Der.: **mrahqia** (adv.), **rahiq(a)**, **ruhqa**.

RHŠ (Aram. & H. רחש, Syr. ܪܚܫ, Ar. حشر, ترخّش from Aram.) to creep, crawl, move, stir, pullulate, bring forth, bring about.

Pe. Pf. **rhiš mana** Oxf. 27 b:bottom the mâna moved; **uplugta bgauaihun rhiš** DC 34. 401 and division took place amongst them; **rihšat mn dukth** DC 34 she stirred from her place; with encl. **rhišalh** Gy 85:9 f. she moved MG 226:6. Pt. **mn dukth larahiš** DC 34. 665 it stirreth not from its place; fem. **rahša nišimta** DC 27. 254, **nišimta rahša** ATŠ II no. 146, **nišimta . . . rahša** ATŠ II no. 108 the soul stirs; pl. **rahšia** Gy 279:20, ATŠ II no. 196 they move. Inf. **mirhaš** DC 12. 52, **ˁšria iardna lmirhaš** DC 12. 52 the jordan is loosed to pullulate with life.

Af. Pt. with encl. **aiar marhišlh mn dukth** DC 34. 665 Ether moveth it from its place.

Der.: **rahša**, **ruhšana**, **rihša**.

RHT (met. of Jew.-Aram. & H. רתח, Syr. & Chr.-Pal. ܪܬܚ) to seethe.

Pe. Pt. pl. **kd bzadanuta umrara rahta libaikun** Gy 39:7 when your hearts seethe with wrath and bitterness; **dudia d-rahtan** DAb seething cauldrons (cf. also s. **rahta**).

Der.: **rahta**.

RWA I (רְוִי, ܪܘܐ & ܪܘܝ, H. רוה, Ar. رَوِيَ, Eth. ረወየ) to drink one's fill, become drunk, intoxicated, to be refreshed by, enjoy.

Pe. Pf. **rua** was drunk MG 257:2; **ruit mn auph** ŠQ 17:6 I was refreshed by its leafiness; (CP 230:8 has **rbit mn auph**) CP 406:4 **uruainin mn mišak** and we were refreshed by thine unction. Impf. **latiruia** Gy 365:4 do not intoxicate thyself (MG 258:ult.); **ništia uniruia** DC 40. 125 f. he will drink his fill. Impt. **rua dul** DC 34. 569 give (him) drink (read af.?), draw water. Pt. pl. with encl. **d-bh rauibh (kulhun) almia** Gy 111:24 f., 112:3 f. by which (all) the worlds are intoxicated.

Af. Pt. pl. with encl. **maruilun b(i)ruita** Gy 60:7, Jb 224:3 they intoxicate them.

Der.: **ruia**, **ruita**.

RWA II (< **RWH** q.v.) = **RHW**. Fem. is used as impersonal verb (differently from Syr. & H. MG 365 n. 4).

Pe.? cf. s. af. impf.

Af. Impf. with encl. **tarualun** Gy 369:4 ff., Gs 105:2 (read pe. **tirualun**?) they shall be relieved MG 247 n. 2, 365:17 f. Part. pres. **qamaruana** Par. xi 23a I provide space MG 379:12.

Der.: cf. s. **RHW** and **RWH**.

ruaha (rt. **RWH**, ܪܘܵܚܵܐ) ease, relief, recovery, refreshment, solace, restoration, revival MG 115:24. Masc. **maria ruaha šaina maria šaina ruaha** Gs 52:20 Lord of sublime bliss MG 319:6; **ruaha šailia** Gy 212:2, Q 57:9 they seek ease; **ruaha naškun** Gy 251:21 they find relief; **ruaha lamaška** Gy 230:1, 232:17 he finds no relief; **ruaha uṭabuta** Gy 233:18 ease and goodness; **nihuia ruaha lnišmata** Gy 251:19 there shall be relief for the souls; **ruaha litlaihun** Gy 252:3 there is no relief for them; **klilia ruaha** Gs 8:17 crowns of solace; **ruaha ḏ-hiia** Gs 8:16 (*&* *often*) = **ruahun ḏ-hiia** Q 41:22, Morg. 242/72:ult., 247/81:12 the ease of Life MG 414:paen.; **laupa uruaha ḏ-hiia** Q 44:17 communion and renewal of Life; **laupa uruaha** Gs 38:5, 74:3; **ʿit ruaha rba ḏ-hiia** s. **ʿit** (*a*); **ruaha ḏ-šušlatun** Gs 113:5 f., 9 relief for their chains; **mn aqa lruaha** DC 41. 236 from distress to relief; **ruaha hua uruaha hauia** JRAS 1937 595: penult. f. there was relief and relief there shall be; **uhauia ruaha** (common final phrase of phylacteries to cure disease) and there will be relief.

ruaz (3rd p. masc. pe. pf. of **RWZ**) used as name of a Vine and of a being of Light: **ruaz gupna** Q. 18:23, 41:1, Oxf. 74 a = CP 42:8, 87:7, 151:6, 209:penult., 231:2, 446:7, ML 108:1, 181:9, 243:10, Gy 211:14, 212:25, 320:14, 321:18; **ruaz nhura rba qadmaia** Oxf. 8 a: middle = ML 181:9.

rubaia (רוּבְעָא, ܪܘܒܥܐ, H. רֹבַע, Ar. رُبْع) Q 7:19, 20:15 a quarter MG 192:bottom.

ruban (Jew.-Aram. רבוון, Sam. ࠓࠁࠅࠀࠍ, Gen. 24:60 cod. BC, Syr. ܪ̈ܒܘܢ, Ar. loan-w. رِبِّيُّون Qur. 3:140 Jeffrey 138 f.; sg. Syr. ܪܒܘ, H. רִבּוֹ) ten thousand, myriad. Indeclinable MG 190:9–12. **šubin ruban** seventy myriads, i.e. 700,000 (Nöld.: 70,000 with a mistaken reference) MG 190:10; **ruban ruban** Gy 210:9, Gs 7:3 myriads on myriads MG 346:15.

rubania 1 = **r(a)bania.** MG 19 footn. **rubanan** Morg. 28:ult., 213/13:6, 236/59:1 our masters (teachers).

rubania 2 a var. of **rubiana** BZ 6 n. 7.

rubiana (rt. **RPA**, cf. **rupiana**, hardly **RBA**) weakness? Varr. **rubania 2**, **rupiana** s.vv. AM trs. 6 n. 7. **rubiana bkraiia** AM 89:16 weakness (?) of the legs; **rubiana uhapapiata** AM 97:18 weakness (?) and sores (cf. **buliana uhapapiata** s. **hapapiata**).

(**RUG** cf. act. pt. pe. of **RGG I & II**).

rugun DC 41:951 read **rugzun**?

rugza 1 (rt. **RGZ**, רוּגְזָא, ܪܘܓܙܐ) anger, wrath, resentment, fury, commotion, excitement MG 104:15. **kulh̠ rugza minh̠ hua** Gy 124:6 all wrath came therefrom; **ʿl rugza btibil mšalṭia** Gy 98:2, 122:2 they are given authority over wrath in the earthly world; **hauma urugza** s. **hauma**; **malkia rugza lmdiniata nišauun** AM 246:2 kings will wreak wrath on the cities; **rugza nasbia** DC 41. 154 are wrathful; **kakia d-rugza** ATŠ II no. 137 teeth of wrath.

rugza 2 (< P. رُخْزَن?) one end of the **burzinqa** (q.v.) which is left hanging down over the left shoulder MMII 30, tip, end (of ritual dress). **qurna ḏ-naṣiph̠ ḏ-hʿ rugza** Lond. roll A 576 the extreme end, that is the tip, of his stole.

rugzana (adj. from **rugza 1**) angry, quick-tempered MG 138:antep.

rugziaiil (rt. **RGZ**) DC 40. 817 an angel.

rud cf. s. **ram.**

RUH (Aram., Syr., H., Ar., Eth. den.) to breathe, blow. Used only in af. s. **RHA** and der.: **ruha, riha.**

RWH (רְוַח, ܪܘܚ, H. רָוַח, Ar. رَوِح, Sab. 𐩠𐩧𐩥𐩢 to amplify) to enlarge, set at large, soften, relieve. Secondary roots **RHW, RWA II** s.vv.

Gl. 119:7 f. (miswritten as **ruha**) عتا *proficere* مالدار كرد.

Der.: **maruaha, ruaha.**

ruh, ruha (רוּחָא, ܪܘܚܐ, H. רוּחַ, Ar. رُوحٌ Jeffrey 40) (*a*) spirit, psyche (CP trs. 246 note 2) (lower than **nišimta**), human spirit, spirit (usually evil) MG 7:10, 63:paen., 65:8, 105:8, about the relation betw. the human spirit and the soul cf. ML 12 n. 1, (*b*) wind (as natural phenomenon), direction, (*c*) wind, flatulence, disease, (*d*) only st. emph. as pr. n. of the mother of devils (usually as **ruha ḏ-qudša** ܪܘܚܐ ܕܩܘܕܫܐ the 'Holy' Ghost as a derisive allusion to the Christian Syr. expression, cf. s. **qudša 1**), identified with the planet Venus (cf. s. **libat**) MG xx 5 f., HpGn 13, Kessler PRE 166, MR 126, 131, Ginzā 189 n. 2, MSt 79 f., Furlani: *I Nomi* 419 f. Fem. MG 159:12. Pl. **-ia**, exceptionally **ruhiata** (**ṭamiata haškata**) DC 40. 245 f. (polluting dark) spirits. (*a*) **pagra uruha unišimta** Oxf. roll g 690 ff., cf. *τὸ πνεῦμα καὶ ἡ ψυχὴ καὶ τὸ σῶμα* I Thess. 5:23; **ruha unišimta** RD B 122 (*&* *often*), pl. **ruhia unišmata** CP 10:14, Q 24:22 = ML 12:2, cf. Q 29:29, 31:17; **zma ḏ-ruha labšia** RD C 27 blood, wherewith they clothe the spirit (cf. H. נֶפֶשׁ Gen. 9:4 f., Lev. 17:11, Deut. 12:23); **ruhia kulhun** Gy 113:8 f. all evil spirits (Lidzb. as (*d*): *alle Rūhās*); **ruh siṭia** Gy 177:20 spirit of seduction; **ruh siṭia umaṣṭia** DC 51. 206 seducing spirit of seduction; (*b*) **mn ruh madna . . . mn ruh marba . . . mn ruh girba . . . mn ruh timia** DC 26. 713 ff. = DC 40. 705 ff. (cf. AM 231:18 f.) from an easterly direction . . . from a westerly direction (&c., &c.); (*c*) **ruha bhandamh̠ nihuilh̠** AM 100:13 she will have wind (i.e. pain) in her limbs; **ruha hʿ ḏ-iatba ʿl** DC 47 (*very often*) the spirit (of illness) that possesses . . .; **ruha tiligth̠** AM 13:12 a demon (: illness) will grasp him; **ruh palga** s. **palga 2**; (*d*) Ruha as mother of Ur Gy 88:1 ff. & often; **ruha uhumra** Gy 81:6 R. and her amulet-spirits; **ruha ḏ-qudša** Gy 27:17, 54:11, 99:19, 132:10, Gs 92:10, Jb 48:8 (*&* *often*); **ruha qadišta** Gy 81:3 f. (cf. Akk. *qadištu* as an epithet of Ištar, Zimmern KAT 423, Ginzā 80 n. 4); **ʿuat ruha, ʿuat ruha ḏ-qudša, ʿuat ruha kadabta** s. **ʿuat**; **arqa ḏ-ruha** RD F 1 = DAb par. the land of R.; **ruha ʿmh̠ ḏ-**

šamiš RD 7 R. the mother of Š.; **ruha mastianita** Gy 100:2, 103:6 seductive R.; **ruha ušuba bnh̲** Gy 339:13 R. and her seven sons (: the planets); **šiṭuata d̲-ruha umšiha** Gy 254:10 (cf. ff.) abominations of R. and Christ; **miša nbiha d̲-ruha** Gy 46:6 Moses the prophet of R.; **abrahim nbiha d̲-ruha** Gy 46:7 Abraham the prophet of R.; **lruha plaglh̲ šiha** Gy 112:5 to R. they allotted voluptuousness; **kd̲ dilik laiit ruha ahat dilia** Gy 146:10 there is no one like thee, R. my sister; **luat ruha azlit** Gy 150:4 I went towards R.; **ruha d̲-minh̲ šuba šibiahia** Gy 381:12 R. from seven planets proceeded; **iurba uruha ualaha d̲-dahlilh̲** Gy 381:20 f. Y. and R. and the god which they worship; **amralun ruha** Gy 226:24 R. spake to them (mistakenly **amarnalun ruha** Gy 226:1, Ginzā 227 n. 4).

ruhaniata pl. female spirits?. **ruhia uruhaniata** DC 40. 826 male (?) and female (?) spirits.

ruhbuia s. **ruhmuia.**

ruhmaia (ܪܗܘܡܝܐ, cf. **rhum 2,** one would then expect ***rhumaia** with Nöld. MG 141:4, but the form is very consistent) Roman, Greek. Pl. **rhumaiia** MG 141:3. **sandar ruhmaiia** Gy 383:15 Alexander the Macedonian; **pirṭauaiia uruhmaiia** Gy 389:21 Parthians and Greeks.

ruhmaita a *malwâša* woman's name.

ruhmuia Morg. 263/16:ult. (var. **ruhbuia** DC 44. 1122) for **ruhmaiia.**

ruhṣana (rt. **RHŠ,** רוּחְצָנָא) trust, confidence, reliance on, safety MG 61:3. **hualan ruhṣana** CP 50:16, ML 66:4 we trust (we have confidence); **lahualh̲ ruhṣana** ATŠ I no. 8 has lost confidence; **ruhṣana ltibil lanihuilkun** DC 27. 230 ye will have no reliance on the earthly world (*& often with* **HUA**).

ruhqa (rt. **RHQ,** ܪܘܚܩܐ) distance. Pl. **-ia** distant places, distant regions. **mn ruhqa** Gy 281:5 from afar; **mn ruhqia** (*often*) from distant regions; **razia . . . d̲-ruhqa uqurba** DC 40. 336 the . . . mysteries of distance and nearness.

ruhqiʿil DC 43 D 20 an angel.

ruhšana (miswritten **ruhṣana** in quotation) (rt. **RHŠ**) creeping creatures, vermin, reptiles. **kulhun ruhšana bgauaihun snʿ dmauatun** AM 197:3 all creeping creatures in them are hideous in appearance.

RWZ (רְוַז, ܪܘܙ) to rejoice, shine, be glad, healthy, fresh, wholesome, flourishing MG 247 n. 2.

Pe. Pf. **ruaz anph̲** Or. 326:23 his face was healthy; **ruaz** as pr. n. s.v., **nišimta riuzat mn ruha** ATŠ II no. 103 the soul rejoiced with the spirit. Impf. **parṣupa d-plan . . . niruaz** Or. 329:9 N.'s countenance is healthy; **niriuzun** Oxf. 59 a, CP 166:6 = ML 201:1 they will be(come) wholesome, (fresh); **aṭšia . . . niriuzun** AM 183:19 the fruits . . . will thrive; **tiriuzun** Gy 18:16 ye shall shine. Act. pt. **rau(u)z** MG 19:5, adjectivally **rauz(i)a** s.v., **(miruaz) rauzia** Jb 167:5 they are fresh; **ʿutria d̲-nhura rauzia batar nhur** Gy 18:17 the uthras of light shine in the place of light; **rauzin nišmatun** ATŠ II no. 106 their souls rejoice (read **rauzan**). Part. pres. **nahrinin urauzinin** DC 34. 22 we shine and exult. Inf. **miruaz** Jb 167:5.

Pa. Pt. **mašqia umrauiz** ATŠ I no. 232 gives to drink and refreshes; pl. with encl. **mrauzibh̲ balma** Gy 12:18 they shine in the world.

Der.: **rauaza, rauz(i)a, ruaz.**

ruzba, ruzb(i)h̲ (P. روزبه) RD D 18, Oxf. 61 b, 111 ab a *malwâša* man's name MG 69:12.

ruṭa = **rauṭa** (q.v.). **ruṭa d̲-asa** Oxf. roll f 681.

ruṭba (rt. **RṬB**) (*a*) Gy 216:11, AM 280:paen. dampness, moisture, (*b*) DC 34. 774 watery matter, saliva?

ruṭna (rt. **RṬN**) JRAS 1937 595:penult. muttered spell, incantation.

ruia (rt. **RWA**) DC 43 J 47 satiety, drunkenness.

ruiaiil DC 13 & 15 an angel MMII 18 n. 8.

ruiana 1 (rt. **RAA II,** Jew.-Aram. רַעְיוֹנָא & רַעְיָנָא, Syr. ܪܥܝܢܐ) thought, reflection, pondering, consideration, meditation, mind, reason, disposition, temperament MG 137:3. Incorrect doublet **riuiana** s.v. Pl. **-ia. ruiana d̲-zidana** Gy 20:21 the mind of an angry one; **bruianh̲ d̲-napšai dahilna** Gs 6:20 in my own mind I fear; **qraba brurbia ruiana nsabth̲** Jb 24:14 I decided to fight against the Great (Life); **ruianh̲ hamimia ubhda ruiana laqaiim** AM 9:15 his temperament is choleric and he does not remain long of one mind; **hamimia ruiania uanašia rahmilh̲** AM 72:7 her temperament is warm, and people love her; **ruianh̲ npišia** AM 27:ult. his opinions are valued; **ruiana ʿmuq ukibša blibh̲** AM 74:2 her mind is darkened and depression is in her heart; **ruianh̲ ʿpika** AM 2:9 his disposition will be warped; **ʿuṣrh̲ uruianh̲** DC 46. 139:3 his thought and his mind.

ruiana 2 (ܪܘܥܢܐ (?) earthquake shock? Doubtf. Pl. **-ia.** AM 219:2.

ruita (rt. **RWA**) (*a*) drunkenness, saturation, intoxication, (*b*) weakness, feebleness, debility, (*c*) overflowing, (*d*) rage, (*e*) personified as a demon of both genders. MG 111:1. (*a*) **ruita d̲-rhamta** s. **rhamta; raz ruita** s. **raz 3** (*a*); **ruitan** Gy 110:11 our intoxication; **maruilun b(i)ruita** s. **RWA I** af.; (*b*) **ʿšata uruita** Or. 325:10 fever and weakness; **marganita uruita** s. **marganita 3; mutana udahalta uruita** AM 242:21 pest, fear, and trembling; (*c*) **mia atraiun ruita hauibun** AM there will be overflowing in the waters of their district; (*d*) **qal aria d̲-bga** (read **bgu**?) **d̲-ruita** DC 46. 16:27 the voice of a lion in a rage; (*e*) **ruita zikria . . . ruita nuqbata** DC 40. 644 male . . . and female weakness-demons.

rukba (rt. **RKB**) (*a*) riding, (*b*) rider, horseman, (*c*) vehicle, chariot, ship, (*d*) running water, stream, course. (*a*) **minaihun nihun lrukba** Gy 124:21 some of them will be for riding; (*b*) **ʿsir hailak rukba rba** DC 37. 479 thy strength is bound, great horseman; (*c*) **rukbaihun d̲-šuba** JRAS 1939 401:4 the chariots (or ships) of the Seven (planets); **rukbaihun bal ularahšia** DC 43 C 58 their chariots were confounded and do not move; (*d*) **nibla brukba d̲-mia** DC 37. 405 will be smitten by a stream of water; **brukba rba d-mia** DC 43 J 11 by a strong stream of water; **brukba ʿpika d̲-mia** DC 43 J 111 by a tortuous stream of water.

RUM I (Aram. & H. רום, Syr. ܪܳܡ, Sab. 𐩧𐩥𐩣 to be high, Ar. رام to desire, رَيْم increase, heap Nöld.: *Neue Beiträge* 70) to be high; af. to raise, exalt; refl. to rise, be set up.

Af. Pf. **arim** Gy 166:14 he raised MG 251:4, but **arim usliq** DC 41. 96 for simple **qam usliq** he arose and went up; **arimat** Q 52:8 MG 251:7, **arimit gbinai** Gy 212:8 I lifted my brows MG 251:9. Impf. **narim, tiarim, ʿiarim** Gy 268:25, 298:1, MG 251:14; with suff. **tarminan** Q 24:8 thou raisest us MG 280:2. Impt. pl. **arimiun ainaikun** DC 50. 48 lift your eyes. Act. pt. **marim** DC 43 E 9 lifting, raising MG 131:paen., 251:18, inflected **marima** Gy 341:20, MG 251:21. Pass. pt. **maram** Gy 3:ult. exalted MG 132:3, 251:24. Inf. **arumia** MG 144:7, 251:25.

Ettaf. Pf. **ʿtaram hanath̲ sradqa . . . binia ruha unišimta** DC 34. 128 that curtain between spirit and soul was raised; **ʿtaram** Gy 280:24, JRAS 1937 594, he extolled himself, was exalted, MG 252:8. Impf. **nitaram** Gy 281:ult. MG 252:9. Pt. pl. **mitarmia** Jb 36:6 they shall be set up.

Gl. (always **arm**, i.e. af. defectively) 7:13 f. ارتفع *elevari* بلند شد; 60:13 f. حمل *portare, rapportare* بر می دارد; 79:9 f. رفع *substare* گرفت; 80:9 f. رفع *exaltare* برداشت; 94:5 f. شال *trahere, tollere* انداخت.

Der.: **(a)ramata, mrauma, (ʿ)mruma, rauma, rama 1, 2, ramta 1, 2, ruma.**

RUM II = **RAM** (q.v.).

Pe. Impf. **rima nirum** AM 250:19, 22 thunder peals. Other forms s. **RAM.**

rum 1 (Ar. روم for Mand. **rhum 2**) Byzantium, Asia Minor, the Levant and Mediterranean territories and their people BZ Ap. II. Often in AM. Later applied specifically to Turks, cf. تاريخ سلاطين الروم Zotb. 222b:bottom, title of a list of Ottoman sultans.

rum 2 AM 275:14 a miswriting of **qum** tribe.

ruma DC 26. 703, DC 40. 687 = **rauma.**

rumaia 1 (adj. from **rum 1**) orig. Roman, then Greek, Byzantine. Pl. **rumaiia 1** Greeks, Byzantines, in late documents Turks (cf. s. **rum 1**). **mšiha rumaia** Gy 54:20, 58:11, **rumaia mšiha** Gy 58:1, or simply **rumaia** Gy 58:3 Christ the Byzantine (or the deceiver? cf. רַמָּיָא MG 121:11, Nöld. ZA xxx 144, Ginzā 49 n. 3, cf. also Lietzmann SBAW xxviii 597, but possibly a pun). Pl. often in AM and other later documents. Gl. 88:3 **rmaia** [sic] روميه *latine* رومانى.

rumaiia 1 pl. of **rumaia 1** (q.v.).

rumai(i)a 2 (by popular etym. from **RMA**, cf. 202:12, Lidzb. ZDMG 694 n. 3; cf. Akk. *ramû* languished, relaxed, *remûtu* laming, paralysis BZ Ap. I; with **d̲-halṣa** cf. ܪܘܡܚܐ, *ῥεῦμα*? ML 36 n. 3; Nöld.'s 'deception' MG 123:10 does not convey the meaning) Q 13:9, 14:11, 17:3, Gy 202:12 (**ramilh̲ rumaiia**), Par. xxvi 236:2, 238:middle, some kind of pains. **rumaiia urabsia** s. **rabsia; ridia urumaiia** CP 30:14, Oxf. roll g 546, 902, Or. 325:7 (text) affliction and pains; **rumaiia d̲-ainh̲** Par. xxvi 107:4 = AM 91:17 rheuminess, (pain(s)?) of the eyes; **šaula urumaiia bišia** Oxf. roll g 800 = Or. 329:16 f. torture and evil pains. The meaning of 'rheumatism' may be contained in **rumaiia d̲-halṣa** Par. xxvi 5:9, 7:2, 25:10, 30:middle, 260:6 (= AM par.) as well as in **rumaiia d̲-burkia** Or. 330:14, **rumaia bhalṣa udupna** Or. 330:13.

rumana (רוּמָּנָא, ܪܘܡܢܐ, H. רִמּוֹן, Ar. رُمَّان, Eth. ሮማን, Fränkel 142, Löw no. 310, Jeffrey 144 f., Nöld.: *Neue Beiträge* 42, Akk. *armannu* from Sum.?) (*a*) pomegranate MG 123:11, (*b*) metaph. (with **d̲-anpa**) high cheekbones, full upper cheeks, full of face, (*c*) metaph. swelling, full feeling (after food). Pl. **-ia.** (*a*) **rumana d̲-mn lbar anpih̲ rauzia** s. **qumana; rumana marira** DC 12:192, Lond. roll B 406 a bitter pomegranate; **rumana d̲-abara** Gy 203:19, 204:8 a pomegranate of lead; **rumana ruman dahba** ŠQ 19:23 pomegranate, a golden pomegranate; **rumana uʿspargila** ATŠ II no. 122 pomegranate and quince; **hurzunia rurbia d̲-rumana** s. **hurzunia; birud lruman** AM 287:19 f. a cooling collyrium of pomegranate (Ar.); (*b*) **rumania d̲-anp(i)h̲** AM 12:9, 18:18, 81:5 etc. he (or she) is full of face; (*c*) **ʿu mindam akil ʿka rumania minh̲** AM 120:15 if he eats anything, there will be swellings (or (*b*)?) from it.

Gl. 87:5 **rmana** [sic] رمان *poma granata* انار.

rumanaiia = **rumaiia 1. arqa d̲-rumanaiia** DC 7 the land of the Romans (i.e. Byzantines).

rumanta (**rumana** with fem. end.) ŠQ 19:23 as symbol of bride.

rumuh̲ (Ar. رُمْح) AM 276:31 etc., lance.

rumia (رومى) = **rumaia 1. dibaš rumia** s. **dibaš.** As name of a people AM 168. **brumia** AM 258:17 in the Greek (reckoning?).

rumil AM 204:8, Rumeli in Turkey? var. **rumin** Ṣâb.'s AM name of a city.

rumqa (Ar. رُمْقَة) scanty measure, a scrap, small quantity. **rmih̲ brumqa d̲-liša** DC 46. 249:8 put it into a bit of wheaten dough.

runza, runzia (ܪܘܙܐ, Ar. رُزّ < P. برنج Löw no. 306) unhusked rice: **ʿsaria urunzia** AM 249:14 barley and rice; **runza šapir nihuia** AM 277 rice will be excellent; **lrunza qiriuih̲** CP 373:6 they created rice.

rus AM 199:7 Russia, Russians.

rus lʿain AM 204:6, **rus lʿin** AM 198:15, **rus d̲-iaman** AM 205:3 f. (var. **rus uiaman** Ṣâb.'s AM) place-names.

rusia (rt. **RSS**?) AM 243:2 scattering abroad, dispersal.

rustam (P. رُسْتَم) AM 106 a man's name. The hero of Firdausī's *Shāhnāma*.

rustaq (ܪܘܣܬܩܐ, Ar. رُسْتَاق < P. روستا Lagarde: *Abhandlungen* 81:211) Gy 385:3 outlying district, outskirt. suburb. Pl. **-ia.** AM 185.

RUP (only Mand., meaning quite opposite to Aram. רפס; **LUP** = **LPP** analogy, cf. Jb ii 150 n. 5) to tie, bind, fasten. Still used with the original meaning 'to loosen' only in one or two places.

Pe. Pf. with encl. **raplh̲ himiana** ATŠ II no. 319 he tied her girdle; with suff. **riph̲ lhalṣh̲** Par. xxvii 50b he tied it to his loins. Impf. **latirup himiana** ATŠ II no. 16 do not tie the girdle; with suff. **niripih̲ lginzih̲** Lond. roll A 775 he ties up his treasures. Impt. **rup bmasa iamina** Par. xxvii 27b, 83b, 85b (cf. 50a) tie on the right forearm; **rup bmasak** Par. xxvii 58a, 82b; **rup bmasik** Par. xxvii 47b tie on thy forearm; **rup bṣuria** Par. xxvii 45b tie to his neck; **rup bṣuraiun** DC 46. 14:paen. tie to their necks; **rup bmiṣai baita** Par. xxvii 38b tie in the middle of the house; with encl. **ruplh̲ bṣaurh̲** DC 43 I 142, DC 46 (*often*) tie it to his neck. Act. pt. **raiip** Par. xxvii 51a (cf. 52a) he ties; with encl. **riša raiiplh̲** RD C 27 = DAb par. he ties his head; pl. **raipia dahba** Lond. roll A 55 they tie gold; pl. with suff. **raipilh̲** DC 38. 26, Oxf. roll f 1339 they tie it; **raipilun bqaina** Jb 148:8 they tie them on a reed. Part. pres. **raiipna daštana minaihun** DC 46. 66:15 (with the orig. meaning:) I detach menstruation from them. Pass pt. **rip** Lond. roll A 103, Oxf. roll f 1376, DC 38. 14; **bʿdh̲ ripa** DC 46. 76:9 tied to her hand; with encl. **riplh̲ zidqa liaminh̲** Oxf. roll f 381 (var. **riplia** DC 42. 19) the oblation is tied to his right hand; **riplak** Lond. roll A 232 is tied to thee; **pandama riplkun** DC 27. 163 the p. (q.v.) was tied on you.

Gl. 23:3 f. اتشدّد (read تشدّد) *invalescere* محكم ساخت; 79:3 f. ربط *alligare, ligare* بست; 89:15 f. شدّ *alligare* بست; 91:15 f. سدّد *claudere* بست; 104:5 f. ضمد *alligare* بست; 134:7 f. قاد *compedibus constringere* زنجير كرد; 151:15 f. منطق [*sic*, taken as a verb: impf. يمنطق] *cingere* ميان بست.

Der.: **rapa, rupa.**

rupa (rt. **RUP**) means of binding. (*a*) protective charm, (*b*) girdle. (*a*) **hazin baba rupa d̲-hšuka kdub** DC 46 write this spell, a protective charm against darkness; (*b*) Gl. 153:11 **rupa** منطقة *zona* ميان بند.

rupana s. **rupiana.**

rupiaiil DC 40. 816 a name given to **adunai ṣbabut.**

rup(i)ana (rt. **RPA**) weakness, convalescence. Varr. **rubania 2, rubiana** s.vv. **man d̲-barqba mikṣar alma ltmania iumia hauilh̲ rupiania** (var. **rupana**) AM 111:16 he who becomes sick in Scorpio, will have weakness up to eight days.

rupi(a)ʿi(i)l (*often*) an angel.

ruṣaṣ (Ar. رَصَاص) lead. **luha d̲-ruṣaṣ** DC 45 a plank of lead.

r(u)ṣip pt. pe. of **RṢP** (q.v.).

RUQ s. **RQQ.**

ruqa (rt. **RQQ,** ܪܘܩܐ, H. רֹק) saliva, spittle, slaver MG 105:5. **raq ruqa** Gs 7:19 he spat out spittle; **ruqh̲ halia bla marira** Gs 3:3 cf. Ginzā 425 n. 2; **ruqa riqa** IM 37:1 spittle is spat out; **atia ruqa mn pumh̲** AM (var. of **riqa** q.v.) 9:17 slaver comes from his mouth; **mn ruqa d̲-atia** DC 43 D 65 from the spittle which comes; **lišana . . . ruqa bgauh̲ škin** ATŠ II no. 116 the tongue . . . saliva is situated in it.

ruqata (rt. **RIQ**) pl. empty words. **ruqata umabadia bišia** Oxf. roll g 792, **ruqata umabadia sainata** Or. 329:13 idle words and hateful acts.

ruqita (ܪܘܩܥܬܐ, ܪܘܩܥܬܐ) strip, rag, piece (of cloth). **bruqita d̲-kitana** DC 37. 285 in a strip of linen.

RWRB (from a reduplicated and dissimilated **RBB**) to make great, exalt, magnify.

Paụpel. Pf. with suff. **rauribtinan** MG 280:10. Impf. (**niraurib** MG 226:24) with suff. **niraurbak** we magnify thee MG 273:24. Pass. pt. **mraurab** exalted MG 49:4, 131:17, 230:23; pl. **anašia d̲-mrauribia** AM 270:3 people of high rank. Part. pres. **mrauribna** Gy 128:5 MG 231:14, **mrauribit** Q 57:31; pass. Q 52:8 MG 232:22. Inf. **raurubia** MG 144:10, 234:8; with suff. **raurubak** Q 53 to magnify thee MG 292:19.

Ethpaụp. Pf. (**ʿtraurab**), **ʿtrauribat** Gy 374:14 she became great (as name of a female genie). Impf. **nitraurbun** they become great MG 227:25. Impt. **ʿtraurab** Gy 70:7 MG 229:18. Pt. **mitraurab** exalted MG 132:25.

Der.: **rurbania, rurbia,** fem. **rurbata.**

rurbania (rt. **RWRB,** cf. foll.) pl. magnates, mighty ones MG 23:10, 137:antep., 170:1. **ʿutria rurbania** DC 53. 390:13 mighty uthras.

rurbia (rt. **RWRB**) pl. of **rba** (*a*) (q.v.) MG 49:3, 127:15, 184:21. Fem. pl. st. emph. **rurbata**; st. abs. **rurban. hiia rurbia** s. **rba** (*a*); **br rurbia** Gy 299:9 (*& often*) son of the Great (Life) MR 152:top; **liliata rurbata** DC 40 powerful liliths; **mihiata rurbata** ATŠ I no. 191 mighty blows; **bauata rurbata** DC 50. 48 mighty prayers; **ainh̲ rurban** AM 9:9 his eyes are large; **rurbia anatun** Oxf. 75 a, ye are great MG 88 n. 1; **rurbia ʿqara** Gs 21:3 Nöld. *von großer Herrlichkeit* MG 311:8, Lidzb. *Wesen* (pl.) *gewaltig an Herrlichkeit*; **ʿburia rurbia** AM 169:7 bumper crops.

RWRT (from a reduplicated and dissimilated **RTT**) to shake, quiver, tremble.

Ethpaụp. Pf. **rat uʿtraurat** (s. **RTT**) MG 85:4, 223:15.

ruš (Iranian *Rašnu*, mod. P. روشن GIPh ii 643) Gy 286:12 a name given to Abathur SsSs i 122, Ginzā 284 n. 2. Doublet **rašna** s.v.

ruš(a)naiia (P. روشنائى) light, radiance (pl.) brilliances. **d̲-rahmalia** (read **rahmanalh̲**) **mn ruš(a)naiia** CP 237:10 = DC 3 & 38 par.

= ŠQ 18:paen. whom I (fem.) love more than brilliant qualities (doubtful).

ruš(u)ma (rt. **RŠM**, רוּשְׁמָא, ܪܘܫܡܐ, Ar. loan-w. روسم wooden seal, Fränkel 137) sign (esp. sacramental, also the name given to the daily ritual ablution), imprint, mark MG 32:23, 104:16. Pl. **-ia.** With suff.: **šum urušum** Q 31:30 = **šumai urušumai** Q 64 (& *often*) my name and my sign MG 175:17 f., **rušumak, rušumh̲** etc.; **rušumaikun rušuma d̲-mia hiia** Gy 18:13 your sign is the sign of living water; **rušuma d̲-hiia** (*often*) the Sign of Life MR 104; **dakia ruš(u)ma, rušumak dakia, rušumia dakiia** s. **dakia, rišman bdakia rušuman** Gy 364:4 (var. **rušuma** BD & DC 22 361, **rušma** C) he signed me with the pure sign.

RUT cf. act. pt. pe. of **RTT.**

ruta for **ʿruta** (after procl.). **bziua unhura uaria uruta** *Florilegium* with brilliance and light and flame and illumination.

RZZ s. **RAZ.**

rziqa (ܪܘܙܩܐ < P. *rōzīk* Lagarde: *Abhandlungen* 81:210, Ar. loan-w. رزق) AM 277:17 supply, provision, livelihood, maintenance. Varr. **raziq, riziq** from Ar. Gl. 79:13 f. **rziqa, arziqa** misinterpreted as a verb ربح *lucrari* فايده كرد.

RZM (Mand. ML 221 n. 2) to be hard on, come down with force, torment, punish. Doubtf.

Pe. Act. pt. **mu šauṭai rama razim ʿlauaikun** CP 181:2 = Oxf. 49a = ML 221:7 is not my lofty lash heavy (or grievous?) upon you.

RṬB (Gen. Sem., Akk. *raṭābu*) to be moist, wet, impregnated with, sappy, juicy, soft.

Pe. Pt. **d̲-bkulhun ruṭbia laraṭib** Gy 216:10 that remains unmoistened (: unsoftened) by all its moisture; **glala bmiša laraṭba** Jb 105:9 (cf. l. 13) stone does not grow soft in oil.

Pa. Pt. **mraṭib** AM 259:5 moist(ening).

Der.: **raṭ(a)buta, raṭuba, raṭiba, ruṭba.**

RṬN (Aram., Syr., Ar. رطن to talk a foreign language) to speak low, talk secretly (in confidence), murmur, mutter, complain; pa. (of birds) to twitter Jb ii 41 n. 5.

Pe. Pf. **puman rṭin kadba** Gy 63:19 our mouth muttered a lie; **kul riṭna d̲-rṭin** Gy 375:4 all murmuring they murmured; **šamiš rṭin** Jb 120:9 the Sun muttered (MG 220:8); **riṭna riṭnit d̲-haršia** Gy 165:10 I muttered many spells. Impf. **lanirṭan ʿlai lbiš** Morg. 264/18:36 he shall not mutter evil about me; **abihdia ʿniš brugza lanirṭun** DC 34. 965 he shall speak to no one in anger. Act. pt. **alaha minaian raṭin** Gy 227:25 God speaketh secretly to us; **mn hilbunh̲ raṭin** Jb 259:1 he mutters from his habitat; **minh̲ raṭin** DC 48. 1 he talks confidentially with him; **kd̲ raṭin** Par. xxvi 17:5 = AM 14:7 when speaking; **šiqra raṭin** Par. xxvi 59:bottom, he mutters a lie; **raṭin bšinta** Par. xxvi **laraṭin abihd(i)h̲ bildbabh̲** Par. xxvi 28:middle = AM 23:14 he should not speak to his enemies; **ʿu raṭin dina hadar dina ʿlh̲** Par. xxvi 28:middle = AM 23:15 if he pleads (in a ?) court of justice, the verdict will turn against him; **arqa raṭna** Jb 68:5 the earth murmurs; pl. **daiuia minaihun raṭnia** Gy 227:24 f. demons speak secretly to them; **minh̲ . . . raṭnia** Jb 72:12, 74:1, 9 they speak to him; **raṭnia** Jb 157:1 they mutter; **raṭnia hdadia** Jb 161:11 they mutter together; **kadba raṭnan** RD C 5 = DAb par. they (fem.) utter a lie. Part. pres. **abihdh̲ laraṭnana** WedF 62:bottom I (fem.) do not speak (secretly) to him.

Pa. Pt. pl. **iatbia sipria umraṭnia** Jb 133:5 the birds sit and twitter.

Der.: **raṭna, ruṭna, riṭna.**

riasia (pl. of Ar. رئيس inst. of رؤساء) chief men. **riasia d̲-hinun rišaiia** AM 265:11 the chief-men which are the first ones.

riba (H. רָעָב?) hunger, famine (doubtf.). V.s. **aqalata.**

ribabia (rt. **RBB**) pl. officials. **šibabia uribabia** DC 40. 340 neighbours and officials.

ribna Jb 40:8 [*bis*], var. **dibna** DC 30 sheep Jb ii 44 n. 1.

rida (rt. **RDA I** Lidzb. ZDMG lxi 694 n. 3) affliction, chastisement. More common in pl. **ridia 1** MG 164:12. **mn ridak blibaihun** DC 37. 39 f. some of thine affliction into their hearts; **ridia urumaiia** Morg. 212/11:9 f., Q 13:9, 14: 11, 17:3, Oxf. roll g 503, 902, DC 51. 78 ff., Or. 325:7 (text) afflictions and pains.

ridia 1 s. **rida.**

ridia 2 for **rdia** pass. pt. pe. of **RDA I** (q.v.).

ridpa (rt. **RDP**) persecution, oppression, affliction, adversity MG 102:4. Pl. **-ia. ridpa d̲-alma** Gy 20:18 persecution of the world; **ana huibun ridpa** Jb 205:10 I persecuted them; **ridpan uandaštan nupša** ATŠ II no. 441 our affliction and anxiety increased; **dina daiina mn ridpia** DC 34. 586, 181 I will give judgement against persecutions.

riha (rt. **RUH**, ܪܝܚܐ, H. רֵיחַ, Ar. رِيح wind) (*a*) breath, smell, scent, perfume, (*b*) incense, frankincense MG 108:ult. Pl. **rihania** perfumes, odours, spices, aromatic herbs MG 169:21. Cf. Jb ii 8 n. 1. (*a*) **marha briha d̲-hiia** Jb 96:7, 99:8 he smells the scent of Life, cf. Jb 6:4, 41:3; **ʿtatna riha d̲-hiia** Jb 252:1 the scent of Life came down; **riha d̲-sruta** Gy 259:10 stinking smell; **rihaihun snia** Gy 25:11 their odour is hateful; **riha d̲-manda d̲-hiia** Morg. 219/26:ult.; (*b*) **dra riha** Oxf. roll f 524, 678 (cf. 527, 630, 681) he took incense; **nirmia riha lnura** Lond. roll A 18 he casts incense on the fire; **riha rma** (*often*) he cast incense; **ruha riha nisbat** Gy 106:9 R. took incense; **azal riha** DC 41. 215 the incense parted; **kapta d̲-riha** RD 44 = DAb par. incense-cup; **qauqa d̲-riha** s. **qauqa**; **b(i)riha** = **bit riha** brazier with a recess for an incenseholder (Lidzb. *Gewürzbehälter*): **riha bbit riha** Lond. roll A 564; **birihak** Lond. roll A 469; **birihia** Lond. roll A 429 (with **bit riha**), Oxf. roll f 159, cf. 180, 258 ff. Pl. **rihania** Morg. 219/26:paen., Q 22:32, Gy 106:18, 107: 2, 146:17, 147:1 f., 351:16, 18, 378:34, Jb 232:2, 4; 254:11; **rihania basimia** Gy 176:23;

rmia šuba rihania DC 40. 74 f. cast in seven aromatic herbs; rihania ubusmania ATŠ II no. 168, 433 (*& often*). Gl. 86:13 riha رايحة *fragrantia* بو; 147:6 riha لبن *thus* حسن لبان.

rihaṭia AM 202 = r(a)haṭia 1.

rihania pl. of **riha** (q.v.).

rihbata s. **rahbata**.

rihua (rt. **RHW**) air, atmospheric conditions, wind, blighting breath. Still used (pron. *rehwā*). Pl. **rihuaiia**. **rihua ḏ-šidta** AM 261:30 = **rihuaiia ḏ-šidta** AM 282:15 f. atmospheric conditions of the year; **ziqa** = **rihua** AM 271: 1 f.; **rihua baina anašia maprina** DC 46. 122:5 I cause an (evil) wind to fly into people's eyes; **ʿnšia baṭanata rihua mamṭina** DC 46. 98:14 I cause 'wind' to come upon pregnant women (: I cause miscarriage?); **rihua mamtana alma ḏ-ʿnta ugabra mištadnḥ** DC 46. 123:3 I bring 'wind' (: evil influence) so that woman and man are crazed; **ʿu rihua našim** AM 276 if an evil wind blows; **ʿl glalia mhaliq ana rihua** DC 46. 125:4 I bring a wind to rocky places; **ʿaliq brihua** DC 46. 190:7 hang it up in the wind.

rihṭa (rt. **RHṬ**) Gs 116:19 running, race, course.

rihmat (rt. **RHM**) in **gabrʿil rihmat** RD 28c a theophorous name.

rihša (rt. **RHŠ**, רִיחְשָׁא, ܪܚܫܐ, doublet **rahša** s.v.) creeping things, vermin, swarms, reptiles MG 61:5, 101:3. Used as collective, but also a pl. form **-ia**. **rihšia bišia** Gy 124: 4 f., 339:12 (cf. Gy 9:1) evil vermin (biting insects etc.); **kul rihšia** DC 27. 240 all living things; **kulhun rihšia uqadahia** ATŠ I no. 4 all creeping creatures and blossoms.

riuana (rt. **RAA III**, from רַעֲנָא) Gy 1:ult., 61:16 etc. clement, merciful MG 139:5. Comforter, Reliever.

riuand 1 (P. ریوند) rhubarb, rue. **riuand ṣinia** DC 46. 87:6, 119:7 f. Chinese rhubarb; **riuand uzma ḏ-šunara** DC 46. 86:8 rhubarb and cat's blood; **riuand umarzanguš** DC 46. 89:7 rue and mouse-ear.

riuand 2 AM 205 name of a city. Var. **rauan 2**. **rauand** s.v.

riuia (rt. **RUA**, Jew.-Aram. רְוָיָה, cf. H. רִי, Ar. رِيّ) (*a*) drunkenness, drinking to repletion, intoxication, (*b*) drinking-place, fountain, water-hole MG 102:23. (*a*) **mištia mn zmaihun lriuia** Gy 174:10 f. drinking their fill of their blood; **štia mn zma . . . lriuia** DC 44. 1993 drink of his blood . . . to repletion; (*b*) **hausia uriuia litlḥ** Gy 216:14, Jb 161:12 there are no cisterns and drinking fountains.

riuiana (rt. **RUA II**, formal influence of preced.) mind, consciousness, faculty. Doublet **ruiana** (s.v.) MG 137:4. Pl. **-ia**. **hašib briuianḥ** Gy 97:3 he cogitated in his mind; **riuiana kšiṭa** Gy 5:8 true mind; **ḏ-iaqid blibia uriuiania** Gy 227:15 that burneth in hearts and senses; **hadia briuianḥ** AM 61 she is of joyful mind.

riziq AM 164, 254, cf. s. **rziqa**.

riṭna (rt. **RṬN**) talk, chatter, murmur(ing), mutter(ing); vernacular, dialect; incantation, spell. MG 102:5. Pl. **-ia**. **riṭna riṭnit ḏ-haršia** s. **RṬN** pe. pf.; **riṭna ḏ-hibil ziua** Gy 221:11 the secret language of H.-Z.; **riṭna ḏ-anania**, **riṭnaiun ḏ-anania** Jb 38:11 f. murmuring of his womenkind; **ḏ-ʿniš ldmutaiun uriṭnaiun lika ḏ-qaiim** Gy 139:16 whose appearance and murmuring no one can stand; **riṭnia ḏ-aula** Gy 218:2 evil murmurs; **riṭna ḏ-abahatḥ** = **riṭnaihun ḏ-abahatḥ** Jb 262:7 f. the speech of his parents; **šuma riṭnaihun ḏ-rbia** Jb 263:9 hear the words of the great (Life); **paš riṭna** Gy 318:5 the murmur remained (doubtf. Ginzā 321 n. 5).

rikša AM 186:7 = **rakša 1**.

rima 1 (rt. **RAM**, ܪܥܡܐ) thunder MG 14:19, 16:14, 101:2. Pl. **-ia** peals. **ram rima** s. **RAM**, **rima nirum** s. **RUM II** (= **RAM**); **rima ubarda** DC 43 I 123 thunder and hail; **rima ubirqa** DC 43 E 41 thunder and lightning; **rimia ubirqa** Gs 12:1 f. peals and lightning; **qal rima ḏ-raiim** DC 46. 15:ult. the noise of thunder that thunders.

rima 2 (H. רִמָּה, Ar. رِمَّة) vermin, worms, maggots MG 102:17. **aqapra urima** Gs 15:7, 15 f. dust and maggots; **rima ʿšiul** Gs 99:12, 132:23 vermin of Sheol MG 313:9.

rimat DC 22. 200, 208, 482 = **ramat** Gy 209:7, 215:19, Gs 99:4.

rimuh AM 276:35 = **rumuḥ**.

rimza (rt. **RMZ**) wink, furtive or secret sign, signal, emblem, symbol, token. Pl. **-ia**. **aina ḏ-ramza rimza** Jb 101:8 eye which winks (signals); **ramzia rimzia** Gy 66:1 f., they give winks; **rimzaiun** Gy 66:2 their winks; **raza urimza** Gy 243:22 a mystery and a symbol, pl. **razia urimzia** Gs 40:6, Jb 166:6; **ainaikun rimza nirimzan** Jb 175:12 your eyes signal; **ṣum ainaikun mn mirmaz rimza** Gy 16:13 f. let your eyes refrain from winking; **bhad rimza pagra mithambal** DC 34. 676 the body is destroyed by a single sign.

rimilan AM 204 name of a city.

rinita occ. for **rnita**.

risa Jb 75:11 a Jewish personal name.

risan (ܪܣܢ, Ar. رَسَن Löw 281) DC 46. 192:7 *Inula Helenium*, fleabane.

risia a var. of **rusia**.

ripa (local ريف) dry land in marsh, river-bank. Pl. **ripia**. **laqaimia bripia** Jb 148:11 they do not stand on the banks.

ripun ripun DC 40. 651 name of a demon.

ripsa (rt. **RPS**) (*a*) kick, beat of the foot Ginzā 208 n. 1, (*b*) a unit of time, (*c*) a malady of some kind. Pl. **-ia**. (*a*) **ripsia rmalḥ ldinanukt bpagrḥ** Gy 207:24 he gave D. body-blows with his foot; (*b*) Gy 196:23, 219:14, ATŠ II no. 135; (*c*) **ripsia uqirsia** Oxf. roll g 901; **ruha hʿ ḏ-iatba lmaṭahiata umitiqria ripsia** Or. 329:29, 332:27 (var. **ripsuia** Oxf. roll g 829) cf. s. **maṭahiata**.

RIQ (Jew.-Aram., Chr.-Pal., H., Syr. ܪܝܩܐ < H., Ar. ريق empty, Akk. *rāqu* to be empty, *rēqu* empty) to be empty. Cf. **ARQ II**.

Der.: **ruqata, riqan, riqin, riqiniata**.

riqa (ܪܩܐ, رَقّ, Akk. *raqqu*) tortoise MG 101:5. **gambḥ ḏ-riqa** Gy 280:3 sides of the tortoise;

miška ḏ-hiuia ulišana ḏ-riqa AM 121–2 a snake-skin and the tongue of a tortoise; **gala uriqa** Lond. roll B 99, DC 12. 46 turtle and tortoise.

riqan(a), riqin (rt. **RIQ**) empty, void, bare, naked, devoid of all; adv. mere, merely MG 109:3, 137:13, 200:21. Fem. pl. st. emph. **riqaniata, riqiniata** MG 21:5, 168:20. **riqan šbaqtḫ lalma** Jb 83:2 devoid of all, thou hast left the world; **ḏ-riqan haka mitagzar** Jb 177:5 f. who is void shall be condemned here; **uailḫ lriqana ḏ-riqin** (var. **riqan** BD) **qaiim bit maksia** Jb 177:6 woe to the empty one that standeth bare in the House of Dues; **qam riqin** (var. **riqan** DC 22. 78) **balma** Gy 83:10 he stood naked in the world; **riqin napqin mn alma** Gs 17:22 naked come they out of the world; **arṭil lalma atalḫ** (read **aitulia**? Ginzā 517 n. 3) **uriqan minḫ apqun** Gs 97:9 f., cf. 83:7 f., 132:19 f. they brought (?) me naked into the world and they took me naked out of it; **minilia riqiniata** Gy 388:24 empty words.

riqata s. **raqata.**

riqin, riqiniata s. riqan(a).

rira (רִירָא, ܪܝܪܐ, H. רִיר, Ar. رِيْر, رِيْل, Akk. *lēru*? Hommel: *Grundr.* 207, 254) spittle, slaver, saliva MG 102:18. **gsa rira mn pumḫ** Gy 143:21 f. he spat forth slaver from his mouth; **atia rira mn pumḫ** Par. xxvi 5:top = AM 4:18 slaver comes from his mouth; **rira daiib** DC 43 E 8, Par. xxiv 8b (*& often*) he dribbles saliva.

riš, riša (רֵישָׁא, ܪܫܐ, Bibl.-Aram. רֵאשׁ, Eg.-Aram. ראשׁ, Palm. רשׁ, רשא, Lidzb. *Hdb. d. nordsem. Epigr.* 366, Ma'lūla *raiša*, H. ראשׁ, Akk. *rēšu*, Sab. 𐩧𐩱𐩪, Ar. رأس, Eth. ርእስ) head, top, end, summit, beginning, extremity, tip, important (thing or person), chief, captain MG 4:26, 17:9, 70:23, 100:25, 149:ult. St. abs. often in idiomatic expressions, st. cstr. to form compound nouns (both similarly to P. سر, cf. examples below). Pl. **rišia, rišata**, more common **riš(a)uata** MG 167: 7. Masc. (*a*) With suff. **brišia** DC 44. 1559, DC 43 C 2 = **brišai** Jb 144:2 etc. on my head; **rišik** Gy 116:14 thy (fem.) head MG 177:16; **riš(i)ḫ** MG 178:1; **prišilḫ lrišiḫ ukinia mia** DC 43 J 125 I separated his watersheds and reservoirs of water; **rišaian** Q 13:23, Oxf. 106 b, our head MG 179:2; **rišaihun ḏ-haršia** Gy 113:3 the chief of wizardry; **rišaihun ḏ-kulhun qrabia** Gy 113:5 the beginning of all wars; (*b*) St. emph. **riša ḏ-qinan** Gy 257:4 the head of our kin; **adam riša ḏ-šurbta haita** Gy 26:7, Jb 146:7 f. the head of the living generation; **riša ḏ-ṭuria** (*often*) mountain-top, summit of range of mountains; **riša ḏ-šidta** AM 258:17 the first day of the year; **riša ḏ-iahra** (*often*) the first day of the month; **riša ḏ-riš** DC 37. 71 the top of the head; **riša ḏ-ʿṣbatḫ** Gy 217:3 his finger-tips. Sometimes replaced by st. abs. (or cstr.): **lriš ḏ-šiša ḏ-miša** ATŠ II no. 160 on the top of the bottle of oil; **riš ḏ-kraiia** (*often in* AM) for **riša ḏ-kraiia** or **riš kraiia** (mod. *rīš-e kərāyī*) the toes; (*c*) St. cstr. (compound nouns): **riš mašknia** Jb 168:1, 8 etc. chiefs of the sanctuary (cf. s. **maškna**); **riš daria** Gy 353:17, 356:4 the head of generations (i.e. the head of the world *ὁ ἄρχων τοῦ κόσμου τούτου*, cf. Ginzā 371 n. 5), different from **riš dara** ML 52:9 (a title of honour) DC 3; **briš iumia** CP 153:5 = ML 183:10 on the first of days (**habšaba**); **riš klila** Gy 334:2 the top of the wreath; **riš kušṭak . . . riš haimanutak** etc. Gy 213 f. the first principle of thy truth . . . of thy faith etc.; **riš almia** Jb 218:10 chief men of the world; **šamiš riš planga** Gy 172:7 Š. (Sun) the commander of the phalanx (cf. P. officer-titles سر لشکر general, سرهنگ colonel etc.); **bauata ḏ-riš haila umadita** Gy 375:3 prayers — 'the first principle of strength and knowledge'; **ʿl riš iardna** Gy 296:11; **briš mia nipqit** CP 124:3, ML 57:8 cf. P. سر آب رفتم ZDMG 1955 p. 361:bottom; **riš šibia rba** Gy 113:3 the beginning of great captivity; **riš kulḫ nkista** Gy 113:5 the head of every slaughter; **briš ziuia ʿtit lhaka briš nhura asgit lka** CP 418:6 f. as leader of beings of light thou camest hither, as a captain of light thou wentest thither; (*d*) St. abs. & idiomatic expressions: **mn riš** Gy 95:4 (*& often*) again (P. از سر, It. *da capo*, Fr. *derechef*); Gs 86:11, 12 first (of all), above all, **mn riš briš** (*very often*) from one end to the other, for ever and ever, completely, fully, continually, utterly; **tisaq lriš** Q 10:10, 63:20 etc. is achieved, completed; **masqitun rahmutkun lriš** Gy 18:11 f. practise a perfect love; **sliq lriš, silqat lriš** (*often in colophons*) was completed (i.e. copied unto the end) MG 303:6–9 (cf. P. idioms MG 303 n. 3); **silqit lbit riš** CP. 44:19 = ML 55:2 I attained my aim; **lbit riš briš** Gy 72:15 cf. MG 309:10, ML 55 n. 2; **ʿl riš ḏ-** Gs 86:13 as soon as MG 462: 24; (*e*) **tinpa nura mn rišatḫ** DC 40. 128 fire will puff out from his heads; **arba rišauata šauitinun** Gy 167:7 I made four ends (extremities); **šuba rišauata** Gs 85:2 (cf. foll.) seven heads. Gl. 71:10 **riša** جمجمه *calvaria* كاس سر; 84:2 **riša** رأس *principium* اوّل; 84:4 **riša** رأس *caput* سر; 85:10 رئيس الجماعه *archisynagogus* رئيس طايفه; 137:3 **riša** قايد *centurio* يوزباشى; 157:3 same as 71:10.

rišaga (**riš** + آغا) chief-lord, head-agha JRAS 1937 610 n. 3.

rišai Jb 75:1, 2 a Jewish personal name.

rišaia (adj. from **riša**) ord. number. first (rarer than **qadmaia**) MG 191:antep. & n. 3; adj. chief, principal, original; subst. head man, person in authority, noble person, person of superior rank. Fem. **rišaita.** Pl. masc. **rišaiia.** **alma ḏ-rišaiia mṭit** Gs 124:23 until I came to the first one(s) (of the planets Ginzā 578 n. 1); **abdḫ ḏ-rišaia** ibid. the servants of the first one(s); **rišaia** (var. **rišaiaia** A, **rišaiia** CD) **ḏ-kulhun kalia** s. **kalia** 3; **ʿštaiia mn hazin rišaia** Gy 194:18 talk to that noble one; **ʿutra niha rišaia** Gy 293:7 mild (and) noble uthra; **mana rba rišaia** Oxf. 57 a the great first *māna*;

rišaia uprišaia Q 61:16 (*& often*) noble and outstanding, pl. **rišaiia uprišaiia** Gy 315:16 f., **prišaiia urišaiia** Gs 27:21; **rišaiia unaṣuraiia** Gy 254:13 (cf. l. 1) noble people and Naṣoraeans; **rišaiia** parallel with **qadmaiia** Q 32:12; **ginzaiia urišaiia** Q 19:15 = ML 52:8, DC 42. 689, Oxf. roll f 32, 335, 415 treasurers (a priestly rank, s.vv.) and men of rank; **rišaiia urišamia** s. **rišama**; **alma rišaia rba** and **alma rišaia zuṭa** titles of two Mand. scrolls (DC 41 & DC 48 = PNC). Fem. RD 10 (*twice*).

rišaiuta s. **rašaiuta.**

rišama, riš ama (cf. **riša** (*c*)) head of the people, ethnarch, a rank higher than *ganzibra* MMII 173. Pl. **-ia. rišama uriš dara** AM 256:14 head of the people and chief of the age; **rišaiia urišamia** Oxf. roll f (often, var. **riš amia** 807, cf. Morg. 94:5).

rišata s. **riša** (*e*).

riš draz (P. ريش دراز) a family-name. Often in colophons.

rišiuta s. **rašiuta.**

rišpa (Ar. رَجْفَة) trembling, agitation. **rišpa ḏ-liba** DC 46 trembling (of) heart.

ristata DC 46. 117:6 corrupt for **riša(ua)ta**?

rkašia (rt. **RKŠ**) DC 26. 347 pl. bindings, harnessings.

RKB (Gen. Sem., Akk. *rakābu*) to mount, ride, get up on.

Pe. Pf. with suff. **rkabtinun** DC 44. 1249 = Morg. 264/18:17 I overrode them. Impf. **nirkab** AM 193:13 he will ride. Act. pt. pl. **bkanpia ḏ-hdadia rakbia** Gy 95:15 they ride on each other's side(s). Part. pres. **rkibna** DC 37:357, DC 44. 516 I ride.

Gl. 81:7 f. **arkb** [sic] ركب *ascendere, equitare* سوار شد.

Der.: **markabta, rukba, rkubia.**

rkubia (rt. **RKB**) Q 52:10 = ML 126:1 pl. riders.

RKA for **RKN** in **nirkia** DC 37. 193 gives way (?), and **ʿtirkia** DC 22. 185 s. **RKN.**

RKK (Aram., Syr., H., Ar.) to be soft, tender, yielding.

Pe. Pass. pt. **rkika** Gl. (see below).

Af. (only doubtf. forms). **miṭra napša tihuia ḏ-arkalun** [sic] **ṭaʿam** AM there will be much rain so that their food becomes soft (?). Pt. **makik umarik ruhia ḏ-ziqia zrizia** DC 44. 630 f. he subdues and softens (?) the spirits of swift storm-winds.

Gl. 87:4 **rkika** رطوبة *humiditas* ترى; 143:9 **rkika** كسلان *piger* كاهل; 147:9 **rkika** لين *tener* ملايم.

Der.: **rakik** (cf. also s. **rgig(a)**).

RKN (Aram., Syr., Ar.) to bend, give way, cede, submit, come down, dismount, fall down, yield.

Ethpe. Pf. **ʿtirkin** Gy 173:8, 362:10, (**ʿtirkia** DC 22. 185) CP 101:15 = ML 127 bent down (sg. & pl.). Pt. **mitirkin** ATŠ I no. 11 is pliant.

Ettaf. Inf. **ltarkunia** Gy 294:7 to give way unto downfall MG 234:6.

RKŠ (H. רָכַס, Ar. رَكَسَ, Akk. *rakāsu*, not H. רָכַשׁ in spite of greater formal resemblance) to bind, harness, tie up.

Pe. Pf. with suff. **rkašṯh bgduliaṯh** Gy 118:11 I bound her by her tresses. Act. pt. pl. **ḏ-rakšia uzaimia utalin** Gy 121:20 that bind and bridle and hang up.

Ethpe. Pf. **ʿtirkiš bʿdḥ uligrḥ** Gy 84:7 f. he was bound hand and foot.

Der.: **rakša 1, 2, rikša, rkašia.**

RMA (רְמָא, ܪܡܐ, H. רמה I, II, Ar. رمى, Eth. ወረየ, Akk. *ramū*) to throw, cast, place, put, pour, set, lay (eggs); (with l and ʿl) to put upon, bring upon, cast on, wear Jb ii 19 n. 1; (with **qala** as obj.) to give out a sound, utter, pronounce, give a cry; (with **ʿniana** as obj.) to answer, address (a hymn) to; (cf. H. II) to be false, betray, deceive; pass. to move about, wriggle, throw oneself about, move from side to side.

Pe. Pf. **qala lbit hiia rma** Morg. 246/80:ult. he raised his voice to the House of Life; **tigra bnhura man rma** Jb 6:10 who cast strife into the light?; **ʿit minaihun ḏ-rma bita** ATŠ I no. 254 some of them laid eggs; (**rmat** Gs 44:19 twice read **ʿmat** why?), **uʿrmat ʿniš ḏ-šatia minḥ bmanaṯh dilḥ** ATŠ II no. 15 and she cast anyone who drinks thereof into her portion; **rmu** Gy 261:7, 22, 265:21, 266:17 they cast, put on etc., **ḏ-rmun lhama uṭabuta rmun ldilkun** CP 293:10 f. who set out bread and ritual food for thee (: Life); **ʿniana ḏ-rminin** ATŠ II no. 177 the hymn which we recited; with encl. **ṣauma rmalun ʿl pumaihun** Gy 356:9 (cf. foll. l.) he imposed fasting on their mouths; **rmatabun** Gy 300:14 she threw amongst them MG 257:16; with suff. **rman** (*often*); **rimian** Gs 67:23 he cast me MG 284: 20, 23; **rimi(i)ḥ** he cast him MG 287:8; **rmaiṯh** Gy 346:15 (var. **rmiṯh**) thou hast cast him MG 288:3; **rmaitun** Gy 365:20, 21 ye cast me (as without suff.); **rmaitunḥ** Gy 349:4, MG 288:7. Impf. **ʿrmia hatma lpumaiun** DC 44. 870 I will place a seal on their mouths; **qudamḥ rmia** ML 213:1 I will cast before him (but see CP trs. 131 n. 4); **nirmun unisigdun** Oxf. 3 b they throw themselves down and worship; with suff. **urminun** Gy 82:13 and I throw them MG 35:9, 290:15; **ʿrminkun** Gy 186:7 I cast you MG 290:3; **bdudia ḏ-nhaša nirimḥ** [*sic*] DC 44. 1007 = Morg. 262/16:4 we will throw him into copper cooking-pots; **nirmunak** Gy 299:21 they throw thee MG 287:4. Impt. pl. **rmu hirba** Jb 11:12 put on the sword; **urmun ʿdaikun lrišaikun** DC 50. 49 place your hands on your heads; sg. with suff. **rminan** Gy 186:1 throw us MG 289:17, pl. with suff. **rumiuia**, but also **rumuia** Gy 101:4, DC 44. 1820 throw him down MG 289:1 f., **rumuia ʿniana** DC 50. 174 recite the hymn. Act. pt. **ramia ʿnianai anuš** Oxf. 2 a:middle, A. giveth me reply; **lahma laramia** RD E 30 (cf. s. pf.); **gaunia ramia** Par xxvi 70:middle, she puts on different colours; **šauṭa ramia** DC 43 J 30 they lay on (apply) the whip; **laramian dahba** Jb 82:9 they (fem.) do not put on (wear) gold; cf. **zahba ramian** RD C 11, 27; **ahuatai ʿniania ramian** Jb 182:9 f. my sisters make the responses; with encl. **kariuta uridpa ramilh̲** AM 53:3 they bring sadness and persecution on him; **ramilak** AM 206:16 they deceive thee; **ramilh̲ rumaiia** Gy 202:12 (s. **rumaiia 2**). Part. pres. **ʿu ana ramina ltigra** Jb 11:5 if I bring about the quarrel; **ramit dahba, ramit kaspa** Gy 116:12 f. thou wearest gold, silver. Pass. pt. **d̲-lpalga d̲-ʿuhra rmia** CP 379:2 lying half-way in the road; **nhura d̲-hiia d̲-rmia** Gy 177:7 the light of Life that is shed abroad; **rmia urapiš** Gy 159:5, Gs 38:ult. it wriggles and jerks about; fem. **rmʿia** Gy 95:1, 216:9 MG 153:27; with encl. **dnab tanina lkadpai rmilia** Morg. 267/24:26 (var. **marminalia** DC 44. 1594 af.) I place the dragon's tail on my shoulders. Pass. part. pres. **rmina** I am thrown MG 260:1; **rminin** Gy 253:4 we are thrown MG 260:7; with encl. **rmitbh̲** Gs 39:20 thou art thrown therein MG 260 n. 1; **rminabh̲** Gy 254:5 we are thrown in it MG 260:8. Inf. with encl. **umirmilun biria** DC 44. 176 to throw them out (or into pits?).

Pa. Pass. pt. **nhura mramai lkadpai** CP 225:paen. = ML 177:8 = ŠQ 16:8 light shed on my shoulders.

Af. Part. pres. with encl. **marminalia** as a var. of **rmilia** (s. pe. pass. pt. with encl.).

Idiom: With **tigra** s. **tigra 1.**

Der.: cf. s. **rumaia 1, rumai(i)a 2, ramia.**

rmaš st. abs. of **ramša,** cf. **br maš** s. **br.**

RMZ (Aram., Syr., Ar., cf. H. with met. רָזַם) to give a (secret) sign, wink, hint at.

Pe. Pf. **ainan rmaz rimza** Gy 63:17 our eye gave (secret) wink(s); **lakirṣit ularimzit** Gs 60:5 I have no secret winks and signs; **rmaznin rimza** Gy 66:4 we gave (secret) sign(s). Impf. **lanirmaz** Gy 66:4 we do not wink; **nirimzan** Q 67:17 etc.; **nirimza** Gy 36:1, cf. Gs 78:1 (var. **nirimzia** BD) they (fem.) wink 228:3, 9 & n. 2. Act. pt. fem. **aina d̲-ramza rimza** Jb 101:8 eye that winks; pl. **ramzia rimza** Gy 66:1 the winkers MG 310: 18 f., Ginzā 60 n. 1. Inf. **mirmaz rimza** Gy 16:14, 41:7 winking.

Der.: **ramaza, rimza.**

RMṬ (for קמט?, cf. **GMṬ**) to pluck.

Pe. Act. pt. fem. pl. **ramṭan uaklan** ATŠ I no. 285 they (fem.: the souls) pluck and eat.

rmiṭa (cf. P. رميده) offended, indignant. BZ 98 n. 2. **qalila urmiṭa** AM 155 hasty tempered and (easily) offended.

RMM (H, רמם II, Ar. رَمّ) the rt. of **rima 2.**

RMŠ (Aram., Syr. den., cf. Ar. رَوَامِس nocturnal animals) the rt. of **ramša, ramšia 1** (abs. **rmaš**), **ramšia 2.**

RNA (Aram., Syr., Ar.) to meditate, consider, ponder, brood, be anxious about.

Pe. Pf. **larna ulaʿtmakak** Jb 8:6 he took no thought, nor did he submit; **larna bbišuta** Gs 43:8 he contemplated no evil; (with encl. **rnabh̲** Gs 43:9 f. read **qrabh̲** he called Ginzā 460 n. 1). Impf. **lau mna qirsa d̲-tirnia** Gs 43:17 thou art not due a portion of suffering that thou shouldst be anxious; **latirnia ulatik(a)ua** Jb 36:11, Gs 43:4, ATŠ II no. 432 be not anxious and fret not; with encl. **nirnibak** Gs 66:16 we will direct our thoughts to thee; **rnibh̲** Gy 366:21 I think on him. Impt. **rnʿ** (var. **rnia** Sh. ʿAbd.'s copy) **mn tibil** Gs 66:16 divert thy thoughts from the earthly world. Act. pt. **rania uamar** Gs 43:1 he pondereth and speaketh; **mhašbana d̲-rania umhašib** Gy 215:12 the thoughtful man that pondereth and planneth; with encl. **d̲-ranibia** Gy 366:20 whoso meditateth upon me.

Der.: **rnita** (var. **rinita**).

RNDD (panp. of **RDD I,** cf. Ar. رَدّ, but also P. راندن MG 75 n. 2, Syr. ܪܢܕ Th. bar Khōnī IM 130:anteantep. from Mand. Nöld. WZKM xii 358) to stir up, rouse, disturb, startle.

Panp. Pf. **randid** MG 75:19; **randid** (var. **radid** Sh. ʿAbd.'s copy) **uaqim šakbia** Gy 361:9 he roused the sleeping ones and caused them to get up; with suff. **randidh̲** Jb 3:2 roused him; **randidun** Gs 47:6 they roused me MG 272:23; **larandidun** Jb 3:2, 128:12 they did not rouse me; **larandidunun mn šintun** Gy 301:10 they roused them not from their sleep; **randidunun** Jb 32:8, 133:12 they roused them; **randidinun** he roused them (Nöld.'s reading of Gy 301:10 MG 281:25). Impf. **nirandidun** Gy 308:11 ff., 319:2, var. **niranddun** Gy 319:5 they rouse them MG 30:14, 227:18; with suff. **nirandidh̲** he rouses him MG 276:8; **tirandidan** Jb 128:13 thou rousest me; **tirandidak** she rouses thee MG 273:anteantep. Impt. with suff. **randiduih̲ uaqmuih̲ mn šinth̲** ATŠ II no. 185 rouse him and raise him from his sleep. Act. pt. **mrandid** Jb 136:1; with encl. **mrandidalun** Jb 137:8 she rouses them; **mrandidabun bharšia d̲-kadba** Gy 81:10 f. she disturbeth them with false magic. Inf. **randudia uaqumia šakbia** Gy 299:11 to rouse and raise the sleeping ones.

Ethpanp. Impf. **nitrandad** Gy 101:12 is roused; **nitrandadun** Par. xi 42 a, CP 275:1 they will be roused; **nitrandidun** AM 193, 207 id. Pt. **mitrandad** CP 275:2 aroused; Pt. fem. **mitrandada** DC 48. 238 she is aroused.

rnita (rt. **RNA**) DC 36 II no. 357, Gy 213:22, AM 178 (*& often*) pondering, meditation, reflection, anxiety, care, worry MG 104:1.

RSA = **RSS alahia ʿtirsin bbahtuta** Gy 174:4, Q 53:10 = CP 103:3 gods are broken down by shame, ML 128:10 (or **ʿtirkin**? cf. ML 128 n. 2, or read **ʿtirsun**?) (from foll.).

RSS (Jew.-Aram., H. II, cf. Ar. رَسّ to dig a well) to crush, break to pieces, crumple up.

Pe. Pf. with suff. **rastinun lgirmh̲** Gy 84:6 I broke his bones into pieces.

Ethpa. Impf. **nitrasas** DC 43 J 209 will be crushed to pieces.

Der.: **rusia**?

rʿia (rt. **RAA I**) (*a*) Gy 268:21 tending, pasturing MG 102:24, (*b*) AM 211:19, var. **rʿiia** Par. xxvi shepherd(s)? Gl. 84:13 **ria** [*sic*] رعاة, رعاى *pastor* چوبان.

RPA (for **RPP**) to loosen, relax, slacken, weaken, undo.

Pe. Act. pt. **gaṭar ularapia** DC 26:621 = DC 44:656 binds and does not loose; **hatmia larapia** DC 46. 234:14 they seal up and do not loose.

Der.: **rup(i)ana, rupiaiil** (& varr.), cf. **rubiana.**

rpila AM 233:9 = **arpila.** Pl. **rpilia** Gy 311:5 BD MG 34:20. **rpilia d̠-hšuka** Jb 99:4, 249:3 clouds of darkness.

RPS (רְפַס, ܪܦܣ, رَفَسَ, rel. to H. רמס) to tread upon, stamp upon Jb ii 69 no. 4, Ginzā 208 n. 1.

Pe. Inf. **mirpas** (in the idiomatic expression **mirpas ainia** s.v.), **lmirpas qaiim** Gs 91:1 it standeth (only) to be trampled down; **kd̠ taqna tibil lmirpas** AM 201:6 when the earth is firm for treading on.

Der.: **mirpas, ripsa.**

RPP (with the orig. meaning of Aram. רפף opposite to Mand. **RUP**) to loosen, detach. Doubtf., only in late texts. **rpupih̠ . . . lplan biša mn baitia** DC 46. 203:paen. detach . . . the wicked N. from his house. Cf. the secondary **RPA** (s.v.) also only in late texts.

RPŠ (Mishn. רפש, der.: Syr. ܪܦܫܐ = Ar. رَفْش winnowing basket < Akk. *rapaštu*?) to jerk about, move (convulsively), flap, flop, flounder. MSchr. 152 n. 3.

Pe. Act. pt. **rmia urapiš** Gy 144:15, 159:5, 17, Gs 38:24 wriggleth and jerketh about.

RṢP (Jew.-Aram., Syr., H., Ar., Akk. *raṣāpu*? Zimmern: *Akk. Fremdw.* 26) to crush, smash.

Pe. Pf. **urṣpit qašth̠** *Florilegium*, and I smashed his bow. Pt. **taqip umarir ur(u)ṣip** DC 43 D 8, 16 overpowering, bitter, and crushing (?).

rqada DC 22. 23 = **rquda** Gy 24:18.

rqahata Zotb. 218b:9 = **arqahata** lands, countries.

rqaqata s. **raqata.**

RQB Gl. 64:11 f. **arqab** خزن *congregare* خزينه ساخت.

RQD (Jew.-Aram. & H. רקד, Syr. ܪܩܕ, Akk. *raqādu*, Ar. رقص) to dance, waggle, rock to and fro, move rhythmically.

Pe. Pf. **rqid** Gy 116:2 danced MG 220:9. Impf. (unknown to Nöld. ibid.) **nirqad unintar** ATŠ I no. 261 will rock and fall down; **latiz(i)mrun ulatiriqdun** Gy 20:14, 39:1 sing not and dance not (pl.). Act. pt. **raqid bsapaqia** RD 22 s. **sapaqa**; pl. **mṭalalia uraqdia** DC 34. 882 they sport and dance; **mnandia uraqdia** Q 52:13 they shake and dance; **raqdia kd̠ ailia** s. **aila.** Part. pres. **ʿnanditun uraqidtun** (read so inst. of **-tin**) Q 52:13 ye shake and dance; **niriqdun ulaniqiršun** DC 12. 114 ff., they shall move (dance) not congeal (stand still).

Pa. Act. pt. **lišanh̠ mraqid** DC 43 E 8 (miscop. as **mbaqid** DC 49. 25) his tongue is waggling.

Der.: **raqada, rqada, rquda.**

rquda (rt. **RQD**) dance, dancing MG 118:15. Var. **rqada** s.v. **zmara urquda** Gy 24:18, ATŠ II no. 64, 253, AM 155:4 song and dance; **šalth̠ rquda qumth̠** Gy 115:24 f. his body desired dance.

rqiha (< רְקִיעָא, ܪܩܝܥܐ, H. רָקִיעַ) sky, firmament MG 71:23, 117:11, 171 n. 3, MR 61:4. Varr. **arqiha, rqʿia, arqa 6.** Masc. pl. **rqihia, rqihata. briša d̠-rqiha** Jb 195:3 at the summit of the firmament; **rqiha ʿlaia . . . rqiha titaia** Jb 195:3 f. the upper sky . . . the lower sky; **(a)rqiha** Jb 197:15 f.; **miṣria** (var. **miṣia** AC) **rqʿia** Gy 80:17 f. the middle of the firmament; **rqiha rba** HG 28 large sky; **šuba rqihia andat** DC 27. 64 f. thou shakest the seven skies; **ṭuria uiardina** (read **iardnia**) **urqihata** ATŠ I no. 83 mountains, rivers, and skies.

rqʿia s. preced.

RQQ (Jew.-Aram., Syr., H.) to spit; ethpa. to cover oneself over? or (cf. ܪܩܥ) to press in, plug in.

Pe. Pf. **raq ruqa** Gs 7:19 f. spat out spittle. Act. pt. **raiig** for **raiiq** see **rgulta, uraiiq** DC 22. 110 & Leid. var. of (**raiim**) Gy 115:19 and spitteth; **minaihun raiqa** Gy 170:15 she spat (hist. pres.) out because of them.

Ethpa. Pf. with encl. **ʿtraqaqlun** ATŠ I no. 254 fixed them in (doubtf.).

Der.: **ruqa, riqa.**

RŠA (רְשֵׁי) to claim a debt, ܪܫܐ to reprehend, cf. Ar. رَشْوة bribe, Akk. *muraššû* Zimmern: *Akk. Fremdw.* 24) to lend, bribe, corrupt.

Pe. Act. pt. **d̠-larašia umitpairia** CP 18:7 = Q 7:12 ML 20:4 (**umitpiria**) who lend not and yet are paid back; **d̠-larašia d̠-ahbilh̠** Jb 148:3 who does not lend what they give him.

Af. Pf. **aršit** Jb 53:16, 54:4 I have lent; with suff. **aršith̠ pudana** (read **purana**) Jb 55:3 s. **pudana.** Pt. **kulman d̠-maršia mitpra** Jb 16:2 whosoever lendeth shall be repaid; pl. **maršin** Jb 114:6 they spend money; **maršin ʿlai** Jb 53:16 they should pay me.

Ettaf. Pt. **lamitaršia** Jb 59:11, Gy 215:6 is not corrupted MG 265:anteantep.

Der.: **rašiuta.**

RŠL (Targ. רשל) to flap wings.

Šaf. Pf. with suff. **šaršilh̠** Jb 142:1 he flapped his wings.

RŠM (Aram. & H. רשם, Syr. ܪܫܡ, Ar. رشم & رسم from Aram. Nöld. ZDMG xxix 237, Fränkel 137, 250) to sign, consecrate by signing, ordain (a priest), seal, imprint.

Pe. Pf. with suff. **rišman** Gy 364:4 he signed me; **nidbai ršiminan** CP 124:penult. f. Nidbai signed us; **ršaminan** ML 150 f. he signed us MG 279:24; **ršamth̠** Gy 332:4 I signed her. Impf. with encl. **niršimubkun** they sign with you MG 228:20. Pass. pt. **ršim(a).** Pass. part. pres. **ršimna** JRAS 1939 401:10 I am signed.

Ethpe. Pf. **ʿtiršim** CP 42:10 = Q 18:23 = ML 50:1 he was signed. Part. pres. **miršimna** I am signed MG 231:10; **miršiminin** Jb 74:6 we are signed MG 214:18, 233:4.

Der.: **mrašmania** (pl.), **ruš(u)ma.**

RTA (*a*) a shortened form of **RTT**? (q.v., cf. also רתע, ܪܬܐ) to tremble, (*b*) a more original but exceptional form of **RHT**? (q.v.).

PE. Pf. **rta iardna** ATŠ the jordan was disturbed. Inf. **udahba ukaspa lmirtia . . . šapir** favourable . . . for smelting gold and silver.
DER.: **rtia**?

rtia (ܪܬܐ) (rt. **RTA**?) heating, exciting, passionate? **zmaria rtia** DC 46. 245:14 exciting (passionate?) songs (doubtf.).

rtitia (rt. **RTT**) (*a*) trembling, shaking, convulsion, ague, fear MG 116:23; (*b*) (anxious) precaution (as semantic development of (*a*)). (*a*) Gy 264:8, Gs 28:3, 32:14, Q 2:7, AM 189, 219:20; always in pl. form. **rtitia d̲-mia** Par. xxvi 6:bottom, 56:8, 62:bottom perh. disturbed (sea-?)water. (*b*) **ʿzdahar utlatma** [quotation, reference, & transl.], Var. **ʿrtitia** s.v.

rtitia 2 (cf. ܪܬܝܬܐ) admonitions, warnings. **ʿzdahar utlatma ušitin alpia zibnia urtitia ʿlnafšak** ATŠ I no. 45 beware 3,600 times take warnings to thyself.

RTT (Jew.-Aram., Syr., cf. H. רְתֵת fright, Akk. *ratātu*?) to shake, tremble, quiver, quake. Reduplicated and dissimilated rt. **RWRT** (s.v.).
PE. Pf. **larat ulaʿtraurat** Gs 1:6, 9, 19 they neither shook nor trembled MG 85:4; **ratat qumat** Gy 272:19 my body trembled MG 248:10; with encl. **laratalhun qumtaihun** Gs 1:7, 9, 19 their body trembled not MG 248:11. Impf. **latirut** Gy 314:21 tremble not MG 249:11. Act. pt. **raiit** MG 250:12.
DER.: (ʿ)**rtitia.**

Š

š the 21st letter of the alphabet. Phonetic value: coronal-alveolar fricative **š**. Phonetic changes: ש > ṣ and s MG § 50. Supplementary letter **š̤** is used to express چ and ج in Ar. and P. words, although the diacritical dots are often omitted MG 2:11 ff.

ša in **ša adiq** DC 32. 249 a miscop. of **saliq** cf. par. passage ibid. 240.

ŠAA I (אִשְׁתְּעֵי, ܐܫܬܥܝ) to talk, discuss, discourse, recite, relate; (cf. Akk. *šeʾū* friend?) to associate. Formally identical with **ŠAA II** Jb ii 11 n. 3.
ETHPA. Pf. **ʿštaiia minh̲** Gy 140:23, 143:3; **ʿštaiia mn . . .** Gy 240:21 he talked with him; **puma laptalh̲ ulaʿštaiia** Gy 244:10 opened not his mouth and spake not (MG 263:24); **ʿštaiat bšuta basimta** Gs 23:6, 12 she spake in lovely speech (MG 263:ult.); **ʿštaiit** DC 34. 111, Gy 143:5, Gs 51:19 I spake; **ʿštaiit minaihun** Gy 157:16 I talked with them (MG 264:13); **ʿštaiun** Gy 125:7 f. they talked; with encl. **ʿštaiilia bšuth̲** Gy 323:10 he spake to me with his speech; **ʿštaiilak** Gy 324:3 (they) spake to thee; **ʿštaiilh̲** Gy 104:1, Gs 21:11, 20 I talked to her; **ʿštaiilun** Gy 91:15, 92:10, Gs 23:14 I related to Him (pl.: the Life) MG 264:15; **ʿštaiilkun** Gs 54:19 I related to Thee (: Life, pl.); **laʿštaiitlia bšuta basimta** Gs 22:9 thou didst not speak to me in lovely voice; **ʿštaiibh̲ bšuta** Gs 42:14 I spake in (lovely?) speech (cf. also Ginzā 459 n. 2). Impf. **ništaiia** Q 25:33, 26:19, 31, Oxf. 83a, Gy 154:2, 311:7 f. (*& often*) MG 70:2, 264:paen.; **tištaiia** AM 57:9, 60:7 she talks; **ʿštaiia** I speak MG 265:3; **ništaiun bšutaiun d̲-labatla** WedF 75a they converse in their immortal speech; with encl. **ʿštaiilun** Gy 326:17 f. I will relate to them. Impt. **ʿštaiia** Gy 194:18 MG 265:15; **ʿštaiun** Gy 125:7 f. MG 265:21; with encl. **ʿštaiilan** Gy 157:4, 258:26 speak to us MG 265:15; **ʿštaiilhun** Gs 54:9, 12 relate to Him (: Life, pl.). Pt. **mištaiia** Gy 129:10, 212:18, 253:20, Gs 19:11, 58:24 etc. MG 132:20, 265:26, fem. **mištaia** Gy 158:16 MG 265:paen.; pl. **mištaiin** Jb 10:7, Gy 148:11, 210:11, 211:11, Gs 36:24, 51:15; **mištaiin bsidria umasqata** Q 35:1; **mištaiin bsidria** Gy 210:15, 22 f. they recite recitations; **mištaiin bzipa . . . . mištaiin bhukumta** Gy 258:23 f. (cf. ff.) they speak in falsehood . . . they speak cunningly; **ʿtlun puma ulamištaiin** Par. xxvii 76a, Morg. 263/16:6 they have a mouth but speak not; **hinun mn ʿniš lamištaiin** ATŠ II no. 53 they associate with no one; with encl. **šuta . . . d̲-mištaiibh̲** Gy 308:21 f. speech . . . with which they converse. Part. pres. **mištaiina** Gy 128:4, 157:10, 168:20, 195:7, 259:2, 264:18, 325:4 (*& often*) I speak MG 266:3; **mištaiit** Gy 211:21 thou relatest MG 266:7. Inf. **ʿštaiuia** Gy 4:24 BCD (miscop. **ʿštaiia** A); **ʿštaiuiia** Gy 143:3 MG 8 n. 1, 144:17 ff.; 266:12–14; **mištaiuia** Gy 69:3, 142:3 MG 266:14 f.
DER.: **šaita 2, šuta 1.**

ŠAA II, ŠUA (prob. Aram. & H. שׁעע, Syr. ܫܥܐ, rel. to שׁוע, ܫܘܐ) to be smooth, pleasant, even, harmonized, glorious. Jb ii 11 n. 3.
PA. Act. pt. pl. with encl. **mšaiilh̲** cf. s. **MŠA II.**
ETHPA. Pf. **ʿštaiubh̲ uʿštababh̲** CP 57:12 = Q 26:17 f. = ML 73:8 (Life) is glorified and praised therein. Pt. pl. **mištaiin hiia** Jb 6:6, Oxf. 34 b, Gy 340:17, 342:1, 345:13, 353:2 f., 358:14, 359:12 f., 366:15, 375:19, Gs 64 ff., Q 64 ff. (*very often*) Life is glorious (? Lidzb. *das Leben ist hochgehalten*) MR 210.
DER.: **šaia, šiuta, tšiuta**?, **tšaia.**

šaba (שְׁבַע, ܫܒܥ) seven. Fem. form, often replaced by masc. **šuba 1** (q.v.) MG 29:8, 188:1; **šaba dmauata** Gy 105:9 seven figures, but **šuba dmu** s. **šuba 1.**

šababata fem. pl. of **š(i)baba. habrata mšailih̲ šababata d̲-qarilai** [*sic*] DC 46. 254:3 her friends question her, neighbours (women) who call to her.

šabadata (rt. **šaf.** of **ABD I**) pl. priestly services, rites performed for the dead. **dukrania ušabadata** DC 27, **adkarata ušabadata** ATŠ II no. 183 commemorations and priestly services.

šabaṭ (Aram. & H. שְׁבָט, Syr. ܫܒܛ, from Akk. *šabāṭu*) Mandaean month under the rule of Aquarius, called colloquially *awwal siṭwa* MMII 84, Ibn Nadīm: شباط SsSs ii 35.

šabaima Gy 384:17, 20 B = **šabima** MG 190 n. 1.

šabaita Jb 144:8 (reed-)boat. Var. **šapaita** B & DC 30.

šabaqa DC 7 for **šabqa**.

šabašta (nom. act. pa. of **ŠBŠ**) Gy 47:5 (*& often*) flattery, infatuation MG 122:4. Pl. **šabašata** trespasses CP 12:ult. = ML 14 n. 2, with suff. **šabašatan** Morg. 209/5:11 f., Q 15:33, 24:7 our trespasses, mistakes (in the commemoration prayers).

šabata (rt. **ŠBA II**) ATŠ II no. 146 (var. **šabhata** DC 6), II no. 345, DC 48. 16 pl. praises. Doubtf. in Gy 272:3, 24, perh. the same, or pl. of **šabta** scrolls, folios? cf. MG 48 n. 3, Ginzā 269 n. 1.

šabhat (Ar. شَبْحَة?) AM 130:14 pegged-out skin.

šabhata s. **šabata.**

šabuia (cf. Ar. شَبْوَة) DC 46. 206:14 scorpion (-sting?).

šabuiia inf. pa. of **ŠBA II** (q.v.).

šabunia (diminutive from שִׁיבָא, cf. H. שְׁבָבִים) Gy 181:12, pl. splinters MG 140:11.

šabur 1 Gy 383:22, 384:1, 3 name of two Persian kings (A.D. 244–72) Ochser ZA xix 76 n. 6, (A.D. 399–420) ibid. 77 n. 2.

šabur 2 a *malwāša* man's name.

šabur 3 AM 205 the district of Šabur Kharnah in Fars BZ Ap. II.

šabiaiil (rt. **ŠBA II**) DC 40. 880 an angel.

šabibtiaiil DC 40. 883 an angel.

šabima seven hundred MG 190:3. Var. **šabaima** s.v.

šabiq haṭaiia s. **ŠBQ** pe. act. pt.

šabqa (ܫܒܩܐ) channel, stream MG 113:5. Var. **šabaqa** s.v. Pl. **-ia. habla ḏ-šabqia** Gy 101:10 the mist (spray) of the streams (var. **šabqa** DC 22 sg.).

šabra DC 47 a more original but exceptional form of **šambra** (q.v.).

šabšuta (rt. **ŠBŠ**) Gy 24:24 flattery, wheedling, cajolery.

šabta (= **šapta 2**) parchment, skin, scroll MG 48:3. Pl. **šabata?** Gy 272:3, 24 (s.v.). **kipruia lšumh mn šabta** Gy 116:1 they erased his name from the scroll; **šabta hiuartia ḏ-mia** DC 37. 189 a white parchment of gut-skin; **miktib ᶜl šabta ḏ-mia** DC 44. 1738 = Morg. 268/26:39 written on a gut-skin.

šaga (שָׁאגָא Löw 64) DC 41 (picture) teak-tree.

šagiana occ. for **šugiana.**

š(a)gira s. **šgira.**

šagra DC 22. 23 & Sh. ʻAbd.'s copy = **šigra** Gy 24:9, cf. **mn šihaiun mn šagraiun šadin lmia** DC 37. 13 f. they shed some of their lust and burning on the entrails.

šagša occ. for **šigša.**

šad (manda), a *malwāša* man's name. Miscop. **šar manda.**

šada s. **šida 2.**

šadai (H. שַׁדַּי) Jewish name given to God. **iahu ṣbabut ᶜl šadai** DC 46. 62:6 & often in talismans.

šad(ai)ia a *malwāša* woman's name.

šadan (P. شادان) Zotb. 217b:4, 220b:9, AM 255:34, RD D 2, 7, 22 (*& often in colophons*) a family-name.

šadana DC 46. 83:10, 120:2 etc. = **šidana.**

šadanak ʿ**adasia** (P. شادنه عدسی BQ s. شادنه, Ar. شاذنج, Syr. ܫܕܢܓ) AM 287:4 a kind of haematite used in preparing medicaments for the eyes.

šadaruan(a) (شادروان BQ) carpet of different colours and designs, curtain of the same kind, possibly fountains. Pl. **šadaruania** DC 43 J 196, DC 34. 1069, RD A 4, **šadaruaniata** RD F 7.

šadarta (nom. act. pa. of **ŠDR**) dismissal, sending away, demission. **šlahta ušadarta lkulh hailh ḏ-hšuka** DC 37 dismissal and sending away for all the host of the Darkness.

šadia = **šad(ai)ia. šadia kisna** Gy 1:6, **šadia mamania** Gy 1:7, 9.

šadid (Ar. شَدِيد) AM 258:19 strong, excessive, extreme.

šadiriata pl. of **šadirta.**

šadilata (שדל, ܫܕܠ) pl. enticements. **ušidia šadilata šadlata** DC 43 J 196 f. and cast (employ) persuasive enticements.

šadirta = **šidirta.** Pl. **šadiriata** DAb for **šidiriata.**

šadlata fem. pl. s. **šadilata.**

šad manda s. **šad.**

šah 1 (Ar. جاه) AM 254:5 honour, glory, greatness, nobility.

šah 2 (P. شاه) Zotb. 221a:34, 227b:34 shah, king.

šahaita (rt. **ŠHA I**) Or. 330:18, DC 51. 453, AM 23:18 etc. (*often*) exhaustion, weakness, wasting away, languishing.

šahal (Ar. جَاهِل) Zotb. 227b:41 imprudent, unwise.

šahalta (nom. act. pa. of **ŠHL**) Gy 270:4, DC 46. 183:1 outflow, issue.

šahana (rt. **ŠHN**, H. שְׁחִין) AM 216 etc. inflammation, ulcers, scabs.

šahara (ܫܗܪܐ Nöld.: *Neue Beiträge* 87) Gy 227:5 vigil-priest.

šahardal (P. شهردار) CP 91:2, Q 43:1 = Morg. 246/79:1 = ML 112:2 ruler, governor.

šaharialia Lond. roll B 144, 591 f., DC 12. 305, DC 7 & 46 (*often*) = **šahrialia** rulers, monarchs.

šaharta (nom. act. pa. of **ŠHR V**) Gy 189:23, 190:10, ML 210:11 slumber Jb ii 225 n. 1. Scr. def. **šhrta** (Montgomery שהרתא) AIT 147:16, 154:11.

šahat s. **šah(u)at.**

šahba 1 = **šahpa.** Pl. **-ia** JRAS 1937 594:3 (cf. s. **ṢRD**).

šahba 2 (cf. Jew.-Aram. שחף & Ar. شَحَبَ to scrape, grate) AM 96 (*& often*) a cutaneous disease, eczema? Var. **šahpa 2** s.v.

šahbana (rt. **ŠHB** = **ŠBA II**) praiseworthy. Fem. **-ita.** **ʿnta š(a)hbanita** AM 75:15 a famous woman.

šah(u)at (ܫܥܘܬܐ) seed(s), progeny, posterity, plants. **šahuat uzira** AM 150:penult. crops (?) and seed; **šah(u)atkun uanašatkun** DC 35 your progeny and your families.

šahupia pl. (of ܫܚܘܦܐ) beestings. **ašqh̲ bmia šahupia** AM 133:6 give him beestings with water to drink.

šahiana, pl. **-ia** Zotb. 230a:1 for **šihiana.**

šahilta (rt. **ŠHL I**) Gy 270:4 overflow, trickling over, discharge.

šahla 1 (rt. **ŠHL II**) ATŠ I no. 247 disrobing, undressing, taking off.

šahla 2 DC 22. 473 = **šihla 2** Gs 88:12.

šahm(a) (Ar. شَحْم) fat, suet. **šahmil qird** AM 129:18 (varr. **šahm al qird, šahma lqird**) monkey's fat.

šahmia a *malwāša* woman's name.

šahpa 1 (cf. **šapta 2**) leaf; fringe? Pl. **-ia** leaves, foliage: **šahpa d̲-asa** Lond. roll B 407 = **šahph̲ d̲-asa** DC 12. 192, 262, Lond. roll B 530 myrtle foliage; **asa bšahph̲** Lond. roll B 188 myrtle with its foliage; **asa sarsin šahpia** s **SRS I**; **ʿlana d̲-šahph̲ nahrin** PD 957 the tree the leaves of which are shining; **šahpia d̲-gupna** Jb 132:10 the vine foliage; **šahph̲ d̲-ʿlana** Jb 131:15 the foliage of the tree; **natria kd̲ šahpia** Gy 203:12, 204:3, ATŠ I no. 238 they fall like leaves; **šahpia d̲-tinia** DC 26. 112 the leaves of fig-trees; **šahpia d̲-lubia** DC 41 foliage of beans; **d̲-šahpia mn ʿlania hun** AM they are (like) leaves from trees; **šahpa mn mia** Gy 381:6 a leaf from the water; **lguṭh̲ . . . bšahpia d̲-šipulh̲ titaia d̲-ligria** JRAS 1937 591:33 seize him . . . by the fringes (?) of the lower skirt of his legs.

šahpa 2 AM 216:11 = **šahba 2.**

šahra RD 28 f. = DAb par. name of a demon.

šahrat ('she–kept–watch') Gy 374:5 name of a cloud; **hdia bšahrat anana** CP 207:penult. rejoice in the cloud Šahrat RD 5, RD A 14 = DAb par. name of a ship bringing the souls from the earth to the House of Abathur.

šahrial(a) (P. شهريار) ruler, governor, potentate, satrap, viceroy. Pl. **šahrialia** Gy 386:3, Morg. 269/29:33 etc. MG xxxii n. 1, Jb ii 81 n. 8, varr. **šaharialia, šihrialia, šahriria 2** s.vv.

šahriria 1 (rt. **ŠHR IV**) Gy 158:11 pains; Gs 20:3 sorrows MG 127:19.

šahriria 2 Jb 75:14 for **šahrialia** Jb ii 81 n. 8.

ṣauaršin s. **ṣaruašin.**

šauat in **bšauat tata** ATŠ I no. 249 = **bṣauat tata** DC 6 in company (?) with the sheep.

ṣauarṣin (P. جوهرچين) DC 46. 126:6 (*& often*) Chinese ink.

šauaršir AM 128 perh. miscop. of preced.

š(a)uṭa (שׁוֹטָא, ܫܘܛܐ, H. שׁוֹט, Ar. سَوْط, Eth. ሰውጥ) whip, scourge, lash, flail MG 23:21. Pl. **-ia.** Masc. **ʿbidata bšauṭa abdia** Gy 19:1 f., Gs 36:20 f. they carry out the(ir) works with the whip, cf. **bšauṭa** Oxf. 55 b, **bšauṭa mhaith̲** Gy 118:14, **bšauṭ(t)a mhaith̲** Gy 119:1 I hit him with the scourge; **mahilak bšauṭa** DC 43 I 123 striking thee with a whip; **šauṭa ušulṭana** Gy 230:3, 13 f., 17, 231:25, 232:19, 233:4, 7, Oxf. 44 b = ML 215:9 scourge and power; **šauṭan ušulṭanan** Gy 368:8 our scourge and our power; **šauṭun ušulṭanun** Gy 17:12, 42:11, 367:9 their scourge and their power; **ia d̲-akla šuṭa ušulṭana** CP 177:1 O ye who eat (are avid of) scourge and despotism; **šauṭa mn ʿdaihun npal** Gy 362:11 the scourge fell out of their hand(s); **šauṭa mn ʿdh̲ npal** Gy 363:6; **šauṭa d̲-nura** Gy 317:12, Gs 26:17, 28:6, 29:18, 31:11 scourge of fire; pl. **šauṭia d̲-nura** Gs 32:17, 34:6, 35:17, **bš(a)uṭia nura** Gy 301:15 with scourges of fire; **šauṭia gildia** Gy 121:19 leathern lashes; **šauṭai rama** Oxford 49 a = CP 185:2, my lofty lash; **šauṭak** ibid. thy scourge; **šauṭa d̲-hibil ziua** RD B 19; **šauṭa umimra** Par. xxvi 174:middle, scourge and command; **lgaṭ šauṭa ʿlh̲** Morg. 264/19:42 = (var. **šuṭa**) DC 44. 1320 took the whip to him (: beat him); **šauṭa ramia daiuia** DC 43 J 30 flail-wielding devils.

šauia (act. pt. pe. of **ŠWA**) equal to, suitable for, fit for; deserving, worthy. **šauia latar nhur** Gy 364:18, CP 165:4, Jb 103:2, ML 200:3 deserving of the place of light. **lašauia** unworthy (s.v.).

šauir Zotb. 218b:23 name of a district.

šauka (Ar. شَوْك) DC 23. 771 thorn.

šaula (< ܫܥܠܐ) AM 103:4, Oxf. roll g 800, Or. 329:16 cough(ing). Var. **šula 2.**

šaupa (cf. mod. Syr. ܫܘܦܐ dwelling-place) byre? **ʿsgira hiua biša bšauph̲** DC 37. 577 the vicious beast is shut up in its byre (?).

šaura (Ar. شُورَى) AM 281:25 counsel.

šaušata (rt. **ŠWŠ**) DC 37. 24 confounding powers.

šautaputa AM 138:2 = **šataputa.**

šauta (ܫܥܘܬܐ) wax. **bšauta uabrišam** DC 12:194 with wax and silk.

šaziria (Ar. جزيرة) DC 46. 85:5, 111:2, Par. xxiv 43b pl. islands?

šaṭama = **šatama** (q.v.). Pl. **šaṭamia** Gs 17:10.

šaṭanuta (abstr. noun from Ar. شطن) AM 168 devilry.

šaṭara (שְׁטָרָא, ܫܛܪܐ from Bab. *šaṭāru* Zimmern: *Akk. Fremdw.* 19) DC 37. 568 document? (or nom. ag. pe. writer?).

šaia (rt. **ŠAA II**) (*a*) subst. lustre, glossiness, smoothness, glory, (*b*) adj. lustrous, smooth, glorious. Written also **šaiia 1.** (*a*) **lašaia ʿtlun** Gs 65:9 MG 432:2 f., **mana d̲-šaia litlh̲** Gy 347:23; **šaia uʿqara** CP 13:14, 253:8, Morg. 198:14, 201:11, 261/14:30, Gy 3:5, ML 15:4, 256:3; **šupra ušaiia uʿqara** Morg. 197:9. Parallel with **sigia** Gs 65:10, parallel with

šlama Oxf. roll g 971; **šaiia upaiia**; (*b*) **ʿutra malka šaia** Jb 256:7.
šaibṭia DC 51. 79 = **šibṭia.**
š(a)iaṭa s. **šiaṭa.**
šaiaiil (theophorous name from **šaia**) DC 40. 1001 an angel.
šaialta (nom. act. pa. of **ŠAL**) question(ing), interrogation, trial MG 122:8. Varr. **šai(i)lta, šaiialta, šialta. šaialta ušargazta** Gy 229:12, ATŠ I no. 239 trial and condemnation; **šaialta hauilan** [*sic*] ATŠ II no. 81 they (fem.) will have questioning (trial); **šaialtẖ bnura ubarda hauia** ATŠ II no. 3 his trial shall be in fire and frost; **šaialtaiun bkupnaiun uṣihiaiun hauia** ATŠ I no. 237 their trial (torment) will consist of hunger and thirst; **šaiialta litlaikun** Gy 68:6 there shall be no trial for you; **šaiiltẖ d̠-almia d̠-nhura (d̠-)minẖ bit** Gy 343: 1 f. I asked him the question of beings of Light, cf. Ginzā 357 n. 1; **šaialta ašualia uarba** Zotb. 231a (2nd text:3) question of the novice and his master.
šai(a)na (ܫܝܢܐ 3 < Av. *šayana*) peace, calm **šaina ušlama** AM 193:4 tranquillity and peace. **šaiania d̠-napšaikun** DC 34. 667 your (own) tranquil minds (?). Varr. **šaina 1, šana 1** s.v.
šaiap (Ar. شياف) AM 287:29 collyrium.
šaiar act. pt. pe. of **ŠRR** (q.v.); RD D 17 (*&* *often*) a *malwāša* man's name.
šaiaš AM 106, RD D 12 (*& often in colophons*) a family name.
šaiata 1 s. **šaiṭa.**
šaiata 2 (ܫܥܝܬܐ, ܫܥܝܬܐ) spectacle, game, sport. **salqia bšaiata sainata** DC 20 they begin (their) hideous sports.
šaibṭia DC 51. 79 = **šibṭia.**
šaid a man's name, prob. for **šai(a)r. iahia šaid** Zotb. 220b:1.
šaiul DC 22. 169 for **ʿšiul** Gy 175:antep.; Jb 114:8 BD for **šiul**; also name of a phylactery DC 43 E.
šaiulia inf. pa. of **ŠAL** (q.v.).
šaiṭa 1 (rt. שוט I H., Jew.-Aram., Chr.-Pal., Akk. *šâṭu*) wandering about, going hither and thither, coming and going. **šaiṭak** (var. **šaiatak** B) **hua bit hiia** Jb 220:12 thy coming and going is in the House of Life.
šaiṭa 2 s. **šiaṭa.**
šaiia 1 s. **šaia.**
šaiia 2 (ܫܥܝܐ) pl. of **šita** 1 MG 70:1, 172:11; used as sg. in mod. Mand. (cf. Syr. st. abs. & Chr.-Pal. ܫܥܝܐ). **šita šaiia purqana** Gy 14:11, 183:14, **šita šaiia d̠-purqana** Gy 35:11, 42:13, 66:15, Gs 19:2 the hour, hour(s) of deliverance MG 320:paen. ff.; **šaba šaiia d̠-iuma** Lond. roll B 124 seven day-hours; **bšaba šaiia d̠-ʿumama ubšaba šaiia d̠-lilia** DC 37. 426 during the seven hours of day and the seven hours of night; **šaiia ušušia** Gy 99:1, 112:18 f., Jb 183:8 hours and twelfths of hours; **šaiia bšaiia** Morg. 220/28:6 f. hour by hour, each hour.
šaiia 3 (rt. **ŠHA**) fading, withering. **šaiia upaiia** s. **paiia 2.**
šaiiz (Ar. جايز) Gy 395:13 licite MG 2: anteantep.
šaii(a)lta s. **šaialta.**
šaina 1 Gy 128:2, AM 220:21 = **šaiana.**
šaina 2 (by epenthesis) = **šania.** Pl. **-ia** DC 37. 571.
šaina 3 (ܫܝܢܐ) mire, filth. **šaina uglala** AM 224:13 mire and hail.
šaina 4 (ܫܢܝܐ) orig. mental alienation, deficiency. **hzuta šaina** AM 233:11 dimness of sight.
šair (cf. **šaiar**) Zotb. 221b:3 a man's name.
šaira (st. emph. of **šaiar**) strong. **šaira uaiar ṣṭunẖ** ATŠ strong and radiant is his body.
šairia pl. (of שֵׁירָא, ܫܝܪܐ, H. pl. שֵׁרוֹת, Ar. سِوَار, Fränkel from Akk. *šewēru* Meissner GGA 1904 756, ZA xvii 242) manacles, chains. **kublia ušairia** DAb fetters and chains.
šaita 1 = **šita 1. hda šaita** DC 42 one hour; **atia bšaita qarak** DC 46. 226:19 he will come to thee within the hour.
šaita 2 (rt. **ŠAA**, שִׁיעֲתָא) AM 99:2 talk, gossip, scandal.
šaka (P. شاخ) branch, twig. Colloquial. Gl. 31:14 **šakai** [*sic*, pl.] اغصان *rami* شاخها; 121:6 **šaka** غصن *ramus* شاخ; 122:6 **šaka** غصون *rami* شاخ.
šakaba (nom. ag. pe. of **ŠKB**) Gy 218:14 sleeper. Pl. **-ia.**
šakaṣta (cf. Ar. شَكِص) adj. fem. niggard, ill-natured, grudging, distressing. **ruh saiantia ʿu šakaṣtẖ** Oxf. roll g 996, Or. 332:16 f. the filthy or distressing spirit.
šakara a var. of **šakra** (q.v.).
šakarnaiia name of a race or tribe. Unknown. **mdinta d̠-šakarnaiia** AM 188:10 (var. **šakirnaiia** Par. xxvi).
šakuba (rt. **ŠKB**) sleeper. Pl. **-ia** DC 43 J 163.
šakin (rt. **ŠKN**) CP 29:14 = Q 12:26, 27:28, 32:3 founding, founder ML 35 n. 1.
šakir (P. شکر) Par. xxiv 43b, DC 46. 111:6 sugar (or sweet syrup).
šakirnaiia s. **šakarnaiia.**
šakra (שִׁכְרָא, ܫܟܪܐ, H. שֵׁכָר, Akk. *šikaru*, cf. *σίκερα* Lewy: *Fremdwörter* 81, Brockelmann i. 336) intoxicating drink, liquor; (cf. **šakir**) syrup. **mlia šakra** Gs 134:3, 11 full of liquor; **ʿu bhamra ʿu bšakra** (var. **bšakara**) **ʿu bmia** Or. 326:9 either in wine, or liquor (or syrup?), or in water; **rmiẖ bšakra** Or. 333:17 put it in liquor (or syrup?).
šakta (cf. ܫܥܘܬܐ) Gy 277:23 sediment, dregs MG 113:2.
ŠAL (Aram. & H. שאל, Syr. ܫܐܠ, South-Ar. 𐩪𐩱𐩡, Ar. سأل, Eth. ሠአለ, Akk. *ša'ālu*) to ask, request, desire, beg, inquire, pray, plead; ethpa. to be put to question (under duress or torture).

PE. Pf. **šal** Gy 241:18; **hiia šal** CP 44:12, ML 55:1 he sought life MG 71:6, 255:paen.; **šalit** Jb 80:1 (for **šalt**) thou didst ask; **šalit** Gy 370:21, 371:7, Par. xi 16b I asked MG 255:

paen.; **šalnin** Gs 112:2, Q 58:11 we asked; **šiltan** Gs 112:8 read **šaltin** ye (fem.) asked MG 255 n. 4; with suff. **šiltan** Gs 124 ff. (fem.) requested from me; **šaltẖ** Gy 115:24 (fem.) requested from him MG 271:paen. & n. 3; **šaltẖ** Gy 358:12 [*bis*], 13 [*bis*] I asked for it. Impf. **nišal** DC 46. 189:14; **tišul** MG 256:1; with suff. **nišilunẖ** Gy 184:14 they ask him MG 256:1, 278:15. Impt. **šul** Oxf. roll f 311, 343, 662, ML 50:4, 53:8. Act. pt. **šaiil** MG 112:13, 256:4; pl. **šailin, šailia** MG 256:4. Part. pres. **šailna šulta** DC 26. 25 I make a request; **šailitun** ATŠ II no. 174 ye ask; with encl. **daiuia šailitulẖ lmuta** DC 43 J 121 demons, ye beseech death. Inf. **mišal** Jb 80:1 MG 129:17.

PA. Pf. **šaiil, šailit** MG 256:10; with suff. **šailu** Gs 95:17 they asked her MG 279:16. Impf. **tišaiil** MG 256:11; with suff. **nišailan** he asks me MG 271:4; **tišailan** ATŠ II no. 45 thou askest me; **ʿšai(i)lẖ** Jb 53:13 I (may) ask him; **nišailun(a)kin** Q 56:20, 93:20 they ask you (fem.) MG 281:11. Impt. **šaiil ʿlauaikun** Gy 68:5 pray for them. Act. pt. **mšaiil** MG 69:19, 131:11; pl. **mšailia** ATŠ II no. 170 they question; pl. with encl. **mšaililẖ** Gs 83:13 they question him MG 397:12; **mšaililun** AM 200:14 they question them. Part. pres. **mšaiilna** Gy 184:7, 10; **mšailitun** Gs 3:21. Inf. **šaiulia** Gs 3:20, 83:13; **mišaiulia** ATŠ I no. 111. Nom. act. **šaialta** s.v.

ETHPA. Pf. **ʿštaial** MG 256:11. Impf. **ništaial** MG 69:20, **ništailun** MG 256:12. Pt. **lamištaial** ATŠ II no. 9 he shall not be questioned; pl. **mištailia** DAb (often), **mištailia ʿl nišmatun** Jb 168:10 they shall be held responsible as regards their souls.

Gl. 89:3 f. **šil** سأل *petere* خواست.

DER.: **šaialta, š(u)iala, šulita 2, šulta 1,** cf. **(a)šualia,** pl. masc. **(a)šualania,** fem. **šualata.**

š(a)lahiata (rt. **ŠLH**) (*a*) emission, sparks (of fire), (*b*) disembodied souls that have left the body Jb ii 181 n. 4. (*a*) **šalahiata ḏ-nura** DC 26. 27 emission(s) of fire; (*b*) **(a)triṣ mana lšlahiata** Jb 185:11 (var. **ʿl šalihiata** B, **ʿl šalahiata** DC 30) a vessel is set up for disembodied spirits; **larmun ʿl mana šalahiata** Jb 186:6 they cast me not on the vessel of disembodied spirits (doubtf.); **ḏ-ʿtibrikibẖ šalahiata ḏ-ganzibria ṭabia** DC 3 & CP 421:7 wherewith the disembodied spirits of good *ganzibras* are blessed.

šalam (P. شَلَم) DC 46. 108:11 darnel-weed.

šalamta (nom. act. pa. of **ŠLM**) forfeiture, yielding. Pl. **-ata. nidria ušalamata** DC 43 D 66, H 40 (& *often*) (forced?) vows and forfeitures.

šalbai Jb 67:13 an (otherwise) unknown Jewish name Jb ii 76 n. 5.

šalgam (P. شَلْغَم) DC 46. 106:11 turnip.

šalda (ܫܠܕܐ) corpse. **ḏ-šalda šaiil** DC 44 who question a corpse.

šalhab(i)ata (שַׁלְהוֹבִיתָא, ܫܠܗܒܝܬܐ, H. שַׁלְהֶבֶת) orig. pl. flames, hence: ardour. **kul ḏ-ʿtlẖ nihuia bšalhabiatik** ŠQ 19:22 all he has will be aflame for thee.

šalhapta (nom. act. of שלחף, šaf. of חלף = **HLP**) ransom. **šalhapta ḏ-mahria** 'Ransom of Disease', title of a phylactery DC 19, DC 43 D etc., cf. DC 20. 4, DC 43 E 2, Par. xxvii 14a.

šalupa (rt. **ŠLP**) priest that removes the fleece from slaughtered victims. Pl. **-ia** Gy 28:14. Fig. extortioner.

šaluq AM 197 name of a city.

šalutania Nöld.'s misreading of **šlutania** Gy 355:16 MG 139 n. 4, cf. Ginzā 371 n. 2.

šalia (rt. **ŠLA I**) (*a*) tranquil, peaceful, calm, (*b*) sudden. Pl. **-iia** MG 164:17. (*a*) **parṣupẖ šalia** Gy 68:1 his tranquil countenance; **šaliia unihia iamamaihun** Gy 9:7 calm and quiet are their seas; **tušlimia šaliia** Gy 373:2 calm perfect ones; **ziuia šaliia** Gy 373:9 perfect beings of light; **ašgandia šaliia** *Florilegium*, tranquil (Lidzb. *seligen*) messengers; (*b*) **mn šalia** DC 22. 175 = **mn šilia** Gy 183:19 suddenly.

šaliṭ(a) (rt. **ŠLṬ**, שַׁלִּיטָא, ܫܠܝܛܐ, H. שַׁלִּיט, Ar. سَلِيط) (*a*) mighty, powerful, (*b*) governor, ruler MG 124:1. Pl. **-ia.** (*a*) **daiua šaliṭa** DC 43 J 77 powerful demon; **šaliṭia umpaqdia** Gy 86:22 powerful and commanding; (*b*) **šaliṭia rurbia** Jb 127:6 mighty rulers; **šaliṭia ḏ-mšalṭia** Jb 181:5 rulers who have authority; **šaliṭa rba ḏ-ʿurašlam** Gy 27:8 f. mighty ruler of Jerusalem; **šaliṭia ḏ-alma** PD 1431 tyrants of the world; **šaliṭun** CP 165:7 = ML 199:8 their ruler.

šaliṭana = **šaliṭa** (*b*). Pl. **-ia** MG 137:12.

šalipa = **šalupa.** Pl. **-ia** Gy 59:22.

šalma Gy 19:2, Gs 80:13, Jb 85:3, Q 38:16 f., 39:28, 45:32, Oxf. roll f 774, 984 = **šlama.**

šalmana (rt. **ŠLM**) peaceful, righteous, honest, perfect. Pl. masc. **-ia,** fem. **-iata.** MG xxviii 15, 137:12, 168:18, MR 120, MSchr. 8 n. 5, 36 n. 1. **šalmana bmahu ḏ-mšalam** Q 57:14 by what a perfect one becometh perfect; **ṭubaihun lšalmania** Gy 5:7 hail to the perfect ones!; **mhaimnia ušalmania** Gy 21:3 faithful and righteous ones; **amarnalun lšalmania** Gy 367:2 I say to the righteous ones; **ʿl šalmania lamagzrit** Gy 367:3 thou condemnest not the righteous ones; **gubria šalmania uʿnšia šalmaniata** Jb 180:13 righteous men and righteous women; **ʿnšia šalmaniata** ATŠ I no. 235. Cf. Gl. 155:7, 157:11, 176:6.

šalmanata in **nidria ušalmanata** CP 199 (m): 24 f. read **šalamata.**

šalmanuta (abstr. noun from **šalmana**) Gy 214:13 f. honesty, righteousness MG xxviii: paen.

šalmʿil (theophorous name from **ŠLM**) RD 17 = DAb par. name of the temple of Ruha.

šalpia DC 22. 55 = **šalipia** Gy 59:22.

šalpta DC 46. 237:3 = **šalhapta.**

šam (Ar. شام) AM 197 Syria, Damascus. Gl. 94:ult. **šam** شام *Syria.*

šamadta (nom. act. pa. of **ŠMD**) DC 26. 73, DC 37. 10, DC 43 A 59, 111, 152 etc. desolation, ban, excommunication, repudiation,

discomfiture. Sometimes confused with **šamarta** (q.v.).
šamaiil, var. **šumaiil** DAb a name given to **samandarʿil.**
šamal (Ar. شمال) AM 275:10 north, left.
šamaluq AM 199 name of a city.
šamaẹan Zotb. 221b:16 (text) a man's name.
šamar urgently, speedily, immediately, s. **ŠMR** (as inchoative verb).
šamaran AM 203, **šamarun** AM 199 name of a Persian town.
šamarta (nom. act. pa. from **ŠMR**) Gs 60:8, DC 40. 530, DC 43 J 130 repudiation, ban(ishment), exile MG 122:5.
šamaša (ܫܡܫܐ, Ar. loan-w. شمّاس Fränkel 276) Gy 227:2 deacon, minister. Var. **šamša 2.**
šamašʿil name given to the stole: see **šamšiil.**
šamašta (rt. ŠMŠ I) (*a*) nom. act. pa.: ministration, ministry, service, (*b*) nom. ag. pe. fem.: prostitute, courtesan, pl. **šamašata.** (*a*) **šamašta d̠-hazin alma** Jb 183:5 the service of this world; **šamaštak** CP 43:ult., ML 54:5 thy service; (*b*) **šamašta d̠-mragaga(n)** Jb 77:10, 246:4 enticing prostitute(s), a surer pl. **šamašata d̠-mragaga** Gy 365:3.
šamat AM 197 name of a town. BZ Ap. II.
šambar AM 128 st. abs. of **šambra.**
šambibia pl. (שְׁבִיבָא, ܫܒܝܒܐ, H. שְׁבִיב, from Akk. *šibūbu*?, cf. *šabābu* to lighten) spark(le)s, rays MG 76:20, 124:20. **šambibia d̠-ziua** Jb 218:15, Gy 198:19, 234:16, Q 55:1, WedF 39:2, DC 27. 217, DC 34. 550, 1070.
šambra (שְׁבָרָא, ܫܒܪܐ Löw no. 317, *Flora* iii 508a, from Akk. *šibburatu, šippuratu*? Thompson: *Herbal* 61) Oxf. roll g 615, 663, 665, 894, 903, 1046, DC 47 (*very often*) rue. St. abs. **šambar** s.v.
šambrania Oxf. roll g 718, 1053, Or. 328:10 some kind of disease or injury to the nose.
šamukṭia (cf. Ar. شمع ML *Nachtr.*, cf. also Wid.: *Hdb. d. Orientalistik*) s.v. WedF 25:12, 26:middle, Oxf. 75 b, 76 a & ff. (wax) candles. Varr. **šimukṭia, šimuktia, šmukṭia, šmuktia** ML 245 footn. *c*, 246 footn. *e*.
šamiaiil DC 40. 1002 an angel. Var. **šamiaʿil.**
šamidai Gy 383:10 name of a king (cf. s. **nuraiṭaš**) Ginzā 411 n. 3.
šamimia Zotb. 225a:2 (text) for **šmimia.**
šamiʿil RD 6 name of a personified arrow.
šamina (rt. **ŠMN**) Gy 183:11, DAb etc. fat MG 124:7. Pl. **-ia** Gy 183:18, 187:7 etc.
šamis Zotb. 223b:2nd text:13 a man's name.
šamiš (Akk. *Šamaš* sun-god, *šamšu* sun, Aram. שִׁמְשָׁא, ܫܡܫܐ, cf. st. emph., H. שֶׁמֶשׁ, Ar. شمس Brockelm. i 234, 260, Wellhausen: *Reste* 60, Nöld. ZDMG xli 712) Šamiš, Sol, sun-god, sun MG 32:33, 150:19. Masc., but st. emph. **šamša 1** (q.v.) sometimes as fem. MG 160:6 f. As pr. n. always in st. abs. MG 300:20. Cf. HpGn Ind. s. Šamaš & Sonne, MMII 75–78, 96 n. 9, MR 126:middle. As god: **šamiš = adunai** Gy 23:15, 120:14, Jb 198:12 (as god of the Jews); **šamiš zidana** Gy 45:11, **šamiš** with **ruha d̠-qudša** Gy 27:16 f., **lšamiš plaglh̠ kadba** Gy 112:10 to Š. they allotted untruth; parallel with other planets Gy 171:21; **šamiš ahun qašiša** Gy 172:2 Š. their (: the planets') eldest brother; **šamiš riš planga** Gy 172:7 (s. **planga**); **daiuia d̠-bit šamiš** Gy 27:21; **šamiš brh̠ d̠-ruha** RD 10, **aṭma d̠-šamiš** RD 7; very frequent in magical documents. As planet: **iahbit šamiš lšamušia ʿl bnat anašia** Gy 210:4 I gave the sun to serve the people (a pun, Ginzā 209 n. 4); **šamiš dahnabh̠** (as fem.) s. **DHN I.** Often.
šamẹa Zotb. 223b:2nd text: 19 a man's name.
šamẹania Zotb. 223a:4, 224b:14 name of a canal.
šamqiʿil DC 50. 657 name of a spirit.
šamša 1 st. emp. of **šamiš** (q.v.) used always as planet-name. Fem. (cf. s. **šamiš**). **atra d̠-larba šamš(i)h̠** Gy 371:17, Gs 11:5, CP 193:4, Jb 45:8, 57:14, Oxf. 56 a = ML 227:8 place, the sun of which doth not set; **šamšia d̠-marai** Jb 128:1, 5 the sun(-rays?) of my Lord.
šamša 2 (var. of **šamaša**) servant.
šamšaṭ AM 199, **šamšin** AM 203 place-names BZ Ap. II.
šamšiil RD 12 = **šamšʿiil** DAb, **šamšʿil** Oxf. 66 a = ML 236:4, **šamašʿil** CP 204:penult. name of a spirit used of a (personified) banner and stola, cf. ML 284.
šana 1 AM 220:19 for **šai(a)na.**
šana 2 AM 101:11 prob. for **šahana.**
šana 3 Morg. 251/89:ult. for **šanai.**
šanai st. abs. of **šania** (q.v.).
šanaia (nom. act. pe. of **ŠNA**) exchanger, broker? **mihla d-qanaia ušanaia** DC 12. 197 f. s. **qanaia.**
šanaiia ATŠ I no. 160 s. **šania.**
šanaita (rt. **ŠNA**) removal, estrangement (cf. **mšaniuta** AM 16). **šanaiita mn ʿnših̠ nihuilh̠** AM 38:4 he will have estrangement from (his) women (or from his wives).
šanan AM 255:30 a man's name.
šanania DC 6 for (ʿ)**šnia.**
šanbur AM 202 name of a town.
šangadia s. foll. & **šangdia.**
šangaria (rt. **ŠGR**?) a throat disease, inflammation? Varr. **šangadia** (cf. ܫܘܢܓܐ phthisis?), **šangiria** Or. 328 n. 5. **šangaria** (var. **šangadia**) **ušangdunia** (var. **šigdunia**) **bapquta** Or. 328:23, var. Oxf. roll g 749 inflammation (? or diphtheria?) and choking (?) in the throat.
šangdunia s. preced.
šangdia (cf. s. **šangaria**) choking?, phthisis?, diphtheria? **tišiqlun . . . šangdia mn apquth̠** DC 51. 447 f. ye shall remove . . . choking (?) from his throat.
šanz AM 198 name of a town BZ Ap. II.
šanziria (cf. שְׁזִירָא twisted cord) **šanziria psiq** JRAS 1937 594:11 the ropes parted (broke).
šanṭiaiil DC 40. 820 an angel.
šania (rt. **ŠNA**) remote, sublime, transcendent, wonderful, strange, different. St. abs. **š(a)nai.** Pl. **šaniia**, abs. **š(a)nin.** MG 114:19, 133 n. 1, 164:18, 174:6–10, Jb ii 1 n. 1, 4 n. 1, MR 121 n. 1. **kukba d̠-šanai mn kulhun kukbia** Gy 224:23 star which is different from all

stars; **šanai liauar barkilh̲** DC 3 & CP 419:5 they bless the Sublime Y. (poetic form for **liauar šania**); **šanai umnakria, šania umnakria** (*very often*) sublime and transcendent (epithets of Life); **ṣauth̲ šnai** Gy 236:14 its radiance is wonderful; **kul had šanai mn habrh̲** Gy 337:10 each different from the other; **birikta d̲-šanai** DC 34. 679 sublime blessing; **brahmia šanaiia** ATŠ I no. 160 (read **šaniia**) sublime devotional prayers; **aiar šania** (*often*) subliminal ether; **ginzia d-šanai** (var. **šanin**) **mn almia** ATŠ II no. 161, var. DC 6 ibid. treasures which transcend the worlds.

šaniuta (abstr. noun from preced.) alienation, estrangement, insanity, madness. Doublet **šanaita** s.v. **šaniuta blibh̲** AM 25:12 derangement of mind, madness; **šaniuta d̲-gubria nihuilh̲** AM 99:ult. she will have men-madness (nymphomania).

šanqia for **šaqia. šauia lšanqia d̲-arqa d̲-hšuka umhalkun** ATŠ I no. 254 making legs of the earth of darkness and making them walk.

šaƐir (Ar. شَاعِر) poet. Var. **šiƐir. šaƐir** (var. **šiƐir**) **hauia** AM 155:9, var. Par. xxvi par. he will be a poet.

šaƐpuria AM 105, Zotb. 226b:35 a family-name.

šapaia Zotb. 217b:16 a family-name.

šapaiia (Ar. شفائي) curative, healing, removing weakness. **šapaiia mn kulhun handamak** DC 46. 136:15 = DC 45 par. (no. 26) removing weakness from all thy limbs.

šapaita DC 30 = **šabaita** Jb 144:8.

šapala 1 (rt. ŠPL) lowland, lower region, valley. Opposed to **ʿlaita** Gy 284:10. **šapala** = **timia** Gy 283:18 BCD (var. **šapla** A); **šapala uzaqapa** DC 12. 261 degradation and raising-up.

šapala 2 (rt. ŠPL, nom. ag. pe.) Jb 42:3, Gy 320:17, DC 51. 715 one who sinks.

šapala 3 (colloquial Lower-ʿIrāqī *šifalaḥ* = P. شَفَلَج) capers. **šapala uzarapa** Lond. roll B 529 = P.A. xiii par. capers and palm-leaf.

šapapa (ܫܦܦܐ) creeper, cripple. Pl. **-ia** Gy 29:11, Jb 274:13.

šapula (rt. ŠPL) lowering, degrading. Pl. **-ia** DC 43 D 65.

šapupa (ܫܦܘܦܐ) crawler, creeper, cripple Jb ii 79 n. 8. Pl. **-ia. man šapupa d̲-qdalh̲ ligria** Jb 72:8 what cripple is there that sprouts legs? **šapupia d̲-šaipia ʿl burkaihun** DC 12. 203, Lond. roll B 433 cripples who creep on their knees; **šapupia ʿl ligraihun asgitinun** Jb 274:13 f. I caused the lame to walk on their feet; **ušapupia lmasguiia** Gy 29:11 and (causeth) the lame to walk. Scr. def. **špupa** *Florilegium* 360:132.

šapur DC 22. 20 = **špur** Gy 21:9.

šapia 1 (rt. ŠPA I pt. pe.) at ease, tranquil, pacified. **pagra šapia** AM 165:6 physical ease.

šapia 2 (rt. ŠPA I cf. ܫܦܝܐ, Ar. شَفًا thorns) edge, fringes? **šapia d̲-šipula** JRAS 1937 591: 33 the edge (or fringes?) of the hem.

šapiut(a) (abstr. noun from **šapia 1**) ease, quiet, comfort. **šapiut pagra** CP 438:9 bodily ease.

šapiqa (cf. Maclean s. ܫܦܩܐ) splendour, brightness. **šapiqa drabša** RD 5 = **šapiqa d̲-drabša** DAb the splendour of the banner.

šapir(a) (rt. ŠPR, שַׁפִּיר, ܫܦܝܪܐ) beautiful, fair, pleasing, lovely, seemly, fine, favourable. St. abs. adverbially: good, well, right, seemly, correct MG 200:20. Fem. **šapirt(i)a** MG 154:17. Pl. masc. **-ia**, fem. **-ata. muta šapira** AM (*often*) seemly death, natural death (opposite of cruel death); **anat šapir sliqt** Gs 64:8 thou didst ascend fairly; **šapir gubria qaiim** AM 14:1, 9:12 f. he is the handsomest of men; **šapir d̲-luataiun azalt** Gy 150:3 it is good that thou didst go to them; **d̲-haizin šapiria znh̲** Gy 369:10 f. he who is so fair (sg.!) by nature; **šapir amria** Gs 70:5 they speak fairly; **lašapir abdia** Gy 96:12 they act not fairly; **rahma mn rahma šapir laqaiim** Gy 388:22 a friend treateth not fairly his friend; **gabra d̲-šapira** Gy 142:15 a man who is comely (st. emph. for abs. MG 307:8); **ʿu haizin ʿubadaikun bišia šapir damia zuadaikun** Gs 100:4 f. if your works are so bad, your viaticum seems to be good (irony); **anpia šapiria** Lond. roll B 341 (& *often*) fair of face. Fem. pl. substantivally: **kulhin šapirata** Gy 217:4 all good things MG 299:22; **mšauiana d̲-šapirata** Gy 2:24 Creator of good things; **haršia d̲-šapirata** DC 12:36 **spells of** fair women.

šapirut(a) (abstr. noun from preced.) good(li)-ness, comeliness. **šapirut pagra** DC 3.219: antep. bodily comeliness.

šapita (rt. ŠPA) DC 44./1746 = Morg. 268/27:4 outflow.

šapla (act. pt. pe. of ŠPL) (*a*) low, mean, bad, despicable, ignoble, (*b*) humble, wretched. St. abs. **špil** MG 152:6 f. (*a*) **bura šapla** Gy 85:6 vile monster; **qarabtana šapla** Gy 96:2 ignoble warrior; (*b*) **maskina hauia ušapla** (var. **šapala** Par. xxvi) **lahauia** AM 26:19 will become poor but not humble (or wretched).

šaplut(a) (abstr. noun from preced.) lowness, humiliation, poverty, misery, meanness. St. abs. adverbially MG 201:17. **šaplut latišauinan** CP 113:11 = Q 57:24 = ML 138:14, DC 41. 220 bring us not into humiliation; **šaplut hauia** AM 49:1 there will be humiliation; neg. **šapluta lahauia** AM 58:20; **šapluta lhabrath̲ lamšauia** AM 59:9 she will not act meanly to her friends; **mn šapluta lmaliuta** DC 51. 590 f. from misery to abundance.

šapta 1 (H. שַׁבָּת, loan-w. ܫܒܬܐ, سَبْت, Eth. ሰንበት, cf. P. شنبه, derived from H. שבת to rest, but cf, Akk. *šabattu, šapattu* day of penitence KAT 592 ff.) Sabbath, Saturday MG 48:3, MR 90:middle. **habšaba qašiš(a) mn šapta** Gy 288:9 Sunday is older, (more revered) than Sabbath; **šapta br maš** Gs 101:4, CP 182:9 and 11 = Oxf. 48 ab Saturday evening; **ium šapta** = **iuma d̲-šapta** AM (often) Saturday. Personified? Jb 104:3, 10. Gl. 34:6 defectively اسبوع *hebdomeda* هفته ; 96:10 **špta** [sic] سبت *sabbatus* شنبه.

šapta 2 (cf. Akk. *šiptu* exorcism?) leaf, folio,

parchment, scroll, skin MG 48:3. Var. **šabta** s.v. Fem. Parallel with **ʿngirta** Jb 70:3, 92:2. **šaptak** Jb 103:12, 105:5, 108:1, 121:6 (par. with **kdabak**) thy scroll; **šaptai** Jb 277:9, PD 41 my scroll; **kaprinalh̲ lšumh̲ mn šaptan** PD 602 we shall erase his name from our scroll; **ʿkiprh̲ lšumh̲ mn šapta** PD 931 I shall erase his name from my scroll; **kiprh̲ lšumaiun mn šapth̲** PD 1091 he erased their names from his scroll (*& often with* **KPR**); **šapta hatiqtia** Q 50:18 an ancient scroll; **hda šapta šauith̲** ATŠ II no. 434 I made it (into) a single scroll; **šapta hiuartia d̲-mia** DC 37. 187 a white parchment of gut-skin; **šapta d̲-pišra d̲-ainia** (title of DC 21) the Scroll of the Exorcism of Eyes.

šapta 3 (rt. **ŠPT**) (*a*) cooking-pot, (*b*) case. (*a*) **bšapta d̲-parzla rimiuk** DC 21 = JRAS 1938 3:21 into a cooking-pot of iron they cast thee; (*b*) **šapta d̲-dahba** DAb a golden case.

šaqa (שָׁקָא & שׁוּקָא, ܫܩܳܐ, H. שׁוֹק, Ar. ساق, Akk. *siqu*?) limb, leg, shin, shank. Pl. **-ia.** **šaqik** Gy 116:12 thy (fem.) legs MG 177:22; **ʿrika šaqh̲** AM 6:ult. her limbs are long; **škiṣia šaqh̲** AM 8:14 his limbs are spare; **šahaita bšaqia** Or. 330:17 f. weakness in the shanks; **d̲-iatba ʿl šaqia** Or. 330:21 situated on the limbs (shanks).

šaqara (nom. ag. pe. of **ŠQR**) liar, deceiver. Fem. **šaqarta.** Pl. masc. **šaqaria. šaqaria** Gs 51:23 f., 52:2 liars; **zapana šaqara** AM 154:13 a cheat, a liar; **ia šaqara** *Florilegium*, O liar!; **ruha šaqarta anat** Gs 117:12 thou art a deceitful spirit (not: Ruha, thou art a liar, as understood by Nöld. MG 307:ult.).

šaquata Gy 106:16 BCD (var. **šiquata** A s.v.) cup-bearers MG 166:21.

šaqip (rt. **ŠQP**) emaciated, pale. **šaqip pagrh̲** AM 8:16 f. his body is emaciated.

šar 1 ('He-was-strong') a name given to heavenly spirits ML 284, Jb ii 6 n. 2. **iušamin ušar ziua** Gy 291:36; **šar gupna** Gy 2:15, 5:1, 322:2, 364:15, 377:22, Morg. 226 = ML 70:3.

šar 2 (Ar. شَرّ?) RD 29 = DAb par. name of a demon.

šar 3 st. cstr. of foll. **bšar mdiniata** AM 208:14 in the location (?) of the cities; **bšar šira d̲-arqa** DC 43 B 15 in (every) inhabited district of the earth.

šara (cf. **mšara**) direction, district, location, locality, neighbourhood, side. St. abs. **šar 3** (see preced.). **lšara d̲-madna** AM 197:14 to the direction of the east; **šara d̲-magrib** AM 257:5 f. direction of the west; **bšara d̲-marba** AM 273:2 in a westerly direction; **lšara d̲-smala** DC 42 to the left side; **šara d̲-iaminh̲** DC 46 134:14 on his right side.

(**šara 2** AM 95:5 for **šaqa** BZ 61 n. 1.)

šarab (Ar. شراب) AM 154:15 wine.

šarahia Zotb. 227a:7 name of a river.

šar(a)uata (rt. **ŠRA**) DC 44. 542 & par. fem. pl. exorcisers.

šaraia 1 (שִׁירָאָה, ܫܺܝܪܳܝܳܐ & ܫܺܐܪܳܝܳܐ, σηρικός) silk MG 17 n. 6. **šaraiia** adj. silken. **lbuša d̲-šaraia** Gy 148:5 garment of silk; **uarda ušaraia** Jb 83:15, Oxf. 44 b rose and silk; **tagia d̲-šaraia** Lond. roll A 31, 35 silken fillets; **ʿuṣṭlia . . . d̲-šaraia** ATŠ I no. 15; **tulita d̲-šaraia** ATŠ I no. 256 silkworm; **kulhun šaraiia** ATŠ I no. 15 all of them silken.

šaraia 2 (rt. **ŠRA**) exorcism. **ardaga d̲-šaraia** s. **ardaga.**

šaraita (nom. act. pa. of **ŠRA**) opening, consecration CP trs. 231 n. 8. **šaraita d̲-taga** CP 351:12, ML 276:9 consecration of the crown; **šaraita d̲-škinta** CP 352:6 consecration of the cult-hut.

šarap (Ar. شَرَف) exaltation (astrol.). **šarap dilh̲ bqaina** AM 286:6, 11, 15, 22, 27, 31, 37 its exaltation is in Libra.

šarapat AM 198 name of a city.

šarat ('She-was-firm') (*a*) name of a female genie, (*b*) a *malwâša* woman's name. (*a*) **šarat niṭupta** Jb 252:6, 256:9; (*b*) **šarat simat** (*often in colophons*).

šarba (شَرْبَة) pitcher, waterpot. **kdub lbuṭa d̲-šarba** DC 46 write on the bottom of a pitcher; **maria šarba** ŠQ 6:2 he who has the pitcher (i.e. the earthenware pot which is broken on the threshold of the marriage-hut).

šargazta (nom. act. šaf. of **RGZ**) anger, fury MG 127:8, confused with the rt. **GZR**: condemnation, retribution, punishment. **šaialth̲ušargazth̲** ATŠ I no. 239 his trial and condemnation.

šargizana (cf. preced.) furious, angry, punitive. **maṭarta d̲-šargizana** DC 35.

šarh̲ (Ar. شَرْح) explanation, commentary, interpretation. **šarh̲ d̲-qabin d̲-šišlam rba** DC 38 (title) The Explanation of the Marriage-Ceremony of the Great Š. (= our ŠQ).

šarhabiil, sarhabʿil (theophorous name from šaf. of **RHB II**) name of a spirit, sometimes male, sometimes female; also as an epithet of Šamiš and a name given to personified scales. Jb ii 229 n. 2. Varr. **šarhabiaiil, šarhabiʿil, šarhabiiil. mana . . . d̲-hu šarhabʿil šumh̲** CP 37:1 and 3, 458:11, 461:17, Gy 238:5 f.; **šarhabʿil gupna** Gy 321:21; **šarhabʿil ziua** Q 16:3 f., Morg. 267/25:27, Gy 250:1; **šurbai ušarhabʿil** Gy 26:21 ff., 262:5, CP 199b:9, Jb 90:8, 277:3, **šurbai ušarhabiiil** Morg. 88:7 f. (first male, second female), cf. **šurbai gabra ušarhabʿil ʿnta** Gy 26:18, 380:5 (ancestors of the human race); **šarhabʿil** RD 10 (var. **šarhabiaiil** DAb) = **šamiš; šarhabʿil** (var. **šarhabiil**) **brh̲ ptahil** RD B 29 (var. DAb par.) as keeper of a purgatory; **šarhabʿ(i)l ubihram muzania** Jb 253:3 f., cf. RD 47.

šarhazta (nom. act. of **ŠRHZ**) Gy 266:14, DC 26. 209 panic, fright MG 127:8.

šarhat (rt. & mean. doubtf. cf. ML 284) see **šahrat.** Oxf. 70 b:bottom = ML 240:7 name of a female genie. In CP 207:penult. **šahrat.**

šaruala (P. شَلْوار) PD 730, 736, 1527, 1553 f., Oxf. 68 ab baggy trousers, leggings of the ritual dress, the *rasta*.

ṣaruašin prob. a miscop. of foll. **spand ʿkuma bšaruašin** (var. **šauaršin**) DC 46 black rue with milk-cream (??).

šaruašir (corruption of P. چربی شیر?) AM 129:15, var. **šaruašar** Par. xxvi milk-cream?

šaruata 1 pl. (of ܫܘܪܘܬܐ, rel. to Jew.-Aram. שירותא) Gs 106:15, PD 1242, 1244 = ATŠ I no. 129 **feasts, festivals.** MG 145:20, 167:18.

šaruata 2 s. **šar(a)uata.**

šaruia (rt. ŠRA I, ܫܪܘܝܐ) releaser, redeemer, deliverer (title given to the death-angel Ṣauriel). MG 113:paen. **ṣaurʿil šaruia** CP 64:ult., Q 29:28, 45:14, Gs 2:3, cf. Q 38:5 ff., 37:6, 45:32, Gs 9:20, 24, 119:10 f., DC 41. 268.

šarukta (a mod. form of ܫܘܪܘܬܐ, cf. s. pl. **šarauata** 1) food, sustenance. **agra lasia iahibna ušarukta lgabra giraia** DC 23. 594 ff. I give the fee to the physician and food to the blood-letter.

šaruqia (rt. ŠRQ I, pl. or inf. pa.?) Or. 327:2 noise(s).

šariaiil (rt. ŠRA I) DC 40. 879. Var. **šariaiʿil** s.v.

šariut(a) (rt. ŠRA I, ܫܪܝܘܬܐ) (*a*) looseness, (*b*) liberty, freedom. (*a*) **šariuta d̲-karsa** AM 146:5 looseness of the belly (diarrhœa); (*b*) **rhamta ušariut** (var. **uširiut**) **ʿdia** Morg. 44:740 ff. (var. Morg. 260/12:17) love and free-handedness (= open-handedness, generosity).

šarim (P. چهارم > چارم) Par. x:coloph. fourth MG 2:13.

šariʿil DC 43 D 32 = **šariaiil.**

šarir(a) (rt. ŠRR, שריר, ܫܪܝܪܐ) strong, powerful, firm, reliable, fit, proper, dependable. Pl. masc. **-ia**, fem. **-ata**. **šarira kul d̲-amria** Gs 85:antep. f. reliable is all that they say; **iaqira ušarira** DC 43 D 49 honoured and powerful; **hauma šarira bgaiṭa** AM 258:25 severe (: excessive) heat in summer; **qurša šarira** AM 258:32 severe (: bitter) cold; **qirsa šarira** AM 178:antepenult. a heavy calamity; **hatmia . . . šariria** DC 37. 296 ff. strong (dependable) seals; **ʿumamata šarirata** DC 40. 419 binding oaths; **luṭata šarirata** DC 12. 36 powerful curses.

šarkana (cf. Syr. ܫܪܟܢܐ remainder, but prob. Talm. שרכא thorn, worthless tree) shrub, any tree. **šarkana hu** DC 41 (picture of a tree).

šarqia (Ar. شرق) AM 203:10 the Levant, or s. AM trs. 11 n. 7; 215:ult.

šarša = **širša** MG 13:19. Pl. **-ia**. **šarša** PD 420, 699, 910, 996, Gs 58:3, Oxf. roll f 1162, 1167 etc., together with **šurša** Gy 311:bottom, 312: 8 f., with **širša** Jb 236:12 ff.; **šaršaihun** PD 525; **ṭuhma ušarša** Gy 142:6 (cf. **ṭuhma uširša** l. 17); **ṭaman ušaršan** Gy 309:3; **šarša br ganinia** DC 34. 943 the cultivated Root (i.e. Mandaeans); **šaršia kabiria** DC 26. 159 mighty tribes. Very often.

šaša s. **ašaša.**

šašba (etym. obscure, cf. Ar. شَبْح?) gate, large door, portals. Pl. **-ia**. **msakralun lšašbia** ATŠ I no. 281 blocks up the portals.

šaškʿil anana Gy 374:19 name of a cloud.

šašq(i)lʿil anana CP trs. 223 n. 1, 342:ult., Lond. roll A 391 f. name of a "cloud".

šata (cf. **ʿšta** 1) buttocks, pubic regions. **manzia d̲-atutia šata uhadiauata** ATŠ I no. 223 the hairs of the pubic regions and breasts.

šataia (nom. ag. pe. of ŠTA) drinker, bibber, guzzler. **aklaia ušataia** AM 39:1 gourmandizer and bibber. Gl. 98:8 **šati** [sic] شريب *potator* آشامنده.

šatama (Lidzb. mistakenly Ar. شَتّام ML 22 n. 6; Akk. *šatammu*), temple-functionary. Pl. **šatamia** Q 8:10 = ML 22:7, also **šaṭamia** s.v.

šataputa (abstr. noun from ŠTP) Gy 388:24, AM (*often*) companionship, partnership, association, alliance, society. Varr. **šauta-puta, šatapta, š(u)taputa.**

šatia 1 act. pe. of ŠTA (q.v.).

šatia 2 Zotb. 218b:16 a city in the district of Mashkun.

šatrin DAb name of a tree in the land of Ptahil.

ŠBA I (שבא, ܫܒܐ, H. שבה, Ar. سبى, Sab. 𐩪𐩨𐩺 prisoner, cf. Akk. *šābû* enemy) to take captive, capture, captivate.

Pe. Pf. with suff. **šibian** Gy 322:23 took me captive; **šibiun** Gs 60:8 they took me captive MG 286:3; **d̲-šibun** [*sic*] **umapikria** DC 37. 498 which bound me and entangle (doubtf.); **šbaitun** Gy 365:19 ye took me captive MG 285:21; **bšibia rba šbaitainun** DC 34. 547 thou didst hold them in dire captivity. Impf. **šibia nišibun** AM 184:15 f. they will take captives; with encl. **nišbilh̲** AM 211:15 will capture it; with suff. **nišibih̲** we capture him MG 287:14. Act. pt. pl. **šibia d̲-šabin** Gy 17:8 prisoners that they capture MG 328:9. Pass. part. pres. **ana huit ašbina bšibia d̲-alma** Zotb. 227b:40 I was captivated by the world.

Ethpe. Pf. **ʿštbun** Jb 267:10 [*twice*] were held captive MG 264:18; **uštbaitun lalma** DC 51. 353 f. and ye are captivated by the world. Impf. **laništbia libaikun** Gy 20:14 let not your hearts be captivated; **ʿlh̲ ništbia umalia ʿlh̲** AM 180:penult. he will shut himself up and mourn for her; **tištbia** Gs 60:11, 13 thou wilt be held captive MG 265:1. Pt. pl. **labšibia mištbin** Gy 8:ult. they are not held in captivity; **mištbin bzimara** Gy 176:21 they are captivated by song; with encl. **bh̲ mišt-bibh̲** Gy 112:8 are captivated by it.

Der.: **šbia, šibia.**

ŠBA II = **ŠBH** (q.v.). Another secondary rt. **ŠHB** s.v.

Pa. **šaba** Morg. 213/14:7 = CP40:2, ML 46:9; **šaba bkasa** he blessed the cup MG 234:20; **šabat** MG 234:27, **šabit** Gs 130:14 MG 235:4; with suff. **šabinun** Gy 349:19 B (var. of **šab-hinun**) he praised them MG 66:7; **šabuk** they praised thee MG 274:13; **šabuia** they praised him MG 278:1; **šabath̲** Q 6:24 I praised him MG 277:10; **šabankun**, var. **šabinkun** Gy 313:11 we praise you MG 281:5; **šabatinun** Q 6:25 etc. (var. **šabitinun** Morg. 229/46:6) I praised them MG 282:anteantep. f.; **šabitinkun** DC 51. 654 I praised you. Impf. **nišaba** MG 235:14; **ʿšaba** MG 235:16; **nišabun, tišabun** Gy 45:8, 59:4, MG 66:4, 235:20; with suff. **nišabak, nʿšabak** Q 53:24 we praise thee MG 273:17 f., **tišabunh̲** ye praise him MG 64:22, 278:14; **tišabuia** Gy 23:11 D, 45:10 id. MG 66:5, 278:21; **nišabunak** they praise thee MG 274:21; **ᶜšabin(h)un** Oxf. III 1 a, 2 b, etc. I praise them MG 282:1. Impt. **šaba** MG 234:25, fem. **šabai** Gy 325:6 MG 237:19; pl. with suff. **šabuia** praise him MG 64:23. Pt. (act. & pass.) **mšaba** MG 16:3, 64:17, 131:10, 16, 236:4 f.; **mšabia, mšabin** MG 64:20; pl. with encl. **mšabilh̲, mšabilun** (*both often*). Part. pres. **mšabana** MG 16:4, 236:14; **mšabit** Gy 208:10 etc., MG 64:20, 236:19; **mšabinin** MG 236:23; **mšabitun** MG 236:27; with encl. **mšabatlun** MG 236:21. Inf. **šabuiia** DC 51:654.

Ethpa. Pf. **ᶜštabit** Q 53:27 thou wert praised MG 16:9, 234:paen. f.; with encl. **uštabab̲h̲** Morg. 230/47:5. Impf. **bnapšh̲ ništaba** Gy 27:11, 50:14 praiseth himself. Pt. **mištaba** praising himself MG 132:18, 236:10.

Der.: s. **ŠBH** and **ŠHB.**

ŠBA III (Targ., H., Moabite, Phoen. שבע, the rt. of the Gen. Sem. 'seven') af. (& doubtf. pa.) to adjure, lay under oath; to bind by oath.

Pa.? Pf. **šabit** (read **ašbit**?) **ᶜlak . . . umauminalak** DC 37. 42 f. I have adjured thee . . . and I bind thee by oath.

Af. Pf. **ašbit ᶜlauaikun umauminalkun** DC 51. 167 I have adjured you and I bind you by oath. Part. pres. **mašbinalak miša umauminalak** CP 30:15, ML 36:6 I adjure thee, oil, and bind thee by oath.

Der.: **šaba, šuba, šabata.**

ŠBA IV = ŠWA.

Pa. Pf. **šabit** DC 22. 113 for **šauith̲** Gy 118:12. Pt. pl. **uminaihun ṭapqia d̲-nhaša mšabin** DAb and some of them make copper plates (13 n. 6).

šbab (Ar. شباب) AM 258:34 youths.

šbania (cf. P. شبانه) **d̲-šaiia** DC 3 (insertion) name of an astrological guide to the fortunes of each of the twenty-four hours.

ŠBD (šaf. of **ABD I** (q.v.)).

ŠBH (Aram. & H. שבח Kautzsch 87, Syr. ܫܒܚ, Ar. سبّح, Eth. ሰብሐ, cf. Akk. *suppū, šuppū* to pray) to praise, give praise, laud, glorify; ethpa. to praise oneself, boast, vaunt. Secondary roots **ŠBA II, ŠHB** s.vv.

Pe. Pass. pt. **šbih** MG 65:5, **bil gabra šbiha** DC 44. 1152 = Morg. 263/17:16 Bel, lauded being; pl. **šbihia** AM 29:5 praiseworthy, excellent.

Pa. Pf. **šabhit** Gs 130:14 (in the same l. with **šabit**) MG 66:5, 235:4; with suff. **šabihth̲** Q 6:24 (var.) I praised him MG 65:17, 277:10; **šabhinun** Gy 349:19 he praised them MG 66:6. Impf. **tišabhun** Gy 23:9 MG 66:4; with suff. **tišabhuia** Gy 23:11 ye praise him MG 278:20. Inf. **šabuhia** CP 115:11, ML 141:1 (*& often*) MG 236:30; with suff. **šabuhak** ML to praise thee MG 292:20.

Ethpa. Only forms from **ŠBA II** (q.v.) found.

Der.: **šbih(a), šubaha.**

šbuqia (rt. **ŠBQ**) divorce. **ᶜngirta d̲-šbuqia** Jb 120:8 (var. **šbuquia** Jb 72:2, **šibquia** BD in both places) a divorce-letter.

šbia (rt. **ŠBA I**) AM 172:penult. depopulation.

šbih(a) pass. pt. pe. of **ŠBH** (q.v.).

šbila (שְׁבִילָא, ܫܒܝܠܐ, H. שְׁבִיל, Ar. سَبِيل) path, way. Var. **ᶜšbila** s.v. Pl. **-ia.** Masc. MG 160 n. 2. **šbila d̲-mhaimnia** Gy 37:5 the path of the believing; **bšbila d̲-šumh̲ d̲-muta** Gy 255:9 on the path of the name of Death; **šbila d̲-saliq latar nhur** Gy 274:13 the path which riseth to the Place of Light (parallel with **dirka . . . d̲-šalmania**); **šbilh̲ bdaria rabut zmar** Gy 274:15 his path (leadeth) through houses of prostitution; **trașt šbila lmhaimnia** Gy 342:19 thou hast set up a path for the believers; **šbila naṭrit** Gs 128:7 ff. thou guardest the path; **aqapra bšbilun laiit** Gy 11:2 there is no dust on their paths; **bhimnu šbila salqia** RD B 88 ff. by which path do they rise?

ŠBQ (שְׁבַק, ܫܒܩ, cf. Ar. سبق Brockelmann i 522) to let, let go, leave, loose, free, pardon, forgive, permit, allow, leave behind, abandon, forsake. Secondary roots **ŠWQ, ŠPQ** s.vv.

Pe. Pf. **šbaq** he le(f)t MG 221:22; with suff. **šbaqth̲** MG 277:1, **šbaqtan** CP 102:3 = Q 52:30 thou hast forsaken me MG 272:3; **šbaqtinun** MG 282:22; **šibqun** MG 272:14; **šibquk** MG 274:9; **šbaqinun** MG 281:18; **šbaqunᶜn, šbaqunin** Gy 375:11 they left them (fem.) MG 283:12; **šibquia** Jb 72:2 BD, 120:8 BD a var. of **šbuqia** (q.v.). Impf. **zma lanišbuq** ATŠ II no. 43 he shall not let blood (MG 218:19, 226:14); **tišbuq** MG 15:2, 226:25; **ᶜšbuq** MG 227:6; with encl. **nišbiqlun** Q 19:28 may he remit them (their sins) MG 218:18; **nišbiqulak** Q 74b:11; **nišbiqulik** Gs 21:ult. they will forgive thee (masc. & fem.); **nišbiqulh̲** ATŠ II no. 345 they will forgive him; **tišbuqlan** Gy 61:15 forgive us; with suff. **ᶜšbiqinun** MG 281:anteantep.; **kd̲ haṭia man nišibqh̲** DC 53. 261:ult. when he sinneth who will forgive him? (MG 275:16); **nišibqak** MG 273:14; **tiš(i)bqan** Gs 116:25 thou lettest me MG 271:2; **ᶜšbiqinkun** MG 30:14; **nišibqunak** Gs 63:23 (var. **nišbqunak** D) MG 274:18 (read **nišbunak** will captivate thee? Ginzā 489 n. 2). Impt. **šbuq** AM 249:3 [*twice*] loose; with suff. **šubqh̲** PD 1043 leave her; **šubqin** Gy 333:3, var. **šubqan** CD let me be! MG 271:19; pl. with encl. **šbuqulh̲ haṭaiih̲** DC 50. 65, **haṭaiih̲ šbuqulh̲** ATŠ II no. 334 forgive him his sins. Act. pt. **šabiq haṭaiia** Jb 1:5, Gy 1:3, 17 f., Gs. 38:5 f., 74:4 (*& very often*) a remitter of sins MG 310:14 & n. 1, MR 172:bottom, MSt 3:24; pl. **qanin ušabqin balma** s. **QNA I**; **d̲-šabqia mn marba lmadna** DC 26. 93 which take to flight from west to east; **ᶜlai hauma urugza šabqia** DC 44. 108 they loose passion and rage against me; with encl. **lašabqilan d̲-nᶜzal** Gy 253:3 f. they do not allow us to go. Part. pres. with encl. **šabqatlh̲** Jb 120:2 thou divorcest her; **šabqatlun** thou leavest them MG 232:22. Pass. pt. pl. **šbiqia** Jb 171:15, 181:5, Gy 357:11 left; with encl. (& act. mean.) **d̲-šbiqilh̲** Gy 60:18 which he left MG 382:7. Inf. **mišbaq hauqa ᶜlh̲** Morg. 216/20:1 to loose fright on him; **lmišbaq mn tihak brišaihun** DC 37. 37 f. to loosen some of thy anxiety in their heads; **mišubiq** [*sic*] **ldukth̲ durdia** DC 3 no. 161 to leave behind in its place the dregs; with suff. **mišibqh̲** Jb 263:13 to loose him.

Ethpe. Pf. **ʿštbiq** DC 34. 255 was expelled; with encl. **haṭaiia . . . ʿštbiqlh̲** DC 48. 278 her sins . . . were remitted. Impf. with encl. **d̲-haṭaikun uhaubaikun ništbiqlkun** Gy 21:12 that your sins and trespasses may be forgiven you; **kul haṭaiih̲ . . . ništbuqlh̲** ATŠ II no. 182 all his sins shall be forgiven him. Pt. **mištbiq** MG 132:10; with encl. **mišt(i)biqlkun** MG 31:16 f.

Gl. 10:11 f. اذن *permittere* گذاشت ; 16:7 f. انتهى *prohibere* منع كرد ; 18:3 f. انزل *deponere* گذاشت ; برگشت ; 46:11 f. ترک *dimittere* گذاشت ; 49:5 f. ترک *permittere* گذاشت ; 56:15 f. جعل *facere* كرد ; 108:9 f. طلق *dimittere* طلاق داد ; ibid. عفى [sic] *parcere, veniam dare, excusare* بخشيد ; 150:5 f. منع *prohibere* منع كرد ; 179:9 f. دع [sic] *ponere* گذاشت ; 179:15 f. دع [sic] *relinquere* گذاشت .

Der.: **šab(a)qa, šbuqia, šbqaiil** (var. **šbqaiail**).

šbqaiail IM no. 14, **šbqaiil** IM no. 13 a genie IM 97/20.

ŠBR (from **TBR** by influence of **ŠMṬ** Jb ii 132 n. 2) to break.

Ethpa. Pf. **ʿštamaṭ uʿštabar** Jb 134:6 they were torn out and broken.

ŠBŠ (Jew.-Aram., Syr., Chr.-Pal.) to confuse, bewilder, befool, lead astray, cozen, cajole. Secondary rt. **ŠMŠ II** s.v.

Pa. Pf. **šabiš** Gs 14:6, 75:4 they befooled me; **mn šabiš ailun lgu pagra** ATŠ II no. 126 (delete **mn**) by cozenry they brought me into the body; **šabšat aiilth̲ lkništa** Gy 115:17 leading astray she brought him into a church; with suff. **šabšan** Gy 369:2 befooled me; **šabšun** Gs 14:18 they befooled me; **šabišth̲** Gy 258:21 I was befooling him; **šabištinkun** Gy 186:15, 233:19 I befooled you (MG 281:2); **šabištun** Gs 11:21, 75:3 ye befooled me (as without suff.). Impf. with suff. **nišabšinun** Gy 257:26 we will cozen them. Act. pt. **mšabiš** Gy 56:9, 186:13 he befooleth, leadeth astray. Part. pres. with encl. **mšabšatlun** Gy 230:17, 233:8 thou befoolest them. Inf. **šabušia** Gy 186:15. Nom. act. **šabašta** s.v.

Ethpa. Pf. **laʿštabaš** Gy 258:22 he was not befooled. Pt. pl. **lamištabšia** Gy 257:27 they are not befooled.

Der.: **šabašta, šabšuta.**

ŠGA (שְׁגָא, ܫܓܐ, H. שׁגה, rel. to **ŠGŠ**) to err, go astray, make a mistake, be amiss, wander.

Pe. Pf. **ʿu šga** ATŠ (very often) if he made a mistake; with encl. **šgulia** cf. s. pass. pt. Impf. **ʿzdahar d̲-lanišgia** DC 41. 284 beware lest he maketh a mistake; **nišga** Gy 33:14 read **-ia**? doubtf. Ginzā 33 n. 1; **latišgia** DC 41. 164 make no mistake; **nišgun** AM 216:ult. they will be amiss. Act. pt. pl. **halin d̲-šagin halalta (bšitin šga)** PD 562 = ATŠ I no. 51 those who make a mistake in the rinsing (have erred sixtyfold); with encl. **šagibun** JRAS 1937 590:20 strayed (?) amongst them. Part. pres. **šagit** CP 95:6 = ML 121:11 AM 206:13, ATŠ II no. 43 thou makest a mistake. Pass. Pt. with encl. **šgilia minaihun** DC 30 (var. **šgulia** Jb 48:12, **gulia** B) some of them were lost to me.

Pa. Impf. **latišagia** DC 48:258 make no mistake.

Der.: **šugiana.**

šganda graphical var. of **ašganda** (q.v.). **(a)šganda šliha d̲-hiia** Jb 52:8 Messenger, Apostle of Life. Often.

šgir(a) (pass. pt. pe. of **ŠGR**) heated, glowing, ardent, enflamed, set alight, kindled. Pl. masc. **-ia**, fem. **-ata. tanura d̲-šgir** AM 134:15 f. = **tanur šgira** DC 46. 179:16 a kindled oven; **duga šgira** Gy 216:14 a glowing oven, pl. **dugia šgirata** Gy 111:7; **kitun** (read **atun** as BC) **d̲-šgiria** Gs 26:13 a heated oven (Nöld.'s emendation to **atunia** MG 304 n. 4 is unnecessary, although Sh. ʿAbd.'s copy indeed has this form).

šgiš(a) (pass. pt. pe. of **ŠGŠ**) (*a*) muddled, confused, (*b*) frightful, violent. Fem. **šgišt(i)a.** Pl. masc. **-ia.** (*a*) **ia šgišia** ATŠ I no. 11 O ye muddleheads! ; **aina šgištia** JRAS 1937 593:29 the confused eye; (*b*) **miṭra šgiš nihuia** AM 250:19 there will be violent rain; **lhilmania šgišia ulhizuania šgišia** DC 40. 462 f. for frightful dreams (: nightmares) and frightful visions.

ŠGM (cf. ܫܓܡ II) to distract (attention), deceive. Doubtf. **nišigmun uašgmun** DC 44. 878 = Morg. 261/16:18 (var. . . . **d̲-šgmun**) they distract their attention having deluded them (?).

ŠGNS in **aqapra nišganas** AM 245:31 for **aqapra nišgaš** Par. xxvi par. dust will be stirred up.

ŠGP (ܫܓܦ, سجف) to cover.

Ethpa. Impf. **ništagap bnura** Par. xxiv 7b = DC 46. 242:1 he shall be covered with fire.

ŠGR I (שְׁגַר I, ܫܓܪ I, H. שׁגר, Ar. سجر) to present oneself, come into existence, be brought to birth.

Ethpa. Impf. **hu bgišmia ništagar** AM 186:14 he will present himself in person; **hiuta nukraita . . . tištagar** AM 221:18 a strange creature . . . will be brought to birth.

ŠGR II (שְׁגַר II, ܫܓܪ II, Ar. سجر) to burn, kindle, flame up, glow, heat.

Pe. Impt. **šgur tanura** AM 134:15 kindle an oven. Pass. pt. **šgir(a)** s.v.

Pa. Nom. ag. **mšagrana** s.v.

Ethpa. Pf. **ʿštagar** Gy 166:15, **ʿštahan uštagar** Gy 282:6 he was hot with lust and enflamed. Impf. **ništagar** Gy 320:5, 377:14, Par. xxiv 7b, DC 46. 166:16 shall burn, be enflamed; **ništagrun** AM 186:3 they will burn. Pt. pl. **mištagria** Gy 225:6 are enflamed.

Der.: **š(a)gira, šagra, šigra.**

ŠGŠ (שְׁגַשׁ, ܫܓܫ, Ar. سجس, Akk. *šagāšu, šaqāšu*) to disturb, cause disturbance, stir up, trouble, perturb, confuse.

Pe. Pf. with suff. **šgašth̲** Jb 20:8 I stirred it

up; **šgaštinun šgašat** Jb 19:8 I disturbed them. Impf. **nišgaš** cf. s. **ŠNGS**. Pass. pt. **šgiš(a)** s.v.

PA. Pf. **šagiš** Jb 7:5, 9:12 he disturbed; **šagiš tigra rmilun** Gy 17:9 f. they cause disturbance and strife (Ginzā 19 n. 2); with suff. **šagšinin ltirata** Gy 151:19 he disturbed their consciences; **šagištinun** Jb 199:10 she confused them (MG 282:19). Impt. with suff. **šagšinin ltirata** Gy 151:17 f. confuse their consciences (var. **šagšinᶜn** MG 282:12). Pt. pl. **mšagšia tigra ramibh̲** Oxf. 55 b they cause disturbance and strife therein; **latirmia mšagšia** (var. **mšagušia** C) **biardna** Jb 10:11 cast not disturbers into the jordan (one would rather expect an abstr. noun Jb ii 17 n. 5).

ETHPE. Pt. **mištigšia ruianh̲** AM 111:9 his reason will be upset (read ethpa.?).

ETHPA. Pf. **ᶜštagaš** Q 52:10, 12, **laštagšun** AM 252:20 (cf. BZ 153 n. 9); **ᶜštagaštun** Q 52:17 MG 224:9; with encl. **ᶜštagašlh̲ ruianh̲** Gy 241:24 his mind was upset; **ᶜštagašlun** Gy 71:13 they were confused; **malkia tištagšun** AM 236:11 kings will be involved in confusion. Pt. **mištagaš** AM 209:18 will be upset; **mazruta lamištagaš** ATŠ II no. 34 (var. **lamištagšia** DC 36) the seed shall not be adulterated; pl. **mdiniata mištagšun** (read **mištagšan**) AM 178:14 cities will be thrown into confusion.

DER.: **mšagašta, šgiš(a), šigša, šigšana, šigšuta.**

ŠDA I (Jew.-Aram., Syr.) to cast, throw, drop, put, pour, shed; idiom: (with **ᶜda**) to lay the hand on, beat; af. to shed, pour; ettaf. to shed tears.

PE. Pf. **šda ᶜda lpumh̲** DC 51. 74 he put his hand to his mouth; **kul d̲-akal šda mn pumh̲** Gy 84:21 whatever he ate he cast out of his mouth; with encl. **ana šilpit ᶜsqta ušdibh̲** Gy 147:13 I drew off the ring and placed it on her; with suff. **lbišna lbuša anuš ᶜlauai šdih̲** Morg. 268/26:20 I wear a dress which A. put on me; **šdun** Gs 60:8 they cast me MG 285: antep.; **šidiuih̲** DC 41. 497 they put him (: inserted his name); **šdaitun šdaitun** Gy 365:21 f. ye cast me (as without suff.) MG 285:22. Impf. **ᶜdh̲ biardna nišdia** ATŠ I no. 34, cf. II no. 15 puts his hand into the jordan; **nišdun ᶜdaihun biardna** ATŠ II no. 15 they put their hands into the jordan; **latišdun bnaikun bit maria** Gy 22:7 f. put ye not your children into a(nother) lord's house; with suff. **tišdinan** Q 57:26 thou castest us MG 289:15. Impt. **šdia** Lond. roll A 237, ML 52:7 insert. Act. pt. **ᶜda lriša šadia** Gy 85:20 she putteth her hand on her head; **ᶜmh̲ qudam abuia šadia** AM 5:15, trs. 8 n. 2 (*& often*) a doubtf. idiom BZ 8 n. 2; with encl. **šadialh̲ barqa** ATŠ I no. 280 she casts it off to the ground; pl. **ᶜda lrišaihun šadin** DC 34. 106 they put their hands on their heads; with encl **šadilia** Gs 75:12 they throw me away. Part. pres. **šadinin** Gy 84:1 we cast. Pass. pt. **bkul had hilbuna ṭaṭka šdiia** DAb in each house a throne is placed.

AF. **halin d̲-ašdia dma** Gy 181:20 those who shed blood; **zmaiun ašdia barqa** Gy 28:14 they shed their blood on the ground; **ašdin uramin durdia** ML 187:2 it (: the water, pl.) they gush forth and cast out the impurities (= read as in CP 155:10 **šadin** etc.).

ETTAF. Pt. **bakia alia umitašida** Gs 74:23 she weepeth, lamenteth, and sheddeth tears; pl. **bakia alia umitašidia** Gy 232:5. Identical with **AŠD** (q.v.).

DER.: **šidaiia.**

ŠDA II, ŠDD (Targ. & H. שדד, Ar. شدّ) to fasten, bind tightly; overpower.

PE. Pf. **karkil šdinun** s. **karkil.** Pt. with encl. **šidiriata šadibun bkulhun** DAb they fasten chains on all of them.

PA. Pf. with suff. **ᶜsir pumh̲ ušadiuih̲** DC 51 his mouth is bound and they bind it fast. Part. pres. **br anašia mšadana alma lišanin** (read **lišanun**) DC 46 I bind human beings as to their tongues (talisman for a tongue-tied person).

šdahaia (rt. **ŠDH**) felling, overpowering, striking down. **giṭra tmanaia d̲-hu šdahaia** DC 43 H 39 eighth knot which is overpowering.

ŠDD s. **ŠDA II.**

ŠDH (cf. **ŠDA I, II**) to strike down, prey upon.

ETHPA. Impf. with suff. **ariauata ništadhunun** AM 222:1 lions will prey upon them.

DER.: **šdahaia.**

šdum a spirit of darkness, one of the rulers of the underworld. Var. **ašdum. (a)šdum qarabtana** Gy 141:21, 23, RD 20 Š. the warrior; **šdum rba br rba d̲-hšuka** Gy 141:11 Š. the great (son?) of darkness; **šdum rba gabara** Gy 144:14 Š. the great and mighty; **hitmit baba banph̲ d̲-šdum** Gy 144:20 f. I sealed the door before Š.; **kursia d̲-šdum** RD 20 the throne of Š.; **baba d̲-šdum** RD E the gate of Š.; **šdum daiua** RD 35 Š. the devil.

šduta for **šidta** in **bšduta tlata habšaba** Zotb. 230a:4 f. in the year beginning on a Tuesday.

ŠDK (Jew.-Aram. שדך to be quiet, pa. to settle down, to negotiate a marriage, Syr. pa. to arrange a marriage) pe. to be quiet, silent, peaceful, settled down; pa. to settle down, smoothe, quieten, make peace, negotiate a marriage, (of a hole) to fill in, level (*idiom*); ethpa. to be settled down, lie quiet.

PE. Impt. **nha ušduk** Gy 350:21 be calm and still (MG 219:ult.). Pass. pt. pl. **nihia ušdikia** Gy 291:37 calm and quiet; **lanihia ulašdikia** Gs 65:10 unrestful and unquiet.

PA. Pf. **ušadik** (var. **šadak**) **bšumh̲ d̲-libat** DC 45 = DC 46. 70:13 and arranged a marriage in the name of Venus. Act. pt. **niqruk mšauia umšadik ᶜutria** CP 279:3, Oxf. 94 b they shall call thee pacifier of uthras; with encl. **mšadiklun lkumṣia** Gy 89:9 he fills in the ditches. Pass. pt. fem. pl. st. emph. **paqata mšadkata** Oxf. roll g 657 peaceful valleys. Nom. ag. **mšadkana** s.v.

ETHPA. Pf. **markabata ᶜštadak** DC 26. 11 the (planetary) ships foundered; **ᶜštadkun kumṣia kulhun** Gy 97:14 all hollows were levelled. Pt. pl. **kulhun kumaṣia mištadkia** Jb 89:7 all pitfalls were removed (filled in).

DER.: **mšadkana.**

ŠDL the rt. of **šadilata šadlata** (q.v.).

ŠDN (den. from **šidana** q.v.) to be(come) mad, crazy, rabid, possessed by a demon.

Pa. Pass. pt. **mšadana** DC 46. 80:10, 109:5 (*& often*) demented.

Ethpa. Pf. **ʿniš d-ʿštadan** DC 46. 20:4 a person who has become crazy. Impf. **kalbia ništadnun** AM 186:3, Par. xxvi 266:8, 275:bottom; dogs will become rabid. Pt. **ʿniš mištadan** DC 46. 76:14, 121:1 a person demented; pl. **ʿnta ugabra d-mištadnia** DC 46. 122:3 woman and man who are demented.

Gl. 28:10 **mšdn** [*sic*] احمق *fatuus*; 157:5 id. مجنون *daemoniacus* ديوانه (cf. MG 84:12).

Der.: cf. **šidana, šadana.**

ŠDP = **ŠTP** (q.v.).

Pa. Impf. **tišadpun** Gy 67:21 ye associate MG 42 & 12. Impt. with suff. **šadpinun** AM 157:2 add them (put them together), (the numerical value of letters).

ŠDQ (< Aram. & H. שתק, Syr. ܫܬܩ) to be silent MG 42:11.

Pe. Impt. **šduq** MG 219:ult. Act. pl. **šadqia** AM 18. Pass. pt. **šdiq** MG 116:14.

Der.: **šidqa.**

ŠDR (Gen. Aram.) to send, send forth, send off, send away, dismiss; to commission, send with a message or on business.

Pa. Pf. **šadar** MG 221:paen., **šadart** MG 222:26; with encl. **šadartulia** (var. **šadirtulia**) Gs 64:5 ye sent to me MG 225:13 f.; with suff. **šadrinan** he sent us MG 279:anteantep.; **šadruia** Gy 143:ult. (var. **šadrunh** D) they sent him MG 277:ult. f.; **šadru** Gs 108:23, 109:4, Q 43:7 they sent her MG 279:14; **šadrun** MG 272:19; **šadrun minṭar dara urandudia** Gy 299:5 He (: Life, pl.) sent me to preserve the generation and to rouse it; **šadrun . . . d-tia ʿbidbh ṭabta** Gy 111:3 He (: Life) sent me . . . that I come to do good therein; **šadruia lparuanqa ʿl adam** Gs 9:7 sent a messenger to A.; **šadrun lalma hazin** Q 13:7 sent me into this world MG 387; **šadarth, šadirth** Gy 346 (: *often*) thou didst send him MG 276:anteantep.; **šadirtan** Gy 338:4 thou didst send me MG 15:28, 272:5 (gives mistakenly **-in** for **-an**); **šadartinun** MG 282:22. Impf. **nišadar** MG 30:5, 226:16; **ʿšadar** MG 227:7. Pt. (act. & pass.) **mšadar** MG 30:5, 131:9, 15, act. Gy 51:8, pass. Gs 2:8, MG 230:8, 9. Part. pres. with encl. **mšadrinalh** Gy 126:ult. we send him (var. **mšadranalh** AB sg.) MG 233:9 f.; **mšadritulh** MG 233:20. Inf. **šaduria** Gs 2:8.

Ethpa. Pf. **ʿštadar ʿutra** Gy 12:3 an uthra was sent; **girmia kulhun ʿbašqar uʿštadar** DC 48. 291 f. all the bones were differentiated and assigned (: given their place or function); **ʿštadrat mazruta** DC 41. 82 the seed was sent forth; with encl. **ʿštadarlh haila** DC 34 strength was assigned him; **ʿštadarlh rahaṭa d-mia hiia** DC 34 a stream of living water was sent to him. Inf. **mištaduria** Jb 167:3 MG 144:20, 234:3.

Gl. 15:7 f., 40:9 f.

Der.: **mšadrana, mšadranuta.**

ŠDR II (Jew.-Aram. שְׁדַר II) to twist.

Der.: **šidiriata, šidra.**

ŠHA I (ܫܗܐ & ܫܗܝ, Jew.-Aram. שְׁהָא, H. שאה I) to fade, wither, languish, dry up by heat.

Pa. Act. pt. **klil almia šahia** CP 76:penult., Q 35:29 a worldly (lit. 'of worlds') wreath withereth; **lašahia ulapaiia** CP 26:1 = DC 34. 452, Q 11:4, Gy 211:14 neither wither nor fade.

Der.: **šahaita, šhunia.**

ŠHA II (cf. Targ. שְׁחֵי, H. שחה = שחח) to bend down?

Pe. Pf. **šihkat ušhit** Oxf. roll g 942 thou wert found bending down (?).

šhaq ('He-harassed'?) name of a spirit (of destruction). **šhaq brh d-iušamin** DAb.

ŠHB (met. of **ŠBH** q.v.) to praise; with **b-** to rejoice in, be proud of, exult in, boast, vaunt, glory in.

Pe. Act. pt. **šahba** MG 235:paen.; pl. **bziuak šahbia** CP 359:antep. they glory in thy radiance; **bgauh šahbia** Gy 10:17, DC 53. 362: 8 (*& often*) are proud of him, glory therein; with encl. **šahibbh** Gy 165:18 is proud of her MG 12:15, 67:2; **šahbabh** Gy 59:8 she is proud of him. Part. pres. **šahbana umšabana** CP 53:22, Q 25:1, Oxf. 7 a, 8 a (var. **šahabana . . .**) I praise and glorify (MG 67:13 f., 236:14 f.).

Der.: **šahbana, šuhba** = **šuba 2, šuhbana.**

šhunia (rt. **ŠHA I**) heat ? (hot flushes: a woman at menopause). **nura masrikna ušhunia** DC 46. 66:14 I kindle fire and heat (?).

ŠHṬ (simplified šaf. of **YHṬ**) pa. to miscarry; ethpa. to fret oneself.

Pa. Pt. **mšahṭa ʿulaihin** Gy 174:14, CP 100: penult., Q 52:15 (they) miscarry their embryos. Part. pres. **mšahṭitin ʿulaikin** CP 101: 8, Q 52:20 did ye miscarry your embryos? MG 233:21.

Ethpa. Pf. **ʿštahaṭ btiniqta** Gy 84:19 he fretted himself with sighing.

ŠHK (met. of שכח, ܫܟܚ af. & refl.) to find, discover. Another secondary rt. **ŠKA I** s.v.

Pe. (but as refl.): Pf. **šihkat ušhit** s. **ŠHA II.**

Ethpe. Pf. **ʿštihkat** ML 60:6 (var. **štikat** n. 3) was found (fem.). Pt. pl. **mištihkin** Gy 386:18 are found.

ŠHL I (Talm. שחל, Syr. ܫܚܠ, Akk. *šaḫālu*, cf. Ar. مِشْخَل filter, strainer Fränkel 167) to drop, exude, discharge (moisture, drops), flow out, slip, trickle away.

Pe. Act. pt. **nišimta mn ligria uburkia šahla** Jb 124:7 the soul slips out by the legs and knees; **diglat šahla mn šihlh** Gs 88:12 the Tigris floweth out of its course; pl. (**mišhal**) **šahlia** Gy 273:11 they slip away. Inf. **mišhal** (just quoted).

Der.: **šahilta, šahla 2, šihla 1, 2.**

ŠHL II (met. of **ŠLH I** q.v.) to send (away), dispatch.

Pe. Pf. with suff. **niṣban šihlan** Gs 67:19 created me and sent me (MG 270:22); **šihlan ušadran** DC 26. 221 dispatched me and sent me; **šihlun** they sent me, He (: Life) sent me MG 272:15; **šihlak** he sent thee MG 273:10; **šihluk** MG 274:10.

Ethpe. Pf. **ʿštihlit** Gs 25:15 I was sent MG 235:5; (**ʿ**)**štihlit uatit** DC 37. 36, DC 44. 330 f.

I was sent and came; **štihlat** (read **štihilt**) **šliha ʿlẖ** DC 43 I 56 thou wert sent to him as a messenger.
Der.: **šihlun.**

ŠHL III (met. of **ŠLH II** = **ŠLA II**) to undress, divest, denude, cast off, take off.

Pe. Act. pt. **šamiš šahla ziuẖ usira šahla tuqnẖ** Gy 203:11 f. the sun strippeth off its radiance and the moon divesteth itself of its gleaming; **hiuia ḏ-šahla lbušiẖ** DC 40. 67 ff. a serpent which slougheth its dress (skin) MG 235:ult.; pl. **šahlia ulabšia** Gy 11:7 they undress and dress; with encl. **kḏ šahlalẖ haza nišimta lilbuš pagria** CP 79:9 = Morg. 234/55: 3 f. = ML 86:2 f. when this soul takes off its bodily garment; **ʿlania ḏ-šahlin ulabšin** DC 34. 342 trees that denude and reclothe (themselves). Part. pres. **šahlana uganiana** DC 46. 191:8 I undress and lie down.
Der.: **šahla 1.**

ŠHL IV (met. of **HŠL**? Ginzā 198 n. 7) in **arqa mišhal šhila** Gy 197:6 Lidzb. *diese Erde wurde festgeschmieden* (doubtf.).

ŠHL V (Ar. جهل) to be ignorant, unwise. Mod. Gl. 61:3 f. **ṣihl** جـهـل *esse insipiens* نميدانست.
Der.: **ṣahal, ṣih(i)l** (fem. **šihiltia**), **ṣihlana.**

ŠHM (Jew. שָׁחַם, שְׁחַם, שְׁחָים, Syr. ܫܚܡ to be black) to be hot; red-hot, to redden, blush.

Pe. Act. pt. pl. **šahmia ubahtia** Jb 161:5 they blush and are ashamed.
Der.: **šuhma,** var. **šihma.**

ŠHN (Jew.-Aram. & H. שחן, Syr. ܫܚܢ, Akk. *šaḫānu*. Ar. سخن) to be(come) hot, grow hot, enraged, be on heat, be inflamed with passion, love, rage, etc.; to have ulcers (cf. der.) Jb ii 128 n. 2.

Pa. Act. pt. pl. with encl. **mšahnilun umšagrilun** DC 37:14 they inflame and make them burn (with lust). Pass. pt. fem. st. emph. **gurita . . . mšahanta** Jb 130:5 f. a bitch on heat.

Ethpa. Pf. **ʿštahan brugziẖ** Gy 281:20 was inflamed with his rage; **ʿštahan uʿštagar** Gy 282:5 (s. **ŠGR**). Impf. **ništahan uništagar** DC 46. 167:1, 189:7; **ništahnun** Gy 112:6; **ništahnun uništhiniun** Gy 258:7 they will be inflamed (MG 227:24); **ništahnun unimitun** Par. xxvi 269:5 = AM par. they will become fever-stricken and will die; **kalbia ništahnun** Par. xxvi 275:ult. = AM 248:2 dogs will become rabid. Pt. fem. **mištahna** DC 46. 16:7 is madly in love; pl. masc. **mištahnia umištagria** Gy 225:6; with encl. **mištahnibẖ** Gy 111:22 are inflamed with it (: the mystery of love).
Der.: **šahana, šana 2?, šhunia, šihana 2.**

ŠHP I (שְׁחַף Levy) to flow.

Pe. Act. pt. pl. **iardnia bziuak šahpia** DC 6 (read **šahbia** as in CP 359:16 i.e. 'rejoice in' and as in ML 267:10) the jordans flow in thy radiance.
Der.: **šahpa 1,** var. **šahba 1.**

ŠHP II the rt. of **šahpa 2** (q.v.) = **šahba 2.**

ŠHQ (Aram. & H. שחק, Syr. & Chr.-Pal. ܫܚܩ, Ar. سَحَقَ, Akk. *šaḫāqu*? Frank OLZ xii 482) to crush, break up, harass, vex, oppress.

Pe. Pf. **šhaq** as pr. n. s.v. Impf. **tišhuq utiṭrud** Oxf. roll g 909, Or. 331:1 (text) thou wilt harass and drive away. Impt. **šhuq uṭrud** Oxf. roll g 552 ff., 681, 688, 704, Or. 325:2 (text) harass and drive away. Act. pt. pl. & inf. **mišhaq šahqia** Gy 259:7 Lidzb. read **mišhar šahria** were troubled (hist. pres.) Ginzā 258 n. 5.

Pa. Impt. with suff. **šahqinun** (var. **šahqilun**) Oxf. roll g 894, Or. 325:6 (text), 333:30 harass them.

Af. Impt. **ašhaq ašhaq asip asip lnbu** DC 43 J. 68 harass, harass, destroy, destroy N.
Der.: **šhaq, šihqa.**

ŠHR I (שְׁהַר, ܫܗܪ, سَهِرَ) to be awake, wake, keep watch, keep vigil, be sleepless.

Pe. Impf. **nišhar** MG 221:3 (without numeric reference, hence doubtf., since identical with **ŠHR V**).

Pa. Pf. **šahrat** as pr. n. s.v.
Der.: **šahara, šahrat.**

ŠHR II (שחר pa. & af., ܫܚܪ I, H. שחר I) to be(come) black.

Af. Pf. **ašhar unasbia ʿukma** Gs 65:12 f. they became black and take on blackness.

ŠHR III (שחר I J., II Ges., Akk. *saḫāru* to search) to search, investigate.

Pe. Part. pres. **šahrana umitaprišana** Gy 161:19 I (fem.) search and meditate (Nöld. as **ŠHR IV**: *ich ängstige mich* MG 231:17).

ŠHR IV (ܫܚܪ III, Ar. سَخَرَ to subdue, Akk. *šuḫaruru* to calm? Jensen in Schulthess HW 78; cf. Nöld. *Neue Beiträge* 87, MSchr. 155 n. 2, 175 n. 5, 181 n. 2) to be anxious, troubled, alarmed, afraid, uneasy, gloomy.

Pe. Impf. **nišhar libẖ** Gy 369:14 his heart will be anxious. Act. pt. **šahra abihdia** Gy 147:14; **šahra bgauẖ** Gy 166:7 she was (hist. pres.) uneasy about it; **šahra udauia** Gy 158:10 she was troubled and wretched; pl. **šahrin udauin** Gy 146:5. Part. pres. **šahrit udauit** Gy 353:19, Gs 21:17 thou art gloomy and mournful.
Der.: **šahriria.**

ŠHR V (consistently used as a synonym with **ŠKB** Jb ii 225 n. 1, Nöld. ZA xxx 159) to slumber, sleep.

Pe. Pf. **šhar uškib** Gy 190:10 he slumbered and slept. Impf. **nišhar uniškub** Gy 189:23 (MG 226:15), **latišhar ulatiškub** Gy 365:23 = Jb 245:13 (MG 226:anteantep.).
Der.: **šaharta** (also def.).

ŠWA (שְׁוִי, ܫܘܐ, H. שוה I to be equal, alike, II to make, Ar. سوى I to be level, smooth, II to make, VIII to become) pe. to be smooth, level, equal, worthy, fit for, deserving; pa. to level, make alike, make, put together, create, appoint, set, prepare, make ready, agree, deem worthy of, suffice. Sometimes written as **ŠBA IV** (q.v.).

Pe. Act. pt. **šauia** (*often*) worthy, equal, with neg. **lašauia** s.v.; pl. **ḏ-šauin ulašanun**

Jb 196:12 which are worthy and did not change (corrupt and out of context Jb ii 191 n. 1); with encl. **šauilia daria ualmia šauilia mn alpa** Jb 200:14, cf. Gy 367:14 is worth to me generations and worlds, worthier than a thousand. Part. pres. **lašauitun lṭabuta** Gy 39:15 ye are worthy of goodness.

Pa. Pf. **šauia** CP 116:4, ML 141:9 he made, **šauiat** she made MG 260:paen.; **šauit napšai gabra hda ḏ-šapir mn dilun** Gy 142:12 I made myself a man who was more pleasing than they (MG 261:6); **šau(u)n** they made MG 261:14, **šauitun** MG 261:21, **šauinin** ATŠ II no. 188 we made; with encl. **šauialh̲** Gy 243:18 she made for him MG 261:2, **šauilh̲** I made him MG 261:8, **šaubin** Gy 110:24 [*twice*] they made in them (fem.) MG 8:21; with suff. **šauian** made me MG 284:26, **šauith̲** Gy 118:22 (*& often*) I made him, her, it MG 288:9, **šauitak** Gy 94:19 I made thee MG 286:27, **šauitinkun** Gy 145:19, 158:1 MG 291:1, **šauiuia** Oxf. 95 a, MG 8 n. 1, 288:24, **šauiun** MG 286:5, **šauiuk** Gy 396:10 (*& often*) MG 287:3, **šauinh̲** Gy 158:5, 244:2, MG 288:16, **šauinan** Gy 116:19 he made us MG 289:14, **šauitun** ye made me (as without suff.) MG 285:22. Impf. **nišauia** MG 261:anteantep., **nišaun** AM 218:20 they will make (Nöld. mistakenly read **nišaun** for **nihaun** Gy 316:5, MG 262:3); **ʿburia nišaun, aṭšia nišaun** AM 224:20 f. crops will prosper, fruits will prosper; **mia nišaun** AM 251:16 there will be enongh water; **tišau(u)n** Gy 317:15 ye prepare MG 262:7; with encl. **nišauilh̲ almia udaria** Gy 15:14 f. is worth to me generations and worlds Ginzā 17 n. 4; **nišauilia** (read **nišaulia** Ginzā 30 n. 5) **almia udaria** Gy 30:3 are worth to me, etc.; **tišauilak** she maketh for thee MG 261:paen.; with suff. **nišauih̲** Gs 62:15 etc. we make her MG 287:14; **tišauian** Gy 147:2 thou makest me MG 285:3; **nišaunan** Gy 258:3 they make us MG 289:antep.; **bʿsura nišauunh̲** AM 191:9 they will commit him in prison; **šaplut latišauinan** Q 57:25 = ML 138:14 = CP 113:11 (s. **šaplut(a)** MG 289:16). Impt. **šauia** (*often*) make; with encl. **šauibh̲** Gy 93:23 create therein, MG 262:10; pl. **šau(u)n** Q 39:ult., MG 262:14. Act. pt. **mšauia** (*often*) he makes MG 262:16, AM 19 he causes; **anat mšauia umšadak ʿutria** CP 279:3 thou makest uthras agree and pacifiest them; **mšauia ruha mn nišimta** Gs 117:15, 128:12, 131:14 he equalizeth the spirit with the soul; pl. **mšauin** they make MG 164:antep.; **mšauiun** (read **mšauiin**) **pihta lnapšaihun** Lond. roll A 91 they make the sacramental bread for themselves; with encl. **mšauilia agra** DC 51. 758 prepares for me reward; **mšauilh̲ ʿutra** Gy 104:20 he will make him an uthra; **mšauilun** (*often*) he makes them; AM 232:22 they will agree with them. Part. pres. **hašta mšauina pisusta** DC 22. 349 (missing in Pet.) now I will make a split; **mšauit** MG 262:22, **pihta umambuha mšauitun** DC 27. 164 ye prepare sacramental bread and drink; with encl. **hzia mšauiatlia** Gy 169:9 beware lest thou comparest thyself to me (MG 262:23); **mšauinalak** MG 262:paen. Pass. pt. **mšauai** MG 263:3 (with a mistaken ref.). Inf. **mšauia ʿdh̲ bʿda ḏ-abahath̲** DC 35. 109 to clasp hands (= put together his hand) with his parents; with suff. **mišauinun** Gy 151:22 to make them MG 293:16. Nom. ag. **mšauiana** s.v.

Ethpa. Pf. **ʿštauia uʿtriṣ bʿqara** CP 465:9 was deemed worthy and established in honour; **škinata ḏ-bgauh̲ štauia** Gy 304:8 the dwellings that are made therein; **ruha ʿštauiat bdmu haua zauh̲** Gy 116:4 R. made herself like his wife Eve (MG 263:ult.); **ʿthambal kḏ ḏ-laʿštauit** Gs 4:9, 21 vanish as as if thou hadst not been created (MG 264:8); **ʿtqrit uhuit uʿštauit** Gy 170:6 I was created, came into being, and was formed (MG 264:13); pl. **ʿštau(u)n** CP 63:15, Q 29:10 = ML 79:6, MG 264:19; fem. pl. **ʿštauaian** Gy 170:ult. and **(ʿ)štauia** Gy 304:8 were made MG 264:25; with encl. **ʿštauilh̲ riša udinba** ATŠ II no. 315 and a beginning and end were made thereto; **ʿštauilun ʿuhrata** DC 7 roads were laid out (levelled) for them. Impf. **mithambal ulaništauia** DC 26. 46 he shall be destroyed and not put together (again). Pt. **mištauia**, pl. **alma ḏ-dahba rhima mištauin** ATŠ II no. 258 (read same II no. 66 for **mištaiin**) until they are worth precious gold.

Der.: **mšauiana, mšauiata, šauia.**

ŠUA (ܫܘܐ, cf. H. שׁעע) = **ŠAA II** pa., cf. s. **MŠA II.**

šualia Jb 168:15, AM 256 (*& very often*) original form of **ašualia** (q.v.). Pl. **šualania, ašualania** Jb 168:13, RD C 6, Q 71:8, 74b:39, Par. xi 23b etc., MG 170:2. Fem. pl. **šualata** RD 10 = DAb par. female attendants.

šub (P. شوب) turban, head-wrap, head-dress. **duktai bšubh̲ ḏ-hidutia** DC 46. 123:1 my place is in the bride's head-dress.

šuba 1 (שִׁבְעָא, ܫܒܥܐ, formally closer to Talm. שׁוּבְעָא, Chr.-Pal. ܫܘܒܥܐ, fem. Nöld. ZDMG xxii 459) seven MG 18:13, 188:1. Masc. form used often for the special fem. **šaba** (s.v.). **šuba šibiahia** Gy 97:24, 98:15, 100:1 ff., 223:13, 381:12 etc., or simply **šuba** a frequent designation of the seven planets (cf. HpGn. 9 ff., 25, 115, 118, 244, 343, 385), **šuba utrisar** Q 48:19, RD B 7 (*& often*) the Seven and the Twelve (: planets and signs of the Zodiac); **šuba utrisar mdabrania ḏ-alma** Gy 23:9 (cf. s. **mdabrana**), **nitharkun biaqdania ḏ-šuba umnata ḏ-šuba nihun** Gy 315:23 they shall burn in the conflagration of the Seven and shall be a portion of the Seven; **šuba bʿuhra lanikatrunh̲** CP 79:10 f. = Q 37:8 the Seven shall not fetter him on the road; **ruha ušuba bnh̲** Gy 339:14 R. and her seven sons (: the planets); **šuba hambagak hun** CP 131:ult., Q 66:31 the Seven were thine enemies; **maṭra ḏ-šuba** CP 91:1, Q 43:1; **maṭarta ḏ-šuba kukbia** Gy 363:17 the purgatory of the seven stars; **šuba daiuia** Gy 27:15 the seven demons; **pura ḏ-purun šuba** s. **pura 3**; **šuba almia bukraiia** PD 999 seven primordial worlds; **šuba šuria ḏ-dahba** Gy 159:11 seven golden walls; **bšuba iamamia ḏ-mia sumaqia** Gy 392:11 f. in seven seas of red water, cf.

ZDMG xlviii 6667:bottom Ginzā 418 n. 4; **šuba razia** Q 62:28 seven mysteries; **šuba dmu** seven figures (cf. P. هفت پيكر) MG 347:22 (apart from **šaba dmauata** s. **šaba**). As ordinal number: **rahmia d̠-šuba šaiia** ML 182:3 the prayer of the seventh hour (CP 151: penult. **d̠-šuba šaiia**). Gl. 100:4 **šuba** سبعة *septem* هفت.

šuba 2 = **šuhba**: **šubai mapraš** DC 41. 540 he teaches my praise.

šuba 3 (ܫܘܒܐ) heat, inflammation. **šuba d̠-riša uhaṣa** DC 46. 106:8 inflammation in head and back.

šubaha (rt. **ŠBH**) praise, glory. **raza hu šubaha** (read **d̠-šubaha**) DC 34. 639 it is the mystery of praise (glory).

šubaia (adj. from **šuba** 1) seventh MG 192:6. Fem. **šubaita** (also a mod. word for 'the week', pron. *šoβeyθa*).

šubana (ܫܘܒܢܐ & ܫܘܒܢܐ Löw no. 314) DC 23. 772, DC 46. 103:1, 119:9 *nigella sativa*, a kind of fennel.

šubasar (שובסר, ܫܒܥܣܪ) seventeen MG 188:18.

šubin (pl. of **šuba** 1, cf. ܫܒܥܝܢ) seventy MG 18:13, 189:15.

ŠUG (ܫܘܓ, Chr.-Pal. ܐܫܝܓ, Pal.-Aram. LS) pe. to rub; af. to wash, rinse.

Pe. Impt. **šig** Gy 68:5 read **ašig** as B (cf. s. af.); with suff. **šugh̠ naᶜim** AM 286:paen. rub it smooth (fine). Act. pt. **šaig ušaiiplh̠ lklila** ŠQ 7:30 (text) he rubs and smears it over the wreath.

Af. Pf. **ašig atutia margna** DC 34. 527 they washed beneath the (ritual) staff; with suff. **lniarak ašigth̠ udakith̠** DC 48. 365 thou hast washed and purified thy (drinking-)bowl. Impf. **našigun** DC 35 they shall wash. Impt. **nkus uašig unaqid uhalil** Gy 68:5 B slaughter, wash, cleanse, rinse; **halil uašig** Gy 18:5, 366:6 rinse and wash; **ašig biardna** Gs 65:23 wash in the jordan (MG 251:16). Act. pt. pl. with encl. **bgapa mašigilin** s. **gapa**. Part. pres. **nasbit umašgit niarak** DC 48. 37 thou takest and washest thy bowl.

Der.: **ašagta** (pl. **ašgata**).

šugda = **šigda**. Pl. **-ia. šugdia uamuza** ŠQ 8:3 almonds and walnuts.

šugiana (rt. **ŠGA**, cf. H. שִׁגָּיוֹן?) DC 50. 872, PD 315, 1726, 1729 error, oversight, mistake MG 137:1. Pl. **-ia** PD 627, 753, 1323, 1731, ATŠ I nos. 69, 129 (*& often*).

šuda (שׁוּחֲדָא, ܫܘܚܕܐ, H. שֹׁחַד) propitiatory gift, bribe(ry) MG 63:10, 104:paen. **latihun nasbia šuda** Gy 35:16 f. be not takers of bribes; **lahuit nasib šuda** Gy 258:16 I was not one that taketh a bribe; **šuda lanasbia** Gs 133:14 they take not a bribe.

ŠUH, ŠIH (Syr. af. & ethpe., cf. Schulthess HW 79, Ar. شاح to do something with great zeal, شيح assiduous, attentive) to be fitting, worthy (of), worth, desirous, zealous Jb ii 20 n. 6.

Pe. Pass. pt. **ših** MG 65:6, **mandaia d̠-ših** RD B 128 a Mandaean (: layman) that is worthy; **d̠-laših** RD B 129 that is unworthy; **kul d̠-ših ših** Gs 24:21 all that is worthy; **kulman d̠-qria uših umzaman** Q 58:1 whosoever is called and worthy and invited; **laših latar nhur** Gy 109:3 is unworthy of the Place of Light; **ših umhaiman** Gy 53:13 worthy and faithful; st. emph. masc. & st. abs. fem. **d̠-šiha ldaura taqna** Gy 319:5 that is worthy of Abiding Abode; **šiha ušauia latar nhur** Gy 299:14, 376:11, Oxf. 27b, 28a are (fem.) worthy of and deserving the Place of Light; **lašiha lbit hiia** Jb 80:6 unworthy of the House of Life; **miša šiha br šušmia** CP 30:7 = Q 13:4, 13 precious sesame-oil; **miša anat šiha** CP 45:13, Q 20:28 fem. pl. **šiha** Gy 299:14; Gs 112:16, 22, 113:1, **nišmata . . . šiha** Gy 364:18 (cf. also examples above); pl. masc. **ᶜqriia ušihia** Gy 256:20 called and worthy; **naṣuraiia d̠-šihia** Gy 315:7 Naṣoraeans that are zealous (worthy); **naṣuraiia d̠-lašihia** Gy 315:12 f., 319:6 Naṣoraeans that are unworthy; **šihia lbit hiia** Gy 251:10 (cf. above); **šihia ldaura taqna** Gy 275:15, 328:22, 341:19 f., DC 53. 395:11 (cf. above); **lašihia latar nhur** Gy 109:3, 111:12, 16, 376:14 (cf. above); **mania šihia** Gy 314:2 zealous *mānas*; **bnai d̠-šihia** Gy 193:20 my children that are zealous; **lašihia** Gy 236:1, 240:24 etc. unworthy; **šihia l-** Q 7:31 fit(ting) for; **ᶜutria d̠-šihia** CP 6:13, Q 2:28 zealous uthras; **almia bmiša šihia** CP 77:9, Q 36:4 worlds are eager for oil; fem. pl. **šihan** DAb (more common **šiha** above) are worthy. With encl. pers. pron. (as part. pres.) **šihu** Gs 83:6 he is worthy MG 65 n. 2; **šihit umšauit** Gy 72:3 thou art worthy and fit (for); **kma šihit iauar** CP 254:14, Oxf. 86b = ML 256:3 how zealous (or deserving) art thou, Yâwar?; **lašihit** Jb 12:10, 13:1, 31:2 thou art unworthy (MG 65 n. 2); followed by encl. prep. **šihatlh̠ lalma hanath̠** Gy 71:20 thou art fit for that (i.e. the other) world; **mahu šihnalik** Gy 187:22 wherefore desirest thou us?; **šihitulia** ibid. I desire you (MG 65 n. 6).

Der.: **ših, šiha** 1, 2.

šuha = **ašuha** 1 (q.v.). Pl. **šuhia** Jb 155:2, Gy 265:12, Gs 111:17 B.

šuhba (rt. **ŠHB**, Syr. ܫܘܒܚܐ) (*a*) praise, fame, reputation, (*b*) pride MG 105:1. Var. **šuba** s.v. (*a*) **šuhba d̠-zadiqia** Q 57:11 (s. **zadiqa**); **šuhba šbiha** Gy 215:3 good (lit. 'praised') reputation (Lidzb. suspected a mis-writing for **šuha** Ginzā 215 n. 3); **šuhba rba** AM 10 (*& often*) great reputation; **ṭapia šuhba ᶜlauaihun** ATŠ II no. 258 and no. 66 fame gathers about them; (*b*) **šuhba urabut karsa** Gy 51:7 pride and high stomach; **bšuhba d̠-napšh̠** Gy 115:2 in his own pride.

šuhbana (adj. from preced.) praiseworthy, famous, splendid MG 138:ult. Fem. **šuhbanita. iatira ušuhbana** AM 87:18 rich and famous; **ᶜnta šuhbanita** AM 85:12 a famous woman.

šuhma (rt. **ŠHM**) AM 179 sultriness, darkness (caused by red dust-storm). Var. **šihma** s.v.

šuza (P. جوز) nut. **šuza d̠-bsaua** DC 46. 125:8 read **šuza d̠-baua** cf. foll.

šuzabaua (P. جوز بوه) AM 92 nutmeg.

ŠWZB (שֵׁיזִב, ܫܘܙܒ < Akk. *ušēzib*, šaf. of עזב Delitzsch: *Prolegomena* 140 n. 4) to save, free, rescue MG 212:7. *Fundamental stem*: Impf. with suff. **ʿšauzbak** MG 273: anteantep.; **ʿšauzbinkun** Gs 25:4, MG 280:ult. Impt. with suff. **šauz(i)ban** MG 271:12; **šauz(i)binan** Gy 62:6, MG 280:3 f.; **šauz(i)binin** Q 19:6, 35:10, MG 282:15. Pt. with encl. **mšauziblh̲** AM 17 he rescues him. Nom. ag. **mšauz(i)bana** s.v. *Reflexive stem*: Impf. **tištauzbun** Gy 36:23 f. MG 247:11. Impt. **ʿštauzab** Gs 21:3 MG ibid. Pt. **mištauzab** Gy 53:22 MG 132:25, 230:24, 247:12.

Der.: **mšauz(i)bana.**

ŠUṬ I (Jew.-Aram. & H. שוט II, Syr. ܫܛ, Akk. *šâṭu* mediae *i* rel. **ŠṬA I**) to take lightly, despise, bring contempt, shame on; af. often for **ŠṬA I** to seduce, cause to commit foolishness MG 272 n. 1, MSchr. 39 n. 2.

Pe. (read af.?): Impf. with suff. **nišiṭh̲** ATŠ II no. 355 he despises it; **tišiṭunh̲** Gy 39:13 ye despise him MG 278:12. Pass. pt. pl. **ʿdaltinun lšiṭia** Gy 94:18 she brought forth the despicable ones.

Af. Pf. **hašṭit** Gs 136:10 I despised MG 211:16, 251:8; with suff. **ašiṭh̲** Gs 95:24 he despised him MG 275:11; **ašiṭtan** Gs 22:6 she seduced me MG 272:1; **ašiṭtinun** Gs 62:15, 63:9 (var. **ašiṭinun** AB), **ašiṭtinʿn** Gs 64:21 I despised them MG 283:1 f.; **ašiṭuia** Gy 231:19 they seduced it; **ašiṭuk** Gs 22:1 they seduced thee. Impf. **kulman d̲-našiṭ raza d̲-abahath̲** ATŠ I no. 3 whosoever despiseth the mystery of his fathers; with suff. **baiin d̲- . . . našiṭh̲ lmiriai** Jb 136:12 they seek . . . to bring contempt on M. Act. pt. **mašiṭ** he despises MG 251:18, irregular **miušaṭ, maušiṭ** s. **YŠṬ**; with encl. **mašiṭilh̲ audia** Gs 39:14 f. the perishable ones despise him; **mašiṭilh̲ lkana d̲-nišmata** Gy 23:10 they seduce the Congregation of Souls. Part. pres. **lamašiṭna** DC 41. 8 I will not take it lightly.

Ethpa. Pf. **ʿštaṭit** Jb 262:13 I have brought contempt on myself.

Der.: **šiuṭa, šiṭuata, šiṭuta, šiṭia.**

ŠUṬ II (Jew.-Aram., H. & mod. H. שוט I, Akk. *šâṭu* mediae *u*, Syr., Ar. & Eth. der. cf. s. **šauṭa**) to draw, move hither and thither, fly, flow; to strike, beat (cf. der.).

Pe. Pf. **anatun raza d̲-mazruta haita ušaṭ** (var. **ušiṭ**) **brazia** ATŠ II no. 143 (var. DC 6) ye are the mystery of the Living Seed and it flowed into the mysteries.

Der.: **šauṭa, šaiṭa 1, 2** (& varr.), **šuṭ(t)a.**

šuṭa s. **š(a)uṭa.**

šuṭta Gy 119:1 for **š(a)uṭa.**

šuiala (rt. **ŠAL**, Syr. ܫܘܐܠܐ, Ar. سُؤَال) question. Pl. **-ia** MG 123:9. **laiadana lhazin šuiala** DC 41. 522 I do not know (the answer to) this question; **alp trisar šuialia** The Thousand and One Questions (title of ATŠ).

šukar (P. شِکَر) sugar, sweetmeats. **šigdia ušukar** ŠQ 8:3, 19:paen. almonds and sugar (sweetmeats).

***šuksa** (P. شِکَست) breaking, catastrophe. Pl. **-ia. šuksia qiriia upigia** DC 40. 637 catastrophes, accidents, and misadventures.

šukṣana (rt. **ŠKṢ**) AM 235:3 scarcity, paucity, sparseness.

šul 1 (cf. H. שׁוּל) lower part (of a garment, or of body), abdomen?. **šul bakia udaurai mitana** DC 37. 487 my abdomen (?) weeps and my habitation groans.

šul 2 Jb 114:8 B for **šiul.**

šula 1 (שְׁעָלָה, ܫܘܥܠܐ, H. שֹׁעַל) handful, palmful MG 70:21, 104:20. Still used (mod. pron. *šolla*). **šula d̲-mia** Gy 302:7, DC 8 a palmful of water.

šula 2 a var. of **šaula** (q.v.).

šula 3 corrupt for **šuiala.** Pl. **-ia. bšulia uminilata** CP 179:12, Oxf. 47 = ML 219:7 cf. MG 432 n. 3.

šulata pl. of **šulta** (q.v.).

šulutana ATŠ I no. 254 etc. = **šultana.**

šulṭa sometimes for **šulṭana.**

šulṭana (rt. **ŠLṬ**, שׁוּלְטָנָא, ܫܘܠܛܢܐ, cf. H. שִׁלְטוֹן, Ar. سُلْطَان) (*a*) power, rule, authority, dominion MG 136:21, (*b*) ruler, governor, one in authority. Pl. of (*b*) **-ia.** (*a*) **šulṭan napšak** Gy 7:4 thine own power; **bšulṭana d̲-napšai** Jb 19:4 by my own power; **aklia šauṭa ušulṭana**; s. **šauṭa, aklia šulṭana** Gy 256:8; **ahbalia šulṭana ʿl** DC 26. 102 (*& often*) he gave me dominion over . . .; (*b*) **kbušiun minai šulṭanh̲** DC 45 subjugate to me those in authority; **ʿubadia d̲-šulṭania** AM 8:penult. government employ, public works.

šulita 1 (rt. **ŠLA II**, Jew.-Aram. שְׁלִיתָא & varr., Syr. ܫܠܝܐ, H. שִׁלְיָה) membrane enveloping the foetus, afterbirth MG 19:20, 164:11. **bšulita uzma** Gy 227:11 with an afterbirth and blood.

šulita 2 (rt. **ŠAL**?) maidservant? **luṭta d̲-rabta ušulita** AO ix 96:8 the curse of mistress and maidservant (Gordon: foetus? doubtf.).

šulta 1 (rt. **ŠAL**, ܫܐܠܬܐ, H. שְׁאֵלָה) question, asking, petition MG 19:21, 110:8. Pl. **šulata** MG 19:21. **šul šulta** CP 42:15, ML 50:4 (*& often*) ask a question; **šulta šailitun d̲-kulhun haṭaiih̲ mitgamrin** ATŠ II no. 174 ye prayed that all her faults might be amended; **kd̲ gabra d̲-iatib bšulta qaiim** RD B 121 = DAb par. as a sitting man gets up on request; **had niqria šulta d̲-iardna** ATŠ II no. 4 one will recite the jordan-prayer.

šulta 2 for **šula 1. šailan šulta d̲-mia** DAb they (fem.) beg for a palmful of water (a pun, cf. Gy 302:7 s. **šula 1** and **šulta 1** with **ŠAL**).

šultana (cf. Mishn. שלל I to hang down) bat. MG 139 n. 4 (read **šlu-**, not **šalu-**) BZ 81 n. 6. Varr. **ašlutina, šulutana, šlutana** s.v. Pl. **-ia. sablh̲ šultana** AM 126:13 take for him a bat; **šultana uaṣlunta raza d̲-aiar lgaṭiun** ATŠ I no. 254 the bat and owl took to the mystery of the air.

šum 1, šuma (Old-Aram., Eg.-Aram., H. & Phoen. שם, Jew.-Aram. שׁוּם, שְׁמָא, Syr. ܫܡܐ, Akk. *šumu*; Sab. 𐩪𐩣, Ar. سِم, اِسم, Eth.

ስም Brockelmann i 333, Nöld.: *Neue Beiträge* 140) name, reputation MG 18:5, 28:ult., 97:10, 185:10; MR 106, 114 f. Varr. ʿ**ušma**, ʿ**šuma** s.vv. Pl. **šumia 1**, **šumhata** (latter as fem. Gy 45:12, 93:20, 159:13 etc.) MG 185:10 f. **šum dilia** Gy 245:12 f. my name; **šum urušum** Q 31:30 = **šumai urušumai** CP 31:11, Q 64 etc. my name and my sign MG 175:17 f.; **bnia šum** CP 110:8, ML 135:10 children of my name; **bšum hiia** = **bšuma d̲-hiia** = **bšumaihun d̲-hiia** in the name (frequent Mandaean *basmala*) MG 314:10 f.; ʿ**l šum d̲-ʿtiglilia** Gy 192:17 in the name of the one who revealed himself to me MG 562 n. 2. St. cstr. in names of higher beings: **šum hai** Gy 195:15, Q 9:2, 30:32, 60:4 = ML 24:21, 83:3, 144:5 = CP 22:12, 67:15, 118:13; **šum ham ziua** Gy 145:21; **šum iauar** PD 351; **šum qašar** DC 43 A 97, 139 (a demon). St. abs. as pr. n. (but different from **šum 2**): **haia šum** (as two words?) **asia d̲-kušṭa** Morg. 116:8 (cf. **haiašum** s.v.); **masiqta d̲-šum rba** PD 834. St. emph. & with suff. **šuma rba qadmaia** Oxf. roll g 556, 905 (*& often*) the First Great Name. With af. of **SLQ I** (q.v.) to give a name, to name; **šuma hauilh̲**, **šuma rba hauilh̲** AM (*often*) he will have a great name (will be famous); **šumh̲ ltlata ʿnšia nizal** AM 12:6 his name will go to (i.e. he will marry) three women BZ 12 n. 2. Pl. **šumia kasiia** Gy 150:23, 159:13 = **šumhata kasiata** Gy 159:13 etc. secret names; **mindam mn šumhata lanadkar** ATŠ II no. 42 he will mention none of the names.

šum 2 (H. שֵׁם II) Shem, Noah's son MR 44 n. 2, MSt 118. **šum br nu** Jb 53:9 ff., 78:13, 90:9, 277:4, Q 18:22, ML 49:11, 52:6, 166:1, Morg. 88:9 = CP 42:7, 43:7, 135:14, Gy 26:24, 381:8; **šum uiam uiapit** Gy 50:1.

šuman AM 202 name of a city BZ Ap. II.

šumai(i)a 1 (adj. from **šuma**) pertaining to name(s), with name(s). Fem. **šumaita 1**. **dukrana d̲-šumaiia** Oxf. roll f 827, DC 25 etc. (var. **d̲-šumaia**), **dukrania u(?)šumaiia** CP 293:17 f. mentioning of names; **šumaita** as a technical term of liturgical praxis, opposite to **zhiraita** (q.v.) DC 27:171 f., 50. 882 f.

šumai(i)a 2 (adj. from **šumia 2**) heavenly, celestial. Fem. **šumaita 2**. Var. **šimaita**. **iumia šumaiia** ATŠ I no. 196 (var. **šimaita** PD) heavenly days (i.e. Panja); **maṣbuta šumaita** ATŠ I no. 67 (var. **šimaita** PD) the heavenly baptism (but cf. s. preced.).

šumbaṭ (prob. from **ŠMṬ**, but cf. also Syr. ܫܡܒܛܐ) long, hanging down MG 77:3, 122:21, or straight (of hair). **manzih̲ šumbaṭ** AM 98:3 (*and often*).

šumbulta, šumbilta, šimbilta (Jew.-Aram. שובלתא & varr., Syr. ܫܒܠܬܐ, H. שִׁבֹּלֶת, Ar. سُنْبُلَة) (*a*) ear of corn, (*b*) Virgo MG 14:2, 19:11, 50:18, 128:4, 172:16. Pl. of (*a*) **šumblia** MG 172:17. (*a*) **pahtilh̲ lhṭita mn šumbilta** ATŠ I no. 285 (var. **šumbilta**) they open up (separate) the grain from the ear; **hapuria mitkil mn qudam šumblia uhaizak mitiklan šumblia** Gs 3:11 f. the green corn is eaten before the (ripe) ears and then the ears are eaten; (*b*) Gy 122:22, 123:24, very often in AM.

šumhata a pl. of **šuma** (q.v.).

šumia 1 a pl. of **šuma** (q.v.).

šumia 2, var. ʿ**šumia** (שְׁמַיָּא, ܫܡܝܐ, H. שָׁמַיִם, Ar. سَمَاء, Sab. 𐩪𐩣𐩺, Eth. ሰማይ, Akk. *šamû*, pl. *šamê* & varr., cf. Brockelmann i 232, Hommel: *Südarabische Chrestomathie* 19, Nyberg MO xiv 210) heavens MG 28:21, 33:7, 109:11. Used as sg. fem. with no further pl. MG 159:paen., 166:11, cf. **šumia** ʿ**ṣṭartia** Oxf. roll f 1232, 1268 = 'little sky' (a blue cloth over roof). ʿ**šumia ṣṭartia** Lond. roll A 9, 67, cf. 204 (the same).

šumka (שְׁמְכָּא, ܫܘܡܟܐ Löw 173, *Flora* ii 186) onion. Still used (colloquial pron. *šomχa*). Gl. 45:11 defectively (pl.?) بصل *caepa* پیاز.

šumna (rt. **ŠMN**) fat. **dakria d̲-šumna** Jb 90:13 f. fat rams.

šumʿil 1 (H. שְׁמוּאֵל) Jb 75:10, 12 Samuel.

šumʿil 2 RD 5 = DAb par. theophorous name given to a (personified) steering-paddle.

***šuna** s. **šunia**.

šunabur AM 198 name of a city.

šunara (שׁוּנְרָא, ܫܘܢܪܐ, Ar. سِنَّوْر Fränkel 112, Akk. *šurānu*) cat. Fem. **šinarta** s.v. **zma d̲-šunara** DC 46. 86:8 blood of a cat; **puma d̲-talia skir bšunara** Morg. 264/19:39 f., cf. DC 44. 1317 the fox's mouth is blocked by a cat.

šunda (according to P.A.) water-fennel Jb ii 154 n. 4. **laklia šunda uṣinda** Jb 151:12 they eat no fennel or fibre.

šundur (P. شوندر) beetroot. **bazra d̲-šundur** DC 45 beetroot seed.

šunia (rt. **ŠNA**?) vicissitude(s), difficulty (-ies), nuisance(s). **šunia uridpa hauilh̲** AM 44:9 he will have vicissitudes and persecution; **šunia bgubria tihuilh̲** AM 64:6 she will have vicissitudes with men; **šunia d̲-liba tihuilh̲** AM 84:antepenult. she will have dementia (?, cf. ܫܢܝܐ); **hiuia ugala mrara šunia** (var. **snia**) **hinun** ATŠ I no. 256 the serpent and tortoise (and?) venom are hateful (?) (doubtful) (read **mraria** 'venomous creatures'?).

šuʿalia Zotb. 218a:14 a family-name.

ŠUP I (Aram., Syr., Akk. *šâpu* den. from *šîpu* = Syr. ܫܝܦܐ collyrium Zimmern ZA xxxii 184, *Akk. Fremdwörter* 61, Langdon OLZ 1909 111) to rub, smear on, scrape, polish, smoothen, sharpen, shove, push aside.

Pe. Pf. **giria šmimia d̲-šap nipquia** (var. **napquia**) **lhazin alma** Gs 114:1, cf. Zotb. 225a:3 (1st text) poisoned (?Lidzb, *flink*?) arrows that they have sharpened (or polished?) and sent out to this world Ginzā 560 n. 4. Impt. **šup** rub; with encl. **šuplh̲ bpagrh̲** DC 46. 97:7 rub it into his body; **šuplh̲ bsipa d̲-baba** DC 44. 2048 rub it on the door-post of his door. Act. pt. **ušaip ainih̲ mn hak mia** DC 46. 9 and he shall rub his eyes with that water; with encl. **ušaig ušaiiplh̲ lklila** s. **ŠUG** pe. act. pt., **šaipalh̲ lpagrh̲** DC 46. 241:2 (*& often*) she shall rub it on her body; pl. **pumaihun šaipia** Gy

45:22 they besmear their mouth; ʿdaiun banpaiun šaipia Gy 224:11 they rub their faces with their hands MG 394:4; with encl. šaipilun Gy 56:2 they rub themselves. Pass. pt. šip rip Oxf. roll f 1376 f. smeared and tied; klila d-asa d-šip d-rip . . . ušip bzaʿparan ŠQ 8:14 the myrtle-wreath that is smeared and tied . . . and smeared with saffron.

Gl. 26:2–4 šap اطاب *ungere* ماليد; 180:1 f. (defectively) روغن ماليد *ungere* دهن.

Der.: šaiap, šupta.

ŠUP II cf. s. ŠPP.

šupura for šipura in pl. šupuria DC 22. 100 = šipuria Gy 105:8.

šupurtaiia Zotb. 218a:19, 220b:30 a family-name.

šupla 1 (rt. ŠPL) (*a*) Or. 330:10 lower parts of the body, (*b*) DC 23. 761–765 a kind of disease.

šupla 2 (cf. ܫܘܦܠܐ) AM 127:20 rump-fat, cf. s. PRQ af.

šupra 1 (rt. ŠPR) beauty, fairness. St. cstr. špur s.v. martia šupra urgaga ŠQ 16:12, CP 226:7 mistress of beauty and grace; šupran urgagan Gy 146:4 our beauty and our grace; midamrabh bšupra Gs 99:10 f. she marvelleth at its beauty; bšupra AM 188 (*& often*) fairly, prosperously.

šupra 2 (Jew.-Aram., H. שׁוֹפָר) = šipura. Pl. šupria Jb 104:4, 105:1.

šupta (rt. ŠUP I) smoothness. tlata razia aina uputa ušupta d-ʿurkh Oxf. xii three mysteries: the eye, the forehead, and the smoothness which is therewith (?).

ŠUṢ, ŠIṢ (cf. Targ. שֵׁיצִי) to cause to go out, drive out, consume.

Pa. Impf. with suff. nišaṣunh uaitunh lbaitai DC 46 they drive him out and bring him to my house. Act. pt. with encl. mšauṣalia [*sic*] umšargizanh DC 46 they consume me and fill me with passion; mšaṣilh umšagrunh DC 46. 238:2 they drive him (?) and inflame him.

Der.: maštuṣia.

ŠUQ (cf. שׁוק to long, desire?) to languish.

Pe. Impf. kišuta tišuq uiabša AM 171 s. kišuta.

ŠWQ occ. for ŠBQ (q.v.).

Pe. Pf. rugza lnišimta šuaq DC 34. 1309 they loosed wrath on the soul. Often, cf. Gl. 179:9 f.

šuqa (שׁוּקָא, ܫܘܩܐ, Ar. loan-w. سُوق Fränkel 187) market, market-place. Pl. -ia. ulšuqa lanizal ATŠ II no. 43 and he shall not go to the market; šuqia malka Jb 128:1, 5 the chief market-places; šidqa bšuqia DC 44. 617 silence in the markets; qiriatkun d-šuqia DC 43 A 89, 132 your mishaps in the markets.

šuqupta (rt. ŠQP) blow, buffeting, rough treatment, blight, plague, murrain. Var. šiqupta s.v. Pl. šqupiata s.v. šuquptaikun uqiriatkun DC 43 A 89, qraiata ušuqupta DC 43 F 25 (& throughout DC 43 F) mishaps and accidents; šuquptaikun d-bit biriata DC 43 A 132 your murrain in the cattle-shed (?); mhita ušqupta (*often*) a smiting and a blow; qiria ušuqupta baqnia hauia AM 170:5 there will be mishaps and murrain amongst sheep. Very often in magic documents.

šuqrak AM 204 name of a town. Doubtf. Varr. šurdak, šurdan (AM 216).

ŠWR (שְׁוַר, ܫܘܪ, Ar. سار, ساور, Akk. *šamāru*) to leap, jump, move suddenly and quickly, spring up, start back, aspire, mount up(wards); to disregard (an oath or vow); pa. to palpitate, make leap. MG 257 n. 2.

Pe. Pf. šuar bdmu dmu DC 43 E 12 they leapt up in various guises; šuar ushiq Gy 191:14 he mounted and leapt up; d-mn tibil šuar CP 166:14, ML 201:8 who sprang out of the earth; hilqak mn daria šuar Gs 79:12 f. thy destiny mounted upwards from the ages; mn qulalan haizak šuart mn pirṣan haizin šuart Gy 362:20 how didst thou leap away from our snares, how didst thou leap away from our debauchery?; haizin šuart mn šihan ušigran uhaizak šuart mn nuran Gy 360:20 f. how didst thou start back from our passion and our lust, how didst thou leap away from our fire?; šuart usliqt DC 21 JRAS 1938 3:5 thou didst leap up and rise up; šiurit (var. šurit A, šurita BD) alit ldibna Jb 42:5 I leapt up and entered the fold. Impf. nišuar uniqum lligrh DC 22. 96 (var. našar Gy 101:7, nišar ibid. D) he will spring up and stand on his feet (var. he will stand firmly on his feet); kukba nišuar AM 231:14 a star shoots; halin ʿumamata nišuar DC 43 A 14 he disregards (: breaks) these oaths (*and often*). Pt. ladiba šauar dibnan Jb 41:5 no wolf leaps into our fold. Part. pres. minaikun šauarna Gs 64: antep. I spring away from you.

Pa. Pt. mšauar DC 43 E 10, DC 49:28 palpitates; transit. with encl. bhinga mšaurilun Gy 225:8 maketh them leap in the dance.

ŠUR (Ar. شار) to give advice, counsel. Foreign. Ar. impf. had iišur šur ʿl anašia AM 283:33 some one will give counsel to the people.

Der.: šur(a) 1.

šur 1, šura 1 (rt. ŠUR q.v.), cf. Gl. 155:5 šura, šurta محافل *concilia* مجلس.

šura 2 (שׁוּרָא, ܫܪܐ, H. שֹׁר, Ar. سُرّ) navel MG 105:5, 484 (Add. to p. 20:5). Masc. šurh ʿl tar šiiriana d-hšuka npal Gy 83:20 f. his navel fell on the door (?) of the Vein of Darkness; kd šurh ʿtgna bšiiriana d-hšuka Gy 83:21 f. when his navel lay (Lidzb. *sich schüttelte*) in the Vein of Darkness; bšura kanilh Gy 84:3 I put a band on his navel; šqul . . . šurak mn šurih DC 37. 605 remove . . . thy navel from his navel; ata lhalṣh ulšuria . . . hauilh AM 36:11 he will have a mark on his loins and on his navel; kiba d-liba ušura hauilh AM 55:18 she will have pain in her heart and navel; niršumunh lšurh ATŠ I no. 201 they shall seal it on his navel; hanath hatma ʿl šura matna DC 41. 522 that seal is placed on the navel; puma qadmaia hu d-hu šura mitiqria ATŠ II no. 383 it is the first mouth which is called navel.

šura 3 (שׁוּרָא, ܫܘܪܐ, H. שׁוּר II, Ar. سُور Fränkel 237) wall MG 105:9. St. cstr. šur,

Pl. **-ia.** Masc. **šur parzla, šura d̲-parzla, šuria d̲-parzla** s. **parzla. tlata šuria d̲-dmasa** DC 34. 252 three walls of diamond; **šuba šuria** DC 27. 100 seven walls; **šuria d̲-dahba** Gy 159:11 golden walls MG 315:8.

šura 4 (P. شوره) marshy ground, foreshore. **ulšura d̲-iardna nhit** DC 34. 309 descended to the foreshore of the Jordan (river).

šura 5 (Ar. شَرّ & شُرّ) war, fight, quarrel. Colloquial pron. *šorra*, st. abs. *šor*. **qaraptania ušur** (var. **ušura**) **hinun** ATŠ I no. 256 (var. DC 6) they are fighters and quarrellers (*abstractum pro concreto*).

šura 6 (cf. Talm. שׁוּרָה line, rule of conduct etc.) road, way? Masc. (Or ܫܘܪܐ leap, spring?). **abar ukšar šurh̲** DC 43 J 52 he crossed over and his leap (?) was successful.

šura 7 (rt. **ŠRR**) chain. Pl. **-ia. tlatma ušitin šuria . . . ukulhin maṣpuṭiata** DAb three hundred and sixty chains . . . and all the fastenings.

šurabta a var. of **šurbta** ML 177 n. 2 (CP. 148: 10 **šurbta**).

šurba st. abs. of **šurbta** (q.v.). Pl. **šurbata** ibid.

šurbai an ancestor of the human race, forming pair with **šarhabʿil** q.v. Both names recall the locution: **šarhib šurbata** (cf. s. šaf. of **RHB II**). **šurbai gabra** Jb 78:12, PD 349, further s. **šarhabʿil.**

šurbuta DC 22. 455 for **šurbta** Gs 68:antep.

šurbina (שׁוּרְבִּינָא, ܫܘܪܒܝܢܐ Löw no. 333, from Bab. *šurmēnu*, Sum. *šurme*) cypress. **qaimunh̲ šurbina** DC 43 I 45 they set up a cypress; **gauaza d̲-šurbina** DC 37 a cypress staff.

šurbiš HG a name given to Ruha.

šurbta, rarely **šurabta, šurubta** (Syr. ܫܪܒܬܐ, also Chr.-Pal., cf. Ar. سُرْبَة row of animals) progeny, species, generation, race, descendants, brood, tribe, family, relatives MG 19:17, 101:24. Fem., but st. abs. **šurba** as masc. **šurbata. šurba rba d̲-hiia** CP 17:6, 63:4, 110:9, 112:6, 392:ult. etc., Q 29:4, 57:7, 58:12 f., Gy 364:2 the great Family of Life; **šurba d̲-hiia** Gy 342:10, MG 315:20; **šurbta d̲-hiia** Gy 105:17; **šurba šania** Jb 191:14 sublime generation; **šurba biša** Gy 119:12 evil generation; **gubria d̲-mqaimia šurbta** Gy 105: 12 men who confirm the generation; **šurbta haita** Q 13:20, 60:11, Jb 146:8 the living generation; **adam riša d̲-šurbta haita** Gy 26:7 Adam, the head of the living generation; **ʿtit misaq šurbta ʿtit šurbta misaq** Gs 68:23 I came to raise (one would expect af.) a generation; **tiklak lak ukulhun šurbatak** DC 37 it will devour thee and all thy progeny; **šarhib šurbata** Gy 240:24; **mšarhib šurbta** Gy 244:24; **ništarhbun šurbata** Gy 251:3 (cf. šaf. & eštaf. of **RHB II**).

šuria 1 pl. of **šura** (cf. esp. 3 and 7).

ṣuria 2 (adj. from جور name of a P. town called later Fīrūzābād, the roses of which were famous, cf. Yāqūt: *Geogr. Wörterbuch* ii 147, ML ix n. 3) of Jur, from Jur. **uarda d̲-ṣuria** ML ix = ŠQ 19:19 roses from Jur.

šuria 3 (cf. Syr. ܫܘܝ to be in astrol. conjunction) conjunction(s astrol.). AM 11:n. 7. **ʿnbu maria . . . pihta nhaša ušuria d̲-šamiš . . . usira** DC 47 Nebo, lord of . . . disclosing predestination and of astrological conjunctions of the sun . . . and of the moon.

ṣurṣan (جُرْجَان arabized form of P. گُرگان) AM 205 Persian province of Jurjan (SE. of Caspian).

ŠWŠ (phon. form of **ŠBŠ**) to put into disorder, confuse, discomfort, put out of gear, disgruntle, confound. MG 49:5 & n. 3.

Pa. Pf. with suff. **šaušaunin lʿbidatun** Gy 110:23 they cast confusion on their deeds. Impf. with suff. **nišaušh̲ liligṭta** Gy 110:17 we will confuse his faction. Impt. defectively **šuš plan** DC 46. 138:1 confound N.; *plene* with suff. **šaušh̲ lplan** DC 45 & 46 (*often*) discomfort N.

Ethpa. Pf. **ʿštauaš radaiia** DC 26. 22 the travellers (: planets) were disconcerted. Impf. **ništauša** Gy 310:21 they (fem.) are cast into confusion. Pt. pl. **mištaušia** Gy 310:16 they are thrown into disorder.

Der.: **tašuiš.**

šuša 1 (Σῶσσος) used of the 12th part of an hour MG xxviii 20 & n. 2. Pl. **-ia. šaiia ušušia** s. **šaiia 2; šuša upalga d̲-šuša** DC 44. 1852 f. = Morg. 269/28:25 five minutes and 2½ minutes; **ušnia ušušia** Gy 196:23 and years and five-minutes; **ṣub šaia** (var. **šaiia** Leid.) **uṣub šušia** Gs 48:21 f. s. **HŠB** pe. pf.

šuša 2 (שׁוּשָׁא, ܫܘܫܐ > Akk. *šūšu*? Löw 378) licorice, liquorice. **usaria ušušadu** DC 46 and barley and their licorice.

šušalta, šuš(i)lta (Jew.-Aram. שַׁלְשְׁלְתָּא, שַׁלְשֶׁלֶת, also varr. with 'שׁו, Syr. ܫܘܫܠܬܐ, Ar. سِلْسِلَة) chain MG 19:18 f., 78:22. Pl. **šušlata. šrath̲ nišimta lšušilth̲** DC 42 the soul loosed its chain; **ʿtpasaq asaria ušušlata** Jb 17:6 bonds and chains were broken; **asartinun lalahia bšušlata d̲-abara** DC 26. 553, DC 40. 571 I fettered the gods with chains of lead; **šušlata d̲-abara** DC 43 A 108; **ʿsira atuat harašata bšušlata d̲-parzla** DC 40. 1102 bound are the women-witches by iron chains; **ahid bšušlata** DC 37. 486 held in chains; **qal šušlata** DC 43 A 53 the sound of chains.

šušban (Jew.-Aram. שׁוֹשְׁבִין, cf. שׁוֹשְׁבִינָא friend, counsellor > Akk. *susabinu*? Del. 506) the bridegroom's best man, the groomsman. Pl. **šušbinia,** var. **šušinia** Jb ii 17, 113 n. 4. **šušban hiduia** DC 3. 380:paen. = CP 226:ult. = ŠQ 16:17 = Par. xv 14b = Par. xxv 19a the bridegroom's groomsman; **d̲-hinun šušbania mitiqrin** ATŠ II no. 315 who are called 'groomsmen'; **kd̲ šušbania maršin bšiul** Jb 114:8 when the groomsmen spend money in Sheol (only C has **šušbinia** omitted in varr. but mentioned in Jb ii 113 n. 4).

šušian a name given to **nauruz zuṭa** the 'Little New Year'. **trin iumia d̲-šušian** ATŠ II no. 16.

šušilta s. **šušalta.**

šušimta (cf. **šušma**) the sesame plant. **šušimta hʿ** DC 41 (first illustration) it is a sesame plant.

šušlata pl. of šušalta, šušilta (q.v.).

šušma (שׁוּשְׁמָא, ܫܘܫܡܐ & ܫܘܫܡܐ, Mishn. שׁוּמְשְׁמִין, Ar. سمسم, Akk. *šamaššamu* >* *šaman šammi*? σήσαμον Löw 376) sesame MG 78:23. Fem. form **šušimta** (s.v.) Pl. **šušmia. miša šiha br šušma hiuara** CP 30:8, Q 13:4, 13 precious oil, product of white sesame; **miša br šušma hiuara** Jb 2:11, 4:13; **asa ušušma hiuara** Jb 41:2 myrtle and white sesame; **šušma hiuara** Jb 269:15; **aitun hiṭia ušušmia** DC 48. 281 they brought wheat and sesame-beans; **šušmia d̲-mqalia bnura** DC 46. 67:3 sesame-seeds parched in fire.

šušmana (שׁוּשְׁמָנָא, שׁוּמְשְׁמָנָא, ܫܘܫܡܢܐ, Ar. سمسم) ant MG 70:24, 139:10. **bizuna d̲-šušmana** s. bizuna; **šduk lqina d̲-šušmana** DC 21 they threw thee on an ant's nest.

ŠWŠQ (šaf. of **YŠQ**?)? Pf. **šaušiq** Par. xiv no. 328 = PD 1447, MG 212:7.

šušta in **bšušta** Gy 382:5 cf. s. **ʿšta I.**

šuštar (P. شوشتر) name of a town on the Karun river, where there used to be a strong Mandaean community. Often in colophons.

ŠUT mod. form of **ŠTA.**

Pe. Impt. **šut** ML 27:10 drink. Pt. **mia lašita** (var. DC 36 **lašatia**) . . . **miša šita** ATŠ II nos. 61 & 248 drinks no water . . . imbibes oil. Mod. pf. *šât*; pres. *qšâyet*.

šuta 1 (rt. **ŠAA I,** שׁוּתָא I = שְׁעוּתָא) talk, speech, conversation, intercourse, saying, word, doctrine MG 146:5. Parallel with **malala** Gy 26:20. **šuta qadmaita** Gy 26:6, 20, 51:4, the first doctrine; **šuta haita** Morg. 235/57:4, Gy 68:20, 79:14 the living doctrine; **šuta haita qadmaita** Gy 125:16, 126:3; **šuta kasita** Morg. 228/43:1 f., Q 25:27, 33, 26:23, **šuta nukraita** Gs 20:ult., MG 318:16 f.; **šuth̲ rhima** AM his conversation is beloved; **uanašia šuth̲ mqablh̲ unihuilh̲ šuta usagia ušulṭana** AM 14:19 and men accept his talk (opinion?) and he will have command and plenty and authority; **ušuta d̲-napšia mnaṭarlh̲** AM 53:6 and he is guarded in conversation; **ušuth̲ msarhib** AM 20:8 his speech is rapid; **šuth̲ mištma** AM 23:5 his word is obeyed; **mn gabra šuta tihuilh̲** AM 28:10 he will have speech of a man (?); **šuth̲ basima umnilh̲ mrauribin** AM 43:penult. his conversation is pleasant and his words are esteemed; **baiarna bšuta d̲-ab** Jb 101:5 f. I shine in the word of my father; **ṭubh̲ d̲-nišma šutai** Jb 237:2 it is well for him that heareth my word; **d̲-šuta d̲-manda d̲-hiia šama** Jb 237:3 who heareth the word of M.–d̲–H., neg. **d̲-šuta d̲-manda d̲-hiia lašama** Jb 237:4; **braza d̲-napšaikun ubšuta d̲-napšaikun ubšuta huilia** DC 26. 701 f., DC 40. 685 f. by your own mysteries and by your own spell, and it shall happen to me according to the word; **bšuta d̲-minh̲ huaitun** DC 26. 549 with the word by which ye came into existence.

šuta 2 (ܫܘܚܬܐ < Akk. *šuḫtu*? Jensen) Gy 182:1 rust, verdigris MG 63, 104:paen. **ṭupša ušuta** s. **ṭupša.**

šuta 3 (שׁוּתָא II, Akk. *šūtu* Delitzsch: *Ass. Handw.* 648) AM 169:penult., 195:13, DC 43 D 47 south wind, south-east wind.

šutapa (Sam. & Jew. ࠔࠅࠕࠐ, שׁוּתָּפָא, ܫܘܬܦܐ; Akk. *šutapû* Meissner ZA viii 82 f., from Sum. ŠU.TAB, cf. Wid. v 172 n. 3) companion, partner, colleague, consort, associate, friend MG 22:17, 128:10. Pl. **šutapia, šutapania. latigizlun mn šutapa** Gy 20:1, **mn šutapa latigizlun** Gy 38:4, **man d̲-gazil mn habrh̲ ušutaph̲** Gy 20:2 cf. s. **GZL** pe.; **šutapa rba d̲-mhaimnia** CP 111:1 = ML 136:8 the Great Comrade of the faithful; **litlh̲ habra btaga ulašutapa bšulṭana** Gy 31:1 f. he has no partner in the crown and no associate in government; **hauit bšutapan** Jb 153:10 thou art become our partner; **zaua šutapa** ATŠ II no. 348 the wife is a partner; **trin šutapania** RD B 115 two partners; **mn šutapanun gazlia** RD C 26 they rob their associates.

šutaputa = **šataputa. abud šataputa** AM 159: 11 form a partnership.

šutla (rt. **ŠTL**) planting, propagation. **amarlan lšutla** ATŠ II 312 tell us about propagation(?).

šutra DC 22. 55 & Sh. ʿAbd.'s copy = **zutra** Gy 60:1.

ŠṬA I (שְׁטָא, שְׁטֵי, ܫܛܐ, mod. H. שטה, Ar. سطا to insult, rel. **ŠUṬ I & YŠṬ**) to act foolishly, go astray; af. to lead astray, seduce, cause to appear foolish, make fools, bring shame upon; to become vile, despicable, contemptible.

Pe. Pf. **atia šiṭia d̲-šṭa** Gs 25:6 there came (hist. pres.) one that acted foolishly. Impf. **mn dilak laništia** CP 247:ult. = ML 253:9 shall not stray away from Thee; **libh̲ laništia bginia d̲-ʿkuria** ATŠ II no. 351 his heart will not go astray in the pollutions of the (pagan) temples; **bdahba ukaspa latištun** Gy 19:3 be not foolish about gold and silver; **mn ʿuhra d̲-hiia latištun** Gy 24:12 stray not from the way of Life. Act. pt. **šiṭia d̲-šaṭia mšiha kulh̲** Gy 120:12 all foolishness that Christ committeth MG 324:9 (with a mistaken ref.); **d̲-šaṭia bšiṭuatun** Gy 121:21 who acteth in their foolish ways.

Af. Pt. **šiṭia maštia balma** Gy 28:10 he bringeth foolishness into the world.

Ethpa. Pf. **ana ʿštaṭit mn ʿutria** Jb 262:13 I was made vile before the uthras.

Der.: s. **ŠUṬ I.**

ŠṬA II (**ŠṬH** q.v.) af. to flay; ethpa. to stretch out, extend, prostrate oneself, cast (oneself) down MG 238:1 & n. 1.

Af. Impf. with encl. **ʿl miškaiun d̲-anašia naštilh̲** Gy 387:15 f. they flay people (MG 363:14 slightly changed).

Ethpa. Pf. **ʿštaṭia qudamai sgid** Gy 306:4 he prostrated himself (and) worshipped; **ʿštaṭia ʿl anph̲ npal** ATŠ I no. 101 = PD 1019 he prostrated himself (and) fell on his face (MG 263:23); **ʿštaṭiat uniplat lqudamh̲** Gs 24:11 f. she prostrated herself and fell down before him (MG 263:paen.); **ʿštaṭit usigdit** Gy 135:19 I prostrated myself and worshipped. Pt. **mištaṭia** Gy 134:11, 136:24 prostrated (hist. pres.) himself MG 237:ult.; pl. **mištaṭin**

ATŠ I no. 112 they cast themselves down. Part. pres. **mištaṭina usagidna** Gy 152:24 I prostrate myself and worship; **sagidna umištaṭina** Gy 157:1 MG 237:ult.

ŠṬH (Aram. & H. שטח, Syr. ܫܛܚ, Ar. سطح, Eth. ሰጠሐ) to stretch out, be prostrate, lie full length.

PE. Pass. pt. pl. fem. **kḏ šamiš šṭiha** Gy 194:1, Q 24:2 they prostrate (themselves) like a servant.

ŠṬM (= ŠTM) the rt. of **šaṭama** (= **šatama**).

ŠṬR (שְׁטַר to draw, spread, strike, Akk. *šaṭāru* to write) to trace (a line), draw, mark out; to spread (out), smear; with **mn** to obliterate, wipe.

PE. Impt. **mia uarda banpia šṭur** DC 46. 116:1 smear (wet) his face with rose-water. Act. pt. **šaṭar dukth̲** RD B 30 = DAb par. marks out its place.

ETHPE. Pf. with encl. **rušumh̲ ḏ-šdum ʿšṭirbh̲** ATŠ II no. 302 the sign of Š, was marked on him. Impf. **šumia tištar** AM 222:17 the heavens are spread out. Pt. **rušuma ḏ-liuiatan minh̲ mištar** ATŠ II no. 289 the sign of Leviathan shall be wiped from him.

šiaṭa 1 (rt. **ŠUṬ II**, hence 'breast-beating') mourning, lamentation Jb ii 115 n. 1. **šaiṭik** (var. **šaiaṭik** B) **hauia bit qubria** Jb 116:6 f. thy mourning will be in the graveyard; **šiiaṭa** (varr. **šaiṭa** A, **šiṭa** D) **ḏ-adam** (var. **ladam**) **matialh̲** Gs 20:4 she brought (hist. pres.) lamentations to Adam; **š(a)iaṭa ḏ-dam matialh̲** Gs 21:19.

šiaṭa 2 (שְׁיָיטָא, שיטא) opinion, system, principle. **šaiilth̲ . . . lhalin šuialia ḏ-šiaṭun dilun** ATŠ II I asked him . . . these questions about their opinion.

šiala = **šuiala**; **šialta** = **šulta** 1. **šiala simat hiia** Zotb. 231a:1 (second text) the question of the 'Treasure-of-Life'; **šialta ḏ-mainia** (read **mania**) **ḏ-dihba rba** ibid. l. 2 the question of the clothes of the Great Feast.

***šiba 1, 2** s. pl. **šibia 2, 3.**

šibaba (שְׁבָבָא, ܫܒܒܐ < Akk. *šabābi*? LS 749 b) neighbour. Pl. **-ia. šibaba ṭaba** Oxf. roll g 615 = Or. 326:18 good neighbour; **aina ḏ-šibabia bišia ubnh̲** JRAS 1937 592:30 the eye of wicked neighbours and their children; **šibabia uribabia** s. **ribabia**; **qal šibabia** DC 45 & 46 the noise of neighbours; **šutapa ušibaba** AM 152:17 partner and neighbour. Gl. 34:12 **šbabai** [sic] اقارب *cognati* نزديكان; 72:11 id. جيران *vicini* همسايه.

šibuia (colloquial) deer. **tirba ḏ-šibuia** DC 46. 132:3 a deer's fat; **ṭupria ḏ-šibui(i)a . . . umiška ḏ-šibuia** Lond. roll B 418 = DC 12:190, 197 a deer's hoofs . . . and a deer's skin.

šibṭa (שִׁבְטָא, ܫܒܛܐ, H. שֵׁבֶט, Akk. *šabbiṭu* rod, staff) used only with figurative meanings. (*a*) plague, disease, pestilence Lidzb. ZDMG lxi 694 n. 3, BZ 108 n. 1, (*b*) disease-demon, Furlani: *I Nomi* 422 f. Pl. **-ia.** (*a*) **šibṭa ukiba nihuilh̲ bpagrh̲** AM 98:14 he will have disease and pain in his body; **kib guara ušibṭa banašia hauia** AM 188:19 f. there will be stomach-ache and disease amongst the people; **kibia ušibṭia** Q 13:9, 14:11, 17:3 pains and diseases; **šibṭa nasgun bmdiniata** AM 249:19 pestilence will go into the cities (read either **šibṭia**, or **nasqia**); (*b*) **šidia ušibṭia** DC 43 D 59; **šibṭia uziqia usaṭania** DC 43 G 5.

šibia 1 (rt. **ŠBA I**, שְׁבְיָא, ܫܒܝܐ) captivity, prison, bondage, depopulation, devastation, marauding, raiding; (as collect. noun) captives MG 102:20, AM p. 178 n. 1. **šibiaikun** your captivity MG 180:9; **br šibia** Gy 15:9, 16:5, Gs 96:1 a captive; **bnia šibia** Gs 11:18 f. captives; **riš šibia rba** Gy 113:3 the head of great captivity; **šibia nišibun** AM 184:15, **šibia ḏ-šabin** Gy 17:8 (s. **ŠBA I**); **šibia uhauqa** AM 169:13 raiding and terrorism; **šibia uqraba** DC 44. 234 captivity and war; **qirsa ušibia** AM 223:16 hardship and devastation; **šibia nišaun** AM 247:12 they will make captives (go on raids); **malka ḏ-miṣraiia bšibia nihuia** AM 276:13 the king of the Egyptians will be in captivity; **bšibia rba šbaitainun** DC 37. 547 thou hast held them in dire bondage; **ʿštbun bšibia ḏ-ruha** Jb 267:10 they were captivated by R.; **šibia umutana** AM 211:4 devastation and pestilence; **kupna ušibia** AM 219:19 famine and desolation; **šibia binia trin malkia napil** AM 273:37 there will be marauding raids between two kings; **qiria ušibia** AM 274:14 disputes and captivity; **šira ušibia** AM 280:11 war and captivity; **šibia uhirba** AM 223:16 captivity and war; **mn šibia atit** ATŠ II no. 125 I came from captivity.

šibia 2 pl. (of colloquial *šebba* MMII 42) sheaf of reeds. **šuba šibia mn šuba rišia** JRAS 1937 591:31 seven bundles of reeds with seven heads (feathery tops?).

šibia 3 pl. (cf. H. & mod. H. שָׁאַב to draw water, absorb, imbibe, Ar. سَأَبَ to drink) streams. **nahria šibia unahrauata nimlun** AM 249:10 brooks, streams, and rivers will fill.

šibiaha (< ܫܒܝܚܐ) planet, demon. Pl. **-ia** MG 56:14, SsSs ii 22, 430, cf. HpGn 22 (& Ind. s. *Planeten*), Furlani: *I Pianeti* (AANL 1948, Serie viii, vol. ii, fasc. 3, pp. 119–87), 'ancora su šibiahia' (*Rivista degli Studi Or.* xxvi 27–33). **šuba šibiahia** (s. **šuba**) MG 327:13, enumerated in Lond. roll B 547 ff., their days Lond. roll B 48 ff.; **ʿu šibiaha hu** DC 26. 43 if he is a demon (the sg. *šiβyāha* is often used in the colloquial); **šibiahia . . . ʿpikia umapkia** Gs 69:1 perverted and perverting . . . planet-demons; **šibiahia ḏ-šuba dmu minaihun npaq** Gy 94:18 planets from which seven shapes issued; **šibiahia bnia ḏ-ruha baṭla** Gy 109:12 the planets, sons of the good-for-nought R. Very often.

šigda (שִׁגְדָּא, ܫܓܕܐ pl. ܫܓܕ̈ܐ, H. שָׁקֵד Löw no. 319, Akk. *šiqdu, šiqittu, šuqdu* Meissner MVAG ix 211) almond. Pl. **-ia.** MG 39 n. 3. **hazin ʿlana ḏ-šigda** DC 7 (illustr.) this is an almond-tree; **šigda** Oxf. roll f 1266, 1318, pl. **šigdia** Oxf. roll f 1389, ŠQ.

šigdunia Oxf. roll g 856 = **šangdunia** s. **šangaria.**

šiglai Zotb. 222b:7 a man's name.

šiglal DC 40. 594 = **šiglat** DC 26. 645 name of a female demon.

šigra 1 (rt. **ŠGR**) heat, fever, inflammation, lust, passion. **šiha ušigra** Gy 28:1, 215:20, Jb 224:2 passion and lust; **šihan ušigran** Gy 362:21 our passion and our lust; **šiha urhamta ušigra** Gy 24:9 passion, love, and lust; **šiha bmia** DC 43 J 139, 150, Oxf. roll g 306, 335, cf. 345 fever in his entrails; **kiba ušigra** AM 29:14 pain and fever; **šihma ušigra** AM 188:4 sultriness and heat.

šigra 2 (شَقِيزَا) almond, pistachio **miša d-šigra** DC 42 almond-oil.

šigša (rt. **ŠGŠ**) disorder, confusion, trouble, upset, tumult, sedition, rebellion, strife; delirium, clouded mind. **šigša uṭirqa** Gy 7:18, 12:10, 31:23, 32:22, AM (*often*) confusion and trouble, cf. Gy 293:11; **šigša ut'ia** Gy 278:3 confusion and error; **alma bšigša niqum** Gy 61:6 the world stayeth in confusion; **šigša d-karsa** AM 114:penult., a disordered stomach; **šigša ušigšana** AM 232:1 confusion and sedition; **qala ušigša** AM 193:17 noise and tumult; **malkia bšigša niplun** AM 236:7 kings will fall into confusion (strife); **šigša d-malkia nihuibun** AM 244:19 there will be disturbance of kings amongst them.

šigšana (from preced.) sedition. **šigša ušigšana** s. **šigša.**

šigšuta (rt. **ŠGŠ**) AM 246:10 f. confusion, disturbance, unrest, tumult. **šigša ušigšuta** AM 246:10 f. confusion and disturbance.

šida 1 (שֵׁידָא, ܫܐܕܐ, H. שֵׁד, Akk. *šēdu*) demon MG 108:paen. Pl. **-ia** MSchr. 91 n. 5, Furlani: *I Nomi* 406 f. **šidia udaiuia** (*often*) demons and devils; **šidia mhamblia** Jb 243:3, 244:6, 245:2 destructive demons; **šidia ulaṭabia** Gy 389:6 demons and monsters; **šidia giṭia** s. **giṭa 1.**

šida 2 (Jew.-Aram. שִׁידָא I & II) (*a*) side, corner, (*b*) chest (var. **šada**). Pl. **-ia.** (*a*) **bšidia d-baita** DC 43 J 71 in the corners of the house; (*b*) **šidik** (var. **šadik** Pet.) **d-mlia mania** DC 22. 513 = Gs 134:5 thy (fem.) chest that is full of garments; **puq ... mn ... kul bazrunia ušidia ugubria** DC 40. 365 depart ... from ... all grain and chests and men.

šidai = **šadai.** **'l šidai** Gy 175:14 (H. אֵל שַׁדַּי).

šidaiia (rt. **ŠDA I**) wateriness (of eyes), overflowing(s). **napṣia ušidaiia uramšia** DC 46. 134:2 = JRAS 1943 p. 170:27 discharges and waterings and dim sight.

šidana (ܫܐܕܢܐ) possessed by a devil, demoniac, mad, diabolic, crazy. Pl. **-ia.** Var. **šadana** s.v. **šidana bla hala hauia** DC 46. 81:2 he will be crazy without mind; **'niš šidana** DC 46. 125:12 a madman; **kalbia šidania nihun** AM 284:18 there will be mad dogs; **mauiana šidana** s. **mauiana.**

šiduia (Ar. جَدّ) grandfather, cf. Gl. 77:4 f. **ansa šiduia d-šiduia d-šiduia** ATŠ colophon (which) my great-great-grandfather copied.

šidiriata pl. (cf. Talm. שׁוֹדְרָא) ropes, chains MG 169:17, Jb ii 197 n. 10. Parallel with **qulalia** Gs 9:9. **kma 'šdia šidiriata** Jb 204:7 how long must I place chains . . .? **hišlit šidiriata** Jb 205:11 I forged chains; **tartin šidiriata** RD 33, 36, 37 two chains; **šitin šidiriata** RD 29 sixty chains; **šidiriata d-dahba** RD 29 golden chains; **šidiriata šadibun bkulhun** RD 23 = DAb par. they fasten all of them with chains.

šidniaiil DAb an angel-name.

šidqa (rt. **ŠDQ**) silence, peace, calm, tranquillity MG 42:11. **šidqa bšuqia uṭulala šibqit 'lauaihun** DC 26. 592, 616 I let silence and shadow fall on the market-places; **ṣauma d-šidqa** Gy 356:14 a fast of silence; **niaha ušidqa** Gy 305:13 calm and peace. Often with **LGṬ** and **NṬR** 'to keep silence', 'hold peace': **lgaṭ šidqa** Jb 122:11, **šidqa lagṭia** DC 3 & CP 422:8; **šidqa nṭar** Gy 71:16, **šidqa niṭrit** Gy 158:20, 295:5, 296:14, **šidqa naṭar** Gy 71:11, **naṭar bšidqa** Jb 29:3, **šidqa naṭrin** Gy 75:23, **šidqa nṭir** Gy 235:19, **šidqa nṭirna** Gy 189:7, **šidqa nṭur** DC 50. 310.

šidra (rt. **ŠDR II**) twisting, spinning (by hand). **gdadia d-panba šidra d-'ma ubrata** DC 45 cotton threads (or cloths) spun by a mother and her daughter.

šidta often for **šita 2** (q.v.) year MG 52:1, 77:10, 98:2, 172:9. St. cstr. **šnat** s.v. Pl. **xxx** (')**šnia** s.v. **šidta d-rhaṭia** AM 288:15 f. the year of (i.e. beginning on a) Friday; **šidta d-habšaba** the year of (: beginning with) Sunday MMII 84, BZ 197 n. 7; **šidta hadita** Gy 228:7 New Year. Often.

ŠIH = **ŠUH.**

ših(a) **1** pass. pt. pe. of **ŠUH** (q.v.).

šiha 2 (rt. **ŠUH**) hot desire, lust, eagerness, concupiscence, lustfulness Jb ii 20 n. 6; lustful, eager. **arqa bšiha aqar** Gy 166:12 they uprooted the earth in (their) lustfulness Ginzā 172 n. 3; **šiha ubišuta** Q 72:3 greediness and evil; **rhamta d-šiha ušigra** Par. xxiv 11a, xxvii 30a, DC 46. 189:10 love that is fervent and burning; **šiha ušigra** Gy 28:1, 215:20 lust and burning; **šiha urhamta ušigra** Gy 24:9, cf. l. 18, **šihan ušigran** Gy 362:21 our lust and our burning; **zmara d-haršia ušiha** Gy 59:5 f. song of sorcery and lust; **haršia ušiha** Gy 225:9; **hamra d-šiha** Gy 6:18 wine of lust; **šiha uzmara** Gy 225:22 f.; **zmara d-šiha** DC 34. 546 lustful music; **ramia šiha balma 'l gubria uligia ušiha 'l 'nšia** Gy 59:11 she casteth lust in the world on men and stammering and lust on women; **mn šihaiun mn šagraiun šadin lmia** DC 37:13 they cast some of their lust and heat on the entrails; **hauma ušiha** Gy 59:16 heat and lust; **raza d-rhamta ušiha** Gy 111:22 the mystery of love and lust; **šiha utiha** Gy 258:6 f. lust and frivolity; **lruha plaglh šiha** Gy 112:5 f. to Ruha (= Venus) they allotted lust; **bšiha d-nisbh lruianh** Gy 116:8 f. in hot desire that occupied his mind; **šiha labišlun** Gy 225:7 they put on lust (: became lustful); **kinar šiha**

Gy 113:6, 187:18 lute of lust MG 309:23, cf. **kinar ušiha** Gy 225:2 (hendiadys); **nišbuqbh̲ šiha unura bgauh̲ d̲-hazin alma** Gy 361:17 f. we will let loose lust and fire in this world; **nirmia šiha uqublia balma** Gy 361:23 we will cast lust and fetters in the world; **hab šiha nišbuq ʿlh̲** Gy 369:13 f. let us loose lust on him; **šiha nisbit minh̲** Gy 91:3 f. I conceived eagerness against him; **bmalalia d̲-šiha bmalala šiha** Jb 239:13 f. with burning words, with passionate speech; **šiha amṭinun lmlakia ušiha amṭinun lalahia** DC 26. 164 f. burning (?) overtook the angels and burning (?) overtook the gods; **akla bšiha** DC 46. 254 she will eat greedily. Very often.

šihana 1 (adj. from **šiha** 2) lustful, greedy, passionate, enraged MG 137:14, Jb ii 20 n. 6. **aria šihana** Gy 282:6 ravening lion; **kalbia šihania** Jb 98:8, Gy 180:7 enraged dogs; **aurus šihana** Gy 59:5, 7 the lustful Oros (Lidzb. Orpheus).

***šihana 2** (rt. **ŠHN**, cf. **šahana**) ulcer. Pl. **šihania** Gy 84:13, MG 115:8.

šihana 3 occ. miscop. of **šihiana.**

šihura (שִׁיחוֹר, שִׁיחוּרָא) coal. **kd̲ šihura mn tapala** DC 40. 271 f. like coal from mud.

šihiana (Ar. شِحْنَة) governor, ruler MG 78:2. Pl. **-ia. gam šihiania uamiraiia uuaziraiia** DC 46. 167:3 for governors, princes, and ministers; **šihiana d̲-huuaiza** ATŠ coloph. the governor of Howeiza; **šihiana d̲-alma** Zotb. 227b:34 the ruler of the world.

Gl. 98:12 **šhiana** [sic] سلطنه *potestas* پادشاهي (*concretum pro abstracto*); 99:12 id. سلطان *imperator* پادشاه; 176:10 id. ولاية *dominium.*

šihianukta (mod. abstr. noun from preced.) Oxf. iii:coloph. governorship, rule MG 78:2.

ṣ̌ih(i)l, ṣ̌ihlana (Ar. جاهل) stupid, impertinent, arrogant. Fem. **ṣ̌ihiltia** JRAS 1943 170:16. Gl. 68:14 **ṣ̌ihl, ṣ̌ihlanai** [sic] جاهل *stultus.*

šihla 1 (rt. **ŠHL I**?) bottom, lowest part, end. **had qaiim briša d̲-dara uhad qaiim bmiṣai dara uhad qaiim bšihla d̲-dara** DC 51. 197 one stands at the beginning of the age and one stands in the middle of the age and one stands at the end of the age; **mn marba lmadna umn daria lšihlia** DC 43 J 67 from the west to the east and from (the beginning of?) ages to the(ir) ends (doubtf.).

šihla 2 (rt. **ŠHL I**) watercourse. **diglat šahla mn šihlh̲** Gs 88:12 s. **ŠHL I.**

šihlun (rt. **ŠHL II**, 'He–(i.e. the Life)–has–sent–me') Morg. 7:2, ML 242:14, 210, Gy 250:1 an uthra, cf. Jb ii 213:12. **šihlun ziua** CP 209:5, 226:6.

šihma (rt. **ŠHM**) AM 171:17, 179:6, 182:1 parching heat, sultriness.

šihqa (rt. **ŠHQ**) DC 23. 177, 205 vexation, anxiety.

šihrilia (cf. **šahrial(a)**) Gy 386:1 pl. rulers, potentates. ATŠ I no. 335.

šiuai a *malwāša* man's name.

šiuṭa (rt. **ŠUṬ I**) scorn, contempt, neglect. **bianquth̲ šiuṭa** (var. **šiṭa** Par. xxvi) **nihuilh̲** AM 81 in his youth he will be treated with contempt (neglect).

šiul (H. שְׁאוֹל, Syr. ܫܝܘܿܠ) Jb 56:9, 114:2 ff. Sheol, underworld, the world of the dead. Var. **ʿšiul** (s.v.) MG xxix 10. Fem. MG 159:20, cf. **šiul titaita** Jb 196:13 the lowest Sheol. Used always in st. abs. as a pr. n. MG 301:5, 305:8.

šiuta (rt. **ŠAA II**) smoothness, comeliness, beauty. **baba d̲-rhamta ualgiṭ bšiuta** DC 46. 234:11 (it is) a love-charm and preserves beauty.

ṣ̌izaiir (Ar. جزاير) DC 12. 336, DC 43 A coloph. = **šizira** (Ar. جزيرة) AM 205 the Jezira, Upper Mesopotamia BZ Ap. II.

šiṭa 1 Gs 20:4 D a var. of **šiaṭa** (q.v.).

šiṭa 2, pl. **-ia.** pass. pt. pe. of **ŠUṬ** (q.v.).

šiṭuta (rt. **ŠUṬ = ŠṬA I**) scorn, contempt, neglect, spoliation, shameful thing or deed. Pl. **šiṭuata** follies, shameful things or deeds MG 146:5, 167:15, nakedness Ginzā 132 n. 8. **alahia bšiṭuta nihun** AM 220:4 the gods will be held in contempt (neglected); **šiṭuta lmdiniata titia** AM 178:13 spoliation will come to the cities; **galiltinun lšiṭuath̲** Gy 118:19 I revealed his shameful parts; **šauith̲ d̲-šiṭuata balma** Gy 118:22 f. I made him despicable in the world Ginzā 133 n. 1; **siṭraiin primlin lšiṭuata** Gy 181:3 f. they (fem.) lay bare their flanks for shameful deeds; **hadiaiin mgalailin lšiṭuata** Gy 225:13 they denude their breasts in libertinism; **kulhin šiṭuata** Gy 218:1; **šiṭuata kulhin** Gy 234:9 all (kinds of) follies; **šiṭuata d̲-napšaiun laiadia** Gy 224:6 f. they know not their own follies; **šiṭuatun** Gy 119:6, 8, 121:21, 222:14, Gs 21:16 etc. their follies (abominations); **šiṭuata d̲-šiṭia lkana d̲-nišmata d̲-ašiṭuia** Gy 231:19 shameful follies to which they (: the planets) seduce the Congregation of Souls; **šiṭuata d̲-abad balma** Gy 231:21 the follies which he committed in the world; **kasun šiṭuatun** Gy 242:10 they covered their nakedness (sexual organs); **bšiṭuata laništun** Gy 240:17 they shall commit no follies; **šuta . . . d̲-šiṭuata mištaiia** Gy 253:19 f. speaketh the speech of follies; **šiṭuata d̲-tibil** Gy 246:4 follies of the earthly world; cf. **šiṭuata d̲-hauian barqa d̲-tibil** ATŠ I no. 93; **šiṭuata d̲-ruha umšiha** Gy 254:10 abominations of Ruha and Christ; **šiṭuata d̲-namrus** Gy 300:15 abominations of Namrus (= Ruha); **ʿuzarh̲ lšiṭuath̲** Gy 382:9 his helpers in shameful deeds; **šiṭuata bnpiš nʿbidubak** (var. **nibidubak, nibidulak**) Gs 2:17, 3:1, 4:7 they may commit many follies on thee; **nipšan šiṭuata d̲-hšuka** ATŠ I no. 253 numerous are the shameful deeds of the Darkness; **šiṭuata unsisuta** AM 242:19 follies and grief.

šiṭia 1 (rt. **ŠṬA I = ŠUṬ I**) folly, foolishness MG 167:15. **šiṭuata d̲-šitia** Gy 231:19 s. **šiṭuata; šiṭia ramibh̲ balma** (often in Gy) casteth folly into the world.

šiṭia 2 pl. of **šiṭa** 2.

šiiaṭa s. **šiaṭa.**

šiik (Ar. شيخ) AM 256:91 f. Sheykh.

šikar (P. شِكَر) AM 287:17 sugar. Var. **šikir** DC 46. 232:1.

šikna (ܫܟܢܐ < Akk. *šiknu* Jb ii 52 n. 4) mire, filth, mud, faeces. **napla bšikna umištikna** Jb 47:1 falls into mire and is stuck there.

šikṣa (rt. ŠKṢ) small quantity, a little. **šikṣa d̲-barnia** DC 24, Oxf. roll f 158 s. **barnia.**

ṣ̌ila (P. چِلّه) bowstring. **iatira d̲-qašta d̲-hu šila** (var. **ṣ̌ila**) DC 44.

šilai Jb 67:13, 74:12 an (otherwise) unknown Jewish name Jb ii 76 n. 5.

šilam DAb a var. of **šišlam** cf. 38 n. 5; also a name given to Sin, cf. 40 n. 6.

šilbai Jb 74:12 = **šalbai** Jb 67:13.

šilia (rt. ŠLA I) peace, calm, ease; with **mn** adverbially: all of a sudden, suddenly, unexpectedly, instantly. **bisra d̲-šilia latikul** AM 60:2 she will not eat meat of ease (bread of idleness); **šilia ukauna** AM 243:13 calm and stability; **mn šilia** Gy 21:9, AM 17:17 suddenly, unexpectedly.

šilmai (Nöld. from H. שְׁלָמִים MG xxix:15, ZA xxx 156, Lidzb. from the name of the Phoen. god שלמן, *Σελαμάνης* ZDMG lxi 691, cf. Brandt: *Die Mandäer* 22 n. 2, Rosenthal AF 242 & nn. 7, 8) one of the pair of guardian spirits of running water, the other being **nidbai** (q.v.). **šilmai unidbai** Gy 125:14, 127:19, Gy 131:11, 285:5, 286:8, 322:9, 374:16, Q 7:6, 14, 8:33, 9:20, 15:18, 21:5, 26:29, 39:10, 40:9, PD 938, 963, Oxf. 35 b; **šilmai . . . unidbai** Q 63:22, Gy 308:9, 16, 309:8, 24, 310:7; **šilmai unidbai ʿutria trin** CP 15:ult., Q 59:32; **šilmai unidbai marh̲ d̲-iardna** Q 62:21, 63:1; **šilmai gabra ganzibra** Gs 8:9; **šilmai marh̲ d̲-baita** Gy 196:14, 197:2, 8, 21 ff.; **šilmai malka** Gy 383:12. Often (esp. in rituals) (see CP index).

šima (rt. ŠMA) hearing MG 102:11. **ʿmra ušima** (*often*) speech and hearing.

šimai(i)a = **šumai(i)a 2** (q.v.). Fem. **šimaita. iumia d̲-šimaiia** PD 1705; **iumia šimaiia** PD 1723 (cf. s. **šumaiia 2**); **aiar šimaita** DC 27. 172 ether is heavenly; **d̲-šimaiia šumh̲** DC 48. 51 whose name is 'Heavenly'.

šimbilta = **šumbilta** MG 14:2.

šimukṭia, šamuktia s.

šmiṭia var. DC 22. 225 **šimṭia** pl. (rt. ŠMṬ, cf. Ar. شَمِيط of mixed colours) Gy 231:1 dresses of mixed colours?, Lidzb. *Schleppkleider* Ginzā 231 n. 6. Doubtf.

šimʿa Zotb. 226b:20 a man's name.

šin (P. چين) AM 199 China, porcelain.

šina 1 (שִׁנָּא, ܫܢܐ, H. שֵׁן, Ar. سِنّ, Eth. ስን, Akk. *šinnu*) tooth; fig. peak, spike. Pl. **šinia.** Fem. MG 157:ult. **šina minh̲ niplat** ATŠ I no. 133 a tooth fell (out) from him; **kakia ušinia** Gy 279:paen., Or. 328:16 molars and tusks (teeth); **kiba d̲-šinia** DC 46. 128:13 toothache; **ušinh̲ hariq** DC 43 E 9 and (he) grinds his teeth; **ʿniš d̲-šinh̲ bihdadia mahia** DC 46. 85:2 one whose teeth strike (= chatter) together; **lšina d̲-ṭura qaiimna** DC 46. 153:6 I stand on the peak of the mountain.

šina 2 = **šai(a)na. šlama ušina** AM peace and tranquillity.

šinarta (fem. of **šunara**) DC 46. 192:7 she-cat.

šingdunia (Talm. שִׁנְדּוּנָא = שִׁגְרוּנָא) Oxf. roll g 871, Or. 330:13 f. hip-disease.

šingilan name of an ʿuthra **malka š. ʿutra** CP 140(d) 9, Jb 9, 16; 229, 19.

ṣ̌inub (Ar. جنوب) AM 275:10 south.

šinia 1 pl. of **šina.**

ṣ̌inia 2 (P. چينى, adj. from **ṣ̌in**) AM 287:3 Chinese.

šinia 3 Oxf. 14 a = CP 155:5, ML 186:9, cf. n. 4, and CP trs. 116:2 before the transmutation (?) of the watersprings.

šinsa AM 204 name of a town (cf. **šanz**).

šinta (שִׁינְתָא, ܫܢܬܐ, H. שֵׁנָה, Akk. *šittu*) sleep MG 52 n. 1, 111:7. **šintai** my sleep MG 176:16; **šintan** our sleep MG 178:antep.; **šintun** CP 148:12, Oxf. 38 b their sleep; **šinta kadirtia** Jb 44:13 heavy sleep; **mšania babia d̲-šinta** Gy 186:12 he changeth the gates of sleep; **šinta lamitiairia škibiun** DC 34. 776 they slept the sleep that is not to be awakened; **akuat šinta d̲-parṭa mn ainh̲** DC 43 J 157 like sleep which departeth from his eyes; **šinta hambaga nišimtaihun** DC 34. 777 sleep is the enemy of their souls; **ulabšinta ulabtirata** DC 43 neither in sleep nor in waking.

šiʿir (Ar. شِعر) Par. xxvi 181 song MG 2:7.

šipan RD 9 = DAb place on the arrow into which the bow-string is fitted (nock).

šipula (rt. ŠPL, ܫܘܦܠܐ) (*a*) skirt, hem, lower part of skirt, (*b*) sexual parts, lower part of abdomen. MG 125:ult. Pl. **-ia.** (*a*) **ligṭuia bšipulh̲** Jb 73:8 they seized him by the skirt; **dirun bšipulun** Jb 127:8 they carried me in their skirts; **šipulh̲ mgargilh̲** Gy 208:6 s. **GRGL**; **ʿl kulhun iamamia šipulh̲** Gs 27:17 his hem is over all the seas; **šipulh̲ bʿda lgiṭlh̲** DC 46. 191:7 he took her skirt in his hand; **kanipiun šipulaikun** DC 50 gather up your skirts; (*b*) **šipulia** of man and woman Lond. roll B 148 ff.; **šipula niṭrat** Q 61:6; **niṭrat šipula** Q 69:27 she preserved her chastity; **šipulia sriqia hauilh̲** Jb 85:7 she will have torn skirts (sexual parts) cf. Jb ii 91 n. 1; **hiduktia d̲-bza razia d̲-šipulh̲** ATŠ I no. 82 a bride whom he deflowered; **ʿl šip(u)lia d̲-atuat ladriklia** Gs 5:4 f., 15 f., 6:12 he had no sexual intercourse with a woman; **ligṭat šipulh̲** Jb 107:5 she preserveth her chastity.

šipulta (rt. ŠPL) lowest part, latter end, decadence. Var. **špulta** s.v. **šipulta udnabta d̲-alma** DC 27 the decadence and end of the world.

šipura (שִׁפּוּרָא, ܫܝܦܘܪܐ, doublet **šupra 2**) trumpet MG 126:5. Pl. **-ia. qarnia ušipuria** Gy 60:5 horns and trumpets; **šipuria uambubia** Gy 105:8 trumpets and flutes; **mamllibh̲ bšipuria** Gy 113:10 they speak therein with trumpets.

šipla = **šipula**, cf. **šiplia** Gs 5:4, 15 = **šipulia** (s. **šipula** (*b*)), **šiplh̲ bʿdh lgaṭlh̲** DC 45 (cf. s. **šipula** (*a*)).

ŠIṢ s. **ŠUṢ.**

šiqana DC 46. 206:14 read **šidana.**
šiquata (rt. **ŠQA**) Gy 106:16, 107:5 cupbearers.
šiqupta = **šuqupta.** Pl. **š(i)qupiata,** cf. s. **šqupiata.** MG 119:11. **mihita ušiqupta** Gy 237:14 blow and affliction; **šiqupta urikša** AM 186:7 assault and (war-)cavalry; **qiria ušiqupta baqnia** AM 170:5 accidents and murrain amongst sheep; **šiqupta umutana** DC 40. 234 f. plague and pestilence; **šiqupta ḏ-baqiata** s. **baqiata 1**; **šiqupiata ḏ-hauin bkul zban** CP 484:3 the blows which occur all the time.
šiqlun ('They–removed–me') Gy 317:6 name of a demon?
šiqra (rt. **ŠQR,** שִׁקְרָא, H. שֶׁקֶר) lie, falsehood, deceit MG 20:1. **qrita ḏ-šiqra** Gy 120:10 deceitful creatures; **pihtḥ . . . lspihatḥ ḏ-šiqra** Jb 67:1, 69:3 he opened . . . his lips of falsehood; **šqul mn arqa . . . šiqra** DC 44. 1242 remove . . . falsehood from earth; **haslḥ lpuma ḏ-nimar šiqra** DC 46. 171:5 heaven prevent his mouth from uttering a lie.
šira 1 AM 22 for **šura 2** navel.
šira 2 (as still used with a double *r* in vernacular pronunciation with the meaning 'quarrel' and 'war' it would represent a natural semantic development of Ar. شِرَّة 'angriness', Lane 1525, 1st col., cf. also **šura 5** [M]; E.S.D. doubts the originality of this pronunciation and suspects a derivation from **ŠRA** [cf. **pira** from **PRA**]) injustice, corruptness, wickedness > quarrel, fight, war (M); dissolution, licence (D). **mirda ušira** AM 184:13 rebellion and fighting; **šira rba nihuia uhdadia nipilgun . . . uniharbun** AM 184:14 f. there will be a great war and they will part from each other . . . and fight; **šira ukṣurta** AM 267:25 war and affliction; **gama ušira** AM 254:11 (Ar. غمّ وشرّ M); **pitna ušira** AM 263:5 (Ar. فتنة وشرّة M); **šira banašia nihuia umalka nimut** AM 264:11 there will be fighting amongst people and a king will die; **mutana ušira** AM 269:ult. mortality and war.
šira 3 (cf. **mšara**) inhabited district, zone, land. **napqia gabaria lšira ḏ-magrib** AM 282:32 mighty men (of war) will set out for a western zone; **bšar šira ḏ-arqa** s. **šar 3.**
širaz (شيراز) AM 198 Shiraz.
širana = **širiana** or (from שִׁיר) poetry, music. **ulzmar šria, širanai ubazirai** PA xii and loose (from spells) my music and my seed.
širasp Gy 391:17 a king of ancient Īrān.
širba (שִׁרְבָא, H. שָׁרָב, cf. Ar. شراب *Fata Morgana*) dry heat, dryness, aridity MG 107: 11. **uazal bširba rhiṭiun** Gy 366:8 they went and ran in dry heat.
širu DC 22. 330 (& Lond.) var. of **širiu** (q.v.).
širupt AM 202 name of a town.
širiana 1 (ܫܪܝܢܐ I, Ar. loan.-w. شِرْيان, Akk. *šer(ḫ)ānu.* (*a*) vein, artery, membrane, fibre, (*b*) fig. channel, flow, river, (*c*) fig. tendency, inclination MG 136:12, MSchr. 138 n. 8, Jb ii 99 n. 6, Ginzā 182 n. 2. Pl. **-ia.** Masc. (*a*) **tlatma ušitin ušita širiania** Lond. roll B 227 (cf. Siouffi 149); **mipta širiana** Par. xxvi 129:middle, 186:bottom = AM par. to open a vein (let blood); **ʿsir širianḥ ḏ-mqardin mn murqa** JRAS 1943 170:28 s. **murqa**; **širianḥ ḏ-sindirka** DC 34. 1283 palm-tree fibres; (*b*) **širiana ḏ-mia** Jb 271:3, 272:3; **širiana ḏ-mia ḏ-arqa ḏ-hšuka** Gy 75:8; **širiana ḏ-hšuka** Gy 83:21 f., 151:12; **širiana ḏ-aina rabtia** Q 21:18; **širiana ḏ-arqa siniauis** Gy 74: 18 f.; **širiana rba ḏ-arqa ḏ-aiar** Gy 178:18; **tana uširiana** Gy 134:16 (doubtf.); (*c*) **lʿuṣriḥ . . . ulširianḥ** DC 46. 139:4 his mind . . . and inclination.
širiana 2 (שִׁרְיָנָא & שִׁרְיוֹנָא, ܫܪܝܢܐ II, H. שִׁרְיוֹן, Ar. سلاح ?, Ass. *sirịām*, Bab. *širịām* Zimmern: *Akk. Fremdwörter* 12) cuirass, coat of mail, armour. **lagṭit bširianḥ ḏ-qumta ḏ-gubḥ** DC 43 I 80 I grasped his armour in which there was his body.
širiana 3 (rt. **ŠRA**) loosening, exorcism, liberation, solution, emanation. **širiana ḏ-saka litlḥ** Jb 98:13, Gy 301:1 (doubtf., Lidzb. *Auflösung* Jb ii 99:20, but *Ader* Ginzā 298:11); **qupla rba ḏ-širiana** DC 26. 154 a great lance of exorcism; **širiana ḏ-kapur** DC 46. 125:8 solution of camphor; **hua mn qudam briša ḏ-ʿtiqria hua briš širiana** DC 40. 290 he was from aforetime, in the beginning of the creation, at the head of the emanation.
širiata 1 pl. (rt. **ŠRA**) (*a*) loosings, freeings, counterspells, exorcisms, (*b*) deconsecration (prayer). Pl. of **šrita** (q.v.). Jb ii 242 n. 2. (*a*) **narga rba ḏ-širiata** Morg. 195:7, 258/7:1 f., 259/9:3, Oxf. roll g 26 f., 72, 239 f., 294 f., 323 f., DC 43 J 11 (*& often in magic documents*) the great axe of exorcisms; pl. **nargia rurbia ḏ-širiata** Morg. 194:3, 195:13 f., **narga rba širiata ʿl qudamai šaria** Jb 273:15 f. the great axe of exorcisms freeing (the way) before me (Lidzb. literally *das Lösungen vor mir löst*); **asaria uširiata** Q 48:1 bonds and liberations; **malalun ḏ-širiata** Morg. 269/39:28 the words of exorcisms; **širiata ḏ-šrit** Morg. 270/ 30:6 exorcisms which thou hast made; (*b*) **ʿniana ḏ-širiata ḏ-taga** Oxf. 113 b responsory of the deconsecration of the crown; **latimrun mindam mn širiata ltagaikun** DC 50 do not repeat any of the deconsecrating prayers for your crown; **kḏ amritun nihušta ušarit širiata** DC 27 when ye have said the whispered prayers and thou hast repeated the deconsecrating prayers, cf. **šarit mindam mn širiata** Q 46:30.
širiata 2 pl. (of שִׁרִיתָא) acc. to Lidzb. 'beams, planks' (*Balken*), ML 98:4 (cf. n. 1); 'loosings', 'exorcisms' E.S.D. (CP trs. 58).
širiata 3 Jb 163:2 doubtf. (perh. 1 (*a*)?).
širiu Gy 384:13, var. **širu** (s.v.) name of a Persian king (beginning of his rule A.D. 628) Ochser ZA xix 79 n. 1, Ginzā 412 n. 2, MG 425 n. 1.
širša (Syr. ܫܪܫܐ, Jew.-Aram. שׁוּרְשָׁא, Chr.-Pal. ܫܘܪܫܐ, H. שֹׁרֶשׁ, Akk. *šuršu*) root, tribe, family, kin, kind, genus; (of water) fount, fountain-head, source MG 13:18, 20:2. Var. **šarša** s.v. Sometimes with religious meaning

(**širša taqna**) referring to Mandaean faith, race or stock, community, orthodox literature etc. HG trs. 11 n. 1. Masc. Pl. **-ia.** **huat mn širšh̲** Gy 145:17 she was from her kin; **širša nṣiba** Gy 79:1 the root (firmly) planted; **širša rba d̲-birkta** Gy 319:6 the great root of benediction; **širšak** Gy 359:8, Gs 59:18, Oxf. 70 a, Lond. roll A 128, Oxf. roll f 1361 etc., thy root, family, origin; **širša d̲-hiia** Gy 107:13 the Root of Life; **saka uširša** DC 51. 165 its end and its origin; **širša uṭuhma uniaka** Gy 143: 14, **širša uniaka** Gy 202:3 (s. **niaka 1**); **širšh̲ kana d̲-nišmata** Gs 37:19 its root is the Congregation of souls; **širša d̲-ab** Gs 71:6 the root (: family) of my father; **širša d̲-hšuka** Gy 316: 15 the root of the Darkness; **širša taqna** Gy 290:27, 317:23 (*& often*) cf. above; **minaiun bširša nasqun** Gy 326:7 some of them will ascend with the root (*idiom*: radically, fundamentally, altogether, to the utmost), cf. **kd̲ ʿmarlak bširša** DC 41. 531 as was told thee radically, and Jb 129:8; **širša d̲-mia hiia** Oxf. 86 b fount of living water; **mipsiq širšh̲ mn almia d̲-nhura** Gy 54:5 his root shall be cut off from the worlds of Light; **širšan utuqnan** Gy 310:3 our root and our stability; **širšaiun ušurbatun** Gy 286:18 their kin and their family; **mn širšaiun** Gy 295:2; **širšia d̲-nhura** Gy 62:12 the roots (: sources) of the light.

šiša (שִׁישָׁא, ܫܝܫܐ, H. שַׁיִשׁ, Akk. *šaššu* alabaster, P. شیشه Lagarde: *Abhandlungen* 83:222) bottle, phial. Masc. **šiša d̲-miša** Q 43:26, ATŠ I no. 248, II no. 160 the phial of oil; **šiša hadta dakia** CP 93:1, Q 44:20 new clean phial; **puma d̲-šiša** CP 92:9 the mouth of the bottle. Often in rituals, cf. Q 45:7 ff.

šišlam (hypocoristic šaf. of **ŠLM**) lit. 'consummated perfection' name of Adam Kasia as Perfect Man, anointed and crowned Priest and Bridegroom. Coron., ML 284, MMII 72 n. 3, 271 n. 3. **šišlam rba** CP 25:11, 140 (*c*):11 and n. 2, 143:14, 140 (*h*):15, 340:6, 16, etc. (see CP Index); RD B 99, Lond. roll A 4, 333, RD 87 ff., 310, 832, Q 10:18, Oxf. 96 b, 97 ab f., 101 b, ML 28:3, 264 ff., Morg. 112:5, Oxf. roll f 52 etc., **malka šišlam rba** Morg. 4:6, ML 171:2, **tarmida šišlam rba** PD 68, **šarh̲ d̲-qabin d̲-šišlam** s. **šarh̲**; **šišlam malka d̲-tagia** PD 1015, **taga nhira šišlam** PD 1004; **lbuša d̲-šišlam gupna** RD 10; **šišlam** = **sin** RD 1.

šišlamʿil var. **šašlamʿil** (theophorous name from preced.) CP 365:2 (CP trs. 240 n. 4), Oxf. roll f 1180, 1182, Oxf. 99a b, 100 b, 101 a, 105 a, 109 b = ML 266:6, 9, 267:4 ff., 270:6, 274:6, 8 name given to the (personified) ritual banner.

šit fem., **šita 1** masc. (שִׁית, ܫܬ, H. שֵׁשׁ, Ar. ستّ, Akk. fem. *šiššit* Brockelmann i 486) six MG 187:.ult.

šita 2 (ܫܢܬܐ Nöld. *Neue Beiträge* 124, Akk. *šattu*) a more original but sporadic form of **šidta** (q.v.) year MG 52:1, 98:2. St. cstr. & pl. s. **šidta** (& s.vv.). **šita d̲-habšaba** Zotb. 231a: 20 the year of Sunday (cf. s. **šidta**). **šita upalga d̲-šita** DC 44. 1850 year and half-year.

šita 3 (שַׁעְתָּא, ܫܥܬܐ, Ar. ساعة, Eth. ሰዐት Nöld. *Neue Beiträge* 44, Can. *šēti* Amarna 138:76) hour MG 16:16, 110:13, 172:12. Pl. **šaiia 2** s.v. **šita šaiia (d̲-)purqana** s. **šaiia 2**; **bšita qadmaita** DC 44. 1098 at the first hour.

šita 4 = **ašita. kd̲ libna bšita** DC 40. 344 like a brick in the wall.

šitaia (adj. from **sita 1**) sixth MG 192:5.

šitasar (Talm. שיתסר, Syr. ܫܬܥܣܪ) sixteen. Orig. masc. form MG 188:17. Special fem. form **asar ušit** MG 189:6.

šitil (Biblical שֵׁת III, ending on the analogy of **hibil**) Seth, Adam's son MR 124, ML 284; used also as a *malwâša* man's name. **hibil ušitil uanuš** (often in CP, see CP Index) Q 60:11, Gy 357:8 (Siouffi 39:16), **hibil ušitil uanuš ʿutra** Gy 101:25, **anuš** and **šitil** RD 42; **šitil rba** Gy 272:2, 23, PD 1259 ff.; **šitil br adam d̲-qaiim bmuzania** RD 51 (cf. Siouffi 42:top); **šitil šitla ṭaba** Gy 108:10 (s. **šitla**); **šitil naṭar dara** Gy 319:2. As Ptahil's son and keeper of a purgatory: **maṭarta d̲-sitil brh̲ d̲-ptahil** RD C 15, 17.

šitin sixty MG 189:14. **masiqta d̲-šitin** CP 95:6, ML 121:12 the *masiqta* of sixty (*faṭiria*); **šitin masqata** ML 121:13 sixty *masiqtas*; **šitin uhda** Gy 317:17 ff., 321:14 f.; **šitin uhda lbuša** Gy 348:5 sixty-one garments; **šitin uhda ʿsura** Gy 348:23 f. sixty-one bonds.

šitla (rt. **ŠTL**) plant, child. Pl. **-ia** plants, offspring. **šitil šitla ṭaba** Gy 108:10 Seth, the good child; **šitlia ništal** (*often*) he will have children; **trin šitlia zikria** ŠQ 5:15[20] two male children; **šitlia d̲-šišlam rba** PD 9 offspring of the Great Šišlam; **šitlia tahmia** Gy 375:14 polluted offspring.

šitlan ('He–planted–me') name of a supernatural being represented with a banner; also a *malwâša* man's name; **drabša d̲-šitlan** RD 1 Šitlan's banner.

šitluia ('He- (i.e. the Life)-planted–him) RD D 21 a supernatural being.

šitma six hundred MG 190:2.

ŠKA I (< Aram. שְׁכַח, ܐܫܟܚ af.) af. to find, discover, acquire, attain; refl. to be present, be at hand, in the possession of. The more orig. form **ŠKH** (q.v.) is sporadic. The rigid form **lʿška** = **liška** and **laniška** only in the idiomatic 'to be (un)able': **laniška d̲-nimar** Gy 11:11 we are unable to say; **kulhun lʿška laqumh̲** Gy 101:15 they could not raise him; **lʿška lazlin** Gy 388:10 they cannot go; **liška labid** Gy 391:23 he cannot do; **lʿška mṣinin bhailaihun** Gy 271:14 we cannot equal them in force; **laiit d̲-lʿška pasqilh̲ lmia** Gy 283:20 no one can cut off water; also **lʿška d̲-** Gy 11:15, 365:24, Gs 61:24, MG 434 f.

Af. Pf. **aška** he, they found MG 64:17 f., 234:20, **hiia aška dilun uaškat nišmat d̲-msakia** CP 133:18 f. = ML 163:4 the Life found His own and my soul found what she expected, but cf. Gs 38:1, 78:11, 90:9 & ML 61 n. 2, **hiia d̲-nafšai aškit** CP 40:11 I found the life of myself; **aškit** MG 3:20, 64:21, 235:5; **aškit mn gabaria** (var. **abaria**?) **d̲-šumia** DC 44. 1404 (var. Morg. 265/21:18) I found some mighty ones of the heavens; **ʿzlit nišmat**

aškit Gy 367:15 I went (and) found my soul (cf. the frequent **aškit nišmat** as a var. of **aškat nišmat** above); **aškun** Gy 381:19 they found MG 237:16; **aškanin, aškinin** Q 22:12 we found MG 64:22, 235:10, 237:1, 3; **aškatun** MG 64:21, 235:9; **laškatun** Jb 59:5 ye have not attained; with suff. **aškh̲** he found him MG 275:9; **aškinun** he found them MG 281:22; **aškitinun, aškatinun** Gy 80:18 (*& often*) I found them MG 282:ult. Impf. **naška** MG 235:14; **kul d̲-baiia mn hiia naška** ATŠ II no. 43 all that he seeks from the Life he will find; **taška** thou findest MG 235:16, 226:paen.; **uaška** [*sic*] Oxf. 59 b and I find (for uʿiaška) MG 235:17 f.; **taškun** MG 235:20; with suff. **naškunh̲** they (will) find him MG 278:16; **kul zban d̲-tibunan taškunan** Gy 260:ult. every time ye seek me ye shall find me. Pt. **maška** MG 4:2, 9:20, 236:7; pl. **maškia, maškin** MG 149:23. Part. pres. **maškit** thou findest MG 236:20; **maškinin** we find MG 236:24; **maškitun** Gy 233:12.

Ethpe. Pf. **ʿštka luatak dilak** Gy 147:21 was found with thee; **d̲-štikat** ML 61:1 that was there. Impf. with encl. **ništkalun lšuba bmnatun** Gy 377:15 f. shall be found as a portion for the Seven.

Ettaf. Pt. **mitaška** is found MG 132:22, 236:11.

Der.: **(a)škita 1.**

ŠKA II (Ar. شكا, but cf. MG 104 n. 1) to complain, lament, cry, cf. Gl. 23:13 f., 132:7 f.

Pe. Pf. **škitun ubkitun** DC 21 ye lamented and wept.

Af. Pf. **aškun** Gy 381:19 they complained MG 104 n. 1 (Lidzb. *sie müßten erdulden* Ginzā 410 n. 4 doubtf.).

Der.: **(a)škita 2, škikta.**

škat dauan AM 199:1 (& varr.) a town in the climate of Venus.

ŠKB (Aram. & H. שכב, Syr. ܫܟܒ, cf. Akk. *sakāpu* Jensen KB vi 306, Eth. ሰከበ, but Ar. سكب trans. to pour out, cf. also Barth WÜ 32) to lie down, sleep, lie with (sexual).

Pe. Pf. **lagna ulaškub** (var. **ulaškib**) Jb 44:13 (var. DC 30) lay not down and slept not (MG 218:12, 219:13); **škib luat ruha** Gy 94:16 he lay with Ruha; **šikbit** thou didst sleep MG 232:12. Impf. **niškub** MG 219:13, 226:15; **luat zauh̲ laniškub** ATŠ I no. 14 he shall not lie with his wife. Impt. **škub, ʿškub** MG 219:13, 229:5; **ʿškub luat ʿmak** Gy 94:14 lie with thy mother. Act. pt. **šakaba d̲-šakib** Gy 218:14 the sleeper that sleepeth; **adam d̲-šakib** (better **d̲-škib** C) **ʿtar** Jb 52:6 f. A. who was sleeping awoke (cf. MG 218:12); **kul arsa d̲-šakib ʿlh̲** DC 43 D 56 and every bed upon which one sleeps; fem. **d̲-šakba luat gabra** JRAS 1939 401:23 one (fem.) who lies with a man; pl. **luat hdadia šakbia** Gy 23:21 they lie with one another (are homosexual); **ʿnšia d̲-bdaštanin hanin bhana gubria šakbia** Gy 23:21 f. those women who are in menstruation sleep in the embrace of men; **arba razia d̲-lašakbian** (read **-bia**) DC 34. 722 four unsleeping mysteries. Part. pres. **šakbitun ulaiit matrana d̲-mitarlkun** DC 34. 704 ye sleep and there is no awakener to wake you up. Pass. pt. **škiba** sleeping, asleep MG 116:15; pl. **razia d̲-škibia atartinun** DC 41. 426 thou hast awakened the dormant mysteries; **ʿtariun razia d̲-škibia** DC 34 the dormant mysteries awoke. Inf. **miškab baiia** Jb 106:ult. f. he wishes to sleep; **traṣlun lmiškab** Gy 243:20 they put them up for sleeping (gave them a bed to sleep on); with suff. **ʿl mišiliak** (var. **lmišlak** DC 30) **uʿl miš(i)kbak** Jb 246:9 f. at thy resting and thy lying down (MG 177:7); **ʿl mišlaikun uʿl mišikbaikun** Gy 17:18, 37:11 at your resting and your lying down. Nom. ag. **šakaba** s.v.

Af. Impf. with suff. **naškbun** Gs 58:8 they let me sleep MG 273:5.

Der.: **šakaba, škibta.**

ŠKH a more orig. but sporadic form of **ŠKA I** (q.v.).

Pe. Pass. pt.: with a prosthetic a and pers. ending **bnahlia d̲-bgauaihun aškihit** Or. 331:17 f. by the ravines in which thou art found; **ʿsiqth̲ škiha** Gy 217:7 his seal-ring is to hand (ready for use, Ginzā 218 n. 1).

škibta (rt. **ŠKB**, pass. pt. fem. st. emph.?) lying down, rest(ing). **arqa škibta titib** AM 238:3 the earth settles down into repose.

škihta ATŠ no. 234, for **škita 2**, complaint.

škinaṣar (< **škina** + **ʿuṣar**) CP 29:13 f., Q 12:26 = ML 35:2 a spirit of light ML 283.

škinta (Jew. שְׁכִינָה, Syr. ܡܫܟܢܐ) (*a*) habitation, dwelling, abode, celestial dwelling MG 52:5, 117:21, MSchr. 9 n. 3, Jb ii 5 n. 2, Ginzā 7 n. 4, (*b*) name given to the cult-hut ML 250 n. 1, MMII 152 f., Furlani: *I Termini* 352 f., (*c*) site, situation, position. St. cstr. **škinat.** Pl. **škinata.** (*a*) **škintai** my dwelling MG 176:17; **škintak** thine abode MG 177:4; **škintik** Gy 220:14 thy (fem.) dwelling MG 177:19; **škinth̲** MG 178:1, **škintan** MG 178:antep.; **bha škinta haza rabtia** Gy 257:17 in this great dwelling, cf. **bh̲ bškinta haza** l. 19 MG 331:13 f.; **škinta škan** Oxf. 32 a he founded a (celestial) dwelling; **škinata d̲-škinbin** Gy 3:21 (celestial) dwellings in which He dwelleth; **škinta bgu škinta** Gy 235:16, 22 a dwelling within a dwelling; **binia škinata tlat** Oxf. 32 a between three (celestial) dwellings; **tlat škinata** Q 63:7, Gy 130:5, 373:10; **škinat ʿutria** Gy 106:21 the abode of uthras; **škinta d̲-adam** RD B 33 A.'s abode; **škinta qadmaita** RD B 31 the first abode; **škinta d̲-ptahil** Gs 92:16 f.; **škinta d̲-abatur** Gs 92:23 = **škinat abatur** Q 4:24; **škinat hibil ušitil uanuš** Q 4:25; **škinat arba gubria** Q 4:23; **škinat hiia** Q 4:22; **škintun d̲-trin ṭuria dakiia** Gy 106:23; **škinata d̲-atar atar** Gy 314:2 dwellings of various places; **škinata d̲-šibiahia** Gy 196:18 dwellings of the planets; **ruban ruban škinata** Gy 69:5, 7 myriads and myriads of dwellings; **škinata titaiata** Gy 54:3 lower abodes; **tlatma ušitin ušit škinata . . . qra mn kul škinta škinta** Gy 128:16 f. three hundred and sixty-six dwellings . . . he called out from every dwelling . . .; **škinata** parallel with **ʿutria** Gs 13:7, parallel with **alma** Gy 70 f., cf. **lika škinata**

ulika d̲-alma Gy 93:22 there are no dwellings and no world, cf. Gy 94:2; **šauit škinata l'utria** Gy 93:14 f. I made dwellings for the uthras; **škinata** Gy 128:15 f., 23 f., 129:1, 3, 136:15, 199:21 ff. and very often; (*b*) Often in rituals; (*c*) **škinat liba uškinat girmia uškinat širiania uškinat marba halin arba škinata** DC 34 the site of the heart, site of the bones, situation of the veins, the site of the womb: these four sites.

škipt diuan AM 204:13 f. name of a town.

škiṣa (pass. pt. pe. of **ŠKṢ**) spare, meagre, lean. Pl. **-ia.** **škiṣia šaqih̲** AM 8:14, Par. xxvi 262:middle = AM par. his legs are lean.

škita 1 = **aškita 1** (q.v.).

škita 2 = **aškita 2.** **bkita uškita** Gs 7:13; **'lita uškita** DC 22. 175 = **'lita uaškita** Gy 183:11 wailing and complaint.

ŠKLL see **KLL.**

ŠKN I (Aram. & H. שְׁכַן, Syr. ܫܟܢ, Ar. سَكَنَ, Akk. *šakānu* to throw and place Brockelmann i 522) to settle in (with **b** or **l**), dwell in, reside, occupy, found a settlement, cause to settle (pe. inst. of af. MG 215:5).

Pe. Pf. **škinata d̲-škan** Gy 304:18 the dwellings which he founded; **škan hiia škinta** Gy 249:9 the Life founded a dwelling; **škinta hanath̲ d̲-hu rba liaminh̲ škan** Gy 12:6 f., 32:19 that dwelling which the Great One founded at his right hand; **arqa d̲-aiar d̲-bh̲ škan hiia napšaihun** Gy 69:21 the earth of ether in which the Life settled Himself, cf. **škan hiia** ML 77:2; **šiknit tlat škinata** Gy 130:4 I founded three dwellings; with encl. **škanbh̲ škinata** Jb 229:13 founded therein dwellings; **škanlia škinta kd̲ dilh̲** Gy 364:17 he founded me a dwelling like his own; **škinta . . . škantlin** DC 48. 398 thou hast provided them with a dwelling; with suff. **šiknan** Gs 41:10 he caused me to dwell; **šiknun bškinata kasiata** Gy 364:8 BCD, DC 22. 361 & Sh. 'Abd.'s copy (only Pet. A has **šaknun**) He (: Life, pl.) gave me habitation in the secret dwellings. Impf. **luath̲ tiškin** (= **tištkin**?) **šitin drabšia** DC 48. 106 f. with it sixty banners are placed (bestowed). Act. pt. **šakin** Q 32:2 he foundeth; pl. **šaknia dmuta qadmaita** Gy 196:5, ML 84:4, CP 69:1, they establish the First Counterpart. Pass. pt. **škina** dwelling, inhabiting MG 116:14; with encl. **bškinatun . . . d̲-škinalh̲ lab** Gy 364:8 in his (: the Life's) . . . dwellings which were founded for my father MG 382:9, Ginzā 386 n. 1; pl. **šrin uškinia** Gy 8:9 they dwell and inhabit; **abahatai d̲-minai škinia** Gy 165:19 my parents who dwelt with me Ginzā 172 n. 1. Inf. **lmiškan škinata** CP 182:ult. to found dwellings; **'tit lmiškan luataikun** Gy 175:9 I came to dwell amongst you; **miškan ruhan . . . bškinta** CP 107:13 f., ML 133:1 that our spirit may rest . . . in the dwelling.

Ethpe. Pf. **diuan d̲-'štiknat luath̲** ATŠ II no. 437 a scroll housed with him; **nišimta 'štiknat briša** ATŠ II no. 118 the soul was placed in the head; **diuan . . . d̲-'štiknat bginza d̲-bihram** ATŠ II no. 438 a scroll . . . that was housed in B.'s library; with encl. **škinta 'štkilh̲** ATŠ II no. 112, **škinta . . . 'štkinlh̲** DC 48. 370 f. (read **'štiknalh̲**) a dwelling was provided for her; **škinta biardna štkinalh̲** DC 27. 96 a *škinta* was provided for her in the jordan. Impf. **bškintai dilia ništkin** Gy 238:23 he shall be lodged in my dwelling; **bškintak dilak ništkin** Gy 364:19; **ništiknan** Par. xi 47a, ATŠ II no. 186 they (fem.) will be given habitation MG 228:5. Pt. **d̲-mištkin hazin ginza luath̲** ATŠ I nos. 158, 207 with whom this treasure is housed; **d̲-raza d̲-abahath̲ . . . luath̲ mištkin** Jb 218:12 f. with whom the mystery of his parents abideth; pl. **bhšuka d̲-atutaiun mištiknia** Gy 252:5 they are made to dwell in the darkness that is beneath them; **bhšuka mištaknia** (ethpa., var. **mištiknia** BD) Jb 181:12; **škinata d̲-ziua mištikna(n)** Jb 218:4 f. the dwellings of light were founded.

Der.: **maškna, škinta.**

ŠKN II (den. from **šikna** q.v.) to be stuck in mud, befouled.

Pa. Pt. **mšakna** s.v.

Ethpe. Pt. fem. **napla bšikna umištikna** Jb 47:1 falls into filth and is stuck there; **mištikna bmia siauia** Gy 170:1 she is stuck in black waters.

Der.: **mšakna, šikna.**

ŠKṢ (Ar. شكص & شكس) to be lean, scarce, indigent, few, in small quantity; to impoverish, make lean.

Pe. Impf. with suff. **latiškiṣunh̲** DC 43 I 126 f. do not impoverish him. Pass. pt. **škiṣa** s.v.

Af?. Part. pres. with encl. **miškiṣatlh̲** DC 37. 491 (read **maškiṣatlh̲**) thou makest him lean.

Gl. 133:7 f. (miswritten af.) قلّل *minuere* كم كرد.

Der.: **šakaṣta, šukṣana, šikṣa, škiṣa.**

ŠLA I (שְׁלָא, ܫܠܐ, H. שלה I, Ar. سلا) to be quiet, still, rest, stay still, be at ease; to desist, be motionless; af. to abandon.

Pe. Impf. **tišilai** DC 43 I 82 thou shalt be quiet. Act. pt. **šalia** s.v.; pass. pt. **šlia** s.v. Part. pres. **šaliana uganiana** DC 46 I (fem.) am at rest and sleep. Inf. with suff. **mišiliak** (var. **mišlak**), **mišlaikun** v.s. **ŠKB** inf. pe. with suff.

Af. Pf. **ašlia markabatun** DC 26. 306 they abandoned their ships.

Der.: **š(a)lia.**

ŠLA II (< **ŠLH I** q.v.) to send (away); to send out a voice, cry.

Af Pf. **ašlia bkaluza qaria ašlia qaria bkaluza** Jb 185:7 he called with a loud voice (lit. sent out a loud proclamation); **ašlia ubgan gabra puha ašlia puha bgan gabra** Gy 85:10 f. the man cried and shouted, 'Woe' cried, 'Woe' shouted the man; **ašliat bqala** Gy 330:2, 363:6 she cried MG 261:1.

Ethpe. Pf. **'štla** Gs 94:23 f. he was sent MG 234:21. Pt. **'l nišmata mištla mištla 'l nišmata** Gy 123:22 is sent against the souls.

Der.: s. **ŠLH I** and the secondary **ŠHL II.**

ŠLA III (< **ŠLH II** q.v.) to take off, undress, divest, disrobe, lay bare, slough off.

Pe. Pf. **šla ulbaš** ATŠ II no. 88 they disrobed and dressed; with suff. **šlat̲h̲** Gs 99:10 she took it off MG 276:19. Impf. **nišla mania** DC 42:4 he shall take off the clothes; **kma ʿšlh̲ ukma ukma ʿlbuš** Gs 43:22 f. how long shall I take it off and put on?; **našlinun ʿl lbuših̲** DC 42. 62 takes off his clothes. Impt. **šla kulhun manak** DC 40. 73 take off all thy clothes (MG 235:25). Pass. pt. **kd̲ šila** ATŠ II no. 70, 269 when unclothed; **kd̲ šlia lbuṭa** DC 46. 167:12 when his arse is bared.

Af. Pf. **ašlit** I took off MG 235:5; with suff. **ašlan** Gy 193:16 he took me off; **ašlh̲ šibqh̲ llbušaihun** Gy 355:15 they took off their garment and left it; **ašlatak** Gy 193:14 B (var. **ašlitak** A, but CD pe.) I cast thee off MG 274:4; **ašlinun** Gy 168:14 he took them off MG 281:22; **ašlun** they took me out MG 272:21. Pt. with encl. **mašlilh̲ lbušh̲ nuqbta** DC 34. 113 they take off her female dress.

Ethpa. Pf. **tibil ʿštaliat** ATŠ II no. 15 the earth was laid bare.

Der.: **šla**, cf. also s. **ŠHL III** and **ŠLH II.**

ŠLA IV (Ar. جلى) to refine, clear. Only one Ar. form in an Ar. context: **iišlia lbaṣar l ʿain** AM 287:15 it clears the sight of the eye.

šla (rt. **ŠLA III**) taking off. **bšla šla** Gs 123:6 = **bšlaha šlaha** Gs 135:9 f. for taking off (and) taking off; **rmun blbuš pagria d̲-hu lbuš uhu šla** Gs 43:21 they threw me into a bodily garment which is clothing and taking off.

šlaha (rt. **ŠLH II**) taking off, casting off, divesting, disrobing (cf. preced.). MG 115:21. Pl. **-ia. bšlaha šlaha** s. **šla**; **šlaha ulbaša** DC 34. 329, 363, 731 taking off and putting on; **šlahia ulbašia** DC 34. 735; **šlahia ulbušia** DC 7 (often) sheaths (?) and coverings; **man d̲-abuih̲ nṣab armalta d̲-šlaha qadmaia** DC 34. 125 one whose father married a widow that lost her first husband.

šlahuta (**ŠLH II**) divesting, shedding, casting-off. **aminṭul d̲-šlahuta lilbuš d̲-ziua** DC 40.67 because of the casting off of the garment of light.

šlahiata s. **šalahiata.**

šlahta (**ŠLH I**). **hua šlahta ušadarta** DC 37. 239 there was dismissal and sending away.

šlam(a) (שְׁלָמָא, ܫܠܡܐ, H. שָׁלוֹם, Phoen. שלם, Ar. سلام, Eth. ሰላም, Akk. *salāmu*) peace, salutation, greeting, wholeness, safety, welfare, perfection MG 115:17. Var. st. emph. **šalma** s.v. **bšlam** Q 65:25, Oxf. 25 b, Jb 52:8, Gy 190:15, Gs 80:24 ff., 81:17 ff. (*& often*) in peace MG 302:ult. **šlama ʿlak** (var. **alak**) Gy 141:22, 147:4 f. peace be with thee MG 483:5; **bnia šlama** Gy 87:9, 93:9, 23, 126:2, 239:20, 22 ff., 240:21 ff., Gs 93:10, Q 30:23, 53:29; **ʿutria bnia šlama** Gs 49:13; **bnia šlama mlakia** Gy 356:7; **gubria bnia šlama** Gy 195:8; **arba gubria bnia šlama** CP 67:14, 118:15, Q 4:23, 40:13, 55:8, 60:5, Gy 195:14, 322:13; **maṭra d̲-bnia šlama** ('sons of perfection' a frequent designation of higher beings HpGn 339 n. 1, Ginzā 89 n. 1). With **YHB** 'to salute': **šlama ʿhablak** Gy 147:6 f. he saluted thee; **šlama laiahbia** Gs 35:10 they salute not. With **QBL**: **šlama qabil minaihun** Gy 154:18 f. receive their salutation; **hakima . . . šlamh̲ qudam sakla . . . šlamh̲ briša d̲-ṣbath̲** Gy 216:ult. f. the wise man . . . his greeting is the first (i.e. is the first to salute); the fool . . . his salutation is with finger-tips; **šušmia nihabian** (= **nihuian**) **bšlama** AM sesame will do well.

šlamana (rt. **ŠLM**) Or. 332:8 health, salvation.

šlamun DC 20. 52, 40. 632 = **šlimun.**

šlanda (שְׁלַנְדָּא, ܫܠܕܐ, Mishn. שְׁלַנְד) (*a*) decayed body, corpse, carcass, (*b*) putridity MG 75:24. Fem. MG 160:12. Var. **ašlanda.** Plu. **-ia.** (*a*) **lahalpa šlanda qudamh̲** Gy 6:21 f. no corpse passeth before him; **(a)šlanda sarita** Gy 283:12 a stinking corpse; **uaških̲ šlanda** Gy 380:ult. and findeth a carcass; **šlanda d̲-lamasgia** Lond. roll B 439 a corpse that does not walk; **kd̲ šlandia** DC 12. 204 like corpses; (*b*) **tibta ušlanda** ATŠ I no. 268 dung and putridity.

ŠLB (perh. Ar. جلب) to attract > catch? in **ʿzlak lašalib mia** Jb 162:5 Lidzb. supposed a corruption of **lašalia bmia** *dein Garn fischt nicht im Wasser* Jb ii 163 n. 7. Doubtf.

ŠLH I (Aram. & H. שׁלח, Syr. ܫܠܚ II, Akk. *tešlītu* order. Secondary roots **ŠHL II** and **ŠLA II**) to send (forth), emit, send away, dismiss.

Pe. Pf. with suff. **lašlahinun lʿutria kulhun** CP 385:9 they sent not all the uthras. Pass. pt. **šlih** MG 65:6, st. emph. **šliha** s.v.; with encl. pers. pron. **šlihit** thou art sent MG 65 n. 2, 236:19.

Pa. Impf. with suff. **nišalhunh̲** Gy 87:11 they shall send him.

Der.: **š(a)lahiata** (*a*), **šlahta, šliha.**

ŠLH II (שְׁלַח, ܫܠܚ I, Ar. سلخ) (Secondary roots **ŠHL III** and **ŠLA III**) to draw off, cast off, take off, undress, disrobe, divest.

Pe. Pass. pt. **minai šliha šliha ʿsira htima** DC 37:417, 431 f. cast off from me, taken off, bound, sealed.

Af. Pf. **ašlhan** Gs 123:9 (in the same l. with **ašlan**) he took me off MG 66:3, 270:31.

Der.: **š(a)lahiata** (*b*), **šlaha, šlahuta.**

ŠLHM (šaf. of ܠܚܡ to menace, cf. H. לחם to fight, Ar. مَلْحَمَة fight, army) to attack, threaten, harm; be(come) pugnacious, dangerous, be a menace (s. AM 139 n. 2, 5 and 6).

Šaf. Impf. with suff. **laštalmat tišalhimin** Or. 332:9 read **(ʿ)štalamt latišalhimim**? thou art perfect, thou doest not harm (??).

Eštaf. Impf. **hiua bira ništalham** AM 229:8 cattle will become ferocious (?); **ganabia ništalhamun** AM 230:3 f. thieves will become a menace; **ariauata ništalhmun** AM 240:6 lions will become a menace.

šlum = **šlam** (s. **šlam(a)**). **bšlum** Gy 125:8; **bišlum** Jb 41:9, 180:4 B, Par. xv 52a:bottom = **bšlam** Jb ii 46 n. 5.

šluq AM 197 name of a town.

šlutana = **šultana.** Pl. **-ia. damin lšlutania d̲-mn hšuka lnhura lanapqia** Gy 355:16 f. they resemble bats that come not forth from darkness to light. Varr. **ašlutana, šulutana.**

šlutinia Leid. varr. of šlutania, ašlutina ATŠ I no. 256 (s. preced.).

ŠLṬ (Aram. & H. שלט, Syr. ܫܠܛ, Akk. *šalāṭu*, Ar. سلط, Eth. ሠለጠ) pa. to give power, endue with might, empower, give authority, appoint; ethpa. to be given power, empowered, authorized, appointed, allowed, permitted.

PA. Pf. **šalṭit** I gave power MG 223:3; **šalṭan** Gy 316:20 he set me in authority MG 270:25; **šaliṭṭak** ATŠ I no. 41, Gy 343:2 f. I gave thee authority MG 274:3; **šaliṭnak** MG 274:7; **šalṭuk lhukmat rbia** Gy 347:6 they appointed thee over the wisdom of the Great (Life). Pt. (act. & pass.) **mšalaṭ** (*often*); pl. **mšalṭia** MG 37:22, **lamšalṭia lmikal** Gy 227:23 they are not allowed to eat (thereof); **šaliṭania ḏ-mšalṭia šbiqia** Gy 357:10 f. rulers who are given power over the abandoned ones. Part. pres. (pass.) **mšalṭit** MG 232:14, **mšalṭinin** MG 233:1. Nom. ag. **msalṭana** s.v.

ETHPA. Pf. **'štalaṭṭ** thou wert set in authority MG 222:paen.; **'štalṭit mimar** Gy 76:15 I was allowed to tell (MG 223:9). Impf. **tištalaṭ** MG 227:4. Pass. pl. **mištalaṭ** (*often*); pl. **'lauaihun lamištalṭia** Gy 9:5 they have no might over them.

DER.: mšalṭana, šaliṭ(a), šaliṭana, šulṭana, (šulṭa).

šlia = šalia, cf. mn šlia s. šalia (*b*).

šliha (pass. pt. of ŠLH I) messenger, apostle, envoy MR 40, 46, Wid. i 77, iii 56, v 57. Pl. -ia. gabrʿil šliha Gy 12:5, 87:10, 93:21; šliha dakia Gy 13:15, 25:5, 32:17 (identified with hibil ziua); šliha qadmaia Gy 24:10, 29:1, 290:4, 14; šliha ḏ-hiia Gy 16:5, 368:16 (& *often*); šliha kušṭana Gy 64:21, 65:5; šliha ḏ-nhura malka Gy 64:10 ff.; šliha naṣba Jb 55:10 (cf. Jb ii 60 n. 6); šlihia unbʿiia Gy 287:12; šlihia uparṣupia Gy 10:9 envoys and personalities; šlihia ḏ-hiia Gy 191:19, DC 26. 351; ʿutria... šlihia Gy 6:12, ʿutria ušlihia Gy 5:3; msadranun ḏ-šlihia ḏ-kušṭa Gy 63:10 sender of Apostles of Truth; šlihia ḏ-husrana Gy 46:15 apostles of perdition; šlihia tlata Gy 47:16; ʿngirta ata mn lʿl bʿdh ḏ-šliha DC 41. 331 a letter came from above in the hand of a messenger.

šlimun (ܫܠܝܡܘܢ, Σολομών, Ar. سليمان, not directly from H. שלמה) Solomon. Var. **šlamun** s.v. šlimun malka br dauid Gy 27:9, 389:12; šlimun malka br daud DC 40. 908, DC 43 E 23, H 30, DC 44. 1694 = Morg. 268/26:7 (& *often*); atuih qudam šlimun DC 46. 61:8 they brought him before Solomon.

ŠLM (Aram. & H. שלם, Syr. ܫܠܡ, Ar. سلم, Akk. *šalāmu*) pe. to (come to an) end, be completed, finished, accomplished; pa. to complete, perfect, accomplish, achieve, acquit oneself, fulfil a vow, recompense, reward; pa. also to greet, salute; af. to complete, give over, hand over, render, give up, surrender; ethpa. to be ended, perfected, purified, surrender, agree, keep oneself pure.

PE. Pf. **šlim** MG 219:19; with suff. **šilman kilai** Gs 98:11 f. my measure came to an end (i.e. I died); **kilai balma šilman** Gy 180:4 (MG 352:paen.); **lgiṭinun ušliminun** DC 43 I 109 they grasped them and put an end to them. Impf. **nišlum** MG 219:19; **kḏ kila ḏ-baita nišlum** Jb 266:3 when the measure of the House is full; **lʿšlum, lišlum** Gs 118:5 is accomplished MG 216:6. Act. pt. **kʿla ḏ-iuhana šalim** Gy 57:17 Yuḥanna's measure (life) cometh to an end; **alma ḏ-šalim kilh** ATŠ II no. 19 until his time (to die) comes; **alma ḏ-ruhh šalma** Jb 97:5 f. until his spirit yields; **alma ḏ-ruhaiun šalma** Gy 119:24, 120:5; pl. **alma ḏ-haṭaiun šalmia** Jb 269:14 until their sins shall be absolved; **andašata ḏ-lašalman** Jb 58:8 anxieties that never cease; **atian dimh ulašalman** Jb 64:6 his tears come and do not cease; **mhašabath lašalman** Gy 12:14 his plans come not to fulfilment. Pass. pt. **ʿuhra šlim** Gy 331:4 the road is at an end; **šlim huit šuba ulaʿbdit mn ʿbadaihun** Gs 123:16 I abstained from the Seven (planets) and did not do any of their works; **akandit kila ḏ-baita lašlim** Jb 266:6 the measure of the House is not full yet; with encl. ṭuria... **lmiklaikun lašlimilkun** CP 110:4, ML 135:7 f. even hills... could not satisfy you as your food (doubtf. ML 135 n. 3). Inf. **lmišlam lkimṣat almia** Gy 175:20 to be consumed at the end of the worlds.

PA. Pf. **šlama ʿlh lašalim** Jb 25:10 he did not greet him; **anin šaliminin luath bkušṭa** ATŠ II no. 326 we have acquitted ourselves towards her with good faith; **kḏ šalmu nidrh** Jb 80:6 when they fulfilled their vow; with suff. **šalmh** CP 45:12 f., ML 57:9 he completed it (Lidzb. *sprach es zu Ende*); **šlama šalimth** Gy 141:ult., 142:14 he greeted him MG 399:23, **šalmuia ldubšaihun** Gs 114:4 they consumed their honey. Impf. **nišalmun lbit maškna** DC 36 no. 235 they hand over (children for instruction) to the sanctuaries. Act. pt. **mšalim** is greeting MG 239:7; with encl. **tušlim(i)a ḏ-šalmania mšalimlun** CP 156:12 ff., ML 188:9 he rewardeth them with the reward of the perfect ones; **mšalimlun lšalmania** Gy 9:ult. he rewardeth the perfect ones. Part. pres. **mšalmit luath bkušṭa** ATŠ II no. 325 I acquit myself towards her in good faith; **kḏ mšalmitun bauatkun** ATŠ II no. 164 when ye finish your prayers. Pass. pt. **mšalam** achieved MG 230:9; **mšalam bkušṭa** Jb 59:12 perfected by the Truth; **ḏ-mšalam mn riš briš** Gy 91:7 which is absolutely perfect; **hakima ḏ-lamšalam** Gy 216:20 a wise man who is not perfect; fem. **mšalma** DAb (& *often*) redeemed; **arqa ḏ-lamšalma** Gy 216:paen. ground that is unredeemed; fem. pl. **nišmata ḏ-lamšalman** RD C I souls that are unredeemed; **kḏ mšalman** Jb 34:8 although they are perfect (women); cf. **ḏ-mšalman** PD 1024 opposed to mṭanpa; st. emph. **tirata mšalmata** Gy 5:8 perfect consciences.

AF. Pf. with encl. **ašlimilun ʿṣtlia** Gy 91:9 I handed them the robes over MG 226:2; with suff. **ašlimh** ML 57:3 = CP 45:6; **ašlmh** he gave him over MG 275:8. Impf. **pagrh lgiṭla našlim** Gy 16:11 he submitteth his body to murder; **mn ʿdh ḏ-smalh našlimh lʿda**

d̲-iaminh̲ DC 50. 281 he hands him over from his left hand to his right hand (MG 275: anteantep. f.). Act. pt. **mašlim nišmata** CP 110:19, ML 136:7 delivereth the souls. Part. pres. **mašlimana napšai** Gs 75:13 I yield myself up. Inf. **lmašlumia hušbana** Gy 312:14, Jb 194:6 to complete the reckoning (MG 234:1).

Ethpa. Pf. **iuma d̲-ṣurta ʿštalmat** ATŠ II no. 196 in the day of ritual uncleanness she was purified; **ʿštalmit** Jb 60:3 I have kept myself pure. Impf. **ništalam** MG 226:20, **bgauh̲ tištalam** ATŠ II no. 141 she will be perfected thereby; **ništalmun** AM 183, 213:12, 247:5 f. they will surrender; with encl. **ništalambak** Gy 98:14 we shall surrender to thee. Pt. **mištalam** RD C 2, Gy 91:13, ATŠ II no. 69, 79 perfected, completed MG 132:17, 230:17; with encl. **d̲-mištalambh̲** Jb 208:8 who keepeth himself pure in it; pl. **mištalmia** RD C 2, Gy 340:15, fem. **d̲-mištalman ud̲-lamištalman** ATŠ I no. 239 (women) who are purified and those who are not purified.

Der.: **ašlamata, šalamata, šalma, šalmana, šalmanata, šišlam, šlam(ana), šlam(a), šlamana, šlum, tušlima, tašlumia.**

ŠLP (Aram. & H. שלף, Syr. ܫܠܦ, Akk. *šalāpu*, Ar. سَلَبَ) to pull out, draw out, extract, unsheathe, pluck out; pa. to fleece MSchr. 228. Gl. 25:13 f.

Pe. Pf. **sipa šlap** Jb 13:2 (cf. pl. 1. 10) he unsheathed the sword; **sipa rba šlap** DC 44. 1462; **šilpit ʿsqta** Gy 147:13 I drew off a ring; **ragala šilpit** DC 26. 613, DC 44. 646 I slipped out of the snare; **sipa šlapnin** Gy 233:16 we unsheathed the sword. Act. pt. **sipa rba šalip** Morg. 260/22:8; pl. with encl. **zaina bgauh̲ šalpilh̲** RD C 14 = DAb par. they draw weapons in it.

Pa. Act. pt. with encl. **mšalpilun** Gy 28:13, 51:24 they fleece them.

Ethpe. Impf. **hirba ništlip** AM 189:ult. the sword will be unsheathed.

Ethpa. Pt. **mištalpia** Gy 59:20 ff., 389:8 they are fleeced; **mištalpia sikia** Gs 17:22 the nails slip out.

Der.: **šalupa, šal(i)pa.**

ŠMA (Aram., H., Phoen. שמע, Syr. ܫܡܥ, South-Ar. 𐩪𐩣𐩲, Ar. سَمِعَ, Eth. ሰምዐ, Akk. *šemū*) to hear, listen, hearken; af. to cause to hear, announce, proclaim; ethpe. to be heard; ethpa. to obey.

Pe. Pf. **š(u)ma** MG 29:1 & n. 1, 90:antep., 234:18, **šimat** Jb 120:6 (*& often*) MG 234:25, **šmit** Oxf. 39 a = Par. xi 55b thou didst hear MG 234:antep., **šimit** I heard MG 235:3, **šmun** Gy 177:1, 282:8 (var. **šumun**) they heard MG 237:14 f., but also **šumaiun** Gy 218:22, 345:1 id. MG 234:23, **šmanin** we heard MG 16:12, **šmatun** ye heard ibid.; with suff. **šimih̲ lqalai** Gs 39:12 he heard my voice; **šman** Gs 135:11 (*twice*) read af. (he caused me to hear) MG 24:antep.; **šmath̲** Gy 133:3 (varr. **šmith̲, šimith̲, šumith̲**) I heard her MG 277: 2 f., **šmitinan** (var. **šmatinan**) Gs 61:3 thou didst hear us MG 280:7 f., **šimun** they heard me MG 272:15, **šimuk** MG 274:9, **šmanh̲** Gy 64:4 we heard her MG 277:19, **šmatunan** Gy 255:10 (**šmitunan** CD) ye heard me MG 272:6. Impf. **nišma** MG 4:antep., 235:11, **ʿšma** Gs 39:8 (*& often*) I listen MG 235:13, **niš(i)mun** MG 26:19, 235:19, **tišimun** MG 235:19; with suff. **tišiman** MG 271:2, **tišmunh̲** MG 278:10. Impt. **š(u)ma** MG 235:23; **ṣut ušuma** Jb 53:5 heed and hearken; special pl. form **š(u)mun** Gy 21:6, MG 237:18; with suff. **šuman** hear me MG 271:8, **šminan** Gy 61:ult. hear us MG 280:3. Act. pt. **šama** MG 16:2, 235: anteantep. Part. pres. **qala šamana** DC 40. 848 I hear the voice; **qal ṭuria šamana** DC 43 J 5 f. I hear the voice of mountains (MG 16:4, 236:13), **šamitun** MG 236:25. Pass. pt. with encl. (& act. mean.) **šmilak** Gs 105:23 thou hast heard, **šmilkun** Gy 392:18 ye have heard MG 236:1, 382:3, 8. Inf. **mišma** Jb 120:6.

Af. Pf. with suff. **ašmh̲ bqalh̲** Gs 39:16 f., **ašmh̲ qalh̲** Gs 45:23 he let his voice be heard (MG 275:9); **ašmitinan** thou didst make us hear MG 280:9, **ašmuia** they let him hear MG 278:2. Impf. with suff. **našmh̲** Jb 58:11 (var. **nišmh̲** BD & DC 30) we will make him hear, **našminun** Gy 73:16 we will make them hear. Impt. fem. with suff. **ašmainan qalik** Jb 140:6 let us hear thy voice. Pt. **mašma** MG 236:7; with encl. **mašmalh̲** Jb 190:7 he let him hear (hist. pres.); pl. **mašmia** ATŠ I no. 45 they cause to hear. Inf. **ašmuiia**, Gy 289:11, MG 236:28.

Ethpe. Pf. **ʿštma** was (or were) heard MG 27:12, 234:19; **ʿmrit uʿštmit** DC 44. 1072 I spoke and was heard; **ʿštmanin** MG 235:10; with encl. **ʿštmialak** Gs 46:2 she was heard by thee MG 234:28; **ʿštmulh̲** Gy 107:6 they were subservient to him; **nimrun uništmun** Gy 289:12 they speak and are heard MG 237:7; with encl. **ništmalan** Gy 244:2 he shall obey us; **ništmulak** Gy 119:14 they shall be subservient to thee MG 237:8. Impt. **amar u(ʿ)štma** (*often*) speak and be heard. Pt. **mištma** AM 23 he will be listened to; **mištma qalaihun** DC 43 D 11 their cry is heard.

Ethpa. Pf. **uštaminin** (for ethpe.) Q 22:13 we were heard MG 237:2. Pf. **naštaimun** (read **ništaimun**) Par. xxvi 59 they will obey MG 24:19. Pt. **mištaima** Q 22 f. obedient MG 24:18; pl. **mištaimia** DC 26. 267, CP 396:12.

Der.: **maštimana** (& varr.), **šima, šmita** (var. **šmata 1**).

šmal (Ar. شمال north). **ziqa smal** AM north wind.

šmata 1 DC 22 = **šmiṭa** Gs 83:4.

šmata 2 (שַׁמְתָּא, ܫܡܬܐ) curse, ban, malediction. **kuba šmata** ATŠ II no. 405 accursed cup.

ŠMD (Jew.-Aram. שמד, Syr. ܫܡܕ, H. שָׁמַד, af. to destroy) to force to apostasy, mislead.

Ethpa. Impf. **d̲-laništamdun brazia mardia** DC 48. 97 so that they are not misled by heretical rites.

Der.: **šamadta.**

šmukta, šmukṭa s. **samukṭa.**

ŠMṬ (Aram., Syr., H., Akk. *šamāṭu*, Ar. سمط) to draw out, tear out, pluck out, pluck off, strip off, uncover, pull off or out, take off, carry off.

Pe. Pf. **šmaṭ uapqan mn alma** Gs 51:9 he plucked me forth and took me out of the world; intrans. **ganpaihun šmaṭ** Jb 133:13 their wings were torn off; similarly **ganpia . . . šmaṭ** Gy 301:1, 6. Impf. **d̲-manzih̲ nišmuṭ** Gy 19:8 who teareth out his hair; **d̲-manzih̲ ʿlh̲ nišmuṭ** Gy 37:20 who teareth out his hair for him MR 80:ult.; with suff. **lišimṭan** Gs 96:5, 7 (var. **nišimṭan**) may he draw me forth MG 216:14, 271:1. Act. pt. **sipa rba qudamai šamiṭ** DC 44. 1470 = Morg. 266/22:15 he draws a great sword before me; pl. **šamṭia** Gy 232:1 they draw forth; **šinaihun harqia uabuṭia samṭia** DC 44. 551 they gnash their teeth and bare (their) fangs. Pass. pt. **šmiṭa** s.v.; with encl. (& pass. meaning) **lašmiṭlh̲** hirba 5:5, 16, 6:13 he drew not a sword.

Pa. Impf. **man d̲-našamiṭ** (read **nišamiṭ**) **pandamh̲** DC 36 no. 73 a person who pulls off his face-veil; **nišamṭun hiua bala bdištata** AM 226:penult. they will carry off (?) wild animals in the prairies. Pt. **ṭaisa uradia ulamšamṭa** Jb 151:16 it flies hither and thither and (its wings) are not torn off; pl. **mšamṭia** JRAS 1937 595:31 are torn out.

Ethpa. Pf. **ganpia . . . ʿštamaṭ** Jb 134:6 the wings . . . were torn off. Impf. **manzih̲ ništamaṭ** Par. xxvi 73:3 her hair will be pulled out.

Der.: **šimṭia, šmiṭa.**

šmiṭa (pass. pt. pe. of preced.) drawn, protracted, long, thin, slender. Pl. **-ia. šmiṭia šaqia** AM 9:1 his limbs are slender; **gaṭinia saqh̲ ušmiṭia** AM 52:17 her limbs are lean and slender.

šmima (rt. **ŠMM**, formed as pass. pt. pe. but of doubtf. mean. Jb ii 19 n. 3) (*a*) adj. destructive? (Lidzb. *flink*), (*b*) subst.? destruction? (Lidzb. *Erstarren, Erstarrung*), (*c*) a weapon? Ginzā 391 n. 2. Pl. **-ia.** (*a*) **giria šmimia** Jb 11:12, 16:1, 11, Gs 114:1, RD B 106 f., DC 44. 26 (poisoned? arrows); (*b*) **ʿndruna šmima nsib** Gs 104:8, 109:19; (*c*) **tlata šmimia bʿdh̲ lgiṭ šmimia niṣbit minh̲** Gy 367:18 f. he grasped three poisoned arrows in his hand, (which) arrows I snatched away from him.

šmimta (different from preced.) adj. fem. an epithet of the Letter, prob. sealed (with wax). Doubtf. **ʿngirta šmimta(i)a** DC 34. 1001, ATŠ II no. 417 a sealed letter.

šmita (rt. **ŠMA**) Gs 83:4 hearing. Var. **šmata 1** s.v.

ŠMN (Aram., Syr., H. Akk. *šamnu* grease, Ar. سمن) to grow fat; pa. to fatten.

Pe. Pf. **šimnit kd̲ ʿlita** DC 44. 1409 f. = Morg. 265/21:21 I waxed as fat as a (fat-tailed sheep's) tail. Part. pres. **baṭnana ušamnana** P.A. xii I have grown a belly and am fat.

Pa. Pass. pt. pl. **mšamnia** Jb 134:9 the fattened ones.

Der.: **šamina, šumna,** cf. **mušmana.**

ŠMṢ (šaf. of **MṢṢ**) to mulct, squeeze, raid, despoil. Only ethpa. (eštaf.) impf. **ništamaṣ** AM 181:21 f. (*& often in* AM) will be despoiled, mulcted.

ŠMR (ܫܡܪ, cf. Ar. سمر) to leave for, set out for, forsake, leave behind (with **ŠBQ**), set out urgently; also as a verb of quick movement forwards (often with **AZL**); pa. to let go, dismiss, dissipate. Jb ii 78 n. 3.

Pa. Pf. **šamar mizal** Gy 114:22, 193:9 he set out forthwith MG 387:10, cf. **šamar bʿurašlam mizlh̲** Jb 70:14 f.; **šamar baiar mizlh̲** Gs 13:23, **šamar mizlaihun balma** Gy 330:24, **šamar mitiaihun balma** Gy 308:14; **šamar šibqh̲** Gy 96:6 he went off and forsook him MG 444:11, cf. **šamar šibquia** Jb 126:3. Impf. **nišamar nišibqh̲** Gy 109:9 we will completely forsake him MG 444:11 f.; **latišamar anania mn duktaihun** Jb 10:9 drive not away the (heavenly) spouses from their places. Pt. **mšamar uazil** Gs 14:1 he speedeth off forthwith; **mšamar unapiq hilph̲** Gs 109:19 urgeth forward and driveth forth its passing; pl. **mšamrin bataiun uazlin** Gs 23 they leave behind their houses and go. Nom. act. **šamarta** s.v.

Ethpa. Pt. **ʿbidath̲ mištamra** Gy 370:11 its works shall be forsaken.

Der.: **šamarta.**

ŠMŠ I (שׁמשׁ, ܫܡܫ) to serve, minister to.

Pa. Pf. **šamišt** Gs 135:24, 136:5 thou didst serve; with suff. **šamištin(h)un** Gs 136:1 thou didst serve them. Pt. with encl. **mšamšalh̲** Gy 208:18, 209:9 ff., **nura mšamšalh̲** Gy 144:16 the fire serves him; pl. **mšamšia** Gy 277:23, 290:1 they serve, with encl **mšamšilh̲** Gy 208:7 they serve him. Pass. pt. pres. **ʿsiritun umšamšitun** DC 43 A 36 ye are bound and brought into servitude. Inf. **iahbit šamiš lšamušia ʿl bnat anašia** Gy 210:3 I gave the sun to serve people (a pun) MG 394:bottom. Nom. act. **šamašta** s.v.

Der.: **šamaša, šamašta, šamiš, šamša.**

ŠMŠ II secondary rt. from **ŠBŠ.**

Pa. Pf. with suff. **lašamšun** Gs 122:25 they could not befool me. Pt. pl. **sahria . . . d̲-mšamšia bpagrh̲** Or. 333:3 demons . . . which befool in his body; with encl. **mšamšilia** Gy 122:23 they try to befool me.

Ethpa. Pt. pl. **lšamiš plaglh̲ kadba d̲-bh̲ mištamšia** Gy 112:10 to Šamiš they allotted a lie by which all the worlds are befooled (pun).

ŠMT (Jew.-Aram. שְׁמַת, Syr. ܫܡܬ) to ban, excommunicate, place a curse on.

Pe. Impf. **tišimtun utišiqlun kulhun kuhrania** DC 51. 461 ban and remove all diseases.

Pa. Pt. with encl. **ruha ušibiahia had lhabrh̲ mšamitlh̲** DC 48. 390 Ruha and the planets curse one another; pl. **mšmtia kakaiun** AO ix 100:antep. f. banned (prob. read **mšamṭia** pulled out) are their teeth; **mbaṭlia umšamtia** AO ix 101:11 f. annulled and banned. Part. pres. **hrimit umšamtit . . . mn baita** DC 21 thou art banned and expelled . . . from the house.

Der.: **šmata 2.**

ŠNA (**שְׁנָא**, **ܫܢܐ**, H. **שנה**, Akk. *šanū*) to change, alter, remove, translate, transmute, transfer; to vanish, disappear, remove oneself.

PE. Pf. **šna** he disappeared MG 257:2; **alma šnat dmutai** Gs 48:3 f. why did my appearance change?; **arqa šnat mn sadanh** DC 26. 199 f. the earth shifted from its axis; with suff. **dkiria bṭabu hiia d-šiniu llbuš** Gs 115:4 f. (var. **d-šiniuih llbušai** DC 22 the Life called to mind, in its goodness, that it would transmute my garment. Pt. **miṭra šania** AM 219:5 the rain will stop, cf. also **šania** s.v., st. abs. **š(a)nai**; pl. **markabata šaniia mn duktaihun** DC 26. 196 f. the (planetary) ships were removed from their places.

PA. Pf. **šania** he transferred MG 260:25; **šaniat** MG 260:paen., **šanit** MG 261:4; **šanun** MG 261:15; **šanun naṣiruta** ATŠ II no. 55, 238 they changed naṣoraeism; **lašaninin** (var. **lašanin**) **d-paqidtinan** CP 32:7, Q 13:23 = ML 38:1 we altered not what thou didst order us MG 260:22; with suff. **šanitinun** Gy 145:19, 158:1 I changed them MG 291:1; **šaniun** Oxf. 51 b they transferred me MG 286:4; **šaninh** Q 63:26 MG 288:16; **šanituia** Q 63:29 MG 288:17. Impf. **tišania** MG 261:paen.; **nišanun** MG 262:3; **tišanun** MG 262:7; with suff. **nišaninun** Gy 145:20 removeth them MG 290:16. Impt. **šania markabatak** DC 43 J 158 remove thy chariots; pl. **šanun markabatun** (read **markabatkun**) DC 32 J 57. Part. pres. fem. **mn kinta lkinta mšaniana** s. **kinta** 1 (MG 262:21); **lamšanit mn mimrak** ATŠ II no. 325 thou shalt not change thy word. Pass. pt. **mšanai**, emph. **mšania** (cf. MG 263:3); with encl. **lamšanailia kudkia** Gs 103:6 I did not alter the boundary stones MG 383:9 f. Inf. **mišanuiia** Gy 214:26, MG 144:3, 263:12, **ulmišanuia hatmia** DC 51. 121 to remove seals.

AF. Pf. **kd qin rabtia ašniat** ATŠ II no. 210 when the great Q. caused perversion; **maṣbuta kulh ašnat** ATŠ II no. 402 all the baptism was dislocated; with suff. **ašnith** Gy 158:ult. she removed him MG 287:ult.

ETHPA. Impf. **mindam minh lamištania** ATŠ I no. 173 (*& often in* ATŠ) nothing shall be removed from him (i.e. he shall not be disqualified from any of his priestly duties); **ʿu pt ṭuhma nautib ligal ništania minh** AM 16:12 if he marries a girl of his family, he will soon put her away (be estranged from her); **ništanun** MG 265:7. Pt. **mištania** MG 132:19, 265:26; pl. id. Q 53:28 removed MG 164:ult.

DER.: **mšauniat, mšaniuta, mšunaiia, mšunia, šana 3 = š(a)nai** emph. **šania, šanaita, šaniuta, šunia, šidta = šita 2** (abs. **šna**, cstr. **šnat**, pl. **šnia, šnʿ**, varr. with **ʿš-**), **šnut**.

šna st. abs. of **šidta = šita 2**. Only distributively **šna bšna** Gy 273:10 year by year MG 301:14.

šnai = š(a)nai.

šnat st. cstr. of **šidta = šita 2**. In colophons to introduce the year of copying.

šnut (rt. **ŠNA**) Gy 218:18 (*twice*) in another way or manner, differently, to the contrary, distortedly MG 146 n. 1, 201:16.

šnia, šnʿ pl. of **šidta = šita 2**. MG 164:2. Var. **ʿšnia**. **bšnia d-piliaṭus** Gy 53:3 in the years of Pilate; **bšnaihun d-hanatun malkia** Gy 387:10 in the years of those kings MG 314:middle; **šnh** his years MG 178:13; **lšnaihun** Gy 9:13 their years; **šnia huit ʿl šnia** Gy 138:10 I stayed years and years; **šnʿ** AM 208 (*& often*).

ŠNQ (**שְׁנַק**, **ܫܢܩ** < Akk. *tašnīqu* Zimmern: *Akk. Fremdw.* 49, rel. **SNQ**) to punish, torture MG 46 n. 4.

PA. Impf. with suff. **nišanqih** DC 3 we shall punish him. Pt. pl. with encl. **mšanqilun lnišmatun** DAb they will torture their souls.

ŠPA I (**שְׁפָא**, **ܫܦܐ**, rel. to **ŠUP**) to be quiet, smooth, clear, at ease; to cleanse, purify; to relax.

PE. Pf. **špit uniṣbit raza d-malakia** DC 44. 429 I cleansed and took away the secret of the angels.

PA. Pf. with suff. **šapitinun qarnai brišai** Morg. 265/21:1 (cf. DC 44. 1379) I smoothened my locks on my head.

AF. Pf. **ašpat . . . ganpak** DC 37 thy wing relaxed.

ETHPE. Pt. pl. **mištpin nauria** Oxf. 44 a = ML 215:7 = CP 176:penult. (but see CP trs. 133 n. 2) mirrors are polished (refers to water-mirror ML 215 n. 2, cf. s. **naura**, hence rel. to **ŠPA II**).

DER.: **šapia 1, 2, šapiut(a), špita 1.**

ŠPA II (Jew.-Aram. **שְׁפַע** & **שְׁפֵי** II, Syr. **ܫܦܥ**, cf. H. **שֶׁפַע** & **שִׁפְעָה** overflow Ar. **سبغ**) to gush, flow out, overflow, pour, tilt, incline MG 237:paen.

PE. Pt. **šapia dmaiun** DAb (var. **šapin dmaiin** RD E 13) their blood gushes out; **mia hiia . . . šapin** Oxf. 14 a:bottom, living waters flow forth; **apkia lmia tahmia ušapin** CP 155:9 = ML 187:2 they transmute stagnant waters and they flow.

ETHPE. Pf. **iardna qadmaia ʿštpia** Gy 70:2 the first jordan flowed forth; **ʿštpun** Gy 69:21, 238:12, 341:6 (the waters) were poured (flowed forth).

ETHPA. Pf. **(ʿ)štapaitun** (var. **(ʿ)štapitun**) Q 22:8 ye were poured MG 264:27. Pt. **aina-niata mištapian** Gs 88:14. Inf. **ʿštapuiia mia ltibil** Q 22:14 when water was poured forth on the earth MG 389:10 f. (cf. 144:17).

DER.: **špita 2** (var. **ʿšpita**).

špaka (cf. **mušpikta**) beam of a pair of scales. **hazin špaka hʿ** DAb this is the beam (of the scales).

špandaiil RD 9 = DAb a theophorous name.

špulta s. **šipulta**. **špulta nbihia d-kadba** DC 9 HG the most degraded of lying prophets.

špur st. cstr. of **šupra**. MG 152:1. Var. **ašpur** Gy 365:14 BCD MG 26:8. **špur pagria** Gy 21:9, 241:9, 243:16, 277:22, Gs 99:11 physical beauty; **d-abdia haršia ušpur anpia** DAb those who perform spells and (practise) flattery (?); **bišpur anpia** Jb 84:1 Lidzb. *mit verschönertem Gesichte*; **(a)špur atuat** Gy 365:14 f. beauty of women.

špinza (P. **سپنج**, **سپنز** Lagarde: *Abhandlungen* 27 f.) temporary lodging, inn, temporary resting-place, refreshment by the way MG 51:22. Var. **ašpinza**. Pl. **-ia. hab lhama umia ušpinza lbnat anaša aniia** Gy 19:24 give bread, water, and lodging to the poor; **špinza baṭla** Gs 47:6 perishable transitory abode; **lšpinzia d̲-pqadlia iatibna** Gy 119:9, Q 38:3 I dwell in the temporary abodes that he ordered for me; **ušpinza mištauilh̲ mn ʿubadih̲** ATŠ I no. 291 a repast shall be provided for her from her (good) deeds.

špikia (**ŠFK**) pourings out (of blood). **qraba . . . uapak špikia** DC 18 war and bloodshed; **qraba . . . uapik špikia mnaihun** DC 43 I:26 war and bloodshed therefrom.

špita 1 (rt. **ŠPA I**) innocence, cleansing, purity, purification. Doubtf. **špil mn špita** HG they fell from innocence (?); **kdabia d̲-mapraš ltuqna d̲-kul špita** HG writings which explain the institution of each purification (?).

špita 2 (rt. **ŠPA II**) outflow, overflow, downpour, gushing flood MG 104:4. Var. **ʿšpita. špita udurdia d̲-anania** CP 373:5, Gy 34:3, 126:17, ZDMG 1955 146(a) 4 overflow and dregs (Lidzb.: *Guß u. Trübung*) of the clouds; **špita d̲-ʿkilta** Gy 33:15 liquid part of the food; **mn špitun d̲-hanatun mia** Gy 87:18 from the outflow of those waters; **špita d̲-kulhun iamamia** Gy 284:5 overflow of all seas; **špita d̲-šapia mn mia** Gy 90:3 the outflow that floweth out of the water; **špita d̲-arqa** Gy 90:4 that which floweth out of the earth.

ŠPK (Jew.-Aram., Syr., Chr.-Pal., H., cf. Ar. سفك) to pour, instil.

Pe. Pf. **špak** Gy 175:4, DC 26.426 he poured; with encl. **špaklik** Gs 76:14; **špaklh̲** Gs 15:2; **špaklun blibaihun hukumta** DC 3. 260:14 = CP 391:7 he poured wisdom into their hearts. Impt. with encl. **špaklia hukumta blibai** CP 291:6 (var. **špukulia** DC 3. 214:14) pour wisdom into my heart.

Ethpe. Pf. **mn ʿšata ʿkilta ʿštpak** DC 43 J 60 was transferred from living fire (doubtf.: read **ʿštpikt** thou wert transferred?), **ʿštipkat blibaihun** DC 34. 426, 428 was poured (fem.) into their hearts. Impf. **nišpik** Gy 387:1 BC, var. **ništpik** Leid. (corrupt **nipšuk** A) is poured MG 214:12.

Ethpa. Pf. **bliba d̲-manu ʿštapkat** DC 3. 256:15 = CP 386:14 into whose heart was it poured?

Der.: **špikia.**

ŠPL (Gen. Sem. exc. Eth.; Akk. *šapālu*, Ar. سَفِلَ) to be low, sink; af. to bring low, degrade, abase; ethpe. to be humiliated, abased; ettaf. id.

Pe. Pf. **nišiplun lʿumqia d̲-arqa** Gy 175:21 they will sink down to the depths of the earth; **tišiplun** MG 26:18. Act. pt. **lhšuka šapla** ATŠ I no. 106 she will sink down to darkness; pl. **šaplin lalma d̲-smala** ATŠ I no. 110 they fall down to the world of the Left.

Af. Impf. **tiašpal** (read **tiašpil**) Par. xxvi 88 she abases MG 226 n. 2; with suff. **ʿiašplinun** I abase them MG 282:4. Act. pt. **hu mašpil hu mdalia** Gy 231:7 f. he casteth down, he raiseth up; pl. **mašpilia umdalia** DC 44. 1816 = Morg. 269/28:4 they degrade and uplift; with encl. **hu mašpililh̲ lkiniana d̲-atar hšuka** DC 34. 1179 they will cast him down to his native place—that is the world of darkness. Pass. pt. **mašpal mn kursih̲** DC 34. 665 is degraded from his throne. Nom. ag. **mašpilana** s.v. Inf. **ašpulia ldaiua** DC 44. 1821 to abase the demon; **mazruta ʿtirat d̲-baiia mašpal bmarba** DC 41. 433 the seed awaked, seeking to be brought down into the womb.

Ethpe. Pf. with encl. **ʿšpilbkun** DC 51. 715 was abased in you. Impf. **ʿštpil** I am abased MG 227:9. Impf. **ništpil lkiniana latar hšuka** ATŠ II no. 355 he will be hurled down etc.; **latuth̲ ništiplun** ATŠ I no. 228 they abase themselves beneath him. Pt. **mištpil** Gs 65:12 falling down.

Ettaf. Pt. **mitašpal** he abases himself MG 230:19; pl. **mištaplia unaplia** DAb they will be abased and fall down.

Der.: **mašpilana, šapala, šapula, šapla, šaplut(a), šip(u)la, šipluta.**

ŠPP I, ŠUP II (ܫܦ, cf. Ar. سفّ) to crawl, creep.

Pe. Act. pt. pl. & inf. **d̲-šaipia mišap ʿl karsatun** Gy 279:19 that crawl on their bellies MG 398:12.

Der.: **š(a)pupa.**

ŠPP II = **ŠPA I. šapapit aina qburtia** JRAS 1937 596:3 thou art made clear, obscured (?) eye.

ŠPQ for **ŠBQ** in **šapqin** Gs 76:21, RD E 11 f. they leave MG 48:14; **nišipqun** RD C 14 id., **nura šapqin** RD C 23 they let loose fire; **hauma uiaqdana špiqia ʿlauaihun** DAb heat and flame are loosed upon them.

ŠPR I (Aram., Syr., H., cf. Ar. سفر to shine) to be fair, beautiful, pleasing; to find pleasing, be pleased; with **banpia** 'to flatter', but pa. (?) with **anpia** as obj. 'to make oneself pleasing', 'find favour'.

Pe. Pf. **šiprit ukaprit anpai** Morg. 264/19:22 read pa.?, cf. par. **šaprit anpai** DC 44. 1300 I beautified my face; **špur** Gy 177:2 they were pleased MG 218:15. Impf. **niquš unišpur** AM 22 he grows old and improves; **banpia latišpur** Q 72:5 do not flatter; **tišpurlh̲** CP 102:18 all will be favourable for her; **latišiprun banpia hdadia** Gy 40:20 do not flatter one another; **ʿbidatak dilak nišipra** Gs 57:4 thy deeds shall be fair; **latišpar atuat d̲-mragaga** Gy 365:1 f. be not pleased by an alluring woman; with encl. **nišiprulun** AM 248:17 they will be pleased by them. Pt. **kul d̲-šapar banpia** Gy 40:21 everyone who flattereth (MSchr. 71).

Pa. Pf. **šaprit anpai** cf. s. pe. pf. Impf. **latišapar** DC 22. 445 = **latišpar** Gy 365:1 (s. pe. impf.).

Der.: **šapir(a), šapirut(a), šupra** (cstr. **(a)špur**).

ŠPR II (Ar. شَفِر) to decrease, diminish, perish. (s. AM p. 203 **ŠPR** and AM p. 18 n. 8). Only post-classical; its use seems to be limited to AM, (s. AM pp. 203–4) where it occurs very often as a confusing homonym of **ŠPR I**, cf. BZ Ap. I s.v. Only pe. impf., us. **nišpar, tišpar** (to keep a difference from **ŠPR I**, which us. has **nišpur, tišpur**): **arbaiia nitun uqiniana nišpar** (read **nišpur**) AM nomads will come and property will be spoilt; **hiua bala bdištata upaqata nišiprun** AM wild animals in the prairies and plains will perish; **malkuta barqa tišpar** AM the kingdom will perish; **malka d̠-mdinta nišania utišpar** AM 239:20 the king of the city will be removed and it will perish; **ʿburia nišiprun . . . ukupna nihuia** AM 207:17 crops will be injured . . . and there will be famine; **abuiih̠ niqum uʿmh̠ tišpar** AM 33:2 his father will live but his mother will perish; **saria uhiṭia nišiprun** AM 270:2 and 268:8 barley and wheat will be injured (by snow); **sidta hanath̠ tišpar** AM 213:19 that year will be lacking; **tišpar kd̠ nura mn ʿšumia** AM 209:10 will be destructive (?) like fire from the sky.

ŠPT (H. שפת) to set, put, place (esp. over fire).

Pe. Pf. with suff. **šiptuk bšapta d̠-parzla rimiuk** JRAS 1938 3:21 they placed thee (over the fire and) cast thee into an iron cooking-pot. Impf. with suff. **nišipth̠ bsilua šarira** JRAS 1907 593:22 we will set it in with a firm shaft. Part. pres. with encl. **kd̠ mnaqdatlh̠ umihla šaptatlh̠** DC 48. 279 when thou cleansest it and puttest salt on it.

Der.: **šapta 3**.

ŠṢA, ŠṢṢ s. **ŠUṢ**.

ŠQA (שקא, ܫܩܐ, H. שקה, Akk. *šaqû*, Ar. سقى, Eth. ሰቀየ) af. to give to drink, give water; to water.

Af. Pf. with suff. **ašqian** he gave me to drink MG 284:26; **ašqitinun** Par. xi 17b I gave them to drink MG 291:2; **ašquia** Gy 115:23 AB (var. **ašquiuia** D) they gave him to drink MG 288:28. Impt. **ašqih̠** MG 287:21; CP 204:4; **ašqinun** Q 10:11, MG 290:19; **ašquia** Gy 15:ult. BD (var. **ašquiuia** A), 36:19, MG 289:5 f. Pt. pl. **mašqia** (for -in) **bit qubria** Jb 114:10 they give drink (refreshment) in the cemetery; with encl. **šilmai unidbai mn mia hiia mašqilh̠** DC 41. 489 Š. and N. give her living water to drink. Part. pres. **dalin umašqin** (var. **dilana umašqana** B, **dalina umašqina** DC 30) **mia lšitlai** Jb 135:4 f. I draw water and water my plants; with suff. **mašqinun** Jb 40:11 I give them to drink MG 291:bottom. Inf. **mašquia mia lšitlai** Jb 135:3 to water my plants; with suff. **mašqinun** Gy 318:24 to give them water MG 293:18.

Der.: **mašqita, šaquata = šiquata**.

šqar DC 46. 254:11, fem. **šqarta** DC 22. 499 def. forms of **šaqara**, fem. **šaqarta**.

ŠQH (šaf. of קְהֵי, קהא?) to make powerless, innocuous? **šqahit aina zruqtia** JRAS 1937 596:1 thou art made innocuous, squinting eye (doubtf.).

šqupta DC 26. 36 = **šuqupta, šiqupta**. Pl. **šqupiata** Q 74b:35, MG 169:12.

ŠQL I (šaf. of **QLL**, Jew.-Aram. שְׁקַל, Syr. ܫܩܠ, Eth. ሰቀለ) to take away, remove, take up, put up, lift up, carry, raise, reject, repel.

Pe. Pf. **šqal ainh̠** Gy 189:10 he raised his eyes; **ainai lmrum šiqlit** CP 40:9, Morg. 214/15:5 f. I raised my eyes to the height; with suff. **šiqlh̠** MG 14:21; Impf. **riših̠ nišqul** ML 22:8 f. he raiseth his head; **riših̠ lanišqul** DC 43 A he shall not lift his head; **taga mn riših̠ lanišqul** ATŠ II no. 39 he does not remove his crown from his head; **zaina alanpai nišqal** DC 44. 1628 = Morg. 267/25:7 f. he takes arms against me; **tišqal** Q 24:6 thou takest; **ʿšqul** Gs 129:ult. I take MG 220:16 f.; **latišiqlun zaina** DC 43 J 8 do not bear arms; with encl. **nišqilulh̠** they raise him MG 228:20. Impt. **šqul** (often in exorcisms) remove; **šqul lkuhrania** Or. 326:4 remove diseases. Pt. pl. **pihta lašaqlia** Gy 285:ult. they do not take the sacramental bread. Part. pres. with encl. **lašaqlanalh̠ umizdahranabh̠** Gy 161:7 I remove him not but preserve him MG 231:25. Inf. **mišqal ainia** Gy 194:24, 280:21, Q 5:16, CP 13:12; **mišqal ainia ukadpia** CP 49:9, Q 23:7 etc. to raise (raising) eyes and shoulders.

Af. Pt. pl. with encl. **mašqililh̠ d̠-diria halin** AM 287:5 they take it out from those seas. Nom. ag. **mašqlana** s.v.

Šaf. (MG 212:7): Pf. **šašqil ganpia d̠-markabatun** ATŠ I no. 100, 161 they hoisted the sails of their ships; **šašqlit** MG 223:12.

Ethpe. Pf. **ʿštqil sipaiun mn ʿdaiun npal** DC 44. 210 ff. their sword was removed (and) fell out of their hands. Impf. **tištqal** (read **tištqil**) **dmuth̠** DC 26. 322 his form will remove itself.

Der.: **mašqlana, mašqlʿil, šašq(i)lʿil, šiqlun**.

ŠQL II (H. שקל) to equal in importance, counterpoise.

Ethpe. Impf. & pt. **d̠-nišqil** (var. **d̠-našqil** PD) **kd̠ gahar** ATŠ I no. 51 so that he shall be as valuable as a jewel.

ŠQP (שְׁקַף, ܫܩܦ) to strike, emaciate, make pale, blight, afflict; to fasten, make a knot.

Pe. Pf. **šqap ʿl** Gy 99:4, Jb 138:2 he beat on; **šiqpat lpumaihun** DC 44. 940 f. she smote their mouths; **giṭra šiqpat** DC 43 I 144 she tied a knot; **šiqpit briših̠** Jb 188:9 AC, I smote his head. Impf. **nitimhia unišqup** ML 23:2 = CP 20:ult. (read **ništqip** he shall be beaten and smitten, cf. n. 1); **tišqup b- . . .** Gs 130:5 thou beatest on . . . Act. pt. pl. **šaqpia bʿda** Gy 353:16 f. they clap their hands; **šaqpia daiaria ualin** Gy 353:15 the inhabitants beat (their breasts) and lament; **šaqpia liardna** Jb 160:11 they strike the jordan (river) Jb ii 161 n. 6.

Der.: **šaqip, š(u)qupta, šiqupta**, pl. **š(i)qupiata**.

ŠQR (Aram., Syr., H., Akk. *tašqirtu* lie, Ar. شُقَر, سقر deceit, from Aram.) to lie, deceive.

Pe. Nom. ag. **šaqara**, fem. **šaqarta** s.v. (often defectively in DC 45 & 46).

Pa. Pf. with encl. **šaqirtbun** (var. **šaqartbun** AC) **bgubria kahnia** Jb 104:1 thou hast deceived men, the priests.

Ethpe.? Impf. **haikin nišiqria** (for **ništiqrun**?) **hinun kabšia** DC 26. 637 (corrupt) those that were deceived, they shall vanquish. Part. pres. **mištiqrit** Gs 117:13 (var.

mištaqrit DC 22. 499 ethpa.) thou tellest lies.

ETHPA. Part. pres. **mištaqrit** cf. s. ethpe.

DER.: **maštiqria, mištiqria, šaqara,** fem. **šaqarta** (also defectively), **šiqra.**

ŠRA I (שְׁרָא, ܫܪܳܐ, H. שָׁרָה, Akk. pi. *šurru* to begin, initiate, Eth. ሰረየ to absolve) pe. to loosen, untie, let loose, submit, agree, open, solve, dissolve, unbind, soften, liquify, free, begin, consecrate, celebrate (a rite), deconsecrate, exorcize; pe. also to dwell, find a dwelling-place, habitation, (and for the rare af.:) to cause to dwell, give a dwelling-place, install, house, cause to rest on, place on, bestow MG 215:5 f.; pa. to open, begin, use, employ, relax; af. (rare) to cause to dwell (*often replaced by* pe., cf. above); ethpe. to be freed, loosened, exorcized.

PE. Pf. **šra ṣauta** Q 26:26, **šra ʿlai mn ṣauth̠** Gy 327:19 (& *often with* **ṣauta** 1 (q.v.) 'to spread lustre'), **šra ṭalia ʿl haua** Gy 242:10 the boy cohabited with Eve; **šrat d̠-tihuia ṣauta** Gy 325:19 f. she agreed to be my companion; **iaminh̠ šru ʿlh̠** Gy 294:22 He (: Life, pl.) put His right hand on him MG 258:5; **mn hukumtun šrun ʿlai** Gy 326:15 (cf. f.) He (: Life) placed on me some of His wisdom; **šrun blilbia haškia** Gy 322:20 they let (it) dwell in dark hearts; **ziua ʿl d̠-ʿtlia šrun ʿlai** Gy 303:12 He (: Life) placed on me more radiance than I had (before); with encl. **šrabun ṣauta** Gy 304:15 (cf. above & s. **ṣauta** 1), **šrititibh̠** Gy 322:19 I dwelt therein MG 257:paen.; **mn niahun šrulia ʿl uṣrai** Gy 342:5 He (: Life) conferred some of His mildness in my mind; with suff. **šran** he let me dwell MG 284:21; **širian** Gs 119:11 he freed me MG 284:23; **širih̠** AM 201 he freed him; **šrath̠** she loosed her MG 287:antep.; **šrith̠ bʿndrunia** Gs 22:16 I installed him in chambers; **šritinun** Gy 346:16 f. I set them (caused them to dwell) MG 290:23; **šrun** Oxf. 51 b MG 285:antep.; **širiuk** Gs 61:12 they caused thee to dwell MG 287:2. Impf. **nišria . . . ʿlauaihun** Gy 361:22 will bestow . . . on them; **atia ṣauta d̠-hiia utišria ʿlh̠** CP 288:13, ATŠ I no. 7; **nišrun ʿlh̠ ṣauta** Gy 308:6 (cf. above and s. **ṣauta** 1); with encl. **tišribin** MG 256 n. 3; with suff. **niširian** Gs 75:6 he will free me MG 285:1; **d̠-nišriuk** Or. 326:6 which (pl.) will free thee (from spells); **tišrunh̠** MG 288:antep. Impt. **šria** (*often in exorcisms*) free, exorcize; with suff. **šrinan** Q 15:29 free us MG 289:18; pl. with suff. **šuriun** Q 74b:32 free me MG 286:13. Act. pt. **ʿu had libna bdukth̠ lašaria** DC 34. 1324 if (but) a single brick does not rest in its place; **šaria d̠-masiqta** CP 207:8, ML 239:7 who celebrateth the *masiqta*; with encl. **lmišria giṭria** DC 51. 120 f. to undo knots; **ulmišaruiia giṭria** DC 51. 121 (same); **šaribun bšurbata šaribun bqarabtania** Gy 83:2 prob. he encamped (hist. pres.) amongst the tribes, he encamped amongst the warriors Ginzā 83 n. 1; **kṣira d̠-šaralh̠** (better var. **šarilh̠**) **zma** AM 141, 147 a sick man whose blood they let; pl. **šarin ʿl ʿuṣria d̠-napšaihun** Gy 246:21 f. they dwell in their own minds; **šarin lmišria hda abatar hda** ATŠ II no. 104 they begin the opening prayers (lit. to open) one after the other s. trsl. 231 n. 6; **haimanuta . . . blibaiun šarilun** Gy 286:2 faith . . . dwelleth in their hearts. Pass. pt. **šria** Gs 8:19 etc. dwelling MG 259:paen., fem. **šrʿia**, irreg. **lašira** ATŠ II no. 198 is not freed, pl. **šri(i)n, šrʿin** Gy 60:8, Q 62:30, MG 165:2, 6, fem. pl. **šrʿiian** Q 62:24, **šrʿia(n)** Gy 378:1, MG 165:antep. f., cf. 166:1. Part. pres. (from pass. pt.) **šrina** I dwell MG 260:1, **šrʿiit** Gy 7:5 thou dwellest MG 260:4; with encl. **šr(ʿ)iatbh̠** Gy 7:6 thou dwellest therein MG 260:6. Inf. **lmišria bbaita ṣauta** Gy 318:21 to spread lustre in the House; **šarin lmišria** s. act. pt. pl.; as pt. **rišaia mišria qala umqarilh̠** DC 51. 587 the First One lets out a voice and calls her; with suff. **miširian** Gs 48:7 to free me MG 292:10; **miširih̠** Gs 48:5 to let her dwell MG 292:paen.

PA. Pf. **šariat** she began MG 260:paen. Act. pt. **mšaria kulhun handamia** AM 122:19 loosens all his limbs. Pass. pt. **šiša hadta d̠-lamšarai** CP 93:1 = Morg. 247/81:16 f. = ML 116:5 a new bottle not yet used; **taga hadta d̠-lamšarai** DC 42. 67 a new crown that is unused; pl. **hiklia hadtia d̠-lamšarin** Gs 22:16 new palaces that were never before used (inhabited).

AF. Pf. with suff. **ašrian** Gs 38:20 f. (& *often*) he let me dwell MG 284:27; **ašriak** Gs 61:15, MG 286:18. Impf. with suff. **ʿiašrh̠ lhibil bʿndruna hadta** Gy 260:17 I will install H. in a new palace. Pt. **mašria mia** Lond. roll A 383 letting water flow.

ETHPE. Pf. **laʿštauun ʿštra** [*sic*] **mn karsauatun** ML 79:6 = CP 63:15 they could not free themselves from their seats (cf. n. 1), **ʿsira hʿ ʿštiriat** DC 44. 1802 = Morg. 268/27:30 she was bound (but?) freed herself (doubtf.); **ʿštrin** (read **ʿštriun**, or **ʿštria** with PD) **mn anania** ATŠ I no. 162 they freed themselves (disembarked) from the clouds; **d̠-mn mruma štirin** [*sic*] DC 37. 49 who were set down from the height (heaven); with encl. **ʿštrialh̠** Gs 10:12 BD (var. **ʿštarialh̠** C, **ʿštrilh̠** A) **bainh̠ dimihta** Gs 10:12 a tear welled out of his eye (MG 264:5). Impf. **mn ʿsura laništria** DC 43 A 66 cannot be freed from the bond; **ʿsir ulamištria** DC 37. 456 is bound and shall not be loosed; **lištria** Gs 113:15 is loosed MG 216:10; with encl. **tištiribin birikta birikta tištiribin** DC 3. 420:10 = CP 274:14 = ŠQ 26:31 (**tištribin**) let blessing rest on them. Impt. **ʿštria** Gy 94:14 free thyself MG 265:12. Pt. **kd̠ mištria nišma mn pagra** Gy 37:16 when a soul is freed from the body; pl. **mištriin** Gy 353:21 A are freed MG 164:20; **kulhun giṭria mištrin** Gy 95:7 all the knots are loosed; **mištria mn dukth̠** ATŠ II no. 395 dislodged from its place. Part. pres. **lamištriit** (var. **lamištriat** D) Jb 64:2 thou wilt not be loosed.

DER.: **šaraita, šaruia, šariaiil, šariaiʿil, šariut(a), širiana** 1, 3, **širiata** 1, **šrita.**

ŠRA II (שְׁרַע, ܫܪܰܥ) to break down, fall into pieces Ginzā 520 n. 8.

Ethpe. Pf. **ʿštra npilia trin ʿuṣṭunia** Gs 85:12 the two columns (: legs) broke and fell down; **hirbia ʿtpagam uʿštra** DC 44 swords were injured and fell to pieces. Pt. pl. **alma ḏ-mištrin ʿuṣṭunia ḏ-šumia uarqa** DC 43 A 63 until the columns (: supports) of sky and earth are broken.

ŠRA III = ŠRR.

Pe. Impf. **nišrun lʿmamatun** AM 177:12 they will hold their pacts; **tiligṭun utišrun** Gy 246:15 take and hold firmly.

Af. certain forms identical with **ŠRR**, cf. **našrun, mašrin.**

Gl. 3:2 ff. **ašrai** [sic] اقام *facere stare* اعدّ ; برخيزانيد *parare.*

šraga 1 (שְׁרָגָא, ܫܪܓܐ < P. چراغ, Ar. loan-w. سراج Lagarde: *Abhandlungen* 31:26) lamp, light. Fem. Gy 281:9, masc. Gs 85:9 ff., 91:10 etc. MG 159:18. Pl. **-ia. šraga nahira** RD G 1 luminous lamp; **šragaian nahira** RD D 4 our luminous lamp; **trin šragia ḏ-minihria ʿumama ulilia** Gs 85:9 f. two lamps (: eyes) that shine day and night; **trin šragia ḏ-iaqdilẖ bainẖ** DC 40. 760 the two lights which burn in his eyes (*double meaning*, s. **šraga 2**); **tlata šragia** Jb 67:6, 69:9, 73:7, DC 26. 647 f., DC 40. 398; **šragia iaqidata** Gy 281:9 burning lamps.

šraga 2 dream, illusion.

šraz AM 204:20 = **širaz.**

šrar (cf. foll.) ML 180:12 name of a personified vine CP 150:14 = ML 284.

šrara (rt. **ŠRR**, ܫܪܪܐ) reality, truth, steadfastness, certainty, reliability, firmness, strength, sound health, stability. MG 115:17, Jb ii xvii n. 3, 34 n. 3. As opposite of **ṭʿia** Gy 15:12, 29:14, 37:1, 63:6, 274:16. **mhauilun šrara lrahmẖ** Gy 53:15 showeth the truth to his friends; **šadartlan šrara** Gy 66:17 thou hast sent us the truth; **ahbalan šrara ḏ-lanipil** Gy 68:2 give us firmness so that we shall not fall; **nitirṣun ligrẖ bšrara** Jb 28:12 his feet will stand firmly; **ligraihun šrara lamaška** Gy 376:20 f. their feet shall not find firm ground; **ligraikun šrara lamaška** Gs 86:1 f., cf. Jb 208:5; **bšrara ligraian** Morg. 256/3:23 in stability of our feet, cf. Lond. roll A 498, **ligraiun šrara lanigišiun** Morg. 255/1:24 s. **GŠŠ**; **bšrara lagašian** Morg. 256/3:33; **dirkia ḏ-šrara** Gy 62:21 ways of truth; **haila ušrara** Jb 1:4, Gy 26:5, 32:9, 315:14, 373:6, 18, 374:22 (*& often*); **haila rama ušrara qašiša** DC 44. 144 f. lofty strength and stern firmness; **haila ušrara ḏ-hšuka** Gy 149:14 strength and firmness of darkness; **šraran uhailan** Gy 149:23, 165:20 our force and strength; **šrarun uhailaiun** Gy 153:20 their force and strength; **naṭarta rabtia ḏ-šrara** Par. xxiv 3ab, xxvii 8a ff. great safeguard of firmness; **atra ḏ-šrara** Gy 188:19, 195:17 the place of truth; **ʿzdaraz bhukumat šrara** Gy 39:4 arm thyself with the wisdom of truth; **hukumta ušrara** Gy 38:13; **rušuma ḏ-šrara** Morg. 267/24:13 the sign of truth; **mitqaiam bqaiamta ḏ-šrara** Gy 45:5 is confirmed by the confirmation of Truth.

ŠRB (Ar. جرب) to (at)tempt. Mod. **atia gabra abatar ʿnta abatar gabra mušarab** DC 46 (a love charm) and the man shall come after the woman tempting the man. Gl. 59:13 f. **ṣ̌rba** [sic] جرب *tentare* تجربه كرد .

ŠRG I (den. from **šraga**) to heat, burn, enflame; to dream, have an illusion.

Pe. Pass. pt. **duga šriga** Gy 216:14 heated oven.

Pa. Pass. pt. **mšarga** DC 23. 515 inflamed.

Der.: **šraga.**

ŠRG II (Talm. שְׁרַג) to glide, slip, or (cf. ܫܪܓ) to hasten.

Pe. Impt. **šrug ʿulbẖ** Oxf. roll g 991, Or. 332:15 slip in, enter.

Ethpa. **kul man ḏ-ništargia** [*sic*] . . . **ʿutra amarlẖ štargit** . . . **ʿu lamištargia** DC 27. 218 f. any man (priest) who makes a slip . . . the *uthra* said to him 'Thou hast slipped' . . . if they do not slip.

ŠRGZ šaf. of **RGZ** (q.v.).

ŠRHB šaf. of **RHB II** (q.v.).

ŠRHZ (šaf. of **RRHZ.** Only Mand.) to tremble, hurry in fright, scare, frighten; refl. to shrink in alarm, be frightened, alarmed MG 212:5.

Šaf. Pf. **šarhiz šibqẖ** Gs 114:23 she left it in alarm, with suff. **minilaihun lašarhizuk** Jb 83:3 their words did not frighten thee away. Inf. **šarhuzia** DC 28, var. **šarhizia** DC 26. 151 to strike panic. Nom. act. **šarhazta** s.v.

Eštaf. Pf. **ʿštarhaz ʿl hdadia miṭarpia** Gy 77:14 were panic-stricken and dashed against each other; **ʿštarhizat** Jb 240:9; **u(ʿ)štarhzat** Gy 341:10 (and) she was frightened MG 222:22; **tibil kulẖ ʿštarhizat** DC 44. 271 the whole earth was aghast; with encl. **ʿštarhazalia** Gy 279:12 she was alarmed MG 226:6. Impf. **ništarhaz** Gy 314:11 MG 226:24; **ništarhaz ʿlẖ rqiha** DC 36. 43 f. the sky will be alarmed by him; **ništarhzun** Gy 315:2, MG 227:24; **maṭaraiia mn qudamẖ ništarhzun** ATŠ II no. 357 purgatory-demons will flee in fright before him. Pt. **mištarhaz** Jb 194:11, MG 230: bottom; **rmʿia arqa umištarhza** Oxf. 11 a the earth fell down in fright; **arqa . . . naida umištarhza** DC 48. 269 the earth . . . trembles and is terrified; pl. **mištarhizia** Jb 41:5, 144:5, Q 68:4, Par. xxvii 23a, **mištarhizia ṭuria** Gy 280:21 the mountains tremble(d); **mištarhzia** Oxf. 72 a, Gy 316:14, 353:14, Gs 82:10, Morg. 266/23:27, ATŠ II no. 79, 303, DC 37. 475, 484.

Der.: **šarhazta.**

ŠRHZL (preced. + encl. l) = **ŠRHZ** MG 86:4, 212 n. 2.

Refl.: Pf. **ʿštarhzal** Gy 294:8, 12 he was, they were, terrified thereat (cf. **ʿštarhzalia** Gy 279:12 s. **ŠRHZ**).

šrznaia diua cf. Jb ii 152 n. 3, Furlani: *I Nomi* 435.

šriga pass. pt. pe. of **ŠRG I** (q.v.).

šrita (rt. **ŠRA I**) (*a*) release, liberation, relief, respite, cure, (*b*) exorcism, spell, charm, (*c*) (dis)solution, diarrhoea, (*d*) liturgical technical term: (de)consecration ML xxiv, but prob. simply performance, perfunctory rite (cf. **šaria d̲-masiqta** s. **ŠRA I** pe. act. pt.). Pl. **širiata** 1 s.v. (*a*) **šrita bdaria litlun** PD 104 there is no release for them in the ages; **šrita ukauna lahauilh̲** DC 46. 188:ult. f. he shall have no respite or resting place; **uhuat šrita** DC 40. 45 and there was relief; **hanath̲ šrita kulhun razia** DC 27. 229 that (*masiqta*) is the liberation of all mysteries; **hauia šrita lman d̲-ʿsir** Lond. roll B, there will be release for one who is bound; (*b*) **šrita abadlh̲** Lond. roll B 252 ff., **šrita abadulh̲** DC 12. 126 f. performed exorcism for him, exorcized him; **pugdana d̲-šrita** JRAS 1937 595:18 exorcizing spell; **šrita d̲-šinta** DC 46 exorcism for sleep(lessness); (*c*) **šrita uruita d̲-ianqia** DC 46 diarrhoea (?) and weakness of infants; (*d*) **buta d̲-šrita** Q 2:22, CP 6:4; **šrita d̲-riha** CP 44:7, Q 19:34; **šrita d̲-pandama** Q 33:15.

ŠRK (= **ŠRG I**) to light, kindle, make fire, burn.

Af. Mod. pf. *ašreχ*. he lit, pres. *qəmašreχ*.

Ethpa. Pf. **markabata ʿštariak** DC 26. 211 (corrupt, better **ʿštarak** DC 28 par.) the (planetary) chariots burnt.

Gl. 92:1 f. **ašrk̦** [sic] شعل *accendere* سوزانيد.

ŠRP (Ar. شرف) to excel, prevail. Postcl.

Ethpa. Impf. **ništarap** AM 187:12 will be paramount; **ʿu mn nirig ništarap zma ništid** AM 187:14 if it be governed (?) by Mars, blood will be shed.

ŠRQ I (Aram., Syr., H.) to utter shrill or disconnected sounds, grunt, squeal, whistle, pipe.

Pe. Impf. **hanik niširqia hinun kibšia** (corrupt) DC 44 those who whistle, they are subdued (doubtf.). Act. pt. **miabib mramiz ušariq** Gy 280:4 f. he whistles, gesticulates and makes noises; **mamlil mištaiia ušariq** AM 124:9 he talks, chatters, and makes noises; **šariq ʿl dardqunia udardiquniata** DC 43 E 10 he whistles to boys and girls. Part. pres. **qarinin ušarqnin** (var. **ušarqinin** B, **ušarqinun** AD) Jb 43:2 I call them and pipe (my pipe) to them; **šariqnin bmašruqtai** DC 42. 3 f. I pipe my pipe to them.

Der.: **šaruqia, mašruqta.**

ŠRQ II (= **ŠRG II**), cf. Talm. שְׁרַק II) to glide down, slip. Doubtf., only in corrupt forms and contexts.

Pe. (var. af.). Pf. with suff. **šraqtan** HG (var. **ašraqtan** DC 36) she made me slip (?). Pt. **bmia d̲-ʿria šraqia** DC 7 into waters that are intermingled and glide on, or better (read **šriqia,** cf. ܫܘܼܪܳܩܳܐ P.-Sm. 4338) that are shining and resplendent.

ŠRR (Aram., Syr., cf. Eth. ሠረረ to found) to be firm, strong, steady, hold strongly. Secondary rt. **ŠRA III** s.v.

Pe. Pf. **šar** 1 as a name given to higher beings (s.v.); **kšar ušar** Gy 135:3 'He–was–successful–and–firm' (also as a name); **šarat** as a name of a female genie and a *malwāša* woman's name (s.v.); **šarat arqa bmsuta** Gy 98:10 earth became firm by condensation (MG 248:9). Impf. **nišar hailak** CP 462:12 thy strength shall be established (cf. the frequent **haila ušrara** s. **šrara**); **tišar** Gs 60:12 (read af.?) MG 249:20; with encl. **nišarlh̲** AM 214:6 (read af.?) he confirms it.

Af. Pf. **ašar** he confirmed MG 251:5; **ašar šban** Q 31:20 (CP 124:17) = ML 49:7, 81:6 he confirmed and baptized me; **ligrai lašar ulaqam** Gy 203:9 my feet stood not firmly; **ašar usbil** PD 944 bore with endurance; **ašar ʿl ʿumamatun** Gy 112:23 (cf. f.) they held firmly to their oaths; **hatma d̲-ahuia ašar ʿlh̲** Gy 144:13 he confirmed on it the seal of his brother; **lalgaṭ ulašar** Gy 315:19 did not hold firmly; **ʿl šuman ašar** Gy 247:1 they held firmly to our name; **iaminh̲ ašariun** (var. **aširiun** D) **ʿlh̲** Gy 292:6 He (: Life, pl.) confirmed him with His right hand MG 251:5 f.; **lhak mamla lašariun** ATŠ I no. 140 they did not hold firmly to that word; **bhailaihun d̲-hiia rbia ašrit alit binataihun** Gs 14:14 by the strength of the Great Life I entered firmly amongst them MG 251:10; **aširtun** MG 251:12, **aširnin** Q 57:24, MG 251:11. Impf. **našar uniqum ʿl ligrh̲** Gy 101:7, 9, 12 he shall stand firmly on his feet MG 251:15; **ialda msakilh̲ lmaṣbuta . . . unašar** DC 41. 504 the babe looketh forward to baptism . . . and becometh (?) strong; **malkalh̲** [*sic*] **našar** AM 218:18 the king will ratify it; **niligṭun unašrun** Gy 246:20 they will hold strongly MG 251:15. Impt. **sbul uašar** Gy 14:24, **ašar bhaimanuta** Gy 36:6, **lguṭ uašar** Q 51:18 (*& often*) MG 251:16. Pt. **mašar** he confirms MG 131:paen., 251:19; pl. **mašrin** Oxf. 23 a, Gy 290:8, 304:24, Gs 25:13 MG 251:22, **mašria** RD B 41, **udmašria šrara maškia** Oxf. 46 b and those who are strong find strength; **brušma d̲-hiia lamašria** RD B 94 they hold not firmly to the sign of Life; **d̲-lagṭia umašria ʿlh̲** CP 46:17, Q 51:17 = ML 60:7 those who hold firmly to it. Nom. ag. **mašrana** s.v.

Der.: **mašrana, šarir(a), šrara.**

ŠRŠ (den. from **širša**) to take root. Only one form found: **ʿlana d̲-šatriš** (read **ʿštaraš**) **mn gauh̲ hahu gupna** DC 22. 398:22 the tree which took root from that vine.

Der.: **širša** & varr.

ŠRŠL (šaf. of Jew.-Aram. רשל to flap, be lax) to relax, slacken, flap (wings) Jb ii 137 n. 8.

Šaf. Pf. with encl. **šaršilh̲ lganph̲ uʿtiblh̲** Jb 142:1 he flapped (or folded) his wings and sat by her.

ŠŠQL šaf. of **ŠQL** (q.v.).

ŠTA I (ܐܶܫܬܺܝ, שְׁתָא, ܫܬܳܐ, שְׁתֵי, H. שתה, South-Ar. 𐩦𐩩𐩺, Eth. ሰትየ, Akk. *šatū*) to drink, imbibe, be satisfied, refreshed. Mod. secondary rt. **ŠUT**, corrupt **ŠTN** s.vv.

Pe. Pf. **šta** MG 257:1, **štit** MG 257:19, **akaliun uštun** DC 41. 185 they ate and drank MG 258:2. Impf. **ništia mištia** Gy 109:18 let us drink MG 258:paen.; **latištia ulatiruia** Jb 246:5 drink not nor become intoxicated; **kd̲ ʿštia ulaʿsba** Gy 86:18 when I drink but am not satisfied. Impt. **štia** MG 259:10. Pt. **šatia,** with encl. **šatilh̲ lhamra** Lond. roll A 328 he drinks wine; pl. **mn mištiaihun šatin** Jb 266:11 they drink of their drink; **ʿnta . . . šatin** Gy

392:12 read **šatla** (sg.) MG 162 n. 1. Part. pres. **mištia lašatina** Gy 148:13, fem. **šatiana** MG 259:21; **aklitun ušatitun** DC 27. 164 ye eat and drink. Inf. **mištia** Gy 109:18, 148:13 (see above); **mištia zmaihun lruia** DC 43 J 47 to drink their blood to intoxication; with suff. **mištiak** Gy 86:16, **ʿl miklaikun uʿl mištiaikun** Gy 17:17 at your eating and at your drinking; **mištiaihun** Jb 266:11 (above s. pt. pl.).

DER.: **šataia.**

ŠTA II (Mishn. שתה II, Jew.-Aram. שְׁתֵי, שְׁתָא, Akk. *šatū*, cf. Jew.-Aram. שְׁתְיָא, Syr. ܫܬܝܐ, H. שָׁתִי I, Ar. ستاة, سَتًى web) to weave.

AF. Pt. pl. **d-maštin ʿzlia** DC 43 J 93 who weave webs; corrupt **ukma triṣ mištaiin . . . maštutin psiq** JRAS 1938 4:26 and "how straightly they weave!" . . . their web was broken.

DER.: **maštuta.**

štaputa AM 23 = **šataputa.**

ŠTL (Aram., Syr., H., coll. Ar., Akk. *šitlu* sprout, offspring) to plant, transplant.

PE. Pf. **štal šitlia** ATŠ I no. 25 (*& often*) he planted plants; **ia bnai ušitlai d-ana biaminai šitlit** ATŠ I no. 74 O my sons and plants which I planted with my right hand! Impf. **šitlia ništal** (*often*), **nišitlun** MG 227:17. Impf. **štul,** with suff. **šutlh̠** ML 244:1, DC 34. 842 plant him; **šutlh̠ lhanath̠ šitlak luatak** DC 34. 843 plant this plant of thine near thee.

DER.: **šutla, šitla.**

ŠTP (Jew.-Aram. שתף, Syr. ܫܘܬܦܐ, Akk. *šatāpu* to help) to join with, associate. Secondary rt. **ŠDP** s.v.

PE. Pf. **štapaitun** Morg. 217/22:ult. f. ye found company. Impf. **tišatpun** Gy 67:21 D var. of **tišadpun** (s. **ŠDP**), with encl. **tišatpulia minaihun** Gy 67:22 ye associate with them (as without the encl.); with suff. **latišatpinan b- . . .** CP 50:13, Q 23:22 = ML 66:3 associate us not with . . . Gl. 93:13 f. **štpa** [sic] شرك *sociari* شريک شد.

DER.: **ša(u)taputa, šutapa.**

ŠTN a corrupt mod. form of **ŠTA I** in **ʿniš mn mirta mištan** DC 46 86:13 a person who drinks some poison.

T

t the 22nd letter of the alphabet. Phonetic value: unvoiced dental plosive or fricative according to pronunciation as non-aspirated *t* or aspirated *θ*. Phonetic changes: **t** > **d** MG 42:2–15; **t** < **d** MG 43:4; of **t** vanishing as verbal ending before encl. and in compound nouns with **bit** (> **bi-**) MG 42:16–22.

ta mod. demonstrative: that. **bta akir dara** CP 354:32 in that last century; **kidbit lta riša** DC 27. 14 I wrote that beginning; **atruk lta bada** Jb 285:6 f. (miswritten as **ltabada** by Lidzb.) they woke thee up for that work.

tababia pl. (rt. אבב, cf. Akk. *abūbu* storm) storms, hurricanes. Us. with **ziqa.** Varr. **tabibia, t(i)babia, tibibia, tbibia** s.vv. Jb ii 130 n. 5. **ziqia utababia** Gs 14:4 D (var. **tibibia** ABC); **tababia birqia uanania** DC 22. 392 = **tibibia** etc. Gs 1:14.

tabara (rt. **TBR**) breaking, collapse. Var. **tbara** s.v. **kušṭa btabara nasba** ATŠ I no. 105 she breaks her oath.

tabula (cf. Jew.-Aram. תבל to spice, season) seasoning. **pt raia tabula** s. **raia 2.**

tabibia Gs 14:4 s. **tababia.**

taga (תָּגָא, ܬܐܓܐ, Ar. loan-w. تاج Fränkel 62) crown, silk fillet worn as the badge of priesthood RO ii 462, Siouffi 123, ML 10 n. 1, 2, MMII 31 n. 8, MR 221 n. 1. Pl. **-ia.** **šišlam malka d-tagia** PD 1016; **taga nahira šišlam** PD (cf. **šišlam** s.v. as a symbol of priesthood); **mara tagia** PD 832, **maria tagia** PD 854 lord of the crowns (Šišlam). Ritual idioms: with **YQR** af. (q.v.) 'to honour the crown'; with **TRṢ** 'to set up, consecrate', cf. **taga d-malka tarṣin** RD C 11 (**malka** = priest), **tagaiun tarṣin** RD C 3, **traṣa d-taga** coronation, Lond. roll A 4 = DC 54 (Coron). Often in rituals.

tahma (Nöld. from ܬܗܡܐ, cf. تَمِهَ & تَهِمَ MG 66:22, Brandt & Lidzb. from תְּהוֹם MR 131: bottom, Jb ii xvi n. 1) (*a*) (of water & earth) brackish, turbid, (*b*) (of words, people, and demons) dull, stupid. Pl. **-ia.** Cf. Nöld. ZA xxx 155; MSt 58. The meaning (*a*) may be confused also with **THM**, meaning 'to keep within bounds, confine' (cf. ܬܚܡ) hence water contained in a receptacle: 'cut-off water'. (*a*) **mia tahmia** Gy 13:2, 84:15, 269:9 f., 297:24, Gs 41:11 ff., Jb 51:11, 204:2, 234:13 ff.; **arqa tahma** Gy 310:17; (*b*) **malalia tahmia** Gy 375:16; **anašia tahmia** Gy 318:4, ATŠ II no. 83; **daiua tahma** Gy 282:8, 13, **daiuia tahmia** DC 26. 127, **tahmia algia** Gy 279:10 (as qualities of demons); **tahmia bahtia** Gy 60:13; **liṭia tahmia** Gs 57:12.

tauma 1 (< תְּחוּמָא, ܬܚܘܡܐ > Akk. *taḫūmu* Delitzsch: *Prolegomena* 42 n. 1) boundary, frontier, limit MG 63:4, 118:22. St. cstr. **ta(u)m.** Pl. **-ia.** Masc. **tauma titaia d-hšuka** Gy 281:23 the lower frontier of darkness, cf. **taum taumia titaiia d-hšuka** DC 12. 220, JRAS 1937 591 n. 1; **tum taumia titaiia** Lond. roll B 466, 473; **razia d-btauma škin** DC 34. 205 mysteries situated in the borderland; **mn rauma ualma ltauma d-almia** ATŠ I no. 224 from the height unto the (uttermost) boundary of the worlds; **unitrahqun d-iatbia**

taumia d̲-ruha DC 51. 498 and those that inhabit the frontiers of R. shall be taken far off.

tauma 2 (from OP *tau(h)ma*, mod. P. تُخْم, cf. Mand. doublet **ṭuhma**) nation, people, race. **amamia taumia ulišania** Gy 220:18, 223:22, 229:19, 232:10, 233:21, Gs 75:11, Q 56:7, RD B 64 (cf. Dan. 3:31, 5:19) MG 325:19; **taumia taumia** Gy 247:15 different peoples; **amamia taumia uqiriata** ATŠ II no. 433 peoples, nations, and cities.

tauma 3 (Jew.-Aram. תְּיוֹם, Syr. ܬܐܘܡܐ, H. תְּאוֹם, Ar. تَوْءَم, تُؤَام, Akk. *tu'āmu, tā'umu*) twins MG 883:8. Pl. **-ia. buṭna tauma zikra unuqbta** Gy 243:5 pregnancy with twins, a male and a female; **iadlat haua tauma zikra unuqbta** Gy 243:7 Eve brought forth twins, a male, a female; **mahunia taumia** s. **mahuna.**

taumia 4 in **gauaza d̲-taumia** DC 44. 513 for **gauazta umia** Morg. 258/8:40.

taumiata 1 Gy 150:21 stoppers, wedges, bolts (DC 22. 146 **tamaita**).

taumiata 2 (rt. **YMA**) Gy 150:21 conjurations, spells MG 133:13, 165:21.

taura (תּוֹרָא, ܬܘܪܐ, South-Ar. ثور, Ar. ثَوْر, Eth. ሰር, H. שׁוֹר, Akk. *šūru*, Gr. *ταῦρος*, Lat. *taurus*, also Zend and Pāzend) (*a*) bull, ox MG 100:17, (*b*) *Taurus*, sign of the Zodiac Siouffi 145, MMII 74. Defectively **tura.** Fem. **t(a)urita, t(a)urta** cow. Pl. masc. **-ia**, fem. **-ata.** (*a*) **gumlia utauria** Gy 387:19 camels and cows; **tauria d̲-piṭra** Gs 130:3 fatted oxen; **aiak taura abatar turta** DC 46. 189:11 like a bull after a cow; **taurta sumaqtia** DC 46. 70:4 a red cow; **azlit lbaqara** (miscop. **laqara**) **d̲-tauria uamart . . . kma šaminia hazin tauria uturata** (var. **utaurata**) DC 21, JRAS 1938 3:16 thou wentest to the herdsman and saidest: . . . how fat these bulls and cows are!; **turata d̲-ʿtbh̲ iamuria** s. **iamuria; qadiaiil taura** RD B 50 ff. name of a deified bull (cf. **taurʿil**); (*b*) Gy 122:17, 123:11, very often in AM.

tauriz AM 204 Tabriz.

taurii(i)l, taurʿi(i)l (theophorous name from **taura**) name of an uthra. ML 284. CP trs. n. 5. **tauriiil ʿutra** Morg. 8:2, CP 117:18; **taurʿil ʿutra** Gy 269:12; **tauriʿil ʿutra** Gy 129:4; **taurʿiil ʿutra** Q 59:26 (Siouffi 40:43, MR 65); **taurʿil gupna** CP 458:2, Gy 321:15. Gy 192: 2 f. as a head of 366 celestial dwellings (**škinata**). Gy 295:11 called **sam smir ziua** and identified with **iauar. alma d̲-turʿil** Gy 306:13 = **alma d̲-taurʿil** ibid. 14 the world of Tauriel (CP s. Index).

tazauin AM 206 name of a city BZ Ap. II.

taiaba (nom. ag. pe. of **TUB**) forgiver, compassionate being MG 120:16, MR 41. **haiasa utaiaba** Gy 1:24, 17:3, 30:20 merciful and forgiving; **taiaba umrahmana** Gy 36:15 compassionate and merciful; **taiaba uriuana** Gy 61:16 compassionate and clement; **taiaba damia lziqa basima** Gy 215:11 a compassionate person resembleth a pleasing wind; **taiaba tub ʿlai** Gy 84:22 Compassionate One, have compassion on me!; **taiaba tub ʿlan** DC 34. 339, DC 41. 268; **taiaba ʿlauaian tub** DC 48. 144 Compassionate One, have compassion on us!

t(a)iabuta (abstr. noun from preced.) forgiveness, forbearance, clemency. Var. **(ʿ)tiabuta** s.v. **taiabuta d̲-marh̲** Gy 17:2 clemency of his Lord.

ta(i)muz s. **tamuz.**

takasar Zotb. 220a:21 read **tšasar** nineteen.

takuna (cf. s. **TKN**) strainer, filter. **mhulta utakuna** DC 48. 281 a sieve and a strainer.

taksata (rt. **KSA**) clothes. Mod. **mindai utaksatai** DC 35:coloph. my things and my clothes.

takta s. **tikta.**

taktuša (rt. **KTŠ**, otherwise used as **KDŠ**, Syr. ܬܟܬܘܫܐ). Pl. **-ia** (DC 22. 40). Gy 17:8, 24: 22, 42:8 fight(ing), strife MG 42:5, 133:9.

taktiha (P. تخت, cf. پايتخت) Zotb. 218b:15 capital city.

tala 1 (תַּעֲלָא, ܬܥܠܐ, Ar. ثَعْلَب & ثُعَال, cf. H. שׁוּעָל, Akk. *šēlibu*) fox. **aiak tala ragala** (var. **dagala**) **šilpit unipqit** DC 26. 613 = DC 44. 645 f., var. Morg. 259/10:paen. f. like a fox I slipped out of the snare (var. like a cunning fox I slipped out) and went forth.

tala 2 AM 218:10 for **talia 1.**

tala 3 (doubtf., cf. Jew.-Aram. תְּלָא hook, or P.A. تَلَوِّى *petite embarcation rapide* Jb ii 162 n. 3) parallel with boat (**arba 1**) in **larbak damia larban ulatalak abinia hʿ** Jb 161:3 thy boat does not resemble our boats, nor is thy fishing-boat (?, hardly fishing-hook) between (them?).

tala 4 (Talm. תְּאלָא Löw 112) young date-palm, seedling-palm. Pl. **-ia. gilita d̲-sindirka d̲-bazira dilh̲ . . . d̲-hu tala šumh̲** DC 34. 366 the date-stone of a palm which is its seed . . . its name is seedling-palm (cf. par. text s. **tala 5**). **hukṣa d̲-tala** s. **hukṣa; talia d̲-ziqla ziburia** JRAS 1937 591:26 male palm(-shoot)s.

tala 5 (appears as a fig. use of **tala 4**, cf. s. (*a*)). (*a*) male, (*b*) strong. (*a*) **br anaša bazira dilh̲ bmiṣai ʿuṣṭunh̲ qaiim hu tala šumh̲ ugabaruta qarilh̲** DC 34. 399 f. (continuation of the text quoted s. **tala 4**) man having seed in the middle of the body is called male and they call it virility; (*b*) **tala ušarir** DC 46 (of an exorcism) it is strong and powerful.

talai ziua s. **talia 2.**

talap (Ar. تلف) AM 280:20 ruin, destruction.

talga 1 (תַּלְגָּא, ܬܠܓܐ, Ar. ثَلْج, H. שֶׁלֶג, Akk. *šalgu*) snow. Still used. **talga ubarda** Gy 283:9 snow and hail; **ṭala utalga banania** DC 40. 275 dew and snow in clouds; **kd̲ talga agambia ṭuria** DC 21, JRAS 1938 2:22 like snow on the mountain-sides; **talga nihuia umiṭra napša** AM 171–9 there will be snow and much rain. Gl. 53:9 missp. with **q** ثلج *nix* برف.

(talga 2) for **taga** in **btalga rba** DC 44. 1956 = **btaga rba** Morg. 270/30:3.

talia 1 (ܛܠܝܐ, Akk. *attalû* Mahler SBWA xcv 363, Nöld. ZA xxv 355 f., Furlani: 'Trattati Astrologici Syriaci', *Rendiconti* 1947 Nov.–Dec.) fictive dragon causing eclipse Ginzā 104 n. 2, BZ 62 n. 2. **talia rba** Gy 98:3 the great dragon, cf. **kbašth ltalia rba d-alahia** DC 23. 743 = DC 40. 753 I subdued the great dragon of the gods, (or **talia** 3?), **riš talia** Par. xxvi 208:middle, 216:bottom = AM par. the head of the dragon; **sira ʿtib btalia** (var. **btilia**) DC 26. 216 the moon was in eclipse; **atuat d-sin kd iatib btalia** AM 211:9 omens of the moon when it is in eclipse; **braz talia** AM 190:15 through the mystery of an eclipse.

talia 2 (act. pt. pe. of **TLA**) one who suspends or hangs up, hanger-up. **ia talia** (var. **talai** CP 214:15, ŠQ 13:18, 25 and ult. = imperat. f. **TLA** q.v.) **ziua** Oxf. 75 b, 76 a ff., WedF 25:11 f., 26:middle, ML 245:2 O lamp-lighter (lit. thou that hangest up light)!

talia 3 (תְּלָיָא hook) sceptre. **malka hurina talia bidh d-napšia ninsib** AM 213:4 another king takes the sceptre into his hand. Cf. **talia rba d-alahia** s. 1.

talia 4 pl. of **tala** 4 (q.v.).

talilia pl. (of תִּלָּא, ܬܠܐ & ܬܠܝܠܐ, H. תֵּל, Ar. تَلّ, from Akk. *tillu* Jensen) Jb 143:6, var. **tallia** B & DC 30, **tililia** Gy 60:2 small hills, mounds.

tam (Talm. תַּם II, Bibl.-Aram. תַּמָּה, Old Aram., Phœn. שם, H. שָׁם, Ar. ثَمَّ, Syr. cf. s. **taman**) there, with prep. **ltam** thither, **mn tam** from there MG 204:8. With **ha-**: **hatam, haltam** s.vv. **qaiim tam luataiun** Gy 238:ult. he stayed (hist. pres.) there with them; **mn tam** ML 14:1 thence.

tamaita (תְּאָם) DC 22. 146 (for **taumiata** Gy 150:21) a fastening.

taman (תַּמָּן, ܬܡܢ) there, in that place (contra MG 204:12). **btaman siba nihuia** AM 184:11 there will be misfortune in that place; **malka rba btaman nihuia** AM 184:11 a great king will be in those parts.

tamuz (Jew. תַּמּוּז month, H. as name of Bab. deity, Syr. ܬܡܘܙ, Ar. تَمُّوز, from Akk. *Ta(u)mûzu, Du'ûzu* Zimmern: *Akk. Fremdwörter* 65) fourth month of the year (corresp. to July) SsSs ii 27. Var. **taimuz.** Often in AM and in colophons.

tamuz(a) (cf. s. preced.) Tammūz, Bab. deity. **halin d-azlin lbit tamuz** Gs 30:20 (var. **tamuza** DC 22 & Sh. 'Abd.'s copy) those who go to the house of T.

tamur hind (Ar. تَمْر هِنْدِى) DC 46. 111:5 tamarind.

tamir AM 256:42 a name.

tamlida (Ar. تَمْلِيد) rejuvenation. **pt tamlida d-nisan** DC 40 daughter of rejuvenescence, that is, of N. (= April).

tana 1 (< Syr. ܬܢܢܐ, תְּנָנָא) a cosmic mist, vapour, or smoke. Pl. **tanania. ham tana pšar tana** Gy 238:8 the mist (or vapour) became warm, the vapour dissolved; **ham ziua pšar tana huat škinta uʿtqaimat bit hiia** CP 17:13 = Q 7:2, ML 19:6 radiance glowed, the vapour melted away, there was an abiding-place (*škinta*) and a House of Life was established; **tana unișibta d-hšuka** Gy 149:11 the fume and product of darkness; **pšar tanania umn kana qadmaia asgun** Gy 292:4 vapours dissolved and went forth from the primal base; **pšar btanania d-iardna** DC 12. 217 melted into the river-mists; **tana šuman** Gy 245:17 parallel with **nihmat hiia šuman d-nihmat. Tanas** are often mentioned as personified female celestial beings like 'clouds' and 'drops', with whom they are often associated.

tana 2 (= **kana**, Akk. *tannu*) a mythological term meaning container, matrix, vessel, or base. The word is used when describing primeval creative processes, MG 163:10, cf. MSchr. 138 n. 7, Kraeling JAOS 1953 pp. 162 ff. Lidzb.'s attempt ML 19 n. 3 to explain **tana** as an abbrev. of **tanura** is unsatisfactory, and in several doubtful instances **tana** 1 might supply the meaning better. **tana qadmaia** Gs 42:9 the first **tana**; **tana kasia** CP 143:12, PD 23, ATŠ I no. 4 the esoteric **tana**; **nibța d-nbaț mn gu tana** Oxf. 48 a the upsurging which burst up from within the **tana**; **tana uširiana** Gy 134:15 the **tana** and artery; **nițupta d-rbat btana urmitibh bgu pagra d-adam** Gy 172:14 f. the drop (sperm ?) which grew in the **tana** and which thou threwest into the body of Adam. The **tana** is said sometimes to have a verge or brink, **utria d-lkiph d-tana iatbia** CP 431:ult. uthras who sit at the verge of the **tana.**

tanania 1 pl. of **tana** (q.v.); **2** rarely for **taninia** (pl. of **tanina**) cf. Gy 375:12.

tang (P. تنگ) tight, narrow, difficult. **tang hauia** AM 110:14 it will be difficult.

tangara 1 (תַּגָּרָא, ܬܓܪܐ < Akk. *tamgāru, tamkāru* Jensen ZA vi 349, Ar. loan-w. تَاجِر Fränkel 181 f., den. verb **TNGR**) dealer, trader, merchant, trafficker MG 76:5, 120:18. Pl. **-ia. tangara d-nišmata** Gy 172:17 merchant (middleman) of souls Ginzā 176 n. 7; **ptula tangara** Gy 273:14, 21 a celibate merchant; **tangaria d-mitangria** Gy 72:14 f. merchants who traffick; **gubria tangaria** Gy 253:16, cf. Q 64:29; **qal tangarun** Jb 145:2 the noise of their traders; **tangaria lazabnia biahud** Jb 82:6 f. the merchants do not trade in Judea; **rgalth ltangarun** Jb 148:2 I bound their merchants; **trisar gubria tangaria** Gy 187:20 the twelve traffickers (= Christian apostles) Ginzā 189 n. 5.

tangara 2 (P. تنگره) copper pot or cauldron. Pl. **-ia. ktub lkasa d-pahara uatna ltangaria bbaita** DC 40. 402 f. write (the charm) on an earthenware bowl and put on copper pots in the house.

tangaruta (abstr. noun from **tangara** 1) (*a*) trade, commerce, wares, merchandize, (*b*) fig. good deeds Ginzā 68 n. 4. (*a*) **țab ltangaruta**

AM 141:12 favourable for trade, cf. Lond. roll B 306, 309; (*b*) **masqia tangarutun lbit riš riš** Gy 72:15 they bring their (good) work to complete achievement.

tanur(a) (תַּנּוּרָא, ܬܢܘܪܐ, H. תַּנּוּר, Akk. *tinūru* Delitzsch: *Prolegomena* 146 n. 3, Zimmern 32, Ar. تَنُّور Fränkel 26) (*a*) oven, (*b*) hollow place, cavity. Masc. MG 159 n. 3. Pl. **-ia.** (*a*) **ʿšata btanur iaqda** DC 43 J 119 flame burns in the oven; **bduq btanur šgira** DC 46. 179:16 put into a heated oven; **qbur btanur šgir** DC 46. 213:paen.; **qbur bqba** (= **bʿqba**) **d-tanura** DC 144. 329 bury (it) in the hind part of the oven; **uʿl hda tanura qaimin** DC 21 no. 276, JRAS 1937 594:18 and they stand by one oven; **giṭma d-šuba tanuria** AM 130:2 the ash of seven ovens; (*b*) **muma btanura dupna nihuilh** AM 82:3 she will have infirmity in the pectoral cavity (?).

Gl. 53:5 **tnura** [*sic*] تَنُّور *clibanus.*

tanihta DC 40. 231 & often for **tinihta.**

tanina (תַּנִּינָא, ܬܢܝܢܐ, H. תַּנִּין, Ar. تِنِّين Fränkel 123, Eth. ተመን, cf. Akk. *dannīnu* earth Jensen ZA vii 174 f., Bittner WZKM xxiii 149, cf. Lewy: *Fremdwörter* 15) dragon. Gy 79:20, 80:17 replaced by **tiniana 2.** Ginzā 80 n. 1 contra MG 122 n. 4. Pl. **taninia 1,** rarely **tanania 2.** MSt 122 f., BZ 96 n. 1. **tanina akla** PD 1171, 1223, 1434 ravenous dragon, pl. **taninia aklia** Gs 53:2; **taninia d-aklilun** RD C 19 dragons which devour them; **liuiatin tanin** ATŠ II no. 355, **liuiatan tanina** Jb 210:5, DC 41. 8 & often; **tanina** (var. **taniana** DC 22) **d-hdirlh lalma** Gs 9:15, cf. 14:9 dragon which encircled the world; **znipta d-tanina** Morg. 257/6:24 = **dnab tanina** Morg. 265/21:40, 267/24:26 the dragon's tail; **tanina d-trin rišauata** RD 36 a two-headed dragon; **tanina . . . d-šuba rišauata** Gs 85:1 a seven-headed . . . dragon; **riša d-tanina** AM 151 the head of the dragon; **mn taninia tiparqun** Gy 43:6 ye shall be freed from the dragons; **ruban ruban taninia bkul had anana ʿka** Jb 48:2 there are myriads and myriads of dragons in each single cloud; **hzaitun ltaninia d-rmin bgauaihun umitapkia** Gy 74:21 f. ye saw the dragons which are cast in them and turn, cf. Gy 75:17 f.

tanina 1 pl. of preced.; **2** occ. for **tanania 1.**

tanʿil DC 50. 719 theophorous name from **tana.**

tasaia in **mauminalak mihla tasaia l- . . .** DC 40:930 f. read **tasia** (impf. of **ASA I**) I adjure thee, Salt, to cure . . .

tasniqa (Syr. ܬܫܢܝܩܐ, Akk. *tašnīqu*, cf. s. **SNQ I**) torture, place of torture, hell MG 46: 20. Pl. **-ia.** **napil btasniqa d-naplibh bišia** Gy 23:3 he shall fall into the place of torture into which the evil ones fall; **raminalun btasniq(i)a d-alma** Gy 220:13 I will throw them into the torture-chambers of the world; **tasniqia d-arqa titaita d-hšuka** CP 52:3, Morg. 223/33:11 f. = ML 67:10 the hells of the lowest world of darkness; **mn rauma ltasniqia tipil** DC 7 thou wilt fall from the heavens to hell.

taʿab (Ar. تَعَب) AM 280:24 fatigue, exhaustion.

taʿlab (Ar. ثَعْلَب) = Mand. **tala 1** fox. **zimta d-taʿlab** Ṣâb.'s AM the hair of a fox.

tapaiia (**TPA IV**) cooks, bakers.

tapala (H. & Jew. תִּפְלָה, cf. **tipla** s.v., Ar. تُفْل & تُفَال saliva) (*a*) mud, slime, (*b*) adhesive, (*c*) lower part, bottom?, (*d*) foolishness, absurdity, frivolity, indecency, grossness. Var. of (*a*) **t(i)pala** s.v., of (*d*) **tipla** s.v. Pl. of (*d*) **tapalia.** (*a*) **kd šihura mn tapala** s. **šihura; ʿuša utapala** (var. **t(i)pala**) CP 51:1, Q 23:27 swamp and mud; (*b*) **tapala rba d-baita kulh bgauh lgiṭ** ATŠ I no. 245 the great uniting element (adhesive) by which the whole edifice is held together; **hanath tapala d-smiklh ukul ʿuṣṭunia** DC 34. 54 that is the adhesive which supports him and all his body; (*c*) **hinun parzla kulh lbar mn tapala titaia** DC 35:coloph.; (*d*) **uarbima uarbin arba tapalia šrʿia ʿlh hanath masgda** DAb = RD 17 and 444,000 indecencies (?) abide in that mosque.

tapukia (inf. ettaf. of **APK**) revolving. **tapukia garglia** Q 54:12 the revolving of the spheres.

tapsaramka s. **tapsramka.**

tapsir (Ar. تَفْسِير) Par. xiv, DC 34. 34:747, ATŠ I no. 48 etc. explanation, treatise, interpretation, commentary MG xxxiii:antep.

tapsramka (אַסְפַּרְמְקָא & varr., ܐܣܦܪܡܟܐ, ܐܦܣܪܡܟܐ & varr.: Löw 152, P. سپرم Lagarde: *Abhandlungen* 65:2) Gy 106:23 *Ocimum basilicum*, odoriferous plant. Varr. **tapsaramka** ibid. D, **ʿtapsramka** Gy 106:24, **ʿtapsaramka** CD.

taqanta 1 (nom. act. pa. of **TQN**) Jb 219:1 f. order, Lidzb. light, illumination (*Erleuchtung*).

taqanta 2 (cf. ܠܒܝܠܐ, ܠܒܝܠܘܬܐ) decrepitude; **taqanta bligrh** DC 43 J 140 (list of physical calamities) decrepitude in his feet.

taqun (rt. **TQN**) steady, unwavering, clear (of light), enduring, steadfast. St. **taqna** (q.v.), but fem. **taqunta**; fem. pl. **taqunata** MG 114: 4 f. & n. 3, 125:11, 174:4. **ziuak taqun** Jb 219:9 thy radiance is clear; **anpiš ziuak utaqun nhurak** ATŠ I no. 162 great is thy radiance and steady thy light; **taqun kd aina hʿ taqunt(i)a** ATŠ II no. 29 he shall be clear as a clear well-spring; **aina taqunta** Gy 215:8, DC 34. 1088 & often; **šurubta . . . rauazta utaqunta** DC 51 flourishing and enduring stock; **halin masqata udukrania haiata ʿrata taqunata** DC 42 these life-giving, light-giving, and restorative *masiqtas* and *dukranas.*

taqup(a) (rt. **TPQ**) strong, overpowering, grievous; (of an odour) pungent, acrid. Fem. **taqupta.** **hda minaihun d-taqip urihh snia** ATŠ I no. 220 (of humours of the body) one of them is acrid and its odour hateful; **hala taqupa** DC 23. 768 (strong) vinegar (cf. mod. *toqfa* vinegar); **taqupa** AM 263:39 bitter; **mšadranuta taqupta** DC 43 D 64 grievous commission.

taqin, fem. **taqintia** sporadically for **taqun,** fem. **taquntia.**

taqip(**a**) (rt. **TQP**) firm, strong, powerful, hard, harsh, severe, stern, unkind, tyrannical. Fem. st. emph. **taqipt**(**i**)**a.** Pl. masc. **-ia,** fem. **-ata.** **libẖ taqipa** AM 27:11 his heart is stern; **maka ltaqipa latatnun** Gy 14:18 surrender not a mild one to a harsh one; **hakima ḏ-lataqip** Gy 216:antep. a wise man who is not firm; **mahra taqipa** AM 44:17 a severe illness; **basima utaqipa** AM 27:penult. pleasant and forcible; **barda taqipa** DC 48. 224 bitter cold; **malakia taqipia** DC 26. 593 powerful angels; **taqipta bharšia hauia** AM 59:1 she will be powerful in magic; **humria taqipata** Or. 326:1 powerful amulet-spirits; **minilia bišata taqipata** DC 44. 1236 = Morg. 264/18:7 wicked, harsh words; **lišania taqipia** DC 44. 1367 = Morg. 265/20:37 harsh tongues.

taqlata pl. (rt. **TQL**) stumbling-blocks, blunders. Var. **tiq**(**i**)**lata** s.vv. **btaqlatkun** (var. **btiqlatikun** C) **lamitqilna** Jb 61:6 f. I am not tripped up by your stumbling-blocks.

taqna (rt. **TQN**) permanent, durable, stable, proper, established, abiding, orthodox, firm, steadfast, well-ordered, reliable, unsullied, clear, lustrous, illustrious, constant, authentic. St. abs. **taqun** s.v. Pl. **taqnia,** fem. st. abs. **taqnan** (emph.) s. **taqun.** **tušbihtẖ taqna** DC 53. 244:14 f. its praise is unsullied; **atra taqna** CP 249:7 unsullied place cf. trsl. 190 n. 1; **daura taqna** Gy 188:11 (*& often*) abiding (i.e. everlasting, eternal) abode, as opposite to **daura baṭla** (Lidzb. *der lichte Wohnsitz*); **hazin maṣbuta taqna umtaqna** DC 50. 176 this is a rightful and confirmative baptism; **zharia taqnia** ATŠ I no. 8 orthodox rubrics; **ruha unišimta upagra taqnia bhdadia** DC 27. 472 spirit, soul, and body are properly integrated; **ginza taqna** Gy 345:19, Gs 58:23 reliable treasure; **ʿbidatun taqnan** DC 53. 271:1 their works are honest; **mia taqnia** (*often*) clear (unsullied) water; **lišana taqna** CP 440:9 honest tongue; **razia taqnia** (*often*) properly performed (authentic) rites.

taqnuta (abstr. noun from preceding) stability etc. Often.

taqpiaiil DC 40. 817, **taqpʿil** Gy 167:9 an angel.

taqriaiil DC 40. 927 an angel.

TAR (secondary rt. from **ATR II**) to be plenteous, abounding, enlarged; to increase; (*less often from* **ATR I**) to rise up, emerge, break through (light), shine. MG 245:4.

Pe. Pf. **mitar tar** Gy 171:9, Gs 41:22 manifested greatness. (**a**)**tar hšuka tar** Gy 83:23 the place (Lidzb. *die Pforte*) of the darkness became enlarged; **mitar tar hšuka** Gy 79:6 the darkness increased (or was enlarged); **daiua tar** (var. **ʿtar** Leid.) **mn siniauis** Gy 134:5 f. there appeared a demon from Siniawis; **tar raza kasia ḏ-tar utar . . . ziuẖ udna** DC 50. 752 Tar, the Secret Mystery, whose radiance rose up and broke through . . . and shone out; **tar ušar iardna kasia** DC 50. 750 the occult jordan emerged and was strong.

tar 1 a var. of **atar** place & of **tir** door. Ginzā 84 n. 2. **tar** (var. **atar** A) **hšuka tar** Gy 83:23 s. **TAR,** cf. **tar** (var. **ʿtar** B) **širiana ḏ-hšuka** Gy 83:21; **hzaiṯẖ ltar** (var. **ltir** BC) **hšuk** Gy 74:18 I saw the door of Darkness.

tar 2 a genie forming a pair with **taruan 1** ML 284, Siouffi 39:20, MMII 76, 245 f. **tar utaruan** Oxf. 57 a = ML 229:1, CP 194:9, Gy 221:4? **tar raza kasia** and **tar ušar iardna** s. **TAR.**

-tar P. comparative suff. تر– frequent in mod. Mand., cf. MG xxv 3.

tarbaṣa (תַּרְבִּיצָא, ܬܪܒܨܐ, < Akk. *tarbaṣu*) (*a*) forecourt, courtyard, house, (*b*) surface or front of certain parts of the body, (*c*) courtyard-demons of both genders. MG 134:4 & n. 2, Jb ii 37 n. 6, Ginzā 106 n. 1. Pl. **-ia.** (*a*) **azil lbaitak ultarbaṣak** DC 40. 1117 go to thy house and thy courtyard; **qbur btarbaṣa ḏ-baiṯẖ** (in several magical documents) bury (it) in the courtyard of his house; (**a**)**btarbaṣa ḏ-napšai** Jb 283:12 in my own house; **btarbaṣa ḏ-ʿustad iaqira** ATŠ coloph. in the house of the respected craftsman . . .; **mn kulhin nišmata ḏ-ʿka btarbaṣai** PA xii from all persons that are in my house; **btarbaṣia ḏ-nhura bit tušlima** Gy 241:13 in the courtyards of light, in the House of Per fection; **tarbaṣia ḏ-qira aklia** Jb 243:5 courtyards impregnated with pitch; (*b*) **tarbaṣia anpaikun** Gy 345:11, **tarbaṣia anpai** Jb 33:3; **tarbaṣia hadiẖ** Gy 99:5, Gs 3:7, **tarbaṣia hadiaiun** Gy 310:24, **tarbaṣia hadiak** Gs 130:5 etc. (cf. s. **hadia 1**); (*c*) **tarbaṣia zikria utarbaṣia nuqbata** DC 37. 394 f.

tarbušnaita DC 43 A 43, 95, 137 a female demon.

tarbuta 1 (rt. **RBA I**) rearing, bringing up, education. **tidal utarbuta tirabia** AM 81:penult. she will bear children and bring them up; **šuma rba nasib utarbuta** AM 8:5 he will acquire a great name and (good) education; **tarbuta nirabia** AM 2:20 he will rear (children); **tarbuta udina nihuilẖ** AM 25:7 he will have education and judgement.

tarbuta 2 name of a lilith. **tarbuta lilita** DC 43 E 75.

targalta (rt. **RGL**) fettering, fetters. **šqul . . . targaltak mn ligrẖ** DC 43 J 155 f. remove . . . thy fetters from his feet.

taruan 1 a genie quoted with **tar 2** (q.v.).

taruan 2 name of an ideal region and hill Jb ii 116 n. 3. **arqa ḏ-taruan dakita** Par. xxvii 69b, Gy 306:3, cf. **taruan dakita** Gy 304:1 f., 6, 21, 305 *passim*, 346:21 etc. (*very often*); **iardna ḏ-taruan dakita** Gy 321:16; **ṭura ḏ-taruan** Jb 189:10 f.; **taruan raza rba ḏ-iardna** Par. xxiv 4b; **taruan nhura** CP 7:5.

tarik (Ar. تاريخ) colophon. **kidbit hazin tarik** DC 12. 344 f., 348, 359, 416 I wrote this colophon.

tarkunia inf. ettaf. of **RKN** (q.v.).

tarmaduta DC 34. 156 read **tarmiduta** priesthood.

tarmud AM 203 name of a town BZ Ap. II.

tarmia AM 255:8 read **tarmidia.**

tarmida (תַּלְמִידָא, ܬܠܡܝܕܐ, H. תַּלְמִיד,

Ar. loan-w. تَلْمِيذ Fränkel 254) orig. disciple (nom. act. used as a concrete noun), hence name now describing all Mandaean priests MG 55:3, 133:16, MR 119, MSchr. 5 n. 2, RO ii 464, MSt 161 f., MMII chapter ix. Pl. **-ia**, fem. **tarmid(i)ata** MG 169:5; **tarmida šišlam rba** PD 68 (Šišlam as a symbol of priesthood); **tarmidak** thy priests MG 177:10; **tarmidiata** Gy 288:5, Jb 45:3, DC 36 II no. 296, cf. **tarmidata umandaiata** ATŠ I no. 239 women of priestly caste and women of lay descent.

tarmiduta (abstr. noun from preced.) priesthood. Var. **tarmaduta** s.v. **hatmia d̲-tarmiduta** DC 34. 18 the seals of priesthood; **šla lbuših̲ d̲-mandaiuta ulbušh̲ d̲-tarmiduta lbaš** DC 34. 601 he took off his lay garments and put on his dress of priesthood; **mn mandaiuta ltarmiduta** ATŠ II no. 358 from lay status to priesthood.

tarnaula (תַּרְנְגָלָא, תַּרְנְגוֹלָא, ܬܪܢܓܠܐ, ܬܪܢܘܓܠܐ, mod. H. תַּרְנְגוֹל, from Akk. *tarlugallu* < Sum. *tarlugal* Oppert ZA vii 339, Zimmern: *Akk. Fremdwörter* 51) cock-bird, cock MG 41:10. Fem. **tarnaulta** hen. **miqria** (var. **mqaria** F & DC 30) **tarnaula** Jb 124:5 at cockcrow (: dawn); **tarnaula d̲-dibra** ATŠ I no. 256 the cock of the wilderness (wild fowl?); **damia kd̲ tarnaulta** DC 46. 66:11, 115:8 resembles a hen; bita **d̲-tarnaula** (read **tarnaulta**?) DC 12 a cock's (hen's?) egg. Masc. often in AM.

taqpʿil Gy 167:12 an angel.

tarṣa (rt. **TRṢ**, cf. **traṣa**) consecration. **nitqaiam tarṣak** = **nitraṣ tarṣak** CP 465:5 thy consecration is confirmed.

tarṣut aina (rt. **TRṢ**) straightness of eye DC 3.

tartin fem. of **trin** (q.v.). **d̲-dimihta bainh̲ kd̲ tartin btartin** DC 44. 1013 who has tears in her eyes, in both of them; **btartinin gasinai** s. **gasina**; **asra utartin** Gy 263:8, 267:7 twelve MG 188:ult.; **dimaihun d̲-tartinin** tears of both of them; **btartinin ʿdh̲** Oxf. 16a with both his hands MG 191:1 f.; but **tartinun** Gy 146:8, 293:13 both of them (masc.); **tartinan** Gy 116:20 etc. both of us MG 191:5 f.; corrupt forms: **tartuinun** Gy 146:8, 147:12, **tartiunan** Gy 116:20 (all three in cod. A) MG 191:10, 12.

tašuan AM 197 name of a town (cf. **tazauin**).

tašuiš (Ar. تَشْوِيش, cf. **ŠWŠ** = **ŠBŠ**) AM 257:16 confusion MG 49 n. 3.

tašlumia Q 56:11 var. of **tušlimia**; **tašlma** Zotb. 229b:5 for **tušlima**. **hin btašlumia taqmilia qudamai** CP 110:5 (= ML **btušlimia**) q.v.

tašrin AM 262:26, 273:19 = **tišrin.**

tata (derivation, uncertain; but cf. Sachau's *Ostracon from Elephantine*, Plate 63:1, & Lidzb. DLZ 1911 col. 2979 = *Ephemeris* iii 256, Jb ii 215 n. 1) lamb, ewe, sheep. **aqamra (d̲-)br tata hiuara** ATŠ I no. 15 = PD 207 wool from a white sheep; **tata hiuartia** Jb 233:2 a white ewe; **alita d̲-tata** ATŠ I no. 248 the tail-fat of a sheep; **damia kd̲ bahima d̲-rišh̲ tata** DC 46 resembles a buffalo with a sheep's head.

tatagmur name given to Yawar, a (personified) tree and a cloud. **iauar tatagmur** Oxf. 57b; **tatagmur ʿlana** Gy 321:17, CP 458:6 = (DC 3. 319:1 **tatagmir**); **tatagmur anana** Gy 374:10.

tatura, taturaqa (תִּיתּוּרָא < Akk. *titurru*; as to the ending -qa cf. Pahl. *vetarak*) bridge MG 134:3. Pl. **taturia**. Masc. **tatura rba d̲-ziua** Gy 272:12, 273:17 great bridge of radiance; **ltatura d̲-ṣar danqa asqh̲** s. **danqa 1**; **taturia** Oxf. 34b. Par. xxiv 28b, 34b, DC 44. 633 ff. = DC 26. 603 ff. = Morg. 259/10: 33 bridges, cf. **batutia taturia** DC 46. 84:9 beneath bridges; **ʿl taturaqa latidun** Q 56:18 = ML 136:4 = CP 110:15 ye shall not pass over the bridge (Lidzb. *ihr werdet am Brückenwächter nicht vorbeigehen*, cf. ML 136 n. 2).

tbaba (rt. תבב to move to and fro) one who dodges, flinches. Doubtf. **ia tbaba zainai** DC 43 J 142 O thou that dodgest (?) my weapon.

tbabia s. **tababia.**

tbara (rt. **TBR**) breaking, fracture, ruin, destruction, breaking down, spoiling, discomfiture. **kušṭa btbara nasba** PD 1045 she breaks her vow; **tbara d̲-mia d̲-buta** PD 595, ATŠ II no. 36 adulteration of the water of prayer; **tbara urgala** DC 43 A 153, DC 37. 10 discomfiture and fettering; **tbara lbnat anašia šabqia** DC 44. 129 they loose discomfiture on the daughters of men.

tbibia Jb 132:8, 12, 133:3, 12, 14, 134:3 = **tababia.**

TBR (תְּבַר, ܬܒܪ, H. שבר I, Sab. 𐩻𐩨𐩧, Ar. ثبر, Eth. ሰበረ, Akk. *šebēru*) to break (down), fracture, weaken, spoil, destroy, adulterate.

Pe. (often also for ethpe.). Pf. **tbar** Q 2:14 for ethpe., **tbar mia d̲-buta** PD 1716 he adulterated the water of prayer; **ʿu tbar hazin raza** DC 43 J 83 if they broke this spell; with suff. **tibrh̲ lmaṭaratun** Gy 324:15 he brake their purgatories. Impf. **nitbar** Gs 119:3 he will break; AM 209 he breaks MG 221:1; **mia d̲-buta (la)nitbar** Q 48:5, 10 he adulterateth (not) the water of prayer. Act. pt. fem. with suff. **tabralh̲ lkušṭa d̲-bgauh̲ nisbat** ATŠ I no. 102 she breaks the vow which she took. Inf. **ulmitbar qublia d̲-baita** DC 51. 122 and to break the chains of the House.

Pa. Pf. **tabar mia d̲-buta** PD 384, 392, 1079 = ATŠ (*often*) par. he adulterated the water of prayer; with suff. **tabirtinun** she broke them MG 282:19; **tabrunun** (var. **tabrinun** B sg., **tarbunun** A corrupt) **lganpia d̲-ʿtlun** Jb 134:5 f. they broke their wings. Impt. **tabar hailaiun** Gy 62:17 break their strength. Pass. pt. pl. **maqim mtabria** Gy 29:10 he raiseth cripples; **mtabria ušapupia** Jb 274:13, 275:14 cripples and the lame. Inf. **taburia hatmia d̲-hšuka** DC 51. 359 f. to break the seals of darkness.

Ethpe. Pf. **ʿtbar kuza** ATŠ II no. 316 the jar was broken; **humarta d̲-halṣai ʿtibrat** Gy 164:18 the joint of my loins was broken. Pt. **mitbir** DC 36 II no. 361 defeated; **mitbar** ATŠ II no. 6 broken.

Ethpa. Pf. ʿ**tabartin** Q 52:18 ye (fem.) were broken MG 224:13.
Der.: **tabara, tbara.**

TGR s. **TNGR.**

THM (Jew.-Aram. & H. תמה; Syr. ܬܗܐ) to be torpid, stupid, stupefied, astounded, dull, inert, listless, inactive, rigid, motionless, senseless, stunned, struck aghast, astonished, amazed, confounded; (of water, cf. Ar. تمه = تهم & Mand. doublet **TMA**) to be brackish, turbid.
Pe.: Act. pt. **tahma** s.v.; pl. with encl. **anašia tahmilẖ** AM 235:15 people will be astounded (?) by him.
Der.: **tahma, tihma, tuhma.**

TUB (תוב, ܬܐܒ > Ar. تاب; cf. H. שוב, Ar. ثاب, Sab. 𐩻𐩥𐩨 to return) to turn back from, repent, forgive, be merciful.
Pe. Pf. **tab hiia lanihuia lmarẖ d̠-baita** Gy 175:12 the Life turned away and will not be a portion of the lords of the House; **hiia tab** ʿ**l iušamin** Gy 294:21 the Life felt compassion for Y. Impt. **tub** 250:6 **tub tub maria ruaha** Gs 52:20 turn thee, turn thee, Lord of restoration; **tub u**ʿ**traham** Gy 61:18; **tub utraham** Jb 163:5 be merciful and compassionate (other examples s. **taiaba**). Act. pt. **taiib** ʿ**l napšẖ** Gy 17:1, 66:10 repenteth; **hin taiib** ATŠ II no. 2 if he should repent. Part. pres. **taibit** ʿ**l bhiria** Gy 275:6 thou forgivest the chosen ones. Inf. **mitab** ʿ**lẖ** Jb 30:12 to forgive him.
Der.: **taiaba, taiabuta,** (ʿ)**tiabuta.**

tuhma (ambiguous) stupefaction, bewilderment, dismay; (if from ܛܘܗܡܐ) restriction, confinement, incarceration. **tuhma l**ʿ**ntẖ** ʿ**u bratẖ** AM 186:12 dismay (or confinement) upon his wife or daughter.

tukia pl. (of תוּכָא, ܬܘܟܐ) (*a*) reproofs, threats, calumnies, (*b*) oppressions, injury, harm, loss, misery. (*a*) **tukia nimrun** ʿ**lẖ** AM 67:16 they will speak calumnies about her; (*b*) **tukia udahalta** AM oppressions and fear.

tuklana (rt. **TKL I**) trust, confidence, faith. **udqaiim** ʿ**l tuklanẖ** Gy 2:7, 31:3 f. and that standeth by faith in him; **sibranan utuklanan** Gy 61:19 our Hope and our Trust.

tulut (Ar. ثُلْث) Zotb. 219a:28 a third.

tulita (תּוֹלַעְתָּא, ܬܘܠܥܬܐ, H. תּוֹלֵעָה, Eth. ቲል, Akk. *tultu*) (*a*) worm, (*b*) embryo. MG 16:21, 22:20, 134:2. Pl. **tulia** (or st. abs. sg.?). (*a*) **urapiš bmia siauia kd̠ tulita** Gy 152:18 and he wriggled in black waters like a worm; **tulita d̠-šaraia, tulita d̠-abrišam** ATŠ I no. 256 silkworm; **tulita lkaka** DC 51. 82 (and bestowed) the worm on the tooth; **unapqa minẖ tulia** DC 46 and the worms will come out of him; (*b*) **tulita d̠-gibilta** ATŠ I no. 257 an embryo, that is a formation.

tum 1 (Talm. תּוּ, Syr. ܬܘܒ, Ar. ثُمَّ) then, after that MG xxxiii n. 1, 49:ult., 204:13, 429:9–15.

tum 2 st. cstr. of **tauma 1** (q.v.).

tum 3 (Ar. ثُوم) garlic: **tum hu** DC 41 (first illustrations) it is a garlic plant.

tumarta (תּוּמַרְתָּא & תְּמַרְתָּא, ܬܘܡܪܬܐ, H. תָּמָר, Ar. تَمْر, Eth. ተምር) DC 23. 55 date. Pl. **tumria** Gs 3:10, MG 18:2, 173:21.

TUN (ܬܐܢ, Eth. ሸነ, Akk. *šânu*, cf. H. שַׁיִן urine, Ar. مَثَانَة urinary bladder) to urinate.
Pe. Act. pt. **taiin** ʿ**lauai** [*sic*] DC 46. 201:13 he shall urinate upon it; **kdub lman taiin bmania** DC 46 write (the charm) for one that urinates in his clothes.
Der.: **tina 1.**

tunba (תּוּנְבָּא, cf. Syr. ܬܘܢܒܐ LS) DC 47,Or. 329:1 rigidity, stupor (name of a disease-spirit), disease of the bowels or anus.

tus name of a mythological dragon. **lriš tuš tanina qaiimna** DC 40. 556 I stand on the head of the dragon T., **ltus tanina qaiimna** DC 40. 672.

tup (onomatopoeic Ar.-P. تُفّ) pah, pooh, ugh, shame! **tup uglila napša** s. **glila.**

tupang (P. تُفَنْگ) DC 43 J 241 gun.

tupiana (rt. **TPA**) (*a*) (of moon) waxing, approaching the full, (*b*) full flow, abundance. (*a*) **hin sin ltupiana d̠-iahra hauia** AM 265:6 should the moon be at its waxing (period) of the month. Var. **tupiata** AM 266:2; (*b*) **hazin baba kdub l**ʿ**nta d̠-halba qarib . . . hauia btupiana** DC 46. 158:5 write this charm for a woman approaching lactation . . . (the milk) will flow abundantly.

tupiata s. **tupiana** (*a*).

tuqna (rt. **TQN**) (*a*) order, stability, construction, establishment, institution, proper or orthodox procedure, (*b*) steady light, constant shining, gleaming (esp. of the moon) MG 49 n. 1, Jb ii 27 n. 2, MR 51 n. 2. (*a*) **širšan utuqnan** Gy 310:3; **masqilẖ ltuqna ušalma** Jb 85:3; **nišimta mn tuqna d̠-tlata razia** ʿ**ṣtarar** HG l. 2652 the soul came into being through the construction of three mysteries; **lman** ʿ**thib tuqna** DC 3 252:12 = CP 382:4. As opposite of **durdia** Gs 41:20, DC 34; (*b*) **ziua lšamiš utuqna lsira** Gy 12:17, 33:3, 23; **šamiš uziuẖ usira utuqnẖ** Gy 289:16; **taqun tuqnẖ mn tuqna d̠-sira** CP 111:10, ML 137:2, Gs 7:3, cf. DC 27. 111; **sira utuqnẖ** Gs 56:3; **ziua utuqna** Gs 56:4, ATŠ II no. 11; **tuqna d̠-giutaikun** Gy 173:22 the splendour of your glory.

tuqpa (rt. **TQP**) AM 233:3, DC 37. 432 might, violence. With suff. **tuqpaihun** Gy 177:7 their wrath.

tura = **taura.** Fem. **turta, turi(k)ta,** pl. **turata. mn taurẖ uturatẖ** DC 46 from his oxen and cows; **kdub lturata ususiata** DC 46. 14 write for cows and mares; **taura abatar turikta** DC 46 (like) a bull after a cow; **ašqiẖ lturta** DC 46. 154:3 make a cow drink it; **miša d̠-turta** DC 45 & 46 butter of a cow. Gl. 34:2 **tura** (& miswritten pl.) بقر ,ابقر *boves* گاوان.

turk (Ar. تُرْك) AM 199 Turk(s).

turkistan AM 198:13 Turkestan.

turṣa (rt. **TRṢ**) uprightness, rightfulness, straightforwardness, honesty, setting upright, evenness, equality. **bturṣa qum** Gy 220:22 be honest; **anašia bturṣa mn hdadia laništaiun** AM 246:19 f. people will not speak honestly; **turṣa amrat** Gy 156:16 (var. **amrit** DC 22, read **amart**) thou art right; **ʿlau d̠-turṣa lahua** Gy 116:18 were there no inequality; **ʿu blilia arqa tinud bmdinta bturṣa laništalam** AM 243:20 if there is an earthquake by night in the city, reconstruction will not be established.

turta s. **tura.**

tušar (Ar. تُجّار) AM 277:17 merchants.

tušbihta (rt. **ŠBH**, תּוּשְׁבַּחְתָּא, ܬܫܒܘܚܬܐ) praise, glory MG 64:8, Ginzā 22 n. 2. St. cstr. **tušbihat** DC 3. 336:13 = CP 342:7. Pl. st. cstr. **tušbihan** Q 55:19 ff., MG 133:9 f.

tušlima (rt. **ŠLM**, Jew. תּוּשְׁלָמָא retribution) (*a*) perfection, perfect(ed) soul, fulfilment, accomplishment, (*b*) recompense MG 133:12. Pl. **-ia** perfected (souls, spirits). (*a*) **bit tušlima** CP 169:16, 170:13, 210:11, 354:15, 456:11, Gy 1:17, 73:17, 326:14, 340:17, Jb 169:5, 241:13 f., 242:11, Oxf. 35, 53 a, 75 b, 114 a the House of Perfection MSchr. 5 n. 1, Ginzā 5 n. 9; **tušlima dakia** Jb 51:7, Gs 69:23 pure perfection, pl. **tušlimia dakiia** Gy 313:23 pure perfect ones (: the uthras); **ʿutria tušlimia** Oxf. 35 b the perfect uthras; parallel with **ʿutria** Gy 7:1, Gs 83:15; **latra d̠-iatbia tušlimia** ŠQ 23:19 to the place where the perfect ones dwell; **tušlimia kasiia** Gy 376:1, Gs 111:4 hidden (: invisible) perfect ones; **tušlimia šaliia** Gy 373:2 peaceful perfect ones; **abuhun d̠-kulhun tušlimia** Gy 306:8 Father of all perfect ones; **ʿutra mqaiim tušlimia** Gy 108:11 uthra confirming the perfect ones; **hin btušlimia tiqmulia** ML 135:8 **hin btašlumia taqmilia** CP (DC 53) 110:5 if ye stand by me as perfect ones; **saliq tušlima** Gs 82:5, 21, CP 134:4 (no. 98) = ML 163:10 the perfected soul ariseth; (*b*) **triṣ qudamh̠ tušlima d̠-šalmania mšalimlun** ML 188:9 = DC 3 (DC 53 differs slightly) there is set up before Him the recompense wherewith He recompenseth the righteous; **rba tušlima rba** Gs 50:21 Lord of great retribution (Lidzb. (*a*)).

tuta 1 (תּוּתָא, ܬܘܬܐ, Mishn. תות, Ar. loan-w. تُوت Löw no. 338, *Flora* i 266, Fränkel 140) DC 6 & 36 no. 279 etc. mulberry. Pl. **tutia d̠-kirmania** AM 286:43 f. mulberries of Kerman. Gl. 54:6 **tuta** توتة *sycomora* توت .

tuta 2 (ܬܘܬܐ) remorse, regret. Soul and silkworm both consume **tuta ututa qarilh̠** ATŠ I no. 279 a play on words. ? Doubtful.

tutba 1 (Ar. ثَوب, hardly from **YTB** MG 133:18–20 & n. 4) (woman's) garment, dress MG 23:13. Pl. **-ia.** Masc. **ʿtlabšat btutba napšh̠** Gy 94:9 she put on a dress; **tutbia hiuaria niṣbh̠** Gy 229:3 dyeth white dresses; **d̠-ašlik minik tutbia d̠-hšuka** DC 40. 87 that divested thee (fem.) of dresses of darkness; **tutbai** Jb 130:4 my dress; **tutbak** Jb 130:7 thy dress.

tutba 2 (from af. of **YTB**; ܬܘܬܒܐ, H. תּוֹשָׁב Brockelmann i 385) immigrant, settler MG 23:13, 133:17. **gabra tutba d̠-mdurta d̠-napših̠ litlh̠** Gy 296:19 an immigrant who hath not his own habitation.

tutia 1 pl. of **tuta** (q.v.).

tutia 2 = **atutia** (q.v.) MG 33:13, 194:8. With or without suff. (Mod. *tūθ*). Gl. 37:6, **tutih̠, tuta** اسفل *dorsum* پائين; 54:15 **tuta** تحت *sub* پائين .

tutia 3 (توتيا) antimony, collyrium. **tutia d̠-ainia** AM 268:37 collyrium for the eyes; **tutia d̠-kirmania** AM 268:37, 287:17 Kirman antimony.

tiabuta 1 = **taiabuta.** Var. **ʿtiabuta** Gy 194:18, Jb 30:7, MG 25:antep. **tiabuta** Gy 21:21, 213:22, 276:5, 345:4, Jb 14:11, 30:7 (var.). **tiabuta d̠-marh̠** Gy 36:14 (cf. Gy 17:2 s. **tabuta**). Parallel with **haiasuta** Gy 2:18. **tiabuta urahmuta** Gy 36:14, 42:16 forgiveness and mercy; **tiabuta d̠-hiia** Gy 194:21 (cf. l. 18) clemency of Life; **ʿtiabutak tihuia ʿlai** Jb 189:1 let thy clemency rest upon me.

tiabuta 2 (Akk. *tibūtu*) AM 224:1 invasion BZ 136 n. 3.

tiaruta 1 (rt. **RAA III**) reconciliation; often as a synonym of **tiabuta 1** mercy, forgiveness. Varr. **atiaruta, ʿtiaruta.** (Nöld. from **YHR** 'shining' MG 145:11). (ʿ)**tiarutkun dilkun** Q 35:11 your mercy; **ʿtiarutkun uʿtrahmutkun** CP 292:10 your mercy and your compassion; **ʿtiarutak tihuia ʿlai** Gs 25:6 pardon me, cf. Q 23:20; **mn hdadia tihuilun tiaruta ʿl abatur uʿl ptahil** Gy 242:4 f. Abathur and Ptahil will forgive one another.

tiaruta 2 (rt. **RAA II**) thought, reflection Ginzā 251 n. 4. **btiaruta d̠-hinun mitraiin** Gy 249:14 according to their thought which they thought out.

tiaruta 3 (ܛܝܪܘܬܐ P. Sm.) bubo, inguinal swelling. **bhamšin utartin šnia tiaruta hauialh̠** AM 88:12 f. at (the age of) fifty-two he will have an inguinal swelling; **mn ʿnta hda tiaruta naška** AM 95:2 from one woman he will contract a bubo.

tiba 1 (cf. **tababia**) storm. Pl. **-ia. ziqa utiba** AM 170:3 = Par. xxvi 196:bottom wind and storms; **tibia urima** Par. xxvi 257:7 storms and thunder.

tiba 2 (Akk. *tibû*, *tibūtu*, Mand. doublet **tiabuta 2**) AM 218:8 attack, assault, invasion.

tibia 1 pl. of **tiba.**

tibia 2 Jb 155:12 pl. of **tibta.**

tibian father of Farīdūn. **paridun br tibian** Gy 382:22 (cf. s. **paridun**).

tibibia Gs 1:14, 20, 14:4, Jb 132:8, Oxf. 46 a = ML 217:6 = **tababia** CP 178:5.

tibid, tibit 1 (Ar. ثَابت) steady, constant, stable, invariable (astrol. term). Bad varr. **tibad, tibat. taura briš tibid hu . . . aria tibit hu . . . arqba tibid hu . . . daula tibit hu** AM 149:18, 19 and ult. Taurus at the beginning is stable . . . Leo is stable . . . Scorpio is stable . . . Aquarius is stable.

tibil (H. תֵּבֵל, Syr. loan-w. ܬܐܒܝܠ) earth, earthly world MG **xxix** 10, MR 60, Ginzā 5 n. 8. Fem. 160:1. Used as a pr. n. always in st. abs. MG 301:4, 305:8. **arqa d̲-tibil** Gy 337:2 f. = **arqa tibil** Gy 90:4 f., 337:11, 338:20, 339:5 = **tibil arqa** JRAS 1937 597:3 (*& often*) the earthly world; **tibil auda** Gy 324:24 the perishing world MG 317:16; **tibil d̲-audia** Gy 328:7 the earth of mortal beings; **tibil d̲-ʿzlat** RD B 34 Ezlat's earth.

tibit 1 s. **tibid.**

tibit 2 a *malwâša* man's name, cf. **sam tibit** RD D 21 f.

tibta (rt. **YTB,** Syr. ܬܐܒܬܐ) dung, excrement. Pl. **tibia 2. kd̲ tibta mn ʿuhra** DC 21 JRAS 1938 6:22 like dung from the road; **kanpa d̲-tibta utinta** ATŠ I no. 216 place where dung and urine is collected; **tibta ušlanda** ATŠ I no. 268 dung and putrefaction; **man d̲-ʿtbh̲ tibta nirmia unidakia napšia** Lond. roll A 166 one who has to excrete shall defecate and purify himself; **lanirmia tibta** ATŠ II no. 381 he must not defecate; **ruqa utibta** Q 72:24 spittle and dung; **tibia turia mlʿia ṣiṣia** Jb 155:12 bulls' excreta full of filth.

tigar s. **tigra.**

tigara (תיגרא Bekh. 9a, var. in Rashi תיגארא read תִּיגָארָא as Mand., from P. تنكيره; loan-words: Syr. ܛܓܝܪܐ, Ar. طنجير MG 51:antep. f., cf. also *Nachtrag* p. 485, Lagarde: *Abhandlungen* 50:135, Fränkel 69) Gy 226:7 bowl, kettle, cauldron. Var. **tigra 2** Gy 226:5, MR 98 n. 3, GGA 1890 401.

tigra 1 (Targ. & Sam. תיגר, תיגרא, Syr. ܬܐܓܪܐ LS 816a, H. תִּגְרָה) quarrel, strife, dissension. St. cstr. **tigar** Gs 91:1, 16 MG 133:21. Pl. **-ia. tigar** my strife MG 175: 22. Often with **RMA**: **nirmia tigra** Gy 114:13 we will pick a quarrel; **minh̲ nirmia tigra** Gy 354:6 we will pick a quarrel with him; **mn gabra tigra ramia** AM 26:17 will pick a quarrel with a man; **ulanašia tigra mšauia** AM 71:5 she will cause dissension amongst people; **kulhun tigria mitpaṣia** RD C 12 all quarrels will be made up; **tigra labuia ulʿm mšauia** AM 51:9 he will quarrel with his father and mother; **ʿkamar tigar** Gs 43:paen. my strife was renewed; **tigra umutana** AM 240:14 strife and pestilence; **tigra hiuara** Gy 386:8 doubtf. Ginzā 413 n. 7.

tigra 2 s. **tigara** basin, bowl: **tigra barqa** DC 22.210 a bowl (or hollow) in the ground.

tigr(?)**niaiil** DC 40. 819 name of an angel.

tidba (rt. **DBA**?) slaughter? **mn tidba napših̲ akla . . . zma d̲-nafših̲ šatia** DC 46. 254:1 she eats of her own slaughter (slaughtered flesh) . . . drinketh her own blood.

tidra (rt. ܚܕܪ?) aid, assistance, help. Doubtf. **tidra buta utušbihta uʿqara** DAb aid (?), prayer, praise, and honour.

tiha (cf. Ar. هَوَاء air) (*a*) breath, steam, vapour, smoke, (*b*) fig. mind, soul, heart, ardour. **Easily confused with tihua.** (*a*) **tiha d̲-npaq mn pumh̲** Gy 83:13 the breath that came out of his mouth; **mn tihh̲ mitih̲ lbuših̲** Gy 83:17 f. (read **lbušai** cf. l. 18) some of his breath reached my garment; **bminilth̲ btihh̲** Gy 280:15 with his word, with his breath; **bihbila d̲-pumh̲ parzla bašil uglala btihh̲ mitharka** Gy 280:20 in the steam of his mouth iron boileth and stone burneth in his breath; **tiha d̲-rbita** Gy 284:2 vapour of the ocean; **tiha d̲-ʿšata ʿkilta** Gy 100:10 the smoke of consuming fire; (*b*) **tihaiun** parallel with **libaihun** Gy 181:4, 209:7; **šiha utiha** Gy 258:6 lust and ardour (?); **atit lbnia d̲-adam lmišbaq mn tihak brišaihun** DC 37. 37 I came to A.'s children to loose some of thy ardour in their heads; **truṣ libak batrh̲ utihak bdukth̲ d̲-ʿzib** DC 51. 400 set thy heart in his home and thy mind in his place which is abandoned.

tihua (met. from תְּוָהּ, ܬܘܗܐ) Gy 173:14, Q 59:28 = ML 143:8 dismay, amazement MG 66:21. **tihua btibil** CP 117:ult. consternation on earth.

tihum (H. תְּהוֹם) ATŠ I no. 11 chaos, abyss, primeval ocean.

tihma (met. of תְּמְהָא, ܬܗܡܐ) Gy 46:18, 175:18 f., 242:24, 335:24, Gs 82:8, Q 68:2, Oxf. 11 b (parallel with **malia** wailing), Jb 51:11, DC 26. 26 etc. bewilderment, dismay MG 102:15, MR 145.

tihrata (ܬܗܪܬܐ) marvels, miracles, wondrous deeds. **d̲-ʿlap btihrahta d̲-mšiha** Gy 227:5 (one) instructed about the messiah's miracles. MG 103:17.

tikia pl. of **tikta** (q.v.).

tikil (rt. **TKL II**) bereavement. **bguara utikil** AM 70:13 in exile and bereavement.

tikla (mod. for **nikla**) falsehood. **zipa utikla** DC 51. 829 lie and falsehood.

tiklana DC 22. 2 for **tuklana** Gy 2:7.

tiksir (Ar. تَكْسِير) DC 44. 759 breaking, destruction. Corrupt. (Or from ܟܣܪ to banish) exile.

tikta (תִּיכְתָּא, ܬܟܬܐ, Ar. loan-w. تِكَّة Fränkel 55) (*a*) draw-string, tie-string, (*b*) zone, ring, halo, circle. Pl. **tikia.** MG 103:1, 172:6. (*a*) **tikta d̲-šarualun** ATŠ II no. 193 the draw-string of their leggings; **ṣailia tikia uhimiania** AM 155 they weave tie-strings and (ritual) girdles; **klila utikta** ŠQ 16:12, CP 226:8 a wreath and a girdle; (*b*) **tikia d̲-nhura** Gy 221:6 haloes of light; **atlata tikia** Jb 79:10 three haloes; **tikia mišal šalit** Jb 80:1 thou askest haloes for thyself.

tilbunia Gy 235:22, Gs 26:1, 27:8, DC 43 A 52, 103 = **hilbunia** Ginzā 236 n. 7.

tilhazata DC 44. 1169 = Morg. 263/17:25 fem. pl. doubtf.

tilia, tililia = **talilia** hills. **tilia d̲-habarauata** GH 2555 mounds of ruins; **ʿl tililia uṭalulia** Gy 60:2 on hills and roof-tops.

timia (for תֵּימָן, ܬܝܡܢܐ, cf. تَيْمَاء and ܬܝܡܐ beside ימן MG 53 n. 3) South, south-east MG 134:1, MR 69 f. **lgirbia mulia qarilh̲ ultimia šapla qarilh̲** Gy 283:17 f. North is called highland and South is called lowland; **daiuia d̲-timia** DC 12. 272 the demons of the South;

šria timia DC 12. 5 loosed is (the evil influence) of the South.

timiaiit (adv. from preced.) southern, southerly, southernmost MG 53 n. 3, 201:3. **timiaiit aith lhah' arqa d-hšuka** Gy 278:10 in the South there is that earth of darkness; **arqa timiaiit raita latutun d-kulhun gabaria haškia** DC 48. 314 the southern earth trembles beneath all the dark Powers.

timria pl. (of תִּימוֹרָא, תִּימוֹרְתָּא, [Mandaic], cf. H. שְׁמֻרָה) (*a*) eyelids, eyelashes, (*b*) twinkling of an eye, blinking of eyes. (*a*) **zapania utimria hiura hinun** DC 41. 457 eyelashes and eyelids became white (?); (*b*) **'tlh timria d-ainia** AM 40:11 he has blinking of the eyes.

tina 1 (rt. **TUN**, [Mandaic]) urine MG 102:19. Also **tinia 1. tina šauilh mištih** Gy 91:2 I made urine his drink; **tinia d-hiuaniata ṭaribin** Gy 224:8 AD, Leid. & Sh. 'Abd.'s copy (Pet. **ṭinia**) they sprinkle the urine of animals on them (cf. Nöld. *Archiv f. Religionswiss.* vii 341 f., Ginzā 225 n. 4); **arib btinia d-hizura** AM 133:ult. mix with urine of a pig; **šuplh mn tina uzma** AM 131:10 rub him with urine and blood; **tinia d-taura hiuara usumaqa** AM 135:2 the urine of a white and red bull.

tina 2 (תִּינְתָּא, [Mandaic], H. תְּאֵנָה, Ar. تين, Akk. *tittu* Löw no. 335 *Flora* i 224 f.) fig. Pl. **-ia 2. natria kd šahpia d-tinia** DC 22. 194 (= Gy 203:12 **d-tinia** missing) they fall like leaves of fig-trees.

tinia 1 s. **tina 1.**

tinia 2 s. **tina 2.**

tinia 3 occ. for **tiniana.**

tiniana 1 (תִּנְיָנָא, [Mandaic], cf. H. שִׁנְיָן doubling, Ar. ثُنْيَان secondary MG 191 n. 4) second, secondary MG 139:3, 191:ult. Fem. **tiniantia** Gy 343:8, MG 153:ult., later also **tinianita**, even **tiniatia** DC 50. 125. Pl. masc. **tiniania. muta tiniana** s. **muta.** Second Life: Gy 93:2, 5, 7 etc., cf. **bit tiniana** Gy 360:13, Ginzā 63:29, **hiia tiniania** s. **hiia**; **biṭnat btiniana** Gy 79:20, cf. 295:24, Nöld. prop. ***tinana** 'smoke' MG 122 n. 4, but cf. Ginzā 78 n. 2; about Gy 80:17 s. **tiniana 2**; **btiniana** Gy 96:13 on the second day, AM 210 in the second season; **tiniana** Gy 342:7, 295:24 of Yušamin, Ginzā 78 n. 2; **sahduta tiniantia stahdat** ATŠ II no. 428 a second testimony was given; **tulita tinianita asqat lnapšh** ATŠ I no. 264 (s. ATŠ trsl. p. 183 n. 6) a second worm reared itself up.

tiniana 2 Gy 80:16 D, var. **-ia** AC var. of **tanina** B & Leid. Ginzā 80 n. 1.

tinihta ([Mandaic] from אִתְאֲנָחָה) Jb 32:11, Gs 49:18, DC 53. 369:6 sighing, groaning, repining, lamenting, misery MG 133:25.

tiniqta (from אִתְאֲנַק) Gy 84:18 sighing, groaning MG 133:25.

tinita a mod. fem. of **tanina**? **damia 'l tinita** DC 46. 90:16 it (: the demon) resembles a she-dragon (?).

tinta 1 ATŠ I no. 13, 216 = **tina 1**, cf. **bit tinta** DC 48. 32 bladder.

tinta 2 DC 6 no. 285 = **tinihta.**

tinta 3 = **tina 2. tinta hu** DC 41 (picture) it is a fig-tree; **rumana uspargla uraz tinta** DC 27. 377 pomegranate, quince and the mystery (symbol) of the fig.

tipla (cf. **tapala** (*d*)) foolishness. Doubtf. **tipla tiplit** Morg. 259/9:5 (**parallel with ruita ruit**). DC 44:32 (or s. [Mandaic] phylactery: I put on? a phylactery) (doubtf.).

tipsiq (rt. **PSQ**) fragment. **mn tipsiq d-bauata d-maṣbuta** DC 3 (a colophon) from a fragment of baptismal prayers.

tiqlata pl. (rt. **TQL**) Jb 172:9, 194:8, 223:8, Gs 9 f. errors, blunders, mistakes, stumblings, MG 103:18; ATŠ II no. 308 stumbling-blocks. Var. **tiqilata** Jb 223:12, **taqlata** s.v. ML 14 n. 1. With suff. **tiqlath** CP 199(c) his blunders, **tiqlatan** Q 24:7 our blunders.

tira (תַּרְעָא, [Mandaic], Ar. loan-w. تُرْعَة Fränkel 15, cf. H. שַׁעַר, Sab. [Sabaic]) door, portal, entrance MG 101:5. St. cstr. **tir, tar 1** (q.v.). Pl. **tiria**, cf. MR 186 n. 4. Masc. **tira baraia** CP 26:5, Q 11:9, 12:22, 20:27, 63:12 the outer door; **tira basima** Gy. 277:4 pleasant entrance; **tira d-muta** Gy 277:24 the gateway of death; **tiria hšuk** Q 65:11, Gy 74:10, 80:10, 86:12, Jb 163:15, 165:1 f., 200:8, 11, 262:9, 264:2, cf. 185:7 the doors of the darkness MSt 23; **tiria kušṭa** Q 24:15 the portals of Truth; **tiria umalkauata** Q 52:10 entrances and kingdoms; **alip alip tiria** Gy 69:7 thousand thousands of doors; **tiria rurbia** Gy 73:22, 295:19 great portals; **tiria iaqdana** Gy 74:13 = portals of flame (cf. **baba d-supat** Jb 17:8).

tirat s. **tirta.**

tirata (cf. תֵּיעַר Pi. תַּעַר to awaken, stir up) waking. **ulabšinta ulabtirata** DC 43, DC 45 neither in sleep nor in waking; **umn qadmu d-tirata** CP 155:6 and before the Awakening without; **lbar** (Lidzb. 186:9 **umn qudam d-tirata lbab** which he translates '*bevor mein Herz . . .*' a misreading).

tirba (תַּרְבָּא, [Mandaic], also Chr.-Pal., Ar. ثَرْب, cf. P. چرب) fat MG 100:antep. **tirba d-hiuaniata** Gy 45:18 fat of animals; **rakik mn tirba** Gy 287:5, Q 14:15 softer than fat; **tirba d-hizura** Lond. roll B 397 pig's fat; **diba utirbh** AM 124:5 wolf and its fat; **had d-glala uhad d-tirba** ATŠ II no. 60, one of stone and one of soft matter.

tirbana (adj. from preced., used also as a subst.) fat, flesh(y). **kul mindam mitlabaš tirbana d-hinun tirbania** ATŠ I no. 268 everything was clothed with flesh, so that they were fleshy; **baiina d-almia tirbana qarilh** ATŠ I No. 268 we seek (read **baiinin**) that which people call flesh(ly).

tiriauis (from **tira**, analogy of **piriauis, siniauis**) the earth of darkness, or its entrance (cf. **tiria hšuk** s. **tira**). **'sir tiriauis** DC 43 A 45, 95, 138.

tiriak (P. تریاک) opium. **hda nukut tiriak** DC 46 one grain of opium.

tirta ([Mandaic], cf. Akk. *têrtu* inner part of the body, Jensen) inner conviction, conscience. Pl. **tirata** MG 101:22. Sg. only with suff. of the 1st p. sg. **tirat** Gy 72:5, 262:16, Gs 124: 21 ff. (parallel with **nišmat**) my conscience; MG 175:ult. **tirata mšalmata** Gy 5:8 sound consciences MG 318:17; **maisit btirata** Morg. 222/32:10 f. = CP 51:13 = Q 24:1 = ML 67:4 (s. **MUŠ**); **šagšinin ltirata** Gy 151:18 f. (impt. & pf.); **tirata umhašbata** Gy 149:24; **kiuan btirath traṣlh b'dh simadra** Gy 115:14 Kiuan conscientiously (?) set a blossom in his hand; **tirata** parallel with **liba** Jb 202:11 f., DC 46. 137:16.

tišilta Zotb. 228b:25 for **tušlima.**

tišrin (תִּשְׁרֵי, ܬܫܪܝܢ, Bab. *tišrîtu* KAT 380, Ar. تشرين) the seventh and eighth months of Mand. calendar (under the rule of Libra and Scorpio, i.e. Oct. and Nov.) SsSs ii 31 f. Var. **tašrin** s.v. **tišrin 'l aual** AM 261:34 = **tišrin aual** AM 262:26 Oct.; **tišrin lakir** AM 266:45 Nov.

tit (< תַּחַת, ܬܚܝܬ, تَحْتُ) Q 71:26 f. down, below MG 16:8; with prep. **ltit** Gy 93:22 downwards, under; **mn tit** Gy 98:11 from down; MG 63:12, 203:15, 360:antep., also **ltitai** (לתתאי Bekh. 8b) Gy 202:14 downwards MG 203:23.

titaia (adj. from preced.) lower, inferior, undermost MG 141:10 & n. 3. Fem. **titaita.** Pl. masc. **titaiia.**

titia occ. for **atutia.**

tkala (rt. **TKL II**, ܬܟܠܐ) Gy 6:21 bereavement, childlessness, Nöld. *Todtenklage* MG 115:18.

TKL I (תְּכַל, ܬܟܠ, Ar. اتّكل from وكل, Akk. *takālu*) to trust.

Pe. Act. pt. with encl. **takilbh tuklanh** Gy 2:6, 7 trusteth in Him; **d-takilbh labahit** Gy 31:3 who trusteth in Him shall not be confounded.

Der.: **tuklana** (var. **tiklana**).

TKL II (Jew.-Aram., Chr.-Pal., Syr. in a der. cf. s. **tkala**, H. שָׁכֹל, Ar. ثَكِل) to be bereaved, become childless.

Der.: **tikil, tkala.**

TKN (Jew. = Aram. תְּכַן to fasten) to squeeze through?, press out?

Der.: **takuna.**

TLA (תלא, ܬܠܐ, H. תלה, Eth. ተለወ, Akk. *tullû*) to lift, hang, suspend, drag, draw, pull; with **nura** to set alight, kindle fire, Jb ii 135 n. 7; with **b** depend on; ethpe. to be seized, grabbed.

Pe. Pf. **nura tlat** Jb 67:7 she kindled fire; **h' šragia tlat** DC 34. 780 she hung up lamps; with encl. **tlalh lsikina lraz ṣaurh** DC 41. 193 he drew the knife across the mystery of its neck; with suff. **tiliu bṣauar nišma** CP 90: penult., Gs 108:22 = Q 42:23 = Morg. 245/77:3 = ML 112:7 they hung it on the soul's neck. Impf. with suff. **nitlunh** CP 7:7 = ML 8:7 they (shall) hang him, her (MG 288: antep.). Impt. fem. **talai** CP 214:15, ŠQ 13: 18, 25 and ult.; **tlai šragia** Jb 139:12 light the lamps; with encl. **šraga d-ziua tlibh** CP 215:8 = ML 245:2 hang on it (or light in it) a lamp of radiance. Act. pt. **talia d-hazin qmaha** DC 37. 276 suspender (i.e. wearer) of this phylactery, cf. **talia 2** s.v.; pl. **zaimia utalin** Gy 121: 20 they restrain and hang up; with encl. **bhadiaiin talilin** Gy 183:13 f. they hang them up by their breasts. Pass. pt. **'lana d-bṭuna tlia** ATŠ I no. 70 a tree hung with fruit; pl. **tl'iia, tliiia** Gy 198:16 MG 165:8.

Af. = Pe. Pf. **nura atlia** Jb 141:13 he set fire.

Ethpe. Impf. **nura titlia** Jb ii 135 n. 7. Pt. **d-mitlia kul daiua d-minaian** DC 40. 121 f. so that each demon is caught by us (?); **d-mitlia** (var. **matlia** PD af.) **nura lhabrh** ATŠ I no. 40 so that fire is set (var. who sets fire) to his neighbour; **bhahu ziua . . . d-mitlia** DC 40. 121 by that . . . radiance which is suspended.

Der.: **talia 2, tlaiia.**

tlaiia (rt. **TLA**) DC 44. 975 = Morg. 272/16:2, DC 44. 1070 = Morg. 263/16:19 gallows.

tlasar (Talm. תליסר = תלתעשׂר, Syr. ܬܠܬܥܣܪ) AM 282:ult. thirteen MG 79:17, 188:19.

tlata masc., **tlat** fem. (תְּלָתָא, תְּלַת, ܬܠܬܐ, ܬܠܬ) three MG 187:anteantep. **tlata** (var. **tlat**) **bauata** Q 6:31 three prayers MG 347:19; **tlata škinata** Q 63:7 three (celestial) dwellings; **tlata ainaniata d-ziua** Q 62:29 three sources of radiance; **tlata mania** Q 62:30; **tlata ginsia . . . utlata razia** DC 34:994; **kukbia tlata** Jb 187:1 ff. (Šâmiš, Sin, and Libat MSt 28 f.); **tlata habšaba** (often in AM) Tuesday. As ordinal: **btlata iumia** Gy 96:13 on the third day; **ltlata zibnia** Gy 71:6 for the third time MG 348:bottom.

tlatin thirty MG 189:11.

tlatma three hundred MG 189:paen. **tlatma ušitin nbihia** Gy 29:15 three hundred and sixty prophets.

tlh AM 275:18 = **'tlh** cf. l. 16.

tliataia third MG 192:1. Fem. **tlitaita.** Pl. **tlitaiia. tlitaia d-ginzaihun** ATŠ II no. 296 the third of their treasures; **hṭimia tlitaiia** s. **TLT. hiia tlitaiia** s. **hiia.**

TLP (Ar. تلف) to be destroyed, ruined. Ar. impf. **iitlip anašia** AM 285:31 people will be destroyed.

Der.: **talap.**

TLT (cf. **tlata**) to do three times, or a third time MG 444 & n. 1.

Pe. Pf. **tlat 'hablia** Jb 173:7 he gave a third time (cf. pa.), **tiltit amarilh lbiša** CP 181:10 thrice I said to the evil one; with suff. **tiniuia utiltuia** Gy 115:23 they did it a second and a third time.

Pa. Pf. **talit 'hablia** Gy 358:9 he gave me for a third time (cf. s. pe.) MG 444:5.

Ethpe Pt. pl. **lišania hṭimia tlitaiia umitlitaiia** DC 40. 165 f., cf. DC 12. 219 f. the tongues are cut in pieces, divided into three, and thrice divided.

Der.: **tlata** etc.

TMA I (secondary rt. from תְּמַה, ܬܡܗ, cf. esp. Ar. تَمِهَ; another secondary rt. **THM** q.v.) to be(come) turbid (of water), dark (opposite of **NHR**) MG 64:14 f., ZA xxx 155.

Pe. Pf. **mia tma ulanahria** Gy 268:1 water became turbid and shineth not; **raza tminaia tma ulanahar** ATŠ I no. 289 the eighth mystery is dark and shineth not (**tminaia tma** for the sake of alliteration?). Inf. **mitm(i)a tahmia** Gs 41:11 they became turbid.

Der.: s. **THM.**

TMA II = **TMM** (q.v.).

tmanaia eighth. Varr. (a)**tminaia** s.vv. MG 192:7. **šuma d̲-tmanaia rba qadmaia** DC 44. 1641 = Morg. 267/25:16 the name of the Great First Eighth [*sic*]; **tmanaia qrun** Jb 38:13 they made me the eighth one; **tmanaia d̲-hšuka** Jb 18:13 (= Yôšamīn, cf. Jb ii p. xxiv); **iuma tmanaia** PD 662, 685, 701 the eighth day; **alma tmanaia** PD 1392 the eighth world.

tmanan eighty MG 22:5, 189:16.

tmanasar eighteen MG 188:19. Fem. **asar utmania** MG 189:7.

tmania (תְּמָנְיָא, ܬܡܳܢܝܳܐ, fem. תְּמָנֵי, ܬܡܳܢܶܐ) eight MG 188:2. The same graphical form for both genders. **tmania maṣbutiata ltmania tarmidia** PD 1234 eight baptisms for eight priests; **tmania maṣbutiata** PD 83; **tmania tarmidia** PD 817; **tmania ʿṣṭunia** Par. xxvii 16a, 19a, 23a eight columns; **tmania bnʿ kukbia** Lond. roll B 168 eight sons of stars; **tmania malkia** PD 819 eight kings; **tmania** (of purgatories) Brandt JPTh 1892 417, 423. Cf. **tmania,** var. **tmanaia** Jb 92:8 f., see ii 95 n. 1.

tmanima eight hundred MG 190:4.

tmima (Gen. Aram., cf. H. תָּמִים) simple(ton), foolish, silly MG 116:19. Pl. **-ia. sakla tmima** Jb 259:9 fool, simpleton, pl. **saklia tmimia** Jb 171:12, 181:10, DC 36 no. 11; **ʿutria tmimia** Gy 92:21 simple-minded (guileless) uthras, cf. Gy 368:1, 12.

tmimuta (abstr. noun from preced.) GRs. 102:4, Q 38:1 = ML 100:3 = CP 81:5 simplicity.

tmina (cf. Ar. ثمين) precious, valuable, dear; value, worth. **tminai tminai mn birkta latibṣar** DC 6. 637 my worth will not detract my value from the blessing. Doubtf. DC 36 omits.

tminaia var. of **tmanaia.** Often in AM. **raza tminaia tma** s. **TMA.**

TMM (Ar. تمّ, cf. frequent colloquial *tamâm tâmmâ*) to be(come), stay, remain. Mod., very often in the colloquial and in colophons.

Pe. Pf. **iahia iuhana tama rba** HG Y.Y. became an initiator, **ana iahia bihram rbai tama ram zihrun** DC 36 (HG) coloph. Ram Zihrun became mine, i.e. Yahia Bihram's, initiator; **tamun bhitin** DC 51. 813 they were ashamed; **tamun arba iahria ṭabuta hzun** DC 12. 392 four months had passed since they saw good food. Impf. **humria uliliata bṣurta nitumun** DC 26. 305 they are surrounded (by) amulet-spirits and liliths.

Gl. 52:9 f. **TM** [sic] تردّد *demorari* هميشه ايستاد; 181:9 f. id. *permorare* هميشه ايستاد.

TMR cf. **tumarta,** pl. **tumria.**

Gl. 22:11 f. **tmra** [sic] أينع *fructificare* ميوه داد.

TNA I (תְּנָא, ܬܢܳܐ, H. שנה I, Ar. ثني, Eth. ሰንየ, Akk. *šanû* to repeat, cf. *šinā* two) to do for a second time, repeat, reiterate MG 444 & n. 1.

Pe. Pf. **(a)tna škib** Gy 245:4 he slept again MG 444:3; **(a)tna uamarlh̲** Gy 71:11 he repeated (it) saying to him MG 445:3; **(a)tna ʿhablia** Jb 713:6 he gave me a second time; **tnat ʿhailat** Gy 95:3 she regained her strength MG 444:4; **tnit ʿthazilh̲** Gy 83:11 I appeared to him for a second time; with suff. **tiniuia** s. **TLT.** Impf. **nitnia nibad** Gy 297:3 he shall repeat it; **nitkamar unitnih̲** ATŠ II no. 347 he shall return and repeat it; **latitnun** Jb 170:7 do not repeat it. Impt. **tnia pšuṭ kušṭa** ML 50:9 give them the hand for a second time; **haizak anat tnia truṣ tagak** DC 34. 1015 then for the second time consecrate thy crown.

Af. Pf. **atna** as var. of **tna** s. pe. Impf. **latatnun** Gy 15:17 repeat it not.

Der.: **tiniana, trin.**

TNA II = **TNH.**

Ethpa. Impf. **ʿtana** I sigh MG 235:17. Pt. pl. (doubtf.) **baitin utanin** (read **mitanin**?) Gy 366:14 they spend the night and sigh (? Ginzā 389 n. 3).

tnat btnat Gy 293:17 doubtf., Lidzb. read **mnat** *Anteil.* Possibly 'were in duplicate'?

TNGR (by dissimil. of the second rad. doubled of **TGR,** den. from **tangara** q.v.) to act as a merchant, trade, barter, traffic, deal with, deal in, profit. Often with fig. mean.: to do good deeds. MG 76:4 f.

Ethpa. Pf. **hla uʿtangar** s. **HLA, laʿtangar btangarutun** Gy 256:5 they bartered not in their commerce; **laʿtangar bkaspaiun** Gy 232:2 they traded not with their silver. Pt. **mitangar** Jb 181:4, MG 132:18, pl. **tangaria d̲-mitangria umasqun tangarutun** Gy 72:14 f. (cf. s. **tangaruta**); **mitangria bagra uzidqa** Q 64:31, **bagra uzidqa mitangria** Gy 340:15 they will deal in gifts and alms.

Der.: **tangara, tangaruta.**

TNH (secondary rt. from אנח = **ANA II,** cf. **tinihta;** another secondary rt. **TNA II** s.v.) to sigh, groan, lament.

Ethpe. Pf. **ʿtnihat** she sighed MG 63:ult.

Der.: **tanihta, tinihta** & varr.

tʿia (a doublet of **ṭʿia,** cf. H. טעה & תעה) error, straying. **mn tʿia lšrara** DC 51. 591 from error to truth; **ruh tʿia** DC 51:591 the spirit of error.

TPA I (תפה II ithpa.) Lidzb.'s conception of **APA II** (q.v.) Jb ii 172 n. 4.

TPA II a mod. form of **ṬPA I.**

Pe. Act. pt. **d̲-ʿdh̲ nakit ukiba tapia** DC 46. 66:2 so that he bites his hand and increases his pain (doubtf.).

Gl. 13:1 f. **atpa** ازداد *augere* زياد كرد; 14:3 f. **atpa** استوا *continere, finire, restituere complere* كامل شد; 78:11 f. **atpa** زاد *adicere*

زياد شد ; 126:13 f. **tpia** فضل *abundare* بسيار شد.

Der.: **tupiana.**

TPA III a mod. form of **ṬPA II.**

Pe. Act. pt. pl. **mia tapin** AM 261:37, 271:1 (var. **tipin** Par. xxvi) the waters will be full to overflowing; **mia bainaniata tapin** AM 262: 11 f. waters in the springs will be full.

TPA IV secondary rt. from **APA I.**

Pe. Impf. **kul man d̲-nitpia unibašil bgauaihun** ATŠ II no. 93 everyone who cooks and boils in them. Pass pt. **tpia bnura** ŠQ 5:14 baked in the fire.

Pa. Inf. **tapuiia** DC 50. 487 to cook.

Der.: **tapaiia.**

tpala ML 66:7 = **tapala** (*a*).

TPL s. **tipla.**

Der.: **t(a)pala, tipla.**

TPT (mod. Syr. ܬܦܛ Macl.) to sneeze.

Pe. Pf. **tpit** Gy 241:18 (var. **tpat**) CP 44:12 = ML 55:1, DC 41. 118 he sneezed.

tqala (rt. **TQL**) DC 20. 120 stumbling-block.

tqina (pass. pt. pe. of **TQN**) Jb 259:10 steady, reliable.

TQL I (תְּקַל I, ܬܩܠ, H. שׁקל, Akk. *šaqālu* Zimmern: *Akk. Fremdwörter* 23, Ar. ثَقُلَ; also **ŠQL** s.v.) to weigh, counterpoise; to smoothen, clear away obstacles.

Pe. Impt. with suff. **tuqlan bmuzaniak** CP 291:2 (defect. var. **tqlan** DC 3. 214:11) weigh me in thy balances (MG 271:7). Act. pt. **taqil ʿubadia uagria** Gs 37:9 (cf. ff.) = ML 17:1 he weigheth deeds and rewards; **taura usarṭana taqil** AM 152:7 Taurus and Cancer counterpoise; **ʿuhrata taqil** ATŠ II no. 343 he smoothens the roads; pl. **taqlia luat hdadia** ATŠ I no. 217 they counterpoise one another.

Ethpe. Impf. **laiit dahba ukaspa d̲-niqrab unitqal banph̲** ATŠ II no. 361 no gold or silver approaches or is commensurate with it. Pt. **mitqil kulh̲ mamla** ATŠ II no. 116 every word is weighed; pl. **bihdadia mitiqlia** Gy 81:3, 96:19 they counterpoise each other.

Der.: **mitqal.**

TQL II (תְּקַל II, ܬܩܠ 5 LS) to stumble, trip up, offend, make mistakes.

Pe. & Ethpe. Impf. **titqil** he stumbles MG 227:2; **mn tiqlatun latitiqlun** CP 126:5 = ML 152:10 stumble not on their stumbling-blocks (or with their stumblings). Pt. **mitqil** he stumbles; pl. **man minaihun d̲-mitiqlin** ATŠ II no. 363 those of them whose feet have tripped. Part. pres. **btaqlatkun lamitqilna** s. **taqlata.**

Der.: **taqlata, tiqlata, tqala.**

TQN (Aram., Syr., H., Akk. *taqānu*, Ar. أتقن to confirm) to be steady, unwavering, firm, orderly; pa. to set in order, arrange, supply, furnish, provide, construct, put on a firm basis, make firm, restore, establish, stabilize, prosper, make prosperous, improve; also to shine, gleam Oxf. 113 a (cf. **taqun, taqna** s.v.).

Pe. Pf. **tqun** Gs 57:9 was firm MG 218:15, **kul mindam tqun** ATŠ II no. 118 everything was in order; **malka tqun basa** Lond. roll A 156 the king was confirmed by the myrtle; **tiqnat dmutai** Gy 101:18 f. my appearance shone; **nihrat utiqnat** Gy 305:19 she shone and glimmered; **bkulhun razia tiqnat** DC 27 she was made ready (qualified) for all the mysteries; **biuma d̲-mahzita tiqnat bainia** Lond. roll A 40 = CP 347:18 on the day on which vision was realized by eyes (?) (s. trsl. CP 227 n. 2); **ʿšata ʿkilta ʿtbihrat utiqnat briša d̲-hanath̲ nišimta** DC 27. 81 f. a crowning (?) flame shone and gleamed on the head of that soul; **baita labnh̲ bana ulatiqnat bʿdh̲ d̲-ardikla** DAb no builder built the House, nor was it framed (constructed) by the hand of an architect; **tiqnit kd̲ libat** DC 44. 1390 (var. **ʿtiqnit** Morg. 265/21:9 ethpe.) I shone like Venus; with suff. **man tiqnh̲** DC 3 no. 375 (var. **taqnh̲** CP 387:9) who set it in order? Impf. **haila lmalka nitqun** AM 245:9 the army will be arrayed for (or against ?) the king; **titqun dmutaian** Gy 30:13 our appearance shall shine MG 218:16; **dmutak titiqun** [*sic*] **utinhar** CP 452:6 thine appearance is effulgent and giveth out light; with encl. **hu nitiqinlia** DC 26. 448 (better var. **nitaqinlia** DC 28 pa.) he shall restore me. Impt. **tqun ginzaikun mn riš briš** ATŠ II no. (?) put your treasure in complete order. Act. pt. replaced by **taqun, taqna** s.vv. Pass. pt. **tqina** s.v.

Pa. Pf. **qra ulataqin** Gs 47:5 he created but did not put into order; **karsauata taqnit taqnit karsauata** DC 53. 266:14 I constructed thrones, I provided thrones; **lminihrh̲ ldmuth̲ ulmitaqnh̲ mn riš briš** CP 222:14 to lighten his countenance and to make him prosper from end to end; **utaqinth̲ ltibil kulh̲** CP 225:13 and improved (made better, made brighter) the whole earth; **taqiniun** Gy 6:5 they established MG 223:23; with encl. **taqnibh̲** Gy 91:6 f. I prepared therein MG 226:1; **lataqnh̲ barba razia** ATŠ II no. 416 he did not confirm him with four mysteries; **taqnu bkulhun šbilia** ATŠ no. (?) they set it firmly upon all its paths; **taqinh̲** we established him MG 277:22; **taqinin** we set them (fem.) in order MG 283:8; **anharth̲ utaqinth̲** Gy 322:18 f. I imparted to it light and lustre. Impf. **manu škinata nitaqin . . . ana škinata ʿtaqin** Jb 261:2, 5 who will establish the dwellings? . . . I will establish the dwellings; **titaqan** (read **titaqin** with Leid.) **ʿbidata kulhin** Gy 92:15 f. thou establishest (appointest) all works; with suff. **nitaqninun** he establishes them MG 281:ult. Impt. with suff. **taqnh̲ uasqh̲ lriš** ML 261:5, CP 275:16 arrange it and complete it successfully; **mtaqnanin d̲-zakauata taqnh̲** CP 210:4, ML 244:2 Confirmer of victories, confirm him! **lataqnih̲ ulatikuih̲** DC 34. 1024 do not correct him and do not reprove him. Pt. **mtaqan bʿbidath̲** RD 11 stable in his works; **makulta mtaqanta d̲-mtaqan ṭama** Gy 215:7 a wholesome meal the taste of which is perfect; **ʿbidata d̲-mtaqna** Jb 11:11 works which are set in order; **maṣbuta taqna umtaqna** s. **taqna**; **taqun lkul šugiania** DC 6 rectify all blunders. Part. pres. **anat hu d̲-mtaqnit ʿutria** Gy 72:1 thou art he who equippest (?) the uthras. Nom. ag. **mtaqnana** s.v. Inf. **ltaqunia ʿutria** CP 442:7 to equip the uthras; with suff. **mitaqninun** Gy 340:12 to equip them MG 293:11.

Ethpe. Pf. **ʿtiqnit** cf. s. pe.

Ettaf. Pf. **bnhurak ʿtaqan kulh̲ alma** DC 53 with thy light the whole world was illumined. Impf. **nitaqnan** they (fem.) are set in order MG 228:6.

Der.: **mtaqnana, taqun, taqna, tuqna, tqina.**

TQP (Aram., Syr., H. from Aram. Nöld. ZDMG xlvii 102, Kautzsch 92, Ar. ثَقُفَ) to be strong, prevail.

Pe. Impf. **malka lbildbaba nitqup** AM 227:7 f. the king will defeat his enemy; **iama taqipa nitqup** AM 236:14 a violent sea will rage.

Der.: **taqup(a), taqip(a), taqpiaiil, tuqpa.**

TRA I (תְּרֵי I, ܐܬܪܝ, cf. Akk. *tārū* guard, supervisor? LS) to warn, admonish, instruct, discipline Jb ii 147 n. 7. Doubtf.

Pe. Pf. **kita lnapšaihun tra** DAb the reproof of themselves which (?) admonished them.

Af. Impf. with suff. **ʿiatria lnunia d̲-ʿumqia** Jb 146:10 Lidzb.: *damit ich die Fische der Tiefe warne*, but more prob. from **ATR**: that I may awaken the fish of the depths.

TRA II (תְּרֵי, תְּרָא II, ܬܪܐ, H. שׁרה, Ar. ثَرِيَ, but cf. P. تَر wet) to wet, moisten, soak, steep in liquid.

Pe. Act. pt. **kita taria bdima** Gs 99:8 she bedeweth the clods with her tears. Pass. pt. **tria bmia** AM 287:24 steeped in water.

Ethpe. Impf. **titira** Or. 331:18 thou wilt be steeped (doubtf.).

tra (only in **d̲-tra**) (תְּרֵי, תְּרָא) to inform, forewarn. **qina d̲-msadra brazia d̲-tra** Or. 6592: 670 a *qina* on which have been set out the mysteries as aforesaid (*or* as was forewarned).

trahmuta (rt. **RHM**) compassion, mercy. **utrahmutkun** Q 73 b (bottom) and your mercy MG 145:9, 13; **trahmut liba** DC 3. 217:antep. compassion of heart.

traṣa (rt. **TRṢ**) setting-up, consecration, celebration (religious). Pl. **-ia. šarh d̲-traṣa d̲-taga d̲-šišlam rba** (title of DC 54 (Cor.) & Lond. roll A) explanation of the coronation (rite) of the Great Šišlam; **traṣa d̲-razia** DC 27. 392 the celebration of mystic rites.

trui both.

trunga (תְּרוּנְגָּא = תְּרוּנָא, H. אֶתְרוֹג Löw) lemon, citron, ethrog; name applied by MM to all citrus fruit. **trunga = atrug** Oxf. roll f 158; **trunga** Lond. roll B 406. **trunga hu** DC 41 (picture) it is a citrous tree; **trunga unargila** ATŠ II no. 217 citron and coconut.

trin (Aram., Syr.) two, both MG 187:bottom. Var. **ʿtrin.** Fem. **tartin** s.v. **asra utrin** Gy 263:8, 267:7 twelve MG 188:ult., 346:ult.; **trin malakia** Gy 13:22 both angels; **trin draiai** Gy 205:3, 23, 206:20 both my arms MG 6:34 bottom; **d̲-masgin trin trin** Gy 65:5 which go two by two MG 348:26; **hauia lhad trin** Gy 95:10, Q 64:2 etc. will be twice as big; **ʿhaial libh̲ had ʿl trin** Gy 95:8 his heart became twice as strong MG 349:4–6.

trisar (Talm. תריסר, Syr. ܬܪܥܣܪ) twelve MG 188:12. Var. **ʿtrisar. šuba utrisar** Q 48:12, RD B 7 the Seven and the Twelve (: the planets and the signs of the Zodiac); **šuba utrisar mdabrania d̲-alma** Gy 23:9 (s. **mdabrana**); **ʿkilta d̲-babia trisar** Q 72:9 (cf. s. **baba**); **trisar kukbia** Gy 99:20 the twelve stars; **trisar maštuṣia** Gy 97:24 (cf. s. **maštuṣia**); **hamša utrisar** Gy 11:1 s. **hamša**; **trisar bnia** Gy 100:3 twelve sons; **amamia trisar** Gy 58:6 twelve peoples (: religions Ginzā 51 n. 7); **trisar buria** Gy 95:11 f. twelve monsters; **trisar dmauata** Gy 95:14 twelve appearances. Of Christ's apostles: **trisar mastiania** Gy 58:2 the twelve seducers; **trisar gubria tangaria** s. **tangara.**

trisaraia, (ܬܪܥܣܪܝܐ) DC 34. 264 twelfth MG 192:25.

triṣ(a) (pass. pt. pe. of **TRṢ**) upright, straight, straightforward, direct, sincere, set right, rectified, straightened, established. Pl. **-ia. triṣ maluašai mn kulhun maluašia** DC 44. 81 my horoscope is more trustworthy than all horoscopes; **blišana triṣa** Gy 5:9 f. with an honest tongue; **gada triṣa** AM 243:20, 64:9 fair fortune; **bturṣa (var. btriṣa) laništalam** AM 243: 20 the rebuilding will not be accomplished; **sahduta d̲-triṣa** ATŠ II no. 172 straightforward (honest) evidence.

triṣuta (abstr. noun from preced.) AM 28:4, DC 50. 17 straightforwardness, uprightness, rectitude.

TRMD (den. from **tarmida**) to instruct, train for priesthood, initiate a novice. MG 84:16.

Parel. Pf. **tarmid tarmidia** DC 12. 408 f. (*& often*) he ordained priests (MG 222:8); **tarmidit** MG 223:12, **tarmidnia tarmidia** DC 50. 934 (mod.) we consecrated priests. Impt. **tarmid** MG 229:17. Act. pt. with encl. **rbania d̲-lamalpilun ltarmidia umitarmidilun** (read **mtarmidilun**) DAb teacher-priests who consecrate novice-priests without instructing them. Pass. pt. **mtarmad hauia tarmida** ATŠ I no. 15 the priest is ordained. Inf. **mitarmudia** CP 183:2, var. **mitarmidia** DC 3. 181: 10 read **(m)tarmudla** to ordain priests (a priest).

Refl.: Pt. pl. **mitarmidin,** var. **mitarmdia** MG 149:13 f. Part. pres. **mitarmadna** (*often in* Jb., cf. 103:10) I become a disciple MG 231:14. Inf. **mitarmudia** with pa.-meaning s. parel.

TRP (cf. ܬܪܦ 2 LS) to bite.

Pe. Act. pt. with encl. **hiuia tariplik** DC 21 a serpent may bite thee (fem.); **d̲-hiuia tariplh̲** ATŠ II no. 77 whom a serpent bites.

TRṢ (Aram., Syr., Akk. *tarāṣu*, Ar. أترص Fränkel 292) to set up, establish, make straight, correct, upright, erect; to consecrate. With **taga**, put on crown, crown as king (priest).

Pe. Pf. **tirṣit** (read ethpe.?) **mn dilkun** CP

262:9 I am corrected (?) by you; with encl. **trașnalun** Gy 247:3 we set them upright (= corrected them) MG 225:11; **trașbh̲** Gy 351:23 he set up in it, wrong var. **traștibh̲** ibid. B MG 226 n. 1; with suff. **tirșh̲** Gy 351:23 he set it up; **traștinan** MG 280:7; **trașnh̲** MG 277:19; **trașunun** MG 283:13; **tirșuia** MG 277: anteantep. Impf. with encl. **taga latitirșulh̲** ATŠ II no. 10 do not crown him (as a priest); with suff. **titirșunh̲** MG 278:8. Impt. **truș drašia** ML 49:3 recite the hymns straightforwardly; **truș libak llibai . . . utruș libak batrh̲** DC 51. 398 f. set thy heart upon my heart . . . and set thy heart in its place; with encl. **ata utrașlia malalai** ML 172:2 come and regulate my speech; pl. with suff. **turșuia ldina ulatipkuia** Gy 14:15 make right judgement and do not pervert it. Pt. pl. **tirșin** (read with var. **tarșin**) **taga barbia bauata** DC 42. 15 they consecrate (put on) the crown with four prayers. Part. pres. **tariștun, tarșitun** ATŠ II no. 168 ye set up; with encl. **tarșinabh̲** Oxf. 34 a I set up therein MG 231:anteantep. Pass. pt. **triș(a)** straight (s.v.) MG 116:12. Pass. part. pres. **trișinin** we are set up MG 232:paen. Inf. **lmitraș iaminaikin** CP 114:14 = **lmitraș iaminaikun** ML 140:1 when setting up your right hands; **ulmitraș ulqaiumia** DC 51. 127 and to set up and to raise up; with suff. **mitrișinkun** Oxf. 5 b to set you up MG 293:4.

Ethpe. Pf. **ʿtriș** MG 212:paen., **ʿtrișt** MG 222:bottom; **ʿtriștun uʿtqaiamtun** ML 95 ye have been set up and established (MG 224:8); **ʿtrișnin** MG 224:20. Impf. **nitriș** DC 53. 352:3 will be established MG 226:18; **tarșak nitraș** CP 465:4 thy consecration is confirmed; **titriș** MG 227:2; **nitirșun** MG 227:20. Pt. **mitriș** MG 132:10. Part. pres. **mitrișit** MG 231: anteantep.

Der.: **tarșa, tarșut, turșa, trașa, triș(a), trișuta.**

TRR (corrupt for **NTR**?) to miscarry: **uialda mitrar** DC 46. 100:1 and the child is miscarried.

tša (תְּשַׁע, ܬܫܥ, H. תֵּשַׁע, Ar. تِسْعٌ, Eth. ተስዑ, Akk. *tišit*, fem. Brockelmann i 486) nine (for both genders) MG 188:3. Var. **ʿtša,** even **ʿša. asar utša** nineteen MG 189:8.

tšasar nineteen MG 188:20. Var. **ʿtšasar.**

tšiaia, var. **tšiiaia** Par. xiv no. 208 ninth MG 192:8.

tšiuta (rt. **ŠAA II,** cf. שְׁעִיעוּתָא smoothness) AM 191 civility, courtesy.

tšima nine hundred MG 190:5. Var. **ʿtšima.**

tšin ninety MG 189:17. Var. **ʿtšin.**

d̲-

d̲- the 23rd letter of the Mand. alphabet used only as relative particle. The sign represents a peculiar development of ܕ or די MG 92:10, Zotb. 225a, AIT 38, AF 228 n. 2; written, as a rule, procliticaIly, but sometimes also (esp. in the codex B of the Ginza) separately MG 12:26, 92:12, hence our transcription as **d̲-**. Actual traditional pronunciations: *ad* and *di* (the latter esp. in **drašia d̲-iahia** pron. *drašidihya*), cf. also MG 25:12 f. Regularly used after st. emph. to express a genitive relation. As relative particle simply, or in **man d̲-** who, **manu d̲-** who is that?, **mahu d̲-** what is that?, **kul d̲-, kulman d̲-** whosoever, **mindam d̲-** something that etc. MG 342 ff. **d̲-la-** Gs 95:24, **d̲-lau** Gy 333:23 without MG 430:paen. f. In relative clauses MG 448–472. Written in a few cases as **ṭ** (q.v.).

A = A

The alphabet is formally closed by the first letter **a,** so that it is supposed to have 24 letters, cf. Morg. 225/1:2 and other magical documents also MII pp. 240–3. (Morg. **257/5**: bottom twice, 265/21:bottom twice, **the final a** is omitted by carelessness of the **copyist**).

www.ingramcontent.com/pod-product-compliance
Lightning Source LLC
Chambersburg PA
CBHW080531300426
44111CB00017B/2677